THE OXFORD
DICTIONARY OF
ENGLISH PROVERBS

THE OXFORD
DICTIONARY OF
ENGLISH PROVERBS

Compiled by
WILLIAM GEORGE SMITH

With an Introduction by
JANET E. HESELTINE

SECOND EDITION
revised throughout by
SIR PAUL HARVEY

OXFORD
AT THE CLARENDON PRESS

Oxford University Press, Ely House, London W. 1

GLASGOW NEW YORK TORONTO MELBOURNE WELLINGTON
CAPE TOWN SALISBURY IBADAN NAIROBI LUSAKA ADDIS ABABA
BOMBAY CALCUTTA MADRAS KARACHI LAHORE DACCA
KUALA LUMPUR HONG KONG

FIRST EDITION 1935
REPRINTED 1936
SECOND EDITION 1948
REPRINTED 1952, 1957, 1960, 1963, 1966

PRINTED IN GREAT BRITAIN
AT THE UNIVERSITY PRESS, OXFORD
BY VIVIAN RIDLER
PRINTER TO THE UNIVERSITY

PREFACE

THE arrangement of a collection of proverbs in such a way that the inquirer may readily find the proverb he is looking for is a matter of some difficulty. The difficulty arises from the fact that many proverbs have not a precise, invariable, and generally known and accepted form. On the contrary, there are frequently variant or uncertain versions, particularly in the opening words and in respect of the use of the definite or indefinite article, the choice between 'He that' and 'He who', the inclusion or exclusion of the first 'as' in proverbs of the type of 'As red as a rose', and similar points of doubt. Who shall say whether it is 'A burnt child' or 'The burnt child' who dreads the fire, or whether, according to the true version, it is 'You' or 'A man' who may lead a horse to the water but cannot make him drink? It follows that no convenient arrangement of proverbs in alphabetical order is possible if the proverbs are set out in their ordinary form.

The proverbs in this collection are arranged in the alphabetical order of some (usually the first) significant word in each, the part (if any) of the proverb preceding the significant word being transferred to the end of the proverb, or, if more convenient, to an intermediate point in it. The transferred part begins with a capital letter, and if placed in the middle of the proverb is terminated by an upright hair-stroke. Thus

> To give a Roland for an Oliver,

becomes

> Roland for an Oliver, To give a;

and

> When you are at Rome, do as Rome does.

becomes

> Rome, When you are at | do as Rome does.

Some proverbs have only one significant word (e.g. 'Blood will have blood'), or a significant word so dominant that, if the inquirer does not know it, he cannot know the proverb at all (e.g. 'Curses like chickens come home to roost'). In these cases nothing further is required. But where, as is more frequent, there are two or more words in a proverb of comparable significance, an inquirer may be uncertain which of these, on the above system, has been chosen as the opening word; or again he may know only the general tenor of the proverb, not its precise wording. Accordingly, under any other word of importance in the proverb a cross-reference has been given showing the opening word under which the proverb appears, together with so much of the rest of it as will indicate its general sense. Thus if the proverb 'He that will play at bowls must expect to meet with rubbers' is looked for under 'Bowls', it will not be found there, but, instead, a cross-reference: 'Bowls, *see* Play at b. must expect rubbers', and the proverb with the relevant quotations will be found under 'Play at bowls'. These cross-references, which are very numerous, should make it possible to trace without difficulty any proverb in the collection.

The cross-references under any word have as a rule been placed immediately after the last proverb beginning with that word. Some slight departures from strict alphabetical order occur here and there, where this appears convenient; but in general the order may be exemplified as follows:

Dog . . .

Dog's . . .

Dogged . . .

Dogs . . .

Dogs' . . .

Dog(s) (cross-references).

It may further be noted that when the alphabetical position of any proverb was being settled, any parenthesis, whether between brackets or between a comma and a vertical stroke, was disregarded. Thus

Necessity (Need) has no law

is placed before

Necessity is a hard dart;

and

Rome, When you are at | do as Rome does

is placed before

Rome was not built in a day.

A certain number of proverbs (mostly Scottish) which appeared in the original edition of *The Oxford Dictionary of Proverbs* have been omitted from the present work because of their somewhat trivial character, and have been replaced by others of greater interest. For many of the latter the publishers are indebted to Professor F. P. Wilson, whose profound knowledge of sixteenth- and seventeenth-century English literature and extensive collections of proverbs and quotations have furnished a multitude of instances of the appearance of proverbs at earlier dates than had previously been recorded. Professor Wilson has also given invaluable advice and assistance on many bibliographical and other points. A number of proverbs and interesting quotations have also been drawn from a collection made by the late G. C. Loane and from notes by Mr. Vernon Rendall.

In the present edition acknowledgement is also due to G. L. Apperson's *English Proverbs and Proverbial Phrases*, published by Messrs. J. M. Dent & Sons Ltd. in 1929, for some early examples which Mr. Apperson's careful researches first made available. These are indicated by (A) after the reference.

P. H.

INTRODUCTION

I

PROVERBS AND POTHOOKS

'To give subtilty to the simple, to the young man knowledge and discretion . . .; the words of the wise and their dark sayings.'

'What is all wisdom save a collection of platitudes? Take fifty of our current proverbial sayings—they are so trite, so threadbare, that we can hardly bring our lips to utter them. None the less, they embody the concentrated experience of the race, and the man who orders his life according to their teaching cannot go far wrong. How easy that seems! Has any one ever done so? Never.'

'Neither may I omit the Significancie of our Proverbs, concise in Words, but plentiful in Number, briefly pointing at many great Matters, and under a Circle of a few Sillables prescribing Sundrie available Caveats.'

'PROVERBS OF CONTENTED TENANTS . . . "Prevention is better than cure".—That is why we keep a Works Department of 500 men maintaining KEY-FLATS in first-class condition.'

A HEBREW sage and a modern novelist, an Elizabethan antiquary and a firm of house-agents in the year of grace 1935—these have all found a 'Significancie' in proverbs. We brood over their words as we turn the pages of Mr. Smith's Dictionary, and memory conjures up for us the picture of a child hunched over her copy-book, struggling with a pen that will waver and a tongue that will protrude, sinking under the desolate certainty of foreknowledge that blots must surely follow upon ink. Slowly her task is finished, pothooks have been laboriously joined, and A BIRD/ IN THE HAND/IS WORTH TWO/IN THE BUSH fills the page in smudgy triumph. The same sentence, perhaps five hundred years before, had been scratched on vellum by a monkish scribe, who added after it the Latin equivalent: *Plus valet in manibus avis unica fronde duabus.* A copy-book maxim to a child in the twentieth century, what did it stand for in the fifteenth? And, still earlier, what would it signify in the days when Solomon collected 'the words of the wise and their dark sayings', with no thought that the young man to whom they were offered might prefer to work out his wisdom for himself?

The proverb is a large subject which can be considered from many angles. The Philosophy of Proverbs, the Origin of Proverbs, the Style or Kinds of Proverbs, Proverbs in Folk-lore and other lores—these have all been examined, and all have their interest. But to us the main interest of proverbs lies in seeing them climb to a popularity that reached its astonishing height in the Elizabethan age, and thereafter declined until the present day, when their use is largely a habit, of which, if we became alive to it, we should probably try to break ourselves, either from a striving after originality, or because sententiousness is one of the bugbears of the modern mind.

There were originally two sources of proverbial wisdom. One was the common man, from whom came the proverbs of distilled experience such as 'A bird in the hand is worth two in the bush'. The other was the wise man, or oracle, whose utterances were the result of reflection, and were received as rules of life by the folk, who had neither time nor mental capacity to meditate upon fundamental truths. The ordinary man was busy making sure that the bird remained in his hand. Once he had discovered the uselessness of two birds in the bush, or ten in the wood, or a hundred in the air, as against the practical satisfaction of one firmly seized hold of, he registered this conviction as a bit of everyday common sense which it would be well to remember, and passed it on. His comment became a familiar saying, a byword, a proverb. In course of time it was quoted by a writer either in its obvious sense, or with a transferred meaning to give point to some quite other subject, thus taking to itself a new characteristic of a proverb. Similarly, as education became more general, the sayings, or *sententiae*, of the wise men were incorporated in books, and gradually penetrated downwards until they were adopted as proverbs by the people. In both cases there is the process of gradual penetration of the spoken word from above to below and below to above, with literature as a kind of eternally moving wheel on which proverbs were caught up, and from which they were thrown off again. Perhaps, therefore, an introduction to a Dictionary of Proverbs which quotes so freely from English literature may be allowed to approach the use of proverbs through English learning, English books, and their writers.

Sayings with a proverbial currency existed in England as far back as the first half of the eighth century, as we know from a letter preserved among the correspondence of Wynfrith, the Northumbrian missionary, perhaps better known as Boniface. The writer, stressing the evils of delay, reminds his correspondent of the Saxon saying (*Memento Saxonicum verbum*): '*Oft dædlata domæ for-eldit sigisitha gahwem; swyltit þi ana.*'[1] (A coward [?sluggard] often misses glory in some high enterprise; therefore he dies alone.) This is surely the 'Delays are dangerous' of later centuries? In an embryonic form, too, proverbs can be traced in the collections of Gnomic verses which appear in the earliest Anglo-Saxon literature. Three such collections form part of the *Exeter Book*, presented to the Cathedral library by Leofric, first Bishop of Exeter, before the year 1050. The sayings are short, sententious, usually moral in purpose, and of a severely practical nature. There was no loafing in the sun for our Anglo-Saxon forbears, no trusting that the next meal would appear of its own accord. '*Seoc se biþ þe to seldan ieteð þeah hine món on sunnan læde . ne mæg he be þy wedre wesan þeah hit sy wearm on sumera.*' (He who eats too seldom will be ill. Though he be led into the sun, he cannot exist upon good weather, though it be warm in summer.)[2] Proverbial utterances such as these transmitted by oral tradition long before they were put on paper, were concrete fragments of wisdom, the result of observation. They were commonplaces in the oldest sense of the word, because they

[1] *Monumenta Germaniae Historica: Epistolarum*, vol. iii, pt. i, p. 428. Mr. Kenneth Sisam, whose translation of the Anglo-Saxon is given above, prefers 'coward', but thinks it is possible that *dædlata* might be taken as sluggard' owing to the context.

[2] *Exeter Book*, pt. ii, p. 40 (E.E.T.S. 1934).

embodied universal truths. They might be shrewd, they may occasionally have been witty; but shrewdness and wit were more often qualities that accrued to the proverb at a later stage of its development, and belonged not so much to the original saying as to the aptness of its application.

Proverbs in a more recognizable form occur in those homilies and chronicles of our early literature which were spoken and preached to the people. They were proverbs of good counsel, the wisdom of the Bible and the early Fathers of the Church made understandable for a simple people by vivid similes taken from everyday life. 'Open not thine heart to every man, lest he requite thee with a shrewd turn' becomes 'Tell never thy foe that thy foot acheth': and the writer of the *Ancrene Riwle*, the *Rules and Duties of Monastic Life*, implores the three devout women to whom his treatise is addressed to subdue the too, too insistent calls of the flesh, for, 'Dear sisters ... The flesh is here at home, as earth upon earth, and therefore, it is brisk and bold, as it is said, 'The cock is brave on his own dunghill".' The *Ancrene Riwle* was written early in the thirteenth century, and by this time the literature of other countries was becoming known. The writings of the Greeks and Romans were eagerly collected and studied in the English monasteries; the French fables and romances had their readers and imitators: and thus proverbs of foreign origin filtered in, were translated into English, and gradually incorporated in the writings in the vernacular.

From a very early date, again, we find short collections of proverbs cropping up in old manuscripts of various types. Three leaves covered with proverbs in Latin and Anglo-Saxon have recently come to light in the middle of an eleventh-century Hymnal, now in the library of Durham Cathedral.[1] Similar collections of a somewhat later date occur in manuscripts in the British Museum, in Oxford, and in Cambridge. Sometimes only half the sentence is written in English, probably because it was so well known, and the whole of the Latin equivalent is given, e.g. 'For my sleve ybroke [men me refuce]: *Pro manica fracta manus est mea sepe redacta.*' We may wonder why the scribes should interrupt their set task, as they did in the Durham MS., to make a copy of some forty-six proverbs. One reason may be that proverbs were of practical use to the medieval clerk. He had to teach Latin grammar to the novices, and what method of teaching could be better than making them familiar with the sayings of everyday life? We know that this system was practised, for at the end of Ælfric's Grammar, dating from the tenth century, there are Latin colloquies, with the Anglo-Saxon written between the lines, describing the daily tasks of life in a monastery.[2] Teaching a language by 'brighter' methods is a recurring novelty!

[1] See note, *The Durham Proverbs*, on p. xxvii. I am indebted to Mr. F. Wormald, Assistant Keeper in the Department of MSS., British Museum, for bringing this manuscript to my notice when it was recently on loan in London.
[2] The colloquies were revised and enlarged by Ælfric Bata, a pupil of Aelfric, and survive only in the edited form. See T. Wright, *Biographia Britannica Literaria*, i. 496 (London, 1842);

But the main reason for these lists of proverbs was more likely to be the growing interest in the art of rhetoric. This, called *þel-cræft*, was taught even in Anglo-Saxon schools. There were many medieval text-books of rhetoric, and according to their doctrines, derived ultimately from Aristotle himself, proverbs, as a stylistic embellishment, were to be used liberally either as beginnings or endings, or still more liberally by way of amplification of subject-matter. This amplification consisted of elaborate descriptions, ornaments, digressions, and other devices; and of these, ornament and digression gave ample scope for the inclusion of proverbs, *sententiae* or *exempla*. Proverbs, again, in rhetorical practice, were employed to round off anecdotes and to point the moral so dear to the Middle Ages; or they became the starting-point of fresh anecdotes and *exempla* by means of which a devious progress was made from one subject to another. They were, too, a necessary part of the equipment of medieval secretaries, who carried on formal and official correspondence on the lines laid down by the *Ars Dictandi* of the schools. In a medieval letter the second part of the framework was the *exordium*, known also as the *proverbium*, or *Benevolentiae Captatio*, and an ambitious young cleric who hankered after a life of worldly success in the secretarial offices of Church or State was well advised to keep a list of proverbs at hand for drafting purposes. He might, indeed, be so fortunate as to possess a reference book in the *Summa de Dictamina* of Ponce de Provence, a complete letter-writer in which proverbs for use upon all occasions had already been collected, even tabulated. 'There is nothing so necessary, says Ponce, as to induce a suitable frame of mind in the reader . . .: and in no way is this so well accomplished as by a proverb. Ponce has the happy thought of providing emollient proverbs for every situation: and for the better convenience of his students these are classified and graded.'[1]

They are dreary, these far-back rhetoricians. *Sit thema*, they say, and wheel their doctrines of precept, definition, and example into place, with all the dragging mechanism of adornment and embellishment. To them matter meant nothing. Fancy and invention less than nothing. But we must linger over them, because it is to their influence on English literature —an influence that lasted till the end of the sixteenth century—that we owe the preservation of so many of our proverbs. To their influence, too, we owe the confusion between proverbs and *sententiae*. A distinction between the two may be exacted in the present day by those who scrutinize collections of proverbs, but it is a distinction that breaks down when rigidly enforced. The mistake lies in forgetting that when the proverb was first caught up into literature, and for a long time afterwards, the two, proverbs and *sententiae*, were one. Literature was under the influence of the rhetoricians, and the proverbs of the people and the *sententiae* or sayings of the philosophers were used alike as precepts and examples, and as the mechanism of style.

also *Early Scholastic Colloquies*, ed. W. H. Stevenson, Anecdota Oxoniensia, Med. and Mod. Ser., pt. xv (Clarendon Press, 1929).

[1] *The Wandering Scholars*, by Helen Waddell, p. 138 (London, 1927).

By the middle of the fourteenth century we may notice how learning
has spread. Books are no longer written only by men who have never
penetrated beyond the four walls of a monastic cell. Their authors move
about in the world, and the men and women who walk their pages mingle
the proverbial expressions of the labourers in the fields and the prentices
in the city with proverbs that have come from classical and foreign
sources. The works of Chaucer and his contemporaries show clearly how
proverbs, proverbial phrases, and proverbial similes, later to become hackneyed, but then in their first freshness, were being disseminated. With
Gower and Lydgate this dissemination meant only that they used a greater
variety of proverbs. Their manner of using them was still that of the homilies and chronicles. They brought them in as similes, to point a moral by
means of a picture: or they simply catalogued proverbs in an orgy of
sententiousness. They wrote, in fact, in the spirit of the Middle Ages.
'What is all wisdom save a collection of platitudes?' says Mr. Norman
Douglas to-day, but we fail to understand the proverb-loving side of the
medieval spirit unless we keep well in our minds that for the people of
Chaucer's time this wisdom was being newly born every day and they were
in at the birth. Chaucer shared the medieval love of sententiousness and
could cater to it, as we find him doing in the tale of *Melibeus*, where he
promises his hearers 'a moral tale vertuous', with 'more of proverbes, than
ye han herd bifore'. But, unlike Gower and Lydgate, he did more than
this. He also knew the doctrines of the rhetoricians well enough to follow
them if he chose, or to mock at them if he chose. He did both: and he went
further. Besides being the poet that he was, the lover of people and life
and beauty, he was a scholar, who loved 'to have at his beddes heed
Twenty bookes clad in blak or reed', and he was a man of affairs, an 'eminent Civil Servant' (the first layman to be Clerk of the Works in England).
In his journeyings on the Continent, as well as from his office at the Customs
and his attendances at Court, he had observed how people acted and spoke.
Above all, he had a sense of humour, a quality possessed by no English
writer before him and very few for a long time after. The greater part of
our early literature is a vast expanse of epics, homilies, and interminable
romances. We wade through narratives of battles, descriptions of courtly
love, descriptions of chivalry, and page after page of moralizing. Occasionally we find passages of surprising beauty and vivid imagery, or again
passages that strike us as unusually modern in their realism, but how seldom we laugh and how still more seldom we smile. Then Chaucer comes
upon the scene, and we watch him discovering that universal truths have
a universal application. He applies his discovery with a sense of humour,
an irony, a faculty for making his men and women spring into life, even
through the proverbs they use, that must have struck his more sophisticated readers with a delighted surprise, and may have disconcerted the
more simple, who knew nothing of the pleasure to be experienced when an
author not only uses his own wits but exacts some liveliness from those of
his reader. What effect did the Wife of Bath have on a people who were

accustomed to steady streams of sententious moralizing? With what relish she explains why her life with her five husbands was not always of the happiest, and comments that the bacon of Dunmow was never fattened for them; while a few minutes later she quotes a proverb of 'the wise astrologien Dan Phtholome'—'Of alle men his wisdom is the hyeste, That rekketh never who hath the world in honde'—in support of her contention that a husband should never begrudge his wife's generosity in matters of love so long as he does not suffer by it. This was pointing a moral with a vengeance.[1]

Down to the middle of the fifteenth century, then, we find the proverbial counsel of the Hebrew prophets, of Greece, Rome, and France, and of the English wise men, given to the people first by the priests and chroniclers, later by the poets and translators. The first dated book to issue from Caxton's press was the *Dictes and Sayings of the Philosophers*. The Earl Rivers, brother-in-law of Edward IV, had gone on a pilgrimage to Spain in the year 1473 to return thanks for restored health. A fellow-pilgrim gave him this book, in its original French version, to enliven the slowly-passing days of the voyage, and it so appealed to him that on his return he made a translation and gave it to Caxton to print. It is a collection of didactic sayings which should be read nowadays only by the unhappy proverb-hunter; but the public of its day called for three editions within twelve years. At the same time, all over the country, local gossip and tradition were coining new proverbs. How did the 'wise men of Gotham' and 'Waltham's calf' come into being? Nobody knows. But by the end of the fifteenth century they were proverbial figures.

Looked at in one way, the history of the use and disuse of proverbs is a progression from the concrete to the abstract. Our economists of to-day theorize about the 'inevitability of gradualness'. Our ancestors of the less cerebral fifteenth century meant much the same thing, but they might say 'Little by little the cat eateth up the bacon flickle', or 'Feather by feather the goose is plucked', making their point by means of the proverbial imagery that was so dear to them. And then, shortly after the opening of the sixteenth century, people and literature became not merely proverb-loving but proverb-conscious. They were to remain so for at least a hundred years, and for this there were two reasons. One was that the folk themselves were now speaking, almost thinking, along canalized lines of proverbs. They had taken what had been given to them in literature, and they had taken the practical maxims of their own daily life, and both were constantly on their lips. When the correspondents of the *Paston Letters* wished to drive home a request, or make some observation more telling, a proverb was at hand. What somebody had said before was the right expression to use again. In the morality plays proverbs were frequent. In the early Tudor drama the stock figures of Virtue and Wisdom opened their

[1] In *Chaucer's Use of Proverbs* (Cambridge, Mass., 1934), Mr. Whiting has given an interesting study of the literary artist at work, using the sayings of the people and the philosophers alike to raise a laugh, to heighten his character drawing, and to give point to his own comments as his narratives proceed.

mouths and strings of proverbs came forth. We turn to the Latin grammar books of the day, the *Vulgaria* of Stanbridge, Whittinton, and Horman, and find that although morning school was hampered by physical discomfort, and the first phrase of the day was *Ova frixa cum petasone quibus vescebar in ientaculo eructare me faciunt* (The fryed egges and bakon that I eate at brekfaste umbraydeth my stomake), the boys went on to learn *Fatuus est cocus qui nescit lambere labia* (He is an euyll coke that can not lycke his owne lyppes), and *Amantium iræ amoris redintegratio est* (The variaunce of lovers (Sayth Terence) is the renuynge of loue). Thus, as education spread, the sayings of Terence and other Latin authors became part of the background of many boys, and were used as proverbs equally with those which might more truly be called English: and some years later Helen's retort to Pandarus, 'Falling in after falling out may make them three', would strike a special chord in an audience who loved to toss proverbs about.

Added to this native fondness for proverbs was the influence of one curious sidestream of the great flood of knowledge let loose by the Renaissance. Erasmus had published his *Adagia* in the year 1500, and it is not too much to say that with this book he acquainted men with the great figures of classical antiquity by means of proverbs. The *Adagia* is a collection of anecdotes running into thousands, each one illustrating a proverb or explaining its origin. It was one of the most widely read books of the first half of the sixteenth century, and the insatiable spirit of the time lapped up old adages together with new knowledge, while with an awakened zest for learning it turned to the sources themselves, translated them, and brought them within reach of the many. As the years passed, the literature of Italy, Spain, and France was brought back to England by the ever-increasing number of men who completed their education as a matter of course by travel on the Continent. Italians, Spaniards, Frenchmen, settled in England, made grammar books and phrase books, translated the writings of their peoples, and put the picturesque proverbial wisdom of their own countries into fresh English words. So we have Sainlien's *French Littelton* (1566), Sandford's *Houres of Recreation* (1572), Minsheu's *Spanish Grammar* (1591), Stepney's *Spanish Schoolmaster* (1591), and above all, Florio's *First* and *Second Fruits* (1578 and 1591), the dialogues which he wrote to acquaint Englishmen with the proverbs from beyond the Alps. 'Proverbs', he says, 'are the pith, the proprieties, the proofes, the purities, the elegancies, as the commonest so the commendablest phrases of a language. To use them is a grace, to understand them a good'; and he ends, with what truth, 'to gather them a paine to me, though gaine to thee'. The *Second Fruits* were published in 1591, twelve years before their author turned the essays of a Frenchman into a classic of English literature. Looking at them we can readily understand how the imagery of these proverbial phrases must have appealed to the people of 'this stirring time, and pregnant prime of invention when everie bramble is fruitefull, when everie molhill hath cast of[f] the winters mourning garment, and when everie man is busilie woorking to feede his owne fancie'. And already the English people had their own collection of proverbs. In 1546 John Heywood had written a *Dialogue conteining Proverbes*, which was so successful that by the year 1598 it had run through six editions.

In 1553 came Thomas Wilson's *Arte of Rhetorique*, one of the earliest and most popular text-books of rhetoric in English. Wilson followed the medieval rhetoricians in recommending the use of proverbs in writing, for emphasis, amplification, adornment, embellishment; and advised his readers to cull their proverbs from the ancient writers and from Master Heywood's book. The *Arte of Rhetorique* was revised in 1560 and went into six editions in fifteen years. It was probably studied by every young writer of the day; and in the many works affected by its teachings we again remark how impossible it is at this time to separate proverbs and *sententiae*. The proverbs and sayings of the people were taken up and used by the writers; the sentences introduced by the writers were so much quoted that they made their way into daily speech and became proverbs.

By the beginning of Elizabeth's reign every one—scholars, wits, courtiers, writers, the queen herself—spoke and wrote in proverbs, even invented them. They welcomed them for their common sense, or because of the 'sweet relished phrases' that struck the wide-open eyes and ears of the time with a delicious novelty; and they used them because writing was still under the influence of the rhetoricians. This taste for proverbs was heightened still more by Lyly and the Euphuists. Lyly did not set a fashion for proverbs. The fashion was already there. But he so exaggerated the fondness of the age for ornate and fanciful language that on a first reading of his *Euphues* we hardly realize how closely packed with proverbial sayings it is, hidden as they are amidst elaborate phrases and similes, play upon words, and strange parallels from natural history. Euphuism—the art of saying a thing and saying it again less clearly—swept over the court, and for a time became the fashionable language of the day. It could not fail to have some reverberations outside the court. Every proverb-collection of later years contains sentences that might have come, very often did come, straight out of Lyly. But they were none the less proverbs. They had been quoted or handed about in general currency long enough to bear the stamp of proverbs and make themselves recognized as such.

In fact, the Elizabethan age was soaked in proverbs. Drayton wrote a sonnet (not a very good one) in proverbs; and when, in the year 1601, a Bill to avoid the Double Payment of Debts was read in the House of Commons, Mr. Thomas Jones even made a speech composed entirely of proverbs. The Honourable Member said:

'It is now my chance to Speak something, and that without Humming or Hawing. I think this Law is a good Law; Even Reckoning makes long Friends; As far goes the *Penny* as the *Penny's* Master. *Vigilantibus non dormientibus jura subveniunt.* Pay the Reckoning over Night, and you shall not be troubled in the Morning . If ready Money be *Mensura Publica*, let every Man cut his Coat according to his Cloth. When his old Suit is in the Wain, let him stay till that his Money bring a new Suit in the Increase. Therefore, I think the Law to be good, and I wish it a good Passage'.[1]

He had said what he wanted to say, said it shortly, and everybody knew what he meant, which is not always the case with parliamentary speeches. Proverbs, too, were woven into tapestries, illustrated in paintings, engraved on cutlery—'For all the world like cutler's poetry Upon a knife'—on posy rings or on beer-mugs. 'When the ale is in the wit is out', 'Soberness conceals what drunkenness reveals', 'Hear much and speak little', may all have preached moderation to the heavy drinker from the rim of his tankard. And the trenchers on the table may have borne the welcome motto, 'Better fill a man's belly than his eye', in strange contrast to the present day, when with each Christmas a calendar exhorts us to 'sell our dole and buy hyacinths to feed the soul'—surely too well-fed a piece of aestheticism?

In the Elizabethan drama proverbs abounded, especially, as Professor Max Förster has pointed out,[2] in the comedies, because the Elizabethans loved a pun, and great play could be made with the literal interpretation of proverbs. Many plays had proverbial titles, *Fast Bind fast Find; Hot Anger soon Cold; 'Tis good sleeping in a Whole Skin; Measure for Measure.* In *The Two Angry Women of Abingdon* one of the characters is called 'Nicholas Proverbs', and lives up to his name by uttering little else. The dialogue is a continual crossing (do we call it *backchat*?) of proverbs.

In private life men scribbled proverbs into their commonplace books, perhaps because it pleased them to have a collection of these sayings to turn to for their own reading, perhaps because writers like Bacon recommended the keeping of notebooks for Formularies and Elegancies—what he also calls Commonplaces—ready to be drawn upon when required.

If we examine the literature of the Elizabethans with an eye merely to the use they have made of proverbs we find one thing common to them all —except Shakespeare. They use proverbs, proverbial similes, adages, wise sayings, what we choose to call them—for their purpose all are alike— either by quoting them directly or by clothing them in more ornate language, but seldom for any effect other than that of emphasis or vivid simile, according to the literary practice of the time. 'A chair there for his Lordship?—Forbear your kindness; an unbidden guest should travel as Dutch women go to church, Bear their stools with them'; 'I do love her just as a man holds a wolf by the ears'; 'It is a dowry, methinks, should make that sunburnt proverb false, "And wash the Aethiop white"'; 'I speak plainly, for plain-dealing is a jewel, and he that useth it shall die a beggar'; 'If one be sicke, what wouldst thou have him doe?—Bee sure that hee make not his physician his heire'; 'As ther can be no bargaine where both be not agreed, neither any Indentures sealed where the one will not consent . . .'

---

[1] *Townshend's Historical Collections*, p. 283 (1680).
[2] 'Das Elisabethanische Sprichwort nach Th. Draxe's Treasurie of Ancient Adagies', in *Anglia*, vol. xlii, p. 361 (1918).

When we come to Shakespeare the case is indeed altered. In his chapter on Shakespeare in the *Cambridge History of English Literature* the late Professor Saintsbury said: 'Euphuism and word-play'—to which we might add, use of proverbs—'of course, are very frequent—shockingly frequent to some people, it would seem. But they are merely things that the poet plays at—whether for his own amusement or his reader's, or both, is a question, perhaps of some curiosity, but of no real importance.' We pause, then, to note that the whole question of the use of proverbs in literature has merely a curious interest, but let us watch Shakespeare at work.

To begin with, he is up to all the tricks of his craft, and it is hard to believe that he was not playing with his material for his own amusement as well as his reader's. As a craftsman he would not be happy until he could use all the new tools that he found to his hand when he came from the country to London. And so the brilliant, light-hearted young Shakespeare must have delighted in throwing off such a *tour de force* as *Love's Labour's Lost*, crammed as it is with puns, allusions, play upon words, and play upon proverbs, which would all at once be caught up by the audience of the day. Was Euphuism the favourite language of the Court? Then that should be the language of his characters, and we get dialogues, for instance whenever Mercutio comes upon the scene, such as might have taken place between any two young Elizabethan courtiers. A few years later we find a parody of Euphuism put into Falstaff's mouth—a sign that Shakespeare was becoming sufficiently independent and conscious of his own powers to mock at literary fashions? 'There is a thing, Harry, which thou hast often heard of, and it is known to many in our land by the name of pitch: this pitch, as ancient writers do report, doth defile; so doth the company thou keepest. . . . If then the tree may be known by the fruit, as the fruit by the tree, then, peremptorily I speak it, there is virtue in that Falstaff.' But Shakespeare goes further than this. He could, of course, and did, make his people quote strings of proverbs or play catch-as-catch-can with them; but when he used them allusively, or as the small change of conversation, they came out transmuted from a contemplative mind that was stored with them. Writers of the Elizabethan age often wrote for writing's sake. They were in love with imagery, with words and fine style. The matter was sometimes secondary. 'As . . .', they begin, and the long, wordy similes go spiralling up, more and more involved, gathering proverbs, ink-horn terms, classical allusions, on their way, 'So . . .', and with leisurely deliberation they unwind themselves from their labyrinth. But what is it all about? Shakespeare's men and women might speak in fine words and fine style, but they also lived and thought. They are the mouthpieces of thoughts tinged with the proverbs that are as surely a part of their background as they were of their creator's.

And so it is that the proverbs in Shakespeare become most interesting when they colour the thoughts of his characters and echo in their words, as in the many forms in which 'Constant dropping wears the stone' recurs; or Hamlet's bitter reply, 'No, nor mine now', to his uncle's 'I have nothing to do with this answer, Hamlet, these words are not mine', reminiscent of 'When the word is out it belongs to another' and 'A word spoken cannot be recalled', both proverbs very much on men's lips at the time. Nothing could more forcibly impress on us the cold-blooded savagery of the Moor in *Titus Andronicus* than his use of a proverb. The nurse has brought in the coal-black fruit of Aaron's and Tamora's lust. Aaron asks how many people have seen the child. The nurse replies 'Cornelia the midwife, and myself, And no one else but the deliver'd empress'. He repeats her words, 'The empress, the midwife, and yourself', then gets up and stands over her, and says very deliberately: 'Two may keep counsel when the third's away. Go to the empress. Tell her this I said', and without an instant's pause stabs her. And can there be anything more poignant than the attempt at a jest made by Lear's poor, shivering fool, when all around him he sees the elements, his master's wits, and his own world dissolving: 'And I'll go to bed at noon'? No one but Shakespeare has dared to let a heart break on a proverb.

In Ben Jonson, who held that 'Figures' were invented for aid, not for ornament, we find a hint that even in speech proverbs should be used with discrimination. For him, 'Ancient proverbs may illuminate a cooper's or a constable's wit', but may not be allowed a person of standing. Downright, in *Every Man in his Humour*, has 'not so much as a good phrase in his belly, but all old iron and rusty proverbs'. In this Jonson was somewhat ahead of his time, but his taste was sound. Gradually, as the seventeenth century wore into the eighteenth, the use of proverbs as a literary fashion died out. Proverbial phrases remained, but they became the idioms of the language and were used insensitively. Neither speculative thought nor an age of reason had a use for proverbs. Men had absorbed the new learning. They had a richer language and they were now interested in teasing out thoughts that could no longer be helped to expression by flashing quotations and proverbs about with all the eager delight of a child displaying a new toy. Motherwell, in his Introduction to Henderson's *Scottish Proverbs* in 1832, summed up the change that had taken place when he said:

'A man whose mind has been enlarged by education, and who has a complete mastery over the riches of his own language, expresses his ideas in his own words; and when he refers to anything beyond the matter under his view, glances towards an abstract principle. A vulgar man, on the other hand, uses those proverbial forms which tradition and daily use have made familiar to him; and when he makes a remark which needs confirmation, he clenches it by a proverb.'

We may take it as a sign that proverbs were on the wane that they now began to be collected so zealously. Each proverb-monger has helped to push them further into the past by finding a new kind of interest in them. They are the concentrated wisdom of the ages, the dark sayings of wise men, 'old sayd saws'. If we wish to study folk-lore, weather lore, popular superstitions, we are to turn to proverbs. If we are interested in philology we may find old forms of speech preserved for us in proverbs, though we must often leave their origin unexplained, or—and sometimes this has its own fascination—choose between several explanations. To this day, if we have pursued an objective by every means known to us, we say that we have left no stone unturned, but we never picture ourselves laboriously moving stones about, or wonder why we should do so. Yet this is a proverbial expression that has descended to us still wrapt in the mists of antiquity. The phrase πάντα λίθον κινεῖν, of which a variant, πάντα κινῆσαι πέτρον, occurs in Euripides, was said by Zenobius, a Roman collector of proverbs, to have originated in the fifth century B.C. After the battle of Salamis a rumour spread that the defeated commander had buried his treasure near the scene of battle. A Theban, on hearing this, hastily bought the ground and started digging. He dug and dug; unearthed no treasure. At last, in the usual trusting manner of the Greeks, he betook himself to the Delphic Oracle for counsel: and the Oracle, in the usual exasperatingly cryptic manner of oracles, told him to move every stone, 'πάντα λίθον κίνει'. So, if we leave no stone unturned are we to think of an avaricious Theban returning tired and hungry from a visit to the Oracle to resume digging operations? Perhaps. But then we learn from Liddell and Scott that the phrase *may* have come from the game of draughts. Did the ancient Greeks spend long hours over their games of draughts, turning every stone not once but several times, and moving it seldom, like any two comfortable Frenchmen sitting over their game and their *fine* in a provincial café? Again, say the painstaking authorities, πάντα λίθον (or πέτρον) κινεῖν may have referred to the fisherman turning over stones as he hunted for crabs. Shall we choose the stooping fisherman, moving slowly from stone to stone as he fills his basket? Has the sun risen to show how golden the sands are, how blue the waters of the Ionian Sea, to warm into iridescent blues and greens, to quicken into an oblique and malevolent activity, the inert masses hidden pale beneath the stones? Or do fishermen hunt for crabs in the early morning hours, when everything is still grey—as grey as those mists in which our phrase is shrouded?

By the first half of the eighteenth century proverbs had considerably depreciated. The dictates of literary style no longer demanded their use; and as they turned into commonplaces and familiar tags to be bandied about in conversation, their wisdom, their pith, and their quaintness were felt to pall. If the drawing-room conversation of his day was at all like the picture Swift gives, he did well to pillory it in *Polite Conversation*; and it is no wonder if the *badinage* of Miss Notable, Mr. Neverout, and their circle left people's ears on the prick for their own and their neighbours' lapses into the inanities of the commonplace. By 1741 Lord Chesterfield was advising his son that 'A man of fashion never has recourse to proverbs and vulgar aphorisms', which were 'so many proofs of having kept bad and low company'.

Of course, proverbs still persisted. The conventions of literary taste and polite usage might frown on them, but they had become a familiar inheritance, and were embodied in literature and traditional speech. The conscious effort for the sophisticated was how not to use them. After all, we cling to our familiar sayings. It is comfortable to repeat what some one has said before. We do not need to defend our own ideas or feel apologetic about our efforts to be amusing. The wise sayings have been accepted from time immemorial: the witty ones have always raised a laugh. It is so easy, too, to find a proverb, or a phrase that with long usage has become proverbial. If we are lazy, or in a hurry, we can always fall back on the wisdom that has been spoon-fed to us, without going through all the painful process of thinking for ourselves, or finding our own words to 'point a moral' and 'adorn a tale'. Perhaps that is why we may count on having at least one proverb served up to us with our daily paper. Leader-writers must work in a hurry.

In the nineteenth century proverbs still occurred frequently in novels and in the writings of the Victorian moralists. Scott used them on principle, because he believed they were too good to be lost, and indeed this is true of many of the Scottish ones. Trollope used them in what we might call good journeyman fashion. He wrote quickly and his output was large. He did not turn aside to find more uncommon ways of expressing himself when there were clusters of good proverbs to his hand. But his proverbs are always pointed and relevant. The readers of his day were content that the inhabitants of Barchester should come alive to them out of a familiar proverbial background such as they all had in their own homes; and if we like Trollope now part of his charm goes if we deny him his proverbs. It is right that we should pause with him to say 'Better the devil you know than the devil you don't know', while the miserable bishop twiddles his thumbs in his easy chair, and half wishes that Mr. Slope may get the better of the battle raging over his head. The moralists used proverbs with all the sententiousness of the Middle Ages and none of their vividness. It was unfortunate that the pithy counsel of the early preachers should later be made an excuse for so much long-windedness.

And to-day? Through the fog of a wintry morning the newspaper-seller at the street corner hardens into shape, slapping warmth into his hands above his bright orange newsbill, and calling 'Pact with Rome'. As we draw nearer he drops into a confidential snarl and tells us 'Rome wasn't built in a day'. If we spend a penny to ask where he got his saying, he replies that it comes from an old song. An 'old song'? Has the building of Rome shared the fate of Milton's sable cloud and become the burden of a music-hall ditty? With a proverb, again, Professor Housman adds a scorpion to his whip and lashes the unfortunate editors of classical texts: 'Misfortunes never come single, and the prattlers about P's authority are afflicted not only with lack of understanding but with loss of memory'; a reviewer begs a novelist 'not, in fact, to launch a splendid ship on a ha'porth of tar'; and a lively fashion writer brings 'According to Cocker' into a discussion of how much hair is to be shown under the newest spring hats.

And then we come across these words in an essay on the author of *Piers*

Plowman: 'He is concerned to be, not pretty, but wide as the whole world —a sun of righteousness shining alike on diadem and dunghill.' Was Mr. F. L. Lucas remembering here that 'The sun is never the worse for shining on a dunghill?' With one sentence he has evoked for us a whole panorama. Chaucer's pilgrims, stilled from their ribaldry, their japes, and their 'worldly vanitees', attend while the good man of religioun expounds Holy Writ to them. 'Holy Writ', he says, 'may nat been defouled.' And, because his business is 'To drawen folk to hevene by . . . good ensample', he adds 'Na-more than the sun that shyneth on the mixen'. The pilgrims fade, and their place is taken by Falstaff and his rascally companions sitting over their cups in the Garter Inn. The fat sinner thinks he spies entertainment and angels to be had from the Merry Wives: 'Page's wife . . . even now . . . examined my parts with most judicious oeilliades; sometimes the beam of her view gilded my foot, sometimes my portly belly.' Whereupon Pistol, weasel-like even when sodden, thrusts 'Then did the sun on dunghill shine'. And is the same saying at the back of Hamlet's thoughts, as another writer has suggested,[1] when he calls the sun a 'good kissing carrion', or from being proverb-minded have we become proverb-haunted? Let us stop before Mr. Smith's legions band themselves into a ghostly army, to make us flee every book that has ever been written and call forlornly for a long-lost yesterday, when proverbs signified pothooks, and the wisdom of the ages straggled inkily across the lines of a child's copy-book.

II

PROVERB COLLECTORS AND PROVERB LITERATURE

THE first collection of English proverbs—*A Dialogue conteining the number in effect of all the proverbes in the Englishe tongue*—appeared in 1546. John Heywood, the author, belonged to the long line of kings' jesters, and may well have invented many of the proverbs set down in his *Dialogue*. His book marked the beginning of an enthusiasm for collecting proverbs which continued more or less steadily for two hundred years. For fifty or sixty years after its issue no fresh collection was published; but we find the antiquaries and topographers of Elizabeth's day zealous in retrieving the sayings of the counties they surveyed. Sometimes these sayings are snatches of weather lore or husbandry current in certain parts of the country; again, they are local pleasantries, what the French call *blasons populaires*, allusions that have a certain quality of the nickname in them, hitting off regional peculiarities or characters, crystallizing ancient gossip. They were specially noticed in the next century by Thomas Fuller, of *Worthies* fame, who seems to have ransacked the pages of his antiquarian predecessors for what he calls 'local' and 'nominal' proverbs.

After Heywood the next notable collector of proverbs[2] is David Fergusson,

---

[1] M. P. Tilley in *Modern Language Review*, vol. xi, p. 462 (1916).

[2] In these pages only the more outstanding collections of proverbs are recorded. Few of the others have more than a bibliographical interest.

minister of the Gospel at Dunfermline, twice Moderator of the General
Assembly of the Church of Scotland, and possessor of the happy talent of
being able 'by his pleasant and facetious conversation' to please and pacify
his peevish king when the latter was in one of his not infrequent furies—
perhaps because the preacher and his most un-royal master had a love of
proverbs in common? Although Fergusson died in 1598, it was not until
1641 that his collection of *Scottish Proverbs* was printed. Some of his
proverbs are definitely Scottish in origin; but many of them are merely
Scotticized forms of those found in Heywood.

In 1614 William Camden brought out a second edition of his *Remaines
Concerning Britaine*. This included a collection of nearly four hundred
proverbs, of which he says: 'Whenas Proverbs are concise, witty, and wise
Speeches grounded vpon long experience, conteining for the most part
good caueats, and therefore both profitable and delightfull; I thought it
not vnfit to set downe heere Alphabetically some of the selectest, and most
vsuall amongst vs, as beeing worthy to haue place amongst the wises[t]
Speeches.' The collection, largely taken from Heywood, was augmented
in the edition of 1623, and again, although Camden had died in the meantime, in the editions of 1629 and 1636.

Early in the seventeenth century, Thomas Draxe, an English clergyman,
interested himself in proverbs. Draxe was something of a scholar, and had
already published, in 1612, a *Collection of Proper, Choice and Elegant Latin
Words and Phrases*. In his view, proverbs gave strength and weight to
sermons and speeches, and were useful for rhetorical adornment (a familiar
phrase, this); also, provided that those *rudia, ridicula et impia proverbia*
were omitted, proverbs were the 'rules of life'. Draxe was a native of
Warwickshire, and may have set down county sayings familiar to his contemporary, Shakespeare,[1] but he explored many fields for his *Bibliotheca
Scholastica Instructissima. Or, A Treasurie of Ancient Adagies, and sententious Prouerbes* (1616), and garnered over two thousand proverbs. They
are arranged under subject headings such as *Anger, Certaintie, Gluttony,
Carnall Loue, Restitution*, &c., a system which always makes for difficulties,
but was nevertheless to be adopted by the next collector of proverbs,
with the sole difference that this time the subject headings would be in
Latin.

Draxe was followed in 1639 by John Clarke, Pastor of the Church of
Fiskerton, near Lincoln, the third of a succession of clergymen who found
the study of proverbs a satisfying hobby. Clarke's interest in the subject
appears to have been mainly that of a grammarian. He had already edited
the *Colloquies* of Erasmus and a Latin Grammar Book or *Phraseologia*;
and in the foreword to his *Paroemiologia* he speaks of it as being specially
intended for use in grammar schools. The *Paroemiologia* is a collection
'gleaned out of all writers, I could read or meet withall . . . beside my owne
observation of many golden proverbs, dropping now and then out of
vulgar mouthes imâ de plebe'. The proverbs, Latin and English, are

---

[1] Professor Max Förster made this suggestion in *Anglia*, vol. xlii, p. 364.

paralleled (and alas! too often buried) under Latin subject headings, modelled on the *Chiliades* of Erasmus.

We next come to George Herbert's collection of *Outlandish Proverbs*. It was not published until 1640, seven years after his death, and contains no foreword. In the second edition, *Jacula Prudentum* (1651), many proverbs have been added by a later editor. We may guess that Herbert collected proverbs for his own edification, and that his interest in them dated from his early, ambitious days, when he learnt French, Spanish, and Italian with a view to devoting himself to a life outside the Church. The foreign grammar and phrase books of his time made a feature of the selection of choice proverbs;[1] and we do, in fact, find many of these repeated in Herbert.

With Herbert we leave the Church for a while, and encounter the next collector of proverbs in James Howell, Historiographer Royal to Charles II. Howell took a real delight in proverbs. 'Though in point of Generation', he says, 'they [proverbs] are a kind of Naturall Children, and of an unknown birth, yet are they no by-blows or bastards, but legitimated by Prescription and long Tract of Ancestriall Time.' His interest in them was partly antiquarian, partly philological (we remember that he revised Cotgrave's Dictionary in 1650, that he wrote Grammars of both the French and Spanish languages, the latter with Remarks upon the Portuguese Dialect, and that his *Proverbs* themselves are bound up with his *Lexicon Tetraglotton*, a lengthy Dictionary of the English, French, Spanish, and Italian tongues), and partly that of a widely travelled man who had the traveller's passion for seeing one thing in relation to another. For him, different races revealed their varying attitudes to life in their proverbs, and he found the comparison an absorbing study. His miscellany, dated 1659, is divided into seven parts: (1) a collection of British Proverbs, which we recognize as being very much a reprint of Camden with additions from other sources; (2) a selection of English proverbs rendered into French, Italian, and Spanish; (3), (4), (5), and (6) selections of French, Italian, Spanish, and British (i.e. Welsh) proverbs with English translations: lastly, with great optimism, he includes a collection of 'New sayings which may serve for Proverbs to Posterity'. Howell reprinted liberally from the collections that had preceded him; but unfortunately he had no method of arrangement, and it is almost impossible to find any given proverb without long search under all of his seven headings.

The first index to a proverb collection, by this time badly needed, was provided by Torriano, who succeeded Howell in 1666 with a large collection of *Italian Proverbs and Proverbial Phrases translated into English*, to which he attached a set of *Dialogues* after the manner of Florio. Giovanni Torriano was a Professor of Italian and a Master of Arts. He had revised and enlarged Florio's *Dictionarie*; and had already, in 1642, issued a small collection of *Select Italian Proverbs*. He, again, pointed out that by means of proverbs the nature and genius of a nation were easily discovered, and

[1] See p. xiii.

that proverbs were 'the Philosophy of a People', as well as a happy method of acquiring proficiency in a foreign tongue. His collection is unwieldy, but includes a vast number of proverbs, which can even be found once the method of the index has been mastered; and the dialogues at the end yield entertainment if not proverbs.

John Ray, who next demands attention, was the first collector to make a manageable book: his *English Proverbs*, first issued in 1670, still remains one of the best and most useful compilations. He was well qualified by training and interests to undertake the task, being a naturalist with a strongly antiquarian bent and keen powers of observation, combined with emphatic views on how best to make use of the information he gathered. Thus, in his introduction to the first edition of his book, he explains the reasons that have led him to classify his proverbs and arrange them under leading words in alphabetical order; and he also gives a list of the sources from which he has drawn. The work is, however, far from being a mere reprint of preceding collections: as well as including many additional proverbs gleaned by Ray and his friends from familiar discourse, it is annotated, as no former collection had been; and the notes, learned, leisurely, and genial, are still invaluable for the study of dialect and folk-lore.

After Ray, we find no noteworthy collection of proverbs until 1721, when James Kelly's *Complete Collection of Scottish Proverbs* made its appearance. Nothing is known about the compiler except that he was by birth and education a Scotsman, and seems to have spent a great part of his life in England. The collection, which he made to give himself 'a Harmless, Innocent, Scholar-like Divertisement in [his] declining Years', was the largest that had so far appeared. It contains over three thousand proverbs, many of them Scottish only in so far as they give the Scottish form of proverbs common to many countries. Kelly too often spoilt the shape and sense of his proverbs in an attempt to adapt them to English understanding, but his work remains a very useful one; and his curiously ungrammatical notes (many of which have been quoted by Mr. Smith) abound in good sense and good, if at times faintly sardonic, humour. Also, he added to his book a workable index.

In 1732 proverbs for the first time made their appeal to the medical profession. Thomas Fuller, M.D., the compiler of *Gnomologia: Adagies and Proverbs*, was a physician practising in Kent. In his introduction he skirted controversial ground by saying that there might be a distinction between adages and proverbs, and refusing to determine which were which. 'All that I take upon me here to do, is only to throw together a vast confus'd heap of unsorted things, old and new, which you may pick over and make use of, according to your Judgment and Pleasure.' He arranges his proverbs in the alphabetical order of the initial word (as Kelly also had done), 'not', as he expressly says, 'as any help to the Reader but to my self, that I might the better avoid Repetitions'. The book is largely made up of proverbs from Ray's and Kelly's collections, with the addition of

'Apothegms, Maxims, Proverbs, acute Expressions, vulgar sayings' which he had noted himself in the course of long years of reading.

Both Ray, who took Scottish proverbs from Fergusson, and Fuller, who with still greater lavishness drew on Kelly, had a regrettable tendency to soften the Scottish tongue for the delicate English ear. Ray had not noticed the printer's foreword to Fergusson's proverbs, which says: 'And whereas there are some old Scottish words not in use now, bear with that, because if ye alter those words, the Proverb will have no grace.' Grace they might have after alteration, but the force had departed. 'You cannot sell the cow and sup the milk', says the Scottish proverb, and we can almost hear the thin lips snap on the last word. Fuller makes it persuasive: 'If you sell the cow you sell her milk too.'

In 1737 'Gentle Shepherd' Ramsay was moved to publish his *Scots Proverbs*, 'More complete and correct than any heretofore published', by indignation at Kelly's collection, which he calls 'a late large Book . . . fou of Errors in a Stile neither *Scots* nor *English*'. We may think he was too well pleased with his own effort, and too hard on Kelly; but he produced a fairly good, typical, Scottish collection, again arranged alphabetically under the first word in each proverb. At the end he put a glossary, quaintly entitled 'Explanation of the Words less frequent amongst our Gentry than the Commons'; and he prefaced the whole by a flowery dedication to the Tenantry of Scotland, Farmers of the Dales, and Storemasters of the Hills, of which the following is a sample: 'On a spare Hour, when the Day is clear, behind a Ruck, or on the green Howm, draw the Treasure [i.e. this book] frae your Pouch, and enjoy the pleasant Companion. Ye happy Herds, while your Hirdsell are feeding on the flowery Braes, you may eithly make your sells Master of the haleware.'

For nearly a century after Ramsay no new collection worthy of note was published, although the older ones, such as Ray's, were reprinted and augmented. In 1823 Isaac D'Israeli included an essay on *The Philosophy of Proverbs* in the second series of his *Curiosities of Literature*. It is discursive, in the style of the author and the day, but still a useful essay—literary, comparative, and anecdotal—and we can see in it the beginning of a critical attitude towards proverbs.

This attitude was developed by William Motherwell, the Scottish poet, who supplied an introduction to Andrew Henderson's *Scottish Proverbs* (Edinburgh, 1832). The collection itself is of little merit; but Motherwell's critical and historical study of proverbs, and the then existing proverb-literature, not only marks an advance on anything that had been done before, but remains one of the soundest pieces of work on the subject. We note a protest in his essay, striking at that date, against the tendency to exclude 'indelicate' proverbs from the collections: 'As a man of the world, studying the taste of his own brief day, our author may be justifiable, but as a philosopher, as an historian of manners, or a severe antiquary, he is most decidedly wrong.'

Next came a little volume of essays on proverbs, *Proverbs and their Lessons*, first published in 1853, by R. C. Trench, 'poet, scholar, and divine', and memorable as one of the principal originators of the *Oxford English Dictionary*. The 'poet'—had taken part, some five and twenty years earlier, in a romantic conspiracy to restore the ill-fated Spanish political exiles from the dreary wastes of Euston Square and Somers Town to their own country. The 'scholar and divine' we take to have been responsible for these essays, which were first framed as lectures to be delivered to working men. They are based on a study of many collections in many languages, and, for all that their manner is slightly 'out of the pulpit', their author has more to say about the form and origin of proverbs than any of his predecessors.

Bohn's *Handbook of Proverbs* and Hislop's *Scottish Proverbs*, published in 1855 and 1862 respectively, may be mentioned in passing, but they were little more than reprints, with some additions, of Rays' *English Proverbs* and the earlier Scottish collections, and show no novelties either of arrangement or annotation.

Next on our list comes Hazlitt's *English Proverbs and Proverbial Phrases*, first published in 1869. This was the most ambitious collection that had yet appeared, as the compiler occasionally gave the sources from which he had taken his proverbs, and added a number of notes and quotations illustrating early uses. But he did not do this consistently enough to make it possible for any one using his book to disregard earlier collections. Also, he omitted many proverbs, either because they had come originally from a foreign language, or because they were too coarse to be perpetuated. The first is an unsound principle of exclusion to adopt when dealing with the English language, which has appropriated words and phrases from all quarters with a catholic readiness: the second overlooks the fact that many of the coarsest proverbs are typically English, and we are more ready to agree with Motherwell's judgement on this point. The arrangement of Hazlitt's proverbs is alphabetical, under the first word of each; there is a long introduction, and a somewhat sketchy index.

In spite of what now seem obvious demerits, Hazlitt's remained the standard collection of proverbs for over half a century. It was reissued, as were older collections, but there was no new compilation of any note until after 1900. The years 1902–4 saw the publication of Lean's *Collectanea*, the four posthumous volumes of *Collections*, by Vincent Stuckey Lean, of *Proverbs (English and Foreign)*, *Folk Lore*, *and Superstitions*, also *Compilations towards Dictionaries of Proverbial Phrases and Words, old and disused*. These collections were the fruit of over fifty years' reading and research upon proverbs, and probably contain a greater mass of information about the subject than has ever been brought together by any other man. Unfortunately, they were printed directly from the manuscript as it stood, and suffer badly from want of arrangement and collation. Their editor supplied an ample index, which does something to remedy this fault; but in spite of this the book is difficult and disappointing to use, and we must regret that a desire for perfection or completeness should in the end have marred so many years of labour.

The most useful collection of proverbs is undoubtedly the one made by G. L. Apperson, *English Proverbs and Proverbial Phrases. A Historical Dictionary*, and published in 1929. It appeared after Mr. Smith had finished work on his own Dictionary, but the wealth of information it contains has been utilized gladly in so far as the limited opportunities of proof-revision have allowed. Mr. Apperson has adopted a novel, twofold method of arrangement: proverbs which classify themselves naturally as referring to months, seasons, places, fools, time, the devil, &c., are grouped under their relative subject-headings, while all other sayings appear alphabetically under their first significant word. This is the first collection to model itself on the *Oxford Dictionary*; each proverb is illustrated with quotations, for which references are given, in historical order; and the compiler expressly points out that he has taken these quotations, wherever possible, from literature rather than from proverb collections. With its many explanatory notes, and its particularly interesting collection of weather lore and 'nominal' proverbs, this book is one which no student of folk-lore can afford to neglect.

During the past twenty-five years particular attention has been devoted to tracing proverbs back to their earliest appearance in English. In 1910 came Skeat's *Early English Proverbs*, a collection of some three hundred proverbs which he had encountered in his readings in early English literature. From time to time Professor Max Förster, one of the most distinguished Anglo-Saxon scholars of the day, to whose generous assistance are due many of the earliest quotations in this Dictionary, has edited early manuscript collections of proverbs; while from frequently-occurring articles in the learned periodicals, and not least from the pages of the *Oxford Dictionary*, we can see how far this branch of the study of the English language and English thought has developed.

In America proverbs find many students. Professor Tilley's *Elizabethan Proverb Lore with Parallels from Shakespeare*, which appeared in 1926, is a collection of over seven hundred proverbs from Lyly's *Euphues* and Pettie's *Petite Pallace*, with parallels from Shakespearian and many other sources. His scholarly introduction on the 'Proverbial Element in Euphues' is also a study of proverb lore since Lyly's day, and it is invaluable to any one who, like the present writer, finds that tracing the popularity of proverbs is not the least of their many interests. Again, Mr. Whiting, whom we mentioned earlier in connexion with his book on *Chaucer's Use of Proverbs*,[1] has written on *The Origin* and *Nature of the Proverb*, and he has lately published a selection of amusing and at times horrifying examples of the use of that over-worked word, 'proverbial'.[2] Another American scholar, Mr. Archer Taylor, has devoted a whole book to *The Proverb* (1931). 'After all', he says, 'we know little or nothing of the

[1] See p. xii, footnote.
[2] *Harvard Studies and Notes on Philology and Literature*, vols. xiii–xvi.

origin, dissemination, and literary style of proverbs'; and from a formidable background of learning he proceeds to make a thorough examination of these aspects of his subject.

Finally, we must not overlook *Proverb Literature*, an excellent bibliography of works, English and foreign, relating to proverbs. The material was mostly gathered by the late T. A. Stephens, a member of the Folk-Lore Society, and the book was edited, with some additions, in 1930 by W. Bonser. It supplies a need which by this time had become acute.

It is a far cry from Heywood's *Dialogue* of 1546 to the present day, and Mr. Taylor's comments on 'the linguistic peculiarities of proverbs', but the twentieth-century proverb-monger must go to many sources—books of proverbs, books about proverbs, even books about books about proverbs —before he can send yet another Dictionary of Proverbs and Proverbial Phrases down the ever-widening stream of literature that deals with these Excellencies of our English Tongue'.

JANET E. HESELTINE.

NOTE ON
THE DURHAM PROVERBS

MS. B. III. 32, from the library of Durham Cathedral, is a Latin hymnal in two, possibly three, very fine hands of the first half of the eleventh century, with interlinear glosses in Anglo-Saxon. The hymnal is followed by Ælfric's grammar.[1]

The collection of proverbs occupies ff. 43*b*–45*b*, coming between a hymn and the Canticles for Matins, and consists of forty-six proverbs, not all complete. Some of them are familiar, such as 'Amicus in necessitate probandus est: *æt pearfe man sceal freonda cunnian*' and '[N]escit suaue diligere qui amarum non gustauerit: *Ne wat swetes ðanc se þe biteres ne onbyrgeð*'. Others, such as 'Nunc in iudicio porci dixit maritus sedens in apro: *Nu hit ys on swines dome cwæþ se ceorl sæt on eoferes hricge*', or '[N]eque confiderem liceat bene ambulasse*t* dixit qu*i* uidit frigas [*read* 'strigas'] capite progredient*es*: *Ne swa þeah treowde þeah þu teala eode cwæþ se þe geseah hægtessan æfter heafde geo*(?)' are of interest both as illustrations of the freakish humour so often expressed in the gargoyles and grotesques of medieval sculpture and illumination, and as surprisingly early examples of the 'quoth the' type of proverb. Again '[C]ecus duob*is* oculis qu*i* pectore non cernit: *Blind byþ bam eagum se þe breostum ne starat*' deserves to be rescued from oblivion for its pleasing sentiment. The Latin seems even more corrupt than the usual medieval Latin; and in the Anglo-Saxon there are forms of words not given in *Bosworth-Toller*.

One interesting feature of the collection is the support it seems to lend to a suggestion made by Wülcker (in *Anglia*, ii. 373) that there was a common source of proverbs from which the fragmentary collections to be found in certain manuscripts were quoted. Two proverbs in the Durham MS. occur also in MS. Royal 2 B. v, with slight differences in the Anglo-Saxon; and MS. Royal 2 B. v in its turn has two proverbs (not in the Durham MS.) that are found also in MS. Cott. Faust. A. x. The first proverb of all in the Durham collection is incomplete. It runs: 'portio beatitudinis: *gepyld byð middes ea*[*des*]'; but it must be a fragment of one of the *Distichs* of Cato: *Forbær oft ðæt ðu eaðe mæʒe wrecan: ʒepyld biþ mihtena mæst* (*middes eades*).[2] Mr. Kenneth Sisam, who has kindly helped me with many of the difficulties that attend even a cursory examination of the Durham collection, tells me also that one or two of the proverbs are echoed in the literature of the time, e.g. '*Ne sceal man to ær forht ne to ær fægen*' recalls the poem *The Wanderer*, line 68: '*Wita sceal gepyldig . . . ne to forht ne to fægen*'.

By the courtesy of the Dean and Chapter of Durham Cathedral I have been enabled to procure a photostat of the proverbs in the Durham MS. I have sent a copy of this to Professor Max Förster in the hope that he will find time at an early date to edit this remarkably interesting collection.

[1] A description of this manuscript is contained in an article on 'Two Anglo-Saxon Miniatures Compared' by F. Wormald, in the *British Museum Quarterly*, vol. ix, no. 4, May 1935.

[2] Bk. 1, no. 38. See 'Metrische Studien' by E. Sievers in *Abhandlungen der . . . sächsischen Gesellschaft der Wissenschaften* (Leipzig), Bd. xxxv, s. 604. I am indebted for this reference to Professor Max Förster.

KEY

TO ABBREVIATED TITLES OF *COLLECTIONS OF PROVERBS,* AS
USED IN THIS WORK

1547 or later ed.	BALDWIN	W. Baldwin, *A Treatise of Moral Philosophy.*
1855	BOHN	H. G. Bohn, *A Handbook of Proverbs.*
1727	BOYER	Abel Boyer, *The Complete French Master.*
1917	BRIDGE	J. C. Bridge, *Cheshire Proverbs.*
1883	BURNE	C. S. Burne, *Shropshire Folk-lore.*
1614 or later ed.	CAMDEN	W. Camden, *Remains concerning Britain.*
1882	CHAMBERLAIN	Mrs. E. L. Chamberlain, *A Glossary of West Worcestershire Words.*
1896	CHEVIOT	A. Cheviot, *Proverbs, Proverbial Expressions, and Popular Rhymes of Scotland.*
1639	CLARKE	J. Clarke, *Parœmiologia Anglo-Latina.*
1664, 1672	CODRINGTON	R. Codrington, *The Second Part of Youth's Behaviour.*
1823	COLLINS	J. Collins, *A Dictionary of Spanish Proverbs.*
1611	COTGRAVE	Randle Cotgrave, *A Dictionary of the French and English Tongues.*
1894	COWAN	F. Cowan, *Dictionary of the Proverbs . . . of the English Language relating to the Sea.*
1611	DAVIES	J. Davies (of Hereford), *The Scourge of Folly,* in *Works* (Grosart), II.
1592 or later ed.	DELAMOTHE	G. Delamothe, *The French Alphabet.*
1846	DENHAM	M. A. Denham, *A Collection of Proverbs . . . relating to the Weather.*
1576	DESAINLIENS	C. Desainliens [= C. Holyband], *The French Littelton* (Curtis) in *Festschrift z. XV Neuphilologentage.* Frankfurt am Main, 1912.
c. 1350	*Douce MS. 52*	*Douce MS. 52* (Förster) in *Festschrift z. XII Deutschen Neuphilologentage.* Erlangen, 1906.
1616 or later ed.	DRAXE	T. Draxe, *Bibliotheca Scholastica.*
1709	DYKES	O. Dykes, *Moral Reflexions upon Select English Proverbs.*
Lugduni, 1550	ERASM. *Ad.*	Erasmus, *Adagiorum Opus.*
1881	EVANS	A. B. Evans, *Leicestershire Words,* &c.
1641	FERGUSSON	David Fergusson, *Scottish Proverbs* (Beveridge).
1830	FORBY	R. Forby, *The Vocabulary of E. Anglia.*
c. 1532	SIR ADRIAN FORTESCUE	Printed from a MS. in the Bodleian in Thomas (Fortescue), Lord Clermont's *A History of the Family of Fortescue* (2nd ed., 1880), pp. 263–5.
1733–58	FRANKLIN	B. Franklin, *Poor Richard's Almanack,* referred to by the year and month.
1662	FULLER	T. Fuller, D.D., *The History of the Worthies of England* (1840).
1732	FULLER	T. Fuller, M.D., *Gnomologia.*
1787 or later ed.	GROSE	F. Grose, *A Provincial Glossary.*
1611	GRUTER	Jan Gruter, *Florilegium Ethicopoliticum.*
1869 or later ed.	HAZLITT	W. C. Hazlitt, *English Proverbs.*

1832	HENDERSON	A. Henderson, *Scottish Proverbs.*
1640	HERBERT	G. Herbert, *Outlandish Proverbs.*
1651	Id.	Id., *Jacula prudentum* (the second ed., slightly expanded, of the *Outlandish Proverbs*). References to both the above are to Vol. I of the 1859 ed. unless another ed. is indicated.
1546 or later ed.	HEYWOOD	J. Heywood, *A Dialogue containing . . . the Proverbs in the English Tongue,* referred to by Part and Chapter, also by page in the 1867 ed.[1]
1555 or later ed.	Id.	Id., *Two Hundred Epigrams upon Two Hundred Proverbs with a third Hundred newly added.*[2]
1862	HISLOP	A. Hislop, *The Proverbs of Scotland* (ed. 3).
1659	HOWELL	J. Howell, *Parœmiographia* (a polyglot collection containing English proverbs and French, Italian, and Spanish proverbs with English translations; also British (Welsh) proverbs with English translations).
1869 or later ed.	INWARDS	R. Inwards, *Weather Lore.*
1721	KELLY	J. Kelly, *A Complete Collection of Scotish Proverbs.*
1902–4	LEAN	V. S. Lean, *Collectanea.*
1707	MAPLETOFT	J. Mapletoft, *Select Proverbs.*
1599	MINSHEU	R. Percyvall, *A Spanish Grammar, now augmented . . . by J. Minsheu.*
1659	N.R.	N.R., *Proverbs English, French, Dutch, [&c.]. All Englished.*
1530	PALSGRAVE	J. Palsgrave, *L'Éclaircissement de la langue française.*
1597	*Politeuphuia*	[J. Bodenham?] *Politeuphuia, Wit's Commonwealth,* first published in 1597 and many times reprinted.
1737	RAMSAY	A. Ramsay, *A Collection of Scots Proverbs* (in *Works,* 1819).
1670, 1678, &c.	RAY	J. Ray, *A Collection of English Proverbs,* several times republished with additions.
1883	ROPER	W. Roper, *Weather Sayings.*
1573	SANDFORD	J. Sandford, *The Garden of Pleasure,* reprinted 1576 as *Hours of Recreation.*
1663	P. STAMPOY	'Pappity Stampoy', *A Collection of Scotch Proverbs* (a plagiarism of one of the editions of Fergusson, above).
1738	SWIFT	J. Swift, *A Complete Collection of Polite and Ingenious Conversation.* References are to the three *Dialogues* which the work comprises and to pages in the 1856 ed. of Swift's *Works,* Vol. II, unless otherwise indicated.
1539 or later ed.	TAVERNER	R. Taverner, *Proverbs or Adages with New Additions, gathered out of the Chiliades of Erasmus.*
1927	TILLEY	M. P. Tilley, *Elizabethan Proverb Lore in Lyly's 'Euphues' and Pettie's 'Petite Pallace'.*
1642	TORRIANO	G. Torriano, *Select Italian Proverbs.*
1666	Id.	Id., *Piazza universale di proverbi italiani* (proverbs given in Italian and English).

[1] It must not be assumed, as is sometimes done, that all the proverbs in the 1562 ed. of the *Dialogue* had appeared in the 1546 ed. of the same. Heywood added many proverbs which are to be found in the ed. printed by Berthelet in 1550, an imperfect copy of which is in the British Museum.

[2] It is a mistake to suppose that the 300 epigrams were printed in 1546. No edition of them earlier than 1555 is known. They were reprinted in 1562. Many of the proverbs in the *Epigrams* had appeared in the *Dialogue* of 1546, but not all.

1853	TRENCH	R. C. Trench (Archb. of Canterbury), *On the Lessons in Proverbs* (1894).
1573	TUSSER	T. Tusser, *Five Hundred Points of Good Husbandry* (1878).
1672	WALKER	W. Walker, *Parœmiologia Anglo-Latina or, English and Latin Proverbs.*
1586 or later ed.	WITHALS	J. Withals, *A Short Dictionary in Latin and English.*
1623	WODROEPHE	J. Wodroephe, *The Spared Houres of a Soldier in His Travels.*

ABBREVIATIONS

a.	*ante,* before.	L.	Latin.
(A)	indicates that the quotation is taken from G. L. Apperson's *English Proverbs and Proverbial Phrases.*	Merm.	Mermaid Series.
		N. & Q.	*Notes and Queries.*
		New Sh. S.	New Shakespeare Society.
		OE	Old English (Anglo-Saxon).
Arb.	Arber's edition.	*O.E.P.*	*Old English Plays* (ed. Hazlitt).
B.S.	Ballad Society.	O.U.P.	Oxford University Press.
C.U.P.	Cambridge University Press.	*P. Pl.*	*Piers Plowman.*
E.D.S.	English Dialect Society.	pr.	printed.
E.E.T.S.	Early English Text Society.	P.S.	Parker Society.
E.P.P.	*Early Popular Poetry* (ed. Hazlitt).	Roxb. Cl.	Roxburghe Club.
		Ser.	Series.
f.	folio.	Sp.	Spanish.
F.L.S.	Folk Lore Society.	S.T.S.	Scottish Text Society.
Fr.	French.	s.v.	*sub voce,* under the word.
Gk.	Greek.	tr.	translation, or translated by.
Gros.	Grosart's edition.	T.T.	Tudor Translations.
Hunt. Cl.	Hunterian Club.	Wks.	Works.

NOTES

A date or a name in brackets following the title of a work indicates the edition referred to.

Plays are referred to by act and scene, or by act alone. Other works are referred to by page unless otherwise indicated.

The absence of a quotation following a reference signifies that in the passage referred to the proverb is given without significant difference. This is indicated by omission marks (. . .) where an explanation of the proverb follows.

A

Ab, *see* Make ab or warp of the business.

Abbey, *see* Bring an a. to a grange; Bury an a.

Abbot, *see* Horner, Popham . . . when the a. went out.

A-bed, All are not | that shall have ill rest.

1509 A. BARCLAY *Ship of Fools* (1874) I. 13 All are nat in bed whiche shall haue yll rest. **1546** HEYWOOD II. vii But take vp in time, or els I protest, All be not a bedde, that shall haue yll rest. **1670** RAY 60 All that are in bed must not have quiet rest.

Abed, *see also* Lies long a.; Name is up (His), he may lie a. till noon; Time for honest folks to be a.

Aberdeen and twelve miles round, Take away | and where are you?

1896 CHEVIOT 309. **1911** *Brit. Wkly.* 27 Jul. 419 A country that has as good a conceit of itself as Scotland, and a city where the best-known proverb is 'Tak' awa' Aberdeen and twal' mile round aboot it, an' far[1] are ye ?' [¹ where.]

Abide a bad market, He that cannot | deserves not a good one.

1678 RAY 173.

Above, *see* Cometh from a. let no man question; Things that are a. us are nothing.

Above-board.

a. **1607** T. MIDDLETON *Family of Love* III. i play fair yet above board. **1616** BEAUM. & FL. *Cust. Country* I. i Yet if you play not fair play, and above-board too, I have a foolish gin here. **1788** BURKE *Sp. agst. Hastings,* Wks. XIII. 293 All that is in this transaction is fair and above-board.

Abra(ha)m, *see* Sham A.

Abraham's bosom, In.

[LUKE xvi. 23 He seeth Abraham afar off, and Lazarus in his bosom.] **1597** SHAKS. *Rich. III* IV. iii. 38 The sons of Edward sleep in Abraham's bosom. *Henry V* II. iii. 10 He 's in Arthur's bosom, if ever man went to Arthur's bosom [malapropism]. *a.* **1797** WALPOLE *Letters* (Toynbee) VI. 310 Two or three old ladies, who are languishing to be in Abraham's bosom.

Abroad, *see* All a. and nothing at home.

Absence sharpens love, presence strengthens it.

1557 TOTTEL *Songs and Sonnets* (Rollins) i. 224 Absence works wonders. *a.* **1633** G. HERBERT *Priest to Temple* (Wks. 1941, 284) Absence breeds strangeness, but presence

5017

B

love. **1732** FULLER no. 755. **1850** T. HAYNES BAYLY *Isle of Beauty* Absence makes the heart grow fonder.

Absence, *see also* Salt water and a. wash away love.

Absent are always in the wrong, The.

c. 1440 LYDGATE *Fall of Princes* III, 1. 3927 For princis ofte . . . Will cachche a quarel . . . Ageyn folk absent. **1640** HERBERT 332 The absent party is still faulty. **1736** FRANKLIN July The absent are never without fault, nor the present without excuse. [Fr. *Les absents ont toujours tort.*]

Absent without fault, nor present without excuse, He is neither.

1616 DRAXE 44.

Absent, *see also* Long a. soon forgotten; Master a. and house dead.

Abstain from beans.

[L. *Abstineto a fabis*, Abstain from beans, i.e. from elections (ERASM., who quotes EMPEDOCLES, κυάμων ἄπο χεῖρας ἔχεσθε).] **1539** TAVERNER f. lv There be sondry interpretacions of thys symbole. But Plutarche and Cicero thynke beanes to be forbydden of Pythagoras, because they be wyndye and do engender impure humours and for that cause provoke bodely lust. **1579** LYLY *Euphues* (Arb.) 148 To absteine from beanes, that is, not to meddle in ciuile affaires or businesse of the common weale, for in the old times the election of Magistrates was made by the pullyng of beanes. **1662** FULLER (*Leics.*) II. 225 I read a Latin proverb, 'A fabis abstineto,' (forbear beans); whereof some make a civil interpretation, 'Meddle not with the matters of state'; because anciently men cast in a bean when they gave their suffrages in public elections.

Absurdities. *See* quotn.

1619 J. FAVOUR *Antiquity triumphing over Novelty* 535 According to the old saying, *Uno absurdo dato, mille sequuntur,* a man may build a thousand absurdities vpon one.

Abundance, like want, ruins many.

1766 *Goody Two-Shoes* v. iii.

Abundance of law breaks no law.

[L. *Abundantia juris non nocet.*] **1721** KELLY 45 . . . Do more than the law requires, rather than leave anything undone that it does.

Abundance of money ruins youth, The.

1670 RAY 18.

Abundance of things ingendereth disdainfulness.

1573 SANDFORD H2ᵛ. **1578** FLORIO *First*

Fruites f. 32 The plenty of things dooth ingender care. 1594 *King Leir III.* ii. 30–1. **1597** DELONEY *I Gentle Craft* (Mann) 121.

Abuse(d), *see* Best things may be a.; No case, a. attorney.

Accidents will happen in the best-regulated families.

1763 COLMAN *Deuce is in him* I (A) Accidents, accidents will happen—no less than seven brought into our infirmary yesterday. **1823** SCOTT *Peveril* xlix, Nay, my lady, . . . such things will befall in the best regulated families. **1850** DICKENS *Dav. Cop.* xxviii 'Copperfield,' said Mr. Micawber, 'accidents will occur in the best-regulated families.'

Accipe, see Better is one *a.*

Accord, There is no good | where every man would be a lord.

1546 HEYWOOD II. vi. 61 Tys sayde there is no good accorde, Where euery man would be a Lorde. Wherefore my wyfe will be no lorde, but lady. **1573** TUSSER 113 *Author's l.* 21 (E.D.S.) 210 But when I spide That Lord with Lord could not accord, . . . Then left I all.

Accordeth, *see* Rhyme (It may), but it a. not.

Account for himself and others, Who must | must know both.

1640 HERBERT 326.

Accounting for tastes, There is no.

[L. *De gustibus non est disputandum.* There is no disputing about tastes.] **1599** MINSHEU (1623) 2V1ᵛ Against ones liking there is no disputing. **1760** STERNE *T. Shandy* I. viii init. *De gustibus non est disputandum*: that is there is no disputing against Hobby-horses. **1779–81** JOHNSON *Lives of Poets* (1908) II. 209 *De gustibus non est disputandum*; men may be convinced, but they cannot be pleased, against their will. **1823** GALT *Entail* xxix 'But you know . . . that there is no accounting for tastes'. **1867** TROLLOPE *Last Chron. Barset* xxxi He had not the slightest objection to recognizing in Major Grantly a suitor for his cousin's hand. . . There was . . . no accounting for tastes.

Accounts, *see* Cast up a.; Short reckonings (a.) long friends.

Accuser, *see* Advocate becomes a. (Woe to him whose).

Ace, *see* Bate me an a.

Ache(s, th), *see* Better eye out than always a.; Head a. (When), all body the worse; Head may never a. till (Wish my); Works after his manner (He that), head a. not.

Achilles, *see* Heel of A.; Spear of A.

Aching teeth, Who hath | hath ill tenants.

1670 RAY 26.

Aching tooth at one, To have an.

1590 LODGE *Rosalynde* 136 (Hunt. Cl.) (A) I have a longing tooth . . . that makes me cry. **1667** L'ESTRANGE *Quevedo's Visions* 201 (1904) (A) You have still . . . an aching tooth at those poor varlets. **1678** BAILEY *Dict.* s.v. 'Ake' (A) To have an aking tooth at one, to be angry at, to have a mind to rebuke or chastise one.

A-cold than a cuckold, It is better to be.

1678 RAY 69.

Acorn, *see* Horse that was foaled of a.; Oak has been an a.

Acorns better than corn, To esteem.

1581 P. BOQUINUS *A Defence of Christianitie* 67 Some, that esteeme Achornes better then corne according to the prouerbe,

Acorns were good till bread was found.

1597 BACON *Ess.* 256 (1862).

Acquaintance, *see* Old a. will be remembered; Short a. brings repentance.

Acquittance, *see* Forbearance is no a.

Acre(s), *see* Half an a. is good land; Reputation is commonly measured by a.; Sits above that deals a.; Three a. and cow.

Act of Parliament, *see* Coach and four; Honest by A. of P. (Cannot make people).

Actions are our security, Our own | not others' judgements.

1640 HERBERT 325.

Actions speak louder than words.

1906 F. MCCULLAGH *With Cossacks* 178 The gallant foreigner, who could not tell them how he sympathized with them, but whose actions spoke louder than words.

Adam, The old.

[= the fallen nature inherited from Adam. *c.* 456 SIDONIUS APOLLINARIS *Op.* p. 561 Veteremque novus . . . Adam.] **1598–9** SHAKS. *Hen. V* I. i. 29 Consideration like an angel came, And whipp'd the offending Adam out of him. **1642** D. ROGERS *Naaman* To Rdr. Corrupt self . . . is (upon point) no other then old Adam; the depravedness and disorder of the appetite before spoken of. **1852** E. FITZGERALD *Polonius* 92 Let him who would know how far he has changed the old Adam, consider his dreams. **1910** G. W. E. RUSSELL *Sketch. & Snap.* 62 As time goes on, we find the old Adam in Manning's nature reasserting itself.

Adam delved and Eve span, When | who was then a (the) gentleman?

c. **1340** HAMPOLE in *Relig. Pieces fr. Thornton MS.* 79 When Adam dalfe and Eve spane . . . Whare was þan þe pride of man? [**1381**]

J. R. GREEN *Short Hist.* (1893) II. 484 A spirit fatal to the whole system of the Middle Ages breathed in the popular rime which condensed the levelling doctrine of John Ball:[1] 'When Adam delved and Eve span, who was then the gentleman?' *c.* 1470 *Harl. MS. 3362*, f. 5*a* When Adam dalf and Eve span, who was then a gentleman? *c.* 1500 *Songs & Carols* (Warton Club) 2 Now bething the, Gentilman How Adam dalf and Eve span. 1605 ROWLANDS *Hell's Broke Loose* 15 For when old Adam delu'd, and Euah span, Where was my silken veluet Gentleman? 1659 HOWELL *Eng. Prov.* 13/2 When *Adam* delv'd and *Eve* span, Who was then a Gentleman? Up starts a churl that gathered good, From whence did spring his noble blood. [[1] executed 1381.]

Adam, *see also* Died half a year ago dead as A.; Know one from A. (Not to).

Add, *see* Insult to injury.

Adder could hear, and the blind-worm could see, If the | neither man nor beast would ever go free.

1856 *N. & Q.* 2nd Ser. I. 331 There is a Kentish proverb about the adder . . . 'If I could hear as well as see, Nor man nor beast should pass by me.' 1869 HAZLITT 228 If I could hear, and thou couldst see, there would none live but you and me, as the adder said to the blindworm. 1879 G. JACKSON *Shropshire Word-Bk.* 135 Shropshire rustics say— 'If the *ether* 'ad the blindworm's ear, An' the blindworm 'ad the *ether's* eye, Neither mon nor beäst could safe pass by'. 1883 BURNE 239 I learnt this version when young—'If the adder could hear, and the blindworm could see, Neither man nor beast would ever go free'. Current near London.

Adder, *see also* Deaf as an a.; March wind kindles the a.; Put your hand in creel and take out either a. or. . . .

Addled egg as an idle bird, As good be an.

1580 LYLY *Euph. & his Eng.* (Arb.) (A) 207. 1601–2 SHAKS. *Troil. & Cres.* I. ii. 145 If you love an addle egg as well as you love an idle head. 1732 FULLER no. 681.

Adlant, *see* Turn a narrow a.

Admonish your friends in private, praise them in public.

[PUB. SYRUS *Secrete amicos admone, lauda palam.*] 1621 BURTON *Anat. Mel.* II. iii. VII (1651) 360.

Ado, *see* Jack-an-apes (More a. with); Make a. and have a.; Much a. about nothing; Much a. to bring beggars to stocks.

Adversity makes a man wise, not rich.

1616 DRAXE 6 In adversitie men finde eies. 1659 N.R. Adversity makes men wise. 1678 RAY 92.

Adversity, *see also* Misery (A.) makes strange bedfellows; Prosperity is blessing of O.T., a. of New; Prosperity makes friends, a. tries them.

Advice, We may give | but we cannot give conduct.

1736 FRANKLIN *Way to Wealth* in Wks. I. 451 (Bigelow).

Advice comes too late, When a thing is done.

1664 CODRINGTON 224. 1670 RAY 1.

Advice, If you wish good | consult an old man.

c. 1386 CHAUCER *Melibeus* B² 2354 For the book seith that 'in olde men is the sapience, and in longe tyme the prudence'. 1813 RAY 1. *Lusit.*

Advice to all; Give | but be security for none.

1855 BOHN 361.

Advice, *see also* First a. of a woman (Take); In vain he craves a.; Woman's a. is no great thing; Write down a. of him who loves you.

Advise none to marry or go to war.

1640 HERBERT 328.

Advise, *see also* Old and wise, yet still a.

Advisement, *see* Good a. (Came never ill of).

Advocate becomes his accuser, Woe be to him whose.

1678 RAY *Adag. Hebr.* 403 . . . God required propitiatory sacrifices of his people . . . But if they offered the blind or lame, &c., they . . . increased their guilt: And thus their advocate became their accuser.

Affairs, like salt fish, ought to be a good while a soaking.

1707 MAPLETOFT 15. 1855 BOHN 305.

Affection blinds reason.

1616 DRAXE 6. 1659 J. HOWELL *Letter of Advice.* 1664 CODRINGTON 205.

Affection, *see also* Heat of a. joined with idleness of brain.

Afraid of far enough.

1670 RAY 161 . . . *Chesh.* Of that which is never likely to happen.

Afraid of him that died last year.

1670 RAY 161. 1732 FULLER no. 810 Are you afraid of him that dy'd last year?

Afraid of his own shadow.

1567 G. FENTON *Bandello* ii. 285 (T.T.) (A) He retorned with more fear of his shadow

then true reaporte of that he had in charge.
1568 GRAFTON *Chron.* II. 659 Whether shee
were afrayed of her owne shadowe . . . the
truth is, that the whole army returned to
their shippes. **1594** SHAKS. *Lucrece* 997 At
his own shadow let the thief run mad. **1670**
RAY 161.

Afraid of the wagging of feathers, He that is | must keep from among wild fowl.

1611 COTGRAVE s.v. 'Fueille'. **1640** HERBERT
no. 48 (Gros.). **1670** RAY 55 . . . Timorous persons must keep as far off from danger as they
can . . . also . . . causeless fear works men unnecessary disquiet.

Afraid of wounds, He that is | must not come nigh a battle.

1639 CLARKE 310. **1670** RAY 56.

Afraid, *see also* Good thing cheap (He will
never have) that is a. to ask price; More
a. than hurt.

Africa always brings something new.

[ARISTOTLE *de Animal. Hist.* 8. 28. 7 Ἀεὶ
Λιβύη φέρει τι καινόν. PLINY (the Elder)
Nat. Hist. 8. 16 *Semper aliquid novi Afri-
cam afferre.* **1500** ERASMUS *Adag.* quoting
PLINY 3. 7. 10 *Semper Africa novi aliquid
apportat.*] **1598** SIR R. BARCKLEY *Of the
Felicitie of Man* 220 Affrica (that accord-
ing to the old proverbe, is accustomed alwayes
to bring forth some new and strange thing).
1601 HOLLAND tr. *Pliny's Nat. Hist.* 8. 16
The Greekes have this common proverbe,
That Affricke evermore bringeth forth some
new and strange thing or other. **1642**
HOWELL *For. Trav.* iii (Arb.) 22 *France,*
which as *Africk* produceth always something
New, for I never knew week passe in *Paris,*
but it brought forth some new kinds of
Authors. **1928** *Daily Mail* 19 Mar. 5/5
'Semper aliquid novi ex Africa'; so runs the
old Latin tag, 'Always something new from
Africa', but the newest . . . is the great
harbour of the Gold Coast.

After a collar cometh a halter.

1583 MELBANCKE *Philotimus* 193 Be ware
you accord not to wear an hempton cord,
For after a collar comes an haulter. **1594-5**
SHAKS. *Rom. & Jul.* I. i. 4 *Sam.* I mean, an
we be in choler, we'll draw. *Greg.* Ay, while
you live, draw your neck out o' the collar.
a. **1596** *K. Edw. IV & Tanner of Tam.* in
PERCY *Reliques* II. i. xv. 171 (Gilfillan) II.
74 'After a coller commeth a halter, I trow
I shall be hang'd to-morrowe'. **1597-8** *1
Hen. IV* II. iv. 356 *Bard.* Choler, my lord, if
rightly taken. *Prince.* No, if rightly taken,
halter.

After a dream of a wedding comes a corpse.

1639 J. CLARKE 236.

After a famine in the stall, comes a famine in the hall.

1678 RAY 353 *Somerset.*

After a lank comes a bank.

1678 RAY 343 . . . said of breeding women.
1727 BOYER *Eng. Fr. Dict.* A lank makes a
bank.

After a sort, as Costlet served the King.

1721 KELLY 44 . . . One Captain Costlet
boasting much of his loyalty, was asked how
he served the King, when he was a captain
in Cromwell's army; answered, After a sort.
1818 SCOTT *Rob Roy* xxvi He's honest after a
sort, as they say . . . Captain Costlett . . .
said that he served him *after a sort.*

After a storm comes a calm [or vice versa].

c. **1200** *Ancrene Riwle* (Morton) 376 Louerd,
þet makest stille efter storme. *c.* **1377** LANG-
LAND *Piers Plowm.* B. xviii. 407 After sharpe
showres most shene is the sonne. *c.* **1387** T.
USK *Test. Love* I. v. 87 After grete stormes
the whether is often mery and smothe. **1576**
DESAINLIENS E i After a storme commeth a
calme. **1576** PETTIE *Petite Pall.* (Gollancz)
II. 91 Calm continueth not long without a
storm. **1580** LYLY *Euph. & his Eng.* Wks.
(Bond) II. 220 Feelyng as it were newe
stormes to arise after a pleasaunt calme.
1614 CAMDEN 303. **1616** DRAXE 23 After a
calme commeth a storm. **1655** FULLER *Ch.
Hist.* IX. viii (1868) III. 169 . . . Wearied with
a former blustering they began now to
repose themselves in a sad silence.

After black clouds, clear weather.

c. **1400** *Tale of Beryn* 1. 3955 After myȝty
cloudis þere comyth a cler sonne. **15** . . J.
REDFORD *Wyt & Sci.* 828 After stormy
clowdes cumth wether clere. **1546** HEYWOOD
I. xi. 30 Be of good chéere. After cloudes
blacke, we shall haue weather cléere.

After cheese comes nothing.

1623 CAMDEN 266. **1639** J. CLARKE 136.
1721 KELLY 52 . . . As being always the last
dish.

After Christmas comes Lent.

1611 COTGRAVE s.v. 'Banquet' After feasting,
fasting. **1632** MASSINGER *City Madam* IV. iv
(Merm.) 472 She hath feasted long, And,
after a carnival, Lent ever follows. **1678** RAY
113.

After death the doctor.

c. **1374** CHAUCER *Troylus* v. 741 Al to late
comth the letuarie [remedy], Whan men the
cors unto the grave carie. **1576** DESAINLIENS
260 We saye in french after death, the
phisitian: and the english sayeth 'after dinner
mustard'. **1612-13** SHAKS. *Hen. VIII* III. ii.
41 All his tricks founder, and he brings his
physic After his patient's death: the King
already Hath married the fair lady. **1670**
RAY 78 . . . *Après la mort le médecin.* Parallel
to . . . Μετὰ πόλεμον ἡ συμμαχία. Post bellum auxilium.

After dinner sit awhile, after supper walk a mile.

[L. *Post prandium stabis, post cœnam ambu-*

labis. Sch. of Health at Salerno.] **1582** G.
WHETSTONE *Heptameron of Civil Discourses*
E 2ᵛ After dinner, talk a-while, After
supper, walk a mile. **1608** BEAUM. & FL.
Philaster II. i As men Do walk a mile,
women should talk an hour After supper:
'Tis their exercise. **1613** WITHER *Abuses* 171
As having sup't 'tis good to walk a mile,
So after dinner men must sit awhile. **1876**
BLACKMORE *Cripps Carrier* IV He neighed
. . . for he felt quite inclined for a little
exercise, . . . 'After supper, trot a mile'.

After Lammas corn ripens as much by night as by day.

[Lammas = 1st of Aug., formerly observed
as harvest festival.] **1678** RAY 352. **1902–4**
LEAN I. 380 . . . from the heavy night dews.

After meat, mustard.

1576 DESAINLIENS 260 The english sayeth
'after dinner, mustard'. **1603** FLORIO tr. *Montaigne* III. x It is even as good as mustard
after dinner. **1670** RAY 119 . . . When there
is no more use of it. **1822** SCOTT *Nigel* iii I
could have gi'en you avisement . . . , but
now its like after meat mustard.

After peascods, *see* Everything is good in its
season (quotn. 1591).

After the house is finished, leave it.

1640 HERBERT 325.

After us the deluge.

[Fr. *Après nous le déluge*: said by Mme de
Pompadour to Louis XV.] **1876** BURNABY
Ride to Khiva Introd. Our rulers did not
trouble their heads much about the matter.
'India will last my time . . . and after me the
Deluge.'

After wit comes ower late.

1594 *King Leir* I. i. 47 After-wishes ever
come too late. **1663** P. STAMPOY 18 Efter
word comes weard. **1683** MERITON *Yorkshire
Ale* 83–7 (1697).

After wit is dear bought.

1590 R. GREENE (Gros.) viii. 125 After wits
are bitten with many sorrowes. **1595** R.
SOUTHWELL 'Love's Delay'. **1709** DYKES 6.

After wit is (is not) the best.

1579 GOSSON *Sch. Abuse* (Arb.) 18 Afterwittes
are euer best. *c.* **1605** COLLIER *Roxb. Ballads*
88 (1847) (A).

'After you' is good manners.

1650 R. HEATH *Clarastella*, Epigrams, 33
Oh! after him is manners. **1658** E. PHILLIPS
Mysteries of Love and Eloquence 158 After
me is manners. **1721** KELLY 42 . . . Spoken
when our betters offer to serve us first.
1738 SWIFT (Dial. ii) 345 O! madam; after
you is good manners.

After your fling, watch for the sting.

1917 BRIDGE 7 . . . After pleasure comes pain.

After-claps, *see* Beware of a.

After-love, *see* Scorn at first makes a. more.

Against the grain.

1607–8 SHAKS. *Coriol.* II. iii. 241 Your
minds, Pre-occupied with what you rather
must do than what you should, made you
against the grain to voice him consul. **1650**
HUBBERT *Pill Formality* 65 O this goes
against the grain, this cannot be indured.
1861 HUGHES *Tom B. at Oxford* xliv (1889)
421 I followed your advice at last, though it
went against the grain uncommonly.

Against the hair.

[= against the grain, inclination. Fr. *À
contre-poil*.] **1387–8** T. USK *Test. Love* II. iv
Ayenst the heere it tourneth. **1579–80**
NORTH *Plutarch* (1676) 388 All went utterly
against the hair with him. **1594–5** SHAKS.
Rom. & Jul. II. iv. 87 Thou desirest me to
stop in my tale against the hair. **1600–1**
Merry W. II. iii. 36 If you should fight, you
go against the hair of your professions.
1601–2 *Troil. & Cres.* I. ii. 26 He is melancholy without cause and merry against the
hair. **1668** HOWE *Bless. Righteous* (1825) 170
Something that crosses them, and goes
against the hair.

Against the shins.

1678 RAY 81 That goes against the shins;
i.e. It's to my prejudice, I do it not willingly.

Agamemnon, *see* Brave men before A.

Age (Winter) and wedlock tames man and beast.

1593–4 SHAKS. *Tam. Shrew* IV. i. 24 But,
thou knowest, winter tames man, woman,
and beast. **1616** DRAXE 231 Marriage and
want of sleep tames both man and beast.
1623 CAMDEN 265 Age and wedlocke, lames
man and beast. **1639** CLARKE 328 Wedding
and ill wintering tame both man and beast.
1670 RAY 47 Age and wedlock bring a man
to his nightcap. **1908** E. PHILLPOTTS *The
Mother* II. v 'Sometimes I feel that desperate
that I could run away' . . . 'Time will tame
you . . . Winter and wedlock tames maids and
beasts.'

Age is jocund, When | it makes sport for death.

1640 HERBERT 347.

Age, *see also* Dies for a. (When he) you may
quake; Look in your mouth to know your
a.; Page of your own a.; Save while you
may (For a.); Youth and a. never agree.

Agony, *see* Pile up the a.

Agree, for the law is costly.

1608 MIDDLETON *Family of Love* v. iii. 24.
1623 CAMDEN 265. **1633** JONSON *T. Tub* IV. i
Come to a composition with him, Turfe,
The law is costly. **1738** SWIFT (Dial. i) 333
Come, agree, agree; the law's costly.

Agree like bells; They | they want nothing but hanging.

1556 G. POYNET *Treatise of Politick Power* E 3ᵛ My lorde and I agree almost like belles. **1629** T. ADAMS *Serm.* (1861-2) I. 186 The great thieves agree one with another. . . . They tune like bells, and want but hanging. **1670** RAY 161. **1802** WOLCOT (P. Pindar) *Middl. Elect.* iii. Wks. (1816) IV. 196 Iss,[1] iss, leek *bells* they all agree, Want nothing now but hanging. [[1] yes.]

Agree like cats and dogs, To.

1557 ERASMUS *A mery Dialogue* B5ᵛ. **1576** PETTIE *Petite Pall.* (Gollancz) II. 85. **1579** GOSSON *Sch. Abuse* (Arb.) 27 He that compareth our instruments, with those that were vsed in ancient times, shall see them agree like Dogges and Cattes. **1616** DRAXE 30 They agree together like cats and dogs. **1692** L'ESTRANGE *Aesop's Fab.* ccccxxviii (1738) 460 In the days of yore, when men and their wives agreed like dog and cat in a house together. **1882** BLACKMORE *Christowell* xxvii They live like cats and dogs, for his lordship has a temper, and so has Mr. G.

Agree like pickpockets in a fair, They.

1813 RAY 178.

Agree like the clocks of London, They.

1589 NASHE *Pasquil's Returne* in Wks. (Gros.) I. 111 The Preachers of England begin to strike and agree like the Clocks of England. **1672** CODRINGTON no. 1206. **1678** RAY 325 . . . I find this among both the *French* and *Italian* proverbs for an instance of disagreement.

Agree like the fiddle and the stick, To.

1589 LYLY *Midas* I. ii. 8.

Agree like two cats in a gutter, They.

1546 HEYWOOD II. i. 44.

Agree, *see also* Hearts may a. though heads differ.

Agreement, *see* Ill a. is better than. . . .

Ague in the spring is physic for a king, An.

1650 A. WELLDON *Secret Hist. Jas. I* (1811) i. 479. **1653** A. WILSON *Hist. Gt. Britain* 285. **1659** HOWELL *Eng. Prov.* 20. **1670** RAY 32 . . . That is if it comes off well. . . . And an ague-fit is not thought to go off kindly, unless it ends in a sweat.

Agues (Diseases) come on horseback, but go away on foot.

1611 COTGRAVE s.v. 'Maladie'. **1678** RAY 33. **1869** HAZLITT 336.

Ague(s), *see also* Autumnal a. . . . mortal; No man dies of an a.; Quartan a. kill old men.

Aid, *see* Minerva to a. (Call).

Air of a window is as the stroke of a cross-bow, The. (*Cf.* Cold wind reach you, &c.)

1642 TORRIANO 11. **1678** RAY 42 [Ital.] Aria di[1] finestra, colpo di balestra. [[1] *da*; Giusti.]

Air, *see also* Ill a. slays sooner than sword; Live on a. like chameleon; Northern wind (a.) brings weather fair.

Ajax, *see* Mad as A.

Akin as Lewson[1] Hill to Pilson[2] Pen, As much.

1662 FULLER (*Dorset*) I. 453 As much akin as Lenson-hill to Pilson-pen. That is no kin at all . . . Spoken of such who have vicinity . . . without the least . . . consanguinity or affinity betwixt them: for these are two high hills. [[1] Lewesdon. [2] Pillesden.]

Akin to the rich man, Every one is.

1642 TORRIANO 82. **1813** RAY 129.

Albion, *see* Perfidious A.

Alchemy to saving, No.

1640 HERBERT 322.

Alderman, *see* Paced like an a.

Ale and history.

a. **1635** R. CORBET *Iter Boreale* in CHALMERS *English Poets* v. 580 Mine host was full of ale and history. **1676** ETHEREGE *Man of Mode* I. i.

Ale (Drink, Wine) is in, When | wit is out.

c. **1386** CHAUCER *Pard. T.* C. 560 In whom that drynke hath dominacioun He kan no conseil kepe. *c.* **1390** GOWER *Conf. Amantis* VI. 555 For wher that wyn doth wit aweie, Wisdom hath loste the rihte weie. **1555** HEYWOOD *Epigr. upon Prov.* no. 163. **1612-15** BP. HALL *Contempl.* XIV. ii (1825) I. 411 We use to say, that when drink is in, wit is out; but if wit were not out, drink would not be in. **1640** HERBERT 325. **1721** KELLY 340 . . . A slender excuse for what people may say, or do in their drink. **1858** SURTEES *Ask Mamma* lviii It was just the wine being in and the wit being out . . . that led him away.

Ale is meat, drink, and cloth, Good.

1602 CAREW *Surv. of Cornwall* 189 (1811) (A) The liquor [ale] is the Englishman's ancientest and wholesomest drink, and serveth many for meat and cloth too. *c.* **1612** BEAUM. & FL. *Scornf. Lady* IV. i In this short sentence ale, is all included: meat, drink, and cloth. **1670** DRYDEN *Almanz. & Alma.* Prol. 15 Like them that find meat, drink, and cloth in ale. **1738** SWIFT (*Dial.* ii) 348 O my lord, my ale is meat, drink, and cloth.

Ale sellers should not be tale-tellers.

1721 KELLY 32 . . . Public-house keepers should not blaze abroad what their guests may say, or do, in their houses.

Ale (Liquor) will make a cat speak, Good.

1565–1618 *Shirburne Ballads* (1907) 93 (A) Who is it but loues good liquor? 'Twill make a catte speak. **1611–12** SHAKS. *Tempest* II. ii. 86 Here is that which will give language to you, cat. **1637** N. BRETON *Pkt. of Letters* in Wks. (Gros.) II. *h* 51 I haue spoken for Ale that will make a Cat speake. **1678** RAY 88 Ale that would make a cat to speak. **1738** SWIFT (Dial. ii) 348 My ale . . . will make a cat speak, and a wise man dumb.

Ale, *see also* Brew good a. (You); Fair chieve good a.; Mends as sour a. in summer; Must be if we sell a. (This); Southwark a.; Water stoups hold no a.

Ale-clout, *see* Wash one's face in a.

Ale-drinkers, *see* Cobblers and tinkers.

Ale-house, *see* Penny to spend; St. Peter's in the Poor, where no a.; Settling an island, first building by Englishman an a.

Alike every day makes a clout[1] on Sunday.

1721 KELLY 46 . . . A reprimand to them who wear their best suit every day, which will soon make them improper to be worn on Sunday. **1732** FULLER no. 785. [[1] rag.]

Alike, *see also* Grooms and householders are a. great (Where), disastrous for houses; Lie all a. in our graves.

Alive, *see* Quite young and all a.

All abroad and nothing at home.

1673 A. MARVELL *Rehearsal Transpros'd* pt. 2, 105.

All came from and will go to others.

1611 COTGRAVE s.v. 'Autruy'. **1640** HERBERT 319.

All complain.

1640 HERBERT 352.

All covet, all lose.

1297 *R. of Gloucester's Chron.* (1724) 306 Wo so coueyteþ al, al leseþ ywys. *c.* **1400** LYDGATE *Isopes* 8. 1 An old prouerbe hath he sayde and shal . . . who al coveiteth, oft he lesith all. **1481** CAXTON *Reynard* xxxiii (Arb.) 95 Who that wold haue all leseth alle Ouer couetous was neuer good. **1546** HEY-WOOD II. ix. 80 Haue ye not heard tell all couet all léese. **1663** J. WILSON *Cheats* IV. i This is it when men must manage their business by themselves:—All covet and all lose. **1692** L'ESTRANGE *Aesop's Fab.* vi (1738) 6 Out of a greediness to get both, he chops at the shadow, and loses the substance. . . . All covet, all lose.

All faults to mend, Hard [it] is for any man.

1546 HEYWOOD I. xi. 29.

All feet tread not in one shoe.

1640 HERBERT 341.

All fellows at football.

1600 *Sir J. Oldcastle* IV. i All friends at football, fellows all in field, Harry, and Dick, and George. **1670** RAY 174 . . . If gentlemen . . . will mingle themselves with rustics in their rude sports; they must look for usage suitable to, or rather coarser than others. **1733** SWIFT *Reas. Repeal. Sacr. Test* Wks. (1856) II. 248 The whole Babel of sectaries joined . . . in a match at football; where the proverb expressly tells us, that *all are fellows*.

All good, and God say Amen.

1616 WITHALS 570.

All Hallows'-tide, Allhallontide, *see* Set trees at A.

All in the day's work, It is.

1738 SWIFT (Dial. i) 336 Will you be so kind as to tie this string for me . . .? it will go all in your day's work. **1820** SCOTT *Monast.* ix That will cost me a farther ride, . . . but it is all in the day's work. **1896** F. E. YOUNG-HUSBAND *Heart of Cont.* 28 The mules merely shook themselves and then stared stonily ahead, as if it were all in the day's work.

All in the seven, It is.

1900 E. J. HARDY *Mr. Thos. Atkins* 4 Soldiers are very philosophical. If anything in their work annoys them they say, 'It's all in the seven,' *i.e.* the seven years for which they join the army.

All is gone, and nothing left, When | what avails the dagger with the dudgeon-heft?

1583 MELBANCKE *Philot.* 28 When all is gone and nothinge lefte, farewell dagger with dudgin haft. **1659** HOWELL *Eng. Prov.* 14/1. [Common daggers had a hilt made of *dudgeon* wood, perhaps boxwood.]

All is over but the shouting.

1842 APPERLEY *Life Sportsman* xvi. 332 It's all over but shouting . . . Antonio's as dead as a hammer. **1869** A. L. GORDON *How we beat the favourite* The race is all over, bar shouting. **1891** J. L. KIPLING *Beast & Man* 226 The Englishman would say the back of a job was broken, or 'All is over but the shouting'.

All meats to be eaten, and all maids to be wed.

1546 HEYWOOD II. ii. 46. **1616** DRAXE 129 That one will nat, another will: so shall all maids bee married, and all meats eaten. **1678** RAY 64.

All men are mortal.

c. **1386** CHAUCER *Melibeus* B² 2803 Deeth is the ende of every man as in this present lyf. *Knight's T.* A 3030 Of man and womman seen we wel also, . . . He moot ben deed, the king as shal a page. *c.* **1430** LYDGATE *Minor Poems* (Percy Soc.) 77 Bothe highe and loughe shal go on dethis daunce. **1597–8** SHAKS. *2 Hen. IV* III. ii. 41 Death, as the Psalmist saith, is certain to all; all shall die. **1598–9** *Much Ado* I. i. 59 Well, we are all mortal. **1599–1600** *A.Y.L.* II. iv. 56 All is mortal in nature. **1600–1** *Hamlet* I. ii. 72 All that live must die. **1616** DRAXE 39.

All men cannot be masters.

1546 HEYWOOD I. xii. 38 Every man may not syt in the chayre. **1604–5** SHAKS. *Othello* I. i. 43 We cannot all be masters. **1732** FULLER no. 537.

All men have what belongs to them, When | it cannot be much.

1640 HERBERT 362.

All men row galley way.

1642 TORRIANO 96. **1813** RAY 16 . . . i.e. Every one draweth towards himself.

All men say you are an ass, When | it is time to bray.

1616 DRAXE 11. **1855** BOHN 2 . . . *Span.*

All men speak, When | no man hears.

1721 KELLY 343 . . . Used when many speak at once in a business.

All men will please, He that | shall never find ease.

[*Cf.* **1509** A. BARCLAY *Ship of Fools* (1874) I. 208.] *a.* **1581** N. WOODES *Conflict of Conscience* G1 He that will seeke eche man to content shall proue himselfe at last most vnwise. **1601** *Historical Collections* (1680) 54 He that seeketh to please All, shall please None. **1639** CLARKE 282.

All men, *see also* True that a. m. say.

All my eye (and Betty Martin).

[= all humbug, nonsense.] **1768** GOLDSMITH *Good-n. Man* III (Globe) 625 That's all my eye. The King only can pardon. **1785** GROSE *Dict. Vulg. T.* s.v. 'Betty Martin', That's my eye betty martin. **1819** MOORE *Tom Crib's Mem. Congress* 2 All my eye, Betty. **1824** SCOTT *St. Ronan's W.* xxxi Sounds of depreciation, forming themselves indistinctly into something like the words, 'My eye and Betty Martin'. **1850** KINGSLEY *Alton L.* xxv Hullo! my eye and Betty Martin! . . . This is too ridiculous. **1894** BLACKMORE *Perlycross* xxi Oh, that's all my eye, and Betty Martin! Nobody believes that, I should hope.

All one (the same) a hundred (thousand) years hence, It will be.

1611 COTGRAVE s.v. 'Fins' All will be one at the latter day, say we. **1738** SWIFT (Dial. i) 338 If people will be rude, I have done: my comfort is, 'twill be all one a thousand years hence. **1839** DICKENS *N. Nickleby* ix Mrs. Squeers . . . frequently remarked when she made any . . . mistake, it would be all the same a hundred years hence. **1855** BOHN 122.

All sorts to make a world, It takes.

1620 SHELTON *Quix.* II. vi (1908) II. 224 In the world there must be of all sorts. **1767** JOHNSON 17 Nov. in *Boswell* (1848) xx. 188 Some lady surely might be found . . . in whose fidelity you might repose. *The World*, says Locke, *has people of all sorts.* **1844** JERROLD *Story of Feather* xxviii Click can't get off this time ? . . . Well, it takes all sorts to make a world. **1891** A. LANG *Ess. in Little* 180 'It takes all sorts to make a world', in poetry as in life. Sir Walter's sort is a very good sort.

All Stuarts are not sib to the king.

1721 KELLY 14 . . . Spoken when people boast of some great man of their name. **1857** DEAN RAMSAY *Remin.* v (1911) 194 Persons may have the name and appearance of greatness without the reality: *A' Stuarts are na sib to the King.*

All that shakes falls not.

1603 FLORIO tr. *Montaigne* III. ix *All that shaketh doth not fall*: the contexture of so vast a frame holds by more than one nail. **1640** HERBERT 364.

All that you get you may put in your eye, and see never the worse.

1545 ASCHAM *Toxoph.* (Arb.) 151 That shoter whiche . . . shooteth . . . in rough wether and fayre, shall alwayes put his wynninges in his eyes. **1546** HEYWOOD I. xi. 34 At end I might put my winnyng in mine eye, And sée neuer the woorse. **1629** T. ADAMS *Serm.* (1861–2) I. 201 Judas . . . sells his Master to the Pharisees, himself to the Devil. Yet when all is done, he might put his gains in his eye.

All the wit in the world, If you had | fools would fell you.

1721 KELLY 185 . . . Spoken disdainfully, to them that think themselves very wise.

All things are good unseyit.[1]

1641 FERGUSSON 14. [[1] untried.]

All things are to be bought at Rome.

1549 LATIMER *5th Serm. bef. Edw. VI* (P.S.) 185 We have the old proverb, *Omnia venalia Romæ*, 'All things are sold for money at Rome'; and Rome is come home to our own doors.

All things have their place, knew we how to place them.

1640 HERBERT 335.

All things in their beginning are good for something.

1640 HERBERT 342.

All things require skill but an appetite.

1640 HERBERT 335.

All things that are sharp are short.

1546 HEYWOOD II. ii. 46.

All things thrive at thrice.

1641 FERGUSSON 12 All things thrives but thrice. **1721** KELLY 26 . . . An encouragement . . . to try the third time. They will say the third's a charm.

All truths are not to be told.

c. **1350** *Douce MS. 52* no. 57 Alle the Sothe is not to be sayde. *c.* **1460** *Passe Forthe, Pilgrime* in Herrig's *Archiv.* 101. 51 Say not all, that wolde the sothe seme. **1640** HERBERT 320. **1670** RAY 150 All truth must not be told at all times. **1721** KELLY 37 *All the truth should not be told.* Because it may be ill-natured, uncharitable, or unseasonable. **1821** SCOTT *Kenilw.* vi A man may, in some circumstances, disguise the truth . . .; for were it to be always spoken, and upon all occasions, this were no world to live in. [Fr. *Toutes les vérités ne sont pas bonnes à dire.*]

All women are good.

1678 RAY 59 All women are good, viz. either good for something or good for nothing. **1836** DICKENS *Pickwick* viii All women are angels, they say.

All 's out is good for prisoners, but naught for the eyes.

1678 RAY 186 . . . 'Tis good for prisoners to be out, but bad for the eyes to be out. This is a droll used by good fellows when one tells them all the drink is out.

All, All are (not), All is (not), All the, All this, *see also under significant words following.*

Allowance, *see* Grains of a.

Almanac, *see* Buchanan's a., long foul long fair; Court hath no a.

Almond for a parrot, An.

a. **1529** SKELTON *Sp. Parrot* 50 (1843) II. 4 An almon now for Parrot, dilycatly drest. **1599** BUTTES *Dyets Dry Dinner* E. 2 *Phillis* was turned into an Almond-tree, for telling tales out schoole: euer sithence, it hath bene a by-word: an Almond for the Parrat: which least it be applied to me, I will leaue my prating. **1601–2** SHAKS. *Troil. & Cres.* V. ii. 191 The parrot will not do more for an almond than he for a commodious drab.

Almost and very (well) nigh saves many a lie.

1639 CLARKE 106. **1670** RAY 56 . . . *Almost* having some latitude, men are apt to stretch it to cover untruths.

Almost was never hanged.

1639 CLARKE 3.

Alms never make poor.

1640 HERBERT 325.

Alms, *see also* Good memory giveth few a.; Preacheth (He that) giveth a.

Almsgiving lessons no man's living, Great.

1640 HERBERT 325.

Alone, *see* Better be a. than . . . ; Eats his cock a. (Who), must saddle horse a.; Man a. either saint or devil; Welcome evil if comest a.; Wise man is never less a.; Woe to him that is a.

Altars, *see* Prosperity no a. smoke (In).

Although it rain, throw not away thy watering-pot.

1640 HERBERT 332.

Although the sun shine, leave not thy cloak at home.

[*c.* **1190** *Li Proverbe au Vilain* (Tobler) 20 no. 44 Et par pluie et par bel tens doit on porter sa chape, ce dit li vilains.] *c.* **1390** CHAUCER *Proverbs* 4 What shul thise clothes thus manyfold, Lo! this hote somers day? After greet hete cometh cold; no man caste his pilche [cloak] away. **1640** HERBERT 332.

Alton, *see* Pass of A. poverty might pass (Through).

Altrincham, *see* Mayor of A.

Always say 'No', If you | you'll never be married.

1721 KELLY 298 Say still no, an' ye'll ne'er be married. **1738** SWIFT (Dial. i) 334 *Miss.* No, I thank your lordship. . . . *Spark.* Well; but if you always say no, you'll never be married.

Always (a) something, There is.

1841 MARRYAT *Poacher* xl There never was anybody . . . who . . . had mixed with the world, who could afterwards say that they were at any time perfectly happy. . . . 'There is always something.' **1883** J. PAYN *Thicker than W.* ii [The marriage] 'upon the whole is very satisfactory; it is true Jeannie hates her gudeman, but then there 's always a something.'

Always taking out of the meal-tub, and never putting in, soon comes to the bottom.

1758 FRANKLIN *Way to Wealth* (Crowell) 20 They think . . . a little to be spent . . . is not worth minding; but *Always taking out,* &c.

Always verify your references.

1918 *Times Lit. Sup.* 26 Apr. 197 Routh's[1] advice, 'Always verify your references' evidently never reached him, or made no impression on him. [[1] M. J. Routh, 1755–1854, President of Magdalen College, Oxford. See Dean Burgon, *Lives of Twelve Good Men* i. 73.]

Amantium irae, *see* Falling out of lovers.

Ambassador, *see* Welsh a.

Ambry, *see* No sooner up but hand in a.

Amend when they cannot appair,[1] Some do.

1555 HEYWOOD *Three Hund. Epig.* nos. 106, 143 He may soone amend, for he can not apeyre. **1611** DAVIES *Prov.* 265. **1616** DRAXE 43 (with 'mend'). [[1] wax worse.]

Amend(s, ed, eth), *see also* Chastiseth one a. many; Every man mend (a.) one (If); Little said soonest a.

Americans, Good | when they die, go to Paris.

1858 O. W. HOLMES *Autocrat of Breakfast Table* vi To these must certainly be added that other saying of one of the wittiest of men [Thomas Appleton, 1812–84]: 'Good Americans, when they die, go to Paris.' **1879** HENRY JAMES *International Episode,* ii. **1882** JOWETT in *Life* II. 208 The Southern climate . . . is, like Paris, 'the heaven to which good Americans go'. **1893** O. WILDE *Woman of No Import.* Act I They say, Lady Hunstanton, that when good Americans die they go to Paris.

Amiss, *see* Thinks a. concludes worse.

Amongst good men two men suffice.

1640 HERBERT 357.

A-mothering, Who goes | finds violets in the lane.

1913 *Spectator* 7 June 967 . . . a popular proverb . . . in Westmoreland. . . . It suggests, I suppose, the blessing which comes of filial affection.

Anchor of a ship, Like the | that is always at sea and never learns to swim.

1894 COWAN 61 . . . The writer frequently has had this proverb applied to him, on account of his inability to resist sea-sickness even after crossing . . . all . . . the waters of the world.

Anchor(s), *see also* Dutchman's a.; Good riding at two a.

Ancum (Ancolme) pike, *see* Witham eel.

Angel visits, Like.

1687 J. NORRIS *Miscellanies* 'The Parting'; 18 How fading are the Joves[1] we dote upon, . . . Like *Angels* visits, *short* and *bright.* **1742** BLAIR *Grave* 589 Its visits, Like those of angels, Short and far between. **1799** CAMPBELL *Pleas. of Hope* II. 377–8 (1807) 77 My wingèd hours of bliss have been, Like angel-visits, few and far between! [[1] joys.]

Angels, On the side of the.

1864 DISRAELI *Sp. on 25 Nov.* Is man an ape or an angel? Now I am on the side of the angels. **1945** 'Watchman' in *Brit. Wkly.* 6 Sept. One might say [of a U.S. magazine] that it was on the side of the angels, if that be understood as meaning that it was on the side of *man.*

Angel(s), *see also* Men are not a.; Oil of a.; Spake an a.; Talk of an a.; Write like a.

Anger and haste hinder good counsel.

1707 MAPLETOFT 8. **1855** BOHN 313.

Anger dieth quickly with a good man.

1664 CODRINGTON 184. **1670** RAY 1.

Anger is a short madness.

[HORACE *Ep.* 1. 2. 62 *Ira furor brevis est.*] *c.* **1200** *Ancrene Riwle* 120 Wreththe[1] is a wodshipe.[2] **1606–7** SHAKS. *Timon of A.* I. ii They say my lords, *Ira furor brevis est.* **1621** BURTON *Anat. Mel.* I. ii. I. ix (1651) 104 Anger, a perturbation, . . . preparing the body to melancholy, and madness itself—*ira furor brevis est.* **1707** SWIFT *Facult. of Mind* Wks. (1904) 416 These orators inflame the people, whose anger is really but a short fit of madness. [[1] wrath. [2] madness.]

Anger punishes itself.

1579 LYLY *Euph. & his Eng.* Wks. (Bond)II. 66 It fell out with him as it doth commonly with all those that are choleric that he hurt no man but himself. **1732** FULLER no. 799.

Anger, *see also* Enter into a house (When you), leave a. at door; Keep yourself from a. of great man.

Angle all day and catch a gudgeon at night, To.

1618 BRETON *Courtier & Countryman* (Roxb. Libr.) 190.

Angle (Fish) with a silver (golden) hook, To.

[ERASM. *Ad. Aureo piscari hamo.* To fish with a golden hook.] **1580** CHURCHYARD *Charge* 28 (Collier) (A) Although you fishe with golden hookes. **1605** BRETON *Honour of Val.* 5/2 Wks. (Gros.) I To fish for honour with a silver hooke. **1678** RAY 226 . . . The Italians by this phrase mean, to buy fish in the market. Money is the best bait to take all sorts of persons with. **1796** M. EDGEWORTH *Par. Asst.* (1903) 422 The servants we might corrupt; but even the old proverb of 'Angle with a silver hook', won't hold good with him.

Angler eats more than he gets, An.

1732 FULLER no. 579. **1823** COLLINS 259 'The fisherman with a rod, eats more than he earns.' Applied to persons who, to avoid work, seek employments of little advantage.

Anglesea is the mother of Wales.

1387 HIGDEN (tr. Trevisa) ii. 39 (Rolls Ser.) A proverbe and an olde sawe . . . Mon moder of Wales. **1613–22** DRAYTON *Polyolb.* ix. 390 Mona . . . Was call'd (in former times) her Country *Cambria's* mother. **1662** FULLER (*Anglesea*) III. 508 *Mon mam Cymbry.* That is, 'Anglesea is the mother of Wales' . . . because, . . . she . . . is said to afford corn enough to sustain all Wales.

Angry as a pismire,[1] As.

c. 1386 CHAUCER *Sum. T.* 118 He is as angry as a pissemyre, Though þat he haue al that he kan desire. [[1] ant.]

Angry as a wasp, As.

c. 1350 *Alexander* l. 738 (A) As wrath as waspe. *a.* 1529 SKELTON *Elyn. Rumming* l. 330 (A) Angry as a waspy. 1546 HEYWOOD I. xi. 25 Nowe mery as a cricket, and by and by, Angry as a waspe. 1659 HOWELL *Eng. Prov.* 3.

Angry as an ass with a squib in his breech, As.

1611 COTGRAVE s.v. 'Asne'.

Angry, When | count a hundred.

1902–4 LEAN IV. 182.

Angry, He that is | is seldom at ease.

1616 DRAXE 9. 1670 RAY 1.

Angry men seldom want woe. (*Cf.* Hasty man, &c.)

1616 DRAXE 9 The angry man neuer wanteth woe. 1732 FULLER no. 801.

Angry without a cause, He that is | shall (must) be pleased without amends.

c. 1510 STANBRIDGE *Vulg.* (E.E.T.S.) Yf thou be angry with me without a cause thou shall be made at one without a mendes. 1641 FERGUSSON 38 He that crabs[1] without cause, should mease[2] without mends. 1670 RAY 56. 1721 KELLY 146 He that is angry without a cause, must mease[2] without amends. [[1] grows angry. [2] settle, grow calm.]

Angry, If you be | you may turn the buckle of your girdle (belt) behind you.

1598–9 SHAKS. *Much Ado* V. i. 144 *D. Pedro.* I think he be angry indeed. *Claud.* If he be, he knows how to turn his girdle. 1621 BURTON *Anat. Mel.* Democ. to Rdr. (1651) 77 If any man take exceptions, let him turn the buckle of his girdle; I care not. 1659 HOWELL *Eng. Prov.* 12/2. 1738 SWIFT (Dial. i) 341 *Lady A.* If miss will be angry for nothing, take my counsel, and bid her turn the buckle of her girdle behind her. 1818 SCOTT *Rob Roy* xxv Nay, never look ... grim at me, man—if ye're angry, ye ken how to turn the buckle o' your belt behind you.

Angry, *see also* Hungry (If thou be), I am a.; Never be a. at (Two things a man should); Short folk are soon a.; Two to one in all things against a. man.

Annuity, *see* Give a man an a.... live for ever.

Anons, *see* Two a. and a by-and-by.

Another yet the same.

[HOR. *Carm. Saec.* 10 *Alme Sol . . . qui alius et idem nasceris.*] 1728 POPE *Dunciad* 3. 40. 1789–91 DARWIN *Botanic Garden* 1. 4. 380. 1814 WORDSWORTH *Excursion* ix A twofold image; on a grassy bank a snow-white ram, and in the crystal flood, Another and the same. 1826 SCOTT *Journ.* 1 Jan. Singular to be at once another and the same.

Another's bread costs dear.

1640 HERBERT 332.

Another, *see also* Fed at a.'s hand (He that is); You are a.

Another man, *see* Conscience is cumbered (Whose), of a. m.'s deeds the worse will deem; Put a. m.'s child in your bosom; Scald not your lips in a. m.'s pottage; Wholesomest meal at a. m.'s cost.

Answer as a man gives, Such | such will he get.

1641 FERGUSSON 90.

Answer (noun), *see also* Get the poor man's a.; Shortest a. is doing; Soft a. turneth away; Wrong hears, wrong a. gives.

Answer(s) (verb), *see* Never a. a question until asked; Understands ill (Who), a. ill.

Ant had wings to her hurt, The.

1620 SHELTON *Quix.* II. xxxiii (1908) III. 55 The proverb says the ant had wings to do her hurt, and it may be Sancho the squire may sooner go to heaven than Sancho the governor.

Antwerp is a pistol pointed at the heart of England.

1903 H. B. GEORGE *Rel. of Geog. & Hist.* 240 'Antwerp', said Napoleon, 'is a pistol pointed at the heart of England'; and he did his best to create a fleet there.

Anvil, When you are an | hold you still; when you are a hammer, strike your fill.

1591 FLORIO *Sec. Frutes* 101. 1640 HERBERT 333. 1902 *Spectator* 24 May As a rule, they make the best of a bad job, remembering the old proverbial rhyme—'When you are', &c.

Anvil, *see also* Many strike on an a. (When), strike by measure.

Any port in a storm.

c. 1780 J. COBB *First Floor* II. ii (Inchbald's *Farces*) (A) Here is a door open, i' faith—any port in a storm, they say. 1821 SCOTT *Pirate* iv As the Scottishman's howf[1] lies right under your lee, why, take any port in a storm. 1882 BLACKMORE *Christowell* I It must be more than twenty years since I saw the inside of a church, ... but any port in a storm, we say. [[1] haunt.]

Any tooth, good barber.

1659 HOWELL *Eng. Prov.* 12. 1678 RAY 91.

Anything for a quiet life.

c. 1621 MIDDLETON *Anything for a Quiet Life*
Title (pr. 1662) 1670 RAY 135. 1738 SWIFT
(Dial. i) 341 *Miss.* Anything for a quiet life:
my nose itch'd. 1836–7 DICKENS *Pickwick*
xliii . . . as the man said wen he took the
sitivation at the lighthouse. 1837 MARRYAT
Diary on Cont. xxxiii A peaceable sort of
man, whose very physiognomy said 'anything for a quiet life'.

Anythingarian, He is an.

a. 1704 T. BROWN *Wks.* (1760) III. 97 Such
bifarious anythingarians, that always make
their interest the standard of their religion.
1738 SWIFT (Dial. i) 338 *Lady S.* What
religion is he of? *Spark.* Why, he is an
Anythingarian. 1850 KINGSLEY *Alton Locke*
xxii They made puir Robbie Burns an
anythingarian with their blethers.

Ape drunk, To be.

[L. *Ebrietas ut vituli et simiae*; Fr. *avoir vin
de singe.* According to tradition, a man when
he begins to drink is like a lamb, but he becomes in turn like the lion, the ape, and the
sow. *See* CHAUCER *Wks.* (Robinson) 871/1.]
c. 1386 CHAUCER *Manc. Prol.* H 44 I trowe
that ye dronken han wyn ape, And that is
whan men pleyen with a straw. 1509 A.
BARCLAY *Ship of Fools* (1874) I. 96 Some are
Ape dronke full of lawghter and of toyes.

Ape's an ape, An | a varlet's a varlet, though they be clad in silk or scarlet.

1539 TAVERNER f. 21 (A) An ape is an ape,
although she wear badges of golde. 1549
CHALONER tr. *Erasmus' Praise of Folly* C 3.
1563 B. GOOGE *Eglogs* iii (Arb.) 40 A prouerbe
olde, hath ofte ben harde and now full true
is tryed: An Ape, wyll euer be an Ape,
thoughe purple gaiments hyde. 1601 JONSON
Poetaster v. iii. 630. 1668 J. WILSON tr.
Moriæ Encomium 24 *Simia, est simia, etiamsi
purpurâ vestiatur* An ape, is an ape, though
clad in scarlet. 1732 FULLER no. 6391.

Ape(s), *see also* Bit and a knock; Higher the
a. goes, the more shows tail; Nuts to an
a.; Old a. hath old eye; Old maids lead
a. in hell.

Apollo, *see* Once in the year A. laughs.

Apothecary's mortar spoils the luter's music, The.

1651 HERBERT 359.

Apothecary, *see also* Broken a., new doctor;
Talk like an a.

Appair, *see* Amend when they cannot a.
(Some).

Apparel makes the man.

c. 1545 *Jacob and Esau*, E 4 Apparell setteth
out a man. 1588 W. AVERELL *Marvellous
Combat of Contrarieties* C 1ᵛ *Vestis virum*

facit, Apparell makes a man. 1591 FLORIO
Sec. Frutes 115 (A) Though manners makes,
yet apparell shapes. 1602 SHAKS. *Hamlet* I.
iii. 73 For the apparel oft proclaims the man.

Appeal from Philip drunk to Philip sober, To.

[VAL. MAX. 6. 2 Ext. 1 *Provocarem ad
Philippum, inquit, sed sobrium.*] 1531 SIR T.
ELYOT *Governour* II. v (Dent) 135 A poure
woman, agayne whom the same kynge had
gyuen iugement; . . . cried, I appele. . . . To
whom appelist thou? said the kyng. I
appele, said she, from the, nowe beinge
dronke, to Kynge Philip the sobre. 1882 W.
BATES *Maclise Port. Gal.* (1898) 1 Kinnaird
. . . retaining the document . . . till he had
an opportunity of appealing 'from Philip
drunk to Philip sober', succeeded in dissuading the poet from his angry purpose. 1906
ALEX. MACLAREN *Exposn., Deut.–1 Sam.* 49
Our appeal is not to men in the flush of
excitement, but to them in their hours of
solitary sane reflection. It is from 'Philip
drunk to Philip sober'.

Appearances, *see* Judge from a. (Never).

Appetite comes with eating.

[RABELAIS i. 5 *L'appétit vient en mangeant.*]
1600–1 SHAKS. *Hamlet* I. ii. 144 Why, she
would hang on him, As if increase of appetite
had grown By what it fed on. a. 1721 PRIOR
Dialog. of Dead (1907) 227 But as we say in
France, the appetite comes in eating; so in
writing you still found more to write. 1906
W. MAXWELL *Yalu to Pt. Arthur* 10 But
appetite comes with eating. Having absorbed
Port Arthur and begun on Manchuria, Russia
saw no reason why she should not have
Korea also.

Appetite, *see also* All things require skill but
a.; Leave (off) with a.; New meat, new a.

Apple, an egg, and a nut, you may eat after a slut, An.

1586 L. EVANS *Revised Withals Dict.* A 7 (A)
Apples, egges and nuttes, a man may eate
thoughe they be dressed by a slute. 1670 RAY
33 . . . .*Poma, ova atque nuces, si det tibi
sordida, gustes.* 1720 *Lady Pennyman's Misc.*
(1740) 18 We got some boiled eggs, and eat
more of our Bacon, which again put me in
Mind of our *English* proverb, of Egg, Apple
and Nut. 1732 FULLER no. 6250.

Apple going to bed, Eat an | make the doctor beg his bread.

1866 *N. & Q.* 3rd Ser. IX. 153. 1911 CROSSING
Folk Rhymes of Devon 122.

Apple of discord.

[The golden apple contended for by Juno,
Minerva, and Venus; whence any subject of
dissension.] a. 1649 DRUMM. OF HAWTH.
Irene Wks. (1711) 173 Who throw the apple
of dissension amongst your subjects. 1867
FREEMAN *Norm. Conq.* I. iv. 195 This great
and wealthy church constantly formed an
apple of discord.

Apple of Sodom.

[= fruit, dissolving into ashes; any disappointing, specious thing.] **1615** BRATHWAIT *Strappado for Div.* (1878) 48 See painted Sodom-apples faire to th'eye, But being tucht they perish instantly. **1634** RAINBOW *Labour* (1635) Those apples of Sodom which dye betwixt the hand and the mouth. **1679–1715** SOUTH *Sermons* (1842) i. 255 An apple of Sodom which, though it may entertain his eye with a florid, jolly white and red, yet, upon the touch, it shall fill his hand only with stench and foulness. **1905** W. J. ROLFE *Shaks. Sonn.* 19 The ashes to which the Sodom-apples of illicit love are turned in the end.

Apple to an oyster, As like as an.

1532 MORE *Works* 724 (1557) (A) No more lyke then an apple to an oyster. **1593–4** SHAKS. *Tam. Shrew* IV. ii. 101 *Tran.* In countenance somewhat doth resemble you. *Bion.* [*aside*] As much as an apple doth an oyster. **1670** RAY 206. **1732** FULLER no. 707 (with 'lobster' for 'oyster').

Apple-cart, To upset the.

1796 GROSE *Dict. Vulg. T.* (ed. 3) s.v. Down with his apple-cart; knock or throw him down. **1796–1801** FESSENDEN *Orig. Poems* (1806) 100 He talketh big words to congress and threateneth to overturn their apple-cart. **1848** in HODDER *Life Shaftesbury* If the Prince goes on like this, why he'll upset our apple-cart. **1896** C. RHODES in *Daily News* 24 July 5/5 Old Jameson has upset my apple-cart.

Apples swim! See how we | quoth the horse-turd.

1616 WITHALS 570 *Nos poma natamus.* Wee apples swimme quoth the horse turds. **1642** D. ROGERS *Naaman* 545 Hypocrites are very glad when God's and their ends concur: as the dung swimming in the same stream with the apples, said, We apples swim. **1692** L'ESTRANGE *Aesop's Fab.* cxxxiv (1738) 150 Upon a . . . fall of rain, the current carried away a huge heap of apples, together with a dung-hill that lay in the watercourse. . . . As they went thus . . . the horse-turds would be . . . crying out still, 'Alack-a-day! How we apples swim!'

Apple(s), *see also* Better an a. given; Choice in rotten a.; Egg to the a. (From the); Good a. on sour stock (No); Lost with an a.; Rotten a. (Not worth a); Rotten a. injures its neighbours.

Approve, *see* See and a. the better course.

April blows his horn, When | it's good both for hay and corn.

1670 RAY 41 . . . That is, when it thunders in April.

April flood carries away the frog and her brood, An.

1639 CLARKE 307. **1670** RAY 41.

April showers bring forth May flowers.

c. **1430** LYDGATE *Reason & Sensuality* 1. 6310 Holsom as the Aprile showr fallyng on the herbes newe. *c.* **1560** WRIGHT *Songs, Philip and Mary* 213 (Roxb. Cl.) (A) When Aprell sylver showers so sweet can make May flowers to sprynge. **1573** TUSSER (1578) 103 Swéete April showers, Doo spring Maie flowers. **1606–7** SHAKS. *Ant. & Cleop.* III. ii. 44 The April's in her eyes ; it is love's spring, And these the showers to bring it on. **1648** HERRICK *Hesper.* Wks. (Gros.) I. 38 First, April, she with mellow showers Opens the way for early flowers ; Then after her comes smiling May, in a more rich and sweet array. **1670** RAY 41 April showers bring forth May flowers. **1821** SCOTT *Kenilw.* xxx. ii I believe, if showers fall in April, that we shall have flowers in May. **1846** DENHAM 36 March winds and April showers bring forth May flowers.

April weather, rain and sunshine both together.

1607 TOURNEUR *Rev. Trag.* v. ii Alas! I shine in tears, like the sun in April. **1824** SCOTT *Redg.* xviii Smiles and tears mingled on Lilias's cheeks, like showers and sunshine in April weather. **1893** INWARDS 23.

April, *see also* Blow in A. (If they [cherries]); Cold A. barn will fill; Dove's flood is worth (In A.); First of A. hunt the gowk;—you may send a fool whither you will; March borrowed from A. ; March the birds begin ; March the cuckoo starts; Men are A. when they woo; Third of A. comes cuckoo ; Windy March and rainy A.

Apron-strings, To be tied to (hold by) (a woman's).

1678 RAY 226 To hold by the Apron-strings, *i.e.* in right of his wife. **1743** FIELDING *Jonathan Wild*, II. iii The hero . . . was not of that low snivelling breed of mortals who, as is generally expressed, *tie themselves to a woman's apron strings*. **1849** MACAULAY *Hist. Eng.* II. 649 He could not submit to be tied to the apron strings even of the best of wives.

Archdeacon Pratt, *see* Jack Sprat.

Archer is not known by his arrows, but his aim, A good.

1580 LYLY *Euph. & his Eng.* Wks. (Bond) II. 104. **1732** FULLER no. 135.

Archer(s), *see also* English a. . . . twenty-four Scots; Speak good of a.

Architect, *see* Every man is the a. of own fortune.

Arden, *see* Black bear of A.

Are you there with your bears?

1594 LYLY *Moth. Bomb.* II. iii. Wks. (1858) II. 96 *Cand.* I . . . come to make choice of a mistresse. *Silena* A ha, are you there with

your beares? **1668** SHADWELL *Sullen Lov.* v.
iii *Rog.* Would she had it, for her own sake,
and yours too. *Co. G.* Faith! are you there
with your bears? Nay, then, I have brought
my hog to a fair market. **1742** RICHARDSON
Pamela III. 335 O ho, Nephew! are you
thereabouts with your bears?

Argument(s), *see* Soft words hard a.

Argus abroad and a mole at home (or vice versa), An.

[Argus, in fable, had 100 eyes.] **1586** PETTIE
Guazzo's Civ. Conv. 74 Doe you not knowe,
that (as the Prouerbe is) we see better a farre
of, than hard by vs, & that at home we see
no more than Moles, but abroade as much as
Argus. **1636** s. WARD *Serm.* (1862) 74 False
zeal loves to be gadding, is eagle-eyed
abroad, and mole-eyed at home. **1642**
TORRIANO 65. **1732** FULLER no. 582.

Argus, *see also* Eyes as A. (As many).

Argyle, Duke of, *see* God bless the D. of A.

Arm(s), *see* Clothe thee in war, a. thee in
peace; Open a. (With); Stretch your a.
no further than sleeve; Weapons of war
will not a. fear; Wide therm had never
long a.

Armour is light at table.

1640 HERBERT 360.

Armour, *see also* Hog in a.; Warm one in
his a. (Absurd to).

Army, like a serpent, goes on its belly, An.

1908 *Times Lit. Sup.* ii. 20 Mar. An army
travels on its belly—and, if the belly be not
well looked after, the pace will be slow.

Army of stags led by a lion would be more formidable than one of lions led by a stag, An.

[PLUTARCH *Chabriae Apophth.* 3 Φοβερώτε-
ρόν ἐστιν ἐλάφων στρατόπεδον ἡγουμένου
λέοντος ἢ λεόντων ἐλάφου. L. *Formidabilior
cervorum exercitus, duce leone, quam leonum
cervo.*] **1890** W. F. BUTLER *Sir C. Napier* 150
Many . . . had seen . . . the fruits of bad
leadership in Cabul, and had learnt to value
the truth of the proverb, . . . that 'a herd of
deer led by a lion was more formidable to
the enemy than a herd of lions led by a deer'.

Aroint, *see* Rynt.

Arrows, Not to know of what wood to make.

1604 R. DALLINGTON *View of France* G 3 As
their prouerbe is here, Il ne scauoit de quel
bois faire ses flesches: He knewe not of what
wood to make his arrowes.

Arrow(s), *see also* Bolt (A.) came never out
of your bag (That); Shoot a second a. to
find first; Wood (Like), like a.

Arsie versie, *see* Kim Kam a. v

Art consists in concealing art.

[L. *Ars est celare artem.*] **1583** MELBANCKE
Philotimus G1 (A) It is a chief point of art to
dissemble art. **1603** BRETON *Packet Mad Lett.*
Wks. (Gros.) II. 11 I have heard scholars
say, that it is art to conceal art, and that
under a face of simplicity, is hidden much
subtlety. **1707** SWIFT *Facult. of Mind* Wks.
(1856) II. 285 In oratory the greatest art is
to hide art. **1907** A. C. BENSON *Upton Lett.*
201 Henry James . . . seems to be so afraid
of anything that is obvious . . . that his art
conceals not art but nature.

Art, He who has an | has everywhere a part.

1666 TORRIANO 14 Who hath a trade, or an
art, every where claims a livelyhood. **1855**
BOHN 399 *Ital.*

Art has no enemy but ignorance.

1599 JONSON *Ev. Man out of Humour*
Induction 219 Arte hath an enemy cal'd
Ignorance. **1653** *Shinkin ap Shone Her Pro-
gnostn. for 1654* 1.

Art improves nature.

1563 R. RAINOLDES *Foundation of Rhetoric*
A1. **1587** UNDERDOWNE *Heliodorus* iii. 94
(T.T.) (A) Arte can breake nature. **1732**
FULLER no. 814 Art helps nature, and
experience art

Art is long, life is short.

[HIPPOCRATES *Aphor.* 1. 1 'Ο βίος βραχύς,
ἡ δὲ τέχνη μακρή. Life is short, and art is
long. L. *Ars longa, vita brevis.*] *c.* **1380**
CHAUCER *Parl. Foules* 1 The lyf so short, the
craft so long to lerne. **1839** LONGFELLOW
Psalm of Life Art is long, and Time is
fleeting. **1869** M. ARNOLD *Culture & Anarchy*,
Our Liberal practitioners. 'Art is long',
says the *Times*, 'and life is short.'

Art, In every | it is good to have a master.

1640 HERBERT 346.

Art(s), *see also* Honours nourish a.; More
matter less a.; Poverty is mother of a.

Arthur could not tame woman's tongue.

1659 HOWELL *Brit. Prov.* 23.

Arthur was not, but whilst he was.

1659 HOWELL *Brit. Prov.* 35 Arthur himself
had but his time. **1662** FULLER *(Cardigan)*
III. 519 'Bu Arthur ond tra fu'. That is,
'Arthur was not, but whilst he was'. It is
sad to say, 'Nos fuimus Trojes'. The greatest
eminency when not extant is extinct.

Arthur, *see also* King A.

As bad as, As fit as, As freely as, As good
(as), As like as, As many, As much, As
well, *see under significant words following.*

Asfordby Bridge, *see* Gone over A. B.

Ash (tree), *see* Oak 's before the a. (If).

Ashamed, *see* Never be a. to eat meat.

Ashes, *see* Divine a. better than earthly meal; Eat a peck of dirt (a.); Lay on more wood, a. give money.

Ashford, *see* Naughty A.

Ask a kite for a feather, and she'll say, she has but just enough to fly with.

1732 FULLER no. 816.

Ask but enough, and you may lower the price as you list.

1642 TORRIANO 46. **1813** RAY 2.

Ask, He that cannot | cannot live.

1616 DRAXE 20. **1639** CLARKE 41.

Ask for bread and be given a stone, To.

[**1611** BIBLE *Matt.* vii. 9 Or what man is there of you, whom if his sonne aske bread, will hee giue him a stone?] **1834** MARRYAT *Jacob Faith.* xxxvii 'We will find you bread, and hard enough you will find it . . . it 's like a flint'. 'So we ask for bread, and you give us a stone.' *a.* **1880** MARQ. SALISBURY in *Life* (1921) I. 120 When asked to support a Church scheme for . . . purely secular . . . work . . . , he refused, with the brief comment, 'They are asking you for bread and you are offering them stones.'

Ask much to have a little.

1539 TAVERNER (1549) E1ᵛ *Iniquum petendum ut aequum feras.* Aske that is unreasonable if thou mayst beare away that is reasonable. **1640** HERBERT 332.

Ask my fellow if I be a thief.

1545 TAVERNER I1ᵛ. **1546** HEYWOOD II. v. **1549** LATIMER *3rd Serm. bef. Edw. VI* (P.S.) 139 Thieves and thieves' fellows be all of one sort. They were wont to say, 'Ask my fellow if I be a thief'. **1614** CAMDEN 303. **1641** FERGUSSON 90 Speir at Jock thief my marrow [i.e. companion] if I be a leal man. **1659** FULLER *Appeal Inj. Innoc.* in *Hist. of Camb. Univ.* (1840) 366 'Ask my fellow if I be a thief'; ask a poetical fable, if a monkish legend be a liar.

Ask no questions and you will be told no lies.

1773 GOLDSMITH *She Stoops to C.* III Ask me no questions and I'll tell you no fibs. **1818** SCOTT *Ht. Midl.* x If ye'll ask nae questions, I'll tell ye nae lees. **1860** DICKENS *Gt. Expect.* ii Drat that boy . . . Ask no questions and you'll be told no lies.

Ask of my fire brown bread, I had rather | than borrow of my neighbour white.

1640 HERBERT 392.

Ask pardon, *see* Never a. p. before accused.

Ask pears of an elm tree, To.

1620 SHELTON *Quix.* II. xl (1908) III. 94 To think that I'll get up on him, either in the saddle or at the crupper, were to ask pears of the elm.

Ask the mother if the child be like the father.

1732 FULLER no. 818.

Ask the price, *see* Good thing cheap (He will never have) that is afraid to.

Ask your neighbour if you shall live in peace, You must.

1639 CLARKE 203. **1721** KELLY 258 *No man can live longer in peace than his neighbour pleases.* For an ill neighbour, with his scolding, noise, complaints, law-suits, and indictments, may be very troublesome. **1732** FULLER no. 5961.

Asketh faintly beggeth a denial, He that.

[SENECA *Hipp. Qui timide rogat, docet negare.*] *a.* **1591** H. SMITH *Serm.* (1866) II. 8 It is an old saying, that he which asketh faintly teacheth us to deny him. **1595–6** SHAKS. *Rich. II* V. iii. 103 He prays but faintly and would be denied. **1633** P. FLETCHER *Pisc. Eclog.* Wks. (1908) II. 202 Cold beggars freeze our gifts: thy faint suit breeds her no. **1732** FULLER no. 2042.

Asking, *see* Lose nothing for a.

Aspen leaf, To quake (tremble) like an.

c. **1374** CHAUCER *Troylus* III. 1151 (A) Right as an aspes leef she gan to quake. *c.* **1386** Id. *Somnour's Prol.* 3 That lyk an aspen leef he quook for yre. ? *a.* **1483** *Mankind* 727 *Mercy.* My body trymmelyth as the aspen leffe. **1593–4** SHAKS. *Titus Andron.* II. iv. 45 O! had the monster seen those lily hands Tremble, like aspen-leaves, upon a lute. **1597–8** *2 Hen. IV* II. iv *Quick.* Feel, masters, how I shake . . . an 'twere an aspen leaf: I cannot abide swaggerers. **1824** D. M. MOIR *Mansie W.* xxv Tommy and Benje trembled from top to toe, like aspen leaves.

Ass climbs a ladder, When an | we may find wisdom in women.

1678 RAY *Adag. Hebr.* 401. **1732** FULLER no. 5546.

Ass endures his burden, but not more than his burden, An.

1599 MINSHEU 83 . . . *El asno sufre la carga, no la sobre carga.* **1620** SHELTON *Quix.* II. lxxi (1908) III. 317 It now sufficeth . . . that the ass endure his charge, but not the surcharge. **1651** HERBERT 367.

Ass falleth, Where-ever an | there will he never fall again.

1642 TORRIANO 48. **1732** FULLER no. 5643.

Ass goes a-travelling, If an | he'll not come home a horse.

1732 FULLER no. 2668. **1852** E. FITZGERALD *Polonius* xlii 'You must swear by Allah, smoke chibouques, and spell Pasha differently from every predecessor, or we shall scarce believe you have been in a hareem!' 'NEVER WENT OUT ASS, AND CAME HOME HORSE.'

Ass in a lion's skin, An.

[The title of one of Æsop's Fables.] **1549** CHALONER tr. *Erasmus' Praise of Folly* A3 Walke lyke Asses in Lyons skinnes, K4 Lyke the asse wrapped in a lyons skinne. **1711** ADDISON *Spect.* No. 13, par. 4 The ill-natured world might call him the Ass in the Lion's Skin. **1748** SMOLLETT *Rod. Rand.* liv He had talked so much of his valour that I had . . . rated him as an ass in a lion's skin.

Ass kicks you, When an | never tell it.

1834 MISS EDGEWORTH *Helen* xxiv Lady Cecilia . . . guessed that Lord Davenant had been circumvented by some diplomatist of inferior talents, and she said to Helen, When an ass kicks you never tell it, is a maxim which mamma . . . always acts upon'.

Ass knows well in whose face he brays, The.

1853 TRENCH iii (1894) 52 What a grave humour lurks in this: *The ass knows well in whose face he brays.* [Sp.] Bien sabe el asno en cuya cara rebozna.

Ass loaded with gold climbs to the top of a castle, An.

[PLUT. *Apoph. Reg.* 178 A.] **1612** CHAPMAN *Widow's Tears* I. iv You must be the ass charged with crowns to make way to the fort, and I the conqueror to follow, and seize it. **1612** T. ADAMS *Gallant's Burden* 52 The Prouerbe sayth, *There is no earthly Gate, but an Asse laden with Gold can enter.* **1620** SHELTON *Quix.* II. xxxv (1908) III. 71 The usual proverb is, 'An ass laden with gold will go lightly uphill'. **1732** FULLER no. 587 An ass laden with gold overtakes everything. Id. No. 588.

Ass loaded with gold still eats thistles, The.

1632 MASSINGER *City Madam* II. i (Merm.) 423 *Luke* Or wilt thou [*to* GOLD.] being keeper of the cash, Like an ass that carries dainties, feed on thistles? *c.* **1645** HOWELL *Lett.* (1903) III. 76 He makes not nummum his numen, money his god. . . . The first . . . is worse than the Arcadian ass, who while he carrieth gold on his back, eats thistles.

Ass must be tied where the master will have him, An.

1642 TORRIANO 15. **1732** FULLER no. 589.

Ass of, To make an.

1595–6 SHAKS. *Mids. N.* III. i. 124 This is to make an ass of me, to fright me, if they could.

Ass of Isis, The.

1598 MARSTON *Sat.* 1 Asse, take off Isis, no man honours thee. **1599** DANIEL *Musophilus* And thinke like Isis Asse, all Honours are Given unto them alone, the which are done Unto the painted Idoll which they bear. **1612** CHAPMAN *Widow's Tears* I. i. 153 And let the beast's dull apprehension take the honour done to Isis, done to himself.

Ass of oneself, To make an.

1865 TROLLOPE *Belton Est.* xx. 241 Don't make such an ass of yourself as to suppose that, &c.

Ass play on a harp (lute)? Did you ever hear an.

13 . . CHAUCER *Boethius* bk. I prose iv Artow lyke an asse to the harpe? *c.* **1390** CHAUCER *Troylus* I. 731. **1549** CHALONER tr. *Erasmus' Praise of Folly* Du^v As inapte as an asse is to finger on harpe. **1549** Ibid. O$_1$ As if an asse were set to plaie on a gitterne.

Ass pricked must needs trot, An.

1573 SANDFORD (1576) 206. **1629** *Book of Meery Riddles* Prov. 58.

Ass (a fool) that brayeth against another ass, He is an.

1616 DRAXE 70 He is an asse that braieth against an asse. **1855** BOHN 375 He is fool enough himself who will bray against another ass.

Ass that brays most eats least, The.

1611 COTGRAVE s.v. 'Asne'. **1670** RAY 3.

Ass thinks himself worthy to stand with the king's horses, Every.

1639 CLARKE 254. **1732** FULLER no. 1405.

Ass to be called a lion? What good can it do an.

1732 FULLER no. 5490.

Ass, *see also* All men say you are an a. (When), time to bray; Angry as an a.; Better ride on an a.; Braying of an a. does not reach heaven; Dispute about shadow of an a.; Drives an a. and leads a whore (Who); Fault of the a. not on packsaddle; Hold the a. by the bridle; Mule (A.) doth scrub another (One); Straw to his dog, bones to a. (Gives); Tell you, you are an a. (If one); Thistle is salad for a.'s mouth; Washeth an a.'s head (He that). *See also* Donkey.

Assault(ed), *see* Man a. is half taken.

Asses bray; Hark! I hear the | we shall have some rain to-day.

1883 ROPER 26. **1893** INWARDS 127.

Astrology is true, but the astrologers cannot find it.

1640 HERBERT 347.

At ease, He that is | seeks dainties.
1640 HERBERT 362.

At hand, quoth Pickpurse.
1575 *App. & Virg.* (Mal. Soc.) l. 531 At hand (quoth picke purse) here redy am I. **1597–8** SHAKS. *1 Hen. IV* II. i. 53 *Gads.* What, ho! chamberlain. *Chamb.* (*within*). 'At hand, quoth pickpurse.'

At hand, All is not | that helps.
1641 FERGUSSON 4. **1721** KELLY 21 . . . Assistance and support may come from whence we cannot foresee. **1732** FULLER no. 526.

At last, *see* Long looked for comes a. l.; Loseth indeed that loseth a. l.; Lost (It is not) that comes a. l.; Never long that comes a. l.

Athanasius against the world.
1597 HOOKER *Eccles. Polity* v. xlii (1830) II. 139 This was the plain condition of those times; the whole world against Athanasius, and Athanasius against it. **1861** DEAN STANLEY *Hist. East. Ch.* (1862) vii. 234–6 In the Nicene Council[1] . . . he was almost the only high ecclesiastic who stood firm against the Arians . . . *Athanasius contra mundum*; a proverb which . . . sets forth the claims of individual . . . judgement. [[1] 325.]

Atheism, *see* Devil divides . . . between a. and superstition.

Atheist is one point beyond the devil, An.
1629 T. ADAMS *Serm.* (1861–2) II. 341 Atheists . . . are in some respects worse than the Devil: he knows and acknowledgeth a Deity; these say, 'There is no God'. **1732** FULLER no. 593 An atheist is got one point beyond the devil.

Atheist(s), *see also* Physicians (Where three), there are two a.

Athens, The modern (*i.e.* Edinburgh).
1822 SCOTT *Nigel* (*Introd. Epist.*) I think our Modern Athens much obliged to me for having established such an extensive manufacture. **1905** J. OXENHAM *White Fire* ii Her husband had been a professor in Edinburgh, and the society he and she had enjoyed in the modern Athens, thirty years before, was her standard of what society ought to be. **1911** *Spectator* 25 Nov. 903 Some of the 'Modern Athenians' look on their unfinished temple on Calton Hill . . . as making the architecture of Edinburgh even more like that of fallen Athens than it would otherwise have been.

Athens, *see also* Owls to A.

Atlantic, *see* Mrs. Partington.

Attain(ed), *see* Hardly a. are longer retained.

Attendance, *see* Dance a.

Attorney(s), *see* Kick an a. downstairs; Two a. can live in a town.

Auger, *see* Wimble will let in a.

August, *see* Born in A.; Dry A. doth harvest no harm; Twenty-fourth of A. be fair (If).

Aunt had been a man, If my | she'd have been my uncle.
1813 RAY 202 . . . Spoken in derision of those who make ridiculous surmises. **1910** A. C. BENSON *Silent Isle* xxii. 145 A speaker recommending a measure . . . that . . . would be a very satisfactory one if only the conditions . . . were different. 'As much as to say', said Whately . . . , 'that if my aunt were a man, he would be my uncle.'

Aunts, She is one of mine | that made mine uncle go a begging.
1678 RAY 227.

Aunts, She is one of my | that my uncle never got any good of.
1855 BOHN 148.

Author, Like | like book.
1646 CODRINGTON 204. **1670** RAY 15.

Autumn fruit without spring blossoms, No.
1732 FULLER no. 3544. **1846** DENHAM 57 No tree bears fruit in autumn that does not blossom in the spring.

Autumn, *see also* Fair things (Of) a. is fair.

Autumnal agues are long or mortal.
1640 HERBERT 323.

Avarice, *see* Poverty is in want of much, a. of everything.

Aver, *see* Holds up her head like hundred pound a.; Inch of a nag worth an a.; Kindly a. never good horse.

Avernus, *see* Descent to A. is easy.

Aw, *see* Well worth a.

Away goes the devil when he finds the door shut against him.
1659 HOWELL *Ital.–Eng.* 4 The devil turns his back at a gate shut. **1666** TORRIANO 67 The devil turns his back, if he find the door shut upon him. **1855** BOHN 323.

Away, *see also* Good that are a. (They are aye); Good wife's a. (When), keys are tint; Hold that will a. (Who can); Once a way (a.) and aye a.

Awe makes Dun draw, *see* Well worth aw, it makes the plough draw.

Awls, *see* Six a. make shoemaker.

Axe to grind, To have an.
[= to have private ends to serve: in reference to a story told by Franklin.] **1815** C. MINER

Who'll turn Grindstones? When I see a merchant over-polite to his customers . . . thinks I, that man has an axe to grind. **1902** W. BESANT *Autobiog.* vii. 123 Sea-captains . . . have no private axe to grind. **1927** *Times* 28 Nov. 14/2 Both Germany and Russia have axes to grind in all that concerns the Lithuanian Republic.

Axe, *see also* Pine wishes herself shrub when a. at her root; Sandal tree perfumes **a.** that fells.

Axle-tree for an oven, A pretty fellow to make an.

1670 RAY 162 (*Chesh.*). **1732** FULLER no. 362.

B

B, *see* Knows not a B from battledore (*or* bull's foot); Say B to battledore.

Babble, *see* Burn does not b. (When).

Babe, *see* Love the b. for her that bare it.

Baby of Beelzebub's bower, Ye be a.

1362 LANGLAND *P.Pl.* A II. 100 A bastard i-boren of Belsabubbes Kunne. **1546** HEYWOOD II. iv. 51.

Baby (-ies), *see also* Empty the b. with the bath; Look b.; Smell of the b.

Babylon, The modern (*i.e.* London).

1835 J. M. WILSON in *Tales of Borders* I. 355, 6 I proceeded to London . . . and . . . found myself . . . in a wilderness. . . . Months passed away, and I was still a wanderer upon the streets of the modern Babylon.

Babylon, *see also* Way to B. will never bring to Jerusalem.

Bacchants, *see* Thyrsus-bearers.

Bacchus hath drowned more men than Neptune.

1732 FULLER no. 830.

Bacchus, *see also* Ceres and B. (Without) Venus grows cold.

Bachelors laugh (grin) and show our teeth, We | but you married men laugh till your hearts ache.

1651 HERBERT 372. **1670** RAY 48. **1732** FULLER no. 5433.

Bachelors' fare: bread and cheese, and kisses.

1738 SWIFT (Dial. i) 338.

Bachelors' wives and maids' children are well taught.

1546 HEYWOOD II. vi. 61. **1614** CAMDEN 304. **1738** SWIFT (Dial. i) 341 Ay, ay! bachelors' wives and maids' children are finely tutored. **1834** MARRYAT *Jacob Faith.* xlii Bachelors' wives are always best managed, they say.

Bachelor(s), *see also* Lewd b. jealous husband; Son of a b.; Two b. drinking to you . . . soon be married.

Back door robs the house, The.

1616 DRAXE 204 The backe doore maketh theeves. **1640** HERBERT no. 474. **1624**

TORRIANO 69. **1659** N.R. 100. **1732** FULLER no. 4402.

Back door, *see also* Nice wife and b. d. make rich man poor; Two daughters and b. d. are thieves. *See also* Postern.

Back is broad enough to bear jests, His.

1639 CLARKE 86. **1670** RAY 163.

Back, *see also* Bear him on my b.; Bear till his b. break; Belly (If it were not for), the b. might wear gold; Claw the b. of; Fall b. fall edge; Fall on his b. and break his nose; God shapes b. for burden; Good for b., bad for head; Rod for his own b.

Backare,[1] quoth Mortimer to his sow.

1546 HEYWOOD I. xi. 34. *a.* **1553** UDALL *Royster D.* I. ii (Arb.) 16. **1593–4** SHAKS. *Tam. Shrew* II. 73 Backare! you are marvellous forward. [[1] stand back.]

Backbiters, *see* Hearers (Were there no), no b.

Bacon, *see* Devil is a hog (When), you shall eat b.; Flitch of b. from Dunmow; Loves b. well that licks; Save one's b.; Sell one's b.; Think there is b. (Where you), there is no chimney.

Bad a Gill, There is not so | but there's as bad a Will.

1678 RAY 146. **1732** FULLER no. 6112.

Bad bush is better than the open field, A.

Cf. c. **1300** *Provs. of Hending,* no. 19 in *Anglia* **51.** 258 Ounder buskes me shal fair weder abide. *cf. c.* **1500** *Sloane MS. 747* f. 66a Under the bosshe yt ys gode fayre weder to abyde. **1670** RAY 58 . . . Better to have a bad friend or relation, than to be quite destitute. **1792** BURNS *Wks.* II. 397 Better a wee bush than nae bield. **1820** SCOTT *Monast.* iii Elspeth . . . will give us houseroom. . . . These evil showers make the low bush better than no bield.

Bad cause that none dare speak in, It is a.

1639 CLARKE 199. **1737** RAMSAY III. 187 It's an ill cause that the lawyers think shame o'.

Bad cloth that will take no colour, It is a.

1546 HEYWOOD II. ix. 76 . . . Ye were neuer so wise, To take specke of colour, of good aduyse. **1580** LYLY *Euph. & his Eng.* (Arb.) 408 Be your cloath neuer so badde it will take some colour, and your cause neuer so false, it will beare some shew of probabilytie. **1670** RAY 71 . . . Cattiva è quella lana che non si puo tingere. *Ital.*

Bad custom is like a good cake, better broken than kept, A.

1611 COTGRAVE s.v. 'Gasteau'. **1670** RAY 76.

Bad day that hath a good night, It is never a.

1608 JOHN DENISON *Three-fold Resolution* (1616) 422 Wee haue an old saying: That is no bad day, that hath a good night. **1641** FERGUSSON 98 They had never an ill day that had a good evening. **1670** RAY 6.

Bad dog never sees the wolf, A.

[**14**. . *Prov. communs* À mauvais chien on ne peut montrer le loup.] **1611** COTGRAVE s.v. 'Loup'. **1640** HERBERT 319.

Bad dog, Into the mouth of a | often falls a good bone.

1639 CLARKE 45. **1670** RAY 82 . . . Souvent à mauvais chien tombe un bon os en gueule. *Gall.*

Bad excuse is better than none at all, A. (*Cf.* Bad shift, &c.)

1551 T. WILSON *Rule of Reason* S 6 This is as thei saie in English, better a badde excuse, then none at all, in Latine it is called, *non causa pro causa posita. a.* **1553** UDALL *Royster D.* v. ii (Arb.) 81 Yea Custance, better (they say) a badde scuse than none. **1579** GOSSON *Sch. Abuse* (Arb.) 42.

Bad is the best.

1564 BULLEIN *Dial. agst. Fever* (E.E.T.S.) 77 Bad is the best, the world amends like sour ale in summer. **1609** SHAKS. *Sonn.* 112. 4 Creating every bad a perfect best. **1678** RAY 96 Where bad 's the best, naught must be the choice. **1800** EDGEWORTH *The Will* ii Bad 's the best, if that be the best of her characters.

Bad money drives out good.

1902–4 LEAN III. 425 Bad money drives out good (money), i.e. inconvertible paper drives out gold.—Gresham's Law.

Bad penny (shilling) always comes back, A.

1824 SCOTT *Redg.* ii Bring back Darsie? little doubt of that—the bad shilling is sure enough to come back again. **1872** BESANT & RICE *Ready-m. Mort.* viii I always said he'd come back like a bad shilling.

Bad sack that will abide no clouting, It is a.

1546 HEYWOOD II. iv. 49. **1670** RAY 23.

Bad shearer never had a good sickle, A.

1721 KELLY 12 An ill Shearer never got a good Hook. **1846** DENHAM 50.

Bad shift is better than none, A. (*Cf.* Bad excuse, &c.)

1599 PORTER *Angry Wom. Abingd.* IV. iii (Merm.) 179 'Tis good to have a cloak for the rain; a bad shift is better than none at all. **1692** L'ESTRANGE *Aesop's Fab.* cxix (1738) 136.

Bad Spaniard makes a good Portuguese, A.

1846 GRANT *Rom. of War* ix The Portuguese are not over nice . . . and we have a proverb among us, 'that a bad Spaniard makes a good Portuguese'. **1853** TRENCH iii 52 The Spaniard's contempt for his peninsular neighbours finds emphatic utterance in: *Take from a Spaniard all his good qualities, and there remains a Portuguese.*

Bad to his own, Who is | is bad to himself.

1855 BOHN 566. *Ital.*

Bad woman is worse than a bad man, A.

1893 LIDDON *Serm. O. Test.* 159 The current . . . proverb, that 'a bad woman is much worse than a bad man', owes its force to the fact that women . . . fall deeper, because they fall . . . from a higher level.

Bad (Ill) workman quarrels with his tools, A.

1568 G. B. GELLI *The Fearful Fancies of the Florentine* tr. W. Barker B 3 All artificers not cunninge, doe impute all the errowrs they do, to the matter they work on. **1611** COTGRAVE s.v. Outil' A bungler cannot find (or fit himself with) good tooles. **1640** HERBERT 320 Never had ill workman good tools. **1670** RAY 158. **1738** SWIFT (Dial. ii) 348 (*Smart*) This knife . . . is so blunt. (*Ans.*) They say, an ill workman never had good tools. **1907** *Japan Times* 26 Feb. General Bildering . . . says it is only a bad workman who quarrels with his tools and repudiates Kuropatkin's criticism of the rank and file.

Bad, *see also* Best go first, b. remain; No man ever . . . b. all at once; Nothing so b. but might have been worse; — in which is not some good.

Badger, *see* Gip with an ill rubbing, quoth B.

Bag (Sack), To give one the.

[= to leave without warning; later, to dismiss.] **1576** *Common Conditions* in Brandl's *Quellen* 599 (A) This tinkerly trade, wee giue it the bagge. **1592** GREENE

Upst. Courtier in *Harl. Misc.* (Malh.) II. 236 To giue **your** masters the bagge. **1629** T. ADAMS *Serm.* (1861–2) II. 250 As [Judas] gave religion the bag for the world, so the world gave him the bag, and turned him a-begging. **1637** SHIRLEY *Hyde Park* I. i *Rid.* If she would affect one of us, for my part I am indifferent. *Vent.* So say I too, but to give us both the canvas! [*Note.* From the practice of journeymen mechanics carrying their tools with them, when dismissed, they were said to get the canvas or the bag.] **1825** C. M. WESTMACOTT *Eng. Spy* I. 178 You munna split on me, or I shall get the zack for telling on ye. **1908** E. M. SNEYD-KYNNERSLEY *H.M.I.* (1910) ii A new minister . . . preached against the war. They had a meeting in the vestry after service, and gave him the sack before dinner.

Bag to hold, To give (one) the.

[= to leave in the lurch.] **1793** T. JEFFERSON *Writ.* (1859) IV. 7 She will leave Spain the bag to hold. **1823** SCOTT *Peveril* vii She gave me the bag to hold, and was smuggling in a corner with a rich old Puritan.

Bag(s), *see also* Beggar beat his b. (Would make); Put him up in a b.; Too much breaks b.; Toom b. rattle; World wags (I wot how), best loved that hath most b.

Bagpipe; He is like a | he never talks till his belly be full.

1616 DRAXE 76 A baggepipe will not lightly speake, untill his belly be full. **1618** D. BELCHIER *Hans Beere-pot* E iv Or Baggepype-like not speake before thou art full. **1678** RAY 291. **1906** QUILLER-COUCH *Sir J. Constantine* xx There 's another saying that even a bagpipe won't speak till his belly be full.

Bagpipes, *see also* Lincolnshire.

Bag-pudding, *see* Deceit in a b. (No); Sweetheart and b.

Bailery, *see* Whiles thou, whiles I, so goes b.

Bailiff of Bedford is coming, The.

1655 FULLER *Hist. Univ. Camb.* v (1840) 105 In the next (being a wet and windy) winter, down comes *the bailiff of Bedford* (so the country-people commonly call the overflowing of the river Ouse), . . . and breaks down all their paper-banks.

Bailiff of the Marshland, The.

1662 FULLER (*Norfolk*) II. 447 'He is arrested by the Bailie of the *Marshland*.' The air of Marshland in this country is none of the wholesomest. . . . Hence . . . strangers coming hither are clapt on the back with an ague. **1897** BP. CREIGHTON *Story of Eng. Shires* 379 The Fenmen . . . counted little of the ague which attacked them, and was called 'the Bailiff of the Marshland'.

Bailiff, *see also* Gerard's b. (Here is).

Bairns o' Falkirk, Like the | they'll end ere they mend.

1862 HISLOP 212 . . . 'This is a proverbial

saying of ill-doing persons, as expressive of there being no hope of them.'

Bairn(s), *see also* Death of a b. is not skailing of house; Fools and b. . . . half-done work; God's b. is eith to lear; Hands off other folks' b.; Sair dung b. that dare not greet; Scant of b. that brought you up; Thrawn faced b. gotten against father's will.

Bait hides the hook, The.

1579 LYLY *Euphues* (Arb.) 77 Beauty . . . was a deceitful bayte with a deadly hooke. **1732** FULLER no. 4403. **1855** BOHN 498.

Bait, *see also* Escaped mouse feels taste of b.; Welsh b.

Bake, *see* Brew (As they), so let them b.

Baker by his bow legs, He should be a.

1607 DEKKER & WEBSTER *Westward Hoe* II. ii (A) Will women's tongues, like bakers' legs, never go straight! **1678** RAY 91.

Baker, Be not a | if your head be of butter.

1640 HERBERT 332.

Baker to the pillory, I fear we part not yet, quoth the.

[There were severe penalties for impurity of bread or shortness of weight.] **1546** HEYWOOD II. ii. 47 And so late met, that I feare we parte not yéet, Quoth the baker to the pylorie. **1659** HOWELL *Eng. Prov.* 11 Ile take no leave of you, quoth the Baker to the Pillory.

Baker's daughter, *see* Three dear years will raise a b. d.

Baking beside meal, It is good.

1641 FERGUSSON 64. **1721** KELLY 181 . . . That is, people may do well enough, when they have some to uphold, and supply them.

Balaam's ass, *see* Mackerel is in season.

Balance distinguisheth not between gold and lead, The.

1640 HERBERT 346.

Bald as a coot, As.

a. **1300** *Gloss. Walter de Biblesworth* in Wright's *Vocab.* 165 *Une blarye*, a balled cote. **1430** LYDGATE *Chron. Troy.* II. xv And yet he was so balde as is a coote. **1546** HEYWOOD I v. 11 What though she be toothlesse, and balde as a coote? **1621** BURTON *Anat. Mel.* III. iii. I. ii (1651) 599 I have an old grim sire to my husband, as bald as a coot.

Bald head is soon shaven, A.

14 . . *Reliq. Antiquae* i. 75 (A) A bare berd wyl sone be shave. **1678** RAY 96. **1802** WOLCOT (P. Pindar) *Middl. Elect.* ii Bald pates be quickly shav'd.

Bald moon, A | quoth Benny Gask; another pint, quoth Lesley.

1721 KELLY 53 . . . Spoken when people encourage themselves to stay a little longer in the ale-house, because they have moon-light. **1818** SCOTT *Rob Roy* xxix Mind the auld saw, man—It's a bauld moon, quoth Benny Gask—another pint, quoth Lesley; we'll no start for another chappin.

Bald, *see also* Believe he's b. till you see his brains (Will not); Mare hath a b. face (When the).

Baldwin's dead, My Lord.

1670 RAY 163 . . . It is used, when one tells that for news which everybody knows. A *Sussex* proverb. But who this Lord *Baldwin* was, I could not learn there.

Bale (Need) is hext (highest), When | boot (help) is next (nighest).

a. **1250** *Owl & Night.* 687–8 Wone þe bale is alre-hecst, þonne is þe bote alre-necst. [When the evil is highest of all, then the remedy is nighest of all.] *a.* **1300** *Cursor M.* 4775 Quen þe bal ys alder hext þen sum time ys bote next. *c.* **1320** *Reliq. Antiquae* (1841) i. 113 When the bale is hest, Thenne is the bote nest. *c.* **1350** *Douce MS. 52* no. 91. *c.* **1400** *Beryn* (E.E.T.S.) l. 3956 So 'aftir bale comyth bote' who-so bydē conne. **1546** HEYWOOD I. xii. 38 Comforte your selfe with this old text, That telth vs, when bale is hekst, boote is next. **1616** DRAXE 24. **1822** SCOTT *Nigel* xxi Did you never hear, that when the need is highest the help is nighest? **1827** HARE *Guess. at Truth* (1859) ii. 316 Though a great and momentous truth is involved in the saying, that, *when need is highest, then aid is nighest*, this comfort belongs only to such as acknowledge that man's waywardness is ever crost and over-ruled by a higher power.

Balk[1] (balks) of good ground, Make not a.

[= don't waste a good chance.] **1636** CAMDEN 302. **1640** FULLER *Joseph's Coat* (1867) 35 The rich Corinthians, in not in-viting the poor, made balks of good ground. **1641** FERGUSSON 78 Make no balkes of good bear land. **1721** KELLY 247 *Make no baulks in good bearland.* Spoken when it is proposed to marry the youngest daughter, before the eldest. [[1] a ridge or piece left unploughed by accident or carelessness.]

Balk(s), *see also* By-walkers (Many), many b.

Ball at one's foot (*or* before one), To have the.

c. **1661** *Papers on Alterat. Prayer-bk.* 24 You have the ball before you, and have the . . . power of contending without controll. **1755** BUBB DODINGTON *Diary* 27 May The Duke of Newcastle had the ball at his foot when his brother died. *c.* **1800** LD. AUCKLAND *Corr.* (1862) 416 We have the ball at our feet, and if the Government will allow us . . . the rebellion will be crushed. **1906** A. T. QUILLER-

COUCH *Cornish Wind.* 126, 7 Relief . . . came with his election as Fellow of Oriel . . . and the brilliant young scholar had . . . the ball at his feet.

Ball does not stick to the wall, If the | it will at least leave a mark.

1732 FULLER no. 2701. **1823** COLLINS 346 . . . It alludes to defamation.

Ball, *see also* Stricken the b. under the line.

Ballast, *see* Sail too big for b. (Make not).

Balm in Gilead.

1560 BIBLE (Geneva) *Jer.* viii. 22 Is there no balme at Gilead? is there no Physition there? **1849** C. BRONTË *Shirley* xi There are two guineas to buy a new frock. Come, Cary, never fear: we'll find balm in Gilead.

Banagher, *see* Bangs B.

Banbury tinkers, who in mending (stopping) one hole make three (two), Like.

1644–7 CLEVELAND *Char. Lond. Diurn.* 8 What did this Parliament ever go about to reforme, but Tinkerwise, in mending one hole they made three? **1647** MILES CORBET *Speech* in *Harl. Misc.* i. 274 (A) The malignants do compare this commonwealth to an old kettle with here and there a fault or a hole . . . in it, and that we (in imitation of our worthy brethren of Banbury) were instructed to mend the said kettle; but, like deceitful and cheating knaves, we have, instead of stopping one hole, made them three or four score. **1659** HOWELL *Eng. Prov.* 14/2. **1663** *A Merry-Conceited Fortune-Teller* A4[v] Tinkers shall have the fortune to stop one hole and make three, and yet they shall be accounted Lads of mettal, and if they escape Banbury they may have a better fortune. **1678** RAY 329. **1738** SWIFT (Dial. i) 341 *Miss* . . . I'm mend-ing . . . *Never.* You have mended as a tinker mends a kettle; stop one hole and make two.

Banbury zeal, cheese, and cakes.

1596 HARINGTON *Anat. Metam. Ajax* liiij b (A) O that I were at Oxenford to eat some Banberie cakes. **1610** CAMDEN *Britannia* tr. Holland 376 The fame of this towne is for zeale, cheese, and cakes. **1662** FULLER (*Oxford*) III. 5 'Banbury zeal, cheese, and cakes'. I admire to find these joined to-gether in so learned an author as Mr. Camden [*Britannia, Oxfordshire*, p. 376] . . . But, . . . no such words are extant in the Latin Camden. . . . In the . . . last edition, anno 1637, . . . the error is continued out of design to nick the town of Banbury, as reputed then a place of precise people.

Banbury, *see also* Hogs to a B. market; Thin as B. cheese.

Band, *see* Old b. is captain's honour.

Bangs (Beats) Banagher! That.

1830–3 CARLETON *Traits & Stories; Three Tasks* (Routledge) 25 'O, by this and by that', says he, 'but that bates Bannagher!'

1885 w. BLACK *White Heather* xl 'Well, that bangs Banagher!' she said with a loud laugh. . . . 'There's a place for twa lovers to foregather!' **1910** P. W. JOYCE *Eng. as We Speak* 192 Banagher is a village in King's Co., on the Shannon. . . . When anything very unusual or unexpected occurs, the people say, 'Well, that bangs Banagher!'

Bank, *see* Safe as the b.

Bankrupt, *see* Sleep soundly (He who desireth to) buy bed of b.

Banning, *see* Be as be may is no b.

Bannock should burn than you should turn it, I had rather my.

1721 KELLY 192 . . . Spoken to those whose intermeddling with our business we think not for our profit.

Bannock, *see also* Grace of gray b. is in baking; Kitty Sleitchock's b.

Banquet, There is no great | but some fares ill.

1640 HERBERT 348.

Bapchild, *see* Live a little while.

Barber learns to shave by shaving fools, A.

1611 COTGRAVE S.V. 'Fol' By shaving a foole one learnes to shave. **1670** RAY 141 . . . He is a fool that will suffer a young beginner to practise first upon him. **1792** WOLCOT (P. Pindar) *Odes to K. Long* v Accept a proverb out of Wisdom's schools, 'Barbers first learn to shave, by shaving fools'.

Barber, One | shaves another gratis.

1654 E. GAYTON *Festivous Notes on Don Quixote* 262 One Barber wipes anothers nose. **1658** E. PHILLIPS *Mysteries of Love and Eloquence* 159 One barber trims another. **1902–4** LEAN IV. 72 . . . L'ung barbier raist l'autre.—Cord., 1538 The custom survives in medical practice. 'Barber' means of course 'barber surgeon'.

Barber shaves so close but another finds work, No.

1640 HERBERT 348. **1732** FULLER no. 3737 One barber shaves not so close but another finds work.

Barber, *see also* Any tooth, good b.; Young b. and old physician.

Barber's chair, *see* Common as a b. c.

Bare as the birch at Yule even, He is as.

1641 FERGUSSON 58 *Of weasters and divers.*[1] . . . He is als bair as the birk on Yule even. [1 bankrupts.]

Bare leg(s), *see* Marriage (More belongs to) than four b. l.; Stocking off a b. l. (Hard to get).

Bare moor that he goes over and gets not a cow, It is a.

1641 FERGUSSON 64.

Bare walls make giddy housewives.

1623 CAMDEN 267. **1639** CLARKE 242. **1655** FULLER *Ch. Hist.* XI. ii (1868) III. 427 If in private houses bare walls make giddy housewives, in princes' palaces empty coffers make unsteady statesmen. **1723** DEFOE *Col. Jack* x Wks. (1912) I. 399 I had . . . a house . . . ; but, as we say, bare walls make giddy hussies. **1732** FULLER no. 839 Bare walls make gadding housewives.

Bare words are (make) no good bargain.

1597 *Politeuphuia* 166 b. **1639** CLARKE 85. **1721** KELLY 72 . . . A preface to the demanding of earnest.

Bare, *see also* More b. than the shoemaker's wife.

Barefoot must not plant thorns, He that goes.

1599 MINSHEU A 3 He that soweth thornes, let him not go barefoot. **1605** S. DANIEL *Philotas* Wks. (Gros.) III. 109 Men must be shod that goe amongst the thornes. **1611** COTGRAVE S.V. 'Pied'. **1640** HERBERT 320. **1670** RAY 2 Barefooted men need not tread on thornes. **1678** RAY 404 While thy shoe is on thy foot tread upon the thorns. **1736** FRANKLIN Oct. He that scatters thorns let him not go barefoot.

Barefoot, *see also* Dance b.; Dead men's shoes (He goes along b. that wears).

Bargain is a bargain, A.

1553 T. WILSON *Arte of Rhet.* 19 A bargain is a bargain, and must stand without all excepcion. **1592** *Arden of Fevers.* II. ii (Shaks. Apoc.) 13 I haue had ten pound to steale a dogge, and we haue no more heere to kill a man; but that a bargane is a bargane, . . . you should do it yourselfe. **1894** BLACKMORE *Perlycross* xi A bargain is a bargain—as we say here.

Bargain is a pick-purse, A good.

1640 HERBERT 317.

Bargains dear bought, Some | good cheap should be sold.

1550 HEYWOOD I. viii. **1611** DAVIES II. 50 Prov. 394.

Bargain(s), *see also* Bare words no b.; Beloved (To be) is above all b.; Best of a bad b.; Good b. (At a) make a pause; Ill b. where no man wins; More words than one to b.; Robin Hood b.; Second word makes b.; Smithfield b.; Two (words) to make a b.

Bark against (at) the moon, To.

1401 *Pol. Poems* (1859) II. 53 Thou, as blynde Bayarde, berkest at the mone. *c.* **1410**

Towneley Plays (E.E.T.S.) xiii. 662 Can ye bark at the mone? **1520** WHITTINTON *Vulgaria* (E.E.T.S.) 72 They playe as the dogge doeth yᵗ barketh at the moon all nyght. **1616** DRAXE 124 He barketh at the moone. **1655** HEYWOOD *Fort. by Land.* I. i. Wks. (1874) VI. 370 He hath such honourable friends to guard him, We should in that but bark against the moon.

Bark and the tree, Put not thy hand between the.

1546 HEYWOOD II. ii 47 It were a foly for mée, To put my hande betwéene the barke and the trée. **1580** TUSSER 10. 30 (1878) 22 Nor put to thy hand betwixt bark and the tree, least through thy owne follie so pinched thou be. **1641** FERGUSSON 86 Put not your hand betwixt the rind and the tree. **1721** KELLY 200 *It is ill meddling between the bark and the rind.* It is a troublesome and thankless office to concern ourselves in the jars, and outfalls of near relations, as man and wife, parents and children. **1813** RAY 118 . . . *i.e.* Meddle not in family matters. **1820** SCOTT *Monast.* iv My Lady . . . differs therein from my Lord. . . . Now is it for me to stir up strife betwixt them, and put as 'twere my finger betwixt the bark and the tree, on account of a pragmatical youngster?

Bark is worse than his bite, His. (*Cf.* Barkers are no biters.)

1663 *Lauderdale Papers* (1884) I. 131 It . . . is intended that that letter shall be a great bark if not a byt. **1816** SCOTT *Antiq.* xxii But they knew the nature of the man. 'Monkbarns's bark', said Miss Griselda Oldbuck . . . , 'is muckle waur than his bite'. **1842** DE QUINCEY *Cicero* Wks. VI. 184 The bark of electioneering mobs is worse than their bite. **1900** G. C. BRODRICK *Mem. & Impress.* 253 [Freeman] was . . . an unscrupulous controversialist. . . . Yet his bark was worse than his bite, and he was essentially a kind-hearted man.

Bark ourselves e'er we buy dogs so dear, We will.

1721 KELLY 357 . . . Spoken when too dear a rate is asked for what we are buying.

Bark up the wrong tree, To.

1833 *Sketches & Eccentr. D. Crockett* (1834) 58 I told him . . . that he reminded me of the meanest thing on God's earth, an old coon dog, barking up the wrong tree. **1841** *Congress. Globe* 25 Jan. App. 153 The stockjobbers were barking up the wrong tree when they wrote those letters.

Bark (of a tree), *see also* Near as b. to tree.

Bark(ing) (of a dog), *see also* Dog's b. (At) seem not to awake; Keep a dog and b. myself; Moon does not heed b. of dogs.

Barkers are no biters, Great.

1387 TREVISA tr. HIGDEN iii. 427 (Rolls Ser.) Hit is þe manere of þe feblest houndes for to berke most. **1584** *Fedele and Fortunio* or *Two Italian Gentlemen* B 2ᵛ Great barkers

are none of the greatest biters. **1599** GREENE *George-a-G.* IV. iii (Merm.) 439 *Shoem.* That will I try. Barking dogs bite not the sorest. **1614** CAMDEN 306. **1721** KELLY 112 . . . Great boasters are not always best performers. **1880** BLACKMORE *Mary Aner.* xlvii Thousands of men threaten, and do nothing, according to the proverb. [*See also* quotations under next proverb.]

Barking dogs seldom bite.

c. **1275** *Prov. of Alfred* (Skeat) B 652 The bicche bitiþ ille þauh he berke stille. **1539** TAVERNER f. xlix Fearfull dogges do barke the sorer. **1595** *Locrine* IV. i (*Shaks. Apoc.*) 56 A barking dog doth seldom strangers bite. **1655** FULLER *Ch. Hist.* VIII. ii (1868) II. 452 [Tunstall's] passion herein may the rather be pardoned, because politicly presumed to bark the more that he might bite the less. **1837** CHAMIER *Saucy Areth.* XXXV Our dogs which bark, Abdallah, seldom bite. [*See also* quotations under preceding proverb. Fr. *Chien qui aboie ne mord pas.*]

Barley straw's good fodder when the cow gives water.

1678 RAY 51.

Barley, *see also* Cry 'B.'; Long in coming as Cotswold b.; Prizing of green b.; St. David's day put b. in clay; Sloe tree is white (When), sow b.

Barley-corn is better than a diamond to a cock, A.

1576 PETTIE *Petite Pall.* (Gollancz) II. 148. **1587** R. GREENE *Euph. his Censure* in Wks. (Gros.) VI. 179 Prefer not a barlie corne before a pretious Jewel, set not a fading content before a perpetuall honor. **1635** QUARLES *Div. Emb.* III. ii We catch at barley-grains, while pearls stand by Despis'd; such very fools art thou and I. **1692** L'ESTRANGE *Aesop's Fab.* i (1738) 1 As a cock was turning up a dunghill, he spied a diamond. Well (says he to himself) . . . a barley-corn had been worth forty on't. **1732** FULLER no. 7.

Barleycorn, *see also* John B.

Barn's full, When the | you may thresh before the door.

c. **1645** HOWELL *Lett.* II. xxiv (A) When the barn was full anyone might thresh in the haggard. **1721** KELLY 354.

Barn, *see also* Robbing the b.

Barnaby bright: the longest day and the shortest night.

[St. Barnabas' Day, the 11th of June, in Old Style reckoned the 'longest day'.] **1595** SPENSER *Epithal.* 266 This day the sunne is in his chiefest hight, With Barnaby the bright. **1659** HOWELL *Eng. Prov.* 20/1. **1670** EACHARD *Cont. Clergy* 32 Barnaby-bright would be much too short for him to tell you all that he could say. **1858** *N. & Q.* 2nd Ser. VI. 522 In some parts of the country the children call the lady-bird Barnaby Bright, and address it thus:—'Barnaby Bright, Barnaby Bright, The longest day and the shortest night'.

Barnaby, see also Dance B.

Barrel the (a) better herring, Never a (Neither).

[= never one better than another: nothing to choose between them.] **1546** HEYWOOD II. xi. 84 A foule olde riche widowe, whether wed would ye, Or a yonge fayre mayde, beyng poore as ye be. In neither barrell better hearyng (quoth hee). *c.* **1550** BALE *K. Johan* 1888 *Eng.* Lyke lorde, lyke chaplayne; neyther barrell better herynge. **1621** BURTON *Anat. Mel.* (1651) 46 Choose out of the whole pack, . . . you shall find them all alike—*never a barrel better herring.* **1680** BUNYAN *Mr. Badman* xii Wks. (Offor) III. 647 'Hang them rogues, there is not a barrel better herring of all the holy brotherhood of them.' **1882** E. GOSSE *Gray* 167 *A Satire upon the Heads, or Never a barrel the better Herring,* a comic piece in which Gray attacked the prominent heads of houses.

Barrel, see also Knock on the hoop, another on b.; Wine by the b. (Cannot know).

Barren sow was never good to pigs, A.

1641 FERGUSSON 78 A yeeld sow was never good to gryses. **1721** KELLY 1 with Yell' and 'Grices'. **1855** BOHN 281.

Barrow, see Bout as B. was.

Barter, see Fond of b. that niffers with Old Nick.

Bashful mind hinders his good intent, His.

1678 RAY 66.

Bashfulness is an enemy to poverty.

[ERASM. *Ad. Verecundia inutilis viro egenti.* Bashfulness is useless to a man in want. HOM. *Od.* 17. 347.] **1670** RAY 2.

Bashfulness, see also Modesty be virtue (Though), b. is vice.

Basket, To go to the.

[= to go to prison.] **1632** MASS. & FIELD *Fatal Dowry* v. i *Pontalier* [to Liladam, who is in custody for debt], Go to the basket and repent.

Basket, You shall have the.

1678 RAY 344 . . . *Taunton.* Said to the journeyman that is envied for pleasing his master.

Basket-justice will do justice right or wrong, A.

1601 in TOWNSHEND *Hist. Coll.* (1680) 268 *A Justice of Peace . . . for half a Dozen of Chickens will Dispence with a whole Dozen of Penal Statutes . . . These be the Basket-Justices.* **1678** RAY 74 A basket Justice; a Jyll Justice; a good forenoon Justice. He'll do Justice, right or wrong.

Bass, The, see Ding doun Tantallon; Tammie Norie o' the B.

Bastard brood is always proud.

1721 KELLY 68. **1736** BAILEY *Dict.* s.v. 'Bastard'.

Bastard, see also Hazelnuts (The more), more b.; Looked on me as cow on b. calf.

Basteth the fat hog, Every man.

c. **1300** *Prov. of Hending* (ed. Schleich) in *Anglia* 51. 271 Euer man fedit þe fat swine for þe smere. **1509** BARCLAY *Ship of Fools* (Jamieson) I. 100. The fat pygge is baast, the lene cony is brent. **1546** HEYWOOD I. xi. 38 Euery man basteth the fat hog we sée, But the leane shall burne er he basted bée. **1641** FERGUSSON in RAY 269 Every man flames[1] the fat sows arse. **1648** HERRICK *Hesper.* 64 Wks. (1893) I. 23 The fattest hogs we grease the more with lard. **1721** KELLY 93 *Every man flamms[1] the fat sow's arse.* They will be sure to get most gifts that least want them. [[1] bastes.]

Baston, see Oil of b.

Bate me an ace, quoth Bolton.

1570 EDWARDS *Damon & Pithias* (Dodsley) IV. 77. *c.* **1590** SIR THOMAS MORE II. i (*Shaks. Apoc.*) 391. **1659** HOWELL *Eng. Prov.* 14/2. **1670** RAY 163 Queen Elisabeth, being presented with a collection of English Proverbs, and being told by the Author, that it contained all the English Proverbs, nay replied she, *Bate me an ace quoth Bolton;* which . . . happened to be wanting in his collection.

Bath, Go to.

[= get away!] **1842–3** W. H. MAXWELL *Hector O'Halloran* xii Curse all parades! Tell Sergeant Skelton to go to Bath, and let the Adjutant go after him!

Bath, see also Beggars of B.

Bath of the blackamoor hath sworn not to whiten, The.

1651 HERBERT 368.

Bathes in May, He who | will soon be laid in clay; he who bathes in June, will sing a merry tune; he who bathes in July, will dance like a fly.

1827 HONE *Table-Book* 315. **1846** DENHAM 45. **1893** INWARDS 27.

Bathon, Jon of, see Speak, spend, quoth J. of B.

Bats in the belfry, To have.

[= to be crazy or eccentric.] **1911** R. D. SAUNDERS *Col. Todhunter* ix. 123 It's a case of bats in the belfry on that one subject. **1927** A. E. W. MASON *No Other Tiger* xix Phyllis Harmer exclaimed . . . 'Dear man, you've got bats in the belfry'.

Battalions, see Providence is always on the side of.

Battersea, Go to | to be cut for the simples.

1787 GROSE (*Glos., Surrey*) 225 ... In Battersea ... market gardeners ... grew medicinal herbs, termed simples, for ... apothecaries, who used to ... see them cut, which they called going to Battersea to have their simples cut; whence foolish people were jocularly advised to go thither for the same purpose.

Battle lost, Next to a | the greatest misery is a battle gained.

[1815] WELLINGTON 1912 *Times Lit. Sup.* 14 June 241 Wellington was the centre of all things ... 'I hope to God', he said one day, that I have fought my last battle ... I always say that, next to a battle lost, the greatest misery is a battle gained'.

Battle, *see also* Ill b. where devil carries colours; Race is not to swift nor b. to strong.

Battledore, *see* Knows not a B from a b.; Say B (or bo) to a b.

Bauchle(s), *see* Rice for good luck.

Bavin[1] is but a blaze, The.

1584 GREENE *Anat. of Fortune* in Wks. (Gros.) III. 194 I went out of my tente ... hoping that hot loue would be soone cold, that the greatest bauin was but a blaze. **1597–8** SHAKS. *1 Hen. IV* III. ii. 61 The skipping king, he ambled up and down With shallow jesters and rash bavin wits, Soon kindled and soon burnt. **1603** H. CROSSE *Vertues Commonw.* (1878) 133 Which like a bauin giueth goodly blaze ... but is soone out. [[1] a bundle of brushwood.]

Bawbee(s), *see* Placks and b. grow pounds.

Bawd, *see* Opportunity is whoredom's b.

Bawdry, *see* Whoring and b. end in beggary.

Bawling, *see* Scolds and infants never lin b.

Bawtry, *see* Hanged for leaving liquor like saddler of B.

Bawty, *see* Bourd not with B.

Bayard, *see* Bold as blind B.; Keep B. in stable.

Be as be may (is no banning).

c. **1386** CHAUCER *Monk's T.* B[2] 3319 Be as be may, I wol hire noght accusen. *c.* **1406** HOCCLEVE *Mâle Règle* 1. 289 Be as be may, no more of this as now. **1546** HEYWOOD II. i. 43 God spéede them, be as be maie is no bannyng. **1594** LYLY *Moth. Bomb.* II. iii. Wks. (1902) III. 188 Well, be as be may is no banning. I think I have charmed my young master. [*Note*, p. 542. Evidently a proverb with folk who think affairs are going well and call for no extraordinary effort.] **1611** DAVIES *Prov.* 20 Be as be may, no banning is: And yet it is a curse To be as now it is; because the world is neuer worse. **1721** KELLY 75 *Be it so, is no banning.*

Spoken when we unwillingly give our consent to a thing.

Be it for better, be it for worse, do you after him that beareth the purse.

c. **1350** *Douce MS. 52* no. 64 Do thow better, do thow worse, Do after hym, that beryth the purse. *a.* **1530** R. *Hill's Commonpl. Bk.* (E.E.T.S.) 130. **1546** HEYWOOD I. v. 10. **1818** SCOTT *Rob Roy* xxvii My puir mither used aye to tell me, Be it better, be it worse, Be ruled by him that has the purse.

Be not, *see* Baker, if head of butter; Bold with your biggers; Hasty to outbid.

Be still, and have thy will.

c. **1450** *Provs. of Wysdom* 100 Suffer and haue þy will. **1853** TRENCH ii 32 That very beautiful [proverb] ... in the writings of Tyndal, *Be still, and have thy will.*

Be what thou wouldst be called (or seem to be).

1547 W. BALDWIN *Treatise of Moral Philosophy* (1550) L 2[v] Thales, be the selfe same that thou pretendest. **1640** HERBERT 351. **1641** FERGUSSON 22. **1721** KELLY 68 *Be what you seem, and seem what you are.* The best way! for hypocrisy is soon discovered.

Beacon Hill, *see* Bore a hole through B. H. (As well).

Beadle, *see* Fear, the b. of the law.

Beads about the neck and the devil in the heart.

1599 MINSHEU (1623) Tt 2[v].

Beads in the hand, The | and the devil in capuch (or, cape of the cloak).

1651 HERBERT 367.

Beam, *see* Kick the b.; Mote and b.

Bean in a monk's hood, Like a.

1546 HEYWOOD II. vi. 62 And she must syt like a beane in a moonkis hood. Bearyng no more rule, than a goose turd in tems [Thames.]

Bean in liberty is better than a comfit in prison, A.

1640 HERBERT 347. **1670** RAY 15. **1732** FULLER no. 9.

Bean hath its black, Every.

a. **1624** BP. M. SMITH *Serm.* (1632) 178. **1639** CLARKE 211. **1818** SCOTT *Rob Roy* xxxviii Ye hae had your ain time o't, Mr. Syddall; but ilka bean has its black, and ilka path has its puddle.

Beans blow before May doth go, Be it weal or be it woe.

1742 *An Agreeable Companion* 33. **1855** BOHN 301.

Bean(s), *see also* Abstain from b.; Crooked man should sow b.; Dunder do gally the b.; Knows how many b. make five; Pea for a b. (To give); Shake a Leicestershire man; Sow b. in the mud; Sow b. in the wind; Sow four b. in a row; Sow or set b. in Candlemas waddle; Sow peas and b. in wane of moon; Three blue b. in blue bladder.

Bear a bull that hath borne a calf, He may.

1539 TAVERNER 10 *Taurum tollet qui uitulum sustulerit.* He that hath borne a calfe, shall also beare a bull, He that accustometh hym selfe to lytle thynges, by lytle and lytle shal be able to go a waye with greater thynges. **1909** A. MACLAREN *Ephesians* 243 The wrestler, according to the old Greek parable, who began by carrying a calf on his shoulders, got to carry an ox by and by.

Bear all his kin on his back, A man cannot.

1721 KELLY 42 . . . Spoken when we are upbraided with some bad kinsman.

Bear and forbear.

[Epictetus' golden rule, ἀνέχου καὶ ἀπέχου.] **1573** SANDFORD (1576). **1573** TUSSER 180 Both beare and forbeare now and then as ye may. **1621** BURTON *Anat. Mel.* II. iii. VII *Sustine et abstine.* **1688** BUNYAN *Bldg. of Ho. of God* X. Wks. (Offor) II. 589 To bear and forbear here, will tend to rest. **1832** HENDERSON 50 Bear and forbear is gude philosophy. **1871** SMILES *Character* 313 The golden rule of married life is, 'Bear and forbear'.

Bear him on my back, I.

1639 CLARKE 303 I bore him all the while on my back. **1670** RAY 164 . . . That is, I remember his injuries done to me with indignation and grief, or with a purpose of revenge.

Bear it away, He will | if it be not too hot or too heavy.

c. **1386** CHAUCER *Friar's T.* D 1436 I spare nat to taken, god it woot, But if it be to hevy or to hoot, What I may gete in conseil prively. **1542** UDALL *Apoph. Cicero* § 50 A taker and a bribing [robbing] feloe, and one for whom nothing was to hotte nor to heauie. **1678** RAY 349 . . *Spoken of a pilferer.*

Bear, If it were a | it would bite you.

1616 DRAXE 4. **1639** CLARKE 6. **1738** SWIFT (Dial. i) 337 *Col.* I have been searching my pockets for my snuff-box, and, egad, here it is in my hand. *Miss.* If it had been a bear, it would have bit you.

Bear picketh muscles, As handsomely as a.

1540 PALSGRAVE *Acolastus* (Carver) 100 It becommeth hym as wel to do, as . . . a beare to pycke muskles. **1546** HEYWOOD II. v. 54 Eche of his iointes against other iustles, As handsomely as a beare picketh muscles.

Bear till his back break, A man may.

1618 FIELD *Amends Ladies* I. i I come not to be scoffed. A woman may bear and bear, till her back burst. **1639** CLARKE 15 A man may bear till his back break.

Bear to a honey-pot, Like a.

1589 [? LYLY] *Pappe w. Hatchet* (1844) 16 Swarm'd . . . like bears to a honie pot.

Bear to the stake, To go like a.

[i.e. to be baited.] *c.* **1430** LYDGATE *Churl & Bird* l. 132 To gon at large, but as a bere at stake, To passe his boundis, but if he leve take. **1546** HEYWOOD I. ix. 17 With as good will as a beare goth to the stake.

Bear wants a tail, and cannot be lion, The.

[*a.* **1588**] **1662** FULLER (*Warwick*) III. 271 Robert Dudley earl of Leicester . . . when he was governor of the Low Countries, . . . signed all instruments with the crest of the Bear and Ragged Staff. He was then suspected . . . [of] an ambitious design to make himself absolute commander (as the lion is king of beasts) over the Low Countries. Whereupon some . . . wrote under his crest. . . . *Ursa caret caudâ. non queat esse Leo.* 'The Bear he never can prevail To Lion it, for lack of tail.' . . . The proverb is applied to such who . . . aspire to what is above their worth to deserve, or power to achieve. **1909** *Times*, *Wkly.* 18 June iii It is not easy to take bears seriously. . . . Their persons end towards the rear with a suddenness which precludes any affectation of dignity. The Bear he never can prevail To lion it for lack of tail.

Bear wealth, poverty will bear itself.

1641 FERGUSSON 10. **1721** KELLY 64 . . . Wealth is subject to a great many more temptations than poverty.

Bear with a sore head, As cross as a.

1785 GROSE *Dict. Vulg. T.* s.v. 'Grumble' He grumbled like a bear with a sore ear. **1870** *N. & Q.* 4th Ser. VI. 321 Thus we say 'As sulky as a bear with a sore head'.

Bear with evil and expect good.

1640 HERBERT 341.

Bear(s) (*noun*), *see also* Are you there with your b.; Black b. of Arden; Call the b. 'uncle'; Carry guts to a b. (Not fit to); Congleton rare sold Bible to pay for b.; Course be fair (If), quoth Bunny to his b.; Fight dog, fight b.; Iron nails that scratcheth b. (Must have); Jack-an-apes (More ado with one); Kings and b. oft worry keepers; One thing thinketh the b.; Sell the b.'s skin before; Shareth honey with b. (He who); Take the b. by the tooth; Tricks as a dancing b. (As many); Young b. with troubles before him.

'Bear' [on Stock Exchange], *see* Price is too low (No).

Bear (*verb*), *see also* Boughs that b. most hang lowest; Devil himself must b. cross; Take no more on you than able to b.; Worthy to b. his books (Not). *See also* Endure.

Bear-garden, He speaks.

1678 RAY 66 . . . That is, such rude and uncivil, or sordid and dirty language, as the rabble that frequent those sports, are wont to use.

Bear-pie, *see* Eaten a b. (He that hath).

Beard that makes the philosopher, It is not the.

[**1654** E. GAYTON *Festivous Notes on Don Quixote* 120 Non barba facit Philosophum.] **1732** FULLER no. 5102.

Beard the lion, To.

[**1611** BIBLE *1 Sam.* xvii. 34, 35 There came a lion, . . . and when he arose against me, I caught him by his beard, and . . . slew him.] **1749** SMOLLETT *Regicide* II. vii (1777) 39 Sooner would'st thou beard The Lion in his rage. **1808** SCOTT *Marmion* VI. xiv And dar'st thou then To beard the lion in his den, The Douglas in his hall? **1894** BLACKMORE *Perlycross* xxii Nothing less would satisfy her than to beard . . . the lion in the den, the arch-accuser, in the very court of judgment.

Beard were all, If the | the goat might preach.

[*Anth. Pal.* 11.430 Εἰ τὸ τρέφειν πώγωνα δοκεῖ σοφίαν περιποιεῖν, καὶ τράγος εὐπώγων αἰψ' ὅλος ἔστι Πλάτων.] **1662** FULLER (*Wales*) III. 484 Goats . . . afterwards put on . . . great gravity. . . . If that ornamental excrement which groweth beneath the chin be the standard of wisdom, they carry it from Aristotle himself. **1690** D'URFEY *Collin's Walk* III. 120 If Providence did Beards devise, To prove the wearers of them wise, A fulsome Goat would then by Nature Excel each other human Creature.

Beard will pay (not pay) for the shaving, The.

1830 FORBY 431 . . . When a person is paid for his labour by taking part, or the whole, of that which he is employed about; as cutting bushes, &c. . . . The work will produce enough to pay for itself. **1917** BRIDGE 111 The beard will not pay for the shaving. When a hedge is trimmed the brushings are called 'beardings'.

Beard(s), *see also* Beild aneath auld man's b.; Fat flits from b.; Long b. heartless . . . England thriftless; Merry in hall when b. wag; Red b. and black head; Ride with b. on shoulder; Teeth are longer than your b.

Bearing, *see* Good b. beginneth worship (In).

Beast that goes always never wants blows, The.

1640 HERBERT 329.

Beast(s), *see also* Keep your feet dry . . . and live like b.; Many-headed b.; Nature of the b.; Strange b. that hath neither head nor tail; Wolf knows what ill b. thinks.

Beat a horse till he be sad, You may | and a cow till she be mad.

1678 RAY 98.

Beat about the bush, To.

[= to approach a subject slowly; shilly-shally.] **1520** WHITTINTON *Vulg.* (E.E.T.S.) 35 A longe betynge aboute the busshe and losse of tyme to a yonge begynner. **1588** GREENE *Pandosto* Prose Wks. (1881–3) IV. 284 Dorastus . . . thought it was vaine so longe to beate about the bush. **1892** STEVENSON & OSB. *Wrecker* xviii I did not know how long he might thus beat about the bush with dreadful hintings.

Beat (any one) black and blue, To.

[Originally *blak and bla*, *blak and blo*: *blo* became obsolete after 1550.] *c.* **1460** *Towneley Myst.* 206 Bett hym blak and bloo **1594** LYLY *Moth. Bomb.* v. iii. Wks. (1902) III. 220 Do you not thinke it would beat my heart blacke and blew? **1600–1** SHAKS. *Merry W.* IV. v. 116 Mistress Ford, good heart, is beaten black and blue.

Beat one like a stockfish, To.

[With reference to the beating of the dried fish before cooking.] **1552** HULOET s.v. 'Beate', Beate often as a stockfyshe is beaten, *retundo*. **1560** BECON *Catech.* vi. Wks. I. 522 b Those parents . . . whiche furiously rage against their children, and . . . beat them as stockfish. **1611–12** SHAKS. *Temp.* III. ii. 81 I'll turn my mercy out o' doors and make a stockfish of thee.

Beat spice it will smell the sweeter, If you.

1576 PETTIE *Petite Pall.* (Gollancz) I. 36 As spices the more they are beaten the sweeter sent they send forth. **1579** LYLY *Euphues* Wks. (Bond) I. 191 If you pownde spices they smell the sweeter. **1732** FULLER no. 2741.

Beat the dog before the lion.

[JACOBUS DE VORAGINE: *Quia quando canis flagellatur, leo domesticatur.*] *c.* **1350** Douce *MS.* 52 no. 63 By the litul welpys me chastys þe lyon. *c.* **1386** CHAUCER *Squire's T.* F¹ 491 And for to maken othere be war by me, As by the whelp chastised is the leon. **1604–5** SHAKS. *Othello* II. iii. 277 Even so as one would beat his offenceless dog to affright an imperious lion. **1640** HERBERT 341.

Beat the horse, He that cannot | beats the saddle.

1573 SANDFORD (1576) 213. **1666** TORRIANO 22 Who cannot strike The Ass may strike The Pack-saddle.

Beat your heels against the ground (or wind), To no more purpose than to.

1670 RAY 190.

Beating proud folks, It is good | for they'll not complain.

1639 CLARKE 31. **1670** RAY 133.

Beats the bush, One | and another catches the birds.

c. **1300** *Ipomadon* 1. 6021 On the bushe bettes one, another man hath the bryde. *c.* **1350** *Douce MS. 52* no. 36 On betyth þe buske anoþer hathe [i.e. hath the] brydde. *c.* **1440** *Generydes* 1. 4524 Some bete the bush ... other men ... catch the burdes. *c.* **1450** *Cov. Myst.* 119 Many a man doth bete the bow, Another man hath the brydde. **1526** *Pilgr. Perf.* (W. de W. 1531) 141 Whiche ... hath ... betten the busshe that you may catche the byrde. **1546** HEYWOOD i. iii. 7 And while I at length debate and beate the bushe, There shall steppe in other men, and catche the burdes. **1614** CAMDEN (*Wise Speeches*) (1870) 289 Thomas Montacute, Earl of Sarisbury,[1] when he besieged Orleans, ... the inhabitants were willing to ... yield themselves to the Duke of Burgundy ... : he ... said in the English Proverb; 'I will not beat the bush, and another shall have the birds'. [[1] Salisbury.]

Beat(en), *see also* Beggar b. his bag (Would make); Better to be b. than in bad company; Friar's b. (When the), then comes James; Roast meat (Give one) and b. him with spit.

Beauchamp, *see* Bold as B.

Beaulieu Fair, *see* Cuckoo goes to B. F.

Beauty and honesty seldom agree.

1580 LYLY *Euph. & his Eng.* (Arb.) 454 Who knoweth not how rare a thing it is (Ladies) to match virginitie with beautie. **1591** FLORIO *Sec. Frutes* 193 Beawtie and honesty seldome agree, for of beautie comes temptation, of temptation dishonour. **1600–1** SHAKS. *Hamlet* III. i. 102 *Oph.* Could beauty, my lord, have better commerce than with honesty? *Ham.* Ay, truly; for the power of beauty will sooner transform honesty from what it is to a bawd than the force of honesty can translate a beauty into his likeness.

Beauty draws more than oxen.

[*Anth. Pal.* 5. 230.] **1591** FLORIO *Sec. Frutes* 183 Ten teemes of oxen draw much lesse, than doth one haire of Helens tresse. **1640** HERBERT 349. **1693** DRYDEN *Persius* 5. 247 She ... can draw you to her with a single hair. **1712** POPE *Rape of Lock* II. 28 And beauty draws us with a single hair.

Beauty is but a blossom.

1616 DRAXE 15. **1732** FULLER no. 947. **1599–1600** SHAKS. *Twelfth N.* I. v. 56 As there is no true cuckold but calamity, so beauty's a flower.

Beauty is but skin-deep.

c. **1606** MIDDLETON & DEKKER *Roaring Girl* (1611) I 3[V] Goodnesse [= beauty] I see is but outside. *a.* **1613** OVERBURY *A Wife*, &c. Wks. (1856) 37 All the carnall beauty of my wife, Is but skin-deep. **1740–1** RICHARDSON *Pamela* (1824) I. xcix. 484 Beauty is but ... a mere skin-deep perfection. **1829** COBBETT *Adv. to Young Men* iii (1906) 122 The less favoured part of the sex say, that 'beauty is but skin deep'; ... but it is very agreeable, though, for all that.

Beauty is no inheritance.

1616 DRAXE 15 Beauty is no heritage. **1670** RAY 2. **1732** FULLER no. 951.

Beauty is potent; but money is omnipotent.

1670 RAY 122. **1732** FULLER no. 952 (with 'more potent' for 'omnipotent'.)

Beauty may have fair leaves, yet bitter fruit.

1580 LYLY *Euph. and his Eng.* Wks. (Bond) II. 169 Beautie may haue faire leaues & foule fruite. **1732** FULLER no. 955.

Beauty, *see also* Fancy passes b.; Poor b. finds more lovers than husbands; Sweet b. with sour beggary.

Because is a woman's reason.

1594–5 SHAKS. *Two Gent.* I. ii. 23 *Jul.* Your reason? *Luc.* I have no other but a woman's reason: I think him so because I think him so. **1601** LYLY *Love's Metam.* IV. i Women's reasons; they would not because they would not. **1721** KELLY 68.

Beck[1] is as good as a Dieu-gard, A.

[O.F. *Dieu vous gard* 'God keep (you)!' a polite salutation.] **1538** BALE *Three Lawes* (1470) As good is a becke, as is a dewe vow garde. **1546** HEYWOOD I. x. 24 And thus with a becke as good as a dieu gard, She flang fro me. **1603** FLORIO tr. *Montaigne* III. v A wink, a cast of the eye ... a becke is as good as a Dew guard. [[1] bow, nod.]

Becomes it as well as a cow doth a cart-saddle, He.

1639 CLARKE 5. **1670** RAY 203 It becomes him as well as a cow doth a cart-saddle.

Bed could tell all it knows, If the | it would put many to the blush.

1659 HOWELL *Eng. Prov.* 2. **1670** RAY 3.

Bed with the lamb, Go to | and rise with the lark.

c. **1555** WRIGHT *Songs &c. Philip and Mary* 38 (Roxb. Cl.) (A) And wythe the larke yche day I ryes. **1580** LYLY *Euph. and his Eng.* (Arb.) 229. **1633** JONSON *T. Tub.* I. iv Madam, if he had couched with the lamb, He had no doubt been stirring with the lark. **1833** LAMB *Elia; Newsp. 35 Yrs. Ago* We were compelled to rise, having been perhaps not above four hours in bed—(for we were no go-to-beds with the lamb, though we anticipated the lark oft times in her rising).

Bed straw, *see* Eaten his b. s. (Look as if had).

Bed, *see also* Go to b. at noon; Goes to b. supperless (Who); Lie in b. and forecast; Lie in b. till meat falls in mouth; Make your b., so lie on it; Put off his clothes before goes to b. (He will not); Put to b.; Sick of the slothful guise; Sluggard's guise, slow to b. *See also* Abed.

Bedfellow(s), *see* Misery (Adversity) makes strange b.

Bedford, *see* Bailiff of B.

Bedpost, *see* Between you and me and b.; Twinkling of a b.

Bee in one's bonnet, To have a.

[= to have a craze on some point.] **1553** *Respublica* I. i (A) Ye must perdonne my wyttes, for I tell you plaine, I have a hive of humble bees swarmynge in my braine. **1681** s. COLVIL *Whiggs Sup.* II. 49 A Scripturest thou proves, as he was, In whose fool bonnet-case a bee was. **1821** SCOTT *Pirate* xxiii As to these Troils . . . there is a bee in their bonnet. **1824** MOIR *Mansie W.* xxiv Things were . . . so queer . . . that I . . . began at length to question . . . whether Taffy's master might not have had a bee in his bonnet. **1863** READE *Hard Cash* xl The doctor had a bee in his own bonnet.

Bee sucks honey, Where the | the spider sucks poison.

1573 G. HARVEY *Letter-bk.* (Camd. Soc.) 25 As ther is matter of poison to the spider where would be matter of honi to the bee. **1575** G. GASCOIGNE *Wks.* (Cunliffe) I. 476 As the venemous spider wil sucke poison out of the most holesome herbe, and the industrious bee can gather honey out of the most stinking weede. **1579** LYLY *Euphues* (Arb.) 35 Ther frequented to his lodging, as well the Spider to sucke poyson of his fine wit, as the Bee to gather Hunny. *a.* **1614** BEAUM. & FL. *Four Plays* Wks. (1905) X. 312 Sweet poetry's A flower, where men, like bees and spiders, may Bear poison, or else sweets and wax away. **1616** DRAXE 124. **1853** TRENCH v. 122 . . . Let the student be as the bee looking for honey, and from . . . classical literature he may store of it abundantly in his hive.

Bee(s), *see also* Busy as a b.; Calf, the goose, the b., world is ruled by; Dead b. makes no honey; Head is full of b.; Honey is sweet (Every b.'s); Honey is sweet but b. stings; Humble b.; May b. don't fly this month; Old b. yield no honey; St. Matthee shut up the b.; Swarm of b. in a churn; Swarm of b. in May; Swine, women, and b. cannot be turned.

Bee-bikes, *see* Scythe cuts (Where), no more b.

Beef, Such | such broth.

1591 T. LODGE *Catharos* (Hunt. Cl.) B 4. **1598** MERES *Palladis* f. 218.

Beef to the heels, like a Mullingar heifer.

1837 LOVER *Rory O'More* ii 'The women in Westmeath, they say, is thick in the legs, . . . and so there's a saying again thim, " You're beef to the heels, like a Mullingar heifer".'

Beef, *see also* Bull b.; No broth . . . no b.; Weavers' b. of Colchester.

Bees are old, When | they yield no honey.

1616 DRAXE 146. **1670** RAY 19. **1732** FULLER no. 3706 Old bees yield no honey.

Bees are, Where | there is honey.

1616 DRAXE 77. **1670** RAY 60 . . . Where there are industrious persons, there is wealth, for the hand of the diligent maketh rich. This we see verified in our neighbours the Hollanders.

Bees that have honey in their mouths have stings in their tails.

c. **1440** *Passe forth, pilgrime* (ed. Förster) in *Archiv f. d. Stud. d. Neueren Sprachen* 101. 29 Favel farith ryght even as dothe the be; Hony-mowthed, full of swetnys is she, But loke behynde and ware ye fro hir stonge. **1660** W. SECKER *Nonsuch Prof.* i (1891) 22 There are some things which are pleasant but not good, as youthful lusts and worldly delights. These bees carry honey in their mouths, but they have a sting in their tails.

Bees, *see also* Bee(s).

Beelzebub, *see* Baby of B.'s bower.

Beer, *see* Heresy and b. came both in a year; New b. . . . make hair grow through hood; Shoulder of mutton and b. make Flemings tarry; Turkeys . . . and b. came into England in one year. *See also* Small beer.

Beer and skittles, *see* Life is not all.

Beery, *see* Sheep of B.

Beetle[1] and the block, Between the.

1589 R. HARVEY *Pl. Perc.*, Thou must come to Knokham faire, and what betweene the block and the beetle, be thumped like a stock fish. **1613** HAYWARD *Norm. Kings* 274 Earle William being thus set, as it were, betweene the beetle and the blocke, was nothing deiected. [[1] mallet.]

Beetle, *see also* Dull as a b.; Shoe the Pasha's horses (They came to), and b. stretched out leg.

Before one can say Jack Robinson.

1778 BURNEY *Evelina* Lett. lxxxii (A) Why, then, 'fore George, I'd do it as soon as say Jack Robinson. **1812** EDGEWORTH *Absentee* ii I'd get her off before you could say Jack Robinson. **1837** SOUTHEY *Doctor* iv. 250 Who was Jack Robinson? . . . the one whose name is in every body's mouth, because it is so easily and so soon said. **1872** BLACKMORE

Maid of Sker x The ship must . . . go to pieces . . . , before one could say Jack Robinson'.

Before St. Chad[1] every goose lays, both good and bad.

1678 RAY 51. **1882** E. L. CHAMBERLAIN 37 By Valentine's[2] day every good goose should lay ; But by David[3] and Chad both good and bad. [[1] 2 March. [2] 14 Feb. [3] 1 March.]

Before the cat can lick her ear.

1593 PEELE *Edward I* ii Wks. (Bullen) I. 101 But go and come with gossip's cheer, Ere Gib our cat can lick her ear. **1665** COTTON *Scarron* 4 Ere a cat could lick her ear. **1670** RAY 168.

Before you make a friend eat a bushel of salt with him.

1539 TAVERNER (1552) 30 *Nemini fidas, nisi cum quo prius modium salis absumpseris.* Trust no man onles thou hast fyrst eaten a bushel of salte with hym. **1621** BURTON *Anat. Mel.* III. iii. IV. ii (1651) 627 As Plutarch adviseth, one must eat *modium salis,* a bushel of salt with him, before he choose his friend.

Before you marry, be sure of a house wherein to tarry.

1642 TORRIANO 66. **1664** CODRINGTON 187. **1670** RAY 17.

Before, *see also* Hires the horse (He that) must ride b.; Kingdom of a cheater (In the) wallet carried b.; Looks not b. (He that) finds himself behind.

Beg at the wrong door, To.

1546 HEYWOOD I. ix Then of truth ye beg at a wrong man's dur. **1616** JONSON *Ev. Man in Humour* II. i. 79 He has the wrong sow by the eare, ifaith: and claps his dish at the wrong mans dore.

Beg from beggars and you'll never be rich.

1721 KELLY 62 . . . Spoken when we ask that from one which they sought from another.

Beg of him who has been a beggar, Neither | nor serve him who has been a servant.

1855 BOHN 458. *Span.*

Beg the question, To.

[= to take for granted the matter in dispute.] **1581** W. CLARKE in *Confer.* iv (1584) Ff iij I say this is still to begge the question. **1680** BURNET *Rochester* (1692) 82 This was to assert or beg the thing in Question. **1788** REID *Aristotle's Log.* v, § 3. 118 Begging the question is when the thing to be proved is assumed in the premises.

Beg, *see also* Learned timely to steal (b.).

Beggar beat his bag, It would make a.

1678 RAY 228.

Beggar can never be bankrupt, A.

1616 WITHALS 572. **1639** CLARKE 243. **1670** RAY 60. **1721** KELLY 36 (as English prov.).

Beggar, One | is enough at a door.

1639 CLARKE 187.

Beggar is never out of his way, The.

1629 T. ADAMS *Works* 120 Vagrant rogues . . . are neuer out of their way. **1659** HOWELL *Eng. Prov.* 15/1.

Beggar is woe that another by the door should go, One.

c. **1350** *Douce MS. 52,* no. 66 On begger is wo þat anothir in-to þe towne goth. **1539** TAVERNER (1552) 9 One begger byddeth wo that another by the dore shuld go. **1608** ARMIN *Nest Ninnies* (1842) 47 One foole cannot indure the sight of another, . . . and one beggar is woe that another by the doore should goe. **1641** FERGUSSON 6.

Beggar knows his dish (bag), As well as the.

1546 HEYWOOD I. xi. **1579** GOSSON *Sch. Abuse* (Arb.) 74 Such as he knew as well as the Begger his dishe. **1638** T. HEYWOOD *Wise W. Hogs.* II. i As well as the beggar knows his dish. **1738** SWIFT (Dial. i) 335 *Never.* Know him! ay, as well as the beggar knows his dish.

Beggar may sing before the thief, The.

[JUVENAL *Sat.* 10. 22 *Cantabit vacuus coram latrone viator.*] **1377** LANGLAND *P. Pl.* B. xiv. 305 An hardy man of herte . amonge an hepe of theues ; *Cantabit pauper coram latrone viator.* *c.* **1386** CHAUCER *W. of Bath's T.* 1192 Juvenal seith of poverte, myrily, 'The pourè man, whan he goth by the weye, Bifore the thevès he may synge and pleye'. *c.* **1440** LYDGATE *Fall of Princes* III. 582 The poore man affor the theeff doth synge. **1546** HEYWOOD I. xii. 38. **1593** PEELE *Edw. I* i A man purse-penniless may sing before a thief. **1614** CAMDEN 312. **1875** J. PAYN *Walter's Word* xxxii 'As to my cheerfulness, there is a proverb that a man with empty pockets is not cast down by falling among thieves'. 'That may be so in England, signor, . . . but with us brigands it is different.'

Beggar on horseback, Set a | and he'll ride a gallop (*for variants see quotations*).

1584 W. AVERELL *A Dyall for Dainty darlings* C 4[v] Set a begger on horsebacke and he will gallop. **1590–1** SHAKS. *3 Hen. VI* I. iv. 127 It needs not, . . . proud queen, Unless the adage must be verified, That beggars' mounted run their horse to death. **1592** NASHE *Pierce Pen.* (Shaks. Soc.) 22 These whelpes . . . drawen vp to the heauen of honour from the dunghill of abiect fortune, haue long been on horsebacke to come riding to your diuellship. **1599** GREENE *Orpharion* in Wks. XII 36 (Gros.), with 'never light'. **1611** GRUTER, with 'run his horse out of breath'. **1616** DRAXE 163 (ditto). **1621** BURTON *Anat. Mel.* II. iii. II (1651) 319 *Nothing so intolerable as a fortunate fool*, . . . Asperius nihil est humili, cum surgit in altum:[1] set a begger on horseback and he will ride a gallop. **1629** T. ADAMS *Serm.* (1861–2) I. 116 He that serves the *flesh* serves his fellow; and a beggar mounted on the back of honour rides post to the devil. **1809** CORBETT *Pol. Reg.* xv. xii. 429 Our own old saying: 'Set a beggar on horse-back, and he'll ride to the devil.' [1 CLAUDIANUS *In Eutrop.* I. 181.]

Beggar, The stoutest | that goes by the way, can't beg through Long[1] on a midsummer's day.

1869 HAZLITT 399 *Higson's MSS. Coll.*, 131. [1 LEAN I. 181 Sharp (*British Gazetteer*, 1852) is doubtless right in assigning it to Longdon in Staffordshire, 'a village of some length'.]

Beggar's-bush, This is the way to.

1564 BULLEIN *Dial. agst. Fever* (E.E.T.S.) 78 (A) In the ende thei go home . . . by weepyng cross, by beggers barne, and by knaues acre. **1592** GREENE *Upst. Courtier* (1871) 6 Walking home by Beggars Bush for a penance. **1662** FULLER (*Hunts.*) II. 98 'This is the way to Beggar's-bush'. It is spoken of such who use dissolute and improvident courses; Beggar's-bush being a tree notoriously known, on the left hand of London road from Huntington to Caxton. . . . King James . . . having heard . . . how Sir Francis [Bacon] had prodigiously rewarded a mean man . . . ; 'Sir Francis', said he, 'you will quickly come to Beggar's-bush; and I may even go along with you, if both be so bountiful'. **1902–4** LEAN I. 103 This is the way to BEGGAR'S BUSH. . . . The primary meaning was a rendezvous for beggars at the bifurcation of two roads.

Beggar's scrip is never filled, A

1539 TAVERNER 39.

Beggars of Bath, The.

1662 FULLER (*Som.*) III. 92 'The beggars of Bath'. Many in that place; some native there, others repairing thither from all parts of the land; the poor for alms; the pained for ease.

Beggars breed, and rich men feed.

1670 RAY 60. **1721** KELLY 75 . . . Poor people's children find a support in the service of the rich and great.

Beggars must (should) be no choosers.

1546 HEYWOOD I. x. 24 Folke saie alwaie, beggers should be no choosers. **1579** GOSSON *Sch. Abuse* (Arb.) 73 Beggars, you know, must bee no choosers. **1593–4** SHAKS. *Tam. Shrew* Ind. I. 41 Lord. Would not the beggar then forget himself? *First Hunt.* Believe me, lord, I think he cannot choose. c. **1612** BEAUM. & FL. *Scornf. Lady* v. i. Wks. (C.U.P.) I. 294 Beggers must be no chusers. **1863** READE *Hard Cash* xxiii So I told him beggars musn't be choosers.

Beggars of Bologna, Like the blind.

1662 J. WILSON *Cheats* II. iv *T. T.* He's like the blind beggars of Bolonia, a man must give 'um a halfpenny to sing, and twopence to hold their tongues.

Beggar(s), *see also* Better to be a b.; Better to die a b.; Dainties love (Who) shall b. prove; Every b. descended from a king; Great as b.; Lady's heart and b.'s purse; Leeful man is b.'s brother; Louse is b.'s companion; Loves the poor but cannot abide b.; Marry a b. and get a louse; Misery may be mother where one b. . . . beg of another; Much ado to bring b. to stocks; Plain of poverty and die b.; Proud b. that makes own alms; Proud mind and b.'s purse; Scratch a b. before you die (You will); Simple man is b.'s brother; Slothful man is b.'s brother; Small invitation will serve b.; Sue a b., get a louse; Wishes were buttercakes (If), b. might bite; Wishes were horses (If) . . . ; Wishes were thrushes (If) . . . ; Wishes would bide (If) . . . ; Young courtier old b.; Young serving-man, old b.

Beggary, *see* Idleness is the key of b.; Sweet beauty with sour b.

Begged for a fool, To be.

1584 D. FENNER *Def. Ministers* (1587) 51 Then would you haue proued vs asses, not begged vs for innocents. **1592** LYLY *Moth. Bom.* I. i He needs not, sir, Ile beg him for a fool. **1736** HERVEY *Mem.* II. 143 Moyle either deserved to be . . . begged for a fool, or hanged for a knave.

Begging, *see* Year sooner to the b. (It is but a).

Begin a journey on Sunday, I love to.

1738 SWIFT (*Dial.* ii) 349 *Col.* Now I always love to begin a journey on Sunday, because I shall have the prayers of the church to preserve all that travel by land or by water.

Begin well, Good to | better to end well.

1664 CODRINGTON 195. **1670** RAY 8.

Beginneth the song, Let him that | make and end.

1616 DRAXE 12.

Beginneth to build too soon that hath not money to finish it, He.

1616 DRAXE 1. **1721** KELLY 50 as English prov.

Beginning, Such | such end.

1546 HEYWOOD II. ix. 77 And such beginnyng such ende we all daie sée.

Beginning(s), *see also* All things in their b. are good; Beware b.; Everything must have b.; Good (Hard) b. makes good ending.

Begins to die that quits his desires, He.

1611 COTGRAVE s.v. 'Abandonner'. **1640** HERBERT 317.

Begin(s), begun, *see also* Better never to b.; Well b. is half done.

Beguile(s, d), *see* Sorrow be in the house that you're b. in; Think none ill (They that) soonest b.; Wily b. with himself (He hath played).

Behind the horseman sits black care.

[HORACE *Odes* 3. 1. 37 *Post equitem sedet atra cura.*] **1603** FLORIO tr. *Montaigne* i. 38 Care, looking grim and black, doth sit behind his back that rides from it. **1861** G. J. WHYTE-MELVILLE *Market Harbor.* ii If Care sits behind the horseman on the cantle of his saddle, Ambition may also be detected clinging somewhere about his spurs. **1857–9** THACKERAY *Virgin.* lxxxv Does not *Atra Cura* sit behind baronets as well as *Equites?*

Behind the mountains there are people to be found.

1861 DEAN STANLEY *Hist. East. Ch.* (1862) i. 2 There is a wise German proverb which tells us that it is good . . . to be reminded that 'Behind the mountains there are people to be found'.

Behind, *see also* Far b. must follow the faster; Far b. that may not follow (They are); Further we go, further b.; Rides b. another (He who) does not travel when he pleases.

Beild[1] aneath an auld man's beard, There is.

1737 RAMSAY III. 196. [[1] shelter, protection.]

Believe he's bald till you see his brains, You will not.

1580 LYLY *Euph. & his Eng.* (Arb.) 267 As incredulous as those, who thinke none balde, till they see his braynes. **1599–1600** SHAKS. *Twelfth N.* IV. ii. 129 I'll ne'er believe a madman till I see his brains. **1639** CLARKE 181.

Believe no tales from an enemy's tongue.

1659 HOWELL *Brit. Prov.* 32.

Believe not all that you see nor half what you hear.

c. **1205** LAYAMON *Brut* (Madden) I. 342 Yif thu ileuest ælcne mon, selde thu sælt wel don. [If thou believest every man, seldom shalt thou do well.] **1858** MULOCK *A Woman's Thoughts* 194 'Believe only half of what you see, and nothing that you hear', is a cynical saying, and yet less bitter than at first appears.

Believe well and have well.

1546 HEYWOOD II. ix. 74 Beleue well, and haue well, men say. **1862** HISLOP (1870) 55 Believe a' ye hear, an' ye may eat a' ye see.

Believe what we desire, We soon. (*Cf.* Wish is father to the thought.)

[CAES. *De Bello G.* 3. 18 *Libenter homines id quod volunt credunt.* Ov. *A.A.* 3. 674 *Prona venit cupidis in sua vota fides.*] *c.* **1386** CHAUCER *Melibeus* B[2] 2473 'Lo, Lo!' quod dame Prudence, 'how lightly is every man enclyned to his owene desyr and to his owene plesaunce!' **1576** PETTIE *Petite Pall.* (Gollancz) I. 177 I did perceive, if desire to have it so did not deceive me. **1597–8** SHAKS. *2 Hen. IV* IV. v. 91 *Prince.* I never thought to hear you speak again. *K. Hen.* Thy wish was father, Harry, to that thought. **1616** DRAXE 191 We soone beleeue that we would haue.

Believe(d), *see also* Do not all you can, b. not all you hear; Easily done soon b.; Husband, don't b. what you see.

Believers, *see* Quick b. need broad shoulders.

Believes all, misseth; He that | he that believes nothing, misseth.

1640 HERBERT 334.

Bell, To bear (*or* carry away) the.

[= to be first.] *c.* **1374** CHAUCER *Troylus* III. 149 And, let us se which of yow shal bere the belle To speke of love aright? *c.* **1460** *Towneley Myst.* 88 Of alle the foles I can telle . . . Ye thre bere the belle. **1594** BARNFIELD *Aff. Sheph.* II. xxxix For pure white the Lilly bears the Bell.—CAREW *Huarte's Exam. Wits* xiii. (1596) 215 Iulius Cæsar . . . bare away the bell (in respect of fortunatenesse) from all other captains of the world. **1621** BURTON *Anat. Mel.* To Rdr. 49 True merchants, they carry away the bell from all other nations. **1817** BYRON *Beppo* x Venice the bell from every city bore.

Bell, book, and candle.

[A form of excommunication closed with the words, 'Doe to the book, quench the candle, ring the bell!'] *a.* **1300** *Cursor M.* 17110 Curced in kirc þan sal þai be wid candil, boke, and bell. *c.* **1548** BALE *K. Johan* 1033 For as moch as Kyng Johan doth Holy Church so handle, Here I do curse hym wyth crosse, boke, bell and candle. **1596–7** SHAKS. *K. John* III. iii. 12 Bell, book, and candle shall not drive me back. **1680** *Spir. Popery* 45 The Field-Preachers damned this Bond with Bell, Book, and Candle. **1896** G. BERNARD SHAW in *The Savoy* Jan. 26 This unseemly wretch should be seized and put out, bell, book, candle and all, until he learns to behave himself.

Bell the cat, To.

[An allusion to the fable of the mice proposing to hang a bell about the cat's neck, to apprise them of her coming.] **1377** LANGLAND *P. Pl.* B. Prol. 168–70 To bugge[1] a belle of brasse . . . And hangen it vp-on the cattes hals. **1482** LD. GRAY IN RAMSAY *Remin.* (1857) v When the nobles of Scotland proposed . . . to take Cochrane, the favourite of James the Third, and hang him, the Lord Gray asked, 'It is well said, but wha will bell the cat?' *a.* **1529** SKELTON *Col. Cloute* 164 Loth to hang the bell aboute the cattes necke. **1721** KELLY 180 It is well said, but who will bell the cat? **1881** JESSOPP *Arcady* 149 Their neighbours . . . wink at much which they would gladly see mended; but who is to bell the cat? . . . He would be a very bold man . . . who would have the pluck to lodge a complaint. **1926** *Times* 1 Nov. 13/2 The taxes are illegal. All are prepared to protest, but none is willing to bell the cat. [[1] buy.]

Belle giant, or devil of Mountsorrel, He leaps like the.

1787 GROSE (*Leics.*) (1811) 190 He leaps like the Belle giant, or devil of Mountsorril. 'About Mountsorrel, or Mounshill', says Peck, 'the country people have a story of a giant or devil, named Bell, who . . . took three prodigious leaps, . . .' This story seems calculated to ridicule . . . shooters in the long bow.

Belled wether break the snow, Let aye the.

1832 HENDERSON 129. **1862** HISLOP 207 . . . A 'bell'd wether' is a ram with a bell round its neck; and the proverb means that a difficult or dangerous undertaking should be led by a person of experience.

Bellerophon, Letters of.

[Proetus sent him to Lycia, γράψας ἐν πίνακι πτυκτῷ θυμοφθόρα πολλά, *Il.* vi. 169, having graved in a folded tablet many deadly things. L. *Literæ Bellerophontis.*] **1742–6** YOUNG *Night Thoughts* VII He, whose blind thought futurity denies, Unconscious bears, Bellerophon! like thee, His own indictment. **1855** BULFINCH *Age of Fable* xvi Bellerophon being unconsciously the bearer of his own death warrant, the expression 'Bellerophontic letters' arose.

Bellows like a bull, He | but is as weak as a bulrush.

1639 CLARKE 142.

Bellows, *see* Windmill go with b. (Cannot make).

Bells call others, but themselves enter not into the church.

1557 NORTH *Diall of Princes* f. 138[v] (A) For men y[t] reade much, and worke litle, are as belles, the which do sound to cal others, and they themselves neuer enter into the church. *a.* **1591** H. SMITH *Serm.* (1866) II. 117 They are like our bells, which can call the people together to the service of God, but cannot perform any service to God. **1640** HERBERT 344 Bells call others, but themselves enter not into the church. **1754** FRANKLIN Feb. The bell calls others to church, but itself never minds the sermon.

Bell(s), *see also* Agree like b., want but hanging; Counsel of fools (To) wooden b.; Cracked b. never sound; Fear not loss of b. more than steeple; Fool thinks (As the),

so b. clinks; God comes to see without a b.; Hang all my b. on one horse; Hear a toll or knell; Silly flock where ewe bears b.; Sound as a b.; Whip and b.

Bell-wether, *see* Flock follow b.

Belly carries the legs (feet), The.

1599 MINSHEU (1623) 273. **1620** SHELTON *Quix.* II. xxxiv (1908) III. 63 The belly carries the legs, and not the legs the belly. **1734** FULLER no. 3194 Let the guts be full, for its they that carry the legs. **1911** A. COHEN *Anct. Jew. Prov.* 39 The stomach carries the feet . . . Similarly it is said 'The heart carries the feet'.

Belly cries cupboard, His (My).

1678 RAY 237. **1738** SWIFT (Dial. ii) 344 *Foot.* Dinner's upon the table. *Col.* Faith, I'm glad of it; my belly began to cry cupboard.

Belly full of gluttony will never study willingly, A.

1586 PETTIE *Guazzo's Civ. Conv.* 190 Know that this proverb is as true as common. That a fat belly doth not engender a subtle wit. **1678** RAY 146 . . . i.e. the old proverbial verse. *Impletus venter non vult studere libenter.* **1845** LOWELL *Conv. on Old Poets* 55 *Impletus venter non vult studere libenter* was the old monkish jingle, and let us be grateful . . . to the critics who have made the poets unwillingly illustrate it.

Belly is full, He whose | believes not him who is fasting. (*Cf.* Full man and a fasting, &c.)

1573 SANDFORD (1576) 211. **1578** FLORIO *First Fruites* f. 29 He that is fed beleeueth not the fasting. **1732** FULLER no. 2399.

Belly is full, When the | the bones would be at rest.

a. **1530** R. Hill's *Commonpl. Bk.* (E.E.T.S.) 129 Whan the beli is fwll, þe bonis wold hawe rest. **1546** HEYWOOD II. ii. 45 Husbande (quoth she) I would we were in our nest. Whan the bealy is full, the bones wold be at rest. **1641** FERGUSSON 106 Quhen the bellie is full, the bones wald have rest. **1738** SWIFT (Dial. ii) 348 *Sir J.* I sometimes take a nap after my pipe; for when the belly is full, the bones would be at rest.

Belly is full, When the | the mind is among the maids.

1607 H. ESTIENNE, *World of Wonders*, tr. R.C., 42 The *Greeke* verse saith proverbially, that when the belly is full, the mind is among the maids. **1611** COTGRAVE s.v. 'Dame' When the belly is full, the breech would be frigging. *c.* **1645** MS. Proverbs in *N. & Q.* vol. 154, 27.

Belly teaches all arts, The.

[**1540** PALSGRAVE *Acolastus* (Carver) 62 The bely which is the master of wytte.] **1855** BOHN 498.

Belly, If it were not for the | the back might wear gold.

1611 COTGRAVE s.v. 'Estat' The bellie is starved by the backe. **1619** W. HORNBY *Scourge of Drunkennes* That by his paunch his backe should fare the worse. **1732** FULLER no. 2690.

Belly thinks the throat is cut, The.

1540 PALSGRAVE *Acolastus* (Carver) 59 My bealy weneth my throte is cutte. **1599** BRETON *Anger & Pat.* Wks. (Gros.) II. 60 *Ang.* My belly will thinke my throat cut that I feede no faster. **1623** CAMDEN 279. **1721** KELLY 379 *Your weime[1] thinks your wizran[2] is cutted.* Spoken to them who have wanted meat long. **1738** SWIFT (Dial. ii) 344 *Miss.* Mr. Neverout, you are in great haste; I believe, your belly thinks your throat's cut. [[1] belly. [2] throat.]

Belly(-ies), *see also* Better b. burst than drink lost; Better fill a man's b. than his eye; Birth follows b.; Eats the calf in cow's b.; Eye is bigger than b.; Full b. neither fights; Hungry b. have no ears; Never good that mind b.

Bellyful is a bellyful, whether it be meat or drink, A.

1666 TORRIANO 321. **1678** RAY 100. **1738** SWIFT (Dial. ii) 347 (*Col.*) I have made my whole dinner of beef. (*Ans.*) . . . A bellyfull's a bellyfull, if it be but of wheat straw.

Bellyful, *see also* Feast and a b. (Little difference).

Bellywark, *see* Sick of the . . . b. in the heel.

Belong(s), *see* All men have what b. to them (When), it cannot be much.

Beloved, To be | is above all bargains.

1640 HERBERT 347.

Beloved, *see also* Well with him who is b.

Below, *see* Things that are b. us are nothing.

Belt, *see* Angry (If you be), turn buckle of b.; Buckles his b. (Every man); Hit below the b.; Thumb under one's b. (To have a man's); Tine the tuppenny b. for the twapenny whang.

Beltanes, *see* Skill of man and beast (You have), born between the B.

Belvoir hath a cap, If | yon churls of the Vale look to that.

1662 FULLER (*Leics.*) II. 226 'If Bevoir have a cap, Yon churls of the vale look to that'. That is, when the clouds . . . hang over the towers of the castle, it is a prognostic of much rain . . . to . . . that fruitful vale, lying in the three counties of Leicester, Lincoln, and Nottingham. **1848** A. B. EVANS *Leics. Words, &c.* (1881) 300 I have heard the proverb . . .

always in the form: 'When Belvoir wears his cap, Yon churls of the Vale look to that'; and . . . when an Albini or a Ros 'wore his cap' in the Manor Court, or rode . . . to the chase . . . there was good cause for the 'churls of the Vale' to look to it.

Bemired, *see* Hog that's b.

Benches, *see* Hall b. are slippery.

Bend while it is a twig, Best to.

1509 A. BARCLAY *Ship of Fools* (1874) I. 47 A lytell twygge plyant is by kynde A bygger braunche is harde to bowe or wynde. *c.* **1532** SIR ADRIAN FORTESCUE no. 12 A bowe is best bowyd, when it is young. **1563** B. GOOGE *Eglogs* vi (Arb.) 53 The tender twyg, that now doth bend at length refuseth cleane. **1650** BAXTER *Saints Everl. Rest* III. xi They are young . . . and flexible . . . You have a twig to bend, and we an oak. **1670** RAY 61.

Bend, *see also* Better b. than break.

Benefice, *see* Gape for a b.

Benefits please, like flowers, while they are fresh.

1651 HERBERT 318.

Benson, *see* Hope better, quoth B. . . . cuckold.

Bent of his bow, I have (know) the.

c. **1430** LYDGATE *Lydgate's Mumming at Hertford* 198 We knowe to well the bent of Jackys bowe. **1546** HEYWOOD I. xi. 30 Though I, hauyng the bent of your vncles bow, Can no way bryng your bolte in the but to stand. **1670** RAY 228. **1783** AINSWORTH *Lat. Dict.* (Morell) 1 s.v. 'Bent' I have got the bend of his bow, *ego illius sensum pulchrè calleo.*

Bermudas let you pass, If the | you must beware of Hatteras.

1840 DANA *Two Years* xxxv We passed inside of the Bermudas; and notwithstanding the old couplet, . . .—'If the Bermudas let you pass, You must beware of Hatteras—' we were to the northward of Hatteras, with good weather.

Bernard did not see everything.

[Usually taken as referring to St. Bernard of Clairvaux, 1091–1153.] *c.* **1385** CHAUCER *L.G.W.* Prol. (1 version) 16 Bernard the monk ne say nat al pardee! **1659** FULLER *Appeal Inj. Innoc.* in *Hist. Camb. Univ.* (1840) 332 *Bernardus non videt omnia;* I could not come to the knowledge of every particular.

Berwick to Dover three hundred miles over, From.

c. **1300** R. BRUNNE tr. LANGTOFT'S *Chron.* (Hearne) 305 (A) Alle Inglond fro Berwick vnto Kent. **1553** T. WILSON *Arte of Rhet.* (1909) 105 Oftentimes they beginne as much from the matter, as it is betwixt Douer and Barwike. **1662** FULLER (*Northumb.*) II. 542

'From Berwick to Dover, three hundred miles over'. That is, from one end of the land to the other. Semnable the Scripture expression, 'From Dan to Beersheba'.

Beside the book, To be.

1605 CHAPMAN *All Fools* II. i. 333 the poor lawyers ... Were fair to rail and talk besides their books Without all order. **1672** WALKER 32.

Beside (Besides) the cushion, To set (*or* put).

[= to depose, or disappoint of an office or dignity.] **1546** HEYWOOD II. ix. 80 I may set you besyde the cushyn yit. And make you wype your nose vpon your sléeue. *a.* **1624** BP. M. SMITH *Serm.* 188 Sometimes putting them besides the cushion, and placing others in their roome.

Beside, *see also* Think all is lost that goes b. your mouth.

Besom, *see* Little for rake after b.; Need of a b. that sweep with turf (They have).

Best among them, There is never a | as the fellow said by the fox cubs.

1678 RAY 228.

Best bred have the best portion, The.

c. **1630** G. HERBERT *Letters* (Wks. ed. Hutchinson 376) take this rule and it is an outlandish one, ... 'the best bredd child hath the best portion'. **1640** HERBERT 361.

Best cart may overthrow, The.

1550 HEYWOOD I. xi. 29 Well (quoth his man) the best cart maie ouerthrowe.

Best cloth may have a moth in it, The.

1576 PETTIE *Petite Pall.* (Gollancz) I. 27 The moth which most of all eateth the best cloth. **1732** FULLER no. 4411.

Best dog leap the stile first, The.

1678 RAY 76 ... i.e. Let the worthiest person take place.

Best foot (*or* leg) foremost (*or* forward), To put (*or* set) one's.

[= to do one's best to get on.] **1593–4** SHAKS. *Titus Andron.* II. iii. 192 Come on, my lords, the better foot before. **1633** JONSON *T. Tub* II. i (Dent) II. 585 Zon Clay, cheer up, the better leg avore. **1678** RAY 245 To set the best foot forward. **1876** BLACKMORE *Cripps* vii Hup! Dobbin there. Best foot foremost kills the hill.

Best general who makes the fewest mistakes, He is the.

1907 SIR I. HAMILTON *Staff Off. Scrap-Bk.* II. 347 The highest authority tells us that he is the best general who makes fewest mistakes.

Best go first, The | the bad remain to mend.

a. **1631** J. DONNE *Sonnet on 'Death'* And soonest our best men with thee doe goe. **1645** *Verney Memoirs* (1892) ii. 75 The best go [= die] first. **1855** BOHN 498. **1859** C. READE *Love me Little* xxi 'She was an angel, ... sent to bear us company a little while, and now she is a saint in heaven'. 'Ah, ma'am! the best goes first, that is an old saying.'

Best gown that goes up and down the house, That is the.

1640 HERBERT 351.

Best is as good as stark naught, The.

1616 WITHALS 581. **1639** CLARKE 14.

Best is behind, The.

c. **1369** CHAUCER *Bk. Duchess* 890 The formest was alway behynde. *a.* **1500** *Robin Hood and the Potter* st. 30 Her es more, and affter ys to saye, The best ys beheynde. *a.* **1529** SKELTON *Wks.* (Dyce) I. 17 Take thys in worth, the best is behynde. **1579** LYLY *Euphues* (Arb.) 146 But the greatest thing is yet behinde. **1605–6** SHAKS. *Macbeth* I. iii. 116 Glamis, and thane of Cawdor: The greatest is behind. **1659** HOWELL *Eng. Prov.* 6/2 The best is behind. **1824** MOIR *Mansie W.* ii In the course of the evening, his lordship whispered to one of the flunkies to bring in some things—they could not hear what.... The wise ones thought within themselves that the best aye comes hindmost.

Best is best cheap.

c. **1532** SIR ADRIAN FORTESCUE, no. 61 Comyngly the best clothe, is best chepe. **1546** HEYWOOD II. vii. **1616** DRAXE 14. **1655–62** GURNALL *Chrn. in Armour* (1865) I. 82 He that sells cheapest shall have most customers, though, at last, best will be best cheap. **1670** RAY 61 ... For it doth the buyer more credit and more service. **1786** WOLCOT (P. Pindar) *Lousiad* v. Wks. (1816) I. 230 'Best is best cheap'—you very wisely cry.

Best is oftentimes the enemy of the good, The.

1608 SHAKS. *Lear* I. iv. 369 Striving to better, oft we mar what's well. **1861** TRENCH *Epist. Seven Ch.* Pref. iii 'The best is oftentimes the enemy of the good'; and ... many a good book has remained unwritten, ... because there floated before the mind's eye ... the ideal of a better or a best. **1925** *Times* 1 Dec. 16/2 This is not the first time in history of the world when the best has been the enemy to the good; ... one single step on ... solid ground may be more profitable than a more ambitious flight. [Fr. *Le mieux est l'ennemi du bien.*]

Best loved furthest off, Men are.

1639 CLARKE 71.

Best men when in the worst health, We are usually the.

1707 MAPLETOFT 79. **1855** BOHN 551.

Best of a bad bargain (market), Make the.

1589 PUTTENHAM *Arte of Eng. Poesie* (Arb.) 195 The figure *Paradiastole* . . . we call the *Curry-fauell*, as when we make the best of a bad thing. **1663** PEPYS *Diary* 14 Aug. I . . . therefore am resolved to make The best of a bad market. **1664** COTTON *Scarron.* i. 465 Let's make the best of a bad market. **1670** RAY 61. **1712** ARBUTHNOT *John Bull* II. xii Matters have not been carried on with due secrecy; however, we must make the best of a bad bargain. **1721** KELLY 247 *Make the best of a bad market.* Since you have faln into a troublesome business, mend it by your cunning and industry. **1775** BOSWELL *Johnson* xlviii (1848) 440 A young lady . . . had married . . . her inferior in rank . . . Mrs. Thrale was all for . . . 'making the best of a bad bargain'. **1829** SCOTT *Journ.* 14 July A rainy forenoon . . . I wrote 4½ pages to make the best of a bad bargain. **1876** E. A. FREEMAN *Norm. Conq.* IV. xvii. 7 Men had made up their minds to submit to what they could not help, and to make the best of a bad bargain.

Best of both worlds, To make the.

1855 KINGSLEY *Westward Ho!* xii Bishop Grandison of Exeter proclaimed . . . 'participation in all spiritual blessings for ever', to all who would promote the bridging of that dangerous ford; and so, consulting alike the interests of their souls and of their bodies, 'make the best of both worlds'. **1871** FROUDE *Calvinism* in *Short Stud.* II (1900) 57 We have learnt . . . to make the best of both worlds, to take political economy for the rule of our conduct, and to relegate religion into the profession of orthodox doctrines.

Best or worst thing to man, for this life, is good or ill choosing his good or ill wife, The.

1546 HEYWOOD I. ii. 4. **1721** KELLY 331 The good or ill hap of a good or ill life, is the good or ill choice of a good or ill wife. **1732** FULLER no. 6413 (*as* 1721).

Best payment is on the peck bottom, The.

1721 KELLY 95 . . . That is, when you have measured out your grain, to receive your payment on the peck that measured it.

Best smell, The | is bread, the best savour salt, the best love that of children.

1640 HERBERT 351.

Best thing for the inside of a man is the outside of a horse, The.

[i.e. riding exercise.] **1906** G. W. E. RUSSELL *Soc. Silhouettes* xxxii. 218 The Squire will wind up . . . with an apocryphal saying which he attributes to Lord Palmerston—'There's nothing so good for the inside of a man as the outside of a horse'.

Best thing in the world is to live above it, The.

1855 BOHN 499.

Best things are worst to come by, The.

1635 SWAN *Spec. Mundi* 465 (A) Excellent things are hard to come by. **1639** CLARKE 87.

Best things (Everything) may be abused, The.

1576 PETTIE *Petite Pall.* (Gollancz) II. 138 There is nothing so good, but by ill using may be made naught. **1579** LYLY *Euphues* (Arb.) 100 There is nothing but through the malice of man may be abused. **1594–5** SHAKS. *Rom. & Jul.* II. iii. 19 Nor aught so good but strain'd from that fair use Revolts from true birth, stumbling on abuse. **1639** CLARKE 5. **1666** TORRIANO 1 Everything may be abused.

Best use of their time, Those that make the | have none to spare.

1732 FULLER no. 5029.

Best wine comes out of an old vessel, The.

1621 BURTON *Anat. Mel.* II. iii. 11 (1651) 312 *Vilis sæpe cadus nobile nectar habet*: the best wine comes out of an old vessell. How many deformed princes, kings, emperours, could I reckon up, philosophers, orators?

Best wine is that a body drinketh of another man's cost, The.

1564 UDALL *Erasm. Apoph.* (1877) 141 To one demanding what wyne he[1] best loued and liked with his good will to drinke, Marie (quoth he) of another mannes purse. [*Margin.* The best wine is that a body drinketh of another mans cost.] [[1] i.e. Diogenes.]

Best, *see also* Good is the enemy of the b.

Bestill [i.e. *be still*] is worth a groat, A good.

c. **1430** LYDGATE *Adv. to Tittle-tattlers* in *Minor Poems* (Percy Soc.) 155 A good be stille is weel wourth a groote. Large language causith repentaunce. **1546** HEYWOOD II. v. 56 A good bestyll is woorth a grote. **1616** DRAXE 191.

Bestows his gifts as broom doth honey, He.

1678 RAY 246 . . . Broom is so far from sweet that it's very bitter.

Bestows, *see also* Plays the whore for apples, then b. them.

Betides, *see* Weel bides, weel b.

Betimes, *see* Rise b. that will cozen devil; Rise b. that would please everybody; Riseth b. hath something in head (He that).

Better a bare foot than none.

1640 HERBERT 320.

Better a castle of bones than of stones.

c. 1350 HY. SAVAGE in [1577] HOLINSHED *Chron.* (1808) VI. 256 In this season dwelled in Vlster . . . sir Robert Sauage . . . 'Father (quoth yoong Sauage) I remember the prouerbe "Better a castell of bones than of stones". Where . . . valiant men are . . . neuer will I . . . cumber my selfe with dead walles.'

Better a clout than a hole out.

1636 CAMDEN 299. 1664 CODRINGTON 188. 1670 RAY 71.

Better a finger off than aye wagging.[1]

c. 1200 *Ancrene Riwle* (Morton) 360 Vor betere is finker offe þen he eke euer. 1641 FERGUSSON 22 Better finger off nor ay warkin.[1] 1721 KELLY 56 *Better finger off as ay wagging.* Better put an end to a troublesome business, than to be always vex'd with it. 1818 SCOTT *Rob Roy* xviii I hae been thinking o' flitting, . . . and now I'm o' the mind to gang in gude earnest . . . better a finger off as aye wagging. [[1] aching.]

Better a lean jade than an empty halter.

1678 RAY 166. 1732 FULLER no. 863.

Better a lean peace than a fat victory.

1578 FLORIO *First Fruites* f. 32 Better is a leane agreement then a fat sentence. 1605 BRETON *Old Man's Lesson* Wks. (Gros.) II. 10 The heart of a wise man will bee better pleased with a poore peace, then a Rich Warre. 1732 FULLER no. 864.

Better a little loss than a long sorrow

1362 LANGLAND *P. Pl.* Prol. 388–9 (Wright) I. 12 For better is a litel los Than a long sorwe.

Better a louse (mouse) in the pot than no flesh at all.

1623 CAMDEN 267 A louse is better than no meat. 1636 *Ibid.* 293 ['mouse']. 1639 CLARKE 249 ['louse']. 1641 FERGUSSON 211 ['mouse']. 1670 RAY 117 ['louse', but adds 'The Scotch proverb saith a mouse']. 1732 FULLER no. 867 ['mouse'].

Better a mischief than an inconvenience.

1572 T. WILSON *Discourse upon Usury* (1925), 237. (As we say) better it is to suffer a mischiefe then an inconvenience. 1639 CLARKE 199 Better once a mischief than ever an inconvenience. 1642 D. ROGERS *Naaman* ix. 255 Redeem a perpetual inconvenience, although by a present mischief (as the proverb saith), pulling down a bad chimney with some cost, rather than enduring a perpetual smoky house. 1670 RAY 121 . . . That is, better a present mischief that is soon over, then a constant grief and disturbance.

Better a portion in a wife than with a wife.

1721 KELLY 70 *Better a togher in her than with her.* Better marry a . . . virtuous woman, . . . than an idle . . . drab, with a much greater portion. 1732 FULLER no. 868. 1886 E. J. HARDY *How to be Happy* iv Better to have a fortune *in* your wife than with her.

Better a snotty child than his nose wiped off.

1611 COTGRAVE s.v. 'Enfant' Better a snottie child then a noselesse. 1640 HERBERT 355.

Better a wee fire to warm us than a mickle fire to burn us.

1721 KELLY 61 . . . An ordinary fortune is safest, and exposes us to less danger. 1824 S. FERRIER *Inheritance* II. xxvii As the old byeword says, 'better a wee ingle to warm ye, than a muckle fire to burn you'.

Better an apple given than eaten.

c. 1300 *Prov. of Hending* 13 Betere is appel y-yeue then y-ete. 1641 FERGUSSON 20 Better apple given nor eaten. 1721 KELLY 42 *An apple is better given than eaten by a time.* A man may get more favour by giving a thing than using it.

Better an egg to-day than a hen to-morrow.

[1546 RABELAIS III. xlii *Ad præsens ova cras pullis sunt meliora.*] 1659 HOWELL *Ital.* 1. 1666 TORRIANO 113 It is better to have an egge to-day, than to-morrow a hen. 1732 FULLER no. 2916 It is better to have a hen to-morrow than an egg to-day. 1734 FRANKLIN Sept. An egg to-day is better than a hen to-morrow. 1777 DIBDIN *Quaker* I. ii An egg to-day is better than a chicken to-morrow. 1860 SURTEES *Plain or Ring?* xiii There is an old adage 'that an egg to-day is worth a hen to-morrow'.

Better an empty house than an ill tenant.

1721 KELLY 67. 1732 FULLER no. 870.

Better an open enemy than a false friend.

c. 1200 *Ancrene Riwle* (Morton) 98 Ueond þet þuncheð freond is swike ouer alle swike. [An enemy who seems a friend is of all traitors the most treacherous.] *c.* 1386 CHAUCER *Merch. T.* E[2] 1784 O famulier foo, that his servyce bedeth! O servant traytour, false hoomly hewe, . . . God shilde us all from youre aqueyntaunce. 1592–3 SHAKS. *Rich. III* III. i. 16 God keep me from false friends. 1655–62 GURNALL *Chrn. in Armour* (1865) ii. 27 A false friend is worse than an open enemy in man's judgment; and a hypocritical Judas more abhorred by God than a bloody Pilate. 1727 GAY *Fables, Shep. Dog & W.* An open foe may prove a curse, But a pretended friend is worse. 1822 SCOTT *Nigel* ix I thank you for your plainness, . . .

an open enemy is better than a hollow friend.
1847 E. BRONTË *Wuthering H.* x 'You are
worse than twenty foes, you poisonous
friend!'

Better are meals many than one too merry.

1546 HEYWOOD II. vii. 69. *c.* **1594** BACON
Promus no. 594. **1616** DRAXE 130 Better
are meales few, then one too merrie. **1616**
Ibid. 67 (with 'feastes fewe'). **1678** RAY 401.

Better are small fish than an empty dish.

1678 RAY 204. **1862** HISLOP 262 Sma' fish
are better than nane. **1905** ASHBY-STERRY in
Graphic Christmas No. You will find that
the spider . . . If he only entangles the tiniest
flies, Thinks '*Small fish are better than none!*'

Better be a fool than a knave.

1595 T. LODGE *A Fig for Momus* (Hunt. Cl.)
B 1 T'is better be a foole then be a fox.
1640 HERBERT 361.

Better be alone than in bad (ill) company.

1477 RIVERS *Dictes and Sayings* (1877) 8 (A)
It is better a man . . . to be a lone than to be
accompayned with euill people. **1586** PETTIE
Guazzo's Civ. Conv. 180 I will withdraw . . .
where with this saying I will remain. It is
better to be alone than in ill company. **1639**
CLARKE 291. **1859** SMILES *Self-Help* 368
Lord Collingwood . . . said, 'Hold it as a
maxim that you had better be alone than in
mean company'.

Better be an old man's darling, than a young man's warling.[1]

1546 HEYWOOD II. vii. 65. **1602** BRETON
Wonders worth Hear. Wks. (Gros.) II. 12 I
see by my neighbours, it is better being an
old mans darling then a young mans world-
ling. **1721** KELLY 74 *Better an old man's
darling, than a young man's wonderling,* say
the Scots, *warling,* say the *English.* **1738**
SWIFT (Dial. i) 342 If I ever be married it
shall be to an old man; . . . it is better to be
an old man's darling than a young man's
warling. **1886** E. J. HARDY *How to be Happy* v
The majority of girls would rather be a young
man's slave than an old man's darling. [[1] one
who is despised or disliked.]

Better be envied than pitied.

[ERASM. *Ad. Praestat invidiosum esse quam
miserabilem,* quoting Greek authors.] **1546**
HEYWOOD I. xi. 26. *c.* **1565** W. WAGER *Enough
is as good as a feast* A 3 A common saying
better is enuy then rueth. *c.* **1592** MARLOWE
Jew of Malta Prol. 27 Let me be envy'd and
not pittied. **1636** CAMDEN 299 It is better to
be spited than pitied. *a.* **1631** DONNE *Verse
Lett.* Wks. (1896) II. 32 Men say, and truly,
that they better be which be envied than
pitied. **1902** G. W. E. RUSSELL *Coll. & Recol.*
2 Ser. (1909) xxxiii Her friend responded
sympathetically, 'My dear, I'd much rather
be envied than pitied'.

Better be first in a village than second at Rome.

[PLUTARCH, *Caesar* 11. 2.] **1542** UDALL
Apoph. of Erasmus (1877) 297 [Julius
Caesar] . . . had lieffer to bee the firste, or the
chief man here, then the seconde man in
Rome. **1605** BACON *Adv. Learn.* II. xxiii.
(1900) 240 Caesar, when he went first into
Gaul, made no scruple to profess *That he had
rather be first in a village than second at Rome.*
1668 COWLEY *Ess.* vi (1904) 78 I should be
like Caesar . . . and choose rather to be the
first man of the village, than second at Rome.

Better be happy than wise.

1546 HEYWOOD II. vi. 62. **1641** FERGUSSON
22.

Better be sure than sorry.

1837 LOVER *Rory O'More* xxi 'Just countin
them,—is there any harm in that?' said the
tinker; 'it's better be sure than sorry'.

Better be the head of a dog (fox, mouse, lizard) than the tail of a lion.

1599 *Master Broughton's Letters* E 2 This is
a common prouerb with them [the Rabbin-
ists], That it is better being the head of a fox,
then the tayle of a lyon; that is, the author
of an addle fancie, then the scholler of a
receiued veritie. **1599** MINSHEU (1623) tt 2
[mouse]. **1640** HERBERT 344 [lizard]. **1670**
RAY 101 [dog]. **1791–1823** I. DISRAELI *Curios.
Lit.* (Chandos) III. 52 The ancient . . . spirit
of Englishmen was once expressed by our
proverb, 'Better be the head of a dog than
the tail of a lion'; i.e. the first of the yeomanry rather than the last of the gentry.

Better be the head of a pike than the tail of a sturgeon.

1659 N. R. 69, 70. **1670** RAY 101.

Better be the head of an ass than the tail of a horse.

1639 CLARKE 105. **1670** RAY 101. **1732**
FULLER no. 928.

Better be the head of the yeomanry than the tail of the gentry.

1639 CLARKE 22. **1670** RAY 101. **1732** FULLER
no. 933 ('yeomen').

Better be unmannerly than trouble-some.

c. **1600** SHAKS. *Merry W.* I. i. 326. **1659**
HOWELL *Eng. Prov.* 5. **1670** RAY 153. **1721**
KELLY 72 *Better my friend think me frame*[1]
than fashious.[2] He that sees his friend too
seldom, errs on the right side. [[1] strange.
[2] troublesome.]

Better belly burst than good drink (meat) lost.

1659 HOWELL *Eng. Prov.* 17. **1678** RAY 100
Better belly burst than good{drink / meat} lost.

Better bend (bow) than break.

c. 1374 CHAUCER *Troylus* I. 257–8 The yerde
is bet that bowen wol and winde, Than that
that brest. c. 1420 *Peter Idle's Instructions
to his Son* (Miessner) **1**. 88 For better is the
tree þat bowe þan breste. c. 1450 *Provs. of
Wysdom* l. 58 Better is to bow þen to brest.
1546 HEYWOOD I. ix. 18 Well (quoth I) better
is to boow then breake. **1642** FULLER *H. &
P. State* v. xviii (1841) 417 Better, for a time,
to bow to our foes, rather than to be broken
by them. **1840** DICKENS *Barn. Rudge* lxxix
I have had . . . sorrows . . . but I have borne
them ill. I have broken where I should have
bent.

Better blue clothes, He is in his.

1678 RAY 66 . . . He thinks himself wondrous
fine.

Better bread than is made of wheat, He would have.

1546 HEYWOOD II. vii. 66 Lyke one of fond
fancy so fyne and so neate, That would haue
better bread than is made of wheate. **1580**
LYLY *Euphues* Ep. Ded. (Arb.) 204 Englishmen deserve to heare finer speech then the
language will allowe, to eate finer bread then
is made of wheat. **1853** TRENCH iv. 87 What
warnings do many contain against . . . a
looking for perfection is a world of imperfection. . . . We say: *He expects better bread
than can be made of wheat.*

Better buy than borrow.

1539 TAVERNER f. 13 I had leuer bye than
begge. **1616** DRAXE 18. **1641** FERGUSSON 24
Better buy as borrow. **1721** KELLY 59 . . .
True! for he that goes a borrowing goes a
sorrowing. **1732** FULLER no. 884.

Better children weep than old (bearded) men.

c. 1350 *Douce MS. 52* no. 103 Better is a
zong chylde wepe than on olde man. **1546**
HEYWOOD I. xi. **1641** FERGUSSON 22 Better
bairnes greit nor bearded men. **1721** KELLY
62 *Better bairns greet as bearded men.* Better
you make your children cry with seasonable
correction, than they make you cry by
their after miscarriage. **1827–30** SCOTT *Tales
Grandf.* xxxii The king burst into tears. 'Let
him weep on', said the Tutor of Glamis[1]
fiercely; 'better that bairns (children) weep,
than bearded men.' [1 to King James VI
after the Ruthven Raid, 1582.]

Better come at the latter end of a feast than the beginning of a fray.

1546 HEYWOOD II. vii. 65 It is yll commyng
. . . to thend of a shot and beginnyng of a
fray. **1597–8** SHAKS. *1 Hen. IV* IV. ii. 86 To
the latter end of a fray and the beginning of
a feast Fits a dull fighter and a keen guest.
1636 MASSINGER *Bashful Lover* III. iii They
said, Haste to the beginning of a feast, There
I am with them; *but to the end of a fray—*
That is apocryphal. **1670** RAY 90. **1721**
KELLY 73 Better the end of a feast than the
beginning of a fray.

Better cut the shoe than pinch the foot.

1580 LYLY *Euph. and his Eng.* Wks. (Bond)
II. 10 Better to cut the shooe, then burne
the last. **1732** FULLER no. 887.

Better day (the day), The | the better deed (the deed).

1607 MIDDLETON *Mich. Term* III. i. **1612**
S. ROWLANDS *Knave of Harts* Wks. (1880)
II. 46 They say, *The better day, the better
deede.* **1655** FULLER *Ch. Hist.* III. i (1868) I.
366 Upon Christmas-day (the better day the
better deed!) he[1] excommunicated Robert de
Broc, because the day before he had cut off
one of his horses' tails. **1721** KELLY *The
better day, the better deed.* I never heard this
used but when people say that they did such
an ill thing on *Sunday.* **1738** SWIFT (Dial. i)
340 *Lady S.* That won't be proper; you
know to-morrow's Sunday. *Ld. S.* What
then, madam! they say, the better day, the
better deed. **1896** J. C. HUTCHESON *Crown
& Anchor* xiii 'The better the day, the better
the deed, . . . it was only the Pharisees who
objected to any necessary work being done
on the Sabbath'. [1 Becket.]

Better end of the string, He has the.

1721 KELLY 157 . . . He has the advantage
in this cause.

Better eye out than always ache.

[Cf. Matt. xviii. 9 And if thine eye offend
thee, pluck it out, and cast it from thee.]
1546 HEYWOOD I. viii. 16 Continuall penurie,
whiche I muste take Telth me, better eye
out then alwaie ake. **1597** BACON *Col. of G. &
E.* 10 (Arb.) 153 Hereof the common fourmes
are, *Better eye out, then alwayes ake.*

Better eye sore than all blind.

c. 1300 *Provs. of Hending* 8 Betere is eye sor,
then al blynd, quoth Hendyng.

Better fed than taught.

1530 PALSGRAVE 557 He is better fostred
than taught. **1546** HEYWOOD I. x. 20 But
ye be better fed then taught farre awaie.
1580 LYLY *Euph. & his Eng.* (Arb.) 420
Better taught than fed. **1602–3** SHAKS. *All's
Well* II. ii. 3 I will show myself highly fed
and lowly taught. **1631** R. BRATHWAIT
Whimzies (Halliw.) 119 His duck will not
swim over with him: which makes him
peremptorily conclude she is better fed than
taught. **1641** FERGUSSON 54 *Of drunkards.*
. . . He is better fed nor nurtured. **1820** SCOTT
Monast. i Those dependents . . . might have
been truly said to be better fed than taught.

Better fill a man's belly than his eye. (Cf. Eye is bigger than the belly.)

1590 GREENE *Mourning Garm.* Wks. (Huth)
IX. 167 Better fill a man's belly than his eye.
1600 J. LANE *Tom Telltroth's Message* (New
Sh. S.) 130. **1636** CAMDEN 293 Better fill a
gluttons belly than his eye.

Better fleech[1] a fool (the devil) than fight him.

1820 SCOTT *Monast.* xiv Keep a calm sough;

better to fleech a fool than fight with him. **1827** Id. *Highl. Widow* ii Those in the Lowland line . . . comforted themselves with the old proverb, that it was better to 'fleech the devil than fight him'. [[1] flatter.]

Better give a shilling than lend and lose half a crown.

1642 TORRIANO 75 It is better to give a shilling away, than lend twenty. **1659** HOWELL *Ital.-Eng.* 14, as 1642 with 'penny' for 'shilling'. **1732** FULLER no. 895.

Better give than take.

c. **1390** GOWER *Conf. Amantis* v. 7725. **1546** HEYWOOD I. v. **1611** DAVIES Prov. 124.

Better give the wool than the sheep.

1573 SANDFORD (1576) 217. **1611** DAVIES Prov. 76 It's better to give the fleece then the sheepe. **1670** RAY 30.

Better go away longing than loathing.

1732 FULLER no. 942.

Better go to bed supperless than to rise in debt.

1659 HOWELL *Span.-Eng.* 6 'Tis wholesomer to go to bed without a supper, then rise in debt. **1670** RAY 7. **1739** FRANKLIN May Rather go to bed supperless than run in debt for a breakfast.

Better go to heaven in rags than to hell in embroidery.

1732 FULLER no. 898.

Better good afar off than evil at hand.

1640 HERBERT 329.

Better half, My.

1590 SIR PHIL. SIDNEY *Arcadia* (1907) III. 357 Argalus came out of his swoon, and . . . forcing up, the best he could, his feeble voice, 'My dear, my better half', said he, 'I find I must now leave thee'. **1667** MILTON *Parad. Lost* v. 95 Best image of myself, and dearer half. [**1926** FOWLER *Mod. Eng. Usage* s.v. *Hackneyed Phrases* My better half.]

Better hand loose than in an ill tethering.

1641 FERGUSSON 20 Better hand louse nor bound to an ill baikine.[1] **1721** KELLY 59 *Better hand loose than on an ill teddering.* Better at liberty, than an ill service. Better a bachelor, than married to an ill wife. [[1] tethering stake.]

Better is one *Accipe*, than twice to say, *Dabo tibi*.

[*c.* **1190** *Li Proverbe au vilain* (Tobler) 22 Mieuz ain un 'tien' que dous 'tu l'avras'.] **1620** SHELTON *Quix.* II. lxxi (1908) III. 320 One 'Take it' is more worth than two 'Thou shalt have it'. **1651** HERBERT 367.

Better keep the devil at the door than turn him out of the house.

1721 KELLY 61 . . . Better to resist the temptations of the Evil One, than to master them when they are comply'd with.

Better kiss a knave than to be troubled with him, It is.

1611 GRUTER. **1614** CAMDEN 308. **1738** SWIFT (Dial. i) 336 *Miss*. Well, I'd rather give a knave a kiss for once than be troubled with him.

Better known than trusted.

c. **1560** HUTH *Anc. Ballads* (1867) 228 (A) They are not so wel trust as knowne. **1648** HERRICK *Hesper.* No. 830 (Saints.) II. 77 Tap (better known then trusted) as we heare. **1818** SCOTT *Rob Roy* xxvi Rashleigh Osbaldistone is better kenned than trusted in Glasgow, for he . . . left debt ahint him.

Better late than never.

c. **1200** *Ancrene Riwle* (Morton) 340 Betere is þo þene no, betere is er. *c.* **1350** *Douce MS. 52* no. 140 Better is late than neuer. *c.* **1386** CHAUCER *Can. Yeom. T.* 1410 Lest ye lese al, for 'bet than never is late'. *c.* **1450** *Assembly of Gods* (Triggs) l. 1204 Vyce to forsake ys bettyr late then neuer. **1546** HEYWOOD I. x. 21 But better late then neuer to repent this. **1786** WOLCOT (P. Pindar) *Lousiad* ii. Wks. (1816) I. 158 But, says the proverb, 'better late than never'. **1836** MARRYAT *Midsh. Easy* ix You made your mind up but late to come to sea. However, . . . 'Better late than never'.

Better learn by your neighbour's skaith than by your own.

c. **1374** CHAUCER *Troylus* III. 329 For wyse ben by foles harm chastysed. **1641** FERGUSSON 20.

Better leave than lack.

1546 HEYWOOD I. v. 10 Praisyng this bargayne saith, better leaue then lacke. **1642** FULLER *H. & P. State* IV. xiv (1841) 291 His book is a worthy work (wherein the reader may rather leave than lack). **1721** KELLY 66 . . . Better to abound in material tools, . . . than be in the least deficient.

Better lose a jest than a friend.

[QUINTILIAN 6. 3. 28 *Potius amicum, quam dictum perdere.*] **1589** G. HARVEY *Pierce's Supererogation* (1593) in Wks. (Gros.) II. 125 It is better to loose a new iest, then an old frend. **1601** JONSON *Poetaster* IV. i A . . . satirical rascal, fly him; he . . . will sooner lose his best friend than his least jest. **1662** FULLER (*London*) ii. 382 John Heiwood . . . was most familiar with Sir Thomas More, whom he much resembled in quickness of parts, both under-valuing their friend to their jest. **1721** KELLY 283 Rather spill[1] your jest than spite your friend. **1816** SCOTT *Antiq.* xlii 'Aweel, Sir Arthur,' replied the beggar, who never hesitated an instant between his friend and his jest, 'mony a wise man sits in a fule's seat, and mony a fule in a wise man's.' [[1] spoil.]

Better lost than found.

1576 PETTIE *Petite Pall.* (Gollancz) II. 68
Knowing him better lost than found, being
no better unto you. **1580** LYLY *Euph. and his
Eng.* Wks. (Bond) II. 66 Better lost they
are with a lyttle grudge, then found with
much griefe. **1599** PORTER *Angry Wom.
Abingd.* IV. iii (Merm.) 175 He is gone to
seek my young mistress; and I think she is
better lost than found. **1650** BROME *Jov.
Crew* IV. (1708) 39 A thing that's better
lost than found; a woman! **1818** SCOTT *Ht.
Midl.* xl We hae but tint a Scot of her, and
that's a thing better lost than found.

Better luck next time.

1834 MARRYAT *Jacob Faith.* ii Better luck
next time, missus', replied I, wiping my eyes.
1866 BLACKMORE *Cradock N.* lv Bob . . .
thought, 'Better luck next time'.

Better my hog dirty home than no hog at all.

1664 CODRINGTON 187. **1670** RAY 13.

Better ne'er been born as have his nails on a Sunday shorn, A man had.

1596 LODGE *Wit's Miserie* (Hunt. Cl.) 12 He
will not . . . paire his nailes while Munday,
to be fortunat in his love. **1695** CONGREVE
Love for L. (Merm.) III. iv. 253 Thou'rt . . .
as melancholic as if thou hadst . . . pared thy
nails on a Sunday. **1846** DENHAM 12. **1848**
Athenæum 5 Feb. Cut your nails on a Sunday, you cut them for evil, For all the next
week you'll be ruled by the devil. **1898** HARE
Shropshire i Sabbatarianism is dying out,
yet—'A man had better ne'er be born Than
on the Sabbath pare his horn' (cut his nails),
is still an adage in vogue.

Better never to begin than never to make an end.

1509 A. BARCLAY *Ship of Fools* (1874) I. 176
Then leue a thynge vnended better nat
begynne. **1616** DRAXE 52. **1639** CLARKE 247.

Better one house troubled (filled) than two (spilled[1]).

1587 GREENE *Penelope's Web* in Wks. (Gros.)
V. 162 (A) Where the old prouerb is fulfild,
better one house troubled then two. *a.* **1590**
LYLY *Moth. Bomb.* v. iii. 106. **1670** RAY 51
Better one house fill'd then two spill'd. This
we use when we hear of a bad Jack who hath
married as bad a Jyll. **1721** KELLY 219 *It
had been a pity to have spoil'd two houses with
them.* Spoken when two ill-natur'd people
are married. [[1] spoiled.]

Better ride on an ass that carries me than a horse that throws me.

1616 DRAXE 223 Better is an asse that
carrieth me, then an horse that layeth me on
the ground. **1640** HERBERT 329 I had rather
ride on the ass that carries me, than on the
horse that throws me. **1670** RAY 2 Better
ride on an asse that carries me, then an asse

that throws me. **1908** J. A. SPENDER *Com. of
Bagshot* xiii. 129 'Better is an ass that
carrieth me than a horse that layeth me on
the ground.' It is the greatest folly to seek
a position to which your abilities are unequal.

Better rue sit than rue flit.

1641 FERGUSSON 22 Better rew sit, nor rew
flit. **1721** KELLY 59 . . . Spoken to them that
long to change masters, servants, houses,
farms and the like. **1818** SCOTT *Ht. Midl.* xx
But ye are of my mind, hinny—better sit
and rue, than flit and rue.

Better say, 'here it is', than, 'here it was'.

1641 FERGUSSON 22. **1721** KELLY 65 . . .
Better be at some pains to secure a thing . . .
than to lament the loss of it when it is gone.

Better side the worse, You make the.

1678 RAY 355. *Som[erset].*

Better sit still than rise and fall.

c. **1410** *Towneley Plays* (E.E.T.S.) 29 (A).
1546 HEYWOOD II. v. 56 Flée thattemtyng
of extremities all. Folke saie, better syt styll
than ryse and fall. **1618** BRETON *Courtier &
Countryman* Wks. (Gros.) II. 9 I haue heard
my father say, that it is better to sit fast,
then to rise and fall. **1623** CAMDEN 266 As
good sit still, as rise vp and fall. **1808** SCOTT
Marmion IV. xxix 'Tis better to sit still and
rest, Than rise, perchance to fall.

Better some of a pudding than none of a pie.

1670 RAY 135.

Better spare at brim than at bottom.

[HESIOD *W. & D.* 367 δειλὴ δ' ἐνὶ πυθμένι
φειδώ.] **1523** FITZHERBERT *Husbandry* (E.D.S.)
100 (A) Thou husbande and huswife, that
intend to . . . kepe measure, you must spare
at the brynke, and not at the bottom. **1546**
HEYWOOD II. v. 54 Better spare at brym than
at bottem, say I. **1573** TUSSER (1878) 23 Some
spareth too late, . . . the foole at the bottom,
the wise at the brim. **1681** W. ROBERTSON
Phraseol. Gen. s.v. Better spare at the brim,
than at the bottom, *sera est in fundo parsimonia* [SENECA *Ep.* I. 5]. **1721** KELLY 59
Better hold at the brim, than hold at the bottom.
Better live sparingly while we have something, than spend lavishly, and afterwards
want.

Better spare to have of thine own, than ask of other men.

1640 HERBERT 329.

Better spared than ill spent.

1616 DRAXE 197. **1670** RAY 144.

Better speak truth rudely, than lie correctly.

1640 HERBERT 352.

Better suffer ill than do ill.

1639 CLARKE 15 Better to suffer wrong than
do wrong. **1640** HERBERT 353.

Better than she is bonny, She is.

1721 KELLY 298 . . . An additional praise of a woman who is commended for her beauty. **1857** DEAN RAMSAY *Remin.* v (1911) 193 This mode of expressing that the worth of a handsome woman outweighs even her beauty has a very Scottish character: *She's better than she's bonny.* **1883** C. READE *Peril. Secret* xiii 'She's the loveliest girl in the county, and better than she's bonny.'

Better the devil (harm) you know than the devil (harm) you don't know.

1576 PETTIE *Petite Pall.* (Gollancz) II. 132 You had rather keep those whom you know, though with some faults, than take those whom you know not, perchance with more faults. **1600–1** SHAKS. *Hamlet* III. i. 81 The dread of something after death . . . makes us rather bear those ills we have Than fly to others that we know not of. **1857** TROLLOPE *Barch. Tow.* xxvi 'Better the d— you know than the d— you don't know', is an old saying, . . . but the bishop had not yet realised the truth of it. **1869** HAZLITT 87 Better the harm I know than that I know not. **1905** B. BURLEIGH *Emp. of East* xxiv Neither the Koreans nor the Chinese love overmuch the Japanese. . . . The Chinese seem to prefer the old Russian devil they know, to the new devil they don't.

Better the foot slip than the tongue.

1573 SANDFORD (1576) 9 Anacarsis . . . was wonte to saye, that it was better to slyde with the feete then with the tong. **1586** PETTIE *Guazzo's Civ. Conv.* 55 Remembring alwaies that it is better to slip with the foote, then with the tongue. **1640** HERBERT 319. **1734** FRANKLIN Jan.

Better the last smile than the first laughter. (*Cf.* Laughs best, &c.)

1550 HEYWOOD II. ix. **1664** CODRINGTON 186. **1670** RAY 24.

Better, the worse, The.

1542 UDALL *Apoph. of Erasmus* (1877) 121. **1584** LYLY *Campaspe* v. i. 5 The better, the worser. **1587** GREENE (Gros.) III. 88. **1625** BACON *Apoph.* Wks. (Chandos) 384 Diogenes said of a young man that danced daintily, and was much commended, 'The better, the worse'.

Better to be a beggar than a fool, It is.

1599 MINSHEU i2ᵛ *Meglio esser mendicamente che ignorante,* Better to bee a beggar then barren of good letters. **1642** TORRIANO 49 It is better to be a beggar than an Ignoramus. **1813** RAY 81.

Better to be a martyr than a confessor, It is.

1586 B. YOUNG *Guazzo's Civ. Conv.* IV. 218 b If I had not giuen credence to that Prouerbe, That it is better to bee a Martyr than a Confessour. **1616** DRAXE 84.

Better to be beaten than be in bad company.

1664 CODRINGTON 188. **1670** RAY 2.

Better to be blind than to see ill.

1640 HERBERT 322.

Better to be half blind than have both his eyes out, A man were. (*Cf.* Better to have one eye, &c., *and* One eye (He that has but), &c.)

1616 WITHALS 576. **1639** CLARKE 86.

Better to die a beggar than live a beggar.

1664 CODRINGTON 188. Better die a beggar, than live a beggar. Remember the golden Mean. **1670** RAY 2. **1732** FULLER no. 888.

Better to go about than to fall into the ditch.

1670 RAY 1.

Better to have a dog fawn on you than bite (bark at) you.

1616 DRAXE 47 As good to haue a dogge fawne vpon him, as barke at him. **1639** CLARKE 219. **1641** FERGUSSON 20 Better a dog fan nor bark on you. **1678** RAY 128. **1721** KELLY 64 *Better a dog fawn on you as bark at you.* It is good to have the good will even of the meanest. **1732** FULLER no. 902.

Better to have one eye than be blind altogether. (*Cf.* Better to be half blind.)

1616 DRAXE 116. **1664** CODRINGTON 187. **1670** RAY 8. **1736** BAILEY *Dict.* s.v. 'Better', Better one eye than quite blind.

Better to have than wish.

c. **1530** *Calisto and Melibea* B 2ᵛ Better is possession than the desyryng. **1670** RAY 29.

Better to wear out than to rust out.

1770 G. WHITEFIELD in SOUTHEY, *Wesley* (1858) ii. 170 (A) I had rather wear out than rust out. **1834** EDGEWORTH *Helen* xxix Helen . . . trembled for her health . . . but she repeated her favourite maxim—'Better to wear out than to rust out'. **1859** SMILES *Self-Help* xi Still we must labour on . . . 'It is better to wear out than to rust out', said Bishop Cumberland.[1] [[1] *ob.* 1718.]

Better two skaiths[1] than one sorrow.

1641 FERGUSSON 22 Better two seils, nor ane sorrow. **1721** KELLY 66 . . . Losses may be repaired, but sorrow will break the heart, and ruin the constitution. [[1] harm, injury.]

Better unborn than unbred (untaught).

c. **1275** *Prov. of Alfred* (Skeat) A 449 For betere is child vnboren þenne vnbeten. *c.* **1300**

Prov. of Hending no. 4 For betere were child ounboren þen ounbeten. *c.* **1300** BRUNNE *Handl. Synne* l. 4855 Better were the chylde unbore than fayle chastysyng and syththen lore. *c.* **1350** *Douce MS. 52,* no. 106 Better is a chylde unborne þen vnlerned. *c.* **1440** *How the Good wife taught her Daughter* (Furnivall) 50 l. 203 For a chyld unbore were better than be untaught. *a.* **1530** *R. Hill's Commonpl. Bk.* (E.E.T.S.) 129 Better it is to be unborne than untaught. **1546** HEYWOOD I. x. 20 Better vnborne than vntought, I haue heard saie. **1662** FULLER (*Shrops.*) III. 68 Unbred! unborn, is better rather.

Better untaught than ill taught.

1678 RAY 345. **1732** FULLER no. 938. **1855** BOHN 330.

Better wear out shoes than sheets.

1663 P. STAMPOY 12. **1721** KELLY 67 . . . Sick men wear sheets and sound men shoes, an excuse of, or for, boys who wear many shoes. **1732** FULLER no. 940.

Better wed over the mixen than over the moor.

1641 FERGUSSON 20 Better wooe over midding nor over mosse. **1662** FULLER (*Chesh.*) I. 266 'Better wed over the mixon than over the moor' . . . that is, hard by or at home, mixon being that heap of compost which lieth in the yards of good husbands. . . . The gentry in Cheshire find it more profitable to match within their county, than to bring a bride out of other shires. **1818** SCOTT *Ht. Midl.* xxxi He might have dune waur than married me . . .—better wed over the mixen as over the moor, as they say in Yorkshire.

Better were within, If | better would come out.

1721 KELLY 217. **1732** FULLER no. 2672.

Better with a rake than a fork, He is.

1580 LYLY *Euph. & his Eng.* (Arb.) 228 Tedding[1] that with a forke in one yeare, which was not gathered together with a rake, in twentie. **1629** T. ADAMS *Serm.* (1861-2) II. 9 Most men now-a-days, as it is in the proverb, are better at the rake than at the pitchfork, readier to pull in than to give out. **1678** RAY 266 He is better with a rake than a fork *& vice versâ.* **1721** KELLY 129 *He comes oftener with the rake than the sho'el.*[2] Spoken of a poor friend, whose business is not to give us, but to get from us. [1 spreading newly-cut grass to dry. 2 shovel.]

Better, *see also* No b. than she should be; See and approve the b. course; Seldom comes a b.; Somewhat is b. than nothing; Useth me b. than he is wont (He that).

Betty Martin, *see* All my eye.

Between the cradle and the grave.

c. **1707** PRIOR (Cambridge) i. 95 Studious the busy moments to deceive That fleet between the cradle and the grave. **1709** STEELE *Tatler* no. 52, ₱ 4 A modest fellow never has

a doubt from his cradle to his grave. **1726** DYER *Grongar Hill* A little rule, a little sway, A sunbeam in a winter's day, Is all the proud and mighty have Between the cradle and the grave.

Between two stools one goes (falls) to the ground.

[SENECA *Controversia* 3. 189 *Duabus sellis sedit.* c. **1026** EGBERT V. LUTTICH *Fecunda Ratis* (Voigt) l. 175 *Labitur enitens sellis herere duabus.* c. **1190** *Li Proverbe au vilain* (Tobler) 84 no. 202 *Entre dous seles chiet cus a terre.*] c. **1390** GOWER *Conf. Amantis* II. 22 Thou farst as he betwen tuo stoles That wolde sitte and goth to grounde. *a.* **1530** *R. Hill's Commonpl. Bk.* (E.E.T.S.) 129 Betwen two stolis, the ars goth to grwnd. **1546** HEYWOOD I. iii. 7 While betweene two stooles, my tayle go to grounde. **1638** T. HEYWOOD *Wise W. of Hogs.* v. iv Here's even the proverb verified—between two stools, the tail goes to ground. **1730** FIELDING *Tom Thumb* II. x While the two stools here sittingpart confound, Between 'em both fall squat upon the ground. **1857** TROLLOPE *Barch. Tow.* xx Truly he had fallen between two stools.

Between you and me and the bedpost.

[= in confidence.] **1805** J. DAVIS *The Post-Captain* xxvi (with 'the post'). **1839** DICKENS *N. Nickleby* x And between you and me and the post, sir, it will be a very nice portrait too. **1875** BROWNING *Inn Album* i A secret's safe between you and me and the gate-post. **1882** BLACKMORE *Christowell* xiii Between you and me and the bed-post, Short—as the old ladies say—I don't want Jack to have her.

Between, *see also under significant words following.*

Bewails himself hath the cure in his hands, He that.

1640 HERBERT 338.

Bewail, *see also* Carrion crows b. dead sheep.

Beware beginnings.

1639 CLARKE 259.

Beware by other men's harms, It is good to.

[PLAUTUS *Merc.* 893 *Feliciter is sapit qui periculo alieno sapit.*] c. **1436** *Libell of Engl. Policy* l. 480 Beware . . . of other mennys perylle. c. **1470** *Harl. MS. 3362* f. la (Förster) in *Anglia* 42. 200 He ys an happy man, þat ys war be anothyr mannys dedys. *Est felix culpa quem castigat aliena.* **1550** HEYWOOD I. xi. 34. **1614** CAMDEN 308.

Beware of a silent dog (man) and still water.

[L. *Cave tibi a cane muto et aquâ silenti.*] **1855** BOHN 331.

Beware of after-claps.

1557 SIR T. MORE *To them that trusteth in*

Fortune But for all that beware of after-claps. **1639** FULLER *Holy War* v. ii (1840) 243 Some therefore in this matter know little, and dare speak less, for fear of after claps.

Beware of breed.

1678 RAY 105 Beware of breed, *Chesh.*, i.e. an ill breed. **1917** BRIDGE 31 Beware of breed; i.e. *bad* breed. A casual allusion to this proverb helped to lose a Cheshire candidate his seat at the General Election of 1857.

Beware of the man of one book.

[L. *Cave ab homine unius libri.*] **1651** HERBERT 370 Woe be to him that reads but one book. **1848** SOUTHEY *Doctor* xlix 113 Upon both subjects he was *homo unius libri*; such a man is proverbially formidable at his own weapon. **1903** J. MCCARTHY *Port. of Sixties* 152 'I fear the man of one book' is a classic proverb.

Beware, *see also* Buyer b.; Had I wist (B. of).

Bewitched, *see* Water b.

Beyond himself, *see* Every man a little b. h. a fool.

Bible is the religion of Protestants, The.

1637 CHILLINGWORTH *Relig. of Protest.* vi (1846) 463 The BIBLE, I say, the BIBLE only, is the religion of protestants! **1921** *Times Lit. Sup.* 19 Aug. 526 The Bible and the Bible only, ... is, according to a well-known saying, the religion of Protestants.

Bible, *see also* Congleton rare sold the B.; Peerage is Englishman's B.

Bidden, *see* Do as you're b.

Bides as fast as a cat bound to a saucer, He.

1641 FERGUSSON 48 He bydes as fast as a cat bound with a sacer.

Bide(s), *see also* Weel b., weel betides; Worth no weal that can b. no woe.

Big(s), *see* Looks as b. as if eaten bull beef; Too b. for one's boots; Two b. will not go in one bag.

Bigger the man, the better the mark, The.

1894 NORTHALL *Folk-phrases* (E.D.S.) 24 The bigger the man, the better the mark, i.e. to aim, or strike at in combat.

Bilberry, *see* Nineteen bits of a b.

Bill under wing.

[= quiet, hidden, like a bird's bill under its wing.] c. **1390** GOWER *Conf. Amantis* v. 6526 What he may get of his michinge [i.e. thieving], It is al bile under the winge. c. **1425** *Seven Sages* (Percy Soc.) 2196. The byrde ... bylle undyr wynge layede. a. **1548** HALL *Chron., Hen. VI*, 174 After this ... the duke of Yorke ... thought it mete neither lenger to

dissimule, nor farther to kepe his bill vnder wyng.

Billesdon, *see* In and out, like B.

Billingsgate for a box on the ear, You shall have as much favour at.

1576 U. FULWELL *Ars adulandi* ❡ 4v A man may buy as much loue at Belinsgate for a box on the eare. **1659** HOWELL *Eng. Prov.* 15. **1670** RAY 215.

Billingsgate language.

1594 *King Leir* III. v. 77 As bad a tongue ... as any oyster-wife at Billingsgate. **1676** WYCHERLEY *Pl. Dealer* III. i (1678) 35 With sharp invectives—*Wid.* (Alias Belin'sgate). **1848** THACKERAY *Vanity F.* xiii Mr. Osborne ... cursed Billingsgate with an emphasis worthy of the place.

Bind the sack before it be full.

1641 FERGUSSON 22 Bind the seck or it be full. **1902–4** LEAN III. 433 Bind the sack ere it be full.—Ferg. Do not tax any person or thing to the utmost.

Bind, *see also* Fast (safe, sure) b., fast find; Hold nor to b. (Neither to); Willows are weak yet they b.

Birch, *see* Bare as the b. at Yule even.

Birchen twigs break no ribs.

1639 CLARKE 75. **1670** RAY 61. **1732** FULLER no. 6380.

Bird in my bosom, I have saved (kept) the.

1550 HALL *Chron.* 2 Saying, when he was dying: I have saved the bird in my bosom: meaning that he had kept both his promise and oath. **1662** FULLER (*Leics.*) II. 253 Burdet [in 1477] patiently and cheerfully took his death, affirming he had a bird in his breast (his own innocency) that sung comfort unto him. **1820** SCOTT *Abbot* viii Thou hast kept well ... the bird in thy bosom. ... Thou hast kept thy secret and mine own amongst thine enemies. *Note.* An expression used by Sir Ralph Percy, slain in the battle of Hedgely-moor in 1464, to express his having preserved unstained his fidelity to the House of Lancaster. **1902** *Spectator* 24 May Queen Christina may say ... that she 'has kept the bird in her bosom', an indefeasible loyalty to her task.

Bird in the hand is worth two in the bush, A.

[c. **1400** in J. WERNER *Lat. Sprichwörter* ... *des Mittelalters* (1912) 70 *Plus valet in manibus avis unica fronde duabus.*] c. **1470** *Harl. MS. 3362*, f. 4a Betyr ys a byrd in þe hond þan tweye in þe wode. a. **1530** R. *Hill's Commonpl. Bk.* (E.E.T.S.) 128 A birde in hond is better than thre in the wode. **1546** HEYWOOD I. xi. 30 Better one byrde in hande than ten in the wood. **1590** LODGE *Rosalynde* in Wks. (1883) I. 32 One birde in the hande is woorth two in the wood; better possesse the love of ALIENA, than catch friuolously at the shadow of ROSALYNDE. **1620** SHELTON *Quix.* II. vii (1908) II. 230 A bird in the hand is worth two in the bush. **1678** BUNYAN *Pilgr.* I (1877) 26 That proverb, *A bird in the hand is worth two in the bush, is* of more authority with them than are all . . . testimonies of the good of the world to come. **1678** RAY *Adag. Hebr.* 404 One bird in the net is better than a hundred flying. **1894** LD. AVEBURY *Use of Life* xv (1904) 92 A bird in the hand is worth two in the bush; but . . . the bird in the bush may never be in the cage, while the future . . . is sure to come.

Bird is known by his note, the man by his words, The.

1642 TORRIANO 6 The bird is known by his note and by speech a man's headpiece. **1569** HOWELL *Ital.-Eng.* 10. **1732** FULLER no. 12.

Bird loves her nest, The.

1640 HERBERT 320.

Bird loves to hear himself sing, Each.

1659 HOWELL *Brit. Prov.* 2 Each bird is well pleased with his own voice. **1855** BOHN 269.

Bird must flighter[1] that flies with one wing, The.

1721 KELLY 308 . . . Spoken by them who have interest only in one side of the house. **1824** SUSAN FERRIER *Inheritance* III. xxxii 'The bird maun flichter that flees wi' ae wing'—but ye's haud up your head yet in spite o' them a'. **1914** K. F. PURDON *Folk of Furry F.* ii He held out a shilling to Hughie. 'A bird never yet flew upon the one wing, Mr. Heffernan!' said Hughie, that was looking to get another shilling. [1 flutter.]

Bird take back its own feathers, If every | he'll (you'll) be naked.

1579–80 LODGE *Def. Poetry* (Shaks. Soc.) 3 Though men . . . polish their writings with others sentences, yet the simple truth will . . . bestowing every feather in the body of the right M. turn out the naked dissembler into his own coat. **1607–8** SHAKS. *Timon of A.* II. i. 30 When every feather sticks in his own wing, Lord Timon will be left a naked gull. **1629** T. ADAMS *Serm.* (1861–2) i. 203 Some he steals from the Jew, . . . much from idolatry, . . . If every bird should fetch her own feathers, you should have a naked Pope. **1732** FULLER no. 2675.

Bird to pick out his own eyes, He hath brought up a.

1590 LODGE *Rosalynde* Wks. (1883) I. 33 In liking Rosalynde thou hatchest vp a bird to pecke out thine owne eyes. **1662** FULLER (*Lancs.*) II. 198 I know you have hatched up some chickens that now seek to pick out your eyes. **1732** FULLER no. 1864.

Bird told me, A.

1546 HEYWOOD II. v. 57 I did lately heere . . . by one byrd that in mine eare was late chauntyng. **1597–8** SHAKS. 2 *Hen. IV* V.

v. 113 I heard a bird so sing. **1611** BIBLE *Eccles.* x. 20 A bird of the air shall carry the voice and that which hath wings shall tell the matter. **1822** SCOTT *Nigel* vi Stone walls have ears, and a bird of the air shall carry the matter.

Birds of a feather flock together.

1578 WHETSTONE *Promos and Cassandra* C 1ᵛ Byrds of a fether, best flye together. **1590–1** SHAKS. *3 Hen. VI* II. i. 170 Clifford and the haught Northumberland, And of their feather many more proud birds. *Ibid.* III. iii. 161 Both of you are birds of self-same feather. **1613** WITHER *Abuses* 72 But as the proverb saith, Birds of a feather Will always use to flock and feed together. **1660** W. SECKER *Nonsuch Prof.* ii (1891) 93 We say, 'That birds of a feather will flock together'. To be too intimate with sinners is to intimate that we are sinners. **1680** BUNYAN *Mr. Badman* iv. Wks. (Offor) III. 615 They were birds of a feather, . . . they were so well met for wickedness. **1828** LYTTON *Pelham* lxxix It is literally true in the systematised roguery of London, that 'birds of a feather flock together'.

Birds of this year in last year's nests, There are no.

1620 SHELTON *Quix.* II. lxxiv (1908) III. 338 I pray you go not on so fast, since that in the nests of the last year there are no birds of this year. Whilom I was a fool, but now I am wise. **1906** A. T. QUILLER-COUCH *From Cornish W.* 5 With what heart Don Quixote . . . in that saddest of all last chapters, bade his friends look not for this year's birds in last year's nests. **1926** *Times* 19 Jan. 15/6 Things may not be as they were; 'there are no birds in last year's nest', and there may be no fish in the old rivers.

Birds were flown, The.

1546 HEYWOOD I. xii. 39 Er the next daie the birdes were flowne eche one, To séeke seruyce. **1575** GASCOIGNE *Posies*; *Flowers*; *A lover* (1907) 94 The Byrdes were flowne before I found the nest. **1855** C. KINGSLEY *Westward Ho!* v The birds are flown, . . . we can do nothing till we raise the hue and cry to-morrow.

Bird(s), *see also* Addled egg as idle b. (As good be); Beats the bush (One), (another catches b.; Bitter b. (Thou art), said raven to starling; Candlemas (As long as b. sings before); Catch b. to-morrow (We shall); Catch old b. with chaff; Child's b. and knave's wife; Destroy the nests, b. fly away; Dow (He will never), egg nor b.; Early b. catches worm; Feather in hand better than b. in air; Forbear not sowing because of b.; Free as b. in air; Fright a b. not the way to catch; Gape long enough ere b. fall in mouth; God builds nest of blind b.; Good egg nor b. (Neither); John Grey's b.; Kill two b. with one stone; Little b. little nest; Little b. that can sing and won't; March the b. begin; May b. aye cheeping; Rough net not best catcher of b.; Small b. must have meat. *See also* Ill bird.

Birth follows the belly, The.

1612–15 BP. HALL *Contempl.* x. vi (1825) I. 284 The mother, as she is more tender over her son, . . . can work most upon his inclination. Whence . . . in the history of the Israelitish Kings, the mother's name is commonly noted; and, as civilly, so also morally, the birth follows the belly.

Birth is much, but breeding is more.

1639 CLARKE 103. **1732** FULLER no. 983.

Birth, *see also* Great b. is a poor dish.

Birthright, *see* Sell one's b.

Bishop has blessed it, The.

1528 TINDALE *Obed. Chrn. Man* (1888) 266 When a thing speedeth not well, we borrow speech, and say, 'The bishop hath blessed it'; because that nothing speedeth well that they meddle withal.

Bishop has put (set) his foot in it, The.

1528 TINDALE *Obed. Chrn. Man* (1888) 266 If the porridge be burned too, or the meat over roasted, we say, 'The bishop hath put his foot in the pot', or, 'The bishop hath played the cook'; because the bishops burn whom they lust, and whosoever displeaseth them. **1573** TUSSER 49 (E.D.S.) 108 Blesse Cisley (good mistris) that Bishop doth ban for burning the milke of hir cheese to the pan. **1641** MILTON *Animad. Rem. Def. Smect.* Prose Wks. (1904) III. 91 I doubt not but they will say, the bishop's foot hath been in your book, for I am sure it is quite spoiled by this just confutation. **1738** SWIFT (Dial. i) 334 *Lady A.* The cream is burnt too. *Betty.* Why, madam, the bishop has set his foot in it. **1917** BRIDGE 112 The Bishop has put his foot in it. Said of burnt milk. '*The milk is bishopped*', is a common phrase in Cheshire.

Bishop, *see also* No b. no king; Once a b. always a b.; Weel's him . . . that has b. in his kin.

Bit and a knock (bob) as men feed apes, A.

1576 GASCOIGNE *Steele Glas* (Arb.) 80 When Fencers fees, are like to apes rewards, A peece of breade, and therwithal a bobbe. **1678** RAY 226.

Bit and the buffet with it, Take the.

1721 KELLY 311 . . . Bear some ill usage of them by whom you get advantage. L. *Asinus esuriens fustem negligit.* **1819** SCOTT *Bride Lam.* xxi A fellow, whom he could either laugh with, or laugh at, . . . who would take, according to Scottish phrase, 'the bit and the buffet'.

Bit draws down another, One.

1639 CLARKE 148.

Bit that one eats no friend makes, The.

1640 HERBERT 323.

Bit(s), *see also* Shoulder of veal . . . good b. (In a); Take the b. in the teeth.

Bitch, *see* God loves (Whom), his b. brings forth pigs; Hasty b. bringeth forth blind whelps.

Bite, If you cannot | never show your teeth.

1639 FULLER *Holy War* II. viii (1840) 59 Bernard, . . . set his title on foot, and then quietly let it fall to the ground, as counting it no policy to show his teeth where he durst not bite. **1670** RAY 63. **1738** SWIFT (Dial. iii) 352 *Miss.* I'm sure you show your teeth when you can't bite. **1906** SIR I. HAMILTON *Staff Off. Scrap. Bk.* 77 The bark-without-preparing-to-bite system of drifting towards war which prevails in England and America.

Bite (or snap) one's nose off, To.

1599 NASHE *Lenten Stuffe* 47 Shee was a shrewish snappish bawd, that wold bite off a man's nose with an answere. **1709** MRS. CENTLIVRE *Busie Bodie* I. i 1 . . . asked him if he was at leisure for his Chocolate, . . . but he snap'd my Nose off; no, I shall be busy here these two Hours.

Bite one's thumbs, To. (*Cf.* Bite the thumb at.)

[An indication of anger or vexation.] **1573** *Satir. Poems Reform.* xlii. 266 The Clerk was like to byte his thowmis. **1594–5** SHAKS. *Rom. & Jul.* I. i. 51 *Abr.* Do you bite your thumb at us, sir? *Sam.* I do bite my thumb, sir. **1608** DEKKER *Dead Term* D iv *b* What shouldering, what Justling, what Jeering, what byting of Thumbs to beget quarrels. **1670** G. H. *Hist. Cardinals* II. ii. 158 The Spaniards were nettled, and bit their thumbs . . . in private.

Bite out of your own hip (arm), You take a.

1721 KELLY 367 . . . What you say reflects upon your self, or family. **1732** FULLER no. 5925 You have taken a bite out of your own arm.

Bite the thumb at, To. (*Cf.* Bite one's thumbs.)

[= to threaten or defy.] **1594–5** SHAKS. *Rom. & Jul.* I. i. 47 I will bite my thumb at them. **1638** T. RANDOLPH *The Muses Looking Glass* III. v. 2 Dags and Pistolls! To bite his thumb at me!

Bite upon the bridle, To.

[= to be impatient of restraint.] *c.* **1390** GOWER *Conf. Amantis* VI. 929 As who seith, upon the bridel I chiewe, so that al is ydel As in effect the fode I have. **1514** BARCLAY *Cyt. & Uplondyshm.* (1847) 41 These courtiers . . . Smelling those dishes, they bite upon the bridle. **1549** LATIMER *7th Serm. bef. Edw. VI* (P.S.) 230 His Father gave him looking on, and suffered him to bite upon the bridle awhile. **1600** ABP. ABBOT *Exp. Jonah* 342 Bite upon the bridle, that . . . he may be wiser afterward. **1612** CHAPMAN *Epicede* 172 The still-feasted arts, which now on bridles bite. **1709** STEELE *Tatler* No. 25 Make the rogue bite upon the bridle', said I; 'pay none of his bills'.

Biter bit, The.

1693 D'URFEY *Richmond Heiress* Epil. (A) Once in an age the biter should be bit. **1710** WARD *Nuptial Dial.* II. 179 I think she merits equal Praise That has the Wit to bite the Biter. **1809** MALKIN *Gil Blas* I. viii I would advise you . . . not to set your wit a second time against the Church: the biter may be bit. **1863** C. READE *Hard Cash* viii He could not sell all the bad paper he had accumulated for a temporary purpose: the panic came too swiftly. . . . The biter was bit: the fox . . . was caught. **1888** MRS. OLIPHANT *Second Son* xliv They should also hear how the tables had been turned upon him, how the biter had been bit.

Bites on every weed must needs light on poison, He that.

1639 CLARKE 211. **1670** RAY 63.

Bite(s) (*noun*), *see also* Bark is worse than his b.; Two b. of a cherry.

Bite(s), bit (*verb*), *see also* Bear (If it were a), it would b. you; Covers me . . . and b. me with his bill; Cur will b. before bark; Dog to b. him (A man may cause own); Drink of the burn when cannot b. of brae; Look on the wall and it will not b.; Mastiff be gentle (Though), b. him not; Never b. unless teeth meet; Once b. twice shy; Trick for trick, . . . when she b. him upon the back and he her upon buttock.

Biteth the mare by the thumb, This.

1546 HEYWOOD II. vi. 62 This biteth the mare by the thumbe, as they say.

Biting and scratching is Scots folk's wooing.

1641 FERGUSSON 24 Byting and scarting is scots folk's wooing. **1832** HENDERSON 87 Scarting and nipping is Scotch folks' wooing.

Bitten by a serpent, He that hath been | is afraid of a rope.

1678 RAY *Adag. Hebr.* 407. **1853** TRENCH iii. 71 The Jewish Rabbis had said long before: *One bitten by a serpent, is afraid of a rope's end*; even . . . a resemblance to a serpent . . . shall now inspire him with terror.

Bitten, Though he be | he's not all eaten.

1639 CLARKE 32.

Bitter bird, Thou art a | said the raven to the starling.

1678 RAY 195.

Bitter in his mouth, Who hath | spits not all sweet.

1640 HERBERT 337. **1732** FULLER no. 2387 (with 'breast' for 'mouth').

Bitter pills may have blessed effects.

c. **1374** CHAUCER *Troylus* III. 1215 O! soth is seyd, that helĕd for to be As of a fevre or other greet syknesse, Men mostĕ drinke, as men may often see, Ful bittre drink. **1579** LYLY *Euphues* (Arb.) 114 The medicine, the more bitter it is, the more better it is in working. **1594–5** SHAKS. *Two Gent.* II. iv. 150 When I was sick you gave me bitter pills. **1601** JONSON *Poetaster* v. iii. 402 They [the pills] are somewhat bitter . . . but very wholesome. **1604–5** SHAKS. *Meas. for Meas.* IV. vi. 8 'Tis a physic That's bitter to sweet end. **1721** KELLY 69 . . . Present afflictions may tend to our future good. **1732** FULLER no. 985 (with 'wholesome' for 'blessed').

Bitter to endure may be sweet to remember, That which was. (*Cf.* Remembrance of past sorrow.)

[SENECA *Herc. Fur.* 656 *Quae fuit durum pati, meminisse dulce est.*] **1732** FULLER no. 4385.

Blab is a scab, He that is a.

1639 CLARKE 132. **1732** FULLER no. 6296 He that is a blab, is a meer scab.

Blab it wist and out it must.

15th Cent. *Harl. MS. 3362* (V. Lean) (A) Labbe hyt whyste, and owt yt must. **1550** HEYWOOD I. x.

Black and blue, *see* Beat (anyone) b. **and b.**

Black and white, In (Under).

[= in writing or in print.] *c.* **1374** CHAUCER *Troylus* II. 1320 And Pandarus gan him the lettre take, And seyde . . . 'Have here a light, and loke on al this blake.' *c.* **1440** LYDGATE *Fall of Princes* (E.E.T.S.) I Prol. l. 465 Hauyng no colours but onli whit & blak. **1598–9** SHAKS. *Much Ado* V. i. 314 *Dogb.* Which, indeed, is not under white and black. **1601** JONSON *Ev. Man in Humour* (Merm.) IV. ii He has basted me rarely, sumptuously! but I have it here in black and white. *a.* **1656** BP. HALL *Rem.* Wks. (1660) 136 We stay not till we have gotten it under black and white. **1712** STEELE *Spect.* No. 286, par. 3 Give us in Black and White your Opinion in the matter. **1866** W. COLLINS *Armadale* IV. xv The whole story of her life, in black and white.

Black as a crow, As.

c. **1320** *Horn Childe* l. 1049 Blac as ani crawe. *c.* **1386** CHAUCER *Knight's T.* A. 2693 Blak he lay as any . . . crowe. **1610–11** SHAKS. *Wint. T.* IV. iii. 221 Cypress black as e'er was crow.

Black as ink.

c. **1510** A. BARCLAY *Egloges* 30 (Spens. Soc.) (A). **1590** SPENSER *F.Q.* I. i. 22 (A). *c.* **1592** SHAKS. *Two Gent.* III. i. 286.

Black as soot (pitch).

c. **1410** *Mirc's Festial* Blake altogether as pitch. **1678** RAY 281.

Black as the devil.

c. **1390** *Romaunt of the Rose* A 973 Blak as

fend in helle. **1509** A. BARCLAY *Ship of Fools* (1874) ii. 269 Defyle their faces . . . more fowle than the blacke Devyll of hell. *c.* 1545 J. REDFORD *Wyt & Sci.* 42 As black as the devyll. **1670** RAY 203.

Black as thunder.

1838 THACKERAY *Yellowplush Papers* (Oxford ed.) 183 Altamont looked as black as thunder.

Black bear of Arden, He is the.

1787 GROSE (*Glos., Warw.*)(1811) 228 He is the black bear of Arden. Guy Beauchamp, Earl of Warwick, was so called, both from his crest . . . a black bear, and from . . . a black and grim countenance, as well as on account of . . . undaunted courage. Arden was a forest [in] . . . this county. . . . The person . . . so denominated, was . . . an object of terror.

Black dog on one's back, To have the.

[= to be in low spirits, or in the sulks.] **1778** MRS. THRALE in *Piozzi Letters* ii. 32 (A) I have lost what made my happiness . . . but the black dog shall not make prey of both my master and myself. **1816** SCOTT *Antiq.* vi ' I think Sir Arthur has got the black dog on his back again', said Miss Oldbuck. **1882** STEVENSON *New Arab. Nts.* ii. 111 He did not seem to be enjoying his luck. . . . The black dog was on his back, as people say, in terrifying nursery metaphor.

Black hen lays a white egg, A.

1616 DRAXE 51 A blacke hen may bring foorth white egges. **1670** RAY 63 . . . This is a French proverb, Noire geline pond blanc œuf. I conceive the meaning of it is, that a black woman may bear a fair child. **1738** SWIFT (Dial. i) 337 Oh! the wonderful works of nature, that a black hen should lay a white egg!

Black, Though I am | I am not the devil.

1592 GREENE *Upst. Courtier* Wks. (1881–3) XI. 259 Marry, quoth hée, that lookte like Lucifer, though I am blacke, I am not the Diuell, but indeed a Colier of Croiden. **1595** PEELE *Old Wiv.* T. 640 Wks. (1888) I. 331 *Cel.* Well, though I am black, I am sure all the world will not forsake me; and, as the old proverb is, though I am black I am not the divel.

Black in the face, *see* Swear till one is b.

Black is any one's eye (eye-brow, nail, &c.), To say.

[= to find fault with, to lay anything to his charge.] *c.* 1412 HOCCLEVE *Reg. Princ.* (1860) 102 The riche and myghty man, thoughe he trespace, No man seithe ones that blak is his eye. **1675** BROOKS *Gold Key* Wks. (1867) V. 250 He knew that the law could not say black was his eye, and that the judge upon the bench would pronounce him righteous. **1749** FIELDING *Tom Jones* IX. iv I defy anybody to say black is my eye. **1828** CARR *Craven Dial.* II. 2 'Thou cannot say

black's my nail'. **1838** MRS. CARLYLE *Let.* to *Miss H. Welsh* 27 May There is none justified in saying with self-complacency, 'black is the eye' of another.

Black is white, To prove that.

1763 CHURCHILL *The Author* 309–10 Wks. (1855) 196 To make most glaring contraries unite, And prove beyond dispute that black is white.

Black man is a pearl (jewel) in a fair woman's eye, A.

1593–4 SHAKS. *Titus Andron.* V. i. 42 This is the pearl that pleas'd your empress' eye. **1594–5** *Two Gent.* V. ii. 10 *Thu.* My face is black. *Pro.* But pearls are fair, and the old saying is, 'Black men are pearls in beauteous ladies' eyes.' **1621** BURTON *Anat. Mel.* III. ii. II. ii (1651) 464 A black man is a pearl in a fair woman's eye, and is as acceptable as lame Vulcan was to Venus. **1670** RAY 51 (with 'jewel').

Black man (men), *see also* God gives b. m. what white forget; Red man (To a) read thy rede. . . .

Black ox[1] has trod on (his, &c.) foot, The.

1546 HEYWOOD I. vii The blacke oxe had not trode on his nor hir foote. **1575** GASCOIGNE *Glass of Govt.* v. 6 They never prove stayed until the blacke oxe hath troden on their toes. **1581** MULCASTER *Positions* xxxvi (1887) 139 Till the blacke oxe, tread vpon his toes, and neede make him trie what mettle he is made of. **1621** BURTON *Anat. Mel.* III. ii. VI. iii (1651) 561 Time, care, rivels[2] her . . . ; after the blacke oxe hath trodden on her toe, she will . . . wax out of favour. **1738** SWIFT (Dial. i) 341 *Lady A.* I hear she's grown a mere otomy.[3] *Lady S.* Poor creature! The black ox has set his foot upon her already. **1850** L. HUNT *Autobiog.* I. iv. 171 The 'black ox' trod on the fairy foot of my light-hearted cousin Fan. **1859** MEREDITH *R. Feverel* xxvii The Black Ox haven't trod on his foot yet. [[1] A symbol for misfortune, adversity, old age. [2] wrinkles. [3] atomy = skeleton.]

Black plum (raisin, grape) is as sweet as a white, A.

1616 DRAXE 15 A blacke raisin as good as a white. (*Ibid.* 16 grape.) **1670** RAY 63 A black plum is as sweet as a white. The prerogative of beauty proceeds from fancy.

Black puddings, *see* Kill hogs (He who does not) will not get b. p.

Black sheep in every flock (fold), There are.

1816 SCOTT *Old Mort.* xxxv The curates . . . know best the black sheep of the flock. **1902** *Spectator* 1 Nov. There is no great movement without its black sheep. **1928** *Times* 17 July 17/5 There is . . . not the slightest intention of impugning the . . . force as a whole, but there are always some black sheep in every fold.

Black sheep is a biting beast, A.

c. **1550** *Six Ballads* (Percy Soc.) 4 (A) The blacke Shepe is a perylous beast. **1591** LYLY *Endym.* II. ii Indeed a black sheep is a perilous beast. **1598** BASTARD *Chrestoleros* IV. xx. 90 Till now I thought the prouerbe did but iest, which said a blacke sheepe was a biting beast.

Black sheep keep the white, Let the.

1639 CLARKE 69.

Black swan, A.

[JUVENAL *Sat.* 6. 165 *Rara avis in terris, nigroque simillima cygno.* A bird rarely seen on earth, and very like a black swan.] **1553** *Respublica* l. 184 Yone the swanne-is-blacke yone. **1569** C. AGRIPPA *Vanity of Arts and Sciences* (1575) 104ᵛ As rare . . . as a black swanne. **1576** PETTIE *Petite Pall.* (Gollancz) I. 89 As rare as a black swan. **1579** LYLY *Euphues* (Arb.) 229 It is as rare to see a rich surety as a black swan. **1614** RALEIGH *Hist. of World* Pref. Only those few black swans I must except who . . . behold death without dread. **1843** DICKENS *Christ. Car.* iii A feathered phenomenon to which a black swan was a matter of course.

Black, Above | there is no colour, and above salt no savour.

1573 SANDFORD (1576) 221 Above God there is no Lord, Above blacke there is no colour; And Above salt there is found no savour. **1659** HOWELL *Ital.–Eng.* 7.

Black velvet, *see* Little gentleman in b. v.

Black will take no other hue.

[PLIN. *H. N.* 8. 193 *Lanarum nigrae nullum colorem bibunt.*] **1546** HEYWOOD II. ix. 76 Folke haue a saiyng bothe olde and trew, In that they say blacke will take none other hew. **1593–4** SHAKS. *Titus Andron.* IV. ii. 100 Coal-black is better than another hue, In that it scorns to bear another hue; for all the water in the ocean Can never turn the swan's black legs to white. **1629** T. ADAMS *Serm.* (1861–2) II. 363 We were wont to say, that black could never be coloured into white; yet the devil hath some painters that undertake it. **1721** KELLY 66 . . . Intimating the difficulty of reclaiming perverse people. Can the Ethiopian change his colour?

Black(s), *see also* Books (To be in a person's b.); Drive b. hogs in the dark; Fair and sluttish, b. and proud; Keep a man out of mud (Way to), b. his boots; Spice is b., but hath sweet smack; Two b. do not make white; Wears b. must hang brush.

Blackamoor, *see* Bath of the b.; Wash a b. white.

Blackberries, *see* Devil sets his foot on b. on Michaelmas; Plenty as b.

Blackbird, *see* Whistle like a b.

Blade wears out the scabbard (sheath), The.

1817 BYRON *So, we'll go no more a roving.* For the sword outwears its sheath, And the soul wears out the breast. **1823** LOCKHART *Reg. Dalton* III. vi There is an old Scots saying . . . that 'the blade wears the scabbard'.

Blad'ry, *see* Shame fall the gear and the b.

Blame, *see* Do as you're bidden, never bear b.

Blames their wife for their own un-thrift, Many a one.

1721 KELLY 250 . . . I never saw a Scottish woman who had not this at her fingers' ends.

Blames would buy, He that.

[BIBLE *Prov.* xx. 14 It is naught, saith the buyer; but when he is gone his way, then he boasteth.] **1640** HERBERT 336. **1854** R. SURTEES *Hand. Cross* xlvi The stables were thrown open. . . . There was Captain Shortflat admiring Artaxerxes, and abusing Dismal Geordy, that he wanted to buy.

Blanch powder land, *see* Killed the blue spider.

Blanket, *see* Wrong side of the b.

Blate[1] cat makes a proud mouse, A.

1641 FERGUSSON 10. **1721** KELLY 25 . . . When parents and masters are too mild and easy, it makes their children and servants too saucy and impertinent. [1 bashful.]

Blaze, *see* Bavin is but a b.; Mare hath bald face (When), filly will have b.

Bleat(s), *see* Every time the sheep b.; Goat must b. where tied.

Bleed your nag on St. Stephen's day, If you | he'll work your work for ever and aye.

1528 MORE *Wks.* (1557) p. 194, col. 2 (A) On Saint Stephen's day we must let al our horses bloud with a knife, because saynt Stephen was killed with stones. **1552** LATIMER *Serm. on St. Stephen's Day Wks.* (1824) II. 321 Upon this day we were wont to let our horses blood. **1846** DENHAM 66 If you bleed your nag on St. Stephen's day, he'll work your wark for ever and ay. Hospinian quotes . . . from Naogeorgus, . . . translated by Barnaby Googe:—Then followeth St. Stephen's day, whereon doth every man, His *horses* jaunt and course abrode, as swiftly as they can, Until they do extremely *sweate,* and then they let them *blood.*

Bless, *see* Cross to b. himself with; Penny to buy . . . (b. him).

Blessed is he who expects nothing, for he shall never be disappointed.

1727 POPE *Let.* to Gay, 6 Oct. *Wks.* (1824) X. 184 I have . . . , repeated to you, a ninth beatitude . . . 'Blessed is he who expects nothing, for he shall never be disappointed.'

1739 FRANKLIN May   Blessed is he that expects nothing, for he shall never be disappointed. **1911** *Times Lit. Sup.* 6 Oct. 359 Evidently Sir Edwin's hope is not too roseate, and he is among those who are accounted blessed because they expect little.

Blessed is the eye, that is betwixt Severn and Wye.

1662 FULLER (*Heref.*) II. 70 'Blessed is the eye, That is betwixt Severn and Wye'. . . . The eyes of those inhabitants are entertained with a pleasant prospect. **1897** BP. CREIGHTON *Some Eng. Shires* 286 Herefordshire . . . throve. owing to its natural fertility and mild climate, so that the proverb ran— 'Blessed is the eye Between Severn and Wye'.

Blessings of the evil Genii are curses, The.

1853 TRENCH vi. 152 An Arabic one . . . is as solemn and sublime in form as it is profound in substance: *The blessings of the evil Genii are curses.* How deep a significance the story of Fortunatus acquires, when regarded as a commentary on this.

Blessing(s), *see also* God's b. make my pot boil (Will); Godfathers oft give b. in a clout; Means (Use the) and God will give b.; Need of a b. that kneel to a thistle; Sorrow wit you wat where a b. may light.

Blessing of your heart, *see* Brew good ale.

Bletherin' coo soon forgets her calf, A.

1330 *Wright's Polit. Songs* (Camd. Soc.) 332 Hit nis noht al for the calf that kow louweth. **1553** T. WILSON *Arte of Rhet.* (1909) 77 The Cowe lacking her Caulf, leaueth lowing within three or fower daies at the farthest. **1895** ADDY *Househ. Tales* 142 In the East Riding they say, 'A bletherin' coo soon forgets her calf', meaning that excessive grief does not last long.

Blind as a bat, As.

1588 J. HARVEY *A Discursive Problem* 40 As blinde as moules, or bats. **1601** T. WRIGHT *The Passions of the Minde* 144 Blinded as battes in their own conceits. **1639** CLARKE 52.

Blind as a beetle.

1548 UDALL *Erasmus Paraphr. Mark* i. 5 Jerusalem . . . albeit she were in very dede as blynde as a betell. **1549** T. CHALENOR *Erasmus, Praise of Folly* N3ᵛ As poreblinde as a bette. **1881** EVANS 102 'As blind as a beetle' is a very common simile, the cockchafer being the beetle referred to.

Blind as a harper, As. (*Cf.* Have among you, blind harpers.)

1584 LYLY *Sapho & P.* IV. iii Harping always upon love, till you be as blind as a harper.

Blind as a mole.

1563 *Mirr. Mag., Rivers* lxiv Blynde as molles. *c.* **1580** J. CONYBEARE *Adagia* (F. C.

Conybeare 1905) 50 **Talpa caecior** blinder than a mole. **1713** BENTLEY *Rem. Disc. Freethink.* II. xlix. 269 In the whole compass and last Tendency of Passages he is as blind as a mole.

Blind as I am blear-eyed, I am not so.

1721 KELLY 199 . . . I may think it proper to hold my tongue, but yet I can very well observe how things go.

Blind as those who won't see, None so.

1546 HEYWOOD II. ix. 75 Who is . . . so blinde, as is hée, That wilfully will nother here nor sée? **1659** HEYLIN *Animadversions* in FULLER *Appeal* (1840) 506 Which makes me wonder . . . that, having access to those records, . . . he should declare himself unable to decide the doubt. . . . But, 'none so blind as he that will not see'. **1852** E. FITZGERALD *Polonius* 58 'None so blind as those that won't see.' Baxter was credulous and incredulous for precisely the same reason. . . . A single effort of the will was sufficient to exclude from his view whatever he judged hostile to his immediate purpose. **1926** *Times* 12 July 15/3 The most charitable thing that can be said . . . is that none are so blind as those who will not see.

Blind eat (eats) many a fly, The.

c. **1430** LYDGATE *Balade* in *Skeat's Chaucer* VII. 295 Men deme hit is right as they see at y; Bewar therfore; the blinde et many a fly. *a.* **1529** SKELTON *Replyc.* 752 The blynde eteth many a flye. **1568** *Jacob & Esau* IV. ix. in HAZL. *O.E.P.* (1874) II. 243 *Mid.* Now I see it true, the blind eat many a fly! I quaked once for fear, that Jacob would be caught. **1636** S. WARD *Serm.* (1862) 99 Blind and ignorant consciences . . . swallow many a fly, and digest all well enough.

Blind enough who sees not through the holes of a sieve, He is.

1620 SHELTON *Quix.* II. i How blind is he who sees not light through the bottom of a meal-sieve! **1670** RAY 3 . . . *Hispan.*

Blind George of Hollowee, *see* Fain see (That would I).

Blind horse, Ever longer the worse looks the.

c. **1350** *Douce MS 52* no. 18 Euer lenger þe wors lokys þe blynde hors.

Blind horse is hardiest, The.

1641 FERGUSSON 98.

Blind Hugh, *see* See (Marry that would I) quoth b. H.

Blind in their own cause, Men are.

1546 HEYWOOD II. v Folk oft tymes are most blind in their owne cause. **1616** DRAXE 150. **1641** FERGUSSON 76. **1678** RAY 384. **1911** *Spectator* 11 Feb. 207 No man should be judge in his own cause, we might add that no man ought to be his own paymaster.

Blind lead the blind, If the | both shall fall into the ditch.

995 *Ang.-Sax. Gosp., Matt.* xv. 14 Se blinda gyf he blindne læt, hig feallaþ begen on ænne pytt. **1389** wyclif—Sothely ȝif a blynd man ȝeue ledynge to a blynd man, bothe fallen doun in to the diche. **1546** heywood ii. v. 55 Where the blynd leadth the blynd, both fall in the dike. **1614** camden 312 The blind leade the blind and both fall into the ditch. **1678** bunyan *Pilgr.* i (1877) 64 That ditch is it into which the blind have led the blind in all ages, and have both there miserably perished. **1868** w. collins *Moonstone* i. x Mr. Franklin . . . said he had often heard of the blind leading the blind, and now . . . he knew what it meant.

Blind man casts his staff or shoots the crow, As the.

1546 heywood ii. ix. 79 Ye cast and coniecture this muche like in show, As the blind man casts his staffe, or shootes the crow. **1608** armin *Nest Ninnies* (Shak. Soc.) 15 This was a flat fool; yet, . . . a blind man may hit a crow. **1641** fergusson 52 He does as the blind man when he casts his staff.

Blind man catches (starts) the hare, As the.

c. **1384** chaucer *Ho. Fame* 172 That been betid, no man wot why, But 'as a blynd man stert an hare'. **1583** p. stubbes *Anat. of Abuses* Pt. II (New Sh. S. ii. 53) *Forte luscus capiat leporem* somtime by chance a blind man may catch a hare. ? *a.* **1630** j. taylor *Kicksey Winsey* Wks. (1872) 6 A blind man may (by fortune) catch a hare.

Blind man's holiday.

1599 nashe *Lent. Stuffe* in *Harl. Misc.* vi. 167 (D.) What will not blind Cupid doe in the night, which is his blindmans holiday. **1678** ray 229 Blindmans holiday, *i.e.* twilight, almost quite dark. **1738** swift (Dial. iii) 352 It is blindman's holiday; we shall soon be all of a colour. **1866** *Aunt Judy's Mag.* Oct. 358 In blindman's holiday, when no work was to be done.

Blind man's peck should be weel measured, The.

1832 henderson 88.

Blind man's wife needs no painting, The.

[Sp. *c.* **1627** correas *Vocab.* (1906) 188 *La mujer del ciego, para quién se afeita?*] **1659** howell *Span.-Eng.* 4. **1670** ray 3 *Hispan.* **1732** fuller no. 1597 For whom does the blind man's wife paint herself? **1736** franklin June Why does the blind man's wife paint herself?

Blind men can (should) judge no colours.

[L. *Caecus non judicat de colore.*] *c.* **1374** chaucer *Troylus* ii. Proem 21 A blynd man ne kan Iuggen wel yn hewys. *c.* **1390** gower *Conf. Amantis* v. 2499 The blinde man no colour demeth. **1546** heywood ii. v. 60 But blinde men should iudge no colours. **1590–1** shaks. *2 Hen. VI* II. i. 125 If thou hadst been born blind, thou mightst as well have known all our names as thus to name the several colours we do wear. **1618** breton *Courtier & Countryman* Wks. (1879) II. 5 You cannot but confess that blind men can judge no colours. **1908** *Christian* 20 Feb. We do not ask the blind their opinion about colours.

Blind man (men), *see also* Kingdom of b. m.

(In the) the one-eyed is king; Let me see, as b. m. said.

Blind that eats his marrow,[1] but far blinder he that lets him, He is.

1641 fergusson 44 He is blind that eats his fellow, but far blinder that lets him. [[1] companion.]

Blind, *see also* Better to be b. than see ill; Better to be half b.; Better to have one eye than be b.; Difference between staring and stark b.; Goose that comes to fox's sermon (B.); Hasty bitch bringeth forth b. whelps; Masters should be sometimes b.; Nod is as good . . . to b. horse.

Blindworm, *see* Adder could hear and b. could see (If).

Blister will rise upon one's tongue that tells a lie, A.

1584 lyly *Sapho & P.* i. ii *Trach.* You have no reason for it but an old report. *Pand.* Report hath not always a blister on her tongue. **1594–5** shaks. *L.L.L.* V. ii. 335 *Ber.* Pay him the due of honey-tongu'd Boyet. *King.* A blister on his sweet tongue, with my heart. **1610–11** *Wint. T.* II. ii. 33 If I prove honey-mouth'd, let my tongue blister. **1625** bacon *Ess., Praise* (Arb.) 355 As we say; That a blister will rise upon one's tongue, that tells a lie. **1732** fuller no. 1127 Common fame hath a blister on its tongue. **1738** swift (Dial. i) 341 I have a blister on my tongue; yet I don't remember I told a lie.

Blithe, *see* Robin that herds . . . can be b. as Sir Robert.

Blithe face, *see* Put a b. f. on black heart.

Blood is alike ancient, All.

1732 fuller no. 505.

Blood is thicker than water.

[= the tie of relationship] *c.* **1180** heinrich der glichessere *Reinhart Fuchs.* Ouch hoer ich sagen, daz sippebluot von wassere niht verdirbet.] **1815** scott *Guy Man.* xxxviii Weel—blude 's thicker than water—she's welcome to the cheeses. **1823** galt *Entail* ii His mother was sib[1] to mine by the father's side, and blood 's thicker than water ony day. **1882** j. m'carthy *Hist. of Own*

Times III. 18 An American naval captain . . . declared that 'blood was thicker than water', and that he could not look on and see Englishmen destroyed by Chinese. **1910** A. M. FAIRBAIRN *Stud. in Rel. & Theol.* 456 Blood is thicker than water; the bond it forms between men is strange and potent and infrangible. [¹ akin.]

Blood of the martyrs is the seed of the church, The.

[TERTULLIAN *Apol.* 50 *Semen est sanguis Christianorum.* The blood of Christians is seed.] **1619** J. FAVOUR *Antiquity* 469 The bloud of the Martyrs was the seed of the Church. **1625** PURCHAS *Pilgrims* (1905–7) I. 168 The seed, the fattening of the Church was the blood of her slain martyrs. **1655** FULLER *Ch. Hist.* I. iv (1868) I. 34 Of all shires in England, Staffordshire was . . . the largest sown with 'the seed of the church', I mean, 'the blood of primitive martyrs'. *a.* **1697** AUBREY *Life of D. Jenkins* And hanged he had been, had not Harry Martyn told them that sanguis martyrum est semen ecclesiae, and that way would do them more mischief. **1887** LD. AVEBURY *Pleas. Life* II. xi The Inquisition has even from its own point of view proved generally a failure. The blood of the martyrs is the seed of the Church.

Blood will have blood.

[*Cf.* **1611** BIBLE *Gen.* ix. 6 Whoso sheddeth man's blood, by man shall his blood be shed.] **1561** NORTON & SACKVILLE *Gorboduc* IV. ii. 364 Blood asketh blood, and death must death requite. **1605–6** SHAKS. *Macbeth* III. iv. 122 It will have blood, they say; blood will have blood. **1798** WORDSWORTH *Hart-Leap Well* Some say that here a murder has been done, And blood cries out for blood.

Blood(s), *see* Come of a b. and so is a pudding; Deer is slain (Where) b. will lie; Difference of b. in a basin (No); Good b. makes bad puddings; Like b. . . . makes happiest marriage; Red as b.; Runs in the b. like wooden legs; Water (B.) from a stone; Welsh b. is up (His).

Bloody bone, *see* Raw head and b. b.

Bloom is off the peach (plum), The.

1738 SWIFT (Dial. i) 341 *Lady A.* She was handsome in her time. . . . *Miss.* She has quite lost the blue on the plum. **1761** A. MURPHY *Old Maid* Wks. (1786) II. 168 *Mr. Harlow.* The bloom has been off the peach any time these fifteen years.

Bloom, *see also* Furze is in b. (When the); Gorse is out of b. (When the).

Blossom in the spring, That which doth | will bring forth fruit in the autumn.

1616 DRAXE 13. **1670** RAY 3. **1732** FULLER no. 3544 No autumn-fruit without spring-blossoms.

Blossom(s), *see also* Autumn fruit without

spring b. (No); Timely b. timely ripe; Vain-glory b. but never bears.

Blot, *see* Fairer the paper fouler b.; Pens may b. but cannot blush.

Blot is no blot unless it be hit, A.

[Metaphor from backgammon.] **1663** J. WILSON *Cheats* V. iii (1671) 72 Provided always, you carry it prudently, for fear of scandal:—a blot, is no blot, till it be hit. **1823** SCOTT *St. Ronans* xvi [A blot is never a blot till it is hit; dishonour concealed is not dishonour in some respects.

Blow first, and sip afterwards.

1678 RAY 103 . . . *Simul sorbere et flare difficile est.* **1732** FULLER no. 995.

Blow great guns, To.

[= to blow a violent gale.] *a.* **1814** C. DIBDIN *Song*; 'The Tar for all Weathers' (1886) 40 But sailors were born for all weathers, Great guns let it blow high or low. **1840** DICKENS *Barn. Rudge* xxxiii It blows great guns indeed.

Blow hot and cold, To.

[In reference to one of Æsop's Fables.] **1549** T. CHALONER *Erasmus, Praise of Folly* G 3 Out of one mouth to blow both hote and colde. **1577** tr. *Bullinger's Decades* (1592) 176 One which out of one mouth, doeth blowe both heat and colde. **1638** CHILLINGWORTH *Relig. of Prot.* I. ii, § 113. 95 These men can blow hot and cold out of the same mouth to serve severall purposes. **1897** M. A. S. HUME *Ralegh* 232 The duplicity of James himself was marvellous. He blew hot and cold with equal facility.

Blow in April, If they | you'll have your fill; but if in May, they'll all go away.

1735 S. PEGGE *Kenticisms, Prov.* (E.D.S.) 75 *Cherries*: . . . In the year 1742 it was otherwise. For, tho' . . . the trees were not in bloom till late in May, I had a great quantity of White and Black Hearts.

Blow (*or* sound) one's own trumpet, To.

[CIC. *de Or.* 2. 20. 86 *Domesticum praeconium.*] **1560** W. FULKE *Antiprognosticon* tr. *W. Painter* C 3 Who shall then be your standard bearer? or who the trompettour to blare out your praise? **1576** FLEMING *Panopl. Epist.* 59 I will . . . sound the trumpet of mine own merits. **1598–9** SHAKS. *Much Ado* V. ii. 91 It is most expedient for the wise, . . . to be the trumpet of his own virtues. **1601–2** *Troil. & Cres.* II. iii. 166 He that is proud eats up himself: pride is his own glass, his own trumpet, his own chronicle. *a.* **1625** J. FLETCHER & MASSINGER *Elder Bro.* I. ii (1905) II. 10 But that modesty forbids, that I should sound the trumpet of my own deserts, I could, &c. **1907** A. C. BENSON *Upton Lett.* 251 It happens too often that biographers of eminent men . . . do a little adventitious self-advertisement. They blow their own trumpet.

Blow the buck's horn, To.

[= to have his labour for his pains.] *c.* 1386 CHAUCER *Miller's T.* 201 Absolon may blowe the bukkes horn.

Blow the wind never so fast, it will fall at last.

1641 FERGUSSON (S.T.S.) no. 169 Blaw the winde never so fast it will lowne at the last. **1721** KELLY no. 83. **1732** FULLER no. 6306.

Blown up,[1] To be.

1607 DEKKER & WEBSTER *North Hoe* B1[v] I will . . . take a faire house in the Citty: no matter tho' it be a Tauerne that has blowne vp his Maister. **1608** DEKKER *Belman of London* B4[v]. **1678** RAY 89. [[1] i.e. a bankrupt.]

Blows best, He that | bears away the horn.

1641 FERGUSSON 44. **1721** KELLY 149 *He that blows best, bear away the horn.* He that does best, shall have the reward, and commendation.

Blows in the dust, He that | fills his eyes with it.

1600 W. SECKER *Nonsuch Prof.* II (1891) 183 He that blows into a heap of dust is in danger of putting out his own eyes. **1640** HERBERT 344.

Blow(s) (*noun*), *see also* Beast that goes always never wants b.; First b.; Word and a b.; Words are but wind, but b. unkind; Words may pass but b. fall heavy.

Blow (*verb*), *see also* Cold (Let them that be) b. at the coal; No man can both sup and b.

Blow point, *see* Boys' play (To leave).

Bloxham, He was born at.

1662 FULLER (*Lincs.*) II. 288 It is a common expression of the country folk in this county, when they intend to character a dull, heavy, blundering person, to say of him, 'he was born at Bloxham'.

Bloxwich[1] bull, Like the.

1867 J. TIMBS *Nooks & Corn. Eng. Life* 261 At Bloxwich, some wag stole the bull [intended for baiting]. The circumstance gave rise to a local proverb still in use. When great expectations are baffled, the circumstance is . . . likened to 'the Bloxwich bull'. [[1] near Walsall, Staffs.]

Blue and better blue, There may be.

1721 KELLY 58 . . . There may be difference between things of the same kind, and persons of the same station. L. *Servus servuum præstat, & dominus dominum.* **1732** FULLER no. 4940.

Blue, *see also* Coventry b.; Stafford b.; Three b. beans; True b.

Blunt, *see* John B.

Blunt wedges rive hard knots.

1539 TAVERNER *Erasm. Prov.* (1552) 5 *Malo nodo malus quærendus cuneus.* To a crabbed knot must be sought a crabbed wedge. A strong disease requireth a strong medicine. A shrewd wife a shrewd husband to tame her. **1601-2** SHAKS. *Troil. & Cres.* I. iii. 316 Blunt wedges rive hard knots.

Blush like a black (blue) dog, To.

[= to have a brazen face.] **1579** GOSSON *Sch. Abuse* (Arb.) 75 We will make him to blush like a blacke Dogge when he is graueled. **1593-4** SHAKS. *Titus Andron.* V. i. 122 *First Goth.* What! canst thou say all this, and never blush? *Aar.* Ay, like a black dog, as the saying is. **1629** T. ADAMS *Serm.* (1861-2) II. 66 A black saint can no more blush than a black dog. **1738** SWIFT (*Dial.* i) 334 *Col.* You'll make Mrs. Betty blush. *Lady S.* Blush! ay, blush like a blue dog.

Blush, *see also* Pens may blot but cannot b.

Blushing is virtue's colour.

1539 R. TAVERNER *Garden of Wisdom* Bk. 2 F 3 Blusshynge is token of an honest nature [Cato]. **1594-5** SHAKS. *Two Gent.* V. iv. 165 I think the boy hath grace in him: he blushes. **1598-9** *Much Ado* IV. i. 35 How like a maid she blushes here . . . Comes not that blood as modest evidence To witness simple virtue? **1605** BACON *Adv. Learn.* I. iii (1900) 20 It was truly said, that *Rubor est virtutis color,* though sometime it come from vice. **1738** SWIFT (*Dial.* i) 336 However, blushing is some sign of grace.

Blustering night, a fair day, A.

1640 HERBERT 331.

Boar, *see* Feeds like a b.; Foam like a b. *See also* Wild boar.

Boast, *see* Great b. and small roast.

Boat without the oar, Ill goes the.

1573 SANDFORD (1576) 207. **1578** FLORIO *First Fruites* f. 28. **1611** DAVIES II. 46 Prov. 229. **1659** HOWELL *Fr.-Eng.* 3.

Boat(s), *see also* Burn one's b.; Same b. (To be in).

Bobtail, *see* Tag, rag, and b.

Bode[1] a robe, and wear it; bode a sack, and bear it.

1721 KELLY 63 . . . Speak heartily, and expect good, and it will fall out accordingly. [[1] expect.]

Bode good, and get it.

1721 KELLY 63.

Bodkin, To ride (*or* sit).

[= to be wedged in between two others where there is proper room for two only.] **1638** FORD *Fancies* IV. i Where but two lie in a bed, you must be—bodkin, bitch-baby— must ye? **1848** THACKERAY *Vanity F.* II. 241

He's too big to travel bodkin between you and me. **1872** FLOR. MONTGOMERY *Thrown Together* ii. 62 The three called a hansom outside, and Cecily . . . sat bodkin.

Bodle, *see* Rake hell for a b.

Bodmin, *see* Out of the world and into B.

Body is more (sooner) dressed than the soul, The.

1616 DRAXE 10 His body is better clothed then his soule. **1640** HERBERT 359.

Body is the socket of the soul, The.

1664 CODRINGTON 218. **1670** RAY 3.

Body, -ies, *see also* Great b. move slowly; Little b. often harbours great soul; Riches increase (When), b. decreaseth.

Boil snow or pound it, Whether you | you can have but water of it.

1640 HERBERT 325.

Boil stones in butter and you may sup the broth.

1721 KELLY 75 . . . Good ingredients will make very coarse meat savoury. **1732** FULLER no. 1003 (with 'sip' for 'sup'). **1895** *Westmr. Gaz.* 22 May 6/1 Like the old saying: 'Boil stones in butter and you shall sup the broth.'

Boil the pot (Make the pot boil), To.

[= to provide one's livelihood.] **1657–61** HEYLIN *Hist. Ref.* (1674) 100 So poor, that it is hardly able to keep the Pot boiling for a parson's dinner. **1812** COMBE *Picturesque* xxiii. 18 No fav'ring patrons have I got, But just enough to boil the pot. **1864** CARLYLE *Fredk. Gt.* XVI. ii (1872) VI. 151 A feeling that glory is excellent, but will not make the national pot boil.

Boil over, *see* Pot's full (When) it will b. o.

Boiling pot, To a | flies come not.

1640 HERBERT 322. **1655–62** GURNALL *Chrn. in Armour* (1865) II. 324 Flies will not so readily light on a pot seething hot on the fire as when it stands cold in the window. Baalzebub . . . the god of a fly . . . will not so readily light on thy sacrifice when flaming . . . with zeal.

Boils his pot with chips, Who | makes his broth smell of smoke.

1813 RAY 19. *Ital.*

Boisterous horse must have a rough bridle, A.

1539 TAVERNER (1545) A5 A boystous horse, a boysteous snaffell. **1616** WITHALS 566. **1616** DRAXE 171. **1639** CLARKE 200.

Bold as a lion, As.

[**1611** BIBLE *Prov.* xxviii. 1 The righteous are bolde as a lyon]. *a.* **1225** *Ancrene Riwle* 274 (A) Herdi ase leun. **1597** SHAKS. 1 *Hen. IV* III. i Valiant as a lion. **1819** SCOTT *Bride Lam.* xi Caleb, to do him justice, was as bold as any lion where the honour of the family of Ravenswood was concerned.

Bold as Beauchamp, As.

1661 FULLER (*Warwick*) III. 271 . . . I conceive that Thomas [Beauchamp, Earl of Warwick] the first of that name [*c.* 1346], gave the chief occasion to this proverb.

Bold as blind Bayard, As.

c. **1350** CLEANNESS l. 886 Thay blustered as blynd as bayard watz euer. *c.* **1386** CHAUCER *Can. Yeom. T.* 1413 Ye been as boold as is Bayard the blynde. *c.* **1390** GOWER *Conf. Amantis* III. 44 But as Bayard the blinde stede . . . He goth there no man will him bidde. **1532** MORE *Confut. Tindale* Wks. 500–1 Bee bolde vpon it lyke blynde bayarde. *c.* **1630** JACKSON *Creed* IV. iv. Wks. III. 33 As . . . boldly as blind bayard rusheth into the battle. **1681** BUNYAN *Come & Welcome* Wks. (1855) I. 289 They presume; they are groundlessly confident. Who so bold as blind Bayard? **1732** FULLER no. 5719 Who so bold as blind Baynard [*sic*]?

Bold man that first ate an oyster, He was a.

1662 FULLER (*Essex*) I. 493 King James was wont to say, 'he was a very valiant man who first adventured on eating of oysters'. **1738** SWIFT (Dial. ii) 344. **1806** WOLCOT (P. Pindar) *Tristia*; *Elegy to the Same* 'Who first an oyster eat', was a bold dog.

Bold (wily) mouse that breeds (builds, nestles) in the cat's ear, It is a.

c. **1430** LYDGATE *Min. Poems* (Percy Soc.) 167 An hardy mowse, that is bold To breede In cattis eeris. **1522** SKELTON *Why not to Court* 753 Wks. (1843) II. 50 Yet it is a wyly mouse That can bylde his dwellinge house Within the cattes eare. *a.* **1530** R. Hill's *Commonpl. Bk.* (E.E.T.S.) 140 It ys a sotyll mouse that slepyth in the cattys eare. **1546** HEYWOOD II. v. 58 I haue heard tell, it had néede to bée. A wyly mouse that should bréede in the cats eare. **1579** LYLY *Euphues* (Arb.) 63 Let *Philautus* behaue himself neuer so craftely, he shal know that it must be a wyly Mouse that shall breede in the Cats eare. **1640** HERBERT 349 It is a bold mouse that nestles in the cat's ear.

Bold than welcome, More.

1591 FLORIO *Sec. Frutes* 53 This house is free, and you are not so bold as welcome. **1721** KELLY 251 *More hamely*[1] *than welcome.* **1738** SWIFT (Dial. i) 336 *Miss.* I'd rather give a knave a kiss for once than be troubled with him; but, upon my word, you are more bold than welcome. [[1] familiar.]

Bold with your biggers, or betters, Be not too.

1659 HOWELL *Eng. Prov.* 3/2.

Bolder than a miller's neck-cloth, What is | which takes a thief by the throat every morning?

1732 FULLER no. 731 As stout as a miller's waistcoat, that takes a thief by the throat every day. **1853** TRENCH iv. 79 'The miller tolling with his golden thumb', has been often the object of malicious insinuations; and of him the Germans have a proverb: *What is bolder than a miller's neck-cloth, which takes a thief by the throat every morning?*[1] [[1] Bebel: *Dicitur in proverbio nostro: nihil esse audacius indusio molitoris, cum omni tempore matutino furem collo apprehendat.*]

Boll, see Love the b. (If you) you cannot hate branches.

Bologna, see Beggars of B. (Like the blind).

Bolt (Arrow) came never out of your bag (bow, quiver), That.

a. **1530** R. Hill's Commonpl. Bk. (E.E.T.S.) 129 Thys arrow comyth never owt of thyn owne bow. **1641** FERGUSSON 98. **1721** KELLY 305 . . . L. *Ex tua faretra*[1] *nunquam venit ista sagitta.* [[1] pharetra, quiver.]

Bolt from the blue, A.

[= a complete surprise] **1875** TENNYSON *Q. Mary* v. ii So from a clear sky falls the thunderbolt! **1911** W. F. BUTLER *Autobiog.* xxi. 380 Like a bolt from the blue came the news of the Jameson raid.

Bolt, see also Fool's b. soon shot; Shaft or a b. of it (I will make a); Shot my b.

Bolton, see Bate me an ace, quoth B.

Bond, see Honest man's word.

Bone between, To cast a.

1546 HEYWOOD II. ii. 47 The diuell hath cast a bone (said I) to set stryfe Betwéene you. **1692** L'ESTRANGE *Josephus' Antiq.* XVI. xi (1733) 439 By this Means she . . . cast in a Bone betwixt the Wife and the Husband.

Bone in one's leg (throat, arm, &c.), To have a.

[An excuse often made when the speaker is unwilling to do what he is asked. On one occasion Demosthenes, who had accepted a bribe, appeared in the assembly of the people with his throat carefully muffled and refused to speak because he 'had a bone in his throat'.] **1542** UDALL *Erasm. Apoph.* 337 b He[1] refused to speake, allegeyng that he had a bone in his throte & could not speake. **1678** RAY 67 I have a bone in mine arm. This is a pretended excuse. **1738** SWIFT (Dial. iii) 351 *Miss.* I can't go, for I have a bone in my leg. **1845** A. SMITH *Fort. Scattergood* F. xxii Mr. Joe Jolit . . . stated that he [had] . . . a bone in his leg, and something green in his eye. [[1] Demosthenes.]

Bone in the leg, Were it not for the | all the world would turn carpenters.

1640 HERBERT 364 Were it not for the bone in the leg, all the world would turn carpenters (to make them crutches).

Bone of contention, A

1562 HEYWOOD II. ii The devil hath cast a bone to set strife between you. **1803** WELLINGTON in GURW. *Disp.* I. 517 A great bone of contention between Scindiah and Holkar.

Bone to pick (bite, gnaw) on, A.

1533 UDALL tr. *Terence, Flowers for Latin Speaking* (1560) I haue geuen hym a bone to gnawe. **1553** T. WILSON *Rule of Reason* Z 3. **1565** CALFHILL *Ans. Treat. Cross.* (1846) 277 A bone for you to pick on. **1602** FULBECKE *Pandectes* 69 He . . . gave them a bone to gnawe.

Bones bring meat to town.

1639 *Berkeley MSS.* (1885) iii. 31 (A) . . . meaninge, Difficult and hard things are not altogether to bee reiected, or things of small consequence. **1642** FULLER *H. & P. State* v. xviii (1841) 'Bones bring meat to town'; and those who are desirous to feast themselves on . . . history, must be content sometimes . . . to feed on hard words, which bring matter along with them. **1721** KELLY 337 *The bones bears the beef home.* An answer to them that complain that there are so many bones in the meat that they are buying.

Bones (or No bones) of (or about), To make.

1459 BRACKLEY, Friar J., in *Paston Letters* (ed. Gairdner, 1901) I. 444 which he promittyd up a certeyn mony, &c., and undirtoke it, &c., and *fond that tyme no bonys* in the matere, &c. (Also *fownde no bonys, ibid.* I. 496.) **1533** UDALL tr. *Terence, Flowers for Latin Speaking* (1560) H 3 I will not shrinke to aduenture it . . . I wyll no bones at it. **1537** *Thersites* A 2. **1542** UDALL *Erasmus Apophthegms* (1877) 133. **1548** UDALL *Erasm. Par. Luke* i. 28 He made no manier bones ne stickyng, but went in hande to offer up his ownly son Isaac. **1589** *Whip for Ape* in LYLY *Wks.* (1902) III. 420 Our *Martin* makes no bones, but plainlie saies, Their fists shall walke, they will both bite and scratch. **1642** D. ROGERS *Naaman* 579 Who make no bones of the Lord's promises, but devoure them all. **1850** THACKERAY *Pendennis* lxiv (1884) 635 Do you think that the Government or the Opposition would make any bones about accepting the seat if he offered it to them?

Bones of a great estate are worth the picking, The.

1721 KELLY 337 . . . Spoken of an estate under burthen, mortgag'd but not sold, that there may be something made of it.

Bone(s), see also Belly is full (When), b. would be at rest; Better a castle of b. than of stones; Bred in the b. will not out of the flesh; Broken b. well set; Carry a b. in mouth; Cast a b. in devil's teeth; Dog gnaws b. (While), companions would he none; Feel in one's b.; Flesh is aye fairest furthest from b.; Give his b. to the dog (He will not); Gnaw the b. fallen to thy lot; Grave (In the) dust and b. jostle not; Joke breaks no b.; Nearer the b. sweeter flesh; Rod breaks no b.; Shirt full of sore b.; Tongue breaketh b.; Try that b. on some other dog.

Bonnet, see Hand twice to your b. for once to pouch; Head will never fill father's b.

Bonny bride is soon buskit,[1] and a short horse is soon wispit, A. (*See also* Short horse is soon curried.)

1641 FERGUSSON 6 *A fair bride is soon buskt, and a short horse soon wispt.* **1721** KELLY 1 *A bony* (sic) *bride is soon busked. A short horse is soon whisked.* . . . What is of itself beautiful, needs but little adorning: . . . a little task is soon ended. **1857** DEAN RAMSAY *Remin.* v (1911) 193 Janet replied . . . 'Ay, weel, a bonny bride's sune buskit.' [[1] dressed, bedecked.]

Bonny, see also Better than she is b. (She is).

Books, To be in a person's (black, bad, good).

[= in disfavour, or favour.] **1592** GREENE *Black Bks. Messenger* Wks. (Gros.) XI. 5 Ned Browne's villanies . . . are too many to be described in my Blacke Booke. **1593-4** SHAKS. *Tam. Shrew* II. 223 A herald, Kate? O! put me in thy books. **1598-9** *Much Ado* I. i. 79 I see, lady, the gentleman is not in your books. **1614** JONSON *Barth. Fair* II. i This is the special day for the detection of these foresaid enormities. Here is my black book for the purpose. *a.* **1627** MIDDLETON *Anything for Quiet Life* I. i She hath . . . her Black Book . . . remembers in it . . . all my misdemeanours. **1861** W. PERRY *Hist. Ch. Eng.* I. xii. 403 The Arminians, who at that time were in his bad books.

Book(s), *see also* Bell, b., and candle; Beside the b.; Great b. great evil; New b. appears (When), read old one; Old wood is best to burn . . . old b. to read; Pictures are the b. of unlearned; Read one like a b.; Speak without b.; Talk like a b.; Wicked b. is the wickeder; Worthy to bear his b. (Not); Years know more than b. *See also* One book.

Boose, see Cherry's b.

Boot and the better horse, He has gotten the.

1721 KELLY 171 . . . That is, he has gotten the advantage in the exchange.

Boot is on the other leg, The.

[= the case is altered.] **1855** G. J. WHYTE-MELVILLE *Gen. Bounce* xvi 'The young woman as owns that house has got *the boot on the other leg.'* **1908** W. S. CHURCHILL *My African J.* iii Here, . . . the boot is on the other leg, and Civilization is ashamed of her arrangements in the presence of a savage.

Boot (=aid), *see* Bale is hext (When), b. is next.

Boot(s), *see also* Grease one's b.; Jogging while your b. are green; Keep a man out of the mud (To), black his b.; Leg warmeth (While) b. harmeth; Over shoes over b.; Too big for one's b.

Booted are not always ready, They that are.

1640 HERBERT 320.

Booty, see Play b.

Borage, see Leaf of b. might buy all they can sell.

Bore a hole through Beacon Hill, You might as well try to.

1855 *N. & Q.* 1st Ser. XI. 223 [Halifax] is overlooked . . . by . . . 'Beacon Hill', and . . . when the inhabitants wished to express the impossibility of any proposal, their reply was, 'You might as well try to bore a hole through Beacon Hill'. . . . A tunnel [now] passes through Beacon Hill.

Bore (Run) him through the nose with a cushion, To.

1597 T. DELONEY 1 *Gentle Craft* 129 . . . and bore him through the nose with a cushin. **1603** *The Bachelor's Banquet* (F. P. Wilson) 66 Thus is he bored through the nose with a cushen. **1672** WALKER 57 (with 'run' for 'bore').

Born for ourselves, We are not.

1639 CLARKE 264

Born in a good hour who gets a good name, He is.

c. **1450** *Prouerbis of Wysdom* 12 Yea, well ys hym, þat hath a gwod name. **1732** FULLER no. 2455.

Born in a mill, He was.

1578 WHETSTONE *Promos and Cassandra* B 3 Were you borne in a myll, curtole? you prate so high. **1678** RAY 76 . . . i.e. He's deaf.

Born in August, He was.

1641 FERGUSSON 46 *Of well skilled persons.* He was born in August. **1662** FULLER (*Northumb.*) II. 544 'He was born in August'. . . . I am informed by a Scottish man, that it is only the periphrasis of a liquorish person, and such said to be born in August, whose tongues will be the tasters of every thing they can come by.

Born to be hanged, He that is | shall never be drowned.

[*Cf. c.* **1598** *MS. Prov.* in FERGUSSON 101 The water will never reave[1] the widdie.[2]] **1540** D. LYNDESAY *Thrie Estaits* 1. 2096 Quha ever bess hangit with his cord needs never to be drowned. **1594-5** SHAKS. *Two Gent.* I. i. 158 Go, go, be gone, to save your ship from wrack; which cannot perish, having thee aboard, Being destin'd to a drier death on shore. **1611-12** *Tempest* I. i. 32

Methinks he hath no drowning mark upon him; his complexion is perfect gallows. *Ibid.* I. i. 62. **1614** CAMDEN 307. **1625** PURCHAS *Pilgrims* (1905-7) XIX. 201 Long with two others escaped (the rest drowned). One of the three ... said nothing, but Gallows claim thy right, which within half a year fell out accordingly. **1723** DEFOE *Col. Jack* vii He had a proverb in his favour, and he got out of the water, ... not being born to be drowned, as I shall observe afterwards in its place. **1738** SWIFT (Dial. i) 337 You know, he that's born to be hang'd will never be drown'd. **1884** BLACKMORE *Tom Upmore* viii Don't tumble into it, ... though you never were born to be drowned, that I'll swear. [¹ rob. ² gallows.]

Born under a three-halfpenny (three penny) planet shall never be worth two pence (a groat), He that was.

1606 DEKKER *News from Hell*, D 1ᵛ All such rich mens darlings are eyther christened by some left-handed Priest, or else borne under a threepenny Planet. **1670** RAY 64 He that was born under a three-halfpenny planet shall never be worth two pence. **1692** L'ESTRANGE *Aesop's Fables* cccxliv (1738) 'No', says Fortune, ... 'I'll ... make good the old saying to ye, *That he that's born under a three-penny planet, shall never be worth a groat.*' **1738** SWIFT (Dial. i) 340 If it rained rich widows, none of them would fall upon me. Egad, I was born under a three-penny planet, never to be worth a groat. **1882** MRS. CHAMBERLAIN *West. Worc. Words* in NORTHALL *Folk-phrases* (1894) 15 He was born under a threepenny planet, i.e. is avaricious, a curmudgeon.

Born when wit was scant, You were.

1670 RAY 199.

Born with a caul, He was.

1540 PALSGRAVE *Acolastus* (Carver) 80 May not men ... thinke, that I was borne in a good howre, or that I was borne with a syly hoffe on myn heed. **1609** JONSON *Alchemist* I. ii. 128 Yo' were borne with a caule o' your head. **1620** J. MELTON *Astrologaster* 46 If a child be borne with a Caule on his head, he shall be very fortunate. **1668** SHADWELL *Sullen Lov.* v. i Sure I was born with a caul on my head, and wrapped in my mother's smock; the ladies do so love me. **1738** SWIFT (Dial. i) 340 Mr. Neverout; I believe you were born with a caul on your head, you are such a favourite among the ladies.

Born with a silver spoon in his mouth, He was.

1639 CLARKE 39 He was borne with a penny in 's mouth. **1721** KELLY 101 *Every man is no born with a silver spoon in his mouth.* Every man is not born to an estate, but must labour for his support. **1762** GOLDSMITH *Cit. World* cxix (Globe) 274 But that was not my chance: one man is born with a silver spoon in his mouth, and another with a wooden ladle. **1849** LYTTON *Caxtons* II. iii I think he is born with a silver spoon in his mouth.

1906 G. W. E. RUSSELL *Soc. Silhouettes* xvii The youth who is born with a silver spoon in his mouth, the heir to entailed acres and accumulated Consols.

Born within the sound of Bow bell, To be. (*See also* London cockney.)

1593 NASHE (McKerrow) II. 95 Some grave Auntients (within the hearing of Bow-bell) would be out of charity with me. **1617** FYNES MORISON *Itinerary* (Harrison *Descr. England* New S. S. IV. 250) Londiners, and all within the sound of Bow-bell, are in reproch called Cocknies. **1638** J. TAYLOR *Bull, Bear, and Horse* B 7 A Young Shee Citizen borne ... having never in her life beene a Traveller further than she could heare the sound of Bow Bell. **1662** FULLER (*London*) II. 344 'He was born within the sound of Bow-bell'. This is perhaps the periphrasis of a Londoner at large, born within the suburbs thereof. ... It is called *Bow-bell*, because hanging in the steeple of *Bow-church*; and *Bow-church* because built upon *bows* or arches. **1738** SWIFT (Dial. ii) 345 You were born within the sound of Bow bell, and don't care to stir so far from London. **1842/3** W. H. MAXWELL *Hector O'H*, XV An artiste ... born and indoctrinated within sound of Bow bells. **1926** *Times* 2 Aug. 11/5 Israel Zangwill ... was born, as he boasted, within the sound of Bow Bells.

Born yesterday, I was not.

1837 MARRYAT *Snarl.* xii The widow read the letter and tossed it into the fire with a 'Pish! I was not born yesterday, as the saying is'. **1871** GILBERT *Pygm. and Galatea* To a suspicious visitor's 'I wasn't born yesterday' Galatea replies 'But I was'. **1894** BLACKMORE *Perlycross* xxi You know that my eyes are pretty sharp, and that I wasn't born yesterday.

Born, *see also* Bloxham (He was b. at); Know where they were b. (Men); Little Witham (He was b. at); Natural to die as to be b.; Once b. once must die; Skill of man (You have), b. between the Beltanes; Soon as man is b. begins to die; Wept when I was b.; Women are b. in Wiltshire.

Borrow, Not so good to | as to be able to lend.

1546 HEYWOOD I. x. 21.

Borrow nor lend, He is well provided within that will neither.

1611 DAVIES *Prov.* 177 The world still he keeps at his staves end that need not to borrow and never will lend. **1641** FERGUSSON 44 He is weill staikit¹ thereben, that will neither borrow nor len. [¹ stocked, provided.]

Borrow when he hath not, Who would | let him borrow when he hath.

1659 N.R. 118. **1855** BOHN 567.

Borrowed garments never fit well.

1732 FULLER no. 1008.

Borrowing days, *see* Put over the b. d.

Borrows must pay again with shame or loss, He that.

1639 CLARKE 246 He that will borrow must pay. **1678** RAY 104 . . . Shame if he returns not as much as he borrowed, loss if more, and it 's very hard to cut the hair.

Borrow(eth, s, ing), *see* Better buy than b.; Contented who needs neither b.; Goes a b. goes a sorrowing; Know the value of a ducat, try to b. one; Know what money is (Would you), b. some; Rath sower never b. of late.

Bosom, *see* Abraham's b.; Bird in my b.

Bossing, *see* Ossing comes to b.

Botch, *see* Patch and long sit.

Both ends (the two ends of the year) meet, To make.

[= to live within one's income.] **1639** CLARKE 242 I cannot make both ends meet. **1662** FULLER (*Cumb.*) I. 343 Worldly wealth he cared not for, desiring only to make both ends meet. **1748** SMOLLETT *Rod. Rand.* x He made shift to make the two ends of the year meet. **1814** JANE AUSTEN *Mansfield P.* iii *Mrs. Norris.* If I can but make both ends meet, that 's all I ask for. **1884** *Graphic* 23 Aug. 198/2 Her mother has to contrive to make both ends meet.

Bottle, *see* Wine in b. does not quench thirst.

Bottom, *see* Spare when b. is bare (Too late to); Tub must stand on own b.; Venture not all in one b.; Wind up your b.

Bottom of the sea, *see* Great way to.

Boughs that bear most, hang lowest, The.

1655 FULLER *Ch. Hist.* x. iii (1868) III. 257 His humility set a lustre on all (admirable that the whole should be so low, whose several parts were so high) . . . like a tree loaden with fruit, bowing down its branches. **1732** FULLER no. 4430. **1856** MRS. BROWNING *Aurora L.* II The vines That bear much fruit are proud to stoop with it.

Bough(s); *see also* Cut not the b. thou standest upon; Short b. long vintage.

Bought a brush, He has.

1813 RAY 56 . . . i.e. He has run away.

Bought and sold.

[= betrayed.] *c.* **1350** *York Plays* (L. T. Smith) 420 Thus schall þe sothe be bought and solde. *c.* **1497** MEDWALL *Fulgens and Lucres* 579 The mater is bought and sold. **1546** HEYWOOD I. x. 19 Than will the pickthanke it tell To your most enmies, you to

bye and sell. **1591–2** SHAKS. *1 Hen. VI* IV. iv. 13 *Som.* Whither were you sent? *Lucy.* Whither, my lord? from bought and sold Lord Talbot. **1592–3** *Com. Err.* III. i. 72 It would make a man mad as a buck to be so bought and sold. *Rich. III* V. iii. 306 *Be not too bold, For Dickon thy master is bought and sold.* **1595–7** *K. John* V. iv. 10 Fly, noble English; you are bought and sold. **1601–2** *Troil. & Cres.* II. i. 51 Thou art bought and sold among those of any wit. **1639** CLARKE 80 You are bought and sold like sheepe in a market.

Bought is cheaper than a gift, What is.

1813 RAY 3 . . . *Lusit. Mais barato he o comprado que o pedido.*

Bought the fox-skin for three pence, and sold the tail for a shilling, He.

1732 FULLER no. 1814.

Bought wit is dear.

1575 GASCOIGNE *Flowers, Posies* (Camb. Clas.) 66 Bought wit is deare, and drest with sower sauce.

Bought wit is the best. (*Cf.* Wit once bought, &c.)

c. **1490** H. MEDWALL, *Nature* I 2 Wyt is nothyng worth tyll yt be dere bought. **1546** HEYWOOD I. viii. 15 But wit is neuer good tyll it be bought. **1599** PORTER *Angry Wom. Abingd.* IV. iii (Merm.) 176 'Tis an old proverb, and not so old as true, bought wit is the best. **1688** BUNYAN *Accept Sacrif.* Wks. (1855) I. 704 We say, Wisdom is not good till it is bought; and he that buys it . . usually smarts for it.

Bought, *see also* Buy.

Boulogne, Our fathers won | who never came within the report of the cannon.

1629 T. ADAMS *Serm.* (1861–2) II. 313 So we make a conquest of peace, as the byword says our fathers won Boulogne; who never came within the report of the cannon.

Bound must obey, They that are.

1205 LAYAMON *Brut.* 1051 Ah heo mot nede beien, þe mon þe ibunden bith. *c.* **1390** GOWER *Conf. Amantis* II, 1. 540 For who is bounden, he mot bowe. *c.* **1410** *Towneley Plays* xiii, 1. 80 Wo is hym that is bun, ffor he must abyde. **1546** HEYWOOD II. v. 55. **1576** PETTIE *Petite Pall.* (Gollancz) II. 46 Alas, they that are bound must obey; he must follow of force his general-captain. **1614** CAMDEN 313.

Bound to see more than he can, One is not.

1653 FULLER *Infants Advocate* xxi in *Sermons* (1891) II. 242 Our English proverb, . . . *One is not bound to see more than he can.* And I conceive I am in no error, because I follow my present light, and all the means of your prescription have made no alteration on my understanding.

Bourbons learn nothing and forget nothing, The.

[TALLEYRAND *Album Perdu* 147 described the *émigrés* as *des gens qui n'ont rien appris ni rien oublié depuis trente ans* (King).] 1861 **G. J.** WHYTE-MELVILLE *Inside Bar* vi The race [of stud-grooms] . . . possesses its own language, its own customs, its own traditions. As Napoleon the First said of the Bourbons, it learns nothing, and forgets nothing.

Bourd[1] not with Bawty,[2] lest he bite you.

1641 FERGUSSON 22. 1721 KELLY 56 . . . Do not jest too familiarly with your superiors, lest you provoke . . . a surlish return. [[1] jest. [2] a watch-dog.]

Bourd[1] wi' cats, They that | maun count on scarts.[2]

1832 HENDERSON 141. [[1] jest. [2] scratches.]

Bourd, *see also* Sooth b. is no b.

Bout as Barrow was, To be.

1678 RAY 66 To be bout, i.e. without, as Barrow was. *Chesh*.

Bow bell, *see* Born within the sound of B. b.

Bow, I have a good | but it is in the castle.

1641 FERGUSSON 64. 1721 KELLY 183 . . . Spoken to them who say that they have a thing very proper for the business, but it is not at hand.

Bow long bent at last waxeth weak, A.

c. 1532 SIR ADRIAN FORTESCUE no. 53 A bowe that is longe bent, will waxe dulle. 1550 HEYWOOD I. xi. 28 But a bow long bent, at length must waxe weake. 1579 LYLY *Euphues* (Arb.) 46 Though the Cammocke the more it is bowed the better it serueth, yet the bow the more it is bent and occupied, the weaker it waxeth. 1614 CAMDEN 302.

Bow of Ulysses.

[*Fig.* a task of great difficulty: see HOMER *Od.* xxi.] 1545 ASCHAM *Toxoph.* (Arb.) 135 Penelope brought Vlixes bowe downe amonges the gentlemen, whiche came on wowing to her, that he which was able to bende it and drawe it, might inioye her. 1678 DRYDEN *All for Love*, Pref. (Merm.) 9 The death of Antony and Cleopatra . . . has been treated by the greatest wits of our nation . . . and . . . their example has given me the confidence to try myself in this bow of Ulysses. 1830 SIR J. HERSCHEL *Stud. Nat. Phil.* III. iii (1851) 273 The bow of Ulysses, which none but its master could bend.

Bow (*noun*), *see also* Bent of his b.; Long b.; Out-shoot a man in his own b.; Yew b. in

Chester (More than one); Young are not always with b. bent.

Bow (*verb*), *see* Better bend (b.) than break.

Bowdon, *see* Vicar of B.

Bowl down hill, It is easy to.

1639 CLARKE 151.

Bowl, *see also* Comes to hand like b. of pint-stoup.

Bowler, *see* Honest man and good b.

Bowling-green, *see* Three things are thrown away in a b.-g.

Bowls, *see* Play at b. must expect rubbers.

Bows and arrows, *see* Man of God is better for having b. and a.

Bows and bills!

[The cry of alarm raised in the English camp in old times.] *a.* 1572 KNOX *Hist. Ref.* 28 (Jam.) The schout ryises, Bowes and Billis! . . . which is a significatioun of extreim defence.

Bows to the bush he gets bield[1] of, Every man.

1721 KELLY 99 . . . Every man pays court to him that he gains by. [[1] shelter.]

Box Harry, To.

[A phrase formerly used by commercial travellers, who had to content themselves at inns with a makeshift meal. HAZLITT.] 1862 BORROW *Wild Wales* xxxiii 'I will have the bacon and eggs with tea and bread-and-butter, . . . in a word, I will box Harry'.

Box (*noun*), *see* Butler's b. at Christmas; Wrong b.

Box (*verb*), *see also* Give (B.) it about.

Box on ear, *see* Billingsgate for b. o. e. (As much favour at).

Boys will be boys.

1681 ROBERTSON *Phraseol. Gener.* 330 (A) Children will do like children. 1853 THACKERAY *Newcomes* xxv We used to call your grandfather by that playful epithet (boys will be boys, you know). 1905 *Almond of Loretto* 358 The devil has got a lot of maxims which his adherents . . . use— . . . 'Boys will be boys.'

Boys (Lads) will be men.

1611 COTGRAVE s.v. 'Enfant' (As we say) boyes will be men one day. 1641 FERGUSSON 72 Laddes will be men. 1732 FULLER no. 1014. 1905 VACHELL *The Hill* 33 I'm sending you to Harrow to study, not books . . . but boys, who will be men when you are a man.

Boys' play, To leave | and go to blow point.

1616 WITHALS 569. 1639 CLARKE 197. 1681 ROBERTSON *Phraseol. Gener.* 997 (A) To leave boys-play and fall to blow point; *Relinquere nuces.*

Boy(s), *see also* Good will (With as) as e'er b. came from school; Least b. carries greatest fiddle; Manned with b. . . . shall have work undone; Miller's b. said so; Naughty b. good men; One b. more trouble than dozen girls.

Brabbling[1] curs never want sore ears.

1611 COTGRAVE s.v. 'Hargneux' A brabling curre is never without torne eares. **1640** HERBERT 319. [1 brawling.]

Brack, *see* Seek a b. where hedge whole.

Bracken bush, *see* Hare or the b. b.

Brackley breed, better to hang than to feed.

1636 *Somers Tracks* vii. 212 (A) Though we be Leicestershire fed, yet we be not Brackley bred, I assure you. **1639** CLARKE 203. **1678** RAY 328 . . . *Brackley* is a decayed market town . . . in *Northamptonshire*, not farre from *Banbury*, which . . . troubling the countrey about with beggers, came into disgrace with its neighbours.

Bradshaw's windmill? What have I to do with.

1678 RAY 317 (*Leics.*) . . . i.e. What have I to doe with another mans business?

Brag is a good dog.

1599 PORTER *Angry Wom. Abingd.* IV. iii (Merm.)176 Ay, Brag's a good dog; threatened folks live long. **1618** *Barnevelt's Apol.* E iv b Bragge is a good Dog still. **1670** RAY 65 Brag's a good dog if he be well set on.

Brag is a good dog, but Holdfast is a better.

1598–9 SHAKS. *Hen. V* II. iii. 55 And holdfast is the only dog, my duck. **1752** JOHNSON *Rambl.* No. 197, par. 3 When I envied the finery of any of my neighbours, [my mother] told me that 'Brag was a good dog, but Holdfast was a better'. **1870** READE *Put Yourself* xxix I wouldn't say a word till it was all settled, for Brag's a good dog, but Holdfast's a better.

Brag is a good dog, but that he hath lost his tail.

1618 BRETON *Courtier & Countryman* Wks. (1879) II. 7 Some of you . . . can scarcely see a penny in your purse, and . . . if Brag were not a good dog, I know not how he would hold up his tail. **1678** RAY 105.

Brag most that can do least, They.

1539 TAVERNER (1545) I 3 Great braggers commonly be least fyghters. *c.* **1598** DELONEY *Gentle Craft* II. vi.

Brag of many goodmorrows, To.

1616 WITHALS 557. **1670** RAY 178.

Brag's a good dog but dares not bite.

1616 DRAXE 48 Bragging mastiues seldome bite. **1732** FULLER no. 1015.

Brain as a burbolt,[1] As much.

a. **1553** UDALL *Royster D.* III. ii (Arb.) 43 As much braine as a burbolt. [1 bird-bolt.]

Brain sows not corn, If the | it plants thistles.

1640 HERBERT 364. **1659** HOWELL *Eng. Prov.* 6/2 The brain that sows not corn plants thistles, viz. *If there be not good thoughts, there are bad.*

Brains are addle, His.

1670 RAY 165.

Brains crow, His.

1678 RAY 230.

Brains don't lie in the beard, The.

1732 FULLER no. 4431.

Brains of a fox will be of little service, if you play with the paw of a lion, The.

1732 FULLER no. 4432.

Brains will work without barm, His.

1678 RAY 230. *Yorksh.*

Brain(s), *see also* Believe he's bald till you see his b. (Will not); Cudgel one's b.; Good manners to offer b. (Not); Guts in his b.; Guts than b. (More); Heat of affection joined with idleness of b.; Idle b. the devil's shop; Pick (Suck) a person's b.; Worm in his b.

Bran, If it be not | it is Bran's brother.

1814 SCOTT *Waverley* xlv You shout . . . as if the Chieftain were just come to your head'. '*Mar e Bran is e a brathair*, If it be not Bran, it is Bran's brother', was the proverbial reply of Maccombich. [Bran was the famous dog of Fingal.]

Bran, *see* Much b. little meal.

Branch(es), *see* Highest b. not safest roost; Love the boll (If you) you cannot hate b.

Brasenose, **Brasen-Nose**, *see* Bred in B. College; Testoons are gone to Oxford.

(Brass) farthing, Not worth a.

1520 R. WHITTINGTON *Vulg.* (E.E.T.S.) 93. **1613** S. ROWLEY *When you see me* D 2 As for the Popes faith (good faith's) not worth a farthing. **1672** WALKER 9 He is not worth a brass farthing.

Brass for gold.

[HOM. *Il.* 6. 236 χρύσεα χαλκείων (exchange of armour).] **1813** BYRON to Gifford 18 June I will not return my brass for your gold by expressing more fully these sentiments of admiration.

Brass kettle, *see* Earthen pot keep clear of b. k.

Brass tacks, To come down to.

1945 *Evening News* 27 Aug. Leader. Europe is a big parish . . . needing . . . parish capacity to come down to brass tacks.

Brave men before Agamemnon, There were.

[HORACE *Odes* 4. 9. 25 *Vixere fortes ante Agamemnona Multi.* Many brave men lived before Agamemnon.] *a.* **1637** JONSON *Underwoods* xii There were brave men before Ajax or Idomen, or all the store that Homer brought to Troy. **1898** G. W. E. RUSSELL *Coll. & Rec.* xiv Brave men have lived since as well as before Agamemnon. **1902** DEAN HOLE *Then & Now* (ed. 7) ix. 116 *Vixere fortes ante Agamemnona*—there was splendid cricket before Grace. **1910** *Times, Wkly.* 21 Jan. Of the *fortes ante Agamemnona,* . . . those Hammurabi, Burnaburiash, Ribaddi, Khuenaten, and even 'Ozymandias, King of Kings', what a happy notion we have!

Brawling booteth[1] not.

1546 HEYWOOD II. ii. 47 Braulyng booted not . . . Alone to bed she went. [[1] profiteth.]

Bray, *see* Vicar of B.

Bray(s, eth) *(verb), see* All men say you are an ass (When), time to b.; Ass that b. against another ass.

Braying of an ass does not reach heaven, The.

1802 WOLCOT (P. Pindar) *Ld. B. & his Motions* Wks. (1816) IV. 236 There is a certain and true saying, Of animals inclin'd to *braying;* . . . 'An ass's voice ne'er reached to Heav'n.'

Brayton bargh, and Hambleton hough, and Burton bream, were all in thy belly, If | it would never be team.[1]

1670 RAY 257 (*Yorks.*) . . . It is spoken of a covetous and unsatiable person, whom nothing will content. *Brayton* and *Hambleton* and *Burton* are places between *Cawood* and *Pontefraict* in this County. *Brayton Bargh* is a small hill. [[1] full.]

Bread and circuses.

[JUVENAL *Sat.* 10. 80 *Duas tantum res anxius optat, Panem et Circenses.* Two things only they earnestly desire, bread and the games of the circus.] **1930** *Times* 11 Nov. 15/4 Processions are good things, and there is never a better time for the circuses than when the bread is dear or scarce.

Bread, butter, and green cheese, is very good English, and very good Friese.

1869 HAZLITT 100.

Bread in one hand, and a stone in the other, You show.

1539 TAVERNER (1545) D1ᵛ *Altera manu fert lapidem, panem ostendit altera.* He beareth a stone in yᵉ one hande, and breade in the other. **1732** FULLER no. 5994.

Bread is buttered on both sides, His.

1678 RAY 232 . . . i.e. He hath a plentiful estate: he is fat and full. **1732** FULLER no. 6044. **1837** LOCKHART *Scott* (1839) i. 206 *note* Wherever Walter goes he is pretty sure to find his bread buttered on both sides.

Bread is the staff of life.

1638 PENKETHMAN *Artach.* A j 6 Bread is worth all, being the Staffe of life. **1704** SWIFT *T. Tub* iv Wks. (1856) I. 105 'Bread', says he, 'dear brothers, is the staff of life.'

Bread men break is broke to them again, What.

1613 DEKKER *Strange Horse-Race* D 2 Such bread as he brake, was but broken to him againe. **1630** TAYLOR (Water-Poet) *Wks.* 2nd pagin. 186.

Bread (Cake) never falls but on its buttered side, The.

1871 *N. & Q.* 4th Ser. VIII. 506 Lancashire Proverbs.—Unlucky persons often remark, 'My cake always falls the butter side down'. **1891** J. L. KIPLING *Beast & Man* 246 We express the completeness of ill-luck by saying, 'The bread never falls but on its buttered side.'

Bread than need, Who hath no more | must not keep a dog.

[L. *Teipsum non alens, canes alis.* Unable to keep yourself, you are keeping dogs.] **1640** HERBERT 322.

Bread and butter, *see* No other meat (They that have); Quarrel with one's b. and b.

Bread, *see also* Acorns were good till b.; Another's b. costs dear; Ask for b. and be given stone; Better b. than is made of wheat; Buying of b. undoes us; Dry b. at home better than; Eat white b. (When shall we); Eaten b. soon forgotten; Every day brings its b.; Fasteth and . . . , spares his b. and goes to hell; Fire is half b.; Griefs with b. are less; Knows on which side b. buttered; Likes not the drink (Who), God deprives of b.; Loveth well sheep's flesh that wets b. in wool; New beer, new b. . . . make hair grow through hood; Second side of b. less time to toast; Take the b. out of one's mouth; Wine by savour, b. by colour. *See also* Brown bread.

Break a butterfly upon the wheel, To.

[To break on the wheel was a punishment for extreme criminals.] **1735** POPE *Prol. Sat.* 308

Who breaks a butterfly upon a wheel? 1889 GOSSE *18th Cent. Lit.* 113 The unfairness of breaking such an exquisite butterfly of art on the wheel of his analysis. 1909 *Times Lit. Sup.* 26 Nov. To dissect in cold blood these specimens of buoyant geniality seems like breaking butterflies upon a wheel.

Break a hog of an ill custom, It is hard to.

1678 RAY 154.

Break a horse's back, be he never so strong, You may.

1639 CLARKE 311.

Break a pasture makes a man; To | to make a pasture breaks a man.

1922 *Spectator* 28 Oct. Much arable land is unsuitable for pasture, and . . . the work of bringing it down to decent pasture would be long and expensive. . . . 'To break a pasture makes a man; to make a pasture breaks a man'.

Break his neck as his fast, A man shall as soon.

1546 HEYWOOD I. xi. 33 In that house commonly such is the cast, A man shall as soone breake his necke as his fast. 1597–8 BP. HALL *Satires* v. ii House-keeping's dead, Saturio: wot'st thou where? Forsooth, they say far hence, in Breck-neck shire. And, ever since, they say, that feel and laste, That men may break their neck soon as their fast. 1641 FERGUSSON 112 Ye will break your neck and your fast alike in his house.

Break one's head and bring a plaster, To.

c. 1430 LYDGATE *Minor Poems* (Percy Soc.) 56 To heke myn hede, and yeve me an houffe. . . . It may wele ryme, but it accordith nought. 1580 LYLY *Euph. & his Eng.* (Arb.) 324 A plaister is a small amends for a broken head. 1608 ARMIN *Nest. Nin.* (Shak. Soc.) 48 The . . . jester . . . lay in durance a great while, till Will Sommers was faine, after he broke his head, to giue him a plaister, to get him out againe. [*a.* 1618] In 1662 FULLER (*Essex*) I. 506 Whilst master of the college, he chanced to punish all the under-graduates therein. . . . The money . . . was expended in new whiting the hall of the college. Whereupon a scholar hung up these verses on the screen: 'Doctor Jegon, Bennet College master, Brake the scholars' heads, and gave the walls a plaister.' 1639 CLARKE 17 He broke my head, and then gave me a plaister. 1738 SWIFT (Dial. i) 341 *Miss.* What! you break my head, and give me a plaster. 1816 J. AUSTEN *Persuasion* xiii 'This is breaking a head and giving a plaster, truly!'

Break, or wear out, If things did not | how would tradesmen live?

1738 SWIFT (Dial. i) 335 *Lady A.* How came you to break your cup? . . . *Lady S.* Why, if things did not break, or wear out, how would tradesmen live?

Break Priscian's head, To.

[= to violate the rules of grammar. Priscian was a Latin grammarian of the 6th cent.] *a.* 1529 SKELTON *Speke, Parrot* in Wks. (Dyce) II. 9 Prisians hed broken now handy dandy. 1589 *Puttenham* (Arb.) 258 *Solecismus . . .* the breaking of Priscian's head. 1594–5 SHAKS. *L.L.L.* V. i. 31 *Nath.* Laus Deo bone intelligo. *Hol. Bone?* bone, for *bene*: Priscian a little scratched; 'twill serve. 1642 FULLER *Holy State* 'Hildegardis' Throwing words at random she never brake Priscian's head. 1663 BUTLER *Hudibras* II. ii. 225 And hold no sin so deeply red As that of breaking Priscian's head. 1728 POPE *Dunciad* iii. 162 Break Priscian's head and Pegasus's neck. 1785 CUMBERLAND *Observer* No. 22, § 6 Observe, how this . . . orator breaks poor Priscian's head for the good of his country. 1785 GROSE *Dict. Vulg. T.* Priscian . . . was so devoted to his favourite study, that to speak false Latin in his company was as disagreeable to him, as to break his head. 1883 *Daily Tel.* 10 Jul. 5/4 Does Shakespeare never break Priscian's head?

Break the egg in anybody's pocket, To.

[= to spoil his plan.] *a.* 1734 NORTH *Exam.* 324 This very circumstance . . . broke the egg . . . in the Pockets of the Whigs.

Break the ice, To.

[= to make a beginning: to break through cold reserve or stiffness.] 1540 PALSGRAVE *Acolastus* (Carver) 31 Philautus . . . cutteth asunder that yee . . . breaketh the way before hym. 1571 L.H. *Dict. French and English* 'To the Reader' Commendable as either breaketh the yce vnto the better seeing, or treadeth the path to the discret and cunning. 1579–80 NORTH *Plutarch* (1676) 89 To be the first to break the Ice of the Enterprize. 1593–4 SHAKS. *Tam. Shrew* I. ii. 270 If you break the ice, and do this feat, Achieve the elder, set the younger free For our access. 1646 J. COOKE *Vind. Prof. Law* To Rdr. I have attempted to break the Ice in a subject concerning reformation in Courts of Justice. 1678 BUTLER *Hudibras* III. i. 493 After he had a while look'd wise, At last broke silence, and the ice. 1741 RICHARDSON *Pamela* (1824) I. ix. 246 You see . . . that I break the ice, and begin first in the indispensably expected correspondence between us. 1893 EARL DUNMORE *Pamirs* I. 226 The ice being thus broken, Ching Dolai put aside the reserve habitual to all Celestials.

Break house, *see* See you in daylight (They that) winna b. the h. for you.

Break(s, eth), broke(n), *see also* Better bend than b.; Cord b. at last by weakest pull; Fair words b. no bones; Pot broken (Your) seems better than my whole; Sung well before he b. shoulder; Thread b. where weakest; Tom pitcher's broken (When), I shall have shards; Too much b. the bag.

Breakfast, *see* Fast for my life (If I were to), I would take good b.; Hare to b. (He that will have).

Breams in his pond, He that hath | is able to bid his friend welcome.

1653 WALTON *Angler* I. x (1915) 165 The French esteem this fish highly, and to that end have this proverb, 'He that hath Breams in his pond, is able to bid his friend welcome'.

Breard[1] like midding[2] breard, There is no.

1721 KELLY 328 *There is no breard like midding breard.* The grains of corn that are carried out unto the dunghill takes root and springs amain; spoken when we see people of mean birth rise suddenly to wealth and honour. [[1] young corn. [2] dung-hill.]

Breast, *see* Thorn against the b.

Breath, One man's | another's death.

1639 CLARKE 253 *Pestilentia.* One man's breath, another's death.

Breath, *see also* First b. is beginning of death; Keep your b. to cool.

Bred in Brasen-Nose College, You were.

[= a play upon the name of a college at Oxford, to denote a person of much assurance.] **1732** FULLER no. 6011.

Bred in the bone will not out of the flesh, What is.

[c. **1290** *Wright's Polit. Songs* (Camd. Soc.) 167 *Osse radicatum raro de carne recedit.*] **1481** CAXTON *Reynard* xii (Arb.) 29 He coude not refrayne hym self that whiche cleuid by the bone myght not out of the flesshe. **1546** HEYWOOD II. viii. 72 This prouerbe prophecied many yeres agone. It will not out of the fleshe that is bred in the bone. **1603** FLORIO tr. *Montaigne* III. xiii (1897) VI. 250 They are effects of custom and use; and *what is bred in the bone, will never out of the flesh.* **1719** DEFOE *Crusoe* (1840) II. i. 1 What is bred in the bone will not go out of the flesh. **1721** KELLY 179 *It is ill to bring out of the flesh that is bred in the bone.* It is hard to leave those ill customs which we have been long inured. **1912** ALEX. MACLAREN *Romans* 231 'You cannot expel nature with a fork', said the Roman. 'What's bred in the bone won't come out of the flesh', says the Englishman.

Bredon-hill puts on his hat, When | ye men of the vale, beware of that.

1869 HAZLITT 474 Bredon-hill is in Worcestershire; the 'hat' is of course . . . the heavy cloud which covers the apex of the hill previously to heavy rain or a thunderstorm.

Breech makes buttons, His (My).

1562–3 *Jack Juggler* in HAZL. *O.E.P.* II. 121 His arse meketh buttons now, and who lusteth to feel, Shall find his heart creeping out at his heel. **1618–19** J. FLETCHER *Bonduca* II. iii. **1670** RAY 165 . . . This is said of a man in fear. . . . Vehement fear causes a relaxation of the *Sphincter ani* and un-voluntary dejection. **1702** *Mouse grown Rat* 23 My Breech began to make Buttons; I dreamt of nothing but Impeachments.

Breech(es), *see also* Breeze in one's b. (To have a); Master wears no b. (Most); Scratch my b.; Wear the b.

Breed in the mud, All that | are not efts (eels).

1580 LYLY *Euph. & his Eng.* Wks. (Bond) II. 89 All things that breede in the mudde, are not Euets. **1732** FULLER no. 549 (with 'eels').

Breed of Lady Mary, You | when you're good you're o'er good.

1721 KELLY 363 . . . A drunken man beg'd Lady Mary to help him on his horse, and having made many attempts to no purpose, . . . at length he jump'd quite over. O *Lady Mary* (said he) *when thou art good, thou art o'er good.*

Breed of the chapman, You | you are never out of your gate.[1]

1721 KELLY 363 . . . Spoken to them that make wherever they go. [[1] way.]

Breed of the good man's mother, You | you are aye in the gate.[1]

1721 KELLY 364 . . . Spoken to them that are in our way. Taken from the ill understanding that is often between mothers in law, and daughters in law. **1862** HISLOP 280 The gude man's mither is aye in the gait. [[1] way.]

Breed of the gowk (cuckoo), Ye | ye have not a rhyme but ane.

1591 FLORIO *Sec. Frutes* 39 Thou haste it euer in thy mouth, even as the cuckoo song. **1641** FERGUSSON 112 We [*sic*] breid of the gouk, ye have not a ryme but ane. **1721** KELLY 362 *You breed of the Gouke, you have ay but one Song.* Spoken to them that always insist upon one thing.

Breed of the miller's daughter, that speered[1] what tree groats[2] grew on, You.

1721 KELLY 364 . . . Spoken when saucy fellows, bred of mean parentage, pretend ignorance of what they were bred with. [[1] inquired. [2] husked oats.]

Breed of the miller's dog, Ye | ye lick your mouth (lips) ere the poke be open.

1641 FERGUSSON 112. **1721** KELLY 361 . . . Spoken to covetous people, who are eagerly expecting a thing, and ready to receive it, before it be proffered.

Breed of the tod's[1] bairns, You | if one be good, all are good.

1721 KELLY 361 . . . Spoken of a bad family, where there are none to mend another. [[1] fox.]

Breed, breeding (*noun*), *see also* Beware of b.; Birth is much, b. is more.

Breed(s), bred (*verb*), *see also* Spins well who b. her children; Where one is b. but . . . (Not).

Breeks, *see* Petticoats woo (When), b. may come speed; Sits full still that has riven b.; Taking the b. off a Hielandman (Ill); Tarry b. pays no fraught.

Breeze in one's breech, To have a.

c. 1630 BEAUM. & FL. *Monsieur Thomas* IV. vi. (A) What, is the breeze in your breech? 1678 RAY 232 To have a breez, i.e. a gad-fly, in his breech. Spoken of one that frisks about, and cannot rest in a place.

Breeze, *see also* Whistle for b.

Brevity is the soul of wit.

1600–1 SHAKS. *Hamlet* II. ii. 90 Brevity is the soul of wit. 1829–30 M. SCOTT *T. Cring. Log* xvi Brevity is the soul of wit,—ahem. 1853 TRENCH i. 8 Brevity, 'the soul of wit', will be eminently the soul of a proverb's wit.

Brew good ale, Blessing of your heart, you.

1594–5 SHAKS. *Two Gent.* III. i. 309 *Speed. Item, She brews good ale. Launce.* And thereof comes the proverb, 'Blessing of your heart, you brew good ale.'

Brew, As they | so let them bake (drink).

c. 1300 *Cursor M.* 1. 2848 Suilk als þai brued now ha þai dronken. *c.* 1350 *Douce MS. 52* no. 97 So brewe, so drynke. *c.* 1390 GOWER *Conf. Amantis* iii. 161 And who so wicked alé breweth Full ofte he mot the worsé drinke. *c.* 1410 *Towneley Plays, 2nd. Shep. Play* 501 Bot we must drynk as we brew. 1546 HEYWOOD I. viii. 15 As I woulde néedes brewe, so must I néedes drynke. 1599 PORTER *Angry Wom. Abingd.* III. ii (Merm.) 158 No, indeed; even as they brew, so let them bake. 1641 FERGUSSON 72 Let him drink as he hes browin. 1652 *Proc. Parliament* no. 138, 2162 The Admirall . . . said, that as they brewed so they should bake. 1721 KELLY 186 *If you brew well, you'll drink the better.* If what you have done be good, and right, you will find the effects accordingly.

Brew, *see also* Must be if we b. (This).

Brewer's horse hath bit, One whom the.

1597–8 SHAKS. *1 Hen. IV* III. iii. 9 An I have not forgotten what the inside of a church is made of, I am a peppercorn, a brewer's horse. 1635 T. HEYWOOD *Philocothonista* 44 To title a drunkard by, wee . . . strive to character him in a more mincing phrase; as thus . . . *One whom the Brewer's horse hath bit.* 1847 HALLIWELL *Dict.* s.v. 'Brewer's horse' A drunkard was sometimes said to be 'one whom the brewer's horse hath bit'. 1917

BRIDGE 100 . . . *One who has had a little too much liquor.*

Brewing, *see* Sairy b. that is not good in newing.

Briars, *see* Leave in the briers; Nip the b. in the bud.

Bribe, nor lose thy right, Neither.

1640 HERBERT 330.

Bribe will enter without knocking, A.

1616 DRAXE 19 A bribe entreth everywhere without knocking. 1639 CLARKE 220.

Bricks without straw, To make.

[Said with allusion to *Exodus* v.] 1616 DEKKER *Villainies Discovered* K 1ᵛ To compell thy Vassall to make more Bricke when strawe and stuffe is taken from him. 1621 BURTON *Anat. Mel.* I. ii. III. xv (1651) 140 Patrons . . . but (hard task-masters they prove) they take away their straw, and compel them to make their number of brick. 1658 *Verney Mem.* (1 907) II. 79 It is an hard task to make bricks without straw. 1661 DK. ORMONDE in *11th Rep. Hist. MSS. Comm.* App. v. 10 If they will not let that [act] passe . . . and yet will have us keepe armys, is it not requiring a tale of bricks, without allowing the straw. 1874 L. STEPHEN *Hours in Library* I. vi. 271 It is often good for us to have to make bricks without straw.

Bricks, *see also* Tale of b. is doubled (When), Moses comes.

Bridal, *see* Man be at his own b. (Meet that).

Bride goes to her marriage-bed, The | but knows not what shall happen to her.

1651 JER. TAYLOR *Holy Dying* I. i (Bohn) 303 Many brides have died . . . according to the saying of Bensirah, the wise Jew, 'The bride went into her chamber, and knew not what should befall her there'. 1678 RAY *Adag. Hebr.* 412 The bride goes to her marriage bed, but knows not what shall happen to her. The meaning is, that we ought not confidently to promise ourselves in any thing any great success.

Bride the sun shines on, and the corpse the rain rains on, Happy is the.

1607 *Puritan Widow* I. i Such a sweet husband have I lost, . . . !—If, Blessed be the corse the rain rains upon, he had it pouring down. 1648 HERRICK *Hesper.* 284 *A Nupt. Song* Blest is the Bride, on whom the Sun doth shine.

Bride, *see also* Bonny b. is soon buskit; Muck-hill on my trencher, quoth the b.; Simpers like a b.

Bridge of one's nose, To make a.

1678 RAY 231 . . . i.e. to intercept ones trencher, cup, or the like; or to offer . . .

kindnesses to one, and then . . . do it to another. *a.* **1700** B. E. *Dict. Cant. Crew* s.v. *You make a Bridge of his Nose,* when you pass your next Neighbour in Drinking or one is prefer'd over another's head. **1738** SWIFT (Dial. ii) 345 *Never.* Pray, my lord, don't make a bridge of my nose.

Bridge, *see also* Cross the b. (Don't) till you get to it; Golden b. (For flying enemy); Good turn will meet another . . . at B. of London; Head (He that will be) let him be b. ; Praise the b. he goes over (Let every man).

Bridges were made for wise men to walk over, and fools to ride over.

1678 RAY 106.

Bridle and spur that makes a good horse, It is the.

1642 TORRIANO 15. **1732** FULLER no. 3021.

Bridle, *see also* Bite upon the b. ; Reason lies between spur and b.; Shake a b. over Yorkshireman.

Bridport, *see* Stabbed with B. dagger.

Bright rain makes fools fain.

1883 ROPER 24. **1917** BRIDGE 162 (A) . . . When a rain-cloud is succeeded by a little brightness in the sky, fools rejoice and think it will soon be fair weather.

Bright that shines by himself, He is only.

1640 HERBERT 350.

Bright, *see also* Look at b. side.

Brill, *see* Deal, Dover, and Harwich, the devil gave.

Brim, *see* Better spare at b.

Brimmer, *see* Deceit in a b. (No).

Bring a cow to the hall and she'll run to the byre.[1]

1641 FERGUSSON 20 Bring a kow to the hall, and she will to the byre again. **1721** KELLY 86 *Drive a cow to the hall and she'll run to the bayer.* Spoken when people of mean breeding . . . do not take to, or become, a more honourable station. [1 cow-shed.]

Bring a noble (shilling) to ninepence, To.

1546 HEYWOOD II. V. 54 He maketh his marts with marchantis likely, To bryng a shillyng to ix. pens quickely. **1568** FULWELL *Like Will to L.* in HAZL. *O.E.P.* (1874) III. 344 For why Tom Tosspot since he went hence, Hath increased a noble just unto nine-pence. **1668** SHADWELL *Sullen Lov.* v. iii (Merm.) 112 I should soon bring a noble to ninepence then, as they say. **1670** RAY 187 To bring a noble to ninepence, and ninepence to nothing. **1721** KELLY 144 He has brought his Noble to Ninepence, and his Nine Pence to nothing (English.)

5017

Bring an abbey to a grange,[1] To.

c. **1480** *Early Miscell.* (Warton Cl. 1855) 26 (A) And nowe that abbay is turned to a grange. *c.* **1548** BALE *K. Johan* 579 *Clargy.* Our changes are soche that an abbeye turneth over horse or male. **1670** RAY 161 . . . We speak it of an unthrift. [1 a country-house.]

Bring an old house on one's head, To.

[= To get oneself into trouble.] *c.* **1566** *The Bugbears* I. ii. **1576** GASCOIGNE *Wks* (Cunliffe) II. 548 My Boye quod he who badd the be so bolde As for to plucke an olde howse on thy hedd? **1608** TOPSELL *Serpents* (1658) 658 You shall pull an old house over your own head by a further provocation. **1670** RAY 188. **1739** J. HILDROP *Regul. Freethinking* 7 He . . . will have good Luck if he does not pull an old House upon his head.

Bring but that's no there ben, It is ill to.

1641 FERGUSSON 62 It is ille to bring butte the thing that is not there benne. **1721** KELLY 194 *It is ill to bring butt, that's no there benn.* One cannot produce what he has not. [*Footnote.* Butt is towards the door. Benn is into the house.]

Bring haddock to paddock, To.

[= to come to destitution.] **1546** HEYWOOD II. X. 82 And thus had he brought haddocke to paddocke. Till they both were not woorth a haddocke. **1577** STANYHURST *Descr. Irel.* in *Holinshed* (1807–8) VI. 23 I had bene like to have brought haddocke to paddocke.

Bring home the wealth of the Indies, He who would | must carry the wealth of the Indies with him.

1778 JOHNSON in *Boswell* (1848) lxv. 597 As the Spanish proverb says, 'He who would bring home the wealth of the Indies must carry the wealth of the Indies with him'. So it is in travelling; a man must carry knowledge with him, if he would bring home knowledge. **1882** J. NICHOL *Amer. Lit.* 6 We can only gather interest on the capital we take with us. 'He that would bring home the wealth of the Indies must carry out the wealth of the Indies.'

Bringeth himself into needless dangers, He that | dieth the devil's martyr.

1639 FULLER *Holy War* II. xxix (1840) Nor will I listen to the unhappy Dutch proverb, 'He that bringeth himself into needless dangers, dieth the devil's martyr'. **1678** RAY 18 Who perisheth in needless danger is the devil's martyr.

Brings good news, He that | knocks hard.

1623 WODROEPHE 487 He knocks boldy at

F

the Gate that brings good Newes in there at. **1640** HERBERT 355.

Brings up his son to nothing, breeds a thief, He that.

1732 FULLER no. 2053.

Bring, *see also* Come with me (If wilt), b. with thee; Evils we b. on ourselves; Take what you find or what you b.; Welcome that b. (They are).

Bristles, *see* Expect of a hog but b. (What can you).

Bristol milk.

1644 PRYNNE & WALKER *Fiennes' Trial* 78 Good store of Bristoll milk, strong wines and waters. **1662** FULLER s.v. 'Bristol' Bristol Milk, (a Prov.) or Sherry-sack. **1848** MACAULAY *Hist. Engl.* I. 335 A rich beverage made of the best Spanish wine and celebrated . . . as Bristol Milk.

Bristol, *see also* Shipshape and B. fashion.

Britain, All countries stand in need of.

1577 W. HARRISON *Descr. of England* (New Sh. S.) ii. 70 It was not said of old time without great reason, that all countries haue need of Britaine, and Britaine itselfe of none. **1580** LYLY *Euph. & his Eng.* (Arb.) 439 (A) Whereof there was an olde saying, all countries stand in neede of Britaine, and Britaine of none.

Britain, *see also* Little B.

Broadgates in Oxford, *see* Verdingales.

Broke his hour that kept his day, He never.

1678 RAY 122.

Broken apothecary, a new doctor, A.

1670 RAY 2.

Broken bones well set become stronger.

1579 LYLY *Euphues* (Arb.) 58 Doth not he remember that the broken bone once set together, is stronger than euer it was? **1597–8** SHAKS. *2 Hen. IV* IV. i. 222 Our peace will, like a broken limb united, Grow stronger for the breaking. **1612** WEBSTER *White Devil* II. i Like bones which, broke in sunder, and well set, knit the more strongly. **1651** WALTON *Sir H. Wotton* in *Lives* (Dent) I. 156 As broken bones well set become stronger, so Sir Henry Wotton did not only recover, but was much more confirmed in his Majesty's estimation.

Broken friendship may be soldered, but will never be sound, A.

1613 R. DALLINGTON *Aphorisms* 201 Friendship once broken is hardly peeced, And peeced Enmity neuer surely sodred. **1732** FULLER no 27.

Broken her elbow, She hath.

1678 RAY 241 She hath broken her elbow. That is, she hath had a bastard.

Broken her elbow at the church (kirk) door, She hath.

1678 RAY 230 She hath broken her elbow at the Church door. Spoken of a housewively maid that grows idle after marriage. **1721** KELLY 293 *She broke her elbow at the kirk door.* Spoken of a thrifty maiden, when she becomes a lazy wife.

Broken her leg above the knee, She hath.

1618 J. FLETCHER *Loyal Subject* III. v (C.U.P.) II. 130 If her foot slip and down fall she, and break her leg 'bove the knee. **1678** RAY 256 She hath broken her leg above the knee, i.e. had a bastard.

Broken reed, To lean upon a (or trust to a broken staff).

[**1611** BIBLE *Isaiah* xxxvi. 6 Lo, thou trustest in the staff of this broken reed, on Egypt; whereon if a man lean, it will go into his hand, and pierce it.] **1509** A. BARCLAY *Ship of Fools* (1874) I. 271 That man . . . lenyth his body vpon a rede. **1580** H. GIFFORD *Posie* (Gros.) 71 To trust her lookes . . . Is nothing els but trust a broken staffe. **1757** SMOLLETT *Reprisal* I. i You lean upon a broken reed, if you trust to their compassion.

Broken sack will hold no corn, A.

1573 SANDFORD A broken bagge can hold no mill. **1611** COTGRAVE s.v. 'Sac' A sacke that's torne, doth shed its corne. **1639** CLARKE 133.

Broken sleeve holdeth the arm back, A.

c. **1470** *Harl. MS. 3362* For my slefe y broke—*Pro manica fracta manus est mea sepe redacta.* *a.* **1530** *R. Hill's Commonpl. Bk.* (E.E.T.S.) 132 For my brokyn sleve, men me refuce—*Pro manica fracta, manus mea est sepe retracta.* **1550** HEYWOOD I. ix. 17 A broken sléeue holdth tharme backe. And shame holdth me backe. **1625** JONSON *Staple of News* I. ii And therefore you've another answering proverb, *A broken sleeve keeps the arm back.*

Broken, *see also* Ship (As b. a) has come to land.

Broo, *see* Ill flesh ne'er made good b.

Brook the weather that love not the wind, Many can.

1594–5 SHAKS. *L.L.L.* IV. ii. 34 *Nath.* Being of an old Father's mind, Many can brook the weather that love not the wind.

Broom, *see* Bestows his gifts as b. honey; Furze (Under the) is . . . , under the b. is silver and gold; New b. sweeps clean.

Broomstick (Besom), To jump (or marry over) the.

[= to go through a *quasi*-marriage ceremony,

in which the parties jump over a broom-stick.] **1774** *Westmr. Mag.* II. 16 He had no inclination for a Broomstick-marriage. **1824** MACAULAY *Misc. Writ.* (1860) I. 95 They were married over a broomstick. **1876** BLACKMORE *Cripps* xix Three or four score of undergraduates . . . had offered her matrimony, and three or four newly elected fellows were asking whether they would vacate, if they happened to jump the broomstick.

Brosten, *see* Welly b.

Broth, *see* Beef (Such), such b.; Boils his pot with chips, makes b. smell of smoke; Cold b. hot again; Eat the devil as the b. (As good); Good b. in old pot; No b. no ball; Sup Simon, here's good b.

Brother had rather see the sister rich than make her so, The.

1611 COTGRAVE s.v. 'Frere' The brother would have his sister rich anyway, but at his own charges. **1678** RAY 203.

Brother, *see also* Younger brother.

Brought an ill comb to my own head, I have.

1721 KELLY 204 . . . That is, I have engaged myself in a troublesome business.

Brown bread, *see* Ask of my fire b. b. (I had rather); Eat your b. b. first; Good small beer, good b. b. (No such thing as).

Brown man, *see* Red man (To a) read thy rede.

Brown study, To be in a.

[= a state of mental abstraction.] *c.* **1300** ROBERT OF BRUNNE tr. LANGTOFT's *Chronicle* (Hearne) 58 (A) Whan Edward perceyued, his herte was in studie. *c.* **1386** CHAUCER *Knight's T.* l. 672 (A) Into a studie he fil sodeynly. **1552** *Dice-Play* 6 Lack of company will soon lead a man into a brown study. **1579** LYLY *Euphues* (Arb.) 80 You are in some brown study, what coulours you might best weare for your Lady. **1712** STEELE *Spect.* No. 286, par. 3 He often puts me into a brown Study how to answer him. **1871** BLACKIE *Four Phases* i. 13 He had been standing there in a brown study.

Browse, *see* Goat must b. where tied.

Brugh, *see* Round the moon there is a b. (When).

Bruit, *see* Much b. little fruit.

Brummagem, *see* Sutton.

Brush, *see* Bought a b. (He has).

Bubble, *see* Man is a b.

Buchanan's almanac, long foul, long fair.

1721 KELLY 69 . . . When weather continues long of one sort, it commonly continues as long of the contrary, when it changes.

Buck of the first head, He is like a.

[**1606** *Return from Parnassus* (Arb.) 30 Now sir, a Bucke the first yeare is a Fawne; the second year a Pricket, The third yeare a Sorell, the fourth yeare a Soare, the fift a Bucke of the first head, the sixt yeare a compleat Buck.] **1678** RAY 67 . . . Brisk, pert, forward. Some apply it to upstart gentlemen.

Buck's horn, *see* Blow the b. h.

Bucket, *see* Kick the b.; Rope in after b. (Throw).

Buckets in a well, Like.

c. **1386** CHAUCER *Knight's T.* l. 675 (A) Now in the croppe, now doun in the breres, Now up, now doun, as boket in a well. **1597** SHAKS. *Rich. II* IV. i. 183 That bucket down and full of tears am I, Drinking my griefs, while you are up on high. **1606** DAY *Ile of Gulls* II. iii Demetrius and Lysander in their hopes and despairs. *a.* **1697** AUBREY *Life of Robert Saunderson* Had his memorie been greater, his judgement had been lesse: they are like two well-bucketts.

Bucking, *see* Smocks than shirts in a b. (He that hath more).

Buckingham, *see* Old man who weds . . . freeman of B.

Buckinghamshire bread and beef: here if you beat a bush it's odds you'll start a thief.

1613–22 DRAYTON *Polyolb.* xxiii. 247 Wks. (1876) III. 95 Rich *Buckingham* doth bear the term of *Bread and Beef,* Where if you beat a Bush, 'tis odds you start a thief. **1662** FULLER (*Bucks.*) I. 194 'Buckinghamshire bread and beef.' The former is as fine, the latter as fat, in this as in any other county. . . . 'Here if you beat a bush, it's odds you'ld start a thief.' . . . But this proverb is now antiquated.

Buckle and bare thong, To come to.

[= to be stripped of everything.] **1546** HEYWOOD II. viii. 73 Little and little he decaied so long, Tyll he at length came to buckle and bare thong. **1678** RAY 232 To bring buckle and thong together.

Buckle and thong.

1599 NASHE (McKerrow) III. 168 As the buckle to the thong. **1631** MABBE *Celestina* (A) Mother and I were nayle and flesh, buckle and thong.

Buckle and thong, *see also* Hold him to it.

Buckle for it, Let them.

1678 RAY 352. *Somerset.*

Buckle, *see also* Angry (If you be) you may turn the b.

Bucklers, To give (one) the.

[= to yield.] **1592** GREENE *Second Pt. of Cony-catching* (Harrison) 12 His maister laught, and was glad . . . to yeeld the bucklers to his prentise, and to become frends. **1598–9** SHAKS. *Much Ado* V. ii. 17 I give thee the bucklers. **1629** T. ADAMS *Serm.* (1861) I. 496 He vies vanities with the slothful, and it is hard to say who wins the game; yet give him the bucklers.

Bucklers, *see also* Take up the cudgels (b.).

Bucklersbury[1] in simple-time, Like.

1600–1 SHAKS. *Merry W.* III. iii. 79 *Fal.* These . . . that come like women in men's apparel, and smell like Bucklersbury in simple-time. [[1] a street in London formerly inhabited chiefly by druggists selling simples, or herbs.]

Buckles his belt his ain gate,[1] Every man.

1721 KELLY 92 *Every man wears his belt in his own fashion.* An apology for a man's acting differently from others. **1818** SCOTT *Ht. Midl.* xxviii Aweel, lass, . . . then thou must pickle in thine own poke-nook, and buckle thy girdle thine ain gate. [[1] way.]

Buffet, *see* Bit and the b. with it (Take the).

Bug, *see* Snug as a b.

Build sandy bowrocks[1] together, We will never.

1721 KELLY 356 . . . That is, we will never be cordial or familiar together. [[1] children's sand-castles.]

Build two chimneys, It is easier to | than to maintain one.

1640 HERBERT 358. **1757** FRANKLIN Jan. 'Tis easier to build two Chimneys than maintain one in Fuel.

Buildeth his house all of sallows, Who that | and pricketh his blind horse over the fallows, and suffereth his wife to go seek hallows,[1] is worthy to be hanged on the gallows.

c. **1386** CHAUCER *W. of Bath's Prol.* D 654 Than wolde he seye right thus, with-outen doute, 'Who-so that buildeth his hous al of salwes, And priketh his blinde hors over the falwes, And suffreth his wyf to go seken halwes, Is worthy to been hanged on the galwes!' **1417** *Reliq. Antiquae* (1841) i. 233 (A) (last line reads, 'God sende hym the blisse of everlasting galos'). [[1] make pilgrimages to shrines.]

Building and marrying of children are great wasters.

1611 COTGRAVE s.v. 'Abandon' The building of houses and making of feasts, are unlimitted wasters of a mans substance. **1616** DRAXE 1 Building is chargeable. **1640** HERBERT 317 Building and marrying of children are great wasters. **1721** KELLY 60 Bigging, and bairns marrying are great wasters.

Building churches, *see* Foreheet nothing but b. c.

Building is a sweet impoverishing.

1602–3 MANNINGHAM *Diary* (Camden Soc.) 9 The proverbe is that building is a thiefe, because it makes us lay out more money than wee thought on. **1640** HERBERT 339.

Build(ing) (*verb*), *see also* Charges of b. are unknown; Patch and long sit, b. and soon flit; Pull down than b. (Easier to); Spirit of b. is come upon him.

Building(s) (*noun*), *see* Good b. without good foundation (No); High b. low foundation; Settling an island, the first b.

Builds a house by the highway side, He that | it is either too high or too low.

1670 RAY 106 . . . Chi fabrica la casa in piazza, ò che è troppo alta ò troppo bassa. *Ital.*

Builds on the people, builds on the dirt, He that.

1616 DRAXE 154 with 'buildeth on the mud'. **1641** JONSON *Timber* '*Principum Varia*' (A) Nor let the common proverb [as in lemma] discredit my opinion. **1666** TORRIANO 212.

Bujalance, *see* Piper of B. (Like the).

Bull beef, *see* Looks as big as . . . eaten b. b.

Bull in a china shop, A.

1834 MARRYAT *Jacob Faith.* xv Whatever it is that smashes, Mrs. T. always swears it was the *most valuable* thing in the room. I'm like a bull in a china-shop. **1863** KINGSLEY *Water Bab.* viii On went the giant . . . like a bull in a china-shop, till he ran into the steeple . . . and knocked the upper half clean off.

Bull's feather, *see* Wears the b.'s f.

Bull's foot, *see* Knows not a B from a b.'s f.

Bull, *see also* Bear a b. that hath borne a calf (He may); Bellows like a b.; Bloxwich b.; Farm full must keep . . . young b.; In time the savage b. bear yoke; Mad as b. of Stamford; Mad b. . . . tied with pack-thread; One dog one b.; Play with a b. till you get horn in eye; Red rag to b.; Take the b. by the horns.

'Bull' [on Stock Exchange], *see* Price is too low (No).

Bull-horn, *see* Show the b.

Bullet has its billet, Every.

1575 GASCOIGNE *Posies, Dulce Bel. Inexp.* (1907) 154 Sufficeth this to prove my theme withal, That every bullet hath a lighting place. **1765** WESLEY *Jrnl.* 6 June He never received one wound. So true is the odd saying of King William, that 'every bullet has its billet'. **1837** DICKENS *Pickwick* xix

It is an established axiom that 'every bullet has its billet'. **1846** J. GRANT *Rom. of War* xx 'Tis the fortune of war; every bullet has its billet—their fate to-day may be ours to-morrow.

Bullimong, *see* Play the devil in the b.

Bulls the cow must keep the calf, He that.

1580 LYLY *Euph. & his Eng.* Wks. (Bond) II. 175 To muse who should father my first childe, wer to doubt when the cowe is mine, who should owe the calfe. **1596–7** SHAKS. *K. John* I. i. 123 In sooth, good friend, your father might have kept This calf bred from his cow from all the world. **1659** HOWELL *Eng. Prov.* (Introd.) In our Common Law there are some Proverbs that carry a kind of authority with them, as that which began in Henry the Fourth's time, He that bulls the cow must keep the calf.

Bully is always a coward, A.

1817 EDGEWORTH *Ormond* xxiv Mrs. M'Crule, who like all other bullies was a coward, lowered her voice. **1826** LAMB *Elia* (in *New Month. Mag.*) Wks. (1898) 220 *Pop. Fal.* THAT A BULLY IS ALWAYS A COWARD. . . . Confront one of the silent heroes with the swaggerer of real life, and his confidence in the theory quickly vanishes. **1909** *Times* (Wkly.) 16 July Like many bullies, it is . . . a coward. A wolf . . . will cower and suffer itself to be killed.

Bulrush, *see* Bellows like a bull, weak as b.; Knot in a b. (Seek).

Bumsted, *see* Crack me that nut.

Bunch, *see* Mother B.

Bungay, *see* Castle of B.

Bung-hole, *see* Spare at the spigot.

Bunny, *see* Course be fair (If), quoth B.

Bunting, *see* Goshawk beats not at b.

Burbolt, *see* Brain as a b. (As much).

Burd(s), *see* Hen goes to the cock (When), b. may gen a knock.

Burden, It is not the | but the over-burden that kills the beast.

1823 COLLINS 231 *No mata la carga sino la sobrecarga*. . . . **1832** HENDERSON 82.

Burdens, The greatest | are not the gainfullest.

1670 RAY 4. **1721** KELLY 336 . . . That is, they who labour sorest, have not the best wages.

Burden(s) (Burthen), *see also* Ass endures his b.; God shapes back for b.; Knows the weight of another's b. (None); Light b. far heavy; Respect the b.; Sad b. to carry dead man's child. *See also* Burthen.

Burford bait.

[= drink.] **1636** TAYLOR (Water-Poet) *Cat. of Taverns* 58 in Wks. 4th Coll. (Spens. Soc.) (A) Beware of a Burfourd bayt, for it may brew the staggers. **1662** FULLER (*Oxon.*) III. 5 'To take a Burford bait.' This . . . is a bait, not to stay the stomach but to lose the wit thereby, as resolved at last into drunkenness.

Burn[1] daylight, To.

c. **1560** *Apius & Virginia* HAZLITT's Dodsley IV. 121. *c.* **1566** *The Bugbears* IV. iii. 21. **1592** KYD *Span. Trag.* (Boas) III. xiia. 29 *Ilier.* Light me your torches then. *Ped.* Then we burne day light. **1594–5** SHAKS. *Rom. & Jul.* I. iv. 43 Come, we burn daylight, ho! . . . I mean, sir, in delay We waste our lights in vain, like lamps by day. **1600–1** *Merry W.* II. i. 54 We burn daylight: here, read, read. **1738** SWIFT (Dial. iii) 352 *Lady A.* No candles yet, I beseech you; don't let us burn daylight. [[1] waste.]

Burn does not babble, When the | it's either ower toom[1] or ower fu'.

1832 HENDERSON 94. [[1] empty.]

Burn his house to warm his hands, He will.

1481 CAXTON *Reynard* (Arb.) 78 They retche not whos[e] hows brenneth so that they may warme them by the coles. **1640** HERBERT 331.

Burn one candle to seek another, To.

1579 GOSSON *Sch. Abuse* (Arb.) 41 I gaue my self to that exercise in hope to thriue but I burnt one candle to seek another, and lost bothe my time and my trauell, when I had doone.

Burn one house to warm another, To.

1881 JESSOPP *Arcady* 28 Such as have pulled down three or four farmhouses and thrown the fields into one large holding . . . may find that it was an evil day for them when they began to 'burn one house to warm another'.

Burn one's boats, To.

[= to commit oneself irrevocably to a course.] **1877** V. L. CAMERON *Across Africa* I. 313 When on the other side I intended—metaphorically speaking—to 'burn my boats', so that there should be no retreating or looking back. **1927** *Times* 26 Aug. 8/1 Burning one's boats, which is often quoted as a sign of strength, is, in essence, much more a sign of weakness.

Burn one's house to get rid of the mice, To.

1629 T. ADAMS *Serm.* (1861–2) I. 434 The empiric to cure the fever, destroys the patient; so the wise man, to burn the mice, set on fire his barn. *a.* **1816** WOLCOT (P. Pindar) *2nd Ep. to Mrs. Clarke* Wks. (1816) IV. 446 Who, but a Bedlamite, would fire his house, To wreak his vengeance on a pilfering mouse? **1865** G. MACDONALD *Alec Forbes* lxxxiii But ye needna burn the hoose to rid the rottans.[1] [[1] rats.]

Burn (Light) the candle at both ends, To.

1592 BACON *Promus* (Potts) no. 1504 To waste that realm as a candle which is lighted at both ends. **1678** RAY 72 A good fellow lights his candle at both ends. **1730** BAILEY *Dict.* s.v. The Candle burns at both Ends. Said when Husband and Wife are both Spendthrifts. **1753** HANWAY *Trav.* (1762) II. I. iii. 19 Apt to light their candle at both ends ; that is to say, they are apt to consume too much, and work too little. **1857** KINGSLEY *Two Yrs. Ago* x By sitting up till two in the morning, and rising again at six. . . . Frank Headley burnt the candle of life at both ends.

Burn the midnight oil, To.

1650 G. DANIEL *Trinarch.*, *Crastini Anim.* 16 As were that worth our Braines, and Midnight Oyle. **1727** GAY *Fables* Introd. 15 Whence is thy learning ? Hath thy toil O'er books consumed the midnight oil?

Burn you for a witch, They that | will lose their coals.

1681 S. COLVIL *Whiggs Sup. Auth. Apol.* I commend their zeal, but not their wisdom ; and who ever shall take the pains to burn them for witches, will lose both coals and labour. **1721** KELLY 332 . . . Eng. *No body will take you for a conjurer.* **1732** FULLER no. 4974. **1816** SCOTT *Antiq.* xvii 'They would burn me, . . . for one great conjurer'. 'They would cast away their coals then', said Oldbuck.

Burn (*noun*), *see* Drink of the b. when cannot bite of brae; Wish the b. dry because it weets our feet.

Burned one candle to St. Michael and another to the Dragon, Like the old woman who.

1603 FLORIO tr. *Montaigne* III. i (1897) V. 5 I could easily for a need, bring a candle to Saint Michael, and another to his Dragon, as the good old woman. I will follow the best side to the fire, but not into it, if I can choose.

Burning, *see* Thole well is good for b.

Burns his house, He that | warms himself for once.

1640 HERBERT 331.

Burns most, He that | shines most.

1640 HERBERT 344. **1852** E. FITZGERALD *Polonius* 84 'He that burns most shines most'. A loving heart is the beginning of all knowledge.

Burn(s, eth) (*verb*), *see* Bannock should b. (Rather my); Candle b. within socket; Neighbour's house is on fire; Reck not whose house b. so they warm them; Turn or b.; Warms too near that b.

Burnt child dreads the fire, The.

c. **1300** *Prov. of Hending* 24 Brend child fur

dredeth. *c.* **1300** *Cursor M.* 1, 7223 Sare man aght to dred the brand, that brint him forwit in his hand. *c.* **1350** *Douce MS. 52* no. 52 Brende chylde fyre dredis. *c.* **1400** *Rom. Rose* 1820 Brent child of fier hath mych drede. *c.* **1450** *Beryn* 78 Brennyd cat dredith feir. *c.* **1470** *Harl. MS. 3362* f. 1 b Onys ybrend euer dret feer—*Ignem formidat adusta manus.* **1546** HEYWOOD II. ii. 45 By that diete a great disease once I gat. And burnt child fyre dredth. **1553** T. WILSON *Arte of Rhet.* (1909) Prol. A v A burnt child feareth the fire, and a beaten dogge escheweth the whippe. **1580** LYLY *Euph. & his Eng.* (Arb.) 319 The burnt childe dreadeth the fire. *a.* **1592** T. WATSON (Arb.) 120 The child whose finger once hath felt the fire, To play therewith will have but small desire. **1670** RAY 66 . . . Almost all Languages afford us sayings and Proverbs to this purpose, such are Παθὼν δέ τε νήπιος ἔγνω [Even the fool knows when he has suffered.] *Hesiod.* **1837** F. CHAMIER *Saucy Arethusa* xxv I have had one turn at starvation . . . : a burnt child dreads the fire.

Burr(s), *see* Cleave like b.; Newcastle b. in his throat; Took her for rose, but breedeth b.

Burr (= halo), *see* Near b. far rain.

Burst, borsten, *see* Give him the other half egg and b. him; Smithwick (You been like), either clemmed or borsten.

Burthen of one's own choice is not felt, A.

1707 MAPLETOFT 7. **1855** BOHN 282.

Burthen, *see also* Burden.

Burton, *see* Brayton.

Bury an abbey, He is able to.

1678 RAY 352 . . . (a spendthrift.)

Bury the hatchet, To. (*Cf.* Hang up one's hatchet.)

[= to proclaim peace, from the custom of the N. Amer. Indians.] **1794** J. GAY *Corr. & Pub. Papers* (1893) IV. 147 To use an Indian figure, may the hatchet henceforth be buried for ever. **1837** W. IRVING *Capt. Bonneville* III. 219 The chiefs met ; the amicable pipe was smoked, the hatchet buried, and peace formally proclaimed. **1890** W. F. BUTLER *Napier* 186 It was usual for the Directors of the [East India] Company to give a banquet. . . . Napier accepted the invitation. The hatchet was to be buried.

Bury (-ies, -ied), *see also* Go after a leech (While men), body is b.; Kills himself with working, b. under gallows; Shovelfuls to b. truth.

Bus, *see* Missed the b.

Bush natural ; more hair than wit.

1550 HEYWOOD II. vii. 68 Thy tales (quoth he) shew long heare, and short wit, wife. **1592-3** SHAKS. *Com. Err.* II. ii. 84 *Dro.* What he [time] hath scanted men in hair he hath given them in wit. *Ant.* . . . Many a man hath more hair than wit. **1594–5** *Two Gent.* III. i. 363 Item, she hath more hair than wit. **1670** RAY 166.

Bush, *see also* Bad b. better than open field; Beat about the b.; Beats the b. (One), another catches the birds; Bows to the b. he gets bield of (Every man); Feareth every b. (He that); Hare or the bracken b.; Rush b. keeps cow; Thinks every b. a boggard; Wag as the b. wags.

Bushel, *see* Hide one's light under b.; Measures another's corn by own b.

Busiest men find (have) the most leisure (time), The.

1884 J. PAYN *Canon's W.* xxxiv It is my experience that the men who are really busiest have the most leisure for everything. **1911** *Times Lit. Sup.* 6 Oct. 365 The busiest men have always the most leisure; and while discharging the multifarious duties of a parish priest and a guardian he found time for travelling.

Business before pleasure.

1837 GORE *Stokeshill Place* (quoted in *N. & Q.* 188, 283). **1857** HEAVYSEGE *Saul* (1869) 141 Business still should alternate with pleasure.

Business, Without │ debauchery.

1640 HERBERT 363.

Business is business.

1797 G. COLMAN *Heir at Law* III. iii Business is business. **1876** BLACKMORE *Cripps* iii Quite right. Business is business. No man can be too particular.

Business is the salt of life.

1672 CODRINGTON 124. **1732** FULLER no. 1026.

Business of life and the day of death, Between the │ a space ought to be interposed.

1651 HERBERT 319.

Business to-morrow.

[PLUTARCH *Pelop.* 10 Εἰς αὔριον τὰ σπουδαῖα.] **379** B.C. ARCHAIAS (the Spartan) in Plutarch *Lives* (1900) II. 10 Archaias laughing, said, 'Serious matters to-morrow'. He took the letter and placed it under the pillow on which he rested. . . . This story, handed down in the form of a proverb, is current among the Greeks even now.

Business. *see also* Citizen is at his b. before he rise; Drive your b.; Every man as his b. lies; Everybody's b. nobody's b.; Great b. turns on little pin; Haste in his b. (Who hath no), mountains seem valleys; Likes not his b., b. likes not him; Love and b. teach eloquence; Mind your b.; Thinks his b. below him; Wind is in north-west (Do b. when).

Busy as a bee, As.

c. **1386** CHAUCER *Mercht.'s T.* 2422 For ay as bisy as bees Been they. **1580** LYLY *Euph. & his Eng.* (Arb.) 252 A comely olde man as busie as a Bee among his Bees.

Busy as a hen with one chicken, As.

1591 W. STEPNEY *Span. Schoolmaster* L 6ᵛ She is as busie as a henne, with two chickins (*Está mas empachada que vna gallina con dos pollos*). **1592** G. DELAMOTHE (1639) 20 He is as busie as a hen that hath but one chicken (*Il est empesché comme une poule qui n'a qu'un poulet*). **1633** SHIRLEY *Witty Fair One* II. ii It has been a proverb, 'as busy as a hen with one chicken'. **1776** WALPOLE *Lett.* (Toynbee) 9. 388 According to the expressive old adage, I am as busy as a hen and one chick. **1914** K. F. PURDON *Folk of Fury F.* v The same as a hen with only one chicken. She'll fuss and cluck as much for it as if she had the whole clutch.

Busy folks are always meddling.

1721 KELLY 72.

Busy, To be too │ gets contempt.

1640 HERBERT 351.

Busy, He that is │ is tempted by but one devil; he that is idle, by a legion.

1732 FULLER no. 2171.

Busy, Who is more │ than he that hath least to do?

1616 DRAXE 20. **1639** CLARKE 20.

Busy will have bands.

1616 DRAXE 19 Busie will haue bondes. **1678** RAY 106 . . . Persons that are meddling and troublesome must be tied short.

Busy, *see also* Ever b. ever bare.

But when? quoth Kettle to his mare.

1678 RAY (*Chesh.*) 276

Butcher does not fear many sheep, One.

1853 TRENCH ii 38 When some of his officers reported . . . the innumerable multitudes of the Persian hosts . . . the youthful Macedonian hero[1] silenced them . . . with the reply: *One butcher does not fear many sheep*. [[1] Alexander the Great.]

Butcher looked for his knife and it was in his mouth, The.

1616 WITHALS 560. **1639** CLARKE 75. *a.* **1654** SELDEN *Table Talk* (Arb.) 104 We look after Religion as the Butcher did after his Knife, when he had it in his Mouth. **1738** SWIFT (*Dial.* i) 337 *Col.* Well; I'm like the butcher that was looking for his knife and had it in his mouth: I have been searching my pockets for my snuff-box, and, egad, here it is in my hand.

Butcher's horse, I think this is a | he carries a calf so well.

1678 RAY 232. 1855 BOHN 492.

Butcher, *see also* Ram to kill a b. (Possible for).

Butler's box[1] at Christmas, Like a.

[[1] A box into which players put a portion of their winnings at Christmas-time for the butler.] 1629 J. TAYLOR *Wit & Mirth* in BRAND *Pop. Ant.* (1870) I. 270 Westminster Hall . . . is like a Butler's Box at Christmas amongst gamesters: for whosoeuer loseth, the Box will bee sure to bee a winner.

Butter in the black dog's hause,[1] Like.

1721 KELLY 236 . . . That is, past recovery. 1816 SCOTT *Antiq.* xxxviii 'Did Dousterswivel know anything about the . . . bullion?' . . . 'Had Dustansnivel kend it was there; it wad hae been butter in the black dog's hause.' 1819 Id. *Leg. Mont.* c. xv You sent me upon a fool's errand to get a buff coat out of the booty taken by the Camerons, whereas you might as well have sent me to fetch a pound of fresh butter out of a black dog's throat. [[1] throat.]

Butter is gold in the morning, silver at noon, lead at night.

1588 COGAN *Haven of Health* (1612) 156 (A) According to the old English Prouerbe: Butter is gold, &c. 1652 FULLER *Com. on Christ's Temp.* in *Sel. Serm.* (1891) II. 89 Some meats are said to be *Gold in the morning, silver at noon, but lead at night.* 1670 RAY 36. 1738 SWIFT (*Dial.* i) 334 They say, butter is gold in the morning, silver at noon, but it is lead at night.

Butter is good for anything but to stop an oven.

1656 L. PRICE *A Map of Merry Conceits* A 5[v] P: (= Proverb) Butter is good for anything: C: (= Crossing) But not to stop ovens with. 1659 HOWELL *Eng. Prov.* 12.

Butter is mad twice a year.

1625 JONSON *Staple of News* II. i So butter answer my expectation, and be not mad butter;—'if it be, It shall both July and December see!' 1678 RAY 50 Butter is said to be mad twice a year; once in summer . . . when it is too thin and fluid; and once in winter . . . when it is too hard and difficult to spread.

Butter is once a year in the cow's horn.

1614 CHAPMAN *Ep. Ded. to Od.* Like winter cows whose milk runs to their horns. 1659 HOWELL *Eng. Prov.* 14. 1678 RAY 50 . . . They mean when the cow gives no milk.

Butter, That which will not be | must be made into cheese.

1678 RAY 107.

Butter that the cow yields, It is not all.

1546 HEYWOOD II. ix. 78 Ye speake now, as ye would créepe into my mouth, . . . But against gaie glosers,[1] this rude text recites, It is not all butter, that the coow shites. 1678 RAY 107 All is not butter the cow shites. Non è tutto butyro che fa la vacca. *Ital.* [[1] flatterers.]

Butter will stick to his (my) bread, No.

1546 HEYWOOD II. vii. 71 But there will no butter cleaue on my breade. 1636 CAMDEN 303. 1721 KELLY 267 *No butter will stick to my bread.* Spoken when all means we use to thrive miscarry. 1727 SWIFT *Pastoral Dial.* Wks. (1856) I. 628 But now I fear it will be said, No butter sticks upon his bread. 1824 SCOTT *Redg.* xv 'No,' replied Nanty; 'the devil a crumb of butter was ever churned that would stick upon my bread'.

Butter, *see also* Boil stones in b.; Demure as if b. would not melt; Fair words b. no parsnips; Fat as b.; Pound of b. among kennel of hounds; Rope and b.; Store of b. (They that have) may lay it thick; Sure as if sealed with b.; That is for that and b.'s for fish.

Butter-cake, *see* 'No, thank you', has lost many a b.

Buttered fagot, *see* Eat a b. f. (He that would).

Buttered side, *see* Bread never falls but on b. s.

Butterfly, *see* Break a b. upon wheel.

Button, Not worth a.

c. 1320 *Sir Beues* 1004 Hauberk ne scheld ne actoun Ne vailede him nouȝt worþ a botoun. 1620 SHELTON *Quix.* II. xxii (1908) II. 338 Whose knowledge and remembrance is not worth a button. 1796 EDGEWORTH *Par. Asst., Simple Susan* (1903) 135 The attorney says the paper's not worth a button in a court of justice. 1860 SURTEES *Plain or Ringlets?* lxviii The Duke's dogs are not worth a button.

Button(s), *see also* Breech makes b.; Care a b. (Not to); Soul above b.; Worth a b. (Not).

Button-hole, *see* Take one down . . . (or a b. lower).

Buy a pig in a poke, To.

c. 1300 *Provs. of Hending* (ed. Schleich) in *Anglia* 51. 263 Wen me bedeþ þe gris, opene þe shet. c. 1350 *Douce MS.* 52 no. 114 When me profereth þe pigge, opon the pogh. 1520 WHITTINGTON *Vulg.* (E.E.T.S.) 107 It is sayd comenly whan the pygge is profered: open the poughen. 1546 HEYWOOD II. ix. 80 Ye love not to bye the pyg in the poke. 1603 FLORIO tr. *Montaigne* I. xlii (1897) II. 154 No man will buy a pig in a poke. If you cheapen a horse, you will take his saddle, and clothes from him, you will see him bare and abroad. **1890** D. C. MURRAY *J. Vale's G.* xxv I can't buy a pig in a poke. . . . Let me know what you've got to sell, and then maybe I'll make a bid for it. [Fr. *acheter chat en poche.*]

Buy an office, They that | must sell something. (*Cf.* Buyeth magistracy, &c.)

1549 LATIMER *5th Serm. bef. Edw. VI* (Arb.) 147 Are ciuile offices bought for monei? . . . If thei bei, thei must nedes sel, for it is wittely spoken. *Vendere iure potest, emerat ille prius*, he may lawefully sel it, he bought it before. **1642** FULLER *H. & P. State* IV. vii (1841) 255 Sir Augustine Nicolls, whom King James used to call 'the Judge that would give no money'. Otherwise, they that buy justice by wholesale, to make themselves savers, must sell it by retail. **1732** FULLER no. 4975.

Buy and sell, and live by the loss, To.

1616 DRAXE 20. **1623** W. PAINTER *Chaucer new Painted* C 6ᵛ Some doe buy and sell and liue by the losse. **1639** CLARKE 81.

Buy at a fair, but sell at home.

1616 DRAXE 21. **1640** HERBERT 324.

Buy dear is not bounty, To.

1640 HERBERT 324.

Buy gold too dear, A man may.

1546 HEYWOOD II. vii. **1662** FULLER (*Kent*) II. 143 He thought that gold might . . . be bought too dear. **1887** LUBBOCK *Pleas. Life* II. ii A wise proverb tells us that gold may be bought too dear.

Buy good cheap that bring nothing home, They.

1641 FERGUSSON 94. **1721** KELLY 318 . . . Spoken to them that think our pennyworth too dear.

Buy in the cheapest market and sell in the dearest, To.

1595 LODGE *Fig for Momus*, Ep. 4 Wks. (1883) III. 59 Buy cheape, sell deare. **1862** RUSKIN *Unto this Last* II (1901) 60 Buy in the cheapest market?—yes; but what made your market cheap? . . . Sell in the dearest? . . . but what made your market dear? **1880** FROUDE *Bunyan* 104 'To buy in the cheapest market and sell in the dearest' was Mr. Badman's common rule in business. . . . In Bunyan's opinion it was knavery in disguise.

Buy no stocks, My son.

1678 RAY 348 . . . *Good counsel at Gleek.*[1] [[1] a game at cards.]

Buy the cow, If you | take the tail into the bargain.

1721 KELLY 190 *It is a shame to eat the cow, and worry on the tail.* It is a shame to perform a great task all but a little, and then give it

over. **1732** FULLER no. 2743. **1824** MOIR *Mansie W.* xxii Peter Farrel was a . . . thorough-going fellow, and did not like half-measures, such as swallowing the sheep and worrying on the tail.

Buy the devil, If we | we must sell the devil.

1838 J. C. APPERLEY *Nimrod's North. Tour* 152 There is a saying amongst horse-dealers . . . namely, 'If we buy the devil, we must sell the devil'; but who was the purchaser of this 'devil' I know not.

Buyer beware, Let the.

[L. *Caveat emptor, quia ignorare non debuit quod jus alienum emit.* Law Maxim—Let a purchaser beware, for he ought not to be ignorant of the nature of the property which he is buying from another party.] **1607** E. SHARPHAM *Fleire* in BANG *Materialen* (1912) II, 1. 36 They are no prouerb breakers: beware the buyer say they. **1927** *Times* 29 Sept. 10/1 We dislike very much, whether it is put in Latin or in English, the phrase 'Let the buyer beware!'

Buyer needs a hundred eyes, The | the seller but one.

[It. *Chi compra ha bisogna di cent' occhi; chi vende n' ha assai di uno.*] **1640** HERBERT 336. **1670** RAY 66 Who buyes hath need of an hundred eyes, who sells hath enough of one. *This is an* Italian *Proverb.* **1745** FRANKLIN July He who buys had need have 100 Eyes, but one's enough for him that sells the stuff. **1796** EDGEWORTH *Par. Asst., Lit. Merch.* i. (1903) 375 He taught him . . . to get . . . from customers by taking advantage of their ignorance. . . . He often repeated . . . 'The buyer has need of a hundred eyes; the seller has need but of one'.

Buyeth dear and taketh up on credit, Who | shall ever sell to his loss.

1573 SANDFORD (1576) 207. **1623** W. PAINTER *Chaucer new Painted* C 6ᵛ Buy not for time those wares that are too deare, For many lose thereby.

Buyeth magistracy, He that | must sell justice. (*Cf.* Buy an office, &c.)

1573 SANDFORD (1576) 10 Pope Urbane the fourthe . . . gave freely for nothyng all offices and benefices, saying, that he that buyeth an office, must needes sell it. **1642** TORRIANO 18 He who buyeth the seat of Justice, must needs make sale thereof.

Buying of bread undoes us, This.

1678 RAY 67. (*Joculatory.*)

Buys a house ready wrought, He that | hath many a tyle·pin[1] (pin and nail, tile and pin) for nought.

1623 CAMDEN 271. **1639** CLARKE 300. **1670** RAY 106. [[1] A peg of hard wood used to fasten the tiles to the laths of a roof.]

Buys and sells is called a merchant, He that.

1678 RAY *Adag. Hebr.* 400 ... This proverb is used in derision of those who buy and sell to their loss. **1911** A. COHEN *Anct. Jewish Pr.* 78 Does a man buy and sell just to be called a merchant? ... The chief aim in trade is to make a profit.

Buys land buys many stones; He that | he that buys flesh buys many bones; he that buys eggs buys many shells; but he that buys good ale buys nothing else.

1678 RAY 211. **1721** KELLY 172 He that buys land, buys stones; He that buys beef, buys bones; He that buys nuts, buys shells; But he that buys good ale, buys nought else.

Buy(s), bought, *see also* All things are to be b. at Rome; Bark ourselves ere we b. dogs so dear; Better b. than borrow; Bought wit is the best; Dear bought and ... dainties for ladies; Difference between will you b. and will you sell; Leaf of borage might b. all they can sell; Ounce of wit that's bought; Penny to b. his dog a loaf; See for your love, b. for your money.

Buzzard, *see* Hawk and b. (Between); Kite

will never be good hawk; Old wise man's shadow better than b.'s sword.

By-and-bye, *see* Street of 'B.' arrives at house of 'Never'; Two anons and a b. is an hour and a half.

Bygones be bygones, Let.

[HOM. *Il.* 18. 112 'Ἀλλὰ τὰ μὲν προτετύχθαι ἐάσομεν, ἀχνύμενοί περ, But we will allow these things to have happened in the past, grieved as we are.] **1546** HEYWOOD II. ix Let all things past pass. **1636** RUTHERFORD *Lett.* lxii (1862) I. 166 Pray ... that byegones betwixt me and my Lord may be byegones. **1648** NETHERSOLE *Parables* 5 Let bygans be bygans. **1706** LD. BELHAVEN *Speech on Union* 2 Nov. I fear not these Articles ... if we ... forgive one another, ... according to our proverb', 'Bygones be bygones'. **1815** SCOTT *Guy Man.* li Let us adopt a Scotch proverb ... 'Let bygones be bygones, and fair play for the future'. **1882** TENNYSON *Prom. May* III. Wks. (1893) 796 *Dora.* Would you beat a man for his brother's fault? ... Let bygones be bygones.

By-walkers, Many | many balks.[1]

1549 LATIMER *2nd Serm. bef. Edw. VI* (P.S.) 112 These men walked by-walks, and the saying is, 'Many by-walkers, many balks':[1] many balks, much stumbling; ... howbeit there were some ... that walked in the king's highway. [¹ ridges of earth.]

C

Cabbage twice cooked (sodden) is death.

[Gk. Δὶς κράμβη θάνατος. L. JUVENAL *Sat.* 7. 154 *Crambe repetita.*] **1545** TAVERNER G 8ᵛ Crambe bis posita mors est Crambe twyse sod is death ... Crambe ... we call Radyshe. **1580** LYLY *Euph. & his Eng.* (Arb.) 391 Which I must omitte, least I set before you, colewortes twice sodden. **1929** *Times* 12 Oct. 6/6 Their havoc is limited to the cabbages; and you know what the opinion of cabbage was amongst the Greeks: Δὶς κράμβη θάνατος.

Cackle like a cadowe,[1] She can.

1549 CHALONER tr. *Erasmus Praise of Folly* L 3ᵛ More Kacling than a menie of dawes. **1579** *Marr. of Wit and Wisdom* (1849) 26. [¹ jackdaw.]

Cackle often, You | but never lay an egg.

1629 T. ADAMS *Serm.* (1861–2) II. 96 Here is one that cackles when he has not laid, and God coming, finds his nest empty. This is to fry in words, freeze in deeds. **1732** FULLER no. 5867 You cackle often, but never lay an egg. **1890** D. C. MURRAY *Jno. V's Guard.* xxxix You're one o' that family o' poultry as does the cackling for other hens' eggs.

Cadbury Castle and Dolbury Hill dolven[1] were, If | all England might plough with a golden share.

1630 T. WESTCOTE *View of Devonshire* (1845) 110 Cadberry, alias Caderbyr. ... The castle [is] ... a high ... hill, ... anciently fortified. ... Of this hidden treasure this rhyming proverb goes commonly and anciently—'If Cadbury Castle and Dolbury Hill dolven[1] were All England might plough with a golden share'. [¹ delved.]

Caddell, *see* Dead (When I am) make no c.

Cadgers[1] are aye cracking o' crook-saddles.[2]

1641 FERGUSSON 26 Cadgers speaks of lead-saddles. **1721** KELLY 77 *Cadgers has ay mind of load saddles.* Spoken when people bring in, by head and shoulders, a discourse of those things they are affected with, and used to. **1818** SCOTT *Rob Roy* xxvi Ye ken cadgers maun aye be speaking about cart-saddles. **1857** DEAN RAMSAY *Remin.* v (1911) 204 *Cadgers are aye cracking o' crooksaddles* ... Professional men are very apt to talk too much of their profession. [¹ pedlars. ² pack-saddles.]

Cadger(s), *see also* King's errand may come c.'s gate; Mickle to do when c. ride.

Caesar's wife must be above suspicion.

1579 LYLY *Euphues* (Arb.) 329 Al women shal be as *Cæsar* would have his wife, not onelye free from sinne, but from suspition. **1827** HARE *Gues. at Truth* (1873) i. 187–8 Cæsar's wife ought to be above suspicion. . . . Yet most . . . would be slow to acknowledge . . . that Cæsar himself ought to be so too.

Caesar, *see also* Render unto C.

Cages for oxen to bring up birds in, He builds.

1678 RAY 352. **1732** FULLER no. 1815.

Cain, *see* Raise C.

Cake hath its make,[1] Every.

1641 FERGUSSON 94 There was never a cake, but it had a make. **1762** SMOLLETT *L. Greaves* x There's no cake, but there's another of the same make. [[1] mate, fellow.]

Cake hath its make; Every | but a scrape cake hath two.

1678 RAY 68 . . . Every wench hath her sweetheart, and the dirtiest commonly the most: make, i.e. match, fellow.

Cake (Meal) is dough, One's.

1559 BECON *Prayers &c.* (P.S.) 277 Or else your cake is dough, and all your fat lie in the fire. **1593–4** SHAKS. *Tam. Shrew* I. i. 110 Our cake 's dough on both sides. *Ibid.* V. i. 145 My cake is dough; but I'll in among the rest, Out of hope of all, but my share of the feast. **1687** SETTLE *Reflect. Dryden* 4 She is sorry his cake is dough, and that he came not soon enough to speed. **1708** MOTTEUX *Rabelais* IV. vi You shall have rare Sport anon, if my Cake ben't Dough, and my Plot do but take. **1721** KELLY 191 *I thought all my meal dough.* I thought all my pains ill bestowed. Spoken when we are disappointed of our expectation.

Cake, *see also* Eat your c. and have it; Poor man turns his c., another takes away; Woos for c. and pudding.

Calends, *see* Greek c.; Janiveer's c. be summerly gay (If).

Cales, *see* Knight of.

Calf love, half love; old love, cold love.

1823 GALT *Entail* xiv Put off for a year or twa this calf love connection. **1876** BLACKMORE *Cripps* xxxiii Calf-love . . . was making a fool of this unfledged fellow.

Calf never heard church-bell, That.

1917 BRIDGE 110 . . . A calf born and killed between two Sundays.

Calf, The | the goose, the bee: the world is ruled by these three.

1635 HOWELL *Lett.* 3 Jul. (1903) II. 103 'Anser, Apis, Vitulus, populos et Regna gubernant.' The goose, the bee and the calf (meaning wax, parchment and the pen), rule the world, but of the three the pen is most predominant.

Calf, The greatest | is not the sweetest veal.

1636 CAMDEN 307. **1732** FULLER no. 4569. **1790** WOLCOT (P. Pindar) *Benev. Ep. to S.U.* Wks. (1816) II. 89 Brudenall who bids us all the proverb feel, 'The largest calves are not the sweetest veal'.

Calf, calves, *see also* Bear a bull that hath borne c. (He may); Cow c. as for bull (As well for); Eat above the tongue, like a c.; Eats the c. in the cow's belly; Kill the fatted c.; Luck (As good) as the lousy c.; Parson's cow (Come home like), with c. at foot; Quey c. dear veal; Suffer a c. to be laid on thee (If thou); Think a c. a muckle beast that never saw cow; Veal will be cheap, c. fall; Wanton as a c. with two dams; Wise as Waltham's c.

Calf's head, *see* Ways of dressing a c. h.

California fever.

1840 DANA *Two Yrs. bef. Mast* xxi The Americans . . . and Englishmen . . . are indeed more industrious . . . than the Spaniards; yet . . . if the 'California fever' (laziness) spares the first generation, it always attacks the second.

Call a man no worse than unthankful, You can.

1639 CLARKE 170.

Call a spade a spade, To.

[= to call things by their real names, without any euphemism. ERASM. *Ad. Ficus ficus, ligonem ligonem vocat.*] **1519** RASTELL *The Four Elements* (Dodsley's *Old Plays* ed. Hazlitt i. 49). **1542** UDALL *Erasm. Apoph.* 167 Philippus aunswered, that the Macedonians wer feloes of no fyne witte in their termes, but altogether grosse, . . . whiche had not the witte to calle a spade by any other name then a spade. **1647** TRAPP *Marrow Gd., Authors in Comm. Ep.* 641 Gods people shall not spare to call a spade a spade, a niggard. **1738** SWIFT (Dial. iii) 351 *Lady A.* You know, I'm old Telltruth; I love to call a spade a spade. **1882** H. A. GILES *Historic China* 55 Chinese prosody is of an extremely complicated character . . . it being an almost unpardonable fault to call a spade a spade.

Call another cause.

1738 SWIFT (Dial. i) 340 *Spark.* Well, so much for that, and butter for fish; let us call another cause.

Call her neighbour *scold*, Who more ready to | than the arrantest scold in the parish?

1639 CLARKE 79.

Call one sir, and something else, To.

1641 W. MOUNTAGU in *Buccleuch MSS.* (Hist.

MSS. Comm.) I. 289 The Bishop saying 'Sir', was mistaken to have said Sirra, and called to the bar. **1678** RAY 269 To call one Sir and something else, i.e. Sirrah.[1] [[1] a contemptuous form of address.]

Call the bear 'uncle' till you are safe across the bridge.

1912 *Times Wkly.* 12 Apr. 287 Critics . . . can quote the excellent Turkish proverb, 'Call the bear "uncle" till you are safe across the bridge', to justify their refusal to add to the Government's difficulties.

Call the king my cousin, I would not.

1721 KELLY 225 . . . Added when we say, Had I such a thing, could I get such a place, or effect such a project: I would think myself so happy, that I would flatter no body. **1914** K. F. PURDON *Folk of Furry F.* i There's the way it is wid women. When they get a daughter marrit, no matter to who, they'll be that proud, . . . that they wouldn't call the King their cousin.

Calm sea, In a | every man is a pilot.

1670 RAY 4. **1732** FULLER no. 2808 In a calm everyone can steer.

Calm sough, *see* Keep a c. s.

Calm weather in June sets corn in tune.

1573 TUSSER xlii. 117. **1732** FULLER no. 6207.

Calm, *see also* After a storm.

Calves are gone down to grass, His.

1678 RAY 232 . . . This is a jeer for men with over-slender legs.

Calves, *see also* Calf, calves.

Cambridge master, *see* Royston horse.

Cambridgeshire camels.

1662 FULLER (*Cambs.*) I. 226 Cambridge-shire Camels'. I cannot reconcile this proverb to any considerable sense. . . . The fen-men . . . on their stilts, are little giants indeed. **1670** RAY 221 Cambridgeshire camels. . . . A nickname . . . perhaps because the three first letters are the same in *Cambridge* and *camel*. **1897** BP. CREIGHTON *Some Eng. Shires* 378 Cambridgeshire camels' was an expression for the marshmen . . . on tall stilts.

Camel going to seek horns, lost his ears, The.

[ERASM. *Ad. Camelus desiderans cornua etiam aures perdidit.* The camel in Aesop's fable asks horns of Jove. Indignant at the foolish request, he deprives it of its ears. TRENCH.] **1608** CHAPMAN *Consp. Byron* IV. i *Creq.* But for a subject to affect a kingdom, Is like the camel that of Jove begged horns. **1621** BURTON *Anat. Mel.* I. ii. III. 14. **1678** RAY *Adag. Hebr.* 399 . . . Against those who being discontented with what they have, in pursuit of more lose what they once had.

Camel(s), *see also* Cambridgeshire c.; Strain at a gnat and swallow c.

Cammock, *see* Crooketh the tree.

Camnethen, *see* Woe worth ill company.

Camomile is trodden on, The more the | the faster it grows.

1576 PETTIE *Petite Pall.* (Gollancz) I. 36 As the herb camomile the more it is trodden down the more it spreadeth abroad, so virtue and honesty the more it is spited the more it sprouteth. **1597-8** SHAKS. *1 Hen. IV* II. iv. 446 Though the camomile, the more it is trodden on the faster it grows, yet youth, the more it is wasted the sooner it wears. **1637** SHIRLEY *Hyde Pk.* III. ii *Mist. C.* For ne'er was simple camomile so trod on, Yet still I grow in love.

Candle burns within the socket, His.

1590-1 SHAKS. *3 Hen. VI* II. vi. 1 Here burns my candle out; ay, here it dies. **1597-8** *2 Hen. IV* I. ii. 179 What! you are as a candle, the better part burnt out. **1633** LD. BROOKE *Caelica* lxxxvii. 235 When as mans life. . . . In soacket of his earthly lanthorne burnes. **1670** RAY 167 . . . That is, he is an old man. Philosophers are wont to compare mans life to the burning of a lamp. **1827** SCOTT *Chron. Canongate* i The light of life . . . was trembling in the socket.

Candle lights others and consumes itself, A.

1599 MINSHEU A 2 with a candle to light others and burn out my self. **1659** N.R. 1. **1742** FRANKLIN Feb. The painful preacher, like a candle bright, consumes himself in giving others light.

Candle, *see also* Burn one c. to seek another; Burn the c. at both ends; Burned one c. to St. Michael (Like woman who); Dance nor hold the c. (Neither); Fly that playeth too long in c.; Game is not worth c.; Go out like c.; Hold a c. (Not able to); Hold a c. to the devil; Punch coal, cut c., neither good housewife; See divine light (Way to), put out own c.; Sun with a c. (Set forth the); *Tace* is Latin for c.; Worst may (He that) shall hold c.

Candle-holder proves a good game-ster, A good.

1670 RAY 4. **1732** FULLER no. 138 A good candle-snuffer may come to be a good player.

Candlemas day[1] be fair and bright, If | winter will have another flight: if on Candlemas day it be shower and rain, winter is gone, and will come not again.

1584 R. SCOT *Witchcraft* XI. xv (A) If Maries purifying-day Be cleare and bright with sunny raie, Then frost and cold shall be much more, After the feast than was before. **1612** WEBSTER *White Devil* V. i Let all that belong to great men remember the old wives' tradition, to be like the lions i' the Tower on Candlemas-day: to mourn if the sun shine, for fear of the pitiful remainder of winter to come. **1653** T. GATAKER, *A Vindication* 125 On *Candlemas* day . . . if it were a close and gloomy day, they [the deer] would come abroad and be frisking upon the lawn, as presaging that winter was in a manner gone, and litle hard weather behind. **1678** RAY 51 . . . This is a translation . . . of that old Latin Distich; *Si Sol splendescat Maria purificante, Major erit glacies post festum quam fuit ante.* **1847** R. CHAMBERS *Pop. Rhymes Scot.* 366 A frosty Candlemas-day is found to be . . . generally indicative of cold for the next six weeks or two months. [[1] 2nd Feb.]

Candlemas Day, On | if the sun shines clear, the shepherd had rather see his wife on the bier.

1830 FORBY 416.

Candlemas-day is come and gone, When | the snow lies on a hot stone.

1678 RAY 43.

Candlemas Day, On | throw candle and candlestick away.

1678 RAY 344. **1875** DYER *Brit. Pop. Cust.* (1900) 55 From Candlemas the use of tapers at vespers and litanies, which had continued through the whole year, ceased until the ensuing *All Hallow Mass,* . . . 'On Candlemas Day, Throw candle and candlestick away'.

Candlemas Day, On | you must have half your straw and half your hay. (*Cf.* Farmer should have, &c.)

1678 RAY 52. **1732** FULLER no. 6487.

Candlemas, As long as the bird sings before | it will greet after it.

1721 KELLY 43. **1846** DENHAM 27.

Candlemas, *see also* Farmer should have on C. day half his hay; Set trees . . . after C.; Wind 's in the east on C. day (When the).

Candlestick, canstick, *see* Coll under c.

Cane, *see* Rotten case (c.) abides no handling.

Cannon, *see* Boulogne (Our fathers won); Cursed in his mother's belly that was killed by c.

Canny Newcastle.

1787 GROSE *Glos., Northumb.* 213 . . . Spoken jocularly to Newcastle-men, . . . for their partiality to their native town. **1854** SURTEES *Hand. Cross* xix 'Where d'ye come from?' 'Canny-newcassel', replied Pigg.

Canoe, *see* Paddle your own c.

Canterbury is the higher rack, but Winchester is the better manger.

1608 HARINGTON *Nugae Antiquae* (1804) ii.

87 (A) A bishop of Winchester one day in pleasant talke, comparing his revenew with the archbishops of Canterburie should say— 'Your Graces will shew better in the racke, but mine will be found more in the maunger.' **1662** FULLER (*Hants*) II. 5 . . . W. Edington, bishop of Winchester, . . . rendering this the reason of his refusal to be removed to Canterbury. . . . The revenues of Winchester . . . are more advantageous to gather riches thereon. . . . Applicable to such who prefer a wealthy privacy before a less profitable dignity.

Canterbury tale, A.

c. **1549** CRANMER *Serm. Rebellion* Wks. (P.S.) II. 198 If we take it for a Canterbury tale, why do we not refuse it? **1608** TOPSELL *Serpents* (1658) 778 To interpret these to be either fables and Canterbury tales, or true historical narrations. **1709** R. STEELE *Tatler* 22 Dec. no. 110, col. 2 I did not care for hearing a Canterbury tale.

Cap after (at) a thing, To throw one's.

(*a*) = to defy.

1601 BRETON *No Whipping* B 8[v] He cast his Cap at sinne in generall. **1609** R. ARMIN *Ital. Tailor and his Boy* A 4 Every Pen & Ink-horne Boy will throwe up his Cap at the hornes of the Moone in censure.

(*b*) = to despair of overtaking.

1592 NASHE (McKerrow) i. 318 *Pierce Pennilesse* May well cast his cappe after it for ever overtaking it. **1603** DEKKER *The Wonderful Year* (Wilson) 19 *Platoes Mirabilis Annus* . . . May throw *Platoes* cap at *Mirabilis*, for that title of wonderfull is bestowed upon 1603. **1607** SHAKS. *Timon of A.* III. iv I perceive our masters may throw their caps at their money. **1670** RAY 168 They may cast their caps at him. When two or more run together, and one gets ground, he that . . . despairs to overtake, commonly casts his hat after the for[e]most, and so gives over the race.

Cap be made of wool, If his.

1633 JONSON *T. Tub* II. ii. (A) Slip, you will answer it, an if your cap be of wool. **1662** FULLER (*Herts.*) II. 68 [In] the reign of King Henry the Eighth, . . . velvet caps becoming fashionable for persons of prime quality, discomposed the proverb, 'If his cap be made of wool', as formerly comprising all conditions of people how high and haughty soever. **1670** RAY 167 If his cap be made of wool . . . was as much to say . . . , As sure as the clothes on his back.

Cap fits, If the | wear it.

1600 BRETON *Pasquil's Foolscap* A 3 Where you finde a head fit for this *Cappe*, either bestowe it *upon* him in charity, or send him where he may haue them for his money. **1748** RICHARDSON *Clarissa H.* (1785) VII. x If indeed thou findest . . . that the cap fits thy own head, why then . . . e'en take and clap it on. **1816** 'QUIZ' *Grand Master* III. 55 If the cap fits him, he may wear it. **1827** SCOTT *Surg. D.* x 'If Captain Middlemas,' he said, 'thought the cap fitted, he was welcome to wear it'. **1887** BLACKMORE *Springhaven* iv Put the cap on if it fits.

Cap is better at ease than my head, My.

1546 HEYWOOD II. vii. 70 Thy toung . . . suche spitefull clappyng haue bred. That my cap is better at ease then my hed.

Cap(s), *see also* Monmouth c.; Pull c.; Put on considering c.; Red c.; Set one's c. at.

Capers like a fly in a tar-box, He.

1678 RAY 68.

Capon, If thou hast not a | feed on an onion.

1611 COTGRAVE s.v. Chapon'. **1670** RAY 4.

Capon(s), *see also* Chickens feed c.; Sairy collop that is off c.

Captain, Such | such retinue.

c. **1390** GOWER *Conf. Amantis* III. 2421 Such Capitein such retenue.

Captain, *see also* Old band is c'.s honour.

Capuch, *see* Beads in hand and devil in c.

Caravan, *see* Dogs bark, but c. goes on.

Carcase is, Wheresoever the | there will the eagles[1] (ravens) be gathered together.

1573 BULLEIN *Dial. agst. Fever* (E.E.T.S.) 19 The Rauen will seeke the carrion. **1611** BIBLE *Matt.* xxiv. 28 For wheresoeuer the carkeise is there will the Eagles bee gathered together. **1853** TRENCH iv. 94 Wheresoever *the carcase is, there will the eagles be gathered together.* . . . Wherever there is a Church or a nation abandoned by the spirit of life, and so a carcase, tainting the air of God's moral world, around it assemble the ministers and messengers of Divine justice, . . . the scavengers of God's moral world. **1855** BOHN 563. [[1] i.e. vultures.]

Cards are the devil's books.

1676 *Poor Robins Alm. Prognost.* C 4 (A) Cards and dice . . . the devil's books and the devil's bones. ?**738** SWIFT (Dial. iii) 350 D— your cards, said he, they are the devil's books. *c.* **1785** BURNS *Twa Dogs* ad fin. Or lee-lang nights, wi' crabbit leuks, Pore owre the devil's pictur'd beuks. **1834** SOUTHEY *Doctor* ii. 249 He thought that cards had not without reason been called the Devil's Books. **1910** *Spectator* 17 Dec. 1073 'The sort that tells you the theatre is the devil's front parlour, and cards is his picture-books.'

Card(s), *see also* Cooling c.; Counted your c. (When you have) . . . gained but little; Outface with a c. of ten; Pack the c. (Many can), yet cannot play; Patience and shuffle the c.; Speak by the c.; Sure c.; Tell thy c., then tell what hast won; Throw up c.

Care a button, Not to.

1861 GEO. ELIOT *Silas M.* iii He did not care a button for cock-fighting.

Care a pin, Not to.

c. **1410** *Towneley Plays* (E.E.T.S.) 34 Thi felowship. Set I not at a pyn. **1590** SPENSER *F.Q.* I. v. 4 Who not a pin Does care for looke of living creatures eye. **1594–5** SHAKS. *L.L.L.* IV. iii. 19 I would not care a pin if the other three were in. **1777** SHERIDAN *Sch. Scandal* III. i 'Tis evident you never cared a pin for me.

Care a straw (three straws), Not to.

c. **1369** CHAUCER *Dethe Blaunche* 718 Socrates . . . ne counted nat thre strees Of noght that fortune koude doo. **1610–11** SHAKS. *Wint. T.* III. ii. 111 I prize it not a straw. **1861** HUGHES *Tom B. at Oxf.* iii Drysdale, who didn't care three straws about knowing St. Cloud. **1887** *Spectator* 1 Oct. 1304 The British Government . . . does not care one straw what religion its subjects profess.

Care and diligence bring luck.

1540 TAVERNER *Flores aliquot sententiarum* A 4 Cura potest omnia, Diligence & study can do al thinges. **1591** W. STEPNEY *Span. Schoolmaster* L 2ᵛ Diligence is the mother of good fortune. **1591** T. LODGE *Catharos* (Hunt. Cl. ed. 13) The prouerbe is, true care preserueth all things. **1612** SHELTON *Quix.* I. iv. 19 Diligence is the mother of good hap. **1732** FULLER no. 1057.

Care is no cure.

1591–2 SHAKS. *1 Hen. VI* III. iii. 3 Care is no cure, but rather corrosive, For things that are not to be remedied. **1678** RAY 108.

Care killed the cat.

1585–1616 *Shirburn Ballads* (1907) 91 (A) Let care kill a catte, Wee'le laugh and be fatte. **1598–9** SHAKS. *Much Ado* V. i. 133 Though care kill'd a cat, thou hast mettle enough in thee to kill care. **1601** JONSON *Ev. Man. in Humour* I. iv. 84 Care'll kill a cat. **1682** N. O. tr. BOILEAU's *Lutrin* iv. 322 Exiling fretting Care, that kills a Cat! **1816** SCOTT *Antiq.* xiv Hang expenses—care killed a cat. **1890** 'R. BOLDREWOOD' *Miner's Right* xxiii He was always ready to enjoy himself . . . 'care killed a cat'.

Care not three skips of a louse, I.

1633 JONSON *T. Tub.* II. i I care not I, sir, not three skips of a louse for you.

Care not would have it.

1670 RAY 67. **1721** KELLY 80 . . . If you ask a man if he will have such a thing, and he answers *I care not*, it is a sign that he would have it.

Care, A pound of | will not pay an ounce of debt.

1599 PORTER *Angry Wom. Abingd.* II. ii (Merm.) 132 Nay, a pound of care will not pay an ounce of debt. **1614** CAMDEN 303.

Care(s) (*noun*), *see also* Behind the horseman sits c.; Light c. speak; Little gear less c.; Little wealth little c.; Much coin much c.; Pains to get, c. to keep; Past cure past c.; Wise fear begets c.

Care(s) (*verb*), *see also* Wise man c. not for what he cannot have.

Careless hussy makes many thieves, A.

1663 P. STAMPOY 4. **1683** MERITON *Yorkshire Ale* (1897) 83–7 (A).

Careless parting between the old mare and the broken cart, A.

1721 KELLY 54 . . . Spoken when a husband or wife dies who did not love one another. **1818** SCOTT *Rob Roy* xxvii 'Gie me my wages . . . , and I'se gae back to Glasgow. There's sma sorrow at our parting, as the auld mear said to the broken cart.'

Careless, The more | the more modish.

1738 SWIFT (Dial. i) 338 *Lady S.* She wears her clothes as if they were thrown on her with a pitchfork. . . . *Never.* Well, that's neither here nor there; for, you know, the more careless the more modish.

Cares not whose child cry, so his laugh, He.

1585–1616 *Shirburn Ballads* (1907) 22 Some care not how others' children cry, So they themselves can prosper well. **1721** KELLY 137 *He cares not whose bairn greet if his laugh.* Spoken of selfish people, whose endeavours terminate upon, and centre in, themselves. **1732** FULLER no. 1823.

Cares, *see also* Care(s).

Car(e)y, *see* Mother C.'s chickens.

Cargo, *see* Flag protects the c.

Carl riches he wretches, As (The more) the.

1641 FERGUSSON 10. **1721** KELLY 24 . . . Many men are found to grow the more niggardly as their wealth increases. **1853** TRENCH v. 111 Mammon . . . given sometimes . . . that under its fatal influence they may grow worse and worse, for *the more the carle riches, he wretches.*

Carl(s), *see also* Kiss a c.; Lairds break (When), c. get land.

Carleton[1] wharlers[2].

1610 HOLLAND *Camden's Brit.* I. 517 As for Carleton, . . . wherein . . . all in manner that are borne . . . have an ill-favoured, untunable, and harsh manner of speech, . . . with a certaine kind of wharling. **1650** FULLER *Pisgah-sight of Pal.* II. ix. par. 3 (1869) 167 It is observed in a village of Charleton in Leicestershire that the people therein are troubled with wharling in their utterance. [[1] Carleton Curlieu, near Leicester. [2] Persons who pronounce the letter *r* with a guttural sound.]

Carpenter, Like (Such) | like (such) chips.

1546 HEYWOOD II. vii. 66 Suche carpenters, such chips (quoth she) folke tell. **1670** RAY 115. **1738** SWIFT (Dial. ii) 347 (*Smart*) You have eaten nothing. (*Ans.*) . . . See all the bones on my plate: they say a carpenter's known by his chips.

Carpenter(s), *see also* Bone in the leg (Were it not for) all would turn c.

Carps, *see* Turkeys, c. . . . came into England.

Carried down the stream, He that is | need not row.

1732 FULLER no. 2280.

Carrier, *see* John (Tom) Long the c.

Carries fire in one hand and water in the other, He.

1412–20 LYDGATE *Troy Bk.* IV. 4988 On swiche folke, platly, is no trist, That fire and water holden in her fist. *c.* **1526** SKELTON *Magnif.* Wks. (1843) I. 248 Two faces in a hood covertly I bear, Water in the one hand, and fire in the other. **1579** LYLY *Euphues* (Arb.) 107 Whatsoeuer I speake to men, the same also I speake to women, I meane not . . . to carye fire in the one hand and water in the other. **1616** DRAXE 46. **1676** BUNYAN *Strait Gate* Wks. (1855) I. 389 He carries fire in the one hand, and water in the other. **1732** FULLER no. 5886.

Carries well to whom it weighs not, He.

1640 HERBERT 336.

Carrieth all his wardrobe about him, He.

1616 WITHALS 573. **1659** HOWELL *Eng. Prov.* 16.

Carrion crows bewail the dead sheep, and then eat them.

1640 HERBERT 339 The crow bewails the sheep, and then eats it. **1670** RAY 6.

Carrion will kill a crow (kite), No.

c. **1610** BEAUM. & FL. *Wit at S. W.* III.i *Fop.* Every one knows the state of his own body, No carrion kills a kite. **1650** Feb. 12–19, *Mercurius Pragmaticus*, 2 T 2ᵛ Hee will make good the Proverb, *no Carrion can kill a Crow.* **1670** RAY 76 No carrion will kill a crow.

Carrion, *see also* Kite will never be good hawk.

Carry a bone in the mouth (*or* teeth), To.

[= said of a ship when she makes the water foam before her.] **1627** CAPT. SMITH *Seaman's Gram.* ii 10 If the Bow be too broad, she will seldom carry a bone in her mouth, or cut a feather, that is, to make a fome before her. **1851** LONGFELLOW *Gold. Leg.* v See how she leaps . . . and speeds away with a bone in her mouth.

Carry a nutmeg in your pocket, If you | you'll be married to an old man.

1738 SWIFT (Dial. i) 342 *Miss, searching her pocket for a thimble, brings out a nutmeg. Never.* O, miss, have a care; for if you carry a nutmeg in your pocket, you'll certainly be married to an old man.

Carry (or bear) coals, To.

[= to do dirty or degrading work, to submit to humiliation.] **1522** SKELTON *Wks.* (Dyce) II. 34 Wyll ye bere no coles? **1594–5** SHAKS. *Rom. & Jul.* I. i. 1 Gregory, o' my word, we'll not carry coals. **1598–9** *Hen. V* III. ii. 50 I knew by that piece of service the men would carry coals. **1600** JONSON *Ev. Man out of Humour* v. i Here comes one that will carry coals, ergo, will hold my dog. **1611** CHAPMAN *May Day* I. i. 430 Above all things you must carry no coals. *a.* **1683** B. WHICH-COTE *Serm.* Those who are sensible that they carry coals, and are full of ill will.

Carry coals to Newcastle, To.

1583 MELVILLE *Autobiog.* (Wodrow S.) i. 163 (A) Salt to Dysart, or colles to Newcastle! *a.* **1661** FULLER (*Northumb.*) 302 To carry coals to Newcastle, that is to do what was done before; or to busy one's self in a need-less employment. **1661** GRAUNT *Bills Mor-tality,* Ded. Ld. Truro I should (according to our English Proverb) . . . but carry Coals to Newcastle. **1822** SCOTT *Let. Joanna Baillie* 10 Feb. in LOCKHART *Life* It would be a sending coals to Newcastle with a ven-geance. **1787** GROSE *Glos.* (1811) 214 To carry coals to Newcastle. . . . In the environs of Newcastle, are most of the coal mines that supply London, and the coal trade to other places.

Carry guts to a bear, Not fit (worthy) to.

1670 RAY 200 Not worthy to carry guts after a Bear. **1786** WOLCOT (P. Pindar) *Lousiad* ii. Wks. (1816) I. 168 George thinks us scarcely fit ('tis very clear) To carry guts, my brethren to a bear. **1840** MARRYAT *Poor Jack* xxviii Well, if I'm a bear, you ar'n't fit to carry guts to a bear. **1904** MRS. HUGHES *Recollections of Scott* vi 'So, sir, I hear you have had the impudence to assert that I am not fit to carry guts to a bear.' 'Oh no!—I defended you, I said you were.'

Carry, *see also* Knows how to c. dead cock home.

Carshalton, *see* Sutton.

Cart before the horse, To set (or put) the.

[= to reverse the natural or proper order.] **1340** *Ayenb.* 243 Moche uolk of religion ȝetteþ þe ȝuolȝ be-uore þe oksen. *c.* **1520**

WHITTINGTON *Vulg.* (1527) 2 That techer setteth the carte before the horse that preferreth imitacyon before preceptes. **1589** PUTTENHAM *Eng. Poesie* (Arb.) 181 We call it in English prouerbe, the cart before the horse, the Greeks call it Histeron proteron, we name it the Preposterous. **1605–6** SHAKS. *K. Lear* I. iv. 246 May not an ass know when the cart draws the horse? **1801** EDGEWORTH *Belinda* iii Esteem ever followed affection, instead of affection following esteem. Woe be to all who in morals preposterously put the cart before the horse! **1863** KINGSLEY *Water Bab.* iv They . . . having, as usual, set the cart before the horse, and taken the effect for the cause.

Cart whemling,[1] If ever I get his | I'll give it a putt.[2]

1641 FERGUSSON 62 If I can get his cairt at a walter,[1] I shall lend it a put. **1721** KELLY 197 . . . If I get him at a disadvantage, I'll take my revenge on him. [[1] overturning. [2] push.]

Carts that come to Crowland are shod with silver, All the.

1662 FULLER (*Lincs.*) II. 268 'All the carts that come to Crowland are shod with silver.' Venice and Crowland, . . . may count their carts alike; that being sited in the sea (this in a morass and fenny ground), so that a horse can hardly come to it.

Cart(s), *see also* Best c. may overthrow; cast at c.'s arse; Make an end of your whistle, though c. overthrow; Old c. well used; Put at the c. that is aye ganging; Time to yoke when c. comes to caples; Un-happy man's c. eith to tumble.

Carter, *see* Swear like a c.

Cart-load, *see* Fall away . . . to a c.

Cart-saddle, *see* Becomes it as cow doth c.

Carver, *see* Worst c. in the world, never make good chaplain.

Case is altered, The.

1594 GREENE *Looking-Glass* II. ii (Merm.) 105 *Lawyer.* Faith sir, the case is altered; you told me it before in another manner: the law goes quite against you. **1609** JONSON *Case Altered* v. vi *Jaq.* I have betrayed myself with my own tongue; The case is altered.

Case is altered, The | quoth Plow-den.[1]

[*a.* **1585**] **1603** DEKKER *Batch. Banq.* in Wks. (Gros.) I. 235 (A) Then is their long warre come to an end, and the case (as Ployden sayth) cleane altered. **1662** FULLER (*Shrops.*) III. 54 'The case is altered', quoth Plowden. This proverb referreth its original to Edmund Plowden, an eminent native and great lawyer of this county, though very various the relations of the occasion thereof. [[1] 1518–85.]

Case(s), *see also* Hard c. bad law; No c., abuse attorney; Rotten c. abides no handling.

Cask savours of the first fill, The.

[HORACE *Ep.* 1. 2. 69 *Quo semel est imbuta recens servabit odorem Testa diu.* A cask will long preserve the flavour with which, when new, it was once impregnated. *c.* 1230 *Contra Avaros* in WRIGHT *Polit. Songs* (Camd. Soc.) 31 Quo semel est imbuta recens servabit odorem.] **1509** A. BARCLAY *Ship of Fools* (1874) I. 47 But fyll an erthen pot first with yll lycoure And euer after it shall smell somwhat soure. **1552** LATIMER *7th Serm. bef. Edw. VI* (P.S.) 431 Where children are brought up in wickedness, they will be wicked all their lives after, . . . 'The earthen pot will long savour of that liquor that is first put into it.' **1591** HARINGTON *Orl. Fur.* Like as the vessell ever beares a taste Of the same juice wherewith it first was fil'd. (*See also* quotations in *England's Parnassus* (1827) 9, 2160.) *c.* **1645** HOWELL *Lett.* 17 Sept. (1903) III. 87 I am not versed in my maternal tongue so exactly as I should be. . . . Yet the old British is not so driven out . . . (for the cask savours still of the liquor it first took in), &c. **1779–81** JOHNSON *Lives Poets* (Bohn) II. 201 A survey of the life and writings of Prior may exemplify a sentence . . . ; *the vessel long retains the scent which it first receives.*

Cask smells of the wine it contains, Every.

1591 FLORIO *Sec. Frutes* 141 The cask gives of that it has in it. **1666** TORRIANO 29 A butt gives such a scent as it hath. **1732** FULLER no. 1473 Every tub smells of the wine it holds.

Cassandra warnings.

[The prophetic warnings of Cassandra, daughter of Priam of Troy, came true, though disregarded at the time.] **1629** T. ADAMS *Serm.* (1861) I. 216 All the prophecies of ill success have been held as Cassandra's riddles. **1928** *Times* 14 Dec. 10/3 His continual 'delay and vacillation', to use Queen Victoria's own words, caused her the gravest anxiety. . . . All her warnings, like those of Cassandra, were neglected, and, like those of Cassandra, were fulfilled in every instance.

Cast a bone in the devil's teeth.

1721 KELLY 79 . . . Gratify some squeezing oppressor, or some unconscionable officer, to save your self from his harm.

Cast at cart's arse, To be.

[= to be in disgrace; offenders were flogged at the tail of a cart.] **1540** PALSGRAVE *Acolastus* B 3 Cast them out at the cartes ars. **1550** HEYWOOD I. ix. 17 I am cast at carts ars.

Cast (Hand) be bad, If thy | mend it with good play.

1732 FULLER no. 2723. **1902–4** LEAN IV. 5 If your hand[1] be bad, mend it with good play. [[1] i.e. at cards.]

Cast beyond the moon, To.

[= to indulge in wild conjectures.] **1546**

G

HEYWOOD I. iv. 9 Feare may force a man to cast beyonde the moone. **1559** *Mirr. Mag.* 529 Beyond the moone when I began to cast . . . what place might be procur'd. **1607** T. HEYWOOD *Wom. K. Kindness* IV. vi (Merm.) 53 But, oh! I talk of things impossible, And cast beyond the moon. **1623** CAMDEN 271 He casts beyond the Moone. **1636** *Ibid.* 296 He casts beyond the Moone that hath p—— on a nettle.

Cast in the teeth, To.

[= to reproach or upbraid.] **1526** TINDALE *James* i. 5 Which geveth to all men . . . withouten doublenes, and casteth no man in the teth. **1546** HEYWOOD I. xi. 36 But therto deuiseth to cast in my téeth, Checks and chokyng oysters. **1579** LYLY *Euph.* (Arb.) 125 The trecheries of his parents . . . wil be cast in his teeth. **1599–1600** SHAKS. *Jul. Caes.* IV. iii. 98 All his faults observ'd, Set in a note-book, learn'd, and conn'd by rote, To cast into my teeth. **1716** HORNECK *Crucif. Jesus* 33 Strangers cast it in his Teeth so often, Where is now thy God?

Cast ne'er a clout till May be out.

[Sp. *c.* **1627** CORREAS *Vocabulario* (1906) 490 Hasta Mayo no te quites el sayo.[1]] **1732** FULLER no. 6193 Leave not off a clout, Till May be out. **1832** HENDERSON 154. [[1] *Do not leave off your coat till May.*]

Cast not out the foul water till you bring in the clean.

1641 FERGUSSON 26 Cast not forth the old water while the new come in. **1721** KELLY 80 . . . Part not with that way of living you have, till you be sure of a better. **1738** SWIFT (Dial. iii) 351 Mrs. Giddy has discarded Dick Shuttle. . . . She was a fool to throw out her dirty water before she got clean. **1842** LOVER *Handy Andy* xxix 'I'll change my clothes' . . . 'You had better wait. . . . You know the old saying, "Don't throw out your dirty wather until you get in fresh".'

Cast of his office, To give one a.

a. **1553** UDALL *Royster D.* I. iv (Arb.) 26 Speake to them: of mine office he shall haue a cast. **1666** TORRIANO 79 The Devil gives him a cast of his Office.

Cast out nature with a fork, Though you | it will still return.

[HORACE *Epist.* 1. 10. 24 *Naturam expellas furca, tamen usque recurret.*] **1539** TAVERNER (1552) 44 Thrust out nature with a croche, yet wyll she styll runne backe agayne. **1594** LYLY *Moth. Bomb.* I. i. Wks. (1902) III. 175 Why though your sons folly be thrust vp with a paire of hornes on a forke, yet being naturall, it will have his course. **1831** PEACOCK *Crotchet Cas.* i Mr. Crotchet . . . seemed . . . to settle down . . . into an English country gentleman. . . . But, though you expel nature with a pitchfork, she will always come back. **1867–77** FROUDE *Short Stud.* (1890) I. 600 Drive out nature with a fork, she ever comes running back.

Cast up accounts (*or* reckoning), To.

c. **1590** LYLY *Moth. Bomb.* II. i. 127 We shall

cast up our accounts, and discharge our stomackes. *c.* **1590** *Ibid.* ii. iv. 5 I must go and cast this matter in a corner. **1630** DEKKER *2 Honest Whore* (1873) ii. 162 The reckonings to cast up. **1678** RAY 87 *Of one drunk* ... He's about to cast up his reckoning or accompts.

Cast your net where there is no fish, It is in vain to.

1732 FULLER no. 2966.

Cast, *see also* Dust in a man's eyes; Lost all who has one c. left (Has not); Rub and a good c.

Casticand, *see* Skiddaw, Lauvellin, and C.

Castle of Bungay, Were I in my | upon the river of Waveney, I would not care for the king of Cockney.

[*King of Cockneys*: a kind of Master of the Revels at Lincoln's Inn on Childermas Day (28 Dec.). The name of this mock king is perhaps referred to in the following saw.] *a.* **1577** HARRISON *England* ii. xiv (1877) I. 266 As for those tales that go of ... the brag of ... [Hugh Bigot] that said in contempt of King Henrie the third ... 'If I were in my castell of Bungeie, Vpon the water of Waueneie, I wold not set a button by the king of Cockneie', I repute them but as toies. **1659** HOWELL *Eng. Prov.* 21/1 Were I near my Castle of *Bungey*, Upon the River of *Wavenley*, I would ne care for the King of *Cockeney*. ... ; *these places are in* Suffolk.

Castles in Spain, To build.

[= to indulge in visionary projects or day dreams: Fr. *Châteaux en Espagne*.] *c.* **1400** *Rom. Rose* 2573 Thou shalt make castels thanne in Spayne, And dreme of joye, alle but in vayne. **1475** CAXTON *Jason* 19 He began to make castellis in Spaygne as louers doo. **1886** W. BLACK *White Heather* xlvi I am less hopeful now; ... my Highland mansion may prove to be a castle in Spain after all.

Castles in the air, To build.

[= to indulge in visionary projects or day dreams. AUGUSTINUS *Sermo* 2. 6. 8 *Sub-tracto fundamento in aere aedificare.*] **1566** PAINTER *Pal. of Pleas.* (Jacobs) i. 266 (A) Alerand ... was a building of castels in the ayre. **1580** NORTH *Plutarch* (1676) 171 They built Castles in the air, and thought to do great wonders. **1612–15** BP. HALL *Contempl.* iv. xi (1825) II. 379 Ye great men, spend not all your time in building castles in the air, or houses on the sand. **1633** MASSINGER *New Way* ii. i (Merm.) 131 *Mar.* Ha! ha! these castles you build in the air Will not persuade me or to give or lend A token to you. **1894** BLACKMORE *Perlycross* xiii His wife ... had seen Jemmy waltzing ... with one of her pretty daughters, and been edified with castles in the air.

Castle(s), *see also* Better a c. of bones; Bow (I have a good), but in the c.; City (C.)

that parleys; Easy to keep c. never besieged; Fair wife and frontier c.; House is his c. (A man's).

Cat, Gloved, Muffled, Muzzled, *see* Cat in gloves.

Cat (*or* kit) after kind. (*See also* Cat will to kind.)

[kind = natural disposition.] **1568** *Jacob & Esau* iv. iv in HAZL. *O.E.P.* ii. 235 Cat after kind (say'th the proverb) sweet milk will lap. **1599–1600** SHAKS. *A. Y. L.* III. ii. 109 If the cat will after kinde, so be sure will Rosalinde. **1670** RAY 183 *Kit* after kind. A chip of the old block.

Cat after kind, good mouse-hunt.

c. **1275** *Provs. of Alfred* (Skeat) A 296 For ofte museth the Kat after hire moder. **1540** *Nice Wanton* 52 For a good mouse-hunt is cat after kynd. **1546** HEYWOOD I. xi. 27. **1678** RAY 109 That that comes of a cat will catch mice ... *Chi da gatta nasce sorici piglia.*

Cat and dog may kiss, yet are none the better friends, The.

c. **1225** *Trin. MS. O. 11. 45* (ed. Förster) in *Eng. Stud.* **31**. 7 Hund and cat kissat, ne beoþ hi no þe bet ifrund. **1855** BOHN 499.

Cat did it, The.

1872 CALVERLEY *Fly Leaves*, 'Sad Memories' Should china fall or chandeliers, or anything but stocks—Nay stocks when they're in flowerpots—the cat expects hard knocks. **1902–4** LEAN I. 433 ... A common shift on puss of unwitnessed smashes.

Cat eateth the flickle,[1] Little and little the.

a. **1500** R. Hill's *Commonpl. Bk.* (E.E.T.S.) 130 (A) A litill and a litill, the cat etith vp the bacon flicke. **1546** HEYWOOD II. vii. 67. [1 flitch.]

Cat; He is like a | fling him which way you will, he'll light on his legs.

1519 HORMAN *Vulgaria* (James) 434 Cattes and dogges when they shal fall from hye so nymbleth therself: that they wyl pitch vpon their fete. *a.* **1616** BEAUM. & FL. *Mons. Thomas* iii. iii Not hurt him, He pitcht vpon his legs like a cat. **1640** TORRIANO *Italian Tutor* 1st dialogue G 2 Like unto so many Cats, come what will, you fall always on your feet. **1678** RAY 282 He's like a cat; fling him which way you will he'll light on 's legs. **1887** S. COLVIN *Keats* 37 Chronically ailing ... but always, in Keats's words, 'coming on his legs again like a cat'.

Cat for lard, Send not a.

1640 HERBERT 347.

Cat, The lickerish[1] (liquorish[1]) | gets many a rap.

1611 COTGRAVE s.v Chat'. **1670** RAY 4. [1 lustful.]

Cat has nine lives, A.

1546 HEYWOOD I. iv. 49 No wyfe, a woman hath nyne lyues like a cat. **1594–5** SHAKS. *Rom. & Jul.* III. i. 81 Good King of Cats, nothing but one of your nine lives. **1894** BLACKMORE *Perlycross* xi If a cat has nine lives, sir; a lie has ninety-nine.

Cat hath eaten her count, The.

1678 RAY 68 . . . It is spoken of women with child, that go beyond their reckoning.

Cat help it, How can the | if the maid be a fool?

1678 RAY 109 . . . Not setting up things securely out of her reach or way.

Cat in gloves (*or* gloved, muffled, muzzled cat) catches no mice, A.

1572 SANDFORD 212 A gloued catte can catche no myse. **1591** W. STEPNEY *Span. Schoolmaster* L 4ᵛ A mauling cat was neuer good hunter. **1611** DAVIES. *Prov.* 333 Cuft Catt 's no good Mouse-hunt. **1623** WODROEPHE *Marrow of French Tongue* 287 A Museld cat is not meete to take Mice. **1623** CAMDEN 266 A mufled Cat was neuer good mouzer. **1629** *Ibid.* 262 A muzzled Cat was neuer good Mouzer. **1636** *Ibid.* 291 A muffled Cat was never good mouser. **1641** FERGUSSON 12 A gloved cat was never a good hunter. **1670** RAY 67 A muffled cat is no good mouser. **1758** FRANKLIN in ARBER *Eng. Garner* v. 580 Handle your tools, without mittens! Remember that *The cat in gloves catches no mice!*

Cat is hungry when a crust contents her, The.

1611 COTGRAVE s.v. 'Chat'. **1670** RAY 4.

Cat is in the cream-pot, The.

1598 T. DELONEY *Gentle Craft* Pt. II (Mann) 208 As well acquainted . . . as the cat in the creame-pan. **1678** RAY 233.

Cat is out of kind that sweet milk will not lap, That.

1678 RAY 108.

Cat jumps, To see (watch) which way the.

[= what direction events are taking.] **1827** SCOTT in *Croker Pap.* (1884) I. xi. 319 Had I time, I believe I would come to London merely to see how the cat jumped. **1863** KINGSLEY *Water Bab.* 289 He . . . understood so well which side his bread was buttered, and which way the cat jumped.

Cat knows whose beard (lips) she licks, The.

[*c.* **1023** EGBERT V. LÜTTICH *Fecunda Ratis* (Voigt) 4 *Ad cuius uenial scit cattus lingere barbam.* *c.* **1190** *Li Proverbe au Vilain* (Tobler) 2 *Li chaz set bien cui barbe il leche.*] *c.* **1225** *Trin. MS. O. 11. 45* (ed. Förster) in *Eng. Stud.* **31.** 7 Wel wot hure cat. whas berd he lickat. *c.* **1300** *Provs. of Hending* (ed.

Schleich) in *Anglia* **51.** 270 Wel wote badde [i.e. *cat*], wose berde he lickith. *c.* **1350** *Douce MS. 52* no. 78 Welle wotys the catte, whoos berde he lykkys. *c.* **1470** *Harl. MS. 3362*, f. 6 Wel wot þe cat whas berd he [likketh]. *c.* **1500** *Sloane MS. 747*, f. 66 a Well wote the cat whos berd he lykt. **1523** SKELTON *Garl. Laurell* 1438 And wele wotith the cat whos berde she likkith. **1550** HEYWOOD II. ix. 81 Kindly he kyst hir, with woords not tart nor tough. But the cat knoweth whose lips she lickth well enough.

Cat loves mustard, As a.

1639 CLARKE 235. **1678** RAY 287.

Cat may look at a king, A.

1546 HEYWOOD II. v. 57 What, a cat maie looke on a King, ye know. **1590** GREENE *Never too late* (1600) 94 A cat may look at a King, and a swain's eye hath as high a reach as a lord's look. **1638** T. HEYWOOD *Wise W. of Hogs.* II. ii A cat may look at a king, and so may I at her. **1893** STEVENSON *Catriona* i 'There is no harm done', said she. . . . 'A cat may look at a king'. [*Cf.* Fr. *Un chien regarde bien un évêque.*]

Cat on hot bricks (a hot bake-stone), Like a.

1678 RAY 285 To go like a cat upon a hot bake-stone. **1861** G. J. WHYTE-MELVILLE *Inside the Bar* ii A well-bred, raking-looking sort of mare . . . Beautiful action she had, stepped away like a cat on hot bricks. **1883** C. READE *Peril. Secret* xxiv. 'Is not a race-horse a poor mincing thing until her blood gets up galloping?' . . . 'You are right, . . . she steps like a cat upon hot bricks.'

Cat round hot milk, Like a.

1855 BOHN 442.

Cat sees not the mouse ever, The.

1640 HERBERT 345. **1670** RAY 67.

Cat shuts its eyes while it steals cream, The.

1853 TRENCH iv. 77 . . . Men become wilfully blind to the wrong which is involved in some pleasing or gainful sin.

Cat speak, Enough to make a.

1611–12 SHAKS. *Temp.* II. ii Open your mouth; here is that will give language to you, cat. **1839** DICKENS *N. Nickleby* xii It's enough to make a Tom cat speak French grammar, only to see how she tosses her head.

Cat, the Rat, and Lovell our Dog, rule all England under an Hog, The.

[**1484**] **1577** HOLINSHED *Chron.* (1808) III. 422 [Richard III executed] a poore gentleman called Callingborne, for making a small rime of three of his . . . councellors, . . . lord Louell, sir Richard Ratcliffe . . . and sir William Catesbie. . . . The Cat, the Rat, and Louell our dog, Rule all England vnder an hog.

Meaning by the hog, the . . . wild boare, which was the King's cognisance. **1816** SCOTT *Antiq.* ii 'His name . . . was Lovel.' 'What! the cat, the rat, and Lovel our dog? Was he descended from King Richard's favourite?'

Cat will to kind. (*See also* Cat after kind.)

c. **1580** G. HARVEY *Letterbk.* (Camd. Soc.) 120 Tis god philosophy: Katt will to kinde. **1692** L'ESTRANGE *Aesop's Fab.* clv (1738) 170 *Cat will to kind,* as they say, and wicked men will be true to their principles.

Cat wink, Let the | and let the mouse run.

1522 *Mundus et Infans* 649 A ha! syrs, let the catte wynke! **1546** HEYWOOD II. iv. 50 But further stryfe to shonne, Let the cat winke, and leat the mouse ronne.

Cat winked when (both) her eyes were out, The.

a. **1535** MORE *Wks.* 241 (R.) It was always that ye cat winked when her eye was oute. **1659** HOWELL *Eng. Prov.* 2/2 The cat winked when both her eyes were out. **1738** SWIFT (Dial. i) 334 I'm told for certain, you had been among the Philistines: no wonder the cat wink'd, when both her eyes were out.

Cat winketh, When the | little wots the mouse what the cat thinketh.

1678 RAY 109. **1732** FULLER no. 6453.

Cat winks a while, Though the | yet sure she is not blind.

1576 *Parad. of Dainty Devices* in *Brit. Bibliog.* (1812) iii. 59 (A) I am not blinde although I winke. **1609** ROWLANDS *Whole crew of Kind Gossips* (Hunt. Cl.) 20 (A) The cat ofte winkes, and yet she is not blinde. **1678** RAY 109. **1802** WOLCOT (P. Pindar) *Middl. Elect.* vi. Wks. (1816) 214 I daant tell all I know; But mum, I'm dumb, I'm dumb, and zo— Cats wink that be not blend.

Cat would eat fish and would not wet her feet, The.

[Med. Lat. *Catus amat piscem, sed non vult tingere plantam (plantas).*] *c.* **1225** *Trin. MS. O. 11. 45* (ed. Förster) in *Eng. Stud.* **31.** 7 Cat lufat visch, ac he nele his feth wete. *Catus amat piscem, sed non vult tangere flumen. c.* **1384** CHAUCER *Ho. Fame* iii. 693 For ye be lyk the slepy cat, That wolde have fish; but wastow what? He woldė no-thyng wete his clowes. *c.* **1390** GOWER *Conf. Amantis* IV. 1108 As a cat wolde etė fisshes Withoutė wetinge of his cles. *c.* **1470** *Harl. MS. 3362,* f. 7 The cat would ete. . . . *Catus vult piscem sed non vult tangere limpham.* **1539** TAVERNER 47 The catte wyll fyshe eate, but she wyl not her feete wette. **1550** HEYWOOD I. xi. 28 But you lust not to doo, that longeth therto. The cat would eate fyshe, and would not wet her féete. **1605–6** SHAKS. *Macbeth* I. vii. 44 Letting 'I dare not' wait upon 'I would', Like the poor cat i' the adage. **1641** FERGUSSON 112 Ye breid of the cat, ye wald fain

eat fish, but yee have na will to weet your feet. **1670** RAY 67 The cat loves fish, but she's loath to wet her feet. Le chat aime le poisson, mais il n'aime pas à mouiller la patte. *Gall.*

Cat's away, When the | the mice will play.

c. **1470** *Harl. MS. 3362* in *Anglia* **42.** 201 The mows lordchypyth, þer a cat ys nawt. *Mus debaccatur, ubi catus non dominatur. a.* **1530** R. Hill's Commonpl. Bk. (E.E.T.S.) 132 The mowse goth a-brode, wher þe cat is not lorde. **1573** SANDFORD (1576) 220 When the Catte is not at home, the Myce daunce. **1598–9** SHAKS. *Hen. V.* I. ii. 172 Playing the mouse in absence of the cat. **1607** T. HEYWOOD *Wom. K. Kindness* IV. iv (Merm.) 51 *Cicely.* Mum; there's an old proverb—when the cat's away, the mouse may play. **1670** RAY 68 When the cat is away, the mice play. *Ital.* Les rats se promenent a l'aise là ou il n'y a point des chats. *Gall.*

Cat's ear, *see* Bold mouse that breeds in.

Cat's foot, *see* Lives under the sign of c. f.

Cat's paw of, To make a.

1831 SCOTT *Journ.* 19 Jan. He [Sir W. S.] will not be made a cat's paw of, look you now. **1844** JOWETT to B. C. Brodie 23 Dec. You must guard against being made a catspaw of.

Cat's paw, *see also* Chestnuts out of the fire.

Cat(s), *see also* Agree like c. and dogs; Agree like two c. in gutter; Ale will make c. speak; Before the c. can lick her ear; Bell the c.; Bides as fast as c. to saucer; Blate cat proud mouse; Bourd wi' c. (They that) maun count on scarts; Every day's no Yuleday—cast the c. a castock; Grin like Cheshire c.; Keep no more c. than will catch mice; Kilkenny c.; Knit . . . my c. a codpiece; Let the c. out of bag; Lives as a cat (As many); Never was c. or dog drowned that could . . . ; No more of a c. but her skin (You can have); Old c. laps as much milk; Old c. sports not; Old c. to an old rat (Put); Playing with straw before old c.; Room to swing c.; Rub a c. on rump (The more), higher she sets tail; Scalded c. fears cold water; Scratching and biting c. and dogs come together; Shoot the c.; Singed c., better than likely (He is like); Strip it as Slack stript the c.; Take your thanks to feed your c.; Teach the c. way to kirn; Tine c. tine game; True as that the c. crew; Turn the c. in pan; Two c. and a mouse never agree; Wanton kittens make sober c.; Watch one as c. mouse; Ways to kill a dog (c.); Weasel and c. make marriage (When), evil presage; Weel kens the mouse when c.'s out; Whip the c.; Wild c. out of a bush (Like); Woe's to them that have the c.'s dish.

Cat-harrow, *see* Draw at the c.

Catch a Tartar, To.

[= to get hold of one who can neither be controlled nor got rid of, or who proves to be too formidable.] **1663** BUTLER *Hudibras* I. iii. 865 Now thou hast got me for a Tartar, To make me 'gainst my will take quarter. **1678** DRYDEN *Kind Keeper* v. i What a Tartar have I caught! **1720** DEFOE *Capt. Singleton* xvi (1906) 260 Tell him, if he should try, he may catch a Tartar. **1861** LD. DUNDONALD *Autobiog.* v. 63 Off Plane Island, we were very near 'catching a Tartar'. . . . We had fallen into the jaws of a formidable Spanish frigate.

Catch a weasel asleep.

1837–47 BARHAM *Ingol. Leg.* (1898) 182 You must be pretty deep to catch weasels asleep.

Catch at, *see* **Never c. at falling knife or friend.**

Catch birds to-morrow, We shall.

1546 HEYWOOD II. viii. 72 Byr lady, than we shall catche byrds to morow.

Catch not at the shadow and lose the substance.

1579 LYLY *Euphues* (Bond) I. 201 In arguing of the shadowe, we forgoe the substance. **1591** SHAKS. *Two Gent.* IV. ii. 120. **1602** *How to Choose a Good Wife from a Bad* (1608) B 2 Ile feed on shadowes let the substance goe. **1612** WEBSTER *White Devil* v. i. 168. **1818** T. L. PEACOCK *Nightmare Abbey* xi Like the dog in the fable, to throw away the substance in catching at the shadow. **1855** BOHN 335.

Catch old birds with chaff, You cannot.

1481 CAXTON *Reynard* xl (Arb.) 110 Wenest thou thus to deceyue . . . I am no byrde to be locked ne take by chaf I know wel ynowh good corn. *c.* **1600** *Timon* IV. ii (1842) 62 Tis well.—An olde birde is not caught with chaffe. **1670** RAY 126. **1824** SCOTT *Redg.* iv Men do not catch old birds with chaff, my master. Where have you got the rhino you are so flush of? **1853** THACKERAY *Newcomes* liii They sang . . . and . . . ogled him as they sang . . . with which chaff our noble bird was by no means to be caught.

Catch (*or* take) one napping, To.

1562 J. PILKINGTON *Expos. Neh.* (1585) 65 Our mortall enemie . . . hopeth to speed at length and take thee napping. **1579** LYLY *Euphues* (Arb.) 87 Although I see the bayte you laye to catch mee, . . . neither are you more desirous to take mee napping, then I willing to confesse my meaning. **1593–4** SHAKS. *Tam. Shrew* IV. ii. 46 Nay, I have ta'en you napping, gentle love. **1594–5** *L.L.L.* IV. iii. 130 I should blush, I know, To be o'rheard and taken napping so. **1633** D. DYKE *Six Evangel. Hist.* 42 Christ coming as a Judge and King . . . finds them in the midst of their disorders, and takes them napping as we say. **1909** *Times* 18 Mar. By the admission of the Government the Admiralty have allowed themselves to be caught napping.

Catch (*or* take) one napping, To | as Mosse took his mare.

1583 MELBANCKE *Philot.* 65 Tooke him napping as Moss did his mare. **1607** *Acc. Christmas Prince* (1816) 40 Now Night growes old, yet walkes here in his trapping Till Daye come catch him, as Mosse his graymare, nappinge. **1611** COTGRAVE *A desprouveu,* at unawares . . . unlooked for; napping, as Mosse tooke his Mare. **1670** RAY 187 I took him napping, as Moss took his mare. **1917** BRIDGE 127 To catch a person napping as Moss caught his mare . . . 'Napping, as Moss caught his mare', is the title of a ballad registered for publication in 1569.

Catch that catch may.

c. **1390** GOWER *Conf. Amantis* VII 394 But cacché who that cacché might. **1555** HEYWOOD *Epigr. upon Prov.* no. 293. *c.* **1612** BEAUM. & FL. *Scornf. Lady* I. i. Wks. (C.U.P.) I. 238 Men, women, and all woo, catch that catch may. **1821** SCOTT *Kenilw.* xi The last words seem to mean 'Catch who catch can'.

Catch the old one on the nest, That is the way to.

1678 RAY 87.

Catch the wind in a net, To.

c. **1580** SIDNEY, First *Arcadia* Wks. (Feuillerat) IV 69 [He] hopes the flickering winde with net to holde. **1592** LYLY *Midas* v. i. Wks. (1902) III. 151 As impossible it is to stay the rumour, as to catch the wind in a net. **1623** WEBSTER *Devil's Law-Case* v. iv. Wks. (1857) 143 Vain the ambition of kings, Who seek . . . To leave a living name behind, And weave but nets to catch the wind.

Catch two pigeons with one bean, To.

1557 NORTH *Diall of Princes* f. 56 (A) For the prouerbe sayeth, that with one beane, a man maye take two pigeons. **1573** SANDFORD 210 È bella cosa pigliar duoi columbi, con una faua. It is a goodly thing to take two pigeons with one beane. **1678** RAY 353.

Catching fish is not the whole of fishing.

1913 *Times Lit. Sup.* 28 Nov. 570 Sportsmen who love sport for the sport's sake: 'Catching fish is not the whole of fishing.'

Catch(ing), *see also* **Craft is in the c.; Dog (Hindmost, Foremost) c. hare; First c. your hare; Lie at c.; Young one squeak (Make the), and you'll c. old one.**

Cater-cousins, They are (not).

[= they are (not) good friends.] **1519** HORMAN *Vulgaria* (Roxb. Cl.) 322 They be cater cosyns: and almoste neuer a sonder. **1596–7** SHAKS. *Merch. V.* II. ii. 143 His master and he, saving your worship's reverence, are scarce cater-cousins. **1598** R. BERNARD tr.

Terence's Andria v. vii They are not now cater cousins [*inimicitia est inter eos*].

Cathkin's covenant with you, I will make | let abee for let abee. (*See also* Let-a-be.)

[= mutual forbearance.] **1857** DEAN RAMSAY *Remin.* v (1911) 204 *I'll mak' Cathkin's covenant with you, Let abee for let abee.* . . . The laird of [Hamilton] had . . . been addicted to intemperance. One of his neighbours, . . . personating the devil, claimed a title to carry him off. . . . The laird showed fight . . . when a parley was proposed, and the issue was, 'Cathkin's covenant, Let abee for let abee.'

Cats and dogs, *see* Agree like c. and d.

Cats are alike grey in the night, All.

1550 HEYWOOD I. v. 10 When all candles be out, all cats be grey. **1721** KELLY 9. **1771** SMOLLETT *Humph. Clink.* 7 Sept. *Wks.* (1871) 556 He knew not which was which; and, as the saying is, *all cats in the dark are gray.* [Fr. *La nuit tous les chats sont gris.*]

Cats eat what hussies[1] spare.

c. **1225** *Trin. MS. O. 11. 45* (ed. Förster) in *Eng. Stud.* 31. 6 Hund eet, þat hen man spelat. Sepe uorat gnarus canis id quod seruat auarus. *c.* **1598** *MS. Proverbs* in FERGUSSON 26 Catis eatis quhilk hussies spairs. **1639** CLARKE 242 What the good wife spares, the cat eats. **1721** KELLY 326· *The things that wives hains,[2] cats eat.* What is too niggardly spared is often as widely squandered. [[1] housewives. [2] spares.]

Cats hide their claws.

1609 DEKKER *Raven's Almanac* G 1 The Tiger when he meanes to prey, then euer hideth his clawes.

Cats, *see also* Cat(s).

Cattle, *see* Hurry no man's c.; Kings are kittle c.; Old c. breed not; Roast meat dões c.

Caudle, *see* Dead (When I am) make me a c.

Caught a knave in a purse-net, There I.

1616 WITHALS 555. **1639** CLARKE 127. **1659** HOWELL *Eng. Prov.* 17/2. **1670** RAY 216. **1732** FULLER no. 4870.

Caul, *see* Born with a c.

Cauld kail[1] het[2] again is aye pat[3] tasted.

1865 G. MACDONALD *Alec Forbes* lvi They all knew as well as he did, that his sermon was only 'cauld kail het again'. [[1] broth. [2] hot. [3] pot.]

Cause, Take away the | and the effect must cease.

1599 MINSHEU (1623) Tt 2[v]. **1620** SHELTON *Quix.* II. lxvii The cause being removed, the sin will be saved.

Cause is good, One | until the other's understood.

1731 *Poor Robins Alm.* Oct. The Proverb is, one Cause is good, Until the other's understood.

Causes to be done, That which a man | he does himself.

[COKE *Qui facit per alium facit per se.* He who does a thing by the agency of another, does it himself.] **1692** L'ESTRANGE *Aesop's Fab.* clxvii (1738) 81 That which a man causes to be done, he does himself, and 'tis all a case whether he does it by practice, precept, or example. **1893** H. P. LIDDON *Serm. O.T.* xv. 217 His acquiescence . . . was virtually a commission, and her acts were, morally, his. . . . What is done through another is done by a man himself. **1916** E. A. BURROUGHS *Val. of Decis.* I. ii His reluctance to give the mobilization order in July, 1870, is . . . a commonplace of history. Still, the consent . . . was given; and *Qui facit per alium, facit per se.*

Cause(s), *see also* Bad c. that none speak in; Call another c.; Grease a c. well; Ill c. (He who hath), sell it cheap; Lion in good c.; Oxford is home of lost c.; Worse appear better c. (Make).

Cave of Adullam.

[**1611** BIBLE 1 *Sam.* xxii. 2 David . . . escaped to the cave Adullam: . . . and every one that was in distress, . . . and every one that was discontented, gathered themselves unto him.] **1866** BRIGHT *Sp.* (1876) 349 The right hon. gentleman . . . has retired into what may be called his political Cave of Adullam, and he has called about him 'every one that was in distress and every one that was discontented'. [The Adullamites led by Lowe, seceded from the Liberal party in 1866.]

Caveat, To put in (*or* enter) a.

[= to give a warning; from L. *caveat*, let him beware.] **1577** tr. *Bullinger's Decades* (1592) 405 It pleased the goodnesse of God by giuing the law to put in a caueat . . . for the tranquilitie of mankinde. **1642** FULLER *H. & P. State* I. xii. 37 She enters a silent caveat by a blush. **1755** YOUNG *Centaur* I. *Wks.* (1757) IV. 116 Putting in a caveat against the ridicule of infidels.

Caveat emptor, *see* Buyer beware.

Cavil will enter in at any hole, and if it find none it will make one.

1616 DRAXE 22.

Cellar, *see* Jack in the low c.

Censure(s), *see* Every man's c. moulded in his nature; Men (So many) so many c.

Cerberus, *see* Sop to C.

Ceres and Bacchus, Without | Venus grows cold.

[TERENCE *Eunuch.* 4. 5. 6 *Sine Cerere et*

Libero friget Venus.] **1593** PEELE *Edw. I.* II.
86–9 *Wks.* (1888) I. 101 I learned in school,
That love's desires and pleasures cool Sans
Ceres' wheat and Bacchus' vine.

Certain, It is | because it is impossible.

[TERTULLIAN *De Carne Christi* 5.] **1642** SIR
T. BROWNE *Religio Med.* I. § ix (1881) 18
Involved Ænigmas and riddles of the
Trinity, with Incarnation and Resurrection.
I can answer all the Objections of Satan . . .
with that odd resolution I learned of Tertullian, *Certum est, quia impossibile est* [generally
given as *Credo quia* . . .]

Certain, *see also* Nothing is c. but death;
Nothing is c. but the unforeseen; Nothing
is so c. as the unexpected.

Certainty, *see* Leaveth surety (c.) and leaneth
to chance; Quit c. for hope (Never).

'Ch was bore at Taunton Dean; where should I be bore else.

['Ch represents *Ich*, the southern form of
pronoun *I*.] **1662** FULLER (*Somerset*) III. 91
'Where should I be born else than in Taunton
Dean.' This is a parcel of ground round about
Taunton, very pleasant and populous. . . .
The peasantry therein . . . conceive it a
disparagement to be born in any other place.
1670 RAY 251.

Chad (Saint), *see* First comes David next
comes C. *See also* St. Chad.

Chaff, *see* Catch old birds with c.; Sift him
. . . and he proveth c.

Chain is no stronger than its weakest link, The.

1908 W. M. RAMSAY in *Expositor* Jan. 7 The
critic who is accustomed to . . . deductive
reasoning (in which, however, the weakness
of even one link in the chain is fatal to the
strength of the whole) is apt to forget that
cumulative reasoning is not of the same kind.

Chains, *see* Old c. gall less than new.

Chalk, By a long.

[= by far, in allusion to the use of chalk in
scoring points, &c.] **1837–40** HALIBURTON
Clockm. (1862) 26 Your factories down East
. . . go ahead on the English a long chalk. *a.*
1859 DE QUINCEY *Syst. Heavens Wks.* III.
171 *note* As regards the body of water . . . the
Indus ranks foremost by a long chalk.

Chalk and cheese.

c. **1390** GOWER *Conf. Amantis* Prol. 1. 416 Lo,
how thei feignen chalk for cheese. **1541**
BARNES *Wks.* (1573) 258 This deffinition
agreeth as well with your key, as chalke and
cheese. *a.* **1555** LATIMER in FOXE *A. & M.*
(1684) III. 413 As though I could not discern
cheese from chalk. **1600** ROWLANDS *Lett.*
Humours Blood vi. 75 Tom is no more like
thee, then Chalks like Cheese. **1672** W.
WALKER *Phras. Anglo-Lat.* 56 I talk of chalk

and you of cheese. **1819** HANNAH MORE *Two
Wealthy F. Wks.* (1830) III. 131 *Brag.* Their
talk was no more like that of my ol landlord, who was a Lord . . . , than chalk is like
cheese. **1849** C. BRONTË *Shirley* v 'You think
yourself a clever fellow, I know, Scott.' 'Ay!
I'm fairish; I can tell cheese fro' chalk.'

Chamber of sickness is the chapel of devotion, The.

1616 DRAXE 190. **1670** RAY 24.

Chameleon, *see* Live on air like c.

Chance in the cock's spur, There is.

1678 RAY 111. **1732** FULLER no. 4890.

Chance it, I will | as Parson Horne (*or* Old Horne) did his neck.

1878 *N. & Q.* 5th Ser. x. 10 'I'll chance it, as
old Horne did his neck', or, 'as parson Horne
did his neck'. Horne was a clergyman in Nottinghamshire. Horne committed a murder.
He escaped to the Continent. After many
years' residence abroad he determined to
return. In answer to an attempt to dissuade
him, . . . , he said, 'I'll chance it' . . . was
tried, condemned, and executed.

Chance, *see also* Grieve when the c. is past
(Too late to); Leaveth surety and leaneth
to c.; Left to c. (Something must be);
Main c.

Chanceth (happens) in an hour, It | that happeneth not in seven years.

c. **1270** *Rawlinson MS. C. 641*, f. 13c in *Eng.
Stud.* **31**. 16 On dai bringd, thet al ier ne
mai. *Quod donare mora nequit annua, dat
brevis hora. Anno cura datur, tamen una dies
operatur. c.* **1350** *Douce MS. 52* no. 44 Oft
bryngeth on day, þat all þe ȝere not may. *c.*
1386 CHAUCER *Knight's T. A.* 1668 Yet
somtyme it shal fallen on a day That falleth
nat eft withinne a thousand yeer. **1546**
HEYWOOD I. xi It hapth in an houre that
hapth not in vii. yéere. *a.* **1553** UDALL
Royster D. IV. iii (Arb.) 61 *Royster.* For such
chaunce may chaunce in an houre, do ye
heare? *M. Mery.* As perchance shall not
chaunce againe in seuen yeare. **1614** CAMDEN
308 It chanceth in an hour, that happeneth
not in seven year. **1641** FERGUSSON 62 It
will come in an houre that will not come in a
year. **1721** KELLY 193 It may come in an
hour, that will not come in a year.

Chancery, *see* Hell and c. always open.

Change a cottage in possession for a kingdom in reversion, I will not.

1639 CLARKE 256. **1678** RAY 116.

Change but the name and the story applies to yourself. *See De te fabula narratur.*

Change his mind, A man will never | if he has no mind to change.

1853 TRENCH iii. 59.

Change his old *Mumpsimus* for the new *Sumpsimus*, He will not.

[In allusion to the story of an illiterate English priest, who when corrected for reading 'quod in ore *mumpsimus*' in the Mass, replied, 'I will not change my old mumpsimus for your new sumpsimus.'] **1531** SIR T. ELYOT *Governour* III. xiv (1880) II. 289 Them whome nothing contenteth out of their accustomed Mumpsimus. **1545** HEN. VIII *Parl. sp.* 24 Dec. in HALL *Chron.*, *Hen. VIII* (1550) 261 b Some be to styff in their old *Mumpsimus*, other be to busy and curious in their newe *Sumpsimus*. **1820** SCOTT *Monast.* Introd. Epist. How many gray heads he hath addled by vain attempts to exchange their old *Mumpsimus* for his new *Sumpsimus*. **1862** KEBLE in LIDDON, &c., *Pusey* (1897) IV. i. 25 I still hold to my old mumpsimus that . . . we cannot be unchurched.

Change my mill, I am loth to.

1678 RAY 349 . . . *Somerset. i.e.* Eat of another dish.

Change of pasture makes fat calves.

1546 HEYWOOD II. iv And some say, chaunge of pasture makth fat calues.

Change of weather is the discourse of fools.

1659 HOWELL *Span.-Eng.* 2. **1664** CODRINGTON 189. **1670** RAY 28.

Change, *see also* Woman's mind and winter wind c. oft.

Change mind, *see* Ladies have leave to c. m.; Wise men c. their m.

Change purpose, *see* Wise man needs not blush for changing his purpose.

Changeful as the moon.

c. **1380** CHAUCER *Rom. Rose* B 3778 And chaunge as the moone. **1588** W. AVERELL *Marvellous Combat of Contrarieties* (STUBBES *Anatomy of Abuses* New Sh. S. I. 253) Women . . . more wauering then the wind, more mutable then the Moone. *a.* **1599** SPENSER *Mutabilitie* c. ii, st. 50 (A) So that as changefull as the moone men use to say.

Changing of words is the lighting of hearts.

[Changing = exchanging.] **1641** FERGUSSON 214 **1855** BOHN 336.

Chapel, *see* God hath his church (Where), the devil will have c.

Chaplain, *see* Lord (Like), like c.; Worst carver in the world, never make good c.

Chapman, *see* Breed of the c., never out of your gate.

Char[1] is char'd, That (This).

[= that job's done.] *c.* **1400** *Seven Sages* (Percy Soc.) 88, 1. 2603 'Sire,' scho sayed, 'this char hys heved.' **1570** *Marriage Wit &*

Sc. IV. iv in HAZL. *O.E.P.* II. 375 This char is char'd well. *c.* **1590** *Sir Thos. More* III. i. 118 (Shaks. *Apoc.*) 398 This charre beeing charde, then all our debt is payd. [[1] piece of work.]

'Char is char'd, That' | **as the boy said when he'd killed his father.**

1917 BRIDGE 111 'That char's charred', as the boy said when he'd killed his father.

'Char is char'd, That' | **as the good wife said when she had hanged her husband.**

1670 RAY 168.

Charge of souls, He that hath | **transports them not in bundles.**

1640 HERBERT 362.

Charge, *see also* Double c. will rive cannon.

Charges of building, and making of gardens are unknown, The.

1640 HERBERT 336.

Charing Cross, *see* Old as C. C.

Charing, Smoky.

1736 S. PEGGE *Kenticisms, Prov.* (E.D.S.) 69 Smoking Charing. [Charing is near Ashford.]

Charitable give out at (the) door and God puts in at the window, The.

1678 RAY 353.

Charity and Pride do both feed the poor.

1597 *Politeuphuia* 211. **1732** FULLER no. 1084.

Charity begins at home.

c. **1380** WYCLIF *Of Prelates* in Wks. (Matthew) 78 Charite schuld bigyne at hem-self. **1616** BEAUM. & FL. *Wit without M.* v. ii Charity and beating begins at home. **1659** FULLER *Appeal Inj. Innoc.* in *Hist. Camb. Univ.* (1840) 317 'Charity begins, but doth not end, at home.' . . . My Church History . . . began with our own domestic affairs, . . . I intended . . . to have proceeded to foreign churches. **1748** SMOLLETT *Rod. Rand* vi The world would do nothing for her if she should come to want—charity begins at home. **1853** TRENCH V. (1894) 102 . . . It is not for nothing that we have been grouped in families, neighbourhoods, and nations.

Charity covers a multitude of sins.

1611 BIBLE *1 Pet.* iv. 8 Charity shall cover the multitude of sins. *a.* **1633** G. HERBERT *Priest to the Temple* xii.

Charles's[1] Wain, The four wheels of | **Grenville, Godolphin, Trevannion, Slanning slain.**

[1643] **1911** CROSSING *Folk Rhymes of Devon*

97 . . . [In] the contest at Bristol, between the Royalists and the troops of the Parliament, . . . Sir Nicholas Slanning and Colonel Trevannion were slain, Sir Bevil Grenville and Sidney Godolphin having fallen in previous engagements. . . . Charles['s] . . . 'wain' made no real progress when the 'wheels' were gone. [[1] Charles I.]

Charon waits for all.

1708 PRIOR *Turtle & Spar*. All that wear feathers first or last Must one day perch on Charon's mast. **1732** FULLER no. 1089.

Charre-folks[1] are never paid.

1678 RAY 112 . . . That is, give them what you will they are never contented. **1732** FULLER no. 1083 Chare folks are never paid enough. [[1] persons hired for jobs.]

Charren, *see* Smoke of C.

Charterhouse, *see* Sister of the C.

Chase, *see* Stern c. long c.

Chasing, *see* Mind's c. mice (Your).

Chastely, If not | yet charily.

1587 GREENE *Penelope's Web* in Wks. (Gros.) V. 209 Offences are not measured by the proportion but by the secrecie: *Si non caste, tamen caute*: if not chastely, yet charely. **1604** WEBSTER &c. *Malcontent* IV. i If not chastely, yet charily.

Chastens one, chastens twenty, He that. (*Cf.* Chastiseth one, &c.)

1640 HERBERT 334.

Chastens, *see also* Happy is he that c. himself.

Chastise with scorpions instead of whips, To.

1611 BIBLE *1 Kings* xii 11 My father hath chastised you with whips, but I will chastise you with scorpions. **1867–77** FROUDE *Short Stud.* (1890) III. 104 'My father chastised you with whips, and I chastise you with scorpions'. So answered a foolish Hebrew king, and lost an empire for his pains. **1879** M. PATTISON *Milton* 153 Prelatry was now scourging the nonconformists with scorpions instead of whips. **1908** *Times Lit. Sup.* 6 Mar. If the Egyptian Pashas had chastised their own people with whips, they had chastised the Sudanese with scorpions.

Chastiseth one amendeth many, He that. (*Cf.* Chastens one, &c.)

1616 DRAXE 32. **1670** RAY 4.

Chatters *to* you, Who | will chatter *of* you.

1853 TRENCH iii. 63 *note*.

Chatting to chiding is not worth a chute.[1]

[= scolding is not worth replying to.] **1546** HEYWOOD II. v. 56. [[1] *chut*, an exclamation of impatience.]

Chawbent, *see* Cheshire.

Cheam, *see* Sutton.

Cheap and nasty.

1831 *Blackw. Mag.* Feb. 416/2 On the top of the 'cheap and nasty', did you never pass through Birmingham? **1885** c. LOWE *Prince Bismarck* (1898) vii [Bismarck] wished to spare his countrymen . . . a repetition of the 'cheap and nasty' verdict which had been pronounced on their products at Philadelphia. **1926** *Times* 31 Mar. 15/4 Official rudeness is cheap, though nasty.

Cheap enough to say, *God help you*, It is.

1732 FULLER no. 2922.

Cheap sitting as standing, It is as.

1666 TORRIANO 277 The English say, it is as cheap sitting as standing, my masters. **1738** SWIFT (Dial. i) 333 *Lady A.* Well, but sit while you stay, 'tis as cheap sitting as standing. **1858** SURTEES *Ask Mamma* xlvii Let 's get chairs and be snug; it 's as cheap sitting as standing.

Cheap (*adj.*), *see also* Best is best c.; Good c. is dear; Good thing c. (He will never have) that is afraid to ask price; Light c., lither yield; Meal c. and shoon dear.

Cheap (*verb*), *see* Heap (The more you), worse you c.

Cheapen, *see* Never c. unless you mean to buy.

Cheapside is the best garden.

1662 FULLER (*London*) II. 333 Natural commodities are not to be expected to grow in this place, . . . Cheapside being called the best garden only by metaphor.

Cheat, and the cheese will show.

1917 BRIDGE 35 . . . That is, if too much cream has been extracted or the cows poorly fed.

Cheat at play, He that will | will cheat you anyway.

1721 KELLY 168. **1732** FULLER no. 6302.

Cheat'em, *see* Starv'em.

Cheat mine own father at cards, I would.

1678 RAY 68.

Cheater, *see* Kingdom of a c. (In the) wallet carried before.

Cheating, *see* Knavery (C.) in all trades.

Cheeks, *see* Little mense o' the c. to bite aff nose.

Cheer, *see* Welcome is best c.

Cheerful look makes a dish a feast A.

1640 HERBERT 319.

Cheese, If you will have a good | and have'n old, you must turn'n seven times before he is cold.

1678 RAY *Somerset* 352.

Cheese and money should always sleep together one night.

1917 BRIDGE 35 . . . Said by farmers in old times, who, immediately the cheese was sold and weighed, demanded payment in gold before the cheese was sent away.

Cheese digests everything but itself.

1584 LYLY *Sapho & P.* III. ii. Wks. (1902) II. 394 *Mol.* It is against the old verse, *Caseus est nequam. Cry.* Yea, but it digesteth all things except itself. **1629** T. ADAMS *Serm.* (1861–2) I. 161 And, as cheese to digest all the rest, yet itself never digested, treason. **1678** RAY 40 Cheese it is a peevish elf, It digests all things but itself. This is a translation of that old rhyming Latin verse, *Caseus est nequam, quia, digerit omnia sequâm.* **1738** SWIFT (Dial. ii) 348 They say, cheese digests everything but itself.

Cheese, *see also* After c. comes nothing; Bread, butter, and green c. very good Friese; Chalk and c.; Cheat and c. will show; Green c. (You see no) but teeth water; Hard c.; Hull c.; King's c. goes away in parings; Moon is made of c.; See his nose c. first; Suffolk c.; Thin as Banbury c.

Cheiny, *see* Philip and C.

Cherry year, a merry year: a plum year, a dumb year, A. (*Cf.* Pear year, &c., Plum year, &c.)

1678 RAY 52. **1732** FULLER no. 6139. **1893** INWARDS 5.

Cherry's boose,[1] He has got into.

c. **1791** PEGGE *Derbicisms* (E.D.S.) 90 (A) When a man weds a second wife, older and perhaps not so handsome as the first, they say 'He has put Browney into Cherry's boose'. **1917** BRIDGE 67 . . . *He has got into good quarters.* A favourite name for a red cow, . . . the most esteemed for milking. [[1] cow-stall.]

Cherry, -ies, *see also* Peas with the King, c. with beggar; Red as a c.; Two bites of a c.; Woman and c. are painted for harm.

Cherry-tree, One | sufficeth not two jays.

1576 LAMBARD *Peramb. of Kent* (1826) 269 It might wel be verified of them, which was wont to be commonly saide, *Unicum Arbustum, non alit duos Erithacos.* One Cherry tree sufficeth not two Iays. **1869** HAZLITT 306.

Cheshire born and Cheshire bred, strong i' th' arm and weak i' th' head.

1917 BRIDGE 36.

Cheshire cat, *see* Grin like C. c.

Cheshire chief of men.

1603 DRAYTON *The Baron's Wars* Wks. (Hebel) II. 19 and V. 71 With those of Cheshire, chiefest for their place. **1613–22** DRAYTON *Polyolb.* viii. 8 (1876) II. 67 For which, our proverb calls her, *Cheshire, chief of men.* **1662** FULLER (*Chesh.*) I. 265 'Cheshire chief of men'. . . . The Cestrians have always demeaned themselves right valiantly in their undertakings.

Cheshire nor Chawbent, Neither in.

1678 RAY 301 . . . That is, nither in *Kent* nor *Christendome. Chawbent* is a town in *Lancashire.* **1917** BRIDGE 96 Neither in Cheshire nor Chowbent. A peculiar kind of saying which is hard to describe—*neither here nor there, neither in the greater nor in the less.* Chawbent or Chowbent, near Manchester, was generally supposed to be much behind the times.

Cheshire, In | there are Lees as plenty as fleas, and as many Davenports as dogs' tails.

1787 GROSE (*Chesh.*) 155 . . . The names of Lee and Davenport are extremely common in this county; the former is, however variously spelt as Lee, Lea, Leigh, Ley, &c. **1917** BRIDGE 18 As many Leighs as fleas, Massies as asses, Crewes as crows, and Davenports as dogs' tails. Four of the great Cheshire families. . . . Another version: Egertons and Leighs As thick as fleas.

Chess-board, *see* World on your c. (Had you the).

Chester, *see* Yew bow in C. (More than one).

Chestnut horse, A.

1838 SOUTHEY *Doctor* v. 58 It is a saying founded on experience that a chesnut horse is always a good one, and will do more work than any horse of the same size of any other colour.

Chestnuts out of the fire with the cat's (dog's) paw, Take the.

[LA FONTAINE ix. 17.] **1640** HERBERT 344 To take the nuts from the fire with the dog's foot. **1657** M. HAWKE *Killing is Murder* These he useth as the monkey did the Cat's paw to scrape the nuts out of the fire. **1662** FULLER (*Surrey*) III. 205 The fable is well known of an ape, which, having a mind to a chestnut lying in the fire, made the foot of a spaniel to be his tongs, by the proxy whereof he got out the nut for himself. **1692** L'ESTRANGE *Aesop's Fab.* clxxxvi (1738) 200 'Tis a court master-piece, to draw chestnuts out of the fire with other peoples fingers. **1868** H. SMART *Breezie Langton* IV You served us all pretty much the same as the monkey did the cat when he wanted the hot chestnuts.

Cheverel, *see* Conscience like a c.'s skin.

Chevin[1] to the trout, Said the | my head's worth all thy bouk.[2]

1496 *Bk. St. Alban's Fishing* 28 The cheuyn

is a stately fysshe: and his heed is a deynty morsell. **1678** RAY 52. [¹ chub. ² belly.]

Chew the cud, To.

[= to ruminate.] **1382** WYCLIF *Hosea* vii. 14 Thei chewiden cud vpon whete, and wyne, and departiden fro me. **1547** *Homilies* 1 *Exhort. Holy Script.* II (1859) 15 Let vs ruminate, and (as it were) chewe the cudde that wee maye haue the sweete iewse . . . & consolation of them. **1749** FIELDING *Tom Jones* XVIII. iii Having left her a little while to chew the cud, if I may use that expression, on these first tidings.

Chicken, To be no.

[= no longer young.] **1720** SWIFT *Stella's Birthday* Pursue your trade of scandal-picking, Your hints that Stella is no chicken. **1761** A. MURPHY *Old Maid* Wks. (1786) II. 158 *Mrs. Har.* Recollect, sister, that you are no chicken. **1877** E. WALFORD *Gt. Families* I. 270 He must have been well forward in years—or at all events, as they say, no chicken.

Chicken is the country's, but the city eats it, The.

1640 HERBERT 322.

Chickens feed capons.

1678 RAY 111 Chickens feed capons . . . Chickens come to be capons. **1732** FULLER no. 1056 Capons were at first but chickens.

Chicken(s), *see also* Children and c. always picking; Count one's c. before hatched; Fox run (Though the), c. hath wings; May c. come cheeping; Michaelmas c. . . . never come to good; Mother Cary's c.

Chick(s), *see* January c.; Love like c. (They).

Chiding, *see* Chatting to c. not worth a chute; Woe to the house where there is no c.

Child, To a | all weather is cold.

1640 HERBERT 351.

Child for the first seven years, Give me a | and you may do what you like with him afterwards.

1902–4 LEAN III. 472 . . . A Jesuit maxim.

Child hath a red tongue, like its father, The.

1678 RAY 234.

Child is christened, When the | you may have godfathers enough.

1639 CLARKE 283 When the child is christ'ned, every man will be godfather. **1670** RAY 69 . . . When a mans need is supplied or his occasions over, people are ready to offer their assistance or service. **1732** FULLER no. 5573 When the christning is over you may have godfathers enough.

Child is father of the man, The.

1802 WORDSWORTH ' *My heart leaps up*' The Child is father of the Man. **1871** SMILES *Character* 33 The influences which contribute to form the character of the child endure through life. . . . 'The child is father of the man'; or, as Milton puts it, 'The childhood shows the man, as morning shows the day.' **1905** MYERS *Wordsworth* 93 'The child is father of the man', . . . and Wordsworth holds that the instincts and pleasures of a healthy childhood sufficiently indicate the lines on which our mature character should be formed.

Child may have too much of his mother's blessing, A.

1639 CLARKE 161 (with 'man' for 'child'). **1670** RAY 122 . . . Mothers are oftentimes too tender and fond of their children. Who are ruined and spoiled by their cockering and indulgence.

Child says nothing, but what it heard by the fire, The.

1640 HERBERT 331. **1721** KELLY 318 The bairn speaks in the fields what he heard by the slett.¹ [¹ fireside.]

Child sleep upon bones, Let not a.

1678 RAY 351 . . . *Somerset.* i.e. The nurses lap.

Child's bird and a knave's (boy's) wife, A.

c. **1400** LYDGATE *Churl & Bird* 374 A childes birrde and a knavis wyfe Have often siethe gret sorowe and myschaunce. **1678** RAY 351 A child's bird and a boy's wife are well used. *Somerset.*

Child's pig but father's bacon.

c. **1350** *Douce MS. 52,* no. 113 Childe is pigge, and fader is the flicche. Porcellus nati fit perna patris veterati. **1678** RAY 111 Child's pig, but father's bacon. Parents usually tell their children, this pig or this lamb is thine, but when they come to be grown up and sold, parents themselves take the money for them. **1914** K. F. PURDON *Folk of Furry F.* ii It would be 'child's pig and Daddy's bacon', . . . with that calf.

Child's service is little, A | yet he is no little fool that despiseth it.

1640 HERBERT 326.

Child(ren), *see* Ask the mother if c. like father; Bachelor's wives and maids' c.; Better a snotty c.; Better c. weep than old men; Burnt c. dreads fire; Cares not whose c. cry; Cockers his c. (He that) provides for enemy; Die like a chrisom c.; Far folks . . . and fair c. die; Give a c. till he craves . . . you'll have foul knave; Good c.; Happy is he that is happy in c.; Harry's c. of Leigh, never one like; Heaven takes care of c.; Horse (The best) needs . . . and aptest c. needs teaching;

Kindness is lost bestowed on c.; Kiss the c. for nurse's sake; Late c. early orphans; Maintains one vice (What) would bring up two c.; *Maxima debetur*; Morning sun, wine-bred c. seldom end well; Past dying of her first c.; Poor man's cow dies, rich man's c.; Praise the c. and make love to mother; Put another man's c. in your bosom; Sad burden to carry dead man's c.; Service a c. does father is to make him foolish; Silly c. is soon ylered; Virtue and a trade best portion for c.; Well for him who has good c.; Wipes the c.'s nose (He that); Wise c. that knows own father.

Children, He that hath | all his morsels are not his own.

1640 HERBERT 337.

Children and chicken must be always picking.

1573 TUSSER 178 Yong children and chickens would ever be eating. **1670** RAY 33.

Children (Drunkards) and fools cannot lie (*or* speak truth). (*Cf.* Fools and madmen, &c.)

1545 TAVERNER 62 Oure common prouerbe . . . Children, drunkers and fooles, can not lye. **1546** HEYWOOD I. xi. 31 Men say also, children and fooles can not ly. **1670** RAY 69 Children and fools speak truth. **1805** SCOTT *Let. to Ellis* in LOCKHART *Life* xiii It is a proverb, that children and fools talk truth.

Children and fools have merry lives.

1639 CLARKE 298. **1670** RAY 69 . . . They are not concern'd either for what is past, or for what is to come.

Children and fools must not play with edged tools. (*See also* Jesting with edged tools.)

a. **1568** ASCHAM *Schoolmaster* (Wks. ed. Wright 266) . . . but fine edge tooles in a fole or mad mans hand. **1642** MILTON *Apol. Smect.* Prose Wks. (1904) III. 114 That he may know what it is to be a child, and yet to meddle with edged tools, I turn his antistrophon upon his own head. **1839** DICKENS *N. Nickleby* xlvii 'Oh dear, what an edged tool you are!' 'Don't play with me then', said Ralph impatiently, 'You know the proverb.'

Children are certain cares, but uncertain comforts.

1639 CLARKE 240 Children are uncertain comforts, but certain cares. **1670** RAY 4. **1886** E. J. HARDY *How to be Happy* xvii Children are *not* 'certain sorrows and uncertain pleasures' when properly managed.

Children are poor men's riches.

1611 COTGRAVE s.v. 'Enfant'. **1670** RAY 4. **1732** FULLER no. 1094.

Children are the parents' riches.

1602–3 SHAKS. *All's Well* I. iii. 28 They say barnes are blessings. **1616** DRAXE 23.

Children are to be deceived with comfits and men with oaths.

[PLUTARCH, *Lysander*, and ERASM. *Ad.*, substituting 'dice' for 'comfits'. HOR. *Sat.* 1. 1. 25 *Ut pueris olim dant crustula blandi Doctores*, As enticing teachers are wont to give pastry to boys.] **1605** BACON *Adv. Learn.* II. xxiii (1900) 246 That other principle of Lysander, *That children are to be deceived with comfits, and men with oaths*: and the like evil and corrupt positions.

Children, He that hath no | feedeth them fat.

1573 SANDFORD (1576) 208 He that hath no children doth bring them up well. **1611** DAVIES. Prov. 236. **1616** DRAXE 59.

Children hear at home, What | doth soon fly abroad.

1611 COTGRAVE s.v. 'Enfant'. **1670** RAY 4. **1732** FULLER no. 5482.

Children in Holland, The | take pleasure in making What the children in England take pleasure in breaking.

1822 SCOTT *Nigel* Introd. Ep. For the critics, they have their business, and I mine; as the nursery proverb goes—'The children in Holland take pleasure in making What the children in England take pleasure in breaking.'

Children, He that has no | knows not what is love.

1666 TORRIANO 89. **1855** BOHN 4.

Children learn to creep ere they can go.

c. **1350** *Douce MS. 52*, no. 116 Fyrst the chylde crepyth and after gooth. **1546** HEYWOOD I. xi. 30 Children learne to créepe er they can learne to go.

Children nowadays, There are no.

1902–4 LEAN IV. 145 . . . This was said 200 years ago: Ah! il n'y a plus d'enfans.— MOLIÈRE, *Mal. Im.* xi.

Children pick up words as pigeons peas, and utter them again as God shall please.

[*Cf.* SHAKS. *L.L.L.* V. ii. 315 This fellow picks up wit as pigeons peas, and utters it again when God doth please. He is wit's pedlar.] **1670** RAY 213.

Children (Maidens) should be seen, and not heard.

c. **1400** *Mirk's Festial* (E.E.T.S.) I. 230 For hyt ys an old Englysch sawe: 'A mayde schuld be seen, but not herd.' **1670** RAY 51 Maidens must be seen and not heard. **1738** SWIFT (Dial. i) 334 Fie, miss; they say maids should be seen and not heard. **1866** E. J. HARDY *How to be Happy* xvii 'Little people should be seen and not heard' is a stupid saying.

Children stand quiet, When | they have done some ill.

1640 HERBERT 341.

Children suck the mother when they are young, and the father when they are old.

1678 RAY 112.

Children to bed and the goose to the fire.

1670 RAY 168. **1710** STEELE *Tatler* No. 263 (1899) IV. 339 We have all of us heard in our infancy, of 'putting the children to bed, and laying the goose to the fire'. This was one of the jocular sayings of our forefathers.

Children when they are little make parents fools, when they are great they make them mad.

1640 HERBERT 360. **1670** RAY 4.

Children, *see also* Child(ren).

Chimneys, Many | little smoke.

1583 STUBBES *Anat.* (New Sh. S.) 105 Many Chimnies, but little smoke. **1603** H. CROSSE, *Virtue's Commonwlth* (Gros.) 89. **1616** DRAXE 93.

Chimney(s), *see also* Build two c. (Easier to) than maintain one; Think there is bacon (Where you), there is no c.

China orange, *see* Lombard Street.

Chin-cough, *see* Tail will catch the c.

Chink, So we get the | we'll bear with the stink.

[L. *Non olet.* 'It doesn't smell'; founded upon a remark of Vespasian after applying to his nose a handful of the gold brought in by his tax on urine. SUET. *Vesp.* 23. JUV. 14. 204. Fr. *L'Argent n'a pas d'odeur.* cf. **1628** EARLE *Microcosm., Phisitian* (Arb.) 25 Of al odors he likes best the smel of Vrine, and holds *Vespatians* rule, that no gain is vnsauory.] **1596** HARINGTON *Metam. of Ajax* (1814) 68 So we get the chinks, We will bear with the stinks. **1639** CLARKE 293 So we get chink, we'll bear with stinke. **1692** DRYDEN *To Mr. Southern* 8 But the gain smells not of the excrement. **1721** KELLY 359 We will bear with the stink, when it brings in the clink. **1888** J. E. T. ROGERS *Econ. Interp. Hist.* (1894) II. xxi. 464 Defoe . . . was ready to take a brief from either of the contending factions. He had accepted as his guide in literary life the adage of Vespasian, *Non olet.* **1902** A. LANG *Hist. Scot.* II. xiii. 335 It did not follow that James need continue to take

money from hands dipped in his mother's blood. Of money, however, from whatever quarter, James thought *non olet.*

Chip in a pottage pot, Like a | doth neither good nor harm.

1619 J. FAVOUR *Antiquity* 234 *Hierome* . . . is made but as a chip in a Keale pot. **1659** N. R. 74. **1670** RAY 168. **1688** *Vox Cleri Pro Rege* 56 A sort of Chip in Pottage, which (he hopes) will not do Popery much good, nor the Church of England much harm. **1880** *Church Times* 25 June (D.) The Burials Bill . . . is thought . . . to resemble the proverbial chip in porridge, which does neither good nor harm. **1910** JOYCE *Eng. as we Speak it in Ireld.* 141 A person who does neither good nor harm . . . is 'like a chip in porridge'; almost always said as a reproach.

Chip of the (same *or*) old block, A.

1627 SANDERSON *Serm.* I. 283 Am not I a child of the same Adam, a vessel of the same clay, a chip of the same block, with him? **1642** MILTON *Apol. Smect.* Prose Wks. (1904) III. 144 How well dost thou now appear to be a chip of the old block, that could find 'Bridge Street and alehouses in heaven'? **1670** RAY 168 . . . He is his father's own son: taken always in an ill sense. **1824** SCOTT *Redg.* xv My father (God bless the old man!), a true chip of the old Presbyterian block.

Chips, *see* Carpenter (Like) like c.; Hew not too high lest c. fall in eye.

Choice in rotten apples, There is small.

1593–4 SHAKS. *Tam. Shrew* I. i. 137 Faith, as you say, there's small choice in rotten apples.

Choice to begin love, but not to end it, A man has.

1855 BOHN 294.

Choice, *see also* Pay your money and take your c.

Choke(s), *see* Hastens a glutton (Who), c. him; Too much pudding c. a dog.

Choleric drinks, The | the melancholic eats, the phlegmatic sleeps.

1640 HERBERT 359. **1670** RAY 5.

Choleric man withdraw a little; From a | from him that says nothing for ever.

1631 MABBE *Celestina* (T.T.) 99 That ancient adage: from an angry man get the gone but for a while; but from an enemy for ever. **1640** HERBERT 324.

Choose a wife on a Saturday rather than a Sunday.

1737 FRANKLIN Oct. If you want a neat wife, chuse her on a Saturday. **1813** RAY 54 If thou desirest a wife, chuse her on Saturday rather than on a Sunday. i.e. see her in an undress. **1846** DENHAM 2.

Choose for yourself and use for yourself.

1616 DRAXE 232 Euery man must chuse and vse his owne wife. **1639** CLARKE 230.

Choose neither a woman nor linen by candle-light.

1573 SANDFORD 101 Choose not a woman, nor linnen clothe by the candle. **1611** DAVIES Prov. 79 'Choose neither women nor lynnen by candle'. **1678** RAY 64 Neither women nor linen by candlelight. **1738** SWIFT (Dial. iii) 352 They say women and linen show best by candle-light. **1737** FRANKLIN May Fine linen, girls and gold so bright Choose not to take by candle-light.

Choose none for thy servant who have served thy betters.

1640 HERBERT 364. **1852** E. FITZGERALD *Polonius* 76 A proverb bids us beware of taking for servant one who has waited on our betters.

Choose not a house near an inn, or in a corner.

1640 HERBERT 330 Choose not a house near an Inn [viz: (for noise); or in a corner (for filth)].

Choosing a wife, and buying a sword, we ought not to trust another, In.

1640 HERBERT 340.

Choose (·ing), *see also* Best or worst to man is c. good or ill wife; Horse made and wife to make (C.); Pays the lawing c. the lodging (Let him that); Wink and c.

Chop and change, To.

[The meaning of *chop* has passed from that of 'to barter' to that of to 'change, alter'.] **1540** COVERDALE *Confut. Standish* Wks. II. 419 Even as ye pervert the words of holy scripture . . . as ye chop and change with it. **1635** QUARLES *Embl.* I. ix (1718) 38 O, who would trust this world . . . That . . . chops and changes ev'ry minute. **1888** *Poor Nellie* 299 It is to be hoped he knows his own mind this time, and does not intend chopping and changing again.

Chop logic, To.

[= to bandy logic, argue.] *c.* **1525** SKELTON *Replyc.* 118 Wolde . . . That wyse Harpocrates Had your mouthes stopped . . . Whan ye logyke chopped. **1577** STANYHURST *Descr. Irel.* in HOLINSHED VI. 49 You charge me . . . that I presume to chop logike with you . . . by answering your snappish Quid with a knappish Quo. **1611** BEAUM. & FL. *Kt. Burn. P.* I. 51 Harke how he chops Logicke with his Mother.

Chopped hay, It goes down like.

1678 RAY 235. **1746** GRAY to Wharton 11 Sept. It [Aristotle] tastes for all the world like chopped hay.

Chough, *see* Cornish c.

Chrisom, *see* Die like a c. child.

Christ (*or* The church) takes not, What | the exchequer carries away.

1855 BOHN 555. *Span.*

Christen the bairn, When you | you (should) know what to call it.

1721 KELLY 347 . . . Spoken in bargain making when we agree on express terms, we know not what to give, and what to expect. **1862** HISLOP 321 When ye christen the bairn ye should ken what to ca't.

Christened with pump water, He was.

1678 RAY 79 . . . It is spoke of one that hath a red face.

Christen(s, ed), *see also* Child is c. (When), godfathers enough; Parson always c. own child first.

Christendom, *see* Kent nor C.

Christian, A complete | must have the works of a Papist, the words of a Puritan, and the faith of a Protestant.

1635 HOWELL *Fam. Lett.* 25 Aug. (1655) II. xi. 23 One who said, That to make one a compleat Christian, he must have the *works of a Papist, the words of a Puritan, and the Faith of a Protestant.*

Christians to the lions! The.

197 TERTULLIAN *Apolog.* xl in RAMSAY *Ch. in Rom. Emp.* (1894) 327 'If the Tiber rises, if the Nile does not rise, if the heavens give no rain, if there is an earthquake, famine, or pestilence, straightway the cry is, "The Christians to the lions!"' **1629** T. ADAMS *Serm.* (1862) I. 466 The Christians . . . made Aurelius's army to prosper . . . ; yet *Christianos ad leones,*—Throw the Christians to the lions.

Christian(s), *see also* Jews spend at Easter; Rain (There is no), the C. are cause.

Christianity, *see* Muscular C.

Christmas comes but once a year.

1573 TUSSER 28 At Christmas play and make good cheere, for Christmas comes but once a yeere. **1622** WITHER 'A Christmas Carroll' in *Faire-Virtue.* And what they want they take in beer, For Christmas comes but once a year. **1931** *Times* 24 Dec. 13/2 'Christmas comes but once a year,' said the old rhyme, 'but when it comes it brings good cheer.' . . . There was a time when Christmas 'good cheer' meant principally a succession of massive meals.

Christmas, *see also* After C. Lent; Coming and so is C.; Talk of C. so long that it comes.

Chronicle small beer, To.

[small beer = trifling matters.] **1604-5** SHAKS. *Othello* II. i. 161 To suckle fools and chronicle small beer. **1880** *Academy* 25 Sept. 219 Two such chroniclers of small beer as Boswell and Erskine.

Church is an anvil which has worn out many hammers, The.

1908 ALEX. MACLAREN *Acts Apost.* I. 136 'The Church is an anvil which has worn out many hammers', and the story of the first collision is, in essentials, the story of all.

Church is not so large but the priest may say service in it, The.

1678 RAY 113.

Church mis-went, If you would go to a | you must go to Cuckstone in Kent.

1736 S. PEGGE *Kenticisms, Prov.* (E.D.S.) 69 ... 'Or very unusual in proportion, as Cuckstone church in Kent, of which it is said— "if you would goe", &c.'. Dr. Plot's Letter to Bp. Fell, in LELAND *Itin.* ii. 137 [. . . It refers to Cuxton, near Rochester.]

Church mouse, *see* Mouse (Mice).

Church (Kirk) stand in the churchyard (kirkyard), Let the.

1678 RAY 113. **1832** HENDERSON 130 . . . Everything in its place.

Church will lose nothing, and defend nothing, The.

1626 OVERBURY *Obs. in Trav.* Wks. (1890) 242 The unproportionable part of the land which the church holds, all which is likewise dead to militarie uses. For, as they say there, *The church will lose nothing, nor defend nothing.*

Church work goes on slowly.

1639 FULLER *Holy War* III. i (1840) 117 Guy ... besieged Ptolemais ... But this siege was churchwork, and therefore went on slowly. **1712** ADDISON *Spect.* No. 383 Wks. (1902) III. 361 The fifty new churches will . . . mend the prospect ; but church-work is slow!

Church(es), *see also* Christ (The c.) takes not (What), exchequer carries away ; Fashion's sake, as dogs go to c. ; Flaming figure in country c. ; Foreheet nothing but building c. ; God hath his c. (Where), the devil . . . ; Good dog who goes to c. ; Houses than parish c. (More) ; Itch of disputing is scab of c. ; Nearer the c., farther from God ; New c. old steeple ; Parsons than parish c. (More) ; *Pater noster* built c. ; Poorer the c. purer the c. ; See a churchman ill (Though you), continue in c. ; Spitting in c. (Some make conscience of), yet . . . ; Three ways, the c., sea, court ; Three wonders of England ; Visible c.

Churchyard, A piece of a | fits everybody.

1640 HERBERT 364.

Churchman, *see* See a c. ill (Though you), continue in church.

Churchyard is so handsome, No | that a man would desire straight to be buried there.

1640 HERBERT 361.

Churchyard, *see also* Green winter fat c. ; Green Yule . . . fat c. ; Hot May fat c. *See also* Kirkyard.

Churl fall out of the moon, Have a care lest the.

c. **1380** CHAUCER *Troylus* I. 1023 Quod Pandarus, 'Thow hast a ful gret care Lest that the cherl may falle out of the moone!' **1846–59** *Denham Tracts* ii. 57 (F.L.S.) (as an 'old, very old proverb').

Churl, *see also* Put a c. upon a gentleman.

Churm, *see* Swarm of bees in a c.

Churning days, I will make him know.

1678 RAY 235.

Cipher in arithmetic, Like a.

1399 LANGLAND *Rich. Redeless* iv. 53 Than satte summe, as siphre doth in awgrym, That noteth a place, and no thing availith. **1547** J. HARRISON *Exhort. Scottes* 229 Our presidentes . . . doo serue but as Cyphers in Algorisme, to fill the place. **1598–9** SHAKS. *Hen. V* Prol. 17 Since a crooked figure may Attest in little place a million ; . . . Let us, ciphers to this great accompt, On your imaginary forces work. **1610–11** *Wint. T.* I. ii. 6 Like a cipher, Yet standing in rich place, I multiply.

Circe, *see* Cup of C.

Circumstances alter cases.

[*Cf.* **1600** DRAYTON *Idea* (Wks. ed. Hebel II. 324) The Circumstance doth make it good or ill. **1642** TORRIANO 60 Conditions break laws.] **1870** C. DICKENS *E. Drood* ix But circumstances alter cases. **1895** J. PAYN *In Market Overt* xxxix Circumstances alter cases even with the best of us, as was shown in a day or two in the conduct of the Bishop.

Circuses, *see* Bread and c.

Cities are taken by the ears.

[= by propaganda.] **1640** HERBERT 361.

Cities seldom change religion only.

1651 HERBERT 320.

Cities, *see also* City (-ies).

Citizen is at his business before he rise, The.

1640 HERBERT 361.

Citizens of Cork are all akin, The.

1654 FULLER *Comment. Ruth* in *Sermons* (1891) I. 100 Camden reports of the citizens of Cork, that all of them ... are of kindred one to the other: but I think, that all wealthy men will hook in the cousin, and draw in some alliance.

City is in a bad case, whose physician hath the gout, That.

1678 RAY *Adag. Hebr.* 397. **1911** A. COHEN *Anct. Jew. Prov.* 107 Unhappy the province whose chancellor of the exchequer is one-eyed.

City (Castle, Woman) that parleys is half gotten, A.

1549 *Complaynt of Scotland* (E.E.T.S.) xiii. 108 Ther is ane ald prouerb that says, that ane herand damysele, and ane spekand castel, sal neuyr end vith honour. **1651** HERBERT 368. **1734** FRANKLIN 40 Neither a fortress nor a m—d will hold out long after they begin to parley.

City (-ies), *see also* Chicken is country's but c. eats it; Great c. great solitude; Men who make c. (It is); No gates no c.; See the c. for the houses (Cannot).

Civility costs nothing.

1841 S. WARREN *Ten Thousand a-Year* iii It may be as well ... to acknowledge the ... fellow's note— ... civility costs nothing. **1873** ALLINGHAM *Rambles* I. 207 Civility costs nothing, ... nothing, that is, to him that shows it; but it often costs the world very dear.

Civility, *see also* Loses anything by c. (One never).

Claps his dish at the wrong man's door, He.

c. **1809** JONSON *Ev. Man in Humour* II. i. 79 An he thinks to be relieved by me, ... he has the wrong sow by the ear, i' faith; and claps his dish at the wrong man's door.

Clartier[1] the cosier, The.

1816 SCOTT *Antiq.* xxvi There was dirt good store. Yet ... an appearance of ... comfort, that seemed to warrant their old sluttish proverb, 'The clartier the cosier'. **1913** A. & J. LANG *Highw. & By. in Border* ix. 239 In an arctic climate, there may perhaps be some excuse for the proverb: 'the clartier the cosier'. [[1] dirtier.]

Claw me, and I'll claw thee.

[Used of mutual flattery.] **1530** PALSGRAVE 486 (A) Clawe my backe, and I wyll clawe thy toe. **1531** TINDALE *Expos.* 1 *John* (1537) 72 We saye, clawe me, clawe y[e]. **1629** J. ADAMS *Serm.* (1861–2) I. 186 'Claw me and I will claw thee'; wink at mine, and I will not see thy faults. **1738** SWIFT (Dial. iii) 350 Ay, claw me, and I'll claw you. **1825** *Blackw. Mag.* XVII. 461 I do not object to Jeffrey's clawing his . . . brother Editor, who so regularly claws him in his New Monthly.

Claw the back of (or claw by the back), To.

[= to 'stroke down', flatter.] *c.* **1394** LANG-

LAND *P. Pl.* Crede 365 Whou þey curry Kinges, & her back claweþ. *a.* **1541** WYATT *Poet. Wks.* (1868) 158 'Take heed of him that by thi back thee claweth'; For none is worse than is a friendly foe.

Claws it as Clayton clawed the pudding when he eat bag and all, He.

1678 RAY 282. **1732** FULLER no. 1826.

Claw(s), *see also* Jaws outrun your c. (Don't let); Scratch (C.) where itches not.

Clay, *see* Sand feeds the c. (When the).

Clayton, *see* Claws it as C. clawed pudding.

Clean as a whistle, As.

1828 *Craven Gloss.* S.V. 'As clean' &c. a proverbial simile, signifying completely, entirely. **1849** W. S. MAYO *Kaloolah* (1850) V. 41 A first rate shot, ... head taken off as clean as a whistle.

Clean breast, To make a.

[= to confess.] **1752** CAMERON in *Scots Mag.* (1753) Oct. 508/1 He pressed him ... to make a clean breast, and tell him all. **1869** C. READE *Foul Play* lxvi I've got a penitent outside, ... he'll make a clean breast. **1891** A. LANG *Ess. in Lit.* 107 The pagan Aztecs only confessed once in a lifetime—... then they made a clean breast of it once for all.

Clean heels, light meals.

1917 BRIDGE 38 ... Refers to the superiority of clay land over sandy land for yielding milk ... On sandy land, cows come to be milked with clean feet; but on clay land the gate places are very muddy.

Clean linen, *see* Wrap up in c. l. (To).

Clean, *see also* Foul (He that has to do with) never comes away c.

Cleanliness is next to godliness.

1605 BACON *Adv. of Learning* II Cleanness of body was ever deemed to proceed from a due reverence to God. *a.* **1791** WESLEY *Serm.* lxxxviii *On Dress* (1838) III. 15 Slovenliness is no part of religion ... 'Cleanliness is indeed next to godliness'. **1876** BURNABY *Ride to Khiva* x 'Cleanliness is next to Godliness'. The latter quality, as displayed in a Russian devotee, is more allied with dirt than anything else.

Cleave the pin, To.

[= in archery, to hit the pin in the centre of the white of the butts.] *c.* **1450** *Coventry Myst.* (Shaks. Soc.) 138 Now, be myn trowthe, ȝe hytte the pynne. **1586** MARLOWE *1st Pt. Tamburl.* II. iv For kings are clouts that every man shoots at, Our crown the pin that thousands seek to cleave. **1594–5** SHAKS. *L.L.L.* IV. i. 140 Then will she get the up-shoot by cleaving the pin. **1594–5** *Rom. & Jul.* II. iv. 15 The very pin of his heart cleft with the blind bow-boy's butt-shaft.

Cleave to the crown though it hang on a bush.

1851 STRICKLAND *Lives of Q. of Eng.* II. 419 The crown [of Richard III] was hidden by a soldier in a hawthorn-bush, but was soon found. . . . To the same circumstance may be referred the loyal proverb of—'Cleave to the crown though it hang on a bush'.

Cleave (Hang, Hold) together like burrs, They.

c. 1330 *Arth. & Merl.* 8290 Togider thei cleued . . . So with other doth the burre. 1514 A. BARCLAY *Cyt. & Uplondyshm.* (1847) 43 Together they cleve more fast then do burres. 1546 HEYWOOD II. v. 59 They cleaue together like burs; that way I shall Pike out no more, than out of the stone wall. 1639 CLARKE 63 They hold together like burres. 1678 RAY 250 They hang together like burs. 1721 ARBUTHNOT *John Bull* (1727) 59 When a fellow stuck like a bur, that there was no shaking him off.

Clemency is cruelty, and cruelty clemency, Sometimes.

1853 TRENCH ii. 43 Catherine de Médicis . . . urged on him . . . a proverb, . . . one of the most convenient maxims for tyrants that was ever framed: *Sometimes clemency is cruelty, and cruelty clemency.*

Clemmed, *see* Smithwick (You been like) either c. or borsten.

Clent,[1] The people of | are all Hills, Waldrons, or devils.

1894 NORTHALL *Folk-phrases* (E.D.S.) 24 The people of Clent are all Hills, Waldrons, or devils. *Worc.* . . . Before 1600, 30 entries of Hills, 18 of Waldron, . . . are registered in the parish books. Afterwards the Hills and Waldrons multiplied exceedingly. [[1] Clent Hills, near Birmingham.]

Clergy, *see* Kittle shooting at c.; Ounce of discretion worth a pound of c.; Three classes of c., Nimrods. . . .

Clergymen's sons always turn out badly.

1886 E. J. HARDY *How to be Happy* xix 'Clergymen's sons always turn out badly'. . . . Because the children are surfeited with severe religion, *not* with the true religion of Christ. 1922 DEAN INGE *Outspoken Ess.* 2nd Ser. 264 An Eton boy . . . when asked why the sons of Eli turned out badly, replied, 'The sons of clergymen always turn out badly'.

Clerk makes the justice, It is the.

1660 A. BROME *Poems* 'The Leveller' (A) 'Tis we commons make the lords, and the clerk makes the justice. 1678 RAY 114.

Clerk of the weather, The.

[= an imaginary official supposed to regulate the weather.] 1841 F. CHAMIER *Tom Bowl.*

xli The wind died away, and . . . Lanyard, who longed for the action . . . cursed the clerk of the weather.

Clerks, The greatest | be not the wisest men.

[Med. L. *Magis magni clerici non sunt magis sapientes.* The greatest scholars are not the wisest men. RABELAIS I. xxxix.] *c.* 1386 CHAUCER *Reeve's T.* A 4054 The gretteste clerkès ben noght wisest men, As whilom to the wolf thus spake the mare.[1] 1481 CAXTON *Reynard* xxvii (Arb.) 63 It is true that I long syth haue redde and herde that the best clerkes ben not the wysest men. *a.* 1603 Q. ELIZABETH in CREIGHTON *Q. Eliz.* (1896) 284 When the Bishop of St. Davids preached . . . on . . . 'Lord teach us to number our days . . .', Elizabeth . . . told him that 'he might have kept his arithmetic for himself: but I see that the greatest clerks are not the wisest men'. 1655 FULLER *Ch. Hist.* III. i (1868) I. 331 Henry Beauclerc . . . crossed the common proverb, 'The greatest clerks are not the wisest men'; being one of the most profound scholars and most politic princes in his generation. [[1] 'The fable of the Wolf and the Mare is found in the Latin Esopean collections.' WRIGHT.]

Clerk(s), *see also* Curate licks the knife (When), bad for c.; Parish c.; Priest (Such as the), such c.; Schools make subtle c.

Cleveland in the clay, bring in two soles and carry one away.

1670 RAY 257 . . . Cleveland is that part of Yorkshire, which borders upon the bishopric of Durham, where the ways in winter time are very foul and deep.

Cleveland, *see also* Roseberry Topping.

Clever, *see* Too c. by half.

Climate(s), *see* Travellers change c.

Climb the ladder must begin at the bottom, He who would.

1821 SCOTT *Kenilw.* vii I was the lowest of the four in rank—but what then?—he that climbs a ladder must begin at the first round.

Climb(s, ed), *see also* Ass c. a ladder (When), may find wisdom in women; Never c. never fell.

Climbers, *see* Hasty c. have sudden falls.

Clink, *see* Kiss the c.

Clip the wings of, To.

[= to check ambition or cripple strength or resources. L. *Pennas incidere alicui* To clip one's wings.] 1590 MARLOWE *Massacre Paris* III. ii Away to prison with him! I'll clip his wings. 1697 DRYDEN *Virg. Georg.* IV. 161 To clip the Wings Of their high-flying Arbitrary Kings. 1874 BLACKIE *Self-cult.* 10 To clip the wings of our conceit.

Clips, *see also* King's English (He c.).

Cloak for his knavery, He hath a.

1678 RAY 235.

Cloak for the rain, A quean hath ever a.

[= an expedient in every difficulty.] **1611** DAVIES Prov. 86.

Cloak for the rain, It is good to have a.

c. **1520** SKELTON *Magnif.* in Wks. (Dyce) I. 225 Ye, for your wyt is cloked for the rayne. **1599** PORTER *Angry Wom. Abingd.* IV. iii (Merm.) 179 *Nich.* 'Tis good to have a cloak for the rain; a bad shift is better than none at all.

Cloak to make when it begins to rain, Have not thy.

a. **1595** *Edward III* III. ii. 20–4. **1639** CLARKE 267 Hee that provides not a cloake before the raine, may chance to be wet to his coste. **1732** FULLER no. 1808.

Cloak, *see also* Although the sun shine leave not thy c.; Hector's c.; Old c. makes new jerkin; Plymouth c.

Clock goes as it pleases the clerk, The.

1629 T. ADAMS *Serm.* (1862) I. 317 Take heed you stay not too long. The devil is a false sexton, and sets the clock too slow, that the night comes ere we be aware. **1678** RAY 114. **1732** FULLER no. 4451.

Clock(s), *see also* Agree like the c. of London; Colne c. always at one; Put back the c.

Clog(s), *see* Nought is to wed with (Where), wise men flee the c.; Twice c., once boots.

Cloister, *see* Go old to the court, young to c.

Close mouth catches no flies, A, *or* **Into a shut mouth flies fly not.**

1599 MINSHEU (1623 Tt 2). **1617** MORYSON *Itin.* (1907–8) III. 400 I must remember the traveller of two good Italian proverbs: *In bocca serrata mai non entrò mosca.* Keep close lips and never fear, Any flies should enter there. **1623** CAMDEN 265. **1640** HERBERT 215. **1659** FULLER *Appeal Inj. Innoc.* (1840) 302 The Spanish proverb . . . is necessary in dangerous . . . times: 'where the mouth is shut, no fly doth enter'. **1700** DRYDEN *Fables, Cock & Fox* Not flattering lies shall soothe me more to sing with winking eyes, And open mouth, for fear of catching flies. **1897** 'H. S. MERRIMAN' *In Kedar's T.* xxiii Concha, remembering . . . that no flies enter a shut mouth, was silent.

Cloth, *see* Bad c. that take no colour; Best c. may have moth in it; Measure his c. by another's yard; Self-edge makes show of c.

Cloth-market, He is in the.

1678 RAY 235 . . . i.e. in bed. **1738** SWIFT (Dial. i) 333 I hope your early rising will do you no harm. I find you are but just come out of the cloth-market.

Clothe thee in war: arm thee in peace.

1640 HERBERT 335.

Clothe thee warm, eat little, drink enough, and thou shalt live.

1573 SANDFORD (1576) 223. **1578** FLORIO *First Fruites* 34.

Clothes, *see* Better blue c. (He is in his); Easter let your c. be new; God sendeth cold after c.; Mend your c. and you may hold out; Put off his c. before goes to bed (He will not); Wear c. (Ever since we), we know not one another.

Cloud, To be under a.

[= in trouble; out of favour; under a slur.] *c.* **1500** *Song Lady Bessy* (Percy Soc.) 79 Then came he under a clowde That some tyme in England was full hee. **1662** FULLER (*Norfolk*) II. 453 When he was under a cloud at court, and ousted of his judge's place, the lands . . . were . . . begged by a peer. **1705** STRYPE *Life of Cheke* (1821) vi, § 1. 138 Thus died Cheke in a cloud; and his name, once most honoured, much eclipsed by his infirmity.

Cloud has a silver lining, Every.

1634 MILTON *Comus* 221 Was I deceived, or did a sable cloud Turn forth her silver lining on the night? **1871** SMILES *Charac.* viii (1876) 218 While we see the cloud, let us not shut our eyes to the silver lining. **1885** GILBERT *Mikado* II. Orig. Plays Ser. III. (1895) 198 Don't let's be downhearted! There's a silver lining to every cloud.

Clouds are upon the hills, When the | they'll come down by the mills.

1678 RAY 49.

Clouds look as if scratched by a hen, If | get ready to reef your topsails then.

1883 ROPER 12. **1893** INWARDS 92.

Cloud(s), *see also* After black c. clear weather; Pryeth into every c. (He that); Red c. in the east.

Cloudy mornings turn to clear afternoons (*or* evenings).

[*Bk. of Tobit* iii. 22: post tempestatem tranquillitatem facis.] *c.* **1200** *Ancrene Riwle* (Morton) 376 Louerd, þet makest stille after storme. *c.* **1374** CHAUCER *Troylus* III. 1060 For I have seyn of a ful misty morwe Folwen ful ofte a merie somer's day. **1546** HEYWOOD II. ix. 81 Thus cloudy mornynges turne to cléere after noones. **1655** FULLER *Ch. Hist.* I. iv. par. 1 (1868) I. 35 Dark . . . was the morning of this century, which afterward cleared up to be a fair day. **1841** CHAMIER *Tom Bowl.* ii Though it's cloudy in the morning, the sun may shine bright enough at noon.

Clout, *see* Alike every day makes c. on Sunday; Better a c. than a hole; Cast ne'er a c. till May be out; Cow is in the c. (When), she's soon out.

Cloven hoof (foot), To show the.

[= to manifest Satanic agency or temptation.] **1594** GREENE *Looking Glass for London* Hath never a cloven hoof; a devil, quoth he. **1604** SHAKS. *Othello* V. ii. 284 I look down towards his feet: but that's a fable. **1662** BUTLER *Hudibras* I. i. 184 Whether the serpent, at the fall, Had cloven feet or none at all. **1822** SCOTT *Nigel* xiv Pleasant communings we had . . . until she showed the cloven foot, beginning to confer with me about some wench. **1822** GALT *Provost* iii The cloven hoof of self-interest was . . . to be seen aneath the robe of public principle. **1910** *Spectator* 19 Nov. 848 Only when [St. Bernard] speaks of household discipline does the cloven hoof of monastic tyranny show.

Clover, To live (*or* be) in.

[= to live luxuriously, clover being good for cattle.] **1710** *Brit. Apollo* II. No. 105. 3/1 I liv'd in Clover. **1813** RAY 57 He's in clover. **1856** R. VAUGHAN *Mystics* (1860) II. VIII. ix. 102 He has been sometimes in clover as a travelling tutor, sometimes he has . . . fared hard. **1864–5** DICKENS *Our Mut. F.* I. xv A man with coals and candles and a pound a week might be in clover here.

Clown, *see* Give a c. your finger.

Clubs are trump.

[= physical force is to decide the matter.] **1588** GREENE *Pandosto* (1843) 27 Taking up a cudgel . . . sware solemnly that she would make clubs trump if hee brought any bastard brat within her dores. **1607** *Widow of Watl. St.* III. i Aye, I knew by their shuffling, clubs would be trump.

Clude, *see* Escape C. and be drowned in Conway.

Coach and four (six) may be driven through any Act of Parliament, A.

a. **1686** SIR STEPHEN RICE in MACAULAY *Hist. Eng.* III. xii (1898) 426 What . . . the law . . . gave them, they could easily infer from a saying which, before he became a Judge, was often in his mouth, 'I will drive', he used to say, 'a coach and six through the Act of Settlement'.

Coaches won't run over him, The.

1813 RAY 186 . . . *i.e.* He is in jail.

Coals of fire on the head, To heap (cast, gather).

[See *Rom.* xii. 20: to produce remorse by requiting evil with good.] **1377** LANGLAND *P. Pl.* B. xiii. 144 To louye . . . þine enemye in al wyse euene forth with þi-selue, Cast coles on his hed. **1526–34** TINDALE *Rom.* xii. 20 In so doynge thou shalt heape coles of fyre on his heed. **1846** DICKENS *Let.* to Landor 22 Nov. I forgive you your reviling of me: there's a shovelful of live coals for your head. **1874** CARLYLE *Let.* to John Carlyle '[Disraeli] . . . I almost never spoke of without contempt . . . and . . . here he comes with a pan of hot coals for my guilty head'.

Coal(s), *see also* Carry c.; Carry c. to Newcastle; Cold (Let them that be) blow at c.; Cold c. to blow at; Glowing c. sparkle; Haul over the c.; Punch c., cut candle, neither good housewife.

Coast is clear, The.

1530 PALSGRAVE 486/2 The kynge intendeth to go to Calays, but we must first clere the costes. *c.* **1566** *The Bugbears* v. v. 4 Are the Costes clere abowte? **1567** HARMAN *Caveat* (ed. Furnivall) 30 Where these rufflares might well beholde the coaste about them cleare. **1590** LODGE *Rosalynde* Wks. (1883) I. 52 Seeing the coast cleare, . . . he sate him downe . . . and there feasted. **1591–2** SHAKS. *1 Hen. VI* I. iii. 90 See the coast clear'd, and then we will depart. **1612–15** BP. HALL *Contempl.* I. vi (1825) II. 192 Herod is now sent home. The coast is clear for the return of that holy family. **1872** C. READE *Wand. Heir* IV The coast was no sooner clear than Philip ran out and invited James into his office.

Coat, He who has but one | cannot lend it.

1855 BOHN 399. *Span.*

Coat that makes the gentleman, It is not the gay.

1615 W. GODDARD *Nest of Wasps* no. 57 Nowe tis cloathes the gentleman doth make. **1616** WITHALS 581. [*cf.* **1623** WODROEPHE *The Marrow of the French Tongue* 276 Often under a poore Wead, Is found a Man that is well-bred.] **1639** CLARKE 124. **1670** RAY 11. **1732** FULLER no. 3002 It is not the fine coat that makes the fine gentleman.

Coat, *see also* Cut the c. according to cloth; Learn to shape Idle a c.; Lost the large c. for the hood; Near is my c. but nearer my skin; Refer my c. and lose a sleeve; Shape a c. for the moon; Shape c. for them, but not their weird; Sure as the c. on back; Turn one's c.

Cob a hat and pair of shoes, Give | and he'll last for ever.

1869 HAZLITT 142 . . . *S. Devon.* Provide a stone foundation and a slate coping for a cob (*mud*) wall.—SHELLY.

Cob's pound, *see* Lob's pound.

Cobble and clout, They that can | shall have work when others go without.

1670 RAY 72. **1732** FULLER no. 6454.

Cobbler go beyond his last, Let not the.

[PLINY THE ELDER *Nat. Hist.* 35. 36 (10)

Ne supra crepidam iudicaret (*sutor*). **1539** TAVERNER f. 17 Let not the shoemaker go beyond hys shoe. **1580** LYLY *Euph. & his Eng.* (Arb.) 203 The shomaker must not goe aboue his latchet, nor the hedger meddle with any thing but his bil. **1594–5** SHAKS. *Rom. & Jul.* I. ii. 40 It is written that the shoemaker should meddle with his yard, and the tailor with his last. **1605** T. HEYWOOD *If you know not me* Wks. (1874) I. 210 Shoomaker, you goe a little beyond your last. **1692–4** L'ESTRANGE *Aesop's Fab.* ccxxv (1708) 245 The Cobler is not to go beyond his last. **1721** KELLY 242 . . . This is from the Latin, *Ne sutor ultra* [Erasmus is responsible for the bad *ultra*] *crepidam*. Taken from the famous story of *Apelles*, who could not bear that the cobler should correct any part of his picture beyond the slipper. **1875** JOWETT *Plato* (ed. 2) III. 53 Great evil may arise from the cobbler leaving his last and turning into . . . a legislator. **1908** LECKY *Hist. & Pol. Ess.* 21 In this, as in most other cases, the proverb was a wise one which bids the cobbler stick to his last.

Cobbler's law; he that takes money must pay the shot.

1678 RAY 90.

Cobblers and tinkers are the best ale-drinkers.

1659 HOWELL *Eng. Prov.* 17. **1670** RAY 5. **1732** FULLER no. 6229.

Cobbler(s), *see also* Higher the plum-tree . . . richer the c., blacker his thumb; Mock not a c.

Cock-a-hoop, To be.

[= in a state of elation.] **1663** BUTLER *Hudibras* I. iii. 14 Hudibras . . . having routed the whole Troop, With Victory was Cock-a-hoop. **1719** *Cordial Low Spirits* 162 The church was very cock-a-hoop, and held up its head and crow'd. **1817** EDGEWORTH *Love & L.* ii. i To make Catty cockahoop, I told her that, &c. **1834** GREVILLE *Mem. Geo. IV* (1875) III. xxiii. 104 The Tories have been mighty cock-a-hoop.

Cock a hoop (*or* the cock on the hoop), To set.

[app. to turn on the tap and let the liquor flow; hence, to drink without stint. By extension: to become reckless, to set all by the ears.] **1519** HORMAN *Vulgaria* (James) 436 He setteth al thyngs at cocke in the hope. **1529** MORE *Comf. agst. Trib.* II. Wks. 1177/2 They . . . set them downe and dryncke well for our sauiours sake, sette cocke a hoope, and fyll in all the cuppes at ones, and then lette Chrystes passion paye for all the scotte. **1538** BALE *Three Lawes* 1806 Cheare now maye I make & set cocke on the houpe. Fyll in all the pottes, and byd me welcome hostesse. **1594–5** SHAKS. *Rom & Jul.* I. v. 85 You'll make a mutiny among my guests! You will set cock-a-hoop. **1621** MOLLE *Camerar. Liv. Libr.* III. i. 147 Resolued . . . to set cock in hoope, and in guzling and good cheere spent all that was left.

Cock-and-bull story, A.

[= a rambling, idle story.] **1608** DAY *Law Trickes* IV. ii (A) What a tale of a cock and a bull he tolde my father. **1621** BURTON *Anat. Mel.* II. ii. IV. (1651) 274 Some mens whole delight is . . . to talk of a Cock and Bull over a pot. **1681** *Trial S. Colledge* 36 You run out in a story of a Cock and a Bull, and I know not what. **1796** BURNET *Mem. Metastasio* II. 77 Not to tire you with the repetition of all the cock and bull stories which I have formerly told you, &c. **1863** KINGSLEY *Water Bab.* vi. 243 They invented a cock-and-bull story, which . . . I never told them.

Cock crows on going to bed, If the | he's sure to rise with a watery head.

1846 DENHAM 18 . . . *i.e.* it will be rain next morning.

Cock is bold (crouse) on his own dunghill (midden), A.

[SENECA *De Morte Claudii: Gallus in sterquilinio suo plurimum potest.* The cock is master on his own dunghill.] *c.* **1023** EGBERT VON LÜTTICH *Fecunda Ratis* I. 1. 239 Confidens animi canis est in stercore noto. *c.* **1200** *Ancrene Riwle* (Morton) 140 As me seith: Thet coc is kene on his owune mixenne. **1387** TREVISA in HIGDEN's *Polychron.* vii. 5 As Seneca seiþ, a cock is most myzty on his dongehille. *c.* **1430** LYDGATE *Pilgr. Life of Man.* 1. 10048 How that every wyht ys bold upon hys owne (erly and late) at the dongel at hys gate [= DEQUILEVILLE, *Pèlerinage* ed. Stürzinger 1. 6351: *Chascun est fort sur son fumier et en sa terre se fait fier.*] **1546** HEYWOOD I. xi. 25 But he was at home there, he might speake his will. Euery cocke is proude on his owne dunghill. **1579** SPENSER *Shep. Cal.* Sept. 46 As cocke on his dunghill crowing cranck. *c.* **1600** DAY *Blind Beggar* II Thou durst not thus in scorn to old Strowd prate, But bock on thine own hill, thus near thy Gate. **1641** FERGUSSON 10 A cock is crouse in his own midding. **1771** SMOLLETT *Humph. Clink.* 13 July Wks. (1871) 534 Insolence . . . akin to the arrogance of the village cock, who never crows but upon his own dunghill.

Cock moult before the hen, If the | we shall have weather thick and thin: but if the hen moult before the cock, we shall have weather hard as a block.

1670 RAY 43.

Cock of hay, The first | frights the cuckoo away.

1846 DENHAM 52.

Cock of the walk.

1688 HOLME *Armoury* II. 251/2 The Cocks Walk is the place where he is bred, which usually is a place that no other Cock comes to. **1823** GROSE *Dict. Vulg. T.* (Egan) Cock, or Chief Cock of the Walk. The leading man in any Society or body; the best boxer in a village or district.

Cock won't fight, That.

1850 THACKERAY *Pendennis* lxvii 'Tell that to the marines, Major', replied the valet, 'that cock won't fight with me'. **1888** 'R. BOLDREWOOD' *Robbery under Arms* 1 My lawyer ... argued that ... no proof had been brought . . . that I had wilfully killed any one. . . . But that cock wouldn't fight. I was found guilty ... and sentenced to death.

Cock's spur, *see* Chance in the c.

Cock(s) (*noun*), *see also* Barley-corn better than diamond to c.; Farm full must keep old c.; Forward c. that croweth in shell; Full flock ... young c.; Jump at it like c. at gooseberry; Knows how to carry dead c. home; Old c. crows, so crows young; Red c. (The); Teague's c., that fought one another; True as that ... c. rocked cradle; Young c. love no coops.

Cock (*verb*), *see* Time to c. your hay and corn.

Cocker, According to.

[= exact, correct: Edw. Cocker (1631–75) published his *Compleat Arithmetician* before 1669.] **1764** A. MURPHY *Apprentice* I. i I have *Cocker's* Arithmetic below stairs . . . I'll ... get it for him. **1882** W. BATES *Maclise Port. Gal.* (1898) 280 This was at the rate of £37 10s. per line, 'according to Cocker'.

Cockers his child, He that | provides for his enemy.

1640 HERBERT 353.

Cockle, *see* Corn is some c. (In much); Sowed c. reaped no corn.

Cockles of the heart, To warm (rejoice) the.

1671 EACHARD *Observ. Answ. Enquiry* This contrivance of his did inwardly rejoice the cockles of his heart. **1747** WARBURTON on *Hamlet* III. ii. 136 The common people say: You rejoice the cockles of my heart, for muscles of my heart; an unlucky mistake of one shell fish for another. **1792** SCOTT *Let.* 30 Sept. in LOCKHART *Life* An expedition . . . which would have delighted the very cockles of your heart. **1834** MARRYAT *Jacob Faith.* xii There's a glass of grog for you. . . . See if that don't warm the cockles of your old heart. **1858** DARWIN in *Life & Lett.* (1888) II. 112 I have just had the innermost cockles of my heart rejoiced by a letter from Lyell. **1910** *Brit. Wkly.* 27 Oct. Poor mothers who gave their babies gin ... 'to warm the cockles of their hearts'.

Cockloft is unfurnished, His.

1621 J. HOWELL *Lett.* 2 Feb. (1903) I. 102 'Sir', said Bacon, 'Tall men are like high houses of four or five storys, wherein commonly the uppermost room is worst furnished.' **1662** FULLER (*Westminster*) II. 413 Edward the First . . . was very high in stature. And though ofttimes such . . . are observed to have little in their cock-loft, yet was he a most judicious man. **1678** RAY 235 His cockloft is unfurnished. *i.e.* He wants brains. **1873** 22 Oct. KILVERT *Diary* ii. 386 To have attics to let unfurnished. **1896** F. LOCKER-LAMPSON *My Confid.* (Nelson) 56 Tall men are like tall houses—often poorly furnished on the top story.

Cockney, *see* Castle of Bungay; London c.

Cockpit, *see* Netherlands are c. of Christendom.

Coelum non animum mutant, *see* Travellers change climates, &c.

Coffin, *see* Nail into c. (Drive).

Coggeshall, *see* Jeering C.

Coin is not common, Where | commons[1] must be scant. (*Cf.* Wine is not common.)

1546 HEYWOOD II. i. 2. **1638** CLARKE 113. [[1] provisions.]

Coin, *see also* Much c. much care.

Colchester, *see* Weavers' beef of C.

Cold April the barn will fill, A.

1659 HOWELL *Span.–Eng.* 21 A cold April, much bread and little wine. **1732** FULLER no. 6356.

Cold as a key.

c. **1390** GOWER *Conf. Amantis* VI. 244 Was nevere Keie Ne posen ys upon the wal More inly cold. **1501** DOUGLAS *Pal. Honour* sig. D ii st. 61 With quakand voce and hart cald as a key. **1546** HEYWOOD II. i. 44 Hotte as a toste it grew cold as a kay. **1592–3** SHAKS. *Rich. III* I. ii. 5 Poor key-cold figure of a holy king! **1594** *Lucrece* 1774 And then in key-cold Lucrece' bleeding stream He falls.

Cold as charity.

[**1380**: WYCLIF *Matt.* xxiv. 12 The charite of many schal wexe cold.] **1572** T. WILSON *Disc. upon Usury* (1925) 201 Charity waxes colde. **1600** NASHE, *Summer's Last Will* l. 932 I see charitie waxes cold. **1609** DEKKER *Gull's Handbook*, ch. 3. **1640** SHIRLEY *St. Pat. for Ireland* III. i (A) Would I were a whale in the frozen sea! charity is not cold enough to relieve me. **1642** SIR T. BROWNE *Relig. Med.* II. iv 'Tis the general complaint . . . that Charity grows cold. **1837** T. HOOK *Jack Brag* xv The wind blows ... about one, and I'm as cold as charity.

Cold, Let them that be | blow at the coal.

c. **1380** *Sir Ferumbras* in *Engl. Charlemagne Romances* (E.E.T.S.) I, 1. 2230 þan saide Lucafere. 'We haue a game in this contray: to blowen atte glede.' **1546** HEYWOOD I. x. 24 Aunt, leat them that be a colde blowe at the cole. **1670** RAY 72 Let him that is cold blow the coal. **1721** KELLY 235 ... Let them drudge about business, that want it, and expect benefit by it.

Cold broth hot again, that loved I never; old love renewed again, that loved I ever.

1721 KELLY 79. **1732** FULLER no. 6429.

Cold coal to blow at, A.

1641 FERGUSSON 66. **1708** M. BRUCE *Lect.* 33 (Jam.) If I had no more to look to but your reports, I would have a cold coal to blow at. **1816** SCOTT *Old Mort.* vii 'Aweel', said Cuddie . . . 'I see but ae gate for't, and that's a cauld coal to blow at, mither'.

Cold comfort.

c. **1325** *E. E. Allit. P.* C 264 Lorde! Colde watȝ his cumfort. **1571** GOLDING *Calvin on Ps.* x. 14 We receive but cold comfort of whatsoever the Scripture speaketh. **1593-4** SHAKS. *Tam. Shrew* IV. i. 33 Shall I complain on thee to our mistress, whose hand . . . thou shalt soon feel, to thy cold comfort. **1596-7** *K. John* V. vii. 42 I beg cold comfort. **1612-15** BP. HALL *Contempl.* IV. xi (1825) II. 380 The cripple . . . looked up, it was cold comfort that he heard, 'Silver and gold have I none'.

Cold hand and a warm heart, A.

1902-4 LEAN III. 380.

Cold May and a windy makes a full barn and a findy,[1] A.

1573 TUSSER May's abst. Cold May and windy, barn filleth up finely. **1670** RAY 41. **1750** ELLIS *Mod. Husb.* III. iii. 9 A cold May and a windy, Makes a full barn and a findy; because a cold and dry May prevents . . . weeds. [[1] solid, full, substantial.]

Cold of complexion, good of condition.

1678 RAY 116. **1732** FULLER no. 1119.

Cold pudding will settle your love.

1685 S. WESLEY *Maggots* 41 Settle the Wit, as *Pudding settles* Love. **1738** SWIFT (Dial. ii) 346 *Miss.* This almond pudding . . . is grown quite cold. *Never* . . . Cold pudding will settle your love. **1848** A. SMITH *Christ. Tadpole* lx The cold plum-pudding too, was a wonder . . . and . . . there was enough of it to settle everybody's love.

Cold shoulder, To give (*or* show) the.

1816 SCOTT *Antiq.* xxxiii 'The Countess's dislike didna gang farther at first than just showing o' the cauld shouther'. **1840** DICKENS *Old C. Shop* lxvi He gives me the cold shoulder on this very matter. **1853** SURTEES *Sponge's Sport.* T. xxxvi Jack . . . was more used to 'cold shoulder' than cordial receptions. **1860** THACKERAY *Lovel* i [She] got to dislike me at last and to show me the cold shoulder.

Cold weather and knaves come out of the north.

1659 HOWELL *Eng. Prov. rendered into French,* &c. 8/2 Cold weather and crafty knaves come out of the north. **1670** RAY 19.

Cold wind reach you through a hole, If | say your prayers, and mind your soul.

1736 FRANKLIN July If wind blows on you through a hole, Make your will and take care of your soul. **1846** DENHAM 16.

Cold, *see also* Child (To a) all weather is c.; Day lengthens c. strengthens; God sendeth c. after clothes; Hour's c. will spoil seven years' warming; May c. thirty days c.; Stuff a c. starve fever.

Coldest flint there is hot fire, In the.

1579 LYLY *Euphues* (Arb.) 79 I, but in the coldest flint there is hot fire. **1594** SHAKS. *Lucrece* 181 As from this cold flint I enforc'd this fire, So Lucrece must I force to my desire. **1601-2** *Troil. & Cres.* III. iii. 256 It lies as coldly in him as fire in a flint, which will not show without knocking. **1607-8** *Timon of A.* I. i. 22 The fire in the flint shows not till it be struck. **1616** DRAXE 193. **1732** FULLER no. 2822. **1837** S. LOVER *Rory O'More* vi Perhaps . . . John Bull is like his own flint-stones, with fire enough in him, only you must strike him hard.

Coldingham common, *see* Conscience like C. c.

Colewort, *see* Cabbage (1580 quotn.).

Coll[1] under canstick.[2]

[a Christmas game; used fig.] **1546** HEYWOOD I. x. 20 Coll vnder canstyk, she can plaie on bothe handis, Dissimulacion well she vnderstandis. [[1] to embrace. [2] candlestick.]

Collar, *see* After a c. a halter.

Collier, *see* Like will to like, quoth devil to c.

Collop, *see* Dear c. cut out of own flesh; Sairy c. that is off capon.

Colne clock, always at one, Like.

1873 HARLAND & WILKINSON *Lancashire Leg.* 194 A steady person is said to be 'like Colne clock—always at one': *i.e.* always the same.

Coloquintida spoils all the broth, A little.

1616 DRAXE 64 A little Coloquintida marreth a whole pot of pottage. **1630** T. ADAMS *Wks.* 711 (A).

Colours of the rainbow, All the.

1600-1 SHAKS. *Merry W.* IV. v. 119 I was beaten myself into all the colours of the rainbow. **1601** LYLY *Love's Met.* IV. i (1902) III. 318 This garland of flowers, which hath all colours of the rainbow.

Colour(s), *see also* Black (Above) there is no c.; Kythe in your own c.; Lie all manner of c. but blue; Nail one's c. to the mast; Sail under false c.; Truth fears no c.; Truth needs no c.

Colt's tooth, A.

c. **1386** CHAUCER *W. of Bath's Prol.* 602 But

yit I had alway a coltis tothe. **1588** GREENE *Perimides* Wks. (Gros.) VII. 91 Hee hath beene a wag, but nowe age hath pluckt out all his Coltes teeth. **1612–13** SHAKS. *Hen. VIII* I. iii. 48 Your colt's tooth is not cast yet? **1709** STEELE *Tatler* no. 151, par. 4 My Aunt Margery had again a Colt's-Tooth in her Head. **1800** WOLCOT (P. Pindar) *Ld. Auck. Tri.* Wks. (1812) IV. 317 His Majesty . . . Had a Colt's tooth and loved another Dame.

Colt(s), *see also* Kick of dam hurts not c.; Ragged as a c.; Ragged c. may make good horse; Ride a young c. (When you), see saddle be girt; Trick the c. gets at first backing; Young c. will canter.

Comb (a person's) head with a three-legged stool, &c., To.

[= to beat, thrash.] **1562** J. HEYWOOD *Epigrams* (ed. Farmer, 1906) 169 *Home is homely*: yea, and too homely sometime Where wives' footstools to their husbands' heads climb. **1567** *Mery Tales* (SKELTON *Wks.*, ed. Dyce I. lix) Hys wife woulde diuers tymes in the weeke kimbe his head with a iii-footed stoole. **1591** *A wonderful Prognostication* (NASHE *Wks.*, ed. McKerrow III. 389). **1593–4** SHAKS. *Tam. Shrew* I. i. 64 To comb your noddle with a three-legg'd stool. **1785** GROSE *Dict. Vulg. T.* s.v. 'Comb' She combed his head with a joint-stool; she threw a stool at him. **1896** LOCKER-LAMPSON *My Confid.* 390 The mother . . . would . . . shy the furniture about. To use her own words of homely vigour, she combed her husband's head with a three-legged stool.

Comb your head backward yet, Somebody will.

1721 KELLY 286 . . . Spoken by mothers to stubborn daughters; intimating they will come under the hands of a step-mother, who, it is likely, will not deal too tenderly with them.

Comb, *see also* Brought an ill c. to my head; Cut the c. of; Scabby heads love not c.

Come after with salt and spoons, To.

1611 DRAYTON *Wks.* (Hebel) I. 500 And I come after bringing Salt and Spoones. *a.* **1700** B.E. *Dict. Cant. Crew*, s.v. 'salt' *To come after with Salt and Spoons*, of one that is none of the Hastings.

Come again, They will | as Goodyer's pigs did.

1678 RAY 235 They'll come again, as Good-yers pigs did, *i.e.* never.

Come and welcome; go by, and no quarrel.

1670 RAY 236.

Come, but come stooping.

1642 TORRIANO 99. **1813** RAY 93.

Come by, *see* Hard to c. b. are much set by (Things).

Come cut and long-tail. (*See also* Tag, rag, and bobtail.)

[= horses or dogs with docked tails and long tails; *fig.* all sorts of people.] **1600–1** SHAKS. *Merry W.* III. iv. 47 Ay, that I will, come cut and long-tail, under the degree of a squire.

Come day, go day, God send Sunday.

1616 DRAXE 194 Come day, goe day, the day is long enough. **1721** KELLY 77 . . . Spoken to lazy, unconscionable servants, who only mind to serve out their time, and get their wages. **1846** DENHAM 15 Come day, gang day, God send Sunday. The sluggard's daily prayer.

Come home, *see* Duck in the mouth (C. h. with); Parson's cow (C. h. like).

Come in at the window, To.

[Said of a bastard.] **1597** SHAKS. *K. John* I. i. 171 In at the window, or else o'er the hatch. . . . I am I, howe'er I was begot. **1605** CHAPMAN *All Fools* III. i. 422 Though he came in at the window, he sets the gates of your honour open. **1629** SHIRLEY *The Ball* II. i I came in at the wicket, some call it the window. **1664** COTTON *Scarron.* i. 517 She [Venus] came in at the window.

Come not to counsel uncalled.

1539 TAVERNER 13 *Ad consilium ne accesseris antequam uoceris.* Come nat to counsayle afore thou be called. *a.* **1585** MONTGOMERIE *Cherrie & Slae* lxxviii (1821) 42 Thair is a sentence said be sum, 'Let nane uncalled to counsell cum, That welcum weins to be.' **1641** FERGUSSON 26.

Come of a blood and so is a pudding, You are.

c. **1598** *MS. Proverbs* in FERGUSSON 113 Ye ar sib[1] to a pudding ye ar com of a blood. **1721** KELLY 368 . . . Spoken to them who boast of their genteel blood. [[1] kin.]

Come, If they | they come not; if they come not, they come.

1662 FULLER (1840) ii. 543 (A). **1670** RAY (*Northumb.*) 248 *If they come they come not* . . . *and If they come not they come.* The cattel of people living hereabout, turn'd into the common pasture, did by custome use to return to their home at night, unless intercepted by the Freebooters and borderers. If therefore those *Borderers* came, their *cattel* came not: if they came not, their cattel surely returned.

Come to, *see* Buckle and bare thong (C. to); See what we must c. to if we live.

Come to himself, Let him | like MacKibbon's crowdy.[1]

1721 KELLY 237 . . . Spoken when people are angry without a cause. **1818** SCOTT *Rob Roy* xxv Ye'll cool and come to yourself, like MacGibbon's crowdy, when he set it out at the window-bole. [[1] brose; porridge.]

Come(s) to light, *see* Nothing c. fairer to l. than long hid.

Come to mickle, It is | but it's no come to that.

1721 KELLY 207 . . . Spoken when we reject the proffer of a mean service, match, or business, we are not come so low as that yet.

Come(s) to pass, *see* Forchets (That which one most) soonest c. to p.

Come with me, If thou wilt | bring with thee.

1573 SANDFORD (1576) 221. **1578** FLORIO *First Fruites* 33. **1732** FULLER no. 6286 Bring something, Lass, along with thee, If thou intend to live with me.

Come with the wind, go with the water.

[Things ill-gotten will be ill-spent.] **1721** KELLY 83 . . . Lat. *Male parta, male dilabuntur.* **1892** HENLEY & STEVENSON *Deac. Brodie* I. ii Onyway, Deacon, ye'd put your ill-gotten gains to a right use: they might come by the wind but they wouldna gang wi' the water.

Comely (Nimble) as a cow in a cage, As.

1399 LANGLAND *Rich. Redeless* iii. 262 (A) As be-cometh a kow to hoppe in a cage! **1546** HEYWOOD II. i. 43 She is in this mariage As comely as is a cowe in a cage. **1678** RAY 287 As nimble as a cow in a cage. **1828** LYTTON *Pelham* lxxvii I have made them as nimble as cows in a cage—I have not learned the use of my fists for nothing.

Comes first to the hill, may sit where he will, He that.

1641 FERGUSSON 42. **1721** KELLY 142 *He that is first on the midding,*[1] *may sit where he will.* He that comes first has commonly the best choice. [[1] dunghill.]

Comes in with his five eggs, He.

[= to break in fussily with an idle story: more fully, *Five eggs a penny, and four of them addle* or *rotten.*] **1542** UDALL *Erasm. Apoph.* 272 Persones comyng in with their fiue egges, how that Scylla had geuen ouer his office of Dictature. **1546** HEYWOOD II. i. 43 In came the thyrde, with his V. egges. **1639** CLARKE 19 He comes in with his five egges, and foure be rotten. **1738** SWIFT (Dial. i) 336 What! and you must come in with your two eggs a-penny, and three of them rotten.

Comes nought out of the sack, There | but what was there.

1640 HERBERT 355.

Comes of a hen, He that | must scrape.

1591 FLORIO *Sec. Frutes* 179 What is hatcht by a hen, will scrape like a hen. **1640** HERBERT 337. **1852** E. FITZGERALD *Polonius* 92 Let him who would know how far he has changed the old Adam, consider his Dreams. 'He that comes of a hen must scrape.'

Comes to (the) hand like the bowl of a pint-stoup, It.

[= is acceptable or opportune.] **1819** SCOTT *Bride Lam.* xi The thunderbolt . . . only served to awaken the . . . inventive genius of the flower of Majors-Domo . . . Caleb exclaimed, 'Heavens be praised!—this comes to hand like the boul of a pint stoup'.

Comes uncalled, He who | sits unserved.

a. **1585** MONTGOMERIE *Cherrie & Slae* lxxviii (1821) 42 Zea, I haif hard another zit, 'Quha cum uncallt, unservd suld sit'. **1721** KELLY 77 . . . They have no reason to expect good usage, who go to a feast uncall'd.

Cometh from above, That which | let no man question.

1662 FULLER (*Leics.*) II. 243 Henry Noel . . . was of the first rank in the Court. And though his lands and livelihood were small, . . . yet in state . . . and expences, did ever equalize the barons of great worth. If any demand whence this proceeded, the Spanish proverb answers him, 'That which cometh from above, let no man question'.

Cometh last to the pot, He that | is soonest wroth.

1546 HEYWOOD II. x. 81 Than was it proued trew, as this prouerbe goth, He that commeth last to the pot, is soonest wroth. **1611** DAVIES *Prov.* 43 'The last at the pot is the first wroth.'

Cometh late, Who | lodgeth ill.

1573 SANDFORD (1576) 209. **1578** FLORIO *First Fruites* 5. **1732** FULLER no. 2381.

Come(s, th), *see also* In time c. whom God sends; Lost (It is not) that c. at last; Never long that c. at last; Old soldier (To c. the); Quickly c. quickly go; Shires (To c. out of the); Take things as they c.; Yorkshire on one (To c.).

Comfort, *see* Cold c.; Want of money want of c.

Comforter's head never aches, The.

1640 HERBERT 336.

Coming, and so is Christmas.

1738 SWIFT (Dial. i) 337 'She's coming, madam.' . . . 'Coming! ay, so is Christmas.' **1854** SURTEES *Hand. Cross* lxii Miss always reported that she saw the offer was coming, but Mama . . . observed that 'Christmas was coming too'.

Coming events cast their shadows before them.

1803 CAMPBELL *Lochiel's Warn.* And coming events cast their shadows before. **1857** TROLLOPE *Barch. Tow.* xxiv The coming event of Mr. Quiverful's transference to Barchester produced a delicious shadow in the shape of new outfit for Mrs. Quiverful.

Coming to heaven with dry eyes, No.

1629 T. ADAMS *Serm.* (1861–2) II. 373 Many saints have now reaped this crop in heaven, that sowed their seed in tears. David, Mary Magdalene, Peter; as if they had made good the proverb, No coming to heaven with dry eyes'.

Command of custom is great, The.

1640 HERBERT 345.

Command others, He is not fit to | that cannot command himself.

c. **1510** STANBRIDGE *Vulg.* (E.E.T.S.) 56 It becometh hym euyll to be a mayster upon seruauntes that cannot ordre hymselfe. **1621** J. FLETCHER *Pilgrim* II. ii How vilely this shows, In one that would command anothers temper, And hear no bound in 's own. **1669** PENN *No Cross, No Crown* xix Cato . . . would say, 'No man is fit to command another, that cannot command himself'.

Command your man, and do it yourself.

1666 TORRIANO 60. **1670** RAY 169. **1692** L'ESTRANGE *Aesop's Fab.* liii (1738) 66 Men are more sensible in their own case than in another's; . . . according to the old saying, *Command your man, and do't yourself.*

Command, *see also* Force hidden in a sweet c.; Obedience learn to c. (Through); Pay well, c. well, hang well.

Commandment: The Eleventh | thou shalt not be found out.

1860 WHYTE-MELVILLE *Holmby H.* xiv Who wink . . . at the infraction of every commandment in the Decalogue, provided you are scrupulous to keep the eleventh, . . . which says, 'thou shalt not be found out!' **1894** DEAN HOLE *More Mem.* xii They stand in awe of but one commandment, 'Thou shalt not be found out'.

Commandments, The ten.

[= the ten finger-nails, esp. of a woman.] *c.* **1520–2** J. HEYWOOD *Four P's* in HAZL. *O.E.P.* I. 381 I beseech him that high sits, Thy wife's ten commandments may search thy five wits. **1542** UDALL *Erasm. Apoph.* (1877) 27. **1590–1** SHAKS. *2 Hen. VI* I. iii. 145 Could I come near your beauty with my nails, I could set my ten commandments in your face. **1814** SCOTT *Wav.* xxx I'll set my ten commandments in the face o' the first loon that lays a finger on him.

Commands enough that obeys a wise man, He.

1640 HERBERT 343. **1650** JER. TAYLOR *Holy Liv.* II. iv (1850) 84 The humble man . . . in all things lets God chose for him . . . He

does not murmur against commands. Assai commanda, chi ubbidisce al saggio.

Commences many things, He who | finishes but few.

1855 BOHN 399. *Ital.*

Commend not your wife, wine, nor house.

1642 TORRIANO 77 (with 'horse'). **1732** FULLER no. 1126.

Commits a fault, He that | thinks everyone speaks of it.

1640 HERBERT 343.

Commodity, *see* Every c. hath its discommodity.

Common as a barber's chair, As.

1554 H. HILARIE *Resurrection of the Mass* A iii I am as common as the Barbours chayre. **1579** GOSSON *Sch. Abuse* (Arb.) 66 Venus . . . that made her self as common as a Barbars chayre. **1602–3** SHAKS. *All's Well* II. ii. 17 He's like a barber's chair that fits all buttocks. **1796** WOLCOT (P. Pindar) *Orson & Ellen* Wks. (1816) IV. 72 Unlike some lasses, common known As is a barber's chair.

Common fame is a liar.

c. **1590** LYLY *Moth. Bomb.* III. iii. 30 Reports are no truths. **1614** W. BROWNE *Shepherd's Pipe* vii Wks. (1869) II. 236 Fame is a liar, and was never other. **1821** SCOTT *Pirate* xxxix But common fame, Magnus considered, was a common liar.

Common fame is seldom to blame.

1670 RAY 88 . . . A general report is rarely without some ground. **1721** KELLY 80 *Common fame sindle[1] to blame.* A man will seldom be under an universal ill report, unless he has given some occasion for it. [[1] seldom.]

Common horse is worst shod, The.

1546 HEYWOOD I. xi. 34.

Common servant is no man's servant, A.

1573 SANDFORD (1576) 209. **1629** *Book of Meery Riddles,* Prov. 85.

Common (*adj.*), *see also* Coin is not c. (Where), commons must be scant; Wine is not c. (Where), commons must be sent.

Common (*noun*), *see* Held together, as men of Marham when they lost their c.

Communications, *see* Evil c. corrupt.

Companion in a long journey and a little inn, A man knows his.

1732 FULLER no. 284 A man knows his companion in a long journey and a little inn. **1908** *Times Lit. Sup.* 25 Dec. 487 When one's brother mortal has stood the searching test

of the long road and the little inn, it is a duty
. . . to regard him with gratitude.

Companion like the penny, There is no.

1670 RAY 21. *Hispan.*

Companion(s), *see also* Dog gnaws bone
(While), c. would he none; Merry c. a
wagon in the way.

Company, As a man is, so is his.

1601 DENT *Plain Man's Pathway* 336. **1616**
DRAXE 25. **1622** C. DUDIN *Grammar Span.
and English* 253 Such as a mans company,
such his manners.

Company in trouble, It is good to have.

c. **1374** CHAUCER *Troylus* I. 708 Men seyn,
to wrecche is consolacioun To have another
felawe in his peyne. *c.* **1386** *Cant. T. G.*
746 For unto shrewes joye it is and ese To
have his felawes in peyne and disese. **1579**
LYLY *Euphues* (Arb.) 96 In misery, Euphues,
it is great comfort to have a companion.
1594 SHAKS. *Lucrece* 790 Fellowship in woe
doth woe assuage. *Ibid.* 1581 It easeth some,
though none it ever cur'd, To think their
dolour others have endur'd. **1620** SHELTON
Quix. II. xiii (1908) II. 269 If that which is
commonly spoken be true, that to have
companions in misery is a lightener of it,
you may comfort me. **1670** RAY 5 . . .
Solamen miseris socios habuisse doloris. [It is
a comfort to the wretched to have had
companions in their woes.]

Company makes the feast, The.

1653 WALTON *Angler* v 'Tis the company and
not the charge that makes the feast.

Company, *see also* Better be alone than in
bad c.; Better to be beaten than in bad c.;
Hell for c. (Nobody will go to); Keep good
men c.; Keep not ill men c.; Keeps his road
who gets rid of bad c.; Kenned folk nae c.;
Knaves (The more), worse c.; Room is
better than his c.; Sike as thou wald be,
draw to sike c.; Two is c., three is none;
Want of c. welcome trumpery; Woe worth
ill c., quoth the kae of Camnethen.

Comparison that makes men happy or miserable, It is.

1732 FULLER no. 5071.

Comparisons are odious.

c. **1440** LYDGATE *Polit. Relig. & Love Poems*
22 Odyous of olde been comparisonis. **1579**
LYLY *Euphues* (Arb.) 68 Livia, though she
be fair, . . . is . . . not so amiable as my
Lucilla . . . ; but lest comparisons should
seem odious, . . . I will omit that. **1598–9**
SHAKS. *Much Ado* III. v. 18 Comparisons are
odorous. *c.* **1600** DONNE *Elegies* viii She and
comparisons are odious. **1724** SWIFT *Drap.
Lett.* v. Wks. (1856) II. 30 A judge . . .
checked the prisoner . . . taxing him with
'reflecting on the court by such a comparison,

because comparisons were odious'. **1859** S. R.
HOLE *Lit. Tour Irel.* xiv Many men . . . forgetting that . . . 'Comparisons are odious',
are never happy but in detecting intelicities.

Complain, *see* All c.

Complains wrongfully on the sea that twice suffers shipwreck, He.

[PUBL. SYRUS 264 (Ribbeck) *Improbe Neptu-
num accusal qui iterum naufragium facit.*]
1579 SPENSER *Shep. Cal.* Feb. The Soveraigne
of the Seas he blames in vain That, once sea-
beate, will to sea again. **1640** HERBERT 350.
1670 RAY 23.

Complexion, *see* Cold of c.

Complies against his will, He that | is of his own opinion still.

1678 BUTLER *Hudibras* III. iii. 547.

Complimentary letter asketh another, One.

1596 NASHE *Saffron W.* S 2 Wks. (McKerrow)
III. 116 One côplementarie Letter asketh
another; & Gabriell first writing to him, and
seeming to admire him and his workes, hee
could doo no lesse . . . but returne him an
answere in the like nature.

Conceal(s), *see* Soberness conceals (What),
drunkenness reveals; Woman c. what she
knows not.

Conceited[1] goods are quickly spent.

1678 RAY 116. [[1] imagined?]

Conduct, *see* Advice (We may give) but
cannot give c.

Conference, *see* Reading maketh a full man,
c. a ready m.

Confess and be hanged.

c. **1592** MARLOWE *Jew of Malta* IV. ii (Merm.)
291 Blame not us but the proverb, Confess
and be hanged. **1604–5** SHAKS. *Othello* IV. i.
37 To confess, and be hanged for his labour.
1665 J. WILSON *Projectors* III. 1 Confess, and
be hang'd!—I am for none of 't! **1821** SCOTT
Pirate xxxix At the gallows! . . . confess
and be hanged is a most reverend proverb.

Confess debt and beg days.

1721 KELLY 79. **1732** FULLER no. 1139.

Confession, *see* Open c. good for soul; Open
c. open penance.

Confessor, *see* Better to be a martyr than c.

Confidence is a plant of slow growth.

1776 EARL OF CHATHAM *Speech* 14 Jan. in
LEAN III. 443 Confidence is a plant of slow
growth in an aged bosom. **1908** SNEYD-
KYNNERSLEY *H.M.I.* iii Confidence is a
plant that for special reasons grows slowly
in that land [Wales]; and occasionally there
were outbursts of fury.

Confidence, *see also* Skill and c. are uncon-
quered army.

**Confuted and yet not convinced, One
may be.**

1732 FULLER no. 3771.

**Congleton rare, Congleton rare, sold
the Bible to pay for a bear.**

1813 RAY 242 Congleton bears. The clerk of
Congleton having taken the old church
Bible . . . sold it to buy a bear. . . . From this,
. . . proceeds the name of Congleton bears.
1917 BRIDGE 39 Congleton rare, Congleton
rare Sold the Bible to pay for a bear. . . . In
the year 1662 the Church Bible was worn out
and money was collected to buy another. . . .
The town bear, kept for baiting, died, and the
keeper applied . . . to the Corporation. They
granted him the 'Bible Money', as . . . the
bear was wanted immediately for the Town
Wakes.

Connaught, *see* Hell or C.

**Conquering weapon as the necessity
of conquering, There is no such.**

1651 HERBERT 366.

Conqueror, He came in with the.

1593–4 SHAKS. *Tam. Shrew* Ind. i. 4 The
Slys are no rogues; look in the chronicles;
we came in with Richard Conqueror. 1639
CHAPMAN *The Ball* I Is he not a complete
gentleman? his family came in with the
conqueror. 1888 J. E. T. ROGERS *Econ.
Interp. Hist.* (1894) ii. xix A good many
people say now, that their families came here
with the Conqueror.

**Conscience as large as a shipman's
hose, A.**

1639 CLARKE 66.

Conscience is a cut-throat.

1616 WITHALS 554. 1639 CLARKE 66.

**Conscience is cumbered and standeth
not clean, Whose | of another
man's deeds the worse will he
deem.**

c. 1500 in *Reliq. Antiquae* (1841) i. 205 Whos
conscience is combred and stondith nott
clene, Of another manis dedis the wursse woll
he deme.

**Conscience like a cheverel's skin, He
hath a.**

1583 STUBBES *Anat. Abus.* ii. 12 The lawiers
have such chauerell consciences. 1594–5
SHAKS. *Rom. & Jul.* II. iv. 90 O! here's a wit
of cheveril, that stretches from an inch
narrow to an ell broad. 1612–13 *Hen. VIII*
II. iii. 33 The capacity Of your soft cheveril
conscience. 1662 FULLER (*Wales*) iii. 484
Cheverel consciences, which will stretch any
way for advantage. 1678 RAY 351 . . . (That
will stretch.) A cheverel is a wild goat.
Somers.

**Conscience like Coldingham[1] com-
mon, Ye hae a.**

1862 HISLOP 328 Ye hae a conscience like
Coldingham common. 'Coldingham moor,
or common, was an undivided waste of above
6,000 acres. The saying is applied to persons
of lax principles.' [[1] Berwick.]

Conscience was hanged long ago.

1596 W. PERKINS *Discourse of Conscience*
(1603) 3 G 4. 1656 L. PRICE *Map of Merry
Conceits* A 5. 1659 N. R. 25.

Conscience, *see also* Friend as far as c. permits; Good c. a feast; Guilty c. needs no
accuser; Nonconformist c.; Once a year
a man may say, on his c.; Quiet c. sleeps;
Term time in the court of c.

Consider(ing), *see* Know what shall be (He
that would) must c.; Put on c. cap.

**Constable for your wit, You might
be a.**

1599 JONSON *Ev. Man out of Humour* i Sog.
Why, for my wealth I might be a justice of
peace. *Car.* Ay, and a constable for your wit.
1678 RAY 236.

**Constable in midsummer watch,
Like a.**

1586 *Eng. Courtier & Count. Gent.* (1868) 67
Vin. When wee come to . . . London, . . . wee
will put on Courtlike garments, and . . . some
of vs weare them with a good grace. *Val.* I
beleeue you, euen like a Constable in Midsommer watch.

**Constable of Openshaw sets beggars
in the stocks at Manchester, The.**

1678 RAY (*Ches.*) 301. 1917 BRIDGE 113
Always given as a Cheshire proverb, but it
can only be so because Openshaw was in the
old Diocese of Chester. 'Openshaw is a
township in the parish of Manchester and
about three and a half miles from the
Cathedral where the stocks were formerly
placed.' [*N. & Q.* iv. 12. 524.]

Constable, *see also* Out-run the c.

**Constancy of the benefit of the year
in their seasons argues a Deity,
The.**

1640 HERBERT 353.

Constant dropping wears the stone.

[OVID *Epist. ex Ponto* 4. 10. 5 *Gutta cavat
lapidem. Cf.* BIBLE *Job* xiv. 19 Little drops
pierce the flint upon which they often fall.]
c. 1200 *Ancrene Riwle* (Morton) 220 Lutle
dropen thurleth thene ulint thet ofte ualleth
theron. *c.* 1387 USK *Test. of Love* i. iii. 101
So ofte falleth the lethy water on the harde
rocke, til it haue thorow persed it. *c.* 1477
CAXTON *Jason* 26 The stone is myned and
holowed by contynuell droppyng of water.
1549 LATIMER *7th Serm. bef. Edw. VI* (P.S.)
232 It is a good wise verse, *Gutta cavat*

lapidem non vi sed sæpe cadendo; 'The drop of rain maketh a hole in the stone, not by violence, but by oft falling'. **1590–1** SHAKS. *3 Hen. VI* III. ii. 50 He plies her hard; and much rain wears the marble. **1594** *Lucrece* 560 Tears harden lust Though marble wear with raining. *Ibid.* 959 Time's office is to ... waste huge stones with little water-drops. **1595–6** *Rich. II* III. iii. 164 Or shall we ... make some pretty match with shedding tears? As thus; to drop them still upon one place, Till they have fretted us a pair of graves Within the earth. **1601–2** *Troil. & Cres.* III. ii. 193 When waterdrops have worn the stones of Troy. **1874** WHYTE-MELVILLE *Uncle John* vi Constant dropping wears away a stone; constant flirtation saps the character.

Consult, *see* Take counsel of (*or* C. with) pillow.

Consume your own smoke.

1843 CARLYLE Letter to Sterling 4 Dec. in FROUDE, *T. Carlyle, History of his Life in London* I. xii I see almost nobody. I ... study to consume my own smoke. *a.* **1893** JOWETT *Life* i. 371 You know Carlyle's saying 'Consume your own smoke', which has perhaps the advantage of increasing the internal heat.

Contemplates, He that | hath a day without night.

1640 HERBERT 345. **1670** RAY 5. **1732** FULLER no. 2069 (with 'on his bed' after 'contemplates').

Contempt pierces even through the shell of the tortoise.

1842 MACAULAY *Ess., Fred. the Gt.* Wks. VI. 689 Contempt, says the eastern proverb, pierces even through the shell of the tortoise; and neither prudence nor decorum had ever restrained Frederic from expressing his measureless contempt for ... Lewis.

Contempt, *see also* Evils are cured by c. (Some); Trust not ... c. of enemy.

Contend, *see* Dispute (C.) about shadow of an ass.

Contending with the master of thirty legions, It is ill.

[SPARTIANUS *Hadr.* 15. 12 *Illum doctiorem omnibus ... qui habet triginta legiones.*] **1605** BACON *Adv. Learn.* I. iii (1900) 27 Accounted ... discretion in him[1] that would not dispute his best with Adrianus Cæsar; excusing himself, *That it was reason to yield to him that commanded thirty legions.* **1629** T. ADAMS *Serm.* (1861–2) III. 285 The philosopher[1] that had shamed himself by weakly disputing with Adrian ... thus excused himself ..., 'Would you have me contend with him that commands thirty legions?' *a.* **1654** SELDEN *Table Talk* (Arb.) 111 'Tis not seasonable to call a man traitor that has an army at his heels. [[1] Favorinus.]

Content in his poverty, He who is | is wonderfully rich.

1613 R. DALLINGTON *Aphorisms* 315 Content is the poore mans riches, and Desire the rich mans povertie. **1623** WODROEPHE 480.

Content is all.

1581 *Howell his devices* (Raleigh) 58 Contented meane exceedeth all. **1639** CLARKE 38.

Content is happiness.

c. **1566** *The Bugbears* IV. ii. 20 Content is agreed. **1579** E. HAKE *News out of Paul's Churchyard* B 1ᵛ Content is pleased. **1591** FLORIO *Sec. Frutes* 28 Content is pleased. **1666** TORRIANO 52. **1732** FULLER no. 1152.

Content is more than a kingdom.

1591 GREENE *Wks.* (Gros.) IX 279 Quiet perswaded her that content was a kingdome. **1597** *Politeuphuia* 204 b Content is more worth then a kingdome. **1607** T. HEYWOOD *Wom. K. Kindness* III. i. 8. **1616** WITHALS A contented mind is a kingdome. **1639** CLARKE 213. **1732** FULLER no. 1153.

Content is the philosopher's stone, that turns all it touches into gold.

1642 FULLER *H. & P. State* III. xvii (1841) 186 Those who seek for the philosopher's stone, ... must not do it with any covetous desire to be rich ... Whosoever would have this jewel of contentment, (which turns all into gold ...) must come ... divested of ... covetous thoughts. **1732** FULLER no. 1154.

Content with his own kevel,[1] Let every man be.

1721 KELLY 232 ... L. *Sorte tuâ contentus abi.* [[1] lot.]

Content (*adj., noun*), *see also* No man is c.; See all, say nought, hold thee c.; Studies his c. (He that).

Content (*verb*), *see* Need much whom nothing will c.

Contented mind is a continual feast, A.

1535 COVERDALE *Bible Prov.* xv. 15 (A) A quiet heart is a continual feast. **1592** WARNER *Alb. England* vii. 37 (A) It is a sweet continuall feast To liue content, I see. **1766** *Goody Two-Shoes* v. iii.

Contented who needs neither borrow nor flatter, He may well be.

1477 RIVERS *Dictes and Sayings* (1877) 69 (A) Some axed him of howe moche goode[s] a man ought to be content, and he answered to haue so moche as he neded nat to flatre nor borowe of other. **1670** RAY 5.

Contented, *see also* Enough who is c. with little; Nothing (He that hath) is not c.

Contentibus, quoth Tommy Tomson, kiss my wife and welcome.

1721 KELLY 81 ... Spoken facetiously when we comply with a project. **1738** SWIFT (*Dial.* iii) 352 With all my heart; kiss my wife and welcome.

Contention, *see* Bone of c.; Hundred ells of c. (In) not inch of love; Spread the table, c. will cease.

Contentment, *see* Wealth (The greatest) is c.

Convenience, *see* Every commodity (1609 quotn.).

Conversation makes one what he is.

1640 HERBERT 359.

Converses not, He that | knows nothing.

1611 COTGRAVE s.v. 'Ville' He that goes not abroad knowes nothing. **1616** DRAXE 60 He that goeth not in company, knoweth nothing. **1664** CODRINGTON 195 He that converseth not with men knoweth nothing. **1670** RAY 5. **1732** FULLER no. 2070.

Convince(s, d), *see* Confuted and yet not c.; Good orator who c. himself.

Conway, *see* Escape Clude and be drowned in C.

Coo, *see* Cow.

Cook any one's goose, To.

[= to 'do for' or ruin a person or thing.] **1851** *Street Ballad* in MAYHEW *Lond. Labour* I. 243 (Hoppe) If they come here we'll cook their goose, The Pope and Cardinal Wiseman. **1853** SURTEES *Sponge's Sport. T.* xxiv 'If he's after either of the Jawley girls, he'll be bad to shake off'. . . . 'I think if he is, I could cook his goose for him.'

Cook-ruffian, able to scald the devil in his feathers.

1670 RAY 169.

Cook that cannot lick his own fingers, He is a poor (ill).

c. **1510** STANBRIDGE *Vulgaria* (E.E.T.S.) 27 He is an euyll coke that can not lycke his owne lyppes. **1545** TAVERNER C 3 He is an euyll cooke that can not lycke his owne fyngers. **1546** HEYWOOD II. viii. 73 A poore cooke that maie not licke his owne fyngers. **1594–5** SHAKS. *Rom. & Jul.* IV. ii. 6 Marry, sir, 'tis an ill cook that cannot lick his own fingers. **1598** PUTTENHAM *Eng. Poesie* (Arb.) 199 A bad cooke that cannot his owne fingers lick. **1642** FULLER *H. & P. State* IV. viii (1841) 260 Sir Thomas Cook . . . had well licked his fingers under queen Margaret (whose wardrober he was, . . .), a man of a great estate. **1721** KELLY 138 *He's a sarry[1] cook that may not lick his own fingers.* Apply'd satyrically to receivers, trustees, guardians, and other managers. Signifying that they will take a share of what is among their hands. [[1] poor, mean.]

Cook's shop, *see* Starve in a c. s.

Cook(s), *see also* French would be best c. in Europe; God sends meat, devil c.; Salt c. bear blame; Too many c. spoil broth.

Cool as a cucumber, As.

a. **1732** GAY *New Song on New Similies* iii I . . . cool as a cucumber could see The rest of womankind. **1838** DE QUINCEY *Greek Lit.* Wks. (1890) X. 318 Thucydides . . . is as cool as a cucumber upon every act of atrocity.

Cool mouth, and warm feet, live long, A.

1611 COTGRAVE s.v. 'Pied' A coole mouth and a dry foot preserve a man long time alive. **1640** HERBERT 318.

Cool one's heels, To

[= to be kept standing or waiting. *c.* **1611** CHAPMAN *Il.* iii. 340 The soldiers all sat down enrank'd, each by his arms and horse That then laid down and cool'd their hoofs.] **1631** DEKKER *Penny-Wise Pound-Foolish* E 3 Bidding him . . . Stand there still and coole his heeles, and (with that) shut the dores upon him. **1633** W. R. *Match at Midnight* III. in HAZL. *O.E.P.* XIII. 52 Let him cool his heels there till morning. **1642** FULLER *H. & P. State* IV. i (1841) 231 O, whilst their heels cool, how do their hearts burn! **1752** FIELDING *Amelia* VI. ix In this parlour Amelia cooled her heels, as the phrase is, near a quarter of an hour.

Cool, *see also* Keep your breath to c.

Cooling card, A.

c. **1566** *The Bugbears* III. i. 51. **1591** SHAKS. *1 Henry VI* V. iii. 84 There all is marr'd: there lies a cooling card. **1621** JAS. I *Answ. Commons* in RUSHW. *Hist. Coll.* (1659) I. 51 God sent us a Cooling-card this year for that heat.

Coot, *see* Bald as a c.; Wit than a c. (No more).

Copy of his countenance, It is but a.

[= not spoken sincerely.] *c.* **1568** WAGER *Longer thou livest* C ii It is but a coppie of his countenance. **1678** RAY 70.

Copyhold with nine lives in it, Like a.

1688 J. SHIRLEY *Triumph of Wit* (1707) I. 19 *Dor.* It is impossible I shou'd survive it. *Tim.* There's no fear of that; y'are like a Copy-hold with Nine Lives in't.

Coral needeth no colouring, Right.

1580 LYLY *Euph. & his Eng.* Ep. Ded. (Arb.) 204 The right Corall needeth no colouring, where the matter it selfe bringeth credit, the man with his glose winneth small commendation. **1732** FULLER no. 4051.

Corbies, *see* Kittle shooting at c. and clergy.

Corby messenger, You are.

c. **1300** *Cursor M.* 1. 1892 For-þi men sais on messanger þat lengs lang to bring answare, He mai be cald, with right resun An of messagers corbun. *c.* **1480** HENRYSON *Wks.* (S.T.S.) II. 86, l. 1152 Schir Corbie Rauin wes maid Apparitour. **1721** KELLY 385 . . .

Taken from the raven sent out of the ark; apply'd to them who being sent an errand do not return with their answer.

Cord breaketh at the last by the weakest pull, The.

1625 BACON *Ess., Seditions* (Arb.) 401 Neither let any Prince, or State, be secure concerning *Discontentments*, because . . . Stormes, though they blow ouer diuers times, yet may fall at last; And as the Spanish Prouerb noteth well; *The cord breaketh at the last by the weakest pull.*

Corinth, It is not given to every man to go to.

[Gk. Οὐ παντὸς ἀνδρὸς εἰς Κόρινθον ἐσθ' ὁ πλοῦς. HORACE *Epist.* 1. 17. 36 *Non cuivis homini contingit adire Corinthum.*] **1542** UDALL *Apoph.* (1877) 379 *Lais* an harlot of *Corinthe* . . . was for none but lordes and gentlemen that might well paie for it. Whereof came vp a prouerbe, that it was not for euery man to go vnto *Corinthe.* **1911** *Times Lit. Sup.* 24 Nov. 471 It is 'not every man who has the luck to go to Corinth', still less is it every man who is able to describe it when he has been there.

Cork, It is nothing but.

1854 *N. & Q.* 1st Ser. x. 128 In Oxfordshire, when a child exhibits an overweening fondness for a parent, with a view to gaining some coveted indulgence, it is usually denominated 'Cork' . . . 'It is nothing but cork' is a common expression from parent to child.

Cork (city), *see* Citizens of C. all akin; Limerick was, . . . C. shall be finest city.

Cork, *see also* Squeeze a c. little juice.

Corn and horn go together.

1678 RAY 116 . . . *i.e.* for prices; when corn is cheap cattle are not dear, and *vice versâ.* **1858** SURTEES *Ask Mamma* xxv Foreign cattle . . . were coming in . . . and the old cry of 'down corn, down horn', frightened the 'stout British farmer'.

Corn hides itself in the snow as an old man in furs, The.

1640 HERBERT 328.

Corn him well, he'll work the better.

1721 KELLY 79 . . . Taken from usage given to horses. Apply'd to the giving of large fees that you may be the better serv'd.

Corn in Egypt.

[In allusion to *Gen.* xlii. 2.] *a.* **1834** LAMB *Let.* in AINGER *Life* vii There is corn in Egypt while there is cash at Leadenhall.

Corn is cleansed with wind, and the soul with chastenings.

1640 HERBERT 324.

Corn is in the shock, When the | the fish are on the rock.

1865 HUNT *Pop. Romances W. of England*

(1896) 428 (A). **1869** HAZLITT 528 . . . *Cornwall.* An allusion to the correspondence of the fishing season with the harvest—more especially the pilchard fishery.

Corn, In much | is some cockle.

1600 NASHE *Summers Last W.* Epil., in DODSLEY *O.E.P.* (1825) ix. 78 In much corn is some cockle; in a heap of coin here and there is a piece of copper.

Corn lies under the straw that is not seen, Much.

1639 CLARKE 145.

Corn, *see also* Acorns better than c. (To esteem); After Lammas c. ripens; Brain sows not c. (If); God sends c. and devil mars sack; Good years c. is hay; Land has its laugh and every c. its chaff; Look at your c. in May; Measures another's c. by own bushel; Muse as they use (Men), measure other folk's c.; Soweth good seed (He that) shall reap good c.; Weeds overgrow c.; Wind shakes no c. (All this).

Cornish chough, A.

1595 *Locrine* v. iii Are the Cornish choughs in such great numbers come to Mercia? **1617** MIDDLETON & ROWLEY *Fair Quarrel* II. ii My name is Chough, a Cornish gentleman. **1824** SCOTT *Redg.* xxii Pengwinion, you Cornish chough, has this good wind blown you north?

Cornish gentlemen are cousins, All.

1602 CAREW *Surv. of Cornwall* (1811) 179 (A). **1724** DEFOE *Journey to Land's E.* (Morley) 138 They generally intermarry . . . from whence they say that proverb upon them was raised, viz., 'That all the Cornish gentlemen are cousins'.

Cornish hug, A.

1617 MIDDLETON & ROWLEY *Fair Quarrel* II. ii I'll show her the Cornish hug. **1662** FULLER (*Cornw.*) I. 306 'To give one a Cornish hug.' . . . The Cornish are masters of the art of wrestling. . . . It is figuratively applicable to the deceitful dealing of such, who secretly design their overthrow whom they openly embrace. *c.* **1802** WOLCOT (P. Pindar) *Invit. to Bonaparte* Wks. (1816) IV. 265 And a warm *Cornish hug,* at thy landing.

Cornish man, men, *see* Tre, Pol, and Pen.

Corntown, *see* Stirling.

Cornwall will bear a shower every day, and two on Sunday. (*Cf.* Hampshire, &c.)

1864 *N. & Q.* 3rd Ser. v. 208.

Cornwall without a boat, To send a husband into.

c. **1566** *The Bugbears* III. i. 29 I hope she wyll not fayle for hys further preferment to send hym in to Cornewayle. **1567** PAINTER *Pal. of Pleasure* (Jacobs) iii. 128 (A) Either of them without shipping sought to send other into Cornouale. **1662** FULLER (*Cornw.*) 198 adding 'This is an Italian Proverb, where it passeth for a *description* (or *derision* rather) of such a Man who is wronged by his Wifes disloyalty. **1670** RAY 223.

Cornwall, *see also* Devil will not come into C.; Saints in C. than in heaven (More).

Cornwallis, *see* Paston poor.

Coronation, *see* Once at a c.

Corporations have neither souls to be saved nor bodies to be kicked.

1886 SALA *Amer. Revis.* 360 You know what Lord Eldon said about Corporate Boards—that they had neither souls to be saved nor bodies to be kicked.

Corpse, *see* After a dream of a wedding comes c.; Bride the sun shines on the c. . . . (Happy the).

Correct *Magnificat,* To.

[A byword for presumptuous fault-finding. *Magnificat* is the hymn of the Virgin Mary, in *Luke* i. 46–55, beginning, in the Vulgate, *Magnificat anima mea Dominum.* L. *magnificare=* to magnify.] **1533** ELYOT *Knowledge* Pref. Accomptyng to be in me no lyttell presumption, that I wylle in notynge other mens vices correct Magnificat. **1540** PALSGRAVE *Acolastus* (Carver) 18 Then Philyp fynde faute which takest vppon the to correct Magnificat. **1659** HEYLIN *Animadv.* in FULLER *Appeal Inj. Innoc.* (1840) 514 This is according to the old saying, to correct *Magnificat.* Assuredly, archbishop Whitgift knew better what he was to write, than to need any such critical emendations.

Correct *Magnificat* before one has learnt *Te Deum,* To.

[= to attempt that for which one has no qualifications.] **1542** UDALL *Erasm. Apoph.* 342 b Suche . . . y^t will take vpon theim to bee doctours in those thynges in whiche theimselfes haue no skille at all, for whiche wee saie in Englyshe, to correcte Magnificat before he haue learned Te Deum.

Corruption of the best becomes the worst.

[L. *Corruptio optimi pessima.*] **1609** SHAKS. *Sonn.* 94 For sweetest things turn sourest by their deeds. *a.* **1612** CHARRON *Of Wisdom* tr. Lennard (1640) 304. **1618** BP. HALL *Contempl.* IV. ix (1825) II. 360 But there is nothing so ill as the corruption of the best. **1856** BRIMLEY *Ess.* on *Angel in the House.* The worst . . . French novels . . . depict a certain kind of real life without reserve . . . *corruptio optimi pessima est.*

Cosier, *see* Clartier the c.

Cost hot water, It will.

1537 *Lisle Papers* XI. 100 (P.R.O.) If they be to be had, I will have of them, or it shall cost me hot water. **1655–62** GURNALL *Chrn. in Armour* (1865) I. 144 If the devil be so

mighty, . . . then sure it will cost hot water before we display our banners upon the walls of that new Jerusalem.

Cost, The more | the more honour.

1641 FERGUSSON 98 The mair cost, the mair honour. **1721** KELLY 317 . . . Spoken to them that propose an expensive thing, when a cheaper would do. **1821** SCOTT *Pirate* xi 'Ay, ay, brother, . . . that's spoken like your wise sell. The mair cost the mair honour—that's your word ever mair.'

Costs little, What | is less esteemed.

1620 SHELTON *Quix.* IV. vii (1908) I. 340 'It is also said as well', quoth Camilla, 'that "that which costeth little is less esteemed".'

Costs more to do ill than to do well, It.

1640 HERBERT 329.

Cost(s) (*noun*), *see also* More c. more worship; Pottage of a stool-foot (With c. make); Woo but c. (Who may).

Cost(s) (*verb*), *see also* Kind (He has it by), it c. him nought; Nothing c. so much as what is given; Three things c. dear, caresses of dog. . . .

Costlet, *see* After a sort, as C. served.

Cotswold lion, A.

[A humorous name for a sheep; perhaps a pun on *leyn* (wool), for which the Cotswold Hills are noted: cf. **1327** PETIT in *Rolls of Parlt.* II 182/1 Unze Sakes & Sys cloves de le meliour Leyn de Coteswold a l'œps nostre dit Seignour.] **1440** Satirical rhymes on Siege of Calais in *Archaeologia* xxxiii. 130 (A) Com renning on him fersly as lyons of Cotteswold. *a.* **1553** UDALL *Royster D.* (Arb.) IV. vi. 70 Then will he looke as fierce as a Cotssold lyon. **?1560** *Thersites* in HAZL. *O.E.P.* I. 400 Now have at the lions on Cots'old. **1600** *Sir J. Oldcastle,* Pt. I. II. i. 228 (*Shaks. Apoc.*) 138 You olde stale ruffin! you lion of Cotswold!

Cotswold, *see also* Long in coming as C. barley.

Cottage, *see* Change a c. in possession.

Couch a hogshead.

[= go to sleep.] c. **1510** *Cock Lorell's Boat* (1841) 18 Some couched a hogges head under a hatche. **1546** HEYWOOD II. ii. 47 In meane time my akyng head to ease, I will couche a hogs hed.

Couch like a quail, To.

c. **1386** CHAUCER *Clerk's T.* 1205–6 In Ialousye I rede eek thou him bynde, And thou shalt make him couche as dooth a quaille.

Cough will stick longer by a horse than half a peck of oats, A.

1678 RAY 117. **1732** FULLER no. 54.

Cough (*noun*), *see also* Dry c. trumpeter of death; Love and a c. cannot be hid.

Cough (*verb*), *see* Drink in your pottage, c. in your grave.

Councils of war never fight.

1891 A. FORBES *Bar. Biv. & Batt.* (1910) 191 Solomon's adage that in the multitude of counsellors there is wisdom does not apply to war. 'Councils of war never fight' has passed into a proverb.

Counsel be good, If the | no matter who gave it.

1732 FULLER no. 2704.

Counsel breaks not the head.

1640 HERBERT 338.

Counsel (Lawyer), He that is his own | has a fool for a client.

1817 EDGEWORTH *Ormond* xviii King Corny . . . has ended . . . by being his own lawyer; he has drawn his will so that any lawyer could drive a coach and six through it. **1850** HUNT *Autob.* xi The proprietor of the *Morning Chronicle* pleaded his own cause, an occasion in which a man is said to have 'a fool for his client' (that is to say, in the opinion of lawyers). **1911** *Brit. Wkly.* 21 Dec. 386 There is a popular impression, for which there is a good deal to be said, that a man who is his own lawyer has a fool for his client.

Counsel is no command.

c. **1390** CHAUCER *W. of Bath's Prol.* l. 67 Conseillyng is no comandement. . . **1721** KELLY 76 . . . That is, I advise you so; but you may do as you please. **1732** FULLER no. 1182.

Counsel must be followed, not praised.

1580 LYLY *Euph. & his Eng.* Wks. (Bond) II. 249–50 The counsel of a friend must be . . . followed, not praised. *c.* **1590** *Id. Moth. Bomb.* II. iii. 26. **1732** FULLER no. 1183.

Counsel nor court, Neither of his.

1546 HEYWOOD I. xi. 35 I was neyther of court nor of counsayle made. **1580** LYLY *Euph. & his Eng.* (Arb.) 377 Howe he imployed it, he shall himselfe vtter, for that I am neither of his counsaile nor court.

Counsel of fools, To the | a wooden bell.

1611 COTGRAVE s.v. 'Bois' For woodden consultations woodden bells. **1640** HERBERT 342.

Counsel over cups is crazy.

1664 CODRINGTON 190 Counsels in Wine do seldome prosper. **1670** RAY 5. **1732** FULLER no. 1184.

Counsel that hath no escape, It is an ill.

1640 HERBERT 350.

Counsel thou wouldest have another keep, first keep it thyself, The.

1623 CAMDEN 279. **1670** RAY 5 Keep counsel thyself first.

Counsel will make a man stick his own mare. (*Cf.* Ill counsel will gar, &c.)

1721 KELLY 82 . . . Spoken when we are over persuaded to do a thing.

Counsel, *see also* Come not to c. uncalled; Court (One of the), but none of the c.; Enemy may chance to give good c.; Give neither c. nor salt; Good c. has no price; Good c. never comes amiss; Good c. never too late; Healthful man can give c. to sick; Ill c. mars all; Ill c. will gar a man stick his mare; Keep c. (Three may) if two away; Keep one's c.; Less of your c. more of your purse; Night is mother of c.; Take c. of pillow; Wiving and thriving should take c.

Counselled, He that will not be | cannot be helped.

1639 CLARKE 22. **1670** RAY 6. **1747** FRANKLIN Aug.

Counsellor, He that is his own | knows nothing sure but what he hath laid out.

1640 HERBERT 363.

Counsellors, Though thou hast never so many | yet do not forsake the counsel of thy own soul.

1678 RAY *Adag. Hebr.* 414. **1907** *Brit. Wkly* 27 June 293 It is very good to take counsel with the wise, but the humblest individual knows his own feeling as no outsider possibly can.

Count not four, except you have them in a wallet.

1640 HERBERT 361. **1666** TORRIANO 229 Count not four, till they be in the bag.

Count one's chickens before they are hatched, To.

a. **1575** T. HOWELL *New Sonnets and pretty Pamphlets* 11 Counte not thy Chickens that unhatched be. **1579** GOSSON *Ephem.* 19 a I woulde not have him to counte his chickens so soone before they be hatcht. **1664** BUTLER *Hudibras* II. iii. 923 To swallow gudgeons ere they're catch'd, And count their chickens ere they're hatch'd. **1678** RAY 117 Count not your chickens before they be hatch't. *Ante victoriam ne canas triumphum.* [Don't sing your triumph before the victory.] **1906** SERJT. MEREWETHER in LADY D. NEVILL *Reminisc.* 306–8 A victory may be snatched, But never count your little chicks, Before they're safely hatched.

Count your gains, *see* Ill luck to.

Count, *see also* Angry (When). c. a hundred

Counted your cards, When you have | you'll find you have gained but little. (*Cf.* Tell thy cards, &c.)

1546 HEYWOOD I. xi. 29 Tell thy cardes, and than tell me what thou hast wonne. **1678** RAY 68.

Countenance, *see* Copy of his c.; Hospitality (Sin against) to open doors, shut c.; Thoughts close and c. loose.

Counter(s) (= prison), *see* Kiss the clink (c.); Slothful is servant of the c.

Counting, *see* Narrow c. culzies no kindness.

Countries, So many | so many customs (laws).

c. **1100** *Anglo-Saxon Gnomic Verses* (Grein) 1. 17 efen-fela bega, þēoda, and þēawa [an equal number both of countries and customs.] *c.* **1300** *Provs. of Hending* 4 Ase fele thedes, ase fele thewes. [So many countries, so many customs.] *c.* **1374** CHAUCER *Troylus* II. 28 In sondry londes, sondry ben usàges. **1670** RAY 73 So many countreys, so many customes. Tant de gens tant de guises. *Gall.*

Country for a wounded heart, The.

1907 A. C. BENSON *From Coll. W.* [ed. 4] 107 'The country for a wounded heart' says the old proverb. . . . I am here inclined to part company with wise men and poets who have spoken and sung of the consoling power of nature.

Country, right or wrong, My (Our).

1816 S. DECATUR *Toast* Our country! . . . may she always be in the right; but our country, right or wrong. **1891** J. E. T. ROGERS *Ind. & Commer. Hist.* 1 The habit . . . of uttering in the treatment of economical questions . . . 'our country, right or wrong', is not patriotism, . . . but . . . a pestilent, economical heresy. **1927** *Times* 5 Feb. 11/5 I would much prefer to enrol myself among those whose motto is 'My country right or wrong' than among those whose motto is 'My country always wrong'.

Country which has no history, Happy is the.

1858–65 CARLYLE *Fred. the Gt.* XVI. i Happy the people whose annals are blank in history. **1871** KINGSLEY *At Last* iii Trinidad ought to have been . . . a happy place from the seventeenth to the nineteenth century, if it be true that happy is the people who have no history. **1880** BLACKMORE *Mary Aner.* vi This land, like a happy country, has escaped, for years and years, the affliction of much history.

Country, *see also* Go into c. to hear news at London; God made the c.; Smoke of a man's own c.; Well with me (Where it is), there is my c.; World (This is the) and the other is c.

Counts all costs, He that | will ne'er put plough in the earth.

1641 FERGUSSON 40. **1721** KELLY 126 . . . He that forecasts all difficulties that he may meet with in his business, will never set about it.

Counts all the pins in the plough, He that | will never yoke her.

1721 KELLY 126.

County Clare payment, A.

1913 LADY GREGORY *New Com.* 96 Only a thank-you job; a County Clare payment, 'God spare you the health!'

Couple are newly married, When a | the first month is honey-moon, or smick smack: the second is, hither and thither: the third is thwick thwack: the fourth, the Devil take them that brought thee and I together.

1670 RAY 53.

Couple is not a pair, Every.

1893 ALLINGHAM *Var. in Prose* III. 318 *Markham.* I'll . . . pass . . . to Doctor Johnson and Horace Walpole. *Frank.* Who by no means formed a pair.

Courage, *see* Dutch c.

Course be fair, If that the | again and again quoth Bunny to his bear.

1616 WITHALS 553 . . . *Bis ac ter quod pulchrum est.* **1639** CLARKE 179. **1670** RAY 163.

Course of true love never did run smooth, The.

1595–6 SHAKS. *Mids. N.* I. i. 134 The course of true love never did run smooth. **1836** M. SCOTT *Cruise Midge* xi 'The course of true love never did run smooth.' And the loves of Saunders Skelp and Jessy Miller were no exception to the rule.

Court, One of the | but none of the counsel.

1546 HEYWOOD I. xi I was neither of court nor of council made. **1639** CLARKE 78. **1721** KELLY *Scot.* 272 . . . One of the party, but not admitted into their secrets, and intrigues.

Court, At | every one for himself.

c. **1386** CHAUCER *Knight's T.* 1181–2 At the kyngès court, my brother, Éch man for hymself. **1640** HERBERT 354.

Court hath no almanac, The.

1640 HERBERT 358. **1710** S. PALMER *Moral Essays on Prov.* 318 All *Europe* has consented to the Proverb, that in a Prince's Court there is no *Almanack*.

Court holy-water.

1519 HORMAN *Vulgaria* (Roxb. Cl.) 333 I

haue many feyre promessis and halywater of court. 1605–6 SHAKS. *K. Lear* III. ii. 10 Court holy-water in a dry house is better than this rain-water out o' door. 1611 COTGRAVE **s.v.** 'Eau'. 1678 RAY 236 . . . Eau beniste de la cour. *Gall.* Fair words and nothing else.

Court, *see also* Counsel nor c. (Neither of his); Dwell in c. (Whoso) must curry favour; Far from c. far from care; Go old to the c.; Highest in c. nearest the widdie; Leave the c. ere c. leave thee; Liveth in c. dieth upon straw; Men in c. (So many), so many strangers; Power seldom grows old at c.; Three ways, the church, sea, c. See *also* Courts.

Courtesies, He may freely receive | that knows how to requite them.

1664 CODRINGTON 195. 1670 RAY 22.

Courtesy is cumbersome to them that ken it not.

1641 FERGUSSON 26. 1721 KELLY 156 *Heigh how*[1] *is heavy some, An old wife is dowisome,*[2] *And courtesy is cumbersome, To them that cannot shew it.* The whole is for the sake of the last, viz. that people who are not used to good breeding, and mannerly behaviour, perform it very untowardly. [[1] an exclamation of sorrow. [2] tedious.]

Courtesy much entreated is half recompensed, A.

1642 TORRIANO 98. 1672 CODRINGTON 106. 1732 FULLER no. 57.

Courtesy on one side only lasts not long.

1640 HERBERT 354. 1732 FULLER no. 1191.

Courtesy, Where there is o'er mickle | there is little kindness.

1721 KELLY 350.

Courtesy (ies), *see also* Full of c. full of craft; Less of your c., more of your purse; Rank c. when forced give thanks for own.

Courtier, *see* Young c. old beggar.

Courting and wooing bring dallying and doing.

1636 CAMDEN 294. 1732 FULLER no. 6264 (with 'canting' for 'courting').

Courts, It is at | as it is in ponds; some fish, some frogs.

1732 FULLER no. 2912.

Cousin, Call me | but cozen me not.

1655 FULLER *Hist. Camb.* (1840) 117 Savill . . ., (to try whether he could make cousens of his aunt's children). 1678 RAY 118. 1790 TRUSLER *Prov. Exempl.* 20 'A truce with your kindness, my good sir',—Call me cousin, but cozen me not.

Cousin(s), *see also* Call the king c.; Kentish c.; Marry come up, my dirty c.; No c. in London no c. at Stonham.

Covenant, *see* Cathkin's c. . . . . let abee for let abee.

Coventry, To send (a person) to.

[= to exclude from society.] 1647 CLARENDON *Hist. Reb.* VI. § 83 At Bromigham a town so generally wicked that it had risen upon small parties of the king's, and killed or taken them prisoners and sent them to Coventry [then strongly held for the Parliament]. 1765 *Club bk. Tarporley Hunt* in EG. WARBURTON *Hunting Songs* Introd. (1877) 16 Mr. John Barry having sent the Fox Hounds to a different place to what was ordered . . . was sent to Coventry, but return'd upon giving six bottles of Claret to the Hunt. 1796 EDGEWORTH *Par. Asst., Eton Mont.* III. ii He'd send me to Coventry, . . . did he but know I was condescending to make this bit of explanation, unknown to him. 1916 E. A. BURROUGHS *Val. of Decis.* II. iv The 'sportsmanship' of the house united against him, and punished his treason by sending him to Coventry.

Coventry blue.

[Blue thread manufactured at Coventry, and used for embroidery.] 1581 W. STAFFORD *Exam. of Certain Complaints* (New Sh. S.) 89 The chiefe trade of Couentry was heretofore in making of blew threde. 1591 's. SMELLKNAVE' *Fearful effects of Two Comets* 28 Knit Nettes of Coventry blewe for Woodcockes. *a.* 1592 GREENE *Jas. IV* (1861) 208 Edge me the sleeves with Coventry blue. 1626 JONSON *Masque of Owls* Wks. (1904) III. 190 And though his hue Be not Coventry blue. Yet is he undone By the thread he has spun. 1662 FULLER (*Warwick*) III 272 'He is true Coventry blue' . . . The best blues . . . are dyed in Coventry. . . . It is applied to . . . a fast and faithful friend.

Cover (*noun*), *see* Cup (Like), like c.

Cover yourself with your shield, and care not for cries.

1640 HERBERT 324.

Coverlet, *see* Honour under c. (Cannot come to).

Covers me with his wings and bites me with his bill, He.

1616 DRAXE 96. 1670 RAY 5.

Covers thee discovers thee, That which.

1620 SHELTON *Quix.* II. v (1908) II. 221 'Would you know why, husband?' answered Teresa: 'for the proverb that says he that covers thee discovers thee. Every one passeth his eyes slightly over the poor, and upon the rich man they fasten them.'

Covet, *see* All c. all lose.

Covetous spends more than the liberal, The.

1640 HERBERT 349.

Covetous was never good, Over.

1481 CAXTON *Reynard* xxxiii (Arb.) 95 It falleth ofte who that wold haue all leseth alle Ouer couetous was neuer good.

Covetous, *see also* Miserable (C.) man maketh a penny of a farthing.

Covetousness breaks (bursts) the bag (sack).

c. **1594** BACON *Promus* (Pott) no. 616 Covetousness breaks the sack. **1620** SHELTON *Quix.* III. vi (1908) I. 148 But, as covetousness breaks the sack, so hath it also torn my hopes. **1651** HERBERT 366. **1821** SCOTT *Kenilw.* iv Be not over greedy, Anthony. Covetousness bursts the sack and spills the grain. **1853** TRENCH v. 111 Our own, *Covetousness bursts the bag.*

Covetousness often starves other vices.

1732 FULLER no. 1178.

Covetousness, *see also* Sins grow old (When), c. is young.

Cow calf as for the bull, As well for the.

1546 HEYWOOD II. iv. 50 As well for the coowe calfe as for the bull.

Cow hath calved, His.

1596 JONSON *Ev. Man in Humour* IV. ii (A) How now! Whose cow has calv'd? **1678** RAY 70 His cow hath calved, or sow pig'd. He hath got what he sought for, or expected.

Cow in a fremit loaning (an uncouth loan),[1] Like a.

1721 KELLY 223 *I was like a cow in an uncouth loan.* That is, everybody look'd strange to me. **1821** SCOTT *Let.* 11 June in LOCKHART *Life* lii (1860) 452 To hear . . . a probationer in divinity, preach his first sermon in the town of Ayr, *like a cow in a fremd loaning.* **1837–9** LOCKHART *Scott* lvi (1860) 488 In the glittering . . . assemblages of that season, the elder bard [Crabbe] was . . . very like *a cow in a fremd loaning.* **1862** HISLOP 136 He's like a cow in a fremit loaning. That is, strange or out of place. [1 strange milking-place.]

Cow is in the clout, When the | she's soon out.

1721 KELLY 342 Eng. *Ready Money will away.* **1832** HENDERSON 58 Put a cow in a clout and she will soon wear out. (The price of a cow is soon spent.)

Cow knows not what her tail is worth till she hath lost it, The.

1640 HERBERT 357.

Cow, Like | like calf.

1564 BULLEIN *Dial. agst. Fever* (E.E.T.S.) 21 *Ambro.* Her son is like the mother . . . , like cow like calf.

Cow little giveth that hardly liveth, The.

1732 FULLER no. 6325. **1855** BOHN 501.

Cow may want her own tail yet, The.

1721 KELLY 321 . . . You may want my kindness hereafter, though you deny me yours now.

Cow that gives a good pail of milk, and then kicks it over, Like the. (*Cf.* Goat gives a good milking, &c.)

1546 HEYWOOD II. vii. 70 Margery good coowe (quoth he) gaue a good méele, But than she cast it downe again with hir héele. **1599** PORTER *Angry Wom. Abingd.* IV. iii (Merm.) 176 *Nich.* Be not you like the cow, that gives a good sop of milk, and casts it down with her heels. **1639** FULLER *Holy War* v. xxii (1840) 280 These Italians . . . as at first they gave good milk, so they kicked it down with their heel, and by their mutual discord caused the loss of all they helped to gain in Syria.

Cow that's first up, The | gets the first of the dew.

1721 KELLY 306 . . . Recommending diligence and industry.

Cow to catch a hare, Set a.

1611 COTGRAVE s.v. 'Vache' A cow may catch a hare. **1678** RAY 342.

Cow with the iron tail, The.

[= the pump.] **1896** J. C. HUTCHESON *Crown & Anchor* xii 'We'll send ashore for a cow for you', . . . put in Mr. Stormcock ironically . . . 'Dobbs, you know the sort of cow the young gentleman wants—one with an iron tail.'

Cow's horn, *see* Tip c. h. with silver.

Cow's tail, *see* Grow like a c. t.

Cow's thumb, To a.

[= exactly, to a hair.] **1681** T. FLATMAN *Heraclitus Ridens* No. 40 (1713) II. 2 Let him alone, he'll trim their whiskers and comb their Perukes for them to a Cow's thumb.

Cow-turd, *see* Humble-bee in c.

Cow(s), coo, *see also* Bare moor he . . . gets not a c.; Barley straw . . . when c. gives water; Beat a horse . . . and a c. till she be mad; Becomes it as c. doth cart-saddle; Bletherin' c. forgets calf; Bring a c. to the hall and she'll run to byre; Butter that the cow yields (Not all); Buy the c. (If you), take the tail; Comely as c. in cage; Crab in a c.'s mouth (No more than); Crooning c.; Curst c. short horns; Devil's c. calves twice a year; Every man as he loveth . . .

when he kissed his c.; God giveth the c.; Good c. hath evil calf (Many); Hackerton's c.; Look to the c. and the sow; Looked on me as c. on bastard calf; Love as . . . between c. and haystack; Luck as had the c. that stuck herself; Old brown c. laid egg; Parson's c. (Come home like) with a calf; Poor man's c. dies; Red c. good milk; Rush bush keeps c.; St. Robert gave his c. (Freely as); Sell the c. and sup the milk; Sell the c. must say the word (Who will); Sheep and a c. (Now I have); Slender in the middle as a c.; Take a man . . . and a c. by horn; Tint a c. (He never) that grat for a needle; Welshman's c., little and good.

Coward to his mettle, Put a | and he'll fight the devil.

1648 HERRICK *Hesper., Feare gets force* (O.U.P.) 302 Despaire takes heart, when ther's no hope to speed: The Coward then takes Armes, and do's the deed. **1721** KELLY 281. **1732** FULLER no. 3980.

Cowards are cruel.

1485 MALORY *Morte d'Arthur* xviii. 24 Ever wylle a coward shewe no mercy. **1616** DRAXE 36 Cruell people are fearefull. **1727** GAY *Fables* i. 33 Cowards are cruel but the brave love mercy. **1849** C. BRONTË *Shirley* xxi The magistrates are . . . frightened, and, like all cowards, show a tendency to be cruel.

Cowards die often.

1596 DRAYTON *Mortimeriados* l. 2723 Every houre he dyes, which ever feares. **1599** SHAKS. *Jul. Caes.* II. ii. 32.

Cowards, Many would be | if they had courage enough.

1695 W. MORGAN *Religio Militis* 19 All men would be Cowards, if they durst. **1732** FULLER no. 3366. **1779–81** JOHNSON *Lives of Poets* (Bohn) i. 224 This was meant of Rochester, whose *buffoon conceit* was . . . a saying often mentioned, that *every Man would be a Coward if he durst.*

Coward(s), *see also* Bully is always a c.; Despair gives courage to c.; Necessity and opportunity make c. valiant; Valiant man's look more than c.'s sword; Virtue of c. is suspicion.

Cowl (Habit, Hood) does not make the monk, The.

[L. *Cucullus non facit monachum.* NECKAM *Non tonsura facit monachum, non horrida vestis.* RABELAIS I. Prol. *Vous mesmes dictes que l'habit ne faict poinct le moine.*] c. 1200 *Ancr. Riwle* 12 Vrom the worlde witen him clene and unwemmed: her inne is religiun and nout iþe wide hod ne iðe blake. c. 1387 USK *Test. of Love* in *Skeat's Chaucer* VII. 91 For habit maketh no monk; ne weringe of gilte spurres maketh no knight. c. 1400 *Rom. Rose* l. 6192 Habite ne maketh monk ne frere; But a clean life and devotion Maketh gode men of religion. **1588** GREENE

Pandosto Pr. Wks. (1881–3) IV. 289 Trueth quoth *Fawnia*, but all that weare Cooles are not Monkes. **1599–1600** SHAKS. *Twelfth N.* I. v. 62 Lady, cucullus non facit monachum; that's as much to say as I wear not motley in my brain. **1604–5** *Meas. for Meas.* V. i. 257 Cucullus non facit monachum: honest in nothing, but in his clothes. **1612–13** *Hen. VIII* III. i. 23 They should be good men. . . . But all hoods make not monks. **1641** FERGUSSON 64 It is not the habite that makes the monk. **1820** SCOTT *Abbot* xxvi 'Call me not doctor, . . . since I have laid aside my furred gown and bonnet.' 'Oh, sir, . . . the cowl makes not the monk.'

Cowped the mickle dish into the little, He has.

1721 KELLY 144 . . . The jest is in the different signification of the word *cowp*, which signifies to buy and sell grain, cattle, &c., and to turn one thing upon another. Spoken when people have fallen behind in dealing.

Cows come home, Till the.

1610 A. COOKE *Pope Joan* in *Harl. Misc.* (Malh.) IV. 95 Drinking, eating, feasting, and revelling, till the cow come home, as the saying is. c. **1612** BEAUM. & FL. *Scornf. Lady* II. i Kiss till the Cow come home. **1738** SWIFT (Dial. ii) 158 I warrant you lay a Bed till the cows came home.

Cows, *see also* Cow(s).

Coy as a croker's[1] mare, As.

1546 HEYWOOD II. i. 43 Of auncient fathers she tooke no cure nor care, She was to them as koy as a crokers mare. **1659** HOWELL *Eng. Prov.* 10/2. [[1] a saffron-dealer.]

Crab[1] in a cow's mouth, It is no more to him than a.

1732 FULLER no. 2990. *Ibid.* no. 5505 What's a crab in a cow's mouth? **1791** WOLCOT (P. Pindar) *Rights of Kings* Wks. (1816) II. 194 Too soon your band its weakness would deplore! A crab in a cow's mouth—no more! [[1] crab-apple.]

Crab of the wood, The | is sauce very good for the crab of the sea, but the wood of the crab is sauce for a drab, that will not her husband obey.

1659 HOWELL *Eng. Prov.* 6/1 The wood of a crab is good for a drab that will not her husband obey. **1670** RAY 210.

Crab, *see also* Sillier than a c.; Runner (Look like a) quoth devil to c.

Crabbed knot must have a crabbed wedge, A.

1539 TAVERNER (1545) A 5 *Malo nodo malus quaerendus cuneus.* To a crabbed knot must be sought a crabbed wedge. **1611** DAVIES *Epigr.* 137.

Crabs, The greatest | be not all the best meat.

1546 HEYWOOD I. xi. 33 We had ... a chéese very greate. But the greattest crabs be not all the best meate.

Crab-tree, The older the | the more crabs it bears.

1856 ABP. WHATELY *Annot. on Bacon's Ess.* 42 (1876) 452 'The older the crab-tree, the more crabs it bears', says the proverb. Unless a correcting principle be *engrafted*, though a man may, perhaps, outgrow the vices and follies of youth, other vices, and even worse, will come in their stead.

Crab-tree where you will, Plant the | it will never bear pippins.

1579 LYLY *Euphues* (Bond) I. 191 Plante and translate the crabbe tree where and whensoever it please you and it will neuer beare sweete apple.

Crab-tree, *see also* Hang a dog on a c.

Crack me that nut (quoth Bumsted). (*Cf.* Hard nut to crack.)

1545 ELYOT *Def. Gd. Wom.* B iv b Nowe knacke me that nut, Maister Candidus. **1546** HEYWOOD II. vii. 66 Knak me that nut. **1678** RAY 69 Crack me that nut, quoth Bumsted.

Cracked bell can never sound well (is never sound), A.

1629 T. ADAMS *Serm.* (1861) I. 73 A wicked man's tongue discovers him. A bell may have a crack, though invisible; take the clapper and strike, and you shall soon perceive it. **1732** FULLER no. 6358. **1823** COLLINS 77 *Campana cascada, nunca sana.* 'A cracked bell is never sound.'—It has a reference to persons of weak minds, arising from natural infirmity or some bodily accident.

Cracked nuts with her tail, She goes as if she.

1678 RAY 291.

Cradle straws are scarce out of his breech.

1678 RAY 346.

Cradle(s), *see also* Between the c. and the grave; Fair in the c., foul in saddle; Foot on c. ... sign of good housewife; Hand that rocks the c.; Knock in the c. (He got a); Plough going (Better have one) than two c.; Shod in c., barefoot in stubble.

Craft against craft makes no living.

1640 HERBERT 358.

Craft bringeth nothing home.

1616 DRAXE 35. **1670** RAY 6. **1732** FULLER no. 1199 Craft counting all things, brings nothing home.

Craft, He that hath not the | let him shut up shop.

1640 HERBERT 356.

Craft in daubing, There is.

1454 *Paston Letters* (1900) I. 269 Her moder ... seyth to her that ther is gode crafte in dawbyng. *c.* **1530** *Hyckescorner* 259, 260 *Imag.* If my handes were smyten of, I can stele with my tethe; For ye knowe well there is crafte in daubynge. **1623** CAMDEN 278. **1678** RAY 120 There is more craft in daubing than in throwing dirt on the wall.

Craft is in the catching, All the.

1608 DEKKER, *The Dead Term* G 2ᵛ All the craft was in the catching. **1616** DRAXE 101. **1631** MABBE *Celestina* 163 (T.T.).

Craft must have clothes, but truth loves to go naked.

1597 *Politeuphuia* 30 b Craft hath neede of cloaking, where truth is euer naked. **1732** FULLER no. 1200.

Craft, *see also* Full of courtesy, full of c.; Gentle c.; Mariners' c.

Crafty knave needs no broker, A.

1546 HEYWOOD I. ii. 135 Two false knaves néede no broker. **1590–1** SHAKS. *2 Hen. VI* I. ii They say,—A crafty knave does need no broker; yet am I Suffolk, and the cardinal's broker. **1598** JONSON *Ev. Man in Humour* III. ii That cannot be, if the proverb hold; for a crafty knave needs no broker. **1611** A. NOWELL *Sword against Swearers* B 3 As two false knaves need no Broker, for they can easily enough agree in wickednesse *Sine mediante.* **1623** CAMDEN 266 A false knaue, needes no broker.

Crafty man, To a | a crafty and a half.

1599 MINSHEU (1623) 2 T 2. **1640** HERBERT 354.

Crambe repetita, see Cabbage twice cooked.

Cranes of Ibycus, The.

[*c.* 540 B.C. Gk. Αἱ ᾿Ιβύκου γέρανοι. Ibycus, a Greek poet, attacked by robbers, called on a flight of cranes to avenge his death. The subsequent sight of these cranes called forth a remark which led to the arrest and execution of the murderers. ERASM. *Ad. Ibyci grues.*] **1853** TRENCH ii. 36 *The Cranes of Ibycus* passed into a proverb, very much as our *Murder will out*, to express the wondrous leadings of God whereby ... secret things of blood are brought to the open light of day. **1905** ALEX. MACLAREN *Genesis* 19 According to the fine old legend of the cranes of Ibycus, a bird of the air will carry the matter.

Crave, *see* Nothing c. nothing have; Nothing have nothing c.; Youth knew what age would c. (If).

Cravers are aye ill payers, Sore.

1721 KELLY 286 ... This proverb, and the

reverse, *viz. Ill payers are sore cravers,* I have never yet seen fail. **1737** RAMSAY III. 186 Ill payers are ay guid cravers.

Craving, *see* Shameful (Shameless) c. must have shameful nay.

Craw flies, When the | her tail follows.
1832 HENDERSON 94.

Crawley brook, *see* Crooked as C. b.

Crazy ship all winds are contrary, To a. (*Cf.* Every wind is ill, &c.)
1640 HERBERT 336. **1670** RAY 6. **1732** FULLER no. 5126.

Creaking door (gate) hangs long on its hinges, A.
1776 T. COGAN *John Buncle, Junior* i. 239 (A) But they say a creaking gate goes the longest upon its hinges; that's my comfort. **1880** BARING GOULD *Mehalah* xxii Your mother . . . may live yet a score of years. Creaky gates last longest.

Cream of the jest, That is the.
1678 RAY 69.

Creampot love, *see* Cupboard love.

Credit, No man ever lost his | but he who had it not.
1664 CODRINGTON 206. **1670** RAY 6.

Credit decayed, and people that have nothing, Take heed of.
1651 HERBERT 371.

Credit is dead, bad pay killed it.
1666 TORRIANO 184 *Trust is dead, ill* payment *kill'd it.*

Credit lost is like a Venice-glass broken.
1664 CODRINGTON 189. **1670** RAY 6. **1796** EDGEWORTH *Par. Asst.* (1903) 411 He found the truth of the proverb, 'that credit lost is like a Venice glass broken—it can't be mended again'.

Credit, *see also* Buyeth dear and taketh up on c. (Who); Honesty (C.) keeps crown of causeway; Lost his c., dead to the world; Religion, c., are not to be touched.

Creditors have better memories than debtors.
1659 HOWELL *Span.-Eng.* 8 The Creditor hath a better memory then the Debtor. **1758** FRANKLIN in ARB. *Eng. Garner* V. 585 When you have got your bargain; you may, perhaps, think little of payment, but . . . *Creditors . . . have better memories than Debtors.*

Creel, *see* Put your hand in c. and take out adder or eel.

Creep into Ebal, and leap into Gerizim, We must.
1853 TRENCH iii. 66 . . . in other words, we must be slow to curse, and swift to bless (Deut. xxvii. 12, 13).

Creep, *see also* Find some hole to c. out at; First c. then go; Kind (Love) will c. where it may not go; Speak as if you would c. into my mouth (You).

Cress, Not worth a.
c. **1387** USK *Test. of Love* in *Skeat's Chaucer* vii. 73 (A) Their might is not worth a cress. **1393** LANGLAND *P. Pl.* C xii. 14 Wysdom and wit now · is nat worth a carse.[1] [[1] cress.]

Cries wine and sells vinegar, He.
1659 HOWELL *Span.-Eng.* 3. **1732** FULLER no. 1831.

Criffel, *see* Skiddaw.

Criminate, *see* No man is bound to c. self.

Cripple, *see* Crooked carlin, quoth the c.; Dwells next door to c. will learn to halt; Halting before a c. (Hard); Mocks a c. ought to be whole.

Cripplegate, *see* Lame as St. Giles, C.

Critics are like brushers of noblemen's clothes.
1625 BACON *Apophthegms* no. 64. **1651** HERBERT 371.

Crock, *see* Part with the c. as the porridge. (As soon).

Crocodile tears.
[= hypocritical sorrow. ERASM. *Ad. Crocodili lacrimae.*] **1579** LYLY *Euphues* (Arb.) 75 The Crocodile shrowdeth greatest treason vnder most pitiful teares. **1590** SPENSER *F. Q.* I. v. 18. **1590–1** SHAKS. *2 Hen. VI* III. i. 226 Gloucester's show Beguiles him as the mournful crocodile With sorrow snares relenting passengers. **1604–5** *Othello* IV. i. 257 If that the earth could teem with woman's tears Each drop she falls would prove a crocodile. **1606–7** *Ant. & Cleop.* II. vii. 56 *Lep.* What manner o' thing is your crocodile? . . . *Ant.* . . . The tears of it are wet. **1625** BACON *Ess., Of Wisdom* (Arb.) 187 It is the Wisedome of Crocodiles, that shed teares, when they would deuoure. **1912** *Times Lit. Sup.* 29 Mar. 128 [Maria Theresa's] crocodile tears over Poland, . . . alienate much of the sympathy which would attach to a good woman.

Croesus, *see* Rich as C.

Croker's mare, *see* Coy as a c. m.

Cromwell, *see* Curse of C.

Crook[1] in the lot of every one, There is a.
a. **1732** T. BOSTON *The Crook in the Lot* (1767

14 The crook in the lot is the special trial appointed for every one. **1818** SCOTT *Ht. Midl.* xii I trust to bear even this crook in my lot with submission. **1880** BLACKMORE *Mary A.* xi In every man's lot must be some crook, since this crooked world turned round. [¹ affliction, trial.]

Crooked as Crawley brook, As.

1662 FULLER (*Beds.*) I. 167 'As crooked as Crawley brook' . . . a nameless brook . . . running by Crawley, and falling . . . into the Ouse.

Crooked carlin, quoth the cripple to his wife.

1721 KELLY 78.

Crooked logs make straight fires.

1611 COTGRAVE s.v. 'Busche'. **1640** HERBERT 319 A crooked log makes a straight fire. **1670** RAY 6.

Crooked¹ man should sow beans, A | and a wud² man peas.

1721 KELLY 42 *A crooked man should sow beans, and a wood man pease.* The one agrees to be thick sown, and the other thin. [¹ lame. ² mad.]

Crooked, *see also* Staff be c. (If), shadow not straight.

Crooketh the tree, Timely (Soon) | that will good cammock¹ (gambrel²) be.

c. **1460** *The Gode Wyfe wold a Pylgr.* (E.E.T.S.) 1. 143 The tre crokothe son that good cambrel wyll be. **1546** HEYWOOD II. ix. 77 Timely crooketh the trée, that will a good camok bée. **1591** LYLY *Endym.* III. i (1902) III. 41 *Tell.* But timely, Madam, crookes that tree that wil be a camock. **1670** RAY 75 Soon crooks the tree, that good gambrel would be. **1721** KELLY 97 *Early crooks the tree that in good cammon³ will be.* . . . Children soon show their propensities and inclinations. [¹ a crooked tree, or bent beam as for the knee of a ship. ² a crooked stick used by butchers for expanding the carcass of a sheep. ³ a crooked stick for playing at shinty.]

Crooning cow, a crowing hen, and a whistling maid boded never luck to a house, A.

1721 KELLY 33 . . . The two first are reckoned ominous, but the reflection is on the third. **1891** J. L. KIPLING *Beast & Man* 40 'A whistling woman and a crowing hen are neither fit for God nor men,' is a mild English saying. **1917** BRIDGE 28 A whistling wife and a crowing hen will fear the old lad¹ out of his den. [¹ the devil.]

Cross and (or) pile.

[Fr. *Croix et* (*ou*) *pile.* The obverse and (or) reverse side of a coin, the *pile* being the under iron of the minting apparatus. *Fig.* The two sides of anything ; one thing and its opposite.]

c. **1390** GOWER *Conf. Amantis* II. 390 Whos tung neither pyl ne crouche mai hyre. *c.* **1450** *Pol. Poems* (1859) II. 240 Crosse and pyle standen in balaunce. *a.* **1613** OVERBURY *Newes, Countrey Newes* Wks. (1856) 175 That good and ill is the crosse and pile in the ayme of life.

Cross as two sticks, As.

1831 SCOTT *Journ.* 2 Nov. Wind as cross as two sticks, with nasty squalls of wind and rain. **1842** S. LOVER *Handy Andy* ii. 24 The renowned O'Grady was according to her account as cross as two sticks. **1855** LD. HOUGHTON in *Life* I. xi. 518 [He] has been as cross as two sticks at not having been asked to dinner at court.

Cross hath its inscription, Each.

1639 CLARKE 16 Every cross has its own inscription. **1670** RAY 75 . . . Crosses and afflictions come not by chance, . . . but are laid on men for some just reason. . . . Many times we may read the sin in the punishment. **1853** TRENCH vi. 140 *Every cross hath its inscription* ; the name . . . inscribed upon it, of the person for whom it was shaped.

Cross on anything, To make a.

[= to reckon as specially happy.] **1546** HEYWOOD I. xi. 36 Come, go we hens friend (quoth I to my mate). And now will I make a crosse on this gate.

Cross on the breast, and the devil in the heart, The.

1598 SIR R. BARCKLEY, *Of the Felicity of Man* 551 *Cruzes de fuera, & diablo de dentro:* crosses without, and the diuell within. **1616** DRAXE 96. **1732** FULLER no. 4462.

Cross the bridge till you get to it, Don't.

1895 ADDY *Househ. Tales* 144 One who anticipates difficulty is told not to cross the bridge till he gets to it.

Cross the stream where it is ebbest.¹

1603 HOLLAND tr. *Plutarch's Morals* 747 (A) There is still a Lancashire proverb 'Cross the stream where it is ebbest'. **1615** BRATHWAIT *Strap. for Div.* 222 O let me now perswade, be not extreame, (*Its easie saies the Prouerb*) *to wade the streame, Where th' foord's at lowest, recollect to minde.* **1859** TRENCH *Sel. Gloss.* (1873) 80 There is still a Lancashire proverb, 'Cross the stream where it is ebbest'. [¹ shallowest.]

Cross (Penny) to bless himself with, He hath never a. (*Cf.* Penny to buy, &c.)

1540 PALSGRAVE *Acolastus* (Carver) 91 He shal be pollyd and shauen by us, tyl he shal not haue a halfepenye lefte to blesse hym wyth. *Ibid.* 140 The moneylesse knaue, (that hath neuer a crosse left him to blesse him with). **1568** FULWELL *Like Will to L.*, in HAZL. *O.E.P.* (1874) III. 346 Not a cross of money to bless me have I. **1638** T. HEYWOOD

Wise W. of Hogs. Wks. (1874) V. 281 Ile play the Franck gamester . . . I will not leave my selfe one Crosse to blesse me. **1670** RAY 170. **1766** GOLDSMITH *Vic. W.* xxi To come and take up an honest house, without cross or coin to bless yourself with. **1819** SCOTT *Bride Lam.* v The Lord Keeper has got all his estates; he has not a cross to bless himself with.

Crosses are ladders that lead to heaven.

1616 DRAXE 36 The Crosse is the ladder of heaven. **1670** RAY 6. **1859** SMILES *Self-Help* 341 If there be real worth in the character, . . . it will give forth its finest fragrance when pressed. 'Crosses', says the old proverb, 'are the ladders that lead to heaven.'

Cross(es), *see also* Cry at the c.; Heads (C.) I win; No c. no crown.

Cross-bow, *see* Fish with a c. (No sure rule to.)

Crouse, *see* Nothing so c. as new washen louse.

Crow in a gutter, Like a.

1579 FULKE *Confut. Sanders* 675 He triumpheth like a crow in a gutter. **1662** J. WILSON *Cheats* III. iv It should be a sweetheart (forsooth)—how it struts, like a crow in a gutter!

Crow is never the whiter for washing herself often, A.

1678 RAY 121. **1732** FULLER no. 1210.

Crow is white, To say the.

1509 A. BARCLAY *Ship of Fools* (1874) II. 212. **1546** HEYWOOD II. v As good than to say the crow is white.

Crow thinks her own bird(s) fairest (whitest), The.

1513 DOUGLAS *Æneis* ix. Prol. 78 The blak craw thinkis hir awin byrdis quhite. **1546** HEYWOOD II. iv. 50 The crow thinkth hir owne birdes fairest in the wood. **1621** BURTON *Anat. Mel.* III. i. II. iii (1651) 421 Another great tye or cause of love, is consanguinity; . . . every crow thinks her own bird fairest. **1670** RAY 76 . . . So the Ethiopians are said to paint the devil white. Every one is partial to . . . his own compositions, his own children, his own country. **1823** GALT *Entail* xxix 'The craw thinks its ain bird the whitest', replied the Leddy.

Crow to pluck (pull) with one, To have a.

[= to have fault to find.] c. **1460** *Towneley Myst.* xviii. 311 Na, na, abide, we haue a craw to pull. **1509** A. BARCLAY *Ship of Fools* (1570) 91 A wrathfull woman . . . He that her weddeth hath a crowe to pull. **1546** HEYWOOD II. v. 58 If he leaue it not, we haue a crow to pul. **1592-3** SHAKS. *Com. Err.* III. i. 83 *Ant. E.* Well, I'll break in. Go borrow me a crow [i.e. bar of iron]. . . . *Dro. E.* If a crow help us in, sirrah, we'll pluck a crow

together. **1665** J. WILSON *Project.* v. Wks. (1874) 266 I've a crow to pluck w' ye. Where 's my coach and the eight horses you talk'd of? **1849** *Tait's Mag.* XVI. 385/1 If there be 'a crow to pluck' between us and any contemporary, we shall make a clean breast of it at once.

Crow(s) (*noun*), *see also* Black as a c.; Carrion c. bewail dead sheep; Carrion will kill c. (No); Evil c. evil egg; Hawks (C.) will not pick out c.'s eyes; High for the pie (Not too) nor too low for c.; Killing a c. with empty sling; Make the c. a pudding; March kill c., pie, . . . and raven. *See also* Craw.

Crows (*verb*), *see* Hen c. louder than cock (Sad house where).

Crow-trodden, You look as if you were.

[= subjected to ignominious treatment.] **1678** RAY 237.

Crowd is not company, A.

1625 BACON *Ess., Friendship* (Arb.) 165 For a crowd is not company; and faces are but a gallery of pictures; . . . where there is no love. **1732** FULLER no. 62.

Crowdy, *see* MacKibbon's c.

Crowing hen, *see* Crooning cow.

Crowland, *see* Carts that come to; Ramsey.

Crown is no cure for the headache, A.

1612-15 BP. HALL *Contempt.* XVIII. iv (1825) I. 565 Yet could not that misgotten crown of his keep his head always from aching. **1757** FRANKLIN *Aug.* The royal crown cures not the headache.

Crown, *see also* Cleave to the c.; Right, master, four nobles a year's a c. a quarter.

Croydon, *see* Sutton.

Cruelty is a tyrant that's always attended with fear.

1616 DRAXE 36 Cruell people are fearefull. **1664** CODRINGTON 190. **1670** RAY 6. **1732** FULLER no. 1213.

Cruelty is more cruel, if we defer the pain.

1651 HERBERT 368.

Cruelty, *see also* Clemency is c. (Sometimes); Mercy to criminal, c. to people.

Crumb(s), *see* Musician hath forgot note (When), c. in throat; Pick up (Gather) one's c.

Crupper, *see* Old mare would have new c.

Cruse, *see* Cup (Such a), such a c.

Crust, *see* Ill dog that deserves not c.; Leap at a c.

Crusty as that is hard baked, She
is as.

1594 LYLY *Moth. Bomb.* II. iii You need not
bee so crustie, you are not so hard bakt.
1678 RAY 352 She is as crousty as that is hard
bak'd. *Somerset.* (One that is surly and
loath to doe any thing.)

Crutch of time does more than the
club of Hercules, The.

1732 FULLER no. 4464.

Crutch(es), *see also* Literature is . . . bad c.;
One foot is better than two c.

Cry at the cross, To.

[The market-cross, at which public announce-
ments were made.] *a.* **1529** SKELTON *Dyuers
Balettys* 36 Wks. (1843) I. 24 It can be no
counsell that is cryed at the cros. **1611** COT-
GRAVE s.v. 'Sing' Thou hast not cried it at
the crosse. **1823** GALT *Entail* xxi As we need
na cry sic things at the Cross, I'm mindit to
hae you and him for the witnesses.

Cry 'Barley',[1] To.

[= to ask for truce, in children's games in
Scotland.] **1757** SMOLLETT *Reprisal* II. x
Macl. I'se no be the first to cry barley.
1814 SCOTT *Waverley* xlii A proper lad o' his
quarters, that will not cry barley in a
brulzie.[2] [[1] parley. [2] fray.]

Cry (out) before one is hurt, To.

1548 *Reliq. Antiquae* (1843) II. 16 Ye may
the better understand that I cry not before
I am pricked. **1611** COTGRAVE s.v. 'Anguille'
Such as . . . crie before their paine approch
them. **1678** RAY 237 You cry before you're
hurt. **1721** KELLY 204 *It is time enough to
cry, Oh, when you are hurt.* Spoken to dissuade people from groundless fears. **1850**
THACKERAY *Pendennis* lxix I . . . took up a
pistol. You see it is not loaded, and this
coward cried out before he was hurt. **1908**
Spectator 6 June The gull's rule is to cry out
before he is hurt.

Cry 'Chuck', *see* Soon enough to c. 'C'.

Cry for the moon, To.

[Typifying something impossible to get.]
1852 DICKENS *Bleak Ho.* vi He was a mere
child in the world, but he didn't cry for the
moon. **1910** *Spectator* 5 Feb. A large section
of the Liberal Party are crying for the moon.

Cry hem and have him.

1599–1600 SHAKS. *A.Y.L.* I. iii. 20 *Cel.* Hem
them away. *Ros.* I would try, if I could
cry 'hem', and have him. **1690** *Dict. Cant.
Crew* F 7 *Hem.* to call after one with an
inarticulate Noise.

Cry (one) Notchel, To.

[= to proclaim publicly that one will not be
responsible for debts incurred by the person
named.] **1681** *Dial. btw. Sam. & Will.* in
Harl. Misc. (1744) II. 101 The King's
Majesty, . . . him they cryed Nochell. *Sam.*
What, as Gaffer Block of our Town cryed his

Wife? **1859** in *N. & Q.* 3rd Ser. (1866) x. 108
On Wednesday there was at Accrington an
extraordinary instance of the disgraceful
practice of 'notchel crying'.

Cry one's eyes out, To.

1613 CHAPMAN *Rev. Bussy* v. i. 144 Those
loveliest eyes . . . she wept quite out. **1704**
CIBBER *Careless Husb.* I. i I could cry my
Eyes out.

Cry *peccavi*, To.

[L. *Peccavi*, 'I have sinned', hence an
acknowledgement of guilt. TER. *Ad.* 2. 4. 12.]
1509 FISHER *Fun. Serm. Hen. VII* Wks.
(1876) 272 Kynge Dauid that wrote this
psalme, with one worde spekynge his herte
was chaunged sayenge *Peccaui*. **1553** T.
WILSON *Arte of Rhet.* (1580) 65 Much soner
shall al other be subiect vnto him, and crie
Peccaui. **1730** SWIFT *Sheridan's Submission*
Wks. (1755) IV. I. 259 Now lowly crouch'd,
I cry peccavi.

Cry quits, To.

1639 FULLER *Holy War* III. xi (1840) 134 This
opportunity was lost by the backwardness
. . . of . . . the English, say the French writers.
To cry quits with them, our English authors
impute it to the envy of the French. **1837**
MARRYAT *Perc. Keene* xix I should have fired
at you, so we may cry quits on that score.

Cry roast meat, To.

[= to be foolish enough to announce to others
a piece of private luck or good fortune.]
1611 GRUTER. *c.* **1612** BEAUM. & FL. *Scornf.
Lady* v. i. Wks. (1905) I. 297 *Lady.* Cannot
you fare well, but you must cry roast meat?
Wel. He that fares well, and will not bless
the founders, is either surfeited or ill taught.
1614 CAMDEN 336 (1870) You cannot fare
well but you must cry rost meat. **1638** SIR
T. HERBERT *Trav.* (ed. 2) 209 At length the
home-bred Chyna cryes roast-meat. **1670**
RAY 88 You can't fare well, but you must
cry roast-meat. Sasse bonne farine sans
trompe ny buccine. *Gall.* Boult thy fine meal,
and eat good past, without report or trumpets
blast. **1673** WYCHERLEY *Gent. Dancing-
Master* I. ii Hark you, madame, can't you
fare well but you must cry 'Roast meat'?
1820 LAMB *Elia.* 1 *Christ's Hosp.* The foolish
beast, not able to fare well but he must cry
roast meat. **1827** SCOTT *Journ.* 1 Jan. My
life has been spent in such day-dreams. But
I cry no roast-meat.

Cry with one eye, and laugh with
the other, To.

c. **1369** CHAUCER *Bk. Duch.* l. 633 She ys
fals ; and ever laughynge With oon eye, and
that other wepynge. *c.* **1460** HENRYSON *Test.
of Cresseid* 230 Thus variant sho was, quha
list tak keip, With ane eye lauch, and with
the uther weip. **1603** SHAKS. *Hamlet* I. ii. 11
With an auspicious and a dropping eye.
1621 BURTON *Anat. Mel.* III. ii. III. iv (1651)
498 They . . . weep with the one eye, laugh
with the other ; or . . . they can both together.
1678 RAY 242. **1732** FULLER no. 4737 The
rich widow cries with one eye, and laughs
with the other.

Cry 'Wolf', To.

[= to raise a false alarm; in allusion to the fable of the shepherd boy who deluded people with false cries of 'Wolf!'] **1692** L'ESTRANGE *Aesop's Fab.* ccclx. 332 The Boy . . . would be Crying *a Wolf, a Wolf,* when there was none, and then could not be Believed when there was. **1858** MRS. CRAIK *Woman's Th.* 281 After crying 'Wolf' ever since . . . seventeen—as some young ladies are fond of doing . . . the grim wolf, old age, is actually showing his teeth in the distance. **1887** BLACKMORE *Springhaven* liii In a matter like that French invasion, . . . 'the cry of wolf' grows stale at last, and then the real danger comes.

Cry you mercy; I | I have killed your cushion.

1530 PALSGRAVE 501 (A) I kry you mercy, I kylled your cussheyn. **1594** LYLY *Moth. Bomb.* IV. ii. Wks. (1902) III. 549 *Half.* On thy conscience tell me what tis a clock? *Silena.* I cry you mercy, I have killed your cushion. [*Note.* Silena is probably garbling the expression 'missed the cushion' or mark in archery.]

Cry you mercy; I | I took you for a joint-stool.[1]

[*cf.* **1670** RAY 68 Cry you mercy, killed my cat . . . spoken to them who do one a shrewd turn, and then make satisfaction with asking pardon or crying mercy.] **1594** LYLY *Moth. Bomb.* IV. ii. Wks. (1902) III. 549 *Accius.* You need not be so lusty, you are not so honest. *Silena.* I cry you mercy, I took you for a joynd stool. [*Note.* Proverb for an unfortunate apology or a pert reply.] **1605–6** SHAKS. *K. Lear* III. vi. 55 *Fool.* Cry you mercy, I took you for a joint-stool. **1634** WITHALS 553 *Ante hoc te cornua habere putabam,* I cry you mercy, I tooke you for a joynd stoole. [[1] A stool made of parts joined or fitted together.]

Cry Yule at other men's cost, It is easy to.

c. **1532** SIR ADRIAN FORTESCUE no. 20 Yt is easy to crye yole at another mans cost. **1550** HEYWOOD I. xi. 28 To flée charge, and fynde ease, ye wold now héere oste. It is easy to cry vle at other mens coste. **1641** FERGUSSON 62 It is eith to cry ȝule on another mans cost.

Cry (*noun*), *see* Great c. little wool.

Cry, cries, cried (*verb*), *see also* Laugh and c. with a breath; Laugh before breakfast, c. before supper; Sing before breakfast, c. before night; Wife c. five loaves a penny.

Crying over spilt milk, It is no use.

1484 CAXTON *Aesope* (Jacobs) ii. 270 (A) The thyrd [doctrine] is that thow take no sorowe of the thynge lost whiche may not be recouered. **1659** HOWELL *Brit. Prov.* 40 No weeping for shed milk. **1738** SWIFT (Dial. i) 335 *Col.* 'Tis a folly to cry for spilt milk. **1884** J. PAYN *Canon's W.* xv There would

be a row, . . . ; but he would say, like a wise man, 'There's no use in crying over spilled milk'.

Cuckold and conceals it, Who is a | carries coals in his bosom.

1659 HOWELL *Span.-Eng.* 14. **1670** RAY 6. *Hispan.*

Cuckold come, If a | he'll take away the meat, if there be no salt on the table.

1678 RAY 69 If a cuckold come he'll take away the meat. *viz.* If there be no salt on the table. **1738** SWIFT (Dial. ii) 344 *Col.* Here's no salt; cuckolds will run away with the meat.

Cuckold is the last that knows of it, The.

1636 CAMDEN 306. **1712** ARBUTHNOT *John Bull* I. viii It is a true saying, that the last man of the parish that knows of his cuckoldom is himself. It was observed by all the neighbourhood that Hocus had dealings with John's wife that were not so much for his honour; but this was perceived by John a little too late.

Cuckold wear his own horns, Let every.

1659 HOWELL *Eng. Prov.* 3. **1670** RAY 6

Cuckolds go to heaven, In rain and sunshine.

1591 FLORIO *Sec. Frutes* 143 All cuckolds shall obtaine Paradise. **1623** WODROEPHE 299 Al Cuckolds shal go to Heauen. **1659** HOWELL *Eng. Prov.* 12/2.

Cuckold(s), *see also* A-cold than a c. (Better be); Hope better, quoth Benson; Mock not, quoth Mumford; Strand on the Green, thirteen houses, fourteen c.

Cuckoo comes, When the | he eats up all the dirt.

[i.e. the mire of winter dries up. LEAN.] **1680** *Yea and Nay Alm.* April. Ladies . . . may walk abroad to take their pleasure, for any old woman will tell you that when the Cuckow comes he eats up all the dirt. **1830** FORBY 430 I will come when the cuckoo has pecked up the dirt. *i.e.* In the spring. **1876** MRS. BANKS *Manch. Man* viii Bush and tree put out pale buds. . . . The cuckoo—to use a village phrase—had 'eaten up the mud'; and the town was alive with holiday-makers.

Cuckoo comes in April, and stays the month of May; sings a song at midsummer, and then goes away, The.

1869 HAZLITT 363.

Cuckoo comes to the bare thorn, When the | sell your cow and buy you corn: but when she comes

to the full bit, sell your corn and buy you sheep. (*Cf.* Cuckoo sitteth, &c.)

1670 RAY 43.

Cuckoo goes to Beaulieu Fair to buy him a greatcoat, The.

1863 J. R. WISE *New Forest* xvi (1895) 180 'The cuckoo goes to Beaulieu Fair to buy him a greatcoat', referring to the arrival of the cuckoo about the 15th of April, whilst the day on which the fair is held is known as the 'cuckoo day'.

Cuckoo singeth all the year, The.

1541 *Schole Ho. Women* 320–1 in HAZL. *E. Pop. Poet* (1866) IV. 117 All beit that few men doo him hear, The cuckoo singeth all the year [*i.e.* cuckoldom continues throughout the year].

Cuckoo sitteth on a dry thorn, When the | sell thy cow and sow thy corn. (*Cf.* Cuckoo comes to the bare thorn.)

1659 HOWELL *Eng. Prov.* 16/2.

Cuckoo, *see also* Breed of the gowk (c.); Cock of hay frights c.; March the c. starts; Nightingale and c. sing both in one month; Third of April comes c.; Three flails and c.; Turn the money when you hear the c.

Cuckstone, *see* Church mis-went.

Cucullus non facit monachum, *see* Cowl (Habit, Hood) does not make the monk.

Cucumber, *see* Cool as a c.

Cudgel one's brains, To.

1600–1 SHAKS. *Ham.* V. i. 63 Cudgel thy brains no more about it. **1849** THACKERAY *Pendennis* xv When a gentleman is cudgelling his brain to find any rhyme for sorrow besides borrow and to-morrow.

Cudgels, *see* Take up c.

Cumber, John à, *see* Devil and J. à C.

Cunning as a dead pig, As | but not half so honest.

1738 SWIFT (Dial. iii) 350 *Miss.* My lady manages him to admiration. *Lady S.* That I believe; for she's as cunning as a dead pig, but not half so honest.

Cunning is no burden.

1520 WHITTINGTON *Vulg.* (E.E.T.S.) 40 Connynge . . . semeth no burden to hym yt hath hit. **1539** TAVERNER f. 22. **1636** CAMDEN 294 Cunning is no burthen. **1642** FULLER *H. & P. State* II. xxv (1841) 138 Cunning is no burden to carry, as paying neither porterage by land, nor pondage by sea. **1732** FULLER no. 4182 Skill is no burthen.

Cunning wife makes her husband her apron, The.

1664 CODRINGTON 215. **1670** RAY 29. *Hispan.*

Cup, Let go the.

1362 LANGLAND *P. Pl.* v. 3162 (Wright) I. 97 And 'lat go the cuppe'; . . . Til Gloton had y-glubbed[1] A galon and a gille. [[1] drunk.]

Cup and can.

[= constant or familiar associates.] **1546** HEYWOOD II. iii. 49 Mery we were as cup and can could holde. **1729** SWIFT *Libel on Dr. Delany* You and he are cup and can. **1738** *Id.* (Dial. iii) 351 Miss, I hear that you and lady Coupler are as great as cup and can.

Cup and the lip, Many things fall (Many a slip) between the.

[Gk. Πολλὰ μεταξὺ πέλει κύλικος καὶ χείλεος ἄκρου. CATO in *Aul. Gell.* 13. 17. 1 *Inter os atque offam multa intervenire posse.* ERASM. *Ad.* *Multa cadunt inter calicem supremaque labra.*] **1539** TAVERNER 16 Manye thynges fall betweene ye cuppe and the mouth **1580** LYLY *Euphues* (Arb.) 471 Manye thinges fall betweene the cup and the lippe. **1591** HARINGTON *Ariosto* xviii. 47 Much falls between the chalice and the chin **1633** JONSON *T. Tub.* III iv. Wks. (1904) II. 463 *Hugh.* *Multa cadunt inter*—you can guess the rest, Many things fall between the cup and the lip. **1712** ARBUTHNOT *John Bull* II. xiii Many things happen between the cup and the lip— witnesses might have been bribed, juries managed, or prosecution stopped. **1824** MOIR *Mansie W.* xxii 'There is many a slip 'tween the cup and the lip', said Peter. **1853** TRENCH ii. 37 Setting down the untasted cup, . . . the master went out to meet the wild boar, and was slain in the encounter; and thus . . . , the proverb, *Many things find place between the cup and the lip*, arose. **1887** T. A. TROLLOPE *What I remember* I. xii. 256 A whole series of slips between the cup and the lip.

Cup in the pate is a mile in the gate, A.

1694 MOTTEUX *Rabelais* IV. ch. 65 (A). **1738** SWIFT (Dial. ii) 349 A cup in the pate is a mile in the gate; and a spur in the head is worth two in the heel.

Cup is fullest, When the | then bear her fairest. (Cf. Full cup, &c.)

c. **1300** *Provs. of Hending* 16 When the coppe is follest, thenne ber hire feyrest. **1721** KELLY 346 *When the cup's full carry it even.* When you have arrived at power and wealth, take a care of insolence, pride, and oppression. **1820** SCOTT *Monast.* Introd. Epist. 'It is difficult', saith the proverb, 'to carry a full cup without spilling.'

Cup, Like (Such) | like (such) cover.

1549 LATIMER *5th Serm. bef. Edw. VI* (P.S.) 181 She was a rich woman, she had her lands by the sheriff's nose. He was a gentleman of a long nose. Such a cup, such a cover! **1655** FULLER *Ch. Hist.* IX. ii, § 20 (1868) II. 552

John Story, . . . a cruel persecutor in the days of Queen Mary, . . . great with the Duke de Alva (like cup, like cover!).

Cup of Circe, The.

[Circe was an enchantress whose cup transformed those who drank it into swine. HOMER *Od.* x; VIRGIL, *Aen.* vii.] **1592–3** SHAKS. *Com. Err.* V. i. 271 I think you all have drunk of Circe's cup. **1861** G. J. WHYTE-MELVILLE *Inside the Bar* i I did not even mistrust the cup of Circe. Ah! she made a pig of her admirer, that ancient enchantress; and in Miss Lushington's presence the admirer makes an ass of himself.

Cup, Such a | such a cruse.

1549 LATIMER *5th Serm. bef. Edw. VI* (Arb.) 142 She was a rych woman, she had hir landes by the Shiriffes nose. He was a gentilman of a longe nose. Such a cup, such a cruse.

Cup, *see also* Full c. must be carried steadily; Kiss the c.; No sooner up but . . . nose in c.

Cupar,[1] He that will to | maun to Cupar.

1721 KELLY 141 *He that will to Cowper, will to Cowper.*[1] A reflection upon obstinate persons, that will not be reclaim'd. **1818** SCOTT *Rob Roy* xxviii The Heccate . . . ejaculated, 'A wilfu' man will hae his way: them that will to Cupar maun to Cupar!' **1893** STEVENSON *Catriona* xiii 'He that will to Cupar, maun to Cupar', said he. [[1] Cupar, a town in Fife.]

Cupboard (*or* Cream-pot) love.

c. **1665** *Roxb. Ball.* vi. 529 And all for the love of the cubbard. **1678** RAY 69 Cream-pot love. Such as young fellows pretend to dairymaids, to get cream and other good things of them. **1757** *Poor Robin* (N.) A cupboard love is seldom true. **1874** DASENT *Tales from Fjeld* 184 To have such a cupboard lover.

Cupboard, *see also* Belly cries c.

Cur will bite before he bark, A.

1623 CAMDEN 265.

Cur(s), *see also* Brabbling c. sore ears; Curst c. must be tied short; Yelping c. will raise mastiffs.

Curate licks the knife, When the | it must be bad for the clerk.

1855 BOHN 560. *Span.*

Curate's egg, good in parts, Like the.

1895 *Punch* cix. 222 'I'm afraid you've got a bad egg, Mr. Jones.' 'Oh no, my Lord, I assure you! Parts of it are excellent!' **1926** *Times* 24 Dec. 11/6 London is architecturally like the curate's egg, 'good in parts'.

Cured her from laying in the hedge,[1] I have | quoth the good man, when he had wed his daughter.

1678 RAY 56. [[1] As hens are inclined to do if allowed free range.]

Cured, What can't be | must be endured.

1377 LANGLAND *P. Pl.* B. x. 439 For *qant oportet vyent enplace . il ny ad que* PATI. [For when MUST comes forward, there is nothing for it but to SUFFER.] 14. . *Grammat. Rules in Reliq. Antiq.* (1843) II. 14 And when *oportet* cums in plas, Thou knawys *miserere*[1] has no gras. c. **1407** LYDGATE *Reson & Sensuality* l. 4757 For the thyng that may nat be eschewed But of force mot be sywed. **1579** SPENSER *Shep. Cal.* Sept. Wks. (Globe) 474 And cleanly cover that cannot be cured: Such ill, as is forced, mought nedes be endured. **1763** CHURCHILL *Proph. of Famine* 363 Patience is sorrow's salve: what can't be cured, So Donald right areads, must be endured. **1870** KINGSLEY *Madam How* i That stupid resignation which some folks preach . . . is merely saying—'What can't be cured Must be endured'. [[1] have mercy.]

Cure(s) (*noun*), *see* Bewails himself that hath c. in hands; Desperate cuts desperate c.; Past c. past care; Pays the physician does the c. (Who).

Cure(s, d) (*verb*), *see also* Ground sweat c. all disorders; Sick of a fever lurden must be c. by hazel gelding.

Curiosity is ill manners in another's house.

1622 C. OUDIN *Grammar in Spanish and English* 271 Curiosity is ill beseeming in an other's house. **1732** FULLER no. 1220.

Curse, Not worth a.

c. **1390** GOWER *Conf. Amantis* iii. 1652. **1820** BYRON *Letters, &c.* v. 57 (Prothero) The Neapolitans are not worth a curse and will be beaten.

Curse of Cromwell, The.

1818 SCOTT *Ht. Midl.* viii The curse of Cromwell, go wi' ye, if ye gie them either fee or bounteth. **1827** *Id. Two Drovers* ii Then the curse of Cromwell on your proud Scots stomach. **1845** CARLYLE *Cromw. Lett. & Sp.* vi. Lr. lxxxv Such is what the Irish common people still call the 'Curse of Cromwell'; this is the summary of his work in that country

Cursed in his mother's belly that was killed by a cannon, He was.

1614 CAMDEN (*Artil.*) (1870) 225 Now he is thought the most unfortunate, and cursed in his mother's womb, who dyeth by great shot. **1662** FULLER (*Sussex*) iii. 241 Yet do I not believe what soldiers commonly say, 'that he was cursed in his mother's belly, who is killed with a cannon'. **1670** RAY 110 Who was kill'd by a cannon bullet, was curst in his mothers belly.

Curses, like chickens, come home to roost.

c. **1275** *Prov. of Alfred* (Skeat) A 84 Eueryches monnes dom [judgement] to his owere dure churreth. c. **1386** CHAUCER *Parson's T.* 620 And ofte tyme swich cursynge wrongfully retorneth agayn to hym that curseth, as a bryd that retorneth agayn to hys owene nest. **1592** *Arden of Fevers.* IV. iv. 40 For curses are like arrowes shot upright, which falling down light on the shuter's head. **1810** SOUTHEY *Kehama* Motto Curses are like young chickens; they always come home to roost. **1880** SMILES *Duty* 89 Their injustice will return upon them. ' Curses, like chickens, come home to roost.'

Curst cow has short horns, A.

[**L.** *Dat Deus immiti cornua curta bovi.*] *c.* **1475** *Eight Goodly Questions* in BELL'S *Chaucer* viii. 189 God sendeth a shrewd cow a short horne. **1546** HEYWOOD I. x. 22 How be it lo god sendth the shrewd coow short hornes. **1588** GREENE *Pandosto* Wks. (1881–3) IV. 247 A curst cow hath oftentimes short hornes, and a willing minde but a weake arm. **1598–9** SHAKS. *Much Ado* II. i. 25 It is said ' God sends a curst cow short horns '; but to a cow too curst he sends none. **1641** FERGUSSON 10 An ill willy kow should have short hornes. **1670** RAY 74 . . . Providence so disposes that they who have the will, want power or means to hurt.

Curst cur (dog) must be tied short, A.

1612 WEBSTER *White Devil* I. ii Women are like curst dogges, civilitie keepes them tyed all day time, but they are let lose at midnight. **1623** CAMDEN 265 A curst dog must be tied short.

Curtain lectures.

1632 *The Pinder of Wakefield* B 1ᵛ Then [after marriage] is the time for curtaine sermons. **1633** T. ADAMS *Exp. 2 Pet.* ii. 5 Often have you heard how much a superstitious wife, by her curtain lectures, hath wrought upon her Christian husband. **1710** ADDISON *Tatler* no. 243 He was then lying under the Discipline of a Curtain-Lecture.

Cushion, *see* Beside the c. (Set); Bore him through nose with a c.; Cry you mercy . . . killed your c.; Kill a man with c.; Miss the c.

Custom (Habit) is a second nature.

[CICERO *De Finibus* 5. 25. 74 *Consuetudine quasi alteram quandam naturam effici.* Custom produces a kind of second nature.] *c.* **1390** GOWER *Conf. Amantis* VI. 664 Usage is the seconde kinde. **1422** J. YONGE *Gov. of Prynces* (E.E.T.S.) 238 For as Ypocras sayth, 'costome is the seconde nature or kynde'. **1629** T. ADAMS *Serm.* (1861–2) I. 263 That custom, being a second nature, the heart hath lost the name of heart. **1712** ADDISON *Spect.* no. 447 Wks. (1902) III. 453 Custom is a second nature. It is indeed able to form the man anew. **1817** SCOTT *Rob Roy* I. x Habit has become a second nature.

Custom without reason is but ancient error.

1567 BALDWIN Y 4. **1597** *Politeuphuia* 58 Custome, though neuer so auncient, without

truth is but an old error. **1732** FULLER no. 1226.

Customs, With | we live well, but laws undo us.

1640 HERBERT 361.

Custom(s), *see also* Bad c. is like a good cake; Command of c. is great; Countries (so many), so many c.; Once a use, ever a c.

Cut a feather, To.

[= to make fine distinctions.] *a.* **1633** AUSTIN *Medit.* (1635) 169 Nor seeke . . . with nice distinctions, to cut a Feather [with the Schoolemen]. **1684** T. GODDARD *Plato's Demon* 317 Men who . . . have not the skill to cut a feather.

Cut and come again.

a. **1700** *New Dict. Cant. Crew* s.v. *Cut and come again,* of Meat that cries come Eat me. **1738** SWIFT (Dial. ii) 344 I vow, 'tis a noble sirloin. Ay; here's cut and come again, Miss. **1823** BYRON *D. Juan* 8. 35 But Johnson was a clever fellow who knew when 'to cut and come again'. **1824** MAGINN *Misc.* 2. 206 A small additional slice of the same genuine honest cut and come again dish. **1853** SURTEES *Sponge's Sport. T.* v Its being all in the funds . . . keeps him constantly in cash, and enables him to ' cut and come again '.

Cut blocks with a razor, To.

[= to waste ingenuity, &c.] **1774** GOLDSMITH *Retal.* 42 'Twas his fate unemployed or in place, sir, To eat mutton cold and cut blocks with a razor.

Cut down an oak and set up a strawberry, To.

1662 FULLER (*Devon*) I. 396 I would not wish this county the increase of these berries, according to the proverb; ' Cut down an oak, and set up a strawberry '.

Cut down the woods, If you | you'll catch the wolf.

1732 FULLER no. 2747.

Cut Falkland wood with a penknife, Long ere you.

1641 FERGUSSON 74. **1662** FULLER (*Northumb.*) II. 544 . . . It is spoken of such who embrace unproportionable and improbable means to effect the means propounded to themselves . . . Falkland . . . in Fife, having a bonny wood . . . about it. **1721** KELLY 241 . . . Spoken when people set about a work without proper tools.

Cut for the simples, To be.

[A play upon the words, *simples* being medicinal herbs.] **1650** in SIMPSON *Documents of St. Paul's* (Camd. Soc.) 148 The Witts of Pauls, Or a Catalogue of those Book-sellers Apprentices, . . . which are to be cut of the simples this next spring. *a.* **1700** *New Dict. Cant. Crew* s.v. *He must be cut of the Simples,* Care must be taken to cure him of Folly.

1738 SWIFT (Dial. i) 334 *Miss.* Indeed, Mr. Neverout, you should be cut for the simples. **1828** CARR *Craven Gloss.* s.v. 'Wants cutting for t' simples', is a ludicrous expression applied to one who has been guilty of some foolish act. **1846** *Jerrold's Shil. Mag.* III. 431 'Get cut for the simples before thou takes promissory notes without dates again'.

Cut large shives of another's loaf, To.

1590 *The Cobbler of Canterbury* (1608) 13 The Prior perceived that the scull had cut a shiue on his loafe. **1670** RAY 162 To cut large thongs of another man's leather. . . . It may pass for a sentence thus, Men cut large shives of others loaves.

Cut large thongs of other men's leather, Men.

[L. *Ex alieno tergore lata secantur lora.*] *c.* **1300** *Provs. of Hending* st. 28 Of un-boht hude men kerueth brod thong. **1456** MARG. PASTON in *P. Lett.* II. 226 Men cut large thongs here of other mens lether. **1550** HEYWOOD II. v. 54 Whyle they cut large thongis of other mens lether. **1605** CHAPMAN *All Fools* IV. i. 147 What huge large thongs he cuts Out of his friend Fortunio's stretching leather. **1641** FERGUSSON 84 Of other mens lether, men takes large whanges. **1655–62** GURNALL *Chrn. in Armour* (1865) I. 251 They then live . . . putting off . . . till the winter of old age. . . . Who gave thee leave to cut out such large thongs of that time which is not thine but God's? **1670** RAY 162. **1853** TRENCH v. 105 The comparative wastefulness wherewith that which is another's is too often used: *Men cut broad thongs from other men's leather.*

Cut not the bough that thou standest upon.

1528 TYNDALE *Obed. of Chrn. M.* (Rel. Tract Soc.) 266 We say, . . . 'Cut not the bough that thou standest upon': whose literal sense is, 'Oppress not the commons'; and is borrowed of hewers.

Cut oats green, If you | you get both king and queen.

1889 E. PEACOCK *Lincolnshire Glos.* (E.D.S.) 379 'If you cut *oats* green You get both king and queen'. That is, if *oats* be not cut before they seem fully ripe, the largest grains which are at the top of the heads will probably fall out and be lost.

Cut off a dog's tail and he will be a dog still.

1573 SANDFORD (1576) 221. **1578** FLORIO *First Fruites* 33.

Cut off one's nose to spite one's face, To.

a. **1200** PETER OF BLOIS *Male ulciscitur dedecus sibi illatum, qui amputat nasum suum.* **1796** GROSE *Dict. Vulg. T.* (ed. 3) s.v. He cut off his nose to be revenged of his face. Said of one who, to be revenged of his neighbour, has

materially injured himself. **1853** SURTEES *Sponge's Sport. T.* xxvii At first I thought of going home, taking the hounds away too. . . . Then I thought that would be only like cutting off my nose to spite my face. **1926** *Times* 25 June 14/4 It was no use cutting off the nose of a Trade Agreement worth £34,000,000 . . . in order to spite the face of a *régime* we did not approve of.

Cut off with a shilling, To.

[= to disinherit by bequeathing a shilling.] **1700** FARQUHAR *Constant Couple* IV. iii. 43 When I die, I'll leave him the Fee-Simple of a Rope and a Shilling. **1762** COLMAN *Mus. Lady* II. 27 I'll disinherit him—I won't leave him a groat—I'll cut him off with a shilling.

Cut one's own throat (with one's own knife), To.

[= to be the means of one's own defeat or destruction.] **1583** GOLDING *Calvin on Deut.* lxxx. 490 They cut their own throtes with their own knife. **1867–77** FROUDE *Short Stud.* (1890) I. 172 They . . . believed that Elizabeth was cutting her own throat, and that the best that they could do was to recover their own queen's favour.

Cut one's thong according to one's leather, To.

1605 CHAPMAN, JONSON & MARSTON *Eastw. Hoe* v. v. 120 Seeke not to goe beyonde your Tether, But cut your Thongs unto your Lether. **1637** R. WHITFORD *Werke for Housholders* F 5 (A) Than (after the commune prouerbe) cute your thong after or accordynge vnto your ledder.

Cut the coat according to the cloth, To.

[= to keep within one's means.] **1546** HEYWOOD I. viii. 16 I shall cut my cote after my cloth. **1580** LYLY *Euph. & his Eng.* (Arb.) 430 Be neither prodigall to spende all, nor couetous to keepe all, cut thy coat according to thy cloth. **1902** *Spectator* 19 Apr. A Prime Minister who will make the financial condition of the nation his prime care . . . will insist on . . . 'cutting his coat according to his cloth'.

Cut the comb of, To.

1548 HALL *Chron. an.* 1 Hen. IV fol. 12 My combe was clerely cut. **1644** JESSOP *Angel of Eph.* 58 The one cuts the combe of Episcopall Dominion. **1670** RAY 169 To cut ones comb. As is usually done to cocks when gelded. **1896** CONAN DOYLE *Rodney S.* x 'That's Dick 'Umphries, the same that was cock of the middleweights until Mendoza cut his comb for 'im'.

Cut the grass (*or* ground) (from) under a person's feet, To.

[= to foil, thwart, trip him up.] **1567** FENTON *Bandello* (T.T.) ii. 10 (A) I find a greater falt in myself in suffring an other to cut the earthe frome under my feete. **1576** PETTIE *Petite Pall.* (Gollancz) I. 121 The other wooer . . . thought the grass had been cut from under his feet. **1659** HOWELL *French Prov.* 9 *Couper l'herbe soubs les pies.* To cut the grass under ones feet. **1672** MARVELL *Reh. Transp.* I. 278 You are all this while cutting the grass under his feet.

Cut (*or* split) the hair, To.

[= to make fine or cavilling distinctions.] **1594–5** SHAKS. *L.L.L.* V. ii. 259 The tongues of mocking wenches are as keen As is the razor's edge invisible, Cutting a smaller hair than may be seen, Above the sense of sense. **1652** SANCROFT *Mod-Policies* in D'OYLY *Life* (1821) II. 241 Machiavel cut the hair when he advised, not absolutely to disavow conscience, but to manage it with such a prudent neglect, as is scarce discernible from a tenderness. **1692** L'ESTRANGE *Josephus, Philo's Emb. to Caius* X (1702) 901 To cut a Hair betwixt Satyr and Flattery. **1732** FULLER no. 6457 It's hard to split the Hair, That nothing is wanted, and nothing to spare.

Cut (*or* slip) the painter, To.

[= to sever a connexion.] *a.* **1700** *New Dict. Cant. Crew* s.v. *I'll cut your Painter for ye*, I'll prevent ye doing me any Mischief. **1867** SMYTH *Sailor's Word-bk.* s.v. 'Cut your painter', make off. **1888** T. W. REID *Life W. E. Forster* II. 99 The sooner we 'cut the painter' and let the Greater Britain drift from us the better it would be for Englishmen.

Cut to unkindness, No.

c. **1599** SHAKS. *Jul. Caes.* III. ii. 188 This was the most unkindest cut of all. **1621** BURTON *Anat. Mel.* I. ii. IV. vii (1651) 169 *No cut, to unkindness,* as the saying is: a frown and hard speech, . . . especially to courtiers, or such as attend upon great persons, is present death. **1659** HOWELL *Eng. Prov.* 13/1 No cutt to unkindness.

Cut(s), *see also* Better c. the shoe; Come c. and long tail; Hold or c. codpiece point; Laugh in one's face and c. his throat; Measure thrice . . . c. but once.

Cut-purse is a sure trade, A | for he hath ready money when his work is done.

1670 RAY 6.

Cutter's[1] law.

1816 SCOTT *Old Mort.* viii This is cutter's law; we must not see a pretty fellow want, if we have cash ourselves. **1826** *Id. Woodst.* xxvii I see, sir, you understand cutter's law—when one tall fellow has coin, another must not be thirsty. [[1] cutter = cut-throat, desperado.]

Cutty, *see* Sup with a c. than want a spoon (Better to).

D

Dabo tibi, *see* Better is one *Accipe*.

Daft that has to do, and spares for every speech, He is but.

a. **1585** A. MONTGOMERIE *Cherrie & Slae* xxvii (1821) 16 He is bot daft that hes ado, And spairis for euery speiche. **1721** KELLY 167.

Dagger hand, *see* Hold up your d. h.

Daggers drawn (drawing), To be at.

[= on the point of fighting; in a state of open hostility.] **1540** PALSGRAVE *Acolastus* F 1 We neuer mete togyther, but we be at daggers drawynge. **1553** GRIMALDE *Cicero's Offices* 12 a They . . . among themselues are wont to bee at daggers drawing. **1668** L'ESTRANGE *Vis. Quev.* (1708) 214 Upon this point were they at Daggers-drawn with the Emperor. **1801** EDGEWORTH *Belinda* xvi Lady Delacour and she are at daggers-drawing. **1870** R. B. BROUGH *Marston Lynch* xxiv. 257 Was Marston still at daggers drawn with his rich uncle?

Dagger(s), *see also* All is gone (When), what avails d.?; Look d.; Playing with short d. (Ill); Wooden d. in painted sheath.

Daimport, *see* Talk as Dutch as D.'s (Darnford's) dog.

Dainties love, Who | shall beggars prove.

1573 TUSSER 33 (1878) 72 Who dainties loue, a begger shall proue.

Dainties of the great are the tears of the poor, The. (*Cf.* Pleasures of the mighty, &c.)

1640 HERBERT 360.

Dainties, *see also* At ease (He that is) seeks d.; Dear bought . . . are d. for ladies; Dinners cannot be long where d. want.

Daisy (-ies), *see* Dock to a d. (As like as); Leap at a d.; Tread on nine d., spring.

Dally not with women or money.

1640 HERBERT 324.

Dam leaps over, Where the | the kid follows.

1732 FULLER no. 5662.

Dam of that was a whisker,[1] The.

1678 RAY 89 *A great Lie.* The dam of that was a whisker. **1681** HICKERINGILL *News fr. Colchester Wks.* (1716) I. 394 With what astonishment the People . . . were struck, when they read . . . this whisking Lye. [[1] something great, excessive.]

Dame, *see* Dorty d. may fa' in the dirt; Holiday d.; Tocherless d. sits long.

Damn with faint praise, To.

1735 POPE *Prol. Sat.* 201 Damn with faint praise, assent with civil leer.

Damocles, *see* Sword of D.

Dan to Beersheba.

[**1611** BIBLE *Judges* xx. 1 The congregation
was gathered together as one man, from Dan
even to Beer-sheba, *i.e.* from north to south.]
1768 STERNE *Sent. Journey* (1888) 65 I pity
the man who can travel from Dan to Beer-
sheba, and cry, 'tis all barren. **1811** SOUTHEY
Let. 8 Sept. to Scott (1912) 183 If you did
not remember that I had been travelling
from Dan to Beersheba.

Dance, They who | are thought mad by those who hear not the music.

1575 H. C. AGRIPPA *Vanity of Arts and Sciences*
tr. Sandford 30ᵛ Daunsing litle differing
from madnes . . . excepte it were tempered
with the sounde of instrumentes. **1927**
Times 16 Feb. 15 col. 4 (A) (Spoken of as an
'old proverb').

Dance attendance, To.

[= to wait obsequiously upon a person.]
1522 SKELTON *Why not to Court* 626 And Syr
ye must daunce attendance, . . . For my
Lords Grace, Hath now no time or space,
To speke with you as yet. **1590–1** SHAKS.
2 Hen. VI. I. iii. 174 Last time I danc'd
attendance on his will Till Paris was besieg'd,
famish'd, and lost. **1592–3** *Rich. III* III. vii.
56 Welcome, my lord: I dance attendance
here; I think the duke will not be spoke
withal. **1612–13** *Hen. VIII* V. ii. 30 Not
thus to suffer A man of his place . . . To
dance attendance on their lordships' pleasures.
1883 GILMOUR *Mongols* xxxi. 362 After
dancing attendance on the court for a month
or two they receive their dismission.

Dance barefoot, To.

[Said of an elder sister when a younger one
was married before her.] **1593–4** SHAKS. *Tam.
Shrew.* II. i. 33 She must have a husband; I
must dance barefoot on her wedding day,
And for your love to her lead apes in hell.
1742 MRS. DELANY *Life & Corr.* (1861) II.
188 The eldest daughter was much disappointed that she should dance barefoot,
and desired her father to find out a match for
her.

Dance Barnaby, To.

[= to dance to a quick movement, move
expeditiously.] **1664** COTTON *Scarron.* 15
Bounce cries the Port-hole, out they fly And
make the world dance Barnaby. **1664**
ETHEREDGE *Com. Revenge* v. ii Widow, here
is music; send for a parson, and we will dance
Barnaby within this half-hour.

Dance (*or* march) in a net, To.

[= to act without concealment, while
expecting to escape notice.] **1532** MORE
Confut. of Tyndale cxxvii (A) I go so bare
dawnsyng naked in a net. **1583** FULKE *Def.
Tr. Script.* vi (1843) 242 Now you have
gotten a fine net to dance naked in, that no
ignorant blind buzzard can see you. **1592**
KYD *Sp. Trag.* IV. iv. 118 Whose reconciled
sonne Marcht in a net, and thought himself
vnseene. *c.* **1599** CHAPMAN *All Fools* II. i. 252

Think not you dance in nets. **1659** HOWELL
Eng. Prov. 11/1 You dance in a nett, and you
think no body sees you. **1679** DRYDEN
Limberham II. i I have danced in a net before
my father, . . . retired to my chamber un-
discovered. **1822** SCOTT *Nigel* xiv (1825) You
must not think to dance in a net before old
Jack Hildebrod.

Dance nor hold the candle, You will neither.

1721 KELLY 367 . . . That is, you will neither
do, nor let do. **1732** FULLER no. 6013.

Dance, When you go to | take heed whom you take by the hand.

1639 CLARKE 24. **1721** KELLY 320 *The next
time you dance, know whom you take by the
hand.* Spoken to them who have imprudently
engag'd with some who have been too cunning, or too hard for them.

Dance the Tyburn jig, To.

[= to be hanged.] **1697** VANBRUGH *Relapse*
Epil. Did ever one yet dance the Tyburn jig
With a free air, or a well-pawdered wig?

Dance to (*or* after) (a person's) pipe (whistle, &c.), To.

[= to follow his lead, act at his instigation.]
1546 HEYWOOD II. vi. 61 That do daunce
after her pipe, I am ny led. **1604** MIDDLETON
Father Hubb. Tales Wks. (1886) VIII. 65 Till
the old devourer . . . death, had made our
landlord dance after his pipe. **1670** RAY 170
To dance to every man's pipe or whistle.
1823 SCOTT *Peveril* vii I thought I had had the
prettiest girl in the Castle dancing after my
whistle. **1845** S. AUSTIN *Ranke's Hist. Ref.* I.
523 That most of these councillors . . . will
'dance to Rome's piping', if they do but see
her gold.

Dance to every fool's pipe, I will not.

1732 FULLER no. 2644.

Dance upon nothing, To.

[= to be hanged.] **1839** H. AINSWORTH *Jack
Sheppard* xxxi (Farmer), 'You'll dance upon
nothing presently', rejoined Jonathan bru-
tally.

Dance without a fiddle (pipe), I will make him.

a. **1625** J. FLETCHER *The Chances* I. viii *Pet.*
Are ye well arm'd? *Ant.* Never fear us.
Here's that will make 'em dance without a
fiddle. **1678** RAY 71 . . . *i.e.* I'll do him an
injury, and he shall not know how.

Dance, If you | you must pay the fiddler.

1638 J. TAYLOR *Taylor's Feast* 94 Those that
dance must pay the Musicke. **1681** *Roxb.
Ballads* v. 67 (B.S.)

Dances well to whom fortune pipes, He.

c. **1390** CHAUCER *Reeve's Prol.* l. 22 We hoppen

alwey whil the world wol pype. **1573** SAND-
FORD *Houres of Recreation* 206 Hee daunceth
well inough, to whom Fortune pipeth. **1636**
CAMDEN 297. **1796** EDGEWORTH *Par. Asst.*
(1903) 410 No doubt of that . . . He always
dances well to whom fortune pipes.

Dancing days are done, His (or My).

1595 SHAKS. *Rom. & Jul.* I. v. 35 You and I
are past our dancing days. **1603** JONSON
Entertainment at Althorp Wks. VII. 129 All
those dauncing days are done. **1604** R.
DALLINGTON *View of Fraunce* V 1ᵛ My
dancing dayes are done. **1721** KELLY 256.

Dance(s, d, -ing), *see* I will make one . . .
when he d. in clogs; Love d. well that d.
among thorns; Merry that d. (All are not);
Take a spring of his fiddle and d. (Let him).

Danes, *see* Kill the D. (It would).

Danger is next neighbour to security.

1607 *Dobson's Dry Bobs* G 1 No man so much
in daunger as he who dreadeth none. **1647**
Countryman's New Commonwealth 5 Security
hath perill. **1721** KELLY 56. **1732** FULLER no.
1233.

Danger itself the best remedy for danger. (*Cf.* Danger, Without | we cannot, &c.)

c. **1580** SIDNEY *First Arcadia* Wks. (Feuillerat) IV. 122 With Daunger to avoyde Daunger. **1651** HERBERT 366. **1666** TORRIANO 202
One danger is not overcome without another.

Danger once, Better pass a | than be always in fear.

1664 CODRINGTON 231. **1670** RAY 9.

Danger (River) past and God forgotten, The.

1611 COTGRAVE s.v. 'Sainct' The danger past
our vowes are soone forgotten. **1640** HER-
BERT 326 (with 'river'). **1670** RAY 6 (with
'danger'). *a.* **1685** T. JORDAN *Epigram* in
Epigrammatists (1876) 261 The danger past,
both are alike requited; God is forgotten, and
the soldier slighted. **1721** KELLY 88 . . . In
time of danger and affliction men will address
themselves earnestly to God for relief; but
too often when relieved forget to be thankful.
1732 FULLER no. 1234. **1853** TRENCH iii. 71
The river past, and God forgotten. . . . He
whose assistance was invoked . . . in the
moment of peril, is remembered no more, so
soon as by his help the danger has been
surmounted.

Danger, Without | we cannot get beyond danger. (*Cf.* Danger itself, &c.)

1631 MABBE *Celestina* (T.T.) 179 Without
danger no danger is overcome. **1640** HERBERT
363.

Danger(s), *see also* Bringeth himself into
needless d. (He that); Lost (All is not)
that is in d.; Naught is never in d.; Out
5017

of debt . . . ; Out of office . . . ; Post of
honour is post of d.; Sail without d. (He
that would); Wars (He that is not in) is not
out of d.; Wisdom (What is not) is d.

Dangerous fire begins in the bed straw, It is a.

c. **1386** CHAUCER *Merch. T.* E² 1783 O perilous fyr, that in the bedstraw bredeth! **1651**
HERBERT 366.

Darby and Joan.

[= an attached couple, espec. in advanced
years and in humble life.] **1735** *Gent. Mag.*
v. 153 has a copy of verses: 'Old Darby, with
Joan by his side, You've often regarded with
wonder: He's dropsical, she is sore-eyed,
Yet they're never happy asunder.' **1773**
GOLDSMITH *She Stoops to C.* I. i You may be
a Darby, but I'll be no Joan, I promise you.
1857 MRS. MATHEWS *Tea-Table Talk* I. 50
They furnished . . . a high-life illustration of
Derby and Joan. **1932** *Daily Mail* 25 Feb.
7/7 Mr. & Mrs. Joseph Ball, both aged more
than 80, . . . were regarded as the village
'Darby and Joan'.

Dare not for his ears, He.

1520 WHITTINTON *Vulg.* (E.E.T.S.) 91 He
durste not for all yᵉ eyen in his head speke to
me after that. **1678** RAY 240.

Dare not show his head, He.

1616 DRAXE 40 Hee dareth not shew his
head for debt. **1678** RAY 89 . . . *A bankrupt.*

Dare, *see also* May if you list, but do if you
d.; Sair dung bairn that d. not greet.

Dark in Dover, When it's | 'tis dark all the world over.

1736 S. PEGGE *Kenticisms, Prov.* (E.D.S.) 70.

Dark, *see also* Drive black hogs in the d.;
Good to be in d. as without light; Gropes
in the d. (He that); Joan is as good as my
lady in the d.

Darkest hour is that before the dawn, The.

1650 FULLER *Pisgah Sight* II. xi It is always
darkest just before the day dawneth. **1849**
C. BRONTË *Shirley* xx This is a terrible hour,
but it is often that darkest point which
precedes the rise of day. **1900** J. MCCARTHY
Hist. Own Times v. 41 Ayoob Khan now laid
siege to Candahar. . . . As so often happens in
the story of England's struggles in India, the
darkest hour proved to be that just before
the dawn. **1906** ALEX. MACLAREN *Expos.*
Deut.—1 *Sam.* 270 The darkest hour is that
before the dawn; and that silent sanctuary,
with the . . . half-blind priest . . . may stand
for . . . the state of Israel.

Darling(s), *see* Better be an old man's d.;
Mothers' d. milksop heroes.

Darnford, *see* Daimport.

Dart, *see* River of Dart.

K

Dartford, *see* Sutton.

Dartmouth, *see* Kingswear.

Dasnell[1] dawcock[2] sits among the doctors, The.

1634 WITHALS 558 The dosnell dawcock comes dropping in among the doctors. **1639** CLARKE 297 The dasnell Dawcock sits among the Doctors. **1659** HOWELL *Eng. Prov.* 15/2 (as 1634). [[1] stupid, clownish. [2] jack-daw, *i.e.* simpleton.]

Date of the devil, The.

[Is opposed to the date of our Lord.] **1362** LANGLAND *P. Pl.* A. ii. 81 In þe Date of þe deuel þe Deede was a-selet.[1] *a.* **1529** SKELTON *Sp. Parrot* 439 Yet the date of ower Lord And the date of the Devyll dothe shrewdlye accord. [[1] sealed, signed.]

Daubing, *see* Craft in d.

Daughter is stolen, When the | shut Pepper Gate.

1662 FULLER (*Chester*) I. 291 'When the daughter is stolen, shut Peppergate'. Peppergate was a postern of this city.... The mayor ... had his daughter (as she was playing at ball with other maidens in Pepper-street) stolen away by a young man, through the same gate; whereupon, ... he caused it to be shut up.

Daughter of the horse-leech, The.

[**1560** GENEVA BIBLE (1586) *Prov.* xxx. 15 The horse leache hath two daughters *which* crie, Giue giue.] **1662** FULLER (*Staffs.*) III. 133 These two wicked instruments, who, with the two 'daughters of the horseleech', were always crying, Give give. **1823** SCOTT *Peveril* xxxviii Such ... were the morning attendants of the Duke of Buckingham—all genuine descendants of the daughter of the horse-leech, whose cry is 'Give, give'. **1882** BESANT *All Sorts* xxviii The habit of demanding remained, because the reformer is like the daughter of the horse-leech, and still cries for more.

Daughter win, He that would the | must with the mother first begin.

1670 RAY 49. **1904** 'H. S. MERRIMAN' *Tomaso's Fortune* ix Felipe was wooing the daughter through the mother, as men have often done before him.

Daughters and dead fish are no keeping wares.

1721 KELLY 86. **1796** WOLCOT (P. Pindar) *Orson & Ellen* Wks. (1816) IV. 68 For daughters and *dead fish*, we find, Were never *keeping* wares.

Daughter(s), *see also* Dawted d. daidling wives; Michaelmas chickens and parsons' d.; Tent thee ... if I can't rule my d.; Two d. and back door are thieves; Vine of a good soil and d. of good mother (Take).

Davenport, *see* Cheshire (In) there are ... D.

David (Saint), *see* First comes D.

David[1] and Chad:[2] sow peas good or bad.

1659 HOWELL *Eng. Prov.* 21/2 *David* and *Chad* sow good or bad. **1670** RAY 43 David and Chad sow pease good or bad. That is about the beginning of March. **1846** DENHAM 40 Sow peas and beans on David and Chad, Be the weather good or bad. [[1] 1 March. [2] 2 March.]

David's sow, *see* Drunk as D. s.

Davy do all things, You are.

1721 KELLY 392 ... Spoken to them that pretend that nothing can be right done unless they be about it.

Davy Jones's locker.

[= the deep, a watery grave.] **1760–2** SMOLLETT *Sir Launcelot Greaves* vii I have seen Davy Jones in the shape of a blue flame, d'ye see, hopping to and fro on the sprit-sail yardarm. **1785** GROSE *Dict. Vulg. T.* David Jones's locker, the sea. **1803** *Nav. Chron.* x. 510 The ... seamen would have met a watery grave; or, to use a seaman's phrase, gone to Davy Jones's locker. **1837** CHAMIER *Saucy Areth.* xiv The boat was capsized, ... and ... all hands are snug enough in Davy Jones's locker.

Dawcock, *see* Dasnell d.

Dawkin, *see* Strike, D.

Dawted daughters make daidling wives.

1862 HISLOP 77 ... Daughters ... much indulged or petted at home before marriage make but indifferent wives.

Day after the fair, A.

[Gk. Κατόπιν ἑορτῆς ἥκεις. L. *Post festum venisti.* You have come after the feast.] **1548** HALL *Chron.* 2186 A daie after the faire, as the common proverb saieth. **1616** N. BRETON *Cross. Prov.* Wks. (1879) II. App. iii He is a fond chapman that comes after the fair. **1676** ETHEREDGE *Man of Mode* III. i You came a day after the fair. **1900** LANG *Hist. Scot.* I. 277 The king was willing to accept the truce, though it came 'a day after the fair'.

Day has eyes, the night has ears, The.

1641 FERGUSSON 96 The day hes eyne, the night hes ears. **1721** KELLY 336.

Day, Oft times one | is better than sometime a whole year.

1481 CAXTON *Reynard* xxvii (Arb.) 66 Oftymes one day is better than somtyme an hole yere.

Day is short, and the work is much, The.

c. **1400** *Beryn* (Chauc. Soc.) l. 3631 The day is short, the work is long. **1678** RAY *Adag.* Hebr. 414 ... *Ars longa vita brevis.*

Day lengthens the cold strengthens, As the.

1639 *Berkeley MSS.* (1885) iii. 30 (A) When the daies begin to lengthen the cold begins to strengthen. **1670** RAY 43. **1721** KELLY 52 ... February and March are much more cold and piercing than December or January. **1899** SIR A. WEST *Recollect.* xxi Bearing out the old adage, ... the cold strengthened as the days lengthened.

Day may bring, What a | a day may take away.

1651 HERBERT 369 What one day gives us, another takes away from us. **1732** FULLER no. 5475.

Day never so long, Be the | at length cometh evensong.

c. **1390** GOWER *Conf. Amantis* VI. 578 (A) Bot hou so that the dai be long, The derke nyht comth ate laste. **1509** HAWES *Pastime of Pleas.* xlii (Percy Soc.) 207 For though the day be never so longe, At last the belles ringeth to evensonge. **1546** HEYWOOD II. vii. 67 Yet is he sure be the daie neuer so long, Euermore at laste they ryng to euensong. **1629** T. ADAMS *Serm.* (1861–2) I. 313 Be the day never so long, yet at last comes evening-song. **1916** SAINTSBURY *Eng. Lit.* 165 We owe to him [Hawes] one of the oldest forms ... of the beautiful saying—Be the day weary, or be the day long, At length it draweth to evensong.

Day passeth without some grief, No.

1664 CODRINGTON 206. **1670** RAY 6.

Day so clear but hath dark clouds, No.

1651 HERBERT 369.

Day still while the sun shines, It is.

1639 CLARKE 294. **1670** RAY 77.

Day that you do well there will be seven moons in the lift,[1] and one in the midden,[2] The.

1721 KELLY 327 ... Intimating that such a one will never do well. **1732** FULLER no. 4468 The Day that you do a good Thing, there will be seven new Moons. [[1] sky. [2] dung hill.]

Day without a line, No.

[L. *Nulla dies sine linea.* No day without a line. *Cf. Pliny* 35. 10. 36, § 84.] **1579** LYLY *Euphues* (Arb.) 153 Follow *Apelles* that cunning and wise Painter, which would lette no day passe ouer his head, without a lyne, without some labour. **1825** SCOTT *Journ.* 1 Dec. *Nulla dies sine linea.* But never a being, from my infancy upwards, hated task-work as I hate it. **1905** A. VAMBÉRY *Story of Strug.* I. iv. 148 True to my principle ... 'Nulla dies sine linea', I had not one lost day to record.

Day(s), *see* All in the d's work; Bad d. that

hath good night (Never); Better d. **better** deed; Blustering night fair d.; Broke his hour that kept his d. (Never); Come d. go d.; Drunken d. have their tomorrows; Every d.; Fair d. in winter; Lucy light shortest d.; Merry as d. is long; One d. gives what another takes; One d. was three till liberty was borrow; One of these d. is none of these d.; Praise a fair d. at night; Rise early (Though you), yet d. comes at his time; Say no more till d. be longer; See d. at a little hole; Sees thee by d. will not seek by night; Twelfth D. the d. are lengthened; Twenty-four hours in d. (Only). *See also* Longest day.

Daylight, *see* Burn d.; Fair fall truth and d.; See you in d. (They that) winna break the house.

De mortuis nil nisi bonum, see Speak well of the dead.

De te fabula narratur.

[HORACE *Sat.* 1. 1. 69 *Mutato nomine de te Fabula narratur*: Change but the name and the story applies to yourself.] **1853** G. J. WHYTE-MELVILLE *Digby G.* xxvi The reader has probably had quite enough of Digby Grand and his autobiography; but to some ... he may say, *Mutato nomine, de te fabula narratur.* **1929** *Times* 12 June 17/4 The eye of fancy catches every seaside place in England pointing the finger at some other with a '*De te fabula*', for fear itself should be accused.

Dead (Deaf, Dumb) as a door-nail (door-tree), As.

[A beam used for fastening the door. *Cf.* OE. næȝl.] *c.* **1350** *Will. Palerne* 628 For but ich haue bote[1] of mi bale[2] I am ded as dorenail. **1362** LANGLAND *P. Pl.* A i. 161 Fey[3] withouten fait[4] is febelore þen nouȝt, And ded as a dore-nayl. **1377** *Ibid.* B i. 185 As ded as a dore-tre. *a.* **1400–50** *Alexander* 4747 Dom as a dorenayle & defe was he bathe. **1590–1** SHAKS. *2 Hen. VI* IV. x. 42 If I do not leave you all as dead as a door-nail. **1597–8** *2 Hen. IV* V. iii. 126 *Fal.* What, is the old King dead? *Pist.* As nail in door. **1843** DICKENS *Christ. Car.* i Old Marley was as dead as a door-nail. **1884** *Pall Mall G.* 29 May 5/2 The Congo treaty may now be regarded as being as dead as a door-nail. [[1] relief, remedy. [2] trouble. [3] faith. [4] deed.]

Dead as a herring, As.

1600–1 SHAKS. *Merry W.* II. iii. 12 By gar, de herring is no dead, so as I vill kill him. **1664** BUTLER *Hudibras* II. iii. 1148 Hudibras, to all appearing, Believ'd him to be dead as Herring.

Dead as Queen Anne, As.

1722 LADY PENNYMAN *Miscell.* (1740) 97 He's as dead as Queen Anne the day after she dy'd. **1837–47** BARHAM *Ingol. Leg.* (1898) 40 Mrs. Winnifred Pryce was as dead as Queen Anne!

Dead bee makes no honey, A.

1573 SANDFORD 206. **1611** DAVIES Prov.
227 'A dead bee will make no honey'; But
from dead bees it's had for money.

Dead dogs bark (bite) not.

c. **1565** R. EDWARDS *Damon and Pithias*
D 3ᵛ A dead dogge can not bite. **1596** A.
COPLEY *Fig for Fortune* (Spens. S.) 23 Dead
dogges barke not. *a.* **1622** J. FLEKKER *Custom
of Country* IV. ii. 26 A dog that's dead, The
Spanish proverb says, will never bite.

Dead donkey nor a dead post-boy, You never see a.

1837 DICKENS *Pickwick* li. **1902–4** LEAN IV.
205.

Dead horse, *see* Flog a d. h.; Work for a d. h.

Dead, When I am | make me a caudle[1] (*altern.* no caddell[2]).

1297 R. GLOUC. (1824) 561 As me seiþ, wan
ich am ded, make me a caudel. *c.* **1598** *MS.
Prov.* in FERGUSSON 107 When I am dead
mak no caddell. **1641** FERGUSSON 106 Quhen
I am dead, make me caddell. **1721** KELLY 351
When I am dead make me Cawdle. Be kind to
me when I am alive, for I shall not value, or
be better for your presents, when I am dead.
[1 a warm drink. 2 disturbance.]

Dead man, *see* Sad burden to carry d. m.'s
child; Speak not of a d. m. at table.

Dead men don't bite (do no harm).

[Gk. Νεκρὸς οὐ δάκνει. ERASM. *Ad. Mortui non
mordent.*] **1548** HALL *Chron.* 128 A prouerbe
... saith, a dead man doth no harme. **1611**
BEAUM. & FL. *Kt. Burn. P.* IV. i Yet am I
glad he's quiet, where I hope He will not bite
again. **1655** FULLER *Ch. Hist.* IX. iv (1868)
III. 24 The dead do not bite; and, being
despatched out of the way, are forgotten.
1882 STEVENSON *Treas. Is.* xi 'Dead men
don't bite', says he. **1902** LANG *Hist. Scot.*
II. 327 The story that Gray 'whispered in
Elizabeth's ear, *The dead don't bite*', is found
in Camden.

Dead men tell no tales.

1663 J. WILSON *Andron. Comn.* I. iv 'Twere
best To knock them i' th' head. ... The dead
can tell no tales. **1703** FARQUHAR *Inconstant*
v Ay, ay, dead men tell no tales. **1850**
KINGSLEY *Alton Locke* iv Where are the
stories of those who have not risen— ...
who have ended in desperation? ... Dead
men tell no tales.

Dead men's shoes, He goes long barefoot that wears (waits for).

1550 HEYWOOD I. xi. 37 Who waitth for dead
men shoen shall go long barefoote. *c.* **1598**
MS. Prov. in FERGUSSON 44 He should hav
Iron shoon quho byds his neighbors dead.
1655 RAY 78 He that waits for dead men
shoes, may go long enough barefoot. A
longue corde tire qui d'autruy mort désire.
He hath but a cord suit who longs for another
man's death. **1721** KELLY 148 ... Spoken to

them who expect to be some man's heir, to
get his place, or wife, if he should die. **1853**
TRENCH 1. 16 The vigorous image of this
proverb: *He who waits for dead men's shoes
may go barefoot.*

Dead men's shoes, *see also* Waiting for
d. m. s.

Dead mouse feels no cold, A.

1678 RAY 123.

Dead, or teaching school, He is either.

[Gk. Ἤ τέθνηκεν ἤ διδάσκει γράμματα.] **1655**
FULLER *Hist. Univ. Camb.* (1840) 237 *Nicias*,
... (having many scholars in his army), had
fought unfortunately against the Sicilians,
and when such few as returned home were
interrogated, what became of their companions, this was all they could return,
'They were either dead, or taught school'.

Dead shot at a yellow-hammer, A.

1796 EDGEWORTH *Par. Asst., Eton Mont.*
(1903) 188 I always took you for 'a dead-
shot at a yellow-hammer'. [*Note.* Young
noblemen at Oxford wear yellow tufts at the
tops of their caps. Hence their flatterers are
said to be dead-shots at yellow-hammers.]

Dead woman will have four to carry her forth, A.

1599 SANDYS *Europæ Spec.* (1629) 194 Seeing
as the Proverbe is, a dead woman will haue
foure to carry her forth. **1678** RAY 354.

Dead, *see also* Ewe is drowned (When) she's
d.; Friendless is the d.; Gives his goods
before he be d. (He that); Praise no man
till he is d.; Speak well of the d.; Stark d.

Deadly disease neither physician nor physic can ease, A.

1573 SANDFORD (1576) 205. **1629** *Book of
Meery Riddles*, Prov. 56.

Deaf as a post.

1540 PALSGRAVE *Acolastus* F 3–F 3ᵛ He
wotteth ful lyttel howe deffe an eare I
intende to gyue him, ... he were as good to
tell his tale to a poste. **1551** CROWLEY
Pleas. & Pain Ye deafe dorepostis, Coulde
ye not heare? *a.* **1845** HOOD *Tale of a
Trumpet* She was deaf as a post.

Deaf as an adder, As.

[*Cf. Psalm* lviii. 4.] **1591** GREENE *Wks.* (Gros.)
IX. 273 The noble men plaide like the deafe
Addar that heareth not the sorcerers charme.
Ibid. 310 No adder so deafe, but had his
charme. **1821** SCOTT *Pirate* xxviii.

Deaf as those who won't hear, None so.

1546 HEYWOOD II. ix. 75 Who is so deafe, or
so blynde, as is hée, That wilfully will nother
here nor sée? *c.* **1560** INGELEND *Disobed.
Child* in HAZLITT *O.E.P.* (1874) II. 285 *Maid.*
I perceive by this gear, That none is so deaf

as who will not hear. 1824 BENTHAM *Bk. of Fallacies* Wks. (1843) II. 412 None are so completely deaf as those who will not hear.

Deaf gains the injury, The, *or* Deaf men go away with the blame.

1640 HERBERT 359. 1664 CODRINGTON 222. 1670 RAY 6. 1732 FULLER no. 1243.

Deaf man, *see* Hae will a d. m. hear; Knock at a d. m.'s door; Sings at a d. m.'s door.

Deaf nuts.

[⇒ nuts with no kernel. ERASM. *Ad. Vitiosa nuce non emam.*] 1613 BP. HALL *Serm. 1 Sam.* xii. 24 He is but a deaf nut therefore, that hath outward service without inward fear. 1637 RUTHERFORD *Lett.* (1862) I. 331 I live upon no deaf nuts, as we use to speak. 1721 KELLY 395 *You are not fed on deaf nuts.* Spoken to those who are plump and in good liking. 1808 SCOTT to C. K. Sharpe 30 Dec. in LOCKHART *Life* The appointments . . . are £300 a year—no deaf nuts. 1858 DE QUINCEY *Autob. Sk.* Wks. I. 88 A blank day, yielding absolutely nothing—what children call a deaf nut.

Deaf, *see also* Mad words d. ears (For); Masters should be . . . sometimes d.

Deal, Dover, and Harwich, the devil gave with his daughter in marriage; and, by a codicil to his will, he added Helvoet and the Brill.

1787 GROSE *Kent* 184 . . . A satyrical squib thrown at the inn-keepers of those places, in return for the many impositions practised on travellers.

Deal fool's dole, To.

1670 RAY 171 . . . To deal all to others and leave nothing to himself.

Deal savage, *see* Dover shark.

Deal wi' the deil, They that | get a dear pennyworth.

1862 HISLOP 302.

Dealest with a fox, If thou | think of his tricks.

1732 FULLER no. 2717.

Dealing, *see* Plain d.

Deals in dirt has aye foul fingers, He that.

1737 RAMSAY III. 183.

Deals in the world needs four sieves, He that.

1640 HERBERT 358.

Deal(s), *see also* Sits above that d. acres.

Dean, *see* Devil and the d. begin with ae letter.

Dear bought and far fetched are dainties for ladies.

c. 1350 *Douce MS. 52* no. 7 Ferre ifet and dere i-bowȝt is goode for ladys. Res longe lata bene fit dominabus amata. *c.* 1470 *Harl. MS. 3362* no. 22 Thyng fer ybrowt ys wel ylouyd. *a.* 1530 *R. Hill's Commonpl. Bk.* (E.E.T.S.) 132 A thyng ferre fett is good for ladyes. 1546 HEYWOOD I. xi. 31 But though we get little, dere bought and far fet. Are deinties for Ladies. 1550 LATIMER *Last Serm. bef. Edw. VI* (P.S.) 253 We must have our power from Turkey, of velvet . . . ; far fetched, dear bought. 1596–7 SHAKS. *Merch. V.* III. ii. 314 Since you are dear bought, I will love you dear. 1609 JONSON *Silent Wom.* Prol. When his cates are all in brought, Though there be none far-fet, there will dear-bought, Be fit for ladies. 1641 FERGUSSON 32 Far sought and dear bought, is good for Ladies. 1738 SWIFT (1892) i. 93 But you know, farfetch'd and dear-bought is fit for Ladies. 1876 MRS. BANKS *Manch. Man* xlii 'Where did these beautiful things come from?' . . . 'India, . . . they are "far-fetched and dear-bought", and so must be good for you, my lady.'

Dear collop that is cut out of thine own flesh, It is a.

1546 HEYWOOD I. x. 23 I haue one of mine owne whom I must looke to. Ye aunt (quoth Alex) . . . I haue heard saie, it is a déere colup That is cut out of thowne fleshe. *c.* 1598 *MS. Provs.* in FERGUSSON 69 It is a neir collop is cut of thy owin flesh.

Dear ship stands (stays) long in the haven (harbour), A.

1641 FERGUSSON 4. 1721 KELLY 50 . . . Apply'd often to nice maids.

Dear year(s), *see* Longer lives good fellow than d. y.; Three d. y. will raise a baker's daughter.

Dear, *see also* Know what would be d. (He that could).

Dearth, *see* Drought never bred d.; Wicked thing to make d. one's garner.

Death and marriage make term day.

1641 FERGUSSON 28 Dead and marriage makes tearm-day. 1721 KELLY 84 . . . Marriage frees a man from his service in Scotland; and death in all countries.

Death come to me from Spain, May my.

1625 BACON *Ess. Despatch* (Arb.) 245 The . . . *Spaniards,* haue been to be noted of Small *Dispatch; Mi venga la Muerte de Spagna; Let my Death come from Spaine;* For then it will be sure to be long in comming. 1853 TRENCH iii. 53 The Italians have a proverb . . . of the tardiness of the despatch of all business in Spain, . . . *May my death come to me from Spain* (Mi venga la morte da Spagna), for so it will come late or not at all.

Death defies the doctor.

[L. *Contra vim mortis non est medicamen in hortis*.] **1721** KELLY 89.

Death devours lambs as well as sheep.

1620 SHELTON *Quix.* II. xx (1908) II. 326 There is no trusting in the Raw-bones, I mean Death, that devours lambs as well as sheep. **1732** FULLER no. 1245.

Death in thy house, Thou hast | and dost bewail anothers.

1640 HERBERT 335.

Death is the grand leveller.

1604–5 SHAKS. *Meas. for Meas.* III. i. 40 Death we fear, That makes these odds all even. **1609–10** *Cymb.* IV. ii. 252 Thersites' body is as good as Ajax' When neither are alive. **1732** FULLER no. 1250.

Death keeps no calendar.

1640 HERBERT 359. **1666** TORRIANO 159 Death hath no Calendar. **1670** RAY 6. **1732** FULLER no. 1251.

Death of a bairn is not the skailing[1] of a house, The.

1721 KELLY 329 . . . The death of a child bears no proportion to the death of a husband or wife. [[1] breaking up.]

Death of a young wolf doth never come too soon, The.

1651 HERBERT 370.

Death of wolves is the safety of the sheep, The.

1573 SANDFORD (1576) 215 (with 'beastes' for 'sheep'). **1578** FLORIO *First Fruites* f. 31 The death of the woolfe, is the health of the sheepe. **1651** HERBERT 367. **1913** A. C. BENSON *Along Road* 270 The Ouseleys have a very curious motto, '*Mors lupi agnis vita*', 'The death of the wolf is life to the lambs'.

Death pays all debts.

1597–8 SHAKS. *1 Hen. IV* III. ii. 157 The end of life cancels all bands. **1603** FLORIO tr. *Montaigne* I. vii (1897) I. 38 The common saying is, that *Death acquits us of all our bonds*. **1609–10** SHAKS. *Cymb.* V. iv. 159 Are you ready for death? . . . The comfort is, you shall be called to no more payments. **1611–12** *Temp.* III. ii. 143 He that dies pays all debts. **1827** SCOTT *Two Drovers* Death pays all debts; it will pay that too.

Death upon wires, Like.

1910 P. W. JOYCE *Eng. as We Speak in Ireld.* 138 An extremely thin emaciated person is *like death upon wires*; alluding to a human skeleton held together by wires.

Death's day is doom's day.

1579 LYLY *Euphues* (Arb.) 181 Euery ones deathes daye is his doomes daye. **1609** SHAKS. *Sonn.* 14. 14 Thy end is truth's and beauty's doom and date. **1732** FULLER no. 1255.

Death's door, To be at.

[= a near approach to death.] **1519** W. HORMAN *Vulg.* H 4[v] He is at dethis dore. **1550** COVERDALE *Spir. Perle* xviii To bring unto deaths door, that he may restore unto life again. **1590–1** SHAKS. *3 Hen. VI.* iii. 105 Even in the downfall of his mellow'd years, When nature brought him to the door of death? **1860** TROLLOPE *Framley P.* xliii Poor Mrs. Crawley had been at death's door.

Deaths foreseen come not.

1640 HERBERT 336.

Death(s), *see also* After d. the doctor; Age is jocund (When), it makes sport for d.; Breath (One man's) another's d.; Business of life and day of d. (Between); Dry cough trumpeter of d.; Enter this life (But one way to), but gates of d. without number; Fair d. honours; Fazarts (To) hard hazards are d.; Fear d. as children the dark; Fears d. lives not (He that); First breath is beginning of d.; Good life makes good d.; Grim d.; Lightening before d.; Lived that lives not after d. (He hath not); Medicine against d. (No); Nothing is certain but d.; Nothing so sure as d.; Old man's staff rapper at d.'s door; Old men go to d., d. comes to young; Old men . . . make much of d.; Owe God a d.; Pale as d.; Peace and patience and d. with repentance; Pulls with a long rope that waits another's d.; Remedy for all but d.; Silent as d.; Silent d.; Welcome d., quoth the rat.

Debauchery, *see* Business (Without), d.

Debt(s), *see* Better go to bed supperless than rise in d.; Care will not pay ounce of d.; Confess d. and beg days; Four things (Of) man has more than he knows . . . d.; Hundred pounds of sorrow pays not d.; Lying rides upon d.'s back; Old d. better than old sores; Old thanks pay not new d.; Out of d., out of danger; Point for d. but not for kindness; Sins and our d. often more than we think; Speak not of my d.; Sturt pays no d.

Debtor's pillow, *see* Sleeps too sound (Let him that) borrow d. p.

Debtors are liars.

1640 HERBERT 324.

Debtors, Of ill | men take oats.

1579 GOSSON *Sch. Abuse* (Arb.) 63 If Players get no better Atturnie to plead their case, I will holde mee contented where the Haruest is harde, too take Otes of yl debters in parte of payment. **1641** FERGUSSON 84 Of ill debtours, men takes eattes.

Deceit in a bag-pudding, There is no.

1584 RICHARD WILSON *Three Ladies of London* D 1 Sirra there is no deceite in a bagge pudding, is there? **1678** RAY 193.

Deceit in a brimmer, There is no.

1659 HOWELL *Eng. Prov.* 5/2.

Deceit, *see also* Trust is mother of d.

Deceive a deceiver is no deceit, To.

c. 1566 W. WAGER *The Cruel Debtor* To deceive such one as is known deceiuable Is no deceyte. 1575 H. C. AGRIPPA *Vanity of Arts and Sciences* tr. Sandford 160 It is no deceipte to deceiue him that deceiueth. 1576 U. FULWELL *Ars Adulandi* L 2ᵛ To deceiue a deceiuer is no disceit.

Deceive oneself is very easy, To.

1640 HERBERT 347.

Deceive the fox must rise betimes, He that will.

1640 HERBERT 334. 1646 J. HOWELL *Lett.* 20 Feb. (1903) III. 4 They must rise betimes that can put tricks upon you. 1721 KELLY 130 *He must rise early, that deceives the tod.* Spoken to those that think to outwit a cunning fellow. 1896 J. C. HUTCHESON *Crown & Anchor* ii You'd have to get up precious early in the morning to take me in, as you know from old experience of me.

Deceives me once, He that | shame fall him; if he deceives me twice, shame fall me.

1650 A. WELLDON *Secret History of James I* (Scott 1811) i. 475 The Italians having a proverbe, He that deceives me once, its his fault, but if twice, its my fault. 1659 N. R. 54. 1721 KELLY 134. 1738 SWIFT (Dial. i) 339 *Never.* Well, miss, if you deceive me a second time, 'tis my fault. 1855 BOHN 415.

Deceive(s, d), *see also* Children are to be d. with comfits, men with oaths; Once d. ever suspected (He that); Trusteth not is not d.

December, *see* May and January (D.); Men are April . . . D. when they are wed.

Declaim against pride, It is not a sign of humility to.

1732 FULLER no. 2994. 1749 FRANKLIN Sept. Declaiming against Pride, is not always a Sign of Humility.

Dee mills, Rent of D. m. (If thou hadst).

Deeds are fruits, words are but leaves.

1616 DRAXE 41. 1670 RAY 7.

Deeds are males, and words are females.

1573 SANDFORD 104 The deeds are manly, and the words womanly. 1598 FLORIO *Worlde of Wordes* Ep. Ded. Our Italians saie, Le parole sono femine, & i fatti sono maschij. Wordes they are women, and deeds they are men. 1621 HOWELL *Lett.* 1 Oct. (1903) i. 86 The Neapolitans . . . make strong, masculine promises, but female performances (for deeds are men, but words are women). 1666 TORRIANO 86. 1796 EDGEWORTH *Par. Asst.* (1903) 415 He does more than he says. Facts are masculine, and words are feminine.

Deeds, not words.

c. 1386 CHAUCER *Canterbury Tales* H. 207 The wyse Plato seith, as ye may rede, The word mot nede accorde with the dede. 1591–2 SHAKS. *1 Hen. VI* III. ii. 49 O! let no words, but deeds, revenge this treason! 1601–2 *Troil. & Cres.* III. ii. 56 Words pay no debts, give her deeds. 1612–13 *Hen. VIII* III. ii. 155 'Tis a kind of good deed to say well: And yet words are no deeds. 1616 DRAXE 41 Doing is better then saying. 1663 BUTLER *Hudibras* I. i. 868 Where we must give the world a proof Of deeds, not words. 1812 EDGEWORTH *Absentee* vi 'Sir James . . . added, "Deeds not words" is my motto'. 1895 PAYN *In Market Overt* xx It is deeds and not words that are required of you.

Deed(s), *see also* Fair words and foul d.; Few words and many d.; Ill d. cannot honour.

Deemeth, *see* Soon d. soon repenteth.

Deep drinketh the goose as the gander, As.

1550 HEYWOOD II. vii. 68. 1580 LYLY *Euphues* (Arb.) 275.

Deeper the sweeter, The.

1580 LYLY *Euph. & his Eng.* Wks. (Bond) II. 219 The honny that lieth in the bottome is the sweetest. 1588 GREENE Wks. (Gros.) VI. 165 Thoughts, the farther they wade, the sweeter. 1596 J. HARRINGTON *Met. of Ajax* (Lindsay) 98 The deeper is the sweeter. *a.* 1601 JONSON *Ev. Man in Humour* II. i. 40.

Deeper, *see also* Farther in, the d.

Deepest water is the best fishing, In the.

1616 DRAXE 67. 1631 MABBE *Celestina* (T.T.) 67 It is an ancient and true received Rule; That it is best fishing in troubled waters. 1637 CAMDEN 300. 1659 N. R. 67. 1664 CODRINGTON 201. 1670 RAY 9.

Deer is slain, Where the | some of her blood will lie.

1721 KELLY 346 . . . Spoken when some of what we have been handling is lost, or when there is some indication of what has been a doing. 1732 FULLER no. 5663.

Deer, *see also* Run like a d.; Stricken d. withdraws to die.

Defects of his qualities, Every man has the.

1887 SYMONS *Introd. to Browning* 19 Mr. Browning has the defects of his qualities. 1911 *Times, Wkly.* 6 Oct. 804 But Lord Curzon, like every other mortal, cannot escape from the defects of his qualities.

Defend (Deliver) me from my friends; God | from my enemies I can (will) defend myself.

[OVID *A. A.* 1. 751 *Non est hostis metuendus amanti. Quos credis fidos effuge: tutus eris.*] 1477 RIVERS *Dictes and Sayings* (1877) 127 Ther was one that praied god to kepe him from the daunger of his frendis. 1594 A. COPLEY *Wits, Fits,* &c. (1614) 50 A fained friend God shield me from his danger, For well I'le saue myselfe from foe and stranger. 1604 MARSTON *Malcontent* IV. iv Now God deliver me from my friends . . . for from my enemies Ile saue myself. 1647 J. HOWELL *Lett.* 14 Feb. (1903) II. 257 There is a saying that carrieth with it a great deal of caution, 'From him whom I trust God defend me, for from him whom I trust not, I will defend myself.' 1666 TORRIANO 7 From my friends God defend me, from my Enemies I can defend myself. 1821 SCOTT *Let.* 20 Apr. in LOCKHART *Life* li (1860) 446 The Spanish proverb says, 'God help me from my friends, and I will keep myself from my enemies; and there is much sense in it. 1850 C. BRONTË *Let. to G. H. Lewes* Jan. I can be on my guard against my enemies, but God deliver me from my friends! 1904 SIR H. HAWKINS *Reminisc.* xxiii The person a prisoner has most to fear when he is tried is too often his own counsel . . . called the *friend* of the prisoner; and I should conclude . . . that the adage 'Save me from my friends' originated in this connexion.

Defend, *see also* Spend me and d. me.

Deil, *see* Devil.

Deity (-ies), *see* Constancy of benefit of year argues D.; Feet of the d. shod with wool.

Delay comes a let, After a.

1721 KELLY 52.

Delayeth, *see* Loses his thanks who promiseth and d.

Delays are dangerous.

c. 1300 *Havelock* l. 1352 Dwelling haueth ofte scathe wrouht. *c.* 1374 CHAUCER *Troylus* III. 852 Thus wryten clerkës wyse, That peril is with drecching in y-drawe. *c.* 1457 *Paston Letters* (Gairdner) I. 414 Taryeng drawyth parell. 1579 LYLY *Euphues* (Arb.) 65 Delayes breede daungers, nothing so perillous as procrastination. 1590–1 SHAKS. *3 Hen. VI* III. ii. 33 Defer no time, delays have dangerous ends. 1620 SHELTON *Quix* II. xli (1908) III. 97 'Tis ordinarily said that delay breeds danger. 1678 OTWAY *Friendship in F.* 39 Come, come, delayes are dangerous.

Delays are not denials.

1907 W. H. G. THOMAS *Comment. on Gen.* i–xxv. 183 God's delays to Abraham were not denials.

Delays (noun), *see also* Desires are nourished by d.

Deliberates, *see* Woman that d. is lost.

Delilah, The lap of.

[Samson disclosed the secret of his strength while dallying with Delilah, a Philistine woman. BIBLE *Judges* xvi. 4–20.] 1616 T. GATACRE *Balm from Gilead* (1862) 99 Ease and prosperity slay some fools; wealth and hearts-ease, like Delilah, rock them asleep on her lap. 1872 G. J. WHYTE-MELVILLE *Satanella* xviii But who, since the days of Samson, was ever able to keep a secret from a woman resolved to worm it out? As the strong man in Delilah's lap, so was Bill in the boudoir of Mrs. Lushington.

Delirant reges, plectuntur Achivi.

[HORACE *Epist.* 1. 2. 14 . . . Kings go mad, the Greeks suffer.] 1928 DEAN INGE in *Times,* 3 Sept. 11/1 The old proverb, *Delirant reges, plectuntur Achivi,* requires to be amended in the light of recent events. It should run, *Delirant Achivi, plectuntur reges,* Nations go mad, and make scapegoats of their rulers.

Deliver, *see* Defend (D.) from my friends.

Deluge, *see* After us the d.

Demands, He that | misseth not, unless his demands be foolish.

1640 HERBERT 334.

Demure as if butter would not melt in his (her) mouth, As.

1530 PALSGRAVE *Lang. Franc.* 620/1 He maketh as thoughe butter wolde nat melte in his mouthe. 1626 J. FLETCHER *Fair M. of Inn* IV. i *For.* A spirit shall look as if butter would not melt in his mouth. 1670 RAY 171. 1850 THACKERAY *Pendennis* lx. (1885) 595 She smiles and languishes, you'd think that butter would not melt in her mouth.

Denial, *see* Asketh faintly beggeth d.

Denies, *see* Gives to all (Who), d. all.

Denshire (*or* Devonshire) land, To.

[= to clear or improve land by paring off turf, &c., burning them, and then spreading the ashes.] 1607 NORDEN *Surv. Dial.* 228 They . . . call it . . . in the South-East parts, Devonshiring. 1662 FULLER (*Devon.*) I. 399 To *Devonshire* land . . . may be said 'to stew the land in its own liquor'. 1799 *Trans. Soc. Encourag. Arts* XVII. 160 The land . . . was denshired, and one crop of oats taken from it.

Depends on another dines ill and sups worse, He who.

1707 MAPLETOFT 57. 1813 RAY 164 Who depends upon another man's table often dines late. 1855 BOHN 399.

Derby ale, *see* Dunmow bacon.

Derby's bands.

1570 *Marriage of Wit and Wisdom* D 1. 1572 T. WILSON *Discourse upon Usury* 227 The poore man, the more he dealeth wyth usurie, the more he is wrapped in Darbyes bandes, as they say. 1576 GASCOIGNE *Steele Gl.* (Arb.) 71 To bind such babes in father Derbies bands.

Descend (Fall) than to ascend (rise), It is easier to.

1611 GRUTER. **1614** CAMDEN *Prov.* 308.

Descent to Avernus[1] is easy, The.

[VIRGIL *Aen.* 6. 126 *Facilis descensus Averno.*] **1697** DRYDEN tr. *Æneid* vi. 192–3 The gates of hell are open night and day; smooth the descent, and easy is the way. **1922** DEAN INGE *Outspoken Ess.* 58 If ever a Church alienates from itself not only the best intellect but the best conscience of the nation, ... the descent to Avernus is easy and the return very difficult. [[1] the entrance to the infernal regions.]

Desert and reward be ever far odd (*or* seldom keep company).

1611 DAVIES *Prov.* 33 Desart and reward be euer farre od. **1670** RAY 7 Desert and reward seldom keep company.

Desert, *see* Get money in a d.

Deserve, *see* First d. then desire.

Deservers grow intolerable presumers, Great.

1651 HERBERT 372.

Deserves not the sweet that will not taste the sour, He.

1539 TAVERNER 59 *Dulcia non meruit qui non gustauit amara.* That is to saye, he hath not deserued yᵉ swete, whiche hath not tasted the sowre. **1659** HOWELL *Eng. Prov.* 13.

Desire hath no rest.

1551 W. BALDWIN *Beware the Cat* (1584) C 2ᵛ Ernest desier banisheth sleep. **1621** BURTON *Anat. Mel.* I. ii. III. 11 A true saying it is, desire hath no rest.

Desires are nourished by delays.

1616 DRAXE 42. **1670** RAY 7.

Desires but little has no need of much, He that.

1588 SIDNEY *Arcadia* (Feuillerat) i. 14 Wanting little, because they desire not much. **1732** FULLER no. 2077.

Desires honour, He that | is not worthy of honour.

1598–9 SHAKS. *Hen. V* IV. iii. 28 But if it be a sin to covet honour, I am the most offending soul alive. **1660** W. SECKER *Nonsuch Prof.* II. (1891) 55 The old maxim is worthy to be revived; he that desires honour, is not worthy of honour.

Desire(s) (*noun*), *see also* Begins to die that quits d.

Desire(s, th) (*verb*), *see also* Believe what we d.; First deserve then d.; Poor that hath little (Not), but that d. much.

Despair gives courage to a coward.

1579 NORTH *Plutarch's Julius Caesar* (Temple Classics) vii. 164 A desperate man feareth no danger, come on. **1612** CHAPMAN *Widow's Tears* v. ii. 190 Despair, they say, makes cowards turn courageous. **1732** FULLER no. 1272.

Despair(ed), *see* Nothing is to be ... d. of.

Desperate cuts (diseases) must have desperate cures.

[L. *Extremis malis extrema remedia.*] **1539** TAVERNER f. 4 Stronge disease requyreth a stronge medicine. **1594–5** SHAKS. *Rom. & Jul.* IV. i. 68 I do spy a kind of hope, Which craves as desperate an execution As that is desperate which we would prevent. **1598–9** *Much Ado* IV. i. 254 To strange sores strangely they strain the cure. **1600–1** *Hamlet* IV. iii. 9 Diseases desperate grown By desperate appliance are reliev'd, Or not at all. **1639** CLARKE 200. **1655** FULLER *Ch. Hist.* IX. ii (1868) II. 559 Seeing desperate diseases must have desperate cures, he would thunder his excommunication against her. **1713** DEFOE *Reas. agst. Suc. Ho. of Han.* Wks (1912) VI. 514 A proverbial saying in physic, desperate diseases must have desperate remedies.

Despises his own life is soon master of another's, He who.

[PUBL. SYR. 205 (Ribbeck) *Heu! quam est timendus qui mori tutum putat.* SENECA *Ep.* 4. 8 *Quisquis vitam suam contempsit, tuae dominus est.*] **1621** BURTON *Anat. Mel.* III. iv. II (1651) 694 How many thousands ... have made away themselves, and many others! For he that cares not for his owne, is master of another mans life. **1642** D. ROGERS *Naaman* x. 295 As one said of a traitor whoso despiseth his own life may easily be master of anothers. **1648** HERRICK *Hesp.* (Muses' Lib.) 488 He's lord of thy life who contemns his own. **1666** TORRIANO 312 He is Master of another's life, who slighteth his own. **1708** SWIFT *Remarks upon 'Rights of Church'* Wks. (1856) II. 183 He that hath neither reputation nor bread hath very little to lose, and hath therefore as little to fear. ... 'Who ever values not his own life, is master of another man's'; so there is something like it in reputation.

Despises pride with a greater pride, There is who.

1546 UDALL tr. *Erasm. Apoph.* (1877) 82 To Diogenes, saiyng I trede the pride of Plato vnder my feete: So thou doest in deede (quoth Plato) but it is with an other kinde of pride, as greate as mine. **1853** TRENCH iv. 81 *There is who despises pride with a greater pride,*[1] a proverb founded ... on the story of Diogenes ... treading under his feet a rich carpet of Plato's. [[1] *It.* Tal sprezza la superbia con una maggior superbia.]

Despond, *see* Slough of.

Destiny is always dark, A man's.

1651 HERBERT 373.

Destroy the lion while he is yet but a whelp.

1732 FULLER no. 1276.

Destroy the nests and the birds will fly away.

1655 FULLER *Ch. Hist.* VI. v. (1868) II. 318 Thacker, being possessed of Repingdon [Repton] abbey . . . plucked down . . . a . . . church belonging thereunto, adding he would destroy the nest, for fear the birds should build therein again. **1721** KELLY 88 Ding down the nests, and the rooks will flee away. Destroy the places where villains shelter, and they will disperse. **1837–47** BARHAM *Ingol. Leg.* (1898) 361 I hear the sacrilegious cry, 'Down with the nests, and the rooks will fly!'

Deuce ace, *see* Size cinque.

Devil always leaves a stink behind him, The.

a. **1591** HY. SMITH *Serm.* (1866) II. 36 Into every shop he [*i.e.* the devil] casts a short measure, or a false balance. . . . Thus in every place where he comes . . . he leaves an evil savour behind him. **1650** FULLER *Pisgah-sight Pal.* IV. vii (1869) 552 The rabbins say he was represented as a he-goat. . . . Indeed, both devils and goats are said to go out in a stink.

Devil always tips at the biggest ruck,[1] The.

1886 R. HOLLAND *Chesh. Gloss.* (E.D.S.) 454 (A). **1917** BRIDGE 113. [[1] heap.]

Devil among the tailors, The.

[= a row going on.] **1834** LD. LONDONDERRY *Let.* 27 May in *Court Will. IV & Victoria* (1861) II. iv. 98 Reports are various as to the state of the enemy's camp, but all agree that there is the devil among the tailors.

Devil and all, The.

[= everything right or wrong, especially the wrong.] **1543** BALE *Yet a Course* Baptyzed bells, bedes, organs . . . the devyll and all of soche idolatrouse beggery. **1811** EARL GOWER 18 Dec. in *C. K. Sharpe's Corr.* (1888) I. 508 I begin to fear that the rheumatism has taken possession of your right arm . . . which would be the devil and all, as the vulgar would say.

Devil (and all) to do, The.

[= much ado.] **1708** MOTTEUX *Rabelais* V. iii There was the Devil and all to do. **1712** ARBUTHNOT *John Bull* III. v Then there was the devil and all to do; spoons, plates, and dishes flew about the room like mad.

Devil and his dam, The.

[*The devil's dam*: applied opprobriously to a woman.] **1393** LANGLAND *P. Pl.* C. xxi. 284 Rys vp ragamoffyn and reche me alle þe barres, That belial þy bel-syre beot with þy damme. **1538** BALE *Thre Lawes* 1070 The deuyll or hys dam. *c.* **1590** MARLOWE *Faustus* II. ii *Luci.* Think on the Devil. *Belz.* And

his dam too. **1591–2** SHAKS. *1 Hen. VI* I. v. 5 Devil, or devil's dam, I'll conjure thee: Blood will I draw on thee, thou art a witch. **1592–3** *Com. Err.* IV. iii. 51 *Ant.* It is the devil. *Dro. S.* Nay, she is worse, she is the devil's dam. **1593–4** *Tam. Shrew* III. ii. 159 Why, she's a devil, a devil, the devil's dam. **1593–4** *Titus Andron.* IV. ii. 66 *Aar.* What hath he sent her? *Nur.* A devil. *Aar.* Why, then she's the devil's dam: a joyful issue. **1600–1** *Merry W.* IV. v. 110 The devil take one party and his dam the other. **1604–5** *Othello* IV. i. 153 Let the devil and his dam haunt you. **1707** J. STEVENS tr. *Quevedo's Com. Wks.* (1709) 350 Such . . . Sayings are a Discredit to your self. As for Instance . . . the Devil and his Dam.

Devil, Bring you the | and I'll bring out his dam.

1616 WITHALS 581. **1639** CLARKE 209.

Devil and John à Cumber, The.

1659 HOWELL *Eng. Prov.* 18/1 The Devil and John of Cumberland. **1660** TATHAM *Rump* IV. i (1879) 253 The devil and John à Cumber go with him.

Devil and the dean begin with ae letter; The | when the devil gets (has) the dean, the kirk will be the better.

1641 FERGUSSON 100 The Devil and the Dean begins with a letter, when the Devil hes the Dean, the Kirk will be the better. **1832** HENDERSON 12.

Devil and the deep (*formerly also* Dead) sea, Between the.

1637 MONRO *Exped.* II. 55 (Jam.) I with my partie, did lie on our poste, as betwixt the devill and the deep sea. **1690** W. WALKER *Idiomat. Anglo-Lat.* 394 Between the devil and the dead sea. **1721** KELLY 58 *Between the Dee'l, and the deep sea.* That is, between two difficulties equally dangerous. **1821** SCOTT *Pirate* xviii Between the Udaller . . . and Captain Cleveland, a man is, as it were, atween the deil and the deep sea. **1859** H. KINGSLEY *Geof. Ham.* xxxix Jack found himself between the devil and the deep sea.

Devil be a vicar, If the | thou wilt be his clerk.

1670 RAY 171. **1721** KELLY 196 *If the Dee'l be Vicar, you'll be Clerk.* Spoken of trimmers, turn-coats, and time-servers.

Devil bides his day, The.

1721 KELLY 303 . . . Taken from a supposition that the Devil, when he enters into a covenant with a witch, sets her a date of her life which he stands to. Spoken when people demand a debt or wages before it be due.

Devil can cite Scripture for his purpose, The.

c. **1592** MARLOWE *Jew of Malta* I What,

bring you Scripture to confirm your wrongs. **1596–7** SHAKS. *Merch. V.* I. iii. 99 The devil can cite Scripture for his purpose. An evil soul, producing holy witness, Is like a villain with a smiling cheek. **1612–15** BP. HALL *Contempl.* II. iii (1825) II. 213 Let no man henceforth marvel to hear heretics or hypocrites quote Scriptures, when Satan himself hath not spared to cite them. **1821** SCOTT *Kenilw.* iv A sort of creeping comes over my skin when I hear the devil quote Scripture.

Devil cannot come, Where the | he will send.

1853 TRENCH vi. 150 *Where the devil cannot come, he will send*;[1] . . . sets out to us the *penetrative* character of temptations, and the certainty that they will follow and find men out in their most secret retreats. [[1] *Note* Wo der Teufel nicht hin mag kommen, da send [et] er seinen Boten hin.]

Devil dances in an empty pocket, The.

c. **1412** HOCCLEVE *De Regim. Princ.* (1860) 25 The feende, men seyne, may hoppe in a pouche, Whan that no crosse[1] therein may appeare. *a.* **1529** SKELTON *Bowge of Court* 365 The deuyll myghte daunce therein for any crowche.[2] **1580** LYLY *Euph. & his Eng.* (Arb.) 238 My Barrell of golde . . . ranne so ower the lees, that the Diuell daunced in the bottome, where he found neuer a crosse. **1636** MASSINGER *Bash. Lov.* III. i Goth. The devil sleeps in my pocket; I have no cross To drive him from it. [[1] coins bore a cross on the reverse. [2] cross.]

Devil ding[1] another, Let one.

1721 KELLY 234 . . . Spoken when two bad persons quarrel. **1857** DEAN RAMSAY *Remin.* v. (1911) 195 *Let ae deil ding anither.* Spoken when two bad persons are at variance over some evil work. [[1] beat.]

Devil divides the world between atheism and superstition, The.

1651 HERBERT 368.

Devil drives, He that the | feels no lead at his heels.

1606 DEKKER *News from Hell* D 3. **1732** FULLER no. 2331.

Devil find a man idle, If the | he'll set him to work.

c. **1386** CHAUCER *Mel.* B[2] 2785 Therfore seith seint Ierome: 'doth somme gode dedes, that the devel which is our enemy ne finde you nat unoccupied.' **1715** WATTS *Divine Songs* 20 For Satan finds some mischief still for idle hands to do. **1721** KELLY 221. **1887** LD. AVEBURY *Pleas. of Life* II. x An old saying tells us that the Devil finds work for those who do not make it for themselves.

Devil gets up to the belfry by the vicar's skirts, The.

1659 HOWELL *Span.-Eng.* 20 By the skirts of the Vicar the Devil climes up to the Steeple. **1732** FULLER no. 4476.

Devil go with thee down the lane, The.

1550 HEYWOOD II. vii. 68 I pray god the deuel go with the, downe the lane.

Devil goes (Deil's gane) ower Jock Wabster, The.

1725 A. RAMSAY *Gent. Shep.* I. ii The 'Deil gaes ower Jock Wabster', hame grows hell; When Pate misca's ye waur than tongue can tell. **1818** SCOTT *Rob Roy* xxvi They will turn desperate—five hundred will rise that might hae sitten at hame—the deil will gae ower Jock Wabster. **1857** DEAN RAMSAY *Remin.* v (1911) 196 *The deil's gane ower Jock Wabster* . . . expresses generally misfortune or confusion, but I am not quite sure . . . who is represented by Jock Wabster.

Devil goes shares in gaming, The.

1707 MAPLETOFT 12. **1855** BOHN 501.

Devil hath cast a bone to set strife, The.

1546 HEYWOOD II. ii. 47 The diuell hath cast a bone (said I) to set stryfe betwéene you.

Devil himself must bear the cross, Where none will, the.

1579 LYLY *Euphues* (Arb.) 53 Where none will, the Diuell himselfe must beare the crosse. **1732** FULLER no. 5652 (with 'none else').

Devil in every berry of the grape, There is a.

1634 HOWELL, *Lett.* 17 Oct. (1903) II. 194 The Turk . . . will . . . drink water, . . . for Mahommed taught them that there was a devil in every berry of the grape. **1649** T. WEAVER *Commend. Verses* in WALTON *Angler* Make good the doctrine of the Turks, That in each grape a devil lurks.

Devil is a busy bishop in his own diocese, The.

1548 LATIMER *Serm. of Plough* (P.S.) 70 Who is the most diligentist bishop and prelate in all England . . . ? . . . It is the devil. He is the most diligent preacher of all other; he is never out of his diocess. **1641** FERGUSSON 96. **1857** DEAN RAMSAY *Remin.* v (1911) 196 *The deil's a busy bishop in his ain diocie.* Bad men are sure to be active in promoting their own bad ends.

Devil is a hog, When the | you shall eat bacon.

1678 RAY 70. [*Joculatory.*]

Devil is an ass, The.

1631 JONSON *Devil is an Ass* Prol. THE DEVIL IS AN ASS: that is, to-day, The name of what you are met for, a new play. **1891** A. LANG *Ess. in Little* 186 Their best plan (in Bunyan's misery) is to tell Apollyon that the Devil is

an ass. **1905** ALEX. MACLAREN *Matthew* I. 83
The title . . . would be coarse if it were not so
true, 'The Devil is an Ass'.

Devil is at home, The.

1620 MIDDLETON *World Tost at Tennis* Wks.
(Bullen) VII. 185 Why, will he have it in 's
house, when the proverb says, The devil's at
home? **1738** SWIFT (Dial. i) 333 *Col.* I must
needs go home for half an hour. *Miss.* Why,
colonel, they say the devil's at home. **1810**
CRABBE *Borough* xix (Oxf.) 184 A foolish
proverb says, 'the devil's at home'; But he is
here and tempts in every room.

Devil is blind, When the.

1659 HOWELL *Eng. Prov.* 12/2. **1678** RAY 70
[*Joculatory*]. **1692** L'ESTRANGE *Aesop's Fab.*
xcix (1738) 114 It happened . . . one day to be
just such a flattering tempting sea again as
that which betrayed him before: *Yes, yes,* says
he, *When the Devil's blind.* **1738** SWIFT (Dial.
i) 336 *Never.* I'll make you a fine present one
of these days. *Miss.* Ay; when the devil's
blind, and his eyes are not sore yet.

Devil is busy in a high wind, The.

1790 BURNS *Tam O' Shanter* The wind blew
as 'twad blawn its last; . . . That night, . . .
The Deil had business on his hand. **1825–6**
PEACOCK *A Mood of Mind* 'The devil in a
gale of wind is as busy as a bee'. **1866**
BLACKMORE *Cradock N.* xxxi The parlour
chimney-stack had fallen . . . Miss Rosedew
. . . was reading . . . the 107th Psalm . . . as the
devil is ever so busy in a gale of wind.

Devil is dead, The.

c. **1470** *Mankind* in MANLY *Spec. of Pre-
Shakesp. Drama* i. 37 (A) Qwyst, pesse! The
deull ys dede! *a.* **1529** SKELTON *Col. Cloute* 36
The deuyll, they say, is dede. **1546** HEYWOOD
II. ix. 75 The diuell is dead wife (quoth he)
for ye sée, I looke lyke a lambe in all your
woordis to mée. **1619** FLETCHER *M. Thomas*
III. i. 222 Bear up, man! Diavolo morte!
1670 RAY 80 In the mouths of the French
and Italians. . . . The Devil is dead [signifies]
that a difficulty is almost conquered, a
journey almost finished, or as we say, The
neck of a business broken. **1709** *Brit. Apollo*
II. No. 56. 3/2 At Play 'tis often said, When
Luck returns—*The Devil's dead.* **1861** H.
KINGSLEY *Ravenshoe* xi I will have my say
when I am in this temper. . . . The devil is
not dead yet. . . . Why do you rouse him?
1861 READE *Cloist. & Hearth,* Denys's catchword, 'The devil is dead'.

Devil is dead, and buried in Kirk-caldy, The.

1837 *Tales of the Borders* III. 379 But the
deil's no buried i' Kirkaldy, if I wadna hae
a blink through Cubby Grindstane's sky-
licht. **1842** R. CHAMBERS *Pop. Rhymes Scot.*
72 A JACOBITE RHYME Some say the deil's
dead, and buried in Kirkaldy!

Devil is dead, When the | he never lacks a chief mourner.

1853 TRENCH iv. 77 When the devil is dead,
he never lacks a chief mourner; . . . there is
no abuse so enormous, no evil so flagrant,
but that the interests or passions of some
will be so bound up in its continuance that
they will lament its extinction.

Devil is dead, When the | there's a wife for Humphrey.

1678 RAY 61. [*Joculatory.*] **1732** FULLER no.
5580 (with 'widow' for 'wife').

Devil is God's ape, The.

1595 *Polimanteia* B 1 (A) Satan desiring in
this to bee Gods ape. **1629** T. ADAMS *Serm.*
(1862) I. 206 Observe how the devil is God's
ape, and strives to match and parallel him,
both in his words and wonders. **1639** FULLER
Holy War IV. xxi These took . . . the name
and habit of *Pastorelli,* poor shepherds; in
imitation belike (as the devil is God's ape) of
those in the gospel. **1905** ALEX. MACLAREN
Matthew II. 236 'The devil is God's ape'.
His work is a parody of Christ's.

Devil is good (kind) to his own, The.

1606 DAY *Isle of Gulls* III. ii You were worse
then the devil els; for they say hee helps his
Servants. **1721** KELLY 310 *The Dee'ls ay
good to his own.* . . . Spoken when they whom
we affect not, thrive and prosper in the world;
as if they had their prosperity from the
Devil. **1738** SWIFT (Dial. iii) 350 *Lady A.*
The fondest father in the world. *Lady S.* Ay,
madam, that's true; for they say, the devil is
kind to his own. **1837** F. CHAMIER *Saucy
Areth.* xiv Weazel was the only midshipman
saved besides myself: the devil always takes
care of his own.

Devil is good to some (somebody), The.

1659 HOWELL *Eng. Prov.* 16/2 The Devil is
good to some body. **1678** RAY 70 The Devil
is good to some.

Devil is good when he is pleased, The.

1581 WOODES *Conflict of Conscience* III. iii (A)
The devil is a good fellow, if one can him
please. **1639** CLARKE 214. **1684** BUNYAN
Seasonable Counsel Wks. (Offor) II. 707 The
devil, they say, is good when he is pleased.
But Christ and his saints, when displeased.
1721 KELLY 333 . . . Spoken to people who
readily take every thing amiss. **1732** FULLER
no. 1916 He is good as long as he's pleased,
and so is the devil. **1738** SWIFT (Dial. ii) 343
Smart. She is very good-humoured. *Never.*
Ay, my lord; so is the devil when he's
pleased.

Devil is in the dice, The.

1678 RAY 70.

Devil is never far off, The.

1642 D. ROGERS *Matr. Hon.* 335 The divell is
never farre off: but presents this butter in so
Lordly a dish, that the soule spies not the
hammer and naile in his hand.

Devil is never nearer than when we are talking of him, The.

1670 RAY 80.

Devil is not always at one door, The.

1592 G. DELAMOTHE (1639) 28 The divell is not alwaies at a poore mans doore. **1640** HERBERT 318.

Devil is not so black as he is painted, The.

1596 LODGE *Margarite Amer.* 84 Devils are not so black as they be painted . . . nor women so wayward as they seem. **1642** HOWELL *For. Trav.* xiv (Arb.) 65 *The Devill is not so black as he is painted,* no more are these Noble *Nations* and *Townes* as they are tainted. **1820** SCOTT *Monast.* xxiv Answer . . . whatever the Baron asks you . . . and . . . show no fear of him—the devil is not so black as he is painted. **1833** MARRYAT *Peter S.* xxix Fear kills more people than the yellow fever. . . . The devil's not half so black as he's painted —nor the yellow fever half so yellow, I presume.

Devil is not so ill as (no worse than) he's called, The.

1721 KELLY 306 *The Dee'l is no worse than he's called.* Apply'd to those who speak worse of bad men than they deserve. **1815** SCOTT *Guy Man.* xxxii 'Well', said the deacon . . . , 'the deil's no sae ill as he's ca'd. It's pleasant to see a gentleman pay the regard to the business o' the county that Mr. Glossin does.'

Devil is subtle, yet weaves a coarse web, The.

1853 TRENCH iii. 57 The ways of falsehood and fraud are so perplexed and crooked, that . . . the wit of the cleverest rogue will not preserve him from being entangled therein. . . . *The devil is subtle, yet weaves a coarse web.*

Devil knows many things because he is old, The.

1586 PETTIE *Guazzo's Civ. Conv.* II. 79 Young men for lack of years and experience, cannot be wise: and thereof cometh the Proverbe, That the Divell is full of knowledge, because he is olde. **1871** C. KINGSLEY *At Last* vii It may have taken ages to discover the Brinvilliers, and ages more to make its poison generally known. . . . 'The devil knows many things, because he is old.'

Devil loves no holy water, The.

1576 LAMBARDE *Peramb. Kent* (1826) 301 The olde Proverbe how well the Divell loveth holy water. **1629** T. ADAMS *Serm.* (1862) I. 165 You wrong Rome's holy water, to think it the devil's drink, when the proverb says, the devil loves no holy water. **1678** RAY 287 To love it as the Devill loves holy water. **1738** SWIFT (Dial. ii) 346 I own I love Mr. Neverout as the devil loves holy water.

Devil lurks (sits) behind the cross, The.

1620 SHELTON *Quix.* I. vi (1908) I. 35 Then was another book opened, . . . *The Knight of the Cross.* . . . Quoth the curate, '. . . it is a common saying, "The devil lurks behind the cross"; wherefore let it go to the fire'.

Devil made askers, The.

1738 SWIFT (Dial. ii) 347 *Smart.* Sir John, will you taste my October? . . . *Sir J.* My lord, I beg your pardon; but they say, the devil made askers.

Devil makes his Christmas-pies of lawyers' tongues and clerks' fingers, The.

1591 FLORIO *Sec. Frutes* 179 Of three things the Deuill makes his messe, Of Lawyers tongues, of Scriueners fingers, you the third may gesse. [i.e. women]. **1629** T. ADAMS *Serm.* (1862) II. 482 Corrupt and conscienceless lawyers you will confess to be sharp and wounding brambles. The Italians have a shrewd proverb against them: 'The devil makes his Christmas-pies of lawyers' tongues and clerks' fingers.' **1669–96** J. AUBREY *Brief Lives* (1898) I. 422 Sir Robert Pye, attorney of the court of wards, . . . happened to die on Christmas day: the news being brought to the serjeant, said he 'The devil has a Christmas pie'.

Devil never assails a man except he find him either void of knowledge, or of the fear of God, The.

1651 HERBERT 372.

Devil never sent a wind out of hell, but he would sail with it, The.

1721 KELLY 333 . . . Spoken of trimmers and time-servers.

Devil on Dun's back, The.

a. **1634** HEYWOOD & BROME *Late Lancashire Witches* II. i The Divell on Dun is rid this way. **1639** CLARKE 197.

Devil on sale, To set the.

1546 HEYWOOD II. vii. 63 Here is a tale, For honestie, méete to set the diuell on sale.

Devil over Lincoln, He looks as the.

1546 HEYWOOD II. ix. 75 Than wold ye looke ouer me, with stomake swolne, Like as the diuel lookt ouer Lincolne. **1662** FULLER (*Linc.*) II. 268 'He looks as the devil over Lincoln'. Lincoln Minster is one of the stateliest structures in Christendom. . . . The devil . . . is supposed to have overlooked this church . . . with a torve and tetric[k] countenance, as maligning men's costly devotion. *Ibid.* (*Oxon.*) III. 6 Some fetch the original of this proverb from a stone picture of the devil, which doth (or lately did) over look Lincoln College. . . . Beholders have since applied those ugly looks to envious persons. **1738** SWIFT (Dial. i) 341 She looked at me as the devil looked over Lincoln.

Devil owed me a good turn, The.

1665 J. WILSON *Projectors* v (1874) 267 *Mrs. Gotam.* I was finely helpt up when I married you. . . . But the devil ow'd me a good turn!

Devil prays, When the | he has a booty in his eye.

1707 MAPLETOFT 73. **1732** FULLER no. 5576.

Devil rides on (upon) a fiddle-stick, The.

[= here's a fine commotion.] **1597–8** SHAKS. *1 Hen. IV* II. iv. 542 Heigh, heigh! the devil rides upon a fiddle-stick: what's the matter? *a.* **1625** BEAUM. & FL. *Hum. Lieut.* IV. iv. Wks. (C.U.P.) II. 349 *Leo.* For this is such a gig, for certain, Gentlemen, The Fiend rides on a Fiddle-stick.

Devil run through thee booted and spurred with a scythe at (on) his back, The.

a. **1625** BEAUM. & FL. *Wom. Prize* v. iii. Wks. (C.U.P.) VIII. 85 *Jaq.* A Sedgly[1] curse light on him, which is, Pedro; The Fiend ride through him booted, and spurr'd, with a Sythe at 's back. [[1] near Dudley, Staffs.]

Devil sets his foot (casts his club) on the blackberries on Michaelmas-day, The.

1727 C. THRELKELD *Synop. Stirp. Hibernicarum* RUBUS MAJOR . . . The Fruit of the *Bramble* is reputed infamous, for causing sore Heads; . . . but I look upon this as a vulgar Error, and that after *Michaelmas* the D——casts his Club over them, which is a Fable. **1852** SIR W. R. WILDE *Irish Pop. Super.* 14 It is a popular belief—kept up probably to prevent children eating them when over ripe—that the *pooca*, as he rides over the country, defiles the blackberries at Michaelmas and Holly-eve. **1902–4** LEAN I. 488 The devil sets his foot on the blackberries on Michaelmas-day. In the Midlands children won't touch them after, because then they are 'gubby', . . . i.e. flies have deposited their eggs in the ripe fruit.

Devil sometimes speaks the truth, The.

c. **1592** SHAKS. *Rich. III* I. ii. 73 O wonderful, when devils tell the truth. **1631** WILLIAM FOSTER *Hoplocrisma Spongus* 20 The Divell is a lyer . . . yet sometimes he tels the truth. **1732** FULLER no. 5308 Truth may sometimes come out of the devil's mouth.

Devil take mocking, The.

1599–1600 SHAKS. *A. Y. L.* III. ii. 227 Nay, but the devil take mocking.

Devil take the hindmost, The.

[HORACE *De Arte Poet.* 417 *Occupet extremum scabies.*] **1608** BEAUM. & FL. *Philas.* v. i (C.U.P.) I. 136 *Thras.* What if . . . they run all away, and cry the Devil take the hindmost. **1725** DEFOE *Everybody's Bus.* Wks. (Bohn) II. 513 In a few years the navigation . . . will be entirely obstructed. . . . Every one of these gentlemen-watermen hopes it will last his time, and so they all cry, The devil take the hindmost. *a.* **1797** NELSON in SOUTHEY *Life* (1813) iii 'From that moment, not a soldier stayed at his post—it was the devil take the hindmost. Many thousands ran away who had never seen the enemy.' **1906** G. W. E. RUSSELL *Social Silh.* xlv He starts in life with a definite plan of absolute and calculated selfishness. . . . His motto is *Extremum occupet scabies*—the devil take the hindmost.

Devil tempts all, The | but the idle man tempts the devil.

1707 MAPLETOFT 110. **1840** MRS. CARLYLE *Let.* (Autumn) to Mrs. C. I am always as busy as possible; on that side at least I hold out no encouragement to the devil. **1887** LD. AVEBURY *Pleas. Life* I. vi There is a Turkish proverb that the Devil tempts the busy man, but the idle man tempts the Devil.

Devil to pay, The.

[Supposed to refer to alleged bargains with Satan, and the inevitable payment to be made to him in the end.] *c.* **1400** *Douce MS. 104* in *Reliq. Antiquae* (1841) I. 257 Beit wer be at tome for ay, Than her to serve the devil to pay. **1711** SWIFT *Jrnl. to Stella* 28 Sept. The Earl of Strafford is to go soon to Holland, and let them know what we have been doing; and then there will be the devil and all to pay. **1820** BYRON in MOORE *Life & Lett.* (1833) III. 63 There will be the devil to pay, and there is no saying who will or who will not be set down in his bill.

Devil to pay and no pitch hot, The.

[Alluding to the difficulty of 'paying' or caulking the seam near a ship's keel called the devil.] **1821** SCOTT *Pirate* xxxvi If they hurt but one hair of Cleveland's head, there will be the devil to pay and no pitch hot. **1872** BLACKMORE *Maid of Sker* xlviii Her pet dog Snap is in the sand, 'with the devil to pay, and no pitch hot', if we take long to get him out again.

Devil was sick, The | the devil a monk would be; the devil was well, the devil a monk was he.

[Med. Lat. *Ægrotavit dæmon, monachus tunc esse volebat; Dæmon convaluit, dæmon ut ante fuit.*] **1586** L. EVANS *Withals Dict. Revised* K 8 (A) The diuell was sicke and crasie; Good woulde the monke bee that was lasie. **1629** T. ADAMS *Serm.* (1862) I. 111 God had need to take what devotion he can get at our hands in our misery, for when prosperity returns, we forget our vows. . . . 'The devil was sick, the devil a monk would be; The devil was well, the devil of monk was he.' **1692** L'ESTRANGE *Aesop's Fab.* cxi (1738) 127 . . . This . . . applies . . . to those that promise more in their adversity than they either intend, or are able to make good in their prosperity. **1881** D. C. MURRAY *Joseph's C.* xvii A prisoner's penitence is a thing the quality of which it is very difficult to judge until you see it . . . tried outside. 'The devil was sick.'

Devil will not come into Cornwall, for fear of being put into a pie, The.

1787 GROSE (*Cornw.*) 160 . . . The people of Cornwall make pies of almost every thing eatable, as squab-pie, herby-pie, pilchard-pie, mugetty-pie, &c.

Devil wipes his tail with the poor man's pride, The.

1659 HOWELL Eng. Prov. rendered into French, &c. 10/2. 1678 RAY 191.

Devil would have been a weaver but for the Temples, The.

1678 RAY 91.

Devil's back, *see* Got over the d. b. spent under his belly.

Devil's child (children) the devil's luck, The.

1678 RAY 126. 1721 KELLY 333 *The Dee'ls bairns have Dee'ls luck.* Spoken enviously when ill people prosper. 1798 NELSON in SOUTHEY *Life* v He . . . obtained everything which he wanted at Syracuse. . . . 'It is an old saying', said he in his letter, 'that the devil's children have the devil's luck.' 1841 F. CHAMIER *Tom Bowl.* xxix The luck of the fellow! . . . not a leg or an arm missing. . . . The devil's children have the devil's luck.

Devil's cow calves twice a year, The.

1721 KELLY 310 . . . Spoken when they whom we affect not, thrive and prosper in the world; as if they had their prosperity from the Devil.

Devil's guts, The.

1678 RAY 72 . . . The surveyours chain.

Devil's martyr, *see* Bringeth himself into needless dangers (He that).

Devil's meal is all (half) bran, The.

1611 DAVIES Prov. 222 'The meal of the devil turns all to bran'. 1611 COTGRAVE s.v. 'Diable' Halfe of the devils meale turns unto branne. 1639 CLARKE 326 The Devils meal is half branne. 1670 RAY 80 The Devils meal is half bran. La farine du diable n'e que bran, or s'en va moitié en bran. *Gall.* 1853 TRENCH vi. 151 *The devil's meal is half bran*; or *all bran*, as the Italians more boldly and more truly proclaim it;[1] unrighteous gains are sure to disappoint the getter. [[1] La farina del diavolo se ne va in semola.]

Devil's mouth is a miser's purse, The.

1589 L. WRIGHT *A Summons for Sleepers* A 3 A couetous mans purse is called the diuels mouth.

Devil's teeth, *see* Cast a bone in d. t.

Devil(s), deil, *see also* Away goes the d. when door shut; Beads about the neck and d. in heart; Beads in hand and d. in capuch; Belle giant or d. of Mountsorrel; Better fleech d. than fight him; Better keep the d. at the door; Better the d. you know; Black as the d.; Black (Though I am), I am not d.; Busy (He that is) is tempted by one d.; Buy the d. (If we), must sell d.; Cook-ruffian, able to scald d.; Cross on breast and d. in heart; Date of the d.; Deal wi' the d. get dear pennyworth; Ding the d. into a wife (You may); Do little for God if d. were dead; Eat the d. as the broth (As good); Every man for himself and d. take hindmost; Garby whose soul neither . . . d. would have; Give the d. his due; God gave no sons (To whom), d. gave nephews; God hath church (Where), d. will have chapel; God made white man, d. made mulatto; God sends corn and d. mars sack; God sends meat and d. sends cooks; God will give (That which) d. cannot reave; Good to fetch d. a priest; Great as the d. and Earl of Kent; Happy is that child whose father goeth to d.; Harrow hell and scum the d.; Hold a candle to the d.; Holyrood day d. goes a-nutting; Hug one as d. hugs witch; Idle brain the d.'s shop; Ill battle (procession) where d. carries colours; Innocent as a d. of two years old; Knows one point more than d.; Leave her . . . and let d. flit her; Lie against d. (Sin to); Like will to like, quoth d. to collier; Long spoon that sups with d.; Man is a . . . d. to his neighbour; Man, woman, and d., three degrees; Marriage (He has a great fancy to) that goes to d. for wife; Marrying the d.'s daughter (As bad as); More like the d. than St. Laurence; Needs must when d. drives; Never go to d. dish-clout in hand; Once a d. always a d.; Patter the d.'s paternoster; Play the d. in the bullimong (*or* horologe); Pull the d. by the tail; Rains when sun is shining (If it), d. is beating wife; Raise no more d. than you can lay; Raise the d. than lay him (Easier to); Rake hell and skim d.; Rise betimes that will cozen d.; Runner (Look like a), quoth d. to crab; Saint abroad, d. at home; Seldom lies d. dead by gate; Serve the d. for God's sake; Shipped the d. (He that hath) must make best; Spite of the d. and Dick Senhouse; Strike, Dawkin, d. is in the hemp; Swallowed the d. swallow his horns; Takes the d. into his boat (He that) must carry; Talk of the d.; Tell truth and shame d.; Wite God (You need not) if d. ding you over; Woman is flax . . . the d. comes; World, the flesh, and the d.; Young saint, old d.

Devonshire dumplings.

a. 1812 WOLCOT (P. Pindar) *Add. to my Bk. Wks.* (1816) II. 250 A servant of Sir Francis Drake, . . . a true Devonshire dumplin. 1902–4 LEAN I. 63 A Devonshire dumpling. A short, thick, and plump young woman.

Devonshire, *see also* Denshire.

Devotion, *see* Chamber of sickness chapel of d.; Prayer but little d. (Has much); Sharp stomach makes short d.

Devour, *see* Little cannot be great unless he d. many.

Dew, *see* Cow that's first up gets first of d.

Diamond cut diamond.

[Used of persons well matched in wit or cunning.] **1628** FORD *Lover's Mel.* I. iii We're caught in our own toils. Diamonds cut diamonds. **1738** SWIFT (Dial. iii) 351 They must rise early that would cheat her of her money . . . ; diamonds cut diamonds. **1863** READE *Hard Cash* xxv He felt . . . sure his employer would outwit him if he could, and resolved it should be diamond cut diamond.

Diamond, *see also* Rough d.

Dice, *see* Devil is in the d.; Throw of the d. (Best) is to throw them away.

Dick's (Nick's) hatband, As queer (tight, odd) as.

1796 GROSE *Dict. Vulg. T.* s.v. 'Dick' I am as queer as Dick's hatband; that is, out of spirits, or don't know what ails me. [*Newcastle form c.* 1850. As queer as Dick's (Nick's) hatband, that went nine times round and wouldn't meet.] **1837** SOUTHEY *Doctor* iv. 252 Who was that other Dick who wore so queer a hat-band that it has ever since served as a standing comparison for all queer things? **1902–4** LEAN II. ii. 865 As queer as Dick's hatband, made of a pea-straw, that went nine times round and would not meet at last.

Dickins *or* Dickson, *see* Gets by that, as D. did.

Die a dog's death (like a dog), To.

1529 RASTELL *Pastyme* (1811) 57 He lyved lyke a lyon, and dyed lyke a dogge. **1607–8** SHAKS. *Timon of A.* II. ii. 91 Thou wast whelped a dog, and thou shalt famish a dog's death. **1894** FENN *In Alpine Valley* I. 22 To die this dog's death, out here under these mountains.

Die by inches, To.

1836 MARRYAT *Midsh. Easy* xvi Hanging they thought better than dying by inches from starvation.

Die in harness, To.

[= to die while still at work.] **1834** MARRYAT *Jacob Faith.* xl I am like an old horse . . . in a mill, that . . . cannot walk straight forward; and . . . I will die in harness.

Die is cast, The.

[= the decisive step is taken; it is beyond recall.] [L. *Alea iacta est* The die is cast, founded upon *Iacta alea esto* (SUETONIUS *Caes.* 1. 32) Let the die be cast! said to have been uttered by Caesar, at the Rubicon, 49 B.C.] **1616** DEKKER *Artillery Garden* C 3ᵛ The Die is throwne to the last chance. **1627** G. HAKEWILL *Apol. of Power and Providence of God* 120 Jacta est alea ; the dice are throwne. **1634** SIR T. HERBERT *Trav.* A iii b Is the die cast, must At this one throw all thou hast gaind be lost? **1712** SWIFT *Jrnl. to Stella* 31 May. I never wished so much as now that I had stayed in Ireland; but the die is cast. **1887** S. COLVIN *Keats* 181 He writes . . . 'I

should like to cast the die for Love or Death' . . . It was for death that the die was cast.

Die like a chrisom[1] child, To.

1598–9 SHAKS. *Hen. V* II. iii. 12 A' made a finer end and went away an it had been any christom child. **1680** BUNYAN *Life Badman* 566 Mr. Badman died like a lamb ; or as they call it, like a chrisom-child, quietly and without fear. [[1] a child newly baptized, still wearing the chrisomer, or christening robe. In the bills of mortality children dying within a month of birth were called *chrisoms*.]

Die well that live well, They.

1639 CLARKE 215.

Die, When I | the world dies with me.

1615 BRATHWAIT *Strap. for Devil* 225 Since as the Prouerbe is, *when he is gone, The world's gone with him, as all in One.* **1639** CLARKE 264.

Die, When you | your trumpeter will be buried.

[Said to one who praises himself.] **1729** FRANKLIN *Busy-Body* no. I in Wks. (Bigelow) I. 29 (A) I am cautious of praising myself, lest I should be told my trumpeter's dead. **1732** FULLER no. 5626. **1751** SMOLLETT *Per. Pickle* ii If so be that I were minded to stand my own trumpeter, some . . . would be taken all aback.

Died half a year ago is as dead as Adam, He that.

1732 FULLER no. 2079.

Dies for age, When he | you may quake for fear.

1721 KELLY 357 . . . Intimating that you are not much younger. **1762** GOLDSMITH *Cit. of World*, Lr. 123 Wks. (Globe) 279 'Who is old, sir? when I die of age, I know of some that will quake for fear.'

Dies like a beast who has done no good while he lived, He.

1640 HERBERT (Gros.) no. 986 Hee a beast doth die, that hath done no good to his country. **1707** MAPLETOFT 112. **1855** BOHN 370.

Dies without the company of good men, puts not himself into a good way, He that.

1640 HERBERT 363.

Die(d, s, st), *see also* Begins to d. that quits desires; Expect to go when you d. (Where do you); Gods love d. young (Whom the); Heathen, when they d., went without candle; Horse must d. in some man's hand; Know not who lives or d.; Know where they were born, not where shall d.; Leave more to do when we d. than have done; Like to d. mends not kirkyard; Live longest must d. at last; Liveth wickedly hardly d. honestly; Man can d.

but once; Natural to d. as to be born; No man d. of an ague; No man knows when shall d.; Old man, when thou d., give me doublet; Sick (Who never was) d. first fit; Soon as man is born, begins to d.; Wife that kept her supper . . . and d. ere day; Young men d. many; Young men may d. but old must d.

Diet, *see* Father of disease (Whatsoever was), ill d. was mother; Little with quiet; Physicians are Dr. D. (Best).

Dieu-gard, *see* Beck is as good.

Difference between *Go* and *Gow*, There is a deal of.

1830 FORBY 432 'There is a deal of difference between go and gow'. *i.e.* between ordering a person to do a thing, and going with him to see him do it, or doing it with him. [Gow, *v.* let us go; an abbrev. of 'go we'.]

Difference between Peter and Peter, There is some.

1620 SHELTON *Quix.* IV. 20 (1908) II. 136 Master barber, you should take heed how you speak; for . . . there is some difference between Peter and Peter. **1732** FULLER no. 4937.

Difference between staring and stark blind (mad), There is.

1546 HEYWOOD II. vii. 67 The difference betwene staryng and starke blynde. The wyse man at all tymes to folow can fynde. **1579** LYLY *Euphues* (Arb.) 39 Consider with thy selfe, the great difference betweene staring and starke blynde. **1616** DRAXE 44. **1629** FORD *Lover's Melan.* II. ii *Mel.* Am I stark mad? *Trol.* No, no, you are but a little staring—there's difference between staring and stark mad. You are but whimsied yet. **1670** RAY 79 There's difference between staring and stark blind (or mad.) . . . If you read it stark mad, it signifies that we ought to distinguish, and not presently pronounce him stark mad that stares a little. . . . If you read it stark blind, then it . . . is a reprehension to those who put no difference between extremes, as perfect blindness and *Lynceus* his sight. **1787** WOLCOT (P. Pindar) *Ode upon Ode* Wks. (1816) I. 322 Peter, there's odds 'twixt staring and stark mad.

Difference between Will you buy? and Will you sell? There is a.

1721 KELLY 317 . . . When people proffer their goods, buyers will be shy: and when people ask to buy, sellers will hold their wares the dearer.

Difference is wide that the sheets will not decide, The.

1678 RAY 201. **1732** FULLER no. 6155 (with 'very' before 'wide').

Difference of bloods in a basin, There is no.

1560 T. BECON *Wks.* II. 18 (LEAN IV. 85). **5017**

1580 LYLY *Euph. & his Eng.* (Arb.) 289 You talke of your birth, when I knowe there is no difference of blouds is [in] a basen. **1602–3** SHAKS. *All's Well* II. iii. 125 Strange is it that our bloods, . . . pour'd all together, Would quite confound distinction. **1732** FULLER 213.

Dig one's grave with one's teeth, To.

[Fr. DE LINCY *Prov. Franç.* I. 214 *Les gourmands font leurs fosses avec leurs dents.*] **1629** T. ADAMS *Serm.* (1861–2) I. 137 Voluptuousness and intemperance, as the French proverb hath it, digs its own grave with the teeth. **1655** FULLER *Ch. Hist.* IV. iii (1868) I. 608 King Edward . . . by intemperance in his diet, in some sort, digged his grave with his own teeth. **1854** SURTEES *Hand. Cross* ii More people dig their graves with their teeth than we imagine.

Dig (*or* take) up the hatchet, To.

[= to take up arms, or declare hostilities, from the custom of the N. Amer. Indians.] **1753** G. WASHINGTON *Jrnl.* Writ. (1889) I. 21 Three Nations of French Indians . . . had taken up the Hatchet against the English. **1861** H. KINGSLEY *Ravenshoe* xlv For Lord Saltire's landed property I shall fight. . . . We will dig up the tomahawk, and be off on the war-trail in your ladyship's brougham. **1889** STEVENSON *Mast. Ball.* xi A dreadful solitude surrounded our steps. . . . 'They must have dug up the hatchet', he said.

Digests, *see* Victuals (Of all) drink d. quickest.

Dighton is pulled down, When | Hull shall become a great town.

1670 RAY 257 Yorkshire. . . . Dighton is a small Town not a mile distant from Hull, and was in the time of the late wars for the most part pull'd down.

Dilemma, *see* Horns of a d.

Diligence, *see* Care and d. bring luck.

Diligent scholar, and the master's paid, A.

1640 HERBERT 325.

Dim Sarsnick with him, It is.

1917 BRIDGE 84 It's Dim Sarsnick with him. '*Dym Sassenach*' = '*I don't understand English*': used by the Welsh when they do not understand, or *pretend* not to understand, what is said to them in English. . . . In Cheshire the saying superseded . . . '*None so deaf as those who won't hear.*'

Dine with Duke Humphrey, To.

[= to go dinnerless.] **1591** *Wonderfull . . . Prognostication* (NASHE Wks. ed. McKerrow III. 393) Sundry fellowes in their silkes shall be appointed to keep Duke Humfrye company in Poules, because they know not wher to get their dinner abroad. **1592** G. HARVEY *Four Lett.* (Nares s.v. *Duke Humphrey*) To seek his dinner in Poules with duke Humphrey. **1592–3** SHAKS. *Rich. III* IV. iv. 175

Duch. What comfortable hour canst thou name That ever grac'd me in thy company? *K. Rich.* Faith, none but Humphrey Hour, that call'd your Grace To breakfast once forth of my company. **1599** BP. HALL *Sat.* III. vii. 6 Trow'st thou where he din'd to-day? In sooth I saw him sit with Duke Humphray. **1604** *Penniless Parl. Threadbare Poets* (Farmer) Let me dine twice a week at Duke Humphrey's table. **1662** FULLER (*Lond.*) II. 345 After the death of good Duke Humphrey . . . to dine with Duke Humphrey [imported] **to** be dinnerless. **1748** SMOLLETT *Rod. Rand.* lv (Farmer) My mistress and her mother must have dined with Duke Humphrey, had I not exerted myself. **1790** GROSE This proverb, Fuller says, has altered its meaning. At first it meant dinner at another man's table: for Humphrey . . . commonly called the good Duke, kept an open table, where any gentleman was welcome to dine. After his decease, to dine with Duke Humphrey meant to go dinnerless. . . . Fuller says, that persons who loitered about in St. Paul's church during dinner-time, were said to dine with Duke Humphrey, from a mistaken notion that he was buried there. **1843** DICKENS *M. Chuz.* i He will have no choice but to dine again with Duke Humphrey.

Dine with St. Giles and the Earl of Murray, To.

[The Earl of Murray was interred in St. Giles's Church, Edinburgh.] **1680** FR. SEMPILL *Banishm. Prov.* 87 I din'd with saints and noblemen, Even sweet St. Giles and the Earl of Murray.

Dined as well as my Lord Mayor of London, I have.

1577 WM. HARRISON *Description of England* (Furnivall i. 151) They thinke . . . themselves to have fared so well, as the lord Maior of London. **1580** LYLY *Euph. & his Eng.* Wks. (Bond) II. 194 Having halfe dyned, they say as it were in a prouerbe, that they are as well satisfied as the Lorde Maior of London. **1602** J. MANNINGHAM *Diary* 40 [Fleetwood the Recorder] imprisoned one for saying he had supt as well as the Lord Maior, when he had nothing but bread and cheese. **1662** FULLER (*Lond.*) II. 346 'I have dined as well as my Lord Mayor of London'. That is, as comfortably, as contentedly, according to the rule, 'satis est quod sufficit' (enough is as good as a feast). **1738** SWIFT (Dial. ii) 347 *Never.* I have dined as well as my lord mayor.

Dines and leaves. He that | lays the cloth twice.

1599 MINSHEU (1623) Tt l**v**. **1640** HERBERT 333.

Dine(s), *see also* Depends on another, d. ill.

Ding[1] doun Tantallon, big[2] a brig[3] to the Bass.

1907 HENDERSON & WATT *Scotland of To-day* xi James V attacked [Tantallon Castle] in 1528 . . . but to no purpose, and so to 'Ding

doun Tantallon Big a brig to the Bass', became a Scots proverb for things impossible. [[1] beat. [2] build. [3] bridge.]

Ding[1] the Deil into a wife, You may | but you'll never ding him out of her.

1721 KELLY 360 . . . That is, a wife is seldom mended by being beaten. [[1] beat.]

Ding, *see also* Devil d. another (Let one); Wand d. him (Let his own).

Dinner, At | my man appears.

1640 HERBERT 318.

Dinners cannot be long where dainties want.

1546 HEYWOOD II. i. 42 Diners can not be long, where deinties want. **1614** CAMDEN 305.

Dinner(s), *see also* After d. sit awhile; Eat a good d. (He that would); Half an hour soon lost at d.; Saveth his d. will have more supper.

Dirk, *see* Never draw d. when dunt will do.

Dirt enough, Fling | and some will stick.

[L. *Calumniare fortiter, aliquid adhærebit.*] **1660** T. HALL *Funebria Florae* 38 (A) Lye lustily, some filth will stick. **1678** B. R. *Letter Pop. Friends* 7 'Tis a blessed Line in Matchiavel—If durt enough be thrown, some will stick. **1706** E. WARD *Hud. Rediv.* I. II. 11 Scurrility's a useful trick, Approv'd by the most politic; Fling dirt enough, and some will stick. **1856-70** FROUDE *Hist. Eng.* xii. 438 No dirt sticks more readily than an accusation of this kind when boldly and positively insisted on.

Dirt into the well that hath given you water, Cast no.

1707 MAPLETOFT 116. **1732** FULLER no. 1067.

Dirt, The more | the less hurt.

1832 HENDERSON 13 The mair dirt, the less hurt.

Dirt, *see also* Deals in d. has aye foul fingers (He that); Eat a peck of d. (Every man must); Falls into the d. (He that); Go through d. (How does he); What serves d. for if it do not stink.

Dirt-bird (Dirt-owl) sings, The | we shall have rain.

1678 RAY 80 . . . When melancholy persons are very merry, it is observed that there usually follows an extraordinary fit of sadness; they doing all things commonly in extremes.

Dirty puddings, *see* Hungry dogs [*also* Scornful dogs] will eat d. p.

Disarmed peace is weak, A.

1640 HERBERT 346.

Discontent is his worst evil, A man's.
1640 HERBERT 331.

Discontented man knows not where to sit easy, A.
1640 HERBERT 333.

Discord, *see* Apple of d.

Discourse makes short days and nights, Sweet.
1640 HERBERT 351.

Discreet advise, While the | the fool doth his business.
1640 HERBERT 330.

Discreet women have neither eyes nor ears.
1640 HERBERT 340. 1670 RAY 7. 1732 FULLER no. 1295 Discreet wives have sometimes neither eyes nor ears.

Discretion is the better part of valour.
[EUR. *Suppl.* 510 Καὶ τοῦτό τοι τὰν δρεῖον ἡ προμηθία.] *c.* 1477 CAXTON *Jason* (E.E.T.S.) 23 Than as wyse and discrete he withdrewe him sayng that more is worth a good retrayte than a folisshe abydinge. 1595-6 SHAKS. *Mids. N.* V. i. 236 *Lys.* This lion is a very fox for his valour. *The.* True; and a goose for his discretion [&c.]. 1597-8 *1 Hen. IV* V. iv. 131 The better part of valour is discretion; in the which better part, I have saved my life. 1607-8 *Coriol.* I. i. 208 For though abundantly they lack discretion, Yet are they passing cowardly. 1611 BEAUM & FL. *A King* IV. iii *Bes.* My sword lost, . . . for discreetly I rendered it. . . . *1st. Sw.* It showed discretion the best part of valour. 1885 C. LOWE *Prince Bismarck* iii Napoleon . . . had vowed that he would free Italy 'from the Alps to the Adriatic', but . . . he acted on the maxim that discretion is the better part of valour.

Discretion, *see also* Offices may be given, not d.; Ounce of d. worth pound of wit; Valour can do little without d.; Valour would fight but d. would run away.

Disdainfulness, *see* Abundance of things.

Disease known is half cured, A.
1694 JAMES WRIGHT *Country Contentments* sect. III Faults, like Diseases, when perfectly discover'd are half cured. 1732 FULLER no. 75.

Disease, The chief | that reigns this year is folly.
1640 HERBERT 352.

Diseases are the price of ill pleasures.
1664 CODRINGTON 190 Diseases are the Interests of Pleasures. 1670 RAY 7. 1732 FULLER no. 1297.

Disease(s), *see also* Agues (D.) come on horseback; Deadly d. neither physician can

ease; Desperate cuts (d.) must have desperate cures; Doctor is often more to be feared; Father of a d. (Whatsoever was), ill diet was mother; Many dishes many d.; Sun rises (When) d. will abate.

Disgraces are like cherries, one draws another.
1640 HERBERT 340.

Disguised, He is.
1562 HEYWOOD *Fifth Hundred of Epigr.* no. 34 Three cuppes full at once shall oft dysgyse thee. 1607 DELONEY *Strange Hist.* (1841) 14 The saylors and the shipmen all, through foule excesse of wine, Were so disguisde that at the sea they shewed themselves like swine. 1678 RAY 87.

Dish, To lay (cast, throw) (a thing) in one's.
[= to reproach or taunt him with it.] 1551 T. WILSON *Logike* (1580) 62 b When wee charge hym with a like fault, and laye some greater matter in his dishe. 1596 NASHE *Saffron Walden* 67 Hee casts the begger in my dish at euerie third sillable. 1615 SWETNAM *Arraignm. Women* (1880), p. xviii Hir dowrie will be often cast in thy dish if shee doe bring wealth with her. 1722 SEWEL *Hist. Quakers* (1795) I. 8 Under the bloody reign of Queen Mary, this was laid in his dish.

Dish(es), *see also* Better are small fish than empty d.; Claps his d. at wrong door; Cowped the mickle d. into the little; First d. aye best eaten; First d. pleaseth all; Hog is never good but in d.; Lost that is put into riven d.; Mair in a mair d.; Many d. many diseases; Speaks as if every word would lift d.

Dish-clout my table-cloth, I will not make my.
1678 RAY 125. 1732 FULLER no. 2646.

Dish-clout, *see also* Never go to devil d. in hand; Thing in it (There is a), quoth . . . when he drank d.

Disorderly, *see* God is made master of family (When), he orders d.

Disputants, Of two | the warmer is generally in the wrong.
1826 LAMB *Elia; Pop. Fallacies* Wks. (1898) 223 OF TWO DISPUTANTS THE WARMEST IS GENERALLY IN THE WRONG. . . . Warmth and earnestness are a proof at least of a man's own conviction of the rectitude of that which he maintains. Coolness is as often the result of . . . indifference to truth . . ., as of . . . confidence in a man's own side in a dispute.

Dispute (Contend) about the shadow of an ass, To.
[ERASM. *Ad. De asini umbrâ disceptare.*] 1896 FROUDE *Counc. of Trent* i. 3 They were often contending, as the Greeks said, for an ass's shadow.

Dispute, *see also* Truth is lost (In too much d.).

Disputing, *see* Itch of d. is scab of church.

Dissemble, *see* Knows not how to d. (Who).

Distaff, *see* Foot on cradle, hand on d. . . . good housewife; Philosophy of the d.; St. D.'s day; Spindle and thy d. ready (Get thy); Spun (If it will not be), bring not to d.; Tow on one's d. (To have).

Distress, *see* Two in d. makes sorrow less.

Distrust, *see* Remember to d.

Ditchwater, *see* Dull as d.

Dived deep into the water, Thou hast | and hast brought up a potsherd.

1678 RAY *Adag. Hebr.* 407.

Divide and rule.

[L. *Divide et impera.*] **1633** PH. FLETCHER *Purple Isl.* VII. lxv In which two swords he [sedition] bore: his word, *Divide and reign*. **1907** *Spectator* 20 Apr. 605 The cynical maxim of 'Divide and rule' has never . . . clouded our relations with the daughter-States.

Divine ashes are better than earthly meal.

1640 HERBERT 349. **1666** TORRIANO 44 Heavenly ashes is more worth, than worldly flower [flour].

Divine grace was never slow (*or* late).

1640 HERBERT 350 Divine grace was never slow. **1666** TORRIANO 108 Divine favours were never too late.

Diviner, *see* Make me a d. and I will make thee rich.

Divinity, *see* Good husbandry good d.; No d. is absent if Prudence present.

Do a foolish thing once in one's life, One cannot | but one must hear of it a hundred times.

1738 SWIFT (Dial. ii) 345 *Lady S.* You have stolen a wedding, it seems? *Sir J.* Well; one can't do a foolish thing once in ones life, but one must hear of it a hundred times.

Do as he would, He that may not | must (will) do as he may. (*Cf.* Do as you may, &c.)

[TER. *Andria* 4. 6. 10 *Ut quimus, aiunt, quando ut volumus non licet.* We must do as we can (as they say) when we can't do as we would.] **1546** HEYWOOD II. v. 55 Who that maie not as they wolde, will as they maie. **1593-4** SHAKS. *Titus Andron.* II. i. 103 And so must you resolve That what you cannot

as you would achieve, You must perforce accomplish as you may. **1598-9** *Hen. V* II. i. 17 When I cannot live any longer, I will do as I may. **1639** CLARKE 129 Men must do as they may, not as they would. **1641** FERGUSSON 38 He that may not as he would, mon do as he may. **1721** KELLY 169 He that may not as he will, must do as he may.

Do as I say, not as I do.

1546 HEYWOOD II. v. 60 It is as folke dooe, and not as folke saie. **1689** SELDEN *Tabletalk* (1887) 145 Preachers say, Do as I say, not as I do. **1911** *Spectator* 24 June 957 It has always been considered allowable to say . . . to children, 'Do as I say rather than as I do'.

Do as the friar saith, not as he doth.

1670 RAY 7.

Do as you may if you can't do as you would. (*Cf.* Do as he would, &c.)

1539 TAVERNER (1545) F 8 *Quando id fieri non potest quod vis id velis quod possis.* Whan that thynge can not be done that thou woldest, will that thou cannest. **1616** DRAXE 32. **1639** CLARKE 267.

Do as you're bidden and you'll never bear blame.

c. **1550** *Howleglas* (F. Ouvry 1868) 47-8 They that do as the be bid: they be worthy to haue thanke. **1678** RAY 101.

Do as you would be done by.

1389 WYCLIF *Luke* vi. 31 And as ʒe wolen that men do to ʒou, and do ʒe to hem in lyk manere. *a.* **1500** *Ratis Raving* (E.E.T.S.) 35 1. 337 Bot that þow pres to do, my sone Rycht as þow wald to the war done. *c.* **1590** *Sir T. More* II. iv A says true: let's do as we may be done by. **1641** FERGUSSON 28 Do as ye wald be done to. **1863** KINGSLEY *Water Bab.* v Be a good boy, and do as you would be done by.

Do better, He that cannot | must be a monk.

1827-30 SCOTT *Tales Grandf.* xxi Douglas was then[1] ordained to be put into the abbey of Lindores, to which sentence he submitted calmly, only using a popular proverb, 'He that cannot do better must be a monk'. [[1] 1484.]

Do good: thou doest it for thyself.

1642 TORRIANO 51. **1658** *Comes Facundus* 176 Do good to yourselves (the Italian beggars word). **1732** FULLER no. 1306 Do good if you expect to receive it.

Do good, *see also* Silly man that can neither d. g. nor ill.

Do ill, Who would | ne'er wants occasion.

1640 HERBERT 322.

Do little for God if the devil were dead, You would.

1641 FERGUSSON 112. **1721** KELLY 364 . . .

That is, you would do little for love, if you were not under fear.

Do much ill, He may | ere he can do much worse.

1550 HEYWOOD I. xi. **1594** BACON *Promus* no. 956 (A).

Do no ill, If thou | do no ill like. (*Cf. Evil do, Whoso will no, &c.*)

1641 FERGUSSON 62.

Do not all you can; spend not all you have; believe not all you hear; and tell not all you know.

1707 MAPLETOFT 36. **1855** BOHN 344.

Do on the hill as you would do in the hall.

1509 A. BARCLAY *Ship of Fools* (1874) II. 266. **1570** Id. *Mirrour of Good Manners* 25 Liue thou vpon hill as thou would liue in hall. **1641** FERGUSSON 28. **1721** KELLY 85 . . . Accustom yourself to act with discretion and good manners at all times. **1732** FULLER no. 1307 Do in the Hole as thou would'st in the Hall.

Do right nor suffer wrong, He will neither.

1678 RAY 266.

Do the likeliest, and God will do the best (*or* hope the best).

1641 FERGUSSON 28 Do the likliest, and God will do the best. **1721** KELLY 90 Do the likeliest, and hope the best. **1732** FULLER no. 1310 (as 1721).

Do the next thing.

1907 A. C. BENSON *Upton Lett.* 322 One's immediate duty is happily, as a rule, clear enough. 'Do the next thing', says the old shrewd motto.

Do these things in a green tree, If they | what shall be done in the dry?

995 *Ang.-Sax. Gosp., Luke* xxiii. 31 Forðám gif hig on grénum treowe ðas þing dóþ, hwæt dóþ hig on ðam drígum? **1389** WYCLIF —For if thei don thes thingis in a grene tree, what schal be don in a drye? **1926** *Times* 12 July 15/4 That is the view . . . which the Labour Party would be wise to accept. 'If they do these things in the green tree, what shall be done in the dry?'

Do well and doubt no man, and do well and doubt all men.

1641 FERGUSSON 28. **1721** KELLY 89 *Do well and doubt no man.* But rest satisfied in the testimony of a good conscience.

Do well and have well.

c. **1350** *Douce MS. 52* no. 32 Do welle and haue welle. **1377** LANGLAND *P. Pl.* B. vii. 113 Dowel, and haue wel . and god shal haue thi

sowle. **1546** HEYWOOD II. ix. 74 Doo well, and haue well, men say also. **1721** KELLY 90 . . . Be a good man, and you will be kindly dealt by. **1732** FULLER no. 1311.

Do well, *see also* Day that you d. w. there will be seven moons; Say w. and d. w. . . . d. w. is better.

Do what he likes with his own, May not a man?

[BIBLE *Matt.* xx. 15 Is it not lawful for me to do what I will with mine own?] **1629** T. ADAMS *Serm.* (1861–2) II. 364 'Relieve the poor', saith the Lord: thou . . . wilt give nothing. Why, may we not do with our own what we list? **1867–77** FROUDE *Short Stud.* (1890) II. 545 These evicting gentlemen claimed the right of all men to do as they would with their own, and they turned the tenants . . . out into the roads. **1891** J. E. T. ROGERS *Ind. & Commer. Hist.* II. ii. 208 That . . . a man may not in the case of land, as the Duke of Newcastle thought, 'do what he wills with his own', is no mere antiquarian utterance.

Do what one's own self wills, It is easy to.

1641 FERGUSSON 62 It is eith till, that the awn self will.

Do what thou oughtest, and come what can.

a. **1633** HERBERT *Priest to Temple* (Wks. ed. Hutchinson 270) Do well and right, and let the world sinke. **1640** HERBERT 355. **1721** KELLY 90 . . . Men should act upon a steady principle of virtue, justice, and honesty, not out of fear, interest, or shame. [Fr. *Fais ce que dois, advienne que pourra.*]

Do wrong once and you'll never hear the end of it.

1633 D. DYKE *Com. upon Philemon* Wks. 201 To hit men in the teeth with that base estate wherein once they were . . . is the common practice of many, insomuch, that the proverb is true, *Once I did ill*, etc.

Do(es, ne, th), *see also* Advice comes too late (When thing done); Causes to be done he d. himself; Easily d. soon believed; Evil do (Whoso will no); Have what he hath not (He that would) should do what he d. not; I do what I can, quoth . . . when he threshed in cloak; Lawfully done which cannot be forborne; Leave more to do when we die; Man has done (Whatever) man may do; No man can do two things at once; Pain to do nothing than something (More); Sport is to do deed and say nothing; Thing that's done is na to do; Thou thyself canst do it (If); Want a thing done (If you); Well done is twice d.; Well done soon d.

Dock to a daisy, As like as a.

1639 CLARKE 96 (A) An odious comparison! a dock to a dazie. **1670** RAY 204 . . . That is, very unlike.

Dock, *see also* In d., out nettle.

Dockyard stroke, *see* Work with d. s.

Doctor cures, If the | the sun sees it; but if he kills, the earth hides it.

[1580 MONTAIGNE II. xxxvii quotes 'le soleil éclaire leur succéz, et la terre cache leur faulte' from Nicocles in Stobaeus.] 1623 WEBSTER *Devil's Law Case* II. iii You that dwell neere these graves and vaults, Which oft doe hide Physicions faults. *a.* 1626 SIR J. DAVIES *Yet other twelve Wonders* The earth my faults doth hide, the world my cures doth see. 1721 KELLY 184 *If the Doctor cures, the Sun sees it; but if he kills, the Earth hides it.* Spoken to dissuade ignorant people from quacking, because they cannot kill with license, as doctors may.

Dr. Fell; I do not like (love) thee | the reason why I cannot tell.

[The translation of Martial's epigram 1. 32 *Non amo te, Sabidi*, &c., made by Thomas Brown on Dr. John Fell, Dean of Christ Ch., Oxford (1660–86), who had threatened to expel him.] 1850 CARLYLE *Lat. D. Pam.*; *Parliaments* (1885) 206 'I do not like thee, Dr. Fell; the reason why I cannot tell'—and perhaps indeed there is no reason. 1906 *Spectator* 5 May The representatives of the Church of England have not thought out a stable basis for their opposition. It is a case of—'I do not like thee, Dr. Fell—The reason why I cannot tell'.

Doctor is often more to be feared than the disease, The.

1621 BURTON *Anat. Mel.* II. iv. I. i (1651) 364 As he said of Adrian, . . . a multitude of physicians hath killed the emperour; *Plus a medico quam a morbo periculi*; more danger there is from the physician, than from the disease. 1660 W. SECKER *Nonsuch Prof.* II (1891) 257 Most that perish, it is not their disease which kills them but their physician. They think to cure themselves, and this leaves them incurable. 1861 C. READE *Cloister & H.* lxxiii Paupers got sick and got well as Nature pleased; but woe betided the rich in an age when, for one Mr. Malady killed three fell by Dr. Remedy.

Doctor, One | makes work for another.

1902–4 LEAN IV. 73.

Doctor's opinion, That is but one.

1721 KELLY 335 . . . Spoken with resentment to them that offer their advice contrary to our interest.

Doctor(s), *see also* After death the d.; Broken apothecary, new d.; Dasnell dawcock sits among d.; Sun enters (Where), d. does not. *See also* Physician.

Doddypoll, *see* Learned as Doctor D.

Dodkin (Doit), Not worth a.

c. 1590 LYLY *Moth. Bomb.* II. ii. 28 Not woorth a dodkin. *c.* 1607 SHAKS. *Timon of A.* I. i. 212 Plain-dealing which will not cost a man a doit. *c.* 1609 J. HEALEY (tr. J. HALL) *Discovery of a New World* (Huntington Brown) 25 Not worth a doit. 1660 BEAUM. & FL. *Faithful Friends* IV. v If my trade then prove not worth a dodkin.

Doers, *see* Ill d. ill deemers.

Does evil, He that | never weens good.

c. 1386 CHAUCER *Cant. Tales* A. 4320 Him thar nat wenĕ wel that yvel dooth. 1641 FERGUSSON 40.

Does ill, He that | hates the light.

[*John* iii. 20 For every one that doeth evil hateth the light.] *c.* 1250 *Owl & Nightingale* 1. 229 Vor everich thing that schuniet right Het luveth thuster and hatiet light. 1629 *Book of Meery Riddles* Prov. 77. 1641 FERGUSSON 38.

Does no good, He who | does evil enough.

1853 TRENCH vi. 147 The world's confession that he who hides his talent is guilty . . . utters itself in the following proverb: *He who does no good, does evil enough.*

Does you an ill turn, He that | will never forgive you.

1721 KELLY 169 . . . The sense and conscience of his injustice, or unkindness, will make him still jealous of you, and so hate you.

Dog at the Nile, Like a.

[ERASM. *Ad. Ut canis e Nilo. i.e.* lapping as they run for fear of crocodiles.] 1581 PETTIE *Guazzo's Civ. Conv.* (1586) 39 You must . . . imitate the dogge of Aegipt, which drinketh at the riuer of Nyle, and then runneth his way. 1606 MARSTON *Sophonisba* I'le . . . trust me as our dogs drinke dangerous Nile. 1791 I. DISRAELI *Curios. Lit.* (1858) I. 11 He[1] read many of these, but not with equal attention—'*Sicut canis ad Nilum, bibens et fugiens*;' like a dog at the Nile, drinking and running. *a.* 1884 PATTISON *Essay on F. A. Wolf* Hayne said of himself that he prelected 'as a dog drinks from the Nile'. [[1] D. Ancillon 1617–92.]

Dog bark, If the old | he gives counsel.

[L. *Prospectandum vetulo latrante.* When the old dog barks it is time to look out.] 1640 HERBERT 326. 1885 E. P. HOOD *World of Prov. & Par.* 229 Some scamp of a fellow . . . might learn something . . . from another old proverb, *If an old dog barks, he gives counsel*'.

Dog bites the stone, not him that throws it, The.

1546 W. HUGH *Troub. Man's Med.* (1831) 5 I would not have thee . . . [ascribe] worldly miseries to the stars, to fate and fortune; playing therein the part of the dog, which bites the stone that is hurled at him . . . ;

but rather imitate . . . David, who blamed not Shimei . . . but imputed his despite unto the Lord. **1580** LYLY *Euph. & his Eng.* (Arb.) 223 They . . . wil[l] not stick to teare Euphues, bicause they do enuie Lyly: Wherein they resemble angry Dogges, which byte the stone, not him that throweth it.

Dog does not eat dog.

[JUVENAL *Sat.* 15. 160 *Parcit cognatis maculis similis fera.*] **1534** POLYDORE VERGIL on the barons rallying to young Henry III *Canis caninum non est* [= *edit.*]. **1598–9** SHAKS. *Much Ado* III. ii. 80 The two bears will not bite one another when they meet. **1601–2** *Troil. & Cres.* V. vii. 19 One bear will not bite another, and wherefore should one bastard? **1651** HERBERT (Gros.) 370 A wolfe will never make war upon another wolfe. **1790** WOLCOT (P. Pindar) *Comp. Epist. to Bruce* Wks. (1816) II. 171 Dog should not prey on dog, the proverb says. **1866** KINGSLEY *Hereward* xxx Dog does not eat dog; and it is hard to be robbed by an Englishman, after being robbed a dozen times by the French.

Dog doff his doublet, It would make a.

1678 RAY 239. *Chesh.*

Dog (Hound) gnaws bone, While the | companions would he none.

[Med. L. *Dum canis os rodit, sociari pluribus odit.* c. **1190** *Li Proverbe au Vilain* (Tobler) no. 10 Chiens en cuisine son per n'i desire.] c. **1225** *Trin. MS. O.* 11. *45* (ed. Förster) in *Eng. Stud.* **31.** 8 Wil ðe hund gnagþ bon, ifere nele he non. Dum canis os rodit, sociari pluribus odit. c. **1470** *Harl. MS. 3362* in *Anglia* 42. 202 Whyl þe dogge gnaweth [bone, companion wold he haue non]. *Dum canis os rodit, sociari pluribus odit.*

Dog has his (a) day, A (Every).

1545 TAVERNER H 7 A dogge hath a day. **1546** HEYWOOD I. xi A dog hath a day. **1550** Q. ELIZ. in STRYPE *Eccl. Mem.* II. xxviii. 234 Notwithstanding, as a dog hath a day, so may I perchance have time to declare it in deeds. **1600–1** SHAKS. *Hamlet* V. i. 315 The cat will mew, and dog will have his day. **1633** JONSON *T. Tub* II. i A man has his hour, and a dog his day. **1670** RAY 80 Every dog hath his day. **1726** POPE *Od.* xxii. 41 Dogs, ye have had your day. **1837** CARLYLE *Fr. Rev.* III. I. i How changed for Marat, lifted from his dark cellar. . . ! All dogs have their day; even rabid dogs. **1851** BORROW *Lavengro* iii. 291 Every dog has his day, and mine has been a fine one.

Dog in a doublet, A.

1577 W. HARRISON *Description of England* (New Sh. S.) i. 168 Except it were a dog in a doublet, you shall not see anie so disguised, as are my countrie men of England. **1620** SHELTON *Quix.* II. i. (1908) III. 173 'And what care I', quoth Sanchica, 'what he says that sees me stately and majestical? "There's a dog in a doublet", and such-like.' **1778** BOSWELL *Johnson* lxvi (1848) 607 BOSWELL. 'I think it is a new thought . . . in a new

attitude.' . . . JOHNSON. 'It is the old dog in the new doublet.'

Dog in a fair: Like a | here, there, and everywhere.

1869 HAZLITT (1882) 270.

Dog in the manger, Like a.

[LUCIAN *Tim.* 14 ἡ ἐν τῇ φάτνῃ κύων. In allusion to Aesop's fable.] c. **1390** GOWER *Conf. Amantis* II. 84 Thogh it be noght the houndes Kinde to ete chaf, yit wol he werne An Oxe which comth to the berne, Therof to taken eny fode. **1564** BULLEYN *Dial. agst. Fever* (1888) 9 Like vnto cruell Dogges liyng in a Maunger, neither eatyng the Haye theim selues ne sufferyng the Horse to feed thereof hymself. **16** . . CHAPMAN (?) *Charlemagne* III. i. 271 Have ye not hearde of Aesopp's dog, that once lay snarling in the oxes maunger? **1621** BURTON *Anat. Mel.* I. ii. III. xii (1651) 115 Like a . . . dog in the manger, he doth only keep it, because it shall do nobody else good, hurting himself and others.

Dog in the morning, A | sailor take warning; a dog in the night is the sailor's delight.

1883 ROPER 6 . . . (A sun-dog in nautical language is a small rainbow near the horizon.)

Dog in the well, There is a.

1641 FERGUSSON 98. **1721** KELLY 305 . . . There is something amiss.

Dog is a lion at home, Every.

1659 N.R. 29. **1666** TORRIANO 36. **1855** BOHN 349.

Dog is allowed his first bite, Every.

1902–4 LEAN I. 439 . . . i.e. is not punished. **1913** *Spectator* 15 Mar. 440 Every dog is allowed by the law one free bite.

Dog is drowning, When a | every one offers him drink.

1611 COTGRAVE s.v. 'Chien'. **1640** HERBERT 320.

Dog is made fat in two meals, A.

1863 WISE *New Forest* xvi (1895) 180 'A dog is made fat in two meals', is applied to upstart or purse-proud people.

Dog is valiant at his own door, Every.

1855 BOHN 349.

Dog, The hindmost (foremost) | may catch (catches) the hare.

1580 LYLY *Euph. & his Eng.* (Arb.) 419 The last dogge oftentimes catcheth the Hare, though the fleetest turne him. **1635** QUARLES *Div. Emb.* IV. iv Be wisely patient; . . . The hindmost hound oft takes the doubling hare. **1659** HOWELL *Eng. Prov.* 16/1 The hindmost hound may catch the hare. **1662** FULLER (*Derb.*) I. 373 As the last dog most commonly catcheth the hare which other dogs have turned and tired before; so such who succeed in dangerous and difficult enterprises, generally reap the benefit of the adventures of those who went before them. **1664** CODRINGTON The foremost dog catches the hare. **1670** RAY 10 The foremost dog catcheth the hare. **1721** KELLY 306 *The foremost hound grips the hare.* Recommending diligence and industry.

Dog returns to his vomit, The.

c. **1400** *Rom. Rose* C. 7285 He is the hound, . . . That to his castyng goth ageyn. **1534** TYNDALE *2 Peter* ii. 22 It is happened vnto them accordinge to the true proverbe: The dogge is turned to his vomet agayne. **1580** LYLY *Euph. & his Eng.* (Arb.) 319 With what face *Euphues* canst thou returne to thy vomit, seeming with the greedy hounde to lap vp that which thou diddest cast vp. **1597-8** SHAKS. *2 Hen. IV* I. iii. 99 Thou common dog . . . now thou wouldst eat thy dead vomit up. **1598-9** *Hen. V* III. vii. 68 Le chien est retourné à son propre vomissement. **1832-8** S. WARREN *Diary of Late P.* xxii His infatuated wife betook herself—'like the dog to his vomit . . .'—to her former . . . extravagance and dissipation.

Dog that fetches, will carry, The.

1830 FORBY 429 . . . *i.e.* A talebearer will tell tales *of* you, as well as *to* you.

Dog that has lost his tail, To look like a.

1678 RAY 286.

Dog that is idle barks at his fleas, The | but he that is hunting feels them not.

1894 DEAN HOLE *More Mem.* xi Honest work is the best cure for all the ills that flesh is heir to, because, according to the Chinese proverb, 'the dog that is idle barks at his fleas, but he that is hunting feels them not'.

Dog that licks ashes trust not with meal, The.

1640 HERBERT 336.

Dog that trots about, The | finds a bone.

1843 BORROW *Bible in Sp.* xlvii As the gipsies say, 'The dog that trots about finds a bone.'

Dog to bite him, A man may cause his own.

1546 HEYWOOD II. vii. 70 A man maie handle his dog so, That he maie make him byte him. **1670** RAY 7.

Dog to follow you, If you would wish the | feed him.

1855 BOHN 422.

Dog under a door, He looks like a.

1678 RAY 70.

Dog who hunts foulest, hits at most faults, The.

1659 HOWELL *Eng. Prov.* 1/2. **1732** FULLER no. 1318 Dogs that hunt foulest hit off most faults.

Dog will bark ere he bite, A.

1550 HEYWOOD II. vii. 70 A dog will barke er he bite, and so thow, After thy barkying wilt bite me.

Dog will not howl if you beat him with a bone, A.

1659 HOWELL *Brit. Eng.* 24 The dog will not bite for being struck with a bone. **1721** KELLY 42 . . . People will bear easily some rough usage, . . . if they see their advantage in it. **1826** SCOTT *Woodst.* xx 'I can bide the bit and the buffet, . . . a hungry tyke ne'er minds a blaud with a rough bane.'

Dog worry my uncle, If I do.

1847 HALLIWELL *Dict.* s.v. 'Dog' (1889) I. 308 *If I do, dog worry my uncle,* a phrase implying refusal on being asked to do anything contrary to one's wishes.

Dog's bark, At every | seem not to awake.

c. **1532** SIR ADRIAN FORTESCUE, no. 56 At every dogge that barkes, one ought not to be anoyd. **1550** HEYWOOD II. v. 56 For little more or lesse no debate make, At euery dogs barke, séeme not to awake.

Dog's dead since you were a whelp, Many a.

1721 KELLY 255. **1732** FULLER no. 3336.

Dog's life, hunger and ease, A.

1660 TORRIANO 276 (A) The English say, hunger and ease is a dogs life. **1670** RAY 172. **1721** KELLY 18 *A dog's life, mickle hunger, mickle ease.* Applied to careless, lazy lubbers, who will not work, and therefore have many a hungry meal.

Dog's nose and a maid's knees are always cold, A.

1639 CLARKE 72 A dog's nose is ever cold. **1670** RAY 51.

Dog's tail, *see* Cut off a d. t.

Dog's trick, That is a.

1678 RAY 344 That's a dog-trick.

Dogged that does it, It is.

1867 TROLLOPE *Last Chron. Barset* lxi Mr. Crawley . . . repeated . . . Giles Hoggett's words. 'It's dogged as does it. It's not thinking about it.' **1877** J. R. GREEN *Lett. to Miss Stopford* 30 Mar. I found that 'dogged does it' had got into my blood, and I knuckled to at my work with a resolve to get it done.

Dogs are fine in the field.

1640 HERBERT 360.

Dogs bark as they are bred.

1721 KELLY 84 . . . Spoken when people, vilely educated, behave themselves accordingly. **1732** FULLER no. 1313.

Dogs bark, but the caravan goes on, The.

1930 *Times* 4 July 17/4 I was struggling to explain the situation to an old Moor. . . . After thinking it over he murmured: 'Dogs bark but the caravan goes on.'

Dogs (Fools) begin in jest and end in earnest.

1612–15 BP. HALL *Contempl.* x. iii (1825) I. 269 As fools and dogs use to begin in jest, and end in earnest, so did these Philistines. **1855** BOHN 345.

Dogs bite, In every country.

1640 HERBERT 346.

Dogs gnaw bones because they cannot swallow them.

1640 HERBERT 339 The dog gnaws the bone because he cannot swallow it. **1670** RAY 7.

Dogs in dough, Like.

1894 NORTHALL *Folk-phrases* 19 . . . *i.e.* unable to make headway.

Dogs run away with whole shoulders.

1622 WITHER *Christm. Car.* Poems (1891) 121 Rank misers now do sparing shun, . . . And dogs thence with whole shoulders run. **1670** RAY 172 . . . Not of mutton, but their own, spoken in derision of a miser's house.

Dogs that bark at a distance bite not at hand.

1623 CAMDEN 268 Dogges barking aloofe, bite not at hand. **1670** RAY 59.

Dogs that put up many hares kill none.

1732 FULLER no. 1319.

Dogs wag their tails not so much in love to you as to your bread.

1611 COTGRAVE s.v. 'Amour' Dogs fawne on a man no longer then he feeds them. **1616** DRAXE 47 The dogge waggeth his tayle, not for you, but for your bread. **1666** TORRIANO 36 A dog wags not his tail for thee, but for the bread. **1670** RAY 7 *Hispan.*

Dogs, Like | when one barks all bark.

[L. *Latrante uno, latrat statim et alter canis.*] **1612** WEBSTER *White Devil* V. iii (Merm.) 99 That old dog-fox, that politician, Florence! . . . I'll be friends with him; for, mark you, sir, one dog Still sets another a-barking. **1639** CLARKE 148. **1732** FULLER no. 3736 One barking Dog, sets all the Street a barking.

Dogs will redd[1] swine.

1641 FERGUSSON 28. **1721** KELLY 85 *Dogs will rid swine.* A third opposite will make two contending parties agree. [[1] to put in order; to part combatants.]

Dog(s), *see* Bad d. (Into mouth of) falls good bone; Bad d. never sees wolf; Bark ourselves ere we buy d. so dear (We will); Barking d. seldom bite; Beat the d. before lion; Best d. leap stile first; Better to have d. fawn than bite; Beware of silent d.; Black d. on one's back (To have); Blush like a black d.; Brag is a good d.; Bread than need (Who hath no more) must not keep d.; Butter in the black d.'s hause (Like); Cat and d. may kiss; Curst cur (d.) tied short; Cut off a d.'s tail, will be d. still; Dead d. bark not; Die a d.'s death; Eat a pudding . . . d. shall have skin; Everybody's d. that whistles; Expect a good whelp from an ill d.; Fashion's sake, as d. go to church; Fast as a d. can trot (*or* will lick); Fells two d. with one stone; Fiddlers, d., and flies come uncalled; Fight d., fight bear; Flesh stands never so high but d. will venture; Folk's d. bark worse than themselves; Gardener's d. that neither eats cabbages; Give a child till . . . and a d. while tail wave; Give a d. an ill name; Give his bone to the d. (He will not); Go to the d.; Good d. deserves good bone; Good d. who goes to church; Hair of d. that bit you; Hang a d. on a crab-tree; Hang his d. (He that would); Help the d. over stile; Hungry as a d.; Hungry d. will eat dirty puddings; Hunt's (Wood's) d. that will neither go to church; Ill d. that deserves not crust; Ill-bred d. that beat bitch; Keep a d. and bark myself; Keeps another man's d. (He that); Knit my d. a pair of breeches; Knows not a pig from a d.; Lazy as Ludlam's d.; Lean d. for hard road; Lean d. to get through hedge; Let sleeping d. lie; Lies down with d. rises with fleas; Little d. have long tails; Little d. start the hare; Living d. better than dead lion; Love me love my d.; Mad d. bites his master; Make a hog or a d. of it; Man has his hour and d. his day; Miller's d.; Moon does not heed barking of d.; Never d. barked against crucifix but . . . ; Never was cat or d. drowned that could . . ; Old d. barks; Old d. bites; One d. one bull; Open doors d. come in; Poor d. that doesn't know 'Come out'; Poor d. that is not worth whistling; Quarrelling d.; Quarrelsome d.; Scalded cat (d.) fears cold water; Scarce of horseflesh where two ride a d.; Scorn a thing as a d. tripe; Scornful d. eat dirty puddings; Scratching and biting cats and d. come together; Sleeps as d. when wives sift meal; Smith's d., so used to sparks; Smith's d. that sleeps at sound of hammer; Staff (Stick) to beat d.; Straw to his d., bones to ass; Strikes my d. (He that) would strike me; Taking wall of a d.; Talk as Dutch as

Daimport's d.; Teach an old d. tricks; Thieves (All are not) that d. bark at; Three things cost, caresses of d.; Thrift of you and wool of d.; Toiling d. comes halting; Toils like a d. in a wheel; Too much pudding will choke d.; Trust not horse's heel nor d.'s tooth; Trust to d. (While you), wolf in sheepfold; Try that bone on other d.; Two cats ... two d. and a bone never agree; Two d. strive for bone, third runs away with it; Use one like a d.; Vex a d. to see pudding creep; Waken sleeping d. (Ill to); Want a pretence to whip a d. (If you); Ways to kill d. than hanging (More); Wolf for his mate (Who hath) needs d. for his man; Women and d. set men by the ears; Word to throw at a d.; Worst d. that is waggeth tail.

Doing nothing we learn to do ill, By.

[CATO MAJOR *Nilne agendo homines male agere discunt.*] **1567** FENTON *Bandello* (T.T.) ii. 63 (A) Plato, who affirmeth that in doynge nothyng men lerne to do evill. **1604** HERBERT 352.

Doing we learn, In.

1640 HERBERT 354.

Doing(s), *see also* Great d. at Gregory's; Saying and d. are two things; Saying is one thing, d. another; Shortest answer is d.; Worth d. at all worth d. well.

Doit, *see* Dodkin (D.).

Dolbury Hill, *see* Cadbury Castle.

Dole, *see* Happy man; Scrambling at a rich man's d.

Dominy (-ies), *see* Mickle to do when d. ride; Pigeons and priests (Doves and d.) make foul houses.

Doncaster daggers, *see* Dunmow bacon.

Done, Lady, *see* Fair as L. D.

Done at any time, What may be | will be done at no time.

1721 KELLY 355.

Done by night appears by day, What is.

c. **1390** GOWER *Conf. Amantis* v. 4597 Bot so prive mai be nothing, That it ne comth to knowleching; Thing don upon the derke nyht Is after knowe on daies liht. **1594** SHAKS. *Lucrece* 747 Day ... night's scapes doth open lay. **1666** TORRIANO 263 That which is done in the dark, appears in the sunshine.

Done cannot be undone, Things.

c. **1369** CHAUCER *Bk. Duchess* 1. 707 For that ys doon ys not to come. *c.* **1460** *The Gode Wyfe wold a Pylgremage* (E.E.T.S.) 1. 119 When dede is doun, hit ys to late. **1546** HEYWOOD I. x. 21 True (quoth Ales) thinges doone can not be vndoone. **1592–3** SHAKS.

Rich. III IV. iv. 292 Look what is done cannot be now amended. **1605–6** *Macbeth* III. ii. 12 Things without all remedy Should be without regard: what 's done is done. *Ibid.* V. ii. 74 What 's done cannot be undone. **1608–9** *Pericles* IV. iii. 1–6 *Dion.* Why, are you foolish? Can it be undone? ... *Cleo.* Were I chief lord of all this spacious world, I'd give it to undo the deed. **1632** MASSINGER *City Madam* V. iii I care not where I go: what's done, with words Cannot be undone. **1818** MISS FERRIER *Marriage* lxvii I hope you will think twice about it. Second thoughts are best. What 's done cannot be undone.

Done ill once, He that hath | will do it again.

1707 MAPLETOFT 53. **1855** BOHN 400.

Done no ill the six days, If you have | you may play the seventh.

1732 FULLER no. 2757.

Done twice, If things were to be | all would be wise.

1640 HERBERT 350.

Done, *see also* Do(es, ne).

Donkey between two bundles of hay, Like a.

[Known as Buridan's ass, but not to be found in his works.] *a.* **1763** BYROM *Fight bet. Figg & Sutton* Dame Victory ... remain'd like the ass 'twixt two bottles of hay, Without ever moving an inch either way. **1824** MOIR *Mansie W.* xxv I swithered,[1] and was like the cuddie[2] between the two bundles of hay. **1850** KINGSLEY *Alton Locke* xxvii You've been off and on lately between flunkeydom and The Cause, like a donkey between two bundles of hay. **1886** E. J. HARDY *How to be Happy* ii Some men ... have almost died of indecision, like the donkey between two exactly similar bundles of hay. [[1] hesitated. [2] ass.]

Donkey, *see also* Dead d. (You never see); Time to cock hay when d. blows his horn. *See also* Ass.

Doomsday, *see* Death's day is d.; Thousand pounds and ... all one at D.

Door, Here is the | and there is the way.

? *a.* **1483** *Mankind* 154 Nought. Her ys *the* dore, her ys *the* wey! **1546** HEYWOOD I. xi. 29 Now here is the doore, and there is the wey, and so ... farewell. **1593–4** SHAKS. *Tam. Shrew* III. ii. 213 The door is open, sir, there lies your way. **1625** JONSON *Staple of News* III. ii *Pen. sen.* There lies your way, you see the door.

Door may be shut but death's door, Every.

1666 TORRIANO 317. **1853** TRENCH i. 17 What is 'All men are mortal', as compared with the proverb: *Every door may be shut but death's door?*

Door must either be shut or open, A.

[Fr. *Il faut qu'une porte soit ouverte ou fermée*. **1691** BRUEYS ET DE PALAPRAT, *Grondeur* 1. 6]. **1762** GOLDSMITH *Cit. World* li There are but the two ways; the door must either be shut, or it must be open. **1896** SAINTSBURY *19th Cent. Lit.* 361 Fiction . . . pleads in vain for detailed treatment. For all doors must be shut or open; and this door must now be shut.

Door of gold, Who will make a | must knock a nail every day.

1640 HERBERT 363.

Door wider than the house, Make not the. (*Cf.* Gate wider than the city.)

1599 R. LINCHE *Fountaine of Ancient Fiction* A 4ᵛ It is an absurd part in an architector to frame a long & vast entry for a little house. **1608** G. WILKINS *Painfull Adventures of Pericles* Preface Nor willing to make a great waie to a little house. **1639** CLARKE 11.

Door(s), *see also* Hatch before the d. (Good to have); Hospitality (Sin against) to open d., shut countenance; One d. shuts (Where) another opens; Open d. dogs come in; Open d. may tempt saint; Postern d. makes thief and whore; Stoop that hath low d.; Sweep before his own d. (If each). *See also* Back door, Stable door.

Door-nail, *see* Dead (Deaf, Dumb) as a d.

Dorty[1] dame may fa'[2] in the dirt, The.

1832 HENDERSON 89. [[1] saucy to her suitors. [2] fall.]

Dot the i's, To.

1849 THACKERAY in *Scribner's Mag.* I. 557/1 I have . . . dotted the i's. **1896** *Daily Chron.* 20 Apr. 4/7 [He] dotted our 'i's' and crossed our 't's' with a vengeance.

Dote more on it than a fool on his bauble, To.

1670 RAY 172.

Doth most at once, He that | doth least.

1707 MAPLETOFT 42. **1855** BOHN 385.

Doth nothing, He that | doth ever amiss.

1531 ELYOT *The Governor* (ed. Croft i. 270) In doing nothinge men lerne to do iuel. **1629** *Book of Meery Riddles* Prov. 75. **1865** Lancs. Prov. in *N. & Q.* 3rd Ser. VIII. 494 Those who are doing nothing are doing ill.

Doth well, He that | wearieth not himself.

1616 DRAXE 32. **1663** F. HAWKINS *Youth's Behaviour* F 8. **1670** RAY 28.

Doth what he should not, He that | shall feel what he would not.

1640 HERBERT 353.

Doth what he will, He that | doth not what he ought.

1640 HERBERT 333. **1747–8** RICHARDSON *Clar. Harlowe* iv let. 24 He who does what he will seldom does what he ought.

Double charge will rive a cannon.

1721 KELLY 86 . . . Spoken when people urge upon you more than you can bear, be it meat, drink, work, or so.

Double, *see also* Work d. tides.

Doublet, *see* Dog doff his d. (Would make); Near is my coat (d.) but nearer my shirt.

Doubt, When in | do nowt.[1]

1917 BRIDGE 389 . . . This shows the cautious Cheshireman at his best. [[1] nought.]

Doubt(s), *see also* Do well and d. no man; Knows nothing, d. nothing.

Doubtful, *see* Persuasion of fortunate sways d.

Dough, *see* Cake is d. (One's).

Dove's flood is worth a king's good, In April.

1610 CAMDEN *Britannia* tr. Holland 587 If it chance to swel above the bankes and overflow the Medowes in April . . . the inhabitants use commonly to chant this joyfull note. In Aprill *Doves* floud, Is worth a Kings good. **1662** FULLER (*Staffs.*) III. 127 Dove, a river parting this and Derbyshire, when it overfloweth its banks in April, is the *Nilus* of Staffordshire.

Dove(s), *see* Noah's d.; Pigeons and priests (D. and dominies); Serpent than d. (To have more of).

Dovecots, *see* Flutter the d.

Dover court: all speakers, and no hearers.

1662 FULLER (*Kent*) II. 124 . . . The proverb is applied to such irregular conferences, wherein the people are all tongue and no ears. **1888** QUILLER-COUCH *Troy Town* xix Then for up ten minutes 'twas Dover to pay, all talkers an' no listeners.

Dover shark and a Deal savage, A.

1787 GROSE (*Kent*) 183 Dover-men have obtained the nickname of shark. The appellation of Deal savage, probably originated from the brutality and exaction of the boatmen.

Dover, *see also* Berwick to D.; Dark in D. (When it 's), dark all world over; Deal, D., and Harwich, the devil gave; Jack of D.

Dow,[1] He will never | egg nor bird. (*See also* Good egg nor bird.)

1678 RAY 355 He'll never dow (i.e. *be good*) egg nor bird. [[1] thrive.]

Dowb, see Take care of D.

Down, He that is | down with him.

c. 1632 *Pepysian Garland* (Rollins) 411 If a man be once downe, the world cryes downe with him still. **1639** CLARKE 115 If a man once fall, all will tread on him. **1678** RAY 129. **1721** KELLY 199 *If a man be once down, down with him.* If fortune frown upon a man, his friends will lessen, and his enemies multiply. **1910** JOYCE *Eng. as We Speak* 109 'When a man is down, down with him': a bitter allusion to the tendency of the world to trample down the unfortunate and helpless.

Down the wind, To go.

1600 N. BRETON *Pasquils Passe and Passeth not* Wks. (Gros.) I. 11 Want and vertue must go downe the wind. **1663** PEPYS *Diary* 25 Jan. So that I perceive he goes down the wind in honor as well as every thing else, every day.

Down, see also Fallen (He that is) cannot help him that is d.; Hit a man when he is d.; Nought lay d., nought take up.

Downham, see Rising was, Lynn is.

Down hill, see Bowl d. h. (Easy to).

Dowry is a bed full of brambles, A great.

1640 HERBERT 352.

Draff[1] is good enough for swine.

1535 *Gentlenes & Nobility* C; Thou sayst trew drafe is good Inough for swyne. **1614** TAYLOR (Water-P.) *Nipping of Abuses* B 4 (A Prouerb old) draffs good enough for hogges. **1623** CAMDEN 268. **1670** RAY 82. **1721** KELLY 85 . . . Spoken jocosely when people refuse what is good, and fine, and feed upon that which is more coarse. [[1] hog-wash.]

Draff is your errand, but drink ye would.

1546 HEYWOOD I. xi. 26. **1580** LYLY *Euph. & his Eng.* (Arb.) 468 Draffe was mine arrand, but drinke I would. **1623** CAMDEN 267 Draft was his errand, but drinke he would. **1721** KELLY 88 *Draff he sought, but drink was his errand.* Spoken of them who make a sleeve-less errand into a house where they know people are at dinner.

Dragon's teeth, To sow.

[= the dragon's teeth fabled by Hyginus (fab. 178) to have been sown by Cadmus, from which sprang armed men.] **1853** MARSDEN *Early Purit.* 290 Jesuits . . . sowed the dragon's teeth which sprung up into the hydras of rebellion and apostasy.

Dragon, see also Serpent, unless . . ., does not become d.

Drank, see Drink.

Draught, see Air of a window stroke of cross-bow; Cold wind reach you (If).

Draw at the cat-harrow,[1] They.

a. **1555** SIR DAV. LINDSAY *Complaynt to K.* 305–8 Wks. (1879) I. 54 For every lord, as he thocht best, Brocht in ane bird to fyll the nest; To be ane wacheman to his marrow, Thay gan to draw at the cat harrow. **1721** KELLY 329 They draw the cat harrow; that is they thwart one another. [[1] A nursery game, played by pulling crossing loops of thread.]

Draw (Pull, Shrink) in (or Shoot out) one's horns, To.

13 . . *Coer de L.* 3835 They . . . gunne to drawen in her hornes, As a snayl among the thornes. *c.* **1374** CHAUCER *Troylus* I. 300 He was tho glad his hornes in to shrinke. **1430–40** LYDGATE *Bochas* I. xx (Bodl. MS.) f. 83/1 Who is knowe outrewe . . . Shrynkith his hornis whan men speake of falsheede. **1589** ? LYLY *Pappe w. Hatchet* Wks. (1902) III. 404 Now the old cuckold hath pulled in his horns. **1662** FULLER (*Kent*) II. 179 The Kentish gentry acquitted themselves so valiantly . . . that Perkin shrunk his horns back again into the shell of his ships. **1818** SCOTT *Rob Roy* xiv The fallow . . . drew in his horns, and . . . acknowledged he might hae been mista'en. **1829–30** M. SCOTT *Tom Cring. Log* xiii She had no sooner gone, than Bang began to shoot out his horns a bit. 'I say, Tom, ask the Don to let us have . . . a tumbler of hot brandy and water.' **1891** *Sat. Rev.* 19 Dec. 682/2 They are imploring the Council to draw in its horns.

Draw the line somewhere, One must.

1887 BLACKMORE *Springhaven* xviii One must draw the line somewhere, or throw overboard all principles; and I draw it . . . against infidels and against Frenchmen. **1896** J. BEALBY *Daughter of Fen* xxix Vulgar, presuming, low-bred upstarts must be kept in their places. . . . The line must be drawn somewhere.

Draw water to (one's) mill, To.

[= to seize every advantage.] **1573** SANDFORD (1576) 222. **1578** FLORIO *First Fruites* 14 Euery man draweth water to hymselfe. **1641** FERGUSSON 30 Every man wishes the water to his own mylne. **1649** HOWELL *Pre-em. Parl.* 10 Lewis the eleventh . . . could well tell how to play his game, and draw water to his owne Mill. **1670** RAY 121 Every miller draws water to his own mill.

Draw, see also Well worth aw, makes plough d.

Draweth his sword against his prince, Who | must throw away the scabbard.

1604 R. DALLINGTON *The View of France* F3[v] His King, against whom when yee drawe the sword, ye must throw the scabberd into the riuer. **1613** R. DALLINGTON *Aphorisms* 331 When the sword of iustice is drawne, . . . throw the scabberd into the fire. **1659** HOWELL *Eng. Prov.* 17/1. **1843** MACAULAY *Ess., Hampden* Wks. V. 583 Hampden . . .

was for vigorous and decisive measures. When he drew the sword, as Clarendon has well said, he threw away the scabbard.

Drawlatch, see John D.

Drawn wells are seldom dry.

1639 CLARKE 107. **1648** HERRICK *Hesper.* 832 Wks. (1893) II. 77 Milk stil your Fountains, and your Springs, for why? The more th'are drawn, the lesse they will grow dry. **1670** RAY 83 . . . *Puteus si hauriatur melior evadit.* . . . All things, especially men's parts, are improved and advanced by use and exercise. **1732** FULLER no. 1327.

Drawn wells have sweetest water.

1639 CLARKE 107.

Dream of a dry summer, To.

1568 W. FULWOOD *Enemie of Idlenesse* (1593) 217 I thinke you dreamed of a drie Summer. **1670** RAY 172.

Dream of a funeral and you hear of a marriage.

1883 BURNE *Shrops. Folk-Lore* 263. **1909** *Brit. Wkly.* 8 July 331 'Dream of a funeral and you hear of a marriage' . . . has probably been verified many times in the experience of ordinary people.

Dreamed (*verb*), *see* Know all (Since you), tell what I d.

Dreams go by contraries.

c. **1400** *Tale of Beryn* prol. 108 Comynly of these swevenys the contrary man shul fynde. **1584** LYLY *Sapho & P.* IV. iii I dreamed last night, but I hope dreams are contrary, that . . . all my hair blazed on a bright flame. **1673** WYCHERLEY *Gent. Dancing Master* IV. i Never fear it: dreams go by the contraries. **1818** FERRIER *Marriage* xxiv Everybody knows dreams are always contrary. **1909** *Brit. Wkly.* 8 July 331 The old saying, 'Dreams go by contraries', is established on a much surer basis of evidence than the telepathic premonitions which find a corresponding fulfilment.

Dream(s) (*noun*), *see also* After a d. of a wedding; Friday night's d.; Morning d. come true.

Dress an egg and give the offal to the poor, To.

1678 RAY 90 *A covetous person.* He'll dress...

Dress up a stick and it does not appear to be a stick.

[Span. *Palo compuesto no parece palo.* A stick dressed up does not look like a stick.] **1620** SHELTON *Quix.* II. li (1908) III. 178 Go well clad, for a stake well dressed seems not to be so. **1640** HERBERT (Gros.) no. 101 Presse[1] a stick, and it seemes a youth. **1666** TORRIANO 187 Clothes set forth poles, and cloth[e] but a pillar, and it shall look like a lady. [[1] A misprint for 'Dress'.]

Dress (*noun*), *see* Whore in a fine d.

Dressing, *see* Fine d. is a foul house swept.

Drift is as bad as unthrift.

1659 HOWELL *Eng. Prov.* 6. **1678** RAY 71.

Drink and drouth come seldom together.

1641 FERGUSSON 28. **1721** KELLY 88 (with 'not always'). **1732** FULLER no. 1329 (with 'not always').

Drink as much after an egg as after an ox, One should.

1608 HARINGTON *Sch. of Salerne* A 7 (A) Remember . . . For every egge you eate you drink as oft. **1659** HOWELL *Eng. Prov.* 13. **1670** RAY 36 . . . This is . . . fond and ungrounded. **1738** SWIFT (Dial. ii) 348 *Sir J.* I take a new-laid egg for breakfast; and faith one should drink as much after an egg as after an ox.

Drink in your pottage, If you | you'll cough in your grave.

1670 RAY 133. **1738** SWIFT (Dial. ii) 347 *Smart.* You ha'n't tasted my cider yet. *Never.* No, my lord; I have been just eating soup; and they say, if one drinks with one's porridge, one will cough in one's grave.

Drink less, and go home by daylight.

c. **1300** *Provs. of Hending* 38 in *Reliq. Antiquae* i. 116 Drynk eft lasse, and go by lyhte hom.

Drink like a fish, To.

1744 THOS. GRAY *Let. to Dr. Wharton* 26 Apr. Mr. Trollope and I are in a course of tar-water . . . I drink like a fish. **1822** SCOTT *Nigel* xxxv He retained the gravity of a judge, even while he drank like a fish.

Drink nettles in March, and eat mugwort in May, If they would | so many fine maidens wouldn't go to the clay.

[**1747** WESLEY *Prim. Physick* (1762) 35 Take an ounce of Nettle juice. **1753** CHAMBERS *Cycl. Supp.* Mugwort has long been famous as an uterine and antispasmodic.] **1846** DENHAM 38.

Drink of the burn, We can | when we cannot bite of the brae.

1641 FERGUSSON 112 Ye may drink of the burn, but not byte of the brae. **1721** KELLY 344 . . . Spoken when people want bread, for none complain for want of drink.

Drink of this water, Don't say, I'll never | how dirty so ever it be.

1710 S. PALMER *Moral Essays on Prov.* 230 (A). **1732** FULLER no. 5016. **1906** CUNNINGHAME GRAHAM *His People* 'Dagos' *fin.* It is not good to say fountain—out of your basin I shall never drink . . . eh, no señor.

Drink only with the duck.

[i.e. drink only water.] **1362** LANGLAND *P. Pl.* A. v. 58 He schulde . . . Drinken bote with þe Doke and dyne but ones

Drink water, Let none say, I will not.

1620 SHELTON *Quix.* II. lv (1908) III. 209 Let . . . no man say, I'll drink no more of such a drink; for where we think to fare well, there is oft ill usage. **1640** HERBERT 331.

Drink wine, and have the gout; drink no wine, and have the gout too.

1584 COGAN *Haven of Health* Ep. Ded. I have heard many gentlemen say ere now: Drink wine, and have the gout: drink none, and have the gout. As who should say, that it maketh no matter what a man eateth or drinketh. **1670** RAY 38 . . . With this saying, intemperate persons that have or fear the gout, encourage themselves to proceed in drinking wine notwithstanding.

Drink (*noun*), *see also* Ale (D.) is in (When), wit is out; Likes not the d. (Who) God deprives of bread; Speak of my d. that never consider my drouth; Speaks in his **d.** what he thought in drouth; Tale of two d.; Victuals (Of all) d. digests quickest; Want in meat (What they), take out in d.; Words would have much d.

Drinking at the harrow when he should be following the plough, He is.

1639 CLARKE 47.

Drinking, *see also* Speak of my great d. (Many).

Drinks not wine after salad, He that | is in danger of being sick.

1611 COTGRAVE s.v. 'Salade' A Sallet without wine is raw, unwholesome, dangerous. **1670** RAY 39 Qui vin ne boit apres salade est en danger estre malade, i.e. He that drinks not wine after salade, is in danger to be sick.

Drinks, The more one | the more one may.

1616 DRAXE 49. **1666** TORRIANO 25 (with 'would' for 'may').

Drink(eth, s), drank (*verb*), *see also* Brew (As they), so let them d.; Clothe thee warm . . . d. enough; Deep d. the goose as the gander; Draff is your errand, but d. ye would; Eat and eat but do not d. (You); Eat at pleasure, d. by measure; Eat thy meat and d. thy d.; Husband d. to the wife (When); Ill guest that never d. to host; Never d. was never athirst; Old man will not d. (When), go to him in another world; Penny in purse will bid me d.; Run as you d. might catch hare; Stay and d. of your browst; Thing in it, quoth . . . when he d. dish-clout; Up hill spare me . . . let me not d. when hot; Walk groundly . . . d. roundly; Whistle and d. at same time.

Drive a snail to Rome, Ye.

1641 FERGUSSON 112.

Drive a top over a tiled house, As soon.

1546 HEYWOOD II. v. 58 I shall as soone trie him or take him this waie, As dryue a top ouer a tyeld house.

Drive black hogs in the dark, It is ill to.

1678 RAY 103. **1732** FULLER no. 2963. **1743** FRANKLIN July How can they advise, if they see but a part? 'Tis very ill driving black hogs in the dark.

Drive out the inch as you have done the span.

1641 FERGUSSON 28. **1721** KELLY 84 *Dree out the inch as you have done the span.* Spoken to encourage people to continue in ill service, or bear ill circumstances, whose end is near at hand.

Drive the nail that will go.

1655 FULLER *Ch. Hist.* II. iv. (1868) I. 201 Thus he drave that nail . . . which would go best for the present. It was *argumentum ad hominem.* **1738** GAY *Fables* Ser. II. ix Hence Politicians, you suggest, Should drive the nail that goes the best.

Drive your business, do not let it drive you.

1672 CODRINGTON 124 Let every one be sure to drive his own business, rather than to let it drive him. **1736** FRANKLIN *Way to Wealth* Wks. (Bigelow) I. 443.

Drive, *see also* Gently over the stones; Lead nor d. (Neither); Three things d. out of house, smoke . . .

Driver, *see* Know your d. (I will make you).

Drives a subtle trade, He.

1678 RAY 91.

Drives an ass and leads a whore, Who | hath toil and sorrow evermore.

1617 MORYSON *Itin.* III. i. 26 (1907–8) III. 403 It is proverbially said, *Chi asini caccia e donne mena, Non è mai senza guai & pena.*[1] Who drives an ass and leads a whore Hath toil and sorrow evermore. **1639** CLARKE 259. [[1] GIUSTI 87 *Chi asino caccia e p . . . mena, non esce mai di pena.*]

Drives fat oxen should himself be fat, Who.

1784 JOHNSON in *Boswell* (1848) lxxx. 767 I cannot agree with you, . . . it might as well be said, 'Who drives fat oxen should himself be fat'. **1902** *Spectator* 8 Nov. Men . . . [jump] to the conclusion that . the Secretary of State for War . . . ought to be a soldier. The principle that 'who drives fat oxen should himself be fat' is one which has always had great attractions for the public mind.

Driving a flock than one, It is better.

1664 J. WILSON *Andron. Comn.* III. v. Wks.

(1874) 172 The people are like sheep—'tis better driving A flock than one.

Driving his hogs over Swarston Bridge,[1] He is.

1787 GROSE (*Derbysh.*) 162 . . . This is a saying used in Derbyshire, when a man snores in his sleep. [[1] Swarkeston Bridge, over the Trent.]

Driving his hogs (pigs) to market, He is.

1738 SWIFT (Dial. ii) 349 He fell asleep, and snored so hard that we thought he was driving his hogs to market. 1903 S. HEDIN *Centr. Asia* II. 318 The sleeping men . . . went on driving their pigs to market for all they were worth.

Driving turkeys to market, He is.

1869 HAZLITT 165 He is driving turkeys to market. i.e. He cannot walk straight.

Drop(s), *see* Gangs up i' sops (When it), it'll fau in d.; Last d. makes cup run over; Many d. make shower.

Dropping(s), *see* Constant d. wears stone; Lose the d. of his nose (He will not).

Dross, *see* No silver without d.

Drought never bred dearth in England.

1533 HEYWOOD *Play of Weather* 1. 364 (A) And it is sayd syns afore we were borne That drought doth neuer make derth of corne. 1640 HERBERT 352 Drought never brought dearth. 1670 RAY 42. 1917 BRIDGE 52 . . . 'It has been proved . . . by practical farmers that in the fine hot years they do the best.'

Drought, Drouth, *see also* Drink and d. seldom together; Mouth (Whoso hath) shall ne'er in England suffer d.; Pedlar's d.; Speak of my drink that never consider my d.

Drowned mouse (rat), Like a.

1542 UDALL tr. *Erasm. Apoph.* 180 b An hedde he had . . . Three heares on a side, like a drouned ratte. 1591-2 SHAKS. *1 Hen. VI* I. ii. 12 Or piteous they will look, like drowned mice. 1678 RAY 286 To look like a drowned mouse. 1697 DAMPIER *Voy.* I. iv. 70 The storm drencht us all like so many drowned Rats. 1778 FRANCES BURNEY *Evelina* xix (1920) 80 You hadn't a dry thread about you . . . and poor *Monseer* French, here, like a drowned rat, by your side!

Drowning man will catch at a straw, A.

1612-15 BP. HALL *Contempl.* XIX. i (1825) I. 609 The drowning man snatches at a side, like twig; . . . the messengers . . . catch hastily at . . . , 'Thy brother Benhadad'. 1748 RICHARDSON *Clarissa* VII. 12 A drowning man will catch at a straw, the proverb well says. 1848 THACKERAY *Vanity F.* xviii 'You fool, why do you catch at a straw?' calm good sense says to the man that is drowning.

Drown(ed, ing), *see also* Dog is d. (When), every one offers him drink; Drunk than d. (Better); Ewe is d. (When the) she's dead; Never was cat or dog d. that could see shore; Pour not water on d. mouse; Safe from the East Indies, d. in Thames; Water where the stirk d. (There was aye some).

Drug in the market, A.

1662 FULLER iv. 54 [He] made such a vent for Welsh cottons, that what he found drugs at home, he left dainties beyond the sea. 1760 MURPHY *Way to Keep Him* I A wife's a drug now; mere tar-water, with every virtue under the sun, but nobody takes it. 1840 HOOD *Up Rhine* 163 Quite a drug in the market.

Drum, Jack *or* Tom, *see* J. D.'s entertainment.

Drums beat, Where | laws are silent.

[CICERO *Pro Milone* 4. 10 *Silent enim leges inter arma.* For the laws are dumb in the midst of arms.] 1655-62 GURNALL *Chrn. in Armour* (1865) I. 553 The church is intended by Christ to be his house. . . . It is his kingdom; and how can his laws be obeyed, if all his subjects be in a hubbub one against another? *Inter arma silent leges*—laws are silent amid arms. 1721 KELLY 358. 1888 J. E. T. ROGERS *Econom. Interp. Hist.* (1894) II. xiii The laws . . . of economical progress, are as silent during warfare as those of the constitution are.

Drunk as a beggar.

1609 J. HALL *Discovery of a new world*, tr. J. Healey (ed. H. Brown) 55 As foxt as forty beggers. 1612 DEKKER *O per se o* M2v. 1616 DRAXE 49 As drunken as a Rat or Beggar.

Drunk as a fiddler.

1607 *The Puritain* v. i. 56 As drunck as a common fiddeler.

Drunk as a fish.

1629 JONSON *New Inn* III. i. 210. 1704 CONGREVE *Way of World* IV. ix.

Drunk as a lord, As.

1654 E. GAYTON *Festivious Notes on Don Quixote* 17 Drunke—as any Lord. 1659 SOMERS *Tracts* (1811) VII. 184 The proverb goes 'As drunk as a lord'. 1731 COFFEY *Devil to pay* I. ii I . . . am now come with a firm Resolution, . . . to be as richly drunk as a Lord. 1869 HAZLITT 61.

Drunk as a mouse, As.

a. 1310 in WRIGHT *Lyric P.* xxxix. 111 When that he is dronke as ase a dreynt mous, thenne we shule borewe the wac ate bayly. *c.* 1386 CHAUCER *W. of Bath's Prol.* 246 Thou comest hoom as dronken as a Mous. 1553 T. WILSON *Arte of Rhet.* (1580) 128 As if one had . . . kepte the Tauerne till he had been as dronke as a Ratte.

Drunk as a wheelbarrow, As.

1678 RAY 87. 1694 MOTTEUX *Rabelais* v. xxxix A . . . sottish Fellow, continually raddled, and as drunk as a Wheelbarrow.

Drunk as David's sow, As.

1652 *A Notable and pleasant History of . . . Hectors, Or, St. Nicholas Clerkes,* 11 As drunk as *David's* Sow. 1671 SHADWELL *Miser* IV (A) I am as drunk . . . as David's sow, as the saying is. 1720 GAY *New Similes* For though as drunk as David's sow, I love her still the better. 1836 MARRYAT *Midsh. Easy* xiv A parcel of fellows . . . who get as drunk as David's sow.

Drunk than drowned, You had better be.

1830 FORBY 430 . . . *i.e.* It is better to exceed in wine now and then, than to be constantly drinking largely of weak liquors.

Drunk, What you do when you are | you must pay for when you are dry (sober).

1721 KELLY 344 . . . The law makes drunkenness no excuse, but rather an aggravation.

Drunk, *see also* Ape d.; Ever d. ever dry; Killeth a man when he is d.

Drunkard alone, Let but the | and he will fall of himself.

1678 RAY *Adag. Hebr.* 407.

Drunkard's purse is a bottle, A.

1640 HERBERT 323.

Drunkard(s), *see also* Children (D.) and fools cannot lie.

Drunken days have all their to-morrows.

1875 SMILES *Thrift* 181 Drunken days have all their to-morrows, as the old proverb says.

Drunken folks seldom take harm.

1591 HARINGTON *Orl. Furioso* xxx. 13 (A) If fortune that helps frantike men and drunke Had not him safe conveyd. 1605 CHAPMAN, &c., *Eastw. Hoe* III. ii They say yet, 'drunken men never take harm'. This night will try the truth of that proverb. 1670 RAY 83.

Drunken man (men), *see* Heaven takes care of . . . d. m.; Stagger like d. m.

Drunkenness, *see* Soberness conceals, d. reveals.

Dry as a kex,[1] As.

1533 UDALL *Flowers for Latin speaking* (1560) U 2 As drie as a kixe. 1891 T. HARDY *Tess* (1892) 139 I should be as dry as a kex with travelling so far. [[1] The dry stem of certain herbaceous plants.]

Dry as dust, As.

[*c.* 1500 *Ludus Coventriae* xiv. 21 (1841) 123 Davy dry dust.] 1600 DEKKER *Shoem. Holiday* II. iii. *a.* 1633 G. HERBERT *Wks.* (Hutchinson) 135 Death is drie as dust.

Dry August and warm doth harvest no harm.

1573 TUSSER 128. 1732 FULLER no. 6209.

Dry bread at home is better than roast meat abroad.

1640 HERBERT 349.

Dry cough is the trumpeter of death, A.

16. . HOWELL *Lett.* (1903) III. 77 Mr. Watts is still troubled with coughing, and . . . as the Turk hath it, 'A dry cough is the trumpeter of death'. 1670 RAY 5.

Dry feet, warm head, bring safe to bed. (*See also* Keep your feet dry.)

1640 HERBERT 336.

Dry light is the best.

1625 BACON *Ess., Friendship* (Arb.) 175 Heraclitus saith well, in one of his Ænigmaes; *Dry light is ever the best.* . . . The Light, that a man receiueth, by Counsell from Another, is Drier, and purer, then that which commeth from his own Vnderstanding. 1907 S. LEE *Gt. Englishmen of 16th C.* 247 The dry light of reason is the only illuminant which permits men to see clearly phenomena as they are.

Dry May and a dripping June bring all things into tune, A.

1742 *An Agreeable Companion* 35 A dripping June Brings all Things in Tune. 1846 DENHAM 50 A good leak in June sets all in tune. 1883 ROPER 22. 1893 INWARDS 29. 1912 *Spectator* 28 Dec. 1094 'A dripping June sets all in tune', and on sandy soils not only farm crops but garden flowers do best in a wet summer.

'Dry meat, It is' | said the country fellow when he lost the hare.

1659 HEYLIN *Animadv.* in FULLER *Appeal* (1840) 496 But it is dry meat, said the country-fellow, when he lost the hare; and so let Calais pass for 'a beggarly town', and 'not worth the keeping', because we have no hope to get it.

Dry summer never made a dear peck, A.

1721 KELLY 8 . . . Though the straw in such years be short, yet the grain is good and hearty.

Dry (*adj.*), *see also* Keep your feet d.; Sow d. and set wet; Wish the burn d. because it weets our feet (We maunna).

Dry (-ies), (*verb*), *see* Nothing d. sooner than tears.

Dublin, *see* Limerick was, D. is, Cork shall be finest city.

Ducat, *see* know the value of d. (If you would know).

Duck in the mouth, To come home with a.

a. 1656 R. CAPEL in SPURGEON *Treas. Dav. Ps.* ix. 18 Money, which lying long in the bank, comes home at last with a duck in its mouth.

Duck swim ? Will a.

1842 s. LOVER *Handy Andy* iv 'What do you say, . . . will you dine with me ?' 'Will a duck swim ?' chuckled out Jack Horan. **1872** G. J. WHYTE-MELVILLE *Satanella* xxix 'Are you game for a day with the stag ?' Will a duck swim !' was the answer.

Duck will not always dabble in the same gutter, A.

1721 KELLY 45. **1732** FULLER no. 82.

Ducks and drakes of (or with), To make.

[= to throw away idly or carelessly.] *c.* **1600** *Timon* v. v I will make duckes and drakes with this my gold. . . . Before your fingers touch a piece thereof. **1768–74** TUCKER *Lt. Nat.* (1852) II. 164 A miser has it in his power to make ducks and drakes of his guineas. **1810** WELLINGTON in GURW. *Desp.* VII. 32 His Majesty's Government never intended to give over the British army to the Governors of this Kingdom to make ducks and drakes with.

Ducks fare well in the Thames, The.

1670 RAY 83.

Ducks have eaten up the dirt, Not till the.

1738 SWIFT (Dial. ii) 349 *Lady S.* When may we hope to see you again in London? *Sir J.* Why, madam, not till the ducks have eat up the dirt, as the children say.

Duck(s), *see also* (Dying) d. in thunder (Like a); Like a duke? like a d.; More rain . . . more water will suit d.; Morley's d., born without notion (Like); Nibbled to death by d. (As good be); Prate . . . but it's d. lays eggs; Take to . . . like d. to water; 'Time enough' lost the d.

Dudgeon-heft, *see* All is gone . . . (When), what avails dagger with d. ?

Dudman[1] and Ramehead[2] meet, When.

[i.e. never.] **1602** R. CAREW *Survey of Cornwall* (1769) 141 Amongst sundrie prouerbs, allotting an impossible time of performance, the *Cornish men* haue this one, When Ramehead and Dudman meet. **1662** FULLER (*Cornwall*) I. 307 'When Dudman and Ramehead meet'. These are two Forelands, well known to sailors, well nigh twenty miles asunder; and the prouerb passeth for the periphrasis of an impossibility. [1 Dodman Point, SW. of St. Austell. 2 Rame Head, the W. horn of Plymouth Bay.]

Due, *see* Loseth his d. gets not thanks

Duke Humphrey, *see* Dine with D. H.

Duke of Exeter's daughter.

[A rack invented by the Duke of Exeter in the reign of Henry VI.] **1642** FULLER *H. & P. State* IV. xiii (1841) 284 A daughter of the duke of Exeter invented a . . . cruel rack . . . often used, in the Tower of London, and commonly called . . . 'the duke of Exeter's daughter'. **1822** SCOTT *Nigel* xxv They threatened to make me hug the Duke of Exeter's daughter. **1878** J. GAIRDNER *Rich. III* iv. 125 Being . . . a prisoner in the Tower, in the severe embrace of 'the Duke of Exeter's daughter'.

Duke, *see also* Like a d. ? like a duck.

Dulcarnon,[1] I am at.

c. **1374** CHAUCER *Troylus* III. 930 I am, til God me bettré mindé sende, At Dulcarnon, right at my wittés ende. **1852** *N. & Q.* 1st Ser. v. 180 The other day . . . a person . . . declaring he was at his wit's end, exclaimed, 'Yes, indeed I am at Dulcarnon'. [1 From Arabic *two-horned*, applied to Euclid i. 47; hence a problem, difficulty.]

Dull as a beetle.

1520 WHITTINTON *Vulg.* (E.E.T.S.) 36. **1670** RAY 204.

Dull (Flat, Dead) as ditchwater, As.

1772 *Garrick Corr.* (1831) i. 465 (A) 'The Grecian Daughter's' being as dead as dishwater after the first act. **1865** DICKENS *Mut. Friend* III. x He'd be sharper than the serpent's tooth, if he wasn't as dull as ditchwater.

Dull, *see also* Work and no play makes . . . d. boy.

Dumb men get no lands.

c. **1390** GOWER *Conf. Amantis* vi. 318 For selden get a domb man londe, Take that proverbe, and understonde. **1406** HOCCLEVE *La Male Règle* 433 The prouerbe is 'the doumb man no lond getith'. **1670** RAY 83 . . . This is parallel to . . . Spare to speak and spare to speed.

Dumb, *see also* Speak with your gold and make other tongues d.

Dummie cannot (will not) lie.

1641 FERGUSSON 28 Dummie (a dumb man) cannot lie. **1721** KELLY 87 . . . Spoken to convince our servants, and others, of their ill usage of what has been among their hands: . . . my horse is lean, my utensils are broken, my grain is eaten. *Nempe res ipsa loquitur.*

Dumpling(s), *see* Devonshire d.; Norfolk d.

Dun [i.e. the horse] is in the mire.

[(a) Things are at a standstill or deadlock; (b) *Dun in the Myre*, an old Christmas game in which a heavy log was lifted and carried off by the players.] *c.* **1386** CHAUCER *Manciple's Prol.* 5 Ther gan our hoost for to lape and pleye, And seyde, sires, what Dun is in the Myre. *c.* **1440** CAPGRAVE *Life St. Kath.* II. 1046 For as wyth me, dun is in the myre, She hath me stoyned and broght me to a bay. *c.* **1529** SKELTON *Garland of Laurell* (Dyce) 1. 1433 Dun is in the myre, dame, reche me my spur. **1594–5** SHAKS. *Rom. & Jul.* I. iv. 41 If thou art Dun, we'll draw thee

from the mire. **1605–6** *K. Lear* II. ii. 5 *Osw.*
Where may we set our horses? *Kent.* I' the
mire. **1640** SHIRLEY *St. Patk. for Ireld.* (N.),
Then draw Dun out of the mire, And throw
the clog into the fire. **1905** *N. & Q.* 10th Ser.
III. 11 An old proverb 'Dun's in the mire'
. . . 'Dun' is evidently the name of a horse,
and the saying no doubt had its origin in the
dreadful state of the roads in early days.

Dun's the mouse.

[A quibble on the word *done*.] **1594–5** SHAKS.
Rom. & Jul. I. iv. 40 *Rom.* The game was
ne'er so fair, and I am done. *Mer.* Tut! dun's
the mouse, the constable's own word. **1600**
Sir John Oldcastle III. ii. Dunne is the
mouse. **1620** *Two Merry Milkmaids* (N.),
Why then 'tis done, and dun's the mouse,
and undone all the courtiers.

Dunder do gally the beans, The.

1678 RAY 347 The dunder do gally [affright]
the beans. *Somers.* Beans shoot up fast after
thunder-storms.

Dunmow bacon, and Doncaster daggers, Monmouth caps and Lemster wool, Derby ale and London beer.

1659 HOWELL *Eng. Prov.* 14/1.

Dunmow, *see also* Flitch of bacon from D.

Dunstable (road), Downright (As plain as).

1546 HEYWOOD II. v. 56 For were ye as
plaine as dunstable by waie. **1549** LATIMER
2nd Serm. bef. Edw. VI (Arb.) 56 Some that
walked in the kynges highe waye ordinarilye,
vprightlye, playne Dunstable waye. **1662**
FULLER (*Beds.*) I. 166 'As plain as Dunstable
Road'. . . . Applied to things plain and simple
. . . Such this road ; being broad and beaten.
1718 PRIOR *Conversation* 49 Sometimes to me
he did apply ; But Down-right Dunstable
was I. **1790** GROSE s.v. 'Beds' As plain as
Dunstable road. Downright Dunstable.
1824 SCOTT *Redg.* xxiv If this is not plain
speaking, there is no such place as downright
Dunstable in being.

Dunt(s), *see* Never draw dirk when d. will do ;
Words are but wind but d. the devil.

Dursley, You are a man of.

1639 *Berkeley MSS.* (1885) iii. 26 (A) Hee'l
proove, I thinke, a man of Durseley. **1662**
FULLER (*Glouc.*) I. 551 'You are a man of
Duresley.' It is taken for one that breaks his
word, and faileth in performance of his
promises ; parallel to *Fides Græca*, or *Fides
Punica.* Duresley is a market and clothing
town in this county. **1902–4** LEAN I. 88 . . .
Murray refers this to the sharping qualities
of the clothier hereabouts.

Dust in a man's (people's) eyes, To throw (cast).

[= to mislead by misrepresentation.] **1581**
PETTIE *Guazzo's Civ. Conv.* (1586) I. 276 They

do nothing else but raise a dust to doe out
their owne eies. **1612** *Crt. & Times Jas. I*
(1849) I. 169 To countermine his underminers,
and, as he termed it, to cast dust in their eyes.
1616 DRAXE 18 To cast dust into a mans eyes.
1767 FRANKLIN *Wks.* (1887) IV. 79 It required
a long discourse to throw dust in the eyes of
common sense. **1926** *Times* 22 Feb. 11/2 The
remedies proposed in the French report are
only an attempt to throw dust in people's
eyes.

Dust is on your feet, While the | sell what you have bought.

1678 RAY *Adag. Hebr.* 401 . . . The meaning
is that we should sell quickly (though with
light gaines) that we may trade for more.

Dust raised by the sheep does not choke the wolf, The.

1732 FULLER no. 4491. **1865** TRENCH *Poems;
Proverbs* xxii. 303 There is no ointment for
the wolf's sore eyes, Like clouds of dust
which from the sheep arise.

Dust, *see also* Blows in the d. (He that) ;
Dry as d. ; Grave (In the) d. and bones
jostle not ; Handful of d. will fill eye ; Kiss
(Lick) the d. ; March d. ; March sun causeth
d. ; Play off your d. ; Rain lays great d.
(Small) ; Shake the d. off one's feet.

Dutch courage.

[= bravery induced by drinking.] **1824** SCOTT
Redg. xvi 'Not the twentieth part of a drop',
said Nanty. 'No Dutch courage for me. . . .
If I live drunk, I should like to die sober.'
1873 H. SPENCER *Stud. Sociol.* viii. 188 A
dose of brandy, by stimulating the circula-
tion, produces 'Dutch courage'.

Dutch uncle, To talk to one like a.

[= to reprove sharply.] **1838** J. C. NEAL
Charcoal Sk. 201 If you keep a cutting
didoes, I must talk to you both like a Dutch
uncle. **1853** *N. & Q.* 1st Ser. VII. 65/2 In
some parts of America, when a person has
determined to give another a regular lecture,
he will often be heard to say 'I will talk to
him like a Dutch uncle'. **1897** CONRAD
Nigger of N. iv To-morrow I will talk to
them like a Dutch Uncle. A crazy crowd of
tinkers!

Dutch, *see also* Talk as D. as Daimport's dog.

Dutchman, I am a.

1848 A. SMITH *Chris. Tadpole* lviii If that
don't do it, I'm a Dutchman! **1866** LES.
STEPHEN in MAITLAND *Life & Lett.* (1906) x.
184 If I don't come out to the United
States next year, I'm a Dutchman.

Dutchman's anchor, It is like the | he has got it at home. (*Cf.* Bow (I have a good), &c.)

1823 J. COLLINS *Dict. Span. Prov.* 67 'I have
a good doublet in France' . . . is said to
ridicule persons who boast of having something which they cannot use or come at.

We say, ' It is like the Dutchman's anchor, he has got it at home.'

Dutchman, *see also* Irishman for a hand.

Dwarf on a giant's shoulders sees further of the two, A.

[L. *Pygmæi gigantum humeris impositi plus quam ipsi gigantes vident.*] **1621** BURTON *Anat. Mel.* Democ. to Rdr. (1651) 8 I say with Didacus Stella (in Luc. 10, tom. 2.) 'A dwarf standing on the shoulders of a giant may see farther than a giant himself'; I may . . . see farther than my predecessors. **1640** HERBERT (Gros.) no. 50. **1642** FULLER *Holy State* (1841) II. 6 Grant them [the moderns] dwarfs, yet stand they on giants' shoulders and may see further. **1895** STEPHENS *Life E. A. Freeman* II. 467 Arnold disparaged by men who . . . had by climbing upon Arnold's shoulders been enabled to see a little farther than Arnold himself.

Dwell at Rotheras, Every one cannot.

1659 HOWELL *Eng. Prov.* 21/2 . . . A delicate seat of the Bodmans in Herefordshire. **1790** GROSE s.v. 'Herefordshire'.

Dwell, Wherever a man | he shall be sure to have a thorn-bush near his door.

1639 CLARKE 165. **1678** RAY 209 . . . No place, no condition is exempt from all trouble. *Nihil est ab omni parte beatum.* [HORACE *Odes* 2. 16. 27 There is nothing that is blessed in every respect.] **1912** *Spectator* 27 July 137 *The Thorn Bush near the Door.* . . . This book is . . . [a] description of every day life in London.

Dwell in court must needs curry favour, Whoso will.

c. **1400** *Beryn* (E.E.T.S.) 1. 362 As þouʒe she had learned cury fauel[1] of some old frere. *c.* **1450** *Provs. of Wysdom* 91 Who so wyll in cowrt dwell, Nedis most he cory fauell.[1] **1616** DRAXE 68 Hee that will in Court dwell, must speake Hauell. [[1] curry-favell = one who solicits favour by flattery.]

Dwells next door to a cripple, He that | will learn to halt.

1579 LYLY *Euphues* (Arb.) 131 It is an olde Prouerbe that if one dwell the next doore to a cre[e]ple he will learne to hault, if one bee conuersant with an hipocrit, he wil soone endeuour to dissemble.

(Dying) duck in thunder (a thunder-storm), Like a.

1785 WOLCOT (P. Pindar) *Lyric Odes* vii. Wks. (1816) I. 68 Gaping upon Tom's thumb, with *me* in wonder, The rabble rais'd its eyes —like ducks in thunder. **1829–30** M. SCOTT *Tom Cring. Log* ix What are you turning your ear for, in that incomprehensible fashion, like a duck in thunder? **1863** KINGSLEY *Water Bab.* v He . . . turned up his eyes like a duck in thunder; for the water was up to his chin. **1880** J. PAYN *Confid. Agent* III. 161 Look less like a duck in a thunderstorm. *a.* **1911** GILBERT *Lost Bab Ballads* (1932) 59 He . . . rolled his eyes of blue As dying ducks in thunderstorms Are often said to do.

Dying, *see also* Past d. of her first child.

Dyke, *see* Earth big the d. (Let the); Leaps over the d. where lowest (Every one).

Dysart, *see* Salt to D. (Carry).

E

Eagles catch no flies.

[ERASM. *Ad. Aquila non captat muscas.*] **1586** PETTIE *Guazzo's Civ. Conv.* 95 That is the right act of a prince, and therefore it is well said, That the eagle catcheth not flies. **1655** FULLER *Ch. Hist.* III. viii (1868) I. 481 When any bishopric, . . . or good living, (*aquila non capit muscas!*) was like to be void, the pope . . . predisposed such places . . . as he pleased. **1786** MRS. PIOZZI *Anec. of S. Johnson* (1892) 76 With regard to slight insults . . . : 'They sting one (says he) but as a fly stings a horse; and the eagle will not catch flies.'

Eagles do not breed doves.

[HOR. *Carm.* 4. 4. 31 *Neque imbellem feroces progenerant aquilae columbam.*] **1593–4** SHAKS. *Titus Andron.* II. iii. 149 'Tis true! the raven doth not hatch a lark. **1613** BEAUM. & FL. *Hon. Man's F.* III. i Doves beget doves; and eagles, eagles, Madam: a citizen . . . seldom at the best proves a gentleman.

Eagles fly alone.

c. **1580** SIDNEY *First Arcadia* (Feuillerat) iv. 12 Egles wee see flye alone, and they are but sheepe which allway heard together. *a.* **1623** WEBSTER *Duch. of M.* v. ii Eagles commonly fly alone: they are crows, daws, and starlings that flock together.

Eagles, *see also* Carcase is (Wheresoever), e. gathered together.

Ear(s), *see* Dare not for his e.; Fields have eyes, woods e.; Harvest e. thick of hearing; In at one e.; Little pitchers have great e.; Nature has given two e., one tongue; Pair of e. draws hundred tongues; Play with the e. than tongue (Better); Set by the e.; Shake your e.; Tell you a tale and find you e.; Two e. to one tongue, hear twice as much as speak; Up to the e.; Walls have e.; Wide e. and short tongue.

Early bird catches the worm, The.

1636 CAMDEN 307. **1670** RAY 84. **1859** H.

KINGSLEY *Geof. Ham.* XXXI A man comes into your room at half-past seven, on a hot morning, . . . and informs you that the 'early bird gets the worm'. **1891** J. L. KIPLING *Beast & Man* 125 Where we should say 'The early bird catches the worm', the Indian rustic says, 'who sleeps late gets the bull-calf, he who rises early the cow-calf'—which is more valuable.

Early master, long (soon) knave.

c. **1350** *Douce MS. 52* no. 68 Erly master, longe knave. *c.* **1450** *Provs. of Wysdom* 1. 33 To erly mayster, the sonner knave. **1641** FERGUSSON 30 Early maister, lang knave. **1721** KELLY 95 *Early master, soon knave.* When a youth is too soon his own master, he will squander his patrimony, and so must turn servant.

Early pricks that will be a thorn, It.

c. **1350** *Douce MS. 52* no. 137 Hit is sone sharpe þat schal be a thorne. *c.* **1450** *Coventry Plays* (E.E.T.S.) 56 Yt ys eyrly scharp thatt wol be thorne. **1523** SKELTON *Garl. of Laurell* 1437 Wks. (Dyce) I. 418 It is sone aspyed where the thorne prikkith. *c.* **1557** *Jacob & Esau* I. ii. in HAZL. *O. E. P.* (1874) II. 196 Young it pricketh (folks do say), that will be a thorn, Esau hath been naught, ever since he was born. **1562** HEYWOOD 143 It prikth betimes, that shalbe a sharpe thorne. **1590** LODGE *Rosalynde* Wks. (1883) I. 18 What sirha, well I see earlie prickes the tree that will prooue a thorne. **1590-1** SHAKS. *3 Hen. VI* V. v. 13 What! can so young a thorn begin to prick? **1636** CAMDEN 295. **1721** KELLY 97 . . . Children soon shew their propensities and inclinations.

Early sow, early mow.

1639 CLARKE 233. **1721** KELLY 96 . . . The sooner a man sets about a business, the sooner he finds the effects of it.

Early to bed and early to rise, makes a man healthy, wealthy, and wise.

1523 FITZHERBERT *Husbandry* (E.D.S.) 101 Erly rysyng maketh a man hole in body, holer in soule, and rycher in goodes. **1599-1600** SHAKS. *Twelfth N.* II. iii. 3 Not to be a-bed after midnight is to be up betimes; and *diluculo surgere*, thou knowest,——. **1639** CLARKE 91. **1766** *Goody Two-Shoes* (3 ed.) II. i Ralph, the raven, composed the following verse, . . . 'Early to bed, and early to rise, Is the way to be healthy, and wealthy, and wise.' **1853** SURTEES *Sponge's Sport. T.* ix Early to bed and early to rise being among Mr. Sponge's maxims, he was enjoying the view . . . shortly after daylight.

Early up and never the nearer.

1546 HEYWOOD I. ii. 5 That they were earely vp, and neuer the nere. **1550** LATIMER *Last Serm. bef. Edw. VI* (P.S.) 275 Poor men put up bills every day, and never the near. **1601** MUNDAY & CHETTLE *Death of Earl of Huntington* F 4 Y'are earely up and yet are nere the neare. **1629** T. ADAMS *Serm.* (1861-2) I. 505 He is early up and never the nearer; saluting Christ in the morning but none of those that stayed with him.

Early wed, early dead.

1615 *The Cold Year, 1614* (*Old Bk. Collector's Miscellany* ed. Hindley ii. 8) Early bridals, make early burials. **1895** *N. & Q.* 8th Ser. VIII. 516.

Early, *see also* Get a name to rise e.; Plaints e. that plaints on his kail; Rises over e. that is hanged ere noon.

Earnest, *see* Mows may come to e.

Ears glow, If your | someone is talking of you.

c. **1374** CHAUCER *Troylus* II. 1021 And we shal speke of thee som-what, I trowe, when thou art goon, to do thyne eres glowe! **1546** HEYWOOD II. i Her ears might well glow, for all the town talked of her.

Ears, *see also* Ear(s).

Earth big[1] the dyke,[2] Let the.

1641 FERGUSSON 84 Of the earth mon the dyke be biggit. **1721** KELLY 235 . . . Let the expense that attends a thing, be taken out of the profit that it yields. [[1] build. [2] ditch.]

Earth, *see also* Pomp the e. covers; Six feet of e. make all equal; Wots not whether he bears the e.

Earthen pot must keep clear of the brass kettle, The.

[= the weaker must avoid a collision with the stronger.] **1586** GENEVA BIBLE, APOCRYPHA *Ecclesiasticus* xiii. 2 For howe agree the kettle and the earthern pot together: for if the one be smitten against the other, it shalbe broken. **1612-15** BP. HALL *Contempl.* XXI. v (1825) II. 133 Now see, what it is for thine earthen pitcher to knock with brass. Now, where is the man that would needs contest with Haman? **1732** FULLER no. 4494 **1822** SCOTT *Nigel* xi Buckingham is Lord of the Ascendant . . .; You are the vase of earth; beware of knocking yourself against the vase of iron. **1909** *Spectator* 8 May 745 A dispassionate explanation of the unfortunate consequences that would inevitably happen should the cracked earthen pot [Russia] come into contact with the iron vessel [Germany].

Ease, If you would be at | all the world is not.

1640 HERBERT 364.

Ease makes thief.

c. **1180** *Hali Meidenhad* 17 Eise makeð þeof. *c.* **1300** *Provs. of Hending* (ed. Schleich) in *Anglia* 51. 272 Wrothelich endit, þat liþir doth. *c.* **1350** *Douce MS. 52* no. 35 Ese makyth thefe.

Ease (*noun*), *see also* All men will please (He that) shall never find e.; Cap is better at e. than head; Honour and e. seldom bedfellows; Itch and e. can no man please; Pennyworth of e.; Sufferance (Of) cometh e.; Take one's e. in one's inn; Think of e.

but work on. World's wealth (If we have not) have world's e. *See also* At ease.

Ease (*verb*), *see* Nothing is (Where), little thing doth e.

Easier (sooner) said than done.

c. 1450 *Religious and Love Poems* [E.E.T.S., cited in Arden ed. of *3 Henry VI* III. ii. 90] Better saide thanne doon. 1483 *Vulg.* (1529) C 8 *Facilius multo est dictu quam factu* It is easyer to saye than to do. 1519 HORMAN *Vulg.* (James) 119. 1546 HEYWOOD II. v. 60 That is (quoth she) sooner said then doone, I dréede. 1681 ROBERTSON *Phraseol. Generalis* 471 'Tis more difficult then you think for; sooner said then done. 1824 MOIR *Mansie W.* ix Easier said than done, howsoever. 1884 BLACKMORE *Tommy Up.* xviii This was easier said than done.

Easier to, *see under significant words following.*

Easily done is soon believed, That which is.

1664 CODRINGTON 216. 1670 RAY 8.

East Indies, *see* Safe from the E. I. and drowned in Thames.

East or west, home is best.

1855 BOHN 347.

East, *see also* Longer e. shorter west; Too far e. is west; Wind's in the e. (When), neither good for man nor beast; Wind's in the e. on Candlemas Day (When). . . .

Easter, At | let your clothes be new, or else be sure you will it rue.

1592 SHAKS. *Rom. & Jul.* III. i (A) Didst thou not fall out with a tailor for wearing his new doublet before Easter? 1875 DYER *Brit. Pop. Cust.* (1900) 160 Poor Robin says: 'At Easter let your clothes be new, Or else be sure you will it rue.'

Easter so longed for is gone in a day.

1642 TORRIANO 84. 1658 *Comes Facundus* 193. 1659 HOWELL *Eng. Prov.* 20/2.

Easter, *see also* Short Lent that must pay at E.; Warrant you for egg at E.

Easterly wind is very unkind, A right.

1855 BOHN 299.

Easterly winds and rain bring cockles[1] here from Spain.

1846 DENHAM 12. [[1] A weed of the cornfields, or a disease which turns the corn black.]

Easy as lying, As.

1600–1 SHAKS. *Hamlet* III. ii. 373 'Tis as easy as lying. 1890 J. PAYN *Burnt Million* xl 'As easy as lying', is a common proverb, but it must have been invented by an optimist.

Easy come, easy go. (*See also* Lightly come, &c., Quickly come, &c.)

1832–8 S. WARREN *Diary of L. Phys.* xxii 'Easy come, easy go', is . . . characteristic of rapidly acquired commercial fortunes. 1861 H. SPENCER *Education* ii 'Easy come easy go', is a saying as applicable to knowledge as to wealth.

Easy to fall into a trap, but hard to get out again, 'Tis.

1580 LYLY *Euph. & his Eng.* Wks. (Bond) II. 157 It is easie to fall into a Nette, but hard to get out. 1732 FULLER no. 5072.

Easy to keep the castle that was never besieged.

1721 KELLY 96 Eith[1] to keep the castle that was never besieged. [[1] easy.]

Easy to praise poverty than to bear it, It is more.

1855 BOHN 432. *Ital.*

Easy to threaten than to kill, It is more.

1855 BOHN 432. *Ital.*

Easy to, *see also under significant words following.*

Eat a buttered fagot, He that would (must) | let him go to Northampton.

1662 FULLER (*Northampt.*) II. 501 'He that must eat a buttered fagot, let him go to Northampton'. Because it is the dearest town in England for fuel, where no coals can come by water, and little wood doth grow on land. 1670 RAY 328.

Eat a good dinner, He that would | let him eat a good breakfast.

1678 RAY 124.

Eat a hen in Janivere; If one knew how good it were to | had he twenty in the flock, he'd leave but one to go with the cock.

1670 RAY 213.

Eat a peck of dirt (*or* ashes) before he dies, Every man must.

1639 CLARKE 165 You must eat a peck of ashes ere you die. 1670 RAY 57. 1738 SWIFT (Dial. i) 337 Poh! you must eat a peck of dirt before you die. 1883 PAYN *Thicker than Water* xlix. It is a sin of omission, . . . a portion of that peck of dirt which we are all said to eat in our lives without knowing it.

Eat a peck of salt, To.

1600 DEKKER, &c. *Patient Grissill* A 3[v] I thinke I shall not eate a pecke of salt: I shall not liue long sure.

Eat a pudding at home, If you | the dog shall have the skin.

1623 CAMDEN 272.

Eat above the tongue, like a calf, You.

1678 RAY 348.

Eat and eat, You | but you do not drink to fill you.

1670 RAY 33 You eat and eat, but you do not drink to fill you. That much drinking takes off the edge of the Appetite to meat, we see by experience in great drinkers, who for the most part do (as we say) but pingle[1] at their meat and eat little. [[1] trifle.]

Eat, and welcome; fast, and heartily welcome.

1678 RAY 84. **1721** KELLY 98 *Eat and welcome, fast and twice as welcome.* A jocose invitation to our known friend to eat. **1732** FULLER no. 1355.

Eat another yard of pudding first, You must.

1830 FORBY 428 . . . *i.e.* You must wait till you grow older.

Eat at pleasure, drink by measure.

c. **1532** SIR ADRIAN FORTESCUE no. 24 Eate & drink by measor, and defye thy leche. **1611** COTGRAVE s.v. 'Pain'. **1670** RAY 38 . . . This is a French proverb, Pain tant qu'il dure, vin à mesure, and they themselves observe it.

Eat his part on Good Friday, He may.

1546 HEYWOOD I. xi. 29 He maie his parte on good fridaie eate, And fast neuer the wurs, for ought he shall geate. **1596-8** SHAKS. *K. John* I. i. 234 Sir Robert might have eat his part in me Upon Good Friday and ne'er broke his fast.

Eat me with (without) salt, He could. (*Cf.* next proverb.)

1580 J. BARET *Alveary* O 33 Odium agreste . . . A Prouerbe vsed, when a man hateth one euen with a deadlie hate, and as our phrase of speach is, He could willingly eate his heart with salt. **1721** KELLY 157 *He could eat me but[1] salt.* . . . The man hates me vehemently. **1738** SWIFT (Dial. i) 338 Does not miss look as if she could eat me without salt? [[1] without.]

Eat my heart with garlic, He could.

1670 RAY 173 . . . That is, he hates me mortally.

Eat of the goose that shall graze on your grave, He hopes to.

1509 A. BARCLAY *Ship of Fools* (1874) II. 170 Suche as they moste gladly dede wolde haue Etyth of that gose that graseth on theyr graue. **1599** PORTER *Angry Wom. Abingd.* I.

ii (Merm.) 113 'The goose that grazeth on the green', quoth he, 'May I eat on, when you shall buried be!' **1639** CLARKE 236.

Eat one's heart (out), To.

[*Il.* 6. 202 *Ὃν θυμὸν κατέδων.* ERASM. *Ad. Cor ne edito.*] **1539** TAVERNER f. 54 (A) Eate not thy harte (that is to saye) consume not thy selfe wyth cares. **1579** LYLY *Euphues* (Arb.) 148 Not to eate our heartes: that is, that wee shoulde not vexe our selues with thoughts. **1596** SPENSER *F. Q.* I. ii. 6 He could not rest; but did his stout heart eat. **1616** DRAXE 125 He eateth his owne heart. **1621** BURTON *Anat. Mel.* I. ii. II. vi (1836) 159 Achilles eating of his own heart in his idleness, because he might not fight. **1625** BACON *Ess., Friendship* (Arb.) 171 The Parable *of Pythagoras* is darke, but true; *Cor ne edito*; *Eat not the Heart.* [Quoted by PLUTARCH *De Educ. Puer.* 17.] **1850** TENNYSON *In Mem.* cviii. 3 I will not eat my heart alone.

Eat one's words, To.

1571 GOLDING *Calvin on Ps. lxii. 12* God eateth not his word when he hath once spoken. *a.* **1618** RALEIGH *Rem.* (1644) Nay wee'le make you confesse . . . and eat your own words. **1670** RAY 173.

Eat (a person) out of house and home, To.

c. **1410** *Towneley Plays* (E.E.T.S.) xiii, 1. 244 Bot were I not more gracyus and rychere befar, I were eten outt of howse and of harbar. **1509** A. BARCLAY *Ship of Fools* (1874) II. 93 And ete theyr mayster out of hous Deuourynge his good tyll he be pore and bare. **1597-8** SHAKS. *2 Hen. IV* II. i. 80 Al I have, he hath eaten me out of house and home. **1712** ARBUTHNOT *John Bull* (1755) 53 John's family was like to be eat out of house and home. **1832** HT. MARTINEAU *Life in Wilds* iv. 54 They would soon eat us out of house and home.

Eat the devil as the broth he is boiled in, As good.

1545 BRINKLOW *Lamentacyon* (E.E.T.S.) 89 (A) If it be so that God, through the kynge, hath caste out the deuell out of this realme, and yet both he and we soppe of the broth in which the deuell was soden. **1670** RAY 80. **1738** SWIFT (Dial. ii) 347 *Sir J.* I seldom eat it . . .; however, . . . send me a little of the crust. *Ld. Spark.* You had as good eat the devil as the broth he is boiled in.

Eat (Have) the fruit, He that would | must climb the tree.

1721 KELLY 141. **1732** FULLER no. 2366.

Eat the kernel, He that will | must crack the nut.

[PLAUTUS *Curc.* 1. 1. 55 *Qui a nuce nucleum esse vult, frangit nucem.*] *c.* **1500** in *Antiq. Repertory* (1809) iv. 416 (A) And yf ye wolde the swetnes haue of the kyrnell, Be content to byte vpon the harde shell. **1539** TAVERNER 47 He that will eat the kernel out of the nut, breaketh the nut. He that loke for profit, may not flee labours. **1670** RAY 84 . . . *Qui nucleum esse vult nucem frangat oportet.* No gains without pains. **1831** MACAULAY *Ess., Johnson* (1872) 183 It is certain that those who will not crack the shell of history will never get at the kernel.

Eat the (or one's) leek, To.

1598–9 SHAKS. *Hen. V* V. i. 10 He is come to me . . . and pid me eat my leek. **1835** DISRAELI *Let.* 20 Aug. in *Cor. Sister* (1886) 43 It was whispered the Whigs meant to swallow the Corporation leek. **1859** *All Year Round* No. 29. 61 The Welshmen very humbly ate their leek. **1902** G. W. E. RUSSELL *Coll. & Recol.* 2 Ser. (1909) 118 A politician who had once professed Republicanism was made to eat the leek in public before he could be admitted to the Cabinet.

Eat thy meat, and drink thy drink, and stand thy ground, old Harry.

1678 RAY 343.

Eat till you sweat and work till you freeze.

a. **1570** *Marriage of Wit and Science* (Shaks. Soc.) 12. **1579** LYLY *Euphues* (Arb.) 111 Neither was I much vnlyke these Abbaie lubbers in my lyfe . . . which laboured till they were colde, eat till they sweat, and lay in bed til their boanes aked. **1580** LYLY *Euph. & his Eng.* Wks. (Bond) I. 251. **1721** KELLY 100 . . . An upbraiding speech to lazy servants who love meat better than work. **1732** FULLER no. 2424.

Eat to live.

c. **1410** *Secreta Secret.* tr. (E.E.T.S.) 67 I will ete so that y leue and noght lyf that y ete. **1577** NORTHBROOKE *Dicing, &c.* (Shaks. Soc.) 40 Thou lyuest not to eate, butte eat as thou mayest lyue. **1621** BURTON *Anat. Mel.* II. ii. I. ii (1651) 235 Eat and live, as the proverb is, . . . *that only repairs man which is well concocted, not that which is devoured.* **1733** FRANKLIN May Eat to live, and not live to eat.

Eat well is drink well's brother.

1721 KELLY 95 . . . Spoken when we have eaten well, and taken a large draught after. **1732** FULLER no. 1357.

Eat white bread? When shall we | When the puttock is dead.

[*Puttock* = a kite; hence, a greedy fellow.] **1629** T. ADAMS *Serm.* (1861–2) II. 329 We may sing, or rather sigh one to another, as little children chant in the streets: 'When shall we eat white bread? When the puttock is dead': when there is not a sacrilegious lawyer left.

Eat your brown bread first, It is a good thing to.

1830 FORBY 429 . . . *i.e.* If you are unfortunate in the early part of life, you may hope for better success in future.

Eat your cake and have your cake (it), You cannot.

1546 HEYWOOD II. ix. 79 I trow ye raue, Wolde ye bothe eate your cake, and haue your cake? **1611** DAVIES *Prov.* 272 'A man cannot eat his cake and have it still'. *a.* **1633** HERBERT *The Size* Wouldst thou both eat thy cake and have it? **1738** SWIFT (Dial. i) 341 *Lady A.* She was handsome in her time; but she cannot eat her cake and have her cake. *a.* **1763** SHENSTONE *Detached Thoughts* 'A person cannot eat his cake and have it' is, as Lord Shaftesbury observed, a proper answer to many splenetic people. **1907** A. C. BENSON *From Coll. Window* (ed. 4) 35 There still remains the intensely human instinct, which survives all the lectures of moralists, the desire to eat one's cake and also to have it.

Eat your nails, You had as good.

1678 RAY 241. **1738** SWIFT (Dial. i) 334 *Miss.* Mr. Neverout, . . . say a word more and you had as good eat your nails.

Eaten a bear-pie, He that hath | will always smell of the garden.[1]

1659 HOWELL *Eng. Prov.* 18/1. **1678** RAY 66. [[1] bear-garden.]

Eaten a horse, and the tail hangs out at his mouth, He hath.

1678 RAY 74.

Eaten a snake, She hath.

1519 HORMAN *Vulg.* (James) 50 Thou hast eate an edders skyn. **1580** LYLY *Euph. & his Eng.* (Arb.) 368 Therefore, hath it growen to a Prouerb in *Italy*, when on[e] seeth a woman striken in age to look amiable, he saith she hath eaten a snake. **1630** DEKKER *Hon. Whore,* Pt. II. I. ii (Merm.) 202 *Hip.* Scarce can I read the stories on your brow, which age hath writ there; you look youthful still. *Orl.* I eat snakes, my lord. **1639** CLARKE 166.

Eaten (swallowed) a stake, He hath.

1546 HEYWOOD I. xi. 29 How be it for any great courtesie he doth make, It séemth the gentill man hath eaten a stake. *a.* **1637** JONSON *Underwoods, Charis* ix. Wks. (1903) III. 283 Drest, you still for man should take him, And not think h' had eat a stake. **1670** RAY 271 He hath swallowed a stake, he cannot stoop.

Eaten bread is (soon) forgotten.

1599 MINSHEU h 4ᵛ. **1623** CAMDEN 268. **1639** CLARKE 169. **1890** CHADWICK *Comment. on Exod.* xvi The bitter proverb that eaten bread is soon forgotten must never be true of the Christian.

Eaten his bed straw, To look as if he had.

1678 RAY 286.

Eaten the hen's rump, He hath

1813 RAY 191 . . . *Ha mangiato il cul della*

gallina.—Ital. Said of a person who is full of talk.

Eaten your dinner off the floor, You might have.

1864 J. PAYN *Lost Sir Massingb.* xxxii [A] spotless kitchen, so exquisitely clean that you might, as the phrase goes, 'have eaten your dinner off the floor'.

Eaters, *see* Nice e. seldom meet with good dinner.

Eating and drinking, He was an ingenious man that first found out.

1738 SWIFT (Dial. ii) 346 Well, he was an ingenious man that first found out eating and drinking.

Eating and drinking takes away one's stomach.

1611 COTGRAVE s.v. 'Mangeant' Eating and drinking will take away any mans stomack. **1670** RAY 84. **1738** SWIFT (Dial. ii) 345 *Lady A.* Well; this eating and drinking takes away a body's stomach. **1785** GROSE *Dict. Vulg. T.* s.v. 'Damper' (A) Eating and drinking being, as the proverb wisely observes, apt to take away the appetite.

Eating and drinking wants but a beginning.

1721 KELLY 98.

Eating and scratching wants but a beginning.

1721 KELLY 286 *Scarting and eating wants but a beginning.* Spoken when people eat more than they thought they could, or to persuade people of weak stomachs to begin. **1732** FULLER no. 5158 To eat and to scratch a man need but begin. **1738** SWIFT (Dial. ii) 344 They say, eating and scratching wants but a beginning: . . . I'll help myself to . . . veal.

Eating, *see also* Often and little e. makes fat; Shameful leaving worse than shameful e.

Eats his cock alone, Who | must saddle his horse alone.

1599 MINSHEU (1623) 2 T 2ᵛ. **1640** HERBERT 333.

Eats least eats most, He that.

a. **1633** HERBERT *Wks.* ed. Hutchinson 295 *He that will eat much, let him eat little* ; because by eating little he prolongs his life.

Eats most porridge, He that | shall have most meat.

1732 FULLER no. 2092.

Eats the calf in the cow's belly, He.

1642 FULLER *H. & P. State* iii. ix (1841) 163 The law of good husbandry forbids us to eat a kid in the mother's belly,—spending our pregnant hopes before they be delivered. **1721** KELLY 138 . . . Applied to them who spend their rent before it be due. **1875** SMILES *Thrift* 277 Interest . . . goes on increasing until . . . it reaches . . . one hundred per cent. This is what is called 'eating the calf in the cow's belly'.

Eats the hard shall eat the ripe, He that.

1640 HERBERT 326.

Eats the king's goose shall be choked with the feathers, He that.

1629 T. ADAMS *Serm.* (1861–2) ii. 507 What family, that hath had but a finger in these sacrileges, hath not been ruinated by them? . . . Remember the proverb: 'He that eats the king's goose shall have the feathers stick in his throat seven years after.' **1670** RAY 15.

Eats the meat, let him pick the bone, He who.

1855 BOHN 399. *Span.*

Eat(s, en), ate, *see also* Apple going to bed; Ass that brays most e. least; Bit that one e., no friend makes; Blind that e. his marrow; Cats e. what hussies spare; Clothe thee warm, e. little; Humble pie; Hungry he could e. a horse; Leeks in Lide; Looks as big as if e. bull beef; Never ate flesh (He that); Never be ashamed to e.; Peas with the King; Work (He that will not) shall not e.

Ebal, *see* Creep into E.

Ebb will fetch off what the tide brings in, The.

1587 CHURCHYARD *Trag. Card. Wolsey* (Dent) 283 Men . . . think all is their own they have in hold. Well, let them say and think what thing they please, This weltering world both flows and ebbs like seas. **1664** CODRINGTON 216. **1670** RAY 26 The tide will fetch away what the ebb brings. **1732** FULLER no. 4495.

Eden (river), *see* Uter-Pendragon.

Edenhall, *see* Luck of E.

Edge, *see* Fall back fall e.

Edged tools, *see* Children and fools must not play with e. t.; Jesting with e. t. (Ill).

Educate our masters, We must.

1867 ROBERT LOWE *Sp. in H. of Commons,* 15 July I believe it will be absolutely necessary that you should prevail on our future masters to learn their letters [popularized as above]. **1871** FROUDE *Short Stud.* Ser. II, on Progress III 'We must educate our masters', said Mr. Lowe sarcastically.

Eel in a sandbag, He is as much out of his element as an.

1600 JONSON *Cynthia's Revels* ii. v. 24 No

better then a dish of eeles in a sand-bagge. **1732** FULLER no. 1912.

Eels, He that will catch | must disturb the flood.

1594 LIPSIUS *6 Books of Politicks* tr. Jones R 1 As Aristophanes saith, it is good catching of Eeles, when the water is stirred. **1607** *Lingua* I. i.

Eel(s), *see also* Breed in the mud (All that) not e.; Hide an e. in sack (Cannot); Hold an e. by tail; Mud chokes no e.; Nimble as e.; Nothing when you are used to it, as e. said; Put your hand in creel and take out adder or e.; Slippery as e.; Witham e.

Eelskins, *see* Merchant of.

Effect speaks, the tongue needs not, The.

1640 HERBERT 350.

Effect, *see also* Cause (take away) and e. must cease.

Efts, *see* Breed in the mud (All that) not e.

Egg and the hen, To have both the.

1573 SANDFORD (1576) 221 There are men in the worlde, that wyll have the egge and the hen. **1578** FLORIO *First Fruites* f. 33 There be many that wyl have both the egge and the hen. **1629** *Book of Meery Riddles* Prov. 118.

Egg, and to bed, An.

1639 CLARKE 113. **1732** FULLER no. 594.

Egg, But one | and that addled.

1732 FULLER no. 1031. **1823** COLLINS 14 Praise thyself chick, thou hast laid an egg, and that a bad one.

Egg to the apples, From the.

[HORACE *Sat.* 1. 3. 6 *Ab ovo usque ad mala: i.e.* from the first to the last dish.] **1580** LYLY *Euph. & his Eng.* Wks. (Bond) II.216 To talke of other thinges in that Court wer to bring Egges after apples. **1616** WITHALS 533 From the beginning to the end: *Ab ovo usque ad mala.* **1619** J. FAVOUR *Antiquity* 595 Let vs repeate, not *ab ouo, ad malum,* from the egge to the apple, but *a nido ad malum.* **1639** CLARKE 3. **1848** BROS. MAYHEW *Image of his Father* ii. 16 'Let me hear all about it, as the Latin phrase runs, *ab ovo usque ad mala*—from beginning to end', said the doctor.

Egg will be in three bellies in twenty-four hours, An.

1678 RAY 131. **1732** FULLER no. 1361.

Egging, *see* Ill e. ill begging.

Eggs, To tread (walk) upon.

[= to walk warily.] **1607** T. HEYWOOD *Wom. K. Kindness* IV. v (Merm.) 152 *Frank.* Tread softly, softly. *Nic.* I will walk on eggs this pace. *a.* **1734** NORTH *Ld. Guilford* (1808) I. 245 This gave him occasion . . . to find if any slip had been made (for he all along trod upon eggs). **1862** CALVERLEY *Verses & Transl.* Charades vi Each treading carefully about, as if he trod on eggs.

Eggs come to be fried, When the.

1620 SHELTON *Quix.* IV. x (1908) II. 26 It shall be perceived at the frying of the eggs, I mean that you shall see it when master inkeeper's worship . . . shall demand the loss and damage. **1823** COLLINS 26 'You will find it out when you are about to fry the eggs'.— A thief, . . . having stolen a frying-pan, was met by the master of the house . . . who asked him his business there; he answered, 'You will know it when you go to fry the eggs'.

Eggs for money, To take.

[= to be put off with something worthless.] **1604** R. DALLINGTON *View of France* M 1ᵛ The [French] Cauallery giues a furious onset at the first charge: but after that first heate, they will take egges for their money. **1610–11** SHAKS. *Wint. T.* I. ii. 161 Mine honest friend, Will you take eggs for money? **1670** G. H. *Hist. Cardinals* II. i. 130 Contented to take Eggs (as it were) for their money.

Eggs in one basket, To have (put) all your.

[= to risk all on a single venture. *Cf.* **1617** J. SWETNAM *School of Defence* 56 He is a foole which will adventure all his goods in one ship.] **1710** S. PALMER *Moral Essays on Prov.* 344 Don't venture all your Eggs in One Basket. **1874** WHYTE-MELVILLE *Uncle John* xxvii 'May I carry your basket all my life?' If you'll put all your eggs in it, yes', answered Annie boldly. **1894** LD. AVEBURY *Use of Life* iii Do not put too many eggs in one basket. However well you may be advised, . . . something may occur to upset all calculations.

Eggs, He that would have | must endure the cackling of hens.

1670 RAY 120 Erasmus saith, they commonly say, He that would have eggs, must endure the cackling of hens. It is I suppose a Dutch proverb. **1721** KELLY 223 *I would not have your cackling for your egg.* I would not have your trouble and noise for all the advantage you bring me.

Eggs on the spit, I have.

1598 JONSON *Ev. Man in Humour* III. iii 1 have eggs on the spit; I cannot go yet, sir. **1678** RAY 241 . . . I am very busie. Egges if they be well roasted require much turning. **1711** SWIFT *Jrnl. to Stella* 27 Dec. We have eggs on the spit, I wish they may not be addle.¹ [¹ rotten.]

Eggs to fry, I have other.

1659 HOWELL *Eng. Prov.* 12/2.

Egg(s), *see also* Addled e. as idle bird (As good be); Apple, an e., and a nut; Better an e. to-day; Break the e. in pocket; Cackle often but never lay e; Comes in with his five e.; Curate's e. (Like the); Dow (He will never), e. nor bird; Dress an e. and give the offal; Drink as much

after an e. as after ox; Evil crow, evil e.;
Fool to roast e. (Set a); Full as an e. of
meat; Give him the other half e.; Good e.
nor bird (Neither); Hen e. goes to the ha'
to bring goose e.; Never take a stone to
break e.; Omelets; Peeled e. (Come to a);
Reason in roasting of e.; Set my house on
fire to roast e.; Shave an e. (Hard to);
Sure as e. is e.; Warrant you for an e. at
Easter; Wild goose never laid tame e.;
Won with the e. and lost with shell.

Egg-shell, see Sail over the sea in e. (Hard to);
Truss up his wit in e. (You may).

Eglinton, Earl of, see God send us some
money.

Egypt, see Corn in E.; Enchantments to E.;
Riches of E. are for foreigners.

Egyptians, see Spoil the E.

Eight(s), see Four E.

Eighth of June it rain, If on the | it foretells a wet harvest men sain.

1732 FULLER no. 6204.

Elbow-grease, It smells of.

1616 WITHALS 562. **1638** J. CLARKE Phraseol.
Puerilis F 3ᵛ. **1670** RAY 173.

Elbow grease gives the best polish.

1672 MARVELL Rehearsal Transpr. I. v Two
or three brawny fellows in a corner with meer
ink and elbow-grease do . . . harm. **1823**
GALT Entail viii He has . . . dintit ma . . .
table past a' the power o' bees-wax and
elbow grease to smooth. **1830** FORBY 431 . . .
i.e. hard rubbing makes furniture look
brighter; generally industry is the surest
road to success.

Elbow(s), see also Broken her e. (She hath);
Eye nor my e. (Neither my); Out at e.;
Rub the e.; Scratch my breech, I'll claw
your e.; Shake the e.; Spring in his e.;
Touch your eye but with your e. (Never).

Elden Hole needs filling.

1670 RAY 173 . . . Spoken of a liar. Elden-
hole is a deep pit in the Peak of Derbyshire.

Elder's white, When | brew and bake a peck; when elder's black, brew and bake a sack.

1678 RAY 252. Somerset.

Element, see Speak ill of others is fifth e.

Elephant, see Fly into an e. (Changes a).

Ell¹ and tell² is good merchandise.

1721 KELLY 95 . . . The best market is to get
ready money for your wares. [¹ ell-wand.
² to count out money.]

Ell, see also Inch in a miss; Inch is as good as
e.; Measure with long (short) e.

Elm has its man, Every.

1928 Times 29 Nov. 10/5 Owing to the
frequency with which this tree sheds its
branches, or is uprooted in a storm, it has
earned for itself a sinister reputation. 'Every
elm has its man' is an old country saying.

Elm, see also Ask pears of an e.

Eloquence, see Love and business teach e.

Emperor of Germany, The | is the King of kings; the King of Spain, king of men; the King of France, king of asses; the King of England, the king of devils.

1647 WARD Simple Cobler 51 There is a
quadrobulary saying, which passes current in
the Westerne World, That the Emperour is
King of Kings, the Spaniard, King of Men,
the French, King of Asses, the King of
England, King of Devils. **1786** WOLCOT (P.
Pindar) Lousiad iii. Wks. (1816) I. 191 I do
not vish myself more greater efils—A king of
Englis be a king of defils.

Empty hands no hawks allure.

[c. **1175** J. OF SALISBURY Polycraticus v. x
Veteri celebratur proverbio: Quia vacuae
manus temeraria petitio est.] c. **1386**
CHAUCER Reeve's T. 214 With empty hand,
men may none haukes tulle [allure]. c. **1430**
LYDGATE Minor Poems (Percy Soc.) 174 With
empty hand may noon haukys lure, And lyke
the audience, so uttir the language. c. **1530**
H. RHODES Bk. Nurture 740 in Babees Bk.
102 For empty fystes, men vse to say, cannot
the Hawke retayne. **1546** HEYWOOD II. v. 54
He hath his haukes in The mew . . . but make
ye sure, With emptie handes men maie no
haukes allure. **1612** WEBSTER White Devil III.
ii 'Tis gold must such an instrument procure;
With empty fist no man doth falcons lure.
1869 HAZLITT 151 Haggard hawks mislike
an empty hand.

Empty purse causes a full heart, An.

1600 DEKKER Old Fortunatus I. ii If his belly
be emptie, his heart is full. **1734** FIELDING
Don Quix. in Eng. I. vi (A).

Empty purse fills the face with wrinkles, An.

1616 DRAXE 161. **1670** RAY 22. **1736** BAILEY
Dict. s.v. 'Purse' (A).

Empty purse that is full of other men's money, That is but an.

1678 RAY 194. **1732** FULLER no. 4352 (with
'folks' for 'men's').

Empty sack cannot stand upright, An.

1642 TORRIANO 90 Sacco vuoto non può star
in piedi. An emptie sack cannot stand upright: NOTA. Applied to such as either pinch
themselves, or are pincht by hard fortune.
1758 FRANKLIN P. Rich. Alm. in ARBER
Eng. Garner v. 584 Poverty often deprives

a man of all spirit and virtue. *'Tis hard for an Empty Bag to stand upright!* **1896** LOCKER-LAMPSON *My Confid.* 395 Gibbs . . . by this artifice . . . made a hundred per cent . . . Gibbs was a needy man, and . . . would often say, 'It's hard for an empty sack to stand upright'.

Empty the baby with the bath, To.

1944 G. B. SHAW *Everybody's Political What's What?* 172 When changing we must be careful not to . . . in mere reaction against the past.

Empty vessels make the greatest sound.

1579 LYLY *Euphues* (Arb.) 45 The emptie vessell giueth a greater sound then the full barrell. **1598-9** SHAKS. *Hen. V* IV. iv. 73 I did never know so full a voice issue from so empty a heart: but the saying is true, 'The empty vessel makes the greatest sound'. **1603** HOLLAND tr. *Plut. Morals* 159 Like empty vessels, void of sense and full of sound. **1612-15** BP. HALL *Contempl.* XIII. i (1825) I. 370 Those vessels yield most sound, that have the least liquor. **1707** SWIFT *Facult. of Mind* Wks. (1856) II. 285 I have always observed that your empty vessels sound loudest.

Empty, *see also* Better an e. house; Fill the mouth with e. spoons; Killing a crow with e. sling.

Enchantments to Egypt.

1853 TRENCH III. 68 The Rabbis [said]: *Enchantments to Egypt,* Egypt being of old accounted the head-quarters of all magic.

End crowns all (*or,* the work), The.

[L. *Finis coronat opus.*] **1590-1** SHAKS. *2 Hen. VI* V. ii. 28 *La fin couronne les œuvres.* **1592** KYD *Span. Trag.* II. vi *Rev.* Thou talk'st of harvest, when the corn is green: The end is crown of every work well done. **1601-2** SHAKS. *Troil. & Cres.* IV. v. 223 The end crowns all, And that old common arbitrator, Time, Will one day end it. **1602-3** *All's Well* IV. iv. 35 *All's well that ends well:* still the fine's the crown; What e'er the course, the end is the renown. **1614-16** *Times Whistle* (E.E.T.S.) 130 Successe by the event is knowne, the end Doth every action praise, or discommend. **1615** CHAPMAN *Od.* v. 58 But th' end shall crown all.

End justifies the means, The.

[**1650** JESUIT HERMANN BUSENBAUM *Medulla theol. Cum finis est licitus, etiam media sunt licita.*] **1721** PRIOR *Hans. C.* (1858) 88 What if to spells I had recourse, 'Tis but to hinder something worse! The end must justify the means. **1820** SCOTT *Abbot* xii It is in the cause of Heaven that I command them to embrace, . . . the end, sister, sanctifies the means we must use. **1897** C. C. KING *Story Brit. Army* 341 The districts annexed, and righteously governed, had recently . . . been 'huge cockpits of slaughter'. The end here unquestionably justified the means. **1907** W. H. G. THOMAS *Genesis I–XXV* 198 How frequently this remarkable combination of

good motive and bad conduct occurs in history and daily life! The end does *not* justify the means, whatever people may say.

End makes all equal, The.

1573 SANDFORD (1576) 214. **1611** DAVIES. Prov. 66. **1732** FULLER no. 4496.

End of an old song, There is an.

1721 KELLY 331 . . . That is, you have all that I can tell you of it.

End of passion is the beginning of repentance, The.

1628 O. FELTHAM *Resolves* viii (Dent) 18 It often falls out, that the end of passion is the beginning of repentance.

End of the rainbow, Go to the | and you'll find a crock of money.

1836 W. D. COOPER *Glos. of Provin. in Sussex* (1853) 40 'Go to the end of the rainbow, and you'll find a crock of money'.

End of the staff (stick), To have (*or* get) the better (*or* worse *or* wrong)

1387 TREVISA *Higden* (Rolls) II. 29 Men of þat side schal haue the wors ende. **1533** UDALL *Flowers for Latin Speaking* (1560) S 6 As we halfe prouerbially saie in englishe, to geue one the worse ende of the staffe. **1534** *Two Coventry C.C. Plays* (E.E.T.S.) 45 (A) He schal be sure, asse God me saue, Eyuer the worse yend of the staff to haue. **1542** UDALL tr. *Erasm. Apoph.* (1877) 340 As often as thei see theim selfes to haue the wurse ende of the staffe in their cause. **1626** JACKSON *Creed* VIII. viii. 71 He having gotten (as wee say) the better end of the staffe, did wrest our wills at his pleasure. **1753** RICHARDSON *Grandison* (1754) II. ii. 12 Miss Byron, I have had the better end of the staff, I believe? **1890** 'ROLF BOLDREWOOD' *Colon. Reformer* xx You will rarely find that the apparently impassive countryman has 'got the wrong end of the stick'.

End tries all, The.

c. **1390** GOWER *Conf. Amantis* VI. 2383 An ende proveth every thing. **1509** A. BARCLAY *Ship of Fools* I. 207 Byde the ende, that onely prouyth all. *c.* **1566** *The Bugbears* II. v The end shall trulye try. **1597** *Wit's Commonwealth* 129 The end of euery thing is the tryall of the action. **1597-8** SHAKS. *2 Hen. IV* II. ii. 52 Let the end try the man.

Ending, *see* Somerton e.

Ends ill which begins in God's name, That never.

1639 CLARKE 109.

End(s) (*noun*), *see also* Better e. of the string; Both e. meet (Make); Everything hath an e.; Game's e. (At the) shall see who gains; Look to the e.; Make an e. of your whistle though cart overthrow; Stay a while . . . e. the sooner; Wills e. wills means.

End(s) (*verb*), *see* Bairns o' Falkirk (Like) they'll e. ere they mend; Well that e. well.

Endure labour in this world, He that will not | let him not be born.

1573 SANDFORD (1576) 103. **1629** *Book of Meery Riddles*, Prov. 28.

Endure to itch, He that will not | must endure to smart.

1550 HEYWOOD I. x He whom in itching no scratching will forbear, He must bear the smarting that shall follow there. **1678** RAY 162.

Endure(d), *see also* Cured (What can't be) must be c.; Mickle maun good heart e.; No man better knows good than he who hath e. evil.

Endures is not overcome, He that.

[VERG. *Aen*. 5. 710 *Superanda omnis fortuna ferendo*.] *c*. **1374** CHAUCER *Troylus* IV. 1584 Men seyn 'the suffrant overcom'th', pardé. *c*. **1382** (?) GOWER *Vox Clam*. iii. 409 *Nobile vincendi genus est pacientia*. **1640** HERBERT 356. **1641** FERGUSSON 40 He that tholes overcomes.

Enemies, If you have no | it's a sign fortune has forgot you.

[PUBL. SYRUS (Ribbeck) 315 *Miserrima est fortuna quae inimico caret*.] **1732** FULLER no. 2759.

Enemy, There is no little.

c. **1386** CHAUCER *Mel*. 2512–13 Ne be nat necligent to kepe thy persone, nat only fro thy gretteste enemys but fro thy leeste enemy. Senek seith: 'a man that is wel avysed, he dredeth his leste enemy'.[1] **1733** FRANKLIN Sept. There is no little enemy. **1887** LD. AVEBURY *Pleas. of Life* I. v Unfortunately, while there are few great friends there is no little enemy. [[1] PUB. SYRUS *Sent*. 255 *Inimicum, quamvis humilem, docti est metuere*.]

Enemy, One | can do more hurt than ten friends can do good.

1711 SWIFT *Jrnl. to Stella* 30 June I have been gaining enemies by the scores, and friends by the couples, which is against the rules of wisdom, because they say one enemy can do more hurt than ten friends can do good.

Enemy, His own | is no one's friend.

1768 GOLDSMITH *Good-nat. Man* iv (Globe) 633 I see that it is in vain to expect happiness from him, who has been so bad an economist of his own; and that I must disclaim his friendship who ceases to be a friend to himself.

Enemy, One | is too much.

1640 HERBERT 342.

Enemy, If you would make an | lend a man money, and ask it of him again.

1813 RAY 7. *Lusit*.

Enemy may chance to give good counsel, An.

1663 F. HAWKINS *Youth's Behaviour* F 8[v] Fas est et ab hoste doceri. Instruction is good, though it come from an enemy. **1732** FULLER no. 600.

Enemy seem a mouse, Though thy | yet watch him like a lion.

1732 FULLER no. 5015.

Enemy, In an | spots are soon seen.

1732 FULLER no. 2813.

Enemy your friend, Make your.

1639 CLARKE 189. **1641** FERGUSSON 40 He is wise that can make a friend of a foe.

Enemy's mouth seldom speaks well, An.

1481 CAXTON *Reynard* iv (Arb.) 7 Sir Isegrym that is eyul sayd it is a comyn prouerbe An Enemyes mouth saith seeld wel.

Enemy (-ies), *see also* Believe no tales from e.; Best is oftentimes e. of good; Better an open e.; *Fas est et ab hoste doceri*; Forgive an e. (If we are to), not bound to trust; Friend to a bosom friend (No), no e. to bosom e.; Gifts from e. dangerous; Gives honour to his e. (He that); Golden bridge (For flying e.); Good is e. of the best; Keep yourself from . . . reconciled e.; Mickle power makes many e.; No man's e. but his own; Nothing worse than familiar e.; Passeth a winter's day (He that) escapes an e.; Reconciled e. (Take heed of); Reconciled friend is double e.; Servants (So many), so many e.; Speak well of friend, of e. say nothing; Strike the serpent's head with e.'s hand; Trust not . . . contempt of e.; Trust not . . . old e.; Wind that comes in . . . and reconciled e.

Engine(s), *see* Great e. on small pivots.

England a good land, and a bad people.

1662 FULLER (*Berks.*) I. 120 'England a good land and a bad people.' This is a French proverb; and we are glad that they . . . will allow any goodness to another country.

England is the paradise of women, the hell of horses, and the purgatory of servants.

[**1583** R. D. *The Mirrour of Mirth* K 1[v] *Paris is a paradise for women, a hel for mens Horses, and a Purgatorye for those that followe suits of Law*.] *c*. **1598** *MS. Provs.* in FERGUSSON 126 England is said to be a hel for horses a purgatorie for servantis ane paradice for wemen. **1617** MORYSON *Itin*. iii. 53 England . . . is said to be the hell of horses, the purgatory of servants, and the paradise of women. **1630** DEKKER *Honest Wh.* Pt. II. iv. i England, they say, is the only hell for horses, and only paradise for women. **1662** FULLER (*Berks.*) I. 116 'England is the paradise of women, hell of horses, purgatory of servants.' For the first, *bilia vera* . . . For the next, . . . *Ignoramus* . . . For the last, . . . we cast it forth as full of falsehood.

England is the ringing island.

1662 FULLER (*Berks.*) I. 115 'England is the ringing island.' Thus it is commonly called by foreigners, as having greater, more, and more tunable bells than any one country in Christendom.

England were but a fling, save for the crooked stick and the grey-goose wing.

1662 FULLER (*Berks.*) I. 116 . . . 'But a fling', . . . not to be valued. . . . 'But for the crooked stick', &c. That is, use of archery. **1874** GREEN *Short Hist. Eng.* P. 261 [At Agincourt] his archers bared their arms . . . to give fair play to 'the crooked stick and the grey goose wing', but for which—as the rime ran—'England were but a fling'.

England win, He that will | must with Ireland first begin.

1567 DIEGO ORTIZ quoted in FROUDE, *Hist. of England* x. 480 (A) There is an English proverb in use among them which says—He who would England win, In Ireland must begin. **1617** MORYSON *Itin.* (1907) II. 170 Incouraged by the blind zeale . . . or animated by an olde Prophesie [:] He that will England winne, Must with Ireland first beginne, did also raise two rebellions. **1662** FULLER (*Berks.*) I. 119 'He that will England win, Must with Ireland first begin'. . . . England . . . is too great a morsel for a foreign foe to be chopped up at once; and therefore it must orderly be attempted, and Ireland be first assaulted.

England wrings, When | Thanet sings.

1892 *Murray's Handbk. Kent* (ed. 5) 219 The Isle of Thanet.—The soil is generally light and chalky, and a wet summer, elsewhere a great evil, is here rather longed for. Hence a local proverb—'When England wrings The island sings'.

England's difficulty is Ireland's opportunity.

1902–4 LEAN I. 35 England's difficulty is Ireland's opportunity. **1914** *Spectator* 8 Aug. 190 That chapter in our history when it could be said that 'England's danger was Ireland's opportunity'.

England's wooden walls.

1605 JONSON, &c. *Eastw. Hoe* II. ii. 100 . . . Expose other mens substances to the mercie of the windes, under protection of a woodden wall. *a.* **1607** DEKKER *Whore of Babylon* (1873) ii. 203 Weele build about our waters wooden walles. **1662** FULLER (*Cumb'ld.*) I. 338 Our wooden walls (so our ships are commonly called) were rough-casted over with a coat of a firmer constitution.

England, *see also* Gluttony is sin of E.; Heart of E.; HEMPE is spun (When), E. is done; Little E. beyond Wales; Long beards heartless . . . makes E. thriftless; Merry E.; Sand feeds the clay (When the); Victuals in E. (More good) than in other kingdoms; War with world, peace with E.; Wonders of E.

Englanders, *see* Little E.

English archer beareth under his girdle twenty-four Scots, Every.

1545 ASCHAM *Toxoph.* (Arb.) 84 The Scottes them selues . . . gyue the whole prayse of shotynge honestlye to Englysshe men, saying thus: that euery Englysshe Archer beareth vnder hys gyrdle .xxiiii. Scottes.

English are a nation of shop-keepers, The.

1766 J. TUCKER *Four Tracts* III (1774) 132 A shop-keeper will never get the more Custom by beating his customers; and what is true of a Shop-keeper, is true of a Shop-keeping Nation. **1776** ADAM SMITH *Wealth Nat.* IV. vii (1828) III. 41 To found a great empire for the sole purpose of raising up a people of customers, may at first sight appear a project fit only for a nation of shopkeepers. **1896** 'H. S. MERRIMAN' *Flotsam* ix We are shop-keepers. . . . But at times we . . . put up the shutters and lock the door—and then there is usually the devil to pay. **1911** *Times, Wkly.* 17 Feb. Napoleon . . . described the English as a nation of shopkeepers. Uttered in a sneering spirit, it embodied . . . the profound truth that our prosperity is based upon our trade.

English are the swearing nation, The.

1713 DEFOE *Reasons agst. Suc. of H. Hanover* Wks. (Bohn) VI. 518 Nay, have we not been called in the vulgar dialect of foreign countries 'the swearing nation'?

English never know when they are beaten, The.

1853 G. J. WHYTE-MELVILLE *Digby G.* iv The name of Englishman [is] a type of all that is resolute, daring, and invincible. We have a high authority in the expression of Napoleon, that 'they never know when they are beaten'. **1911** J. H. A. MACDONALD in *Spectator* 30 Sept. 489 The British subject has a repute for not knowing when he is beaten, and it is a valuable quality for a martial race. . . . But it has often been an injurious hindrance where the question was [one] . . . of progress in things practical, especially in mechanical developments.

English summer, An | three (two) hot days and a thunderstorm.

1854 SURTEES *Hand. Cross* li Summer was merely inserted as a sort of compliment,— three hot days and a thunderstorm being the general amount of an English summer. **1909** *Times* 28 May People speak of the English summer as consisting of three fine days ending in a thunderstorm.

English, *see also* **Wardour-street.**

Englishman, One | can beat three Frenchmen.

1598-9 SHAKS. *Hen. V.* III. vi. 161 When they were in health, . . . I thought upon one pair of English legs Did march three Frenchmen. **1745** HOR. WALPOLE *Let.* to G. Montagu 13 Jul. We, who formerly . . . could any one of us beat three Frenchmen, are now so degenerated, that three Frenchmen can evidently beat one Englishman. **1748** BOSWELL *Johnson* (on the French Academy) This is the proportion . . . As three to sixteen hundred, so is the proportion of an Englishman to a Frenchman. **1762** GOLDSMITH *Cit. World* cxx (Globe) 274 We had no arms; but one Englishman is able to beat five Frenchmen at any time. **1833** MARRYAT *P. Simple* xlvi My men, . . . there are three privateers . . . it's just a fair match for you—one Englishman can always beat three Frenchmen.

Englishman is never happy but when he is miserable, An | a Scotchman never at home but when he is abroad, and an Irishman never at peace but when he is fighting.

1865 ABP. WHATELY *Commonpl.-Bk.* 293 It has been said that 'an Englishman is never happy but when he is miserable, a Scotchman never at home but when he is abroad, and an Irishman never at peace but when he is fighting.'

Englishman Italianate is a devil incarnate, The.

[Ital. *Inglese italianato è un diavolo incarnato.*] **1570** ASCHAM *Scholemaster* (Arb.) 78 The *Italian* sayth of the English Man, . . . *Englese Italianato, è un diabolo incarnato,* that is to say, you remaine men in shape and facion, but becum deuils in life and condition. **1591** GREENE *Disc. Coosnage* (N.) I am Englishe borne, and I have English thoughts; not a Devill incarnate because I am Itallanate. **1659** HOWELL *Ital. Prov.* 1 An Englishman Italionat is a Devill Incarnat. **1873** J. R. GREEN *Lett.* 7 Feb. Don't think I am getting 'Italianate', which according to Ascham is pretty much the same as 'a devil incarnate'.

Englishman knows not when a thing is well, A right.

1616 WITHALS 561 You are a right Englishman, you cannot tell when a thing is well. **1670** RAY 85. **1738** SWIFT (Dial. ii) 347 Well, Mr. Neverout, I find you are a true Englishman; you never know when you are well.

Englishman loves a lord, An.

1909 *Spectator* 3 July 9 It is always said that an Englishman loves a lord. It would be more exact to say that he is in love with lordliness.

Englishman weeps, The | the Irishman sleeps; but the Scottishman gangs while[1] he gets it.

1721 KELLY 323 . . . A pretended account of the behaviour of these three nations, when they want meat. [[1] till.]

Englishman's (Briton's) privilege to grumble, It is an.

1866 BLACKMORE *Cradock N.* lxiv Sir Cradock grumbles . . . now and then, because, like all of us Englishmen, he must have his grievance. **1871** C. KINGSLEY *At Last* iii Trinidad is loyal (with occasional grumblings, of course, as is the right of free-born Britons). **1881** W. WESTALL *Old Factory* xxxvii We are like to grumble a bit sometimes—it is an Englishman's privilege, you know.

Englishman, *see also* **Heart of an E. towards Welshman; House is his castle; Irishman for a hand . . . the E. for a face; Peerage is E.'s Bible; Settling an island, the first building . . . by an E. an alehouse; Way to an E.'s heart.**

Enjoy, *see* **Goods are theirs that e. them; Name (He that hath the) may e. the game.**

Enough, and none to spare, Like Madam Hassell's feast.

1856 *N. & Q.* 2nd Ser. I. 313 Like Madam Hassell's feast, enough, and none to spare. *Ibid.* II. 339 This proverb is changed only in name in Ireland. In Dublin . . . it originated at the table of a Mrs. Casely, who . . . was accustomed to say, 'Well, I declare; just enough and none to spare'. [*Cf.* **1917** BRIDGE 54 (A) Enough and no more, like Mrs. Milton's feast.]

Enough for one is enough for two, What's.

1902-4 LEAN IV. 178.

Enough is as good as a feast.

[EURIPIDES *Phoen.* 554 ἐπεὶ τά γ' ἀρκοῦνθ' ἱκανὰ τοῖσι σώφροσιν.] c. **1420** LYDGATE *Ass. Gods* (E.E.T.S.) 59 l. 2035 As good ys ynough as a gret feste. **1546** HEYWOOD II. xi. 85 Folke saie, enough is as good as a feast. **1594-5** SHAKS. *L.L.L.* V. i. 1 *Hol.* Satis quod sufficit. **1662** FULLER (*Lond.*) II. 346 According to the rule, 'satis est quod sufficit' (enough is as good as a feast). **1738** SWIFT (Dial. i) 334 No, I thank your lordship, enough's as good as a feast. **1826** LAMB *Ess., Pop. Fallacies* Wks. (1898) 223 That enough is as good as a feast. Not a man, woman, or child in ten miles round Guildhall, who really believes this saying.

Enough is enough.

1546 HEYWOOD II. xi. **1570** *Marriage of Wit and Science* D 4. **1834** SOUTHEY *Doctor* i. 199 As for money, enough is enough.

Enough, Of | men leave. (*Cf.* Enough where nothing left.)

1641 FERGUSSON 82. **1721** KELLY 272 . . .

They who leave no scraps can hardly be said to have enough.

Enough one day, He will have | when his mouth is full of mould.

1583 P. STUBBES *Anatomy of Abuses* Pt. II (New Sh. S.) ii. 27 Greedy gentlemen, who will neuer have inough, till their mouths be full of clay, and their bodie full of grauell. **1670** RAY 173. **1721** KELLY 161 *He'll get enough one day, when his mouth's full of mools.* Spoken of covetous people, who will never be satisfied while they are alive.

Enough where nothing [was] left, There was never. (*Cf.* Enough (Of) men leave.)

1639 CLARKE 38.

Enough who is contented with little, He hath.

1551 W. BALDWIN *Beware the Cat* (1584) B 3 A little sufflseth him that hath inough. **1658** E. PHILLIPS *Mysteries of Love and Eloquence* 159 He hath enough that's pleased. **1659** N. R. 41 (as 1658).

Enough, *see also* Knoweth when he hath e. (He that); More than e. too much.

Enough to, *see* Cat speak; Saint swear; Wolf from the door.

Enriched, *see* Pension never e. young man.

Enter into a house, When you | leave the anger ever at the door.

1640 HERBERT 358.

Enter into Paradise must have a good key, He that will.

1640 HERBERT (Gros.) no. 889. **1732** FULLER no. 2347 (with 'must come with the right key').

Enter this life, There is but one way to | but the gates of death are without number.

1603 FLORIO tr. *Montaigne* II. iii (1897) III. 32 Nature . . . hath left us the key of the fields. She hath appointed but one entrance into life, but many a thousand ways out of it. *c.* **1628** FULKE GREVILLE, LD. BROOKE *Alaham* IV. i. Wks. (Gros.) III. 257 If Nature saw no cause of suddaine ends, She that but one way made to draw our breath, Would not haue left so many doores to Death.

Enter(s), *see also* Nothing e. into close hand.

Enterprise, *see* Examined e. goes boldly

Entertainment, *see* Jack Drum's e.

Envied, *see* Better be e. than pitied.

Envious man shall never want woe, The.

1636 CAMDEN 307.

Envy never dies.

1523–5 BERNERS tr. *Froissart* ch. 428 (A) There is a Comune proverb, the whiche is true, and that is, howe envy never dyeth. **1616** DRAXE 53 Enuie is neuer dead. **1624** BURTON *Anat. Mel.* 91 Hatred hath an end, envy never ceaseth (*from* Cardan). **1658** C. HOOLE *Sententiae Pueriles* 15 Envy ceaseth after death.

Envy never enriched any man.

1616 DRAXE 53 A man shall neuer bee enriched by enuie. **1670** RAY 8.

Epsom, *see* Sutton.

Erasmus laid the egg of the Reformation, and Luther hatched it.

1877 TRENCH *Mediev. Ch. Hist.* xxvi (1879) 399 [Erasmus] had too earnestly denounced the corruptions of the Church not to be regarded with dislike and suspicion by all who clung to these;—it was he, they said, who laid the egg which Luther hatched.

Ermine, In an | spots are soon discovered.

1642 TORRIANO 78. **1732** FULLER no. 2814.

Err is human, To.

[L. *Humanum est errare.*] **1542** UDALL tr. *Erasm. Apoph.* (1877) xiii Bothe wer men, and might erre. **1575** C. AGRIPPA, *Vanity of Arts and Sciences* tr. Sandford ¶3ᵛ Tullie . . . in the first of his *Offices* . . . sayth . . . to erre . . . is mans propertie. **1576** PETTIE *Petite Pall.* (Gollancz) I. 6 *Errare humanum esl; in errore perseverare, belluinum.* **1594** HOOKER *Eccles. Polity*, Preface, ch. ix Think ye are men, deem it not impossible for you to err. **1655–62** GURNALL *Chrn. in Armour* (1865) I. 298 The first shows thee a weak man —*humanum est errare*, to err is human. **1711** POPE *Ess. Crit.* 525 To err is human; to forgive, divine. **1908** *Times Lit. Sup.* 27 Mar. The modern moralist pardons everything, because he is not certain of anything, except that to err is human.

Errand, *see* Draff is your e., but drink ye would; Go twenty miles on your e.; King's e. may come cadger's gate; Sleeveless e.; Tod never sped better than . . . own e.; Wise man on an e. (Send).

Error, *see* Show a good man his e. he turns it to virtue.

Errs and mends, Who | to God himself commends.

1620 SHELTON *Quix.* II. xxviii (1908) III. 20 Pardon me, sir, and pity my youth . . . 'Who errs and mends, to God himself commends.'

Err(s), *see also* Talk much and e. much; War (In) it is not permitted twice to e.

Escape a scouring, To.

1560 T. PALFREYMAN *A Mirror or clear glass* D 5 Thou hast escaped a scouringe, or passed thorough the pykes. **1639** CLARKE 80. **1721** DEFOE *Mem. Cavalier* x (1840) 187 Aylesbury escaped a scouring for that time.

Escape Clude, and be drowned in Conway, To.

1662 FULLER (*Carnarvon*) I. 527 'To 'scape Clude, and be drowned in Conway' . . . Scylla [and] Charibdis . . . were near, . . . whereas the two rivers of Clude and Conway are twenty miles asunder.

Escape, *see also* Counsel that hath no e. (Ill).

Escaped mouse ever feels the taste of the bait, The.

1640 HERBERT 349.

Escaped the thunder, and fell into the lightning, I.

1599 MINSHEU (1623) 2S 6ᵛ. **1612** N. POWNOLL *The Yg. Divine's Apology* A 5 For so to shunne shame, and seeke glorie, what were it else, but (as the Spaniard speaketh) to escape the thunderbolt, and fall into the lightning's flash. **1651** HERBERT 367.

Essex calves.

1573 G. HARVEY *Letter-Book* (Camden Soc.) 135 (A) Foes must be frende, quoth an Essex kalfe. **1605** CHAPMAN, &c. *Eastw. Hoe* II. iii. 26 These women, sir, are like Essex calves. **1617** MORYSON *Itin.* III. i. 53 (1907–8) III. 463 Essex men are called calves (because they abound there). **1719** D'URFEY *Pills* IV 43 It prov'd an Essex Calf. **1909** *Times Lit. Sup.* 26 Nov. As a rule these men have been Scots or Cornishmen rather than 'Essex calves'.

Essex miles.

1606 DEKKER *News from Hell* B 4ᵛ The miles are not halfe so long as those betweene *Colchester* and *Ipswich*. **1662** FULLER (1840) I. 497 (A).

Essex stiles, Kentish miles, Norfolk wiles, many a man beguiles.

15th c. in *Reliq. Antiquae* i. 269 (A) Suffolk full of wiles, Norffolk full of giles. **1617** MORYSON *Itin.* III. i. 53 (1907–8) III. 463 *Norfolk* wiles (for crafty litigiousness): *Essex* stiles (so many as make walking tedious): *Kentish* miles (of the length). **1670** RAY 86 Essex stiles, Kentish miles, Norfolk wiles many a man beguiles. For stiles *Essex* may well vie with any county of England. . . . Length of miles I know not what reason *Kent* hath to pretend to . . . but for cunning in the law and wrangling, *Norfolk* men are justly noted.

Estate, He has a good | but that the right owner keeps it from him.

1678 RAY 78. **1738** SWIFT (Dial. i) 338 Well, however, they say he has a great estate, but only the right owner keeps him out of it.

Estate in two parishes is bread in two wallets.

1640 HERBERT 327.

Estate(s), *see also* Bones of a great e. worth the picking; Hard thing to have great e. and not love it; Many e. are spent in the getting; Near of kin to an e. (Good to be.)

Esteem(ed), *see* Costs little (What) less e.

Ethiopian, *see* Wash an E. white.

Ettle, *see* Oft e. whiles hit.

Eve, *see* Say to pleasure, Gentle E.

Even reckoning makes long friends.

1546 HEYWOOD II. iv. 53 Euen reeknyng makth longe freendis. **1670** RAY 136 Even reckoning keeps long friends. **1760** COLMAN *Polly Honeycombe* 16 Right Reckoning makes long friends, you know.

Evening brings all home, The.

[SAPPHO *Ἕσπερε πάντα φέρων ὅσα φαίνολις ἐσκέδασ' Αὔως, | φέρεις οἶν, φέρεις αἶγα, φέρεις ἄπυ μάτερι παῖδα.*] **1857** DEAN RAMSAY *Remin.* v (1911) 200 *The e'ening brings a' hame* is an interesting saying, meaning that the evening of life, or the approach of death, softens many of our political and religious differences.

Evening crowns (praises) the day, The.

1545 TAVERNER G 5ᵛ Our englyshe prouerbe —At euen men shulde the fayre day preisen. **1612–15** BP. HALL *Contempl.* XIX. v (1825) I. 633 The evening praises the day, and the chief grace of the theatre is in the last scene. 'Be faithful to the death, and I will give thee a crown of life.' **1615** M. R. *President for Young Pen. Men* B 1ᵛ It is the Euening praiseth the Day, and he is only happy that holds out to the end. *a.* **1619** DANIEL *A Funeral Poem* 380 For 'tis the evening crowns the day. **1692** L'ESTRANGE *Aesop's Fab.* ccxciv (1738) 307 'Tis matter of humanity . . . to be tender one of another: for no man living knows his end, and 'tis *the evening crowns the day.* **1721** KELLY 336 *The evening crowns the day.* For as our success appears then, it is good or bad.

Evening orts are good morning fodder.

1639 CLARKE 114. **1721** KELLY 96 *Evening oarts is good morning fodder.* Spoken when a man breakfasts upon what he left for supper. **1732** FULLER no. 1401 (with 'oats' for 'orts').

Evening praises the day, and the morning a frost (*in error for* mine host?), The.

1640 HERBERT 347. **1642** TORRIANO 70 The evening commendeth the morning, but the morning commendeth mine hoste.

Evening red and morning grey help the traveller on his way: evening grey and morning red bring down rain upon his head.

1586 L. EVANS *Withals Dict. Revised* N 7 (A) The euening red, the morning gray, Foreshewes a cleare and summers day. **1611** COTGRAVE s.v. 'Matin' . . . presage a fair succeeding day. **1639** CLARKE 263 An evening red and a morning gray, Are sure signs of a fair day. **1846** DENHAM 8 An evening red and morning grey, Will set the traveller on his way; But if the evening's grey, and the morning red, Put on your hat or you'll wet your head. **1893** INWARDS 54 Evening red and morning grey Help the traveller on his way, Evening grey and morning red Bring down rain upon his head.

Evening words are not like to morning.

1611 COTGRAVE s.v. Parole' The evening chat is not like the mornings tattle. **1640** HERBERT 320.

Evensong, *see* Day never so long cometh e.

Event(s), *see* Coming e. cast their shadows.

Ever busy, ever bare.

1721 KELLY 91 . . . It is not always found that they who pursue the world most eagerly, gets the greatest share of it.

Ever drunk, ever dry.

1509 A. BARCLAY *Ship of Fools* (1874) I. 51 The more that some drynke: the more they wax drye. **1605** CHAPMAN, &c. *Eastw. Hoe* I. ii He that's most drunken may soonest be athirst. **1614** CAMDEN 305.

Ever, *see also* Blind horse (E. the worse looks the); Sick of the slothful guise (E.); Wear clothes (E. since we).

Every beggar is descended from some king, and every king is descended from some beggar.

1602 *Thomas Lord Cromwell* I. ii There's legions now of beggars on the earth, That their original did spring from kings: And many monarchs now whose fathers were The riff-raff of their age. **1631–59** FULLER *Infants Advoc.* xix in *Collected Serm.* (1891) II. 222 We have a saying, *Every beggar is descended from some king, and every king is descended from some beggar.*

Every block will not make a Mercury.

[L. *Ex quovis ligno non fit Mercurius.*] **1629** T. ADAMS *Serm.* (1861–2) II. 300 It was wont to be said, *Ex quolibet ligno non fit Mercurius,* —Every block is not fit to make an image. **1689** SHADWELL *Bury Fair* II. i *Ex quovis ligno,* &c. Mercury's statue is not made of every wood. **1732** FULLER no. 1410.

Every commodity hath its discommodity.

1576 PETTIE *Petite Pall.* I. 76. **1581** *Id. Guazzo's Civ. Conv.* 9. **1616** DRAXE 24. **1672** WALKER 36 No convenience without its inconveniency.

Every day braw[1] makes Sunday a daw.[2]

1851–63 *Ulster Jrnl. Arch.* ii in LEAN I. 347. [[1] fine. [2] a drab.]

5017

Every day brings its bread with it.

1640 HERBERT 317.

Every day cometh night.

1573 SANDFORD (1576) 219. **1578** FLORIO *First Fruites* 33.

Every day is holiday with sluggards.

1539 TAVERNER (1545) E 8 *Ignauis semper feriae sunt.* With sluggers or vnhardy persons, it is alwayes holy daye. **1611** DAVIES *Epigr.* 42 'With sluggards eu'ry day is holy day'; And so it is with some that seldome sleepes.

Every day of the week a shower of rain, and on Sunday twain.

1659 HOWELL *Eng. Prov.* 11/2 . . . a proverb in many shires of England.

Every day of thy life is a leaf in thy history.

1902–4 LEAN III. 455.

Every day's no Yule-day—cast the cat a castock.[1]

1721 KELLY 94. **1846** DENHAM 62. [[1] = kale stock, cabbage stump.]

Every evil under the sun, For | there is a remedy or there is none: if there be one, try and find it; if there be none, never mind it.

1869 HAZLITT 135.

Every extremity is a fault.

1573 SANDFORD (1576) H 3ᵛ. **1583** P. STUBBES *Anatomy of Abuses* (New Sh. S.) i. 33 *Omne extremum uertitur in uitium,* every extreme is turned into vice. **1629** *Book of Meery Riddles* Prov. 30 (A).

Every fault, In | there is folly.

1707 MAPLETOFT 126. **1878** J. PLATT *Morality* 34 (A).

Every hand fleeceth, Where | the sheep goes naked.

1639 CLARKE 187. **1732** FULLER no. 5645.

Every light is not the sun.

1670 RAY 15.

Every little helps.

1791 O'KEEFFE *Wild Oats* v. iii (A) Here— it's not much! but every little helps. **1840** MARRYAT *Poor Jack* xiii That's a very old saying, that every little helps.

Every maid is undone.

1678 RAY 172.

Every man a little beyond himself is a fool.

1677 YARRANTON *Engl.'s Improvement* 105 Every Man is a Fool when he is out of his own way. **1855** BOHN 350.

Every man as he loveth, quoth the good man when he kissed his cow.

1546 HEYWOOD II. i. 43 And in this case euery man as he loueth Quoth the good man, whan that he kyst his coowe. **1675** COTTON *Poet. Wks.* (1745) Why each one as he likes, you know, quo' th' good man when he kissed his cow. **1721** KELLY 91 Every man to his mind, quoth the carle when he kiss'd his cow. **1738** SWIFT (Dial. i) 333 Why, every one as they like, as the good woman said when she kiss'd her cow. **1741** CHESTERFIELD 25 July Every one as they like, as the good man said when he kissed his cow. **1842** E. FITZGERALD *Lett.* 22 Sept. (1901) I. 136 Every one to his taste, as one might well say to any woman who kissed the cow pastured there.

Every man as his business lies.

1597 SHAKS. *1 Henry IV* II. ii. 75 Every man to his business. **1678** RAY 107.

Every man for himself, and God (the devil) for us all (take the hindmost).

c. **1386** CHAUCER *Knight's T.* A 1182 At the Kynges court, my brother, Ech man for hymself, ther is noon oother. *c.* **1514** A. BARCLAY *Eclogues* i. 1009 Eche man for him selfe, and the fiende for all. **1562** HEYWOOD *Three Hundred Epig.* no. 96 Euery man for him self, and god for vs all. **1572** SANDFORD *Houres of Recreation* 219 Euery man for him self, and the Deuill for all. **1629** T. ADAMS *Serm.* (1861–2) II. 90 That byword, 'Every man for himself, and God for us all', is uncharitable, ungodly. **1830** MARRYAT *King's Own* liii The captain . . . ordered the sailor to leave the boat. 'Every man for himself, and God for us all!' was the cool answer of the refractory seaman. **1858** D. MULOCK *A Woman's Thoughts* 39 The world is hard enough, for two-thirds of it are struggling for the dear life—'each for himself, and de'il tak the hindmost'. [Fr. *Chacun pour soi et Dieu pour tous.*]

Every man gets his own, When | the thief will get the widdie.[1]

1721 KELLY 352. [[1] gallows.]

Every man has his price.

a. **1745** WALPOLE in W. COXE, *Memoirs of Sir R. W.* (1798) i. 757 All those men have their price. *a.* **1761** J. RICH *Corr.* v. 308 It is said, but not to the credit of human nature, that every man has his price. **1790** WESLEY *Serm.* 123 That politician . . . whose favourite saying was, 'Do not tell me of your virtue. . . .: I tell you, every man has his price'. **1845** JAMES *Smuggler* x 'Oh! every man has his price', rejoined Mr. Radford. **1892** LIDDON *Some Words of Christ* 23 That shallow maxim of worldly cynicism, which tells us that 'every man has his price'.

Every man hath his faults.

1593 *Tell-Trothes New Year's gift* (New. Sh. S.) 32 I knowe that euery one hath his faulte. **1600–1** SHAKS. *Merry W.* I. iv. 15 He is something peevish that way, but nobody but has his fault. **1607–8** *Timon of A.* III. i. 31 Every man hath his fault, and honesty is his. **1639** CLARKE 80. **1666** TORRIANO 68. **1902–4** LEAN IV. 64 Nobody is faultless.

Every man (thing) in his (its) way.

1653 A. WILSON *History of Gt. Britain* 185 Every man in his *Profession*! **1677** YARRANTON *Engl.'s Improvement* 105 (A) Now I see the old saying is true, Every man is a fool when he is out of his own way. **1678** RAY 84. **1693** W. FREKE *Select Essays* A 6 Every thing in its way.

Every man is best known to himself.

1616 DRAXE 27. **1639** CLARKE 65.

Every man is mad on some point.

a. **1721** PRIOR *Dialog. of Dead* (1907) 267 As you were saying, every man is mad, but in a different manner, and upon some particular objects.

Every man is master, Where | the world goes to wrack.[1]

1639 CLARKE 218. [[1] wreck.]

Every man is the architect of his own fortune.

[SALLUST *De Rep.* 1. 1 *Faber quisque fortunae suae.*] **1533** UDALL *Flowers for Latin Speaking* (1560) 24 A prouerbiall speakyng: *Fortunam sibi quisque fingit,* Every man maketh . . . is causer of his own fortunes. **1539** TAVERNER f. 37 A man's owne maners do shape hym hys fortune. **1605** BACON *Adv. of Learn.* Bk. II It grew to an adage, *Faber quisque Fortunae propriae.* **1613** BROWNE *Brit. Past.* iii. 585 Each man the workman of his fortune is. **1620** SHELTON *Quix.* II. lxvi (1908) III. 285 Hence 'tis said that every man is the artificer of his own fortune. **1649** MILTON *Eikon.* xxi Architects of their own happiness. **1687** DRYDEN *Hind and Panther* iii. 1268 Smiths of their own foolish fate. **1818** FERRIER *Marriage* lii As every man is said to be the artificer of his own fortune, so every one . . . had best be the artificer of their own friendship.

Every man mend (amend) one, If | all shall be mended (amended).

1555 HEYWOOD *Epigr. upon Prov.* no. 1 If euery man mende one, all shall be mended. **1579** LYLY *Euphues* (Arb.) 142 Let vs endeauour euery one to amend one, and we shall all soone be amended. **1641** FERGUSSON 64 Ilk man mend ane, and all will be mended. **1670** RAY 20. **1852** E. FITZGERALD *Polonius* cxi To two bad verses which I write Two good shall be appended: If every man would mend a man, Then all mankind were mended.

Every man should take his own.

1595–6 SHAKS. *Mids. N.* III. ii. 458 And the country proverb known, That every man should take his own.

Every man to his taste. (*Cf.* Every man as he loveth, &c.)

1580 LYLY *Euph. & his Eng.* Wks. (Bond) II.

161 Euery one as he lyketh. **1611** COTGRAVE s.v. 'Chascun' Every one as hee likes. **1849** LYTTON *Caxtons* XVII. i Every man to his taste in the Bush.

Every man to his trade.

[AR. *Vesp.* 1431 ἔρδοι τις ἥν ἔκαστος εἰδείη τέχνην, Each man should do the art he knows. CIC. *Tusc.* 1. 18. 41 *Quem quisque norit artem, in hac se exerceat.*] **1539** TAVERNER 33 Let euerye man exercise hym selfe in the facultie that he knoweth. **1597-8** SHAKS. *1 Hen. IV* II. ii. 85 Every man to his business. *a.* **1721** PRIOR *Dialog. of Dead* (1907) 221 Every man to his trade, Charles, you should have challenged me at long pike or broad sword. **1721** KELLY 97 *Every man to his trade, quoth the boy to the Bishop.* A Bishop asked a cabin boy if he could say his prayers; he asked the Bishop if he could say his compass, the Bishop said, No; Why then, says the boy, *Every man* to his trade. **1902** *Spectator* 15 Mar. However, every man to his trade.

Every man's censure is first moulded in his own nature.

1651 HERBERT 373.

Every man's man had a man, and that made the Treve fall.

1721 KELLY 94 . . . The Trave was a strong castle built by Black Douglas. The governor left a deputy, and he a substitute, by whose negligence the castle was taken and burned: spoken when servants employ other servants to do the business that they were entrusted with, and both neglect it.

Every man('s), *see also under significant words following.*

Every one after his fashion.

1546 HEYWOOD I. xi. **1614** CAMDEN 305.

Every one is weary: the poor in seeking, the rich in keeping, the good in learning.

1640 HERBERT 349.

Every one is witty for his own purpose.

1640 HERBERT 352.

Every one puts his fault on the times.

1640 HERBERT 348. **1872** BLACKMORE *Maid of Sker* i I pray you to lay the main fault thereof on the badness of the times.

Every one (horse) thinks his sack (pack) heaviest.

1611 COTGRAVE s.v. Fardeau' Every one finds his owne burthen heavy enough. **1640** HERBERT 352. **1732** FULLER no. 1420 Every horse thinks his own pack heaviest.

Every one's faults are not written in their foreheads.

1678 RAY 141. **1721** KELLY 214 *It is well, that all our faults are not written in our face.*

Spoken to them who upbraid us with some faults that we have been guilty of; alleging if theirs were known, they would look as black. **1855** BOHN 417 *Gaelic.* If the best man's faults were written on his forehead, it would make him pull his hat over his eyes.

Every one, *see also under significant words following.*

Every pleasure has a pain.

1591 GREENE *Wks.* (Gros.) IX. 256-7 Euerie bliss hath his bane, . . . euerie pleasure hath his paine. **1598** CHAPMAN *Blind Beggar of Alex.* Sc. v (A).

Every time the sheep bleats it loses a mouthful.

1599 MINSHEU (1623) 2 X 3. **1623** WODROEPHE *Spared Houres* 476 The yewe that doth bleate doth loose the most of her meate. **1666** TORRIANO 28 The sheep, for offering to bleat, loseth her bit. **1732** FULLER no. 1471. **1861** HUGHES *Tom B. at Oxford* xxiii He said something about a bleating sheep losing a bite; but I should think this young man is not much of a talker.

Every wind is ill to a broken ship. (*Cf.* Crazy ship, &c.)

1616 DRAXE 171. **1869** SPURGEON *John Ploughman* ch. vii (A) Every wind is foul for a crazy ship.

Every, *see also under significant words following.*

Everybody's business is nobody's business.

[AR. *Pol.* 2. 1. 10 ἥκιστα γὰρ ἐπιμελείας τυγχάνει τὸ πλείστων κοινόν.] **1611** COTGRAVE s.v. 'Ouvrage' Every bodies work is no bodies work. **1653** WALTON *Angler* I. ii A wise friend of mine did usually say, 'that which is everybody's business is nobody's business'. **1725** DEFOE *Everybody's business is nobody's business*, Title. **1829** COBBETT *Adv. to Y. Men* vi (1906) 294 Public property is never so well taken care of as private property; . . . 'that which is everybody's business is nobody's business'.

Everybody's dog that whistles, I am not.

1616 WITHALS 570. **1639** CLARKE 232. **1826** SCOTT *Woodstock* (1908) ix. 138 'You are sure he will come, like a dog at a whistle,' said Wildrake.

Everybody's somebody, When | then no one's anybody.

1889 W. S. GILBERT *The Gondoliers* II When everyone is somebodee, Then no-one's anybody! **1902** *Spectator* 8 Nov. If it is taken by theatre managers as a settled matter . . . that such 'criticism' shall be favourable, then 'criticism' becomes the wrong word to use . . . 'When everybody's somebody, then no one's anybody.'

Everything comes to him who waits.

c. **1514** A. BARCLAY *Eclogues* 2. 843 Somewhat

shall come who can his time abide. **1642**
TORRIANO 26 He who can wait, hath what he
desireth. **1847** DISRAELI *Tancred* IV. viii
Everything comes if a man will only wait.
1863 LONGFELLOW *Wayside Inn* ii All things
come round to him who will but wait. **1894**
LD. AVEBURY *Use of Life* xv (1904) 93 Do
not expect too much, and do not expect it
too quickly. 'Everything comes to those
who know how to wait.' **1908** S. PAGET
Confes. Med. 114 Nature . . . is not in any
hurry . . . ; everything comes to her, who
waits. [Fr. *Tout vient à point à qui sait
attendre.*]

Everything hath an end.

c. **1374** CHAUCER *Troylus* III. 615 But at the
laste, as every thing hath ende. *c.* **1490**
Partonope (E.E.T.S.) 1. 11144 Ye wote wele,
of all thing moste be an ende.

Everything hath an end, and a pudding hath two.

1592 NASHE *Four Lett. Confut.* (1593) 28
Every thing hath an end, and a pudding hath
two. **1611** BEAUM. & FL. *Kt. Burn. P.* I. i As
writers say, all things have end, And that we
call a pudding, hath his two. **1738** SWIFT
(Dial. i) 341 Well, all things have an end, and
a pudding has two. **1826** SCOTT *Woodst.* x
'Everything hath an end', said the Mayor,
'and that which we call a pudding hath
two.'

Everything hath its seed.

1616 DRAXE 12.

Everything hath its time.

c. **1380** CHAUCER *Troilus & Cressida* II. 989
Every thing hath tyme. *c.* **1390** GOWER
Conf. Amantis v. 7187 Alle thing hath time
and stede. **1666** TORRIANO 283. **1732** FULLER
no. 1466 . . . and that time must be watched.

Everything helps, quoth the wren, when she pissed into the sea.

[**1590** G. MEURIER *Deviz. familier.* 'Peu ayde',
disçoit le formy, pissant en mer en plein
midy.] **1623** CAMDEN 268.

Everything in turn, except scandal, whose turn is always.

1887 BLACKMORE *Springhaven* xviii You
know the old proverb—'Everything in turn,
except scandal, whose turn is always'.

Everything is as it is taken. (*Cf.* Things are as they be taken.)

1531 ELYOT *The Governor* i. 278 Euerything
is to be estemed after his value. **1542** A.
BORDE *Dietary* (E.E.T.S.) 260 Euery thyng
as it is handled. **1616** BRETON *Cross. of Prov.*
Wks. (1879) II. App. iii.

Everything is good in its season.

1591 W. STEPNEY *Span. Schoolmaster* L 3ᵛ
Euery thing in his season, & after pescods
come peasen. **1616** DRAXE 184. **1639** CLARKE
237.

Everything is of use to a housekeeper.

1640 HERBERT 320.

Everything is the worse for wearing.

c. **1520** SKELTON *Magnyf.* 1. 456 All thynge is
worse whan it is worne. **1639** CLARKE 190.
1670 RAY 159.

Everything is yours, You think | but a little the king has.

1738 SWIFT (Dial. ii) 350 *Never.* I'm sure 'tis
mine. *Miss.* What! you think everything is
yours, but a little the King has.

Everything must have a beginning.

c. **1374** CHAUCER *Troylus* II. 671 For every
thing a ginning hath it nede. **1575** GASCOIGNE
Gl. Govt. II. iii (1910) 37 All thinges have a
beginning, shee is a woman, and nothing is
unpossible. *a.* **1627** MIDDLETON *Mayor of
Queenb.* IV. iii I'll be the first then: Everything has beginning. **1641** FERGUSSON 4 All
things hath a beginning (God excepted).
1840 MARRYAT *Poor Jack* xxxi You've never
been to sea before.' 'No . . . ; but there must
be a beginning to everything.'

Everything new is fine.

1611 COTGRAVE s.v. 'Nouveau' Euery new
thing looks fair. **1640** HERBERT 320.

Everything would fain live.

1670 RAY 116. **1721** KELLY 94 . . . Spoken in
excuse of man or beast, who make their best
endeavour to get a living. **1732** FULLER no.
1469.

Evil communications corrupt good manners.

[MENANDER, *Thais Fragment* 2 Φθείρουσιν
ἤθη χρήσθ' ὁμιλίαι κακαί.] **1582** *Anglo-Rhem-
ish N.Test., 1 Corinth.* xv. 33 Euil communications corrupt good maners. **1829** COBBETT *Adv.
to Y. Men* v (1906) 264 'Evil communications
corrupt good manners'. . . . Jails, barracks,
factories, do not corrupt by their walls, but
by their condensed numbers.

Evil crow, An | an evil egg.

1536 LATIMER *2nd Serm. bef. Conv.* (P.S.) 42
Ye know this is a proverb much used: 'An
evil crow, an evil egg'. Then the children of
this world . . . cannot choose but be evil.

Evil do, Whoso will no | shall do nothing that belongeth thereto. (*Cf.* Do no ill, If thou, &c.)

1537 R. WHITFORD *Werke for Housholders* D 7
(A) The olde prouerbe sayth, who so wyll
none euyll do, shulde do nothynge that
longeth therto. **1539** TAVERNER (1545) G 8
Oure Englishe prouerbe He that woll no
hurte do, muste do nothynge that longe
there to. **1546** HEYWOOD II. V. *c.* **1577** J.
NORTHBROOKE *Treat. agst. Dicing* (Shaks.
Soc.) 173 Come you away from it, and vse it
no more, . . .: as the olde saying is, He that
will none euill do, Must do nothing belonging
therto. **1732** FULLER no. 6305 . . . must do
nought that's like there to.

Evil grain, Of | no good seed can come.

1616 DRAXE 13 Of euill graine, no good seede. 1670 RAY 8.

Evil hour, see Put off the e. h.

Evil (Naught) is soon learned, That which is.

1639 CLARKE 260 That which is naught is soon learned. 1670 RAY 8 That which is evil is soon learn't.

Evil (ill) manners, Of | spring good laws.

[MACROBIUS 3. 7. 10 *Vetus verbum est; leges inquit, ex malis moribus procreantur.* ERASM. *Ad. Bonae leges ex malis moribus procreantur.*] 1539 TAVERNER (1545) D 4ᵛ Good lawes be gendred of euyll maners. 1578 TIMME *Caluine on Gen.* 70 According to the common Proverb 'Of evil manners spring good laws'. 1619 J. FAVOUR *Antiquity* 406 Good laws proceed from euill manners. 1655 FULLER *Hist. Camb.* iii. 54 Ill Manners occasion Good laws, as the Handsome Children of Ugly Parents.

Evil that cometh out of thy mouth flieth into thy bosom.

1616 DRAXE 192 The euill that commeth out of the mouth, returneth (or falleth) into the bosome. 1670 RAY 8.

Evil there is odds, In.

1616 DRAXE 55. 1639 CLARKE 197.

Evils are cured by contempt, Some.

1651 HERBERT 366.

Evils (Harms, Ills, Mischiefs), Of two | choose the least.

c. 1374 CHAUCER *Troylus* II. 470 'Of harmès two the lesse is for to chese'. 1461 *Paston Lett.* (Gairdner) II. 73 Of ij. harmys the leste is to be take. 1546 HEYWOOD I. v. 10 Of two yls, choose the least whyle choyse lyth in lot. 1549 *Complaynt of Scotland* (E.E.T.S.) 163 Be suld cheis the smallest of thir tua euillis. 1580 LYLY *Euph. & his Eng.* (Arb.) 338 Of two mischiefes the least is to be chosen. 1602 *Thos. Ld. Cromwell* III. ii (*Shaks. Apoc.*) 177 Crom. But of two euils, 'tis best to shun the greatest, and better is it that he liues in thrall, Then such a Noble Earle as he should fall. 1891 A. FORBES *Bar. Biv. & Bat.* (1910) 187 Either the Turks would make a prisoner of me . . . or I must . . . take my chance of the Russian fire as I galloped for . . . shelter. . . . 'Of two evils choose the less', says the wise proverb.

Evils have their comfort; good none can support (to wit) with a moderate and contented heart.

1640 HERBERT 326.

Evils we bring on ourselves are the hardest to bear, The.

1902–4 LEAN IV. 119 . . . Bien est malheureux qui est cause de son malheur.—Cordier, 1538.

Evil (*adj. adv.*), see Blessings of the e. Genii are curses; Helpeth the evil hurteth the good (He that); Ill (E.) gotten ill (e.) spent; Ill (E.) will never said well.

Evil(s) (*noun*), see Bear with e.; Does e. (He that) never weens good; Every e. under the sun (For), there is remedy; Good is to be sought out and e. attended; Welcome e. if alone; Women (Wives and wind) are necessary e.

Evil, see also Ill.

Ewe and a lamb, Now I have got an | every one cries, Welcome Peter. (*Cf.* Sheep and a cow, &c.)

1732 FULLER no. 3690.

Ewe is drowned, When the | she 's dead.

1721 KELLY 354 . . . Spoken when a thing is gone, and past recovery.

Ewe(s), Yowe(s), see also Lamb where it's tipped, the e. where she's clipped; Many frosts . . . make rotten y.; Old e. lamb fashion; Silly flock where e. bears bell; Stamps like a e.

Ewell, see Sutton.

Examined enterprise goes on boldly, An.

1640 HERBERT 346.

Example is better than precept.

c. 1400 *Mirk's Festial* (E.E.T.S.) 216 Then saythe Seynt Austeyn that an ensampull yn doyng ys mor commendabull then ys techyng other prechyng. a. 1568 ASCHAM *Scholem.* (Mayor) 61 One example is more valuable . . . than twenty preceptes written in bookes. 1708 PRIOR *Turtle & Spar.* Example draws where precept fails, And sermons are less read than tales. 1824 MOIR *Mansie W.* xix Example is better than precept. 1894 LD. AVEBURY *Use of Life* xix Men can be more easily led than driven: example is better than precept.

Example to another, He is in ill case that gives.

1573 SANDFORD (1576) 222. 1629 *Book of Meery Riddles* Prov. 125.

Example, see also Good e. best sermon; Like me, God bless the e.

Exception proves the rule, The.

[*Exceptio firmat regulam in non exceptis*, shortened from CIC. *pro Balbo* 14. 32.] 1662 J. WILSON *Cheats* To Rdr. Wks. (1874) 11 I think I have sufficiently justified the brave man even by this reason, that the exception proves the rule. 1827–48 HAVE *Gues. at*

Truth ii (1859) 510 *The exception proves the rule* . . . has often been greatly abused. As it is usually brought forward, the exception in most cases merely proves the rule to be a bad one. **1896** w. w. skeat *Stud. Pastime* 78 'Exceptio probat regulam' . . . means, 'The exception tests the rule'. . . . The older English equivalent, 'The exception proves the rule', had once the same signification, the use of *prove* for *test* being familiar to all readers of the Bible.

Exception, *see also* Rule without some e. (No general).

Exchange (A fair exchange) is no robbery.

1546 heywood ii. iv. 51 Though chaunge be no robbry for the chaunged case. **1655** fuller *Ch. Hist.* i. v (1868) I. 61 In lieu of what he left behind him, (exchange is no robbery), he carried along with him some of St. Alban's dust. **1784** smollett *Rod. Rand.* xli Casting an eye at my hat and wig, . . . he took them off, and clapping his own on my head, declared that a fair exchange was no robbery. **1819** scott *Leg. Mont.* xiv This sword is an Andrew Ferrara, and the pistols better than my own. But a fair exchange is no robbery.

Exchequer, *see* Christ takes not (What), the e. carries away.

Excuses himself, accuses himself, He who.

[hieronymus *Ep.* 4 *ad virginem* c. 3 *Dum excusare credis, accusas.* Fr. *Qui s'excuse, s'accuse.*] **1611** cotgrave s.v. 'excuser' Some when they meane to excuse, accuse, themselues. **1616** draxe 58 To excuse is to accuse. **1664** codrington 191 Excusing is oftentimes accusing. **1884** j. payn *Canon's Ward* xxxi It is very difficult for a person in my position to excuse without accusing himself.

Excuse(s), *see also* Bad e. better than none; Find a woman without e.; Idle folks lack no e.; Ill paymaster never wants e.; Naught is that muse that finds no e.; Woman need but look on apron-string.

Exeter, *see* Duke of E.'s daughter.

Exhorts others to give, Let him who | give of his own.

1929 dean inge *Assessm. & Antic.* 136 There is nothing generous in voting away other people's money. . . . There is a Latin proverb: *Qui suadet, sua det*—'Let him who exhorts others to give, give of his own'.

Exon, *see* Kirton.

Expect a good whelp from an ill dog, We may not.

1678 ray *Adag. Hebr* 398.

Expect from a hog but a grunt? What can you.

1731 *Poor Robins Alm.* If we petition a Hog,

what can we expect but a grunt. **1827** scott *Two Drovers* i If he had not . . . been but a Dumfriesshire hog . . . he would have spoken more like a gentleman, But you cannot have more of a sow than a grumph. **1910** p. w. joyce *Eng. as we Speak* 137 Of a coarse, ill-mannered man, who uses unmannerly language: 'What could you expect from a pig but a grunt.'

Expect of a hog but his bristles? What can you.

1813 ray 201. **1855** bohn 166.

Expect to go when you die? Where do you.

1809 malkin *Gil Blas* iii. iii There is usury! . . . unconscionable dogs! Where do they expect to go when they die?

Expect(s), *see also* Bear with evil, e. good; Blessed is he who e. nothing; Suffer and e.

Experience is good, if not bought too dear.

1721 kelly 91. **1732** fuller no. 1479.

Experience is sometimes dangerous.

1573 sandford (1576) 212. **1578** florio *First Fruites* f. 30 (a) Experience sometymes is perilous.

Experience is the mistress of (*or* teaches) fools.

a. **1568** ascham *Scholem.* Erasmus . . . saide wiselie that experience is the common scholehouse of foles. **1579** lyly *Euphues* (Arb.) 123 It is commonly said, yet doe I thinke it a common lye, that experience is the mistresse of fooles, for . . . they be most fooles that want it. **1618** breton *Courtier & Countryman* Wks. (1879) II. 8 Let ignorance be an enemy to wit, and experience be the mistress of fools. **1641** fergusson 30 Experience may teach a fool. **1670** ray 86 *Experientia stultorum magistra.* Wise men learn by others harms, fools by their own. **1874** whytemelville *Uncle John* x Experience does not make fools wise. . . . Most proverbs are fallacious. None greater than that which says it does.

Experience is the mother (father) of wisdom (knowledge) (and memory the mother).

1539 taverner tr. *Erasm. Garden of Wisdom* C 8ᵛ Experience is mother of prudence. **1573** sandford H 4ᵛ Experience is the mother of things. **1578** florio *First Fruites* f. 32 Tyme is the father of truth, and experience is the mother of al things. **1594** lipsius *6 Bks. of Politics* tr. Jones 12 Vse begot me, and Memorie my mother brought me forth [Afranius on Wisdom]. **1616** draxe 58 Experience the mother of wisedome. **1707** mapletoft 34. **1732** fuller no. 1480 Experience is the Father of Wisdom, and Memory the Mother.

Experience keeps a dear school, but fools learn in no other.

[*Cf.* **1604** drayton *Owle* 1. 1088 Fooles still

too deare have sound Experience bought.]
1758 FRANKLIN *Way to Wealth* (Crowell) 24
*Experience keeps a dear school, but fools will
learn in no other,* as Poor Richard says. **1855**
LEWES *Life of Goethe* Experience is the only
Schoolmaster; although, as Jean Paul says,
the school fees are somewhat heavy. **1897**
C. C. KING *Story of Brit. Army* 112 But the
British leaders were to learn the fact, they
might have foreseen, in the 'only school fools
learn in, that of experience'.

Experience without learning is better than learning without experience.

1707 MAPLETOFT 77. **1855** BOHN 352.

Extreme will hold long, No.

1616 BRETON *Cross. Prov.* Wks. (1879) II.
App. iii.

Extremes meet.

1606-7 SHAKS. *Ant. & Cleop.* III iv. 19 No
midway 'Twixt these extremes meet. **1770**
WALPOLE *Letters* (Cunningham) vii. 395 (A)
We seem to be plunging into the horrors of
France . . . yet, as extremes meet, there is
at this moment amazing insensibility. **1809**
MALKIN *Gil Blas* I. v Gentlemen, extremes
are said to meet. **1822** SCOTT *Nigel* xxvii
This Olifaunt is a Puritan?—not the less
likely to be a Papist, . . . for extremes meet.
1853 TRENCH iv. 96 *Extremes meet* . . . Roman
Emperors would one day have blasphemous
honours paid to them, . . . on the next day
. . . to be flung at last into the common sewer.

Extremes, *see also* Sturt follows all e.

Extremity of right is wrong.

1539 TAVERNER (1545) D 4 *Summum ius
summa iniuria* Extreme lawe is extreme
wronge. **1569** GRAFTON *Chron.* (1809) II. 228
The extremitie of iustice is extreme iniustice.
1580 LYLY *Euph. & his Eng.* (Arb.) 461
Justice without mercie were extreame
iniurie. *a.* **1634** CHAPMAN *Chabot* II. iii. 17
Extreme justice is . . . the extreme of injury.
1639 CLARKE 172.

Extremity, *see also* Every e. a fault.

Eye behind him (or in the back of his head), He has an.

[PLAUT. *Aul.* 1. 1. 25 *In occipitio quoque oculos
habet.*] *c.* **1575** *Gammer Gurton's Needle* II. ii
She hath an eie behind her. **1721** KELLY 170
He has an eye in his neck. Spoken of wary
and cautious people.

Eye is a shrew, The.

a. **1591** HY. SMITH *Serm.* (1866) I. 283 It is a
true proverb, The eye is a shrew; although it
shew light, yet it leadeth many into darkness.
If Eve had not seen, she had not lusted.
1678 RAY 354.

Eye is bigger than the belly, The.

1580 LYLY *Euph. & his Eng.* (Arb.) 327 Thou
art like the *Epicure,* whose bellye is sooner
filled then his eye. **1640** HERBERT 364. **1726**
SWIFT *Gulliver* II. viii. Wks. (1856) I. 40 The
captain . . . replied with the old English

proverb, 'That he doubted mine eyes were
bigger than my belly'. **1738** *Id.* (Dial. ii) 347
Miss. I thought I could have eaten this wing
of a chicken; but my eye's bigger than my
belly.

Eye nor my elbow, Neither my.

1894 NORTHALL *Folk-phrases* 20 . . . i.e.
neither one thing nor the other.

Eye, One | of the master sees more than ten of the servants.

1640 HERBERT 349. **1732** FULLER no. 3749
(with 'man's' for 'servants').

Eye of the master will do more work than both his hands, The.

1758 FRANKLIN *Poor Rich. Alm.* in ARBER
Eng. Garner v And again, The Eye of the
master will do more work than both his Hands.
1876 MRS. BANKS *Manch. Man* xiv She was
wont to say, 'The eye of a master does more
work than both his hands', accordingly in
house or warehouse her active supervision
kept other hands from idling.

Eye sees not, What the | the heart craves not.

1620 SHELTON *Quix.* II. lxvii (1908) III. 293
The heart dreams not of what the eye sees
not. **1669** PENN *No Cross, no Crown* v No
thanks if they commit not what they are not
tempted to commit. What the eye views not,
the heart craves not, as well as rues not.

Eye sees not, What the | the heart rues not. (Cf. Far from eye, &c.)

1539 TAVERNER (1552) 13 That the eye seeth
not, yᵉ herte rueth not. **1546** HEYWOOD II. vii.
64 That the eie séeth not, the hert rewth not.
1603 FLORIO tr. *Montaigne* III. xiii (1897) VI.
286 I never desire or find fault with that I
see not: that proverb is verified in me; *What
eye seeth not, the heart rueth not.* **1721** KELLY
341 . . . Men may have losses, but if they be
unknown to them they give them no trouble.
1853 TRENCH vi 146 On the danger of overlooking and forgetting all the suffering of
others . . . which is not actually submitted
to our eyes: *What the eye does not see, the
heart does not rue.*

Eye sees only what it has the power of seeing, The.

1906 G. W. E. RUSSELL *Soc. Silh.* xlvi The
difference is not in our circumstances but in
ourselves. 'The eye sees in all things that
which it brought with it the power to see.'

Eye that sees all things else sees not itself, The.

a. **1591** HY. SMITH *Serm.* (1866) I. 284 As the
eye seeth all things and cannot see itself;
so we can see other men's faults, but not our
own. **1594** NASH *Unf. Trav.* (1920) Ded. 3
How wel or ill I have done in it, I am
ignorant: (the eye that sees round about it
selfe, sees not into it selfe).

Eye will have his part, The.

1640 HERBERT 339.

Eyes about him, He has all his.

1813 RAY 60 . . . i.e. He looks well after his affairs.

Eyes are upon the King, Many.

1616 DRAXE 106.

Eyes as Argus, As many.

[Argus, in fable, had a hundred eyes.] *c.* **1374** CHAUCER *Troylus* IV. 1459 Youre fader is in sleght as Argus eyed. *c.* **1548** BALE *K. Johan* 244 Nay, ye can not, thowgh ye had Argus eyes. **1575** GASCOIGNE *Posies, Supposes* II. i (1907) 199 If I had as many eyes as Argus, I could not have sought a man more narrowly.

Eyes draw (gather, pick) straws, His.

[= to be sleepy.] **1691** MRS. D'ANVERS *Academia* 36 Their Eyes by this time all drew straws. **1738** SWIFT (Dial. iii) 352 *Miss.* Indeed my eyes draw straws. *She's almost asleep.* **1796** WOLCOT (P. Pindar) *Orson & Ellen* v. 125 Their eyelids did not once pick straws. **1824** MOIR *Mansie W.* xxiv As I had been up since five in the morning . . . my een were gathering straws.

Eyes have one language every where, The.

1640 HERBERT 361.

Eyes on letters nor hands in coffers, Neither.

1573 SANDFORD (1576) 218 Neither the eye in the letter, nor the hande in the purse of an other. **1578** FLORIO *First Fruites* f. 33. **1640** HERBERT (Gros.) no. 284.

Eye(s), *see* All 's out is good for prisoners; All that you get you may put in your e.;

Better e. out; Better e. sore; Better fill a man's belly than his e.; Better to have one e.; Bird to pick out his own e. (Brought up); Buyer needs hundred e.; Cry one's e. out; Cry with one e., laugh with other; Day has e., night has ears; Fair wife (Who hath) needs more than two e.; Far from e. far from heart; Fields have e.; Forehead and e. (In) lecture of mind; Four e. see more; Greedy e. to have leal heart (Hard for); Handful of dust will fill e.; Hawks will not pick hawk's e. out; Heart's letter is read in e.; I was by . . . when my e. was put on; Jaundiced e. all things look yellow (To); Jest not with the e.; Keep your e. open before marriage; Keep your mouth shut and e. open; Light is naught for sore e.; Little troubles e., less the soul; Master's e. fattens horse; Master's e. maketh horse fat; Miller's e.; Nature has given two e.; One e. (He that has but) sees better; ―― must be afraid to lose it; Pipe one's e.; Please your e. and plague heart; Proud e., open purse . . . bring mischief; Religion, credit, the e. not to be touched; Rolling e. roving heart; Sight for sore e.; Sleep with one e. open; Touch your e. but with elbow; Twinkling of an e.; Two e. see more than one; War and physic governed by e.; Wash their throats before they washed their e.; Water is the e. of landscape; Whirl the e. shows kite's brain; Winketh with one e. (He that) I will not trust; Wool over e. (Draw). *See also* Goose's eye; Jew's eye; Weather-eye.

Eyewitness, One | is better than two hear-so's.

1539 TAVERNER (1552) f. 43 *Pluris est oculatus testis unus q auriti decem.* One eye wytnesse, is of more value, then ten are [ear] wytnesses. **1639** CLARKE 309.

F

Face as long as a fiddle, To have a.

[= to look dismal.] **1903** A. T. QUILLER-COUCH *Hetty Wesley* II. iv All looked at her; even Johnny Whitelamb looked, with a face as long as a fiddle.

Face is the index of the heart (mind), The.

[L. *Vultus est index animi.*] **1586** L. EVANS *Withals Dict. Revised* L 7 (A) Your face doth testifie what you be inwardly. **1614–16** *Times Whistle* ii. 630–2 Man is to man a subject of deceite; And that olde saying is vntrue, 'the face Is index of the heart'. **1837** LOVER *Rory O'More* xlii 'Your brow and your mouth are playing at cross purposes; for while gloom sits on the one, mirth is twitching at the other.' 'The face is the index of the mind . . . : it is a true saying.'

Face made of a fiddle, To have one's.

[= to be irresistibly charming.] **1678** RAY 243 I think his face is made of a fiddle, every one that looks on him loves him. **1762** SMOLLETT *Sir L. Greaves* (1780) I. viii. 84 Your honour's face is made of a fiddle; every one that looks on you loves you. **1816** SCOTT *Old Mort.* xxxvii How could I help it? His face was made of a fiddle.

Face the music, To.

[= to face boldly the consequences of one's actions, to accept the inevitable.] *a.* **1851** J. F. COOPER in SCHELE DE VERE *Americanisms* (1872) 601 Rabelais' unpleasant 'quarter' is by our more picturesque people called *facing the music.* **1897** RHODES in *Westm. Gaz.* 6 Jan. 5/1 I will not refer to the vulgar colloquialism that I was afraid to face the music.

Face to face, the truth comes out.

1732 FULLER no. 1485. **1852** E. FITZGERALD *Polonius* 53 'Face to face truth comes out apace.' (If you have but an eye to find it by.)

Face to God, He has one | and another to the devil.

1641 FERGUSSON in RAY (1670) 281. **1721** KELLY 152. **1732** FULLER no. 1878.

Face(s), *see also* Fair f. cannot have crabbed heart; Fair f. foul heart; Fair f. half a fortune; Foul f. (Never a) but there's foul fancy; Good f. needs no band; Good f. on a thing (Put); Good f. recommendation; Good fame better than good f.; Joy of the heart makes f. merry; Laugh in one's f. and cut his throat; Set one's f. like a flint; Truth has a scratched f.; Truth hath good f., bad clothes; Two f. in one hood; Woman, the more curious about her f. *See also* Blithe face; Smiling face.

Facilis descensus Averno, see Descent to Avernus.

Fact (Truth) is stranger than fiction.

1823 BYRON *Juan* XIV. ci Truth is always strange; Stranger than fiction. **1863** C. READE *Hard Cash* xxx Sampson was greatly struck with the revelation: he . . . said truth was stranger than fiction. **1881** A. JESSOP *Arcady* 98 The world at large does not believe that there ever did live . . . such a beneficed clergyman as Parson Chowne. . . . In this particular case fact is stranger than fiction. **1910** A. M. FAIRBAIRN *Stud. in Relig. & Theol.* 395 Forgetting the fact which is stranger than fiction, that the sagest man in the theory of the State may be the unwisest man in statecraft.

Facts, So much the worse for the.

1902–4 LEAN IV. 96.

Facts are stubborn things.

1749 SMOLLETT *Gil Blas* x. i (A). **1756–66** AMORY *John Buncle* 124 Facts are things too stubborn to be destroyed by laughing and doubting. **1866** BLACKMORE *Cradock N.* li Facts, however, are stubborn things, and will not even make a bow to . . . young ladies. **1867** FROUDE *Short Studies* I 'Homer' Facts, it was once said, are stubborn things; but in our days we have changed all that.

Fagot, see Eat a buttered f. go to Northampton.

Fail(s, ed), *see* Good that f. never; Mickle f. that fools think.

Failure teaches success.

1902 G. BALFOUR *Life of Stevenson* I. 101 It is an old . . . saying that failure is the only high-road to success.

Failures, *see also* Three f. and a fire make a Scotsman's fortune.

Fain see, That would I | said blind George of Hollowee.

1633 JONSON *T. Tub* II. i That I would fain

zee, quoth the blind George of Holloway. **1678** RAY 268.

Fain, *see also* Fowl of a fair day (As f. as).

Faint at the smell of a wallflower, He will.

1787 GROSE (*London*) 198 . . . Intimating that the person so spoken of had been confined in the gaol of Newgate; formerly styled the wall-flower, from the wall-flowers growing up against it.

Faint heart never won fair lady (*or* castle).

c. **1390** GOWER *Conf. Amantis* v. 6573 Bot as men sein, wher herte is failed, Ther schal no castell ben assailed. **1569** W. ELDERTON *Ballad, Brittain's Ida* v. i Faint hearts faire ladies neuer win. **1580** LYLY *Euph. & his Eng.* (Arb.) 364 Faint heart, Philautus, neither winneth castle nor lady. **1593** SHAKS. *Venus & Adon.* 569 Affection faints not like a pale-fac'd coward But then woos best when most his choice is froward. **1614** CAMDEN 306 Faint heart neuer wonne fair lady. **1753** RICHARDSON *Grandison* I. xvi (1812) 28 Then, madam, we will *not* take your denial. . . . Have I not heard it said, that *faint heart never won fair lady*? **1802** EDGEWORTH *Irish Bulls* xi But 'faint heart never won fair lady', so I made bold to speak to Rose. **1839** DICKENS *N. Nickleby* liii Faint heart never won fair lady.

Faintly, *see* Asketh f. beggeth denial.

Fair and sluttish (*or* foolish), black and proud, long and lazy, little and loud.

c. **1598** *MS. Proverbs* in FERGUSSON 105 Of the culloris of women. Fair & foolish, litil & loud, Long & lusty, black & proud. Fat & merry, lean & sad, Pale & pettish, Red & bad, High cullour (in a woman) choler showes; And shee's unholsome that lyk sorrell growes. Nought ar the peeuish, proud, malitious, But worst of all the Red shrill, jealious. **1670** RAY 51. **1732** FULLER no. 6409.

Fair and softly, as lawyers go to heaven.

1670 RAY 193. **1845** A. SMITH *Scatterg. Fam.* xv You buy as slowly as lawyers go to heaven, and that takes a long time for 'em to do.

Fair and softly goes far.

c. **1350** *Douce MS. 52* no. 50 Fayre and softe me ferre gose. *c.* **1374** CHAUCER *Troylus* v. 347 Thei take it wisely faire and softe. *c.* **1400** *Tale of Beryn* (E.E.T.S.) 28 But feir and sofft with ese, homward they hir led. *c.* **1450** *Coventry Plays* (E.E.T.S.) 50 For soft and essele men goo far. **1576** DESAINLIENS E 1 Softe passe goeth farre. **1598–9** SHAKS. *Much Ado* V. iv. 72 *Friar* To the chapel let us presently. *Bene.* Soft and fair, friar. **1607** TOPSELL *Four-f. Beasts* (1673) 210 The proverb is old and true, 'Fair and softly goeth far'. **1639** CLARKE 3 Soft and fair goes far. **1641** FERGUSSON 42 Hulie[1] and fair men rides far journeys. **1670** RAY 87 . . . He that spurs on too fast at first setting out, tires before he comes to his journey's end. *Festina lente.* **1818** SCOTT *Ht. Midl.* xlv 'Fair and softly gangs far', said Meiklehose; 'and . . . I wad hae him think twice or he mells wi' Knockdunder.' **1914** K. F. PURDON *Folk of Furry F.* ii I'm slow, but fair and easy goes far in a day. [[1] softly.]

Fair as Lady Done, As.

1678 RAY 283 . . . *Chesh.* The Dones were a great family in Cheshire, living at Utkinton . . .: Nurses use there to call their children so if girls. **1917** BRIDGE 12 . . . The wife of Sir John Done (*d.* 1629), of Utkinton, hereditary bow-bearer of Delamere Forest.

Fair chieve[1] all where love trucks.[2]

1670 RAY 47. [[1] See quotation under next proverb. [2] = deals.]

Fair chieve good ale, it makes many folks speak as they think.

1678 RAY 93 . . . Fair chieve is used in the same sense here as . . . Good speed, Good success have it.

Fair day in winter is the mother of a storm, A.

1639 CLARKE 171 A faire day is mother of a storme. **1651** HERBERT 370.

Fair day, To a | open the window, but make you ready as to a foul.

1640 HERBERT 322.

Fair death honours the whole life, A.

1640 HERBERT 342.

Fair face and a foul heart, A.

1598 JONSON *Ev. Man in Humour* IV. vi I have known fair hides have foul hearts ere now, sister. **1659** HOWELL *Eng. Prov.* 3 A fair face, and a foul heart. **1866** READE *G. Gaunt* xl A mob . . . shouting, 'Murderess . . . Fair face but foul heart!'

Fair face cannot have a crabbed heart, A.

c. **1590** LYLY *Love's Metam.* III. i. 52 Faire faces should have smoothe hearts. **1593** *Passionate Morrice* (New Sh. S.) 92 (A) Building vpon the prouerbe, A fair face, &c.

Fair face is half a portion, A.

1616 DRAXE 15 Shee that is faire, hath halfe her portion. **1639** CLARKE 120.

Fair fall nothing once by the year.

1639 in *Berkeley MSS.* (1885) iii. 30 (A). **1678** RAY 182 . . . It may sometimes be better to have nothing than something.

Fair fall truth and daylight.

1678 RAY 211.

Fair field and no favour, A.

1883 E. PENNELL-ELMHIRST *Cream Leicestersh.*

202 He . . . asked only for a fair field and a clear course.

Fair gainings make fair spendings.

1573 SANDFORD (1576) 210. **1629** *Book of Meery Riddles* Prov. 99.

Fair in love and war, All is.

1606 MARSTON *The Fawn* IV. i. 716 An old saw hath bin, Faith's breach for love and kingdoms is no sin. *c.* **1630** BEAUM. & FL. *Lovers' Progress* v. ii (A) All stratagems In love, and that the sharpest war, are lawful. **1801** EDGEWORTH *Belinda* xx In love and war, you know, all stratagems are allowable. **1845** G. P. R. JAMES *Smuggler* xvii But after all, in love and war, every stratagem is fair, they say. **1884** J. PAYN *Canon's Ward* xviii When she reminded him of his solemn promise . . . , he hinted that 'all things were fair (lies included) in love or war'.

Fair in the cradle, and foul in the saddle (*or* vice versa).

1614 CAMDEN 306 Foul in the cradle proveth fair in the saddle. **1670** RAY 87. **1732** FULLER no. 6119.

Fair is not fair, but that which pleaseth.

1640 HERBERT 340. **1670** RAY 9

Fair lasts all the year, The.

1541 *Sch. House of Women* l. 348 in HAZLITT, *Early Pop. Poetry* iv. 118 (A) He need go no farther, the fair is heer; Bye when ye list, it lasteth ouer yeer. **1546** HEYWOOD II. ii. 136. **1611** DAVIES Prov. 1.

Fair March is worth a king's ransom, A.

1598 JONSON *Case is Altered* v. iv March fair all, for *a fair March is worth a king's ransom*!

Fair offer is no cause of feud, A.

1721 KELLY 109 . . . Spoken when one refuses what we proffer them. **1818** SCOTT *Ht. Midl.* xxvi A fair offer, Jeanie, is nae cause of feud.

Fair (Good) pawn never shamed his master, A.

1623 CAMDEN 265. **1631** BRATHWAITE *Whimzies. A Wine-soaker* (1859) 103 Howsoever, a good pawn never sham'd his master. **1670** RAY 130 A fair pawn never sham'd his master. **1721** KELLY 7 *A good pawn never sham'd its master.* It is no shame for a man to borrow on a good pawn.

Fair play's a jewel.

1824 SCOTT *Redg.* xxi No, no, friend—fair play's a jewel—time about, if you please. **1837** CHAMIER *Saucy Areth.* ix Fair play's a jewel. Molly, let go my hair, and I'll fight till I die.

Fair play, *see also* Hands off and f. p.

Fair shop and little gain, A.

1573 SANDFORD (1576) 207 Waxe, linnen

doath, and Fustiane, A fayre shoppe and little gayne. **1629** *Book of Meery Riddles* Prov. 69.

Fair thing full false, There is many a.

1641 FERGUSSON 96.

Fair things, Of | the autumn is fair.

1640 HERBERT 344.

Fair way, To be in a.

a. **1618** RALEIGH *Ess.* (1650) E. v The Caliphes . . . obtained . . . a mighty Empire, which was in faire way to have enlarged. **1814** D. H. O'BRIEN *Captiv. & Escape* 101 Being in a fair way of succeeding.

Fair weather after you.

1594–5 SHAKS. *L.L.L.* I. ii. 150 *Arm.* And so farewell. *Jaq.* Fair weather after you! **1599** PORTER *Angry Wom. Abingd.* II. i (Merm.) 127 *Phil.* Shall I fling an old shoe after ye? *Nich.* No; you should say, God send fair weather after me!

Fair weather in winter on one night's ice, Expect not.

1640 HERBERT 339 Trust not one night's ice. **1670** RAY 28.

Fair weather prepare for foul, In.

1732 FULLER no. 2818.

Fair weather should do any harm, It is a pity that.

1616 DRAXE 45. **1639** CLARKE 79. **1738** SWIFT (Dial. ii) 343 *Col.* The day is finely cleared up. *Smart.* . . . 'Tis a pity that fair weather should ever do any harm.

Fair weather when the shrews have dined, It will be.

1546 HEYWOOD I. xiii. 41 When all shrews haue dind, Chaunge from foule weather to faire is oft enclind. **1678** RAY 243.

Fair weather, *see also* Farewell frost, f. w. next; Full moon brings f. w.

Fair wife and a frontier castle breed quarrels, A.

1640 HERBERT 321.

Fair wife, Who hath a | needs more than twó eyes.

1664 CODRINGTON 226. **1670** RAY 9.

Fair without, false (foul) within. (*Cf.* Fair face and a foul heart.)

c. **1200** *Old Eng. Homilies* (Morris) I. 25 Als swa is an eppel . . . wið-uten feire and frakel wið-innen. *c.* **1275** *Provs. of Alfred* (Skeat) 30 Mony appel is bryht wiþ-vte And bitter wiþ-inne. *c.* **1386** CHAUCER *Canterbury Tales* G. 964 Ne every appel that is fair at yë Ne is nat good, what so men clappe or cryë. *c.* **1430** LYDGATE *Minor Poems* (Percy Soc.) 43 Appeles and peres that semen very gode, Ful

ofte tyme are roten by the core. **1596–7** SHAKS. *Merch. V.* I. iii. 102 A goodly apple, rotten at the heart. **1621** BRATHWAITE *Omphale* (1877) 277 As spotted as the Ermine, whose smooth skin, Though it be faire without, is foule within.

Fair woman and a slashed gown find always some nail in the way, A.

1642 TORRIANO 14. **1658** *Comes Facundus* 234 A fair woman and a pink'd garment is ever meeting with some tenter-hook. **1670** RAY 9.

Fair woman without virtue is like palled wine, A.

1707 MAPLETOFT 5. **1855** BOHN 285.

Fair word in flyting,[1] There was never a.

1641 FERGUSSON 96 There was never a fair word in chiding. **1683** MERITON *Yorks. Ale* (1697) 83–7 (A) Neay, faire words in flighting. **1721** KELLY 303 . . . An excuse for what a man might say in his passion, upon provocation. [[1] scolding.]

Fair words and foul deeds cheat wise men as well as fools. (*Cf.* Good words and ill deeds, &c.)

1573 SANDFORD (1576) 206. **1578** FLORIO *First Fruites* f. 25. 46 **1589** L. WRIGHT *A Summons for Sleepers* C 3 Faire words and wicked deeds deceive both wise men and fooles. **1616** DRAXE 46.

Fair words and foul play cheat both young and old.

1707 MAPLETOFT 69. **1855** BOHN 353.

Fair (Soft) words break no bones.

c. **1450** *How the Good Wife* 1. 43 Ne fayre wordis brake neuer bone. **1611** DAVIES Prov. 52. **1641** FERGUSSON 32 Faire words brake never bane, foule words breaks many ane. **1662** FULLER (*York*) III. 467 Expounding Scripture in a typical way . . . crowded his church with auditors, seeing such soft preaching breaks no bones. **1670** RAY 158 Soft words break no bones.

Fair (Fine) words butter no parsnips.

1638 CLARKE *Phras. Puerilis* A 6. **1639** CLARKE 12 Fair words butter noe parsnips, *verba non alunt familiam.* **1676** WYCHERLEY *Pl. Dealer* v. iii Fair words butter no cabbage. **1692** L'ESTRANGE *Aesop's Fab.* cccxl (1738) 353 Relations, friendships, are but empty names of things, and *Words butter no parsnips.* **1797** G. COLMAN *Heir at Law* III. iii Business is business, and fine words, you know, butter no parsnips. **1847–8** THACKERAY *Vanity F.* xix Who . . . said that 'fine words butter no parsnips?' Half the parsnips of society are served and rendered palatable with no other sauce.

Fair words did fet gromwell[1] seed plenty.

1546 HEYWOOD II. i. 44 His wife was set In

suche dotage of him, that fayre woordes did fet, Gromelséede plentie. [[1] hard seeds used in medicine.]

Fair words fill not the belly.

1580 LYLY *Euph. & his Eng.* (Arb.) 476 Fayre words fatte few. **1670** RAY 61 The belly is not filled with fair words. **1732** FULLER no. 1491.

Fair words hurt not the mouth (tongue).

1550 HEYWOOD I. ix. 18 It hurteth not the tounge to geue fayre wurdis. **1605** CHAPMAN, &c. *Eastw. Hoe* IV. i O, madam, 'Fair words never hurt the tongue'. **1614** CAMDEN 306 Fair words hurt not the mouth. **1659** HOWELL *Eng. Prov.* 5/2 Smooth language grates not the tongue. **1670** RAY 158 Soft words hurt not the mouth. Douces *or* belles paroles ne scorchent pas la langue. *Gall.* Soft words scald not the tongue.

Fair words make fools fain.

[*c.* **1023** EGBERT V. LÜTTICH *Fecunda Ratis* (Voigt) 116 Promissis uacuis spes luditur irrita follis.] *c.* **1225** *Trin. MS. O. 11. 45* (ed. Förster) in *Eng. Stud.* **31.** 5 Beau premettere e poy doner fet le fol conforter. *c.* **1390** GOWER *Conf. Amantis* VII. 1564 Word hath beguiled many a man. *c.* **1400** *Rom. Rose* 1. 4446 Fair biheeste desceyveth fule. **1471** RIPLEY *Comp. Alch.* v. in *Ashm.* (1652) 157 Fayre promys makyth folys fayne. **1546** HEYWOOD II. v. 56 Fayre woordes make fooles fayne. **1599–1600** SHAKS. *Jul. Caes.* III. i. 42 That which melteth fools, I mean sweet words. **1641** FERGUSSON 32 Fair heghts[1] makes fools fain. **1829** SCOTT *Anne of G.* iv Fine words to make foolish maidens fain. [[1] promises.]

Fair words make me look to my purse.

1640 HERBERT 343.

Fair words will not make the pot play.[1]

1721 KELLY 106. [[1] boil.]

Fair words, *see also* Keep off and give f. w.

Fair (*adj. adv.*), *see also* Blustering night, f. day; Fat, f., and forty; Fowl of a f. day (As fain as); Plays you as f. as if picked pocket; Praise a f. day at night.

Fair (noun), *see also* Day after the f.; Speak of the f. as things went with them.

Fairer the hostess, the fouler the reckoning, The.

a. **1635** CORBET *Poems* in CHALMERS, v. 579 (A) A handsome hostess makes the reckoning deare. **1659** HOWELL *Eng. Prov.* 2/1.

Fairer the paper, the fouler the blot, The.

1732 FULLER no. 4513.

Fairest flower in his crown (garden, garland), It is the.

1546 HEYWOOD II. viii. 72 And she is scand Not onely the fairest floure in your garland, But also she is all the faire flowers thereof. **1592** KYD *Span. Trag.* (Boas) I. iv. 4 Don Andreas . . . Who, liuing was my garlands sweetest flower. **1670** RAY 176 It's the fairest flower in his crown or garden.

Fairy (-ies), *see* Scythe cuts (Where), no more f.

Faith with heretics, No.

c. **1592** MARLOWE *Jew of Malta* II. iii (Merm.) 269 *Bar.* It's no sin to deceive a Christian; For they themselves hold it a principle, Faith is not to be held with heretics. **1596–7** SHAKS. *K. John* III. i. 174 And blessed shall he be that doth revolt From his allegiance to a heretic. ? *a.* **1630** J. TAYLOR (Water-P.) *Kicksey Winsey* Wks. (1872) 11 They being Romists, I a Protestant: Their apostatical injunction saith, To keep their faith with me, is breach of faith. **1753** RICHARDSON *Grandison* (1812) VII. iii. 562 I remember the hint he gave to Father Marescotti; but would even *that* good man have thought himself bound to observe faith with heretics in such a case?

Faith, *see also* Love ask f. and f. asks firmness; Love is (Where) there is f.; Money, wisdom, and good f. less than men count upon; Pins his f. upon another's sleeve; Punic f.

Faithful friend is hard to find, Remember man and keep in mind, a.

1721 KELLY 285.

Falcon, *see* Kite will never be good hawk.

Falconer, *see* Swear like a f.

Falkirk, *see* Bairns o' F. (Like the).

Falkland, *see* Cut F. wood with a penknife.

Fall away from a horse-load to a cart-load, To.

1630 DEKKER *Honest Whore Pt. II.* v. i (Merm.) 269 Any woman that has fallen from a horse-load to a cart-load,[1] . . . can direct you to her. [*Note.* [1] An allusion to the carting of prostitutes.] **1738** SWIFT (Dial. i) 339 *Lady S.* Don't you think the colonel's mightily fall'n away of late? *Spark.* Ay, fall'n from a horseload to a cartload.

Fall back, fall edge.

[= Whatever may happen.] *c.* **1535** LYNDSAY *Three Estates* 1. 403 We sall neuer sleip one wink till it be back or eadge. **1553** *Respublica* V. v Fall backe fall edge I am ons at a poincte. **1622** MABBE tr. *Aleman's Guzman d'Alf.* I. 9 Fall back, fall Edge, goe which way you will to work. **1830** SCOTT *Jrnl.* 21 Dec. Fall back, fall edge, nothing shall induce me to publish what [etc.].

Fall into sin is human, To | to remain in sin is devilish.

[ST. CHRYSOST. *Adhortatio ad Theod. lap-*

sum, l. 14: 'Humanum enim est peccare, diabolicum uero perseuerare.'] *c.* **1386** CHAUCER *Mel.* B² 2454 The proverbe seith: that 'for to do sinne is mannish, but certes for to persevere longe in sinne is werk of the devel'. **1655-62** GURNALL *Chrn. in Armour* (1865) I. 298 It is bad enough to fall into an error, but worse to persist. The first shows thee a weak man . . . but the other makes thee too like the devil, who is to this day of the same mind he was at his first fall.

Fall not out with a friend for a trifle.

1639 CLARKE 25. **1670** RAY 9.

Fall on his back and break his nose, He would.

1853 TRENCH i. 21 Of the man . . . to whom the most unlikely calamities . . . befall, they say: *He would fall on his back, and break his nose.* **1912** *Spectator* 18 May 788 'He who is born to misfortune falls on his back and fractures his nose' says a misanthropic humorist.

Fall to pieces, To.

[= to give birth to a child.] **1781** BENTHAM *Wks.* (1843) X. 111 Mrs. Dunning . . . is just ready to fall to pieces.

Fall, *see also* **Fall(s).**

Fallen, He that is | cannot help him that is down.

1640 HERBERT 352.

Falling master makes a standing servant, A.

1721 KELLY 15 . . . Men fall behind in the world by negligence . . . which knavish servants will be sure to take their advantage of; it is no new thing to see a receiver buy his master's estate.

Falling out of lovers is the renewing of love, The.

[TERENCE *Andria* 3. 3. 23 *Amantium irae amoris integratio est.*] **1520** WHITTINTON *Vulg.* (E.E.T.S.) 39 The variaunce of louers (sayth Terence) is the renuynge of loue. **1578** R. EDWARDES *Parad. D. Deuises* 49 *Amantium iræ amoris redintigratia est.* . . . I have found, this prouerbe true to proue, The falling out of faithfull frends, renuing is of loue. **1601-2** SHAKS. *Troil. & Cres.* III. i. 112 Falling in after falling out may make them three. **1621** BURTON *Anat. Mel.* III. ii. III. iv (1651) 489 She would . . . pick quarrels upon no occasion, because she would be reconciled to him again. *Amantium iræ amoris redintegratio,* . . . the falling out of lovers is the renewing of love. **1753** RICHARDSON *Grandison* III. xviii (1812) 229 'The falling out of lovers,' says he, . . . 'is the renewal of love.' Are we not now better friends, than if we had never differed?

Falling, *see also* **Never catch at f. knife or f. friend.**

Falls into the dirt, He that | the longer he stays there the fouler he is.

1640 HERBERT 336. **1721** KELLY 130 . . .

Spoken to those who lie under a slander, urging them to get themselves clear'd as soon as they can. **1732** FULLER no. 2096.

Falls to-day may rise to-morrow, He that.

1620 SHELTON *Quix.* II. lxv (1908) III. 282 He that falls to-day may rise to-morrow, except it be that he mean to lie a-bed. **1732** FULLER no. 2097 He that falls to-day may be up again to-morrow.

Fall(s) (*noun*), *see* **Higher standing lower f.;** **Higher the fool greater the f.;** **Highest tree hath greatest f.;** **Stumble may prevent f.**

Fall(s), fell (*verb*), *see also* **All that shakes f. not;** **Ass f. (Wherever), there will never f. again;** **Better sit still than f.;** **Better to go about than f.;** **Cup and the lip (Many things f. between);** **Descend (F.) than to ascend (Easier to);** **Never climbed never f.;** **Never rode never f.;** **Rides sure that never f.;** **Sooner f. than rise (One may);** **Struck at Tib, down f. Tom;** **Take me not up before I f.**

False as a Scot, As.

1670 RAY 204. **1701** DEFOE *True-born Englishman* ii. Wks. (1911) V. 444 False from the Scot, and from the Norman worse.

False as hell, As.

1604 SHAKS. *Othello* IV. ii. 39 Heaven truly knows that thou art false as hell. **1611** BEAUM & FL. *A King and No King* III. i. 147. **1680** D'URFEY *Virtuous Wife* IV. iii (A).

False colours, *see* **Sail under f. c.**

False tongue will hardly speak truth, A.

1616 DRAXE 11.

False with one can be false with two.

1604 SHAKS. *Othello* I. iii. 294 She has deceived her father and may thee. **1902-4** LEAN III. 463.

False, *see also* **Fair thing full f. (Many a).**

Falsehood in fellowship, There is.

c. **1470** G. ASHBY *Poems* (E.E.T.S.) 26 Be wele ware of falsehode in felawship. **1546** HEYWOOD II. v If he plaie falsehed in felowship, plaie yee. **1594** NASHE *Unf. Trav.* (1920) 95 What is there in *Fraunce* to bee learned more than in *England*, but falshod in fellowship. **1614** CAMDEN 313.

Falsehood never made a fair hinder end.

1641 FERGUSSON 32.

Fame is a magnifying glass.

1732 FULLER no. 1495.

Fame is but the breath of the people.

1611 CORYAT *Crudities* (1905) i. 60 (A) Fame is but winde. **1650** JER. TAYLOR *Holy Liv.*

i. ii (1875) 17 That which would purchase heaven for him he parts with for the breath of the people; which at best is but air, and that not often wholesome. **1732** FULLER no. 1497 Fame is but the breath of the people; and that often unwholesome.

Fame, *see also* Common f. a liar; Common f. seldom to blame; Good f. better than good face; Soweth virtue shall reap f.; Ways to f. (Many).

Familiarity breeds contempt.

[PUB. SYRUS 102 *Parit contemptum nimia familiaritas.* AUGUSTINE (?) *Scala Paradisi* cap. 8 (Migne 40. 1001) *Nimia familiaritas parit contemptum.*] 12th cent. ALANUS DE INSULIS in Wright *Minor Anglo-Latin Satirists* Record Ser. ii. 454 (A). *c.* **1386** CHAUCER *Mel.* B² 2876 Men seyn that 'over-greet homlinesse engendreth dispreysinge'. *c.* **1449** PECOCK *Repr.* 184 Ouermyche hom-lines with a thing gendrith dispising toward the same thing. 1548 UDALL, &c. *Erasm. Par. John* 34a Familiarity bringeth contempt. **1600–1** SHAKS. *Merry W.* I. i. 256 *Slen.* I hope upon familiarity will grow more contempt. **1641** FERGUSSON 82 Over great familiaritie genders despite. **1654** FULLER *Comment on Ruth* in *Serm.* (1891) I. 86 With base and sordid natures familiarity breeds contempt. **1869** TROLLOPE *He Knew He Was Right* 311 Perhaps, if I heard Tennyson talking every day, I shouldn't read Tennyson. Familiarity does breed contempt.

Family, *see* Poor kin (f.) that has neither whore nor thief.

Famine in England begins at the horse-manger, A.

1636 CAMDEN 302 No dearth but breeds in the horse-manger. **1670** RAY 44 . . . In opposition to the rack: for in dry years when hay is dear, commonly corn is cheap: but when oats . . . is dear, the rest are seldom cheap.

Famine, *see also* After a f. in the stall; Under water, f.

Fancy flees before the wind.

1721 KELLY 105 . . . Love and liking are not always well grounded.

Fancy may bolt[1] bran and think it flour.

1546 HEYWOOD II. iv. 51 Fancy may boult bran, and make ye take it floure. **1611** DAVIES *Prov.* 358 'Fancy may boult bran till it be floure.' **1670** RAY 88. [¹ sift.]

Fancy may kill or cure.

1721 KELLY 111 . . . There are many stories of the power of imagination to do good or evil, and . . . the efficacy of these things they call charms depend[s] entirely upon it. **1732** FULLER no. 1500.

Fancy passes beauty.

1678 RAY 136. **1732** FULLER no. 1501 (with 'surpasses').

Fanned fires and forced love never did well yet.

1721 KELLY 108 . . . Both flames burn brightest when they come freely. **1824** FERRIER *Inheritance* xxxiv There's an old byword, 'Fanned fires and forced love ne'er did weel'; and some people will maybe not crack quite so crouse by and by.

Fans in hell, There are no.

1853 TRENCH iv 75 This Arabic [proverb] . . . worthy of Mecca's prophet himself, and of the earnestness with which he realized Gehenna: *There are no fans in Hell.*

Far about, *see* Go f. a. seeking the nearest.

Far behind must follow the faster.

1721 KELLY 107 . . . People whose business and labour is behind their neighbours, must be the more busy and industrious.

Far behind that may not follow, They are.

1721 KELLY 324 . . . Spoken when people do not despond, though behind others.

Far cry to Lochow, It is a.

1819 SCOTT *Leg. Mont.* xii This menace was received with a scornful laugh, while one of the Campbells replied, 'It is a far cry to Lochow'; a proverbial expression of the tribe, meaning that their ancient hereditary domains lay beyond the reach of an invading army. **1850** *Tait's Mag.* XVII. 75/1 In those days it was a 'far cry' from Orkney to Holyrood. **1890** 'ROLF BOLDREWOOD' *Miner's Right* xxiii Because it was 'a far cry to Lochow', or, in other words, a long way from the Oxley to Pekin, no protest on the part of his Celestial Highness reached us.

Far fetched, *see* Dear bought and f. f. are dainties.

Far folk fare best.

1616 DRAXE 45. **1639** CLARKE 177.

Far folks fare well, and fair children die.

1678 RAY 136 . . . People are apt to boast of the good and wealthy condition of their far-off friends, and to commend their dead children.

Far fowls have fair feathers.

c. **1508** DUNBAR *Schir, yit remimbir* 21 (1907) 129 Ay farest faderis hes farrest fowlis Suppois thay haif no sang but youlis. **1721** KELLY 102 . . . Spoken when people extol what they have heard or seen elsewhere, as giving little credit to them. **1789** BURNS *Five Carlins* For far aff fowls have feathers fair.

Far from court, far from care.

1639 CLARKE 205. **1732** FULLER no. 1503.

Far from eye, far from heart. (*Cf.* Eye sees not, What the, &c.)

c. **1300** *Provs. of Hending* 27 Fer from eye,

fer from herte. *c.* **1300** *Cursor M.* l. 4508
Hert sun for-gettes that ne ei seis. *c.* **1336**
CHAUCER *Miller's T.* A 3392 Men seyn right
thus 'Alwey the nye slye Maketh the ferre
leeve to be looth'. *c.* **1400** *MS. Latin no.
344, J. Rylands Libr.* (ed. Pantin) in *Bull.
J. R. Libr.* XIV. 24 Ferre from ye, ferre from
hert.

Far from Jupiter, far from thunder.

1580 LYLY *Euph. & his Eng.* (Arb.) 351 My
dealyngs about the Courte shall be fewe, for
I loue to stande aloofe from *Ioue* and lyght-
ning. **1629** T. ADAMS *Serm.* (1861–2) III. 43
Procul a Joue, procul a fulmine [ERASM. *Ad.*]
was the old saying: Far from Jupiter, far
from his thunder. **1692** L'ESTRANGE *Aesop's
Fab.* xi (1738) 14 *Far from Jupiter* (says the
adage) *far from the thunder.* What signifies
the splendour . . . of courts . . . , considering
the . . . frowns of princes.

Far shooting never killed bird.

1640 HERBERT 336.

Far, *see also* Goes f. that never returns;
Goeth f. (He that) hath many encounters;
So f. so good.

Fare (*noun*), *see* Hard f. makes hungry
bellies.

Fare best, Fare well, *see* Far folk(s).

Fared worse than when I wished for my supper, I never.

1623 CAMDEN 272. **1670** RAY 157.

Fare(s, d), (*verb*), *see also* Banquet (There is
no great) but some f. ill; Go farther f.
worse; Well f. nothing once a year.

Farewell and be hanged.

1575 G. HARVEY *Letter-Book* (Camden Soc.)
95 (A) Farewell and be hanged, good man
cowe. **1608** MIDDLETON *Trick to Catch* IV. i
Farewell, and be hang'd, you . . . rascals.
1670 RAY 174 Farewell and be hang'd, friends
must part.

Farewell, fieldfare!

c. **1374** CHAUCER *Troylus* III. 861 The harm
is don, and far-wel feldéfare! *c.* **1400** *Rom.
Rose* 5510 And syngè 'Go fare-wel, feldefare'.
All suchè freendis I beshrewe. **1878** *N. & Q.*
5th Ser. IX. 136–7 in LEAN IV. 225 That the
fieldfare is a migrant seems to have been
accepted in Chaucer's time from the proverbial phrase, 'Farewell, fieldefare!'

Farewell, forty pence! Jack Noble is dead (a-bed).

[= contemptuous dismissal.] *c.* **1500** MED-
WALL *Nature in 'Lost' Tudor Plays* (1907) 98
She opened a window and put forth her head
—Hence, Forty Pence! quo' she, Jack Noble
is a-bed. *c.* **1600** DAY *Begg. Bednall Gr.* V.
(1881) 114 Why, farewell 40 pence! **1631**
F. LENTON *Characters* (1663) no. 17 Her
Purse . . . seldome exonerats its selfe till the
Maulster appeares, and then farwel forty

pence. **1639** CLARKE 68 Farewell, forty
pence! Jack Noble is dead.

Farewell frost.

1564 BULLEIN *Dial. agst. Fever* (1888) 72
Hitherto hath not been found neither cow
nor man, and all the milk is gone. Farewell
frost! **1670** RAY 174 Farewell frost: nothing
got, nor nothing lost.

Farewell frost, fair weather next.

1721 KELLY 104 *Farewell frost, fair weather
nest.*[1] Spoken when they go off, whom we are
glad to part with. [[1] next.]

Farewell, gentle Geoffrey!

c. **1475** *Mankind* l. 155. *c.* **1520** J. RASTELL
Four Elements C 5 Farewell gentyll John.
1546 HEYWOOD I. xi. **1565** *King Darius* F 3
Farewell gentle Hary.

Farewell, *see also* Welcome (Such), such f.

Fare-ye-weel, Meg Dorts, and e'en's ye like.

1725 A. RAMSAY *Gentle Shep.* I. i 'Then fare
ye weel, Meg Dorts, and e'en's ye like,' I
careless cry'd, and lap in o'er the dyke. **1862**
HISLOP 94 Fare-ye-well, Meg Dorts, and e'en's
ye like. A jocose adieu to those who go away
in the sulks.

Farlie(s), *see* Fault (If it be), it is no f.;
Longer we live more f. we see. *See also*
Ferlies.

Farm full, He that will have his | must keep an old cock and a young bull. (*But cf.* Full flock, &c.)

1750 W. ELLIS *Mod. Husbandman* III. 94
When a bull comes to be four, he is heavy
and sluggish. . . . The old verse says, 'He
that will have his farm full, Must keep an old
cock and a young bull'.

Farm(s), *see also* Flitting of f. makes mailings
dear; Hold the greatest f. (They that) pay
least rent; Sell a f. and go to sea.

Farmer should have on Candlemas Day, half his stover[1] and half his hay, The.

1639 in *Berkeley MSS.* (1885) III. 30 (A) At
Candlemas a provident husbandman should
have half his fodder and all his corne remain-
inge. **1732** FULLER no. 6487 On Candlemas
day, you must have half your straw and half
your hay. **1869** HAZLITT 367. [[1] fodder.]

Farmer(s), *see also* Feed like a f.; Pigeons go
a benting (When), f. lie lamenting.

Farther in, the deeper, The.

1721 KELLY 324 *The farrer in the deeper.*
Spoken to people engag'd into an intricate
business: the more they struggle the more
they are entangled. **1824** MOIR *Mansie W.*
xx This astonished us more and more, and

. . . I thought there surely must be some league and paction with the Old One; but the further in the deeper.

Farther the sight the nearer the rain, The.

1883 ROPER 23. 1893 INWARDS 105.

Farther, Further, *see also* Go f. fare worse.

Farthest (Longest) way about is the nearest way home, The.

1580 LYLY *Euph. & his Eng.* Wks. (Bond) II. 96 Thou goest about (but yet the neerest way) to hang me vp for holydayes. 1600 KEMP *Nine Days' Wonder* (*Social England*, Lang 156) Getting so into Master Mayor's gates a nearer way, But, at last, I found it the further way about. 1635 QUARLES *Emblems* IV. ii. 2 The road to resolution lies by doubt: The next way home's the farthest way about. 1642 FULLER *H. & P. State* IV. ix. 11 When . . . he privately tells his prince of his faults, he knows, by Nathan's parable, to go the nearest way home by going far about. 1670 RAY 95 . . . What is gained in the shortness, may be lost in the goodness of the way. 1905 ALEX. MACLAREN *Matthew* i. 166 The longest way round is sometimes the shortest way home.

Farthing(s), *see* Brass f. (Not worth); Four f. and a thimble; Loses his wife and a f. (He that); Miserable man maketh a penny of a f., and the liberal of a f. sixpence; Thinks his penny (f.) good silver.

Fas est et ab hoste doceri.

[ARISTOPHANES *Aves* 376 Ἀλλ' ἀπ' ἐχθρῶν δῆτα πολλὰ μανθάνουσιν οἱ σοφοί. And yet wise men learn much from enemies. OVID *Metamorph.* iv. 428 *Fas est et ab hoste doceri*; it is lawful to learn even from an enemy.] 1911 *Spectator* 21 Sept. 594 It is lawful, declares the old Latin proverb, to be taught by one's foe.

Fash one's thumb, To.

[= to give oneself trouble.] 1786 BURNS *Ernest Cry & Prayer* v Speak out, an' never fash your thumb. 1818 SCOTT *Ht. Midl.* xvi It was lang syne, . . . and I'll ne'er fash my thumb about it.

Fashion's sake, For | as dogs go to church (the market).

1599–1600 SHAKS. *A.Y.L.* III. ii. 271 *Jaq.* I had as lief have been myself alone. *Orl.* And so had I; but yet, for fashion' sake, I thank you too for your society. 1721 KELLY 109 *For fashions sake, as dogs goes to the market.* Spoken when we see people declare for a party, or make a profession, which we suppose they would not do, if it were not in vogue. 1732 FULLER no. 1590.

Fashion, *see also* Every one after his f.; Out of the world out of f.; Plain f. is best; Tailors and writers must mind f.

Fast and loose, *see* Play f. and l.

Fast as a dog can trot, As.

1678 RAY 89 He lies as fast as a dog can trot.

Fast as a dog will lick a dish, As.

1546 HEYWOOD II. vii. 64 She will lie as fast as a dogge will licke a dishe. 1721 KELLY 151 He can lie as fast as a dog can lick a dish.

Fast (thick) as hops, As.

1590 NASHE *Pasquil's Apol.* 1 c They must be throwne ouer the Pulpit as thicke as hoppes. 1599 PORTER *Angry Wom. Abingd.* IV. iii The water drops from you as fast as hops. 1690 D'URFEY *Collin's Walk* i. 7 To make him sprout as fast as hops.

Fast as one goeth another cometh, As.

1546 HEYWOOD I. iii. 7.

Fast (Safe, Sure) bind, fast (safe, sure) find.

1484 CAXTON *Æsope* v. 4 Who that wel byndeth well can he vnbynd. 1546 HEYWOOD I. iii. 7 Than catche and holde while I may, fast bind, fast find. *c.* 1548 BALE *K. Johan* 1897 As the saynge is, he fyndeth that surely bynde. 1573 TUSSER 83 *Washing* (1878) 173 Drie sunne, drie winde, safe binde, safe finde. 1596–7 SHAKS. *Merch. V* II. v. 53 Shut doors after you: 'Fast bind, fast find', A proverb never stale in thrifty mind. 1622 J. FLETCHER *Span. Cur.* II. ii So, so, fast bind, fast find. 1655 FULLER *Ch. Hist.* IV. iv (1868) I. 611 Because 'sure bind, sure find', he [i.e. Richard III] is said, and his queen, to be crowned again in York with great solemnity. 1824 SCOTT *Redg.* xiii Mr. Trumbull, . . . muttered something about fast bind, fast find, turned the key, and put it into his pocket. 1890 D. C. MURRAY *J. Vale's Guard* vi 'Safe bind, safe find,' said Uncle Robert, locking the door and pocketing the key.

Fast for [fear of] breaking your shins (falling), Not too.

1580 BARET *Alvearie* (*Cante* A 59) A Prouerbe applyed vnto those, that take no deliberation in bringing any thing to passe: and as we say: not to[o] fast for breaking your shinnes. 1599 PORTER *Angry Wom. Abingd.* II. i (Merm.) 125 *Nich.* Haste makes waste; soft fire makes sweet malt; not too fast for falling.

Fast for my life, If I were to | I would take a good breakfast in the morning.

1678 RAY 67. 1738 SWIFT (*Dial.* ii) 346 If I were to fast for my life, I would take a good breakfast in the morning, A good dinner at noon, and a good supper at night.

Fast, Fastest (*adj. adv.*), *see also* Over f. over loose; Runs f. gets most ground; Runs f. gets the ring; Runs f. will not run long.

Fast (*noun*), *see* Break his neck as his f. (As soon).

Fastens where there is gain, Every one.

1640 HERBERT 341.

Fasteth and doeth no other good, Who | spares his bread and goes to hell.

1650 JER. TAYLOR *Holy Liv.* IV. v (Bohn) 190 The devil . . . will be as tempting with the windiness of a violent fast as with the flesh of an ordinary meal. . . . Fasting alone will not cure this devil. Chi digiuna ed altro ben non fa, Sparagna il pane, ed al inferno va. 1659 HOWELL *Ital.* 1.

Fasting when the table is covered with fish, It is good.

1855 BOHN 270. [*Danish.*]

Fasting, *see also* Belly is full (He whose) believeth not the f.; Full man and a f. (It is ill speaking between); Never well, full nor f.; Speak to a f. man (Never).

Fasts enough that has had a bad (slender) meal, He.

1611 COTGRAVE s.v. 'Assez' He that feeds barely fasts sufficiently. 1650 JER. TAYLOR *Holy Liv.* IV. v (1850) 190 A diet of fasting, a daily lessening of our portion of meat and drink, . . . which may make the least preparation for the lusts of the body. Digiuna assai chi mal mangia. 1732 FULLER no. 1844.

Fat as a fool.

1575 *Apius and Virginia* B 1 1. 228. 1579 LYLY *Euphues* 118 (Arber). 1678 RAY 283.

Fat as a hen in the forehead, As.

[*Ironical.*] 1618–19 J. FLETCHER *Bonduca* I. ii Will feed ye up as fat as hens i' th' foreheads. 1738 SWIFT (Dial. iii) 357 *Miss.* Fat! ay, fat as a hen in the forehead.

Fat as butter, As.

1584 LYLY *Campaspe* I. ii. 76 I would make mine eyes fatte as butter. 1597–8 SHAKS. *1 Hen. IV* II. iv. 560 A gross fat man.—As fat as butter. 1604 DEKKER *News from Gravesend* (*Plague Pamphlets*, ed. Wilson 72). 1621 BURTON *Anat. Mel.* II. ii. v Alpine mice . . . sleeping under the snow . . . as fat as butter.

Fat drops from fat flesh.

1597–8 SHAKS. *1 Hen. IV* II. ii. 119 Falstaff sweats to death And lards the lean earth as he walks along. 1678 RAY 137.

Fat, fair, and forty.

1795 O'KEEFFE *Irish Minnie* II. iii (A) Fat, fair, and forty were all the toast of the young men. 1824 SCOTT *Redg.* vii Fat, fair, and forty, . . . that is all I know of her.

Fat flits from (a man's) beard, The.

[*i.e.* he lets go the advantage he has gained.] 1546 HEYWOOD I. iii Blame me not to haste, for feare mine eie be blerde. And therby the fat cleane flit fro my berde.

5017

O

Fat hens lay few eggs.

1629 T. ADAMS *Serm.* (1861–2) I. 191 Midnight revels, morning junkets, . . . but add new to their indigested surfeits. They are the devil's crammed fowls, like Aesop's hens, too fat to lay, to produce the fruits of any goodness.

Fat hog, *see* Basteth the f. h. (Every man).

Fat housekeepers make lean executors.

1611 COTGRAVE s.v. 'Testament' Great house-keepers leave poor executors. 1721 KELLY 111 . . . Because they spend all in their lifetime. 1732 FULLER no. 1505. 1758 FRANKLIN *Poor Rich. Alm.* in ARBER *Eng. Garner* v. 582 A fat kitchen makes a lean Will.

Fat is in the fire, (All) the.

[In early use expressing failure, but now meaning there will be an explosion.] *c.* 1374 CHAUCER *Troylus* III. 710 This night shal I make it wel, Or casten al the gruwel in the fyre. 1399 LANGLAND *Rich. Redeles* II. 51 That shente all the browet, And cast adoun the crokk the colys amyd [ruined the pottage and cast down the pot amidst the coals.] 1546 HEYWOOD I. iii. 6 Then farewell riches, the fat is in the fire. 1578 SIDNEY *Lady of May Rhombus the schoolmaster.* O tace, tace, or all the fat will be liquefied. 1633 JONSON *Love's Welc. at Welb.* Wks. (1904) III. 217 Else all the fat i' the fire were lost. 1797 WOLCOT (P. Pindar) *Livery of London* Wks. (1812) III. 449 Should we once complain The fat will all be in the fire. 1902 *Autobiog. of W. Besant* 164 Ganneau asked permission to see the MS., and then all the fat was in the fire.

Fat land grow foulest weeds, On.

1393 LANGLAND *P. Pl.* C. xiii. 224 On fat londe and ful of donge · foulest wedes groweth. 1597–8 SHAKS. *2 Hen. IV.* IV. iv. 54 *K. Hen.* Most subject is the fattest soil to weeds; And he, the noble image of my youth, is overspread with them.

Fat man, *see* Little knoweth f. m. what lean thinketh.

Fat paunches have lean pates.

[Gk. Παχεῖα γαστὴρ λεπτὸν οὐ τίκτει νόον. JEROME *Pinguis venter non gignit sensum tenuem.* (A fat paunch does not produce fine sense.)] 1586 B. YOUNG tr. *Guazzo's Civ. Conv.* f. 190 (A) The prouerbe is as true as common. That a fat bellie doth not engender a subtill witte. 1594–5 SHAKS. *L.L.L.* I. i. 26 Fat paunches have lean pates, and dainty bits Make rich the ribs, but bankrupt quite the wits. 1639 CLARKE 192 Fat paunches and lean pates. 1721 KELLY 106 *Fat paunches bode lean pates.* A groundless reflection upon fat men. 1732 FULLER no. 1506 (with 'make' for 'have').

Fat sorrow is better than lean sorrow.

1678 RAY 137 . . . Better have a rich husband

and a sorrowful life than a poor husband and a sorrowful life with him; spoken to encourage a maid to marry a rich man, though ill conditioned. **1732** FULLER no. 1507. **1902** DEAN HOLE *Then & Now* [7 ed.] viii They forget awhile the 'mighty difference' which one of them suggested, when told by a rich neighbour that we all had our troubles, 'between fat sorrow and lean'.

Fat, *see also* Drives f. oxen should be f.; Laugh and be f.; Lick the f. from the beard; Little knoweth the f. sow what lean doth mean; Swine over f. cause of own bane; Take the f. with the lean.

Fate leads the willing, but drives the stubborn.

[SENECA *Epist.* 107. 11 *Ducunt volentem fata, nolentem trahunt.* From a quatrain by Cleanthes, quoted by Epictetus at the end of his *Enchiridion.*] **1629** T. ADAMS *Serm.* (1861–2) II. 94 What thou must do, do willingly. *Fata volentem ducunt, nolentem trahunt.* God gently leads thee coming, but drags thee on withdrawing. *a.* **1657** LOVELACE (Everyman) 369 Fates lead the willing, but the unwilling draw. **1732** FULLER no. 1508.

Fate, *see also* Flying from f. (No); Sure as f.

Father, That is for the | but not for the son.

1721 KELLY 322 ... Spoken when a thing is done with slight materials, and consequently will not be lasting.

Father buys, The | the son bigs,[1] the grandchild sells, and his son thigs.[2]

1721 KELLY 312 ... A proverb much used in *Lowthian*, where estates stay not long in one family. **1862** HISLOP 280 The grandsire buys, the father bigs, the son sells, and the grandson thigs. [[1] builds. [2] begs.]

Father, One | can support ten children; ten children cannot support one father.

1853 TRENCH iv. 82 This Spanish: *One father can support ten children*; *ten children cannot support one father*; ... attesting the comparative weakness of the filial as set over against the paternal affection.

Father, One | is enough to govern one hundred sons, but not a hundred sons one father.

1640 HERBERT 336.

Father is judge, He whose | goes safe to his trial.

1620 SHELTON *Quix.* II. xliii (A) For according to the proverb, 'He that hath the judge to his father, &c.' and I am governor, which is more than judge. **1732** FULLER no. 2400.

Father, One | is more than a hundred schoolmasters.

1640 HERBERT 349.

Father, Like | like son.

[ERASM. *Ad. Hodie vulgo dicitur ex Athanasii symbolo detortum, Qualis pater, talis filius.*] **1362** LANGLAND *P. Pl.* II. 934 (Wright) I. 29 And Mede is manered after hym, Right as kynde asketh *Qualis pater talis filius. c.* **1386** CHAUCER *Leg. Good Women* l. 2448 It com hym of nature As doth the fox Renard, [so doth] the foxes sone. **1509** A. BARCLAY *Ship of Fools* (1874) I. 236 An olde prouerbe hath longe agone be sayde That oft the sone in maner lyke wyll be Vnto the Father. **1616** DRAXE 23 Like father, like sonne: like mother like daughter. **1708** DYKES *Mor. Reflect. Provs.* 30 Like Father, Like Son. ... How many *Sons* inherit their *Fathers Failings*, as well as *Estates?* **1841** S. WARREN *Ten Thous. a Year* xxvi Two such bitter Tories ... for, like father, like son.

Father of a disease, Whatsoever was the | an ill diet was the mother.

1651 HERBERT 365.

Father to the bough, the son to the plough, The.

1576 LAMBARDE *Peramb. of Kent* (1826) 497 (A). **1662** FULLER (*Kent*) II. 124 'The father to the bough, The son to the plough.' That is, though the father be executed for his offence, the son shall nevertheless succeed to his inheritance. **1787** GROSE (*Kent*) 182 ... One of the privileges of gavel-kind, ... whereby ... only the goods and chattels, but not the lands, are forfeited to the crown, on the execution of a criminal.

Father was a bad (*or* no) glazier, Your.

1738 SWIFT (Dial. i) 334 *Lady S.* You stand in your own light. ... *Spark.* I'm sure he sits in mine. Pr'ythee, Tom, sit a little further; I believe your father was no glazier. **1910** P. W. JOYCE *Eng. as We Speak* 113 'Your father was a bad glazier': said to a person who is standing in one's light.

Father, *see also* Give it about ... come to f. at last; Happy is he whose friends (f.) born before him; Happy is that child whose f. goeth to devil; Head will never fill f.'s bonnet; Speak good of archers for your f. shot; Speak good of pipers, your f. was fiddler; Teach your f. to get children; Thank God your f. born before you.

Fault confessed is half redressed, A.

1592 *Arden of Fevers.* IV. iv (*Shaks. Apoc.*) A fault confessed is more than half amends. **1622** BEAUM. & FL. *Prophetess* v. iii For faults confess'd, they say, are half forgiven. **1732** FULLER no. 1140 Confession of a fault makes half amends. **1822** SCOTT *Nigel* xxix Indeed, to confess is, in this case, in some slight sort to redress.

Fault, He hath but one: | he is nought.

1546 HEYWOOD I. xi. 29. **1732** FULLER no.

6054 Your main fault is, you are good for nothing.

Fault is as great as he that is faulty, The.

1640 HERBERT 335.

Fault is, Where no | there needs no pardon.

1616 DRAXE 28. **1617** *Machivels Dugge* f. 8 (with 'excuse' for pardon'). **1639** CLARKE 208.

Fault, If it be a | it is no farlie.[1]

1721 KELLY 190 . . . Spoken in excuse for doing a thing, bad indeed, but common, and usual. [[1] miracle, wonder.]

Fault of a wife, He has | that marries mam's pet. (*Cf.* Dawted daughters, &c.)

1721 KELLY 153 . . . Maids that have been much indulged by their mothers, and have had much of their will, seldom prove good wives.

Fault of the ass must not be laid upon the pack-saddle, The.

1620 SHELTON *Quix.* II. lxvi (1908) III. 286 According to the opinion of wise men, the fault of the ass must not be laid upon the pack-saddle.

Fault of the horse is put on the saddle, The.

1640 HERBERT 328.

Faults are theirs that commit them, The first | the second theirs that permit them.

[**1592** G. DELAMOTHE (1647) 56 A second fault ought not to be pardoned.] **1707** MAPLETOFT 10. **1732** FULLER no. 4528.

Faults are thick where love is thin.

1616 DRAXE 119 Where Loue is not, there is hatred. **1659** HOWELL *Brit. Prov.* 2. **1886** E. J. HARDY *How to be Happy* vi There is another way in which people make the worst . . . of their bad matrimonial bargains. 'Faults are thick where love is thin', and love having become thin they exaggerate the badness of their bargains.

Faults on both sides, There are.

1902 DEAN HOLE *Then & Now* [ed. 7] xiii My convictions are, after sixty years of intercourse with clergy and laity . . . , that there are faults on both sides.

Fault(s), Fauts, *see also* All f. to mend (Hard for any man); Commits a f. (He that) thinks every one speaks of it; Every f. there is folly (In); Every man hath his f.; Every one puts his f. on times; Every one's f. not written in foreheads; Find f. if you knew how; Find f. with fat goose;

Foolish in the f., wise in punishment; Great men have great f.; Hantle o' f. (Some hae); Love fails (Where), we espy f.; Men's years and f. more than they own; Punishment (Many without), but none without f.; Spy f. if eyes were out (You would); Wants a mule without f. (He who); Wink at small f. *See also* Mend-fault.

Faultless, *see* Lifeless that is f.

Faulty stands on his guard, The.

1640 HERBERT 353. **1670** RAY 9.

Favour, Without | none will know you, and with it you will not know yourself.

1640 HERBERT 324.

Favour will as surely perish as life.

1651 HERBERT 366.

Favour(s), *see also* Grace will last, f. blast; Great men's f. uncertain.

Fawn like a spaniel, To. (*Cf.* Flattering as a spaniel.)

c. **1592** MARLOWE *Jew of Malta* II. iii *Bar.* We Jews can fawn like spaniels when we please. **1599–1600** SHAKS. *Jul. Caes.* III. i. 43 That which melteth fools; I mean sweet words, Low-crooked curtsies, and base spaniel fawning. **1611** MIDDLETON *Roar. Girl* v. i He hath been brought up in the Isle of Dogs, and can both fawn like a spaniel, and bite like a mastiff, as he finds occasion. **1612–13** SHAKS. *Hen. VIII* V. iii. 126 You play the spaniel, And think with wagging of your tongue to win me.

Fawn, *see also* Better to have dog f. than bite; Spaniels that f. when beaten.

Fazarts,[1] To | hard hazards are death ere they come there.

a. **1585** MONTGOMERIE *Cherrie & Slae* 377 To fazarts, hard hazarts Is deid or they cum thair. **1721** KELLY 332 . . . Cowardly people are almost kill'd at the sight of danger. [[1] cowards.]

Fear death as children to go in the dark, Men.

1607–12 BACON *Ess., Death* (Arb.) 382 Men feare death as Children feare to goe in the darke. **1670** RAY 7.

Fear hath a quick ear.

1609 JONSON *Silent Woman* IV. v. 98. **1654** GAYTON *Pleasant Notes Don Q.* 65 (A).

Fear is bondage, All.

1573 SANDFORD (1576) H 4. **1629** *Book of Meery Riddles* Prov. 35.

Fear is stronger than love.

1624 BURTON *Anat. Mel.* III. ii. v. 4 N 3 margin, Vehement Feare expells Loue. **1732** FULLER no. 1513.

Fear keeps and looks to the vineyard, and not the owner.

1599 MINSHEU (1623) Tt 2 **1651** HERBERT 366.

Fear keeps the garden better than the gardener.

1640 HERBERT 329.

Fear not the loss of the bell more than the loss of the steeple.

1855 BOHN 7.

Fear nothing but sin.

1640 HERBERT 331.

Fear, the beadle of the law.

1650 STAPYLTON *Strada's Low-C. Wars* ii. 33 Fear, the beadle of the law, terrified them from the beginning. **1651** HERBERT 366.

Fear the Greeks, even when bringing gifts, I.

[VIRGIL *Aen.* 2. 49 *Timeo Danaos, et dona ferentes.*] **1777** JOHNSON *Let.* 3 May in *Boswell* (1848) lvii. 530 Tell Mrs. Boswell that I shall taste her marmalade cautiously at first. *Timeo Danaos et dona ferentes.* Beware, says the Italian proverb, of a reconciled enemy. **1929** *Times* 26 Oct. 13/3 MR. MOSES . . . must now be reflecting on the wisdom of the advice to 'fear the Greeks even when they bring gifts'.

Fear the worst, It is good to | the best will save itself (be the welcomer).

[L. *Grata superveniet quae non sperabitur hora.* The hour of happiness will be the more welcome, the less it is expected.] **1616** DRAXE 65 (with 'will save itself'). **1670** RAY 89. **1721** KELLY 200 . . . Fearing the worst will make us careful, and cautious; and if things succeed better than we expected, the surprise will be pleasant.

Feareth every bush must never go a-birding, He that.

1580 LYLY *Euph. & his Eng.* (Arb.) 354 He that feareth euery bush must neuer goe a birding, he that casteth all doubts, shall neuer be resolued in any thing. *c.* **1598** *MS. Provs.* in FERGUSSON 56 He that is afrayd of every bush wil never proue good huntsman.

Feareth every grass must not walk (p—) in a meadow, He that.

c. **1412** HOCCLEVE *Reg. of Princes* (Furnivall) 1. 1887 Men seyn, who-so of every grace hath drede, let hym beware to walk in any mede. *c.* **1566** *The Bugbears* (ed. Bond) I. iii. 14 He shall never p— in medow that fearethe every grasse. **1614** CAMDEN 730.

Fearful as Plutus, As.

1621 BURTON *Anat. Mel.* I. ii. III. 13 (1651) 116 *Timidus Plutus*, an old proverb, As fearful as Plutus; . . . trusting no man. 1853 TRENCH v. 112 A Latin proverb on the

moral cowardice which it is the character of riches to generate, Timidus Plutus.

Fears are divided in the midst.

1640 HERBERT 347.

Fears death lives not, He that.

1553 ERASMUS *Precepts of Cato* (1560) G 1ᵛ He yᵗ so sore feareth his death, . . . it were as good to haue no life at all. **1640** HERBERT 353.

Fears leaves, He that | let him not go into the wood.

1611 COTGRAVE s.v. 'Peur' Let him thats skar'd by leaues keepe from the Wood. **1616** DRAXE 65 He that is afraid of leaues, must not go to the wood. **1640** HERBERT 352. **1670** RAY 55 . . . This a French proverb Englished. Qui a peur de feuilles ne doit aller au bois.

Fears the gallows shall never be a good thief, He that.

1592 GREENE *Disput.* 3.

Fears you present will hate you absent, He that.

1732 FULLER no. 2101.

Fear(s) (*noun*), **see also** Danger once (Better pass) than be always in f.; Dies for age (When he) you may quake for f.; Gold (When we have) we are in f.; Lives ill (He that) f. follows; Medicine for f. (No); Money (To have) is a f.; Pains to get . . . f. to lose; Travelleth not by sea knows not f.; Weapons of war will not arm f.; Wise f. begets care.

Fear(s) (*verb*), **see also** Hopes not for good f. not evil; Right (He that hath) f.; Truth f. no colours; Tyrants seem to kiss (Time to f. when).

Feast and a bellyful, Little difference between a.

1659 HOWELL *Eng. Prov.* 13/2. **1678** RAY 100. **1790** TRUSLER *Prov. Exempl.* 169 When hunger is satisfied, even the sight of meat is disgusting. *Little difference between a feast and a bellyful*; and when our inclinations are gratified, what more can we need?

Feast or a fast, Either a.

1732 FULLER no. 3113 Is there no mean, but fast or feast? **1912** *Daily Tel.* 26 July 12 Dock labour has been graphically described as 'either a feast or a fast'. Good wages may be earned in a short time. . . . On the other hand, work is not always obtainable.

Feast to a miser's (churl's), No.

1611 DAVIES *Prov.* 349 'A man shall as soone breake his necke as his fast In a miser's house': Yet stay, . . . it is confest That there is no cheare to a miser's feast. **1639** CLARKE 192 No feast to a churls. **1678** RAY 137 No feast to a Misers. Il n'est banquet que d'homme chiche. *Gall.*

Feast, *see also* Better come at end of f.; Cheerful look makes f.; Company makes f.; Contented mind; Good conscience; Yule f. done at Pasch.

Feather by feather, the goose is plucked.

1666 TORRIANO 174 A penna a [penna] si pela l'oca. *Quill by quill, is a goose pluck'd.* **1732** FULLER no. 1514. **1790** TRUSLER *Prov. Exempl.* 183 The weak man . . . hair by hair . . . got off the whole tail without much labour; for, according to the Italian proverb, *Feather by feather, the goose is plucked.* **1856–70** FROUDE *Hist. Eng.* XII. 414 Howard, whose notion was to 'pluck the feathers of the Spaniards one by one', sent his own launch . . . to take her.

Feather in hand, A | is better than a bird in the air.

1640 HERBERT 344.

Feather in one's cap, A.

1661 DR. DENTON to Sir R. Verney *Verney Memoirs* iv (1899) 7 A feather in my capp. **1678** RAY 342 He put a fine feather in my cap, i.e. Honour without profit. **1808** SCOTT in LOCKHART *Life* (1860) xvii. 163 Literary fame, he always said, was a bright feather in the cap. **1824** L. HUNT in *Examiner* 28 Mar. Gresset wrote other poems, . . . but the Parrot is the feather in his cap.

Feather one's nest, To.

[= enrich oneself.] **1553** *Republica* in '*Lost' Tudor Plays* (1907) 183 Now is the time come . . . to feather my nest. **1583** STUBBES *Anat. Abus.* II (1882) 38 By this meanes . . . they feather their nests well inough. **1612** T. TAYLOR *Comm. Titus* i. 7 Yet all this worke is neglected, that his owne neast may be well feathered. **1680** BUNYAN *Mr. Badman* (1929) 142 When *Mr. Badman* had well feathered his Nest with other mens goods and money, after a little time *he breaks.* **1721** KELLY 161 *He has feathered his nest, he may fly when he will.* Spoken of them who have had a good place so long, that they have gotten estates. **1753** SMOLLETT *Ct. Fathom* (1784) 41/2 His spouse . . . was disposed to feather her own nest, at the expense of him and his heirs. **1884** J. PAYN *Canon's Ward* 1 Adair . . . had feathered his nest . . . , had laid his hands upon everything that could be realized, and turned it into portable property.

Feather(s), *see also* Afraid of the wagging of f.; Ask a kite for a f.; Bird take back own f. (If every); Cut a f.; Fine f. make fine birds; Knocked me down with a f. (Might have); Light as a f.; Meet-mate and you meet (If your) . . . two men bear a f.; Words and f. wind carries away.

Featherbed, *see* Go to heaven in f.

February fill dyke.

1557 TUSSER cii Feuerell fill dyke, doth good with his snowe. **1670** RAY 40 February fill dike Be it black or be it white; But if it be white, It's the better to like. **1721** KELLY 107 *February fill dike either with black or white.* February brings commonly rough weather, either snow or rain. **1879** R. JEFFERIES *Wild Life South. Co.* xvii February 'fill ditch', as the old folk call it, on account of the rains.

February hath one and thirty days, Reckon right, and.

1640 HERBERT 327. **1670** RAY 9.

February makes a bridge, and March breaks it.

1640 HERBERT 351. **1732** FULLER no. 1516. **1914** *Brit. Wkly.* 12 Mar. 690 The wintry weather of Tuesday . . . did its best to justify the old English saying, 'February makes a bridge, and March breaks it'.

Februeer doth cut and shear.

1633 JONSON *T. Tub.* I. i Februere Doth cut and shear.

February (Februeer), *see also* Months in the year curse a fair F.; Welshman had rather see . . . than fair F.

Fed at another's hand (table), He that is | may stay long ere he be full.

1640 HERBERT 338. **1813** RAY 164 Who depends upon another man's table often dines late. *Chi per altrui mano s'imbocca, tardi si satolla.* Ital.

Fee, *see* Lean f. fit reward for lazy clerk.

Feed by measure and defy the physician.

1550 HEYWOOD II. vii. 67. **1670** RAY 39 Feed sparingly, and defy the physician. **1721** KELLY 236 *Live in measure, and laugh at the mediciners.* Nothing contributes more to Health, than a temperate Diet. Whereas, *Nimia gula morborum Mater.*

Feed like a farmer, To.

1655 FULLER *Ch. Hist.* VI. ii (v. 13) (A) On which the abbot fed as the farmer of his grange. **1670** RAY 202. **1738** SWIFT (Dial. ii) 348 *Lady A.* I have fed like a farmer: . . . my jaws are weary of chewing.

Feeding out of course makes mettle out of kind.

1721 KELLY 103 . . . Good pasture will make a small breed of cattle larger.

Feeds like a boar in a frank,[1] He.

1597–8 SHAKS. *2 Hen. IV* II. ii. 160 Where sups he? doth the old boar feed in the old frank? **1631** F. LENTON *Characters* (1663) no. 15 His greatest study is how he may . . . feed at ease like a Boar in a Frank. [[1] sty.]

Feeds like a freeholder of Maxfield (or Macclesfield) who hath neither corn nor hay at Michaelmas, He.

1678 RAY (*Chesh.*) 301 . . . *Maxfield is a*

market town . . . , where they drive a great trade of making and selling buttons. When this came to be a proverb, it should seem the inhabitants were poorer or worse husbands then now they are.

Feed(s), fed, *see also* Better f. than taught; Strike as ye f.; Well for him who f. a good man; Where one is bred (Not), but where f.

Feel in one's bones, To.

1607–8 SHAKS. *Timon of A.* III. v. 131 *Sec. Lord* Lord Timon's mad. *Third Lord* I feel't upon my bones. **1841** DICKENS *Barn. Rudge* liii I seem to hear it, Muster Gashford, in my very bones. **1875** HOLLAND *Sevenoaks* xxiii. 315 I can feel the thing in my bones.

Feel, *see also* Doth what he should not shall f. what he would not.

Feeling hath no fellow.

1678 RAY 138.

Feet of the (avenging) deities are shod with wool, The.

[MACROB. *Proverbium . . . deos laneos pedes habere. Cf.* PETRON. *Dii pedes lanatos habent.*] **1853** TRENCH vi. 148 . . . Here . . . is introduced —the noiseless approach and advance of these judgments, as noiseless as the steps of one whose feet are wrapped in wool.

Feet under another man's table, To thrust one's.

1589 L. WRIGHT, *A Summons for Sleepers,* *2ᵛ The prelacie which these new devising church-founders are now so desirous to have established . . . must liue popularly with their feet vnder other mens tables, and their tongues tyed to other mens purses. **1678** RAY 272. **1732** FULLER no. 5247.

Feet, *see also* Foot.

Fell (*noun*), *see* Fleece and f.

Fell swoop, *see* Swoop (At one fell).

Felled, *see* Oak is not f. at one stroke.

Fellow-ruler, He that hath a | hath an over-ruler.

1611 COTGRAVE s.v. 'Avoir'. **1670** RAY 9.

Fellows, *see* All f. at football.

Fellowship, *see* Falsehood in f.

Fells two dogs with one stone, He.

1721 KELLY 131 . . . Spoken when a man with one and the self same pains effects two different businesses.

Fence against a flail, No.

1670 RAY 89 . . . Some evils and calamities assault so violently, that there is no resisting of them. **1730** SWIFT *On Stephen Duck*[1] *Wks.* (1856) I. 637 The thresher Duck[1] could o'er the queen prevail, The proverb says, 'no fence against a flail'. [[1] a farm-labourer,

advanced by Queen Caroline; rector of Byfleet, 1752.]

Fence against ill fortune, No.

1623 CAMDEN 279 There is no fence for ill fortune. **1670** RAY 89 . . . Some evils and calamities assault so violently, that there is no resisting of them.

Fence, *see also* Nigger in the f.

Fencer hath one trick in his budget more than ever he taught a scholar, A.

1616 WITHALS 566. **1639** CLARKE 127.

Ferlies[1] make fools fain.

1821 SCOTT *Pirate* iv 'I had only some curiosity to see the new implements he has brought.' 'Ay, ay, ferlies make fools fain.' [[1] wonders.]

Ferlie(s), *see also* Farlie.

Fern grows red, When | then milk is good with bread.

1659 HOWELL *Eng. Prov.* 11/2. **1670** RAY 35 When Fern begins to look red Then milk is good with brown bread. It is observed by good housewives, that milk is thicker in the Autumn then in the Summer.

Fern is as high as a ladle, When the | you may sleep as long as you are able.

1670 RAY 35.

Fern is as high as a spoon, When the | you may sleep an hour at noon.

1670 RAY 34. **1732** FULLER no. 6186.

Fern-bush, *see* Fox from a f. (Know a).

Ferret, *see* Rabbit hunting with dead f.

Festina lente, see Make haste slowly.

Fetch fire, You are come to.

c. **1374** CHAUCER *Troylus* v. 485 'Be we comen hider To fecchen fir, and rennen hom ayein?' **1579** LYLY *Euphues* (Arb.) 72 Comming to *Naples* but to fetch fire, as the byword is, not to make my place of abode. **1721** KELLY 374 . . . Spoken to them who make short visits.

Fetch the five pounds? When do you.

[A man of Poole, it is said, may claim £5, if he gets a certificate of honesty at the end of his apprenticeship.] **1787** GROSE (*Dorset.*) 169 It is a common water joke to ask the crew of a Pool ship, whether any one has yet received that five pounds.

Fetch(ed), *see also* Dear bought and far f. are dainties for ladies; Good to be sent for (or f.) sorrow; Lives longest (He that) must f. wood farthest.

Fetters, *see* Loveth his f. be they gold (No man).

Feud, *see* What rake the f. where friendship dow not?

Fever, *see* Stuff a cold and starve f.

Few lawyers die well, few physicians live well.

1569 c. AGRIPPA *Vanity of Arts and Sciences* tr. Sandford (1575) 179[v] It is growne to a prouerbe: *Neither the Phisition lyueth well, nor the Lawer dyeth well.* **1598** SIR R. BARCKLEY *Of the Felicity of Man* 384 There is a common prouerbe, that neither a Phisition liueth well, nor a lawyer dieth well. **1636** CAMDEN 295.

Few words and many deeds.

1616 DRAXE 41.

Few words to the wise suffice (are best). (*Cf.* Word is enough, &c.)

c. 1275 *Provs. of Alfred* (Skeat) A 38 Mid fewe worde wis mon fele biluken wel con. *c.* 1475 *Mankind* l. 102 Few wordis: few and well sett! **1546** HEYWOOD II. vii. 67 Fewe woord is to the wise suffice to be spoken. *c.* 1568 V. FULWELL *Like will to like* B 2[v] Few words are best among freends. **1576** DESAIN-LIENS 261 Few wordes among wise men suffiseth. **1578** SIDNEY *Wks.* (Feuillerat) III. 124 Few wordes are beste. **1594** *King Leir* III. v. 109. *c.* 1600 *Roxb. Ballads* (Hindley) I. 157 It is an old saying that few words are best. **1614** CAMDEN 306. **1678** RAY 220 Few words are best. . . . A fool's voice is known by multitude of words.

Fewer his years, The | the fewer his tears.

1732 FULLER no. 6233. **1855** BOHN 504.

Fewer, *see also* More the merrier, f. the better cheer.

Fickle, *see* Praise none too much, for all f.

Fiction, *see* Fact is stranger than f.

Fiddle, but not the stick, He has got the.

1653 WALTON *Angler* 106 I lent you indeed my Fiddle, but not my Fiddlestick. **1678** RAY 86 He hath got the fiddle, but not the stick, i.e. The books but not the learning, to make use of them, or the like.

Fiddle for shives,[1] Go | among old wives.

1639 CLARKE 68 (with 'good' for old'). **1670** RAY 175. [[1] slices of bread.]

Fiddle while Rome is burning, To.

[= to be occupied with trifles in face of a crisis.] **1649** G. DANIEL *Trinarch.* To Rdr. 163 Let Nero fiddle out Rome's Obsequies. **1855** KINGSLEY *West. Ho!* x It is fiddling while Rome is burning, to spend more pages over the sorrows of . . . Rose Salterne, while

the destinies of Europe are hanging on the marriage between Elizabeth and Anjou. **1926** *Times* 28 June 10/5 I should like to remind . . . Liberals . . . that 'Nero fiddled while Rome burned'.

Fiddle, *see also* Agree like f. and stick; Face as long as f.; Face made of a f. (To have one's); Fine as a f.; Fit as a f.; Good tune on old f.; Least boy carries greatest f.; Play first (second) f.; Sow to a f.; Take a spring of his own f.

Fiddlers, dogs, and flies, come to feasts uncalled.

1641 FERGUSSON 34. **1721** KELLY 111 . . . Fiddlers for money, the flies for a sip, and the dogs for a scrap.

Fiddler's fare; meat, drink, and money.

1599 *Soliman and Perseda* I. iv. 51 Fiddler's fee. **1606** *Return from Parn.* I. i. 380 Fiddlers' wages. **1608** *Dumb Knight* III in HAZLITT O.E.P. x. 169 You have had more than fidler's fare, for you have meat, money, and cloth. **1639** CLARKE 161 Meat, drink, and money, a fidler's life. **1659** HOWELL *Eng. Prov.* 16/2. **1721** KELLY 111 . . . Spoken often when we have din'd with our friend, and after won some money from him at play. **1738** SWIFT (Dial. iii) 350 *Miss.* Did your ladyship play? *Lady S.* Yes, and won; so I came off with fiddler's fare, meat, drink, and money.

Fiddler(s), *see also* Dance (If you) you must pay f.; Fools and f. sing at their meat; House of a f. (In the) all fiddle; More fool than f.

Fiddlestick, *see* Devil rides on f.

Fiddlestrings, *see* Fret one's self to f.

Fidging mare should be well girded, A.

1721 KELLY 8 . . . A cunning tricky fellow should not be trusted without great caution.

Fie upon hens! quoth the fox, because he could not reach them.

1678 RAY 142.

Field requires three things; A | fair weather, sound seed, and a good husbandman.

1642 TORRIANO 96. **1846** DENHAM 3.

Field, *see also* Fair f. and no favour; Hard-fought f. where no man escapeth.

Fieldfare, *see* Farewell f.

Fields (Hedges) have eyes, and woods (walls) have ears. (*Cf.* Walls have ears.)

c. 1225 *Trin. MS. O. 11. 45* (ed. Förster) in *Eng. Stud.* **31.** 8 Veld haued hege, & wude haued heare—Campus habet lumen et habet nemus auris acumen. *c.* **1386** CHAUCER *Canterbury Tales* A 1522 But sooth is seyd, go sithen many yeres, That 'field hath eyen and the wode hath eris'. *c.* **1430** *K. Edward & the Shep.* (Hartshorne, A.M.T.) 46 Wode has erys, felde has siʒt. *c.* **1470** *Harl. MS. 3362* (ed. Förster) in *Anglia* 42. 202 Feld haþ eye, wode haþ ere. **1546** HEYWOOD II. v. 57 But féelds haue eies, and woodes haue eares, ye wot. **1611** COTGRAVE s.v. 'Bois' Woods haue their eares, & fields their eyes, euerie thing hath some instrument of, or helpe for, discouerie. **1664** J. HOWELL *Dodona's Grove* A 4[v] Hedges have eares, the rurall Proverb sayes. **1738** SWIFT (Dial. iii) 351 Ay, madam; but they say hedges have eyes, and walls have ears. **1822** SCOTT *Nigel* vi It is not good to speak of such things . . . ; stone walls have ears. **1905** WEYMAN *Starvecrow F.* xxviii Heedful of the old saying, that fields have eyes and woods have ears.

Fifth wheel to a coach, A.

1631 DEKKER *Match me in London* I ad fin. (A) Thou tyest but wings to a swift gray hounds heele, And addest to a running charriot a fift wheele. **1913** *Spectator* 22 Mar. 499 These local bodies are . . . useless, a fifth wheel in a coach which runs none too smoothly . . . at the best.

Fig, Not worth a.

1528 MORE *Wks.* (1557) 241 (A). **1600** ROWLANDS *Let. Humours Blood* i. 7 All Beere in Europe is not worth a figge. **1852** THACKERAY *Esmond* III. ii Nor . . . is the young fellow worth a fig that would.

Fig(s), *see also* Name of the Prophet—f. (In the); Peach will have wine and f. water; Peel a f. for friend.

Fight dog, fight bear.

1583 STUBBES *Anat. of Abuses* (New Sh. S.) 178 (A) Some . . . will not make anie bones of xx . . . pound at once to hazard at a bait, with 'fight dog, feight beare (say they), the deuill part all!' **1623** MIDDLETON *Span. Gip.* IV. iii A match; we'll fight dog, fight bear. *a.* **1642** SIR W. MONSON *Naval Tracts* III. (1704) 350/2 You must fight according to the old saying, Fight Dog, Fight Bear; that is, till one be overcome. **1678** RAY 244 . . . *Ne depugnes in alieno negotio.* [Fight not in another person's concerns.] **1831** SCOTT *Diary* 5 Mar. A resolution to keep myself clear of politics, and let them 'fight dog, fight bear'.

Fight for one's own hand, To.

[**1396**] HAL O' THE WYND, or Henry Gow, in SCOTT *F. M. Perth* (1828) xxxiv 'I fought for my own hand', said the Smith indifferently; and the expression is still proverbial in Scotland. **1879** FROUDE *Cæsar* ix. 92 Lesbos was occupied by adventurers, who were fighting for their own hand. **1900** A. LANG *Hist. Scot.* IX. 291 The Celt recognized no part in Lowland patriotism. . . . He fought, like Hal of the Wynd, for his own hand.

Fight like Kilkenny cats, To.

[= to engage in a mutually destructive

struggle.] [*a.* **1850**] in LEAN I. 276 The Kilkenny cats, who fought till there was nothing but their tails left of either. **1864** *N. & Q.* 3rd Ser. v. 433 It has become a proverb, 'as quarrelsome as the Kilkenny cats'—two of the cats in which city are asserted to have fought so long and so furiously that nought was found of them but two tails! **1866** BLACKMORE *Cradock N.* li When shall we men leave off fighting, cease to prove . . . the legends of Kilkenny (by leaving only our tails behind us, a legacy for new lawsuits) . . .?

Fight tooth and nail, To.

1579 W. WILKINSON *Confut. Familye of Love* 51 M. Harding fighteth for it tooth and nail. **1909** *Times Wkly.* 14 May Herr von Holstein . . . fought tooth and nail for the acquisition of Samoa.

Fight with (one's own) shadow, To.

[Gk. Σκιαμαχία. A fighting with shadows.] **1580** WILLIAM CHARKE *An answer to a seditious pamphlet lately cast abroad by a Jesuit* C 8 The prouerbe maketh it a uayne fight to fight with a shadowe. **1596–7** SHAKS. *Merch. V.* I. ii. 66 He will fence with his own shadow. **1608** R. WOODCOKE *Goodly Answer* B 2. **1659** FULLER *Appeal Inj. Innoc.* in *Hist. Camb. Univ.* (1840) 592 To fight with a shadow (whether one's own or another's) passeth for the proverbial expression of a vain and useless act. **1670** RAY 175 . . . To be afraid of his own fancies, imagining danger or enemies, where there are none.

Fight(s), *see also* Better fleech a fool than f. him; Full belly neither f.; Sore f. wrens as cranes; Speaks well f. well (He that).

Fighting cocks, To live like.

1826 COBBETT *Rur. Rides* (1885) II. 107 [They] live like fighting-cocks upon the labour of the rest of the community. **1858** SURTEES *Ask Mamma* xxiv The servants here seem to live like fighting-cocks, . . . breakfasts, luncheons, dinners, teas, and suppers.

Fighting, *see also* Painting and f. look aloof (On).

Fights and runs away, may live to fight another day, He that.

[Gk. Ἀνὴρ ὁ φεύγων καὶ πάλιν μαχήσεται.] *a.* **1250** *Owl & Night.* 176 'Wel fiʒt þat wel fliʒt', seiþ þe wise. ? *a.* **1300** *Salomon & Sat.* (1848) 272 Wel fyþt þat wel flyþ quoþ Hendyng. *c.* **1440** *Gesta Rom.* lvii. 420 (Add. MS.) It is an olde sawe, He feghtith wele that fleith faste. **1602–3** SHAKS. *All's Well* III. ii. 40 *Clo.* Your son will not be killed so soon as I thought he would. *Count.* Why should he be killed? *Clo.* So say I, madam, if he run away . . . ; the danger is in standing to't. **1621** BURTON *Anat. Mel.* II. iii. VII (1651) 357 He that runs away in a battle, as Demosthenes said, may fight again. **1678** BUTLER *Hudibras* III. ii. 243 For those that fly may fight again, which he can never do that's slain. **1750** J. RAY *Hist. Rebell.* 50 The Dragoons . . . thought proper . . . a sudden retreat; as knowing that, *He that fights and runs away, May turn and fight another Day.*

File, *see* Time is a f. that wears.

Fill the mouth with empty spoons, To. (*Cf.* Gives fair words, &c.)

1639 CLARKE 314. **1664** CODRINGTON 230. **1670** RAY 175. **1721** KELLY 384 *You have put a toom*[1] *spoon in my mouth.* You have rais'd, and disappointed my expectation. [1 empty.]

Fills, *see also* Little and often f. purse.

Filth under the white snow the sun discovers, The.

1640 HERBERT 341.

Find a woman (you) without an excuse, and find a hare without a meuse.[1]

1592 GREENE *Disp. bet. Conny-Catch.* (Bodley Hd.) 22 Come but to the olde Prouerbe . . . , Tis as hard to find a Hare without a Muse, as a woman without a scuse. **1659** HOWELL *Eng. Prov.* 12/1 Take a Hare without a muse, and a Knave without an excuse, and hang them up. **1670** RAY 174 Find you without an excuse, and find a hare without a muse. [1 A gap through which a hare is wont to pass.]

Find ease, *see* All men will please (He that) shall never f. e.

Find fault if you knew how, You would.

1639 CLARKE 80.

Find fault that cannot mend, He may.

1721 KELLY 171. **1732** FULLER no. 1985 He may find fault, but let him mend it if he can.

Find fault with a fat goose, You.

1678 RAY 248. **1732** FULLER no. 5902.

Find fault with my shoes, and give me no leather, I never loved them that.

1721 KELLY 224 . . . Apply'd to them that find fault with some part of our habit, yet contribute nothing to make it better.

Find guilty Gilbert[1] where he had hid the brush, To.

1608 ARMIN *Nest Nin.* (Shaks. Soc.) 39 Not I, says another; but by her cheeks you might find guilty Gilbert, where he had hid the brush. [1 a N. country name for a dog.]

Find it where the Highlandman found the tongs, To.

1721 KELLY 383 A Highlandman being challenged for stealing a pair of tongs, said he found them; and being asked where? He

said, Hard by the fire side. Spoken when boys have pick'd something, and pretend they found it.

Find not that you do not seek, Take heed you.

1546 HEYWOOD II. v. 58 But whan she seemed to be fixed in mynde, Rather to seeke for that she was lothe to fynde. **1596** HARINGTON *Metam. of Ajax* (1814) 122 If a man had no light to work, yet he would feel, to seek that he would not find, for fear lest they should find that they did not seek. **1670** RAY 9. *Ital.*

Find (Found) out, *see* Eating and drinking (Ingenious man that first f. o.).

Find some hole to creep out at, He will.

1678 RAY 253.

Find what was never lost, To.

1536 LATIMER *2nd Serm. bef. Conv.* (P.S.) 51 This, to pray for dead folks, this is not found, for it was never lost. How can that be found that was not lost. **1546** HEYWOOD I. xi If ye seeke to fynd thynges er they be lost, Ye shall fynde one daie you come to your cost. **1609** ARMIN *Two Maids Tab.* How can ye find the glove was never lost? **1732** FULLER no. 5918 You have found what was never lost.

Find(eth, s), found, *see also* Grind or f.; Lost all, f. myself; Nothing seek nothing f.; Seeketh f. (He that); Take things as you f. them; Take what you f. or what you bring.

Finder(s), *see* Losers seekers, f. keepers.

Finding's keeping.

1863 SPEKE *Discov. Source Nile* v The scoundrels said, Findings are keepings by the laws of our country; and as we found your cows, so we will keep them'.

Fine as a fiddle, As.

1603 *The Bachelors Banquet* (Wilson) 28 As fine as a farthing fiddle. **1862** *Dialect of Leeds* 407 (A).

Fine as fivepence, As.

1564 BULLEIN *Dial. agst. Fever* (E.E.T.S.) 62 (A) Out of the countree . . . as fine as fippence! **1575** *App. & Virginia* (Mal. Soc.) l. 225 As fine as phippence, as proude as a Pecocke. **1659** HOWELL *Eng. Prov.* 11 As fine as fippence, as neat as ninepence.

Fine as if you had a whiting hanging at your side, or girdle, You are as.

1678 RAY 345.

Fine dressing is a foul house swept before the doors.

1640 HERBERT 328. **1732** FULLER no. 1538 (with 'usually' after 'is').

Fine (Fair) feathers make fine birds (fair fowls).

[SPONDANUS (1557–95) on *Od.* 6. 29 quotes *proverbium apud meos Vascones 'speciosae plumae avem speciosam constituunt'*.] 1611 DAVIES Prov. 162 The faire Feathers still make the faire Fowles. But some haue faire feathers that looke but like Owles. 1670 RAY 87 Fair feathers make fair fowls. Fair clothes, ornaments and dresses set off persons . . . God makes and apparel shapes. 1714 MANDEVILLE *Fab. Bees* (1725) I. 130 Fine feathers make fine birds. 1853 SURTEES *Ask Mamma* x Mrs. . . . essayed to pick her to pieces, in-timating that she was much indebted to her dress—that fine feathers made fine birds. 1917 BRIDGE 57 Fine feathers make fine birds, but they don't make *lady*-birds.

Fine words dress ill deeds.

c. 1303 BRUNNE *Handl. Synne* 4179 Wyth feyre wurdys he shal the grete; But yn hys herte he shal thynke For to do the a wykked blynke. 1640 HERBERT 340.

Fine words, *see also* Fair words.

Fine, *see also* Makes a thing too f., breaks it; Whore in a f. dress.

Finger and thumb, They are.

[= on intimate terms.] 1579 LYLY *Euphues* (Arb.) 68 In that thou cravest my aide, assure thyselfe I will be the finger next thy thombe. 1659 HOWELL *Eng. Prov.* 13 You two are finger and thumb. 1730–6 BAILEY (folio) s.v. They are Finger and Thumb, that is, they are so great together, there is no parting them.

Finger in one's mouth, With one's.

[= (*a*) helplessly inactive, (*b*) with nothing accomplished, 'looking foolish'.] 1649 CROM-WELL *Lett.* 14 Nov. To stand with our fingers in our mouths. 1874 *Spectator* (1891) 28 Mar. 443 He returned to Ireland with his finger in his mouth.

Finger in the pie, To have a.

1553 *Respublica* in '*Lost' Tudor Plays* (1907) Bring me in credit that my hands be in the pie. 1612–13 SHAKS. *Hen. VIII* I. i. 52 No man's pie is freed From his ambitious finger. 1659 B. HARRIS *Parival's Iron Age* 75 Lusatia . . . must needs, forsooth, have her Finger in the Pye. 1678 RAY 244 He had a finger in the pie when he burnt his nail off. 1886 MISS TYTLER *Buried Diamonds* xii Susie . . . liked to have a finger in every pie.

Fingers are all thumbs, His.

1546 J. HEYWOOD II. v. 54 Whan he should get ought, eche fynger is a thumbe. *a.* 1553 UDALL *Royster D.* I. iii (Arb.) 22 Ah, eche finger is a thombe to day me thinke. 1899 A. T. QUILLER-COUCH *Ship of Stars* xiii I think my fingers must be all thumbs.

Fingers are lime twigs, His.

a. 1500 J. SKELTON *The Bowge of Courte* l. 509 Lyghte lyme fynger, he toke none other

wage. *a.* 1534 *Hyckescorner* 651, 2 All my fyngers were arayed with lyme, So I con-vayed a cuppe manerly. 1596 HARINGTON *Metam. Ajax* (1814) 65 A certain gentleman that had his fingers made of lime-twigs, stole a piece of plate. 1611–12 SHAKS. *Tempest* IV. i. 246 Come, put some lime upon your fingers. 1670 RAY 175 . . . Spoken of a thievish person.

Fingers (*or* hands) in mortar, To have one's.

[= to have building going on.] 1665 GERBIER *Brief Disc.* 3 Those who say, That a wise man never ought to put his finger into Morter. 1738 SWIFT (Dial. ii) 343 *Lady S.* You are come to a sad dirty house; I am sorry for it, but we have had our hands in mortar.

Fingers were made before forks, and hands before knives.

1567 *Loseley MSS.* (ed. Kempe 1836) 212 As God made hands before knives, So God send a good lot to the cutler's wives. 1738 SWIFT (Dial. ii) 345 Here, miss; they say fingers were made before forks, and hands before knives.

Fingers' ends, At one's.

1542 UDALL tr. *Erasm. Apoph.* (1877) 39. 1549 CHALONER tr. *Erasm. Praise of Folly* C IV. 1550 W. HARRYS *The market or fair of Usurers* A 6 Judas lesson . . . what wyll ye gyue, is learned at the fyngers endys. 1711 STEELE *Spect.* No. 156 Names which a man of his learning has at his Fingers-Ends. 1862 CARLYLE *Fredk. Gt.* (1865) III. IX. ii. 82 All manner of Military Histories . . . are at his finger-ends.

Finger(s), *see also* Better a f. off; Fish on one's f. (To find); Give a clown your f.; Put one's f. in fire; Put your f. in fire and say it was fortune; Turn round one's f.; Wet f. (With a); Wit in his little f. (He has more).

Finglesham Church, *see* Married at F. C.

Finishes, *see* Commences many things f. few.

Fire and tow, All.

c. 1303 BRUNNE *Handl. Synne* 7924 But of wymmen hyt ys grete wundyr, Hyt fareth wyth hem as fyre and tundyr. *c.* 1635 BEAUM. & FL. *Elder Brother* I. ii For he is fire and tow; and so have at him. 1670 RAY 175.

Fire and water, To go through.

c. 825 *Vesp. Psalter* lxv[i]. 12 We leordun ðorh fyr & weter. 1534 HERVET tr. *Xeno-phon's Householde* 61 b They wolde gladly folowe theym through fire and water, and throughe all maner of daunger. 1600–1 SHAKS. *Merry W.* III. iv. 107 A woman would run through fire and water for such a kind heart. *Ibid.* III. v. 131 Master Brook, I will be thrown into Etna, as I have been into Thames, ere I will leave her thus.

Fire and water are good servants, but bad masters.

1562 BULLEIN *Bulwarke of Defence* f. 12 (A) Water is a very good seruaunt, but it is a cruell maister. **1662** FULLER (*Cornw.*) I. 314 Philosophy being in divinity as fire and water in a family—a good servant, but bad master. **1738** SWIFT (Dial. ii) 349 *Col.* Why, fire and water are good servants, but they are very bad masters.

Fire and water have no mercy.

1577 PEACHAM *Garden of Eloquence* (1593) 87. **1584** A. MUNDAY *Two Italian Gentlemen* G 1ᵛ They say fire and water hath no mercy. **1599** NASHE *Lenten Stuff* Wks. (McKerrow) III. 164.

Fire away, Flanagan!

1841 S. WARREN *Ten Thous. a Year* xxxi And you won't be angry? . . . Then fire away, Flannagan!' cried Titmouse joyfully.

Fire is as hurtful as healthful.

1579 GOSSON *Sch. Abuse* (Arb.) 23 Fyre is as hurtfull, as healthie. **1597** *Politeuphuia* 166 b.

Fire is good for the fireside.

1862 HISLOP 96 . . . All things are good in their proper places.

Fire is half bread.

1908 C. M. DOUGHTY *Wand. in Arabia* I. x. 196 Cheerful is the gipsy fire of . . . bushes: there is a winter proverb of the poor in Europe, 'Fire is half bread!'

Fire is never without heat, The.

1611 DAVIES Prov. 220.

Fire of London¹ was a punishment for gluttony, The.

1787 GROSE (*London*) 206 The fire of London was a punishment for gluttony. For Iron-monger-lane was red-fire-hot, Milk-street boiled over; it began in Pudding-lane, and ended at Pye-corner. [¹ 1666.]

Fire of straw (hay), A.

1573 SANDFORD (1576) 207. **1577** PEACHAM *Garden of Eloquence* (1593) 30 He that maketh his fire with hay, hath much smoke and litle heate. **1578** FLORIO *First Fruites* f. 28. **1629** *Book of Meery Riddles* Prov. 71 A fire of straw yields naught but smoke. **1666** TORRIANO 97. **1732** FULLER no. 2236 He that maketh a Fire of straw, hath much Smoke and but little warmth.

Fire, Make no | raise no smoke.

1546 HEYWOOD II. v. 57 There is no fyre without some smoke, we sée. Well well, make no fyre, reyse no smoke, (sayd shée).

Fire so low, You cannot make the | but it will get out.

1640 HERBERT 361.

Fire that does not warm me shall never scorch me, The.

1642 TORRIANO 63. **1855** BOHN 504.

Fire that's closest kept burns most of all.

[OVID *Met.* 4. 64 *Quoque magis tegitur, tectus magis aestuat ignis.*] *c.* **1374** CHAUCER *Troylus* II. 538 Wel the hotter been the gledes rede, That men hem wryen with asshen pale and dede. *c.* **1385** Id. *Leg. Good Women* 735 Wry the gleed, and hotter is the fire. **1579** LYLY *Euphues* (Arb.) 61 He that stoppeth the streame, forceth [causeth] it to swell higher . . . he that casteth water on [in] the fire in [at] the Smithes forge, maketh it to flame fiercer. **1593–4** SHAKS. *Titus Andron.* II. iv. 36 Sorrow conceal'd, like to an oven stopp'd, Doth burn the heart to cinders where it is. **1594–5** *Two Gent.* I. ii. 30 Fire that's closest kept burns most of all. *Ibid.* II. vii. 24 *Luc.* I do not seek to quench your love's hot fire, But qualify the fire's extreme rage . . . *Jul.* The more thou damm'st it up, the more it burns. **1593** *Ven. & Adon.* 331 An oven that is stopp'd, or river stay'd Burneth more hotly, swelleth more with rage. **1611** COTGRAVE s.v. 'Feu' The more that fire's kept downe the more it burns.

Fire to flax, Put not.

c. **1386** CHAUCER *W. of Bath's Prol.* D 89 For peril is bothĕ fyr and tow t'assemble. **1639** CLARKE 197.

Fire which lights (warms) us at a distance will burn us when near, The.

c. **1374** CHAUCER *Troylus* I. 449 And ay the ner he was, the more he brende. For ay the ner the fir, the hotter is. **1580** LYLY *Euph. & his Eng.* (Arb.) 351 Fire giueth lyght to things farre off, and burneth that which is next to it. The Court shineth to me that come not there, but singeth those that dwell there. **1584** Id. *Campaspe* IV. iv *Camp.* The love of kings is like . . . fire, which warmeth afar off, and burneth near hand. **1869** HAZLITT 368 The fire which lighteth us at a distance will burn us when near.

Fire(s), *see also* Better a wee f. to warm us; Carries f. in one hand; Coals of f. on the head (Heap); Coldest flint there is f.; Dangerous f. begins in bedstraw; Fanned f. and forced love; Fetch f. (You are come to); Freets fail (When), f.'s good for fiercy; Green wood makes hot f.; House, a wife, and a f. to put her in; Kindle not a f. you cannot extinguish; Little f. burns deal of corn; Little sticks kindle f.; Little wind kindles, much puts out f.; Longest at f. soonest finds cold; Love of lads and f. of chats soon out; Make a f. (He that can) can end quarrel; Nail (F.) drives out another; Neighbour's house on f.; No f., no smoke; No smoke without f.; Oil on the f. is not way to quench; Oil to f. (Bring); Own f. is pleasant (*under* Own hearth); Play at chess when house on f.; Poke a

man's f. after known him seven years;
Put one's finger in f.; Quenching of f. with
tow (No); Set my house on f. to toast eggs;
Silks and satins put out the f.; Sit near the
f. when chimney smokes; Skeer your own
f.; Skirts of straw (Who hath) fear the f.;
Smell f. (Well may he) whose gown burns;
Smoke of a man's own country, better
than f. of another; Soft f., sweet malt;
Spend much (If you can), put the more to
the f.; Three failures and a f. make fortune;
Three removes as bad as f.; Water afar
quencheth not f.; Water, f., quickly make
room; Well to work and make a f. care
and skill require; Woman is flax, man is
f.; Working and making f. discretion
require.

First advice of a woman and not the second, Take the.

1853 TRENCH iv. 89 . . . for in processes of
reasoning, out of which the second counsels
spring, women may and will be inferior to us.
[Fr. *Prends le premier conseil d'une femme, et
non le second.*]

First, I am not the | and shall not be the last.

c. 1200 *Ancrene Riwle* 86 Nert tu nout, i
þisse þinge, þe uorme,[1] ne þe laste. 1678 RAY
74. [[1] first.]

First blow is as much as two, The.

1640 HERBERT 359.

First blow is half the battle, The.

1773 GOLDSMITH *She Stoops to C.* II. i *Mar.*
I have been thinking, George, of changing
our travelling dresses. . . . *Hast.* . . . The first
blow is half the battle. I intend opening the
campaign with the white and gold. 1790
BURNS *Prol. at Dumfries* He bids you mind,
amid your thoughtless rattle, That the first
blow is ever half the battle.

First blow makes the wrong, The | but the second makes the fray.

1597 BACON *Col. of G. & E.* 10 (Arb.) 154 In
such cases the second degree seemes the
worthyest, as . . . *The second blow makes the
fray.* a. 1631 DONNE *Serm.* xl (Alford) 306
The first blow makes the Wrong, but the
second makes the Fray. 1676 HALE *Contempl.*
I. 242 It is a true Proverb, It is the second
blow makes the fray. 1898 A. J. C. HARE
Shropshire viii. 257 'It takes two blows to
make a battle', is a local proverb.

First born, first fed.

1616 DRAXE 144. 1659 HOWELL *Fr.-Eng.* 4.

First breath is the beginning of death, The.

1576 PETTIE *Petite Pall.* I. 62. 1732 FULLER
no. 4524.

First catch your hare.

[c. 1300 BRACTON *De legibus et consuetudini-*
bus Angliae IV. xxi. §4 (Rolls ed. III. 234) *Et
vulgariter dicitur quod primo oportet cervum
capere, et postea, cum captus fuerit, illum
excoriare.* (quot. in 1931 A. TAYLOR *The
Proverb* 79).] 1853 BRIMLEY *Ess. on 'My
Novel'* The sagacious Mrs. Glasse prefaces her
receipt for hare-soup by the pithy direction,
first catch your hare. 1855 THACKERAY *Rose
& Ring* xiv 'To seize wherever I should light
upon him—' 'First catch your hare! . . .'
exclaimed his Royal Highness. 1896 *Daily
News* 20 July 8/2 The familiar words, 'First
catch your hare', were never to be found in
Mrs. Glasse's famous volume.[1] What she really
said was, 'Take your hare when it is cased.'
[[1] *Art of Cookery*, 1747.]

First chapter of fools is, to hold themselves wise, The. (*Cf.* First degree of folly, &c.)

1573 SANDFORD (1576) 211. 1578 FLORIO
First Fruites f. 29. 1659 HOWELL *Eng. Prov.*
1/1.

First chapter of fools themselves magnifies, The.

1611 DAVIES *Prov.* 61.

First come, first served.

[ERASM. gives as modern proverb *Qui primus
venerit, primus molet.*] c. 1386 CHAUCER *Canterbury Tales* D. 389 'Who so first cometh to
the mille first grynt.' 1599 PORTER *Angry
Wom. Abingd.* IV. iii (Merm.) 175 So, first
come, first served; I am for him. 1608 ARMIN
Nest Nin. (1842) 25 He found the sexton . . .
making nine graves, . . . and whoso dies next,
first comes, first served. 1819 SCOTT *Leg. Mont.*
XX All must . . . take their place as soldiers
should, upon the principle of—first come, first
served.

First comes David,[1] next comes Chad,[2] and then comes Winneral (Winnold)[3] as though he was mad.

1846 DENHAM 34. [[1] 1st March, [2] 2nd March
[3] 3rd March. A corruption of Winwaloe.]

First creep, and then go.

c. 1410 *Towneley Plays* (E.E.T.S.) 103 Fyrst
must vs crepe and sythen go. 1639 CLARKE
116. 1670 RAY 75 You must learn to creep
before you go. 1854 SURTEES *Hand. Cross*
xvii But we must all creep afore we can
walk, and all be bitten afore we can bite.

First cut, The | and all the loaf besides.

1662 FULLER (*Kent*) II. 122 Kent and Christendom (parallel to Rome and Italy) is as
much as the first cut, and all the loaf besides.
1732 FULLER no. 4526.

First degree of folly, The | is to hold one's self wise, the second to profess it, the third to despise counsel. (*Cf.* First chapter of fools, &c.)

1640 HERBERT 339.

First deserve, and then desire.
1636 CAMDEN 296.

First dish is aye best eaten, The.
1721 KELLY 336.

First dish pleaseth all, The.
1640 HERBERT 352. 1732 FULLER no. 4527.

First glass for thirst, The | the second for nourishment, the third for pleasure, and the fourth for madness.
1586 PETTIE *Guazzo's Civ. Conv.* 195 A certaine wise man was wont to saie: That the first cup of Wine was of thirst: The second of merrinesse: The third of temptation: The fourth of foolishnesse. 1621 BURTON *Anat. Mel.* Democr. to Rdr. (1651) 44 The first pot quencheth thirst (so Panyasis the poet determines in Athenæus): *secunda Gratiis, Horis, et Dionysis*—the second makes merry: the third for pleasure: *quarta ad insaniam,* the fourth makes them mad.

First impressions are half the battle (or are most lasting).
1796-97 JANE AUSTEN *First Impressions,* the original of *Pride and Prejudice* (W. and R. A. Austen-Leigh, *Jane Austen,* 1913, 96). 1843-4 DICKENS *M. Chuz.* v First impressions, you know, often go a long way, and last a long time.

First learn, What we | we best can.
1721 KELLY 340.

First of April, On the | hunt the gowk another mile.
1846 DENHAM 41 [April gowk = April fool.]

First of April, On the | you may send a fool (gowk[1]) whither you will.
1732 FULLER no. 6135 The first day of April, You may send a Fool whither you will. 1869 HAZLITT 304 On the first of Aperill, you may send a gowk[1] whither you will. [[1] *i.e.* a fool.]

First of March, On the | the crows begin to search.
1846 DENHAM 39 . . . Crows are supposed to commence pairing on this day.

First of July, If the | it be rainy weather, 'twill rain more or less for four weeks together.
1732 FULLER no. 6467.

First of November, On the | if the weather holds clear, an end of wheat-sowing do make for this year.
1573 TUSSER 90 (1878) 181 Seede cake. Wife, some time this weeke, if the wether hold cleere, an end of wheat sowing we make for this yeare. 1846 DENHAM 61.

First pig, but the last whelp (puppy) of the litter, is the best, The.
1659 HOWELL *Ital.* 2 The first pig, the last puppy is best. 1678 RAY 53 Primo porco, ultimo cane. i.e. *The first pig, but the last whelp of the litter is the best.* 1732 FULLER no. 4530.

First think, and then speak.
1639 CLARKE 133.

First thrive and then wive.
1608-9 SHAKS. *Pericles* V. ii. 9 So he thriv'd that he is promis'd to be wiv'd to fair Marina. 1639 CLARKE 230.

First try and then trust. (Cf. Try your friend before you trust him.)
1639 CLARKE 305.

First wife is matrimony, the second company, the third heresy, The.
1855 BOHN 505. *Ital.*

First word of flyting,[1] You have got the.
1721 KELLY 374 . . . Spoken to them that blame us lest we should blame them. [[1] scolding.]

First word stand, Let the.
1599 PORTER *Angry Wom. Abingd.* II. ii. (Merm.) 131 *Coomes.* Shall we be merry? an we shall, say but we shall, and let the first word stand.

First, *see also* Best go f.; Better be f. in a village; Comes f. to the hill may sit where he will; Let your house to your enemy (F. year); Riseth f. is f. dressed. *See also under significant words following* 'First'.

Fish (fair, well) and catch a frog, To. (Cf. Fond fisher that angles for frog.)
1546 HEYWOOD I. xi. 26 But now he hath well fysht and caught a frog. *a.* 1555 LATIMER in FOXE *A. & M.* (1684) III. 413 Well, I have fished and caught a frog; brought little to pass with much ado. 1605 CHAPMAN, &c. *Eastw. Hoe* IV. i (1889) 474 Your ladyship hath 'fished fair, and caught a frog' as the saying is. 1678 RAY 245.

Fish begins to stink at the head.
[Gk. Ἰχθὺς ἐκ τῆς κεφαλῆς ὄζειν ἄρχεται. ERASM. gives as vulgar proverb *Piscis primum a capite foetet.*] 1611 COTGRAVE S.V. 'Poisson' The head of a fish is euer tainted first. 1860 BOHN *Dict. L. Quot.* 538 . . . The corruption of a state is first discernible in the higher classes.

Fish follow the bait.
1640 HERBERT 345 The fish adores the bait. 1670 RAY 9 The fish follow the bait.

Fish for a herring and catch a sprat, To.

1639 CLARKE 2. **1670** RAY 180. **1732** FULLER no. 5165 (reading 'with a herring').

Fish in the sea as ever came out of it, There are as good (*or* The sea hath fish for every man).

c. **1374** CHAUCER *Troylus* III. 35 Whan they kan nought construe . . . whi this fish, and naught that, comth to were [weir]. **1576** PETTIE *Petite Pall.* (Gollancz) I. 33 The sea hath fish for every man. **1636** CAMDEN 308 The sea hath fish for every man. **1822** SCOTT *Nigel* xxxv Here be as bonny lasses in London as this Peg-a-Ramsay . . . there is as good fish in the sea as ever came out of it. **1881** GILBERT *Patience* (Dragoons' chorus) There's fish in the sea, no doubt of it, As good as ever came out of it. **1905** HOUSMAN ed. *Juvenalis Saturae* Pref. xxi But there are as bad fish in the sea as ever came out of it.

Fish in troubled waters, To (*Cf.* Fishing in troubled waters.)

1568 GRAFTON *Chron.* II. 102 Their perswasions, whiche alwayes desyre your unquietnesse, whereby they may the better fishe in the water when it is troubled. **1722** SEWEL *Hist. Quakers* (1795) I. iv. 276 You delight to fish in troubled waters.

Fish is cast away that is cast in dry pools.

c. **1374** CHAUCER *Troylus* IV. 765 How sholde a fish withoute water dure? *c.* **1390** LANGLAND *P. Pl.* C. vi. 149 Right as fishes in flood . . . whanne hem faileth water, Deyen for drouthe whenne thei drye liggen. **1550** HEYWOOD I. xi. **1605** CHAPMAN, &c. *Eastw. Hoe* v. i Do not importune me . . . Master Wolf, 'Fish is cast away that is cast in dry pools'. Tell hypocrisy it will not do. **1670** RAY 90 Fishes are cast away, that are cast into dry ponds.

Fish is caught, When the | the net is laid aside.

1629 T. ADAMS *Serm.* (1861–2) II. 112 On a sudden, these 'sons of thunder' are as mute as fishes. What is the matter? . . . Oh, sir, they have the promotion already. You may perceive the fish is caught, by their hanging aside their nets.

Fish, The best (greatest) | keep (swim near) the bottom.

1616 BRETON *Cross Prov.* Wks. (1879) II. App. iii The greatest sort of fish keep the bottom. **1639** CLARKE 212 The best fish swim near the bottom.

Fish mars water, and (but) flesh mends it.

1573 SANDFORD (1576) 211. **1578** FLORIO *First Fruites* f. 29 Fish marreth the water, and flesh doth dresse it. **1629** *Book of Meery Riddles* Prov. 104 Fish marreth water, and flesh mendeth it. **1678** RAY 41 Fish spoils water, but flesh mends it.

Fish must swim thrice.

1611 COTGRAVE s.v. 'Poisson' We say flsh must ever swim twice [water, wine] (A). **1638** BRAITHWAIT *Barnabees Jrnl.* iii With carouses I did trimme me, That my fish might swim within me. **1670** RAY 38 . . . Once in the water, a second time in the sauce, and a third time in wine in the stomach. Poisson, gorret & cochin vie en l'eau, & mort en vin [*sic*]. *Gall.* Fish and young swine live in water and die in wine. **1738** SWIFT (Dial. ii) 344 *Smart.* Tom, they say fish should swim thrice. . . . First it should swim in the sea, (do you mind me?) then it should swim in butter; and at last, sirrah, it should swim in good claret.

Fish nor flesh (nor good red herring), Neither.

1528 *Rede me & be nott wrothe* I. iij b Wone that is nether flesshe nor fisshe. **1546** HEYWOOD I. x. 20 She is nother fyshe nor fleshe, nor good red hearyng. **1597–8** SHAKS. *1 Hen. IV* III. iii. 144 *Fal.* Why? she's neither fish nor flesh; a man knows not where to have her. **1600** HOLLAND *Livy* xxiv, xlv (1609) 540 He had the party himselfe in jelousie and suspition, as one neither fish nor flesh, a man of no credit. **1682** DRYDEN *Dk. Guise* Ep., Poems (O.U.P.) 247 Damn'd Neuters, in their middle way of steering, Are neither Fish nor Flesh nor good Red-Herring. **1816** SCOTT *Old Mort.* xxx Langcale cannot be suitably or preceesely termed either fish, flesh, or gude red herring; whoever has the stronger party has Langcale. **1902** DEAN HOLE *Then & Now* (7 ed.) vi Behold an hermaphrodite, neither 'fish, flesh, fowl, nor good red herring', the demolition of a woman, the caricature of a man, ridiculed as 'our friend from Middle Sex'.

Fish of one and flesh (*or* fowl) of another, To make.

[to make an invidious distinction; to show partiality.] **1639** CLARKE 182 I will not make fleshe of one and fish of the other. **1670** RAY 9 I'll not make *fish* of one and flesh of another. **1725** DEFOE *Everybody's Business* Wks. (Bohn) II. 510 The complaints alleged against the maids are . . . very applicable to our gentlemen's gentlemen; I would, therefore, have them under the very same regulations, and . . . would not make fish of one and flesh of the other. **1885** *Manch. Exam.* 21 May 5/2 This is making fish of one and fowl of another with a vengeance.

Fish on one's fingers, To find.

1583 GREENE *Wks.* (Gros.) II. 85 *Pharicles* . . . found fish on his fingers, that he might be the last should take his leave of *Publia*. **1590** LODGE *Rosalynde* 122 (Hunt, Cl.) (A) Ganimede rose as one that would suffer no fish to hang on his fingers.

Fish out of water, Like a.

[attrib. to St. Athanasius: not later than A.D. 373. *See* SKEAT *Early Eng. Prov.* 89.] *c.* **1374** CHAUCER *Troylus* IV. 765 How sholde a fish with-outĕ water dure? *c.* **1386** Id. *Prol.* 180 Ne that a Monk whan he is recchĕless Is

likned til a fissh that is waterlees. *c.* **1390**
LANGLAND *P. P. C.* vi. 149–50 Right as
fishes in flod whanne hem faileth water,
Deyen for drouth whenne thei drye liggen.
1613 PURCHAS *Pilgrimage* vi. xii. 636 The
Arabians out of the desarts are as Fishes out
of the Water. **1655–62** GURNALL *Chrn. in
Armour* (1865) I. 215 A tradesman out of his
shop . . . is as a fish out of the water, never in
his element till he be in his calling again.
1851 KINGSLEY *Yeast* xi A navvy drops into
a church by accident, and there he has to sit
like a fish out of water. **1876** BURNABY *Ride
to Khiva* ii A diplomatist in a land where he
cannot read the newspapers or converse with
all classes of society, . . . is rather like a fish
out of water.

Fish that comes to net, All is.

c. **1520** in *Ballads from MSS.* (B.S.) i. 95 (A)
Alle ys ffysshe that commyth to the nett.
1523 LD. BERNERS *Froiss.* I. ccccxvi. 727 Such
as came after toke all . . . for all was fysshe
that came to net. **1578** BULLEIN *Dial. agst.
Fever* (1888) 90 Taking up every commodity,
refusing nothing: all is fish that cometh to
the net. **1680** BUNYAN *Mr. Badman* i. Wks.
(1855) III. 598 What was his father's could
not escape his fingers, all was fish that came
to his net. **1826** LAMB to J. B. Dibdin, 14
July All jests were fish that to his net came.

Fish that will not some time or other bite, It is rare to find a.

1732 FULLER no. 5114.

Fish to fry, I have other.

[= other business to attend to.] **1660**
EVELYN *Mem.* (1857) III. 132 I fear he hath
other fish to fry. **1710–11** SWIFT *Jrnl. to
Stella* 8 Feb. I have other fish to fry; so
good morrow my ladies all. **1889** MRS.
OLIPHANT *Poor Gent.* xliv I've got other
things in hand . . . I've got other fish to fry.

Fish to fry than snigs[1] without butter, I have other.

1917 BRIDGE 78. [[1] eels.]

Fish will soon be caught that nibbles at every bait, That.

1633 PHIN. FLETCHER *Pisc. Eclog.* v. Wks.
(1908) II. 201 The fish long playing with the
baited-hook, At last is caught: Thus many a
Nymph is took. **1660** W. SECKER *Nonsuch
Prof.* II (1891) 241 If you . . . be found
nibbling at the bait, you may justly expect
the hook to enter into your bowels! **1732**
FULLER no. 4342.

Fish with a cross-bow, It is no sure rule to.

1640 HERBERT 331.

Fisherman's walk: A | three steps and overboard.

1829 M. SCOTT *T. Cringle's Log* i Walking to
and fro on the confined decks of the little
vessels . . . 'a fisherman's walk, two steps and
overboard'. **1896** F. LOCKER-LAMPSON *My*

Confid. 77 The river-pilots . . . at anchor,
taking a fisherman's constitutional ('three
steps and overboard').

Fishes that catches one, Still he.

1592 DELAMOTHE (1647) 54 Still fisheth he
that catches one. **1611** COTGRAVE s.v. 'Pescher'
And yet he fishes who catches one. **1639**
CLARKE 294. **1670** RAY 91 . . . Tousjours
pesche qui en prend un. *Gall.*

Fish(es) (*noun*), *see also* Better are small f.
than empty dish; Cast your net where no
f. (Vain to); Catching f. not whole of
fishing; Corn is in shock (When), f. are on
rock; Courts (It is at) as in ponds, some f.;
Daughters and dead f. no keeping wares;
Fasting when table covered with f. (Good);
Fresh f. and new-come guests; Fresh f. and
poor friends; Good f. if it were caught;
Gravest f. is oyster; Great f. eat up small;
Great river great f. (In a); Gut no f. till
you get; Had I f. is good without mustard;
Had I f. never good with garlic; Herring
is king (Of all f. in sea); Little f. are sweet;
Little f. slip through nets; No man cries
stinking f.; Old f. and young flesh; Old f.,
old oil, old friend; Raw pulleyn . . . and
f. make churchyards fat; Sea has f. for
every man; Silly f. caught twice; Taken
by a morsel, says the f.; Unsonsy f. gets
unlucky bait; Venture a small f. to catch
great one; Wind is south (When) . . . bait
into f.'s mouth. Wind is west (When)
f. bite best. *See also* Salt fish.

Fish (*verb*), *see also* Angle (F.) with silver
hook.

Fisher, *see* Fond f. that angles for frog;
March whisker never good f.; Mock no
pannier men; Wind's in north (When), f.
goes not forth.

Fisher's folly, *see* Kirkbie's castle.

Fish-guts, *see* Keep your ain f.

Fishing before the net, It is ill.

c. **1410** *Towneley Plays* (E.E.T.S.) 104 Ye
fysh before the net. *c.* **1480** HENRYSON *Wks.*
(S.T.S.) II. 130 l. 1755 The Lark . . . said,
'Scho fischit lang befoir the Net.' **1546**
HEYWOOD I. xi. 31. **1641** FERGUSSON 44 He
that fishes afore the net, lang or he fish get.
1721 KELLY 148 *He that fishes before the net,
long e'er he fish get.* Spoken to those who
devour by expectation, what they have not
in possession, for the fish are not gotten till
the net be drawn ashore.

Fishing in troubled waters, It is good.

[PETER OF BLOIS (Migne) 154 *Vulgo enim
dicitur, Aqua turbida piscosior est.* MAP *De
Cur. Nug.* (Camden Soc.) 242 *In aqua turbida
piscantur uberius.*] **1568** GRAFTON *Chron.* II.
102 Their persuasions whiche alwayes desyre
your quietnesse, wherby they may the
better fishe in the water when it is troubled.

1590 SIDNEY *First Arcadia* (Feuillerat) 242 The waters beeying as the Proverb saythe trubled and so the better for his fisshing. **1595** DANIELL *Civ. Wars* i st. 82 They thought best fishing still in troubled streams. **1612–15** BP. HALL *Contempl.* XVIII. i (1825) I. 548 Jeroboam had secretly troubled these waters, that he might fish more gainfully. **1641** FERGUSSON 64 It is good fishing in muddy waters. **1670** RAY 90 It's good fishing in drumling[1] waters. Il n'y a pesche qu'en eau troublé. *Gall.* In troubled waters; that is, in a time of publick calamity, when all things are in confusion. **1682** DRYDEN *Abs. & Achit.* II. 314 Who Rich and Great by past Rebellions grew, and long to fish the troubled Waves anew. **1722** SEWEL *Hist. Quakers* (1795) I. iv. 276 You delight to fish in troubled waters. **1902** A. LANG *Hist. Scot.* II 335 Arran had been trying to fish in the troubled waters. [[1] turbid, muddy.]

Fishing, The end of | is not angling, but catching.

1580 LYLY *Euphues & his Engl.* (Arb.) 396 (A). **1732** FULLER no. 4497. **1910** *Spectator* 5 Nov. 723 Mr. Sheringham recognizes that the business of fishing is to catch fish if possible.

Fishing to fishing in the sea, No.

1575 CHURCHYARD *Chippes* 41 (Collier) (A) Some say there is no fishing to the seas. **1577** PEACHAM *Garden of Eloquence* (1593) 87 I haue heard my father say, and eke my mother sing, There is no fishing to the sea, nor service to the King. *c.* **1580** HARVEY *Marginalia* (1913) 142 No fisshing to the Sea, nor service to A King. **1591** LYLY *Wks.* (Bond) I. 428 [as Harvey]. *c.* **1591** GREENE *James IV* I. ii 436 [as Harvey]. **1602** BRETON *Wonders w. Hearing* Wks. (Gros.) II. 9 *Fran.* Oh sir, nothing venture nothing have, there is no fishing to the sea, the gain of one voyage will bear the loss of many. **1625** PURCHAS *Pilgrims* (1905–7) XIX. 251 I am none of Neptune's secretaries; yet know this, that there is no fishing to the sea, and no country so strong by sea as that which findeth most employment in this kind. **1659** HOWELL *Eng. Prov.* 18/2 There is no fishing to the Sea, nor service to the Kings. **1670** RAY 90 No *fishing* to fishing in the sea. Il fait beau pescher en eau large. *Gall.* It's good fishing in large waters.

Fishing-rod has a fool at one end and sometimes a fish at the other, A.

1819 L. HUNT in *The Indicator*, 17 Nov. *Angling* The good old joke . . . that angling is . . . 'a stick and a string, with a fly at one end and a fool at the other'.

Fishing, *see also* Deepest water best f.

Fist, *see* Fool that makes a wedge of f.

Fit as a fiddle, As.

1616 HAUGHTON *Eng. for my money* IV. 1. (A) This is excellent, i' faith; as fit as a fiddle. **1882** MISS BRADDON *Mt. Royal* III. xi. 253 'Is Salathiel pretty fresh?' asked the Baron. 'Fft as a fiddle.' See also, for a discussion of this proverb, *N. & Q.*, vol. 192, no. 8, 159.

Fit(s, ted) (*verb*), *see* Suit is best that best f.; Well f. abide (Things).

Fitting, *see* Suffered to do more than is f. (He that is) will do more than lawful.

Five pound note, There never was a | but there was a ten pound road for it.

1862 HISLOP 287 There ne'er was a five pound note but there was a ten pound road for't. Such was the reply of a lady . . . when asked what she did with all the money she got.

Five pounds, *see* Fetch the f. p. (When do you)?

Five shillings, *see* Follow him long ere f. s. fall from him.

Fivepence, *see* Fine as f.

Flag protects the cargo, The.

1902–4 LEAN IV. 122 The flag protects the cargo.—(Sea.) Le pavillon couvre la marchandise.

Flag, *see also* Trade follows f.

Flail(s), *see* Fence against a f. (No); November take f.; Three f. and cuckoo.

Flame, *see* Fuel (Take away), take away f.

Flaming figure (Fair show) in a country church, It will make a.

1670 RAY 192 To make a fair show in a countrey Church. **1721** KELLY 207 *It will make a bra*[1] *show, in a landward*[2] *kirk.* A jest upon a girl when we see her fond of a new suit. **1738** SWIFT (Dial. ii) 344 *Spark.* Your ladyship has a very fine scarf. *Lady S.* Yes, my lord; it will make a flaming figure in a country church. [[1] braw, fine. [2] country.]

Flanagan, *see* Fire away, F.!

Flanders mares, fairest afar off, Like.

1717 *Six N. Count. Diaries* (Surtees Soc.) 82 (A) Uncle told me now we are to see yon damsel of Mr. Collingwood's. She's like a Flanders mare. **1732** FULLER no. 3229.

Flannel, *see* Patience and f. for gout.

Flap with a fox's tail, To give one a.

1530 PALSGRAVE 563 (A) I flatter hym to begyle him, or I gyve one a slappe with a foxe tayle. **1553** T. WILSON *Arte of Rhet.* (1909) 37 So that he gaineth alwaies, . . . whereas the other get . . . a flappe with a Foxe taile. **1602** *Thos. Lord Cromwell* IV. ii. 33 (*Shaks. Apoc.*) 181 I, we shall haue now three flappes with a Foxe taile. **1633** JONSON *T. Tub.* II. i But a man may break His heart out in these days, and get a flap With a fox-tail when he has done. **1670** RAY 176 . . . That is, to cozen or defraud. **1808** SCOTT *Let.* 19 Nov. in LOCKHART *Life* xviii (1860) 172 I owe Jeffrey a flap with a fox-tail on account of his review of Marmion.

Flat, That is.

[(a) formerly = that's the undeniable truth; (b) a defiant expression of one's determination.] **1594–5** SHAKS. *L.L.L.* III. i. 107 The boy hath sold him a bargain, a goose, that's flat. **1597–8** *1 Hen. IV* I. iii. 218 Nay, I will; that's flat. *Ibid.* IV. ii. 43 I'll not march through Coventry with them, that's flat. **1665** *Surv. Aff. Netherl.* 120 Its the greatest Bogg of Europe . . . that's flat. **1716** ADDISON *Drummer* I. i I'll give Madam warning, that's flat. **1852** SMEDLEY *L. Arundel* i. 15 'I won't then, that's flat', exclaimed Rachel.

Flat as a flounder, As.

1611 COTGRAVE s.v. 'Nez' A nose as flat as a Flooke (say we). *c.* **1625** BEAUM. & FL. *Women pleased* II. iv (A). **1659** HOWELL *Eng. Prov.* 5/1. **1720** GAY *New Similes* Flat as a flounder when I lie.

Flat as a pancake, As.

1542 UDALL tr. *Erasm. Apoph.* (1877) 250 (A) His nose as flat as a cake, bruised or beaten to his face. **1599** PORTER *Angry Wom. Abingd.* II. iii (Merm.) 133 And makes him sit at table pancakewise, Flat, flat. **1836** LEIGH HUNT *Visit to Zoolog. G.* in *New Month. Mag.* Aug. One tread of his foot would have smashed the little pertinacious wretch as flat as a pancake.

Flatter, *see* Contented who needs neither borrow nor f.

Flatterer as a man's self, There is no such.

1732 FULLER no. 4922.

Flatterer's throat is an open sepulchre, A.

1640 HERBERT 345.

Flatterer, *see also* Foe to a f. (No); Friend and your f. (I cannot be).

Flattering as a spaniel. (*Cf.* Fawn like a spaniel.)

1585 GREENE *Wks.* (Gros.) V. 103 Like Spanyels flattering with their tayles. **1616** WITHALS 553. **1639** CLARKE 285. **1670** RAY 204.

Flattery (Fraud) in friendship, There is.

1576 PETTIE *Petite Pall.* (Gollancz) I. 101 Alas! my Germanicus, are you to know . . . the falsehood in friends! **1579** LYLY *Euphues* (Arb.) 69 Here you may see, Gentlemen, . . . the fraude in friendshippe. **1598–9** SHAKS. *Hen. V* III. vii. 129 I will cap that proverb with 'There is flattery in friendship'.

Flavour, *see* Nothing hath no f.

Flax, *see* Fire to f. (Put not); Spindle and distaff ready, God will send f.; Woman is f.

Flay a flea for the hide and tallow, To.

1820 SCOTT *Abbot* xix The falconer observed, that . . . it had got harder and harder . . . to

    P

the poor gentlemen and yeoman retainers, but that now it was an absolute flaying of a flea for the hide and tallow. **1837** CHAMIER *Saucy Areth.* xxi 'Well', said the boatman, as he looked at the money, '. . . you would skin a flea for its hide and tallow!'

Flay (*or* Skin) a flint (groat), To.

[= to act meanly in order to get or save money.] **1640** HERBERT (Gros.) no. 760 You cannot flea[1] a stone. **1659** *Burton's Diary* (1828) IV. 398 Some of them were so strict that they would flea a flint. **1678** RAY 245 He would *flay* a flint, *or flay* a groat, spoken of a covetous person. **1884** BESANT *Childr. Gibeon* II. xxxi Just as the toper squeezes the empty bottle and the miser skins the flint. [[1] flay.]

Flay, *see also* No man can f. a stone.

Flea, a fly, and a flitch of bacon, A.

1902–4 LEAN (*York.*) I. 219 (Arms of the County.) A flea, a fly, and a flitch of bacon. The flea will suck any one's blood; the fly drink out of any one's cup; and the bacon is no good till it is hung.

Flea in March, If you kill one | you kill a hundred.

1902–4 LEAN III. 512.

Flea in one's ear, A.

[= a stinging reproof, which sends one away discomfited. Fr. *avoir la puce en l'oreille*, in the sense of being tormented by the desires and cares of love, occurs in *a.* **1465** CHARLES D'ORLÉANS *Chanson* I and in **1546** RABELAIS III. vii.] *c.* **1430** *Pilgr. Lyf. Manhode* (1869) II. xxxix. 91 And manye oothere grete wundres . . . whiche ben fleen in myne eres. **1546** HEYWOOD I. xi. 29 He standth now as he had a flea in his eare. . . . **1577** tr. *De L'Isle Legendarie* B vj 6 Sending them away with fleas in their eares, vtterly disappointed of their purpose. *a.* **1625** BEAUM. & FL. *Love's Cure* III. iii He went away with a flea in 's ear, Like a poor cur. **1712** ARBUTHNOT *John Bull* III. vi We being stronger than they, sent them away with a flea in their ear. **1887** RIDER HAGGARD *Jess* xiii I sent him off with a flea in his ear, I can tell you.

Flea (Fly) stick in the wall, Let that.

1757 SMOLLETT *Reprisal* II. iii *Macl.* Let that flie stick i' the wa'—when the dirt's dry it will rub out. **1818** SCOTT *Rob Roy* xxiii 'It will be a shame . . . to me and mine, . . . for ever.' 'Hout tout, man! let that flee stick in the wa', answered his kinsman; 'when the dirt's dry it will rub out.' **1824** MOIR *Mansie W.* xxvi Keh, keh, let that flea stick to the wa'; it's a' ye ken about it. **1866** READE *G. Gaunt* xvi 'Let that flea stick in the wall', said Betty contemptuously.

Flea(s), *see also* Flay a f. for hide and tallow; Dog that is idle barks at f., hunting feels not; Lies down with dogs, rise with f.; Nothing must be done hastily but killing f.

Flea-bitten horse never tires, A.

1577 *Heresbach's Husb.* (1586) ii. 116b (A)

The fleabitten horse prooveth alwaies good in travell. **1614** JONSON *Barthol. Fair* IV. iii Why, well said, old flea-bitten; thou'lt never tire, I see.

Flee never so fast you cannot flee your fortune.

1721 KELLY 108 . . . Spoken by them who believe that all things come by fatality.

Flee, *see also* Nought is to wed with (Where) . . . f. the clog.

Fleece and fell, To have both. (*Cf.* Shepherd must fleece his sheep, &c.)

1616 WITHALS 553 A good shepheard must take the fleece, and not ye fel. **1639** CLARKE 39 Will you have both fleece and fell?

Fleeceth, *see* Every hand f. (Where), sheep go naked.

Fleech, *see* Better f. a fool than fight him.

Fleet, *see* Whet his knife on . . . the F.

Flemings, *see* Shoulder of mutton and English beer make F. tarry.

Flesh is aye fairest that is farthest from the bone, The. [*But cf.* The nearer the bone the sweeter the flesh.]

1721 KELLY 325 . . . Spoken to them who are plump and look well.

Flesh, All | is not venison.

1592 DELAMOTHE (1647) 56. **1640** HERBERT 368. **1670** RAY 91 . . . Toute chair n'est pas venaison.

Flesh stands never so high but a dog will venture his legs.

1678 RAY 139. **1732** FULLER no. 1553.

Flesh, *see also* Fish nor f. (Neither); Fish of one and f. of another (Make); Ill f. ne'er made good broo; Never ate f. thinks pudding dainty; Old fish and young f.; Take away the salt, throw f. to dogs; Way of all f.; World, the f., and the devil.

Fletcher, *see* Like than Jack f. and his bolt (No more); Mends as the f. mends bolt.

Flies haunt (go to) lean horses.

1573 SANDFORD 205 The Flyes goe to leane horses. **1611** DAVIES Prov. 45 'The flyes haunt leane horses.' **1640** HERBERT 320 Flies are busiest about lean horses.

Fling at the brod[1] was ne'er a good ox.

1721 KELLY 107 . . . Taken from a drawing ox, who kicks when he is prick'd by the goad. Apply'd to them who spurn at reproof. [1 goad.]

Fling, *see also* After your f. watch for sting.

Flint, *see* Coldest f. there is fire (In); Flay a f.; Hard as a f.; Set one's face like a f.; Water from a f.

Flitch of bacon from Dunmow, He may fetch a.

1362 LANGLAND *P. Pl.* ix. 5515 (Wright) I. 169 And though thei do hem to Dunmowe, But if the devel helpe, To folwen after the flicche, Fecche thei it nevere. *c.* **1386** CHAUCER *W. of Bath's Prol.* 217 The bacoun was nat fet for hem, I trowe, That som men han in Essexe at Dunmowe. **1662** FULLER (*Essex*) I. 498 'He may fetch a flitch of bacon from Dunmow.' This proverb dependeth on a custom practised in the priory of Dunmow. . . . Any person . . . might demand . . . a gammon or flitch of bacon, upon the solemn taking of the ensuing oath [that husband and wife had not quarrelled since marriage]. **1708** PRIOR *Turtle & Sparrow* 233 Few married folk peck Dunmow-bacon. **1912** *Daily Tel.* 6 Aug. 3 Six years have passed since the Dunmow flitch of bacon has been bestowed on any couple who could truthfully take oath that neither had 'offended each other in deed or word, Or in a Twelvemonth and a Day repented not in thought any way'.

Flitch, *see also* Flea, a fly, and a f.

Flitting of farms makes mailings dear.

1721 KELLY 8 As one flits, another sits, and that makes the Mealings [farms] dear. **1846** DENHAM 3.

Flitting, *see also* Moonlight f. (Make a).

Flock follow the bell-wether, The.

1655 FULLER *Ch. Hist.* IV. ii (1868) I. 567 I am little moved with what T. Walsingham writes, (whom all later authors follow, as a flock the bell-wether). **1709** SWIFT in *Tatler* No. 66 Daniel can . . . grow fat by voluntary subscription, while the parson of the parish goes to law for half his dues. Daniel will tell you, it is not the shepherd, but the sheep with the bell, which the flock follows. **1896** 'H. S. MERRIMAN' *Flotsam* xxiii Others soon followed her ladyship, . . . for most women are like sheep in their visits, especially if the bell-wether carries a title.

Flock, *see also* Driving a f. than one (Better); Full f. (He who will have); Silly f. where ewe bears bell.

Flodden, *see* Mair tint at F.

Flog (*also* to mount on) a dead horse, To.

1879 TRENCH *Med. Ch. Hist.* [ed. 2] x. 145 The passion . . . never embodied itself in the shape of an eighth Crusade; and those who tried to quicken it again . . . were doomed to discover the truth . . . that it is no use to flog a dead horse. **1926** *Times* 19 July 13/6 By this time, however, Count Metternich was flogging a dead horse.

Flog (a person) within an inch of his life, To.

1872 C. READE *Wand. Heir* V They . . . bound Regulus to a tree, and flogged him within an inch of his life.

Flogged, The man who has not been | is not educated.

[MENANDER *Monosticha* 422 'Ο μὴ δαρεὶς ἄνθρωπος οὐ παιδεύεται. The man that has never been flogged has never been taught.] **1929** *Times* 29 June 13/5 I hailed with delight the letter . . . in defence . . . of punishing boys . . . with the rod. . . . As the Greek poet said of old, 'A man who has not been flogged is not educated'.

Flood(s), *see* April f. carries away frog; Dove's f. worth a king's good; May f. never did good; Michaelmas Day (So many days old the moon is), so many f.; Winter's thunder and summer's f. never boded good.

Floor, *see* Eaten your dinner off f. (Might have).

Flounder, *see* Flat as a f.; Frying-pan into fire (Like f.).

Flow hath its ebb, Every.

c. **1420** LYDGATE *Troy Bk.* II. 1. 2013 After a flowe, an ebbe folweth ay. **1576** PETTIE *Petite Pall.* (1908) II. 91 The sun being at the highest, declineth: and the sea being at full tide, ebbeth. **1639** CLARKE 123 A flow will have an ebb. **1721** KELLY 97 . . . There is a time when families, and single persons thrive, and there is a time when they go backward.

Flowers in May, As welcome as.

1540 PALSGRAVE *Acolastus* R 2 Howe do al thinges shewe pleasantly (as do flowres in May, or in the sprynge tyme)? **1591** FLORIO *Sec. Frutes* 55 Welcome Maie with his flowres. **1623** WODROEPHE 251. **1645** HOWELL *Lett.* 28 Apr. (1903) II. 97 Yours of the fifth of March, . . . was as welcome to me as flowers in May. **1840** DICKENS *Old C. Shop* xlviii He's as welcome as flowers in May.

Flower(s), *see* Fairest f. in his crown; Fresh as f. in May; One f. makes no garland.

Flutter the dovecots, To.

1607–8 SHAKS. *Coriol.* V. v Like an eagle in a dove-cote, I fluttered your Volscians in Corioli. **1864** FROUDE *Short Stud. Sc. Hist.* (1867) 2 A work which . . . fluttered the dovecotes of the Imperial Academy of St. Petersburg.

Fly, Not worth a.

1297 R. GLOUCESTER (1724) 428 Wat was þy strengþe worþ ? . . . ywys noȝt worþ a flye. *c.* **1352** LAU. MINOT *Songs* K. Ed. *Wars* in WRIGHT *Pol. Poems* (1859–61) I. 59 And all thaire fare noght wurth a flye. *c.* **1470** HENRYSON *Mor. Fab.,* 'Fox, Wolf, Cadg.'

(1917) 97 For he that will not laubour and help himself, . . . he is not worth ane fle.

Fly and eke a friar will fall in every dish and matter, A.

c. **1386** CHAUCER *W. of Bath's Prol.* 835 Lo, goode men, a flye, and eek a frere, Wol falle in every dysshe and eek mateere.

Fly, He would fain | but he wanteth feathers.

1550 HEYWOOD I. xi. 29 He would fayne flée, but he wanteth fethers. **1591–2** SHAKS. *1 Hen. VI* I. i. 75 Another would fly swift, but wanteth wings. **1611** DAVIES Prov. 344 Some would faine flie but feathers they want'. **1670** RAY 91 . . . *Sine pennis volare haud facile est.* PLAUT. in *Pœnulo.* Nothing of moment can be done without necessary helps, or convenient means.

Fly, If you must | fly well.

1640 HERBERT 364.

Fly followeth the honey, A.

c. **1412** HOCCLEVE *De Reg. Princ.* 110 A flye folowethe the hony.

Fly hath a spleen, A.

[L. *Habet et musca splenem.* Even a fly has anger. ERASM. *Ad. Formicae inest sua bilis.*] **1584** LYLY *Alex. & Campaspe* V. iv Sparkes have their heate, ants their gall, flies their spleene. **1623** CAMDEN 265. **1662** FULLER (*Rutl.*) III. 41 [Jeffrey] shewed to all, that *habet musca suum splenum*; and they must be little indeed that cannot do mischief.

Fly in amber, A.

1735 POPE *Ep. Arbuthnot* 169 Pretty! in amber to observe the forms Of hairs, or straws, or dirt, or grubs, or worms! **1778** WALPOLE *Letters* (Toynbee) X. 319 A line of yours [Mason] will preserve me like a fly in amber. **1847** BLACKWELL Malet's *North. Antiq.* 374 Byron caught him up, and . . . preserved him, like a fly in amber, for future generations to wonder at.

Fly in the face of Providence, To.

1894 BARING-GOULD *Queen of L.* II. 59 I am not one to fly in the face of Providence. **1911** *Spectator* 3 June 840 Knox . . . says: 'God hath determined that His Kirk . . . should be taught not by angels but by men.' That being so, we do but fly in the face of Providence when we provide not for men but for angels.

Fly in the ointment, A.

BIBLE *Eccles.* x. 1 Dead flies cause the ointment of the Apothecary to send forth a stinking savour. **1833** LAMB *Poor Relations* A fly in your ointment, a mote in your eye.

Fly into an elephant, He changes a.

1549 CHALENOR tr. *Erasm. Praise of Folly* A 2 Labour of a sely fly to make an Elephante. **1736** BAILEY *Dict.* s.v. 'Elephant' (A) To make of a fly an elephant. **1813** RAY 75.

Fly, The | sat upon the axletree of the chariot-wheel and said, What a dust do I raise!

1586 PETTIE *Guazzo's Civ. Conv.* 71 According to the example of the Flye, which sitting vppon a cart that was driuen on the waye, sayde, he had raysed a very great dust. **1612** BACON *Ess., Vain-glory* (Arb.) 462 It was pretily deuised of *Æsop*, The Flie sate vpon the Axletree of the Chariot wheele, and said, What a dust doe I raise! So there are some vaine persons, that whatsoeuer goeth alone, or moues vpon greater meanes, they thinke it is they that carry it. *a.* **1721** PRIOR *The Flies* (Says t' other, perched upon the wheel) Did ever any mortal Fly Raise such a cloud of dust as I! **1823** SYD. SMITH Speech at Thirsk 24 Mar. 'Here we are, a set of obscure country clergymen, . . . like flies on the chariot-wheel; perched upon a question of which we can neither see the diameter, nor control the motion, nor influence the moving force.'

Fly, The | that playeth too long in the candle, singeth his wings at last.

a. **1591** HY. SMITH *Serm.* (1866) I. 279 As the fly, by often dallying with the candle, at last scorcheth her wings with the flame; so taking, he[1] was taken, and at last was drunk. **1596–7** SHAKS. *Merch. V.* II. ix. 79 Thus hath the candle sing'd the moth. [[1] Noah.]

Fly that (the) pleasure which paineth afterward (*or* bites to-morrow).

1573 SANDFORD (1576) H 3ᵛ Flee that present pleasure, whiche afterwarde maketh thee sory. **1629** *Bk. Meery Rid.* (Halliw.) 97 Fly that pleasure which paineth afterward. **1640** HERBERT 338 Fly the pleasure that bites to-morrow.

Fly up with Jackson's hens, I will make him.

1678 RAY 86 . . . i.e. undo him. **1887** T. DARLINGTON *Folk-Speech of S. Chesh.* (E.D.S.) 192 Fly up . . . to be bankrupt. The full phrase 'to *fly up* with Jackson's hens' is more frequently heard.

Fly with the owl, To.

1622 MALYNES *Anc. Law-Merch.* 426 There is a Custome that no Officer may arrest after Sun set; such therefore as goe abroad at those times, are said to Fly with the Owle, by a common prouerbe.

Fly, flies, *see also* Boiling pot (To a) f. come not; Capers like a f. in a tar-box; Close mouth catches no f.; Fiddlers, dogs, and f. come uncalled; Flea, a f. and a flitch; Flea (F.) stick in the wall (Let that); Honey (Make yourself) and f. will devour; Hungry f. bite sore; Kill two f. with one flap; Laws catch f. but let hornets free; Light as a f.; Lose a f. to catch trout; Swallowed a f.

Flying enemy, *see* Golden bridge.

Flying from fate, No.

1732 FULLER no. 3568. **1910** *Spectator* 17 Dec. 1074 'All went well enough till a circus come to the town, and then I was mad to join it. . . . I was called to it, and you can't go against your fate'.

Flying without wings, No.

[PLAUTUS *Poenulus* 4. 2. 49 *Sine pennis volare haud facile est.* It is not easy to fly without feathers.] **1605** CHAPMAN, &c. *Eastw. Hoe* II. i (1889) 459 *Quick.* We must have trades to live withal; for we cannot stand without legs, nor fly without wings. **1670** RAY 91 No flying without wings. He would fain fly, but he wants feathers. . . . Nothing of moment can be done without necessary helps, or convenient means. **1721** KELLY 267 . . . A man cannot thrive and prosper in the world, that has no stock, or support.

Flyting, *see* Fair word in f. (Never a); First word of f. (Got the).

Foal amble if the horse and mare trot? How can the.

1550 HEYWOOD I. xi. 27 The litter is lyke to the syre and the damme. How can the fole amble, if the hors and mare trot? **1553** T. WILSON *Arte of Rhet.* 61 Trotte sire and trotte damme, how should the fole amble? **1621** BURTON *Anat. Mel.* III. iii. IV. ii (1651) 628 If the dam trot, the foale will not amble. **1641** FERGUSSON 96 Trot mother, trot father, how can the foal amble?

Foam like a boar, To.

1546 HEYWOOD I. xi. 36 She fometh lyke a bore.

Foe to a flatterer, No.

1578 M. HUNNIS in *Paradyse dayntye dev.* (1868) 97 *No foe to a flatterer* [Title]. **1629** T. ADAMS *Serm.* (1861–2) I. 188 *Plus nocet lingua adulatoris quam manus persecutoris.*[1] There is no foe to the flatterer. [[1] AUGUST. in Ps. lxvi.]

Foe(s), *see also* Four things (Of) man has more than he knows . . . f.; Misfortune makes f. of friends; One f. is too many; Secret f. gives sudden blow; Tell thy f. that thy foot acheth (Never); Truth finds f.; Woes unite f.

Fog cannot be dispelled with a fan, A.

1846 DENHAM 1.

Folk's dogs bark worse than themselves.

1721 KELLY 102 . . . Spoken when our neighbour's servants resent a thing we have done, worse than they would do themselves.

Folks grow old, When | they are not set by.

1639 CLARKE 280.

Folk(s), *see also* Far f. fare best; Far f. fare well.

Follow him long ere five shillings fall from him, You will.

c. **1598** *MS. Proverbs* in FERGUSSON 117 Ye will follow him long or 5*s.* fall from him. **1721** KELLY 378 . . . Discouraging from paying court and attendance upon those by whom you will never be bettered. **1732** FULLER no. 5944 You may follow him long e're a shilling drop from him.

Follow love (pleasure) and it will flee thee: flee love (pleasure) and it will follow thee.

c. **1400** *Rom. Rose* B. 4783 If thou flee it [love], it shal flee thee; Folowe it, and folowen shal it thee. **1550** HEYWOOD I. xi. 27 Folowe pleasure, and then will pleasure flée. Flée pleasure, and pleasure will folowe thée. **1641** FERGUSSON 32 Follow love and it will flee thee, flee love and it will follow thee. **1670** RAY 21 Fly pleasure and it will follow thee. **1678** *Ibid.* 55 Follow love and it will flee, Flee love and it will follow thee. This was wont to be said of glory, *Sequentem fugit, fugientem sequitur.* Just like a shadow.

Follow not truth too near the heels, lest it dash out thy teeth.

1614 SIR W. RALEGH *Hist. of the World* Preface Who-so-ever in writing a moderne Historie, shall follow truth too neare the heeles, it may happily strike out his teeth. *a.* **1634** S. ROWLEY *The Noble Soldier* C 3ᵛ I will follow Truth at the heeles, tho her foot beat my gums in peeces. **1651** HERBERT 370. **1655** FULLER *Ch. Hist.* IX. viii (1868) III. 166 I know how dangerous it is to follow truth too near the heels; yet better it is that the teeth of an historian be struck out of his head for writing the truth, than that they . . . rot in his jaws, by feeding . . . on the sweetmeats of flattery. **1827** HARE *Gues. at Truth* (1873) i. 283 Circumstantial accuracy with regard to facts is a very ticklish matter . . . As Raleigh says in a different sense . . . 'if we follow Truth too near the heels, it may haply strike out our eyes'.

Follow one's nose, To.

[= to go straight on, without reflection or preconceived plan.] *c.* **1350** *Cleanness* 1. 978 in *Allit. Poems* (E.E.T.S.) 67 Loth and tho lulywhite his lefly two deȝter, Ay folȝed ȝere face bifore her bothe yȝen. *c.* **1510** STANBRIDGE *Vulgaria* (E.E.T.S.) 24 Ryght forthe on thy nose. Recta via incede. **1635** SHIRLEY *Lady of Pleas.* II. ii (Merm.) 291 Give him leave To follow his nose, madam, while he hunts In view—he'll soon be at fault. **1650** B. *Discolliminium* 19 I'le follow Providence, or my Nose, as well as I can.

Follow the old fox, It is good to.

1639 CLARKE 268.

Follow the river and you'll get to the sea.

a. **1595** *Edward III* v. i. 92 All riuers haue recourse unto the Sea. **1608** J. HALL *Epistles* I. v (p. 37) Euen little streams empty them-

selues into great rivers, and they againe into the sea. **1732** FULLER no. 1556. [Fr. *Suivez la rivière et vous gagnerez la mer.*]

Follows (Looks to) freits, He that | freits will follow him.

? 17 . . *Adam o' Gordon* xxvii in PINKERTON *Select. Sc. Ballads* (1783) I. 49 Wha luik to freits, my master deir, Freits will ay follow them. **1721** KELLY 128 . . . He that notices superstitious observations (such as spilling of salt, . . .) it will fall to him accordingly. **1804** MUNGO PARK in LOCKHART'S *Scott* xiii (1860) 117 He answered, smiling, '*Freits* (omens) follow those who look to them'. . . . Scott never saw him again. **1914** *Times Lit. Sup.* 10 Apr. 178 The Kings of Scots have always been beset by omens, and . . . to him who follows freits, freits follow.

Follows Nature, He that | is never out of his way.

1576 PETTIE *Petite Pall.* (Gollancz) I. 14 and I. 83. **1579** LYLY *Euphues* Wks. (Bond) I. 192 Doth not Cicero conclude and allow that if we follow and obey Nature we shall neuer err? **1732** FULLER no. 2108.

Follows the Lord, He that | hopes to go before.

1640 HERBERT 363.

Follow(s), *see also* Dam leaps over (Where), kid f.; Far behind that may not f.

Folly grows without watering.

1640 HERBERT 344. **1732** FULLER no. 1574 Fools grow without watering. **1853** TRENCH iv. 78 *Fools grow without watering;* no need therefore of adulation or flattery, to quicken them to a ranker growth.

Folly is a bonny dog.

1641 FERGUSSON 32. **1857** DEAN RAMSAY *Remin.* v (1911) 200 *Folly is a bonny dog.* Meaning, I suppose, that many are imposed upon the false appearances and attractions of vicious pleasures.

Folly of one man is the fortune of another, The.

1607 BACON *Ess., Fortune* in Wks. (1858) VI. 472 The folly of one man is the fortune of another. **1855** BOHN 505.

Folly to being in love, No.

1768 RAY 50 No folly to being in love, or where loves in the case, the Doctor is an Ass.

Folly were grief, If | every house would weep.

1640 HERBERT 335.

Folly, *see also* Disease (Chief) that reigns is f.; Every fault (In) there is f.; First degree of f. is to hold self wise; Jollity but hath smack of f. (No); Wisdom to find out own f.

Fond[1] fisher that angles for a frog,
He is a. (*Cf.* Fish and catch a frog.)

1616 BRETON *Cross Prov..* Wks. (1879) II.
App. iii. [[1] foolish.]

Fond of barter that niffers with Old Nick, He is.

1834 A. CUNNINGHAM *Wks. of Burns* VIII. 278
Glossary. He's fond o' barter that niffers wi'
Auld Nick. (Scot. Say.)

Fond of gape-seed, She is.

1598 FLORIO *World of Words* s.v. 'anfanare'
To go seeking for a halfepeny worth of gaping
seede. **1600** NASHE *Summers Last Will* Wks.
(McKerrow) III. 275. **1602** *Entertainment at
Harefield* (NICHOL'S *Progresses* 1823 iii. 586)
You come to buy gape seed. **1603** FLORIO tr.
Montaigne (F. A. YATES *Florio* 233) Such as
gather stubble (as the common saying is) or
looke about for gape-seed. **1830** FORBY
431 . . . i.e. Of staring at everything that
passes.

Fool always rushes to the fore, A.

1853 TRENCH iii. 59.

Fool and his money are soon parted, A.

1573 TUSSER X. 19 A foole and his monie be
soone at debate, which after with sorrow
repents him too late. **1629** HOWELL *Fam.
Lett.* 20 Oct. T.B. intends to give money for
such a place . . . I fear it will be verified in
him that a fool and his money is soon parted.
1670 RAY 91. **1748** SMOLLETT *Rod. Rand.* xi
Well, fools and their money are soon parted.
1816 SCOTT *Antiq.* xxxix A fool and his
money is soon parted, nephew.

Fool as he looks, Not such a.

1888 MRS. OLIPHANT *Second Son* ix Oh, I am
not such a fool as I look. My father always
said so. **1905** VACHELL *The Hill* 70 I shan't
forget either that you're not half such a fool
as you look.

Fool asks much, The | but he is more fool that grants it.

1616 DRAXE 21. **1640** HERBERT 330.

Fool does in the end, What the | the wise man does at the beginning.

1853 TRENCH V. 121 *That which the fool does
in the end, the wise man does at the beginning;*
the wise with a good grace what the fool with
an ill. **1866** KINGSLEY *Hereward* v 'It's a
fool's trick', answered the stranger . . . , 'to
put off what you must do at last.'

Fool doth think he is wise, The | but the wise man knows himself to be a fool.

1599–1600 SHAKS. *A.Y.L.* V. i. 35 I do now
remember a saying, 'The fool doth think he is
wise, but the wise man knows himself to be a
fool.'

Fool finds a horseshoe, When a | he thinks aye the like to do.

1721 KELLY 348 . . . Spoken when they, who
have had some fortune, think always to be as
successful. **1732** FULLER no. 6415.

Fool hath bethought himself, When a | the market's over.

1732 FULLER no. 5530.

Fool: I am a | I love anything (everything) that is good.

1678 RAY 247. **1738** SWIFT (Dial. i) 335 *Col.*
I'm like all fools; I love everything that's
good.

Fool in his sleeve, Every one hath a.

1640 HERBERT 357.

Fool is fulsome, A.

1659 HOWELL *Eng. Prov.* 10/2. **1670** RAY 10.

Fool is never cured, He who is born a.

1642 TORRIANO 22. **1732** FULLER no. 2391.

Fool knows more in his own house than a wise man in another's, A.

1620 SHELTON *Quix.* II. xliii (A). **1640**
HERBERT 329.

Fool, One | makes many (a hundred).

[L. *Unius dementia dementes efficit multos.*
The madness of one makes many mad.]
1617 J. SWETNAM *School of Defence* 11 The
olde Prouerbe, One foole makes many. **1640**
HERBERT 342 One fool makes a hundred. **1659**
HOWELL *Eng. Prov.* 9/1 One fool
maketh many fools. **1738** SWIFT (Dial. i) 336
Never. Well, I see one fool makes many.
1813 SCOTT *Let.* to Byron 6 Nov. in LOCK-
HART's *Life* As to those who . . . take my
rhapsodies for their model . . . they have
exemplified the ancient adage, 'one fool
makes many'.

Fool may ask more questions in an hour than a wise man can answer in seven years, A.

1670 RAY 91. **1738** SWIFT (Dial. ii) 347 *Miss.*
They say a fool will ask more questions than
the wisest body can answer. **1821** SCOTT
Pirate xviii Bryce Snailsfoot is a cautious
man . . .; he knows a fool may ask more
questions than a wise man cares to answer.

Fool may give a wise man counsel, A.

c. **1374** CHAUCER *Troylus* i. 630 A fool may
eek a wis-man ofte gyde. **1509** A. BARCLAY
Ship of Fools (1874) I. 58 Oft a folys counsayle Tourneth a wyse man to confort and
auayle. **1721** KELLY 25 . . . An apology of
those who offer their advice to them who
may be supposed to excel them in parts and
sense. **1818** SCOTT *Ht. Midl.* xlv If a fule
may gie a wise man a counsel, I wad hae him
think twice or he mells wi' Knockdunder.

Fool may sometimes speak to the purpose, A.

[Gk. Πολλάκι τοι καὶ μωρὸς ἀνὴρ κατακαίριον εἶπε. L. *Interdum stultus benè loquitur.*] 1613 WITHER *Abuses* Title-page A fool to purpose speaks some time you know. 1668 J. WILSON tr. *Moriæ Encomium* 160 Remembering in the mean time, that Greek proverb . . . *Sometimes a fool may speak a word in season.*

Fool may throw a stone into a well, A | which a hundred wise men cannot pull out.

1640 HERBERT 342.

Fool of the family: The | make a parson of him.

1545 ASCHAM *Toxoph.* (Arb.) 154 This boye is fit for nothynge els, but to set to lerning and make a prest of. 1648 JOHN HALL *Sat.* i. 133–6 But if it chance they have one leader sone Born for to number eggs, he must to school; Especiall' if some patron will engage Th' advowson of some neighbouring vicarage. 1905 J. OXENHAM *White Fire* ix I was at Eton with B— and at Oxford. He always was a fool. . . . He ought to have gone into the Church.

Fool of thyself, Make not a | to make others merry.

1621 BURTON *Anat. Mel.* II. iii. VII (1651) 360.

Fool or a physician at forty (thirty), Every man is a.

[TAC. *Ann.* 6. 46 [*Tiberius*] *solitus eludere medicorum artes atque eos, qui post tricesimum aetatis annum ad internoscenda corpori suo utilia vel noxia alieni consilii indigerent.*] 1594 O. B. *Questions* G 1 This old prouerbe; Either a foole or a Phisition. 1601 HOLLAND tr. *Pliny* xxviii. 5 [ii. 304] Every man is to be his owne Physician: whereupon might rise this proverbe, *A foole or a Physician.* 1601 JONSON *Poetaster* III. iv. 8–10. 1607 BARNES *Divils Charter* L 3 Eyther mere fooles or good physitions all. 1659 HOWELL *Eng. Prov.* 6/2 Every one a fool or a physitian to himself after thirtie. 1670 RAY 35 Every man is either a fool or a physician after thirty years of age. 1721 KELLY 101 *Every man at thirty is a fool or a physician.* He is a fool who at that age knows not his constitution. 1742 GRAY to West Jan. quoting Cheyne [Dr. George, 1671–1743] Every man after fourty is either a fool or a physician. 1851 HELPS *Compan. of Sol.* x A man learns certain rules of health, so that it is said that at forty he is either a fool or a physician.

Fool praises another, One.

1740 FRANKLIN Nov. Who knows a fool must know his brother; For one will recommend another.

Fool saith, The | Who would have thought it?

1540 TAVERNER tr. *Erasm. Flores sententiarum* B 2ᵛ Indecora sapienti vox est. Non putaram,

aut non expectaram. It is an uncourtly sayeing for a wise man to say, I wold not have thought it, or I wolde not have loked that it should have come so to passe. c. 1590 LYLY *Moth. Bomb.* IV. ii. 38. 1608 J. DAY *Law Tricks or Who would have thought it?* 1616 DRAXE 13 It is the part of a foole to say, I had not thought. 1639 CLARKE 320 Who would have thought it? 1732 FULLER no. 4539.

Fool sometimes, Every man is a | and none at all times.

1640 HERBERT 324 None is a fool always, every one sometimes. 1721 KELLY 99 . . . An apology for an imprudent action, in ourselves, or others.

Fool that forgets himself, He is a.

c. 1374 CHAUCER *Troylus* v. 98 I have herd seyd ek tymes twelve, ' He is a fool that wole foryete hymselve.' 1596–7 SHAKS. *K. John* III. iv. 48 I am not mad ; I would to heaven I were! For then, 'tis like I should forget myself. 1641 FERGUSSON 42.

Fool that is not melancholy once a day, He is a.

1678 RAY 346.

Fool that kisseth the maid when he may kiss the mistress, He is a.

1659 HOWELL *Eng. Prov.* 15/2. 1670 RAY 111 If you can kiss the mistress, never kiss the maid.

Fool that makes a wedge of his fist, He is a.

1611 COTGRAVE s.v. 'Coing'. 1640 HERBERT 344.

Fool that marries his wife at Yule, He is a | for when the corn's to shear the bairn's to bear.

1721 KELLY 167 . . . If a woman be got with child in Christmas, it is like that she may lye in harvest, the throngest time of the year.

Fool, He hath great need of a | that plays the fool himself.

1611 COTGRAVE s.v. 'Fol'. 1640 HERBERT 319. 1721 KELLY 161 He would fain have a fool that makes a fool of himself.

Fool that thinks not that another thinks, He is a.

1640 HERBERT 330.

Fool thinks, As the | so the bell clinks.

c. 1390 GOWER *Conf. Amantis* i. 75 For as it seemeth that a bell Like to the wordés that men tell Answereth right so. 1607 *Lingua* III. vii (A) As the fool thinketh, so the bell clinketh. I protest I hear no more than a post. 1621 BURTON *Anat. Mel.* I. iii. III (1651) 211 He that hears bells, will make them sound what he list, *As the fool thinketh, so the bell clinketh.* 1732 FULLER no. 6121. 1850

CARLYLE *Latter-Day Pamph.* viii (1885) 285–6 It is a true adage, 'As the fool thinks, the bell clinks'.

Fool to roast eggs, Set a | and a wise man to eat them.

1678 RAY 241.

Fool to the market (far, to France), Send a | and a fool he will return again.

1586 G. WHITNEY *Emblems* 178 The foole that farre is sente some wisedome to attaine; Returnes an idiot, as he wente, and bringes the foole againe. **1678** RAY 140 Send a fool to the market and a fool he will return again. The Italians say, Chi bestia va a Roma bestia retorna. He that goes a beast to Rome returns thence a beast. Change of place changes not men's minds or manners. **1832** HENDERSON 22 Send a fool to France and he'll come a fool back.

Fool to the old fool, No.

1546 HEYWOOD II. ii. 46 But there is no foole to the olde foole, folke say. **1594** LYLY *Moth. Bomb.* IV. ii. Wks. (1902) III. 211 *Acc.* In faith I perceive an olde sawe and a rustic, no foole to the old foole. **1614** CAMDEN 313. **1721** KELLY 256 . . . Spoken when men of advanc'd age behave themselves, or talk youthfully, or wantonly. **1859** TENNYSON *Grandmother* Wks. (1893) 226 I . . . spoke I scarce knew how; Ah, there's no fool like the old one—it makes me angry now. **1893** H. P. LIDDON *Serm. on O. T.* xi. 162 'No fool is so bad as the old fool', for . . . he is less capable of improvement than a young one.

Fool, A | unless he knows Latin, is never a great fool.

1853 TRENCH iv. 78 The Spaniards [have] . . . on the folly of a pedant as the most intolerable of all follies: *A fool, unless he knows Latin, is never a great fool.*

Fool wanders, The | the wise man travels.

1732 FULLER no. 4540. **1837** LD. AVEBURY *Pleas. Life* I. vii 'He that would make his travels delightful must first make himself delightful' (Seneca). According to the old proverb, 'the fool wanders, the wise man travels.'

Fool who makes his physician his heir, He is a.

[PUB. SYRUS *Male secum agit aeger, medicum qui haeredem facit.* A sick man does badly for himself who makes the physician his heir.] **1553** *Precepts of Cato* (1560) Ff 4ᵛ He is not lyke long to prosper, Who maketh a phisicion his heyer. **1584** LYLY *Campaspe* v. iv. Wks. (1902) II. 355 *Alex.* If one be sick, what wouldest thou haue him do? *Diog.* Be sure that he make not his Phisition his heire. **1648** HERRICK *Hesper.* 316 *On Leech.* Wks. (1893) I. 161 He knows he must of Cure despaire, Who makes the slie Physitian his Heire. **1733** FRANKLIN Feb. He's a fool that makes his doctor his heir.

Fool will not give his bauble for the Tower of London, A.

a. **1500** in *R. Hill's Commonpl. Bk.* (E.E.T.S.) 130 (A). **1577** GRANGE *Gold. Aphrod.* Ep. Ded. (Being somewhat wedded as most fools are) to mine owne opinion, who would hardly forgoe their bable for the Tower of London. **1599** PORTER *Angry Wom.* Abingd. IV. iii (Merm.) 178 Well, I see the fool will not leave his bauble for the Tower of London. **1641** FERGUSSON 12.

Fool's bell is soon rung, A.

c. **1400** *Rom. Rose* 5266 And fooles can not holde his tunge; A fooles belle is soone runge.

Fool's bolt is soon shot, A. (*Cf.* Shot one's bolt.)

c. **1225** *South. Legendary* (E.E.T.S.) I. 93 Ouwer [ʒoure al] bolt is sone ischote. *c.* **1275** *Provs. of Alfred,* A. 421 Sottes bolt is sone i-schote. *c.* **1300** *Provs. of Hending* xi Sottes bolt is sone schote. **1375** *Ywain & Gawain* (Ritson) I l. 2168 For fole bolt es sone shot. *c.* **1450** *Proverbis of Wysdom* in HERRIG's *Archiv.* 90 l. 113 A fole is bolt is sone i-shote. **1546** HEYWOOD II. iii. 48 She maie saie (quoth I) a fooles bolte soone shot. **1598–9** SHAKS. *Hen. V* III. vii. 132 You are the better at proverbs, by how much—A fool's bolt is soon shot. **1599–1600** *A.Y.L.* V. iv. 67 *Duke S.* By my faith, he is very swift and sententious. *Touch.* According to the fool's bolt, sir. **1653** (?) FORD *The Queen* (ed. Bang) in *Mat. zur Kunde des Eng. Drames* XIII l. 1012 A wise mans bolt is soon shot. **1748** SMOLLETT *Rod. Rand.* liii 'Your bolt is soon shot, according to the old proverb', said she.

Fool's bolt may sometimes hit the mark, A.

1580 FULWELL *Ars Adul.* Dial. 7 Fools bolts (men say) are soonest shot yet oft they hit the mark. **1732** FULLER no. 107 A fool's bolt may sometimes hit the white.

Fool's haste is no speed.

1641 FERGUSSON 32. **1721** KELLY 102 . . . Spoken when people make a great bustle, and . . . often by their too much haste spoil what they are about.

Fool's paradise, A.

1462 W. PASTON in *Paston Lett.* No. 457 II. 109 I wold not be in a folis paradyce. **1528** ROY *Rede Me* (Arb.) 86 Thus my lady, not very wyse, Is brought in to foles paradyse. **1594–5** SHAKS. *Rom. & Jul.* II. iv. 175 If ye should lead her into a fool's paradise, as they say, it were a very gross kind of behaviour. **1728** POPE *Dunc.* iii. 9. **1856** MRS. BROWNING *Aur. Leigh* iv. 341 Love's fool-paradise Is out of date, like Adam's.

Fool's tongue is long enough to cut his own throat, A.

1732 FULLER no. 108.

Fool(s), *see also* All the wit in the world (If you had), f. would fell you; Ass (F.) that brayeth against other ass; Barber learns shaving f.; Begged for a f.; Better be a f. than knave; Better fleece a f. than fight him; Bridges were made for . . . f. to ride over; Change of weather the discourse of f.; Child's service . . . f. that despiseth; Children and f. cannot lie; —— have merry lives; —— must not play with edged tools; Counsel (He that is own) has f. for client; Counsel of f. (To) wooden bell Deal f.'s dole; Discreet advise (While), f. does his business; Dote more on it than f. on bauble; Dogs (F.) begin in jest; Every man a little beyond himself a f.; Experience is mistress of f.; Experience keeps a dear school . . .; Fat as a f.; Ferlies make f. fain; First chapter of f.; Fishing-rod has f. at one end; Fortune favours f.; God help the f.; God sendeth fortune to f.; Higher the f. greater fall; Hood for this f.; House-top (On the) in anger soon is f.; Knaves and f. divide the world; Lawyers' houses built on f.; Lend and lose, so play f.; Love makes a wit of the f.; Man at five, f. at fifteen; Many a one for land takes f. by hand; Mickle fails that f. think; More f. than fiddler; More knave than f.; More know Tom F.; No play without f.; Nod for a wise man, rod for f.; Nod from a lord breakfast for f.; Oil of f.; Play with a f. at home; Promise and give nothing, comfort to f.; Riches serve wise man, command f.; Sends a f. expects one (or means to follow); Success makes f. seem wise; Talks to himself speaks to a f.; Teaches himself has f. for master; Too much of nothing but f.; Two f. in one house too many; Two f. met; Vicar of f. is his ghostly father; Want of a wise man (For) f. set in chair; Whip for a f.; White wall is f.'s paper; Who's the f. now; Wisdom sometimes to seem f.; Wise erred not (If), go hard with f.; Wise man must carry the f.; Wise men change their minds, f. never; —— have their mouth in their heart, f. . . . ; —— learn by other men's harms, f. . . . ; —— make proverbs, f. repeat; —— propose, f. determine; —— silent, f. talk; Wise (None is so) but f. overtakes; Woman she is fair (Tell a); Woman's advice . . . who won't take is f.; Words are money of f.; Young men think old men f. *See also* Fools, Play the fool.

Foolish in the fault, He that is | let him be wise in the punishment.

1640 HERBERT 343.

Foolish man, *see* Hope often deludes f. m.

Foolish (Peevish) pity mars a city.

1556 J. HEYWOOD *Spider & Flie* (Farmer) 307 This . . . Is either not pity, or peevish pity, which (as th'old saying saith) marreth the city. **1639** CLARKE 181. **1723** CAMDEN 275 Peevish pitty, marres a Citty.

Foolish sheep that makes the wolf his confessor, It is a.

1642 TORRIANO 53 There is a silly sheep that goeth to the woolf to shriue her self. **1664** CODRINGTON 222. **1670** RAY 23.

Foolish tongues talk by the dozen.

c. **1380** CHAUCER *Parl. Fowles* 1. 574 But sooth is seyd 'a fool can noght be stille'. *c.* **1400** *Rom. Rose* 1. 5265 Fooles can not hold hir tunge. **1640** HERBERT 347.

Foolish, *see also* Do a f. thing once (One cannot) but one must hear of it; Least f. is wise; Service a child doth his father (The first) is to make him f.

Fools and bairns should not see half-done work.

1721 KELLY 108. **1818** SCOTT in LOCKHART'S *Life* xliii (1860) 386 'Bairns and fools' . . . according to our old canny proverb, should never see half-done work. **1913** A. &. J. LANG *Highw. & By. in the Border* ix To the lay eye improvement is yet barely perceptible. 'Fools and bairns', however, they tell us, 'should never see half-done work'.

Fools and fiddlers sing at their meat, None but.

1813 RAY 9.

Fools and madmen speak the truth. (*Cf.* Children and fools, &c.)

1549 CHALENOR tr. *Erasmus Praise of Folly* Q 4ᵛ That priuilege fooles haue to speake trouthe without offence. **1602** DEKKER *Satiro-Mastix*, Dram. Wks. (1873) I. 198 A foole will confesse truth. **1634** *Cacoethes Leaden Legacy* A 9 The English Proverbe saith, that truth by fooles is onely told.

Fools are fain of flitting.

[HOR. *Ep.* 1. 14. 43 *Optat ephippia bos: piger optat arare caballus.* The ox covets the horse's trappings, the lazy horse wishes to plough.] **1641** FERGUSSON 32. **1721** KELLY 105 *Fools are fain of flitting, and wise men of sitting.* Spoken to them who are fond of altering their place, station, or condition, without good reason.

Fools are fain of nothing (right nought).

1641 FERGUSSON 32 Fools are fain of right nought. **1721** KELLY 111 *Fools are fain of nothing.* Spoken when we see people much taken up with fair promises, or improbable expectations.

Fools bite one another, but wise men agree together.

1640 HERBERT 339.

Fools build houses, and wise men buy (or live in) them.

1670 RAY 91 Fools build houses, and wise men buy them. **1721** KELLY 110 *Fools big houses* *and wise men buy them.* I knew a gentleman buy £2000 worth of land, build a house upon it, and sell both house and land to pay the expenses of his building. **1732** FULLER no. 1573 (with 'enjoy' for 'buy'). **1911** SIR W. F. BUTLER *Autobiog.* xix The adage says that fools build houses for other men to live in. Certainly the men who build the big house of Empire for England usually get the attic or the underground story in it for their own lodgment.

Fools cut their fingers, but wise men cut their thumbs.

1738 SWIFT (Dial. i) 335 *Lady S.* 'Tis only fools cut their fingers, but wise folks cut their thumbs. **1902–4** LEAN III. 467 Fools cut their fingers, but wise men cut their thumbs . . . i.e. the follies of the wise are prodigious.

Fools exult when Governments change, Only.

1928 *Times* 19 Nov. 15/3 A somewhat cynical proverb current among the Rumanian peasants, who say that 'Only fools exult when Governments change'.

Fools give to please all but their own.

1640 HERBERT 351.

Fools grow without watering.

1707 MAPLETOFT 43. **1732** FULLER No. 1574. **1853** TRENCH (1905) 73.

Fools had baubles, If all | we should want fuel.

c. **1350** *Douce MS. 52* no. 109 A fole sholde neuer haue a babulle in hande. **1640** HERBERT 320.

Fools have the wit to keep themselves warm (*or* out of the rain).

1599 H. BUTTES *Dyets Drie Dinner* B. iv Fools . . . have the wit to keep themselves out of the rain. **1599–1600** SHAKS. *Twelfth N.* I. iii. 78 I am not such an ass but I can keep my hand dry.

Fools lade the water, and wise men catch the fish.

c. **1450** *Babees Bk.* (Furnivall) 332 Folus lade polys,[1] wisemenn ete þe fysshe. *c.* **1520** SKELTON *Magnyf.* 1. 300 Wel, wyse men may ete the fysshe, when ye [i.e. Fancy] shal draw the pole.[1] **1636** CAMDEN 296. [[1] pools.]

Fools live poor to die rich.

1659 N.R. 32. **1855** BOHN 356.

Fools make feasts, and wise men eat them.

1573 SANDFORD 214 Fooles make feastes, and wyse menne enioy them. **1639** CLARKE 186. **1721** KELLY 110 . . . This was once said to a great man in Scotland, upon his giving an entertainment. Who readily answer'd, *Wise men make proverbs and fools repeat them.* **1832–8** S. WARREN *Diary of Late Phys.* xxii Her trembling husband . . . suggested . . . the

old saying, 'that fools make feasts, and wise men eat them'.

Fools one to another, We are.

1640 HERBERT 335.

Fools set far (long) trysts.

1641 FERGUSSON 32 Fooles sets far trystes. **1721** KELLY 102 *Fools sets long trysts.* Spoken when people promise to do a thing a good while hence.

Fools set stools for wise folks to stumble at.

1623 CAMDEN 269.

Fools should not fool it, If | they shall lose their season.

1640 HERBERT 350.

Fools should not have chapping sticks.[1]

1641 FERGUSSON 32 Fooles should have no chappin sticks. **1681** S. COLVIL *Whigs Sup.* I. 68 It is the simplest of all tricks To suffer fools have chopping sticks. **1721** KELLY 104 . . . Spoken when we take a stick from a child, or when others are doing harm with what they have taken up. **1818** SCOTT *Rob Roy* xxxiv Deil tak him . . . that gies women either secret to keep or power to abuse —fules shouldna hae chapping sticks. [[1] dangerous tools or weapons.]

Fools tie knots, and wise men loose them.

1639 CLARKE 88. **1721** KELLY 107 . . . Spoken when people . . . have spoil'd and entangled a business, which will require wisdom to set right again.

Fools went not to market, If | bad wares would not be sold.

1640 HERBERT 320 Were there no fools, bad ware would not pass. **1670** RAY 10. *Hispan.*

Fools will be fools still.

1575 *Gam. Gurton's N.* I. iv Might ha kept it when ye had it! but fooles will be fooles styll.

Fools will be meddling.

1611 BIBLE *Prov.* xx. 3 Every fool will be meddling. **1670** RAY 91. **1738** SWIFT (Dial. i) 338 *Miss.* Why, madam, fools will be meddling; I wish he may cut his fingers.

Fools wore white caps, If all | we should seem a flock of geese.

1640 HERBERT 341.

Fools, *see also* Fool(s).

Foot on the cradle and hand on the distaff is the sign of a good housewife, The.

1659 HOWELL *Span.-Eng.* 2. **1670** RAY 14. *Hispan.* **1721** KELLY 307 *The foot at the* *cradle, and the hand at the roke[1] is the sign of a good housewife.* Spoken jocosely when we see a woman spinning, and rocking the cradle with her foot. **1737** RAMSAY III. 195 The foot at the cradle an' the hand at the reel, Is a sign o' a woman that means to do weel. [[1] distaff.]

Foot out of the langel,[1] You have aye a.

1721 KELLY 292 . . . Spoken to them that perversely oppose every thing. [[1] a tether.]

Foot, feet, *see* All f. tread not in one shoe; Best f. foremost; Better a bare f.; Better the f. slip; Cool mouth and warm f.; Dry f. warm head bring safe; Foul f. makes full wame; Foul f. (You have o'er) to come so far ben; God comes with leaden f.; Going (Walking) f. aye getting; Head and f. keep warm; Keep your f. dry and head hot; Lame f. overtakes swift one; Length of person's f. (Find); Measure another man's f. by own last; One f. in grave (To have); One shoe not fit all f.; Open your mouth but you put your f. in it (Never); Seek in a sheep five f.; Steal the hog and give the f.; Tell thy foe that thy f. acheth (Never); Thinketh his f. be where his head; White f. (One), buy him; Will is ready (Where), f. is light. *See also* **Feet, Hind foot.**

Football, *see* All fellows at f.

Footsteps, *see* Master's f. fatten soil.

Forbear not sowing because of birds.

1640 HERBERT 348.

Forbear, forborne, *see also* Lawfully done which cannot be f.

Forbearance (Omittance, Sufferance) is no acquittance.

[L. *Quod defertur non aufertur.* What is deferred is not relinquished.] **1546** HEYWOOD II. iv. 53 But sufferance is no quittance in this daiment. **1592** *Arden of Fevers.* II. ii Arden escaped us. . . . But forbearance is no acquittance; another time we'll do it. **1599–1600** SHAKS. *A.Y.L.* III. v. 133 But that's all one; omittance is no quittance. **1667** MILTON *P.L.* X. 52 But soon shall find Forbearance no acquittance ere day end.

Forbid a thing, and that we will do.

[ov. *Am.* 3. 4. 17 *Nitimus in vetitum semper, cupimusque negata.*] c. **1386** CHAUCER *W. of Bath's Prol.* D. 519 Forbede us thing, and that desyren we. **1641** FERGUSSON 32. **1721** KELLY 107 Forbid a fool a thing, and that he will do.

Forbidden fruit is sweet.

[**1611** BIBLE *Gen.* iii. 6.] c. **1386** CHAUCER *Parson's T.* I. 332 The flessh hadde delit in the beautee of the fruyt defended. **1629** T. ADAMS *Serm.* (1861–2) I. 53 But as the proverb hath it, apples are sweet when they are plucked in the gardener's absence. Eve liked no apple in the garden so well as the forbidden. **1855** BOHN 357

Force hidden in a sweet command, There is great.

1586 PETTIE *Guazzo's Civ. Conv.* 173 Threatning words, wherewith they make all the house to shake: not knowing that (as the Poet saith) Great force lies hid in gentle Soueraigntie. **1640** HERBERT 345.

Force without forecast is of little avail.

1721 KELLY 106. **1732** FULLER no. 1589.

Force, *see also* Subtlety is better than f.

Forced put, He is at a.

1657 G. STARKEY *Helmont's Vind.* 328 In expectation that Nature being forced to play a desperate game, and reduced to a forc't put, may [&c.]. **1678** RAY 79. **1772** NUGENT *Hist. Friar Gerund* I. 526 He thought that it might pass for a case of necessity, or forced-put. **1876** in *N. & Q.* 5th Ser. v. 266 A tradesman [of Torquay] told me . . . that he had left his house very early . . . 'but not from choice, 'twas a force-put'.

Forchets,[1] That which one most | soonest comes to pass.

1678 RAY 71. [[1] anticipates.]

'Ford', In | in 'ham', in 'ley', and 'ton', the most of English surnames run.

1605 R. VERSTEGAN *Restit. of Dec. Intell.* (1673) 326 Ton . . . I take to be one of the greatest terminations we have, and . . . [it] may be said, In *foord,* in *ham,* in *ley,* and *tun,* The most of English Surnames run. **1879** C. W. BARDSLEY *Rom. of Lond. Direct.* 32 The rhyme . . . is true, that 'In "ford", in "ham", in "ley", and "ton", The most of English surnames run'. All names with this termination are local, and comprise a large proportion of our national nomenclature.

Ford, *see also* Praising a f. till a man be over (Not good).

Forecast is better than work-hard.

1612 CHAPMAN *Widow's Tears* II. iv Acknowledge forecast is better than labour. **1670** RAY 92. **1721** KELLY 106 Force, without forecast, is little worth. Strength, unless guided by skill and discretion, will avail but little. **1732** FULLER no. 1588.

Forecasts all perils, He that | will never sail the sea.

a. **1585** MONTGOMERIE *Cherrie & Slae* xxxviii (1821) 22 'And I haif hard', quod Hope, 'that he Sall nevir schaip to sayle the se, That for all perrils castis'.

Forecasts all perils, He that | will win no worship.

1721 KELLY 167 . . . Because he will be frightened from any noble attempt.

Forecast(s), *see also* Force without f. of little avail; Lie in bed and f.

Forehead and the eye, In the | the lecture of the mind doth lie.

1595–6 SHAKS. *Rich. II* I. iii. 208 Uncle, even in the glasses of thine eyes I see thy grieved heart. **1616** DRAXE 61 (with 'heart is read'). **1670** RAY 92.

Forehead, *see also* Penny in the f.

Foreheet (Foreswear) nothing but building churches and louping[1] over them, I will.

1678 RAY (*Northern*) 355 I'll foreheet (i.e. predetermine) nothing but building churches and louping over them. **1738** SWIFT (Dial. ii) 349 *Lady S.* I hear . . . you have foreswore the town. *Sir. J.* No, madam; I never foreswore anything but the building of churches. [1 leaping.]

Fore-horse, *see* Ride the f.

Forelock, *see* Time by the f. (Take).

Foremost, *see* Dog (Hindmost, F.) may catch (catches) hare.

Forenoon(s), *see* Longer f. shorter afternoon; Two f. in the same day (Cannot have).

Foreswear, *see* Foreheet (F.) nothing but building churches.

Foretold, *see* Long f. long last.

Forewarned, forearmed.

[L. *Praemonitus, praemunitus.*] *a.* **1530** R. *Hill's Commonpl. Bk.* (E.E.T.S.) 132 He that is warned ys half armed. *c.* **1530** REDFORD *Play Wit & Sci.* 1021 *Wyt.* 'Once warne[d], half-armd' folk say. **1546** HEYWOOD II. vi. 63 Halfe warnd halfe armde. **1590–1** SHAKS. *3 Hen. VI* IV. i. 113 I will arm me, being thus forewarn'd. **1592** *Arden of Fevers.* I. 583 Forewarned, forearmed; who threats his enemy, Lends him a sword to guard himself withal. **1662** FULLER (*Devon*) I. 442 Let all ships passing thereby be forearmed because forewarned thereof. **1883** PAYN *Thicker than W.* xii But she was forewarned and forearmed.

Forewit, One good | is worth two afterwits.

1546 HEYWOOD I. viii. 15 Howbeit when bought wits to best price bée brought, Yet is one good forewit woorth two after wits.

Forfeits, *see* Plays more than he sees (He that) f. his eyes.

Forge, *see* Water in a smith's f.

Forget(s), forgot(ten), *see* Fool that f. himself; Forgive and f.; Friar f. feud (Never); Knows (What one) it is useful sometimes to f.; Learneth young f. not; Musician hath f. his note (When), crumb in throat; Seldom seen, soon f.

Forgive an enemy, If we are bound to | we are not bound to trust him.

1732 FULLER no. 2728.

Forgive and forget.

a. **1225** *Ancrene Riwle* 124 Al þet hurt and al þet sore were uorȝiten and forȝiuen uor glednesse. **1377** LANGLAND *P. Pl. B.* xvii 241 So wil Cryst of his curteisye · and men crye hym mercy, Bothe forȝiue and forȝete. **1546** HEYWOOD II. ix. 74 Praiyng hir, to forgeue and forget all frée. **1590–1** SHAKS. *3 Hen. VI* III. iii. 200 I forgive and quite forget old faults. **1595–6** *Rich. II* I. i. 156 Forget, forgive; conclude and be agreed. **1602–3** *All's Well* V. iii. 9 I have forgiven and forgotten all. **1605–6** *K. Lear* IV. vii. 84 Pray you now, forget and forgive: I am old and foolish. **1621** BURTON *Anat. Mel.* Democr. to Rdr. (1651) 78 If . . . I have said amiss, let it be forgotten and forgiven. **1775** SHERIDAN *Rivals* v. iii Give me your hand, Sir Lucius, forget and forgive. **1894** LD. AVEBURY *Use of Life* ii Individuals often forget and forgive, but Societies never do.

Forgive any sooner than thyself.

1553 *Precepts of Cato* Cleobulus 4 (1560 Q 6) Forgeue other, to thee ofte offendynge, But thy selfe forgiue not in any euel doynge. **1664** CODRINGTON 192. **1670** RAY 10.

Forgive(n), *see also* Fristed is not f.; Vengeance is to f. (Noblest).

Forgotten, *see* Long absent soon f.

Fork is commonly the rake's heir, The.

1732 FULLER no. 4536.

Fork, *see also* Better with a rake than a f.

Forsake not the market for the toll.

1623 CAMDEN 269. **1670** RAY 119.

Forsakes measure, He that | measure forsakes him.

1641 FERGUSSON 38 He that forsakes missour, missour forsakes him. **1721** KELLY 158 . . . That is, he who is immoderate in anything, design, or action, shall meet with treatment accordingly.

Forth bridles the wild Highlandman.

[The River Forth was a restraint upon Highland raids.] **1818** SCOTT *Rob Roy* xxviii Bailie Jarvie suggested, in his proverbial expression, that 'Forth bridles the wild Highlandman'. **1886** STEVENSON *Kidnapped* xxvi Forth is our trouble; ye ken the saying, 'Forth bridles the wild Highlandman'.

Fortunate head that never ached, It is a.

1855 BOHN 427.

Fortunate, If you are too | you will not know yourself; if you are too unfortunate, nobody will know you.

1732 FULLER no. 2733.

Fortunate, *see also* Wicked (The more), more f.

Fortunatus' purse.

[= the inexhaustible purse of a fairy tale hero.] **1600** DEKKER *Old Fortunatus* III. ii If this strange purse his sacred virtues hold, We'll circle England with a wall of gold. **1626** JONSON *Fortun. Isles* Wks. (1904) III. 194 Where would you wish to be now, or what to see, Without the Fortunate Purse to bear your charges. **1910** *Times, Wkly.* 8 July 515 The Chancellor of the Exchequer . . . regards it as the bag of FORTUNATUS in which he has only to dip his hand to draw out as much as he pleases.

Fortune can take from us nothing but what she gave us.

[PUB. SYRUS *Nihil eripit Fortuna nisi quod et dedit.*] **1732** FULLER no. 1598.

Fortune favour I may have her, If | for I go about her: if fortune fail, you may kiss her tail, and go without her.

1670 RAY 212.

Fortune favours fools.

[L. *Fortuna favet fatuis.*] *c.* **1560** L. WAGER *The Longer thou Livest* D 4 Fortune can exalte fooles. **1563** GOOGE *Epytaphes* (Arb.) 74 But Fortune favours Fooles as old men saye. **1603** N. BRETON *Pkt. of Letters* in Wks. (Gros.) II *h* 33 Because Fortune fauors few fooles this yeare, weé must tarry longer to play our game. **1643** T. BROWNE *Religio Medici* pt. i. § 18 That contemptible Proverb, That fools only are Fortunate.

Fortune favours the bold (brave).

[VIRGIL *Aen.* 10. 284 *Audentes fortuna iuvat.*] *c.* **1374** CHAUCER *Troylus* IV. 600 Thenk eek Fortune, as wel thiselven woost, Helpeth hardy man to his enprise. *c.* **1390** GOWER *Conf. Amantis* VII. 400 And saith, 'Fortúne unto the bolde Is favoráble for to helpe'. **1481** CAXTON *Reynard* xxvii (Arb.) 66 Who that is hardy th[e] auenture helpeth hym. **1539** TAVERNER (1552) 10 Audaces fortuna iuuat. Fortune helpeth men of good courage. **1622** FLETCHER *Prophetess* IV. vi He is the scorn of Fortune: but you'll say, That she forsook him for his want of courage, But never leaves the bold. *c.* **1724** A. RAMSAY *The Widow can Bake* For fortune aye favours the active and bauld. **1841** CHAMIER *Tom Bowl.* xi Fortune, they say, favours the brave; . . . and Bowling . . . ran the vessel close to the fort.

Fortune is blind.

1588 GREENE *Pandosto* Prose Wks. (1881–3) VI. 245 Fortune although blind, . . . sent them . . . a good gale of winde. **1596–7** SHAKS. *Merch. V.* II. i. 36 So may I, blind fortune leading me, Miss that which one unworthier may attain. **1593–9** *Hen. V* III. vi. 33 *Flu.* Fortune is painted plind, with a muffler afore her eyes, to signify to you that Fortune is plind. **1601** JONSON *Poetaster* V. i

All human business fortune doth command without all order; and with her blind hand, She, blind, bestows blind gifts.

Fortune is variant.

c. **1390** GOWER *Conf. Amantis* VIII. 585 Fortune hath euer been muable and mai no while stande stable. *c.* **1420** LYDGATE *Assembly of Gods* st. 46 p. 10 (E.E.T.S.) (A) Varyaunt she [Fortune] was. **1509** A. BARCLAY *Ship of Fools* I. 126 (1874) (A) Fortune euer hath an incertayne end.

Fortune knocks once at least at every man's gate.

1567 FENTON *Bandello* (T.T.) ii. 148 Fortune once in the course of our life dothe put into our handes the offer of a good torne. **1869** HAZLITT 136. **1889** W. F. BUTLER *C. G. Gordon* 51 Fate, it is said, knocks once at every man's door . . . Gordon had just passed his thirtieth year when Fortune . . . knocked at . . . the door which was to lead him to fame.

Fortune knocks, When | open the door.

1620 SHELTON *Quix.* II. v (1908) II. 220 It is not fit that whilst good luck is knocking at our door we shut it: let us therefore sail with this prosperous wind.

Fortune smiles, When | embrace her.

1664 CODRINGTON 224. **1670** RAY 10 When Fortune smiles on thee, take the advantage. **1732** FULLER no. 5553.

Fortune to be pictured on a wheel, Not only ought | but every thing else in the world.

1651 HERBERT 367.

Fortune to one is mother, to another is stepmother.

1573 SANDFORD A 3 True it is as Hesiodus saith, time is otherwhile a mother, otherwhile a stepdame. **1581** T. HOWELL *Devices* (1906) 52 My stepdame strange, I Fortune yet doe finde. **1651** HERBERT 369.

Fortune(s), *see also* Dances well to whom f. pipes; Every man is the architect of own f.; Flee never so fast, cannot flee f.; Gaineth enough whom f. loseth; Give a man f.; God sendeth f. to fools; Good man whom f. makes better; Great f. brings misfortune; Industry is f.'s right hand; Manners make often f.; Put your finger in fire and say it was f. *See also* Good fortune, Ill fortune.

Forty pence, *see* Farewell f. p.

Forward cock that croweth in the shell, It will be a.

1591 LYLY *Endym.* II. ii *Favil.* Away, peevish boy, a rod were better under thy girdle, than love in thy mouth: it will be a forward cock that croweth in the shell.

Forward, *see also* Go f. and fall.

Foster, *see* No longer f., no longer lemman.

Foul dirty ways, and a long sickness, Take heed of.

1651 HERBERT 371.

Foul face, There is never a | but there's a foul fancy.

1917 BRIDGE 119 There's never a fou' face but there's a fou' fancy. Ugly people have ugly thoughts.

Foul feet, You have o'er | to come so far ben.[1]

c. **1598** *MS. Proverbs* in FERGUSSON 115.
1721 KELLY 372 . . . That is, you are too mean to pretend to such a courtship. [[1] into the house.]

Foul foot makes a full wame, A.

1721 KELLY 27 . . . Industry will be sure of a maintenance. A man that carefully goes about his business will have foul feet.

Foul morning may turn to a fair day, A.

1624 BURTON *Anat. Mel.* II. iii. III. 275 A lowring morning may turne to a faire after noone. **1732** FULLER no. 115.

Foul, He that hath to do with what is | never comes away clean. (*Cf.* Toucheth pitch, &c.)

c. **1250** *Owl & Night.* 299 z ʒet Alured seide an oþer side a word þat is isprunge wide: 'þat wit þe fule haueþ imene, ne cumeþ he neuer from him cleine.'

Foul water as soon as fair will quench hot fire.

1546 HEYWOOD I. v. 10. **1594** LYLY *Moth. Bomb.* III. iv.

Foul (*adj.*), *see also* Good land where there is f. way.

Foul(s) (*verb*), *see* No man f. hands in own business.

Found out, *see* Commandment (Eleventh); Eating and drinking (Ingenious who f. o.).

Foundation, *see* Good building without good f. (No); High buildings low f.

Four Eights, The.

1886 FROUDE *Oceana* xiv The good people of Auckland[1] . . . had little to complain of. . . . The four eights, that ideal of operative felicity, are here a realized fact! (*Note.* Eight [hours] to work, eight to play, eight to sleep, and eight shillings a day.) [[1] New Zealand.]

Four eyes see more than two.

[L *Plus. vident oculi quam oculus.* The eyes see more than one eye.] **1599** MINSHEU (1623) Tt 2 Foure eies see better then two.

1600 HAKLUYT *Navig. & Disc. of Eng. Nat.* (2 ed.) III. Ep. Ded. (1903) I. lxxvi Commonly a souldier observeth one thing, and a mariner another, and as your honour knoweth, Plus vident oculi, quàm oculus. **1898** F. MAX MÜLLER *Auld Lang Syne* 80 But who has ever examined any translation from any language, without finding signs of . . . carelessness or ignorance? Four eyes see more than two.

Four farthings and a thimble, will make a tailor's pocket jingle.

1659 HOWELL *Eng. Prov.* 15/1.

Four pence to a groat, As like as.

1678 RAY 286.

Four things, Of | every man has more than he knows: of sins, of debts, of years, and of foes.

1853 TRENCH iv. 82 In the same rank of unwelcome proverbs . . . this Persian one: *Of four things every man has more than he knows: of sins, of debts, of years, and of foes.*

Four, *see also* Count not f. except in wallet.

Fowey, The gallants of.

1587 HARRISON's *Descr. of Britain* in HOLINSHED i. 62 The ships of Fawy sailing on a time by Rhie and Winchelseie in the time of king Edward the third, refused stoutlie to vale anie bonet there, . . . Herevpon the Rhie and Winchelseie men made out vpon them with cut and long taile: but so hardlie were they interteined by the Fawy pirates (I should saie adventurers) that they were driven home againe . . . in token of their victorie . . . the Foyens were called the gallants of Fawy or Foy. **1602** R. CAREW *Survey of Cornwall* (1769) 135. **1787** GROSE (*Cornwall*) 161 The gallants of Foy. The inhabitants of Foy were, in the time of King Edward IV, famous for their privateers, and their gallant behaviour at sea; whence they obtained that denomination. **1920** F. MUIRHEAD *England* 179 It was . . . one of the foremost seaports of the kingdom, and the achievements of the 'Gallants of Fowey' rank with those of the 'Sea-Dogs of Devon'.

Fowl of a fair day, As fain (glad) as a.

1377 LANGLAND *P. Pl.* B. x. 153 Thanne was I also fayne, as foule of faire morwe. **1678** RAY 285 As glad as a fowl of a fair day. **1862** HISLOP 40 As fain as a fool[1] o' a fair day. [[1] fowl.]

Fowl(s), *see* Far f. fair feathers; Fish of one and f. of another (Make).

Fowler's pipe sounds sweet till the bird is caught, The.

1732 FULLER no. 4542.

Fox, He has caught a.

[= is drunk.] **1599** MINSHEU (1623) 2 X 2 To be turned into a Fox, To be drunk. **1690**

New Dict. Canting Crew E 7 He has caught a fox, he is very drunk.

Fox cubs, *see* Best among them (Never a), as fellow said by f. c.

Fox fares best when he is banned (cursed), The.

1548 A. BORDE *Introduction* (E.E.T.S.) 166 The more the fox is cursed, the better he doth fare. *c.* **1565** W. WAGER *Enough is as good as a feast* E 4ᵛ. **1592** CHETTLE *Kindhartes Dreame* (1874) 70 But I perceiue you fare as the Fox, the more band, the better hap. **1602** *Thomas Ld. Cromwell* II. iii (*Shaks. Apoc.*) 173 Praie thy worst; The Fox fares better still when he is curst. **1605** JONSON *Volpone* v. iii. 119 The Foxe fares ever best, when he is cursed. **1614** CAMDEN 312 The Fox fareth well when he is cursed. **1655** FULLER *Ch. Hist.* III. v (1868) I. 411 These Caursines[1] were generally hated for their extortions. . . . [They] cared not what they were called, being akin to the cunning creature, which fareth best when cursed. **1721** KELLY 331 *The tod[2] never fares better than when he's ban'd.* Spoken when we are told that such people curse us, which we think the effect of envy, the companion of felicity. The fox is cursed, when he takes our poultry. [[1] Lombard bankers of Cahors. [2] fox.]

Fox for his mate, He that hath a | hath need of a net at his girdle.

1640 HERBERT 337.

Fox from a fern-bush, He does not know a.

1580 LYLY *Euph. & his Eng.* Wks. (Bond) II. 92 It is a blynde Goose that knoweth not a Foxe from a Fearne-bush. **1587** BRIDGES *Def. of Govt. in C. of E.* 99 (A) It seemed (as the saying is) either a foxe or a fearne brake. **1616** WITHALS 574. **1639** CLARKE 143 He spoke of a fox but . . . it was but a ferne brake. **1846–59** *Denham Tracts* ii. 107 (A) (F.L.S.).

Fox hath once got in his nose, When the | he'll soon find means to make the body follow.

1590–1 SHAKS. *3 Hen. VI* IV. vii. 25 I challenge nothing but my dukedom . . . *Glo.* [*Aside*] But when the fox hath once got in his nose, He'll soon find means to make the body follow.

Fox is brought to the furrier, At length the.

1640 HERBERT 320. **1796** EDGEWORTH *Par. Asst., Lit. Merchts.* iii (1903) 409 Still at your old tricks . . . No fox so cunning but he comes to the furrier's at last. **1818** SCOTT *Rob Roy* xxvii They'll be upsides wi' Rob at the last . . . the fox's hide finds aye the flaying knife.

Fox is known by his brush (furred tail), The.

1545 BRINKLOW *Compl.* xxiv As yᵘ mayest

knowe a foxe by his furred taile. **1607** WALKINGTON *Opt. Glass* 38 A fox is known by his brush.

Fox knows much, The | but more he that catcheth him.

1631 MABBE *Celestina* (T.T.) 207 (A) If the fox be crafty, more crafty is he that catches him. **1640** HERBERT 330.

Fox lick a lamb, It is an ill sign to see a.

1678 RAY 142.

Fox may grow grey, but never good, The.

1572 J. PARINCHEF *Extract of Examples* 18 The Foxe may change his cote, but neuer will leaue his crafte (From Brusonius lib. I. cap. 1.) **1631** MABBE *Celestina* (T.T.) 207 (A) Though the fox change his haire, yet he never changeth his nature. **1721** KELLY 361 *You breed of the tod, you grow gray before you grow good.* Spoken to old gray headed sinners who will not reform their lives. **1749** FRANKLIN Mar. Many foxes grow grey, but few grow good. **1855** BOHN 505.

Fox preacheth, When the | then beware your geese.

c. **1460** *Towneley Myst.* (Surtees) 10 Let furth youre geyse, the foxe wille preche. **1546** HEYWOOD II. vii. 67 For though this appéere a proper pulpet péece, Yet whan the fox preacheth, then beware your géese. **1614** CAMDEN 304 Beware the geesse when the Fox preaches. **1721** KELLY 344 *When the tod[1] preaches, look to the geese.* When wicked men put on a cloak of religion, suspect some wicked design. [[1] fox.]

Fox preys farthest from home, The.

1629 T. ADAMS *Serm.* (1861–2) II. 317 The fox seldom preys near home, nor doth Satan meddle with his own. **1659** HOWELL *Eng. Prov.* 2/2. **1670** RAY 92 The fox preys furthest from's hole. Crafty thieves steal far from home.

Fox run, Though the | the chicken hath wings.

1640 HERBERT 343. **1732** FULLER no. 5008.

Fox should not be of the jury at a goose's trial, A.

1732 FULLER no. 116. **1802** WOLCOT (P. Pindar) *Middl. Elect.* i A fox should not be of the jury Upon a goose's trial.

Fox smells his own stink first, The.

1738 SWIFT (Dial. i) 339 *Col.* Here's a very bad smell. *Miss.* . . . The fox is the finder. **1914** K. F. PURDON *Folk of Furry F.* vii 'Dan Grennan . . . had a great deal to say . . . about a bullock that is missing. But I can't help thinking of a saying . . . how that the fox always smells his own smell!'

Fox that had lost its tail would persuade others out of theirs, The.

a. **1581** N. WOODES *Conflict of Conscience*

G 3ᵛ The Foxe . . . caught in snare, and scapt with losse of tayle, To cut off theirs, as burthenous, did all the rest counsayll. **1658** FLECKNOE *Enigm. Characters* 78 (A) Like the fox, who having lost his own taile, would needs perswade all others out of theirs.

Fox to keep the (his) geese, He sets the.

1638 J. CLARKE *Phraseologia Puerilis* E 2. **1639** CLARKE 9. **1672** WALKER 31. **1709** O. DYKES *Eng. Prov.* 45 He sets the Fox to keep his Geese . . . reflects upon . . . men . . . intrusting either *Sharpers* with their *money*, *Blabs* with their *Secrets*, or *Enemies* . . . with their *Lives*. **1822** SCOTT *Nigel* xxix Come, damsel, now I will escort you back to the Lady Mansel, and pray her . . . that when she is again trusted with a goose, she will not give it to the fox to keep.

Fox turns monk, At length the.

1611 COTGRAVE S.V. 'Moine'. **1640** HERBERT 320.

Fox was sick, The | and he knew not where: he clapped his hand on his tail, and swore it was there.

1678 RAY 71. **1738** SWIFT (Dial. ii) 345 *Miss.* I have cut my finger . . . this finger: no, 'tis this: I vow I can't find which it is. *Never.* Ay; the fox had a wound, and he could not tell where, &c. **1830** LYTTON *Paul C.* xviii 'The fox had a wound, and he could not tell where'—we feel extremely unhappy, and we cannot tell *why*.

Fox's tail, *see* Flap with a f. t. (Give one a).

Fox's wiles will never enter the lion's head, The.

1580 LYLY *Euph. & his Eng.* (Arb.) 337 The Foxes wiles shal neuer enter into ye Lyons head, nor *Medeas* charmes into *Philautus* heart.

Fox(es), *see also* Brains of a f. of little service if . . . paw of lion; Dealest with a f. (If thou); Deceive the f. must rise betimes; Fie upon hens, quoth f.; Follow the old f.; Goose that comes to f.'s sermon (Blind); Lion's skin cannot (If), the f.'s shall; Long runs the f. as he has feet; No more of the f. than the skin (You can have); Old f. not easily snared; Old f. want no tutors; Red as a f.; Sleeping f. catches no poultry; Tail doth often catch f.; Take hares with f.; Wolf and f. privateers. *See also under* Tod.

Fox-skin, *see* Bought the f. for three pence.

France is a meadow that cuts thrice a year.

[Fr. *France est un pré qui se tond trois foys l'année.*] **1640** HERBERT 358.

France (*or* England) win, He that will | must with Scotland first begin.

1548 HALL *Chron.* (1890) 55 (A) The old auncient prouerbe . . . whiche saieth he that will Fraunce wynne, muste with Scotlande firste beginne. **1577** HOLINSHED *Chron.* (1808) 66 Rafe Neuill . . . thought good to mooue the King to begin first with Scotland; . . . concluding . . . with this old saieng: that who so will France win, must with Scotland first begin. **1598–9** SHAKS. *Hen. V* I. ii. 166 But there's a saying . . . ; *If that you will France win, Then with Scotland first begin.* **1902** A. LANG *Hist. Scot.* II. 363 Father Creighton and other Scots held that 'He who would England win Must with Scotland first begin', and credulously believed that James would be converted.

France's ruin, The day of | is the eve of the ruin of England.

1626 SIR T. OVERBURY *Obs. Trav.* Wks. (1890) 245 Now the only entire body in Christendome that makes head against the *Spanish* monarchy, is *France*; and therefore they say in *France*, that the day of the ruine of *France*, is the eve of the ruine of England.

Franciscans' hackney, *see* Go upon F. h.

Fraud, *see* Frost and f. end in foul.

Fray, *see* Better come at end of feast than beginning of f.; First blow makes . . . the second makes a f.

Free and easy.

1699 LISTER *Journ. Paris* 41 In a very free and easy posture. **1711** *Spectator* no. 119 ¶ 3 The fashionable world is grown free and easy. **1764** COWPER to Mrs. Hill 5 Jan. Reading over what I have written, I find it perfectly free and easy. **1864** NEWMAN *Apol.* I had a lounging free-and-easy way of carrying things on.

Free as a bird in air.

1533 J. HEYWOOD *Pardoner and Friar* A 1 As free As be the byrdes that in the ayre flee. **1631** T. POWELL *Tom of all Trades* (New. Sh. S.) 166 He may trade as free as bird in ayre.

Free as the wind.

1607 HEYWOOD *Fair Maid of the Exchange* (1874) ii. 18 As free as aire. **1609** SHAKS. *Coriol.* I. ix Were he the butcher of my son, he should Be free as is the wind.

Free country, This is a.

1889 WESTALL *Birch Dene* (1891) 243 It would never do to make th' cottages too comfortable. . . . And this is a free country. Them as doesn't like 'em can leave 'em'. **1911** *Spectator* 2 Sept. 339 I can leave off work when I please, and so can Smith, Brown, Jones, and Robinson. . . . This is a free country!'

Free of fruit that wants an orchard, He is.

1721 KELLY 134 . . . Spoken to them who tell how free and liberal they would be, if they had such things, or were such persons.

Free of her lips, free of her hips.

1576 PETTIE *Petite Pall.* (1908) II. 32 They are as loose of their lips and as free of their flesh. **1678** RAY 62. **1732** FULLER no. 6269.

Free of his gift as a poor man is of his eye, He is as.

1546 HEYWOOD I. xi As free of gift as a poor man of his eye. **1659** HOWELL *Eng. Prov.* 14/1.

Free of horse that never had one, He is.

c. **1300** *Provs. of Hending* xxvii He is fre of hors þat ner nade non, quoþ Hendyng. **1641** FERGUSSON 94 They are good willie of their horse that hes nane.

Free, He is not | that draws his chain.

1640 HERBERT 355.

Freedom is a fair thing.

1375 BARBOUR *Bruce* I. 1. 225 A! fredome is A noble thing! **1641** FERGUSSON 32.

Freer, see Nothing f. than a gift.

Freets[1] fail, When all | fire's good for the fiercy.[2]

1641 FERGUSSON 34 Fire is good for the farcie. **1721** KELLY 353 . . . Spoken when after ordinary attempts, we betake ourselves to extraordinary. [[1] charms. [2] glanders.]

Freezes who does not burn, He.

1907 *Brit. Wkly.* 19 Dec. 321 That old saying, Alget qui non ardet'—'he freezes who does not burn', is true . . . , and wherever we find . . . success, it has been attained as the result of . . . whole-hearted enthusiasm.

Freight, see Many ventures make full f.

Freit(s), see Follows f. (He that).

French leave, To take.

[= to depart, act, without asking leave or giving notice.] **1771** SMOLLETT *Humph. Clink.* (1895) 238 He stole away an Irishman's bride, and took a French leave of me and his master. **1816** SCOTT *Antiq.* iii I began to think you had . . . taken French leave, as . . . Mac-Cribb, did, when he went off with one of my Syrian medals. **1841** CHAMIER *Tom Bowl.* ii I kept thinking of Susan, and . . . made up my mind to take French leave and visit her.

French soldier carries a marshal's baton in his knapsack, Every.

[*Tout soldat français porte dans sa giberne le bâton de maréchal de France.* Attributed (in a slightly different form) to Louis XVIII (*Moniteur Univ.* Aug. 8, 1819) and to Napoleon (E. BLAZE, *La vie militaire sous l'Empire* (1837) I. v).] **1867–77** FROUDE *Short. Stud.* (1890) III. 204 It was said a few years ago that every French drummer-boy knew that he carried a marshal's baton in his knapsack.

French would be the best cooks in Europe if they had got any butcher's meat, The.

1881 BAGEHOT *Biog. Stud., Guizot* 358 Pari-
5017

sian literature . . . generally reminds its readers of the old saying, 'That the French would be the best cooks in Europe if they had got any butcher's meat'.

French, see also Jack would be gentleman if could speak F.; Pedlar's F.; Tottenham is turned F.

Frenzy, heresy, and jealousy, seldom cured.

a. **1529** SKELTON *Replycacion* l. 406 (A) For be ye wele assured That frensy nor ielousy nor heresy wyll neuer dye. **1651** HERBERT 365.

Frequent (*verb*), **see** Well used (Where men are) they'll f.

Fresh as a rose.

c. **1390** CHAUCER *W. of Bath's Prol.* 448 As fressh as is a rose. **1412–20** LYDGATE *Troy Book* V. 2897 (A) with swetenes freshe as any rose. **1590** SPENSER *F. Q.* II. ix. 36 (A) That was right faire and fresh as morning rose.

Fresh as flowers in May.

c. **1370** CHAUCER *Knights T.* 1037 Fressher than the May with flowres newe. *c.* **1380** Id. *Troilus & Cressida* V. 884 (A) As fressh as braunches in May. *c.* **1440** *Lyf of our Lady* G 2 (Caxton) Fayrer than Floure in maye. **1631** HEYWOOD *Fair Maid of West* II. I (A) You shall meete some of them sometimes as fresh as flowers in May.

Fresh as paint.

1850 THACKERAY *Pendennis* vii (Oxf.) 983.

Fresh fish and new-come guests smell in three days.

1580 LYLY *Euph. & his Eng.* (Arb.) 305 As we say in *Athens*, fishe and gesse in three dayes are stale. **1648** HERRICK *Hesper.* 378 Wks. (1893) I. 189 Two dayes y'ave landed here; a third yee know, Makes guests and fish smell strong; pray go. **1670** RAY 90 Fresh fish and new come guests, smell by they are three days old.

Fresh fish and poor friends become soon ill savoured.

1721 KELLY 106 . . . Spoken when we see poor relations slighted.

Fret like gummed taffeta (velvet), To.

[The material being stiffened with gum, quickly rubbed and fretted itself out.] **1597–8** SHAKS. *1 Hen. IV* II. ii. 1 I have removed Falstaff's horse, and he frets like a gummed velvet. **1604** DEKKER *News from Graves-end* (*Plague Pamphlets* ed. Wilson 67) Fret not worse than gumd Taffety. **1629** T. ADAMS *Serm.* (1861–2) II. 361 Shall the black coat carry away the tithe-shock? The gummed taffeta gentlemen would fret out at this. **1738** SWIFT (*Dial.* ii) 348 *Col.* [*Whispers Neverout.*] Smoke miss; faith, you have made her fret like gum taffeta.

Fret one's self to fiddlestrings, To.

1835 MRS. CARLYLE *Lett.* I. 43 I do but . . .
fret myself to fiddlestrings. **1876** MRS. BANKS
Manch. Man xliii She was fretting herself
to fiddle-strings for a fellow younger than
herself.

Friar, a liar, A.

1381 WALSINGHAM *Historia Anglicana* (Rolls
Ser.) II. 13. *Nota Contra Fratres Mendicantes.*
. . . In diebus istis . . . bonum [erat] argumentum. . . . 'Hic est Frater, ergo mendax.'
1647 TRAPP *Comm.* I. *Tim.* iv. 2 It was grown
to a common proverb, A friar, a liar.

Friar forgot feud, Never.

1820 SCOTT *Monast.* x The devil was in me
when I took this road—I might have
remembered the proverb, 'Never Friar forgot
feud'.

Friar never loved, What was good the.

1619 J. FAVOUR *Antiquity* 412 It is an old said
saw, *Was good, neuer loued the Frier.* a. **1633**
JONSON *T. Tub* III. vii. 13 What should
have beene, that never lov'd the Friar. **1670**
RAY 94.

Friar preached against stealing, and had a goose (pudding) in his sleeve, The.

[*Cf.* the story of the friar in *Hundred Mery
Tales* (Oesterley 1866) no. lxx. 120.] **1640**
HERBERT 351. **1659** HOWELL *Eng. Prov.* 2/1
The Frier preacht against stealing, when he
had a pudding in his sleeve.

Friar's beaten, When the | then comes James.

1639 CLARKE 282.

Friars observant spare their own and eat other men's.

1573 SANDFORD (1576) 212. **1578** FLORIO
First Fruites 30. **1629** *Book of Meery Riddles*
Prov. 112.

Friar(s), *see also* Do as the f. saith; Fly and
eke a f. will fall in every dish; Pudding for
a f.'s mouth.

Friday and the week is seldom aleek.

c. **1386** CHAUCER *Knight's T.* 1539 Selde is the
Friday al the wyke y-like. **1874** W. PENGELLY
in *N. & Q.* 5th Ser. II. 184 (A) [Corn.] Friday
and the week are seldom aleek.

Friday look (or face), A.

1583 MELBANCKE *Philotimus* (British Bibliographer ii. 446) Friday faced scoulds. **1592**
GREENE *Wks.* (Gros.) XII 120 (A) The foxe
made a Friday face, counterfeiting sorrow.
1846 DENHAM 6 Has a Friday look (sulky,
downcast).

Friday night's dream on the Saturday told, is sure to come true be it never so old.

1846 DENHAM 11. **1898** HARE *Shropshire* ii
Friday, in this neighbourhood, is still called
Cross Day. 'A Friday night's dream, on
Saturday told, Is sure to come true, be it
never so old.'

Friday will be either king or underling.

1587 W. HARRISON *Description of England*
(New Sh. S.) ii. 90 The fridaie being com-
monlye called among the vulgar sort either
King or worling, because it is either the
fairest or foulest of the seauen. **1875** A. B.
CHEALES *Proverb Folk-Lore* 19 (A).

Friday's hair, and Saturday's horn, goes to the D'ule[1] on Monday morn.

[i.e. unlucky to cut hair on Friday and nails
on Saturday.] **1678** RAY 294. [[1]dole, grief.]

Friday's moon, come when it will comes too soon.

1869 HAZLITT 138.

Friday, *see also* Sings on F. will weep Sunday;
Thursday at three . . . see what F. will be.

Friend and your flatterer too, I cannot be your.

1669 PENN *No Cross, No Crown* II. xix
Phocion . . . was honest and poor . . . Anti-
pater, pressing him to submit to his sense, he
answered, 'Thou canst not have me for thy
friend and flatterer too'. **1732** FULLER no.
2592. **1744** FRANKLIN *Sept.* The same man
cannot be both friend and flatterer.

Friend as far as conscience permits, A.

1547 WM. BALDWIN *Treatise Moral Philosophy*
(1550) P 3ᵛ It is lawfull to be a frende, but
no further then to the aulter: that is we ought
not for our frendes sake to transgresse our
religion. **1736** BAILEY *Dict.* s.v. 'Conscience'.

Friend asks, When a | there is no tomorrow.

1611 COTGRAVE s.v. Demain'. **1640** HERBERT
318 (A).

Friend at a sneeze; He is a | the most you can get of him is a *God bless you.*

c. **1566** *The Bugbears* I. ii When he happen-
ethe to sneese in the nighte hath he not ned
of on to saie Christe helpe. **1651–3** JER.
TAYLOR *Sunday Serm.* XIII (1850) 162 'A
friend at a sneeze and an alms-basket full of
prayers', a love that is lazy . . . and a pity
without support, are the images and colours
of that grace, whose very constitution and
design is beneficence and well-doing. **1732**
FULLER no. 2436.

Friend at (in) court, A.

1655 DICKSON *On Ps.* cv. 16 When the Lord was to bring his people into Egypt He provided so as they should have a friend at court before they came. **1848** DICKENS *Dombey* xxxviii I shouldn't wonder—friends at court you know.

Friend in court is better than (or worth) a penny in purse, A.

c. **1400** *Rom. Rose* 5541 For freend in court ay better is Than peny in [his] purs. *a.* **1534** *Hyckescorner* 659 [Frewyll] But a frende in courte is worth a peny in purse. **1580** LYLY *Euph. & his Eng.* (Arb.) 476 I know that a friende in the court is better then a penney in the purse. **1597–8** SHAKS. *2 Hen. IV* V. i I will use him well: a friend i' the court is better than a penny in purse. **1670** RAY 73 A friend in court, is worth a penny in a man's purse.

Friend in need is a friend indeed, A.

c. **1275** *Provs. of Alfred* (Skeat) 50 A such fere þe is help in mode. **1599** SHAKS. *Pass. Pilgr.* 423 He that is thy friend indeed, He will help thee in thy need. **1641** FERGUSSON 96 There is no friend to a friend in mister.[1] **1678** RAY 142. **1802** EDGEWORTH *Rosanna* iv I thank you heartily. . . . A friend in need is a friend indeed. **1866** READE *G. Gaunt* xlvi *You* came to my side when I was in trouble. . . . A friend in need is a friend indeed! [[1] need.]

Friend in the market is better than money in the chest, A.

1664 CODRINGTON 184 A Friend in the way is better than a penny in the purse. **1732** FULLER no. 119.

Friend is another self, A.

[ARIST. *Eth.* 4. 4 ἔστι γὰρ ὁ φίλος ἄλλος αὐτός.] **1539** TAVERNER tr. *Erasm. Garden of Wisdom* F 2 A frende . . . One soule . . . in two bodyes. **1542** UDALL tr. *Erasm. Apoph.* (1877) 233 The prouerbe *amicus alter ipse* . . . two frendes are one soul and one body. **1567** WM. BALDWIN *Treatise of Moral Phil.* P 6[v] A frende is properlye named thother I. **1576** PETTIE *Petite Pall.* (Gollancz) i. 157 Of all griefs is most griping when friends are forced to part from each other . . . when own's self is separated from himself, or at least his second self. **1579** LYLY *Euphues* (Arb.) 48 A friend is . . . at al times an other I. **1631** F. LENTON *Characters* (1663) sig. H *A true friend*, . . . He is a mans second selfe.

Friend is my nearest relation, A good.

1732 FULLER no. 151.

Friend is never known till a man have need, A.

[ENN. ap. Cic. *Am.* 17. 64 *Amicus certus in re incerta cernitur.* *c.* **1190** *Li Proverbe au Vilain* (Tobler) 32 Au besoing voit on qui amis est, ce dit li vilains.] *c.* **1300** BRUNNE *Handl. Synne* 1. 2251 At nede shul men proue here frendys. *c.* **1340** DAN MICHEL *Ayenbite* (Morris) 186 Ate niede: me yȝiȝþ

Friend is not so soon gotten as lost, A.

1567 PAINTER *Pal. of Pleasure* (Jacobs) ii. 177 (A) As the common prouerbe and wise sayinge reporteth, that the vertue is no lesse to conserue frendship gotten, than the wisedome was great to get and win the same. **1599** PORTER *Angry Wom. Abingd.* viii. 386 By lady, a friend is not so soone gotten as lost. **1732** FULLER no. 1612.

Friend that grindeth at my mill, He is my.

1616 DRAXE 75. **1639** CLARKE 16.

Friend thy foe, Make not thy.

c. **1327** *Chester Plays, Crucifixion* (Shaks. Soc.) ii. 63 *Sec. Latro.* Ah! man, be still, I thee praye, . . . Make not thy frende thy foe.

Friend to a bosom friend ; No | no enemy to a bosom enemy.

1721 KELLY 261.

Friend to everybody is a friend to nobody, A.

1623 WODROEPHE 475 (A) All men's friend, no man's friend. **1645** FULLER *Gd. Thts. Bad T.; M. Cont.* xiii I cannot conceive how he can be a friend to any, who is a friend to all. **1727** GAY *Fables, Hare & many Fr.* Friendship, like love, is but a name, Unless you stint the flame. **1778** JOHNSON in *Boswell* lxiv (1847) 593 An old Greek said, 'He that has *friends* has *no friend*'.[1] [[1] οὐθεὶς φίλος ᾧ πολλοὶ φίλοι. ARISTOTLE, *Eud. Eth.* 7. 12.]

Friend to thyself, Be a | and others will befriend thee.

1721 KELLY 57 . . . Men's friends commonly bear a proportion to their circumstances in the world. **1732** FULLER no. 847.

Friend too cheap to thee, nor thyself too dear to him, Make not thy.

1659 HOWELL *Eng. Prov.* 18/2.

Friend will help at a dead lift, A.

1636 CAMDEN 290.

Friendless is the dead.

c. **1300** *Provs. of Hending* 37 Frendles ys the dede. **1611** COTGRAVE s.v. 'Ami' The dead haue no friends, the sicke but faint ones.

Friends agree best at a distance.

? **1622** J. TAYLOR (Water-P.) *Trav. Twelvepence* But there's no great loue lost 'twixt them and mee, We keepe asunder, and so best agree. **1721** KELLY 103.

huet þe urend is. **1380** GOWER *Conf. Amantis* v. 4912 Thou schalt finde At nede fewe frendes kinde. *c.* **1489** CAXTON *Sonnes of Aymon* xix. 433 It is sayd, that at the nede the frende is knowen. **1546** HEYWOOD I. xi. 38. **1614** CAMDEN 302.

Friends are like fiddle-strings, they must not be screwed too tight.

1855 BOHN 358.

Friends are thieves of time.

1605 BACON *Adv. Learn.* II. xxiii (1900) 218 We use to advise young students from company keeping, by saying, *Amici fures temporis*. *a.* **1612** CHARRON *Of Wisdom* (1640) 217 Friends steal away time. **1783** BOSWELL *Johnson* lxxv (1848) 727 He may love study, and wish not to be interrupted by his friends: *Amici fures temporis*.

Friends both in heaven and hell, It is good to have some.

1640 HERBERT 369.

Friends fail fliers.

a. **1548** HALL *Chron.* (1809) 361 (A) Frendes fayle fliers. **1577** HOLINSHED *Chron.* (1808) III. 381 We might . . . make them true by our going, if we were caught and brought back, as friends fail fliers. **1636** CAMDEN 296.

Friends in general, Many | one in special.

1640 HERBERT 330.

Friends may meet, but mountains never greet.

1530 PALSGRAVE 635 (A) Hylles do never mete, but acquayntaunce doth often. **1568** FULWELL *Like will to L.* (1906) 13 It is an old saying, that mountains and hills never meet; But I see that men shall meet, though they do not seek. **1594** LYLY *Moth. Bomb.* v. iii Then we four met, which argued we were no mountains. **1599–1600** SHAKS. *A.Y.L.* III. ii. 196 It is a hard matter for friends to meet; but mountains may be removed by earthquakes, and so encounter. **1670** RAY 94 . . . *Mons cum monte non miscebitur. Pares cum paribus.* Two haughty persons will seldom agree together. **1757** SMOLLETT *Rehearsal* II. ii *Mac.* But, he and I sall meet before mountains meet.

Friends (The best of friends) must part.

c. **1380** CHAUCER *Troilus & Cressida* v. 343 Alwey freendes may nought been y-fere. *c.* **1602** CHAPMAN *May-Day* IV. iv. 51 Friends must part. **1620** *Roxb. Ballads* (Hindley) I. 253 For friends, you know must part. **1731** SWIFT *On Death of Dr. Swift* But dearest friends, they say, must part. **1821** SCOTT *Kenilw.* xi The best friends must part, Flibbertigibbet. **1910** G. W. E. RUSSELL *Sketch & Snap.* 212 But the best of friends must part, and it is time to take our leave of this . . . high-souled cavalier.

Friends round the Wrekin, All.

1700 CONGREVE *Way of World* III. xv (A) You could intreat to be remember'd then to your friends round the Rekin. **1706** FARQUHAR *Recruit. Off.* Ded. To all Friends round the Wrekin. **1787** GROSE 220 To all friends round the Wrekin. A mode of drinking to all friends, wheresoever they may be, taking the Wrekin as a centre. The Wrekin is a mountain in the neighbourhood of Shrewsbury. **1813** RAY 72 All friends round the Wrekin, not forgetting the trunk-maker and his son Tom.

Friends, All are not | that speak us fair.

1580 LYLY *Euph. & his Eng.* Wks. (Bond) II. 95 Nor [are] all friends that beare a faire face. **1639** CLARKE 128.

Friends, Have but few | though many acquaintains.

1659 HOWELL *Eng. Prov.* 5/2. **1670** RAY 11 Have but few friends though much acquaintaince.

Friends tie their purse with a cobweb thread.

1855 BOHN 358.

Friend(s), *see also* Admonish your f.; Before you make a f. eat . . . with him; Better an open enemy; Better lose a jest than a f.; Bit that one eats no f. makes; Breams in his pond, f. welcome; Cat and dog may kiss, yet none the better f.; Defend me from my f.; Enemy your f. (Make your); Even reckoning long f.; Faithful f. is hard to find; Fall not out with a f.; Fresh fish and poor f. become soon ill savoured; Full purse never wanted f.; Go down ladder . . . up when choosest f.; Good cheer is lacking (When) f. will be packing; Good f. that speaks well of us; Grow howbackit bearing your f. (You will never); Happy is he whose f. born before him; Hatred with f. succour to foes; Kindred (Wheresoever you see), make much of your f.; Knave is in plum-tree (When) he hath neither f. nor kin; Lend your money lose f.; Lent (When I), I had a f.; Life without f. is death; Little intermeddling makes good f.; Live without our f. (We can), but not our neighbours; Lost (It is not) that f. (neighbour) gets; Love your f. but look to yourself; Love your f. with his fault; Many f. (He that hath); Many kinsfolk few f.; Marriages and funerals (At) f. are discerned; Merry when f. meet; Mirror (Best) is an old f.; Misfortune makes foes of f.; Near f. better than far kinsman; No longer foster, no longer f.; No man hath a worse f. than he brings; Old f. are best; Old fish, old oil, old f.; One foe is too many, a hundred f. too few; One God, no more, but f.; Physician like f. (No); Poor folks' f. soon misken them; Prosperity (In time of) f. will be plenty; Prove thy f. ere need; Put off the person of a judge . . . of a f.; Quits his place well that leaves f.; Reconciled f. is double enemy; Rich folk have many f.; Rich knows not who is f.; See your f. (Whensoever you), trust to yourself; Short reckonings long f.; Speak well of f., of enemy nothing; Strength enough to bear misfortunes of f.; Things of f. are in common; Thunder lasted (While), bad men f.; Trust not new f.; Trust not praise of f.; Try your f. before you trust; Two f. have a common purse (When); Two f. with one gift (Make); Wanted me and your meat (If you) would want one good f.

Friended, *see* Man is f. (As a), so law ended.

Friendship cannot stand always on one side.

1641 FERGUSSON 34 Friendship stands not in one side. **1721** KELLY 103 *Friendship cannot stand ay on one side.* Friendship is cultivated by mutual good offices; spoken to urge some instances of kindness on them, to whom we have been formerly obliged.

Friendship, *see also* Broken f. may be soldered; Flattery in f.; Hedge between keeps f. green; Love puts in (When) f. is gone; Sudden f. sure repentance; What rake the feud where f. dow not?

Friese, *see* Bread, butter, and green cheese.

Fright a bird is not the way to catch her, To.

1616 DRAXE 2. **1639** CLARKE 311. **1640** HERBERT 319 He that will take the bird must not scare it. **1670** RAY 95. **1721** KELLY 106 *Flaying[1] a burd is no the way to grip it.* A vile intimation! that a man should conceal his ill intentions upon any, lest they provide against it, and so prevent it. **1732** FULLER no. 1627. [[1] frightening.]

Frighted, frightened, *see* Lived too near a wood to be f. by owls; More afraid (f.) than hurt; Nothing (He that has) is f. at nothing.

Fristed[1] is not forgiven, The thing that's.

[L. *Quod defertur non aufertur.* That which is deferred is not relinquished.] **1641** FERGUSSON 94. **1721** KELLY 305. **1824** SCOTT *Redg.* xii He was murdered in cold blood, with many a pretty fellow besides.—Well, we may have our day next—what is fristed is not forgiven. [[1] delayed, or sold on credit.]

Frog cannot out of her bog, The.

1659 N.R. 13. **1670** RAY 95. **1732** FULLER no. 6113.

Frog in the well knows nothing of the great ocean, The.

1909 A. LLOYD *Every-day Japan* (1911) 147 The Japanese peasant has a narrow horizon. 'The frog in the well', says his proverb, 'knows nothing of the great ocean.'

Frog on a chopping block, To sit like a.

1678 RAY. 288. **1732** FULLER no. 723 As pert as a frog upon a washing-block.

Frog (Toad) said to the harrow, The| cursed be so many lords.

[*c.* **1290** *Wright's Polit. Songs* (Camd. Soc.) 166 Dixit bufo crati [sic], 'maledicti tot dominati!'] *c.* **1380** WYCLIF *Serm.* Sel. Wks. II. 280 Cristene men may seye, as þe poete seiþ in prouerbe—þe frogge seide to þe harwe, cursid be so many lordis. **1641** FERGUSSON 76 Mony masters, quoth the poddock to the harrow, when everie tind took her a knock. **1721** KELLY 243 *Many masters, quoth the poddock to the harrow, when every tin gave her a tig.[1]* Spoken by those whom persons, inferior to their masters, presume to reprove, command, or correct. **1818** SCOTT *Rob Roy* xxvii Andrew was compelled to submit, only muttering between his teeth, 'Ower mony maisters,—ower mony maisters, as the paddock said to the harrow, when every tooth gae her a tig.' [[1] twitch.]

Frog, *see also* April flood carries away f.; Fish and catch f.; Fond fisher that angles for f.; Gossips are f.; Look to him, jailer . . . f. in stocks.

Froize, *see* Pudding (If it won't) it will f.

From home, *see* Good man is f. h. (When) . . table soon spread.

Frost and fraud both end in foul (have always foul ends).

1607 *A True Report of the . . . Murder . . . in the house of Sir Jerome Bowes* C 3. **1614** CAMDEN 306 Frost and fraud have always foul ends. **1621** BURTON *Anat. Mel.* I. ii. III. xv (1651) 138 They do manifestly perceive, that (as he said) frost and fraud come to foul ends. **1662** FULLER (*Chesh.*) 1. 271 It was an ordinary speech in his mouth to say, 'frost and fraud both end in foul.' **1721** KELLY 103 Frost and falsehood has ay a foul hinder end.

Frost never lasts more than three days, A white.

1883 ROPER 17 adding 'A long frost is a black frost'. **1893** INWARDS 114.

Frosts, The first and last | are the worst.

1640 HERBERT 361.

Frosts in March, So many | so many in May.

1659 HOWELL *Eng. Prov.* 16/1 If frost in March there will be some in May. **1678** RAY 344.

Frost(s), *see also* Farewell f.; God will (What) no f. can kill; Hail brings f. in tail; Hunger in f. that will not work in heat; Many f. and many thowes make rotten yowes; Surprised with the first f.

Frugality, *see* Industry is fortune's right hand, f. her left.

Fruit fails, When all | welcome haws.

1721 KELLY 350 . . . Spoken when we take up with what's coarse, when the good is spent.

1914 K. F. PURDON *Folk of Furry F.* vii 'Lame of a leg, and grey in the head! . . . that's a fancy man for a girl to take!' 'Marg was none too young herself, . . . and when all fruit fails, welcome haws! She wanted someone'.

Fruit have, If you would | you must bring the leaf to the grave.

1678 RAY 53 . . . That is, you must transplant your trees just about the fall of the leaf, . . . not sooner, because of the motion of the sap, nor later, that they may have time to take root before the deep frosts.

Fruit ripens not well in the shade.

1732 FULLER no. 1632.

Fruit, *see also* Autumn f. without spring blossoms (No); Eat the f. (He that would) must climb tree; Forbidden f.; Free of f. that wants orchard; No root no f.; Tree (Like) like f.; Tree loaded with f. people throw stones.

Fry (Stew) in one's own grease (juice), To.

13 . . *Coer de L.* Better it is that we out renne, Thenne . . . frye inne oure owne gres! *c.* **1386** CHAUCER *W. of Bath's Prol.* D. 486 I made folk swich chere, That in his owene grece I made him frye For angre, and for verray Ialousye. **1546** HEYWOOD I. xi. 37 She fryeth in hir owne grease, but as for my parte, If she be angry, beshrew her angry harte. **1656** EARL MONM. tr. *Boccalini's Advts. Parnass.* (1674) 204 [He] could not better discover Hypocrites, than by suffering them (like Oysters) to stew in their own water. **1664** COTTON *Scarron.* iv. 987 I stew all night in my own grease. **1885** SIR W. HARCOURT *Sp. at Lowestoft* 14 Dec. Liberals must not be in a hurry to turn the Tories out. He would let them for a few months stew in their own Parnellite juice.

Frying-pan into the fire, Like the flounder, out of the.

1528 MORE *Wks.* (1557) 179 col. 2 (A) Lepe they lyke a flounder out of a frying-panne into the fyre. **1546** HEYWOOD II. v. 59 Coulde make ye dooe, but as the flounder doothe, Leape out of the friyng pan into the fyre. **1623** CAMDEN 273.

Frying-pan into the fire, Out of the.

1514 A. BARCLAY *Egloges* (E.E.T.S.) 10 Out of the water thou leapest into the fyre. **1546** HEYWOOD II. v. 59 Leape out of the friyng pan into the fyre. And chaunge from yll peyn to wurs. **1599–1600** SHAKS. *A.Y.L.* I. ii. 304 Thus must I from the smoke into the smother. **1625** PURCHAS *Pilgrims* (1905–7) I. 14 Out of the frying-pan of Paynim rites, into the fire of Mahometry. **1875** SMILES *Thrift* 275 The man in debt . . . tries a money-lender; and, if he succeeds, he is only out of the frying-pan into the fire.

Frying-pan said to the kettle, The | 'Avaunt, black brows!'

1620 SHELTON *Quix.* II. lxvii (1908) III. 293 'Methinks, sir, . . . you are like what is said that the frying-pan said to the kettle, "Avaunt, blackbrows"; you reprehend me for speaking of proverbs, and you thread up yours by two and two.'

Fuel, Take away | take away flame.

1639 CLARKE 192. **1670** RAY 95 . . . Remove the tale-bearer, and contention ceaseth.

Fuel, *see* Laid in his f. before St. John (Never rued that).

Full as an egg is of meat, As.

1520 WHITTINGTON *Vulg.* (E.E.T.S.) 96 As ful . . . as an egge is of oote mele. **1575** *Gammer Gurton's N.* v. ii. 57 An egge is not so ful of meate, as she is ful of lyes. **1594–5** SHAKS. *Rom. & Jul.* III. i. 24 Thy head is as full of quarrels as an egg is full of meat. **1639** CLARKE 69 As full of knavery as an egge of meat. **1719** PRIOR *Bibo & Charon* Wks. (1858) 419 As full of champagne as an egg's full of meat.

Full belly neither fights nor flies well, A.

1640 HERBERT 320. **1844** E. FITZGERALD *Lett.* 22 Aug. (1901) I. 173 It is a grievous thing to grow poddy: the age of chivalry is gone then . . . 'a full belly neither fights nor flies well'.

Full cup must be carried steadily, A.

c. **1300** *Provs. of Hending* xvi When the coppe is follest, then ber hire feyrest. **1732** FULLER no. 122. **1820** SCOTT *Monast.* Introd. Ep. 'It is difficult', saith the proverb, 'to carry a full cup without spilling.' The wealth of the community . . . was . . . a snare to the brethren. **1903** G. H. KNIGHT *Master's Qns.* 145 All hands are not steady enough to carry a full cup.

Full flock, He who will have a | must have an old stag[1] and a young cock. (*But cf.* Farm full, &c.)

a. **1697** J. AUBREY in HALLIWELL *Dict. Arch. & Prov. Wds.* (1889) II. 794 Aubrey gives the following Lancashire proverb. . . . He that will have a full flock Must have an old *stagge* and a young cock. *MS. Royal Soc.* p. 298. [[1] gander.]

Full man and a fasting, It is ill speaking between a. (*Cf.* Belly is full, He whose, &c.)

c. **1598** *MS. Proverbs* in FERGUSSON 101 Thair is nothing betuix a bursten body and a hungered. **1824** SCOTT *Redg.* Lett. xi Ye maun eat and drink, Steenie, . . . for we do little else here, and it's ill speaking between a fou man and a fasting.

Full moon, Like a.

1882 BESANT *All Sorts & C.* i This ornament of the Upper House was a big, fat man, with a face like a full moon.

Full moon brings fair weather, The.

1855 BOHN 505. **1893** INWARDS 64.

Full of courtesy, full of craft.

1594 NASHE *Unfort. Trav.* (1902) 8 As true as that olde adage, Much curtesie, much subtiltie. **1639** CLARKE 139 The more courtesie the more craft. **1670** RAY 73 . . . Sincere and true hearted persons are least given to compliment and ceremony. It's suspicious he hath some design upon me, who courts and flatters me. **1796** EDGEWORTH *Par. Assl.* (1903) 392 We have been finely duped. . . . Full of courtesy, full of craft!

Full of himself that he is quite empty, He is so.

1732 FULLER no. 2472.

Full purse, He that has a | never wanted a friend.

1721 KELLY 161.

Full(est), *see also* Cup is f. (When), bear her fairest; Foul foot makes f. wame; Never well, f. nor fasting; Son f. and tattered; Well is f. (When), it will run over.

Funeral, One | makes another (many).

1894 BLACKMORE *Perlycross* vii It has been said, and is true too often . . . that one funeral makes many. A strong east wind . . . whistled through the crowd of mourners.

Funeral(s), *see also* Dream of f., hear of marriage; Marriages and f. (At) friends are discerned.

Fur (= furrow), *see* Whip and whirr never made good f.

Furmity kettle, *see* Simpers like a f. k.

Further than the wall he cannot go.

1528 MORE *Wks.* (1557) 187 col. 1 (A) I am in this matter euen at the harde walle, and se not how to go further. **1546** HEYWOOD II. v. 58 That déede without woords shall driue him to the wall. And further than the wall he can not go.

Further we (you) go, The | the further behind.

1477 RIVERS *Dictes and Sayings* (1877) 144 He that goth owte of his weye, the more he goth, the ferther is he behinde. **1546** HEYWOOD II. viii. 72 Ye maie walke this waie, but sure ye shall fynde, The further ye go, the further behynde. **1659** HOWELL *Eng. Prov.* 5/2.

Further, *see also* Farther.

Furthest, *see* Best loved f. off.

Furze, Under the | is hunger and cold; under the broom is silver and gold.

1678 RAY 348.

Furze is in bloom, When the | my love's in tune.

1752 *Poor Robin Alm.* (A) August, Joan says: Furze in bloom still', and she'll be kiss'd if she's her will. **1903** *Spectator* 9 May At almost any season of the year gorse can be found in . . . flower . . . 'When the furze is in bloom, my love's in tune'.

G

Gabriel blows his horn, When | then this question will be decided.

? *a.* **1384** (?) WYCLIF *Eng. Wks.* (E.E.T.S.) XXVI. vii. 382 And I wote wel þat gabriel schal blow his horne or þai han preuyd þe mynor. **1659** HOWELL *Eng. Prov.* 21/2 When *Gabriel* blowes his horn, then this question will be decided; *viz. Never.*

Gad, *see* Tribe of Levi . . . tribe of G.

Gain is to lose, Sometimes the best.

1640 HERBERT 327.

Gain teacheth how to spend, To.

1640 HERBERT 339.

Gain, All is not | that is put in the purse.

1639 CLARKE 187. **1670** RAY 194 All is not won that is put in the purse. **1760–7** STERNE *T. Shandy* III. xxx.

Gaineth enough whom fortune loseth, He.

1573 SANDFORD (1576) 206. **1611** COTGRAVE s.v. 'Gaigner' Assez gaigne qui malheur

perd; He gets enough that misses an ill turn. **1629** *Book of Meery Riddles* Prov. 60.

Gains time gains all things, He that.

1628 SIR EDWARD CECIL, Viscount Wimbledon (*The Times* 19 April 1943, p. 6, Col. 5) As the proverb saith, Gain time gain life. **1710** S. PALMER *Moral Essays on Proverbs* 380 (A).

Gains well and spends well, He that | needs no account book.

1640 HERBERT 356.

Gain(s) (*noun*), *see also* Fastens where there is g.; Great g. makes work easy; Great pain and little g.; Ill luck to count your g.; Ill-gotten goods (g.); Lacketh a stock (Who), his g. not worth chip; Light g. heavy purses; Lose your time (If you). cannot get g.

Gain(ed) (*verb*), *see also* Gear is easier g. than guided; Knows what may be g. never steals (He that); Lightly g. quickly lost.

Gainfullest, *see* Burdens (Greatest) are not g.

Gaining(s), *see* Fair g. make fair spendings; Sparing is first g.

Galen, *see* Suppers (By) more have been killed than G. cured.

Gallants, *see* Fowey (G. of).

Galled horse will not endure the comb, A, *see* Rub a galled horse, &c.

Galley-slave, *see* Work like g.

Gallop, *see* Kick in one's g.

Gallows groans for him (you), The.

1577 *Misogonus* I. iv (A) The gallowes grones for this wage as iust rope ripe. **1585–1616** *Shirburn Ballads* xxxii (1907) 131 Thus, then he scaped hanging, And made no more moan; But yet for his presence the gallows did groan. **1738** SWIFT (Dial. i) 341 *Miss.* Well, go hang yourself in your own garters, for I'm sure the gallows groans for you.

Gallows in his face, He has the.

1768 GOLDSMITH *Good-nat. Man.* v. (Globe) 637/1 Hold him fast, the dog: he has the gallows in his face. **1819** SCOTT *Bride Lam.* vi As to Craigie, . . . he had gallows written on his brow in the hour of his birth.

Gallows will have its own at last, The.

c. **1592** WM. PERKINS *Salve for a Sick Man* (1603) f. 528 b In the daies of King Edward . . . one . . . desperatly minded to . . . cried out saying, O gallowse claime thy right. **1707** MAPLETOFT 72. **1855** BOHN 506.

Gallows, *see also* Buildeth his house all of sallows; Fears the g. (He that) never good thief; Kills himself with working . . . buried under g.; Save a thief from g. and he will . . .; Sea and the g. refuse none; Show the g. before the town.

Gambrel, *see* Crooketh the tree.

Game is cheaper in the market than in the fields and woods.

1732 FULLER no. 1641.

Game is not worth the candle, The.

1602 *The Jesuits' Catechism* 27 b As good fellowes vse to say, The sport is worthy of a candle. **1603** FLORIO tr. *Montaigne* II. xvii (1897) IV. 153 The horror of a fall doth more hurt me, than the blow. The play is not worth the candle. **1640** HERBERT 352 It is a poor sport that is not worth the candle. **1668** COWLEY *Ess.* x (1904) 105 When the light of life is so near going out, and ought to be so precious, *le jeu ne vaut pas la chandelle*, the play is not worth the expense of the candle. **1874** P. BAYNE in *Contemp. Rev.* Oct. 706 The game would not be worth the candle.

Game that two can play at, That is a.

1845 E. FITZGERALD *Lett.* 12 June (1901) I. 193 I . . . told him two could play at that game. **1896** J. C. HUTCHESON *Crown &*

Anchor xx I tried retaliation, commencing now to hit out with my fists in return. 'Two can play at that game, old fellow.'

Game's end, At the | we shall see who gains.

1640 HERBERT 342.

Games, In all | it is good to leave off a winner.

1732 FULLER no. 2812.

Game(s), *see also* Name (He that hath the) may enjoy the g.; Play small g. before he will sit out (He will); Play the g.; Tine cat tine g.

Gamester, The better | the worser man.

1639 CLARKE 96.

Gamesters and race-horses never last long.

1640 HERBERT 352.

Gamester(s), *see also* Candle-holder good g.; Hasty g. oversee.

Gaming, women, and wine, while they laugh, they make men pine.

1640 HERBERT 345.

Gaming, *see also* Devil goes shares in g.

Gander, *see* Man among the geese when g. away; Sauce for the goose.

Gangs up i' sops, When it | it'll fau down i' drops.

1828 CARR *Craven Dialect* ii. 147 (A). **1869** HAZLITT 458 . . . A North Country proverb, the sops being the small detached clouds hanging on the sides of a mountain.—HALLIWELL.

Gap(s), *see* Stop g. with rushes; Stop two g. with one bush.

Gape for a benefice, To.

1670 RAY 246. **1738** (*see* Gapeth until he be fed).

Gape for gudgeons, You.

1670 T. W. *The Optic Glass of Humours* ¶ 7ᵛ Thou vsest not to gape after gougins. **1659** HOWELL *Eng. Prov.* 15/2.

Gape like an oyster, To.

1614 JONSON *Barth. Fair* v. iii I have gaped as the oyster for the tide, after thy destruction. **1618–19** J. FLETCHER *Bonduca* I. ii Thou want'st drink. Did I not find thee gaping like an oyster For a new tide.

Gape long enough ere a bird fall in your mouth, You may.

1540 PALSGRAVE *Acolastus* L 1 Do thou but gape, and I shall make larkes fall in to thy mouthe. **1639** CLARKE 153. **1738** (*see* Gapeth until he be fed).

Gape-seed, *see* Fond of g,

Gapeth until he be fed, He that | well may he gape until he be dead.

1550 HEYWOOD I. ix. 17 Nay, he that gapeth till he be fed, Maie fortune to fast and famishe for honger. **1611** DAVIES Prov. 399. **1721** KELLY 119 *Gape while you get it.* Spoken to those who expect a thing without reason. **1738** SWIFT (Dial. ii) 350 *Col.* Do you gape for preferment? *Never.* Faith, I may gape long enough, before it falls into my mouth.

Gaping against (before) an oven, It is ill.

a. **1250** *Owl & Night.* 292 (1922) 28 Ne wit¹ þan ofne² me ne ʒonie.³ **1577–87** HOLINSHED *Chron.* (1807–8) II. 389 A man ought not to chide with a foole, nor gape over an oven. **1659** HOWELL *Eng. Prov.* 12/1 It is ill gaping before an oven. **1670** RAY 96 No gaping against an oven. [¹ against. ² oven. ³ yawn.]

Garb of old Gaul, The.

a. **1817** SIR H. ERSKINE *In the garb of old Gaul,* In the garb of old Gaul, wi' the fire of old Rome (in the *Scottish Students' Song Book*). **1889** E. B. TYLOR *Anthrop.* [ed. 2] 251 Many ancient nations wore trousers, as . . . the Gauls and Britons, so that it is a mistake to call the present Highland costume the 'garb of old Gaul'.

Garby whose soul neither God nor the devil would have, He is like.

1732 FULLER no. 2461.

Garden without its weeds, No.

1579 LYLY *Euphues* (Arb.) 196 No doubt it is in the courte . . . as in all gardeins, some flowers, some weedes. **1621** BURTON *Anat. Mel.* III. iv. I. iii (1651) 676 The divel . . . will never suffer the church to be quiet or at rest: no garden so well tilled but some noxious weedes grow up in it. **1732** FULLER no. 3576 No Garden without its weeds. *Ibid.* no. 152 A good garden may have some weeds. **1826** SOUTHEY *Lett.* (to daughters) 19 July (1912) 414 But the best dispositions require self-watchfulness, as there is no garden but what produces weeds.

Garden(s), *see also* Charges of building and . . . g. are unknown; Fear keeps the g. better than gardener; Land (You may be on), yet not in g.; Market is best g.; Patience grow in g. (Let).

Gardener's dog, that neither eats cabbages himself, nor lets anybody else, Like the.

[**1640** OUDIN *Curios. franç.* 97 Comme le chien du jardinier qui ne mange pas des choux et ne veut pas que personne en mange.] **1732** FULLER no. 3235.

Garland, *see* One flower makes no g.

Garlic makes a man wink, drink, and stink.

1594 NASHE *Unfort. Trav.* in Wks. (Gros.) V. 71 (A). **1607** SIR J. HARINGTON *Englishman's Doctor* (1922) 86 And scorne not Garlicke like to some that thinke It onely makes men winke, and drinke, and stinke.

Garments, *see* Borrowed g. never fit.

Garner, *see* Says his g. is full (None).

Garters, *see* Hang himself in own g.

Gate of horn, The. (*Cf.* Ivory gate.)

[In classical legend (*Od.* 19. 562 ff; *Aen.* 6. 893) that through which true dreams came forth.] **1662** FULLER (*Cornw.*) I. 302 'Dreams have two gates: one made (they say) of horn; By this port pass true and prophetic dreams.' **1831** MACAULAY *Ess., Hampden* Wks. V. 557 [Archbishop Laud] dreamed that he had turned Papist; of all his dreams the only one, we suspect, which came through the gate of horn.

Gate wider than the city, Make not the. (*Cf.* Door wider than the house.)

1597 N. BRETON *Wit's Trenchmore* Dedn. To make a large gate of a little Towne. **1603** H. CHETTLE *England's Mourning Garment* (Harl. Misc. 1745 iii. 501) My Epistle to you is like the little Town that the *Cynick* would have persuaded the Citizens was ready to run out at the great Gates. **1635** E. LEIGH *Selected . . . Observations* *8ᵛ Least I should bee vp-brayded with the city of *Myndus,* for making my porch too bigge.

Gate(s), *see also* Breed of the chapman, never out of your g.; Breed of the good man's mother, aye in the g.; Ivory g.; Lies not in your g., breaks not your shins; No g. no city; Withy tree would have new g. (Old). *See also* Yate.

Gath, Tell it not in.

[= publish it not to the enemy, or to the Philistine, or to the world.] **1382** WYCLIF 2 Sam. i. 20 Woleth ʒe not telle in Geth, ne telle ʒe in . . . Aschalon. **1751** RICHARDSON 11 July (*Corresp.* iii. 169) A wise man to be in love! Tell it not in Gath. **1904** MARIE CORELLI *God's Gd. Man* xx The fact is—but tell it not in Gath—I was happier without them!

Gather(s, ed), *see* Hand that gives g.; Narrow g. widely spent; Pick up (G.) one's crumbs; Scatter with one hand, g. with two; World is unstable, therefore g. in time.

Gathering, *see* Little good comes of g.

Gaudy morning bodes a wet afternoon, A.

a. **1595** *Edward III* IV. ix. 17 The proverbe . . . Too bright a morning breeds a lowring daie. **1624** BURTON *Anat. Mel.* 96 A fair morning turns to a lowring afternoone. **1893** INWARDS 50.

Gaul, *see* Garb of old G.

Gauntlet, To throw (cast, fling) down the.

[= to give a challenge.] **1590** *Pasquil's Apol.* I. D iv 6 I cast them my Gauntlet, take it vp who dares. **1806** SURR *Winter in Lond.* (ed. 3) II. 204 The duchess of Drinkwater appeared upon the field of fashion, and threw down the gauntlet of defiance to Belgrave. **1867** TROLLOPE *Last Chron. Barset* II. lxvii. 249 [She] had thrown down her gauntlet to him, and he had not been slow in picking it up.

Gauntlet of a hedging glove, Make not a.

1639 CLARKE 5. **1732** FULLER no. 3318.

Gauntlet, *see also* Run the g.

Gave, *see* Give(s).

Gay, *see also* Merry (G.) as a lark.

Gay that is green,[1] All is.

1546 HEYWOOD II. i. 44 Some laught, and said, all thing is gay that is gréene. [[1] fresh.]

Gazed at the moon and fell in the gutter, You. (*Cf.* Glower at the moon, &c.)

1721 KELLY 377 with 'midden'. **1732** FULLER no. 5904.

Gear[1] is easier gained than guided.

1721 KELLY 115 *Geer is easier gotten, than guided.* It may be gotten by chance, or inheritance, but must be guided by discretion. [[1] wealth, property.]

Gear that is gifted[1] is never so sweet as the gear that is won, The.

1875 SMILES *Thrift* 177 A penny earned honestly is better than a shilling given. A Scotch proverb says, 'The gear that is gifted is never sae sweet as the gear that is won'. [[1] given.]

Gear, *see also* Little g. less care; Shame fall the g. and the blad'ry.

Geese are swans, All (his).

a. **1529** SKELTON *Magnyfycence* l. 302 (A) In faythe, els had I gone to long to scole, But yf I coulde knowe a gose from a swanne. **1589** *Pasquil's Ret.* C 1 Euery Goose . . . must goe for a Swan, and whatsoeuer he speakes, must be Canonicall. **1621** BURTON *Anat. Mel.* Democ. to Rdr. 29 All his Geese are Swannes. **1777** BOSWELL *Johnson* lxi (1848) 558 Taylor, who praised every thing of his own to excess, . . . 'whose geese were all swans', . . . expatiated on . . . his bull-dog.

Geese slur on the ice, To as much purpose as the.

1670 RAY 190. *Chesh.*

Geese, *see also* Goose.

General, *see* Best g. who makes fewest mistakes; One bad g. better than two good.

Generations to make a gentleman, It takes three.

1881 BAGEHOT *Biograph. Stud.* (1899) 47 'It takes', it is said that Sir Robert Peel observed, 'three generations to make a gentleman'. **1902** DEAN HOLE *Then & Now* (ed. 7) iii. 37 Whatever may be the causes . . . the dictum, 'It takes three generations to make a gentleman', is no longer in quotation.

Genii, *see* Blessings of evil G.

Genoa has mountains without wood, sea without fish, women without shame, and men without conscience.

1642 HOWELL *For. Trav.* viii (Arb.) 41 It is proverbially said, there are in *Genoa, Mountaines without wood, Sea without fish, Women without shame, and Men without conscience,* which makes them to be termed the *white Moores.* **1666** TORRIANO *Ital. Prov.* 102 Genoa *Sea without fish, Air without fouls, Mountains without woods, and Women without shame.*

Gentility without ability is worse than plain beggary.

1670 RAY 96.

Gentility, *see also* Honour (G.) is but ancient riches.

Gentle (Mild) as a lamb.

c. **1362** LANGLAND *P. Pl.* A vi. 43 He is as louh as a lomb. louelich of speche. *c.* **1440** LYDGATE *Fall. Princes* I. 6934 Stille as a lamb, most meek off his visage. **1520** WHITTINGTON *Vulg.* (E.E.T.S.) 99 I shall make hym as styll as a lambe or euer I haue done with hym. **1594–5** SHAKS. *Rom. & Jul.* II. v. 44 I'll warrant him, as gentle as a lamb. **1595–6** *Rich. II* II. i. 175 In peace was never gentle lamb more mild. **1670** RAY 206.

Gentle craft, The.

[= the trade of shoemaking.] **1592** R. GREENE *Quip for an Upstart Courtier* Wks. (Gros.) XI. 264. **1592** T. NASHE *Pierce Penilesse* Wks. (McKerrow) I. 201. *a.* **1593** *George-a-Greene* (1599) F 4 b You shall be no more called Shoomakers. But you and yours to the worlds ende, Shall be called the trade of the gentle craft. **1688** R. HOLME *Armoury* III. 99/1 A Man on a Seat [a Shooe-maker] . . . exercising of the Gentle Craft. **1845** LONGFELLOW *Poems* 90 Hans Sachs, the cobbler-poet, laureate of the gentle craft.

Gentle hawk half mans herself,[1] The.

1640 HERBERT 318. [[1] i.e. becomes tractable.]

Gentle heart is tied with an easy thread, A.

a. **1633** G. HERBERT *The Glimpse* l. 20. **1640** HERBERT 351. **1666** TORRIANO 58 A gentle heart is tied with a twine threed.

Gentle horse that never cast his rider, He is a.

1721 KELLY 166 He's a gentle horse that never cust[1] his rider. He is a good servant that never disobliged his master. [[1] threw.]

Gentle housewife mars the household, A.

1611 COTGRAVE s.v. 'Femme' The over-gentle houswife marres her houshold. **1640** HERBERT I. 319.

Gentle is that gentle does.

c. **1390** CHAUCER *W. of Bath's T.* l. 1168 He is gentil that dooth gentil deedis. **1854** J. W. WARTER *Last of Old Squires* 43 (A) His common saying was 'Gentle is that gentle does'.

Gentle puddocks[1] have long toes.

1721 KELLY 114 *Gentle poddocks has long toes.* Spoken to dissuade you from provoking persons of power and interest; because they can reach you, though at a distance. [[1] probably = puttocks = kites.]

Gentleman but his pleasure, What's a.

1573 G. HARVEY *Letter-Book* (Camden Soc.) 15 (A). **1670** RAY 96. **1732** FULLER no. 5506.

Gentleman, He that would be a | let him go to an assault (storm a town).

1640 HERBERT 357. **1664** CODRINGTON 230. **1670** RAY 11 Who would be a gentleman let him storm a town.

Gentleman of the first head, A.

1509 A. BARCLAY *Ship of Fools* (1874) I. 36 A fox furred Jentelman: of the fyrst yere or hede. **1552** HULOET *Abced.* N 5 (A) Gentleman of the first head, or *ironice* be applyed to such as would be estemed a gentleman, having no poynt or qualitie of a gentleman, nor gentleman borne. **1611** COTGRAVE s.v. 'Gentilhomme de ville' A gentleman of the first head, an vpstart gentleman.

Gentleman that pays the rent, The.

[= the pig.] **1837** LOVER *Rory O'More* xxiii A pig wallows on a dunghill . . . until a starved cur . . . drives him for shelter into the house, whose mistress protects 'the gintleman that pays the rent'. **1907** G. B. SHAW *John Bull's Other Island* That's what they call a pig in England.

Gentleman will do like a gentleman, A.

1623 MINSHEU T t 2. **1630** BRATHWAIT *Eng. Gent.* (1641) 148 (A).

Gentleman without an estate is like a pudding without suet, A.

1659 HOWELL *Eng. Prov.* 12 (with 'money' for

'an estate'). **1670** RAY 96 (with 'living'). **1732** FULLER no. 129.

Gentleman's greyhound and a salt box, seek them at the fire, A.

1640 HERBERT 326.

Gentlemen and rich men are venison in heaven. (*See also* Princes are venison, &c.)

c. **1577** J. NORTHBROOKE *Treat. agst. Dicing* (1843) 22 I pray God the olde prouerbe be not found true, that gentlemen and riche men are venison in Heauen (that is), very rare and daintie to haue them come thither. **1616** T. ADAMS *Gallant's Burden* 52 A wealthy and great man, served vp to Gods table in his kingdome, is as rare as Venison at our Boardes on earth.

Gentleman (-men), *see also* Coat that makes the g. (Not); Generations to make g. (Takes three); Jack would be a g. if could speak French; —— if he had money; Jack-out-of-doors (Not) nor yet g.; King can make . . . not a g.; Little g. in black velvet; Manchester men and Liverpool g.; Manners and money make g.; Meant for a g. but spoilt; Presbyterianism no religion for g.; Put a churl upon a g.; Swear like a g.

Gentles, Where there are | there are aye off-fallings.

1721 KELLY 348 . . . Spoken jocosely to our children, when they have forgot something where they were last; as their gloves, knives, &c. **1862** HISLOP 322 . . . There is such abundance of good prepared, that something may be reasonably expected for the poor. It may also be a delicate allusion to the failings of the aristocracy.

Gently over the stones, Drive.

1711 SWIFT *Jrnl. to Stella* 30 June A gallop! sit fast, sirrah, and don't ride hard upon the stones. **1843–4** DICKENS *M. Chuz.* xxix Gently over the stones, Poll. Go a-tiptoe over the pimples. **1886** E. J. HARDY *How to be Happy* xi 'Drive gently over the stones!' This piece of advice, . . . given to inexperienced whips, may be suggested metaphorically to the newly-married.

Gentry sent to market will not buy one bushel of corn.

a. **1598** LORD BURGHLEY in PEEK *Desid. Curiosa* (1779) 47 (A) For a man can buy nothing in the market with gentility. **1662** FULLER (*Yorks.*) III. 441 Seeing gentry alone . . . (as the plain proverb saith) 'sent to market will not buy a bushel of wheat', it is good even for those of the best birth to acquire some liberal quality. **1670** RAY 96. **1721** KELLY 119 *Gentry sent to the market will not buy a peck of meal.* Spoken when a bare gentlewoman is proffered in marriage to the son of a wealthy yeoman. *Ibid.* 293 Send your gentle blood to the market and see what it will buy. **1858** SURTEES *Ask Mamma* x Marry him to some . . . young woman in his own rank of life, . . .: gentility is all very well to talk about, but it gets you nothin' at the market.

George-a-Green, As good as.

1590 *Tarlton's News out of Purgatory* (1844 ed. J. O. Halliwell, 56). **1597** DELONEY *Jack of Newbury* Wks. (Mann) 16. **1599** GREENE *George-a-Greene* IV. i Many in manner of a proverb say, 'Were he as good as George-a-Greene, I would strike him sure'. **1648** HERRICK *Hymn to Bacchus* Wks. (1893) II. 60 Yet he'le be thought or seen, So good as *George-a-Green.*

Gerard's bailiff, Here is | work or you must die with cold.

1678 RAY 355 *Somerset.*

Gerizim, *see* Creep into Ebal.

German's wit is in his fingers, The.

1605 SYLVESTER, *Du Bartas* Week II, Day ii, Pt. 3, l. 616 (A) The Northern man, whose wit in's fingers settles. **1640** HERBERT 318.

German, *see also* Jump as G.'s lips.

Get a name to rise early, and you may lie all day. (*Cf.* Name is up, &c.).

1617 SWETNAM *School of Defence* 41. **1659** N.R. 47 He that hath a fame of rising early may sleep till dinner. **1672** CODRINGTON 379 Get a good name and go to sleep. **1721** KELLY 112 . . . I would not have a man depend too much upon this proverb; for a good name is soon lost, and hardly to be retrieved.

Get him where you left him, You will.

1721 KELLY 388 . . . Spoken of even tempered people.

Get money in a desert, He would.

1813 RAY 196 . . . He would thrive where another would starve.

Get the poor man's answer, He will.

1721 KELLY 165 . . . That is, a flat denial; spoken when it is said that such a man will court a woman, whom we suspect he will not get.

Gets by that, He | as Dickins (Dickson) did by his distress.

1579 R. GALIS *A Brief Treatise contayning the cruelty of Elizabeth Style* (*Library*, 1938, xviii. 278) I was constrained to take half the money they cost mee gaining by them as Dickins did by his Dishes Who bying fiue for twopence solde six for a peny. *c.* **1599** MIDDLETON *Old Law* v. i No more is got by that than William Dickins got by his wooden dishes. **1639** CLARKE 82. **1670** RAY 171 To get by a thing as *Dickson* did by his distress. That is, over the shoulders, as the vulgar usually say. **1837** SOUTHEY *Doctor* iv. 251 Who was William Dickins, whose wooden dishes sold so badly that when any one lost by the sale of his wares, the said Dickins and his dishes, were brought up in scornful comparison?

Gets doth much, He who | but he who keeps doth more.

1707 MAPLETOFT 113. **1855** BOHN 399.

Gets little thanks for losing his own, A man.

1721 KELLY 53 . . . If a man do not exact those perquisites that he has a title to, people will think them not due.

Get(s), got, *see* All that you g. you may put in your eye; Seek mickle, g. something; So g. so gone; Who are you for? him I g. most by. *See also significant words following* 'get'.

Giants in the earth in those days, There were.

[BIBLE *Gen.* vi. **4.**] **1858** GLADSTONE *St. on Homer* i. 38.

Giant(s), *see also* Belle g.; Dwarf on g.'s shoulders.

Giblets, *see* Steal a goose and give the g. *See also* Goose giblets.

Giddy, He that is | thinks the world turns round.

1593–4 SHAKS. *Tam. Shrew* V. ii. 20 He that is giddy thinks the world turns round. **1621** BURTON *Anat. Mel.* III. iv. I. iii (1651) 672 Though . . . the whole world contradict it, they care not, . . .: and as Gregory well notes *of such as are vertiginous, they think all turns round and moves.*

Giff gaff was a good fellow.

1549 LATIMER *3rd Serm. bef. Edw. VI* (P.S.) 140 Somewhat was given to them before, and they must needs give somewhat again, for Giffe-gaffe was a good fellow. **1624** BP. R. MONTAGU *New Gagg* 92 Giff-gaff is a good fellow. **1636** CAMDEN 296 Give gave was a good man. **1818** SCOTT *Ht. Midl.* xvi Gif-gaf makes gude friends, ye ken. **1895** *Dundee Advertiser* in *Daily News* 22 Mar. 7/2 The 'giff-gaff' principle of making friends.

Giff gaff was a good man, but he is soon weary.

1670 RAY 96 . . . *Giffe gaffe* is one good turn for another.

Gift (Given) horse in the mouth, Look not a.

[*a.* **420** ST. JEROME *Comment Epist. Ephes.,* Praef. *Noli* (*ut vulgare est proverbium*) *equi dentes inspicere donati.* Med. Lat. *Si quis dat mannos, ne quaere in dentibus annos.* RABELAIS I. xi *De cheval donné tousjours reguardoit en la gueulle.*] *c.* **1510** STANBRIDGE *Vulg.* (E.E.T.S.) 27 A gyuen hors may not [be] loked in the tethe. **1539** TAVERNER lxvii A gyuen horse (we saye) maye not be loked in the mouthe. **1546** HEYWOOD I. v. 11 Where gyftis be geuen fréely, est west north or south, No man ought to looke a geuen hors in the mouth. **1620** SHELTON *Quix.* II. iv (1908)

II. 215 I am not so very an ass as to refuse it, according to the proverb, 'Look not a given horse in the mouth'. **1662** BUTLER *Hudibras* I. i. 490 He ne-er considered it, as loth to look a gift . . . **1826** LAMB *Pop. Fallacies* Wks. (1898) 227 THAT WE MUST NOT LOOK A GIFT-HORSE IN THE MOUTH. . . . Some people have a knack of putting upon you gifts of no real value, to engage you to substantial gratitude. **1873** ALLINGHAM *Rambles* Wks. II. 74 The policy of not looking a gift horse in the mouth may easily be carried too far . . . and the guardians of . . . York Minster ought to be particular.

Gift makes room for him, A man's.

[**1611** BIBLE *Proverbs* xviii. 16 A man's gift maketh room for him, and bringeth him before great men.] **1732** FULLER no. 308.

Gift much expected is paid, not given, A.

1597 WARNER *Albion's England* v. 26 *To loiter well deserued Gifts, is not to giue but sell, When to requite ingratitude, were to do euill well.* **1640** HERBERT 344. **1666** TORRIANO 76 A gift long look'd for, is sold, not given. **1732** FULLER no. 130 A gift long waited for is sold, not given.

Gift of the gab, The.

[= fluency of speech.] **1695** COLVIL *Whigs Supplic.* To Rdr. A v [Pretended quot. from Z. Boyd]. There was a Man called Job, . . . He had a good gift of the Gob.[1] **1794** GODWIN *Caleb Williams* 29 He knew well enough that he had the gift of the gab. **1853** G. J. WHYTE-MELVILLE *Digby G.* x The sturdy yeoman has not . . . 'the gift of the gab'. [[1] mouth.]

Gifted, *see* Gear that is g. never so sweet.

Gifts enter everywhere without a wimble.

1616 DRAXE 19 A bribe entreth euery where without knocking. **1640** HERBERT 361.

Gifts from enemies are dangerous.

1545 TAVERNER G 5 *Hostium munera, non munera.* The gyftes of enemyes be no gyftes. **1580** WM. CHARKE *An answer to a seditious pamphlet* D 1 If the giftes of enemies be giftlesse gifts (as the prouerbe noteth) . . . **1614** D. DYKE *Mystery of Self-Deceiving* 15 As in the prouerbe, there are giftlesse gifts. **1732** FULLER no. 1650.

Gift(s), *see also* Bestows his g. as broom honey; Bought is cheaper than g.; Free of his g. as poor man of eye; Great g. from great men; Little given seasonably excuses great g.; Nothing freer than a g.; Takes g. (She that), herself she sells; Throw no g. at giver's head; Wicked man's g.

Giglot, *see* Peas (The smaller the) . . . the fairer the woman the more the g.

Gilbert, *see* Find guilty G.

Gilead, *see* Balm in G.

Gileynour, *see* Greedy man and g. soon agreed.

Gill, *see* Bad a G. (There is not so) but there's as bad a Will.

Gilt, *see* Take the g. off gingerbread; Try your skill in g. first.

Gimmingham, Trimmingham, Knapton, and Trunch, North Repps and South Repps are all of a bunch.

1678 RAY (*Norfolk*) 327 . . . These are names of parishes lying close together.

Gingerbread, *see* Take the gilt off.

Gip with an ill rubbing, quoth Badger, when his mare kicked.

1678 RAY 85 . . . A ridiculous expression, used to persons that are pettish and froward.

Girdle, *see* Angry (If you be) you may turn buckle of g.; Head under one's g. (To have a man's); M under one's g. (To have an).

Gist of a lady's letter is in the postscript, The.

1801 EDGEWORTH *Belinda* xx The substance of a lady's letter, it has been said, always is comprised in the postscript. **1887** BLACKMORE *Springhaven* liv Watching . . . the last communication of the sun, and his postscript (which, like a lady's, is the gist of what he means).

Give a child till he craves, and a dog while his tail doth wave, and you'll have a fair dog, but a foul knave.

1303 *Handlyng Synne* 7240 (SKEAT *E. E. Prov.* 39) Yyue thy chylde when he wyl kraue, And thy whelpe whyl hyt wyl haue, Than mayst thou make, yn a stounde, A foule chylde and a feyre hounde. **1670** RAY 82. **1721** KELLY 112 *Give a bairn his will, and a whelp his fill, and none of these two will thrive.* The whelp will be fat and lazy; and the child will be perverse and froward.

Give a clown your finger, and he will take your hand.

1640 HERBERT 322. **1721** KELLY 118 . . . Suffer an unmannerly fellow to intrude upon you, and he will intrude more and more.

Give a dog an ill name and hang him.

1721 KELLY 124 . . . Spoken of those who raise an ill name on a man on purpose to prevent his advancement. **1815** SCOTT *Guy Man.* xxiii It is pithily said, 'Give a dog an ill name and hang him', and . . . if you give a man, or a race of men, an ill name, they are very likely to do something that deserves hanging. **1888** MRS. OLIPHANT *Second Son* xli Give a dog an ill name and hang him, they say; call a woman a mother-in-law, and it's the same thing.

Give a groat for an owl, He is in great want of a bird that will.

1678 RAY 101. **1802** WOLCOT (P. Pindar) *Pitt & his S.* Wks. (1816) IV. 230 'A man must be hard driv'n to find a bird, Who offers two-pence for an owl.'

Give a lie twenty-four hours' start, and you can never overtake it.

1902–4 LEAN III. 471.

Give a loaf, and beg a shive.[1]

1678 RAY 247. [[1] slice.]

Give a man an annuity and he'll live for ever.

1824 BYRON *Juan* II. lxv 'Tis said that persons living on annuities Are longer lived than others, . . . Some . . . *do* never die. **1851** G. OUTRAM *The Annuity* She 's some auld Pagan mummified, Alive for her annuity.

Give a man fortune (luck) and cast (throw) him into the sea.

1576 *Parad. of Dainty Devices*, no. (A) 27 Geve me good Fortune all men sayes, and throw me in the seas. **c. 1600** *Edmond Ironside* l. 1737 Give a man luck and cast him over the gallous. **1620** SHELTON *Quix.* II. xlii (1908) III. 108 Here the proverb comes in, and joins well, that 'Give a man luck, and cast him in the sea'. **1639** CLARKE 125. **1721** KELLY 113 . . . Spoken when a man is unexpectedly fortunate.

Give a slave a rod, and he'll beat his master.

1639 CLARKE 193.

Give a thing, and take a thing, to wear the devil's gold ring.

1611 COTGRAVE s.v. 'Retirer' To give a thing and take a thing; to weare the diuell's gold-ring. **1629** T. ADAMS *Serm.* (1861–2) II. 288 Things dedicated to God are not to be transferred to the uses of men; . . . [it is] a proverb among our children. To give a thing and take a thing is fit for the devil's darling. **1642** FULLER *Holy State* III. xxv (1841) 220 Plato saith, that in his time it was a proverb amongst children: Τῶν ὀρθῶς δοθέντων, οὐκ ἔστιν ἀφαίρεσις. 'Things that are truly given must not be taken away again.' **1721** KELLY 120 *Give a thing, and take a thing, Is the ill man's good*[1] *ring.* A cant among children, when they demand a thing again, which they had bestowed. [[1] gold.]

Give a thing and take again, and you shall ride in hell's wain.

1678 RAY 146.

Give a Yorkshireman a halter, and he'll find a horse.

1869 HAZLITT 141.

Give and spend, and God will send. (*See also* Spend and God will send.)

1855 BOHN 361.

Give and take.

1519 HORMAN *Vulg.* (James) 98 A man muste somtyme gyue and somtyme take. **1662** FULLER (*Surrey*) III. 234 The king, who in this kind would give and not take, being no good fellow in tart repartees, was . . . highly offended. **1778** FRANCES BURNEY *Evelina* xxv (1920) 135 Give and Take is fair in all nations. **1832** MARRYAT *N. Forster* xlvii Give and take is fair play. All I say is, let it be a fair stand-up fight.

Give gave, *see* Giff gaff.

Give him an inch and he'll take an ell.

1546 HEYWOOD II. ix When I gave you an inch ye took an ell. **1599** PORTER *Angry Wom. Abingd.* IV. iii (Merm.) 177 Give an inch, and you'll take an ell. **1612–15** BP. HALL *Contempl.* IV. ix (1825) III. 358 It is the fashion of our bold nature, upon an inch given to challenge an ell. **1798** CANNING & FRERE *Anti-Jacobin* xxxv Though they still took an ell, when we gave them an inch, They would all have been loyal—like Ballynahinch.

Give him one and lend him another, I thought I would.

1670 RAY 177 . . . *i.e.* I would be quit with him.

Give him the other half egg and burst him.

1678 RAY 241.

Give his bone to the dog, He will not.

1721 KELLY 154 . . . Spoken of sturdy people, who will not readily part with their interest, or be bullied out of it.

Give (Box) it about, it will come to my father at last.

[*c.* **1680** The story is told of young Ralegh and his father in a passage omitted from A. Clark's edition of Aubrey's *Brief Lives* ii. 194: 'Box about, 'twill come to my Father anon.'] **1721** KELLY . . . A young fellow was sitting in company with his father, who . . . gave him a blow; who immediately gave his left hand man as much, and bad[e] him give it about. Spoken when we would have some ill turn done to somebody, but not immediately by ourself. **1738** SWIFT (Dial. iii) 352 Methinks you are very witty upon one another: come, box it about; 'twill come to my father at last.

Give little to his servant, He can | that licks his knife (trencher).

c. **1400** *Rom. Rose* C. 6502 What shulde he yeve that likketh his knyf? **1640** HERBERT 356. **1813** RAY 14 (*Ital.*) He can give little to his servant who licks his own trencher.

Give neither counsel nor salt till you are asked for it.

1855 BOHN 4 *Ital.*

Give never the wolf the wether to keep.

[TERENCE *Eunuchus* 5. 1. 16 *Lupo ovem*

commisisti. You have entrusted the sheep to the wolf.] 1639 CLARKE 95 You have given the wolf the weather to keep. 1641 FERGUSSON 36. 1670 RAY 200 You give the wolf the weather to keep. 1863 READE *Hard Cash* xli A lunatic . . . protected by that functionary, is literally a lamb protected by a wolf.

Give one's head for the washing (nought), To.

c. 1500 MEDWALL *Nature* 1. 721 in '*Lost*' *Tudor Plays* (1907) 66 A well-drawn man is he; and a well-taught, That will not give his head for nought. 1596 NASHE *Saffron Walden* L 4 But the time was, when he would not haue guien his head for the washing. 1663 BUTLER *Hudbras* I. iii. 256 For my Part it shall ne'er be sed, I for the washing give my Head. 1721 KELLY 154 *He will not give the head for the washing.* Spoken of sturdy people, who will not readily part with their interest, or be bullied out of it. 1738 SWIFT (Dial. i) 336 *Lady S.* I find, Mr. Neverout, you won't give your head for the washing, as they say.

Give the devil his due.

1589 ? LYLY *Pappe w. Hatchet* D i j Giue them their due though they were diuels. 1597–8 SHAKS. *1 Hen. IV* I. ii. 132 He was never yet a breaker of proverbs: he will give the devil his due. 1598–9 *Hen. V* III. vii. 131 I will take that vp with 'Give the devil his due'. 1618 J. FLETCHER *Loyal Subj.* I. iii *Theo.* Whose doubts and envies—But the Devil will have his due. 1642 *Prince Rupert's Declarat.* 2 The Cavaliers (to give the Divell his due) fought very valiantly. 1751 SMOLLETT *Per. Pick.* xv You always used me in an officer-like manner, that I must own, to give the devil his due.

Give what he hasn't got, A man cannot.

1775 JOHNSON in *Boswell* 1. (1848) 455 This is an old axiom which no man has yet thought fit to deny. *Nil dat quod non habet.*

Given him turnips, She has.

1845 FORD *Handb. Spain* i. 27 *note.* This gourd forms a favourite metaphor . . . she has refused him; it is the 'giving cold turnips' of Suffolk. 1869 HAZLITT 346 . . . *Devonshire, i.e.* Jilted him.

Given them green stockings, She has.

1862 HISLOP 259 . . . Spoken when a young woman marries before her elder sisters.

Gives fair words, He who | feeds you with an empty spoon. (*Cf.* Fill the mouth with empty spoons.)

1855 BOHN 399.

Gives his goods before he be dead, He that | take up a mallet and knock him on the head.

1640 HERBERT (Gros.) no. 849 He that gives all before hee dies provides to suffer. 1641

FERGUSSON 44 He that takes all his geir fra himself, and gives to his bairns, it were weill ward to take a mell and knock out his harmes.[1] 1670 RAY 78 Who gives away his goods before he is dead, Take a beetle and knock him on the head. 1721 KELLY 156 *He that gives all his geer to his bairns, Take up a beetle, and knock out his harns*[1]. . . John Bell, having given his whole substance to his children, was by them neglected; after he died there was found . . . a mallet with this inscription, I John Bell, leaves here a mell, the man to fell, who gives all to his bairns, and keeps nothing to himself. 1912 *Times Lit. Sup.* 31 May 222 The rhyme on an almshouse in the Bargates at Leominster[2]— He that gives away all before he is dead, Let 'em take this hatchet and knock him on y[e] head. [[1] brains. [2] founded 1735.]

Gives honour to his enemy, He that | is like to an ass.

1678 RAY *Adag. Hebr.* 413.

Gives me small gifts, He that | would have me live.

[*c.* 1190 *Li Proverbe au Vilain* (Tobler) 8 Qui petit me done, il veut que je vive.] *c.* 1300 *Provs. of Hending* no. 20 That me lutel yeueth, he my lyf ys on. 1640 HERBERT 363.

Gives thee a bone, He that | would not have thee die.

1640 HERBERT 334. 1650 JER. TAYLOR *Holy Liv.* IV. § 8 (1850) 219 A cup of water, if it be but love to the brethren, . . . shall be accepted. Chi ti da un'ossa, non ti verrebbe morto.

Gives thee a capon, He that | give him the leg and wing.

1640 HERBERT 322.

Gives to all, denies all, Who.

1611 COTGRAVE s.v. 'Donner' He that gives me all denies me all; viz. He that offers me all meanes to give me nothing. 1640 HERBERT 318.

Gives to another bestows on himself, He who.

1664 CODRINGTON 197 He that giveth discreetly, gaineth directly. 1684 RYCAUT tr. *Gracian's Critick* 240 (A). 1732 FULLER no. 2114 He that gives to a worthy person bestows a benefit upon himself.

Gives to be seen, He that | will relieve none in the dark

1732 FULLER no. 2115 He that gives to be seen, would never relieve a man in the dark.

Gives twice who gives quickly, He.

[PUBL. SYRUS 235 (Ribbeck) *Inopi beneficium bis dat qui dat celeriter. Cf.* SENECA *Ep.* 108. 9.] *c.* 1385 CHAUCER *Leg. Good Wom.* Prel. G 441 For whoso yeveth a yifte, or doth a grace, Do it by tyme, his thank is wel the more. 1553 T. WILSON *Arte of Rhet.* (1909) 119 He giueth twise, that giueth sone and cherefully. **1620** SHELTON *Quix.* IV. vii (1908) I. 340 It is an old proverb, 'that he that gives quickly, gives twice'. **1670** RAY 11. He giveth twice that gives in a trice. **1775** JOHNSON 19 Jan., in *Boswell* (1848) xlvii. 427 I did really ask the favour twice; but you have been even with me by granting it so speedily. *Bis dat qui cito dat.* **1907** *Spectator* 22 June 979 The Union Jack Club ... needs £16,000. ... He gives twice who gives quickly.

Give(s), gave, *see also* Better g. a shilling than lend; Better g. than take; Exhorts others to g. (Let him who); Good mother says not . . . but g.; Grateful man (To) g.; Hand that g. gathers; Handsome head ... pray g. tester; Hard g. more than he that hath nothing; Long a giving knows not how to g.; Losers leave to speak (G.); One day g. (What) another takes away; Piper a penny to play (G. the); Spent we had (What we), what we g. we have. *For To give, see also under significant words following.*

Giving and taking, In | it is easy mistaking.

1855 BOHN 424.

Giving is dead, restoring very sick.

1573 SANDFORD 103 Giuen is dead, and restored is nought. **1640** HERBERT 344.

Giving much to the poor, doth enrich (increase) a man's store.

1640 HERBERT 325. **1678** RAY 146 (with increase').

Gladness, A man of | seldom falls into madness.

1659 HOWELL *Eng. Prov.* 17/1. **1670** RAY 11.

Gladness, *see also* Sadness and g. succeed each other.

Glasgow people, Greenock folk, and Paisley bodies.

1842 R. CHAMBERS *Pop. Rhymes of Scot.* 20 ... These words imply gradations of dignity, the Paisley bodies being ... at the bottom of the scale.

Glass houses, *see* Head (House) of g. (He that hath) must not throw stones.

Glass tells you, What your | will not be told by counsel.

1640 HERBERT 329.

Glass, *see also* First g. for thirst; Loves g. without G (He that); Luck of Edenhall (If g. break); Woman and g. in danger; Women look in their g. (The more).

Glasses and lasses are brittle ware.

1576 PETTIE *Petite Pall.* (Gollancz) II. 106 Women having lost their chastity are like broken glasses which are good for nothing. **1579** LYLY *Euphues* Wks. (Bond) I. 234 After all his strife he wan but a Strumpet, that for all his trauails he reduced (I cannot say reclaymed) but a straggeler: which was as much in my iudgement, as to strive for a broken glasse which is good for nothing. **1599** SHAKS. *Pass. Pilgr.* 87 Fair is my love ... Brighter than glass, and yet, as glass is, brittle. **1621** HOWELL *Lett.* 1 June (1903) I. 63 A saying ... , 'That the first handsome woman ... was made of Venice glass', ... implies beauty, but brittleness with all (and Venice is not unfurnished with some of that mould, for no place abounds more with lasses and glasses). **1721** KELLY 113 *Glasses and lasses are bruckle[1] wares.* Both apt to fall, and both ruined by falling. [[1] brittle.]

Glastonbury Tor, *see* Old as G. T.

Glazier, *see* Father was a bad g.

Glean before the cart has carried, To.

1550 HEYWOOD I. xi Thou goest a-gleaning ere the cart have carried.

Gled[1] whistled, It was never for nothing that the.

1721 KELLY 199 ... People who officiously offer their service may be suspected to have some selfish end in it. [[1] kite.]

Glimmer in the touch-box,[1] There is a.

1678 RAY 247. [[1] a musketeer's box for priming-powder.]

Gloucestershire kindness.

1894 NORTHALL *Folk-phrases of Four Co.* 14 Gloucestershire kindness, giving away what you don't want yourself.

Gloucestershire, *see also* Sure as God's in G.

Glove(s), *see* Gauntlet of a hedging g. (Make not); Hand and g.; Shoeing-horn to help on g.

Glower[1] at the moon and fall on the midden,[2] To. (*Cf.* Gazed at the moon, &c.)

1721 KELLY 377 *You look'd at the Moon, and fell on the Midding.* Spoken to them, who pretended and design'd great things, but afterwards took up with less. [[1] stare. [2] dunghill.]

Glowing coals sparkle oft.

1616 DRAXE 85. **1670** RAY 72 ... When the mind is heated with any passion, it will often break out in words and expressions, *Psalm* 39.

Glow-worm lights her lamp, When the | the air is always damp.

1883 ROPER 31. **1893** INWARDS 145.

Glue did not hold, The.

1813 RAY 196 ... i.e. You were baulked in

your wishes: you missed your aim. **1855**
BOHN 162.

Glutton, *see* Hastens a g. (Who), chokes him;
Meals (Two hungry) make third a g.

Gluttony is the sin of England.

1640 FULLER *Joseph's Parti-col. Coat* Sermons
(1891) I. 203 Gluttony is the sin of England;
for though . . . we may entitle ourselves to the
pride of the Spanish, jealousy of the Italian,
wantonness of the French, drunkenness of
the Dutch, and laziness of the Irish; . . . yet
our ancientest carte is for the sin of gluttony.

Gluttony kills more than the sword.

1509 A. BARCLAY *Ship of Fools* (1874) II. 266
Mo dye By glotony, excesse and lyuynge
bestyall Than by hunger, knyfe, or deth
naturall. **1601** T. WRIGHT *Passions of the
Mind* 206 Gluttonie must be the nursse of
Physitians, since, *plures occidit gula quam
gladius.* **1617** MORYSON *Itin.* I. I. i (1907–8)
I. 20 A round table . . . with many inscrip-
tions persuading temperance, such as . . .
Plures crapula quam ensis. **1641** FERGUSSON 90
Surfeit slayes mae nor the sword. **1721**
KELLY 299 Surfeits slay more than swords.
Plures necat gula quam gladius.

Gluttony, *see also* Belly full of g. will never
study.

Gnat, *see* Strain at a g.

Gnaw the bone which is fallen to thy lot.

1678 RAY *Adag. Hebr.* 411 . . . That is, He
that hath an ill wife must patiently bear with
her: it may also be applied to other things.

Go a long way after one is weary, One can (may).

1853 TRENCH iv *One can go a long way after
one is weary.*[1] . . . [has] the poetry of an
infinite sadness about it, so soon as one gives
it that larger range of application which it is
capable of receiving. **1913** *Brit. Wkly.* 2 Jan.
454 In a paragraph on the Austrian Emperor
. . . the words occur, 'We keep going a long
time after we are tired'. [[1] *On va bien loin
depuis qu'on est las.*]

Go about, *see* Better to g. a. than to fall.

Go after a leech, While men | the body is buried.

1837–8 USK *Test. Love* III. vii. 79 While men
gon after a leche, the body is buryed.

Go down the ladder when thou marriest a wife; go up when thou choosest a friend.

1678 RAY *Adag. Hebr.* 400 . . . The meaning
is, that we should not marry a wife above our
rank, though we choose such a friend.

Go far about seeking the nearest, You.

1721 KELLY 370 ... . Spoken to them who, out

5017   R

of design, speak not directly to the business,
or who take an improper course to obtain
their end.

Go farther and fare worse.

1546 HEYWOOD II. iv. 51 And might haue
gone further, and haue faren wurs. **1614** BP.
HALL *Recoll. Treat.* 412 That ancient check
of going far and faring worse. **1738** SWIFT
(*Dial.* ii) 344 Come, Sir John, you may go
further and fare worse. **1847–8** THACKERAY
Vanity F. iv She's just as rich as most of the
girls who come out to India. I might go
farther and fare worse.

Go forward and fall, go backward and mar all.

1639 CLARKE 250.

Go here away, go there away, quoth Madge Whitworth when she rode the mare in the tedder.

1678 RAY 85.

Go home, and say your prayers.

1637 SHIRLEY *Hyde Pk.* I. ii Go home, and
say your prayers, I will not look For thanks
till seven years hence.

Go in God's name, so ride no witches.

1678 RAY 247.

Go into the country to hear what news at London, You must.

1678 RAY 345.

Go not for every grief to the physician, nor for every quarrel to the lawyer, nor for every thirst to the pot.

1640 HERBERT 330.

Go old to the court, and young to a cloister, A man must | that would go from thence to heaven.

1678 RAY 117.

Go out and kill? What shall we.

1896 'H. S. MERRIMAN' *The Sowers* xxi 'The
Prince', continued De Chauxville, . . . 'is a
great sportsman, . . . a mighty hunter. I
wonder why Englishmen always want to kill
something.' **1902–4** LEAN I. 19 What shall
we go out and kill? (The after-breakfast
inquiry.) An Englishman's idea of happiness
is to find something he can kill and to hunt it.

Go out like a candle in a snuff (or the snuff of a candle), To.

a. **1618** SYLVESTER (1621) 1162 Forgotten all
their Storie . . . Went out in Snuffe and left
ill sent behind. *a.* **1618** RALEIGH in HANNAH,
Poems of Wotton and Raleigh 74 Cowards
[may] fear to die; but Courage stout, Rather
than live in Snuff, will be put out. **1654**
WARREN *Unbelievers* 252 His Arguments
should go out like a snuffe of a candle in the

socket. **1687** WINSTANLEY *Eng. Poets* (Milton) in GOSSE *Gossip in Lib.* (1893) 110 But his Fame is gone out like a Candle in a Snuff, and his Memory wil always stink. **1841** S. WARREN *Ten Thous. a Year* ix 'Bess dropped off sudden, like, at last, didn't she?' . . . 'She went out, as they say, like the snuff of a candle.'

Go over the stile, He that will not | must be thrust through the gate.

1678 RAY 206.

Go snacks, To.

[= to have a share; divide profits.] **1701** FARQUHAR *Sir H. Wildair* IV. ii Well, monsieur! 'tis about a thousand pounds; we go snacks. **1809** MALKIN *Gil Blas* x. xi You shall go snacks in all that we can squeeze out of the old fellow. **1884** BLACKMORE *Tom. Upmore* xvi If John Windsor would go snacks, I should feel half inclined to consider about consulting a Solicitor.

Go the whole hog, To.

1830 GALT *Lawrie T.* II. i (1849) 43 I reckon Squire Lawrie may go the whole hog with her. **1837** TH. HOOK *Jack Brag* v He determined to 'go the whole hog', and follow up this feint . . . which might . . . be turned into a real attack. **1905** VACHELL *The Hill* 147 You're not prepared to go the whole hog? You want to pick and choose.

Go through dirt? How does he.

1917 BRIDGE 75 . . . *How does he bear suffering or temptation?*

Go to a goat for wool, You.

[ERASM. *Ad. De lana caprina.*] **1629** T. ADAMS *Serm.* (1861–2) I. 330 He shall hardly get from his patron the milk of the vicarage; but if he looks for the fleeces of the parsonage, he shall have, after the proverb, *lanam caprinam.*[1] **1721** KELLY 364 You come to the goat's house to thig[2] wool. **1802** WOLCOT (P. Pindar) *Middle. Elect.*, Let. ii. Wks. (1816) IV. Vor he that goeth vor *manners* there, Goeth **to** a goat vor *wool.* [[1] goats' wool. [2] beg.]

Go to bed at noon, Ye would make me.

1546 HEYWOOD II. vii. 69 It semeth ye wolde make me go to bed at noone. **1605–6** SHAKS. *K. Lear* III. vi. 92 *Lear.* We'll go to supper i' the morning: so, so, so. *Fool.* And I'll go to bed at noon.

Go to heaven in a featherbed, To. (*Cf.* Going to heaven in a sedan.)

c. **1520** SIR THOS. MORE in HARPSFIELD *Life* (E.E.T.S.) 75 If his wife or any of his children had beene diseased or troubled, he would say vnto them: 'We may not locke at our pleasures to goe to heauen in Fetherbeddes.' **1630** BRATHWAIT *Eng. Gent.* (1641) 152 Wee cannot goe to heaven on beds of down. **1678** RAY 243 . . . *Non est e terris mollis ad astra via.* [Not easy is the passage from the earth to the stars.]

Go to heaven in a string, To.

[= to be hanged: referred originally to the Jesuits who were hanged in the reign of Elizabeth.] **1592** GREENE *2nd Pt. Connycatching* B 26 The quest went vpon him and condemned him, and so the priggar went to heauen in a string. *a.* **1708** T. WARD *England's Reform.* II (1710) 47 Then may he boldly take his Swing, and go to Heaven in a string.

Go to heaven in a wheelbarrow, To.

[= to go to hell.] **1629** T. ADAMS *Serm.* (1861–2) I. 144 This oppressor must needs go to heaven. . . . But it will be, as the byword is, in a wheelbarrow: the fiends, and not the angels, will take hold on him.

Go to hell for the house profit, He will.

1641 FERGUSSON 54 *Of hypocrites.* . . . He will go to hell for the house profit. **1721** KELLY 156 . . . Spoken of them that will do any thing for gain.

Go to pot (*also* to the pot), To.

[= to be cut in pieces like meat for the pot; to be ruined or destroyed.] **1531** ELYOT *Governor* (Croft) i. 196 Kylling of dere . . . serueth well for the potte (as is the commune saynge). **1542** UDALL tr. *Erasm. Apoph.* (1877) 129 The ryche . . . went daily to the potte. **1546** HEYWOOD II. v. 56 The weaker goeth to the pot. **1678** RAY 190. **1757** SMOLLETT *Reprisal* I. viii. Wks. (1871) 610 All our fine project gone to pot! *a.* **1812** WOLCOT (P. Pindar) *Peter's Pension* Wks. (1816) I. 417 What if *my* good friend Hastings goes to pot?

Go to the dogs, To.

[= to be ruined.] **1865** LES. STEPHEN *Let.* to Lowell 13 Jan. An elderly Tory . . . added that we were all going to the dogs in consequence of that . . . Reform Bill. **1909** E. PHILLPOTTS *The Haven* I. xiv None agreed together save in this: that Brixham was going to the dogs a good deal quicker than the rest of the world.

Go to the well against his will, If the lad | either the can will break or the water will spill.

1721 KELLY 185 . . . Spoken when people mismanage a business, that they were forc'd to go about against their mind.

Go twenty miles on your errand first, I will.

1670 RAY 177.

Go up like a rocket and come down like the stick, To.

1909 *Brit. Wkly.* 7 Jan. We know the talk about a man going up like a rocket and coming down like a stick. . . . It is generally the man's own fault.

Go up the ladder to bed, You will.

1678 RAY 256 . . . *i.e.* be hang'd.

Go upon the Franciscans' hackney; *i.e.* on foot, To.

1651 HERBERT 365.

Go, goes, goest, goeth, gone, *see also* All is g. (When), what avails dagger; Beast that g. always never wants blows; Difference between *go* and *gow*; Expect to go when you die (Where do you); Fast as one g. another cometh; First creep then go; House and land are g. (When), learning is excellent; Tell me with whom thou g.; Thither as I would go I can go late; Way to be g. is not to stay; Welcome when thou go.; World (Thus fareth), that one g. up, another down. *For* To go, To go through, To go to, *see also under significant words following.*

Goat gives a good milking, but she casts it all down with her foot, The. (*Cf.* Cow that gives a good pail of milk, &c.)

1721 KELLY 310 ... Spoken when they who do a piece of good service, by their after behaviour spoil the good grace of it.

Goat must browse (bleat) where she is tied, The.

1611 COTGRAVE S.V. 'Chevre'. **1640** HERBERT 319. **1721** KELLY 343 *Where the buck is bound there he must bleat.* Men must bear these hardships to which they are bound, either by force or compact. **1852** E. FITZGERALD *Polonius* 59 'The goat must browse where she is tied'. Poverty ... surrounds a man with ready-made barriers, which, if they do mournfully gall and hamper, do at least prescribe for him, and force on him, a sort of course and goal.

Goats, You have no | and yet you sell kids.

1732 FULLER no. 5922. **1855** BOHN 527 They that sell kids, and have no goats, how came they by them?

Goat(s), *see also* Beard were all (If), g. might preach; Go to a g. for wool; Stink like a g.

God, and parents, and our master, can never be requited.

1640 HERBERT (Gros.) no. 800. **1658** *Comes Facundus* 237. **1659** N.R. 38. **1670** RAY 12.

God bless the Duke of Argyle!

1859 HOTTEN *Slang Dict.* (1874) 178 God bless the Duke of Argyle! A Scottish insinuation made when one shrugs his shoulders ... Said to have been . the thankful exclamation of the Glasgow folk, at finding ... iron posts, erected by his grace in that city to mark ... his property, very convenient to rub against. **1877–80** E. WALFORD *Tales of Gt. Fam.* (1890) 36 A Scotchman has good reason occasionally to cry out 'God bless the Duke of Argyll', for reasons best known north of the Tweed.

God bless you, *see* Friend at a sneeze.

God builds the nest of the blind bird.

1909 *Spectator* 2 Jan. 12/2 Will these men from the country ... be able to hold their own ...? *Inshallah.* God builds the nest of the blind bird, says the Turkish proverb.

God comes at last when we think he is farthest off.

1659 HOWELL *Ital. Eng.* 7. **1670** RAY 11.

God comes to see without a bell.

1640 HERBERT 335. **1823** COLLINS 385 'God came to visit him without a bell'.—It intimates, that a man has had some unexpected good fortune. It is the custom in Spain, when a person is dying, to carry the viaticum to the house, preceded by an attendant ringing a bell; ... which gave rise to the proverb of God paying a visit.

God comes with leaden feet, but strikes with iron hands.

1579 LYLY *Euphues* (Arb.) 172 Though God haue leaden handes which when they strike pay home, yet hath he leaden feete which are as slow to ouertake a sinner. **1629** T. ADAMS *Serm.* (1861–2) I. 214 Though these punishments fall not suddenly, yet certainly, if repentance step not between ... God hath leaden feet, but iron hands. **1670** RAY 11.

God complains not, but doth what is fitting.

1640 HERBERT (Gros.) no. 178.

God gave no sons, the devil gives nephews, He to whom.

1855 BOHN 398. *Spanish.*

God gives black men what white men forget.

1804 EDGEWORTH *Pop. Tales; Gratef. Negro* (1805) III. 205 Do what you please for a negro, he will cheat you.... You know what their maxim is: 'God gives black men what white men forget.'

God gives his wrath by weight, and without weight his mercy.

1651 HERBERT 369.

God gives the milk, but not the pail.

1912 *Spectator* 18 May 788 In the wisdom of the West, the necessity for hard work and for initiative is continually emphasised. 'God gives the milk, but not the pail', is typical of many sayings of the people.

God giveth the cow, but not by the horn.

c. **1366** no. 120 of *Cod. Philol.* (Göttingen Univ. Libr.) f. 169 a–180 b, quoted by E. VOIGT in *Romanische Forschungen* iii (1887), 281–314 *Ipse laborato! non dicas dat deus aurum'; Dat deus omne bonum, sed non per cornua taurum. Ibid.* foot-note, *Regimen *moralitatis*, Dist. 31 ; 120. 2 *schon mit unwesentlichen Abweichungen in Prora* 145 *Dat deus ipse boues nulli per cornua duclos. c.* **1400** *Cloud of Unknowing* (E.E.T.S. 1944) For þei sey þat God sendeþ þe kow, bot not by þe horne. *A ladder of foure Rongys* (*Douce MS.* 322[1], f. 55 b) quoted in preceding, p. 57 n. He yeveth the Oxe by the horne . . . when he not called offerth hys grace. [[1]said to be tr. of the *Scala Claustralium* of Guigo II, Prior of the Grande Chartreuse towards the end of the 12th cent.]

God hath his church (temple), Where | the devil will have his chapel.

1560 BECON *Catechism* (P.S.) 361 (A) For commonly, wheresoever God buildeth a church, the devil will build a chapel just by. **1621** BURTON *Anat. Mel.* III. iv. i (1651) 640 Blind zeale . . . is religions ape. . . . For where God hath a temple, the divel will have a chappel. **1670** RAY 70. **1701** DEFOE *Trueborn Englishman* II. Wks. (Bohn) V. 434 Wherever God erects a house of prayer, The Devil always builds a chapel there: And 'twill be found upon examination, The latter has the largest congregation. **1903** G. H. KNIGHT *Master's Questions* 90 Nowhere does the devil build his little chapels more cunningly than close under the shadow of the great temple of Christian liberty. A thing in itself completely right and good, may be, in its effects on others, completely evil.

God have mercy, horse, *see* Godamercy, &c.

God heals, and the physician hath the thanks.

1640 HERBERT 325. **1736** FRANKLIN Nov. God heals and the doctor takes the fee.

God help the fool, quoth Pedley.

1678 RAY 72 . . . This Pedley was a natural fool himself, and yet had usually this expression in his mouth. Indeed none are more ready to pity the folly of others, than those who have but a small measure of wit themselves.

God help the poor, for the rich can help themselves.

1609 DEKKER *Work for Armourers*, title-page God helpe the Poore, The rich can shift. **1721** KELLY 124 . . . Spoken in case of famine or scarcity of bread.

God help the rich, the poor can beg.

1659 HOWELL *Eng. Prov.* 16/2. **1721** KELLY 124 . . . Spoken . . . in case of public disturbances.

God help us (*or* you), *see* Cheap enough to say, *G. h. y.*; Lie down and cry, *G. h. u.*

God (Heaven) helps them that help themselves.

[L. *Dii facientes adjuvant*.] **1545** TAVERNER H1[v] Dii facientes adiuuant. The goddes do helpe the doers. **1580** BARET *Alveary* s.v. 'Induce' God doth helpe those in their affaires, which are industrious: according to

Homere. **1640** HERBERT 342 Help thyself, and God will help thee. **1736** FRANKLIN June God helps them that help themselves. **1841** S. WARREN *Ten Thous. a Year* xxi Never, never despair, Mr. Aubrey! Heaven helps those who help themselves. **1892** LIDDON *Serm. Wds. of Christ* 43 As the proverb most truly says, He helps them that help themselves.

God is a good man.

15— WEVER *Lusty Juventus* in HAZL. *O.E.P.* II. 73 He will say that God is a good man. **1526** *Hund. Mery Tales* (Oesterley) no. 85, p. 140 (A) There came one which sayde y[t] God was a good man. **1598–9** SHAKS. *Much Ado* III. v. 39 Well, God's a good man.

God is a good worker, but He loves to be helped.

1853 TRENCH V. 115 *God helps them that help themselves* . . . appears with a slight variation in the Basque: God is a good worker, but He loves to be helped.

God is a sure paymaster.

1639 CLARKE 325.

God is at the end, when we think he is furthest off it.

1640 HERBERT 345.

God is made the master of a family, When | he orders the disorderly.

1640 HERBERT 362.

God (Nature) is no botcher.

1546 HEYWOOD II. i. 43 God is no botcher syr, saide an other. He shapeth all partes, as eche part maie fytte other. **1639** CLARKE 224 Nature is no botcher.

God is where He was.

1530 PALSGRAVE 519 (A) Never dispayre, man, God is there as he was. **1546** HEYWOOD I. xii. 38 Take no thought in no case, God is where he was. **1678** RAY 147 . . . Spoken to encourage people in any distress. **1841** BROWNING *Pippa Passes* God's in his heaven, all 's right with the world.

God keep me from four houses, a usurer's, a tavern, a spital, and a prison.

1640 HERBERT 354.

God keep me from the man that has but one thing to mind.

1721 KELLY 115 . . . Because he will mind that thing to purpose. Spoken by great men, when poor people importune them about some special interest, which they have at heart.

God knows well which are the best pilgrims.

1611 COTGRAVE s.v. Pelerin' God knowes who 's a good pilgrim. **1678** RAY 147.

God loathes aught, When | men presently loathe it too.

1853 TRENCH vi. 141 That ancient German proverb: *When God loathes aught, men presently loathe it too.* He who first uttered this must have watched long . . . how it ever came to pass that even worldly honour tarried not long with them from whom the true honour whereof God is the dispenser had departed.

God loves, Whom | his bitch brings forth pigs.

1813 RAY 45 . . . Under the blessing of heaven all things co-operate for his good, even beyond his expectations. [Span.]

God made me, I am as.

1738 SWIFT (Dial. i) 339 *Spark.* They said that you were a complete beauty. *Miss.* My lord, I am as God made me.

God made the country, and man made the town.

[VARRO *Nec mirum, quod divina natura dedit agros, ars humana aedificavit urbes.*] **1783** COWPER *Task* I. 749 God made the country, and man made the town. **1869** LECKY *Hist. Europ. Mor.* (1905) I. ii. 265 Varro expressed an eminently Roman sentiment in that beautiful sentence which Cowper has introduced into English poetry, 'Divine Providence made the country, but human art the town.' **1903** AINGER *Crabbe* 118 The Borough . . . reminds us of a saying of Tennyson's, that if God made the country, and man made the city, then it was the devil who made the country-town.

God made the white man, God made the black man, the devil made the mulatto.

1901 *Chamb. Encyc.* VI. 22 The saying 'God made the white man, God made the black man, the devil made the mulatto', expresses a feeling as to the frequently inconvenient variability of variety-hybrids.

God makes and man (apparel) shapes.

1621 BURTON *Anat. Mel.* III. ii. III. iii (1651) 473 The greatest provocations of lust are from our apparel; God makes, they say, man shapes, and there is no motive like unto it. **1650** BULWER *Anthropomet.* 256 God makes, and the Tailor shapes. **1678** RAY 177 God makes and apparel shapes; but money makes the man. Pecunia vir. Χρήματα ἀνήρ· Tanti quantum habeas sis. Horat.

God never sendeth mouth but He sendeth meat.

1377 LANGLAND *P. Pl.* B. xiv. 39 (A) For lente neuere was lyf but lyflode were shapen. **1546** HEYWOOD I. iv. 8 God neuer sendth mouth, but he sendeth meat. *c.* **1612** FLETCHER *Scornf. Lady* I. i They say nature brings forth none but she provides for them. **1641** FERGUSSON 36 God sends never the mouth but the meat with it. **1894** LD.

AVEBURY *Use of Life* xii Children are sometimes spoken of as 'sent', and improvident parents excuse themselves by saying that 'if God sends mouths, He will send food to fill them'. **1905** A. MACLAREN *Expos. of Script., Matt.* I. 103 God never sends mouths but He sends meat to fill them. Such longings prophesy their fruition.

God oft hath a great share in a little house.

1640 HERBERT 319.

God or a painter, He is either a | for he makes faces.

1594–5 SHAKS. *L.L.L.* V. ii. 645 He 's a god or a painter; for he makes faces. **1732** FULLER no. 1914.

God provides for him that trusteth.

1640 HERBERT 351.

God reaches us good things by our own hands.

1732 FULLER no. 1683.

God save the mark.

[prob. originally a formula to avert an evil omen, hence used by way of apology when something horrible, &c., has been mentioned.] **1592** SHAKS. *Rom. & Jul.* III. ii. 53 I saw the wound, I saw it with mine eyes, God save the mark. **1761** STERNE *T. Shandy* III. xxxiii My father . . . had no more nose, my dear, saving the mark, than there is upon the back of my hand. **1815** HUGG *Pilgrims of the Sun,* Dedn to Byron Not for . . . thy virtues high (God bless the mark!) do I this homage plight.

God say Amen, *see* **All good, and G. say Amen.**

God, The most high | sees, and bears: my neighbour knows nothing, and yet is always finding fault.

1813 RAY 324. *Per.*

God send us of our own when rich men go to dinner.

1639 CLARKE 37.

God send us some money, for they are little thought of that want it, quoth the Earl of Eglinton at his prayers.

1721 KELLY 113.

God send you joy, for sorrow will come fast enough.

1605 *London Prodigal* III. iii God give you joy, as the old zaid proverb is, and some zorrow among. **1616** DRAXE 120. **1639** CLARKE 185.

God send you more wit, and me more money.

1616 WITHALS 555. **1659** HOWELL *Eng. Prov.*

15/2. **1721** KELLY 120 *God send you more wit, and me more silver, for we have both need of it.* Spoken when people propose, or say, what we think foolish and improper. **1732** FULLER no. 1689. **1738** SWIFT (Dial. iii) 350 *Lady A.* A dull unmannerly brute! well, God send him more wit, and me more money.

God send you readier meat than running hares.

1721 KELLY 113 . . . Spoken to those who have improbable expectations.

God sendeth cold after clothes.

1546 HEYWOOD I. iv. 8 God sendth colde after clothes. **1603** FLORIO tr. *Montaigne* III. vi (1897) V. 190 God sends my cold answerable to my cloths. **1641** FERGUSSON 34 God sends men cauld as they have clothes to. **1721** KELLY 113 *God sends men cloth, according to their cold.* God supports and supplies men, according to their circumstances.

God sendeth fortune to fools.

1546 HEYWOOD II. vi. 62 That they saie as ofte, God sendeth fortune to fooles. **1592** KYD *Soliman* (Boas) II. ii. 1 God sends fortunes to fools. **1599–1600** SHAKS. *A.Y.L.* II. vii. 19 'Call me not fool till heaven hath sent me fortune.' **1614** CAMDEN 306 God sendeth fortune to fools.

God sends corn and the devil mars the sack.

1616 DRAXE 4 (with asketh' for 'sends'). **1664** CODRINGTON (with 'giveth' for 'sends'). **1670** RAY 97.

God sends meat and the devil sends cooks.

1542 BOORDE *Dyetary* (E.E.T.S.) 260 (A) It is a common prouerbe, 'God may send a man good meate, but the deuyll may send an euyll coke to dystrue it'. **1545** ASCHAM *Toxoph.* II (Arb.) 132 He maye . . . haue cause to saye so of his fletcher, as . . . is communelye spoken of Cookes; . . . that God sendeth vs good fethers, but the deuyll noughtie Fletchers. **1617** J. TAYLOR (Water-Poet) *Obs. & Trav.* Wks. (1872) 26 Such diet we had, that the proverb was truly verified *God sent meat, and the Devil sent Cooks.* **1738** SWIFT (Dial. ii) 347 *Smart.* This goose is quite raw; well, God sends meat, but the devil sends cooks. **1822** SCOTT *Nigel* xxvii That homely proverb that men taunt my calling with,—'God sends good meat, but the devil sends cooks.'

God shapes the back for the burthen.

1822 COBBETT *Rur. Rides* 2 Jan. (1914) 55 As 'God has made the back to the burthen', so the clay and coppice people make the dress to the stubs and bushes. **1883** BARING-GOULD *John Herring* vi The sisters worried these men a good deal. They all took it in good part. Their backs were made to bear their burden.

God stint all strife.

1546 HEYWOOD II. viii. 72 I can no more herin, but god stint all strife.

God strikes not with both hands, for to the sea he made havens, and to rivers fords.

1640 HERBERT 332.

God strikes with his finger, and not with all his arm.

1592 G. DELAMOTHE (1647) 8 God strikes with his finger and not with all his arme. *Dieu nous frappe du doigts & non de tout le bras.* **1605** J. SYLVESTER *Bartas* 390. **1651** HERBERT 369.

God take the sun out of the heaven, Though | yet we must have patience.

1640 HERBERT 362.

God tempers the wind to the shorn lamb.

[*cf.* **1594** H. ESTIENNE *Premices* 47 Ces termes, *Dieu mesure le froid à la brebis tondue,* sont les propres termes du proverbe. Vray est qu'on le dit encore en deux autres sortes: (dont l'une est, *Dieu donne le froid selon la robbe*).] **1640** HERBERT 357 To a close shorn sheep, God gives wind by measure. **1768** STERNE *Sent. Journ.* II. 175 God tempers the wind, said Maria, to the shorn lamb. **1880** GOLDW. SMITH *Cowper* 59 It seems that the book found its way into the dictator's hands, . . . and that he even did something to temper the wind of criticism to the shorn lamb.

God when all is done, There is.

1546 HEYWOOD I. vii. 14 Ye there was God (quoth he) whan all is doone.

God will give, That which | the devil cannot reave.[1]

1641 FERGUSSON 66 It that God will give, the devil cannot reave. **1721** KELLY 320 . . . Spoken when we have attain'd our end in spite of opposition. [[1] rob us of.]

God will have see, That | shall not wink.

1560 *Nice Wanton* in HAZL. *O.E.P.* (1874) II. 182 But it is an old proverb, you have heard it, I think: That God will have see, shall not wink.

God will help, Where (Whom) | nothing does harm (none can hinder).

c. **1300** *Havelock* 647 Soth it is, þat men seyt and suereth:[1] 'þer god wile helpen, nouth no dereth'.[2] *c.* **1450** MERLIN 524 Ther-fore is seide proverbe, that god will haue a saued, no man may distroye. *a.* **1533** LD. BERNERS *Huon.* cxxx. 480 It is a commune prouerbe sayde, 'whome that god wyll ayde, no man can hurt'. **1721** KELLY 357 Whom God will help none can hinder. [[1] swear. [2] injures.]

God will, What | no frost can kill.

1639 CLARKE 225. **1732** FULLER no. 6106.

God will, When | no wind but brings rain.

1616 DRAXE 82 When God will, at all windes it will raine. **1640** HERBERT 333.

God will send time to provide for time.

1546 HEYWOOD I. xii. 39 Well (quoth I) God will sende Tyme to prouyde for tyme.

God's bairn is eith[1] to lear.

1721 KELLY 112 ... A child endowed with grace and good nature will be easily taught. [[1] easy.]

God's blessing make my pot boil, or my spit go? Will.

1721 KELLY 351 ... A great oppressor .. when poor people offered him all that they could get, and bid him take it with God's blessing, ... would stormingly say, *Will God's blessing make my pot play, or my spit go?*

God's grace and Pilling Moss[1] are boundless.

1662 FULLER (Lancs.) II. 220 Pyllyn-moss is the fountain of fuel [turf] in this county, and is conceived inexhaustible by the vicinage. ... May God's grace (which the vulgar, in their profane proverb, equally yoke therewith)... never be drained ...! [[1] Near Fleetwood; in 1920 a breeding-ground for vast flocks of sea-gulls.]

God's help is nearer than the fair even.

1641 FERGUSSON 36. **1721** KELLY 117 ... God's immediate providence may sooner assist us, than any second causes that we may propose.

God's lambs will play.

1830 FORBY 432 ... An apology for riotous youth.

God's mill grinds slow but sure.

[SEXTUS EMPIRICUS Ὀψὲ θεῶν ἀλέουσι μύλοι, ἀλέουσι δὲ λεπτά. The mills of the gods grind slowly, but they grind small. PLUT. *De sera num. vind.* Οὐχ ὁρῶ τι χρήσιμον ἔνεστι τοῖς ὀψὲ δὴ τούτοις ἀλεῖν λεγομένοις μύλοις τῶν θεῶν. I don't see any use in these 'late-grinding' mills of the Gods.] **1640** HERBERT 352. **1870** LONGFELLOW tr. *von Logau, Retribution* Though the mills of God grind slowly, yet they grind exceeding small. **1899** A. WHITE *Modern Jew* 98 [The] capture and destruction of the Spanish fleet ... satisfied them that though the mills of God grind slowly the ruin of Spain was an equitable adjustment of her debt to the Jews.

God's poor and the devil's poor, There are.

1629 T. ADAMS *Serm.* (1861-2) II. 232 There are God's poor and the devil's poor: those the hand of God hath crossed; these have forced necessity on themselves by a dissolute life.

Gods love die young, Whom the.

[MENANDER *Dis Exapaton, Frag.* 4 *Ὅν οἱ θεοὶ φιλοῦσιν ἀποθνῄσκει νέος.* PLAUTUS *Bacchides* 4. 7. 18 *Quem di diligunt Adolescens moritur, dum valet, sentit, sapit.* Whom the gods love die young, while still he can enjoy health, tastes and senses.] **1546** W. HUGH *Troub. Man's Med.* II (1831) 46 But among all others, saith the Greek poet Menander, most happy are they, and best beloved of God, that die when they are young. **1553** T. WILSON *Arte of Rhet.* (1909) 73 Whom God loueth best, those he taketh soonest. **1651** HERBERT 368 Those that God loves do not live long. **1821** BYRON *Juan* IV. xii 'Whom the gods love die young', was said of yore.

God, gods, *see also* Charitable give out and G. puts in; Danger past, G. forgotten; Do little for G. if devil were dead; Do the likeliest, G. will do best; Ends ill which begins in G.'s name (Never); Every man for himself and G. for all; Face to G. (He has one), another to devil; Garby whose soul neither G. would have; Give and spend, G. will send; Grace of G. is enough; —— is worth a fair; Guided that G. guides (They are well); Have G. have all; Heaven (G.) is above all; In time comes whom G. sends; Like me, G. bless the example; Likes not the drink, G. deprives of bread; Loseth nothing who keeps G. for friend; Lost be for G. (Let that which is); Make a poor man knight (Little of G.'s might); Man doth what he can, G. what He will; Man is a g. to his neighbour; Man is to man a g.; Man is to man either g. or wolf; Man punishes action, G. intention; Man's extremity G.'s opportunity; Many meet the gods, few salute; Nearer the church, farther from G.; Not G. above gets all men's love; One G., no more, but friends; Out of G.'s blessing into the warm sun; Owe G. a death; Peace (Where there is) G. is; Pleaseth not G. (When it); Poor that G. hates; *Quos Deus vult perdere* (Whom G. would ruin); Serves G. for money (He that); Serves G. (He who) serves good master; Sooth as G. is king; Spender (To good) G. is treasurer; Spindle and distaff ready, G. will send flax; Sure as G.'s in Gloucestershire; Thrives he whom G. loves; True as G. is in heaven; Trust in G. but keep powder dry; Wite G. (You need not) if Deil ding you over.

Godalming rabbits.

[**1762** C. CHURCHILL *Ghost* i. 435-8 But if such things no more engage The taste of a politer age, To help them out in time of need Another Tofts must rabbits breed.] **1787** GROSE (*Surrey*) 226 Godalmin rabbits. A term of reproach to the inhabitants of this place, ... for the well-known deception practised by a Mrs. Tofts, who pretended to be delivered of live rabbits.

Godamercy (Gramercy) horse.

1546 HEYWOOD II. vii God have mercy, horse!

1595 J. PAYNE *Royal Exchange* As the hostes reckonyng with her gest less willing to lodge in her hows then his tyred horse, made a low curtesy . . . to the beaste, and seyd 'Gathamercy horse'. *c.* **1600** COLLIER *Roxb. Ballads* 29 (1847) The hostler, to maintaine himself with money in 's purse, Approves the proverbe true, and sayes, gramercy horse. **1659** HOWELL *Eng. Prov.* 14/1. **1710** *Brit. Apollo* III. no. 118. 3/1 I find I'm whole, *God a mercy Horse.*

Godfathers oft give their blessings in a clout.

[= money wrapped up in a cloth.] **1546** HEYWOOD II. ix. 79 Well (quoth he) if ye list to bring it out, Ye can geue me your blessyng in a clout. **1611** DAVIES *Prov.* 268.

Godfathers, *see also* Child is christened (When) g. enough.

Godly, *see* Peter is so g. that God don't make him thrive.

Godolphin, *see* Charles's Wain; Never a Granville wanted.

Goes a borrowing, goes a sorrowing, He that.

c. **1470** *Harl. MS. 116* (*Rel. Antiq.* I. 316) f. 125 a He that fast spendyth must nede borowe; but whan he schal paye a3en, then ys al the sorowe. **1545** TAVERNER F6. **1573** TUSSER XV. 31. **1678** RAY 104. **1836** MARRYAT *Midsh. Easy* viii You had made your request for the loan . . . fully anticipating a refusal (from the feeling that he who goes a borrowing goes a sorrowing). **1894** LD. AVEBURY *Use of Life* iii (1904) 24 Debt is slavery. 'Who goes a-borrowing goes a-sorrowing.'

Goes a great voyage that goes to the bottom of the sea, He. (*Cf.* Great way to the bottom of the sea.)

1732 FULLER no. 1850.

Goes and comes, He that | maketh a good voyage.

1573 SANDFORD (1576) 209. **1578** FLORIO *First Fruites* f. 29 (A) [with 'returneth' for 'comes'.] **1629** *Book of Meery Riddles* Prov. 90.

Goes far that never returns (*or* turns not again), He. (*Cf.* Runneth far, &c.)

1545 TAVERNER D 4ᵛ The English prouerbe . . . He runneth farre, that neuer commeth agayn. **1546** HEYWOOD II. ix He runneth far that never turneth again. **1579** LYLY *Euphues* Wks. (Bond) I. 322 He runneth farre that neuer retourneth. **1629** T. ADAMS *Serm.* (1861–2) II. 95 They go far that never return. We heard this son at the highest stair of rebellion, now . . . 'he repented and went'. **1662** FULLER (*Surrey*) III. 207 'But they go far who turn not again'; and in him the proverb was veirfied, 'Naughty boys sometimes make good men'.

Goes not out of his way that goes to a good inn, He.

1611 COTGRAVE s.v. 'Fourvoyer'. **1640** HERBERT 355.

Goes to bed supperless, Who | all night tumbles and tosses.

1567 PAINTER *Pal. of Pleasure* (Jacobs) iii. 215 (A) Accordynge to the prouerbe: He that goeth to bed supperlesse, lyeth in his bed restlesse. **1670** RAY 37 . . . This is an Italian Proverb. *Chi va à letto senza cena Tutta notte si dimena.*

Goes to bed thirsty, He that | riseth healthy.

1640 HERBERT 363. **1678** RAY 37. . . . *Qui couche avec la soif se leve avec la santé.*

Goes, goeth, *see also* Go.

Goeth far, He that | hath many encounters.

1640 HERBERT 346.

Goeth out with often loss, He that | at last comes home by weeping cross.

1564 BULLEIN *Dial. agst. Fever* (E.E.T.S.) 78 (A) In the ende thei go home . . . by weepyng cross. **1579** GOSSON *Sch. Abuse* (Arb.) 46 They . . . returne home by weeping Crosse, and fewe of them come to an honest ende. **1603** FLORIO tr. *Montaigne* III. v. (1897) V. 108 Few men have wedded their . . . paramours or mistresses, but have come home by weeping cross. **1670** RAY 28.

Going (Walking) foot is aye getting, A.

c. **1300** *Cursor M.* 28939 (Cott. Galba) Gangand fote ay getes fode. **1670** RAY 262 A walking foot is ay getting. **1721** KELLY 11 *A going foot is ay getting, if it were but a thorn.* A man of industry will certainly get a living: though this proverb is often applied to those who went abroad, and got a mischief. **1914** PURDON *Folk of Furry F.* vi It's better for a body to be moving somewhere, even if it's only to get you a prod of a thorn in the toe!

Going to grass with his teeth upwards, He is.

1813 RAY 196 . . ., i.e. He is going to be buried.

Going to heaven in a sedan, There is no. (*Cf.* Go to heaven in a featherbed.)

1732 FULLER no. 4910.

Gold do? What cannot. (*Cf.* Money do, &c.)

1639 CLARKE 221.

Gold goes in at any gate except heaven's.

1629 T. ADAMS *Serm.* (1861–2) I. 143 Philip

was wont to say that an ass laden with gold would enter the gates of any city; but the golden load of bribes and extortions shall bar a man out of the city of God. 1660 W. SECKER *Nonsuch Prof.* ii (1891) 134 The gates of heaven . . . are not unlocked with a golden key. 1670 RAY 97.

Gold is an orator.

1592 SHAKS. *Rich. III* IV. ii. 38 Gold were as good as twenty orators. 1594 BARNFIELD *Affect Shep.* (Percy Soc.) 48 (A) Gold is a deepe-perswading orator.

Gold is but muck.

1589 LYLY *Midas* II. ii. 5 Gold is but the earths garbadge. *c.* 1598 JONSON *Case is altered* IV. iv (A) [Cited as 'the old proverb'.]

Gold, The purest | is the most ductile.

1620–8 FELTHAM *Resolves, Humility* (1904) 285 I will (in things not weighty) submit freely: the purest gold is most ductile: it is commonly a good blade that bends well.

Gold knew what gold is, If | gold would get gold, I wis.

1640 HERBERT 364.

Gold may buy land, He that has.

1641 FERGUSSON 44. 1683 MERITON *Yorks. Ale* (1697) 83–7 (A).

Gold mines, *see* Parnassus has no g. m.

Gold of Toulouse.

1621 BURTON *Anat. Mel.* I. ii. III. xv (1651) 138 It is *aurum Tholosanum*, and will produce no better effects. 1629 T. ADAMS *Serm.* (1861–2) II. 507 What family, that hath had but a finger in these sacrileges, hath not been ruinated by them? They have been more unfortunate to the gentry of England than was the gold of Tholossa to the followers of Scipio. 1871 LIDDELL *Stud. Hist. Rome* 1 *Q.* Servilius Cæpio . . . gained an evil reputation by the sack of Tolosa. . . . The plunder he took was immense: but the greater part was seized by robbers on the way to Marseilles, and 'Toulouse gold' became a proverbial expression for ill-gotten but unprofitable gains.

Gold, All is not | that glitters.

[L. *Non omne quod nitet aurum est.*] *c.* 1220 *Hali Meidenhad* (E.E.T.S.) 9 (A) Nis hit nower neh gold al þat ter schineþ. *c.* 1300 *Provs. of Hending* no. 18 Hit nis nout al gold, þat shineþ. *c.* 1386 CHAUCER *Can. Yeom. Prol. & T.* 409 But al thyng which that shyneth as the gold, Nis nat gold, as that I have herd it told. *c.* 1430 LYDGATE *Fall Princes* IV. 15 All is not gold that shineth bright. 1553 BECON *Reliques of Rome* (1563) 207 All is not golde that glistereth. 1596–7 SHAKS. *Merch. V.* II. vii. 65 All that glisters is not gold; Often have you heard that told. 1614 CAMDEN 303 All is not gold that glisters. 1638 DRUMM. OF HAWTH. *Biblioth. Edinb. Lectori* Wks. (1711) 222 All is not gold which glittereth. 1784 JOHNSON 2 Oct. in *Boswell* (ed. 2) All is not gold that glitters, as we have been often told.

Gold, When we have | we are in fear; when we have none we are in danger. (*Cf.* Money, To have | is a fear.)

1616 DRAXE 45. 1642 TORRIANO 99. 1664 CODRINGTON 226 with 'trouble' for 'danger'. 1670 RAY 12.

Gold which is worth gold, That is.

1611 COTGRAVE S.V. 'Or'. 1640 HERBERT 355. 1655–62 GURNALL *Chrn. in Armour* (1865) I. 531 We say, 'That is gold which is worth gold'—which we may anywhere exchange for gold.

Gold, *see also* Ass loaded with g.; Balance distinguisheth not between g. and lead; Belly (If were not for) the back might wear g.; Brass for g.; Buy g. too dear; Door of g. (Who will make) must knock nail every day; Good as g.; Labours and thrives (He that) spins g.; Lock will hold against g. (No); Look to a gown of g.; No silver (g.) without dross; Old friends . . . and old g. are best; Ounce of state requires pound of g.; Pour g. on him, he'll never thrive; Speak with your g. (You may); Touchstone tries g. (As the); Trust him with untold g. (You may); Try your skill . . . then in g.; Win g. and wear g.

Golden age never was the present age, The.

1732 FULLER no. 4556. 1880 BLACKMORE *Mary Anerley* xliv She began . . . to contemplate the past as a golden age . . . and to look upon the present as a period of steel.

Golden (silver) bridge, For a flying enemy make a.

[ERASM. *Apoph.* viii. 14, quoting Alphonso of Aragon, *Hostibus fugientibus pontem argenteum exstruendum esse.* 1534 RABELAIS I. xliii.] 1576 LAMBARDE *Peramb. of Kent* (1826) 371 (A) It was well said of one . . . If thine enemie will flie, make him a bridge of golde. *a.* 1601 NASHE (McKerrow) ii. 179 I thought to make my foe a bridge of gold, or faire words, to flie by. 1620 SHELTON *Quix.* II. lviii (1908) III. 231 One only knight expects you, who is not of that mind or opinion of those that say, To a flying enemy a silver bridge. 1633 MASSINGER *Guardian* I. i For a flying foe, Discreet and provident conquerors build up A bridge of gold. 1889 STEVENSON *Mas. of Ball.* iv. A military proverb: that it is a good thing to make a bridge of gold to a flying enemy.

Golden calf, The.

[*Exodus* xxxii.] 1732 FULLER no. 4704 The People will worship even a Calf, if it be a Golden one. 1827 HARE *Guesses at Truth* i (1859) 164 Millions . . . who fancy that happiness may be attained by riches, . . . may be numbered among the idolaters of the golden calf. 1902 G. W. E. RUSSELL *Col. & Recol.* 2

Ser. (1909) ii The worship of the Golden Calf is the characteristic cult of modern Society.

Golden life in an iron age, We must not look for a.

1616 DRAXE 209 A golden life is not to be expected in an yron world. *Ibid.* 243 A man must not looke for a golden life in an yron world. 1639 CLARKE 124. 1670 RAY 14. 1732 FULLER no. 5450.

Golden mean, The.

[HOR. *Od.* 2. 10. 5 *Aurea mediocritas.*] *c.* 1200 *Ancrene Riwle* 336 Þe middel weie of mesure is euer guldene. *a.* 1591 HY. SMITH *Serm.* (1866) I. 162 The golden mean is good for all things. Solomon doth not forbid to eat honey, but eat not too much, lest thou surfeit. 1642 MILTON *Apol. Smect.* Prose Wks. (Bell) III. 164 If they, for lucre, use to creep into the church undiscernibly, . . . provide that no revenue there may exceed the golden mean. 1901 R. G. MOULTON *Shaks. as Dram. Art.* 46 Proverbs like 'Grasp all, lose all', . . . express moral equilibrium, and the 'golden mean' is its proverbial formula.

Golden, *see also* Angle with silver (g.) hook.

Goldfinch, *see* Makes his mistress a g.

Golgotha are skulls of all sizes, In.

a. 1591 HY. SMITH *Serm.* (1866) I. 261 As many little skulls are in Golgotha as great skulls. 1660 W. SECKER *Nonsuch Prof.* II. (1891) 294 As there are none too old for eternity, so there are none too young for mortality. In Golgotha there are skulls of all sizes.

Gone over Asfordby Bridge backwards, He has.

1678 RAY (*Leics.*) 317 . . . Spoken of one that is past learning. 1881 EVANS 299 . . . In modern usage it is applied to one who 'sets the cart before the horse' in word or deed.

Gone, *see also* Go.

Good advisement, There came never ill of.

1641 FERGUSSON 96. 1721 KELLY 334 . . . A persuasion to consider well of a thing before you go about it.

Good against evil, Set.

1640 HERBERT 355.

Good and quickly seldom meet.

1640 HERBERT 344. 1790 TRUSLER *Prov. Exempl.* 138 According to the Italians, Hastily and well never met. A man of sense may be expeditious, but is never in a hurry.

Good apple on a sour stock, No.

1393 LANGLAND *P. Pl.* C. xi. 206 For god seith hit hym-self . . . 'shal neuere good appel Thorw no sotel science on sour stock growe'.[1] [[1] *Matt.* vii. 18.]

Good as a play, As.

1579 GOSSON *Sch. Abuse* (Arb.) 35 It is a right Comedie, to marke their behaviour. 1606 DEKKER *News from Hell* Prose Wks. (Gros. II. 118) It was a Comedy, to see what a crowding . . . there was. 1638 TAYLOR (Water-Poet) *Bull, Beare, &c.* 43 in *Wks.* 3rd coll. (Spens. S.) (A) It was as good as a comedy to him to see the trees fall. 1845 DICKENS *Cricket* Chirp 2 (A) John had such a lively interest . . . that it was as good as a play.

Good as gold, As.

1841 DICKENS *Old Cur. Shop* xxxix There was the baby, too [at Astley's], who had never closed an eye all night, but had sat as good as gold, trying to force a large orange into its mouth.

Good bargain (pennyworth), At a | make a pause (think twice).

1640 HERBERT 342 On a good bargain think twice. 1666 TORRIANO 65 At a good pennyworth pause a little while. 1753 FRANKLIN *P. Rich. Alm.* in ARBER *Eng. Garner* v. 583 *At a great pennyworth, pause a while!* . . . perhaps the cheapness is apparent only. 1796 EDGEWORTH *Par. Asst., Lit. Merchts.* ii (1903) 391 'Think twice of a good bargain', says the proverb.

Good bearing beginneth worship, In.

1597 *How the Goode Wif* in HAZL. *Early Pop. Poet.* (1856) I. 181 In thi gode berynge begynnythe thy worschipe, my dere childe.

Good (Hard) beginning makes a good ending, A. (*Cf.* Well begun, &c.)

c. 1300 *Provs. of Hending* ii God beginning maketh god endynge. *c.* 1350 *Douce MS.* 52 no. 22 Of a gode begynnyng comyth a gode endyng. *c.* 1390 GOWER *Conf. Amantis* Prol. l. 86 But in proverbe I have herd seye That who that wel his werk begynneth The rather a good ende he wynneth. 1546 HEYWOOD I. x. 21 Ye Ales, of a good begynnyng comth a good end. 1614 CAMDEN 302 A hard beginning hath a good ending.

Good blood makes bad puddings without groats or suet.

1665 J. WILSON *Projectors* II. i I have so often heard him protest against your great matches, as he calls 'em, and compares 'em to an ill pudding—all blood and no fat. 1678 RAY 66 . . . Χρήματα ἀνήρ. Nobility is nothing but ancient riches: and money is the idol the world adores. *Ibid.* 230 He hath good blood in him if he had but groats to it. 1869 *Lonsdale Glos., Groats* . . . The proverb current in Lonsdale, 'Blood without groats is nowt', meaning that family without fortune is of no consequence.

Good broth may be made in an old pot.

1601 J. CHAMBER *Treatise agst. Judicial Astrologie* B 1ᵛ As good broth may come out of a woodden ladle, as out of a siluer spoone. 1666 TORRIANO 111 (A) (with 'sops' for 'broth'). 1880 SPURGEON *Ploughman's Pictures* 84 (A).

Good building without a good foundation, No.

1599 MINSHEU (1623) 2 X_2^v Vpon a good foundation a good building is made. **1732** FULLER no. 3578.

Good cheap is dear.

[good cheap = a bargain.] c. **1375** *Cato Major* I. xxix in *Anglia VII* þat is a good chep may beo dere, And deore good chep also. **1640** HERBERT 329.

Good cheap, *see also* Buy g. c. that bring nothing home; Good cheer and g. c. gars many haunt the house; Saying goes g. c. *See also* Good thing cheap.

Good cheer and good cheap gars[1] many haunt the house.

1670 FERGUSSON 34. [1 causes.]

Good cheer is lacking, When | our friends will be packing.

1639 CLARKE 12. **1732** FULLER no. 6299.

Good child, *see* Well for him who has g. c.

Good conscience is a continual feast, A.

[Cf. *Prov.* xv. 15 But he that is of a merry heart hath a continual feast.] **1605** BACON *Adv. Learn.* II Whereunto the wisdom of that heavenly leader hath signed, also hath affirmed that a good conscience is a continual feast. **1616** DRAXE 28. **1621** BURTON *Anat. Mel.* II. iii. VII (1651) 358 When they have all done, *a good conscience is a continual feast.* **1655** WILL ROADES to Sir Ralph Verney, *Verney Memoirs* (1894) iii. 234. **1834** PROUT *Fraser's Mag.* Dec. A good conscience was the *juge convivium* of his mind.

Good cope, *see* Segging is g. c.

Good counsel has no price.

1855 BOHN 363.

Good counsel never comes amiss.

1616 DRAXE 33 Good counsell will doe no harme. **1732** FULLER no. 1708.

Good counsel never comes too late.

1633 JONSON *T. Tub* III. iv Good counsels lightly never come too late.

Good cow hath an evil (bad) calf, Many a.

1520 WHITTINGTON *Vulg.* (E.E.T.S.) 72 It is comenly sayd: many a good kowe bryngeth for the a sory calfe. **1546** HEYWOOD I. x. 23 But many a good coowe hath an euill caulfe. I speake this doughter in thy mothers behalfe. **1605** CHAPMAN, &c. *Eastw. Hoe* IV. i Why dost thou weep now? Thou art not the first good cow hast had an ill calf. **1670** RAY 74 Many a good cow hath but a bad calf. Ἀνδρῶν ἡρώων τέκνα πήματα. Heroum filii noxii. . . . Men famous for learning, vertue, valour, success have for the most part either

left behind them no children, or such as that it had been more for their honour and the interest of humane affairs, that they had died childless. **1721** KELLY 7 *An ill cow may have a good calf.* Bad people may have good children.

Good dog deserves a good bone, A.

1611 COTGRAVE s.v. 'Bon'. **1633** JONSON *T. Tub* II. i A good dog Deserves, sir, a good bone of a free master.

Good dog who goes to church, He is a.

1826 SCOTT *Woodst.* i Bevis . . . fell under the proverb which avers, 'He is a good dog which goes to church'; for . . . he behaved himself . . . decorously. **1896** F. LOCKER-LAMPSON *My Confid.* 44 'Tis said, by men of deep research, He's a good dog who goes to church.

Good egg nor bird, Neither (Never). (See also** Dow, egg nor bird.)**

1591 W. STEPNEY *Span. Schoolmaster* L 5[v] Neither good egge nor good bird. **1629** T. ADAMS *Serm.* (1861-2) I. 170 But sin of itself is good neither in egg nor bird, neither in root nor branch. **1670** RAY 173. **1721** KELLY 262 *Never good egg, or burd.*[1] Spoken of bad boys, when they become worse men. [1 chicken.]

Good enough for the parson unless the parish were better, It is.

1678 RAY 187 . . . It's here supposed that if the Parish be very bad the Parson must be in some fault, and therefore any thing is good enough for that Parson whose parishioners are bad, either by reason of his ill example, or the neglect of his duty.

Good enough is never ought.

1678 RAY 148.

Good even, good Robin Hood.

1522 SKELTON *Why not to Court* 192–4 Wks. (1843) II. 32 He sayth, How saye ye, my lords? Is nat my reason good? Good euyn, good Robyn Hood! **1879** C. W. BARDSLEY *Rom. Lond. Direct.* 61 'Good even, Robin Hood', . . . implied civility extorted by fear.

Good example is the best sermon, A.

1732 FULLER no. 146.

Good face is a letter of recommendation, A.

[PUBL. SYR. 169 *Formosa facies muta commendatio est.*] **1620** SHELTON *Quix.* II. lxiii (1908) III. 270 His beauty giving him in that instant, as it were, a letter of recommendation. **1768** STERNE *Sent. Journ.* Amiens. There was a passport in his very looks. **1771** SMOLLETT *Humph. Clink.* 11 Oct. Wks. (1871) 580 His honest countenance was a good letter of recommendation.

Good face needs no band, and a bad one deserves none, A.

1579 LYLY *Euphues* Wks. (Bond) I. 181

Where the countenance is fair there need no colours. **1639** CLARKE 131. A good face needs no band. **1678** RAY 97 . . . Some make a rhyme of this, by adding, *And a pretty wench no land.* **1738** SWIFT (Dial. i) 337 *Col.* Oh, Madam! a good face needs no band. *Miss.* No; and a bad one deserves none.

Good face on a thing, To put a.

1387 TREVISA tr. Higden (Rolls S.) vii. 25 (A) And made good face to þe eorle and semblant *c.* **1489** CAXTON *Sons of Aymon* ix. 227 Lete vs . . . bere oute a good face as longe as we ben alyve. **1867** FREEMAN *Norm. Conq.* (1876) I. iv. 231 Richer puts as good a face as he can on Hugh's discomfiture.

Good fame is better than a good face.

1721 KELLY 71. **1732** FULLER no. 150.

Good fellow is a costly name, A.

1721 KELLY 16, 17 . . . Because it requires a great deal to procure it, and more to uphold it; spoken when people urge us to spend, that we may be reckoned good fellows.

Good fellow, *see also* Longer lives g. f. than dear year.

Good finds good.

1640 HERBERT 339.

Good fish if it were but caught, It is.

1659 HOWELL *Eng. Prov.* 12/1 Good fish, but all the craft is in the catching. **1678** RAY 71 . . . It's spoken of any considerable good that one hath not, but talks much of, sues for, or endeavours after. **1732** FULLER no. 2936.

Good for the back, That which is | is bad for the head.

1670 RAY 58.

Good for the head, That which is | is evil for the neck and the shoulders.

1604 JAMES I *Counterblaste* (Arb.) 107 There is almost no sort either of nourishment or medicine, that hath not some thing in it disagreeable to mans bodie, . . . according to the olde prouerbe, That which is good for the head, is euill for the necke and the shoulders.

Good for the liver may be bad for the spleen.

1732 FULLER no. 1711.

Good fortune, *see* Ounce of g. f. worth pound of forecast.

Good Friday, *see* Eat his part on G. F.

Good friend that speaks well of us behind our backs, He is a.

1678 RAY 143. **1732** FULLER no. 2465 He's my friend that speaks well of me behind my back.

Good gear that lasts aye, It is.

c. **1384** CHAUCER *Ho. Fame* III. 57 Men seyn, what may ever laste. *c.* **1598** *MS. Provs.* in FERGUSSON 69 It is good geir quhilk lasts ay. **1602–3** SHAKS. *All's Well* II. 60 Things may serve long but not serve ever.

Good goose, do not bite.

1594–5 SHAKS. *Rom. & Jul.* II. iv. 85 Nay good goose, bite not. **1599** PORTER *Angry Wom. Abingd.* IV. iii (Merm.) 178 Good goose, bite not.

Good goose that's ay dropping, It is a.

1641 FERGUSSON 64. **1721** KELLY 190 *It's a good goose that's ay dropping.* It is a good friend that is always giving; spoken to dissuade us from too much importuning a friend.

Good hand, good hire.

1639 CLARKE 92.

Good harvest, He that hath a | may be content with some thistles.

1639 CLARKE 198. **1721** KELLY 150 *He that has a good crop, may be doing with some thistles.* If a man hath had a great deal of good conveniencies, he may bear with some misfortunes.

Good harvests make men prodigal, bad ones provident.

1611 COTGRAVE S.V. 'Année'. **1670** RAY 13.

Good health, He who hath | is young; and he is rich who owes nothing.

1707 MAPLETOFT 12. **1855** BOHN 400.

Good heart cannot lie, A.

1640 HERBERT 354.

Good heart conquers ill fortune, A.

1620 SHELTON *Quix.* II. XXXV (1908) III. 72 A good heart conquers ill fortune, as well thou knowest.

Good heed hath good hap.

[*Cf. c.* **1540** N. UDALL *Ralph Roister Doister* III. iii. 104 Good happe is not hastie.] **1638** J. CLARKE *Phraseol. Puerilis* C 7 Good heed hath as good hap. **1681** W. ROBERTSON *Phraseol. Generalis* 719 (A).

Good horse cannot be of a bad colour, A.

1653 WALTON *Angler* V It is observed by some, that 'there is no good horse of a bad colour'. **1721** KELLY 126 Horses are good of all hues. **1891** J. L. KIPLING *Beast & Man* 179 'A good horse is never of a bad colour' . . . is wildly irreverent from the Oriental point of view. **1912** *Spectator* 28 Dec. 1094 Virgil . . . did not hold that 'a good horse cannot be of a bad colour'.

Good horse oft needs a good spur, A.

1639 CLARKE 93.

Good horse should be seldom spurred, A.

1616 DRAXE 234 A running horse needeth no spurre. **1641** FERGUSSON 43 A gentle horse would not be over sair spurred. **1732** FULLER no. 156.

Good horse that never stumbles, It is a.

1530 PALSGRAVE 742 (A) He is a good horse that stumbleth nat sometyme. **1546** HEYWOOD I. viii. 16 Though it be a good hors That neuer stumbleth. **1599** PORTER *Angry Wom. Abingd.* II. ii (Merm.) 132 *Nich.* Well, 'tis a good horse never stumbles. **1670** RAY 105 It's a good horse that never stumbles: and a good wife that never grumbles. **1721** KELLY 126 *He's a good horse that never stumbled, And a better wife that never grumbled.* Both so rare, that I never met with either.

Good horses make short miles.

1640 HERBERT 360.

Good house, In a | all is quickly ready.

1611 COTGRAVE S.V. Maison'. **1640** HERBERT 319.

Good house-wife that will not wind up her bottom, She is not a.

[i.e., literally, wind up her 'bottom' or skein of yarn.] **1678** RAY 88 . . . *i.e.* take off her drink.

Good hurler[1] that's on the ditch, He is a.

1856 ABP. WHATELY *Annot. Bacon's Ess.* (1876) 495 'Lookers-on many times see more than gamesters' . . . has a parallel in an Irish proverb: 'He is a good hurler that's on the ditch.' [[1] hockey-player.]

Good husband makes a good wife, A. (Cf. Good Jack, &c.)

1616 DRAXE 233. **1621** BURTON *Anat. Mel.* III. iii. IV. i. (1836) 648 (A) For as the old saying is, a good husband makes a good wife. **1702** FARQUHAR *Inconstant* II. i (A) A good Husband makes a good Wife at any time.

Good husbandry is good divinity.

1707 MAPLETOFT 108. **1846** DENHAM 2.

Good in the maw that is sweet in the mouth, That is not always.

1579 LYLY *Euphues* Wks. (Bond) I. 313 Manye meates which are sowre in the mouth and sharpe in the mawe. **1592** G. DELAMOTHE (1647) 6 What is sweet in the mouth, is oft bitter at the heart. **1594** SHAKS. *Rape of Lucrece* 699 His taste delicious, in digestion souring. *c.* **1594** *Rich. II* I. iii. 236 Things sweet to taste prove in digestion sour. **1669** *Politeuphuia* 172 (A) What is sweet in the mouth is bitter in the stomach. **1678** RAY 174. **1732** FULLER no. 5511.

Good is good, but better carries it.

1640 HERBERT 339. **1670** RAY 148 Though good be good, yet better is better (*or* better carries it).

Good is the enemy of the best, The.

1912 J. KELMAN *Thoughts on Things Eternal* 108 Every respectable Pharisee proves the truth of the saying that 'the good is the enemy of the best'. . . . Christ insists that we shall not be content with a second-best, though it be good.

Good is to be sought out and evil attended.

1640 HERBERT 322.

Good Jack makes a good Jill, A. (Cf. Good husband, &c.)

1636 CAMDEN 291. **1670** RAY 108 . . . Inferiors imitate the manners of superiors; . . . wives of their husbands. **1876** MRS. BANKS *Manch. Man* xlvii Justifying her daughter's flight with . . . 'A good Jack makes a good Jill'.

Good judgement that relieth not wholly on his own, He hath a.

1642 TORRIANO 57. **1707** MAPLETOFT 1. **1732** FULLER no. 1882.

Good kail is half a meal (half meat).

1670 RAY 36 Good keal is half a meal. **1721** KELLY 118 *Good kail is half meat.* Good broth will, in some measure, supply the want of bread. **1732** FULLER no. 6252 (as 1670).

Good land: evil way.

1633 DONNE *Poems* (Grierson) i. 81 (A) There is best land where there is foulest way. **1640** HERBERT 354 Good land: evil way. **1653** WALTON *Angler* II. i (1915) 256 The foul way serves to justify the fertility of the soil, according to the proverb, 'There is good land where there is foul way'.

Good land where there is foul way, There is, *see* Good land: evil way.

Good language which all understand not, That is not.

1640 HERBERT 331.

Good lasses, All are | but whence come the bad wives?

1721 KELLY 19 *All are good lasses, but, where comes the ill wives from?* Nobody can blame young women for putting the best side outmost, and concealing their bad humours 'till they get husbands.

Good lawyer, *see* Lawyer.

Good life, A handful of | is better than a bushel of learning.

1640 HERBERT 317.

Good life makes a good death, A.

1592 DELAMOTHE (1647) 58 A good life

causeth a good death. **1629** *Book of Meery Riddles* Prov. 27. **1616** DRAXE 114.

Good luck, More by | than by good guiding (management).

1616 DRAXE 72 More by chance then by any good cunning. **1721** KELLY 248 . . . Spoken when a thing, ill managed, falls out well. **1852** MRS. CARLYLE *Lett.* to T. C., 10 Aug. Mazzini . . . made my hair stand on end with his projects. If he is not shot, or in an Austrian fortress within the month, it will be more by good luck than good guiding.

Good maid, but for thought, word, and deed, She is a.

1678 RAY 258.

Good man can no more harm than a sheep, A.

[*Cf.* **1546** HEYWOOD I. x. 23 She can no more harm than can a she ape.] **1614** CAMDEN 302.

Good man is from home, When the | the good wife's table is soon spread.

1678 RAY 61. **1721** KELLY 352 *When the good man's away the board cloth is tint.*[1] Because the commons will then be short. [[1] lost.]

Goodman is the last who knows what's amiss at home, The.

1658 *Comes facundus* 21. **1670** RAY 52. **1707** MAPLETOFT 106.

Goodman saith, As the | so say we; but as the good woman saith, so must it be.

1639 *Berkeley MSS.* (1885) iii. 33 (A) [with 'so it should be' for so say we']. **1670** RAY 51.

Good man thrive, If a | all thrive with him.

1640 HERBERT 349.

Good man whom fortune makes better, He is a.

1732 FULLER no. 2438.

Good man (men), *see also* Amongst g. m. two men suffice; Show a g. m. his error; Well for him who feeds g. m.

Good man's mother, *see* Breed of the g. m.'s m.

Good manners to except my Lord Mayor of London.

[**1655** FULLER *Church Hist.* III. vi (14) (A) The richest and proudest (always good manners to except Cardinal Wolsey).] **1662** FULLER (*Lond.*) II. 346 'Good manners to except my lord mayor of London'. This is a corrective for such, whose expressions are of the largest size, and too general in their extent. . . . It is

not civil to fill up all the room in our speeches of ourselves, but to leave an upper place void . . . for our betters.

Good manners to offer brains, It is not.

1738 SWIFT (Dial. ii) 346 *Lady S.* Then, madam, shall I send you the brains? I beg your ladyship's pardon; for they say, 'tis not good manners to offer brains.

Good manners to show your learning before ladies, It is not.

1738 SWIFT (Dial. ii) 347 *Never. Tace* is Latin for a candle. *Miss.* Is that manners, to show your learning before ladies.

Good manners, *see also* 'After you' is g. m.; Know g. m. but use but few (You); Nurture and g. m. maketh man. *See also* Manners.

Good memories have ill judgements.

1721 KELLY 119 . . . Spoken to them who call to mind a past thing, at an unseasonable time, or before improper company.

Good memory, He that hath a | giveth few alms.

1662 FULLER (*Devon*) I. 408 The Welch have a proverb . . . 'He that hath a good memory, giveth few alms'; because he keepeth in mind what and to whom he had given before.

Good men (folks) are scarce.

1638 D. TUVIL *Vade Mecum* (3rd ed.) 96 (A). **1660** TATHAM *Rump* II. i *Lady Bert.* Could you find no better company? 1 *Lady.* Good men were scarce. **1721** KELLY 124 *Good folks are scarce, you'll take care of one.* Spoken to those who carefully provide against ill weather, or cowardly shun dangers. **1738** SWIFT (Dial. i) 336 Come, come, miss, make much of nought; good folks are scarce. **1821** SCOTT *Pirate* v Triptolemus . . . knew good people were scarce, . . . and had . . . that wisdom which looks towards self-preservation as the first law of nature.

Good morrow, *see* Sheep and a cow (Now I have) everybody bids g. m.

Good mother says not, Will you? but gives, The.

1640 HERBERT 339.

Good name keeps its lustre in the dark, A.

1664 CODRINGTON 184. **1670** RAY 18.

Good name, *see also* Born in a good hour who gets g. n.; Take away my g. n. take away life.

Good neighbour, A | a good morrow.

c. **1470** *Harl. MS. 116* in *Rel. Antiq.* I. 316 He that hath a good neyghboure hath a good morowe. **1594** *Mirr. Policy* (1599) Oiij The common proverb saith, That who so hath a

good neighbour, hath a good morrow. **1598–9**
SHAKS. *Hen. V* IV. i. 6 Our bad neighbour
makes us early stirrers. **1670** RAY 124 A
good neighbour, a good good-morrow.

Good news may be told at any time, but ill in the morning.

1640 HERBERT 357.

Good news, *see also* Brings g. n. (He that)
knocks hard.

Good night(s), *see* Many G. n. is loth away.

Good or ill hap of a good or ill life, is the good or ill choice of a good or ill wife.

1721 KELLY 331. **1732** FULLER no. 6413.

Good orator who convinces himself, He is a.

1707 MAPLETOFT 16. **1855** BOHN 374.

Good painter can draw a devil as well as an angel, A.

1592 DELAMOTHE (1647) 56. **1639** CLARKE
311.

Good payer is master of another's purse, A.

1640 HERBERT 345.

Good paymaster needs no surety, A.

1620 SHELTON *Quix.* II. xiv (1908) II. 274 A
staid voice answered and said: 'A good paymaster needs no surety.' **1640** HERBERT 322
A good paymaster starts not at assurances.

Good pedigrees, In | there are governors and chandlers.

1640 HERBERT 327.

Good reason and part cause.

1721 KELLY 122. *Good reason, and part of
cause.* An ironical approbation of some foolish
saying, action, or design. **1862** HISLOP 108.
1902–4 LEAN III. 475 Good reason and part
cause.—Quoted by Dean Church . . . (1887)
as a subtle Scotch proverb, meaning that the
good reasons for a decision are often only
part of the cause of its being adopted.

Good riding at two anchors, men have told, for if one break the other may hold.

[PROPERTIUS 3. 13. 41 *Nam melius duo
defendunt retinacula navim.*] **1550** HEYWOOD
II. ix. 76 Good ridyng at two ankers men
haue tolde, For if the tone faile, the tother
maie holde. **1579** LYLY *Euphues* (Arb.) 116
It is safe riding at two ankers. **1599–1600**
SHAKS. *Twelfth N.* I. v. 25 *Clo.* I am resolved
on two points. *Mat.* That if one break, the
other will hold.

Good ruler, No man can be a | unless he hath first been ruled.

1539 TAVERNER 2 *Nemo bene imperat, nisi qui*

paruerit imperio. No man can be a good ruler,
onles he hath bene first ruled.

Good saver is a good server, A.

1598 R. CLEAVER *A Godly Form of Household
Government* 76–90 A good saver is as good
as a good getter [L. B. WRIGHT *Middle-class
Culture* 212]. **1678** RAY 350.

Good service is a great enchantment.

1616 DRAXE 186 No such enchantment as a
good seruice. **1640** HERBERT 330.

Good shape is in the shears' mouth, A.

1721 KELLY 46. **1855** BOHN 289.

Good shepherd must fleece his sheep, not flay them, A.

[SUET. *Tib.* 32 fin. *Boni pastoris est tondere
pecus, non deglubere.*] **1539** TAVERNER 48
It is the parte of a good shepherde or pastor
to sheare the shepe and nat to plucke of theyr
skynes. **1616** WITHALS 553 A good shepheard
must take the fleece, and not the fel. **1616**
DRAXE 148.

Good small beer, good brown bread, or a good old woman, There is no such thing as. (*Cf.* Good things I do not love.)

1738 SWIFT (Dial. ii) 345 *Col.* Pray, friend,
give me a glass of small beer, if it be good.
Smart. Why, colonel, they say there is no
such thing as good small beer, good brown
bread, or a good old woman.

Good spear, He that hath a | let him try it.

1573 SANDFORD (1576) 208. **1578** FLORIO *First
Fruites* f. 28 (A) (with 'prove it against a wal'
for 'try it'). **1629** *Book of Meery Riddles*
Prov. 74.

Good sport that fills the belly, That is.

1721 KELLY 190. **1732** FULLER no. 4354.

Good swimmers at length are drowned.

1611 COTGRAVE s.v. 'Nageur' Good swimmers
at the length feed Haddocks. **1640** HERBERT
354. **1907** *Illust. Lond. News* 1 June He was
a strong swimmer; but, as the Eastern
proverb has it, 'The fate of the swimmer is to
be taken by the sea'.

Good that are away, They are aye.

1721 KELLY 338 . . . Spoken when people
lavishly commend those of their friends that
are abroad or dead.

Good that does me good, That is my.

1639 CLARKE 109 That's good that doth us
good. **1678** RAY 148.

Good that failed never, He is.

1641 FERGUSSON 42. **1721** KELLY 163 . . . A
persuasion to bear the neglects of a friend

who has, on other occasions, been beneficial to you.

Good that he is good for nothing, So.

1607–12 BACON *Ess., Goodness* (Arb.) 200 The *Italians* haue an vngracious proverbe *Tanto buon che val niente, So good that he is good for Nothinge.* **1639** CLARKE 78 So good as good for nothing. **1738** SWIFT (Dial. ii) 348 *Lady S.* How do you like these preserved oranges? *Lady A.* . . . They are too good. *Lady S.* O, madam, I have heard 'em say, that too good is stark naught. **1871** SMILES *Character* 301 It is still . . . the practice to cultivate the weakness of woman rather than her strength. . . . She incurs the risk of becoming the embodiment of the Italian proverb—'so good that she is good for nothing'.

Good that knows not why he is good, He cannot be.

c. **1580** SIDNEY (First) *Arcadia* (Feuillerat) iv. 5 Hee can not bee good, that knowes not whye hee ys good. **1602** CAREW *Survey of Cornwall* (1769) 87. **1732** FULLER no. 1819.

Good that mends, It is.

1721 KELLY 205 . . . Spoken when we hear that a person, or thing, is better, or does better.

Good thing cheap, He will never have a | that is afraid to ask the price.

1616 DRAXE 4. **1670** RAY 56 He'st ne're have thing good cheap, that's afraid to ask the price. Il n'aura ja[mais] bon marché qui ne le demande [pas]. *Gall.*

Good thing is soon caught up, A.

1611 COTGRAVE s.v. 'Beau' A goodly thing is quickly snatched up. **1664** CODRINGTON 184 (with 'snatch'd' for 'caught'). **1670** RAY 12 (as 1664). **1732** FULLER no. 181.

Good things are hard.

[Gk. Χαλεπὰ τὰ καλά. Attributed to Solon and Pittacus; Socrates quotes as an old proverb (PL. *Crat.* 1. 384 A).] **1603** HOLLAND tr. *Plutarch's Morals* 6 Whatsoever is faire and goodly, the same also is hard and difficult. **1664** JOS. MEDE Wks. I. Gen. Pref. That all excellent things are hard, is so confessed a truth, that it has passed into a vulgar proverb. **1853** TRENCH vi. 136 With the proverb, *Good things are hard,* [Socrates] continually rebuked their empty pretensions; and made suspicious at least their delusive promises.

Good things I do not love; Some | a good long mile, good small beer, and a good old woman.

1678 RAY 148.

Good time coming, There is a.

1818 SCOTT *Rob Roy* xxxii 'I could have wished it had been . . . when I could have better paid the compliments I owe your Grace;—but there's a gude time coming'.

1851 KINGSLEY *Yeast* xvii Your very coster-monger trolls out his belief that 'there's a good time coming'.

Good tither, a good thriver, A.

1678 RAY 352. *Somerset.*

Good to be good in your time, for you know not how long it will last, It is.

1721 KELLY 193 . . . Spoken to those who are now in credit, power, and authority; that they should not be proud or insolent; for they may meet with a change.

Good to be in the dark as without light, It is as.

1670 RAY 77.

Good to be sent for sorrow (*or* to fetch sorrow), You are.

1670 RAY 194 Good to fetch a sick man sorrow and a dead man woe. *Chesh.* KELLY 379 *You are good to be sent for sorrow.* Spoken to them who tarry long when they are sent an errand. *Ibid.* 122 Good to fetch sorrow to a sick wife. **1738** SWIFT (Dial. i) (A) You are fit to be sent for sorrow, you stay so long by the way. **1917** BRIDGE He's good to fetch a sick man sorrow and a dead man woe. There are plenty of people ready to convey sorrowful tidings. It also applies to anyone going about his business in a lazy or slovenly manner.

Good to fetch the devil a priest, You are.

1721 KELLY 379 . . . Spoken to them who tarry long when they are sent an errand.

Good tongue is a good weapon, A.

1721 KELLY 8. **1732** FULLER no. 180.

Good tongue, Who has not a | ought to have good hands.

1816 RAY 166.

Good tongue that says no ill, and a better heart that thinks none, It is a.

1721 KELLY 222 . . . Used when we have no inclination to speak our minds freely, concerning courts, or great men.

Good trade, He that hath no | it is to his loss.

1640 HERBERT 343.

Good trade, Who hath a | through all waters may wade.

1659 HOWELL *Fr.-Eng.* 23 He that hath a good trade will have his share. **1732** FULLER no. 2386 He who hath a trade hath a share every where. **1855** BOHN 566.

Good tree is a good shelter, A.

1674 J. SMITH, *Grammatica Quadrilinguis* 205

He that leans on a good Tree, a good shadow covers him. *i.e.* It is good to have a great mans Protection. **1732** FULLER no. 182.

Good tree that hath neither knap[1] nor gaw,[2] It is a.

1721 KELLY 218 . . . There is nothing altogether perfect. [[1] knob. [2] want, blemish.]

Good tune played on an old fiddle, There's many a.

1903 S. BUTLER, *Way of All Flesh*, ch. 61. **1917** BRIDGE 117.

Good (Ill, Shrewd) turn asks (deserves, requires) another, One.

c. **1400** MS. *Latin 394, John Rylands Libr.* (ed. Pantin) in *Bull. J. R. Libr.* XIV 92 O good turne asket another. **1509** A. BARCLAY *Ship of Fools* (1874) II. 38 One yll turne requyreth, another be thou sure. **1550** HEYWOOD I. xi. 34 One good tourne askth an other. **1602** *Lord Cromwell* II. ii (*Shaks. Apoc.*) 172 *Hod.* As indeede one good turn asketh another. **1612–15** BP. HALL *Contempl.* XIV. ii (1825) I. 408 One good turn requires another. . . . David's soldiers were Nabal's shepherds; . . . justly should they have been set at the upper end of the table. **1654** H. L'ESTRANGE *Chas. I* (1655) 15 One good turn deserves another. **1670** RAY 20 One shrewd turn asks another. **1824** SCOTT *St. Ronans* xvii But one good turn deserves another—in that case, you must . . . dine with me. **1894** STEVENSON & OSBOURNE *Ebb-Tide* i 'One good turn deserves another . . . Say the word and you can have a cruise upon the carpet.'

Good turn, He that will do thee a | either he will be gone or die.

1651 HERBERT 367.

Good turn, One | will meet another, if it were at the Bridge of London.

1721 KELLY 275 . . . Spoken by them who make a return for former favours.

Good turn, *see also* Loses by doing g. t. (One never).

Good ware makes quick markets.

[PLAUTUS *Poenulus* 1. 2. 128 *Proba merx facile emptorem repperit.* Good wares easily find a buyer.] **1611** COTGRAVE S.V. 'Marchand' Good chaffer cannot want a chapman. **1611** DRAXE 226 Good ware maketh good markets. **1616** BRETON *Cross. Prov.* (1879) II. App. iii Good ware makes quick markets.

Good watch prevents misfortune.

1591–2 SHAKS. *1 Hen. VI* II. i. 58 Had your watch been good, This sudden mischief never could have fall'n. **1611** COTGRAVE S.V. 'Bon' Good watch prevents misfortune. **1664** CODRINGTON 194. **1670** RAY 28.

Good wife and health is a man's best wealth, A.

1721 KELLY 31. **1732** FULLER no. 6313.

Good wife in the country, There is one | and every man thinks he hath her.

1620 SHELTON *Quix.* II. xxii (1908) II. 334 It was an opinion of I know not what sage man, that there was but one good woman in the world; and . . . that every man should think, that was married, that his wife was she. **1670** RAY 49. **1738** SWIFT (Dial. i) 342 *Lady S.* They say, that every married man should believe there's but one good wife in the world, and that's his own. **1852** MRS. CARLYLE *Let.* to T. Carlyle 24 Jul. Kingsley told me about his wife—that she was 'the adorablest wife man ever had!'

Good wife makes a good husband, A.

1546 HEYWOOD II. viii. 72 A good wife makth a good husbande, (they saie). **1614** CAMDEN 302.

Good wife's a goodly prize, Saith Solomon the wise, A.

1678 RAY 58.

Good wife's away, When the | the keys are tint.[1]

1721 KELLY 352 . . . For if she be not at home you'll get no drink. [[1] lost.]

Good will, One ought to have (show).

c. **1300** *Havelok* 600 (Skeat) 19 For man shal god wille haue.

Good will, With as | as e'er boy came from school.

1593–4 SHAKS. *Tam. Shrew* III. ii. 153 *Tra.* Signior Gremio, came you from the church? *Gre.* As willingly as e'er I came from school. **1639** CLARKE 186.

Good will, *see also* Killed her for g. w.; Welcome (G. w.) is the best cheer.

Good wind that blows a man to the wine, It is a.

1594 LYLY *Moth. Bomb.* II. v. Wks. (1892) II. 100 *Stel.* It was an olde proverbe, when his great-grandfather was a childe, that it was a good wind that blew a man to the wine.

Good wine engendreth good blood.

1568 G. B. GELLI *Fearful Fancies of the Florentine Cooper* tr. W. Barker C 7[V] with 'Good drink'. *c.* **1584** LYLY *Alex. & Campaspe* V. iii. 12 Good drinke makes good bloud. **1594** NASHE *Unfort. Trav.* Wks. (McKerrow) II. 308 Good drinke makes good blood. **1597–8** SHAKS. *2 Hen. IV* IV. iii. 94 This same young sober-blooded boy doth not love me; . . . but that's no marvel, he drinks no wine. **1598–9** *Much Ado* I. i. 261 Prove that ever I lose more blood with love than I will get again with drinking. **1616** DRAXE 236.

Good wine needs no bush.

[A bunch of ivy was the sign of a vintner's shop.] *c.* **1426** LYDGATE *Pilgr. Life of Man*

l. 20415 And at tavernys (with-outĕ wene)
Thys tooknys nor thys bowys grene, . . .
The wyn they mende nat. **1539** TAVERNER
F 2ᵛ (1552, 42). Wyne that is saleable & good
nedeth no bushe or garlande of yuye to be
hanged before. **1579** LYLY *Euphues* (Arb.)
204 Where the wine is neat, there needeth no
Iuie-bush. **1599–1600** SHAKS. *A.Y.L.* Epil.
If it be true that good wine need no bush, 'tis
true, that a good play needs no epilogue.
1623 CAMDEN 269 Good wine needes no Iuybush. **1641** FERGUSSON 34 Good wine needs
not a wispe. **1674** R. GODFREY *Inj. & Ab.
Physic* 168 As good Wine needs no Bush, no
more do good Medicines a printed Bill. **1845**
FORD *Handbk. Spain* I. 30 Good wine needs
neither bush, herald, nor crier.

Good winter brings a good summer, A.

1616 DRAXE 12. **1670** RAY 29.

Good wit, Such a one hath a | if a wise man had the keeping of it.

1636 CAMDEN 305.

Good wits jump.

1659 HOWELL *Eng. Prov.* 17/1 Good wits
commonly jump. **1688** SHADWELL *Squire Als.*
III. i Say'st thou so my girl! good wits jump.
I had the same thought with thee. **1738**
SWIFT (Dial. i) 340 *Miss.* Well, I had that at
my tongue's end. *Lady A.* Why, miss, they
say good wits jump. **1760–7** STERNE *T.
Shandy* liii Great wits jump.

Good word costs no more than a bad one, A.

1692 L'ESTRANGE *Aesop's Fab.* (1738) cclxxvi.
292 *A good word*, they say, *costs no more than
a bad.* **1732** FULLER no. 1735.

Good words and ill deeds deceive wise and fools. (Cf. Fair words and foul deeds, &c.)

1601 T. WRIGHT *The Passions of the Mind* 141
Wordes good, and workes ill, Makes fooles
and wisemen leese their skill. **1611** DAVIES
Prov. 228.

Good words anoint us, and ill do unjoint us.

1573 SANDFORD (1576) 216 Good wordes doe
annointe, the shrewde doe pricke. **1578** FLORIO
First Fruites f. 31 (A) Good woords annoynt
a man, the yl woordes kyl a man. **1611** DAVIES
Prov. 72.

Good words are good cheap.

1639 CLARKE 194.

Good words cool more than cold water.

1616 DRAXE 241 A good word doeth coole
more then a cauldron of water. **1640** HERBERT
329 Good words quench more than a bucket
of water. **1670** RAY 158.

Good words cost nought.

1542 SIR T. WYATT *Throughout the world* Fair
words . . . be good cheap, they cost right
nought. **1599** PORTER *Angry Wom. Abingd.*
IV. iii (Merm.) 175 Good words cost nought.
1640 HERBERT 324 Good words are worth
much, and cost little. **1721** KELLY 124 . . .
And therefore may be the freelier given.

Good words fill not a sack.

1678 RAY 220. **1732** FULLER no. 1737.

Good words without deeds are rushes and reeds.

1659 HOWELL *Eng. Prov.* 17/1. **1670** RAY 30.
1732 FULLER no. 6247.

Good workmen are seldom rich.

1640 HERBERT 352.

Good world, It is a | but they are ill that are on it.

1721 KELLY 191 . . . The word World is sometimes taken for the universe, and sometimes
for mankind; in the first sense it is good, in
the second bad.

Good world, if it hold, It is a.

1721 KELLY 191 . . . Spoken to them who
take their ease and pleasure now, without
respect to their future condition.

Good years corn is hay, In | in ill years straw is corn.

1640 HERBERT 327.

Good (*adj.*), *see also* All g., and God say Amen;
All things are g. unseyit; All women are
g.; Breed of Lady Mary, when you're g.
you're o'er g.; Every one is weary, the g.
in learning; Everything is g. in season;
Evil manners (Of), g. laws; Friar never
loved what was g.; George-a-Green (G. as);
No man so g. but another as g.; Nothing
but is g. for something; Presumed g. till
found in fault; Some g., some bad, as
sheep; Tale ill told is marred (G.); Tale
is none the worse twice told (G.); Too g.
is stark naught; Too g. to be true. Year
(A g.) will not make him.

Good(s) (*noun*), *see also* Better g. afar off;
Bode g. and get it; Conceited g. quickly
spent; Do g., thou doest it for thyself;
Does no g. (He who) does evil; Evils have
their comfort, g. none can support; Ill
that doth not hurt (So great is) as the g.
that doth not help; Ill-gotten g.; Little g.
comes of gathering; Little g. soon spent;
Little g. to stark nought; Man far from his
g. is near harm; Man has no more g. than
gets g. of; No man better knows what g. is;
Plenty of g. (He that hath) shall have
more; See no g. near home (Some can);
Swine (He is like), never do g. while he lives.

Good, It is, *see also under significant words
following.*

Goodness is not tied to greatness.

1631 WM. FOSTER *Hoplocrisma Spongus* **A4** Better is goodnesse without greatnesse, than greatnesse without goodnesse. **1639** CLARKE 226 Greatness and goodnesse goe not alwey together. **1655** T. MUFFETT *Healths Improvement* 161 (A) As the Greek proverb saith, Goodness is not tied to greatness, but greatness to goodness.

Goodness of a horse goes in at his mouth, The.

1861 G. J. WHYTE-MELVILLE *Inside the Bar* iv The Arabs . . . have a saying, that 'the goodness of a horse goes in at his mouth', and it is incredible . . . what improvement may be made in the animal by . . . old oats and exercise.

Goods are theirs that enjoy them.

1578 FLORIO *First Fruites* f. 31 (A) The ware is not his that gathers it, but his that enjoyes it. **1579** SPENSER *Shep. Cal.* May Wks. (Globe) 459 Good is no good, but if it be spend. **1603** FLORIO tr. *Montaigne* I. xlii (1897) II. 160 Whatsoever the goods of fortune are, a man must have a proper sense to savour them: it is the enjoying and not the possessing of them, that makes us happy. **1640** HERBERT 356.

Goods, see also Good(s).

Goodwin Sands,[1] To set up shop upon.

1550 HEYWOOD II. ix. 76 But you leaue all anker holde, on seas or lands. And so set vp shop vpon Goodwins sands. **1678** RAY 72 Let him set up shop on Goodwins sands. This is a piece of country wit; there being an equivoq; in the word *Good-win*, which is a surname, and also signifies gaining wealth. **1748** FRANKLIN May Sell-cheap kept shop on Goodwin Sands, and yet had store of custom. [1 Sandbanks off the coast of Kent, exposed at low water.]

Goodwin Sands, see also Tenterden steeple.

Goodyer's pig, Like | never well but when he is doing mischief.

1670 RAY 209. *Cheshire.*

Goodyer, see also Come again, as G.'s pigs did.

Goom, see Soon in the g. quick in womb.

Goose and gander and gosling, are three sounds but one thing.

1659 HOWELL *Span.–Eng.* 20. **1678** RAY 148.

Goose cannot graze after him, A.

1611 CHAPMAN *May-Day* III. i. Plays (1889) 290 The pasture is so bare with him that a goose cannot graze upon't. **1670** RAY 178.

Goose so grey in the lake, There is no | that cannot find a gander for her make.[1]

c. **1386** CHAUCER *W. of Bath's Prol.* 269 Ne noon so grey a goos gooth in the lake, As,

selstow, wol been withouté make. **1594** LYLY *Moth. Bomb.* III. iv. Wks. (1902) III. 200 *Half.* He loues thee well that would run after. *Rix.* Why, *Halfpenie*, there's no goose so gray in the lake, that cannot finde a gander for her make. **1883** J. PAYN *Thicker than W.* i She was . . . by no means averse to a third experience in matrimony. 'There swam no goose so gray', they were wont to quote. [1 mate.]

Goose that comes to the fox's sermon, It is a blind (silly).

1580 LYLY *Euph. & his Eng.* (Arb.) 327 It is . . . a blinde Goose that commeth to the Foxes sermon, *Euphues* is not entangled with *Philautus* charmes. **1584** GREENE *Arbast's Anatomy of Fortune* Wks. (Gros.) III. 208 It is . . . a blind goose that runneth to the foxe's sermon. **1732** FULLER no. 2881 It is a silly goose that comes to a fox's sermon.

Goose that will eat no oats, Young (or Old) is the.

1580 LYLY *Euph. & his Eng.* (Arb.) 366 Truely *Camilla* I haue heard, that young is the Goose yat wil eate no Oates. **1591** Id. *Endym.* v. ii *Epi.* Why she is so cold, that no fire can thaw her thoughts. *Top.* It is an old goose, Epi, that will eat no oats. **1732** FULLER no. 6037 Young is the Goose, that will not eat Oats.

Goose that will not baste herself, It is a sorry.

1670 RAY 218. **1732** FULLER no. 2886.

Goose, He that has a | will get a goose.

1721 KELLY 132 . . . A man that is wealthy, will be sure to get gifts, whereas he that is poor will remain so.

Goose, geese, see Before St. Chad every g. lays; Calf, the g., bee, world is ruled by; Children to bed and g. to fire; Cook anyone's g.; Deep drinketh g.; Eat of the g. that shall graze on your grave; Eats the king's g. (He that); Feather by feather g. is plucked; Find fault with fat g.; Fox to keep the g. (Sets); Fox should not be of jury at g.'s trial; Good g., do not bite; Good g. that's ay dropping; Gosling flew . . . and came back g.; Goslings lead the g. to grass; Kill the g. that lays golden eggs; Know a g. from a gridiron; Macfarlane's g. that liked play better than meat; Man among the g. when gander away; Many women, many words, many g. . . .; Rain raineth and g. winketh (When), little wots gosling . . .; Reason pist my g. (Such a); Sauce for the g.; Say *bo* to a g.; See a woman weep (No more pity) than g. go barefoot; Shoe the g.; Skill in horseflesh to buy g.; Steal a g. and give giblets; —— and stick down feather; Tittle-tattle, give the g. more hay; Valentine's Day will good g. lay; Walsall man's g.; Widecombe folk are picking g.; Wild g.; Winchester g.; Wise as a g.; Women and g. (Where) wants no noise.

Goose giblet(s), *see* Hare's head against the g.g. (Set the).

Goose's eye, *see* Meat in a g. e.

Gooseberry, *see* Jump at it like cock at g.

Gordian knot, To cut the (*or* a).

[An intricate knot tied by Gordius, a Phrygian king. Whoever loosed it was to rule Asia, so Alexander the Great cut it through with his sword. The phrase means to get rid of a difficulty by force or by evading the supposed conditions of solution. ERASM. *Ad.* 1. 9. 48.] **1579** FULKE *Heskin's Parl.* 396 Hee had found out a sworde to cutt in sunder this Gordian knot. **1598-9** SHAKS. *Hen. V* I. i. 46 Turn him to any cause of policy, The Gordian knot of it he will unloose. **1682** SIR T. BROWNE *Chr. Mor.* II, § 13 Death will find some ways to unty or cut the most Gordian knots of Life. **1841** S. WARREN *Ten Thous. a Year* iii Suicide ... is a way ... of cutting the Gordian knot of the difficulties of life.

Gordon(s), *see* Miscall a G. in raws of Strathlogie; Tender G. that dow not be hanged.

Gorse is out of bloom, When the | kissing's out of fashion. (*Cf.* Furze is in bloom, &c.)

c. **1225** *Trin. MS. O. 11. 45* (ed. Förster) in *Eng. Stud.* **31.** 5 Whanne bloweþ þe brom, þanne wogeþ þe grom; Whanne bloweþ þe furs, þanne wogeþ he wurs. *Lixa uel opilio procus est florente mirica; Rusco florente minus hic gaudebit amica.* **1752** *Poor Robin's Alm.* Aug. Dog-days are in he'll say's the reason why kissing now is out of season: but *Joan* says furz in bloom is still, And she'll be kissed if she's her will. **1847** DENHAM 12 When whins are out of bloom, kissing's out of fashion. Whins are *never* out of bloom. **1860** G. J. WHYTE-MELVILLE *Holmby H.* ii 'When the gorse is out of bloom, young ladies', quoth Sir Giles, 'then is kissing out of fashion!' ... There is no day in the year when the blossom is off the gorse.

Goshawk beats[1] not at a bunting,[2] A.

1616 WITHALS 556. **1639** CLARKE 69. [[1] flies. [2] woodlark.]

Gosling flew over the Rhine and came back a goose, A.

1929 DEAN INGE *Assessments* 220 As a German proverb says: 'A gosling flew over the Rhine and came back a goose.' Leisure is necessary for wisdom; and the faster we travel, the less leisure we have.

Goslings lead the geese to grass (water).

[**1640** OUDIN *Curios. franç.* 398 Les oisons veulent mener paistre leur mère (The goslings would lead their mother out to grass).] **1642** TORRIANO 60 Goslings haue the geese to watering. **1732** FULLER no. 1740 Goslins lead the geese to water.

Gosling(s), *see also* May-day is ... gone, thou art a g.; Rain raineth (When the) ... little wots the g.; Shoe the g.

Gospel, With the | one becomes a heretic.

1666 TORRIANO 81 With the Gospel sometimes a body becomes an Heretick. **1853** TRENCH iii. 56 How curious ... the confession ... that the maintenance of the Roman system and the study of Holy Scripture cannot go together. ... *With the Gospel one becomes a heretic.*[1] [[1] *Con l'Evangelo si diventa eretico.*]

Gospel, All is (*or* is not) | that comes out of (his) mouth.

a. **1250** *Owl & Night* 1268 For thi seide Alfred swithe wel And his worde was godd spel, That [&c.]. *c.* **1374** CHAUCER *Troylus* v. 1265 God wot I wende ... That every word was gospel that ye seyde. *c.* **1386** Id. *Leg. Good Women* G. 326 Al ne is nat gospel that is to yow pleyned. *c.* **1400** *Rom. Rose* l. 7609 Alle is not gospel oute of doute, that men seyn in the towne aboute. **1546** HEYWOOD II. ii. 46 Gospell in thy mouth (quoth he) this strife to breake. How be it, all is not gospell that thou doest speake. **1579** LYLY *Euphues* (Arb.) 67 Philautus thinking ... all to be gospel that *Euphues* uttered. **1670** RAY 178. **1880** E. A. FREEMAN in *Life & Lett.* (1895) II. 467 I ... don't take as Gospel either all that you say or all that the *Beamish boys* say.

Gospel, *see also* True (Sooth) as g.

Gossips are frogs, they drink and talk.

1640 HERBERT 330.

Gossip(s), *see also* Merry when g. meet; Up to one's g.

Got over the devil's back is spent under his belly, What is.

1600 J. BAXTER *A Toile for Two-Legged Foxes* 188 As it hath been gotten ouer the deuills backe, so shall it be spent vnder his dammes belly. **1607** MIDDLETON *Mich. Term* IV. i *Quo* What's got over the devil's back (that's by knavery), must be spent under his belly (that's by lechery). **1670** RAY 80 What is gotten over the *Devil's* back, is spent under his belly. *Malè parta male dilabuntur.* What is got by oppression or extortion is many times spent in riot and luxury. **1821** SCOTT *Pirate* xxxi You shall not prevail on me to go farther in the devil's road with you; for ... what is got over his back is spent—you wot how.

Gotham, *see* Wise as a man of G.

Gout, With respect to the | the physician is but a lout.

1666 TORRIANO 107 In the gout the Physician sees no cure. **1855** BOHN 31 ... *Span.*

Gout, *see also* Drink wine and have the g.; Pain like g. (No); Patience and flannel for the g.

Government(s), *see* Fools exult when g. change.

Government stroke, *see* Work with G. s.

Gowk, *see* Breed of the g. (cuckoo), ye have not a rhyme but ane; See the g. in your sleep.

Gown is his that wears it, and the world his that enjoys it, The.

1573 SANDFORD (1576) 216 The gowne is not his that maketh it, but his that enioyeth it. 1640 HERBERT 340. 1736 BAILEY *Dict.* s.v. 'World'.

Gown(s), *see also* Best g. that goes up and down house; Fair woman and a slashed g.; Green g.; Look to a g. of gold; Maid oft seen and g. oft worn; Puts on a public g. (He that).

Grace of a gray bannock is in the baking of it, The.

1721 KELLY 303 . . . The setting out of an ordinary thing to best advantage will make it look well.

Grace of God is (gear) enough, The.

1377 LANGLAND *P. Pl.* B. ix. 176 And thanne gete ȝe the grace of god . and good ynogh to lyue with. 1590 SPENSER *F. Q.* I. x. 38 The grace of God he laid up still in store . . . He had enough. 1596–7 SHAKS. *Merch. V.* II. ii. 166 The old proverb is very well parted between my master Shylock and you, sir: you have the grace of God, sir, and he hath enough. 1641 FERGUSSON 100 The grace of God is gear enough.

Grace of God is worth a fair, The.

c. 1350 *Douce MS. 52* no. 41 The grace of God is better þen. iii. feyrys. 1546 HEYWOOD I. xii. 38 Though eueryman may not syt in the chayre. Yet alwaie the grace of God is woorth a fayre. 1616 DRAXE 82.

Grace of God, *see also* O Master Vier . . . we had no g. of G., no shipwreck upon our coast.

Grace will last, favour (beauty) will blast.

c. 1450 *Prouerbis of Wysdom* 28 Owte take grace all thyng shall passe. 1639 CLARKE 119 Grace will last, favour will blast. 1732 FULLER no. 6292 (with 'beauty').

Grace, *see also* Divine g. never slow; Pride and g. dwelt never in one place; Seek g. at graceless face; Space cometh g. (In); Whoredom and g. ne'er in one place.

Grafting on a good stock, It is good.

1678 RAY 354. 1732 FULLER no. 5082.

Grafts be very good, Let the | or the knife be where it stood.

1855 BOHN 441.

Grain by grain, and the hen fills her belly.

1653 MIDDLETON & ROWLEY *Span. Gipsy* II. i

(A) Grain picked up after grain makes pullen fat. 1732 FULLER no. 1744.

Grain, One | fills not a sack, but helps his fellow.

1640 HERBERT 327. 1855 BOHN 529. Though one grain fills not the sack, it helps.

Grain of salt, To take a thing with a.

[mod. L. *cum grano salis* = to accept a statement with a certain amount of reserve.] 1647 TRAPP *Comm. Rev.* vi. 11 This is to be taken with a grain of salt. 1908 *Athenaeum* 1 Aug. 118/1 Our reasons for not accepting the author's pictures of early Ireland without many grains of salt.

Grains of allowance, He must have his.

1678 RAY 248.

Grain(s), *see also* Against the g.; Evil g. (Of) no good seed.

Gramercy, *see* Godamercy.

Grampus, To puff and blow like a.

1826 SCOTT *Woodst.* xxxiv The bulky Corporal . . . puffed and blew like a grampus that has got into shoal water.

Grandame, *see* Teach your g. to grope ducks; ——to sup sour milk.

Grandfather's servants are never good.

1732 FULLER no. 1745.

Grandmother, *see* Teach your g.

Grange, *see* Bring an abbey to a g.

Grantham gruel, nine grits and a gallon of water.

1662 FULLER (*Lincs.*) II. 269 'Grantham gruel, nine grits and a gallon of water'. . . . The proverb is applicable to those who in their speeches or actions multiply what is superfluous.

Grantham steeple stand awry, It is height makes.

1591 *Simon Smell-Knave* C 1 Grantam steeple by the assistance of learned Masons, may perhappes be taught to holde uppe his head manly againe. 1638 BRATHWAIT *Barnabees Jrnl.* iii Thence to Grantham I retiring, Famous for a Spire aspiring. 1647 CLEVELAND *Elegy on Archb. of Canterbury.* 'Tis height makes Grantham steeple stand awry. 1662 FULLER (*Lincs.*) II. 268 ''Tis height[1] makes Grantham steeple stand awry'. This steeple seems crooked unto the beholders . . . though some conceive the slenderness at such a distance is all the obliquity thereof. Eminency exposeth the uprightest persons to exception; and such who cannot find faults in them, will find faults at them, envying their advancement. 1732 FULLER no. 5086. [1 280 ft.]

Granville, *see* Never a G. wanted loyalty.

Grapes are sour, The.

[Said proverbially with allusion to Æsop's fable of 'The Fox and the Grapes'.] 1484 CAXTON *Fables of Æsop* iv. 1 [The fox] sayd these raysyns ben sowre. 1602–3 SHAKS. *All's Well* II. i. 73 O! will you eat no grapes, my royal fox? Yes, but you will my noble grapes an if My royal fox could reach them. 1629 T. ADAMS *Works* 69 The foxe dispraiseth the grapes he cannot reach. 1640 HERBERT 323 The fox, when he cannot reach the grapes, says, They are not ripe. 1721 KELLY 287 *Soure plumbs quoth the tod,[1] when he could not climb the tree.* 1857 TROLLOPE *Barch. Tow.* xlvi Mr. S. . . . said, as plainly as a look could speak, that the grapes were sour. [1 fox.]

Grape(s), *see also* Black plum (g.) sweet as white; Devil in every berry of g.; Woman that loves to be at window like bunch of g.

Grasp all, lose all.

c. 1205 LAYAMON *Brut* (Madden) I. 278 For þe mon is muchel sot: þe nimeð to him-seoluen Mare þonne he maȝen waldë. *c.* 1386 CHAUCER *Mel.* B² 2405 For the proverbe seith, He that to muche embraceth, distrey-neth litel. 1790 TRUSLER *Prov. Exempl.* 189 *Grasp all, lose all.* The known fable of the Dog and the Shadow is a true emblem of covetousness. 1901 R. G. MOULTON *Shaks. as Dram. Art.* 46 Proverbs like 'Grasp all, lose all', . . . exactly express moral equilibrium. [Fr. *Qui trop embrasse mal étreint.*]

Grass grows not upon the highway (at the market cross).

1659 HOWELL *Brit.-Eng.* 24 In market grows no grass or grain. 1678 RAY 149 Grass grows not upon the high way. 1721 KELLY 309 *There grows no grass at the market cross.* An invective against the barrenness of whores.

Grass grows on his (my) heel, No.

1553 UDALL *Royster D.* iv. v (Arb.) 67 *Tru.* Ye are a slow goer sir . . . Maistresse since I went no grasse hath growne on my hele. 1580 LYLY *Euph. & his Eng.* (Arb.) 240 There will . . . no grasse hang on [the] heeles of *Mercury.* 1737 RAMSAY 24 He'll no let Grass grow at his Heels.

Grass grows, While the | the horse starves.

[Simeon of Chieti 1243: *Timemus ne illius vulgaris proverbii locus adveniat: . . . Dum herba crescit equus moritur, & dum fugans canis mingit fugiens lupus evasit.*] *c.* 1350 *Douce MS. 52* no. 20 While þe grasse growes, þe goode hors sterues. *c.* 1440 CAPGRAVE *Life St. Kath.* II. 253 The gray hors, whyl his gras growyth, May sterue for hunger, þus seyth þe prouerbe. *a.* 1530 R. *Hill's Commonpl. Bk.* (1858) 140 Whyle the grasse growyth the hors stervyth. 1600–1 SHAKS. *Ham.* III. ii. 365 Ay, sir, but 'While the grass grows'— the proverb is something musty. 1614 CAM-DEN 314. 1820 GALT *Ayrshire Leg.* x I under-stand, sir, . . . that you have a notion of Miss Bell Tod, but that until ye get a kirk there

can be no marriage. But the auld horse may die waiting for the new grass. 1884 J. PAYN *Canon's Ward* 1 What's to become of me . . . while our schemes are ripening? While the grass grows the steed starves. 1896 FROUDE *Counc. of Trent* ii. 27 Thinkers are a minority in this world. Thought works slowly, and while the grass grows the steed starves.

Grass look green (grow) in Janiveer, If | 'twill look (grow) the worser all the year.

1670 RAY 40 If the grass grow in Janiveer, It grows the worse for't all the year. 1732 FULLER no. 6147.

Grass (Summer) on the top of the oak tree, Look for.

1670 RAY 44 You must look for grass on the top of the oak tree. Because the grass seldom springs well before the oak begins to put forth. 1882 CHAMBERLAIN 38 Look for summer on the top of an oak tree.

Grass, *see also* Cut the g. under feet; Feareth every g. (He that); Going to g. with teeth upwards; Higher the hill, lower the g.; March g. never did good; Pluck the g. to know the wind; Turk's horse doth tread (Where), g. never grows.

Grateful man, To a | give money when he asks.

1640 HERBERT 322.

Grave as a judge, As.

1685 S. WESLEY *Maggots* 2 (A) As grave as judge that's giving charge. *a.* 1870 DICKENS *Reprinted Pieces* The Detective Police Filey walks round it [a horse and cart] as grave as a judge—me too.

Grave, In the | dust and bones jostle not for the wall.

1732 FULLER no. 2826.

Grave(s) (*noun*), *see also* Between the cradle and g.; Dig one's g. with one's teeth; Eat of the goose that shall graze on your g.; Lie all alike in our g.; More thy years nearer thy g.; One foot in g. (To have); Sleeping enough in g. (There will be); Turn in his g.; Walking over my g.; White man's g.

Gravel pit, *see* Live in a g. p.

Gravest fish is an oyster; the gravest bird's an owl; the gravest beast's an ass; and the gravest man's a fool, The.

1737 RAMSAY III. 194.

Gravest man, *see* Gravest fish . . . g. m a fool.

Gray (*adj.*), *see* Grey.

Gray's Inn for walks, Lincoln's Inn for a wall, the Inner Temple for a garden, and the Middle for a hall. (*Cf.* Inner Temple rich, &c.)

[The four great Inns of Court, in London, are legal societies having the exclusive right of calling persons to the English Bar.] 1659 HOWELL *Eng. Prov.* 21/2.

Gray's Inn, *see also* Inner Temple.

Graze on the plain, To.

[= to be turned out of doors.] 1605 CHAPMAN, &c. *Eastw. Hoe* IV. ii. 26 Or else go graze o' the common. 1611 COTGRAVE S.V. 'Sac' and 'Soleil' He is turned out to grazing. 1869 HAZLITT A 18.

Graze, *see also* Eat of the goose that shall g. on your grave.

Grease a cause well, it will stretch, If you.

1732 FULLER no. 2753.

Grease a man in the fist (hand), To.

a. 1529 SKELTON *Magnyf.* 437–8 Wyth golde and grotes they grese my hande, In stede of ryght that wronge may stande. 1583 STUBBES *Anat. Abus.* (Furnivall) I. 117 If you have argent . . . to grease them in the fist withall, than your sute shall want no furtherance. 1670 RAY 178 . . . That is to put money in his hand, to fee or bribe him. 1690 D'URFEY *Collin's Walk* iii. 93 Where many a Client Verdict miss'd, For want of greazing in the fist.

Grease one's boots, To.

1813 RAY 198 To grease one's boots. *Ungere gli stavile* [*stivali*]. *Ital.* To cajole or flatter.

Grease the fat sow, To.

1550 HEYWOOD I. xi. 32 What should we (quoth I) grease the fat sow in thars. 1611 DAVIES *Prov.* 18 'All men do grease the fatt sowe in the taile'. 1786 WOLCOT (P. Pindar) *Lousiad* iii. Wks. (1816) I. 199 To greaze a vat ould pig in the tail.

Grease, *see also* Fry in one's own g.

Greases his wheels helps his oxen, He who.

1666 TORRIANO 241 Grease the wheel, if thou intend the cart shall go. 1732 FULLER no. 2384.

Great and the little have need one of another, The.

1732 FULLER no. 4564.

Great as beggars, As.

1639 Letter of EDMUND VERNEY, *Verney Memoirs* (1892) i. 170 My Colonel and I are as great as two beggers. 1682 BUNYAN *Holy War* 260 When Cerberus and Mr. Profane met, they were presently as great as beggars.

Great as the devil and the Earl of Kent,[1] As.

a. 1704 T. BROWN Wks. (1760) II. 194 We became as great friends as the Devil and the Earl of Kent. 1738 SWIFT (Dial. iii) 351 *Lady A.* Ay, Miss, as great as the devil and the Earl of Kent. [[1] Earl Godwin, *d.* 1053.]

Great birth is a very poor dish at table.

1707 MAPLETOFT 37. 1855 BOHN 365.

Great boast and small roast (makes unsavoury mouths).

c. 1532 R. COPLAND *Spyttel House* l. 978 (A) Grete boost and small roost. 1546 HEYWOOD I. xi. 30 I thanke you (quoth I) but great bost and small roste, Maketh vnsauery mouthes, where ever men oste. *a.* 1591 HY. SMITH *Serm.* (1866) II. 57 Every one is good to the poor, . . . but they will give them nought but words. Then I say, great boast and small roast makes unsavoury mouths. 1614 CAMDEN 306 Great boast small roast. 1648 HERRICK *Hesper.* 221 *Great Boast, Small Roast* Wks. (1893) I. 115 Of flanks and chines of beef doth Gorrel boast He has at home; but who tastes boiled or roast? 1670 RAY 64 . . . Grands vanteurs petits faiseurs. *Gall.* 1907 *Spectator* 16 Nov. 766 As a matter of fact boasting is joined to meagre performance. . . . 'Much boast, small roast', is both English and Italian.

Great bodies move slowly.

1612–15 BP. HALL *Contempl.* XXI. ii (1825) II. 102 Great bodies must have slow motions: as Jerusalem, so the church of God, whose type it was, must be finished by leisure. 1721 KELLY 124 . . . Spoken of the deliberations of parliaments, and other great assemblies; or in jest to them that go slowly on in their business.

Great book is a great evil, A.

[CALLIM. Μέγα βιβλίον μέγα κακόν.] 1621 BURTON *Anat. Mel.* Democ. to Rdr. (1651) 7 Oftentimes it falls out (which Callimachus taxed of old) a great book is a great mischief. 1909 *Brit. Wkly.* 8 Apr. 13 It may be . . . said in reference to this unhappy production that a great book is indeed a great evil.

Great businesses turn on a little pin. (*Cf.* Great engines, &c.)

1640 HERBERT 351.

Great city, a great solitude, A.

[Gk. Μεγάλη πόλις μεγάλη ἐρημία. ERASM. *Magna civitas magna solitudo.*] 1625 BACON *Ess., Friendship* (Arb.) 165 The Latin adage meeteth with it a little; *Magna ciuitas, magna solitudo*; because in a great town, friends are scattered. 1723 FULLER no. 191. 1845 A. SMITH *Scatterg. Fam.* xv There is no solitude so terrible and dreary as that felt in the very heart of a vast, unsympathizing city.

Great cry and little wool.

c. 1475 FORTESCUE *Govt. of Eng.* (Plummer)

x. 132 His hyghnes shall haue þeroff, but as hadd þe man þat sherid is hogge, much crye and litil woll. **1579** GOSSON *Sch. Abuse* (Arb.) 28 As one said at the shearing of hogs, great cry and little wool, much adoe and smal help. **1659** HOWELL *Eng. Prov.* 13 A great cry and little wool, quoth the Devil when he sheard the hog. **1663** BUTLER *Hudibras* I. i. 852 Or shear swine, all cry and no wool. **1678** RAY 237 Here's a great cry and but a little wool (as the fellow said when he shear'd his hogs). Assai romor & poca lana. *Ital.* **1711** ADDISON *Spect.* No. 251 Wks. (1902) III. 150 Those . . . make the most noise who have least to sell, . . . to whom I cannot but apply that old proverb of 'Much cry, but little wool'. **1721** KELLY 165 *Humph, quoth the Dee'l, when he clip'd the Sow, A great Cry, and little Woo.* Spoken of great pretences, and small performances. **1804** WOLCOT (P. Pindar) *Lyric Odes* iii Exclaim, 'Great *cry,* and little *wool!*' As Satan holla'd, when he shaved the pig. **1827** SCOTT *Journ.* 24 Feb. As to the collection, it was much cry and little woo', as the deil said when he shore the sow. **1891** J. L. KIPLING *Beast & Man* 93 For 'great cry and little wool' rustics say, 'The goat bleated all night and produced only one kid',—two being the usual number.

Great doings at Gregory's; heat the oven twice for a custard.

1678 RAY 72. **1732** FULLER no. 1755.

Great engines turn on small pivots. (*Cf.* Great businesses, &c.)

1658 *Comes Facundus* 183 Great engines turn on little pins. **1855** BOHN 366.

Great fish eat up the small, The.

c. **1410** *Pride of Life* (*Non-Cycle Mystery Plays*, ed. O. Waterhouse 100). **1509** A. BARCLAY *Ship of Fools* (1874) I. 101 The wolfe etis the shepe, the great fysshe the small. **1608–9** SHAKS. *Per.* II. i. 30 *3 Fish.* Master, I marvel how the fishes live in the sea. *1 Fish.* Why, as men do a-land; the great ones eat up the little ones. **1616** DRAXE 143.

Great fortune brings with it great misfortune.

1642 TORRIANO 6. **1651** HERBERT 370. **1659** N. R. 37.

Great gain makes work easy.

1721 KELLY 119 with gains'. **1732** FULLER 1756.

Great gifts are from great men.

1670 RAY 98.

Great honours are great burdens.

1547 WM. BALDWIN *Treatise of Moral Philosophy* (1550) O 8 He that desyreth great charges, desyreth great troubles. **1576** PETTIE *Petite Pall.* (Gollancz) I. 101 In greatest charge are greatest cares. **1611** JONSON *Catiline* III. i Great honors are great burdens. **1670** FLECKNOE *Epigrams* 53 (A).

Great journey to the world's end, It is a.

1639 CLARKE 3. **1670** RAY 158.

Great loss but[1] some small profit, No.

1670 RAY 117 As for instance, he whose sheep die of the rot, saves the skins and wool. [1 without.]

Great man and a great river are often ill neighbours, A.

1657 E. LEIGH *Select Observations* 276 A great Lord, A great Bell, A great River are three ill Neighbours. **1732** FULLER no. 198. **1813** RAY 117 A great lord is a bad neighbour.

Great memory without learning, A man of a | hath a rock[1] and a spindle, and no stuff to spin.

1651 HERBERT 367. [1 distaff.]

Great men have great faults.

1616 DRAXE 128. **1639** CLARKE 160 Great mens faults are never small.

Great men would have care of little ones, If | both would last long.

1640 HERBERT 350.

Great men's favours are uncertain.

1612 A. STAFFORD *Meditations* 104 A great mans fauor is hardly got, & easily lost. **1736** BAILEY *Dict.* s.v. 'Favour'.

Great men's sons seldom do well.

1539 TAVERNER 58 Heroum filii noxæ. The children of most renowned and noble personages be for most part destructions to a common wealth. **1621** BURTON *Anat. Mel.* III. ii. VI. iii (1651) 568 Think but of that old proverb, 'Ἡρώων τέκνα πήματα, Heroum filii noxæ, great men's sons seldome do well.

Great men (man), *see also* Great gifts are from g. m.; Keep yourself from anger of g. m.; Serve a g. m. you will know sorrow.

Great nose, He that has a | thinks everybody is speaking of it.

1721 KELLY 172 *He that has a mickle nose, thinks every body is speaking of it.* People that are sensible of their guilt, are always full of suspicion. **1826** SCOTT *Diary* 24 Jan. I went to the Court for the first time to-day, and, like the man with the large nose, thought everybody was thinking of me and my mishap.

Great ones if there were no little ones, There would be no.

1640 HERBERT 331. **1732** FULLER no. 4868.

Great pain and little gain will make a man soon weary.

1616 DRAXE 222. **1639** CLARKE 154.

Great pains quickly find ease.

1640 HERBERT 342.

Great put the little on the hook, The.

1640 HERBERT 360.

Great river, In a | great fish are found: but take heed lest you be drowned.

1640 HERBERT 324.

Great ship asks deep waters, A.

1732 FULLER no. 203 ('must have deep water').

Great shoe fits not a little foot, A.

1581 PETTIE Guazzo's Civ. Conv. (1586) 61 Agesilaus finding fault [with over-emphasis of small matters] said he liked not of that shoemaker, who made a great shoe for a little foot. 1616 DRAXE 3. 1639 CLARKE 138.

Great strokes make not sweet music.

1580 LYLY Euph. & his Eng. (Arb.) 473 Instruments sound sweetest when they be touched softest. 1640 HERBERT 318. 1670 RAY 12 The greatest strokes make not the best music.

Great thieves hang little ones.

1597–8 SHAKS. 1 Hen. IV I. ii. 75 Fal. Do not thou, when thou art king, hang a thief. Prince No; thou shalt . . . Thou shalt have the hanging of the thieves. 1660 SECKER Nonsuch Prof. iii (1891) 276 It was formerly the complaint of a certain person, 'That the greatest thieves did execution upon the least.' 1692 L'ESTRANGE Aesop's Fab. ccccxcviii (1738) 545 Thus goes the world, the little thieves hang for 't, while the great ones sit upon the bench.

Great trees are good for nothing but shade.

1640 HERBERT 343.

Great trees keep down (under) the little ones.

1642 FULLER H. & P. State iv. iii (1841) 240 Most of the clergy (more pitying his profession than person) were glad, that the felling of this oak would cause the growth of much underwood. 1732 FULLER no. 1769.

Great way to the bottom of the sea, It is a. (Cf. Goes a great voyage, &c.)

1639 CLARKE 4.

Great weights hang on small wires.

1639 CLARKE 109. 1642 FULLER H. & P. State iv. viii (1841) 260 The counsel for the king, hanging as much weight on the smallest wire as it would hold, aggravated each particular. 1732 FULLER no. 1773 Great weight may hang [&c.]. 1898 ALEX. WHYTE Bib. Char., Gid. to Abs. 34 They have suspended excellent New Testament sermons on these adapted texts; hanging great weights on small wires.

Great winds blow upon high hills.

c. 1200 Ancrene Riwle (Morton) 178 Euer so the hul is more and herre, so the wind is more theron. 1578 CHURCHYARDE Mirr. Mag., Shore's Wife 47 The wind is great vpon the highest hills, The quiet life is in the dale below. 1670 RAY 107 Huge winds blow on high hills.

Great without small makes a bad wall.

1887 LD. AVEBURY Pleas. of Life I. ii The importance of small things has been pointed out by philosophers. . . . 'Great without small makes a bad wall', says a quaint Greek proverb, which seems to go back to cyclopean times.

Great wits have short memories.

1668 DRYDEN Sir M. Mar-all IV. i (A) Good wits, you know, have bad memories. a. 1763 SHENSTONE Detached Thoughts on Writing and Books 'Great wits have short memories' is a proverb; it undoubtedly has some foundation.

Great would have none great, and the little all little, The.

1640 HERBERT 360.

Great, see also Barkers are no biters (G.); Dainties of g. are tears of poor; Grooms and householders are alike g. (Where) disastrous for houses; Little cannot be g. unless devour many; Wise and g. (He that is truly) lives too early. See also under significant words following 'Great'.

Greater the truth, The | the greater the libel.

c. 1787 BURNS Lines &c. Wks. (Globe) 150 Dost not know that old Mansfield, who writes like the Bible, Says the more 'tis a truth, sir, the more 'tis a libel? 1828 LYTTON Pelham XXV 'The greater the truth, the greater the libel', said Warburton, with a sneer. 1882 S. A. BENT Fam. Short Say. (ed. 8) 371 The greater the truth, the greater the libel. A maxim of the law in vogue . . . while Mansfield[1] presided over the King's Bench. . . . The maxim is said to have originated in the Star Chamber. [1 1705–93.]

Greatest hate springs from the greatest love, The.

1579 LYLY Euphues Wks. (Bond) I. 197 Ye deepest loue tourneth to the deadliest hate. 1581 PETTIE Guazzo's Civ. Conv. (1586) 162 Know you not that where is great love, from thence proceedeth great hate. 1732 FULLER no. 4573.

Greatest, see also under significant words following.

Greatness, see Goodness is not tied to g.

Greed, see Need makes g.

Greedy eating horse. To a | a short halter.

1651 HERBERT 368.

Greedy eye to have a leal[1] heart, It is hard for a.

1721 KELLY 209 . . . Because such act against the bent of their inclinations. [[1] loyal, honest.]

Greedy folks have long arms.

1721 KELLY 122 . . . People will make strange shifts to get what they have a desire for.

Greedy is the good-less.

c. **1300** *Provs. of Hending* 15   Gredy is the godles.

Greedy man and the gileynour[1] are soon agreed, The.

1721 KELLY 307 . . . The covetous man will be glad of a good offer, and the cheat will offer well, designing never to pay. [[1] cheat.]

Greek Calends, At (On) the. (*Cf.* Latter Lammas.)

[L. *Ad Graecas kalendas*, humorous for 'never', since the Greeks used no calends in their reckoning of time. Due to the Emperor Augustus; SUET. *Div. Aug.* 60.] **1540** PALS-GRAVE *Acolastus* V[1] (A)   At the Grekish calendes... or a daye after domesday. *a.* **1649** DRUMM. OF HAWTH. *Consid. Parlt.* Wks. (1711) 185   That gold, plate, and all silver, given . . . in these late troubles, shall be paid at the Greek Kalends.

Greek meets Greek, When | then comes the tug of war.

[The now usual perversion of Nath. Lee's line:—'When Greeks join'd Greeks then was the tug of war', from his tragedy *The Rival Queens* (IV. i.) first published in 1677.] **1824** SCOTT *St. Ronans* xviii Mowbray had . . . some reason to admit that, When Greek meets Greek, then comes the tug of war. The light skirmishing betwixt the parties was ended, and the serious battle commenced. **1863** C. READE *Hard Cash* xxxv Meantime, . . . Greek was meeting Greek only a few yards off. Mr. Hardie was being undermined by a man of his own calibre.

Greek to me (him), It is (was).

1575 GASCOIGNE *Posies, Supposes* I. 1 (1907) 190 *Balia*. This gear is Greek to me. **1599-1600** SHAKS. *Jul. Caes.* I. ii. 282-7 *Cas.* Did Cicero say anything? *Casca.* Ay, he spoke Greek... but, for mine own part, it was Greek to me. **1688** SHADWELL *Squire of Als.* iv. i All this fine language had been heathen Greek to me. **1705** STRYPE *Life Sir J. Cheke*[1] (1821) i, § 2. 14 This language was little known or understood hitherto in this realm. And if any saw a piece of Greek they used to say, *Græcum est; non potest legi*, i.e. 'It is Greek, it cannot be read'. **1840** DICKENS *Barn. Rudge* i I am a stranger, and this is Greek to me. [[1] Prof. of Greek, Cambridge, 1540-51.]

Greek(s), *see also* Fear the G.

Green as a leek, As.

c. **1370** CHAUCER *Romaunt of the Rose* A 212 Al-so grene as any leek. **1585** *Nomenclator*

180 (A) A colour as greene as a leeke. **1595** SHAKS. *Mids. N.* V. i (A) His eyes were green as leeks.

Green cheese, You see no | but your teeth must water.

1546 HEYWOOD II. ix. 80 Haue ye not heard tell all couet all léese: A sir, I sée, ye may sée no gréene chéese But your téeth must water. **1639** CLARKE 39 He sees no green cheese but his mouth waters after it.

Green cheese, *see also* Moon is made of.

Green gown, To give a woman a.

[= to roll her in sport on the grass; hence euphemistically, see quot. 1825-80.] *a.* **1586** SIDNEY *Arcadia* I (1598) 84 Then some greene gownes are by the lasses worne In chastest plaies. **1599** GREENE *Geo. a Greene* Wks. (Gros.) XIV. 140 Madge pointed to meet me in your wheate-close. . . . And first I saluted her with a greene gowne and after fell as hard a-wooing as if the Priest had been at our backs, to haue married vs. *a.* **1700** B. E. *Dict. Cant. Crew, Green Gown*, a throwing of young lasses on the grass and kissing them. **1825-80** JAMIESON, *Green Gown*, the supposed badge of the loss of virginity, Roxb.

Green[1] in my eye? Do you see any.

1851 MAYHEW *Lond. Labour* II. 41 'I'm not a tailor, but I understands about clothes, and I believe that no person ever saw anything green in my eye.' **1894** BLACKMORE *Perlycross* xxi Serjeant, do you see any green in my eye? [[1] gullibility.]

Green stockings, *see* Given them g. s. (She has).

Green tree, *see* Do these things in a g. t. (If they).

Green winter (Yule) makes a fat churchyard (kirkyard), A. (*Cf.* Green Yule and a white Pasch, &c.)

1659 N. R. A hot Winter makes a full Church-yard. **1670** RAY 42 A green winter makes a fat churchyard. This proverb was sufficiently confuted *anno* 1667, in which the winter was very mild; and yet no mortality . . . ensued the summer or autumn following. **1721** KELLY 30 *A green yule makes a fat churchyard.* This, and a great many proverbial observations upon the seasons of the year, are groundless. **1816** SCOTT *Antiq.* xxiii It cam a green Yule, and the folk died thick and fast—for ye ken a green Yule makes a fat kirkyard.

Green wood makes a hot fire.

1477 RIVERS *Dictes* (1877) 65 The grene wode is hotter than the other whan it is wel kyn-deled. **1553** R. WILSON *Arte of Rhet.* (1909) 84 In greene wood we may see, that where as the fuell is not most apt for burning, yet the fire lasteth longer. **1640** HERBERT 356.

Green wound is soon healed, A.

c. **1532** SIR ADRIAN FORTESCUE no. 43   A

wound when it is grene, is best to be healid. **1579** LYLY *Euphues* Wks (Bond) I. 249 Searche the wounde while it is greene; too late commeth the salue when the sore festereth. **1590–1** SHAKS. *2 Hen. VI* III. i. 287 Stop the rage betime, Before the wound do grow uncurable; For, being green, there is great hope of help. **1593** *Tell Truth's New Years Gift* (New Sh. S.) 34 It is easy to cure a greene wound. **1670** RAY 31.

Green Yule and a white Pasch[1] make a fat churchyard, A. (*Cf.* Green winter, &c.)

1931 *Times* 8 Jan. 8/3 If fully stated, 'A green Yule and a white Pasch make a fat churchyard', there is no fallacy, as a mild winter followed by a severe spring is so often fatal to old and delicate people. [[1] Easter.]

Green, *see also* Gay that is g.; Grey and g. worst medley; Hoar head and a g. tail; Lincoln g.; Marry in green . . . sorrow; Strew g. rushes for stranger; Thraw the wand while g.; Yellow's forsaken and g.'s foresworn.

Greenland, *see* Northerly wind and blubber.

Greenock, *see* Glasgow people, G. folk.

Greet(s) (i.e. weep), *see* Laugh at leisure, you may g. ere night; No play where one g. and another laughs; Sair dung bairn that dare not g.; See a woman g. (No more pity) than goose go barefoot.

Gregory, *see* Great doings at G.'s.

Grenville, *see* Charles's Wain.

Grey (*proper name*), *see* John G.'s bird.

Grey and green make the worst medley.

c. **1386** CHAUCER *Cant. T.* A 3878 For in oure wyl ther stiketh evere a nayl, To have an hoor heed and a grene tayl, As hath a leek. **1597–8** BP. HALL *Satires* IV. iv The maidens mock, and call him withered leek, That with a green tail hath an hoary head. **1678** RAY 149 Gray and green make the worst medley. *Turpe senex miles, turpe senilis amor.* Ovid.

Grey as a badger, As.

1707 THOS. BROWN, *Letters from the Dead to the Living*, 'Lilly to Cooley' (*Amusements*, ed. A. L. Hayward, 1927, 413). **1720** SWIFT Wks. (Scott) xiv. 134 (A) Though she lives till she's grey as a badger all over.

Grey before he is good, He is.

1678 RAY 249.

Grey (White) hairs are death's blossoms.

c. **1386** CHAUCER *Cant. T.* A 3869 This whyte top wryteth myne olde yeres. **1588** GREENE *Pandosto* Prose Wks. (1881–3) IV. 271 Thou seest my white hayres are blossoms for the grave. **1678** RAY 149 Gray hairs are death's blossoms.

Grey hairs, *see also* Horns and g. h. do **not** come by years.

Grey head is often placed on green shoulders, A.

1814 *Intrigues of a Day* III. iii As the proverb says, a grey head is often placed on green shoulders.

Grey mare is the better horse, The.

[= the wife rules the husband.] **1546** HEYWOOD II. iv. 52. *c.* **1645** HOWELL *Lett.* I. iv. ix To suffer the Gray-mare sometimes to be the better Horse. **1726** *Adv. Capt. R. Boyle* 2 She began to tyrannize over my master, . . . and soon prov'd, as the Saying is, The grey Mare to be the better Horse. **1847** TENNYSON *Princ.* v. 441 The gray mare Is ill to live with, when her whinny shrills From tile to scullery.

Grey (*adj.*), *see also* Evening red and morning g.

Greyhound, *see* Gentleman's g. and a salt box.

[Greyhound, shape of a], *see* Head like a snake.

Grice(s), *see* Barren sow was never good to pigs (g.); Lay the head of sow to tail of g.

Grief of the head is the grief of griefs, The.

1659 HOWELL *Eng. Prov.* 10/2.

Griefs with bread are less, All.

1620 SHELTON *Quix.* II. xiii (1908) II. 266 And yet not so bad if we might eat at all, for good fare lessens care. **1640** HERBERT 335.

Grief(s), *see also* Day passeth without some g. (No); Folly were g. (If); Honour (Where no), there is no g.; Master a g. (Every one can); Time (and thinking) tame g.; Whither goest, g.

Grieve for that (what) you cannot help, Never.

1639 CLARKE 292.

Grieve when the chance is past, It is too late to.

1636 CAMDEN 300.

Grim death, *see* Hold on like g. d.

Grin and abide (bear it), To.

a. **1775** W. HICKEY *Memoirs* I. 196 'I recommend you to grin and bear it' (an expression used by sailors after a long continuance of bad weather.) **1794–6** E. DARWIN *Zoon.* (1802) II. 114 Thus we have a proverb where no help could be had in pain, 'to grin and abide'. **1834** MARRYAT *P. Simple* liv The best plan is to grin and bear it. **1876** BLACKMORE *Cripps* x All things are dead against me; I must grin, as you say, and bear it.

Grin like a Cheshire cat, To.

1803 C. LAMB *Let.* to Manning 26 Feb. I made a pun the other day, and palmed it upon

Holcroft, who grinned like a Cheshire cat. **1855** THACKERAY *Newcomes* xxiv. Mamma is smiling with all her might. In fact Mr. Newcome says . . . , 'That woman grins like a Cheshire cat'.

Grind or find, I will either.
1670 RAY 178.

Grind(s, eth), *see also* Friend that g. at my mill; Miller g. more men's corn than one.

Grindstone, *see* Nose to the g. (To hold); Scot, a rat, and a Newcastle g.

Grisel(l), *see* Mares in the wood than g. (More); Patient G.

Grist to the (one's) mill, To bring.
1583 GOLDING *Calvin on Deut.* cxxiii. 755 There is no lykelihoode that those thinges will bring gryst to the mill. **1655** FULLER *Ch. Hist.* III. vi (1868) I. 444 And here foreign casuists bring in a bundle of mortal sins, all grist for their own mill. **1822** GALT *Provost* iv By which . . . no little grist came to his mill.

Groaning horse and a groaning wife never fail their master, A.
1546 HEYWOOD II. iv A gronyng horse, and a gronyng wyfe, Neuer fayle their maister. **1670** RAY 51 A grunting horse and a groaning wife seldom fail their master.

Groat, Not worth a (grey).
1509 A. BARCLAY *Ship of Fools* (1874) I. 159 Skant worth a grote. **1546** HEYWOOD I. xi. 31 And I knew him, not woorth a grey grote. . . . Poore as the poorest. **1694** *The Brothers in Terence made English* 189 The woman's not worth a Groat.

Groat is ill saved that shames the master, The.
1614 CAMDEN 306. **1670** RAY 23. **1853** TRENCH 110 Others . . . forbid this frugality from degenerating into a sordid and dishonourable parsimony; such . . . as . . . *The groat is ill saved which shames its master.*

Groat, *see also* Flay (Skin) a g.; Four pence to a g. (As like as); Hole in the g. to-day (Will be a); Penny is well spent that saves g.

Groats, *see* Kens his g. among other folk's kail.

Groby pool, For his death there is many a wet eye in.
1678 RAY (*Leics.*) 317. **1902–4** LEAN I. 124 . . . *i.e.* eyot or little isle, implying that no tears are shed by his friends. [It is the largest sheet of water in the county.]

Groby Pool, *see also* Thatch G. P. with pancakes.

Groin (= grumbler), *see* Like a hog hangeth the g. on her husband.

Gromwell seed, *see* Fair words did fet.

Groom is a king at home, Every.
1611 DAVIES *Prov.* 54.

Grooms and householders are all alike great, Where | very disastrous will it be for the houses and all that dwell in them.
1399 LANGLAND *Rich. Redeles* i. 65–7 ffor, as it is said . by elderne[1] dawis,[2] 'Ther gromes and the goodmen . beth all eliche grette, Well wo beth the wones[3] . and all that woneth ther-in!' [[1] ancestors'. [2] days. [3] dwellings.]

Gropes in the dark finds that he would not, He that.
1659 HOWELL *Eng. Prov.* 13/1. **1670** RAY 12.

Ground, He is on the.
1641 FERGUSSON 52 *Of weasters and divers.*[1] . . . He is on the ground. [[1] bankrupts.]

Ground is not good enough for her (&c.) to walk on, The.
1864 BLACKMORE *Clara V.* xxxix Mrs. Shelfer (who had Irish blood in her veins) used to declare that the ground was not good enough for them to walk on.

Ground sweat cures all disorders, A.
c. **1816** FARMER *Musa Pedestris* 81 (A) We . . . sent him to take a ground-sweat [buried him]. **1830** FORBY 434 'A ground sweat cures all disorders', i.e. In the grave all complaints cease from troubling.

Ground, *see also* Kiss (Lick) the g.; Lies upon the g. (He that) can fall no lower; Love the g. he treads on; Remedy against ill man is much g. between.

Groundsel[1] speaks not, The | save what it heard at (of) the hinges.
1640 HERBERT 331. **1670** RAY 12 (with 'of'). [[1] threshold.]

Grow howbackit[1] bearing your friends, You will never.
1862 HISLOP 334 . . . From this we can infer that the person addressed does not allow himself to be troubled by his friends. [[1] humpbacked.]

Grow like a cow's tail, To.
1678 RAY 249 To grow like a cows tail, *i.e.* downwards. **1721** KELLY 361 *You breed of the cow's tail, you grow backward.* Spoken to boys who do not improve at school. **1829** G. GRIFFIN *Collegians* xii 'Grew?—If she did, it's like the cow's tail, downwards.'

Grow, *see also* Many things g. in garden never sown; One for the mouse . . . and one to g.

Growed by night, This.
1678 RAY 72 . . . Spoken of a crooked stick or tree, it could not see to grow. (*Joculatory.*)

Growing youth has a wolf in his belly, A.

[*Cf.* **1886** JOWETT *Life* III. 220 No man will be pacified when he hath the wolf in his belly. (Said of the Irish.)] **1611** COTGRAVE s.v. 'Ieune' A youth in growing hath a wolfe in his guts. **1666** TORRIANO 56 *A young man who still* groweth, *hath a woolf in his belly.* **1823** COLLINS 214 . . . That is, he is a great eater.

Gruel, *see* Grantham g.

Grumble, *see* Englishman's privilege.

Grunt, *see* Expect from a hog but a g. (What can you).

Grunting horse, *see* Groaning horse.

Guard, *see* Faulty stands on his g.; Welt or g. (Without).

Gudgeon(s), *see* Angle all day and catch g.; Gape for g.; Swallow a g.

Guest(s), *see* Fresh fish and new-come g.; Ill g. that never drinks to host; Unbidden g. knoweth not where to sit.

Guide (*noun*), *see* No man before his g.; Takes the raven for g. (He that).

Guided that God guides, They are well.

1721 KELLY 337 . . . Spoken when some person has committed some malefice.

Guide(d) (*verb*), *see also* Gear is easier gained than g.

Guilty conscience needs no accuser (is a thousand witnesses), A.

1578 FLORIO *First Fruites* 32 Conscience serveth instead of a thousand witnesses. **1592** GREENE *Philomela* in Wks. (Gros.) XI. 200 I see, and with trembling I feele, that a guiltye conscience is a thousand witnesses. **1592–3** SHAKS. *Rich. III* V. iii. 193 My conscience hath a thousand several tongues, And every tongue brings in a several tale, And every tale condemns me for a villain. **1744** *Life & Adv. Mat. Bishop* 106 It is an old saying, *a guilty conscience needs no accuser.* **1881** D. C. MURRAY *Joseph's Ct.* viii 'Where are *you* off to?' asked George with a great effort . . . a guilty conscience needs no accuser.

Guilty, *see also* Find g. Gilbert; Truest jests sound worst in g. ears.

Gull comes against the rain, The.

1616 DRAXE 190 The gull commeth not, but against a tempest. **1664** CODRINGTON 214 The gull is alwayes seen against a tempest. **1670** RAY 98.

Gull(ed) (*verb*), *see* World will be g. (If).

Gummed taffeta (velvet), *see* Fret like g. t.

Gun(s), *see* Highlandman's g. that needed new lock; Stand to one's g.; Sure as a g.

Gunner to his linstock, The | and the steersman to the helm.

1748 SMOLLETT *Rod. Rand.* xlii I meddle with nobody's affairs but my own; the gunner to his linstock,[1] and the steersman to the helm, as the saying is. **1894** SIR H. MAXWELL *Life W. H. Smith* 262 He . . . never showed any disposition to trespass on the province of science or literature. . . . There is sound sense in the adage, 'The cobbler to his last and the gunner to his linstock'. [[1] a staff with a forked head to hold a lighted match.]

Gunner's daughter, *see* Married to g. d.

Gunshot, *see* Out of g.

Gut no fish till you get them.

1721 KELLY 114 . . . Spoken to them who have pregnant expectations, and boast of them as if they had them in possession. **1824** MOIR *Mansie W.* xx The doing so might not only set them to the sinful envying of our good fortune, . . . but might lead away ourselves to be gutting our fish before we get them.

Guts (No guts) in his brain, He has.

1601–2 SHAKS. *Troil & Cres.* II. i. 79 This lord . . . who wears his wits in his belly, and his guts in his head. **1663** BUTLER *Hudibras* iii. 1091 Truly that is no Hard Matter for a Man to do, That has but any Guts in's Brains. **1678** RAY 249 He has no guts in's brains. The *anfractus* of the brain, look'd upon when the *Dura mater* is taken off, do much resemble guts. **1694** MOTTEUX *Rabelais* v. Prol. (1737) 53 One without Guts in his Brains, whose Cockloft is unfurnish'd. **1738** SWIFT (Dial. i) 340 The fellow's well enough, if he had any guts in his brains.

Guts than brains, He has more.

1678 RAY 249.

Guts uphold the heart, The | and not the heart the guts.

1732 FULLER no. 4585.

Guts, *see also* Carry g. to a bear (Not fit to).

Gutter Lane, All goeth down.

1628 RICHARD RAWLIDGE *A Monster hate Found Out and Discovered* C₂ᵛ an hundred Kanns of Beere . . . were filled in a trice, and almost all sodainly turned downe Guttur lane. **1662** FULLER (*Lond.*) II. 348 'All goeth down Gutter-lane' . . . a small lane, leading out of Cheapside, . . . which orthography presents . . . [as] *Guthurun-lane*, from him the once owner thereof. . . . The proverb is applicable to those who spend all in drunkenness and gluttony.

Gutter, *see also* Gazed at moon and fell in g.; Repairs not his g. (Who) repairs whole house.

Gyges, *see* Ring of G.

H

Hab or nab.

[= get or lose, hit or miss, at random.] **1542**
UDALL tr. *Erasm. Apoph.* (1877) 209 Put to
the plounge of ... habbe or nhabbe, to wynne
all, or to lese all. **1580** LYLY *Euph. & his Engl.*
(Arb.) 354 Philautus determined, hab, nab, to
sende his letters. **1599–1600** SHAKS. *Twelfth
N.* III. iv. 265 Hob, nob, is his word: give't
or take't. **1664** BUTLER *Hudibras.* II. iii. 990
Cyphers, Astral Characters ... set down Hab-
nab at random. **1831** SCOTT *Jrnl.* II. 388 It is
all hab-nab at a venture.

Habit(s), *see* Custom (H.) is second nature;
Holy h. cleanseth not foul soul; Pursuits
become h.

Hackerton's cow, That is.

[Hackerton was a lawyer who when told that
his heifer had been gored by an ox, claimed
the ox in recompense; but when told that the
reverse of this had happened, replied, 'The
case alters there'.] **1721** KELLY 326 ...
Spoken when people alter their opinions when
the case comes home to themselves.

Hackney mistress, hackney maid.

1616 WITHALS 579. **1639** CLARKE 217 **1670**
RAY 99 ... Ὁποία ἡ δέσποινα τοῖαι καὶ θερα-
παινίδες. CIC. *Epist. Att.* 5. Qualis hera tales
pedissequæ. [Like mistress, like maid.] **1732**
FULLER no. 1780.

Had I fish, is good without mustard (butter).

1623 CAMDEN 271 Had I fish is good without
butter. **1670** RAY 99 Had I fish is good without mustard. **1721** KELLY 145 Had I fish was
never good to eat with mustard. An answer
to them that say, had I such a thing, I would
do so, or so.

Had I fish, was never good with garlic.

1641 FERGUSSON 38.

'Had I wist', Beware of.

c. **1350** *Douce MS. 52* no. 98 Holde þy
thombe in thi fyst, And kepe þe welle fro
'Had I wyst'. *c.* **1390** GOWER *Conf. Amantis*
II. 102 And is all ware of *had I wist*. *c.* **1400**
Arthur (Furnivall) l. 545 Ther nys no man
wel nye, y tryste, y þat can be waar of hadde
wyste. *c.* **1500** *Percy Provs.* in *Anglia* XIV.
486 Of had I wyst all way beware. **1526**
SKELTON *Magnyf.* Wks. (1843) I. 232 Hem,
syr, yet beware of Had I wyste! **1546** HEY-
WOOD I. ii And that deliberation doth men
assist, Before they wed, to beware of Had I
wist. **1732** FULLER no. 976.

Had I wist, comes too late.

c. **1400** BERYN (E.E.T.S.) l. 2348 (A) But
nowe it is to late to speke of had-I-wist. **1639**
CLARKE 281.

Had I wist, was a fool.

[L. *Stultum est dicere, Non putarem.*] **1599**

BRETON *Anger & Pat.* Wks. (Gros.) II. 60
Had I wist was a foole. **1721** KELLY 131 *Had
I wist, quoth the fool* ... Spoken when people
say, *Had I wist* what would have been the
consequence of such an action, I had not
done it.

Haddock, Not worth a.

1546 HEYWOOD II. x. 82 And thus had he
brought haddocke to paddocke. Till they
both were not woorth a haddocke.

Haddock, *see also* Bring h. to paddock;
Leaped a h.

Hae[1] lad and run lad.

1721 KELLY 131 ... Give ready money for
your service, and you will be sure to be well
served. [[1] Here, take.]

Hae[1] will a deaf man hear.

1721 KELLY 133. [[1] Here, take.]

Hail brings frost in the tail.

1670 RAY 42 Hail brings frost i' th' tail. **1882**
CHAMBERLAIN 38 Hail brings frost in its tail.

Hail fellow well met (with one), To be.

[= to be intimate (too intimate) with.] **1519**
HORMAN *Vulg.* f. 148 (A) He made so moche
of his servaunt that he waxed hayle felowe
with hym. **1581** PETTIE *Guazzo's Civ. Conv.*
III (1586) 171 The maister ... being as you
say haile fellow well met with his servant.
1586 J. HOOKER *Girald. Irel.* in *Holinshed* II.
105/2 He ... placed himselfe ... hard at the
earle of Ormond his elbow, as though he were
haile fellow well met. **1616** WITHALS 567 *Ne
cuivis porrigas dextram.* Be not hail fellow
well met with every one. **1670** EACHARD
Cont. Clergy 74 The multitude did not go hail
fellow well met with Him. **1888** RIDER HAG-
GARD *Col. Quaritch* I. i. 4 He was popular ...
though not in any hail-fellow-well-met kind
of way.

Hair, Not worth a.

1509 A. BARCLAY *Ship of Fools* (1874) I. 177
Skantly worth a here. **1565** *King Darius* A4
Not worth the valour of a heare. **1613** WITHER
Abuses Stript Epigr. 10 (A) To call you best,
or the most faire ... is now not commenda-
tions worth a haire.

Hair and hair makes the carle's head bare.

[HOR. *Ep.* 2. 1. 45.] **1639** CLARKE 10 Pull
hair and hair and you'll make the carle bald.
1641 FERGUSSON 40. **1721** KELLY 136 ... An
estate may be ruined by small diminutions.

Hair grows through his hood, His.

c. **1450** in *Rel. Antiq.* (1843) II. 67 He that
lovyth welle to fare, Ever to spend and never
spare But he have the more good His here
wol grow throw his hood. *c.* **1550** INGELEND
Disob. Child in HAZL. *O.E.P.* II. 301 Therefore
let him look his purse be right good, That

it may discharge all that is spent, Or else it will make his hair grow through his hood. **1587** FULWELL *Like Will to L.* in HAZL. *O.E.P.* (1874) III. 325 So that my company they think to be so good, That in short space their hair grows through their hood. **1678** RAY 73 ... He is very poor, his hood is full of holes.

Hair in one's neck, A.

[= a cause of trouble or annoyance.] *a.* **1450** *Ratis Raving* III. 199 Think one the har is in thi nek. **1818** SCOTT *Rob Roy* xxiii An Bailie Grahame were to get word o' this ... it wad be a sair hair in my neck!

Hair of the dog that bit you, A.

1546 HEYWOOD I. xi. 37 I pray the leat me and my felow haue A heare of the dog that bote vs last night. **1611** COTGRAVE S.V. 'Beste' Our ale-knights often ... say, Give us a hair of the dog that last bit us. **1661** PEPYS April 3 Up among my workmen, my head akeing all day from last night's debauch. ... At noon dined with Sir W. Batten and Pen, who would needs have me drink two good drafts of sack to-day, to cure me of my last night's disease, which I thought strange but I think find true. **1738** SWIFT (Dial. ii) 348 Our way is, to take a hair of the same dog next morning. **1824** SCOTT *Redg.* xiv He took a large glass of brandy. 'A hair of the dog that bit me', he continued.

Hair so small but hath his shadow, No.

[PUBLILIUS SYRUS 138 *Etiam capillus unus habet umbram suam.* Even a single hair has its shadow.] **1584** LYLY *Sapho & Phao* Prol., Wks. (1902) II. 372 There is no needles point so smal, which hath not his cōpasse: nor haire so slender, which hath not his shadowe. **1590** LODGE *Rosalynde* Wks. (1883) I. 130 Affirming, that as ... the smallest haires have their shadowes: so the meanest swaines had their fancies. **1596** Id. *Wits Miserie* Wks. (1883) IV. 24 If you say that (as PUBLIUS MIMUS saith) the smallest haire hath his shadow (& with Rabin BEN-AZAI) that no man liuing is to bée contemned. **1651** HERBERT 369.

Hair to make a tether of, A.

[= a slight pretext of which to make a great deal.] **1809** SCOTT *Let. to G. Ellis* 3 Nov. in LOCKHART *Life* Those who wish to undermine it want but, according to our Scotch proverb, a hair to make a tether of.

Hair(s), *see also* Against the h.; Bush natural, more h. than wit; Cut (Split) the h.; Friday's h. and Saturday's horn; Grey h. death's blossoms; Horns and grey h.; Horse lies down (Where), h. will be found; Maidens (All are not) that wear bare h.

Hake, *see* Lose in h. (What we), shall have in herring.

Hale pow[1], He should have a | that calls his neighbour nitty know.[2]

1641 FERGUSSON 42. **1721** KELLY 133 ... A

man ought to be free of these faults that he throws up to others. [[1] head. [2] hillock.]

Half a loaf is better than no bread.

1546 HEYWOOD I. xi. 30 For better is halfe a lofe than no bread. **1567** *Appius & Virg.* (Mal. Soc.) l. 1109 And well this prouerb commeth in my head, Birlady halfe a loaf is better then nere a whit of bread. **1642** D. ROGERS *Naaman to Rdr.* He is a fool who counts not half a loaf better than no bread, or despiseth the moonshine because the sun is down. **1850** KINGSLEY *Alton L.* x We must live somehow, and half a loaf is better than no bread.

Half a tale is enough for a wise man.

1641 FERGUSSON 38

Half an acre is good land.

1659 HOWELL *Eng. Prov.* 2/1. **1670** RAY 99. **1721** KELLY 143 *Half acres bears good corn.* Alluding to the half acre given to the herd, and commonly spoken in gaming, when we are but half as many as our antagonists.

Half an hour is soon lost at dinner.

1738 SWIFT (Dial. ii) 344 Sir John, fall to: you know half an hour is soon lost at dinner.

Half an hour's hanging hinders five miles' riding.

1678 RAY 150.

Half an hour, *see also* Hour.

Half-done work, *see* Fools and bairns.

Half is more than the whole, The.

[HESIOD *Works & Days* 40 Πλέον ἥμισυ παντός. ERASM. *Ad. Dimidium plus toto.*] **1550** LATIMER *Serm. Stamford* (P.S.) 277 There is a proverb ... , *Dimidium plus toto*; 'The half sometimes more than the whole.' The mean life is the best life and the most quiet life of all. **1791** I. DISRAELI *Cur. Lit.* (1858) III. 35 The admonition of the poet ... to prefer a friendly accommodation to a litigious lawsuit, has fixed a paradoxical proverb ... Πλέον ἥμισυ παντός, The half is better than the whole! **1907** A. C. BENSON *From Coll. W.* (ed. 4) 80 It is true of conversation as of many other things, that the half is better than the whole. People who are fond of talking ought to beware of being lengthy.

Half-seas over, To be.

[= half-drunk.] **1692** DRYDEN *Cleom.* v. ii I'm half-seas o'er to death. *a.* **1700** B.E. *Dict. Cant. Crew* Half Seas over, almost Drunk. **1714** *Spectator* No. 616, par. 4 Our friend the alderman was half seas over before the bone-fire was out. **1730** FIELDING *T. Thumb* I. ii I already half-seas over am.

Half sheweth what the whole meaneth, The.

c. **1530** *Calisto and Meliboea* Now know ye by the half tale what the hole doth meane. **1546** HEYWOOD II. vii. **1616** DRAXE 78 *bis.*

Half the battle, *see* First blow.

Half the truth is often a great lie.

1758 FRANKLIN July. **1859** TENNYSON *The Grandmother* VIII That a lie which is half a truth is ever the blackest of lies, That a lie which is all a lie may be met and fought with outright, But a lie which is part a truth is a harder matter to fight.

Half the way to know the way.

1659 HOWELL *Brit. Prov.* 11.

Half (One half of) the world knows not how the other half lives.

[**1532** RABELAIS II. xxxii *La moytié du monde ne sçait comment l'autre vit.*] **1633** R. ASHLEY *Cochin-China* A₁ the one moity [of the world] is in a maner unknowne to the other. **1640** HERBERT 359. **1721** KELLY 274 *One half of the world kens not how the other lives.* Men bred to ease and luxury are not sensible of the mean condition of a great many. **1755** FRANKLIN Pref. It is a common saying, that *One Half of the World does not know how the other Half lives.* **1830** MARRYAT *King's Own* x It is an old proverb that 'one half of the world do not know how the other half live'. Add to it, nor *where* they live.

Half, halves, *see also* Better h.; Never do things by h.; Take h. in hand (Best to).

Halfpenny (ies, ce), *See* Hand on another h. (To have); Hand on my h. (I will lay); Hand on one's h.; Hap and h. goods enough; Heart is on h.; Know by a h. if priest will take offering; Look twice at a h.; Put two h. in a purse; Thinks his penny (h.) good silver; Three halfpence.

Halfpennyworth, Ha'porth, *See* Hang saving, bring us a h. of cheese; Ship (To lose) for h. of tar.

Halgaver, *see* Summoned before Mayor of H.

Halifax Law.

1577 W. HARRISON *Description of England* (New. Sh. S.) i. 227. **1586** LEICESTER in MOTLEY *United Netherlands* (1860) i. 444 (A) I have had Halifax law—to be condemned first and inquired upon after.

Halifax, *see also* Heading H.; Hell, Hull, and H.

Hall benches (binks) are slippery (sliddery).

c. **1450** HENRYSON *Mor. Fab.* 154 (1845) 209 Be war in welth, for hall-benkis ar rycht slidder. **1641** FERGUSSON 40 Hall binks are sliddrie. **1721** KELLY 133 *Hall binks are slippery.* Great men's favour is uncertain.

Hall, *see* Bring a cow to the h.; Do on the hill as in the h.

Hallamshire¹ shall be God's croft, When all the world shall be aloft, then.

1678 RAY 340 (Yorks.). [¹ Sheffield and its surroundings.]

Halloo (Whistle) until one is out of the wood, Not to.

1792 D'ARBLAY *Diary* (1876) iii. 473 (A) Mʳ Windham says we are not yet out of the wood, though we see the path through it. **1801** W. HUNTINGTON *Bank of Faith* 85 But, alas! I hallooed before I was out of the wood. **1866** KINGSLEY *Hereward* iii Don't halloa till you are out of the wood. This is a night for praying rather than boasting. **1876** FAIRBAIRN in *Contemp. Rev.* June 137 He halloos, not only before he is out of the wood, but before he is well into it. **1922** MRS. MEYNELL Feb. I whistled before I was out of the wood when I said my cold was better.

Halt before you are lame, You.

1670 RAY 179.

Halter to hang himself, He hath made a.

1616 WITHALS 582. **1626** JONSON *Staple of News* v. iii. 16 In mine owne halter, I haue made the *Noose.* **1639** CLARKE 200.

Halter, *see* After a collar cometh a h.; Better a lean jade than empty h.; Give a Yorkshireman a h.; Hang together like pebbles in h.; Rope (H.) (Name not) in his house that hanged himself; Stretch without a h.

Halting (To halt) before a cripple, It is hard.

c. **1374** CHAUCER *Troylus* IV. 1457–9 'It is ful hard to halten unespyed Bifore a crepil, for he can the craft: Your fader is in sleighte as Argus ȳed.' **1546** HEYWOOD II. v. 59 It is harde haltyng before a créeple ye wot. **1581** B. RICH *Farewell to the Militarie Prof.* (Sh. Soc.) 44 Wee have a proverbe—it is ill haultyng before a creeple. **1655** FULLER *Ch. Hist.* IV. iv (1868) I. 614 Buckingham . . . pretending very fair in his behaviour. But, hard it is to halt before a cripple, and dissemble before King Richard.

Hambleton, *see* Brayton.

Hamlet without the Prince of Denmark, Like.

1818 BYRON to Murray 20 Aug. My autobiographical Essay wᵈ resemble the tragedy of Hamlet at the country theatre, recited 'with the part of Hamlet left out by particular desire'. **1859** G. MEREDITH, *Ordeal of Richard Feverel*, ch. 4, What have you been doing at home, Cousin Rady?' 'Playing Hamlet, in the absence of the Prince of Denmark.' **1910** *Times, Wkly.* 17 June 452 The Army without Kitchener is like *Hamlet* without the Prince of Denmark. **1932** A. HUXLEY in *Letters of D. H. Lawrence* Introd. x His book is *Hamlet* without the Prince of Denmark. **1941** R. R. MARETT *A Jerseyman at Oxford* viii But all this sounds like Hamlet with its leading part [Jowett] left out.

Hammer and the anvil, Between the.

[ERASM. *Ad. Inter malleum et incudem.*

Jerome's Latin of Origen's saying.] **1534** LD.
BERNERS *Gold Bk. M. Aurel.* (1546) Eij, My
spyrite is betwene the harde anuielde and
the importunate hammer. **1892–3** J. A.
FROUDE *Council of Trent* (1896) v. 110 Fate
had dealt hardly with [Pope Clement VII].
For half his reign, as he said, he had been
between the anvil and the hammer.

Hammer, *see also* Anvil (When you are) . . . ,
when you are h., strike.

Hampden, *see* Tring, Wing, and Ivinghoe.

Hampshire ground requires every day in the week a shower of rain, and on Sunday twain. (*Cf.* Cornwall, &c.)

1813 RAY 248. **1790** GROSE s.v. ' Hants '.

Hampshire hog.

[= a native of Hampshire.] **1622** DRAYTON
Polyolb. II. xxiii. 240 As *Hamshire* long for
her, hath had the term of *Hogs*. **1720** *Vade
Mecum for Malt-worms* (1850?) I. 50 Now
to the sign of *Fish* let's jog, There to find out
a *Hampshire Hog*, A man whom none can lay
a Fault on, The Pink of Courtesie at *Alton*.
1866 BLACKMORE *Cradock N.* vii ' Naw oose
Hampshire hogs, But to zhow the way in
bogs.' So John Rosedew quoted . . . from an
old New Forest rhyme.

Hand and glove.

1654 E. GAYTON 129 . . . had been Hand and
Glove. **1680** R. MANSEL *Narr. Popish Plot* 103
Mrs. Collier, to whom Mr. Willoughby was
such a Croney, that they were hand and glove.
1780 COWPER *Table T.* 173 As if the world
and they were hand and glove. **1881** BESANT
& RICE *Chapl. of Fleet* I. iv The Doctor is . . .
hand-in-glove with the bishop.

Hand in the lion's mouth, He that hath his | must take it out as well as he can.

[*Cf. Ps.* xxii. 21 ; *2 Tim.* iv. 17.] **1721** KELLY
171 . . . He that is under the distress of a severe
person, must extricate himself as well as he is
able. **1819** SCOTT *Ivanhoe* xliv Thy hand is in
the lion's mouth.

Hand like a foot, You have made a.

1721 KELLY 386 . . . Spoken to those who are
disappointed of their expectations.

Hand of man, Whatever is made by the | by the hand of man may be overturned.

1651 HERBERT 373.

Hand on another half-penny, To have one's.

[= to have another object in view.] **1577**
GASCOIGNE *Hearbes*, &c. Wks. (1587) 255 But
his mystresse having hyr hand on another
halfpenny gan thus say unto him.

Hand on my halfpenny ere I part with it, I will lay my.

1678 RAY 250.

Hand (*or* Heart) on one's halfpenny, To have one's. (*See also* Heart is on, &c.)

[= to have a particular object in view.] **1542**
UDALL tr. *Erasm. Apoph.* (1877) 72 Aristippas
. . . whose mind was more on his halfpenie,
then Pluto had set his. **1546** HEYWOOD I. vi.
11 So harde is your hande set on your half-
peny, That my reasonyng your reason setteth
nought by. **1589** GREENE *Menaphon* (Arb.)
49 Twere necessarie he tolde us how his heart
came thus on his halfepence.

Hand over head.

[= recklessly] *c.* **1440** *Bone Florence* 475
Than they faght hand ovyr hedd. **1549**
LATIMER *7th Serm. bef. Edw. VI* (P.S.) 218
These doctors we . . . thank God for . . . but
yet I would not have men to be sworn to
them, and so addict, as to take hand over
head whatsoever they say. **1655–62** GURNALL
Chrn. in Armour (1865) I. 293 The Bereans
. . . did not believe hand over head, but their
faith was the result of a judgment . . . convinced by scripture evidence. **1839** JAMES
Louis XIV III. 240 A lavish guardian, who . . .
spent the estate hand-over-head.

Hand over head, as men took the Covenant.

1678 RAY 250. **1791–1823** I. DISRAELI *Curios.
Lit.* (Chandos) III. 59 *Hand over head, as the
men took the Covenant* . . . preserves the
manner in which the Scotch covenant . . .
was violently taken by above sixty thousand
persons about Edinburgh, in 1638.

Hand play, churls' play.

[Span. *Juego de manos juego de villanos.*
Sport with the hands is the sport of peasants.]
1689 SHADWELL *Bury Fair* II. i (Merm.) 389
Sir Humph. Is not that a pretty clinch, Jack?
[*He gives him a rap on the back.*] *Trim.* Sir,
let me tell you, there is a Spanish proverb,
which says, Whego[1] *de manos, whego de
Vilanos.* [[1] Phonetic for *juego*, 'joke' or
'play'.]

Hand that gives, gathers, The.

1659 HOWELL *Brit. Prov.* 34.

Hand to mouth, *see* Live from h. to m.

Hand that rocks the cradle rules the world, The.

a. **1881** W. R. WALLACE *John o'London's
Treasure Trove.* The hand that rocks the
cradle Is the hand that rules the world.

Hand twice to your bonnet for once to your pouch,[1] Put your.

1737 RAMSAY III. 192. [[1] purse.]

Hand, One | washeth another (the other) and both the face. (*Cf.* following proverb.)

[ERASM. *Ad. Manus manum lavat,* quoting

χεὶρ χεῖρα κνίζει.] **1573** SANDFORD (1576)
223. **1578** FLORIO *First Fruites* f. 34. **1580**
LYLY *Euph. & his Eng.* (Arb.) 221 One hand
washeth an other but they both wash the
face. **1596** SPENSER, *F.Q.* IV. i. 40 Myself will
for you fight, As ye have done for me, The
left hand rubs the right. **1617** MORYSON *Itin.*
III. I. ii. 17 He that writes often, shall often
receive letters for answere: for one hand
washeth another. **1640** HERBERT 328 **1881**
DEAN PLUMPTRE *Eccles.* iv. 9 Two are better
than one. . . . So the Greek proverb ran as to
friends χεὶρ χεῖρα νίπτει, δάκτυλός τε δάκτυλον.
'Hand cleanseth hand, and finger finger helps.'

Hand, One | will not wash the other for nothing.

1721 KELLY 275.

Hand(s), *see also* Bark and tree (Put not h.
between); Better h. loose than in ill
tethering; Cold h. warm heart; Fingers
were made . . . and h. before knives; Good
h. good hire; Good tongue (Who has not)
ought to have good h.; Help, h., for I have
no lands; Kiss the h. they wish cut off;
Many h. light work; Mouth hath beguiled
your h. (Your); Nothing enters into close
h.; Pleased (If you be not), put h. in
pocket; Right h. from his left (Knows not);
Stretch your arm (h.) no further than
sleeve; Two h. in dish, one in purse;
Washing his h. (For) none sells lands;
White h. cannot hurt; Wise h. doth not all
foolish mouth speaks. *See also* At hand.

Hand (at cards), *see* Cast (H.) be bad (If),
mend by good play.

Handful of dust will fill the eye of man, Nothing but a.

1853 TRENCH iv. 75 This Arabic, on the never
satisfied eye of desire: *Nothing but a handful
of dust will fill the eye of man.*

Handful of trade is an handful of gold, An.

1721 KELLY 13. **1732** FULLER no. 603.

Handful, *see also* Know by a h. the sack.

Handkerchief, To fling (throw) one's.

[= to express condescending preference for
a person.] **1622** J. FLETCHER *Sea-Voyage* III.
i Like the Grand Signior . . . then draw I
forth My handkercher, and having made my
choice, I thus bestow it. **1718** (O.S.) LADY
M. W. MONTAGU *Let.* Countess of Mar 10 Mar.
The Sultana . . . assured me, that the story
of the Sultan's throwing a handkerchief is
altogether fabulous. **1850** THACKERAY *Pendennis* lxv 'And so, . . . you condescend to
fling to me your royal pocket handkerchief',
said Blanche.

Handle without mittens, To.

[= to treat unmercifully.] **1659** HOWELL
Fr.-Eng. 16 (A) They will not be caught
without mittains. **1678** RAY 76 To handle
without mittins. **1699** R. L'ESTRANGE *Erasm.*

Colloq. (1711) 178 He handled the Reverend
Fathers without Mittens.

Handles a nettle tenderly is soonest stung, He that.

1579 LYLY *Euphues* (Arb.) 66 True it is
Philautus that hee which toucheth the Nettle
tenderly, is soonest stoung. **1660** W. SECKER
Nonsuch Prof. II. (1891) 158 Sin is like a
nettle, which stings when it is gently touched,
but hurts not when it is roughly handled.
1732 FULLER no. 2126. **1753** AARON HILL *The
Nettle's Lesson* Tender-handed stroke a nettle,
And it stings you for your pains; Grasp it like
a man of mettle, And it soft as silk remains.
1830 FORBY 430 'Nip a nettle hard, and it
will not sting you'—*i.e.* Strong and decided
measures prevail best with troublesome
people.

Handles thorns shall prick his fingers, He that.

1616 BRETON *Wks.* (Gros.) II. e 6 (A). **1670**
RAY 148.

Handle(s), *see* Most things have two h.

Hands off and fair play.

1639 CLARKE 273. **1815** SCOTT *Guy Man.* xl
Hands off is fair play.

Hands off other folks' bairns, Hold your | till you get some of your own.

1855 BOHN 408.

Hands, *see also* Hand(s).

Handsaw is a good thing, but not to shave with, A.

1732 T. FULLER no. 210. **1746** FRANKLIN Dec.
Tim and his handsaw are good in their place,
Tho' not fit for preaching or shaving a face.
1802 WOLCOT (P. Pindar) *Middl. Elect.* i A
*handsaw is a useful thing, But never made for
shaving.*

Handsome at twenty, He that is not | nor strong at thirty, nor rich at forty, nor wise at fifty, will never be handsome, strong, rich, or wise.

1640 HERBERT 333.

Handsome head of hair; You have a | pray give me a tester.[1]

1678 RAY 73 You have a handsome head of
hair, pray give me a tester. When Spendthrifts come to borrow money they commonly
usher in their errand with some frivolous discourse in commendation of the person they
would borrow of, or some of his parts or
qualities: The same be said of beggers. [[1] sixpence.]

Handsome is that handsome does.

1580 MUNDAY *Sunday Examples* (Sh. S.) 78 (A)
But as the auncient adage is, goodly is he that
goodly dooth. **1670** RAY 99 He is handsome

that handsome doth. **1766** GOLDSMITH *Vicar of W.* i They are as heaven made them, handsome enough if they be good enough; for handsome is that handsome does. **1829** COBBETT *Adv. to Y. Men* iii (1906) 122 'Handsome is that handsome does', used to say to me an old man, who had marked me out for his not over-handsome daughter. **1896** SKEAT *Stud. Pastime* 79 In the proverb Handsome is as handsome does', *handsome* means *neat*, with reference to skilfulness of execution.

Handspike, *see* Purser's shirt on a h. (Like a).

Handwriting, *see* Writing (H.) on the wall.

Hang a dog on a crab-tree, and he'll never love verjuice.[1]

1670 RAY 81 ... This is a ludicrous and nugatory saying, for a dog once hang'd is past loving or hating. But generally men and beasts shun those things, by or for which they have smarted. **1692** L'ESTRANGE *Aesop's Fab.* lix (1738) 74 Affliction makes a man both honest and wise; for the smart brings him to a sense of his error, and the experiment to the knowledge of it. ... *Hang a dog upon a crab-tree* (we say), *and he'll never love verjuice.* [1 The juice of sour fruit, formerly much used in cooking.]

Hang a nose, To.

[= to have an inclination or hankering.] **1649** G. DANIEL *Trinarch. Hen. V* cxxv Chuse his Bread, And hang a Nose to Leekes, Quaile-Surfetted. **1655** tr. *Sorel's Com. Hist. Francion* VIII. 19 If there be in my Kitchin any thing better than another . . . this Gallant wil hang a nose after it.

Hang all my bells upon one horse, I must (will) not.

1659 HOWELL *Eng. Prov.* 14/2 . . .; *viz. Give all away to one son.* **1732** FULLER no. 1786 Hang not all your bells upon one horse.

Hang by the heels, Let him.

1678 RAY 353 Let him hang by the heels. *Som.* (Of a man that dies in debt: His wife leaving all at his death, crying his goods in three markets and three Parish Churches is so free of all his debts.)

Hang him that hath no shifts.

1639 CLARKE 42.

Hang him that hath no shift (shifts) and him that hath one too many.

1616 WITHALS 584 **1721** KELLY 128 . . . He that has no shift, is not worth hanging; and he that has too many, may be hanged in time. **1732** FULLER no. 1785. **1738** SWIFT (Dial. i) 341 *Never.* The loop of my hat is broke, how shall I mend it? [*He fastens it with a pin.*] Well, hang him, say I, that has no shift. *Miss.* Ay, and hang him that has one too many.

Hang himself in his own garters, He may go.

1596 T. LODGE *Wit's Misery* E 4 I will make

the moule warpe hang himselfe in his owne garters. **1597–8** SHAKS. *1 Hen. IV* II. ii. 46 Go, hang thyself in thine own heir apparent garters. **1599–1600** *Twelfth N.* I. iii. 13 These clothes are good enough to drink in, and so be these boots too: an they be not, let them hang themselves in their own straps. **1605** JONSON *Volpone* v. iii. 20. **1611** TOURNEUR *Ath. Trag.* II. v And as I ran, indeed I bid him hang himself in his own garters. **1652** 'G. ALBUMAZAR' *Mercurius Phreneticus* 2 Potes pendere in tuo Gartero, you may hang yourself in your own Garters. **1678** RAY 246. **1692** T. D'URFEY *The Marriage-Hater Match'd* v. iii. **1738** SWIFT 341 Well, go hang yourself in your own garters.

Hang his dog, He that would | gives out first that he is mad.

1530 PALSGRAVE 450 (A) He that wyll kyll his neyghbours dogge beareth folkes in hande he is madde. **1670** RAY 81. ... He that is about to do any thing disingenuous, unworthy, or of evil fame, first bethinks himself of some plausible pretence. **1732** FULLER no. 2362.

Hang in your light, *see* Horns; Lips; Maidenhead.

Hang one's harp on the willows, To.

1611 BIBLE *Ps.* cxxxvii. 1, 2 We wept, when we remembered Zion. We hanged our harps upon the willows. **1633** P. FLETCHER *Pisc. Eclog.* iv No marvel if I hate my jocund rhymes, And hang my pipe upon a willow bough. **1757** SMOLLETT *Reprisal* I. 8 All our fine project gone to pot!—We may now hang up our harps among the willows.

Hang saving: bring us a ha'porth of cheese.

c. **1630** *Hang Pinching* [title of ballad] in *Roxb. Ballads* (B.S.) iii (A). **1738** SWIFT (Dial. ii) 348 Come, hang saving; bring us up a half-p'orth of cheese.

Hang than to hold, Better to.

1567 HARMAN *Caveat* (Viles & Furnivall) 76 He is better to hang then to drawe forth. **1624** T. BREWER *A Knot of Fools* Better to hang, then to feed. **1639** CLARKE 86. **1635** MERITON *Yorks. Ale* 48 (A) Sike fowkes are fitter to hang than hawd.

Hang the groin (a leg, an arse), To.

[= to hesitate or hold back.] **1577–87** HOLINSHED *Chron.* (1807–8) III. 163 At this answer The duke hoong the groin. **1596** HARINGTON *Metam. Ajax* (1814) 61 Some of our rude countrymen english this hanging an arse. **1883** STEVENSON *Treas. Isl.* I. v. You have thousands, you fools, and you hang a leg!

Hang together like pebbles in a halter, They.

1678 RAY 250.

Hang up one's hatchet, To.

[= to cease from one's labours, to rest.] *a.* **1327** *Pol. Songs* (Camden Soc.) 223 Hang up thyn hachet ant thy knyf Whil him lasteth the lyf with the long shonkes. *c.* **1430** *Hymns Virg.* (1867) 69 Hang up þin hatchet & take þi reste. *a.* **1530** *R. Hill's Common Pl. Bk.* (1858) 140 When thou hast well done hang up thy hatchet.

Hang yourself for a pastime.

1678 RAY 73.

Hanged for a sheep as a lamb, As good (well) be.

1678 RAY 350 As good be hang'd for an old sheep as a young lamb. *Somerset.* **1721** KELLY 46 ... Used at a game at tables, when I venture high in order to recover my game which otherwise would be lost. **1836** MARRYAT *Midsh. Easy* xvii We may as well be hanged for a sheep as a lamb, ... I vote that we do not go on board.

Hanged for leaving his liquor, like the saddler of Bawtry,[1] He will be. (*Cf.* Hanged that left his drink, &c.)

1790 GROSE S.V. Yorkshire' (A). **1818** S. PEGGE *Curialia Mix.* 340 This saying, often applied ... to a man who quits his friends too early, and will not stay to finish his bottle; 'That he will be hanged for leaving his liquor, like the saddler of Bawtry'. [1 Yorks.]

Hanged, If I be | I'll choose my gallows.

a. **1633** JONSON *T. Tub* IV. vi. 97–8 Hang'd ...? yes sure; unlesse, as with the Proverbe, You meane to make the choice of your own gallowes. **1659** HOWELL *Eng. Prov.* 16/2 If I be hang'd Ile chuse my gallowes. **1738** SWIFT (Dial. ii) 343 *Never.* Well, miss, if I must be hanged, I won't go far to choose my gallows; it shall be about your fair neck.

Hanged in May, He that is | will eat no flannes[1] in midsummer.

1820 SCOTT *Abbot* xxxiii He that is hanged in May will eat no flannes in Midsummer. [1 custards, pancakes.]

Hanged, He that hath had one of his family | may not say to his neighbour, Hang up this fish. (*Cf.* Rope, Name not, &c.)

1678 RAY *Adag. Hebr.* 408 ... The meaning is, we must abstain from words of reproach, ... especially when we are not free from the crimes which we reproach others for.

Hanged that left his drink behind him, He was. (*Cf.* Hanged for leaving his liquor, &c.)

c. **1640** *Roxb. Ballads* (B.S.) 416 (A) He was hang'd that left his drinke behinde. **1678** RAY 71 ... Good fellows have a story of a certain malefactor, who came to be suspected upon leaving his drink behind him in an Alehouse, at the News of an Hue and cry. **1738** SWIFT

(Dial. ii) 349 Stay till this bottle's out; you know, the man was hang'd that left his liquor behind him.

Hangeth himself on Sunday, He that | shall hang still uncut down on Monday.

1546 HEYWOOD I. xi. 27 Well, he that hangth him selfe a sondaie (said hée) Shall hang still vncut downe a mondaie for mée.

Hanging and wiving (wedding) go by destiny.

1546 HEYWOOD I. iii. 7. Be it far or nie, weddyng is desteny, And hangyng likewise, saith that prouerbe, said I. **1596–7** SHAKS. *Merch. V.* II. ix. 82 The ancient saying is no heresy: 'Hanging and wiving goes by destiny.' **1599** DEKKER *Shoem. Hol.* IV. iii *Firk.* Well, God sends fools fortune, and ... he may light upon his matrimony by such a device; for wedding and hanging goes by destiny. **1641** FERGUSSON 40 Hanging ganges be hap. **1664** BUTLER *Hudibras* II. i. 839 If matrimony and hanging go By dest'ny, why not whipping too? **1738** SWIFT (Dial. i) 340 'Twas her fate; they say, marriage and hanging go by destiny.

Hanging's stretching; mocking's catching. (*See also* Mocking is catching.)

1678 RAY 200.

Hanging, *see also* Agree like bells, want but h.; Half an hour's h. hinders ... riding; Thieves and rogues have the best luck, if they but scape h.; Ways to kill dog than h. (More).

Hangs by jommetry, It.

1738 SWIFT (Dial. i) 341 *Miss.* My petticoat! how it hangs by jommetry! *Never.* Perhaps the fault may be in your shape.

Hang(s, ed, eth), *see also* Almost was never h.; Born to be h. never be drowned; Boughs that bear most h. lowest; Confess and be h.; Haste to h. true men (No); Ill deemed half h.; Killeth a man when drunk shall be h.; Live to be old (If you would not), be h. young; Luck goes on (If your), you may hope to be h.; Men of all trades (Of), they especially h. thieves; Over holy was h.; Pay well ... h. well; Rich before night, h. before noon; Rich man's money h. him; Rises over early that is h. ere noon; Rope enough ... h. himself (h. his mare); Rope (Name not) in his house that h. himself; Scant of news that told father was h.; Sheep h. by his own shank (Let every); Suits h. half a year in Westminster Hall; Tender Gordons that dow not be h.; Worst use can put man to is h. him.

Hankering and hinging on is a poor trade.

1721 KELLY 142 ... Spoken of the miserable

condition of those who depend upon great men's promises for places and preferments.

Hans-in-kelder.

[Dutch, lit. Jack-in-cellar: an unborn child.] **1635** BROME *Sparagus Garden* III. iv. Wks. (1873) III. 159 Come here's a health to the Hans in Kelder, and the mother of the boy, if it prove so. **1816** SCOTT *Let.* 12 Nov. in LOCKHART *Life* xxxvii (1860) 337 I think of sending you one day . . . a little drama. . . . It is yet only in embryo—a sort of poetical Hans in Kelder.

Hantle[1] o' fauts, Some hae a | ye're only a ne'er-do-weel.

1862 HISLOP 264 . . . Some, though very bad, still have some redeeming qualities; the party addressed has none. [[1] a considerable number.]

Hap and halfpenny goods enough.

1639 CLARKE 126. **1641** FERGUSSON 44 Hap and a half-pennie, is warlds geir enough. **1670** RAY 100 . . . i.e. Good luck is enough, though a man hath not a penny left him.

Hap, Some have the | some stick in the gap.

1639 CLARKE 125. **1721** KELLY 296.

Hap, *see also* Good or ill h. of a good or ill life; No man can make his own h.

Happen(eth, s), *see* Chanceth (H.) in an hour that h. not in seven years; Unforeseen that h.

Happiness takes no account of time.

1718 PRIOR *Alma* iii. 257 Holds that the happy know no hours; So, through the street at midnight scours.

Happiness, *see* Talks much of his h. (He that).

Happy (Merry) as a king.

c. **1512** *Hickscorner* C 3ᵛ. *c.* **1554** *Enterlude of Youth* in BANG *Materialien* B. 12, p. 8 I wyll make as mery as a kynge. **1595** PEELE *Old Wiues Tale* A 3 This Smith leads a life as merrie as a king. **1720** GAY *New Similes* Full as an egg was I with glee; And happy as a king. **1840** LEVER *Chas. O'Mal.* lxxv My father mixed a jug of . . . punch, and sat down as happy as a king.

Happy for a day, Let him that would be | go to the barber; for a week, marry a wife; for a month, buy him a new horse; for a year, build him a new house; for all his life time, be an honest man.

1662 FULLER *(Wales)* III. 487 'Italian'.

Happy is he that chastens himself.

1640 HERBERT 155.

Happy is he that is happy in his children.

1732 FULLER no. 1787.

Happy is he whose friends were (father was) born before him. (*Cf.* Thank God that your father, &c.)

1670 RAY 99 Happy is he whose friends were born before him, i.e. Who has *rem non labore parandum sed relictam.* **1721** KELLY 379 *You may thank God that your friends were born before you.* Spoken to inactive thriftless people, who, if their parents had left them nothing must have begg'd. **1732** FULLER no. 1790. **1738** SWIFT (Dial. iii) 350 Why, madam, 'tis happy for him that his father was born before him.

Happy is she who marries the son of a dead mother. (*Cf.* Well married who has neither, &c.)

1721 KELLY 162 . . . There is rarely a good understanding between a daughter-in-law, and her husband's mother.

Happy is that child whose father goeth to the devil.

1552 LATIMER *Serm. Lord's Prayer* v. (P.S.) 410 There is a common saying amongst the worldlings, Happy is that child whose father goeth to the devil. . . . Many a father goeth to the devil for his child's sake; in that he . . . scraped for his child, and forgat to relieve his poor miserable neighbour. **1590–1** SHAKS. *3 Hen. VI* II. ii. 47 And happy always was it for that son Whose father for his hoarding went to hell? **1670** RAY 100 Happy is the child whose father went to the devil. For commonly they who first raise great estates, do it either by usury and extortion, or by fraud and cozening, or by flattery and ministering to other men's vices.

Happy is the, *see also* Bride the sun shines on; Country which has no history; Wooing that is not long.

Happy man cannot be harried,[1] The.

1721 KELLY 313 . . . Spoken when a feared misfortune happened for the best. [[1] ruined.]

Happy man, happy dole (be his dole).

[= may happiness be his portion.] **1546** HEYWOOD I. iii. 7 Than wed or hang (quoth he) what helpeth in the whole To hast or hang aloof, happy man happy dole. **1593–4** SHAKS. *Tam. Shrew* I. i. 144 Sweet Bianca! Happy man be his dole. **1597–8** *1 Hen. IV* II. ii. 84 Now my masters, happy man be his dole, say I. **1600–1** *Merry W.* III. iv. 68 If it be my luck, so; if not, happy man be his dole. **1610–11** *Wint. T.* I. ii. 163 Mam. No, my lord, I'll fight. Leon. You will? Why, happy man be his dole. **1660** TATHAM *Rump.* I. i A short life and a merry life, I cry. Happy man be his dole. **1809** MALKIN *Gil Blas* VIII. ix Happy man be his dole who can get them to dinner or supper.

Happy man, happy kevel.[1]

1641 FERGUSSON 42 Happie man, happie

cavil. KELLY 159 ... Jocosely spoken when people are drawing lots, or when it has fallen out well with us, or our friend. [¹ lot.]

Happy, Call no man | till he dies.

[AESCH. *Ag.* 928. SOPH. *Oed. Rex*, last words. EUR. *Androm.* 100. HDT. 1. 32 (Solon and Croesus). OV. *Met.* 3. 135.] **1603** FLORIO tr. *Montaigne* I. xviii (1897) I. 83 We must expect of man the latest day, Nor e'er he die, be's happy, can we say. **1891** *Times* 5 Dec. 'Call no man happy till he dies' is the motto ... suggested by the career of Dom Pedro [of Brazil].

Happy whom other men's perils make wary, He is.

1539 TAVERNER 3 Fœlix quem faciunt aliena pericula cautum. He is happy, whom other mens perils maketh ware. **1636** CAMDEN 299 He is happy can beware by others' harms.

Happy, *see also* Better be h. than wise; Hour wherein a man might be h. could he find it; Misery enough to have once been h.

Harborough field, I will throw you into.

1678 RAY 317 (*Leics.*) ... A threat for children, Harborough having no field.

Harbory, *see* Ill of his h. is good of way-kenning.

Hard as a flint (*or* stone), As.

c. **1390** CHAUCER *Merchant's T.* 746 An herte as hard as any stoon. *c.* **1400** *Pety Job* 318 in *26 Pol. Poems* 131 He thynketh myn hert ys harder than a ston. **1720** GAY *Poems* (Underhill) ii. 278 (A) Hard is her heart as flint or stone.

Hard baked, *see* Crusty as that is h. b.

Hard cases make bad law.

[SALL. *Cat.* 51. 27 *Omnia mala exempla ex bonis* (i.e. good special cases) *orta sunt.*] **1902–4** LEAN III. 479 Hard cases make bad law, i.e. lead to legislation for exceptions. **1909** *Spectator* 809 Even so bad a case ... does not ... alter our attitude ... 'Hard cases make bad law', and also bad policy. **1945** CHURCHILL (Premier) 12 June (in H. of Commons) Hard cases do not make good law.

Hard cheese.

1876 MRS. BANKS *Manch. Man* xlii It's hard cheese for a man to owe everything to his father-in-law.

Hard fare makes hungry bellies.

1616 BRETON *Wks.* (Gros.) II. e 6 (A) Hard fare makes hungry stomackes. **1639** CLARKE 241. **1732** FULLER no. 1796.

Hard-fought field, where no man escapeth unkilled, A.

1546 HEYWOOD I. xi. 37 Olde men say that are skyld, A hard foughten féeld, where no man skapth vnkylld. **1639** CLARKE 103 'Tis

an hard battle where none scape. **1641** FERGUSSON 66 It's a sair field where all are dung¹ down. [¹ beaten.]

Hard gives more than he that hath nothing, The.

1599 MINSHEU (1623) Ss 6ᵛ More giueth the hard than the naked. **1640** HERBERT 329.

Hard heart against hard hap (Stout heart to a stey¹ brae), Set.

a. **1585** ALEX. MONTGOMERIE *Cherrie & Slae* xxxvi (1821) 21 So gets ay, that sets ay, Stout stomackis to the brae. **1639** CLARKE 15. **1721** KELLY 287 *Set a stout heart to a stay brea.* Set about a difficult business with courage and constancy. **1821** GALT *Annals of Par.* i I began a round of visitations; but oh, it was a steep brae that I had to climb, and it needed a stout heart. For I found the doors ... barred against me. **1830** CARLYLE *Let. to Brother John* 11 Feb. 'Stout heart to a stay brae' then, my brave boy! There is nothing in this world to frighten a clear heart. [¹ steep.]

Hard-hearted as a Scot of Scotland, As.

1678 RAY 285.

Hard nut to crack, A. (*Cf.* Crack me that nut.)

1655 FULLER *Hist. Camb.* (1840) 95 Why was this Hall first visited ? ... But the nut is not worth the cracking. **1745** FRANKLIN *Lett.* Wks. 1887 II. 16 Fortified towns are hard nuts to crack. **1888** J. PAYN *Myst. Mirbridge* You will find Robert Morris a hard nut to crack.

Hard task to be poor and leal, It is a.

1721 KELLY 211 ... Because poverty is a great tentation to steal.

Hard thing to have a great estate, and not fall in love with it, It is a.

1721 FULLER no. 2862.

Hard to come by are much set by, Things that are. (*See also* Hardly attained, &c.)

c. **1400** *Rom. Rose* 2737 May no man have good, but he it by. A man loveth more tendirly The thyng that he hath bought most dere. **1587** GREENE *Wks.* (Gros.) IV. 101 Hardlie come by, warilie kept. **1629** T. ADAMS *Serm.* (1861–2) II. 545 Benefits common to all ... are little regarded: but *quæ rarissima carissima*—things hard to come by are much set by.

Hard to please a knave as a knight, It is as.

1639 CLARKE 275. **1670** RAY 111.

Hard winter when one wolf eats another, It is a.

1579 LYLY *Euph.* (Arb.) 78 Men themselues haue by vse obserued, yat it must be harde

Winter when one Wolfe eateth another. **1651** HERBERT 369 A wolf will never make war against another wolf. **1670** RAY 156 ... Mauvaise est la saison quand un loup mange l'autre.

Hard with hard makes not the stone wall.

[Med. L. *Durum et durum non faciunt murum.*] **1573** SANDFORD 210 Harde with hard neuer made good wall. **1629** T. ADAMS *Serm.* (1861-2) II. 317 The Italians have a proverb, 'Hard without soft, the wall is nought'. Stones ... without mortar ... make but a tottering wall ... The society that consists of nothing but stones, intractable and refractory spirits, ... soon dissolves. **1655** FULLER *Ch. Hist.* II. iii. (1868) I. 143 'Hard with hard', saith the proverb, 'makes no wall'; and no wonder if the spiritual building went on no better, wherein the austerity and harshness of the pastor met with the ignorance and sturdiness of the people.

Hard words break no bones.

1867 TROLLOPE *Last Chron. Bars.* II. xii I often tell 'em how wrong folks are to say that soft words butter no parsnips, and hard words break no bones. **1882** BLACKMORE *Christow.* xlix 'Scoundrel, after all that I have done—'. 'Hard words break no bones, my friend.'

Hard, *see also* Row to hoe (H.); Three things ... h. to be known; Work h., live h. ... would be h. indeed.

Hard, It is; Hard to make, It is. *See also under significant words following.*

Hardly attained are longer retained, Things. (*See also* Hard to come by, &c.)

1639 CLARKE 101.

Hardships, *see* Misfortunes (H.) never come alone.

Hare, He hath devoured a. (*Cf.* Hare is melancholy meat.)

1577 T. KENDALL *Flowers of Epigrams* B 2 Thou didst neuer eate an hare. **1599** H. BUTLER *Diet's Dry Dinner* K 2 It is a receiued opinion, that vse of Hares procureth beautie, fresh colour, and cheerfull countenance, for a seuenight space: in so much as the Italians haue a by-word, which speaketh thus of a faire man, He hath eaten an Hare.

Hare always returns to her form, The.

1818 SCOTT *Ht. Midl.* xxxiv I have no thought of stirring from the house I was born in; like the hare, I shall be worried in the seat I started from.

Hare is melancholy meat. (*Cf.* Hare, He hath devoured a.)

1558 BULLEIN *Govt. of Health* f. 90 (A) The fleshe of hares be hoote and drye, ingenderers of melancholye. **1621** BURTON *Anat. Mel.* I. ii.

II. 1 (1651) 67 Hare, a black meat, melancholy, and hard of digestion. **1738** SWIFT (Dial. ii) 346 *Lady S.* Will your ladyship have any of this hare? *Lady A.* No, madam, they say 'tis melancholy meat.

Hare (Tod[1]) or the bracken bush, Either the.

1659 T. PECKE *Parnassi Puerp.* 143 (A) He can't discern a hare from a brake-bush. **1670** RAY 179 It's either a hare or a brake-bush ... something if you knew what. **1721** KELLY 97 *Either the tod or the bracken bush.* Spoken to silly people when they speak with uncertainty. [[1] fox.]

Hare to breakfast, He that will have a | must hunt over-night.

1636 CAMDEN 297. **1732** FULLER no. 2365.

Hare went (goes) away, Here (There) the.

[= here or there the matter ended.] *c.* **1500** MEDWALL *Nature* pt. II. l. 589 (BRANDL *Quellen* 134) (A) There went the hare away. **1546** HEYWOOD II. v. 60 And here gothe the hare awaie. **1579** GOSSON *Sch. Abuse* (Arb.) 70 *Hic labor, hoc opus est,* there goeth the hare away. **1592** KYD *Span. Trag.* III. xii. 24 Here's the king ... there goes the hare away. **1600** HOLLAND *Livy* XXXV. xlv. 914 And here went the hare away. **1620** SHELTON *Quix.* II. xxx (1908) III. 31 But where we least think there goes the hare away.

Hare's foot, *see* Kiss the h. f.

Hare's head against the goose giblet(s), Set the.

1545 TAVERNER 26 As I say in our Englyshe prouerbe: Set the hares head against the gose gyblet. **1546** HEYWOOD II. iv. **1599** DEKKER *Shoem. Hol.* II. i (Merm.) 17 I'd set my old debts against my new driblets, And the hare's foot against the goose giblets. **1633** ROWLEY *Match. Midn.* v in HAZL. *Old Eng. Plays* XIII. 88 As I have been bawd to the flesh, you have been bawd to your money, so set the hare-pie against the goose-giblets. **1670** RAY 179 ... That is, balance things, set one against another. **1732** FULLER no. 4109.

Hares may pull dead lions by the beard.

[ERASM. *Ad.* IV. vii. 82 *Mortuo leoni et lepores insultant.*] **1586** PETTIE *Guazzo's Civ. Conv.* 31 Of these this saying rose, That the Lion being dead, the verie Hares triumph over him. *c.* **1589** KYD *Span. Trag.* I. ii. 172 So hares may pull dead lions by the beard. **1596-7** SHAKS. *K. John* II. i. 138 You are the hare of whom the proverb goes Whose valour plucks dead lions by the beard.

Hare(s), *see* Cow to catch a h. (Set a); Dog (Hindmost) may catch h.; Dry meat ... when he lost the h.; Find a woman ... and a h. without meuse; First catch your h.; God send you readier meat than running h.; Hunt for a h. with tabor; Mad as a h.; Run after two h. (If you); Run with the h. and hunt with hounds; Seek a h. in a hen's nest; Take h. with foxes; Tortoise to catch h. (Set); Two h. afoot (To have).

Harlot, *see* Silk and scarlet (In).

Harm watch, harm catch.

1481 CAXTON *Reynard* xx (Arb.) 50 I shal vnbynde my sack. yf he wil seche harm he shal fynde harme. **1614** JONSON *Barthol. Fair* v. iii *Harm watch, harm catch*, he says. **1663** J. WILSON *Cheats* II. v And to our seeming, it said again—Harm watch, harm catch.

Harm(s), *see also* Better the devil (h.) you know; Beware by other men's h.; Hate not at first h.

Harp and harrow, To agree like.

[= things entirely different, though their names alliterate.] **1563** BECON *Displ. Pop. Masse* (1637) 299 The Lords Supper and your peevish, popish private masse do agree together . . . as the common proverbe is, like harpe and harrow, or like the hare and the hound. **1624** GATAKER *Transubst.* 203 These things hang together like harp and harrow, as they say. **1639** CLARKE 94 They agree like harpe and harrow. **1700** T. BROWN tr. *Fresny's Amusem. Ser. & Com.* 34 [Beth- lehem] Bedlam . . . whether the Name and Thing be not as disagreeable as Harp and Harrow.

Harp on (upon) one string, To.

c. **1374** CHAUCER *Troylus* II. 1033 For though the beste harpour upon lyve Wolde on the beste sowned joly harpe . . . Touche ay o streng. . . . It sholde maken every wight to dulle. **1579** LYLY *Euphues* (Arb.) 137 He shoulde moreouer talke of many matters, not alwayes harp vpon one string. **1592–3** SHAKS. *Rich. III* IV. iv. 365 Harp not on that string, madam; that is past. **1600–1** *Hamlet* II. ii. 191 How say you by that? Still harping on my daughter. **1607–8** *Coriol.* II. iii. 260 Say you ne'er had done 't—Harp on that still— but by our putting on. **1662** FULLER (*Somers.*) III. 96 Which harping on that one string of his fidelity . . . was harmonious to queen Elizabeth.

Harp on the string that giveth no melody, You.

1546 HEYWOOD II. iv. 52 Ye harpe on the stryng, that geueth no melody. Your tounges run before your witis. **1580** LYLY *Euph. & his Eng.* (Arb.) 387 Thou harpest on that string, which long since was out of tune, but now is broken.

Harp, *see also* Ass play upon a h.; Hang one's h. on willows.

Harper(s), *see* Blind as a h.; Have among you, blind h.

Harried, *see* Happy man cannot be h.

Harrington (*i.e.* a farthing), Not worth a.

[A patent to coin farthings was granted in

1613 to Lord Harrington of Exton, hence the name.] **1628** SIR H. WOTTON *Let.* 12 Aug. in *Reliq. Wott.* (1672) 558 I have lost four or five friends, and yet I thank God, not gotten the value of one *Harrington*.

Harrogate Wells, Said the Devil when flying o'er | I think I am getting near home by the smells.

1902–4 LEAN I. 222. [Harrogate, in Yorkshire, is noted for its sulphurous, chalybeate and saline springs.]

Harrow (Rake) hell, and scum the devil. (*See also* Rake hell, &c.)

1670 RAY 180 Harrow or rake hell, and scum the Devil. **1732** FULLER no. 1798 Harrow hell and rake up the devil.

Harrow (*noun*), *see* Drinking at the h.; Frog said to the h., cursed be so many lords; Harp and h.; Toad under a h.

Harry's children of Leigh, never an one like another.

1670 RAY 217 (*Cheshire*).

Harry, *see also* Box H.; King H.

Hartlepool, *see* Mayor of H. (Like the).

Harvest ears, thick of hearing.

1546 HEYWOOD II. ix. 74 You had on your haruest eares, thicke of hearyng. **1608** WITHALS 46 Thine eares be on a pilgrimage . . . as they say commonly, thou hast on thy haruest eares.

Harvest follows seed-time.

1639 CLARKE 183.

Harvest(s), *see also* Eighth of June it rains (If on) wet h.; Good h. (He that hath) may be content with some thistles; Good h. make men prodigal; Long h. of little corn; Short h. make short adlings.

Harwich, *see* Deal, Dover, and H., the devil gave.

Has an hundred and one, He that | and owes an hundred and two, the Lord have mercy upon him.

1732 FULLER no. 2132.

Hassell's feast (Madam), *see* Enough and none to spare.

Haste and wisdom are things far odd.

1546 HEYWOOD I. ii. 5 Than seeth he hast and wisdome thingis far od.

Haste but good (speed), No.

a. **1553** UDALL *Royster D.* I. iii (Arb.) 20 *Tib.* No haste but good, Madge Mumblecrust, for whip and whurre[1] The olde prouerbe doth say, neuer made good furre.[2] **1639** CLARKE 115 No haste but good speed. **1721** KELLY 261 *No more haste than good speed. . . .* Spoken when we are unreasonably urged to make haste. [¹ hurry. ² furlong.]

Haste comes not alone.

1611 COTGRAVE s.v. 'Haste' Haste never comes alone, viz. hath ever some trouble or other t'accompany it. **1640** HERBERT 355.

Haste in his business, Who hath no | mountains to him seem valleys.

1640 HERBERT 363.

Haste is from hell (the devil).

1633 HOWELL *Fam. Lett.* 5 Sept. (1903) II. 140 As it is a principle in chemistry that *Omni festinatio est a Diabolo*, All haste comes from Hell, so in . . . any business of State, all rashness and precipitation comes from an ill spirit. **1929** *Times* 12 Sept. 14/3 Listening patiently to the views . . . [f]or he understood the East; he knew that for an Intelligence officer 'haste is from the devil'.

Haste like a snail, In.

1546 HEYWOOD I. ix. 17 And thytherward hye me in haste lyke a snayle.

Haste makes waste.

c. **1386** CHAUCER *Cant. Tales* B² 2244 The prouerbe seith . . . 'in wikked haste is no profit'. **1546** HEYWOOD I. ii. 5 Show after weddyng, that hast maketh waste. **1663** BUTLER *Hudibras* iii. 1253 *Festina lente*, Not too fast; For haste (the proverb says) makes waste. **1853** TRENCH i. 16 Many excellent proverbs, such as *Haste makes waste* . . . have nothing figurative about them.

Haste makes waste, and waste makes want, and want makes strife between the goodman and his wife.

1678 RAY 151.

Haste, The more | the less (worse) speed.

c. **1350** *Douce MS. 52* no. 86 The more hast, þe worse spede. *c.* **1430** LYDGATE *Minor Poems* (Percy Soc.) 75 The slowar paas, the further in rennyng; The more I renne, the more wey I lese. **1546** HEYWOOD I. ii. 5 Moste times he seeth, the more haste the lesse speede. **1594–5** SHAKS. *Rom. & Jul.* II. iii. 94 Wisely and slow; They stumble that run fast. **1595** *Locrine* I. ii (*Shaks. Apoc.*) 43 *Strum.* My penne is naught; gentlemen, lend me a knife. I thinke the more haste the worst speed. **1611** DAVIES *Prov.* 48 'The more haste, the worse speede.' **1887** BLACKMORE *Springhaven* lvii Some days had been spent by the leisurely Dutchman in providing fresh supplies, and the stout bark's favourite maxim seemed to be, 'the more haste the less speed'. **1894** LD. AVEBURY *Use of Life* xii (1904) 77 Do nothing in a hurry. Nature never does. 'Most haste, worst speed.' **1896** SKEAT *Stud. Pastime* 79 'The more haste, the worse speed.' . . . When we remember that *speed* really meant *success* in Old English, the sense becomes 'The more haste, the worse success', which is a perfectly wise and sensible saying.

Haste, The more | the worse speed, quoth the tailor to his long thread.

1721 KELLY 313.

Haste to hang true men, No.

c. **1550** *Jacke Juggeler* in HAZLITT, *Old Plays* ii. 120 (A) I fear hanging, whereunto no man is hasty. **1599** PORTER *Angry Wom. Abingd.* II. i (Merm.) 126 *Nich.* There's no haste to hang true men. **1662** FULLER (*London*) II. 341 As if Londoners . . . aim more at dispatch than justice; and, to make quick riddance (though no haste to hang true men), acquit half, and condemn half.

Haste trips up its own heels.

1732 FULLER no. 1801.

Haste when you come down than when you went up, Make no more.

1604 *Pasquils Jests* (1864) 42 (A) Take heed that you never get faster downe then you go up. **1678** RAY 151 As the man said to him on the tree top, Make no more haste when you come down than when you went up. **1692** L'ESTRANGE *Aesop's Fab.* ccclxix (1738) 388 Have a care . . ., whenever you climb another tree, that you come no faster down than you went up.

Haste, *see also* Anger and h. hinder good counsel; Fool's h. no speed; Make h. slowly; Make h. to an ill way; More h. than speed; No man makes h. to the market; Thrive in all h. (You would).

Hastens a glutton, Who | chokes him.

1640 HERBERT 356.

Hasteth well that wisely can abide, He, *see* Make haste slowly.

Hastily, *see* Nothing must be done h. but killing fleas.

Hastings, He is none of the.

1546 HEYWOOD I. xi. 35 Toward your woorkyng (quoth he) ye make such tastingis, As approue you to be none of the hastingis. **1662** FULLER (*Sussex*) III. 243 'He is none of the Hastings'. . . . There is a noble and ancient family of the Hastings . . . earls . . . of Huntingdon. Now men commonly say, They are none of the Hastings, who being slow and slack go about business with no agility.

Hasty bitch bringeth forth blind whelps, The.

[ERASM. *Ad.* (quoting Aristotle and Galen) *Canis festinans cæcos parit catulos.*] **1556** R. ROBINSON tr. *More's Utopia* 2nd ed. To Reader (Arb.) 19 (A) But as the latin prouerbe sayeth: the hastye bitche bringeth forth blind whelpes. For when this my worke was finished, the rudenes thereof shewed it to be done in poste haste. **1575** GASCOIGNE *Posies, Flowers* 68 The swiftest bitche brings foorth the blyndest whelpes. **1755** FRANKLIN *Mar.* The hasty Bitch brings forth blind Puppies.

Hasty climbers have sudden falls.

c. **1480** *Digby Plays* (E.E.T.S.) 54 (A) Who clymyth high, his ffalle grett is. **1579** SPENSER *Shep. Cal.* Jul., Wks. (Globe) 466 Great clymbers fall unsoft. *a.* **1607** SIR E. DYER *My mind to me* And hasty climbers soon do fall. **1670** RAY 71 Hasty climbers, have sudden falls. Those that rise suddenly from a mean condition to great estate or dignity, do often fall more suddenly, as . . . many Court-favourites.

Hasty gamesters oversee.

1678 RAY 151. **1732** FULLER no. 1803 (adding themselves').

Hasty love is soon hot and soon cold. (*See also* Soon hot soon cold.)

1546 HEYWOOD I. ii Then perceive they well, hot love soon cold. *c.* **1570** *Wyt & Science* 645 Thys proverbe old: Hastye love is soone hot and soone cold!

Hasty man never wants woe, A. (*Cf.* Angry man, &c.)

c. **1374** CHAUCER *Troylus* IV. 1568 For hastif man ne wanteth never care! *c.* **1390** GOWER *Conf. Amantis* III. 1861 Folhaste is cause of mochel wo. *c.* **1420** *Peter Idle's Instructions to his son* (Miessner) l. 238 An hasty man wanteth neuer woo. *c.* **1450** *Prov. of Wysdom* in HERRIG'S *Archiv.* 90 l. 125 Hastye man lackype no sorow. **1546** HEYWOOD I. ii. 5. **1614** CAMDEN 302. **1640** HERBERT 342 The choleric man never wants woe. **1721** KELLY 2 A wilful man never wanted woe.

Hasty man, *see also* Keep out of a h. m.'s way.

Hasty meeting, a hasty parting, A.

1721 KELLY 19. **1736** BAILEY *Dict.* s.v. 'Woo'.

Hasty people will never make good midwives.

1659 HOWELL *Eng. Prov.* 3/2. **1670** RAY 101.

Hasty to outbid another, Be not too.

1664 CODRINGTON 188. **1670** RAY 3.

Hasty, *see also* Too h. to be parish clerk.

Hat covers his family, His.

1858 SURTEES *Ask Mamma* xvi His hat had so long covered his family, that he hardly knew how to set about obtaining his own consent to marry. **1894** BLACKMORE *Perly-cross* xl Jakes . . . sat down, thanking the crown of his hat that it covered the whole of his domestic interests.

Hat is not made for one shower, A.

1640 HERBERT 348.

Hat, *see also* Cob a h. and a pair of shoes (Give); Head (He that has no) needs no h.; Pull down your h. on wind side.

Hatband, *see* Dick's h. (Queer as).

Hatch[1] before the door, It is good to have (keep, set) a.

[= to keep silence.] **1546** HEYWOOD I. xi. 26 Well I will no more sturre. It is good to haue a hatche before the durre. **1555** R. SMITH in FOXE *A. & M.* (1684) III. 336/2 Seeing God hath given a Tongue, And put it under power: The surest way it is to set A hatch before the door. **1579** GOSSON *Sch. Abuse* (Arb.) 53 I wish that euery rebuker shoulde place a hatch before the door. [[1] a half-door; small gate or wicket.]

Hatch, match, and despatch.

1878 J. PAYN *By Proxy* xix First came the Births, Deaths, and Marriages, . . . the female mind . . . takes an interest in the 'Hatch, Match, and Despatch' of its fellow-creatures.

Hatch(eth), *see also* Mischief h. (He that).

Hatchet, To throw (fling, sling) the.

[= to make exaggerated statements.] **1780** G. PARKER *Life's Painter* xii. 85 Many . . . habituate themselves by degrees to a mode of the hatchet-flinging extreme. **1893** T. B. FOREMAN *Trip to Spain* 97 The ladies titter, knowing, as we do the skipper's habit of slinging the hatchet.

Hatchet, *see also* Bury the h.; Dig up the h.; Hang up one's h.; Helve after h. (Throw); Pap with a h.

Hate (one) like poison, To.

1812 EDGEWORTH *Absentee* xiii I know she hates me like poison.

Hate not at the first harm.

1639 CLARKE 235.

Hate, *see also* Greatest h. from greatest love; Love as in time thou shouldest h.

Hated man, *see* Seldom does the h. m. end well.

Hated of his subjects, He that is | cannot be counted a king.

1641 FERGUSSON 44.

Hates not the person, but the vice, One.

1604–5 SHAKS. *Meas. for Meas.* II. ii. 37 Condemn the fault, and not the actor of it? **1666** TORRIANO 313.

Hath it and will not keep it; He that | he that wants it and will not seek it; he that drinks and is not dry, shall want money as well as I.

1659 HOWELL *Eng. Prov.* 21. **1670** RAY 211.

Hatred is blind, as well as love.

1732 FULLER no. 1805. **1903** MERRIMAN *Barlasch* xxi Love, it is said, is blind. But hatred is as bad.

Hatred with friends is succour to foes.

1573 SANDFORD (1576) 219. **1578** FLORIO *First Fruites*, f. 33 (A) Hatred among friendes is succour vnto strangers. **1616** DRAXE 30.

Hatter, *see* Mad as a h.

Hatteras, *see* Bermudas.

Haul (Fetch, Bring, *or* Call) over the coals, To.

[= to call to account: originally in reference to the treatment of heretics.] **1565** CDL. ALLEN in FULKE *Confut.* (1577) 372 S. Augustine, that knewe best how to fetche an heretike ouer the coles. **1639** FULLER *Holy War* v. ii (1840) 243 If they should say the Templars were burned wrongfully, they may be fetched over the coals themselves. **1658** J. SMITH *Wit Restor'd* (Hotten) 283 Your Smith can fetch em over the coales. **1804** EDGEWORTH *Pop. Tales*; Contrast i 'This is by way of calling me over the coals for being idle, I suppose!' said Sally. **1832** MARRYAT *Newton F.* xiii Lest he should be 'hauled over the coals' by the Admiralty.

Have among you, blind harpers.

[= a drinking pledge.] **1546** HEYWOOD II. vii. 65 I came to be mery. wherwith merily, Proface. Haue among you blynd harpers (sayde I). **1608** DAY *Hum. out of B.* IV. iii *Page* Are you blind, my lord? *Horl.* As a purblind poet: have amongst you, blind harpers. **1664** COTTON *Scarronides* i. 170 Quoth he, Blind Harpers, have among ye.

Have at it, and have it.

1852 E. FITZGERALD *Polonius* 112 'Have at it, and have it'. One might add many capital English proverbs of this kind, all so characteristic of the activity and boldness of our forefathers.

Have God and have all.

1641 FERGUSSON 44.

Have his muck for his meat, You will.

1670 RAY 186 You'st have his *muck* for his meat.

Have is have.

1596-7 SHAKS. *K. John* I. i. 173 Have is have, however men do catch. **1599–1600** *A.Y.L.* V. i. 44 Learn this of me: to have, is to have.

Have to say, What you | will keep cold, I warrant.

1733 SWIFT (Dial. ii) 349 *Miss.* Don't ask questions with a dirty face: I warrant, what you have to say will keep cold.

Have what he hath not, He that would | should (would) do what he doth not.

1546 HEYWOOD II. ix. 78 Ye (quoth she) who

had that he hath not, woulde Doo that he dooth not, as olde men haue tolde. **1640** HERBERT 343.

Have, *see also* Better to h. than wish; Nothing crave, nothing h.; Nothing h., nothing crave.

Have, To, *see also under significant words following.*

'Haves' and the 'have nots', The.

1742 JARVIS *D. Quix.* II. xx The Haves and Have-nots. **1911** W. F. BUTLER *Autobiog.* ix The have's and the have-not's were always face to face, ready to shoot down or to rush in. **1927** *Daily Mail* 26 Apr. 8/3 People ... argue that society is divided by a kind of wicked, cunning provision into the 'haves' and the 'have nots'.

Havocks, He that | may sit, he that improves must flit.

1891 J. E. T. ROGERS *Ind. & Commer. Hist.* II. iv 'He that havocks may sit, He that improves must flit', . . . current up to the middle of the eighteenth century, . . . meant that a man who racked his land could stay, while he who cultivated it well would have his rent raised . . . and be made to pay interest on his improvements, or go.

Haw, Not worth a.

c. **1280** *Castle of Love* in *Vernon MS.* (E.E.T.S.) 368 (A) Ne wisdam nis not worth an hawe. **1297** R. GLOUC. (1724) 254 Al nas wurth an hawe. *c.* **1386** CHAUCER *W. of Bath's Prol.* 659 I setté noght an haw Of his proverbès. *a.* **1399** *Complaint of Ploughman* in WRIGHT *Pol. Poems* (1861) I. 312 An harlots sonne not worth an hawe. **1593** *Jack Straw* II. in HAZL. *O.E.P.* V. 394 We'll not leave a man of law, Nor a paper worth a haw.

Haw(s), *see also* Fruit fails (When) welcome h.; Many h. many snaws; Many h. . . . many cold toes.

Hawk and buzzard, Between.

c. **1613** MIDDLETON *No Wit, No Help* I. i. 263. **1631** DEKKER *Match me in London* (Wks. 1873, iv. 192) Whether to recoyle or aduance on, I am betweene Hawke and Buzzard. **1638** BRATHWAIT *Barnabees Jrnl.* (1876) M 2 Like a semidormant, and semivigilant, betwixt hawke and buzzard. **1692** L'ESTRANGE *Aesop's Fab.* ccclii (1738) 365 A fantastical levity that holds us *off and on, betwixt hawk and buzzard*, as we say. **1832** J. P. KENNEDY *Swallow B.* (1860) 17 I entered Richmond between hawk and buzzard.

Hawk of the right nest, He's a.

1721 KELLY 138. **1732** FULLER no. 2439.

Hawking, The first point of | is hold fast.

c. **1450** *Booke of Hawkyng* in *Reliq. Antiq.* (1841) I. 296 In the begynnyng of termes of hawkyng. . . . The first is holde fast when abatith. **1546** HEYWOOD II. iv. 52. The fyrst point of haukyng is holde fast. And holde

ye fast I red you. **1665** J. WILSON *Projectors*
II. i *Suck.* 'Tis the first point of falconry to
hold fast; and if the young master has that
good quality, I dare trust him for the rest.

Hawks (Crows) will not pick out hawks' (crows') eyes.

1573 SANDFORD (1576) 210 One crowe neuer
pulleth out an others eyes. **1818** SCOTT *Rob
Roy* xxx I wadna . . . rest my main dependence on the Hielandmen—hawks winna pike
out hawks' een. They may quarrel amang
themsells, . . . but they are sure to join . . .
against a' civilised folk. **1883** PAYN *Thicker
than W.* xli Members of his profession . . .
while warning others of the dangers of the
table, seem to pluck from them the flower
safety. Is it . . . that, since 'hawks do not
peck out hawks' een', they know they can be
cured for nothing?

Hawk(s), *see also* Empty hands no h. allure;
  Gentle h. half mans herself; Highflying h.
  fit for princes; Kite will never be good h.;
  Know a h. from a handsaw; One point of
  a good h. (She hath); Ware h.

Hawse-hole, To come (creep) in through the.

1898 W. C. RUSSELL *Romance of Midsh.* xi
Bowser . . . had come in through the hawse-
pipe, by which is signified he had begun his
career in the forecastle. . . . But he was . . . a
safe . . . commander. **1902** A. B. LUBBOCK
Round the Horn vi The mate . . . [is] a man
who came through the hawsehole, and has
seen some very hard times.

Hay in (on) one's horns, To carry.

[= to be ill-tempered or dangerous.
HORACE *Sat.* 1. 4. 34 *Faenum habet in cornu,*
from an ox apt to gore, whose horns were
bound about with hay.] **1601** JONSON
Poetaster IV. i *Tuc.* A sharp thorny-toothed
satirical rascal, fly him; he carries hay in his
horn. **1648** HERRICK *Hesper., Oberon's Pal.*
(1869) 176 He's sharpe as thorn, And fretfull
carries hay in's horne. **1769** BOSWELL *Johnson* xxii (1848) 202 Horace . . . compares one
who attacks his friends . . . to a pushing ox,
that is marked by a bunch of hay put upon
his horns: '*Fænum habet in cornu.*'

Hay, *see also* Chopped h.; Cock of h. frights
  cuckoo; Lim h.; Make h. while sun shines;
  Orts of good h. (Make not); Web of a
  bottle of h. (Hard to make).

Hazel, *see* Sick of a fever lurden cured by h.

Hazelnuts, The more | the more bastard children.

1844 NORTHALL *Folk-phrases* (E.D.S.) 24.
Glouc.

He can ill (be), *see* Master that never was
  scholar; Pipe that lacketh lip.

He cannot (be), *see under significant words
  following.*

He that, He that cannot, He that hath (no),
  He that is, He that will, He who, He will

(not), He would (have), He would not, *see
under significant words following.*

Head acheth, When the | all the body is the worse.

[L. *Si caput dolet, omnia membra languent.*
If the head aches, all the members languish.]
c. **1230** WRIGHT *Pol. Songs John to Edw. II*
(Camden Soc.) 31 (A) *Cui caput infirmum
cetera membra dolent.* c. **1399** GOWER *Pr. of
Peace* in SKEAT *Chaucer* VII. 212 Of that the
heed is syk, the limmes aken. **1546** HEYWOOD
II. vii. 70 God sende that hed (said she) a
better nurs. For whan the head aketh, all
the bodie is the wurs. **1620** SHELTON *Quix.*
II. ii (1908) II. 201 According to the saying,
"Quando caput dolet", . . . I mean . . . that
when the head aches, all the body is out of
tune; . . . I, being thy lord and master, am
thy head'.

Head and feet keep warm, The | the rest will take no harm.

1611 COTGRAVE s.v. 'Demeurant' The foot
and head kept warme, no matter for the rest.
1670 RAY 39. **1832** HENDERSON 128 Keep the
head and feet warm, and the rest will take
nae harm.

Head, You have a | and so has a pin (nail).

1709 STEELE *Tatler* No. 83 My boy breaks
glasses and pipes; and . . . I only say, 'Ah,
Jack! thou hast a head, and so has a pin'.
1738 SWIFT (Dial. i) 337 *Bet.* Madam, I can't
go faster than my legs will carry me. *Lady S.*
Ay, thou hast a head, and so has a pin. **1823**
GALT *Entail* viii Girzy, t'ou has a head, and
so has a nail.

Head is all of a lump, His.

1738 SWIFT (Dial. i) 342 Nay, she must be
hurt for certain; for you see her head is all
of a lump.

Head is down, When my | my house is theekit (thatched).

1721 KELLY 342 . . . Spoken by those who are
free from debts, concerns, or future projects;
as common tradesmen, day labourers, and
servants who work . . . and get their wages.

Head is full of bees, His.

1513 DOUGLAS *Æneis* viii. Prol. 120 Quhat
bern be thou in bed with heid full of beis?
1546 HEYWOOD I. xii Their heads be full of
bees. *a.* **1553** UDALL *Royster D.* I. iv (Arb.) 29
Who so hath suche bees as your maister in
hys head, Had neede to haue his spirites with
Musike to be fed. **1641** FERGUSSON 54 *Of
drunkards.* His head is full of bees.

Head is screwed on the right way, His.

1843 *Life & Lett. of Mandell Creighton* (1904)
I. 3 The father . . . had a . . . contempt for
those without force of character or capacity
. . . who . . . had not 'their head screwed on
the right way'.

Head, He that will be a | let him be a bridge.

1662 FULLER (*Cardig.*) III. 520 'He that will be a head, let him be a bridge' . . . is founded on a fictitious tradition [that] . . . Benigridran, a Briton, . . . came to a river over which neither was bridge nor ferry; hereupon he was fain to carry all his men over . . . on his own back.

Head like a snake, A | a neck like a drake, a back like a beam, a belly like a bream, a foot like a cat, a tail like a rat.

1670 RAY 212. [The shape of a good greyhound.]

Head may never ache till that day, I wish my.

1738 SWIFT (Dial. i) 336 *Lady A*. Miss is in love. *Miss*. I wish my head may never ache till that day.

Head, He that hath no | needs no hat.

1611 COTGRAVE s.v. Chaperon' He that hath no head needs no hood. **1616** DRAXE 140 (with 'cap'). **1640** HERBERT (Gros.) no. 989 with 'hat'. **1670** RAY 101 . . . Qui n'a point de teste n'a que faire de chaperon. *Gall.*

Head, Who hath no | needs no heart.

1640 HERBERT 363.

Head (House) of glass, He that hath a | must not throw stones at another.

c. **1374** CHAUCER *Troylus* II. 867 And for-thy, who that hath a hed of verre, For cast of stonès war him in the werre! **1640** HERBERT 326 Whose house is of glass, must not throw stones at another. **1660** SECKER *Nonsuch Prof.* II (1891) 183 What do you get by throwing stones at your enemys windows, while your own children look out at the casements? **1666** TORRIANO 45 Who hath his brains of glass let him not go into a battel of stones. **1754** SHEBEARE *Matrimony* (1766) II. 102 Thee shouldst not throw stones, who hast a Head of Glass thyself. **1891** J. E. T. ROGERS *Ind. & Commerc. Hist.* 36 I am not sure that we in modern times can decently charge the Roman people with the lust of conquest, for . . . most of the European monarchies would be throwing stones from glass houses.

Head of hair, *see* Handsome h. of h., pray give me a tester.

Head of wax, He that hath a | must not walk in the sun.

1640 HERBERT 337 He that hath a head of wax must not walk in the sun. **1749** FRANKLIN July If your head is wax, don't walk in the Sun.

Head under one's girdle, To have a man's.

[To have him in subjection, under control.]

1546 HEYWOOD II. v. 58 And if ye chaunce in aduoutrie to catche him, . . . Then haue ye his head fast vnder your gyrdell. **1629** T. ADAMS *Serm.* (1861–2) I. 330 If he may not have his head under his girdle, and his attendance as servile as his livery-groom's, he thinks himself indignified.

Head will never fill your father's bonnet, Your.

1721 KELLY 372 . . . That is, you will never be so wise a man as your father.

Head's running upon Jolly Robins, Your.

1596 T. LODGE *Wit's Misery* (Hunt. Cl.) E 2ᵛ He [the usurer] casts Jolly Robbins in his head how to cousin the simple fellow. **1629** *Merchandise of Popish Priests* Of him whom we see very lively and pleasantly disposed, we say, his head is full of jolly Robins [cited in Mann's ed. of Deloney p. 537]. **1917** BRIDGE 159.

Heading Halifax.

1613–22 DRAYTON *Polyolb.* xxvii. 59 And travelling along by Heading-*Halifax*. **1787** GROSE (*Yorks.*) 231 At Halifax persons taken in the act of stealing cloth, were instantly, and without any process, beheaded, with an engine called a maiden.

Heads as Hydra, As many.

[A fabulous monster with a hundred heads.] *a.* **1647** BEAUM. & FL. *Lawes of Candy* I. i. Wks. (1905) III. 247 Supposing that their adversaries grew Like *Hydra's* head. **1690** DRYDEN *Don Sebas.* I. i (Merm.) II. 306 The fruitful heads of Hydra.

Heads (Cross) I win, tails (pile) you lose.

[From deciding a matter by spinning a coin in the air and seeing whether the obverse or reverse falls uppermost.] **1678** BUTLER *Hudibras* III. iii. 685 For matrimony, and hanging here, Both go by destiny so clear. That you as sure may pick and choose, As cross I win, and pile you lose. **1846** DK. RUTLAND in *Croker Papers* (1884) III. xxiv. 59 A game which a sharper once played with a dupe, intituled, 'Heads I win, and tails you lose.' **1926** *Times* 28 May 14/7 A better exposition of the unbusinesslike principle of 'heads you win; tails we lose', would be hard to conceive.

Head(s), *see also* Better be h. of a dog (ass, pike, yeomanry); Break one's h. and bring plaster; Bring an old house on h.; Cap is better at ease than h.; Coals of fire on h.; Comb h. with three-legged stool; Comb your h. backward; Comforter's h. never aches; Dare not show his h.; Dry feet warm h. bring safe; Fortunate h. that never ached; Give one's h. for the washing (for nought); Good for back bad for h.; Good for h. evil for neck; Grey h. green shoulders; Hit the nail on h.; Hoar h. and green tail; Holds up her h. like a hen

drinking (a hundred pound aver); Idle h.
box for wind; Keep one head for reckoning; Keep one's h. above water; Keep
your feet dry and h. hot; King Charles's
h.; Many h. better than one; Men (H.)
(So many), so many censures (minds, wits);
Mickle h. little wit; Old h. and young
hands; Old h. young shoulders; Over h.
and ears; Raw h. and bloody bone; Red
beard and black h.; Run one's h. against
stone wall; Scabby h. love not comb;
Scald h. soon broken; Scratches his h.
with one finger; Soft place in one's h.;
Sound h. that has not soft piece; Staff to
break his own h.; Stoop when the head is
off (No time to); Strange beast that hath
neither h.; Two faces (h.) in one hood;
Two h. better than one; Windmills in the
h.; Wise h. close mouth; Wit in his h. (He
hath no more).

Heal[1] sail is good sail.

1721 KELLY 143 . . . It is good merchandising
when we can put off all our wares in one bulk.
Spoken jocosely when we take all that is
before us. [[1] whole.]

Healed as hurt, A man is not so soon.

1599 PORTER Angry Wom. Abingd. IV. ii.
(Merm.) 176 A man is not so soon whole
as hurt. **1614** CAMDEN 302. **1721** KELLY 48
. . . Misfortunes come suddenly, but their
remedies by more slow degrees.

Healing of an old sore, It is ill.

1509 A. BARCLAY Ship of Fools (Jamieson) I.
164 In olde sores is grettest ieopardye. **1546**
HEYWOOD II. viii. 71 She hath (they say)
bene styffe necked euermore. And it is yll
healyng of an olde sore. **1579** LYLY Euphues
(Arb.) 109 Search the wound while it is
greene, too late commeth the salue when the
sore festereth. **1732** FULLER no. 3727 Old
sores are hardly cured.

Health and money go far.

1640 HERBERT 338.

Health and sickness surely are men's double enemies.

1640 HERBERT 363.

Health is better than wealth.

[Ecclesiasticus XXX. 15 Health and strength
is above all gold (Geneva).] **1584** COGAN
Hav. of Health, Ep. Ded. Health and strength
is above all gold (as saith Jesus Syrach).
1678 RAY 153. **1855** BOHN 364 Good health
is above wealth.

Health is not valued till sickness comes.

1600 Maid's Metamorphosis E 4[V] They know
the want of health that haue bene sick. **1631**
DEKKER, Penny-wise, Pound-foolish A 3 Life
. . . knowes not her owne pretious value, till
Sicknesse layes it in the Ballance. **1666**
TORRIANO 119 In sickness health is known.
1732 FULLER no. 2478.

Health, The chief box of | is time.

1640 HERBERT 359.

Health without money is half an ague.

1640 HERBERT 341.

Health, see also Best men when in worst h.;
Good h. (He that hath); Good wife and
h.; Kent (Some places of) have h. and no
wealth; Little labour much h.; Pledge
your own h. (Must not); Poverty is the
mother of h.

Healthful man can give counsel to the sick, The.

1539 TAVERNER (1545) C 3[V] Facile cum
valemus recta consilia ægrotis damus. When
we be hayle, we easely gyue good counsayles
to the sycke. This sentence of Terence. . . .
a. **1581** N. WOODES Conflict of Conscience I i.
1651 HERBERT 369.

Heap, The more you | the worse you cheap.

1670 RAY 102 . . . The more you rake and
scrape, the worse success you have.

Heap (noun), see Strike all of a h.

Hear a toll or knell, When thou dost | then think upon thy passing bell.

1659 HOWELL Eng. Prov. 6/1.

Hear all parties (both sides).

[ST. AUGUSTINE De Duabus Animabus, XIV.
ii Audi alteram partem.] **1481** CAXTON Reynard (Arb.) XXV. 57 There ben many that
complayne on other and ben in the defaute
them self. Audi alteram partem, here that
other partye. **1546** HEYWOOD I. xiii. 40 A
man should here all partis, er he judge any.
1641 FERGUSSON 40. **1692** L'ESTRANGE
Aesop's Fab. xi (1738) 14 'Tis against
common justice to pass sentence without
hearing both sides. **1883** READE Peril. Secret
vi I should wish you to hear both sides.

Hear and see and be still (say but little).

c. **1430** LYDGATE Minor Poems (Percy Soc.)
155 Here al thyng and kepe thy pacience.
c. **1450** Provs. of Wysdom 99 Hyre and se,
and be styll. Ibid. 95 Hyre and se, and say
nowght. Ibid. 119 Hyre and se, and say but
lyte. c. **1470** Harl. MS. 3362 (ed. Förster) in
Anglia 42. 199 Here ȝe and sey nawt [all].
1509 A. BARCLAY Ship of Fools (1874) I. 200
They that wyll liue in quyetnes and rest must
here and se and hasty wordes refrayne. **1578**
FLORIO First Fruites f. 10 Who heares, sees,
and holds his peace, may alway liue in peace.

Hear and see and do (say) the best.

c. **1450** Provs. of Wysdom 127 Hyre and se,
say and do the best. **1639** CLARKE 102 Hear
and see and say the best.

Hear much, speak little.

c. **1420** Peter Idel's Instructions (E.E.T.S.)

l. 59 Telle neuer the more, though þou moche hire. **1562** HEYWOOD *Epigr.* (1867) 96 Who hereth oft, And speaketh séeld, Be witte aloft, He wynth the féeld. **1600–1** SHAKS. *Ham.* I. iii. 68 Give every man thine ear, but few thy voice. **1621** BURTON *Anat. Mel.* II. iii. VII (1651) 360 Out of humane authors take these few cautions ... *Hear much: speak little.*

Hear on that ear, He cannot.

1641 FERGUSSON 46 He hears not at that ear. **1670** RAY 180 **1721** KELLY 150 *He is deaf on that side of his head.* Spoken of those who like not, and therefore take no notice of, your proposals.

Hear the lark sing than the mouse cheep (squeak), It is better to.

1306–7 DOUGLAS in SCOTT *Tales Grandf.* (1827–30) ix [Douglas] set fire to the castle; and ... took refuge with his followers in the hills and forests. 'He loved better,' he said, 'to hear the lark sing than the mouse squeak.' **1855** BOHN 435. **1891** A. LANG *Ess. in Little* 4 Like the good Lord James Douglas, we had liefer hear the lark sing over moor and down, with Chicot, than listen to the starved-mouse squeak ... with M. Zola.

Hear(s), *see also* All men speak (When), no man h.; Child says nothing but what it h.; Children h. at home (What) soon fly abroad; Do a foolish thing once (One cannot) but one must h. of it; Love to h. well of themselves (Men); Speaks the thing he should not; Strike but h.; Wrong h., wrong answer gives.

Heard a pin drop, You might have.

1824 SUSAN FERRIER *Inheritance* II. xiv You might have heard a pin drop in the house while that was going on. **1893** MONT. WILLIAMS *Leaves of a L.* xxx Mr. Gladstone began to speak. That great crowd ... became ... profoundly silent. You actually might have heard the proverbial pin drop.

Heard where he is not seen, He may be.

1670 RAY 180.

Hearers, Were there no | there would be no backbiters.

1640 HERBERT 320.

Hearing, From | comes wisdom; from speaking, repentance.

1707 MAPLETOFT 31. **1855** BOHN 359.

Hearing, *see also* Ill h. ill rehearsing.

Hearken to reason, or she will be heard.

1611 COTGRAVE S.V. Mettre' Mets raison, adding 'Let reasons rudder steere thy prow, least thou make wrecke on woes enow.' **1640** HERBERT 320. **1758** FRANKLIN *Way to Wealth* (Crowell) 24 Remember ... further, that *If you will not hear Reason, she will surely rap your knuckles.*

Hearken to the hinder end of it.

1721 KELLY 144 Spoken when we suspect that such a project, or action, will have an ill consequence.

Hears much and speaks not at all, He that | shall be welcome both in bower and hall.

1586 G. WHITNEY *Emblems* 191 (A) Heare much; but little speake. **1670** RAY 102.

Hears, *see also* Hear(s).

Heart hath its own ache, Every.

[BIBLE *Prov.* xiv. 10 The heart knoweth his own bitterness.] **1732** FULLER no. 1418.

Heart is a fire, When the | some sparks will fly out of the mouth.

1520 WHITTINGTON *Vulg.* (E.E.T.S.) 77 Whan the herte is full of pryde, ye tongue is full of boost and braggynge. **1732** FULLER no. 5589.

Heart is caught in the rebound, Many a.

1872 G. J. WHYTE-MELVILLE *Satanella* viii On Satanella's refusal of her veteran admirer, she calculated. ... In such an ignominious state men are to be caught on the rebound. **1902–4** LEAN IV. 41 Many a heart is caught in the rebound. *i.e.* after a repulse by another.

Heart is full of lust, When the | the mouth's full of leasings.

1721 KELLY 352 A reflection upon these damnable lies, enforc'd with horrid oaths, by which poor maids are deceiv'd.

Heart is full, When the | the tongue will speak.

1721 KELLY 356.

Heart is in his boots (shoes), His. (*Cf. the following proverbs.*)

1863 SPEKE *Disc. of Nile* ii With 'my heart in my shoes', I gave what I thought their due ... and motioned them to be off. **1891** A. FORBES *Barracks Biv. & Bat.* (1910) 2 Cholera was decimating the troop, and the hearts of brave men were in their boots.

Heart is in his heels, His.

[HOM. *Il.* 15. 280 πᾶσιν δὲ παραὶ ποσὶ κάππεσε θυμός. Their heels took in their dropping hearts (Chapman).] **1548** UDALL tr. *Erasm. Par. Luke* xxii 174 b Petur beeyng feared with this saiyng of a woman ... as if his herte had been in his hele clene gon. **1563–87** FOXE *A. & M.* (1631) III. xi. 253/2 When the Bishop heard this, ... his heart was in his heeles, and ... he with the rest of the Court betooke them to their legges.

Heart is in his hose, His.

c. **1410** *Towneley Plays* (E.E.T.S.) 113 A, thy hart is in thy hose! **1546** HEYWOOD I. xi. 30 Your hert is in your hose all in dispaire.

c. **1600** *Timon* I. v My hart is at the bottome of my hose. **1641** FERGUSSON 56 *Of fleyit*[1] *persons.* His heart is in his hose. [[1] frightened.]

Heart is in his mouth, His.

[HOM. *Il.* 22. 452 παλλέται ἦτορ ἀνὰ στόμα To my throat my heart bounds (Chapman).] **1537** *Thersites* B 4. **1548** UDALL tr. *Erasm. Par. Luke* xxiii. 199 Hauyng their herte at their verai mouth for feare. **1716** ADDISON *Drummer* I. i And faith my heart was in my mouth; I thought I had tumbled over a spirit. **1856** WHYTE-MELVILLE *Kate Cov.* xiii A ring at the door-bell brings everybody's heart into everybody's mouth.

Heart is on his halfpenny, His. (*See also* Hand on one's halfpenny.)

1590 LODGE *Rosalynde* Wks. (1883) I. 21 Saladin . . . thought to shake him out of his dumps thus . . . 'What, is your heart on your half penie, or are you saying a Dirge for your father's soule?' **1639** CLARKE 36 His heart's on 's halfpenny.

Heart of an Englishman towards a Welshman, The.

1662 FULLER (*Cardig.*) III. 519 'The heart of an Englishman' (whom they call Saxons) 'towards a Welchman'. It is either applied to such who are possessed with prejudice, or only carry an outward compliance without cordial affection. **1902–4** LEAN I. 233 Calon y Sais wrth Cymro. The heart of an Englishman (or Saxon) towards a Welshman, *i.e.* open or secret hatred.

Heart of England, The.

1897 BP. CREIGHTON *Story Eng. Shires* 309 It was not accidental that Warwickshire produced the greatest of Englishmen. 'The heart of England', as the county has been called, summed up all that was most purely English in its scenery and associations.

Heart of gall, *see* Honey tongue.

Heart of grace, To take.

[= to pluck up courage.] **1530** PALSGRAVE 748 (A) They lyved a great whyle lyke cowardes, but at the laste they toke herte a gresse to them. **1546** HEYWOOD II. viii. 71 She takth such hert of grace. **1548** UDALL tr. *Erasm. Par. Matt.* xxii. 106 They takyng hart of grace agayne. **1555** HEYWOOD *Three Hund. Epigrams* no. 92 Thou takest hart of grasse wyfe, not hart of grace. **1712** ARBUTHNOT *John Bull* IV. iv He was afraid to venture himself alone with him. At last he took heart of grace. **1890** *Times* 14 Oct. 6/2 The non-union labourers . . . took heart of grace and applied for work.

Heart of oak, He is.

1591 *The Speeches and Honourable Entertainment at Cowdrey* (LYLY *Wks.* ed. Bond I. 425) All heartes of Oke. **1602** DEKKER *Satiro-Mastix* (1873) i. 265 My tough hearts of Oake that stand too 't so valliantly. **1609** *Old Meg of Herefordsh.* Yonkers that have hearts of oake at fourscore yeares. **1691** WOOD *Ath. Oxon.* II. 221 He was . . . a heart

of oke, and a pillar of the Land. **1870** DICKENS *E. Drood* xii A nation of hearts of oak.

Heart that makes the theologian, It is the.

1908 A. MACLAREN *Expos., Acts* I. 340 Every one that loveth is born of God and knoweth God. *Pectus facit Theologum.*

Heart thinketh, What the | the tongue speaketh.

1477 RIVERS *Dictes &c.* (1877) 26 The mouth sheweth often what the hert thinketh. **1583** GREENE *Mamillia* in Wks. (Gros.) II. 116 Gonzaga . . . thought, what the heart did think, the tongue would clink. **1598–9** SHAKS. *Much Ado* III. ii. 14 What his heart thinks his tongue speaks. **1614** CAMDEN 314.

Heart's letter is read in the eyes, The.

1640 HERBERT 327.

Hearts may agree, though heads differ.

1732 FULLER no. 2480.

Heart(s), *see also* Cockles of the h.; Cold hand warm h.; Country for wounded h.; Eat one's h. out; Eye sees not (What the) h.; craves not (rues not); Faint h. never won; Fair face cannot have crabbed h.; Fair face foul h.; Gentle h. is tied; Good h. cannot lie; Good h. conquers fortune; Good tongue that says no ill, better h. thinks none; Guts uphold the h.; Hard (Stout) h. against hard hap (to stey brae); Head (Who hath no) needs no h.; Joy of h. makes face merry; Kind h. soonest wronged; Lady's h. and beggar's purse; Lay sorrow to your h. (Never); Leal h. lied never; Long day (Not a), but good h. rids work; Loyal h. . . . Traitors' Bridge; Mickle maun good h. endure; Nearest the h. nearest the mouth; Please your eye and plague your h.; Poor h. that never rejoices; Prolong thy life, quiet h. loving wife; Put blithe face on black h.; Rolling eye roving h.; Send you away with a sore h.; Set your h. at rest; Short folk's h. soon at their mouth; Tine h. tine all; Velvet true h.; Way to an Englishman's h.; Wears his h. upon sleeve; Wise men have mouth in h., fools h. in mouth.

Hearth, *see* Keystone under the h.; Own h. is gowd's worth.

Heat nor cold abides always in the sky, Neither.

1678 RAY 47 *Ne caldo, ne gelo resta mai in cielo.* Ital. Neither heat nor cold abides always in the sky.

Heat of affection, There is no | but is joined with some idleness of brain, says the Spaniard.

1651 HERBERT 365.

Heat (Sunshine) that melts the wax will harden the clay, The same.

1579 GASCOIGNE *Hemetes* Wks. (C.U.P.) II. 476 We see that one self same sunshine doth both harden the clay, and dissolve the wax. **1629** T. ADAMS *Serm.* (1861–2) II. 476 As by the heat of the sun wax is softened, and yet clay is hardened; so by the preaching of the word the hearts of such as shall be saved are mollified; but the hearts of the lost are further obdurate. **1660** SECKER *Nonsuch Prof.* II. (1891) 25 The same heat that melts the wax, will harden the clay.

Heathen, when they died, went to bed without a candle, The.

1732 FULLER no. 4589.

Heather-bells grow cockle-shells, When | the miller and the priest will forget themsels.

1842 R. CHAMBERS *Pop. Rhymes of Scot.* 72 ... Intimating that, till some natural impossibility shall take place, the miller will not neglect to exact his multure, nor the priest his tithes.

Heaven and hell is not known till hereafter, All of.

1732 FULLER no. 540.

Heaven (God) is above all.

1595–6 SHAKS. *Rich. II* III. iii. 17 *York.* The heavens are o'er our heads. *Boling.* I know it uncle; and oppose not myself Against their will. **1604–5** *Othello* II. iii. 105 Well, God's above all; and there be souls must be saved, and there be souls must not be saved. **1612–13** *Hen. VIII* III. i. 99 Heaven is above all yet; there sits a judge That no king can corrupt.

Heaven takes care of children, sailors, and drunken men.

1861 HUGHES *Tom B. at Oxford* xii Heaven, they say, protects children, sailors, and drunken men; and whatever answers to Heaven in the academical system protects freshmen. **1865** G. MACDONALD *A. Forbes* lxxvi They say there's a special Providence watches ower drunk men and bairns.

Heaven will make amends for all.

1732 FULLER no. 2483.

Heaven, *see also* Better go to h. in rags; Coming to h. with dry eyes (No); Friends both in h. and hell; Going to h. in a sedan (No); Go to h. in a feather-bed (string, wheelbarrow); God (H.) helps them that help themselves; Order is h.'s first law; Way to h. is alike; —— is as ready by water as land.

Heavy purse makes a light heart, A.

1631 JONSON *New Inn* I. i *Host.* A heavy purse makes a light heart. There 'tis exprest.

Heavy, *see also* Bear it away (He will) if not too h.

Hector's cloak, To take.

1662 FULLER (*Northumb.*) II. 542 When Thomas Percy, earl of Northumberland, anno 1569, was routed in the rebellion ... against queen Elizabeth, he hid himself in the house of Hector Armstrong, of Harlow, ... who for money betrayed him to the Regent of Scotland ... 'To take Hector's cloak', is continued to this day ..., when they would express a man that betrayeth his friend who trusted him.

Hedge between keeps friendship green, A.

1707 MAPLETOFT 47. **1710** G. PALMER *Moral Essays on Proverbs* 168 A wall between preserves love. **1917** BRIDGE 3.

Hedge have, If you would a good | carry the leaves to the grave.

[For meaning *see* Fruit have, &c.] **1678** RAY 350.

Hedge(s), *see also* Cured her from laying in the h.; Fields (H.) have eyes; Leap over h. before come at stile; Leap over nine h. (Ready to); Leap over where h. lowest; Love your neighbour, yet pull not down h.; Low h. easily leaped over; Seek a brack where h. is whole; Sheltering under an old h. (Good); Side of the h. (To be on right or wrong).

Heed, *see* Good h. hath good hap; Take h. doth surely speed; Take h. is fair thing (good rede); Too much taking h. is loss.

Heel of Achilles.

[=the only vulnerable spot (in allusion to the story of the dipping of Achilles in the river Styx).] **1810** COLERIDGE *Friend* 431 Ireland, that vulnerable heel of the British Achilles. **1864** CARLYLE *Fred. Great* XVII. ii. IV. 522 Hanover ... the Achilles'-heel to invulnerable England. **1944** *Times* 19 June 5/6 Military observers have dubbed Viipuri the Achilles' heel of the Finnish defences.

Heel(s), *see also* Beat your h. against the ground (As good); Clean h. light meals; Cool one's h.; Grass grows on his h. (No); Heart is in his h. (His); Lay sorrow to your heart (Never) when others to their h.; Pair of h. is often worth two of hands; Pair of h. (Show a fair); Scorn with the h.; Touch me not on sore h.; Trust not a horse's h.

Height, *see* Grantham steeple.

Heir, *see* Ill man lie in thy straw (Let an), looks to be thy h.; Fool who makes physician h.; Land was never lost for want of h.

Held together, They | as the men of Marham when they lost their common.

1662 FULLER (*Lincs.*) II. 269 They held together as the men of Marham when they lost their common'. Some understand it ironically; that is, they were divided with several factions. . . . Others use this proverb only as an expression of ill success. . . . Though this Proverb be frequent in this shire Marham is in Norfolk. **1818** SCOTT *Ht. Midl.* xxix 'Since they hae lost Jim the Rat, they hold together no better than the men of Marsham when they lost their common'.

Hell and chancery are always open.

1732 FULLER no. 2486.

Hell for company, There is nobody will go to.

1651 HERBERT 373.

Hell, Hull and Halifax, From | good Lord deliver us.

1594 A. COPLEY *Wits, Fits, etc.* (1614) 112 (A) It is proverbiall in our countrie; From Hull, Hell, and Halifax, Good Lord deliver us. **1623** J. TAYLOR (Water-P.) *Mer. Wher. Fer. Voy.* Wks. (1872) 22 There is a Proverb, and a Prayer withall, That we may not to three strange places fall: From *Hull*, from Halifax, from *Hell*, 'tis thus, From all these three, *Good Lord deliver us.* **1662** FULLER (*Yorks.*) III. 398 'From Hell, Hull, and Halifax, —— deliver us.' This is part of the beggar's and vagrant's litany. . . . Hull is terrible unto them, as a town of good government. . . . Halifax is formidable unto them for . . . thieves . . . stealing cloth, are instantly beheaded with an engine.

Hell is broke loose.

1577 *Misogonus* II. v. 15 I thinke hell breake louse when thou gatst the this poste. **1594** GREENE *Friar Bacon* IV. i (Merm.) 283 Hell's broken loose; your Head speaks; and there's such a thunder and lightning, that I warrant all Oxford is up in arms. **1611-12** SHAKS. *Temp.* I. ii. 214 Hell is empty, And all the devils are here. **1623** JONSON *Time Vind.* Wks. (1904) 171 How now! what's here! Is hell broke loose? **1738** SWIFT (Dial. i) 339 Hey, what a clattering is here! one would think hell was broke loose. **1821** BYRON *Vis. Judg.* lviii Their . . . cries . . . realised the phrase of 'hell broke loose'. **1857** READE *White Lies* xxi A furious cannonade roared . . . till daybreak. Hell seemed broke loose.

Hell is full of good meanings and wishes.

1574 E. HELLOWES *Guevara's Epistles* 205 Hell is full of good desires. **1629** T. ADAMS *Serm.* (1861-2) II. 489 One said, that hell is like to be full of good purposes, but heaven of good works. **1640** HERBERT 325. **1655-62** GURNALL *Chrn. in Armour* (1865) I. 412 The proverb saith, 'Hell is full of good wishes',—of such, who now, when it is too late, wish they had acted their part otherwise . . . than they did. And do you not think there are . . . good meanings also?

Hell is paved with good intentions.

1736 WESLEY *Journ.* 10 July It is a true saying, Hell is . . . **1775** JOHNSON in *Boswell* (1848) xlix. 450 No saint . . . was more sensible of the unhappy failure of pious resolves than Johnson. He said one day, . . . 'Sir, hell is paved with good intentions'. **1819** SCOTT *Bride Lam.* vii 'Hell is paved with good intentions'—as much as to say, they are more often formed than executed. **1839** SIR C. NAPIER in BUTLER *Life* (1890) 96 Hell may be paved with good intentions, but it is assuredly hung with Manchester cottons. **1865** RUSKIN *Ethics of Dust* v Their best intentions merely make the road smooth for them . . . You can't pave the bottomless pit; but you may the road to it.

Hell is wherever heaven is not.

1597 *Politeuphuia* 260 Hell is euery where, where heauen is not. **1732** FULLER no. 2489.

Hell or Connaught.

1896 W. O'C. MORRIS *Ireland 1494-1868* 154 Cromwell resolved . . . to compel the 'rebel' owners of land to take refuge in Connaught . . . 'Hell or Connaught', a phrase that has come down to this time. **1911** *Autobiog. of Sir W. F. Butler* xvi. 266 The alternative was like that which Cromwell gave, . . . only that Connaught was left out.

Hell, They that be in | ween there is none other heaven.

1546 HEYWOOD I. xi. 33 They that be in hell, wene there is none other heuen. **1590** SIR J. SMYTH *Disc. Weapons* Proeme *iij b They verifie the olde Proverb, which is, That such as were never but in Hell, doo thinke that there is no other Heaven. **1597** BACON *Col. of G. & E.* 6 (Arb.) 146 The formes to make it conceyued that that was euill which is chaunged for the better are, *He that is in hell thinkes there is no other heauen.*

Hell will never be full till you be in it.

1721 KELLY 160 . . . A bitter reflection upon them who are very covetous, or very malicious.

Hell will never have its due, till it have its hold of you.

1855 BOHN 405.

Hell, *see also* Better go . . . than to h. in embroidery; False as h.; Fans in h. (No); Fasteth and doeth no other good . . . goes to h.; Friends both in heaven and h.; Go to h. for the house profit; Harrow h. and scum devil; Heaven and h. not known till hereafter; Hopers go to h.; Lackey comes to h.'s door (When) devils lock gates; Rake h. and skim the devil; Rake h. for a bodle; Redemption from h. (No); Sel, sel, has half-filled h.; War begins (When), h. openeth; Wicked man his own h.; Work hard . . . and go to h., hard indeed.

Helmet of Pluto, The.

1625 BACON *Ess., Delays* (Arb.) 525 For the

Helmet of Pluto, which maketh the Politicke Man goe Inuisible, is, *Secrecy* in the Counsell, and *Celerity* in the Execution.

Help, for help in harvest.

1721 KELLY 170 ... That is, help me now, and I will help you on your throngest[1] occasion. [[1] busiest.]

Help, hands; for I have no lands.

1591 *Troub. Raigne K. John* (1611) 19 Help hands, I have no lands, Honor is my desire. **1608** ARMIN *Nest. Nin.* (1842) 47 Fool, says the jester, use thy hands, help hands, for I have no lands. **1754** FRANKLIN Jan. Help, Hands; For I have no Lands.

Help one to salt, help one to sorrow.

1666 TORRIANO 34, 182 Offer not to present salt, or the head of any creature. **1872** J. GLYDE, jr. *Norfolk Garland* 44 (A). **1903** W. A. DUTT *Norfolk Broads* 338 That 'to help one to salt is to help one to sorrow' is as firmly credited as the belief that good luck attaches to the picking up of pins or cast horseshoes.

Help the (lame) dog over the stile.

1546 HEYWOOD I. xi. 32 As good a déede, As it is to helpe a dogge ouer a style. **1638** CHILLINGWORTH *Relig. Prot.* I. III. § 33. I once knew a man out of courtesy, help a lame dog over a stile, and he for requital bit him by the fingers. **1738** SWIFT (Dial. i) 339 I know I shall always have your good word; you love to help a lame dog over the stile. **1857** KINGSLEY *Two Years Ago* XXV 'I can . . . help a lame dog over a stile'.

Help (*noun*), *see also* Bale (Need) is hext (When), boot (h.) is next; God's h. is nearer than the fair even; Mickle ado and little h.; Thou thyself canst do it (If), attend no other's help.

Helpeth the evil hurteth the good, He that.

1547 WM. BALDWIN *Moral Philosophy* (1550) P 3ᵛ. **1669** *Politeuphuia* 186 (A) He that helpeth an evil man hurteth him that is good. **1732** FULLER no. 2163.

Helps little that helpeth not himself, He.

1573 SANDFORD (1576) H 2ᵛ. **1629** *Book of Meery Riddles* Prov. 16.

Help(s, ing) (*verb*), *see also* At hand (All is not) that h.; Everything h. quoth the wren; God h. the fool (poor, rich); God h. them that h. themselves; God will h. (Where or Whom) nothing does harm (or can hinder); Never be angry at (Two things), what he can h. and what he cannot h.; Three h. one another bear burthen of six.

Helve after the hatchet, To throw the.

[⬟ to add new loss to that already incurred.] *c.* 1200 MAP *De Nugis Cur.* I. x *Manubrium post securim iacere.* **1546** HEYWOOD II. ix For

here I sende thaxe after the helue awaie. **1577–87** HOLINSHED *Chron.* (1807–8) IV. 338 Rather throw the helve after the hatchet, and leave your ruines to be repaired by your prince. **1685** COTTON tr. *Montaigne* (1711) 222 I abandon myself through despair . . . and as the saying is, throw the Helve after the Hatchet. **1824** SCOTT *St. Ronan's* XXVI Monsieur Martigny will be too much heart-broken to make further fight, but will e'en throw helve after hatchet.

Helvoet, *see* Deal, Dover, and Harwich, the devil gave.

Hemp, *see* Stalk of carl h. in you (You have a).

HEMPE is spun, When | England is done.

1625 BACON *Ess., Prophecies* (Arb.) 536 The triuiall *Prophecie*, which I heard, when I was a Childe, . . . was; *When Hempe is sponne; England's done.* Whereby, it was generally conceived, that after the *Princes* had Reigned, which had the Principiall *Letters*, of that Word *Hempe* (which were *Henry, Edward, Mary, Philip, Elizabeth*) *England* should come to utter Confusion.

Hempstead, *see* Raw H.

Hen crows louder than the cock, It is a sad house where the.

1573 SANDFORD (1576) 222. **1578** FLORIO *First Fruites* f. 33 They are sory houses, where the Hennes crowe, and the cock holdes his peace. **1621** QUARLES *Ester*, Med. III. Wks. (1880–1) II. 50 Ill thriues the haplesse Family, that showes A Cocke that's silent, and a Hen that crowes. **1625** J. HOWELL *Lett.* 5 Feb. (1903) I. 250 I remember a French proverb: 'La maison est miserable et mechante Ou la poule plus haut que le cocq chante.' 'That house doth every day more wretched grow Where the hen louder than the cock doth crow.' **1678** RAY 64 ... *Trista è quella casa dove le galline cantano e 'l gallo tace.* Ital. **1866** C. READE *G. Gaunt* XX This house is no place for us that be women: . . . where the hen she crows and the cock do but cluck.

Hen does not prate, If the | she will not lay.

1642 TORRIANO 68 The hen that cakels is she that hath laid. **1659** N. R. 121. **1732** FULLER no. 2799 If you would have a Hen lay, you must bear with her cackling. **1830** FORBY 427 If the hen does not prate, she will not lay': *i.e.* Scolding wives make the best housewives.

Hen egg goes to the ha',[1] The | to bring the goose egg awa'.

1721 KELLY 316 ... Spoken when poor people give small gifts to be doubly repaid. [[1] hall, the great house.]

Hen goes to the cock, When the | the burds[1] may gen a knock.

1721 KELLY 350 ... Spoken when widows who design a second marriage prove harsh to their children. [[1] chickens.]

Hen, Like | like chicken.

1632 MASSINGER *City Madam* I. i (Merm.) 405 *Anne.* He's grown Rebellious, madam. *Gold.* Nay, like hen, like chicken.

Hen live, Let the | though it be with her pip.

1620 SHELTON *Quix.* II. v (1908) II. 218 Let the hen live, though it be with her pip; live you, and the devil take all the governments in the world.

Hen on a hot girdle (griddle), Like a.

1812 W. TENNANT *Anster F.* VI liv As would a hen leap on a fire-hot griddle. **1824** MOIR *Mansie W.* viii I began to be . . . uneasy, and figeted on the board like a hen on a hot girdle. **1895** J. BARLOW *Maureen's Fairing* 42 The misthress had been like a hin on a hot griddle ever since.

Hen that cackles in your house and lays in another's, It is no good.

1586 WITHALS A7 A badde henne is that which layeth egges for our neighbours, and not for them that keepe her. **1732** FULLER no. 2987.

Hen's nest, *see* Seek a hare in a h. n.

Hen(s), *see also* Black h. lays white egg; Busy as a h. with one chicken; Cock moult before h. (If); Comes of a h. must scrape (He that); Crooning cow, a crowing h.; Eat a h. in Janivere; Eaten the h.'s rump; Eggs and the h. (To have both); Fat as a h. in the forehead; Fat h. lay few eggs; Fie upon h. quoth fox; Grain by grain and the h. fills; Nice as a nun's h.; Offer your h. for sale on rainy day (Never); Pecked to death by a h. (As good be); Poor h. that can't scrat for one chick; Sell his h. on a rainy day; Son of the white h.; Thrift goes by the profit of a yeld h. (Your); Women and h. through gadding are lost. *See also* Hens.

Hende[1] as a hound in a kitchen, As.

1377 LANGLAND *P. Pl.* B. v. 261 'I am holden', quod he, 'as hende as hounde is in kychyne. [[1] well-behaved.]

Hengsten Down well ywrought, is worth London town dear ybought.

1602 R. CAREW *Survey of Cornwall* (1811) 272 The country people have a bye-word, that Hengsten Down, well yrought, Is worth London Town, dear ybought, Which grew from the store of tin, in former times, there digged up.

Henley, *see* More fools in H.

Henry the Eighth pulled down monks and their cells, Henry the Ninth should pull down bishops, and their bells.

1608 J. HARINGTON *Brief View State of Ch. Eng.* (1653) Title page. Written for the private use of Prince Henry, upon occasion of that Proverb, *Henry the eighth pull'd down Monks and their Cells. Henry the ninth should pull down Bishops, and their Bells.*

Henry VIII, *see also* King Henry.

Henry[1] was the union of the roses,[2] In | in James[3] of the kingdoms.

1629 T. ADAMS *Serm.* (1861–2) II. 326 We are not shuffled into a popular government, nor cut into cantons by a headless, headstrong, aristocracy; but *Henricus Rosas, Regna Jacobus*—in Henry was the union of the roses, in James of the kingdoms. [[1] Henry VII. [2] Houses of York and Lancaster. [3] James I.]

Hens are free of horse corn.

1721 KELLY 170 . . . Spoken of those who are free of what is not their own.

Hens, *see also* Hen(s).

Heraldry, *see* Metal upon metal false h.

Herb will cure love, No.

[ov. *Met* I. 523 Hei mihi, quod nullis amor est sanabilis herbis!] *c.* **1386** CHAUCER *Leg. Good Women* 1187 Love wol love, for nothing will it wonde [cease]. **1832** HENDERSON 40.

Herb-John,[1] Without | no good pottage.

[**1658** GURNALL *Chrn. in Armour* II. 12 (in DAVIES *Suppl. Eng. Gloss.* 309) *Herb-John* in the pot does neither much good nor hurt.] **1614** T. ADAMS *Devil's Banquet* 307 Balme, with the destitution of Gods blessing, doth as much good as a branch of hearb-John in our pottage. **1659** HOWELL *Eng. Prov.* 13/1 Without herb-*John*, no good pottage. [[1] some tasteless pot-herb.]

Hercules could contend against two, Not even.

[Gk. Οὐδὲ Ἡρακλῆς πρὸς δύο. L. ERASM. *Ad. Ne Hercules quidem adversus duos.*] **1539** TAVERNER f. 17 (A) Not Hercules against two, that is to say. **1576** GASCOIGNE *Grief of Joy* iii (C.U.P.) 540 But two to one, can be no equal lot, For why? the Latin proverb, saith, you wot, *Sit quisque similis inter suos, Ne Hercules enim contra duos.* **1590–1** SHAKS. *3 Hen. VI* II. i. 53 *Mess.* But Hercules himself must yield to odds. **1607** CHAPMAN *Rev. of Bus.* III. i (Merm.) 271 Two are enough to encounter Hercules.

Hercules was not begot in one night.

1674 MILTON *Dec. for Elect. of John III.* Prose Wks. (1890) III. 481 It was not right that a hero . . . should in a moment . . . be made a king, whenas antiquity by an ancient proverb has delivered, 'that Hercules was not begot in one night'.

Hercules with the distaff.

1778 JOHNSON in *Boswell* (1848) lxiv. 592 'You shall see what a book of cookery I shall make . . . ' *Miss Seward* 'That would be Hercules with the distaff indeed'.

Hercules, *see also* Crutch of time . . . club of H.

Herds (= shepherds), *see* Ill h. fat wolves.

Here a little and there a little.

1555 HEYWOOD *Epigr. upon Proverbs* no. 237 Here sum and theare sum. **1601** A. DENT *Plain Man's Pathway* 367. **1616** DRAXE 13.

Here to-day and gone to-morrow.

1616 DRAXE 133 Alive to day, and dead to morrow. **1638** J. TAYLOR *Bull Bear and Horse* A 6ᵛ. **1721** KELLY 166 Here to Day, and away to Morrow. **1731** *Poor Robins Alm.* The *world is full of Vissitudes, we are here to-day, and gone to-morrow,* as the Shoe-maker said when he was going to run away.

Here, *see also* Better say, Here it is; Neither h. nor there.

Hereafter comes not yet.

1546 HEYWOOD II. vii. 67 Though hereafter comes not yit. **1611** DAVIES *Prov.* 84 Her-after comes not. **1660** TATHAM *Rump.* III. i. Wks. (1879) 234 *Bert.* We'll think on that herafter. *Hus.* Hereafter comes not yet, then, it seems? **1721** KELLY 144 . . . Spoken when we suspect that such a project, or action, will have an ill consequence.

Heresy and beer came hopping into England both in a year.

1599 BUTTES *Dyets Dry Dinner* G 4 I know not how it happened (as he merrily saith) that heresie and beere came hopping into England both in a yeere. **1646** *Ex-ale-tation of Ale* 6 For with this same beere came up heresies here, the old Catholike drink is a [pot of good Ale].

Heresy is the school of pride.

1651 HERBERT 366.

Heresy may be easier kept out than shook off.

1651 HERBERT 366.

Heresy, *see also* Frenzy, h., and jealousy seldom cured.

Heretic and a good subject, For the same man to be a | is incompossible.

1651 HERBERT 366.

Heretic, *see also* Faith with h. (No); Gospel (With the) one becomes h.

Hermit Kingdom, The (*i.e.* Korea).

1911 *Times Lit. Sup.* 15 Sept. 330 The con-sequences . . . must eventually be the same in the Middle as in the Hermit Kingdom; and . . . Manchuria . . . must shortly share the fate which has overtaken Korea.

Hero, *see* No man is a h. to valet.

Herring is the king, Of all the fish in the sea.

1598 JONSON *Ev. Man in Humour* I. iii. 12

Herring the king of fish. **1599** NASHE *Lenten Stuff* Wks. (McKerrow) III. 149. **1639** CHAP-MAN *Chabot* III. ii. 80 Herrings, which some say is the King of fishes. **1659** HOWELL *Eng. Prov.* 21/1.

Herring must hang by its own gill, Every.

1639 CLARKE 20 Every herring must hang by th'owne gill. **1670** RAY 102. **1721** KELLY 240 *Let every herring hing by its own head.* Every man must stand by his own endeavour, industry, and interest. **1818** SCOTT *Rob Roy* xxvi Na, na! let every herring hing by its ain head, and every sheep by its ain shank.

Herrings in a barrel, Like.

1881 D. C. MURRAY *Joseph's Coat* xii The hall of justice was small . . . and there were fifty or sixty people packed into it like herrings in a barrel.

Herring(s), *see also* Barrel the better h. (Never a); Dead as a h.; Fish for h. and catch sprat; Lean as a shotten h.; Lose in hake (What we), shall have in h.; Poke savour of the h.; Red h.; Sprat nowadays calls itself h.; Sprat to catch h.

Hertfordshire clubs and clouted shoon.

1613–22 DRAYTON *Polyolb.* xxiii. 249, 50 (1876) III. 95 So *Hartford* blazon'd is, *The Club, and clowted Shoone.* **1662** FULLER (*Herts.*) II. 39 'Hertfordshire clubs and clouted shoon'. Some will wonder how this shire, lying so near to London, should be guilty of so much rusticalness. But the finest cloth must have a list, and the pure peasants are as of coarse a thread in this county as in any other place.

Hertfordshire kindness.

1662 FULLER (*Herts.*) II. 40 'Hertfordshire kindness'. The people in this county at entertainments drink back to those who drank to them. **1738** SWIFT (Dial. ii) 345 *Never.* This moment I did myself the honour to drink to your lordship. *Ld. S.* Why, then, that's Hertfordshire kindness.

Hesky's library—all outside, Like.

1917 BRIDGE 90 Like Hesky's library—all outside. Anything pretentious or unreal. A common saying in Cheshire and North Wales in the middle of last century. When Mr. Bamford Hesketh erected Gwrych Castle . . . the owner had not a tithe of the books necessary to fill [the library shelves].

Hew (Climb, Look) not too high lest the chips fall in thine eye.

c. **1330** BRUNNE *Chron.* (Hearne) I. 91 Sorow þan is his pyne, þat he wis ouer his heued, þe chip falles in his ine. *c.* **1350** *Douce MS. 52* no. 128 Whoso heweth to hye, þere falle chippis in his ye. *c.* **1370** *Sir Eglamour* (Schleich) l. 70 The man þat hewes ouer-hey, þe chyppis fallis in his eye. *c.* **1390** GOWER *Conf. Amantis* i. 75 Full ofte he heweth up so highe, That chippes fallen in his eye. *c.* **1433**

LYDGATE *Edmund & Tremund* iii. 5 I am ferful aboue myn hed to hewe, lyst froward chippis of presumpcioun sholde blynde myn eyen in ther fallyng doon. *a.* 1530 *R. Hill's Commonpl. Bk.* (1858) 140 Clyme not to hye lest chypys fall yn thyn eie. 1546 HEYWOOD II. vii. 67 But this prouerbe precheth to men haute or hye, Hewe not to hye, lest the chips fall in thine iye. 1580 LYLY *Euph. & his Eng.* (Arb.) 467 In the choyce of a wife . . . one looketh high as one yat feareth no chips. 1641 FERGUSSON 38 He that hewes over hie, the spaill will fall into his eye. 1670 RAY 102 Look not too high, lest a chip fall in thine eye. *Noli altum sapere.*

Heyden, *see* Paston poor.

Hiccup, To cure one of the.

1635 SHIRLEY *Lady of Pleas.* III. ii (Merm.) 314 I am not troubled with the hickup, gentlemen, You should bestow this fright upon me. 1744 BIRCH *Life Boyle* in *Boyle's Wks.* I. 83 (R.) Some are freed from the hiccough, by being told of some feigned ill news. 1910 JOYCE *Eng. as We Speak* 202 'To cure a person's hiccup' means to . . . bring him to his senses. . . . [It] is the general belief through Ireland that . . . hiccup may be cured by suddenly making some . . . alarming announcement to the person.

Hickledy pickledy, one among another.

1678 RAY 349 Hickledy pickledy, one among another. We have in our language many the like . . . reduplications to signifie any confusion or mixture.

Hide an eel in a sack, You cannot.

1640 HERBERT 352. 1732 FULLER no. 5875.

Hide nothing from thy minister, physician, and lawyer.

1573 SANDFORD H 2 *Al Medico & Auuocato Non tener il ver' celato,* Conceale not the truth From the Phisition and Lawyer. 1578 FLORIO *First Fruites* f. 27 From the Phisition & Attorney, Keepe not the truth hidden. 1640 HERBERT 321 Deceive not thy physician, confessor, nor lawyer. 1670 RAY 103 . . . He that doth so, doth it to his own harm or loss, wronging thereby either his soul, body, or estate. 1748 FRANKLIN July To friend, lawyer, doctor, tell plain your whole case; Nor think on bad matters to put a good face. 1834 EDGEWORTH *Helen* xxi Always tell your confessor, your lawyer, your physician, your friend, your whole case.

Hide one's light (candle) under a bushel, To.

[1526–34 TINDALE *Matt.* v. 15 Nether do men lyght a candell, and put it vnder a busshell, but on a candelstick, and it lighteth all them which are in the housse.] *a.* 1873 LYTTON *Kenelm C.* VII. vii Slothfully determined to hide his candle under a bushel.

Hide (*noun*), *see* Horns go with h. (Let).

Hide, hid (*verb*), *see* Nothing comes fairer to light than long h.

Hides can find, He that.

c. 1400 *Seven Sages* (Percy Soc.) 68 He may wel fynde that hyde him selven. 1646 FULLER *Wounded Consc.* (1841) 339 Our English proverb saith, he that hath hid can find. 1678 RAY 137 They that feal (i.e. hide) can find. 1842 MARRYAT *Perc. Keene* iii Yes, yes, those who hide can find. 1855 BOHN 406 Hiders are good finders.

Hielandman, *see* Taking the breeks off a H. (Ill).

High and dry.

1894 DEAN HOLE *More Mem.* ii. 29 The clergy, . . . described by their critics as 'High and Dry', high in their self-esteem, and 'dry as a Monday bun' in their discourses. 1910 *Times Lit. Sup.* 9 Dec. What is usually called the 'High and Dry' section was in fact . . . a 'Low Church or Latitudinarian party, . . . content to leave things as they were'.

High as a hog, all but the bristles, As.

1670 RAY 202 . . . Spoken of a dwarf in derision.

High as two (three) horse loaves,[1] As.

[A jocular standard of measurement.] 1546 HEYWOOD I. x. 20 As high as twoo horse loues hir person is. 1670 RAY 202 As high as three horse loaves . . . spoken of a dwarf in derision. [[1] made of beans and wheat.]

High buildings have a low foundation.

1623 CAMDEN 265 A high building, a low foundation. 1670 RAY 103 A high building, a low foundation. 1855 BOHN 406.

High for the pie, Not too | nor too low for the crow.

1546 HEYWOOD II. vii. 67 Measure is a mery meane, as this doth show, Not to hye for the pye, nor to lowe for the crow.

High horse, *see* Ride the h. h.

High in the instep, To be.

[= haughty, proud.] 1542 BOORDE *Introd.* (E.E.T.S.) xxvi. 189 (A) They be hyghe in the instep, and stondeth in theyr owne consayte. 1546 HEYWOOD I. xi. 31 He is so hy in thinstep. 1617 MORYSON *Itin.* II. 26 Now the Gentleman was growne higher in the instep, as appeared by the insolent conditions he required. 1828 *Craven Dial.* s.v. 'She is rather high in her instep', she is proud and haughty.

High places have their precipices.

1732 FULLER no. 2501. 1813 RAY 121.

High regions are never without storms.

1855 BOHN 406.

High ropes, To be on the.

[= in an elated, disdainful, or enraged mood.]

a. **1700** B.E. *Dict. Cant. Crew* s.v. *Rope*, upon the High-ropes, Cock-a-hoop. **1711** SWIFT *Jrnl. to Stella* 6 Dec. The Duke of Marlborough ... is one day humble, and the next day on the high ropes. **1773** GOLDSMITH *Stoops to Conq.* II. Wks. (Globe) 653/2 All upon the high rope! His uncle a colonel. **1838** DICKENS *N. Nickleby* xxxi I went there the night before last, but she was quite on the high ropes about something.

High, *see also* Hew (Climb, Look) not too h. lest chips fall in eye.

Higher standing, The | the lower fall.

c. **1430** LYDGATE *Minor Poems* (Percy Soc.) 24 Who sitteth highest moost like to fall soon. **1549** *Compl. of Scotland* (E.E.T.S.) 170 The mair eleuat that ane person be in superfleu digniteis, his fal and ruuyn sal be the hauyar. Quanto gradus altior, tanto casus grauior. **1641** FERGUSSON 98 The higher up, the greater fall. **1670** RAY 102. **1721** KELLY 319 The higher up, the lower fall.

Higher the ape goes, The | the more he shows his tail.

c. **1594** BACON *Promus* 309, no. 924 He doth like the ape that the higher he clymbes the more he shows his ars. **1640** HERBERT 352. **1670** RAY 57 ... The higher beggars or base bred persons are advanced, the more they discover the lowness and baseness of their spirits and tempers. **1861** C. READE *Cloister & H.* lii Margaret retorted: '... Your speech betrays you. 'Tis not till the ape hath mounted the tree that she shows her tail so plain.'

Higher the fool, The | the greater the fall.

1707 MAPLETOFT 125 (Welsh).

Higher the hill, The | the lower the grass.

1509 A. BARCLAY *Ship of Fools* (1874) I. 188 On hyest places most gras doth not ay growe. **1721** KELLY 330 ... People of the most greatest fortunes are not the most liberal.

Higher the plum-tree, The | the riper (sweeter) the plum: the richer the cobbler, the blacker his thumb.

1579 GOSSON *Ephemerides* 76 b Rich Coblers, haue blacke Thumbes. **1639** CLARKE 88 The higher the plum-tree the sweeter the plumme. **1659** N.R. 112. **1670** RAY 210. **1732** FULLER no. 6420.

Higher the tree, The | the sweeter the plum, the better the shoe, the blacker the thumb.

1659 HOWELL *Eng. Prov.* 17/2.

Highest branch is not the safest roost, The.

1855 BOHN 507.

Highest in court (Nearest the King) nearest the widdie.[1]

1641 FERGUSSON 82 Nearest the King, nearest the widdie. **1721** KELLY 126 *Highest in court nearest the widdie.* Witness the fatal fall of many courtiers. [[1] gallows.]

Highest tree hath the greatest fall, The.

c. **1374** CHAUCER *Troylus* II. 1380–6 Whan that the sturdy ook, Receyvĕd hath the happy falling strook, The gretĕ sweigh doth it come al at ones. ... For swifter cours com'th thing that is of wighte, Whan it descendeth, than don thinges lighte. **1639** CLARKE 122. **1670** RAY 13.

Highflying hawks are fit for princes.

1670 RAY 101.

Highgate, *see* Sworn at H.; Water his horse at H.

Highlandman's gun, Like the | that needed a new lock, stock, and barrel.

1817 SCOTT *Let. to Terry* 29 Oct. in LOCKHART *Life* Like the Highlandman's gun, she wants stock, lock, and barrel, to put her into repair.

Highlandman, *see also* Find it where H. found tongs; Forth bridles the H. *See also* Hielandman.

Highlands, Speak well of the | but dwell in the Laigh.[1]

1896 CHEVIOT 303. [[1] Lowlands.]

Highway is never about, The.

1623 J. CHAMBERLAIN *Letters* (McClure) ii. 508 Commonly the high way is both safest and shortest. **1639** CLARKE 202.

Highway, He that leaves the | to cut short, commonly goes about. (*Cf.* Highway is never about.)

1707 MAPLETOFT 74. **1732** FULLER no. 2213.

Highway, *see also* Grass grows not upon h.; Silent H.; Sows in the h. (He that).

Hilary term, *see* Keep H. t.

Hill in King Harry's day, This was a.

1678 RAY 73. (*Joculatory.*)

Hills (*proper name*), *see* Clent (People of).

Hills are green (blue) far away.

1887 H. CAINE *Deemster* v 'What's it saying'; they would mutter; 'a green hill when far from me; bare, bare when it is near'. **1914** *Spectator* 6 June, 955 It is the habit of the Celt to create fanciful golden ages in the past —'Blue are the faraway hills', runs the Gaelic proverb.

Hill(s), *see also* Clouds are upon h. (When); Do on the h. as in the hall; Higher the h.

lower the grass; Hop against h.; Mist comes from the h. (When); Praise a h. but keep below; Up h. spare me; Up the h. favour me.

Hilt(s), *see* Loose in the h.

Hinckley field, *see* Last man that he killed.

Hind foot, *see* Ill paut with her h. f. (She has).

Hinder end, *see* Hearken to the h. e.

Hindmost, *see* Dog (H.) may catch hare.

Hindostan, *see* Pepper to H.

Hinge(s), *see* Groundsel speaks not save . . . heard at h.

Hinging on, *see* Hankering and h. o. is a poor trade.

Hip, To have one on the.

[= have one at a disadvantage.] **1546** HEY-WOOD II. v. 58 Then haue ye him on the hyp, or on the hyrdell. **1596–7** SHAKS. *Merch. V.* IV. i. 335 Now, infidel, I have thee on the hip. **1604–5** *Othello* II. i. 317 I'll have our Michael Cassio on the hip. **1639** FULLER *Holy War* II. viii (1840) 59 Arnulphus . . . fearing to wrestle with the king, who had him on the hip, and could out him at pleasure.

Hip, *see also* Bite out of your own h. (Take a).

Hire, *see* Good hand good h.

Hired horse tired never, A.

1641 FERGUSSON 102. **1683** MERITON *Yorks. Ale* 83–7 (1697) (A).

Hires the horse, He that | must ride before.

1639 CLARKE 99. **1670** RAY 106.

History repeats itself.

1885 A. JESSOPP *Daily Life in a Med. M.* 163 That age has passed away for ever. History repeats itself, it is true, but history will not bear mimicry. **1902** J. K. LAUGHTON in *Lect. Hist. 19th Cent.* 87 Should we again be at war with France, history would repeat itself in many of its phases.

History, *see also* Ale and h.; Country which has no h.; Every day of thy life is a leaf.

Hit (Kick) a man when he is down, To.

1712 SWIFT *Jrnl. to Stella* 8 Jan. The Duke of Marlborough says there is nothing he now desires so much as to . . . soften Dr. Swift. . . . Now he is down, I shall not trample on him. **1853** THACKERAY *Newcomes* xxix I don't know whether it is very brave in you to hit a chap when he is down. **1870** J. R. GREEN *Let.* to Freeman 31 Aug. I can't kick France now she's down, as Jupiter does.

Hit a man your own size.

1850 SMEDLEY *Frank Fairlegh* xxxiii Hit a man your own size, you great big monster.

Hit (Strike) below the belt, To.

1890 S. BARING-GOULD *Arminell* II. xxxiv. 265 You have behaved infamously towards your benefactor, you have hurt him where he is most sensitive—hitting, you contemptible little coward, below the belt. **1926** *Times* 13 Jul. 10/3 In England we did not believe in stabbing a man in the back or hitting him below the belt.

Hit him hard: he has no friends.

1850 D. M. MULOCK *Woman's Thoughts* 156 The poor costermonger, who shouts after the little pugilistic sweep the familiar tragic-comic saying: 'Hit him hard; he's got no friends!'

Hit one over the thumbs, To.

[= to punish, or reprove sharply.] **1540** PALSGRAVE *Acolastus* B 4 (A) Haue men hytte the vpon the thombes? *a.* **1548** HALL *Chron., Hen. VII* 33 In the later ende of hys oracion, he a little rebuked the lady Margaret and hyt her of [Grafton on] the thombes. **1553** T. WILSON *Arte of Rhet.* (1580) 3 The Philosopher . . . did hit a yong man ouer the Thumbes verie handsomely, for vsyng ouer old, and ouer straunge woordes.

Hit or miss.

1560 T. WILSON *Arte of Rhet.* (1909) 87 (A) Which shot in the open and plaine fields at all adventures hittie missie. **1601–2** SHAKS. *Troil. & Cres.* I. iii. 384 But, hit or miss, Our project's life this shape of sense assumes. **1705** HICKERINGILL *Priest-cr.* I. (1721) 14 Do we all march towards Heaven hit or miss, and by guess? **1873** OUIDA *Pascarèl* II. 42 It is not the happy-go-lucky hit-or-miss sort of thing that you may fancy.

Hit or miss for a cow-heel.

1678 RAY 73.

Hit the nail on the head, To.

[= to come at the point of the matter.] *c.* **1520** STANBRIDGE *Vulg.* B 5 (A) Thou hyttest the nayle on the head. *a.* **1529** SKELTON *Col. Cloute* 34 And yf that he hyt The nayle on the hede, It standeth in no stede. **1599** H. BUTTES *Dyets Drie Dinner* E vj His chiefe pride resteth in hitting the nayle on the head with a quainte Epithite. **1614** CAMDEN 305 Euery man cannot hit the naile on the head. **1662** FULLER (*Linc.*) II. 295 James Yorke . . . set forth a book of heraldry. . . . And although there be some mistake (no hand so steady as always to hit the nail on the head) [&c.]. **1852** E. FITZGERALD *Polonius* 15 Where the writer has gone to the heart of a matter, the centre of the circle, hit the nail on the head and driven it home. **1903** BRYCE *Stud. Contemp. Biog.* 461 Mr. Gladstone showed in argument a knack of hitting the nail not quite on the head.

Hit (Shoot nigh) the prick (mark), To.

c. **1400** *Sowdone Bab.* 2260 Thou kanste welle hit the prikke.[1] **1546** HEYWOOD I. vi. xii Ye mary (quoth he) nowe ye shoote nie the pricke. [[1] mark in shooting with bow.]

Hit(s), *see also* Oft ettle, whiles h.; Once h. (He that) is ever bending; Shoots oft at last shall h. mark; Vulgar will keep no account of your h.

Hitch your wagon to a star.

1870 EMERSON *Society and Solitude* Civilization'.

Ho, *see* Out of all whooping (*or* h.).

Hoar head and a green tail, To have a.

c. **1386** CHAUCER *Reeve's Prol.* 25 To have an hoor heed and a grene tayl, As hath a leek; for thogh our might be goon, Our wil desireth folie ever in oon.

Hoardeth up money, He that | taketh pains for other men.

1567 W. BALDWIN *Treatise Moral Philosophy* A 5ᵛ. **1669** *Politeuphuia* 130 (A). **1732** FULLER no. 2165.

Hob's pound, *see* Lob's pound.

Hobby runs away with him, His.

1834 EDGEWORTH *Helen* xvii Beauclerc's hobbies, I plainly see, will always run away with him headlong.

Hobby, *see also* Ride a h. to death.

Hobby-horse, Every man hath his.

1676 HALE *Contempl.* I. 201. Almost every person hath some hobby horse or other wherein he prides himself. *a.* **1791** WESLEY *Serm.* lxxxiii. II. 2 Wks. (1811) IX. 434 Every one has (to use the cant term of the day . . .) *his hobby-horse*! Something that pleases the great boy for a few hours.

Hobgoblin reads his own writing, The.

1853 TRENCH iii. 59.

Hobson's choice.

[Tobias Hobson, the Cambridge carrier, who let out horses, compelled customers to take the horse which happened to be next the stable-door, or go without.] **1649** *Somers Tracts* (1811) vii. 87 (A) I had Hobson's choice, either be a Hobson or nothing. **1660** S. FISHER *Rustick's Alarm* Wks. (1679) 128 If in this Case there be no other (as the Proverb is) then Hobson's choice . . . which is, chuse whether you will have this or none. *a.* **1708** T. WARD *Eng. Ref.* (1716) 326 Where to elect there is but one, 'Tis Hobson's choice, Take that or none. **1714** *Spectator* 509. **1858** R. SURTEES *Ask Mamma* xliii It was a case of Hobson's choice with them.

Hoe, *see* Row to h. (Hard); Tickle it with a h.

Hog hath its Martinmas, Every.

1620 SHELTON *Quix.* II. lxii (1908) III. 265 I thought . . . it had been . . . turned to ashes for an idle pamphlet; but it will not, like hogs, want its Saint Martin. [*Note.* That saint's day is hogs' searing.]

Hog his own apple, Every.

1748 SMOLLETT *Rod. Rand.* xli I let them have share and share while it lasted. Howsomever, I should have remembered the old saying, *Every hog his own apple.*

Hog in armour, A.

[= a stiff clumsy person.] **1659** HOWELL *Eng. Prov.* 19/1 He looketh like a Hogg in armour. **1774** *Westmr. Mag.* II. 457 I never see Alderman —— on horseback, but he reminds me of an hog in armour. **1857** TROLLOPE *Three Clerks* (1860) 289 But he did not carry his finery like a hog in armour, as an Englishman so often does when an Englishman stoops to be fine.

Hog is never good but when he is in the dish, The.

1587 MASCALL *Govt. Cattle* (1627) 270 Wherefore the common saying is, the hog is never good but when he is in the dish.

Hog never looks up to him that threshes down the acorns, The.

1654 FULLER *Comment. on Ruth* in *Serm.* (1891) I. 9 In prosperity, we are commonly like hogs feeding on the mast, not minding his hand that shaketh it down. **1732** FULLER no. 4599.

Hog that's bemired endeavours to bemire others, A.

1599 MINSHEU (1623) 2Y6ᵛ One hog that hath wallowed in the mire will beray another. **1732** FULLER no. 214.

Hogs Norton, where Pigs play on the Organ.

c. **1554** *Interlude of Youth* in HAZL. *O.E.P.* (1874) II. 31 Wert thou born in Trumpington, And brought up at Hoggesnorton? **1616** WITHALS 580. **1639** CLARKE 7 A pig playes on the organs. **1640** *Wits Recreation* (Hotten) 88 You your garden may Hogs Norton call, here Pigs on organs play. **1659** HOWELL *Eng. Prov.* 16/1 I think thou wast born at *Hoggs-Norton*, where piggs play upon the Organs. **1662** FULLER (*Oxf.*) III. 5 'You were born at Hogs-Norton.' This is a village, properly called Hoch-Norton, whose inhabitants (it seems formerly) were so rustical in their behaviour, that boorish and clownish people are said to have been born at *Hogs-Norton.* **1881** EVANS 301 'Hogs Norton, where Pigs play on the Organ'. . . . To say that a man comes from Hog's Norton is simply equivalent to saying that he snores.

Hogs to a Banbury market, He hath brought his.

1639 CLARKE 201.

Hogs (Pigs) to a fair (fine) market, He hath brought his.

1600 DAY & CHETTLE *The Blind Beggar of Bednal-Green* v. i I have brought my hogs to a fair Market. **1618–19** J. FLETCHER *Bonduca*

v. ii You have brought your hogs to a fine market; you are wise, Sir. **1638** CLARKE *Phraseol. Puer.* 76 *Triticum advexi & hordeum vendo* . . . I have brought my hogges to a faire market. **1659** HOWELL *Eng. Prov.* 5 You have brought your hogs to a fair market. Spoken in derision when a business hath sped ill. **1748** SMOLLETT *Rod. Rand.* XV Strap . . . observed that we had brought our pigs to a fine market. **1805** LAMB *Mr. H——*. II. Wks. (1898) 641 Your Honour has had some mortification . . . ; you have brought your pigs to a fine market. **1890** D. C. MURRAY *John Vale's G.* xvi Mr. Orme . . . felt that he had brought his pigs to a poor market.

Hogs to the honey pots, The.

1678 RAY 354.

Hog(s), *see also* Basteth the fat h. (Every man); Better my h. dirty home; Break a h. of ill custom (Hard to); Drive black h. in dark; Driving his h. . . . (He is); Expect of a h. but bristles (a grunt) (What can you); High as a h.; Kill h. (He who does not) will not get black puddings; Last man he killed keeps h.; Like a h. hangeth the groin on her husband; Like a h. he never does good till his death; Make a h. or a dog of it; One h. (He that hath) makes him fat; Routing like a h.; Steal the h. and give feet.

Hogshead, *see* Couch a h.

Hoist with his own petard.

1600–1 SHAKS. *Hamlet* III. iv. 207 For 'tis the sport to have the enginer Hoist with his own petar. **1826** SCOTT *Woodst.* xxxiii 'Tis sport to have the engineer Hoist with his own petard, as our immortal Shakespeare has it. **1885** C. LOWE *Bismarck* (1898) 322 The Chancellor had been caught in his own trap, hoist, so to speak, with his own petard.

Hoist your sail when the wind is fair.

1583 MELBANCKE *Philotimus* 24 Yt is well, therefore, to make hay while the sunne shines, when winde is at will to hoyse vp saile. **1732** FULLER no. 2518. **1822** SCOTT *Nigel*, Introd. Ep. A man should strike while the iron is hot, and hoist sail while the wind is fair.

Hoistings, or Hustings, You are all for the.

1662 FULLER (*Lond.*) II. 349 'You are all for the Hoistings, or Hustings.' It is spoken of those who by pride or passion are mounted or elated to a pitch above the due proportion of their birth, quality, or estate. . . . It cometh from the hustings, the principal and highest court in London.

Holborn, *see* Ride backwards up H. Hill.

Hold a candle to, Not able (fit) to.

1861 G. J. WHYTE-MELVILLE *Market Harbor.* xviii The Reverend . . . always declared . . . that Cissy could not hold a candle to what her mother had been in her best days. **1882** BLACKMORE *Christowell* xxxvi Some one . . .

intending ill to my poor pears. . . . That man . . . who . . . had nothing fit to hold a candle to my *Léon Leclerc.* **1883** W. E. NORRIS *No New Thing* I. vii. 175 Edith is pretty, very pretty; but she can't hold a candle to Nellie.

Hold a candle to the devil, To.

[= to assist in wrong-doing.] **1461** *Paston Lett.* (Gairdner) II. 73 It is a comon prouerbe, 'A man must sumtyme set a candel before the Devyle.' **1520** WHITTINGTON *Vulg.* (E.E.T.S.) 107 Thou art aboute to please a shrewe (I haue espyed) as a man that offereth a candell to the deuyll. **1546** HEYWOOD I. X. 20 I fearyng She would spit her venym, thought it not euyll To sette vp a candle before the deuyll. **1599** PORTER *Angry Wom. Abingd.* IV. iii (Merm.) 176 Yet I'll give him good words; 'tis good to hold the candle before the devil. **1649** HOWELL *Pre-em. Parl.* 20 According to the Italian Proverb, That one must sometimes light a candle to the Devil. **1828** SCOTT *F. M. Perth* II. 213 (D.) Here have I been holding a candle to the devil, to show him the way to mischief.

Hold a candle to the sun, To, *see* Sun with a candle (To set forth the).

Hold an eel by the tail, To.

1546 HEYWOOD I. x Her promise of friendship for any auayle Is as sure to hold as an ele by the tayle. *c.* **1612** BEAUM. & FL. *Scornf. Lady* II. i. Wks. (1905) I. 246 I will end with the wise man, and say; He that holds a woman, has an eel by the tail.

Hold by the apron-strings, To.

1678 RAY 226 To hold by the Apron-strings. *i.e.* in right of his wife.

Hold fast when you have it.

1546 HEYWOOD I. X. 24 Hold fast whan ye haue it (quoth she) by my lyfe. **1639** CLARKE 233 Hold fast while you have it. **1876** MRS. BANKS *Manch. Man* X Then, . . . rang, clear and distinct, Humphry Chetham's motto—— 'Quod tuum tene!' (What you have, hold!)

Hold fast, *see also* Hawking (First point of).

Hold him to it buckle and thong.

1658 *Wit Restor'd* in *Mus. Deliciae* (Hotten) i. 280 (A) When one is held to it hard, buckle and thong. **1678** RAY 73.

Hold(s) his peace, *see* Speaks sows (He that) . . . h. h. p. gathers.

Hold his tongue, *see* Knows not how to h. h. t. (He that); Leave to speak (Must have) who cannot h. h. t.; Speak well (He cannot) that cannot h. h. t. *See also* Hold one's tongue.

Hold nor to bind, Neither to.

1824 SCOTT *St. Ronan's* xv A lord! . . . a lord come down to the Waal—they will be neither to haud nor to bind now. **1824** MOIR *Mansie W.* ii The old lady was neither to hold nor bind, and nothing would serve her but having . . . the old woman . . . committed to the Tolbooth. **1900** J. MCCARTHY *Hist. Own Times*

V. 144 King Theebaw was ... a madman, ... like Caligula.... He was a man, ... 'Neither to haud nor to bind.'

Hold on like grim death, To.

1837 TH. HOOK *Jack Brag* xx 'Delightful breeze!' said Mr. Buckthorne to Jock, who was holding on, like grim death, by the companion. **1861** READE *Cloister & H.* iv He would seize it with his teeth, and . . . hold on like grim death by his huge ivories.

Hold one's tongue in an ill time, One may.

1616 DRAXE 191. **1670** RAY 103.

Hold or cut codpiece point.

1595 SHAKS. *Mids. N.* I. ii. 113 Hold or cut bowstrings. **1678** RAY 73.

Hold that will away? Who can (or may).

c. **1374** CHAUCER *Troylus* IV. 1628 For who may holde a thing that wol awey? **1546** HEYWOOD II. vi. 62 Saieth an other, who maie holde that will awaie. **1614** JONSON *Barth. Fair* I. i *Cokes.* Who can hold that will away? I had rather lose him than the Fair, I wusse. **1721** KELLY 352 . . . Spoken when our friends will not be prevail'd upon to tarry with us.

Hold the ass by the bridle, It is good to.

1639 CLARKE 161.

Hold the candle, *see* Dance nor h. the c. (Neither).

Hold the greatest farms, They that | pay the least rent.

1651 HERBERT 368 . . . applied to rich men that are unthankful to God.

Hold up your dagger hand.

1639 CLARKE 46. **1678** RAY 88 *Phrases . . . belonging to . . . drinking.* Hold up your dagger hand.

Hold your tongue, husband, and let me talk that have all the wit.

1678 RAY 84. **1732** FULLER no. 2521.

Holdfast, *see* Brag is a good dog but H. better.

Holds his peace and gathers stones, Who | will find a time to throw them.

1903 A. T. QUILLER-COUCH *Hetty Wesley* I. iii These Hindus are the devil . . . for nursing a grudge. 'Keep a stone in your pocket seven years: turn it, keep it for another seven; 'twill be ready at your hand for your enemy' —that's their way.

Holds up her head like a hen drinking (a hundred pound aver[1]), She.

1721 KELLY 294 Spoken of a woman who affectedly holds her head high. [[1] horse.]

Hole calls the thief, The.

1640 HERBERT 326.

Hole in the groat to-day, and the supper to seek, There will be a.

1721 KELLY 325 . . . A saying of labourers, when they fear a rainy afternoon.

Hole in the house, There is a.

1721 KELLY 315 . . . Spoken when some are present, before whom it is not proper to speak our mind.

Hole in the water, To make a.

[= to commit suicide by drowning.] **1813** RAY 201. **1853** DICKENS *Bleak Ho.* xlvi Why I don't go and make a hole in the water I don't know.

Hole under his nose that all his money runs into, He has a.

1611 COTGRAVE S.V. 'Soulier' The hole too open under the nose, breeds tattered shooes, and ragged hose. **1659** HOWELL *Fr.-Eng.* 10. **1732** FULLER no. 1858.

Hole(s), *see also* Find some h. to creep out at; Pick a h.; See day at a little h.; Tell how many h. be in a scummer; Tod keeps his own h. clean; Wish your skin full of h. (Long ere you).

Holiday dame, She is an.

1678 RAY 73 She's an holy day dame. (*Joculatory.*)

Holiday(s), *see also* Every day is h. with sluggards; Lay up for h.

Holland, *see* Children in H. take pleasure in making.

Holloway, Blind George of, *see* Fain see (That would I).

Holmesdale, The vale of | never won nor never shall.

1576 W. LAMBARDE *Peramb. of Kent* (1596) 520, 904 The Danes were ouerthrowne and vanquished. This victorie, . . . begate, as I gesse, the common byword, vsed amongst the inhabitauntes of this vale, . . . The vale of Holmesdale, Neuer wonne, nor neuer shale. **1659** HOWELL *Eng. Prov.* 21/1 . . . *Holmesdale is near Rigat[1] in Surrey.* [[1] Reigate.]

Holy habit cleanseth not a foul soul, A.

1640 HERBERT 348.

Holy I'll be, I, marry will I.

1616 WITHALS 560. **1639** CLARKE 139.

Holy, *see also* Over h. was hanged.

Holyrood Day[1] the devil goes a-nutting, On.

1693 *Poor Robin* Sept. **14,** 26 in LEAN II. i. 242

The devil, as some people say A-nutting goes Holy Rood Day; Let women, then, their children keep At home that day. **1830** FORBY 418. [¹ 14 Sept.]

Holy-water, *see* Court h.; Public money is like h.

Home is home, though it be never so homely.

1670 RAY 103 Home is home though it be never so homely. **1692** L'ESTRANGE *Aesop's Fab.* clxxxv (1738) 198 'Why truly', says the tortoise, 'I was at home, . . . and *Home is home let it be never so homely*'. **1826** LAMB *Pop. Fallacies* no. 12. **1883** J. PAYN *Thicker than W.* ix 'Home is home, no matter how homely', and the sitting-room and two bedrooms . . . were as much their home as though they possessed a house in the neighbouring square.

Home is homely.

1546 HEYWOOD I. iv. 9 And home is homely, though it be poore in syght. **1611** COTGRAVE s.v. 'Pouvoir' When all is done home's homelie. **1732** KELLY 132 Hame is a hamely word. **1832** MOTHERWELL Introd. to HENDERSON's *Scot. Prov.* (1881) xix Nothing more bitter was ever uttered . . . against our Supreme Court of Judicature, than the saying . . . *Hame is hamely, quo' the Deil, when he fand himself in the Court of Session.*

Home Rule, Rome Rule.

1911 *Spectator*, Suppt. 29 Apr. 628 Ireland is now ruled partially by the priests, and may be so entirely in the near future if it is true that 'Home Rule is Rome Rule'.

Home, *see also* Dry bread at h. better than; East or west, h. is best; Farthest way about nearest way h.; Go h. and say prayers; Little journeys . . . bring safe h.; Long h.; Place like h. (No); Tarry-long brings little h. *See also* From home.

Home-keeping youths have ever homely wits.

1594–5 SHAKS. *Two Gent.* I. i. 2 Home-keeping youth have ever homely wits. **1830** MARRYAT *King's Own* xxxvii 'Home-keeping youths have ever homely wits', they say.

Homer sometimes nods.

[HORACE *Ars P.* 359 *Quandoque bonus dormitat Homerus.*] **1530** PALSGRAVE 897 (A) And ther where they shall se the good Homer have ben aslepe to be wyllyng by good maner to wake him, in correctyng the fautes in the whiche by cause of the same he is fallin. **1621** BURTON *Anat. Mel.* Democr. to Rdr. (1651) 78 The very best may sometimes err; *aliquando bonus dormitat Homerus.* **1674** DRYDEN *Apol. Heroic Poetry* Horace acknowledges that honest Homer nods sometimes: he is not equally awake in every line. **1887** HUXLEY in *19th Cent.* Feb. 196 Scientific reason, like Homer, sometimes nods.

Homo homini lupus, see Man is to man a wolf.

Honest a man as any is in the cards if (when) the kings are out, As.

1583 MELBANCKE *Philotimus* 191 Yes sure, you are as honest a man, as any is in the cardes if the kinges were out. **1678** RAY 291. **1732** FULLER no. 697.

Honest a man as ever broke bread (lived by bread), As.

1598–9 SHAKS. *Much Ado* III. v. 42 An honest soul . . . as ever broke bread. **1600–1** *Merry W.* I. iv. 161 An honest maid as ever broke bread. **1631** T. HEYWOOD *Fair Maid of W.* II. i My father was a baker; . . . as honest a man as ever lived by bread.

Honest a man as ever trod on neat's (shoe-)leather, As.

1595 PEELE *Old Wives' T.* 476 Our Jack, sir? as good a fellow as ever trod upon neat's leather. **1599–1600** SHAKS. *Jul. Caes.* I. i. 27 As proper men as ever trod upon neat's leather have gone upon my handiwork. **1670** RAY 181. As honest a man as ever trod on shoe leather.

Honest as the skin between his brows, As.

1598–9 SHAKS. *Much Ado* III. v. 13 An old man, . . . but, in faith, honest as the skin between his brows.

Honest (Sober) by Act of Parliament, You cannot make people.

1631 JONSON *Devil is an Ass* IV. i *Lady T.* This act may make him honest. *Man.* If he were To be made honest by an act of parliament, I should not alter in my faith of him. **1905** ALEX. MACLAREN *Expos. Math.* II. 185 The people who do not believe in certain . . . restrictions of the liquor traffic say, 'You cannot make people sober by Act of Parliament'.

Honest look covereth many faults, An.

1642 TORRIANO 99 {with covers an infinite faults'). **1732** FULLER no. 609.

Honest man and a good bowler, An.

1594–5 SHAKS. *L.L.L.* V. ii. 584 He is a marvellous good neighbour, faith, and a very good bowler. **1635** QUARLES *Emb.* I. x The vulgar proverb's crost, he hardly can Be a good bowler and an honest man.

Honest man's word is as good as his bond, An.

1642 FULLER *H. & P. State* v. xiii (1841) 382 He hath this property of an honest man, that his word is as good as his bond. **1753** RICHARDSON *Grandison* Let. v I am no flincher . . . the word of Sir Rowland Meredith is as good as his bond. **1859** SMILES *Self-Help* ix David Barclay . . . was a mirror of . . . honesty; . . . his word was always held to be as good as his bond.

Honest man, *see also* North-west wind (H. m. and a); Thread will tie.

Honest men marry soon, wise men not at all.

1659 HOWELL *Ital.* 1 Honest men use to marry, but wise men not. **1670** RAY 17 *Ital.*

Honest woman, *see* Name of an h. w. is mickle worth.

Honest, *see also* Poor but h.; Turn the (an h.) penny.

Honesty is the best policy.

1599 SANDYS *Europæ Spec.* (1632) 102 Our grosse conceipts, who think honestie the best policie. **1607-8** SHAKS. *Coriol.* III. ii. 42 I have heard you say, Honour and policy, like unsever'd friends, I' the war do grow together. **1662** FULLER (*Warwicks.*) III. 274 This his plain-dealing so wrought on his adversaries (honesty at long running is the best policy) that he was . . . continued . . . in his bishopric. **1773** BYROM *Poems* (*The Nimmers*) I. 75 I'll filch no filching;—and I'll tell no lye; Honesty's the best Policy—say I. **1904** *Spectator* 18 June 953 Archbishop Whately's saying that 'honesty is the best policy, but he is not an honest man who is honest for this reason'.

Honesty (Credit) keeps the crown of the causeway.

1721 KELLY 155 . . . An honest man has nothing to be asham'd of, and so cares not whom he meets. *Ibid.* 317 Truth and honesty, &c. **1832** HENDERSON 9 Credit keeps the crown o' the causey.

Honesty may be dear bought, but can never be an ill pennyworth.

1721 KELLY 162 . . . For it will be sure to make a man a gainer at the last.

Honesty, *see also* Beauty and h. seldom agree; Knavery may serve, but h. is best; Surfeits of too much h. (A man never).

Honey, Make yourself all | and the flies will devour you.

1620 SHELTON *Quix.* II. xlix (1908) III. 157 Ay, ay, cover yourselves with honey, and you shall see the flies will eat you. **1791-1823** I. DISRAELI *Curios. Lit.* (Chandos) III. 51 The Italian proverbs have taken a tinge from their deep and politic genius . . . 'Make yourself all honey, and the flies will devour you.' **1853** TRENCH iii. 69 We say: *Daub yourself with honey, and you'll be covered with flies.*

Honey cloys the maw, Much.

[BIBLE *Proverbs* xxv. 27.] **1377** LANGLAND *P. Pl.* B. 54–6 Salomon . . . seith, *sicut qui mel comedit multum, non est ei bonum:* . . . To Englisch-men this is to mene. . . . The man that moche hony eteth. . . . his mawe it engleymeth.[1] *c.* **1386** CHAUCER *Mel.* B² 2606 And Salomon seith, 'If thou hast founden hony, ete of it that suffyseth; for if thou ete of

it out of measure, thou shalt spewe'. **1579** LYLY *Euphues* (Arb.) 157 The Bee though she delight to suck the faire flower, yet is she at last cloyed with Honny. **1595-6** SHAKS. *Mids. N.* II. ii. 137 A surfeit of the sweetest things The deepest loathing to the stomach brings. [1 cloys.]

Honey in his pot, He that hath no | let him have it in his mouth.

1616 DRAXE 161 He that hath no honie in his pot, hath none in his mouth. **1640** HERBERT 334.

Honey in the mouth saves the purse.

1855 BOHN 408. *Ital.*

Honey is not for the ass's mouth.

1620 SHELTON *Quix.* IV. xxv (1908) II. 177 'Honey is not made for the ass's mouth', quoth Sancho; 'wife, thou shalt know it in good time'. **1732** FULLER no. 2537.

Honey is sweet, Every bee's.

1640 HERBERT 346.

Honey is sweet, but the bee stings.

1576 G. WAPULL *Tide Tarrieth No Man* A 3 In the Bee . . . we see, Sweete honey and sting. **1640** HERBERT (Gros.) no. 208 **1670** RAY 13.

Honey that is licked from the thorn, Dear bought is the.

c. **1175** *Old Eng. Homilies* (Morris) I. 185 Nis nan blisse . . . thet ne beo To bitter aboht; thet et huni ther-in, beoth licked of thornes. *c.* **1240** *Ureisun* Huni þer-in beoþ liked of þornes. *c.* **1300** *Provs. of Hending* 31 Dere is boht the hony that is licked of the thorne. *c.* **1350** *Douce MS. 52* no. 79 Hit is harde to lykke hony fro the thorne. *Ibid.* no. 80 Dere is þe hony bouȝt þat on thornes is souȝt. *c.* **1390** GOWER *Conf. Amantis* vi. 324 And thus as I have said a-forn, I lické hony on the thorn. **1678** RAY 379 **1732** FULLER no. 2215 He that licks honey from a nettle pays too dear for it. **1902** *Spectator* 11 Jan. Cases of plant poisoning . . . are . . . caused by mistaking fungi for mushrooms, . . . of which Gerard quaintly says: 'Beware of licking honey among the thorns.'

Honey tongue, a heart of gall, A.

c. **1300** *Cursor M.* l. 25729 Hony pai bede and gif us gall. **1580** LYLY *Euph. & his Eng.* (Arb.) 384 A dissembler hath evermore honey in his mouth, and gall in his mind. *a.* **1599** RALEIGH *Nymph's Reply* A honey tongue, a heart of gall, Is fancy's spring, but sorrow's fall. **1614** CAMDEN 302.

Honey, *see also* Bee sucks honey (Where) spider sucks poison; Bees are old (When) yield no h.; Bees are (Where), there is h.; Bestows his gifts as broom h.; Lick h. through cleft stick; Lick h. with little finger; Milk and h.; Saying H. (Not with) sweetness comes; Shareth h. with bear (He who); Steals h. should beware of sting; Sweet as h.; Wine (Of) the middle, of h. the bottom.

Honey-bird, *see* 'Sweet-heart' and 'H.' keeps no house.

Honey-moon, It will not always be.

1639 CLARKE 123.

Honey-moon, *see also* Couple are newly married (When) first month is h.

Honey-pot(s), *see* Bear to a h. (Like a); Hogs to the h. p.

Honi soit qui mal y pense, see Ill be to him, &c.

Honour a physician before thou hast need of him.

1678 RAY *Adag. Hebr.* 411 Honour a Physitian before thou hast need of him. That is, we must honour God in our health and prosperity that he may be propitious to us in our adversity.

Honour among thieves, There is.

1703 MOTTEUX *Quixote* II. lx (A) The old proverb still holds good, Thieves are never rogues among themselves. **1828** LYTTON *Pelham* lxix I have often heard . . . that there is *honour* among thieves. **1891** A. LANG *Ess. in Little* 140 [Capt. Morgan[1]] was indeed a thief, and bilked his crews . . . Who would linger long when there is not even honour among thieves? [[1] the buccaneer, c. 1635–88.]

Honour and ease are seldom bedfellows.

1599 MINSHEU (1623) 2 T 2[v] **1639** CLARKE 137.

Honour and profit lie not in one sack.

1640 HERBERT 327.

Honour buys no beef in the market.

1668 SHADWELL *Sullen Lov.* v. iii I am not ambitious of that. As the excellent proverb says, 'Honour will buy no beef'.

Honour ceaseth, Where | there knowledge decreaseth. (*See also* Honours nourish arts.)

1616 WITHALS 558. **1639** CLARKE 137. **1670** RAY 104.

Honour (Gentility) is but ancient riches.

c. **1386** CHAUCER *W. of Bath's T.* D 117 Crist wol, we clayme of him our gentillesse, Nat of our eldres for his old richesse. *a.* **1598** LD. BURGHLEY in PECK *Desid. Curiosa* (1779) 48 (A) For gentility is nothing else but antient riches. **1618** N. BRETON *Courtier & Countryman* (Roxb. rep.) 190 An-other of an excellent worlds wit, . . . would say, that honour was but ancient riches. **1651** HERBERT 365 Gentility is nothing but ancient riches.

Honour shows the man.

[BIAS (Ar. *Eth.* 5. 3) ἀρχὴ ἄνδρα δείκνυσι] 1597

BACON *Essays*, No. 11 A place sheweth the man. **1612–15** BP. HALL *Contempl.* XIII. v (1825) I. 389 Honour shows the man; and if there be any blemishes of imperfection, they will be seen in the man that is unexpectedly lifted above his fellows.

Honour, Where there is no | there is no grief.

1616 DRAXE 92. **1640** HERBERT 325.

Honour under coverlet, We cannot come to.

1640 HERBERT 342.

Honour without maintenance is like a blue[1] coat without a badge.

1660 TATHAM *The Rump* III. i (1879) 239 I have heard some say, that honour without maintenance is like a blew coat without a badge. [[1] blue was the common colour for a servant's livery.]

Honour without profit is a ring on the finger.

1611 COTGRAVE s.v. 'Seigneurie' (A) Honour without profit is like a six-penny rent to one that hath nothing else to live upon. **1640** HERBERT 327.

Honours change manners.

[L. *Honores mutant mores.*] **1548** HALL *Chron.* (1809) 387 But when he[1] was once crouned king . . . he cast a way his old cōdicions as y[e] adder doeth her skynne, verefieng y[e] old prouerbe, honoures chaunge maners. **1629** T. ADAMS *Serm.* (1861–2) II. 418 Honours change manners; and we will not know those in the court who often fed us in the country. **1670** RAY 104 . . . As poverty depresseth and debaseth a man's mind. So great place and estate advance and enlarge it; but many times corrupt and puff it up. **1757** JOHNSON 21 June in *Boswell* (1848) xii. 108 You might write to me now and then, . . . But *honores mutant mores.* Professors forget their friends. [[1] Richard III.]

Honours nourish arts. (*See also* Honour ceaseth, &c.)

[CICERO *Tusc.* 1. 2. 4. *Honos alit artes.*] **1539** TAVERNER (1545) D 2 *Honos alit artes.* Honowre mayntayneth Kunnyng. *c.* **1600** F. THYNNE *Pride and Lowliness* (Sh. S.) 22 (A) Sayeth not the proverbe, honors norishe artes?

Honour(s), *see also* Cost (The more), more h.; Desires h. (He that) is not worthy; Gives h. to his enemy (He that); Great h. great burdens; Ill deed cannot bring h.; Jest not with . . . h.; No profit to h.; Post of h. is post of danger. *See also* Lip-honour.

Hoo, Kent.

1587 HARRISON *Descr. of Britain* (in HOLINSHED, i. 30) There goeth an old proverbe in rime . . . He that rideth into the hundred of How, Beside pilfering sea-men shall find durt

ynow. **1735** PEGGE *Kent. Prov.* in E.D.S. no.
12, p. 73 (A) He that rideth into the Hundred
of Hoo, Besides pilfering seamen, shall find
dirt enow.

Hood for this fool, A.

1509 A. BARCLAY *Ship of Fools* (1874) i. 38 To
kepe you from the rayne, ye shall haue a foles
hode. *c.* **1566** COLLMAN *Ball. and Broadsides*
(Roxb. Cl.) 93 (A) A hood, a hood, for such a
foole.

Hood, *see also* Hair grows through his h;
Lost the large coat for the h.; Two faces in
one h.

Hook, On one's own.

1845 *N. Y. Herald* Oct. (Bartlett) The time is
fast approaching when we shall have our
American Pope . . . and American Catholic
everything, on our own hook. **1849** THACKE-
RAY *Pendennis* lxix Do we come out as
Liberal Conservative, or as Government men,
or on our own hook? **1861** HUGHES *Tom B. at
Oxford* ii I thought today I would go on my
own hook, and see if I couldn't make a better
hand of it.

Hook or by crook, By.

[= by fair means or foul.] *c.* **1380** WYCLIF
Eng. Wks. (E.E.T.S.) 250 (A) Comynly thei
schulle bie hem with pore mennes goodis with
hook or with crook. *c.* **1390** GOWER *Conf.
Amantis* v 251 So what with hoke and what
with croke They make her maister ofte winne.
1550 HEYWOOD I. xi. 36 By hooke or crooke
nought could I wyn there. **1649** MILTON
Eikonoklastes Prose Wks. (1904) I. 397
Master of almost two millions yearly, what by
hook or crook, was still in want.

Hook's well lost to catch a salmon, A.

1616 DRAXE 5. **1639** CLARKE 41. **1670** RAY
104.

Hook(s), *see also* Great put the little on the
h.; Off the h.

Hoop, *see* Knock on the h. another on
barrel.

Hop against the hill, To.

[= to strive against an unsurmountable
obstacle. HAZL.] **1575** GASCOIGNE *Posies,
Hearbes* (1907) 335 So strive I now to shewe,
my feeble forward will, Although I know my
labour lost, to hop against the Hill.

Hop the twig, To.

[= to go off, die.] **1785** GROSE *Dict. Vulg. T.*
Hop the twig, to run away (*cant*) **1797** MARY
ROBINSON *Walsingham* IV. 280 [He] kept his
bed three days, and hopped the twig on the
fourth. **1828** *Craven Dial., Hop,* to die. *Ibid.,
Hop*, 'to hop the twig', to run away in debt.
1870 MISS BRIDGMAN *R. Lynne* II. iv. 289 If
old Campbell hops the twig.

Hop whore, pipe thief.

1546 HEYWOOD II. vii. 71 Now go to thy
derlyngis, and declare thy gréefe. Where all
thy pleasure is, hop hoore, pipe théefe.

Hope (well) and have (well).

1540 PALSGRAVE *Acolastus* Q 1 Hope welle
and haue well. *c.* **1566** *The Bugbears* IV. v. 28.
1576 W. HUNIS in *Paradise Dayntie Deuises*
(1810) 57 Hope well and haue well (Title).
1600 A. FRAUNCE in *Eng. Parnassus* (1913)
107 Hope and haue, in time a man may
gaine any woman. **1614** CAMDEN 307 Hope
well, and haue well. **1721** KELLY 290 *Spee[1]
well and hae well* . . . That is, hope and expect
good things, and it will fall out accordingly.
[[1] bode.]

Hope better, I | quoth Benson, when his wife bade him, Come in, cuckold.

1678 RAY 86. **1732** FULLER no. 2608.

Hope deceiveth, Too much.

1573 SANDFORD (1576) 222. **1578** FLORIO *First
Fruites* f. 33. **1629** *Book of Meery Riddles* Prov.
126.

Hope deferred maketh the heart sick.

1382 WYCLIF *Prov.* xiii. 12 Hope that is
deferrid tormenteth the soule. **1616** DRAXE
42 Long hope is the fainting of the soule.
1836 MARRYAT *Midsh. Easy* xxix How true it
is that hope deferred maketh the heart sick!
. . . the buoyant calculations of youth had
been . . . crushed, and now, . . . he dared not
hope.

Hope for the best.

1590 SPENSER *F.Q.* IV. vi. 37 (A) Its best to
hope the best, though of the worst affrayd.
1726 *Adv. Capt. R. Boyle* 16 Come, hope for
the best, said I.

Hope is a good breakfast but a bad supper.

1625 BACON *Apoph.* in *Mor. & Hist. Wks.*
(1894) 170 Saith the fisherman, 'We had
hope then to make a better gain of it'. Saith
Mr. Bacon, . . . 'Hope is a good breakfast, but
it is a bad supper'.

Hope is a lover's staff.

1855 BOHN 408.

Hope is but the dream of those that wake.

[ARISTOTLE in DIOG. LAERT. 5. 18 ἐρωτηθεὶς τί
ἐστὶν ἐλπίς; Ἐγρηγορότος, εἶπεν, ἐνύπνιον.]
1718 PRIOR *Solomon* iii. 102.

Hope is the poor man's bread.

1640 HERBERT 340. **1650** JER. TAYLOR *Holy
Liv.* II. vi (1850) 98 Please thyself with hopes
of the future. La speranza è il pan de' poveri.

Hope of long life beguileth many a good wife.

c. **1300** *Provs. of Hending* 39 Hope of long lyf
Gyleth mony god wyfe.

Hope often deludes the foolish man.

c. **1300** *Havelock* 307 (E.E.T.S.) 10 Hope
maketh fol man ofte blenkes'.

Hope, If it were not for | the heart would break.

c. **1200** *Ancrene Riwle* 80 Ase me seið, ʒif hope nere, heorte to breke. *c.* **1350** *Douce MS. 52* no. 127 Hope ne were, hert brostun were. *c.* **1440** *Gesta Rom.* (E.E.T.S.) 228 Yf hope were not, hert shulde breke. *c.* **1470** *Harl. MS. 3362* f. 4*a* Ʒyf hope nere hert wolde toberste. **1614** CAMDEN 314 Without hope the heart would break. **1636** S. WARD *Serm.* (1862) 60 Were it not for hope in small pressures, we say heart would burst. **1660** TATHAM *The Rump* II. i (1879) 222 If it were not for hope, the heart would break, they say. **1894** LD. AVEBURY *Use of Life* XV There is an old proverb that if it were not for Hope the heart would break. Everything may be retrieved except despair.

Hopers go to hell.

1721 KELLY 164 ... Spoken when they, whom we are reproving for their carelessness, and negligence, say they hope to do well enough.

Hopes not for good, He that | fears not evil.

1640 HERBERT 343. **1732** FULLER no. 2166 He that hopes no good fears no ill.

Hope(s) (*noun*), *see also* Lives by h. will die by hunger; Lives in h. (He that) danceth; Lives on h. hath slender diet; Quit certainty for h. (Never).

Hope(s) (*verb*), *see also* Do the likeliest, h. the best.

Hops make or break.

1869 HAZLITT 208. **1902–4** LEAN I. 419 ... The yield is most uncertain and the cultivation most expensive; the value of the land may be won in a single year or its whole expenditure lost.

Hops, *see also* Fast as h.; Ladybirds (Plenty of), plenty of h.; St. James's Day be come ... you may have h.; Turkeys, carps, h. ... came into England.

Horn mad (wood).

1546 HEYWOOD II. x. 82 She was (as they say) horne wood. **1592–3** SHAKS. *Com. Err.* II. i. 57 Why, mistress, sure my master is hornmad.... I mean not cuckold-mad; but, sure, he is stark mad. **1598–9** *Much Ado* I. i. 280 If this should never happen, thou wouldst be horn-mad. **1600–1** *Merry W.* I. iv. 51 If he had found the young man, he would have been horn-mad. *Ibid.* III. v. 155 If I have horns to make me mad, let the proverb go with me; I'll be horn-mad.

Horn of a pig's tail, You cannot make a.

1670 RAY 104.

Horn spoon holds no poison, A.

1721 KELLY 43 ... They who cannot procure better spoons are not worth poisoning.

Horn(s), *see also* April blows his h.; Blows best (He that) bears away h.; Camel going to seek h. lost ears; Corn and h. go together; Curst cow short h.; Draw in one's h.; Friday's hair and Saturday's h.; Gabriel blows his h. (When); Gate of h.; God giveth cow; Hay in one's h. (Carry); Make a spoon or spoil h.; New tout in old h.; Nicks in her h. (She has many); Old oxen have stiff h.; Ox is taken by the h.; Play with a bull till get h. in eye; Right as a ram's h.; Wear a h. and blow it not. *See also* Buck's horn, Cow's horn.

Horne (Old *or* Parson), *see* Chance it, as P.H. did his neck.

Horner, Popham, Wyndham, and Thynne, when the abbot went out, then they went in.

1669–96 AUBREY *Lives* (Clark) i. 279 (A) Hopton, Horner, Smyth, and Thynne, when abbots went out, then they came in. **1902–4** LEAN I. 187 Horner, Popham, Wyndham, and Thynne, when the Abbot went out, then they went in.—Higson [*MSS. Coll.*] 173.—The four families to whom Glastonbury Abbey estate was granted at the Dissolution. **1927** *Times* 1 Apr. 16/3 John Horner, traditionally said to have been steward to the Abbot of Glastonbury.... An old local rhyme records that—'Wyndham, Horner, Popham, and Thynne, When the Abbot went out, they came in'.

Horner, *see also* Portman.

Horns and grey hairs do not come by years.

1599 MINSHEU (1623) 2 T 6. **1678** RAY 156.

Horns go with the hide, Let the.

1855 BOHN 441. **1862** HISLOP 209 Let the horns gang wi' the hide. The horns bearing but insignificant value in comparison with the hide, they should be thrown into the purchase of the latter free of charge.

Horns hang in your light, Your.

1583 MELBANCKE *Philot.* 36 A gentlewoman ... gotten by stealth by the wicked aspect of a beggerly micher, whom her mothers husband ... could not see for hornes growing ouer his eyes. **1678** RAY 346.

Horns in his bosom, He that hath | let him not put them on his head.

1624 BURTON *Anat. Mel.* III. iii. IV. i. 3 S 1 *Sapientes portant cornua in pectore, stulti in fronte,* saith *Nevisanus,* wise men beare their hornes in their hearts, fooles on their foreheads. **1640** HERBERT 344. **1670** RAY 104 ... Let a man hide his shame, not publish it. **1732** FULLER no. 5704 (with 'forehead').

Horns in his pocket than wind them, He had better put his.

1678 RAY 74. **1732** FULLER no. 1852.

Horns of a dilemma, To be on the.

[Each of the alternatives of a dilemma—in

scholastic Lat. *argumentum cornutum*—on which one is figured as liable to be caught or impaled.] 1647 COWLEY *Mistr., Agst. Hope* i And both the Horns of Fates Dilemma wound. 1887 FOWLER *Deduct. Logic* v. 121 In disputation, the adversary who is refuted by a dilemma is said to be 'fixed on the horns of a dilemma'.

Horns, *see also* Horn(s).

Horologe, *see* Play the devil in the h.

Horse, a wife, and a sword may be shewed, but not lent, A.

1574 F. HELLOWES *Guevara's Epistles* 509 It is an old prouerb that the wife and the sword may bee shewed, but not lent. 1576 DESAINLIENS D 5ᵛ. 1591 W. STEPNEY *Span. Schoolmaster* M 6ᵛ Four things cannot be lent, a good horse, a wise woman . . . a faithful seruant . . . a good sword. 1623 CAMDEN 297.

Horse and man (or foot).

[= completely.] 1599 CHAPMAN *An Humorous Days Mirth* vi. 51 Then is he ouerthrown both horse and foot. 1603 DEKKER *Wonderful Year* (*Plague Pamphlets* ed. Wilson 35) It . . . ouer-turnd them . . . horse and foote. 1607 MIDDLETON *The Phœnix* Wks. (Bullen) I. 180 I hope I shall overthrow him horse and foot. 1639 CLARKE 86. 1666 TORRIANO 134.

Horse break his halter (bridle), It would have made a.

1546 HEYWOOD II. i. 44 To sée his swéete lookes, and here hir swéete wurdes. And to thinke wherfore they bothe put both in vre, It wolde haue made a hors breake his halter sure. 1670 RAY 165 'Twould make a horse break his bridle, or a dog his halter.

Horse cast a shoe, Your.

1678 RAY 349.

Horse corn, *see* Hens are free of h. c.

Horse drink when he will, not what he will, Let a.

1678 RAY 157.

Horse in a mill, Like a.

1611 MIDDLETON *Roaring G.* I. i *Sebas.* My thoughts must run As a horse runs that's blind round in a mill. 1679 SHADWELL *True Widow* I had rather suffer, by venturing to bring new things upon the stage, than go on like a mill-horse in the same round. [Note by Shadwell, in first ed., at the back of the 'Dramatis Personæ'.]

Horse is troubled with corns, That.

1678 RAY 74 . . . *i.e.* foundered.

Horse lies down, Where the | there some hair will be found.

a. 1530 R. Hill's *Commonpl. Bk.* (E.E.T.S.) 129 Whan the hors waloweth, som heris be loste. 1639 CLARKE 216 Where the horse rubbs some haire is left behind. 1662 FULLER

5017

(*Cornw.*) I. 299 Foreigners . . . sometimes are driven hither against their will, but never without the profit of the inhabitants, according to the common proverb, 'where the horse lieth down, there some hairs will be found'.

Horse loaves, *see* High as two h. l.

Horse made and a man to make, A. (*Cf.* the following proverb.)

1611 COTGRAVE s.v. 'Cheval' A made horse, and a man unarm'd are fittest for use. 1640 HERBERT 318.

Horse made, and a wife to make, Choose a.

1640 HERBERT 357.

Horse, Who hath no | may ride on a staff.

1444 LYDGATE in *Pol. Poems* (1859) II. 219 Whoo hath noon hors on a staff may ride.

Horse must die in some man's hand, The old.

1641 FERGUSSON 60 In some mens aught[1] mon the auld horse die. 1721 KELLY 312. [1 ownership.]

Horse must smell to a pixy, The good.

1869 HAZLITT 370 The good horse must smell to a pixy. *S. Devon. i.e.* must know by smelling where the pixy (ignis fatuus), and therefore, the bog, is.—SHELLY.

Horse, The best | needs breaking, and the aptest child needs teaching.

1639 CLARKE 100.

Horse next the mill carries all the grist, The.

1623 CAMDEN 279. 1670 RAY 121. 1732 FULLER no. 4601.

Horse of another (the same) colour, A.

1599–1600 SHAKS. *Twel. N.* II. iii. 181 My purpose is indeed a horse of that colour. 1599–1600 *A.Y.L.* III. ii. 435 Boys and women are, for the most part cattle of this colour. 1867 TROLLOPE *Last Chron. Barset* I. xxiv. 216 What did you think of his wife? That's a horse of another colour altogether.

Horse of thine own, Have a | and thou may'st borrow another.

1659 HOWELL *Brit. Prov.* 34 Have a horse of thy own, thou maist borrow another.

Horse, One | stays for another.

1738 SWIFT (Dial. ii) 344 *Never.* You see, sir John, we stayed for you as one horse does for another.

Horse stumbles that has four legs, A.

1640 HERBERT 351. 1678 RAY (Scottish) 360

A horse may stumble on four feet. 1721 KELLY 26. *A horse with four feet may snapper,[1] by a time.* An excuse for those who inadvertently misplace their words. [[1] stumble.]

Horse that draws after him his halter, The | is not altogether escaped.

1639 CLARKE 250. **1651** HERBERT 369. **1732** FULLER no. 4602. **1853** TRENCH vi. 147 *The horse which draws its halter is not quite escaped*; . . . so long as any remnant of a sinful habit is retained by us, so long as we draw this halter, we make but an idle boast of our liberty.

Horse that was foaled of an acorn, A.

1678 RAY 253 You'll ride on a horse that was foal'd of an acorn. That is the gallows. **1708** MOTTEUX *Rabelais* v. xxviii. (1737) 128 May I ride on a horse that was foal'd of an acorn. **1828** LYTTON *Pelham* iii. xviii. 296 As pretty a Tyburn blossom as ever was brought up to ride a horse foaled by an acorn.

Horse that will not carry a saddle must have no oats, A.

1642 TORRIANO 9. **1732** FULLER no. 218.

Horse will not void oats, A.

1721 KELLY 84 It is hard to make a Horse shite Oats that never eat any [given as an English proverb]. **1745** FRANKLIN *Wks.* (Bigelow) II. 35–6 (A) If, as the proverb says, it is unreasonable to expect a horse should void oats, which never eat any.

Horse's head is swollen so big that he cannot come out of the stable, His.

[= He can't pay the ostler.] **1659** HOWELL *Eng. Prov.* 6/1.

Horses, As good | draw in carts, as coaches.

1621 BURTON *Anat. Mel.* ii. iii. vii. (1651) 350.

Horse(s), *see also* Ass goes a-travelling, he'll not come home h.; Beat a h. till he be sad; Beat the h. (He that cannot) beats the saddle; Best thing for inside of man is outside of h.; Blind h. (Ever the worse looks); Blind h. is hardiest; Boisterous h. must have rough bridle; Boot and the better h. (He has gotten); Break a h.'s back (You may); Brewer's h. hath let (One whom); Bridle and spur makes good h.; Butcher's h., he carries calf; Chestnut h.; Common h. is worst shod; Cough will stick by a h.; Dead h.; Eaten a h. and tail hangs out; Every one (h). thinks his sack heaviest; Fault of h. put on saddle; Flea-bitten h. never tires; Flog a dead h.; Foal amble if h. trot (How can); Free of h. that never had one; Galled h. not endure comb; Gentle h. that never cast rider; Gift h. in the mouth (Look not); Give a Yorkshireman halter, he'll find h.; Good h. cannot be bad colour; Good h. good spur; Good h. make short miles; Good h. should be seldom spurred; Good h. that never stumbles; Goodness of a h. goes in at mouth; Grass grows (While) the h. starves; Greedy eating h. (To) short halter; Groaning h. . . . never fail master; High h.; Hired h. tired never; Hires the h. (He that) must ride before; Hounds and h. devour masters; Hungry h. makes clean manger; Ill h. that can neither whinny nor wag tail; Kindly aver never good h.; Know the h. by his harness (You may); Latin, a h., and money (With) thou wilt pass; Lead a h. to water; Lend thy h. for long journey, return with skin; Lets his h. drink at every lake (He that); Like to like, scabbed h. to old dike; Live h. and you'll get grass; Loader's h. that lives among thieves (Like a); Luck in h. . . . kiss parson's wife; Man is not a h. because born in stable; Mettle is dangerous in a blind horse; Mule (h.) doth scrub another (One); Nod is as good . . . to blind h.; Old wood is best . . . old h. to ride; One thing thinketh the h.; Ox before, of a h. behind (Take hold of); Proud h. that will not bear provender; Ragged colt . . . good h.; Ride a free h. to death; Royston h.; Rub a galled h., he will wince; Running h. open grave; Saddle on right h.; Scabbed horse cannot abide comb; Scald h. for scabbed squire; Scholar as my h. Ball (As good); Set their h. together (They cannot); Short h. soon curried (*also under* Bonny bride); Shortly as a h. will lick; Shoulder of mutton for a sick h.; Spur a hamshackled h. (Idle to); Spur and whip for dull h.; Spurring a free h. (Ill); Steal a h. (One man may); Steal the h. and carry home bridle; Strong as a h.; Swap h. when crossing; Taken my h. and left me the tether; Trust not h.'s heel; Turk's h. doth tread (Where); Walking with a h. in hand (Good); Water his h. at Highgate (Make him); White h.; White h. and a fair wife (He that hath); Willing h. (All lay load on); Win the h. or lose the saddle; Work like a h.; Wrong h.; Young trooper, old h.

Horse, *see also* Fore-horse, Jade, Mare, Nag.

Horse(d) (*verb*), *see* Manned with boys and h. with colts.

Horseback, When one is on | he knows all things.

1640 HERBERT 362.

Horseback, *see also* Agues (Diseases) come on h.

Horseflesh, *see* Scarce of h. where two ride on dog; Skill in h. to buy a goose.

Horse-leech, *see* Daughter of h.

Horseman, *see* Behind the h. sits care.

Horseshoe that clatters wants a nail, The.

1855 BOHN 508. *Span.*

Horseshoe, *see also* Fool finds a h. (When) he thinks like to do; Wear like a h. (She will).

Horse-turd, *see* Apples swim (See how we).

Hose (*proper name*), *see* Whores in H. than . . . in Long Clawson (More).

Hose, *see* Man is a man though h. on his head; Welshman's h.

Hosed and shod, He came in.

1678 RAY 74 . . . He was born to a good estate. He came into the world as a bee into the hive: or into an house, or into a trade, or employment.

Hospital, *see* Suit at law and urinal bring to h.

Hospitality, It is a sin against | to open your doors and shut up your countenance.

1605 BACON *Adv. Learn.* II. xxiii. 3 (1900) 218 Saith Cicero, . . . ; *Nil interest habere ostium apertum, vultum clausum*; it is nothing won to admit men with an open door, and to receive them with a shut and reserved countenance. **1732** FULLER no. 2883. **1746** FRANKLIN *Dec.* Half Hospitality opens his Door and shuts up his Countenance.

Host's invitation is expensive, An.

1642 TORRIANO 66 An hosts invitation is not without expence. **1732** FULLER no. 612.

Host, *see also* Reckons without his h.

Hostages, *see* Wife and children . . . h. to fortune.

Hostess, *see* Fairer the h. fouler the reckoning.

Hot as coals, As.

1533 UDALL *Flowers for Latin Speaking* (1560) E 4. **1540** PALSGRAVE *Acolastus* O 2ᵛ He loueth ye as hot as coles. **1542** UDALL tr. *Erasm. Apoph.* (1877) 38. **1563** FOXE *Actes* (1846) V. 19 (A) The bishop and all his doctors were as hot as coals.

Hot love, hasty vengeance.

1721 KELLY 163 . . . The love that's too violent will not last long.

Hot love is soon cold.

1537 R. WHITFORD *Werke for Housholders* D7 (A) Hote loue is sone colde. **1546** HEYWOOD I. ii. 5 Than perceiue they well, hotte loue soone colde. **1579** LYLY *Euphues* (Arb.) 95 I hope that such hot loue cannot be so soone colde. **1670** RAY 46. **1732** FULLER no. 2549.

Hot May makes a fat churchyard, A.

1659 HOWELL *Eng. Prov.* 11/2. **1670** RAY 42.

Hot sup, hot swallow.

c. **1400** *MS. Latin no. 394*, J. Rylands Libr. (ed. Pantin) in *Bull. J. R. Libr.* XIV 26 Drynke hoot and swolow hoot. **1639** CLARKE 239.

Hot water, *see* Cost h. w. (It will); Seek h. w. under ice.

Hot, *see also* Bear it away if not too h. or too heavy; Too h. to hold.

Hounds and horses devour their masters.

1639 CLARKE 325.

Hound(s), *see also* Dog (H.) gnaws bone (While), companion would he none; Hende as a h. in a kitchen; Many h. may soon worry one hare; Masterless h. (Like a); Pound of butter among kennel of h.; Run with hare and hunt with h.; We h. slew the hare.

Hour in a day between a good housewife and a bad, There is but an.

1678 RAY 74 . . . With a little more pains, she that slatters might do things neatly.

Hour in the morning is worth two in the evening, An.

1827 HONE *Ev. Day Book* ii. 477 (A) [Cited as 'an old and a true saying']. **1855** BOHN 311.

Hour to-day, One | is worth two to-morrow.

1732 FULLER no. 3761.

Hour wherein a man might be happy all his life could he find it, There is an.

1651 HERBERT 370..

Hour's cold, One | will spoil seven years' warming.

1721 KELLY 276.

Hour's sleep before midnight, One | is worth three (two) after.

1640 HERBERT 357. **1670** RAY 37. **1829** COBBETT *Adv. to Y. Men* i (1906) 35 It is said by the country-people that one hour's sleep before midnight is worth more than two are worth after midnight; and this I believe to be a fact.

Hour, *see also* Broke his h. that kept day (He never); Chanceth in an h.; Darkest h. is that before dawn; Evil h.; Half an h. soon lost at dinner; Half an h.'s hanging hinders . . . riding; Man has his h.

House, a wife, and a fire to put her in, A.

1721 KELLY 264 *Never look for a wife, till you have a house, and a fire to put her in.* The jest is in *a fire to put her in*, a house to put her in, and a fire to set her by. **1738** SWIFT (Dial. i) 342 *Lady S.* But, colonel, when do you design to get a house, and a wife, and a fire to put her in?

House and home, *see* Eat out of h. and h.

House and land are gone and spent, When | then learning is most excellent.

1753 s. FOOTE *Taste* (ed. 2) I. i. 12 *Lady*. It has always been my Maxum . . . to give my Children Learning enough; for, as the old saying is, *When House and Land are gone and spent, Then Learning is most excellent*. **1896** s. BARING-GOULD *Broom-Squire* xxvi I have . . . got Simon to write for me, on the fly-leaf. . . . When land is gone, and money is spent, Then learning is most excellent.'

House built by the wayside is either too high or too low, A.

1642 TORRIANO 29. **1658** *Comes Facundus* 181. **1670** RAY 106. **1732** FULLER no. 220.

House goes mad when women gad.

1822 SCOTT *Nigel* iv Let your husband come to me, good dame, . . . The proverb says, ' House goes mad when women gad '.

House is a fine house when good folks are within, The.

1640 HERBERT 361.

House is burned down, When the | you bring water.

1575 G. GASCOIGNE *Glass of Government* 4th Chorus All too late the water comes, when house is burned quite. **1732** FULLER no. 5592.

House is his castle, A man's (Englishman's).

1581 H. ÉTIENNE, *Stage of Popish Toys*, tr. G.N. 88 [The English papists owe it to the Queen that] youre house is youre Castell. *cf.* **1640** HERBERT 337 My house, my house, though thou art small, thou art to me the escurial. **1642** FULLER *Fast Serm., Innoc. Day Sermons* (1891) I. 260 It was wont to be said *A man's house is his castle* ; but if this castle of late hath proved unable to secure any, let them make their conscience their castle. **1670** RAY 106 A man's house is his castle. This is a kind of law proverb, *Jura publica favent privato domus*. **1779** JOHNSON in *Boswell* (1848) lxviii. 626 In London, . . . a man's own house is truly his *castle*, in which he can be in perfect safety from intrusion. **1836–7** DICKENS *Pickwick* xxiv Some people maintain that an Englishman's house is his castle. That's gammon. **1893** R. HEATH *Eng. Peasant* 33 The popular notion of every Englishman's house being his castle was conspicuously demonstrated to be a fallacy, by 22 and 23 Car., 2.15.

House of a fiddler, In the | all fiddle.

a. **1633** G. HERBERT *Priest to the Temple* Wks. (Hutchinson) 240. **1640** HERBERT 327. **1732** FULLER no. 2809 In a fidlers house all are dancers.

House out of the windows, To throw (fling) the.

[= to put everything into confusion.] **1562** BULLEIN *Bulwarke of Defence* f. xxviii Haue

at all, . . . caste the house out at the window. **1604** DEKKER *Honest Whore* v. ii To throw the house out at window will be the better and no man will suspect that we lurk here to steal mutton. **1611** BEAUM. & FL. *Kt. Burn. P.* III. v We are at home now; where, I warrant you, you shall find the house flung out of the windows. **1844** W. H. MAXWELL *Sport & Adv. Scott.* vi (1855) 77 Would not . . . Stubbs throw the house out of the windows?

House shows the owner, The.

1611 COTGRAVE s.v. 'Maison' The house discovers the owner. **1640** HERBERT 317.

House stands on my lady's ground, His.

1678 RAY 75.

Houses than parish churches, There are more.

1579 GOSSON *Sch. Abuse* (Arb.) 37 There are more houses then Parishe Churches.

House(s), *see also* After the h. is finished leave it ; Best gown that goes up and down h. ; Better an empty h. ; Better one h. filled ; Better one h. troubled ; Bring an old h. on one's head ; Burn one h. to warm another ; Burn one's h. to rid of mice ; Buys a h. ready wrought (He that) ; Choose not a h. near an inn ; Commend not your . . . h. ; Good h. (In a) all quickly ready ; Head is down (When my), h. is thatched ; Head (H.) of glass ; Hole in the h. (There is a) ; Lawyers' h. built on fools ; Let your h. to your enemy (First year) ; Little h. has wide mouth ; Little h. well filled ; Love his h. yet not ride on ridge ; Master absent and h. dead ; Neighbour's h. on fire ; Reck not whose h. burneth so they may warm ; See the city for the h. (Cannot) ; Seest thine h. in flames (When), warm thyself by it ; Set my h. on fire to roast eggs ; Small h. ·has wide throat ; Thatches his h. with turds (He that) ; Woe to the h. where there is no chiding ; Woman the more . . . careless about her h. *See also* Glass house.

House-going parson makes a church-going people, A.

1913 *Brit. Wkly.* 2 Jan. 445 If anyone was missed at church, the next morning he went to the truant's house. . . . He firmly believed that a house-going parson makes a church-going people.

Household, *see* Woeful is the h. that wants a woman.

Householders, *see* Grooms and h. are all alike great (Where).

Housekeeper(s), *see* Everything is of use to h. ; Fat h. make lean executors ; Noble h. need no doors.

Housekeeping, *see* Marriage is honourable, but h. a shrew,

House-top, On the | in anger soon is a fool.

1546 HEYWOOD II. v. 54 He is at three woordis vp in the house roufe. **1611** DAVIES Prov. 290.

Housewife, -wives, see Bare walls . . . giddy h.; Foot on cradle . . . sign of good h.; Gentle h. mars household; Good h. that will not wind up her bottom (Not a); Hour in a day between good h. and bad; Punch coal, cut candle . . . neither good h.; Rouk-town seldom good h.; Sweet in the bed . . . was never good h.

How doth your Whither go you?

1678 RAY 346 . . . (*Your wife.*)

Howbackit, see Grow h. bearing your friends (You will never).

Howl with the wolves, One must.

1578 TIMME *Calvin on Gen.* vi. 181 This diuelishe prouerbe . . . we must howle among the Wolues. **1649** BP. HALL *Cases Consc.* (1650) 187 What do you howling amongst Wolves, if you be not one? **1853** TRENCH V. 107 *One must howl with the wolves*; . . . when a general cry is raised against any, it is safest to join it, lest we be supposed to sympathize with its object. . . . In the whole circle of proverbs there is scarcely a baser or more cowardly than this. **1897** A. C. DOYLE *Uncle Bernac* i Napoleon's power is far too great to be shaken. This being so, I have tried to serve him, for it is well to howl when you are among wolves.

Hug one as the devil hugs a witch, To.

1678 RAY 286. **1738** SWIFT (Dial. i) 342 *Lady A.* Why she and you were as great[1] as two inkle-weavers. I've seen her hug you as the devil hugged the witch. [1 intimate.]

Hugger-mugger,[1] In.

a. **1529** SKELTON *Magnyf.* 392 As men dare speke it hugger mugger. **1589** [? LYLY] *Pappe w. Hatchet* Wks. (1902) III. 401 He would not smother up sin, and deal in hugger mugger against his conscience. **1600–1** SHAKS. *Hamlet* IV. v. 84 We have done but greenly, In hugger-mugger to inter him. **1678** BUTLER *Hudibras* III. iii. 123 Where I, in hugger-mugger, hid, Have noted all they said or did. **1762** C. CHURCHILL *The Ghost* III. Wks. (1868) 289 It must not, as the vulgar say, Be done in hugger-mugger way. **1882** BLACKMORE *Christowel* xlvi By assenting to a hugger-mugger style of slapdash. [1 secretly.]

Hull cheese.

1678 RAY 340 You have eaten some Hull cheese. *i.e.* Are drunk, Hull is famous for strong ale.

Hull, see also Dighton is pulled down (When), H. great town; Hell, H., and Halifax; Oxford for learning . . . H. for women.

Human nature in man, There is a great deal of.

1871 KINGSLEY *At Last* ii 'There is a great deal of human nature in man' . . .; and one's human nature . . . will persist in considering beauty and ugliness as absolute realities.

Humble hearts have humble desires.

1640 HERBERT 317.

Humble pie, To eat.

[= to submit to humiliation: it may possibly be derived from the *umbles* (entrails) of the deer, which were the perquisite of the huntsman, and *umble-pie* would be the food of inferiors.] **1830** FORBY App. 432 'To make one eat humble pie'—*i.e.* To make him lower his tone, and be submissive. **1855** THACKERAY *Newcomes* I. xiv. 136 'You drank too much wine last night, and disgraced yourself. . . . You must get up and eat humble pie this morning'. **1861** H. KINGSLEY *Ravenshoe* xxx He had . . . to eat humble pie, to go back . . . and accept their offers.

Humble, see also Noble (The more), more h.

Humble-bee in a cow-turd thinks himself a king, An.

1576 PETTIE *Petite Pall.* (Gollancz) II. 124. **1659** HOWELL *Eng. Prov.* 1. **1670** RAY 14.

Humble bee, see also H. b. in a churn, *under* Swarm of bees all in a churn.

Humility, see Declaim against pride.

Humours, see Stillest h. are the worst.

Humphrey, see Devil is dead (When), there 's a wife for H.

Hunchback does not see his own hump, but sees his companion's, The.

1648 HERRICK *Hesper., Our own sinnes* Wks. (1921) 248 Other mens sins wee ever beare in mind; *None sees the fardell[1] of his faults behind.* **1758** FRANKLIN Mar. Happy Tom Crump ne'er sees his own Hump. **1905** ALEX. MACLAREN *Expos. Matthew* I. 327 Every body can see the hump on his friend's shoulders, but it takes some effort to see our own. [1 burden.]

Hundred ells of contention, In an | there is not an inch of love.

1640 HERBERT 355.

Hundred pounds of sorrow pays not one ounce of debt, An.

1640 HERBERT (Gros.) no. 410 A hundred loade of thought will not pay one ounce of debts. **1642** TORRIANO 18. *a.* **1704** T. BROWN *Wks.* (1760) III. 247 (A) [cited as 'the country proverb'].

Hundred, see also All one a h. years hence; Has an h. and one and owes h. and two;

Lost in the h. found in the shire; One man is worth h.; Sluggard takes an h. steps.

Hunger breaks (pierces) stone walls.

c. 1350 *Douce MS. 52* no. 28 Hungur brekyth stone and walle. 1546 HEYWOOD I. xii. 39 Some saie, and I feele hunger perseth stone wall. 1607–8 SHAKS. *Cor.* I. i. 211 They said they were an-hungry; sigh'd forth proverbs: That hunger broke stone walls. 1634 *P.R.O. State Papers Dom.* CCLXXI, July 1, no. 3, 128 Capt. Henry Bell to Abp. Laud . . . Beseeches the Archbishop to . . . consider the old proverb 'Hunger breaketh stone walls'. 1677 YARRANTON *England's Improvement* 179 Hunger will brake stone walls. 1787 GROSE (*Glos., Suff.*) 224 Hunger will break through stone walls, or any thing except a Suffolk cheese. Suffolk cheese is, from its poverty, the subject of much low wit. It is by some represented as only fit for making wheels for wheelbarrows. 1839 T. C. CROKER *Pop. Songs of Ireld.* 38 A facetious essayist . . . observes . . . 'the Irish might have attempted to satisfy hunger with trefoil,[1] . . . for hunger will break through a stone wall'. [[1] shamrock.]

Hunger drops out of his nose.

1546 HEYWOOD I. xi. 32 Hunger droppeth euen out of bothe their noses. 1605 CHAPMAN, &c. *Eastw. Hoe* IV. i Come away, I say, hunger drops out at his nose. 1611 COTGRAVE s.v. 'Chiche-face' A . . .∕ wretched fellow, one out of whose nose hunger drops.

Hunger fetches the wolf out of the woods.

1567 PAINTER *Pal. of Pleasure* (Jacobs) III. 216 Now I well perceiue that Hunger forceth the Woulf oute of his Denne. 1666 TORRIANO 83 Hunger drives the woolf out of the forest. 1748 SMOLLETT tr. *Gil Blas* XII. vii (1907) II. 385 This one . . . I own is the child of necessity. Hunger, thou knowest, brings the wolf out of the wood.

Hunger finds no fault with the cookery.

1659 N.R. 50 Hunger hath alwaies a good Cook. 1732 FULLER no. 2566.

Hunger in frost that will not work in heat, They must.

c. 1532 SIR ADRIAN FORTESCUE, no. 21 A shall hunger in froste, that in hete will not wyrke. 1550 HEYWOOD I. xi. 28.

Hunger is good kitchen[1] meat.

1641 FERGUSSON 38. 1721 KELLY 127 . . . The same with the English, *Hunger is good sauce.* [[1] anything eaten with bread as a relish.]

Hunger is the best sauce.

[CICERO *Fames optimum condimentum.*] 1362 LANGLAND *P. Pl.* VI. 4324 (Wright) I. 133 Er hunger thee take, And sende thee of his sauce. 1555 EDEN *Decades* 62 *marg.* Hunger is the best sauce. 1564 UDALL tr. *Erasm. Apoph.* (1877) 2 Socrates said, the best sauce in the world for meates, is to bee

houngrie. 1642 FULLER *H. & P. State* II. xix (1841) 109 God is not so hard a Master, but that he alloweth his servants sauce (besides hunger) to eat with their meat. 1850 KINGSLEY *Alton L.* ix If hunger is, as they say, a better sauce than any Ude invents.

Hunger knows no friend.

1719 DEFOE *Crusoe* II. ii Hunger knows no friend.

Hunger makes dinners, pastime suppers.

1640 HERBERT 355.

Hunger makes hard beans sweet.

c. 1350 *Douce MS. 52* no. 29 Hungur makyth harde benys swete. *a.* 1530 *R. Hill's Commonpl. Bk.* (E.E.T.S.) 133 Hungre maketh hard bones [read *benes*] softe. Dura licet faba denti sic salus esurienti. 1550 HEYWOOD I. x. 24. 1670 RAY 107 Hunger makes hard bones sweet beans . . . Erasmus relates as a common Proverb . . . Hunger makes raw beans rellish well or taste of Sugar.

Hunger waits only eight days.

1837 A. LEIGHTON in *Tales of Borders* III. 239 'Hunger waits only eight days, as the sayin' is', replied he, 'an' ye'll live mair than that time, I hope'.

Hunger, *see also* Lie down for love (They that) should rise for h.; Lives by hope will die by h.

Hungry as a dog.

c. 1590 SIR J. DAVIES Epigram no. 19. 1607 DEKKER *Jests to make you merry* C I[v]. 1862 *Dialect of Leeds* 405 (A).

Hungry as a hunter, As.

1818 LAMB to Mrs. Wordsworth 18 Feb. Up I go, mutton on the table, hungry as a hunter. 1855–7 MAGINN *Misc.* i. 358.

Hungry bellies have no ears.

[CATO THE ELDER *Venter famelicus auriculis caret.* A hungry belly hath no ears.] 1539 TAVERNER 47 Venter auribus caret. The belly hath no ears. When the belly's matter is in hand, honest reasons be not admitted, nor heard. 1653 WALTON *Angler* 144 It is a hard thing to perswade the belly, because it hath no ears. *a.* 1673 ABP. LEIGHTON *Theol. Lect.* xxii. Wks. (1819) IV. 230 Consider 'that, as Cato said, the belly has no ears', but it has a mouth, into which a bridle must be put. 1853 TRENCH ii. 27 When we have . . . the English, *Hungry bellies have no ears,* and . . . the Latin, Jejunus venter non audit verba libenter, who can doubt that the first is the proverb, and the second only the versification of the proverb? [Fr. 1678 LA FONTAINE *Fables* IX. xviii *Ventre affamé n'a pas d'oreilles.*]

Hungry dogs will eat dirty puddings. (*See also* Scornful dogs, &c.)

1538 J. BALE *Three Laws* B4. 1546 HEYWOOD I. v. 11 What, hungry dogges will eate durty

puddyngs man. **1600** DEKKER *Old Fort.* II. ii
The horse . . . has his head ever in the manger;
. . . and a hungry dog eats dirty puddings.
1670 RAY 82 . . . *Jejunus rarò stomachus
vulgaria temnit.* **1830** G. COLMAN (Jr.) *Random
Rec.* I. 37 'Hungry dogs eat dirty pudding',
which is a satire upon the distress of epicures,
during the scarcity of provisions. **1832**
HENDERSON 34 Hungry dogs are blythe o'
bursten puddins.

Hungry flies bite sore.

1546 HEYWOOD II. ix On suche as shewe, that
hungry flies byte sore. **1678** RAY 159 . . . The
horse in the fable with a gall'd back desired
the flies that were full might not be driven
away, because hungry ones would then take
their place.

Hungry forties, The.

1911 *Times, Wkly.* 25 Aug. 683 A . . . complete refutation of the legend that the food-
prices of the 'hungry forties' were immediately reduced by the abolition[1] of the Corn
Laws. [[1] 1846.]

Hungry he could eat a horse behind the saddle, He is so.

1678 RAY 253.

Hungry horse makes a clean manger, A.

1659 HOWELL *Eng. Prov.* 2/2.

Hungry, If thou be | I am angry; let us go fight.

1678 RAY 65.

Hungry man, an angry man, A.

1659 HOWELL *Eng. Prov.* 13/2. **1738** SWIFT
(Dial. ii) 344 *Miss* . . . I'm hungry. *Never.*
And I'm angry; so let us both go fight. **1909**
Spectator 22 May 824 The *Acharnians* . . .
made fun of the Athenians. . . . 'A hungry
man is an angry man' . . . and the Athenians
were certainly hungry.

Hungry man smells meat afar off, A.

1641 FERGUSSON 19 A hungry man sees far.
1721 KELLY 3. **1732** FULLER no. 224.

Hungry, *see also* Hard fare h. bellies; Poor
(H.) as a church mouse.

Hunt for (*or* Catch) a hare with a tabor,[1] To.

[= to seek to do something almost impossible.] **1399** LANGLAND *Rich. Redeles* I. 58
Men myȝtten as well haue hunted an hare
with a tabre As aske ony mendis ffor þat þei
mysdede. *c.* **1430** LYDGATE *Minor Poems*
(Percy Soc.) 154 Men with a tabour may
lyghtly catche an hare. **1546** HEYWOOD I. ix.
17 And yet shall we catche a hare with a
taber, As soone as catche ought of them.
1579 LYLY *Euphues* (Arb.) 44 You shal
assoone catch a Hare with a taber as you shal
perswade youth . . . to such seueritie of life.
1624 CAPT. J. SMITH *Virginia* IV. 155 Will any
goe to catch a Hare with a Taber and a Pipe?
[[1] a small drum.]

Hunt squirrels, and make no noise, You must.

1830 FORBY 429 'You must hunt squirrels
and make no noise'. *i.e.* If you wish to
succeed in an inquiry, you must go quietly
about it.

Hunt, *see also* Hare to breakfast (He that
will have) must h. overnight.

Hunt's (Wood's) dog that will neither go to church (out) nor stay at home, Like.

1678 RAY 291 Like Hunts dog, that will
neither goe to Church nor stay at home. **1732**
FULLER no. 3241 Like Wood's dog, he'll
neither go to church nor stay at home. **1880**
N. & Q. 6th Ser. II. 166 'Why', said the old
man, 'it has been a say as long ago as I was a
child, Contrary as Wood's dog, that wouldn't
go out nor yet stop at home.' **1917** BRIDGE
90 . . . *Impossible to please* . . . 'Hunt was
a Shropshire labourer, whose dog when shut
up at home during service-time howled . . . ;
but when his master took him with him . . .
the dog would not enter the church'.

Hunters, All are not | that blow the horn.

[Med. Lat. *Non est venator quivis per cornua
flator.*] **1586** L. EVANS *Withals Dict. Revised*
E6 (A) Every horne blower is not a hunter.
1678 RAY 160

Hunter(s), *see also* Hungry as a h.

Hunting, hawking, and paramours, for one joy a hundred displeasures.

1641 FERGUSSON 42.

Hunting morning, *see* Southerly wind.

Hunting, *see also* Dog that is idle barks at
fleas; War, h. . . . full of trouble.

Hurdle, *see* Looks as if he sucked dam
through h.

Hurleburle-swyre, *see* Little kens the wife.

Hurler, *see* Good h. that's on the ditch.

Hurry no man's cattle; you may come to have a donkey of your own.

1822 SCOTT *Pirate* ix 'A' in gude time, replied
the jagger, 'hurry no man's cattle'. **1869**
HAZLITT (1907) 236 Hurry no man's cattle;
you may come to have a donkey of your own.
Sometimes said to an impatient child.

Hurry, *see also* Old man in h.

Hurts another hurts himself, He that.

1573 SANDFORD (1576) 209. **1578** FLORIO
First Fruites f. 29. **1629** *Book of Meery
Riddles* Prov. 84.

Hurt(s, eth), *see also* Dirt (The more), less h.;

Healed as h. (Not so soon); Helpeth the evil (He that) h. the good; Ill that doth not h. me (So great is); No man, though never so little, but can h.; Offended (H.) but by himself (None is).

Husband be not at home, If the | there is nobody.

1640 HERBERT 364.

Husband, don't believe what you see, but what I tell you.

1732 FULLER no. 2577.

Husband drinks to the wife, When the | all would be well; when the wife drinks to the husband, all is well.

1659 HOWELL *Eng. Prov. Rend. into Fr.* 9 (7) (A) When the good wife drinketh to the husband all is well in the house. 1670 RAY 53. 1732 FULLER no. 5593.

Husband, In the | wisdom, in the wife gentleness.

1640 HERBERT 348.

Husbandry, *see* Good h. good divinity.

Husbands are in heaven whose wives scold (chide) not.

1550 HEYWOOD II. vii. 70. 1670 RAY 14.

Husband(s), *see also* Cornwall without a boat (Send h. into); Good h. good wife; Good wife good h.; Ill h. who is not missed; Lewd bachelor jealous h.; Marriage (In) the h. should have two eyes; Usurers good h.; Workman (The better), the worse h.; Wrongs of a h. not reproached.

Hussy (-ies), *see* Careless h. makes many thieves; Cats eat what h. spare.

Hustings, *see* Hoistings (You are for the) or H.

Hydra, *see* Heads as H. (As many).

Hyena, *see* Laugh like a h.

I

I do what I can (my endeavour, good will), quoth the fellow, when he threshed in his cloak.

1602 MANNINGHAM *Diary* (Camd. Soc.) 131 ' I will doe myne endeavor' quoth he that thrasht in his cloke. 1639 CLARKE 155. 1670 RAY 247 I'll do my good will, as he said that thresht in's cloak. This was some Scotchman, for I have been told, that they are wont to do so.

I proud (stout) and thou proud (stout), who shall bear the ashes out?

1550 HEYWOOD I. x. 22 I proud, and thou proud, who shall beare thashes out. 1732 FULLER no. 6284 I stout, and thou stout; Who shall carry the dirt out? 1853 TRENCH iv. 83 The Gallegas proverb, *You a lady, I a lady who shall drive the hogs a-field?* ... So too our own: *I stout and you stout, who will carry the dirt out?*

I to-day, you to-morrow.

[L. *Hodie mihi, cras tibi.* To-day it is my turn, to-morrow yours. Lady Jane Grey scratched, when imprisoned in the Tower, *Sors hodierna mihi cras erit illa tibi.*] *c.* 1200 *Ancrene Riwle* 278 ' Ille hodie, ego cras'; pet is, 'He to daie, ich to morwen.' *c.* 1592 MARLOWE *Jew of Malta* IV. iv Whom I saluted with an old hempen proverb, *Hodie tibi, cras mihi.* 1596 SPENSER *F.Q.* VI. i. 41 What haps to-day to me, to-morrow may to you. 1639 CLARKE 124. 1721 KELLY 350 What is my turn to-day, may be yours to-morrow. 1927 E. V. LUCAS in *Times* 11 Mar. 15/6 To-morrow ... hardly occupies the Jamaican mind at all.... There is even a native proverb: To-day fo' me; to-

morrow fo' you.' 1927 *Times* 15 Mar. 16/5 The Upper House of Congress ... when the dignity and privileges of a Senator are concerned ... can translate *Hodie mihi, cras tibi* as well as any Latinist.

I was by, quoth Pedley, when my eye was put on.

1678 RAY 242 ... This Pedley was a natural fool, of whom go many stories.

I will make one, quoth Kirkham, when he danced in his clogs.

1670 RAY 182. *Chesh.*

Ibycus, *see* Cranes of I.

Ice, *see* Break the i.; Seek hot water under i.

Iceland, *see* Snakes in I.

Idle, Be not | and you shall not be longing.

1640 HERBERT 331.

Idle brain is the devil's shop, An.

1629 T. ADAMS *Serm.* (1861–2) II. 450 The slothful person is the devil's shop, wherein he worketh engines of destruction. 1678 RAY 161. 1859 SMILES *Self-Help* ix Steady employment ... keeps one out of mischief, for truly an idle brain is the devil's workshop.

Idle folks have the least leisure.

1853 SURTEES *Sponge's Sport* T. liii 'Got a great deal to do', retorted Jog, who, like all thoroughly idle men, was always dreadfully busy. 1908 *Spectator* 10 Oct. The difference between leisureliness and laziness runs parallel with that between quickness and haste. 'Idle people', says the proverb, 'have the least leisure'.

Idle folks (people) have the most labour (or take the most pains).

1678 RAY 161 Idle folks have the most labour. **1732** FULLER no. 3056 Idle people take the most pains.

Idle folks lack no excuses.

1616 WITHALS 559 Idleness is never to seeke for an excuse. **1639** CLARKE 234.

Idle head is a box for the wind, An.

1640 HERBERT 347.

Idle man, see Devil tempts all, but i. m. tempts devil.

Idle person is the devil's cushion (or playfellow), An.

1624 BURTON Anat. Mel. 73 Idleness . . . the Diuells cushion, as Gualter calls it, his pillow, and chiefe reposall. **1630** T. ADAMS Wks. 197 (A) The idle man is the devil's cushion, whereupon he sits and takes his ease. **1732** FULLER no. 620 (with 'playfellow').

Idle youth, An | a needy age. (Cf. Lazy youth, &c.)

1611 COTGRAVE s.v. 'Jeunesse', An idle youth a needie age. **1642** TORRIANO 54 A young man idle, an old man needy. **1651** HERBERT 365. **1657** E. LEIGH Select Observations 266. **1659** N. R. 16.

Idle(s), see also Lazy (I.) folks take most pains; Learn to shape I. a coat; Sick of the i.; Sick of the i. crick.

Idleness, Of | comes no goodness.

1611 COTGRAVE s.v. 'Gueule'. **1678** RAY 161. **1732** FULLER no. 3698 Of idleness never comes any good.

Idleness is the key of beggary.

1670 RAY 14.

Idleness is the root (mother) of all evil (sin, vice).

1205 LAYAMON Brut (Madden) II. 624 Idelnesse maketh mon His monscipe leose. Idelnesse maketh cnihte For-leosen his irihte. c. **1386** CHAUCER Sec. Nun's Tale l. 1 The ministre and the norice un-to vyces. which that men clepe in English Ydelnesse. c. **1430** LYDGATE Fall of Princes (E.E.T.S.) I. ii. 2249 First this kyng ches to been his guide Moodir off vices, callid idilnesse. **15.** . REDFORD Wyt & Sci. 347 For that common strumpet, Idellnes, The verye roote of all vyciousnes? **1599** JAMES VI Basil. Dor. (Arb.) 155 For banishing of idleness (the mother of all vice). **1856** FROUDE Hist. Eng. I. 54 Every child . . . was to be trained up in some business or calling, 'idleness being the mother of all sin'.

Idleness must thank itself if it go barefoot.

1813 RAY 126.

Idleness turns the edge of wit.

1579 LYLY Euphues Wks. (Bond) I. 263 Sloth tourneth the edge of wit, Study sharpeneth the mind. **1616** DRAXE 96 Sloth turneth the edge of wit. **1670** RAY 14.

'If' and 'An' spoils many a good charter.

[L. Suppositio nihil ponit in re.] **1721** KELLY 209 . . . Spoken when a thing is promised upon such a condition, If they can, If they have time. Taken from the Clauses Irritant in a Conveyance.

If ifs and an's were pots and pans, there'd be no trade for tinkers.

1850 KINGSLEY Alton Locke x 'If a poor man's prayer can bring God's curse down . . .' 'If ifs and ans were pots and pans.' **1886** N. & Q. 7th Ser. I. 71 There is also the old doggerel— If ifs and ands Were pots and pans Where would be the work for Tinkers' hands?

'Ifs' and 'ands'. (See also If ifs and an's.)

1513 MORE Rich. III (1883) 47 What, quod the protectour, thou seruest me, I wene, with iffes and with andes. **1592** KYD Span. Trag. (Boas) II. i. 77 What, Villaine, ifs and ands? **1678** CUDWORTH Intell. Syst. 723 Absolutely, and without any ifs and ands.

Ignorance is bliss, Where | 'tis folly to be wise.

1742 GRAY Ode Prospect Eton Coll. 98–9 Thought would destroy their paradise! No more; where ignorance is bliss, 'Tis folly to be wise. **1900** E. J. HARDY Mr. Thos. Atkins 291 Never did soldiers set out for a war in better spirits than did ours for this . . . against the Boers. They . . . afforded a pathetic illustration of the proverb: 'Where ignorance is bliss 'tis folly to be wise.'

Ignorance is the mother of devotion.

1559 BP. JEWELL Wks. (P.S.) III. ii. 1202 (A) Ignorantia enim, inquit, mater est verae pietatis quam ille appellavit devotionem. **1573** New Custom I. i. in HAZL. O.E.P. III. 10 That I, Ignorance, am the mother of true devotion. **1590** SIDNEY First Arcadia (Feuillerat) 5 Yt comes of a very yll grounde, that ignorance should bee ye mother of faithfullnes. **1621** BURTON Anat. Mel. III. iv. I. ii (1651) 653 The best meanes . . . is to keep them still in ignorance: for Ignorance is the mother of devotion, . . . This hath been the divels practice. **1629** T. ADAMS Serm. (1861–2) II. 411 Sing not, thou Roman siren, that ignorance is the dam of devotion, to breed it.

Ignorance is the mother of impudence.

1573 SANDFORD (1576) B 1v Socrates . . . helde, that ignorance was the mother of presumption. **1589** L. WRIGHT, A Summons for Sleepers G₂v Ignorance hath alwayes the boldest face. **1597** Politeuphuia 56 Ignorance hath euer the boldest face. **1666** TORRIANO 116. **1732** FULLER no. 3067. **1855** BOHN 422.

Ignorance of the law excuses no man.

[Law Maxim *Ignorantia legis neminem excusat.*] **1629** T. ADAMS *Works; Med. upon Creed* 1099 But if the King make speciall lawes, . . . euery subject is bound to know that. *Ignorantia Iuris* will excuse no man.

Ignorance, *see also* Art has no enemy but i.

Ignorant hath an eagle's wings and an owl's eyes, The.

1616 DRAXE 27 [The ignorant] is Eagle eyed in other mens matters, but as blind as a buzzard in his owne. **1616** *Ibid.* 98 The ignorant hath the wings of an Eagle, and the eyes of an Owle. **1640** HERBERT 358.

Ignotum per ignotius.

[The unknown explained by that which is more unknown.] *c.* **1386** CHAUCER *Can. Yeo. T.* 1457 'Which is that?' quod he. '*Magnasia* is the same', Seydè Plato. 'Ye, sire, and is it thus? This is *ignotum per ignocius.* What is Magnasia, . . . ?' **1827** HARE *Gues. at Truth* (1859) i. 359 We too often find those who have to teach children, explaining *ignotum per ignotius*; and at times one is much puzzled to do otherwise.

Ill agreement is better than a good judgement, An. (*Cf.* Lean compromise.)

1573 SANDFORD (1576) 217 A leane agreement is better than a fatte sentence. **1640** HERBERT 329.

Ill air slays sooner than the sword.

a. **1450** *Ratis Raving* i. 167 (1870) 30 Tras weil the philosophur *is* word, Than sonar slais ill air na suord. **1576** PETTIE *Petite Pall.* (Gollancz) ii. 52 The air whereby we live, is death to the diseased or wounded man.

Ill bargain where no man wins, It is an.

[L. *Flet victus, victor interiit.* The conquered mourns, the conqueror is undone.] **1721** KELLY 182.

Ill battle (procession) where the devil carries the colours (candle, cross), It is an.

1608 BEAUM. & FL. *Philas.* iv. i *Dion.* O there's a Rank Regiment where the Devil carries the Colours, and his Dam Drum major. **1616** DRAXE 87 It is an euill procession, where the Deuill beareth the Crosse. *Ibid.* 212 It is an euill countrey where the deuill rules, or carieth the Crosse. **1627** DRAYTON *Agincourt* 82 Ill's the procession (and foreruns much loss), wherein men say the devil bears the cross. **1670** RAY 7 It's an ill battel where the Divel carries the colours. *Ibid.* 22 It is an ill procession where the devil holds the candle. **1678** RAY 192 It's an ill procession where the Devil carries the cross. **1853** TRENCH iv. 77 *When rogues go in procession, the devil holds the cross;*[1] when evil men have all their own way, . . . in the inverted hierarchy which is then set up, the foremost in badness is foremost also in such honour as is going. **1909** *Spectator* 2 Oct. 488 Colet . . . warned the King . . . that they who were fighting through hatred and ambition were warring under the banner . . . of the Devil. [[1] It. *Quando i furbi vanno in processione, il diavolo porta la croce.*]

Ill be to (Shame take) him that thinketh ill.

[*Honi soit qui mal y pense.*] *c.* **1460** SIR R. ROS *La Belle Dame* in SKEAT *Chaucer* VII. 397 Who thinketh il, no good may him befal. **1546** HEYWOOD I. ix. 17 And shame take him that shame thinkth ye thinke none. **1589** PUTTENHAM (Arb.) 116 Commonly thus Englished, Ill be . . . , but in mine opinion better thus, Dishonoured is he who meanes dishonorably. **1596** SPENSER *F.Q.* IV. 66 Shame be his meede, quoth he, that meaneth shame. **1600–1** SHAKS. *Merry W.* V. v. 75 And, *Honi soit qui mal y pense* write In emerald tufts, flowers purple, blue, and white. **1668** DENHAM in DRYDEN, *Misc.* v. 76 Who evil thinks, may evil him confound.

Ill (Foul) bird that bewrays (defiles, fouls) its own nest, It is an.

[*c.* **1023** EGBERT V. LÜTTICH *Fecunda Ratis* (Voigt) l. 148 *Nidos commaculans inmundus habebitur ales: Pelex nec factis claret nec nomine digna.*] *a.* **1250** *Owl & Night.* 99–100 (1922) 10 'Dahet habbe þat ilke best þat fuleþ his owe nest'. *c.* **1320** N. BOZON *Contes Moralisés* 205 Hyt ys a fowle brydde that fylyȝth hys owne nest. *c.* **1378** GOWER *Mir. de l'Omme* l. 23413 Trop est l'oisel de mesprisure Q'au son ny propre fait lesure. *c.* **1440** CAPGRAVE *Life St. Kath.* v. 1594 It is neyther wurshipful ne honest On-to mankeende to foule soo his nest. **1509** A. BARCLAY *Ship of Fools* (1570) 65 It is a lewde birde that fileth his own neste. **1546** HEYWOOD II. v. 58 It is a foule byrd, that fyleth his owne nest. I wold haue him . . . leaue lewde tickyng. *a.* **1591** HY. SMITH *Serm.* (1866) I. 26 It becometh not any woman to set light by her husband, nor to publish his infirmities: for they say, That is an evil bird that defileth her own nest. **1599–1600** SHAKS. *A.Y.L.* IV. i. 216 We must have your doublet and hose plucked over your head, and show the world what the bird hath done to her own nest. **1614** CAMDEN 308 It is a fowle bird that fileth his owne nest. **1670** RAY 62 It's an ill bird that beraies its own nest. **1701** DEFOE *Trueborn Englishman* Explan. Pref. I am taxed with bewraying my own nest, and abusing our nation, by discovering the meanness of our original. **1818** SCOTT *Rob Roy* xxvi Where's the use o' vilifying ane's country, and bringing a discredit on ane's kin, before southrons and strangers? It's an ill bird that files its ain nest. **1926** *Times* 7 Sept. 17/5 Nothing . . . can excuse the bad taste of Samuel Butler's virulent attack upon his defenceless family . . . It's an ill bird that fouls its own nest.

Ill bird that pecks out the dam's eyes, It is an.

1639 CLARKE 272.

Ill cause, He who hath an | let him sell it cheap.

1707 MAPLETOFT 59. 1855 BOHN 399.

Ill, Of one | come many.

1641 FERGUSSON 84.

Ill comes in by ells, and goes out by inches.

1640 HERBERT 325.

Ill (Ill news) comes often on the back of worse.

1721 KELLY 201 . . . Spoken when one misfortune succeeds another. 1737 RAMSAY III. 186 Ill comes upon waur's back.

Ill counsel mars all.

1639 CLARKE 22.

Ill counsel will gar[1] a man stick his ain mare.

1737 RAMSAY III. 186. [¹ cause.]

Ill deed cannot bring honour, An.

1640 HERBERT 354.

Ill deemed, half hanged. (Cf. Ill name, He that hath, &c.)

1641 FERGUSSON 38 He that is evil deemed is half hanged. 1721 KELLY 195 . . . A man that is vehemently suspected, will soon be found guilty.

Ill doers are ill deemers (dreaders).

1509 A. BARCLAY Ship of Fools (1874) I. 297 Yll doers alway hate the lyght. a. 1568 ASCHAM Schoolmaster Wks. (Wright) 230 Ill doinges, breed ill thinkinges. 1576 PETTIE Petite Pall. (Gollancz) II. 119 For mala mens, malus animus, an evil disposition breedeth an evil suspicion! 1721 KELLY 176. 1737 RAMSAY III. 186 Ill doers are ay ill dreaders. 1738 SWIFT (Dial. i) 341 Never. Madam, they say ill-doers are ill-deemers. 1815 SCOTT Guy Man. l. It is the ill-doers and ill-dreaders. 1824 FERRIER Inheritance II. xxxiv 'They say ill-doers are ill-dreaders', retorted his antagonist. 1828 SCOTT Fair Maid xvii Put me not to quote the old saw, that evil doers are evil dreaders. 1886 STEVENSON Kidnapped xxvii If you were more trustful, it would be better befit your time of life. . . . We have a proverb . . . that evil doers are aye evil-dreaders.

Ill dog that deserves not a crust, It is an.

1670 RAY 81 . . . Digna canis pabulo. Ἀξία ἡ κύων τοῦ βρώματος. Eras. ex Suida.

Ill egging[1] makes ill begging.

1623 CAMDEN 272. 1670 RAY 84 . . . Evil persons by enticing and flattery, draw on others to be as bad as themselves. [¹ urging on.]

Ill fame, see Keep yourself from . . . man of i. f.

Ill flesh (beef) ne'er made good broo[1].

1721 KELLY 198 Ill flesh was never good bruise.[1] Signifying that ill natur'd people seldom do a good thing: The Scots call an ill natured boy, Ill Flesh. 1862 HISLOP 172 Ill flesh ne'er made gude broo, Bad meat never made good soup; or, a bad man cannot be expected to do a good act. [¹ broth.]

Ill for the rider, good for the abider.

1639 CLARKE 18 . . . The best ground 's the dirtiest. 1670 RAY 43 The worse for the rider, the better for the bider. Bon pais [i.e. pays] mauvais chemin. Gall. Rich land, bad way.

Ill fortune, He that hath no | is troubled with good.

1640 HERBERT 334. 1670 RAY 10 He who hath no ill fortune is cloyed with good.

Ill fortune, see also Good heart conquers i. f.; Ill marriage is a spring of i. f.; Fence against i. f. (No)

Ill-gotten (Evil-gotten) goods (gains) never (seldom) prosper.

[HESIOD Opera et Dies l. 349 Κακὰ κέρδεα ἶσ' ἄτῃσι. Dishonest gains are losses.] 1519 HORMAN Vulg. f. 77 (A) Euyll goten ryches wyll neuer proue longe. 1539 TAVERNER 25 Male parta male dilabuntur.[1] Euyl gotten good go euyll awaye. It is commonly sene by the hyghe prouydēce of God that goodes vnlaufully gotten vanishe awaye, no man knoweth howe. 1575 GASCOIGNE Dulce Bellum in Wks. (1907) II. 146 Since goods ill got, so little time endure. 1590–1 SHAKS. 3 Hen. VI II. ii. 45 K. Hen. Didst thou never hear That things ill got had ever bad success? 1609 JONSON Case Altered v. vi Ill-gotten goods ne'er thrive; I played the thief, and now am robbed myself. 1761 A. MURPHY The Citizen I. ii. Wks. (1786) II. 233 The moment young master comes to possession, 'Ill got, ill gone', I warrant me. 1826 LAMB Elia, Pop. Fallacies ii THAT ILL-GOTTEN GAIN NEVER PROSPERS. . . . It is the trite consolation administered to the easy dupe, when he has been tricked out of his money or estate. [¹ CICERO Phil. 2. 27. 65.]

Ill-gotten goods thrive not to the third heir.

[L. De male quaesitis non gaudet tertius haeres. A third heir does not enjoy property dishonestly got.] c. 1303 BRUNNE Handl. Synne l. 9477 For thys men se, and sey alday, 'The threde eyre sellep alle away'. 1564 BULLEIN Dial. agst. Fever (1888) 72 They had no power in law to be-will unto their children that which was gotten in serving the Devil, which would not prosper to the third heir.

Ill (Evil) gotten, ill (evil) spent (gone).

[Quot. by CICERO Phil. 2. 27. 65. Male parta male dilabuntur.] 1481 CAXTON Reynard (Arb.) 8 Male quesisti et male perdidisti; hit is ryght that it be euil lost that is evil wonne. c. 1500 Harl. MS. 2331, f. 147 a (Rel. Ant. I. 20) Euil gotten, wors spent. 1555 HEYWOOD

Epig. upon Prov. no. 126 Ill gotten ill spent.
1564 BULLEIN *Dial. agst. Fever* (1888) 72 For
evil gotten goods are evil spent. **1614** CAMDEN
305 Evil gotten, evil spent. **1641** FERGUSSON
60 Ill win, ill warit.[1] [[1] laid out.]

**Ill guest that never drinks to his
host, He is an.**

1678 RAY 86. **1855** BOHN 375.

**Ill hearing makes ill (wrong) re-
hearsing.**

1721 KELLY 187 . . . Spoken when we hear one
give a wrong account of a matter of fact.
1820 SCOTT *Monast.* XXXV 'I thought you
said this youth had been a stranger.' 'Ill
hearing makes ill rehearsing,' said the land-
lady.

Ill herds make fat wolves (foxes).

1641 FERGUSSON **1721** KELLY 220 . . . It
signifies that careless keepers give thieves
occasion to steal. **1737** RAMSAY III. 186 Ill
herds mak fat foxes.

**Ill horse can neither whinny nor wag
his tail, It is an.**

1593 B.R. *Greene's News* (McKerrow) E 1[v] It is
a tyred Iade that cannot cry weehee, and a
sorry Mare that cannot wag her taile. **1594**
LYLY *Moth. Bomb.* IV. ii. Wks. (1902) III. 213
Dro. And I restored him so gently, that he
neither would cry *wyhie,* nor wag the tail.
1670 RAY 105. **1732** FULLER no. 2882 (with
'silly horse').

**Ill husband who is not missed, He is
an.**

1614 Letter to John Hoskyns (*Life* by L. B.
OSBORN 41) 'Tis a bad husband that a wife
and child . . . not miss. **1616** DRAXE 2.

**Ill language, There were no | if it were
not ill taken.**

1640 HERBERT 331. **1732** FULLER no. 4945.

Ill layers up make many thieves.

1721 KELLY 196.

Ill life, An | an ill end.

c. **1300** *King Alisaunder* (Weber) 753 Soth
hit is, in al[le] thyng, Of eovel lif comuth
eovel eyndyng. **1678** RAY 261.

Ill look among lambs, He has an.

1721 KELLY 155 . . . Applied to wanton
young fellows casting an eye to the girls;
alluding to a superstitious fancy among the
Scots, that an ill eye may do harm. **1732**
FULLER no. 1861.

Ill luck? What is worse than.

1639 CLARKE 166. **1641** *Organ's Echo* in
WILKINS *Polit. Ballads* (1860) I. 5 The proverb
says, *What's worse than ill luck.* **1664** WILSON
Projectors II. i Wks. (1874) 234 Then our
business is done already. What's worse than
ill luck? **1721** KELLY 354 . . . Spoken when
a thing miscarries purely by misfortune.

Ill luck is good for something.

1636 CAMDEN 300. **1732** FULLER no. 3074.

Ill luck is worse than found money.

1591 GREENE *Art of Coney-Catching* (Harrison)
21 Tis ill luck to keep founde money.

**Ill luck to count your gains during
the game.**

1773 BYROM *Misc. Poems,* 'The Pond' I. 72
He knew a wise old Saying, which maintain'd,
That 'twas bad Luck to count what one had
gain'd.

Ill luck, *see also* Picture of i. l. (Look like).

Ill man hath his ill day, Every.

1640 HERBERT 321.

**Ill man lie in thy straw, Let an | and
he looks to be thy heir.**

1640 HERBERT 329.

Ill man, *see also* Remedy against an i. m.

**Ill marriage is a spring of ill fortune,
An.**

1616 DRAXE 224.

**Ill name, He that hath an | is half
hanged. (***Cf.* **Give a dog an ill
name, &c.,** *and* **Ill deemed, half
hanged.)**

1546 HEYWOOD II. vi. 63 He that hath an
yll name, is halfe hangd, ye know. **1629**
T. ADAMS *Serm.* (1861–2) I. 224 It is a very
ominous and suspicious thing to have an ill
name. The proverb saith, he is half-hanged.
1641 FERGUSSON 38 He that is evil deemed
is half hanged. **1897** M. A. S. HUME *Raleigh*
270 'Were not *fama malum gravius quam res,*
and an ill name half hanged, . . . he would
have been acquitted.'

Ill name, *see also* Give a dog an i. n.; Ill
wound is cured, not i. n.; Nothing to be
got without pains (but i. n.).

**Ill natures, the more you ask them,
the more they stick.**

1640 HERBERT 321.

**Ill news comes apace (unsent for,
never comes too late).**

1574 HELLOWES *Guevara's Ep.* (1577) 58
Euil newes neuer comes too late. **1603**
DRAYTON *Baron's Wars* II. xxviii Ill news
hath wings, and with the wind doth go.
1623 CAMDEN 272 Ill newes commes too
soone. **1639** CLARKE 123 Ill news comes
unsent for. **1671** MILTON *Samson Ag.* 1538
For evil news rides post, while good news
baits. **1678** RAY 161. **1685** DRYDEN *Thren.
Aug.* 49 Ill news is winged with fate and flies
apace.

Ill news is too often true.

1611 DAVIES *Prov.* 47 Ill newes are commonly
true. **1639** CLARKE 228. **1721** KELLY 221 Ill
news are ay o'er true.

Ill news, *see* Ill (I. n.) comes often on the back of worse.

Ill of his harbory is good of his way-kenning, He that is.

1641 FERGUSSON 40. **1721** KELLY 143 *He that's ill of his lodging, is well of the waykenning.* Spoken when I ask my neighbour a loan, and he tells me that he cannot, but such an one can.

Ill paut[1] with her hind foot, She has an.

1721 KELLY 297 . . . Signifying that such a woman is stubborn. Taken from cows who kick when they are milked. [[1] back stroke.]

Ill paymaster never wants excuse, An.

1622 CÉSAR BUDIN *Grammar Span. and Eng.* tr. I. W. 217 An ill paymaster neuer wants excuses. **1732** FULLER no. 627.

Ill plea should be well pleaded, An.

1721 KELLY 20. **1855** BOHN 312.

Ill said that was not ill taken, It was never. (*Cf.* Ill language, There were no, &c.)

1721 KELLY 189 . . . Intimating that we had no ill design in what we said, only the man took it ill.

Ill servant will never be a good master, An.

1641 FERGUSSON 101. **1683** MERITON *Yorks. Ale* 83–7 (A).

Ill spun weft[1] will out either now or eft,[2] An.

c. **1300** *Provs. of Hending* 35 Euer out cometh euel sponne web. *c.* **1350** *Douce MS. 52* no. 31 Euyl spunnen ȝerne comyth euyll oute. *c.* **1460** *Towneley Myst. 2nd. Shep. Play* 587 Ill spon weft, iwys, ay commys foull owte. **1670** RAY 154 . . . This is a Yorkshire proverb. [[1] web. [2] afterwards.]

Ill that doth not hurt me, So great is the | as is the good that doth not help me.

1573 SANDFORD (1576) 102. **1578** FLORIO *First Fruites* f. 32 (A). **1629** *Book of Meery Riddles* Prov. 1.

Ill to himself will be good to nobody, He that is.

1721 KELLY 125. **1732** FULLER no. 2284.

Ill turn is soon done, An.

1721 KELLY 125. **1732** FULLER no. 631.

Ill turn, *see also* Does you an i. t., never forgive you.

Ill vessels seldom miscarry.

1611 COTGRAVE s.v. 'Vaisseau' A course

glasse neuer falls vnto the ground. **1640** HERBERT 320.

Ill ware is never cheap.

1611 COTGRAVE s.v. 'Mauvais' Bad ware is neuer cheape enough. **1640** HERBERT 319.

Ill way, *see* Make haste to an i. w.

Ill weather, *see* Sorrow (and i. w.) come unsent for.

Ill weed (Crop of a turd) mars a whole pot of pottage, One.

1546 HEYWOOD II. vi. 62 For were ye . . . The castell of honestée in all things els. Yet should this one thing . . . Defoyle and deface that castell to a cotage. One crop of a tourd marrth a pot of potage. **1579** LYLY *Euphues* (Arb.) 39 One leafe of *Colloquintida*, marreth and spoyleth the whole pot of porredge. **1614** CAMDEN 310 One ill weed marreth a whole pot of pottage.

Ill weeds grow apace (fast).

c. **1470** *Harl. MS. 3362* (ed. Förster) in *Anglia* 42. 200 Wyl[d] weed ys sone y-growe. *Creuerat herba satis, que nil habet utilitatis.* **1546** HEYWOOD I. x. 22 Ill wéede growth fast Ales: wherby the corne is lorne. **1578** FLORIO *First Fruites* 31 An yl weede groweth apace. **1592–3** SHAKS. *Rich. III* II. iv. 13 'Ay,' quoth my uncle Gloucester, 'Small herbs have grace, great weeds do grow apace': And since, methinks, I would not grow so fast, Because sweet flowers are slow and weeds make haste. *Ibid.* III. i. 103 You said that idle weeds are fast in growth. **1614** CAMDEN 308 Ill weeds grow fast. **1660** TATHAM *The Rump* I. i Ill weeds grow apace, brother. **1738** SWIFT (Dial. i) 335 *Col.* Don't you think miss is grown? *Lady A.* Ay, ill weeds grow apace. **1905** A. MACLAREN *Matt.* II. 208 'Ill weeds grow apace'; and these, as is their nature, grow faster than the good seed.

Ill weeds wax well.

1641 FERGUSSON 60 Ill weids waxes weill.

Ill (Evil) will never said well.

c. **1400** *Rom. Rose* B. 3802 For Wikkid-Tunge seith never well. **1566** L. WAGER *Mary Magdalene* (1902) Prol. l. 22 For euill will neuer said well, they do say. **1598–9** SHAKS. *Hen. V* III. vii. 126 *Con.* 'Tis a hooded valour; and when it appears, it will bate. *Orl.* 'Ill will, never said well.' **1623** CAMDEN 268 Euill will, neuer sayes well. **1721** KELLY 176 *Ill will never spoke well.* When people are known to have an aversion to any person, or party, what they say of them, must be received with some abatement.

Ill wind that blows nobody (no man) good (to good), It is an.

1546 HEYWOOD II. ix. 77 An yll wynde that blowth no man to good, men say. **1573–80** TUSSER 29 It is an ill winde turnes none to good. **1590–1** SHAKS. *3 Hen. VI* II. v. 55 Ill blows the wind that profits nobody. **1597–8** *2 Hen. IV* V. iii. 88 *Fal.* What wind blew you hither, Pistol? *Pist.* Not the ill wind which blows no man to good. **1640** HERBERT 357 It is an ill air where we gain nothing. **1655** FULLER *Ch. Hist.* II. ii (1868) I. 157 It is an ill wind which bloweth no man profit. He is cast on the shore of Friezland . . . , where the inhabitants . . . were by his preaching converted to Christianity. **1660** TATHAM *Rump* II. i. Wks. (1879) 220 'Tis an ill wind, they say, bloughs nobody good. **1832–3** S. WARREN *Diary of Phys.* i My good fortune (truly it is an ill wind that blows *nobody* any good) was almost too much for me. **1839** DICKENS *N. Nickleby* lvi But it 's a ill wind as blows no good to nobody. **1928** *Times* 7 Jan. 6/2 It is an ill wind that blows nobody any good, and cannot we all learn a lesson from the recent great snowstorm?

Ill word, One | asketh another.

1550 HEYWOOD I. ix. 18 One yll woord axeth an other, as folkis speake. **1614** CAMDEN 310 One ill word asketh another.

Ill word meets another, One | and it were at the Bridge of London.

1641 FERGUSSON 6. **1662** FULLER (*Lond.*) II. 343.

Ill workers are aye guid to-putters[1] (onlookers).

1737 RAMSAY III. 186. **1862** HISLOP 176 Ill workers are aye gude onlookers. [[1] taskmasters.]

Ill workman, *see* Bad workman.

Ill wound is cured, An | not an ill name.

1640 HERBERT 328. **1664** CODRINGTON 218. **1670** RAY 18 The evil wound is cured, but not the evil name.

Ill year, *see* Nothing between poor man and rich but . . . i. y.

Ill(s), *see also* Cook that cannot lick (I.); Costs more to do i.; Do i. (Who would) ne'er wants occasion; Do much i. (He may) ere he can do worse; Do no i. (If thou), do no i. like; Does i. hates light (He that); Done i. once will do again; Done no i. the six days, play the seventh; Evils (I.) (Of two) choose the least; Say no i. of the year till past; Suffer the i., look for the good; Three i. come from north.

Ill, It is, *see under significant words following.*

Ill-bred dog that will beat a bitch, It is an.

1732 FULLER no. 2898.

Imitation is the sincerest flattery.

1820 COLTON *Lacon* ccxvii Imitation is the sincerest of flattery. **1901** S. LANE-POOLE *Sir H. Parkes* viii. 138 No sincerer flattery exists than imitation.

Impossibilities, *see* No one is bound to i.

'Impossible' is not in my dictionary, The word.

1855 BOHN 519 . . . *Used by Napoleon*. **1910** *Spectator* 10 Dec. 1031 Edison . . . is . . . the Napoleon of inventors. His assistants say . . . that he is one of those who have no use for the word impossible.

Impossible, *see also* Certain because it is i.; Naught 's i. as t'auld woman said; Nothing is i. to willing heart.

Impressions, *see* First i.

Improve(s), *see* Havocks (He that) may sit, i. must flit.

In and out, like Billesdon I wote.

1678 RAY (*Leic.*) 317. **1848** EVANS 115 'In and out, like Billesdon, I wote.' A scattered irregular village [between Leicester and Uppingham].

In at one ear and out at the other.

c. **1374** CHAUCER *Troylus* IV. 434 Oon ere it herde, att' other out it wente. **1546** HEYWOOD II. ix. 76 Thaduyse of all fréends I say, one and other Went in at the tone eare, and out at the tother. **1641** FERGUSSON 64. **1738** SWIFT (Dial. iii) 352 *Miss.* All they can say goes in at one ear and out at t'other for me.

In dock, out nettle.

[Originally a charm uttered to cure nettlestings by dock-leaves, became a proverbial expression for changeableness and inconstancy.] *c.* **1374** CHAUCER *Troylus* IV. 460 But canstow pleyèn raket, to and fro, Netle in, dokke out, now this, now that. **1546** HEYWOOD II. i. 45 For in one state they twayne could not yet settle. But waueryng as the wynde, in docke out nettle. *a.* **1553** UDALL *Royster D.* II. iii (Arb.) 34 I cannot skill of such chaungeable mettle, There is nothing with them but in docke out nettle. **1655** FULLER *Ch. Hist.* I. v, §§ 47, 48 (1868) I. 246 'Monks for their insolency were driven out of their seats, and secular clerks brought into their room.' Thus was it often, 'in dock, out nettle', as they could strengthen their parties. **1861** T. HUGHES *Tom B. at Oxford* xxiii The constable . . . found some dock leaves, . . . rubbed her hands with the leaves, repeating the old saw Out nettle, In dock: Dock shall ha' A new smock; Nettle shan't Ha' narrun.

In for a penny, in for a pound.

1695 RAVENSCROFT *Canterbury Guests* v. i Well, than, O'er shooes, o'er boots. And In for a penny, in for a Pound. **1815** SCOTT *Guy Man.* xlvi 'I will', quoth Sampson . . . for he thought to himself, in for a penny, in for a pound; and he fairly drank the witch's health in a cup of brandy. **1827** HARE *Gues. at Truth* i (1859) 230 No propagation or multiplication is more rapid than that of evil. . . . He who is in for a penny, . . . will find he is in for a pound. **1839** DICKENS *N. Nickleby* lvii If you're in for a penny, you're in for a pound. **1894** BLACKMORE *Perlycross* xv In for a penny, in for a pound. Throw the helve after the hatchet. . . . These and other reckless maxims . . . were cited.

In time comes he (she) whom God sends.

1640 HERBERT 336. **1670** RAY 51 (with 'she'). **1732** FULLER no. 2831.

In time the savage bull doth bear the yoke.

[OVID *Ars Amatoria* 1. 472 *Tempore lenta pati frena docentur equi. Ibid.* 2. 184 *Rustica paulatim taurus aratra subit.*] **1592** KYD *Span. Trag.* (Boas) II. i. 3 In time the sauage Bull sustains the yoake. **1598–9** SHAKS. *Much Ado* I. i. 271 In time the savage bull doth bear the yoke.

In vain he craves advice that will not follow it.

1611 COTGRAVE s.v. 'Croire'. **1670** RAY 1.

In vain is the mill-clack, if the miller his hearing lack.

1640 HERBERT 332.

In vain the net is spread in the sight of any bird.

1611 BIBLE *Proverbs* i. 17 Surely in vain the net is spread in the sight of any bird. **1888** J. E. T. ROGERS *Econ. Interp. Hist.* (1894) II. xxi. 473 The landowners in Pitt's time foresaw this. . . . They would certainly be caught, and the net was spread in vain in sight of the bird.

In vain, *see also* Rise early.

Inch breaks no square, An.

1555 HEYWOOD *Epigr. upon Prov.* no. 4 An inche breakth no square. **1636** S. WARD *Serm.* (1862) 104 A good conscience . . . says not, an inch breaks no square, and small faults must be winked at. **1760–7** STERNE *T. Shandy* II. v This fault in Trim broke no squares with them. **1771** SMOLLETT *Humph. Clink.* 17 May Wks. (1871) 492 Eastgate understood the hint; and told him that one day should break no squares.

Inch in a miss is as good as an ell, An.

1614 CAMDEN 303. **1659** HOWELL *Eng. Prov.* 7 An inch in a miss is as bad as an ell. **1721** KELLY 35 *An inch of a miss is as good as a span.* Spoken when a thing was near the effecting, and yet did not hit. **1732** FULLER no. 635.

Inch is as good as an ell, An.

1546 HEYWOOD II. ix. 78 As good is an inche As an ell. **1818** SCOTT *Ht. Midl.* xliii His great surprise was, that so small a pistol could kill so big a man . . . an inch was as good as an ell.

Inch of a nag is worth a span of an aver,[1] An.

1641 FERGUSSON 16. **1721** KELLY 28 . . . A

little man, if smart and stout, is much preferable to an unwieldy lubber. [[1] workhorse.]

Inch of his will, for a span (an ell) of his thrift, He will not give an.

1520 R. WHITTINTON *Vulg.* (E.E.T.S.) 91 Many a man setteth more by an ynche of his wyl than an ell of his thryfte & thou art one of them. **1641** FERGUSSON 46. **1721** KELLY 150 . . . Spoken of wilful and obstinate people, who will not comply with your most advantageous proposals, if contrary to their perverse humours.

Inch, *see also* Drive out the i. as you have the span; Flog (a person) within i. of his life; Give him an i. and he'll take ell; Man every i.; Sees an i. before his nose.

Inconvenience, *see* Better a mischief.

Indentures, To make.

[= to stagger as when drunk.] **1598** I. M. *A Health to the Gentlemanly Profession of Servingmen* (W. C. Hazlitt) 138 Making Indentures all along the ditches. **1603** DEKKER *The wonderful year* E 4ᵛ His legges drew a paire of Indentures, betweene his bodie and the earth. **1681** *Roxb. Ballads* (B.S.) vi. 3 (A) Being so drunk that he cutteth indentures.

Indian summer.

[A period of calm, dry, mild weather, with hazy atmosphere, occurring in the late autumn in the Northern United States.] **1794** E. DENNY *Milit. Journ.* (1859) 198, Oct. 13th Pleasant weather. The Indian summer here [near Presqu. Isle]. **1830** DE QUINCY *Bentley* Wks. VI. 180 An Indian summer crept stealthily over his closing days. **1898** BOLDREWOOD *Rom. Canvass Town* 71 Mild Indian-summer-like days.

Indies, *see* Bring home wealth of the I.

Indulgences to Rome.

1853 TRENCH iii. 68 In the Middle Ages they had this proverb: *Indulgences to Rome*, Rome being the centre and source of this spiritual traffic.

Industry is fortune's right hand, and frugality her left.

1670 RAY 14. **1799** EDGEWORTH *Pop. Tales; Lame Jervas* ii . . . a proverb which has been worth ten times more to me than all my little purse contained.

Ingleborough,[1] Pendle,[2] and Penyghent,[3] are the highest hills between Scotland and Trent.

1586 CAMDEN *Britannia* 430–1 Horum libentius meminerim, quod in Apennino nostro sunt eminentissimi; inde vulgo vsurpatur, Ingleborrow, Pendle, and Penigent, Are the highest hils between Scotland and Trent. **1613–22** DRAYTON *Polyolb.* xxviii. 115 (1876) III. 189 That *Ingleborow* Hill, *Pendle*, and *Penigent*, Should naméd be the high'st

betwixt our *Tweed* and *Trent.* 1670 RAY 256
Pendle, Penigent *and* Ingleborough, *Are the
three highest hills all England thorow.* These
three hills are in sight of each other, *Pendle*
on the edge of *Lancashire, Penigent* and
Ingleborough near *Settle* in *Yorkshire,* and
not far from *Westmorland.* [¹ Yorks. 2,373 ft.
² Lancs. 1,830 ft. ³ Yorks. 2,273 ft.]

Inheritance, *see* Beauty is no i.

Injuries don't use to be written on ice.

1732 FULLER no. 3096.

Injury is to be measured by malice.

1732 FULLER no. 3099.

Injury (-ies), *see also* Neglect will kill an i.
sooner than revenge; Patience under old i.
invites; Remedy for i. is not to remember.

Ink, *see* Wash out i. with i.

Inkhorn, *see* Smell of the i.

Inn, *see* Companion in a . . . little i. (A man
knows his); Goes not out of way . . . to
good i.; Take one's ease in one's i.

Inner Temple rich, the Middle Temple poor; Lincoln's Inn for law, and Gray's Inn for a whore, The. (*Cf.* Gray's Inn for walks, &c.)

1813 RAY 237.

Inner Temple, *see also* Gray's Inn.

Innocence is no protection.

1605 B. JONSON *Sejanus* IV. i. 40 No innocence
is safe, When power contests. 1732 FULLER
no. 3100.

Innocent actions carry their warrant with them.

1573 SANDFORD (1576) 215. 1578 FLORIO
First Fruites f. 31 (A) Innocencie beareth her
defence with her. 1732 FULLER no. 3102.

Innocent as a devil of two years old, As.

1678 RAY 286. 1738 SWIFT (Dial. i) 341
Spark. I meant no harm. *Lady S.* No, to be
sure, my lord! you are as innocent as a devil
of two years old.

Innocent as a new-born babe (*or* as child unborn).

1606 O. ORMEROD *The Picture of a Papist* 191
As innocent as the childe newelie borne.
1608 MIDDLETON *The Family of Love* Wks.
(Bullen), iii. 115 I am as innocent in this as
the child new-born. 1745 SWIFT *Dir. to
Servants* (A) 'Chambermaid', offering to take
her oath . . . that she was innocent as the
child unborn.

Innocent until he is proved guilty, Every one is held to be.

1910 *Spectator* 6 Aug. 205 The rule that a
man must be assumed to be innocent till
proved guilty is thoroughly sound.

Inquisition, *see* King and the I. (With the),
hush!

Insatiable, *see* Three things are i.

Inside, *see* Best thing for i. of a man.

Instep, *see* High in the i.

Insult to injury, To add.

1748 E. MOORE *The Foundling* v. ii (A) This
is adding insult to injuries. 1805 *Ann. 8th
Cong.* 2 Sess. 1072 It was adding insult to
injury, and expenses to both. 1837 DICKENS
Pickwick xxxv 'Not content vith writin' up
Pickwick, they puts "Moses" afore it, vich
I call addin' insult to injury.'

Intent, *see* Bashful mind hinders good i.

Intents and purposes, To all.

1546 *Act* 37 *Hen. VIII, c.* 9, § 1 To all
intents, constructions, and purposes. 1629
STRATFORD *Let.* in *Slingsby's Diary* (1836) 321
Your self [being] as formerly vice president
to all intentts. 1716 ADDISON *Drummer* i
Sir George is as dead at present, to all Intents
and Purposes, as he will be a Twelve-month
hence. 1879 M. ARNOLD *Ess. Porro unum* 162
The rest of the nation consists, for all intents
and purposes, of one immense class.

Interest will not lie.

1688 BUNYAN *Work of Jesus Christ* Wks.
(1855) I. 164 Our English proverb is, Interest
will not lie; interest will make a man do that
which otherwise he would not do.

Intermeddling, *see* Little i. good friends.

Invented the Maiden first hanselled it, He that.

[OVID *Ars Am.* 1. 655 *Neque enim lex aequior
ulla, Quam necis artifices arte perire sua.*]
1652 TATHAM *Scots. Fig.* II. Wks. (1879) 141
I'm sworn to cheat my father, and 'tis fit He
that first made the gin should hansell it.
1721 KELLY 140. 1853 TRENCH ii. 37 . . . The
Regent Morton, the inventor of . . . 'The
Maiden', a sort of . . . guillotine, was himself
the first upon whom the proof of it was made.
Men felt . . . that 'no law was juster than that
the artificers of death should perish by their
own art'.

Invitation, *see* Host's i. is expensive; Small
i. will serve beggar.

Invite not a Jew either to pig or pork.

[1596–7 SHAKS. *Merch. V.* I. iii. 34 *Bass.* If it
please you to dine with us. *Shy.* Yes, to smell
pork . . . I will buy with you, sell with you, . . .
and so following; but I will not eat with you.]
1732 FULLER no. 3106.

Invited you to the roast ? Who.

1721 KELLY 351 ... Spoken when people put their hand uninvited to what is not theirs.

Invite(s), see also Sign i. you in, money redeem you out.

Ipswich, a town without inhabitants, a river without water, streets without names, where asses wear boots.

1787 GROSE (Suffolk) 224 ... This description of Ipswich was given to King Charles II by the Duke of Buckingham. ... The town, having no manufactory, was thinly inhabited; the streets at that time were not named; at low water the bed of the river is left dry; and the bowling-green of Christ-church priory ... was rolled by asses, in a sort of boots, to prevent their feet sinking into the turf.

Ique, see Words ending in *i.* mock physician.

Ira furor brevis est, see Anger is a short madness.

Ireland, see England win (He that will) must with I. begin; England's difficulty I.'s opportunity.

Irish, see More I. than the I.; Weep I.

Irishman before answering a question always asks another, An.

1910 P. W. JOYCE Eng. as We Speak 109 'An Irishman before answering a question always asks another': he wants to know why he is asked.

Irishman for a hand, The | the Welshman for a leg, the Englishman for a face, and the Dutchman for a beard.

1630 DEKKER Honest Whore, Pt. II. I. i (Merm.) 195 Lod. There's a saying when they commend nations. It goes, the Irishman for his hand, the Welshman for a leg, the Englishman for a face, the Dutchman for a beard.

Irishman on the spit, Put an | and you can always get another Irishman to baste him.

1907 G. B. SHAW John B's Other Is. (1912) Pref. xxxiii To thump the Nationalist or Orange tub ... puts a premium on the rancour or callousness that has given rise to the proverb that if you put an Irishman on a spit you can always get another Irishman to baste him.

Irishman's obligation, Like an | all on one side.

1894 NORTHALL Folk-phrases 19.

Irishman, see also Englishman is never happy ... I. never at peace; Englishman weeps ... I. sleeps.

Iron age, see Golden life in i. a. (Not look for).

5017   Y

Iron entered into his soul, The.

[L. *Ferrum pertransiit animam ejus, Ps.* civ (cv) 18, a mistranslation in the Vulgate of the Heb. (lit. 'his person entered into the iron', i.e. fetters, chains).] c. 825 Vesp. Psalter civ. 18 Iren ðorhleorde sawle his. a. 1340 HAMPOLE Psalter civ. 17 Yryn passid thorgh his saule. **1539** BIBLE (Great) Ps. cv. 18 Whose fete they hurt in the stockes: the yron entred in to hys soule. **1768** STERNE Sent. Journ. (1778) II. 32 (Captive), I saw the iron enter into his soul. **1843** MACAULAY Ess., Mad. D'Arblay (1865) II. 304/2 She was sinking into a slavery worse than that of the body. The iron was beginning to enter into the soul.

Iron hand in a velvet glove, An.

1850 CARLYLE Latter-Day Pamph. ii (1885) 48 Soft of speech and manner, yet with an inflexible vigour of command ... 'iron hand in a velvet glove', as Napoleon defined it. **1882** PIDGEON Engineer's Holiday (1883) 167 Whose hand of iron was never ungloved with velvet.

Iron nails that scratches a bear, He must have.

1678 RAY 98. **1801** WOLCOT (P. Pindar) Out at Last A man must have, the proverb says, Good iron nails that scratches a bear. **1828** LYTTON Pelham lxxvii He must have iron nails who scratches a bear. You have sent me a challenge, and the hangman shall bring you my answer.

Iron(s), see also Cow with i. tail; Many i. in the fire; Strike while i. hot.

Isis, see Ass of I.

Island, see Settling an i., the first building.

Isle of Saints, The.

1875 KILLEN Eccles. Hist. Ireland I. 40 In the seventh century Ireland was known by the designation of 'The Isle of Saints'. ... Its missionaries laboured with singular success in France, Germany, Switzerland, and Italy, as well as in Great Britain.

Isle of Wight hath no monks, lawyers, or foxes, The.

1586 CAMDEN Britannia (Hants.) (1722) I. 153 Isle of Wight. ... The inhabitants facetiously boast, how much happier they are than their Neighbours, since they never had either Monks, or Lawyers, or Foxes.

Italianate, see Englishman I.

Italians are wise before the deed, The | the Germans in the deed, the French after the deed.

1640 HERBERT 360.

Italy, see Live in I.

Itch and ease can no man please.

1546 HEYWOOD II. iv. 51 But all thyng male

be suffred sauyng welth. An olde saide sawe, itche and ease, can no man please. **1732** FULLER no. 6237.

Itch of disputing is the scab of the church, The.

[c. **1639**] **1651** *Reliquiæ Wottonianæ* (1672) I. 135 *Panegyrick to K. Charles. Disputandi pruritus fit Ecclesiarum Scabies.* [p. 147] In my opinion (if I may have pardon for the phrase) *The Itch of disputing, will prove the Scab of Churches.* **1651** HERBERT 370 The itch of disputing is the scab of the Church [transln. of the saying *Disputandi prurigo est ecclesiæ scabies*].

Itch(es), *see also* Endure to i. (He that will not); Scratch where it i. not.

Ithuriel's spear.

[A touch of the angel Ithuriel's spear exposed deceit.] **1667** MILTON *Par. Lost* iv. 810 Him thus intent Ithuriel with his spear Touched lightly; for no falsehood can endure Touch of celestial temper. **1926** A. CLUTTON-BROCK *Ess. on Relig.* vi. 157 The new weapon of psychology . . . may become for us an Ithuriel's spear. When the Devil within us pretends to be an angel . . . at a touch of that spear the disguise will fall away.

Ivinghoe, *see* Tring.

Ivory gate, The. (*Cf.* Gate of horn.)

[In classical legend that through which false dreams came forth; *Od.* 19. 564; *Aen.* 6. 895.] **1870** MORRIS *Earthly Par.* I. Apol., Let it suffice me that my murmuring rhyme Beats with light wing against the ivory gate.

Ivy-leaf, Not worth an.

c. **1390** GOWER *Conf. Amantis* IV. 586 That all nys worth an yvy lef.

Ivy leaf, *see also* Pipe in an i. L

J

Jack-a-lent, A.

1553 H. MACHYN *Diary* (Camden Soc.) 33 And then shreyffing Jake-of-lent on horssbake, and a doc[tor] ys fezyssyoun, and then Jake-of-lent[s] wyff. . . . c. **1560** WRIGHT *Songs etc. Philip and Mary* (Roxb. Cl.) 191 (A) Then Jacke-a-lent comes justlynge in, with the hedpeece of a herynge. **1598** SHAKS. *Merry W.* V. v. 134 See now how wit may be made a Jacke-a-Lent when 'tis vpon ill employment. **1633** JONSON *T. Tub* IV. iii Thou . . . Travell'dst to Hampstead Heath on Ash Wednesday. Where thou didst stand six weeks the Jack-of-Lent For boys to hurl, three throws a penny, at thee. **1813**–49 *Brand's Pop. Antiq.* I. 101 **1863** *Chambers' Bk. of Days* I. 240/2.

Jack among the maids.

[= a gallant, a ladies' man.] **1785** J. TRUSLER *Mod. Times* I. 160 The Mayor . . . was a pleasant man, and Jack among the maids.

Jack-an-Ape be merry, Can | when his clog is at his heel?

c. **1440** *Book of Curtasye* (Furnivall) l. 108 Thou art like an ape tey3ed with a dogge. c. **1450** *Polit. Poems* (Wright) II. 232 Jac Napes wolde one the see a maryner to ben, with his cloge and his cheyn. **1636** CAMDEN 294.

Jack-an-apes is no gentleman.

1639 CLARKE 226.

Jack-an-apes than all the bears, More ado with one.

1616 DRAXE 70. **1639** CLARKE 73. **1732** FULLER no. 3464.

Jack and Gill (Jill). (*Cf.* Jack has, &c.; Jack shall have, &c.)

14 . . LYDGATE *London Lyckpeny* 83 Some songe of Ienken and Iulyan for there mede. e. **1450** *Cov. Myst.* (Shaks. Soc.) 340 And I wole kepe the feet this tyde Thow ther come both Iakke and Gylle. **1661** NEEDHAM *Hist. Eng. Rebell.* 74 Princes are brav'd by Jack and Jill. **1852** LYTTON *My Novel* III. 10 If Gill was a shrew, it was because Jack did not . . . stop her mouth with a kiss.

Jack at a pinch.

1622 MABBE tr. *Aleman's Guzman d'Alf.* I. 130 When there was neede of my seruice . . . I was seldome or neuer wanting; I was Iacke at a pinch. a. **1700** B. E. *Dict. Cant. Crew, Jack at a Pinch*, a poor Hackney Parson. **1883** WHITCHER *Widow Bedott Papers* ii Miss Coon . . . knows that the Major took her [to wife] 'Jack at a pinch'—seein' he couldent get such as he wanted, he took such as he could get.

Jack (Tom) Drum's entertainment.

[= a rough reception, turning an unwelcome guest out of doors.] **1577**–87 HOLINSHED *Hist. Irel.* B ij (N.) 1 Tom Drum's entertainment, which is, to bale a man in by the head, and thrust him out by both shoulders. **1579** GOSSON *Sch. Abuse* (Arb.) 22 Plato when he sawe the doctrine of these Teachers, . . . gaue them all Drummes entertainment, not suffering them once to shew their faces in a reformed common wealth. **1602**–3 SHAKS. *All's Well* III. vi. 41 If you give him not John Drum's entertainment, your inclining cannot be removed. **1607** DAY *Parl. of Bees* V With Jack Drum's entertainment he shall dance the jig called Beggar's Bush. **1649** J. TAYLOR (Water-P.) *Wand. to West* 16 The Hostess being very willing to give the courteous entertainment of Jack Drum, commanded me very kindley to get me out of doors.

Jack has (must have) his Jill, Every. (*Cf.* Jack shall have Jill.)

1611 COTGRAVE s.v. 'Demander' (A) Like will to like; a Jacke lookes for a Gill. **1619**

Satyricall Epigr., in BARDSLEY's Puritan Nomen. (1897) 104 The proverb is, each Jacke shall have his Gill. **1670** RAY 108 Every Jack must have his Gill. Chascun demande sa sorte. Gall. Like will to like. It ought to be written Jyll. **1738** SWIFT (Dial. i) 340 Miss. You are a saucy Jack, to use such expressions. Never. Why, then, miss, . . . I must tell you there's ne'er a Jack but there's a Gill. **1855** G. J. WHYTE-MELVILLE Gen. Bounce ii 'Every Jack has his Gill', if he and she can only find each other out at the propitious moment.

Jack-hold-my-staff.

[= a servile attendant.] **1625** BP. MOUNTAGU App. Cæsar ii. xvi. 217 As if . . . the man [were not] to bee made any more account of than Iack hold my staffe, by these Rabbies. **1678** MRS. BEHN Sir Patient Fancy v Madam, in plain English I am made a . . . Jack-hold-my-staff, . . . to give Leander time to marry your Daughter.

Jack in a box.

1570 Satir. Poems Reform xxii. 78 Jak in the bokis, for all thy mokis a vengeance mot the fall! **1577** Misogonus iii. i Its no tale of Iacke a male [= Jack in the male or trunk.] **1583** MELBANCKE Philotimus (British Bibliographer ii. 446). **1592** NASHE Wks. (McKerrow) III. 1467. **1690** New Dict. Cant. Crew G 2 (A) Jack in a box, a sharper or cheat.

Jack in office.

[= a consequential petty official.] c. **1608** SHAKS. Coriol. V. iii You shall perceive that a jack guardant cannot office me from my son Coriolanus. **1670** RAY 214 To be Jack in an office. a. **1700** B. E. Dict. Cant. Crew, Jack in an Office, of one that behaves himself Imperiously in it. **1742** FRANKLIN Mar. Two upstart Jacks in Office, proud and vain. **1732** FULLER no. 3050 Jack in an office is a great man. **1895** D. C. MURRAY Martyred Fool ii. ii. 169 A jack in office of the average juge d'instruction type, who barked at him in the common imperative way of his tribe.

Jack in the low cellar.

[a rendering of Dutch Hans-in-Kelder, an unborn child.] **1751** SMOLLETT Per. Pick. x When his companions drank to the Hans en Kelderr, or Jack in the low cellar, he could not help displaying an extraordinary complacence of countenance.

Jack is as good as his master.

1869 C. READE Foul Play xl Is it the general opinion of seamen before the mast? Come, tell us. Jack's as good as his master in these matters. **1895** R. GARNETT Age of Dryden 245 The simple discovery that for the novelist's purpose, Jack was as good as his master. **1905** W. C. RUSSELL Old Harb. T. xi If the crew are to be carried away to an unknown place, they all go below to a man, for Jack's as good as his master when it comes to his having to do something which he didn't agree for.

Jack (John) of all trades.

1618 MYNSHUL Ess. Prison 24 Some broken Citizen, who hath well plaid Iack of all trades. **1639** MAYNE City Match ii. v You mungrel, you John of all Trades. **1712** ARBUTHNOT John Bull iv Old Lewis Baboon was a sort of Jack of all trades, which made the rest of the tradesmen jealous. **1813** SCOTT Let. to Joanna Baillie 21 Mar. in LOCKHART Life Being a complete jack-of-all-trades, from the carpenter to the shepherd, nothing comes strange to him.

Jack of all trades, and master of none.

1800 EDGEWORTH Pop. Tales, Will l 'How comes it that I am so unlucky?' 'Jack of all trades, and master of none!' said Goodenough, with a sneer. **1878** S. WALPOLE Hist. Eng. I. 311 It would be unfair to say of Lord Brougham that he was 'Jack of all trades and master of none'.

Jack of all trades is of no trade.

1732 FULLER no. 3051. **1770** Gent. Mag. xl. 61 Jack at all trades, is seldom good at any.

Jack of (on) both sides.

1562 (title) A Godly and necessary Admonition concerning Neutres, such as deserve the grosse name of Iack of both sydes. **1656** EARL MONM. Advt. fr. Parnass. 338 That he hath won this universal good will by the vice of playing Jack of both sides. **1759** DILWORTH Pope 59 That he was a papist, a jack o' both sides. **1882** BLACKMORE Christowell xxiii Rose Arthur . . . wondered at his impartiality about a gentleman whom he had longed so lately to put upon a bonfire. Somehow or other, . . . now he seemed a Jack of both sides.

Jack of Dover.

['The name of some dish, probably a pie that had been cooked more than once.' (Skeat.)] c. **1386** CHAUCER Cook's Prol. 23 Many a Iakke of Douere hastow soold That hath been twies hoot and twies coold.

Jack-out-of-doors, Not | nor yet gentleman.

1639 CLARKE 206.

Jack (John) out of office.

1546 HEYWOOD ii. iii. 48 And Iack out of office she maie bid me walke. **1591-2** SHAKS. 1 Hen. VI I. i. 175 Win. I am left out; for me nothing remains. But long I will not be Jack-out-of-office. **1668** L'ESTRANGE Vis. Quev. (1708) 65 We should be but so many Jacks out of Office.

Jack Robinson, see Before one can say.

Jack shall have Jill, All shall be well. (Cf. Jack and Jill; Jack has his Jill.)

c. **1516** SKELTON Magnificence l. 287 What auayleth Lordshyp yourself for to kyll With care and with thought how Jacke shall have Gill? **1546** HEYWOOD II. iii. 48 Come chat at home, al is wel. Iack shall haue gill. **1595–6** SHAKS. *Mids. N.* III. ii. 461 Jack shall have Jill; Naught shall go ill; . . . And all shall be well. **1623** CAMDEN 266.

Jack Sprat (Archdeacon Pratt) he loved no fat, and his wife she loved no lean: And yet betwixt them both, they licked the platters clean.

1639 CLARKE 57 Jack will eat no fat and Jill doth love no lean. **1659** HOWELL *Eng. Prov.* 20/1 Archdeacon Pratt would eat no fatt, His wife would eat no lean; Twixt Archdeacon Pratt and Joan his wife, The meat was eat up clean. **1670** RAY 211.

Jack Sprat would teach his grandame.

1639 CLARKE 4 Jack sprat teacheth his grandame. **1670** RAY 108 . . . *Ante barbam doces senes.*

Jack West.

1856 *N. & Q.* 2nd Ser. II. 289 It is common to hear in Hampshire a stye on the eyelid called a *Jack West.*

Jack would be a gentleman if he could speak French.

c. **1515** SKELTON *Coyst.* in *Wks.* (Dyce) I. 16 For Jak wold be a jentylman that late was a grome. **1550** HEYWOOD I. xi. 29. **1662** FULLER (*Berks.*) I. 118 We ape the French . . . in their language ('which if Jack could speak, he would be a gentleman'). **1670** RAY 108 . . . This was a proverb, when the gentry brought up their children to speak French. **1732** FULLER no. 3052.

Jack would be a gentleman if he had money.

1639 CLARKE 98.

Jack would wipe his nose if he had it.

1659 HOWELL *Eng. Prov. Rend. into Fr.* 8. **1670** RAY 108.

Jack's in love, If | he's no judge of Jill's beauty.

1732 FULLER no. 2681.

Jack, *see also* Good J. good Jill; Play the J.; Work and no play makes J. dull boy.

Jackdaw, *see* Says nothing (Though he) . . . like Welshman's j.

Jacks[1] are common to all that will play.

1598 JONSON *Ev. Man in Humour* II. iii *Pros.* I can compare him to nothing more happily than a barber's virginals; for every one may play upon him. **1611** DAVIES *Prov.* 174 'Some Jackes[1] are common to all that will play'. [[1] The parts of virginals which twanged the wires; used for the keys of a musical instrument.]

Jackson, *see* Fly up with J.'s hens.

Jade eats as much as a good horse, A.

1640 HERBERT 342.

Jade, *see also* Better a lean j.

Jam, *see* Powder in j.

James, *see* Friar's beaten (When the), then comes J.; Henry was union of roses, J. of kingdoms.

Janiveer[1] freeze the pot by the fire.

1557 TUSSER in *Brit. Bibliog.* (1812) iii. 20 (A) As Janeuer fryse pot, bidth corne kepe hym lowe. **1670** RAY 40. [[1] January.]

Janiveer sows oats, Who in | gets gold and groats; who sows in May, gets little that way.

1732 FULLER no. 6149. **1813** RAY 36. **1869** HAZLITT (1882) 228 If in January you sow oats, it will bring golden groats.

Janiveer's calends be summerly gay, If | 'twill be winterly weather till the calends of May.

1686–7 J. AUBREY *Rem. Gent. & Jud.* (1881) 7 There is a proverb in Welsh of great antiquity, sc. Haf hyd gatan Gaiaf hyd Fay. That is, if it be somerly weather till the Kalends of January, it will be winterly weather to the Kalends of May. **1732** FULLER no. 6483.

January, A summerish | a winterish spring.

1742 *An Agreeable Companion* 4 It is an ancient Saying, among the Welch, 'If it be Summerly Weather, at the beginning of *January,* it will be Winterly Weather, till the beginning of May'. **1893** INWARDS 10.

January chicks, To have.

1813 RAY 202 To have January chicks. [Ital.] *Aver i pulcini di gen[n]aio.* To have children in old age.

January commits the fault, and May bears the blame.

1659 HOWELL *Ital.–Eng.* 14. **1893** INWARDS 11.

January, Janiveer, Janivere, *see also* Eat a hen in J.; Grass look green in J. (If); March in J., J. in March; May and J.

Jardines, *see* Johnstons.

Jaundiced eye, To the | all things look yellow.

c. **1386** CHAUCER *Mel.* B² 2891 The prophete
seith that 'troubled eyen han no cleer sighte'.
1612 WEBSTER *While Devil* I. ii (Merm.) 12
Cam. The fault . . . is not in the eyesight.
Flam. True; but they that have the yellow
jaundice think all objects they look on to be
yellow. **1660** W. SECKER *Nonsuch Prof.* II.
(1891) 184 Nero thought no person chaste,
because he was so unchaste himself. Such as
are troubled with the jaundice see all things
yellow. **1709** POPE *Ess. Crit.* II. 359 All looks
yellow to the jaundic'd eye.

Jaw (= rush of water), see Jouk and let the j. gae by.

Jaws outrun your claws, Don't let your.

1577 W. HARRISON *Description of Eng.* (New
Sh. S.) i. 151 The artificers in cities and good
townes . . . some of them doo suffer their
iawes to go oft before their clawes. **1917**
BRIDGE 50.

Jay(s), see Cherry-tree sufficeth not two j.

Jealousy, see Frenzy, heresy, and j., seldom cured; Love is never without j.

Jedwood or Jeddart¹ justice.

[= trial after execution.] **1605–9 in** P. H.
BROWN *Hist. Scot.* (1902) II. 263 In associa-
tion with the Earl of Dunbar, who in 1606
was appointed chief Commissioner, [Cran-
stoun] plied his task so effectually that . . .
their work is significantly commemorated in
the Border phrase 'Jeddart Justice'—hang
first and try afterwards. **1706** A. SHIELDS
Eng. Ch. Commun. Pref. 8 Guilty of Couper
Justice and Jedburgh Law as the proverb is.
1828 SCOTT *F. M. Perth* xxxii We will have
Jedwood justice—hang in haste and try at
leisure. **1831** MACAULAY *Essay on Byron's
Life* True Jedwood justice was dealt out to
him. [¹ Jedburgh.]

Jeering Coggeshall.

1662 FULLER (*Essex*) I. 498 'Jeering Coxhall'.
How much truth herein, I am as unable to
tell, as loth to believe. . . . No town in
England, of its bigness, afforded more
martyrs in the reign of queen Mary, who did
not jeer or jest with the fire.

Jenny, see Silly Jockey (Never was) but there was as silly J.

Jeopardy, see Joy (With all your) join your j.

Jerdans, see Johnstons.

Jericho, Go to.

[= get away!] **1575** *Apius and Virginia* D 1
Haue with ye to Jerico. a. **1633** *A Tale of a
Tub* II. iv. 30 An' you say the word, send me
to *Iericho.* **1635** HEYWOOD *Hierarch.* iv. 208
Who would . . . I know. Bid such young
boyes to stay in Iericho Vntill their Beards

were growne, their wits more staid. **1694**
Terence made English 146 Ay let him be
jogging to Jericho for me. **1837–46** BARHAM
Ingol. Leg., Mis. at Margate (1898) 389 She
with her apron wiped the plates, and, as she
rubb'd the delf, Said I might 'go to Jericho,
and fetch my beer myself!'

Jericho, see also Wish one at J.

Jerusalem, see Way to Babylon.

Jest not with the eye, or with religion (honour).

1640 HERBERT 324. **1721** KELLY 64 *Bourd¹
not with my eye, nor with my honour.* Both
these are too tender points to be jested with;
and the honour often more nice than the eye.
[¹ jest.]

Jest, If you give (make) a | you must take a jest.

1738 SWIFT (Dial. i) 338 *Col.* I'll give you as
good as you bring: what! if you give a jest
you must take a jest.

**Jest(s), see also Back broad enough to bear j.;
Better lose a j.; Cream of the j.; Dogs
begin in j. end in earnest; Leave a j. when
pleases best; True word spoken in j.;
Truest j. sound worst in guilty ears. *See
also* Bourd.**

Jesting with edged tools, It is ill. (*See also* Children and fools must not, &c.)

c. **1510** STANBRIDGE *Vulg.* (E.E.T.S.) 20 It is
shrewed to iape with naked swordes. **1588**
GREENE *Pandosto* Pr. Wks. (1881–3) IV. 293
It is ill iesting with edged tooles, and bad
sporting with kinges. **1613** BEAUM. & FL.
Honest M. Fort. II. i I do not love to see a
sword drawn in the hand of a man that looks
so furious, there's no jesting with edge tools.
1623 CAMDEN 272 Its not good iesting with
edg'd tooles. **1662** FULLER (*Westmr.*) II. 413
A place . . . by the Exchequer Court . . .
commonly called Hell; I could wish it had
another name, seeing it is ill jesting with
edge-tools, especially such as are sharpened
by Scripture. **1721** KELLY 267 *No jesting
with edg'd tools.* It is no safe jesting with
powerful men, or sacred things.

Jesting, see also Long j. never good.

Jew, To look like a.

1611 CORYAT *Crudities* (1776) I. 299 Our
English prouerbe: To looke like a Iewe
(whereby is meant sometimes a weather
beaten warp-faced fellow, sometimes a phren-
ticke and lunaticke person, sometimes one
discontented).

Jew's eye, see Worth a J. e.

Jews spend at Easter, The | the Moors at marriages, the Christians in suits.

1640 HERBERT 328. **1651–3** JER. TAYLOR

Sunday Serm. xxi (1850) 585 Is it not a sad thing that . . . it should become a proverb that 'the Jew spends all in his passover, the Moor in his marriage, and the Christian in his lawsuits'?

Jew(s), *see also* Invite not a J. to pig; No J., no wooden shoes; Use one like a J.

Jill *see* Jack and J.; Jack shall have J.

Joan is as good as my lady in the dark.

[Gk. Λύχνου ἀρθέντος, γυνὴ πᾶσα ἡ αὐτή. ERASM. *Ad.* Sublata lucerna nihil interest inter mulieres. When the light is removed, every woman is the same.] *c.* 1530 *Of Gentleness and Nobility* C 1ᵛ As good is the foule as the fayre in the dark. 1594 SHAKS. *L.L.L.* III. i. 207 Some men may love my lady, and some Joan. 1595 *K. John* I. i. 184 Now can I make any Joan a lady. 1599 A. MUNDAY *Joan as good as my Lady* (play-title, Henslowe's *Diary* ed. Greg i. 102). 1601 A. DENT *Plain Man's Pathway* 59. 1620 SHELTON *Quix.* II. xxxiii (1908) III. 55 Here is as good bread made as in France; and in the night Joan is as good as my lady. 1648 HERRICK *Hesper.* 865 Wks. (1893) II. 86 Night makes no difference 'twixt the Priest and Clark; *Jone* as my Lady is as good i' th' dark.

Job's Comforter, A.

[= a comforter who aggravates distress.] 1611 BIBLE *Job* xvi. 1, 2 Then Job answered . . . miserable comforters, are ye all. 1630 BRATHWAIT *Eng. Gent.* (1641) 132 (A) Iob called his friends miserable comforters. 1654 FULLER *Serm., Comfort in Calamity* This *If,* . . . is likely to prove with Job's friend, but a miserable comforter. 1738 SWIFT (Dial. iii) 351 *Lady S.* Your ladyship looks thinner than when I saw you last. *Miss.* Your ladyship is one of Job's comforters. 1836 MARRYAT *Midsh. Easy* xxix You are one of Job's comforters, Martin.

Job, *see also* Patient as J.; Poor as J.

Jock the laird's brother, He is but.

1721 KELLY 139 . . . The Scottish lairds' concern and zeal for the standing and continuance of their families, makes the provision for their younger sons very small.

Jock's news, That is.

1721 KELLY 339 . . . Spoken when people tell that for news which everybody knows.

Jock, *see also* Little J. gets the little dish.

Jockey, *see* Silly J. (Never was) but there was as silly Jenny.

Jogging while your boots are green, Be.

1596 SHAKS. *Tam. Shrew* III. ii. 214 You may be jogging whiles your boots are green. 1777 C. DIBDIN *Quaker* I. i You may as well be jogging, Sir, While yet your boots are green.

John à Cumber, *see* Devil and J.

John-a-dreams.

[= a dreamy fellow.] 1600–1 SHAKS. *Hamlet* II. ii. 603 I . . . peak, Like John-a-dreams, unpregnant of my cause, And can say nothing. 1876 HENLEY *Bk. Verses* (1888) 91 Kate-a-Whimsies, John-a-Dreams, Still debating, still delay.

John-a-droyne.

1562 HEYWOOD 214 Yet hogis head in hogstowne is no Iohn a droyne. 1596 NASHE *Saffron Walden* P j b That poor Iohn a Droynes his man, . . . a great big-boand thresher.

John-a-nods.

[= one who is nodding or not quite awake.] 1603 HARSNET *Pop. Impost.* xxiii. 160 Hee would say The Apostle wrote like a good plain Iohn a nods.

John-a-nokes (i.e. *John* who dwells at the oak).

[A fictitious name for one of the parties in a legal action (usually coupled with *John-a-stiles* as the name of the other); hence sometimes used indefinitely for any individual person.] 1531 *Dial. on Laws Eng.* II. ix. 19 If a man haue lande for terme of lyfe of Iohan at Noke and make a lease. 1581 SIDNEY *Apol. Poetrie* (Arb.) 53 Doth the Lawyer lye then, when vnder the names of Iohn a stile and Iohn a noakes [*Wks.* (1622) 520 Iohn of the Stile, & Iohn of the Nokes] hee puts his case? 1678 MRS. BEHN *Sir Patient Fancy* v Madam, in plain English I am made a John-A-Nokes of. 1815 SCOTT *Guy Man.* xlii Adventurers who are as willing to plead for John o' Nokes as for the first noble of the land.

John-a-stiles.

1531 *Dial. on Laws Eng.* I. vi. 12 If a man be outlawed, and after by his wyll byqueth certayne goodes to Iohn at Style. 1714 *Spectator* No. 577, par. 6 The humble Petition of John a Nokes and John a Stiles, Sheweth, That your Petitioners have had Causes depending in Westminster-Hall above five hundred years.

John Barleycorn.

[= the personified spirit of malt liquor.] *c.* 1620 (*title*) in Pepysian Library, A pleasant new ballad . . . of the bloody murther of Sir John Barleycorn. 1670 RAY 59 Sr John Barley-corn's the strongest knight. 17 . . *John Barleycorn* in PERCY's *Reliques*, John Barleycorn has got a beard Like any other man. 1786 BURNS *Scotch Drink* iii John Barleycorn, Thou king o' grain.

John (Jack) Blunt.

[= a blunt fellow.] 1508 DUNBAR *Twa mariit wemen* 142 For all the buddis of Iohne Blunt, quhen he abone clymis. 1898 *Daily News* 17 Nov. 5/4 He was at once a Jack Blunt and equal to a trick.

John Bull.

[= Englishmen collectively, or the typical Englishman.] 1712 ARBUTHNOT (*title*) Law is a Bottomless Pit. Exemplified in the Case of the Lord Strutt, John Bull, Nicholas Frog and Lewis Baboon: who spent all they had in a Lawsuit. *a.* **1791** BOSWELL *Johnson* xxx (1848) 269 [Johnson] was, indeed, if I may be allowed the phrase, at bottom much of a John Bull: much of a blunt true-born Englishman. **1898** G. W. E. RUSSELL *Coll. & Recoll.* v The typical John Bull—Lord Palmerston's 'Fat man with a white hat in the twopenny omnibus'. **1910** *Times Lit. Sup.* 29 July Our peculiarly English and prosaic idol of John Bull ... is a creation of the English mind in its grossest mood.

John Company.

[A humorous appellation of the East India Company, taken over from the name *Jan Kompanie,* by which the Dutch E.I.C., and now the Dutch Government, are known to natives in the East.] **1785** *Sparrmann's Voy. Cape G. Hope,* &c. x. II. 21 I ordered my interpreter to say farther, that we were the children of *Jan Company,* who had sent us out to view this country. **1808** *Life Ld. Minto in India* (1880) 184 (Y.) Preparations to save Johnny Company's cash. **1893** W. C. RUSSELL *Emigr. Ship* iii One of the handsomest of John Company's ships. **1910** *Times, Wkly.* 21 Jan. Great Moguls who sat on the peacock throne at Delhi ..., till the Mutiny ended them and 'John Company' together.

John Doe and Richard Roe.

[John Doe (*Eng. Law*), the name given to the fictitious lessee of the plaintiff, in the (now obsolete) mixed action of ejectment, the fictitious defendant being called *Richard Roe.*] **1768** BLACKSTONE *Comm.* III. xviii. 274 The security here spoken of ... is at present become a mere form: and John Doe and Richard Roe are always returned as the standing pledges for this purpose. **1841** S. WARREN *Ten Thous. a Year* viii John Doe further says that one Richard Roe (who calls himself—'a Casual Ejector') came and turned him out, and so John Doe brings his action against Richard Roe.

John Drawlatch.

[= thief, loafer, ne'er-do-well.] **1546** HEYWOOD II. viii. 72 Why will ye (quoth he) I shall folow hir will? To make me Iohn drawlache, or such a snekebill.[1] [[1] *sneakbill,* a word of contempt.]

John Grey's bird.

c. **1575** GASCOIGNE *Fruites Warre* cxxxi The Green Knight was amongst the rest Like John Greys bird that ventured with the best.

John (Tom) Long the carrier.

1550 HEYWOOD I. xi I will send it him by John Long the carrier. **16 .** HOWELL *Lett.* 5 June (1903) III. 116 That yours should be a whole month in making scarce 100 English miles ... is strange to me, unless you purposely sent it by John Long the carrier. **1834-7** SOUTHEY *Doctor* iv. 136 Who was Tom Long the carrier? ... what road did he travel?

John o' Groats, *see* Land's End to J. o' G.

John[1] Thomson's man.

[= a man who is guided by his wife.] **1500-20** DUNBAR *Poems* lxii. 4 God gif ȝe war Johne Thomsounis man. **1637** R. MONRO *Exp. Scots Regim.* II. 30 Some will allege, he was Iohn Thomsons man. ... All stories esteeme them happie, that can live together, man and wife, without contention. **1681** S. COLVIL *Whiggs Supp.* I. 18 So the imperious Roxalan, made the Great Turk John Thomson's man. **1721** KELLY 72 *Better be John Tomson's man, than Ring and Dinn's, or John Knox's. John Thomson's man is he that is complaisant to his wife's humours, Ring and Dinn's is he whom his wife scolds, John Knox's is he whom his wife beats.* **1816** SCOTT *Old Mort.* xxxviii D'ye think I am to be John Tamson's man, and maistered by women a' the days o' my life? [[1] Joan.]

John Trot.

[= an uncultured person, bumpkin.] **1753** FOOTE *Eng. in Paris* Epil. The merest John Trot in a week you shall zee *Bien poli, bien frizé.* **1762** COLMAN *Mus. Lady* II. i Our travelling gentry ... return from the tour of Europe as mere English boors as they went— John Trot still. **1827** HOOD *John Trot* (Ballad) John Trot he was as tall a lad As York did ever rear.

Johnny Newcome.

1837 CHAMIER *Saucy Areth.* xv You always know a Johnny Newcome by his getting his back to the breeze.

Johnny Raw.

1813 COL. HAWKER *Diary* (1893) I. 68 A grand attack was made on the Johnny raws of Blandford. **1823** in HONE *Every-day Bk.* II. 1395. There were some Johnny Raws on board. **1886** STEVENSON *Kidnapped* (1888) 39 You took me for a country Johnnie Raw, with no more mother-wit or courage than a porridge-stick.

Johnson, *see* Venture it, as J. did his wife.

Johnstons, We are as many | as you are Jerdans (Jardines).

1721 KELLY 347 ... Taken from two families who were always on one side; though now the proverb signifies that we have as many to take our part, as you have to take yours, yet I am inclined to believe that at first it signified that we contribute as much to the common cause as you do. **1832** HENDERSON 140 There's as mony Johnstones as Jardines. (As many on one side as on the other.)

Joint-stool, *see* Cry you mercy, I took you for j.

Joke breaks no bones, A.

1819 BYRON *Wks.* 748 A joke, the proverb says, breaks no bones; but it may break a bookseller.

Jollity but hath a smack of folly, There is no.

1640 HERBERT 340.

Jolly, *see* Over j. dow not.

Jolly Robins, *see* Head's running upon J. R.

Jommetry, *see* Hangs by j.

Jouk[1] and let the jaw[2] gae (gang) by.

1721 KELLY 189 *Juck, and let a jaw go o'er you.* That is, prudently yield to a present torrent. **1818** SCOTT *Rob Roy* xxv Gang your ways hame, like a gude bairn—jouk[1] and let the jaw[2] gae by. [[1] stoop. [2] rush of water.]

Journey(s), *see* Begin a j. on Sunday; Companion in a long j. (A man knows his); Great j. to world's end; Little j. . . . bring safe home; Long j. (In a) straw weighs; Meat and matins hinder no j.; Prayers and provender hinder no j.; Sports and j. men are known (In); World is long j.

Jove (Jupiter) laughs at lovers' perjuries.

[TIBULLUS 3. 6. 49 *Periuria ridet amantum Jupiter.* OVID *A.A.* 1. 633 *Jupiter ex alto periuria ridet amantum.*] **1567** *Lady Lucres* in *Plasidas*, &c. (Roxb. Cl.) 143 (A) Jupiter rather laughethe then takethe angerlye the periurynge of louers. **1580** GREENE *Mamillia* in Wks. (Gros.) II. 92 Dooe not the Gods, saye the Poets, laugh at the periurie of Louers? and that Iupiter smyles at the crafte of Cupyd. **1594–5** SHAKS. *Rom. & Jul.* II. ii. 92 At lovers' perjuries, They say, Jove laughs. **1700** DRYDEN *Pal. & Arcite* II. 140 And Jove but laughs at lovers' perjury!

Joy, With all your | join all your jeopardy.

1546 HEYWOOD II. xi. 83.

Joy of the heart makes the face merry, The.

1601 T. WRIGHT *The Passions of the Mind* 50 According to the old prouerb, *Cor gaudens exhilerat faciem,* a rejoycing heart maketh merry the face. **1611** DAVIES *Prov.* 224 The ioy of the heart fairly coulors the face. **1629** *Book of Meery Riddles* Prov. 54 The heart's mirth doth make the face fayre. **1616** DRAXE 130.

Joy without annoy (alloy), No.

[L. *Extrema gaudii luctus occupat.* Grief borders on the extremes of gladness.] c. **1386** CHAUCER *Nun's Priest's T.* B[2] 3205 For evere the latter ende of joye is wo. **1639** CLARKE 134. **1855** BOHN 524 There is no joy without alloy.

Joy(s), *see also* Hunting, hawking . . . for one j. hundred displeasures; One year of j.; Sorrow (Of thy) be not . . . of thy j. be not too glad; Weep for j. is kind of manna.

Judas kiss, A.

1382 WYCLIF *Luke* xxii. 48 And Jhesus seide to hym, Judas, with a Coss thou bytrayest mannys son. c. **1548** BALE *K. Johan* 2109 A false Judas kysse he hath gyven and is gone. **1618** J. FLETCHER *Loy. Subj.* IV. vi The Judas way, to kiss me, bid me welcome, And cut my throat. **1865** DICKENS *Our Mut. Fr.* III. v Sophronia . . . found it necessary to . . . give Bella a kiss. A Judas order of kiss.

Judas might have repented before he could have found a tree to have hanged himself upon, had he betrayed Christ in Scotland.

1659 HOWELL *Eng. Prov.* 21/1.

Judge but himself, He who will have no | condemns himself.

1707 MAPLETOFT 12. **1855** BOHN 401.

Judge conceives quickly, judges slowly, A good.

c. **1386** CHAUCER *Mel.* B[2] 2221 And eek men seyn that thilke iuge is wys that soone understandeth a matiere and juggeth by leyser. **1640** HERBERT 345.

Judge from appearances, Never.

1526 TINDALE *John* vii. 24 Judge not after the vtter aperaunce, but iudge rightewes iudgement. **1890** MONTAGU WILLIAMS *Leaves of a L.* xx (1893) 144 Little did the audience know what subsequently transpired as to her character. . . . She wore . . . every appearance of innocence, but in her person she illustrated the truth of the old adage that one should not judge by appearances. **1896** J. C. HUTCHESON *Crown & Anchor* xv I learnt . . . not to judge by appearances and from hasty conclusions as to the character of my messmates.

Judge in his own cause, No man ought to be.

1845 H. BROOM *Legal Maxims* 418 It is unreasonable, that, if wrong be done to a man, he should be his own judge thereof, according to the maxim, *nemo debet esse judex in propriâ causâ.* **1928** *Times,* 22 Aug. 9/4 The principle that no judge could be a judge in his own case was generally accepted. The chairman of a meeting was in a quasi-judicial capacity.

Judge not, that ye be not judged.

1611 BIBLE *Matt.* vii. 1 Judge not, that ye be not judged. **1925** A. CLUTTON-BROCK *Ess. on Life* x. 109 The saying, 'Judge not, that ye be not judged', is . . . a statement of fact. Nothing makes us dislike a man so much as the knowledge that he is always judging us and all men.

Judges others, Who | condemns himself.

1882 W. BESANT *All Sorts* xlv Aurelia . . . says she is afraid that splendour may make me forget old friends; . . . perhaps she judged others by herself.

Judges' wigs.

1823 COBBETT *Rural Rides* 2 Aug. I saw . . . several parcels of those white, curled clouds that we call *Judges' Wigs.*

Judge(s), *see also* Father is j. (He whose) goes safe to trial; Grave as j.; Put off the person of a j.

Judgement, *see* Good j. that relieth not on his own.

Juice, *see* Fry (Stew) in their own grease (j.).

July, *see* First of J. it be rainy (If); No tempest, good J.; Shower in J. . . . worth plow of oxen.

Jump¹ (*or* Just) as German's lips, As.

1546 HEYWOOD II. ii. 46 The hen (quoth she) the cocke (quoth he) iust (quoth she) As Iermans lips. **1579** GOSSON *Sch. Abuse* (Arb.) 27 Shall see them agree like Dogges and Cattes, and meete as iump as Germans lippes. **1659** HOWELL *Eng. Prov.* 3/1 As just as Jerman's lips; *spoken in derision.* [¹ exactly (here used in sarcasm).]

Jump (*or* leap) at it like a cock at a gooseberry, To.

1813 SCOTT *Let. to Southey* 4 Sept. in LOCK-HART *Life* XXVI I . . . beg you think before you reject the offer . . . I should have jumped at it like a cock at a gooseberry. **1824** Id. *St. Ronan's* ii He just jumped at the ready penny, like a cock at a grosert.¹ **1836** M. SCOTT *Cruise of Midge* viii Ancient maidens, who at forty loup like a cock at a grousart¹ . . . at the *homo* they turned up their noses at at twenty. [¹ gooseberry.]

Jump, *see also* Broomstick (To j. the).

June, *see* Calm weather in J. sets corn in tune; Dry May and dripping J.; Eighth of J. it rain (If) foretells wet harvest.

Jupiter, *see* Far from J. far from thunder.

Jury, *see* London j. hang half, save half.

Just as a square, As.

[= as exact as a measuring-square.] *c.* **1386** CHAUCER *Sum. T.* 2090 Thou shalt me fynde as just as is a squyre.

Just before you are generous, Be.

1777 SHERIDAN *Sch. for Scandal* IV. i 'Be just before you're generous'.—Why, so I would if I could. **1833** MARRYAT *P. Simple* xi I owe every farthing of my money. . . . There's an old proverb—be just before you're generous. **1908** *Spectator* 4 Apr. A likeable man is tempted to be generous before he is just.

Just war is better than an unjust peace, A.

[TAC. *Ann. Miseram pacem vel bello bene mutari.* For the opposite see CIC. *ad Fam.* 6. 6. 5 *Vel iniquissimam pacem iustissimo bello antiferrem.*] **1595** DANIEL *Civ. Wars* I. 73 Since wise men ever have preferred farre Th' unjustest peace before the justest warre. **1605** DANIEL *Ulys. & Siren* For oft we see a wicked peace To be well chang'd for war. **1629** T. ADAMS *Serm.* (1862) II. 87 There is enough in every man to keep him from idleness; if at least he do not prefer an unjust peace to a just war.

Justice pleaseth few in their own house.

1640 HERBERT 336.

Justice, *see also* Basket-justice will do j.; Buyeth magistracy must sell j.; Clerk makes the j.; Much law little j.; Poetical j.

K

Ka me, ka thee.

[= implies mutual help, or mutual flattery.] **1550** HEYWOOD I. xi. 34 Ka me, ka the, one good tourne askth an other. **1608** ARMIN *Nest Nin.* (Shak. Soc.) 34 Kay me I'll kay thee; give me an inch to-day I'll give thee an ell to-morrow. *a.* **1658** FORD, &c. *Witch Edmonton* II. i If you'll be so kind to ka me one good turn, I'll be so courteous to kob you another. **1721** KELLY 227 *Kae me, and I'll kae thee.* Spoken when great people invite and feast one another, and neglect the poor. **1821** SCOTT *Kenilw.* v Bear this in upon her . . . and let me alone for extolling you in her ear . . . *Ka me, ka thee.* **1823** BYRON *Juan* XI. lxxviii Caw me, caw thee.

Kae, *see* Woe worth ill company, quoth the k.

Kail spares bread.

1641 FERGUSSON 70. **1721** KELLY 227 *Kail hains¹ bread.* Good broth will, in some measure, supply the want of bread. [¹ saves.]

Kail through the reek, To give one his.

[= to let a person 'have it'.] **1757** SMOLLETT *Reprisal* II. i *Macl.* Guid faith! you and I

man ha' our kail through the reek. **1816** SCOTT *Old Mort.* xiv When my mither and him forgathered they set till the sodgers, and I think they gae them their kale through the reek! **1836** M. SCOTT *Cruise of Midge* xi Was it not a proud thing for a parritch-fed laddie . . . to gie them their kail through the reek, and cry 'anathema marantha' against the vices of the rich.

Kail, *see also* Cauld k. het again; Good k. is half a meal; Sup k. with him (He would not).

Kalends, *see* Calends.

Keep a calm sough.

[= say little or nothing.] **1820** SCOTT *Abbot* xvii Keep a calm sough, as the Scots say —hear every man's counsel, and keep your own. **1823** J. GALT *Entail* xx I'll keep a calm sough—least said's soonest mendit—I'll haud my tongue. **1880** MRS. LYNN LINTON *Rebel Family* xiii Keeping a calm sough was the best wisdom.

Keep a dog and bark myself, I will not.

1583 MELBANCKE *Philotimus* 119 It is smal

reason you should kepe a dog, and barke your selfe. **1670** RAY 81 What? Keep a *dog* and bark myself. That is, must I keep servants, and do my work myself. **1721** KELLY 203 . . . If I keep servants, they shall do my work for me. **1738** SWIFT (Dial. i) 334 *Lady A.* Good miss, stir the fire. . . . *Miss.* Indeed, your ladyship could have stirred it much better. *Lady A.* . . . I won't keep a dog and bark myself.

Keep a man out of the mud, The way to | is to black his boots.

1909 M. LOANE *An Englishman's Cas.* vii Mothers firmly believe in the old saying, 'The way to keep a man out of the mud is to black his boots', and always dress their sons as well as they possibly can.

Keep a penny, Who will not | never shall have many.

1639 CLARKE 129.

Keep a thing seven years and you will find a use for it.

1663 KILLIGREW *Parson's Wedding* II. vii (A) According to the proverb, keep a thing seven years, and then if thou hast no use on't, throw't away. **1826** SCOTT *Woodst.* xxviii Two lines of Horace, which I have carried in my thick head several years, . . . have come pat to my purpose. . . . If you keep a thing seven years you are sure to find a use for it at last. **1863** C. READE *Hard Cash* xxix It is the very thing . . . I . . . put it away, and forgot it. They say if you keep a thing seven years.

Keep Bayard[1] in the stable, To.

c. **1400** *Beryn* (E.E.T.S.) l. 3183 Ful trewe is that byword, 'a man to seruesabill, Ledith offt[e] beyard [Bayard] from his owne stabill.' **1546** HEYWOOD I. xii. 39 Their landlorde came to their house to take a stresse For rent, to haue kept Bayard in the stable. **1623** CAMDEN 273. [[1] a (bay) horse.]

Keep cold, *see* Have to say (What you) will k. c.

Keep counsel, Three (Two) may | if two (one) be away.

c. **1400** *Rom. Rose* 2529 For tweyne of noumbre is bet than thre In every counsell and secre. **1546** HEYWOOD II. v. 53 We twayne are one to many (quoth I) for men say, Thrée maie a kepe counsayle, if two be away. *c.* **1558** W. WEDLOCKE *Image of Idlenesse* (1574) F 1ᵛ The common Prouerb . . . two may chaunce to keep councel but the third neuer. **1578** WHETSTONE *Promos & Cassandra* E 3ᵛ. **1579** LYLY *Euphues* (Arb.) 67 I would haue swallowed mine own sorrow in silence, knowing . . . that two may keepe counsaile if one be away. **1593–4** SHAKS. *Titus Andron.* IV. ii. 145 Two may keep counsel when the third's away . . . [*stabbing her*]. **1594–5** *Rom. & Jul.* II. iv. 211 Is your man secret? Did you ne'er hear say, Two may keep counsel, putting one away? **1640** HERBERT 350 Three can hold their peace if two be away. **1670**

RAY 148 Three may keep counsel, if two be away. The French say, Secret de deux secret de Dieu, secret de trois secret de tous.

Keep good men company, and you shall be of the number.

1640 HERBERT 322.

Keep Hilary term, To.

[= to be cheerful or merry.] **1629** T. ADAMS *Serm.* (1861–2) I. 68 This joy . . . overcomes the world, nonsuits the devil, and makes a man keep Hilary-term all his life.

Keep my mind to myself, and tell my tale to the wind, I will.

1721 KELLY 182 . . . I will . . . conceal my resentments; but I will watch an opportunity for retaliation.

Keep no more cats than will catch mice, I will.

1678 RAY (*Somerset*) 350 I will keep no more cats then will catch mice (*i.e.* no more in family then will earn their living). **1861** C. READE *Cloister & H.* lii Now, Martin, you must help. I'll no more cats than can slay mice. **1898** F. T. BULLEN '*Cachalot*' 25 In the ordinary merchantman there are decidedly 'no more cats than can catch mice'.

Keep not ill men company, lest you increase the number.

1640 HERBERT 332.

Keep off and give fair words.

1818 SCOTT *Rob Roy* xxvi He tried if Mac Vittie and Co. wad gie him siller on them— but . . . they keepit aff, and gae fair words.

Keep one head for the reckoning, It is good to.

1573 *New Custom* III. i. in HAZL. *O.E.P.* (1874) III. 43 *Perv. Doc.* But, as the proverb saith, it is good to keep still One head for the reckoning, both sober and wise.

Keep one's head above water, To.

[= to avoid ruin by a continued struggle.] **1742** FIELDING *J. Andrews* III. xiii If I can hold my head above water it is all I can. **1809** MALKIN *Gil Blas* v. i, par. 7 To carry me discreetly through the world, and keep my head above water. **1860** SURTEES *Plain or Ring?* xxxix I'm . . . just able by the greatest caution and prudence to keep my head above water and no more.

Keep one's own counsel, To.

1598–9 SHAKS. *Much Ado* III. iii. 91 Keep your fellows' counsels and your own. **1600–1** *Hamlet* IV. ii. 11 That I can keep your counsel and not mine own. **1639** CLARKE 67 Keep counsell first thy selfe. **1711** ADDISON *Spect.* No. 12, par. 1 I am the best Man in the World to keep my own Counsel. **1855** MACAULAY *Hist. Eng.* IV. 584 William kept his own counsel so well that not a hint of his intention got abroad.

Keep one's tongue within one's teeth, To.

1660 TATHAM *Rump.* I. i (1879) 212 You know, my lord, I can keep my tongue within my teeth sometimes. **1721** KELLY 225.

Keep out of a hasty man's way for a while; out of a sullen man's all the days of your life.

1855 BOHN 436.

Keep sheep by moonlight, To.

[= to be hanged in chains.] **1898** A. E. HOUSMAN *Shropsh. Lad* ix [Lads] That shepherded the moonlit sheep A hundred years ago.

Keep sheep, *see also* Who wats who may k. s.

Keep some till furthermore come.

1670 RAY 110.

Keep something for him that rides on the white horse.[1] (*Cf.* Save something for the man, &c.)

1721 KELLY 226. (Given as *English.*) [[1] age, distress, and necessity.]

Keep something for the sore foot.

1721 KELLY 226 . . . Preserve something for age, distress, and necessity. **1830** CARLETON *Traits &c., Three Tasks* Jack would feel a little consarn for not being able to lay past anything for the *sore foot.*

Keep the keepers? Who shall.

[JUVENAL *Sat.* 6. 347 *Quis custodiet ipsos custodes?*] *c.* **1550** POPE PIUS II, *Goodly History of the Lady Lucres* (1560) D 2 (cited in E.E.T.S. ed. of Boorde's *Introduction,* p. 342) In vayne doth the husband set kepers ouer her; for who shal kepe those kepers? **1567** *Plasidas,* &c. (Roxb. Cl.) 132 (as previous quotation). **1611** JONSON *Catiline* III. i. 108 And watch the watcher. **1732** FULLER no. 5718 Who shall keep the keepers?

Keep the pot boiling.

1825 BROCKETT *N. C. Gloss., Keep-the-pot-boiling,* a common expression among young people, when they are anxious to carry on their gambols with spirit. **1837** DICKENS *Pickwick* xxx Mr. Pickwick . . . went slowly and gravely down the slide . . . 'Keep the pot a bilin', sir!' said Sam.

Keep the staff in your own hand.

1737 RAMSAY III. 188.

Keep the wolf from the door, To.

[= to avert starvation.] *a.* **1529** SKELTON *Col. Cloute* 152–5 Lyke Aaron and Ure,[1] The wolfe from the dore To werryn[2] and to kepe From theyr goostly shepe. **1546** HEYWOOD II. vii. 68 I would haue ye stur Honestly, to kepe the wolfe from the dur. **1645** HOWELL *Lett.* 28 Apr. (1903) I. 99 *He* or *she* should have wherewith to support both, . . . at least to keep the wolf from the door, otherwise it were a mere madness to marry. **1885**

J. ORMSBY *Don Quixote* I Introd. 30 [Cervantes] married . . . a lady . . . who brought him a fortune which may possibly have served to keep the wolf from the door, but if so, that was all. [[1] Hur. [2] guard.]

Keep thy shop and thy shop will keep thee.

1605 CHAPMAN, &c. *Eastw. Hoe* I. 1 *Touch.* I . . . garnished my shop . . . with thrifty sentences; as, 'Touchstone, keep thy shop, and thy shop will keep thee'. **1712** *Spectator* 14 Oct. [He, Sir W. Turner] would say, *keep your Shop, and your Shop will keep you.* **1759** GOLDSMITH *Bee* vii I would earnestly recommend this adage to every mechanic in London, 'Keep your shop, and your shop will keep you'. **1831** MACAULAY *Ess., Boswell's Johnson* Richardson, like a man of sense, kept his shop; and his shop kept him.

Keep your ain fish-guts to your ain sea-maws.[1]

1721 KELLY 118 *Give your own sea maws your own fish guts.* If you have any superfluities give them to your poor relations, friends, or countrymen, rather than to others. **1816** SCOTT *Antiq.* xv My gude man likes to ride the expresses himsell: we maun gie our ain fish-guts to our ain sea-maws. It's a red half-guinea to him every time he munts his mear. **1857** DEAN RAMSAY *Remin.* v (1911) 197 . . . This was a favourite proverb with Scott when he meant to express the policy of first considering the interests that are nearest home. [[1] gulls.]

Keep (Save) your breath (wind) to cool your broth (porridge).

1599 PORTER *Angry Wom. Abingd.* II. i (Merm.) 127 *Nich.* You may speak when you are spoken to, and keep your wind to cool your pottage. **1605** CHAPMAN, &c. *Eastw. Hoe* III. ii *Touch.* My speeches were ever in vain . . . ; and therefore, . . . I will save my breath for my broth anon. **1721** KELLY 229 *Keep your breath to cool your brose.* Spoken to them who talk much to little purpose. **1738** SWIFT (Dial. i) 337 *Miss.* Pray keep your breath to cool your porridge. **1796** EDGEWORTH *Par. Asst.* (1903) 262 None of your flummery stuff will go down with his worship . . . ; so you may . . . spare your breath to cool your porridge. **1813** J. AUSTEN *Pride & Prej.* vi (1895) 21 There is a very fine old saying, . . . 'Keep your breath to cool your porridge', and I shall keep mine to swell my song. **1816** SCOTT *Old Mort.* xxxv Hold your peace and keep your ain breath to cool your ain porridge.

Keep your eyes wide open before marriage, and half shut afterwards.

1738 FRANKLIN June Keep your eyes wide open before marriage, half shut afterwards.

Keep your feet dry, and your head hot; and for the rest live like a beast.

1603 FLORIO tr. *Montaigne* II. xii (1897) III.

242 This common saying is always in the people's mouth: *Tenez chauds les pieds et la teste, Au demeurant vivez en beste.* (With marginal gloss: JOUBERT *Err. Pop.* [1570] pur. ii. pag. 140 Keepe warme (t'is meete) thy head and feete: In all the rest, live like a beast). **1678** RAY 42 Asciuto il piede calda la testa, e dal resto vive da bestia, i.e. *Keep your feet dry and your head hot, and for the rest live like a beast.*

Keep your mouth shut and your eyes open.

1710 S. PALMER *Moral Essays on Prov.* 143 (A). **1737** RAMSAY III. 188 Keep your mouth close an' your een open.

Keep your pecker[1] up.

1853 'C. BEDE' *Verdant Green* I. xii Keep your pecker up. **1857** DICKENS *Lett.* 17 Aug. Keep your pecker up with that. [[1] courage, resolution.]

Keep your weather-eye open.

1867 ADML. SMYTH *Sailor's Word-Bk.* 724 Keep your weather-eye open', be on your guard; look out for squalls.

Keep yourself from the anger of a great man, from the tumult of a mob, from a man of ill fame, from a widow that has been thrice married, from a wind that comes in at a hole, and from a reconciled enemy.

1707 MAPLETOFT 67. **1855** BOHN 437.

Keep(s), kept, *see also* Counsel thou wouldest another k., k. thyself; Gets doth much, . . . k. doth more; Hath it and will not k. it; Wife that k. her supper . . . died ere day.

Keeping is harder than winning.

c. **1374** CHAUCER *Troylus* III. 1634 As gret a craft is kepé wel as winne.

Keeps another man's dog, He that | shall have nothing left him but the line.

1623 CAMDEN 270. **1670** RAY 81 . . . This is a Greek proverb. *Ὃς κύνα τρέφει ξένον τούτῳ μόνον λίνος μένει.* The meaning is, that he who bestows a benefit upon an ungrateful person loses his cost. For if a dog break lose, he presently gets him home to his former master, leaving the cord he was tied with.

Keeps company with the wolf, Who | will learn to howl.

1591 FLORIO *Second Frutes* 57 (A) Who is bread among wolfes will learn to houle. **1670** RAY 30.

Keeps his own, He that | makes war.

1640 HERBERT 356.

Keeps his road well enough who gets rid of bad company, He.

1707 MAPLETOFT 2. **1855** BOHN 378.

Keeps, *see also* Keep(s).

Keer, *see* Kent and K.

Kelly, *see* King may come to K.

Kenned folks are nae company.

1737 RAMSAY III. 128.

Kenned, *see also* Little k. less cared for.

Kennel, *see* Look not for musk in a k.

Kennington, *see* Naughty Ashford.

Kens his groats among other folk's kail, He.

1641 FERGUSSON 50 *Of weillie persons.* . . . He kens his groats among other folks kail. **1721** KELLY 153 . . . Spoken of those who are sharp and sagacious in knowing their own. **1857** DEAN RAMSAY *Remin.* vi (1911) 238 An old lady . . . from whom the 'Great Unknown[1]' had derived many an ancient tale, . . . protested, 'D'ye think, sir, I dinna ken my ain groats in ither folk's kail?' [[1] Scott.]

Kent and Keer[1] have parted many a good man and his mere.

1873 HARLAND & WILKINSON *Lancashire Leg.* 193 Kent and Keer Have parted many a good man and his mere [mare] . . . Many have perished in fording both rivers when swollen, and in crossing the adjacent sands. [[1] Two rivers flowing into Morecambe Bay.]

Kent, Some places of | have health and no wealth, some wealth and no health, some health and wealth, some have neither health nor wealth.

1586 CAMDEN *Brit., Kent* (1722) I. 215 The Inhabitants, . . . distinguish it into three . . portions . . . the *upper*, lying upon the Thames, . . . healthy, but not altogether so rich; the *middle*, . . . both healthy and rich; the *lower*, . . . rich, but withal unhealthy, because of the wet marshy soil. **1659** HOWELL *Eng. Prov.* 20/2 **1678** RAY 315 Some part of *Kent* hath *health and no wealth*, viz. East *Kent*. Some *wealth and no health*, viz. The weald of *Kent*. Some both *health and wealth*, viz. the middle of the Country and parts near *London*.

Kent nor Christendom, Neither in.

c. **1492** Carol (R. L. GREENE *Early English Carols* 4) Come thou no more here nor in Kent. *a.* **1542** SIR T. WYATT Satire I But here I am in Kent and Christendom. **1579** SPENSER *Shep. Cal.* Sept. (Kelmscott) 69 Hob. Sith the Saxon king Never was woolfe seene, many nor some, Nor in all Kent, nor in Christendome. **1662** FULLER (*Kent*) II. 122 'Neither in Kent nor Christendom'. . . . This home proverb . . . ought to be restrained to English Christendom, whereof Kent was first converted to the faith. So then Kent and Christendom (parallel to Rome and Italy) is as much as the first cut, and all the loaf besides. **1876** W. W. SKEAT in PEGGE *Kenticisms*

(E.D.S.) 62 [*Neither in Kent nor Christendom.*]
Kent is obviously singled out as containing
the metropolis (Canterbury) of all English
Christendom.

Kentchester Hill, *see* Sutton Wall.

Kentish Cousins.

1736 s. PEGGE *Kenticisms, Prov.* (E.D.S.) 64
Kentish Cousins. The sense of this is . . .
cousins germans quite remov'd. . . . The
inhabitants are kept at home more than they
are in the inland counties. This confinement
naturally produces intermarriages amongst
themselves.

Kentish Longtails.

c. **1600** DELONEY *Wks.* (Mann) 383 (A) The
valiant courage and policie of the Kentish-
men with long tayles. **1613–22** DRAYTON
Polyolb. xxiii. 237 (1876) III. 95 *Kent* first in
our account, doth to itself apply, (Quoth he)
this Blazon first, *Long Tails and Liberty.*
1617 MORYSON *Itin.* III. i. 53 (1907–8) III. 463
The Kentish men of old were said to have
tails, because trafficing in the Low Countries,
they never paid full payments of what they
did owe, but still left some part unpaid. **1662**
FULLER (*Kent*) II. 123 'Kentish long-tails' . . .
To come closer to . . . this proverb, I conceive
it first of outlandish extraction, and cast by
foreigners as a note of disgrace on all the
English, though it chanceth to stick only on
the Kentish at this day.

Kent, -ish, *see also* Essex stiles, K. miles;
Great as the devil and the Earl of K.;
Knight of Cales; Lithe as a lass of K.;
Men of K.

Kentshire, hot as fire.

1736 s. PEGGE *Kenticisms, Prov.* (E.D.S.) 61
Kentshire, Hoot as fyre. . . . This country is
remarkably hot on account of its chalk hills
and chalky as well as gravelly roads.

Kernel, *see* Eat the k. must crack nut.

Kettle (*proper name*), *see* But when? quoth K.

Kettle of fish, A pretty (fine).

[= a muddle, or awkward state of things.]
1742 FIELDING *J. Andrews* I. xii 'Here's a
pretty kettle of fish', cries Mrs. Tow-wouse.
1800 WELLINGTON *Let. to Close* 2 Oct. in
GURW. *Desp.* (1837) I. 245 If so, we shall
have a fine kettle of fish at Seringapatam.

Kettle, *see also* Frying-pan said to k.,
'Avaunt . . .'; Pot and k.; Simpers like a
furmity k. *See also* Brass kettle.

Kevel, *see* Happy man, happy k.

Kex, *see* Dry as a k.

Keys hang not at one man's girdle, All the.

c. **1400** MS. *Latin no.* 394, *J. Rylands Libr.*
(ed. Pantin) in *Bull. J.R. Libr.* XIV f. 3v
Not all keyes hongen atte oo wyues gyrdell.
1546 HEYWOOD I. xi. 30 The kays hang not all

by one mans gyrdell man. **1579** GOSSON *Sch.
Abuse* (Arb.) 45 But all the keyes hang not at
one man's girdle. **1641** FERGUSSON 8 All the
keys of the countrey hangs not at ane belt.
1721 KELLY 62 *All the keys of the world hings
not at your belt.* Spoken to those who refuse
us their help, . . . intimating that others may
afford what they deny us.

Keys in the bunch, He tries all the.

1616 DRAXE 189 s.v. 'Shifting'.

Key(s), *see also* Good wife's away (When) k.
are tint; Kit hath lost her k.; Like punishment . . . k. and keyhole sustain; Silver k.
open iron lock; Used k. always bright.

Keystone under the hearth, key-stone under the horse's belly.

1863 J. R. WISE *New Forest* (1895) xv. 170
The smuggler's real proverb, 'Keystone
under the hearth, keystone under the horse's
belly'. That is to say, the smuggled spirits
were concealed either below the fireplace or
in the stable, just beneath where the horse
stood.

Kick against the prick(s),[1] To.

[= to resist to one's own hurt. *Acta apost.*
ix. 5 *Durum est contra stimulum calcitrare.*]
c. **1300** *Cursor M.* 1. 19626 Hit is to þe ful
harde & wik for to wirk a-gaine þe prik. **1380**
WYCLIF *Acts* ix. 5 It is hard to thee: to kike
aȝens the pricke. *c.* **1380** CHAUCER *Truth* l. 11
And eek be war to sporne ageyn an al. *c.* **1390**
GOWER *Conf. Amantis* III. 16 And thus myn
hand again the pricke I hurte. *c.* **1430** LYD-
GATE *Pilgr. Life of Man* (E.E.T.S.) 390,
l. 14459 Hard ys to sporne ageyn an hal.
1546 HEYWOOD II. v. 55 Foly it is to spourne
against a pricke. **1641** FERGUSSON 64 It is
hard to fling at the brod[1] or kick at the prick.
a. **1677** BARROW *Serm.* III. 394 To blow
against the wind, to kick against the pricks.
1926 *Times* 29 June 17/3 The West Ham
Board of Guardians persist in kicking against
the pricks. [[1] goad.]

Kick an attorney downstairs and he'll stick to you for life.

1902–4 LEAN IV. 24. (A Bar proverb.)

Kick down the ladder, To.

1655 FULLER *Ch. Hist.* v. iii (1868) II. 65
[Polydore Virgil] is said to have burned all
those rare authors, which he could compass
into his possession. Thus . . . he cut down
those stairs whereby he ascended the throne
of his own knowledge. **1794** NELSON in
NICOLAS *Disp.* (ed. 2) I. 449 Duncan is, I
think, a little altered; there is nothing like
kicking down the ladder a man rises by. **1848**
THACKERAY *Book of Snobs* vii (1872) 27 She
has struggled so gallantly for polite reputation that she has won it: pitilessly kicking
down the ladder as she advanced degree by
degree. **1882** s. R. GARDINER *Introd. Eng.
Hist.* 68 The Great Council . . . might be
inclined, if they proved successful, to kick
over the ladder by which they had risen to
power.

Kick in one's gallop, To have a.

1809 MALKIN *Gil Blas.* III x My fairy queen, . . . you have an ugly kick in your gallop. I have observed you with the players. **1836** M. SCOTT *Cruise of Midge* i A grapeshot . . . had shattered his left thigh, and considerably shortened it, thereby giving him a kick in his gallop.

Kick of the dam hurts not the colt, The.

1732 FULLER no. 4611.

Kick one's heels, To.

[= to stand waiting idly or impatiently.] **1760** FOOTE *Minor* II (1781) 51 To let your uncle kick his heels in your hall. **1833** MARRYAT *P. Simple* xiii I'll trouble him [not] to leave me here kicking my heels.

Kick over the traces, To.

[= to throw off the usual restraints.] **1861** H. KINGSLEY *Ravenshoe* xlii I'll go about with the rogue. He is inclined to kick over the traces. **1876** L. STEPHEN *Hours in Library* II. 354 The effervescence of genius which drives men to kick over the traces of respectability.

Kick the beam, To.

1667 MILTON *Par. Lost* IV. 1004 The latter quick up flew and kickt the beam. **1712** ADDISON *Spect.* No. 463 The latter, to show its comparative lightness, immediately flew up and kickt the Beam.

Kick the bucket, To.

[The beam on which a slaughtered pig is suspended by the heels is called in Norfolk a 'bucket', hence the phrase signifies 'to die'.] **1785** GROSE *Dict. Vulg. T.* s.v. *To kick the bucket*, to die. **1806** WOLCOT (P. Pindar) *Tristia* Wks. (1816) IV. 309 Pitt has kick'd the bucket. **1810** TANNAHILL *Poems* (1846) 57 Till time himsel' turn auld and kick the bucket. **1899** W. P. RIDGE *Son of the State* xi A man that's getting near to kicking the bucket can't be too cautious of what he says.

Kick the wind, To.

1598 FLORIO *Worlde of Wordes* 96/1 *Dar de' calci a Rouaio*, to be hang'd, to kicke the winde.

Kick(s), *see also* Ass k. you (When), never tell; Monkey's allowance, more k. than halfpence.

Kid in her kilting,[1] She has got a.

1721 KELLY 300 . . . That is, she has got a bastard about her. [[1] trussed-up petticoats.]

Kid that keeps above is in no danger of the wolf, The.

1732 FULLER no. 4612.

Kid, *see also* Dam leaps over (Where), k. follows; Piece of a k. worth two of a cat.

Kilkenny cats, *see* Fight like K. c.

Kill a man for a mess of mustard, He will.

1555 HEYWOOD *Epigr. upon Prov.* no. 207.

Kill a man with a cushion, To.

1616 WITHALS 575. **1639** CLARKE 310. **1670** RAY 218.

Kill a pig every day, We don't.

1877 E. PEACOCK *Gloss. of Lincolnshire Wds.* (1889) 403 'We don't kill a *pig* every day', that is, we have not every day a merrymaking.

Kill another in jest and be hanged in earnest, A man may.

1599 PORTER *Angry Wom. Abingd.* v. 1 (Merm.) 192 Hear, and make an end; you may kill one another in jest, and be hanged in earnest.

Kill hogs, He who does not | will not get black puddings.

1855 BOHN 399. *Span.*

Kill the Danes, It would.

1842 LEVER *Jack Hinton* xlviii Comfortable! The ways of this place would kill the Danes! Nothing but ringing bells from morning till night: carriages drivin' like wind up to the door.

Kill the fatted calf, To.

1526 TINDALE *Luke* xv. 23 And brynge hidder that fatted caulfe, and kyll hym, and lett vs eate, and be mery. **1647** COWLEY *Mistress, The Welcome*, i Go. let the fatted calf be kill'd. **1810** J. MOORE *Post-Captain* (ed. 4) viii. 34 The whole family crowded round him: the fatted calf was killed; and all was joy, mirth, and jubilee.

Kill the goose that lays the golden eggs, To.

1484 CAXTON *Æsope* (Jacobs) II. 245 This fable sayeth of a man whiche had a goos that leyd euery day an egge of gold. [The whole fable is given.] **1589?** LYLY *Pappe w. Hatchet* Wks. (1902) III. 404 A man . . . had a goose, which euerie daie laid him a golden egge, hee . . . kild his goose, thinking to haue a mine of golde in her bellie, and finding nothing but dung, . . . wisht his goose aliue. **1824** SCOTT *St. Ronan's* xi You must draw the neck of the goose which lays the golden eggs; you must lend me the whole stock. **1911** *Spectator* 22 Apr. 592 Capital already committed to an industry can sometimes be 'held up' by the State and forced to accept, not the market price, but a price artificially fixed. . . . Such treatment soon kills the goose that lays the golden eggs. **1925** *Times* 19 Dec. M. Bratiano, the Finance Minister, is 'killing the goose that lays the golden eggs'.

Kill two birds with one stone (bolt, sling), To.

[OVID *A.A.* 3. 358 *Unus cum gemino calculus hoste perit.*] **1611** COTGRAVE s.v. Coup'

D'une pierre faire deux coups. To kill two birds with one stone. 1656 HOBBES *Liberty, &c.* (1841) 117 T. H. thinks to kill two birds with one stone, and satisfy two arguments with one answer. 1659 HEYLIN *Animadv.* in FULLER *Appeal Inj. Innoc.* (1840) 656 That two birds might be killed with the same bolt, no sooner was Dr. Price deceased, but the bishop of Lincoln . . . calls the prebends together. 1662 FULLER (*Kent*) II. 151 Thus have I (not killed two birds with one bolt, but) revived two men's memories with one record. 1670 RAY 197 To kill two birds with one shaft (stone). D'une pierre faire deux coups, *Gall.* 1843 DICKENS *M. Chuz.* vi It was their custom, . . . whenever such a thing was practicable, to kill two birds with one stone. 1902 *Spectator* 11 Jan. It will be convenient and economical to kill two birds with one stone, and to use the same men for garrisoning the country and for settling on the land.

Kill two flies with one flap, To.

1678 RAY 275.

Kill with kindness (as fond apes do their young), To.

a. 1557 *Wealth and Health* D1ᵛ With kindnes my her ye do kyll. 1580 LYLY *Euph. & his Eng.* Wks. (Bond) II. 5 I should resemble the Ape, and kill it by cullying it. 1582 WHETSTONE *Heptameron of Civil Discourses* T 4. 1583 GREENE *Wks.* (Gros.) II. 26 Jason . . . in lieu of her loue, killed her [Medea] with kindnesse. 1593 *Tell-Truths New Years Gift* (New Sh. S.) 43 Thou kilst by kindnesse, if thou kilst. 1593-4 SHAKS. *Tam. Shrew* IV. i. 211 This is a way to kill a wife with kindness. 1601 LYLY *Love's Met.* IV. ii. *Pro.* That young cruel resembleth old apes, who kill by culling:[1] . . . never smiling but when she meaneth to smite. 1607 T. HEYWOOD *Woman killed with Kindness* [title]. 1629 T. ADAMS *Serm.* (1861-2) II. 57 These are Satan's white boys, or rather black boys, whom he kills, like the ape her young, with kindness, and damns with indulgence. 1670 RAY 2 The ape so long clippeth her young that at last she killeth them. 1698 FRYER *Acc. E. India & P.* 100 Tom Coriat . . . was killed with kindness by the English Merchants. [1 hugging.]

Killed her for good will, I | said Scot, when he killed his neighbour's mare.

1678 RAY 85.

Killed the blue spider in Blanch powder land, This is he that.

a. 1553 UDALL *Royster D.* I. iv (Arb.) 28 *M. Mery.* This is hee vnderstand, That killed the blewe Spider in Blanchepouder lande.

Killeth a man when he is drunk, He that | shall be hanged when he is sober.

1550 HEYWOOD I. x. 23 He that kylth a man, when he is dronke (quoth she) Shalbe hangd when he is sobre. 1659 HOWELL *Eng. Prov.* 13/2.

Kill(s, ed, eth), *see also* Burden (It is not) that k. the beast; Cursed in his mother's belly that was k. by cannon; Go out and k. (What shall we); Last man that he k. keeps hogs; Leeches k. with licence; March, k. crow, pie, and cadow; Ways to k. dog than hanging (More).

Killing a crow with an empty sling, It is.

1678 RAY 120.

Killing no murder.

1657 SEXBY & TITUS *Killing no Murder* [Title of a pamphlet to prove that the assassination of the Protector, Cromwell, was lawful and laudable.] 1836 MARRYAT *Midsh. Easy* xviii In this case killing's no murder . . . by the laws of society, any one who attempts the life of another has forfeited his own. 1908 *Times Lit. Sup.* 5 June The exception is the share which he took in the conspiracy of Orsini against Napoleon III. . . . It was probably a case to which Holyoake would have applied the doctrine of 'killing no murder'.

Kills himself with working, He that | must be buried under the gallows.

1678 RAY 221. 1854 A. E. BAKER *Northants. Glos.* 264 Those who kill themselves with hard work, it is said, 'will be buried under the gallows'.

Kills that thinks but to hurt, He often.

1607 H. ESTIENNE *World of Wonders* tr. R.C. 160 He often killeth who thinkes but to hurt. c. 1645 MS. proverbs in *N. & Q.* 154, 27 (A).

Kiln calls the oven burnt-hearth, The.

1603 FLORIO tr. *Montaigne* (1634) 503 Which some say prouerbially 'Ill may the Kill call the ouen "burnt taile"!' 1853 TRENCH iii. 67 We say . . . *The kiln calls the oven, Burnt house*; . . . the Germans: *One ass nicknames another, Long-ears*—Ein Esel schimpft den andern, Langohr.

Kiln of malt is on fire, My.

1636 CAMDEN 302.

Kiln, *see also* Peck of malt (For my) set k. on fire.

Kilting, *see* Kid in her k. (She has got a).

Kim Kam arsie versie.

1539 TAVERNER 62 Cleane contrarily and arsy versy as they say. 1607-8 SHAKS. *Coriol.* III. i. 302 *Sic.* This is clean Kam. *Bru.* Merely awry. 1616 DRAXE 3. 1639 CLARKE 7.

Kin, *see* Bear all his k. (A man cannot); Knave is in plum-tree (When) he hath . . . nor k.; Near of k. to land (Good to be); Poor k. that has neither whore nor thief.

Kin-cough, *see* Tail will catch the chin-cough.

Kind as a kite, As | all you cannot eat you'll hide.

1639 CLARKE 287. **1670** RAY 202.

Kind hearts are soonest wronged.

1616 BRETON *Cross. Prov.* Wks. (1879) **II.** App. iii.

Kind, He has it by | it costs him nought.

c. **1374** CHAUCER *Boethius* (Robinson) 421/1 Thou nilt nat thanne denye', quod sche, 'that the moevement of goynge nys in men by kynde?' **1616** DRAXE 138 It commeth to him by kind, it cost him nought. **1623** CAMDEN 272. **1639** CLARKE 111. **1670** RAY 182 It comes by kind: it costs him nothing. **1732** FULLER no. 5484 What cometh by kind costeth nothing.

Kind (Kindness, Love) will creep where it may not go.

[Kind (= nature) was mistaken variously for Kinship and Kindness or Love. See quotations.] *c.* **1350** *Douce MS. 52* no. 85 Kynde crepus ther hit may no go. **1460** *Towneley Myst.*, *2nd Shep. Play* 591, *I Pastor* I trow, kynde will crepe Where it may not go. *c.* **1500** *Everyman* l. 316 To my kynnesmen I wyll truely, prayenge them to helpe in my necessyte. I beleve that they wyll do so, for kynde will crepe where it may not go. **1546** HEYWOOD I. xi. 27 Men saie, kinde will créepe where it maie not go. **1548** E. HALL *Chron.* f. 190. He ... rode in poste to his kinsman ... verefying the old proverbe kynne [*sic*] will crepe where it maie not go. **1594–5** SHAKS. *Two Gent.* IV. ii. 20 You know that love Will creep in service where it cannot go. **1614** CAMDEN 309 (with 'Kindnesse'). **1635** QUARLES *Div. Emb.* IV. iii. 3 Thy thoughts are swift, although thy legs be slow; True love will creep, not having strength to go. **1641** FERGUSSON 70 (with 'kindnesse'). **1753** RICHARDSON *Grandison* II. xvi (1812) 132 Lean upon me, my dear, and *creep*: love will creep, they say, where it cannot go. **1857** DEAN RAMSAY *Remin.* v (1911) 203 *Kindness creeps where it canna gang* prettily expresses that where love can do little, it will do that little though it cannot do more.

Kindle not a fire that you cannot extinguish.

1584 B. R. *Euterpe* (Lang) 136 (A) I will kindle no moe coales then I may well quenche. **1855** BOHN 437.

Kindle(d), *see also* Wood half-burnt is easily k.

Kindly[1] aver[2] will never make a good horse, A.

1599 JAMES VI *Basil. Doron* (Arb.) 128 It is an old and true saying, that a kindly aver will never become a good horse: for ... it is evil to get out of the flesh that is bred in the bone. **1678** RAY 95 ... In our ancient writings *Averium* signifies any labouring beast. **1721** KELLY 40 *A kindly aver was never a good nag.*

Those who are naturally of a low, mean mind, will make but a sorry figure in a higher station. [[1] natural; [2] work-horse.]

Kindness cannot be bought for gear.

1641 FERGUSSON 70. **1721** KELLY 227 ... But rather by mutual good offices.

Kindness comes of will.

1641 FERGUSSON 70. **1721** KELLY 226 *Kindness comes awill.* That is, love cannot be forc'd.

Kindness is lost that's bestowed on children and old folks (men).

1509 A. BARCLAY *Ship of Fools* (1874) II. 182 All is lost that thou dost gyue to fynde. Four sortis of people: the first is a vylayne. Or chorle, for agayne thou shalt hym proue vnkynde. The seconde a childe, for his forgetfull mynde Expellyth kyndnes, the thirde a man in age The fourth a woman varyable as the wynde. **1629** T. ADAMS *Serm.* (1861–2) I. 135 We have a saying from Aristotle, *Nec in puerum, nec in senem collocandum esse beneficium,*—That our beneficence should not be fixed upon a child or an old man; for the child, before he comes to age will forget it, and the old man will die before he can requite it. **1639** CLARKE 45. **1641** FERGUSSON 60 It is tint[1] that is done to childe and auld men. [[1] lost.]

Kindness lies not aye in one side of the house.

1641 FERGUSSON 70. **1721** KELLY 227 *Kindness cannot stand ay on one side.* Spoken when you offer an instance of kindness to them who have been formerly kind to you.

Kindness, *see also* Courtesy (Where o'er mickle), little k.; Gloucestershire k.; Kill with k.; Kind (K.) will creep where it may not go; Milk of human k.; Poind for debt, not for k.

Kindred, Wheresoever you see your | make much of your friends.

1659 HOWELL *Eng. Prov.* 11/2. **1732** FULLER no. 5660.

Kindred, *see also* Shame in a k.

King and pope, the lion and the wolf, The.

1659 HOWELL *Eng. Prov.* 12/2 ... *A Proverb used in King Johns time, in regard of the great exactions.*

King and the Inquisition, With the | hush!

1855 BOHN 570. *Span.*

King Arthur did never violate the refuge of a woman.

1662 FULLER (*Cardigan*) III. 519 King Arthur did never violate the refuge of a woman.' Arthur is ... the mirror of manhood. By the woman's refuge, many understand her tongue, and no valiant man will revenge her words with his blows.

King can do no wrong, The.

1689 SELDEN *Table-Talk* (Arb.) 61 The King can do no wrong, that is no Process can be granted against him. **1763** BOSWELL *Johnson* xvi (1848) 144 Goldsmith . . . disputed . . . against the well-known maxim of the British constitution, 'the King can do no wrong'. **1765** BLACKSTONE *Comm.* I. vii. 246 The king can do no wrong. . . . The prerogative of the crown extends not to do any injury: it is created for the benefit of the people, and therefore cannot be exerted to their prejudice. **1908** E. M. SNEYD-KYNNERSLEY *H.M.I.* xix The Canons were appointed by the Crown. The King can do no wrong, but he may be misguided.

King can (may) make a knight, but not a gentleman, The.

1689 SELDEN *Table-Talk* (Arb.) 52 The King cannot make a Gentleman of Blood . . . but he can make a Gentleman by Creation. **1902–4** LEAN IV. 128 The king may make a knight, but not a gentleman.

King can make a serjeant,[1] but not a lawyer, The.

1732 FULLER no. 4613. [[1] Serjeant-at-law.]

King Charles's head.

[The type of an obsessing notion.] **1849–50** DICKENS *D. Copperfield* xiv As I looked along the lines [of Mr. Dick's Memorial] I thought I saw some allusion to King Charles the First's head again in one or two places.

King cometh to Wogan, It shall be done when the.

1659 HOWELL *Eng. Prov.* 21/1 It shall be done when the King cometh to Wogan; a little Village; *viz.* An impossibility. **1787** GROSE (*Worcs.*) 231 . . . Wogan is a small village, . . . quite out of any thoroughfare, and therefore very unlikely to be ever visited by the king.

King goes as far as he can, and not so far as he would, The.

1855 BOHN 508. *Span.*

King Harry loved a man.

c. **1600** *Return from Parnassus* I. 735 *Ficus pro diabolo* Kinge Harrie loued a man! *a.* **1635** NAUNTON *Fragm. Reg.* (Arb.) 28 The people hath it to this day in proverb, King Harry loved a man. **1636** CAMDEN 301. **1662** FULLER (*Sussex*) III. 263 These three were knighted for their valour by King Henry the Eighth (who never laid his sword on his shoulders who was not a man). **1845** CARLYLE *Cromwell* Introd. iii Tourneying successfully before King Harry, who loved a man.

King Harry[1] robbed the church, and died a beggar.

1678 RAY 354. [[1] Henry VIII.]

King Harry, *see also* Hill in K. H.'s day (This was a).

King is dead. The | Long live the King!

1859 LD. DUFFERIN *Lett. from High Lat.* (1895) 116 The last fiery segment had disappeared beneath the purple horizon, and all was over. 'The King is dead . . . the King is dead! Long live the King!' And up from the sea . . . rose the young monarch of a new day.

King may come to Kelly yet, and when he comes he'll ride, The.

1721 KELLY 323 . . . The time may come, that I may get my revenge upon such people; and then I will do it to purpose.

King never dies, The.

[L. *Rex nunquam moritur.* Law Max.] **1760** H. WALPOLE *Let.* 25 Oct. I had already begun to think that the lawyers for once talked sense, when they said the *King never dies.* He[1] probably got his death . . . by viewing the troops. **1911** H. BROOM *Legal Max.* [ed. 8] 36 *The king never dies.* ' It is true', said Lord Lyndhurst, 'that the king never dies; the demise is immediately followed by the succession; . . . The sovereign always exists; the person only is changed.' [[1] Geo. II.]

King of England (of France, of Spain), *see* Emperor of Germany.

King of France and twenty thousand men went up the hill, and so came home again, The.

1649 J. TAYLOR (Water-P.) *Wonders of West* (1872) 28 *In imitation of a mighty king, Whose warlike acts, good fellows often sing.* The King of France and twenty thousand men, Went up the hill, and so came home again.

King of France get wot of that, Long ere the.

1721 KELLY 231 . . . Spoken when people make a great talk of some little accident.

King of good fellows is appointed for the queen of beggars, The.

c. **1565** *The Bugbears* I. ii. 4 The king of good felowes that didst lie with the queene of beggars. **1636** CAMDEN 307. **1732** FULLER no. 4616.

King of your word, Ye should be a.

1641 FERGUSSON 112.

King over the water, The.

[= the representative of the exiled Stuart dynasty.] **1824** SCOTT *Redg. Let.* v He so far compromised his loyalty, as to announce merely 'The King', as his first toast. . . . Our guest made a motion with his glass so as to pass it over the water-decanter . . . , and added, 'Over the water'.

King, Whosoever is | thou wilt be his man.

1670 RAY 183.

Kings' chaff is worth other men's corn.

1641 FERGUSSON 70. **1721** KELLY 226 . . . The perquisites that attend kings service is better than the wages of other persons. **1818** SCOTT *Rob Roy* xxxiv They say . . . that kings' chaff is better than other folk's corn; but I think that canna be said o' kings' soldiers, if they let themselves be beaten wi' a wheen auld carles.

King's cheese goes half away in parings, The.

1659 HOWELL *Eng. Prov.* 1/1 The King's cheese goes half away in parings; *viz. among so many Officers.* **1709** DYKES 299 . . . The courts of princes . . . are seldom free from pilferers, pick-pockets, and thieves . . . in places of trust. **1735** FRANKLIN June The King's cheese is half wasted in parings; but no matter, 'tis made of the peoples milk.

King's coat, *see* Wear the k. c.

King's English, He clips the.

[= is drunk.] **1603** DEKKER *The Wonderful Year* E 4ᵛ If he [a drunkard] had clipt but a quarter so much of the King's siluer, as he did of the Kings English, . . . **1745** FRANKLIN *Drinker's Dict.* in Wks. (Bigelow) II. 24.

King's English, The.

1391 CHAUCER *Astrolabe* Prol. 65 And preie God save the King, that is lord of this langage. **1553** T. WILSON *Arte of Rhet.* (1909) 162 These fine English clerkes will say, they speake in their mother tongue, if a man should charge them for counterfeiting the Kings English. **1600–1** SHAKS. *Merry W.* I. iv. 6 Abusing of God's patience, and the King's English. **1714** *Spectator* 3 Nov. Mrs. Mayoress clip'd the King's *English.* **1876** MRS. BANKS *Manch. Man* xv In her attempt to appear . . . a lady, she 'clipped the King's English', and made almost as glaring errors as Mrs. Malaprop.

King's errand may come the cadger's[1] gate[2] yet, The.

1721 KELLY 311 . . . A great man may want a mean man's service. **1827** SCOTT *Let.* 30 Nov. in LOCKHART *Life* lxxiv Would to God *the King's errand might lie in the cadger's gait,* that I might have some better way of showing my feelings than merely by a letter of thanks. [[1] pedlar, gipsy, beggar. [2] way.]

King's face should give grace, A.

1827–30 SCOTT *Tales Grandf.* xxvi Henry VIII . . . blamed the implacability of James . . . , and quoted an old proverb—A King's face should give grace.

King's horse, He shall have the.

1678 RAY 89 *A lier* . . . He shall have the kings horse.

King's horses, *see* Ass thinks himself worthy.

King(s), *see* Call the k. cousin; Eats the k.'s

goose (He that); Emperor of Germany is the K. of k.; Every beggar descended from some k.; Every thing is yours (You think) but a little the k. has; Eyes are upon the k.; Groom is a k. at home; Happy (Merry) as a k.; Hated of his subjects cannot be counted k.; Highest in court (Nearest the k.), nearest the widdie; Kingdom whose k. a child (Woe to); Laws go as the k. likes; Must is for the k.; Nothing is (Where) k. must lose his right; Sail, quoth the k.; Subject's love is k.'s lifeguard; Two k. in one kingdom.

Kingdom come.

[From the clause *Thy kingdom come* in the Lord's Prayer.] **1785** GROSE *Dict. Vulg. T.* s.v. He is gone to Kingdom come, he is dead. **1789** WOLCOT (P. Pindar) *Subj. Paint.* Wks. (1812) II. 180 Sending such a Rogue to Kingdom-come. **1836** MARRYAT *Midsh. Easy* xxx They will all be in Kingdom come to-morrow morning, if the breeze comes more on the land. **1870** MISS BRIDGMAN *R. Lynne* I. xii. 184 So old aunt Duncan has gone to kingdom come at last.

Kingdom of a cheater, In the | the wallet is carried before.

1640 HERBERT 339.

Kingdom of blind men, In the | the one-eyed is king.

[ERASM. *Ad.* 2.4.96.] **1522** SKELTON *Why not to Court* 529–32 But haue ye nat harde this, How an one eyed man is Well syghted when He is amonge blynde men? **1640** HERBERT 339. **1665** MARVELL *Satires, Char. of Hol.* Among the blind the one-eyed blinkard reigns, So rules among the drownèd he that drains. **1779–81** JOHNSON *Lives of Poets, Milton* (1908) I. 147 He might still be the giant of the pygmies, the one-eyed monarch of the blind. **1871** A. B. MITFORD *Tales of Old Japan* (1886) 26 I know but one warbler whose note has any music in it, the *uguisu,* . . . at best, a king in the kingdom of the blind.

Kingdom whose King is a child, Woe to the.

Ecclesiastes x. 16. **1509** A. BARCLAY *Ship of Fools* (1874) II. 14. **1594** SHAKS. *Rich. III* II. iii (A) Woe to that land that's govern'd by a child.

Kingdom, *see also* Change a cottage in possession for k. in reversion; Mind to me a k. is.

Kings and bears oft worry their keepers.

1641 FERGUSSON 70 Kings and Bares oft worries their keepers. **1721** KELLY 226 . . . Witness the tragical end of many courtiers.

Kings are kittle cattle to shoe behind.

[*Kittill to scho behind* = Not to be depended upon.] **1818** SCOTT *Ht. Midl.* xxxviii 'Kings are kittle cattle to shoe behind, as we say in the north', replied the Duke; 'but . . . the matter is quite certain'.

Kings are out of play.

1641 FERGUSSON 70. **1721** KELLY 225 . . . It is not right, in subjects, to jest upon kings, or to pry narrowly into their determinations, and actions.

Kings go mad, *see Delirant reges.*

Kings have long arms (hands).

[Gk. Μακραὶ τυράννων χεῖρες. L. OVID *Heroides* 17. 166 *An nescis longas regibus esse manus?* Knowest thou not that kings have long arms?] **1539** TAVERNER 4 Longæ regum manus. Kynges haue longe handes. They can brynge in men, they can plucke in thynges, though they be a great waye of. **1579** LYLY *Euphues* (Arb.) 76 Knowest thou not *Euphues* that kinges haue long armes, and rulers large reaches? **1642** FULLER *H. & P. State* iv. xxi (1840) 326 They stand in daily fear lest Darius Longimanus (such a one is every king) should reach them, and revenge himself. **1752** FRANKLIN Jan. Kings have long arms, but misfortune longer: let none think themselves out of her reach. **1823** SCOTT *Peveril* xlv They say kings have long hands —I think they have as much occasion for long memories.

Kings have many ears and many eyes.

[LUCIAN *Adversus Indoctum* 23 Ὦτα καὶ ὀφθαλμοὶ πολλοὶ βασιλέως.] **1539** TAVERNER 4 Multæ regum aures, atque oculi. Kynges haue many eares and manye eyes, as who shulde saye, nothynge can be spoken, nothynge doone so secretly againste kynges and rulers, but by one meanes or other at lengthe it wyll come to theyr knowledge. **1641** FERGUSSON 70 Kings hes long ears.

Kings, *see also* King(s).

Kingswear[1] was a market town When Dartmouth[1] was a furzy down.

1926 *Times* 4 Feb. 13/4 Some little local jealousy, as in the old rhyme: Kingswear was a market town When Dartmouth was a furzy down. [[1] in Devon.]

Kinsfolk, *see* Many k. few friends; Marriages and funerals (At) friends discerned from k.

Kinsman helps kinsman, but woe to him that hath nothing.

1573 SANDFORD (1576) H 3. **1578** FLORIO *First Fruites* f. 32 (A) Kinsfolkes with kinsfolke, wo to hym that hath nothing. **1629** *Book of Meery Riddles* Prov. 19.

Kinsman, *see also* Near friend better than far k.

Kippen, *see* Out of the world and into K.

Kirby, *see* Sutton.

Kirk and a mill of it, Make a.

1721 KELLY 252 . . . That is, make your best of it. **1823** J. GALT *Entail* xviii The property

is my own . . . and surely I may mak a kirk and a mill o't an I like.

Kirk is aye greedy, The.

1721 KELLY 314 . . . Clergymen have perquisites and tithes due from every man in the parish, and because they demand these small sums they are called covetous.

Kirk is mickle, The | but you may say mass in one end of it.

1721 KELLY 314 . . . Spoken when people say something is too much, intimating that they need take no more than they have use for. **1824** SCOTT *Redg.* Let. xiii 'Better have a wine-glass, Mr. Peebles, . . .' 'If the kirk is ower muckle we can sing mass in the quire', said Peter, helping himself in the goblet out of which he had been drinking the small beer.

Kirk, *see also* Church (K.) stand in churchyard (Let the); Love the K. yet not ride on ridge; Physic do not work, prepare for k.; Rives the k. to theek the quire.

Kirkbie's castle, and Fisher's folly; Spinola's pleasure, and Megse's glory.

1598 STOW *Survey of London* 128 Bishopsgate Ward. . . . This house, being so largely and sumptuously builded by a man[1] of no greater calling or possessions, was mockingly called Fishers Folly, and a Rithme was made of it, and other the like in this manner, Kirkebies Castle, and Fishers Folly, Spinilas Pleasure, and Megses glorie. [[1] Iasper Fisher free of the Goldsmithes. STOW 128.]

Kirkcaldy, *see* Devil is dead and buried in K.

Kirkham, *see* I will make one, quoth K.

Kirkyard, *see* Like to die mends not k.

Kirtle, *see* Near is my coat (k.) but nearer is.

Kirton was a borough town When Exon was a vuzzy down.

1876 *N. & Q.* 5th Ser. VI. 364 (A) When Kirton wuz a borough town, Ex'ter was a vuzzy-down. **1911** CROSSING *Folk Rhy. of Devon* 13 Kirton was a borough town When Exon was a vuzzy down. . . . Crediton, or Kirton as it is still frequently called, was once of greater importance than it is to-day.

Kiss (Knock) a carle, and clap (ding[1]) a carle, and that's the way to tine[2] (win) a carle.

1721 KELLY 228 *Kiss a carle, and clap a carle, and that's the way to tine a carle.* People of mean breeding are rather to be won by harsh treatment, than civil. *Ibid.* 228 *Knock a carle, and ding a carle; and that's the way to win a carle.* [[1] beat. [2] lose.]

Kiss and be friends.

c. **1300** BRUNNE *Chron.* (Hearne) 64 Kisse and be gode frende in luf and in wille. **1419** *Twenty-six Poems* (E.E.T.S.) 69 Make hem

kyssen and be frende, þat were fou [foes] feynt.
1635 QUARLES *Div. Emb.* II. viii Come, buss[1]
and friends; . , . what ails my babe to cry?
1689 SELDEN *Table-Talk, Money* (Arb.) 76
The People and the Prince kist and were
Friends, and so things were quiet for a while.
1738 SWIFT (Dial. i) 341 *Col.* [*To Neverout.*]
Tom, miss and you must kiss and be friends.
1778 FRANCES BURNEY *Evelina* (1920) II. 269
He'll do you no harm, man!—come, kiss and
be friends! [[1] kiss.]

Kiss, Do not make me | and you will not make me sin.

1707 MAPLETOFT 56. **1855** BOHN 292.

Kiss than spin, She had rather.

1678 RAY 255. **1732** FULLER no. 4123.

Kiss the child for the nurse's sake, Many.

13th cent. MS. quoted in **1846** WRIGHT
Essays on the Middle Ages i. 150 (A) *Osculor
hunc ore natum nutricis amore. c.* **1470** *Harl.
MS. 3362* (ed. Förster) in *Anglia* **42.** 199
Ofte me kessyt þe chil(d) for [the nurse's
sake]. *Osculor hunc ore puerum nutricis
amore.* **1546** HEYWOOD II. vii. 69. **1594**
BACON *Promus* (Pott) 216, no. 495. **1655–62**
GURNALL *Chrn. in Armour* (1865) I. 82 Some
will kiss the child for the nurse's sake, and
like the present for the hand that brings it.
1721 KELLY 243 *Many one kisses the bairn for
love of the nurrish.* That is, shows their kindness to the companions, friends, or relations,
of those upon whom they have a design,
which they hope by their influence to effect.
1823 SCOTT *Peveril* viii. Among men, dame,
many one caresses the infant that he may
kiss the child's maid.

Kiss the clink[1] (or counter[1]), To.

[= to be confined in prison.] *c.* **1560** HUTH
Ancient Ballads, &c. (1867) 227 (A) Then
some the Counter oft doo kisse, If that the
money be not paid. **1588** J. UDALL *Diotrephes* (Arb.) 22 I will make thee kiss the
Clinke for this geare. **1620** ROWLANDS *Night
Raven* (1872) 11 You kisse the Counter sirra.
[[1] prison.]

Kiss the cup, To.

[= to drink.] *c.* **1412** HOCCLEVE *De Reg.
Princ.* 3815 More is . . . honurable, a man
compleyne of thirst, Than dronken be, whan
he þe cuppe haþ kist. **1579** GOSSON *Sch. Abuse*
(Arb.) 25 Kissing the cupp too often.

Kiss (Lick) the dust (ground), To.

1589 *Pasquil's Ret.* B Ouerthrow the state,
and make the Emperiall crowne of her
Maiestye kisse the ground. **1605–6** SHAKS.
Macbeth V. vii. 57 I will not yield To kisse the
ground before young Malcolm's feet. **1610–11**
Wint. T. V. i. 199 They kneel, they kiss the
earth. **1782** COWPER *Boadicea* 19 Soon her
pride shall kiss the ground. **1835** I. TAYLOR
Spir. Despot. x. 410 To kiss the dust before
monstrous superstitions. **1867** TROLLOPE
Last Chron. Barset II. lvi. 129 She had yielded
and *nad* kissed the dust,

Kiss the hand they wish cut off, Many.

1599 MINSHEU (1623) 2 Z 5[v] **1634** HOWELL
Lett. 28 Feb. (1903) II. 135 An Italian . . . will
tell you that he kisseth your hand . . . a thousand
times over, when he wisheth them both cut
off. **1640** HERBERT 330 **1897** 'H. S. MERRI-
MAN' *In Kedar's Tents* xxiv 'A Carlist . . .
rag whose readers are scarcely likely to be
interested for a good motive in . . . the Queen
Regent. . . . Many kiss the hands they would
fain see chopped off.'

Kiss the hare's foot, To.

[= to be late (a different sense in quot.
1818).] **1598** *Servingmans Comfort* in *Inedited Tracts* (Hazlitt, 1868) 112 (A) Vpon
payne to dyne with Duke Humfrie or kisse
the Hares foote. **1613–16** W. BROWNE *Brit.
Past.* II. ii We had need Make haste away,
unlesse we meane to speed With those that
kisse the Hares foot. **1738** SWIFT (Dial. ii)
344 *Sir John Linger comes in. . . . Lady S.*
I doubt you must kiss the hare's foot. *Sir J.*
I see you are fast by the teeth. **1818** SCOTT
Let. to Croker 5 Feb. in LOCKHART *Life* xl
The poor clergyman [got] nothing whatever,
or, as we say, *the hare's foot to lick.*

Kiss the post, To.

[= to be shut out in consequence of being too
late.] *c.* **1514** BARCLAY *Egloges* ii (1570) B
iv/2 Thou shalt lose thy meat and kisse the
post. **1600** T. HEYWOOD *1st Pt. Edw. IV*, Wks.
(1874) IV. 47 Make haste thou art best, for
feare thou kiss the post. **1681** W. ROBERTSON
Phraseol. Gen. (1693) 475 You must kiss the
post, or hare's foot, *Sero venere bubulci.*

Kiss the rod, To.

[as children formerly had to do before
chastisement.] *a.* **1586** SIDNEY *Arcadia* II
(1867) 190 Yet he durst not but kiss his
rod and gladly make much of his entertainment. **1594–5** SHAKS. *Two Gent.* I. ii. 57
Foolish love That, like a testy babe, will
scratch the nurse And presently all humbled
kiss the rod! **1595–6** *Rich. II* V. i. 32 Wilt
thou, pupil-like, Take thy correction mildly,
kiss the rod. **1628** SHIRLEY *Witty Fair One* I.
iii Come, I'll be a good child, and kiss the rod.
1800 I. MILNER in *Life* xii (1842) 209 When
the fits of illness come, I do not, I believe,
properly kiss the rod.

Kiss till the cow come home.

c. **1612** J. FLETCHER *Scornf. Lady* II. i. Wks.
(C.U.P.) I. 248 *Young L.* Kiss till the Cow
come home, kiss close, kiss close knaves.

Kisses are keys.

1616 N. BRETON *Cross. Prov.* ii. Wks. (1879)
II. App. iii Wanton kisses are the keys of sin.
1639 CLARKE 28.

Kisseth his wife (Sits to work) in the market-place, He that | shall have many teachers.

1659 HOWELL *Eng. Prov.* 13/1 He that kisseth
his wife in the market-place shall have many
teachers. **1670** RAY 110 He that kisseth his

wife in the market-place shall have enough
to teach him. **1721** KELLY 173 *He that kisseth
his wife at the market cross, will have many to
teach him.* Spoken when people are officiously
instructing us in doing what we are about.
1732 FULLER no. 2303. He that sits to work
in the market-place shall have many teachers.

Kiss(ed, es, eth), *see also* Better k. a knave;
Contentibus ... k. my wife; Every man as
he loveth ... when he k. his cow; Fool
that k. the maid; Luck in horses must k.
parson's wife; Never k. a man's wife;
Tyrants seem to k. (Time to fear when);
Wipes the child's nose (He that) k. mother.

Kissing goes by favour.

1616 DRAXE 64 Kissing commeth by fauour.
1621 BURTON *Anat. Mel.* II. iii. VII footnote.
1639 CLARKE 28 **1659** HEYLIN *Animadversions* in FULLER *Appeal Inj. Innoc.* (1840) 618
But 'kissing goes by favour', as the saying
is; and therefore let him favour whom he
pleases, and kiss where he favoureth. **1721**
KELLY 225 . . . Men shew regard, or do
service, to people as they affect. **1880** BLACK-
MORE *Mary Aner.* xxi ' I should like . . . to
give you one kiss, Insie' . . . Before he could
reason in favour of a privilege which goes
proverbially by favour, the young maid was
gone.

Kissing, *see also* Gorse is **out of bloom**
(When), k. **out of fashion.**

Kit[1] hath lost her key.

1533 MORE *Apol.* xxiv. Wks. 888/2 Certaine
letters which some of the brethrene let fall of
late, and lost theim of likelyhedde as some
good kitte leseth her kayes. **1548** W. PATTEN
Exp. Scott. Pref. in *Eng. Garner* III. 71 Obla-
tions and offerings ... for deliverance of bad
husbands . . ., to keep down the belly, and
when 'Kit had lost her key'. [[1] Catherine or
Kate.]

Kit, *see* Cat (K.) after kind.

Kitchen boys, *see* Laird slight lady (If), so
will k. b.

Kitchen physic is the best physic.

1542 A. BORDE *Dietary* (E.E.T.S.) 277 The
chefe physycke . . . dothe come from the
kytchyn. **1562** BULLEIN *Bulwark of Def.* (*Bk.
of Comp.*) 48 With kitchin phisicke: whiche
kitchin, I assure thee, is a good Poticaries
shop. **1738** SWIFT (Dial. ii) *Col.* Well, after
all, kitchen physic is the best physic.

Kitchen, *see also* Little k. makes large house;
Said in the k. should not be heard in hall;
Take tea in the k.

Kite will never be a good hawk, A carrion. (One cannot make a falcon of a buzzard.)

c. **1300** *King Alis.*1. 3047 Nultow never, late
ne skete A goshawk maken of a Kete, No
faucon mak[en] of busard, No hardy knyht
mak of coward. *c.* **1400** *Rom. Rose* l. 4031
Man [ne] may, for no daunting, Make a

sperhauke of a bosarde. **1576** DESAINLIENS 260
A carreine kite will neuer bee good hawke—
On ne sauroit faire d'une buse un esprevier.
1614 CAMDEN 302. **1820** SCOTT *Monast.*
xix For seldom doth a good hawk come out
of a kite's egg.

Kite, *see also* Ask a k. for a feather; Carrion
will kill k. (No); Kind as a k.; Leg of a lark
better than a k.; Whirl the eyes shows k.'s
brain; Yellow as k.'s foot.

Kitten(s), *see* Wanton k. make sober cats.
Playful as a k.

Kittle cattle, *see* Kings are k. c. **to shoe**
behind.

Kittle[1] shooting at corbies and clergy, It is.

1737 RAMSAY III. 187. **1787** BURNS *Brigs of
Ayr* As for your Priesthood I shall say but
little, Corbies and Clergy are a shot right
kittle. **1855** STIRLING-MAXWELL in *Misc. Ess.
& Addr.* (1891) 28 Against our divines I have
not met with any but these three—' It's
kittle shooting at corbies and clergy'.
[[1] difficult.]

Kitty Sleitchock's[1] bannock, You have gotten a piece of.

1721 KELLY 373 . . . Spoken when young ones
flatter us for something. [[1] Kate the
Flatterer.]

Knapton, *see* Gimmingham.

Knave is in a plum-tree, When a | he hath neither friend nor kin.

1640 HERBERT 341.

Knave than a fool, I'd rather have a.

1659 N. R. 15 A man had better have a knave,
than a fool, to his Servant. **1913** *Folk-Lore*
xxiv. 77 (A).

Knave, The more (worse) | the better luck.

1636 CAMDEN 307 The more knave the better
luck. **1660** TATHAM *The Rump* IV. i (1879) 250
What says Pluck?—The worser knave, the
better luck!

Knave to the learned knave, No.

1617 MORYSON *Itin.* III. i. 5 (1907–8) III. 358
Thus the English Proverb saith. No knave
to the learned knave.

Knave to the old knave, No. (*Cf.* Old knave is no babe.)

1571 R. EDWARDS *Damon & Pithias* in HAZL.
O.E.P. IV. 78 *Will.* You are a wily collier and
a brave, I see now there is no knave, like to
the old knave.

Knave(s), *see also* Better be a fool than k.;
Better kiss a k.; Caught a k. in a purse-net;
Cold weather and k. come out of the north;
Crafty k. needs no broker; Know a k. (If

ye would); Merry when k. meet; More k. than fool; Mortar (No more) . . . cunning k. has cunning trick; Old k. no babe; Once a k. ever a k.; Pack of cards without k. (No); Stool in the sun (Put), when one k. rises . . . .

Knavery (Cheating) in all trades, but most in tailors, There is.

1632 MARTIN PARKER *Knavery in all Trades* (title). **1654** 12–19 July *Mercurius Fumigosus* 49 If there be not Knavery in *All Trades*, I shrewdly am mistaken. **1658** *Comes Facundus* 192. **1666** TORRIANO 19 As the English in Drollery will say, There's cheating in all Trades, but ours. **1692** L'ESTRANGE *Æsop's Fab.* clxxxiii (1738) 195 Jupiter appointed Mercury to make him a composition of fraud and hypocrisy, and to give every artificer his dose on't. . . . Mercury . . . gave the tailors the whole quantity that was left, and from hence comes the old saying, *There's knavery in all trades, but most in tailors.*

Knavery may serve for a turn, but honesty is best at long run.

1678 RAY 164.

Knavery, *see also* Cloak for his k.

Knaves and fools divide the world.

1659 N. R. 71. **1670** RAY 111.

Knaves, The more | the worse company.

1519 *Four Elements* in HAZLITT *O.E.P.* (1874) I. 35 What, art thou here? I see well, I, The mo knaves the worse company. **1550** HEYWOOD I. xi. 29 But the mo knaues the woorse company to gréete.

Knaves, *see also* Knave(s).

Knees of the gods, On the.

[= beyond human control. HOM. *Il.* 17. 514; *Od.* 1. 9 θεῶν ἐν γούνασι] **1879** BUTCHER & LANG *Odyssey* I. 9 Howbeit these things surely lie on the knees of the gods, whether he shall return or not. **1886** FROUDE *Oceana* vii If the several provinces continue to increase their numbers at the present rate, there will be more than fifty millions then. There is a proverb that 'nothing is certain but the unforeseen'. . . . ταῦτα θεῶν ἐν γούνασι κεῖται. **1900** *Daily News* 17 Aug. 6/5 Such things are yet upon the knees of the gods.

Knees, *see also* Dog's nose and maid's k.

Knell, *see* Hear a toll or k. (When dost), think on passing bell.

Knife into a person, To have one's.

1890 D. C. MURRAY *John V's. Guard.* xxxvi I reckon you've got your knife into Mr. Jousserau. **1911** *Spectator* 3 June 854 The dislike of the Socialists for Mr. John Burns . . . has never been disguised, and they seldom lose an opportunity of 'getting their knife' into him.

Knife, knives, *see also* Butcher looked for his k.; Ox falls (If), whet your k.; Oxford k. and London wives; Same k. cuts bread and fingers; Smith forges weak k. (Often); Stuck a k. to my heart (If you had); Whet a k. for own throat.

Knight of Cales, A | and a gentleman of Wales, and a laird of the north countree; a yeoman of Kent, with his yearly rent, will buy them out all three.

[Cadiz, formerly *Cales*, in Spain, was captured by Essex in 1596.] *a.* **1658** F. OSBORNE *Tradit. Memoirs* (*Secret History of James I*, 1811, i. 41). **1659** HOWELL *Eng. Prov.* 17. **1662** FULLER (*Kent*) II. 121 . . . *Cales Knights* were made in that voyage, by Robert earl of Essex, anno Domini 1596, to the number of sixty, whereof . . . some were of low fortunes.

Knight of the post.

[= a perjurer; one who got his living by giving false evidence.] **1580** E. KNIGHT *Trial Truth* 39 b Men, . . . who will not let to sweare vpon a booke, . . . beyng hyred therevnto for money . . . called Knightes of the poste. **1599** KYD *Sol. & Pers.* V. iii *Piston.* Faith, two great Knights of the post swore vpon the Alcaron that he would haue firde the Turkes Fleete.

Knight, *see also* Make a poor man k. (Little of God's might to).

Knit my dog a pair of breeches and my cat a codpiece.

1678 RAY 255.

Knit, *see also* Know well ere thou k.

Knock at a deaf man's door, To.

1601 A. DENT *Plain Man's Pathway* 55 It is but euen to plough the Sea, or knocke at a deafe mans doore. **1616** B. RICH *Ladies Looking Glasse* 3 (A). **1639** CLARKE 7 You knock at a deafeman's doore or wrong doore.

Knock in the cradle, He got a.

1611 DONNE *Anat. of World; First Anniv.* 195 Poems (1896) II. 111 Then first of all The world did in her cradle take a fall, And turn'd her brains. **1678** RAY 255.

Knock on the hoop, and another on the barrel, He giveth one.

1813 RAY 13 . . . *Ital.* i.e. he speaks now to the purpose, now on matters wholly extraneous.

Knock under the board.

[= succumb in a drinking-bout.] **1678** RAY 74. . . . *He must do so that will not drink his cup.* **1691–2** *Gentl. Jrnl.* 10 Mar. He that flinches his glass and to Drink is not able, Let him quarrel no more, but knock under the Table.

Knocked me down with a feather, You might have.

[= overcome with surprise.] **1821** COBBETT

Rural Rides 6 Nov. I asked the ostler the name of the place; and, as the old women say, 'you might have knocked me down with a feather', when he said, 'Great Bedwin'. **1891** A. FORBES *Barracks, Biv. & Bat.* (1910) 95 You might have knocked him down with a feather—he was stricken absolutely dumb.

Knock(ed, s), *see also* Fortune k. (When), open the door; Kiss (K.) a carle and ding a carle; Young men's k. old men feel.

Knot in a bulrush, To seek (find) a.

[TER. *And.* 5.4.38 *Nodum in scirpo quaerere* = to find difficulties where there are none.] **1340** *Ayenbite* 253 þet zekþ þet uel ine þe aye oþer þane knotte ine þe resse. **1581** J. BELL *Haddon's Answ. Osor.* 436 Myne opposed adversary will seeke after a knott in a Bullrush as the Proverbe is. *a.* **1601** NASHE Wks. (McKerrow) I. 373 Cares enough the ordinarie course of our life tythes of his own accord to us, though we seeke not a knot in a bulrush. **1748** EDWARDS *Can. of Criticism* Can. 8 Ex. 30 Here our profess'd Critic ... is searching after knots in a bulrush.

Knot is loose, Where the | the string slippeth.

1579 GOSSON *Ephemerides* 28 Where the Knot is loose the string slippes. **1597** *Politeuphuia* 166 Where the Knot is loose, the string slypeth. **1639** CLARKE 248.

Knot(s), *see also* Blunt wedges rive hard k.; Crabbed k. must have crabbed wedge; Tailor that makes not a k. loseth stitch; Tied a k. with his tongue.

Knotty timber.

1616 DRAXE 188 A knottie peece of timber must have sharpe wedges. **1664** CODRINGTON 203 Knotty pieces of Timber must have sharp Wedges. **1670** RAY 15 A knotty piece of timber must have smooth wedges. **1855** BOHN 438 Knotty timber requires sharp wedges.

Know a goose from a gridiron, To.

1896 J. C. HUTCHESON *Crown & Anch.* vi He's quite a contrast to the sucking Nelsons ... who don't, as a rule, know a goose from a gridiron!

Know a hawk from a handsaw, To.

[In the following, *handsaw* is generally explained as a corruption of *heronshaw*, or *hernsew*, dial. *harnsa*, heron.] **1600–1** SHAKS. *Hamlet* II. ii. 367 I am but mad north, north-west; when the wind is southerly, I know a hawk from a handsaw. **1850** KINGSLEY *Alton L.* iv Wasn't there enough in that talk ... to show anybody that, who can tell a hawk from a hand-saw?

Know a knave, If ye would | give him a staff.

1640 HERBERT 318.

Know a trick worth two of that, To.

1837 DICKENS *Pickwick* xxvii He knows a trick worth a good half dozen of that.

Know all, Since you | and I nothing, tell me what I dreamed last night.

1640 HERBERT 333.

Know by a halfpenny if the priest will take an offering, They will.

1721 KELLY 321 ... A small experiment will discover a covetous inclination.

Know by a handful the whole sack, You may. (*Cf.* Sack is known, &c.)

1732 FULLER no. 5949.

Know by a penny how a shilling spends, You may.

1678 RAY 78 [*Joculatory.*]

Know by your nose (looks) what pottage (porridge) you love, One may.

1564 BULLEIN *Dial. agst. Fever* (1888) 79 *Roger.* I see by his nose that of al potage he loueth good Ale. **1590** LODGE *Rosalynde* Wks. (1883) I. 42 Her colour chaungde, and she said to Aliena, See, Mistresse, where our iolly Forrester comes. And you are not a little glad thereof, quoth Aliena; your nose bewrayes what porredge you loue. **1610** FIELD *Woman is a W.* I. ii (Merm.) 351 *Pen.* One may see by her nose what pottage she loves. **1639** CLARKE 179. **1670** RAY 125.

Know good manners, You | but you use but a few.

1520 R. WHITTINTON *Vulg.* (E.E.T.S.) 95 Ye have seen more good maners then ye have borne awaye. **1639** CLARKE 2. **1670** RAY 185. **1732** FULLER no. 5919 You have good manners, but never carry them about you.

Know him as well as if I had gone through him with a lighted link, I.

1721 KELLY 202, with 'candle' for 'link'. **1732** FULLER no. 2611.

Know him not, I | should I meet him in my pottage dish.

1672 WALKER 13. **1678** RAY 265. **1732** FULLER no. 2613 (with 'porridge' for 'pottage dish').

Know how the market goeth, Men | by the market men.

1546 HEYWOOD I. xi. 31 Men know (quoth I) I haue herd now and then, How the market goth by the market men. *a.* **1591** HY. SMITH *Serm.* (1866) I. 11 If thou wilt know a godly man, ... mark ... report, because as the market goes, so they say the market-men will talk.

Know no more than the Pope of Rome about it, I.

1664 BUTLER *Hudibras* II. iii. 195 That durst upon a *truth* give doom He knew no more then th' *Pope of Rome.* **1678** RAY 255 To know one no more than he does the Pope of

Rome. **1863** *N. & Q.* 3rd Ser. III. 470 Persons when professing entire ignorance of any subject, exclaim, ' I know no more than the Pope of Rome about it '; . . . the expression [is] especially current . . . **in Pembrokeshire.**

Know not me, If you | you know nobody.

1605–6 T. HEYWOOD *If you know not me, you know no bodie.* (Title of play.)

Know not who lives or dies, We.

1640 HERBERT 361.

Know one another, They that | salute afar off.

1640 HERBERT 325.

Know one from Adam, Not to.

1861 G. J. WHYTE-MELVILLE *Market Harbor.* vii ' Who's that fellow? Is he staying with you at Harborough?' . . . 'Don't know him from Adam,' he replied.

Know the horse by his harness, You may.

1639 CLARKE 64. **1670** RAY 105. [But *cf.* **1732** FULLER no. 5883 You can't judge of the horse by the harness.]

Know the ropes, To.

[= to be acquainted with ways of doing things.] **1840** R. H. DANA *Bef. Mast* ix The captain, who . . . 'knew the ropes', took the steering oar. **1874** *Slang Dict.* 271 'To know the ropes', is to be conversant with the minutiae of metropolitan dodges. **1892** STEVENSON *Wrecker* xxii Anywhere from Tonga to the Admiralty Isles, he knew the ropes and could lie in the native dialect.

Know the value of a ducat, If you would | try to borrow one. (*Cf.* Know what money is, &c.)

1732 FULLER no. 2801.

Know the worst is good, To.

1639 CLARKE 199.

Know the worth of water till the well is dry, We never.

1721 KELLY 351. **1758** FRANKLIN *Poor Rich Alm.* in ARBER *Eng. Garner* v. 583 *Always taking out of the meal tub, and never putting in, soon comes to the bottom.* Then, as *Poor* DICK says, *When the well's dry, they know the worth of water!*

Know thyself.

[THALES in DIOGENES LAERTIUS, 1. 1. 13, 40. Γνῶθι σαυτόν. JUVENAL 11. 27 *E coelo descendit γνῶθι σεαυτόν.*] **1531** SIR T. ELYOT *Governour* III. iii (Dent) 202 The words be these in latine, *Nosce te ipsum,* whiche is in englysshe, know thy selfe. **1545** ASCHAM *Toxoph.* (Arb.) 155 That wise prouerbe of Apollo, *Knowe thy selfe:* that is to saye, learne to knowe what thou art able, fitte, and

apt vnto, and folowe that. **1660** W. SECKER *Nonsuch Prof.* II (1891) 186 The heathen tell us that 'know thyself' was an oracle that came down from heaven. Sure I am it is this oracle that will lead us to the God of heaven. **1737** RAMSAY III. 188 Ken yoursel, and your neighbours winna misken you. **1850** LYTTON *Caxtons* XVI. X 'Know thyself', saith the old philosophy. 'Improve thyself', saith the new. **1905** A. MACLAREN *Exposn., Matthew* I. 113 The proud old saying of the Greeks, 'Know thyself', if it were followed out unflinchingly . . . would result in this profound abnegation of all claims. [See more in *N. & Q.* Vol. 180, 177.]

Know well ere thou knit.

c. **1450** *Prouerbis of Wysdom* 39 Know well, ore þou knyt to fast; Fore ofte rape[1] rewyþe at last. [[1] haste.]

Know what I know, I.

c. **1592** MARLOWE *Jew of Malta* IV. i Do nothing; but I know what I know; he's a murderer. **1905** WEYMAN *Starvecrow F.* xxviii Therefore I'll spare speech, But—I know what I know.

Know what money is, Would you | go borrow some. (*Cf.* Know the value of a ducat, &c.)

1640 HERBERT 335 Would you know what money is, go borrow some. **1841** S. WARREN *Ten Thous. a Year* iv ' If you want to learn the value of money, try to borrow some', . . . and Titmouse was now going to learn that useful but bitter lesson.

Know what shall be, He that would | must consider what hath been.

1732 FULLER no. 2367.

Know what to do, When you don't |— wait.

1874 G. J. WHYTE-MELVILLE *Uncle John* xx I should wait. When in doubt what to do, he is a wise man who does nothing.

Know what would be dear, He that could | need be a merchant but one year.

1546 HEYWOOD I. i. 3 Who so that knew, what wolde be dere, Should neede be a marchant but one yeere. *a.* **1585** MONTGOMERIE *Cherrie & Slae* xciv (1821) 50 Quha wist quhat wald be cheip or deir, Sould neid to traffique but a ȝeir, Gif things to cum were kend. **1670** RAY 78 . . . Such a merchant was the Philosopher Thales . . . he foreseeing a future dearth of Olives, the year following, bought up at easie rates all that kind of fruit then in mens hands.

Know what you can do till you try, You never.

1829 MARRYAT *Frank Mild.* vii I have often heard my poor old uncle say that no man knows what he can do till he tries. **1893** MONT. WILLIAMS *Leaves of a Life* xiii On hearing the verdict he . . . shouted out: 'I told you so. . . . ! You never know what you can do till you try.'

Know what's o'clock, To.

1837 DICKENS *Pickwick* xliii I know what's o'clock, Sir. Wen I don't, I'll ask you, Sir. **1878** BROWNING *Two Poets of Croisic* xciv You've learnt your lesson, found out what's o'clock.

Know when to spend and when to spare, and you need not be busy; you'll ne'er be bare.

1664 CODRINGTON 203 Know when to spend and when to spare is great wisdom. **1721** KELLY 225. **1732** FULLER no. 6437.

Know where they were born, Men | not where they shall die.

1639 CLARKE 108.

Know which way the wind blows, To.

1546 HEYWOOD II. ix. 75 I know, And knew, which waie the winde blewe, and will blow.

Know wine by the barrel, You cannot.

1640 HERBERT 318. **1732** FULLER no. 5884 (with 'cask' for 'barrel').

Know your driver, I will make you.

1678 RAY 345 (*Somerset*).

Know your meaning by your mumping (gaping),[1] I.

1639 CLARKE 64 I know your meaning by your winking. **1659** HOWELL *Eng. Prov.* 21/1 You may know his meaning by his gaping. **1670** RAY 186 One may know your meaning by your gaping. **1721** KELLY 183 *I know your meaning, by your mumping.* I know by your motions and gestures what you would be at, and what you design. *a.* **1734** NORTH *Exam.* I. iii, § 46 We are to understand his Meaning by his Mumping. [[1] grimacing.]

Know your thoughts as well as if I were within you, I.

1738 SWIFT (Dial. iii) 350 *Lady S.* Madam, I fancy I know your thoughts, as well as if I were within you.

Knoweth when he hath enough is no fool, He that.

1550 HEYWOOD II. vii.

Know(eth, n, s), knew, *see also* Better k.

than trusted; Better the devil you k.; Every man is best k. to himself; Favour (Without) none will k. you; Goodman is last who k. what's amiss; Little k. the fat sow what lean doth mean; No man better k. what good is; No man k. when he shall die; Shirt k. my design (If my); Shuns the man that k. him; Speers the gate he k.

(Many); Sports and journeys men are k. (In); Three things there be hard to be k.; Twyford my name is, I k. nothing of matter; Wretched (Hard to be), but worse to be k. so.

Knowledge is folly, except grace guide it.

1640 HERBERT 328.

Knowledge is no burthen.

1616 WITHALS 582. **1640** HERBERT 349. **1641** FERGUSSON 70 Knowledge is eith[1] borne about. [[1] easily.]

Knowledge is power.

[BIBLE *Prov.* xxiv. 5 A wise man is strong; yea, a man of knowledge increaseth strength.] **1590-1** SHAKS. *2 Hen. VI* IV. vii. 79 Ignorance is the curse of God, Knowledge the wing wherewith we fly to heaven. **1620** BACON *Nov. Organ.* Aphor. iii Scientia et potentia humana in idem coincidunt, quia ignoratio causae destituit effectum. [Knowledge and human power are synonymous, since the ignorance of the cause frustrates the effect.] **1853** LYTTON *My Novel* I. iii Well, KNOWLEDGE IS POWER. **1859** SMILES *Self. Help* xi 'Knowledge is power'; but . . . knowledge of itself, unless wisely directed, might merely make bad men more dangerous. **1907** S. LEE *Gt. Englishmen 16th Cent.* 4 [Bacon's] Latin apophthegm, 'nam ipsa scientia potestas est'[1]—'for knowledge is power'—might be described as the watchword of the intellectual history of England . . . in the sixteenth century. **1908** J. A. SPENDER *Com. Bagshot* ix. 84 Women understand men . . . better than any man understands women. Since knowledge is power, woman has a control over man which man never has over her. [[1] *De Haeresibus* x. 329.]

Knowledge makes one laugh, but wealth makes one dance.

1640 HERBERT 361.

Knowledge without practice makes but half an artist.

1616 DRAXE 242 Knowledge without practice, is nothing. **1732** FULLER no. 3141.

Knowledge, *see also* Honour ceaseth (Where), k. decreaseth; Zeal without k.

Knows enough that can live and hold his peace, He.

1573 SANDFORD (1576) H 3 He knoweth inough that knoweth nought, if he knoweth how to holde his peace. **1586** PETTIE *Guazzo's Civ. Conv.* f. 55 (A) It is likewise saide, That he knoweth ynough who knoweth nothing if he know how to holde his peace.

Knows how many (blue) beans make five, He.

1830 GALT *Laurie T.* (1849) II. i. 42 Few men who better knew how many blue beans it takes to make five. **1894** NORTHALL *Folk-*

phrases 16 To say of a man that 'He knows how many beans make five' is to speak highly of his shrewdness. **1909** *Times Wkly.* 11 June 377 But the Bishop . . . knew how many beans make five, and he soon found out about Margaret.

Knows how to carry the dead cock home, He.

1869 HAZLITT 193 A correspondent of *Notes and Queries* says: . . . This . . . was in common use in the Derbyshire village where I was born. It was said of lads and men who . . . in . . . games, trials of strength, or fights, knew how to bear defeat manfully. . . . 'He knows how to carry the dead cock home!'

Knows, What one | it is useful sometimes to forget.

[PUB. SYRUS *Etiam oblivisci quod scis, interdum expedit.* It is sometimes as well to forget what you know.] **1855** BOHN 555.

Knows little, He that | often (soon) repeats it.

1707 MAPLETOFT 22 He who knows but little presently outs with it. **1732** FULLER no. 2209. **1813** RAY 124 *Quien poco sabe presto lo reza.* He that knows little soon repeats it.

Knows most, Who | speaks least.

1666 TORRIANO 189 Who knows most, speaks least.

Knows not a B from a battledore,[1] He.

1563–87 FOXE *A. & M.* II. 474 He knew not a B from a battledore nor ever a letter of the book. **1609** DEKKER *Guls Horne-Bk.* 3 You shall not neede to buy bookes, no, scorne to distinguish a B from a battle dore. **1639** CLARKE 297 [[1] A horn-book.]

Knows not a B from a bull's foot, He.

[= entirely illiterate.] **1401** *Polit. Poems* (Wright) II. 57 I know not an A from the wyndmylne, ne a B from a bole foot. **1721** KELLY 159 *He knows not a B by a bull's foot.* That is, he is illiterate. **1824** MOIR *Mansie W.* xxi One who . . . could distinguish the difference between a B and a bull's foot. **1887** BLACKMORE *Springhaven* v But the opinion of the men was different, because they knew a bee from a bull's foot.

Knows not a pig from a dog, He.

1678 RAY 264.

Knows not how to dissemble, Who | knows not how to live.

a. **1576** PETTIE, *Petite Pall.* (Gollancz) I. 116 He who knoweth not how to dissemble knoweth not how to live. **1589** G. PULTENHAM, *Art of English Poesy* III. xviii The great Emperour [Vespasian] that had it vsually in his mouth tc say, *Qui nescit dissimulare nescit regnare.* **1654** E. GAYTON *Pleasant Notes on Don Quixote* 163 **1892** SIR H. MAXWELL *Meridiana* 61 THE ART OF COMPLAISANCE . . .

(London, 1697) . . . **bears on** the title the forbidding aphorism—' Qui nescit dissimulare nescit vivere'[1]—(he who knows not how to dissemble, knows not how to live). [[1] Louis XI said this was all the Latin the Dauphin need learn. (From *Politica* of Justus Lipsius (*a.* 1591) citing Vincentius Lupanus.)]

Knows not how to hold his tongue, He that | knows not how to talk.

1669 *Politeuphuia* 157 (A) He that knows not when to hold his peace knows not when to talk. **1732** FULLER no. 2210.

Knows not to swim goes to the bottom, In the world, who.

1640 HERBERT 330.

Knows not whether his shoe goes awry, He.

1678 RAY 81. [*To tread a shoe awry* = To make a lapse from virtue.]

Knows nothing, He that | doubts nothing.

1611 COTGRAVE s.v. 'Rien'. **1640** HERBERT 356. **1853** TRENCH iv. 78 Here is excellently unfolded to us the secret of the fool's confidence: *Who knows nothing, doubts nothing.*[1] [[1] Fr. *Qui rien ne sait, de rien ne doute.*]

Knows on which side his bread is buttered, He.

1546 HEYWOOD II. vii. 71 I know on which syde my bread is buttred. **1564** BULLEIN *Dial. agst. Fever* (1888) 112 He knoweth upon which side his bread is buttered well enough. **1819** SCOTT *Bride Lam.* xviii No man knows so well as Bittlebrains on which side his bread is buttered. **1882** BLACKMORE *Christowell* ix You know . . . upon which side your bread is buttered. And you think to make a good thing of what you have got out of me.

Knows one point more than the devil, He.

1620 SHELTON *Quix.* II. xxviii (A) I know that you know an ace more than the devil in all you speak or think. **1813** RAY 204.

Knows the weight of another's burden, None.

1640 HERBERT 357.

Knows what may be gained in a day, He that | never steals.

1640 HERBERT 338.

Knows who's a good maid? Who.

1678 RAY 172.

Knows, *see also* Know(eth, n, s).

Kythe[1] in your own colours, that folk may ken you.

1832 HENDERSON 129 Kythe in your ain colours. **1862** HISLOP 202. [[1] appear.]

Kythe, *see also* Love me (If you), k. that.

L

Labour as long lived, pray as even dying.

1640 HERBERT 340.

Labour for one's pains, To have nothing but one's.

1589 NASH *Pref. to Greene's Menaphon* Wks. (1905) III. 314 They haue nought but . . . (to bring it to our English Prouerbe) their labour for their trauell. **1601–2** SHAKS. *Troil. & Cres.* I. i. 73 I have had my labour for my travail. **1655–62** GURNALL *Chrn. in Armour* (1865) I. 224 They are but few that carry away the prize in the world's lottery; the greater number have only their labour for their pains. **1670** RAY 183.

Labour is light where love doth pay.

1582 T. WATSON *EKATOMΠAΘIA* (Arb.) 138 The Labour is light, where Loue is the Paiemistres. **1600** DRAYTON *Idea* (Hebel) iii. 340.

Labour younger, Ye shall never.

1546 HEYWOOD I. ix. 17 Set forward, ye shall neuer labour yonger. **1579** LYLY *Euphues* (Arb.) 65 Take heart at grasse, younger thou shalt neuer be. **1593–4** SHAKS. *Tam. Shrew* Ind. II. 146 Let the world slip: we shall ne'er be younger.

Labour, *see also* Endure l. in this world (He that will not); Idle folks have most l.; Land (He that hath some) must have l.; Little l. much health; Ox go where he shall not l. (Whither shall); Pride of rich makes l. of poor; Six days shalt thou l. and the seventh . . . ; Think no l. slavery.

Labourer is worthy of his hire, The.

[**1611** BIBLE *Luke* x. 7.] **1824** SCOTT *St. Ronans* x Your service will not be altogether gratuitous, my old friend, the labourer is worthy of his hire. **1880** MYERS *Wordsworth* 100 Wordsworth . . . was far from expecting . . . to make a rapid fortune; but he felt that the labourer was worthy of his hire.

Labours and thrives, He that | spins gold.

1640 HERBERT 333.

Labyrinth, If you go into a | take a clew with you.

1580 LYLY *Euph. & his Eng.* (Arb.) 393 Theseus woulde not goe into the Laborinth without a threede that might shew him the way out. **1732** FULLER no. 2752.

Lachrymae, see Sing *l.*

Lack to a wife, No.

1639 CLARKE 329.

Lack to lack a wife, No.

1546 HEYWOOD II. xi. 84 Suche kynde of lyuyng, for suche kynde of lyfe, As lackyng the same, no lacke to lacke a wife.

Lack[1] what they would fain have in their pack, Many men.

1641 FERGUSSON 76. **1721** KELLY 249 . . . Men will seem to discommend what they have a great mind to, in order to get it cheaper. [[1] discommend.]

Lack, *see also* Better leave than l.; What d'ye l.

Lacketh a stock, Who | his gain is not worth a chip.

1546 HEYWOOD II. ix. 77. **1614** CAMDEN 314.

Lackey comes to hell's door, When a | the devils lock the gates.

1640 HERBERT 362.

Lacking[1] breeds laziness, praise breeds pith.[2]

1721 KELLY 237 . . . Discommend a boy and you discourage him, but commend him and it will spur him on. [[1] discommending. [2] force.]

Lackland, Sir John.

[= one who has no landed possessions.] **1594** GREENE *Looking Glass* Wks. (Gros.) XIV. 40 How cheere you, gentlemen? you crie 'no lands' too; the Judge hath made you a knight for a gentleman, hath dubbed you sir John Lack-land.

Lack-latin, Sir John.

[= a name for an ignorant priest.] *c.* **1535** SIR F. BYGOD *Treat. concern. impropriations* C vj Is it nat great pitye to se a man to haue thre or foure benefyces . . . which he neuer cometh at, but setteth in euery one of them a syr John lacke latin, that can scarce rede his porteus.[1] **1614** JACKSON *Creed* III. iii, § 5 We are bound to believe the Church's decisions read or explained unto us (by the pope's messenger though a Sir John Lack-latin). [[1] breviary.]

Lacks[1] my mare would buy my mare, He that.

1721 KELLY 130 . . . Buyers commonly discommend what they have a mind to; apply'd when a man discommends a maid, whom he would gladly marry, if he could get her [[1] discommends.]

Lads, *see* Boys (L.) will be men.

Ladder(s), *see* Climb the l. must begin at bottom; Crosses are l. to heaven; Go down the l. when marriest; Go up the l. to bed; Kick down the l.; Step after step l. is ascended; World is a l.

Ladies have leave to change their minds.

1905 WEYMAN *Starvecrow* F. xxi 'But perhaps . . . the young lady will still change her mind. To change the mind'—with a feeble grin—'is a lady's privilege'.

Ladies, *see also* Lady (-ies).

Ladle, *see* Wife that never cries for l. till pot runs over.

Lads love[1] is lassies' delight, and if lads won't love, lassies will flite.[2]

1828 w. CARR *Dial. of Craven* I. 273 '*Lads love*[1] is lassies delight', a vulgar phrase common in Craven, to which is frequently added ... 'And if *lads* don't *love*, lassies will flite.[2]' [[1] The Shrub Southernwood: *Artemisia Abrotanum*, also known as 'Old Man'. [2] scold.]

Lad's love's a busk of broom, hot awhile and soon done.

1670 RAY 46 *Chesh.*

Lady Day the latter,[1] On | the cold comes on the water.

1732 FULLER no. 6217. [[1] Formerly 'Lady Day' was used to denote not only the Annunciation (25 Mar.) but also other festivals of the Virgin,'including her Conception (8 Dec.).]

Lady falls in our Lord's lap, When our | then let England beware a sad clap (mishap).

1654 E. GAYTON *Pleasant Notes upon Don Quixote* 47 Those yeares most joyfull where our Ladies day (being Rent-day) fals out late, when the Lady lies in the Lords lap. **1662** FULLER (*Berks.*) I. 113 'When our Lady falls in our lord's lap Then let England beware a sad clap/mishap', alias, 'Then let the clergyman look to his cap'. It ... would intimate ... as if the blessed Virgin ... watcheth an opportunity of revenge. ... And when her day (being the five and twentieth of March ...) chanceth to fall on the day of Christ's resurrection, then ... some signal judgement is intended to our state, and churchmen especially.

Lady's (Lord's) heart and a beggar's purse, Nothing agreeth worse than a.

1546 HEYWOOD I. x. 22 There is nothing in this worlde that agréeth wurs, Then dooeth a Ladies hert and a beggers purs. **1562** Ibid. *Epig.* 47 (p. 134) There is nothing in this world that agréeth wurse, Then doth a lordes harte and a beggers purse.

Lady (-ies), *see also* Gist of l.'s letter in postscript; House stands on my l.'s ground; Joan is as good as my l. in dark; Laird slight the l. (If the); Lord doth lie in our L.'s lap (When our), England beware; Prayers are done (When), my l. is ready.

Ladybirds, Plenty of | plenty of hops.

1869 HAZLITT 317.

Laid in his fuel before St. John,[1] Never rued the man that.

1732 FULLER no. 6205. [[1] Dec. 27.]

Laird of pity, He looks like the.

1641 FERGUSSON 48 *Of fleyit*[1] *persons*. ... He looks like the laird of pity. [[1] frightened.]

Laird slight the lady, If the | so will all the kitchen boys.

1721 KELLY 185 ... If people despise their own, so will other persons.

Lairds break, When | carles get land.

1721 KELLY 348 ... When a great estate is sold, mean people, who have a little money, will buy each a share.

Laird's brother, *see* Jock the l. b.

Lamb where it's tipped, and the ewe where she's clipped, The.

1721 KELLY 307 ... A proverbial rule about tithes; signifying that the lamb shall pay tithes in the place where the ewe was when she took the ram, but the old sheep where they were shorn.

Lambs, Like | you do nothing but suck and wag your tail.

1721 KELLY 386 *You have nothing to do but suck, and wag your tail.* Taken from young lambs; spoken to them who have got a plentiful condition, place, or station. **1732** FULLER no. 3230.

Lamb(s), *see also* Bed with the l.; Ewe and a l. (Now I have) ... Welcome Peter; Fox lick a l. (Ill sign); Gentle as a l.; God tempers the wind; God's l. will play; Ill look among l.; Life of wolf is death of l.; Old ewe l. fashion; Soon goeth the young l.'s skin to market.

Lame as St. Giles, Cripplegate, As.

1662 FULLER (*Lond.*) II. 349 'As lame as St. Giles Cripplegate'. ... This proverb ... is spoken ... of such who for some light hurt lag behind, and sometimes is applied to those who out of laziness ... counterfeit infirmity.

Lame foot overtakes the swift one in the end, The.

1867–77 FROUDE *Short Stud.* II (1900) 43 The laws of Heaven are long-enduring. ... But the lame foot, as the Greek proverb said, overtakes the swift one in the end; and the longer the forbearance the sharper the retribution when it comes.

Lame goes as far as your staggerer, The.

1640 HERBERT 342.

Lame messenger, *see* Stay till the l. m. come.

Lame post brings the truest news, The.

1659 N. R. 115. **1732** FULLER no. 4620.

Lame tongue gets nothing, The.

1636 CAMDEN 307.

Lame traveller should get out betimes, A.

1732 FULLER no. 235.

Lame, *see also* Halt before you are l. (You); Retreat (In a) the l. are foremost; See which leg you are l. of.

Lament, *see* Short pleasure long l.

Lamentation of a bad market, The.

1678 RAY 345.

Lammas, *see* After L. corn ripens; Latter L.

Lammermoor lion,[1] You look like a.

1721 KELLY 380 . . . Lammermoor is a large sheep walk in the east of Scotland. The English say, An Essex lyon. [[1] i.e. a sheep.]

Lamp, *see* Smells of the L.

Lancashire fair women.

1609 DEKKER *The Raven's Almanack* G 1 A wench of a good bone and a lusty complexion, much like to Lancashire breed. **1613–22** DRAYTON *Polyolb.* xxvii. 65 (1876) III. 175 Ye lusty lasses then, in *Lancashire* that dwell, For beauty that are said to bear away the bell. **1662** FULLER (*Lancs.*) II. 191 'Lancashire fair women' . . . God having given fair complexions to the women in this county, art may save her pains . . . in endeavouring to better them.

Lancashire law—no stakes, no draw.

1828 W. CARR *Dial. of Craven* I. 274 'Lancashire law, no stakes, no draw', a saying whereby a person who loses a wager endeavours to evade payment when the wager was merely verbal and no stake deposited.

Lancashire man at any time, or tide, He that would take a | must bait his hook with a good egg, or an apple with a red side.

1613 DRAYTON *Polyolb.* xxvii. 65, 68 (1876) III. 175 Ye lusty lasses then, in *Lancashire* that dwell, . . . As ye the Egg-pie love, and Apple cherry-red. [Foot-note: He that will fish for a *Lancashire* man, at any time or tide, Must bait his hook with a good Egg-pie, or an Apple with a red side.] **1678** RAY 316 He that would take a Lancashire man at any time or tide, Must bait his hook with a good egge-pie or an apple with a red side.

Lancashire thinks to-day, What | all England will think to-morrow.

1902–4 LEAN I. 116 . . . This was in the days of the Anti-Corn-Law League. Since then the initiative in political movements proceeds from Birmingham.

Lancashire witches.[1]

1634 T. HEYWOOD & BROME *Lancashire Witches*[1] (Title of Play). **1787** GROSE (*Lancs.*)
186 Lancashire witches . . . at the same time as it records the beauty of the Lancashire females, carries with it a kind of reflection on the males, for . . . executing a number of poor innocent people, under the denomination of witches. **1880** J. NICHOL *Byron* 57 Of Cadiz . . . [Byron] writes with enthusiasm . . . The belles of this city, he says, are the Lancashire witches of Spain. [[1] In 1612 nine witches were hanged in Lancashire; and in 1633 seventeen were sentenced, but not executed.]

Land has its laugh,[1] Every | and every corn has its chaff.

1641 FERGUSSON 30 Every land hes the lauch, and everie corne hes the caffe. **1721** KELLY 92 . . . Every country hath its own laws, customs, and usages. **1916** *Brit. Wkly.* 2 Nov. 84 'Every land', says the old Scottish proverb, 'has its ain lauch'. And every class has its own mode of thought and expression. [[1] law.]

Land, He that hath some | must have some labour.

1639 CLARKE 59. **1670** RAY 112. **1732** FULLER no. 2161.

Land of cakes, The.

[Refers to the *oatcakes* of Scotland and is applied (originally in banter) to Scotland or the Scottish Lowlands.] **1669** SIR R. MORAY in *Lauderdale Papers* (1885) II. cxiv. 171 If you do not come out of the land of cakes before New Year's day. *c.* **1730** BURT *Lett. N. Scotl.* (1760) II. xxiv. 271 The Lowlanders call their part of the Country the Land of Cakes. *a.* **1846** J. IMLAH *Song, Land o' Cakes,* An' fill ye up and toast the cup, The land o' cakes for ever.

Land of Nod, The.

[= sleep. A pun on the Biblical place-name, *Gen.* iv. 16.] **1738** SWIFT (*Dial.* iii) 352 *Col.* I am going to the land of Nod. **1818** SCOTT *Ht. Midl.* xxx There's queer things chanced since ye hae been in the land of Nod. **1863** READE *Hard Cash* xviii [It] had my lady into the land of Nod in half a minute.

Land was never lost for want of an heir.

1678 RAY 165 Land was never lost for want of an heir. Ai ricchi non mancano parenti. *Ital.* The rich never want kindred.

Land, You may be on | yet not in a garden.

1640 HERBERT 361.

Land's end.

1550 HEYWOOD, II. vii. 68 Thou gossepst at home to meet me at landis ende.

Land's End to John o' Groat's, From the.

[= through Great Britain.] **1823** SCOTT *St. Ronan's* X (A) I can beat Wolverine from the Land's-End to Johnnie Groat's. **1827** HARE *Gues. at Truth* (1873) i. 232 From the Land's

End to John of Groat's House, scarcely a man any longer remembers that the business of governors is to govern. **1890** PAYN *Burnt Mil.* xiv If you laid it down in sovereigns, . . . it would have reached from the Land's End to John o' Groat's.

Lands, He that hath | hath quarrels (war).

1640 HERBERT 363. **1666** TORRIANO 284 Who buies land buies war. **1855** BOHN 566 Who has land, has war.

Land(s), *see also* Fat l. grow foulest weeds; Gold may buy l. (He that has); Good l., evil way; Good l. where there is foul way; Little house well filled, little l. well tilled; Many a one for l. takes a fool by the hand; Near of kin to l. (Good to be); Prate is but prate, it's money buys l.; Talk is but talk, money buys l.

Landscape, *see* Water is eye of a l.

Lane, *see* Long l. that has no turning.

Langel, *see* Foot out of the l. (You have a).

Language(s), *see* Eyes have one l.; Good l. which all understand not (That is not); Ill l. if not ill taken (No); Nothing so necessary for travellers as l.

Lank, *see* After a l. a bank.

Lanthorn, *see* Light (To great) a great l.

Lapped (Wrapped) in his mother's smock, He was.

1590 GREENE *Never too Late* in Wks. VIII. 198 How should I be vsed: but as one that was wrapt in his mothers smock when hee was borne. **1668** SHADWELL *Sullen Lov.* v. i Sure I was born with a caul on my head, and wrapped in my mother's smock; the ladies do so love me. **1670** RAY 184. **1704** STEELE *Lying Lover* II. ii I can't believe there's anything in that old whim of being wrapt in one's mother's smock. . . . But . . . I have strange luck with the women. **1721** KELLY 139 He was wrap'd in his mother's sark tail. **1738** SWIFT (Dial. ii) 347 Indeed, miss, I believe you were wrapt in your mother's smock, you are so well beloved.

Lapwing cries farthest from her nest, The.

1580 LYLY *Euph. & his Eng.* (Arb.) 214 In this I resemble the Lappwing who . . . flyeth with a false cry farre from their nestes. **1592** GREENE *Art Conny Catching* II. 4 Who . . . cry with the Lapwing farthest from their nest. **1592–3** SHAKS. *Com. Err.* IV. ii. 27 Far from her nest the lapwing cries away: My heart prays for him, though my tongue do curse. **1607** CHAPMAN *Rev. of Bus.* V. i (1874) 210 Trust not his oath. He will lie like a lapwing, when she flies Far from her sought nest, still 'here 'tis', she cries. **1670** RAY 256.

Larder but hath its mice, No.

1732 FULLER no. 3587.

Large as life, As.

1799 EDGEWORTH *Lame Jervas* ii I see the puppets, the wheelbarrows, everything as large as life! **1853** C. BEDE *Verdant Green* vi An imposing-looking Don, as large as life and quite as natural. **1894** BLACKMORE *Perlycross* xxi To be sure I was, as large as life, and twice as natural!

Larks fall there ready roasted, The.

[Fr. **1640** OUDIN *Curios. franç.* 10 *Les allouetes luy tomberont tousic rosties dans la bouche.*] **1659** HOWELL *Fr.-Eng.* 3 *He thinks that roasted larks will fall into his mouth;* spoken of a sluggard. **1855** BOHN 168.

Lark(s), *see also* Bed with the lamb, rise with l.; Hear the l. than the mouse (Better); Leg of a l. better than; Lovers live by love as l. by leeks; Merry (Gay) as a l.; Sing like a l.; Sky falls we shall catch l.

Lass in the red petticoat shall pay for all, The.

1662 J. WILSON *Cheats* I. ii *Afterwit.* Come— the red petticoat must piece up all. **1678** RAY 80 The lass i' th' red petticoat shall pay for all. Young men answer so when they are chid for being so prodigal and expensive, meaning, they will get a wife with a good portion, that shall pay for it.

Lass with the tear in her eye, Take a.

1823 GALT *Entail* III. xxviii 'Bell Father-lans', resumed the Leddy, 'I'll tak you wi' the tear in your ee'. **1827** SCOTT *Surg. Dau.* iv 'I may be brought up by a sabre, . . . then your road to Menie will be free and open, and . . . you may take her "with the tear in her ee", as old saws advise.'

Lasses are lads' leavings.

1670 RAY 217 (*Chesh.*)

Lass(es), Lassy (-ies), *see also* Glasses and l. brittle; Good l. (All are), but whence bad wives? Lads love is l.' delight; Lisping l. good to kiss; Lithe as a l. of Kent.

Last, but not least.

1580 LYLY *Euph. & his Eng.* (Arb.) 343 Of these three but one can stand me in steede, the last, but not the least. **1599–1600** SHAKS. *Jul. Cæs.* III. i. 189 Though last, not least in love. **1605–6** *K. Lear* I. i. 85 Although our last, not least. *a.* **1627** MIDDLETON *Mayor of Queenb.* III. iii *Ol.* Though I speak last, my lord, I am not least. **1853** SURTEES *Sponge's Sport. T.* lxvii Though last not least, here's Facey Romford.

Last drop makes the cup run over, The.

1655 FULLER *Ch. Hist.* XI. ii (1868) III. 449 When the cup is brimfull before, the last (though least) super added drop is charged alone to be the cause of all the running over. **1876** J. PAYN *Halves* x An application of her brother-in-law for a five-pound note . . . was the last drop that caused Mrs. Raeburn's cup of bitterness to overflow.

Last garment is made without pockets, Our.

1853 TRENCH v. 113 This Italian . . . teaches . . . with an image Dantesque in its vigour, that 'a man shall carry nothing away with him when he dieth', *Our last robe*, that is, our winding sheet, *is made without pockets.*[1] **1909** ALEX. MACLAREN *Expos., Ephesians* 41 There is nothing that is truly our wealth which remains outside of us, and can be separated from us. 'Shrouds have no pockets.' [[1] *L'ultimo vestito ce lo fanno senza tasche.*]

Last in bed to put out the light.

1902–4 LEAN IV. 27.

Last legs, To be (go) on one's.

[= the end of one's life; fig. the end of one's resources.] **1599** MASSINGER, &c. *Old Law* v. i *Eugenia*. My husband goes upon his last hour now. *1st Courtier*. On his last legs, I am sure. **1678** RAY 89 *A Bankrupt*. He goes on's last legs. **1846** DE QUINCEY *Syst. Heavens Wks.* (1854) III. 174 If the Earth were on her last legs. **1857** A. TROLLOPE *Barch. Tow.* i The bishop was quite on his last legs.

Last make fast.

c. **1350** *Douce MS. 52* no. 48 Who-so comyth late to his in, shall erly forthynke. **1576** DESAINLIENS E i He that cometh last, maketh the dore fast. **1659** HOWELL *Eng. Prov.* 6/2 Last make fast, *viz. shut the dore.* **1881** A. B. EVANS *Leicest. Words* (E.D.S.) 302 'Last make fast'. . . . It is a recognized rule in passing through a gate that has been opened.

Last man that he killed keeps hogs in Hinckley field, The.

1678 RAY 317 (*Leics.*) . . . Spoken of a coward that never durst fight. **1881** A. B. EVANS *Leicest. Wds.* (E.D.S.) 301. . . . It is now, and I imagine always was, applied rather to a boaster of the 'Ancient Pistol' type.

Last my time, It will.

1856 FROUDE *Hist. Eng.* I. 222 Such thoughts . . . were thrust aside as an uneasy dream, . . . or with the coward's consolation, 'It will last my time'.

Last prayers, She is at her.

1678 RAY 79 (*Joculatory*).

Last straw breaks the camel's back, The.

[**1645** ABP. BRAMHALL *Wks.* IV. 59 in LEAN IV. 20 It is the last feather that breaks the horse's back.] **1848** DICKENS *Dombey* ii As the last straw breaks the laden camel's back, this piece of underground information crushed the sinking spirits of Mr. Dombey. **1881** D. C. MURRAY *Joseph's Coat* iv Young Joe's resolve to emigrate . . . had been the last straw which broke the camel's back, and they were now irreconcilable. **1902** G. W. E. RUSSELL *Coll. & Recoll.* (1909) 116 Palmerston's contumacy was the last straw, and he was . . . dismissed from the Foreign Office.

Last suitor wins the maid, The.

1611 COTGRAVE s.v. 'Aimé' (with 'wench' for 'maid'). **1670** RAY 15. **1732** FULLER no. 4624.

Last word (though one talk bilk for it), To have the.

1633 JONSON *T. Tub* I. i *Tub*. He will have the last word, though he talk bilk for 't. *Hugh*. Bilk! What's that? *Tub*. Why, nothing: a word signifying Nothing; and borrowed here to express nothing. **1678** RAY 228 He will have the last word, though he talk bilk for it. **1738** SWIFT (*Dial*. i) 338 *Never*. Miss, you have shot your bolt: I find you must have the last word.

Last word, *see also* Women will have the l. w.

Last (*adj., adv.*), *see also* Better the l. smile; Cometh l. to the pot soonest wroth; Pays l. never pays twice. *See also* At last.

Last (*noun*), *see* Cobbler go beyond his l. (Let not).

Last(s) (*verb*), *see* Good gear that l. aye.

Latch-key, *see* Liberty but no l.

Late children, early orphans.

1742 FRANKLIN *Mar*. Late Children, early Orphans.

Late-comers are shent.[1]

1599 PORTER *Angry Wom. Abingd.* II. iv (Merm.) 136 *Phil*. Tush, there is no good luck in this delay . . .; late-comers, man, are shent. [[1] ruined.]

Late repentance is seldom true.

1552 LATIMER *Wks.* (P.S.) II. 193 (A) It is a common saying, *Pœnitentia sera raro vera.* **1639** CLARKE 255. **1732** FULLER no. 3145.

Late, *see also* Better l. than never; Riseth l. must trot. *See also* Too late to.

Λάθε βιώσας, *see* Live in the shade.

Latin, a horse, and money, With | thou wilt pass through the world.

1666 TORRIANO 91 With a Florin. Latin and a good Nag, one may find out the way in any Country. **1809** MALKIN *Gil Blas* x. x Those who can talk Latin may always find their way to Rome. **1855** BOHN 570.

Latin, *see also* Speak false L.; *Tace* is L. for candle.

Latter Lammas, At. (*Cf.* Greek Calends.)

[= never] **1553** *Respublica* III. v (A) Faith youer Mars-ship will thrive att the latter Lammas. **1567** GASCOIGNE *Instruct. Making Verse, Posies* (1575) Uij Many writers . . . draw their sentences in length, & make an ende at latter Lammas. **1642** FULLER *Holy & Prof. St.* IV. xv. 316 This your will At latter lammas wee'l fulfill [his translation of *Ad Graecas, bone rex, fient mandata, Calendas,* a line by Q. Elizabeth]. **1857** KINGSLEY *Two Yrs. Ago* vii A treatise . . . which will be published probably . . . in the season of Latter Lammas, and the Greek Kalends.

Laugh and be (grow) fat.

1596 HARINGTON *Metam. of Ajax* (1814) 68 (A) Many of the worshipful of the city, that make sweet gains of stinking wares; and will laugh and be fat. **1599** JONSON *Ev. Man out of Humour* III. i *Clove.* When shall we sup together, and laugh and be fat with those good wenches, ha? **1682** N. O. tr. *Le Lutrin* iv. 40 There will we . . . laugh, grow fat. **1737** GREEN *Spleen* 93 Laugh and be well. Monkeys have been extreme good doctors for the spleen. **1823** SCOTT *Peveril* xxxiii He seems to have reversed the old proverb of 'laugh and be fat'. **1844** T. HOOD *Lett. to a Child*, Apr. I mean ... to laugh till I grow fat, or at least streaky.

Laugh and cry both with a breath, It is hard to.

1593 SHAKS. *Venus & Adon.* 412 For I have heard it [love] is a life in death, That laughs and weeps, and all but with a breath. **1616** DRAXE 46 He doeth laugh and weepe with one breath. **1616** WITHALS 581 It is a hard thing to laugh and cry both with a breath. **1639** CLARKE 147. **1670** RAY 184 He can laugh and cry and both in a wind. **1732** FULLER no. 4120 She can laugh and cry both in a wind.

Laugh and lay (lie) down.

[An obsolete game at cards.] **1522** SKELTON *Why not to Court* 928 Now nothynge but pay, pay, With, laughe and lay downe, Borowgh, cyte, and towne. **1591** FLORIO *Second Fruites* 67 What game doo you plaie at cardes? At primero, at trump, at laugh and lie downe. **1606** CHAPMAN *Gent. Usher* IV. ii. 83 Sweet lady, if you will laugh and lie down, I am pleased. **1634** S. R. *Noble Soldier* II. ii. in BULLEN *O. Pl.* I. 268 Sorrow becomes me best. A suit of laugh and lye downe would wear better. *a.* **1825** FORBY *Laugh-and-lay-down*, a childish game at cards.

Laugh at leisure, you may greet[1] ere night.

1721 KELLY 240 . . . A reprimand to them that laugh immoderately. [[1] weep.]

Laugh before breakfast, you'll cry before supper. (*Cf.* Sing before breakfast.)

1721 KELLY 332 They that laugh in the morning may greet e'er night. **1902–4** LEAN IV. 28 . . . Tel rit au matin qui pleure au soir. Cotgrave, 1611

Laugh in one's face and cut his throat, To.

1629 T. ADAMS *Serm.* (1861–2) III. 267 It is a dissembling falsehood in man to smile and betray, as Judas began his treachery with a kiss. Such are likened to those bottled windy drinks, that laugh in a mans face, and then cut his throat. **1670** RAY 184 . . . As bottled Ale is said to do. Da una banda m'onge, da l'altra me ponge. *Ital.* **1738** SWIFT (Dial. ii) 345 *Ld. Smart.* I have some excellent cider. . . How is it treacherous? *Ld. Spark.* Because it smiles in my face, and cuts my throat.

Laugh in one's sleeve, To.

[= to be secretly amused.] **1506** DAUS tr. *Sleidane's Comm.* 64 If I coveted nowe to avenge the injuries that you have done me, I myght laughe in my slyve. **1546** HEYWOOD II. v. 58 To that I saide nought but laught in my sleeue. **1642** D. ROGERS *Naaman* 228 Thou . . . hast fleerd and laught in the sleeve at the sincere. **1799** WOLCOT (P. Pindar) *Nil Admirari* Wks. (1816) III. 443 With smiles her eulogy Miss Hannah hears; Laughs in her sleeve at all thy pompous praise. **1836** MARRYAT *Midsh. Easy* xxiii Mr. Hicks laughed in his sleeve, so did Jack.

Laugh like a hyena, To.

1599–1600 SHAKS. *A.Y.L.* IV. i. 163 I will laugh like a hyen, and that when thou art inclined to sleep. **1837** TH. HOOK *Jack Brag* xiv The purser of the ship—a great coarse creature, who used to laugh all day long like a hyæna. **1857** TROLLOPE *Barch. Tow.* xxxiii Mrs. Proudie smiled as a hyena may probably smile before he begins his laugh. . . . And then the hyena laughed out.

Laugh (smile) on the other (wrong) side (of one's face, mouth), To.

1666 TORRIANO 173 The English say, when one hath conveniently reveng'd ones self on another; Now you can laugh but on one side of your mouth, friend. **1809** MALKIN *Gil Blas* II. v, par. 2 We were made to laugh on the other side of our mouths by an unforeseen occurrence. **1834** EDGEWORTH *Helen* xxvi Ladies may smile, but they would smile on the wrong sides of their pretty little mouths if they had been treated as I have been. **1842** S. LOVER *Handy Andy* iii 'I'll make him laugh at the wrong side of his mouth', thought the Squire . . . and began a very smart horsewhipping of the attorney. **1905** WEYMAN *Starvecrow F.* vii He'll drub you . . . till you smile on the other side of your face!

Laugh that win, They.

1546 HEYWOOD I. v He laugheth that winneth. **1604–5** SHAKS. *Othello* IV. i. 126 *Cas.* Ha, ha, ha! *Oth.* So, so, so, so. They laugh that win. **1622** MAY *Heir* III. i Let them laugh That win the prize. **1670** RAY 184 Let them laugh that win. **1836** MARRYAT *Midsh. Easy* xxiii 'To-morrow morning what a laugh we shall have!' 'Let those laugh who win', thought Jack.

Laughed at, He is not | that laughs at himself first.

1732 FULLER no. 1936. **1786** MRS. PIOZZI *Anec. of S. Johnson* (1892) 99 Thinking I suppose that the old maxim, of beginning to laugh at yourself first where you have anything ridiculous about you, he . . . called his girl *Trundle* when he spoke of her. **1927** *Times*, 17 Sept. 11/4 Any man who laughs at his own misfortunes has . . . saved himself from being laughed at by others.

Laughing to girn[1] in a widdy,[2] It is nae.

1737 RAMSAY III. 187. [[1] grin. [2] gallows.]

Laughs best who laughs last, He. (*Cf.* Better the last smile, &c.)

[*Cf.* **1591** *Troublesome Reign Kg. John* Part I C 3 Let them reioyce that at the ende doo win. **1659** N. R. 54 He laugheth that winneth.] **1715** VANBRUGH *Country House* II. v But mum, he laughs best that laughs least. **1823** SCOTT *Peveril* xxxviii Your Grace knows the French proverb,[1] 'He laughs best who laughs last'. **1904** 'H. S. MERRIMAN' *The Last Hope* xvi Men must have . . . laughed at the astounding simplicity of the French people. But he laughs best who laughs last. [[1] Rira bien qui rira le dernier.]

Laughs ill that laughs himself to death, He.

1616 DRAXE 130. **1639** CLARKE 201. **1670** RAY 15. **1732** FULLER no. 1962.

Laugh(s), *see also* Bachelors l. and show our teeth (We); Jove l. at lovers' perjuries; No play where one greets and another l.

Laughter, *see* Better the last smile than first l.

Laurence bids wages, *see* Lazy Laurence.

Lauvellin, *see* Skiddaw.

Lavender, *see* Lay (up) in l.

Lavishly, *see* Speaks l. shall hear knavishly.

Law for lying, No.

1678 RAY 172 . . . A man may lie without danger of the law.

Law for the rich, One | and another for the poor.

1830 MARRYAT *King's Own* xi Is there nothing smuggled besides gin? Now, if the husbands and fathers of these ladies—those who have themselves enacted the laws—wink at their *infringement*, why should not others do so? . . . There cannot be one law for the rich and another for the poor. **1888** J. E. T. ROGERS *Econ. Interp. Hist.* (1894) II. xxi There is an objection to the taxation of the inheritance of personal property of a very serious kind. It is that it is one law for the rich and another for the poor. **1913** *Spectator* 8 Nov. 757 The idea prevails abroad that there is one law for the 'rich' Englishman and another for the 'poor' foreigner.

Law for wagging of a straw, He will go to.

1548 A. BORDE *Introduction* (E.E.T.S.) 122. **1616** WITHALS 563. **1670** RAY 184.

Law groweth of sin, and doth punish it, The.

1573 SANDFORD (1576) H 4 (with chastiseth').

5017

1578 FLORIO *First Fruites* f. 32. **1639** *Book of Meery Riddles* (as 1573).

Law is a bottomless pit.

1712 ARBUTHNOT *John Bull* vi Law is a bottomless pit; it is a cormorant, a harpy, that devours everything. **1823** J. GALT *Entail* III xxii But what lawyer would laugh, even in his own 'bottomless pit'?

Law is a lickpenny.

a. **1633** JONSON *T. Tub* IV. i. 57 The Law is costly, and will draw on charge. **1638** J. TAYLOR *Bull Bear & Horse* B 6ᵛ The proverbe says truly, *The Law is costly.* **1818** SCOTT *Ht. Mdl.* xxxviii But law licks up a', as the common folk say. **1824** Id., *St. Ronans* xxviii You talked of a law-suit—law is a lick-penny, Mr. Tyrrel.

Law is a pickpurse.

1621 HOWELL *Lett.* 20 Mar. (1903) I. 109 Law is a pickpurse.

Law is an ass, The.

a. **1634** CHAPMAN *Revenge for Honour* III. ii I am ashamed the law is such an ass. **1838** DICKENS *Ol. Twist* li 'If the law supposes that', said Mr. Bumble . . . 'the law is a ass—a idiot.'

Law is not the same at morning and at night, The.

1640 HERBERT 358.

Law makers should not be law breakers.

c. **1386** CHAUCER *Cant. T.* B 43–4 For swich lawe as man yeveth another wight He sholde hym-selven usen it by right. **1669** PENN *No Cross, No Crown* xix Xenophanes being jeered for refusing to play at a forbidden game, answered, '. . . They that make laws, must keep them.' **1721** KELLY 232 . . . Lat. *Patere legem quam tulisti.* **1830** MARRYAT *King's Own* xi You'll allow also that lawmakers should not be law-breakers.

Law of the Medes and Persians, The.

[Often used, with allusion to *Daniel* vi. 12, as the type of something unalterable.] **1382** WYCLIF *Dan.* vi. 15 The lawe of Medis and Persis. **1762** CHURCHILL *Ghost* ii. 657 For what his greatness hath decreed, Like laws of Persia and of Mede, . . . Must never of repeal admit. **1853** 'C. BEDE' *Verdant Green* I. ii His word is no longer the law of the Medes and Persians, as it was at home.

Law(s), *see also* Abundance of l. breaks no l.; Agree for the l. is costly; Cobbler's l.; Customs (With) we live well, but l. undo us; Cutter's l.; Drums beat (Where) l. are silent; Evil manners (Of) good l.; Fear, the beadle of l.; Halifax l.; Hard cases bad l.; Ignorance of the l. excuses no man; Loves l. (He that) will get his fill; Man is friended (As a) so l. is ended; Many lords many l.; Much l. little justice; Order is heaven's first l.; Pennyweight of love worth pound of l.;

A a

Pleaing at the l. is like fighting through whin; Possession is nine points of l.; Show me the man and I'll show the l.; Stafford l.; Stopford l.; Suit at l. and urinal; Suit of l. (One) breeds twenty; Take the l. into own hands; Thousand pounds of l. not ounce of love; Uncertainty of l. (Glorious); Vengeance of the l.; War, hunting, and l. full of trouble; Wrong l. make short governance.

Lawful, *see* Suffered to do . . . will do more.

Lawfully done which cannot be forborne, That may be.

1779–81 JOHNSON *Lives of Poets*, Pope (Bohn) III. 183 It must be remembered that *necessitas quod cogit defendit*; that may be lawfully done which cannot be forborn. Time and place will always enforce regard.

Lawing, *see* Pays the l. choose the lodging.

Lawn, *see* Sell l. before he can fold it (He that will).

Lawrence, *see* Laurence.

Laws catch flies but let hornets go free.

c. **1412** HOCCLEVE *De Reg. Princ.* (1860) 101 Right as lop-webbes flyes smale and gnattes Taken, and suffren grete flyes go, For alle this world lawe is reulede so. *a.* **1591** HY. SMITH *Serm., Mem. for Mag.* (1866) I. 348 Our laws have been a long time like to spiders' webs, so that the great buzzing bees break through, and the little feeble flies hang fast in them. **1625** BACON *Apoph.* Wks. (Chandos) 381 One of the Seven [Solon, *Diog. La.* I. 57] was wont to say; That laws were like cobwebs; where the small flies were caught, and the great break through. *a.* **1628** FULKE GREVILLE *Treatise of Monarchie* I, st. 10 All laws like cobwebs catching little flies, but never great ones without princes' eyes. **1707** SWIFT *Facult. of Mind* Wks. (1856) II. 285 After which, laws are like cobwebs, which may catch small flies, but let wasps and hornets break through.

Laws go as kings like.

1885 J. ORMSBY tr. *Quixote* xlv (II. 301) 'May I never share heaven', said the poor barber, 'if your worships are not all mistaken; but, "laws go"—I say no more.' [Alfonso VI at Toledo settled the question as to which of the rival rituals, the French or the Musarabic, was to be adopted, by flinging the latter into the fire. Hence the proverb.]

Laws, The more | the more offenders (sins).

[TACITUS *Annals* 3. 27 *Corruptissima republica plurimae leges.* The more corrupt the state, the more numerous the laws.] **1667** MILTON *Par. Lost* xii. 283 So many Laws argue so many sins Among them. **1732** FULLER no. 4663.

Laws, *see also* Law(s).

Lawsuit, *see* Lean compromise better than fat l. *See also* Suit at law.

Lawsuits consume time, and money, and rest, and friends.

1640 HERBERT 353.

Lawton gate a clap, She hath given.

1678 RAY (*Chesh.*) 300 . . . Spoken of one got with child and going to London to conceal it. *Lawton* is in the way to *London* from several parts of *Cheshire*.

Lawyer, A good | an evil neighbour.

1604 R. DALLINGTON *The View of Fraunce* B 4 I haue heard some poore Countreyman say, He loues not to haue his house too neere a Lawyer. It should seeme they bee ill Neighbours. **1611** COTGRAVE s.v. 'Advocat'. **1670** RAY 15.

Lawyer must be a great liar, A good.

1674 J. SMITH *Grammatica Quadrilinguis* (Fr.-Eng.), 65 Lawyers are oftentimes lyars. **1703** E. WARD *Writings* ii. 319 (A) [cited as 'a common saying'].

Lawyer never goes to law himself, A.

1666 TORRIANO 206 No good Attorney will ever go to law. **1902–4** LEAN III. 393.

Lawyer's opinion is worth nothing unless paid for, A.

1605–6 SHAKS. *K. Lear* I. iv. 142 *Kent.* This is nothing, fool. *Fool.* Then 'tis like the breath of an unfee'd lawyer, you gave me nothing for't. [Cf. **1616** DRAXE 25 A Lawyer will not pleade but for money.] **1902–4** LEAN III. 393.

Lawyers' gowns are lined with the wilfulness of their clients.

1707 MAPLETOFT 17. **1855** BOHN 439.

Lawyers' houses are built on the heads of fools.

1640 HERBERT 360.

Lawyer(s), *see also* Counsel (L.) (He that is his own) has fool for client; Fair and softly as l. to heaven; Few l. die well; Go not for every . . . quarrel to l.; Hide nothing from thy l.; King can make . . . not a l.; Old physician, young l.; Wimple in a l.'s clew.

Lay by, *see* L. things by, may come to use; Rainy day.

Lay down, *see* Laugh and l. d.; Lick and l. d.; Nought l. d. nought take up.

Lay (up) in lavender, To.

[= (a) to lay aside carefully for future use, (b) *slang* to pawn, (c) to put out of the way of doing harm.] **1592** GREENE *Upst. Courtier* (1871) 34 He is ready to lend . . . upon rings . . . or any other good pawn, but the poor gentleman pays so dear for the lavender it is laid up in that . . . **1599** JONSON *Ev. Man out* *of Humour* III. iii. 40 Which sute . . . new lies in lauander. **1605** CHAPMAN, &c. *Eastw. Hoe* G 2 Good faith rather then thou shouldest pawne a rag more il'e lay my ladiship in lauender. *a.* **1628** EARLE *Microcosm., Yng. rawe Preacher* (Arb.) 23 He . . . ha's a jest still in lavender for Bellarmine. *a.* **1639** WOTTON *Let. to Walton* in *Relig.* (1651) 512 Yours hath lyen so long by me (as it were in lavender) without an answer. **1664** COTTON *Scarron.* She laid him [Julus] up in lavender. *a.* **1700** B.E. *Dict. Cant. Crew* s.v. *Laydup-in Lavender,* when any Cloaths or other Moveables are pawn'd or dipt for present Money. **1822** SCOTT *Nigel* xxiii Lowestoffe is laid up in lavender only for having shown you the way into Alsatia.

Lay it on with a trowel, To.

[= to express a thing coarsely ; now *spec.* to flatter grossly.] **1599–1600** SHAKS. *A.Y.L.* I. ii. 112 Well said, that was laid on with a trowel. **1650** FULLER *Pisgah-sight* II. vi (1869) 142 Flattery of the Roman emperors, . . . so gross that it seems . . . daubed with a trowel. **1732** FULLER no. 5930 You lay on your Butter, as with a Trowel. **1898** G. W. E. RUSSELL *Coll. & Recoll.* xxiii He [Lord Beaconsfield] said to Mr. Matthew Arnold . . . 'Every one likes flattery ; and when you come to Royalty you should lay it on with a trowel.'

Lay on more wood; ashes give money.

1642 TORRIANO 75. **1658** *Comes Facundus* 194 Do, lay on more wood, hang it, the Ashes will yeeld money. **1678** RAY 65.

Lay sorrow to your heart when others lay it to their heels, Never.

1871 *N. & Q.* 4th Ser. VIII. 506 LANCASHIRE PROVERBS.—'Never lay sorrow to your heart when others lay it to their heels.' This is said when any one is grieved by the desertion of children or friends.

Lay the head of the sow to the tail of the grice.[1]

1721 KELLY 62 . . . That is, balance your loss with your gain. **1818** SCOTT *Rob Roy* xxiv An I am to lose by ye, I'se ne'er deny I hae won by ye mony a fair pund sterling—Sae, an it come to the warst, I'se e'en lay the head o' the sow to the tail o' the grice. [[1] pig.]

Lay the reins on the neck, To.

c. **1600** *Edmund Ironside* l. 157 Yf you lay the teame vppon theire neckes and lett them have but any scope to runne . . . **1607** R. C[AREW] tr. *Estienne's World of Wonders* 58 Youth is set at libertie, and haue the reine laid in their necks to runne at randon. **1807** OPIE *Lect. on Art* iv (1848) 332 No man ever more completely laid the reins on the neck of his inclinations.

Lay the stool's foot in water, To.

1830 FORBY 433 . . . To make preparation for company. It is derived from the custom of washing brick floors.

Lay the sweet side of your tongue to it.

1721 KELLY 239 . . . An answer to them that ask what they will get to their hasty-pudding.

Lay things by, they may come to use. (*Cf.* Keep a thing seven years, &c.)

1642 TORRIANO 75 Lay up thy goods in a corner, there will be a time, they will be usefull. **1732** FULLER no. 3154.

Lay up for holidays, To.

1546 HEYWOOD II. x. 83 In condition they differde so many waies That lightly he layde hir up for hollie daies. **1580** LYLY *Euph. & his Eng.* (Arb.) 323 Thou goest about . . . to hang me up for holydayes, as one neither fitting thy head nor pleasing thy humour.

Lay up, *see also* Lay (up) in lavender ; Rainy day.

Lay your wame to your winning.

1832 HENDERSON 16 . . . Let not your household expenditure exceed your income. **1862** HISLOP 247 Poor folk maun fit their wame to their winning.

Layer(s) up, *see* Ill l. u. make thieves.

Laying, *see* Cured her from l. in the hedge.

Layton, *see* Prayers (They shall have) . . . quoth vicar of L.

Laziness, *see* Lacking breeds l. ; Pride and l. would have mickle upholding.

Lazy as Ludlam's dog, As | that leaned his head against a wall to bark.

1670 RAY 202. **1801** WOLCOT (P. Pindar) *Out at Last* Wks. (1816) III. 385 Lazy as Ludlam's lazy dog, That held his head against the wall to bark. **1891** J. L. KIPLING *Beast & Man* 287 English rustics talk of a man 'as lazy as Ludlam's dog that leaned his head against the wall to bark'.

Lazy-bones.

[= a lazy person.] **1592** G. HARVEY *Pierce's Super.* (1593) 185 Was . . . legierdemane a slowewome, Viuacitie a lasie-bones. **1809** MALKIN *Gil Blas* II. i. par. 6 Master lazy-bones did not like sitting up!

Lazy (Idle) folks (people) take the most pains (*or* have the most labour).

1678 RAY 161 Idle folks have the most labour. **1707** MAPLETOFT 112 Idle lazy Folks have most labour. **1732** FULLER no. 3056 Idle people take the most pains. **1890** D. C. MURRAY *J. Vale's Guard.* xix It is as true in morals as it is in business that lazy people take the most pains.

Lazy Laurence.

[= an idle person ; possibly mere alliteration, or in allusion to the heat prevalent about St.

Laurence's day, Aug. 10.] **1784** *Gent. Mag.*
II. 349 (A) When a person in hot weather
seems lazy, it is a common saying that Lawrence bids him high wages. **1796** EDGEWORTH
Par. Asst., '*Lazy Lawrence*' (1903) 53 He
was found early and late at his work, established a new character, and . . . lost the name
of 'Lazy Lawrence'. **1796** PEGGE *Anonym.*
VIII. xix (1809) 348 *Laurence bids wages*; a
proverbial saying for *to be lazy*; because St.
Laurence's day is the 10th of August within
the dog-days. **1821** CLARE *Vill. Minstr.* II. 23
When . . . the warm sun smiles And 'Lawrence wages bids' on hills and stiles. **1836**
W. D. COOPER *Glos. Sussex Provinc.* 24 'I ha'e
got a touch o' ol' Laurence todae, I be
troubled to git ane wud me work'. **1863**
J. R. WISE *New Forest* xvi (1895) 174 If a
peasant is lazy, it is proverbially said,
'Laurence has got upon him', or, 'He has
got a touch of Laurence'. **1880** *E. Cornwall
Gloss.* He's as lazy as Larence. One wad
think that Larence had got hold o'n.

Lazy ox is little better for the goad, A.

1732 FULLER no. 236.

Lazy sheep thinks its wool heavy, A.

1727 GAY *Fables, Hare & Friends* The sheep
was feeble, and complain'd His sides a load
of wool sustain'd. **1732** FULLER no. 237.

Lazy youth, a lousy age, A. (*Cf.* Idle youth, &c.)

1672 CODRINGTON 107. **1736** BAILEY *Dict.* s.v.
'Youth' (A).

Lazy, *see also* Lean fee fit reward for l. clerk;
Long and l.

Lea, *see* Leave her on a l.

Lead a horse to the water, A man may | but he cannot make him drink.

c. 1175 *Lambeth Hom.* (Morris) 9 Hwa is þet
mei þet hors wettrien þe him self nule
drinken? **1546** HEYWOOD I. xi. 27 A man
maie well bring a horse to the water, But he
can not make him drinke without he will.
1647 FULLER *C. Wounded Consc.* One may
bring them down to the spring of life, but
cannot make them drink of the waters thereof. **1763** JOHNSON in *Boswell* xvi. (1848) 146
You need not be afraid of his forcing you to
be . . . a lawyer; . . . 'One man may lead a
horse to the water, but twenty cannot make
him drink.' **1857** TROLLOPE *Barch. Tow.*
xxxv 'Well,' said she . . . , 'one man can take
a horse to water, but a thousand can't make
him drink.'

Lead nor drive, Neither.

1667 L'ESTRANGE *Quevedo's Visions* (1904)
80 (A) Another . . . would neither lead nor
drive. **1678** RAY 75 . . . An untoward, un-
manageable person.

Lead one by the nose, To.

[LUCIAN, *Hermos.* 168: οὐδὲν κωλύσει σε τῆς
ῥινὸς ἕλκεσθαι ὑφ' ἑκάστου = L. *naribus tra-*
here, as was done with bears.] **1581** T. LUPTON
A Persuasion from Papistry 149 (T 3) He
maye leade them by the noses whiche waye
he liste. **1598** FLORIO *Worlde of Wordes* s.v.
Menar per il naso, to leade by the nose, to
make a foole of one. **1604–5** SHAKS. *Othello* I.
iii. 407 The Moor . . . will as tenderly be led
by the nose As asses are. **1610–11** *Wint. T.*
IV. iii. 835 Though authority be a stubborn
bear, yet he is oft led by the nose with gold.
1621 BURTON *Anat. Mel.* III. iv. I. ii (1651)
648 They will make others most devout and
superstitious, . . . and lead them by the nose
like so many bears in a line. **1689** FULLER
Holy War II. xxxi (1840) 90 Manasses, . . .
under pretence of opening the queen's eyes,
did lead her by the nose, captivating her judgment instead of directing it. *a.* **1687** COTTON
Poet. Wks. (1765) 198 He master is of thee
indeed, and thee still by the nose does lead.

Lead (*noun*), *see* Balance distinguisheth not
between gold and l.

Lead(s) (*verb*), *see also* Fate l. the willing.

Leaden sword in an ivory sheath, A.

[L. *In eburna vagina plumbeus gladius.*] **1533**
UDALL *Flowers for Latin Speaking* (1560) Z 2
A latine prouerbe: *Plumbeo iugulare gladio*, to
cutte ones throte with a sworde of lead, that
is to saie, to goe about . . . to conuince a man
with a vayne . . . argument. **1540** TAVERNER
tr. *Erasm. Flores sententiarum* O 1 *Qui forma
decorus indecore loquitur, ex eburnea uagina
plumbeum educit gladium* A goodlye person
that speaketh vngoodly wordes, draweth
forth a leaden swerd out of an Iuery skaberd.
1542 UDALL tr. *Erasm. Apoph.* (1877) 163
Hearyng a young strieplyng, of a verie well
fauoured and honeste face, vsyng vnhonest
communicacion, Art thou not ashamed,
quoth he, to drawe a sword of lead out of an
ieuorie sheathe? **1592** LYLY *Midas* I. ii
That's a leaden dagger in a velvet sheath, to
have a black tongue in a fair mouth.

Leaden, *see also* God comes with l. feet.

Leaf of borage might buy all the substance that they can sell, A.

1546 HEYWOOD I. x. 21 But wed of corage
They must in all haste, though a leafe of
borage Might by all the substance that they
can sell.

Leaf (-ves), *see also* Every day of . . . a l. in thy
history; Fears l. (He that) . . . not go into
wood; Take a l. out of book; Turn a new l.

Leak like a sieve, To.

1861 C. READE *Cloister & H.* lvii The captain
left the helm and came amidships pale as
death. . . . 'She leaks like a sieve.' **1903**
A. T. QUILLER-COUCH *Hetty Wesley* II. i The
kettle . . . began to leak like a sieve.

Leak will sink a great ship, A small.

1732 FULLER no. 407. **1745** FRANKLIN *Jan.*
Beware of little expenses, a small leak will
sink a great ship.

Leak, *see also* Old vessels must l.

Leal folks never wanted gear.

1721 KELLY 231.

Leal heart lied never.

1768 A. ROSS *Helenore* (1778) 89 Her dowie pain she could no more conceal; The heart, they'll say, will never lie that's leal. **1862** HISLOP 206.

Leal, *see also* Hard task to be poor and l.

Lean as a rake, As.

c. **1386** CHAUCER *Prol.* 287 As lene was his hors as is a rake. **1659** HOWELL *Prov.* 10. *a.* **1732** GAY *New Song New Sim.* Songs, &c. (1784) II. 115 Lean as a rake with sighs and care.

Lean as a shotten herring.

1593 G. HARVEY *Wks.* (Gros.) II. 130 His conceit is as lank, as a shotten herring. **1607** T. W. *The Optic Glass of Humours* C 6. **1659** HOWELL *Fr.–Eng.* 18.

Lean compromise is better than a fat lawsuit, A. (*Cf.* Ill agreement, &c.)

1666 TORRIANO 1 A sorry agreement is better than a good sute in Law. **1753** FRANKLIN Aug. A lean award is better than a fat judgment.

Lean dog for a hard road, A.

1917 BRIDGE 4.

Lean dog to get through a hedge, A.

1902–4 LEAN III. 393 . . . Spare people most easy to pull through an illness. (Lancashire.)

Lean fee is a fit reward for a lazy clerk, A.

1579 GOSSON *Ephemerides* (*Sch. Abuse* [Arb.] 11) A leane fee is fitte for a lazie Clarke.

Lean liberty is better than fat slavery.

1732 FULLER no. 3158.

Lean to the wrong shore, To.

1546 HEYWOOD II. ii. 47 Ye leane (quoth he) to the wrong shore.

Lean, *see also* Snapping so short makes you look so l.

Leap an inch from a slut (shrew), She cannot.

1648 25 Jan.–3 Feb. *Mercurius Aulicus*, Numb. 1, A 2ᵛ Not one of 'em are able to leap three foot from a knave. **1678** RAY 256 She doth not leap an inch from a shrew. **1732** FULLER no. 4121 (with 'slut').

Leap at a crust, To.

1612 T. JAMES *Jesuits Downfall* 23 You shall see them all leape at a crust, ere it be long. **1616** WITHALS 566. **1616** DRAXE 95 Hee will leape at a crust.

Leap at a daisy, To.

[= to be hanged.] **1553** *Respublica* v. ii (A) Some of vs erelong maie happe leape at a daisie. **1575** *Gamm. Gurton* v. ii. 235 I will go neare for this to make ye leape at a dasye.

Leap in the dark, A.

1697 VANBRUGH *Prov. Wife* v. vi Now I am in for Hobbes' voyage; a great leap in the dark.[1] **1721** DEFOE *Moll Flanders* (1840) 75 Make matrimony, like death, a leap in the dark. **1903** BRYCE *Biograph. Stud.* 57 The Act of 1867 was described at the time as 'a leap in the dark'. [1 referring to traditional last words of Thomas Hobbes (d. 1679), 'I am going to take a great leap into obscurity'. Cf. traditional last words of Rabelais (d. 1553) *Je m'en vais chercher un grand peut-être.*]

Leap into a well, If you | Providence is not bound to fetch you out.

1732 FULLER no. 2795.

Leap over nine hedges, He is ready to.

1678 RAY 353.

Leap over the hedge before you come at the stile (*or vice versa*), To.

1546 HEYWOOD II. ix Ye would be over the stile before you come at it. **1566** GASCOIGNE *Supposes* II. i. (1907) 202 You would fayne leape over the stile before you come at the hedge. **1670** RAY 184.

Leap over where the hedge (dyke) is lowest, Men.

1546 HEYWOOD II. v. 56 Where the hedge is lowest, men maie soonest ouer. **1639** CLARKE 172. **1655–62** GURNALL *Chrn. in Armour* (1865) I. 296 The devil chose rather to assault Eve than Adam . . . He labours to creep over where the hedge is lowest, and the resistance likely to be weakest. **1721** KELLY 250 *Men loup the dike where it is leaghest.*[1] That is, oppress and over-run those who are least able to resist them. [1 lowest.]

Leap year is never a good sheep year, A.

1601 J. CHAMBER *Treatise against Judicial Astrology* 110 Shepheards and heardsmen . . . report that their flockes and cattell those yeares [in leap years] either conceiue not at all, or if they do, yet go not out their time, or if they go out, yet they bring forth certain weake and crossed ware. **1846** DENHAM 17.

Leaped a haddock (*or whiting*), There.

[= an opportunity was missed.][1] **1546** HEYWOOD II. vii. 64 There lepte a whityng (quoth she). *c.* **1612** BEAUM. & FL. *Scornf. Lady* IV. 1 *Abig.* My little Levite hath forsaken me . . . : well fool, you leapt a Haddock when you left him. **1670** RAY 199 To let leap a whiting, *i.e.* To let slip an opportunity.

Leaps over the dyke where it is lowest, Every one.

1721 KELLY 97 *Every one loups o'er the dike where it is laighest.* . . . Signifying that poor people are run down by every body.

Leap(s), *see also* Dam l. over (Where), kid follows; Recoil a little . . . l. the better; Stumble at straw and l. over block.

Learn at other men's cost, It is good to.

1573 TUSSER *Husb.* x (1878) 23 Then happie is he by example that can take heede by the fall of a mischieued man.

Learn to pray, He that will (would) | let him go to sea.

1576 GASCOIGNE *Steele Glas* (Arb.) 79 For towarde shipwracke, many men can pray. *a.* **1631** DONNE *Sat.* vii Poems (1896) II. 209 Friends, like land soldiers in a storm at sea, Not knowing what to do, for him did pray. **1640** HERBERT (Gros.) no. 84. **1655–62** GURNALL *Chrn. in Armour* (1865) I. 577 The proverb indeed is, 'He that would learn to pray, let him go to sea'. **1659** N. R. 42. **1678** BUTLER *Hudibras* III. ii. 537 (As carnal seamen, in a storm, Turn pious converts, and reform.) **1694** R. SOUTH *Twelve Sermons* 199 1a. **1908** *Spectator* 13 Aug. 452 These sailors . . . can only call upon the Most High. . . . There is a Basque proverb, 'Let him who knows not how to pray, go to sea'.

Learn to say before you sing.

1639 CLARKE 116.

Learn to shape Idle a coat, You will soon.

1602 CAREW *Surv. of Cornwall* (1769) f. 56 To reproue one of laziness, they will say, Doest thou make Idle a coate? that is, a coate for idlenes? **1678** RAY 254.

Learn weeping, and thou shalt gain laughing.

1640 HERBERT 322.

Learn wisdom by the follies of others.

1855 BOHN *Ital.*

Learn young, learn fair.

1641 FERGUSSON 72.

Learn your goodam to make milk kail.

1721 KELLY 233 . . . Spoken to them who officiously offer to teach them who know more than themselves.

Learned as Doctor Doddypoll,[1] As.

c. **1410** *Towneley Plays* (E.E.T.S.) 173 (A) ffy, dotty-pols, with your bookys! *a.* **1534** *Hyckescorner* 695 What, mayster doctour Dotypoll, Can you not preche well in a blacke boll, Or dispute ony dyvynyte? **1659** HOWELL *Eng. Prov.* 17 [[1] a blockhead.]

Learned timely to steal (beg) that could not say 'Nay', He.

c. **1460** *Towneley Myst., 2nd Shep. Play* 524 He lernyd tymely to steyll that couth not say nay. **1641** FERGUSSON 42 He gangs earlie to steal, that cannot say na. **1721** KELLY 170 *He gangs early to beg that cannot say nay.* Because men will make a prey of his liberal disposition.

Learned (*adj.*), *see also* Lives well is l. enough.

Learneth young, Whoso | forgets not when he is old.

c. **1275** *Provs. of Alfred* (Skeat) A 100–5 The mon þe on his youhþe yeorne leorneþ . . . he may beon on elde wenliche lorþeu. [The man who learns eagerly in youth . . . may be an excellent teacher when he is old.] *c.* **1300** *Provs. of Hending* 6 Whose yong lereth,[1] olt[2] he ne leseth.[3] *c.* **1400** *Beryn* (E.E.T.S.) l. 938 For thing I-take in [youthe, is] hard to put away. [[1] learneth. [2] old. [3] loseth.]

Learning is the eye of the mind.

1616 DRAXE 110.

Learning makes a good man better and an ill man worse.

1611 GRUTER. *c.* **1612** P. CHARRON *Of Wisdom* tr. S. Lennard (1640) 507 One . . . hath said . . . That learning marreth weake wits, and spirits, perfiteth the strong and naturall. **1614** CAMDEN. **1707** MAPLETOFT 96. **1732** FULLER no. 3162.

Learning, *see also* Experience without l.; Good life better than bushel of l. (Handful of); Good manners to show l. before ladies (Not); Great memory without l.; House and land are spent (When), l. is excellent; Little l. dangerous; Love of money and of l. rarely meet; Much science (l.) much sorrow; Ounce of discretion worth pound of l.; Pay more for schooling than l. is worth; Wit without l. tree without fruit.

Learns a trade, He that | hath a purchase made.

1611 COTGRAVE s.v. 'Mestier' He that hath a good trade hath a goodly revenue. **1640** HERBERT 362.

Learn(s, t, ed), *see also* Better l. by neighbour's skaith; Doing nothing we l. to do ill; Doing we l.; Evil is some l.; *Fas est et ab hoste doceri*; First l. (What we) we best can; Live and l.; Never too old to l.; Nothing questioneth nothing l.; Wise men l. by other men's harms.

Lease, *see* New l. of life; No man hath l. of his life.

Least boy always carries the greatest fiddle, The.

1670 RAY 112 . . . All lay load upon those that are the least able to bear it. For they that are least able to bear, are least able to resist the imposition of the burden. **1732** FULLER no. 4629 (omitting 'always').

Least foolish is wise, The.

1640 HERBERT 359.

Least said, soonest mended. *See also* Little (Least, Nothing) said is soon amended.

1776 T. COGAN *John Buncle, Junior* I. 237–8 (A) But mum's the word; least said is soonest mended. **1837** DICKENS *Pickwick* xlviii The old lady . . . ventured to approach Mr. Benjamin Allen with a few comforting reflections, of which the chief were that . . . the least said the soonest mended.

Leather, Nothing like.

1692 L'ESTRANGE *Aesop's Fab.* ccccxlviii (1738) 484 There was a council of mechanics called to advise about the fortifying of a city. . . . Up starts a currier; Gentlemen, says he, when y'ave said all that can be said, there's nothing in the world like leather. **1837** SIR F. PALGRAVE *Merch. & Friar* (1844) 147 Depend upon it, Sir, there is nothing like leather. **1905** WEYMAN *Starvecrow F.* ii 'My lords would not sleep in their beds . . . if it were not for the yeomanry and the runners.' . . . Mrs. Gilson coughed drily. 'Leather's a fine thing', she said, 'if you believe the cobbler.'

Leather, *see also* Cut large thongs of other men's l.; Cut one's thong according to one's l.; Find fault with my shoes and give no l.; Raw l. will stretch; Tongue is made of loose l. (Your); Tough as l.

Leave a jest when it pleases you best.

1640 HERBERT 321. Leave jesting while it pleaseth, lest it turn to earnest. **1732** FULLER no. 6357. **1855** BOHN 440.

Leave her on a lea and let the devil flit her.

1599 PORTER *Angry Wom. Abingd.* IV. iii (Merm.) 175 *Nich.* But an they would be ruled by me, they should set her on the leeland, and bid the devil split her. **1659** HOWELL *Eng. Prov.* 16/2 Leave her on a ley, and let the Devil flitt her; *A Lincolnshire proverb spoken of a scolding wife; viz. Tye her to a Plow-ridge, and lett the Devill remove her to a better Pasture.*

Leave in the briers, To.

[in troubles, difficulties.] **1520** WHITTINGTON *Vulg.* (E.E.T.S.) 98 Thou art a sure spere at nede · that leues a man stykkynge in the breres. **1563** FOXE *A. & M.* I. 208/1 Leaving the Bishops, and such others, in the Briers. **1670** RAY 166 To leave one in the briers (or suds).

Leave in the lurch, To.

[= to leave in adverse circumstances, or unexpected difficulty.] **1576** G. HARVEY *Letter-Book* (Camden Soc.) 163 (A) Lest he fail in his reckning . . . and so leave himself in the lurch. **1596** NASHE *Saffron Walden* 119 He . . . left both of them in the lurtch for him. **1600** HOLLAND *Livy* 222 The Volscians seeing themselves abandoned and left in the lurch

by them, . . . quit the campe and field. **1705** STRYPE *Life of Cheke* v. ii (1821) 94 The Lords . . . proclaimed Mary Queen, . . . and thus was poor Sir John Cheke left in the lurch. **1879** BROWNING *Martin Relph* 66 He has left his sweetheart here in the lurch.

Leave is light.

1546 HEYWOOD I. x Ye might have knocked ere ye came in; leave is light. **1631** JONSON *New Inn* v. i *Host.* But you must ask my leave first, . . . Leave is but light. **1670** RAY 113 . . . It's an easie matter to ask leave. **1721** KELLY 230 . . . A reproof to them who intrude upon your interest, without your permission.

Leave more to do when we die, We | than we have done.

1640 HERBERT 361.

Leave no stone unturned, To.

[= to try every possible means. EUR. *Heracl.* 1002 πάντα κινῆσαι πέτρον. PLINY *Ep.* 1. 20. 15 . . . *omnia pertempto, omnia experior,* πάντα denique λίθον κινῶ. ERASM. *Ad. Omnem movere lapidem.*] *c.* **1550** *Dice-Play* B vj He will refuse no labour nor leaue no stone vnturned, to pick up a penny. **1655** FULLER *Ch. Hist.* XI. iii (1868) III. 471 They did whatsoever good men could, . . . leaving no stone unturned which might advantage them herein. **1926** *Times* 17 Apr. 14/3 The Government . . . would leave no stone unturned to avoid the catastrophe of a stoppage.

Leave off while the play is good.

c. **1350** *Douce MS. 52* no. 58 When game is best, Hit is tyme to rest. *c.* **1390** GOWER *Conf. Amantis* VIII. 3087 In his proverbe seith the wise, whan game is best, is best to leave. *c.* **1450** *Provs. of Wisdom* (ed. Zupitza) in *Archiv. f. d. Stud. d. Neueren Sprachen* **90.** 245 When game is best, is tyme to lete. **1721** KELLY 233 . . . Lest, if it be continued, it may come to earnest. Spoken also by people of age and gravity, when young people jest upon them, intimating that they will not bear it. **1820** SCOTT *Monast.* xiii When I saw our host break ranks, . . . I e'en pricked off with myself while the play was good. **1832** W. BATES *Maclise Port. Gal.* (1898) 280 James Smith . . . laid down the principle . . . that when a man had played a good game, he should retire from the tables, and leave off a winner.

Leave off, *see also* Piper of Bujalance who got . . . ten [maravedi] to l. o.

Leave the court ere the court leave thee.

1641 FERGUSSON 72. **1721** KELLY 234 . . . A good advice in its literal sense, if courtiers would take it, but it signifies that we should mortify our vicious inclinations, by consideration and religion, before old age make them forsake us.

Leave to speak who cannot hold his tongue, He must have.

1641 FERGUSSON 38 He mon have leave to speak that cannot had his tongue. **1683**

MERITON *Yorks. Ale* (1697) 83–7 (A). 1721 KELLY 145 . . . Spoken against impertinent and indefatigable baublers.

Leave to thrive for throng,[1] You cannot get.

1721 KELLY 365 . . . That is, your too much haste spoils your business. [[1] press of business.]

Leave (Let) well alone.

c. **1396** CHAUCER *Envoy to Bukton* l. 27 Unwys is he that kan no wele endure. If thou be siker, put the nat in drede. **1834** MARRYAT *Jacob Faith.* xxxiii You're well off at present, and 'leave well alone' is a good motto. **1849** LYTTON *Caxtons* VI. vi We have been happy for more than eighteen years without them, Kitty! . . . To leave well alone is a golden rule worth all in Pythagoras. **1863** C. READE *Hard Cash* liii Colt cast a glance of triumph, and declined to re-examine. He always let well alone.

Leave (off) with an appetite.

1558 BULLEIN *Govt. of Health* 37 And so leue w̄ an appetite, passinge the time wyslie betwene dinner and supper.

Leave (*noun*), *see also* French l. (Take); Losers l. to speak (Give).

Leaves the old way for the new, Who | will find himself deceived.

1573 SANDFORD (1576) 103. **1666** TORRIANO 271.

Leaveth surety (certainty) and leaneth to chance, He that | when fools pipe he may dance.

1546 HEYWOOD II. xi. 83 Who that leaueth surety and leaneth vnto chance, Whan fooles pype, by auctoritée he maie daunce. **1670** RAY 68 He that leaves certainty and sticks to chance, When fools pipe he may dance.

Leave(s), leaving, left (*verb*), *see also* Better l. than lack; Dines and l. lays cloth twice; Get him where you l. him; Shameful l. worse than shameful eating.

Lecher, *see* Old man l.

Lecture(s), *see* Curtain l.; Forehead and eye (In) l. of mind.

Lee(s) (*proper name*), *see* Cheshire there are L. (In).

Leech, *see* Go after a l. (While men), body is buried.

Leeches kill with licence.

1721 KELLY 232 . . . An argument dissuading people of no skill from quacking; for if any that they administer to die, they will be blam'd; but if any die under the hands of a physician, no notice is taken of it.

Leeful[1] man is the beggar's brother, The.

1721 KELLY 315 . . . Spoken when we have

lent something that we now want, and must be forced to borrow. [[1] The man that is ready to lend.]

Leek, Not worth a.

c. **1350** *Alexander* l. 4229 (A) And your lare of a leke suld nevir the less worth. *c.* **1400** *Rom. Rose* B. 4830 Sich love I preise not at a lek. *c.* **1412** HOCCLEVE *De Reg. Princ.* (1860) 60 Love on luste groundede is not worthe a leeke. *a.* **1529** SKELTON *Col. Cloute* 183 Wks. (1843) I. 318 But it is not worth a leke.

Leeks in Lide, and ramsins[1] in May, Eat | and all the year after physicians may play.

1686–7 AUBREY *Rem. Gent. & Jud.* 13 The vulgar in the West of England doe call the month of March, Lide [= O.E. Hlyde]. A proverbiall rhythme—'Eate Leekes in Lide, and Ramsins in May, And all the yeare after Physitians may play.' [[1] Garlic.]

Leek(s), *see also* Eat the l.; Green as a l.

Leeward for fine weather, Look not, like the Dutchman, to.

1883 ROPER 13.

Left his purse in his other hose (breeches), He hath.

1616 WITHALS 584. **1639** CLARKE 244. **1721** KELLY 138 *He left his money in his other breeks.* A taunt to him that wants money to pay his reckoning.

Left to chance, Something must be.

1903 W. C. RUSSELL *Overdue* ii 'Something must be left to chance', was a condition of Lord Nelson's tactics, and a clear recognition of the limits of human penetration.

Left (*adj.*), *see* Over the l. shoulder.

Leg bail, To give (take).

[= to run away, decamp.] **1774** FERGUSSON *Poems* (1807) 234 They took leg-bail and ran awa With pith and speed. **1775** ADAIR *Amer. Ind.* 277 I had concluded to use no chivalry, but give them leg-bail instead of it, by . . . making for a deep swamp. **1785** GROSE *Dict. Vulg. T.* s.v. 'Leg' To give leg bail and land security, to run away. **1842–3** W. H. MAXWELL *Hector O'Hal.* iv The priest and my lady will hear all in the morning, and, i' faith, I'll give them leg-bail in the mean time.

Leg of a lark is better than the body of a kite, A.

1546 HEYWOOD I. iv. 9 She, by lacke of substance séemyng but a sparke, Steynth[1] yet the stoutest, For a leg of a larke Is better than is the body of a kyght. **1605** CHAPMAN, &c. *Eastw. Hoe* V. i. 153 The legge of a larke is better then the body of a kight. **1670** RAY 112 One leg of a lark's worth the whole body of a kite. **1684** BUNYAN *Pilgr.* II (1867) 192 Yea, with delight, Say my lark's leg is better than a kite. [[1] checks.]

Leg warmeth, While the | the boot harmeth.

a. **1500** R. *Hill's Commonpl. Bk.* (E.E.T.S.) 128 (A) While the fote warmith, the sho harmith. **1546** HEYWOOD II. ii. 46 Long liyng warme in bed is holsome (quoth shée) While the leg warmeth, the boote harmeth (quoth hée). **1721** KELLY 251 Mickle sorrow comes to the screa,[1] e'er the heat come to the tea[2]. [[1] shoe. [2] toe.]

Leg(s), *see also* Belly carries the l.; Bone in the l. (Were it not for); Lies have short l.; Long be thy l. and short thy life; Lose a l. rather than life; Old use and wont, l. about the fire; Right as my l.; Runs in the blood like wooden l.; See which l. you are lame of; Set a person on his l.; Shake a loose l.; Stretch your l. according to coverlet; Talk the hind l. off a donkey; Thought hath good l.; Understanding (Who has not) let him have l.; Use l. and have l.; White l. would aye be rused.

Legion(s), *see* Contending with master of l. (Ill).

Leicestershire, *see* Shake a L. man . . . beans rattle.

Leigh, *see* Harry's children of L.

Leighton Buzzard, *see* Tring, Wing, and Ivinghoe.

Leisure, *see* Busiest men have most l.; Idle folks have least l.; Luck in l.

Leman *or* **Lemman,** *see* No longer foster no longer l.; Tender as a parson's l.

Lemster [Leominster] bread and Weabley ale.

1586 CAMDEN *Britannia* 352 *Frumento item ideo est fælix, & pane e purissimo polline, vt huius panis & Weabliæ potus . . . in prouerbium cesserint.* **1610** *Ibid.* tr. Holland 620 So renowned also it is for wheat, and head of the finest floure, that Lemster bread and Weabley Ale . . . are growne unto a common proverbe.

Lemster [Leominster] ore.[1]

1514 BARCLAY *Egloges* (E.E.T.S.) iv. l. 316 Cornewall hath tinne and lymster wools fine. **1613–22** DRAYTON *Polyolb.* vii. 145 (1876) I. 176 At *Lemster,* for whose wool whose staple doth excell.—vii. 151 Where lives the man so dull, on Britain's further shore, To whom did never sound the name of *Lemster* Ore? That with the silkworm's web for smallness doth compare. **1648** HERRICK *Hesper., Oberon's Pal.* (1901) I. 215 A bank of mosse . . . farre more Soft then the finest Lemster Ore. [[1] wool.]

Lemster ore, *see also* Webley ale.

Lemster wool, *see* Dunmow bacon.

Lend and lose; so play fools.

1678 RAY 347.

Lend thy horse for a long journey, thou mayest have him return with his skin.

1670 RAY 14.

Lend your money and lose your friend.

1600–1 SHAKS. *Hamlet* I. iii. 75 Neither a borrower or lender be; For loan oft loses both itself and friend. **1611** COTGRAVE S.v. Ami' *Qui preste à l'ami perd au double:* Prov. viz. both friend and money. To which purpose we haue a . . . Ryme, which begins with, I lent my money to my friend, and ends with I lost both money, and my friend. **1721** KELLY 240 . . . It is not the lending of our money that loses our friend; but the demanding it again.

Lends, gives, He that.

1640 HERBERT 353.

Lends his pot may seethe his kail in his loof,[1] He that.

1737 RAMSAY III. 184. [[1] palm of hand.

Lend(s), *see also* Better give a shilling than l.; Borrow (Not so good to) as to l.; Borrow nor l.; Coat (He who has but one) cannot l. it; Enemy (If you would make), l.; Give him one and l. him another.

Length begets loathing.

1742 JARVIS *Don Quixote* II. xxvi Length begets loathing. **1896** F. LOCKER-LAMPSON *My Confid.* 43 'Length begets loathing'. I well remember the sultry Sunday evenings when . . . we simmered through Mr. Shepherd's long-winded pastorals.

Length of a person's foot, To find (*or* know) the.

1580 LYLY *Euph. & his Eng.* (Arb.) 290 You shal not know the length of my foote, vntill by your cunning you get commendation. *a.* **1591** HY. SMITH *Serm.* (1866) II. 37 [Satan] marks how every man is inclined, . . . and when he hath the measure of his foote, then he fits him. **1594–5** SHAKS. *L.L.L.* V. ii. 475 Do not you know my lady's foot by the Squire? [i.e. square, measure.] **1616** DRAXE 108 I know the length of his foot. *a.* **1617** BAYNE *On Eph.* I. 15 (1643) 156 Persons who can humour them, and find the length of their foot. **1826** SCOTT *Woodst.* xix I think I know the length of this man's foot. We have had a jollification or so together.

Lent, When I | I had a friend; but, when I asked, he was unkind.

c. **1450** *Provs. of Wysdom* 163 When I lent, I had a frend; But when I askyd, he was vnkynd. **1639** CLARKE 169 When I lend I am his friend, when I ask I am unkind.

Lent (*noun*), *see* After Christmas comes L.; Marry in L., live to repent; Short L. that must pay at Easter·

Lent (*verb*), *see also* Lippens to l. ploughs, his land will lie ley.

Leominster, *see* Lemster.

Leopard, In a | the spots are not observed.

1640 HERBERT 348.

Less of your counsel (courtesy) and more of your cost (purse).

1629 T. ADAMS *Serm.* (1861–2) II. 407 With a show of spiritual counsel, they neglect corporal comfort; and ... the poor might well reply, More of your cost, and less of your counsel. **1670** RAY 74 Less of your courtesie and more of your purse. *Re opitulandum non verbis.*

Let-a-be for let-a-be. (*See also* Cathkin's covenant, &c.)

[= mutual forbearance.] **1821** SCOTT *Pirate* xxxvii I am for let-a-be for let-a-be, as the boys say.

Let-a-be for let-a-be with mad dogs and daft folk.

1836 M. SCOTT *Cruise Midge* ii The Scotch corporal ... took the liberty of putting in his oar. 'Beg pardon, Mr. Brail, but let abee for let abee with mad dogs and daft folk, is an auld but very true adage.'

Let anybody lie by him, He will not.

1678 RAY 89 *A Liar* ... He'll not let any body lye by him.

Let me see, as the blind man said.

1864–5 DICKENS *Our Mut. Fr.* II. ii 'What's the news in-doors?' ... 'Let me see, said the blind man. Why the last news is, that I don't mean to marry your brother.'

Let sleeping dogs lie. (*Cf.* Waken sleeping dogs, It is ill to.)

c. **1386** CHAUCER *Franklin's T.* F² 1472 Lat slepen that is stille. **1681** S. COLVIL *Whiggs Sup.* II. 27 It's best To let a sleeping mastiff rest. **1824** SCOTT *Redg.* lett. xi Take my advice, and speer as little about him as he does about you. Best to let sleeping dogs lie. **1882** BLACKMORE *Christowell* xxvi He laughed at the maxim of antiquity, *quieta noli movere*; which is, in our vernacular, 'let sleeping dogs lie'. **1902** A. LANG *Hist. Scot.* II. 509 It was the error of James that in ecclesiastical matters he could not obey the proverb, 'Let sleeping dogs lie'.

Let the cat out of the bag, To.

[= to disclose a guarded secret.] **1760** *Lond. Mag.* xxix. 224 We could have wished that the author ... had not let the cat out of the bag. **1796** EDGEWORTH *Par. Asst., Eton M.* III. ii I forgot, I was nigh letting the cat out o' the bag again. **1836** MARRYAT *Midsh. Easy* xxi Gascoigne closed his chair to Jack's, who, he was afraid, being a little affected with wine, would 'let the cat out of the bag'.

1847–8 THACKERAY *Vanity F.* xix Letting the cat of selfishness out of the bag of secrecy.

Let your house to your enemy; The first year | the second, to your friend; the third, live in it yourself.

1869 HAZLITT 382.

Let (= hindrance), *see* Little l. lets ill workman.

Let (a, every, him, &c.), *see also under the significant words following.*

Lets his horse drink at every lake, and his wife go to every wake, He that | shall never be without a whore and a jade.

1591 FLORIO *Second Frutes* 41 Who lets his wife go to euerie feaste, And lets his horse drinke at euerie puddle, Shall haue of his horse, a starke iadish beast And of his best wife, a twang with a huddle. **1640** HERBERT (Gros.) no. 430 Who lets his wife goe to every feast, and his horse drinke at every water, Shall neither have good wife nor good horse. **1670** RAY 29.

Letter stay for the post, Let your | not the post for the letter.

1642 TORRIANO 14. **1664** CODRINGTON 203. **1670** RAY 15. *Ital.*

Letter(s), *see* Complimentary l. asketh another; Eyes on l. (Neither) nor hands in coffers; Gist of a lady's l. in postscript; *Littera scripta manet.*

Lettuce, *see* Lips (Like), like l.

Level, *see* Line and l. (By).

Levi, *see* Tribe of l.

Lewd bachelor makes a jealous husband, A.

1707 MAPLETOFT 26.

Lewisham, Long, lazy, lousy.

1787 GROSE (*Kent*) 183 ... Lewisham is certainly a very long town or village, and, ... was once a very poor one. ... The alliteration of this proverb, rather than the truth of it, has preserved it to the present time.

Lewson Hill, *see* Akin as L. H. to Pilson Pen.

Liar is not believed when he speaks the truth, A.

[CICERO *De Div.* 2. 71. 146 *Mendaci homini, ne verum quidem dicenti, credere solemus.* We are accustomed to give no credit to a liar, even when he tells the truth.] **1477** RIVERS *Dictes, &c.* (1877) 117 (A) The reward of a lyar is that he be not beleuid of that he reherseth. **1692** L'ESTRANGE *Aesop's Fab.* (1738) lxxiv A common liar (says the old moral) shall not be believed even when he speaks true.

Liar is worse than a thief, A.

1623 W. PAINTER *Chaucer new Painted* B 5 A
Lyar is counted in a common-wealth, Worse
then a thiefe that liueth vpon stealth. **1639**
CLARKE 150.

Liar, lick dish.

1575 *Gamm. Gurton* v. ii. 252 Thou lier lick-
dish, didst not say the neele wold be gitten?
1631 CHETTLE *Trag. Hoffman* v *Luc.* Lyer,
lyer, licke dish.

Liars begin by imposing upon others, but end by deceiving themselves.

1622 BACON *Hen. VII* Wks. (Chandos) 446
Perkin . . . with oft telling a lie, was turned
by habit almost into the thing he seemed to
be; and from a liar to a believer. **1718** PRIOR
Alma iii As folks, quoth Richard, prone to
leasing, Say things at first because they're
pleasing, . . . Till their own dreams at length
deceive 'em, And, oft repeating, they believe
'em. **1855** BOHN 441.

Liars have need of good memories.

[QUINT. 4. 2. 91 *Mendacem memorem esse
oportet.*] *a.* **1555** LATIMER in *Godly Confer.
w. Ridley* (1556) b 2 b Lyers had nede to
haue good memories. **1692** L'ESTRANGE
Aesop's Fab. cccliii (1738) 366 Wherefore
parasites and liars had need of good
memories. **1710–11** SWIFT *Examiner* There
is one essential point wherein a political liar
differs from others of the faculty, that he
ought to have but a short memory. **1721**
KELLY 50 . . . Lest he tell the same lie different ways.

Liar(s), *see also* Common fame is a l.;
Lawyer must be great l.; Show me a l. and
I will show thief; Vaunter and l. near akin.

Libel, *see* Greater the truth.

Liberal [man], *see* Miserable man maketh a
penny of a farthing.

Liberty, but no latch-key.

1902 A. R. COLQUHOUN *Mastery of Pacific* 129
In the Philippines . . . finances are to be
controlled by the Americans . . . But that a
man . . . fit for self-government . . . cannot be
entrusted with public funds is . . . equal to
'liberty, but no latch-key'!

Liberty hall.

1773 GOLDSMITH *Stoops to C.* II (Globe) 652/1
Hard. This is Liberty-hall, gentlemen. You
may do just as you please here. **1845** JAMES
Smuggler vii Let every man do as he likes.
Have I not heard you, a thousand times, call
your house Liberty Hall?

Liberty is not licence.

a. **1645** MILTON *Sonnet* vii Licence they mean
when they cry liberty. *a.* **1720** SHEFFIELD
(Dk. Buckhm.) *Wks.* (1753) I. 272 They are
for licence, not for liberty. **1852** DAVIES &
VAUGHAN tr. *Republic of Plato* Analysis of
Bk. viii Liberty, degenerating into licence,
is the chief feature of such a state [demo-
cracy].

Liberty, *see also* Bean in liberty . . . comfit in
prison; Lean l. better than fat slavery;
Loses his l. loses all; Too much l. spoils all.

Library, *see* Hesky's l.

Licence, *see* Liberty is not l.

Lick and lay down.

1824 SCOTT *St. Ronans* xiv What for suld I
no have a Corpus delicti, . . . or any other
Corpus that I like, sae lang as I am willing
to lick and lay down the ready siller? **1862**
HISLOP 210 . . . A proverbial form of expression of a man's being able to pay his way.

Lick honey through a cleft stick, To.

1670 RAY 184. **1732** FULLER no. 5197.

Lick honey with your little finger.

1586 PETTIE tr. *Guazzo's Civ. Conv.* f. 118 (A)
That olde saying, that we must tast honie
but with our fingers end. **1639** CLARKE 306.

Lick (a person or thing) into shape, To.

[= to give form and regularity to; to mould,
make presentable. DONATUS *Life of Virgil
Carmen se more ursae parere dicens, et
lambendo demum effingere.*] **1413** *Pilgr. Sowle*
(Caxton 1483) IV. xxiv. 70 Beres ben brought
forthe al fowle and transformyd and after
that by lyckynge of the fader and the moder
they ben brought in to theyr kyndely shap.
1612 CHAPMAN *Widowes T.* Wks. (1873) III.
31 He has not licked his whelp into full shape
yet. **1621** BURTON *Anat. Mel.* Democr. to
Rdr. (1676) 7/2 Enforced, as a Bear doth her
Whelps, to bring forth this confused lump, I
had not time to lick it into form. **1780**
WESLEY *Wks.* (1872) IX. 509 Mr. Law, by
taking immense pains, has licked it into some
shape. **1862** MRS. CARLYLE *Lett.* III. 132 I
shall have trouble enough in licking her [a
young servant] into shape.

Lick it up like Lim hay, To.

1670 RAY 206 . . . *Lim* is a village on the river
Mersey, that parts *Cheshire* and *Lancashire*,
where the best hay is gotten.

Lick the fat from the (a person's) beard, To.

[= to forestall the results of (a person's)
enterprise or industry.] **1548** HALL *Chron.*
169 b Other . . . merchants . . . sore abhorr-
yng the Italian nacion for lickyng the fat
from their beards, and taking from them their
accustomed livyng. **1579** SPENSER *Shep. Cal.*
Sep. 123 But they that shooten neerest the
pricke Sayne, other the fat from their beards
doen lick. **1888** DOUGHTY *Arabia Deserta*
(1923) i. 311 It irked the lean Beduin souls
to see the parasite grow fat of that which he
licked vilely from their beards.

Lick whole, To.

[= to heal of wounds or sores by licking.
c. **1550** *Disc. Common Weal Eng.* (1893) 32
If anie men haue licked theim selues whole
youe be the same. **1596** BP. W. BARLOW *Three
Serm.* i. 129 Who vnder a show of licking

them whole, suck out euen their hart blood.
1670 RAY 184 To lick ones self whole again.
1712 ARBUTHNOT *John Bull* IV. vi He would
quickly lick himself whole again, by his vails.

Lick your dish.

1678 RAY 88.

Lick(s, ed), *see also* Cook that cannot l. his
fingers; Curate l. the knife (When), bad
for clerk; Give little to his servants that l.
his knife (He can); Kiss (L.) the dust; Loved
mutton well that l.; Loves bacon well that
l.; Loves roast meat well that l.

Lickerish of tongue, light of tail.

c. **1386** CHAUCER *W. of Bath's Prol.* D. 466
For al so siker as cold engendreth hayl, A
likerous mouth moste han a likerous tayl.
1539 TAVERNER f. xxxvi Our Englysh
prouerbe . . . sayeth A lycourouse mouthe,
a lycourouse tayle. **1553** T. WILSON *Arte of
Rhet.* 66 Likeryshe of tongue, lighte of taile.

Lickerish (liquorish), *see also* Cat (The l.) gets
many a rap.

Lide, *see* Leeks in L. (Eat).

Lidford[1] (Lydford) law.

1399 LANGLAND *Rich. Redeless* iii. 145 (A)
Be the lawe of Lydfford. **1565** JEWEL *Repl.
Harding* (1611) 356 But heere he thought . . .
to call vs Theeues, and wicked Judges, and
to charge vs with the Law of Lydford. **1629**
T. ADAMS *Serm.* (1861–2) II. 120 As it is reported of a judge of the Stannery at Lydford,
in Devonshire, who having hanged a felon
among the tinners in the forenoon, sat in
judgment on him in the afternoon. *c.* **1644**
W. BROWNE *Lidford Journey* Wks. (Roxb.)
II. 352 I ofte haue heard of Lidford Lawe,
How in the Morne they hang & drawe, And
sitt in iudgment after. **1710** *Brit. Apollo* II.
No. 3. 5/2 First Hang and Draw, Then hear
the cause by Lidford Law. [[1] A village
between Tavistock and Okehampton.]

Lie abed, *see* Name is up (His), he may l. a.

Lie against (on) the devil, It is a sin to.

a. **1555** RIDLEY *Wks.* 10 It is also a true
common proverb, that it is even sin to lie
upon the devil. **1641** FERGUSSON 62 It is a sin
to lye on the Devil. **1678** RAY 125 It's a sin
to belie the Devil.

Lie all alike in our graves, We shall.

1639 CLARKE 13. **1670** RAY 56. **1732** FULLER
no. 5455.

Lie all manner of colours but blue, Thou'lt | and that is gone to the litting.

1678 RAY 75 Thou'lt lie all manner of colours
but blew, and that is gone to the litting. *i.e.*
dy[e]ing. (*Jocularly.*)

Lie at (the) catch (*or* upon the catch), To.

[= to set oneself to entrap a person to be

captious.] **1605** T. RYVES *Vicar's Plea* (1620)
141 That hee seeme not to lie at catch for
an aduantage against his inferiour fellow
minister. **1659** FULLER *Appeal Inj. Innoc.*
in *Hist. Camb. Univ.* (1840) 405 I have to do
with an adversary who lieth at catch for the
least advantage. **1678** BUNYAN *Pilgr.* I.
(1877) 88 *Talk.* You lie at the catch, I perceive. *Faith.* No, not I; I am only for setting
things right.

Lie be well drest, Though a | it is ever overcome.

1640 HERBERT 323.

Lie could have choked him, If a | that would have done it.

1678 RAY 89.

Lie down, and cry, *God help us,* We must not.

1611 CHAPMAN *May-Day* I. i (1889) 278 *Lod.*
Do not lie in a ditch, and say God help me;
use the lawful tools he hath lent thee. **1732**
FULLER no. 5449.

Lie down[1] for love, They that | should rise for hunger.

1721 KELLY 339 . . . Alleging if they had not
been too well fed, they would not be troubled
with that disease. Lat. *Sine Cerere & Baccho,
friget Venus.* [[1] fall sick.]

Lie had worried you, If a | you had been dead long since.

1721 KELLY 201.

Lie in bed and forecast, To.

1678 RAY 75.

Lie in bed till meat falls in one's mouth, To.

1550 HEYWOOD I. ix. 17 Tyl meate fall in
your mouth, will ye ly in bed.

Lie, One | makes (calls for) many.

1642 FULLER *H. & P. State* v. xii (1841) 379
Having made one lie, he is fain to make more
to maintain it. **1732** FULLER no. 3766 One
lie calls for many.

Lie or two may escape, In many words a.

1548 HALL *Chron. Ded. to Edw. VI* (1809) vi
I might beleue all written in his greate
volumes to bee as trewe as the Gospell. But
I haue redde an olde Prouerbe, which saithe,
that in many woordes, a lye or twayne sone
maie scape.

Lie upon roses when young, If you | you'll lie upon thorns when old.

1635 QUARLES *Emblems* I. vii And he repents
in thorns, that sleeps in beds of roses. **1732**
FULLER no. 2764.

Lie where he was slain, He will not.

a. **1585** MONTGOMERIE *Cherrie & Slae* xxiv

(1821) 20 He will not ly quhair he is slaine, That douttis befoir he dies. **1721** KELLY 135 ... Spoken of timorous people, as if their corpse would flee from the place where they should be kill'd.

Lie will steal, He that will. (*Cf.* Show me a liar, &c.)

1607 R. WEST *Court of Conscience* F 1ᵛ (as the Prouerbe saith) He that will lie will steale. **1607** DEKKER & WILKINS *Jests to make you Merry* F 1 Lyers, and such commonly are theeues. **1630** J. TAYLOR *Wks.* R r 1 He that will lie will steale. **1656** L. PRICE *Map of Merry Conceits* A 4.

Lie with a latchet, That is a.

[= a great lie.] **1600** A. COOKE *Pope Joane* 20 He writes, that, in as much as she was a Germaine, no Germaine could euer since be chosen Pope. Which is a lie with a latchet. **1678** RAY 257 That's a lie with a latchet, All the dogs i' th' town cannot match it. **1694** MOTTEUX *Rabelais* v. xxx. 152 That's a Lye with a Latchet.

Lie with a witness, That is a.

1593–4 SHAKS. *Tam. Shrew* V. i. 122 Here's packing, with a witness, to deceive us all. **1678** RAY 89 *A great Lie.* That's a lie with a witness.

Lief go to mill as to mass, Ye had as.

1636 CAMDEN 310. **1732** FULLER no. 5909 You had rather go to Mill than to Mass.

Lies down (Sleeps) with dogs, He that | must rise up with fleas.

[SENECA *Qui cum canibus concumbunt cum pulicibus surgent.*] **1573** SANDFORD 209 *Chi va dormir con i cani, si leva con i pulici.* He that goeth to bedde with Dogges, aryseth with fleas. **1612** WEBSTER *White Devil* v. i They have a certain spice of the disease; For they that sleep with dogs shall rise with fleas. **1640** HERBERT 333 He that lies with the dogs, riseth with fleas. **1670** RAY 82 ... Chi con cane dorme con pulce se leva. *Ital.* Qui se couche avec les chiens se leve avec des puces. *Gall.* **1721** KELLY 129 ... If you keep company with base and unworthy fellows, you will get some ill by them. **1791** WOLCOT (P. Pindar) *Rights of Kings* viii To this great truth, a universe agrees, 'He who lies down with dogs, will rise with fleas'. **1842** LEVER *Jack Hinton* xxii If you lie down with the dogs, you'll get up with fleas, and that's the fruits of travelling with a fool.

Lies have short (no) legs (wings).

1573 SANDFORD (1576) 216 A lye hath one lame legge. *Ibid.* Lies haue short legs. **1578** FLORIO *First Fruites* f. 31 Lyes have short legges. **1611** DAVIES *Prov.* 73 Lies have short wings. **1666** TORRIANO 22 A lye hath no feet. *Ibid.* Lyes have short legs. **1732** FULLER no. 263 A lie has no leg, but a scandal has wings. **1853** TRENCH vi. 128 *A lie has no legs.* ... Its priests may prop it up from without, ... after it has once fallen before the presence of the truth, yet this all will prove labour in vain.

Lies like truth, He.

1841 CHAMIER *Tom Bowl.* v He lied so much like truth that she was deceived.

Lies long abed, He that | his estate feels it.

1640 HERBERT 325. **1761** A. MURPHY *Citizen* i. ii He that lies in bed, his estate feels it.

Lies not in your gate, It that | breaks not your shins.

1641 FERGUSSON 62.

Lies upon the ground, He that | can fall no lower.

[ALAIN DE LILLE (1114–1203) *Doctrinale Altum* p. 8 *Qui jacet in terrâ, non habet unde cadat.*] **1570** A. BARCLAY *Mirrour of Good Manners* (Spens. S.) 46 (A) A man on grounde resting can not much lower fall. **1629** T. ADAMS *Serm.* (1861–2) ii. 192 We say, *Qui jacet in terris, non habet unde cadat,*— He that lies on the ground hath no lower descant to fall to. **1663** BUTLER *Hudibras* i. iii. 877 I am not now in Fortune's power, He that is down can fall no lower. **1678** BUNYAN *Pilgr.* ii (Shepherd's Boy's Song) He that is down needs fear no fall.

Lie(s) (*noun*), see also Ask no questions told no l.; Blister ... upon tongue that tells a l.; Give a l. start; Long ways long l.; Misunderstanding brings l.; Slander (It may be) but no l.; 'They say so' is half a l.; Trusts in a l. (He that) shall perish in truth.

Lie(s, d) (*verb*), see also Better speak truth rudely than l. correctly; Dummie cannot l.; Leal heart l. never; Let anybody l. by him (He will not); Old men and travellers l. by authority; Painters and poets have leave to l.; Soldiers and travellers l. by authority; Swear (He that will) will l.; Tell a l. and find truth; Tongue doth l. that speaks in haste; Traveller may l. with authority.

Life for a living man, There is aye.

1721 KELLY 323 ... Spoken when we are disappointed of something that we expected; intimating that we can, and will, live without it. **1834** CARLYLE *Let.* to John C. 22 July This being my task *till* the end of the year, why should I curiously inquire what is to become of me next? 'There is aye life for a living body.'

Life is a pilgrimage.

1579 LYLY *Euphues* (Arb.) 181 Dost thou not knowe that ... the whole course of life is but a ... pilgrymage, a warfare? **1595–6** SHAKS. *Rich. II* II. i. 155 His time is spent; our pilgrimage must be. **1599–1600** A.Y.L. III. ii. 139 How brief the life of man Runs his erring pilgrimage. **1604–5** *Meas. for Meas.* II. i. 36 See that Claudio Be executed by nine to-morrow morning: ... For that's the utmost of his pilgrimage. *a.* **1626** SIR J. DAVIES version of *Ps.* xxxix. 12 On earth

a pilgrim as my fathers were (*Vulg.* pere-
grinus). *a.* **1633** G. HERBERT *The Church* 113
The Pilgrimage (title).

Life is a shuttle.

1560 BIBLE (Genevan) **1586** *Job* vii. 6 My
dayes are swifter thē a weauers shittle.
1600–1 SHAKS. *Merry W.* V. i. 25 *Fal.* I know
also life is a shuttle. **1855** BOHN 442.

Life is a span.

[*Ps.* xxxix. 6 (Prayer-Book) Behold, thou
hast made my days as it were a span long.]
c. **1100** *Beowulf* 2727 ða wæs eall sceacen
dogor-gerimes. [Now the span (*lit.* the
number) of his days was all run out.] **1599**
DAVIES *Immort. Soul* Introd. xlv (1742) 12
I know my Life's a Pain, and but a Span.
1604–5 SHAKS. *Othello* II. iii. 75 A life's but
a span. **1607–8** *Tim. of Athens* V. iii. 13
Timon is dead, who hath outstretch'd his
span. **1836** O. W. HOLMES *My Aunt* in *Poems*
(1846) 86 Her waist is ampler than her life,
For life is but a span.

Life is half spent before we know what it is.

1640 HERBERT 359. **1732** FULLER no. 3208.

Life is made up of little things.

1902–4 LEAN IV. 33.

Life is not all beer and skittles.

1836–7 DICKENS *Pickwick* xli It's a regular
holiday to them—all porter and skittles.
1857 T. HUGHES *Tom Brown* I. ii Life isn't
all beer and skittles. **1888** R. KIPLING, *Drums
Fore & Aft* The men ... fell in for their first
march, when they began to realize that a
soldier's life was not all beer and skittles.

Life is sweet.

c. **1350** *Patience* l. 156 in *Allit. Poems*
(E.E.T.S.) 96 (A) For þe monnes lode neuer
so luther, the lyf is ay swete. *c.* **1390** GOWER
Conf. Amantis v 239 Crist diedé him self for
the feith; But now our ferful prelate saith;
'The life is swete'. **1601** LYLY *Love's Metam.*
III. i. Wks. (1902) 315 *Eris.* Life is sweet,
hunger sharp; between them the contention
must be short. **1668** J. WILSON tr. *Moriæ
Encomium* 49 Old women ... ever mumbling
in their mouths (φῶς ἀγαθὸν) Life is sweet.
1863 C. READE *Hard Cash* xxxi He came up
gurgling ... and swimming for his life ...
Life is sweet.

Life lieth not in living, but in liking.

1639 CLARKE 322. **1670** RAY 113 ... Martial
saith, *Non est vivere, sed valere vita.*

Life of man is a winter way, The.

1640 HERBERT 359.

Life of man is a winter's day and a winter's way, The.

1670 RAY 16.

Life of the wolf is the death of the lamb, The.

1616 DRAXE 101. **1639** CLARKE.

Life, Such a | such a death.

1639 CLARKE 322.

Life, While there is | there is hope.

[CICERO *Ad Atticum* 9. 10. 3 *Aegroto, dum
anima est spes esse dicitur.* As the saying is,
while there is life there is hope. ERASM *Ad.
Aegroto, dum anima est spes est.*] **1539**
TAVERNER f. xxxvi The sycke person whyle
he hath lyfe, hath hope. **1670** RAY 113. **1727**
GAY *Fables* I. xxvii. 49 'While there is life,
there's hope', he cried; 'Then why such
haste?' so groaned and died. **1841** CARLYLE
Heroes v (1896) 248 One should have toler-
ance for a man, hope of him. ... While life
lasts, hope lasts for every man. **1869**
C. READE *Foul Play* xi They lost, for a few
moments, all idea of escaping. But, ...
while there's life there's hope': and ... their
elastic minds recoiled against despair.

Life without a friend, is death without a witness.

1640 HERBERT 335. **1732** FULLER no. 3211
(... death with a vengeance).

Life you loved me not, In | in death you bewail me.

1640 HERBERT 327.

Life, *see also* Art is long, l. short; Business
of l. and day of death (Between); Despises his own l. master of another's;
Enter this l. (But one way to); Good l.
better than learning; Good l. makes good
death; Hope of long l. beguileth; Ill l. ill
end; Large as l.; Long be thy legs, short
thy l.; Lose a leg rather than l.; New lease
of l.; No man hath lease of his l.; Prolong
thy l. (Two things), quiet heart loving
wife; Short l. and merry; Speaks ill (Of
him that) consider the l.; Spies (The l. of);
Time (He that hath) hath l.; Unworthy of
l. that causes not l.

Lifeguard, *see* Subject's love is king's l.

Lifeless that is faultless, He is.

1546 HEYWOOD I. xi. 29 He is liueles, that is
fautles, olde folkes thought. *c.* **1598** *MS.
Proverbs* in FERGUSSON 34 Faultles lifles.

Lift, *see* Lout so low and l. so little.

Light, To a great | a great lanthorn.

1640 HERBERT 351.

Light a torch gives, The more | the shorter it lasts.

1732 FULLER no. 4664 The more light a
torch gives, the less while it lasts.

Light as a feather.

c. **1535** SIR D. LYNDSAY *Three Estates* l. 3527
Lichter nor ane fidder. **1629** SHIRLEY
Wedding II. iii (A) Light as a feather, hanging
will never kill you.

Light as a fly.

1509 A. BARCLAY *Ship of Fools* (1874) II. 290
Light as fle. *c.* **1560** *Tom Tyler* l. 112. **1616**
WITHALS 580. **1670** RAY 206.

Light burdens far heavy.

1546 HEYWOOD II. ix. 80 A sir light burdeine far heauy (quoth she) This light burdein in longe walke welny tryeth me. **1640** HERBERT 318 Light burdens, long borne, grow heavy. **1670** RAY 114 . . . Petit fardeau poise à la longue, or, Petite chose de loing poise, *Gall.* **1682** BUNYAN *Greatness of the Soul* Wks. (1855) I. 124 We use to say, light burdens far carried are heavy.

Light cares speak, great ones are dumb.

[SENECA *Hippol.* 607 *Curae leves loquuntur, ingentes stupent.*] *a.* **1618** SYLVESTER (1621) 1209 Small griefes speake, but great are dumb. **1864** FRISWELL *Gentle Life* 164 Not one of us is there but would exchange all his little troubles for some heavy one . . . 'Light cares cry out: the heavier are dumb'.

Light cheap, lither[1] yield.

[i.e. That which is cheaply bought brings a poor return]. *c.* **1300** *Provs. of Hending* 30 Lyht chep, luthere yeldes. *c.* **1400** *MS. Latin no. 394 John Rylands Libr.* (ed. Pantin) in *Bull. J. R. Libr.* XIV. 103 Lyȝt chepe, lyther forȝeldes. *c.* **1460** *Towneley Myst., 2nd Shep. Play* 170 And men say 'Lyght chepe Letherly foryeldys'. **1670** RAY 114 . . . That that costs little, will do little service; for commonly the best is best cheap. [1 bad.]

Light(ly) come, light(ly) go.

c. **1374** CHAUCER *Troylus* II. 1238 For-why men seith, 'Impressiounès light Ful lightly ben ay redy to the flighte'. *c.* **1386** Id., *Pard. T. C.* 781 And lightly as it comth so wol we spende. **1546** HEYWOOD II. ix. 77 Light come, light go. **1616** R. C. *Times' Whistle* vi. 2828 (E.E.T.S.) 89 'But lightly come', we say, 'doth lightly goe'. **1712** ARBUTHNOT *John Bull* II. iv A thriftless wretch, spending the goods and gear that his forefathers won with the sweat of their brows: light come, light go. **1861** C. READE *Cloister & H.* xxxvii Our honestest customers are the thieves . . . with them and with their purses 'tis lightly come, and lightly go.

Light gains (winnings) make heavy purses.

1546 HEYWOOD I. xi. 30 Euer more light gaynes make heauy purses. **1594** BACON *Promus* f. 89a. **1614** CAMDEN 309. **1641** FERGUSSON 90 Small winning makes a heavie purse.

Light is naught for sore eyes, The.

1579 GOSSON *Ephemerides* 19 Sore eyes maye not view the light, without a scarfe. **1580** LYLY *Euph. & his Eng.* (Arb.) 411 Why . . . suffer them to eate their meate by a candle that have sore eyes? **1639** CLARKE 161. **1670** RAY 114 . . . A l'œil malade la lumière nuit, *Gall.* He that doth evil hateth the light, &c.

Light, In your own | like the Mayor of Market-Jew.

1864 *N. & Q.* 3rd Ser. v. 275. In your own light, like the Mayor of Market-Jew. The pew of the Mayor of Marazion[1] (or Market-Jew) was so placed, that he was in his own light. [1 Cornwall.]

Light purse makes a heavy heart, A.

[*Cf. c.* **1514** A. BARCLAY *Eclogues* iv. 20 When purse is heauy oftetime the heart is light.] **1595** H. CHETTLE *Piers Plainnes* E 1ᵛ They made manie light purses and heavye hearts. **1732** FULLER no. 241.

Light, *see also* Does ill (He that) hates **l.**; Dry l.; Every l. is not the sun; Hide one's l. under a bushel; Horns hang in your l.; Lips hang in your l.; Little is the l. seen far in the night; Maidenhead hangs in your l.; See divine l. (Way to) put out own candle; Stand in one's own l.

Lighted upon a lime[1] twig, He.

1732 FULLER no. 1964. [1 bird-lime.]

Lightening before death, A.

1584 COGAN *Haven of Health* (1612) 135 A Lating prouerbe, *Cygnea cantio,* which among the common people is termed, a lightning before death. **1594–5** SHAKS. *Rom. & Jul.* V. iii. 90 How oft when men are at the point of death Have they been merry! which their keepers call A lightning before death. **1615** CHAPMAN *Od.* xviii. 230 Th'utmost lightning that still ushers death. **1641** BROME *Jov. Crew* v. Wks. (1873) III. 441 If it be a lightning before death, the best is, I am his heir. **1670** RAY 76 . . . A little before they die . . . their understanding and memory return to them; as a candle just before it goes out gives a great blaze. **1712** ADDISON *Spect.* No. 517, par. 2 We were once in great Hopes of his Recovery . . . but this only proved a light'ning before Death. **1785** WALPOLE *Lett.* (Toynbee) 13. 322 I hope this revival of wit is not lightning before death. **1840** HOOD *Up Rhine* 7 The old saying about a lightening before death. **1876** TENNYSON *Harold* 3. 1 This lightning before death plays on the word.

Lightens and thunders beware of a tree, When caught by the tempest, wherever it be, if it.

1846 DENHAM 19. [It is dangerous, in a thunderstorm, to shelter under a tree.]

Light-heeled mother makes a heavy-heeled daughter, A.

1670 RAY 53 . . . Because she doth all her work herself, and her daughter the mean time sitting idle, contracts a habit of sloth. **1721** KELLY 22 An olight[1] mother makes a sweir[2] daughter. [1 nimble. 2 lazy.]

Lightly gained quickly lost. (*Cf.* Quickly come, &c.; Easy come, &c.)

1576 U. FULWELL *Ars Adulandi* E 4ᵛ Experience taught me that easely woone was lightly loste. **1583** GREENE *Wks.* (Gros.) II. 25 (A) He wil iudge that is lightly to bee gained, is as quickly lost.

Lightning lightly before thunder, There is.

1611–12 SHAKS. *Tempest* I. ii. 201 Jove's lightnings, the precursors O' the dreadful thunder-claps. **1616** DRAXE 228 Lightly before thunder, lightning. **1639** CLARKE 209.

Like a duke? like a duck.

1546 HEYWOOD II. vii. 71 Then euery daie to fare lyke a duke with thée. Lyke a duke, lyke a duck (quoth she) thou shalt fare, except thou wilt spare.

Like a hog hangeth the groin[1] on her husband.

1546 HEYWOOD II. vi. 61 Euermore like a hog hangeth the groyne, On hir husbande, except he be hir slaue. [[1] grumbler.]

Like a hog (swine) he never does good till his death. (*See also* Swine (He is like a), &c.)

a. **1600** *Gernutus* in PERCY *Reliques* I. ii (1857) 106 His life was like a barrow hogge, that liveth many a day, Yet never once doth any good, until men will him slay. **1621** W. MASON *Handf. Essaies* 47 *Of Couetousnes* . . . Vntil this earthworme come vnto the earth, hee minds nothing but earthly things, like a Swine he neuer doth good till his death.

Like blood, like good, and like age, makes the happiest marriage.

1639 CLARKE 28.

Like cures like.

[L. *Similia similibus curantur.* KING quotes SAMUEL HAHNEMANN, *Organon der Heilkunst*, 1810.] **1853** 'C. BEDE' *Verdant Green* viii On the homœopathic principle of 'like cures like', a cigar was the best preventative against . . . smoke.

Like is the same, No.

[L. *Nullum simile est idem.*] **1638** ROWLEY *Shoemaker a Gent.* II. *Leo.* Why wouldst not have her like me? *Cris.* Because no like's the same.

Like it, If you don't | you may look off it.

1738 SWIFT (Dial. i) 335 *Never.* I don't much like the colour of that ribbon. *Miss.* . . . If you don't much like it, you may look off it.

Like it, If you don't | you may lump[1] it.

1833 NEAL *Down Easters* I. vii. 104 Let 'em lump it if they don't like it. **1864–5** DICKENS *Our Mut. Fr.* IV. iii 'I'm a-going to call you Boffin, for short, . . . If you don't like it, it's open to you to lump it.' [[1] put up with it.]

Like loves like.

1539 TAVERNER 8 Simile gaudet simili. The lyke delytethe in the lyke . . . Symylytude (as Aristotle sayeth) is mother of loue.

Like me, God bless the example.

1670 RAY 184.

Like one as if he had been spit out of his mouth, As.

c. **1400** *Beryn* (E.E.T.S.) 97 l. 3232 Be-hold thy sone! it semeth crope out of þy mowith. **1602** BRETON *Wonders worth Hear.* (1879) 8/1 Twoo girles, . . . the one as like an Owle, the other as like an Urchin, as if they had been spitte out of the mouthes of them. **1738** SWIFT (Dial. iii) 350 *Miss.* She's as like her husband as if she were spit out of his mouth.

Like punishment and equal pain, both key and keyhole do sustain.

1639 CLARKE 239.

Like than Jack fletcher[1] and his bolt,[2] No more.

1576 L. TWYNE *Pat. of Painefull Adv.* (1903) 75 There is no more likenesse betweene them sauing that the childe hath the generall shape and proportion of a man, than is betweene Jack fletcher and his bolt. [[1] arrow-maker. [2] arrow.]

Like that they are the worse for it, They are so.

1678 RAY 354.

Like to die mends (fills) not the kirkyard.

1641 FERGUSSON 72. **1721** KELLY 233.

Like to like. (*See also* Like will to like.)

c. **1375** *Sc. Leg. Saints* (Petrus) I. 543 Lyk to lyk accordis wele. **1586** G. WHITNEY *Choice of Emblems* (Green) 164 Then like to like or best alone remains. **1818** SCOTT *Ht. Midl.* xvii He wad be ravished to hae a crack wi' you—like to like, ye ken—it's a proverb never fails—and ye are baith a pair o' the deevil's peats. **1824** Id., *St. Ronan's* xi I wad hae like draw to like.

Like to like, a scabbed horse to an old dike.

1639 CLARKE 287. **1721** KELLY 231.

Like to like, and Nan for Nicholas.

1670 RAY 15.

Like will to like.

[HOM. *Od.* 17. 218 ὡς αἰεὶ τὸν ὁμοῖον ἄγει θεὸς ὡς τὸν ὁμοῖον. CICERO *De Senect.* 3. 7 Pares autem vetere proverbio cum paribus facillime congregantur.] *c.* **1375** *Scottish Legendary* (Horstmann) *Matthias* xii. 134 Lyke to lyk draw ay. *c.* **1386** CHAUCER *Squire's T.* F[1] 608 I trowe he hadde thilke text in minde, That 'alle thing, repeiring to his kinde, Gladeth him-self.' *c.* **1430** LYDGATE *Minor Poems* (Percy Soc.) 55 Alle thynge in kynde desirith thynge i-like. *c.* **1460** *Provs. of Good Counsel* (Furnivall) 70 This proverbe dothe specify: Lyke wyll to lyke in eche company. **1509** A. BARCLAY *Ship of Fools* (1874) II. 35 For it is a prouerbe and an olde sayd sawe that in euery place lyke to lyke wyll drawe. **1539** TAVERNER 8 As the Englyshe man sayeth. Lyke wyll to lyke. Symylytude (as Aristotle sayeth) is mother of loue. **1579** LYLY *Euphues* (Arb.) 48 Doth not the simpathy of manners make the coniunction of mindes? Is it not a by word lyke will to lyke? **1648** HERRICK *Hesper.* No. 1044 Wks. (1893) II. 138 Like will to like, each Creature loves his kinde. **1823** SCOTT *Peveril* xiv How could I help it? like will to like—the boy would come—the girl would see him.

Like will to like, quoth the devil to the collier.

1568 FULWELL *Like Will to L.* (1906) 24 Like will to like, quoth the Devil to the Collier. **1680** BUNYAN *Mr. Badman* xii. Wks. (1855) III. 647 *Wise.* Hang them rogues . . . Like to like, quoth the devil to the collier, this is your precise crew.

Like (a, the), Like as, *see also under significant words following.*

Like(s) (*verb*), *see* Do what he l. with his own; Says what he l. (He who).

Likeliest, *see* Do the l., and hope the best (*or* God will do best).

Likely lies in the mire, and unlikely goes by it (gets over).

1641 FERGUSSON 72 Likelie lies in the myre, and unliklie goes by it. **1721** KELLY 238 *Likely lies in the mire, and unlikely gets over.* Good likelihood is not always an infallible token of great strength, skill, or fortune. **1732** FULLER no. 3242 (with 'gets over').

Likeness causeth liking.

1539 TAVERNER (1545) A 8ᵛ *Æqualis æqualem delectat* Lyke delyteth the lyke. **1593** SIDNEY *Arcadia* To the Reader (Feuillerat) i. 524 Likeness is a great cause of liking. **1605** *The Countess of Lincoln's Nursery* A 4ᵛ *Likenesse* is Mother & Nurse of liking. **1639** CLARKE 27. **1732** FULLER no. 3243. Likeness begets love, yet proud men hate one another.

Likes not his business, Who | his business likes not him.

1846 T. WRIGHT *Essays on Middle Ages* i. 140 (A) We have the saying 'Who likes not . . .', &c. **1869** HAZLITT 471.

Likes not the drink, Who | God deprives him of bread.

1640 HERBERT 336. **1664** CODRINGTON 228. **1670** RAY 11.

Likes, *see also* Like(s).

Lim hay, *see* Lick it up like L. h.

Lime makes a rich father and a poor son.

1846 DENHAM 6. **1917** BRIDGE 92 Lime enriches the father and beggars the son. Lime is not . . . a manure, but it renders

available the inert matter in the soil, and it is therefore necessary to follow it up with manure.

Lime twig(s), *see* Fingers are l. t.; Lighted upon l. t.

Limerick was, Dublin is, and Cork shall be, the finest city of the three.

1859 DEAN HOLE *Lit. Tour in Ireld.* xviii To my fancy the old prophecy is fulfilled— 'Limerick was, Dublin is, and Cork shall be The finest city of the three.'

Lincoln green.

[= a bright green stuff made at Lincoln.] *c.* **1510** *Gest R. Hode* ccccxxii in CHILD *Ballads* III. 77 Whan they were clothed in Lyncolne grene, They kest away theyr graye. **1613–22** DRAYTON *Polyolb.* xxv. 262 (1876) III. 150 Whose swains in shepherds' gray, and girls in *Lincolne* green. *a.* **1845** HOOD *Forge* I. xiii With little jackets . . . Of Lincoln green.

Lincoln shall be hanged for London's sake.

c. **1590** *Sir Thomas More* III. i (Shaks. Apocr.) 397 *Lin.* This the olde prouerbe now compleate dooth make, That Lincolne should be hangd for London's sake.

Lincoln was, London is, and York shall be.

1588 J. HARVEY *Discursive Prophecies* 56. **1607** DEKKER & WEBSTER *Northward Ho* A2. **1623** J. TAYLOR (Water-P.) *Mer. Wher. Fer. Voy.* Wks. (1872) 17 There is a Proverb, part of which is this, They say that *Lincoln was, and London is.* **1662** FULLER (*York*) III. 461 'Lincoln was, London is, and York shall be' . . . That *Lincoln was,* namely a fairer, greater, richer city . . . doth plainly appear by the ruins thereof . . . That *London is,* we know; that *York shall be,* God knows.

Lincoln's Inn, *see* Gray's Inn; Inner Temple.

Lincoln, *see also* Devil over L. (He looks as); Tom of Lincoln.

Lincolnshire bagpipes.

1590 *Three Lords, &c.* in HAZLITT *Old Plays* vi. 393 (A) The sweet ballad of the Lincolnshire bagpipes. **1597–8** SHAKS. *1 Hen. IV.* I. ii. 85 *Fal.* I am as melancholy as a gib cat, . . . or the drone of a Lincolnshire bagpipe. **1617** MORYSON *Itin.* III. i. 54 (1907–8) III. 463 Lincolnshire bells and bag-pipes . . . are proverbially spoken of.

Lincolnshire, where hogs sh— soap, and cows sh— fire.

1659 HOWELL *Eng. Prov.* 21. **1670** RAY 236 Lincolnshire, *where hogs shite sope and cows shite fire.* The inhabitants of the poorer sort washing their clothes with hogs dung, and burning dried cow-dung for want of better fuel.

Line and level, By.

1573 TUSSER xlvi (1878) 101 Through cunning

with dible, rake, mattock, and spade, by line and by leauell, trim garden is made. **1589** PUTTENHAM *Art of Engl. Poesy* (*Eliz. Crit. Essays* ed. Gregory Smith ii. 173) This decencie is therfore the line & leuell for al good makers to do their busines by. **1605** J. CHAMBERLAIN *Letters* (McLure) i. 200. **1611** COTGRAVE s.v. 'A Pied' By line and leuell, by compasse and measure, proportionably. **1611–12** SHAKS. *Tempest* V. i. 238 We steal by line and level, an't like your grace. **1639** CLARKE 92. **1892** *see quot. under* Silk and Scarlet.

Line one's pockets, To.

[= to amass a comfortable fortune.] *c.* **1514** A. BARCLAY *Cyt. & Uplondyshm.* (Percy Soc.) lxi He had a pautner with purses manyfold And surely lined with siluer and with golde. **1604–5** SHAKS. *Othello* I. i. 53 Others there are Who, . . . throwing but shows of service on their lords, Do well thrive by them, and when they have lin'd their coats Do themselves homage. **1731** W. BOWMAN *Serm.* xxix Tho' such change would line our breeches.

Line to the wall, Bring your | not the wall to the line.

[ERASM. *Ad.* II. v. 36 *Ad amussim applica lapidem, non ad lapidem amussim*]. **1604** CHAPMAN *Bussy* III. i. 70 To the line the stone, Not to the stone, the line should be oppos'd. **1732** FULLER no. 1021.

Line, *see also* Day without a l. (No); Peace beyond the l. (No); Straight as a l.; Stricken the ball under the l.

Linen often to water, soon to tatter.

1678 RAY 347 Often to the water often to the tatter (*of linen*). **1732** FULLER no. 6378. **1855** BOHN 444.

Linen, *see also* Choose neither a woman nor l. by candle-light; Wash dirty l. in public.

Lion in a good cause, He is a.

1663 P. STAMPOY 8 with 'his own cause'. **1732** FULLER no. 1907.

Lion in the way (path), A.

1611 BIBLE *Prov.* xxvi. 13 The slothful man saith, There is a lion in the way. **1641** MILTON *Reform.* II. Wks. (1847) 18/1 They fear'd not the bug-bear danger nor the lion in the way that the sluggish and timorous politician thinks he sees. **1868** BRIGHT *Sp. Ireland* 1 Apr. You have always . . . lions in the path.

Lion is known by his claws (paw), The.

[Gk. 'Εκ τῶν ὀνύχων τὸν λέοντα γιγνώσκειν. To judge of the lion from his claws. ERASM. *Ad.* I. ix. 34 *Leonem ex unguibus aestimare.*] **1579–80** LODGE *Def. Poetry* (Shaks. Soc.)3 The Rubie is discerned by his pale rednes; and who hath not hard that the Lyon is known by hys clawes? **1639** CLARKE 131 A Lion is known by his pawe. **1642** D. ROGERS *Naaman* 158 By the paw we may judge of the lion, and perceive how far sanctification lies above self. **1861** DEAN STANLEY *Eastern Ch.* iii Many

more stories might be told of him [Spyridion], but (to use the words of an ancient writer who has related some of them) 'from the claws you can make out the lion'.

Lion is not so fierce as he is painted (as they paint him), The.

1599 MINSHEU (1623) 2 T 2. **1639** FULLER *Holy War* v. xxx (1840) 300 But the lion is not so fierce as he is painted, nor this empire so formidable as fame giveth it out. **1640** HERBERT 330 The lion is not so fierce as they paint him. **1670** RAY 114 The lion 's not half so fierce as he is painted. . . . Things are represented at a distance . . . beyond their just proportion and merit. Fame is a magnifying glass.

Lion kicked by an ass, The.

1874 SWINBURNE *Let.* 23 Feb. in *Times Lit. Sup.* 28 May 1909; 196 The last . . . public voice that reached him [Landor] from England must have been . . . obloquy and insult. It is true that the lion at whom those asses' kicks were aimed was by no means maimed or clipped as to the claws and teeth.

Lion may come to be beholden to a mouse, A.

1613 BEAUM. & FL. *Honest Man's Fort.* III. i Pray you accept My will to do you service: I have heard The mouse once saved the lion in his need. **1732** FULLER no. 264. **1842** MARRYAT *Perc. Keene* xvii A mouse may help a lion, as the fable says.

Lion's mouth, The.

[**1560** GENEVA BIBLE *Ps.* xxii. 21 Saue me from the lyons mouth. *2 Tim.* iv. 17 I was deliuered out of the mouth of the Lion.] **1601** DENT *Pathw. Heaven* 62 What doth hee else, but (as it were) put his finger into the Lion's mouth. **1726** CAVALIER *Mem.* iv. 289 He wou'd not lay down his Arms, saying it was better to die, than to run into the Lion's mouth.

Lion's provider, The.

[= jackal, *lit. & fig.*] [The jackal was formerly supposed to go before the lion and hunt up his prey for him.] **1667** DRYDEN *Ann. Mir.* st. 82 Their fireships like jackals appear, Who on their lions for the prey attend. **1672** W. DE BRITAINE *Dutch Usurp.* 33 They must not be like the Joecaul, which provides food for the Lyon. **1808** SCOTT *Let. to W. Gifford* 25 Oct. in LOCKHART *Life* If you will accept of my services as a sort of jackal or lion's provider. *a.* **1822** SHELLEY *Daemon of World* 426 There man was long the train-bearer of slaves . . . The jackal of ambition's lion-rage.

Lion's share, The.

[Fable of Aesop, PHAEDR. l. 5.] **1790** BURKE *Fr. Rev.* Wks. V. 252 Nor when they were in partnership with the farmer . . . have I heard that they had taken the lion's share. **1823** SCOTT *Peveril* xxi 'The goodman has . . . come to wait on you himself. He always does so when company drink wine.' 'That he may come in for the host's, that is, the lion's share. **1897** M. A. S. HUME *Ralegh* 42 The confiscated lands of the departed Desmonds in Munster were to be scrambled for, and Ralegh naturally came in for the lion's share.

Lion's skin cannot, If the | the fox's shall.

[ERASM. *Ad. Si leonina pellis non satis est, vulpina addenda.*] **1573** SANDFORD (1576) 117 If the Lions skin be not enough, take the Wolfes too. *Erasmus* attributeth this last saying also to *Lisander* Capteyne of the *Lacedemonians* [Here given to King Antigonus]. **1579** NORTH *Plutarch's Alexander & Caesar* (Temple Classics vii. 231) He might haue sewed (as they say) the case of the fox with the skin of the lion. **1594** *Selimus* 1733 I like Lysander's counsel passing well; ' If that I cannot speed with lion's force, To clothe my complots in a fox's skin'. **1621** HOWELL *Lett.* 30 Nov. (1903) I. 95 The Duke of Savoy . . . though he be valiant enough, yet he knows how to patch the lion's skin with a fox's tail. **1670** RAY 184 . . . *Si leonina pellis non satis est, assuenda vulpina.* . . . To attempt or compass that by craft, which we cannot obtain by force. **1700** TYRRELL *Hist. Eng.* II. 847 When the Lyon's Skin alone would not serve turn, he knew how to make it out with that of the fox. **1906** ALEX. MACLAREN *Expos., Deut.* 1 *Sam.* 359 He had a streak of oriental craft, and stood on the moral level of his times and country, in his readiness to eke out the lion's skin with the fox's tail.

Lion's skin is never cheap, A.

1611 COTGRAVE s.v. 'Lion' *Il n'y eut iamais bon marché de peaux de lions,* . . . a Lyons skinne was neuer bought good cheape. **1640** HERBERT 319.

Lions, To see (*or* show) the.

[= the sights worth seeing, from the practice of taking visitors to see the lions which used to be kept in front of the present entrance to the Tower of London.] **1590** GREENE *Wks.* (Gros.) VIII. 6 (A) This countrey Francesco was no other but a meere nouice, and that so newly, that to vse the old prouerb, he had scarce seene the lions. **1630** CAPT. J. SMITH *True Trav.* xviii (Arb.) 872 After, one Master John Bull . . . , with divers of his friends, went to see the Lyons [in the Tower]. **1709** STEELE *Tatler* No. 30 16 June I took three lads, . . . to show them . . . the lions, the tombs, Bedlam, and the other places which are entertainments to raw minds. **1840** HOOD *Up Rhine* 96 The rest of the day was spent in seeing the Lions—and first the Cathedral.

Lion(s), *see also* Army of stags led by l.; Ass in l.'s skin; Ass to be called a l. (What good can it do); Bear wants tail and cannot be l.; Beard the l.; Beat the dog before the l.; Bold as a l.; Brains of fox of little service if . . . paw of l.; Christians to the l.; Destroy the l. while a whelp; Fox's wiles never enter l.'s head; Hand in the l.'s mouth (He that hath); Hares may pull dead l.; Lammermoor l.; Living dog . . . dead l.; Man is a l. in own cause; One, but a l.; Sell the bear's (l.'s) skin before; Sight of a man hath force of a l.

Lip-honour costs little, yet may bring in much.

1642 TORRIANO 82. **1732** FULLER no. 3245.

Lippens[1] to lent ploughs, He that | his land will lie ley.[2]

1641 FERGUSSON 38 He that lippens to bon plowes, his land will ly ley. **1721** KELLY 145. **1862** HISLOP 146 He that lippens to lent plows may hae his land lang lea. He that relies on favours being granted is liable to disappointment. [[1] trusts. [2] unploughed.]

Lips hang in your light, Your.

a. **1529** SKELTON *Magnyfycence* l. 1061 (A) Tusshe, thy lyppes hange in thyne eye. **1546** HEYWOOD II. iv. 51 Your lips hang in your light, but this poore man sées how blindly ye stand in your owne light. Your looking-glass will tell you what none of your friends will. *c.* **1594** BACON *Promus* (Pott) 119, no. 107. **1855** BOHN 582.

Lips, however rosy, must be fed.

1855 BOHN 444.

Lips, Like (Such) | like (such) lettuce.

[L. *Similem habent labra lactucam*, an alleged saying of M. Crassus, when he heard a description of an ass eating thistles. *See* JEROME *Ep.* l. 7 and at length *N. & Q.* 175. 99.] *a.* **1540** BARNES *Wks.* (1573) 189/1 No doubt the prouerbe is true, such lippes, such lectuce, such saintes such miracles. **1568** FULWELL *Like will to L.* in HAZL. *O.E.P.* (1874) III. 330 And as the wise man said, such letuce such lips. **1587** FLEMING *Contn. Holinshed* III. 1017/2 Like lips, like lettice, as is their cause so are the rulers. **1631** JONSON *New Inn* II. ii *Ld. Beauf.* Lætitia! a fair omen, and I take it: Let me have still such Lettice for my lips. **1670** RAY 114 . . . *Similes habent labra lactucas.* . . . As when a dull scholar happens to a stupid or ignorant master; a froward wife to a peevish husband.

Lip(s), *see also* Free of her l.; Pipe that lacketh his upper l. (He can ill); Stiff upper l. (Keep).

Liquor, *see* Ale (L.) will make cat speak; Hanged for leaving his l.

Lisping lass is good to kiss, A.

1639 FORD *Lady's Trial* IV. ii. *Fut.* Your lips are destined to a better use, Or else the proverb fails of lisping maids. *Am.* Kithing you mean. **1678** RAY 349.

List, *see* May if you l., but do if you dare.

Listeners hear no (never hear) good of themselves.

26 Jan.–2 Feb. **1647** *Mercurius Elencticus* 76 The old Proverb is, Hearkners never heare good of them selves. **1678** RAY 75. **1692** L'ESTRANGE *Aesop's Fab.* clxx (1738) 183 'Tis an old saying, that *Listeners never hear well of themselves*; and Mercury's curiosity

sped accordingly in this fable. **1836** MARRYAT *Midsh. Easy* xvii 'If I mistake not, . . . your conversation refers to me'. 'Very likely it does,' replied the boatswain. Listeners hear no good of themselves.' **1839** DICKENS *N. Nickleby* xlii 'If it is fated that listeners are never to hear any good of themselves', said Mrs. Browdie, 'I can't help it and I am very sorry for it'.

Literature is a good staff but a bad crutch.

1835 *Poor Scholar* in WILSON *Tales of Borders* I. 199 I found that literature was a good staff but a bad crutch; and . . . I used it accordingly. **1859** SMILES *Self-Help* iv [Sir Walter Scott] said: 'I determined that literature should be my staff, not my crutch, and that the profits of my literary labour . . . should not . . . become necessary to my ordinary expenses.'

Lith[1] and selthe[2] are fellows.

c. **1300** *Havelok* 1338 (E.E.T.S.) 41 Lith and selthe felawes are. (*Note*, p. 141: Goldborough tells him to avoid delay, since rest may accompany success, but cannot precede it.) [[1] rest. [2] success.]

Lithe as a lass of Kent.

1579 SPENSER *Shep. Cal.* Feb. 74 His dewelap as lythe, as lasse of Kent. **1593** DRAYTON *Dowsabell* Her features all as fresh above, As is the grass that grows by Dove; And lyth as lasse of Kent.

Lither, *see* Long as he is l., he might thatch.

Litter is like to the sire and the dam, The.

1550 HEYWOOD I. xi. 27 Commenly all thyng shewth fro whens it camme. The litter is lyke to the syre and the damme.

Litter, *see also* First pig . . . of l. is the best.

Littera scripta manet.

[The written letter remains.] *a.* **1347** MURIMUTH *Chron.* 1 quotes *Res audita perit, littera scripta manet.* **1642** HOWELL *For. Trav.* iii (Arb.) 20 For *the* Penne *maketh the deepest furrowes, and doth fertilize, and enrich the memory more than any thing else,* Littera scripta manet.

Little and good fills the trencher, A.

1640 HERBERT 341. **1670** RAY 16 That little which is good fills the trencher.

Little and loud.

1648 HERRICK *Hesper.*, No. 601 '*Little & Loud*' Wks. (1893) I. 277 Little you are; for Womans sake be proud; For my sake next, (though little) *be not loud.*

Little and often fills the purse.

1658 *Comes Facundus* 23. **1666** TORRIANO 211 **1732** FULLER no. 3249. **1790** TRUSLER *Prov. Exempl.* 183 As *Little and often fills the purse,* he who begins to save, will soon find himself rich.

Little bird is content with a little nest, A.

1616 DRAXE 116 For a little bird, a little nest. **1732** FULLER no. 244.

Little birds that can sing and won't sing should be made to sing.

1678 RAY 343 The bird that can sing and will not sing must be made to sing. **1721** KELLY 320 *The bird that can sing, and will not sing, should be gar'd sing.* Spoken when we use rough means to perverse people. **1845** DICKENS *Cricket on H.* ii. 'The bird that can sing and won't sing, must be made to sing, they say,' grumbled Tackleton. **1890** D. C. MURRAY *J. Vale's Guard.* vii Your uncle is very little pleased with the progress you have been making. . . . Little birds that can sing and will not sing will have to be made to sing.

Little body often harbours a great soul, A.

1611 COTGRAVE s.v. 'Lievre' A little bush may hold a great hare, a little body a great heart. **1670** RAY 16. **1888** QUILLER-COUCH *Troy Town* vi She bore a great soul in a little body.

Little Britain.

[L. *Britannia minor* (Geoff. of Monmouth) = Brittany, in France.] **1662** FULLER (*Wales*) III. 493 The Danes woefully harassed the land, which caused him to ship himself over into Little Britain in France; the inhabitants whereof may be termed cousin-Germans to the Welch.

Little can a long tongue lein.[1]

1721 KELLY 240 . . . Spoken as a reproof to a baubler [*i.e.* babbler]. [[1] conceal.]

Little cannot be great unless he devour many, The.

1616 DRAXE 148 A little body cannot be great, except he eate many. **1640** HERBERT 359.

Little dogs have long tails.

1721 KELLY 233.

Little dogs start the hare, the great get her.

1640 HERBERT 345. **1732** FULLER no. 3254.

Little England beyond Wales.

1586 CAMDEN *Britannia* 373 (A). **1662** FULLER (*Pembrokeshire*) III. 553 A part of this county is peopled by Flemings, placed there by King Henry the First, . . . and their country is called Little England beyond Wales. **1670** RAY 258 . . . so called because the inhabitants speak good English.

Little Englanders.

1895 *Westm. Gaz.* 1 Aug. 2/2 The error so often made by Little Englanders. **1910** *Times, Wkly.* 10 June 420 Goldwin Smith was . . . a Little Englander of the Little Englanders. He saw nothing in the Empire . . . but a burden on England and an obstacle to the full civic development of the Colonies.

Little fire burns up a great deal of corn, A.

1586 *La Primaudaye* tr. T. BOWES (**1589**) 123 A little fire consumeth a great wood. *c.* **1592** SHAKS. *3 Hen. VI* IV. viii. 7 A little fire is quickly trodden out, Which being suffered rivers cannot quench. **1595** *A pleasant Satyre* (*A Satyre Menippized*) 99 A little fire maketh a great flame. **1678** RAY *Adag. Hebr.* 413 A little fire burns up a great deal of corn. . . . To be understood of the mischief which an evil and slandering tongue does, and is exemplified in Doeg who by this means brought destruction upon the priests.

Little fish are sweet.

1830 FORBY 434 . . . It means small gifts are always acceptable. **1914** K. F. PURDON *Folk of Furry F.* vii 'They'll sell at a loss', he went on, with a sigh, 'but sure, little fish is sweet! and the rent has to be made up'.

Little fishes slip through nets, but great fishes are taken.

1509 A. BARCLAY *Ship of Fools* (1874) I. 191. **1598** MERES *Palladis* f. 246 (A).

Little for the rake after the besom, There is.

1641 FERGUSSON 94. **1721** KELLY 319 . . . There is little to be gotten of such a thing, when covetous people have had their will of it.

Little gear, less care. (*Cf.* Little wealth little care.)

1721 KELLY 236.

Little gentleman in black velvet, The.

[= a mole.] [A Jacobite phrase, referring to the belief that the death of William III was caused by his horse's stumbling over a mole-hill.] **1814** SCOTT *Wav.* xi The little gentleman in black velvet who did such service in 1702. **1928** *Times* 11 Oct. 19/6 One may recognize him as 'the little gentleman in black velvet' of Jacobite toasts, whose hillock gave William III his fatal fall from his horse.

Little given seasonably, excuses a great gift, A.

1640 HERBERT 355.

Little good comes of gathering.

a. **1450** *Tale of Colkelbie Sow* 19–21 in HAZLITT *Pop. Poetry of Scot.* (1895) I. 185 For in old prouerbe we sing Cumis littill gud of gaddering Quhair wrechit awerice birnis.

Little good (gear) is soon spent.

1555 HEYWOOD *Epigr. upon Proverbs* no. 169 Lyttel good, soone spended. **1639** CLARKE 242. **1641** FERGUSSON 71. **1721** KELLY 231.

Little good to stark nought, To come from.

1639 CLARKE 83. **1670** RAY 178.

Little house has a wide mouth, A.

1721 KELLY 6 A small house has a wide throat. **1865** *Lancs. Proverbs* in *N. & Q.* 3rd Ser. viii. 494 (A) (as 1721). **1883** BURNE *Shropsh. Folk-Lore* 589 (A).

Little house well filled, a little land well tilled, and a little wife well willed, A.

1539 TAVERNER (1545) I 2ᵛ The english . . . sayeth in this wyse.

> A lyttle house well fylled
> A lytle ground wel tylled ⎱ is best.
> And a little wife well wylled ⎰

1670 RAY 53. **1738** SWIFT (Dial. ii) 347 *Ld. S.* What do you think of a little house well filled? *Sir J.* And a little land well tilled? *Col.* Ay; and a little wife well willed?

Little intermeddling makes good friends (fair parting).

1641 FERGUSSON 71 Little intrometting maks good freinds. **1721** KELLY 233 Little intermeddling makes fair parting.

Little, He that hath | is the less dirty.

1640 HERBERT 338.

Little is the light will be seen far in a mirk night.

1819 SCOTT *Bride Lam.* xxvi But the . . . blaze which might have been seen ten miles off . . .?' 'Hout awa! it's an auld saying and a true,—"Little's the light Will be seen far in a mirk night".'

Little Jock gets the little dish, and it holds him aye long little.

1721 KELLY 230 . . . Poor people are poorly serv'd, which prolongs their poverty. **1862** HISLOP 216.

Little journeys and good cost bring safe home.

1640 HERBERT 341.

Little kenned, less cared for.

1721 KELLY 237 .. Spoken of such of our relations as dwell at a distance. Lat. *Non sunt amici, amici qui vivunt procul.*

Little kens the wife that sits by the fire, how the wind blows cold in Hurleburle-swyre.

1641 FERGUSSON 74. **1721** KELLY 229 . . . *Hurle-burle-swyre* is a passage through a ridge of mountains, that separate Nithsdale from Twadale,[1] and Clydsdale[2]: where . . . there is a perpetual blowing . . . They that are at ease, know little of the trouble that others are expos'd to. **1819** SCOTT *Bride Lam.* vi Keep you the cheek of the chimney-nook till I come back. . . . Little kens the auld wife that sits by the fire, How cauld the wind blaws in hurle-burle swire. [¹ Tweeddale. ² Clydesdale.]

Little kitchen makes a large house, A.

1614 SIR T. OVERBURY *Characters* Wks. (1890) 144 A *French cooke*. He is the prime cause why noblemen build their houses so great: for the smalnesse of their kitchin, makes the house the bigger. **1640** HERBERT 339.

Little knoweth the fat sow (man) what the lean doth mean (thinketh).

c. **1350** *Douce MS. 52* no. 115 Lytyl wote þe full what þe hungry aylyz. *c.* **1480** *The lytylle Childrenes lytil Boke* in *Babees Book* (Furnivall) 16 For the fulle wombe without any faylys wot fulle lytyl what the hungry aylyȝ. **1546** HEYWOOD I. x. 24 Littell knoweth the fat sow, what the leane dooth meane. **1550** BECON *Fort. Faith* Prol. A ii According to the common Prouerbe, Lyttel wote the ful sow that is in yᵉ stye, What the hungrye sow ayleth, that goeth by. **1640** HERBERT 345 The fat man knoweth not what the lean thinketh. **1852** E. FITZGERALD *Polonius* xi 'The Fat Sow knows not what the Lean one thinks' . . . Swollen Wealth is well enacted by the fat Sow reclining in her sty, as a Dowager in an opera-box, serenely unconscious of all her kindred's leanness without.

Little labour, much health, A.

1640 HERBERT 349.

Little learning is a dangerous thing, A.

1711 POPE *Ess. Crit.* 215 A little learning is a dangerous thing. **1830** G. COLMAN *Rand. Rec.* I. 100 'A little learning is a dangerous thing';—and a great deal cannot be hammer'd into the heads of vulgar men.

Little let¹ lets an ill workman, A.

1640 HERBERT 352. [¹ hindrance.]

Little London beyond Wales.

1670 RAY 258 . . . i.e. *Beaumaris* in the Isle of *Anglesey*: so called because the inhabitants speak good *English*.

Little losses amaze, great tame.

1640 HERBERT 364.

Little mead, little need.

1678 RAY 352 . . . *Somerset*. (A mild winter hoped for after a bad summer.)

Little meddling maketh much rest.

c. **1386** CHAUCER *Manciple's T.* H. 350 That litel jangling causeth muchel rest. *c.* **1450** *Prouerbis of Wysdom* 128 Lytyll medlyng makype mych rest. **1546** HEYWOOD II. ii. 47 To meddle little for me it is beste. For of little medlyng cometh great reste. **1635** SWAN *Spec. Mundi* (1670) 368 In little medling is much rest. **1659** HOWELL *Eng. Prov.* 9/1 Of little medling cometh great ease.

Little mense¹ o' the cheeks to bite off the nose.

1862 HISLOP 216 . . . It is bad policy for a person to injure another with whom he is intimately connected, or upon whom he is depending. [¹ discretion.]

Little money as you have manners, If you had as | you would be the poorest man of your kin.

1721 KELLY 205 . . . Spoken to wealthy people, when they behave themselves rudely, haughtily, or insolently. **1732** FULLER no. 2754.

Little (Small) pitchers have great (long, wide) ears.

1546 HEYWOOD II. v Auoyd your children, small pitchers haue wide eares. **1592–3** SHAKS. *Rich. III* II. iv. 37 *Arch.* Good madam, be not angry with the child. *Q. Eliz.* Pitchers have ears. **1593–4** *Tam. Shrew* IV. iv. 52 Not in my house, Lucretio; for you know Pitchers have ears, and I have many servants. **1640** HERBERT 335 Little pitchers have wide ears. **1837–47** BARHAM *Ingol. Leg., St. Dunstan* A truth Insisted on much in my earlier years, To wit, 'Little pitchers have very long ears!' **1915** *Lit. Digest* 4 Sept. 475/1 The little pitchers with big ears have been taking in a good deal of war talk.

Little pot is soon hot, A.

1546 HEYWOOD I. xi. 25 It is wood¹ at a woorde, little potte soone whot. **1593–4** SHAKS. *Tam. Shrew* IV. i. 6 Now were I not a little pot and soon hot, my very lips might freeze. **1606** DAY *Isle of Gulls.* III. ii *Vio.* Nay, though I be but a little pot, I shall be as soon hot as another. **1670** RAY 115 . . . Little persons are commonly choleric. **1883** READE *Peril. Secr.* xv Cheeky little beggar, But . . . 'a little pot is soon hot'. [¹ mad, furious.]

Little (Least, Nothing) said is soon (soonest) amended (mended). (*See also* Least said, &c.)

c. **1460** *Parl. of Byrdes* in HAZL. *Early Pop. Poetry* III. 169 Who sayth lytell he is wyse and fewe wordes are soone amended. **1555** HEYWOOD *Epigr. upon Prov.* no. 169 Lyttle sayde, soone amended. **1599** PORTER *Angry Wom. Abingd.* III. ii (Merm.) 158 *Nich.* Little said is soon amended. **1634** FORD *Per. Warb.* IV. ii. Wks. (1869) II. 182 *J. a-Wat.* It is good to consider . . . , otherwise— . . . little said is soon amended. **1635** SWAN *Spec. Mundi* (1670) 368 In little medling is much rest; and 'nothing said is soonest amended'. **1721** KELLY 231 Little said soon mended. **1818** SCOTT *Rob Roy* xxix About treason and all that, it's lost time to speak of it—least said is sunest mended. **1917** BRIDGE 89 Least said soonest mended, but nowt said needs no mending.

Little sap in dry pease hulls, There is.

1641 FERGUSSON 98 There [is] little sap in dry peis hoo

Little, He that hath | shall have less.

1639 CLARKE 82.

Little sticks kindle the fire; great ones put it out.

c. **1300** BRUNNE *Handl. Synne* l. 12438 Thou seest stykkẽs that are smale, They brenne fyrst feyre. **1640** HERBERT 332.

Little stream drives a light mill, A.

1579 GOSSON *Ephemerides* (*Sch. Abuse* Arber 10–11) A little streame serves to drive a light Mill. **1597** *Politeuphuia* 166. **1639** CLARKE 129.

Little thieves are hanged, but great ones escape.

1639 CLARKE 172.

Little thing, Of a | a little displeaseth.

1640 HERBERT 354.

Little thing, *see also* Nothing is (Where), a little thing doth ease.

Little things are great to little men.

1764 O. GOLDSMITH *The Traveller* l. 42 These little things are great to little men. **1765** JOHNSON *Preface to Shakespeare* (*Johnson on Shakespeare*, ed. Raleigh 51) Small things make mean men proud. *a.* **1792** SIR JOSHUA REYNOLDS *Two Dialogues* (*Johnsonian Miscellanies*, Birkbeck-Hill ii. 235). **1827** HONE *Table-Book* 110 (A).

Little things are pretty.

1539 TAVERNER f. 50 (A) Vnto lyttle thynges is a certayne grace annexed. **1678** RAY 169 ... Χάρις βαιοῖσιν ὀπηδεῖ.

Little things please (affect, attract) little minds.

[OVID *Ars Amatoria* 1. 159 *Parva leves capiunt animos.*] **1845** DISRAELI *Sybil* III. ii Little things affect little minds. Lord Marney ... was kept at the station which aggravated his spleen.

Little tit,[1] all tail.

1546 HEYWOOD I. x. 20 But little titte all tayle, I haue heard er this. [[1] a small animal or object.]

Little to sew, when tailors are true.

1721 KELLY 235 ... Lat. *Raro, ad tempus, fidem præstant artifices.*

Little troubles the eye, but far less the soul.

1641 FERGUSSON 74.

Little wealth little care. (*Cf.* Little gear, less care.)

1616 DRAXE 160. **1640** HERBERT (Gros.) no. 497.

Little wind kindles, much puts out the fire, A.

1586 B. YOUNG tr. *Guazzo's Civ. Conv.* f. 193

(A). **1593–4** SHAKS. *Tam. Shrew* II. i. 135 Though little fire grows great with little wind, yet extreme gusts will blow out fire and all. **1640** HERBERT 349.

Little wit, You have a | and it doth you good sometimes.

1664 CODRINGTON 230. **1670** RAY 30.

Little wit in the head makes much work for the heel (feet). (*Cf. the following proverb.*)

1832 HENDERSON 83 Little wit in the head maks muckle travel to the heel. **1855** BOHN 445 Little wit in the head makes much work for the feet.

Little wit makes meikle travel. (*Cf. the preceding proverb.*)

1641 FERGUSSON 70. **1707** MAPLETOFT 121 Little wit makes mickle travel. **1721** KELLY 230 *Little wit as mickle travell.* Spoken when people for want of skill, put themselves to more trouble than they need.

Little wit will serve a fortunate man, A.

1573 SANDFORD (1576) 220 A little wit is inough for him to whome fortune pipes. **1707** MAPLETOFT 27. **1855** BOHN 293.

Little with quiet is the only diet, A.

c. **1300** *King Alis.* (Weber) l. 7365 Beter is, lyte to have in ese Then muche to have[n] in malese. **1611** COTGRAVE s.v. 'Pen' A little with quietnesse is Gods owne gift. Id. s.v. 'Paix' A little with peace is a great blessing. **1640** HERBERT 332.

Little Witham, He was born at.

1562 HEYWOOD *Fifth Hund. of Epig.* no. 19 (1867) 182 Whens come great breeches? from little wittam. **1662** FULLER (*Lincs.*) II. 269 'He was born at Little Wittham'. This village in this county by orthography is Witham.... But such nominal proverbs take the advantage of all manner of spelling as due unto them. It is applied to such people as are not overstocked with acuteness.

Little wood will heat a little oven, A.

1642 TORRIANO 4. **1732** FULLER no. 254.

Little, *see also* Every l. helps; Fair and sluttish ... l. and loud; Here a l. there a l.; Tarry-long brings l. home; Woman were as l. as she is good (If a), peascod would make her a gown.

Live a little while, If you will | go to Bapchild; if you'd live long, go to Tenham or Tong.

1736 S. PEGGE *Kenticisms, Prov.* (E.D.S.) 67 ... Bapchild is indeed a bad and unhealthy situation. [It is adjacent to Tong, which adjoins Teynham.]

Live and learn.

1575 GASCOIGNE *Glass of Government* (Cunliffe) 88 We live to learne, for so Sainct Paule doth teach. **1579** LYLY *Euphues* (Arber) 44 You have lived long and learned little. **1639** CLARKE 267. **1659** HOWELL *Eng. Prov.* 13/2 One may live and learn, and be hanged and forget all. **1662** J. WILSON *Cheats* III. iii *Scru.* I see a man may live and learn every day. **1704** STEELE *Lying Lov.* I. i *Y. Bookw.* Don't stand gaping, but live and learn, my lad. **1894** LD. AVEBURY *Use of Life* vi No doubt we go on learning as long as we live: Live and learn.'

Live and let live.

1622 MALYNES *Anc. Law-Merch.* 229 According to the Dutch prouerbe . . . Leuen ende laeten leuen, to liue and to let others liue. **1641** FERGUSSON 72. **1678** RAY 170 . . . *i.e.* Do as you would be done by. Let such pennyworths as your tenants may live under you. **1692** L'ESTRANGE *Aesop's Fab.* cxxxix (1738) 154 *Live and let live*, is the rule of common justice. **1902** J. H. ROSE in *Lect. Hist. 19th Cent.* 77 Napoleon had no conception of the maxim—'Live and let live'. His commercial ideas were narrowly national. **1906** HERBERT PAUL *Stray Leaves* Bp. Creighton, 'Live and let live' was his motto.

Live, I | and lords (the best) do no more.

1599 PORTER *Angry Wom. Abingd.* II. ii (Merm.) 131 *Fran.* Well, how doth thy master? *Nich.* Forsooth, live, and the best doth no better. **1721** KELLY 400 Even living, and Lairds do no more. **1732** FULLER no. 2616 I live; and Lords do no more.

Live, He will (would) | as long as old Rosse (Russe) of Pottern,[1] who lived till all the world was weary of him.

1659 HOWELL *Eng. Prov.* 14/2 (with 'will' and 'Russe'). **1678** RAY *Prov.* 80 (with 'would' and 'Rosse'). [[1] near Devizes, Wilts.]

Live as they would die, Let all.

1640 HERBERT 351.

Live by selling ware for words, One cannot.

1639 CLARKE 156. **1670** RAY 154. **1732** FULLER no. 3741 (with 'goods' for ware').

Live by the quick (living), not by the dead, We must.

1545 TAVERNER B 3 Oure Englyshe prouerbe —we ought to lyue by the quycke and not by the deade. **1576** PETTIE *Petite Pall.* (Gollancz) I. 109 You are to know that we must live by the living, not by the dead. **1605** T. HEYWOOD *If you know not me* (Shaks. Soc.) 52 *Tame.* 'Twere fit To spend some funeral tears upon her hearse. . . . *Clown.* Ay, but do you not know the old proverb? We must live by the quick, and not by the dead. **1614** SIR T. OVERBURY *Characters* Wks. (1890) 145 *A Sexton.* Of all proverbs, hee cannot endure to heare that which sayes, We ought to live by the quick, not by the dead. **1738** SWIFT (Dial. ii) 349 *Never.* Well; rest his soul: we must live by the living, and not by the dead.

Live ever, If you would | you must wash milk from your liver.

1611 COTGRAVE s.v. 'Laict' Wash thy milke off thy liver (say we). **1678** RAY 36 . . . Vin sur laict c'est souhait, Laict sur vin c'est venin. *Gall.* This is an idle old saw, for which I can see no reason but rather the contrary.

Live for aye, He that would | must eat sage in May.

1588 COGAN *Haven of Health* (1612) xi. 32 (A) In *Schola Salerni* it is demanded *Cur moriatur homo cui saluia crescit in horto?* As who should say, such is the vertue of sage, that if it were possible, it would make a man immortall. **1678** RAY 36 . . . 'That Sage was by our ancestours esteemed a very wholesome herb, and much conducing to longevity appears by that verse in *Schola Salernitana, Cur moriatur homo cui Salvia crescit in horto?* [Why should the man die in whose garden sage grows?] **1732** FULLER no. 6253 He that would live for aye, must eat butter and sage in May.

Live from hand to mouth, To.

[= to live improvidently.] **1549** CHALENOR tr. *Erasm. Praise of Folly* G 1 Lyue from hande to mouthe. **1580** J. CONYBEARE *Adagia* 50 They liue from hande to mouthe. **1603** FLORIO tr. *Montaigne* III. iii (1897) V. 68 I live from hand to mouth, and . . . I live but to myself. **1712** ARBUTHNOT *John Bull* xv Poor Frog . . . is in hard circumstances, he has a numerous family, and lives from hand to mouth. **1910** *Spectator* 6 Aug. 199 Other women . . . waste by living in a needlessly hand-to-mouth fashion.

Live, horse, and you'll get grass.

1738 SWIFT (Dial. i) 342 *Nev.* I hope to have a rich . . . wife yet before I die. *Col.* Ay, Tom; live, horse, and thou shalt have grass.

Live in a gravel pit, He would.

1678 RAY 72 . . . Spoken of a wary, sparing, niggardly person.

Live in Italy, A man would | but he would choose to die in Spain.

1651 HERBERT 365 A man would live in Italy (a place of pleasure), but he would choose to die in Spain, where they say the Catholic Religion is professed with great strictness.

Live in peace and rest, He that would (will) | must hear, and see, and say the best.

c. **1450** *Prov. of Good Counsel* (E.E.T.S.) l. 52 (A) Yf thou wylte leve in peas and reste, here, and see, and sey the beste. **1611** DAVIES *Prov.* 69. **1670** RAY 130 . . . Oy, voy, & te tais, si tu veux vivre en paix, *Gall.* Ode, vede, tace, Se vuoi viver in pace, *Ital.* **1796** EDGEWORTH *Par. Asst.* (1903) 410 It is not our affair, however. Let him make himself happy his way, and we ours. He that would live in peace and rest, Must hear, and see and say the best.

Live in the shade.

1896 DEAN PLUMPTRE *Ecclesiastes* 1:3 *Λάθε*

βιώσας, 'live in the shade', was the Epicurean rule of wisdom. Pleasure was not found in feasts and sensual excess but in sobriety of mind.

Live longest, They that | must die at last.

1670 RAY 116.

Live longest,They who | will see most.

1620 SHELTON *Quix.* II. lii (A) My mother was used to say that it was needful to live long to see much. **1837** TH. HOOK *Jack Brag* xvii I'll watch her pretty closely. . . . Never mind; them as lives longest sees the most.

Live on air like the chameleon, To.

1594-5 SHAKS. *Two Gent.* II. i. 181 The chameleon Love can feed on the air. **1600-1** *Hamlet* III. ii. 101 Of the chameleon's dish: I eat the air, promise-crammed. **1629** T. ADAMS *Serm.* (1862) I. 361 Is he ever the fuller or fatter for our word? Not unless, like a chameleon, he can live by air. **1670** RAY 56 A man cannot live by the air. *a.* **1812** WOLCOT (P. Pindar) *Lyric Odes* v. (1816) I. 18 No matter, verily, how slight their fare; Nay, though camelion-like, they fed on air.

Live peaceably with all breeds good blood, To.

1640 HERBERT 361.

Live to be old, If you would not | you must be hanged when you are young.

1670 RAY 126.

Live well for a week, If you would | kill a hog; if you would live well for a month, marry; if you would live well all your life, turn priest.

1666 TORRIANO 151 (A) Who intends to have a good Month, let him to the bath, a good year, let him marry, a good week, let him kill a hog, who will be happy alwaies, let him turn priest. **1809** S. PEGGE *Anonymiana* II. xix. 64 If you would live well for a week, kill a hog; if you would live well for a month, marry; if you would live well all your life, turn priest. . . . Turning priest . . . alludes to the celibacy of the Romish Clergy, and has a pungent sense, as much as to say, do not marry at all.

Live without our friends, We can | but not without our neighbours.

1721 KELLY 348. **1732** FULLER no. 5435.

Live(s), *see also* Clover (L. in); Everything would l.; Fighting cocks (L. like); Hen l. (Let the) though with her pip; Know not who l. or dies (We); Long (Not how) but how well we l.; Longer l. a good fellow than dear year; Longer we l. more farlies we see; Man l. (As a), so shall he die; Mind what you must l. by; See what we must come to if we l.; Soul is not where it l. but where loves; Too wise to l. long; Trades l. (Let all); Unworthy to l. who l. for himself.

Lived that lives not after death, He hath not.

1640 HERBERT 357.

Lived too near a wood to be frightened by owls, I have.

1738 SWIFT (Dial. iii) 352 *Spark.* Never fear him, miss. *Miss.* . . . Do you think I was born in a wood, to be afraid of an owl? **1855** BOHN 411.

Liver, *see* Good for the l. bad for spleen.

Liverpool, *see* Manchester men and L. gentlemen.

Lives as a cat, As many.

c. **1625** BEAUM. & FL. *Mons. Thomas* III. i. Wks. (1905) IV. 127 There be as many lives in't, as a cat carries. **1684** BUNYAN *Pilgr.* II (1862) 331 He had, as they say, as many lives as a cat. **1738** SWIFT (Dial. i) 342 *Col.* They say a woman has as many lives as a cat.

Lives by hope will die by hunger, Who. (*Cf.* Lives on hope, &c.)

1616 DRAXE 92 Hope will make a man neither eat nor drinke. **1623** WODROEPHE 302 Hee who lives of Hope makes a thinne Belly. **1711** ADDISON *Spect.* No. 191 Wks. (Bohn) III. 63 The man who will live above his present circumstances, is in great danger of living in a little time much beneath them; or, as the Italian proverb runs, The man who lives by Hope will die by Hunger.

Lives by love, and lumps in corners (the cupboard), She.

1678 RAY 75 (*Joculatory*). **1738** SWIFT (Dial. i) 339 *Col.* Miss lives upon love. *Miss.* Yes, upon love and lumps of the cupboard.

Lives ill, He that | fear follows him.

1640 HERBERT 322.

Lives in hope, He that | danceth without music.

1591 FLORIO *Second Frutes* 149 (A) He that dooth liue in hope, dooth dance in narrow scope. **1640** HERBERT 363. **1670** RAY 13 He that lives in hope danceth without a minstrel.

Lives long suffers much, He that.

1620 SHELTON *Quix.* II. xxxii (1908) III. 45 'Tis good to live long, to see much; although 'tis said also that he that lives long suffers much.

Lives long that lives well, He.

1553 T. WILSON *Arte of Rhet.* (1909) 83 They liued long enough, that haue liued well enough. **1642** FULLER *H. & P. State*, I. vi (1841) 15 If he chance to die young, yet he lives long that lives well. **1721** KELLY 168 He that liveth well, liveth long.

Lives longest, He that | must fetch his wood farthest.

1608 J. NORDEN *Surveyors Dialogue* (Harrison, *Description of England*, New Sh. S. iii. 191) As the Prouerbe is, Let them that liue longest, fetch their wood farthest. **1623** CAMDEN 271. **1625** PURCHAS *Pilgrims* (1905–7) XIX. 247 Herein we may verify the old proverb, That he which liveth longest, shall fetch his wood furthest. **1670** RAY 116.

Lives most, dies most, He that.

1640 HERBERT 338.

Lives not well one year, He that | sorrows seven after.

1640 HERBERT 343. **1748** RICHARDSON *Clarissa* iv, let. 24 He that lives ill one year will sorrow for it seven.

Lives on hope hath a slender diet, He that. (*Cf.* Lives by hope, &c.)

[L. *Qui spe aluntur, pendent, non vivunt*.] **1689** SHADWELL *Bury Fair* III. i Hope is a very thin diet, fit for love in a fever. **1721** KELLY 129.

Lives under the sign of the cat's foot, He.

1678 RAY 68 . . . He is hen-peckt, his wife scratches him.

Lives unsafely that looks too near on things, He.

1611 COTGRAVE S.V. 'Esplucher' (with 'to matters' for 'on things'). **1640** HERBERT 319.

Lives well is learned enough, He that.

1611 COTGRAVE S.V. 'Vivre' He that lives well enough hath skill enough. **1640** HERBERT 320.

Lives well, sees afar off, He that.

1640 HERBERT 334.

Lives, *see also* Live(s).

Liveth in Court dieth upon straw, He that.

1573 SANDFORD (1576) 209. **1629** *Book of Meery Riddles* Prov. 131.

Liveth wickedly can hardly die honestly, He that.

1616 DRAXE 114. **1664** CODRINGTON 198. **1670** RAY 16.

Living dog is better than a dead lion, A.

1382 WYCLIF *Eccl.* ix. 4 Betere is a quyc dogge than a leoun dead. **1595** DANIEL *Civ. Wars* 4. st. 3 Their wisedom . . . Live dogges before dead Lyons estimates. **1655** FULLER *Ch. Hist.* III. i (1868) I. 322 Doth not Solomon say true, 'A living dog is better than a dead lion'; when such a little cur durst snarl at the corpse of a king? **1906** IAN HAMILTON *Staff-*

Off. Scrap-Bk. I. 197 To the Japanese soldier . . . the dead lion is one thousand times more enviable than the live dog.

Living man all things can, No.

[VIRGIL *Eclog.* 8. 63 *Non omnia possumus omnes*. We cannot any of us do all things.] **1639** CLARKE 147. *Ibid.* 97 No man is good at all things.

Living well is the best revenge.

1640 HERBERT 342.

Living, *see also* Live by the l. (We must); Remember the l.

Lizard(s), *see* Rock L.; Serpent has bitten (Whom a), l. alarms.

Load, *see* Willing horse (All lay l. on).

Loader's horse that lives among thieves, Like a.

[loader = carrier; carriers were not noted for honesty.] **1678** RAY 350 . . . (*The countrey man near a town.*) *Som.*

Loaf (-ves), *see* Cut large shives of another's l.; First cut and all l. besides; Give a l. and beg shive; Half a l. better than . . .; Set not your l. in till oven hot; Shive of a cut l. (Safe taking); Shive of my own l.; Traitors at the table; Wife cries five l. a penny.

Loan, *see* Seldom cometh l. laughing home.

Loaning, *see* Cow in a fremit l. (Like a).

Loathe, Loathing, *see* Better go away longing than l.; Length begets l.

Loaves and fishes.

[= material benefits rather than spiritual blessings.] **1389** WYCLIF *John* vi. 9, 26 O child is here, that hath fyue barley looues and tweye fysches. . . . ʒe seken me, not for ʒe syʒ the tokenis, but for ʒe eeten of looues, and ben fillid. **1614** BP. HALL *Recoll. Treat.* 954 If it were not for the loaves and fishes, the traine of Christ would bee lesse. **1905** G. O. TREVELYAN *Interludes* 124 A Mohammedan foundation, something between a college and a monastery. . . . It is very richly endowed, and the loaves and fishes are kept strictly among the founder's kin.

Loaves, *see also* Loaf (-ves).

Lob's (Cob's, Hob's) pound.

[= prison, lock-up; also *fig.* an entanglement, difficulty.] **1597** B. S. *Discov. Knights of Post* B, Knightes of the Poste, Lords of lobs pound, and heires apparant to the pillory. **1639** CLARKE 188 Hee's in Cobs pound. **1663** BUTLER *Hudibras* I. iii. 910 Crowdero, whom in Irons bound, Thou basely threw'st into Lob's pound. **1796** MAD. D'ARBLAY *Camilla* IV. iii What! are you all in Hob's pound? **1829** BENTHAM *Justice & Cod. Petit. Wks.* (1843) V. 494 Pass on to the dependant, when the time came for his finding himself in Lob's pound. **1895** *E. Angl. Gloss.* Lobs-pound, to be in any difficulty or perplexed state.

Lobster, *see* Runner (Look like a), quoth devil to l.

Lochaber axe, He looks like a.

1641 FERGUSSON 48 *Of fleyit[1] persons.* . . . He looks like a Lochwhaber axe. **1721** KELLY 373 *You look like a Lochaber ax new come from the grindstone.* Us'd when people look sillily, demurely, foolishly, or wildly. [[1] frightened.]

Lochow, *see* Far cry to.

Lock will hold against the power of gold, No.

1580 LYLY *Euph. & his Eng.* Wks. (Bond) II. 71 And who is so ignorant that knoweth not, gold be a Key for euery locke? **1640** HERBERT 332.

Lock, *see also* Highlandman's gun that needed l., stock, and barrel; Silver key open iron l.; Stock, l., and barrel.

Lockerby lick, A.

[= a face-blow.] [**1593**] in HUME BROWN *Hist. Scot.* (1902) II. 219 The two forces met at Dryfe Sands, near Lockerby;[1] and . . . the Johnstones gained a decisive victory. . . . From the number of face-wounds given in the battle, a 'Lockerby lick' passed into the common speech of the country. **1882** A. CUNNINGHAM *Tradl. Tales* (1887) 232 If ye lay a hand . . . on the poor demented lassie, I'se land ye a Lockerby lick. [[1] Dumfries.]

Lockington, *see* Put up your pipes and go to L.

Lockit, Bessie, *see* Rynt you witch, quoth B. L.

Lodgeth, *see* Cometh late l. ill (Who).

Log nor a stork, Neither a | good Jupiter.

[In allusion to Æsop's fable of the frogs who appealed to Jupiter for a king, and being dissatisfied with the log given them found him replaced by a stork.] **1620–8** FELTHAM *Resolves* (Dent) 169 I like neither a devouring Stork, nor a Jupiter's log. **1732** FULLER no. 3521. **1907** *Spectator* 16 Nov. 744 The rise of the Mahdi in 1881, and the subsequent liberation of . . . the Soudan from Egyptian rule, was only a substitution of King Stork for King Log.

Log(s), *see also* Crooked l. straight fires.

Logic, *see* Chop l.

Lombard Street to a China orange, All.

[Lombard Street, in London, has many banks.] **1752** MURPHY *Gray's Inn Journ.* No. xi 30 Dec. (A) I'll lay all Lombard-Street to an egg-shell that it is true. **1832** MARRYAT *N. Forster* xlvii 'All Lombard Street to a China orange, 'tis Surcœuf', replied Captain Oughton. **1848 9** LYTTON *Caxtons* IV. iii 'It is Lombard Street to a China orange', quoth Uncle Jack. 'Are the odds . . . so great?'

Lombard, *see also* Sick of the L. fever.

London Bridge had fewer eyes, If | it would see better.

1869 HAZLITT 246 . . . In allusion to the numerous and narrow openings for vessels.

London Bridge was built upon woolpacks.

1607 BEAUMONT *K. Burn. P.* Induction The rearing of London Bridge upon wool-sacks. **1659** *London Chaunticleers* viii in HAZL. *O.E.P.* VI 341 *Curds.* When we kept the Whitson ale, when we danced *The Building of London Bridge upon woolpacks.* **1812** J. BRADY *Clavis Calendaria* I. 194 'That London Bridge was built upon wool-sacks'; that is, the expense of the fabric . . . about the end of the 12th century, was defrayed by an impost, . . . upon the wool brought to the metropolis.

London Bridge was made for wise men to go over, and fools to go under.

1639 CLARKE 249. [LEAN I. 140 The present bridge was built in 1825. The danger to light wherries in shooting the bridge was appreciable.]

London Bridge, *see also* Good turn (One) will meet another.

London cockney, A. (*See also* Born within the sound of Bow bell.)

1600 ROWLANDS *Lett. Hum. Blood* iv. 65 I scorne . . . To let a Bow-bell Cockney put me downe. **1617** MINSHEU *Ductor* s.v. *A Cockney* . . . , applied only to one borne within the sound of Bow-bell, that is, within the City of London. **1617** MORYSON *Itin.* III. 53 Londiners, and all within the sound of Bow-bell, are in reproch called Cockneis, and eaters of buttered tostes.

London jury; A | hang half, and save half.

1608 MIDDLETON *Trick Catch Old One* IV. V Thou that goest upon Middlesex juries, and wilt make haste to give up thy verdict because thou wilt not lose thy dinner. **1662** FULLER (*London*) II. 340 'A London jury; hang half, and save half' . . . as if Londoners, frequently impannelled on juries, . . . to make quick riddance . . ., acquit half, and condemn half. **1732** FULLER no. 231 (with 'A Kentish jury').

London lickpenny.

14 . . ? LYDGATE (title) *London Lyckpeny. c.* **1600** DAY *Begg. Bednall Gr.* II. ii. (1881) 34 London lick penny call ye it—t'as licked me with a witness. **1662** FULLER (*Lond.*) II. 342 'London lick-penny.' The countryman coming up hither, by his own experience, will easily expound the meaning thereof. **1710–11** SWIFT *Jrnl. to Stella* 15 Jan. It has cost me three guineas to-day for a periwig. . . . Well, London lickpenny; I find it true.

London, She hath been at | to call a strea a 'straw', and a waw a 'wall'.

1670 RAY 218 . . . *Chesh.* This the common people use in scorn of those who having been at London are ashamed to speak their own country dialect.

London, *see also* Dunmow bacon . . . L. beer; Lincoln shall be hanged for L.'s sake; Lincoln was, L. is; Little L. beyond Wales; No cousin in L.; Nobody's nails can reach L.; Oxford for learning, L. for wit; Oxford knives and L. wives; Which way to L.? A poke full of plums. *See also* Clocks, Lord Mayor of London.

Londoner like, ask as much more as you will take.

1678 RAY 349.

Lone sheep is in danger of the wolf, The.

[1611 COTGRAVE s.v. 'Homme seul' The lone man is Wolues meat.] 1639 CLARKE 117.

Long (*proper name*), *see* Beggar that goes by the way can't beg through L.; John (Tom) L. the carrier.

Long a giving knows not how to give, He that is.

1640 HERBERT 340.

Long a widow weds with shame.

1659 HOWELL *Brit. Prov.* 19.

Long absent, soon forgotten.

1611 COTGRAVE s.v. 'Ami' Long absence alters affection. 1616 DRAXE 2. 1670 RAY 55 . . . Parallel to this are, *Out of sight, out of mind,* and *Seldom seen, soon forgotten.*

Long and lazy.

1648 HERRICK *Hesper.* No. 358 Long and Lazy. That was the Proverb. Let my mistress be Lasie to others, but be long to me. 1872 BLACKMORE *Maid of Sker* xiii You are long enough, and lazy enough; put your hand to the bridle.

Long and lazy, little and loud; fat and fulsome, pretty and proud.

1591 FLORIO *Second Frutes* 189 If long, she is lazy, if little, she is lowde. 1659 HOWELL *Eng. Prov.* 10/2 Long and lazy, little and loud, Fatt and fulsome, prety and proud; *in point of women.*

Long and the short of it, The.

c. 1330 BRUNNE *Chron.* (Hearne) 222 To say longly or schorte, alle [that] armes bare. 1589 NASHE *Death of Martin Mar-Prelate* in Wks. (Gros.) I. 185 This is the short and the long, and the somme of all. 1589–9 SHAKS. *Hen. V* III. ii. 130 That sal I suerly do, that is the breff and the long. 1681 W. ROBERTSON *Phraseol. Gen.* 837/2 *The* LONG *and the short of a business*; Summa rei.

Long as a Welsh pedigree, As.

1662 FULLER (*Wales*) III. 489 'As long as a Welsh pedigree', Any Welch gentleman . . . can presently climb up, by the stairs of his pedigree, into princely extraction. 1846 J. GRANT *Rom. of War* xviii Señor Sancho . . . has a name as long as a Welsh pedigree.

Long as he is lither,[1] If he were as | he might thatch a house without a ladder.

1678 RAY *Chesh.* 257. [[1] lazy.]

Long as I live, I'll spit in my parlour, As.

1721 KELLY 53 As long as I live I'll fart at my own Fire-side. 1732 FULLER no. 710.

Long as Meg of Westminster, As.

c. 1589 LYLY *Pap with a Hatchet* Wks. (Bond) III. 403. 1590 *Stationers' Register* 18 Aug. 1590. 1593 G. HARVEY *Pierce's Supererogation* (cited Deloney, ed. Mann 532). 1662 FULLER (*Westmr.*) II. 413 'As long as Meg of Westminster', . . . Applied to persons very tall, especially if they have hop-pole height, wanting breadth proportionable thereto. That such a giant woman ever was in Westminster, cannot be proved. [A cannon in Dover Castle and a flagstone in Westminster Abbey were called after her. Her life and merry pranks were printed in 1582. LEAN II. 850.]

Long a-tuning your pipes, You are as | as another would play a spring.[1]

1721 KELLY 371 . . . You are as long a setting about a thing, as another would actually do it. [[1] tune.]

Long be thy legs and short be thy life.

1550 HEYWOOD II. vii. 68 Thy tales (quoth he) shew long heare, and short wit, wife. But long be thy legs, and short be thy lyfe.

Long beards heartless; painted hoods witless; gay coats graceless; makes England thriftless.

1580 STOW *Chron. of Eng., Edwd. III.* 359 The Scottes made manye taunting rimes against the *Englishmen* . . . amongst the which was . . . Long beardes hartlesse, Painted hoodes witlesse, Gay coates gracelesse, Makes England thriftlesse.

Long bow, To draw (pull) the.

[= to exaggerate, to lie.] 1678 RAY 89 *A Lier.* He's a long-bow-man. 1824 BYRON *Juan* xvi. i They . . . draw the long bow better now than ever. 1853 THACKERAY *Newcomes* lii It was not much of a fib that Barnes had told. . . . But if he had recollected . . . [he] would not have pulled that unlucky long-bow. 1908 C. M. DOUGHTY *Wand. in Arabia* I. ii. 13 Pity Mohammed had not seen Petra! he might have drawn another long-bow shot in Wady Mûsa.

Long, It is not how | but how well we live.

1664 CODRINGTON 200 It is not how long we live, but how well we live. **1670** RAY 16.

Long Clawson, *see* Whores in Hose than . . . in L. C. (More).

Long day, Not a | but a good heart rids work.

1611 COTGRAVE S.V. 'Grand' Not long dayes, but strong hearts, dispatch a work. **1640** HERBERT 318.

Long day that never pay, They take a.

1678 RAY 188.

Long foretold, long last; short notice, soon past.

1866 A. STEINMETZ *Man. of Weathercasts* 155 Old saws about the barometer. . . . 'Long foretold, long last: Short notice, soon past.' **1889** JEROME *Three Men in Boat* v The barometer is . . . misleading. . . . Boots . . . read out a poem which was printed over the top of the oracle, about 'Long foretold, long last; Short notice, soon past'. The fine weather never came that summer.

Long harvest of (for) a little corn, A.

1550 HEYWOOD I. xii Surely . . . ye have in this time thus worne, Made a long haruest for a little corne. **1579** LYLY *Euphues* (Arb.) 97 Euphues (quoth shee) you make a long Haruest for a lyttle corne, and angle for the fish that is alreadie caught. **1614** CAMDEN 302 **1670** RAY 180 To make a long harvest of a little corn. **1786** *Har'st Rig* cxlii (1794) 43 Lang was the har'st and little corn!

Long home, The.

[= the grave.] [**1611** BIBLE *Eccles.* xii. 5 Man goeth to his long home.] **1303** BRUNNE *Handl. Synne* l. 9195 (A) And thy traueyle shalt thou sone ende, For to thy long home sone shalt thou wende. **1662** FULLER (*Warwickshire*) III. 273 Some think she went her own pace to the grave, while others suspect a grain was given her, to quicken her in her journey to her long home.

Long in coming as Cotswold barley, It is as.

1662 FULLER (*Glos.*) I. 552 'It is long in coming as Cotswold barley.' It is applied to such things as are slow but sure. The corn, in this cold county on the Wolds, . . . is very backward at the first; but afterwards overtakes the forwardest in the county. **1670** RAY 228 *Gloucestershire*.

Long jesting was never good.

1640 HERBERT 349.

Long journey, In a | straw weighs.

1640 HERBERT 355.

Long lane (run) that has no turning, It is a.

8 July **1633** *Stationers' Register* (Arb.) iv. 299 (ballad) Long runns that neere turnes. **1670** RAY 117 It is a long run that never turns. **1778** FOOTE *Trip Calais* II. Wks. (1799) II. 355 It is a long lane that has no turning. **1827** SCOTT *Chron. Canongate* v It is a long lane that has no turning. . . . He has sown his wild oats, . . . and has settled into a steady respectable man. **1894** LD. AVEBURY *Use of Life* iii (1904) 24 If money comes in slowly at first, do not be discouraged; it is a long lane which has no turning; . . . lay up some for a rainy day, remembering that good lanes have their turnings as well as bad ones.

Long liveth a merry man as a sad, As.

[PUB. SYRUS 438: *O vita misero longa, felici brevis.*] c. **1300** *Vernon MS.* (E.E.T.S.) 347 (A) Lenger liueth a glad mon then a sori. c. **1350** *Douce MS. 52*, no. 57 As long lyeuth a mery man as a sory. a. **1553** UDALL *Royster D.* I. i (Arb.) 11 As long lyueth the mery man (they say) As doth the sory man, and longer by a day. **1594–5** SHAKS. *L.L.L.* V. ii. 18 She might ha' been a grandam ere she died; And so may you, for a light heart lives long. **1597–8** *2 Hen. IV.* V. iii. 48 A merry heart lives long-a. **1602** D. LYNDSAY *Thrie Estaits* l. 106 Als lang leifis the mirrie man As the sorie for ocht he can. **1614** CAMDEN 302 As long liveth a merry man as a sad.

Long looked for comes at last.

c. **1483** *Quatuor Sermones* (Roxb. Cl.) 53 A thynge that is long desyred at the last it comyth. **1593–4** SHAKS. *Tam. Shrew* II. 327 Now is the day we long have looked for. **1608** ARMIN *Nest Ninnies* (Shak. Soc.) 15 Though long lookt for comes at last, yet they shoot short that aim to hit this mark. **1655** FULLER *Ch. Hist.* II. ii (1868) I. 130 Long-looked-for comes at last. King Edwin, almost three years a candidate-at-large of Christianity, embraceth the same. **1846** DICKENS *Bat. of Life* II A gay day . . . for us. . . . Long looked forward to, dearest, and come at last.

Long man, *see* Seldom is l. m. wise.

Long mint, little dint.

1721 KELLY 237 . . . Spoken when men threaten much, and dare not execute. **1832** HENDERSON 129 . . . (Long attempted or threatened, little executed.)

Long pull, a strong pull, and a pull all together, A.

1822 BYRON *Vision of Judg.* st. 1 The devils had ta'en a long, strong pull, and a pull all together, as they say at sea. **1834** MARRYAT *Jacob Faith.* xii 'A long pull, a strong pull, and a pull altogether', sang out old Tom.

Long run, In (At) the.

[= in the end.] **1627** J. CARTER *Plain Exposition* (F. Hall) 117 At the long run. **1656** CROMWELL *Speech* 17 Sept. They [the discontented] must end at the interest of the Cavalier at the long run. **1804** EDGEWORTH

Contrast ix At the long run, these fellows never thrive. **1842** MRS. CARLYLE *Lett.* I. 156 Compromises never are found to answer, I think, in the long run.

Long runs the fox as he has feet, As.

c. **1450** HENRYSON *Mor. Fab.* 29 Aye runnes the Foxe as long as hee feete hes. **1641** FERGUSSON **4**.

Long spoon, He should have a | that sups with the devil.

c. **1386** CHAUCER *Sqr.'s T.* 594 Therefore bihoueth hire a ful long spoon that shal ete with a feend. **1539** TAVERNER 9 He had nede to haue a longe spone that shulde eate with the deuyl. **1592–3** SHAKS. *Com. Err.* IV. iii. 62 Marry, he must have a long spoon that must eat with the devil. **1611–12** *Temp.* II. ii. 107 This is a devil, and no monster: I will leave him; I have no long spoon. **1641** FERGUSSON 42 He should have a long shafted spoon that sups kail with the devil. **1818** SCOTT *Ht. Midl.* xlv I wad hae him think twice or he mells wi' Knockdunder. He suld hae a lang-shankit spune that wad sup kail wi' the deil. **1853** TRENCH vi. 151 *He had need of a long spoon that eats with the devil* . . . men fancy . . . they can cheat the arch-cheater, . . . being sure in this to be miserably deceived.

Long standing and small offering maketh poor parsons.

1546 HEYWOOD II. ix. 80 Men saie (said he) long standyng and small offring Maketh poore persons. **1641** FERGUSSON 72 Lang Standing, and little offering makes a poore prise. **1721** KELLY 235 *Long standing, and little offering, makes a poor priest.* Spoken by hucksters, pedlars, and the like, when they have an ill market.

Long-tail, *see* Come cut and l. t.

Longtails, *see* Kentish L.

Long tarrying takes all the thanks away.

1641 FERGUSSON 70.

Long time to know the world's pulse, There needs a.

1640 HERBERT 357.

Long tongue is a sign of a short hand, A.

1640 HERBERT 328. **1721** KELLY 43 *A long tongue has a short hand.* They who are lavish in their promises are often short in their performances.

Long-tongued wives go long with bairn.

1670 RAY 49. **1721** KELLY 239 . . . Baubling wives will tell every tattling gossip that they have conceived; which makes them long expect their lying in. Apply'd to those who discover their projects, designs, and intentions, long before they are put in execution.

Long ways, long lies.

1614 CAMDEN *Rem., Art.* (1870) 224 Some have sailed . . . as far as China, . . . to fetch the invention of guns from thence, but we know the Spanish proverb, 'Long ways, long lies'.

Long (*adj.*, *adv.*), *see also* Buchanan's almanac, l. foul l. fair; Fair and sluttish . . . l. and lazy; Never l. that comes at last; Row to hoe (L.).

Longer east, the shorter west, The.

1546 HEYWOOD I. xiii. 41 Alwaie the longer east the shorter west.

Longer forenoon, the shorter afternoon, The.

1546 HEYWOOD I. xiii. 41.

Longer lives a good fellow than a dear year.

1678 RAY 170.

Longer we live, the more farlies[1] we see, The.

1641 FERGUSSON 94. **1721** KELLY 313. [[1] wonders.]

Longer you look at it the less you will like it, The.

1872 G. J. WHYTE-MELVILLE *Satan.* xxiii It's no use being shifty about it. You've got to jump, and the longer you look, the less you'll like it.

Longest at the fire soonest finds cold.

1721 KELLY 238 . . . Those who are used to ease, softness, and plenty, will soon be sensible of a contrary condition.

Longest day hath an (his) end (must have an end), The.

c. **1390** GOWER *Conf. Amantis* I. 578 Bot hou so that the dai be long. The derke nyht comth ate laste. **1580** LYLY *Euph. & his Eng.* (Arb.) 250 (A) The longest summers day hath his euening. **1599–1600** SHAKS. *Jul. Caes.* V. i. 125 But it sufficeth that the day will end. **1612–15** BP. HALL *Contempl.* XX. v (1825) II. 33 The longest day must have his evening. Good Elisha, that had lived some ninety years, . . . is now cast upon the bed of his . . . death. **1614** CAMDEN 313 The longest day hath his end. **1659** HOWELL *Eng. Prov.* 10/1 The longest day hath an end. **1670** RAY 77 The longest day must have an end. **1721** KELLY 337 *The longest day will have an end.* Spoken when men now in power oppress us, signifying that there may be a turn. **1841** CHAMIER *Tom Bowl.* ii The longest day will have an end, and though it's cloudy in the morning, the sun may shine bright enough at noon.

Longest day, *see also* Barnaby bright.

Longest night will have an end, The.

1613 WITHER *Abuses* I. xvi. *Sorrow* Calmes

doe the roughest stormes that are attend, And th' longest night that is will haue an end.

Longest night, *see also* St. Thomas gray.

Longest, *see also* Farthest (L.) way about is nearest way home.

Longing, *see* Better go away l. than loathing.

Look at (on) the bright side.

1864 J. PAYN *Lost Sir Mas.* xx No news is good news, you know, . . . We should always look upon the bright side of things. **1905** G. O. TREVELYAN *Interludes* 150 Englishmen are always inclined to look at the bright side of things, as long as there is a bright side at which to look.

Look at your corn in May, If you | you'll come weeping away; if you look at the same in June, you'll come home in another tune.

1639 CLARKE 307 They that go to their corn in May may come weeping away: they that go in June may come back with a merry tune. **1670** RAY 41. **1846** DENHAM 46.

Look babies, To.

[i.e. the small image of oneself reflected in the pupil of another's eye.] *c.* **1566** *The Bugbears* IV. v. 40 Some one or other lookt babies in here eie. **1580** T. CHURCHYARD *Churchyard's Chance* E 1 And loe amid my laughing eyen, twoo pretie babes did plaie. **1589** T. LODGE *Glaucus and Scilla* (Hunt. Cl.) C 2ᵛ She lookes for babies in his eies. **1599** BRETON *Wit's Will* (1860) 44 Chinning and embracing, and looking babies in one anothers eyes. **1621** BURTON *Anat. Mel.* III. ii. VI. v (1651) 576 They may kiss and coll, lye and look babies in one anothers eyes.

Look before (ere) you leap.

c. **1350** *Douce MS. 52*, no. 150 First loke and aftirward lepe; Avyse the welle, or thow speke. **1528** TINDALE *Obed. Chrn. Man* (1888) 266 We say, . . . 'Look ere thou leap': whose literal sense is, 'Do nothing suddenly, or without advisement'. **1546** HEYWOOD I. ii. 6 Ye may learne good cheape, In weddyng and al thing, to looke or ye leape. **1579** LYLY *Euphues* (Arb.) 193 In things of great importance, we commonly looke before we leape. **1597** MONTGOMERIE *Cherrie & Slae* xxiv (1821) 20 Luik quhair to licht, before thou loup. **1664** BUTLER *Hudibras* II. ii. 503 (1854) I. 156 And look before you ere you leap. **1836** MARRYAT *Midsh. Easy* vi Look before you leap is an old proverb. . . . Jack . . . had pitched into a small apiary, and had upset two hives of bees.

Look daggers, To.

1833 MARRYAT *P. Simple* lii Lord Privilege . . . looked daggers at me as he walked up-stairs.

Look for your money where you lost it.

1902–4 LEAN IV 36 . . . Stock Exchange maxim, *i.e.* wait for a further fall.

Look in your mouth to know your age, They need not.

[JUVENAL *Sat.* 6. 199 *Facies tua computat annos.* Your face shows your years.] **1616** WITHALS 557. **1639** CLARKE 280. **1670** RAY 188. **1721** KELLY 359 Eng.

Look nine ways, To.

[= asquint, askew.] **1542** UDALL tr. *Erasm. Apoph.* (1877) 203 Squyntied he was, and looked nyne wayes. **1649** G. DANIEL *Trinarch., Rich. II*, 326 Passion flyes Squinting, and, as wee say, Nine wayes at Thrice. **1653** *Verney Memoirs* iii (1894) 58 When I told her of your question, she looked nine waies at once, and gave you noe answer.

Look not for musk in a dog's kennel.

1611 COTGRAVE s.v. 'Chien' (with 'civet' for 'musk'). **1640** HERBERT 318. **1655–62** GURNALL *Chrn. in Armour* (1865) I. 468 Who would look for musk in a dog's kennel? That thou mayest sooner find there than any true sweetness . . . in unholiness.

Look not on pleasures as they come but as they go.

a. **1633** G. HERBERT 'The Church Porch' l. 458. **1707** MAPLETOFT 103. **1855** BOHN 339.

Look on the wall, and it will not bite you.

1678 RAY 83 . . . Spoken in jeer to such as are bitten with mustard.

Look through the (*or* one's) fingers (at, upon), To.

1532 TYNDALE *Expos. St. Mathew* (P.S.) 127 (A) They either look through the fingers, or else give thee a flap with a fox-tail, for a little money. **1549** LATIMER *4th Serm. bef. Edw. VI* (Arb.) 105 If the kynge . . . shoulde loke through his fingers, and wynke at it. **1691** J. WILSON *Belphegor* III. i. Enough to make a modest woman look through her fingers.

Look to a gown of gold, and you will at least get a sleeve of it.

1824 SCOTT *Redg. Let.* ii My visions of preferment, . . . are . . . capable of being realised. . . . What says my father's proverb? 'Look to a gown of gold, and you will at least get a sleeve of it.' **1859** SMILES *Self-Help* 386 He who has a high standard . . . will certainly do better than he who has none at all. 'Pluck at a gown of gold', says the Scotch proverb, 'and you may get a sleeve o't.'

Look to him, jailer; there's a frog in the stocks.

1678 RAY 72. **1732** FULLER no. 3274.

Look to the cow, and the sow, and the wheat mow, and all will be well enow.

1678 RAY 347. *Somerset.*

Look to (Mark) the end.

[L. *Respice finem*. *Gesta Rom.* ch. 103 *Quidquid agas, prudenter agas, et respice finem.*] *c.* 1300 *Cursor M.* l. 4379 For qua bigin wil ani thing He aght to thinc on the ending. *c.* 1350 *Royal MS.* 8 E *xvii* f. 107a Er þu do eny þing, þenk one þe ending. 1550 LATIMER *Serm. Stamford* (P.S.) 294 *Respice finem*, mark the end'; look upon the end. The end is, all adversaries of the truth must be confounded and come to nought. 1592–3 SHAKS. *Com. Err.* IV. iv. 43 Mistress, *respice finem*, respect your end; or rather, . . . 'Beware the rope's end'. *c.* 1593 MARLOWE *Edw. II* II. i. 16 He is banish'd . . . Ay, for a while; but, Baldock, mark the end. 1816 SCOTT *Antiq.* viii A pedigree of a hundred links is hanging on a tenpenny tow ; . . . , *respice finem*—look to your end.

Look to (in) (a person's) water, To.

[To scrutinize a person's conduct rigorously, in reference to the inspection of a patient's urine as a means of diagnosis.] 1377 LANGLAND *P. Pl.* B II. 223 Thanne loured leches . and lettres thei sent, That he sholde wonye with hem . wateres to loke. 1546 HEYWOOD I. xi. 33 By my faith you come to look in my water. 1597–8 SHAKS. *2 Hen. IV* I. ii. 1 *Fal.* Sirrah, . . . what says the doctor to my water? *Page.* He said, sir, the water itself was a good healthy water; but for the party that owed it, he might have more diseases than he knew for! 1600 ROWLANDS *Lett. Humours Blood* vi Heele looke vnto your water well enough. 1700 T. BROWN *Amusem. Ser. & Com.* iii. Wks. (1720) III. 36 I . . . judged he had been whipping it in with the Gentlewoman before mentioned, tho' 'twas not convenient to tell him so, lest his Wife should watch his Waters more narrowly than she had done.

Look twice at (both sides of) a penny (halfpenny), To.

1824 MOIR *Mansie W.* xx He was . . . Aberdeen-awa like, and looking at two sides of a halfpenny; but . . . he behaved to me like a gentleman. 1861 READE *Cloister & H.* xxxvi Gerard . . . always looked at two sides of a penny, and he tried to purchase this mass a trifle under the usual terms. 1863 Id. *Hard Cash* xii I look twice at a penny; but she looks twice at both sides of a halfpenny before she will let him go.

Look where it is not, as well as where it is, You must.

1732 FULLER no. 5964.

Looked for, *see* Long l. f. comes at last.

Looked on me as a cow on a bastard calf, She.

1678 RAY 353 . . . *Somerset.* [*i.e.* coldly, suspiciously.]

Lookers-on see more than players (most of the game).

cf. 1578 G. WHETSTONE *Promus and Cassandra* I 2 As at Cheastes, though skylfull players play, Skyllesse vewers may see what they omyt. 1589 PUTTENHAM *Art of Poetry* (*Eliz. Crit. Essays* Gregory Smith ii. 184) No lesse then doth the looker on or beholder of a game better see into all points of auantage, then the player himselfe. *c.* 1595 BACON *Promus* no. 145 with 'standers by'. 1597–8 Id. *Ess., Followers* (Arb.) 38 To take aduise of friends is euer honorable: For *lookers on many times see more then gamesters.* 1635 HOWELL *Lett.* 1 May (1903) II. 138 There is a true saying, that the spectator ofttimes sees more than the gamester. 1884 J. PAYN *Canon's Ward* xxiv In love affairs, . . . when the love is . . . on one side, it is the looker-on who sees most of the game.

Lookers-on, *see also* Standers-by.

Looks as big as if he had eaten bull beef, He.

1579 GOSSON *Ephemerides* They haue eaten bulbief. 1580 J. BARET *Alveary* T 270 Such as haue a terrible and frowning countenance, and (as our common byword saith) which looke as though they had eaten Bulbeefe. 1670 RAY 164.

Looks as if he had neither won nor lost, He.

1590 LODGE *Rosalynde* (Hunt. Cl.) 190 (A) The shepherde stoode as though hee had neither won nor lost. 1678 RAY 257 He looks as if he had neither won nor lost. He stands as if he were mop't, in a brown study, unconcern'd.

Looks as if (though) he had sucked his dam through a hurdle, He.

1670 RAY 170.

Looks as the wood were full of thieves, He.

1641 FERGUSSON 48 *Of fleyit*[1] *persons.* . . . He looks as the wood were full of thieves. [1 frightened.]

Looks breed love.

[ERASM. *Ad. Amor ex oculo.*] 1539 TAVERNER xii Ex aspectu nascitur amor. Of syght is loue gendred. 1596–7 SHAKS. *Merch. V.* III. ii. 63 Tell me where is fancy bred? . . . It is engender'd in the eyes, With gazing fed. 1639 CLARKE 28.

Looks not before, He that | finds himself behind.

1640 HERBERT 326.

Looks not well to himself that looks not ever, He.

1611 COTGRAVE s.v. 'Garder' He lookes not, that still lookes not, to himselfe. 1640 HERBERT 355.

Looks one way and rows another, He.

1579 GOSSON *Ephemerides* (*Sch. Abuse*, Arb. 87) Hee shewed him selfe a cunning sculler that rowes his Bote forwarde, thoughe hee haue turned his face too the sterne. **1621** BURTON *Anat. Mel.* Democr. to Rdr. (1651) 29 Teach others to fast, and play the gluttons themselves ; like watermen, that row one way and look another. **1655** FULLER *Ch. Hist.* III. iv (1868) I. 389 The clergy looking at London, but rowing to Rome, carrying Italian hearts in English bodies. **1867–77** FROUDE *Short Stud.* (1890) I. 155 Bunsen . . . could not get inside the English mind. He did not know that some people go furthest and go fastest when they look one way and row the other.

Look (*noun*), *see also* Cheerful l. makes a feast ; Honest l. covereth faults ; Ill l. among lambs ; Pitiful l. asks enough.

Look(s, ed, ing) (*verb*), *see also* Leeward for fine weather (L. not to) ; Longer you l. the less you will like ; Loving comes by l. ; Show me not (L. not on) the meat ; Trust me, but l. to thyself ; Women l. in their glass (The more).

Look(s) as (*or like*), *see under significant words following.*

Loose in the hilts, She is.

[= conjugally unfaithful.] **1623** WEBSTER *Duch. of M.* II. v. (Merm.) 168 *Fer.* Read there—a sister damned : she's loose i' the hilts ; Grown a notorious strumpet. **1650** HOWELL *Cotgrave's Dict.* Ep. Ded. In French *Cocu* is taken for one who's wife is loose in the hilts. **1682** VILLIERS (Dk. Buckhm.) *Chances* Wks. (1714) 136 It's no matter, she's loose i' th' Hilts, by Heaven.

Loose, *see* Better hand l. than in ill tethering.

Lord doth lie in our Lady's lap, When our | then, O England, beware of a clap.

1629 T. ADAMS *Serm.* (1861–2) I. 501 He dreams . . . of a Popish curse. 'And Our Lord lights in our lady's lap, And therefore England must have a clap.' **1659** HOWELL *Eng. Prov.* 16/2 When Christ falleth in our Ladies lapp, Then lett *England* look for a clapp. **1910** *Times Wkly.* 13 May How strange Good Friday should have fallen on Lady Day[1] this year ! The old proverb has come too true : 'If our Lord falls in our Lady's lap, England shall have a great mishap.' [1 Feast of Annunciation, 25 Mar.]

Lord, Like | like chaplain.

c. **1550** BALE *K. Johan* (Camden Soc.) 73 Lyke Lorde, lyke chaplayne.

Lord(s), *see also* Accord (No) where every man would be l. ; Drunk as a l. ; Follows the L. (He that) ; Lady falls in our L.'s lap (When our) ; Lady's (L.'s) heart and beggar's purse ; Many l. many laws ; New l. new laws ; Nod from a l. breakfast for fool ; Rich as a l.

Lord Mayor of London, *see* Dined as well as ; Good manners to except.

Lordship, One good | is worth all his manners.[1]

1639 CLARKE 168. [1 manors.]

Lordships changes manners.

1641 FERGUSSON 72. **1721** KELLY 237 . . . When people grow rich, and powerful, they grow proud.

Lordship(s), *see also* Love and l. like no fellowship.

Lose a fly to catch a trout, You must.

1640 HERBERT 355.

Lose a leg rather than a life.

1607 DAY, &c. *Travels of three English Brothers* Wks. (Bullen) 65 To saue the body we must loose a lim. **1732** FULLER no. 3278.

Lose a Scot, We will not.

1662 FULLER (*Northumb.*) II. 542 'We will not lose a Scot'. That is, 'we will lose nothing, however inconsiderable soever, which we can save or recover. . . .' The proverb began in the English borders, when . . . they had little esteem of, and less affection for, a Scotchman.

Lose his goods for want of demanding them, A man may.

1616 DRAXE 18. **1670** RAY 7.

Lose in hake, What we | we shall have in herring.

1602 R. CAREW *Survey of Cornwall* (1811) 105 The hakes . . . haunted the coast in great abundance ; but now, being deprived of their wonted bait, are much diminished ; verifying the proverb, 'What we lose in hake, we shall have in herring'.

Lose nothing for asking.

1586 PETTIE tr. *Guazzo's Civ. Conv.* 218 Nothing is lost for asking. **1640** HERBERT 361 Many things are lost for want of asking. **1670** RAY 58. **1721** KELLY 381 You will let nothing be bint[1] for want of craving. [1 lost.]

Lose the droppings of his nose, He will not.

1659 HOWELL *Eng. Prov.* 12/1.

Lose what you never had, You cannot.

1653 WALTON *Angler* I. v (1915) 108 *Pis.* He has broke it ; there's half a line and a good hook lost. *Ven.* Aye, and a good Trout too. *Pis.* Nay, the Trout is not lost ; for . . . no man can lose what he never had.

Lose your time, If you | you cannot get money or gain.

1616 DRAXE 206 In loosing time, a man getteth no money. **1640** HERBERT 332.

Lose(s), losing, *see also* All covet all l. ; Gain is to l. (Sometimes) ; Gets little thanks for l. his own ; Grasp all l. all ; Lend your money, l. friend; Merry as he that hath nought to l.; Play well if you l. (It signifies nothing to); Win at first, l. at last.

Losers are always in the wrong.

1855 BOHN 446. *Spanish.*

Losers leave to speak (talk), Give.

1533 MORE *Wks.* (1557) 1018 (A) Hit is an olde curtesye at the cardes perdy, to let the leser haue hys wordes. **1546** HEYWOOD II. vi. 62 And where reason and custome (they say) afoords, Alwaie to let the loosers haue their woords. **1590–1** SHAKS. *2 Hen. VI* III. i. 185 And well such losers may have leave to speak. **1592** NASHE *Pierce Pen.* Wks. (1904) I. 160 I, I, we'll give losers leave to talk. **1593–4** SHAKS. *Titus Andron.* III. i. 232 Losers will have leave To ease their stomachs with their bitter tongues. **1655** FULLER *Ch. Hist.* IV. i (1868) I. 540 Give winners leave to laugh, and losers to speak, or else both will take leave to themselves. **1665** J. WILSON *Projectors* IV You've saved your money, and the loser may be allow'd the liberty of speaking. **1721** KELLY 123 *Give losing gamesters leave to talk.* Suffer men who have had losses and wrongs, to express their resentments. **1818** SCOTT *Ht. Midl.* xlviii The captain, who had lost . . . at backgammon, was in the pouting mood not unusual to losers, and which, says the proverb, must be allowed to them.

Losers seekers, finders keepers.

1824 MOIR *Mansie W.* xi According to the auld Scotch proverb of 'He that finds keeps, And he that loses seeks'. **1856** C. READE *Never Too Late* lxv I told them we have a proverb—'Losers seekers, finders keepers'.

Loses anything by politeness (civility), One never. (*See also* Civility costs nothing.)

1902–4 LEAN IV. 75.

Loses by doing a good turn, One never.

1842 TORRIANO 78. **1664** CODRINGTON 207. **1670** RAY 12. **1721** KELLY 275 . . . Spoken by them who make a return for former favours.

Loses his thanks who promiseth and delayeth, He.

1616 DRAXE 42. **1670** RAY 7 . . . *Gratia ab officio, quod mora tardat, abest.*

Loses his wife and a farthing, He that | hath a great loss of his farthing. (*See also* Loseth his wife and sixpence.)

1678 RAY 58 . . . *Che perde* [la] *moglie & un quatrino, hà gran perdita del quatrino.* Ital.

Loses, loseth, see also Lose(s).

Loseth his due gets not thanks, He that.

1640 HERBERT 334.

Loseth his liberty loseth all, Who.

c. **1430** LYDGATE *Churl & Bird* 92–5 And thowe my cage forged were with golde, . . . I remembre a proverb said of olde, 'Who lesethe his fredam, in faith! he loseth all'.

Loseth his wife and sixpence, He that | hath lost a tester.[1] (*See also* Loses his wife and a farthing.)

1670 RAY 49. **1738** SWIFT (Dial. i) 342 They say, he that has lost his wife and sixpence, has lost a tester. [1 sixpence.]

Loseth indeed that loseth at last, He.

1732 FULLER no. 1975.

Loseth is merchant, He that | as well as he that gains.

1640 HERBERT 342.

Loseth nothing who keeps God for his friend, He.

1611 COTGRAVE s.v. 'Perdre' Hee that keepes God to friend can nothing loose. **1640** HERBERT 318. He loseth nothing that loseth not God. **1670** RAY 16.

Loss embraceth shame.

1640 HERBERT 345.

Loss(es), see also Better a little l.; Buy and sell and live by l.; Fear not l. of bell more than l. of steeple; Great l. but some profit (No); Little l. amaze.

Lost all and found myself, I have.

1639 CLARKE 198.

Lost all who has one cast left, He has not.

1664 CODRINGTON 197 He hath not lost all who hath one throw to cast. **1670** RAY 16 [as 1664]. **1732** FULLER no. 1876.

Lost as found, As good.

1546 HEYWOOD I. x. 23 A gest as good lost as founde. **1576** U. FULWELL *Ars Adulandi* vii. 36 As good such frendes were lost as found that helpeth not at neede. **1670** RAY 184 Better lost than found.

Lost be for God, Let that which is.

1853 TRENCH ii. 39 The father of a family, making his will . . . , ordained concerning a certain cow which had strayed, . . . that, if it was found, it should be for his children, if not found, for God: and hence the proverb,[1] *Let that which is lost be for God,* arose. [1 Spanish.]

Lost his credit, He that hath | is dead to the world.

1640 HERBERT 334.

Lost his taste, To him that has | sweet is sour.

1576 PETTIE *Petite Pall.* (Gollancz) i. 172 The sight of meat is very loathsome to him whose stomach is ill, or hath already eaten

his fill. **1579** LYLY *Euphues* Wks. (Bond) I.
194 To the stomacke quatted with daynties
all delycates seeme quesie. **1580** Id.
Euph. & his Eng. Wks. (Bond) II. 101 A sick
man's mouth, who can realish nothing by the
taste, not that the fault is in the meat, but
in his malady. **1616** DRAXE 29. **1670** RAY
26. **1732** FULLER no. 5182 (with 'has a bad
taste' and 'bitter').

Lost (Won) in the hundred[1] will be found (lost) in the shire, What is.

1520 WHITTINTON *Vulg.* (E.E.T.S.) 93 For
what so euer thou wynnes in the shyre Thou
shall lese it in the hondreth. **1546** HEYWOOD
II. ix. 76 But towne or féelde, where most
thrift did apéere, What ye wan in the hundred
ye lost in the shéere. **1629** T. ADAMS *Serm.*
(1861–2) II. 531 Some have objected . . . that
. . . this sitting of Antichrist in Rome proves
them to be a true church. But I am sure, . . .
what they get in the hundred they lose in the
shire. **1662** FULLER (*Northants*) II. 538 He
had not one foot of land . . . in the whole
county . . . [but] had a very fair estate elsewhere. And, as our English proverb saith,
'What is lost in the hundred will be found
in the shire'; so what was lost in the shire
would be found in the land. **1670** RAY 155
What is got in the county, is lost in the
hundred. What is got in the whole sum is
lost in particular reckonings; or . . . What is
got one way, is lost another. **1732** FULLER
no. 5522 What they lose in the hundred they
gain in the county. [1 subdivision of a county.]

Lost (Tint), It is not │ that a friend (neighbour) gets.

1641 FERGUSSON 64 It is not tint that is done
to friends. **1721** KELLY 198 It is no tint, a
friend gets. **1891** J. L. KIPLING *Beast & Man*
188 The public at large have reaped much of
the crop sown by Government for its own
army, but, . . . What a neighbour gets is not
lost'.

Lost, It is not │ that comes at last.

1620 SHELTON *Quix.* IV. iv (1908) I. 297 But
it is not lost that comes at last; I will see her,
and then all things shall be amended. **1648**
HERRICK *Hesper.* No. 655 Wks. (1893) II. 118
Though long it be, years may repay the debt;
None loseth that, which he in time may get.

Lost, All is not │ that is in danger.

1670 RAY 117 . . . As for instance, he whose
sheep die of the rot, saves the skins and the
wool. **1721** KELLY *All is not tint[1] that 's in
peril.* . . . Our affairs may come to a better
effect than is now expected. [1 lost.]

Lost that is put into a riven dish, All is.

1611 MIDDLETON *Roaring Girl* IV. ii When
we have done our best, all's but put into a
riven dish; we are but frumped at and libelled
upon. **1670** RAY 137 . . . All is lost that is
bestowed on an ungrateful person.

Lost that is unsought, It is.

1546 HEYWOOD I. xi. **1659** HOWELL *Eng.
Prov.* 14/1.

Lost the large coat for the hood, Oft times for sparing of a little cost a man has.

c. **1390** GOWER *Conf. Amantis* v. 4785 For
sparinge of a litel cost Fulofte time a man
hath lost The large cote for the hod.

Lost the ring, If I have │ yet the fingers are still here.

1853 TRENCH v. 117 This Italian and
Spanish . . . , *If I have lost the ring, yet the
fingers are still here.* In it is asserted the
comparative indifference of that loss which
reaches but to things external to us, so long
as we ourselves remain, and are true to ourselves.

Lost (Tint) the tongue of the trump,[1] You have.

1721 KELLY 389 . . . That is, you want the
main thing. [1 Jew's harp.]

Lost with an apple and won with a nut (*or vice versa*).

1546 HEYWOOD I. x. 20 She is lost with an
apple, and woon with a nut. **1579** LYLY
Euphues (Arb.) 59 If he perceiue thee to be
wonne with a Nut, he will imagine that thou
wilt be lost with an Apple. **1623** SANDERSON
Serm. (1681) I. 95 Of a wavering and fickle
mind; as we say of children: won with an
apple, and lost with a nut. **1659** HOWELL
Eng. Prov. 15 He may be gott by an Apple,
and lost by a Nutt. **1732** FULLER no. 2201.

Lost, *see also* Better l. than found; Lucky
John Toy, l. a shilling; Think all is l. that
goes beside your mouth; Tint (Lost) thing
(For a) care not.

Lot, *see* Crook in the l. of everyone.

Loth to bed, *see* Sick of the slothful guise.

Loud as Tom of Lincoln,[1] As.

1639 J. FLETCHER *Woman's Prize* III. iv
Mixt with a learned lecture of ill language,
Louder than Tom o' Lincoln. **1662** FULLER
(*Lincs.*) II. 267 'As loud as Tom of Lin-
coln'. . . . Tom of Lincoln may be called the
Stentor (fifty lesser bells may be made out of
him) of all in this county. **1818** SCOTT *Ht.
Midl.* xxx Madge, who is as loud as Tom of
Lincoln, is somewhat still. [1 the great
cathedral bell.]

Loud one, That is a.

1678 RAY 89 *A great Lie.* That's a loud one.

Loud, *see also* Little and l.

Louse is a beggar's companion, A.

1594 R. WILSON *Coblers Proph.* (Malone Soc.)
l. 836 What thinke ye as the Prouerb goes
that beggers haue no lice? **1616** N. BRETON
Cross of Prov. in Wks. (Gros.) II A Louse is a
Begger's companion.

Louse, lice, *see also* Better a l. in a pot; Care
not three skips of a l.; Nits will be L.;

Nothing so crouse as a new washen l.; Skin a l. and send hide to market; Sure as a l. in Pomfret.

Lout[1] so low and lift so little, I will never.

1721 KELLY 184 *I will never lout so leagh,[2] and lift so little.* . . . Returns of a haughty maid to them that tell her of an unworthy suitor. [[1] stoop. [2] low.]

Love a woman, He that does not | sucked a sow.

1667 L'ESTRANGE *Quevedo's Visions* (1904) 144 (A) 'My officious friend', said I, 'he that does not love a woman sucked a cow'. 1732 FULLER no. 2083. 1738 SWIFT (Dial. i) 342 And they say he that hates woman, sucked a sow.

Love and a cough (light) cannot be hid.

[L. *Amor tussisque non celantur.*] *c.* 1300 *Cursor M.* l. 4276 Luken luue at the end wil kith. 1573 SANDFORD 196 Foure things cannot be kept close, Loue, the cough, fyre, and sorowe. 1600 DEKKER *Old Fort.* II. ii *Fort.* Age is like love, it cannot be hid. 1611 COTGRAVE s.v. 'Amour' Loue, and the Cough cannot be hidden. 1640 HERBERT 319. 1670 RAY 47 . . . The French and Italians add to these two the itch. 1721 KELLY 242. Love and light cannot be hid. 1737 FRANKLIN April Love, cough, and a smoke, can't well be hid. 1863 G. ELIOT *Romola* vi If there are two things not to be hidden—love and a cough—I say there is a third, and that is ignorance.

Love and be wise, One cannot (or To be wise and eke to love is granted scarce to God above).

[PUBL. SYRUS 22 *Amare et sapere vix Deo conceditur.*] 1553 *Precepts of Cato* (1560) T I[v]. 1579 LYLY *Euphues* (Croll) 46 To love and to live well is not granted to Jupiter. 1580 G. HARVEY, *Three Letters* (Oxford Spenser, 627), To be wise, and eke to Love, Is graunted scarce to God aboue. *c.* 1603 SHAKS. *Troil. & Cres.* III. ii. 163 To be wise and love Exceeds man's might; that dwells with gods above. 1605 BACON *Adv. of Learning* II. Wks. (J. M. Robertson) 79 It is not granted to man to love and to be wise. *a.* 1612 CHARRON *Of Wisdom* tr. Lennard (1640) 239 It was impossible even for *Iupiter* himselfe to love, . . . and to be wise at one time.

Love and business teach eloquence.

1640 HERBERT 350.

Love and lordship like no fellowship.

(1) In the sense that they brook no rivals: *c.* 1386 CHAUCER *Knight's T.* 1625 Ful sooth is seyd that love ne lordshipe Wol nought, his thankès, have no felaweshipe. 1591 SPENSER *M. Hubberd* 1026 But either (algates[1]) would be Lord alone; For Love and Lordship bide no paragone. 1639 CLARKE 27. 1670 RAY 46 . . . Lovers and Princes cannot endure

rivals or partners. 1721 KELLY 242 Love and lordship like no marrows.[2] [[1] always. [2] partners.]

(2) In the sense that they agree not together: [OVID *Metam.* 2. 846 *Non bene conueniunt nec in una sede morantur Maiestas et Amor.* Love and high Majestie agree not well, nor will together in one bosom dwell (Sandys), of Jupiter as a bull.] 1859 LEIGH HUNT in Blunden 195, on Shelley's style, It disproves the adage of the Latin poet. Majesty and love do sit on one throne in the lofty buildings of his poetry.

Love and pease-pottage will make their way (are two dangerous things).

1654 E. GAYTON *Pleasant Notes upon Don Quixote* 46 Love and Pease-pottage are a dangerous surfet. 1670 RAY 47 . . . Because one breaks the belly, the other the heart. 1721 KELLY 231 Love, and raw pease, are two ill things, the one breaks the heart, and the other brusts the belly. 1738 SWIFT (Dial. i) 339 *Lady A.* Ay; they say love and pease-porridge are two dangerous things; one breaks the heart; and the other the belly.

Love as in time to come thou shouldest hate, and hate as thou shouldest in time to come, love.

[Gk. Old men, according to the counsel of Bias, καὶ φιλοῦσιν ὡς μισήσοντες καὶ μισοῦσιν ὡς φιλήσοντες, ARIST. *Rhet.* 2.13.4, both love as if they were going to hate, and hate as if they were going to love. L. PUBL. SYRUS 245 *Ita amicum habeas, posse ut facile fieri hunc inimicum putes.* Regard your friend as if you thought that he might easily become your enemy.] 1539 TAVERNER xxxi *Ama tanquam osurus, oderis tanquam amaturus.* Loue as in tyme to come thou shuldest hate, & hate as thou shuldest in tyme to come loue. 1605 BACON *Adv. Learn.* II. xxiii (1900) 245 That ancient precept of Bias, construed not to any point of perfidiousness but only to caution and moderation, *Et ama tanquam inimicus futurus, et odi tanquam amaturus.* 1625 Id. *Apoph.* Wks. (Chandos) 359 Bias gave in precept, 'Love as if you should hereafter hate: and hate as if you should hereafter love'. 1651 HERBERT 369 We must love as looking one day to hate. 1844 KINGLAKE *Eothen* xxv Treat your friend, says the proverb, as though he were one day to become your enemy, and your enemy as though he were one day to become your friend.

Love as there is between the old cow and the haystack, As much.

1738 SWIFT (Dial. iii) 351 *Lady S.* I am told you meet together with as much love as there is between the old cow and the haystack.

Love asks faith, and faith (asks) firmness.

1640 HERBERT 343. 1670 RAY 16. *Ital.*

Love at first sight.

1598 MARLOWE *Hero & L.* i. 174 Where both deliberate the loue is slight: Who euer lou'd, that lou'd not at first sight? **1611–12** SHAKS. *Temp.* I. ii. 437 At the first sight They have changed eyes. **1913** G. W. E. RUSSELL *Half-Lengths* 152 At the top he found a wonderful view. . . . It was a case of love at first sight. The estate . . . passed into Baron Ferdinand's hands.

Love at the door and leave at the hatch, To.

1678 RAY 258. **1732** FULLER no. 5200 To love the door and leave the hatch.

Love begets love.

[L. *Amor gignit amorem.*] **1648** HERRICK *Hesper.* No. 47. Wks. (1900) II. 51 Love love begets; then never be Unsoft to him who 's smooth to thee. **1909** A. MACLAREN *Ephesians* 275 Love begets love, and . . . if a man loves God, then that glowing beam will glow whether it is turned to earth or turned to heaven.

Love being jealous, makes a good eye look asquint.

1640 HERBERT 342 Love makes a good eye squint. **1670** RAY 16.

Love best, Whom we | to them we can say least.

1576 PETTIE *Petite Pall.* (Gollancz) II. 29 As I have heard, those that love most speak least. **1594–5** SHAKS. *Two Gent.* I. ii. 32 *Jul.* They do not love that show their love. *Luc.* O! they love least that let men know their love. **1670** RAY 47.

Love cannot be compelled.

c. **1390** CHAUCER *Franklin's T.* 36 Love wol nat ben constreyned by maistrye. **1590** SPENSER *F.Q.* III. i. 25 Ne may loue be compeld by maisterie. **1591** LYLY *Endym.* v. iii *Cynth.* I will not command love, for it cannot be enforced: let me entreat it. **1621** BURTON *Anat. Mel.* III. ii. VI. v (1651) 577 You must consider that *Amor cogi non potest*, love cannot be compelled, they must affect as they may.

Love comes as goes, As good.

c. **1470** HENRYSON *Mor. Fab.* III. xvii in *Anglia* ix. 357 The prouerbe sayis 'als gude luif cummis as gais'.

Love comes in at the window and goes out at the door.

1611 GRUTER. **1614** CAMDEN 309. **1670** RAY 47 [with 'windows' and 'doors'].

Love dancing well that dance among thorns, They.

1623 CAMDEN 279. **1670** RAY 77.

Love does much, money does everything (*or more*).

[Fr. **1612** GRUTER *Floril.* III. 186 Amour peut moult; argent peut tout. Sp. *c.* **1627** CORREAS *Vocab.* (1906) 68 Amor faz molto, argen faz todo.] **1587** GREENE *Wks.* (Gros.)

III. 61 (A). **1666** TORRIANO 9 Love can do much, but money can do more. **1732** FULLER no. 3286.

Love expels another, One.

1579 LYLY *Euphues* Wks. (Bond) I. 255. **1624** BURTON *Anat. Mel.* III. ii. v. ii. 3 M 1 Driue out one loue with another . . . one loue driues out another.

Love fails, Where | we espy all faults.

1670 RAY 16.

Love his house well, and yet not ride on the ridge,[1] A man may.

1553 T. WILSON *Arte of Rhet.* (1580) 192 A man maie love his house well, and yet not ride vpon the ridge. **1614** CAMDEN 302. **1738** SWIFT (*Dial.* ii) 349 So I do still, Colonel; but a man may love his house very well without riding on the ridge. **1853** TRENCH iv. 76 *A man may love his house well, without riding on the ridge*; it is enough for a wise man to know what is precious to himself, without . . . evermore proclaiming it to the world. [1 top of the roof.]

Love his little finger more than thy whole body, I.

1659 HOWELL *Eng. Prov.* 15/1.

Love in his breast, He that hath | hath spurs in his sides.

1640 HERBERT 337.

Love is a sweet torment (bitter-sweet).

1616 DRAXE 121 Loue is a sweet torment. *a.* **1637** JONSON *Underwoods* (1640) 206 Love is a bitter-sweet.

Love is blind.

c. **1386** CHAUCER *Merch. T.* 1598 For love is blynd al day, and may nat see. *c.* **1390** GOWER *Conf. Amantis* i. 47 ffor loue is blind and may noght se. **1583** MELBANCKE *Philotimus* G 11 Loue is blind. **1594–5** SHAKS. *Two Gent.* II. i. 76 *Speed.* If you love her you cannot see her. *Val.* Why? *Speed.* Because Love is blind. **1594–5** *Rom. & Jul.* II. i. 33 If love be blind, love cannot hit the mark. *Ibid.* III. ii. 9 If love be blind, it best agrees with night. **1596–7** *Merch. V.* II. vi. 36 But love is blind, and lovers cannot see The pretty follies that themselves commit. **1598–9** *Hen. V* V. ii. 327 Yet they [maids] do wink and yield, as love is blind and enforces. **1885** G. BRIMLEY *Ess.*, 'Tennyson' (1882) 52 There is profound beauty and truth in the allegory that represents love as a blind child.

Love is blind, Though | yet 'tis not for want of eyes.

1732 FULLER no. 5004.

Love is foul, No | nor prison fair.

1611 DAVIES *Prov.* 215 There was never fair prison nor love with foul face. **1651** HERBERT 369.

Love is free.

c. **1386** CHAUCER *Knight's T.* ii. **1606** Thynk wel that love is fre! And I wol love hire mawgree al thy myght.

Love is full of fear (trouble).

[*ov. Her.* l. 12 *Res est solliciti plena timoris amor.*] *c.* **1374** CHAUCER *Troylus* IV. **1644** For I am evere a-gast, for-why men rede That 'love is thing ay ful of bisy drede'. **1593** SHAKS. *Ven. & Ad.* 1021 Fie, fie, fond love! thou art so full of fear. **1616** DRAXE 122 Loue is full of trouble.

Love is lawless.

c. **1380** CHAUCER *Troilus & Criseyde* IV. 618 Through love is broken al day every lawe. *c.* **1386** Id. *Knights T.* 1163–6 Wostow nat wel the oldè clerkès sawe,[1] That *who shal yeve a lovere any lawe*; *Love is a gretter lawe, by my pan, Than may be yeve of any erthely man?* *c.* **1390** GOWER *Conf. Amantis* I. 18 For loves lawe is out of reule. **1576** PETTIE *Petite Pall.* (Gollancz) I. 177 If loue had law. **1579** LYLY *Euphues* Wks. (Bond) I. 228 As loue knoweth no lawes. **1581** RICH *Farewell to Militarie Prof.* (Shaks. Soc.) 131 As love is without lawe, so it is without respect, either of friende or foe. **1639** CLARKE 27 Love is lawless. **1700** DRYDEN *Pal & Arcite* I. 326 (Globe) 519 And knowst thou not, no law is made for love? [[1] BOETHIUS, *De Consolatione Philosophiae*, lib. III. met. xii. 47 *Quis legem det amantibus? Maior lex amor est sibi.*]

Love is never without jealousy.

1576 PETTIE *Petite Pall.* (Gollancz) II. 102 Love, they say, is light of belief, and jealousy is grounded upon love. **1593** SHAKS. *Venus & Adon.* 1137 It [love] shall be waited on with jealousy. **1594–5** *Two Gent.* II. iv. 178 For love, thou know'st, is full of jealousy. **1603** N. BRETON *Pkt. Mad Lett.* Wks. (1879) II. 21 I perceive it is true, . . . that love is not without jealousy. **1721** KELLY 241 . . . Lat. *zelotypiam parit amor.* **1732** FULLER no. 4731 The reward of love is jealousy. **1837** THEO. HOOK *Jack Brag* iii. None who have not felt jealousy—and, since there never can be love without it, who has not?

Love is no lack, In.

c. **1400** *Mirk's Festial* (E.E.T.S.) 165 For loue haþe no lake. **1546** HEYWOOD I. iv One shewth me openly in loue is no lacke. **1593** *Tell-trothes New-Yeares Gift* (1876) 7 Contentment in loue . . . according to the saying, *Loue hath no lacke.* **1614** CAMDEN 308. **1650** BROME *Jov. Crew* III (1708) 36 *Amie.* That's a most lying proverb that says, Where love is there's no lack: I am faint, and cannot travel further without meat. **1721** KELLY 240 Love has no lack, if the dame was ne'er so black.

Love is not found in the market.

1640 HERBERT 336.

Love is sweet in the beginning but sour in the ending.

1579 LYLY *Euphues* (Arb.) 108 Though the beginning of loue bring delight, the ende bringeth destruction. **1593** SHAKS. *Venus & Adon.* 1138 It [love] shall . . . Find sweet beginning, but unsavoury end. **1616** DRAXE 121.

Love is the loadstone of love.

1666 TORRIANO 10 Love is wont to be the loadstone of love. **1732** FULLER no. 3288.

Love is the reward of love.

1700 DRYDEN *Pal. & Arcite* II. 373 (Globe) 533 For 'tis their maxim, love is love's reward.

Love is the true price of love.

c. **1420** *Twenty-six Poems* (E.E.T.S.) 76 (A) Loue for loue is euenest boughte. **1569** E. FENTON *Wonders of Nature* 66 Loue . . . can not be payed but wyth loue. **1640** HERBERT 342. **1852** E. FITZGERALD *Polonius* xix Healthy, happy English labourers . . . Not, however, to be bought wholly by money wages—'Love is the true price of love.'

Love is, Where | there is faith.

1586 PETTIE tr. *Guazzo's Civ. Conv.* 221 According to the common saying, where loue is there is faith.

Love is without reason.

1509 A. BARCLAY *Ship of Fools* I. 81 He that louyth is voyde of all reason. **1581** B. RICH *Farewell to Militarie Prof.* (Shaks. Soc.) 191 Love is without lawe, so it maketh the pacientes to bee as utterly voide of reason. **1616** DRAXE 121 Loue an unruly passion.

Love lasts as long as money endures.

1474 CAXTON *Chesse* III. iii Hereof men say a comyn proverbe in englond, that loue lasteth as longe as the money endurith.

Love laughs at locksmiths.

1593 SHAKS. *Venus & Adon.* 576 Were beauty under twenty locks kept fast, Yet love breaks through and picks them all at last. **1803** G. COLMAN (Jun.) *Love Laughs at Locksmiths* Title of Play. **1877** E. WALFORD *Tales of Our Gt. Fam.* (1890) 261 Dorothy [Vernon] was . . . Kept almost a prisoner . . . Love, however, laughs at locksmiths.

Love like chick, They.

[*Chick* = a term of endearment.] **1648** HERRICK *Hesper.*, *For Duke of Yorke* 8 And so dresse him up with love, As to be the chick of Jove. **1678** RAY 347. *Somerset.*

Love like pig and pie, They.

1621 BURTON *Anat. Mel.* III. ii. III. iii (1651 478 If she be rich, . . . they love her dearly, like pig and pye, and are ready to hang themselves if they may not have her.

Love lives in cottages as well as in courts.

1590 LODGE *Rosalynde* (Hunt. Cl.) 95 Loue lurkes assoone about a Sheepcoate as a

Pallaice. **1670** RAY 16.   **1721** KELLY 236 ... Conjugal love much more, for they who live in cottages . . . seldom marry for interest, wealth, or court favour.

Love locks no cupboards.

1639 CLARKE 26.

Love lost between them, There is no.

(a) Their affection is mutual. *Obs. c.* **1640** R. DAVENPORT *Surv. Sci.* Wks. (Bullen 1890) 327 Oh my sweete! Sure there is no loue lost when you two meete. **1823** LAMB *Elia* Ser. II. *New Year's Coming of Age, Shrove Tuesday* was helping the *Second of September* . . . which courtesy the latter returned . . .— so that there was no love lost for that matter. (b) They have no love for each other. ?**1622** J. TAYLOR (Water-P.) *Trav. Twelve-pence* Wks. (1630) I. 71 But there's no great love lost 'twixt them and mee, We keepe asunder and so best agree. **1889** T. A. TROLLOPE *What I remember* III. 91 Between Italian and French radicals there is really no love lost.

Love lost betwixt sailors and soldiers, There is no.

1599 NASHE *Lenten Stuffe* Wks. (McKerrow 1905) III. 230 There is no more loue betwixt them then betwixt saylers and land souldiours.

Love makes a wit of the fool.

1624 BURTON *Anat. Mel.* III. ii. III. iii. I 4 As it [love] makes wisemen fooles, so many times it makes fooles become wise. **1774** C. DIBDIN *Quaker* I. viii (A) According unto the proverb, love maketh a wit of the fool.

Love makes all hard hearts gentle.

1640 HERBERT 342.

Love makes one fit for any work.

1640 HERBERT 347.

Love makes the world go round.

[JACOPONE DA TODI *Cielo e terra per te* [*amor*] *si conduce.* DANTE, *Paradiso* fin. Love . . . that moves the sun in heaven and all the stars (Cary).] **1656** COWLEY *David.* 'Tis thou that mov'st the world through every part. **1712** BLACKMORE *Creation* V refers the belief to Aristotle. **1865** DODGSON *Alice in W.* ix. **1882** GILBERT *Iolanthe* In for a penny, in for a pound, 'Tis love that makes the world go round.

Love me for little that hate me for naught, They.

1813 RAY *Scot. Prov.* 310.

Love me, If you | kythe[1] that.

1721 KELLY 187 . . . If you have a value for me, show it by your deeds. When one professeth kindness for another, he will answer, *What says the bird?* alleging that there is a bird whose note is *kythe that.* [[1] make it appear.]

Love me little, (and) love me long.

1546 HEYWOOD II. ii Old wise folk say: love me little, love me long. *a.* **1548** HALL *Chron.*

(1809) 444 The olde Proverbe love me little and love me long. **1594–5** SHAKS. *Rom. & Jul.* II. vi. 14 Therefore love moderately; long love doth so. **1629** T. ADAMS *Serm.* (1861–2) II. 418 Men cannot brook poor friends. This inconstant charity is hateful, as our English phrase premonisheth: 'Love me little and love me long'. **1721** KELLY 229 . . . A dissuasive from shewing too much, and too sudden kindness. **1907** *Times Lit. Sup.* 8 Mar. Mrs. Bellew is a lady who cannot love either little or long. She . . . tires very quickly of the men who are irresistibly drawn to her.

Love me, love my dog.

[*a.* 1153 ST. BERNARD *Serm., In Festo S. Mich.,* iii *Qui me amat, amat et canem meum.*] *c.* **1480** *Early Miscell.* (Warton Cl.) 62 He that lovythe me lovythe my hound. **1546** HEYWOOD II. ix Ye haue bene so veraie a hog, To my fréendis. What man, loue me, loue me dog. **1612** CHAPMAN *Widow's Tears* I. ii *Eud.* Love me? love my dog. *Thar.* I am bound to that by the proverb, madam. **1692** L'ESTRANGE *Aesop's Fab.* cvi (1738) 122 *Love me, love my dog,* . . . for there are certain decencies of respect due to the servant for the master's sake. **1826** LAMB *Pop. Fallacies* Wks. (1898) 231 THAT YOU MUST LOVE ME, AND LOVE MY DOG. . . . We could never yet form a friendship . . . without the intervention of some third anomaly, . . . —the understood *dog* in the proverb.

Love most are least set by, They who.

1659 HOWELL *Eng. Prov.* 12/2. **1670** RAY 16.

Love my lady, Some men must | and some Joan.

1594–5 SHAKS. *L.L.L.* III. 215 Some men must love my lady and some Joan. **1855** BOHN 489.

Love needs no teaching.

a. **1618** RALEIGH *Rem.* (1664) 35 Love needs no teaching.

Love not at the first look.

1639 CLARKE 28.

Love of lads and fire of chats[1] is soon in and soon out.

c. **1460** *Good Wyfe wold a Pylgr.* in *Q. Eliz. Acad.* (E.E.T.S.) 41 A fyre of sponys, and louve of gromis, Full soun woll be att a nende. **1670** RAY 46 *Derbyshire.* [[1] chips.]

Love of money and the love of learning rarely meet, The.

1651 HERBERT 372.

Love of the wicked is more dangerous than their hatred, The.

1732 FULLER no. 4636.

Love one like pie, To.

1738 SWIFT (Dial. ii) 346 *Miss.* I love him like pie, I'd rather the devil had him than I.

Love or money, For.

1590 C. S. *Right Relig.* 18 Then should not men eyther for loue or money have pardons. **1712** SWIFT *Jrnl. to Stella* 7 Aug. No more ghosts now for love or money. **1801** EDGE-WORTH *Cas. Rackrent* (1890) 13 Many gentlemen . . . made it their choice . . . when there was no room to be had for love or money, to sleep in the chicken-house.

Love puts in, When | friendship is gone.

1576 PETTIE *Petite Pall.* (Gollancz) II. 96 Where love leadeth . . . no friend is forced of . . . **1579** LYLY *Euphues* Wks. (Bond) I. 209 Where loue beareth sway, friendshippe can haue no shew. c. **1630** BEAUM. & FL. *Lovers' Progress* I. i (quoted as proverb) (A).

Love, Next to | quietness.

1678 RAY 194.

Love rules his kingdom without a sword.

1640 HERBERT 342. **1834** EDGEWORTH *Helen* vi What a pretty proverb that was, . . .— 'Love rules his kingdom without a sword.'

Love the babe for her that bare it.

1639 CLARKE 285.

Love the boll, If you | you cannot hate the branches.

1639 CLARKE 285.

Love (Worship) the ground he (*or* she) treads on, To.

c. **1612** BEAUM. & FL. *Scornf. Lady* v. i 'Tis a shame you should use a poor Gentlewoman so untowardly; she loves the ground you tread on. **1856** DICKENS, &c. *Wreck Golden Mary* ii. 19 I worshipped the very ground she walked on!

Love the Kirk well and yet not ride on the ridge,[1] A man may.

1721 KELLY 37 . . . A man may love a thing, or person, very well, and yet not show too much fondness. **1824** SCOTT *Redg.* xiii One may love the Kirk, and yet not ride on the rigging of it; and one may love the king, and yet not be cramming him eternally down the throat of . . . folk that may . . . like another king better. **1857** DEAN RAMSAY *Remin.* v. (1911) 202 *He rides on the riggin o' the kirk.* The rigging being the top of the roof, the proverb used to be applied to those who carried their zeal for church matters to the extreme point. [1 top of the roof.]

Love thee like pudding, I | if thou wert pie I'd eat thee.

1678 RAY 349.

Love to a father's, No.

1640 HERBERT 322.

Love to hear well of themselves. Men.

1639 CLARKE 12.

Love too much that die for love, They.

1611 COTGRAVE s.v. 'Mourir'. **1670** RAY 16.

Love what nobody else loves, I.

1738 SWIFT (Dial. ii) 344 *Col.* [*To Neverout.*] Prithee, Tom, send me the two legs . . . of that pigeon; for, you must know, I love what nobody else loves.

Love will creep where it cannot go, *see* Kind (L.) will creep.

Love will find out the way.

c. **1597** DELONEY *Gentle Craft* XV (A) Thus loue you see, can find a way to make both men and maids obey. **1661** T. B. *Love Will Find out the Way* (Title of play). a. **1765** PERCY *Reliques* III. iii (1857) 517 Over the mountains, And over the waves; . . . Love will find out the way.

Love without end hath no end.

1625 BACON *Apoph.* Wks. (Chandos) 358 There is a Spanish adage, 'Love without end hath no end': meaning, that if it were begun not upon particular ends it would last.

Love your friend, but look to yourself.

1721 KELLY 238.

Love your friend with his fault.

1650 JER. TAYLOR *Holy Liv.* II. iv (1850) 78 Cyrus, . . . amongst his equals in age, . . . would never play at any sport . . . in which he knew himself more excellent than they. Ama l'amico tuo con il difetto suo. **1852** E. FITZGERALD *Polonius* civ A modern Greek proverb says, 'Love your friend with his foible'. **1853** TRENCH iii. 49 The Latin proverb, Mores amici novens, non oderis [see HORACE, *Sat.* 1. 3. 24–93] . . . finds its grateful equivalent in the Italian, Ama l'amico tuo con il difetto suo (*Love your friend with his fault*).

Love your neighbour, yet pull not down your hedge.

1640 HERBERT 322. **1761** A. MURPHY *The Citizen* I. ii *Geo.* You have taught me to be cautious in this wide world. Love your neighbour, but don't pull down your hedge. **1889** MRS. OLIPHANT *Neighb. on Green* i They were so friendly that it was once proposed to cut it down, . . . but . . . the end of it was that the hedge remained.

Loved mutton well that licked where the ewe lay, He.

1721 KELLY 125 . . . Spoken to them who will sip the bottom of a glass where good liquor was, or scrape a plate, after good meat. **1816** SCOTT *Antiq.* xliv That German devil was glowering at the lid of the kist (they liked mutton weel that licket whare the yowe lay).

Love's wars, In | he who flieth is conqueror.

1642 TORRIANO 77. **1732** FULLER no. 2819.

Love (*noun*), *see also* Absence sharpens l.; Best smell is bread . . . best l. of children; Calf l. half l.; Choice to begin l. (A man has); Cold broth . . . old l. renewed again; Course of true l. never run smooth; Cupboard l.; Fair chieve all where l. trucks; Fair in l. and war; Fanned fires and forced l.; Faults are thick where l. thin; Follow l. and it will flee; Folly to being in l. (No); Furze is in bloom (When), l. in tune; Hasty l. soon cold; Herb will cure l. (No); Hot l. hasty vengeance; —— soon cold; Hundred ells of contention (In) not inch of l.; Jack's in l. (If) he's no judge; Kind (L.) will creep where it may not go; Labour is light where l. doth pay; Lad's l. a busk of broom; Lie down for l. (They that) should rise for hunger; Lives by l. and lumps; Looks breed l.; Marrieth for l. without money (Who); Marry first and l. will follow; Merry as be can, for l. ne'er delights in sorrowful man; Nail (L.) drives out another; Off with the old l. (Best to be); Old l. not forgotten; Pennyweight of l. worth pound of law; Poverty comes in (When) l. leaps out; Presents of l. fear not to be ill taken; Remedy for l. is land between; Salt water . . . wash away l.; Sound l. not soon forgotten; Soup and l. (Of) first is best; Subject's l. is king's life-guard; Thousand pounds of law (In a) not ounce of l.; True l. kythes in need; War, hunting, and l. full of trouble; Wine and youth increase l.

Love(s, d, th) (*verb*), *see* Best l. furthest off; Every man as he l.; Fool (I am a), I l. anything good; Good things I do not l.; Life you l. me not (In), in death bewail; Like l. like; Soul is . . . where it l.; Speaks me fair and l. me not; World wags (I wot how), best l. that hath most bags.

Lovell, *see* Cat, the Rat, and L.

Lovers live by love, as larks live by leeks.

1546 HEYWOOD I. x. 20 Louers liue by loue, ye as larkes liue by léekes Saied this Ales, muche more then halfe in mockage. **1670** RAY 46 . . . This is I conceive in derision of such expressions as living by love. **1721** KELLY 367 *You live on love as laverocks*[1] *do on leeks.* A jest upon them that eat little. [[1] larks.]

Lover(s), *see also* Falling out of l. is renewing of l.; Jove laughs at l.'s perjuries; Poor beauty finds more l.

Loves bacon well that licks the swine-sty door, He.

1678 RAY 96. **1732** FULLER no. 1978 (with 'sow's breach' for 'swine-sty door').

Loves glass without G, He that | take away L and that is he.

1669 *New Help to Discourse* 265 (A). **1678** RAY 55. **1746** FRANKLIN Jan. He that whines for Glass without G Take away L and that's he.

Loves law, He that | will get his fill of it.

1721 KELLY 165 . . . For such are sure of two things, an uneasy life, and a broken fortune.

Loves noise, He that | must buy a pig.

1813 RAY 143 . . . *Quien quiere ruydo, compre un cochino. Hisp.*

Loves roast meat well that licks the spit, He.

1670 RAY 137.

Loves the poor well, She | but cannot abide beggars.

1678 RAY 350 . . . *Somerset.* (*of pretenders to charity.*)

Loves the tree, He that | loves the branch.

1639 CLARKE 285 (A) If you love the boll you cannot hate the braunches. **1640** HERBERT 356.

Loveth his fetters, No man | be they made of gold.

1550 HEYWOOD I. viii. 15 No man loueth his fetters, be they made of gold. Were I loose from the louely lynkes of my chayne, I would not daunce in such fayre fetters agayne. **1605** CHAPMAN, &c. *Eastw. Hoe* IV. i *Touch.* Wife, no man loves his fetters, be they made of gold. I list not ha' my head fastened under my child's girdle. **1894** LD. AVEBURY *Use of Life* iii (1904) 27 All fetters are bad, even if they be made of gold . . . in the case of many rich men, they are really the slaves . . . of money.

Loveth well sheep's flesh, He | that wets his bread in the wool.

c. **1460** *Gode Wyfe wd. a Pylgr.* in Q. Eliz. *Acad.* (E.E.T.S.) 41 He wyll lowys scheppis flesche, That wettytt his bred in woll. a. **1530** R. Hill's *Commonpl. Bk.* (E.E.T.S.) 131 He loveth well moton, pat weteth his bred in wool—Optat eius carnem, tangens in vellere panem. **1546** HEYWOOD II. v. 58 He loueth well shéeps flesh, that wets his bred in the wul. **1670** RAY 123 He loves mutton well that dips his bread in the wool.

Loves, loveth, *see also* Love(s).

Loving comes by looking.

1539 TAVERNER xii Ex aspectu nascitur amor. Of syght is love gendred. c. **1577** NORTHBROOKE *Treat. agst. Dicing* (1843) 89 She must needes fire some . . . According to the olde prouerbe, *ex visu amor.* **1639** CLARKE 28.

Low ebb at Newgate, He that is at a | may soon be afloat at Tyburn.

1562 HEYWOOD *Three Hundred Epigrammes* Ep. 56 Thou art at an ebbe in Newgate, thou hast wrong. But thou shalt be a flote at Tyburne ere long. **1662** FULLER (*Middlesex*) II. 314 'He that is a low ebb at Newgate, may soon be afloat at Tyburn'. I allow not this satirical proverb, as it makes mirth on men in misery. **1670** RAY 238.

Low hedge is easily leaped over, A.

1611 GRUTER. **1614** CAMDEN 302. **1670** RAY 16. **1732** FULLER no. 259.

Low man, *see* Seldom is ... l. m. lowly.

Lower, *see* Mill-stone (The l.) grinds as well; Stone (The l.) can do no good.

Lowly sit, richly warm.

1670 RAY 117 ... A mean condition is both more safe and more comfortable, then a high estate.

Loyal heart may be landed under Traitors' Bridge, A.

1662 FULLER (*Lond.*) II. 347 'A loyal heart may be landed under Traitors' Bridge.' This is a bridge under which is an entrance into the Tower.... Passive innocence, ... may be accused without cause, and disposed at the pleasure of others.

Lubberland, where the pigs run about ready roasted, and cry, Come eat me!

1614 JONSON *Barthol. Fair* III. ii *Lit.* Good mother, how shall we finde a pigge, if we doe not looke about for't? will it run off o' the spit, into our mouths thinke you? as in Lubberland? and cry, *we, we?*

Lubberland, where they have half-a-crown a day for sleeping.

1813 RAY 64 You would do well in lubberland, where they have half-a-crown a day for sleeping.

Lucifer, *see* Proud as L.

Luck, As good | as had the cow that stuck herself with her own horn.

1678 RAY 287. **1828** LYTTON *Pelham* lv Things ... grew worse with me, who have had 'as good luck as the cow that stuck herself with her own horn'.

Luck, As good | as the lousy calf, that lived all winter and died in the summer.

1678 RAY 287.

Luck goes on at this rate, If your | you may very well hope to be hanged.

1732 FULLER no. 2806.

Luck in horses, He that would have good | must kiss the parson's wife.

1621 JONSON *Gipsies Met.* Wks. (1904) III. 152 You'll have good luck to horseflesh, o' my life, You ploughed so late with the vicar's wife. **1678** RAY 86. **1738** SWIFT (Dial. ii) 345 *Sir J.* I have had devilish bad luck in horse-flesh of late. *Smart.* Why, then, Sir John, you must kiss a parson's wife.

Luck in leisure, There is.

1683 G. MERITON *Yorks. Dialogue* 9. **1855** BOHN 522.

Luck in odd numbers, There is.

[VERG. *Ecl.* 875 *Numero deus impare gaudet.*] **1600–1** SHAKS. *Merry W.* V. i. 3 This is the third time: I hope good luck lies in odd numbers. **1826** S. LOVER *Rory O'More* 'Then here goes another', says he, 'to make sure, For there's luck in odd numbers', says Rory O'More. **1883** J. PAYN *Thicker than W.* i She was ... by no means averse to a third experiment in matrimony.... 'There was luck in odd numbers.'

Luck of Edenhall, If that glass either break or fall, farewell the.

[See LONGFELLOW's tr. of UHLAND *Das Glück von Edenhall*; also SCOTT *Border Minstrelsy* ii. 196.] **1794** W. HUTCHINSON *Hist. Cumberland* I. 269 An old painted drinking glass, called the Luck of Edenhall, is preserved with great care [in the Musgrave family].... The legendary tale is, that the butler, going to draw water, surprised a company of fairies ... near the well: he seized the glass ... they tried to recover it; but, after an ineffectual struggle, flew away, saying: If that glass either break or fall, Farewel the luck of Edenhall.

Luck, *see also* Better l. next time; Care and diligence bring l.; Give a man l.; Knave (The more), better l.; Properer man, worse l.; Shitten l. is good l.; Thieves and rogues have best l.; Voyage never has l. where each has vote; Worse l. now, the better another time. *See also* Good luck, Ill luck.

Lucky at cards, unlucky in love.

1738 SWIFT (Dial. iii) 352 *Lady S.* Well, miss, you'll have a sad husband, you have such good luck at cards. **1865** T. W. ROBERTSON *Society* II. ii *Chodd. Jun.* I'm always lucky at cards! *Sid.* Yes, I know an old proverb about that ... Lucky at play, unlucky in——.

Lucky in life, unlucky in love.

1908 E. PHILLPOTTS *The Mother* II. xiii One might almost think the old saying 'Lucky in life, unlucky in love' was true.

Lucky John Toy: Like | lost a shilling and found a tupenny loaf.

1856 N. & Q. 2nd Ser. II. 327 At Penryn, in West Cornwall, I frequently used to hear this proverb applied to any one who rejoiced over a small gain, though purchased at the expense of a greater loss: 'Like lucky Jahn Toy—lost a shilling and found a tupenny loaf'.

Lucky men need no counsel.

1642 TORRIANO 78. **1707** MAPLETOFT 12. **1855** BOHN 447.

Lucky pudding, If ever you make a | I shall eat the prick.[1]

1641 FERGUSSON 66. **1721** KELLY 198 If ever you make a good pudding, I'll eat the prick. That is, I am much mistaken if ever you do good. [1 skewer.]

Lucky, *see also* Wicked (The more), more l.

Lucy light, the shortest day and the longest night.[1]

1611 DONNE *Anat. of World. Prog. of S.*, *2nd An.* 119 (1896) II. 131 Think that they bury thee, and think that rite Lays thee to sleep but a Saint Lucy's night. **1629** T. ADAMS *Med. Creed* Wks. (1861–2) III. 239 Under the law they had short days and long nights. . . . Theirs was a St Lucy's day, short and cloudy, ours is a St Barnaby's day. **1678** RAY 52. [1 St. Lucy's day, O.S., was 21 Dec.]

Ludlam, *see* Lazy as L.'s dog.

Lugs, *see* Pint stoups hae lang l.

Lump(s), *see* Head is all of a l.; Lives by love and l.

Lundy, *see* Padstow Point **to** L. **light.**

Lurch, *see* Leave in the l.

Lurden, *see* Sick of a fever l.

Lust, *see* Heart is full of l. (When), **mouth's** full of leasings; Man is known **mortal** by . . . l.

Lute, *see* Ass play on l.

Luther, *see* Erasmus laid egg of Reformation.

Lydford, *see* Lidford.

Lying rides upon debt's back.

1758 FRANKLIN *Way to Wealth* (Crowell) 22 If you cannot pay . . . you will make . . . sneaking excuses, and . . . sink into . . . **lying;** for, . . . *Lying rides upon debt's back.*

Lying, *see also* Easy as l.; Law for l. (No); Whispering but there is l. (No).

Lynn, *see* Rising.

M

M under one's girdle, To have (*or* carry) an.

[= to use a respectful prefix (Mr., Mrs.) when addressing or mentioning a person.] *a.* **1553** UDALL *Royster D.* III. iii (Arb.) 48 *M. Mery.* Ralph Royster Doister were hir owne I warrant you. *R. Royster* Neare an M by your girdle? **1605** CHAPMAN, &c. *Eastw. Hoe!* IV *Quick.* Must Golding sit upon us? *Con.* Yod might carry an M under your girdle, to Mr. Deputy's worship. **1738** SWIFT (Dial. i) 335 *Lady A.* What, plain Neverout! methinks you might have an M under your girdle, miss. **1816** SCOTT *Old Mort.* xxix Ye might hae had an M under your belt for Mistress Wilson of Milnwood.

Macclesfield, *see* Feeds like a . . . of M. *See also* Maxfield.

Macfarlane's geese, Like | that liked their play better than their meat.

1721 KELLY 361 *You breed of MacFarlan's geese, you have more mind of your play, than your meat.* Spoken to our children, when their earnestness upon their play, keeps them from dinner. **1820** SCOTT *Monast.* xiii The Miller . . . intimating . . . some allusion to the proverb of MacFarlane's geese, which 'liked their play better than their meat'. [Note.— Wild geese . . . in Loch Lomond . . . were supposed to have some connection with the ancient family of MacFarlane . . . James VI . . . had been much amused by the geese pursuing each other . . . When one which was brought to table, was found to be tough and ill-fed, James observed—'that MacFarlane's geese liked their play better than their meat'.]

Mackerel is in season when Balaam's ass speaks in church.

1902–4 LEAN I. 442 . . . The lesson in the old Lectionary (Numbers xxii) for 2nd Sunday after Easter.

Mackerel sky.

1669 WORLIDGE *Syst. Agric.* (1681) 295 In a fair day, if the sky seem to be dapled with white Clouds, (which they usually term a Mackarel-sky) it usually predicts rain. **1895** ADDY *Househ. Tales*, &c. 119 Yorkshire farmers . . . call a sky which is flecked with many small clouds a 'mackerel sky': A mackerel sky Is never long dry.

Mackerel sky and mares' tails make lofty ships carry low sails.

1869 INWARDS 59.

Mackerel, *see also* Sprat to catch m.

MacKibbon's crowdy, *see* Come to himself (Let him).

Mackissock's cow did, I will do as | I'll think more than I say.

1721 KELLY 183 I . . . will . . . conceal my resentments; but I will watch an opportunity for retaliation.

Macwhid, *see* Make a shift.

Mad action, One | is not enough to prove a man mad.

1732 FULLER no. 3767.

Mad as a (March) hare, As.

c. **1386** CHAUCER *Friar's T.* D 1327 For
though this somnour wood were as an hare.
1529 MORE *Supp. Soulys* Wks. 299/2 As mad
not as a march hare, but as a madde dogge.
1602 DEKKER *Honest Wh.* v. ii They're
madder than March hares. **1863** KINGSLEY
Water Bab. v A very clever old gentleman:
but . . . as mad as a March hare.

Mad as a hatter.

1837–40 HALIBURTON *Clockm.* (1862) 109
Sister Sal . . . walked out of the town, as mad
as a hatter. **1857** HUGHES *Tom Brown* II. iii
He's a very good fellow, but as mad as a
hatter.

Mad as Ajax, As.

1594–5 SHAKS. *L.L.L.* IV. iii. 7 This love is
as mad as Ajax: it kills sheep; it kills me.
1607 CHAPMAN *Bussy d'Amb.* III. i Quarrel
with sheep, and run as mad as Ajax.

Mad as the baiting bull of Stamford, As.

1662 FULLER (*Lincs.*) II. 268 'As mad as the
baiting bull of Stamford.' Earl Warren . . .
gave all those meadows . . . on condition that
they find a mad bull . . . six weeks before
Christmas day, for . . . that sport every year.

Mad bull is not to be tied up with a packthread, A.

1732 FULLER no. 266. **1746** FRANKLIN Oct.
Mad kings and mad bulls are not to be held
by treaties and packthread.

Mad dog bites his master, The.

1732 FULLER no. 4644.

Mad folks in a narrow place, Take heed of.

1651 HERBERT 371.

Mad words deaf ears, For.

[Fr. **1558** MEURIER *Colloq. A folles paroles
oreilles sourdes.* Sp. *c.* 1627 CORREAS *Vocab.*
(1906) 17 *A palabras locas, orejas sordas.*]
1616 DRAXE 70 For foolish talke deafe eares.
1732 FULLER no. 1593. **1853** TRENCH vi. 140
Of words . . . wrung out from moments of
agony, may we not hope that . . . , *For mad
words deaf ears,* is often graciously true, even
in the very courts of heaven?

Mad, You will never be | you are of so many minds.

1580 LYLY *Euph. & his Eng.* Wks. (Bond)
II. 185 Loue quoth Euphues kil neuer make
thee mad, for it commeth by fits, not like a
quotidian, but a tertian. **1670** RAY 118. **1738**
SWIFT (Dial. i) 338 *Lady S.* Well, Mr. Neverout, you'll never be mad, you are of so many
minds.

Mad, *see also* Dance (They who) are thought
m.; Difference between staring and stark
m.; Every man is m. on some point;
Horn m.; House goes m. when women gad;
Oppression maketh wise man m.

Madame Parnell,[1] crack the nut and eat the kernel.

1659 HOWELL *Eng. Prov.* 21/2 . . . *This alludes
to labor.* [[1] *Parnel,* M.E. *Peronelle,* a Christian
name from St. *Petronilla,* came to signify a
wanton young woman.]

Made a song of, She is not to be.

1721 KELLY 296 . . . An abatement to a
woman's commendation for beauty.

Made, *see also* Many a thing's m. for money.

Madge Whitworth, *see* Go here away.

Madman (-men), *see* Fools and m. speak the
truth; Naked sword in m.'s hand.

Madness, *see* Anger is short m.; Gladness
(A man of) seldom falls into m.; Method
in his m.; Midsummer moon (m.)

Madrid air is so still, yet so keen, that it will not blow out a candle but will extinguish a life.

1928 *Times* 24 Apr. 18/2 The Madrid climate
. . . has been calumniated . . . ever since the
invention of the proverb that Madrid air is
so still, yet so keen, that it will not blow out
a candle but will extinguish a life.

Maggot[1] bites, When the.

1687 MIEGE *Gt. Fr. Dict.* II. s.v. I shall do
it, when the magget bites. *Je le ferai, quand
il m'en prendra envie.* [[1] a whimsical or perverse fancy.]

Magistracy makes not the man, but discovers what metal is in him.

1539 TAVERNER (1545) D 5 *Magistratus virum
indicat* Authoritie declareth a man. **1540** Id.
tr. *Erasm. Flores aliquot sententiarum* A 2
Magistratus virum arguit. Authoritie or office
vttereth what the man is. **1642** D. ROGERS
Matrim. Honour 45 (A) The old speech is,
Magistracy makes not the man, but discovers
what mettell is in him.

Magnificat at Matins, Like.

c. **1580** J. CONYBEARE 45 As farre from the
purpose as Magnificat from mattines. **1588**
BP. ANDREWES *Serm. at Spital* (1629) 24 (A)
Their note comes in like magnificat at
Matins. **1611** COTGRAVE (A) s.v. 'Magnificat'
Chanter Magnificat à matines. To doe things
disorderly, or use a thing unseasonably.

Magnificat, see also Correct M. (To).

Magnificent but it is not war, It is.

1854? CANROBERT C'est magnifique mais ce
n'est pas la guerre. [Of the charge of the
British Light Brigade, at Balaklava, 25 Oct.]
1909 *Times Wkly.* 30 Apr. We admire . . .
the pioneer who is at once priest, evangelist,
carpenter, printer, schoolmaster, physician.
It is magnificent, but it is not war. What he
needs is . . . our support.

Magpie, *see* One [m.] for sorrow.

Mahomet's coffin (tomb),[1] Like.

1649 MILTON *Eikon*. Prose Wks. (1904) I. 394 We meet next with a comparison . . . , 'that the parliament have hung the majesty of kingship in an airy imagination of royalty, between the privileges of both houses, like the tomb of Mahomet.' **1718** PRIOR *Alma* ii. 719 The balance always would hang even, Like Mahomet's tomb, 'twixt earth and heaven. **1818** SCOTT *Rob Roy* xxx Would not suffer the honest Bailie to remain suspended, like the coffin of Mahomet, between heaven and earth. **1894** STEVENSON & OSBOURNE *Ebb-Tide* vii Birds whisked in the air above, . . . fishes in the scarce denser medium below ; between, like Mahomet's coffin, the boat drew away on the surface. [[1] fabled to be kept in suspension by loadstones.]

Mahomet, *see also* Mountain will not come to M.

Maid oft seen, A | and a gown oft worn, are disesteemed and held in scorn.

1611 COTGRAVE s.v. 'Fille'. **1670** RAY 17. **1732** FULLER no. 6395.

Maid that laughs is half taken, A.

1664 CODRINGTON 183. **1670** RAY 16. **1732** FULLER no. 269.

Maid was born odd, This.

1678 RAY 77 Spoken of a maid who lives to be old, and cannot get a husband.

Maiden (The), *see* Invented the M. (He that).

Maiden with many wooers often chooses the worst, A.

1721 KELLY 32 . . . Often true literally, but applied to those who having many things in their proffer, choose the worst.

Maidenhead hangs in your light, Your.

1738 SWIFT (Dial. ii) 347 *Miss*. Where's my knife? sure I ha'n't eaten it. . . . *Sir J*. No, miss ; but your maidenhead hangs in your light.

Maidenhood, *see* Malkin's m.

Maidens must be mild and meek, swift to hear and slow to speak.

1721 KELLY 247 . . . A rhyme much canted by Mothers to their Daughters in former Times ; but now almost antiquated. **1732** FULLER no. 6410.

Maidens should be meek while[1] they be married.

1641 FERGUSSON 76. **1917** BRIDGE 93 (with 'mim till' for 'meek while'). [[1] until.]

Maidens should be mim till they're married, and then they may burn kirks.

1721 KELLY 253 . . . Spoken often by way of reflection, when we say that such a one is a good humour'd Girl, as if you would say, observe how she'll prove when she is married. **1855** W. STIRLING-MAXWELL *Prov. Philos. Scot*. Wks. (1891) VI. 31 Our own country . . . is hardly . . . less cynical . . . 'Maidens should be mim till they're married, and then they may burn kirks'.

Maidens, All are not | that wear bare hair.

1641 FERGUSSON 16 All are not maidens that wears bair hair. **1721** KELLY 4 *All is not gold that glitters, nor maidens that wear their hair*. It was the fashion some years ago for virgins to go bare headed ; . . . every thing is not so good as its appears.

Maidens' tochers and ministers' stipends are aye less than they are called.

1721 KELLY 248 . . . Maidens portions are magnified to procure them suiters. And ministers livings are call'd larger, by them who grudge that they are so large.

Maids say 'Nay' and take.

c. **1535** LYNDSAY *Three Estates* l. 305 We will tak it . . . Howbeit that wee say nay. **1562** HEYWOOD *Three Hundr.Epig.* no. 223 Say nay and take it. **1592–3** SHAKS. *Rich. III* III. vii. 49 *Buck*. And be not easily won to our requests ; Play the maid's part, still answer nay, and take it. **1594** GREENE *Looking-Glass* II. i (Merm.) 98 *Alv*. Tut, my Remilia, be not thou so coy ; Say nay, and take it. **1648** HERRICK *Hesper*. 676 Wks. (1893) II. 28 Women, although they ne'er so goodly make it, Their fashion is, but to say no, to take it. **1738** SWIFT (Dial. i) 334 *Lady A*. Give her a dish ; for they say maids will say no, and take it. **1896** F. LOCKER-LAMPSON *My Confid*. 16 Maids, in modesty, say 'No' to that which they would have the profferer construe 'Ay'.

Maids than Malkin, There are more | (and more men than Michael).

1546 HEYWOOD I. xi. 26 Tushe, there was no mo maydes but malkyn tho. **1579** GOSSON *Sch. Abuse* (Arb.) 37 There are . . . more maydes then Maulkin. *a*. **1625** FLETCHER *Woman's Prize* I. iii *Petru*. Well there are more Maides than Maudlin, that's my comfort. *Mar*. Yes, and more men than Michael. **1636** CAMDEN 308 There's more Maids than Maukins. **1678** RAY 172 There are more maids then Maukin, and more men then Michael.

Maids want nothing but husbands, and when they have them they want everything.

1678 RAY 347. *Somerset*.

Maid(s), maiden(s), *see* All meats . . . all m. to be wed ; Belly is full (When the) ; Cat help it (How can) if m. a fool ; Children (M.) should be seen not heard ; Crooning cow . . . and whistling m. boded never luck ; Every m. is undone ; Good m. but for thought, word, and deed ; Knows

who's a good m. (Who); Mealy-mouthed
m. stands long at the mill; Meeterly as
m. in fairness; Mope-eyed by living a m.;
Nineteen nay-says of a m. half a grant;
Old m. lead apes in hell; Suffolk fair m.;
Tall m. is stooping (While), little one hath
swept; Will not (If one), another will;
Worst store, m. unbestowed.

Main-brace, see Splice the m.

Main chance, Look (Have an eye) to the.

1580 LYLY *Euph. & his Eng.* (Arb.) 430 (A)
Alwayes haue an eye to the mayne, what soeuer
thou art chaunced at the buy. **1584** R. W. *Three
Ladies Lond.* I. E ij b Trust me thou art as
craftie to haue an eye to the mayne chaunce:
As the Taylor that out of seuen yardes stole
one and a halfe of durance. **1590–1** SHAKS.
2 Hen. VI I. i. 212 *Sal.* Then let's make
haste away, and look unto the main . . . *War*
. . . Main chance, father, you meant; but I
meant Maine. **1625** HOWELL *Lett.* 6 Jan.
(1903) I. 247 Bacon . . . scarce left money
to bury him, which, . . . did argue no great
wisdom, it being . . . essential . . . to provide
for the main chance. **1670** RAY 117. **1843–4**
DICKENS *M. Chuz.* viii The education of Mr.
Jonas had been conducted . . . on the strictest principles of the main chance. The very
first word he learnt to spell was 'gain'.
1879 W. MINTO *Daniel Defoe* 135 [Defoe] was
a man of business, and practised the profession of letters with a shrewd eye to the main
chance.

Maintains one vice, What | would bring up two children.

1758 FRANKLIN in ARBER *Eng. Garner* V. 582
Away, then, with your expensive follies! . . .
For, as *Poor* DICK says, . . . *What maintains
one vice, would bring up two children.*

Mair[1] in a mair[2] dish.

1721 KELLY 247 . . . That is, a great deal more;
an answer to them who ask you if you will
have any more, when you have gotten but
very little. [[1] more. [2] bigger.]

Mair lost at Sherramuir, There was | where the Hielandman lost his faither and his mither, and a gude buff-belt worth baith o' them.

1814 SCOTT *Waverley* xlvii His death was
lamented by few. Most . . . agreed in the
pithy observation . . . that there 'was mair
tint (lost) at Sheriff-Muir'.[1] [[1] where a battle
was fought, near Stirling, in the Jacobite
rebellion of 1715.]

Mair tint[1] at Flodden,[2] There was.

1820 SCOTT *Monast.* x The Fife men say, an
the whole pack of ye were slain, there were
more lost at Flodden. [[1] lost. [2] Battle of
Flodden, 1513.]

Make a fire well, He that can | can end a quarrel.

1640 HERBERT 343.

Make a hog or a dog of it (a thing).

1670 RAY 217. **1721** KELLY 252 *The English,
Make a hog or a dog of it:* . . . means, bring it
either to one use, or another.

Make a poor man a knight, It is little of God's might to.

[JUVENAL *Sat.* 7. 197. *Si fortuna volet, fies
de rhetore consul.*] **1641** FERGUSSON 64. **1721**
KELLY 182.

Make a shift, I will | as Macwhid did with the preaching.

1721 KELLY 188 . . . Alexander Macwhid was
a knowing countryman. . . . At the Restora-
tion, clergymen being scarce, Bishop Taylor
ask'd him if he thought he could preach, he
answered that he could *Make a shift.* . . . The
proverb is spoken when we promise to do as
well as we can.

Make a spoon or spoil a horn, He will.

[= achieve success or be a failure.] **1818**
SCOTT *Rob Roy* xxii Mr. Osbaldistone is a
gude honest gentleman; but I aye said he was
ane o' them wad make a spune or spoil a horn.
1820 BYRON to Murray 23 Apr. I can't
cobble: I must make a spoon or spoil a horn—
and there's an end. **1892** *Boys Own Paper*
Dec. 87/1 Your son . . . will turn out something some day. He'll make a spoon or spoil
a horn.

Make ab or warp of the business as soon as you can.

1659 HOWELL *Eng. Prov.* 17/1 . . . *A metaphor
taken from weavers.*

Make ado and have ado.

1678 RAY 70.

Make an end of your whistle, though the cart overthrow, You will.

1678 RAY 276.

Make faces, see God or a painter, for he m. f.

Make haste slowly.

[Gk. Σπεῦδε βραδέως. L. *Festina lente.* AUGUS-
TUS in *Suet.* 2. 25] *c.* **1374** CHAUCER *Troylus*
I. 956 He hasteth wel that wisly can abide.
1590 LODGE *Rosalynde* Wks. (1883) I. 123
Festina Lente, especially in Loue: for momen-
tarie fancies are ofttimes the fruites of follies.
1663 BUTLER *Hudibras* I. iii. 1253 (1854) 107
Festina lente, Not too fast; For haste (the
proverb says) makes waste. **1694** SOAME in
Dryden Misc. 4. 157 Gently make haste.
1744 FRANKLIN Apr. Make haste slowly.
1907 *Spectator* 12 Jan. 43 'Hasten slowly'
is a very good motto in Imperial politics.

Make haste to an ill way, that you may get out of it.

1640 HERBERT 322.

Make hay while the sun shines.

1509 A. BARCLAY *Ship of Fools* (1874) II. 46
Who that in July whyle Phebus is shynynge

About his hay is nat besy labourynge . . .
Shall in the wynter his negligence bewayle.
1546 HEYWOOD I. iii. 6 Whan the sunne
shinth make hay. **1583** MELBANCKE *Philotimus* 24 Yt is well therefor to make hay
while the sunne shines. **1590–1** SHAKS. *3 Hen.*
VI IV. viii. 61 The sun shines hot; and, if
we use delay, Cold biting winter mars our
hop'd-for hay. **1636** CAMDEN 302 Make hay
while Sun shines. **1835** MRS. CARLYLE *Lett.*
July 'It is good to make hay while the sun
shines', which means, in the present case, . . .
to catch hold of a friend while she is in the
humour. **1853** TRENCH iii. 64 *Make hay while*
the sun shines, is truly English, and could
have had its birth only under such variable
skies as ours.

Make me a diviner and I will make thee rich.

1573 SANDFORD (1576) 212. **1578** FLORIO
First Fruites f. 30 (A). **1629** *Book of Meery*
Riddles Prov. 111. **1732** FULLER no. 3315
(with 'Sooth-sayer' for 'diviner').

Make much of nought.

1639 CLARKE 314. **1678** RAY 347 You love to
make much of naught (*your self*). **1738** SWIFT
(Dial. i) 336 *Never*. Come, come, Miss, make
much of nought; good folks are scarce.

Make much of one, good men are scarce.

1631 PHIN. FLETCHER *Sicelides* III. iv. Wks.
(1908) I. 224 *Can.* Good men are scanty,
make much of one, Cancrone. **1670** RAY 118.

Make much of what you have.

1639 CLARKE 129.

Make or mar.

c. **1420** LYDGATE *Assembly of Gods* 556
Neptunus, that dothe bothe make & marre.
1542 UDALL tr. *Erasm. Apoph.* 267 b Declaring that he was vtterly mynded to put al in
hasards to make or marre. **1594–5** SHAKS.
L.L.L. IV. iii. 191 *Cost.* Nay, it makes
nothing, sir. *King* If it mar nothing neither.
1599–1600 *A.Y.L.* I. i. 32 *Orl.* I am not
taught to make anything. *Oli.* What mar
you then Sir? **1604–5** *Othello* V. i. 4 It
makes us, or it mars us. **1613** DAY *Festivals*
vii (1615) 206 That Part of a Woman which
either makes all, or marres all, I meane her
Tongue. **1885** MRS. C. PRAED *Affinities* II. xii.
5 As for Lady Romer's scheme, it is not my
business to make or mar it.

Make sport, He that cannot | should mar none.

1662 J. WILSON *Cheats* II. ii (1874) 37 If I can
make no sport, I'll mar none. **1721** KELLY
143.

Make the crow a pudding, You look as if you would.

c. **1598** DELONEY *Gentle Craft* II. iii Let no
man . . . say thou gauest the crow a pudding,
because loue would let thee liue no longer.
1598–9 SHAKS. *Hen. V* II. i. 91 By my troth,
he'll yield the crow a pudding one of these

days . **1678** RAY 237 You look as if you
would make the crow a pudding, *i.e.* die.
1721 KELLY 167 *He owes a pudding to the*
glade.[1] Spoken of a poor weak beast which
we suspect to be a dying. [[1] kite.]

Make up one's mouth, To.

1546 HEYWOOD I. xi Here with all his wife to
make vp my mouthe, Not onely hir husbandes
tauntyng tale auouthe, But therto deuiseth
to cast in my téeth, Checks and chokyng
oysters. **1584** COGAN *Haven Health* (1636) 170
Commonly at great feasts . . . they use to
serve vp sturgeon last, as it were to make up
the mouth.

Make your bed, As you | so you must lie on it.

c. **1590** G. HARVEY *Marginalia* (1913) 88
Lett them . . . go to there bedd, as themselues
shall make it. **1640** HERBERT 333 He that
makes his bed ill, lies there. **1721** KELLY 16
As you make your bed, so you lie down. According to your conditions you have your bargain.
1881 D. C. MURRAY *Joseph's Coat* XXX 'You
have made your bed', says the . . . proverb
. . . lie upon it.' But it is no easier to lie upon
it because the briars between the sheets were
put there by your own hands.

Make, To, *see also under significant words*
following.

Make (a, the, your), *see also under significant*
words following.

Make not (a, the, thy), *see also under significant words following.*

Makes a good war, He that | makes a good peace.

1640 HERBERT 337. **1732** FULLER no. 2230.

Makes a thing too fine, He that | breaks it.

1640 HERBERT 338.

Makes himself a sheep, He that | shall be eaten by the wolf.

1583 MELBANCKE *Philotimus* Bb 4 (A) He . . .
that needes be a sheep, cannot greatly grudge
to be bitten with a fox. **1611** DAVIES Prov. 55
'If men become sheepe, the wolfe will
deuoure them'. **1617** MORYSON *Itin.* III. i. 25
(1907–8) III. 400 According to the Italian
proverb: *Chi pecora si fa, il Lupo se la*
mangia. The man who makes himself a
sheep, The wolf will eat, whilst he doth sleep.
1651 HERBERT 367. **1670** RAY 141 . . . Qui se
fait brebis le loup le mange. *Gall.* He that is
gentle and puts up affronts and injuries shall
be sure to be loaden.

Makes his mistress a goldfinch, He that | may find her a wagtail.

1589 LYLY *Midas* I. i. 82 If therfore thou
make not thy mistres a goldfinch, thou mayst
chance to find her a wagtaile. **1647** *Countrym.*
New Commonwealth 8 He that makes his
Mistresse a goldfinch, may perhaps finde her

a wagtaile. **1832** HENDERSON 61 Mak your
wife a goodspink and she'll turn a water-
wagtail.

Makes much of his painted sheath (sheets), He.

c. **1520** WHITTINGTON *Vulg.* (E.E.T.S.) 105 He
is not a lytle proude of his paynted sheythe
and loketh of a heyght. **1562** HEYWOOD *Three
Hundred Epigrams* no. 71 Thou makst much
of thy peynted sheathe, and wylt do, It
hauynge not one good knyfe longyng therto.
1641 FERGUSSON 52 *Of proud persons.* He
makes meikle of his painted sheits.

Makes no mistakes, He who | makes nothing.

1911 *Times Wkly.* 3 Nov. 883 Of course, he
has made mistakes such as all men make who
ever make anything. **1925** *Times* 9 Nov. 17/4
The comforting assurance that 'a man who
never makes mistakes never makes anything'.

Malady, *see* Much meat much m.

Malice hurts itself most.

1572 HARVEY *Marginalia* 103 Malice drinkith
upp the greatist part of her owne poyson.
1639 CLARKE 197. **1732** FULLER no. 3327 (as
1572).

Malice is mindful.

c. **1600** *Edmund Ironside* l. 1387 Remember
this, malice hath a perfect memory. **1639**
CLARKE 196. **1721** KELLY 249 . . . Spoken
when people rip up old sores, and think, with
resentment, upon old disobligations. **1732**
FULLER no. 3329.

Malice, *see also* Injury is measured by m.;
More m. than matter.

Malkin's[1] maidenhood.

1377 LANGLAND *P. Pl.* B. i. 181–2 Ʒe ne haue
na more meryte. in masse ne in houres,[2]
Than Malkyn of hire maydenhode. that no
man desireth. *c.* **1386** CHAUCER *Cant. T.* B[1] 30
Tyme . . . wol nat come agayn, withouten
drede, Namoore than wole Malkynes mayden-
hede. [[1] a wanton slattern. [2] services of the
church.]

Malkin, *see also* Maids than M. (More).

Malt is above meal (wheat) with him.

[= he is drunk.] **1546** HEYWOOD I. xi. 25
Malt is aboue wheate with him market men
saie. **1626** BRETON *Fantastickes* B 3 Haruest.
Malt is now aboue wheat with a number of
mad people. **1641** FERGUSSON 98 The malt
is above the beir. **1824** SCOTT *Redg.* xii
'Come, Provost,' said the lady rising, 'if the
maut gets abune the meal with you, it is
time for me to take myself away.' **1891**
A. FORBES *Bar. Biv. & Bat.* (1910) 62 As he
marched home from the little public-house . . .
with 'the malt abune the meal', his effort to
appear preternaturally sober was quite a
spectacle.

Malt, *see also* Kiln of m. is on fire; Sit in
the chair that have m. to sell; Soft fire
sweet m.

Malt-man comes on Monday, The.

1600 DRAYTON *Oldcastle* III. iii. 27 Be mery,
wench, the mault-man comes on munday.
? **1622** J. TAYLOR (Water-P.) *Trav. Twelve-
pence* (1630) 70 The Malt-man came on
Munday, & would haue me. **1659** HOWELL
Eng. Prov. 9/2.

Malt-man (men), *see also* Merry when m.
meet; Worst world that ever was, m. got
his sack again.

Malvern Hill, Go dig at.

1564–5 *Stationers' Register* (Arb.) i. 270 . . . to
men of suche Willes that are so Redy to
Dygge vp Malbron hilles [a ballad]. **1659**
HOWELL *Eng. Prov.* 20. **1790** GROSE s.v.
Worcestershire.

Malvern, *see also* Sip up the Severn and
swallow M.

Man alone is either a saint or a devil, A.

1621 BURTON *Anat. Mel.* I. ii. II. vi. (1651) 90
As the saying is; *homo solus aut deus, aut
dæmon*; a man, alone, is either a saint or a
devil.

Man among the geese when the gander is away, You are a.

1670 RAY 177. *Chesh.*

Man assaulted is half taken, A.

1573 SANDFORD (1576) H 3ᵛ. **1629** *Book of
Meery Riddles* Prov. 22. **1642** TORRIANO 59
(with 'set upon' for 'assaulted'). [Cf. A man
surprised is half beaten, **1732** FULLER no. 310.]

Man at five may be fool at fifteen, A.

1721 KELLY 10 . . . A pregnant, pert, witty
child, may prove but a heavy worthless man.

Man at the wheel, *see* Speak to.

Man be at his own bridal, It is meet that a.

c. **1390** LANGLAND *P. Pl.* C. III. 56 And al the
riche retynaunce . that roteth hem on fals
lyuynge Were bede to that brudale. **1546**
HEYWOOD I. vi. 12 Ye know well it is, . . .
Méete, that a man be at his owne brydale.
1579 LYLY *Euphues* (Arb.) 85 But me thinkes
it is good reason, that I shoulde bee at mine
owne brideall, and not giuen in the Church,
before I knowe the Bridegroome.

Man before his mother, He will be a.

1721 KELLY 174 . . . Spoken to ill grown
children. **1888** STEVENSON *Black Arrow* iii
'I do but jest', said Dick. 'Ye'll be a man
before your mother, Jack.'

Man but his mind? What is a.

1639 CLARKE 16.

Man can die but once, A.

1597–8 SHAKS. *2 Hen. IV* III. ii. 250 A man
can die but once. **1606–7** *Ant. & Cleop.* IV.

xiv. 27 Death of one person can be paid but once. **1616** DRAXE 44 A man can die but one maner of death. **1708** PRIOR *Turlle & Spar.* With great submission I pronounce, That people die no more than once. **1840** MARRYAT *Olla Pod.* xii 'A man cannot die more than once', is an old apophthegm, ... but ... a man can die ... once professionally or legally, and once naturally.

Man can do no more than he can, A.

1530 PALSGRAVE 474 (A) No man can do above his power. **1670** RAY 67.

Man doth what he can, and God what He will.

1616 DRAXE 81. **1639** CLARKE 87.

Man every inch of him, A.

1605–6 SHAKS. *K. Lear* IV. vi. 109 Ay, every inch a king. **1630** CLARKE 247. **1678** RAY 76. **1892** HENLEY & STEVENSON *Adml. Guinea* I. ii He's a man every inch of him; but he can't endure Kit French.

Man far from his good is near his harm, A.

c. **1350** *Douce MS. 52* no. 12 Who is ferre from his disshe is nyhgh his harme. *c.* **1400** *MS. Latin no. 394 J. Rylands Libr.* (ed. Pantin) in *Bull. J. R. Libr.* XIV f. 6*v.* Who so is fer from his disch is nyȝe his harm. **1546** HEYWOOD II. ix. 75. **1614** CAMDEN 302. **1641** FERGUSSON 38 He that is far from his geir, is neir his skaith.

Man has done, Whatever | man may do.

1863 C. READE *Hard Cash* xxix 'Whatever man has done man may do', said Dr. Sampson stoutly.

Man has his hour, and a dog his day, A. (See also Dog has his day.)

c. **1525–9** *Godly Queen Hester* (Greg) 26. **1633** JONSON *T. Tub* II. i Right! vor a man has his hour, and a dog his day.

Man has no more goods than he gets good of, A.

1641 FERGUSSON 10. **1721** KELLY 25 ... What a man enjoys of his substance is really his, the rest he has only the keeping of.

Man hath his mare again, All is well, and the.

1595–6 SHAKS. *Mids. N.* III. ii. 463 The man shall have his mare again, And all shall be well. **1647** J. FLETCHER *Chances* III. iv Why, the man has his mare again, and all's well. **1678** RAY 259. **1712** ADDISON *Spect.* No. 481 I am pleased with a porter's decision ... upon ... a virtuous woman's marrying a second husband, while her first was yet alive. ... [He] solves it ... by the old proverb, that if his first master be still living, 'The man must have his mare again.'

Man in the moon.

a. **1310** in WRIGHT *Lyric P.* xxxix. 110 This ilke mon upon heh when er he were, wher he were ythe mone boren ant y-fed. *c.* **1374** CHAUCER *Troylus* I. 1024 þou hast a ful grete care Lest þat þe Cherl wole falle out of þe mone. *c.* **1449** PECOCK *Repr.* II. iv (Rolls) 155 A man which stale sumtyme a birthan of thornis war sett in to the moone there forto abide for euere. *a.* **1548** HALL *Chron. Rich. III* 37 When the quene had heard this frendely mocion (which was as farre from her thought as the man that the rude people saie is in the moone). **1594–5** SHAKS. *L.L.L.* V. ii. 215 Yet still she is the moon, and I the man. **1595–6** *Mids. N.* V. 249 Myself the man i' the moon do seem to be. **1611–12** *Tempest* II. i. 257 The man i' the moon's too slow. *Ibid.* II. ii. 142 I was the man in the moon, when time was. **1621** LAUD *Serm.* 19 June 24 These conuerted Iewes must meet out of all Nations: the ten Tribes as well as the rest ... Men in the Moone. **1778** FRANCES BURNEY *Evelina* (1920) I. 202 'He'd no more right to our money than the man in the moon'. **1866** *John Bull* 1 Sept. 584/1 Mr. Mum, the man in the moon, who, he said was a necessary consequence of a Totnes election.

Man in the oak.

[= a spirit supposed to inhabit an oak.] **1584** R. SCOT *Discov. Witchcr.* VII. xv (1886) 122 Robin Goodfellow, the spoorne,[1] the mare, the man in the oke. **1604** MIDDLETON *Witch* I. ii Dwarfes, Imps, ... the Man i' th' oake. [[1] spectre, phantom.]

Man in the street, The.

1831 GREVILLE *Mem.* 22 Mar. (1874) II. 131 The other [side affirms] that the King will not consent to it, knowing, as 'the man in the street' (as we call him at Newmarket) always does, the greatest secrets of kings. **1844** EMERSON *Essays* II Self-reliance. But the man in the street, finding no worth in himself which corresponds to the force which built a tower or sculptured a marble god, feels poor when he looks on these. **1850** Id. *Representative Men* VI Napoleon. The man in the street finds in him [Napoleon] the qualities and powers of other men in the street. **1854** Id. *Lett. and Soc. Aims.* Wks. (Bohn) III. 192 The speech of the man in the street is invariably strong. **1909** *Spectator* 22 May 808 The Socialist party ... are concerned only with the facts which meet the eye of 'the man in the street'.

Man is a bubble.

[Gk. Πομφόλυξ ὁ ἄνθρωπος. ERASM. *Ad. Homo bulla.*] **1539** TAVERNER 34 *Homo bulla.* Man is but a bubble, or bladder of the water. **1651** JER. TAYLOR *Holy Dying* (1850) I. i. 299 A man is a bubble, (said the Greek proverb) which Lucian represents ... saying, that all the world is like a storm, and men rise up in their several generations, like bubbles descending à *Jove pluvio*, from God and the dew of heaven, from a tear and a drop of rain, from nature and Providence.

Man is a god or a devil to his neighbour. (Cf. Man is to man a god.)

1639 CLARKE 137.

Man is a lion in his own (a good) cause, A.

1641 FERGUSSON 12. **1721** KELLY 6 . . . No man so zealous for, or assiduous in, a man's business, as himself. **1732** FULLER no. 1907 He is a lion in a good cause.

Man is a man though he have but a hose on his head, A.

c. **1386** CHAUCER *Can. Yeom. T.* 724 Now may I were an hose upon myn heed. **1599** PORTER *Angry Wom. Abingd.* II. i (Merm.) 126 I am your father's man, and a man's a man, an a have but a hose on his head. **1620** SHELTON *Quix.* II. lxv (1908) III. 282 'No more of that, sir,' said Sancho; 'a man is a man, though he have but a hose on his head.' **1708** DYKES *Mor. Reflect. Prov.* 255 A man is a man still, if he hath but a hose on his head. . . . We may sometimes chance to meet with a Diogenes in rags.

Man is as old as he feels, and a woman as old as she looks, A.

1907 *Illus. Lond. News* 25 May The adage that a man is as old as he feels, and a woman as old as she looks, may be said to contain much inherent truth.

Man is friended, As a | so the law is ended.

1538 T. STARKEY *England* (Cowper) I. iii. 86 For (as hyt ys commynly and truly also sayd) 'materys be endyd as they be frendyd'. **1614** CAMDEN 303.

Man is known to be mortal by two things, sleep and lust, A.

1651 HERBERT 371.

Man is not a horse because he was born in a stable, A.

1829–30 M. SCOTT *T. Cring. Log* iv An Englishman . . . born in Buenos Ayres . . . having joined the patriots, this brought treason home to him. . . . 'Truly, . . . *a man does sometimes become a horse by being born in a stable.*' **1906** *Times Lit. Sup.* 27 Apr. Except on the principle that the man who is born in a stable is a horse, [Lever] was not an Irishman at all.

Man is the head, but woman turns it.

1875 A. B. CHEALES *Prov. Folk-Lore* 12 (A). **1917** BRIDGE 93.

Man is the measure of all things.

[PLATO *Cratylus* 4. Πάντων χρημάτων μέτρον εἶναι ἄνθρωπον.] **1631** CHAPMAN *Caesar & Pompey* II. iv. 117 As of all things man is said the measure, So your full merits measure forth a man. **1908** A. C. BENSON *At Large* iv. 72 The old world . . . held that all things were created for man. . . . This philosophy was summed up in the phrase that *man was the measure of all things.* **1924** R. W. LIVINGSTONE *Greek Genius* 111 It is the human standpoint towards life; . . . we may sum it up in the

saying attributed to Protagoras, ἄνθρωπος μέτρον πάντων—Man is the measure of all things.

Man is to man a god.

[Gk. *Ἄνθρωπος ἀνθρώπῳ δαιμόνιον*. CAECILIUS STATIUS *Fragment* 16, *Homo homini deus est, si suum officium sciat,* Man is a god to his fellow-man, if he know his duty.] **1548** HALL *Chron.* (1809) 324 The olde Greke prouerbe . . . that a man, to a man shall sometyme be as a God, for the young erle Henry[1] . . . by the labor of Ihon Cheulet, . . . was preserued, saved, and deliuered. [[1] Henry of Richmond.]

Man is to man a wolf (*Homo homini lupus*).

[PLAUTUS *As.* 2. 4. 88. ERASM. *Ad.*] **1569** C. AGRIPPA *Vanity of Arts & Sciences* tr. Sandford (1575) 124 Man (as the Prouerbe saith) is a woulfe to man. **1596** T. LODGE *Wit's Misery* B 1 The old Prouerbe . . . that *Homo est homini dæmon,* Man vnto man is a deuill. **1621** BURTON *Anat. Mel.* I. i. I. i. (1651) 4 The greatest enemy to man is man, who, by the devil's instigation, is . . . a wolf, a devil to himself and others. **1662** FULLER (*Merioneth*) III. 547 It is my desire, that . . . the people . . . give no longer occasion to the proverb, 'Homo homini lupus'. **1785** COWPER *The Task* iv Wks. (1836) VII. 38 I mourn the pride and avarice that make man a wolf to man. **1888** J. E. T. ROGERS *Econ. Interp. Hist.* (1894) II. xvi. 341 '*Homo homini lupus*', said Plautus. . . . This is the comment in which the historical relations of man to man have been . . condensed.

Man is to man either a god or a wolf.

1603 FLORIO tr. *Montaigne* III. v (1897) V. 106 It is a match whereto may well be applied the common saying, *homo homini aut Deus aut Lupus* (ERAS. *Chil.* i. cent. i. 69, 70). *Man unto man is either a God or a Wolf.* **1612** WEBSTER *White Devil* IV. i (Merm.) 70 *Brach.* Thou hast led me, . . . To my eternal ruin. Woman to man Is either a god or a wolf.

Man is worth, As the | his land is worth.

1853 TRENCH vi. 133 *As the man is worth, his land is worth.* Man is lord of the outward conditions of his existence to a far greater extent than is commonly assumed; even climate, . . . it is in his power immensely to modify.

Man lives, As a | so shall he die, as a tree falls, so shall it lie.

[**1611** BIBLE *Eccles.* xi. 3 If the tree fall toward the south, or toward the north, in the place where the tree falleth, there it shall be.] **1549** LATIMER *Seven Sermons* (Arb.) 118 (A) Wheresoeuer the tree falleth . . . there it shall rest. *c.* **1550** *Howleglas* (Ouvry) 84 As men liue so is their end. **1669** PENN *No Cross, No Crown* xii As the tree falls, it lies; and as death leaves men, judgment finds them. **1678** RAY 296. **1836** M. SCOTT *Cruise of Midge* xiv It is of no use, . . . as the tree falls, so must it lie—it is a part of my creed.

Man of God is better for having his bows and arrows about him, The.

1659 HOWELL *Eng. Prov.* 2/1.

Man of straw is worth a woman of gold, A.

1591 FLORIO *Second Frutes* 173 (A) (with 'more worth than' for 'worth'). 1615 DANIEL *Hymen's Tri.* Idolatrize not so that sex but hold A man of straw more than a wife of gold. 1670 RAY 49 A man of straw is worth a woman of gold. . . . *Un homme de paille vaut une femme d'or.*

Man of, *see also* Beware of m. o. one book; Gladness seldom falls into madness; Great memory without learning; Many trades begs on Sunday; Three letters; Words and not deeds is like a garden full of weeds.

Man on the raft who thought the river-banks were moving and himself standing still, Like the.

1894 F. COWAN *Sea Provs.* 61 . . . Said of a man who sees everybody around him growing older and not himself.

Man or mouse.

1542 UDALL tr. *Erasm. Apoph.* 267 b He was vtterly mynded to put al in hasard to make or marre, & to bee manne or mous. *c.* 1622 FLETCHER *Love's Cure* II. ii I will make a man, or a mouse on you. 1869 TENNYSON *North. Farmer,* N.S. ii Doesn't thou know that a man mun be either a man or a mouse?

Man proposes, God disposes.

[*Prov.* xvi. 9 (Vulgate) *Cor hominis disponit uiam suam; sed Domini est dirigere gressus eius.*—*De Imitatione Christi,* Rib. i. c. 19 *Homo proponit, sed Deus disponit.*] 1377 LANGLAND *P. Pl.* B. xi. 36, 37 *Homo proponit,* quod a poete . and Plato he hyght, And *Deus disponit,* quod he . lat God done his wille. *c.* 1450 tr. *De Imitatione* I. xix For man purposiþ & god disposiþ. 1612 SHELTON *Quix.* II. lv But man purposeth and God disposeth. 1625 PURCHAS *Pilgrims* (1905–7) XIX. 506, 7 The Zelanders . . . coined . . . money . . . with this sentence: Man purposeth, God disposeth. 1641 FERGUSSON 78 Man propous, but God dispous. 1655–62 GURNALL *Chrn. in Armour* (1865) II. 360 Whatever will thou makest, God is sure to be thy executor. Man may propose and purpose, but God disposeth. 1853 TRENCH iii. 66 *Man proposes, God disposes;* . . . every nation in Europe possesses.

Man punishes the action, but God the intention.

1732 FULLER no. 3332.

Man sleeps, When a | his head is in his stomach.

1640 HERBERT 362.

Man that sought his mare, and he riding on her, You are like the.

1721 KELLY 363 . . . Spoken to them that are seeking what they have about them.

Man without a smiling face must not open a shop, A.

1928 *Times* 29 May 10/1 The Chinese, who are masters of condensed philosophy, have a maxim which runs: 'A man without a smiling face must not open a shop.'

Man without money is no man at all, A.

1592 G. DELAMOTHE (1647) 56 (with '. . . is a body without a soule'). 1659 N. R. 17 A man without money is a bodye without life. 1732 FULLER no. 317.

Man without reason is a beast in season, A.

1659 HOWELL *Eng. Prov.* 11/2. 1670 RAY 22. 1732 FULLER no. 6244.

Man without religion is like a horse without a bridle, A.

[L. *Homo sine religione, sicut equus sine fraeno.*] 1621 BURTON *Anat. Mel.* III. iv. I. ii (1651) 646 Justice and religion are the two chief props . . . of a . . . commonwealth: . . . as Sabellicus delivers, *a man without religion is like an horse without a bridle.*

Man, woman, and devil, are the three degrees of comparison.

1732 FULLER no. 3335.

Man's extremity is God's opportunity.

1629 T. ADAMS *Serm.* (1861–2) I. 96 Here is now a delivery fit for God, a cure for the almighty hand to undertake, Man's extremity is God's opportunity. 1706 LD. BELHAVEN *Speech in Scot. Parl. on Union,* 2 Nov. Man's extremity is God's opportunity. . . . Some unforeseen providence will fall out, that may cast the balance. 1916 E. A. BURROUGHS *Valley of Decis.* (1920) viii. 197 This was . . . a typical case of 'Man's extremity, God's opportunity'.

Man (men), *see also* Hand of m. (Whatever is made by) . . . may be overturned; Living m. (No) all things can; Remember thou art but a m.; Show me not (Look not on) the meat but the m.; Show me the m., and I'll show the law; To-day a m., to-morrow a mouse.

Man (men), *see also these preceded by one of the following adjectives:* All, Angry, Another, Black, Blind, Bold, Brown, Busiest, Choleric, Cornish, Crafty, Crooked, Dead, Deaf, Discontented, Drowning, Drunken, Dumb, Envious, Every, Fat, Foolish, Full, Good, Grateful, Gravest, Great, Greedy, Happy, Hasty, Hated, Healthful, Honest, Hungry, Idle, Ill, Ingenious, Last, Leeful, Liberal, Long, Low, Manchester, Married, Mercenary, Merry, Mighty, Miserable, Moneyless (Silverless), Naked, Nine, No, Old, One, Other, Pale, Patient, Poor, Properer, Rich, Sick, Silent,

Silly, Simple, Singing, Slothful, Sober, Solitary, Sullen, True, Two, Unhappy, Valiant, Waking, White, Wicked, Wight, Wilful, Wise, Wisest, Wrong, Young.

Man (cannot, had, has, is, may, must, never, shall as soon, were, will never, would), *see also under significant words following*.

Man's, A, *see* Destiny always dark; Discontent his worst evil; Gift makes room for him; House is his castle; Studies pass into character.

Manchester bred: long in the arms, and short in the head.

1869 HAZLITT 273. **1902–4** LEAN I. 119 Higson [*MS. Coll.*] 51.

Manchester men and Liverpool gentlemen.

1881 *N. & Q.* 6th Ser. III. 148 There is a common saying in Lancashire: 'A Liverpool gentleman, a Manchester man, a chap fra' Bought'n (Bolton), and a fella fra' Wiggin' (Wigan). **1908** E. M. SNEYD-KYNNERSLEY *H.M.I.* xxviii The commercial travellers, and others, speak of Manchester *men*, and Liverpool *gentlemen*.

Manchester, *see also* Constable of Openshaw.

Manful, *see* Mickle but not m.

Manger, *see* Dog in m.; Hungry horse clean m.; Rack and m.

Manned with boys, and horsed with colts, He that is | shall have his meat eaten, and his work undone.

1623 CAMDEN 270. **1670** RAY 118. **1721** KELLY 169 . . . Because the boy will neglect his business, and the horse will throw him.

Manners and money make a gentleman.

1732 FULLER no. 3333.

Manners know distance.

1648 HERRICK *Hesper., To Sir L. Pemb.* Wks. (Aldine) I. 189 Manners knowes distance, and a man unrude, Wo'd soon recoile, and not intrude His Stomach to a second Meale.

Manners make often fortunes.

1539 TAVERNER (1545) E 5ᵛ *Sui cuique mores fingunt fortunam.* A mans owne maners do shape hym his fortune. **1597** *Politeuphuia* 166 b A mans owne manners doth shape him his fortunes. **1664** CODRINGTON 206. **1670** RAY 17.

Manners maketh (make the) man.

c. **1350** *Douce MS. 52* no. 75 Maner makys man. *c.* **1460** *Prov. of Wisdom* (ed. Zupitza) in *Archiv. f. d. Stud. d. Neueren Sprachen* 90. 245 Euer maner and clothyng makyth man. **1509** BARCLAY *Ship of Fools* 118 An olde prouerbe . . . Sayth that good lyfe and maners makyth man. **1605** *London Prodigal* I. ii

(*Shaks. Apoc.*) 196 *Wea.* For thers an old saying: . . . Be he borne in barne or hall, Tis maners makes the man and all. **1662** FULLER (*Hants*) II. 5 'Manners make a man' quoth William Wickham'.[1] This generally was his motto, inscribed frequently on the places of his founding. **1701** DEFOE *True-born Eng.* II. Wks. (Bohn) V. 444 Now, Satire, if you can, Their temper show, for manners make the man. **1721** KELLY 246 *Meat feeds, cloth cleeds, but manners makes the man* . . . Good meat, and fine clothes, without good breeding, are but poor recommendations. **1902** A. R. COLQUHOUN *Mastery of Pacif.* 252 It is the gravest mistake to . . . introduce the freedom of speech and laxity of manners characteristic of modern Europe and America into the East, whose people are still under the impression that 'manners makyth man'. [1 Bishop of Winchester, 1367–1404, founder of Winchester College and New College, Oxford.]

Manners, *see also* Evil m. (Of) spring good laws; Honours change m.; Little money as m. (If you had); Lordship (One good) is worth all his m.; Lordships change m.; Meat is much, m. is more; Men (Like) like m.; Mend his m. (Let him); Other times, other m. *See also* Good manners.

Manors, *see* Lordship (One good) is worth all his manners [= manors].

Many a little makes a mickle.

c. **1200** *Ancrene Riwle* 54 Thus ofte, ase me seith of lutel wacseþ muchel. **1614** CAMDEN 310. **1655** FULLER *Ch. Hist.* VI. v (1868) II. 311 Vast was the wealth accruing to the crown by the dissolution of chantries. 'Many a little', saith the proverb, 'make a mickle'. These foundations, though small in revenue, yet being many in number, mounted up a great bank. **1712** *Spectator* 14 Oct. **1721** KELLY 254 Many littles make a mickle. *Lat. Ex granis fit acervus.* **1758** FRANKLIN *Way to Wealth* (Crowell) 19 Remember, *Many a little makes a mickle*. **1844** CARLYLE to his mother, 24 Apr., in FROUDE, *Carlyle's Life in London* xii.

Many a man (one) serves a thankless master.

1620 SHELTON *Quix.* II. lxvi (1908) III. 286 That it may not be said, So a good servant, an ungrateful master. **1641** FERGUSSON 78. **1721** KELLY 248.

Many a man singeth that wife home bringeth; wist he what he brought, weep he might.

c. **1275** *Provs. of Alfred* A 15 264–7 (1907) 26 Monymon singeþ þat wif hom bryngeþ; wiste he hwat he brouhte, wepen he myhte. *c.* **1300** *Provs. of Hending* 18 Monimon syngeth, When he hom bryngeth Is yonge wyf; Wyste [he] whet he broghte, Wepen he mohte.

Many a one for land takes a fool by the hand.

c. **1300** *Provs. of Hending* 36 Monimon for

londe, Wyueth to shonde. **1639** CLARKE 99
For a little land, take a fool by the hand.
1678 RAY 56 Many an one for land takes a
fool by the hand, *i.e.* marries her or him.
1732 FULLER no. 6263.

Many a one says well that thinks ill.

1738 SWIFT (Dial. i) 335 *Never.* Well,
miss—— *Miss.* Ay, ay; many a one says well
that thinks ill.

Many a thing's made for money (the penny).

1591 LYLY *Endym.* II. ii *Epi.* Why it is a
squirrel. *Top.* A squirrel? O Gods, what
things are made for money! **1857** DEAN
RAMSAY *Remin.* V (1911) 203 *Mony a thing's
made for the pennie, i.e.* Many contrivances
are thought of to get money. *Ibid.* A ridiculous addition used to be made to the common
Scottish saying, *Mony a thing's made for the
pennie,* . . . 'As the old woman said when she
saw a black man'—taking it for granted that
he was an ingenious and curious piece of
mechanism made for profit.

Many dishes make many diseases.

1622 H. PEACHAM *The Complete Gentleman*
(1634, ed. G. S. Gordon) 228 Many dishes
breed many diseases. **1655** T. MUFFETT
Healths Improvement 272 (A) (quoted as
proverb).

Many drops make a shower.

1576 PETTIE *Petite Pall.* (Gollancz) I. 171.
1600 *The Maid's Metamorphosis* Prologue
Drops not diminish, but encrease great floods.
1624 BURTON *Anat. Mel.* I. ii. IV. vii (p. 151)
with 'make a flood'. **1846** DENHAM 1.

Many estates are spent in the getting, since women, for Tea, forsook spinning and knitting; and men, for Punch, forsook hewing and splitting.

1758 FRANKLIN in ARBER *Eng. Garner* V. 582.

Many fair promises in marriage making, but few in tocher[1] paying.

1641 FERGUSSON 98 There are many fair
words in the marriage making, but few in the
tochergood paying. **1721** KELLY 246 . . .
People will flatter you with fair promises and
proposals; till they get you engag'd in some
project for their interest, but after alter their
tune. [1 portion, dowry.]

Many friends, He that hath | eateth too much salt with his meat.

1659 HOWELL *Eng. Prov.* 19/1.

Many frosts and many thowes[1] make many rotten yowes.[2]

1846 DENHAM 62 [1 thaws. 2 ewes.]

Many 'Good nights' is loth away.

a **1721** PRIOR *Thief & Cord.* Wks. (1858) 190
And often took leave; but was loth to depart.

1721 KELLY 251 . . . Spoken by those who,
by reason of some accident, return after they
have taken their leave.

Many hands make light (quick, slight) work.

[ERASM. *Ad. Multae manus onus levius reddunt.*
Many hands make a burden lighter.] *c.* **1350**
Douce MS. 52 no. 70 Many hondys makyn
lygth worke. **14** . . *Sir Beues* 3012 (MS. M.)
Though Ascaparde be neuer so starke, Many
handes make lyght warke! *c.* **1470** *Harl. MS.
3362*, f. 76. Many handis makith lyth werk—
Multorum manus alleuiatur opus. **1539**
TAVERNER 36 Many handes make a lyghte
burthen. **1546** HEYWOOD II. v. 54 Many
handis make light warke. **1599** JAMES VI
Basil. Dor. (Roxb.) II. 60 Establish honest,
diligent, but few searchers (for manie handes
make slight worke). **1614** CAMDEN 309. **1616**
BRETON *Cross. Prov.* Wks. (1879) II, App. iii
Many hands make quick work. **1663** F.
HAWKINS *Youth's Behav.* 90 Many hands
make light work. **1678** BUTLER *Hudibras* III.
ii. 261 Most hands dispatch apace, and make
light work (the proverb says). **1721** KELLY
244 *Many hands make slight work.* Because,
while every one trusts to another, the work is
neglected. **1830** W. CARLETON *Irish Peasantry*
(1864) I. 37 Many hands make light work,
and . . . it wasn't long till they had cleared
a way for themselves.

Many haws, many sloes: many cold toes.

1846 DENHAM 16.

Many haws, many snaws.

1842 R. CHAMBERS *Pop. Rhymes Scot.* 37 Mony
hawes, Mony snaws. It is thus inferred that,
when there is a great exhibition of blossoms
on the hedgerows, the ensuing winter will be
remarkable for snowstorms. . . . A provi-
dential object, . . . to supply food for the
birds in the coming season. **1846** DENHAM 24
Many hips and haws, many frosts and snaws.

Many-headed beast [= the multitude], The.

1531 ELYOT *The Governor* (Crofts) i. 9 A
monster with many heedes. **1539** R. TAVERNER
Garden of Wisdom Bk. ii F.V That beast of
manye heddes I meane . . . the people, for
so . . . Horace calleth them. **1734** POPE *Imit.
Horace* Ep. I. i. 121 (A) The people are a
many-headed beast.

Many heads are better than one.

1721 KELLY 247.

Many hounds may soon worry[1] one hare.

1639 CLARKE 56 Many dogs may easily worry
one. **1721** KELLY 245 . . . Spoken when a
potent family, with their friends, relations,
and followers, bear hard upon a poor man.
[1 kill.]

Many irons in the fire, part (some) must cool.

1549 SIR W. PAGET *Let. to Somerset* 7 July

(P.R.O., St. Pap. Dom. Edw. VI. viii. No. 4) Put no more so many yrons in the fyre at ones. **1624** CAPT. SMITH *Virginia* iv. 159 They that have many Irons in the fire, some must burne. **1641** FERGUSSON 76 Mony yrons in the fire part mon coole. **1721** KELLY 255 ... When men have too many works in hand, too many offices, or employments, some must be neglected. **1881** WESTALL *Old Factory* iii Dr. Leatherlad was ... by no means a bad teacher, but having many irons in the fire ... he had to leave his scholars ... pretty much to their own devices.

Many kinsfolk and few friends.

1546 HEYWOOD I. xi Many kynsfolke and few fréends, some folke saie. But I fynde many kynsfolke, and fréende not one. **1621** BURTON *Anat. Mel.* III. i. II. ii (1651) 421 The love of kinsmen is grown cold, 'many kinsmen (as the saying is) few friends'. **1670** RAY 94 ... Ones kindred are not always to be accounted ones friends. **1721** KELLY 251 *Many aunts, many emms,[1] many kinsfolk, few friends.* Spoken by them that have many rich friends, and are little the better for them. [[1] relations.]

Many lords, many laws.

1616 DRAXE 7.

Many means to get money.

1639 CLARKE 191.

Many meet the gods, but few salute them.

[L. *Occurrit cuicunque Deus paucique salutant.*] **1853** TRENCH vi. 134 *Many meet the gods, but few salute them.* How often do the gods ... meet men in ... a sorrow which might be a purifying one, ... a joy which might elevate their hearts to thankfulness and praise; and yet how few ... *salute* them.

Many men have many minds.

[TER. *Phorm.* 2. 4. 14. *Quot homines tot sententiae.*] *c.* **1387** CHAUCER *Squire's T.* 202 As many hedes, as many wittes ther ben. **1596** SPENSER *F. Q.* IV. v. 11 Diverse wits affected divers beene.

Many rains, many rowans;[1] many rowans, many yawns.[2]

1846 DENHAM 54 [[1] Rowans are the fruit of the mountain ash; and an abundance thereof is held to denote a deficient harvest. [2] Light grains of wheat, oats, or barley.]

Many small make a great.

c. **1386** CHAUCER *Parson's T.* 362 For the proverbe seith that 'manye smale maken a greet'. **1546** HEYWOOD I. xi. 30 Here some and there some, many small make a great.

Many strike on an anvil, When | they must strike by measure.

1670 RAY 17.

Many things grow in the garden that were never sown there.

[Sp. *c.* **1627** CORREAS *Vocab.* (1906) 207 Nace en la güerta lo que el hortelano no siembra. (*In the garden more grows than the gardener sows.*)] **1659** HOWELL *Span.-Eng.* 6. **1670** RAY 12. **1709-10** ADDISON *Tatler* No. 146 (1899) III. 174 That spurious crop of blessings and calamities which were never sown by the hand of the Deity, but grew of themselves. **1853** TRENCH iv. 92 *More springs in the garden than the gardener ever sowed* ... is a proverb ... for parents and teachers, that they lap not themselves in a false dream of security.

Many trades, A man of | begs his bread on Sunday.

1721 KELLY 5 ... A man of many trades seldom thrives so well, as he that sticks closely to one.

Many ventures make a full freight.

1616 DRAXE 5. **1670** RAY 17.

Many wells, many buckets.

1550 HEYWOOD II. vii. 70 But well wif well. Well well (quoth she) many wels, many buckets.

Many women, many words; many geese, many turds.

c. **1350** *Douce MS. 52* no. 69 There ben women, there ben wordis; there ben gese, there ben tordys. **1541** *Schoolho. of Women* 481 in HAZLITT *Early Pop. Poet.* iv. 123 Where many geese be, be many t—ds, And where be women, are many woords. **1678** RAY 64 Where there are women and geese there wants no noise.

Many words, many buffets.

1546 HEYWOOD II. vii. 70 Ye (quoth he) and many woords, many buffets. Had you some husband, and snapte at him thus, I wys he would geue you a recumbentibus.[1] [[1] knockdown blow.]

Many words, In | the truth goeth by.

1545 TAVERNER B₅ᵛ Oure *Englyshe* prouerbe ... where many wordes be, the truth goeth by. **1548** HALL *Chron.* Dedn. (A) I haue redde an olde proverbe, whiche saithe, that in many woordes, a lye or twayne sone maie escape. **1616** DRAXE 11 Where many words are the truth often goeth by.

Many (a, a man, a one, can, have been, men), *see also under significant words following.*

Mar, *see* Make or m.

March borrowed from April three days, and they were ill.

1646 BROWNE *Pseudo. Epi.* VI. iv (A) So it is usual among us ... to ascribe unto March certain borrowed days from April. **1670** RAY 41 April borrows three days from March and they are ill. **1721** KELLY 252 *March borrowed from Averil Three days, and they were ill.* It is alleg'd that the first three days of *April* are commonly rough and intemperate, like *March*, and these we call the borrowing days. **1731** *Poor Robin's Alm.* Obs. on April ... There is an old proverb . . . viz. *March borrow'd of April three Days and they were ill, They kill'd three Lambs were playing on a hill.* **1847** R. CHAMBERS *Pop. Rhymes Scot.* 368 March borrowed from April Three days, and they were ill: The first o' them was wind and weet; The second o' them was snaw and sleet; The third o' them was sic a freeze, It froze the birds' nebs to the trees.

March comes in like a lion and goes out like a lamb.

1624 J. FLETCHER *Wife for Month* II. i *Me.* I would chuse March, for I would come in like a Lion. *To.* But you'ld go out like a Lamb, when you went to hanging. **1640** HOWELL *Dodona's G.* 10 Like the moneth of March, which entreth like a Lion, but goeth out like a Lamb. **1670** RAY 41 March hack ham comes in like a lion, goes out like a lamb. **1849** C. BRONTË *Shirley* xv Peter . . . had sense to feel that . . . he had better be civil. Like March, having come in like a lion, he purposed to go out like a lamb.

March comes in with adder heads, and goes out with peacock tails.

1721 KELLY 251.

March dust, A peck of | and a shower in May, makes the corn green and the fields gay.

1721 KELLY 43. **1732** FULLER no. 6476.

March dust (wind) and May sun, makes corn (clothes) white and maids dun.

1670 RAY 41 (with 'wind' and 'clothes'). **1846** DENHAM 39.

March dust is worth a king's ransom, A bushel (peck) of.

c. **1530** HEYWOOD *Play of Wether* 622 (Brandl) One bushell of march is worth a kynges raunsome. **1557** TUSSER cii A bushel of Marche dust, worth raunsomes of gold. **1662** FULLER (*Berks.*) I. 120 In England a bushel of March dust is worth a king's ransom. . . . A general good redounds to our land by a dry March. **1885** D. C. MURRAY *Rainbow G.* v. iv A neighbour . . . quoted the proverb that a peck of March dust is worth a king's ransom.

March grass never did good.

1678 RAY 44. **1732** FULLER no. 6475. **1908** *Sphere* 14 Mar. 233 Weather saws which the wintry weather has brought home . . . to us. 'March grass', says one of them, 'never did good'.

March in Janiveer, Janiveer in March I fear.

1678 RAY 44. **1908** *Sphere* 14 Mar. 233 'Janiveer in March I fear'. . . . This reminds one of . . . saws which the wintry weather has brought home . . . to us.

March, In | kill crow, pie,[1] and cadow,[2] rook, buzzard, and raven; or else go desire them to seek a new haven.

1846 DENHAM 35. [[1] magpie. [2] jackdaw.]

March many weathers.

1678 RAY 44.

March many weathers rained and blowed; but March grass never did good.

1732 FULLER no. 6475.

March sun causeth dust, The | and the winds blow it about.

1664 CODRINGTON 220. **1670** RAY 17.

March sun raises, but dissolves not, The.

1640 HERBERT 346.

March, In | the birds begin to search; in April the corn begins to fill; in May, the birds begin to lay.

1869 HAZLITT 233.

March, In | the cuckoo starts; in April, a' tune his bill; in May, a' sing all day; in June, a' change his tune; in July, away a' fly; in August, away a' must; in September, you'll *allers* remember; in October, 'ull never get over.

1849 HALLIWELL *Pop. Rhymes & Nurs. T.* 160 In April the cuckoo shows his bill; in May, he sings all day; in June, he alters his tune; in July, away he'll fly; in August, away he must. **1869** *N. & Q.* 4th Ser. III. 94. [East Anglia.]

March whisker[1] was never a good fisher.

1641 FERGUSSON 78 **1721** KELLY 255 . . . A windy March is a token of a bad fish year. **1732** FULLER no. 6127. **1842** R. CHAMBERS *Pop. Rhymes Scot.* 74 March whisker Was ne'er a gude fisher—. . . A blustering March is unfavourable to the angler, although good for the farmer. [[1] blusterer.]

March wind kindles (wakes) the adder and blooms the thorn (whin).

1846 DENHAM 39 March wind, kindles the ether,[1] and blooms the whin. [[1] adder.]

March, *see also* Fair M. king's ransom; February makes bridge, M. breaks it; First of M. crows begin to search; Frosts in M., so many in May; Mad as a M. hare; Windy M. and rainy April.

Mare hath a bald face, When the | the filly will have a blaze.[1]

1659 HOWELL *Eng. Prov.* 2/2. **1732** FULLER no. 5596. [[1] white mark on face.]

Mare's nest, To find a.

[= an illusory discovery.] **1576** R. PETERSON *Galateo* (1892) 111 (A) Nor stare in a mans face as if he had spied a mares nest. **1582** N. BRETON in *Works* (Gros.) I a 6 To laughe at a horse nest, and whine too like a boy. *a.* **1619** FLETCHER *Bonduca* V. ii Why dost thou laugh? What Mares nest hast thou found? **1721** KELLY 385 *You have found a horse nest.* Spoken to them who laugh without a cause. **1738** SWIFT (Dial. i) 337 *Nev.* What! you have found a mare's nest, and laugh at the eggs? **1892** *Times Wkly.* 21 Oct. 18/2 Colonel S.'s discovery is a mere mare's nest.

Mare's shoe and a horse's shoe are both alike, A.

1721 KELLY 34. **1732** FULLER no. 318.

Mare's tails, *see* Mackerel sky and m. t.

Mares in the wood than Grisell, There are more.

1678 RAY 173.

Mare(s), mear (*Scot.*), *see also* Biteth the m. by the thumb; Careless parting . . . m. and broken cart; Coy as a croker's m.; Fidging m. should be well girded; Flanders m.; Gip . . . quoth Badger, when his m. kicked; Grey m. is better horse; Lacks my m. (He that) would buy my m.; Man hath his m. again; Man that sought his m., and he riding on her; Miller's m. (Like a); Nag with a weamb, m. with nean; Old m. leave flinging (Hard to make); Old m. would have new crupper; Proo naunt your m. puts; Put the man to the mear that can manage; Ride who will, the m. is shod; Shoe the wild (mockish) m.; Whose m. is dead?

Marham, *see* Held together, as the men of M.

Mariners' craft is the grossest, yet of handicrafts the subtillest.

1573 SANDFORD (1576) 211.

Mariners, *see also* St. Paul's m.

Marines, *see* Tell that to the m.

Mark after her mother, She hath a.

1678 RAY 259 . . . That is, she is her mother's own daughter. *Patris est filius.*

Mark with a white stone, To.

[= to reckon as specially fortunate or happy, in allusion to the use of a white stone among the ancients as a memorial of a fortunate event. ERASM. *Ad. Creta notare, carbone notare.*] **1540** PALSGRAVE *Acolastus* K 1 O festyuall daye . . . worthye to be marked with a stone as whyte as snowe. *c.* **1645** HOWELL *Lett.* I. i. xiii (1890) 38 You are one . . . whose Name I haue mark'd with the whitest Stone. **1748** SMOLLETT *Rod. Rand.* lii 'God be praised! a white stone!' . . . he alluded to the *Dies fasti* of the Romans, *albo lapide notati.* **1885** HORNADAY *Two Yrs. in Jungle* xxvii. 318 I have marked that day with a white stone as being the one on which I ate my first durian.

Mark, *see also* Bigger the man, better the m.; God save the m.; Hit the prick (m.).

Marked, *see* Person m. (Take heed of).

Market cross, *see* Grass grows not at the m. c.

Market days, *see* Mickle between m. d.

Market goes, As the | wives must sell.

[*cf.* **1659** N.R. 78 Men must make there market as the time serves.] **1721** KELLY 52 with 'wares'. **1732** FULLER no. 734.

Market is the best garden, The.

1640 HERBERT 351. **1670** RAY 17 . . . *At London they are wont to say,* Cheapside is the best garden.

Market(s), *see also* Abide a bad m. (He that cannot); Buy in cheapest m.; Driving hogs (pigs, turkeys) to m.; Fool hath bethought himself (When), m.'s over; Fools went not to m. (If) bad wares not sold; Forsake not m. for the toll; Friend in the m.; Gentry sent to m. will not buy . . . corn; Good ware quick m.; Hogs to a fair m. (He hath brought); know how the m. goeth (Men); Lamentation of a bad m.; No man makes haste to m. where nothing . . . but blows; Run before one's horse to m.; Sell his ware after the m.; Three women make m.

Market-Jew, *see* Light (In your own), like the Mayor of M.

Market-place, *see* Kisseth his wife (*or* Sits to work) in the m. (He that).

Marls sand, He who | may buy the land.

1753 *Gent. Mag.* 120 (A) We have an old saying [Lancs.]: He that marls sand may buy land. **1917** BRIDGE 72 . . . The marl acted as manure and was . . . of most value on sandy soil. . . . The whole proverb stands thus: 'He that marls sand may buy the land, He that marls moss, shall have no loss, He that marls clay, flings all away.'

Marriage halves our griefs, doubles our joys, and quadruples our expenses.

1902–4 LEAN IV. 44.

Marriage is a lottery.

1605 MARSTON *The Dutch Courtesan* III. i. 73 Husbands are like lots in the lottery: you may draw forty blanks before you find one that has any prize in him. **1633** JONSON *T. Tub* I. i *Hugh.* I smile to think how like a lottery These weddings are. **1642** FULLER *H. & P. State* III. xxii (1841) 203 Marriage shall prove no lottery to thee, when the hand of Providence chooseth for thee; who, if drawing a blank, can turn it into a prize, by sanctifying a bad wife unto thee. **1875** SMILES *Thrift* 266 'Marriage is a lottery'. It may be so if we abjure the teachings of prudence. *a.* **1898** BURNE-JONES in his *Life* Isn't marriage a lottery? . . . Then shouldn't it be prohibited by law?

Marriage (Matrimony) is (comes by) destiny.

1548 HALL *Chron.* (1809) [Edw. IV] 264 Bot now consider the old prouerbe to be true yt saieth: that marriage is destinie. **1602-3** SHAKS. *All's Well* I. iii. 67 *Clo.* Your marriage comes by destiny. **1605** CHAPMAN *All Fools* v. i (1874) 74 *Go.* Give me your hand, there is no remedy, Marriage is ever made by destiny.

Marriage is honourable.

[*Hebrews* xiii. 4 Marriage is honourable in all, and the bed undefiled.] **1576** PETTIE *Petite Pall.* (Gollancz) I. 11 As amongst all the bonds of benevolence and goodwill there is none more honourable, ancient, or honest than marriage. **1598-9** SHAKS. *Much Ado* III. iv. 30 Is not marriage honourable in a beggar? *Ibid.* V. iv. 30 This day to be conjoin'd In the state of honourable marriage. **1616** BRETON *Cross. of Provs.* in Wks. (Gros.) II e 8 Marriage is honourable.

Marriage is honourable, but housekeeping is a shrew.

1670 RAY 48 Marriage is honourable, but house-keeping's a shrew. **1738** SWIFT (Dial. i) 340 *Lady S.* Mr. Neverout, marriage is honourable, but housekeeping is a shrew.

Marriage makes or mars a man.

1625 HOWELL *Lett.* 5 Feb. (1903) I. 248 You are upon a treaty of marriage. . . . A work of such consequence that it may make you or mar you. **1666** TORRIANO 143 *Who* marries, *either makes himself, or mars himself.* **1841** CAPT. MARRYAT *Poacher* xxviii Neither my Ophelia nor Amelia should marry . . . without I was convinced the gentleman considered it a very serious affair. It makes or mars a man, as the saying is.

Marriage, More belongs to | than four bare legs in a bed.

1550 HEYWOOD I. viii. 16 In house to kepe housholde, whan folks wyll néedis wed, Mo thyngs belong, than foure bare legs in a bed. **1631** JONSON *New Inn* v. i *Host.* Four thousand pound! that's better Than sounds the proverb, *four bare legs in a bed.* **1721** KELLY 234 *Long e'er four bare legs heat in a bed.* To dissuade people who have no stock from marrying. **1738** SWIFT (Dial. i) 340 *Lady A.* Consider, Mr. Neverout, four bare legs in a bed: and you are a younger brother. **1823** J. GALT *Entail* vii Now-a-days it's no the fashion for bare legs to come thegither—The wife maun hae something to put in the pot as well as the man.

Marriage, He has a great fancy to | that goes to the devil for a wife.

1732 FULLER no. 1856.

Marriage, In | the husband should have two eyes, and the wife but one.

1580 LYLY *Euph. & his Eng.* (Arb.) 284 In mariage, as market folkes tel me, the husband should haue two eies, and the wife but one.

Marriages and funerals, At | friends are discerned from kinsfolk.

1573 SANDFORD (1576) 205. **1629** *Book of Meery Riddles* Prov. 55. **1732** FULLER no. 829

Marriages are made in heaven.

1567 PAINTER *Pal. of Pleasure* (Jacobs) iii. 24 (A) True it is that marriage be don in heauen and performed in earth. **1580** LYLY *Euph. & his Eng.* (Arb.) 471 Mar[r]iages are made in heauen, though consum[m]ated in yearth [earth]. **1662** FULLER (*Westmr.*) II. 415 But that motion died with her father, heaven (wherein marriages are made) re-serving that place for Margaret. **1721** KELLY 183 If marriages be made in heaven, some had few friends there. **1738** SWIFT (Dial. i) 340 *Spark.* They say, marriages are made in heaven; but I doubt, when she was married, she had no friend there. **1853** TRENCH iii. 48 A proverb of such religious depth and beauty as . . . *Marriages are made in heaven*, it would have been quite impossible for all heathen antiquity to have produced.

Marriages in May, Of the | the bairns die of a decay.

[OVID *Fasti* 5. 490 *Mense malum Maio nubere vulgus ait.* People say it is ill to marry in the month of May.] **1821** GALT *Annals of Par.* vi [We] were married on the 29th day of April . . . on account of the dread that we had of being married in May, for it is said, 'Of the marriages in May, The bairns die of a decay'.

Marriage(s), *see also* Death and m. make term day; Ill m. spring of ill fortune; Keep your eyes open before m.; Like blood . . . makes happiest m.; Money makes m.; Motions are not m.; Weasel and cat make m. (When), evil presage.

Married at Finglesham Church, To be.

1736 PEGGE *Kenticisms, Prov.* (E.D.S.) 71 . . . There is no church at Finglesham; but a chalk-pit celebrated for casual amours; of which kind of rencounters the saying is us'd.

Married man turns his staff into a stake, A.

1640 HERBERT 334. **1670** RAY 17 The married man must turn his staff into a stake.

Married men, *see* Bachelors laugh.

Married to the gunner's daughter, To be.

[= to be lashed to a ship's gun for punishment.] 1821 BYRON in MOORE *Lett.* (1833) 139 As ... Captain Whitby ... used to say to his seamen (when 'married to the gunner's daughter')—'two dozen, and let you off easy'. 1833 MARRYAT *P. Simple* xxxii I'll marry some of you young gentlemen to the gunner's daughter.

Married woman has nothing of her own but her wedding-ring and her hair-lace, A.

1738 SWIFT (Dial. iii) 351 *Lady S.* They say a married woman has nothing of her own but her wedding-ring and her hair-lace: but if women had been the law-makers, it would have been better.

Marries a widow and three children, He that | marries four thieves.

1670 RAY 51. 1721 KELLY 137 *He that marries a widow, and two daughters, marries three stark thieves.* Because his wife will put things away to them, or for them.

Marries a widow and two daughters, He that | has three back doors to his house.

1721 KELLY 137 ... Because his wife will put things away to them, or for them.

Marries a widow, He that | will often have a dead man's head thrown in his dish.

1546 HEYWOOD II. vii. 66 For I neuer méete the at fleshe nor at fishe, But I haue sure a deade mans head in my dishe. 1813 RAY 15 *Hisp.* 1884 J. PAYN *Canon's Ward* xxvii It is always dangerous to marry a widow, because of the unpleasant comparisons which she may make.

Marries between the sickle and the scythe, Who | will never thrive.

1678 RAY 352.

Marries ere he be wise, He that | will die ere he thrive.

1546 HEYWOOD I. viii. 15 Who wedth or he be wise shall die ere he thriue. 1641 FERGUSSON 42. 1721 KELLY 148 ... For want of skill to manage a family, he will put himself so far behind, that he will not easily recover.

Marries for wealth, He that | sells his liberty.

1640 HERBERT 353. 1732 FULLER no. 2238.

Marries late, He that | marries ill.

1589 NASHE *Wks.* (Gros.) I. 17 (A) Thys common prouerbe, he that marrieth late marrieth euill. 1640 HERBERT 356.

Marrieth for love without money, Who | hath good nights and sorry days.

1642 TORRIANO 37. 1664 CODRINGTON 226. 1670 RAY 17. 1732 FULLER no. 5710.

Marry a beggar, and get a louse for your tocher-good[1].

1721 KELLY 245 ... A dissuasive from joining in trade, or farm, with a poor man, where the whole loss must lie on you. [1 portion.]

Marry a widow before she leaves mourning.

1640 HERBERT 328.

Marry a widow, Never | unless her first husband was hanged.

1721 KELLY 260 ... Lest she upbraid you with him, and sing you an old Scottish song: *You will never be like our old good man.*

Marry a wife of thine own degree. (*Cf.* Marry thy like.)

[CALLIMACHUS in Diog. Laert. 1. 4. 80 *Τὴν κατὰ σαυτὸν ἔλα.*] 1577 tr. *Bullinger's Decades* (1592) 228 That vsuall Prouerbe: Marrie a wife of thine owne degree.

Marry come up.

1594–5 SHAKS. *Rom. & Jul.* II. v. 64 *Nurse.* Marry, come up, I trow; Is this the poultice for my aching bones? 1608–9 *Pericles* IV. vi 164 Marry, come up, my dish of chastity with rosemary and bays! 1642 J. EATON *Honey-c. Free Justif.* 14 Taunting and reproachfull terms, as, *Marry come up.* 1862 BORROW *Wild Wales* I. xxiv. 276 Unworthy? marry come up! I won't hear such an expression.

Marry come up, my dirty cousin.

1674 T. DUFFET *Empress of Morocco* 4 *Q Moth.* Marry come up, my durty Cozen, He may have such as you by th' Dozen. 1678 RAY 68 ... Spoken by way of taunt, to those who boast themselves of their birth, parentage, or the like. 1721 KELLY 82 ... A reprimand to mean people, when they propose a thing that seems too saucy. 1738 SWIFT (Dial. ii) 346 *Miss.* A kiss! marry come up, my dirty cousin.

Marry first, and love will come afterwards (follow).

1699 *Poor Robin's Alm.* Jan. O this Devilish thirst of Gold, which shall cause many to Marry where they do not fansie, relying upon the *Sunday-Penny's Proverb, Marry first and love will come afterwards.* 1780 MRS. H. COWLEY *Belle's Strat.* III. i. Wks. (1813) 265 *Mrs. R.* Then you wont trust to the good old Maxim—'Marry first, and Love will follow'?

Marry in green, They that | their sorrow is soon seen,

1847 R. CHAMBERS *Pop. Rhymes Scot.* (1870) 341 Green ... [has] been connected by superstition with calamity and sorrow. . . . They that marry in green, Their sorrow is soon seen. . . . In the north of Scotland, no young woman would wear such attire on her wedding day.

Marry in haste, and repent at leisure.

[PHILEMON *Fab. Incertae, Frag.* 105 Γάμειν ὃς ἐθέλει, εἰς μετάνοιαν ἔρχεται. He who would marry is on the road to repentance.] **1566** PAINTER *Pal. of Pleasure* (Jacobs) i. 115 (A) Leaste in making hastie choise, leasure for repentaunce shuld folow. **1576** PETTIE *Petite Pall.* (Gollancz) II. 61 Bargains made in speed are commonly repented at leisure. **1590–1** SHAKS. *3 Hen. VI* IV. i. 18 Hasty marriage seldom proveth well. **1598–9** *Much Ado* II. i. 77 Wooing, wedding, and repenting, is as a Scotch jig, a measure, and a cinque-pace: the first suit is hot and hasty, . . . the wedding, mannerly-modest, as a measure, . . . and then comes Repentance, and, with his bad legs, falls into the cinque-pace faster and faster, till he sink into his grave. **1614** DAY *Festivals* (1615) 282 Marrying in hast, and Repenting at leisure. **1670** RAY 47 *Ital.* **1734** FRANKLIN *May* Grief often treads upon the heels of pleasure, Marry'd in haste, we oft repent at leisure. **1872** SIR W. STIRLING-MAXWELL *Rector. Addr.* in *Wks.* (1891) VI. 425 'Marry in haste and repent at leisure' is a proverb that may be borne in mind with advantage in the choice of a party as well as of a wife. **1883** J. PAYN *Thicker than W.* xxxi She had married in haste, and repented, not at leisure, but with equal rapidity.

Marry in Lent, and you'll live to repent.

1876 MRS. G. L. BANKS *Manch. Man* xviii The double fees of Lent, and the ill-luck supposed to follow a couple united during the penitential forty days. **1929** *Daily Mail* 6 March 11/5 A London registrar told a *Daily Mail* reporter yesterday: The fixed idea that marriages should not take place in Lent seems to have disappeared.

Marry in May, repent alway.

[OVID *Fasti* 5. 490 *Mense malum Maio nubere vulgus ait.* To marry in the month of May is unlucky, they say.] **1675** *Poor Robin's Alm.* May (A) The proverb saies . . . Of all the moneths 'tis worst to wed in May. **1841** CHAMIER *Tom Bowling* lvii Mrs. Talbot, in this month, in spite of Ovid's declaration, that 'the girls were good for nought who wed in May', was to be married.

Marry late or never, It is good to.

[*cf.* **1616** DRAXE 230 It is good to marry late.] **1639** CLARKE 329. **1670** RAY 47.

Marry not an old crony, or a fool, for money.

1621 BURTON *Anat. Mel.* II. iii. VII (1651) 428.

Marry, He who is about to | should consider how it is with his neighbours.

1707 MAPLETOFT 78. **1855** BOHN 400.

Marry thy like. (*Cf.* Marry a wife of thine own degree, *and* Marry with your match.)

1539 TAVERNER 65 *Aequalem tibi vxorem quære.* Mary thy lyke.

Marry with your match. (*Cf. the preceding proverb, and* Marry a wife of thine own degree.)

[OVID *Heroides* 9. 32 *Siqua voles apte nubere, nube pari.* If you would wed fitly, wed in your station.] **1639** CLARKE 230 . . . *Si vis nubere, nube pari.* **1721** KELLY 252 *Marry above your match, and you get a master.* A wife, above our station and condition, will be apt to despise us, think herself disgraced, and prove insolent.

Marry your daughters betimes, lest they marry themselves.

a. **1598** LORD BURLEIGH *Precepts* (1637) 9. **1621** BURTON *Anat. Mel.* III. ii. VI. v (1651) 577 'Tis good to get them husbands betimes . . . ; they perchance will marry themselves else, or do worse. **1651** HERBERT 372.

Marry your son when you will, your daughter when you can.

1640 HERBERT 324.

Marry (-ies, -ied), *see* Advise none to m.; Always say 'No' (If you), never be m.; Before you m. be sure of a house; Broomstick (To m. over the); Carry a nutmeg (If you), m. to old man; Couple are newly m. (When a), first month is; Fool that m. wife at Yule; Happy is she who m. son of dead mother; Honest men m. soon, wise not at all; Live well for a . . . month (If you would), m.; Needles and pins, when a man m.; Needy when he is m. shall be rich when buried; No man is a match for woman till m.; Promising and performing (Between) man may m. his daughter; Shrew than a sheep (Better to m.); Two bachelors drinking to you . . . soon be m.; Well m. who has neither mother-in-law; Young man should not m. yet.

Marrying the devil's daughter, and living with the old folks, As bad as.

1830 FORBY 434 . . . Commonly applied to a person who has made unpromising connexions in marriage.

Marrying, *see also* Building and m. of children are great wasters.

Marshal's bâton, *see* French soldier carries.

Marshland (The), *see* Bailiff of the M.

Martin, *see* Robin and the wren.

Martinmas, *see* Hog hath its M. (Every); Wind is on M. Eve (Where the).

Martyr(s), *see* Better to be a m. than confessor; Blood of the m. is seed of Church; Devil's m.; Religion but **can** boast m. (No); Suffering (Not the) but the cause makes m.

Mary (Lady), *see* Breed of L. M., when you're good you're o'er good.

Mass nor mattins, Neither.

[= nothing of very serious import.] **1528** SIR T. MORE *Dial. conc. Heresyes* I. xx. Wks. 145/2 It maketh no matter they saye, ye may beginne agayne and mende it, for it is nother masse nor mattyns.

Mass, *see also* Lief go to mill as to m.; Meat and m. never hindered; No priest no m.

Master a grief but he that has it, Every one can.

1598-9 SHAKS. *Much Ado* III. ii. 29.

Master absent and the house dead, The.

1640 HERBERT 360.

Master and servant, Every one is a. (*Cf.* Master must serve, &c.)

1640 HERBERT 364.

Master in an house, One | is enough.

1639 CLARKE 218.

Master, Like | like man.

[ERASM. *Ad. Qualis hera, talis pedissequae*, from CIC. *ad Att.* 5. 11. *Qualis dominus, talis et servus*, PETRONIUS ARBITER *Satyricon* 58.] **1548** UDALL tr. *Erasm. Par. Luke* xxiii. 177 Beeyng lyke men lyke maister accordyng to the prouerbe. **1568** FULWELL *Like Will to L.* (1906) 24 *Newf.* For, like master, like man. **1620** SHELTON *Quix.* II. x (1908) II. 248 This master of mine . . . is a bedlam . . . , and I . . . am the greater coxcomb of two, . . . if the proverb be true that says, 'like master, like man'. **1840** MARRYAT *Poor Jack* i They say, 'Like master, like man'; and I may add, 'Like lady, like maid'. Lady Hercules was fine, but her maid was still finer.

Master must serve [another], He that is a. (*Cf.* Master and servant, &c.)

1640 HERBERT 362.

Master of himself, He that is | will soon be master of others.

1732 FULLER no. 2182. **1855** BOHN 389 He that is master of himself will soon be master of others.

Master of straw eats a servant of steel, A.

1640 HERBERT 364.

Master one than engage with ten, Better.

1721 KELLY 72. **1732** FULLER no. 916.

Master that never was scholar, He can ill be.

1616 WITHALS 567 He can ill play the master, that hath not been a scholler. **1639** CLARKE 284.

Master wears no breeches, Most.

1588 GREENE *Pandosto* Prose Wks. (Huth) IV. 267 His wife . . . taking up a cudgel (for the most maister went breechles) sware solemnly that shee would make clubs trumps. **1590-1** SHAKS. *2 Hen. VI* I. iii. 148 Though in this place most master wear no breeches, She shall not strike Dame Eleanor unreveng'd. **1623** CAMDEN 274.

Master's eye fattens the horse, and his foot the ground, The.

1537 R. WHITFORD *Werke for Housholders* sig. F 5 The steppe of the husbande: maketh a fatte donghyll and the eye of the mayster a fatte horse. **1640** HERBERT 340.

Master's eye maketh the horse fat, The.

[PLUTARCH *Moralia*, Bk. I. Οὐδὲν οὕτω πιαίνει τὸν ἵππον ὡς βασιλέως ὀφθαλμός. Nothing fattens the horse so much as the master's eye.] **1552** LATIMER *5th Serm. Lord's Prayer* (P.S.) 394 A fellow asked a philosopher. . . . 'How is a horse made fat?' The philosopher made answer, . . . 'With his master's eye' . . . meaning . . . that the master should . . . take heed to the horse-keeper, that the horse might be well fed. **1579** LYLY *Euphues* (Arb.) 104 It is the eye of the master that fatteth the horse, and the loue of the woeman, that maketh the man. **1631** BRAITHWAIT *Whimzies* (1859) 69 The masters eye feeds his horse; but the ostlers starves him.

Master's footsteps fatten the soil, The.

1648 HERRICK *Hesper., Country Life* 23 Wks. (1921) 226 The best compost for the Lands Is the wise Masters Feet, and Hands. **1659** HOWELL *Eng. Prov.* 10/2. **1721** KELLY 308 *The master's foot is the best foulzie*[1] . . . The other asked, what was the best gooding[1] for ground? and was answered, The master's foot. . . . The care and concern of a man will make his business prosper. [[1] manure.]

Master's Yorkshire too.

1787 GROSE (*Yorks.*) 95 A Yorkshire hostler . . . in London, being asked . . . [why he] remained so long without becoming master . . . answered, *Measter's Yorkshire too!* A saying used by persons, on discovering the design of any one to impose on them, implying that they are a match for them.

Master-blow, *see* Reserve the m.-b.

Masterless hound, Like a.

c. 1530 REDFORD *Play Wit & Sci.* 542 (1903) 440 Lyke a masterles hownde Wandryng all abowt seakyng his master.

Masters should be sometimes blind, and sometimes deaf.

1732 FULLER no. 3376. **1895** J. PAYN *In Market O.* ix He . . . weil knew when to be deaf, as it behoves a good tutor, above all men to know.

Master(s), *see also* All men cannot be m.; Art (In every) it is good to have m.; Diligent scholar, m.'s paid; Early m. long knave; Educate our m.; Every man is m. (Where) world to wrack; Eye of the m. sees more (One); Eye of the m. will do more work; Falling m. standing servant; God and parents and our m. never requited; God is made m. of family (When), he orders disorderly; Jack is as good as his m.; Jack of all trades, m. of none; Mistress (Such) . . . such m. such man; No man is his craft's m. first day; Purse be your m.; Scholar may waur the m.; Servants make worst m.; Share not pears with your m.; Sleepy m., servant a lout; Trim tram, like m. like man; Wrongs of a . . . m. not reproached.

Mastery mows the meadows down.

1641 FERGUSSON 76. **1721** KELLY 251 . . . Spoken when people of power and wealth effect a great business in a short time. **1818** SCOTT *Ht. Midl.* xlv The Captain . . . keeps a high hand over the country, . . . and maistry, ye ken, maws the meadows doun.

Mastery, *see also* Use makes m.

Mastiff be gentle, Though the | yet bite him not by the lip.

1640 HERBERT 323.

Mastiff(s), *see also* Spit in his mouth and make him m.; Yelping curs will raise m.

Match, *see* Meddle with your m.; No man is a m. for woman till married.

Matins, *see* Meat and m. hinder no journey.

Matrimony, *see* Marriage (M.) is destiny; Pulse beats m. (Her).

Matter, *see* More malice than m.; More m. less art; Much m. of wooden platter.

Maw, *see* Good in the m. which is sweet in mouth.

Maxfield[1] measure, heap and thrust (thrutch).

1670 RAY 217 Macklesfield measure, heap and thrust. *Chesh.* **1787** GROSE (*Ches.*) 156 Maxfield measure, heap and thrutch (thrust). At some places the measure is . . . heaped above the top. . . . That of Maxfield was of this kind. **1878** *N. & Q.* 5th Ser. x. 284 We have an old colloquial saying; . . . Maxfield measure, upyeped and thrutched', that is, it is heaped up and pressed down. [[1] Macclesfield.]

Maxfield, *see also* Feeds like a freeholder of M.

Maxima debetur puero reverentia.

[JUVENAL *Sat.* 14. 47 The greatest reverence is due to a child.] **1892** H. P. LIDDON *Serm. Wds. Christ* 12 There is the warning . . . 'Maxima debetur pueris reverentia'. Children should be treated with the respect which is due to their innocence of the world.

May, The merry month of.

1412–20 LYDGATE *Troy. Bk.* I. 1293 And May was com, þe monyth of gladnes. **1579** SPENSER *Shep. Cal.* May Wks. (Globe) 458 Is not thilke the mery moneth of May. **1598** BARNFIELD *Ode* As it fell vpon a Day, In the merrie Month of May.

May and January (*or* December).

c. **1386** CHAUCER *Merch. T.* E[2] 1693 That she, this mayden, which that Mayus highte, . . . Shal wedded be unto this Januarie. **1581** T. HOWELL *Devises* I ij In fayth doth frozen Ianus double face, Such fauour finde, to match with pleasant Maye. **1606** DEKKER *Sev. Sins* (Arb.) 44 You doe wrong to Time inforcing May to embrace December. **1891** R. BUCHANAN *Coming Terror* 267 When asthmatic January weds buxom May.

May be hath a may not be, Every.

1678 RAY 174.

May be, What | may not be.

1721 KELLY 358.

May-bee was ne'er a gude honey bee.

1832 HENDERSON 131.

May bees don't fly this month.

1721 KELLY 252 *May bees fly not this time o' the year.* A return to them that say, *May be,* such a thing will come to pass. **1738** SWIFT (Dial. i) 334 *Miss.* Maybe there is, colonel. *Col.* Ay, but May bees don't fly now, miss.

May birds are aye cheeping.

1862 HISLOP 223 . . . This refers to the popular superstition against marrying in . . . May, the children of which marriages are said to 'die of decay'.

May chickens come cheeping.

1895 S. O. ADDY *Househ. Tales, &c.* 116 Children born in the month of May require great care in bringing up, for 'May chickens come cheeping'.

May cold is a thirty-day cold, A.

1876 BLACKMORE *Cripps Carrier* xxxv This is the worst time of year to take cold, 'A May cold is a thirty-day cold'.

May-day is come and gone; thou art a gosling and I am none.

1846 DENHAM 44 . . . Should an attempt be made, to make any one a May-gosling [the equivalent of an 'April fool'] on the 2nd of May, this rhyming saying is retorted upon them.

May-day, pay-day, pack rags and go away.

1883 C. S. BURNE *Shropshire Folk-Lore* 465 A good deal of hiring is still done . . . on the first of May. . . . The saying runs—'May Day, pay day, Pack rags and go away!'

May flood never did good, A.

1639 CLARKE 307. **1678** RAY 45.

May-hill, If he can climb over | he'll do.

2. Jan. **1619** J. CHAMBERLAIN *Letters* (McLure) ii. 197 We cannot be out of the feare [of the safety of the Queen] till we see her past the top of May-hill. **1846** DENHAM 43 He'll never climb May-hill; or, If he can climb over May-hill he'll do. May is considered a *trying month* for health.

May if you list, You | but do if you dare.

1678 RAY 350.

May makes or mars the wheat.

1822 COBBETT *Rural Rides* 19 June (1914) 79 The old remark of the country people in England, that '*May* makes or mars the wheat'; for it is May that the ear and the grains are *formed*.

May never goes out without a wheat-ear.

1830 FORBY 417.

May (*noun*), *see also* April showers M. flowers; Beans blow before M.; Cast ne'er a clout till M. be out; Cold M. and windy; Dry M. and dripping June; Hot M., fat churchyard; January commits fault, M. bears blame; Leeks in Lide and ramsins in M.; Look at your corn in M. (If you); March dust and a shower in M.; March dust and M. sun, corn white maids dun; March (In) the birds . . . in M. the birds; March (In) the cuckoo . . . in M. a' sing; Marriages in M. (Of) bairns die; Marry in M. repent; Sage in M. (Set); Shear your sheep in M.; Town in M. (He that is in).

Maynooth, *see* Pardon of M.

Mayor of Altrincham The | and the mayor of Over; the one is a thatcher, the other a dauber.[1]

1678 RAY 301 Cheshire . . . These are two petty Corporations whose poverty makes them ridiculous to their neighbours.[2] **1917** BRIDGE 115 . . . A good thatcher was a very skilled workman. . . . The Mayoralty of Altrincham (. . . created by Charter in 1290) has been held by members of the best families in the district. [[1] a plasterer, builder of clay walls. [2] In 1920 the population of Altrincham was 18,000.]

Mayor of Altrincham lies in bed while his breeches are mending, The.

1678 RAY 301 *Cheshire*. **1787** GROSE (*Ches.*) 157 . . . As the mayor of every other town must do, if he had but one pair, as is said to have been the case with this worshipful magistrate. **1818** SCOTT *Ht. Midl.* xlv 'I was like the Mayor of Altringham, who lies in bed while his breeches are mending, for the girl did not bring up the right bundle to my room till she had brought up all the others by mistake.'

Mayor of Hartlepool, Like the | you cannot do that.

1678 RAY 317. **1787** GROSE (*Leics.*) 190 . . . It seems to belong to Durham, Hartlepool being within that bishopric. The sense of it is, you cannot work impossibilities. . . . A mayor of a poor corporation, . . . told them, that though he was mayor of that corporation, he was still but a man, there being many things that he could not do.

Mayor of London (Lord), *see* Dined as well as; Good manners to except.

Mayor of Northampton opens oysters with his dagger, The.

1662 FULLER (*Northants*) II. 500 The mayor of Northampton opens oysters with his dagger.' This town being eighty miles from the sea, sea-fish may be presumed stale therein.

Mead, *see* Little m. little need.

Meadow, *see* Thin m. soon mowed.

Meal cheap and the shoon dear, The | quoth the souter's wife, that would I hear.

1721 KELLY 317.

Meals, Two (Three) hungry (ill) | make the third (fourth) a glutton.

1546 HEYWOOD I. xi. 37 At breakfast and diner I éete little meate. And two hongry meales make the thyrd a glutten. **1623** CAMDEN 278 Three hungry meales, makes the fourth a glutton. **1640** HERBERT 344 Two ill meals make the third a glutton. **1655** FULLER *Ch. Hist.* VI. ii (1868) II. 218 At last a sirloin of beef was set before him, on which the abbot fed . . . and verified the proverb, that 'two hungry meals make the third a glutton'. **1721** KELLY *Two hungry meals make the third a glutton.* Spoken when one eats greedily after long fasting. Applied also to other things of the like nature, where long wanting sharpens the appetite.

Meal(s), *see also* Better are m. many than one too merry; Much bran little m.; Wholesomest m. at another man's cost.

Meal-tub, *see* Always taking out of the.

Mealy-mouthed maidens stand long at the mill.

1737 RAMSAY III. 190.

Mean (*noun*), *see* Measure is a merry m.; Merry m.

Meaning, *see* Know your m. by your mumping.

Means, Use the | and God will give the blessing.

1580 LYLY *Euph. & his Eng.* Wks. (Bond) II. 67 Vse the meane, if you desire to haue the ende. **1633** DRAXE 109. **1670** RAY 17. **1732** FULLER no. 5413 (with 'and trust to God for the blessing').

Means, *see* Many m. to get money.

Meant for a gentleman, He was | but was spoilt in the making.

1738 SWIFT (Dial. i) 338 I think she was cut out for a gentlewoman, but she was spoil'd in the making. **1830** FORBY 434.

Meant, *see also* Take things as m.

Mear, *see* Mare.

Measure another man's foot by one's own last, To.

[*Cf.* **1545** TAVERNER H 4 *Tuo te pede metiri.* Mesure youre selfe by youre owne fote]. **1598** R. BERNARD *Terence in English* 70 He measures another man's foot by his own last.

Measure for measure.

1595 *True Trag. Rich. D. of York* (Sh. S.) 151 (A) Measure for measure must be answered. **1604–5** SHAKS. *Meas. for Meas.* (title).

Measure his cloth by another's yard, To.

1579 LYLY *Euphues* (Arb.) 63 Did not *Gyges* cut *Candaules* a coat by hys owne measure? **1678** RAY 260.

Measure in all things, There is a.

c. **1380** CHAUCER *Troylus* II. 715 In every thyng, I woot, there lith mesure. **1509** A. BARCLAY *Ship of Fools* (1874) I. 97. **1547** WM. BALDWIN *Treatise Moral Philosophy* (1550) L₄ Vse measure in all things. **1580** LYLY *Euph. & his Eng.* Wks. (Bond) II. 152 In all things I know there must be a meane. **1598–9** SHAKS. *Much Ado* II. i. 73 If the prince be too important, tell him there is measure in everything. **1616** DRAXE 131.

Measure is a merry mean.

1399 *Richard Redeles* II. 139 Mesure is a meri mene. *a.* **1529** SKELTON *Magnyf.* 385 Wks. (1843) I. 238 Yet mesure is a mery mene. **1546** HEYWOOD II. vii. 67 Measure is a mery meane, as this doth show, Not to hye for the pye, nor to lowe for the crow.

Measure is medicine.

1362 LANGLAND *P. Pl.* A. I. 33 Measure is Medicine þauh þou muche ʒeor[n]e.

Measure is treasure.

c. **1200** *Ancrene Riwle* 286 Euerich thing me mei ouerdon. Best is euer i-mete. *c.* **1350** *Douce MS. 52* no. 81 Mesure is tresure. *c.* **1430** LYDGATE *Minor Poems* (Percy Soc.) 208 Men wryte of oold how mesour is tresour. *a.* **1529** SKELTON *Sp. Parrot* 64 In mesure is tresure. **1641** FERGUSSON 76.

Measure the meat by the man, To.

[**1533** HEYWOOD *Play of Love* l. 1230 (BRANDL, *Quellen* 198) (A) Look not on the meat but on the man.] **1678** RAY 354.

Measure thrice what thou buyest; and cut it but once.

1591 FLORIO *Sec. Frutes* 97 Alwaies measure manie, Before you cut anie. **1670** RAY 17 *Ital.* **1721** KELLY 255 *Measure twice, cut but once.* Take good deliberation before you fall to actual execution. **1853** TRENCH iv. 88 A word of timely caution . . . lies in the . . . Russian proverb: *Measure thy cloth ten times; thou canst cut it but once.*

Measure with the long ell (with the short ell), To.

[= to measure unfairly as buyer or seller respectively.] **1474** CAXTON *Chesse* 119 In hys right hand an elle for to mesure wyth. **1580** SIDNEY *Arcadia* (1622) 62 The night measured by the short ell of sleepe. **1637** R. MONRO *Exped.* II. 46 Sometimes the Souldiers (the worst sort of them) measured the packes belonging to the Marchants with the long ell.

Measure yourself by your own foot.

[HOR. *Ep.* l. 7. 98 *Metiri se quemque suo modulo ac pede verumst.*] **1539** TAVERNER 60 . . . The iust measure of euery man consisteth in seuen of his owne fete. By this prouerbe we be therefore warned that we delyte not of selues beyond our condition and state, neyther yet esteme our selues by the prayses of flatterours, or opinion of the people.

Measure (*noun*), *see also* Feed by m. and defy physician; Forsakes m. (He that); Man is the m. of all; Mete and m. make all wise; Sin to sell dear (It is no) but to give ill m.; Vessel (The greatest) hath but its m.; Weening is not m.; Weight and m. take away strife.

Measure(d) (*verb*), *see also* Men are not to be m. by inches; Muse as they use (Men), m. corn by their own bushel.

Measures another's corn by his own bushel, He.

1631 W. SALTONSTALL *Picturae Loquentes* F 1ᵛ Her corne stands not long for the sellers sake, and she crosses the proverbe, for shee measures it out by anothers bushell. **1644** MILTON *Areop.* (Arb.) 72 We shall know nothing but what is measur'd to us by their bushel? **1670** RAY 186 You measure every ones corn by your own bushel. **1738** SWIFT (Dial. i) 343 Mr. Neverout, . . . you measure my corn by your bushel. **1881** TYLOR *Anthropology* (1889) 410 The student of history must avoid that error which the proverb calls measuring other people's corn by one's own bushel.

Measures not himself is measured, He that.

1640 HERBERT 338.

Measureth oil shall anoint his fingers, He that.

1611 COTGRAVE s.v. 'Huile' (with 'besmeares' for 'shall anoint'). **1616** DRAXE 169 (with 'anointeth'). **1670** RAY 126 . . . Qui mesure l'huile il s'en oingt les mains. *Gall.*

Meat and good drink, If it wasn't for | the women might gnaw the sheets.

1539 TAVERNER (1545) E 4 *Sine Cerere et Baccho friget Venus.* Without meate and drynke the lust of the body is colde. **1598** R. BERNARD *Terence in English* 96 (2nd ed.) [quoted as 'the old saying'] (A).

Meat and mass never hindered any man.

1641 FERGUSSON 78. **1721** KELLY 253. **1818** SCOTT *Rob Roy* xxix 'What the deevil are ye in sic a hurry for?' said Garschattachin; 'meat and mass never hindered wark'. **1893** STEVENSON *Catriona* xix Meat and mass never hindered man. The mass I cannot afford you, for we are all good Protestants. But the meat I press on your attention. **1900** R. B. CUNNINGHAME GRAHAM *Thirteen Stories* 'A Hegira.' Not that the halt lost time, for travellers all know that 'to hear mass and to give barley to your beasts loses no tittle of the day'.

Meat and matins hinder no man's journey. (*Cf.* Prayers and provender, &c.)

1639 CLARKE 273. **1670** RAY 120 . . . In other words, Prayers and provender, &c. **1732** FULLER no. 3382 (with 'not a' for 'no man's').

Meat (morsel) for mowers, No.

[= unsuitable to, or unobtainable by, people of low degree.] **1542** UDALL tr. *Erasm. Apoph.* 342 Lais an harlot of Corinthe . . . so dere & costely that she was no morsel for mowyers. **1581** MULCASTER *Positions* xxxviii (1887) 179 To hope for hie mariages, is good meat, but not for mowers. **1616** DRAXE 101 It is not for your mowing. **1639** CLARKE 72. **1738** SWIFT (Dial. iii) 352 *Col.* Let's kiss and be friends. *Miss.* Hands off! that's meat for your master. **1876** J. PAYN *Halves* i He was wholly unsuspicious of her design, imagining her to be meat for his masters.

Meat in a goose's eye, There's.

1621 J. TAYLOR (Water-P.) *Wks.* (1630) pagin. I, 105 (A) For the old prouerbe I must here apply, Good meate men may picke from a gooses eye. **1641** FERGUSSON 98 There is meickle hid meat in a goose eye. **1678** RAY 148.

Meat, One man's | is another man's poison.

[*Quod cibus est aliis, aliis est acre venenum,* from LUCR. 4. 637. What is food for some is black poison to others.] **1614** W. BARCLAY *Nepenthes, or the Vertues of Tobacco* in ARBER *Counterblaste* 116 As concerning the hatred of Princes, one mans meate is another mans poyson. *a.* **1721** PRIOR *Dial. of Dead* (1907) 246 *Mont.* May I not nauseate the food which you covet; and is it not even a proverb, that what is meat to one man is poison to another. **1908** ALEX. MACLAREN *Acts Apos.* I. 382 It is we ourselves who settle what God's words and acts will be to us. The trite proverb, 'One man's meat is another man's poison', is true in the highest regions.

Meat is much, but manners (mense[1]) is more (better).

1639 CLARKE 93. **1641** FERGUSSON 76 Meat is good, but mense is better. **1721** KELLY 244 *Meat is good, but mense is better.* Let not one's greediness on their meat intrench upon their modesty. [[1] modesty.]

Meat(s), *see* After m. mustard; All m. to be eaten; Crabs (Greatest) be not all best m.; Dry m. . . . when he lost the hare; Eats the m. let him pick bone; God send you readier m. than hares; God sends m. and the devil sends cooks; Loves roast m. that licks; Measure the m. by the man; Merry at m. (Good to be); Morn come and m. with it (Let); Much m. much malady; New m. new appetite; No other m. (They that have), bread eat; Poor men seek m. for their stomach; Reconciled enemies and m. twice boiled (Take heed of); Roast m. does cattle; Show me not (Look not on) the m. but the man; Stomach (To have) and lack m.; Sweet m. . . . sour sauce; Want in m. (What they) let them take in drink.

Medal hath its reverse, Every.

1603 FLORIO tr. *Montaigne* III. xi (1897) VI. 164 *Ogni medaglia ha il suo riverscio; Each outside hath his inside,* saith the Italian. **1842** LEVER *Jack Hinton* ii Happily, there is a reverse to the medal. **1908** W. S. CHURCHILL *My African J.* iii That there is a rude reverse to the East African medal . . . cannot be disputed.

Meddle nor make,[1] I will neither (not).

1564 *Child Marr.* (1897) 123 I will neither make nor medle with her. **1598-9** SHAKS. *Much Ado* III. iii. 55 The less you meddle or make . . . the more is for your honesty. **1600-1** *Merry W.* I. iv. 114 I vil teach a . . . priest to meddle or make. **1601-2** *Troil. & Cres.* I. i. 14 I'll not meddle nor make no further. *Ibid.* I. i. 85 I'll meddle nor make no more in the

matter. **1661** PEPYS *Diary* 7 Nov. Pegg kite
now hath declared she will have the beggarly
rogue the weaver; and so we are resolved
neither to meddle nor make with her. **1678**
RAY 68 Quoth the young Cock, I'll neither
meddle nor make. When he saw the old
cocks neck wrung off, for taking part with
the master, and the old hens, for taking part
with the dame. *Ibid.* 260 I will neither
meddle nor make, said Bill Heaps, when he
spilled the buttermilk. **1849** c. BRONTË
Shirley xxi Moore may settle his own
matters henceforward for me; I'll neither
meddle nor make with them further. [¹ interfere.]

Meddle with your match.

1598 JONSON *Ev. Man in Humour* III. ii *Cob.*
Nay, he will not meddle with his match.
1612–15 BP. HALL *Contempl.* VI. ii (1825) I.
140 We meddle not with our match, when
we strive with our Maker. **1721** KELLY 246 ...
Spoken by people of age, when young people
jest upon them too wantonly: or by weak
people, when insulted by the more strong and
robust. **1738** SWIFT (Dial. iii) 352 *Spark.*
Miss, you are too severe; you would not
meddle with your match.

Meddle with your old shoes.

1577 *Misogonus* II. v (A) What, are you his
spoksman? Meddle you with your old
showes. **1670** RAY 186.

Meddlesome Matty.

1804–5 ANN & J. TAYLOR *Orig. Poems* (1877)
169 'Meddlesome Matty' (Title) In vain you
told her not to touch, Her trick of meddling
grew so much. **1927** *Times* 17 Aug. 11/5 My
warning was addressed to those who would
make of the League 'a kind of international
Meddlesome Matty'.

Meddleth in all things may shoe the gosling, Who. (*Cf.* Shoe the goose.)

[*To shoe the goose, gosling* = to spend one's
time in trifling or unnecessary labour.]
c. **1434** Whoso melles of wat men dos, Let
hym cum hier and shoo the ghos. *Inscription*
in Whalley Church cited in Farmer's ed. of
Heywood's *Proverbs.* **1546** HEYWOOD II. iii.
49. **1659** HOWELL *Eng. Prov.* 3/1 Who
medleth with all things. may goe and shooe
Goslings. **1804** EDGEWORTH *Pop. Tales,
Lame Jervas* iii A blacksmith once said to
me, when . . . asked why he was not both
blacksmith and whitesmith, 'The smith that
will meddle with all things may go shoe the
goslings'.

Meddling, *see* Little m. much rest.

Medea's¹ kettle.

a. **1616** JONSON *Mercury Vind.* Wks. (1903)
III. 97 To have Medea's kettle hung up, that
they may souse into it when they will, and
come out renewed. **1695** CONGREVE *Love
for L.* IV. iii (Merm.) 279 *Val.* Change the
shape and shake off age; get thee Medea's
kettle, and be boiled anew. [¹ a sorceress of
Colchis.]

Medicine against death, There is no.

[Med. **L.** *Contra malum mortis, non est*

medicamen in hortis. Against the evil of
death there is no remedy in the gardens.]
1787 COWPER *Yearly Bill of Mortality* No
medicine, though it oft can cure, Can always
balk the tomb. **1902** DEAN HOLE *Then &
Now* (ed. 7) viii. 103 But ... we hold our own
at bowls, not forgetting that *Contra vim
mortis non est medicamen in hortis.*

Medicine (remedy) for fear (but cut off the head), There is no.

1641 FERGUSSON 96 There is na medicine for
fear. **1721** KELLY 319 *There is no remedy for
fear but cut off the head.* For a panic fear is
beyond all arguments.

Medicines are not meant to live on.

1545 ASCHAM *Toxoph.* (Arb.) 60 Aristotle
him selfe sayeth, that medicines be no meate
to lyue withall.

Medlar(s), *see* Time and straw make m. ripe.

Medley bells, *see* Webley ale.

Medusa's head.

1726 J. ARMSTRONG *Imit. of Shaks.* So ...
wrought the grisly aspect Of terrible Medusa,
... When wandering through the woods she
frown'd to stone Their savage tenants. **1900**
LES. STEPHEN *Lett.* in MAITLAND *Life* (1906)
ix. 150 When I introduced theological topics
... my 'Medusa's head' petrified the company. **1908** SIR F. TREVES *Cradle of Deep* iii.
14 She can see in the lazar-house, ... the
future of her days.... The fresh young face
will become the Medusa's head.

Meet troubles half-way, Don't.

1598–9 SHAKS. *Much Ado* I. i. 99 You are
come to meet your trouble: the fashion of the
world is to avoid cost, and you encounter it.
1896 HUTCHESON *Crown & Anch.* xvi I can't
see the use of anticipating the worst and
trying to meet troubles half-way.

Meet (*verb*), *see also* Know him not should I
m. him.

Meet as, *see* Rope for a thief; Sow to bear
saddle; Thief for the widdy.

Meeterly as maids are in fairness.

1678 RAY 355 Northern Proverbs ... Meeterly
(*indifferently*) as maids are in fairness.

Meeting, *see* Hasty m. hasty parting; Sorrow
is at parting if at m. laughter.

Meet-mate and you meet together, If your | then shall we see two men bear a feather.

1546 HEYWOOD I. xi. 35 [Of means employed
altogether disproportionate to the end in
view. Farmer's ed. of Heywood, 140.]

Meg Dorts, *see* Fare-ye-weel, M. D.

Meg of Westminster, *see* Long as M.

Megse's glory, *see* Kirkbie's castle.

Melancholic, *see* Choleric drinks, m. eats.

Melancholy as a cat, As.

1592 LYLY *Midas* v. ii. Wks. (1902) III. 155
I am as melancholy as a cat. **1597–8** SHAKS.
1 Hen. IV I. ii. 83 I am as melancholy as a
gib cat. **1720** GAY *New Similes* I melancholy
as a cat, am kept awake to weep.

Melancholy as a collier's horse, As.

c. **1602** *Return from Parnassus* IV. i. 1512.
1659 HOWELL *Eng. Prov.* 10/2.

Melancholy as a dog, As.

1594 NASH *Unf. Trav.* (1920) 16 The dice of
late are growen as melancholy as a dog.

Melancholy as a hare, As.

1597–8 SHAKS. *1 Hen. IV* I. ii. 86 What say-
est thou to a hare, or the melancholy of
Moorditch? **1738** SWIFT (Dial. ii) 346
Lady S. Will your ladyship have any of this
hare? *Lady A.* No, madam, they say 'tis
melancholy meat.

Melancholy, *see also* Fool that is not m. (He
is a).

Melt like wax, To.

[BIBLE *Ps.* xxii. 14 My heart is like wax; it
is melted in the midst of my bowels. *Ibid.*
Ps. xcvii. 5 The hills melted like wax at the
presence of the Lord.] **1596–7** SHAKS. *K. John*
V. iv. 24 Life, Which bleeds away, even as a
form of wax Resolveth from his figure 'gainst
the fire? **1866** KINGSLEY *Hereward* xxxi It
made their hearts . . . melt like wax within
them.

Melts, *see* Heat that m. wax harden clay.

Melverley[1], {God help me. / and what do you think?

1850 *N. & Q.* 1st Ser. I. 325 Melverley, by
Severn side . . . is frequently inundated in
winter, and, consequently, very productive
in summer. . . . If a Melverley man is asked
in winter where he belongs, the . . . reply is,
'Melverley, God help me'; but . . . in summer,
. . . Melverley, and what do you think?'
[[1] 11 m. from Shrewsbury.]

Memory (-ies), *see* Good m. (He that hath)
giveth few alms; Good m. have ill judge-
ments; Great m. without learning; Great
wits, short m.; Wolf may lose teeth but
not m.

Men are April when they woo, December when they are wed.

c. **1600** SHAKS. *A.Y.L.* IV. i. 147. **1855** BOHN
451.

Men are not angels.

1612–13 SHAKS. *Hen. VIII* V. iii. 10 But we
are all men . . . few are angels. **1639** CLARKE
80.

Men are not to be measured by inches.

1603 FLORIO tr. *Montaigne* I. xix (1897) I. 113
A little man is a whole man as well as a great
man. Neither men nor their lives are
measured by the ell. **1721** KELLY 116 *God
doth not measure men by inches.* People of
small stature may have stout hearts. **1732**
FULLER no. 3390. **1858** C. READE *Jack of All
T.* viii Five feet four . . . did not come up to
her notion . . . I should have . . . told her the
pluck makes the man, and not the inches.

Men in court, So many | and so many strangers.

1640 HERBERT 357.

Men, Like | like manners.

1842 TENNYSON *Walking to the Mail* 55 *Jas.*
Like men, like manners: like breeds like,
they say.

Men of all trades, Of the | they especially hang thieves.

c. **1300** *Provs. of Hending* 34 Of alle master[1]
men, mest me[n] hongeth theues. [[1] trade,
occupation.]

Men of Kent, The.

1662 FULLER (*Kent*) II. 122 'A man of Kent'.
This may relate either to the liberty or to the
courage of this county men. **1787** GROSE
(*Kent*) 181 All the inhabitants of Kent, east
of the river Medway, are called Men of Kent,
from the story of their having retained their
ancient privileges, particularly those of
gavel-kind, by meeting William the Conqueror, at Swanscomb-bottom. . . . The rest
of the inhabitants of the county are stiled
Kentish men. **1861** C. BEDE *New Rector* x. 104
The 'Men of Kent', you know, were never
conquered! **1926** *Times* 5 July 24/7 Handley
Cross Spa . . . lay . . . in the heart of the
country of Men of Kent and Kentish Men.

Men (Heads), So many | so many censures.[1]

1590 TARLTON *News Purgat.* (Shaks. Soc.) 73
I could not learn for whom this torment were
provided, for that so many men, so many
censures. **1616** GREENE *Mourning Garm.*
Wks. (Huth.) IX. 174 So many heads, so
many censures, euery fancy liketh a sundry
friend. [[1] opinions.]

Men (Heads), So many | so many minds (wits).

[TERENCE *Phorm.* 2. 4. 14 *Quot homines
tot sententiae.*] *c.* **1386** CHAUCER *Squire's T.*
203 As many hedes, as many wittes ther
been. **1539** TAVERNER 13 Quot homines, tot
sententiæ. So many heads, so many judgments. **1546** HEYWOOD I. iii. 7 All this no
further fits, But to shew, so many heds so
many wits. **1579** LYLY *Euphues* (Arb.) 40
But so many men so many mindes, that may
seeme in your eye odious, which in an others
eye may be gracious. **1621** BURTON *Anat.
Mel.* Democr. to Rdr. (1651) 9 So many
men, so many minds: that which thou con-
demnest, he commends. **1692** L'ESTRANGE
Aesop's Fab. ccclviii (1738) 374 *So many
men, so many minds*; and this diversity of
thought must necessarily be attended with
folly, vanity, and error.

Men who make a city, It is the.

[THUCYD. *Hist.* 7. 77. 7. Ἄνδρες γὰρ πόλις καὶ οὐ τείχη, οὐδὲ νῆες ἀνδρῶν κεναί. It is men who make a city, not walls, or ships without crews.] 1732 FULLER no. 5121 'Tis the men, not the houses, that make the city. 1927 *Times* 13 Oct. 15/2 In the old Greek saying it is the men who make a city: so with a public school. *Ibid.* 28 Oct. 15/5 It is useless to reform the slums, unless you reform the slum landlord and the slum tenant. ἄνδρες γὰρ πόλις.

Men's years and their faults are always more than they are willing to own.

1707 MAPLETOFT 20. 1855 BOHN 452.

Men, *see also* Man (men).

Men, Men are, Men use to, *see also under significant words following.*

Mend but not grow worse, He may.

1616 DRAXE 43 Some doe mend, when they cannot appaire. 1659 HOWELL *Eng. Prov. Rend. into Fr.* 7/2.

Mend his manners, Let him | 'twill be his own another day.

1678 RAY 76.

Mend or end, Either.

1603 FLORIO Dedn. of his *Montaigne* to Lady Rich, Your all praise-exceeding father . . . lived not to mend or end it [the Arcadia]. 1605 DANIEL *Queen's Arcadia* IV. iv All extremities must end or mend. 1605–6 SHAKS. *Macbeth* III. i. 114 I would set my life on any chance, To mend it or be rid on't. 1639 CLARKE 223. 1759 WESLEY *Journ.* 30 Aug. I took knowledge what manner of teachers they had been accustomed to, and determined to mend them or end them. 1884 J. MORLEY in *Times* 31 July 11/4 The . . . question of mending or ending the H. of L.

Mend your clothes, and you may hold out this year.

1640 HERBERT 321.

Mend-fault, One | is worth twenty spy-faults.

1882 CHAMBERLAIN 39.

Mends as sour ale mends in summer, He.

1546 HEYWOOD II. ix. 75 Then wolde ye mend, as the fletcher mends his bolte. Or as sowre ale mendth in summer. 1639 FULLER *Holy War* v. xvi (1840) 271 They lost none of their old faults, and got many new, mending in this hot country like sour ale in summer. 1738 SWIFT (Dial. iii) 351 Manners, indeed! I find you mend like sour ale in summer.

Mends as the fletcher[1] mends his bolt, He.

1546 HEYWOOD II. ix. 75 Then wolde ye

mend, as the fletcher mends his bolte. Or as sowre ale mendth in summer. [[1] arrow-maker.]

Mends is worth misdeeds.

1641 FERGUSSON 78. 1721 KELLY 320 *There is nothing but 'mends for misdeeds.* If I have done you harm, I will make reparation.

Mend(s, ed), *see also* All faults to m. (Hard for any man); Bairns o' Falkirk (Like) they'll end ere they m.; Errs and m. (Who) to God commends; Every man m. one (If); Find fault that cannot m.; Good that m. (It is); Little said soon m.; Never too late to m.; Stumbles and falls not, m. his pace; Things at worst m.; Young enough to m.

Mens sana in corpore sano, *see* Sound mind in a sound body.

Mercenary man, *see* Virtue flies from heart of m. m.

Merchandise, *see* Ell and tell good m.

Merchant bare, He is not a | that hath money, worth or ware.

1664 CODRINGTON 200. 1670 RAY 17. 1721 KELLY 171 . . . A good merchant may want ready money. 1732 FULLER no. 6240 (with 'money-worth and').

Merchant of eelskins, A.

1545 ASCHAM *Toxoph.* (Arb.) 151 He that wyll . . . use the seas knowinge no more what is to be done in a tempest than in a caulme, shall soone becumme a marchaunt of Eele skinnes.

Merchant that gains not, loseth, A.

1607 H. ESTIENNE *World of Wonders* tr. R. C. 114 The merchant that is no gainer, is a loser. 1611 COTGRAVE s.v. 'Gaigner' The marchant loses when he gaines not. 1640 HERBERT 319.

Merchant, *see also* Buys and sells (He that) called m.; Know what would be dear (He that could) need be m. but one year; Loseth (He that) is m. as he that gains.

Merciful, *see* Stout be m. (As you are).

Mercury, *see* Every block will not make M.

Mercy surpasses justice.

c. 1374 CHAUCER *Troylus* III. 1282 'Here may men see that mercy passeth[1] right'. 1387–8 T. USK *Test. Love* III. i. 137 Mercy bothe right and lawe passeth.[1] [[1] surpasses.]

Mercy to the criminal may be cruelty to the people.

[COKE *Minatur innocentibus qui parcit nocentibus.* He threatens the innocent who spares the guilty.] 1711 ADDISON *Spect.* No. 169 In the public administration of justice, mercy to one may be cruelty to others.

Mercy, *see also* God gives his wrath by weight.

Mere scholar, a mere ass, A.

1621 BURTON *Anat. Mel.* I. ii. III. xv. (1836) 202 Because they cannot ride an horse, . . . they are . . . accounted silly fools . . . : a meer scholar, a meer ass. **1732** FULLER no. 332 A mere scholar at court is an ass among apes.

Merry and wise, It is good to be.

c. **1540** UDALL *Roister D.* I. i. 6. **1546** HEYWOOD I. ii. 5 Whan hasty witlesse mirth is mated weele, Good to be mery and wise, they thinke and feele. **1611** BEAUM. & FL. *Kt. Burn. P.* II. i *Wife.* Come, come, George, let's be merry and wise. **1662** L'ESTRANGE *A Whipp* 21 You are merry, sir; be wise too; and do not mind the King too much of the Act of Oblivion. **1721** KELLY 123 . . . Spoken when peoples mirth border[s] too much upon folly.

Merry as a cricket, As.

1546 HEYWOOD I. xi. 25. **1597-8** SHAKS. *1 Hen. IV* II. iv. 101 As merry as crickets, my lad. **1659** HOWELL *Eng. Prov.* 3/1. **1857** KINGSLEY *Two Yrs. Ago* iv I have not had all the luck I expected ; but am . . . as merry as a cricket.

Merry as a grig,[1] As.

1566 DRANT *Horace Sat.* I. iii (A) A merry grig, a iocande frende. **1720** GAY *New Similes* She . . . merry as a grig is grown. **1760** GOLDSMITH *Ess.* vi (Globe) 304 I grew as merry as a grig, and laughed at every word that was spoken. **1887** BLACKMORE *Springhaven* xxxix 'General', cried Charron, now as merry as a grig. [[1] small eel.]

Merry (Gay) as a lark, As.

1606 CHAPMAN *Sir Giles Goosecap* IV. i. 221 Merry as the morning lark. **1835** SOUTHEY *Doctor* iii. 57 Always gay as a lark and busy as a bee. **1838** THACKERAY *Yellowplush Papers* (Oxford ed. 240) As merry as a lark. *Ibid.* 197 Gay as a lark.

Merry as a pie.

c. **1386** CHAUCER *Shipman's T.* B² 1399 And forth she gooth as jolif as a pye. **1546** HEYWOOD II. iii. 49 And she for hir parte, made vs chéere heauen hye. The fyrst parte of dyner mery as a pye.

Merry as be can, Aye be as | for love ne'er delights in a sorrowful man.

1678 RAY 55.

Merry as he that hath nought to lose? Who so.

1663 F. HAWKINS *Youth's Behaviour* F 7ᵛ Cantabit vacuus . . . He that has least, lives merriest. **1672** WALKER 39.

Merry as mice in malt, As.

1639 CLARKE 185. **1659** HOWELL *Eng. Prov.* 3/1.

Merry as the day is long, As.

c. **1598-9** SHAKS. *Much Ado* II. i. 54. **1688** L'ESTRANGE *Quevedo's Visions* (1708) 43.

Merry as the maids, As.

1630 *Roxb. Ballads* (B.S.) i. 448 (A) For with joviall blades I'm as mery as the maids. **1684** BUNYAN *Pilgr. P.* II. (1877) 210 At Madam *Wanton's*, where we were as merry as the maids. **1818** SCOTT *Rob Roy* ix We will . . . have old Cobs the fiddler, and be as merry as the maids.

Merry as three chips, As.

1546 HEYWOOD I. vii. 14 So pleyde these twayne, as mery as thrée chipps.

Merry at meat, It is good to be.

c. **1532** SIR ADRIAN FORTESCUE no. 46 Be blythe at thy mete, devout at thy masse. **1616** DRAXE 130 It is good to bee merry at meate, or meales. **1670** RAY 18.

Merry companion is a waggon in the way, A.

1553 *Precepts of Cato* (1560) X 4ᵛ A mery companion that can talke and clatter, Vpon the highewaye, is insteade of an horse lytter. **1579** LYLY *Euphues Wks.* (Bond) I. 323 A pleasant companion is a bayte in a iourney. **1583** STUBBES *Anat. of Abuses* (New Sh. S.) i. 22 *Comes facundus in via, pro vehiculo est* . . . A good Companion to trauayle withall is insteade of a Wagon or Chariot. **1616** N. BRETON *Cross. of Prov.* (Gros.) II. 8 A merry Companion is a Wagon in the way. **1621** BURTON *Anat. Mel.* II. ii. VI. iv (1651) 302 A merry companion is better than music, and, . . . *comes jucundus in viâ pro vehiculo*,[1] as a wagon to him that is wearied on the way. **1639** CLARKE 291 Good company is a good coach. **1838** APPERLEY *Nimrod's North T.* 10 A pleasant companion is said to shorten the road, and . . . I always endeavour to find the 'comes jucundus', which the facetious Publius Syrus says, is as good as a coach itself. [[1] Pub. Syrus.]

Merry England.

c. **1300** *Cursor M.* 8 First conquerour of meri Ingland. **1436** *Siege Calais* in *Pol. Poems* (Rolls) II. 156 The crown of mery Ynglland. **1590** SPENSER *F.Q.* I. x. 61 Saint George of mery England the signe of victoree. **1819** SCOTT *Ivanhoe* xxxvii It cannot be that in merry England, the hospitable, the generous, the free . . . there will not be found one to fight for justice. *a.* **1830** HAZLITT *Merry England* (Title of an essay) Pleasures in the open air 'were sufficient to justify the well-known appellation of Merry Sherwood' and in like manner we may apply the phrase to Merry England.

Merry in hall when beards wag all, It is.

a. **1300** *King Alis.* 1164 Swithe mury hit is in halle, When the burdes wawen alle! **1550** BECON *Fort. Faith.* Prol. A ii They remember thys olde sayinge: It is mery in hal, Whē berdes wag al. **1593** PEELE *Edwd. I* xiii.

41–3 Wks. (Bullen) I. 180 *Longs.* Set these lords and ladies to dancing; so shall you fulfil the old English proverb, '`'Tis merry in hall when beards wag all`'. **1597–8** SHAKS. *2 Hen. IV* V. iii. 35. **1616** JONSON *Masque of Christmas* Wks. (1903) III. 105 Let me be brought before my Lord Chamberlain, . . . : '*Tis merry in hall, when beards wag all.* **1738** SWIFT (Dial. ii) 348 *Smart.* Come, they say, 'tis merry in the hall when beards wag all.

Merry is the feast-making till we come to the reckoning.

1678 RAY 175. **1732** FULLER no. 3409.

Merry man, *see* Long liveth a m. m. as a sad.

Merry mean.

[= a happy medium.] *a.* **1575** GASCOIGNE *Posies, Flowers* 41 Thus learne I by my glasse, that merrie meane is best. **1616** SURFL. & MARKH. *Country Farm* 580 So greatly . . . is the merrie meane commended.

Merry meet, merry part.

1678 RAY 175. **1732** FULLER no. 3410.

Merry Monarch.[1]

? c. 1665 ROCHESTER *Sat. on King* 19 Restless he rolls about from Whore to Whore. A merry Monarch, scandalous, and poor. **1712** STEELE *Spect.* No. 462, par. 5 This very Mayor afterwards erected a statue of his merry Monarch in Stocks-Market. [1 Charles II.]

Merry pin,[1] To be in a.

c. **1386** CHAUCER *Merchants T.* E[2] 1516 Youre herte hangeth on a joly pyn. *c.* **1485** *Digby Myst.* v. 492 I wyll sett my soule on a mery pynne. **1661** BLOUNT *Glossogr.* (ed. 2) s.v. He is in a merry Pin. **1670** RAY 189 . . . Probably this might come from drinking at pins. The Dutch and English . . . were wont to drink out of a cup marked with certain pins. **1782** COWPER *Gilpin* 178 Right glad to find His friend in merry pin. **1887** A. RILEY *Athos* 210 Our prelate was in merry pin. [1 humour.]

Merry that dance lightly, All are not.

1380 CHAUCER *Parl. Fowls* 592 Daunseth he murye that is myrtheles? *c.* **1425** LYDGATE *Daunce Macabre* 392 Alle be not mery wich that men se daunce. **1640** HERBERT 354.

Merry Wakefield.

1615 R. BRATHWAIT *Strappado for Div.* 203 The first whereof that I intend to show, Is merry *Wakefield* and her *Pindar*[1] too. **1662** FULLER (*Yorks.*) III. 399 'Merry Wakefield'. What peculiar cause of mirth this town has above others I do not know. [1 George-a-Green.]

Merry when friends meet, It's.

1564 W. BULLEIN *Dial. agst. Fever* (E.E.T.S.) 1578 66 Marie when frendes dooe meete. **1600** BRETON *Pasquil's Foolscap* E 3ᵛ. **1616** DRAXE 74. **1639** CLARKE 26.

Merry when gossips meet, 'Tis.

1602 S. ROWLAND *Tis Merrie when Gossips meet* (title). **1639** CLARKE 184.

Merry when knaves meet, It is.

c. **1520** *Cock Lorells Bote* (Percy Soc.) 14 (A) But mery it is whan knaues done mete. **1540** PALSGRAVE *Acolastus*, S 2 It is merye . . . Whan Knaues in graine mete. **1550** HEYWOOD I. xi. 29 **1602** S. ROWLAND *Tis Merrie when Gossips Meet* in *Wks.* (Hunt. Cl.) I Ther's a Booke cal'd *T'is merry when Knaues meete.* And ther's a Ballad, *'T'is merry when Malt-men meete*: and besides, there's an old Prouerbe, *The more the merrier.*

Merry when maltmen meet, It is.

1601 B. BARNES *The Devil's Charter* l. 1555. **1602** *see* quotation under preceding proverb. *c.* **1630** *Roxb. Ballads* (B.S.) i. 59 (A).

Merry (-ier), *see also* Happy (M.) as a king; Jack-an-Ape be m. (Can); More the m. (The); Sing so m. a note (Who can) as who cannot change groat.

Merryman, *see* Physicians are . . . Dr. M. (Best).

Messan, *see* We hounds . . . quoth the m.

Messengers should neither be headed nor hanged.

1641 FERGUSSON 76. **1721** KELLY 246 . . . An excuse for carrying an ungrateful message. L. *Legatus nec violatur, nec læditur.*

Messenger(s), *see also* Corby m.; Lame m.

Messmate before a shipmate; shipmate before a stranger; stranger before a dog.

1867 ADML. W. H. SMYTH *Sailor's Word-Bk.* 478 Comrades in many ways; whence the *saw* 'Messmate before a shipmate, shipmate before a stranger, stranger before a dog'. **1898** W. C. RUSSELL *Rom. of Midsh.* xiv There's no love lost between you . . . I remember a sailor reciting . . . : 'A messmate before a shipmate, a shipmate before a stranger, a stranger before a dog, but a dog before a soldier'.

Metal to the back, He is.

1593–4 SHAKS. *Titus Andron.* IV. iii. 47 No big-bon'd men. . . . But metal, Marcus, steel to the very back. **1678** RAY 76 . . . *A metaphor taken from knives and swords.* **1687** T. BROWN *Saints in Uproar* Wks. (1730) I. 73 A notable fellow of his inches, and metal to the back.

Metal upon metal is false heraldry.

1651 CLEVELAND *Upon Sir Thos. Martin* 24 Metal upon metal is ill armoury. **1659** FULLER *Appeal Inj. Innoc.* in *Hist. Camb. Univ.* (1840) 400 What? Doth he[1] allege himself to prove his own opinion? My bad heraldry was never guilty of such a fault,—metal upon metal! *c.* **1725** SWIFT *Poem upon W. Wood*[2] Wks. (1856) I. 718 I cannot agree; For metal on metal is false heraldry. Why that may be true; yet Wood[2] upon Wood,[3] I'll maintain with my life, is heraldry good. [[1] P. Heylin. [2] W. Wood obtained a patent for coining halfpence for Ireland. [3] i.e. the gallows.]

Mete and measure make all men wise.

1721 KELLY 247 . . . Spoken when people would have what they buy weighed, or measured.

Method in his madness, There's.

1603 SHAKS. *Hamlet* II. ii. 211 Though this be madness, yet there is method in it. **1895** TYRRELL *Latin Poetry* vii Moreover, furious though he [Juvenal] always appears to be, there is method in his madness.

Mettle is dangerous in a blind horse.

1636 S. WARD *Serm.* (1862) 76 It would grieve a man, indeed, to see zeal misplaced, like mettle in a blind horse. **1670** RAY 18. **1721** KELLY 244 *Metal is dangerous in a blind mare.* And so is bigotry, and blind zeal, in an ignorant fellow. **1832** HENDERSON 83 Mettle is kittle in a blind horse.

Mettle, *see also* Feeding out of course makes m. out of kind.

Meum and *tuum*.

[L. = Mine and Thine.] **1550** POLYDORE VERGIL 438 *Illæ duæ semper religiosi pestiferæ voces, Meum et Tuum.* **1594** GREENE & LODGE *Looking-gl.* (1598) C ii j *Rasni.* What, wooe my subiects wife that honoureth me? *Radag.* Tut, kings this *meum, tuum* should not know. **1606** DANIEL *Queen's Arc.* 1001 These proprieties of *meum* and *tuum.* a. **1667** J. TAYLOR *Serm.* 17 Let the husband and wife infinitely avoid a curious distinction of mine and thine. **1820** LAMB *Two Races of Men* in *Lond. Mag.* Dec. Wks. (1898) 20 What a careless, even deportment hath your borrower! . . . What a liberal confounding of those pedantic distinctions of *meum* and *tuum.* **1827** HARE *Gues. at Truth* (1873) i. 3 The first thing we learn is *Meum,* the last is *Tuum.* None can have lived among children without noticing the former fact; few have associated with men and not remarkt the latter. **1876** BURNABY *Ride to Khiva* vii My friend and self . . . brought up the rear, with a careful eye upon our effects, as the people . . . were said to have some difficulty in distinguishing between *meum* and *tuum.*

Meum, Tuum, Suum, set all the world together by the ears.

[L. = mine, thine, his.] **1902–4** LEAN IV. 48.

Mezentian union.

[Mezentius, a mythical Etruscan king, bound living men face to face with corpses, and left them to die: VERG. *Aen.* 8. 485–8.] **1659** FULLER *Appeal Inj. Innoc.* III. 81 A piece of Mezentism in his joyning of the Dead and Living together. **1874** STUBBS *Const. Hist.* i. I. 6 England . . . spared from the curse of the . . . Mezentian union with Italy, . . . developed its own common law.

Mice, *see* Mouse.

Michael, *see* Maids than Malkin (More) and more men than M.

Michaelmas chickens and parsons' daughters never come to good.

1894 NORTHALL *Folk Phrases* (E.D.S.) 19.

Michaelmas Day, So many days old the moon is on | so many floods after.

1661 M. STEVENSON *Twelve Moneths* 44 They say so many dayes old the Moon is on Michaelmas day, so many Floods after.

Michaelmas moon rises aye alike soon, The.

1721 KELLY 334 . . . The moon . . . rising more northerly, rises more early. My country people believe it to be a particular providence of God that people may see to get in their grain.

Michaelmas rot comes never in the pot.

1639 CLARKE 307. **1639** J. SMYTH *Berkeley MSS.* in LEAN I. 381 Sheep . . . rotting at Michaelmas, die in Lent after, when that season of the year permitted not the poor man to eat them.

Michaelmas, *see also* Spends his M. rent in midsummer.

Mickle ado, and little help.

1670 RAY 120.

Mickle between market days, There is.

1721 KELLY 325 . . . Times, modes, prices, and other circumstances are mutable.

Mickle, but not manful.

1721 KELLY 253.

Mickle fails that fools think.

c. **1374** CHAUCER *Troylus* I. 217 But alday faileth thing that fooles wenden. **1721** KELLY 243.

Mickle head, little wit.

1641 FERGUSSON 78. **1721** KELLY 253 . . . A groundless reflection; an eminent instance to the contrary was John, Duke of Lauderdale.

Mickle maun (must) a good heart endure (thole).

1641 FERGUSSON 78 Meikle mon a good heart endure. **1721** KELLY 253 Mickle must a good heart thole.

Mickle power makes many enemies.

1721 KELLY 253 . . . Occasion'd partly by envy, partly by fear. L. *Necesse est ut multos timeat, quem multi timent.*

Mickle spoken, part maun spill.

1641 FERGUSSON 76.

Mickle to do when cadgers (dominies[1]) ride, There is.

1721 KELLY 315 . . . For such are not well provided for riding, nor expert at it. **1836** MRS. CARLYLE *Let.* to Mrs. Welsh 5 Sept. The proverb says 'there is much ado when cadgers ride'. . . . I do not know precisely what 'cadger' means, but . . . the friends . . . of cadgers should therefore use all soft persuasions to induce them to remain at home. [¹ pedagogues.]

Mickle, *see also* Come to m. (It is), but no to that; Seek m. and get something.

Midden, *see* Glower at the moon.

Middle Temple, *see* Gray's Inn; Inner Temple.

Middlesex clowns.

1662 FULLER (*Midsx.*) II. 313   A Middlesex clown'. . . . The multitude of gentry here . . . discover the *clownishness* of others, and render it more conspicuous. However, . . . there are some of the yeomanry in this county as completely civil as any in England.

Midnight oil, *see* Burn the m. o.

Midshipman's half-pay.

1856 C. KINGSLEY *Lett.* May in DAVIES *Sup. Eng. Glos.* 406 You fellows worked like bricks, spent money, and got midshipman's half-pay (nothing a-day and find yourself).

Midsummer moon (madness).

1588 *Martin Marprelate Epitome* (*Tracts,* Pierce 129) You may demand whether it be midsummer moon with him or no. **1590** *An Almond for a Parrot* Nashe's *Wks.* (McKerrow) III. 363. **1596** NASHE *Have with you* Wks. (Gros.) III. 55 Ere hee bee come to the full Midsommer Moone, and raging Calentura of his wretchedness. **1599–1600** SHAKS. *Twelfth N.* III. iv. 62 *Oli.* Why, this is very midsummer madness. **1678** RAY 76 'Tis midsummer moon with you *i.e.* You are mad. **1691** DRYDEN *Amphitryon* IV. Plays (1701) II. 428 *Amp.* What's this Midsummer-Moon? Is all the World gone a madding?

Midsummer, *see also* Mile to m. (To have but a); Spends his Michaelmas rent in m.

Midwife (-ves), *see* Hasty people never good m.; Ride as if to fetch m.

Might is (makes, overcomes) right.

[PLATO *Rep.* 1. 338 Φημὶ γὰρ ἐγὼ εἶναι τὸ δίκαιον οὐκ ἄλλο τι ἢ τὸ τοῦ κρείττονος ξυμφέρον. For I [Thrasymachus] say that justice is nothing else than the interest of the stronger. LUCAN 1. 174 *Mensuraque iuris vis est.*] *a.* **1327** *Pol. Songs* (Camden) 254 For miht is right, the lond is laweles. *c.* **1390** GOWER *Conf. Amantis* v. 2021 ffor wher þat such on is of myht, His will schal stonde in stede of riht. **1546** HEYWOOD II. v. 56 We sée many tymes, might ouercomth right. **1597–8** SHAKS. *2 Hen. IV* V. iv. 26 *Mrs. Quick.* O, that right should thus overcome might! **1639** CLARKE 172 Might overcomes right. **1790** TRUSLER *Prov. Exempl.*

78 The law is so expensive, . . . that those who have not sufficient money to support perhaps a just cause, must give it up . . . ; for *might* too often overcomes right. **1876** TENNYSON *Showday at Battle Abbey* We stroll and stare Where might made right eight hundred years ago. **1892** J. NICHOL *Carlyle* 77 [In] *Chartism* . . . he clearly enunciates 'Might is right'— one of the few strings on which . . . he played through life.

Might or by sleight, Either by.

1639 CLARKE 127. **1670** RAY 186. **1721** KELLY 179 If I cannot do by might, I'll do by sleight. If I dare not attack my enemy openly, I'll do him an injury in a private, and clandestine way.

Mighty man, *see* Wrath of a m. m. (Take heed of).

Mighty, *see also* Pleasures of m., tears of poor.

Mild, *see* Gentle (M.) as a lamb.

Mile is two in winter, Every.

1640 HERBERT 360.

Mile to midsummer, To have but a.

[= to be somewhat mad.] *c.* **1465** *Eng. Chron.* (Camden Soc.) 92 Tho bestys that thys wroughte to mydsomer have but a myle.

Mile(s), *see also* Essex m.; Good things I do not love, good long m.; Robin Hood's m.; Sit awhile and go a m.

Milk and honey.

[BIBLE *Exodus* iii. 8] *c.* **1000** Ælfric *Numbers* xvi. 13 Of þam lande, þe weoll meolc and hunie. **1382** WYCLIF *Ezek.* xx. 6 The loond which Y hadde purueide to hem, flowynge with mylk and hony. **1783** J. KING *Th. on Difficulties,* &c. ii. 28 America is now the fancied land of milk and honey. **1826** DIS-RAELI *Viv. Grey* II. i The milk and honey of the political Canaan.

Milk bowl, *see* Wheamow (I am very), quoth old woman when she stepped into m. b.

Milk is white, and lieth not in the dyke, but all men know it good meat.

1546 HEYWOOD II. iv. 51.

Milk kail, *see* Learn your goodam to make m. k.

Milk of human kindness.

1605–6 SHAKS. *Macbeth* I. v. 18 *Lady M.* I fear thy nature; It is too full o' the milk of human kindness To catch the nearest way. **1763** CHURCHILL *Ep. to Hogarth* Candour, . . . With the sweet milk of human kindness bless'd, The furious ardour of my zeal repressed. **1796** BURKE *Lett. to Noble Ld.* Wks. (1901) V. 130 These gentle historians . . . dip their pens in nothing but the milk of human kindness. **1908** E. M. SNEYD-KYNNERSLEY *H.M.I.* ix Bishop Wilberforce . . . after meeting with a brother Bishop . . . said he had often heard of the milk of human kindness, but never hitherto had he met the cow.

Milk says to wine, Welcome friend.
1640 HERBERT 325.

Milk sod[1] over, Their.
1678 RAY 354. **1732** FULLER no. 2510 His milk boil'd over. [[1] boiled.]

Milk, see also Bristol m.; Cow that gives good pail of m., and kicks it over; Crying over spilt m.; Fern grows red (When), m good with bread; God gives the m., not the pail; Live ever (If you would), wash m. from liver; Nothing turns sourer than m.; Suffolk m.

Milking, see Goat gives a good m. but casts it down.

Milksop, see Mothers' darlings m. heroes.

Mill cannot grind with the water that is past, The.
1616 DRAXE 151 The water that is past, cannot make the mill goe. **1640** HERBERT 324. **1865** ABP. TRENCH Poems, Proverbs xix. 303 Oh seize the instant time; you never will With waters once passed by impel the mill.

Mill gets by going, The.
1651 HERBERT 8. **1897** 'H. S. MERRIMAN' In Kedar's T. xxx 'The mill gains by going, and not by standing still,' he said, and added, ... 'But it is always a mistake to grind another's wheat for nothing.'

Mill that is always going grinds coarse and fine, The.
1910 P. W. JOYCE Eng. as We Speak 115 A person who talks too much cannot escape saying things now and then that would be better left unsaid:—'The mill that is always going grinds coarse and fine.'

Mill will go with all winds, His.
1625 JONSON Staple of News III. i He ... is turned The Church's miller, grinds the catholic grist With every wind. **1689** SELDEN Table-Talk (Arb.) 32 Collonel Goring serving first the one side and then the other, did like a good Miller that knows how to grind which way so ever the Wind sits. **1732** FULLER no. 2511.

Mill(s), see also Born in a m.; Draw water to m.; God's m. grinds slow; Kirk and a m. of it (Make a); Lief go to m. as to mass; Little stream drives light m.; No m. no meal; Sacks to the m. (More); Safe as a thief in a m.; Water goes by m. that miller knows not of (Much).

Mill-clack, see In vain is the m.

Miller got never better moulter[1] than he took with his own hands, The. (Cf. Millers take aye, &c.)
1721 KELLY 313 ... Spoken to them who have a thing at their own taking. [[1] toll.]

Miller grinds more men's corn than one, The.
1596 NASHE Saffron W. (1870) To Reader 18 O! good brother Timothie, rule your reason; the miller gryndes more mens corne than one.

Miller hath a golden thumb, An honest.
c. **1386** CHAUCER Prol. 562 Wel coude he stelen corn and tollen thriès, And yet he hadde a thombe of gold, pardee. **1678** RAY (Som.) 354 Every honest miller hath a golden thumb. They reply, None but a cuckold can see it. **1820** SCOTT Monast. xiii Beside that which the miller might have amassed by means of his proverbial golden thumb, Mysie was to inherit . . . land.

Miller, Many a | many a thief.
1533 J. HEYWOOD Play of Weather B 4ᵛ Who wolde be a myller as goode be a thefe. **1634** T. HEYWOOD & BROME Late Lancashire Witches (1874) iv. 195 They say we Millers are theeves. **1673** Vinegar & Mustard 19 in HINDLEY, Old Book Coll. Miscell. iii (A).

Miller's boy said so, The.
1830 FORBY 431 ... It was matter of common report.

Miller's daughter, see Breed of the m. d. who speered. . . .

Miller's dog, see Breed of the m. d. (Ye).

Miller's eye, see Put out m. e.

Miller's mare, Like a.
1620 BEAUM. & FL. Lit. Fr. Law. IV. i. Wks. (1906) III. 430 Nurse. I can jump yet, Or tread a measure. Lam. Like a Millers Mare.

Miller's neck-cloth, see Bolder than a m. n. (What is).

Millers take aye the best multar[1] with their own hand. (Cf. Miller got never better moulter, &c.)
1641 FERGUSSON 78. [[1] toll.]

Miller(s), see also Draw water to one's mill (1670 quotation); Heather-bells grow (When) ... m. and priest forget themsels; In vain is mill-clack if m. hearing lack; Muckle water rins while m. sleeps; Put a m. . . . in bag, first that comes out will be a thief; Sure (Good to be), toll it again, quoth m.; Wight (Stout) as m.'s waistcoat.

Mill-post, see Thwitten a m.-p. to pudding-prick.

Mills and wives are ever wanting.
1586 PETTIE Guazzo's Civ. Conv. 137 Women, though never so honest, are insatiable of such trifles. Whereupon it is said, that mills and women ever want something. **1640** HERBERT 335 Mills and wives ever want. **1670** RAY 18. **1721** KELLY 249 ... It requires much to keep a mill useful, and a wife fine.

Mills will not grind if you give them not water.

1636 s. WARD *Serm.* (1862) 128 Such mercenary lawyers . . . only keep life in the law so long as there is money in the purse, and when this golden stream ceaseth the mill stands still. **1642** TORRIANO 64 A mill will not grind without wind or water. **1659** HOWELL *Brit. Prov.* 33 The mill stands that wants water. **1732** FULLER no. 3414.

Mills, *see also* Mill(s).

Millstone, I can see as far into a | as another man.

[= to display acuteness; but it is often used ironically.] **1546** HEYWOOD I. x. 21 She thought Ales, she had séene far in a milstone, Whan she got a husbande. **1577** STANYHURST *Descr. Irel.* in HOLINSHED (1808) vi. 18 He would see further in a milstone than others. **1625** HART *Anat. Ur.* II. vii. 92 They . . . could see as farre into a milstone as any of our . . . Physitians. **1668** SHADWELL *Sullen Lov.* IV. 1 He's resolved to have satisfaction . . . ; and, if I can see as far into a millstone as another, he's no bully Sandy. **1738** SWIFT (Dial. i) 338 I'd hold a wager there will be a match between her and Dick Dolt: and I believe I can see as far into a millstone as another man.

Mill-stone, The lower | grinds as well as the upper.

1678 RAY 172.

Millstone(s), *see also* Seaman, if he carries m., will have a quail; Trusted with a house full of m.; Weep m. *See also* Stone.

Mim¹ as a May puddock², As.

1823 GALT *Entail* III. viii. 76 You sitting as mim as a May puddock, when you see us . . . met for a blithesome occasion. [¹ demure. ² frog.]

Mince matters (the matter), To.

[= to extenuate.] **1604–5** SHAKS. *Othello* II. iii. 249 Thy honesty and love doth mince this matter, Making it light to Cassio. *Ant. & Cleop.* I. ii. 114 Speak to me home, mince not the general tongue. **1649** BP. HALL *Cases Consc.* (1650) 160 Some Doctors . . . would either excuse, or mince the matter. **1741** RICHARDSON *Pamela* II. 82 Well, Tom, said he, don't mince the matter. Tell me, before Mrs. Andrews, what they said. **1840** CARLYLE *Heroes* ii (1858) 239 A candid ferocity, if the case call for it, is in him; he does not mince matters.

Mind is the man, The.

[CICERO *Rep.* 6. 24. 26 *Mens cuiusque est quisque.* Each man's mind is himself.] **1642** D. ROGERS *Naaman* 163 The mind of every man is the man: be it the spirit of the miser, the mind of the drunkard . . . they are more precious to them than life itself!

Mind other men, but most yourself.

1639 CLARKE 217.

Mind to me a kingdom is, My.

[SENECA *Thyestes* 380 *Mens regnum bona possidet.*] **1588** SIR E. DYER *My Mind to Me a Kingdom is* (Title of Poem). **1606** CHAPMAN *Mons. d'Olive* II. ii. 21 His mind is his kingdom. **1609** JONSON *Case Altered* I. i *On.* I am no gentleman born, I must confess; but *my mind to me a kingdom is. Ant.* Truly a very good saying.

Mind what you must live by.

1639 CLARKE 21.

Mind your (own) business.

1639 CLARKE 11. **1882** H. H. ALMOND in R. J. MACKENZIE *Life* (1905) 358 The Devil has got a lot of maxims which his adherents . . . are not slow to use—'Mind your own business'. . . . You can't do more good than by putting down . . . evil . . . without being too nice as to whether you have a right to interfere or not. **1890** J. PAYN *Burnt Mil.* xxv When people ask me . . . what is the meaning of this reformation, I shall tell them . . . to mind their own business.

Mind's chasing mice, Your.

1721 KELLY 384 . . . Eng. *Your wit's a wool gathering.*

Mind(s) (*noun*), *see also* Bashful m. hinders intent; Change his m. if he has no m. to change (Will never); Forehead and eye (In) lecture of m.; Keep my m. to myself (I will); Mad (You will never be), you are of so many m.; Man (What is a) but his m.; Many men have many m.; Men (So many), so many m.; Month's m. (To have a); Proud m. and beggar's purse; Resolved m. hath no cares; Sound m. in sound body; Unsound m. . . . if you feed you poison; Woman's m. change oft.

Mind (*verb*), *see also* God keep me from the man that has but one thing to m.; Never m. what people say.

Mine is yours (mine own), What's | and what is yours is mine.

1576 PETTIE *Petite Pall.* (Gollancz) I. 116 But that which is mine should be yours, and yours your own. **1604–5** SHAKS. *Meas. for Meas.* V. i. 536 Dear Isabel, I have a motion . . . Whereto if you'll a willing ear incline, What's mine is yours, and what is yours is mine. **1606–7** *Ant. & Cleop.* V. ii. 150 O, behold, How pomp is follow'd; mine will now be yours; And, should we shift estates, yours would be mine. **1666** TORRIANO 278 A Man may make bold with what's ones own, one would think: The English ever say, That which is mine, is my own. **1738** SWIFT (Dial. ii) 350 *Never.* Why, what's yours is mine, and what's mine is my own.

Mine, *see also* So much is m. as I enjoy.

Minerva to aid, Call | but bestir thyself.

[Gk. Σὺν Ἀθήνῃ καὶ χεῖρα κίνει. ERASM. *Ad.*

Cum Minerva manum quoque move.] **1853**
TRENCH V. 115 It was current long ago in
Greece: *Call Minerva to aid, but bestir thyself.*

Minerva, *see also* Sow teaching M.

Minister(s), *see* Hide nothing from thy m.;
Maidens' tochers and m.' stipends aye
less than called.

Mint[1] ere you strike.

1641 FERGUSSON 76. **1721** KELLY 251 . . .
Spoken to them that threaten us; give me
fair warning, and do your best. [[1] warn.]

Mint (= threatened), *see also* Long m. little
dint.

Mire, *see* Dun is in the m.; Likely lies in the
m.; Town but had a m. (Never a good).

Mirror, The best | is an old friend.

1640 HERBERT 331. **1902–4** LEAN IV. 149
There is no better looking-glass than an old
true friend. [Span.] No ay mejor espejo que
el amigo viejo.—NUÑEZ. 1555.

Mirror, *see also* Wine is the m. of the mind.

**Mirth of the world dureth but a
while, The.**

1573 SANDFORD (1576) H 2ᵛ. **1629** *Book of
Meery Riddles* Prov. 11.

Mirth, *see also* Ounce of m. worth pound of
sorrow.

**Miscall a Gordon in the raws of
Strathbogie, Never.**

1832 HENDERSON 6 . . . Strathbogie was the
district of the Gordons. Never speak ill of a
man on his own ground.

**Mischief comes by the pound and
goes away by the ounce.**

1573 SANDFORD (1576) 211. **1589** L. WRIGHT
Display of Dutie 29 Though mischiefe and
misery do come by pounds, and go away by
ounces: yet a pound of sorrow will not pay
an ounce of debt. **1639** CLARKE 165 Mis-
chiefs come by the pound but go away by
ounces. **1670** RAY 121. **1732** FULLER no. 3417.

Mischief has swift wings.

1605 *Sir T. Smith's Voyage into Russia* L 2ᵛ–
L 3 Mischiefe hath the winges of Thought and
Resolution. **1609** J. MELTON *Six-fold Politician* 13 (A) Mischiefe is well saide to haue
swift winges.

**Mischief hatcheth, mischief catcheth,
He that.**

1623 CAMDEN 271.

Mischief, The more | the better sport.

1721 KELLY 337 . . . A common, but wicked
and foolish saying. **1747** LD. LOVAT in
CHAMBERS *Hist. Rebel. Scot.* (1828) II. xii. 265
When informed . . . that a scaffold had fallen
near the place of execution, by which many

persons were killed . . . , he only remarked,
'The mair mischief, the better sport.'

Mischief, *see also* Better a m. than incon-
venience; Money for m. (They can find);
Mother of m. no bigger than midge's wing;
No m. but a woman . . . at bottom;
Women in m. are wiser.

Misdeeds, *see* Mends is worth m.

Miser, *see* Feast to a m.'s (No).

**Miserable (Covetous) man maketh a
penny of a farthing, and the liberal
of a farthing sixpence, The.**

1640 HERBERT 326. **1707** MAPLETOFT 55.
1855 BOHN 284.

Miserere, *see* Oportet comes in place (When).

**Misery enough to have once been
happy, It is.**

1562 BULLEIN *Bulwark of Defence* (*Book of
Compounds* f. 76) (Lean iv. 150) There is no
greater adversity than in misery to remember
prosperity. **1576** PETTIE *Petite Pall.* (Gollancz) I. 28 Adversity is ever most bitter to
him who hath long time lived in prosperity.
1619 J. FAVOUR *Antiquity* 413. **1624** BURTON
Anat. Mel. II. iii. III. *Miserum est fuisse
felicem* . . . it is a great miserie to have beene
happy. **1639** CLARKE 166. [See the sentiment
illustrated at large in *N. & Q.* 174. 436.]

**Misery (Adversity) makes (acquaints
men with) strange bedfellows.**

1611–12 SHAKS. *Tempest* II. ii. 42 My best
way is to creep under his gaberdine; there is
no other shelter hereabout: misery acquaints
a man with strange bedfellows. **1837–9**
LOCKHART *Life Scott* xii (1860) 112 Literature, like misery, makes men acquainted with
strange bed-fellows. **1861** DEAN STANLEY
Hist. East. Ch. v (1862) 160 As increasing
troubles made strange bedfellows, the Meli-
tian schismatics and the Arian heretics, once
deadly enemies, became sworn allies against
. . . Athanasius. **1927** *Times* 27 Aug. 12/1
The . . . alliance of 1923–5 was an illustration
of the adage that adversity makes strange
bedfellows.

**Misery may be mother where one
beggar is driven to beg of another.**

1546 HEYWOOD II. x. 82 But as men saie,
misery maie be mother, Where one begger is
dryuen to beg of an other.

Misfortune makes foes of friends.

c. **1386** CHAUCER *Monk's T.* 3434–6 For what
man that hath freendes thurgh Fortúne
Mishape wol maken hem enemys, as I gesse;
This proverbe is ful sooth and ful commúne.

**Misfortunes (Hardships) never (sel-
dom) come alone (single).**

[*Ezekiel* vii. 5.] *c.* **1300** *King Alisaunder* l. 1282
Men telleth in olde mone, 'The qued[1] comuth
nowher alone'. *c.* **1350** IPOMADON l. 1623

Come never sorow be it one, But there come mo full gryme. *c.* **1490** *Partonope* (E.E.T.S.) I. l. 5542 For efter won euylle comythe mony mo. **1509** A. BARCLAY *Ship of Fools* (1874) II. 251 For wyse men sayth, and oft it fallyth so . . . That one myshap fortuneth neuer alone. *c.* **1580** SPELMAN *Dial.* (Roxb. Cl.) 3 A man cannot have one losse, but more will ffollowe. **1600–1** SHAKS. *Hamlet* IV. v. 78 When sorrows come, they come not single spies, But in battalions. *Ibid.* IV. vii. 164 One woe doth tread upon another's heels. **1622** MABBE tr. *Aleman's Guzman d'Alf.* I. iii. 29 *marg.* Misfortunes seldome come alone. **1721** KELLY 143 Hardships sindle (i.e. seldom) come single. **1837** MARRYAT *Diary on Con.* xxxii People will agree in the trite observation that misfortunes never come single. **1894** BLACKMORE *Perlycross* xxv As misfortunes never come single, the sacred day robbed him of another fine resource. **1905** HOUSMAN ed. *Juvenalis Satvrae* (1931) Pref. xvi Misfortunes never come single, and the prattlers about P's authority are afflicted not only with lack of understanding but with loss of memory. [¹ harm.]

Misfortune(s), *see also* Strength enough to bear m. of friends; Worst m. are those which never befall.

Misreckoning (Wrong reckoning) is no payment.

1546 HEYWOOD II. iv. 53 No (quoth she) nor misrecknyng is no paiment. **1639** CLARKE 126 Wrong reckoning is no payment. *Ibid.* 156 (Misreckoning). **1721** KELLY 348 *Wrong count is no payment.* And therefore all accounts pass, errors excepted.

Miss is as good as a mile, A.

[Formerly *An inch in a miss is as good as an ell.*] **1825** SCOTT *Jrnl.* 3 Dec. (1890) I. 32 He was very near being a poet—but a miss is as good as a mile, and he always fell short of the mark. **1872** BLACKMORE *Maid Sker* xxxii A miss is as good as a mile, your reverence. Many a cannon ball has passed me nearer than your horse's hoof.

Miss the bus, To.

[= to miss an opportunity.] **1915** C. J. DENNIS *Sentimental Bloke* 118 The deeds and words of some un'appy bloke Who's missed the bus. **1922** *Daily Mail* 28 Oct. 3/3 The Prime Minister has missed the bus' . . . He has thrown away the greatest opportunity ever offered . . . to any statesman. **1945** *Evening Standard* 4 Aug. All Spaniards I spoke to realized that their government had missed the bus.

Miss the cushion, To.

[= to miss the mark, err.] *c.* **1525** SKELTON *Col. Cloute* 998 And whan he weneth to syt Yet maye he mysse the quysshyon. **1571** HANMER *Chron. Irel.* (1623) 168 He was elected Archbishop of St. Davids, but at Rome he was outbid, by him that had more money, and missed the Cushin. **1608** HIERON *Defence* II. 157 He hath missed the cushen and sitteth bare.

Miss, *see also* Inch in a m. as good as ell.

Mist comes from the hill, When the | then good weather it doth spill: when the mist comes from the sea, then good weather it will be.

1846 DENHAM 18.

Mist, *see also* Scottish m. will wet Englishman.

Mistakes, *see* Makes no m. makes nothing.

Mistaking, *see* Giving and taking easy m.

Mrs. Grundy say? What will.

[*Mrs. Grundy* is an imaginary personification of the tyranny of conventional propriety, first appearing in:—] **1798** T. MORTON *Speed the Plough* II. iii (1801) 29 *Dame Ashfield.* If shame should come to the poor child [her daughter]—I say, Tummas, what would Mrs. Grundy say then? **1813** *Examiner* 15 Mar. 170/2 What will Mrs. Grundy say? **1857** LOCKER *Lond. Lyrics* (1874) 102 And many are afraid of God—And more of Mrs. Grundy. **1875** SMILES *Thrift* 249 Custom, habit, fashion, use, and wont, are all represented in her . . . 'What will Mrs. Grundy say?' quells many a noble impulse, hinders many a self-denying act.

Mrs. Partington mopping up the Atlantic, Like.

1831 SYD. SMITH *Speech at Taunton on Reform Bill* The attempt of the Lords to stop the progress of reform, reminds me of . . . Mrs. Partington . . . trundling her mop, . . . and vigorously pushing away the Atlantic Ocean [during an inundation of sea-water at Sidmouth, in 1824]. **1894** F. COWAN *Sea Prov.* 60 Like Mrs. Partington mopping against the tide of the Atlantic.

Mistress, Such | such Nan; such master, such man.

1573 TUSSER 47 (E.D.S.) 103.

Mistress, *see also* Hackney m. hackney maid; Three things cost, . . . love of m. . . . .

Misty morning may have a fine day, A.

1721 KELLY 48. **1732** FULLER no. 327.

Misunderstanding brings lies to town.

1639 CLARKE 2. **1670** RAY 121 . . . Lies and false reports arise most part from mistake and misunderstanding.

Mitcham, *see* Sutton.

Mittens, *see* Handle without m.

Mix your liquor, Never.

a. **1831** C. DIBDIN JR. *Ben the Boatswain* (1886) 266 By drinking grog I lost my life; so, lest my fate you meet, Why, never mix your liquor, lads, but always drink it neat.

Mixture, *see* Right m. good mortar.

Mob has many heads, but no brains, The.

1732 FULLER no. 4653. 1747 FRANKLIN Nov. A mob's a monster; heads enough but no brains.

Mob, *see also* Keep yourself from . . . tumult of m.

Mobberley hole, *see* Rain always comes out of.

Mock no pannier men; your father was a fisher.

1678 RAY 78. 1732 FULLER no. 3425 (with if' before 'your').

Mock not a cobbler for his black thumbs.

1642 FULLER *H. & P. State* III. ii (1841) 146 Neither flout any for his profession, if honest, though poor and painful. Mock not a cobbler for his black thumbs.

Mock not, quoth Mumford, when his wife called him cuckold.

1659 HOWELL *Eng. Prov.* 9/1. 1732 FULLER no. 3426.

Mocking (Scorning) is catching.

1533 J. HEYWOOD *Play of Love* l. 568 (BRANDL, *Quellen* 177) (A) For who so that mocketh shall surely stur This olde prouerbe mockum moccabitur. 1678 RAY 200 *Scorning* is catching. He that scorns any condition, action or employment, may come to be . . . driven upon it himself. 1721 KELLY 255 *Mocking is catching.* Spoken to discourage people from mimicking any man's imperfections, lest you contract a habit of them. 1738 SWIFT (Dial. i) 340 *Miss.* [*imitating Lady Answerall's* tone.] Very pretty! one breaks the heart, and the other the belly. *Lady A.* Have a care, they say, mocking is catching.

Mocking, *see also* Hanging's stretching, m.'s catching.

Mocks a cripple, ought to be whole, He that.

1586 PETTIE *Guazzo's Civ. Conv.* 76 For as the Prouerbe is, Hee that mocketh the lame, must take heede that he himselfe go vpright. 1640 HERBERT 343.

Modesty be a virtue, Though | yet bashfulness is a vice.

1732 FULLER no. 5006.

Modesty sets off one newly come to honour.

1651 HERBERT 366.

Modish, *see* Careless (The more), more m.

Mole, *see* Argus abroad, m. at home.

Moment, *see* Spur of the m.

Monday for wealth, Tuesday for health, Wednesday the best day of all; Thursday for crosses, Friday for losses, Saturday no luck at all.

1850 N. & Q., 1st Ser. II. 515. [*Days of the Week.—Marriage.*]

Monday, *see also* St. M.; Saturday is working day, M. holiday of preachers.

Money, All things are obedient to.

[HORACE *Sat.* 2. 3. 94–6 *Omnis enim res, Virtus, fama, decus, divina humanaque pulchris Divitiis parent.*] c. 1390 CHAUCER *Tale of Melibee* B 2740 Salomon seith that alle thynges obeyen to moneye. c. 1390 GOWER *Conf. Amantis* v. 244 All the world to gold obeieth. 1539 TAVERNER f. 14 (A).

Money answers all things.

1611 BIBLE *Eccles.* x. 19.

Money be not thy servant, If | it will be thy master.

1666 TORRIANO 64 Money is a Servant to him who can make use of it, otherwise it is a Master. 1732 FULLER no. 2694. 1887 LD. AVEBURY *Pleas. of Life* II. ii This is of course on the supposition that you are master of money, that the money is not master of you.

Money begets (breeds, gets) money

1572 T. WILSON *Discourse upon Usury* (1925) 248 Money getteth money. 1593 SHAKS. *Venus & Adon.* 767 Gold that's put to use more gold begets. 1666 TORRIANO 64 Moneys beget moneys. 1689 SELDEN *Table-Talk* (Arb.) 114 'Tis a vain thing to say, Money begets not Money; for that no doubt it does. 1841 MARRYAT *Poacher* xxxvii Seven hundred pounds; eh, youngster? . . . Money breeds money. 1861 TRAFFORD *City & Suburb* xiv Money makes money, it is said. 1872 BESANT & RICE *Ready-m. Mort.* ii Money gets money. If you have but much, you must, in spite of yourself, have more.

Money burns (a hole) in your pocket, Your.

[= clamours to be spent.] c. 1530 MORE *Wks.* (1557) 195 (A) A little wanton money which . . . burned out the bottom of his purse. 1573 TUSSER X (E.D.S.) 19 Sonne, think not thy monie purse bottom to burn, but keepe it for profite, to serue thine owne turn. 1846 CAPT. MARRYAT *Privateersman* viii How could I get rid of my money, which burns in my pocket, if I did not spend as much in one day as would suffice for three weeks? 1875 SMILES *Thrift* 139 A man who has more money about him than he requires... is tempted to spend it. . . . It is apt to 'burn a hole in his pocket'.

Money comes from him like drops of blood, His.

1678 RAY 90 *A covetous person.* . . . 1688 BUNYAN *Jer. Sinner Saved* Wks. (1855) I. 87

Niggardly rich men, whose money comes from them like drops of blood.

Money do ? What will not. (*Cf.* Gold do, &c.)

1567 HARMAN *Caveat* (Viles & Furnivall) 60 What can not be hadde for money, as the prouerbe sayth (*Omnia venalia Romæ*). **1681** ROBERTSON *Phraseol. Generalis* 892 (A).

Money draws money.

1666 TORRIANO 239 Wealth goes to wealth. **1880** MRS. OLIPHANT *Greatest Heir* ii Others ... insisted on leaving their money to Lucy on the ... principle that to those who have shall be given ... 'Money draws money', the proverb says.

Money for mischief, They can find | when they can find none to buy corn.

1678 RAY *Adag. Hebr.* 409.

Money in his purse, He that hath | cannot want a head for his shoulders.

1659 HOWELL *Eng. Prov.* 13/2.

Money in thy purse, Put (Keep).

1604–5 SHAKS. *Othello* I. iii. 345, &c. Put money in thy purse. **1659** HOWELL *Eng. Prov.* 17/1 My friend keep money in thy purse; '*Tis one of Solomon's Proverbs said one.* **1855** BOHN 456 My son, put money in thy purse and then keep it.

Money, To have | is a fear, not to have it a grief. (*Cf.* Gold, when we have, &c.)

[*Anth. Pal.* 9. 394 χρυσέ ... τὸ ἔχειν σε φόβος καὶ μὴ ἔχειν ὀδύνη.] **1640** HERBERT 345.

Money is a good servant, but a bad master.

1633 MASSINGER *New Way* IV. i (Merm.) 173 L. *All.* I must grant, Riches, well got, to be a useful servant, But a bad master. **1855** BOHN 453.

Money is often lost for want of money.

1616 DRAXE 69. **1855** BOHN 453.

Money is round, and rolls away.

1619 *Helpe to Discourse* (1640) 120 (A) Why is the forme of money round? Because it is to runne from every man. **1659** HOWELL *Ital. Prov.* 2 Money is round, and so quickly trills away. **1902–4** LEAN I. 424 Bawbees are round and rin away: a grip o' th' ground is gude to hae. [*N. Fife F. L. Journal*, ii. 91.] **1905** A. MACLAREN *Expos., Matt.* II. 256 It is not for nothing that sovereigns are made circular, for they roll very rapidly, and 'riches take to themselves wings and fly away'.

Money is that which art hath turned up trump.

1659 HOWELL *Eng. Prov.* 18/1. **1670** RAY 18.

Money is the sinews of (love as well as of) war.

[LIBANIUS orat. 46 τὰ νεῦρα τοῦ πολέμου. CIC. *Philippica* 5. 2. 5 *Nervos belli pecuniam* (*largiri*).] **1573** SANDFORD (1576) 138 K4 *Timotheus* affirmeth, that money is the sinewes of all things. *c.* **1590** G. HARVEY *Marginalia* 101. **1592** BACON in Parliament (H. TOWNSHEND *Historical Collections* (1680) 60) Laws are the sinews of peace, money of war. **1592** LYLY *Midas* I. i. Wks. (1902) III. 117 *Mel.* I would wish that everything I touched might turn to gold: this is the sinews of war. **1599** JAMES VI *Basil. Dor.* II (Roxb. Cl.) 68 Before ye take on warres, ... remember, that money is *Nervus belli*. **1625** BACON *Ess., Greatness of K.* (Arb.) 473 Neither is Money the Sinewes of Warre, (as it is trivially said) where the Sinewes of Mens Armes, in Base and Effeminate People, are failing. **1642** FULLER *H. & P. State* II. xx (1841) 114 (*The Good Soldier*) Moneys are the sinews of war; yet if these sinews should chance to be shrunk, and pay casually fall short, he takes a fit of this convulsion patiently. **1732** FULLER no. 3442 Money is the sinew of love as well as of war. **1829–30** M. SCOTT *T. Cring. Log* vii A stream of gold and silver flowing into the Bank of England, ... thus supplying the sinews of war to the government. **1890** J. PAYN *Burnt Mil.* xxii These debts ... must be prejudicial indeed to any matrimonial project. Yet here was this young fellow actually offering to supply his rival with the sinews of war—and love.

Money is welcome though it come in a dirty clout.

1629 HOWELL *Lett.* 3 Aug. (1903) I. 309 Nor would I receive money in a dirty clout, if possibly I could be without it. **1659** Id. *Eng. Prov.* 13/2 Money is welcome, though it come in a shitten clout. **1721** KELLY 249 Money is welcome in a dirten clout. L. *Dulcis odor lucri ex re quâlibet.* **1723** DEFOE *Col. Jack* ii. Wks. (1912) I. 280 People say, when they have been talking of money that they could not get in, I wish I had it in a foul clout.

Money is wise, it knows its way.

1678 RAY 352 ... (*Som.*) Sayes the poor man that must pay as soon as he receives.

Money like hay, To make.

1835 J. M. WILSON in the *Tales of Borders* I. 17 Robin Paterson rented a farm ... of fifty acres, in which, as his neighbours said, he was 'making money like hay'.

Money makes a man free (recommends a man) everywhere.

1542 BECON *Early Wks.* (P.S.) 223 Whosoever hath money may go where he list, and do whatsoever he will at his own pleasure. **1731** *Poor Robin's Alm*, Expln. of Alm. *Eat boil'd or roast, or drink good Wine or Beer, But,* Money recommends you every where. **1737**

RAMSAY III. 190 Money maks a man free
ilka where.

Money makes marriage (the match).

1592 GREENE *Groatsworth of Witte* (Harrison)
26 Money now a dayes makes the match, or
else the match is marde. **1621** BURTON *Anat.
Mel.* III. ii. III. iii (1651) **478** There is another
great allurement, . . . and that is mony;
veniunt a dote sagittæ, mony makes the match.
1732 FULLER no. 3445.

Money makes the man.

[L. *Divitiae virum faciunt.*] **1542** BECON *Early
Wks.* (P.S.) 222. **1616** DRAXE 131. **1662**
FULLER (*Hants*) II. 5 We commonly say, . . .
In the *Change*; 'Money makes a man', which
puts him in a solvable condition. **1828**
LYTTON *Pelham* xxxv The continent only
does for us English people to see. . . . Here,
as you know, 'money makes the man'. **1850**
KINGSLEY *Alton L.* ii Money most truly and
fearfully 'makes the man'. A difference in
income, as you go lower, makes more and
more difference . . . in all which polishes the
man.

Money makes the mare to go.

1573 SANDFORD 213 Money makes the horse
to goe. **1670** RAY 122. **1690** T. D'URFEY
Collin's Walk iii. 96 As Money makes the
Mare to go, Even so it makes the Lawyer too.
1809 MALKIN *Gil Blas* I. viii My business on
the high road is not to hear sermons. Money
makes my mare to go. **1914** K. F. PURDON
Folk of Furry F. iii It's a true saying,
'Money makes the mare to go'! Of course
every one had to give in to Julia on account
of the fortune she had.

Money, He that hath no | needeth no purse.

1616 DRAXE 140. **1666** TORRIANO 63. **1813**
RAY 139.

Money never comes out of season.

1616 DRAXE s.v. 'Golde' 83. **1639** CLARKE
220.

Money or your life! Your.

1864 J. PAYN *Lost Sir Massingb.* xxix A
pistol was protruded into the carriage. 'Your
money or your life! . . . ,' said a rough voice.

Money refused loseth its brightness.

1640 HERBERT 338.

Money wants no followers.

1651 HERBERT 373.

Money will do anything.

1613 W. GAMAGE, *Linsey-Woolsey* C 1 The
prouerbe is, Dame Mony can do All. **1616**
DRAXE 131. **1623** WODROEPHE 475 Mony
doth all Things.

Money will do more than my lord's letter.

c. **1609** JONSON *Ev. Man in Humour* II. v. 50.
1678 RAY 177. **1732** FULLER no. 3447.

Money, wisdom, and good faith, Of | there is commonly less than men count upon.

1605 BACON *Adv. Learn.* II. xxiii (O.U.P.) 232
It is an error frequent for men to shoot over,
and to suppose deeper ends and more compass
reaches than are: the Italian proverb being
. . . for the most part true: Di danari, di seno,
e di fede, Cè nè manco che non credi:[1] There
is commonly less money, less wisdom, and
less good faith, than men do account upon.
[[1] GIUSTI *Proverbi Toscani* 263 Danari, senno
e fede, ce n'è manco l'uom crede.]

Money, wit, and virtue, Of | believe one-fourth of what you hear.

1707 MAPLETOFT 8. **1855** BOHN 466.

Money would be gotten if there were money to get it with.

1721 KELLY 250 . . . Intimating that the man
would thrive, if he had a stock.

Money you refuse will never do you good, The.

1707 MAPLETOFT 2. **1855** BOHN 510.

Money, *see also* Abundance of m. ruins
youth; Bad m. drives out good; Beauty
is potent, m. omnipotent; Dally not with
women or m.; Eggs for m. (Take); Get m.
in a desert; God send us some m. quoth
Earl of Eglinton; God send you . . . and
me more m.; Hath it and will not keep
it (He that), . . . shall want m.; Health and
m. go far; Health without m. half ague;
Hole under his nose that his m. runs into;
Know what m. is (Would you), borrow;
Latin, a horse, and m. (With), thou wilt
pass; Little m. as manners (If you had);
Look for your m. where you lost it; Lose
your time (If you), you cannot get m.;
Love does much, m. everything; Love
lasts as m. endures; Love of m. and of
learning rarely meet; Love or m. (For);
Man without m. no man at all; Many a
thing's made for m.; Many means to get
m.; Marrieth for love without m. (Who);
Merchant bare that hath m. (He is not);
Moyen does mickle but m. does more;
Much m. makes a country poor; Muck and
m. go together; No m. no Swiss; Patience,
time, and m. accommodate; Pay your m.
and take your choice; Plays his m.
ought not to value it (He that); Prate . . .
but it's m. buys lands; Public m. is like
holy water; Put one's m. on wrong horse;
Ready m.; Rich man's m. hangs him;
Sign invites you in, m. redeem you out;
Skilfullest wanting m. is scorned; Talk is
but talk, m. buys lands; Tell m. after your
father; Throw good m. after bad; Trade
is mother of m.; Travel through world
(To) . . . m. and patience; Trust him with
untold m. (You may); Turn the m. when
hear cuckoo; Want of m. want of comfort:

Will buyeth, m. payeth; Words are but sands, m. buys lands.

Moneyless (Silverless) man goes fast through the market, A.

1721 KELLY 10 *A silverless man goes fast through the market.* Because he does not stay to cheapen or buy. **1732** FULLER no. 330 A moneyless man goes fast thro' the market.

Monk out of his cloister is like a fish out of water, A.

[L. *Sicut piscis sine aqua caret vita, ita sine monasterio monachus.* Decretal of Gratian.] *c.* **1386** CHAUCER *Prol.* 179–81 Ne that a Monk when he is recchélees Is likned til a fissh that is waterlees ; This to seyn, a Monk out of his cloystre.

Monk's hood, *see* Bean in a m. h. (Like a).

Monk(s), *see also* Cowl does not make m.; Do better (He that cannot) must be m.; Ox before . . . m. on all sides (Take heed of); Portman, Horner . . . when the m. went out they came in; Runaway m. never praises convent; Three things are insatiable.

Monkey's allowance, more kicks than halfpence.

1824 SCOTT *St. Ronan's* xxxiv Which is like monkey's allowance, I suppose', said the traveller, 'more kicks than halfpence'. **1833** MARRYAT *P. Simple* ii When you get on board, you'll find monkey's allowance— more kicks than half-pence. **1900** E. J. HARDY *Mr. Thomas Atkins* 297 On active service kicks are more plentiful than halfpence.

Monmouth caps.

[= a flat round cap.] **1585–1616** *Shirburn Ballads* xxix (1907) 118 'The miller in his best array'.—He puts on His Monmouth cap. **1598–9** SHAKS. *Hen. V* IV. vii. 104 *Flu.* Welshmen . . . wearing leeks in their Monmouth caps. **1662** FULLER (*Monmouthshire*) II. 432 The best caps were formerly made at Monmouth. . . . The trade was . . . removed hence to Beaudly . . . yet . . . they are called Monmouth caps unto this day.

Monmouth caps, *see also* Dunmow bacon.

Month of Sundays, It will not happen in a.

1842–3 W. H. MAXWELL *Hector O'Hal.* xviii If she's not married till she marries me, she'll be single for a month of Sundays.

Month's mind to a thing, To have a.

[= a strong inclination.] **1575** GASCOIGNE *Glass of Govt.* II. v. (A) She hath a monethes minde vnto Phylosarchus. **1594–5** SHAKS. *Two Gent.* I. ii. 134 I see you have a month's mind to them. **1598** HALL *Virgidemiarum The Three last Bookes. Of byting Satyres* Lib. 4 Sat. 4 sig. D 1 *b.* He thaws like Chaucer's frosty Ianiuere, And sets a Months minde vpon smyling May. **1605** *London Prodigal* I. ii. 143 (*Shaks. Apoc.*) 197 He hath a moneths mind

here to mistresse *Francesse.* **1631** BRATHWAITE *Whimzies* (1859) 118 This hath made him sometimes to have a month's mind to go for Virginia. **1670** RAY 186 . . . In ancient wills, we find often mention of a moneths mind. . . . The meaning was, because the party deceased, used to appoint a second lesser funeral solemnity for remembrance of him. **1738** SWIFT (Dial. i) 342 *Col.* She had a month's mind to Dick Frontless, and thought to run away with him.

Months in the year curse a fair Februeer, All the.

1670 RAY 40. **1847** R. CHAMBERS *Pop. Rhymes Scot.* 364 Good weather in February is regarded as an unfavourable symptom of what is to come: A' the months o' the year curse a fair Februar.

Moon does not heed the barking of dogs (wolves), The.

[L. *Latrantem curatne alta Diana canem?* Does Diana on high care for the dog that barks at her?] **1580** LYLY *Euph. & his Eng.* (Arb.) 386 Eager Wolues bark at ye Moone, though they cannot reach it. **1599** MINSHEU 4 i 2ᵛ For all the dogs barking the moone will stand where it did. **1621** BURTON *Anat. Mel.* II. iii. vii (1651) 358 Doth the moon care for the barking of a dog? They detract, scoffe, and raile (saith one), and bark at me on every side; but I . . . vindicate myself by contempt alone. **1660** W. SECKER *Nonsuch Prof.* II (1891) 74 Believers resemble the moon, which emerges from her eclipse by keeping her motion; and ceases not to shine because the dogs bark at her.

Moon is made of green cheese, He thinks (or would make me believe) the.

a. **1529** FRITH *Antith.* (1829) 315 They would make men believe . . . that the moon is made of green cheese. **1546** HEYWOOD II. vii. 69 Ye fet circumquaques to make me beleue Or thinke, that the moone is made of a gréene chéese. **1611** COTGRAVE S.V. 'Arain' (Wee say of such an Idiot) hee thinkes the Moone is made of greene cheese. **1641** FERGUSSON 48 *Of false persons* . . . He wald gar a man trow that the moon is made of green cheis, or thet the cat took the heron. **1783** AINSWORTH *Lat. Dict.* (Morell) 1. s.v. *Moon,* Tell me the moon is made of green cheese! **1863** KINGSLEY *Water Bab.* iv. 195 Writing a great book, . . . in which he proved that the moon was made of green cheese.

Moon shows a silver shield, If the | be not afraid to reap your field; but if she rises haloed round, soon we'll tread on deluged ground.

1883 ROPER 8. **1893** INWARDS 64.

Moon's in the full, When the | then wit's in the wane.

c. **1621** DEKKER, &c. The Witch of Edmonton (*Dramatic Wks.* 1873 IV. 367). **1846** DENHAM 4.

Moon's not seen where the sun shines, The.

1576 PETTIE *Petite Pall.* (Gollancz) II. 109 When sun shineth, the light of the stars is not seen. **1594–5** SHAKS. *L.L.L.* IV. iii. 230 My love, her mistress, is a gracious moon; She, an attending star, scarce seen a light. **1616** DRAXE 128 Where the Sunne shineth, the Moone hath nought to doe. **1678** RAY 178.

Moon(s), *see* Bald m. . . . another pint; Bark against m.; Cast beyond the m.; Changeful as the m.; Churl fall out of m. (Care lest); Cry for the m.; Day that you do well there will be seven m.; Friday's m. comes too soon; Full m. (Like a); Full m. brings fair weather; Gazed at m. and fell in gutter; Glower at m. and fall on midden; Man in the m.; Michaelmas Day (So many days old the m. is); Michaelmas m. rises soon; Midsummer m.; No m. no man; Old of the m. (In the) cloudy morning bodes; Once in a blue m.; Pale m. doth rain; Round the m. there is a brugh (When); Saturday's m. . . . comes too soon; Shape a coat for the m.; Shoot the m.; Sun, m. . . . against us; Sussex m.

Moonlight flitting, To make a.

[= to remove by night, or by stealth.] **1721** KELLY 145 . . . to signify that a man has run away for fear of his creditors. **1821** GALT *Annals of Par.* xxxi He was fain to make a moonlight flitting, leaving his wife for a time to manage his affairs. **1824** MOIR *Mansie W.* xvii The whole covey of them, no better than a set of swindlers, . . . made that very night a moonlight flitting. **1892** STEVENSON *Wrecker* v I made a moonlight flitting, a thing never dignified.

Moonlight, *see also* Keep sheep by m.

Moonrakers, *see* Wiltshire m.

Moonshine in the mustard-pot.

1639 CLARKE 68. **1678** RAY 76 Thou shalt have moonshine i' th' mustard-pot for it, *i.e.* nothing.

Moonshine in the water.

1468 *Paston Letters* (Gairdner) II. 326 If Sir Thomas Howys wer . . . made byleve and put in hope of the moone shone in the water and I wot nat what. **1546** HEYWOOD I. xi. 36 I will as soone be hylt, As waite againe for the mooneshine in the water. **1594–5** SHAKS. *L.L.L.* V. ii. 209 O vain petitioner! beg a greater matter; Thou now request'st but moonshine in the water.

Moonshine, *see also* Mouthful of m.

Moor, *see* Bare m. that he goes over and gets not cow.

Moore, *see* Scratch a M.

Moors, The more | the better victory.

1678 RAY 351. **1813** *Ibid.* 140 A saying used by the Spaniards, when the Moors were in Spain.

Moors, *see also* Jews spend at Easter; Three M. to a Portuguese.

Mope-eyed[1] by (with) living so long a maid, You are.

1648 HERRICK *Hesper., Upon Himselfe* Mopey'd I am, as some have said, Because I've liv'd so long a maid. **1678** RAY 346. **1721** KELLY 394 . . . Spoken to those who overlook a thing before them. [1 purblind.]

Morally wrong can never be politically right, That which is.

1902–4 LEAN IV. 109.

Moraoh downs, hard and never ploughed, Like.

1864 *N. & Q.* 3rd Ser. v. 275. *Cornish Provs.*

More afraid (frightened) than hurt.

1530 PALSGRAVE 558 (A) He was sorer frayed than hurt. **1546** HEYWOOD I. iv. 9 Shall feare all thyng, that he shall let fall all, And be more fraid then hurt. **1579** LYLY *Euph.* (Arb.) 189 Certeinly thou art more afraide then hurte. **1641** FERGUSSON 48 He is war fleyit[1] nor he is hurt. **1725** A. RAMSAY *Gent. Shep.* v. i Bauldy's more afraid than hurt. **1827** LAMB *Lett.* to Patmore 19 Jul. Down went my sister through a crazy chair . . . Mary was more frightened than hurt. [1 frightened.]

More bare (Worse shod) than the shoemaker's wife and the smith's mare, None.

1546 HEYWOOD I. xi. 32 But who is wurs shod, than the shoemakers wyfe, With shops full of newe shoes all hir lyfe? **1603** FLORIO tr. *Montaigne* I. xxiv. (1897) I. 197 When we see a man ill shod, if he chance to be a shoemaker, we say . . . commonly none goes worse shod than they. Even so . . . experience doth often shew us, a physician less healthy, a divine less reformed, . . . a wise man less sufficient than another. **1641** FERGUSSON 94 The Sowter's wife is worst shod. **1678** RAY 202. **1721** KELLY 258 None worse sho'd than the shoemaker's wife, and the smith's mare. **1876** SMILES *Scotch Naturalist* 380 His large family . . . were all . . . well shod, notwithstanding the Scottish proverb to the contrary. 'The Smith's mare and the shoemaker's bairns are aye the worst shod.'

More cost, more worship.

1591 HARINGTON *Orl. Furioso*, Adv. to Reader All their figures are cut in wood, & none in metall, and in that respect inferior to these, at least (by the old prouerbe) the more cost, the more worship. **1639** CLARKE 134. **1855** BOHN 511 The more worship, the more cost.

More folks are wed than keep good houses.

1683 MERITON *Yorks. Ale* 17.

More fool than fiddler.

1678 RAY 245.

More fools in Henley.

1894 NORTHALL *Folk-phrases* 19 . . . Used by natives of Henley-in-Arden, co. *Warw.*, when strangers of remarkable appearance tarry in the main street. It might be made to cut both ways certainly.

More haste than good speed.

1542 UDALL tr. *Erasm. Apoph.* (1877) 41 (A) Soche persones, as do make moste hast in the beginning, haue commonly (accordyng to our Englishe prouerbe) worst spede toward the endyng. **1546** HEYWOOD I. viii. 16 I am taught to know, in more hast than good spéede How *Judicare* came into the Créede. **1642** FULLER *H. & P. State* v. xviii (1841) 438 Anna . . . made more haste than good speed, marrying Andronicus some weeks after the death of Alexius.

More Irish than the Irish themselves.

1860 RILEY *Dict. Lat. Quot.* (Bohn) 146 *Hibernicis ipsis Hibernior.*—'More Irish than the Irish themselves'. A specimen of modern dog Latin, quoted against those who are guilty of bulls or other absurdities. **1871** C. M. YONGE *Cameos from Eng. H.* 2nd Ser. xviii (1899) 189 In the . . . fourteenth century . . . the great feudal chiefs, descended usually from the Norman and English conquerors, . . . greatly contemning . . . 'the mere Irish', though other people pronounced them . . . '*Hibernis ipsis Hiberniores*' (more Irish than the Irish). **1929** *Times* 30 Jan. 10/3 The Norman-Irish de Burghs, often 'more Irish than the Irish themselves'.

More knave than fool.

1624 T. BREWER *A Knot of Fools* More Knaue than foole. *c.* **1630** In *Roxburghe Ballads* (Hindley) I. 72 This man's more knaue than foole. **1738** SWIFT (Dial. ii) 349 *Nev.* I take him to be more knave than fool.

More know Tom Fool than Tom Fool knows.

1656 S. HOLLAND *Wit and Fancy in a Maze* 63 In all Comedies more know the Clown, then the Clown knows. **1723** DEFOE *Col. Jack* xvii. Wks. (Bohn) I. 506 It was no satisfaction to me that I knew not their faces, for they might know mine . . . , according to the old English proverb, 'that more knows Tom Fool, than Tom Fool knows'. **1896** J. C. HUTCHESON *Crown & Anchor* xxxiii Some fellow . . . accosts me . . . as if I were an old friend . . . illustrating the truth of the adage, . . . 'More people know Tom Fool than Tom Fool knows'!

More like the devil than St. Laurence.

1678 RAY 256.

More malice than matter.

1678 RAY 352. (*Som.*).

More matter, less art.

1600–1 SHAKS. *Hamlet* II. ii. 95 More matter, with less art.

More nice than wise.

1581 B. RICH *Farewell to Militarie Prof.*

(Shaks. Soc.) 139 I warrant you, thei can make it more nice then wise. **1682** BUNYAN *Greatness of Soul* Wks. (1855) I. 128 Calling those that cry out so hotly against it, men more nice than wise. **1721** KELLY 249 . . . Spoken when people out of bashfulness leave a thing unsaid, or a person unspoken to, which would have contributed to their interest.

More rain, more rest; more water will suit the ducks best.

1864 *N. & Q.* 3rd Ser. V. 208 *Cornish Provs.*

More royalist than the king.

1904 'H. S. MERRIMAN' *The Last Hope* xxxv The Duchess of Angoulême, . . . who had despised . . . Louis XVIII and Charles X, for the concessions they had made—who was more Royalist than the King.

More sauce than pig.

28 June **1624** *Ballad* entered in Stationers' Register (Arb. iv. 119). **1659** N.R. 77, with 'meat' for 'pig'. **1738** SWIFT Dial. ii (A).

More than enough is too much.

1562 HEYWOOD, *First Hundred of Epigrams* no. 52 More then enough were wast. **1573** SANDFORD (1576) 212 Superfluitie, or that which is more than is inough, breaketh the couer. **1629** *Book of Meery Riddles* Prov. 107. **1732** FULLER no. 3461.

More than he is worth doth spend, Who | he makes a rope his life to end.

1670 RAY 24.

More the merrier; The | the fewer the better cheer (fare).

1530 PALSGRAVE 885 (A). **1546** HEYWOOD II. vii. 65 The mo the merier, we all daie here and sée. Ye, but the fewer the better fare (said hée). **1614** JONSON *Barth. Fair* I. i *Litt.* Ay, and Solomon too, Win, the more the merrier. **1629** T. ADAMS *Serm.* (1862) I. 244 The company is . . . all the patriarchs, prophets, saints. . . . Here, the more the merrier, yea, and the better cheer too. **1738** SWIFT (Dial. ii) 344 *Lady S.* Sir John, I beg you will sit down; come, the more the merrier. *Sir J.* Ay; but the fewer the better cheer. **1855** KINGSLEY *Westw. Ho!* xxiv 'The more the merrier: but the fewer the better fare.' I think we will do without our red friends for this time.

More there's in it, The | the more there's of it.

1738 SWIFT (Dial. i) 337 *Never.* There's some dirt in my teacup. *Miss.* Come, come, the more there's in't, the more there's on't.

More thy years, The | the nearer (nigher) thy grave.

1611 GRUTER. **1614** CAMDEN 313. **1639** CLARKE 308.

More words than one go to a bargain. (*Cf.* Two (words) to make bargain.)

1590 LODGE *Rosalynde* (Greg) 92 There goes more words to a bargain than one. **1670** RAY 58. **1732** FULLER no. 3465.

More, There are more, *see also under significant words following.*

Morley's ducks, born without a notion, Like.

1878 *N. & Q.* 5th Ser. x. 10 'Like Morley's ducks, born without a notion'.... A Nottinghamshire saying ... spoken of some one ... committing a stupid action. A public-house at Sneinton ... had been kept by generations of Morleys, and one of them, in answer to a complaint of their straying into a neighbour's garden, said his ducks were 'born without a notion'.

Morn come and the meat with it, Let the.

1721 KELLY 231 ... Spoken to them who are solicitous for to-morrow's provision.

Morning dreams come true.

[HORACE *Sat.* 1. 10 *Post mediam noctem visus, cum somnia vera.* He appeared to me after midnight, when dreams are true.] **1540** PALSGRAVE *Acolastus* II (A) After Mydnyght men saye, that dreames be true. **1681** DRYDEN *Span. Friar* III. ii. Wks. (1701) II. 281 *Qu.* At break of Day, when Dreams, they say, are true. **1810** W. B. RHODES *Bombas. Fur.* This morn, ... I dreamt (and morning dreams come true, they say). **1912** A. MACLAREN *Exposn., Romans* 87 Our highest anticipations and desires are not unsubstantial visions, but morning dreams, which are proverbially sure to be fulfilled.

Morning hour has gold in its mouth, The.

1853 TRENCH V. 121 *The morning hour has gold in its mouth*;[1] ... the earlier hours given to toil will yield larger and more genial returns than the later, ... [and it] is true in respect of moral no less than mental acquisitions. [[1] Morgenstund hat Gold im Mund.]

Morning mountains, In the | in the evening fountains.

1640 HERBERT 340. **1855** BOHN 511 The morning to the mountain, the evening to the fountain.

Morning rain, For a | leave not your journey.

a. **1530** R. *Hill's Commonpl. Bk.* (E.E.T.S.) 131 He is no good swayn, þat lettith his jorney for þe rayn. **1640** HERBERT 362.

Morning sun, A | and a wine-bred child, and a Latin-bred woman, seldom end well.

1640 HERBERT 357.

Morning sun never lasts a day, The.

1640 HERBERT 335. **1754** FRANKLIN Nov. For age and want save while you may; No morning sun lasts a whole day.

Morning sun, *see also* Save while you may, no m. s. lasts whole day.

Morning(s), *see also* Cloudy m. turn to clear; Evening praises the day, m. a frost; Evening red and m. grey; Foul m. fair day; Gaudy m. wet afternoon; Misty m. fine day; Old of the moon (In the), cloudy m. bodes; Pride of the m.; Rely on glory of the m. (Never); Work in the m. may trimly be done.

Morsel, *see* Taken by a m.

Mortal, *see* All men are m.; Man is known m. by two things.

Mortar, No more | no more brick, a cunning knave has a cunning trick.

1678 RAY 296.

Mortar, *see also* Apothecary's m. spoils music; Fingers in m. (To have); Right mixture good m.

Mortimer, *see* Backare, quoth M.

Morton's[1] Fork (*or* Crutch).

[*a.* 1500] **1874** J. R. GREEN *Short Hist.* 296 'Mortons fork', extorted gifts to the exchequer from men who lived handsomely on the ground that their wealth was manifest, and from those who lived plainly on the plea, that economy had made them wealthy. **1894** *Dict. Nat. Biog.* XXXIX. 152 [Morton] has been traditionally known as the author of 'Morton's Fork' or 'Morton's Crutch', but ... he and Richard Foxe ... did their best to restrain Henry's[2] avarice. **1932** *Times* 11 Apr. 13/5 There is no alternative but to pay this 'benevolence' ... Nothing is said as to any payment by the Commissioners [of Inland Revenue] by way of interest ... Could 'Morton's fork' be more sharply pronged than this? [[1] Lord Chancellor, 1487. [2] Henry VII.]

Mort-stone, *see* Remove M.

Moses, *see* Stand M.; Tale of bricks is doubled (When) M. comes.

Moss, *see* Wood in a wilderness, m. in a mountain, are little thought of.

Mosse (*proper noun*), *see* Catch one napping, as M. did his mare.

Most take all.

a. **1633** G. HERBERT 'The Quidditie' *Wks.* (Hutchinson) 70. **1678** RAY 347.

Most things have two handles.

[EPICTETUS *Ench.* 63 Πᾶν πρᾶγμα δύο ἔχει λαβάς.] **1650** TAYLOR *Holy Living* ii. § 6 (A) There is nothing but hath a double handle, or at least we have two hands to apprehend it. **1732** FULLER no. 3472 Most things have two handles; and a wise man takes hold of the best. *a.* **1734** R. NORTH, *Lives* (Bohn) i. 361 The public . . . seldom or never takes such matters by the right handles. **1791–1823** I. DISRAELI *Curios. Lit.* (Chandos) III. 334 But everything hath two handles, saith the ancient adage. **1881** CANON AINGER *Chas. Lamb* 176 Lamb . . . loved paradox. . . . As Hartley Coleridge adds, it was his way always to take hold of things 'by the better handle'.

Mote and beam.

[*Luke* vi. 41] *c.* **1387** CHAUCER *Reeve's T.* prol. fin. He can wel in myn yĕ seen a stalke, But in his owne he can nat seen a balke. **1598** SHAKS. *L.L.L.* IV. iii. 161 You found his mote; the King your mote did see; But I a beam do find in each of three.

Moth, *see* Best cloth may have m. in it.

Mother Bunch.

1861 G. J. WHYTE-MELVILLE *Market Harb.* viii I *have* seen mammas whom the fairest of Eve's daughters might be proud to resemble; but it is sometimes hard upon the young Phœbe to have perpetually at her side the shapeless Mother Bunch, into the facsimile of which she must eventually grow.

Mother Car(e)y's chicken(s).

[A name given by sailors to the Stormy Petrel; also (in *pl.*) applied to falling snow.] **1767** CARTERET in HAWKSWORTH *Voy.* (1773) I. 318 The peterels, to which sailors have given the name of Mother Carey's chickens. **1836** MARRYAT *Midsh. Easy* xxvi 'You ought to be thrown overboard', said Gascoigne; 'all this comes from your croaking—you're a Mother Carey's chicken'. **1864** *Athenaeum* 558/2 'Mother Carey's Chickens'.

Mother, Like | like daughter (child).

1509 A. BARCLAY *Ship of Fools* (1874) I. 236 An olde prouerbe hath longe agone be sayde That oft . . . the mayde Or doughter, vnto the mother wyll agre. **1611** BIBLE *Ezekiel* xvi. 44 Every one . . . shall use this proverb against thee, saying, As is the mother, so is her daughter. **1835** MARRYAT *Jacob Faith.* xxiii But like mother like child, they say.

Mother of mischief is no bigger (more) than a midge's wing, The.

1641 FERGUSSON 98 The mother of mischief is na mair nor a midge wing. **1721** KELLY 310 . . . Spoken when a great quarrel has risen from a small occasion. **1796** EDGEWORTH *Par. Asst.*, '*Barring Out*' (1903) 307 'The mother of mischief', says an old proverb, 'is no bigger than a midge's wing'. **1858** MRS. CRAIK *A Woman's Thoughts* 177 Fatal and vile as her progeny may be, 'the mother of mischief', says the proverb, 'is no bigger than a midge's wing.'

Mother says, It is not as thy | but as thy neighbours say.

1678 RAY *Adag. Hebr.* 398 . . . The meaning is that we are not to regard the praises of a near relation, but to listen to what is said by the neighbourhood.

Mother wit, *see* Ounce of discretion (m. w.) worth pound of wit (clergy).

Mother's breath is aye sweet, The.

1721 KELLY 332 . . . Spoken of the tender affection of mothers.

Mother's (or Woman's) side is the surest, The.

[**1420** HENRY V.] **1548** HALL *Chron.* (1809) 101 Was not my great grandmother . . . of the noble house of Valoys ? . . . if the old and trite proverb be true that the woman's side is the surer side and that the child followeth the womb, . . . the surer part is French. **1607** MIDDLETON *Mich. T.* I. i. Wks. (1885) I. 222 Yet the mother's side Being surer than the father's, it may prove, Men plead for money best, women for love.

Mother's smock, *see* Lapped in his m. s.

Mother's son, Every.

c. **1300** *King Alisaunder* (Weber) l. 2098 For mekely ilka modir soun. **1485** MALORY *Morte d'Arthur* II. x And there were slain many mothers' sons. **1545** ASCHAM *Toxoph.* (Arb.) 69 The Romaynes . . . slewe them euery mother son. **1595–6** SHAKS. *Mids. N.* I. ii. 80 That would hang us, every mother's son. *Ibid.* III. i. 75 Come, sit down, every mother's son. **1837** MARRYAT *Snarl.* ix I'd have flogg'd each mother's son.

Mother, *see also* Ask the m. if child like father; Child may have too much m.'s blessing; Good m. says not, Will you? but gives; Light-heeled m.; Mark after her m. (She hath a); Pitiful m. . . . scald head; Trade is m. of money.

Mothering Sunday, On | above all other, every child should dine with its mother.

1854 A. E. BAKER *Northamptonshire Glos.* 33. **1875** DYER *Brit. Pop. Cust.* (1900) 116 In the *Gent. Mag.* (vol. liv, p. 98) a correspondent tells us that whilst he was an apprentice the custom was to visit his mother on Mid-Lent Sunday (thence called Mothering Sunday) for a regale of excellent furmety.

Mother-in-law and daughter-in-law are a tempest and hail storm.

1707 MAPLETOFT 30. **1855** BOHN 455.

Mother-in-law, There is but one good | and she is dead.

1863 J. R. WISE *New Forest* (1895) 179 'There is but one good mother-in-law, and she is dead'. . . . It exactly corresponds with the German saying, 'There is no good mother-in-law but she that wears a green gown', that is, who lies in the churchyard.

Mother-in-law remembers not that she was a daughter-in-law, The.

1659 HOWELL *Brit. Prov.* 36 The mother in law doth not remember that she hath been a daughter in law by her lease. **1732** FULLER no. 4675.

Mother-in-law, *see also* Rely on the . . . smile of m. (Never); Well married who has neither m.

Mothers' darlings make but milksop heroes.

1732 FULLER no. 3474.

Motions are not marriages.

1678 RAY 56.

Mould, *see* Enough one day (He will have) when mouth full of m.

Moulter, Multar, *see* Miller got never better m. than he took with own hands; Millers take aye the best m. with own hand.

Mountain and a river are good neighbours, A.

1640 HERBERT 330.

Mountain (out) of a molehill, To make a.

c. **1557** ROPER *Life of More* (Hitchcock) 63 Thus was the great mountayne turned scant to a litle mole hill. **1570** FOXE *A. & M.* (ed. 2) II. 1361/1 Too much amplifying thinges yᵗ be but small, makyng mountaines of Molehils. **1633** P. FLETCHER *Purple Is.* vii. 65 (1908) II. 101 And molehill faults to mountains multiply. **1778** T. HUTCHINSON *Diary* 5 May I told him his nerves were affected: every mole-hill was a mountain. **1861** DEAN STANLEY *Hist. East. Ch.* Introd. iii The higher and wider is the sweep of vision, the more difficult it is to stumble at trifles, and make mountains out of mole-hills.

Mountain will not come to Mahomet, If the | Mahomet must go to the mountain.

1625 BACON *Ess., Boldness* (Arb.) 519 *Mahomet* cald the Hill to come to him, . . . And when the Hill stood still, he was neuer a whit abashed, but said; *If the Hill will not come to Mahomet, Mahomet wil go to the hil.* **1732** FULLER no. 2707. **1757** GOLDSMITH *Lett. to D. Hodson,* 27 Dec. As the mountain will not come to Mahomet, why Mahomet shall go to the mountain; . . . as you cannot . . . pay me a visit, . . . next summer . . . I shall spend three [weeks] among my friends in Ireland. **1849** LYTTON *Caxtons* VI. iv Neither Kitty nor I can change our habits, even for friendship. . . . Mountains cannot stir, . . . but Mahomet can come to the mountain as often as he likes.

Mountaineers are always freemen.

1803 WORDSWORTH *To Highland Girl* Thou wear'st upon thy forehead clear The freedom of a mountaineer. **1921** M. HEWLETT *Wiltshire Ess.* 41 That last . . . sentiment has disappeared in Kentucky. As my correspondent says, 'Montani semper liberi', Class-distinctions are not effective in the art of the free-born.

Mountains have brought forth a mouse, The.

[HORACE *De Arte Poet.* 139 *Parturiunt montes, nascetur ridiculus mus.* The mountains are in labour, a ridiculous mouse will be born. (An allusion to Æsop's fable of the Mountain in Labour.)] *c.* **1390** GOWER *Conf. Amantis* VII. 3553–75 For so it fell that ilke day, This hell [hill] on his childinge lay, . . . The nerr this hell was upon chance To taken his deliverance, The more unbuxumliche he cride; . . . And ate laste it was a Mous, The which was bore. **1549** LATIMER *1st Serm. bef. Edw. VI* (P.S.) 92 For all their boasts, little or nothing was done; in whom these words of Horace may well be verified, . . . 'The mountains swell up, the poor mouse is brought out.' **1589** NASHE *Pref. to Greene's 'Menaphon'* Wks. (McKerrow) III. 312 Let other men . . . praise the Mountaine that in seauen yeares bringeth forth a Mouse . . . ; but giue me the man whose extemporall veine . . . will excell our greatest Art-maisters deliberate thoughts. **1885** D. C. MURRAY *Rainbow G.* III. i After the mountain has been in labour, the kindliest commendations the mouse can deserve can hardly be satisfactory to the mountain.

Mountain(s), *see also* Behind the m. there are people; Friends may meet, but m. . . .; Haste in his business (Who hath no), m. to him seem valleys; Morning m. (In the); Promises m. performs molehills.

Mountsorrel, *see* Belle giant or devil of M.

Mouse a hole, I gave the | and she is become my heir.

1640 HERBERT 321.

Mouse [do] against the cat, What may the.

c. **1390** GOWER *Conf. Amantis* III. 1643 What mai the Mous ayein the Cat?

Mouse in a cheese, To speak like a.

1670 RAY 186. **1686** EDMUND VERNEY to his son Edmund, *Verney Memoirs* (1899) IV. 381 I pray when you speak in the [Sheldonian] Theatre doe not speak like a mouse in a chees for that will be a great shame instead of an honour, but speak out your words boldly and distinctly.

Mouse in a mill, Like a.

1584 *Three Lords & Three Ladies of London* in HAZL. *O.E.P.* VI. 392 *Simpl.* Nor I need sell no ballads, but live like a mouse in a mill, and have another grind my meal for me.

Mouse in pitch, A.

[HERODAS 2. 63 μῦς ἐν πίσσῃ. ERASM. *Mus picem gustans.*] *c.* **1522** ERASMUS in FROUDE

Counc. of Trent (1892–3) iii 'Alas! that I in my old age should have fallen into such a mess, like a mouse into a pot of pitch.' **1603** FLORIO tr. *Montaigne* III. xiii (1897) VI. 221 She doth but quest and ferret, . . . turning, winding, building, and entangling herself in her own work . . . *Mus in pice. A mouse in pitch.*

Mouse in time may bite in two a cable, A.

1546 HEYWOOD II. vii. 67 Little losse by length maie growe importable. A mouse in tyme, maie byte a two, a cable. **1605–6** SHAKS. *K. Lear* II. ii. 79 Rogues . . . Like rats, oft bite the holy cords a-twain Which are too intrinse t' unloose. **1758** FRANKLIN in ARBER *Eng. Garner* v. 580 Stick to it steadily! and you will see great effects, for . . . *By diligence and patience, the mouse ate in two the cable.*

Mouse that hath but one hole is quickly taken, The.

[PLAUTUS *Truc.* 4. 4. 15 *Mus non uni fidet antro.* The mouse does not trust to one hole only. *Epp. Obsc. Vir.* i. 3 *Mus miser est antro qui tantum clauditur uno.*] *c.* **1386** CHAUCER *W. of Bath's Prol.* 572–4 I holde a mouses herte nat worth a leek, That hath but oon hole for to stertë to; And if that faillë, thanne is al y-do. **1651** HERBERT 370. **1866** BLACKMORE *Cradock N.* xvii Biddy . . . took to her brogue as a tower of refuge. Bilingual races are up to the tactics of rats with a double hole. **1897** 'H. S. MERRIMAN' *In Kedar's T.* xvii The house seemed to have two staircases of stone and two doors. There is a Spanish proverb which says that the rat which has only one hole is soon caught. Perhaps the architect . . . had built his house to suit his tenants.

Mouse (Mice), *see also* Better a louse (m.) in the pot; Blate cat, proud mouse; Bold m. that breeds in cat's ear; Burn one's house to get rid of m.; Cat wink (Let the) and m. run; Cat winketh (When) little wots m. what cat thinketh; Dead m. feels no cold; Drowned m. (Like a); Drunk as a m.; Dun's the m.; Escaped m. feels taste of bait; Hear the lark than the m. (Better); Hungry as a church m.; Larder but hath m. (No); Lion may come to be beholden to m.; Man or m.; Mind's chasing m. (Your); Peace and catch a m.; Plough stand to catch a m. (Let); Poor as a church m.; Pour not water on drowned m.; Scatter her m. (To); To-day a man, to-morrow a m.; Weel kens the m. when cat's out of house.

Mouse-hunt, *see* Cat after kind.

Mouse-trap smell of blood (cheese), Let not the.

1659 HOWELL *Eng. Prov.* 11/1 (with 'cheese'). **1732** FULLER no. 3189 (with 'blood'). **1802** J. WOLCOT (P. Pindar) *Middl. Elect.* i He made poor work o' Cold-bath howze. The

trap that wishth to catch a mowze, Shud never smell of *blood.*

Mouth, One | doth nothing without another.

1640 HERBERT 364.

Mouth hath beguiled your hands, Your.

1678 RAY 260. **1732** FULLER no. 6057.

Mouth of his own, He that hath a | must not say to another, blow.

1640 HERBERT 334. **1732** FULLER no. 2130.

Mouth, Whoso hath but a | shall ne'er in England suffer drouth.

1670 RAY 85 . . . For if he doth but open it, its a chance but it will rain in. . . . We seldome suffer for want of rain.

Mouth(s), *see also* Butcher looked for knife . . . in his m.; Close m. catches no flies; Cool m. and warm feet; Devil's m. is miser's purse; Duck in the m. (Come home with); Enemy's m. seldom speaks well; Enough one day (He will have) when m. full of mould; Evil that cometh out of thy m.; Fill the m. with empty spoons; God never sendeth m. but sendeth meat; Good in the maw that is sweet in m.; Heart is a fire, sparks out of m.; Heart is full of lust (When), m.'s full of leasings; Keep your m. shut; Look in your m. to know your age; Make up one's m.; Nearest the heart, nearest the m.; Open one's m. wide (To); Open your m. but you put foot in it; Ready m. for cherry; Speak (You never) but your mouth opens; Stop every man's m. (He who will); Stop two m. with one morsel; Wise hand doth not all foolish m. speaks; Wise head makes close m.; Wise men have their m. in their heart; Wry m. (Make a).

Mouthful of moonshine, To give one a.

1785 GROSE *Dict. Vulg. T.* s.v. A matter or mouthful of moonshine, a trifle, nothing.

Mower(s), *see* Meat for m. (No).

Mows[1] may come to earnest.

1721 KELLY 254 . . . What you speak in jest, may come to be done in reality. [[1] jesting.]

Mows (*verb*), *see* Mastery m. the meadows.

Moyen[1] does mickle, but money does more.

1721 KELLY 243. [[1] interest.]

Much ado about nothing.

1598–9 SHAKS. *Much Ado about Nothing* (Title of Play).

Much ado to bring beggars to stocks; and when they come there, they'll not put in their legs.

1616 DRAXE 14 Much a doe to bring Beggars to the stockes. 1670 RAY 60.

Much bran and little meal.

1616 DRAXE 17. 1670 RAY 65. 1732 FULLER no. 3477 (with 'flour' for 'meal').

Much bruit, little fruit.

1639 FULLER Holy War II. xxix (1840) 87 The French proverb was verified by this voyage, 'Much bruit and little fruit'. They not only did no good in the Holy Land . . . but also did much harm.

Much coin, much care.

[HORACE Odes 3. 16 Crescentem sequitur cura pecuniam. Care follows increasing wealth.] 1639 CLARKE 292.

Much law, but little justice.

1732 FULLER no. 3482.

Much matter of a wooden platter.

1616 WITHALS 565 Much matter of a treene platter. 1639 CLARKE 133. 1670 RAY 185 . . . Δεινὰ περὶ φακῆς. [Terrible talk about a lentil.] Mira de lente, A great stir about a thing of nothing.

Much meat, much malady (many maladies).

1597 Politeuphuia 250 It is an old prouerbe, much meate, much maladie. 1603 H. CROSSE Virtue's Commonwealth (Gros.) 146 As the prouerbe saith, much meate much maladie. 1619 Keepe within Compasse C,ᵛ. 1629 T. ADAMS Serm. (1861–2) II. 28 Multa fercula, multos morbos,—Many dishes, many diseases. 1647 TRAPP Marrow Gd. Authors in Comm. Ep. 614 Q. Elizabeth . . . knew, that much meat, much malady. 1670 RAY 120 . . . Our nation . . . hath been noted for excess in eating, and it was almost grown a Proverb, That English men dig their graves with their teeth.

Much money makes a country poor, for it sets a dearer price on every thing.

1651 HERBERT 373.

Much of a muchness.

1727 VANBRUGH & CIBBER Prov. Husband I Man. I hope at least, you and your good woman agree still. J. Mood. Ay, ay! much of a muchness. 1837 T. HOOK Jack Brag ii I never had two horses that suited me better. I have . . . nine—much of a muchness. 1912 SIR EVELYN WOOD Midsh. to F. Marshal xxxiv The Commander-in-Chief . . . said more than once, 'Men are much of a muchness; I find officers very much on a par'.

Much science (learning), much sorrow.

1607–40 Politeuphuia s.v. Proverbs' Much learning much sorrow. 1639 CLARKE 101.

Much would (shall) have more.

c. 1350 Douce MS. 52 no. 65 Mykulle wulle more. 1594 SHAKS. Lucrece 98 Cloy'd with much, he pineth still for more. 1613–22 DRAYTON Polyolb. xv. 293 (1876) II. 191 Then Loddon next comes in, contributing her store; As still we see, 'The much runs ever to the more'. 1639 CLARKE 99 Much shall have more. 1721 KELLY 245 Mickle would ay have more. . . . Spoken of the insatiable desire that rich men have after wealth. 1900 J. MC. CARTHY Hist. Own. T. v. 94 Expedition after expedition has been sent out to extend the Egyptian frontier. . . . 'Much will have more'; but in this case . . . much is compelled, for the sake of . . . security, to try to have more.

Much, see also Make much of.

Much, see also under significant words following.

Muck, Not worth his.

1639 CLARKE 70.

Muck and money go together.

1678 RAY 179 . . . Those that are slovenly and dirty usually grow rich, not they that are nice and curious in their diet, houses, and clothes.

Muck and truck.

[= miscellaneous articles of trade.] 1898 Daily News 22 July 4/7 'Sufficient attention is not paid to muck and truck.' So says the British Consul at Shanghai.

Muck of the world.

c. 1390 GOWER Conf. Amantis v. 4854 Bot forto pinche and forto spare, Of worldes muk to gete encress. 1546 HEYWOOD I. xi. 36 To disdeygne me, who mucke of the worlde hoordth not. As he dooth. 1607–8 SHAKS. Coriol. II. ii. 131 Look'd upon things precious as they were The common muck o' the world.

Muck, see also Have his m. for his meat; Riches are like m. . . . spread abroad.

Muck-hill at his door, He hath a good.

1678 RAY 261 . . . i.e. he is rich.

Muck-hill on my trencher, You make a | quoth the bride.

1678 RAY 77 . . . You carve me a great heap. 1732 FULLER no. 5936.

Muck-hill(s), see also Old m. will bloom.

Muckle water rins while the miller sleeps, There's.

1814 HOGG to Byron 11 Oct.

Mud chokes no eels.

1732 FULLER no. 3488.

Mud, see also Breed in the m. are not efts (All that); Keep a man out of the m. (Way to) is black his boots.

Mugwort, *see* Drink nettles in March, eat m. in May.

Mulatto, *see* God made the white man . . . the devil made m.

Mulberry-tree, *see* Time and art (With) leaf of m. becomes satin.

Mule (Ass, Horse), One | doth scrub another.

[ERASM. *Ad. Mutuum muli scabunt.*] **1540** PALSGRAVE *Acolastus* (Carver) 129 Mules scratche of eche other scabbes or scurffes. **1545** TAVERNER I 1ᵛ One moile claweth another. **1549** CHALONER tr. *Erasm. Pr. of Folly* 13. **1580** J. CONYBEARE 25 Mules do gnap or rubbe one another. **1584** COGAN *Haven of Health* (1636) 6 Why (quoth the Emperor[1]) one of you might claw and rub anothers back well enough. So wisely did he delude the practise of parasites, according to the old proverb, Muli mutuum scabunt. **1614** OVERBURY *Characters. An Ostler* Hee puffes and blowes ouer your horse, . . . and leaues much of the dressing to the prouerbe of *Muli mutuo scabunt*, one horse rubs another. **1616** CORYAT *Traueller for Eng. Wits* 37 In Latine, *Mulus mulum scabit*, one Mule scratcheth another; by which the Ancients signified, that courtesies done vnto friends, ought to be requited with reciprocall offices of friendship. **1635** RANDOLPH *Muses Looking-Gl.* III. iv I need not flatter these, they'le doe't themselves, And crosse the Proverb that was wont to say One Mule doth scrub another. **1738** SWIFT (Dial. iii) 350 *Lady S.* Well, she and Tom Gosling were banging compliments backward and forward: it looked like two asses scrubbing one another. [[1] Augustus.]

Mule, *see also* Wants a m. without fault (He who).

Mulligrubs, *see* Sick of the m.

Mullingar heifer, *see* Beef to the heels.

Multar, *see* Moulter.

Mum[1] for that.

1687 MONTAGUE & PRIOR *Hind & P. Transv.* 7 It has cost me some pains to clear Her Title. Well but Mum for that, Mr. Smith. [[1] silence.]

Mum is counsel.

c. **1374** CHAUCER *Troylus* III, l. 294. These wyse clerkes that ben dede wil yet pro-verbed to us yonge, That 'firste vertu is to kepe tonge'. **1546** HEYWOOD II. v. 53 I will say nought but mum, and mum is counsell.

Mum's the word.

1590–1 SHAKS. *2 Hen. VI* I. ii. 89 Give no words but mum. **1599** GREENE *Alphonsus* I. i (Merm.) 11 *Car.* What ne'er a word but mum? Alphonsus, speak. a. **1704** T. BROWN *Walks round Lond., Coffee-Houses* Wks. (1709) III. III. 39 But Mum's the Word—for who wou'd speak their Mind among Tarrs and commissioners. **1837** T. HOOK *Jack Brag* xii All quiet and snug—mum's the word, and

no mistake. **1894** BLACKMORE *Perlycross* xxi Mum's the word.

Mumbo Jumbo.

1738 F. MOORE *Trav. Afr.* 40 A dreadful Bugbear to the Women, call'd Mumbo-Jumbo, which is what keeps the Women in awe. **1837** HOOD *Ode to Rae Wilson* xxiv You might have been High Priest to Mumbo-Jumbo. **1876** GEO. ELIOT *Dan. Der.* xxviii The name of Mompert had become a sort of Mumbo-Jumbo. **1907** A. C. BENSON *Upton Lett.* 259 Erudition . . . a hideous idol, a Mumbo-Jumbo, a Moloch in whose honour children have still to pass through the fire in . . . dark academic groves.

Mumchance (Mumphazard) that was hanged for saying nothing, He looks like.

1579 GOSSON *Ephemerides* 7 Ready as a man desperate . . . to forsweare my country, to sette the hares heade to the goose gyblettes, and al that I haue at a mumme chaunce. **1670** RAY 290 (with 'Mumphazard') *Chest.* a. **1700** B.E. *Dict. Cant. Crew* 'Mumchance', One that sits mute. He looks like Mum-chance that was Hang'd for saying of nothing. **1738** SWIFT (Dial. i) 335 Methinks you look like Mumchance, that was hanged for saying nothing.

Mumford, *see* Mock not, quoth M.

Mumphazard, *see* Mumchance.

Mumpsimus, see Change his old *M.*

Murder is out, The.

[Said when something is suddenly revealed or explained.] **1706** FARQUHAR *Recruit. Off.* III. i Now the murder's out. **1831** MACAULAY *Let.* 29 June Barnes . . . pretended that all the best strokes were his. I believed that he was lying. . . . And now the murder is out. **1837** DICKENS *Pickwick* xliii fin. Now the murder's out, and, damme, there's an end on't.

Murder will out (cannot be hid).

c. **1300** *Cursor M.* 1084 (Gött) For-þi sais into þis tyde, Is no man þat murthir may hide. c. **1386** CHAUCER *Nun's Pr. T.* 232 Mordre wol out that se we day by day. **1433** LYDG. *St. Edmund* II. 225 in Horstm. Altengl. Leg. (1881) 400 Moordre wil out, thouh it abide a while. **1592** KYD *Span. Trag.* (Boas) II. vi. 58 The heauens are iust, murder cannot be hid. **1592–3** SHAKS. *Rich. III* I. iv. 293 Well, I'll go hide the body in some hole, . . . And when I have my meed, I will away; For this will out. **1596–7** *Merch. V.* II. ii. 86 Truth will come to light; murder cannot be hid long. **1600–1** *Hamlet* II. ii. 630 For murder, though it have no tongue, will speak With most miraculous organ. **1604–5** *Othello* V. i. 109 Nay, guiltiness will speak, Though tongues were out of use. **1664** COTTON *Scarron* i. 675 Murder at some odd time will out.

Murray, Earl of, *see* Dine with St. Giles and E. of M.

Muscles, *see* Bear picketh m.

Muscular Christianity.

[A term applied (from about 1857) to the ideal of religious character exhibited in the writings of Chas. Kingsley.] 1858 *Edin. Rev.* Jan. cvii. 190 It is a school of which Mr. Kingsley is the ablest doctor; and its doctrine has been described . . . as 'muscular Christianity'. 1880 DISRAELI *Endym.* xiv Nigel . . . was also a sportsman. His Christianity was muscular.

Muse as they use, Men.

1583 MELBANCKE *Philotimus* G 3 Use not, as you muse, and good inough. 1670 RAY 123.

Muse as they use, measure other folk's corn by their own bushel, Men.

1678 RAY 179.

Muse (*noun*), *see* Naught is that m. that finds no excuse.

Music helps not the toothache.

1640 HERBERT 342.

Music is the eye of the ear.

1616 DRAXE 136.

Music on a wheelbarrow, You may make as good.

1678 RAY 276.

Music, *see also* Apothecary's mortar spoils luter's m.; Face the m.; Great strokes make not m.; Voice is best m.; Women and m. should never be dated.

Musician hath forgot his note, When a | he makes as though a crumb stuck in his throat.

[Gk. Ἀπορία ψάλτου βήξ. The musician slurs his mistake with a cough.] 1639 CLARKE 108. 1670 RAY 123 . . . When a singing-man or musician is out or at a loss, to conceal it he coughs.

Musk, *see* Look not for m. in a kennel.

Musselbrogh[1] was a brogh when Edinbrogh was nane; and Musselbrogh 'ill be a brogh, when Edinbrogh is gane.

1842 R. CHAMBERS *Pop. Rhymes of Scot.* 14 This is a pun or quibble. *Brogh* is a term for a mussel bed, one of which exists at the mouth of the Esk and gives name to the burgh. [[1] Musselburgh in Midlothian.]

Must be if we brew (sell ale), This.

1678 RAY 87 . . . That is if we undertake mean and sordid, or lucrative employments, we must be content with some trouble, inconvenience, affronts, disturbance, &c. 1721 KELLY 295 Sik things will be, if we sell drink. 1738 SWIFT (Dial. iii) 352 *Miss.* Well, thus it must be, if we sell ale.

Must be must be, What.

1841 S. WARREN *Ten Thous. a Year* i It's really very inconvenient . . . for any of my young men to be absent . . . but—I suppose—what must be must be.

Must is for the king.

1599 CHAPMAN *Hum. Day's M.* (1889) 26 *Lab.* Must she, sir; have you brought the king's warrant for it? 1603 DEKKER, &c. *Grissil* iv. ii Must is for kings, And low obedience for underlings. 1659 FULLER *Appeal Inj. Innoc.* (1840) 354 'MUST is for a king', and seeing the doctor and I are both kings alike, I return, 'He *must not* be so understood'. 1681 BUNYAN *Come and Welcome* Wks. (1855) I. 257 'Must is for the king.' If they shall come, they shall come. 1738 SWIFT *Pol. Conversat.* Introd. Wks. (1856) II. 332 I have taken care to enforce loyalty by an invincible argument, . . .—'MUST is for the king.'

Mustard, *see* After meat m.; Cat loves m. (As a); Kill a man for a mess of m.; Tewkesbury m.

Mute as a fish.

c. 1450 BURGH (& LYDGATE) *Secrees* (E.E.T.S.) st. 330 p. 73 (A) Dowmbe as þe ffysh. 1601 JONSON *Poetaster* iv. i *Gal.* What, mute? *Tib.* Ay, as fishes. 1688 BUNYAN *Build. Ho. God* ix. Wks. (1855) II. 586 Meek as a lamb, mute as a fish.

Mute as a mackerel.

1760 FOOTE *Minor* I. Wks. (1799) I. 238 You can be secret as well as serviceable? . . . Mute as a mackrel. 1819 *Metropolis* III. 154 We were as mute as mackarel for exactly seven minutes and a half.

Mutton is sweet, and gars folk die ere they be sick.

1721 KELLY 250 . . . That is, makes people steal sheep and so be hang'd.

Mutton, *see also* Loved m. well that licked; Shoulder of m. and beer make Flemings tarry; Shoulder of m. draws down another; — is going (When), good to take slice; — for a sick horse; Sow is good m. (Your). *See also* Sheep's flesh.

Muxy, He got out of the | and fell into the pucksy.

1616 DRAXE 55 He is gotten out of the myre and is fallen into the river. 1869 HAZLITT 158 . . . i.e. He got out of the dunghill and fell into the slough.

Myrtle standing among nettles, A | does notwithstanding retain the name of a myrtle.

1678 RAY *Adag. Hebr.* 397.

N

Nab¹ me, I'll nab thee.

1678 RAY 351. **1678** BUTLER *Hudibras* III. ii. **1457** To nab the itches of their sects, as jades do one another's necks. [¹ to bite gently.]

Naboth's vineyard.

[= the coveted possession of a neighbour.] **1611** BIBLE *1 Kings* xxi. 2 And Ahab spake unto Naboth, saying, Give me thy vineyard, . . . because it is near unto my house. **1709** SWIFT *The Garden Plot* Wks. (1856) I. 701 When Naboth's vineyard look'd so fine, The king cried out, 'Would this were mine!'

Nag with a weamb¹ and a mare with nean², A.

1670 RAY 44. [¹ belly. ² none.]

Nag, *see also* Bleed your n. on St. Stephen's day; Inch of a n. worth span of aver.

Nail, On the.

[= on the spot, at once; chiefly used of making money payments.] **1596** NASHE *Saf. Walden* Wks. (Gros.) III. 59 Tell me, haue you a minde to anie thing in the Doctors Booke! speake the word, and I will help you to it vpon the naile. **1600** HOLLAND *Livy* VI. xiv. 225 [He] paid the whole debt downe right on the naile, unto the creditour. **1720** SWIFT *Run of Bankers* Wks. (1755) IV. i. 22 We want our money on the nail. **1804** EDGEWORTH *Pop. T., Will* ii The bonnet's all I want, which I'll pay for on the nail.

Nail (Fire, Love), One | drives out another.

[AR. *Pol.* 5. 11. 3 ἥλῳ ὁ ἧλος (sc. ἐκκρούεται).] *c.* **1200** *Ancrene Riwle* (Morton) 404 Vor, al so as on neil driueð ut þen oðerne. . . . *c.* **1374** CHAUCER *Troylus* IV. 415 The newë love out chaceth ofte the olde. **1555** HEYWOOD *Epigr. upon Prov.* no. 111 One nayle driueth out an other. **1579** LYLY *Euphues* (Arb.) 116 One loue expelleth an other. **1580** Id. *Euph. & his Eng.* (Arb.) 356 The fire that burneth, taketh away the heate of the burn. **1594–5** SHAKS. *Rom. & Jul.* I. ii. 46 Tut man, one fire burns out another's burning. *Two Gent.* II. iv. 192 Even as one heat another heat expels, Or as one nail by strength drives out another, So the remembrance of my former love Is by a newer object quite forgotten. **1596–7** *K. John* III. i. 277 And falsehood falsehood cures, as fire cools fire Within the scorched veins of one newburn'd. **1599–1600** *Jul. Caes.* III. i. 171 As fire drives out fire, so pity pity. **1607–8** *Coriol.* IV. vii. 54 One fire drives out one fire; one nail, one nail. **1606** CHAPMAN *Mons. d'Olive* v. i. Wks. (1874) III. 134 *Va.* For one heat, all know, doth drive out another, One passion doth expel another still. *c.* **1645** HOWELL *Lett.* 17 Sept. (1903) III. 87 Languages and words . . . may be said to stick in the memory like nails on pegs in a wainscot door, which used to thrust out one another oftentimes. **1666** TORRIANO 10 One love expels another. **1836** MRS. CARLYLE *Let.* April 1 One feels soaked to the very heart. . . .

As one fire is understood to drive out another, I thought one water might drive out another also; and so . . . I took a shower-bath. **1855** BOHN 469 One love drives out another. **1900** *Athenaeum* 27 Oct. 547/2 Nail drives out nail.

Nail into any one's coffin, To drive (*or* put) a.

[= to do a thing that tends to shorten his life.] **1789** WOLCOT *Wks.* (1795) ii. 100 (A) Care to our coffin adds a nail, no doubt. **1836** A. FONBLANQUE *Eng. under 7 Administr.* (1837) III. 321 A dram which . . . drives nails into the victim's coffin, according to the expressive vulgar saying. **1885** LOWE *Prince Bismarck* (1898) iii. 51 Frederick William IV renounced all his sovereign rights over Neuchâtel. . . . But the incident preyed deeply on the sensitive spirit of the King. It drove a nail into his coffin.

Nail one's colours to the mast, To.

[= to adopt an unyielding attitude.] **1841** CHAMIER *Tom Bowl.* lv If ever we get athwart hawse of a Frenchman, Captain Bowling need not nail his colours to the mast, for there will not be one man on board who would haul them down. **1848** DICKENS *Dombey* v Mrs. Chick had nailed her colours to the mast and repeated 'I know it isn't'. **1926** *Times* 28 May 16/5 The present negotiators . . . had nailed their colours to the mast, and it was very difficult . . . to take out any of the nails.

Nail to the counter, To.

[= to expose as false, in allusion to the practice of dealing thus with spurious coins.] **1573** C. DESAINLIENS *French Schoolmaster* (1615) N 3ᵛ There is a counterfeit shilling: nayle it at the threshold of the door. *a.* **1590** LYLY *Moth. Bomb.* II. i. 52 I shall goe for siluer though, when they shall bee nailed vp for slips. **1601–2** *Blurt Master Constable* (Middleton Wks. (Bullen) i. 40) If he be counterfeit, nail him vp upon one of your posts. **1842** O. W. HOLMES *Med. Ess.* Wks. (1891) IX. 67 A few familiar facts . . . have been suffered to pass current so long that it is time they should be nailed to the counter. **1890** *Spectator* 9 Aug. It was a good deed to nail all this to the counter.

Nail, *see also* Drive the n. that will go; Hit the n. on the head; Want of a n. the shoe is lost.

Nails (*of fingers*), *see* Better ne'er been born as have n. Sunday shorn; Eat your n. (Had as good); Iron n. that scratches bear; Nobody's n. can reach London; Paring of his nails (Part with); Pearl on your n.

Naked as a frog.

1626 J. FLETCHER *Fair M. of Inn* IV. i. Wks. (C.U.P.) IX. 201 *For.* I will make you dance a new dance call'd leap-frog. . . . And as naked as a frog.

Naked as a needle.

1350 *Alexander* l. 4027 (A) And aye is naked a nedill as natour tham schapis. **1377** LANGLAND *P. Pl.* B. XII. 162 Take two stronge men, and in themese[1] caste hem, And bothe naked as a nedle. **1470–85** MALORY *Morte d'Arthur* XI. i. 572 There syr launcelot toke the fayrest lady by the hand . . . and she was naked as a nedel. [[1] Thames.]

Naked as a robin.

1883 BURNE *Shropsh. Folk-Lore* 595 (A). **1890** D. C. MURRAY *J. Vale's Guard.* xxxviii Time was I wouldn't ha' married her . . . without her lands. You can send her now as naked as a robin, if you like.

Naked as a worm.

c. **1400** *Rom. Rose* l. 454 (A) For naked as a worm was she. *a.* **1467** *Gregory's Chron.* (Camd. Soc.) 211 The Lorde Schalys . . . was slayne at Synt Mary Overeyes . . . , and laye there dyspoyly nakyd as a worme.

Naked as he was born.

1564 UDALL tr. *Erasm. Apoph.* (1877) 59 Either of them as naked as euer thei wer borne. **1621** BURTON *Anat. Mel.* III. ii. III. iii (1651) 469 At our coming to Brazil, we found both men and women naked as they were born. **1829–30** M. SCOTT *T. Cring. Log* xii There lay the canoe . . . with her crew . . . as naked as the day they were born.

Naked as my nail.

1533 HEYWOOD *Play of Wether* l. 922 (A) Thou myghtest go as naked as my nayle. **1540** PALSGRAVE *Acolastus* (Carver) 144. **1559** *Mirr. Mag.* (1562) Bb vij We . . . were led in prysoners naked as my nayle. **1633** T. HEYWOOD *Eng. Trav.* II. i. C iij b He . . . did . . . so Plucke them and Pull them till hee left them as naked as my Naile.

Naked man is sought after to be rifled, No.

[L. *Nemo potest nudo vestimenta detrahere.* No one can strip a naked man of his garment.] **1651** HERBERT 366.

Naked man, *see also* Need makes the n. m. run.

Naked sword in a madman's hand, It is ill putting a.

1539 TAVERNER E 7 Truely, quoth the Kyng [Henry VII], me thought that a naked sworde was comytted to the handes of a madde man. **1546** HEYWOOD II. viii. 71 It is (as olde men right well under-stande) Ill puttyng a nakt swoord in a mad mans hande. **1590–1** SHAKS. *2 Hen. VI* III. i. 347 You put sharp weapons in a madman's hands. **1681** S. COLVIL *Whiggs Sup.* I. 69 A sword put in a wood[1] man's hand, Bred meikle trouble to the land. **1721** KELLY 264 Never put a sword in a wood[1] man's hand. *L.* Ne puero gladium. [[1] mad.]

Name for nothing, You had not your.

1616 DRAXE 137 He hath not his name for naught. **1678** RAY 261.

Name is up; His | he may lie abed till noon. (*Cf.* Get a name, &c.)

1611 COTGRAVE s.v. 'Bruit' He that is thought to rise betime, may lye abed till noone. **1617** J. SWETNAM *School of Defence* 41 Hee which is accounted for an early riser, may lie a bed till eleauen of the clocke. **1659** HOWELL *Eng. Prov.* 3/2 Who hath once the fame to be an early riser, may sleep till noon. **1688** BUNYAN *Jer. Sinner Saved* Wks. (1855) I. 75 He that can do thus, . . . he shall have the name and fame he desires; he may lie a-bed till noon. **1729** SWIFT *An Epistle* (*Christmas-Box for Dr. Delany*) Wks. (1856) I. 667 How different is this from Smedley! (His name is up, he may in bed lie.)

Name, He that hath the | may as well enjoy the game.

1894 BLACKMORE *Perlycross* xv He that hath the name may as well enjoy the game.— These and other reckless maxims of our worthy grandsires . . . were cited.

Name no names, I.

1614 BEAUM. & FL. *Wit at S.W.* II. i. *Clown.* So serving-man Pompey Doodle may be respected as well with ladies (though I name no parties) as Sir Gregory Fop. **1633** SHIRLEY *Witty Fair One* V. iii *Brains.* Somebody hath been cozened, I name nobody. **1858** C. READE *Jack of All T.* V Mr. Yates, who could play upon the public ear better than some fiddles (I name no names).

Name of an honest woman is mickle worth, The.

1721 KELLY 334 . . . A reason given for a woman, who has borne a bastard, for marrying an inferior person.

Name of the Prophet—figs! In the.

[= a pompous introduction to some triviality.] **1812** H. & J. SMITH *Rejected Addr.* x The pious hawkers of Constantinople, who solemnly perambulate her streets, exclaiming, 'In the name of the Prophet—figs!'

Names and natures do often agree.

1611 BIBLE *1 Sam.* xxv. 25 As his name is, so is he; Nabal[1] is his name, and folly is with him. **1639** CLARKE 287. **1760** STERNE *T. Shandy* I. xix. **1791** I. DISRAELI *Curios. Lit.* (1858) II. 48 Milton . . . condescends to insinuate that their barbarous names are symbolical of their natures,—and from a man of the name of *Mac Collkittok*, he expects no mercy. [[1] i.e. fool.]

Names are debts.

1827–48 HARE *Gues. at Truth* (1859) I. 134, 5 No people . . . ever had so lively a feeling of the power of the names as the Romans. . . . Every member of a great house had a determinate course markt out for him . . . : his name admonisht him of what he owed to his country. **1901** ALEX. WHYTE *Bib. Char., Stephen* 15 *Nomina debita*, says John Donne; that is to say, 'Every man owes to the world the signification of his name, and of all his name. Every new addition of honour or of office lays a new obligation upon him, and his Christian name above all.'

Name(s), (*noun*), *see also De te fabula narratur*; Get a n. to rise early; Sticks and stones . . . but n. never hurt. *See also* Good name, Ill name.

Name (*verb*), *see also* Rope (N. not) in his house that hanged himself.

Named, *see* Sooner n. sooner come; Worthy to be n. same day (Not).

Nan, *see* Like to like and N. for Nicholas.

Naples, *see* See N. and die.

Napping, *see* Catch one n. (as Mosse did his mare).

Narrow counting culzies[1] no kindness, Over.

1641 FERGUSSON 84. **1721** KELLY 273 . . . When people deal in rigour with us, we think ourselves but little oblig'd to them. [[1] elicits.]

Narrow gathered, widely spent.

1721 KELLY 257 . . . Wealth, gotten by too much sparing, comes often to be widely squander'd.

Narrow, *see also* Turn a n. adlant; Wide will wear, but n. tear.

Natural to die as to be born, It is as.

1732 FULLER no. 2911. **1910** *Spectator* 7 May 'Men fear death', says Bacon, '. . . but the fear of it, as a tribute due unto nature, is weak'. . . . It is as natural to die as to be born.

Nature abhors a vacuum.

[PLUT. *De Plac. Phil.* l. 18]. **1603** HOLLAND, *Plutarch's Mor.* 1021 There is no voidness or vacuity in nature. **1606–7** SHAKS. *Ant. & Cleop.* II. ii. 216 The air . . . but for vacancy Had gone to gaze on Cleopatra too, and made a gap in nature. **1642** FULLER *H. & P. State* v. ii (1841) 340 Queen Joan . . . (hating widowhood as much as nature doth *vacuum*) married James King of Majorca. **1771** JOHNSON 20 June in *Boswell* (1848) xxv. 224 Whatever philosophy may determine of material nature, it is certainly true of intellectual nature, that it *abhors a vacuum*: our minds cannot be empty. **1841** ABP. TRENCH *Notes on Par.* xxi (1889) 368 Since grace will as little as nature endure a vacuum, he receives a new . . . commission: *Go out . . . and compel them to come in, that my house may be filled.*

Nature does nothing in vain.

[AR. *Pol.* 1. 2. 10 Οὐθὲν γάρ, ὡς φαμέν, μάτην ἡ φύσις ποιεῖ, For, as we say, Nature does nothing in vain.] *c.* **1580** G. HARVEY *Marginalia* 128 . . . *Naturam: quae . . . nihil facit frustra.* **1605** BACON *Adv. of Learning* (Robertson) 163 Nature which doth nothing in vain. **1642** SIR T. BROWNE *Relig. Med.* I. xv *Natura nihil agit frustra*, is the only indisputable Axiome in Philosophy. There are no Grotesques in Nature; not anything framed

to fill up empty Cantons, and unnecessary spaces. **1822** ABP. WHATELY *Use Ab. of Party F.* (1859) 8 No . . . inherent principle of our nature is in itself either mischievous or useless. The maxim that Nature does nothing in vain, is not more true in the material, than in the moral world.

Nature draws more than ten teams.

1640 HERBERT 353. **1670** RAY 18 Nature draws more than ten oxen.

Nature has given us two ears, two eyes, and but one tongue; to the end we should hear and see more than we speak.

1605 *London Prodigal* III. ii (*Shaks. Apoc.*) 205 *Lance.* Euery man hath one tongue, and two eares: nature, in her building, is a most curious worke-maister. *Flow.* That is as much (as) to say, a man should heare more then he should speake. *c.* **1635** HOWELL *Lett.* to G. G. (1903) II. 109 You have two eyes and two ears, but one tongue. You know my meaning. **1855** BOHN 457 . . . *Socrates.*

Nature hates all sudden changes.

[**1613** TISSOT *Natura nihil facit per saltum*, applied to the law, by Linnaeus to vegetation.] **1721** KELLY 267 . . . It is not safe for a man to change in his diet, behaviour, or way of living suddenly, from one extreme to another. **1924** R. W. LIVINGSTONE *Greek Genius* 206 We have watched the obscure beginnings of philosophy, and now we must pass over nearly two centuries; remembering, however, that though we can take leaps, nature *nihil facit per saltum.*

Nature is conquered (governed) by obeying her.

1827–48 HARE *Gues. at Truth* (1859) I. 166 Bacon has declared it: *Natura non nisi parendo vincitur*: and the triumphs of Science since his days have proved how willing Nature is to be conquered by those who will obey her. **1916** E. A. BURROUGHS *Val. of Decis.* (1920) III. iv. 285 'God resisteth the proud but giveth grace unto the humble' is only a theological version of the scientific truism, To conquer Nature you must obey her'.

Nature is the true law.

1573 SANDFORD (1576) H4.

Nature of the beast, It is the.

1678 RAY 77 It's the nature o' th' beast. **1683** JOHN VERNEY to his wife, *Verney Memoirs* (1899) iv. 254 I'me very Sorry John my Coachman Should be soe greate a Clowne to you . . . but t'is the nature of the Beast.

Nature passes[1] nurture (art). (*But cf.* Nurture is above nature.)

1519 HORMAN *Vulg.* X 4 No craft can make a thynge so plesaunt as nature. **1579** LYLY *Euphues* (Arb.) 41 Education can have no show where the excellencye of Nature doth bea sway. **1606** CHAPMAN *Gentleman*

Usher I. i. 231 Nature yields more than Art.
1641 FERGUSSON 80. [[1] surpasses.]

Nature, time, and patience are the three great physicians.

1707 MAPLETOFT 15. **1855** BOHN 457.

Nature will have its course.

c. **1400** BERYN (E.E.T.S.) 105 (A) ffor kynde
woll have his cours'. **1590** LYLY *Moth. Bomb.*
I. i. 101 Your son's folly . . . being naturall;
it will haue his course. **1616** DRAXE 137.

Nature, *see also* Art improves n.; Cast out n.
with a fork, will return; Follows n. (He
that); God (N.) is no botcher; Ill n., the
more you ask, more they stick; Names and
n. often agree; Nurture is above n.

Naught is never in danger.

[L. *Malum vas non frangitur.* A worthless
vessel does not get broken.] **1639** CLARKE
126. **1738** SWIFT (Dial. i) 335 *Lady S.* Well,
well, nought's never in danger. I warrant
miss will spit in her hand, and hold fast.
1853 SURTEES *Sponge's Sport. T.* lvi 'He was
nearly killed last time'. . . . 'Oh, nought's
never in danger!' observed Bob Spangles.

Naught is that muse that finds no excuse.

1573 SANDFORD (1576) 222.

Naught will be naught.

1573 TUSSER *Husb., Housw. Adm.* 77 (E.D.S.)
169 As rod little mendeth where maners be
spilt, so naught will be naught say and do
what thou wilt.

Naught's impossible, as t'auld woman said when they told her cauf had swallowed grindlestone.[1]

1917 BRIDGE 96. [[1] grindstone.]

Naught, *see also* Best is as good as stark n.;
Old n. will never be aught. *See also*
Nothing, Nought.

Naughty Ashford, surly Wye, poor Kennington hard by.

1736 S. PEGGE *Kenticisms, Prov.* (E.D.S.) 67.

Naughty boys sometimes make good men.

1662 FULLER (*Surrey*) III. 207 Nicholas West[1]
was born at Putney. . . . In him the proverb
was verified, 'Naughty boys sometimes make
good men'. He seasonably retrenched his
wildness, turned hard student, became an
eminent scholar and most able statesman.
[[1] Bishop of Ely, 1515–33.]

Nay-says, *see* Nineteen n. of a maiden half
a grant.

Nay, stay, quoth Stringer, when his neck was in the halter.

1678 RAY 82. **1732** FULLER no. 3512.

Ne supra crepidam, see Cobbler go beyond
his last (Let not).

Neapolitan shrug, To give one the.

1594 NASH *Unfort. Trav.* (1920) 93 It is
growen to a common prouerbe, *Ile give him
the Neapolitan shrug*, when one intends to play
the villaine, and make no boast of it.

Near as bark to tree, As.

1580 LYLY *Euph. & his Eng.* (Arb.) 313 As
neere is Fancie to Beautie, . . . as the stalke
to the rynde, as the earth to the root. **1639**
CLARKE 286.

Near burr, far rain.

1830 FORBY 417 'Near bur, far rain.' The
'bur' is the halo round the moon, and . . .
when it appears near the moon there will be
fine weather.

Near friend is better than a far-dwelling kinsman, A.

1545 TAVERNER G 1 An englysshe prouerbe
. . . A nere neyghbour is better than a farre
frende. **1607–40** *Politeuphuia* s.v. 'Proverbs'.

Near is my coat (doublet, kirtle, petticoat) but nearer is my shirt (smock).

[PLAUTUS *Trin.* 5. 2. 30 *Tunica propior
pallio est.*] **1461** *Paston Lett.* I. 542 Nere is
my kyrtyl, but nerre[1] is my smok. **1539**
TAVERNER 15 The Englysshe prouerbe
sayethe thus: nere is my cote, but nerer is
my shyrt. **1546** HEYWOOD I. x. 23 Though
ny be my kyrtell, yet nere[1] is my smocke.
I haue one of mine owne whom I must looke
to. **1612** JONSON *Alchem.* III. ii *Sub.* And
though to fortune near be her petticoat, Yet
nearer is her smock, the queen doth note.
1622 HOWELL *Lett.* 1 May (1903) I. 125 That
king . . . having too many irons in the fire at
his own home, . . . answered them that his
shirt was nearer to him than his doublet.
1641 FERGUSSON 82 Neir is the kirtle, but
neirer is the sark. **1732** FULLER no. 4745
The shirt is nearer than the coat. **1894**
NORTHALL *Folk-phrases* (E.D.S.) 25 The
smock is nearer than the petticoat. [[1] nearer.]

Near is my coat (shirt) but nearer is my skin.

c. **1570** *Ballads* (Percy Soc.) I. 99 (A)
Neerer is my skin then shirte. **1596** LODGE
Marg. Amer. 103 My shirt is neare me, my
lord, but, my skin is nearest. **1614** CAMDEN
305 Close sitteth my shirt, but closer my skin.
1636 HENSHAW *Horæ Sub.* 72 His charity
begins at home, and there it ends: neare is
his coat, but neerer is his skin. **1712** ARBUTH-
NOT *John Bull* II. xix 'My shirt', quoth her,
'is near me, but my skin is nearer. Whilst I
take care of the welfare of other folks, nobody
can blame me to apply a little balsam to my
own sores.' **1817** LAMB to Kenneys, Oct.
Dear is my shirt, but dearer is my skin.

Near of kin to land (an estate), It is good to be.

1662 FULLER (*Leics.*) II. 227 Our English

proverb, ' It is good to be near a-kin to land', holdeth in private patrimonies, not titles to crowns. **1670** RAY 110 It's good to be near of kin to an estate. **1721** KELLY 197 *It is something to be sib[1] to a good estate.* Because at the long run it may fall to us. [[1] akin.]

Near, *see also* Lives unsafely that looks too n.

Nearer the bone, The | the sweeter the flesh. (*But cf.* The flesh is aye fairest that is farthest from the bone.)

1559 *Ballads* (Percy Soc.) I. 21 The nigher the bone, the flesh is much sweeter. **1639** CLARKE 163. **1662** FULLER (*Wales*) III. 480 As the sweetest flesh is said to be nearest the bones, so most delicious valleys are interposed betwixt these mountains. **1824** LAMB *Lond. Mag.* Nov. in *Elia*, 'Capt. Jąckson' (1921) 255 Sliding a slender ratio of Single Gloucester upon his wife's plate, . . . he would convey the remanent rind into his own, with a merry quirk of 'the nearer the bone', &c.

Nearer the church, The | the farther from God.

c. **1303** BRUNNE *Handl. Synne* l. 9242 Tharfor men seye, an weyl ys trowed, 'þe nere þe cherche, þe fyrþer fro God'. *c.* **1350** *MS. Douce 52* no. 15 The nerer the chyrche the fer fro Crist. **1546** HEYWOOD I. ix. 17 The nere to the churche, the ferther from God. **1579** SPENSER *Shep. Cal.* Jul. Wks. (Globe) 467 To Kerke the narre, from God more farre, Has bene an old-sayd sawe. **1611** TOURNEUR *Ath. Trag.* I. iv. *Bel.* Come, set forward to the church. . . . *Seb.* And verify the proverb—The nearer the church the further from God. **1620** SHELTON *Quix.* II. xlvii (1908) III. 142 Eat nothing of all this meat . . . for this dinner was presented by nuns, and it is an old saying, 'The nearer the church, the farther from God'. **1641** FERGUSSON 82 Neirest the kirk, farrest fra God. **1819** SCOTT *Ivanhoe* xx It makes good the old proverb, The nearer the church. . . .

Nearest the heart, nearest the mouth.

1641 FERGUSSON 82. **1721** KELLY 265 . . . Spoken to them who, designing to name one person, by mistake names another, perhaps a mistress or sweetheart.

Nearest way is commonly the foulest, The.

c. **1595** BACON *Promus* no. 1247 In actions as in wayes the nearest the fowlest. **1605** Id. *Advancement of Learning* ii (J. M. Robertson) 164. **1625** Id. *Apophthegms* no. 245. **1732** FULLER no. 4921 There is no short cut of a way, without some foul way.

Nearest, *see also* Farthest way about n. way home; Go far about seeking the n.

Neat as a new pin, As.

1796 WOLCOT *Orson & Ellen* Wks. (1816) IV. 71 How neat was Ellen in her dress! As neat as a new pin! **1849–50** THACKERAY *Pendennis*

I. xii Major Pendennis, whom Miss Costigan declared to be a proper gentleman entirely . . . as neat as a pin.

Neat but not gaudy.

c. **1601** SHAKS. *Hamlet* I. iii. 71 Costly thy habit as thy purse can buy, But not express'd in fancy; rich, not gaudy. **1631** BRATHWAIT *Eng. Gentlewoman* (1641) 399 (A) Making this her impreze: *Comely not gaudy.* **1850** THACKERAY *Pendennis* xiii.

Necessity and opportunity may make a coward valiant.

1611 COTGRAVE s.v. 'Necessité' Necessitie addes mettall to the meacocke; makes the coward couragious. **1613** R. DALLINGTON *Aphorisms* 120 Necessitie makes the most cowards valiant. **1732** FULLER no. 3514.

Necessity (Need) has (knows) no law.

[SIMONIDES 8. 20 Ἀνάγκᾳ δ' οὐδὲ θεοὶ μάχονται. Even the gods war not with necessity. PLUTARCH *De Def. Orac.* Ἄπαντα τἀναγκαῖα συγχωρεῖ θεός. *Law Max.—Necessitas non habet legem.*] **1377** LANGLAND *P. Pl.* B. xx. 10 Nede ne hath no lawe, ne neure shal falle in dette. *c.* **1440** *Jacob's Well* 206 þanne nede hath no lawe. *a.* **1529** SKELTON *Col. Cloute* 864 Wks. (1843) I. 344 But it is an olde sayd sawe, That nede hath no lawe. **1546** HEYWOOD I. x. 20 But neede hath no lawe, néede maketh hir hither iet. *a.* **1555** RIDLEY *Lament. Ch.* (1566) D iv The latter reason . . . includeth a necessitie which, after the common sayinge, hathe no law. **1653** H. COGAN *Pinto's Trav.* xlvi. 268 Necessity, which hath no law, compelled us thereunto. **1837** CARLYLE *Fr. Rev.* III. I. iii Your Hessian forager has only 'three sous a day': . . . women . . . are robbed; . . . for Necessity, on three half-pence a day, has no law.

Necessity is a hard dart.

1539 TAVERNER (1545) E 2[v] *Ingens telum necessitas.* Necessitie is a sore weapon. **1540** PALSGRAVE *Acolastus* 35 b Necessitie is a harde weapon. **1560** BECON in *Catechism*, &c. (P.S.) 601 (A).

Necessity is coal black.

1678 RAY 180.

Necessity is the mother of invention.

1519 HORMAN *Vulg.* f. 52 (A) Nede taught hym wytte. **1545** ASCHAM *Toxoph.* (Arb.) 134 Necessitie, the inuentour of all goodnesse (as all authours in a maner, doo saye) . . . inuented a shaft heed. **1608** CHAPMAN *Byron* IV. ii. 35 The great mother of all productions, grave Necessity. **1641** FERGUSSON 76 Mister[1] makes men of craft. **1726** SWIFT *Gul. Trav.* IV. x. Wks. (1856) I. 75 I sold my shoes with wood, which I cut from a tree. . . . No man could more verify the truth. . . . 'That necessity is the mother of invention'. *a.* **1763** SHENSTONE *Detached Thoughts on Writing* Necessity may be the mother of lucrative invention, but it is the death of poetical invention. **1891** J. E. T. ROGERS *Indust. & Com. Hist. Eng.* v We have got an old proverb,

. . . for the extension of it in detail is the substance of a good part of the Plutus of Aristophanes, 'that necessity is the mother of invention'. Take away the necessity and the invention goes with it. [¹ Necessity.]

Necessity, *see also* Conquering weapon as n. of conquering (No such); Virtue of n. (Make).

Neck and crop.

[= bodily, completely.] **1816** HONE *Ev. Day Book* i. 461 (A) Explain the terms . . . neck and crop. . . . **1833** M. SCOTT *T. Cring. Log* xvi Chuck them neck and crop . . . down a dark staircase. **1890** S. BARING-GOULD *Arminell* xxix So he is turned out of the house, neck and crop.

Neck or nothing (nought).

1678 RAY 347. **1715** M. DAVIES *Athen. Brit.* I. 321 Worth venturing Neck or nothing for. **1738** SWIFT (Dial. i) 342 [*The Footman . . . falls down stairs*] *Lady A.* Neck or nothing; come down or I'll fetch you down. **1782** COWPER *Gilpin* 89 Away went Gilpin, neck or nought. **1810** CLARKE *Trav. Russia* 333 She rides, to use the language of English sportsmen, 'neck or nothing'. **1834** EDGE-WORTH *Helen* xxv But, neck or nothing. I am apt to go through with whatever I once take into my head. **1892** A. DOBSON *S. Richardson* 121 Miss Mulso . . . was not one of Richardson's neck-or-nothing flatterers. **1908** W. S. CHURCHILL *My African Journey* ii Three or four daring Britons . . . gallop . . . neck or nothing—across rocks, holes, tussocks, nullahs.

Neck out of the collar, To slip one's.

1583 GOLDING *Calvin on Deut. cxxv* 772 Albeit we . . . would slippe our heades out of the coler seeking to shift off yᵉ matter. **1592-3** SHAKS. *Rich. III* IV. iv. 112 Now thy proud neck bears half my burden'd yoke; From which even here, I slip my wearied head. **1616** DRAXE 189 He draweth his necke out of the coller. **1633** D. DYKE *Wks. Philemon* 242 Religion . . . will not teach thy servant to slip his neck out of the collar, and to deny thee service and subjection. **1655** FULLER *Ch. Hist.* IX. viii. 30 (1868) III. 168 [Parsons] having got his neck out of the collar, accused others for not drawing weight enough.

Neck, *see also* Break his n. as his fast (As soon); Chance it, as Horne did his n.; Good for the head evil for n.; See thy n. as long as my arm.

Neck-cloth, *see* Bolder than miller's n. (What is).

Need makes greed.

1721 KELLY 265 . . . Want is a temptation to covetousness.

Need makes the naked man run (and sorrow makes websters spin).

1639 CLARKE 225. **1641** D. FERGUSSON 82 Need gars naked men run, and sorrow gars websters spin. **1670** RAY 124.

Need makes the old wife trot.

c. **1225** *Trin. MS. O.* 11. 45 (ed. Förster) in *Eng. Stud.* **31.** 8 Neode makad heald wif eorne. *c.* **1470** *Harl. MS. 3362*, f. 3 *a* Nede makyth an old wyfe [rame]. *a.* **1530** *R. Hill's Commonpl. Bk.* (1858) 140 Nede makyth the old wyffe to trotte. **1546** HEYWOOD II. x Néede makth tholde wyfe trot. **1608** TOPSELL *Serpents* (1658) 780 Hunger breaketh stonewalls, and hard need makes the old wife trot. **1821** SCOTT *Pirate* xxiv Stimulated by the spur which maketh the old woman proverbially to trot, Swertha posted down to the hamlet, with all the speed of threescore.

Need much whom nothing will content, They.

1639 CLARKE 38. **1670** RAY 124. **1732** FULLER no. 4969.

Need of a besom that sweep the house with a turf, They have.

1678 RAY 101.

Need of a blessing who kneel to a thistle, They have.

1580 MUNDAY *Zelauto* Their courtesie is overmuch that will kneele to a Thystle. **1623** CAMDEN 279 They haue need of a blessing, will kneele to a thistle. **1664** CODRINGTON 223 (with 'who pray to a Thief'). **1670** RAY 103. **1732** FULLER no. 4964. [See *N. & Q.* 180. 237.]

Need will have its course.

1598 JONSON *Ev. Man in Humour* II. ii. 53. **1678** RAY 180.

Need, *see also* Bale (N.) is hext (When) boot is next; Great and little have n. one of another; Necessity (N.) has no law; Once in ten years man hath n. of another; See him n. but not see him bleed.

Needham.

1575 G. GASCOIGNE *Posies Wks.* (Cunliffe) I. 73 Saint needam be their speede. **1603** H. CROSSE *Virtue's Commonwealth* (Gros.) 63 Come home by Needham-crosse, not fooles aere. **1629** T. ADAMS *Serm.* 466 Idlenesse is the coach to bring a man to *Needome*, prodigality the post-horse. **1662** FULLER (*Suffolk*) III. 161 'You are in the highway to Needham'. Needham is a market-town in this county. . . . They are said to be in the highway to Needham who hasten to poverty.

Needingworth, It comes from.

1639 CLARKE 68.

Needle, Not worth a.

c. **1200** *Ancrene Riwle* 400 And alle þeos þinges somed, agean mine bode, ne beoð nout worð a nelde.¹ *a.* **1399** *Complaint of Ploughman* in WRIGHT *Pol. Poems* (1861) I. 327 Soche willers witte is not worth a nelde.¹ [¹ needle.]

Needle in a bottle¹ of hay, Like a.

1532 MORE *Wks.* (1557) I. 837 To seke out

one lyne in all hys bookes wer to go looke a nedle in a medow. **1592** GREENE *Upst. Courtier* (1871) 4b He ... gropeth in the dark to find a needle in a bottle of hay. **1610** FIELD *Woman is a W.* I. ii (Merm.) 351 *Pouts.* That little old dried neat's tongue. ... Methinks he in his lady should show like a needle in a bottle of hay. **1690** W. WALKER *Idiom. Anglo. Lat.* (1695) Pref. A labour much like that of seeking a needle in a Bottle of Hay. **1711** SWIFT *Jrnl. to Stella* 22 Oct. I must rout among your letters, a needle in a bottle of hay. **1742** GRAY *Lett.* (1900) I. 105 A coach that seem'd to have lost its way, by looking for a needle in a bottle of hay. [¹ bundle.]

Needle's eye.

1389 WYCLIF *Matt.* xix. 24 It is liȝter a camel for to passe thorwȝ a nedelis eiȝe, than a riche man to entre into the kyngdam of heuenes. **1579** GOSSON *Sch. Abuse* (Arb.) 27 Euerie one of them may ... daunce the wilde Morice in a Needles eye. **1595–6** SHAKS. *Rich. II* V. v. 17 It is hard to come as for a camel To thread the postern of a needle's eye. **1622** FITZGEFFREY *Elisha* 46 He had learned also how to make the Camell passe through the needles eye, namely by casting off the bunch on the back. **1872** BESANT & RICE *Ready-m. Mort.* xlvi A single-hearted ... rich man, for whom the needle's eye is as easy to pass, as for the poorest pauper.

Needles and pins, needles and pins: when a man marries his trouble begins.

1843 HALLIWELL *Nursery Rhymes* 122 (A). **1876** BLACKMORE *Cripps* lii Cripps ... was sadly singing ... that exquisite elegiac— 'Needles and pins, needles and pins, When a man marries, his trouble begins!'

Needle(s), *see also* Put it together with hot n. and burnt thread; St. Peter's n. (Go through); Sharp as a n.; Steel in my n. eye, though little; Tine n. tine darg; Tint a cow that grat for n. (He never).

Needs must.

c. **1390** GOWER *Conf. Amantis* I. 291 For it is seid thus overal, That nedes mot that nede schal. **1604** E. GRIMSTONE *Hist. Siege Ostend* 195 We beleeue them no more then needs must. **1871** BROWNING *Balaustion* 2287 She shall go, if needs must.

Needs must when the devil drives.

c. **1420** LYDGATE *Ass. of Gods* (E.E.T.S.) 1. 20 For hit ys oft seyde by hem that yet lyues He must nedys go that the deuell dryues. **1523** SKELTON *Garl. Laurel* 1434 Nedes must he rin that the deuyll dryuith. **1546** HEYWOOD II. vii. 64 And that he must néedes go, whom the diuel dooth driue. **1592** KYD *Sp. Trag.* III. xii. 81 For needs must he go that the devils drive. **1602–3** SHAKS. *All's Well* I. iii. 32 He must needs go that the devil drives. **1613** PURCHAS *Pilgrimage* I. xv. 71 Needs must they goe whom the diuell driueth. **1664** COTTON *Scarron.* i. 14 He needs must go, the Devil drives. **1839** DICKENS *N. Nickleby* v. Needs must, you know, when

somebody drives. Necessity is my driver and that is only another name for the same gentleman. **1853** R. S. SURTEES *Sponge's Sport. T.* xxv 'Well', said he, 'needs must when a certain gentleman drives'.

Needy when he is married, He that is | shall be rich when he is buried.

1616 DRAXE 230. **1670** RAY 48. **1707** MAPLETOFT 112 (with 'Poor' for 'needy').

Ne'er-do-weel, *see* Hantle o' fauts (Some hae), ye're only n.

Negatives, *see* Two n. make affirmative.

Neglect will kill an injury sooner than revenge.

1620–8 FELTHAM *Resolves* (Dent) 213.

Neighbour-quart is good quart.

1678 RAY 180 ... *i.e.* Giffe gaffe is a good fellow.

Neighbour's house is on fire, Look to thyself when thy.

[VIRGIL *Aen.* 2. 311 *Proximus ardet Ucalegon.* Your neighbour Ucalegon is on fire. HORACE *Ep.* 1. 18. 84 *Tua res agitur, paries cum proximus ardet.* Your own property is at stake, when your neighbour's house is on fire.] **1519** HORMAN *Vulg.* (Roxb. Cl.) 184 Whan my neybours house is a fyre: I can nat be out of thought for myn owne. **1594** GREENE *Looking-Glass* V. v. (Merm.) 164 O proud adulterous glory of the west! Thy neighbours burn, yet dost thou fear no fire. **1636** CAMDEN 299. **1639** CLARKE 250. **1662** FULLER (*Cumberland*) I. 340 'When thy neighbour's house doth burn, Take heed the next be not thy turn.' **1891** J. E. T. ROGERS *Ind. & Com. Hist.* iv The true cause ... of a credit panic is the close interlacing of monetary interests. If Ucalegon's house catches fire, his neighbours are in extreme risk of the conflagration extending.

Neighbour's scathe is my present peril, My next. (*Cf. preceding proverb.*)

1721 KELLY 245 ... L. [*Nam*] *tua res agitur paries quum proximus ardet.*

Neighbours, He dwells far from (*or* hath ill) | that is fain to praise himself.

1509 A. BARCLAY *Ship of Fools* (1874) II. 68 Men ... In theyr olde prouerbes often comprehende That he that is amonge shrewyd neyghbours May his owne dedes laufully commende. **1593–4** SHAKS. *Titus Andron.* V. iii. 118 When no friends are by, men praise themselves. **1598–9** *Much Ado* V. ii. 82 *Beat.* There's not one wise man among twenty that will praise himself. *Bene.* An old, an old instance, Beatrice, that lived in the time of good neighbours. **1599** PORTER *Angry Wom. Abingd.* IV. iii (Merm.) 178 You dwell by ill neighbours, Richard; that makes ye praise yourself. **1659** HOWELL *Eng. Prov.* 16/1 Who commendeth himself, wanteth good neighbours. **1670** RAY 125 ... *Proprio laus sordet in ore.* Let another man praise thee, and not thine own mouth; a stranger, and not thine own lips. [*Prov.* xxvii. 2.] **1721** KELLY 375 *You live beside ill neighbours.* Spoken when people commend themselves. **1738** SWIFT (Dial. i) 337 I find you live by ill neighbours, when you are forced to praise yourself.

Neighbour(s), *see also* Ask of my fire (Rather) than borrow of n.; Ask your n. if you shall live in peace; Better learn by n.'s skaith; God sees and bears, n. finds fault; Good n. good morrow; Hale pow that calls n. nitty know; Live without our friends but not our n.; Lost (It is not) that a friend (n.) gets; Love your n., yet pull not down hedge; Marry (He about to) should consider n.; Mother says (It is not as), but as n. say; Well with him beloved of n.

Neither here nor there.

1581 A. MANUTIUS *Phrases Linguae Latinae* 62 It is neither here nor there, or I passe not what you thinke of me. **1594** T. NASHE *Unfort. Trav.* Wks. (McKerrow) II. 210. **1600–1** SHAKS. *Merry W.* I. iv. 110 But notwithstanding that, I know Anne's mind, that's neither here nor there. **1604–5** *Othello* IV. iii. 59 *Des.* Doth that bode weeping? *Emil.* 'Tis neither here nor there. **1722** STEELE *Consc. Lov.* IV. i (Merm.) 349 *Boy.* Nay, nay! that's neither here nor there: what's matter whether she is within or no, if she has not a mind to see anybody? **1760–7** STERNE *T. Shandy* VI. vi But this is neither here nor there: why do I mention it? **1815** SCOTT *Guy Man.* iv And I had a wee bit of law business besides, but that's neither here nor there.

Neither (a, in, my, of his, to), *see under significant words following.*

Nemesis.

[Gk. Νέμεσις, the goddess of retribution, = one who avenges or punishes.] **1576** GASCOIGNE *Philomene* (Arb.) 114 She calls on Nemesis ..., The Goddesse of al iust reuenge. **1591–2** SHAKS. *1 Hen. VI* IV vii. 78 Is Talbot slain ..., Your kingdom's terror and black Nemesis? **1621** BURTON *Anat. Mel.* II. iii. VII *Nemesis* comes after, *sero sed serio,* stay but a little and thou shalt see God's just judgment overtake him [the wicked man]. **1642** H. MORE *Song of Soul* III. II. xiii Thus sensuall souls do find their righteous doom which Nemesis inflicts. **1901** R. G. MOULTON *Shakespeare as Dram. Art.* 46 This Nemesis is deeply embedded in the popular mind and repeatedly crops up in its proverbial wisdom.

Nemo repente fuit turpissimus, see No man ever became thoroughly bad all at once.

Neptune, *see* Bacchus hath drowned more than N.

Nertown was a market town, when Taunton was a furzy down.

1851 *N. & Q.* 1st Ser. IV. 149 'Nerton was a

market town When Taunton was a furzy down'. This Nertown is a village adjoining Taunton. ... It's name is ... a corruption of ... Nethertown.

Nessus, *see* Shirt of N.

Nest(s), *see* Birds of this year in last year's n. (No); Catch the old one on the n.; Destroy the n., birds fly away; Feather one's n.; God builds the n. of blind bird; Little bird content with little n. *See also* Mare's nest.

Net of the sleeper catches fish, The.

[Gk. Εὕδοντι κύρτος αἱρεῖ. ERASM. *Ad. Dormientis rete trahit.*] **1683** WHITE-KENNETT tr. *Erasm. Pr. of Folly* (8th ed.) 135 (A) Thus Timotheus, the Athenian commander, in all his expeditions was a mirror of good luck, because he was a little underwitted; from him was occasioned the proverb, *The net fills though the fisherman sleeps.* **1853** TRENCH V. 119 The following [is] often quoted or alluded to by Greek and Latin authors: *The net of the sleeping (fisherman) takes.*

Net, *see also* Cast your n. where no fish (Vain to); Dance in a n.; In vain the n. is spread; Rough n. not best catcher of birds.

Netherlands are the cockpit of Christendom, The.

1642 HOWELL *For. Trav.* xiii (Arb.) 60 For the *Netherlands* have been for many yeares, ... the very *Cockpit of Christendome,* the *Schoole of Armes,* and *Rendezvous of all adventurous Spirits.*

Nettle(s), *see* Drink n. in March; Handles a n. tenderly (He that); In dock out n.; Stung by a n. (Better to be).

Neust (Newst) of a neustness (newstness).

1813 RAY 274 Neust of a neustness. *i.e.* Almost the same. An expression very current in Berkshire, about Binfield.

Never a Granville¹ wanted loyalty, a Godolphin wit, or a Trelawny courage.

1869 HAZLITT 290 *Cornw.* [¹ Sir Rich. Grenville, *d.* Azores, 1591; and Sir Bevil Grenville, *d.* Lansdowne, 1643, belonged to this family.]

Never a whit as never the better, As good.

1546 HEYWOOD II. xi. **1599** BRETON *Anger & Patience* Wks. (Gros.) II. 60 As good never a whit, as never the better. **1652** FULLER *Com. on Christ's Temp.* in *Sel. Serm.* (1891) II. 73 *As good never a whit as never the better*; and in effect it was never shown which was so soon removed. **1732** FULLER no. 687.

Never answer a question until it is asked.

1902–4 LEAN IV. 56.

Never ask pardon before you are accused.

1855 BOHN 458.

Never ate flesh, He that | thinks a pudding a dainty.

1721 KELLY 126 . . . A man not us'd to what is good, thinks much of what is indifferent.

Never be angry at, Two things a man should | ; what he can help, and what he cannot help.

1721 KELLY 322. **1732** FULLER no. 5335.

Never be ashamed to eat your meat.

1639 CLARKE 269. **1670** RAY 57 . . . *Apud mensam verecundari neminem decet. Erasmus* takes notice, that this Proverb is handed down to us from the Ancients. . . . Yet some there are who out of a rustick shamefacedness or over-mannerliness are very troublesome at table, expecting to be . . . often invited to eat, and refusing what you offer them.

Never be weary of well doing.

[**1534** TINDALE *Galat.* vi. 9 Let vs not be weary of wel doyng.] **1616** DRAXE 32. **1670** RAY 154.

Never bite, unless you make your teeth meet.

1721 KELLY 258 . . . This . . . savour[s] too much of malice and revenge. . . . The more noble way is to forget and to forgive.

Never but once at a wedding.

1678 RAY 263. **1738** SWIFT (Dial. i) 336 *Never.* Did you ever see the like? *Miss.* Never, but once at a wedding.

Never catch at a falling knife or a falling friend.

1864 J. H. FRISWELL *Gentle Life* 79 The Scotch . . . have a like proverb . . . , 'Never catch at a falling knife or a falling friend.'

Never cheapen unless you mean to buy.

1902-4 LEAN IV. 56.

Never climbed never fell, He that.

1546 HEYWOOD I. xii. 38. **1659** HOWELL *Eng. Prov.* 15/1.

Never do things by halves.

1753 HANWAY *Trav.* (1762) II. XIV. i. 343 Nadir, who did nothing by halves, was determined to pull off the mask. **1883** C. READE *Peril Secr.* viii 'Oh, never do things by halves', said the ready girl.

Never dog barked against the crucifix but he ran mad.

1642 FULLER *H. & P. State* v. vi (1841) 355 He scoffs . . . at sacred things.—This . . . ulcers men's hearts with profaneness. The Popish

proverb, well understood, hath a truth in it: 'Never dog barked against the crucifix, but he ran mad.'

Never drank was never athirst, He that.

1659 HOWELL *Eng. Prov.* 13/2.

Never draw your dirk when a dunt[1] will do.

1832 HENDERSON 51 [[1] blow.]

Never go to the devil and a dishclout in your hand.

1721 KELLY 264 . . . If you will be a knave, be not in a trifle, but in something of value.

Never good that mind their belly so much.

1678 RAY 347. *Somerset.*

Never is a long day (term).

c. **1386** CHAUCER *Canon's Yeoman's T.* G. 1411 Nevere to thryve were to long a date. **1721** KELLY 260 . . . Spoken to them that say they will never get such a thing effected. **1884** J. PAYN *Canon's Ward* xxv I will never, never marry again.' 'Never is a long day . . .', said Jeanette cheerfully. **1887** BLACKMORE *Springhaven* xvii She never could pay her rent. But 'never is a long time,' . . . and . . . she stood clear of all debt now.

Never kiss a man's wife, nor wipe his knife, for he will be likely to do both after you.

1639 CLARKE 45 To kiss a man's wife, or wipe his knife, is a thankless office. **1721** KELLY 263.

Never long that comes at last, It is.

1639 CLARKE 295.

Never-mass, At.

[= never] **1537** *Thersites* D 4. **1639** CLARKE 229.

Never mind what people say.

1855 C. KINGSLEY *Lett.* to Ludlow in *Lett. & Mem.* (1882) I. xiii. 358 To make my children . . . scoffing radicals . . . would be perfectly easy . . . if I were to make the watch-word of my house, 'Never mind what people say.'

Never rode never fell, He that.

1641 FERGUSSON 82. **1721** KELLY 139.

Never say die.

[= never give in.] **1837** DICKENS *Pickwick* ii (1867) 6 Never say die—down upon your luck. **1838** *Wilson's Tales of Borders* IV. 142 Never say 'die', while there's a shot[1] in the locker, Bill; we'll weather many a Friday's sailing yet. **1848** A. SMITH *Christ. Tadpole* 1 Never say die, mother: that's the line of business. [[1] money.]

Never sigh, but send.

1678 RAY 348 Never sigh but send. *Ibid.* 81 Sigh not, but send, he'll come if he be unhanged. **1721** KELLY 89 *Do not sigh for him. but send for him; if he be unhang'd he'll come,* Spoken when a young maid sighs, alleging that it is for a sweetheart. **1738** SWIFT (Dial. i) 336 MISS *sighs . . . Spark.* Come, miss, never sigh, but send for him.

Never take a stone (forehammer) to break an egg, when you can do it with the back of your knife.

1721 KELLY 266. **1737** RAMSAY III. 191 Ne'er tak a forehammer to break an egg when ye can do it wi' a pen knife.

Never take the tawse[1] when a word will do the turn.

1721 KELLY 266 . . . Severity ought never to be used where fair means will prevail. [[1] a leather strap with a fringed end, used instead of a rod.]

Never the nearer, *see* Early up.

Never too late to mend.

1590 GREENE *Never too Late* [title] (A). *c.* **1645** HOWELL *Lett.* 9 Nov. (1903) III. 139 We have both of us our failings that way : . . . but it is never over late to mend. **1837** T. HOOK *Jack Brag* i. Ah, Johnny, . . . you never will mend till it is too late. **1883** J. PAYN *Thicker than W.* x It is never too late to mend, . . . and . . . his recantation has been a very full one.

Never too late to repent.

a. **1591** HY. SMITH *Serm.* (1866) I. 218 It is an old saying, Repentance is never too late ; but it is a true saying, Repentance is never too soon. **1670** RAY 112 . . . *Nunquam sera est,* &c.

Never too old (late) to learn.

[SENECA *Epist.* 76. 3. *Tamdiu discendum est quamdiu nescias : si proverbio credimus, 'quamdiu vivis'.* We must go on learning as long as we are ignorant ; or, if we believe the proverb, as long as we live.] *a.* **1627** MIDDLETON *Mayor Queenb.* v. i (Merm.) II. 383 *Simon.* A man is never too old to learn. **1670** RAY 112. **1712** ARBUTHNOT *John Bull* i. vii A lawyer I was born, and a lawyer I will be ; one is never too old to learn. **1721** KELLY 266 Never too late to learn. L. *Nunquam sera est ad bonos mores via.*

Never was cat or dog drowned, that could but see the shore.

c. **1594** BACON *Promus* no. 590 (A) A catt will never drowne if she sees the shore. **1666** TORRIANO 36 Neither dog nor cat ever drown, so long as they can discern the shore. **1732** FULLER no. 3532.

Never was strumpet fair.

1640 HERBERT 338.

Never well (pleased) full nor fasting.

1603 *The Bachelor's Banquet* (F. P. Wilson) 77 You were never other . . . never pleased full nor fasting. **1608** J. HALL *Characters,* 'Malcontent' He is neither well full nor fasting. **1617** J. SWETNAM *School of Defence* 13 Some are neuer well full nor fasting. **1639** CLARKE 34 Neither pleased full nor fasting. **1670** RAY 176. **1692** L'ESTRANGE *Aesop's Fab.* CCXCV (1738) 307. **1721** KELLY 376 You are never pleas'd fow[1] or fasting. [[1] full.]

Never, *see also* Street of 'By-and-bye' house of 'N'.

Never, *see also under significant words following.*

New beer, new bread and green wood, will make a man's hair grow through his hood.

1750 W. ELLIS *Mod. Husbandm.* i. 91 For as the Verse or Proverb says—New Beer, new Bread, and green Wood will make a Man's Hair grow through his Hood. [i.e. reduce him to poverty.]

New book appears, When a | read an old one.

1907 A. C. BENSON *From Coll. Window* (ed. 4) 297 What [Walter Pater] is condemning is the . . . encrusting of the mind with prejudices and habits, the tendency, as Charles Lamb wittily said, whenever a new book comes out, to read an old one.

New broom sweeps clean, A.

1546 HEYWOOD II. i. 44 Some thereto said, the gréene new brome swéepth cléene. **1579** LYLY *Euphues* (Arb.) 89 Ah well I wot that a new broome sweepeth cleane. **1721** KELLY 15 *A new besom sweeps clean.* Spoken of new servants, who are commonly very diligent ; and new officers, who are commonly very severe. **1867–77** FROUDE *Short Stud.* III. 77 New brooms sweep clean. Abbot Thomas, like most of his predecessors, began with attempts at reformation.

New church, old steeple: poor town and proud people.

1873 HARLAND & WILKINSON *Lancashire Leg.* 202 As to the prosperous and beautiful village of Bowness, on Windermere—'New church, old steeple, Poor town, and proud people.'

New College, *see* Thrive as N.C. students.

New is not true, What is | and what is true is not new.

[**1772** J. H. VOSS in *Vossischer Musenalmanach* 71 (King), Dein redseliges Buch lehrt mancherlei Neues und Wahres: Wäre das Wahre nur neu, wäre das Neue nur wahr.] **1880** J. NICHOL *Byron* 167 We are told . . . that he knew little of art or music. . . . It is true but not new. Hunt proceeds to say that Byron had no sentiment . . . ; it is new enough, but is manifestly not true. **1928** *Times* 4 Feb. 8/2 Sir Arthur Evans has fallen a victim . . . to the old slogan 'What is new cannot be true'.

New lease of life, To take out a.

1809 SCOTT *Let. to Ellis* 8 Jul. in LOCKHART
Life xix My friend has since taken out a new
lease of life, and . . . may . . . live as long as I
shall;—such odious deceivers are these in-
valids. **1867–77** FROUDE *Short Stud.* (1890) I.
161 Had the popes and cardinals been wise
they would have . . . cleared their teaching of
its lumber, and taken out a new lease of life
both for it and for themselves.

New lords, new laws.

a. **1548** HALL *Chron.*, *Hen. VI* 169 Tholde
spoken proverbs, here toke place: New
Lordes, new lawes. **1721** KELLY 260 . . . L.
Novus Rex, nova lex. **1824** SCOTT *St. Ronans*
xiv But new lords new laws—naething but
fine and imprisonment, and the game no a
feather the plentier.

New meat begets a new appetite.

1616 DRAXE 24 New meate bringeth a new
appetite. **1670** RAY 18.

New presbyter is old priest writ large.

c. **1646** MILTON *New Forcers Consc.* 20 When
they shall read this clearly in your charge:
New Presbyter is but Old Priest writ Large.
1876 D. MACLEOD *Mem. Norman Macleod* I.
183 Knowing how easily 'presbyter' might
become 'priest writ large', he was . . . afraid
of the tyranny of Church Courts and ecclesiastical majorities. **1880** FROUDE *Bunyan* 66,
67 When Elizabeth died,[1] the . . . High
Church party . . . abused their power. . . . The
Bishops were displaced by Presbyterian
elders. The Presbyterian elders became
themselves 'hireling wolves', 'old priest'
written in new characters. [[1] 1603.]

New prince, Of a | new bondage.

1651 HERBERT 369.

New Testament, *see* Testament.

New things are fair.

c. **1380** CHAUCER *Leg. of Good Women* l. 1077
To som folk ofte newe thyng is sote. *c.* **1386**
CHAUCER *Squire's T.* F[1] 610 Men loven of
propre kynde newefangelnesse. *c.* **1412** LYD-
GATE *Troy Bk.* IV. 572 Here men may se
how it is natural then to delite in þing[e] þat
is newe. **1651** HERBERT 369.

New tout[1] in an old horn, A.

1678 RAY 361 A new sound in an old horn.
1721 KELLY 28 *An old tout in a new horn.*
Spoken when we hear (perhaps in other words)
what we have heard before. **1822** SCOTT
Nigel xxvii There are . . . Puritans of papisti-
cal principles—it is just a new tout on an old
horn. [[1] blast.]

New, *see also* Everything n. is fine; Nothing
n. under sun.

Newcastle burr in his throat, He has the.

1760 FOOTE *Minor* (1781) Introd. 9 An Aunt
just come from the North, with the true

New Castle bur in her throat. **1787** GROSE
(*Northumb.*) 212 . . . The people of Newcastle, Morpeth, and their environs, have a
peculiar guttural pronunciation.

Newcastle, *see also* Canny N.; Carry coals to
N.; Scot, a rat, and a N. grindstone.

Newcome, *see* Johny N.

Newer is truer.

1546 HEYWOOD II. iv. 51 Thy ryme (quoth
he) is muche elder then mine. But myne
beyng newer is truer then thine.

Newgate, *see* Low ebb at N. (He that is at).

News are like fish.

1616 BRETON *Cross. Prov.* ii. Wks. (1879) II.
App. iii.

News, *see also* Go into country to hear n.;
Jock's n.; Lame post brings truest n.; No
n. is good n.; Scant of news that told his
father was hanged; Stay a little and n.
will find you. *See also* Good news, Ill news.

Next, *see* Do the n. thing; Thank you for the
n. (I will).

Next to (a, no), *see* under *significant words
following.*

Niagara, *see* Shoot N.

Nibbled to death by ducks, One had as good be.

1678 RAY 240.

Nice as a nun's hen, As.

15th cent. *Reliq. Antiq.* (1841) i. 248 (A) Some
[women] be nyse as a nanne bene. **1546** HEY-
WOOD II. i. 43 She tooke thenterteinment of
the young men All in daliaunce, as nice as a
nun's hen. **1553** T. WILSON *Rhet.* (1580) 223
I knewe a Prieste that was as nice as a Nonnes
Henne, when he would saie Masse.

Nice eaters seldom meet with a good dinner.

1732 FULLER no. 3540.

Nice wife, A | and a back door oft do (will soon) make a rich man poor.

c. **1450** *Prov. of Good Counsel* (Furnivall) l. 33
A nyse wyfe & A backe dore, Makyth oftyn
tymus A ryche man pore. **1551** W. BALDWIN
Beware the Cat (1584) E 7[v] A wanton wife
and a back-door wil soon make a rich man
poor. **1639** CLARKE 218. **1640** HERBERT 340
The back-door robs the house. **1721** KELLY
45 . . . The wife will spend, and the servants
purloin.

Nice, *see also* More n. than wise.

Nichils in nine pokes.

[*Nichil* (med. L.) or *Nihil* (class. L.) = nothing
is 'a word which the Sheriff answers, that is
opposed concerning Debts illeviable, and that

are nothing worth, by reason of the insufficiency of the Parties from whom they are due'. See **1684** MANLEY *Cowell's Interpreter.*] **1584** R. SCOT *Discov. Witches* (1886) XVI. vi. 406 The witches . . . that . . . give their soules to the divell . . . and their bodies to the hangman to be trussed on the gallows, for nichels in a bag. **1670** RAY 188 . . . *Chesh. i.e.* Nothing at all. **1678** *Ibid.* 261 *Nichils* in nine pokes *or* nooks. **1917** BRIDGE 97 Nichills in nine holes. Nothing at all. Absolutely empty. . . . There are two variants, the first of which is fairly common in Cheshire:— *Nichills in nine pokes* (sacks or bags). *Nichills in nine nooks.*

Nick (of time), In the.

1577 HANMER *Anc. Eccl. Hist.* VI. vi The Romane navie . . . arrived at the very pinch, or as commonly we say, in the nicke. **1594** LYLY *Moth. Bomb.* III. iii *Dromio.* My device was, . . . that he should come in the nick when she was singing. **1604–5** SHAKS. *Othello* V. ii. 316 Iago in the nick came in and satisfied him. [Ff. 'interim'.] **1642** *Declar. Lords & Comm. to Gen. Assembly Ch. Scot.* 12 In this nick of time. **1681** DRYDEN *Span. Friar* I. i *Lorenzo.* A seasonable girl, just in the nick now. *a.* **1707** S. PATRICK *Autobiogr.* (1839) 179 I look upon it as a singular providence of God, that Dr. Harris . . . should come in at that nick of time. **1775** SHERIDAN *Rivals* IV. iii To be sure I'm just come in the nick. **1877** BESANT & RICE *Son of Vulcan* Prol. ii This grand-uncle had 'gone over to the majority' in the very nick of time.

Nick, *see* Dick's (N.'s) hatband.

Nicks (Wrinkles) in her horn, She has a good many.

[JUVENAL *Sat.* 6. 199 *Facies tua computat annos.* Your face reckons your years.] **1721** KELLY 359 *We may know your age by the wrinkles of your horn.* Spoken to old maids when they pretend to be young. **1910** P. W. JOYCE *Eng. as We Speak* 113 'She has a good many nicks in her horn': said of a girl who is becoming an old maid. A cow is said to have a nick in her horn for every year.

Nigger in the wood-pile (fence), A.

[= a private reason or motive for action, which is not divulged.] **1862** *Congress. Globe* 3 June 2527/1 [These gentlemen] spoke two whole hours . . . in showing—to borrow an elegant phrase, the paternity of which belongs, I think, to their side of the House— that there was 'a nigger in the wood-pile'. **1888** BRET HARTE *Phyllis of Sierras* I. iii. 90 There's another Englishman coming up from 'Frisco . . . he'll guess there's a nigger in the fence somewhere. **1911** WOODROW WILSON in *Outlook* 11 Aug. 944 If you go through the schedules you will find some nigger in every wood pile.

Nigh, *see* Almost and very n. saves many a lie.

Night cometh, The | when no man can work.

1526 TINDALE *John* ix. 4 The nyght commeth,

when no man can worke. **1791** BOSWELL *Johnson* xxi (1847) 192 I observed upon the dial-plate of his watch a short Greek inscription . . . *Νὺξ γὰρ ἔρχεται,* . . . 'the night cometh when no man can work'. **1902** FAIRBAIRN *Philos. Chrn. Rel.* (ed. 2) I. iv. 143 Men thought of themselves more worthily and of their deeds more truly when they saw that a night came when no man could work.

Night is no man's friend, The.

1853 TRENCH iii. 45 The old German proverb: *The night is no man's friend* (Die Nacht ist keines Menschen Freund) . . . rests . . . on the wide-spread feeling in the northern mythologies of the night as an unfriendly and, indeed, hostile power to man.

Night is the mother of counsel.

[MENANDER *Monosticha* 150 *Ἐν νυκτὶ βουλὴ τοῖς σοφοῖσι γίγνεται.* By night counsel comes to the wise. ERASM. *Ad. In nocte consilium.* **1573** SANDFORD (1576) 215. **1590** SPENSER *F. Q.* I. i. 291 Untroubled night, they say, gives counsell best. **1640** HERBERT 352 Night is the mother of Councils. **1660** DRYDEN *Astraea Red.* 93 Well might the ancient poets then confer On Night the honoured name of Counseller.

Night, *see also* Blustering n., fair day; Day has eyes, n. ears; Done by n. appears by day; Every day cometh n.; Growed by n. (This); Longest n. will have end; Lucy light . . . longest n.; Runs in the n. stumbles; Sun has set, no n. followed.

Nightingale and cuckoo sing both in one month, The.

1639 CLARKE 106.

Nightingale, *see also* Owl sings (When), n. hold her peace; Third of April comes . . . n.

Nil admirari (Wonder at nothing).

[HORACE *Epist.* 1. 6. 1 *Nil admirari, prope res est una, Numici, Solaque, quae possit facere et servare beatum.* To wonder at nothing is about the one and only thing, Numicius, which can make a man happy, and keep him so.] *a.* **1626** SIR JOHN DAVIES *Acrostic on Q. Elizabeth* Brave spirit, large heart, admiring naught. **1821** BYRON *Juan* V. 100 I ne'er could see the very Great happiness of the 'Nil Admirari'. **1855** TENNYSON *Maud* iv. 7 Not to admire or desire. **1881** DEAN PLUMPTRE *Ecclesiastes* V. 8 The words 'wonder not' tells us . . . who had been his teachers. In that counsel we have a distinct echo from one of the floating maxims of Greek proverbial wisdom, from the *Μηδὲν θαυμάζειν* ('wonder at nothing') of Pythagoras . . . which has become more widely known through the *Nil admirari* of Horace. **1883** J. PAYN *Thicker than W.* xiv The Aglaia Club, which . . . was a somewhat 'used up' and *nil admirari* society.

Nile, *see* Dog at the N. (Like a); Throw him into N. . . . fish in his mouth.

Nimble as an eel, As.

c. **1594** SHAKS. *L.L.L.* I. ii. 28 An eel is quick.

c. **1595** *Thomas of Woodstock* l. 295 As nimble
as an Eele. **1732** FULLER no. 719 As nimble
as an eel in a sandbag.

Nimble ninepence.

1851 MAYHEW *Lond. Labour* (1864) II. 263/1
The nimble ninepence' being considered
'better than the slow shilling'. **1894** ASTLEY
50 Years Life II. 68 Not a bad instance of
the nimble ninepence.

Nimble, *see also* Quick and n.

Nimrod(s), *see* Three classes of clergy, N.

Nine days, *see* Wonder.

Nine men, *see* Run to work as if n. m. held
you.

Nine tailors make a man.

1607 DEKKER & WEBSTER *Northw. Hoe* II (A)
They say three taylors go to the making vp of
a man. **1615** CLEVELAND *Poems* 23 Like to
nine Taylors, who if rightly spell'd, Into one
man, are monosyllabled. **1663** BUTLER
Hudibras. I. ii. 22 Compos'd of many Ingredient Valors Just like the Manhood of nine
Taylors. **1771** SMOLLETT *Humph. Clink.*
18 Jul. Wks. (1871) 539 Made her believe I
was a tailor, and that she was going to marry
the ninth part of a man. **1819** SCOTT *Lett.*
26 July in LOCKHART *Life* They say it takes
nine tailors to make a man—apparently, one
is sufficient to ruin him. **1908** H. B. WALTERS
in *Church Bells* 96 'Nine Tailors make a
man', is *said* to be really 'nine tellers',
'tellers' being the strokes for male, female, or
child, in a funeral knell or passing bell. 3 × 3
for male. [In Dorset these strokes are said
to be called tailors: *Acad.* 11 Feb. 1899,
190/1.]

Nine words at once, To talk.

1509 A. BARCLAY *Ship of Fools* (1874) I. 96
Some speketh .IX. wordes at thryse. **1611**
COTGRAVE S.V. 'Tost' To speak thick, or fast,
or (as we say) nine words at once.

Nine Worthies.

[Nine famous personages, viz. Three Jews
(Joshua, David, Judas Maccabæus); three
Gentiles (Hector, Alexander, Julius Cæsar);
three Christians (Arthur, Charlemagne,
Godfrey of Bouillon).] *c.* 1417 *Agincourt* 13
Though thou be not set amorge yᵉ worthyes
nyne, Yet wast thou a conqueroure in thy
tyme. **1594–5** SHAKS. *L.L.L.* V. i. 128 Sir,
you shall present before her the Nine
Worthies. *Ibid.* V. ii. 486, &c. **1597–8**
2 Hen. IV II. iv. 238 Thou art as valorous
as Hector of Troy . . . and ten times better
than the Nine Worthies. **1619** J. TAYLOR
(Water-P.) *Kicksey Winsey* C 1 b Forgot had
bin the thrice three worthies names, If thrice
Muses had not writ their fames.

Nine-pence to the shilling.

1889 B. PEACOCK *Glos. Lincs.* (E.S.D.) 370
Nine-pence-to-the-shilling.—Below the average in common sense. 'How's Mr. . . .?
Thaay do saay as he's nobut nine-pence-to-
th'-shilling.'—M. F., Scotton, 1876.

Ninepence, *see* Bring a noble to n.; Nimble n.

Nineteen bits of a bilberry, He will make.

1678 RAY 229 . . . Spoken of a covetous
person.

Nineteen nay-says of a maiden are a half a grant.

1721 KELLY 268 . . . Spoken to encourage
those who have had a denial from their
mistress to attack them again.

Nineteen, *see also* Tongue runs n. to dozen.

Nip the briar in the bud, It is good to.

1613 DALLINGTON *Aphorisms* 100 If they be
not nipped in the bud. **1721** KELLY 211 . . .
It is good to prevent, by wholesome correction, the vicious inclinations of children.
1732 FULLER no. 3543.

Nippence, nopence, half a groat wanting twopence.

1659 HOWELL *Eng. Prov.* 12/1.

Nits will be lice.

a. **1700** *New Dict. Cant. Crew* H7 Nitts will
be Lice. **1791** I. DISRAELI *Curios. Lit.* (1858)
III. 44 Oliver Cromwell's coarse but descrip-
tive proverb conveys the contempt which
he felt for some of his mean and troublesome
coadjutors: 'Nits will be lice!'

'No', *see* Say 'No' till you are asked (Don't).

No better than she (they) should be.

[= of doubtful moral character.] **1604**
Pasquils Jests (1864) 35 A man whose wife
was no better then she should be. **1712**
STEELE *Spect.* No. 503 Some say, 'A very
fine lady'; others, 'I'll warrant you, she is
no better than she should be.' **1882** J. C.
MORRISON *Macaulay* 105 He goes up to the
dignified dames . . . and finishes by telling
them roundly that in his opinion they are all
no better than they should be.

No bishop, no king.

1589? LYLY *Whip for Ape* Wks. (1902) III.
420 Yes, he that now saith, Why should
Bishops be? Will next cry out, Why Kings?
The Saints are free. **1604** JAMES I in FULLER
Ch. Hist. (1655) X. i (1868) III. 201 *His
Majesty.*—I approve the calling and use of
bishops in the church; and it is my aphorism,
'No bishop, no king.' **1641** 'SMECTYMNUUS'
Vind. Answ. § 16, 208 King James of blessed
memory said, *no Bishop no King*: it was not
he, but others that added, *No Ceremony, no
Bishop.*

No broth, no ball; no ball, no beef.

1853 MRS. GASKELL *Cranford* iv We used to
keep strictly to my father's rule, 'No broth,
no ball; no ball, no beef'; and always began
dinner with broth. Then we had suet puddings, boiled in the broth with the beef; and
then the meat itself. If we did not sup our
broth, we had no ball.

No case: abuse the plaintiff's attorney.

1662 J. WILSON *Cheats* I. iv. Wks. (1874) 28 *Runter.* Then, if at any time you find you have the worst end of the staff, leave off your cause and fall upon the person of your adversary. **1890** *Times* 6 Dec. [Biog. notice] Mr. Huddleston . . . attacked the police as severely as if his instructions had been similar to the time-honoured 'No case, abuse the opposing attorney'. **1913** *Times Lit. Sup.* 5 Sep. 365 All kinds of irrelevancies of the proverbial 'abuse-the-plaintiff's-attorney' type, are calmly brushed aside by such Judges as the Lords of Appeal in Ordinary.

No cousin in London, no cousin at Stonham.

1830 FORBY 429 [A Londoner who had failed to reciprocate the hospitality of a cousin at the village of Stonham in Suffolk, again went there.] The Londoner . . . was instantly repulsed with the answer, 'No cousin in London, no cousin at Stonham.'

No cross, no crown.

1621 QUARLES *Ester; Med.* ix The way to Blisse lyes not on beds of Downe, And he that had no Crosse, deserues no Crowne. **1669** W. PENN (title) No Cross no Crown; a Discourse shewing . . . that the . . . daily bearing of Christ's Cross, is the alone way to the rest and kingdom of God. **1910** ALEX. MACLAREN *Expos., Hebrews* xiii 10, 15 Jesus Christ, and Jesus Christ's servants . . . obey the same law, and that law is, no cross, no crown.

No divinity is absent if Prudence is present.

[JUVENAL *Sat.* 10. 365 and 14. 315. *Nullum numen abest si sit prudentia.* Sandys, OVID *Met.* 11 (Comm.) Where wisdom, there the God; quoted by Chesterfield, Letter 28.] **1783** JOHNSON in *Boswell* lxxv (1848) 717 Though the proverb *Nullum numen abest, si sit prudentia*, does not always prove true, we may be certain of the converse of it, *Nullum numen adest, si sit imprudentia.* Note. Mrs. Piozzi gives a more classical . . . variation: *Nullum numen adest ni sit prudentia.*— CROKER. **1837** LOCKHART *Life Scott* xxxvii (1860) 333 Scott . . . seldom failed to introduce some passing hint of caution—such as *Nullum numen abest si sit prudentia.* **1880** BLACKMORE *Mary Aner.* xlix 'If prudence be present, no divinity is absent', according to high authority; but the author of the proverb must have first excluded love from the list of divinities.

No fire, no smoke (without smoke). (*Cf.* No smoke without some fire.)

1386 CHAUCER *Mel.* B² 2375 'It may nat be' seith he [Seneca] 'that, where greet fyr hath longe tyme endured, that ther ne dwellth som vapour of warmnesse. **1546** HEYWOOD II. v. 57 There is no fyre without some smoke. **1580** LYLY *Euph. & his Eng.* (Arb.) 328 No fire made of wood but hath smoake. **1641** WENTWORTH *Ld. Strafford Speech bef. Ho. of Lords,* 13 April Where hath this fire lain hid for so many hundred years, without smoke to discover it? **1659** HOWELL *Eng. Prov.* 15/1 No fire without smoak. **1869** TROLLOPE *He knew he was right* xv Mrs. MacHugh said that there was never fire without smoke.

No gates, no city.

1662 FULLER (*Worc.*) III. 386 The great and ancient gates of London town (No gates, no city) now are voted down, And down were cast.

'**No, I thank you**', *see* Would No, I t. *you* had never been made.

No Jews, no wooden shoes.

[*c.* 1754] **1861** H. MAYHEW *Lond. Labour* II. 117 'No Jews! No wooden shoes!!' Some mob-leader . . . had in this distich cleverly blended the prejudice against the Jews with the easily excited but vague fears of a French invasion.

No longer foster,[1] no longer lemman[2] (friend).

c. 1412 HOCCLEVE *De Regim. Princ.* (1860) 60 Ne lenger forster, ne lenger lemman. Love on luste groundede is not worth a leeke. **1546** HEYWOOD II. ix. 79 I saie to suche (said she) no longer foster, No longer lemman. **1639** CLARKE 33. [¹ nourish, support. ² lover, mistress.]

No longer pipe, no longer dance.

1620 SHELTON *Quix.* II. vii (1908) II. 233 It shall not be said, master, for me, 'No longer pipe no longer dance.' **1623** CAMDEN 274 No longer pipe, no longer daunce. **1641** Letter of EDMUND VERNEY, *Verney Memoirs* (1892) ii. 131. **1721** KELLY 257 . . . A reflection on those who have been advantaged by us heretofore, whose kindness continues no longer than they are getting by us. **1796** EDGEWORTH *Par. Asst., Lit. Merchts.* iii (1903) 410 'He always pleases well to whom fortune pipes.' 'Yes, no longer pipe, no longer dance', replied Francisco; and here they parted.

No man before his guide.

1639 CLARKE 6.

No man better knows what good is than he who hath endured evil.

1597 *Politeuphuia* 5 'of Heaven'. **1616** DRAXE 60. **1670** RAY 8.

No man can both sup and blow at once.

1597 N. BRETON *Wits Trenchmour* Wks. (Gros.) II. *b* 11 Contraries cannot at one time be in one subiect: which we see otherwise doe fall out in a man, that warmes his hands and cooles his pottage, and all with one breath. **1641** FERGUSSON 80. **1721** KELLY 359.

No man can do two things at once.

1509 A. BARCLAY *Ship of Fools* (1874) I. 160 No man can be atonys in euery place. **1547** WM. BALDWIN *Treatise of Moral Philosophy*

(1550) L 5 Attempte not two thynges at once for the one will hynder the other. **1611** COT-GRAVE s.v. 'Moulin' One cannot be in two places or follow two businesses at once.

No man can flay a stone.

1670 RAY 9.

No man can make his own hap.

1641 FERGUSSON 82. **1721** KELLY 267.

No man can play the fool so well as the wise man.

[HORACE *Odes* 4. 12. 27 *Misce stultitiam consiliis brevem; Dulce est desipere in loco.* And be for once unwise. While time allows, 'Tis sweet the fool to play.—Conington. *Don Quix.* II. iii He must not be a fool that would well counterfeit to be so.] **1599–1600** SHAKS. *Twelfth N.* III. i. 68 This fellow's wise enough to play the fool, And to do that well craves a kind of wit. **1601** JONSON *Poetaster* IV. iii *Alb.* I have read in a book, that to play the fool wisely, is high wisdom. **1611** DAVIES *Prov.* 56 None plaies the foole well without wit. **1641** FERGUSSON 82. **1721** KELLY 267.

No man can serve two masters.

c. **1330** WRIGHT *Pol. Songs* (Camden Soc.) 325 (A) That no man may wel serve tweie lordes to queme. **1389** WYCLIF *Matt.* vi. 24 No man may serue to two lordis. **1526** TINDALE *Ibid.* No man can serve two masters. **1642** D. ROGERS *Naaman* 166 You cannot have your will ... and Christ too ; no man can serve two masters. **1853** TRENCH vi. 143 Our Lord ... has said: 'No man can serve two masters' ... ; compare the Spanish proverb: *He who must serve two masters, must lie to one.* **1907** S. LEE *Gt. Eng. of 16th Cent.* 22 [Sir T. More] made ... a working reconciliation between the old religion and the new learning.... There was inconsistency in the endeavours to serve two masters.

No man cries stinking fish.

1656 L. PRICE *A Map of Merry Conceits* A 4 You never heard a fish wife Cry stinking fish. **1660** JER. TAYLOR *Duct. Dubit.* (1671) 805 Does ever any man cry stinking fish to be sold? **1732** FULLER no. 3596. **1806** WOLCOT (P. Pindar) *Tristia* Wks. (1816) IV. 309 But no one, to be sure, cries 'Stinking fish'. **1912** *Spectator* 29 June, 1033 It is always foolish to cry 'stinking fish' or to lower one's prestige in the international market by appearing to confess to a weakness which does not exist.

No man dies of an ague, or without it.

1629 T. ADAMS *Serm.* (1861–2) II. 455 But as physicians say, no man dies of an ague, or without it ; so seldom any soul dies of pride, or without pride.

No man ever became thoroughly bad all at once.

[JUVENAL *Sat.* 2. 83 *Nemo repente fuit turpissimus.*] **1590** SIDNEY *Arcadia* I. xii There is no man sodainely excellentlie good, or extremely evill. **1601** JONSON *Cynth. Rev.* VI. i No man is presently made bad with ill. **1629** T. ADAMS *Serm.* (1861–2) I. 7 The violence and virulence of this venomous quality comes not at first. *Nemo fit repente pessimus*—No man becomes worst at the first dash. **1832** LYTTON *Eug. Aram* v. iv Mankind are not instantaneously corrupted. **1850** Id. *Caxtons* III. vii (1854) 52 'Done his duty, and reformed the unhappy wretch, ... *Nemo repentè turpissimus semper fuit*—No man is wholly bad all at once'. **1892** H. P. LIDDON *Serm. Wds. of Christ* 126 The old saying that no man becomes very bad all of a sudden—*nemo repente fuit turpissimus*—applies to the life of faith as well as of conduct.

No man fouls his hands in his own business.

1632 HERBERT *Priest to Temple* xxxii. Wks. (1859) I. 241 The *Italian* says, *None fouls his hands in his own business* ; and it is an honest, and just care, so it exceed not bounds, for every one to employ himself to the advancement of his affairs.

No man hath a lease of his life.

1377 LANGLAND *P. Pl.* B. x. 89 (Skeat) I. 292 For we haue no lettre of owre lyf . how longe it shal dure. **1590–1** SHAKS. *2 Hen. VI* IV. x. 6 If I might have a lease of my life for a thousand years I could stay no longer. **1721** KELLY 266. **1862** HISLOP 232 Nae man has a tack[1] o' his life. [[1] lease.]

No man hath a worse friend than he brings from home.

1623 CAMDEN 280 Where shall a man haue a worse friend, than hee brings from home. **1678** RAY 351. **1738** SWIFT (Dial. i) 333 Well, I see there's no worse friend than one brings from home with one ; and I am not the first man has carried a rod to whip himself. **1853** TRENCH vi 146 This one ... telling of the enemy whom every one of us has the most to fear: *No man has a worse friend than he brings with him from home* ; ... in striking agreement with Augustine's remarkable prayer, 'Deliver me from the evil man, from myself'.[1] [[1] *Libera me ab homine malo, a meipso.*]

No man is a hero to his valet.

[Fr. ... *qu'il n'y avait point de héros pour les valets de chambres.* MADAME CORNUEL, 1605–94.] **1685** COTTON *Montaigne* III. ii Few men have been admired by their domestics. **1764** FOOTE *Patron* II (1774) 30 *Jul.* It has been said ... that no man is a hero to his valet de chambre ; now I am afraid when you and I grow a little more intimate, ... you will be horribly disappointed in your high expectations. **1818** BYRON *Beppo* xxxiii And to his very valet seemed a hero. **1824** SIR J. PRIOR *Life of Burke* xvi (Bohn) 490 No man, it has been said, is a hero to his valet-de-chambre ; and ... few men perhaps however great in the estimation of the world, carry the same impression of greatness into the bosoms of their own families. **1841** CARLYLE *Heroes* V (1896) 258 We ... deny altogether ... that no man is a Hero to his *valet-de-chambre*. Or if so, it is not the Hero's blame, but the Valet's. **1910** *Times Wkly.* 21 Jan. Many men have been heroes to their valets, and most (except Pope and Poe) to their biographers.

No man is a match for a woman till he's married.

1854 SURTEES *Handley Cross* lvii That no man is a match for a woman till he's married, is an axiom that most Benedicts will subscribe to.

No man is bound to criminate himself.

[A Law maxim. L. *Nemo tenetur seipsum accusare.*] **1724** DEFOE *Behav. Servts.* 94 *Ed.* I hope your Worship will not be angry, . . .; *am I obliged to accuse myself? Just.* Why no, you are not. [**1868**] MONTAGUE WILLIAMS *Leaves of Life* xviii (1893) 125 Mr. Baron Bramwell said . . . that the witnesses might have refused to give evidence on the ground that, by so doing, they might incriminate themselves.

No man is content.

[L. *Nemo suâ sorte contentus.* No man is content with his lot.] **1639** CLARKE 73.

No man is his craft's master the first day.

1540 PALSGRAVE *Acolastus* (Carver) 70 No man is borne a craftsman. **1580** LYLY *Euph. & his Eng.* Wks. (Bond) II. 68 *Appelles* was no good Paynter the first day. **1580** J. BARET *Alveary* V 95 One daie is not sufficient to attaine to learning. **1639** CLARKE 35. **1640** HERBERT 347 None is born master. **1678** RAY 120 . . . *Nessuno nasce maestro.* Ital.

No man is wise at all times.

[PLINY *H. N.* 7. 40. 2 *Nemo mortalium omnibus horis sapit.* No one of mortals is wise at all times.] **1639** CLARKE 266. **1766** GOLDSMITH *Vic. W.* x (Globe) 19 I was tired of being always wise, and could not help gratifying their request, because I loved to see them happy.

No man knows when he shall die, although he knows he must die.

c. **1386** CHAUCER *Clerk's T.* E[1] 124 And al so certein as we knowe echoon That we shul deye, as uncerteyn we alle Been of that day whan deeth shal on us falle. *c.* **1450** *Provs. of Wisdom* (ed. Schleich) in Anglia **51.** 224 We schal dye, we note, how sone. **1590** GREENE *Never too Late* Wks. (Gros.) VIII. 125 Wee haue nothing more certaine than to dye, nor nothing more vncertaine than the houre of death. **1599–1600** SHAKS. *Jul. Caes.* III. i. 99 That we shall die, we know ; 'tis but the time And drawing days out, that men stand upon.

No man lives so poor as he was born.

[PUBL. SYR. *Nemo ita pauper vivit, quam pauper natus est.*] **1732** FULLER no. 3604.

No man makes haste to the market where there's nothing to be bought but blows.

1670 RAY 119.

No man may poind[1] for unkindness. (*See also* Poind for debt, &c.)

1641 FERGUSSON 82. [[1] distrain.]

No man so good, but another may be as good as he.

1662 FULLER (*Ches.*) I. 265 Some will oppose to this narrow county-proverb, an English one of greater latitude, viz. No man so good, but another may be as good as he'.

No man, There is | though never so little, but sometimes he can hurt.

1651 HERBERT 369.

No man was ever made more healthful by a dangerous sickness, or came home better from a long voyage.

1617 MORYSON *Itin.* III. i. 5 (1908) III. 357 The wiser sort, . . . see many returne from forraine parts corrupted with vices proper to them, according to the Flemings Proverb : that no man was ever made more healthfull by a dangerous sicknesse, or came home better from a long voyage.

No man will another in the oven (kirn) seek, except that himself have been there before.

1520 W. DE WORDE *Seven Wise Masters* 40 (A) Yr fader soughte neuer his sone in ye ouen but yf he had bin therin hymselfe. **1546** HEYWOOD II. vii. 69 And as for yll places, thou sekest me in mo, And in woorse to, than I into any go. Wherby this prouerbe shewth the in by the wéeke. . . . **1596** NASHE *Saffron W.* 151 Of the Good-wife . . . finding her daughter in the ouen, where she would neuer haue sought her, if she had not been there first her selfe. **1640** HERBERT 349 If the mother had not been in the oven, she had never sought her daughter there. **1641** FERGUSSON 82 Na man can seek his marrow in the kirne, sa weill as he that hes been in it himself.

No man's enemy but his own, He is.

1592 GREENE *A Quip for an upstart courtier* Wks. (Gros.) xi. 290 I think him an honest man if he would but liue within his compasse, and generally no mans foe but his own. **1629** T. ADAMS *Serm.* (1861–2) III. 80 The prodigal is no man's foe but his own, saith the proverb. **1639** CLARKE 21. **1749** FIELDING *Tom Jones* (1805) I. IV. v Sophia . . . discerned that Tom . . . was nobody's enemy but his own. **1881** A. JESSOPP *Arcady* 183 Ben's life . . . has been singularly inoffensive. As the saying is, 'He has been no man's enemy but his own'.

No Man's Land.

[**1348–9**] **1662** FULLER (*Warwick*) III. 277 There happened so grievous a pestilence in London, that . . . the dead might seem to justle one another. . . . Whereupon this bishop[1] bought . . . ground near Smithfield. It was called *No-man's-land,* . . . as designed and consecrated for the general sepulture of the deceased. **1719** DEFOE *Crusoe* II (Globe) 563 This was a kind of Border, that might be called *no Man's Land*, being a Part of . . . *Grand Tartary.* **1896** R. S. S. BADEN-POWELL *Downfall of Prempeh* 68 The Adansis . . . have been removed . . . and the district remains a No Man's Land, and practically a bush desert. **1928** *Times*, 10 Dec. 15/6 There are to-day . . . zones of what may be called, economically, No Man's Land. . . . They are too far from the market. **1929** 16 April 22/4 The narrator begins by losing him while on patrol, and then undergoes . . . dreadful experiences in 'No Man's Land'. . . . Before he can escape from his shell-hole, the French launch a minor attack. [[1] Ralph de Stratford, d. 1354.]

No matter how but whether.

1639 CLARKE 216.

No mill, no meal.

[Gk. *Ὁ φεύγων μύλον ἄλφιτα φεύγει.* He who shuns the millstone shuns the meal. L. *Qui fugit molam farinam non invenit.* He who flies from the mill gets no meal.] **1639** CLARKE 163 No milne, no meale. **1732** FULLER no. 3613.

No mischief but a woman or a priest is at the bottom of it.

[JUVENAL *Sat.* 6. 242 *Nulla fere causa est in qua non femina litem moverit.* There is scarcely any dispute but a woman has been at the bottom of it.] **1549** LATIMER *2nd Serm. bef. Edw. VI* (Arb.) 57 He called . . . one Abiather the hyghe prieste. For it is maruayle if any mischyefe be in hand, if a priest be not at some ende of it. **1629** T. ADAMS *Medit. upon Creed* 1169 When he would peruert a whole family to superstition, hee teaches his Iesuite to begin with the woman. **1659** HOWELL *Eng. Prov.* 15/1 There is no mischief in the world done, But that a woman is alwayes one. **1670** RAY 50 There's no mischief in the world done, But a woman is always one. **1754** RICHARDSON *Grandison* Lett. 24 Such a plot must have a woman in it. **1830** SCOTT *Note K* in *Ht. Midl.* The journal . . . proceeds thus: '. . . No doubt the daughter and parson would endeavour to persuade him to decline troubling himself in the matter . . . *No mischief but a woman or a priest in it*—here both.'

No money, no Swiss.

1652 E. PEYTON *Secret Hist. of James I* (1811) ii. 428 As the proverb is, no money no Swiss: no money no obedience. **1670** RAY 143 No silver no servant. The *Suisses* have a Proverb among themselves, parallel to this. Point d'argent point de Suisse. No money no *Suisse*. The *Suisses* for money will serve neighbouring princes in their wars. **1738** GAY *Fables* II. ix. 61 For these, like Swiss attend; No longer pay, no longer friend. **1840** MARRYAT *Olla Pod.* XXXV What a pity . . . that a nation so brave . . . should be . . . so *innately* mercenary. There never was a truer saying than Point d'argent, point de Suisse'.

No moon, no man.

1878 T. HARDY, *Return of the Native*, bk. 1,

ch. 3, 'No moon, no man'. 'Tis one of the truest sayings ever spit out. The boy never comes to anything that's born at new moon. **1878** DYER *Eng. Folk-Lore* 41 (A) In Cornwall, when a child is born in the interval between an old moon and the first appearance of a new one, it is said that it will never live to reach the age of puberty. Hence the saying No moon, no man'.

No more of a cat but (than) her skin, You can have.

1564 BULLEIN *Dial. agst. Fever* (1888) 9 In my fantasie it is happy to the Huntman when he haue nethyng of the Catte but the sillie skinne. **1721** CLARKE 163 You can have no more of a cat but her skin. **1721** KELLY 371 *You'll get no more of the cat, but the skin.* You can have no more of a person, or thing, than they can afford. **1738** SWIFT (Dial. ii) 349 *Col.* He . . . snored so hard that we thought he was driving his hogs to market. *Spark.* Why, what! you can have no more of a cat than her skin.

No more of a fox than the skin, You can have.

c. **1514** A. BARCLAY *Eclogues* ii. 1074. **1546** HEYWOOD II. ix. 79 Ye haue had of me all that I might make. And be a man neuer so greedy to wyn, He can haue no more of the foxe but the skyn.

No news is good news.

1616 JAMES I in *Losely MSS.* (Kempe) 403 (A) No newis is better then evill newis. *c.* **1645** HOWELL *Lett.* II. xviii I am of the Italians mind that said, *Nulla nuova, buona nuova*, no news, good news. **1850** SMEDLEY *Frank Fairlegh* X Arguing . . . (on the 'no news being good news' system) that I should have heard again if anything had gone wrong, I dismissed the subject from my mind. **1864** J. PAYN *Lost Sir Massingb.* XX Well, no news is good news, you know.

No one is bound to do impossibilities.

1655 FULLER *Hist. Univ. Camb.* (1840) 236 Though divines, they were presumed to have so much of civil law, yea, of the law of nature, as to know, *Nemo tenetur ad impossibilia,* 'No man is tied to impossibilities'.

No other meat, They that have | bread and butter are glad to eat.

1670 RAY 66.

No pains, no gains.

1577 J. GRANGE *Golden Aphroditis* M[1] (A) Who will the fruyte that haruest yeeldes must take the payne. **1605–6** SHAKS. *Macbeth* IV. i. 39 O! well done! I commend your pains, And every one shall share i' the gains. **1648** HERRICK *Hesper.* Wks. (O.U.P.) 248 *No Paines, No Gaines.* If little labour, little are our gaines: Mans fortunes . . . are according to his paines. **1721** KELLY 259 No profit but[1] pains. **1853** TRENCH V. 114 For the most part they courageously accept the law of labour, *No pains, no gains,* . . . as the appointed law and condition of man's life. **1864** R. BROWNING

Death in Desert 207 When pain ends, gain ends too. [¹ without.]

No paternoster, no penny.

[= no work, no pay.] **1707** HICKERINGILL *Priest-cr.* II. ii. 22 Once was—No Pater Noster, No Penny; now—No Sermons, not a Penny, not a farthing.

No penny, no pardon.

1531 TINDALE *Expos. 1 John* in Wks. (1573) 395/1 O Popishe forgiuenesse with whom it goeth after the comon prouerbe, no peny no pardon. **1641** FERGUSSON 82.

No penny, no paternoster.

[= priests insist on being paid as a condition of performing service.] **1528** TINDALE *Obed. of Christ. Man.* (P.S.) 245 (A) After the common saying, No peny, no paternoster'. **1546** *Suppl. Commons* (1871) 87 Theyr couetouse is growne into this prouerbe, 'No peny, no pater noster'. **1621** BURTON *Anat. Mel.* 'No penny . . .', as the saying is. **1640** BASTWICK *Lord Bps.* vi. E iv b No penny, no Pater noster; they looke more to their tithes, then to their taske. **1648** HERRICK *Hesper., The Peter-penny* Wks. (O.U.P.) 251 Who at a dead lift, Can't send for a gift A Pig to the Priest for a Roster, Shall heare his Clarke say, . . . *No pennie, no Pater Noster.*

No penny, no *placebo.*

c. **1548** BALE *K. Johan* 1930 Sed. No grote no pater noster, no penye no *placebo.*¹ [¹ Vespers in the Office for the Dead, from first word in first antiphon, *Placebo,* I shall be pleasing or acceptable; *Ps.* cxiv. 9 Vulg.]

No play where one greets¹ and another laughs, It is.

1641 FERGUSSON 62. **1721** KELLY 198 . . . Spoken when a patrimony is unequally divided. [¹ weeps.]

No play without a fool, There is.

1615 W. GODDARD *Nest of Wasps* B 4ᵛ Without Divells, plaies are nothing worth. **1626** JONSON *The Staple of News* 1st Intermean 35 My husband . . . was wont to say, there was no play without a *Foole,* or a *Diuell* in it. **1639** CLARKE 149.

No priest, no mass.

[a. **1585**] **1662** FULLER (*Shropshire*) III. 54 Plowden¹ being of the Romish persuasion, some setters² trepanned him . . . to hear mass. But afterwards Plowden understanding that the pretender to officiate was no priest, . . . 'Oh the case is altered', quoth Plowden: 'no priest, no mass'. **1732** FULLER no. 3618. [¹ 1518–85. ² decoys.]

No profit to honour, no honour to religion.

1640 HERBERT 352.

No purchase, no pay.

[a. **1700**] **1867** ADML. W. H. SMYTH *Sailor's Word-Bk.* 521 A buccaneering principle of hire, under the notion of plunder and sharing in prizes, was, *no purchase no pay.*

No receiver, no thief.

c. **1386** CHAUCER *Cook's T.* A 4415 Ther is no theef with-oute a louke¹ That helpeth him to wasten and to souke. **1546** HEYWOOD I. xii. 40 For this prouerbe préeues, Where be no receiuers, there be no théeues. **1629** T. ADAMS *Serm.* (1861–2) I. 187 The calumniator is a wretched thief, and robs man of the best thing he hath. . . . But if there were no receiver there would be no thief. **1639** CLARKE 233 The receiver makes the thief. **1641** FERGUSSON 94 There is na thief without a resetter. **1670** RAY 136. **1926** *Times* 22 Nov. 11/3 It had often been said in those Courts that if there were no receivers there would be no thieves. [¹ accomplice.]

No reply (plie¹) is best.

1641 FERGUSSON 82 Na plie is best. **1721** KELLY 267 *No reply is best.* Spoken by sedate and even temper'd men, when abused by others. [¹ lawsuit.]

No root, no fruit.

c. **1374** CHAUCER *Troylus* IV. 770 For which ful ofte a by-word here I seye, That 'rooteles moot grenè soonè deye'. **1640** J. DYKE *Worthy Commun.* 176 No roote no fruite.

No silver, no servant.

1616 DRAXE 179. **1639** CLARKE 243. **1670** RAY 143.

No silver (gold) without his dross.

1611 COTGRAVE s.v. 'Or' No Gold without some drosse. **1616** DRAXE 63 (with 'siluer'). **1639** CLARKE 80 (with 'silver').

No smoke without some fire. (*Cf.* No fire, no smoke.)

c. **1375** BARBOUR *Bruce* (E.E.T.S.) IV, l. 123 And thair may no man fire sa covir, [Bot] low or reyk sall it discovir. c. **1440** LYDGATE *Wks.* (E.E.T.S.) I. 134 Wher no fyr maad is may no smoke aryse. **1579** LYLY *Euphues* (Arb.) 153 Ther can no great smoke arise, but there must be some fire, no great reporte without great suspition. **1655** FULLER *Ch. Hist.* II. v (1868) I. 232 Dunstan, by looking on his own furnace, might learn thence, there was no smoke but some fire: either he was dishonest or indiscreet, which gave the ground-work to their general suspicion. **1869** TROLLOPE *He knew he was right* lii He considered that . . . Emily . . . had behaved badly. He . . . repeated . . . the old adage, that there was no smoke without fire.

No song, no supper.

1611 BEAUM. & FL. *Kt. Burn. P.* II.1 Mist. M. No, Michael, . . . let him stay at home and sing for his supper. **1894** STEVENSON & OSBORNE *Ebb-Tide* vii If you're not there by the time named, there will be no banquet; no song, no supper, Mr. Whish!

No sooner said than done.

[TER. *And.* 2.3.7 *Dictum factum,* Said [and] done.] **1824** MOIR *Mansie W.* xvii The lassie

... cried out, 'Hide me ... for yonder comes my old father!' No sooner said than done. **1888** 'ROLF BOLDREWOOD' *Robbery under Arms* xl No sooner said than done. We went to work and got everything ready.

No sooner up, but hand (head) in the ambry,[1] and nose in the cup.

1580 TUSSER lxxv. ii Some slouens from sleeping no sooner get vp, But hand is in aumbrie, and nose in the cup. **1639** CLARKE 136. **1721** KELLY 263 *No sooner up, but her head in the ambry.* Spoken of, or to maidens, who have too early a stomach. [[1] store-closet, or cupboard in a pantry.]

No sport, no pie.

a. **1625** J. FLETCHER *Wom. Prize* I. iv *Petr.* I'll devil 'em: by these ten bones I will: I'll bring it to the old proverb, no sport no pie. **1678** RAY 205.

No tempest, good July, lest corn look ruely.

1580 TUSSER 55 xliv (E.D.S.) 122 Julies husbandrie. No tempest, good Julie, Least corne lookes rulie. **1732** FULLER no. 6208 No Tempest, good July; Lest corn come off bluely.

'No, thank you', has lost many a good butter-cake.

1873 HARLAND & WILKINSON *Lancashire Leg.* 201.

No, No man, No more, *see also under significant words following.*

Noah's Ark.

[A cloud-formation having some resemblance to the outline of a ship's hull.] **1787** BEST *Angling* (ed. 2) 145 Small black fragments of clouds like smoke, flying underneath, which some call messengers, and others Noah's Ark. **1821** CLARE *Vill. Minstr.* II. 27 As oft from 'Noah's Ark' great floods descend. **1866** BLACKMORE *Cradock Now.* xxxi Daubed with lumps of vapour which mariners call 'Noah's arks'.

Noah's dove.

1560 BIBLE Geneva (1586) *Genesis* viii. 6–9 Noah ... sent a doue from him. ... But the doue found no rest for the sole of her foote: therefore she returned vnto him into the Arke (for the waters were vpon the whole earth). **1599** SIR J. DAVIES *Nosce Teipsum* xxx. st. 26 When the soule findes heere no true content, And like *Noah's Doue*, can no sure footing take, She returne from whence shee first was sent. **1853** J. MONT-GOMERY *For ever with the Lord* st. 5 Like Noah's dove, I flit between Rough seas and stormy skies.

Nobility, without ability, is like a pudding wanting suet.

1721 KELLY 259 ... Both want the principal ingredient.

Nobility, *see also* Virtue is the only true n.

Noble housekeepers need no doors.

1640 HERBERT 321.

Noble plant suits not with a stub-born ground, A.

1640 HERBERT 346. **1670** RAY 21 Noble plants suit not a stubborn soil.

Noble, The more | the more humble.

1616 DRAXE 142. **1670** RAY 19.

Noble, Jack, *see* Farewell, forty pence! J. N. is dead.

Noble (*adj.*), *see also* Serve a n. disposition ... he will repay.

Noble(s), (*noun*), *see* Bring a n. to ninepence; Right, master, four n. a year's a crown a quarter; Yellow as the golden n.

Nobody's nails can reach the length of London.

1818 SCOTT *Ht. Midl.* iv (1852) 51 When we had a king, and a chancellor, and parliament-men o' our ain, we could aye peeble them wi' stanes when they werena gude bairns— But naebody's nails can reach the length o' Lunnon. **1896** A. CHEVIOT *Prov. Scotl.* 258 Naebody's nails can reach the length of Lunnon. ... This saying arose after the Union of the English and Scottish Parliaments in 1707.

Nod for a wise man, A | and a rod for a fool.

1678 RAY *Adag. Hebr.* 413. **1732** FULLER no. 337.

Nod from a lord, A | is a breakfast for a fool.

1732 FULLER no. 338. *a.* **1816** WOLCOT (P. Pindar) *Odes of Condol.* Wks. (1816) II. 338 As nods of lords are dinners for a *fool.*

Nod is as good as a wink to a blind horse, A.

1802 D. WORDSWORTH *Journal* (Knight) i. 129 (A) A wink's as good as a nod with some folks. **1809** MALKIN *Gil Blas* II. ix (Dent) I. 128 I shall say no more at present, a nod is as good as a wink. **1818** SCOTT *Ht. Midl.* xvi 'Ye understand my meaning?' 'Ay, ... sir; a wink's as gude as a nod to a blind horse.' **1837–47** BARHAM *Ingol. Leg.* (1898) 488 'To a blind horse a Nod is as good as a Wink!' Which some learned Chap, ... Perhaps would translate by the words '*Verbum Sap!*'

Noise is greater than the nuts, The.

1651 HERBERT 366.

Noise is so great, The | one cannot hear God thunder.

1853 TRENCH vi. 135 The divine voices ... being drowned for too many by the deafening tumult and hubbub of the world: *The noise is so great, one cannot hear God thunder.* (Le bruit est si fort, qu'on n'entend pas Dieu tonner.)

Noise, *see also* Hunt squirrels and make no n.;
Loves n. must buy pig.

Nolens volens.

[L. — willing or unwilling.] **1593** PEELE
Edw. I Wks. (Rtldg.) 394/2 A little serves the
friar's lust When *nolens volens* fast he must.
1665 SIR T. HERBERT *Trav.* (1677) 124 He
would profer them a little money for what he
liked, which if they refused, then *nolens
volens* he would have it. **1815** SCOTT *Guy
Man.* l Well, *nolens volens* You must hold
your tongue. **1837** HOOD *Ode to Rae Wilson*
455 Tugg'd him neck and crop Just *nolens
volens* thro' the open shop.

Noli me tangere.

[L. *Noli me tangere*, 'touch me not', occurring
in the Vulgate, *John* xx. 17.] *c.* **1475** *Mankind* in '*Lost Tudor Plays*' (1907) 23 He is a
noli-me-tangere. **1634** w. WOOD *New Eng.
Prosp.* (1865) 24 The Porcupine . . . stands
upon his guard, and proclaims *Noli me
tangere*, to man and beast. *a.* **1635** NAUNTON
Fragm. Reg. (Arb.) 18 He was wont to say of
them, that they were of the Tribe of Dan, and
were *noli me tangeres*; implying, that they
were not to be contested with. **1806** J. BERES-
FORD *Miseries Hum. Life* x. xxi (ed. 5) I. 219
Every dish, as it is brought in, carrying a
'noli me tangere' on the face of it. [*Cf.* Fr.
Sainte nitouche.]

Nolo episcopari.

[L. *Nolo episcopari*, I do not wish to be made
a bishop'; now applied commonly to those
who profess a reluctance for promotion
which they do not feel.] **1678** DRYDEN
Limberham III. i Plays (1701) II. 127 *Lim.*
But you wou'd be intreated, and say, *Nolo,
nolo, nolo*, three times, like any Bishop, when
your Mouth waters at the Diocese. *a.* **1816**
WOLCOT (P. Pindar) *2nd Ep. to Mrs. C.* Wks.
(1816) IV. 450 For, unlike Bishops, 'tis my
firm intention To cry out, 'Yes, my Liege',
for Place or Pension. **1827** SCOTT *Journ.*
16 July, There may be something like affectation and *nolo episcopari* in seeming to under-
rate my own Labours. **1884** TENNYSON
Becket Prol. Wks. (1893) 696 *Becket*. Take
thou mine answer in bare commonplace—
Nolo episcopari. **1941** R. R. MARETT *A
Jerseyman at Oxford* xv I should have
deemed it cowardly to plead a *nolo episcopari*.

Nomen, omen.

[L. *nomen*, a name.] **1662** FULLER (*Devon*) I.
407 John Jewel[1] . . . was born . . . 24th of
May 1552 . . . It may be said of his surname,
nomen, omen; Jewel his name and precious
his virtues. [[1] Bp. of Salisbury.]

Non est inventus.

[L. *Non est inventus* — 'He was not found'.
The answer made by the sheriff in the return
of the writ when the defendant is not to be
found in his bailiwick. In 16th–17th cent.
often used allusively.] *c.* **1475** *Mankind* 774
in *Macro Plays* 29 ȝe must speke to þe
schryne for a 'cepe coppus', Ellys ȝe must be
fayn to retorn with 'non est inventus'. **1583**
STUBBES *Anat. Abus.* Kj Sheriffes & officers
wil returne writs with a *tarde venit* or with a

non est inuentus. **1590** GREENE *Never too
Late* (1600) H 3 So long put he his hand into
his purse, that at last the empty bottome
returned him a writ of *Non est inuentus*. **1827**
DE QUINCEY *Murder* Wks. (1854) IV. 50 He
inquired after the unfortunate reporter . . .;
the answer was . . . from the under-sheriff
of our county—'Non est inventus'. **1850**
THACKERAY *Pendennis* lx Mrs. Montague
Rivers hoff to Boulogne—non est inwentus,
Mr. Morgan.

Non placet.

[L. *Non placet*, 'it does not please'; the formula used in the older universities and in
ecclesiastical assemblies, in giving a negative
vote upon a proposition.] **1589** GREENE
Menaphon (Arb.) 42 When I craued a finall
resolution to my fatal passions, shee . . .
shooke me off with a *Non placet*. *a.* **1635**
SIBBES *Christian's End* (1639) v. 110 When
flesh and bloud shall put up a petition, . . .
give it a *Non placet*, deny the petition. **1890**
Echoes from the Oxford Magazine ed. 2
'L'Envoy' We have assisted the Hebdo-
madal Council in the establishment of the
Non-Placet Society.

Non-apparent must be treated as non-existent, Things which are.

[*De non apparentibus, et non existentibus,
eadem est ratio.* Law Maxim.] **1845** H. BROOM
Legal Max. (1870) 164 *Quod non apparet non
est*—that which does not appear must be
taken in law as if it were not. **1906** MAITLAND
Life Les. Stephen xx. 438 People who rigorously refuse 'to trot out their feelings' . . .
must not be surprised if a good old legal
maxim about the non-apparent and non-
existent is applied to their case. **1909** ALEX.
MACLAREN *Philippians* i. 27, 28 We are . . .
foolish slaves of mere sense, shaping our lives
on the legal maxim that things which are non-
apparent must be treated as non-existent.

Nonconformist conscience.

1890 *Let.* in *Times* 28 Nov. 8/6 The minimum
demand of the great Nonconformist party is
the . . . abdication of Mr. Parnell. . . . Nothing
less will satisfy the Nonconformist conscience
now. **1896** MAX BEERBOHM *King George the
Fourth* The Nonconformist Conscience makes
cowards of us all. **1929** *Times* 23 April 12/2
There is in the bones of the British people a
reverence for God and the things of God.
You may call it 'the Non-Conformist Conscience' or whatever you like, but it is there.

None (but, is, is so, so), *see under significant
words following.*

Non-existent, *see* Non-apparent.

Nonsuch, He is a.

1670 BROOKS *Wks.* (1867) VI. 30 Job was a
non-such in his day for holiness. **1753**
RICHARDSON *Sir C. Grandison* I. xxii (1781)
152 Then you are, as indeed I have always
thought you, a nonsuch of a woman. **1895**
'SARAH TYTLER' *Macdonald Lass* 172 As for
your Prince, . . . he's not a nonsuch.

Nopence, *see* Nippence, n.

Norfolk dumplings.

c. **1600** DAY *Begg. Bednall Gr.* I. ii (1881) 35
Y. *Str.* I was as naked as your *Norfolk*
Dumplin. **1608** ARMIN *Nest Nin.* (Shaks. Soc.)
17 Nothing was undone that might be done
to make Jemy Camber a tall, little, slender
man, when yet he lookt like a Norfolke
dumpling, thicke and short. **1662** FULLER
(*Norfolk*) II. 446 'Norfolk dumplings'. This
cannot be verified of any dwarfish . . . stature
of people in this county. . . . But it relates to
the fare they commonly feed on.

Norfolk, *see also* Essex stiles . . . N. wiles.

Norman, *see* Row the boat, N.

North, Out of the | all ill comes forth.

1597 DRAYTON *England's Heroical Epistles*
Wks. (Hebel) II. 188 They say, all Mischiefe
commeth from the North. **1598** SIR R.
BARCKLEY *Felicitie of Man* (1631) IV. iii. 339
There hath beene an old saying, that all evils
rise out of the North. **1656** FORD & DECKER
Sun's Darling v. 35 *Wint.* What such mur-
murings does your gall bring forth, Will you
prove't true, no good coms from the North.
1670 RAY 19 Three ills come from the North,
a cold wind, a shrinking cloth, and a dissembling man.

North country, *see* Knight of Cales.

North for greatness, The | the east for health; the south for neatness, the west for wealth.

1662 FULLER (*Dorset*) I. 453 The houses of the
gentry herein are built rather to be lived in,
than to be looked on. . . . Indeed the rhyme
holds generally true of the English structures,
'The north for greatness, the east for health;
The south for neatness, the west for wealth'.

North of England for an ox, The | the south for a sheep, and the middle part for a man.

1662 FULLER (*Wilts.*) III. 314 I have heard
a wise man say, that an ox . . . would, of all
England, choose to live in the north, a sheep
in the south . . . , and a man in the middle
betwixt both.

North wind doth blow, The | and we shall have snow.

1846 DENHAM. **1883** ROPER 9. **1893** INWARDS
78.

North, *see also* Cold weather and knaves
come out of n.; Three ills come from n.;
Wind's in n. (When), fisher goes not forth.

North-east, *see* Wind is n.-e. (If the).

North-west wind, An honest man and a | generally go to sleep to-gether.

1883 ROPER 11. **1893** INWARDS 79.

North-west, *see also* Wind is in n.-w. (Do
business when).

Northampton stands on other men's legs.

1662 FULLER (*Northamp.*) II. 498 The town
of Northampton may be said to stand chiefly
on other men's legs; where . . . the most and
cheapest boots and stockings are bought in
England. **1897** BP. CREIGHTON *Some Eng.
Shires* 343 It was this central position that
gave Northampton its trade of shoemaking,
. . . and hides could easily be obtained from
the rich grazing meadows . . . on every side.
It was an old saying that 'Northampton
stood on other men's legs'.

Northampton, *see also* Eat a buttered fagot;
Mayor of N.

Northamptonshire for squires and spires.

1869 HAZLITT 297. **1878** *Murray's Guidebk.
to Northamp.* xix Northamptonshire has
been called a land of 'Squires and Spires';
and it is undoubtedly preeminent in noble
examples of the latter.

Northerly wind and blubber, brings home the Greenland lubber.

1846 DENHAM 20 . . . A satirical proverb
made use of by sailors.

Northern wind (air) brings weather fair, A.

1846 DENHAM. **1883** ROPER 9. **1893** INWARDS
77.

Nose of wax, A.

[= a thing or person easily moulded.] **1532**
TINDALE *Expos. Matt.* vi. 23 If the Scripture
be contrary, then make it a nose of wax and
wrest it this way and that till it agree. **1621**
SYLVESTER 1055 Words wax-nosed. **1686**
HORNECK *Crucif. Jesus* ix. 167 Oral Tradition, that nose of wax, which you may turn
and set, which way you list. **1815** SCOTT *Guy
Man.* v I let . . . the constable . . . manage the
business his ain gate, as if I had been a nose
o' wax. **1821** GALT *Annals Parish* xii Her
ladyship . . . said that I was a nose-of-wax.

Nose out of joint, To put (*or* thrust) one's.

[= to displace or supplant one; to dis-
concert.] **1581** RICH *Farew. Milit. Profess.*
K iv It could bee no other then his owne
manne, that had thrust his nose so farre out
of ioynte. **1598** R. BERNARD tr. *Terence,
Eunuch* I. ii Fearing now lest this wench . . .
should put your nose out of joynt. **1662**
PEPYS *Diary* 31 May The King is pleased
enough with her: which, I fear, will put
Madam Castlemaine's nose out of joynt. **1860**
THACKERAY *Lovel* vi My dear, I guess your
ladyship's nose is out of joint.

Nose swell, To make one's.

[= to make one jealous or envious.] **1678**
RAY 77 Doth your nose swell (or eek, *i.e.*
itch) at that? **1743** in HOWELL *St. Trials*
(1813) XVII. 1187 He heard lord Altham

say, . . . my wife has got a son, which will make my brother's nose swell.

Nose to make a poor man's sow, He hath a good.

1639 CLARKE 239. **1678** RAY 262 . . . Il seroit bon truy à pauvre homme. *Gall.* **1738** SWIFT (Dial. iii) 352 Tom, you have a good nose to make a poor man's sow.

Nose to the grindstone, To hold (keep, bring, put) one's.

1532 FRITH *Mirr. to know Thyself* (1829) 273 This Text holdeth their noses so hard to the grindstone, that it clean disfigureth their faces. **1546** HEYWOOD I. v. 10 I shall to reueng former hurtis, Hold their noses to grinstone. **1621** BURTON *Anat. Mel.* III. i. III (1651) 429 We . . . contemn, insult, vex, torture, molest, and hold one anothers noses to the grindstone hard. **1801** EDGEWORTH *Pop. Tales, Contrast* i I would not let my nose be kept to the grindstone, as yours is, for any one living. **1823** GALT *Entail* III. xx Leave no stone unturned till you hae brought Mr. Milrookit's nose to the grindstone. **1901** S. LANE-POOLE *Sir H. Parkes in C.* i. 14 Morrison . . . kept his nose to the grindstone, and taught him the value of hard work.

Nose warp, You make his.

1678 RAY 262.

Nose will abide no jests, His.

1588 *Mar-Prelate Epit.* (1843) 9 (A) I am sure their noses can abide no iest. **1593** PEELE *Edward 1st* (1883) 382 *Rice ap. Mer.* We are . . . disposed to be pleasant with thee a little; but I perceive, friar, thy nose will bide no jest. **1659** HOWELL *Eng. Prov.* 6/1 His nose will abide no jests.

Nose will not make a shoeing horn, Every man's.

1576 GASCOIGNE *Grief of Joy* i (1910) 518 Full well wot you, that Corinth shoeing horns May not be made, like every noddy's nose. **1670** RAY 125. **1721** KELLY 91 . . . Spoken to them who have found the man with whom they were dealing, more sagacious and cunning than they expected.

Nose, *see also* Better a snotty child than n. wiped off; Bite one's n. off; Bore him through n. with cushion; Bridge of one's n. (Make a); Cut off one's n. to spite; Dog's n. always cold; Fall on his back and break n.; Follow one's n.; Fox hath got in his n. (When), body follow; Great n. (He that has) thinks everybody speaking of it; Hang a n.; Jack would wipe his n. if had it; Know by your n. what pottage you love; Lead one by the n.; Little mense o' the cheeks to bite off n.; Lose the droppings of his n. (He will not); Pepper in the n. (Take); Plain as the n. on man's face; See his n. cheese first; Sees an inch before n.; Tell where to turn his n. (Cannot); Wipe one's n. with sleeve; Wiped his n. on it.

Nosegay to him as long as he lives, It will be a.

1678 RAY 262 . . . It will stink in his nostrils, spoken of any bad matter a man hath been engaged in.

Not God above gets all men's love.

[THEOGNIS 26 Οὐδὲ γὰρ ὁ Ζεὺς Οὔθ' ὕων πάντεσσ' ἀνδάνει οὔτ' ἀνέχων. For not even Jove can please all, whether he rains or does not rain. ERASM. *Ad. Ne Juppiter quidem omnibus placet.*] **1616** WITHALS 568. **1639** CLARKE 147. **1721** KELLY 267 . . . L. *Jupiter neque pluens neque abstinens omnibus placet.*

Not guilty—but don't do it again.

1902–4 LEAN IV. 64.

Not (a, a word of, able to, even, fit to, made of, only ought, so good to, such a, till the, to, to be, too), *see under significant words following.*

Not worth (a, an, his), *see* (Brass) farthing, Button, Cress, Curse, Dodkin, Doit, Fig, Fly, Groat, Haddock, Hair, Harrington, Haw, Ivy-leaf, Leek, Muck, Needle, Nutshell, Pin, Plack, Rotten apple, Shoebuckles, Straw, Taking the wall of dog, Three halfpence.

Notchel, *see* Cry N.

Nothing between a poor man and a rich but a piece of an ill year.

1721 KELLY 335 . . . Because, in that space, many things may fall out, that may make a rich man poor.

Nothing but is good for something.

1639 CLARKE 72. **1681** DRYDEN *Span. Friar* III. ii (Merm.) 164 They say everything in the world is good for something . . . but I never knew what a friar was good for, till your pimping showed me.

Nothing but up and ride?

1639 CLARKE 116 What? no more but up and ride? **1670** RAY 198. **1732** FULLER no. 5497.

Nothing comes fairer (sooner) to light than that which has been long hid.

1641 FERGUSSON 82 (with sooner'). **1721** KELLY 260 . . . Spoken when people unexpectedly find what has been long hid, or discovers what has been long conceal'd.

Nothing comes of (from) nothing.

[L. *Ex nihilo nihil fit.*] *c.* **1380** CHAUCER *Boece* (Robinson) v. i. 46 For this sentence is verray and soth, that 'no thing hath his beynge of naught'. *c.* **1592** MARLOWE *Jew of Malta* I. ii (Merm.) 243 *Bar.* Christians, what or how can I multiply? Of naught is nothing made. **1605–6** SHAKS. *K. Lear* I. iv. 146 Why, no, boy; nothing can be made out of nothing. **1610** FIELD *Woman is a W.* II. i (Merm.) 372 *Page.* I remember thus much philosophy of my schoolmaster, *ex nihilo nihil fit.*

Nothing costs so much as what is given us.

1732 FULLER no. 3660.

Nothing crave, nothing have.

1732 FULLER no. 6242.

Nothing dries sooner than tears.

[CICERO *De Part. Orat.* 17. 57 *Cito enim exarescit lacrima.*] **1560** T. WILSON *Arte of Rhet.* (1909) 134 (A) For as Cicero doth say, nothing drieth soner then teares. **1612** WEBSTER *White Devil* v. iii (Merm.) 103 *Flam.* These are but moonish shades of griefs or fears; There's nothing sooner dries than women's tears. **1670** RAY 147 . . . Niente più tosto se secca che lagrime. *Ital.* **1757** FRANKLIN Jan. Nothing dries sooner than a tear.

Nothing enters into a close hand.

1641 FERGUSSON 80. **1721** KELLY 263 . . . Niggardly people will not procure much good will.

Nothing for nothing (naught).

c. **1400** *Rom. Rose* 4476 Withoute yift, is not to prise. **1608** SHAKS. *K. Lear* I. i. 89 Nothing will come of nothing: speak again. a. **1704** T. BROWN to *Author of Address* in *Collect. of Poems* 97 Thou know'st the Proverb: Nothing due for naught. **1860** SURTEES *Plain or Ringlets?* li Some of the greatest screws . . . 'nothing for nothing', and uttermost-farthing men, are . . . spendthrifts in the matter of electioneering expenses. **1863** G. ELIOT *Romola* i Nothing for nothing, young man. **1882** BLACKMORE *Christowell* ix I forgot that nothing is to be had for nothing. **1904–10** ALEX. MACLAREN *Expos., Amos* 172 The last touch in the picture is meanness, which turned everything into money. . . . Is not 'nothing for nothing' an approved maxim to-day?

Nothing for nothing, and very little for a halfpenny.

1858 G. J. WHYTE-MELVILLE *Interpreter* xxv Sir Harry . . . recollected the old-established principle of himself and his clique, 'Nothing for nothing, and very little for a halfpenny'.

Nothing freer than a gift.

c. **1451** *Paston Letters* (J. Gairdner 1904) ii. 256 And askyd here Wat was freer than gyfte. c. **1470** HENRYSON *Mor. Fab., Fox, Wolf, and Husb.* 38 (1917) 107 And is thair oucht, sayis thow, frear than gift? **1639** CLARKE 222 What's freer than gift? **1721** KELLY 267. **1832** HENDERSON 28.

Nothing hath no savour (flavour).

1546 HEYWOOD I. viii. 16 But now I can smell, nothyng hath no sauer. **1614** CAMDEN 310 Nothing hath no sauour. **1738** SWIFT (Dial. i) 343 *Lady A.* Has he got a good fortune with his lady? for they say something has some savour, but nothing has no flavour.

Nothing have, nothing crave.

1659 HOWELL *Eng. Prov.* 16/2.

Nothing ill in Spain but that which speaks.

1642 HOWELL *For. Travel* vii (Arb.) 38 *Spaine* yeeldeth to none of her neighbours in perfection of anything, but only in *Plenty*; which I beleeve was the ground of a Proverbe . . . , *No ay cosa mala en Espana, sino lo que habla*, there is nothing ill in *Spaine*, but that which speakes.

Nothing is, Where | a little thing doth ease.

1546 HEYWOOD I. x. 24. **1614** CAMDEN 314.

Nothing is certain but death and quarter day (the taxes).

1902–4 LEAN 153 There is nothing sure but death and quarter day. **1912** *Spectator* 18 May, 785 It is not merely the . . . amount of the taxes. . . . It is their compulsory and irresistible incidence. . . . 'There are only two evils from which no man can escape—death and the king's taxes'.

Nothing is certain but the unforeseen. (*Cf.* Nothing is so certain as the unexpected.)

1886 FROUDE *Oceana* vii There is a proverb that 'nothing is certain but the unforeseen', and in fact few things turn out as we expect them. **1905** ALEX. MACLAREN *Expos., Matthew* I. 322 There is nothing certain to happen, says the proverb, but the unforeseen. To-morrow *will have* its cares.

Nothing, He that has | is frighted at nothing.

c. **1557** ROPER *Life of More* (Hitchcock) 7 He nothinge having, nothing could loose. **1592** NASHE *Summer's Last Will* Wks. (McKerrow) III. 242 *Cui nil est, nil deest*: he that hath nothing, wants nothing. **1639** CLARKE 41 They that have nothing, need feare to lose nothing. **1732** FULLER no. 2150.

Nothing is impossible to a willing heart.

1546 HEYWOOD I. iv. 9 Who hopeth in Gods helpe, his helpe can not starte: Nothing is impossible to a willyng hart. **1641** FERGUSSON 82 Nothing is difficile to a well willit man. **1670** RAY 29 Nothing is impossible to a willing mind.

Nothing, He that hath | is not contented.

1670 RAY 19.

Nothing is so certain as the unexpected. (*Cf.* Nothing is certain but the unforeseen.)

1885 C. LOWE *Bismarck* ix (1898) 320 The fall of Bismarck was . . . one of the wonders of the century; and . . . no more unexpected event ever happened, though the French . . . will have it that nothing is so certain as the unexpected. **1909** ALEX. MACLAREN *Expos.*,

Ephesians 338 The temptation comes stealthily, 'as a thief in the night'. Nothing is so certain as the unexpected.

Nothing is stolen without hands.

1616 BRETON *Cross. Prov.* Wks. (1879) II. App. iii There is nothing stolen without hands. **1639** CLARKE 149.

Nothing is, Where | the king must lose his right.

1546 HEYWOOD I. xii. 39 Where as nothing is, the kynge must lose his right. **1605** *Lond. Prodigal* iii. iii (*Shaks. Apoc.*) 208 Alas, what good . . . To imprison him that nothing hath to pay? And where nought is, the king doth lose his due. **1721** KELLY 358 . . . And so must the subject but with this difference, that the king loseth his right in no other case.

Nothing is to be presumed on, or despaired of.

1651 HERBERT 319.

Nothing like, *see under significant words following.*

Nothing must be done hastily but killing of fleas.

1678 RAY 151. **1721** KELLY 261 *Nothing to be done in haste, but gripping of fleas.* . . . Spoken when we are unreasonably urged to make haste.

Nothing new under the sun.

1382 WYCLIF *Eccl.* i. 10 No thing vndir the sunne *is* newe. *c.* **1386** CHAUCER *Knight's T.* A 2125 Ther nys no newë gyse, that it nas old. **1816** WOLCOT (P. Pindar) *Ode on Ancients* Wks. IV. 131 Alas! there's nothing new beneath the sun: The ancients with their hooks have reap'd the field. **1850** KINGSLEY *Alton L.* There is nothing new under the sun; all that is stale and trite to a Septuagenarian, who has seen where it all ends.

Nothing patent in the New Testament that is not latent in the Old.

1902–4 LEAN IV. 153 . . . In vetere novum latet, in novo vetus patet.

Nothing questioneth, He that | nothing learneth.

1579 GOSSON *Ephemerides* 61 b. **1732** FULLER no. 2241.

Nothing seek, nothing find.

1581 RICH *Farewell to Militarie Prof.* (1846) 128 As the proverbe is (he that sekes shall finde). **1614** COCKS in *Cal. Col. P., E. Indies* 342 As the saying is, nothing seek nothing find.

Nothing so bad but it might have been worse.

1876 MRS. BANKS *Manch. Man* xliii However, there is nothing so bad but it might be worse. **1886** E. J. HARDY *How to be Happy* xxi Let us resolve to look at the bright side of things. . . .

'Nothing so bad but it might have been worse'. **1908** *Times Wkly.* 9 Oct. Farmers . . . will regard the . . . meteorological changes as illustrating the ancient axiom to the effect that circumstances are never so bad that they cannot be worse.

Nothing so bad in which there is not something of good.

1678 RAY *Adag. Hebr.* 408.

Nothing so crouse,[1] as a new washen louse.

1641 FERGUSSON 100. **1721** KELLY 263 . . . Spoken of them who have been ragged, and dirty, and are proud, and fond of new, or clean cloaths. [[1] brisk.]

Nothing so necessary for travellers as languages.

1616 BRETON *Cross. Prov.* Wks. (1879) II. App. iii.

Nothing so sure as death.

c. **1300** *King Alisaunder* l. 918 N'is in this world so siker thyng So is deth, to olde and yyng. **1639** CLARKE 214.

Nothing stake, nothing draw. (*Cf.* Nought lay down, &c.)

1678 RAY 206.

Nothing succeeds like success.

1872 BESANT & RICE *Ready-money M.* ix In Mr. Mortiboy's judgment, no proverb could be better than . . . 'Nothing succeeds like success'. Success dazzled him. **1903** J. MCCARTHY *Portr. of Sixties* xxi Robson's . . . dazzling success led to the waste of his physical powers and to his early death. . . . In certain cases at least, nothing fails like success. **1919** DEAN INGE *Outspoken Ess.* 88 Aristocracies do not maintain their numbers. The ruling race rules itself out; nothing fails like success.

Nothing that is violent is permanent.

1576 PETTIE *Petite Pall.* (Gollancz) ii. 62 Nothing violent is permanent. **1594** SHAKS. *Lucrece* 894 Thy violent vanities can never last. **1595–6** *Rich. II* II. i. 34 For violent fires soon burn out themselves. **1600–1** *Hamlet* II. i. 103 This is the very ecstasy of love, Whose violent property fordoes itself. **1613** WITHER *Abuses* ii. i As if all euils they would quite reforme Within a moment: But things *violent* Cannot you know be long time *permanent*. **1623** J. TAYLOR (Water-P.) *Mer. Wher. Fer. Voy.* Wks. (1872) 4 But nothing violent is permanent, and in short space away the Tempest went. **1861** G. J. WHYTE-MELVILLE *Inside Bar* iv There is a good old rule in mechanics which affirms 'nil violentum est perpetuum'.

Nothing tickles that pinches not.

1603 FLORIO tr. *Montaigne* iii. xii (1897) VI. 184 *Nothing tickles that pincheth not.* And good historians avoid calm narrations, . . . to retreeve seditions and find out wars, whereto they know we call them.

Nothing to be got without pains.

1573 SANDFORD (1576) 218 No good thing is
without payne. **1611** COTGRAVE s.v. 'Peine'
Nor bread, nor ought is gotten without
paines. **1616** WITHALS 562 Nothing proues
well except it be plyed. **1721** KELLY Nothing
gotten but [= without] pains, but an ill
name. **1732** FULLER no. 3677 . . . but poverty.

Nothing turns sourer than milk.

1830 FORBY 428 . . . *i.e.* A mild, good-
humoured man is most determined, when he
is thoroughly provoked.

Nothing (Nought) venture, nothing (nought) have.

c. **1374** CHAUCER *Troylus* II, l. 807 And seyde,
he which that no-thing under-taketh, Nothing ne acheveth, be him looth or dere. *c.*
1386 *Reeve's T.* A 4210 'Unhardy is unsely',[1]
thus men sayth. **1546** HEYWOOD I. xi. 31
Nought venter nought haue. **1602** BRETON
Wonders in Wks (Gros.) **II. 9** *Fran.* The
young man replyed: Oh sir, nothing venter
nothing haue. **1777** BOSWELL *Johnson* lxi
(1848) 558 I observed, 'I am, however,
generally for trying: "Nothing venture,
nothing have".' **1850** LYTTON *My Novel* IV.
iv 'Learn whist—sixpenny points to begin
with'. . . . Shaking my head, I called for my
bill. . . . 'Poor spirit, sir! . . . Nothing venture, nothing have.' [[1] unfortunate.]

Nothing venture, nothing win.

1481 CAXTON *Reynard* (Arb.) 27 He that wil
wynne he muste laboure and auenture. **1668**
SEDLEY *Mulberry Gard.* III. ii Who ever
caught any thing with a naked hook? Nothing
venture, nothing win. **1876** BLACKMORE
Cripps xliii We must all have been in France
. . . if—well, never mind. Nothing venture
nothing win. But happily we have won.

Nothing when you are used to it, It is.

1738 SWIFT (Dial. ii) 350 *Miss.* I would not
keep such company for the world. *Lady A.*
O, miss, 'tis nothing when you are used to it.

Nothing when you are used to it, It is | as the eels said when they were being skinned alive.

1829–30 M. SCOTT *T. Cring. Log* i Who says
that eels cannot be made used to skinning?
The poor girls continued their little preparations with alacrity. **1902–4** LEAN IV. 19 'Tis
nothing when you are used to it, as the eels
said when they were being skinned alive.

Nothing worse than a familiar[1] enemy.

[**1526** TINDALE *Matt.* x. 36 And a mannes
fooes shalbe they of his owne housholde.]
c. **1386** CHAUCER *Merch. T.* E[2] 1784 O famulier
foo, that his service bedeth! *c.* **1400** *Test.
Love* II. 343/1 Nothyng is werse . . . than . . . a
famyliar enemye. *c.* **1538** *Lisle Papers* XII.
art. 43 in *N. & Q.* 4th Ser. IX. 423 It hath
been an old proverbe that there is no worse
pestilence than a famylyar enemy. [[1] of one's
own household.]

Nothing, *see also* Enough where n. was left (Never); Fair fall n.; Pain to do n. than something (More); Put n. into purse (If you); Say n. than not to purpose (Better); Too much of n. but fools; Well fare n. once a year.

Notice, *see* Long foretold . . . short n. soon past.

Nottingham, *see* Smith of N.

Nought is to wed with, Where | wise men flee the clog.

1546 HEYWOOD I. xi. 26. **1614** CAMDEN 314
Where nought is to wend whit [1636 *with*],
wise men flee the clog.

Nought lay down, nought take up. (*Cf.* Nothing stake, &c.)

1546 HEYWOOD I. xi. 34 He can . . . no tyme
assine, In whiche he hath laied downe one
peny by myne, . . . And . . . nought lay
downe, nought take vp. **1659** HOWELL *Eng.
Prov.* 5/1 Nothing down, nothing up.

Nought, He that hath | shall have nought.

1509 A. BARCLAY *Ship of Fools* (1874) I. 100
He that nought hathe, shall so alway byde
poor, But he that ouer moche hath, yet shall
haue more. *c.* **1550** *Parl. of Byrdes* l. 221 in
HAZLITT, *Early Pop. Poetry* iii. 179 (A).

Nought won by the one, nought won by the other.

1550 HEYWOOD I. xi. 34.

Nought, *see also* Fault (He hath but one), he
is n.; Play for n. as work for n. (As good);
Well fare n. once a year. *See also* Naught,
Nothing.

November take flail, let ship no more sail. (*Cf.* Thresher take his flail.)

1573 TUSSER 21. xix (1878) 55. **1732** FULLER
no. 6221.

November, *see also* First of N. . . . an end of
wheat-sowing.

Now I have, *see* Ewe and a lamb; Sheep and
a cow.

Now is now, and Yule's in winter.

1615 R. BRATHWAIT *A Strappado for the
Devil* (Ebsworth) 89 The time is chang'd,
now's now, and then was then. **1721** KELLY
268 . . . A return to them that say *Now*, by
way of resentment; a particle common in
Scotland. **1846** DENHAM 6.

Now or never.

1590–1 SHAKS. *2 Hen. VI* III. i. 331 Now,
York, or never, steel thy fearful thoughts.
1608 DAY *Humour* IV. iii (Merm.) 319 *Flor.*
You shall find us at the south port.—Now or
never, my lord. **1712** ADDISON *Spect.* No. 403
Wks. (1902) III. 381 Sharp's the word. Now

H h

or never boy. Up to the walls of Paris directly. **1847-8** THACKERAY *Vanity F.* vi Now or never was the moment, Miss Sharp thought, to provoke the declaration which was trembling on **the** timid lips of Mr. Sedley.

Nullum numen abest si sit prudentia, see No divinity.

Number one.

[= oneself. *cf.* **1721** KELLY 124 *Good folks are scarce, you'll take care of one.* Spoken to those who . . . cowardly shun dangers.] **1796** EDGEWORTH *Par. Asst.* (1903) 322 I'm only talking of number one, you know. I must take care of that first. **1839** DICKENS *N. Nickleby* lx The only number in all arithmetic that I know of, as a husband and a father, is number one. **1849** DARWIN in *Life & Lett.* I. 369 I do not see my way clearly, beyond humbly endeavouring to reform Number one.

Nun of Sion, with the friar of Sheen, The.

1659 HOWELL *Eng. Prov.* 17/1 The Nun of *Sion* with the Frier of *Shean,* Went under the water to play the quean. **1787** GROSE (*Middlesex*) 209 The nun of Sion, with the friar of Shean. A saying, meant to express birds of a feather. Although the river Thames runs between these two monasteries, there is a vulgar tradition that they had a subterraneous communication.

Nun, see also Nice as a n.'s hen.

Nunc dimitis, see Sing *N. d.*

Nunky[1] pays for all.

1815 *Zeluca* III. 232 ' *There my dear!* "Nunky pays for all",' said Mr. Bessaly in a parenthesis. [[1] *nuncle, i.e.* uncle.]

Nurse is valued till the child has done sucking, The.

1732 FULLER no. 4688.

Nurse's tongue is privileged to talk, The.

1659 HOWELL *Brit.-Eng.* 4. **1670** RAY 19.

Nurses put one bit in the child's mouth and two in their own.

1639 CLARKE 39 .

Nurse(s), see also Kiss the child for n.'s sake; One year a n. and seven the worse.

Nurture and good manners maketh man. (*Cf.* Manners maketh man.)

c. **1460** *Vrbanitatis* 33 in *Babees Bk.* (E.E.T.S.) 14 In halle, in chambur, ore where þou gon, Nurtur & good maners makeþ man.

Nurture is above nature. (*But see* Nature passes nurture.)

1579 LYLY *Euphues* (Arb.) 127 But you see how Education altereth Nature. **1611** COTGRAVE s.v. 'Nourriture' Nurture surpasseth nature. **1639** CLARKE 167.

Nuts to an ape, It is like.

1711-12 SWIFT *Jrnl. to Stella* 8 Jan. Lord Keeper and Treasurer teased me for a week. It was nuts to them. **1732** FULLER no. 2970 **1809** MALKIN *Gil Blas* VI. i His disgrace or ruin will be nuts to me. **1843** DICKENS *Christmas C.* i It was the very thing he liked. To edge his way along . . . warning all human sympathy to keep its distance, was . . . 'nuts' to Scrooge.

Nut(s), see also Apple, **an** egg, and a n.; Crack me that n.; Cracked n. with her tail (As if she); Deaf n.; Eat the kernel must crack n.; Hard n. to crack; Lost with an apple, won with a n.; Madame Parnell, crack the n.; Noise is greater than the n.; Sweet as a n.; Sweet n. if you were well cracked.

Nut-crack, see Windmill dwindles into n.-c.

Nutmeg, see Carry a n. in pocket, married to old man.

Nutshell, Not worth a.

a. **1300** *Cursor M.* 23828 þair spede es noght a nute-scell. *c.* **1390** GOWER *Conf. Amantis* II. 20 Bot al nys worth a note schale. *a.* **1529** SKELTON *Agst. Venemous Tongues* Wks. (1843) I. 135 All is not worth a couple of nut shalis.

Nutting on Sundays, If you go | the devil will come to help and hold the boughs for you.

1894 A. J. C. HARE *Sussex* 43 Hazel copses . . . are . . . abundant. 'If you go nutting on Sundays, the devil will come to help, and hold down the boughs for you', is an old Sussex proverb.

Nutting, see also Holyrood Day the devil goes a-n.; Speak in clusters, begot in n.

O

O Master Vier, we cannot pay you your rent, for we had no grace of God this year; no shipwreck upon our coast.

1659 HOWELL *Eng. Prov.* 12/2 . . . A saying of the *Cornish.*

Oak has been an acorn, Every.

1732 FULLER no. 4576 The greatest oaks have

been little acorns. **1852** E. FITZGERALD *Polonius* v 'Every oak must be an acorn.' **1908** *Times Lit. Sup.* 26 June We always forget that the oak grew from an acorn.

Oak is not felled at one stroke, An.

c. **1400** *Rom. Rose* 3687 For no man at the firstè stroke Ne maye nat fellè downe an oke. *c.* **1430** LYDGATE *Fall Princes* I. 96 These ookis grete be nat douníhewe First at a strok. *a.* **1530** *R. Hill's Commonpl. Bk.*

(E.E.T.S.) 128 Hit is a febill tre that fallith at the first strok. **1621** BURTON *Anat. Mel.* I. ii. IV. vii (1651) 172 An old oak is not felled at a blow. **1641** FERGUSSON 96 The tree falls not at the first stroke.

Oak's before the ash, If the | then you'll only get a splash; if the ash precedes the oak, then you may expect a soak.

1852 *N. & Q.* 1st Ser. v. 581 When the oak comes out before the ash, there will be fine weather in harvest. I . . . find it generally correct. **1911** *Times Lit. Sup.* 4 Aug. 285 One of the commonest weather rhymes in most parts of England deals with the budding of the oak and the ash:—When the oak's before the ash Then you'll only get a splash, When the ash is before the oak Then you may expect a soak. But in North Germany the signs are exactly inverted, and also in Cornwall.

Oaks may fall when reeds stand the storm.

c. **1374** CHAUCER *Troylus* II. 1387 'But reed that boweth doun for every blast Ful lightly, cessé wind, it wol arise; But so wil not an ook whan it is cast'. **1577** TUSSER liii (1878) 149 Like as in tempest great, where wind doth beare the stroke, Much safer stands the bowing reede then doth the stubborn oke. **1621** BURTON *Anat. Mel.* II. iii. III. (1651) 329 Though I live obscure, yet I live clean and honest; and when as the lofty oke is blown down, the silly reed may stand. **1660** FULLER (*Hants*) II. 13 Though our Lord Powlet enjoyed his place not so many years, yet did he serve more sovereigns, in more mutable times, being (as he said of himself) 'no oak, but an osier'. **1732** FULLER no. 3692.

Oak(s), *see also* Cut down o. and set strawberry; Grass on the top of o. tree (Look for); Man in the o.; Strokes fell great o.; Willow will buy horse before o. saddle.

Oar in every man's boat (barge), To have an.

[= to have a hand in every one's affairs.] *c.* **1500** *Cocke Lorell's Bote* (Percy Soc.) 11 In Cocke's bote eche man had an ore. **1543** UDALL tr. *Erasm. Apoph.* II. 180 In eche mannes bote, would he haue an ore. **1546** HEYWOOD I. x. 19 She must haue an ore in euery mans barge. **1606** *Ret. from Parnassus* Lodge [open to criticism] for his oare in every paper boate. **1631** BRATHWAITE *Whimzies* (1859) 86 He loves to fish in troubled waters, have an oar in every mans boat.

Oar(s), *see also* Boat without the o. (Ill goes); Put in one's o.

Oath is better broken than kept, An unlawful.

1640 HERBERT 364 An oath that is not to be made, is not to be kept. **1670** RAY 126.

Oatmeal, *see* Store of o. (Where there is), you may put enough in crock.

Oats will mow themselves.

1750 W. ELLIS *Mod. Husbandm.* v. 52 Oats are so heavy a Grain as to lie close with a little Trouble. We say, Oats will mow themselves.

Oat(s), *see also* Cut o. green; Debtors (Of ill) men take o.; Janiveer sows o. (Who in); Rough o.; St. David's day put o. in clay; Water trotted is as good as o.; Wild o.

Obedience is much more seen in little things than in great.

1732 FULLER no. 3693.

Obedience is the first duty of a soldier.

1846–7 J. GRANT *Rom. of War* lix 'What do the wiseacres at headquarters mean in sending a detachment there?' 'I suppose they scarcely know themselves. But obedience—we all know the adage.' **1872** G. J. WHYTE MELVILLE *Satanella* xxiv 'The first duty of a soldier is obedience', he answered in great glee.

Obedience learn to command, Through.

[SENECA *de Ira* 2. 14. 4 *Nemo regere potest nisi qui et regi.*] **1671** MILTON *P.R.* iii. 194 [He can] best reign who first Hath well obeyed. **1841** CHAMIER *Tom Bowl.* xliii Many instances of oppression and tyranny . . . had originated in Curlew's ignorance, both of the duties of a seaman and of an officer. It was evident he had never learnt to obey, and thus was unfit for command.

Obey(s), *see* Bound must o.; Commands enough that o. a wise man.

Obligation, *see* Irishman's o.

Occam's razor.

[*Entia non sunt multiplicanda praeter necessitatem,* the leading principle of the nominalism of William of Occam, an Eng. scholastic philosopher of first half of 14th cent., that for purposes of explanation things not known to exist should not, unless it is absolutely necessary, be postulated as existing; usually called the Law of Parcimony.] **1836–7** W. HAMILTON *Metaph.* xxxix (1859) II. 395 We are, therefore, entitled to apply Occam's razor to this theory of causality. **1929** *Let. to Times* 2 May 12/2 Is it to be a universal denomination *ante rem,* or a still more universal (!) denomination *post rem?* Has the noble lord forgotten Occam's razor?

Occasion is bald behind, *see* Time by the forelock.

Occasion lost cannot be redeemed, An.

1616 DRAXE 144 An occasion lost, cannot easily bee redeemed. **1813** RAY 144.

Occasion, *see also* Do ill (Who would) ne'er wants o.; Time (O.) by the forelock (Take).

O'clock, *see* Know what's o.

Odds, *see* Evil there is o. (In); Two to one is o.

Off the hooks.

[(a) = out of condition, order.] 14 Nov. **1616** J. CHAMBERLAIN *Letters* (McLure) ii. 34 The Lord Cooke [= Coke] is now quite of the hookes. **1626** JONSON *Staple of News* iii. ii. 24 To hang the States on, h' has heau'd off the hookes. a. **1659** CLEVELAND *Pet. Poem* 22 My Doublet looks Like him that wears it, quite off o' the Hooks. **1684** H. MORE *Answer* 240 But the application is, methinks, much off the Hooks. [(b) = out of bounds.] **1612** *North's Plutarch* 1214 Agrippina began . . . to flye off the hookes: and coming to Nero himself, threatned to take his Empire from him. [(c) = out of humour or spirits, or crazy.] **1621** FLETCHER *Pilgrim* iii. vi What fit's this? The Pilgrim's off the hooks too. **1662** PEPYS *Diary* 28 Apr. One thing that hath put Sir William so long off the hooks. **1824** SCOTT *St. Ronan's* xxx Everybody . . . is a little off the hooks . . . in plain words, a little crazy, or so. [(d) = crestfallen.] **1639** DAVENPORT *New Trick* I. ii. [(e) = dead or dying.] **1842** BARHAM *Ingol. Leg., Blk. Mousq.* II Our friend . . . has popp'd off the hooks! **1894** BLACKMORE *Perlycross* 293 Is it true that old Fox is dropping off the hooks?

Off with the old love before you are on with the new, It is best to be.

1571 R. EDWARDS *Damon and Pithias* in HAZLITT *Old Plays* iv. 447 (A) 'Tis good to be off wi' the old love Before you are on wi' the new. **1819** SCOTT *Bride Lam.* xxix Bucklaw, half humming, half speaking the end of the old song—' It is best to be off wi' the old love Before you be on wi' the new'. **1857** TROLLOPE *Barch. Tow.* xxvii There is an old song which gives us some very good advice about courting: 'It's gude to be off with the auld luve Before ye be on wi' the new.' **1891** A. LANG *Ess. in Little* 6 Dumas . . . met the great man at Marseilles, where . . . Alexandre chanced to be 'on with the new love' before being completely 'off with the old'.

Offended (Hurt) but by himself, None is.

[L. *Nemo laeditur nisi a seipso.* No man is hurt but by himself.] **1640** HERBERT 348.

Offender never pardons, The.

[TAC. *Agric.* 42. 4 *Proprium humani ingenii est odisse quem laeseris.*] **1640** HERBERT 343. **1666** TORRIANO 176 (18) Who offends, ne'er forgives [pardons]. **1672** DRYDEN *Conq. Gran.* Pt. 2. I. ii *Zul.* Forgiveness to the injur'd does belong, But they ne'er pardon who have done the wrong. **1876** MRS. BANKS *Manch. Man* xlv He was of Mrs. Ashton's mind that, 'as offenders never pardon', Augusta needed a friend.

Offer much, To.

1611 COTGRAVE s.v. 'Beaucoup' To offer much to him that asketh little, is flatly to denie him the little he asketh. **1631** MABBE *Celestina* (T.T.) 116 (A) It is a common saying; To offer much to him that asketh but a little, is a kinde of deniall.

Offer your hen for sale on a rainy day, Never.

1721 KELLY 373. **1846** DENHAM 3.

Offer, *see also* Fair o. no cause of feud.

Offering, *see* Long standing and small o. maketh poor parsons; Priest (Such), such o.; Saint (Like), like o.

Off-fallings, *see* Gentles (Where there are), there are o.-f.

Office, He hath a good | he must needs thrive.

1678 RAY 263.

Office, *see also* Buy an o. (They that) must sell; Cast of his o. (Give one a); Out of o. out of danger. *See also* Magistracy.

Offices may well be given, but not discretion.

1573 SANDFORD (1576) 221. **1578** FLORIO *First Fruites* f. 33. **1629** *Book of Meery Riddles* Prov. 116.

Offspring of those that are very old, or very young, lasts not, The.

1640 HERBERT 358.

Oft ettle,[1] whiles hit.

1721 KELLY 269 . . . People who have made many tryals to do a thing, may hit right at last. [1 aim.]

Often and little eating makes a man fat.

1657 E. LEIGH *Select & Choice Observations* 275. **1659** N. R. 84. **1670** RAY 38.

Often, *see also* Little and o. fills purse.

Oil of angels.[1]

[= gold as gifts or bribes.] **1592** GREENE *Upst. Courtier* E j b The palms of their hands so hot that they cannot be coold vnlesse they be rubed with the oil of angels. **1623** MASSINGER *Dk. Milan* iii. ii I have seen . . . his stripes wash'd off With the oil of angels. [1 a gold coin worth 10s.]

Oil of baston.[1]

[= a beating.] **1608** WITHALS 308 They call it vulgarly the oyle of Baston, or a sower cudgell. [1 stick.]

Oil of fool.

[= flattery used to befool a person.] **1785** WOLCOT (P. Pindar) *9th Ode to R.A.'s*, Reynolds . . . prithee, seek the Courtier's school And learn to manufacture oil of fool.

Oil of whip (strap).

1662 FULLER (*Somerset*) iii. 92 Although oil of whip be the proper plaister for the cramp of laziness, yet some pity is due to impotent persons. **1693** *Poor Robin* Now for to cure such a disease as this, The oyl of whip the surest medicine is. **1847** HALLIWELL *Dict.* (1889) II. 816 Strap-oil. A severe beating. It is a common joke on April 1st to send a lad for a pennyworth of strap-oil, which is generally ministered on his own person.

Oil on the fire is not the way to quench it, Pouring.

1607-8 SHAKS. *Coriol.* III. i. 196 This is the way to kindle, not to quench. **1608-9** *Pericles* I. iv. 4 That were to blow at fire in hope to quench it. **1623** CAMDEN 275. **1670** RAY 126 To cast oil in the fire's not the way to quench it. **1875** CARLYLE *Early K. of Norway* vii Wretched Ethelred . . . offered them Danegelt . . .: a dear method of quenching fire by pouring *oil* on it.

Oil to the fire, To bring.

c. **1386** CHAUCER *Phys. T.* C 60 For wyn and youthe dooth Venus encresse, As men in fyr wol casten oille or greesse. *c.* **1550** INGELEND *Disob. Child* in HAZL. *O.E.P.* (1874) II. 280 *The Father.* And, after the proverb, we put oil to the fire. **1605-6** SHAKS. *K. Lear* II. ii. 82 Bring oil to fire, snow to their colder moods.

Oil upon the waters, To pour.

[= to smooth matters over.] **1847** W. B. BARING in *Croker Papers* (1884) III. xxv. 103 Lord G. [Bentinck] . . . spoke angrily. D'Israeli poured oil and calmed the waves. **1864-5** DICKENS *Mutual Friend* III. xii 'His wife . . . would throw oil on the waters . . . I should fail to move him to an angry outburst, if his wife was there'.

Oil, *see also* Measureth o. (He that) shall anoint fingers; Midnight o.; Old fish, old o., old friend; Smooth as o.; Truth and o. are ever above; Wine (Of) the middle, of o. the top.

Ointment, *see* Fly in the o.

Old acquaintance will soon be remembered.

c. **1550** R. WEVER *Lusty Juventus* in HAZL. *O.E.P.* II. 70 *Juv.* I never knew, That you and I together were acquainted: But nevertheless, if you do it renew, Old acquaintance will soon be remembered.

Old age, *see* Dies for age (When he) you may quake for fear.

Old and cold.

1327-8 *Chester Plays, Salut. & Nativ.* (Shaks. Soc.) I. 98 For I am bouth oulde and coulde. **1721** KELLY 160 *He is old and cold, and ill to lye beside.* Spoken by a young maid, when jeer'd with an old man.

Old and tough, young and tender.

1678 RAY 85. **1855** THACKERAY *Little Billee* There's little Bill as is young and tender, We're old and tough.

Old and wise, Though | yet still advise.

1640 HERBERT 323. **1732** FULLER no. 6227.

Old ape hath an old eye, An.

1636 CAMDEN 291. **1639** CLARKE 267. **1738** SWIFT (Dial. i) 338 *Miss.* I must beg your pardon a thousand times; but they say, an old ape hath an old eye.

Old as Charing Cross, As.

1598 DELONEY 2 *Gentle Craft* Wks. (Mann) 188.

Old as Glastonbury Tor, As.

[The Tor (550 ft.) is crowned with the tower of a chapel destroyed in 1271.] **1678** RAY 344 . . . *Somerset.* This torre, *i.e.* tower, so called from the Latin *Turris*, stands upon a round hill.

Old as my tongue and a little older than my teeth.

1738 SWIFT (Dial. i) 336 *Miss.* Why, I'm as old as my tongue, and a little older than my teeth.

Old as Pauls (*or* Paul's steeple), As.

[The steeple of Old St. Paul's cathedral was destroyed by lightning in 1561 and never re-erected.] **1659** HOWELL *Prov.* Dedn. (A) Some of them may be said to be as old as Pauls steeple. **1662** FULLER (*London*) II. 346 'As old as Paul's steeple'. . . . This proverb . . . serveth . . . to be returned to such, who pretend those things to be novel, which are known to be stale . . . and almost antiquated. **1670** RAY 206 As old as *Pauls* (or *Pauls* steeple). **1738** SWIFT (Dial. i) 340 *Lady A.* How do you like Lady Fruzz? *Never.* . . . She's as old as Poles'.

Old band is a captain's honour, An.

1573 SANDFORD (1576) 207. **1578** FLORIO *First Fruites* f. 28 (A) An old ensigne is the honor of a captaine. **1629** *Book of Meery Riddles* Prov. 65.

Old be, or young die.

1678 RAY 182.

Old bees yield no honey.

1670 RAY 19 When bees are old they yield no honey.

Old bones, She will never make.

1872 C. READE *Wandering H.* ix She is too good to last. . . . I fear she is like her father, and will ne'er make old bones.

Old brown cow laid an egg, The.

1917 BRIDGE 117 . . . Used as an answer to importunate questioners.

Old cart well used may outlast a new one abused, An.

1550 HEYWOOD I. xi Cartis well driuen . . . go longe vpright. **1732** FULLER no. 6287.

Old cat laps as much milk as a young (kitten), An.

1623 CAMDEN 266. **1670** RAY 68 An old cat laps as much as a young kitlin.

Old cat sports not with her prey, An.

1640 HERBERT 364.

Old cat to an old rat, Put an.

1668 DAVENANT *Man's the Master* I. i. Wks. (1874) V. 16 As the proverb says, put an old cat to an old rat.

Old cattle breed not.

1629 T. ADAMS *Serm.* (1861–2) I. 485 Old cattle breed no longer, doted trees deny fruit, the tired earth becomes barren. 1670 RAY 127.

Old chains gall less than new.

1907 *Spectator* 12 Jan. 50 Prayer-book revision . . . might . . . end in a narrowing . . . of the Church. The late Master of Balliol once reminded Liberal Churchmen that old chains gall less than new'.

Old cloak makes a new jerkin, An.

c. 1592 KYD *Span. Trag.* III. vi Doost thou think to liue till his olde doublet will make thee a new trusse? 1594 BACON *Promus* 212, no. 469 Old treacle new losange. *c.* 1598 MS. *Proverbs* in FERGUSSON 85 Often hath it bein sein that Eva's old Kirtl hath maid old Adam a pair of new breeches. 1600–1 SHAKS. *Merry W.* I. iii. 18 An old cloak makes a new jerkin; a withered serving-man, a fresh tapster.

Old cock crows, As the | so crows the young (*or*, the young one learns).

c. 1350 *Douce MS.* 52 no. 43 As þe cocke croweth, so þe chekyn lernyth. 1509 BARCLAY *Ship of Fools* (Jamieson) 235 The yonge Cok lerneth to crowe hye of the olde. 1546 HEYWOOD I. x. 19 Their folkis glomd on me to, by which it apéereth. The yonge cocke croweth, as he the olde héereth. 1615 BRATHWAIT *Strappado for Div.* 176 Which by the proverb every man discerns, *Since as the old cock crows, the young cock learns.* 1821 SCOTT *Pirate* xviii As the old cock crows the young cock learns . . . the father declares against the king's customs, and the daughter against the king's crown. 1834 MARRYAT *Jacob Faith.* xxv There's an old adage which saith, 'As the old cock crows, so doth the young'.

Old debts are better than old sores.

1721 KELLY 274 . . . The one may be paid, and the other will ache.

Old dog barks not in vain, An.

1573 SANDFORD 207. 1651 HERBERT 368.

Old dog bites sore, An.

1539 TAVERNER (1545) A 3ᵛ The englysh prouerbe sayth thus An olde dogge byteth sore. 1546 HEYWOOD II. vi. 61 It is saide of olde, an olde dog byteth sore. 1721 KELLY 23 . . . Spoken to discourage one from provoking a man of advanc'd years; for . . . he will give a desperate blow.

Old enough and ugly enough to take care of oneself.

1872 G. J. WHYTE-MELVILLE *Satanella* x Are you quite alone, on your own hook?' 'What a question!' she laughed. 'I suppose you think I'm old enough and ugly enough to take care of myself!'

Old enough to lie without doors.

1678 RAY 77.

Old ewe dressed lamb fashion, An.

1891 J. L. KIPLING *Beast & Man* 201 Of an old woman in gay attire they say, 'An old mare in a red rein'. Our brutal saw says, 'Old ewe, lamb fashion'.

Old fish and young flesh do feed men best.

c. 1386 CHAUCER *Merch. T.* E² 1418 Oold fissh and yongè flessh wolde I have fayn. . . . Bet than olde boef is the tendrè veel. I wol no womman thritty yeer of age. 1546 HEYWOOD II. iv. 50 Olde fish and yong flesh (quoth he) dooth men best féede. 1670 RAY 39 Jeun chair & vieil poisson, *i.e.* Young flesh and old fish are best.

Old fish, old oil, and an old friend are the best.

1678 RAY 41 Pesce, oglio & amico vecchio. *Old fish, old oil and an old friend are the best.*

Old folks, *see* Kindness is lost bestowed on o. f.

Old fox is not easily snared, An.

1539 TAVERNER 27 An olde foxe is not taken in a snare. 1621 BURTON *Anat. Mel.* II. iii. vi (1651) 348 A little experience and practice will inure us to it; *vetula vulpes*, as the proverb saith, *laques haud capitur*; an old fox is not so easily taken in a snare. 1809 MALKIN *Gil Blas* IV. xi Justice . . . is coming . . . to lay her paw upon my person. But an old fox is too cunning to be caught in a trap.

Old foxes want no tutors.

1670 RAY 127 An old fox need learn no craft. 1732 FULLER no. 3712 Old foxes want no tutors. *Ibid.* no. 644 An old fox needs not to be taught tricks. 1792 WOLCOT (P. Pindar) *Odes to Pitt* V Wks. (1816) II. 263 What, preach to *me* on *money*-wit! Old foxes want no tutors', Billy Pitt.

Old friends and old wine and old gold are best.

1576 PETTIE *Petite Pall.* (Gollancz) II. 132 You ought to like those friends best which last longest, and have lived longest with you . . . like many wines, which the older they are the better they are! *c.* 1594 BACON *Promus* 508. 1612 Vin vieux, amy vieux et or vieux sont aimez en tous lieux. 1640 HERBERT 323 Old wine and an old friend are good provisions. 1670 RAY 19.

Old head and young hands.

1678 RAY 347. *Somerset.*

Old head on young shoulders, An. (*Cf.* Grey head . . . green shoulders.)

1595 SHAKS. *Merch. V.* IV. i. 162 I neuer

knew **so** young a body with so olde a head. **1639** CLARKE 7 You set an old mans head on a yong mans shoulders. **1842** MARRYAT *Perc. Keene* xix You appear to have an old head upon very young shoulders; at one moment to be a scampish boy . . . , and at another a resolute . . . man.

Old knave is no babe (child), An.

1528 MORE *Wks.* (1557) p. 242 col. 1 (A) They shal for al that fynde in some of us yt an olde knaue is no chylde. **1546** HEYWOOD II. ii. 47 I shall make hir knowe, an olde knaue is no childe. **1555** Id. *Epigr. upon Prov.* no. 148 An olde knaue is no babe. **1641** FERGUSSON 10 An old knave is na bairne. **1721** KELLY 35 *An old knave is no bairn* . . . Cunning old companions, who are thoroughly versed in cheating and deceit.

Old long, He that would be | must be old betimes.

1539 TAVERNER f. 10 (A) Become an olde man betyme yf thou wylt be an olde man longe. **1672** W. WALKER *Parœm.* 39 He that would be old, must be old betimes. **1691** R. CROMWELL *Let.* in *Eng. Hist. Rev.* (1898) xiii. 109 There is an old proverb 'old yong, yong old' **1711** STEELE *Spect.* No. 153, 25 Aug. 'It was prettily said, 'He that would be long an old man must begin early to be one'. . . . It is necessary that before the arrival of age we bid adieu to the pursuits of youth.

Old love will not be forgotten.

1634 T. HEYWOOD & R. BROME *Late Lancashire Witches* Heywood's *Wks.* (1874) iv. 201 and 216. **1675** *Letter* to Sir R. Verney *Verney Memoirs* iv (1899) 311 Ould love will not be forgotten.

Old maids lead apes in hell.

1575 GASCOIGNE *Posies* in *Wks.* (Cunliffe) I. 430 (A) I am afrayde my marryage will bee marred, and I may go lead apes in hell. **1579** LYLY *Euphues* (Arb.) 75 But certes I will either lead a virgins life in earth (though I lead Apes in hel) or els follow thee. **1593-4** SHAKS. *Tam. Shrew* II. i. 34 I must dance bare-foot on her wedding-day, And, for your love to her, lead apes in hell. **1598-9** *Much Ado* II. i. 43 Therefore I will . . . lead his apes into hell . . . and there will the devil meet me . . . and say, Get you to heaven, Beatrice, get you to heaven; here's no place for you maids:' so deliver I up my apes. **1605** *London Prodigal* I. ii (*Shaks. Apoc.*) 196 *Wea.* But tis an old prouerbe, and you know it well, That women dying maides lead apes in hell. **1738** SWIFT (Dial. ii) 342 *Col.* Miss, you may say what you please; but faith you'll never lead apes in hell.

Old man in a house is a good sign, An.

1678 RAY *Adag. Hebr.* 403 . . . Old men are fit to give wise counsel.

Old man in a hurry, An,

1886 LORD RANDOLPH CHURCHILL on Gladstone, *To the Electors of South Paddington, June 1886.* [*Cf.* WELLINGTON in Greville,

Aug. 1840 I have not time not to do what is right.]

Old man is a bed full of bones, An.

1678 RAY 184. **1732** FULLER no. 648.

Old man lecher, young man liar.

c. **1250** *Ten Abuses* in *O. E. Misc.* 184 Old mon lechur, ȝunch mon lieȝer [*2nd texi* lyere.]

Old man never wants a tale to tell, An.

1732 FULLER no. 649.

Old Man of the Sea.

[In the *Arabian Nights*, the Old Man of the Sea, once seated on the shoulders of Sindbad, refused to dismount.] **1809** SCOTT *Let.* 7 Aug. in LOCKHART *Life* xix The old incumbent . . . reminds me of Sindbad's Old Man of the Sea, and will certainly throttle me if I can't somehow dismount him. **1909** *Spectator* 4 Dec. 931 If the Budget were passed, 'an Old Man of the Sea' would be sat upon the shoulders of the respectable and reputable classes in the community. **1927** *Times* 22 July 15/4 The bad habit into which we slip almost unconsciously fixes itself about our necks as firmly as any Old Man of the Sea.

Old man, when thou diest, give me thy doublet.

1678 RAY 77.

Old man who weds a buxom young maiden, An | bids fair to become a freeman of Buckingham.

1787 GROSE 152 . . . The fabricator of this proverb, by a freeman of Buckingham, meant a cuckold.

Old man will not drink, When an | go to see him in another world.

1664 CODRINGTON 227. **1666** TORRIANO 298. **1670** RAY 20. *Ital.*

Old man's staff is the rapper of death's door, An.

c. **1386** CHAUCER *Pardoner's T.* C. 727–31 And on the ground, which is my moodres gate, I knokke with my staf, bothe erly and late, And seye 'leeve mooder, leet me in!' **1640** HERBERT 359. **1732** FULLER no. 4690.

Old mare leave flinging,[1] It is hard to make an.

1721 KELLY 193 . . . It is hard to reclaim those who have been long and habitually wicked. [[1] kicking.]

Old mare would have a new crupper, My.

1546 HEYWOOD II. i. 43 What mine olde mare would haue a new crouper. **1611** DAVIES *Prov.* 185 'The old mare would have a new crupper.' **1659** HOWELL *Eng. Prov.* 2/1 Old mares lust after new cruppers.

Old men and travellers may lie by authority. (*See also* Soldiers and travellers; Traveller may lie, &c.)

a. 1607 *Lingua* D 1 Mendacio *loq.* old men ... challenge my Company by authority. 1623 CAMDEN 275 (with 'farre trauellers'). 1639 CLARKE 316.

Old men are twice children.

[ARISTOPH. *Nub.* 1417 'Εγὼ δέ γ' ἀντεί-ποιμ' ἄν, ὡς δὶς παῖδες οἱ γέροντες. I would reply that old men are twice boys. ERASM. *Ad. Bis pueri senes.*] 1539 TAVERNER f. 16 (A) Olde folke are twyse chyldren. 1549 LATIMER 2nd *Serm. bef. Edw. VI* (Arb.) 56 Kynge Dauid beynge . . . in hys second chyldhode, for al old men are twise chyldren, as the Prouerb is. *Senex bis puer.* 1600-1 SHAKS. *Hamlet* II. ii. 403 They say an old man is twice a child. 1605-6 *K. Lear* I. iii. 19 Now by my life, Old fools are babes again. 1609-10 *Cymb.* V. iii. 57 Two boys, an old man twice a boy. 1662 FULLER (*Berks.*) I. 129 In such cases native air may prove cordial to patients, as mothers' milk to (and old men are twice) children. 1821 GALT *Annals of Par.* xvi Lady Macadam; in whom the saying was verified, that old folk are twice bairns, for ... she was as play-rife as a very lassie at her sampler.

Old men go to death, death comes to young men.

1625 BACON *Apoph.* Wks. (Chandos) 379 One of the fathers saith, 'That there is but this difference between the death of old men and young men; that old men go to death, and death comes to young men'. 1732 FULLER no. 3719.

Old men, when they scorn young, make much of death.

1640 HERBERT 345.

Old man (men), *see also* Advice (If you wish good) consult o. m.; Better be an o. m.'s darling; Kindness is lost bestowed on o. m.; Wrongs not an o. m. that steals supper; Young man should not marry yet, o. m. not at all; Young man would (If) and o. m. could; Young men's knocks o. m. feel.

Old muck-hills will bloom.

1678 RAY 77.

Old naught will never be aught, An.

1678 RAY 184.

Old Nick.

[= the Devil.] 1641 MARMION *Antiquary* III (Hazlitt's Dodsley, xiii. 458), Old Nick Machiauel. *a.* 1643 in EBSWORTH *Merry Drollery* App. (1875) 394 For Roundheads Old Nick stand up now. 1668 R. L'ESTRANGE *Vis. Quev.* (1708) 84 They were all sent to Old Nick. 1774 GOLDSMITH *Retal.* 58 We wished him full ten times a day at Old Nick. 1886 BESANT *Childr. Gibeon* I. viii When you ...

made us laugh with your conceit, being always conceited as Old Nick.

Old Nick, *see also* Fond of barter that niffers with O. N.

Old of the moon, In the | a cloudy morning bodes a fair afternoon.

1639 *Berkeley MSS.* (1885) iii. 31 (A) A misty morne in th' old o' th' moone doth alwaies bring a faire post-noone. An hilly proverb about Simondsall (Glouc.). 1678 RAY 48.

Old ox makes a straight furrow, An.

1659 HOWELL *Span.-Eng.* 9 (with the streightest'). 1666 TORRIANO 30 An old oxe, a streight [furrow]. 1732 FULLER no. 650. 1823 COLLINS 69 . . . Applicable to those persons, who, guided by their judgment and experience, conduct their affairs . . . with success.

Old ox will find a shelter for himself, An.

[L. *Bos senior caute consulit ipse sibi.*] 1732 FULLER no. 651. 1823 COLLINS 4 'Do not seek a shelter for an old ox.' Alluding to old persons, who know from experience what they require.

Old oxen (stots) have stiff horns.

1832 HENDERSON 102 Auld stots hae stiff horns.

Old physician, An | and a young lawyer. (*Cf.* Young barber and an old physician.)

1640 HERBERT 347. 1642 FULLER *H. & P. State* II. i (1841) 50 Commonly, physicians, like beer, are best when they are old; and lawyers, like bread, when they are young and new. 1670 RAY 36 . . . An old physician because of his experience; a young lawyer, because he . . . will have leisure enough to attend to your business.

Old poacher makes the best keeper, An.

c. 1386 CHAUCER *Physician's T.* C. 83 A theef of venisoun, that hath forlaft His likerousnesse, and al his olde craft, Can kepe a forest best of any man. 1655 FULLER *Ch. Hist.* IX. iii (1868) II. 596 Always set a — to catch a —; and the greatest deer-stealers make the best park-keepers. 1864 PAYN *Lost Sir Massingb.* xiv If you want to find a gentleman who in his youth . . . has been a poacher . . ., look you among the game-preservers on the bench of justice.

Old pottage (porridge) is sooner heated than new made.

1670 RAY 47 . . . Old lovers fallen out are sooner reconciled then new loves begun. Nay the Comedian saith, *Amantium iræ amoris redintegratio est.* [The quarrels of lovers are the renewal of love. TER. *Andria* 3. 3. 23.] 1732 FULLER no. 3724 (with 'porridge' and 'warmed').

Old praise dies, unless you feed it.

1640 HERBERT 350.

Old sack asketh much patching, An.

1546 HEYWOOD II. ii. 47 I promise you an olde sacke axeth much patchyng. 1641 FERGUSSON 10 An old seck is ay skailing.[1] [[1] spilling.]

Old Sarbut says (told me) so.

1894 NORTHALL *Folk-phrases* (E.D.S.) 20 Old Sarbut told me so. *Warw.* A local version of 'A little bird told me so'. The mythical Sarbut . . . is credited with the revealing of secrets, and as the originator of malicious statements.

Old Scratch.

[= the Devil.] 1762 SMOLLETT *L. Greaves* II. x He must have sold himself to Old Scratch. 1843 DICKENS *Christmas C.* iv 'Well!' said the first. 'Old Scratch has got his own at last, hey?'

Old Serpent.

[= the Devil.] 1382 WYCLIF *Rev.* xx. 2 The olde serpent, that is the deuel. 1629 T. ADAMS *Med. upon Creed* Wks. (1861–2) III. 178 A serpent . . . is still his emblem. Every serpent is (as it were), a young devil, and the devil is called an 'old serpent'. 1817 MOORE *Lalla Rookh; Par. & Peri* 206, 'Some flowerlets of Eden ye still inherit, But the trail of the Serpent is over them all!'

Old sin makes new shame.

c. 1300 *Havelok* 2461 (E.E.T.S.) 69 Old sinne makes newe shame. *c.* 1350 *Douce MS. 52* no. 119 Olde synnys makyn new shamys. *c.* 1390 GOWER *Conf. Amantis* III. 2033 Men sein: 'Old Senne newe schame.' *a.* 1470 HARDYNG *Chron.* cxiv. xviii Thus synnes olde make shames come full newe. 1623 WODROEPHE 522. 1721 KELLY 269 Old sins breed new Shame.

Old soldier over one, To come the.

[= to impose on one.] 1824 SCOTT *St. Ronan's* xviii I should think he was coming the old soldier over me. 1861 HUGHES *Tom B. at Oxford* II. xvii. 331 But you needn't try to come the old soldier over me. I'm not quite such a fool as that.

Old springs[1] give no price.

1721 KELLY 273 . . . Spoken when old people or things are despised. [[1] tunes.]

Old Testament, *see* Testament.

Old thanks pay not for a new debt.

1642 TORRIANO 1 Old thanks beseem not a new gift. 1732 FULLER no. 3728.

Old, None so | that he hopes not for a year of life.

[CICERO *De Senect.* 7. 24 *Nemo enim est tam senex, qui se annum non putet posse vivere.* There is no one so old but he thinks he can live a year.] *c.* 1520 *Calisto & Mel.* in HAZL. *O.E.P.* (1874) I. 78 None so old but may live a year. 1629 T. ADAMS *Serm.* (1861–2) II. 135 Though *tam senex nemo, quin putet se annum posse vivere,*—no man is so old but still he thinks he may live another year. And therefore lightly the older, the more covetous. 1678 RAY 353.

Old thief deserves (desires) a new halter, An.

1623 CAMDEN 265. 1670 RAY 127 (desires).

Old use and wont, legs about the fire.

1721 KELLY 273 . . . A reflection on them who persevere in a bad custom.

Old vessels must leak.

1613 *Scoggins Jests* D 7 Olde vessels must needs leake. 1666 TORRIANO 163. 1732 FULLER no. 3729.

Old way, *see* Leaves the o. w. for the new.

Old wife that wats[1] her weird,[2] She is an.

1721 KELLY 285 . . . None can know what may come of them. [[1] knows. [2] fortune.]

Old wise man's shadow is better than a young buzzard's sword, An.

1640 HERBERT 321.

Old wives' tales.

c. 1200 *Ancrene Riwle* 88 Me seið upon ancren, þat euerich mest; haueð on olde cwene to ueden hire earen; ane maðelild þ maðeleð hire all þe talen of þe londe: [People say of anchoresses that almost every one hath an old woman to feed her ears; a prating gossip who tells her all the tales of the land.] 1387 TREVISA tr. *Higden* (Rolls Ser.) III. 265 And useþ telynges as olde wifes dooþ. 1509 A. BARCLAY *Ship of Fools* I. 72 A fole he is . . . to byleue the tales of an olde wife. 1542 UDALL tr. *Erasm. Apoph.* (1877) Pref. xxv Old wiues foolishe tales of Robin Hoode.

Old wives were aye good maidens.

1721 KELLY 271 . . . Old people will always be boasting what fine feats they did when they were young.

Old (Auld) wife (wives), *see also* Need makes o. w. trot; Sorrow and an evil life maketh o. w.; Tough sinew in a. w.'s heel (There is a).

Old woman in a wooden ruff, An.

1678 RAY 77 An old woman in a wooden ruff; *i.e.* in an antique dress.

Old woman, *see also* Good small beer, good o. w. (No such thing as); Good things I do not love, good o. w.

Old wood is best to burn, old horse to ride, old books to read, and old wine to drink. (Cf. Old friends, &c.)

c. 1580 SIDNEY First *Arcadia* (Feuillerat) iv

91 Old wood makes the best fire. **1589** LEO. WRIGHT *Displ. Dutie* 19 As olde wood is best to burne: old horse to ride, old bookes to reade, and old wine to drinke: so are old friends alwayes most trusty to use. **1625** BACON *Apoph.* Wks. (Chandos) 366 Alonso of Arragon was wont to say . . ., 'That age appeared to be the best in four things: old wood best to burn; old wine to drink; old friends to trust; and old authors to read. **1773** GOLDSMITH *She Stoops to C.* I. Wks. (Globe) 645 I love everything that's old: old friends, old times, old manners, old books, old wine; and . . . I have been pretty fond of an old wife.

Old young and old long. (*Cf.* Old long, &c.)

[CICERO *De Senec.* 32 *Mature fieri senem, si diu velis senex esse.* You must be an old man young, if you would be an old man long.] **1670** RAY 34 . . . This is alleged as a Proverb by Cicero.

Old, *see also* Folks grow old (When) they are not set by; Live to be o. (If you would not), be hanged young; Man is as o. as he feels'; Offspring of very o. lasts not; Sins grow o. (When) covetousness young; Well o. (He that would be) must be o. betimes.

Older and wiser.

1639 CLARKE 84 The older the wiser. **1670** RAY 126.

Olive, Call me not an | till thou see me gathered.

1640 HERBERT 331.

Omelets are not made without breaking of eggs.

[**1815** B. HAYDON *Autobiography* ch. 15 *On ne peut pas faire des omelettes sans casser les œufs.*] **1859** GEN. P. THOMPSON *Audi Alt.* II. xc. 65 We are walking upon eggs and . . . the omelet will not be made without the breaking of some. **1898** *Times* 10 Jan. 13/3 Omelettes cannot be made without breaking eggs, and war cannot be made without losses of this kind occurring.

Omittance is no quittance.

1596 SPENSER *F.Q.* IV. iii. 11 But to forbeare doth not forgive the debt. *c.* **1600** SHAKS. *A.Y.L.* III. v. 133 I marvel why I answer'd not again, But that's all one: omittance is no quittance.

Omittance, *see also* Forbearance.

Omne ignotum pro magnifico.

[TACITUS *Agricola* xxx. *Omne ignotum pro magnifico est.* Everything unknown is taken for magnificent.] **1819** LEIGH HUNT *Indicator* 8 Dec. It is better to verify the proverb, and take everything unknown for magnificent, rather than predetermine it to be worthless. The gain is greater. **1909** A. LLOYD *Every-day Japan* (1911) 235 *Omne ignotum pro mirifico....* The Japanese . . . flock to the Hibiya Park, that they may see . . . gay-coloured flowers in the trim beds, for the park is laid out in the Western style of gardening.

Once a bishop, always a bishop.

1655 FULLER *Ch. Hist.* VII. i. 28 (1868) II. 379 Latimer, by the courtesy of England ('once a bishop and ever a bishop'), was in civility saluted 'lord'.

Once a devil, always a devil.

1903 A. C. PLOWDEN *Grain or Chaff?* xxiii When a Counsel has two cases coming on at the same time in different Courts, he asks a friend to attend to one of them. Such a friend immediately becomes a 'devil'. . . . With some men it is, 'Once a devil, always a devil'; they never become anything else.

Once a knave, and ever a knave.

1659 HOWELL *Eng. Prov.* 13/1.

Once a parson (priest), always a parson (priest).

1859 G. A. SALA *Round the Clock* (1878) 290 The great case of Horne Tooke *versus* the House of Commons—'Once a priest for ever a priest.' **1865** LES. STEPHEN *Let.* 13 Jan. in *Life* (1906) ix. 158 As in this . . . country we stick to the maxim, 'once a parson, always a parson', I could not . . . go in for law. **1920** *Bookman* Sept. 192 No former celibate, with Boris's incapacity for blotting out his past, could be happy until he returned to his cell —once a priest always a priest, is a true enough motto so far as he is concerned. [On 9 Aug. 1870, an act enabling the clergy to unfrock themselves was passed. LEAN IV. 71.]

Once a use and ever a custom.

1594–5 SHAKS. *Two Gent.* V. iv. 1 How use doth breed a habit in a man. **1623** CAMDEN 275. **1670** RAY 153. **1732** FULLER no. 3733 Once in use, and ever after a custom.

Once a way (away) and aye a way (away).

1721 KELLY 274 . . . As a proverb it signifies that no private authority can stop that which has once been allowed to be a public road. As a phrase, it signifies that a thing is quite gone.

Once a whore and ever a whore.

1613 H. PARROT *Laquei Ridiculosi* ii epi. 121 (A). **1659** HOWELL *Eng. Prov.* 15/1.

Once a year a man may say, on his conscience.

1640 HERBERT 361.

Once, and use it not.

1598 DELONEY 2 *Gentle Craft* (Mann) 149. **1678** RAY 263.

Once at a coronation.

1678 RAY 263.

Once bit (bitten), twice shy.

1853 SURTEES *Sponge's Sport.* T. xxxiii

Jawleyford had been bit once, and he was not going to give Mr. Sponge a second chance. **1899** SIR A. WEST *Recoll.* xiii Mr. Thomas ... answered: 'Once bitten twice shy. I have tried one gentleman [as an apprentice] and will never try another.' **1909** *Times* 18 March The Admiralty have allowed themselves to be caught napping once, and ... they must not be caught napping again. Once bit, twice shy.

Once born, He that is | once must die.

1651 HERBERT 367.

Once deceives, He that | is ever suspected.

1640 HERBERT 337.

Once hits, He that | is ever bending.

1640 HERBERT 353.

Once in a blue moon.

1869 E. YATES *Wrecked in Port* xxii. 242 That indefinite period known as a 'blue moon'. **1876** MISS BRADDON *Josh. Haggard's Dau.* xxiv. 246 A fruit pasty once in a blue moon. **1891** A. FORBES *Barracks Biv. & Bat.* (1910) 107 It was only once in a blue moon that he was seen in the saddle.

Once in ten years, one man hath need of another.

1578 FLORIO *First Fruites* f. 33. **1732** FULLER no. 3732.

Once in the year Apollo laughs.

[L. *Semel in anno ridet Apollo.*] **1638** R. BRATHWAIT *Barnabees Jrnl.* iv. Cc (1820) 11. 401 Thou err'st (*Mirtilus*) so doe mo[1] too, If thou think'st I never goe to *Bacchus* temple, which I follow, 'Once a yeare laughs wise *Apollo.*' [[1] more.]

Once out and always out.

1654 E. GAYTON *Pleasant Notes upon Don Quixote* 5 Once out and ever out. **1678** RAY 77.

Once paid (and) never craved.

1639 CLARKE 182. **1641** FERGUSSON 8. **1721** KELLY 270 ... In the Scottish dialect, *Anes pay't ne'er cree't*; pay your debts, and prevent dunning.

Once wood[1] and aye the waur[2] (never wise).

1641 FERGUSSON 8 Anes wood, never wise. **1721** KELLY 271 ... They who have once been mad will seldom have their senses sound and well again. [[1] mad. [2] worse.]

One and all.

1662 FULLER (*Devon*) I. 416 The English nation ... had learnt also from the soldiers ... to cry out 'one and all'; each shire setting forth a remonstrance of their grievances. **1725** DEFOE *New Voy. round World* Wks. (Bohn) VI. 222 Some bold rogues upon the forecastle ... cried out, One and all, which

was a cry ... of mutiny and rebellion. **1850** KINGSLEY *Alton L.* x Mind, 'One and all', as the Cornishmen say, and no peaching.

One and none is all one.

1664 CODRINGTON 208. **1670** RAY 20. [*Hispan.*]

One and one, *see* Spindles are made (By o. and o.).

One (Two) and thirty, He is.

1593-4 SHAKS. *Tam. Shrew* I. ii. 33 Was it fit for a servant to use his master so; being, perhaps, for aught I see, two-and-thirty, a pip out? **1678** RAY 87 *Of one drunk.* ... He is one and thirty.

One bad general is better than two good ones.

1902-4 LEAN IV. 72 ... To escape divided counsels.

One book, *see* Beware of man of o. b.

One boy is more trouble than a dozen girls.

1848 BROS. MAYHEW *Image of his Father* ix. 109 She was 'dratting that young monkey', and vowing that one boy was more trouble than a dozen girls.

One, but (that one) a lion.

[AESOP *Fables* 240 (*The Lioness and the Fox*)"Ἕνα ... ἀλλὰ λέοντα.] **1692** L'ESTRANGE *Aesop's Fab.* cxxii (1738) 138 A fox cast it in the teeth of a lioness, that she brought forth but one whelp at a time. 'Very right,' says the other, 'but then that one is a lion.' **1884** H. D. TRAILL *Coleridge* iii. 48 The one long poem[1] which Coleridge contributed to the collection is alone sufficient to associate it for ever with his name. *Unum sed leonem.* To any one who should have taunted him with the infertility of his muse he might have returned the haughty answer of the lioness in the fable. [[1] *Ancient Mariner.*]

One day gives us, What | another takes away from us.

1651 HERBERT 369.

One day was three till liberty was borrow.

1546 HEYWOOD I. x. 22 Eche one daie was thrée, tyll lybertée was borow, For one monthis ioie to bryng hir hole liues sorow.

One dog, one bull.

1879 G. F. JACKSON *Shropshire Wd.-Bk.* 309 One dog, one bull, *phr.* signifies 'fair play'. This saying had its rise in the practice of bull-baiting ... which lingered in Shropshire till about ... 1841.

One door shuts, Where | another opens.

1586 D. ROWLAND tr. *Lazarillo* (1924) 32 (A) This proverb was fulfild, when one doore is shut the other openeth. **1620** SHELTON *Quix.* III. vii (1908) I. 159 They are all sentences taken out of experience itself, . . . specially that proverb that says, 'Where one door is shut, another is opened.' **1821** GALT *Annals of Par.* xxvi As one door shuts another opens; for scarcely were we in quietness by the decease of . . . Lady Macadam, till a full equivalent for her was given in this hot and fiery Mr. Cayenne. **1853** SURTEES *Sponge's Sport. T.* xliii 'When one door shuts another opens', say the saucy servants. **1853** TRENCH v. 116 To the brave and bold the world will not always be adverse. *Where one door shuts another opens.*[1] [[1] Span. *Donde una puerta se cierra, otra se abre.*]

One doth the scathe, and another hath the scorn.

1611 COTGRAVE s.v. 'Faire'. **1659** HOWELL *Eng. Prov.* 6/1. **1678** RAY 186 . . . *i.e.* One doth the harm and another bears the blame.

One eye, He that hath but | must be afraid to lose it.

1651 HERBERT 367. **1721** KELLY 128 *He that hath but one eye, must look well to that.* Spoken when a man hath but one thing of a kind, and therefore shy to lend it.

One eye, He that has but | sees the better for it.

1678 RAY 134 . . . Better than he would do without it: a ridiculous saying.

One-eyed, *see* Kingdom of blind men (In the).

One flower makes no garland.

1640 HERBERT 342.

One foe is too many; and a hundred friends too few.

1640 HERBERT (Gros.) no. 519 One enemy is too much. **1853** TRENCH iv. 81 The . . . German proverb: *One foe is too many; and a hundred friends too few.*[1] . . . The hundred friends will *wish* you well; but the one foe will *do* you ill. Their benevolence will be ordinarily passive; his malevolence will be constantly active. [[1] *Ein Feind ist zu viel; und hundert Freunde sind zu wenig.*]

One foot in the grave, To have.

[= to be near death.] **1509** A. BARCLAY *Ship of Fools* (1874) I. 44 Thy graue is open, thy one fote in the pyt. **1566** PAINTER *Pal. of Pleasure* (Jacobs) II. 109 Takyng paines to visite him, who hath one of his feet alreadie within the graue, the other stepping after with conuenient speede. **1632** MASSINGER & FIELD *Fatal Dowry* I. ii When one foot 's in the grave. **1655** FULLER *Ch. Hist.* IX. vii (1868) III. 115 A pious and godly life, which increased in his old age; so that, . . . whilst he had one foot in the grave, he had the other in heaven. **1726** SWIFT *Voy. to Laputa* x He observed long life to be the universal desire . . . of mankind. That whoever had one foot in the grave was sure to hold back the other as strongly as he could. **1886** J. PAYN *Luck Darrells* xv He has twenty thousand a year . . . And one foot in the grave.

One foot in the straw, He that hath | hath another in the spittle.[1]

1640 HERBERT 338. [[1] hospital.]

One foot is better than two crutches.

1640 HERBERT 353.

One [magpie] for sorrow: two for mirth: three for a wedding: four for a birth: five for silver: six for gold: seven for a secret, not to be told: eight for heaven: nine for hell: and ten for the devil's own sel.

a. **1846** B. HAYDON *Autobiography* Pt. 1 ch. 5 (anno 1808) The old saw, One for sorrow, two for mirth, three for a wedding, and four for death (Devonshire). **1846** DENHAM 35 One for sorrow: two for mirth: three for a wedding: four for a birth: five for silver: six for gold: seven for a secret, not to be told: eight for heaven: nine for hell: and ten for the devil's own sel. **1865** *N. & Q.* 3rd Ser. VII. 304 We shall now proceed to the magpies: II. *Cornish* 'One for sorrow, two for mirth, Three for a wedding, four for a birth'. *Welsh.* 'Piogen â chroesdra.'—A magpie and disappointment. . . . It is always an evil omen, and invariably 'one for sorrow' in this locality. [Cardigan.] **1913** A. C. BENSON *Along the Road* 162 I never see magpies myself without repeating the old rhyme: 'One for sorrow, Two for mirth, Three for a death, Four for a birth; Five, you will shortly be In a great company.'

One for the mouse, one for the crow, one to rot, and one to grow.

1850 *N. & Q.* 1st Ser. II. 515 *How to sow Beans.* 'One for the mouse, One for the crow, One to rot, One to grow.'

One God, no more, but friends good store.

1616 WITHALS 583. **1639** CLARKE 26. **1670** RAY 94.

One hog, He that hath | makes him fat; and he that hath one son makes him a fool.

1640 HERBERT 338. **1732** FULLER no. 2138.

One is no number.

[MACROB. *Comm. Somn. Scip.* 2. 8 *Monas numerus esse non dicitur.*] **1598** MARLOWE *Hero & L.* i. 255 One is no number, maides are nothing then Without the sweet societie of men. **1609** SHAKS. *Sonnets* 136. 8 Among a number one is reckoned none (cf. 8. 14). *a.* **1649** DRUMMOND (Muses *Lib.* 1. 155 Poor one no number is.

One man is worth a hundred and a hundred is not worth one.

1573 SANDFORD (1576) H 4. **1578** FLORIO *First Fruites* f. 32. **1629** *Book of Meery Riddles* Prov. 42.

One man no man.

[Gk. *Εἷς ἀνήρ, οὐδεὶς ἀνήρ.*] **1539** TAVERNER 17 Vnus uir nullus uir. One man no man. *a.* **1591** H. SMITH *Serm.* (1866) I. 8 ('A Preparative to Marriage'). We say that one is none, because he cannot be fewer than none, . . . less than one, . . . weaker than one . **1853** TRENCH vi. 135 *One man no man* . . . rests on that great truth upon which the deeper thinkers of antiquity laid so much stress—namely; that *in the idea* the state precedes the individual, man not being merely accidentally *gregarious*, but essentially *social*.

One man's will is another man's wit.

1597 J. BODENHAM *Politeuphuia* 37 b. **1647** *Countrym. New Commonwealth* 14 (A).

One of these days is none of these days.

1658 *Comes Facundus* 185. **1855** BOHN 470.

One point of a good hawk, She hath | she is hardy.

1546 HEYWOOD II. iv. 52.

One shoe will not fit all feet.

1602 J. H., *Work for Chimney-sweepers* B 3ᵛ no more then one shooe can wel serue all mens feete. **1672** WALKER 47 To make one shoe serve for all feet.

One soweth and another reapeth.

1526 TINDALE *John* iv. 37 And here in ys the sayinge true, that won soweth, and another repeth. **1590–1** SHAKS. *2 Hen. VI* III. i. 381 From Ireland come I with my strength And reap the harvest which that rascal sow'd.— **1853** TRENCH i. 5 He declares, 'Herein is that saying', or that proverb, true, *One soweth and another reapeth*'.

One tale (story) is good till another is told.

1601 WEEVER *Mirr. Mart.* A iij b One tale is good, untill anothers told. **1662** FULLER (*Kent*) II. 125 But one story is good till another is heard. . . . I met since with a supplement thereunto. **1831** MACAULAY *Ess., Sadler's Ref.* Wks. V. 482 A theory is not proved . . . merely because the evidence in its favour looks well at first sight. . . . 'One story is good till another is told!'

One thing at a time.

1825 SYD. SMITH in *Edinb. Rev.* Wks. (1839) II. 266 *Snail's Pace Argument.*—'*One thing at a time! Not too fast!*' **1868** W. W. COLLINS *Moonstone* I. xviii 'One thing at a time' said the Sergeant, . . . 'I must attend to Miss Verinder first'. **1926** *Times* 27 Feb. 13/3 'One thing at a time', as Lord Grey said . . . yesterday.

One thing at a time, and that done well, is a very good thing, as many can tell.

1885 D. C. MURRAY *Rainbow Gold* IV. vi I'm not going to have too many irons in the fire.

You know the old saying, Sarah: One thing at a time, and that done well, Is a very good thing, as many can tell.

One thing said twice deserveth a 'trudge'.

1579 LYLY *Euphues* (Arb.) 137 It is varietie that mooueth the minde of al men, and one thing said twice (as we say commonly) deserueth a trudge.[1] [[1] meaning uncertain.]

One thing thinketh the bear, and another he that leadeth him.

c. **1374** CHAUCER *Troylus* IV. 1453 And thus men seith, that 'oon thenketh the bere, But al another thenketh his ledére!' *c.* **1400** *MS. Latin no. 364, J. Rylands Libr.* (ed. Pantin) in *Bull. J. R. Libr.* XIV, f. 24 The berewarde and the bere thenken not alle on.

One thing thinketh the horse, and another he that saddles (rides) him.

1622 CÉSAR OUDIN *A Grammar Spanish and English* tr. I. W. 251. **1631** MABBE *Celestina* (T. T.) 264 (A). **1640** HERBERT 335 The horse thinks one thing, and he that saddles him another. **1670** RAY 14 The horse thinks one thing, and he that rides him another. **1732** FULLER no. 3799.

One tongue is enough for a woman.

1659 N. R. 84. [*c.* **1670**] M. PATTISON *Milton* (1883) 147 [Milton] did not allow his daughters to learn any language, saying with a gibe that one tongue was enough for a woman. **1738** SWIFT (Dial. ii) 344 *Miss.* Will you please to send me a piece of tongue? *Never.* By no means, madam: one tongue is enough for a woman. **1837** T. HOOK *Jack Brag* xi I am no great linguist. I am very much of the opinion that one tongue is sufficient for one woman.

One, two, three, four, are just half a score.

1678 RAY 86.

One year a nurse, and seven years the worse.

1641 FERGUSSON no. 31 A year a nurish, seven years a da.[1] **1663** P. STAMPOY 4. **1678** RAY 182 . . . Because feeding well and doing little she becomes liquorish and gets a habit of idleness. **1721** KELLY 270 *One year a nurse, and seven years a daw.*[1] Because that year will give her a habit of idleness. **1732** FULLER no. 6377. [[1] slut.]

One year of joy, another of comfort, and all the rest of content.

1678 RAY 63 . . . *A marriage wish.*

One year's seeding makes seven years' weeding.

1873 HARLAND & WILKINSON *Lancashire Leg.* 190 One year's seeding makes seven years weeding. **1917** BRIDGE 100 One year's seed

Seven years' weed. If weeds are neglected they increase very fast and give much trouble in eradicating them.

One's too few, three too many.
1678 RAY 342. *Somerset.*

One (can, cannot, drop of, good, had as good be, has always, is not, man may, man's, may, may be, must, never, ought to have, should, whom the), one's, *see also under significant words following.*

Onion, It will do with an.
1659 HOWELL *Eng. Prov.* 1. **1678** RAY 78.

Onion, *see also* Capon (If thou hast not a), feed on an o.

Open arms, With.
[= welcoming any chance or anybody. ERASM. *Ad. Obviis ulnis, manibus.*] *a.* **1687** COTTON *Poems* (1923) 186 I, for thy bounty well prepar'd, with open arms my blessing meet. **1735** POPE *Ep. to Arbuthnot* 142 With open arms received one Poet more. *a.* **1761** RICHARDSON *Corr.* v. 332 By whom she was received with open arms.

Open confession is good for the soul.
1721 KELLY 270 . . . Spoken ironically, to them that boast of their ill deeds. **1881** J. PAYN *Grape from Thorn* xxxix Confession may be good for the soul; but it is doubtful whether the avowal of incapacity to the parties desirous of securing our services is quite judicious.

Open confession, open penance.
1608 ARMIN *Nest Ninnies* (1842) 46 Take thy forfeit (Harry) says the foole; open confession, open penance.

Open door may tempt a saint, An.
1659 HOWELL *Span.–Eng.* 16. **1732** FULLER no. 655.

Open doors dogs come in, At.
c. **1200** *Ancrene Riwle* 60 Hund wule in bliðeliche hwar se he ivint hit open. **1641** FERGUSSON 8. **1721** KELLY 23 *At open doors dogs come benn.* And so will thieves and impertinent persons. **1826** SCOTT *Woodst.* xxxvii They say in my country, when doors are open dogs enter.

Open one's mouth wide, To.
[= to ask a high price.] **1891** C. ROBERTS *Adrift Amer.* 251 To use a vulgarism, he did not open his mouth so wide as the other, but at once offered me a through ticket to Liverpool for $72. **1898** *Daily News* 28 Oct. 3/1 Directly the word England is mentioned, the mouths of the Continental artists are opened so unconscionably wide.

Open Sesame.
[The charm used to open the door of the robbers' den in the tale of 'Ali Baba and the Forty Thieves'; hence a magic password.] **1785** *Arab. Nts. Entert.* 562 Ali Baba . . . perceiving the door, . . . said 'Open, Sesame'. **1806** SCOTT *Let.* to Ld. Dalkeith 11 Feb. in LOCKHART *Life* xv Your notoriety becomes a talisman—an 'Open Sesame' before which everything gives way. **1876** BURNABY *Ride to Khiva* ii 'From hall porters to the mistresses of those officials who give out the railway contracts, all have their price. You will find gold . . . an open sesame throughout the Russian Empire.'

Open thy purse, and then open thy sack.
1678 RAY *Adag. Hebr.* 402 Open thy purse (viz. *to receive thy money*) and then open thy sack, *i.e.* then deliver thy goods.

Open your mouth but you put your foot in it, You never.
1910 P. W. JOYCE *Eng. as We Speak* 128 To a person who habitually uses unfortunate blundering expressions: 'You never open your mouth but you put your foot in it.'

Open your pack, and sell no wares, Never.
1721 KELLY 262 . . . Never proffer your service where it is not likely to be accepted.

Openshaw, *see* Constable of O.

Opinion(s), *see* Complies against his will, of same o. still; Doctor's o. (That is but one); Plant an o. they seem to eradicate (Some); Speers all o. comes ill speed.

Oportet comes in place (When) thou knowest *miserere* has no grace, *see* Cured (What can't be) must be endured.

Opportunity is whoredom's bawd.
1617 T. HEYWOOD *Fair Maid of W.* I. iii (Merm.) 85 *Good.* Then put her to't; win Opportunity, She's the best bawd. **1636** CAMDEN 303.

Opportunity makes the thief.
c. **1220** *Hali Meidenhad* (E.E.T.S.) 17 (A) Man seið þat eise makeð þeof. *c.* **1440** in HIGDEN *Polychron.* (1865) VII. 379 At the laste bischop seide to hym 'Me thenke that oportunite makethe a thefe'. **1576** PETTIE *Petite Pall.* (Gollancz) II. 93 As a pleasant prey soon enticeth a simple thief. **1623** CAMDEN 275. **1670** RAY 129 . . . *Occasio facit furem.* Therefore, masters . . . ought to secure their moneys and goods under lock and key; that they do not give . . . a temptation to steal. **1791** I. DISRAELI *Cur. Lit.* (1858) III. 42 At another *entrée* the proverb was—*L'occasion fait le larron.* Opportunity makes the thief.

Oppression maketh a wise man mad.
1611 BIBLE *Eccles.* vii. 7. **1616** BRETON *Cross. Prov.* Wks. (1879) II. App. iii. **1895** DEAN PLUMPTRE *Eccles.* 162 *Surely oppression maketh a wise man mad.* . . . The oppressive exercise of power is so demoralizing even then the wise man, skilled in state-craft, loses his wisdom. There comes upon him, as the history of crime so often shews, something like a mania of tyrannous cruelty.

Oracle, *see* Speak like an o.

Orange that is too hard squeezed yields a bitter juice, The.

1732 FULLER no. 4696.

Orator, *see* Good o. who convinces himself; Sorrow makes silence best o.

Orchard, *see* Free of fruit that wants o.; Rob an o. when none keeps (Easy to).

Order is heaven's first law.

1734 POPE *Ess. Man.* iv. 49 Order is Heav'n's first Law. **1858** MRS. CRAIK *Woman's Thoughts* 247 'Order is Heaven's first law', and a mind without order can by no possibility be either a healthy or a happy mind. **1886** E. J. HARDY *How to be Happy* xxiv In the home more than anywhere else order is heaven's first law.

Order reigns at Warsaw.

[**1831**] **1882** BENT *Fam. Short Say.* (ed. 8) 478 After the insurrection of Warsaw . . . was subdued, . . . Sebastiani . . . announced in the Chamber of Deputies, Sept. 16, 1831, . . . 'My letters from Poland announce that order reigns in Warsaw' (*Des lettres que je reçois de Pologne m'annoncent que la tranquillité règne à Varsovie*). **1892** J. NICHOL *T. Carlyle* 202 He has no word of censure for the more settled form of anarchy which announced, 'Order reigns at Warsaw'. **1908** *Times Wkly.* 30 Oct. Sir Theodore Martin . . . said . . . 'We may yet see the glitter of the bayonet in Piccadilly. . . . Peace may only be restored in London as in Warsaw.'

Orestes, *see* Pylades and O.

Orphans, *see* Late children early o.

Orts[1] of good hay, Make not.

1639 CLARKE 262. **1670** RAY 188. [[1] leavings.]

Orts, *see also* Evening o. morning fodder.

Ossa upon Pelion, To heap (cast, pile).

[VIRGIL *Georgics* 1. 281 *Imponere Pelio Ossam.* The allusion is to the attempt of the giants, in mythology, to scale heaven by piling Mount Ossa upon Mount Pelion.] **1609** DEKKER *Gull's Horn-book* E 3v You heape *Pelion* vpon *Ossa*, glory vpon glory. **1633** T. HEYWOOD *Eng. Trav.* iv. iii (Merm.) 223 And, to suppress Your souls yet lower, without hope to rise, Heap Ossa upon Pelion. **1668** COWLEY *Essays; Of Greatness* (1906) 433 The old Gyants are said to have made an Heroical attempt of scaling Heaven in despight of the gods, and they cast *Ossa* upon *Olympus* and *Pelion* upon *Ossa*.

Ossing comes to bossing.

c. **1350** *Douce MS. 52* no. 117 Ossyng comys to bossyng. **1670** RAY 52 . . . *Chesh.* Ossing, *i.e.* offering or aiming to do. The meaning is the same, with *Courting and woing brings dallying and doing.*

Ostrich policy.

1623 *Someth. Written by Occas. Accid. Blacke Friers* 14 Like the Austridge, who hiding her little head, supposeth her great body obscured. **1837** CARLYLE *Fr. Rev.* I. i. iv Louis XV . . . would not suffer Death to be spoken of; avoided the sight of churchyards, funereal monuments, and whatever could bring it to mind. It is the resource of the Ostrich; who, hard hunted, sticks his foolish head in the ground, and would fain forget that his foolish unseeing body is not unseen too. **1891** *Pall Mall G.* 12 Sept. 1/2 The facts . . . are too damning to leave much room for an ostrich policy.

Ostrich, *see also* Stomach (Digestion) like an o.

Other man (men), *see* Beware by o. m.'s harms; Cry Yule at o. m.'s cost; Learn at o. m.'s cost.

Other people, *see* Toils like a dog, who roasts for o. p.'s eating.

Other times, other manners.

[Fr. *Autres temps, autres mœurs.*] **1892** A. DOBSON *S. Richardson* 101 Notwithstanding the favourite explanation of 'other times, other manners', contemporary critics of Clarissa found very much the same fault with her history as people do to-day.

Other(s), *see also* All came from . . . o.

Otherwise, *see* Some are wise and some o.

Ounce of discretion (mother wit), An | is worth a pound of wit (learning, clergy).

1629 T. ADAMS *Serm.* (1861–2) I. 123 The proverb is true, An ounce of discretion is worth a pound of learning. **1641** FERGUSSON 16 An ounce of mothers wit is worth a pound of clergy. **1670** RAY 79 An ounce of discretion, is worth a pound of wit. **1882** SYD. SMITH *Persecuting Bishops* in *Edinb. Rev. Wks.* (1850) 359 We are convinced of the justice of the old saying, that an ounce of mother wit is worth a pound of clergy.

Ounce of (good) fortune is worth a pound of forecast (discretion), An.

1611 COTGRAVE, s.v. 'Sagesse' An ounce of lucke excells a pound of wit. **1672** WALKER 42 (with 'discretion'). **1732** FULLER no. 657 (with 'forecast').

Ounce of mirth is worth a pound of sorrow, An.

1576 PETTIE *Petite Pall.* (Gollancz) I. 141. **1579** LYLY *Euphues* Wks. (Bond) I. 247 For euerye dramme of pleasure, an ounce of payne. *a.* **1594** *Locrine* iv. i. 102 One dramme of ioy, must haue a pound of care. **1619** B. RICH *Irish Hubbub* 4 (A) A little mirth (they say) is worth a great deale of sorrow.

Ounce of practice is worth a pound of precept, An.

1866 BLACKMORE *Cradock N.* xxxvii Remember that rigid probity, and the strictest punctuality ..., are the very soul of business, and that an ounce of practice is worth a pound of precept.

Ounce of state requires a pound of gold, An.

1573 SANDFORD (1576) H 3ᵛ. **1629** *Book of Meery Riddles* Prov. 26.

Ounce of wit that's bought is worth a pound that's taught, An.

1732 FULLER no. 6495.

Our Lady, *see* Lady.

Our Lord, *see* Lord.

Ourselves, *see* Born for o. (We are not).

Out at elbow(s), To be.

[= to be ragged.] **1590** NASHE *Almond for a Parrot* (1846) 26 Your witte wilbe welny worn thredbare, and your banquerout in-uention cleane out at the elbowes. **1604–5** SHAKS. *Meas. for Meas.* II. i. 61 He cannot [speak] Sir; he's out at elbow. **1771** SMOLLETT *Humph. Clink.* (1815) 55 Sir Ulic Mackilligut ... is said to be much out at elbows.

Out of all whooping (*or* ho).

c. **1374** CHAUCER *Troylus* II. 1083. And after that, than gan he telle his woo; But that was endeles, withouten hoo. **1546** HEYWOOD I. xi. 33 She is one of them, to whom God bad who. **1577** *Misogonus* in BRANDL *Quellen* II. iii. 442 Thoughe you thinke him past whoo, He may yet reduce him. **1599–1600** SHAKS. *A.Y.L.* III. ii. 204 O wonderful ... I out of all whooping! **1639** CLARKE 38 He hath noe whoe with him. **1711** SWIFT *Jrnl. to Stella* Lett. xx When your tongue runs, there's no ho with you, pray.

Out of debt, out of danger.

1551 ROBINSON tr. *More's Utop.* ii (Arb.) 104 Whyche to those riche men, in whose debte and daunger they be not, do giue almost diuine honoures. **1636** CAMDEN 304 Out of debt, out of deadly sinne. **1639** CLARKE 82 Out of debt and deadly danger. **1641** H. PEACHAM *Worth of a Penny* (1667) in ARBER'S *Garner* VI. 256 How bold, confident, merry, lively, and ever in humour, are Moneyed Men. [*For being out of debt, they are out of danger!*] **1908** E. M. SNEYD-KYNNERSLEY *H.M.I.* (1910) xxi Call it distributing capital expenditure over a term of years', and even a rural dean succumbs. Out of debt, out of danger', but out of debt, out of progress'.

Out of doors, *see* Step (The greatest) is that o. of d.

Out of God's blessing into the warm sun.

[i.e. from better to worse.] **1546** HEYWOOD II. v. 55 In your rennyng from him to me, ye runne Out of gods blessing into the warme sunne. **1576** PETTIE *Petite Pall.* (Gollancz) II. 146 You would ... bring me ... out of God's blessing into a warm sun. **1605–6** SHAKS. *K.*

Lear II. ii. 168 Thou out of heaven's benediction comest to the warm sun. **1616** DRAXE 6. **1655** FULLER *Ch. Hist.* III. iv (1868) I. 398 But small reason had King John to rejoice, being come out of God's blessing (of whom before he immediately held the crown), into the warm sun, or rather scorching heat of the pope's protection. **1670** RAY 177 ... *Ab equis ad asinos.* **1738** SWIFT (Dial. i) 340 *Never.* Well, she's got out of God's blessing into the warm sun.

Out of gunshot.

1551 ROBINSON tr. *Utopia* (Arb.) 26 Being themselves ... as sayeth the prouerbe, oute of all daunger of gonneshotte. **1678** RAY 249.

Out of office, out of danger.

1633 MASSINGER *New Way* II. i (Merm.) 126 *Over.* In being out of office I am out of danger; Where, if I were a justice, ... I might. ... Run myself finely into a *premunire.*

Out of season, out of price.

1595 SOUTHWELL *Losse in Delaye* Wks. (1872) 76 Tyme and place give best advice, Out of season, out of price.

Out of sight, out of languor.[1]

1641 FERGUSSON 84. **1721** KELLY 269. [1 desire.]

Out of sight, out of mind.

a. **1275** *Provs. of Alfred* B. 554 For he þat is ute bi-loken he is inne sone for-ȝeten. *c.* **1450** tr. *De Imitatione* I. xxiii. 30 Whan man is oute of siȝt, sone he passiþ oute of mynde. **1539** TAVERNER 30 Oure Englysshe prouerbe. ... Oute of syght, oute of mynde. **1608** DAY *Hum. out of B.* III. i (Merm.) 299 *Flo.* Clean out of sight? *Page.* And out of mind too, or else you have not the mind of a true woman. **1704** M. HENRY *Friendly Visits* 16 Though they are out of sight they are not out of mind. **1807–8** SYD. SMITH *Peter Plym.* iii. Wks. (1839) III. 298 Out of sight, out of mind, seems to be a proverb which applies to enemies as well as friends.

Out of the world and into Bodmin.

1893 *Murray's Handbk. Cornwall* 66 Bodmin ... seems always to have been regarded as somewhat remote and difficult of approach; and an old saw runs, 'Out of the world and into Bodmin'.

Out of the world and into Kippen.

1862 HISLOP 244 ... Kippen, in Stirlingshire, was formerly so very remote and little frequented by strangers, that a visit to it was jocularly deemed equivalent to going out of the world altogether.

Out of the world as out of the fashion, As good be.

1639 CLARKE 171. **1738** SWIFT (Dial. ii) 343 *Never.* My lord, it is better to be out of the world than out of the fashion. **1837** HOOK

Jack Brag xvi 'Yes', said Salmon, 'one may as well be out of the world as out of the fashion.'

Out of the, *see also under significant words following.*

Out, *see also* Once o. always o.

Outbid, *see* Hasty to o. another (Be not).

Outface with a card of ten, To.

[To brag, put on a bold front. 'Face' was a term at the game of Primero, see HALLIWELL *Dict.*] 1520 WHITTINGTON *Vulg.* (E.E.T.S.) 93 I set very lytle or nought by hym y^t can not face oute his ware with a carde of .x. 1593-4 SHAKS. *Tam. Shrew* II. i. 399 Yet I have fac'd it with a card of ten.

Out-Herod Herod, To.

[= To outdo Herod, represented in old Mystery Plays as a blustering tyrant, in violence.] 1600-1 SHAKS. *Hamlet* III. ii. 16 I would have such a fellow whipped for o'er-doing Termagant; it out-herods Herod. 1800 EDGEWORTH *Belinda* (1832) I. iii. 57 She out-Heroded Herod upon the occasion. 1819 *Metropolis* I. 172 Out-heroding the French cavaliers in compliment and in extravagance. 1904 H. BRADLEY *Making of English* 231 One Shaksperian phrase, 'to out-Herod Herod', . . . has become the model after which a large number of other expressions have been framed.

Out-run (*or* Over-run) the constable, To.

[At first in literal sense, later = to run into debt.] 1600 KEMP *Nine Daies Wonder* 15 (A) I far'd like one that had . . . tride the use of his legs to out-run the constable. 1663 BUTLER *Hudibras* I. iii. 1367-8 Quoth Hudibras, Friend Ralph, thou hast Outrun the constable at last. 1670 RAY 169 To outrun the constable. To spend more then ones allowance or income. 1689 SELDEN *Table-Talk* (Arb.) 76 There was another trick found out to get money, and . . . another Parliament was call'd . . . , &c. But now they have so out-run the Constable——. 1748 SMOLLETT *Rod. Rand.* xxiii 'Harkee, my girl, how far have you overrun the constable?' I told him that the debt amounted to eleven pounds. 1906 *Times Lit. Sup.* 27 April The Englishman . . . has it . . . in his mind that the natural Irishman . . . drinks hard, outrunning the constable, living from hand to mouth.

Out-shoot a man in his own bow, To.

a. 1585 MONTGOMERIE *Cherrie & Slae* lxxix. (1821) 42 In your awin bow ʒe are owreshot, Be mair than half ane inch. 1639 FULLER *Holy War* IV. vi (1840) 185 Because Rome maketh her universality such a masterpiece to boast of, let us see if the Greek church may not outshoot her in her own bow.

Oven, *see* Axle-tree for an o.; Gaping against an o. (Ill); Great doings at Gregory's; Kiln calls o. burnt-hearth; Little wood heat little o.; No man will another in o. seek; Set not your loaf till o. hot; Time to set in when o. comes to dough.

Over, Mayor of, *see* Mayor of Altrincham.

Over fast (sicker) over loose.

1641 FERGUSSON 82. 1721 KELLY 271 *O'er sicker, o'er lose.* The method taken to secure a thing often makes it miscarry.

Over head and ears.

c. 1514 BARCLAY *Eclogues* iv. 76. 1530 PALS-GRAVE 725/2 He souced him in the water over head and eares. 1533 J. HEYWOOD *Play of Love* B 4^v. Quyte ouer the eares in loue. *c.* 1540 UDALL *Roister D.* I. i. 40 Up is he to the harde eares in debt. 1665 MANLEY *Grotius' Low C. Warres* 875 The Commonwealth . . . would run over head and ears in debt. 1749 FIELDING *Tom Jones* IV. iii The poor lad plumped over head and ears into the water.

Over holy[1] was hanged, but rough and sonsy[2] wan[3] away.

1721 KELLY 271 *O'er hally[1] was hang'd[2] but rough and sonsie wan away.* Spoken against too precise people; as if those of less pretensions were more to be trusted. [[1] softly. [2] lucky. [3] got.]

Over jolly dow not.[1]

1641 FERGUSSON 84 [[1] doesn't last.]

Over shoes, over boots.

1556 J. POYNET *A Treatise* He maye bringe them ones in to the puddle ouer the shoen. 1578 G. WHETSTONE, *Promos and Cassandra* G 4 Ouer the shooes . . . yu loue. 1594-5 SHAKS. *Two Gent.* I. i. 24 *Pro.* For he was more than over shoes in love. *Val.* 'Tis true; for you are over boots in love. 1607 E. SHARP-HAM *Cupid's Whirligig* E 2. 1615 M. R. *A President for Young Pen-Men* D 1^v Not ouer bootes though ouer shoes, not gone so farre but I can come home againe. 1616 BRETON *Cross. Prov. Wks.* (1879) II. App. iii *P.* Over shoes, over boots. 1648 SANDERSON *Serm.* (1681) II. 248 Over shoes, over boots; I know God will never forgive me, and therefore I will never trouble myself to seek His favour . . . this is properly the sin of despair. 1818 SCOTT *Rob Roy* xxvi I hae taen sae muckle concern wi' your affairs already, that it maun een be ower shoon ower boots wi' me now. 1854 R. S. SURTEES *Hand. Cross* xiv Considering how far he had gone, and how h° would be laughed at if he backed out, he determined to let it be 'over shoes over boots'.

Over the left shoulder.

[= the words used express the reverse of what is really meant.] 1611 COTGRAVE S.V. 'Espaule', Ouer the shoulder, or the wrong way. 1654 E. GAYTON *Festivous Notes on Don Quixote* 186 You shall . . . fetch your enemies over the left shoulder. 1659 HOWELL *Eng. Prov.* 17 I have gott it ore the left shoulder. 1692 L'ESTRANGE *Aesop's Fab.* cccxxxviii (1738) 351 This good office over the left shoulder, is the civility that he values himself upon. He gives her his good word (as we call it) to the very end that she may be eaten. 1837 DICKENS *Pickwick* xlii Each gentleman pointed with his right thumb over his left shoulder . . . 'over the left' . . . its expression is one of light and playful sarcasm. **1838** J. C. APPERLEY *Nimrod's North. T.* 12 'Well, Mr. Guard, you made a pretty business of your last Leger'. *Guard.* 'All over the left shoulder; they drawed me of forty pound'.

Over the stile ere you come at it, You would be.

1546 HEYWOOD II. ix. 80 Like one halfe lost, till gredy graspyng gat it, Ye would be ouer the style, er ye come at it.

Overcome, *see* Endures is not o. (He that).

Over-run, *see* Out-run (O.-r.) the constable.

Overtakes, *see* Lame foot o. swift one.

Owe God a death, To.

[HOR. *A.P.* 63 *Debemur morti nos nostraque.*] **1588** G. D. *A Briefe Discovery* 125 We do all owe God a death: how shall we better pay it, then in his quarrell? **1592** *The Repentance of Robert Greene* (Harrison) 11. *a.* **1593** *Jack Straw* (Hazlitt's Dodsley V. 381). **1597–8** SHAKS. *1 Hen. IV.* V. i. 127 Why, thou owest God a death. **1681** ROBERTSON *Phraseol. General.* 969/1 I ow God a death; Debemur morti nos nostráque.

Owe(s), *see also* Has an hundred and one and o. (He that).

Oweth, He who | is in all the wrong.

1642 TORRIANO 32 He who oweth is in all the wrong [*Chi deve, hà tutti i torti*]. **1732** FULLER no. 2398.

Owing, *see* Sleep without supping, wake without o.

Owl flies, The.

1549 T. CHALONER tr. *Erasm. Praise of Folly* P 4 This other prouerbe, *The howlate flieth* (whereby was ment, that lyke as *Pallas*, to whome the howlate is consecrate, was wont to geue good . . . successe to . . . *Atheniens* purposes vnaduisedly enterprised: So that armie which had *Timotheus* ones for captaine, was euer victorious though tenne to one it should haue chaunced otherwise).

Owl in an ivy-bush, An.

c. **1540** UDALL *Roister D.* II. i. 23 With toodleloodle poope As the howlet out of an yvie bushe shoulde hoope. **1579–80** LODGE *Def. Poet.* (Shaks. Soc.) 8 Your day Owl . . . hath brought such a lot of wondering birds about your ears, as . . . will chatter you out of your ivy bush. *a.* **1611** BEAUM. & FL. *Four Plays in One* Induct. Could not you be content to be an owl in such an ivy-bush? **1738** SWIFT (Dial. i) 341 *Col.* He look'd . . . like an owl in an ivy-bush.

Owl is the king of the night, An.

1616 DRAXE 69. **1639** CLARKE 1.

Owl on stock.

[G. C. Macaulay explains as a reference to recriminations between the owl and the stock upon which he sits, on the matter of cleanliness. The application is to a man who

quarrels with his own performances. It seems to be nearly equivalent to the saying about 'the bird that fouls his own nest'.] *c.* **1390** GOWER *Conf. Amantis* III. 585 Bot Oule on Stock and Stock on Oule; The more that a man defoule, Men witen wel which hath the werse.

Owl sings, When the | the nightingale will hold her peace.

1603 BRETON *Packet Mad Let.* Wks. (1879) II. 12.

Owl thinks her own young fairest, The.

1576 U. FULWELL *Ars Adulandi* E 1 Thou knowest the fable in Æsope, that the Oule thought her owne birdes faierest. **1732** FULLER no. 4698 (with 'young ones beauties').

Owl was a baker's daughter, The.

1600–1 SHAKS. *Hamlet* IV. v. 42 They say the owl was a baker's daughter. Lord! we know what we are, but know not what we may be. [She was transformed, according to a story 'among the vulgar in Gloucestershire', for begrudging bread to Christ.]

Owls to Athens.

[Ar. *Av.* 301 Γλαῦκ' εἰς Ἀθήνας.] **1545** *Bibliotheca Eliotæ Noctuæ Athenis* Oules to Athenes. *c.* **1580** J. CONYBEARE 46. **1590** SWINBURNE *Testaments* Pref. I may be thought . . . to carrie owles to Athens, and to trouble the reader with a matter altogether needlesse and superfluous. **1591** HARINGTON *Ariosto* 40. 1 Pots to Samos, owls to Athens, crocodiles to Nile. **1853** TRENCH iii. 68 Expressing well the absurdity of sending to a place that which already abounds there, . . . the Greeks said: *Owls to Athens.*

Owl(s), *see also* Fly with the o.; Give a groat for an o. (He is in great want that will); Lived too near wood to be frightened by o.

Own hearth is gowd's worth, One's, or Own fire is pleasant, One's.

c. **1300** *Provs. of Hending* 14 Este bueth oune brondes. *c.* **1350** *Douce MS. 52* no. 54 Hit is merry a man to syt by his owne fyre. **1862** HISLOP 34 Ane's ain hearth is gowd's worth.

Own is own.

c. **1300** *Provs. of Hending* 26 Owen ys owen, and other mennes edueth. *c.* **1450** *Provs. of Wysdom* 103 Own is own and opere men is edwyte. **1546** HEYWOOD II. iv. 53 For alwaie owne is owne, at the recknyngis éend. **1659** HOWELL *Eng. Prov.* 7/1 Own is own, and home is home.

Own, *see also* Rod for his o. back; Wise that hath wit for o. affairs.

Ox before, Take heed of an | of a horse behind, of a monk on all sides.

1640 HERBERT 358. **1670** RAY 20 (with 'ass' for 'horse').

Ox falls, If the | whet your knife.

1678 RAY *Adag. Hebr.* 405 When the Ox falls, there are many that will help to kill him. The meaning is, that there are many ready to trample upon him that is afflicted. **1855** BOHN 276.

Ox go where he shall not labour?[1] Whither shall the.

1631 MABBE *Celestina* (T.T.) 78 (A) Which way shall the oxe goe, but he must needs plough? **1640** HERBERT 321. **1853** TRENCH v. 114 *Where wilt thou go, ox, that thou wilt not have to plough?[2]* is the Catalan remonstrance addressed to one, who imagines by any outward change of condition to evade the inevitable task and toil of existence. [[1] Span. *Adonde irá el buey, que no are?* [2] Cat. *Ahont anirás, bou, que no llaures?*]

Ox is never woe, till he to the harrow go, The.

1523 FITZHERB. *Husb.* § 15 It is an olde sayinge, The oxe is neuer wo, tyll he to the harowe goo.

Ox is taken by the horns, and a man by the tongue, An.

1611 COTGRAVE s.v. 'Homme' An oxe (is bound) by the horne, a man by his word. **1640** HERBERT 361.

Ox on his tongue, He has an.

[Of one who keeps silence for some weighty reason. AESCH. *Ag.* 36 τὰ δ' ἄλλα σιγῶ, βοῦς ἐπὶ γλώσσῃ μέγας βέβηκεν. L. *Bos in linguâ.* 1911 *Times Wkly.* 24 Nov. 473 [Borrow] got to know the importance of maintaining an ox upon his tongue.

Ox, An | when he is loose, licks himself at pleasure.

1732 FULLER no. 659.

Ox when weariest treads surest, The.

[*a.* 420 JEROME *Bos lassus fortius figit pedem.*] 1539 TAVERNER 3 Bos lassus fortius figit pedem. An old beaten ox fasteneth his foot the stronger. Jerome used this proverb writing to S. Augustine to fear him that he a young man should not provoke S. Jerome at that time old. **1678** RAY 186.

Ox(en), *see also* Black o. has trod on his foot; Cages for o. to bring up birds; Drives fat o. (Who); Fling at the brod ne'er a good o.; Lazy o. little better for goad; Old o. have stiff horns; Old o. straight furrow; Old o. will find shelter; St. Luke's day the o. have leave to play; Swallow an o. and be choked with tail.

Oxford draws knife, When | England's soon at strife.

1662 FULLER (*Oxford*) III. 8 *Chronica si penses, cum pugnent Oxonienses Post aliquot menses volat ira per Angliginenses.*' 'Mark the chronicles aright, When Oxford scholars fall to fight, Before many months expir'd England will with war be fir'd.' **1874** J. R. GREEN *Short Hist.* (1892) I. iii. 255 Every phase of ecclesiastical controversy or political strife was preluded by some fierce outbreak in this turbulent, surging mob.... A murderous town and gown row preceded the opening of the Barons' War. 'When Oxford draws knife', ran the old rime, England's soon at strife'.

Oxford for learning, London for wit, Hull for women, and York for a tit.[1]

a. 1871 HIGSON *MSS. Coll.*, 209 in HAZLITT 326. [[1] horse.]

Oxford is half-way to Rome.

1872 W. BLACK *Adv. Phaeton* vi 'They say that Oxford is halfway to Rome'.... But knowing what effect this reference to her theological sympathies was likely to have on Tita, I thought it prudent to send the horses on.

Oxford is the home of lost causes.

1865 M. ARNOLD *Ess. in Criticism* Pref. xix Oxford . . . Adorable dreamer . . .! home of lost causes, and forsaken beliefs, and unpopular names, and impossible loyalties. **1914** *Times Lit. Sup.* 7 Aug. 378 Oxford has often been called 'the home of lost causes', or, as Mr. Cram puts it, 'of causes not lost but gone before'.

Oxford knives, and London wives.

1659 HOWELL *Eng. Prov.* 14/1.

Oyster is a gentle thing, and will not come unless you sing, The.

1776 HERD *Scot. Songs*, '*The Dreg Song*' II. 165 The oysters are a gentle kin, They winna tak unless you sing. **1816** SCOTT *Antiq.* xl Elspeth chanting . . . 'But the oyster loves the dredging sang, For they come of a gentle kind'. **1869** HAZLITT 381.

Oysters? How do you after your.

1678 RAY 78.

Oysters are a cruel meat, because we eat them alive; an uncharitable meat, for we leave nothing to the poor; and an ungodly meat, because we never say grace. (See also Oysters are ungodly.)

1738 SWIFT (*Dial.* ii) 344 *Lady S.* They say oysters are a cruel meat, because we eat them alive: then they are an uncharitable meat, for we leave nothing to the poor; and they are an ungodly meat, because we never say grace.

Oysters are only in season in the R months.

1577 W. HARRISON *Description of England* (New Sh. S.) ii. 22 Our oisters are generallie forborne in the foure hot moneths of the yeare, that is, Maie, Iune, Iulie, and August ['which are void of the letter R' added 1587].

1599 H. BUTTES *Dyets Dry Dinner* N The Oyster . . . is vnseasonable and vnholesome in all monethes, that haue not the letter R in their name. **1678** RAY 349 Oysters are not good in a moneth that hath not an R in it. **1764** CHESTERFIELD *Lett.* cccxlvi Here is no domestic news of changes and chances in the political world, which like oysters, are only in season in the R months, when the Parliament sits. **1906** A. T. QUILLER-COUCH *Mayor of T.* xii We were talking of oyster shells. . . . You can't procure 'em all the year round. . . . You can work at your beds whenever there's an 'r' in the month, and then, during the summer, take a spell.

Oysters are ungodly, because they are eaten without grace; un-

charitable because we leave nought but shells; and unprofitable because they must swim in wine.

1611 *Tarlton's Jests* (Shaks. Soc.) 6 Oysters . . . be ungodly meate, uncharitable meat, and unprofitable meate. . . . They are ungodly, sayes Tarlton, because they are eaten without grace; uncharitable, because they leave nought but shells; and unprofitable, because they must swim in wine.

Oyster(s), *see also* Apple to an o. (As like as an); Bold man that first ate o.; Gape like an o.; Gravest fish is o.; Mayor of Northampton opens o. with dagger.

P

P's and Q's, To mind (be on), one's.

[= to be very particular as to one's words or behaviour.] **1602** DEKKER *Satiro-mastix* in Wks. (1873) I. 211 Now thou art in thy Pee and Kue. **1779** MRS. H. COWLEY *Who's the Dupe?* I. i You must mind your *P*'s and *Q*'s with him, I can tell you. **?1800** W. B. RHODES *Bomb. Fur.* iv. 30 My sword I can well use So mind your P's and Q's. *a.* **1814** *Apollo's Choice* in *Mod. Brit. Drama* IV. 208 I must be on my P's and Q's here, or I shall get my neck into a halter. **1888** C. BLATHERWICK *Uncle Pierce* i He was rather on his p's and q's.

Pace that kills, It is the.

1850 THACKERAY *Pendennis* xix You're going too fast, and can't keep up the pace, . . . it will kill you. You're livin' as if there was no end to the money . . . at home. **1901** S. LANE-POOLE *Sir H. Parkes* 365 There is an old proverb about the pace that kills, and . . . Sir Harry was killing himself by work at high pressure.

Pace, *see also* Soft p. goes far.

Paced like an alderman, He is.

1583 MELBANCKE *Philotimus* I 4 (A) Vsing an aldermans pace before he can wel gange. **1639** CLARKE 32.

Pack of cards without a knave, There is no.

1600 BRETON *Pasquils Fooles-Cappe* 26/1 Wks. (Gros.) I. 26 And yet is it in vaine such *world* to wish: There is no packe of Cardes without a *Knaue*.

Pack the cards, Many can | yet cannot play well.

1659 HOWELL *Eng. Prov.* 19/1 . . . *viz. Witty men seldom wise.*

Pack to the pins, You have brought the.

a. **1585** MONTGOMERIE *Cherrie & Slae* xciii

(1821) 49 'Suppose the pack cum to the pins, Quha can his chance eschew?' **1721** KELLY 368 . . . That is, you have dwindled away your stock.

Pack, *see also* Every one thinks his p. heaviest; Lack what they would have in their p. (Many men); Open your p. and sell no wares (Never); Silly p. that may not pay the custom; Small p. becomes small pedlar; Take part of pelf when p. a-dealing.

Pack-saddle, *see* Fault of the ass not on p.

Pad in the straw, A.

[= a lurking or hidden danger.] **1530** PALS-GRAVE 595/1 Though they make no never so fayre a face, yet there is a padde in the strawe. **1650** FULLER *Pisgah* III. II. viii. § 3 *Latet anguis in herbâ*, there is a pad in the straw, and invisible mischief lurking therein.

Paddle one's own canoe, To.

[= to make one's way by one's own exertions.] **1844** MARRYAT *Settlers in Canada* I think it much better as we all go along together that every man paddle his own canoe. **1854** SARAH T. BOLTON *Song* 'Paddle Your Own Canoe'.

Paddocks, *see* Weather meet to set p. abroad in.

Padstow Point to Lundy Light, From | is a watery grave from day to night.

1911 CROSSING *Folk Rhymes of Devon* 125 From Padstow Point to Lundy Light, Is a watery grave from day to night. . . . The coast . . . to Trevose Head, near Padstow, offers no shelter. . . . The line from Trevose to . . . the light on Lundy Island . . . is . . . regarded by the fishermen and sailors as a fatal one.

Page of your own age, Make a.

1608 ARMIN *Nest Nin.* (Shaks. Soc.) 53 The

next bootes Ile make a page of my own age, and carry home myselfe. **1616** DRAXE 30 Let him make a page of his age. **1670** RAY 189. **1738** SWIFT (Dial. i) 343 *Miss.* Make a page of your own age, and do it yourself. **1818** SCOTT *Rob Roy* xxxii Folk may just mak a page o' their ain age, and . . . gang their ain errands.

Pagoda tree, *see* Shake the p. t.

Paid, He is well | that is well satisfied.

1596–7 SHAKS. *Merch. V.* IV. i. 416 He is well paid that is well satisfied.

Paigle [= cowslip], *see* Yellow as a p.

Pail, *see* God gives the milk not the p.

Pain both to pay and pray, It is a.

1641 FERGUSSON 64.

Pain is forgotten where gain follows.

1636 CAMDEN 304. **1732** FULLER no. 3836.

Pain is gain.

1881 DEAN PLUMPTRE *Eccles.* vii. 3 *Sorrow is better than laughter.* . . . We are reminded of the Greek axiom, παθεῖν, μαθεῖν ('Pain is gain'). . . . There is a moral improvement rising out of sorrow which is not gained from enjoyment however blameless.

Pain like the gout (and toothache), There is no.

1616 BRETON *Cross. Prov. Wks.* (Gros.) II. App. iii *P.* There is no paine like the Gowt. *C.* Yes, the Tooth-ach.

Pain to do nothing than something, It is more.

1640 HERBERT 357.

Pains is the price that God putteth upon all things.

[EPICHARMUS τῶν πόνων πωλοῦσιν ἡμῖν πάντα τἀγάθ' οἱ θεοί.] **1648** HERRICK *Hesp.* (Muses Lib.) 471 Jove will not let his gifts go from him if not bought with sweat. **1659** HOWELL *Eng. Prov.* 19/2.

Pains to get, care to keep, fear to lose.

1616 DRAXE 181 There is paine in getting, care in keeping, and griefe in losing riches. **1651** HERBERT 362.

Pain(s), *see also* Great p. and little gain soon weary; Great p. quickly find ease; Labour for one's p. (To have one's); Like punishment and equal p. key and keyhole sustain; No p. no gains; Nothing to be got without p.; Take a p. for a pleasure.

Painted pictures are dead speakers.

1616 BRETON *Cross. Prov. Wks.* (Gros.) II. e 5 Painted creatures are dead speakers. **1678** RAY 20.

Paint(s, ed), *see also* Fresh as p.; Makes much

of his p. sheath; Woman and a cherry are p. for harm; Woman that p. puts up a bill.

Painter, *see* God or a p. (He is either a); Good p. can draw a devil.

Painter (of a boat), *see* Cut the p.

Painters and poets have leave to lie.

[HOR. *A.P.* 9 *Pictoribus atque poetis quidlibet audendi semper fuit aequa potestas.*] **1591** HARINGTON *Apol. of Poetrie* par. 3 According to that old verse . . . Astronomers, painters, and poets may lye by authoritie. **1639** CLARKE 131. **1641** FERGUSSON 86.

Painting and fighting look aloof, On.

1640 HERBERT 328. **1721** KELLY 273 *On painting and fighting look abigh.*[1] It is dangerous to be near the one, and if we look near the other it loseth much of its advantage. [1 at a distance.]

Painting. *see also* Blind man's wife needs no p.; Woman's p. breed stomach's fainting (Let no).

Pair of ears draws dry a hundred tongues, One.

1640 HERBERT 342.

Pair of heels, One | is often worth two pair of hands.

1575 *Gamm. Gurton* IV. ii. 77 *Chat.* If one pair of legs had not bene worth two paire of hands He had had his bearde shaven if my nayles wold have served. **1659** HOWELL *Eng. Prov.* 2/1. **1678** RAY 153 . . . Always for cowards. The *French* say, Qui n'a cœur ait jambes; and the *Italian* . . . , Chi non ha cuore habbi gambe. He that hath no heart let him have heels. **1820** SCOTT *Monast.* xiii I . . . made two pair of legs (and these were not mine, but my mare's) worth one pair of hands. . . . I e'en pricked off with myself.

Pair of heels, *see also* Show a fair p. of h.

Pair of shears between them, There went but a.

[They match each other as if cut from the same piece of cloth.] **1579** LYLY *Euphues Wks.* (1902) I. 195 The *Sympathie* of affections and as it were but a payre of sheeres to go betweene their natures. **1604–5** SHAKS. *Meas. for Meas.* I. ii. 29 *Luc.* Thou thyself art a wicked villain, despite all grace. *First Gent.* Well, there went but a pair of shears between us. **1632** *Star Chamber Cases* (Camden) 98 There went but a paire of sheeres between a Papist and a Protestant, and not a pinne to choose of what religion a man is.

Paisley, *see* Glasgow people . . . P. bodies.

Palate, *see* Purse and his p. ill met.

Pale as death, As.

1567 PAINTER *Pal. of Pleasure* (Jacobs) iii. 9 (A) The colour whereof is more pale than death. **1751** FIELDING *Amelia* VI. ix She turned as pale as death. **1818** SCOTT *Ivanhoe* ix 'Over God's forebode!' said Prince John, involuntarily turning . . . as pale as death.

Pale man, *see* Red man (To a) read thy rede.

Pale moon doth rain, red moon doth blow: white moon doth neither rain nor snow.

1639 CLARKE 263.

Paleness of the pilot is a sign of a storm, The.

1594 GREENE *Looking-Glass* IV. i (Merm.) 130 *Mast.* Our bark is batter'd by encountering storms, . . . The steersman, pale and careful, holds his helm. **1666** TORRIANO 169 (31).

Palm oil.

[= bribery.] **1907** H. DE WINDT *Through Savage Europe* xviii My mission . . . was eventually accomplished, chiefly by the aid of 'palm oil'. **1929** *Times* 12 Jan. 14/3 With a little 'palm oil' you have been able to . . . get back the stolen property.

Paltock's Inn.

[= a poor place.] **1579** GOSSON *Sch. Abuse* (Arb.) 52 Comming to *Chenas* a blind village, in comparison of *Athens* a Paltockes Inne.

Pan, *see* Turn the cat in p.

Pancake(s), *see* Flat as a p.; Thatch Groby Pool with p.

Pandora's Box.

[Jupiter gave Pandora a box containing all human ills, which flew forth when the box was opened: but at the bottom was Hope.] **1579** GOSSON *Sch. Abuse* (Arb.) 44 I cannot lyken our affection better than to . . . *Pandoraes* boxe, lift vppe the lidde, out flyes the Deuill. **1621** BURTON *Anat. Mel.* I. i. I. i (1651) 2 The sin of our first parent Adam . . . shadowed unto us in the tale of Pandoras box, which, being opened through her curiosity, filled the world full of all manner of diseases. **1679** J. GOODMAN *Penit. Pardoned* II. i (1713) 264 There may be some hope left in the bottom of this Pandora's box of calamities. **1888** J. E. T. ROGERS *Econ. Interp. Hist.* (1894) xvii The favours of Government are like the box of Pandora, with this important difference, that they rarely leave hope at the bottom.

Panem et circenses, *see* Bread and circuses.

Pannier, *see* Mock no p. men.

Pantofles,[1] To stand (be, &c.) upon (one's).

[= to be on one's dignity.] **1573** G. HARVEY *Letter-bk.* (Camden) 14 He was now altogither set on his merri pinnes and walked on his stateli pantocles. **1579** LYLY *Euphues* (Arb.) 47 For the most part they stand so on their pantuffles. **1616** DRAXE 214 He standeth too much on his pantofles. **1685** BUNYAN *Pharisee & Publ.* Wks. (1845) 140 Thou standest upon thy points and pantables, thou wilt not bate God on all of what thy righteousness is worth. [1 slippers, pattens.]

Pap with a hatchet.

1589? LYLY (*title*) Pappe with an Hatchet. **1592** G. HARVEY *Foure Lett.* ii. Wks. (Gros.) I. 164 I neither name Martin-mar-prelate: nor shame Papp wyth a hatchet. **1594** LYLY *Moth. Bomb.* I. iii. 104 They give us pap with a spoone before we can speake, and when we speake for that we love, pap with a hatchet. **1615** A. NICCHOLES *Disc. Marr.* ix. 30 He that so olde seekes for a nurse so yong, shall have pappe with a Hatchet for his comfort. **1909** M. LOANE *Englishman's Castle* viii The poor are extremely sensitive to small amenities. . . . 'Pap with an hatchet' may be all very well among social equals, but more ceremony is needed when there is a gap . . . between the persons concerned.

Paper, *see* Fairer the p. fouler blot; Youth and white p. take any impression.

Papist, *see* Christian (A complete) must have works of a P.

Paradise, *see* Enter into P. must have good key.

Paramour(s), *see* Hunting, hawking, and p.; Puddings and p. should be hotly handled.

Parched pea on a griddle, Like a.

1896 J. C. HUTCHESON *Crown & Anchor* iv The wiry little . . . waiter . . . was hopping about the room 'like a parched pea on a griddle'.

Pardon all but thyself.

1611 COTGRAVE S.V. 'Pardonner'. **1640** HERBERT 349.

Pardon makes offenders.

1604–5 SHAKS. *Meas. for Meas.* II. i. 307 Pardon is still the nurse of second woe. **1639** CLARKE 182.

Pardon of Maynooth.

[1535] FROUDE *Hist. Eng.* (1856–70) II. viii The prisoners . . . under the ruins of their own den,[1] were hung up for a sign to the whole nation. . . . In the presence of this 'Pardon of Maynooth', as it was called, the phantom of rebellion vanished on the spot. [1 the castle of Maynooth.]

Pardoning the bad is injuring the good.

1732 FULLER no. 3842.

Pardons and pleasantness are great revenges of slanders.

1640 HERBERT 334.

Pardon(s) (*noun*), *see also* Fault is (Where no) needs no p.; Never ask p. before you are accused; No penny no p.

Pardon(s) (*verb*), *see also* Offender never p.

Parent(s), *see* God, and p. . . . can never be requited.

Paring of his nails, He will not part with the.

1546 HEYWOOD I. xi. 33 She will not part with the paryng of hir nayles. **1639** CLARKE 37. **1670** RAY 184 He'll not lose the pairing of 's nails.

Parings of a pippin are better than a whole crab, The.

1732 FULLER no. 4701.

Paris, *see* Americans when they die.

Parish(es), *see* Estate in two p.

Parish clerk, *see* Too hasty to be p. c.

Parish priest forgetteth that ever he hath been holy water (parish) clerk, The.

1533 J. HEYWOOD *John, Tyb, &c.* (Farmer) 86 (A) But now I see well the old proverb is true; That parish priest forgetteth that ever he was clerk. **1546** HEYWOOD I. xi. 31 And now nought he setteth By poore folke, For the paryshe priest forgetteth That euer he hath bene holy water clarke. **1548** HALL *Chron.* (1809) 387 But when he was once crouned King . . . he cast aside his old cōdicions . . . verefieng ye old prouerbe, honoures chaunge maners, as the parishe prest remembreth that he was neuer parishe clerck. **1599** PORTER *Angry Wom. Abingd.* II. i (Merm.) 120 Hark, mother, hark! The priest forgets that e'er he was a clerk: When you were at my years, . . . Your mind was to change maidenhead for wife.

Parish top,[1] Like a.

1599–1600 SHAKS. *Twelfth N.* I. iii. 45 *Sir To.* He's a coward . . . that will not drink . . . till his brains turn o' the toe like a parish-top. *c.* **1616** FLETCHER & MASS. *Thierry & Theod.* II. iii A boy of twelve Should scourge him hither like a parish-top. [[1] a large top provided for the use of peasants in frosty weather.]

Parleys, *see* City (Castle, Woman) that p.; Valour that p.; Virtue which p.

Parliament can do everything but turn a boy into a girl.

1902–4 LEAN IV. 79.

Parnassus has no gold mines in it.

1732 FULLER no. 3844.

Parnell, *see* Madame P. crack the nut; Tender as P. that broke her finger.

Parrot, *see* Almond for a p.; Prate like a p.

Parsley bed.

1622 MABBE tr. *Aleman's Guzman d'Alf.* I. 25 *margin* That phrase which we vse to little children, when we tell them they were borne in their mothers Parsly-bed. **1796** PEGGE *Anonym.* I, § 91 (1809) 52 The child, when new-born, comes out of the persley bed, they will say in the North.

Parsley fried will bring a man to his saddle, and a woman to her grave.

1678 RAY 345.

Parsley, *see also* Welsh p.

Parson (Priest) always christens his own child first, The.

1670 RAY 129 'Tis good christening a man's own child first. **1721** KELLY 310 *The priest christens his own bairn first.* An apology for serving ourselves before our neighbours. **1738** SWIFT (Dial. i) 335 *Never.* Miss, will you be so kind as to fill me a dish of tea? *Miss* . . . I'm just going to fill one for myself; and, you know, the parson always christens his own child first. **1927** E. V. LUCAS in *Times* 15 Mar. 18/1 Jamaican proverbs . . . I quote a few . . . 'Parson christen him own piccanniny first.'

Parson of Saddleworth,[1] Like the | who could read in no book but his own.

1670 RAY 209 . . . *Chesh.* [[1] In Yorkshire, but belonging, ecclesiastically, to the parish of Rochdale, Lancs.]

Parson Smith, *see* Smith.

Parson's cow, To come home like the | with a calf at her foot.

1670 RAY 209 . . . *Chesh.* **1917** BRIDGE 333 . . . Said of a girl returning home with an addition to the family. Sometimes said of one who has succeeded well in business and greatly increased his store.

Parson's pig, *see* Poor and peart like p.'s p.

Parsons are souls' waggoners.

1640 HERBERT 360.

Parsons than parish churches, There are more.

1894 NORTHALL *Folk-phrases* (E.D.S.) 25.

Parson(s), *see also* Good enough for the p. unless parish better; House-going p., church-going people; Long standing . . . maketh poor p.; Michaelmas chickens and p.'s daughters; Once a p. always a p.; Pinch on the p.'s side; Tender as a p.'s leman.

Part with the crock as the porridge, She will as soon.

1678 RAY 352 *Somerset.*

Part with, *see also* Paring of his nails.

Part (*verb*), *see also* Baker to the pillory (Fear we p. not yet, quoth).

Parthian shaft (shot).

[The Parthians discharged their arrows while retreating; now used figuratively.] **1902** GREENOUGH & KITTREDGE *Words* 380 A

'Parthian shot' was very literal to Crassus[1] . . .: to us it is only an elegant and pointed synonym for our method of 'having the last word'. [[1] 53 B.C.]

Parthian war.

1629 T. ADAMS *Serm.* (1861–2) I. 222 The best way to conquer sin is by Parthian war, to run away. So the poet—'Sed fuge; tutus adhuc Parthus ab hoste fuga est.'

Parting of the ways, To be (stand) at the.

1611 BIBLE *Ezek.* xxi. 21 For the King of Babylon stood at the parting of the way, at the head of the two ways, to use divination. **1928** *Times* 29 May 8/4 India is at the parting of the ways, and needs the services of her best sons.

Parting, *see also* Careless p. between mare and cart; Little intermeddling fair p.; Sorrow is at p. if at meeting laughter.

Partington, Mrs., *see* Mrs. P. mopping up Atlantic.

Partridge had the woodcock's thigh If the | it would be the best bird that ever did fly.

1670 RAY 44. **1732** FULLER no. 6400.

Pasch, *see* Green Yule and white P. . . . fat churchyard; Yule feast may be done at P.

Pass of Alton, Through the | poverty might pass without peril of robbing.

['The wooded pass of Alton, on the borders of Surrey and Hampshire, . . . was a favourite ambush for outlaws.' Quoted in SKEAT *P. Pl.* II. 213.] **1393** LANGLAND *P. Pl.* C. xvii. 139 Thorw the pas of Altoun Pouerte myghte passe · with-oute peril of robbynge.

Pass (through) the pikes, To.

[= to pass through difficulties or dangers.] **1560** T. PALFREYMAN *A Mirror or clear glass* D 5 Thou hast escaped a scowringe, or passed thorough the pykes. **1567** G. FENTON *Bandello* (T.T.) I. 239 At the leaste, hee wolde graunte him dispence and saffe conduit To passe thorow the pikes of his infortunat dangers. **1611** CHAPMAN *May-Day* III. ii (1874) 291 Y'ave past the pikes i' faith, and all the jails of the love-god swarm in yonder house, to salute your recovery. **1616** JONSON *Masque of Christmas* Wks. (1903) III. 106 I bring you a masque . . . Which say the King likes, I ha' passed the pikes. **1785** COWPER *Let. to Lady Hesketh* 30 Nov. Wks. (1836) V. 187 So far, therefore, I have passed the pikes. The Monthly Critics have not yet noticed me.

Passage, *see* Worse the p., more welcome port.

Passeth a winter's day, He that | escapes an enemy.

[**14..** Fr. *Prov. communs.* Qui passe un jour

d'yver si passe un de ses ennemis mortelz.] **1640** HERBERT 356.

Passing bell, *see* Hear a toll or knell.

Passion, *see* End of p. beginning of repentance.

Past cannot be recalled, Things.

1546 HEYWOOD I. x. 21 But thingis past my handis, I can not call agein. **1594** LYLY *Moth. Bomb.* IV. i *Dro.* I am sure you are not angry, seeing things past cannot be recalled. **1616** DRAXE 151 That that is past, cannot be recalled or helped. **1802** EDGEWORTH *Pop. Tales, Rosanna* iii Since a thing past can't be recalled, . . . we may be content.

Past cure, past care.

1593 GREENE *Wks.* (Gros.) II. 154 (A) Remember the olde prouerbe, past cure, past care. **1594–5** SHAKS. *L.L.L.* V. ii. 28 Great reason; for 'past cure is still past care'. **1595–6** *Rich. II.* II. iii. 171 Things past redress are now with me past care. **1598** DRAYTON *Her. Epist., Rich. II to Q. Isabel* (1603) 40 Comfort is now vnpleasing to mine eare, Past cure, past care, my bed become my Beere. **1609** SHAKS. *Sonn.* 147, 9 Past cure I am, now Reason is past care. **1610–11** *Wint. T.* III. ii. 223 What's past help Should be past grief.

Past dying of her first child, She is.

1678 RAY 240 . . . *i.e.* she hath had a bastard.

Past shame, past amendment (grace).

c. **1530** REDFORD *Wit & Sci.* 840 As the sayeng is, and daylye seene—Past Shame once, and past all amendment. **1609–10** SHAKS. *Cymb.* I. i. 136 *Cym.* O disloyal thing . . . Past grace? obedience? *Imo.* Past hope, and in despair; that way, past grace. **1692** J. RAY *Dissoln. & Changes of World* 214 Doth not the Scripture condemn a Whore's forehead? Is it not a true Proverb, Past Shame, past Grace?

Paston poor, There never was a | a Heyden a coward, nor a Cornwallis a fool.

1678 RAY 327. Norfolk.

Pasture, *see* Break a p. makes a man (To); Change of p. makes fat calves.

Patch and long sit, build and soon flit (*or* Botch and sit, build and flit).

1618 W. LAWSON *New Orchard & Garden* (1676) 9 Tenants who have taken up this proverb *Botch and*, &c. **1664** CODRINGTON 209. **1670** RAY 16.

Patch by patch is good housewifery, but patch upon patch is plain beggary.

1639 *Berkeley MSS.* (1885) iii. 33 (A) Patch by patch is yeomanly; but patch vpon patch is beggerly. **1670** RAY 129. **1732** FULLER no. 6181.

Patent, see Nothing p. in New Testament.

Pater noster built churches, and *Our Father* pulls them down.

1616 T. ADAMS *Gallant's Burden* 35 Common Prophane persons . . . that make the profession of the Gospell haue an euill name: hence that Prouerbe, *Pater noster*, set vp Churches, *Our Father*, pulles them downe. **1644** FULLER *Jacob's Vow* in *Sel. Serm.* (1891) I. 426 Will yourselves . . . suffer the houses of God to lie waste? Shall *Pater noster* build churches, and *Our Father* pull them down (as the proverb is)? or suffer them to fall? **1670** RAY 70 . . . I do not look upon the building of Churches as an argument of the goodness of the Roman religion, for . . . its easier to part with ones goods then ones sins.

Paternoster, He may be in my | but he shall never come in my creed.

1546 HEYWOOD II. ix. 79 He maie be in my Pater noster in déede. But be sure, he shall neuer come in my Créede. **1629** T. ADAMS *Serm.* (1861–2) II. 247 [Flatterers] are . . . the commonwealth's wolves. Put them in your *Paternoster*, let them never come in your creed: pray for them, but trust them no more than thieves.

Paternoster, see also No p. no penny; No penny no p.; Patter the devil's p.

Path hath a puddle, Every.

1640 HERBERT 327. **1818** SCOTT *Rob Roy* xxxviii Ye hae had your ain time o't, Mr. Syddall; but . . . ilka path has its puddle.

Patience and flannel for the gout.

1732 FULLER no. 3856 Patience is good for abundance of things besides the gout. **1738** SWIFT (Dial. iii) 351 *Lady A.* He's laid up with the gout . . . I hear he's weary of doctoring it, and now makes use of nothing but patience and flannel.

Patience, and shuffle the cards.

1620 SHELTON *Quix.* II. xxiii (1908) II. 345 If it be otherwise, O cousin, I say, patience and shuffle. [*Note.* Card-players . . . when they lose, cry to the dealer, 'Patience and shuffle the cards.'] **1810** SCOTT *Let. Joanna Baillie* 23 Nov. in LOCKHART *Life* xxi But, as Durandarte says. . . . —'Patience, cousin, and shuffle the cards.'

Patience[1] grow in your garden alway, Let.

1550 HEYWOOD I. xi. 37. **1611** DAVIES Prov. 374 'Let patience still in your garden appeare.' [[1] a species of Dock; *Rumex Patientia*, Linn.]

Patience, He that hath | hath fat thrushes for a farthing.

1640 HERBERT 337.

Patience in adversity bringeth a man to the Three Cranes in the Vintry.

1599 PORTER *Angry Wom. Abingd.* IV. iii

(Merm.) 177 *Nich.* I am patient, I must needs say, for patience in adversity brings a man to the Three Cranes in the Vintry. **1616** DRAXE 152.

Patience is a flower that grows not in every one's garden.

1616 DRAXE 152 Patience is an excellent hearbe, but it groweth not in a womans head. **1644** HOWELL *Lett.* 1 Dec. (1903) I. 96 No more, but that I wish you patience, which is a flower that grows not in every garden. **1670** RAY 21 . . . *Herein is an allusion to the name of a Plant so called*, i.e. Rhabarbarum Monachorum.

Patience is a plaster for all sores.

c. 1390 GOWER *Conf. Amantis* III. 614 Pacience . . . is the leche of alle offence, As tellen ous these olde men. **a. 1591** H. SMITH *Serm.* (1866) I. 230 Among the strange cures of patience, David may report of his experience what this plaster has done for him. **1639** CLARKE 15. **1885** E. P. HOOD *World of Prov.* 72 The large store of proverbs inculcating a cheerful endurance of the ills of life. . . . 'Patience is a plaister for all sores.'

Patience is a virtue.

1377 LANGLAND *P. Pl.* B xi. 370 (A) Suffraunce is a souereygne vertue. **c. 1386** CHAUCER *Franklin's T.* 773 Pácience is an heigh vertú, certeyn. **1594** LYLY *Moth. Bomb.* v. iii *Memp.* Well, patience is a virtue, but pinching is worse than any vice! **1618** BEAUM. & FL. *Loy. Sub.* III. ii *Theo.* Study your Vertue, Patience, It may get Mustard to your Meat. **1753** RICHARDSON *Grandison* (1812) II. xvii. 137 Aunt Prue in Yorkshire . . . will be able to instruct you, that patience is a virtue; and that you ought not to be in haste to take a first offer, for fear you should not have a second.

Patience is the best remedy (medicine).

1578 FLORIO *First Fruites* f. 44 Pacience is the best medicine that is, for a sicke man, the most precious plaister that is, for any wounde. **a. 1763** SHENSTONE *Detached Thoughts on Men and Manners* Patience is the Panacea; but where does it grow and who can swallow it?

Patience perforce.

c. 1570 *Marriage of Wit and Wisdom* (Halliwell) 2. **1575** GASCOIGNE *Patience Perforce* [title of poem]. **1584** *Three Ladies of London* in HAZLITT *O.E.P.* VI. 303 He must have patience perforce, seeing there is no remedy. **1592–3** SHAKS. *Rich. III* I. i. 116 *Glo.* Meantime, have patience. *Clar.* I must perforce. **1594–5** *Rom. & Jul.* I. v. 93 Patience perforce with wilful choler meeting Makes my flesh tremble in their different greeting. **1596** SPENSER *F. Q.* II. iii. 3 Patience perforce: helplesse what may it boot To frett for anger, or for griefe to mone? **1837** SOUTHEY *Lett. Mrs. Hughes* 7 Dec. 'Patience perforce' was what I heard of every day in Portugal,— . . . it *must* be practised at last, whether you like it or not.

Patience perforce is medicine for a mad dog.

1606–7 SHAKS. *Ant. & Cleop.* IV. xiii Patience is sottish and impatience does become a dog that's mad. **1659** HOWELL *Eng. Prov.* 9/2.

Patience, time and money accommodate all things.

1640 HERBERT 341.

Patience under old injuries invites new ones.

1617 MORYSON *Itin.* III. i. 25 (1907–8) III. 400 Some dissuade men from being patient in their conversation, saying that he invites a new injury, who bears the old patiently.

Patience with poverty is all a poor man's remedy.

14 Sept. **1605** J. CHAMBERLAIN *Letters* (McLure) i. 207 Patience is the poore mans vertue. **1639** CLARKE 15. **1670** RAY 130.

Patience, *see also* God take the sun (Though), we must have p.; Nature, time and p. . . . physicians; Peace and p., and death with repentance; Preacheth p. that never knew pain; Remedy but p. (No); Travel through world necessary to have . . . money and p.

Patient as Job, As.

1509 A. BARCLAY *Ship of Fools* (1874) I. 113. **1597–8** SHAKS. *2 Hen. IV* I. ii. 145 I am as poor as Job, my lord, but not so patient. **1643** MILTON, *Divorce* I. viii. Wks. (1851) 39 Job the patientest of men. **1908** *Confessio Medici* 83 *Talk of the patience of Job*, said a Hospital-nurse, *Job was never on night-duty.*

Patient Grisel.

c. **1386** CHAUCER *Clerk's T.* 1177 Grisilde is deed, and eek hire pacience. **1593–4** SHAKS. *Tam. Shrew* II. i. 289 For patience she will prove a second Grissel. **1818** SUSAN FERRIER *Marriage* xlvii Your patient Grizzles make nothing of it, except in little books: in real life they become perfect packhorses, saddled with the whole offences of the family. **1892** SIR H. MAXWELL *Meridiana* 155 The part she had to play in life is known to have been the patient Grizel' business.

Patient men win the day.

c. **1382** GOWER *Vox Clam.* iii. 409 *Vincit qui patitur; si vis vincere, disce pati.* c. **1386** CHAUCER *Franklin's T.* F² 773 Patience . . . venquysseth, as thise clerkes seyn, Thynges that rigour sholde nevere atteyne. **1393** LANGLAND *P. Pl.* C. xvi. 138 Quath Peers the Plouhman . '*pacientes uincunt*'. **1639** CLARKE 242 . . . Vincit qui patitur. **1853** TRENCH v. 116 As the Italians say: *The World is for him who has patience.*[1] [¹ Il mondo è di chi ha pazienza.]

Patient (*adj.*), *see also* Served must be p. (He that will be).

Patient (*noun*), *see* Physician owes all to p.

Patriotism is the last refuge of a scoundrel.

1775 JOHNSON in *Boswell* (1848) xlix. 446 Johnson suddenly uttered . . . an apophthegm, at which many will start: 'Patriotism is the last refuge of a scoundrel.'

Patter the devil's paternoster, To.

c. **1386** CHAUCER *Pars. T.* I. 434 Yet wol they seyn harm and grucche and murmure priuely for verray despit, whiche wordes men clepen the deueles Pater noster. **1530** PALSGRAVE 642/1 I murmure, I make a noyse, I bydde the dyuels Paster noster. **1546** HEYWOOD I. xi. 32 Pattryng the diuels Pater noster to hir selfe. **1665** J. WILSON *Projectors* II. i (1874) 231 How he mumbles the devil's *paternoster*! **1678** RAY 264 He is pattring the Devils *Pater Noster*. When one is grumbling to himself and it may be cursing those that have angred or displeased him.

Paul Pry.

[*Paul Pry*; a very inquisitive character in comedy of same name by John Poole; 1825.] **1829** MACAULAY *Ess., Southey* v. 348 He conceives that . . . the magistrate . . . ought to be . . . a Paul Pry in every house, spying, eaves-dropping. **1902** A. E. W. MASON *Four Feathers* xiii Blindness means to all men . . . continual and irritable curiosity—there is no Paul Pry like your blind man.

Paul's pigeons.

[= scholars of St. Paul's School, London.] **1662** FULLER (*London*) II. 357 Nicholas Heath was . . . one of St. Anthony's pigs therein (so were the scholars of that school commonly called, as those of St. Paul's, Paul's pigeons).

Paul's will not always stand.

1593 G. HARVEY *Wks.* (Gros.) i. 297 (A) Powles steeple, and a hugyer thing is doune. **1659** HOWELL *Eng. Prov.* Dedn. *We live in those destructive fatall Times, that are like to verifie a very ancient Proverb of that stately Temple*[1] . . . viz. Pauls cannot alwayes stand, *alluding to the lubricity of all sublunary things. Ibid.* 6/1 *Pauls* will not always stand. [¹ St. Paul's Cathedral.]

Paul's, *see also* Old as P.; Westminster for a wife, P. for a man (Who goes to).

Paunches, *see* Fat p. have lean pates.

Paut, *see* Ill p. with her hind foot (She has).

Pawn, *see* Fair p. never shamed his master.

Paws off, Pompey.

1834 MARRYAT *Jacob Faith.* xii Although she liked to be noticed so far by other chaps, yet Ben was the only one she ever wished to be handled by—it was 'Paws off, Pompey', with all the rest.

Pax Britannica.

1896 R. S. S. BADEN-POWELL *Downf. of Prempeh* 17 Mr. Chamberlain . . . put it thus: . . . 'I think the duty of this country . . . is to establish . . . *Pax Britannica*, and force these people to keep the peace amongst themselves.' **1911** *Spectator* 10 June 882 Nearly half the revenue of [South Nigeria] is derived from the duty imposed on spirits. . . . Is this to be the result of the boasted *Pax Britannica*?

Pay beforehand was never well served.

1591 FLORIO *Sec. Frutes* 39 He that paieth afore hand, hath neuer his worke well done. **1721** KELLY 278 . . . It is common to see tradesmen, and labourers, to go about a piece of work with great uneasiness, which is to pay a just debt. **1732** FULLER no. 2245. **1819** SCOTT *Bride Lam.* iii 'Your honour is the bad paymaster', he said, 'who pays before it is done.'

Pay, He that cannot | let him pray.

1611 COTGRAVE s.v. 'Argent'. **1670** RAY 130. **1732** FULLER no. 6362.

Pay (Paid) for, *see* Drunk (What you do) you must p. f. sober; Purse opened not when it was p. f. (Your).

Pay more for your schooling than your learning is worth, You.

1639 CLARKE 59. **1732** FULLER no. 5955 You may pay for your schooling more than your learning is worth.

Pay not a servant his wages, If you | he will pay himself.

1732 FULLER no. 2778.

Pay one in his own coin, To.

1589 GREENE *Tullies Loue* in Wks. (Gros.) VII. 133 Lentulus . . . paide hir his debt in hir owne coine. **1639** FULLER *Holy War* II. xxiv (1840) 80 [Baldwin] played on them freely to their faces; yea, and never refused the coin he paid them in, but would be contented . . . to be the subject of a good jest. **1655–62** GURNALL *Chrn. in Armour* (1865) I. 391 Now when he [Joseph] might have paid them in their own coin, . . . this holy man is lift above all thoughts of revenge. **1867–77** FROUDE *Reynard* in *Short Stud.* (1890) I. 607 If the other animals venture to take liberties with him, he will repay them in their own coin.

Pay (a person off) scot and lot, To.

[= to pay out thoroughly, to settle with.] **1494** in *Eng. Gilds* (1870) 189 I shalbe redy at scotte and lotte, and all my duties truly pay and doo. **1597–8** SHAKS. *1 Hen. IV* V. iv. 115 'Twas time to counterfeit, or that hot termagant Scot had paid me scot and lot too. **1844** DICKENS *Mart. Chuz.* xxiv I'll pay you off scot and lot by and bye.

Pay the piper, To.

[= to bear the cost.] **1638** J. TAYLOR (Water-P.) *Taylor's Feast* 98 in *Wks.* 3rd Coll. (Spens. S.) (A) Alwayes those that dance must pay the musicke. **1681** T. FLATMAN *Heraclitus Ridens* No. 29 (1713) I. 190 After all this Dance he has led the Nation, he must

at last come to pay the piper himself. **1753** CHESTERFIELD *Lett.* (1792) II. 39 The other Powers cannot well dance, when neither France nor the maritime Powers can . . . pay the piper. **1829–30** M. SCOTT *T. Cring. Log* xvi I don't defend slavery . . . but am I to be the only one to pay the piper in compassing its extinction?

Pay through the nose, To.

[= to be overcharged.] **1672** MARVELL *Reh. Transp.* I. 270 Made them pay for it most unconscionably and through the nose. **1782** MISS BURNEY *Cecilia* x. vi She knows nothing of business, and is made to pay for everything through the nose. **1878** J. PAYN *By Proxy* xvii '¡You have been paying through the nose.' 'No doubt. They are all cheats.'

Pay too dear for one's whistle, To.

[= to pay much more for something than it is worth: in allusion to a story of Benj. Franklin (*Wks.* 1840 II. 182).] **1851** TICKNOR *Life, Lett. & Jrnls.* (1876) II. xiii. 271 Too much, he thought, for the price of such a whistle. **1854** R. S. SURTEES *Hand. Cross* vii I should not like to pay too dear for my whistle. **1876** GEO. ELIOT *Dan. Der.* xxxv If a man likes to do it he must pay for his whistle.

Pay well, command well, hang well.

[**1643**] RALPH, LORD HOPTON[1] in DAV. LLOYD *Memoires* (1668) 343 His three words were, *Pay well, Command well,* and *Hang well.* [[1] a General in Charles I's army.]

Pay with the same dish you borrow.

1639 CLARKE 14.

Pay your money and you take your choice, You.

1902–4 LEAN IV. 205 Whichever you please my little dears: You pays your money and you takes your choice. You pays your money and what you sees is A cow or a donkey just as you pleases. **1910** *Times Lit. Sup.* 30 Sept. 350 California with its many climates (you pay your money and take your choice, . . .) is now the chief playground of well-to-do Americans.

Pay (*noun*), *see* No purchase no p.

Pay(s), paid (*verb*), *see also* Long day that never p. (They take); Nunky p. for all; Once p. never craved; Pain both to p. and pray; Pitch and p.; Promiseth like merchant, p. like man of war; Samson was strong, yet could not p. money; Short Lent that must p. at Easter; Silly pack that may not p. custom; Small sum will p. short reckoning; Solomon was a wise man and Sampson . . . yet neither could p.; Sweet appears sour when we p.; Take all and p. all; — and pay the baker.

Payer(s), *see* Cravers are aye ill p.; Good p. is master of another's purse.

Paymaster, *see* Good p. needs no surety; Ill p. never wants excuse.

Payment, *see* Best p. is on peck bottom.

Pays last, He that | never pays twice.

1659 HOWELL *Eng. Prov. Rend. into Fr.* 4/1 Who payeth last payeth but once. **1670** RAY 130. **1721** KELLY 150 . . . Spoken in jest to one who is loth to pay his reckoning, as if it was out of a principle of prudence. **1732** FULLER no. 2246.

Pays the lawing[1] choose the lodging, Let him that.

1827 SCOTT *Chron. Canong.* v I'm nane of thae heartsome land leddies that can . . . make themsells agreeable ; . . . but if it is your will to stay here, he that pays the lawing[1] maun choose the lodging. [[1] reckoning.]

Pays the physician does the cure, Who.

1616 DRAXE 132 They that pay the Physition, shall bee cured. **1640** HERBERT 357.

Pays the piper may call the tune, He who. (*See also* Pay the piper, *and quotations there.*)

1895 *Daily News* 18 Dec. 9/1 Londoners had paid the piper, and should choose the tune, **1910** *Spectator* 22 Oct. 643 How the Irish Nationalist leader can combine 'loyalty' with the acceptance of Patrick Ford's dollars is a question. . . . 'He who pays the piper calls the tune.'

Pays the rent, *see* Gentleman that p. the r.

Pays, *see also* Pay(s).

Pea for a bean, To give a.

c. **1390** GOWER *Conf. Amantis* v. 4408 He wol ayeinward take a bene, Ther he hath lent the smale pese. **1896** *Folk-Lore* vii. 377 (A).

Pea, *see also,* Peas.

Peace and catch a mouse.

1659 HOWELL *Eng. Prov.* 11/1.

Peace and patience, and death with repentance.

1640 HERBERT 332.

Peace, If you wish for | be prepared for war. (*Cf.* Peace, In time of | prepare for war.)

[VEGETIUS *Mil.* Qui desiderat pacem, praeparet bellum. Generally quoted as *Si vis pacem, para bellum.*] **1885** C. LOWE *Bismarck* (1898) vii Lord Beaconsfield had acted on the maxim that 'if you want peace, you must prepare for war'.

Peace beyond the line, No.

1821 SCOTT *Pirate* xxi There is never peace with Spaniards beyond the Line—I have heard Captain Tragendeck and honest old Commodore Rummelaer say so a hundred times, and they have both been down in the Bay of Honduras and all thereabouts.

Peace, He that will not have | God gives him war.

1640 HERBERT 351.

Peace, Where there is | God is.

1640 HERBERT 351.

Peace makes plenty.

c. **1425** *MS. Digby* 230 lf. 223 b (*Reliq. Ant.* (1841) i. 315) Pees makith Plente Plente makith Pride Pride maketh Plee[1] Plee makith Pouert Pouert makith Pees. *a.* **1590** PUTTENHAM (Arb.) 217 Peace makes plentie, plentie makes pride. **1598–9** SHAKS. *Hen. V* V. ii. 34 Peace, Dear nurse of arts, plenties, and joyful births. **1610** *Histriomastix,* the six acts: Peace, Plenty, Pride, Envy, War, Poverty—then Peace again. **1659** HOWELL *Eng. Prov.* 19/1 Through peace cometh plenty. [[1] plea.]

Peace, In time of | prepare for war.

c. **1535** LYNDSAY *Three Estates* 2560 Into peace, ye sould provyde for weirs. **1548** HALL *Chron. Edward IV,* an. 9, 209 He forgat the olde adage, Saynge in tyme of peace prouyde for warre. **1581** W. STAFFORD *Examn. ordinary complaints* (New Sh. S.) 65 In peace, tendes for warre. **1617** J. SWETNAM *School of Defence* 61 Wee find the wise to prouide . . . in time of peace for wars. **1624** BURTON *Anat. Mel.* II. iii. VI. 264.

Peace with sword in hand, 'Tis safest making.

1594 LIPSIUS *6 Books of Politics* tr. Jones 2 A 3 The olde prouerbe . . . It is best treating of peace, with weapons in ones hand. **1699** FARQUHAR *Love & a Bottle* v. iii (A).

Peace, *see also* Ask your neighbour if you shall live in p.; Better a lean p. than fat victory; Clothe thee in war, arm thee in p.; Disarmed p. is weak; Just war better than unjust p.; Live in p. and rest (He that would); Pipe of p.; Soldiers in p. like chimneys in summer; War (Of all) p. is end; Wisdom p. (By).

Peaceably, *see* Live p. with all breeds good blood.

Peacemaker, *see* Stick is surest p.

Peach will have wine and the fig water, The.

1573 SANDFORD (1576) 211. **1629** *Book of Meery Riddles* Prov. 103.

Peach, *see also* Peel a . . . p. for enemy.

Peacock hath fair feathers, but foul feet, The.

1599 DAVIES *Nosce Teipsum* fin. Compare thy peacock's feet with thy gay peacock's traine. **1616** DRAXE 10.

Peacock loudly bawls, When the | soon we'll have both rain and squalls.

1883 OPER 28. **1893** INWARDS 135.

Peacock, *see also* Proud as a p.

Pear year, a dear year, A. (*Cf.* Cherry year, &c.)

1742 *An Agreeable Companion* 65 A Pear Year, a dear Year, A cherry Year, a merry year, A plumb year, a dumb year. **1893** INWARDS 5.

Pear(s), *see also* Ask p. of an elm; Plant p. for your heirs; Share not p. with your master; Worst pig gets best p.

Pearl on your nail, Make a.

1592 NASH *Pierce Pen.* (Collier) 58 marg. Drinking super nagulum, a devise . . . which is, after a man hath turnde up the bottom of the cup, to drop it on hys nayle, and made a pearle with that is left; which, if it slide, . . . he must drinke againe for his penance. **1868** *N. & Q.* 4th Ser. I. 460 At the tables of . . . friends in Scotland and in London . . . the custom was to turn the glass with the mouth downwards, and to tap it with the thumb-nail—repeating . . . *Supernaculum.*

Pearls before swine, To cast.

1340 *Ayenbite* (E.E.T.S.) 152 (A) þet we ne þrauwe naȝt oure preciouse stones touore þe zuyn. **1362** LANGLAND *P. Pl.* A. xi. 9 *Noli mittere Margeri*—perles Among hogges. *c.* **1430** LYDGATE *Minor Poems* (Percy Soc.) 188 Men should not put . . . perles whight, To-fore rude swyne. **1526** TINDALE *Matt.* vii. 6 Nether caste ye youre pearles before swyne. **1645** MILTON *2nd Sonn. Tetrach.* This is got by casting Pearl to Hoggs. **1655** FULLER *Ch. Hist.* II. i (1868) I. 93 The people of Rome, accounting him a precious jewel, . . . would 'not cast this pearl before swine', by hazarding him to the insolency of the Pagans. **1848** DICKENS *Dombey* xxiii Oh, I do a thankless thing, and cast pearls before swine!

Pearls dissolved in wine (vinegar).

1580 LYLY *Euph. & his Eng.* (Arb.) 312 I but there is no Pearle so hard but Vinegar breaketh it. **1600–1** SHAKS. *Hamlet* V. ii. 285–96 The king shall drink to Hamlet's better breath; And in the cup an union shall he throw, Richer than that which four successive kings In Denmark's crown have worn. . . . Hamlet, this pearl is thine; Here's to thy health. Give him the cup. **1605** JONSON *Volpone* III. See, here, a rope of pearl; and each more orient than the brave Egyptian queen caroused: Dissolve and drink them. **1616** BRETON *Cross. Prov.* Wks. (Gros.) II e 6 Pearles are restorative.

Peas, The smaller the | the more to the pot; the fairer the woman, the more the giglot.[1]

c. **1350** *Douce MS. 52* no. 99 The smaller pesun, the more to pott; the fayrer woman, the more gylott. *c.* **1470** *Harl. MS. 3362,* f. 7 b The smellere pesyn, þe mo to þe pot. *c.* **1470** *Slo. MS. 1210,* f. 134a in *Rel. Antiq.* II. 40 The smaller pese, the mo to the pott; the fayrere woman, the more gylott. **1541** *Schoolho. of Women* 558 in HAZL. *Early Pop.*

Poetry IV. 126 The smaller pease, the mo to the pot, The fairer woman the more gillot. **1546** HEYWOOD I. v. 10 Who hath many pease maie put the mo in the pot. [1 a wanton.]

Peas with the King, and cherries with the beggar, Eat.

c. **1530** *Dialogues of Creatures* xx I counsell not seruantis to ete churyes with ther bettyrs. For they wyl haue the rype and leue them the harde. **1642** FULLER *H. & P. State* III. v *He that eats cherries with noblemen shall have his eyes spirted out with the stones.*—This outlandish proverb hath in it an English truth, that they who constantly converse with men far above their estates, shall reap shame and loss thereby. **1721** KELLY 100 . . . Peas are best when young, and cherries when ripe. **1732** FULLER no. 1356.

Pea(s), pease, *see also* Crooked man should sow beans, wud man p.; David and Chad, sow p.; Little sap in dry p. hulls; Parched p. on a griddle; St. Benedick sow thy p.; Sow peas . . . in wane of moon; Two p. (As like as).

Pease, *see* Pea(s).

Pease-cod(s), *see* Everything is good in its season (*quotation* 1591); Winter-time . . . , p. time for wooing; Woman were as little as good (If a), a p. would make her hood.

Pease-field, He is going into the.

1678 RAY 264 . . . i.e. falling asleep.

Pease-pottage, *see* Love and p.

Peat-pot[1] into the mire, Out of the.

1721 KELLY 268. [1 the hole out of which peat is dug.]

Pebbles, *see* Hang together like p. in halter.

Peccavi, see Cry p.

Peck of malt, For my | set the kiln on fire.

1616 WITHALS 566. **1638** J. TAYLOR *Bull, Bear, and Horse* A 6. **1639** CLARKE 254. **1917** BRIDGE 58 . . . Our proverb seems to mean 'I mustn't be hasty—I am not such a fool as to burn the kiln down to get my paltry peck'.

Peck of troubles, To be in a.

1533 UDALL *Flowers of Latin Speaking* (1560) M 5ᵛ As we saie in inglish prouerbially, in a whole pecke of troubles. *c.* **1535** in *Archæologia* xxv. 97 The said George . . . told hym that Mr. More was in a pecke of troubles. **1857** HUGHES *Tom Brown* I. viii A pretty peck of troubles you'll get into.

Peck, *see also* Best payment is on the p. bottom; Eat a p. of dirt (Every man must).

Pecked to death by a hen, One had as good be.

1678 RAY 240.

Pecker, *see* Keep your p. up.

Pedigree(s), *see* Good p. (In) there are . . . chandlers; Long as Welsh p.

Pedlar carry his own burden (pack), Let every.

1659 HOWELL *Eng. Prov.* 17/2. **1670** RAY 21. **1732** FULLER no. 3176.

Pedlar's drouth.

1821 SCOTT *Pirate* vi My certie, . . . there is the chapman's drouth and his hunger baith, as folks say. (*Footnote.*—The chapman's drouth, that is the pedlar's thirst, is proverbial in Scotland because those pedestrian traders were in the use of modestly asking only for a drink of water, when, in fact, they were desirous of food.)

Pedlar's French.

1530 PALSGRAVE 727/1 They speke a pedlars frenche amongest them selfe. *c.* **1536** R. COPLAND *Highway to the Spittle house* And thus they babble . . . with theyr pedlyng frenche. **1567** HARMAN *Caveat* 23 Their languag— which they terme peddelars Frenche or Canting. **1613** WITHER *Abuses* II. i. L 3 Besides as I suppose their lawes they pen'd, In their old *Pedlers French* vnto this end. **1620** SHELTON *Quix.* II. xix (1908) II. 312 All this to the husbandmen was heathen Greek or pedlar's French.

Pedlar, *see also* Small pack becomes small p.

Pedley, *see* God help the fool, quoth P.; I was by, quoth P.; Rope enough . . . said P.; Slow and sure like P.'s mare.

Peebles for pleasure.

1890 F. ANSTEY *Pariah* I. ii 'I think Littlehampton must be ever so much more amusing than France is'. 'Peebles for pleasure!' remarked Margot at hearing Lettice's opinion on the comparative merits of France and Littlehampton. **1919** DEAN INGE *Outspoken Ess.* 36 The local patriot thinks that Peebles, and not Paris, is the place for pleasure, or asks whether any good thing can come out of Nazareth.

Peel a fig for your friend and a peach for your enemy.

1573 SANDFORD (1576) 205. **1629** *Book of Meery Riddles* Prov. 53. **1678** RAY 53 Al amico cura [g]li il fico, Al inimico il Persico. *Pill a fig for your friend, and a peach for your enemy.*

Peeled egg, You have come to a.

1721 KELLY 369 . . . Spoken to those who have got an estate, place, or preferment ready prepar'd for their hand.

Peeps through a hole, He who | may see what will vex him.

1707 MAPLETOFT 75. **1710** PALMER *Moral Essays on Proverbs* 135 (A). **1855** BOHN 401.

Peerage is the Englishman's Bible, The.

1850 CARLYLE *Lat.-Day Pam.* No. 7 (1885) 241 Collins's old Peerage-Book . . . is properly all we English have for a Biographical Dictionary;—nay, . . . for a National Bible. **1883** W. BATES *Maclise Port.-Gallery* 68 That bulky volume which has been called the Englishman's Bible—*Burke's Peerage.*

Peers, *see* Play with your p.

Peg, *see* Round p. in square hole; Take one down a p.

Pelf, *see* Take part of the p. when pack a-dealing.

Pelion, *see* Ossa.

Pen and ink is wit's plough.

1639 CLARKE 35.

Pendle, *see* Ingleborough.

Pendulum, *see* Swing of the p.

Penelope's web.

[Penelope undid at night what she had woven during the day, to defer her choice of a husband in the absence of Ulysses.] **1591** FLORIO *Sec. Frutes* 195 If this be all you say, a fayre threed she hath sponne, For what she wrought all day, at night was all vndone. **1607–8** SHAKS. *Coriol.* I. iii. 92 You would be another Penelope; yet they say all the yarn she spun in Ulysses' absence did but fill Ithaca with moths. **1614** SIR T. OVERBURY *Characters* (1890) 73 *A Melancholy Man.* He winds up his thoughts often, and as often unwinds them; Penelope's web thrives faster. **1629** T. ADAMS *Serm.* (1861–2) I. 459 Examples teach soonest. . . . The force of a hundred good sermons is lost by one enormity; so easy is it to weave Penelope's web. **1707** SWIFT *Facult. of Mind* Wks. (1856) II. 285 Else we shall be forced to weave Penelope's web, unravel in the night what we spun in the day. **1910** *Times Lit. Sup.* 14 Oct. 'A Penelope, who unravels by night the web she has woven all day long; . . . such', says Anthero de Quental, 'is History'.

Penniless Bench.

[A covered open-air seat for destitute wayfarers. To sit on Penniless Bench = to be in extreme poverty.] **1560–1** in W. H. TURNER *Select. Rec. Oxf.* (1880) 284 Item, to . . . for mending the peneles benche. **1580** LYLY *Euph. & his Eng.* (Arb.) 244 Every stoole he sate on was Penniles bench. **1604** MIDDLETON *Works* (Bullen) VIII. 27 The time was at hand, like a pickpurse, that Pierce should be called no more Pennyless, like the Mayor's bench at Oxford. [Ed. note: At the east end of old Carfax church at Oxford there was a seat for loungers which was known as *Penniless Bench.* Hence came the proverb 'To sit on Penniless Bench'.] **1632** MASSINGER *City Madam* IV. i. Bid him bear up; he shall not Sit long on Penniless-Bench. **1860** WARTER *Seaboard* II. 43 Though he have sometimes to sit on the Penniless Bench.

Penniless souls maun[1] pine in purgatory.

1823 HENDERSON 46. [[1] must.]

Penny and penny laid up will be many.

1591 W. STEPNEY The Span. Schoolmaster One penie here, and in another place another, makes two pence. 1639 CLARKE 35. 1670 RAY 130.

Penny at a pinch is worth a pound, A.

1616 WITHALS 553. 1639 CLARKE 45.

Penny for your thoughts, A.

1546 HEYWOOD II. iv. 50 Wherwith in a great musyng he was brought. Fréend (quoth the good man) a peny for your thought. 1738 SWIFT (Dial. i) 333 Never. Here's poor miss has not a word to throw at a dog. Come, a penny for your thought. 1870 READE Put Yourself xxiv Always in the clouds, . . . A penny for your thoughts, sir!

Penny in purse will bid me drink, when all the friends I have will not.

1678 RAY 130.

Penny in the forehead, A.

[Allusion to a nursery joke in which a coin is pressed to the forehead so as to be felt as if still there after removal.] 1607 SHARPHAM Cupid's Whirligig K 3 Holde vp your head Tobias, and looke and you can see a penny in my browe. 1658/9 T. BURTON Diary 9 March (A) Sir A. Haslerigge . . . said 'I am not bound always to look you in the face like children, to see if you have a penny in your forehead'.

Penny is well spent that saves a groat, That.

1611 COTGRAVE s.v. 'Bon' Well is that half-penie spent that saues a penie. 1614 CAMDEN 312. 1670 RAY 130. 1732 FULLER no. 4369. 1749 FRANKLIN March 'Tis a well spent penny that saves a groat.

Penny more buys the whistle, A.

1721 KELLY 8 . . . Spoken when one gets a bargain for a little more than was offer'd for it; or at cards, when a card is taken by a card just bigger by one. 1732 FULLER no. 341.

Penny saved is a penny gained (got), A. (But cf. Penny that's saved is not gotten.)

1640 HERBERT 341 A penny spared is twice got. 1662 FULLER (Hunts.) II. 103 By the same proportion that a penny saved is a penny gained, the preserver of books is a mate for the compiler of them. 1695 RAVENSCROFT Canterbury Guests II. iv This I did to prevent expenses, for . . . A penny sav'd, is a penny got. 1712 Spectator 14 Oct. I think a speculation upon Many a Little makes a Mickle; a Penny saved is a penny got . . . would be

very useful to the World. 1748 THOMSON Castle Ind. i st. 50 A penny saved is a penny got . . . this scoundrel maxim. 1811 BYRON Hints fr. Horace 516 A penny saved, my lad, 's a penny got. 1838 Chamb. Edin. Jrnl. 45 A penny saved is a penny gained.

Penny soul never came to twopence, A.

1844 Chamb. Jrnl. II. 225 A penny soul never came to twopence. 1859 SMILES Self-Help ix (1860) 235 Narrow-mindedness in living and in dealing . . . leads to failure. The penny soul never came to twopence.

Penny that's saved is not gotten, Every. (But cf. Penny saved is a penny gained.)

1670 RAY 139.

Penny to buy his dog a loaf (or to bless him), He has not a. (Cf. Cross (Penny) to bless himself with.)

1546 HEYWOOD II. viii. 73 Money, and money woorth, did so misse him, That he had not now one peny to blisse him. 1641 FERGUSSON 50. Of weasters and divers.[1] . . . [[1] bankrupts.]

Penny to spend at a new ale-house, Every one has a.

1678 RAY 181. 1732 FULLER no. 1445.

Penny wise and pound foolish.

1607 TOPSELL Four-f. Beasts 609 If by covetousnesse or negligence, one withdraw from them their ordinary foode, he shall be penny wise, and pound foolish. 1612–15 BP. HALL Contempl. IV. xxvii (1825) II. 495 Worldly hearts are penny-wise, and pound-foolish: they . . . set high prices upon . . . trash of this world; but . . . heavenly things, . . . they shamefully undervalue. 1712 ADDISON Spect. No. 295, par. 6 I think a Woman who will give up herself to a Man in marriage, where there is the least Room for such an Apprehension, . . . may very properly be accused . . . of being Penny Wise and Pound foolish. 1827 HARE Gues. at Truth (1873) i. 239 Many . . . are said to be penny-wise and pound-foolish: but they who are penny-foolish will hardly be pound-wise.

Penny (-ies), pence, see also Bad p. always comes back; Companion like the p. (No); Cross (P.) to bless himself with; In for a p.; Keep a p. (Who will not); Know by a p. how shilling spends; Look twice at a p.; No paternoster no p.; No p. no pardon; No p. no paternoster; No p. no placebo; Piper a p. to play (Give); Put the poor man's p. and the rich man's p. in ae purse; Put two halfpennies (p.) in a purse; Smith and his p. both are black; Take care of the p., and the pounds . . .; Thinks his p. good silver; Touch pot touch p.; Turn the (an honest) p.; Unrighteous p. corrupts righteous pound.

Penny-weight of love is worth a pound of law, A.

1721 KELLY 17 . . . A dissuasive from law-suits among neighbours; used also when we value a man more for his good humour than his skill in the laws. **1732** FULLER no. 343.

Pennyworth of ease is worth a penny, A.

1636 CAMDEN 291. **1732** FULLER no. 344.

Pennyworth(s), *see also* Good bargain (p.) (At a) make pause; Robin Hood's p.; Ruined by buying good p.

Pens may blot, but they cannot blush.

1577 J. GRANGE *Gold Aphrod.* K ij If needes you would haue opend (quoth she) your budget of villany unto me, yet better mighte you haue done it with penne and inke, who (as the Prouerbe goeth) neuer blusheth, then with that shamefull tongue of yours. **1616** DRAXE 12 Pennes may blot, but they cannot blush.

Pension never enriched a young man.
1640 HERBERT 341.

Penyghent, *see* Ingleborough.

Penzance, Not a word of.

1678 RAY 350 Not a word of Pensants. **1750** R. HEATH *Acct. of Islands of Scilly* 405 July 20, 1595, . . . *four Gallies* of the *Spaniards* appeared . . . against Mousehole. . . . *Ibid.* 407 *note The Cornish Inhabitants*, at this Time, behaving so ill in making Defence against the Enemy, added a Proverb more to this County.[1] *Not a Word of Pensance.* [1 Cornwall.]

People, *see* Priest (Like) like p.; Prince (Like) like p.; Voice of the p. voice of God; Wrath of . . and tumult of p. (Take heed of).

Pepper Gate, *see* Daughter is stolen (When), shut P. G.

Pepper in the nose, To take.

[= to take offence, be vexed.] **1377** LANG-LAND *P. Pl.* B. xv. 197 And to þere peple han peper in the nose. *c.* **1450** *Provs. of Wysdom* in *Anglia* 51. 222, l. 53 Have not pepir in þi nose. **1520** WHITTINGTON *Vulg.* (1527) 24 If ony man offende hym, he may not forthwith take peper in the nose, and show by rough words . . . that he is angred. **1579** LYLY *Euphues* (Arb.) 118 I would not that al women should take pepper in the nose, in that I haue disclosed the legerdemaines of a fewe. **1682** BUNYAN *Holy War* 267 The peevish old gentleman took pepper in the nose.

Pepper is black and hath a good smack.

a. **1530** R. *Hill's Commonpl. Bk.* (1858) 140 Though peper be blek yt hath a gode smek. **1546** HEYWOOD ii. iv. 51 Pepper is blacke And hath a good smacke And euery man doth it bye.

Pepper to Hindostan.

1791 I. DISRAELI *Cur. Lit.* (1858) iii. 46 In the 'Bustan' of Sadi we have *Infers piper in Hindostan*; 'To carry pepper to Hindostan'. **1853** TRENCH iii. 68 The Greeks said: *Owls to Athens*, Attica abounding with these birds; . . . the Orientals: *Pepper to Hindostan*.

Perfect, *see* Use (Practice) makes p.

Perfidious Albion.

a. **1821** NAPOLEON I in *N. & Q.* (1921) 12th Ser. VIII. 216 Bossuet's reference to 'La perfide Angleterre' occurs in his 'Premier Sermon pour la Circoncision'. The alteration from 'Angleterre' to 'Albion' has been usually attributed to Napoleon I, who used it as the Romans used *Punica fides*. **1908** *Sphere* 28 March 270 Most of the continental states seem to recognize the disinterested nature of the British proposal. 'Perfidious Albion' it is coming to be seen has no selfish interest in reducing Macedonia to peace and order.

Perfidious, *see also* Tie can oblige p. (No).

Performance, One acre of | is worth twenty of the Land of Promise.

1596 NASHE *Saffron W.* T 3 Wks. (1905) III. 126 Consil. *He saith in one leafe* that one acre of performance is worth twentie of the Land of Promise.

Peril(s), *see* Forecasts all p. (He that) will never sail sea; —— will win no worship; Happy whom other men's p. make wary; Neighbour's scathe is my p.; Profit (What is none of my) shall be none of my p.

Perish by permitted things, We.

[L. *Perimus licitis.*] **1853** TRENCH vi. 141 Sir Matthew Hale[1] . . . had continually in his mouth the modern Latin proverb, We perish by permitted things. . . . Nearly as much danger threatens the soul from things per-mitted as from things unpermitted. [1 Lord Chief Justice of England, 1671–6.]

Perjuries, *see* Jove laughs at lovers' p.

Permitted, *see* Perish by p. things (We).

Pershore { **where do you think? God help us!**

1894 NORTHALL *Folk-phrases* (E.D.S.) 21 Pershore { where do you think? God help us! Pershore, *Worc.*, is noted for its fruit. When there is a particularly fine crop, any native vendor, if asked where his fruit was grown, says boastingly, 'Parshur, where do you think but Parshur?' If asked the same question in a bad season, he replies, 'Parshur, God help us!'

Person marked, Take heed of a | and a widow thrice married.

1651 HERBERT 371. **1721** KELLY 311 *Take*

a care of that man whom God has set a mark on. . . . The Scots generally have an aversion to any that have any natural defect or redundancy. **1914** *Lady's Pict.* 21 Nov. 713 The . . . crippled sword-arm was very noticeable. A Frenchman said: 'Distrust those that are marked by the Creator.'

Persuasion of the fortunate sways the doubtful, The.

1640 HERBERT 347.

Pert as a sparrow, As.

1610 *Histriomastix* II. i. 311. **1837** J. F. & M. PALMER *Devonshire Dialect* 30 (A).

Perverseness makes one squint-eyed.

1640 HERBERT 347.

Pet, *see* Take p.

Petard, *see* Hoist with his own p.

Peter is so godly, that God don't make him thrive.

1732 FULLER no. 3870.

Peter of Wood, church and mills are all his.

1670 RAY 217. *Chesh.* **1917** BRIDGE 103 . . . I have failed to find any solution of this saying.

Peter, *see also* Difference between P. and P.; Rob P. to pay Paul.

Peterborough, *see* Ramsey.

Petticoats woo, When | breeks may come speed.

1721 KELLY 346 . . . Spoken when maids court young men.

Petticoat(s), *see also* Lass in the red p. shall pay; Near is my coat (p.) but nearer is. . . .

Philip and Cheiny.

[i. Two or more of common people taken at random.] **1542** UDALL tr. *Erasm. Apoph.* (1877) 311 It was not his entent to bryng vnto Sylla philip and cheinie, mo then a good meiny, but to bryng hable souldiours of manhood approved and well tried to his handes. **1573** TUSSER 2 (E.D.S.) 8 Loiterers I kept so meanie, both Philip, Hob, and Cheanie. [ii. A woollen stuff of common quality.] **1614** FLETCHER *Wit at S. W.* II. i *Lady R.* Thirteene pound . . . 'Twill put a Lady scarce in Philip and Cheyney.

Philip and Mary on a shilling, Like.

[On the shilling of 1554 the two busts are face to face.] **1678** BUTLER *Hudibras* III. i. 688 Wks. (1854) I. 231 Still amorous, and fond, and billing, Like Philip and Mary on a shilling.

Philip, *see also* Appeal from P. drunk.

Philosopher, *see* Beard that makes p. (It is not).

Philosopher's stone, *see* Content is the p. s.; Thrift is the p. s.

Philosophy of the distaff, It is the.

1651 HERBERT 365.

Phlegmatic, *see* Choleric drinks, p. sleeps.

Physic before he is sick, He takes.

1616 WITHALS 575. **1639** CLARKE 283. **1670** RAY 189.

Physic do not work, If | prepare for the kirk.

c. **1386** CHAUCER *Knight's Tale* A. 2759 And certeinly, ther nature wol nat wirche, Farwel, phisyk! go ber the man to chirche! **1678** RAY 189.

Physic, *see also* Ague in the spring is p. for king; Kitchen p. is best p.; Temperance is best p.; War and p. governed by eye.

Physician, heal thyself.

[ERASM. *Ad. Aliorum medicus.*] **1389** WYCLIF *Luke* iv. 23 Sothli ȝe schulen seie to me this liknesse, Leeche, heele thi silf. *c.* **1412** HOCCLEVE *De Regim. Princ.* (1860) 7 Cure, godeman? ye, thow art a faire leche; Cure thy self, that tremblest as thou goste. **1526** TINDALE *Luke* iv 23 Ye maye very wele saye vnto me this proverbe, Visicion, heale thy silfe. **1579** LYLY *Euphues* (Arb.) 118 If thou saye to mee, Phisition heale thy selfe. I aunswere, that I am meetly well purged of that disease. **1590–1** SHAKS. *2 Hen. VI* II. i. 53 *Medice, teipsum*; Protector, see to't well, protect yourself. **1616** DRAXE 154 Physition heale thy selfe. **1882** BLACKMORE *Christowell* xxiv 'Physician, heal thyself', is the hardest, and most unanswerable of all taunts.

Physician, A | is an angel when employed, but a devil when one must pay him.

1820 SCOTT *Abbot* xxvi I cured him . . . and now he talks of the chargeableness of medicine. . . . Old saying and true, Prœmia cum poscit medicus, Sathan est. We are angels when we come to cure—devils when we ask payment.

Physician like a true friend, No.

c. **1386** CHAUCER *Mel.* 2495 Catoun seith, 'If thou hast nede of help, axe it of thy freendes, for ther nys noon so good a phisicien as thy trewe freend'. [SKEAT footnote: *Cato, De Moribus*, iv. 13: 'Auxilium a nobis petito, si forte laboras. Nec quisquam melior medicus quam fidus amicus.'

Physician, The | owes all to the patient, but the patient owes nothing to him but a little money.

1616 DRAXE 155 The physitian oweth all to the disease, and the disease nothing to the physition. **1640** HERBERT 359.

Physicians, The best | are Dr. Diet, Dr. Quiet, and Dr. Merryman.

1558 BULLEYN *Govt. of Health* 50 Cousaill was geuen me, that I should not staye myselfe vpon the pinion of any one phisicion, but rather vpon three. . . . The first was called doctor diet, the seconde doctor quiet, the thirde doctor mery mã. **1621** BURTON *Anat. Mel.* II. ii. VI. iv (1651) 301 This is one of the three Salernitan doctors, D. Merryman, D. Diet, and D. Quiet, which cure all diseases —*Mens hilaris, requies, moderata diæta.* **1738** SWIFT (Dial. ii) 347 *Lady S.* The best doctors in the world are doctor diet, doctor quiet, and doctor merryman. **1909** *Spectator* 30 Jan. A proverb prescribes for sickness Dr. Diet, Dr. Quiet, and Dr. Merryman. The merry heart goes all the way in all but the worst sickness.

Physicians kill more than they cure.

1624 BURTON *Anat. Mel.* II. iv. I. i. 2 P4[v] Physitians kill as many as they saue. **1703** E. WARD *Writings* ii. 328 (A) ('an old maxim ').

Physicians, Where there are three | there are two atheists.

1643 SIR K. DIGBY *Observations upon Religio Medici* It is a common speech (but only amongst the unlearned sort) *ubi tres medici duo athei.* **1656** T. KECK *Crit. Notes app. to Sir T. Browne's 'Religio Medici'* § 1 Physicians . . . are commonly ill spoke of in this behalf. It is a common saying, *Ubi tres medici, duo athei.* **1837** SOUTHEY *Doctor* iv. 181 (citing the passage from Digby.) **1853** TRENCH iv. 79 A Latin medieval proverb boldly proclaims: *Where there are three physicians, there are two atheists.*

Physicians' faults are covered with earth.

1547 WM. BALDWIN *Treatise Moral Philosophy* (1550) D 6 Anarcharsis to a painter that had become a physician: The faultes that thou madest before in thy workes, might sone bee espied: but them if thou makest now, are lyd under the yearthe. **1595** A. COPLEY *Wits, Fits, and Fancies* (1614) C 2[v] The faultes you made before (when a painter) might easily be seene, but those you commit now (you are a physician) are hidden under the earth. **1597** *Politeuphuia* 161 *Nicocles* called Phisitions happy men, because the sun made manifest what good successe so ever happened in their cures, and the earth buried what fault soeuer they committed.

Physician(s), *see also* City is in bad case whose p. has gout; Deadly disease neither p. can ease; Feed by measure and defy p.; Few lawyers . . . few p. live well; Fool or p. at forty; Fool who makes p. heir; Go not for every grief to p.; God heals and p. hath thanks; Gout (With respect to) p. but a lout; Hide nothing from thy p.; Honour a p. before need of him; Nature, time, and patience p.; Old p., young lawyer; Pays the p. (Who) does the cure; Pitiful surgeon (p.) spoileth sore; Words ending in *ique* mock p.; Young barber, old p. *See also* Doctor.

Pick a hole (*or* holes) in something, To.

1588 *Mar-Prelate's Epitome* (1843) 3 (A)

There is a deuice to fynde a hole in the coat of some of you puritanes. **1598–9** SHAKS. *Hen. V* III. vi. 89 If I find a hole in his coat I will tell him my mind. **1600–1** *Merry W.* III. v. 144 There 's a hole made in your best coat, Master Ford. **1616** T. ADAMS *Three Divine Sisters* 5 *Satan* is a subtill Lawyer, . . . and will soone picke holes in it [the evidence]. **1632** *Pinder of Wakefield* D 2. **1639** CLARKE 80 It 's easie to pick a hole in another man's coat, if he be disposed. **1648** NEEDHAM *Plea for King* 21 Every ambitious popular person would be ready to pick holes in their Coates, to bring them into disfavour of the People. **1655–62** GURNALL *Chrn. in Armour* (1865) I. 85 Nor is it hard for Satan to pick some hole in the saint's coat, when he walks most circumspectly. **1894** *Aspects Mod. Oxford* 93 Any one can pick holes in the University system of teaching and examination.

Pick (*or* suck) a person's brains, To.

[= to elicit and appropriate the results of his thought.] *a.* **1893** JOWETT *Life* i. 435 Do you possess the art of picking other people's brains? **1907** A. C. BENSON *From Coll. Window* [4 ed.] 48 He had an astonishing memory. . . . If one wanted to know what books to read in any line, one had only to pick his brains.

Pick out, *see* Bird to p. o. his own eyes (Hath brought up); Hawks will not p. o. hawks' eyes.

Pick up (*or* Gather) one's crumbs, To.

[= to pick up or recover strength or health.] **1474** *Paston Letters* (Gairdner) III. 114 But, God thanke yow, I toke so my crommys whyl[s] I was wyth yow, that I feled my sylfe . . . stronger than I wenyd that I had ben. **1588** A. INGRAM in HAKLUYT *Voy.* II. II. 130 Our men beganne to gather vp their crums and to recouer some better strength. *c.* **1645** HOWELL *Lett.* 2 Feb. an. 1621 Thank God, I . . . am recovering and picking up my crums apace. **1840** R. H. DANA *Before Mast* xxvii [He] had 'picked up his crumbs' . . . and [was] getting strength and confidence daily. **1888** W. *Somerset Word-bk.* s.v. A person or animal improving in appearance is said to be picking up his crumbs.

Pick(ed), *see also* Plays you as fair as if he p. your pocket; Wit to p. a lock.

Pickerel, *see* Turkeys . . . p. and beer came into England.

Pickpockets, *see* Agree like p.

Pickpurse, *see* At hand, quoth P.; Purgatory p.

Picture of ill luck, To look like the.

1678 RAY 286.

Pictures are the books of the unlearned.

1660 FULLER (*Canterb.*) II. 181 According to the maxim, 'pictures are the books', painted windows were in the time of popery the library of lay-men; and after the Conquest grew in general use in England.

Picture(s), *see also* Painted p. are dead speakers.

Pie(s), *see* Finger in the p.; No sport no p.; Prayers (They shall have no more of our) than we of their p.

Pie (bird), *see* High for the p. (Not too); Preach like a p.

Piece of a kid is worth two of a cat, A.

1550 HEYWOOD II. vii. 70 A péece of a Kyd is woorth two of a cat. Who the diuell will chaunge a rabet for a rat? **1547** BORDE *Introd. of Knowledge* (Furnivall) 274 Yonge kyddes flesshe is praysed aboue all other flesshe. **1614** CAMDEN 303.

Piece, *see also* Churchyard (A p. of) fits every body.

Pie-lid makes people wise.

1592 LYLY *Midas* IV. iii *Lic.* He hath laid the plot to be prudent: why 'tis pasty crust, eat enough and it will make you wise, an old proverb. **1678** RAY 79 . . . Because no man can tell what is in a pye till the lid be taken up.

Pig of my own sow, A.

c. **1535** *Gentleness and Nobility* A IV (A) That is euyn a pyg of our own sow. **1546** HEYWOOD II. vii. 64 A pyg of myne owne sowe. **1579** GOSSON *Sch. Abuse* (Arb.) 40 The last, because it is knowen too be a Pig of myne owne Sowe, I will speake the lesse of it. **1731** FIELDING *Grub St. Op.* III. xiv If you come to my house I will treat you With a pig of your own sow.

Pig of the worse pannier, A.

1533 J. HEYWOOD *John, Tyb, &c.* (Farmer) 89 (A) And, peradventure, there, he and she Will make me cuckold, even to anger me; and then had I a pig in the worse panyer. **1546** HEYWOOD II. xi. 84 Who that hath either of these pygs in vre, He hathe a pyg of the woorse panier sure.

Pig's tail, Like a | going all day and nothing done at night.

1865 *Lancs. Proverbs* in *N. & Q.* 3rd Ser. VIII. 494 (A). **1869** HAZLITT (1882) 271. *Lancashire.*

Pig's tail, Of a | you can never make a good shaft.

1651 HERBERT 368. **1742** FRANKLIN April Tom, vain's your Pains; They all will fail: Ne'er was good Arrow made of a Sow's Tail.

Pig's tail, *see also* Horn of a p. t. (Cannot make a).

Pig, *see also* Pig(s).

Pigeon never knoweth woe, but when she doth a-benting go, The.

1609 T. RAVENSCROFT *Deuteromelia* F 3 (A)

The pigion is neuer woe, till abenting she goe. **1611** *Melismata* in LEAN I. 432 The pigeon is never woe Till a-benting she doth go. **1670** RAY 44. **1750** W. ELLIS *Mod. Husbandman* III. 134 At this time of the year . . . the pigeons have had hardly any other field-meat besides, except the seed of bent-grass; which occasioned the old verse: The pigeon never knows more woe, Than when he does a-benting go.

Pigeons and priests (Doves and dominies) make foul houses.

[**1386** CHAUCER *Cant. T., Shipman–Prioress Link* B² 1632 Draweth no monkes moore unto youre in. **1530** BAIF *Mimes II* IV. 85 Chi vuol tener la casa monda Non tenga mai ne prete ne colomba.] **1610** B. RICH *New Descript. Ireland* xiii. 47 I could wish them to bee well aware of this holy brood of the *Popes* Cockrels, the prouerbe is old, and not so old as true: *That Pigeons and Priests do make foule houses.* **1641** FERGUSSON 86 Priests and doves makes foule houses. **1721** KELLY 86 *Doves and domine's leave ay a foul house.* Pigeons will dirty everything where they are: and these little fellows, whom gentlemen bring in to educate their children, will be intriguing with the maids.

Pigeons go a benting,[1] When the | then the farmers lie lamenting.

1830 FORBY 417. [[1] feeding on the seeds of grasses.]

Pigeon(s), *see also* Catch two p. with one bean; Paul's p.; Shoot at a p. and kill crow.

Pigmarket, *see* Silence in the p.

Pigs fly in the air with their tails forward.

1616 WITHALS 583. **1639** CLARKE 147.

Pigs love that lie together.

1678 RAY 189 . . . A familiar conversation breeds friendship among them who are of the most base and sordid natures.

Pigs may fly; but they are very unlikely birds.

1862 HISLOP 179 It may be that swine may flee, but it's no an ilka day's bird. An emphatic expression of incredulity at an extraordinary, or . . . improbable statement. **1885** E. P. HOOD *World Prov. & P.* 352 Here is the passage . . . with its succession of hypotheses and suppositions. . . . And so, . . . '*Pigs might fly, but they are very unlikely birds.*'

Pigs may whistle, but they hae an ill mouth for't.

1832 HENDERSON 135. **1846** J. GRANT *Rom. of War* xii 'I dare say the Spanish sounds very singular to your ear'. 'Ay, sir, it puts me in mind o' an auld saying o' my faither the piper. "A soo may whussle, but its mouth is no made for't."'

Pigs see the wind.

1678 BUTLER *Hudibras* III. ii. 1107 Had lights where better eyes were blind, As pigs are said to see the wind. **1823** BYRON *Juan* VII. lxxxiv Ask the pig who sees the wind! **1902–4** LEAN I. 437 Pigs see the wind, *i.e.* the coming tempest, which makes them the most restless of animals.

Pig(s), *see also* Buy a p. in a poke; Child's p. father's bacon; Come again as Goodyer's p. did; Cunning as a dead p.; First p. . . . is the best; God loves (Whom), his bitch brings forth p.; Goodyer's p. . . . doing mischief (Like); Hogs Norton; Hogs (P.) to a fair market; Kill a p. every day (We don't); Knows not a p. from dog; Lubberland where the p. run about; More sauce than p.; Parson's p.; Please the p.; Pretty p. makes ugly sow; Proud as a p.; St. Anthony's (Tantony) p.; Snug as a p.; Stare like a stuck p.; Swine (P.) (He is like a), he'll never do good while he lives; Wilful as a p.; Worst p. gets best pear; Young p. grunts like old sow.

Pike(s), *see* Ancum p.; Pass the p.; Witham p.

Pikestaff, *see* Plain as a p.

Pilate's voice.

[The loud voice belonging to the part of Pilate in the mystery plays.] **1530** PALSGRAVE 837 In a pylates voyce, *a haulte voyx.* **1542** UDALL tr. *Erasm. Apoph.* (1877) 382 He heard a certain oratour speaking out of measure loude and high, and altogether in Pilates voice. **1546** HEYWOOD I. x. 20 Streight after diner myne aunte had no choice, But other burst, or burst out in pilat's voice.

Pile up the agony, To.

1835–40 HALIBURTON *Clockm.* (1862) 444 I was actilly in a piled-up-agony. **1839** MARRYATT *Diary Amer.* Ser. 1. II. 235 I do think he piled the agony up a little too high in that last scene. **1852** C. BRONTË in *Mrs. Gaskell's Life* (1857) II. xi. 267 I doubt whether the regular novel-reader will consider the 'agony piled sufficiently high' (as the Americans say).

Pilgrim(s), *see* God knows well which are best p.

Pilgrimage, *see* Life is a p.

Pillar to post (*or* Post to pillar), From.

[i.e. from whipping-post to pillory.] *c.* **1420** LYDGATE *Ass. of Gods* 1147 Thus fro poost to pylour he was made to daunce. **1514** A. BARCLAY *Cyt. & Uplondysshm.* (Percy Soc.) 67 From poste unto piller tossed shalt thou be. **1549** LATIMER *7th Serm. bef. Edw. VI* (P.S.) 230 A wonderful thing, how he was tost from post to pillar. *a.* **1550** *Vox Populi* 185 in HAZL. *E.P.P.* III. 274 From piller vnto post the powr man he was tost. **1605** CHAPMAN *All Fools* III. i This light sex is tumbled and tossed from post to pillar. **1670** RAY 190 To be tost from post to pillory. **1882** BLACKMORE *Christowell* lii Mr. Greatorex . . . had been sent from pillar to post, for a fortnight, to find out such a hole as this.

Pilling Moss, *see* God's grace.

Pillory, *see* Baker to the p. (Part not yet, quoth).

Pillow, *see* Debtor's p.; Take counsel of p.

Pills were pleasant, If the | they would not want gilding.

1616 DRAXE 58 If the Apothecaries pilles had a good taste, they would neuer gilde them ouer. **1639** CLARKE 108 Apothecaries would not give pills in sugar unless they were bitter. **1732** FULLER no. 2711.

Pills, *see* Bitter p. blessed effects.

Pillvall, *see* Remedy (If there be no), welcome P.

Pilot, *see* Calm sea every man a p.; Paleness of p. is sign of storm.

Pin, Not worth a (Flanders).

c. **1492** *Thrie Priests of Peblis* in *Early Pop. Poet. Scot.* 1189 (1895) I. 163 To thé thow thocht I was not wort ane prene. *c.* **1530** H. RHODES *Bk. Nurture* 420 in *Babees Bk.* 93 Yet he is not worth a pin. *c.* **1550** WEVER *Lusty Juv.* in HAZL. *Old Eng. Plays* II. 64 If I had not been, Thou haddest not been worth a Flanders pin At this present day. **1590** LODGE *Rosalynde* Wks. (1883) I. 37 Aliena . . . said, the wedding was not worth a pinne, vnles there were some cheere. **1594–5** SHAKS. *Two Gent.* II. vii. 55 A round hose, madam, now's not worth a pin. **1600–1** *Hamlet* I. iv. 65 I do not set my life at a pin's fee.

Pin a day is a groat a year, A.

1712 ADDISON *Spect.* No. 295, par. 4 A Pin a Day, says our frugal proverb, is a Groat a Year. **1827** HARE *Gues. at Truth* (1873) i. 238 Thrift is the best means of thriving. . . . A pin a-day is a groat a-year.

Pin, See a | and let it stay (lie), you'll want a pin another day (before you die); see a pin and pick it up, all the day you'll have good luck.

1843 HALLIWELL *Nursery Rhymes* 120 (A) See a pin and let it lay, Bad luck you'll have all the day! **1872** *N. & Q.* 4th Ser. x. 477 (A) I have frequently heard the following in Cornwall 'To see a pin and let it lie, You'll want a pin before you die'. **1883** BURNE & JACKSON *Shropshire Folk-Lore* 279.

Pin, *see also* Pin(s).

Pinch on the parson's (priest's) side.

[= reduce your almsgiving, or tithes.] **1530** *Proper Dyaloge* in *Rede me*, &c. (Arb.) 169 Let him ones begynne to pynche Or withdrawe their tithinge an ynche, For an heretike they will him ascite. **1576** U. FULWELL *Ars Adulandi* M 3ᵛ Pinch on the parsons side my Lorde, the whorsons haue too much. **1629** T. ADAMS *Serm.* (1861–2) I. 466 This is a common slander when the hell-hound (the covetous wretch) pincheth on the priest's side: 'No matter, let him talk for his living'.

Pinch(es), *see also* Nothing tickles that p. not; Penny at a p. worth a pound.

Pine wishes herself a shrub when the axe is at her root, The.

1692 L'ESTRANGE *Aesop's Fab.* ccxxxvii (1738) 253 'Tell me, however, when the carpenter comes next with the axe into the wood, to fell timber, whether you had not rather be a bramble than a fir tree'. **1732** FULLER no. 4705.

Pins and needles, To be on.

1897 STEVENSON *St. Ives* xxix He was plainly on pins and needles. **1910** P. W. JOYCE *Eng. as We Speak* 141 I was *on pins and needles* till you came home: *i.e.* I was very uneasy.

Pins his faith upon another man's sleeve, He.

1579 LYLY *Euphues* Wks. (Bond) I. 249 Art thou so pinned to their sleeves. . . . **1584** *Sapho & Phao* II. iv. 97 Be not pinned always on her sleeves. **1590** GREENE *Wks.* (Gros.) IX. 173 What is it for mee to pinne a fayre meacocke and a witty milksop on my sleeve, who dare not answere with their swords in the face of the enemy? **1594–5** SHAKS. *L.L.L.* V. ii. 321 This gallant pins the wenches on his sleeve. **1660** SECKER *Nonsuch Prof.* iii (1891) 274 That was a good saying of Sir Thomas More: 'I will not pin my faith upon any man's sleeve, because I know not whither he will carry it.' **1678** RAY 342 I'll not pin my faith on your sleeve. **1824** FERRIER *Inheritance* II. xi There are those who pin their faith upon the sleeve of some favourite preacher. **1867–77** FROUDE *Short Stud.* (1890) III. 140 The Protestant . . . refused to pin his faith upon the Church's sleeve thenceforward.

Pin(s), *see also* Care a p. (Not to); Cleave the p.; Heard a p. drop (Might have); Neat as a new p.; Pack to the p. (Brought the); Silvered p. fair without foul within; Stoop for a p. (He that will not); Takes not up a p. slights wife (He that).

Pint stoups hae lang lugs.

1818 SCOTT *Rob Roy* xxvi Not that I wad speak ony ill of this MacCallum More— 'Curse not the rich in your bedchamber, . . . For a bird of the air shall carry the clatter, and pint stoups hae lang lugs.' **1862** HISLOP 247 . . . For a great deal is said over them, which, but for their influence, would not be heard.

Pint stoup(s), *see also* Comes to the hand like p. s.

Pint, *see also* Bald moon . . . another p.

Pipe in (*or* with) an ivy leaf, To.

[= to console oneself (for failure, &c.) with some frivolous employment.] *c.* **1370** WYCLIF *Eng. Wks.* (E.E.T.S.) 372 (A) The Seculer party may go pipe with an yuy lefe for any lordeschipis that the clerkis will geue hem agen. *c.* **1374** CHAUCER *Troylus* v. 1433 But, Troylus, thou mayst now, este or weste, Pipe in an ivy leefe, if that the leste. **1387–8** T. USK *Test. Love* III. vii (Skeat) l. 50 Far wel the gardiner, he may pipe with an yue leafe, his fruite is failed. *c.* **1430** LYDGATE *Churl & Bird* 276 *Minor Poems* (Percy Soc.) 189 Thou mayst go pype in an yve-leffe.

Pipe of peace, To smoke the.

1762 FOOTE *Lyar.* I. (1786) 17 I had the first honour of smoaking the pipe of peace with the little Carpenter. **1789** WOLCOT (P. Pindar) *Subj. for Paint.* Wks. (1816) II. 3 I come to bid the hatchet's labour cease, And smoke with friends the calumet of peace. **1870** MISS BRIDGMAN *Rob. Lynne* II. xii. 261 They had better smoke the pipe of peace.

Pipe one's eye (*or* eyes), To.

[Orig. Naut. slang = to weep.] **1789** C. DIBDIN *Song, Poor Jack* iii What argufies sniv'ling and piping your eye? *a.* **1814** *Sailor's Ret.* II. i in *New Brit. Theatre* II. 337 Lucy and he must have piped their eyes enough by this time. **1826** HOOD *Faithless Sally Brown* xv in *Whims & Odd* (1861) 44 He heav'd a bitter sigh, And then began to eye his pipe, And then to pipe his eye.

Pipe that lacketh his upper lip, He can ill.

1546 HEYWOOD II. ix. 77 **1621** JONSON *Gip. Metam.* Wks. (1904) III. 154 Marry, a new collection, there's no music else, masters; he can ill pipe that wants his upper lip, money. **1670** RAY 131 . . . Things cannot be done without necessary helps and instruments.

Pipe(s) (*noun*), *see also* Fowler's p. sweet till bird caught; Long a-tuning your p. (You are as); Put that in your p.; Put up your p.

Pipe (*verb*), *see also* No longer p. no longer dance.

Piper a penny to play, Give the | and two pence to leave off.

1732 FULLER no. 1660.

Piper of Bujalance, Like the | who got one maravedi to strike up and ten to leave off.

1846 LONGFELLOW *Span. Studt.* I. ii Art thou related to the bagpiper of Bujalance, who asked a maravedi for playing, and ten for leaving off? **1885** J. ORMSBY *D. Quixote* II. 345 Note B. That peculiarly humorous one . . . , 'The piper of Bujalance, (who got) one maravedi to strike up and ten to leave off'.

Piper wants mickle that wants the nether chaft(s),[1] The.

1641 FERGUSSON 94. **1721** KELLY 310 . . . Spoken when a thing is wanting that is absolutely necessary. [[1] lower jaw.]

Piper(s), *see also* Pays the p. call the tune; Speak good of p.

Pippin(s), *see* Crab-tree where you will (Plant), never bear p.; Parings of a p. better than whole crab.

Pirate gets nothing of another but his cask, One.

1666 TORRIANO 54 'Twixt Pirate and Pirate, there's nothing to be had but empty barrels. **1732** FULLER no. 3790.

Pisgah sight, A.

[BIBLE *Deut.* xxxiv. 1–3.] **1650** FULLER *A Pisgah-sight of Palestine* (title). **1829** SCOTT *Journal* 7 Mar. This extrication of my affairs, though only a Pisgah prospect, occupies my mind more than is fitting.

Pismire, *see* Angry as a p.

Piss clear, and defy the physician.

1591 FLORIO *Sec. Frutes* 61 I knowe no better phisick then to pisse cleare, that so a man may bid a figg for the phisition. **1678** RAY 42 Piscia chiaro & incaca al medico, i.e. Pisse clear and defie the physician.

Piss down one's back, To.

1813 RAY 66 . . . *i.e.* to flatter.

Piss in the same quill, To.

1678 RAY 265. *a.* **1734** NORTH *Exam.* I. ii, § 78 (1740) 70 So strangely did Papist and Fanatic, or . . . the Anticourt Party, p—s in a Quill; agreeing in all Things that tended to create Troubles and disturbances.

Piss not against the wind.

1642 TORRIANO 19 He who pisseth against the wind, wetteth his shirt. **1670** RAY 131 . . . Chi piscia contra il vento si bagna la commiscia, *Ital.* He that pisseth against the wind, wets his shirt. It is to a man's own prejudice, to strive against the stream.

Pissed on a nettle, He has.

1546 HEYWOOD II. x. 82 It seemed to him she had pissed on a nettle. **1592** GREENE *Upst. Courtier* B 3 All these women that you heare brawling . . . and skolding thus, have seuerally pist on this bush of nettles. **1641** FERGUSSON 50 *Of angry persons.* He hes pisht on a nettle. *a.* **1700** B.E. *Dict. Cant. Crew* s.v. *He has pist upon a Nettle*, he is very uneasy or much out of Humor. **1828** *Craven Gloss.* s.v. 'Thou's p—d of a nettle this morning', said of a waspish, ill-tempered person.

Pissed tallow, He has.

c. **1450** *M. E. Med. Book* (Heinrich) Take talow of an hert, suche as he pysseþ by twene two seynt mary dayes. **1600–1** SHAKS. *Merry W.* V. v. 16 For me, I am here a Windsor stag, . . . send me a cool rut-time, Jove, or who can blame me to piss my tallow. **1678** RAY 78 . . . This is spoken of bucks who grow lean after rutting time, and may be applied to men. **1694** MOTTEUX *Rabelais* v. xxviii

(1737) 132 He's nothing but Skin and Bones; he has piss'd his Tallow.

Pitch and pay.

14. . *Piers of Fulham* 206 in HAZL. *E.P.P.* II. 9 Yt ys full hard bothe to pyche and paye. **1559** *Mirr. Mag., Warwick* xiv I vsed playnnes, euer pitch and pay. **1598–9** SHAKS. *Hen. V* II. iii. 51 The word is, Pitch and pay: trust none. **1608** H. CLAPHAM *Errour on Left Hand* 102 But you your promise once did breake. Give me your hand, that you will pitch and pay.

Pitch, *see also* Devil to pay and no p. hot; Toucheth p. (He that) shall be defiled.

Pitcher (Pot) goes so often to the well (water), The | that it is broken at last.

1340 *Ayenb.* 206 Zuo longe þeþ pot to þe wetere, þet hit comþ to-broke hom. *c.* **1350** *Douce MS. 52* no. 88 The pot goth so longe to the water þat he comyth broke home. *a.* **1450** *Knt. de la Tour* 82 It is a trew prouerbe, that 'the potte may goo so longe to water, that atte the laste it is broken'. **1546** HEYWOOD II. vii. 67 The pot so long to the water gothe. Tyll at the laste it comthe home broken. **1591** GREENE *Art Conny Catch.* II (1592) 15 Yet at last so long the pitcher goeth to the brooke, that it commeth broken home. *c.* **1645** HOWELL *Lett.* I. i. vi That the Pot which goes often to the water, comes home crack'd at last. **1670** RAY 131 The pitcher doth not go so often to the water, but it comes home broken at last. **1826** SCOTT *Woodst.* xxii The pitcher goes oft to the well——. **1883** *Pall Mall G.* 3 Oct. 3/2 The pitcher, however, has gone once too often to the well, and yesterday . . . the panorama caught fire in earnest, and was reduced to ashes.

Pitcher goes so often to the well, The | that it leaves its handle or its mouth.

1851 SIR A. HELPS *Compan. of Sol.* vi (1907) 65 The Spaniards . . . express it prettily . . . The little pitcher that goes often to the fountain, either leaves the handle, or the spout, behind some day. The dainty vase . . . kept under a glass case . . ., should not be too proud of remaining without a flaw, considering its great advantages.

Pitcher strikes the stone, Whether the | or the stone the pitcher, it is bad for the pitcher.

1620 SHELTON *Quix.* III. vi (1908) I. 158 After what way soever I grow angry with thee, it will be bad for the pitcher. *Ibid.* II. xliii (1908) III. 116 And 'If the pot fall upon the stone, or the stone on the pot, ill for the pot, ill for the stone'. **1911** A. COHEN *Anct. Jew. Prov.* 103 If the stone falls on the pot, woe to the pot; if the pot falls on the stone, woe to the pot; in either case woe to the pot. . . . The weak always suffers. A proverb . . . current in Spain, borrowed in all probability from the Jews.

Pitcher(s), *see also* Little p. have great ears; Tom p.'s broken (When), I shall have shards.

Pities another remembers himself, He that.

1640 HERBERT 353. **1748** RICHARDSON *Clarissa* iv let. 24 Another proverb that I picked up at Madrid . . . 'he that' &c.

Pitiful look asks enough, A.

1640 HERBERT 353.

Pitiful mother makes a scald[1] head, A.

1640 HERBERT 347. [[1] scabby.]

Pitiful surgeon (physician) spoileth a sore, A.

1573 SANDFORD (1576) 217 A pitiful physition maketh a deadly wounde. **1578** FLORIO *First Fruites* f. 32 (A) A pitifull physition maketh a scabed wound. **1604** MARSTON *Malcontent* IV. ii. 95 A pitiful surgeon makes a dangerous sore.

Pity is akin to love.

1599–1600 SHAKS. *Twelfth N.* III. i. 136 *Vio.* I pity you. *Oli.* That's a degree to love. **1696** SOUTHERNE *Oroonoko* II. i Do pity me; Pity's akin to love. **1896** F. LOCKER-LAMPSON *My Confid.* 95 They say that Pity is akin to Love, though only a Poor Relation; but Amy did not even pity me.

Pity (*noun*), *see also* Foolish p. mars a city; Laird of p. (Looks like).

Pity (-ied) (*verb*), *see also* Sick man is not to be p. who hath cure.

Pivot(s), *see* Great engines.

Pixy, *see* Horse must smell to a p. (Good).

Place for everything, and everything in its place, A.

1875 SMILES *Thrift* 78 Order is most useful in the management of everything. . . . Its maxim is, A place for everything and everything in its place. **1902–4** LEAN III. 401.

Place in the sun, One's.

1727 B. KENNET *Pascal's Thoughts* (ed. 2) 291 This Dog's *mine*, says the poor Child: this is *my* Place, in the Sun. From so petty a Beginning, may we trace the Tyranny and Usurpation of the whole Earth. **1911** *Times* 28 Aug. 6/3 (Wilhelm II's Speech at Hamburg, 27 Aug.) No one can dispute with us the place in the sun that is our due.

Place like home, There is no.

1822 J. H. PAYNE *Song*, 'Home, Sweet Home' Be it ever so humble, there's no place like home. **1859** LD. DUFFERIN *Lett. High Lat.* (1895) 241 My . . . infant walrus . . . would . . . come . . . among us again with a contented grunt, as much as to say, 'Well, after all, there's no place like *home*!' **1876** J. PAYN *Halves* xxi

When one was sick there was no place like home.

Place(s), *see also* All things have their p.; Quits his p. well that leaves friend; Sit in your p., none can make you rise; Two p. at once (One cannot be in); Women think p. a sweet fish.

Placebo, *see* No penny no p.; Sing p.

Plack,[1] Not worth a.

a. **1550** in DUNBAR *Poems* (S.T.S.) 307 He wald nocht mend thame worth ane plack. *a.* **1585** A. MONTGOMERIE *Cherrie & Slae* lxxxiii (1821) 44 ʒe are nae prophet worth a plak. [[1] a small copper coin current in Scotland in 15th and 16th cents.]

Placks and bawbees grow pounds.

1832 HENDERSON 16.

Plain as a pikestaff, As.

[An alteration of the earlier phrase *as plain as a packstaff*, in reference to its plain surface.] **1532** MORE *Wks.* (1557) 814 (A). **1542** BECON *David's Harp* Early *Wks.* (P.S.) 276 He is as plain as a pack-staff. **1591** GREENE *Disc. Coosnage* (1592) 4 A new game . . . that hath no policie nor knauerie, but plaine as a pike-staffe. **1719** D'URFEY *Pills* III. 22 When a Reason's as plain as a Pikestaff. **1818** SCOTT *Rob Roy* xxvi I'll make it as plain as Peter Pasley's pike-staff. **1867** TROLLOPE *Last Chron. Barset* I. xlii. 367 The evidence against him was as plain as a pikestaff.

Plain as the nose on a man's face, As.

1586 PETTIE *Guazzo's Civ. Conv.* The simple soules not perceiving that their transformation, or rather deformation, is no more seene than a nose in a man's face. **1592** SHAKS. *Two Gent.* II. i. 131–2 O jest unseen, inscrutable, invisible, As a nose on a man's face. **1639** CLARKE 188 As plaine as the nose on a mans face. **1655** H. MORE *Second Lash* 200 As plain as the nose on a man's face. **1868** W. COLLINS *Moonstone* xv On evidence which is as plain as the nose on your face!

Plain dealing is a jewel.

1607–8 SHAKS. *Timon of A.* I. i. 216 *Tim.* How dost thou like this jewel, Apemantus? *Apem.* Not so well as plain-dealing. **1685** DRYDEN *Albion & Alban.* Epil. *Plain Dealing* for a Jewel has been known; But ne'er till now the Jewel of a Crown.

Plain dealing is a jewel, but he that useth it shall die a beggar.

1583 MELBANCKE *Philotimus* Epist. Ded. (A) Plaine dealing is a jewel (though they that vse it commonly die beggers). **1599** PORTER *Angry Wom. Abingd.* IV. iii (Merm.) 176 *Nich.* I speak plainly, for plain-dealing is a jewel, and he that useth it shall die a beggar. **1660** W. SECKER *Nonsuch Prof.* II (1891) 284 That is but an hall-made proverb: plain dealing is a jewel, but he who adheres to it shall die a beggar.

Plain dealing is dead, and died without issue.

1616 B. RICH *Ladies Looking Glasse* 60 (A) Plaine dealing: honesty is dead. **1732** FULLER no. 3879. **1750** FRANKLIN Sept. Poor Plain dealing! dead without Issue.

Plain dealing is praised more than practised.

1639 CLARKE 138.

Plain fashion is best, The.

1555 HEYWOOD *Epigr. upon Prov.* no. 201.

Plain of poverty and die a beggar.

1678 RAY 191.

Plaints (Tarrows) early that plaints (tarrows) on his kail, He.

1641 FERGUSSON 42. **1721** KELLY 135 *He tarrows early that tarrows on his kail.* The Scots, for their first dish have broth (which they call kail) and their flesh-meat . . . after. Spoken when men complain before they see the utmost that they will get.

Planet(s), *see* Born under a three-halfpenny p.; Rains by p.

Plant an opinion they seem to eradicate, Some men.

1640 HERBERT 372.

Plant pears for your heirs.

1869 HAZLITT 330 . . . A proverb which no longer holds true, since pears are now made to yield well after a few years.

Plant (*noun*), *see* Noble p. suits not stubborn ground.

Plant(ed), (*verb*), *see also* Crab-tree where you will (P.); Pluck not where never p.

Plants a walnut-tree, He who | expects not to eat of the fruit.

1732 FULLER no. 2401.

Plaster for so small a sore, That is a prodigious.

1732 FULLER no. 4347.

Plaster, *see also* Break one's head and bring p.

Platter, *see* Much matter of wooden p.

Play at bowls, He that will | must expect to meet with rubbers.

1594–5 SHAKS. *L.L.L.* IV. i. 142 *Cost.* Challenge her to bowl. *Boyet.* I fear too much rubbing. **1595–6** *Rich. II* III. iv. 4 *First Lady* Madam, we'll play at bowls. *Queen* 'Twill make me think the world is full of rubs. **1771** SMOLLETT *Humph. Clink.* 3 Oct. Wks. (1871) 572 The lieutenant had carried his resentment too far, . . . but, according to the proverb, *he that will play at bowls must expect to meet with rubbers.* **1824** SCOTT *Redg.* xx

'And how if it fails?' said Darsie. 'Thereafter as it may be', said Nixon; 'they who play at bowls must meet with rubbers.'

Play at chess when the house is on fire, To.

1651 HERBERT 370. **1732** FULLER no. 5539 When a man's house is on fire, it's time to break off chess.

Play booty, To.

[= to act as decoy for confederates, practise collusion.] **1540** PALSGRAVE *Acolastus* T 4 (A) Shall not I be boty or party felow with the? **1561** AWDELAY *Frat. of Vacabondes* 9 And consent as though they will play booty against him. **1592** GREENE *Art Conny Catch.* II. 8 The bowlers cast euer booty and doth win or loose as the bet of the gripe leadeth them. **1622** MABBE tr. *Aleman's Guzman d'Alf.* I. 222 Wee are three of vs, let vs all play booty, and joyne together to coozen the Cardinall. **1771** P. PARSONS *Newmarket* I. 108 Bribing the rider to play booty, to lose the race. **1813** *Examiner* 17 May 319/1 I gave a jockey a handsome premium to play booty.

Play (at) fast and loose, To.

[= to be unreliable or inconsistent. Fast-and-loose was an old cheating game played by gipsies and vagrants. *See* 1847 HALLIWELL Dict.] **1557** *Tottel's Misc.* (Arb.) 157. [Title of Epigram] Of a new married student that plaid fast or loose. **1594–5** SHAKS. *L.L.L.* I. ii. 162 *Cost.* Let me not be pent up, sir: I will fast, being loose. *Moth.* No, sir; that were fast and loose. *Ibid.* III. 109 To sell a bargain well is as cunning as fast and loose. **1596–7** *K. John* III. i. 242 Play fast and loose with faith? **1606–7** *Ant. & Cleop.* IV. x. 41 This grave charm, . . . Like a right gipsy, hath, at fast and loose, Beguil'd me. **1630** *R. Johnson's Kingd. & Commw.* 369 The French playing fast and loose with their Salick Law. **1712** STEELE *Spect.* No. 320, par. 1 A little . . . playing fast and loose, between Love and Indifference. **1829** *Westm. Rev.* x. 185 Doctrines . . . which play at fast and loose with truth and falsehood. **1860** THACKERAY *Lovel the Wid.* vi (1869) 252 She had played fast and loose with me.

Play first (*or* second) fiddle, To.

[= to take a leading (or subordinate) place.] **1778** *Learning at Loss* II. 79 Our Friends . . . returned, with Jack Solecism the first Fiddle as usual. **1809** MALKIN *Gil Blas* x. xi I am quite at your service to play second fiddle in all your laudable enterprises. **1822** O'MEARA *Napoleon in Exile* I. 227 He was of opinion that Prussia should never play the first fiddle in the affairs of the Continent. **1850** THACKERAY *Pendennis* (1878) II. xvii. 19 'I've played a second fiddle all through life', he said with a bitter laugh. **1909** *Times* 17 May Austria-Hungary . . . last autumn took the initiative on her own account. For the first time during . . . her alliance with Germany . . . she has played the first fiddle.

Play for nought as work for nought, As good.

1533 UDALL *Flowers for Latin Speaking*

Better contented (according to the accustomed prouerbe) to plaie for naught then to werke for naught. **1546** HEYWOOD I. xi. 36 As good play for nought as woorke for nought, folke tell. **1721** KELLY 60 Better play for nought, than work for nought. **1808** SCOTT *Let. to Sharpe* 30 Dec. in LOCKHART *Life* The fee is ten guineas . . . —as good play for nothing, you know, as work for nothing.

Play off your dust.

1670 RAY 216 *Drinking Phrases* Play off your dust.

Play one's cards well, To.

[= to make good use of one's resources or opportunities.] **1753** FOOTE *Eng. in Paris* I. i If Lucinda plays her cards well, we have not much to fear from that Quarter. **1894** MRS. STEEL *Potter's Thumb* xxv 'He is a fool, and yet he is playing his cards well'.

Play providence, To.

1886 W. BLACK *White Heather* xlvii His pet hobby was playing the part of a small, beneficent Providence; and he had already befriended Ronald. **1909** *Spectator* 11 Dec. 988 The rôle of Providence is intensely attractive. We doubt whether there is any woman who does not hope to play it . . . Match-making on the part of a mother is . . . part of her regular work.

Play rex, To.

[= to act as lord or master. L. *Rex*, a King.] **1578** FOXE in *Bk. Chr. Prayers* 28 b Needs would haue . . . an Italian stranger, the Bishop of Rome to play Rex ouer them. **1597** BEARD *Theatre God's Judgem.* (1612) 529 The Scots that were so curbed in his fathers dayes, now played rex through his negligence. **1651** N. BACON *Disc. Govt. Eng.* II. xxxvii (1739) 168 The Prelacy . . . played Rex all the while with the people.

Play small game before he will sit out, He (The devil) will.

1578 G. WHETSTONE *Promus & Cassandra* D 4ᵛ He will playe at Small game, or he sitte out. *a.* **1591** HY. SMITH *Serm.* (1866) II. 108 The devil, or the world, or the flesh, will play small game, as we use to say, before they will sit out. If they cannot get full possession of our hearts, then they are content to have some part of our love. **1623** CAMDEN 270. **1631** R. BRAITHWAIT *Whimzies* (1859) 148 Now for the divel, he ha's so much to do With roaring boys, he'll slight such babes as thou. Yet be not too secure, but put him to't, For he'll play at small game, e'er he sit out. **1655–62** GURNALL *Chrn. in Armour* (1865) I. 294 They would make us think, that here men played but at small game, and their souls were not at stake, as in other sins. **1721** KELLY 391 You will play small game before you stand out. **1827** SCOTT *Cannongate* i Some stuck to cards, and though no longer deep gamblers, rather played small game than sat out.

Play, The less | the better.

1641 FERGUSSON 98.

Play the devil in the bullimong, To.

1678 RAY 239 To play the *Devil* i' th' bulmong, *i.e.* corn mingled of pease, tares, and oats [sown together for feeding cattle.]

Play the devil in the horologe, To.

[= to play pranks with the works of a clock; a type of the confusion caused by a mischievous agent in any orderly system.] **1519** HORMAN *Vulg.* 232 b Some for a tryfull pley the deuyil in the orlege. *a.* **1553** UDALL *Royster D.* III. ii (Arb.) 43 *Cust.* What will he? *Me.* Play the deuill in the horologe.

Play the fool.

1612 P. CHARRON *Of Wisdom* tr. Lennard (1640) 139 That Proverbe . . . a man must not play the foole by halfes. **1732** FULLER no. 2849 It is a cunning part to play the fool well.

Play the fool, *see also* No man can p. the f. as wise man; Wise man who cannot (He is not); Wise men p. the f. (If).

Play the game.

c. **1386** CHAUCER *Clerk's T.* Prol. 10–11 For what man that is entred in a pley, He nedès moot unto the pley assente. **1898** KIPLING *Day's Work* 248 (*Maltese Cat*) 'Play the game, don't talk'. **1904** *Daily Chron.* 2 May 4/5 Men do not talk about their honour nowadays —they call it 'playing the game'.

Play the jack, To.

[= to play the knave, to do a mean thing.] **1567** GOLDING *Ovid* xiii. 289 (A) Yit durst Thersites bee So bold as rayle uppon the kings, and he was payd by mee For playing so the sawcye Jacke. **1611** BEAUM. & FL. *Kt. Burn. P.* Induct. If you were not resolved to play the Jacks, what need you study for new subjects, purposely to abuse your betters? **1611–12** SHAKS. *Temp.* IV. i. 198 Your fairy . . . has done little better than played the Jack with us. **1668** PEPYS *Diary* 23 Feb. Sir R. Brookes overtook us coming to town; who played the jacke with us all, and is a fellow that I must trust no more.

Play well if you lose, It signifies nothing to.

1732 FULLER no. 3045.

Play with a bull till you get his horn in your eye, You may.

1917 BRIDGE 158 . . . Another form of 'Do not play with edged tools'.

Play with a fool at home, and he will play with you in the market.

1640 HERBERT 323. **1670** RAY 10. **1732** FULLER no. 2763 If you let a fool play with you at home, he'll do so with you in the market.

Play with fire, To.

1655 H. VAUGHAN *Garland* in *Silex Scint.* II. (1847) 132 I played with fire, did counsell spurn, . . . But never thought that fire would burn, Or that a soul could ake.

Play with the ears than the tongue, It is better to.

1611 DAVIES Prov. 217.

Play with you for shoe-buckles, I will not.

1639 CLARKE 195 We play not for shooe-buckles. **1678** RAY 347.

Play with your peers.

1629 A. MONTGOMERIE *Flyting* (1821) 107 Play with thy peir, or I'll pull thee like a Paipe. **1641** FERGUSSON 86. **1721** KELLY 281 *Play with your playfeers.*[1] Spoken to young people when they offer to be roguish upon, or play too saucily with, old people. [[1] fellows.]

Play, women, and wine undo men laughing.

1579 LYLY *Euphues* (Arb.) 118 It is play, wine and wantonnesse, that feedeth a lover as fat as a foole. **1655–62** GURNALL *Chrn. in Armour* (1865) II. 239 The Italians say that 'play, wine, and women consume a man laughing'. It is true of all pleasurable sins. **1670** RAY 21.

Play(s) (*noun*), see also Boys' p. (To leave); Cast be bad (If), mend by good p.; Good as a p.; Hand p. churls' p.; Leave off while p. good; No p. without fool.

Play(s) (*verb*), see also Children and fools must not p. with edged tools; Done no ill the six days (If you have), p. the seventh; Jacks are common to all that will p.; Wily beguiled (P.).

Playful as a kitten, As.

1825 SCOTT *Journ.* 21 Dec. I never saw Byron so full of fun, frolic, wit, and whim; he was as playful as a kitten.

Playing with a straw before an old cat, No.

c. **1450** HENRYSON *Mor. Fab.* 65 It is ane olde Dog . . . that thou begyles, Thou weines to draw the stra before the Cat. **1546** HEYWOOD II. viii. 72 No plaiyng with a strawe before an olde cat, Euery tryflyng toie age can not laugh at. **1641** FERGUSSON 64 It is ill to draw a strea before an auld cat. **1721** KELLY 180 *I am o'er old a cat, to draw a straw before my nose* . . . I am too old to be imposed upon. A young cat will jump at a straw drawn before her, but not an old one. **1818** SCOTT *Rob Roy* xxvi He tried if Mac Vittie and Co. wad gie him siller on them . . . but they were ower auld cats to draw that strae afore them.

Playing with short daggers, It is ill.

1546 HEYWOOD I. xii. 39 It be ill playing with short daggers, Whiche meaneth, that euery wise man staggers, . . . to be busie or bolde With his biggers or betters.

Plays best (well) that wins, He.

1555 HEYWOOD *Epigr. upon Prov.* no. 230. **1639** CLARKE 122 He plays well that wins.

Plays his money, He that | ought not to value it.

1640 HERBERT 326.

Plays more than he sees, He that | forfeits his eyes to the king.

1614 CAMDEN 307. **1670** RAY 132. **1721** KELLY 172 . . . An excuse for overlooking an advantage at game.

Plays the whore for apples, She | and then bestows them upon the sick.

1678 RAY *Adag. Hebr.* 407 . . . This Proverb is used against those who give Almes of what they get unjustly.

Plays you as fair as if he picked your pocket, He.

1678 RAY 79.

Plea, see Ill p. should be well pleaded.

Pleaing[1] at the law is like fighting through a whin[2] bush,—The harder the blows, the sairer[3] the scarts.[4]

1832 HENDERSON 39. [[1] pleading. [2] furze. [3] sorer. [4] scratches.]

Please all parties, It is hard to.

1721 KELLY 220 . . . *Durum est omnibus placere.*

Please the pigs.

[= please the fates; if circumstances permit.] **1702** T. BROWN *Lett. fr. Dead* Wks. (1760) II 198 I'll have one of the wigs to carry into the country with me, and [i.e. an't] please the pigs. **1891** *Blackw. Mag.* June 819/1 There I'll be, please the pigs, on Thursday night.

Please, I will | what so betide.

c. **1450** *Provs. of Wysdom* 19 'I wyll please, what so betyde'. If thou wylt please, lay truthe, a syde.

Please your eye and plague your heart.

1655 A. BREWER *Love-sick King* III in BANG, *Materialen* B. 18 p. 38 (A) She may please your eye a little . . . but vex your heart. **1748** SMOLLETT *Rod. Rand.* xl Many a substantial farmer . . . would be glad to marry her; but she was resolved to please her eye, if she should plague her heart. **1829** COBBETT *Adv. to Y. Men* iii (1906) 122 'Please your eye and plague your heart' is an adage that want of beauty invented, I dare say, more than a thousand years ago. **1876** MRS. BANKS *Manch. Man* xxxviii But I WILL marry him, mamma—*I'll please my eye, if I plague my heart.*

Please(s), *see also* All men will p. (He that) shall never find ease; Hard to p. a knave as a knight; Rise betimes that would p. everybody; Sport best p. that does least know how.

Pleased as Punch, As.

1854 DICKENS *Hard Times* I. vi. (A) When Sissy got into the school here . . . her father was as pleased as Punch. **1942** EVELYN WAUGH *Put out More Flags,* Spring iii Believe it or not, she's as pleased as Punch.

Pleased, If you be not | put your hand in your pocket and please yourself.

1678 RAY 79 . . . A jeering expression to such as will not be pleased with the reasonable offers of others. **1732** FULLER no. 2739 (with 'content' for 'pleased').

Pleased, *see also* Never well (p.), full nor fasting.

Pleaseth not God, When it | the saint can do little.

1664 CODRINGTON 223. **1670** RAY 23.

Pleasing ware is half sold.

1611 COTGRAVE S.V. 'Chose'. **1640** HERBERT 317. **1721** KELLY 235 *Lik'd geer is half bought.* For in that case a man will give a little more for his fancy.

Pleasure long expected is dear enough sold, A.

1640 HERBERT 357.

Pleasure refrain, Who will in time present | shall in time to come the more pleasure obtain.

1550 HEYWOOD I. xi. 27.

Pleasure without pain (repentance), No.

1576 PETTIE *Petite Pall.* (Gollancz) I. 142 Pleasure must be purchased with the price of pain. *c.* **1590** MARLOWE *Faustus* V. iv. His store of pleasure must be sauced with pain. **1599–1600** SHAKS. *Twelfth N.* II. iv. 71 *Duke.* I'll pay thy pleasure then. *Clo.* Truly, sir, and pleasure will be paid, one time or another. **1639** CLARKE 326 Never pleasure without repentance.

Pleasures of the mighty are the tears of the poor, The. (*Cf.* Dainties of the great, &c.)

1616 DRAXE 143. **1670** RAY 21. **1732** FULLER no. 4707 The pleasures of the rich are bought with the tears of the poor.

Pleasure(s), *see also* Diseases are the price of ill p.; Every p. has a pain; Fly that p. which paineth after; Follow love (p.) and it will flee; Gentleman but his p. (What's a); Look not on p. as they come; Say to

p., *Gentle Eve*; Short p. long lament; Toil of a p.

Pledge your own health, You must not.

1599 JONSON *Ev. Man out of Humour,* Induction 359 There's an old rule; *No pledging your own health.* **1678** RAY 152.

Plenty as blackberries, As.

1597–8 SHAKS. *1 Hen. IV* II. iv. 265 It reasons were as plenty as blackberries, I would give no man a reason upon compulsion. **1841** CARLYLE *Heroes* v (1896) 426 Though you had constitutions plentiful as blackberries.

Plenty breeds pride.

1589 PUTTENHAM *Art of Poetry* Bk. III ch. 19. **1639** CLARKE 33.

Plenty is no dainty.

c. **1449** PECOCK *Repr.* 184 Experience wole weel schewe that plente is no deinte, and ouermyche homelines with a thing gendrith dispising toward the same thing. **1542** RECORDE *Gr. Artes* B ij Plentie is no deintie, as the common saieying is. **1546** HEYWOOD II. iv. 51 Plentie is no deintie, ye sée not your own ease.

Plenty is no plague.

1616 DRAXE 159 Plentie is no sore. **1832** HENDERSON 85.

Plenty makes dainty.

1678 RAY 190. **1721** KELLY 281 . . . When people have variety of many meats, or abundance of one sort, they are nice and delicate. **1732** FULLER no. 6375.

Plenty makes poor.

[ov. *Met.* 3. 466 *Inopem me copia fecit.*] **1596** SPENSER *F.Q.* I. iv. 29 Whose wealth was want, whose plenty made him poor. **1621** BRATHWAIT *Omphale* in *Nat. Embas.* (1877) 269 Forced now to surfet on her store, She prou'd this true: Much plentie made her poore. **1623** FLETCHER *Lover's Progress* I. ii Abundance makes me poor.

Plenty of good(s), He that hath | shall have more.

1546 HEYWOOD I. xi. 38. **1614** CAMDEN 307.

Plenty will take no heed, He who of | shall find default in time of need.

c. **1450** *Prov. of Wysdom* 159, 160.

Plie, *see* No reply (p.) is best.

Plough be jogging, If your | you may have meat for your horses.

1659 HOWELL *Eng. Prov.* 11/1.

Plough deep, while sluggards sleep; and you shall have corn to sell and to keep.

1758 FRANKLIN in ARBER *E. Garner* V. 580

Then *Plough deep, while sluggards sleep; And you shall have corn to sell and to keep*, says *Poor* DICK.

Plough goes not well if the plough-man hold it not, The.

1616 WITHALS 573. **1639** J. CLARKE 92. **1732** FULLER no. 4710.

Plough going than two cradles, It is better to have one.

1580 LYLY *Euph. & his Eng.* (Arb.) 229 Be not hastie to marry, it is better to haue one plough going, then two cradells. **1732** FULLER no. 905.

Plough stand to catch a mouse, Let (*or* Never let) the.

1678 RAY 265 Let the plough stand to catch a mouse. **1721** KELLY 234 *Let the plough stand, and slay a mouse.* Lay aside, for a little, that business that you are so earnest upon; and take a little divertisement. *Ibid.* 234 Master *Palmer*[1] has one.... *Never let the plough stand to slay a mouse* . . . to wit, that we be not taken off from our proper business, by every obvious divertisement. [[1] S. Palmer, author of *Moral Essays*, 1710.]

Plough the sands, To.

[= fruitless labour. OVID *ex Ponto* 4. 2. 16 *Siccum sterili vomere litus aro.* ERASM. *Ad. Arare litus.*] *a.* **1529** SKELTON *Speke, Parrot* in Wks. (Dyce) II. 17 To sowe corne in the see sande, ther wyll no crope growe. **1590** GREENE *Never too late* Wks. (Gros.) VIII. 166 With sweating browes I long haue plowde the sands . . . Repent hath sent me home with emptie hands. **1605** SYLVESTER (1621) 19 On thankless furrows of a fruitless sand Their seed and labour lose, with heedless hand. **1647** JER. TAYLOR *Lib. Proph.* Ep. Ded. 5 That I had as good plow the Sands, or till the Aire, as perswade such Doctrines, which destroy mens interests. **1775** WESLEY *Jrnl.* 15 Nov. I preached at Dorking. But still I fear we are ploughing upon the sand: we see no fruit of our labours.

Plough would thrive, He that by the | himself must either hold or drive.

1678 RAY 191. **1758** FRANKLIN *Way to Wealth* (Crowell) 18 We must . . . not trust too much to others; for, . . . *He that by the plough would thrive, Himself must either hold or drive.*

Plough with an ox and an ass to-gether, To.

1560 GENEVA BIBLE (1586) *Deut.* xxii. 10 Thou shalt not plowe with an oxe and an asse together. **1813** RAY 212 . . . *i.e.* To sort things ill.

Plough with any one's heifer (ox, calf), To.

[After *Judges* xiv. 18.] **1535** COVERDALE *Judg.* xiv. 18 Yf ye had not plowed with my calfe [1611 heifer], ye shulde not haue founde out my ryddle. **1584** *G.*B. *Beware the Cat* Ded. I doubt whether M. Stremer will be contented that other men ploughe with his oxen. **1632** MASSINGER *City Madam* II. iii I will undertake To find the north passage to the Indies sooner Than plough with your proud heifer.

Plough with such oxen as he hath, A man must.

1678 RAY 191. **1732** FULLER no. 5968.

Plough (*noun*), *see also* Counts all costs (He that) will ne'er put p.; Counts all the pins in the p. will never yoke (He that); Lippens to lent p. his land will lie ley; Pen and ink is wit's p.; Scythe cuts and p. rives (Where), no more fairies; Speed the p.; Well worth aw, it makes p. draw.

Plough (*verb*), *see also* Whistling to going to p. (Belongs more than).

Pluck not where you never planted.

1639 CLARKE 270.

Pluck the grass to know where the wind sits, To.

[= to interpret the signs of the times.] **1596–7** SHAKS. *Merch. Ven.* I. i. 18 I should be still Plucking the grass to know where sits the wind. *a.* **1670** HACKET *Abp. Williams* II (1692) 16 No Man could pluck the Grass better, to know where the Wind sat; no Man could spie sooner from whence a Mischief did rise.

Plum year a dumb year, A. (*See also* Pear year, &c., Cherry year, &c.)

1678 RAY 52. **1732** FULLER no. 6139.

Plum, *see also* Black p. sweet as white; Higher the tree sweeter the p.

Plum-tree, *see* Higher the p. riper the plum; Knave is in a p. (When).

Pluto, *see* Helmet of P.

Plutus, *see* Fearful as P.

Plymouth cloak, A.

[= a cudgel or staff carried by one who walked without cloak, and thus facetiously assumed to take the place of the latter.] **1608** DEKKER *2nd Pt. Honest Wh.* III. ii Shall I walke in a Plimouth Cloake, (that's to say) like a rogue, in my hose and doublet, and a crabtree cudgell in my hand? **1662** FULLER (*Devon*) I. 399 'A Plymouth Cloak'. That is, a cane or a staff.... Many a man ... coming home from far voyages, may chance to land here, and ... [be] unable ... to recruit himself with clothes.

Plymouth was a vuzzy[1] down, When | Plympton was a borough town.

1850 *N. & Q.* 1st Ser. II. 511 (A). **1911** W. CROSSING *Folk Rhymes of Devon* 12 When

Plymouth was a vuzzy down Plympton was a borough town. Plympton is more ancient than Plymouth, although it had not become a 'borough town', until long after the latter had sprung into existence. [¹ furzy.]

Plympton, *see* Plymouth.

Poacher, *see* Old p. best keeper.

Pocket (up) an injury, To.

[= to take an affront without showing resentment.] **1589** GREENE *Span. Masquerado* Wks. (Gros.) V. 273 Thus the great Generall of Spaine was content to pockette vppe this Dishonour to saue his life. **1596–7** SHAKS. *K. John* III. i. 200 Well ruffian, I must pocket up these wrongs. **1597–8** *1 Hen. IV* III. iii. 183 And yet you will stand to it, you will not pocket up wrong. **1598–9** *Hen. V* III. ii. 54 They would have me as familiar with men's pockets as their gloves or their handkerchers . . ., it is plain pocketing up of wrongs. **1622** MABBE tr. *Aleman's Guzman d'Alf.* I. 214 If he . . . pocket a wrong, and hold his hands, he is a coward. **1769** *Polit. Register* v. 229 Your grace would have pocketed the affront.

Pocket(s), *see also* Last garment is made without p.; Line one's p.; Money burns in your p.

Poet is born not made, A.

[L. *Poeta nascitur, non fit.*] *c.* **1581** SIDNEY *Apologie* (Arb.) 62 Therefore is it an old prouerbe, *Orator fit; Poeta nascitur.* **1620** SHELTON *Quix.* II. xvi (1908) II. 292 It is a true opinion that a poet is born so ; . . . a poet is naturally born a poet from his mother's womb. **1662** FULLER (*Warw.*) III. 284 Shakespeare . . . was an eminent instance of the truth of that rule, 'Poeta non fit sed nascitur' (one is not made but born a poet). **1827** HARE *Gues. at Truth* (1873) 194 It is impossible to devise any scheme of education . . . for promoting the development of poetical genius. . . . *Poeta nascitur, non fit.*

Poets, *see* Painters and p. have leave to lie.

Poetical justice.

1711 *Spectator* Apr. 16, no. 40 *King Lear* is an admirable tragedy of the same kind [in which calamities are not relieved], as Shakespeare wrote it ; but as it is reformed according to the Chymerical Notion of Poetical Justice, in my humble opinion it has lost half its beauty. **1712** *Ibid.* 28 Nov. no. 548 That late invented term called *Poetical Justice.* **1765** JOHNSON *Observ. on Plays of Shakesp.* Hamlet. The poet is accused of having shown little regard to poetical justice. **1938** E. I. FRIPP *Shakesp. Man and Artist* ii. 1606 Notwithstanding painful features, it [*K. Lear*] is comedy in the sense that 'poetic justice' is done.

Poind¹ for debt but not for kindness, We can.

1721 KELLY 349 . . . If our friends will not be kind to us, we have no remedy at law. [¹ distrain.]

Poind, *see also* No man may p. for unkindness.

Poison, One drop of | infects the whole tun of wine.

c. **1175** *Old Eng. Homilies* (Morris) Ser. 1. 23 A lutel ater¹ bitteret muchel swete. **1579** LYLY *Euphues* (Arb.) 39 One droppe of poyson infecteth the whole tunne of Wine. [¹ venom.]

Poison is poison though it comes in a golden cup.

1576 PETTIE *Petite Pall.* (Gollancz) II. 80 As in fair painted pots poison oft is put. **1579** LYLY *Euphues* (Bond) i. 202 Doe we not commonly see that in paynted pottes is hidden the deadlyest poyson? **1584** RICH *Don Simonides* Part ii O 3 The painted pot [shrowdeth] the deuowrying poyson. **1584** W. WARNER *Pan his Syrinx* E 3 Out of golden cuppes you will drinke poisoned draughts. **1587** GREENE *Wks.* (Gros.) III. 206 Fond were that person that would think wel of him that proferreth poyson though in a golden pot. **1600** N. BRETON *Melancholique Humours* (Harrison) 36 Poys'ned broth, in silver dishes. **1616** DRAXE 61 In golden pottes are hidden the most deadly poison.

Poison, *see also* Bee sucks honey (Where), spider sucks p.; Bites on every weed (He that) must light on poison; Horn spoon holds no p.; Meat (one man's) is another's p.; Unsound minds . . . if you feed, you p.

Poke a man's fire, You may | after you've known him seven years, but not before.

1902–4 LEAN IV. 204 . . . You must be a seven years' friend of the house before you dare stir the fire. [*N. & Q.*]

Poke savour of the herring, It is kindly¹ that the.

1641 FERGUSSON 62 It is kindlie that the poke sare² of the herring. **1721** KELLY 197 . . . It is no uncommon thing to see children take after their parents. Always meant in ill things. [¹ natural. ² savour, smell.]

Poke(s), *see also* Toom p. will strive; Which way to London? A p. full of plums.

Poker, *see* Stiff as a p.

Politeness, *see* Loses anything by p. (One never).

Politically, *see* Morally wrong cannot be p. right.

Polycrates, *see* Ring of P.

Pomfret, *see* Sure as a louse in P.

Pomp the earth covers, All our.

1640 HERBERT 350.

Pompey, *see* Paws off, P.

Pompous provision cometh not all, alway of gluttony, but of pride some time.

1550 HEYWOOD II. vii. 67.

Pond(s), *see* Breams in his p. . . . friend welcome; Courts (It is at) as in p.

Pons asinorum.

[= bridge of asses. A humorous name for the 5th prop. of the 1st bk. of Euclid, found difficult by beginners, hence used allusively.] **1751** SMOLLETT *Per. Pic.* I. xviii. 130 Peregrine . . . began to read Euclid . . . but he had scarcely advanced beyond the *Pons Asinorum* when his ardor abated. **1845** FORD *Handbk. Spain* I. 217/2 This bridge was the *pons asinorum* of the French, which English never suffered them to cross. **1870** *Eng. Mech.* 4 Feb. 502/1 He knows the operation . . . to be the *pons asinorum* of incompetent workmen.

Pontifical fellow, He is a.

1528 TINDALE *Obed. Chrn. Man* (1888) 266 We say, . . . 'He is a pontifical fellow'; that is, proud and stately.

Pool(s), *see* Standing p. gather filth.

Poole was a fish-pool, and the men of Poole fish, If | there'd be a pool for the devil and fish for his dish.

1787 GROSE (*Dorset*) 169 . . . This satyrical distich was written a long time ago. Pool is, at present, a respectable place, and has in it several rich merchants trading to Newfoundland.

Poor and liberal, rich and covetous.

1631 MABBE *Celestina* (T.T.) 212 When I was poore, then was I liberall; when I was rich, then was I covetous. **1640** HERBERT 333.

Poor and peart like the parson's pig.

1887 T. DARLINGTON S. *Cheshire Folk Speech* (E.D.S.) 289 (A) He's poor an' peart, like the parson's pig. **1903** *Eng. Dialect Dict.* IV. 446 *Cheshire* . . . probably refers to the times when the parson collected his tithe in kind. The pig reserved for him, being a small one and not overfed, was consequently brisk and active.

Poor and proud, fie, fie.

1599–1600 SHAKS. *Twelfth N.* III. i. 141 O world! how apt the poor are to be proud. **1611** GRUTER. **1614** CAMDEN 311.

Poor, To be | and seem poor is the very devil.

1847–59 SIR A. HELPS *Friends in Council* (Ser. 2) vi 'To *be* poor and *seem* poor is the very devil'. . . . That that should be a favourite proverb in a Christian country . . . tells a good deal about the inhabitants of that country.

Poor (Hungry) as a church mouse, As.

1659 HOWELL *Eng. Prov.* 13/2 As hungry as a church mouse. **1670** RAY 205. **1731** *Pol. Ballads* (1860) II. 222 The owner, 'tis said, was once poor as church-mouse. **1848** THACKERAY *Vanity F.* xxiii The young couple are as poor as church mice. **1857** DICKENS *Litlle Dorr.* xxxiii 'As poor as Thingummy'. 'A church mouse', Mrs. Merdle suggested with a smile.

Poor as a (church) rat, As.

1672 CORYE *Gen. Enemies* I. 1 All that live with him Are as poor as Church-Rats. **1703** WARD *Writings* ii. 120 As poor as rats. **1833** MARRYAT *P. Simple* xxxi He's as poor as a rat.

Poor as Job, As.

c. **1300** BRUNNE *Chron.* 323 As Job þe pouere man. *c.* **1390** GOWER *Conf. Amantis* v. l. 2505 To ben for evere til I deie As pooere as Job, and loveles. **1553** T. WILSON *Arte of Rhet.* (1580) 210 Tushe, thou art as poore as Iob. **1597–8** SHAKS. *2 Hen. IV* I. ii. 145 I am as poor as Job, my lord. **1600–1** *Merry W.* V. v. 168 *Ford.* One that is as slanderous as Satan? *Page.* And as poor as Job? **1822** BYRON *Werner* I. i. 401 He's poor as Job, and not so patient.

Poor beauty finds more lovers than husbands, A.

1640 HERBERT 340.

Poor but honest.

c. **1540** UDALL *Roister D.* III. iv. 2 May not folks be honest, pray you, though they be poore? *a.* **1577** *Misogonus* III. i. 253 Though wear poore yet wear true and trusty. *c.* **1595** BACON *Promus* no. 120 Poore and trew. **1640** *Verney Memoirs* (1892) i. 179 Beleeve the proverbe of me, though poore yet honest. **1654** E. GAYTON *Festivous Notes on Don Quixote* 92.

Poor dog that does not know 'Come out', It is a.

1830 FORBY 428 . . . *i.e.* He is foolish, who does not know when to desist.

Poor dog that is not worth the whistling, It is a.

1546 HEYWOOD I. xi It is, as I haue lerned in lystnyng, A poore dogge, that is not woorth the whystlyng. **1603** BRETON *Packet Mad Lett.* Wks. (1879) II. 19 There are more maids than Maulkin, and I count myself worth the whistling after. **1614** CAMDEN 303. **1738** SWIFT (*Dial.* i) 336 *Never.* Because, miss, you never asked me: and 'tis an ill dog that's not worth whistling for.

Poor folk (men) are fain of little.

1641 FERGUSSON 86 Poor men are fain of little thing. **1721** KELLY 279 . . . Because they have no hopes to get much.

Poor folk fare the best.

1639 CLARKE 205.

Poor folks are glad of porridge (pottage).

1576 U. FULWELL *Ars Adulandi* K 3 Poore men are pleasde with potage ay til better vittailes fall. **1639** CLARKE 225. **1659** HOWELL *Eng.*| *Prov.* 4/1 Poor folks must be glad of pottage.

Poor folks' friends soon misken them.

c. **1386** CHAUCER *Man of Law's Prol.* B¹ 121 If thou be poore, thy brother hateth thee, And alle thy freendes fleen fro thee, alas! **1721** KELLY 279.

Poor heart that never rejoices, It is a.

1833 MARRYAT *Peter Simple* v 'Well', continued he, 'it's a poor heart that never rejoiceth'. He then poured out half a tumbler of rum. **1843–4** DICKENS *M. Chuz.* v 'Let us be merry'. Here he took a captain's biscuit. 'It is a poor heart that never rejoices.'

Poor hen that can't *scrat*¹ for one chick, It is a.

1721 KELLY 181 *It is a sary hen that cannot scrape to one burd.* Spoken of them that have but one child to provide for. **1882** E. L. CHAMBERLAIN *West Worc. Wds.* (E.D.S.) 39. [¹ scratch.]

Poor indeed that can promise nothing, He is.

1616 DRAXE 242. **1639** CLARKE 142. **1670** RAY 132. **1732** FULLER no. 1941.

Poor kin (family) that has neither whore nor thief in it, It is a.

1659 HOWELL *Prov. Span.-Eng.* 1 There's no family but there's a whore or a knave of it. **1721** KELLY 186 ... Spoken when some of our relations, who have done an ill thing, is cast in our teeth.

Poor man is aye put to the worst, The.

[OVID *Fast.* I. 218 *Pauper ubique iacet.* Everywhere the poor man is despised.] **1721** KELLY 314.

Poor man pays for all, The.

1639 CLARKE 99. **1721** KELLY 323.

Poor man turns his cake, The | and another comes and takes it away.

1678 RAY *Adag. Hebr.* 402.

Poor man's cow dies, a rich man's child, A.

1640 HERBERT 357.

Poor man's shilling is but a penny, The.

1721 KELLY 337 . . . Because he must buy everything at the dearest rate.

Poor man's table is soon spread, A.

1616 DRAXE 138. **1670** RAY 132.

Poor man's tale cannot be heard, A.

1616 DRAXE 162. **1639** *Berkeley MSS.* (1885) iii. 31 (A) A poare mans tale may now be heard; vizt when none speakes the meanest may (Gloucest.).

Poor men go to heaven as soon as rich.

1639 CLARKE 98.

Poor men have no souls.

1555 HEYWOOD *Epigr. upon Prov.* no. 167 Poore men haue no soules, no but poore men had soules: Tyll the drunken soules, drownd theyr soules in ale boules. **1641** FERGUSSON 86 Poor men they say hes na souls. **1721** KELLY 281 . . . This is an old proverb in the time of Pop'ry when the poor had no masses, or *Dirige's* said for them.

Poor men seek meat for their stomach; rich men stomach for their meat.

1595 A. COPLEY *Wits, Fits and Fancies* (1614) 105 (with 'want' for 'seek'). **1659** HOWELL *Eng. Prov.* 10/2 The difference twixt the poor man and the rich, is that the one walketh to gett meat for his stomach, the other to get a stomack to his meat. **1678** RAY 79 (with 'walketh to get'). **1732** FULLER no. 3895. **1862** HISLOP 248.

Poor man (men), *see also* Get the p. m.'s answer; Make a p. m. a knight (Little of God's might to); Nothing between p. m. and rich but . . . ill year; Put the p. m.'s penny and the rich man's in ae purse.

Poor that God hates, He is.

1615 M. R. *A President for Young Pen-Men* C 4 He is poore whom God hateth. **1633** DRAXE 162. **1641** FERGUSSON 40. **1721** KELLY 138 . . . A surlish reply to them who, tauntingly, call us poor.

Poor that hath little, He is not | but he that desireth much.

1547 WM. BALDWIN *Treatise Moral Philosophy* (1550) K 7 Not he that hath lyttle, but he that desyreth muche is poore. **1595** DANIEL *Civil Wars* bk. iii Wks. (Gros.) II. 125. **1640** HERBERT 331. **1732** FULLER no. 1937 (with 'craves' for 'desireth').

Poor thing but mine own, A.

Usual misquoting of *c.* **1600** SHAKS. *A.Y.L.* V. iv. 60 An ill-favoured thing, Sir, but mine own. **1885** MEREDITH *Diana of Crossways* xxx Touchstone's 'poor thing but mine own' is godlike in its enveloping fold.

Poor, *see also* Charity and pride feed the p.;
Every one is weary, the p. in seeking;
Giving much to the p. doth enrich; God
help the p.; God's p. and devil's p.; Hard
task to be p. and leal; Loves the p. but
cannot abide beggars; Much money makes
country p.; No man lives so p. as he was
born; Pleasures of mighty, tears of p.;
Reasons of p. weigh not; Serves the p.
with thump on the back.

Poorer the church, the purer the church, The.

1869 HAZLITT 396.

Pope, If you would be | you must think of nothing else.

[*Cf.* **1659** N. R. 68 If thou mindest to be
Pope, thou must have him to write in thy
forehead.] **1707** MAPLETOFT 53. **1855** BOHN
422.

Pope, *see also* King and p., lion and wolf;
Know no more than P.; Sit in Rome and
strive against P. (Hard to); Turk and the
P. (Here is a talk of).

Popham, *see* Horner; Portman.

Porpoise plays before a storm, The.

1605 CHAPMAN, &c. *Eastw. Hoe* III. ii (1874)
469 *Dr.* There was a porpoise even now seen
at London-bridge, which is always the messenger of tempests, he says. *a.* **1613** OVER-
BURY *Newes* Wks. (1890) 198 That the
wantonnesse of a peaceable common-wealth,
is like the playing of the porpesse before a
storme. **1623** WEBSTER *Duch. Malfi* III. iii
(Merm.) 188 That cardinal . . . lifts up 's nose,
like a foul porpoise before a storm.

Porridge, *see* Eats most p. (He that); Keep
your breath to cool p.; Old pottage (p.) is
sooner heated; Part with the crock as the
p. (As soon); Poor folks are glad of p. *See
also under* Pottage.

Port, *see* Any p. in a storm; Worse the passage, more welcome p.

Portion, *see* Best bred have best p.; Better a
p. in a wife.

Portman, Horner, Popham and Thynne, when the monks went out, they came in.

[**15.**] **1876** *Preface* to THYNNE *Animadv. on
Chaucer* ix Sir John Thynne[1] . . . [built] the
beautiful family seat[2] . . . doubtless aided
indirectly by the Reformation, for, says the
old couplet, 'Portman, Horner, Popham, and
Thynne, When the monks went out, they
came in'. **1669-96** AUBREY *Lives* (Clark) i.
279 (A) (with 'Hopton, Horner, Smyth, and
Thynne'). [[1] *d.* 1580. [2] Longleat, Wilts.]

Portuguese, *see* Bad Spaniard makes good P.;
Three Moors to a P.

Positive, One | weighs more than twenty negatives.

1689 PRIOR *Epist. to F. Shepherd* 131 Wks.
(1858) 21 One single positive weighs more,
You know, than negatives a score.

Possession is nine (*formerly* eleven) points of the law.

a. **1596** *Edward III* III. i. 109 Tis you are in
possession of the Crowne, And thats the
surest poynt of all the Law. **1616** DRAXE 163
Possession is nine points in the Law. **1623**
CAMDEN 275 Possession is eleven points of
the Law. **1639** FULLER *Holy War* v. xxix
(1840) 297 At this day the Turk hath eleven
points of the law in Jerusalem, I mean possession. **1678** RAY 191 *Possession* is eleven
points of the Law, *and they say there are but
twelve.* **1712** ARBUTHNOT *John Bull* IV. iii
Possession . . . would make it much surer.
They say 'it is eleven points of the Law!'
1796 EDGEWORTH *Par. Asst., Simple S.* (1903)
89 'Pardon me', said the attorney, . . .
'possession . . . is nine points of the law'.
1880 BLACKMORE *Mary Aner.* 1 There is a
coarse axiom . . . that possession is nine points
of the law. We have possession.

Possession is worth an ill charter.

1641 FERGUSSON 86. **1721** KELLY 278 . . .
The law supposes the person in possession to
be the right owner, till the contrary appear.

Possession, *see also* Change a cottage in p.;
Prospect is often better than p.

Posset-drink, *see* Twittle twattle, drink up
your p.

Post of honour is the post of danger, The.

1624 J. FLETCHER *Rule a Wife* IV. i. Wks.
(1905) III. 209 For I remembered your old
Roman axiom, The more the danger, still the
more the honour. **1670** RAY 117 The more
danger, the more honour. **1832** HENDERSON
32. **1905** *Brit. Wkly.* 14 Dec. The Chancellor-
ship of the Exchequer . . . is pre-eminently the
post of danger, and therefore the post of
honour in the new Government.

Post, *see also* Kiss the p.; Lame p. brings
truest news; Letter stay for the p. (Let
your); Pillar to p.

Post-boy, *see* Dead donkey nor dead p.
(Never see).

Postern door makes thief and whore, The. (*See also* Nice wife and back door, &c.)

1573 SANDFORD (1576) 216 The posterne
dore marreth the house. **1611** DAVIES *Prov.*
71. **1616** DRAXE 143 The posterne doore
maketh theeues. **1623** CAMDEN 334. **1732**
FULLER no. 6176.

Postscript, *see* Gist of lady's letter in p.

Pot and kettle.

[= equally black.] **1620** SHELTON *Quix.* II.

lxvii (A) You are like what is said that the frying-pan said to the kettle, 'Avant, black-brows'. 1639 CLARKE 8 The pot calls the pan burnt-arse. *a.* 1700 *Dict. Cant. Crew* s.v. 'The Pot calls the kettle black A—', when one accuses another of what he is as Deep in himself. 1841 S. WARREN *Ten Thous. a Year* ii 'Come, you know you're a liar, Huck . . .' 'The pot and kettle, anyhow, Tit, as far as that goes.'

Pot broken, Your | seems better than my whole one.

1640 HERBERT 329.

Pot's full, When the | it will boil over.

1721 KELLY 357.

Pot, *see also* Boil the p. (Make the p. boil); Cometh last to the p. (He that) soonest wroth; Earthen p. must keep clear brass kettle; Go not for every thirst to p.; Go to p.; God's blessing make my p. boil (Will); Good broth in old p.; Honey in his p. (He that hath no); Ill weed mars a whole p.; Keep the p. boiling; Little p. soon hot; Pitcher (P.) goes so often to the well; Touch p. touch penny; Watched p. long boiling; Wife that never cries for ladle till p. runs over; Year is (As the), your p. must seethe.

Potato, Like a | the best part of him (you) underground.

1841 CHAMIER *Tom Bowl.* i What does it signify who your father was? if he had been better than you, . . . I'm blessed if you would not have been like a potato, the best part of you underground.

Potatoes and point.

1825 J. NEAL *Bro. Jonathan* I. 75 The potatoes and point of an Irish peasant. 1890 W. F. BUTLER *Napier* 81 The boasted 'wealth of England', he scornfully remarks, 'is to her vast poor and pauper classes as the potato and the "pint" of the Irish labourer'. 1910 P. W. JOYCE *Eng. as We Speak* 247 You will sometimes read . . . that each person, before taking a bite, *pointed* the potato at a salt herring or a bit of bacon hanging in front of the chimney: but this . . . never occurred in real life.

Potsherd, *see* Dived deep . . . and brought up p.

Pottage of a stool-foot, With cost one may make.

1678 RAY 70.

Pottage pot, *see* Chip in a p. p. (Like a).

Pottage, *see also* Herb-John (Without) no good p.; Know by your nose what p. you love; Old p. is sooner heated; Rain p. (If it should), he would want dish; Scald not your lips in another's p. *See also under* Porridge.

Potter envies another, One.

[HESIOD *Works & Days* 25 Καὶ κεραμεὺς κεραμεῖ κοτέει. L. *Figulus figulo invidet, faber fabro.* The potter envies the potter, and smith the smith.] 1633 D. DYKE *Wks. Philemon* 23 In the most men the proverb is verified, *Figulus figulo invidet*; One potter envies another. But far be this envy from all Christians of what calling soever, especially of the ministry. 1891 A. LANG *Ess. in Little* 105 Artists are a jealous race. 'Potter hates potter, and poet hates poet', as Hesiod said so long ago.

Pouch, *see* Hand twice to bonnet for once to p.

Poultry, *see* Women, priests, and p. have never enough.

Pound of butter among a kennel of hounds? What is a.

1670 RAY 66. 1732 FULLER no. 5498.

Pound, *see also* Care (A p. of) will not pay debt; Lob's p.; Mischief comes by the p.

Pour gold on him, and he'll never thrive.

1639 CLARKE 220.

Pour not water on a drowned mouse.

1639 CLARKE 9. 1670 RAY 133 . . . *i.e.* Add not affliction to misery. 1721 KELLY 267 . . . Never insult over those who are down already. 1738 SWIFT (Dial. i) 334 *Never.* Take pity on poor miss; don't throw water on a drowned rat. 1832 HENDERSON 81 It's needless to pour water on a drowned mouse.

Poverty breeds strife. (Cf. Want makes strife, &c.)

1678 RAY 354. *Somerset.*

Poverty comes in at (the) doors, When | love leaps out at (the) windows.

1631 BRATHWAIT *Eng. Gentlewoman* (1641) 346 (A) It hath been an old maxime; that as poverty goes in at one doore, love goes out at the other. 1639 CLARKE 25. 1721 KELLY 346 (with 'friendship' for 'love'). 1732 FULLER no. 5565. 1823 GALT *Entail* xiv 'Tak thy tocherless bargain to thee. . . . But mind my words—when poverty comes in at the door, love jumps out at the window.' 1869 READE *Foul Play* 1 When Mr. Wylie urged her to marry him . . . she spoke out . . . 'I've seen poverty enough in my mother's house, it shan't come in at my door to drive love out of window'.

Poverty is hateful good.

1377 LANGLAND *P. Pl.* B. xiv 275 '*Paupertas*', quod Pacience '*est odibile bonum*'. *c.* 1386 CHAUCER *Wife's T.* 1195 Povert is hateful good, and, as I gesse, A ful greet bringer out of bisinesse.

Poverty is in want of much, avarice of everything.

[PUB. SYRUS 121 *Desunt inopiae multa, avaritiae omnia.*] 1668 COWLEY *Ess.* vii (1904) 82 One line of Ovid: *Desunt luxuriæ multa, avaritiæ omnia.* Much is wanting to luxury, all to avarice. To which saying, I have a mind to add . . . ; Poverty wants some, luxury many, avarice all things. 1669 PENN *No Cross, No Crown* xiii Poverty wants many things, but covetousness all.

Poverty is (a pain, but) no disgrace.

1721 KELLY 278 *Poortha[1] is a pain, but no disgrace.* Unless it be the effects of laziness, and luxury. 1827–48 HARE *Gues. at Truth* (1859) i. 148 *La pobreza no es vileza*, Poverty is no disgrace, says the Biscayan proverb, *Paupertas ridiculos homines facit*, says the Roman satirist. . . . Which is the wiser and better saying. . . ? [1 poverty.]

Poverty is no sin.

1640 HERBERT 356. 1641 PEACHAM *Worth of a Penny* in ARBER *Garner* VI. 260 Women of the meanest condition may make good wives; since *Paupertas non est vitium*; Poverty is no vice. 1832–8 S. WARREN *Diary of Phys.* (1854) xxvii You know, sir, poverty's no sin.

Poverty is not a shame; but the being ashamed of it is.

1732 FULLER no. 3908. 1749 FRANKLIN July. Having been poor is no shame, but being ashamed of it, is. 1824 SCOTT *St. Ronans* xxxv 'From shame, brother?' said Clara. 'No shame in honest poverty, I hope.'

Poverty, He that is in | is still in suspicion.

1553 *Precepts of Cato* (1556) S 4ᵛ They that be in pouertie and myserye Be alwayes suspected of iniquitie. 1573 SANDFORD (1576) 207. 1629 *Book of Meery Riddles* Prov. 73.

Poverty is the mother of all arts.

1666 TORRIANO 214 (A). 1855 BOHN 475.

Poverty is the mother of health.

1377 LANGLAND *P. Pl.* B xiv. 298 Þe fyfte [pouerte] is moder of helthe. 1598 SIR R. BARCKLEY *Felicitie of Man* (1631) IV. iii. 335 A poore table is the mother of health. 1640 HERBERT 339.

Poverty parteth fellowship (friends, good company).

c. 1350 *Douce MS. 52* no. 107 Poverte brekys company. *c.* 1386 CHAUCER *Mel.* B² 2749 And if thy fortune change that thou wexe povre, farewel freendshipe and felawshipe. 1406 HOCCLEVE *Male Regle* (E.E.T.S.) l. 133 Fy! Lak of coyn departith conpaignie. 1546 HEYWOOD I. xii. 40 Yet pouertie parteth felowship we sée. 1594 NASHE *Unf. Trav.* (1920) 8 But pouertie in the end partes friends. 1616 BRETON *Cross Prov.* Wks. (1879) II. App. iii Poverty parts good company. 1641 FERGUSSON 86 Povertie parts good

company, and is an enemie to vertue. 1721 KELLY 278 *Poortha[1] parts friends.* At least makes them very coldrife. 1842 LOVER *Handy Andy* ii As the old song says, 'Poverty parts good company'; . . . he can't afford to know you any longer, now that you have lent him all the money you had. [1 poverty.]

Poverty takes away pith.

1822 SCOTT *Nigel* xxxv I ken weel, by sad experience, that poortith[1] takes away pith. . . . But courage, man. [1 poverty.]

Poverty, *see also* Bashfulness enemy to p.; Bear wealth, p. bear itself; Content in his p.; Easy to praise p. than bear it (More); Pass of Alton (Through) p. might pass; Patience with p. poor man's remedy; Plain of p. and die beggar; Riches bringeth oft harm where p. passes; Sloth the key to p.; Virtue that p. destroyeth not (No).

Powder in jam.

[Powders, disguised by a covering of jam, are given to children.] 1925 A. CLUTTON-BROCK *Ess. on Life* ix The poet, it has been said . . . , is to be respected if he makes agreeable to us moral lessons which otherwise we might find repulsive. This is the powder-in-jam theory.

Powder, *see also* Trust in God but keep p. dry.

Power behind the throne, The.

1905 VACHELL *The Hill* 198 It was his habit to consult his wife in emergencies. The chief cutter . . . said that Amelia was the power behind the throne. 1909 *Times Lit. Sup.* 23 July 269 The Duc de Morny . . . far more than the . . . Empress, was the power behind the Throne.

Power seldom grows old at court.

1651 HERBERT 366.

Power, *see also* Mickle p. makes many enemies.

Powys is the paradise of Wales.

1662 FULLER (*Montgomeryshire*) III. 549 'Pywys Paradwys Cymry'. That is, 'Powis is the paradise of Wales'. This proverb referreth to Teliessen[1] the author thereof, at what time Powis had far larger bounds than at this day, as containing all the land interjacent betwixt Wye and Severn. [1 Taliesin, a British bard, perhaps mythic, of 6th cent.]

Practice makes perfect, *see* Use (P.) makes perfect.

Practice, *see also* Knowledge without p. makes but half artist; Ounce of p. worth pound of precept.

Practise what you preach.

1377 LANGLAND *P. Pl.* B. v. 45 'If ȝe lyuen as ȝe leren vs . we shal leue[1] ȝow the bettere.' 1596–7 SHAKS. *Merch. V.* I. ii. 15 It is a good divine that follows his own instructions. **1639** FULLER *Holy War* I. xxiii (1840) 42 The Levites . . . had forty-eight cities, . . . being better provided for than many English ministers, who may preach of hospitality to their people, but cannot go to the cost to practise their own doctrine. **1812** COMBE (*Dr. Syntax*) *Consolation* xxvii 'Tis not for me, my friend, to teach You; you should practise what you preach. **1853** THACKERAY *Newcomes* xiv Take counsel by an old soldier, who fully practises what he preaches, and beseeches you to beware of the bottle. [¹ believe.]

Praise a fair day at night.

c. **1350** *Douce MS. 52* no. 10 At euene prayse þe fayre day. **1481** CAXTON *Reynard* xxix (Arb.) 75 Me ought not preyse to[o] moche the daye . tyl euen be come. **1616** ADAMS *Gallant's Burden* 38 Your Life is in the Noone of pride, but (we say) Prayse a faire day at Night. **1640** HERBERT 321 Praise day at night, and life at the end. **1721** KELLY 282 *Ruse¹ the fair day at night.* Commend not a thing, or project, till it has had its full effect. **1853** TRENCH iv. 89 This is Spanish: *Call me not 'olive', till you see me gathered*; being nearly parallel to our own: *Praise a fair day at night.* [¹ praise.]

Praise a hill, but keep below.

1591 FLORIO *Sec. Frutes* 99 Wonder at hills, keepe on the plaine. **1640** HERBERT 340.

Praise at parting.

c. **1410** *Towneley Plays* (E.E.T.S.) 108 Now prays at the partyng. *c.* **1440** *Gesta Romanorum* (E.E.T.S.) 39 'Preyse at þe parting', seide þe knyȝt. **1580** LYLY *Euph. & his Eng.* (Arb.) 363 I but *Philautus* prayse at the parting, if she had not liked thee, she would neuer haue aunswered thee. **1611–12** SHAKS. *Tempest* III. iii. 38 *Alonso.* . . . A kind of excellent dumb discourse. *Prosp.* Praise in departing.

Praise is not pudding.

1728 POPE *Dunc.* I. 54 Where, in nice balance, truth with gold she weighs, And solid pudding against empty praise. **1750** FRANKLIN Pref. Since 't is not improbable, that a Man may receive more solid Satisfaction from *Pudding*, while he is *living*, than from *Praise*, after he is *dead*. **1837–48** BARHAM *Ingol. Leg., House-Warming* (1898) 581 An old proverb says, Pudding still before praise!' **1885** D. C. MURRAY *Rainbow Gold* II. i Even the empty praise is problematical just yet, and the solid pudding is denied me altogether. They consent to publish . . . but they pay nothing.

Praise makes good men better, and bad men worse.

1732 FULLER no. 3918.

Praise no man till he is dead.

1540 TAVERNER A 6ᵛ *Vitae finem spectato.* Praise no man for blessed and happy till thou se the ende of his life. **1567** WM. BALDWIN *Treatise Moral Philosophy* S 6 Praise no man before death, for death is the discouerer of all his woorkes.

Praise none too much, for all are fickle.

1640 HERBERT 353.

Praise nor dispraise thyself; Neither | thy actions serve the turn.

1640 HERBERT 353.

Praise (Speak well of) the bridge he goes over (that carries him over), Let every man.

1678 RAY 106 . . . *i.e.* Speak not ill of him who hath done you a courtesie, or whom you have made use of to your benefit; or do commonly make use of. **1721** FULLER no. 3175. **1850** KINGSLEY *Alton Locke* x Every one speaks well of the bridge which carries him over. Every one fancies the laws which fill his pockets to be God's laws. **1886** G. DAWSON *Biog. Lect.* 22 Our love of compromise . . . is our little weakness, and it has also been our great strength; . . . and of course we speak well of the bridge that carries us over.

Praise the child, and you make love to the mother.

1829 COBBETT *Adv. to Y. Men* iv (1906) 154 It is an old saying, 'Praise the child, and you make love to the mother'; and it is surprising how far this will go. **1886** E. J. HARDY *How to be Happy* xix 'Praise the child and you make love to the mother'; and it is a thing no husband ought to overlook.

Praise the sea, but keep on land.

1591 FLORIO *Sec. Frutes* 99 Praise the sea, on shore remaine. **1640** HERBERT 340.

Praise the wine before ye taste of the grape, Ye.

1550 HEYWOOD I. X.

Praise to the face is open disgrace.

1869 BRET HARTE *Lonely Ride in* HARTE *Stories & Poems* (1915) 79 'Praise to the face is open disgrace'. I heard no more. **1902–4** LEAN IV. 85.

Praise without profit puts little in the pot.

1666 TORRIANO 131 (A) Praises fill not the belly. **1721** KELLY 280. **1732** FULLER no. 3922.

Praise(s) (*noun*), *see also* Damn with faint p.; Lacking breeds laziness, p. breeds pith; Old p. dies unless you feed it; Stinking p. comes of own mouth; True p. roots and spreads; Trust not p. of friend.

Praise(s) (*verb*), *see also* Evening p. the day; Neighbours (He dwells far from) that p. himself.

Praiseth himself, He that | spattereth himself.

1640 HERBERT 362.

Praiseth Saint Peter, Who | doth not blame Saint Paul.

1640 HERBERT 356.

Praising a ford till a man be over, It is not good.

1575 GASCOIGNE *Posies* (Cunliffe) 6 Yet is it true that I must take the foord as I finde it. **1616** DRAXE 52 It is not good praysing of a foord, vntill a man be ouer. **1641** FERGUSSON 86 Ruse[1] the foord as ye find it. **1670** RAY 92. **1818** SCOTT *Rob Roy* xxvii But it's an ill wind blaws naebody gude—Let ilka ane ruse the ford as they find it. [[1] praise.]

Prate is but prate; it's money buys land. (*Cf.* Talk is but talk, &c.)

1678 RAY 177.

Prate is prate; but it's the duck lays the eggs.

1659 HOWELL *Eng. Prov.* 13/2. **1670** RAY 215.

Prate like a parrot, To.

1630 B. JONSON *New Inn* I. i He prates Latin, An it were a parrot, or a play-boy. **1639** CLARKE 133 He prates like a parrot.

Pray for yourself, I am not sick.

1550 HEYWOOD II. vii. 68.

Pray, *see also* Labour as long lived, p. as dying; Learn to p., go to sea; Pain both to pay and p.

Prayer but little devotion, He has much.

1546 HEYWOOD II. ix. 79 Aue Maria (quoth he) how much mocion Here is to praiers, with how littell deuocion. **1641** FERGUSSON 54. **1721** KELLY 170 ... Spoken of those men who make great pretences to religion, but shew little of it in their practice.

Prayer should be the key of the day and the lock of the night.

1620-8 O. FELTHAM *Resolves* lxvii (Dent) 353 Though prayer should be the key of the day, and the lock of the night, yet I hold it more needful in the morning, than when our bodies do take their repose.

Prayers and provender hinder no man's journey. (*Cf.* Meat and matins, &c.)

1632 HERBERT *Country Parson* xvii. Wks. (1859) I. 200 At going to bed ... he will have prayers in the hall ... The like he doth in the morning, using pleasantly the outlandish proverb, that *Prayers and Provender never hinder Journey.* **1670** RAY 133.

Prayers are done, When | my lady is ready.

1611 COTGRAVE s.v. 'Messe' When prayers were ended, Madame ends her pranking' (A). **1640** HERBERT 20.

Prayers of the wicked won't prevail, The.

1738 SWIFT (Dial. ii) 349 *Col.* I wish you may be wet to the skin. *Sir J.* Ay; but they say the prayers of the wicked won't prevail.

Prayers, They shall have no more of our | than we of their pies, quoth the vicar of Layton.

1678 RAY 191.

Prayer(s), *see also* Go home and say p.; Last p. (She is at her); Said my p. in other corner; Says anything but his p.

Preach at Tyburn Cross,[1] To.

[= to be hanged.] **1576** GASCOIGNE *Steele Glas* (Arb.) 55 That Souldiours sterue, or prech at Tiborne crosse. [[1] the place of execution.]

Preach like a pie, To.

a. **1607** *Chester Whitsun Plays; Proc. Prophet.* 273 BALAACK. Popelard! thou preachest as a pie.[1] [[1] magpie.]

Preached, *see* Friar p. against stealing.

Preacher(s), *see* Saturday is working day ... of p.; Saved (He that will not be) needs no p.

Preaches well that lives well, He.

1620 SHELTON *Quix.* II. xxi (1908) II. 326 'He preaches well that lives well', said Sancho. **1732** FULLER no. 2006.

Preacheth, He that | giveth alms.

1640 HERBERT 353.

Preacheth patience that never knew pain, He.

1855 BOHN 381.

Preacheth war, Who | is the devil's chaplain.

1664 CODRINGTON 229. **1670** RAY 27. **1732** FULLER no. 2251 (with 'preacheth up war when it might well be avoided').

Precept, *see* Ounce of practice worth pound of p.

Precipices, *see* High places have p.

Presbyter, *see* New p. is old priest.

Presbyterianism is no religion for a gentleman.

1660 CHARLES II in CARLYLE *Cromwell* (1845) VI. cxxiv [Lauderdale] ... knelt before his now triumphant Sacred Majesty ...; learned from his Majesty, that 'Presbyterianism was no religion for a gentleman'; gave it up, not without pangs. **1913** *Times Lit. Sup.* 21 Nov. 544 Charles II is credited with the remark that Presbyterianism is no religion for a gentleman.

Present (*adj.*), see Absent without fault nor p. without excuse (Neither); Fears you p. (He that) will hate you absent; Pleasure refrain (Who will in time p.), shall more pleasure obtain; Things p. are judged by things past.

Presents of love fear not to be ill taken of strangers.

1651 HERBERT 321.

Preston, see Proud P.

Presumed good, All are | till they are found in a fault.

1640 HERBERT 360.

Presumed, see also Nothing is to be p. on.

Presumers, see Deservers grow p.

Pretence, see Want a p. to whip dog.

Prettiness dies first.

1640 HERBERT 340.

Prettiness dies quickly.

1670 RAY 21.

Prettiness makes no pottage.

1678 RAY 192. **1732** FULLER no. 3931.

Pretty fellow, see Axle-tree for oven.

Pretty pig makes an ugly old sow, A.

1721 KELLY 42. **1732** FULLER no. 363.

Pretty that have pretty conditions, They are.

1616 DRAXE 15.

Pretty, see also Long and lazy...p. and proud.

Prevention is better than cure.

c. **1240** BRACTON *De Legibus* (Rolls Ser. vi. 104) bk. v, c. 10, § 14 (A) Cum melius et utilius sit in tempore occurrere quam post causam vulneratam quaerere remedium. **1630** T. ADAMS *Wks.* 598 (A) Prevention is so much better than healing. **1732** FULLER no. 3932 Prevention is much preferable to Cure. **1751** N. COTTON *Vis. Verse, Health* 31 Prevention is the better Cure, So says the Proverb, and 'tis sure. *a.* **1863** SIR G. C. LEWIS in BAGEHOT *Biog. Stud.* (1881) 212 'In *my* opinion, in nine cases out of ten, cure is better than prevention. . . . By looking forward to all possible evils, we waste the strength that had best be concentrated in curing the one evil which happens.'

Price is too low for a 'bear'[1] or too high for a 'bull',[2] No.

[Stock Exchange.] **1884** *Times* 28 June No price is too low for a 'bear' or too high for a 'bull' (LEAN IV. 62). [[1] one who sells stock for future delivery hoping to buy it cheap meanwhile, and therefore tries to bring prices down. [2] person trying to raise prices.]

Price, see also Ask but enough . . . lower the price; Every man has his p.; Good thing cheap (He will never have) that is afraid to ask p.; Much money makes country poor, for it sets dearer p.

Prick(s) (*noun*), see Hit the p.; kick against p.

Prick(s) (*verb*), see Early p. that will be thorn.

Pride and grace dwelt never in one place.

1721 KELLY 276. **1732** FULLER no. 6273.

Pride and laziness would have mickle upholding.

1641 FERGUSSON 86. **1721** KELLY 277 . . . Pride requires ornament, and laziness service.

Pride and poverty are ill met, yet often seen together.

1660 *The Rump Despairing, or the Rump's Proverbs*, p. 2 You know Pride and Poverty make a double affliction. **1732** FULLER no. 3933.

Pride breakfasted with plenty, dined with poverty, and supped with infamy.

1758 FRANKLIN in ARBER *Garner* v. 584 Pride that *dines on Vanity, sups on Contempt*, as *Poor* RICHARD says. And in another place, *Pride breakfasted with Plenty, dined with Poverty and supped with Infamy.*

Pride, but[1] profit, wear shoon[2] and go bare foot.

1721 KELLY 277 . . . Spoken when people have something fine about them, but the rest shabby. [[1] without. [2] shoes.]

Pride feels (finds, knows) no cold (pain).

1629 T. ADAMS *Serm.* (1861–2) I. 190 Pride is never without her own pain, though she will not feel it; be her garments what they will, yet she will never be too hot nor too cold. **1631** JONSON *New Inn* II. i *Lady F.* Thou must make shift with it; pride feels no pain. Girt thee hard, Prue. **1650** SIR J. BIRKENHEAD, *Two Centuries of Pauls Church-yard* 59 Pride feels no cold. **1670** RAY 133 Pride feels no cold. **1721** KELLY 277 *Pride finds no cold.* Spoken heretofore to young women, when, in compliance with the fashion, they went with their breasts and shoulders bare. **1732** FULLER no. 3935 Pride feels no frost. **1837** T. HOOK *Jack Brag* xviii Truly, indeed, does the proverb say that 'pride knows no pain'.

Pride goeth before, and shame cometh after. (See also Pride rides, &c.)

c. 1350 *Douce MS. 52* no. 135. *c.* 1440 *Jacob's Well* 70 Pride goth beforn, & schame folwyth after. *a.* 1529 SKELTON *Agst. Garnesche* 165 Wks. (Dyce) I. 131. 1546 HEYWOOD I. x. 22 Pryde wyll haue a fall. For pryde goeth before, and shame cometh after. 1732 FULLER no. 3936.

Pride goeth before destruction.

1560 GENEVA BIBLE *Prov.* xvi. 18 Pride goeth before destruction, and an high mind before the fall. 1816 SCOTT *Antiq.* xxix I think [it] . . . has made me proud o' my ain lot; but I wuss it bode me gude, for pride goeth before destruction.

Pride is as loud a beggar as want, and a great deal more saucy.

1732 FULLER no. 3941.

Pride may lurk under a threadbare cloak.

1542 UDALL tr. *Erasm. Apoph.* (1877) 24 Pride maie as well be in sack cloth as in rich araie. 1732 FULLER no. 3947.

Pride must be pinched.

1894 NORTHALL *Folk-phrases* (E.D.S.) 21 Pride must be pinched. A reproof to one who complains of tight boots, garments, &c.

Pride of the morning, The.

1827 KEBLE *Christ. Yr.*, *25th S. aft. Trin.* Pride of the dewy morning, The swain's experienced eye From thee takes timely warning Nor trusts the gorgeous sky. 1891 A. FORBES *Bar. Biv. & Bat.* (1910) 9 There had been a shower as the sun rose—the 'pride of the morning' the soldiers call the sprinkle—just sufficient to lay the dust.

Pride of the rich makes the labour(s) of the poor, The.

1616 BRETON *Cross. Prov.* Wks. (1879) II App. iii. 1639 CLARKE 18.

Pride rides, When | shame lacqueys. (See also Pride goeth before, &c.)

1573 SANDFORD (1576) 40 Lewis the eleuenth of *Fraunce* . . . was woonte to saye, when pryde rydeth, loue and shame goe behynde. 1597 *Politeuphuia* 234 b When pride dooth ride, shame & danger doe follow on foote. 1732 FULLER no. 5567.

Pride that apes humility.

1799 COLERIDGE *Devil's Thoughts* vi And the Devil did grin, for his darling sin Is pride that apes humility. 1858 SURTEES *Ask Mamma* xvii [He] divested himself of his paletot in which he had been doing 'the pride that apes humility'. 1910 *Spectator* 10 Dec. 1028 Browning's . . . simplicity was very real . . . and he was wholly free from the pride that apes humility.

Pride will have (never left his master without) a fall.

c. 1390 GOWER *Conf. Amantis* I. 3066 Pride . . . schal down falle and ouer the owe. 1509 BARCLAY *Shyp of Folys* (1874) II. 159 For it hath be sene is sene, and euer shall That first or last foule pryde wyll haue a fall. 1546 HEYWOOD I. x. 22 Well well !(quoth mine aunte) pryde wyll haue a fall. 1595–6 SHAKS. *Rich. II* V. v. 88 *Rich.* Would he not stumble ? Would he not fall down.—Since pride must have a fall. 1646 J. WHITAKER *Uzziah* 26 That pride will have a fall, is from common experience grown proverbiall. 1721 KELLY 276 *Pride never left his master without a fall.* Proud people often meet with very humbling circumstances. 1784 JOHNSON *Let.* 2 Aug. in *Boswell* I am now reduced to think . . . of the weather. Pride must have a fall.

Pride, *see also* Charity and p. feed the poor; Declaim against p. (Not sign of humility to); Despises p. with greater p.; Pompous provision cometh of p.

Priest in his own house, Every man is a.

1894 DEAN HOLE *More Mem.* xxi When I was asked to officiate, I reminded my kind host that every man is a patriarch and priest in his own household, and I begged him to conduct the service according to his custom.

Priest, Like | like people.

1606 G. CLOSSE *The Parricide Papist* B 4 The prouerbe was well shared amongst them, such a priest, such people. 1611 BIBLE *Hosea* iv. 9 And there shall be like people, like priest. [1382 WYCLIF as the peple so the prest.] 1664 JOS. MEDE Wks. *Disc.* xxxvi. 276 *Ita populus, sicut sacerdos,* Such as the priest is, such will the people be; the priest cannot err, but he causeth others to err also. 1670 RAY 114. 1893 R. HEATH *Eng. Peasant* 329 He had so deep a reverence for the clergy, that it never entered into his mind that perhaps, after all, it was 'like people, like priest'.

Priest praises his own relics, Each.

c. 1400 *MS. Latin no. 394, J. Rylands Libr.* (ed. Pantin) in *Bull. J. R. Libr.* XIV f. 18 Eche preste preyseth his awgh relikes.

Priest, Such as the | such is the clerk.

[*Cf. Isaiah* xxiv. 2.] 1622 C. OUDIN *A Grammar Spanish & English* 269 Such as the Priest, such is the Clarke. 1624 BURTON *Anat. Mel.* 123, I. ii. III. xv Such a Patrone, such a Clearke. 1732 FULLER no. 4279.

Priest, Such | such offering.

1641 FERGUSSON 90 Sike[1] priest, sike offering. [[1] such.]

Priest(s), *see also* Good to fetch the devil a p.; Heather-bells . . . (When), miller and p. forget themsels; Know by a half-penny if p. take offering; Live well (If you would)

... turn p.; New presbyter is old p.; No mischief but p. at bottom; No p. no mass; Once a parson (p.) always a p.; Parish p. forgetteth he hath been clerk; Parson (P.) always christens own child first; Pigeons and p. make foul houses; Pinch on the p.'s side; Three things are insatiable; Women, p., and poultry have never enough.

Prince, Like | like people.

1616 DRAXE 88. **1621** BURTON *Anat. Mel.* Democr. to Rdr. (1651) 49 As the princes are, so are the people; *qualis rex, talis grex.* **1648** HERRICK *Hesper.* No. 760 *Like Prince, Like People.* Examples lead us, and wee likely see, Such as the Prince is, will his people be.

Princes are venison in heaven. (*See also* Gentlemen and rich men, &c.)

1651 HERBERT 371.

Princes have no way.

1640 HERBERT 361.

Prince(s), *see also* New p. new bondage; Punctuality is politeness of p.

Print, In.

1576 FLEMING *Panoplie of Epistles* 357 What soeuer is uttered in such mennes hearing, must bee done in printe; as wee say in oure common Prouerbe. **1594–5** SHAKS. *Two Gent.* II. i. 177 All this I speak in print, for in print I found it. **1594–5** *L.L.L.* III. i. 182 Most sweet gardon! I will do it, sir, in print. **1599–1600** *A.Y.L.* V. iv. 94 O sir, we quarrel in print. **1616** DRAXE 56 In print, rarely, admirably, finically.

Priscian, *see* Break P.'s head.

Prison, *see* Bean in liberty better than comfit in p.; God keep me from ... a p.; Love is foul (No), nor p. fair.

Prisoner(s), *see* All's out is good for p.; Secret is thy p. (Thy).

Prizing of green barley, It is ill.

1721 KELLY 218 ... It is ill prizing these things who have not yet had an occasion of shewing themselves; spoken of boys, colts, &c.

Probabilities do not make one truth, A thousand.

1707 MAPLETOFT 32. **1855** BOHN 302.

Procession, *see* Ill battle (p.) where devil carries colours.

Procrastination is the thief of time.

1742 YOUNG *Night Thoughts* I. 393 Procrastination is the thief of time; Year after year it steals, till all are fled. **1850** DICKENS *Dav. Cop.* xii Never do to-morrow what you can do to-day. Procrastination is the thief of time.

Procrustes' bed.

[Procrustes, a fabulous robber of Attica.] **1563** FULKE *Defence* i (P.S.) 97 You play manifestly with us the lewd part of Procrustes, the thievish host, which would make his guest's stature equal with his bed's, either by stretching them out if they were too short, or by cutting off their legs if they were too long. **1618** JONSON, *Conv. with Drummond* (ed. Patterson, 1924) 6 He cursed Petrarch for redacting verses to Sonnets, which he said were like that Tirrants bed, wher some who were too short were racked, others too long cut short. **1769** BURKE *Observ. on 'The Present State of Nat.'* Wks. (Bohn) I. 258 *Procrustes* shall never be my hero of legislation; with his iron bed, the allegory of his government. ... Such was the state-bed of uniformity. **1796** LAMB to Coleridge, June Who shall go about to bring opinion to the bed of Procrustes? **1827** HARE *Gues. at Truth* (1873) i. 258 The man of the world is the Procrustes, who lays down his bed across the high-road, and binds all passers-by to it.

Proffered service (ware) stinks.

[ST. JEROME *Merx ultronea putet*; and so ERASM. *Ad.*] c. **1350** *Douce MS. 52* no. 33 Bodun seruycys stynkys—Omnibus oblatus sordere solet famulatus. c. **1386** CHAUCER *Canon's Yeom. T.* G 1066 Ful sooth it is that swiche profrèd servyse Stynketh, as witnessen thise oldè wyse. **1546** HEYWOOD II. iv. 50 I wene (quoth she) proferd seruyce stynkth. **1584** LODGE *Alarum agst. Usurers* (Shaks. Soc.) 45 For that I see so good a nature in you (if preferred service stinke not) I will verye willynglye ... further you in what I may. **1612** CHAPMAN *Widow's Scars* I. ii. 53 But offered ware is not so sweet, you know. **1641** FERGUSSON 20 Bodin geir stinkes. **1670** RAY 134 Proffer'd service (and so ware) stinks. **1710** SWIFT *Jrnl. to Stella* 22 Oct. I stopped short in my overture, and we parted very drily. ... Is there so much in the proverb of proffered service? When shall I grow wise? **1771** SMOLLETT *Humph. Clink.* 26 Apr. (1871) 481 When I go to market to sell, my commodity stinks; but when I want to buy ... it can't be had for love or money.

Profit, What is none of my | shall be none of my peril.

1721 KELLY 343 ... I will not engage myself deep in a business in which I have no concern. L. *Mihi istic nec seritur nec metitur.* [PLAUTUS *Epidicus* 2. 2. 80.]

Profit(s), *see also* Go to hell for the house p.; Honour and p. not in one sack; No p. to honour; Small p. quick returns; Thrift goes by the p. of a yeld hen (Your).

Profitable, *see* Shrew p. may serve.

Prolong thy life: Two things doth | a quiet heart and a loving wife.

1607 T. DELONEY *Strange Histories; Wise Sentences* (Percy Soc.) 70 Two things doth prolong thy lyfe: A quiet heart and a loving wife.

Promise, To | and give nothing, is comfort to a fool.

1616 DRAXE 167 To promise, and to give nought, is to comfort a foole. **1670** RAY 22.

Promise is debt.

c. **1386** CHAUCER *Man of Law Head-link* B[1] 41 Biheste is dette. **14.**. *Everyman* 821 Yet promyse is dette, this ye well wot. *c.* **1500** *Young Children's Bk.* 49 in *Babees Bk.* (E.E.T.S.) 19 Fore euery promys, it is dette, That wi*th* no falsed muste be lette. **1639** CLARKE 194 Promise is a due debt. **1813** RAY 19 He who promises runs in debt. *Hisp.*

Promises are either broken or kept.

1692 L'ESTRANGE *Aesop's Fab.* ccclxvi (1738) 383 *All promises are either broken or kept* . . . Here's a reproof to all religious cheats and impostures, that promise more than they are able to perform. **1738** SWIFT (Dial. i) 337 *Lady S.* One thing is certain, that she has promised to have him. *Spark.* Why, madam, you know promises are either broken or kept.

Promises are like pie-crust, made to be broken.

1598–9 SHAKS. *Hen. V* II. iii. 54 For oaths are straws, men's faiths are wafercakes. **1706** WARD *Hud. Rediv.* v. vii. 9 (A) Fair promises avail but little, Like too rich pye-crust they're so brittle. **1738** SWIFT (Dial. i) 337 *Lady A.* Promises and pie-crust are made to be broken. **1739** 'R. BULL' tr. *Dedekindus' Grobianus* 162 Then all the Vengeance of the Gods invoke, In case this Pye-crust Promise should be broke. **1871** TROLLOPE *Ralph the H.* xxiii 'Promises like that are mere pie-crusts', said Ralph.

Promises mountains and performs molehills, He.

1573 SANDFORD (1576) 211 He promiseth seas and mountaynes. **1576** PETTIE *Petite Pall.* (Gollancz) I. 75 Will he not promise golden hills and perform dirty dales? **1578** FLORIO *First Fruites* f. 29. **1629** *Book of Meery Riddles* Prov. 105.

Promises too much, He that | means nothing.

1616 DRAXE 167 He that promises all, deceiueth all. **1732** FULLER no. 2253.

Promises (*noun*), *see also* Many fair p. in marriage making.

Promiseth like a merchant, and pays like a man of war, He.

1639 CLARKE 194. **1670** RAY 22.

Promise(s, -th, -d) (*verb*), *see also* Loses his thanks who p. and delayeth; Performance (One acre of) is worth twenty of p.; Poor indeed that can p. nothing.

Promising and performing, Between | a man may marry his daughter.

1670 RAY 22.

Promising is the eve of giving.

1573 SANDFORD (1576) 211 (with 'vigil' for 'eve'). **1578** FLORIO *First Fruites* f. 29 The eue to geue, is to promise. **1640** HERBERT 356.

Proo[1] naunt[2] your mare puts.

1678 RAY 79 *Proo* naunt your mare puts, *i.e.* pushes. [[1] a call to a cow or horse, inviting it to stand still or come near. [2] aunt.]

Proof of the pudding is in the eating, The.

c. **1300** *King Alisaunder* l. 4042 (A) Hit is y-writein, every thyng Himseolf shewith in tastyng. **1623** CAMDEN 266 All the proofe of a pudding, is in the eating. **1682** N. O. tr. BOILEAU *Le Lutrin* 23 To spight his foes, yet for all's feating, The proof of th' pudding's seen i' th' eating. **1738** SWIFT (Dial. ii) 345 *Lady A.* Do you love pudding? *Nev.* I love everything that is good; but the proof of the pudding is in the eating. **1830** G. COLMAN (Jr.) *Rand. Records* I. 37 'The proof of the pudding is in the eating', which is a precept to trust only to absolute experience.

Proper that hath proper conditions,[1] He is.

1599 PORTER *Angry Wom. Abingd.* IV. iii (Merm.) 176 But he is proper that hath proper conditions. **1614** CAMDEN 307. [[1] disposition.]

Properer man, The | the worse luck.

1606 J. DAY *Isle of Gulls* ii. 2 (Bullen) 34 You may see the prosperer women the worse luck. **1613** J. CHAMBERLAIN *Letters* 18 Feb. (McLure) i. 426 The old proverb the roperer men the worse luck. **1633** JONSON *T. Tub* III. iv (1904) 463 The properer man, the worse luck. **1670** RAY 134 The properer man (and so the honester) the worse luck.

Property has its duties as well as its rights.

1891 J. E. T. ROGERS *Ind. & Commer. Hist.* II. iv It is very injurious . . . that a man should have the nominal ownership of land when . . . he cannot . . . satisfy Mr. Drummond's famous dictum, that property has its duties as well as its rights.

Prophet is not without honour save in his own country, A.

1389 WYCLIF *Matt.* xiii. 57 A prophete is nat with outen wirshipe, no but in his owne cuntree. **1526** TINDALE *ibid.* There is no prophet with out honoure, save in hys awne countre. **1603** FLORIO tr. *Montaigne* III. ii (1897) V. 33 No man hath been a prophet, not only in his house, but in his own country, saith the experience of histories. **1771** SMOLLETT *Humph. Clink.* 15 Sept. The captain, like the prophets of old, is but little honoured in his own country. **1823** GALT *Entail* III. xxviii That's just as I might hae expectit—a prophet ne'er got honour in his own country. **1879** M. PATTISON *Milton* 153 The homage which was wanting to the prophet [i.e. Milton] in his own country was more liberally tendered by foreigners.

Prophet, *see also* Name of the P.—figs (In the).

Prospect is often better than possession.

1732 FULLER no. 3958.

Prosperity, In time of | friends will be plenty; in time of adversity, not one amongst twenty.

1659 HOWELL *Eng. Prov.* 20/1. **1732** FULLER no. 6394.

Prosperity is the blessing of the Old Testament, adversity the blessing of the New.

a. **1626** BACON *Ornamenta Rat.* Wks. (Chandos) 115 Prosperity is the blessing of the Old Testament, adversity the blessing of the New, which carrieth the greater benediction and the clear revelation of God's favour. **1908** A. C. BENSON *At Large* xii. 222 The Bishop seemed to have forgotten the ancient maxim that prosperity is the blessing of the Old Testament, and affliction the blessing of the New.

Prosperity lets go the bridle.

1640 HERBERT 351. **1754** FRANKLIN May Nay When Prosperity was well mounted, she let go the Bridle, and soon came tumbling out of the Saddle.

Prosperity makes friends, adversity tries them.

1597 *Politeuphuia* 161 Prosperitie getteth friends, but aduersitie tryeth them. **1598** SIR R. BARCKLEY *Felicity of Man* 538 Prosperitie winneth friendes, but aduersitie proueth them. **1732** FULLER no. 3962 (with 'followers' for 'friends' and 'distinguishes' for 'tries'). **1853** TRENCH iii. 59.

Prosperity no altars smoke, In.

1853 TRENCH iv. 88 On the danger of being overset by prosperity: . . . another Italian which says: *In prosperity no altars smoke.*

Prosperity, *see also* Swells in p. shrink in adversity.

Protestant Rome, The.

[= Geneva.] **1912** *Spectator* 27 Jan. 128 During the period of religious persecution the 'Protestant Rome' became a city of refuge into which flowed a constant stream of emigration from France. In the eighteenth century Geneva became something of a cosmopolitan centre.

Protestant(s), *see also* Bible is religion of P.; Christian must have . . . faith of a P.

Proteus, *see* Shapes as P. (As many).

Proud as a peacock, As.

c. **1290** *Polit. Songs* (Wright) 159 A pruest[1]

proud ase a po[2]. *c.* **1386** CHAUCER *Reeve's T.* 3926 As eny pecok he was proud and gay. **1560** DAUS tr. *Sleidane's Comm.* 119 They are as bragge and as proude as pecockes. **1592–3** SHAKS. *Com. Err.* IV. iii. 181 'Fly pride', says the peacock: mistress, that you know. **1753** RICHARDSON *Grandison* Lr. 137 Lord L., proud as a peacock, is . . . come for me. [[1] priest. [2] peacock.]

Proud as a pig with two tails, As.

1837 T. HOOK *Jack Brag* xvi 'No', interrupted Mrs. Salmon, '. . . you are as proud as a pig with two tails.'

Proud as Lucifer, As.

c. **1394** *Polit. Poems* (Wright) I. 318 As proud as Luciferre. **1450** *Partonope* (E.E.T.S.) l. 9740 As prowde as Lucifere. **1782** MISS BURNEY *Cecilia* ix. vi They say he's as proud as Lucifer.

Proud beggar that makes his own alms, He is a.

c. **1430** LYDGATE *Minor Poems* (Percy Soc.) 56 A prowde hert in a beggers brest . . . It accordith nought. **1721** KELLY 152 . . . *Eng. Beggars should not be chusers.*

Proud (*or* Stout) comes behind as goes before, As.

1575 *Gam. Gurton's N.* v. ii. 331 As proude coms behinde, they say, as any goes before! **1655** FULLER *Ch. Hist.* iii. iii (1868) I. 374 York was rather quiet than contented, pleasing itself that 'as stout came behind as went before'.

Proud eye, A | an open purse, and a light wife, bring mischief to the first, misery to the second, and horns to the third.

1597 *Politeuphuia* 236 b. **1647** *Countrym. New Commonwealth* 35.

Proud horse that will not bear his own provender, It is a.

1546 HEYWOOD II. ix. 81 With good will wife, for it is (said he to her) A proude horse that will not beare his own prouander. **1599** PORTER *Angry Wom. Abingd.* IV. iii (Merm.) 177 *Nich.* He's a proud horse will not carry his own provender. **1670** RAY 105 It's an ill horse will not carry his own provender. **1721** KELLY 131 *He's a proud horse that will not bear his own prowan.*[1] An excuse for doing our own business ourselves. [[1] provender.]

Proud mind and a beggar's purse agree not well together, A.

c. **1430** LYDGATE *Minor Poems* (Percy Soc.) 56 A prowde hert in a beggers brest . . . it accordith nought. **1670** RAY 133. **1732** FULLER no. 369 A proud mind and a poor purse are ill met. *Ibid.* no. 6386 There's nothing agrees worse Than a prince's heart and a beggar's purse.

Proud Preston.

1727 DEFOE *Tour* iii. 221 The Town . . . is full of Gentlemen, Attorneys, Proctors, and Notaries. . . . The People are gay here, though not perhaps the richer for that; but it has on this Account obtained the name of Proud Preston. **1818** SCOTT *Rob Roy* xxxvii Wilfred . . . was slain at Proud Preston, in Lancashire, on the day that General Carpenter attacked the barricades.

Proud Preston, poor people, high church, and low steeple.

1852 *N. & Q.* 1st Ser. VI. 496 The old lines . . . are, 'Proud Preston, Poor people, High church, And low steeple'. The name in the first line yet adheres to us; . . . the second is no longer applicable; . . . [and] in 1815 the tower of the church . . . was pulled down, and . . . one of proportionate size erected.

Proud tod[1] that will not scrape his own hole, He is a.

1641 FERGUSSON 40. **1721** KELLY 146 . . . A reproof to them who refuse to do their own proper business, or an excuse in them that do it. [[1] fox.]

Proud, *see also* Beating p. folks (It is good); I p. and thou p.; Long and lazy . . . pretty and p.; Poor and p.

Prove thy friend ere thou have need.

c. **1400** *Cato's Morals* in *Cursor M.* (E.E.T.S.) III. 1672 Be scarske of þi louing til hit come to prouing of þi gode frende. **1546** HEYWOOD I. xi. 38.

Prove, *see also* Black is white (P. that).

Provender pricketh him, His.

1546 HEYWOOD I. xi. 27 For when provender prickt them a little tyne, they did as thy wife and thou did, both dote each one on other. **1650** BROME *Jov. Crew* I. (1708) 7 I left the merry grigs (as their provender has prickt 'em) in such a *Hoigh* yonder! such a frolic! **1670** RAY 190.

Provender, *see also* Prayers and p. hinder no journey.

Proverbs, *see* Wise men make p.

Proves too much, That which | proves nothing.

1732 FULLER no. 4384.

Provide for the worst; the best will save itself.

1528 SIR T. MORE *Wks.* (1557) 105 b . . . deme the best . . . prouide for the worst. **1546** HEY-WOOD I. v. 10 To prouyde for the woorst, whyle the best it selfe saue. **1599–1600** SHAKS. *Jul. Caes.* V. i. 97 But since the affairs of men rest still uncertain, Let's reason with the worst that may befall. **1659** HOWELL *Eng. Prov.* 17/1. **1670** RAY 89 It's good to fear the worst, the best will save itself. **1885** E. P. HOOD *World of Prov.* 477

'*Provide for the worst, and the best will look after itself*', says caution.

Providence is always on the side of the strongest battalions.

[**1770** VOLTAIRE *Let.* 6 Feb. *On dit que Dieu est toujours pour les gros bataillons.*] **1842** ALISON *Hist. Europe* X. lxxviii. 1013 Moreau expressed a fact of general application, explained according to the irreligious ideas of the French Revolution, when he said, that 'Providence was always on the side of dense battalions'. **1867–77** FROUDE *Short Stud.* (1890) II. 397 If Providence, as Napoleon scornfully said, is on the side of the strongest battalions, it provides also, as Napoleon himself found at Leipsic, that in the times of these tremendous visitations the strong battalions shall be found in defence of the cause which it intends shall conquer. **1906** ALEX. MACLAREN *Expos., Deut.–1 Sam.* 238 The old sneer, that 'Providence is always on the side of the strongest battalions', is . . . the very opposite of the truth.

Providence is better than rent.

1640 HERBERT 328.

Providence, *see also* Fly in the face of P.; Leap into a well (If you), P. not fetch you out; Play p.

Providing is preventing.

1883 GEORGINA JACKSON *Shropshire Folk-Lore* 588 A collier's wife at Kelley heard that her father-in-law . . . was dangerously ill, so having an opportunity of buying cheaply, she got mourning for all her family . . . ; but the old man recovered. '*Pervidin's perventin.*' The proverb may also be taken in the sense of 'forewarned is forearmed'.

Provision in season makes a rich house.

1641 FERGUSSON 86 Provision in season, makes a rich meason.[1] **1721** KELLY 281 . . . Because every thing is gotten at the easiest rate. [[1] house.]

Provision, *see also* Pompous p. cometh not alway of gluttony.

Prudence, *see* No divinity is absent if P. present.

Pry, *see* Paul P.

Pryeth into every cloud, He that | may be stricken with a thunderbolt.

1670 RAY 134.

Psalms, *see* Whistle p. to taffrail.

Public gown, *see* Puts on a p. g. (He that).

Public money is like holy water, every one helps himself to it.

1857 BOHN *Polyglot For. Prov.* 101. [Italian.

Public, *see also* Serves the p. (He who).

Pucksy, see Muxy (He got out of the).

Pudding for a friar's mouth, As fit as a.

1568 FULWELL *Like Will to L.* (1906) 13 I will find one as fit for you as a pudding for a friar's mouth. **1602–3** SHAKS. *All's Well* II. ii. 29 As fit as . . . the nun's lips to the friar's mouth; nay, as the pudding to his skin. **1659** J. DAY *Blind Beg. Bethnal Green* IV Thou com'st as fit for the purpose as a Pudding for a Fryers mouth.

Pudding, If it won't | it will froize.

1830 FORBY 427 . . . *i.e.* If it won't do for one thing, it will for another.

Pudding time, He (It) comes in.

1546 HEYWOOD II. ix. 80 This geare comth euen in puddyng time rightlie. **1568** FULWELL *Like Will to L.* (1906) 14 Even in pudding time Yonder cometh Ralph Roister, an old friend of mine! **1611** DAVIES *Prov.* 41 Oft things fall out in pudding time. **1738** SWIFT (Dial. ii) 344 Will you do as we do? You are come in pudding time.

Puddings and paramours should be hotly handled.

1641 FERGUSSON 86. **1721** KELLY 277 . . . Puddings, when cold, are uneatable, and love, when coldrife, is near the breaking off.

Pudding(s), see also Better some of a p.; Claws it as Clayton clawed p.; Cold p. will settle love; Come of a blood and so is a p.; Dirty p.; Eat a p. at home, dog have skin; Eat another yard of p. first; Good blood makes bad p.; Lucky p. (If ever you make), I'll eat the prick; Make the crow a p.; Never ate flesh (He that) thinks p. dainty; Proof of the p. in the eating; Salt to Dysart and p. to Tranent (Carry); Too much p. will choke dog; Vex a dog to see p. creep; Woos for cake and p.

Pudding-prick, see Thwitten a mill-post to p. *See also* Lucky pudding.

Puddle, see Path hath a p. (Every).

Puddock(s), see Gentle p. have long toes; Mim as a May p.

Puero, see *Maxima debetur.*

Puff and blow, see Grampus.

Puff not against the wind.

1614 CAMDEN 311.

Pull caps, To.

[= to quarrel, wrangle.] **1754** RICHARDSON 12 Sept. (*Corresp.* v. 27) She scrupled not . . . to pull caps in good-humoured roguery. **1778** FRANCES BURNEY *Evelina* (1920) II. 238 If either of you have any inclination to pull caps for the title of Miss Belmont, you must do it with all speed. **1826** SCOTT *Journ.* 3 Aug. So the two Duties may go pull caps about it.

1853 SURTEES *Sponge's Sport. T.* vii 'There's nothin' talked of . . . but the rich stranger that's a comin', and the gals are all pulling caps, who's to have the first chance.'

Pull devil, pull baker.

1759 COLMAN *Rolliad* can. ii (A) Pull Tom, pull Nick, pull baker, and pull devil. **1819** SCOTT *Let.* to Ld. Montagu 4 Mar. in LOCKHART *Life* xliv A most disagreeable see-saw— a kind of pull-devil, pull-baker contention. **1853** SURTEES *Sponge's Sport T.* 1 Mr. Sponge was now engaged with a game of 'pull devil, pull baker', with the hounds for the fox. **1909** *Spectator* 28 Aug. 293 In China . . . in financial matters there has been a game of ' Pull devil, pull baker' between the central Government and the provincial Governments, the central Government exacting as much as possible and the provincial Governments withholding as much as possible.

Pull down than to build, It is easier to.

1587 J. BRIDGES *Def. of Govt. in C. of E.* 518 It is a true say of olde, *Facilius est destruere quam construere,* We may quicklier pull downe with one hande, than wee can easilie builde againe with both. **1855** BOHN 88. **1909** *Times* 28 Apr. Turkey and her new rulers . . . have astonished those who thought they knew the Turks best by . . . the vigour . . . with which the great change has been conducted. . . . But it is easier always and everywhere to pull down than to build up.

Pull down your hat on the wind['s] side.

1640 HERBERT 333. **1721** KELLY 19 *As the wind blows seek your beel.* . . . Advising us to make our interest as the times change. . . . Eng. *Pull down your hat on the wind side.*

Pull not out your teeth but with a leaden instrument.

1678 RAY 351.

Pull out one tooth and pull out more.

1552 A. BORDE *Brev. of Health* 97. xxxviii And beware of pullyng out any toth for pul out one, and pul out mo.

Pull the devil by the tail, To.

[= to be in difficulties or straits. Fr. *tirer le diable par la queue.*] *a.* **1832** BENTHAM *Wks.* (1838–43) X. 25 So fond of spending his money on antiquities, that he was always pulling the devil by the tail.

Pull the thorn out of your foot and put it into my own, I will not.

1633 D. DYKE Wks. *Philemon* 279 When thou . . . becomest surety for another, let it be for no more than thou art willing and well able to part withall. A man is not bound to pluck a thorn out of another man's foot, to put it into his own. **1678** RAY 273.

Pull, *see also* Long p., and p. all together.

Pulleyn, *see* Raw p. . . . make churchyards fat.

Pulls with a long rope that waits for another's death, He.
1640 HERBERT 318.

Pulse beats matrimony, Her.
1678 RAY 265. **1732** FULLER no. 2492.

Pulse, *see also* Long time to know world's p.

Pun, He that would make a | would pick a pocket.
1729 in POPE *Dunc.* i. 63 *note* A great Critick [Dennis] formerly . . . declared He that would pun would pick a Pocket. **1907** HAMMERTON *Eng. Humourists* 111 If there were any truth in that ancient saw, . . . 'He who would make a pun, would pick a pocket', what a capacity for pocket-picking had Francis Burnand!

Punch coal, cut candle, set brand on end, neither good housewife, nor good housewife's friend.
1678 RAY 295.

Punch (*noun*), *see* Many estates are spent . . . since men for P. forsook. . . .

Punctuality is the politeness of princes.
[LOUIS XVIII *L'exactitude est la politesse des rois.*] **1834** EDGEWORTH *Helen* xxv She dreaded, when the General quoted 'Punctuality is the virtue of princes', that Mr. Harley . . . would have ridiculed so antiquated a notion. **1854** SURTEES *Hand. Cross* xxxv Punctuality is the politeness of princes, and I don't like keeping people waiting. **1879** DOWDEN *Southey* 104 Verbeyst, the prince of booksellers, had not a prince's politeness of punctuality.

Punctuality is the soul of business.
1855 BOHN 477. **1911** W. CROSSING *Folk Rhy. of Devon* 16 Punctuality is the soul of business, and in these days of cheap watches there can be no excuse for anybody failing to cultivate the habit.

Punic faith.
[= faithlessness. L. *Fides Punica*, The faith of Carthaginians, who were supposed to be systematically false; cf. LIVY 21. 4 (of Hannibal) *Perfidia plus quam Punica.*] **1631** MASSINGER *Believe as you List* II. ii The Punicque faith is branded by Our enemies. **1768–74** TUCKER *Lt. Nat.* (1852) II. 318 French faith became the same among us, as Punic faith had been among the Romans. **1824** SCOTT *Redg.* xvii A devout belief in whatever had been said of the punic faith of Jesuits.

Punish(es), *see* Man p. the action, God the intention.

Punishment, Many without | but none without fault (sin).
1616 DRAXE 63. **1670** RAY 17 (with 'sin').

Punishment is lame, but it comes.
[HOR. *Od.* 3. 2. 31 *Raro antecedentem scelestum Deseruit pede poena claudo.*] **1640** HERBERT 328. **1853** TRENCH vi. 147 *Punishment is lame, but it comes,* . . . rests on an image derived from antiquity.

Punishment, *see also* Like p. . . . key and keyhole sustain; Sin brings its p.

Puppy, *see* First pig but last p. best.

Purchase, *see* No p. no pay.

Purgatory pickpurse.
[= the use made of the doctrine of purgatory to obtain payment for masses for departed souls.] **1537** tr. *Latimer's Serm. bef. Convoc.* D ij They that begotte and brought forth, that one old ancient purgatorie pycke pourse. *a.* **1591** H. SMITH *Arrow agst. Ath.* (1622) 60 It may be well and justly called Purgatorie Pickpurse; . . . wealth and great riches of the clergy, was the only mark they aimed at. **1721** M. HENRY *Popery* Wks. (1853) II. 346/2 'Purgatory pick-purse', so it has been called. **1922** DEAN INGE *Outspoken Ess.* 33 The reformers in the sixteenth century complained of 'Purgatory Pickpurse'; our revolutionists think that heaven and hell are made to discharge the same function of bolstering up social injustice.

Purgatory, *see also* Penniless souls maun pine in p.

Puritan, *see* Christian must have . . . words of a P.

Purple, *see* Win p. and wear p.

Purse and his palate are ill met, His.
1721 KELLY 154 . . . Spoken when a poor man loves to eat good meat. **1732** FULLER no. 2513.

Purse be your master, Let your.
1616 WITHALS 564. **1639** CLARKE 129. **1670** RAY 135. **1672** WALKER 47.

Purse is made of a toad's skin, His.
1678 RAY 90 *A covetous person.* His purse is made of a toads skin.

Purse opened not (was steekit[1]) when it (that) was paid for, Your.
1721 KELLY 385 . . . A reproof to those who abuse what is not their own. **1832** A. HENDERSON 151 Your purse was steikit when that was paid for. [[1] shut.]

Purse to your wife, If you sell your | give your breeks into the bargain.
1721 KELLY 195 . . . For if your wife command your purse, she will certainly have the mastery in everything else.

Purse, *see also* Be it for better . . . do after him that beareth the p.; Empty p. causes full heart; Empty p. fills face with wrinkles; Empty p. that is full of other men's money; Fortunatus' p.; Full p. (He that has) never wanted friend; Gain that is put in p. (All is not); Heavy p. light heart; Left his p. in his other hose; Less of your counsel, more of your p.; Light p. heavy heart; Money (He that hath no) needeth no p.; Open thy p. then thy sack; Proud eye, open p. bring; Proud mind and beggar's p.; Put nothing into p. (If you); Put two halfpennies in a p.; Rusty sword and empty p. plead performance; Shows his p. bribes thief; Shows his p. longs to be rid of it; Sickness soaks the p.; Silk p. of a sow's ear; Smiles of a pretty woman are tears of p.; Toom p. makes blate merchant; Two friends have a common p. (When); Two hands in a dish, one in a p.

Purse-net, *see* Caught a knave in a p.

Purser's shirt on a handspike, Like a.

1810 J. MOORE *Post-Captain* V. 23 There is nothing of him left but ribs and trucks. His coat fits him like a purser's shirt upon a handspike.

Pursuits become (*or* grow into) habits.

[L. *Abeunt studia in mores.*] **1605** BACON *Adv. Learn.* I. iii (Oxf.) 21 *Abeunt studia in mores,* studies have an influence and operation upon the manners of those that are conversant in them. **1926** *Times* 1 Feb. Rushbrooke . . . acquired . . . a particular bent to New Testament studies, not on their exegetical side only but also as a foundation for life. *Abierunt studia in mores.*

Put a blithe face on a black heart, It is ill to.

1721 KELLY 216 . . . It is hard to pretend mirth, when the heart is sorrowful.

Put a churl (carl) upon a gentleman, I will never (not).

1586 L. EVANS *Withals Dict. Revised* D 7 Lay not a Churle upon a Gentleman, drinke not beere after wine. **1721** KELLY 186 *I will never put the carle above the gentleman.* Spoken when we offer ale to them that have been drinking claret. **1738** SWIFT (Dial. ii) 348 *Smart.* Will you taste a glass of October[1]? *Never.* No, faith, my lord; I like your wine, and won't put a churl upon a gentleman; your honour's claret is good enough for me. [[1] ale.]

Put a miller, a weaver, and a tailor in a bag, and shake them; the first that comes out will be a thief.

1659 HOWELL *Eng. Prov.* 3/2.

Put another man's child in your bosom, and he'll creep out at your elbow.

1670 RAY 52 . . . *Chesh.* That is, cherish or love him, he'll never be naturally affected towards you.

Put[1] at the cart that is aye ganging, They.

1641 FERGUSSON 96. **1721** KELLY 371 . . . Spoken to them whom we have been very ready to serve, when our readiness that way encourages them to put the sorer upon us. [[1] push.]

Put back the clock, To.

1907 A. C. BENSON *Upton Lett.* [ed. 2] 61 The attempt to put back the clock, and to try and restore things as they were. **1928** *Times* 23 Oct. 12/2 This means . . . the abandonment of the idea of an All-Indian Parliament. Can the clock be put back?

Put him up in a bag, He is able to.

1662 FULLER (*Cardigan*) III. 520 They had a kind of play, wherein the stronger . . . put the weaker into a sack; and hence we have borrowed our English by-word . . . 'He is able to put him up in a bag.'

Put in one's oar, To.

c. **1779** R. CUMBERLAND in *Lett. Lit. Men* (Camden) 412 Whilst I have such a friend to act for me, why should I put in my oar? **1809** MALKIN *Gil Blas* I. vii. par. 1 I . . . put in my oar whenever I thought I could say a good thing. **1886** BESANT *Childr. Gibeon* II. xxx 'Now, don't you put your oar in, young woman. You'd best stand out of the way, you had!'

Put it on thick, and a little will stick.

1841 F. CHAMIER *Tom Bowl.* iii Captain Cornish . . . had also imbibed the vulgar but correct notion of 'put it on thick, and a little will stick', so that in plaster and in compliments the proverb is verified.

Put it together with a hot needle and burnt thread, You.

1678 RAY 350.

Put no faith in tale-bearers.

c. **1450** *Provs. of Wysdom* 123 Be ware of hym, þat tel-þe talis. **1560** DAUS tr. *Sleidane's Comm.* 21 b He admonisheth him to gyue no credit to talebearers. **1855** BOHN 477.

Put not your trust in princes.

[*Ps.* cxlvi. 3.] **1641** LD. STRAFFORD in PROTHERO *Psalms in Hum. L.* (1903) 238 May 12th, 1641 Strafford met his death courageously on Tower Hill. The news that Charles had deserted him had come to him with the shock of surprise. . . . It was to the Psalms that, in bitterness of spirit, he turned for their expression: 'O put not your trust in princes, nor in any child of man'.

Put nothing into your purse, If you | you can take nothing out.

1732 FULLER no. 2781.

Put off his clothes (doublet) before he goes to bed, He will not.

1603 FLORIO tr. *Montaigne* II. viii (1897) III. 102 That answer . . . which fathers have commonly in their mouths: *I will not put off my clothes before I be ready to go to bed.* **1662** FULLER (*Cumb.*) I. 343 Archbishop Grindall . . . was willing to put off his clothes before he went to bed, and in his lifetime to resign his place to doctor Whitgift. **1678** RAY 239 He'll not put off his doublet before he goes to bed, *i.e.* part with his estate before he die. **1888** FREEMAN *Wm. the Conq.* x. 176 Robert . . . demand[ed] . . . Normandy and Maine. William refused with many pithy sayings. It was not his manner to take off his clothes till he went to bed.

Put off the evil hour as long as you can.

1738 SWIFT (Dial. ii) 349 *Smart.* Come, sit down; let us put off the evil hour as long as we can.

Put off the person of a judge, He hath | that puts on the person of a friend.

1629 T. ADAMS *Serm.* (1861–2) II. 550 Tully tells us of a proverb: *Exuit personam judicis, quisquis amici induit*—He hath put off the person of a judge, that puts on the person of a friend.

Put off till to-morrow what may be done to-day, Never.

c. **1386** CHAUCER *Mel.* B² 2984 'An old proverbe,' quod she, 'seith: that "the goodnesse that thou mayst do this day, do it; and abyde nat ne delaye it nat till to-morwe".' **1576** PETTIE *Petite Pall.* (Gollancz) I. 6 Qui paratus non est hodie, cras minus aptus erit. **1616** DRAXE 42 Deferre not vntill to morrow, if thou canst do it to day. **1633** J. HOWELL *Lett.* 5 Sep. (Dent) II. 140 Secretary Cecil . . . would ofttimes speak of himself, 'It shall never be said of me that I will defer till to-morrow what I can do to-day'. **1712** ADDISON *Spect.* No. 487 Wks. (Bohn) III. 469 The maxim . . . should be inviolable with a man in office, never to think of doing that to-morrow which may be done to-day. **1846** DENHAM 3 Never put off till to-morrow, what you can do to-day. **1906** W. MAXWELL *From Yalu to Port A.* 7 It was added that the Chinese Government 'would not reply in haste', but would take advantage of its reputation for never doing to-day what could be put off till the morrow.

Put on one's considering (or thinking) cap, To.

[= to take time for thinking over something.] **1607** H. ESTIENNE *World of Wonders* tr. R. C. 25 A man had need to put on his considering

cap. **1657** R. LIGON *Barbadoes* (1673) 42 They fall back, and put on their considering caps. **1738** SWIFT (Dial. i) 341 *Never.* Guess who it was that told me; come, put on your considering cap.

Put one to (upon) his trump (or trumps), To.

[= to oblige a card player to play out his trumps; *fig.* to put to the last expedient.] **1559** *Mir. Mag., Jack Cade* xx Ere he took me, I put him to his trumps. **1584** LYLY *Campaspe* III. iv Doeth not your beauty put the painter to his trump? **1697** DAMPIER *Voy.* (1729) I. 526 The Wind . . . oft put us to our trumps to manage the Ship. **1907** W. JAMES *Pragmatism* iv. 142 A bit of danger or hardship puts us agreeably to our trumps.

Put one's finger in the fire, To.

1546 HEYWOOD II. ii. 47 It were a foly for mee . . . to put my finger to far in the fyre, Betweene you. **1600–1** SHAKS. *Merry W.* I. iv. 91 I'll ne'er put my finger in the fire. **1670** RAY 175 . . . *Prudens in flammam ne manum injicito*, Hieron. . . . Put not your finger needlessly in the fire. Meddle not with a quarrel voluntarily. **1828** SCOTT *F. M. Perth* vii You will needs put your finger in the fire.

Put one's money upon the wrong horse, To.

1897 MARQ. SALISBURY in *Ho. Lords* 19 Jan. Many members of this House will keenly feel the nature of the mistake that was made when I say that we all put our money upon the wrong horse.

Put out the miller's eye, To.

1678 RAY 343 . . . Spoken by good housewives when they have wet their meal for bread or paste too much. **1834** ESTHER COPLEY *Housekpr's Guide* x. 233 If after . . . 'putting out the millers eye' by too much water, you add flour to make it stiff enough for rolling out [&c.].

Put out your tubs when it is raining.

1721 KELLY 176 *It is good to have our coag¹ out, when it rains kail.* It is good to be in the way when things are a going. **1909** ALEX. MACLAREN *Expos. Hebrews* 353 There is a vulgar old proverb that says, 'Put out your tubs when it is raining'. Be sure that when the gift is falling you fling your hearts wide for its acceptance. [¹ dish.]

Put out, see also Silks and satins p. o. the fire.

Put over the borrowing days, He will.

[i.e. the last three days of March (Old Style), said in Scottish folk-lore to have been borrowed by March from April, and supposed to be especially stormy.] **1721** KELLY 174 . . . Spoken upon some hopes of our sick friend's recovery; taken from weak cattle, who if they outlive the first nine days of April, we hope, they will not die.

Put that in your pipe and smoke it.

[= digest or put up with that if you can.] **1836** DICKENS *Pickwick* ii Put that in his pipe. **1840** BARHAM *Ingol. Leg.* Ser. 1 *St. Odille* Put that in your pipe, my lord Otto, and smoke it! **1884** W. E. NORRIS *Thirlby Hall* xxv It don't do to let them get the whip-hand of you, according to my experience. Put that in your pipe and smoke it, Master Charley.

Put the man to the mear[1] that can manage the mear.

1862 HISLOP 250. [[1] mare.]

Put the poor man's penny and the rich man's penny in ae purse, and they'll come out alike.

1832 HENDERSON 86.

Put to bed with a shovel, He is.

1785 GROSE s.v. 'Bed' Put to bed with a mattock, and tucked up with a spade. **1813** RAY 75 ... He is going to be buried.

Put tricks upon travellers, Don't.

1611–12 SHAKS. *Tempest* II. ii. 60 Have we devils here? Do you put tricks upon us with savages and men of Ind? **1738** SWIFT (Dial. i) 341 *Never.* I know better things, miss and I are good friends; don't put tricks upon travellers. **1870** READE *Put Yourself* xxix 'That's a lie! ... none of your tricks upon travellers.'

Put two halfpennies (pennies) in a purse, and they will draw together.

1641 FERGUSSON 86. **1721** KELLY 281 ... When people have purchased any little sum of money it will easily encrease. Apply'd sometimes when rich men marry rich women.

Put up your pipes.

[= desist; 'shut up'.] **1556** OLDE *Antichrist* 148 Then maye the B[ishop] of Rome put up his pypes. **1594–5** SHAKS. *Rom. & Jul.* IV. v. 96 Faith, we may put up our pipes, and be gone. **1604–5** *Othello* III. i. 20 Then put up your pipes in your bag, for I'll away. **1639** CLARKE 155.

Put up your pipes, and go to Lockington wake.[1]

1678 RAY 317 Leicestershire. *Put up your pipes, and goe to Lockington wake.* **1787** GROSE

(*Leics.*) 189 Put up your pipes, and go to Lockington-wake. Lockington stands . . . upon the confines of Derby and Nottingham shires. [[1] festival, fair.]

Put your finger in the fire, and say it was your fortune.

1721 KELLY 280 ... Spoken to them who lay the blame of their crimes, and mismanagements, on their hard fortune.

Put your hand in the creel,[1] and take out either an adder or an eel.

a. 1610 A. MONTGOMERIE *Misc. Poems; The poet reasons* (1821) 203 Bot put ʒour hand, by hazard in the creill; Zit men hes mater vharvpon to muse, For they must drau ane adder or ane eill. **1721** KELLY 278 ... Spoken of taking a wife, where no cunning, art, or sense can secure a good choice. **1823** GALT *Entail* xxv Watty, my lad, ... 'Marriage is a creel, where ye maun catch', as the auld byword runs, 'an adder or an eel'. [[1] wicker basket for fish, &c.]

Put yourself in his place.

1870 READE *Put Yourself in His Place* (Title).

Put, Put a (an), Put not, Put your, *see also under significant words following.*

Puts on a public gown, He that must put off a private person.

1642 FULLER *H. & P. State* iv. vii (1841) 255 The Good Judge . . . gives sentence with uprightness. For when he put on his robes, he put off his relations to any; and, like Melchisedec, becomes without pedigree. **1732** FULLER no. 2257.

Puttock, *see* Eat white bread (When shall we)? When the p. is dead.

Pylades and Orestes died long ago, and left no successors.

[Two inseparable friends. Orestes was the son of Agamemnon and of Clytemnestra, whom, by the help of Pylades, he killed.] **1732** FULLER no. 3987.

Pyrrhic victory.

[A victory gained at too great a cost; in allusion to the exclamation attributed to Pyrrhus, King of Epirus, after the battle of Asculum in Apulia, in 279 B.C. ... , 'One more such victory and we are lost.'] **1885** *Daily Tel.* 17 Dec. Although its acceptance might secure for the moment the triumph of a party division, it would be indeed a Pyrrhic victory.

Q

Quail, *see* Couch like a q.

Quake, *see* Aspen leaf.

Quality, without quantity, is little thought of.

1721 KELLY 282.

Quandary, To be in a.

[= extreme perplexity or difficult situation.] **1579** LYLY *Euphues* (Arb.) 45 *Euphues* hauing thus ended his talke, departed leauing this olde gentleman in a great quandarie. **1600–1** SHAKS. *Merry W.* II. ii. 63–5 *Quick.* You have brought her into such a canaries as 'tis wonderful: the best courtier of them all ... could never have brought her to such a canary. **1616** DRAXE 153. **1875** JOWETT *Plato* (ed. 2) I. 229 Now I was in a great quandary at having to answer this question.

Quarrel with one's bread and butter, To.

[= to fall out with one's means of support.] **1738** SWIFT (Dial. i) 334 *Miss*. I won't quarrel with my bread and butter for all that; I know when I'm well. **1780** CRAIG *Mirror* No. 69 par. 1 How did she show superior sense by thus quarrelling with her bread and butter? **1883** J. PAYN *Thicker than W.* xxxviii He thought that Edgar had shown his wisdom in not 'quarrelling with his bread and butter'.

Quarrel, *see also* Come and welcome, go by, no q.; Make a fire (He that can) can end q.; Two to make q.

Quarrelling dogs come halting home.

1721 KELLY 309 Tulying[1] dogs come halting home. **1732** FULLER no. 3988. [[1] fighting.]

Quarrelsome dogs get dirty coats.

1842 S. LOVER *Handy Andy* xlvi 'You're a stout fellow, Ratty', said he, 'but remember this old saying, "Quarrelsome dogs get dirty coats".'

Quart, *see* Neighbour-q. is good q.

Quartan agues kill old men, and cure young.

1659 HOWELL *Ital.-Eng.* 15. **1678** RAY 41. **1732** FULLER no. 3991.

Quarter day, *see* Nothing is certain but ... q. d.

Quarter-master wherever he comes, He'll be.

1572 T. WILSON *Discorse upon Usury* (1925) 210 He ... wilbee quarter master wyth mee I tell you, do what I can [of a forward young fellow]. **1678** RAY 266. **1732** FULLER no. 2414 He would be quarter-master at home, if his wife would let him.

Quatre trey, *see* Size cinque.

Queen Anne is dead.

[= stale news.] **1722** Ballad in LADY PENNY-MAN *Miscellanies* 1740 (A) He's as dead as Queen Anne the day after she dy'd. **1840** BARHAM *Ingol. Leg.* Ser. 1. *Acc. New Play* Lord Brougham, it appears isn't dead, though Queen Anne is. **1859** THACKERAY *Virgin.* lxxiii On which my lady cried petulantly, 'Oh, Lord, Queen Anne's dead, I suppose.' **1885** D. C. MURRAY *Rainbow G.* III. v May happen thee hasn't heard th' other piece o' news. Queen Anne's dead.

Queen Anne, *see also* Dead as Q. A.

Queen Elizabeth is dead.

1738 SWIFT (Dial. i) 333 *Lady S.* What news,

Mr. Neverout. *Never*. Why, madam, Queen Elizabeth's dead.

Queen of beggars, *see* King of good fellows.

Queen's weather.

[= fine weather.] **1902** GUGGISBERG *The Shop* 177 On the 22nd June, 1897, the cadets ... proceeded to London to take part in Her Majesty's Diamond Jubilee celebration. ... Never did the expression 'Queen's weather' more thoroughly deserve its meaning. **1910** *Times Wkly.* 9 Dec. The Coronation of King Edward took place in weather as bright as that which had come to be known as 'Queen's weather'.

Queer Street.

[An imaginary street where people in diffi-culties are supposed to reside; hence any difficulty, &c.] **1836** DICKENS *Pickwick* lv You would have found yourself in Queer Street before this. **1837** LYTTON *E. Maltrav.* IV. vii You are in the wrong box—planted in Queer Street, as we say in London. **1865** Id. *Mut. Fr.* III. i Queer Street is full of lodgers just at present.

Queer, *see also* Dick's hatband (Q. as).

Quench, *see* Wine in bottle does not q. thirst.

Quenching of fire with tow, There is no.

1616 DRAXE 143. **1813** RAY 153.

Question for question is all fair.

1773 GOLDSMITH *She Stoops to C.* I. ii (Globe) 648 *Tony*. No offence; but question for question is all fair, you know.

Question(s) (*noun*), *see also* Ask no q., told no lies; Beg the q.; Fool may ask more q.; Spur a jade a q., she'll kick an answer; Two sides to every q.

Question(eth) (*verb*), *see* Cometh from above let no man q.; Nothing q., nothing learneth.

Quey[1] calves are dear veal.

1737 RAMSAY III. 192 Quey caufs are dear veal. [[1] Heifer. Female calves should be kept for breeding.]

Qui facit per alium facit per se, *see* Causes to be done.

Quick and nimble, more like a bear than a squirrel.

1732 FULLER no. 3992. **1813** RAY 66 In some places they say, in drollery, *Quick and nimble, more like a bear than a squirrel*.

Quick and nimble, 'twill be your own another day.

1678 RAY 345.

Quick at meat, quick at work.

1611 COTGRAVE s.v. 'Bon' A good beast eats apace; or, as we say, good at meat good at

worke. **1616** DRAXE 44. **1639** CLARKE 92
1738 SWIFT (Dial. ii) 348 *Miss.* I have dined
this half hour. *Lady S.* What! quick at meat,
quick at work, they say.

Quick believers need broad shoulders.

1640 HERBERT 318.

Quick returns make rich merchants.

1721 KELLY 282 . . . Often ironically apply'd
to them, who having been drunk, and having
slept themselves sober, go to it again.

Quick, *see also* Live by the q. (We must);
Touched him on the q.

Quickly come, quickly go.

1578 G. WHETSTONE *Promus & Cassandra* I i[v]
Who gets a pace as meryly may spend. **1583**
MELBANCKE *Philotimus* V 2[v] Quickly spent,
thats easely gotten. **1631** MABBE *Celestina*
(T.T.) 29 Quickly be wonne, and quickly be
lost. **1869** HAZLITT 322.

Quickly too'd[1] and quickly go, quickly will thy mother have moe.

1659 HOWELL *Eng. Prov.* 4/1 Soon todd,[1]
soon with God. *A Northern Proverb when a
child hath teeth too soon.* **1670** RAY 52 Quickly
too'd and quickly go, Quickly will thy mother
have moe. *Yorksh.* Some have it quickly
to'd, quickly with God, as if early breeding
of teeth, were a sign of a short life, whereas
we read of some born with teeth in their
heads, who have yet lived long enough to
become famous men. [[1] toothed.]

Quickly, *see also* Good and q. seldom meet.

Quiet as a wasp in one's nose, She is as.

1616 WITHALS 566 A woman is as quiet, as a
waspe in a mans nose. **1659** HOWELL *Eng.
Prov.* 16/1. **1670** RAY 215. **1732** FULLER
no. 4130 (with 'ear' for 'nose').

Quiet conscience sleeps in thunder, A.

1721 KELLY 14 *A safe conscience makes a
sound sleep.* And doubtless a bad conscience
will have the contrary effect. **1732** FULLER
no. 374. **1747** FRANKLIN July A quiet conscience sleeps in thunder, but rest and guilt
live far asunder.

Quiet sow, quiet mow.

1850 *N. & Q.* 1st Ser. II. 512 . . . A saying
with reference to land or lease held on lives.
If the seed is sown without notice of the death
of the life, the corn may be reaped, although
the death took place before the sowing.

Quiet, *see also* Anything for q. life; Little
with q.; Physicians (Best) are Dr. Diet,
Dr. Q.

Quietness is best.

a. **1599** *George a Green* 1150. **1664** CODRING-
TON 209 Quietnesse is a great treasure. **1832**
HENDERSON 135.

Quietness is best, as the fox said when he bit the cock's head off.

1886 R. HOLLAND, *Cheshire Gloss.* (E.D.S.)
453 (A). **1917** BRIDGE 104.

Quietness, *see also* Love (Next to), q.

Quietus, To give a.

[Med. L. *Quietus est* = he is quit. A discharge, acquittance; death.] **1600–1** SHAKS.
Hamlet III. i. 75 For who would bear the
whips and scorns of time, . . . When he himself might his quietus make With a bare
bodkin? **1609** *Sonn.* 126. 12 Her [Nature's]
audit, though delay'd, answer'd must be,
And her quietus is to render thee. **1618**
BEAUM. & FL. *Loy. Subj.* II. v You have . . .
eas'd mine age, Sir; And to this care a fair
Quietus given. **1775** SHERIDAN *Rivals* v. iii
If an unlucky bullet should carry a quietus
with it. **1872** BAKER *Nile Tribut.* v. 65 The
shot, far from producing a quietus, gave rise
to a series of convulsive struggles.

Quinine is made of the sweat of ship carpenters.

1894 F. COWAN *Sea Prov.* 67 Quinine is made
of the sweat of ship carpenters. Hence it is
very dear.

Quis custodiet, see Keep the keepers.

Quit certainty for hope, Never.

[HESIOD Νήπιος ὃς τὰ ἕτοιμα λιπών τ'
ἀνέτοιμα διώκει. He is a fool who leaves a
certainty to pursue an uncertainty.] **1546**
HEYWOOD II. xi. 83 Who that leaveth surety
and leaneth unto chance, when fools pipe, by
authority he may dance. **1855** BOHN 459.

Quite young and all alive, like an old maid of forty-five.

1869 HAZLITT 336.

Quits his place well that leaves his friend there, He.

1640 HERBERT 357.

Quits, *see* Cry q.

Quits (*verb*), *see also* Begins to die that q.
his desires.

Quittance, *see* Omittance.

Quos (*Quem*) *Deus vult perdere prius dementat.* (Whom God would ruin, he first deprives of reason.)

[SOPHOCLES *Ant.* 622 Τὸ κακὸν δοκεῖν ποτ'
ἐσθλὸν τῷδ' ἔμμεν ὅτῳ φρένας θεὸς ἄγει πρὸς
ἄταν. LYCURGUS 159. 20 Οἱ θεοὶ οὐδὲν πρότερον
ποιοῦσιν ἢ τῶν πονηρῶν ἀνθρώπων τὴν διά-
νοιαν παράγουσι. PUB. SYRUS *Sentent.* (Orelli)
741 *Stultum facit Fortuna quem vult perdere.*
1694 JOSHUA BARNES *Euripides* Index Prior,
letter D *Deus quos vult perdere dementat
prius. Ibid.* p. 515, l. 436 Ὅταν δὲ δαίμων
ἀνδρὶ πορσύνῃ κακὰ τὸν νοῦν ἔβλαψε πρῶτον

▪ Trag. adesp. 455 N².] **1640** HERBERT 349 When God will punish, he will first take away the understanding. **1687** DRYDEN *Hind & Panther* iii. 1093 For those whom God to ruine has design'd, He fits for Fate, and first destroys their Mind. **1783** BOSWELL *Johnson* lxxv (1848) 718 I once talked to him of some of the sayings which every body repeats, but nobody knows where to find, such as *Quos* DEUS *vult perdere, prius de-*

mentat. **1885** C. LOWE *Bismarck* (1898) iv Either driven mad by the gods who meant to destroy them, or deluded with hopes of succour from friends who could do nothing but leave them in the lurch, the Danes remained stone-deaf to the moderate proposals of the allies.

Quot homines tot sententiae, see Men (So many), so many minds.

R

'R' is the dog's letter.

[= has the sound of a snarl. PERSIUS *Sat.* i. 109 *Sonat hic de nare canina Littera.* Here from the nostril sounds the canine letter.] **1509** A. BARCLAY *Ship of Fools* (1874) I. 182 This man malycious . . . Nought els soundeth but the hoorse letter R . . . , he none answere hath saue the dogges letter. **1594–5** SHAKS. *Rom. & Jul.* II. iv. 225 *Rom.* Both with an R. *Nurse.* Ah! mocker; that's the dog's name. **1629** T. ADAMS *Serm.* (1861–2) I. 484 Because *R* is a dogged letter, . . . all terms with *R* in them, shall be put out. **1636** B. JONSON *Eng. Gram.* (1640) 47 R is the Dogs Letter and hurreth[1] in the sound. **1645** FULLER *Good Thoughts* (1841) 186 This scholar . . . made a Latin oration . . . without an R therein . . . to show that men might speak without being beholden to the dog's letter. [¹ snarls.]

Rabbit, He is like a | fat and lean in twenty-four hours.

1678 RAY 288. **1738** SWIFT (Dial. i) 339 I am like a rabbit, fat and lean in four-and-twenty hours.

Rabbit for a rat? Who will change a.

1550 HEYWOOD II. vii. 70 A péece of a kyd is woorth two of a cat. Who the diuell will chaunge a rabet for a rat?

Rabbit hunting with a dead ferret, To go.

1732 FULLER no. 5170 To go a coney-catching with a dead ferrit. **1813** RAY 213 . . . *Andar a caça con huron muerto. Hisp.* **1897** 'H. S. MERRIMAN' *In Kedar's T.* vii The innkeeper next door displays a branch of pine, which, I notice, is more attractive. . . . One does not catch rabbits with a dead ferret.

Rabbits, *see* Godalming.

Race is got by running, The.

1732 FULLER no. 4728.

Race is not to the swift, The | nor the battle to the strong.

[**1560** GENEVA BIBLE *Eccl.* ix. 11 I saw vnder the sunne that the race is not to the swift, nor yᵉ battell to the strong.] **1621** BURTON *Anat. Mel.* II. iii. VII (1651) 351 It is not honesty, learning, worth, wisdom, that prefers men, (*the race is not to the swift, nor the battle to the strong*) but . . . chance.

Race-horses, *see* Gamesters and r. never last.

Rack and manger, To lie (live) at.

[= to live in reckless abundance.] *c.* **1378** WYCLIF *Works* (Matthew) 435 It is yuel to kepe a wast hors in stable, . . . but it is worse to haue a womman at racke and at manger. *a.* **1625** J. FLETCHER *Lit. Fr. Law* v. i (1905) III. 451 God help the Courtiers, That lye at rack and manger. **1679** MRS. BEHN *Feign'd Curtizan* III. i Danger, . . . once o'recome, I lie at rack and manger. **1825** SCOTT *Journ.* 9 Dec. Harriet Wilson . . . who lived with half the gay world at rack and manger. **1843** CARLYLE *Past & Pr.* II. i John Lackland . . . tearing out the bowels of St. Edmundsbury Convent . . . by living at rack and manger there.

Raddleman, *see* Rutland R.

Raft, *see* Man on the r. who thought riverbanks moving.

Ragged as a colt, As.

1537 *Thersites* C 2ᵛ As ragged as a colt. **1863** WISE *New Forest* ch. xvi (A) The proverb 'as ragged as a colt Pixey' is everywhere to be heard, and at which Drayton seems to hint in his *Court of Faerie*: 'This Puck seems but a dreaming dolt, Still walking like a ragged colt.'

Ragged colt may make a good horse, A.

a. **1500** R. *Hill's Commonpl. Bk.* (E.E.T.S.) 128 (A) Of a rwgged colte cwmeth a good hors. **1546** HEYWOOD I. xi. 27 Colts (quoth his man) may proue well with tatches yll. For of a ragged colte there comth a good horse. **1605** CHAPMAN, &c., *Eastw. Hoe* v. i (1874) 483 Heaven pardon my severity! 'The ragged colt may proue a good horse'. **1670** RAY 72 . . . An unhappy boy may make a good man. . . . Children which seem less handsome when young, do afterwards grow into shape and comeliness. **1721** KELLY 48 . . . And so may an untoward slovenly boy prove a decent and useful man.

Rain always comes out of Mobberley hole, The.

1917 BRIDGE 117 The rain always comes out of Mobberley hole. [Wilmslow.] . . . The direction from which an unpleasant wind or rain comes is almost invariably termed a 'hole'.

Rain before seven: fine before eleven.

1853 N. & Q. 1st Ser. VIII. 218. **1909** *Spectator* 20 Mar. 452 'Rain before seven, shine before eleven', is one of the most trustworthy of all country saws.

Rain cats and dogs, To.

[= to rain violently.] **1653** R. BROME *City Wit* IV. i It shall raine ... dogs and polecats, and so forth. **1738** SWIFT (Dial. ii) 349 *Spark.* Sir John will go, though he was sure it would rain cats and dogs. **1819** SHELLEY *Let. to Peacock* 25 Feb. It began raining cats and dogs. **1882** BLACKMORE *Christow.* XX It was raining cats and dogs ... when Parson Short ... rode up the lane.

Rain comes before the wind, If the | lower your topsails, and take them in; if the wind comes before the rain, lower your topsails, and hoist them again.

1853 N. & Q. 1st Ser. VIII. 218.

Rain comes scouth when the wind's in the south, The.

1862 HISLOP ... 'To rain scouth', is to rain abundantly or heavily.

Rain from the east: wet two days (twenty-four hours) at least.

1830 FORBY 417 When it rains with the wind in the east, it rains for twenty-four hours at least. **1869** HAZLITT 337.

Rain lays great dust, Small.

1670 RAY 135. **1732** FULLER no. 4193.

Rain lays great winds, Small.

1639 CLARKE 204. **1670** RAY 135 Petite pluye abat grand vent. Small rain, or a little rain lays a great wind. *Gall.*

Rain pottage, If it should | he would want his dish.

1670 RAY 191. **1732** FULLER no. 2687.

Rain, rain, go to Spain: fair weather come again.

1659 HOWELL *Eng. Prov.* 20/1.

Rain raineth and the goose winketh, When the | little wots the gosling what the goose thinketh.

1523 SKELTON *Garl. Laurel* 1431 Whan the rayne rayneth and the gose wynkith, Lytill wotith the goslyng what the gose thynketh.

Rain, Some | some rest.

1678 RAY 80 ... *A harvest proverb.*

Rain, There is no | —the Christians are the cause.

[a. 413] **1869** LECKY *Hist. Europ. Mor.* (1905) I. iii 'There is no rain—the Christians are the cause', had become a popular proverb in Rome. (ST. AUG. *De Civ. Dei* ii. 3.)

Rain(s) (*noun*), *see also* Asses bray, we shall have r.; Bright r. makes fools fain; Cloak for the r. (Good to have); Dirt-bird sings, we shall have r.; Easterly winds and r. bring cockles; Every day of the week a shower of r.; Farther the sight, nearer the r.; God will (When) no wind but brings r.; Gull comes against r.; Many r. many rowans; More r. more rest; Morning r. (For a) leave not journey; Near burr far r.; Peacock loudly bawls (When); Right as r.; Snails on the road you see (When); Sun goes pale to bed, r. tomorrow; Three things drive man out of house; Wind's in the south, it's in r.'s mouth.

Rain(s, ing) (*verb*), *see also* Although it r. throw not away watering-pot; Cloak to make when r. (Have not thy); Put out your tubs when r.

Rainbow at morn, A | put your hook in the corn: a rainbow at eve, put your head in the sheave.

1883 ROPER 11. **1893** INWARDS 112.

Rainbow in the eve, If there be a | it will rain and leave; but if there be a rainbow in the morrow, it will neither lend nor borrow.

1670 RAY 43.

Rainbow in the morning, A | is the shepherd's (sailor's) warning; a rainbow at night is the shepherd's (sailor's) delight.

1555 L. DIGGES *Prognostication* B 2 If in the mornyng the raynebow appere, it signifieth moysture ... If in the evening it spend it self, fayre weather ensueth. **1828** SIR H. DAVY *Salmonia* (1851) vi. 164 I have often observed that the old proverb is correct—A rainbow in the morning is the shepherd's warning; A rainbow at night is the shepherd's delight. **1898** R. INWARDS *Weather Lore* (ed. 3) 135 Rainbow at night, Sailor's delight; Rainbow in morning, sailors take warning.

Rainbow, *see also* End of the r. (Go to the).

Rains but it pours, It never.

1726 SWIFT & POPE *Prose Miscellanies* [title of paper] (A) It cannot rain but it pours. **1809** MALKIN *Gil Blas* I. ix As it never rains but it pours, I was in the front of the battle, hemmed in between the captain and the lieutenant. **1851** KINGSLEY *Yeast* vi 'It never rains but it pours', and one cannot fall in with a new fact or a new acquaintance but next day twenty fresh things shall spring up as if by magic. **1913** *Spectator* 26 Apr. 687 'It never rains but it pours' might be said ... of the number of books on Japan which have appeared in the last few years.

Rains by planets, It.

1662 FULLER (*Westmr.*) II. 421 Rain (which country people say goeth by planets) goeth by Providence. **1670** RAY 45 ... This the country people use when it rains in one place and not in another; meaning that the showers are governed by the planets, which ... cause such uncertain wandering of clouds and falls of rain. Or ... the falls of showers are as uncertain as the motions of the planets are imagined to be. **1882** in LUCAS *Stud. Nidderdale* 206 That no two floods in Nidderdale are alike in effect, which is locally accounted for by saying, 'that the rain falls in planets'.

Rains when the sun is shining, If it | the devil is beating his wife.

1738 SWIFT (*Dial.* i) 334 *Col.* It rained and the sun shone at the same time. *Never.* Why, then the devil was beating his wife behind the door with a shoulder of mutton. **1828** LYTTON *Pelham* lxi Sharp shower coming on. 'The devil will soon be beating his wife with a leg of mutton', as the proverb says.

Rains, *see also* Rain(s).

Rainy day, Lay up (Lay by *or* Keep something) against (for) a.

c. **1566** *The Bugbears* III. ii. 23 Wold he haue me kepe nothyng agaynst a raynye day? **1582** C. FETHERSTON *A Dialogue against light dancing* ¶ 4 It is good sauing a penny against a wet day. **1639** CLARKE 93 Lay up for a rainie day. **1677** YARRANTON *Eng. Impr.* 115 In the Time of Plenty, then lay up for a Rainy-day. **1841** F. CHAMIER *Tom Bowl.* xxxix. I have got some money that I put by for a rainy day.

Rainy, *see also* First of July (If the) it be r.; Offer your hen for sale on r. day (Never).

Raise Cain, To.

[= to make a disturbance.] **1852** MRS. STOWE *Uncle Tom's C.* xx. 212 Topsy would hold a perfect carnival of confusion ... in short as Miss Ophelia phrased it, raising Cain' generally. **1882** STEVENSON *Treasure Is.* iii If I get the horrors, I'm a man that has lived rough, and I'll raise Cain.

Raise no more devils (spirits) than you can lay (conjure down).

1631 JONSON *New Inn* III. ii *Prud.* Beware you do not conjure up a spirit You cannot lay. **1655** FULLER *Ch. Hist.* x. iv (1868) III. 300 The boy, having gotten a habit of counterfeiting, ... would not be un-deviled by all their exorcisms; so that the priests raised up a spirit which they could not allay. **1670** RAY 135 Raise no more spirits then you can conjure down. **1721** KELLY 282 ... Do not stir up a strife, that you will not afterward be able to appease. **1845** MACAULAY *Speech on Maynooth* Wks. VIII. 314 All

those fierce spirits, whom you hallooed on ... now ... worry you. ... Did you think, when ... you called the Devil up, that it was as easy to lay him as to raise him?

Raise the devil, To.

[= to create trouble, uproar.] **1705** VANBRUGH *Confed.* v. ii Sir, give me an account of my Necklace, or I'll make such a Noise in your House I'll raise the Devil in't. **1841** LEVER *C. O'Malley* lxiii He was going to raise the devil.

Raise the devil than to lay him, It is easier to.

1655 FULLER *Ch. Hist.* x. iv (1868) III. 300 The boy, having gotten a habit of counterfeiting, ... would not be un-deviled by all their exorcisms; so that the priests raised up a spirit which they could not allay. **1777** GARRICK Prol. to *Sch. for Scandal* Alas! the devil's sooner raised than laid. **1845** MACAULAY *Speech on Maynooth* Wks. VIII. 314 Did you think, when, to serve your turn, you called the Devil up, that it was as easy to lay him as to raise him? **1890** 'ROLF BOLDREWOOD' *Miner's Right* xxi But exorcists of all kinds ... have ever found the fiend more easy to invoke than to lay.

Raise the wind, To.

[= to procure money.] **1789** *Loiterer* No. 42 10 He ... never offered to pay earnest. I suppose, poor fellow, he could not raise the wind. **1857** TROLLOPE *Three Clerks* xxxiv He came to me this morning to raise the wind.

Raisin, *see* Black plum (r.) sweet as white.

Rake hell and skim the devil, you can't find another such man. (*See also* Harrow hell, &c.)

c. **1700** *Dict. Cant. Crew* s.v. 'Scumm'. **1754** BERTHELSON *Eng.–Dan. Dict.* s.v. 'Rake' (A).

Rake hell for a bodle,[1] He would.

1832 HENDERSON 2. [1 one-sixth of a penny.]

Rake, *see also* Better with a r. than a fork; Fork is commonly r.'s heir; Lean as a r.; Little for the r. after besom.

Ram to kill a butcher, It is possible for a.

1670 RAY 22. **1828** LYTTON *Pelham* xiii Don't think of fighting the man; he is a tradesman. ... Remember that '*a ram may kill a butcher*'.

Ram, *see also* Right as a r.'s horn.

Ramehead, *see* Dudman.

Ramsey the rich.

[A Benedictine Abbey, near Huntingdon, built 969. *See* LEAN I. 103.] **1662** FULLER (*Huntingd.*) II. 98 'Ramsey the Rich'. This was the ... Crœsus of all our English abbeys; for, having but sixty monks to maintain therein, the revenues thereof, ... amounted unto seven thousand pounds a year.

Ramsey, the rich of gold and of fee; Thorney, the flower of the fen country. Crowland, so courteous of meat and of drink; Peterborough the proud, as all men do think. And Sawtrey, by the way, that old abbaye Gave more alms in one day than all they.

1852 N. & Q. 1st Ser. VI. 350.

Ramsins, *see* Leeks in Lide and r. in May.

Rancour sticks long by the ribs.

1616 WITHALS 561. **1639** CLARKE 178. **1659** HOWELL *Eng. Prov.* 16/1.

Rank courtesy when a man is forced to give thanks for his own, It is a.

1664 CODRINGTON 203. **1670** RAY 20.

Rap, Not a.

[*Rap*, a counterfeit coin passing current for a halfpenny in Ireland in the 18th cent. Taken as a type of the smallest coin.] **1830** MARRYAT *King's Own* XXXV 'You must fork out.' 'Not a rap.' **1834** AINSWORTH *Rookwood* III. V For the mare-with-three-legs [the gallows], boys, I care not a rap. **1881** MISS BRADDON *Asphodel* XIV. 158 A man who dies and leaves not a rap behind him.

Rape[1] rueth, Oft.

c. **1300** *Prov. of Hending* XXXI in *Salomon & Sat.* (1848) 278 Ofte rap reweþ, quoþ Hendyng. *c.* **1390** GOWER *Conf. Amantis* III. 1625 Men sen alday þat rape reweþ. **1473** MARG. PASTON in *P. Lett.* III. 78 Bydde hym that he be not to hasty of takyng of orderes . . . for oftyn rape rewith. *c.* **1580** SPELMAN *Dialogue* (Roxb. Cl.) 2 I mynde to go safelye, least in goyinge to hastelye, we Repente more speedely. And thinges dunne in haste Bringeth spedye Repentance. [[1] haste.]

Rape (= rope), *see* Whaup in the r. (There is a).

Rath[1] sower never borroweth of the late, The.

1659 HOWELL *Eng. Prov.* 17/1. [[1] early.]

Rather sell than be poor.

1678 RAY *Adag. Hebr.* 400.

Rats desert (forsake, leave) a falling house (sinking ship).

1579 T. LUPTON *A Thousand Notable Things* ii. 87 Rats and dormice will forsake old and ruinous houses, three months before they fall [cited in note to WEBSTER *Duchess of Malfi* (Lucas) V. ii. 219–20]. *a.* **1588** DR. RECORD (quoted J. HARVEY *Concerning Prophesies* (1588) 81) When a house will fall, the Mice right quicke Flee thence before. **1601** PLINY tr. Holland viii. 28, When an house is readie to tumble downe, the mice goes out of it before. **1607** TOURNEUR *Rev. Trag.* v. ii *Bos.* Like the mice That forsake falling houses, I would shift to other dependance. **1611–12** SHAKS. *Tempest* I. ii. 147 A rotten carcass of a boat, . . . the very rats Instinctively have quit it. **1625** BACON *Ess., Wisd. for Man's Self* (Arb.) 187 It is the *Wisedome of Rats*, that will be sure to leaue a House, somewhat before it fall. **1738** GAY *Fables* Ser. II. ix As rats, before the mansion falls, Desert late hospitable walls, In shoals the servile creatures run, To bow before the rising sun. **1824** SCOTT *St. Ronans* xxv They say a falling house is best known by the rats leaving it— a falling state, by the desertion of confederates and allies—and a falling man, by the desertion of his friends. **1895** J. PAYN *In Mark. Ov.* xxvi This is bad news indeed about Barton's pupils. . . . It is a case of the rats leaving a sinking ship, I fear.

Rat(s), *see also* Drowned mouse (r.); Poor as a r.; Rhyme r. to death; Scot, a r., travel world over; Smell a r.; Welcome death, quoth the r.

Rat-trap, Like a | easier to get into than out of.

1897 L. J. TROTTER *Life of J. Nicholson* xi November passed away before John Nicholson found himself free to quit. . . . India, he wrote, was 'like a rat-trap—easier to get into than out of'.

Raven(s), *see* Bitter bird (Thou art) said r. to starling; Carcase is (Where the), r. will gather; Takes the r. for guide (He that).

Ravine (= rapine), *see* Ruin of one r.

Raw, *see* Johnny R.

Raw head and bloody bone.

[= a bugbear.] **1598** FLORIO *Worlde of Wordes* s.v. *Mani* . . . imagined spirits that nurces fraie their babes withall to make them leaue crying, as we say bug-beare, or else rawe head and bloodie bone. **1622** FLETCHER *Prophetess* IV. V But now I look Like Bloody-Bone and Raw-head, to frighten children. **1824** SCOTT *St. Ronans* xix I had . . . to walk to the Spa, bleeding like a calf, and tell a raw-head-and-bloody-bone story about a footpad.

Raw Hempstead.[1]

1902–4 LEAN I. 152 The rawness of Hempstead may possibly be attributed to its position on one of the bleakest portions of our eastern coast, and not from any want of polish on the part of its inhabitants. [[1] Norfolk.]

Raw leather will stretch.

1611 DAVIES *Prov.* 213.

Raw pulleyn,[1] veal, and fish, make the churchyards fat.

1623 WODROEPHE 522 Ill sodden Veale, and rawe Hennes, make swollē Churchards Lust, & Death. **1678** RAY 41 Vitello, pullastro & pesce crudo ingrassano i cimiterii.[2] i.e. *Raw pulleyn, veal and fish make the churchyards fat.* [[1] poultry. [2] Vitello, pollastro e pesci crudi ingrassano i cimiteri.]

Razor, *see* Cut blocks with r.; Occam's; Sharp as a r.

Read one like a book, To.

1594–5 SHAKS. *Rom. & Jul.* I. iii. 81 Read o'er the volume of young Paris' face And find delight writ there with beauty's pen. **1601–2** *Troil. & Cres.* IV. v. 238 O! like a book of sport thou'lt read me o'er; But there's more in me than thou understand'st. **1874** WHYTE-MELVILLE *Uncle John* v That lady, who read him like a book, preserved an appearance of complete unconsciousness.

Read, try, judge, and speak as you find, says old Suffolk.

1813 RAY 71. **1855** BOHN 62.

Read, *see also* New book appears (When) r. old one; Parson of Saddleworth (Like the) who could r. no book but his own.

Reading maketh a full man, conference a ready man, and writing an exact man.

1597–8 BACON *Ess., Studies* (Arb.) 10 Reading maketh a full man, conference a readye man, and writing an exacte man. **1738** FRANKLIN Oct. Reading makes a full man—meditation a profound man—discourse a clear man.

Ready money is a ready medicine.

c. **1580** J. CONYBEARE *Adagia* in *John Cony-beare* (1905) 46 Pecunia praesens, medicamen est praesentaneum: Redie money, redie medicine. **1640** HERBERT 365.

Ready money will away.

? **1622** J. TAYLOR (Water-P.) *Trav. Twelve-pence* Wks. (1630) I. 72/2 The Prouerbe true doth say That ready money euer will away. **1659** HOWELL *Eng. Prov.* 12/1.

Ready mouth for a ripe cherry, A.

1641 FERGUSSON 112. **1721** KELLY 366 . . . Spoken to those who are ready to catch at what we have. **1732** FULLER no. 5913.

Ready, *see also* Booted are not always r.; Rides ere he be r. (He that).

Reap, *see* Sow (As they), so let them r.

Reason binds the man.

1641 FERGUSSON 86.

Reason governs the wise man and cudgels the fool.

1707 MAPLETOFT 24. **1855** BOHN 479.

Reason in roasting of eggs, There is.

1659 HOWELL *Eng. Prov.* 12/2. **1773** BURKE in BOSWELL *Johnson* xxx *note* 'Your defini-tion is good', said Mr. Burke, 'and I now see the full force of the common proverb, "There is *reason* in roasting of eggs".' **1867** TROL-LOPE *Last Chron. Bar.* lxxv But there's reason in the roasting of eggs, and . . . money

is not so plentiful . . . that your uncle can afford to throw it into the Barchester gutters.

Reason, One | is as good as fifty.

1718 PRIOR *Alma* i. 513 Wks. (1858) 233 Examples I could cite you more; But be contented with these four: For, when one's proofs are aptly chosen, Four are as valid as four dozen.

Reason laboureth will.

1546 HEYWOOD I. v. 10 Reason laboureth wyll, to wyn wyls consent, To take lacke of beautie but as an eye sore.

Reason lies between the spur and the bridle.

1640 HERBERT 350.

Reason pist my goose, Such a.

1616 WITHALS 560 You speake like a Potte-cary, such a reason pist my goose. **1639** CLARKE 70.

Reason rules all things.

1616 DRAXE 175 Let reason rule all your actions. **1659** HOWELL *Eng. Prov.* 9/2.

Reasons of the poor weigh not, The.

1616 DRAXE 162 A poor mans tale cannot be heard. **1640** HERBERT 347.

Reason(s), *see also* Affection blinds r.; Be-cause is a woman's r.; Good r. and part cause; Hearken to r.; Man without r. a beast; Rhyme nor r. (Neither).

Rebound, *see* Heart is caught in r. (Many).

Recalled, *see* Past cannot be recalled (Things).

Receiver is as bad as the thief, The.

1650 SIR J. BIRKENHEAD *Two Centuries of Pauls Church-yard* 5 A Receiver is worse then a thief. **1662** FULLER (*Notts.*) II. 569 But, seeing the receiver is as bad as the thief, . . . the cheap pennyworths of plundered goods may in fine prove dear enough to their consciences. **1721** KELLY 15 *A receipter is worse than a thief.* If there were none to receive stol'n goods, thieves would be dis-couraged. **1830** MARRYAT *King's Own* xi The receiver is as bad as the thief. . . . If there were no demand there would be no supply.

Receiver, *see also* No r. no thief.

Reck not whose house burneth, They | so that they may warm them by the coals.

1481 CAXTON *Reynard* xxx (Arb.) 78 They retche not whos[e] hows brenneth · so that they may warme them by the coles.

Reckless youth makes rueful age.

c. **1520** DUNBAR *Wks.* (S.T.S.) II. 309 Mis-governit yowth makis gowsty[1] age. **1641** FERGUSSON 86 Rackless youth, makes a goustie[1] age. **1721** KELLY 284 . . . People who live too fast when they are young, will neither have a vigorous, nor a comfortable old age. [¹ dreary, wasted.]

Reckons without his host, He that | must reckon again (twice).

c. **1489** CAXTON *Blanchardyn* lii. 202 It ys sayd in comyn that 'who soeuer rekeneth wythoute his hoste, he rekeneth twys for ones'. **1533** MORE *Debell. Salem* Wks. 991/2 He fareth lo lyke a geste, that makyth hys rekening himselfe without hys hoste. **1579** LYLY *Euphues* (Arb.) 84 In that *Philautus* . . . shoulde accompt me his wife before he wo[o]e mee, certeinly he is lyke for mee to make his rec[k]oning twice, bicause he reckoneth without his Hostesse. **1670** RAY 136 . . . Chi fa conto senza l'hoste fa conto due volte, *Ital.* Qui compte sans son hoste, il lui convient compter deux fois, *Gall.* **1824** SCOTT *St. Ronans* xv But hostess as she was herself, . . . she reckoned without her host in the present instance. **1909** *Spectator* 3 July 9 Any man who counts upon such a desire as a political asset reckons without his host.

Reckon(s), *see also* Tell (R.) money after your father.

Reckoning(s), *see* Cast up accounts (r.); Even r. long friends; Fairer the hostess, fouler r.; Keep one head for r.; Merry is feast-making till r.; Misreckoning is no payment; Short r.; Small sum will pay short r.

Recks not who is rich, Wisest is he who.

[L. (in Ellesmere MS., margin) *Inter omnes altior existit, qui non curat in cuius manu sit mundus.*] *c.* **1386** CHAUCER *W. of Bath's Prol.* 326 The wyse astrologien Dan Ptholome, that seith this proverbe in his Almageste, 'Of alle men his wisdom is the hyeste, That rekketh never who hath the world in honde'.¹ [¹ i.e. who has abundant wealth.]

Recoil a little, We must | to the end we may leap the better.

1611 COTGRAVE s.v. 'Saulter' *Il recule pour mieux saulter.* He goes backe to take burre, or to leape the better. **1616** DRAXE 245. **1651** HERBERT 369. **1827** HARE *Gues. at Truth* (1859) i. 328 We must not overlook the numerous examples which history furnishes in proof that, according to the French proverb, *il faut reculer pour mieux sauter.*

Reconciled enemies (and of meat twice boiled), Take heed of.

c. **1386** CHAUCER *Mel.* B² 2371 And eek thou shalt eschewe the conseilling of thyne olde enemys that been reconsiled. **1613** R. DALLINGTON *Aphorisms* 181 There is no Sinceritie in reconciled enemies. **1621** BURTON *Anat. Mel.* II. iii. VII (1651) 360 Take heed of a reconciled enemy. **1670** RAY *Prov.* 22 Take heed of enemies reconcil'd, and of meat twice boil'd. **1733** FRANKLIN Sept. Beware of meat twice boiled and an old foe reconcil'd. **1777** JOHNSON 3 May in *Boswell* (1848) lvii.

530 Tell Mrs. Boswell I shall taste her marmalade cautiously at first. . . . Beware, says the Italian proverb, of a reconciled enemy.

Reconciled friend is a double enemy, A. (*Cf.* the preceding proverb.)

c. **1622** CHAPMAN ? *Alphonsus of Germany* Trust not a reconciled friend. **1732** FULLER no. 379.

Recumbentibus, To give one a.

[= a knock-down blow.] *c.* **1400** *Laud Troy Bk.* 7490 He ʒaff the Kyng Episcropus Suche a recumbentibus, He smot In-two both helme & mayle. **1546** HEYWOOD II. vii. 70 Had you some husbande, and snapt at him thus, I wys he would geue you a recumbentibus. **1599** *Nashe's Lenten Stuffe* in *Harl. Miscell.* VI. 153 Which leesing, had I bene let alone, I would have put to bed with a *recumbentibus.* *a.* **1687** COTTON *Poet. Wks.* (1765) 294 Which Recumbentibus he [Hercules] got By being of an Argonaut.

Red as a cherry, As.

c. **1425** *Disput. Mary & Cross* in *Leg. Rood* (1871) 217 Dropes rede as ripe cherrees. *c.* **1440** *Bone Flor.* 1763 Wyne redd as Cherye. *c.* **1520** SKELTON *Magnificence* l. 1558. *c.* **1550** *Robin Conscience* iii. 243.

Red as a fox, As.

c. **1386** CHAUCER *Prol.* 552 His berd, as any sowe or fox, was reed. **1837** LEVER *Harry Lorr.* vi Father Malachi's dark; but . . . the coadjutor's as red as a fox.

Red as a rose, As.

c. **1260** *King Horn* (Camb.) l. 16 (Hall) (A) Rose red was his colour. *c.* **1374** CHAUCER *Troylus* ii. 1256. 'Nay, nay!' quod she, and wex as red as rose. **1597–8** SHAKS. *2 Hen. IV* II. iv. 27 Your colour, . . . is as red as any rose. **1863** KINGSLEY *Water Bab.* ii A fine old English gentleman, with a face as red as a rose. **1798** COLERIDGE *Anc. Mariner* i. 34 Red as a rose is she.

Red as a turkey-cock, As.

1596 T. LODGE *Wit's Misery* (Hunt. Cl.) L 1 He lookes red in the gils like a Turkie cocke. *c.* **1630** BEAUM. & FL. *Faithful Friends* III. ii (A) Blush as red as a turkey-cock.

Red as blood, As.

c. **1205** LAYAMON 15940 þe oder [drake] is milc-whit . . . þe oðer is ræd alse blod. *c.* **1386** CHAUCER *Prol.* 635 To drynken strong wyn, reed as blood. **1886** STEVENSON *Kidnapped* vi The cardinal bird that is as red as blood.

Red beard and a black head, A | catch him with a good trick and take him dead.

1659 HOWELL *Eng. Prov.* 12/2. **1670** RAY 212. **1732** FULLER no. 1915 He is false by nature that has a black head and a red beard.

Red cap, You shall have the.

1678 RAY 352 . . . *Somerset.* (Said to a marriage-maker.)

Red clouds in the east, rain the next day.

1883 ROPER 14. **1893** INWARDS 88.

Red cock, The.

[= incendiarism. Probably taken from the German *roter Hahn* used already by H. SACHS in this sense.] **1815** SCOTT *Guy Man.* iii 'We'll see if the red cock craw not in his bonnie barnyard ae morning before day-dawing.' . . . 'What does she mean?' . . . 'Fire-raising', answered the laconic Dominie.

Red cow gives good milk, A.

1917 BRIDGE 5 . . . In old medical books, when milk was ordered to be given, it was frequently specified that it should be taken from a red cow. . . . 'A draught of red cow's milk'. Walton's *Compleat Angler.*

Red herring across the track, To draw a.

[= to attempt to divert attention from the real question.] **1890** W. F. BUTLER *Sir C. Napier* 60 Englishmen, so long diverted from their own affairs by the red herring of foreign politics so adroitly drawn across the trail, would [&c.]. **1928** *Times* 7 Apr. 8/1 These ladies . . . then calmly proceed to draw various red herrings of their own across the track.

Red herring ne'er spake word but een, broil my back, but not my weamb.[1]

1678 RAY 52. [1 belly.]

Red man, To a | read thy rede[1]; with a brown man break thy bread; at a pale man draw thy knife; from a black man keep thy wife.

c. **1470** *Harl. MS. 3362,* f. 17*a* To þe blak draw þy knyf; with þe brown led þy lyf. **1573** SANDFORD (1576) 213 Greete a redde man and a bearded woman three myles off. *c.* **1598** *MS. Proverbs* in FERGUSSON 104 Of the cullouris of men that is: To a Red man read thy Reade. With a Broune man break thy bread At a pale man draw thy knyf From a blak man keip thy wyfe The Red is wise, the Broun trusty The pale envyous, & the black lusty. **1615** R. TOFTE tr. of B. VARCHI *Blazon of Jealousie* 21 The sallow complectioned fellow, with a blacke beard, . . . [is] to be suspected about Womens matters, according to the old saying: *To a Red man reade thy Reade,*[1] With *a Browne man breake thy Bread, At a Pale man draw thy Knife, From a Blacke man keepe thy Wife.* Which wee expound after this manner: *The Red is wise, the Browne trusty, The Pale enuious, and the Blacke lusty.* **1659** HOWELL *Eng. Prov.* 16/2 At a pale man draw thy knife, from a black man keep thy wife. [1 declare thy counsel, plan.]

Red rag to a bull, Like a.

[OVID *Met.* 12. 103 *Sua irritamina* . . *poeniceas uestes.*] **1580** LYLY *Euph. & his*

Eng. (Arb.) 474 He that commeth before an Elephant will not weare bright colours, nor he that commeth to a Bull red. **1899** SIR A. WEST *Recollect.* II. xiv. 87 His appointment . . . was looked on as a job, and Mr. Gladstone, to whom a job was like a red rag to a bull, thought so. **1928** *Times* 27 June 15/1 Cyrillic type is like a red rag to a bull to the Croats in their present frame of mind.

Red sky, *see* Sky red in the morning.

Red the sun begins his race, If | expect that rain will flow apace. (*Cf.* Sky red in the morning.)

1846 DENHAM 11.

Red wood maks gude spindles.

1862 HISLOP 253 . . . 'Red wood', the name given to the reddish . . . and more incorruptible wood found in the heart of trees.— *Jamieson.*

Red, *see also* Evening r. and morning grey; Lass in the r. petticoat; Rowan tree and r. thread; Sun in r. should set (If).

Redd[1] for windlestraws, He that is | should not sleep in lees[2].

1641 D. FERGUSSON 40. **1721** KELLY 134 *He that's redd for windle straws, should not pish in lays.* Spoken to those who are afraid of small and far distant dangers. [1 afraid. 2 unploughed land.]

Redder's (Redding)[1] stroke, The.

1721 KELLY 159 He who meddles with quarrels, gets the ridding stroke. **1737** A. RAMSAY (1750) 45 He that meddles with toolies[2] comes in for the redding streak. **1816** SCOTT *Old Mort.* iv 'If they come to lounder ilk ither, . . . suldna I call on you?' 'At no hand, Jenny; the redder gets aye the warst lick in the fray.' **1888** MRS. OLIPHANT *Second Son* v After receiving this redding stroke, which is inevitably the recompense of the third party, Edmund drew back a little. **1900** LANG *Hist. Scot.* I. 325 The Earl of Crawford was mortally wounded—'got the redder's stroke'—in an attempt to stop the fighting. [1 The redder is one who attempts to settle a dispute. 2 quarrels.]

Rede, *see* Short r. good r.

Redemption from hell, There is no.

1377 LANGLAND *P. Pl.* B. xviii. 152 That thyng that ones was in helle · out cometh hit neuere. For Iob[1] the parfit patriarke · repreoueth thy sawes, *Quia in inferno nulla est redempcio.* **1622** J. TAYLOR (Water-P.) *Mer. Wher. Fer.* Wks. (1872) 23 From *Hell* each man says, *Lord deliver me,* Because from *Hell* can no redemption be. **1662** FULLER (*Westmr.*) II. 413 'There is no redemption from Hell'. There is a place . . . partly by the Exchequer Court, commonly called Hell. . . . Formerly this place was . . . for the king's debtors, who never were freed thence, until they had paid their uttermost due. . . . This proverb is applied to moneys paid into the Exchequer, which thence are irrecoverable. [1 VULGATE *Job* vii. 9 Sicut consumitur nubes, et pertransit; sic qui descenderit ad inferos, non ascendet.]

Reeds, Where there are | there is water.

c. 1700 *Dict. Cant. Crew* s.v. 'Smoke' No Reeds but there is some Water. 1732 FULLER no. 5674.

Reed(s), *see also* Broken r. (Lean upon); Oaks may fall when r. stand storm.

Reek comes aye doun again however high it flees.

1837 A. LEIGHTON in *Tales of Borders* III. 335 'Set a beggar on horseback an' he'll ride to the deevil'.... Anither o' the same kind— 'Reek comes aye doun again, however high it flees'—is just as pithy and pertinent to your case.

Reek, *see also* Kail through the r. (Give one his).

Refer my coat and lose a sleeve.

1721 KELLY 283 ... Arbitrators, for the better accommodation of business, make both parties abate of their pretensions.

References, *see* Always verify r.

Refrain, *see* Pleasure r. (Who will in time present).

Refuse a good offer, Never.

1670 RAY 136. 1824 SCOTT *Redg.* xxi 'You shall have a bellyful for love....' 'I shall never refuse a fair offer', said the poverty-stricken guest.

Refuse a wife with one fault, and take one with two.

1659 HOWELL *Brit. Prov.* 13.

Reins, *see* Lay the r. on the neck.

Reivers[1] should not be ruers.

1641 FERGUSSON 88. 1721 KELLY 284 ... They who are so fond of a thing as to snap greedily at it, should not repent that they have got it. [1 robbers.]

Religion a stalking-horse to shoot other fowl.

1604 WEBSTER &c. *Malcontent* IV. i A fellow that makes religion his stalking-horse. 1651 HERBERT 366. 1678 BUNYAN *Pilgr.* I. (1877) 115 *Chr.* If it be unlawful to follow Christ for loaves, ... how much more abominable is it to make of him and Religion a Stalking-horse, to get and enjoy the world.

Religion an ill man is of, It matters not what.

1732 FULLER no. 3038.

Religion but can boast of its martyrs, No.

1732 FULLER no. 3621.

Religion, credit, and the eye are not to be touched.

1616 DRAXE 61 Faith and the eye are tender. 1640 HERBERT 355.

Religion is the rule of life.

1616 BRETON *Cross. Prov.* Wks. (1879) II. App. iii.

Religion, *see also* Bible is r. of Protestants; Cities seldom change r. only; Jest not with ... r.; Man without r. like a horse.

Rely on the glory of the morning or on the smile of your mother-in-law, Never.

1922 J. W. R. SCOTT *Foundations of Japan* 121 We spoke of weather signs, and he quoted a proverb, 'Never rely on the glory of the morning or on the smile of your mother-in-law'.

Remedy, The best | against an ill man, is much ground between.

1640 HERBERT 324.

Remedy but patience, No.

[HOR. *Od.* 1. 24. 19 *Durum: sed levius fit patientia Quidquid corrigere est nefas.*] 1557 *Letter of Muscovy Company* (Hakluyt, Everyman i. 381). 1566 GASCOIGNE *Supposes* I. ii. 1578 R. W. *Three Ladies of London* C 3. 1592 SHAKS. *Two Gent.* II. ii. 2. 1624 BURTON *Anat. Mel.* III. iii. IV. i 3 R 3ᵛ & III. iii. iv. i 3 S 1. 1631 T. BREWER *Merry Devil of Edmonton* F 2 He saw there was no remedy but patience. 1616 DRAXE 151. 1670 RAY 190 1680 L'ESTRANGE *Citt & Bumpkin* 6 *Citt.* Well, there's no remedy but patience. 1692 Id. *Aesop's Fab.* cxciii (1738) 209 The silly ass stood preaching to himself upon the text of *No remedy but patience.*

Remedy for all things (everything) but death, There is a.

c. 1430 LYDGATE *Daunce Mac.* 1. 432 Aʒens deeth is worth no medicine. 1573 SANDFORD 99. 1620 SHELTON *Quix.* II. lxiv (1908) III. 275 'There is a remedy for everything but death', said Don Quixote. 1641 FERGUSSON 96 There is a remeid for all things but stark deid. 1896 F. LOCKER-LAMPSON *My Confid.* 95 There is a remedy for everything except Death..., so the bitterness of this disappointment has long passed away.

Remedy for everything, could men find it, There is a.

1576 *Paradise of Dainty Devices* (Lean) iv. 60 The ancient proverb saith that none so fester'd grief Doth grow, for which the gods themselves have not ordain'd relief. 1579 LYLY *Euphues*, Wks. (Bond) I. 208 O ye gods haue ye ordayned for euerye maladye a medicine, for euery sore a salue, for euery payne a plaister. 1624 BURTON *Anat. Mel.* II. iv. I. ii. 298. 1642 TORRIANO 4. 1651 HERBERT 370.

Remedy for injuries, is not to remember them, The.

1855 BOHN 514. *Ital.*

Remedy for love is—land between, The.

1855 BOHN 514. *Sp.*

Remedy is worse than the disease, The.

1582 MULCASTER *Elementary* (Campagnac) 107. 1597 7 Nov. *Calendar Hatfield MSS.* vii. 541–3. 1601 DANIEL 'To Sir Thomas Egerton' l. 20. 1607–12 BACON *Ess., Seditions* (Arb.) 414 Lett Princes . . . not be without some great person of Militarye valew . . . for the repressing of seditions. . . . But lett such one, be an assured one, . . . orels[1] the remedy is worse then the disease. 1896 FROUDE *Council of Trent* i. 5 Rebellion against an unjust and corrupt government may be a remedy worse than the disease. [1 or else.]

Remedy, If there be no | then welcome Pillvall.

1670 RAY 189.

Remedy, *see also* Every evil under sun (For) there is r.; Medicine (R.) for fear (No); Wrong without r. (No).

Remember the living, We ought to.

1539 TAVERNER 11 *Viuorum oportet meminisse.* We ought to remember the lyuynge. There may be many that loue to talke of dead men, yea and wyth dead mē as much as in them lyeth.

Remember thou art but a man.

1673 DAV. LLOYD *Dying & Dead Men's Words* 83 *Philip of Macedon* had one every morning to call upon him to remember that he was a man. 1732 FULLER no. 4014.

Remember to distrust.

[EPICHARMUS Νᾶφε καὶ μέμνασ' ἀπιστεῖν (in CIC. *ad Att.* 1. 19. 8). ERASM. *Ad. Sobrius sis ac memineris nemini confidere.*] 1664 J. WILSON *Andron. Com.* III. iii. Wks. (1874) 165 *Mam.* You forget our proverb—Remember to distrust! This easy faith Has done more mischief than it e'er did good.

Remember(s), *see also* Bitter to endure may be sweet to r.; Faithful friend hard to find (R. man); St. Vincent's Day (R. on); Youth is used to (What) age r.

Remembrance of past sorrow is joyful, The. (*Cf.* Bitter to endure, &c.)

1576 PETTIE *Petite Pall.* (Gollancz) I. 79 The

remembrance of the peril past delighteth. 1594–5 SHAKS. *Rom. & Jul.* III. v. 52 All these woes shall serve For sweet discourses in our time to come. 1639 CLARKE 206. 1827 POLLOK *Course of Time* i. 464 Sorrows remembered sweeten joy.

Remove an old tree and it will wither to death.

1523 A. BARCLAY *Mirr. of Good Manners* (Spenser Soc.) 67 An olde tree transposed shall finde small auantage. 1670 RAY 22. 1721 KELLY 284 . . . Spoken by a man who is loth to leave a place in his advanc'd years, in which he had long lived. 1831 W. M. PRAED *The Old Tory* I'm near threescore; you ought to know You can't transplant so old a tree.

Remove Mort-stone, He may.

1662 FULLER (*Devon*) I. 399 'He may remove Mort-stone'. There is a bay in this county called Mort-bay;[1] but the harbour in the entrance thereof is stopped with a huge rock, called Mort-stone; and the people merrily say that none can remove it, save such who are masters of their wives. [1 SW. of Ilfracombe.]

Remove stones, bruise their fingers, Who.

1640 HERBERT 318.

Remove Tottenham Wood, You shall as easily.

1631 W. BEDWELL *Brief Descript.* Tottenham iii *You shall as easily remoue Tottenham wood.* This is, of some spoken of things impossible, or not likely to be effected. For the Hill is not only very high, but also it's very great.

Remove(s), *see also* Three r. as bad as fire.

Render unto Caesar the things which are Caesar's.

[1611 BIBLE *Matthew* xxii. 21 Render therefore unto Cæsar the things which are Cæsar's; and unto God the things that are God's.] 1601 BP. BARLOW *Serm. Paules Crosse* 27 The things due from subjects to their Cæsar.

Rent of Dee mills, If thou hadst the | thou wouldst spend it.

1670 RAY 171 . . . *Chesh. Dee* is the name of the river on which the city *Chester* stands: the mills[1] thereon yield a very great annual rent. [1 Pulled down in 1910.]

Rent, *see also* Hold the greatest farms pay least r. (They that); O Master Vier, we cannot pay your r.; Providence is better than r.; Spend a whole year's r. at one meal.

Repairs not a part, He that | builds all.

1640 HERBERT 333.

Repairs not his gutter, Who | repairs his whole house.

1849 RUSKIN *Seven Lamps.* VI. xix (1880) 196

A few dead leaves and sticks swept in time out of a water-course, will save both roof and walls from ruin. **1855** BOHN 567 ... *Span.*

Repay, *see* Serve a noble disposition ... he will r.

Repeats, *see* Knows little (He that) often r. it.

Repent, *see* Never too late to r.

Repentance comes too late. *(But cf. Never too late to repent.)*

c. **1440** LYDGATE *Fall of Princes* III, l. 915 Harm doon, to late folweth repentaunce. **1575** GASCOIGNE *Posies; Flowers* (1907) I. 66 Bought witte is deare, and drest with sower salte, Repentaunce commes to late. **1670** RAY 22 When all is consumed, repentance comes too late.

Repentance, *see also* End of passion beginning of r.; Hearing (From) comes wisdom, from speaking r.; Late r. seldom true; Peace and patience and death with r.

Repented speech than silence, More have.

1640 HERBERT 349 More have repented speech than silence. **1872** BLACKMORE *Maid of Sker* xxxiv Seldom need any man repent for not having said more than he did; and never so needeth a Welshman.

Reply, *see* No r. is best.

Repps, *see* Gimmingham.

Reproach, *see* Sting of a r. is the truth.

Reputation is commonly measured by the acre.

1732 FULLER no. 4023.

Reserve the master-blow.

1642 TORRIANO 90. **1659** HOWELL *Ital.-Eng.* 13 Reserve thy master-piece. **1813** RAY 20 ... *i.e.* Teach not all thy skill, lest the scholar over-reach or insult the master.

Resolute, *see* Things that must be (In) ... be r.

Resolved mind hath no cares, The.

1640 HERBERT 339.

Respect a man, he will do the more.

1659 HOWELL *Brit. Prov.* 16.

Respect the burden.

[*a.* **1821** NAPOLEON I.] **1902–4** LEAN IV. 89 ... (A saying of Napoleon at St. Helena when, going up a narrow ascent, he met a heavily-burthened peasant, who was told to give place.—Emerson, *Representative Men.*) **1910** *Spectator* 26 Nov. 902 No one ... can look at the portraits hanging there without feeling how profound is Van Gogh's ... respect for the human burden.

Respects not is not respected, He that.

a. **1633** G. HERBERT *Priest to the Temple,* Wks. (Hutchinson) 268. **1640** HERBERT 337.

Respice finem, *see* Look to the end.

Rest, *see* A-bed (All are not) that shall have ill r.; Sufferance (Of) cometh r.

Restoring, *see* Giving is dead, r. sick.

Retained, *see* Hardly attained longer r. (Things).

Retinue, *see* Captain (Such) such r.

Retreat, In a | the lame are foremost.

1640 HERBERT 357.

Returns, *see* Goes far that never r.; Quick r. make rich merchants; Small profits quick r.

Revenge is a dish that should be eaten cold.

1885 C. LOWE *Bismarck* (1898) iii. 36 [Bismarck] had defended Olmütz, it is true, but ... with a secret resolution to 'eat the dish of his revenge cold instead of hot'. **1895** J. PAYN *In Mark. Ov.* xvii Invective can be used at any time; like vengeance, it is a dish that can be eaten cold.

Revenge is a morsel for God.

1629 T. ADAMS *Serm.* (1861–2) II. 325 When the Italians hear how God hath reserved vengeance to himself, they say blasphemously, 'He knew it was too sweet a bit for man, therefore, kept it for his own tooth'. **1853** TRENCH iii. 55 Italian history ... shows them no empty words, but truest utterances of the nation's heart.... One of them ... declares, *Revenge is a morsel for God.* [Vendetta, boccon di Dio.]

Revenge is sweet.

1566 PAINTER *Pal. of Pleasure* (Jacobs) ii. 35 (A) Vengeance is sweet. **1609** B. JONSON *Sil. Wom.* IV. V O reuenge, how sweet art thou! **1667** MILTON *Par. Lost* ix. 171 Revenge, at first, though sweet, Bitter ere long, back on itself recoils. **1775** SHERIDAN *St. Pat. Day* II. iv Revenge is sweet.... And though disappointed of my designs upon your daughter, ... I am revenged on her unnatural father. **1861** H. KINGSLEY *Ravenshoe* xxxvi Revenge is sweet—to some. Not to him.

Revenge of a hundred years hath still its sucking teeth.

[*It.* Vendetta di cent' anni ha ancor i lattaiuoli.] **1666** TORRIANO 299. **1853** TRENCH iii. 56 Another [Italian proverb] proclaims an immortality of hatred, ... *Revenge of a hundred years hath still its sucking teeth.*

Revenge(s), *see also* Living well best r.; Neglect will kill an injury sooner than r.; Pardons and pleasantness are great r. *See also* Vengeance.

Revenged all (every) wrong, Had I | I had not worn my skirts so long.

a. **1500** *R. Hill's Commonpl. Bk.* (E.E.T.S.) 140 (A) He that will venge euery wreth, tho longer he levith the lesse he hath. **1575** GASCOIGNE *Posies, Dulce Bel. Inex.* (1907) 147 But sit at home and learn this old-said saw, *Had I revenged been of every harm, My coat had never kept me half so warm.* **1670** RAY 136.

Reverend are ever before, The.

1640 HERBERT 358.

Reverentia, see Maxima debetur.

Revolutions are not made with rose-water.

1819 BYRON *Letters* (Prothero) iv. 358 (A). **1830** *Morn. Chron.* 4 Aug. But for the 1500 killed and wounded . . . this would almost have been what Mirabeau [in 1789] said was impossible: a revolution of rose-water. **1873** LYTTON *Parisians* v. vii Did I not imply . . . that we commence our journal with politics the mildest? Though revolutions are not made with rose-water, it is rose-water that nourishes their roots. **1894** LD. AVEBURY *Use of Life* xi It is sometimes said that Revolutions are not made with rose-water. Greater changes, however, have been made in the constitution of the world by argument than by arms.

Reward, see Desert and r. ever far odd; Wise who first gave r.

Rex, see Play r.

Rheum, see Wealth is like r.

Rhyme, It may | but it accordeth not.

c. **1387** T. USK *Test. of Love* in SKEAT *Chaucer* VII. 51 These thinges . . . mowe wel, if men liste, ryme; trewly, they acorde nothing. *c.* **1430** LYDGATE *Inconsistency* in *Minor Poems* (Percy Soc.) 55 It may wele ryme but it accordith nought. **1546** HEYWOOD I. xi. 36 To disdeygne me, who mucke of the worlde hoordth not, As he dooth, it may ryme but it accordth not.

Rhyme nor reason, Neither.

a. **1529** SKELTON in *Wks.* (Dyce) I. 123 For reson can I non fynde Nor good ryme in yower mater. **1592–3** SHAKS. *Com. Err.* II. ii. 49 Neither rime nor reason. **1599–1600** *A.Y.L.* III. ii. 418 Neither rime nor reason can express how much. **1600–1** *Merry W.* V. v. 135 In despite of the truth of all rime and reason. **1625** BACON *Apoph.* Wks. (Chandos) 381 'Now it is somewhat, for now it is rhyme: whereas before it was neither rhyme nor reason'. **1664** H. MORE *Myst. Iniq.* 415 Against all the Laws of Prophetick Interpretation, nay indeed against all rhyme and reason. **1678** RAY 349 Heer's nor rhythm, nor reason. **1888** 'R. BOLDREWOOD' *Robbery under Arms* II. xi. 181 This won't do. There's neither rhyme nor reason about it.

Rhyme rats to death, To.

[With reference to the alleged killing or expulsion of Irish rats by riming.] **1581** SIDNEY *Apol.* (Arb.) 72 I will not wish vnto you . . . to be rimed to death, as is sayd to be doone in Ireland. **1599–1600** SHAKS. *A.Y.L.* III. ii. 188 I was never so be-rimed since Pythagoras' time, that I was an Irish rat. **1660** (title) Rats Rhimed to Death, or, The Rump-Parliament Hang'd up in the Shambles. **1735** POPE *Donne Sat.* II. 22 Songs no longer move; No rat is rhym'd to death, nor maid to love.

Rhymed, see Well r., tutor, brains, and stairs.

Rib(s), see Stick by the r.

Ribchester was as rich as any town in Christendom, It is written upon a wall in Rome.

1586 CAMDEN *Britannia, Lancs.* (1722) I. 971 A village call'd at this day *Rible-chester*, where so many marks of Roman Antiquity . . . are commonly dug-up, that this hobbling rhyme of the Inhabitants does not seem to be altogether groundless: It is written upon a wall in Rome, Ribchester was as rich as any Town in Christendome.

Rice for good luck, and bauchles[1] for bonny bairns.

1896 CHEVIOT 285 . . . Refers to the custom of throwing rice and old shoes after a newly married couple. [[1] old shoes.]

Rich as a lord, As.

1837 DISRAELI *Venetia* I. v Your la'ship knows tis quite a saying, As rich as a lord.

Rich as a new-shorn sheep, As.

c. **1520** *Cock Lovells Bote* (Percy Soc.) 1 (A) The next that came was a coryar, And a cobeler, his brother, As ryche as a newe shorne shepe. **1546** HEYWOOD I. xi. 35 Till time ye be ryche as a new shorne shéepe. **1631** BRATHWAITE *Whimzies* (1859) 62 His speculation in time will make him as rich as a new-shorn sheep.

Rich as Croesus, As.

1577 KENDALL *Flow. of Epigrams* (Spens. Soc.) 57 (A) As riche as Cresus Affric is. **1849** THACKERAY *Pendennis* I. ch. 12 [*Miss Costigan*] If he had a good coat, you fancied he was as rich as Crazes. As Croesus, said Mr. Bowles.

Rich before night, He that will be | may be hanged before noon.

1607 H. ESTIENNE *World of Wonders,* tr. R.C. 39 This . . . prouerbiall saying, He that would quickly be rich, must turne his backe on God. *a.* **1679** J. DUPORT in interleaved copy of RAY (1670) at Trin. Coll., Cambridge. **1692** L'ESTRANGE *Aesop's Fab.* ccclxix (1738) 388 Slow and sure . . . is good counsel. 'Tis a roguey kind of a saying, that *He that will be rich before night, may be hanged before noon.*

Rich enough that wants nothing, He is.

c. **1387** T. USK *Test. of Love* in SKEAT *Chaucer* VII. 88 Is he nat riche that hath suffisaunce. **1640** HERBERT 336.

Rich enough who lacks not bread, He is.

[S. HIERON. *Epist.* cxxv *Satis diues, qui pane non indiget.*] **1377** LANGLAND *P. Pl.* B. vii 86 He hath ynough that hath bred ynough · though he haue nouȝt elles: *Satis diues est, qui non indiget pane.*

Rich folk have many (routh[1] of) friends.

c. **1386** CHAUCER *Mel.* B² 2748 Pamphilles seith also '. . . if thou be right riche, thou shalt find a greet nombre of felawes and freendes'. **1721** KELLY 283 . . . Many of whom are but flatterers. **1832** HENDERSON 54 Rich folk hae routh[1] o' friends. [¹ plenty.]

Rich knows not who is his friend, The.

1640 HERBERT 357.

Rich man steal? Why should a.

1678 RAY 196. **1732** FULLER no. 5736.

Rich man's money hangs him often-times, A.

1616 WITHALS 562. **1639** CLARKE 98.

Rich men are stewards for the poor.

1552 LATIMER *Serm. Lord's Prayer* v (Parker Soc.) 399 You rich men, when there cometh a poor man unto you, . . . remember that thy riches be not thy own, but thou art but a steward over them. **1616** BRETON *Cross. Prov.* Wks. (1879) II. App. iii. **1735** POPE *Moral Essays* iii. 173 Who sees pale Memnon pine amidst his store, Sees but a backward steward for the poor.

Rich men may have what they will.

1617 J. SWETNAM *School of Defence* 66 As the olde Prouerbe goeth, The rich men haue the Lawe in their owne hands. **1639** CLARKE 99 Rich men may doe any thing. **1869** HAZLITT 325.

Rich man (men), *see also* Akin to the r. m. (Every one); Gentlemen and r. m. are venison in heaven; Poor man's cow dies and r. m.'s child; Put the poor man's penny and the r. m.'s . . . ; Scrambling at a r. m.'s dole.

Rich rogue; A | two shirts and a rag.

1678 RAY 80. **1738** SWIFT (Dial. i) 338 Ay a rich rogue, two shirts and a rag.

Rich, *see also* Brother had rather see sister r.; Every one is weary, the r. in keeping; God help the r.; Handsome at twenty nor r. at forty will never be; Law for the r. (One); Make me a diviner, I will make thee r.;

Poor and liberal, r. and covetous; Pride of r. makes labour of poor; Quick returns make r. merchants; Recks not who is r. (Wisest who); Tithe and be r.

Richer the cobbler, The | the blacker his thumb, *see* Higher the plum-tree.

Riches are but the baggage of virtue (fortune).

1607–12 BACON *Ess., Riches* (Arb.) 230 I cannott call *Riches* better than the baggage of *Vertue* (the Romaine word is better, *Impedimenta*) For as the *Baggage* is to an Army, so is Riches to vertue. **1670** RAY 18 Riches are but the baggage of fortune. **1732** FULLER no. 4042 (as 1670).

Riches are like muck, which stink in a heap, but spread abroad make the earth fruitful.

1564 BULLEIN *Dial. agst. Fever* (1888) 9 *Mend.* Couetous vsurers . . . like vnto great stinkyng mucle medin hilles, whiche neuer doe pleasure vnto the Lande . . . vntill their heapes are caste abroade to the profite of many. **1599** JONSON *Ev. Man out of Humour* III. ii *Sord.* I have lived, Like an unsavoury muck-hill to myself, Yet now my gathered heaps being spread abroad, Shall turn to better and more fruitful uses. **1625** BACON *Apoph.* Wks. (Chandos) 369 Mr. Bettenham . . . used to say, that riches were like muck; when it lay in a heap it gave but a stench . . . ; but when it was spread upon the ground, then it was cause of much fruit. **1670** RAY 22.

Riches bringeth oft harm and ever fear, where poverty passeth without grudge of grief.

1546 HEYWOOD I. xii. 38.

Riches have wings.

1560 GENEVA BIBLE (1586) *Proverbs* xxiii. 5 For riches taketh her to her wings, as an eagle, & flieth into the heauen. **1607–12** BACON *Ess., Riches* (Arb.) 238 Riches have winges, and sometymes they fly away of themselves. **1855** BOHN 480.

Riches increase, When | the body decreaseth.

1670 RAY 22 . . . *For most men grow old before they grow rich.*

Riches of Egypt are for the foreigners therein, The.

1875 BURCKHARDT *Arab. Provs.* 83 . . . Since the time of the Pharaohs Egypt has never been governed by national rulers, but constantly by foreigners.

Riches serve a wise man but command a fool.

a. **1612** CHARRON *of Wisdom* tr. Lennard (1640) 84 Riches serves wise men, but command a foole. For a covetous man serves his riches, not they him. **1669** PENN *No Cross,*

No Crown xiii **Peter Charron,**[1] a famous Frenchman, wrote . . . 'Riches serve wise men, but command a fool; for a covetous man serveth his riches, and not they him.' **1732** FULLER no. 4047. [[1] *d.* 1603.]

Riches (*noun*), *see also* Honour is but ancient r.; Small r. hath most rest.

Riches (*verb*), *see* Carl r. he wretches (As the).

Riddle, *see* Sib as sieve and r.

Ride a free horse to death, One may.

1633 JONSON *T. Tub* III. iv (A) Spur a free horse, he'll run himself to death. **1750** W. ELLIS *Mod. Husbandm.* VII. 95 The roots will after this often cutting . . . wear out and die before their natural Time, according to the Proverb, *One may ride a free Horse to Death.*

Ride a hobby to death, To.

[= to overdo some pet subject.] **1881** A. JESSOPP *Arcady* 197 They got astride of this favourite hobby-horse of the doctrinaires, and . . . a hobby may be ridden to death.

Ride a horse and mare on the shoulders, an ass and mule on the buttocks.

1678 RAY 53.

Ride a young colt, When you | see your saddle be well girt.

1659 HOWELL *Eng. Prov.* 13/2.

Ride an inch behind the tail, You shall.

1678 RAY 266.

Ride as if you went to fetch the midwife, You.

1678 RAY 266.

Ride backwards up Holborn Hill, He will.

1785 GROSE *Classical Dict.* s.v. 'London' (A). **1787** Id. *Prov. Glos.* (*London*) 197 He will ride backwards up Holborn-hill. He will come to be hanged. Criminals . . . were, till about the year 1784, executed at Tyburn, the way to which from Newgate, was up Holborn-hill. They were generally conveyed in carts . . . with their backs towards the horses.

Ride fair, and jaup[1] none.

1721 KELLY 283 . . . Taken from riding through a puddle: but apply'd to too home jesting. [[1] to bespatter with mud.]

Ride so near the rump, You | you'll let none get on behind you.

1721 KELLY 365 . . . You go sharply to work, that you will let none get any advantage by you.

Ride softly, that we may come sooner home.

1678 RAY 204. **1732** FULLER no. 4050.

Ride the fore-horse, To.

1664 ETHEREGE *Comical Revenge* III. v (A) *Palmer* [*coming late to duel ground*] I see you ride the fore-horse, gentlemen. **1738** SWIFT (Dial. i) 340 *Never.* Well, miss, you ride the fore-horse to-day.

Ride (*or* Mount) the high horse, To.

[= to put on airs.] **1721** KELLY 173 He is upon his high Horse. **1805** F. AMES *Wks.* I. 339 I expect reverses and disasters, and that Great Britain, now on the high horse, will dismount again. **1824** MISS FERRIER *Inheritance* III. xii Fred seems to be on his high horse to-day, . . . I told you he would give himself airs. **1855** TROLLOPE *Warden* vii Though Eleanor Harding rode off from John Bold on a high horse, it must not be supposed that her heart was so elate as her demeanour.

Ride the water with, He is not a man to.

1857 DEAN RAMSAY *Remin.* v. (1911) 202 *He's not a man to ride the water wi'.* A common Scottish saying to express you cannot trust such an one in trying times. May have arisen . . . where fords abounded, and the crossing them was dangerous.

Ride to Romford[1] on it, You might.

1738 SWIFT (Dial. ii) 348 *Smart.* [*Carving a partridge.*] Well, one may ride to Rumford upon this knife, it is so blunt. **1901** *N. & Q.*, 9th Ser. VIII. 306 'You might ride to Romford on it'. When a youngster I often heard my old grandmother make this remark *à propos* any blunt carving or other knife which failed to come up to expectations. [[1] Romford, in Essex, famous for breeches-making.]

Ride who will, the mare is shod.

1541 *Sch. house of Women* 571–3 in HAZL. *Pop. Poet. Eng.* (1866) IV. 127 Our fly is fetled vnto the saddle; Ride who wil, shod is the Mare, And thus they exchaunge ware for ware.

Ride with the beard on the shoulder, To.

1823 SCOTT *Peveril* vii They rode, as the Spanish proverb expresses it, 'with the beard on the shoulder', looking around, . . . and using every precaution to have the speediest knowledge of any pursuit.

Rides a tiger, He who | is afraid to dismount.

1902 A. R. COLQUHOUN *Mastery of Pacific* 410 These colonies are a constant and ever-increasing drain on France. They are for her the tiger which she has mounted (to use the Chinese phrase), and which she can neither manage nor get rid of.

Rides behind another, He who | does not travel when he pleases.

1855 BOHN 401.

Rides ere he be ready, He that | wants some of his gear.

1641 FERGUSSON 48. **1721** KELLY 154 . . . Apply'd to him who goes about a business without proper tools to accomplish it.

Rides not ay when he saddles his horse, He.

1721 KELLY 175 . . . Spoken of them who make great pretences to haste, but yet linger long enough.

Rides sure that never fell, He.

1641 FERGUSSON 38 He rides sicker that fell never. **1721** KELLY 133 . . . A man has gone through the world with a strange even hand, that never committed a blunder. **1732** FULLER no. 2011 He rode sure indeed, that never caught a fall in his life.

Ride(s), rode, *see also* Better r. on an ass that carries me; Mickle to do when cadgers r.; Never r. never fell; Nothing but up and r.; Two men r. on a horse (If).

Rider, *see* Ill for the r. good for abider.

Ridge, *see* Love his house (*or* the Kirk), yet not ride on r.

Ridiculous, *see* Sublime to the r.

Riding, *see* Good r. at two anchors; Half an hour's hanging hinders r.; Safe r. in good haven.

Rig, *see* Run a r.

Right as a ram's horn, As.

c. **1320** *Reliq. Antiquae* (1843) ii. 19 (A) As ryt as rams orn. *a.* **1529** SKELTON *Col. Cloute* 1200 They say many matters be borne By the right of a ram's horn. **1659** HOWELL *Eng. Prov.* 11/2.

Right as a trivet, As.

1835 HOOD *Dead Robbery* x I'm right' thought Bunce, 'as any trivet'. **1837** DICKENS *Pickwick* l 'I hope you are well, Sir.' 'Right as a trivet, Sir,' replied Bob Sawyer.

Right as my leg, As.

c. **1630** *Roxb. Ballads* (B.S.) iii. 338 (A) That are as right's my leg. **1638** 12 Feb. *Stationer's Register* (Arb.) iv. 455 *The New Married Couple or as right as my leg.* **1639** CHAPMAN & SHIRLEY *The Ball* iv Wks. (1889) 506 Good! right as my leg again. **1663** J. WILSON *Cheats* II. iv *T.T.* All's well, and as right as my leg. *Bil.* And that's crooked to my knowledge.

Right as rain, As.

[PLAUTUS *Capt.* 2. 2. 86 *Tam hoc tibi in proclivi quam imber est quando pluit.*] **1894** W. RAYMOND *Love & Quiet Life* 108 (A) '"Tes so right as rain, Zir,' sez I.

Right at Rome, No.

1639 CLARKE 172.

Right, He that hath | fears; he that hath wrong, hopes.

1640 HERBERT 337.

Right hand from his left, He knows not his.

1619 J. FAVOUR *Antiquity triumphing over Novelty* 376 A child of Nineueh, that scarce knew his right hand from his left. **1681** ROBERTSON *Phraseol. Generalis* 1079.

Right, master, right; four nobles a year's a crown a quarter.

1670 RAY 217 . . . *Chesh.* **1917** BRIDGE 105 . . . It seems to be a sarcastic answer to one who is very positive in asserting an inaccuracy.

Right mixture makes good mortar.

1721 KELLY 284. **1732** *Fuller* no. 4052.

Right side.

1664 CODRINGTON 201 I will not take from my left side to give to my right. **1670** RAY 195 To take from ones right side, to give to ones left.

Right wrongs no man.

1832 HENDERSON 86.

Right, *see also* Bribe nor lose thy r. (Neither); Do r. nor suffer wrong (He will neither); Extremity of r. is wrong; Take from the r. hand.

Rigorous, *see* Virtuous that is not r. (He cannot be).

Riners, *see* Shed r. with a whaver (To).

Ring of a rush.

[i.e. of no value.] *c.* **1449** PECOCK *Repr.* II. v. 166 It is weel allowid . . . that he make a ring of a rische and putte it on his fynger. **1546** HEYWOOD I. iii. 7 I hoppyng without for a ryng of a rushe. **1602–3** SHAKS. *All's Well* II. ii As fit . . . as Tib's rush for Tom's forefinger. **1641** FERGUSSON 22 Better na ring nor the ring of a rashe. **1732** FULLER no. 918 Better no Ring, than a Ring of a Rush. **1813** ELLIS *Brand's Pop. Antiq.* II. 38 A custom . . . appears antiently to have prevailed, . . . of marrying with a Rush Ring; chiefly practised, however, by designing men.

Ring of Gyges.

[An ancestor of Gyges, a Lydian, found a gold ring, which, worn on the finger, rendered him invisible (PLATO *Rep.* 2. 359). ERASM. *Ad. Gygis anulus.*] **1586?** LYLY *Triumphs of Trophes* Wks. (Clar. Press) III. 430 To walke vnseene with *Giges* ring faine they would. **1606** CHAPMAN *M. d'Olive* II. ii. 86 Thought myself as private as if I had had King Giris [sic] ring and could have gone invisible. **1662** FULLER (*Heref.*) II. 70 Civil war . . . will trace all corners, except they be surrounded with Gyges' ring. **1710** STEELE *Tatler*, No. 138 (1896) 71 Gyges . . . had an enchanted ring, . . . making him who wore it visible or invisible, as he turned it to or from his body.... Tully ... says ..., 'that a man of honour who had such a ring would act just in the same manner as he would without it'.

Ring of Polycrates.

[HDT. 3. 41, 42. PLINY *H.N.* 33. 6.] **1908** A. C. BENSON *At Large* xii. 225 Polycrates of Samos ... was the tyrant with whom everything went well ..., so that to avoid the punishment of undue prosperity he threw his great signet-ring into the sea; but when he was served a day or two later with a slice of fish at his banquet, there was the ring.

Ring, *see also* Lost the r. (If I have), fingers still here.

Rip not up old sores.

1573 G. HARVEY *Letterbk.* (Camd. Soc.) 18 Besides sutch ripping up of ould matters ... as I suppose there have sildum been seen the like. *c.* **1592** NASH *Summer's Last Will* l. 410. **1639** CLARKE 303. **1679** J. GOODMAN *Penit. Pard.* III. vi (1713) 393 He will not rake in men's wounds, nor rip up old sores. **1830** GALT *Lawrie T.* IV. ix It's little my part to rip up old sores.

Ripon, *see* True steel as R. rowels.

Rise betimes that will cozen the devil, He must.

1659 HOWELL *Eng. Prov.* 19/1.

Rise betimes that would please everybody, He had need.

1639 CLARKE 34 They must rise betimes that please all. **1670** RAY 132. **1732** FULLER no. 1854.

Rise early that used to rise late, In vain they.

1611 DAVIES *Prov.* 216. Wks. **1616** DRAXE 37.

Rise early, Though you | yet the day comes at his time, and not till then.

1640 HERBERT 333.

Rise on the right (*or* wrong) side, To.

[A happy, or unhappy, augury.] **1540** PALS-GRAVE *Acolastus* (Carver) 90. **1546** HEYWOOD II. iv. 51 You rose on your right syde here right. **1633** JONSON *T. Tub.* IV. iii We are like men that wander in strange woods, and lose ourselves in search of them we seek. *Hilts.* This was because we rose on the wrong side. **1824** SCOTT *Redg.* xx Why, brother Nixon, thou art angry this morning ... hast risen from thy wrong side, I think. **1894** BLACKMORE *Perlycross* xxxii I have heard of people getting out of bed the wrong side; and you can't make it right all day.

Rises not early, He that | never does a good day's work. (*Cf.* Riseth late, &c.)

1616 DRAXE 144 ('in the morning loseth his journey'). **1846** DENHAM 5.

Rises over early, He | that is hanged ere noon.

1641 FERGUSSON 40.

Riseth betimes, He that | hath something in his head.

1640 HERBERT 328.

Riseth first, He that | is first dressed.

1640 HERBERT 326.

Riseth late, He that | must trot all day. (*Cf.* Rises not early, &c.)

1659 HOWELL *Span.-Eng.* 17. **1758** FRANKLIN Pref. *He that riseth late, must trot all Day, and shall scarce overtake his Business at night.*

Rise(s, th), *see also* Bed with the lamb (Go to), rise with lark; Get a name to r. early; Thrive (He that will) must r. at five.

Rising sun, *see* Worship the r. s.

Rising was a seaport town, and Lynn it was a wash, but now Lynn is a seaport town, and Rising fares the worst.[1]

1851 N. & Q. 1st Ser. III. 206. [[1] Norfolk. See **1902-4** LEAN I. 150 Castle Rising is described in ... 1672, as utterly decayed and its havens filled with sand.]

Rising was, Lynn is, and Downham shall be, the greatest seaport of the three.

1851 N. & Q. 1st Ser. III. 206.

Riven breeks, *see* Sits full still that has r. b.

Riven dish, *see* Lost that is put into r. d.; Simpers like a r. d.

River of Dart! O river of Dart! every year thou claimest a heart.[1]

1850 N. & Q. 1st Ser. II. 511 ... It is said that a year never passes without the drowning of one person, at least, in the Dart. The river ... is liable to sudden risings, when the water comes down with great strength and violence. **1912** *Spectator* 3 Aug. 163 Perhaps it is ... the huge stones ... which sets a certain cruelty about the Dartmoor landscape; perhaps ... it is the name of the river, and the legend of its toll, 'every year a heart', to rhyme with its name. [[1] Devon.]

Rivers need a spring.

1640 HERBERT 345.

Rivers run into the sea, All.

a. **1595** *Edward III* V. i. 92 All riuers haue recourse vnto the Sea. **1608** J. HALL, *Epistles* I. v. 37 Euen little streames empty themselues into great riuers; and they againe into the Sea. **1616** DRAXE 180 All riuers runne into the sea. **1732** FULLER no. 541 All rivers do what they can for the sea.

River, *see also* Danger (R.) past, God forgotten; Follow the r. get to the sea; Great man and great r. ill neighbours; Great r. great fish (In a); Mountain and r. good neighbours.

River-banks, *see* Man on the raft who thought r. moving.

Rives the kirk to theek[1] the quire, He.

1641 FERGUSSON 48. 1721 KELLY 276 Peel the kirk, and thick the quire. 1857 DEAN RAMSAY *Remin.* v (1911) 202 *He rives the kirk to theik the quire.* Spoken of unprofitable persons who, in the English proverb, 'rob Peter to pay Paul'. [1 thatch.]

Rivington Pike do wear a hood, If | be sure that day will ne'er be good.

1670 RAY (*Lancs.*) 236 ... A mist on the top of that hill is a sign of foul weather.

Roads lead to Rome, All.

c. 1391 CHAUCER *Astrolabe* Prol. 45 Right as diverse pathes leden diverse folk the righte way to Rome. 1872 BLACK *Strange Adv. Ph.* vi You know all roads lead to Rome, and they say that Oxford is halfway to Rome. 1893 BP. MOULE *Comment. Rom.* 3 As 'all roads led to Rome', so all roads led from Rome.

Road(s), *see also* Keeps his r. who gets rid of bad company; Royal r. to learning (No).

Roar like a bull, To.

1545 ASCHAM *Toxoph.* (Arb.) 42 Roring lyke a bull, as some lawyers do. 1840 MARRYAT *Poor Jack* xiii There was one of our men hanging on the main-stay, and roaring like a bull.

Roast a stone, To.

1522 SKELTON *Why not to Court?* 109 Pescoddes they may shyll, Or elles go rost a stone. 1546 HEYWOOD II. ii. 46 Her carrain carkas (saide he) is so colde, ... I do but roste a stone. In warmyng hir.

Roast meat, To give one (a dog) | and beat him with the spit.

[To follow hospitality with harshness.] 1553 T. WILSON *Arte of Rhet.* (1909) 72 Such are not to be lyked that geue a man a shoulder of mutton, and breake his head with the spitte when they haue doen. 1636 CAMDEN 296 Give a dog roast and beat him with the spit. 1674 WOOD *Life* (O.H.S.) II. 296 He gave me roast meat and beat me with the spit. *a.* 1700 B. E. *Dict. Cant. Crew* s.v. *To give one Roast-meat, and Beat him with the Spit,* to do one a Curtesy, and Twit or Upbraid him with it. 1876 ROBINSON *Whitby Gloss.* 182/1 'Never invite a friend to a roast and then beat him with the spit', do not confer a favor and then make the obligation felt.

Roast meat does[1] cattle.

1877 E. LEIGH *Chesh. Gloss.* 63 (A) ... which means that in dry seasons cattle, if they can only get plenty of water, often milk better than in cold wet seasons, when there is more grass. 1917 BRIDGE 105 ... In a very dry season, grass which is half burnt is more fattening than grass in a rainy season. [1 fattens.]

Roast meat, You are in your | when others are in their sod.

1616 WITHALS 575. 1639 CLARKE 115. 1670 RAY 176. 1732 FULLER no. 5849.

Roast meat, *see also* Cry r. m.

Rob an orchard when none keeps it, It is easy to.

1670 RAY 23.

Rob, He that doth not | makes not a robe or garment.

1573 SANDFORD (1576) 209. 1629 *Book of Meery Riddles* Prov. 83.

Rob Peter to (give to, clothe) pay Paul, To.

c. 1380 WYCLIF *Sel. Wks.* III. 174 Lord, hou schulde God approve þat þou robbe Petur, and gif þis robbere to Poule in þe name of Crist? *c.* 1440 *Jacob's Well* 305 þei robbyn seynt petyr & ȝeuyn it seynt Poule. 1514 BARCLAY *Egloges* i Fewe Princes geue that which to them selfe attayne ... They robbe saint Peter therewith To cloth S. Powle. 1546 HEYWOOD I. xi. 26 Lyke a pyckpurs pilgrim, ye prie and ye proule At rouers, to rob Peter and paie Poule. 1581 PETTIE *Guazzo's Civ. Conv.* III (1586) 168 *b* That in my iudgement is a shameful thing ... to uncloath Peter to cloath Paule. 1640 HERBERT 352 Give not St. Peter so much, to leave St. Paul nothing. 1655 FULLER *Ch. Hist.* XI. vi (1868) III. 550 Much he[1] expended on the repair of Westminster Abbey church; and his answer is generally known, when pressed by Bishop Laud to a larger contribution to St. Paul's, that he would not rob Peter to pay Paul. 1737 *Gent. Mag.* VII. 172/1 This Scheme is ... calculated ... to Rob Peter to pay Paul, or, to remove ye Burthen from one Part of the Community, and lay it upon another. 1926 *Times* 7 Jan. 9/6 Martin and Martin had been in low water for a long time and had recourse to the method of robbing Peter to pay Paul. [1 Dean Williams.]

Rob(s), *see also* Table r. more than a thief.

Robbing the barn.

1869 HAZLITT 325 ... The good wife sometimes does this to pay for extra finery.

Robe, *see* Bode a r. and wear it; Rob (He that doth not) makes not r.

Rob'em, *see* Starv'em.

Robert, Sir, *see* Robin that herds ... can be as blithe as S. R.

Robin (Sparrow), The | and the wren are God's cock and hen : the martin and the swallow are God's mate and marrow.

a. **1508** SKELTON *Phil. Sparrow* 598–601 Wks. (1843) I. 69 That Phyllyp may ... treade the prety wren, That is our Ladyes hen. **1826** R. WILBRAHAM *Chesh. Glos.* 105 The following ... is common in Cheshire: The Robin and the Wren Are God's cock and hen, The Martin and the Swallow are God's mate and marrow. **1908** *Times Wkly.* 7 Feb. iii The rhyme ... which asserts that the robin and the wren 'are God's cock and hen' expresses a belief ... that the robin and the wren are actually the male and female of one species.

Robin Goodfellow.

[= a sportive elf or goblin.] **1531** TINDALE *Wks.* (P.S. 1849) 139 The Scripture ... is become a maze unto them, in which they wander as in a mist, or (as we say) led by Robin Goodfellow, that they cannot come to the right way. **1595–6** SHAKS. *Mids. N.* II. i. 34 That shrewd and knavish sprite Call'd Robin Goodfellow.

Robin Goodfellow has been with you to-night.

1567 *Caueat for Commen Cursetors* (E.E.T.S.) iii. 36 I verely suppose that when they wer wel waked with cold, they suerly thought that Robin goodfellow (accordige to the old saying) had bene with them that night.

Robin Goodfellow was a strange man.

1639 CLARKE 69.

Robin Hood bargains.

1709 *Brit. Apollo* No. 58 3/1 When ... a Purchase you reap, that is wondrous Cheap, They Robin-Hood Bargains are call'd.

Robin Hood could bear (stand) any wind (anything) but a thaw wind.

c. **1855** *Life & Ballads of Robin Hood* ii (A) Every Yorkshireman is familiar with the observation that Robin Hood could brave all weathers but a thaw wind. **1917** BRIDGE 105 Robin Hood could stand anything but a thaw wind. A *thaw* or *tho'* wind is a cold piercing wind from the S. or SE. which often accompanies the breaking up of a long frost.

Robin Hood robbed the rich and gave to the poor.

1930 *Times* 24 Oct. 10/1 On what economic or ethical principle is it right for Robin Hood, whether Robin Hood is an individual or a nation, to rob rich men and give the proceeds (or part of them) to the poor? Can any one imagine that that is honest?

Robin Hood's mile.

[= one of several times the recognized length.] **1559** W. CUNNINGHAM *Cosmogr. Glasse* 57 These are Robin Hode's miles, as the prouerbe is.

Robin Hood's pennyworth.

[= a thing or quantity sold at a robber's price, i.e. far below the real value.] **1565** *Col. S. P. Dom. Eliz.* i. 262 at St. John's Cambridge 'Making Robin Hoodes pennyworthes of their copes and vestments'. **1582** G. WHETSTONE *Heptameron of Civil Discourses* T2 The cunning Lawier, that buyeth Robin hoodes penneworthes, & yet with some nice forfaitures, threatneth the seller, with continuall bondage. **1600** W. HAUGHTON *Robin Hood's Pen'orths* (play title, Henslowe's *Diary*, ed. Greg, ii. 215). **1629** T. ADAMS *Serm.* (1861–2) I. 201 The devil ... makes the world believe that he sells Robin Hood's pennyworths; that he hath ... a prodigal hand, and gives all *gratis.* **1677** W. HUGHES *Man of Sin* II. viii. 122 In Germany, there is a Robin-Hood's pennyworth to be had, ... 8000 years of Pardon both from punishment and fault.

Robin Hood, *see also* Good even, good R. H.; Speak of R. H. (Many) that never shot; Tales of R. H. are good among fools.

Robin sings in the bush, If the | then the weather will be coarse ; but if the robin sings on the barn, then the weather will be warm.

1830 FORBY 416.

Robin that herds on the height can be as blithe as Sir Robert the knight.

1862 HISLOP 253.

Robs a scholar, He that | robs twenty men.

1616 WITHALS 553. **1639** CLARKE 243. **1670** RAY 23 ... *For commonly he borrows a cloak of one, a sword of another, a pair of boots of a third, a hat of a fourth, &c.*

Robs, *see also* Rob(s).

Rock,[1] Thus rid the.

[= so was the distaff managed.] **1546** HEYWOOD II. ix. 76 What ye wan in the hundred ye lost in the shéere. In all your good husbandry, thus ryd the rocke. [[1] distaff.]

Rock (= distaff), *see also* Tow on one's r. (To have).

Rock Lizards.

1842 BORROW *Bible in Spain* (1843) III. xiv. 269 He was ... what is called a rock lizard, that is, a person born at Gibraltar of English parents.

Rock Scorpions.

1867 ADM. SMYTH *Sailor's Word-bk. Rock Scorpion*, a name applied to persons born at Gibraltar. **1891** A. FORBES *Barracks, Biv. & Bat.* (1910) 105 The Smytches, Rock Scorpions, Cypriotes, ... and other miscellaneous scum of the Levant who were serving as mule-drivers.

Rocket, *see* Go up like r.

Rod breaks no bones, The.

1616 DRAXE 182. **1639** CLARKE 75.

Rod for his own back (breech, tail), He makes a.

c. **1374** CHAUCER *Troylus* I. 740 For it is seyd, man maketh ofte a yerde With which the maker is himself y-beten. **1533** FRITH *Disp. Purg.* (1829) 110 Then hath he made a rod for his own breech. **1546** HEYWOOD I. ii. 5 Whan haste proueth a rod made for his owne tayle. **1650** BAXTER *Saints' Everl. Rest* III. ix And so make a rod for their own backs.

Rods in pickle (*or* piss), To have.

[= to have punishment in store.] **1553** *Respublica* III. v. 820 Some would in no wyse to owre desyres applye. But we have Roddes in pysse for them. **1648** J. DILLINGHAM in *Ld. Montagu of Beaulieu's P.* (Hist. MSS. Comm.) 163 No doubt there are many rods in pickle against many great ones. **1714** MANDEVILLE *Fab. Bees* (1733) I. 331 I see a thousand rods in piss, and the whole posse of diminutive pedants against me. **1911** W. F. BUTLER *Autobiog* xxi The visit of Sir Alfred Milner . . . was . . . for . . . the preparation and pickling of rods for the Republic.

Rod(s), *see also* Give a slave a r.; Kiss the r.; Spare the r. spoil child; Whip for fool and r. for school.

Roger, *see* Sow is good mutton (Your).

Rogue like to the godly rogue, No.

1732 FULLER no. 3624.

Rogue, *see also* Rich r., two shirts and a rag.

Roint, *see* Rynt.

Roland for an Oliver, To give a.

[= tit for tat. Roland and Oliver were two of the paladins of Charlemagne, both famous for their exploits.] **1548** HALL *Chronicle* (1809) 266 (A) To haue a Rowland for an Olyuer. **1549** CHALONER tr. *Erasm. Praise of Folly* M 3 Set one enchaunter against an other, or an Oliver for a Rolande. **1577** HOLINSHED *Chron.* (1808) III. 205 Bicause he knew the French King would not take the matter well, to haue a Roland for an Oliuer; he sente solemne ambassadours to the King of England, offering him his daughter in mariage. **1670** RAY 191 . . . That is, *quid pro quo,* to be even with one. **1692** L'ESTRANGE *Aesop's Fab.* xxxi (1738) 38 'Tis allowable in all the liberties of conversation to give a man a Rowland for his Oliver, and to pay him in his own coin. **1816** SCOTT *Antiq.* xxxv He gave my termagant kinsman a *quid pro quo*—a Rowland for his Oliver, as the vulgar say.

Rolling eye, a roving heart, A.

1629 T. ADAMS *Serm.* (1861–2) II. 219 The eye is the pulse of the soul: as physicians judge of the heart by the pulse, so we by the eye; a rolling eye, a roving heart.

Rolling stone gathers no moss, A.

[ERASM. *Ad. Λίθος κυλινδόμενος τὸ φῦκος οὐ ποιεῖ.* Musco lapis volutus haud obducitur.] **1362** LANGLAND *P. Pl. A.* x. 101 Selden Moseþ þe Marbelston þat men ofte treden. *c.* **1460** in *Q. Eliz. Acad.* (1869) 39 Syldon mossyth the stone þat oftyn ys tornnyd & wende. **1546** HEYWOOD I. xi. 26. **1618** BRETON *Courtier & Countryman* Wks. (Gros.) II. 8/2 I haue heard that roling stones gather no mosse. **1709** A. PHILIPS *Pastoral* 2 A rolling stone is ever bare of moss. **1720** T. BOSTON *Fourfold State* (1797) 305 A rolling stone gathers no fog. **1886** E. J. HARDY *How to be Happy* xiv Servants are now rolling stones that gather no moss. **1917** BRIDGE 5 A rolling stone gathers no moss, but a tethered sheep winna get fat. Cheshiremen are rather fond of putting a tag to an ordinary proverb. In Surrey and Sussex we have the addition:— 'And a sitting hen never grows fat'.

Rome brick, I found | I leave it marble.

[L. *Urbem lateritiam invenit, marmoream reliquit.*[1]] **1783** JOHNSON *Life of Dryden* What was said of Rome, adorned by Augustus, may be applied by an easy metaphor to English poetry embellished by Dryden, *lateritiam invenit, marmoream reliquit.* He found it brick and left it marble. **1828** (Feb.) BROUGHAM *Speech in Ho. of Commons on Law Reform* It was the boast of Augustus . . . that he found Rome of brick, and left it of marble . . . Much nobler will be the sovereign's boast . . . that he found law dear, and left it cheap. [[1] Adapted from SUETONIUS *Aug.* 28.]

Rome, When you are at | do as Rome does.

[s. AMBROSE *Quando hic sum, non ieiuno Sabbato; quando Romae sum, ieiuno Sabbato* (s. AUGUSTINE, *Ep.* 36, ch. 14). JER. TAYLOR, *Si fueris Romæ, Romano vivito more; Si fueris alibi, vivito sicut ibi.* If you are at Rome, live after the Roman fashion; if you are elsewhere, live as they do there.] *a.* **1530** R. Hill's *Commonpl. Bk.* (E.E.T.S.) 130 When thou art at Rome, do after the dome; And whan þou art els wher, do as they do ther. **1586** PETTIE *Guazzo's Civ. Conv.* 26 He had so readie a wit to frame himselfe to the diuersitie of the life and manners of other Countries, and according to the saying, When one is at Rome, to liue as they doe at Rome. **1669** PENN *No Cross, No Crown* ix Her fashions, as those of France now, were as laws to the world, at least at Rome: whence it is proverbial, *Cum fueris Romæ, Romano vivito more.* 'When thou art at Rome, thou must do as Rome does. **1849** C. BRONTË *Shirley* v Don't put on the sabots again. I told you . . . they were not quite the thing for this country . . . do at Rome as the Romans do.

Rome was not built in a (one) day.

[*c.* **1190** *Li Proverbe au Vilain* (Tobler) 43 Rome ne fut pas faite toute en un jour, ce dit li vilains.] **1545** TAVERNER D 1ᵛ. **1546** HEYWOOD I. xi. 30 Rome was not built in one daie (quoth he) and yet stood. Till it was

finisht. **1622** BEAUM. & FL. *Prophetess* I. iii
Delph. You must have patience, *Rome was not
built in one day.* **1641** FERGUSSON 88 Rome
was not biggit on the first day. **1660** TATHAM
Rump. I. i (1879) 214 Why, gentlemen,
Rome was not built in a day. **1748** SMOLLETT
Rod. Rand. li Mounting by gradual steps to
the summit of your fortune. Rome was not
built in a day. **1901** S. LANE-POOLE *Sir H.
Parkes* xvii. 316 The Japanese ... went too
fast and fell into grave commercial, monetary, and administrative troubles. Neither
Rome nor New Japan could be built in a day.

Rome, *see also* All things are to be bought at
R.; Better be first in a village than second
at R.; Drive a snail to R.; Fiddle while R.
burning; Home rule R. rule; Indulgences
to R.; Protestant R.; Ribchester; Right
at R. (No); Roads lead to R. (All); Sit in
R. and strive against Pope (Hard to);
Traveller to R. must have. ...

Romford, *see* Ride to R. on it.

Room is better than his company, His.

1579 *Marr. of Wit & Wisdom* (Sh. S.) iii. 27
(A) I had rather haue your roome as your
companie. **1591** GREENE *Farewell to Forty* in
Wks. (Gros.) IX. 329 I had a liefe haue their
roome as their companie. **1633** D. DYKE
School of Afflict. 216 Many, ... are rather
like the Gadarenes, loving the ministers'
room better than their company. **1662** FUL-
LER (*Lancs.*) II. 211 Worthington perceiving
his room more welcome than his company,
embraced the next opportunity of departure.
1822 SCOTT *Nigel* xxvi The waterman declared he would rather have her room than
her company.

Room to swing a cat, Not.

a. **1679** J. DUPORT, MS. note in Trin. Coll.
Camb. copy of RAY 1670 A good large conscience—you may swing a cat in it. **1771**
SMOLLETT *Humph. Clink.* II 8 June, At
London, I am pent up in frouzy lodgings,
where there is not room to swing a cat. **1927**
Times 11 Feb. 10/3 The working rooms ...
are crowded with store cases, and not a man
... has room to swing a cat.

Roost, *see* Highest branch not safest r.

Root (*noun*), *see* No r. no fruit.

Root(s) (*verb*), *see* Tree r. more fast which has
stood blast.

Rope and butter; if one slip t'other will hold, A.

1652 *A New Model* (single sheet) A rope and
butter. **1678** RAY 267. **1732** FULLER no. 384.

Rope enough and he'll hang himself, Give a thief (him).

1639 FULLER *Holy War* v. vii (A) They were
suffered to have rope enough, till they had
haltered themselves in a *præmunire.* **1670**
RAY 148 Give a thief rope enough and he'll
hang himself. **1732** FULLER no. 1657 Give
him but rope enough, and he'll hang himself.

Rope enough, I thought I had given her | said Pedley, when he hanged his mare.

1670 RAY 191. **1732** FULLER no. 2627.

Rope for a thief, As meet as a. (*Cf.* Worth it as a thief worth a rope.)

1540 PALSGRAVE *Acolastus* (Carver) 88 As
mete for him as a rope is for a thefe. **1546**
HEYWOOD I. x. 20.

Rope in after the bucket, Throw the.

1599 MINSHEU (1623) 2 S 6ᵛ To cast the rope
after the caldron. **1631** MABBE *Celestina*
(T.T.) 24 The rope will go after the Bucket:
and one losse follow another. **1732** FULLER
no. 5042.

Rope (Halter), Name not a | in his house that hanged himself (was hanged).

1599 MINSHEU (1623) 2 T 5ᵛ. **1620** SHELTON
Quix. III. xi (1908) I. 220 Why do I name an
ass with my mouth, seeing one should not
mention a rope in one's house that was
hanged? **1640** HERBERT 348 Mention not a
halter in the house of him that was hanged.
1670 RAY *Prov.* 138 Name not a rope in his
house that hang'd himself. **1890** J. PAYN
Burnt Mil. xxxii Miss Grace, whom he
pictured ... as sensitive upon the matter, as
though if her parent had been hung she
would have been to an allusion to a rope.

Ropes of sand, To make (*or* twist).

[ERASM. *Ad. Ex arena funiculum nectis.* You
are for making a rope of sand.] **1576** E.
PATRIZI *Civil Policy* tr. R. Robinson 60ᵛ The
prouerbe: Of Sand an infinite quantitie take,
And yet vnpossible it is a coarde to make.
1594 LIPSIUS *6 Books of Politics* tr. Jones X 2
There are manye other things, which I can
not easilie tye together with this corde of
sand. *c.* **1594** BACON *Promus* (Pott) 275 To
knytt a rope of sand. **1608** CHAPMAN *Byron's
Trag.* v. iv. 55 These are but ropes of sand.
1621 BURTON *Anat. Mel.* I. ii. IV. vii (1651)
167 Make a rope of sand; to what end? **1631**
JONSON *Devil is an Ass* I. i. *Sat.* Get you e'en
back, sir, To making of your rope of sand
again. **1662** BUTLER *Hudibras* I. i. 51 For he
a rope of sand could twist As tough as learned
Sorbonist. **1800** J. ADAMS Wks. (1854) IX. 87
Sweden and Denmark, Russia and Prussia,
might form a rope of sand, but no dependence
can be placed on such a maritime coalition.
1909 ALEX. MACLAREN *Ephesians* 305 Men
... are doing what ... evil spirits were condemned to do—spinning ropes out of sea-
sand.

Rope(s), *see also* Bitten by a serpent afraid
of a r.; High r. (To be on the). *See also*
Rape.

Rose, The fairest | at last is withered.

1591 FLORIO *Sec. Frutes* 105 The fairest and
the sweetest Rose, In time must fade and
beauty lose. **1623** CAMDEN 279 The fairest
rose in three dayes is withered. **1670** RAY 138.

Rose without a thorn, No.

1430–40 LYDGATE *Bochas* Prol. ix There is no rose . . . in garden, but there be sum thorne. **1579** LYLY *Euphues* (Arb.) 33 The sweetest Rose hath his prickell. **1591–2** SHAKS. *1 Hen. VI* II. iv. 69 Hath not thy rose a thorn, Plantagenet? **1603** FLORIO tr. *Montaigne* III. iii (1897) V. 68 But no good without pains; no roses without prickles. **1609** SHAKS. *Sonn.* 35. 2 Roses have thorns and silver fountains mud. **1647** HERRICK *Noble Numb.*; *The Rose* (O.U.P.) 386 But ne're the Rose without the Thorn. **1670** RAY 138. **1855** BOHN 129 For the rose the thorn is often plucked. **1866** C. READE *Griffith G.* xli There was a thorn in the rose of their wedded life: he was of the Church of England; she . . . a Roman Catholic.

Rose(s), *see also* Fresh as **a r.**; Lie upon **r.** when young; Red as **a r.**; Stung by a nettle than a **r.** (Better be); Took her for **a r.**; Truths and **r.** have thorns; Under the **r.**

Rose-water, *see* Revolutions.

Roseberry Topping wears a cap, When | let Cleveland then beware a clap.

1621 P. HOLLAND tr. CAMDEN *Brit.* 721 (A). **1659** E. LEIGH *Eng. Described* 232 Yorkshire; North Riding—*Ounsbery-Hill*, or *Roseberry-Topping*, . . . maketh a goodly shew. . . . So often as the Head therof hath his cloudy Cap on, lightly there followeth rain: whence they have a proverbial Rhime, *When Roseberry-Topping wears a Cop, Let Cliveland then beware a clap.*

Rosse (Russe) of Potterne, *see* Live as long as old R. of P.

Rot, *see* Michaelmas **r.**

Rotheras, *see* Dwell at R. (Every one cannot).

Rotten apple, Not worth a.

c. **1370** CHAUCER *Romaunt of the Rose* B 4531 Ne worth an appel. *c.* **1489** CAXTON *Sons of Aymon* (E.E.T.S.) 544 (A) The sones of a traytour whiche ben not worthe a roten apple.

Rotten apple injures its neighbours, The.

[L. *Pomum compunctum cito corrumpit sibi iunctum.*] **1340** *Ayenbite* 205 A roted eppel amang þe holen, makeþ rotie þe y-зounde. *c.* **1386** CHAUCER *Cook's T.* 4406 Wel bet is roten appel out of hord Than that it rotie al the remenaunt. **1736** FRANKLIN July The rotten apple spoils his companion. **1855** BOHN 514.

Rotten apples, *see* Choice in **r. a.** (Small).

Rotten case (cane) abides no handling, A.

1597–8 SHAKS. *2 Hen. IV* IV. i. 161 'We shall admit no parley'. . . . 'That argues but the shame of your offence: A rotten case abides no handling'. **1855** BOHN 299 A rotten cane abides no handling.

Rough and ready.

1855 BROWNING *Bp. Bloug. Apol.* You, . . . The rough and ready man, who write apace, Read somewhat seldomer, think perhaps even less. **1880** S. BARING-GOULD *Mehalah* I. v Glory was the girl for him, rough and ready, who could row a boat, and wade in the mud.

Rough as it runs, as the boy said when his ass kicked him.

1687 T. BROWN in *Dk. Buckingham's Wks.* (1705) II. 129 If you don't like me rough, as I run, fare you well, Madam. **1763** J. BOSWELL *Let. Ld. Hailes* 16 Jul. Take me just as I am, good, or bad, or indifferent; or (as Sir Francis Dashwood said of the Cyder Bill) *rough as I run.* **1813** RAY 231.

Rough diamond, A.

[= a person of intrinsic worth but rough manners.] **1624** FLETCHER *Wife for Month* IV. ii She is very honest, And will be hard to cut as a rough diamond. **1700** Dryden *Pref. Fables* (Globe) 503 Chaucer, I confess, is a rough diamond. **1908** *Spectator* 21 Nov. 807 Benbow . . . was a rough diamond— . . . and a gallant tar.

Rough net is not the best catcher of birds, The.

1550 HEYWOOD I. ix. 18 It hurteth not the tounge to geue fayre wurdis. The rough net is not the best catcher of burdis. **1614** CAMDEN 313.

Rough oats, To take.

c. **1580** J. CONYBEARE 14 Rather I hadde to take rough otes (as they saye) of a bad debter then nothynge at all.

Rough with the smooth, Take the.

c. **1400** *Beryn* (E.E.T.S.) 37 Take yeur part as it comyth, of roughe and eke of smooth. **1882** BLACKMORE *Christowell* xvi To take the rough and smooth together, is a test of magnanimity; but Howell took the rough without the smooth.

Rouk-town's seldom a good housewife at home, A.

1670 RAY 52 . . . A Yorkshire proverb. A rouk-town is a gossiping housewife.

Round of beef, *see* Tomtit on **r. of b.** (Like a).

Round peg in a square hole (*or vice versa*), A.

1804–6 SYDNEY SMITH *Lecture* ix We shall generally find that the triangular person has got into the square hole, the oblong into the triangular, and a square person has squeezed himself into a round hole. **1836** FONBLANQUE *Eng. under Seven Administr.* (1837) III. 342 Sir Robert Peel was a smooth round peg in a sharp-cornered square hole, and Lord Lyndhurst is a rectangular square-cut peg, in a smooth round hole. **1901** *Westm. Gaz.* 24 Dec. 2/2 Was there ever a more glaring case of square peg in round hole and round peg in square?

Round table, At a | there's no dispute of place.

1623 WODROEPHE 483 A round table yealds no debate. **1670** RAY 138.

Round the moon there is a brugh,[1] When | the weather will be cold and rough.

1631 BRATHWAIT *Whimzies* (1859) 104 (A) A burre[1] about the moone is not halfe so certain a presage of tempest as . . . **1846** DENHAM 17. [[1] halo.]

Roundabouts, *see* Swings (To lose on).

Roundheads, *see* Wellington R.

Routing[1] like a hog.

c. **1386** CHAUCER *Reeve's T.* A. 4163 This millere hath so wisely bibbed ale That as an hors he snorteth in his sleep, . . . Men myghte hir rowtyng heere two furlong. **1546** HEYWOOD I. x. 24 But where was your vncle . . .? A sléepe by (quoth she) routyng lyke a hog. [[1] snoring.]

Row the boat, Norman, row.

[**1453**] **1598** STOW *Survey of Lond.* (1633) 567 Sir Iohn Norman . . . was the first Maior that was rowed by water to *Westminster*, to take his Oath. . . . The Watermen made a Song in his prayse beginning, *Row thy Boate, Norman*, &c. *a.* **1529** SKELTON *Bowge* 252 Wks. (1843) I. 40 Heue and how rombelow,[1] row the bote, Norman, rowe! [[1] a cry of rowers.]

Row to hoe, To have a hard (long).

1835 D. CROCKETT *Tour Down East* 69 I never opposed Andrew Jackson for the sake of popularity. I knew it was a hard row to hoe. **1848** LOWELL *Biglow P.* Ser. 1. Wks. (1884) 213 You've a darned long row to hoe.

Row(s) (*verb*), *see also* All men r. galley way; Carried down the stream need not r.; Looks one way r. another.

Rowan tree and red thread make the witches tine[1] their speed.

1846–59 *Denham Tracts* (F.L.S.) ii. 329 (A) (with 'haud the witches a' in dread'). **1896** CHEVIOT 287 . . . It was at one time common in Scotland to attach a cross of this wood to the byre-door with a red thread, as a security to the cattle against witches. [[1] lose.]

Rowan(s), *see also* Many rains many r.

Royal road to learning, There is no.

[PROCLUS *Comm. in Eucl.* 68 (Teubner) μὴ εἶναι βασιλικὴν ἀτραπὸν ἐπὶ γεωμετρίαν, quoting Euclid to Ptolemy I.] **1857** TROLLOPE *Barch. Tow.* xx There is no royal road to learning; no short cut to the acquirement of

any valuable art. **1894** LD. AVEBURY *Use of Life* vii In the earlier stages of Education . . . neither rank nor wealth gives any substantial advantage. . . . It was long ago remarked that there was no royal road to learning.

Royalist, *see* More r. than the king.

Royet[1] lads (may) make sober men.

1832 HENDERSON 64. [[1] wild.]

Royston horse and a Cambridge master of arts will give way to nobody, A.

1662 FULLER (*Cambs.*) I. 226 A Boisten[1] horse and a Cambridge Master of Art, are a couple of creatures that will give way to nobody.' This proverb we find in the letter of William Zoon written to George Bruin, in his 'Theatre of Cities'. [[1] misprint for Royston, Cambs.]

Rub, There is (Here lies) the.

[= inconvenience, difficulty; comes from the game of bowls.] **1600–1** SHAKS. *Hamlet* III. i. 65 To sleep! perchance to dream! ay, there's the rub; For in that sleep of death what dreams may come. **1629** T. ADAMS *Serm.* (1861–2) I. 216 The proverbs are . . . joined . . . with a *but* . . . All runs smooth, and inclines to the bias of our own affections, till it lights upon this rub. **1712** STEELE *Spect.* No. 533, par. 1 But her Relations are not Intimates with mine. Ah! there's the rub. **1821** SCOTT *Pirate* xxxiv Here lies the rub . . . When she hears of you she will be at you. **1830** LYTTON *Paul Clif.* xx Expense! . . . Ay! there's the rub!

Rub a cat on the rump, The more you | the higher she sets up her tail.

1678 RAY 109. **1853** TRENCH iv. 78 No need . . . of adulation or flattery to quicken [fools] to a ranker growth; for *The more you stroke the cat's tail, the more he raises his back.*

Rub a galled (scabbed) horse on the back (gall) and he will wince.

a. **1384** WYCLIF *Wks.* (Arnold) III. 231 (A) As a horse unrubbed, that haves a sore back, wynses when he is oght touched or rubbed on his rugge. *c.* **1386** CHAUCER *W. of Bath's T.* D 939 For trewely, there is noon of us alle, If any wight wol clawe us on the galle, That we nil kike. **1523** SKELTON *Gar. Laur.* 97 Yet wrote he none ill Sauynge he rubbid sum vpon the gall. **1541** *Schole-Ho. Women* 1013 in HAZL. *E.P.P.* IV. 145 Rub a scald horse vpon the gall, And he wil bite, wins and went, So wil all people that are maleuolent. **1570** EDWARDS *Damon & Pithias* (Dodsley) 28 I know the galled horse will soonest wince. **1600–1** SHAKS. *Hamlet* III. ii. 232 Let the gall'd jade wince, our withers are unwrung. **1640** HERBERT 369 A scabbed horse cannot abide the comb. **1659** HOWELL *Eng. Prov.* 6/2. **1670** RAY 95. **1738** SWIFT (Dial. i) 336 *Lady S.* Touch a gall'd horse, and he'll wince. **1869** HAZLITT 372.

Rub and a good (great) cast.

[Comes from the game of bowls.] **1608** DEKKER *Bellman of London* F 3ᵛ Rub & a Great one. **1614** T. FREEMAN *Rubbe, and a great Cast* (Title). **1678** RAY 81 . . . Be not too hasty, and you'll speed the better.

Rub (*or* Scratch) the elbow, To.

[= to show oneself pleased.] **1594** NASHE *Unfort. Trav.* Wks. (McKerrow) III. 219 Had you seene him how he . . . scratcht his scabd elbowes at this speach. **1594–5** SHAKS. *L.L.L.* V. vii. 109 One rubb'd his elbow thus, and fleer'd, and swore A better speech was never spoke before. **1597–8** *1 Hen. IV* V. i. 77 Fickle changelings and poor discontents, Which gape and rub the elbow at the news Of hurlyburly innovation. **1598** E. GILPIN *Skial.* (1878) 25 He'le . . . scratch the elbow too To see two butchers curres fight.

Rubicon, To cross (*or* pass) the.

[= to take a decisive step, especially at the outset; Caesar's crossing of this stream, in N. Italy, marked the beginning of war with Pompey.] **1626** J. MEAD in BIRCH *Crt. & Times Chas. I* (1848) I. 180 Queen Dido did never more importune Æneas's stay at Carthage, than his mother and sister do his continuance here at London. . . . But now he is past the Rubicon. **1643** J. OWEN *Death of Death* Wks. (1852) X. 150 The die being cast and Rubicon crossed. **1827** SCOTT *Napoleon* iv. 21 [Bonaparte] would, . . . like Cæsar, have crossed the Rubicon at the head of the popular party.

Rudder, *see* Ruled by the r. (Who will not be); Tongue is the r. of our ship.

Rue and thyme grow both in one garden.

1721 KELLY 283 . . . A persuasion to repent and give over an attempt before it be too late, alluding to the sound of the two herbs here nam'd. **1824** S. FERRIER *Inheritance* III. vi I wish it may last; but 'rue and thyme grow baith in ae garden'.

Rue in thyme should be a maiden's posie.

1721 KELLY 284. [A play upon the word *thyme* (time).]

Rue (*noun*), *see also* Take the r.

Rue(th) (*verb*), *see* Better r. sit than r. flit; Rape rueth (Oft).

Ruff, *see* Old woman in wooden r.

Ruffian's-hall, He is only fit for.

1592 NASHE Wks. (McKerrow) I. 187 Make Ruffians hall of Hell. **1631** STOW *Annals* 1023 West Smithfield for many years called Ruffians Hall. **1662** FULLER (*Lond.*) II. 347 'He is only fit for a Ruffian's hall'. A ruffian is the same with a swaggerer. . . . West Smithfield . . . was formerly called Ruffian's-hall, where such men met casually and otherwise. . . . The proverb [is] only appliable to quarrelsome people . . . who delight in brawls and blows.

Rugged stone grows smooth from hand to hand, A.

1640 HERBERT 332.

Ruin of one ravine.[1]

1546 HEYWOOD II. ix. 77 And sure sens we were borne, Ruine of one rauine, was there none gretter. [[1] act of rapine.]

Ruin(s), *see also* Abundance like want r.; France's r. is eve of r. of England; *Quos Deus vult perdere* (Whom God would r.).

Ruined by buying good pennyworths, Many have been.

1732 FULLER no. 3349. **1758** FRANKLIN *Way to Wealth* (Crowell) 20 The bargain, by straitening thee in thy business, may do thee more harm than good. . . . Many have been ruined by buying good pennyworths.

Rule a shrew save he that hath her, Every man can.

1546 HEYWOOD II. vi. 61. **1621** BURTON *Anat. Mel.* II. ii. vi. i (1651) 291 Every man, as the saying is, can tame a shrew, but he that hath her. **1721** KELLY 92 *Every man can guide an ill wife, but he that has her.* Often . . . applied in a literal sense; but in a general when one apprehends that he could order such a station, post, or business, better than he that has it.

Rule of thumb.

[= a roughly practical **method** without scientific basis.] **1692** SIR W. HOPE *Fencing-Master* 157 What he doth, he doth by rule of Thumb, and not by art. **1721** KELLY 257 *No rule so good as rule of thumb, if it hit.* But it seldom hits! Spoken when a thing falls out to be right, which we did at a venture. **1865** M. ARNOLD *Ess. Crit.* v. 159 The English . . . have in all their changes proceeded, . . . by the rule of thumb. **1909** *Times Wkly.* 1 June 363 His scientific method he shares with his countrymen, who have long discarded the rule of thumb which we are just discovering to be inadequate in modern conditions.

Rule the roast, To.

[= to have full sway; to be master.] **14 . .** *Carpenter's Tools* 176 in HAZLITT *E.P.P.* I. 85 What so uer ȝe brage ore boste, My mayster ȝet shall reule the roste. **1526** SKELTON *Magnyf.* 805 *Cra. Con.* In fayth, I rule moche of the rost. *Clo. Col.* Rule the roste! thou woldest, ye. **1577–87** HOLINSHED *Chron.* II. 23/1 These were Irish potentates, and before their discomfiture they ruled the rost. **1590–1** SHAKS. *2 Hen. VI* I. i. 110 Suffolk, the new-made duke that rules the roast. **1778** FOOTE *Trip Calais* II The ladies always rule the roast in this part of the world.

Rule with a rod of iron, To.

1526 TINDALE *Rev.* ii. 27 And he shall rule them with a rodde of yron: and as the vessels

of a potter, shall he breake them to shevers.
1871 C. KINGSLEY *At Last* iii Trinidad became
English; and Picton ruled it, for a while with
a rod of iron.

Rule without some exception, There is no general.

1579 NORTH *Plutarch's Alexander & Caesar*
(Temple Classics) vii. 220 All rules have their
exceptions. **1608** T. HEYWOOD *Lucreece* I. ii
(Merm.) 335 A general concourse of wise
men!... Tarquin, if the general rule have no
exceptions, thou wilt have an empty con-
sistory. **1621** BURTON *Anat. Mel.* I. ii. II. iii
(1651) 76 No rule is so general, which admits
not some exception. **1738** SWIFT (Dial. i) 342
Lady A. But I hope you won't blame the
whole sex because some are bad ... *Col.* O
madam; there's no general rule without an
exception.

Rule youth well, and (for) age will rule itself.

1641 FERGUSSON 88 Rule youth weill, and
eild[1] will rule the sell. **1721** KELLY 283 ...
Youth is rash and headstrong, but age sober
and steadfast. [[1] age.]

Rule, *see also* Tent thee (I will) ... if I can't
r. my daughter, I'll r. my good.

Ruled by his own dame, He that will not be | shall be ruled by his step-dame.

1509 A. BARCLAY *Ship of Fools* (1874) I. 203
But who that of his moders doctryne hath
disdayne: Shall by his stepdame endure wo
care and payne. *a.* **1530** *R. Hill's Commonpl.
Bk.* (E.E.T.S.) 128 He that will not be
warned bi his owne fader, he shall be warned
bi his stepfader. **1546** HEYWOOD II. ix. 76.
1641 FERGUSSON 38 He that will not hear
mother head, shall hear stepmotherhead.
1721 KELLY 158 *He that will not hear mother
hood, shall hear step-mother hood.* That is,
they who will not be prevailed upon by fair
means, shall meet with harsher treatment.

Ruled by the rudder, Who will not be | must be ruled by the rock.

1666 TORRIANO 286 That ship which will
have no rudder, must have a rock. **1823**
DISRAELI *Cur. of Lit.* (1824) 2nd Ser. i. 454
(A) [Cited as 'a Cornish proverb']. **1853**
TRENCH iii 64 Obstinate wrongheads, who
will take no warning except from calamities
... : *Who will not be ruled by the rudder, must be
ruled by the rock.* **1911** B. WILBERFORCE *Secret
of Quiet Mind* 79 The spiritual blindness of the
people made the ... destruction of Jerusalem,
and its attendant horrors inevitable. 'He who
will not be ruled by the rudder must be ruled
by the rock', but ruled he must be.

Ruler, *see* Fellow-ruler; Good r. (No man
can be) unless.

Rump, *see* Eaten the hen's r.; Ride so near
the r. (You) let none get on behind.

Run a (*or* the) rig, To.

[= to play pranks.] **1782** COWPER *Gilpin* xxv

He little dreamt, when he set out, Of running
such a rig! **1797** B. HAMILTON in BEDDOES
Contrib. Phys. & Med. Knowl. (1799) 315 To
run the rig with the boys in the street in place
of going on my errand.

Run after two hares, If you | you will catch neither.

[ERASM. *Ad. Duos insequens lepores neutrum
capit.*] **1509** A. BARCLAY *Ship of Fools* (1874)
I. 153 A fole is he whiche with one hande
tendyth to take two hares in one instant.
1573 SANDFORD (1576) 207. **1580** LYLY *Euph.
& his Eng.* (Arb.) 394 Yet one thing maketh
[mee] to feare, that in running after two
Hares, I catch neither. **1658–9** BURTON
Diary 9 Mar. (1828) IV. 108 Keep to your
debate. You have two hares a-foot. You
will lose both. **1732** FULLER no. 2782.

Run amuck, To.

[= a headlong course of attack.] **1672**
MARVELL *Reh. Transp.* I. 59 Like a raging
Indian ... he runs a mucke (as they cal it
there) stabbing every man he meets. **1735**
POPE *Hor. Sat.* II. i. 70 I'm too discreet To
run a muck, and tilt at all I meet. **1880**
W. R. SMITH in *Manch. Guard.* 29 Oct. In their
alarm they were determined to run amuck of
everything.

Run as you drink, If you could | you might catch a hare.

1640 HERBERT 335.

Run (*or* Go) before one's horse to market, To.

[= to count one's chickens before they are
hatched.] **1592–3** SHAKS. *Rich. III* I. i. 160
But yet I run before my horse to market:
Clarence still breathes, Edward still lives and
reigns, When they are gone, then must I
count my gains. **1709** R. KINGSTON *Apop.
Curiosa* 79 Resolution without Deliberation
... is like running before ones Mare to the
Market.

Run like a deer, To.

1594–5 SHAKS. *L.L.L.* V. ii. 310 Whip to
your tents, as roes run over land. **1620**
SHELTON *Quix.* II. xix (1908) II. 313 He is
the activest youth we have, ... he runs like
a deer. **1859** H. KINGSLEY *Geof. Hamlyn* xl
The black lad ... running like a deer, sped
... across the plain.

Run one's head against a stone wall, To.

1589 ? LYLY *Pappe w. Hatchet* in Wks. (1902)
III. 410 But if like a restie Iade thou wilt
take the bitt in thy mouth, ... thou shalt ...
haue thy head runne against a stone wall.

Run over, *see* Coaches wont r. o. him.

Run tap, run tapster.

1678 RAY 86 ... This is said of a tapster that
drinks so much himself, and is so free of his
drink to others that he is fain to run away.

Run that cannot go, He may ill.

1546 HEYWOOD II. ix. 77 Men saie he maie yll renne, that can not go. *c.* **1610** BEAUM. & FL. *Kt. Burn. P.* II. v. 41 Though I can scarcely go, I needs must run. **1636** CAMDEN 308 They hardly can run, that cannot go. **1721** KELLY 130 . . . In vain he attempts an uneasy task, who is not equal to an easy one.

Run the gantlope (*or* gauntlet), To.

[Orig. a military punishment in which the culprit ran, stripped to the waist, between two rows of men, who struck at him with sticks or knotted cords.] **1649** T. FORD *Lus. Fort.* *2 Being now exposed to run the Gantelope of the Worlds censure. **1709** POPE *Let. to Wycherley* 17 May Hitherto your miscellanies have safely run the gauntlet, through all the coffee-houses. **1836** *Edin. Rev.* lxiv. 71 No doubt he ran the usual gantelope of jokes. **1839** LD. BROUGHAM *Statesm. Geo. III, Eldon* (ed. 2) 254 The case had run the gauntlet of the courts.

Run to work in haste, You | as [if] nine men held you.

1546 HEYWOOD I. xi. 35.

Run (Hold) with the hare and hunt (*or* run) with the hounds, To.

c. **1440** *Jacob's Well* (E.E.T.S.) 263 þou hast a crokyd tunge heldyng wyth hownd and wyth hare. **1546** HEYWOOD I. x. 19 There is no mo such titifyls in Englands ground, To holde with the hare, and run with the hound. **1579** LYLY *Euphues* (Arb.) 107 Whatsoeuer I speake to men, the same also I speake to women, I meane not to run with the Hare and holde with the Hounde. **1690** *Turn-Coat of Times* in *Roxb. Ball.* (1883) IV. 515 I can hold with the Hare, and run with the Hound: Which no body can deny. **1896** M. A. S. HUME *Courtships of Q. Eliz.* 261 Leicester, as usual, tried to run with the hare and hunt with the hounds, to retain French bribes and yet to stand in the way of French objects. **1943** HOWELL SMITH *In search of real Bible* This very dogmatic scholar [Sayce] was wont to run. . . .

Run (*noun*), *see* Long lane (r.) no turning; Long r. (In the).

Run(s) (*verb*), *see also* Hae lad and r. lad; Need makes naked man r.; Rough as it r.

Runaway monk never praises his convent, A.

1666 TORRIANO 156 A vagrant Monk ne'r spoke well of his Convent. **1855** BOHN 299.

Runner, You look like a | quoth the devil to the crab (lobster).

1721 KELLY 389 *You look like a runner, quoth the Dee'l to the lobster.* Spoken to those who are very unlikely to do what they pretend to. **1802** WOLCOT (P. Pindar) *Middl. Elect.* i. *Wks.* (1816) IV. 174 *He* conquer *us,* the scab! *He,* that ne'er renn'd a race before; 'Yes, you're a *racer,* to be sure,' Cried the Devil to the crab.

Runneth far that never turneth again, He. (*Cf.* Goes far, &c.)

1546 HEYWOOD II. ix. 74. **1579** LYLY *Euphues* (Arb.) 197 He runneth far that neuer returneth.

Running horse, an open grave, A.

1573 SANDFORD (1576) 207. **1578** FLORIO *First Fruites* f. 28. **1611** COTGRAVE S.V. 'Sepulchre'. **1629** *Book of Meery Riddles* (Halliw.) 99. **1666** TORRIANO 43. **1732** FULLER no. 376 (with 'race-horse').

Running leather, *see* Shoes be made of r. l.

Runs fast will not run long, He that.

1855 BOHN 392.

Runs fastest gets most ground, He that.

1670 RAY 138.

Runs fastest, He that | gets the ring.

1546 HEYWOOD I. iii. 7 Where wooers hoppe in and out, long time may bryng Him that hoppeth best, at last to haue the ryng. **1593–4** SHAKS. *Tam. Shrew* I. i. 144 He that runs fastest gets the ring. How say you, Signior Gremio?

Runs in the blood like wooden legs, It.

1917 BRIDGE 81 . . . Said of any family peculiarity.

Runs in the night, He that | stumbles.

1616 DRAXE 98 Hee that runneth in the night, stumbleth. **1664** CODRINGTON 196. **1670** RAY 19.

Runs, *see also* Run(s).

Rush bush keeps the cow, The.

a. **1542** SIR. D. LINDSAY *Complaynt to K.* 407–8 Wks. (1879) I. 57 Jhone Upeland bene full blyith, I trow, Because the rysche bus kepis his how. [*Note,* p. 256, James V[1] had made such an example of the thieves, . . . that it was a common saying, 'That he made the rush bush keep the cow'.—CHALMERS.] **1827–30** SCOTT *Tales Grandf.* xxvii James was said to have made 'the rush bush keep the cow'; that is to say, . . . cattle might remain on their pastures unwatched. [[1] 1513–42.]

Rush(es), *see also* Ring of a r.; Strew green r. for stranger.

Russia is always defeated, but never beaten.

1913 *Spectator* 26 Apr. 687 We come to the Russo-Japanese war. . . . The campaign . . . furnishes another proof of the saying that Russia is always defeated but never beaten.

Russian, *see* Scratch a R.

Rusty sword and empty purse plead performance of covenants, The.

1664 CODRINGTON 216. **1670** RAY 23.

Rutland Raddleman.

1613–22 DRAYTON *Polyolb.* xxiii. 268 (1876) III. 95 And little *Rutlandshire* is terméd *Raddleman.* **1662** FULLER (*Rutland*) III. 38 'Rutland Raddleman.' . . . *Radleman* is a *Reddleman*, a trade . . . only in this county, whence men bring . . . a pack of red stones, or ochre, which they sell . . . for the marking of sheep.

Rye, *see* Sow wheat . . . and r. in dust.

Rynt you witch, quoth Besse Lockit to her mother.

c. **1605** SHAKS. *Lear* III. iv Aroint thee, witch. *Macbeth* I. iii Aroint thee, witch! the rump-fed ronyon cries. **1674** RAY *Collectn. Eng. Words* 52 *Rynt* ye: By your leave, stand handsomely. As, Rynt you Witch, quoth *Besse Locket* to her Mother, Proverb, *Chesh.* **1917** BRIDGE 106 Roint ye! witch, as Bessie Lockit said to her mother. Roint, Rynt, Runt . . . = away with you. . . . 'Runt thee' is an expression used by milkmaids to a cow when she has been milked, to get out of the way. *Wilbraham.*

S

Sack is known by the sample, The.

1732 FULLER no. 5949 You may know by a Handful the whole Sack. **1869** HAZLITT 397.

Sacks to the mill, More.

[*To bring more sacks to the mill* = to supplement argument with argument or weight with weight.] **1590** NASHE *Pasquil's Apol.* I. Cij b To the next, to the next, more sacks to the Myll. **1594–5** SHAKS. *L.L.L.* IV. iii. 81 More sacks to the mill! O heavens! I have my wish. **1623** MIDDLETON *Span. Gipsy* IV. i (Merm.) I 419 *Alv., Guim., &c.* Welcome welcome, welcome! *Soto.* More sacks to the mill. **1738** SWIFT (Dial. i) 338 [NEVEROUT, *as* MISS *is standing, pulls her suddenly on his lap.*] *Never.* Now, colonel, come sit down on my lap; more sacks upon the mill.

Sack(s), *see also* Bad s. that abide no clouting; Bag (S.) (To give the); Bind the s. before full; Broken s. hold no corn; Comes nought out of s. but was there; Empty s. cannot stand; Every one thinks his s. heaviest; Know by a handful the s.; Old s. asketh much patching; Tying the s. before it be full.

Sad burden to carry a dead man's child, It is a.

1655 FULLER *Ch. Hist.* II. v. § 29 (1868) I. 237 Our women have a proverb, 'It is a sad burden to carry a dead man's child'; and, surely, a historian hath no heart . . . to exemplify dead canons.

Sad, *see also* Long liveth a merry man as a s.

Saddle on the right horse, Set the.

1607 DEKKER & WEBSTER *Westward Ho* G 4 How say you wenches, haue I set the Sadle on the right horse? **1616** DRAXE 105 The right saddle must bee set on the right horse. 19 June **1619** J. CHAMBERLAIN *Letters* (McLure) ii. 246 Yt wilbe . . . difficult . . . to set the right saddle upon the right horse. *a.* **1653** GOUGE *Comm. Hebr.* xi. 37 To remove this scandal, the apostle setteth the saddle on the right Horse, and sheweth, that [&c.]. **1660** W. SECKER *Nonsuch Prof.* III

(1891) 276 God . . . will bring every sinner to the bar. . . . Then He will set the saddle on the back of the right horse. **1670** RAY 138 . . . This Proverb may be variously applied; either thus, Let them bear the blame that deserve it: or thus, Let them bear the burden that are best able. **1678** DRYDEN *All for Love* Pref. (Merm.) II. ii I suppose he would think it a wiser part to set the saddle on the right horse, and choose rather to live with the reputation of a plain-spoken, honest man, than to die with the infamy of an incestuous villain.

Saddles lack, Where | better ride on a pad than on the horse bareback.

1550 HEYWOOD I. x. 24. **1732** FULLER no. 6464.

Saddle(s) (*noun*), *see also* Cadgers are aye cracking of s.; Fair in cradle foul in s.; Fault of horse put on s.; Ride a young colt (When you) . . . s. well girt; Sow to bear s. (Meet as).

Saddle(s) (*verb*), *see* Eats his cock alone (Who) must s. alone; Rides not ay when he s. horse.

Saddleworth, *see* Parson of S. (Like the).

Sadness and gladness succeed each other.

1639 CLARKE 326. **1670** RAY 139.

Safe as a thief in a mill, As.

1606 J. DAY, &c. *The Isle of Gulls* II. ii (Bullen) 37. **1663** J. WILSON *Cheats* I. i As safe in the constable's house, as a thief in a mill. **1738** SWIFT (Dial. i) 337 *Col.* Then, I warrant, you'll be as safe as a thief in a mill.

Safe as the bank, As.

1857–8 DICKENS *Little Dorrit* ix As trustworthy as the Bank of England. **1862** Id. *Letters* (1880) ii. 183 (A).

Safe bind, safe find.

1824 SCOTT *St. Ronan's* xxxvi Safe bind, Safe find—it may be once away and aye away.

Safe from the East Indies, He came | and was drowned in the Thames.

1732 FULLER no. 1817.

Safe is the word.

1721 KELLY 291 ... Taken from the watchword given among soldiers, spoken when we have gotten over some great difficulty. **1733** SWIFT *On Poetry* Wks. (1856) I. 652 If still you be disposed to rhyme, Go try your hand a second time. Again you fail: yet Safe's the word; Take courage, and attempt a third.

Safe riding in a good haven, It is.

1659 HOWELL *Eng. Prov.* 16/2. **1732** FULLER no. 5083 'Tis good riding in a safe harbour.

Safe side, Nothing like being on the.

1902–4 LEAN IV. 152.

Safe, *see also* Way to be s.

Safely, *see* Wisely walketh that s. go.

Safety first.

1929 DEAN INGE *Assess. & Anticip.* 87 'Safety first' is all very well when we are preparing to cross a street or board an omnibus.

Saffron Walden, God help me!

1851 *N. & Q.* 1st Ser. III. 167 Many of the mendicants who ramble the county of Suffolk in search of relief, when asked where they come from, reply in a pitiful tone, 'Saffron Walden, God help me'.

Sage in May, Set | and it will grow alway.

1661 M. STEVENSON *Twelve Moneths* 23 I shall conclude with the old Proverb, Set Sage in *May*, and it will grow alway.

Sage, *see* Live for aye eat s. in May.

Said in the kitchen, All that is | should not be heard in the hall.

1721 KELLY 9 ... Every thing that a man may say of his neighbour, ... should not be whisper'd to him.

Said my prayers in the other corner, I have.

1869 HAZLITT 221 ... *Devon.* This phrase is in common use in cases where a person only partially fills any utensil, as a jug or a milk-bowl.

Sail near the wind, To.

[= to come near transgressing a law or moral principle.] **1840** H. COLERIDGE *Int. to Massinger & Ford* xxxvii [Shakespeare's] nurse is not a very discreet guardianess for a beauty ... her language sails a little too near the wind. **1902** A. R. COLQUHOUN *Mastery of Pac.* 192 In Australia ... steps are to be taken against natives of India by means of an education test. As the Hindoos are British subjects, this is sailing rather near the wind.

Sail over the sea in an egg-shell, It is hard to.

1639 CLARKE 5.

Sail, quoth the king: hold, quoth the wind.

1721 KELLY 285 ... That unaccountable creature, which God brings out of his treasures, cannot be commanded by mortal power. **1732** FULLER no. 4064. **1820** SCOTT *Monast. Ans. to Introd. Epist.* Mr. Watt ... affording the means ... of sailing without that wind which defied the commands ... of Xerxes himself. *Note.*—Probably the author alludes to the national adage: The king said sail, But the wind said no.

Sail too big for the ballast, Make not thy.

1577–87 W. HARRISON *Description of England* (New Sh. S.) i. 129 No man hath hurt by it but himselfe, who ... will ... as our prouerbe saith, now and then beare a bigger saile than his boat is able to sustaine. *a.* **1609** JONSON *Ev. Man in Humour* I. i. 83 Not that your sayle be bigger then your boat. **1732** FULLER no. 3322.

Sail under false colours, To.

1897 STEVENSON *St. Ives* xxviii If it could be managed without ... the mention of my real name. I had so much wisdom as to sail under false colours in this foolish jaunt of mine.

Sail without danger, He that would | must never come on the main sea.

1639 CLARKE 250. **1670** RAY 139.

Sail(s), *see also* Heal s. is good s.; Hoist your s. when wind fair.

Sailing in a sow's ear, To come.

1670 RAY 192. **1732** FULLER no. 5146.

Sailor's warning, *see* Rainbow in the morning; Sky red in the morning.

Sailors get money like horses, and spend it like asses.

1751 SMOLLETT *Per. Pick.* ii I make good the old saying, 'We sailors get money like horses, and spend it like asses'. *a.* **1814** C. DIBDIN *Songs,* 'At Sea' (1886) 16 'Tis said that, with grog and our lasses Because jolly sailors are free, Our money we squander like asses Which like horses we earn'd when at sea.

Sailors go round the world without going into it.

1829 MARRYAT *Frank M.* xxvii You know her character, and you should know something about our sex; but sailors, they say, go round the world without going into it.

Sailors' fingers must be all fish-hooks.

1902 A. B. LUBBOCK *Round the Horn* vi Frenzied men tore at the sail with both hands, hanging on by their eyelids .... Truly a sailor must have each finger a fishhook, as they say.

Sailors, *see also* Heaven takes care of s.; Love lost betwixt s. and soldiers (No); Souters shouldna be s.

Saint abroad and a devil at home, A.

1633 P. FLETCHER *Purp. Is.* VII. xxxvi (1908) II. 94 A saint abroad, at home a fiend; and worst a saint. **1678** BUNYAN *Pilgr.* I. (1877) 84 Thus say the common people that know him, *A saint abroad, and a devil at home.*

St. Andrew the King, three weeks and three days before Christmas comes in.

1830 FORBY 418.

St. Anthony's (*or* Tantony) pig, To follow one like a.

[Pigs under the protection of St. Anthony, the patron of swineherds, were allowed to roam the streets, and followed any one who fed them.] **1598** STOW *Surv. Lond.* (1603) 185 Whereupon was raised a prouerbe, such a one will follow such a one, and whine as it were an Anthonie pig. **1606** CHAPMAN *Gent. Usher* IV. i Plays (1874) 100 I have followed you up and down like a Tantalus pig. **1709** *Brit. Apollo* II. No. 62 3/2 Whom all the Town follow, Like so many St. Anthony's pigs. **1738** SWIFT (Dial. i) 340 *Lady A.* She made me follow her last week through all the shops like a Tantiny pig. **1765** BICKERSTAFFE *Love in Village* I. ix To see you dangling after me every where, like a tantony pig.

St. Augustine, *see* Sermon without St. A.

St. Bartholomew[1] brings the cold dew.

1678 RAY 52. **1846** DENHAM 55 At St. Barthol'mew, Then comes cold dew. **1859** *N. & Q.* 2nd Ser. VIII. 242 St. Barthŏlomew, Bring'st the cold dew. [[1] 24 Aug.]

St. Benedick,[1] sow thy pease, or keep them in thy rick.

1678 RAY 52. [[1] 21 March.]

St. Bernard, *see* Bernard did not see every thing.

St. Chad, *see* Before St. C. every goose lays; St. Valentine's Day cast beans ... but on St. C. sow. *See also* Chad.

St. David's day,[1] put oats and barley in the clay.

1678 RAY 346 ... With us it is accounted a little too early to sow barley (which is a tender grain) in the beginning of March. [[1] 1 March.]

St. David, *see also* David.

St. Distaff's Day neither work nor play, On.

1648 HERRICK *Hesper.* Wks. (O.U.P.) 308 *Saint Distaffs day, or the morrow after Twelfth day.* Partly worke and partly play He must on S. *Distaff's* day. **1846** DENHAM 23 On St. Distaff's Day—neither work nor play. Jan. 7th: called St. Distaff's Day, or Rock Day, because (the Christmas holidays having ended) good housewives resumed ... the distaff.

St. George to borrow.

[(i) St. G. being security for one's good faith; (ii) an asseveration, By St. G.!] **1529** SKELTON *Albany* 506 Sainct George to borrowe, Ye shall have schame and sorrowe. **1548** HALL *Chron.* (1809) 416 Now sent George to borowe, let us set forward. **1566** UDALL *Royster D.* IV. viii. 77 What then? Sainct George to borow, our Ladies Knight.

St. George, Like | who is always on horseback and never rides.

1579 LYLY *Euphues* (Bond) II. 260 (A) Lyke St. George, who is euer on horse backe yet neuer rideth. *a.* **1591** HY. SMITH *Serm.* (1866) II. 32 [*Satan*] is not called a tempter, ... a murderer, and a compasser, in vain; like St. George, which is always on horseback, and never rides. **1592** NASHE *Pierce Pen.* Wks. (1904) I. 174 These whelpes of the first Litter of Gentilitie, ... I knowe not howe, like Saint *George*, they are alwaies mounted, but neuer moue. **1596–7** SHAKS. *K. John* II. i. 288 Saint George, that swing'd the dragon, and e'er since Sits on his horse back at mine hostess' door. **1738** FRANKLIN *Aug.* Defer not thy well doing; be not like St. George, who is always a-horseback, and never rides on.

St. Giles's breed; fat, ragged and saucy.

1787 GROSE (*Lond.*) 197 St. Giles's[1] breed; fat, ragged and saucy. The people of that parish, particularly those resident in Newton and Dyot streets, still retain their rags and impudence. [[1] A district in west-central London, long notorious for poverty and vice.]

St. Giles's cup.

[Criminals on their way to the gallows at Tyburn were presented with a cup of water at or near the church of St. Giles in the Fields.] *a.* **1580** *Death's Dance* in COLLIER *Roxb. Bal.* (1847) 3 If Death would ... briefly say, '... I bring to you Saint Giles his bowle', 'twould put them all in feare. **1594** CHURCHYARD *Mirror of Man* 'Trusting in friendship makes some be trust up, Or ride in a cart to kis Saint Giles his cup'.

St. Giles, *see also* Dine with St. G.; Lame as St. G.

St. Hugh's bones.

[= shoemakers' tools.] **1597** DELONEY *1 Gentle Craft,* Wks. (Mann) 87. **1600** DEKKER *Gentle Craft* iv (1862) 15 Skoomaker, have you all your tools ... your hand- and thumbleathers and good Saint-Hughs bones to smooth up your work. **1688** R. HOLME *Acad. Armory* III. viii. 349 Let not any of ... the Gentle Craft, take it in ill part, that all their

Tools were not set together, seeing St. Hughs Bones ought not to be separated.

St. James's Day[1] be come and gone, Till | you may have hops or you may have none.

1670 RAY 44. [[1] July 25.]

St. John to borrow.

[St. John being security for good faith.] *c.* **1386** CHAUCER *Squire's T.* 596 I hydde fro hym my sorwe And took hym by the hond, Seint John to borwe, And seydè thus: 'Lo, I am yourès al.'

St. John to borrow!

[A Scottish formula at parting = *au revoir.*] **1423** JAS. I *Kings Q.* xxiii With mony 'fare wele' and 'sanct Iohne to borowe'. *c.* **1470** HENRY *Wallace* III. 336 Thar leyff thai tuk, with conforde. . . . Sanct Iohne to borch, thai suld meyt haille agayne.

St. John, *see also* Laid in his fuel before St. J.

St. Johnston's riband (tippet).

[Sc. A halter or hangman's rope. *St. Johnston* = Perth.] **1638** H. ADAMSON *Muse's Threnodie* (1774) 119 Hence of St. Johnston's ribband came the word. **1816** SCOTT *Old Mort.* vii To be sent to Heaven wi' a Saint Johnstone's tippit about my hause.

St. Laurence, *see* More like the devil than St. L.

Saint (Shrine), Like | like offering.

1550 BALE *Eng. Votaries* II. 105 b These adages myght then haue bene founde true, suche saynt, suche shryne, suche bere, suche bottell. **1639** CLARKE 46.

St. Luke was a saint and a physician, and yet he died (is dead).

1616 DRAXE 133. **1640** HERBERT 363.

St. Luke's Day[1] the oxen have leave to play, On.

[The ox was the medieval symbol of St. Luke.] **1732** FULLER no. 6220. [[1] 18 Oct.]

St. Luke's (little) summer.

[Occurring about St. Luke's Day, 18 Oct.] **1828** T. FORSTER *Circle Seasons* 293 Fair, warm, and dry weather, often occurs about this time, and is called St. Luke's Little Summer. **1855** *N. & Q.* 1st Ser. XII. 366/1 A few fine days, . . . called St. Luke's little summer; which the good folks of Hants and Dorset always expect about the 18th of this month.

St. Martin's rings.

[= imitation gold rings.] **1589** R. HARVEY *Pl. Perc.* 4 I doubt whether all be gold that glistereth, sith Saint Martins rings be but Copper inside.

St. Martin's stuff (ware).

[= counterfeit goods.] **1598** GILPIN *Skial.*

(1878) 41 I had thought the last mask. . . . Had . . . Taught thee S. Martins stuffe from true gold lace. **1648** C. WALKER *Hist. Independ.* I. 122 These letters may be St. Martins ware, counterfeit stuffe.

St. Martin's summer.

[Fine, mild weather occurring about Martinmas.] **1591–2** SHAKS. *I Hen. VI* I. ii. 161 Expect Saint Martin's summer, halcyon days. **1864** TENNYSON *Aylmer's F.* 560 Then ensued A Martin's summer of his faded love. **1880** MAHAFFY *Hist. Gr. Lit.* i. 97 The martinmas summer of Greek literature in Plutarch. **1888** A. T. QUILLER-COUCH *Troy Town* vii She was . . . not young, but rather in that St. Martin's Summer when a woman learns for the first time the value of her charms. **1896** H. S. MERRIMAN *Flotsam* ii The carriage was . . . in the shadow of the trees in Trinity Square, for it was St. Martin's summer and a hot October.

St. Matthee[1] shut up the bee.

1678 RAY 52. [[1] St. Matthias, 24 Feb.]

St. Matthew[1] get candlesticks new.

1830 FORBY 418. [[1] 21 Sept.]

St. Matthi[1] lay candlesticks by.

1830 FORBY 418. [[1] St. Matthias, 24 Feb.]

St. Matthias[1] both leaf and grass.

1659 HOWELL *Eng. Prov.* 21/2. [[1] 24 Feb.]

St. Matthie[1] all the year goes by.

1678 RAY 52 . . . Because in Leap-year the supernumerary day is then intercalated. [[1] St. Matthias, 24 Feb.]

St. Matthie[1] sends saps into the tree.

1678 RAY 50. [[1] St. Matthias.]

St. Mattho,[1] take thy hopper,[2] and sow.

1678 RAY 52. [[1] St. Matthias. [2] seed-basket.]

St. Michael, *see* Burned one candle to St. M.

St. Monday.

[Used with reference to workmen being idle on Monday, as a consequence of drunkenness on the Sunday.] **1753** *Scots. Mag.* Apr. 208/1 (*title*) St. Monday; or, the tippling tradesmen. **1804** EDGEWORTH *Pop. Tales, To-morrow* vii (1856) 408 *note* It is a custom in Ireland among shoemakers, if they intoxicate themselves on Sunday, to do no work on Monday; and this they call making a Saint Monday. **1857** GEN. P. THOMPSON *Audi Alt.* I. vii. 22 An assemblage of artisans keeping Saint Monday.

St. Nicholas'(s) clerks.

[i. = poor scholars.] **1553** T. WILSON *Arte of Rhet.* (1580) 155 Thei are no Churchmen, thei are maisterlesse men, or rather S. Nicolas clerkes that lacke liuyng. [ii. = highwaymen.] **1570** FOXE *A. & M.* (ed. 2) 2287 I haue heard of men robbed by S. Nicolas clerkes. **1597–8** SHAKS. *1 Hen. IV* II. i. 67 Sirrah, if they meet not with Saint Nicholas' clerks, I'll give thee this neck. **1662** J. WILSON *The Cheats* I. i Who should I meet with but our old Gang, some of St. Nicholas's Clerks.

St. Paul[1] be fair and clear, If | then betides a happy year.

14th cent. ROBERT OF AVESBURY *Hist.* (Hearne) 266 (A) *Clara dies Pauli bona tempora denotat anni.* **1584** R. SCOT *Witchcraft* XI. xv (A) If Paul th' apostles day be clear, it doth foreshew a lucky year. **1686–7** J. AUBREY *Rem. Gent. & Jud.* (1881) 94 The old verse so much observed by Countrey people: 'If Paul's day be faire and cleare It will betyde a happy yeare.' **1732** FULLER no. 6142 If *St. Paul* be fair and clear, Then betides a happy Year; If the Wind do blow aloft, Then of Wars we shall hear full oft; If the Clouds make dark the Sky, Great store of People then will die; If there be either Snow or Rain, Then will be dear all sorts of Grain. **1846** DENHAM 24 If St. Paul's day be fine and clear, It doth betide a happy year; But if by chance it then should rain, It will make dear all kinds of grain; And if the clouds make dark the sky, Then neat[2] and fowls this year shall die; If blustering winds do blow aloft, Then wars, shall trouble the realm full oft. **1866** *N. & Q.* 3rd Ser. IX. 118 A Huntingdonshire cottager said to me: 'We shall have a fine spring, Sir. There is an old proverb that says: "If Paul's day is fine, it will be a fine spring".' [[1] 25 Jan. [2] cattle.]

St. Paul's mariners, He is one of.

1662 FULLER (*Kent*) II. 119 Navigation is much improved . . . since Saint Paul's time; insomuch that, when a man goes bunglingly about any work in a ship, I have heard our Englishmen say, 'Such a man is one of St. Paul's mariners'.

St. Paul, *see also* Praiseth St. Peter (Who) doth not blame St. P. *See also* Paul's.

St. Peter's in the Poor, where no tavern, alehouse, or sign at the door.

1662 FULLER (*Lond.*) II. 345 'St. Peter's in the poor, Where no tavern, alehouse, or sign at the door.' Under correction, I conceive it called 'in the poor', because the Augustinian friars, professing wilful poverty, for some hundreds of years, possessed more than a moiety thereof. . . . This parish[1] . . . was (not to say is) one of the richest in London. [[1] Old Broad Street. LEAN I. 142.]

St. Peter's needle, To go through.

1917 BRIDGE 134 . . . To have serious misfortune. Applied to a man who has become a bankrupt and is sold up.

St. Peter, *see also* Praiseth St. P. (Who) doth not blame St. Paul.

St. Robert gave his cow, As freely as.

1670 RAY 208 . . . This Robert was a Knareburgh[1] saint. [[1] Knaresborough, Yorks.]

St. Stephen, Blessed be | there is no fast upon his even.

1659 HOWELL *Eng. Prov.* 21/1 . . . *Because 'tis Christmas night.*

St. Stephen, *see also* Bleed your nag on S.'s day; Yule is young . . . and as old in S.

Saint swear, Enough to make a.

c. **1560** *Tom Tyler* 809. **1577** *Misogonus* II. v We . . . could anger him an he were a verye Saynt *c.* **1599** JONSON *Case is Altered* I. vii. 17. **1608** BEAUM. & FL. *Philas.* IV. ii This would make a saint swear like a soldier. **1842** MARRYAT *Perc. Keene* xxvi The remonstrances . . . the badgering I have received . . . have been enough to make a saint swear. **1903** CONRAD *Typhoon* 27 The weather's awful. It would make a saint swear.

St. Swithin[1] is christening the apples.

1813 BRAND *Pop. Antiq.* (Ellis, 1895) i. 342 (A) There is an old saying that when it rains on St. Swithin's Day, it is the Saint christening the apples. **1846** DENHAM 50 . . . A common observation on this (St. Swithin's) day, should it chance to be a rainy one. [[1] 15 July.]

St. Swithin's day, if thou dost rain, for forty days it will remain; St. Swithin's day, if thou be fair, for forty days 'twill rain na mair.

[St. Swithun (or Swithin), bishop of Winchester, d. 862.] **1599** JONSON *Ev. Man out of Humour* I. i Sord. O, here, *Saint Swithin's*, the 15 *day, variable weather, for the most part rain*, . . . why, it should rain forty days after, now, more or less, it was a rule held afore I was able to hold a plough. **1697** *Poor Robin's Alm.* in DENHAM 53 In this month is St. Swithin's day; On which, if that it rain, they say, Full xl days after it will, Or more or less some rain distill. **1716** GAY *Trivia* I. 183–6 How if on Swithin's feast the welkin lowers, And ev'ry pent-house streams with hasty showers, Twice twenty days shall clouds their fleeces drain, And wash the pavements with incessant rain. **1846** DENHAM 52 St. Swithin's day, if thou dost rain, For forty days it will remain: St. Swithin's day, if thou be fair, For forty days 'twill rain na mair.

St. Thomas à Waterings.

[A place used for executions in Surrey, on the Kent road, where horses were watered; dedicated to Thomas à Becket.] *c.* **1386** CHAUCER *Prol.* 826 And forth we riden, . . . Unto the wateryng of Seint Thomas. **1631** JONSON *New Inn* I. i *Host.* He may, perhaps, take a degree at Tyburn, . . . come, to read a lecture . . . at St. Thomas à Waterings.

St. Thomas[1] divine, brewing, baking, and killing of fat swine.

1742 *An Agreeable Companion* 59 Thomas Divine, Brewing and Baking, and Killing of Swine. **1797–1811** *Agricult. Com. to Bd. of Agric.* in LEAN I. 383. [[1] 21 Dec.]

St. Thomas[1] gray! St. Thomas gray! the longest night and the shortest day.

1859 *N. & Q.* 2nd Ser. VIII. 242. [[1] 21 Dec.]

St. Valentine,[1] On | all the birds of the air in couples do join.

c. **1380** CHAUCER *Parl. of Foules* l. 309 For this was on seynt Valentynes day, When every foul cometh ther to chese his make.[2] **1477** *Paston Letters* (Gairdner) III. 169 And, cosyn, uppon Fryday is Sent Volentynes Day, and every brydde chesyth hym a make. **1595-6** SHAKS. *Mids. N.* IV. i. 145 Saint Valentine is past: Begin these woodbirds but to couple now? **1714** GAY *Shep. Wk.*, *Thurs.* 37 Last *Valentine*, the Day when Birds of Kind Their Paramours with mutual Chirpings find, I rearly[3] rose. **1830** FORBY 418 On St. Valentine, all the birds of the air in couples do join. [[1] 14 Feb. [2] mate. [3] early.]

St. Valentine,[1] set thy hopper[2] by mine.

1678 RAY 52. [[1] 14 Feb. [2] seed-basket.]

St. Valentine's Day[1] cast beans in clay, On | but on St. Chad[2] sow good or bad.

1639 SMYTH *Berkeley MSS.* in LEAN I. 376 [[1] 14 Feb. [2] 2 March.]

St. Valentine, *see also* Valentine.

St. Vincent's Day,[1] Remember on | if the sun his beams display, be sure to mark the transient beam, which through the casement sheds a gleam; for 'tis a token bright and clear of prosperous weather all the year.

1584 R. SCOT *Witchcraft* XI. xv (A). **1846** DENHAM 24. [[1] 22 Jan.]

St. Vitus's day[1] be rainy weather, If | it will rain for thirty days together.

1846 DENHAM 49. [[1] 15 June.]

Saints in Cornwall than in heaven, There are more.

1864 *N. & Q.* 3rd Ser. V. 275 *Cornish Proverbs.*—There are more Saints in Cornwall than in Heaven. The process of creation is continued.... I lately, in a Cornish paper, met with *Saint Newlyn*.

Saint(s), *see also* Pleaseth not God (When it), s. can do little; Young s., old devil.

Sair dung[1] bairn that dare not greet,[2] It is a.

1641 FERGUSSON 66. **1721** KELLY 177 . . .

They are under great awe, that may not complain. [[1] beaten. [2] cry.]

Sairs[1] should be sair handled.

1862 HISLOP 255 . . . That is, delicate or painful subjects should be cautiously alluded to. [[1] sores.]

Sairy brewing that is not good in the newing,[1] It is a.

1641 FERGUSSON 60. **1721** KELLY 181 . . . Spoken when people are much taken with new projects. [[1] when it is new.]

Sairy collop that is taken off a capon, It is a.

1641 FERGUSSON 60. **1721** KELLY 189 . . One cannot take much where there is but little.

Sairy wood that has never a withered bough in it, It is a.

1721 KELLY 186 . . . Spoken when some of our relations, who have done an ill thing, is cast in our teeth.

Salad may be the prologue to a bad supper, A good.

1642 TORRIANO 100. **1659** N.R. 19 A good Sallet the beginning of a bad Supper. **1664** CODRINGTON 184. **1732** FULLER no. 174.

Salad, *see also* Drinks not wine after s. (He that); Thistle is fat s. for ass.

Salisbury Cathedral was built upon wool-packs.

1656-91 J. AUBREY *Nat. Hist. Wilts.* (1847) 98 The old tradition is, that this church was *built upon wooll-packs.* . . . It might be that . . . when Salisbury Cathedral was building, . . . an imposition might be putt on the Wiltshire wool-packs towards the carrying on of this magnificent structure.

Salisbury Plain is seldom (never) without a thief or twain.

1656-91 J. AUBREY *Nat. Hist. Wilts.* (1847) xiv. 69 A PROVERB: 'Salisbury Plain Never without a thief or twain.' **1659** HOWELL *Eng. Prov.* 17/1 Salisbury Plain, is seldome without a theef or twain.

Sallows, *see* Buildeth his house all of s.

Salmon and sermon have their season in Lent.

1659 HOWELL *Fr.-Eng.* 21. **1670** RAY 23 . . . *Gall.* **1917** BRIDGE 106 . . . Not exclusively a Cheshire saying but often used in the County, the Dee being a salmon river.

Salmon, *see also* Hook's well lost to catch s.

Salt, Below (Above) the.

[A large salt-cellar in the middle of a dining-table formerly marked off the less honoured guests from those more honoured.] **1597** BP. HALL *Sat.* II. vi That he do, on no default,

Euer presume to sit aboue the salt. **1599**
B. JONSON *Cynthia's Rev.* II. ii (1616) 200 Hee
neuer drinkes below the salt. **1658** *Wit
Restor'd* 43 Hee . . . humbly sate Below the
Salt, and munch'd his sprat.

Salt cooks bear blame, but fresh bear shame.

1670 RAY 73. **1732** FULLER no. 6300.

Salt fish, *see* Affairs, like s. f., ought to be . . .
soaking.

Salt on a bird's tail, To cast (lay, throw).

[In allusion to the jocular advice given to
children to catch birds by putting salt on
their tails.] **1580** LYLY *Euph. & his Eng.*
(Arb.) 327 It is . . . a foolish bird that staieth
the laying salt on hir taile. **1639** CLARKE 155
You catch birds by laying salt on their tayles.
1664 BUTLER *Hudibras* II. i. 78 Such great
achievements cannot fail, To cast salt on a
woman's tail. **1704** SWIFT *T. Tub* vii Men
catch knowledge by throwing their wit on the
posteriors of a book, as boys do sparrows by
flinging salt upon their tails. **1721** KELLY 380
You will ne'er cast salt on his tail. That is, he
has clean escap'd. **1813** SOUTHEY *Nelson* viii
If they go on playing this game, some day
we shall lay salt upon their tails.

Salt seasons all things.

1591 FLORIO *Sec. Frutes* 53 (A) Salt savoureth,
and seasoneth all things. **1659** HOWELL *Eng.
Prov.* 9/2.

Salt to Dysart and puddings to Tranent, Carry.

[= to send things to a place where they are
already plentiful.] *c.* **1598** *MS. Proverbs* in
FERGUSSON 47 He cals[1] salt to Dysart. **1822**
SCOTT *Let.* 10 Feb. in LOCKHART *Life* lv (1860)
472 It would be sending coals to Newcastle . . . , not to mention salt to Dysart, and
all other superfluous importations (&c.). **1862**
HISLOP 70 Carry saut to Dysart and puddings
to Tranent. [[1] drives.]

Salt water and absence wash away love.

a. **1805** NELSON in SOUTHEY *Life* (1813) ii
'Have you not often heard', says he in
another letter, 'that salt water and absence
always wash away love? Now I am such a
heretic as not to believe that faith.' **1840**
MARRYAT *Poor Jack* xxxviii I'm very glad
that we're off to-morrow—salt water cures
love, they say, sooner than anything else.

Salt water never gives cold.

1837 T. HOOK *Jack Brag* xii 'Wet clothes!'
said Jack. 'Nothing—a mere flea-bite—salt
water never gives cold.'

Salt, *see also* Before you make friend eat . . .
s. with him; Black (Above) there is no
colour; Come after with s. and spoons;
Eat a peck of s.; Give neither counsel nor
s.; Help one to s., help to sorrow; Take

away the s., throw flesh to the dogs;
Worth one's s.

Salute, *see* Know one another (They that) s.
afar.

Salve for every sore, There is a.

1542 *Sch. House of Women* 1. 401 (A) A salve
there is for euery sore. **1579** LYLY *Euphues*
(Arb.) 61 O ye Gods, have ye ordeyned for
every malady a medicine, for every sore a
salve, for every paine a plaster, leaving only
love remedilesse? **1590–1** SHAKS. *3 Hen. VI*
IV. vi. 88 But let us hence, my sovereign, to
provide A salve for any sore that may betide.
1639 CLARKE 44. **1908** C. M. DOUGHTY
Wander. Arabia I. vi. 102 Some specific must
he have for every disease, because 'there is a
salve in nature for every sore'.

Salve, *see also* Seek your s. where you get
your sore; — where you got your ail.

Same boat, To be all in the.

[CIC. *ad Fam.* 12. 25 *Una navis est iam
bonorum omnium.*] **1584** HUDSON *Judith*
(J. Craigie) 51 Haue ye pain? So likewise
pain haue we; For in one boat we both im-
barked be. **1857** HUGHES *Tom Brown* 131
'But my face is all muddy', argued Tom.
'Oh, we're all in one boat for that matter.'

Same knife cuts bread and fingers, The.

1579 GOSSON *Sch. Abuse* (Arb.) 46 The goodness of a Knife cuts the owner's fingers. **1580**
LYLY *Euph. & His Eng.* Wks. II. 28
That were as fond as not to cut ones meate
with that knife yt an other hath cut his
finger. **1616** DRAXE 224. **1659** HOWELL
Sp.–Eng. 19.

Sample, *see* Sack is known by s.

Sampson than of Solomon in him, There is more of.

1830 FORBY 430 . . . *i.e.* Great bodily strength,
but little sense.

Samson was a strong man, yet could he not pay money before he had it. (*Cf.* Solomon was a wise man.)

1659 HOWELL *Eng. Prov.* 21/1. **1678** RAY 76.
1732 FULLER no. 4066.

Samson, *see also* Solomon was a wise man.

Sand feeds the clay, When the | England cries Well-a-day: but when the clay feeds the sand, it is merry with England.

1577 W. HARRISON *Description of Eng.* (New
Sh. S.) iii. 139–140 According to the old rude
verse set downe of England . . . When the
sand dooth serue the claie Then may we sing
well awaie; But when the claie doth serue the
sand, Then is it merie with England. **1662**
FULLER (*Berks.*) I. 116 'When the sand feeds
the clay, England cries Well-a-day: But

when the clay feeds the sand, it is merry with England.' As Nottinghamshire is divided into . . . the sand and the clay, all England falls under the same *dicotomy*; yet . . . the sand hardly amounteth to the fifth part thereof. Now a wet year, which drowneth and chilleth the clay, makes the sandy ground most fruitful with corn, and the general granary of the land.

Sand, *see also* Sowing on the **s**.

Sandal tree perfumes the axe that fells it, The.

1853 TRENCH iv. 75 This Indian [proverb], suggesting that good should be returned for evil: *The sandal tree perfumes the axe that fells it.* **1865** Id. *Poems* 302 The sandal tree, most sacred tree of all, Perfumes the very axe which bids it fall.

Sands will sink a ship, Many.

1621 BURTON *Anat. Mel.* I. ii. iv. vii (1651) 172 As Austin said,[1] *many grains and small sands sink a ship,* . . . Often reiterated, many dispositions produce an habit. **1670** RAY 118 . . . We must have a care of little things. [[1] Numquid minutissima sunt grana arenae? sed si arena amplius in navem mittatur, mergit illam.]

Sandy bowrocks, *see* Build **s. b.** together (We will never).

Sap and heart are the best of wood.

1917 BRIDGE 106 . . . Outside and inside are equally useful.

Sap, *see also* Little **s.** in dry pease hulls.

Sarbut, *see* Old S. says so.

Sarum, *see Secundum usum S.*

Satan reproves sin.

1666 TORRIANO 60 The devil corrects sin. **1721** KELLY 287 . . . Spoken when we are reproved by wicked men. **1822** SCOTT *Nigel* xxxii I am afraid . . . I might have thought of the old proverb of 'Satan reproving sin'. **1897** C. C. KING *Story of Brit. Army* 176 Napoleon . . . induced his ally, the Czar, to address King George a letter, asking him to make peace 'in the name of humanity!' It was like 'Satan reproving sin'.

Satisfied, *see* Paid that is well **s**.

Saturday is the working day and Monday the holiday of preachers.

1661 FULLER (*Cambs.*) I. 240 Andrew Marvail[1] . . . preached what he had pre-studied some competent time before; insomuch that he was wont to say, that he would cross the common proverb, which called 'Saturday the working day, and Monday the holiday of preachers'. [[1] Marvell.]

Saturday servants never stay, Sunday servants run away.

1851 STERNBERG *Dialect of Northants* 169 (A). **1917** BRIDGE 107 Servant maids do not like to go to a new place on Saturday . . . Northamptonshire:—*Saturday servants never stay, Sunday servants run away.*

Saturday without some sunshine, There is never a.

1835 SOUTHEY *Doctor* iii. 165. **1866** *New Suffolk Garland* 166 (A) There is also a saying that 'the sun is always seen on a Saturday'.

Saturday's flittings light sittings.

1854 BAKER *Northants Gloss.* s.v. 'Flit' (A) 'Saturday's flit will never sit' is a proverb of prediction with superstitious servants, who reluctantly enter upon a new service on that day. **1917** BRIDGE 107 Saturday's flittings, Light sittings. Servant maids do not like to go to a new place on a Saturday as it forebodes a short stay.

Saturday's moon, A | if it comes once in seven years, it comes too soon.

1732 FULLER no. 6491. **1864** *N. & Q.* 3rd Ser. v. 209 A Saturday or a Sunday moon Comes once in seven years too soon.

Saturday's new, and Sunday's full, was never fine and never wool.[1]

1823 E. MOOR *Suffolk Words* 494 We have a local antipathy to a Saturday *new* and Sunday *full* moon, . . . Saturday's new and Sunday's full, Was never fine, nor never *wool*. **1830** FORBY 417. [[1] will.]

Sauce for the goose is sauce for the gander, What 's.

1670 RAY 98 That that's good sawce for a goose, is good for a gander. This is a woman's Proverb. **1692** L'ESTRANGE *Aesop's Fab.* cccii. 264 Sauce for a Goose is Sauce for a Gander. **1738** SWIFT (Dial. ii) 350 *Miss gives Neverout a smart pinch.* . . . *Never.* [*Giving Miss a pinch.*] Take that, miss; what's sauce for a goose, is sauce for a gander. **1823** BYRON *Juan* xiv. lxxxiii Teach them that 'sauce for goose is sauce for gander'. **1894** BLACKMORE *Perlycross* xxxv A proverb of large equity, . . . declares . . . that 'sauce for the goose is sauce for the gander'.

Sauce, *see also* More **s.** than pig; Seek your salve (**s.**) where you get ail; Sweet meat . . . sour **s.**; Sweet **s.** wax sour.

Saul also among the prophets? Is.

1611 BIBLE *1 Sam.* x. 11 Is Saul also among the prophets? **1815** SCOTT *Guy Man.* xxi Is Saul, you will say, among the prophets? Colonel Mannering write poetry! **1853** TRENCH ii. 35 'Is Saul also among the prophets' . . . finds its application as often as any one reveals suddenly . . . a nobleness which had been latent in him until now. **1882** 'F. ANSTEY' *Vice Versâ* iv This is indeed finding Saul among the prophets; your sentiments, if sincere, Bultitude . . . are very creditable.

Save a stranger from the sea, and he'll turn your enemy.

1599–1600 SHAKS. *Twelfth N.* II. i. 24 *Seb.*

Before you took me from the breach of the sea was my sister drowned. . . . *Ant.* If you will not murder me for my love, let me be your servant. **1822** SCOTT *Pirate* vii 'Are you mad . . . to risk the saving of a drowning man? Wot ye not . . . he will be sure to do you some capital injury?'

Save a thief from the gallows and he shall hate (never love) you.

13 . . *Sir Beues* (A.) 1217 Deliure a þef fro þe galwe, He þe hateþ after þe alle halwe! **1484** CAXTON *Fables of Aesop* I. x Yf ye kepe a man fro the galhows he shalle neuer loue yow after.

Save a thief from the gallows and he will be the first shall do thee a mischief.

1583 MELBANCKE *Philot.* 163 True is the Prouerbe, saue a Thiefe from the gallowes and he will be the firste shall doe thee a mischiefe. **1721** KELLY 61 *Buy a thief from the gallows, and he'll help to hang your self.* A very worth clergyman in Scotland, . . . saved a villain from the gallows: and twelve years after, he was the first that rabbled him, and the sorest upon him.

Save a thief from the gallows, and he will be the first to show the way to St. Giles's.[1]

1593 NASHE *Christ's T.* Pref. Ep. Saue a thief from the gallows, and hee'le be the first to shew the way to Saint Gilesesse. [1 The church of St. Giles in the Fields was on the way to the gallows.]

Save a thief from the gallows and he will cut your throat.

1614 CAMDEN 311. **1692** L'ESTRANGE *Aesop's Fab.* cccxi (1738) 334 The mouse gnawed a hole in't, and set her at liberty; and the kite eat up the mouse for her pains. . . . *Save a thief from the gallows,* and he'll cut your throat. **1723** DEFOE *Col. Jack* ix Whence else came the English proverb, That if you save a thief from the gallows, he shall be the first to cut your throat.

Save a thief from the gallows and he will help to hang you.

1583 GOLDING *Calvin on Deut.* li. 307 Saue a theefe from the gallowes and hee will helpe to hang thee. **1622** MASSINGER *Virg. Mar.* II. iii *Spun.* She saved us from the gallows, and, only to keep one proverb from breaking his neck, we'll hang her.

Save one's bacon, To.

[= to escape injury to one's body.] **1675** DICK HALS to Sir R. Verney *Verney Memoirs* (1899) iv. 312 My last reprive . . . came durante bene placito Regis. Iff soe, itt will still save my bacon. **1691** *Weesils* i. 5 No, they'l conclude I do't to save my Bacon. **1812** COMBE (Dr. Syntax) *Pictur.* vi. 22 But as he ran to save his bacon, By hat and wig he was forsaken.

Save something for the man that rides on the white horse.

1670 RAY 139 . . . For old age, wherein the head grows white.

Save while you may: For age and want | no morning sun lasts a whole day.

1758 FRANKLIN in ARBER *Eng. Garner* v. 585 You may think yourself in thriving circumstances; . . . but *For Age and Want, save while you may! No morning sun lasts a whole day.*

Saved, He that will not be | needs no preacher.

1670 RAY 21.

Save(s, d), *see also* Groat is ill s. that shames; Penny is well spent that s. groat.

Savers in a house do well, Some.

1678 RAY 198.

Saver(s), *see also* Good s. is good server.

Saveth his dinner will have the more for his supper, He that.

1616 DRAXE 197. **1639** CLARKE 241. **1670** RAY 79 . . . This is a French proverb, Qui garde son disne il a mieux à souper. He that spares when he is young, may the better spend when he is old. **1732** FULLER no. 2288.

Saving, Of | cometh having. (*Cf.* Sparing is the first getting.)

1580 LYLY *Euph. & his Eng.* (Arb.) 229 Sparing, is good getting. **1616** DRAXE 197. **1670** RAY 139. **1732** FULLER no. 6102.

Saving your presence.

1611 BEAUM. & FL. *Kt. Burn. P.* II. ii You lookt so grim, and, as I may say it, saving your presence, more like a Giant than a mortal man. **1907** ELIZ. ROBINS *Convert.* ii. 24 There's nothing I should quite so much hate talking about as politics—saving your presence.

Saving your (one's) reverence.

c. **1400** MAUNDEV. (1839) xvii. 185 But aftre my lytylee wytt, it semethe me, savynge here reverence, that it is more. **1455** *Rolls of Parlt.* v. 285/1 Defaime untruly (savyng youre reverence) leyed upon us. *a.* **1593** MARLOWE *Edw. II* I. i. Saving your reverence, you must pardon me. **1596–7** SHAKS. *Merch. V.* II. ii. 27 To run away from the Jew, I should be ruled by the fiend, who, saving your reverence, is the devil himself. *Ibid.* II. ii. 142 His master and he, saving your worship's reverence, are scarce cater-cousins. **1597–8** *1 Hen. IV* II. iv. 522 But that he is, saving your reverence, a whore master, that I utterly deny. **1598–9** *Much Ado* III. iv. 32 I think you would have me say, 'saving your reverence, a husband'. **1604–5** *Meas. for Meas.* II. i. 95 Sir, she came in, great with child, and longing,—saving your honour's reverence—for stewed prunes.

Saving, *see also* Alchemy to s. (No); Hang s.

Savour (*noun*), *see* Best smell is bread, the best s. salt; Nothing hath no s.; Something hath some s.

Savours (*verb*), *see* Cask s. of first fill.

Saws, *see* Sooth s. be to lords lothe.

Sawtrey, *see* Ramsey.

Say as men say, but think to yourself.

1639 CLARKE 327.

Say B to a battledore, He cannot.

1565 J. HALL *Hist. Expostulation* (Percy Soc.) 16 (A) He . . . knew not a letter or a b from a bateldore. **1599** NASHE *Lent. Stuffe* Wks. (1885) V. 197 Euery man can say Bee to a Battledore, and write in prayse of Vertue. **1896** SKEAT *Stud. Past* 62 A hornbook . . . was shaped something like a battledore. . . . To be able to say B when B was pointed to in the hornbook, was called 'to say B to a battledore'.

Say before they say.

1857 BOHN *Pol. For. Prov.* 517 . . . (Tell your own story first.)

Say *bo* to a battledore, He cannot.

1621 BP. MONTAGU *Diatribæ* 118 Some . . . will . . . conclude, that the Clergy of this time were blind Bayards, and not able to say bo to a battledore.

Say *bo* to a goose, He cannot.

1588 *Marprel. Ep.* (Arb.) 43 He is not able to say bo to a goose. **1603** T. HEYWOOD *Wom. K. Kindness* III. ii Unless it be Nick and I, there's not one amongst them all can say bo to a goose. **1748** SMOLLETT *Rod. Rand.* liv I could not say Bo to a goose. **1866** BLACKMORE *Cradock N.* xxx (1883) 166 Bob could never say 'bo' to a gosling of the feminine gender.

Say little (nothing), I | but I think the more.

1546 HEYWOOD II. ii. 47 I say little (said she) but I thinke more. **1599** PORTER *Angry Wom. Abingd.* IV. iii (Mermaid) 176 Well, I say little, but I think the more. **1721** KELLY 182 *I will say nothing, but I will yerk[1] at the thinking* . . . I will at present conceal my resentments; but I will watch an opportunity for retaliation. **1738** SWIFT (Dial. i) 336 *Never.* Miss says nothing; but I warrant she pays it off with thinking. **1861** G. J. WHYTE-MELVILLE *Market Harb.* xviii Cissy . . . said nothing; perhaps she thought the more. [[1] be busy.]

Say 'Nay', *see* Learned timely to steal that could not say 'Nay'.

Say 'No', *see* Always say 'No' (If you), you'll never be married.

Say no ill of the year till it be past.

1640 HERBERT 331. **1732** FULLER no. 4071.

Say no more till the day be longer, I Will.

1562 HEYWOOD *Three Hundred Epigr.* no. 168. **1616** DRAXE 148.

Say 'No' till you are asked, Don't.

1738 SWIFT (Dial. i) 337 *Miss.* Pray, don't say no, till you are asked.

Say nothing, Better | than not to the purpose.

30 April **1605** J. CHAMBERLAIN *Letters* (McLure) i. 205 As goode say nothing as to no purpose. **1732** FULLER no. 921.

Say nothing when you are dead.

1813 RAY 67 Say nothing when you are dead, *i.e.* Be silent.

Say to pleasure, *Gentle Eve*, I will none of your apple.

1651 HERBERT 370.

Say true, You | will you swallow my knife?

1678 RAY 255.

Say well, and do well, end with one letter; say well is good, but do well is better.

1536 *Remedy for Sedition* (cited Elyot's *Governor*, ed. Croft, ii. 41) Men say wel that do wel. **1639** CLARKE 194. **1732** FULLER no. 6447.

Say well or be still.

c. **1480** *Early Miscell.* (Warton Cl., 1855) 63 (A) Ewyre say wylle, or hold the[e] styll. a. **1529** SKELTON *Agst. Comely Coyst.* 64 Wks. (1843) I. 17 A prouerbe of old, say well or be styll.

Saying and doing are two things. (*See also* Saying is one thing.)

1550 HEYWOOD II. v. 60 But it is as folke dooe, and not as folke saie. For they saie, saiyng and dooyng are two thingis.

Saying goes good cheap.

1641 FERGUSSON 88.

Saying, Honey, Honey, It is not with | that sweetness will come into the mouth.

1853 TRENCH v. 114 They courageously accept the law of labour . . . This is Turkish: *It is not with saying, Honey, Honey, that sweetness comes into the mouth.*

Saying is one thing, and doing another. (*See also* Saying and doing.)

1603 FLORIO tr. *Montaigne* II. xxxi (1897) IV. 264 *Saying is one thing and doing another.* A man must consider the sermon apart and

the preacher several. **1620** SHELTON *Quix.*
II. lxiv (1908) III. 275 'You do prettily
facilitate the matter', said Sancho; 'but 'tis
one thing to say and another to do.' **1812**
H. & J. SMITH *Rej. Addr., Drury L. Hust.* 'Tis
just like the hustings, We kick up a bother,
But saying is one thing and doing 's another.

Says anything but his prayers, He | and those he whistles.

1732 FULLER no. 2014. **1738** SWIFT (Dial. i)
335 Miss will say anything but her prayers,
and those she whistles. **1802** WOLCOT (P.
Pindar) *Middl. Elect.* iii Zay ev'ry thing
bezides their pray'rs, And those, agosh! they
whistle.

Says his garner is full, None.

1640 HERBERT 348.

Says nothing, Though he | he pays it with thinking, like the Welsh-man's jackdaw.

1855 BOHN 60.

Says what he likes, He who | shall hear what he does not like.

[TERENCE *Qui pergit ea quae vult dicere, ea
quae non vult audiet.*] **1539** TAVERNER 2 He
that speaketh what he woll, shall heare what
he woll not. Let men beware how they rail.
1588 GREENE *Pandosto* Wks. (1881–3) IV. 293
Peace husband . . . : speake no more than
you should, least you heare what you would
not. **1853** TRENCH iv. 86 *Who says what he
likes, shall hear what he does not like,* gives a
further motive for self-government in speech.

Say(s), saith, said, *see also* Crow is white
(To s.); Easier s. than done; Goodman s.
so s. we (As the); Ill s. that was not
ill taken (Never); Learn to s. before you
sing; Little (Least, Nothing) s. soon
amended; Love best (Whom we), to
them can s. least; Many a one s. well
that thinks ill; No sooner s. than done;
See all, s. nought; See much (I) but I s.
little; Sell the cow (Who will) must s. the
word; So s. so done; Sport is to do deed
and s. nothing; 'They s. so' is half a lie;
They s. — What s. they; Though I s. it that
should not.

Scab in the end, It will prove a.

1639 CLARKE 109.

Scabbard, *see* Blade wears out s.; Draweth
sword against prince (Who), must throw
away s.

Scabbed horse cannot abide the comb, *see*
Rub a galled horse, &c. (1640 quotn.).

Scabbed sheep, One | will mar a whole flock.

[JUVENAL *Sat. 2. 79 Grex totus in agris
Unius scabie cadit.* The entire flock dies in
the field of the disease introduced by one.]
c. **1350** *Douce MS. 52,* no. 87 Oon scabbyd

shepe makyth a fowle flock. **1520** WHITTING-
TON *Vulg.* (E.E.T.S.) 116 One scabbed shepe
(as they say) marreth a hole flocke. *a.* **1530**
R. Hill's Commonpl. Bk. (E.E.T.S.) 129 One
skabbid shepe infectith all the folde. **1611**
DAVIES Prov. 68. **1616** BRETON *Cross.
Prov.* Wks. (1879) II. App. iii One rotten
sheep will mar a whole flock. **1629** T. ADAMS
Serm. (1861–2) I. 76 They report, that once
one scabbed sheep from Spain rotted all the
sheep of England. In this manner is this
poison of adultery spread from a harlot. **1715**
ISAAC WATTS *Divine Songs* (1728) xxi. 30
From one rude Boy that's us'd to mock,
Ten learn the wicked Jest; One sickly Sheep
infects the Flock, And poysons all the rest.

Scabby heads love not the comb.

1623 WODROEPHE 516 A scabbed Head doth
never loue the Combe. **1732** FULLER no. 4072.
1796 WOLCOT (P. Pindar) *Orson & Ellen* Wks.
(1816) IV. 83 But George disliketh much to
hear About his Scottish home; Thus *scabby
heads*, the proverb says, For ever hate a *comb*.

Scald[1] head is soon broken, A.

c. **1350** *Douce MS. 52* no. 47 A scald mannys
hede is lefe to breke. *c.* **1470** *Harl. MS.
3362,* f. 1a Frangitur exfacile caput infantis
glabriosi—A scallyd mannys hed ys good to be
broke. **1546** HEYWOOD II. iii. 49 But a scalde
head is soone broken, and so they, As ye shall
streight here, fell at a new frey. **1721** KELLY
11 *A scal'd head is eith[2] to bleed.* A thing that
was but tender before, will easily be put out
of order. [[1] scabby. [2] easy.]

Scald[1] horse is good enough for a scabbed squire, A.

1540 *Acolastus* M 2[v] For such a scalde squier
as he is, a scabbed horse. **1546** HEYWOOD
I. xi. 33 But hakney men saie, at mangy
hackneis hyer, A scald hors is good inough
for a scabde squyer. **1611** DAVIES Prov.
169 A scald horse is good enough for a
scab'd squire; But not if that scabb pays well
for the hire. [[1] scabby.]

Scald not your lips in another man's pottage.

1598 *Servingmans Comfort* in *Inedited Tracts*
(Hazlitt) 99 (A) It is not good to scalde ones
lyppes in other mens pottage. **1629** T. ADAMS
Serm. (1861–2) III. 502 He busieth himself
in other men's commonwealths: . . . he scalds
his lips in every neighbour's pottage. **1670**
RAY 56. **1766** *Goody Two-Shoes* [3 ed.] v. i
Don't burn your lips with another man's
broth. **1823** GALT *Entail* III. xxiv If ye'll tak
my advice, ye'll no sca'd your lips in other
folks' kail.

Scalded cat (dog) fears cold water, A.

1611 COTGRAVE s.v. 'Chien' The scaulded
dog feares euen colde water. Id. s.v. 'Chat'.
1670 RAY 140. **1796** EDGEWORTH *Par. Asst.*
(1903) 381 As my father said to you once—
the scalded dog fears cold water. [Fr. *Chat
échaudé craint l'eau froide.*]

Scandal, *see* Everything in turn except s.

Scanderbeg's[1] sword must have Scanderbeg's arm.

1655–62 GURNALL *Chrn. in Armour* (1865) II. 239 Not another arm could use this sword to have done thus much with it, besides the Spirit of God. . . . None could do such feats with Scanderbeg's sword as himself. **1732** FULLER no. 4077. **1779–81** JOHNSON *Lives of Poets* (Bohn) II. 212 [Congreve] . . . has the sword without the arm of Scanderbeg; he has his antagonist's coarseness, but not his strength. [[1] George Castriota, the Albanian hero, 1403–68.]

Scant of bairns that brought you up, They were.

1721 KELLY 321 . . . Spoken to ill thriven, or ill mannered children.

Scant (Scarce) of news that told his father was hanged, He was.

1707 MAPLETOFT 119. **1721** KELLY 136 . . . Spoken to them that say something that may tend to the disparagement of themselves, or family. **1732** FULLER no. 2378. **1852** E. FITZ-GERALD *Polonius* 35 Cobbett used to say that people never should sit talking till they didn't know what to talk about. *He was scant o' news wha tauld his father was hanged.*

Scar(s), *see* Wars bring s.

Scarborough warning.

[= very short notice, or no notice at all; a surprise.] **1546** HEYWOOD I. xi. 35 A daie er I was wedde, I bad you (quoth I) Scarbrough warnyng I had (quoth he) wherby, I kept me thens. **1573** TUSSER X (1878) 22 Or Skarborow warning, as ill I beleeue, when (sir I arest yee) gets hold of thy sleeue. **1582** STANYHURST *Aen.* 3 (Arb.) 81 Hym by his syers altars killing with skarboro warning [*incautum*]. **1603** BP. T. MATTHEW *Let.* 19 Jan. in CARDWELL *Confer.* (1840) 166 I received a message . . . that it was his Majesty's pleasure that I should preach before him upon Sunday next; which Scarborough warning did not only perplex me, but [&c.]. **1832** SCOTT *Redg.* xix The true man for giving Scarborough warning—first knock you down, then bid you stand.

Scarce of horseflesh, They are | where two and two ride on a dog.

1678 RAY 157.

Scarce, *see also* Scant (S.) of news.

Scarlet fever.

[= the attraction of a soldier's red coat.] **1846** J. GRANT *Rom. of War.* xxxiv Louis . . . appeared . . . in the uniform of the Gordon Highlanders; and . . . all the young ladies were quite in love with him, fairly touched with the scarlet fever. **1876** MRS. BANKS *Manch. Man* IV Glory's scarlet fever was as rife an epidemic in Manchester as elsewhere. The town bristled with bayonets.

Scathe, *see* Neighbour's s. is my peril; One doth the **s.**, another hath scorn; Scorn comes with **s.**

Scatter her mice, To.

1869 HAZLITT 446 . . . Said of a woman who has had a baby, and goes about to see her friends. There is a supposed liability to catch the same complaint.

Scatter with one hand, gather with two.

1659 HOWELL *Brit. Prov.* 2.

Sceptre is one thing, A | and a ladle another.

1573 SANDFORD N 5[v] The common prouerbe: *Aliud est sceptrum, aliud plectrum*: that is, the scepter is one thing, and the harp is an other. **1640** HERBERT 343.

Scholar as my horse Ball, As good a.

1639 CLARKE 145.

Scholar may waur[1] the master, The.

1721 KELLY 310 The scholar may war the teacher by a time. L. *Meliorem præsto magistro discipulum.*[2] [[1] be better than. [2] Juvenal.]

Scholar, *see also* Diligent s., the master's paid; Mere s. mere ass; Robs a s. robs twenty.

School, *see* Good will (With as) as e'er boy came from s.

Schoolboys are the reasonablest people in the world; they care not how little they have for their money.

1678 RAY 81.

Schooling, *see* Pay more for s. than learning is worth.

Schoolmaster is abroad, The.

1828 LD. BROUGHAM *Speech* 29 Jan. The schoolmaster is abroad! and I trust more to the schoolmaster . . . than to the soldier. **1841** MARRYAT *Poacher* xxxiii That is very polite for a mender of old kettles; but the schoolmaster is abroad, which, I presume, accounts for such strange anomalies.

Schools make subtle clerks, Sundry.

c. **1386** CHAUCER *Mercht's T.* E[2] 1427 For sondry scolès maken sotile clerkis.

Science, *see* Much s. much sorrow.

Scoggin[1] is a doctor, Among the common people.

1616 WITHALS 559. **1639** CLARKE 143. [[1] a jester, *temp.* Edw. IV.]

Scold, Who hath a | hath sorrow to his sops.

1659 HOWELL *Eng. Prov.* 15/1. **1732** FULLER no. 5705.

Scold like a wych-waller, To.

1670 RAY 208 . . . *Chesh.* That is, a boiler of salt; wych houses are salt houses, and walling is boiling. **1917** BRIDGE 142 . . . Women were formerly exclusively employed in this operation, hence the 'scolding.'

Scold, *see also* Call her neighbour s. (Who more ready to).

Scolding wife, *see* Three things drive out of house, . . . s. w.

Scolds and infants never lin[1] bawling.

1616 BRETON *Cross. Prov. Wks.* (1879) II. App. iii. [[1] cease.]

Scone of a baking is enough, One.

1721 KELLY 273 . . . It is unreasonable to expect two gratuities out of one thing.

Score twice before you cut once.

1688 R. HOLME *Acad. of Armory* III. vi. 292 The point on the back of the Shoomakers pareing knife is to Score, or Trace out the Leather before he venture to cut it, according to the saying, *Score twice before you Cut once.* **1917** BRIDGE 107 . . . Don't cut your leather until you feel sure that you have selected the right place, Used by the shoemakers of Chester.

Scorn a thing as a dog scorns tripe, To.

1670 RAY 207.

Scorn at first makes after-love the more.

1594–5 SHAKS. *Two Gent.* III. i. 95 For scorn at first makes after-love the more. **1855** BOHN 482.

Scorn comes commonly with scathe.

a. **1585** MONTGOMERIE *Cherrie & Slae* xvi (1821) 11 As skorne cummis commonlie with skaith, Sa I behufit to bide them baith. **1721** KELLY 288 . . . Spoken when one gets a hurt, and another laughs at it.

Scorn with (at) the heels, To.

c. **1599** SHAKS. *Much Ado* III. iv. 50 I scorn that with my heels. **1611** HEYWOOD *Golden Age* To scorn acorns with their heels. **1612** FIELD *Woman a Weathercock* IV. ii He contemns you, he scorns you at his heels. **1827** SCOTT *Journ.* 10 Apr. Some incivility from Leith Bank, which I despise with my heels.

Scorn, *see also* One doth the scathe another hath s.

Scornful dogs will eat dirty puddings. (See also Hungry dogs, &c.).

1709 MANDEVILLE *Virgin Unmask'd* (1724) 32 (A) Dirty puddings for dirty dogs. **1738** SWIFT (Dial. i) 335 *Miss.* I scorn your words. *Never.* Well, but scornful dogs will eat dirty

puddings. **1816** SCOTT *Antiq.* xliii The messenger (one of those dogs who are not too scornful to eat dirty puddings) caught in his hand the guinea which Hector chucked at his face.

Scorning, *see* Mocking (S.) is catching.

Scorpion under every stone, There is a.

[SOPH. *Frag.* 35 Ἐν παντὶ γάρ τοι σκορπίος φρουρεῖ λίθῳ. Under every stone a scorpion lies hid. ERASM. *Ad. Sub omni lapide scorpius dormit.* Under every stone a scorpion sleeps.] *c.* **1522** ERASMUS *Let.* Pope Adrian VI in FROUDE *Council Trent* (1896) iii. 66 Then there was only approval and encouragement, where now there is a scorpion under every stone. People seem as if they wished to drive me into rebellion.

Scorpion(s), *see also* Chastise with s.; Rock S.

Scot (*proper name*), *see* Killed her for good will, said S.

Scot, A | a rat, and a Newcastle grindstone travel all the world over.

1662 FULLER (*Northumb.*) II. 543 'A Scottish man and a Newcastle grindstone, travel all the world over.' The Scots (gentry especially), . . . travel into foreign parts, most for maintenance, many for accomplishment. . . . No grindstone so good as those of Newcastle. **1821** A. CUNNINGHAM in LOCKHART *Scott* lii (1860) 457 [Mr. Bolton] said, That's like the old saying,—in every quarter of the world you will find a Scot, a rat, and a Newcastle grindstone'.

Scot and lot, *see* Pay s. and l.

Scot will not fight till he sees his own blood, The.

1822 SCOTT *Nigel* i 'The Scot will not fight till he sees his own blood', said Tunstall, whom his north of England extraction had made familiar with all manner of proverbs against those who lay yet farther north than himself.

Scotch ordinary, The.

1678 RAY 81 The *Scotch* ordinary. *i.e.* The house of office.

Scot-free, To go.

[= free from payment of 'scot', tavern score, fine, &c., *fig.* exempt from injury, punishment; &c.] **1531** TINDALE *Expos. 1 John* (1537) 22 The poore synner shulde go Skot fre without oughte at all. **1546** *St. Papers Hen. VIII* XI. 129 What damages their cuntrey and people had suffred by this warre, and that Your Majestie went not all scott free. *a.* **1548** HALL *Chron. Edw. IV* 233 They payed no money, but were set scot free. **1740** RICHARDSON *Pamela* (1824) I. 117 She should not, for all the trouble she has cost you, go away scot-free. **1877** BLACK *Green Past.* xiii When some notorious offender has got off scot free.

Scotland, *see* France win (He that will) must with S. begin.

Scotsmen aye reckon frae an ill hour.

1832 HENDERSON 87.

Scotsmen take their mark from a mischief.

1721 KELLY 292 . . . Spoken when we say such a thing fell out, when such an ill accident came to pass. A Scottish man solicited the Prince of Orange to be made an Ensign, for he had been a sergeant ever since his Highness run away from Groll.

Scot(s), Scotchman, Scottishman, *see also* Biting and scratching is S. wooing; Englishman is never happy . . . S. never at home; Englishman weeps . . . S. gangs while he gets it; False as a S.; Hard-hearted as a S.; Lose a S. (We will not).

Scottish mist will wet an Englishman to the skin, A.

1589 [? LYLY] *Pappe w. Hatchet* Ded., Wks. (1902) III. 394 We care not for a Scottish mist, though it wet us to the skin. 1662 FULLER (*Northumb.*) II. 543 'A Scottish mist may wet an Englishman to the skin' . . . Mists . . . have their fountain north, but fall short of Tweed. 1721 KELLY 18 . . . I never knew the meaning of this . . . unless it be, that a Scottish man will bear more foul weather than an English.

Scouring, *see* Escape a s.

Scrambling at a rich man's dole, It is brave.

1639 CLARKE 39. 1732 FULLER no. 5069.

Scrape, *see* Comes of a hen (He that) must s.

Scratch (*proper name*), *see* Old S.

Scratch, To come (bring) up to the.

[= the line drawn across the ring, to which boxers are brought for an encounter; often used fig.] 1821 *John Bull* 7 Jan. 29/3 He started a few seconds before the time and came up . . . to the scratch at the moment appointed. 1824 SCOTT *St. Ronan's* xii A dogged look of obstinacy, expressive, to use his own phrase, of a determined resolution to come up to the scratch. 1905 SIR G. O. TREVELYAN *Interludes* 155 When once natives have given way, it is almost impossible to bring them again to the scratch.

Scratch a beggar one day before you die, You will.

1639 CLARKE 209 You'l scratch a beggar one day before you die. 1910 P. W. JOYCE *Eng. as We Speak* 194 Tom Hogan is managing his farm in a way likely to bring him to poverty. . . . 'Tom, you'll scratch a beggarman's back yet': meaning that Tom will himself be the beggarman.

Scratch a Moore and your own blood will flow.

1913 *Times Lit. Sup.* 15 Aug. 336 George Moore . . . was . . . of impetuous temper, which vented itself in fierce and unguarded words, if not deeds. 'Scratch a Moore and your own blood will flow' is a proverb in Mayo.

Scratch a Russian and you'll find a Tartar.

1876 BURNABY *Ride to Khiva* ix Grattez le Russe et vous trouverez le Tartare. . . . It requires but little rubbing to disclose the Tartar blood so freely circulated through the Muscovite veins. 1888 MRS. OLIPHANT *Second Son* xiv I don't put any faith in Russians. . . . 'Scratch a Russian and you'll come to the Tartar.' 1911 *Spectator* 2 Dec. 964 Until a short time ago the aphorism, 'Scratch a Russian and you find a Tartar', was the sum of British comprehension of the Russian character.

Scratch me (my back) and I'll scratch you (yours).

[DIOGENIANUS τὸν ξύοντα δ᾽ ἀντιξύειν.] 1868 W. COLLINS *Moonstone* viii We are all getting liberal now; and (provided you can scratch me if I scratch you) what do I care . . . whether you are a Dustman or a Duke? 1929 *Times* 8 Aug. 9/1 Its members bargain among themselves to support the pet schemes of each on the principle of 'you scratch my back and I'll scratch yours'.

Scratch my back and I'll scratch your face.

1887 *Cornhill Mag.*, Nov. in LEAN I. 66 If you scratch my back, I'll scratch your face. Said by 'The Demon of Dartmoor[1]' to speculators who have attempted to reclaim the moor and come to grief. [[1] Devon.]

Scratch my breech and I'll claw your elbow.

1611 COTGRAVE s.v. Contrelouĕr' To scratch the backe of one who hath alreadie clawed his elbow. 1616 WITHALS 564. 1670 RAY 140 . . . *Mutuum muli scabunt*. Ka me and I'll ka thee. When undeserving persons commend one another.

Scratch (Claw) where it itches not, I.

1514 A. BARCLAY *Egloges* (E.E.T.S.) 143 But Codrus I clawe oft where it doth not itche. 1546 HEYWOOD II. vii. 70 Thou makest me claw where it itcheth not. 1589 PUTTENHAM *Eng. Poesie* III. xxiii (Arb.) 279 The French King . . . said somewhat sharply, I pray thee good fellow clawe me not where I itch not with thy sacred maiestie. 1636 CAMDEN 299. 1678 RAY 296 It would make a man scratch where it doth not itch, To see a man live poor to die rich, *Est furor haud dubius simul et manifesta phrenesis, ut locuples moriaris egenti vivere fato.*—Juvenal [14. 136].

Scratches his head with one finger, He.

1542 UDALL tr. *Erasm. Apoph.* (1877) 360 *Uno digito caput scalpere.* 1855 BOHN 381.

Scratch(ed), *see also* Rub (S.) the elbow; Truth has a s. face.

Scratching and biting, By | cats and dogs come together.

1546 HEYWOOD II. i. 45. **1623** CAMDEN 267.

Scratching, *see also* Eating and s. wants but beginning.

Screw loose somewhere, There is a.

[= something wrong in the condition of things; a dangerous weakness in some arrangement.] **1810** *Sporting Mag.* XXXVI. 166 The others . . . had got a screw loose. **1833** E. FITZGERALD *Lett.* (1889) I. 21 In fact, a genius with a screw loose, as we used to say. **1837** DICKENS *Pickwick* xlix Something dark and mysterious was going forward, or, as he always said himself, 'there was a screw loose somewhere'.

Scripture, *see* Devil can cite S.

Scruffel, *see* Skiddaw.

Scylla and Charybdis, Between.

[A monster on a rock, and a whirlpool, on opposite sides of the Straits of Messina; HOMER *Od.* xii. *c.* 1180 *Walter of Lille* v. 301 Incidis in Scyllam cupiens vitare Charybdin.] **1576** PETTIE *Petite Pall.* (Gollancz) II. 89 But running from Charybdis he rushed upon Scilla. **1579** GOSSON *Sch. Abuse* (Arb.) 61 Lest that laboring to shun Sylla you light on Charibdis. **1579** LYLY *Euphues* Wks. (Bond) I. 189 Thou arte heere amiddest the pykes betweene Scilla and Caribdis. **1596–7** SHAKS. *Merch. V.* III. v. 17 When I shun Scylla, your father, I fall into Charybdis, your mother. **1662** FULLER (*Carnarvon*) iii. 527 That pilot is to be pitied, who, to shun Scylla, doth run on Charibdis. **1824** SCOTT *St. Ronan's* xxviii The Nabob made a considerable circuit to avoid . . . this filthy puddle . . . and by that means fell upon Scylla as he sought to avoid Charybdis . . . and fell into the channel of the streamlet. **1896** M. A. S. HUME *Courtships of Q. Eliz.* 226 [Elizabeth] said, My lord, here I am between Scylla and Charybdis.

Scythe cuts and the plough rives, Where the | no more fairies and bee-bikes.[1]

1846 DENHAM 17. [[1] bees' nests.]

Scythe, *see also* Marries between the sickle and the s. (Who).

Sea and the gallows refuse none, The.

1614 T. GENTLEMAN *England's Way to Win Wealth* (*Social England* ed. Lang 271) The sailor's proverb, The sea and the gallows refuse none. **1703** NED WARD *Trip to New Eng.* Wks. II. 141 A man on Board cannot but be thoughtful on two Destinies, *viz.* Hanging and Drowning. . . . It often put me in mind of the old Proverb, *The Sea and the Gallows* refuses none. **1866** BROGDEN *Lincolnsh. Words* 79 There is an old adage, that 'The Kirk-garth, like the gallows and the sea, receives all without asking questions'.

Sea complains it wanteth water, The.

1639 CLARKE 6. **1732** FULLER no. 4740 The sea complains for want of water.

Sea has fish for every man, The.

1576 PETTIE *Petite Pall.* (Gollancz) I. 33. **1636** CAMDEN 308.

Sea refuses no river, The.

1605 *London Prodigal* I. i (*Shaks. Apoc.*) 193 *Vnck.* Brother, he is one that will borrow of any man. *Fath.* Why, you see, so doth the sea: it borrowes of all the smal currents in the world, to encrease himselfe. **1732** FULLER no. 4741.

Sea, Being on | sail; being on land, settle.

1640 HERBERT 337.

Sea, *see* Calm s. (In) every man a pilot; Complains wrongfully on the s.; Fish in the s. (As good) (*or* The s. hath fish for every man); Forecasts all perils (He that) will never sail s.; Goes a great voyage to the bottom of s.; Great way to the bottom of the s.; Learn to pray, go to s.; Mist comes from the . . . s. (When); Praise the s. but keep on land; Save a stranger from the s. and he'll . . .; Sell a farm and go to s.; Send him to the s., he will not get water; Three things are insatiable; Three ways, the Church, s., court; Travelleth not by s. knows not fear of God.

Seal(ed), *see* Sure as if s. with butter.

Seaman, A | if he carries a millstone, will have a quail out of it.

1670 RAY 218 . . . *Spoken of the common mariners, if they can come at things that may be eat or drunk.*

Season(s), *see* Constancy of the benefit in s. argues Deity; Everything is good in s.; Out of s. out of price.

Seasonable as snow in summer, As.

c. **1568** WAGER *Longer thou livest* F 3(A) As snow in harvest is untimely. **1670** RAY 202.

Seasonably, *see* Little given s. excuses great gift.

Second side of the bread takes less time to toast, The.

1887 BLACKMORE *Springhaven* xviii 'The second side of the bread takes less time to toast'. We must not let the first side of ours be toasted; we will shun all the fire of suspicion.

Second thoughts are best.

[EUR. *Hipp.* 436 Ἀι δεύτεραί πως φροντίδες σοφώτεραι. ERASM. *Ad. Posterioribus melioribus.*] **1586** PETTIE *Guazzo's Civ. Conv.* 23 Wherby I finde verified the Prouerbe, That the second thoughts are euer the best. **1738** swift (Dial. ii) 346 *Smart*. What do you say to my wine? *Sir J*. I'll take another glass first: second thoughts are best. **1821** SCOTT *Pirate* iv Second thoughts are best; . . . take any port in a storm. **1852** E. FITZGERALD *Polonius* 13 'Second thoughts are best'. 'No', says the Guesser at Truth, 'First thoughts are . . . those of generous impulse'.

Second word makes the bargain, The. (*Cf.* Two (words) to make bargain.)

1597 BACON *Col. of G. & E*. 10 (Arb.) 154 In such cases the second degree seemes the worthyest, as . . . *The second word makes the bargaine.*

Second, *see also* First blow makes wrong, s. makes fray; Shoot a s. arrow to find first.

Secret foe gives a sudden blow, A.

1721 KELLY 50. **1736** BAILEY *Dict.* s.v. 'Foe'.

Secret is thy prisoner; Thy | if thou let it go, thou art a prisoner to it.

1678 RAY *Adag. Hebr.* 408 . . . We ought to be as careful in keeping a secret as an officer in keeping his prisoner, who makes himself a prisoner by letting his prisoner go.

Secret, Wherever there is a | there must be something wrong.

1696 ROGER NORTH *Lives* (Bohn) iii. 233 Secrecy is never without guile. **1837** LOCKHART *Life of Scott* ii. 42 (A) (cited as 'an old saying').

Secret, *see also* Tells a s. (He that) is another's servant.

Secrets, If you would know | look for them in grief or pleasure.

1640 HERBERT 334. **1670** RAY 23.

Secundum usum Sarum, It is done.

1589 [? LYLY] *Pappe w. Hatchet* Wks. (1902) III. 400 For the winter nights the tales shall be told *secundum usum Sarum*. **1662** FULLER (*Wilts.*) III. 319 'It is done *secundum usum Sarum*. . . . Many offices or forms of service were used . . . in England . . . until Osmond bishop of Sarum,[1] about the year . . . 1090, made that . . . office, which was generally received all over England. . . . It is now applied to . . . patterns of unquestionable authority. [1 1½ m. from Salisbury, the present seat of the bishopric.]

Secure is not safe, He that is too.

1732 FULLER no. 2195. **1748** FRANKLIN *Aug.* He that's secure is not safe.

Security, *see* Actions are our s. (Our own); Advice to all, s. for none.

Sedan, *see* Going to heaven in a s. (No).

See a churchman ill, Though you | yet continue in the church still.

1640 HERBERT 350.

See a woman weep (greet), It is no more pity to | than to see a goose go bare foot.

c. **1275** *Prov. of Alfred* (Skeat) 31 Wummen wepeð for mod Ofter þanne for eni good. *c.* **1548** BALE *K. Johan* 173–5 *Sed.* Yt is as great pyte to se, a woman wepe As yt is to se a sely dodman[1] crepe, Or, as ye wold say, a sely goose go barefote. **1621** BURTON *Anat. Mel.* III. ii. III. iv. (1651) 498 And as much pitty is to be taken of a woman weeping, as of a goose going barefooted. **1641** FERGUSSON 64 It is na mair pittie to see a woman greit, nor to see a goose go bair fit. **1857** DEAN RAMSAY *Remin.* v (1911) 197 . . . A . . . reference to the facility with which the softer sex can avail themselves of tears to carry a point. [1 snail.]

See all, say nought, hold thee content.

1578 M. EDWARDES *Parad. D. Deuises* (reprint) 134 Wherefore in all as men are bent, Se all, saie nought, holde thee content.

See, and approve, the better course; I | [but] I follow the worse.

[OVID *Metamorph.* 7. 20 *Video meliora proboque; Deteriora sequor*.] **1592** DANIEL *Complaint of Rosamond*, ll. 433–4 We see what's good, and therto we consent, But yet we choose the worst, and soone repent. **1616** T. ADAMS *Gallant's Burden* 33. **1751** FIELDING *Amelia* VIII. X. **1827** HARE *Gues. at Truth* (1859) i. 139 The mind, when allowed its full and free play, prefers moral good, however faintly, to moral evil. Hence the old confession, *Video meliora, proboque*: and hence are we so much better judges in another's case than our own.

See, To | and to be seen.

[OVID *A.A.* 1. 99 *Spectatum veniunt, veniunt spectentur ut ipsae*.] *c.* **1387** CHAUCER *W. of Bath Prol.* 552 And for to see and eek for to be seye. **1609** JONSON *Epithal.* (1633) 20 And they came all to see and to be seen. **1828** SCOTT *Journ.* 3 May After the dinner I went to Mrs. Scott of Harden, to see and be seen by her nieces. *a.* **1911** GILBERT *Lost Bab Ballads* 31 To see and be seen is for what we pay At Islington on the half-crown day.

See day at a little hole, One may.

1546 HEYWOOD I. x. 21 I sée daie at this little hole. For this blood Shewth what fruite will folow. **1590** LODGE *Rosalynde* Wks. (1883) I. 68 Aliena (that spied where the hare was by the hounds, and could see day at a little hole), thought to be pleasant with her Ganimede. **1594–5** SHAKS. *L.L.L.* V. ii. 732 I have seen the day of wrong through the little hole of discretion. **1623** CAMDEN 275.

See divine light, The way to | is to put out thine own candle.

1855 BOHN 518.

See for your love (and) buy for your money.

1639 CLARKE 79. **1721** KELLY 299 *See for love,*

and buy for money. A cant among pedlars and hucksters.

See him need, I may | but I'll not see him bleed.

1670 RAY 187 . . . Parents will usually say this of prodigal or undutiful children; meaning, I will be content to see them suffer a little hardship, but not any great calamity.

See his (your) nose cheese first, I will.

1721 KELLY 224 *I would sooner see your nose cheese, and my self the first bite.* A disdainful rejecting of an unworthy proposal. **1738** SWIFT (Dial. ii) 343 *Miss.* I'll see your nose cheese first and the dogs eating it. **1816** SCOTT *Let.* 29 Apr. in LOCKHART *Life* xxxvii (1860) 334 He proposes they shall have the copyright *for ever.* I will see their noses cheese first.

See me, and see me not.

1546 HEYWOOD II. v. 57 If he plaie falsehed in felowship, plaie yée, Sée me, and sée me not . to woorst part to flée.

See much, I | but I say little and do less.

a. **1451** LYDGATE cited E. K. CHAMBERS *Close of the Middle Ages* 116 See myche, say lytell, & lerne to suffer in tyme. **1546** HEYWOOD I. xi. 34.

See Naples and then die.

1882 G. A. SALA *America Rev.* 284 'See Naples and then die', says the proverb. My view . . . is that you should see Canal-street, New Orleans, and then try to live as much longer as ever you can. **1890** MRS. OLIPHANT *Kirsteen* viii This was the Highland girl's devout belief; *Vedi Napoli e poi morire;*[1] earth could not have anything to show more fair. [[1] *Vedi Napoli e poi muori.*]

See no good near home, Some people can.

1902–4 LEAN IV. 97.

See not what is in the wallet behind, We.

1602 *The Jesuit's Catechism* ¶ ¶ 1ᵛ You see not that part of the wallet that hangs at your owne backes. **1732** FULLER no. 5453.

See not what sits on our shoulder, We.

1616 WITHALS 569. **1639** CLARKE 52.

See, Marry, that would I | quoth blind Hugh.

1533 J. HEYWOOD *Pardoner & Friar* in HAZLITT *O.E.P.* (1874) I. 232 *Friar.* I'sh knock thee on the costard, I would thou it knew—*Pard.* 'Marry that I would see, quod blind Hew.' **1738** SWIFT (Dial. i) 336 *Never.* O! 'tis the prettiest thing. . . . *Miss.* Would I could see it, quoth blind Hugh.

See the city for the houses, You cannot.

1597–8 BP. HALL *Satires* IV. i That *Lyncius*[1]

may be match't with *Gaulard's* sight. That sees not *Paris* for the houses' height. **1877** ABP. TRENCH *Med. Ch. Hist.* i The countryman . . . having gone for the first time to see some famous city, complained on his return home that he could not see the city for the houses. [[1] Lynceus, one of the Argonauts, famed for his sight.]

See the gowk[1] in your sleep, You will.

1846 JAMIESON *Scot. Dict.* 298 To SEE THE GOWK in one's sleep. . . . A proverbial phrase denoting a change of mind. [[1] cuckoo.]

See the wood for trees, You cannot.

1546 HEYWOOD II. iv. 51. **1612–15** BP. HALL *Contempl.* IV. xii (1825) II. 389 Let me not seem . . . an abettor of those Alcoran-like fables of our Popish doctors, who, not seeing the wood for trees, do *hærere in cortice;* 'stick in the bark'. **1738** SWIFT (Dial. i) 333 *Spark.* Tom, how is it that you can't see the wood for trees. **1912** *Spectator* 27 Jul. 121 We never get from it the sweep of narrative and the view as from a high place which we get from the greater historians. Once again, it is a case of the trees obscuring the wood.

See thy neck as long as my arm, I will first.

1678 RAY 261.

See what we must all come to, if we live, You.

1678 RAY 65.

See what we shall see, We shall.

1895 J. PAYN *In Market Overt* xiv 'Well, we shall see what we shall see, when Miss Bryce comes in for her own', said Avis doggedly.

See which leg you are lame of, I now.

1586 D. ROULAND *Lazarillo* (1924) 40 (A) As for me, when I perceiued upon which foot hee halted, I made hast to eat. **1732** FULLER no. 2623.

See with one's own eyes, To.

1707 J. STEVENS tr. *Quevedo's Com. Wks.* (1709) 350 I have seen it with my own Eyes. **1776** *Trial of Nuncomar* 24/2 I have seen him . . . with my own eyes take off his seal.

See you in daylight, They that | winna break the house for you at night. (*Cf.* Sees thee by day, &c.)

1832 HENDERSON 93 . . . (Spoken to ugly women.)

See your friend, Whensoever you | trust to yourself.

1616 BRETON *Cross Prov.* II. Wks. (1879) II. App. iii.

See(s), *see also* Bound to s. (One is not); Fain s. (That would I), said blind George; God will have s. (That) shall not wink; Let me s., as blind man said; Live longest will s. most; Lives well (He that) s. afar.

See, *see also under significant words following.*

Seed, *see* Every thing hath its s.; Evil grain (Of) no good s.; Soweth good **s.** shall reap good corn.

Seeding, *see* One year's s. makes seven years' weeding.

Seeing is believing.

1619 J. FAVOUR *Antiquity* 419 *Seeing is no leeving* with these men, they will take no witnesse of their owne eyes. **1639** CLARKE 90. **1678** RAY 200 . . . Chi con l'occhio vede, col cuor crede. *Ital.* **1712** ARBUTHNOT *John Bull* II. xviii There's nothing like matter of fact; seeing is believing. **1721** KELLY 298 Seeing is believing all the world over. **1827–48** HARE *Gues. at Truth* (1859) ii. 497 *Seeing is believing,* says the proverb. . . . Though, of all our senses, the eyes are the most easily deceived, we believe them in preference to any other evidence. **1909** *Times Lit. Sup.* 28 May 198 Seeing is believing; . . . only art can make history really credible, or a great name more than a label to an abstraction.

Seek a brack[1] where the hedge is whole, You.

1580 LYLY *Euph. & his Eng.* Wks. (Bond) II. 150 Wild horses breake high hedges though they cannot leap over them. **1616** WITHALS 568 (as Clarke). **1639** CLARKE 80 You'd break a gap where the hedge is whole. **1670** RAY 165. [[1] breach, gap.]

Seek a hare in a hen's nest, To.

1599 PORTER *Angry Wom. Abingd.* IV. iii (Merm. 175 He is gone to seek a hare in a hen's nest, . . . which is as seldom seen as a black swan.

Seek grace at (of) a graceless face, You.

[**1530**] JOHN ARMSTRONG of Gilnockie in SCOTT *Tales of Grandf.* (1827) I. xxvii When the King[1] would listen to none of his offers, the robber-chief said, very proudly, 'I am but a fool to ask grace at a graceless face'. **1641** FERGUSSON 112. [[1] James V.]

Seek hot water under cold ice, You.

1641 FERGUSSON 112. **1721** KELLY 364 . . . You court for friendship from them that will not befriend you.

Seek in a sheep five feet where there are but four, To.

1640 HERBERT 369.

Seek mickle, and get something; seek little, and get nothing.

1721 KELLY 291.

Seek that which may be found.

1621 BURTON *Anat. Mel.* II. iii. VII (1651) 360 Out of humane authors take these few cautions, . . . Seek that which may be found.

Seek till you find, and you'll not lose your labour.

1678 RAY 200. **1738** SWIFT (Dial. i) 341 *Miss.* I have lost the finest needle—*Lady A.* Why, seek till you find it, and then you won't lose your labour.

Seek your salve (sauce) where you get your sore (ail).

c. **1400** *Rom. Rose* l. 1965 The helthe of love mot be founde Where as they token first her wounde. **1580** LYLY *Euph. & his Eng.* (Arb.) 296 There is none that can better heale your wound than he that made it. **1641** FERGUSSON 90 Seik your sauce where you get your ail. **1721** KELLY 292 . . . Spoken to them who are sick after drink, *alias,* Take a hair of the dog that bit you. **1732** FULLER no. 4090.

Seek your salve where you got your ail, and beg your barm where you buy your ale.

1862 HISLOP 257 . . . The surly reply of a person who has been shunned for some trivial or mistaken reason by one who is compelled by circumstances to apply to him for information or assistance.

Seeketh findeth, He that.

[BIBLE *Matt.* vii. 7]. **1533** J. HEYWOOD *Play of Love* C 2. **1546** HEYWOOD I. x. 20.

Seeks trouble, He that | it were a pity he should miss it.

1721 KELLY 131 . . . Spoken to, and of, quarrellers, who commonly come by the worst.

Seeks trouble, He that | never misses.

c. **1460** *Pol., Rel., and Love Poems* (E.E.T.S.) 69 (A) Who sechith sorwe, is by [his be] the receyte. **1649** HERBERT 337.

Seek(s), sought, *see also* Find not that you do not s. (Take heed you); Man that s. his mare, and he riding on her; No man will another in the oven s.; Nothing s. nothing find.

Seem not greater than thou art.

1621 BURTON *Anat. Mel.* II. iii. VII (1651) 360 Out of humane authors take these few cautions, . . . Seem not greater than thou art.

Seen, *see* Gives to be s. (He that); Seldom **s.** soon forgotten.

Sees an inch before his nose, He.

1641 FERGUSSON 46 *Of well skilled persons.* He sees an inch before his nose.

Sees thee by day will not seek thee by night, Who. (*Cf.* See you in daylight, &c.)

1573 SANDFORD (1576) 209. **1659** HOWELL *Ital.-Eng.* 2.

Sees, *see also* See(s).

Seest thine house in flames, When thou | approach and warm thyself by it.

1853 TRENCH iii. 52 How proud a looking of calamity in the face, speaks out in . . . : *When thou seest thine house in flames, approach and warm thyself by it.*[1] [[1] Quando verás tu casa quemar, llegate á escalentar.]

Segging is good cope.

[Used in echoes of the Dutch proverb *zeggen is goedkoop, 'saying is cheap'.*] **1546** HEYWOOD II. ix. 77 The Ducheman saieth, that seggyng is good cope. **1613** F. ROBARTS *Revenue Gosp.* 104 Alasse, alasse, segging is no good coping.

Seill[1] comes not while (till) sorrow be gone (over).

1641 FERGUSSON 90. **1721** KELLY 294 . . . Eng. *When bale is highest boot is next.* [[1] happiness.]

Sel, sel, has half-filled hell.

1862 HISLOP 257 . . . 'Sel, sel', that is, the sin of selfishness.

Seldom comes (cometh) a (the) better.

a. 1272 *MS. Temp. Hen. III* in DOUCE *Illust. of Shaks.* (1807) II. 34 [The story is related of the monks who, discontented with the gifts of their abbot, prayed that he might die. He did die and the gifts of the next abbot were less satisfactory than those of his predecessor. This abbot likewise died, whether in answer to the prayers of the monks or not, and a third abbot brought disappointment again. One of the monks then suggested that they should pray for this abbot to live, for who could say what a fourth one would do?] Unde solet dici 'Seilde comed se betere'. **1546** HEYWOOD I. iv. 8. **1592–3** SHAKS. *Rich. III* II. iii. 4 Ill news by'r lady; seldom comes the better. I fear, I fear, 't will prove a giddy world. **1599** PORTER *Angry Wom. Abingd.* II. i (Merm.) 127 *Nich.* I pray God save my master's life, for seldom comes the better! **1820** SCOTT *Abbot* vi Though he may be a good riddance in the main, yet what says the very sooth proverb, 'Seldom comes a better'.

Seldom cometh loan laughing home.

c. 1300 *Prov. of Hending* 25 Selde cometh lone lahynde hom. **c. 1350** *Douce MS. 52* no. 82 Seldun comyth lone law3yng home. **1721** KELLY 6 *A borrow'd loan should come laughing home.* What a man borrows he should return with thankfulness.

Seldom does the hated man end well.

a. 1250 *Owl & Night* 942–4 (C.U.P.) 80 For hit seide þe king Alfred: 'Sel[d]e endeð wel þe loþe, an selde plaideð wel þe wroþe.' [The hated man seldom ends well, and the angry man seldom pleads well.]

Seldom is a long man wise, or a low man lowly.

1583 MELBANCKE *Philot.* U 3 I have red that in an old smokie authour, . . . and here I meane to insert . . . I haue seldome sene a long man wise, or a lowe man lowlie.

Seldom lies the devil dead by the gate (*or* in a ditch).

c. 1460 *Towneley Myst., 2nd Shep. Play* 229 III PASTOR Seldom lyys the dewyll dede by the gate. **c. 1470** HENRYSON *Mor. Fab., Fox, Wolf & C.* 113 'Heir lyis', quod he, 'the devill deid in a dyke. Sic ane selcouth[1] saw I not this sevin yeir.' **1641** FERGUSSON 88 Seldome lies the Devil dead by the dyke side. **1670** RAY 79 Seldom lies the *Devil* dead in a ditch. We are not to trust the Devil or his children, though they seem . . . without all power or will to hurt. . . . Perchance this Proverb may allude to the fable of the fox, which escaped by feigning himself dead. **1721** KELLY 230 *Long e'er the Dee 'l lye dead by the dikeside.* Spoken when people make a great talk of some little accident. [[1] strange thing.]

Seldom seen, soon forgotten.

c. 1350 *Douce MS. 52* no. 89 Seldun sey, sone for3ete. **c. 1375** *Vernon MS.* (Furnivall) 715 That selden i-sei3e is sone for3ete. **1377** *Pol. Poems* (Rolls) I. 215 He that was ur most spede Is selden seye and sone for3ete. **c. 1450** *Prouerbis of Wysdom* 25 Seld i-say ys sone fore-yete. **c. 1470** *Harl. MS. 3362* (ed. Förster) in *Anglia* 42. 201 3elde y-sey3e, sone for3ete. *Res raro visa procul est a corde rescisa.* **a. 1530** *R. Hill's Commonpl. Bk.* (E.E.T.S.) 129 Seld sene, sone forgotin. **1546** HEYWOOD I. xi. 25 I haue séene this gentleman, if I wist where. Howe be it lo, seldome séene, soone forgotten. **1614** CAMDEN no. 467. **1721** KELLY 297 Sindle[1] seen, soon forgotten. [[1] Seldom.]

Self do, self have.

1546 HEYWOOD I. viii. 16 For I did it my selfe: and selfe do, selfe haue. **1579** GOSSON *Sch. Abuse* (Arb.) 46 Selfe doe, selfe haue, they whette their Swoords against themselues. **1605** CHAPMAN, &c., *Eastw. Hoe* v. i. *Mist. T.* 'Tis better than thou deservest. . . . Thou wert afire to be a lady, and now your ladyship and you may both blow at the coal, for aught I know. 'Self do, self have.' **1641** FERGUSSON 90 Self deed, self fa.[1] **1721** KELLY 300 *Self deed, self fa.*[1] That is, as you do to others, so it will befall you. [[1] come to your share.]

Self-defence, *see* Self-preservation.

Self-edge makes show of the cloth, The.

1670 RAY 141. **1732** FULLER no. 4744.

Self-love is a mote in every man's eye.

1616 WITHALS 564.

Self-praise comes aye stinking ben.[1]

1832 HENDERSON 47. [[1] home.]

Self-praise is no recommendation.

[L. *Laus in proprio ore sordescit.* Praise in one's own mouth is offensive.] **1612** SHELTON

Quix. I. III. ii (A) Which is such that if I do not praise it, it is because men say that proper praise stinks. **1614–16** *Times Whistle* iii. 1088–9 Hast thou that auncient, true saide sawe forgot, That 'a man's praise in his owne mouth doth stinke'? **1854** SURTEES *Hand. Cross* xxxix 'Self-praise is no commendation', muttered our Master. **1864–5** DICKENS *Our Mut. Fr.* IV. ii 'Mr. and Mrs. Boffin will remind you of the old adage, that self-praise is no recommendation.'

Self-preservation is the first law of nature.

1613 R. DALLINGTON *Aphorisms* 160 Custom hath taught nations, and Reason men, and Nature beasts, that self-defence is alwaies lawfull. *a.* **1614** DONNE Βιαθάνατος (1644) sig. AA It is onely upon this reason, that selfe-preservation is of Naturall Law. *a.* **1678**? MARVELL *Hodge's Vision* Self-preservation, Nature's first great law. **1681** DRYDEN *Span. Friar* IV. ii *Bert.* If one of you must fall, Self-preservation is the first of laws. **1821** SCOTT *Pirate* v *Triptolemus* . . . had a reasonable share of that wisdom which looks towards self-preservation as the first law of nature. **1858** MRS. CRAIK *A Woman's Thoughts* 71 That 'first law of nature', self-preservation, is—doubtless, for wise purposes—imprinted pretty strongly on the mind of the male sex.

Sell a farm and go to sea? Who would.

1903 W. C. RUSSELL *Overdue* ii. 28 Are not sailors right . . . when they hold that a man touches the extreme of idiocy when he sells a farm and goes to sea?

Sell his hen on a rainy day, He will not.

1721 KELLY 373 *You will not sell your hen in a rainy day.* You will part with nothing to your disadvantage, for a hen looks ill on a rainy day. **1766** GOLDSMITH *Vicar W.* xii. Wks. (Globe) 24/1 He knows what he is about. I'll warrant we'll never see him sell his hen of a rainy day. **1831** SCOTT *Journ.* 13 Mar. I will not sell on a rainy day, as our proverb says. **1846** DENHAM 3 Never offer your hen for sale on a rainy day.

Sell his ware after the rates of the market, A man must.

1584 GREENE *Wks.* (Gros.) III. 224 (A) If thou bee wise . . . make thy market while the chaffer is set to sale. **1670** RAY 23. **1732** FULLER no. 5969 You must sell as markets go.

Sell, If it will not | it will not sour.

1721 KELLY 214 . . . Spoken when people will not give a price for those wares that will keep without loss.

Sell (Buy) lawn before he can fold it, He that will | he will repent him before he have sold it.

[Ital. *Chi fa mercantia e no la cognosce, se trova le mane piene di mosche.*] **1546** HEY-

WOOD I. viii. 15. **1580** LYLY *Euph. & his Eng.* (Arb.) 290 He that will sell lawne must learne to folde it. **1670** RAY 112 He that buys lawn before he can fold it, Shall repent him before he have sold it.

Sell one's bacon, To.

[i.e. one's flesh or body.] **1825** CARLYLE *Schiller* III (1845) 163 To the Kaiser, therefore, I sold my bacon, And by him good charge of the whole is taken.

Sell one's birthright, To.

1560 BIBLE (Geneva version) chapter-heading to *Genesis* xxv Esau selleth his birthright for a messe of pottage. **1611** BIBLE *Hebrews* xii. 16 Lest there be any . . . prophane person, as Esau, who for one morsell of meat sold his birthright. **1629** T. ADAMS *Serm.* (1861–2) II. 537 There be some that *sell* their birthright: it is said of the lawyer that he hath *linguam venalem,* a saleable tongue; the covetous, *venalem animam,* a saleable soul; the harlot, *venalem carnem,* a saleable flesh.

Sell the bear's (lion's) skin before one has caught the bear (lion), To.

1580 LYLY *Euph. & his Eng.* Wks. (Bond) ii. 53 I trusted so much, that I solde the skinne before the Beaste was taken. **1598–9** SHAKS. *Hen. V* IV. iii. 93 The man that once did sell the lion's skin While the beast liv'd, was kill'd with hunting him. **1662** FULLER (*Cornw.*) I. 304 Medina Sidonia . . . resolved [Mount-Edgecombe] for his own possession in the partage of this kingdom.[1] . . . But he had catched a great cold, had he had no other clothes to wear than those which were to be made of a skin of a bear not yet killed. **1721** KELLY 376 You sell the bear skin on his back. [[1] 1588.]

Sell the cow and sup the milk, You cannot.

1721 KELLY 379. **1732** FULLER no. 2786 If you sell the cow, you sell her milk too.

Sell the cow must say the word, Who will.

1640 HERBERT 353.

Sell(s, ing), *see also* Buy at a fair, s. at home; Dust is on your feet (While), s. what have bought; Live by selling ware for words (One cannot); Open your pack and s. no wares (Never); Rather s. than be poor; Sin to s. dear (It is no), but to give ill measure; Takes gifts (She that) herself she s.; Washing his hands (For) none s. lands; Weigh justly, s. dearly.

Selthe, *see* Lith and s. are fellows.

Send and fetch.

1641 FERGUSSON 90. **1721** KELLY 288 . . . Lat. *Da, si vis accipere.*

Send him (you) to the sea and he (you) will not get (salt) water.

1641 FERGUSSON 90. **1683** MERITON *Yorks.*

Ale (1697) 83–7 (A). **1721** KELLY 287 . . . Spoken when people foolishly come short of their errand.

Send you away with a sore heart, He will never.

1721 KELLY 165 . . . Spoken of those who are ready at their promises, but slow in their performance.

Send, *see also* Never sigh, but s.

Send, Send a, Send not a, *see also under significant words following.*

Sends a fool, He that | expects one.

1640 HERBERT 356.

Sends a fool, He that | means to follow him.

1640 HERBERT 319.

Senhouse, Dick, *see* Spite of the devil and D. S.

September blow soft till fruit be in loft.

1573 TUSSER xv. 34 Septembre blowe soft, Till fruite be in loft. **1732** FULLER no. 6214. **1928** *Daily Mail* 3 Sept. 10/2 'September blow soft till the apple's in the loft' is what we desire of this traditionally beautiful month.

Sermon without St. Augustine is like a stew without bacon, A.

1853 TRENCH iii. 65 A traveller . . . could make no mistake about the following: *A sermon without Augustine is as a stew without bacon.*

Sermon, *see also* Good example best s.; Salmon and s. have season in Lent.

Serpent has bitten, Whom a | a lizard alarms.

1666 TORRIANO 257 *Whom an* adder *bites, dreads a lyzard.* **1853** TRENCH iii. 70 Another [Italian proverb] which could only have had its birth in the sunny South, where the glancing but harmless lizard so often darts across your path: *Whom a serpent has bitten, a lizard alarms.*

Serpent than the dove, To have more of the.

[**1526** TINDALE *Matt.* x. 16 Be ye therfore wyse as serpentes, and innocent as doves.] *c.* **1592** MARLOWE *Jew of Malta* II. iii (Merm.) 260 Now will I show myself To have more of the serpent than the dove; That is—more knave than fool. **1642** D. ROGERS *Naaman* 210 Many professors defile the ointment of sweete Christianity, with their overmuch pollicy. . . . They put more of the Serpent, then the Dove into the confection. **1910** A. M. FAIRBAIRN *Stud. Relig. & Theol.* 167 If Lightfoot had had more of the serpent and less of the dove in him, he would have kept clear himself of the Clementine literature.

Serpent, A | unless it has devoured a serpent, does not become a dragon.

[ERASM. *Ad.* "Οφις εἰ μὴ φάγοι ὄφιν, δράκων οὐ γενήσεται. Serpens, ni edat serpentem, draco non fiet.] **1613** BEAUM. & FL. *Honest Man's Fort.* III. i The snake that would be a dragon and have wings, must eat. **1625** BACON *Ess., Fortune* (Arb.) 375 No Man prospers so suddenly, as by Others Errours. *Serpens nisi Serpentem comederit non fit Draco.* **1679** DRYDEN *Oedipus* III. i A serpent ne'er becomes a flying dragon, Till he has eat a serpent.

Serpent, *see also* Bitten by a s. afraid of rope; Old S.; Strike s.'s head with enemy's hand; Stung by a s.; Trail of the s.

Servant before that he can be a master, One must be a.

1616 DRAXE 18.

Servant is known by his master's absence, A.

1642 TORRIANO 78. **1659** HOWELL *Ital.–Eng.* 12. **1732** FULLER no. 390.

Servant, He that has no | must serve himself.

c. **1386** CHAUCER *Reeve's T.* 4027 Hym boês[1] serve hym-self that has na swayn, Or elles he is a fool, as clerkès sayn. [[1] behoves.]

Servant, A good | should have the back of an ass, the tongue of a sheep, and the snout of a swine.

1589 L. WRIGHT *Display of Dutie* 37 It is required in a good seruant, to haue the backe of an Asse, to beare all things patiently: the tongue of a sheepe, to keepe silence gently: and the snout of a swyne, to feede on all thinges heartily.

Servant, A good | should never be in the way and never out of the way.

[Said by Chas. II of Sidney Godolphin: *see* LEAN III. 389.] **1896** F. LOCKER-LAMPSON *My Confid.* 403 Margaret, . . . was . . . a good servant (never in and never out of the way).

Servant, If you would have a good | take neither a kinsman nor a friend.

1640 HERBERT 354 A kinsman, a friend, or whom you entreat, take not to serve you, if you will be served neatly. **1855** BOHN 422.

Servants make the worst masters.

1902–4 LEAN IV. 93.

Servants (Slaves), So many | so many enemies.

[CATO *Quot servi, tot hostes.*] **1539** TAVERNER f. 34 *Quot seruos habemus, tottidem habemus hostes.* Loke how many bondmen we haue and so many enemyes we haue. **1603** FLORIO tr. *Montaigne* II. viii (1897) III. 110 Old Cato was wont to say, So many servants, so many enemies. **1869** LECKY *Hist. Eur. Mor.* (1905) I. ii. 302 The servile wars . . . had shaken Italy to the centre, and the shock was felt in every household. 'As many enemies as slaves', had become a Roman proverb. **1892** BP. LIGHTFOOT *Philemon* 320 The universal distrust had already found expression in a common proverb, 'As many enemies as slaves'. [*Note.*—Senec. *Ep. Mor.* 47 '. . . *totidem hostes esse quot servos*'.]

Servant(s), *see also* Beg of . . . a beggar (Neither) nor serve s.; Choose none for thy s. who have served betters; Common s. no man's s.; Give little to his s. (He can) that licks his knife; Grandfather's s. never good; Ill s. never good master; Master of straw eat s. of steel; No silver no s.; Pay not a s. his wages (If you), will pay himself; Saturday s. never stay, Sunday s. run away; Sleepy master, s. a lout; Smiling boy seldom good s.

Serve a great man, and you will know what sorrow is.

1855 BOHN 483.

Serve a noble disposition, though poor, the time comes that he will repay thee.

1611 COTGRAVE s.v. 'Bon' He that serues a good master looks for a good reward. **1640** HERBERT 334.

Serve the devil for God's sake, To.

1820 SCOTT *Abbot* xxiv Do you suppose I would betray my mistress, because I see cause to doubt of her religion?—that would be a serving, as they say, the devil for God's sake.

Serve the tod[1], As long as you | you must bear up his tail.

1641 FERGUSSON 12 As long as ye serve the tod, ye man bear up his tail. **1721** KELLY 26 . . . When you have engaged in any man's service, you must not think yourself too good for anything he employs you in. [[1] fox.]

Served, He that will be | must be patient.

1640 HERBERT 334.

Served, He that would be well | must know when to change his servants.

1707 MAPLETOFT 27. **1855** BOHN 396.

Serves God for money, He that | will serve the devil for better wages.

1692 L'ESTRANGE *Aesop's Fab.* cv (1738) 121 It is a kind of a conditional devotion for men to be religious no longer than they can save,

or get by't. . . . The . . . moral is . . . comprised in the old saying, *He that serves God for money, will serve the devil for better wages.*

Serves God, serves a good master, He who.

1611 COTGRAVE s.v. 'Maistre' The servant of God hath a good master. **1853** TRENCH vi. 146 We might . . . remind our hearers of that word: *He who serves God, serves a good master.*

Serves is preserved, He who.

1917 *Record* 7 June 414 There is an old Latin proverb—'He who serves is preserved'. It is profoundly true. The useless is cast aside— the useless man, the useless code, the useless people.

Serves, He that | must serve.

1640 HERBERT 353.

Serves the poor with a thump on the back with a stone, He.

1678 RAY 90 *A covetous person. . . .*

Serves the public, He who | hath but a scurvy master.

1855 BOHN 401.

Serves well, He that | needs not [be afraid to] ask his wages.

1640 HERBERT 354. **1732** FULLER no. 2296 (with 'be afraid to').

Serve(s, d), *see also* After a sort, as Costlet s. the King; Beg of . . . a beggar (Neither) nor s. servant; Many a man s. thankless master; No man can s. two masters.

Service a child doth his father is to make him foolish, The first.

1640 HERBERT 339.

Service is no inheritance.

1412 HOCCLEVE *Reg. of Princes* (E.E.T.S.) 31 l. 841 Seruyse, I wot well, is non heritage. **1509** A. BARCLAY *Ship of Fools* (1874) I. 106 Thus worldly seruyce is no sure herytage. **1602-3** SHAKS. *All's Well* I. iii. 25 In Isbel's case and mine own. Service is no inheritance. **1631** BRATHWAIT *Whimzies* (1859) 98 But service is no inheritance, lest therefore . . . he should grow weary of his place, or his place of him; . . . he begins to store up against winter. **1721** KELLY 298 . . . An argument for servants to seek out for some settlement. **1824** SCOTT *St. Ronan's* x '[You] call yourself the friend and servant of our family'. . . . 'Ay, . . . —but service is nae inheritance; and as for friendship, it begins at hame.' **1830** MARRYAT *King's Own* x There was a club established for servants out of place. . . . Our seal was a bunch of green poplar rods, with '*Service is no inheritance*' as a motto.

Service to the king's, No.

1484 CAXTON *Chartier's Curial* (E.E.T.S.) 19 Ne seruyse lyke to the kyng souerayn. *c.* **1580** G. HARVEY *Marginalia* (1913) 142 No fisshing

to yᵉ Sea . nor seruice to A King. **1618**
N. BRETON *Courtier & Countryman* Wks.
(Gros.) II. 10 Though there is no service to
the King, nor no fishing to the Sea, yet there
are [&c.]. **1639** CLARKE 98. [*See also quotations under* Fishing to fishing in the sea.]

Service without reward is punishment.

1616 DRAXE 187 Seruice vnrewarded is a
punishment. **1640** HERBERT 364.

Service, *see also* Child's s. is little, yet fool
that despiseth; Good s. great enchantment; Proffered s. stinks; Trade is better
than s.; Yeoman's s.

Serving-man, *see* Young s. old beggar.

Sesame, *see* Open S.

Set a person on his legs, To.

1679–1715 SOUTH *Serm.* 2 fin. The excellency
of Christian religion ... to set fallen man upon
his legs again.

Set (Fall together) by the ears, To.

[= to put or be at variance.] **1546** HEYWOOD
II. i. 45 Together by the eares they come
(quoth I) chéerely. **1553** T. WILSON *Arte of
Rhet.* (1909) 37 When is the law profitable?
Assuredly, ... especially in this age, when
all men goe together by the eares, for this
matter, and that matter. **1602–3** SHAKS.
All's Well I. ii. 1 The Florentines and Senoys
are by the ears. **1603** KNOLLES *Hist. Turkes*
1184 They fell together by the eares about
the matter. **1607–8** SHAKS. *Coriol.* I. i. 239
Were half to half the world by the ears ...
I'd revolt. **1636** S. WARD *Serm.* (1862) 77 The
devil ... threw in these bones to set us together by the ears. **1725** DEFOE *Voy. round
W.* (1840) 67 They would fall together by the
ears about who should go with you. **1868**
G. DUFF *Pol. Surv.* (1868) 40 Does it [Turkey]
fancy that it will obtain security for itself by
setting Greek and Bulgarian by the ears?

Set in, *see* Time to s. i. when oven comes to
dough.

Set my house on fire only to roast his eggs, He.

1612 BACON *Ess., Of Wisdom* (Arb.) 186 And
certainly it is the nature of extreme selfelouers, as they will set an house on fire, and
it were but to rost their egges. **1629** T. ADAMS
Serm. (1861–2) II. 259 They ... would set
their neighbour's house on fire and it were
but to roast their own eggs. **1692** L'ESTRANGE
Aesop's Fab. clxviii (1738) 181 Those that ...
*set their country afire for the roasting their own
eggs.* **1751** FRANKLIN Jan. Pray don't burn
my House to roast your Eggs.

Set not your loaf in till the oven's hot.

1732 FULLER no. 4110.

Set one's cap at, To.

[Said of a woman who sets herself to gain the
affections of a man.] **1822** BYRON *Juan* xi.

lxxx Some, who once set their caps at
cautious dukes. **1848** THACKERAY *Vanity F.*
I. iii That girl is setting her cap at you.

Set one's face like a flint, To.

[= firmly, steadfastly.] **1611** BIBLE *Isaiah* l. 7
Therefore have I set my face like a flint, and
I know that I shall not be ashamed. **1688**
BUNYAN *Wk. of Jesus Christ as Adv.* Wks
(1855) I. 180 He ... sets his face like a flint
to plead for me with God. **1859** KINGSLEY
Misc. (1860) I. 321 Set his face like a flint.

Set the Thames on fire, To.

[= to do something remarkable.] **1778** FOOTE
Trip Calais III. iii Matt Minnikin ... an
honest *burgoise*, ... won't set fire to the
Thames. **1785** GROSE *Dict. Vulg. T.* s.v.
'Thames' He will not find out a way to set
the Thames on fire; he will not make any
wonderful discoveries. **1863** KINGSLEY *Water
Bab.* viii The Pantheon of the Great Unsuccessful, ... in which ... projectors [lecture]
on the discoveries which ought to have set
the Thames on fire. **1909** *Times Lit. Sup.*
27 Aug. The vast majority ... are decidedly
unimaginative ... The Thames will never be
set on fire ... by the ... [Masonic] Grand
Lodge of England.

Set their horses together, They cannot.

1639 CLARKE 94 (with 'i' th' same stable' for
'together'). **1670** RAY 181.

Set trees at Allhallontide[1] and command them to prosper: set them after Candlemas[2] and entreat them to grow.

1678 RAY 52 ... This Dr. J. Beal alledgeth
as an old English and Welch Proverb, concerning Apple and Pear-trees, Oak and
Hawthorn quicks. **1822** SCOTT *Letter* 15 May
in LOCKHART *Life* lvi (1860) 479 Except
evergreens, I would never transplant a tree
betwixt March and Martinmas. ... Plant a
tree before Candlemas, and *command* it to
grow—plant it after Candlemas, and you
must *entreat* it. [[1] All Hallows'-tide, the
season of All Saints, the first week in November. [2] Feast of Purif. of Virg. Mary, 2 Feb.]

Set trees poor and they will grow rich, set them rich and they will grow poor.

1678 RAY 350 ... Remove them always out
of a more barren into a fatter soil.

Set up (or in) one's staff (of rest), To.

[= to settle down in a place.] **1573** HARVEY
Letter-Book (Camden Soc.) 4 (A) He hath set
down his staf, and made his reckning. **1576**
LAMBARDE *Peramb. of Kent* (1826) 430 (A)
She resolved ... to set up her last rest, in
hope to recover her losses again. **1592–3**
SHAKS. *Com. Err.* III. i. 51 Have at you with
a proverb: Shall I set in my staff? **1594–5**
Rom. & Jul. V. iii. 110 O! here Will I set
up my everlasting rest. **1594** NASHE *Unf.
Trav.* Wks. (Gros.) V. 46 Here I was in good

hope to set vp my staffe for some reasonable time. **1609** BODLEY *Life* (1647) 15 I concluded at the last to set up my Staffe at the Library doore in Oxford. **1815** SCOTT *Guy Man.* xix. Here, then, Mannering resolved, for some time at least, to set up the staff of his rest. **1860** TROLLOPE *Framley P.* xlviii They appeared in London and there set up their staff.

Set your heart at rest.

1595–6 SHAKS. *Mids. N.* II. i. 121 Set your heart at rest. **1670** RAY 190.

Set your wit against a child, Don't.

1738 SWIFT (Dial. i) 334 *Never.* Why so hard upon poor miss? Don't set your wit against a child.

Set, *see also* Sow dry and s. wet.

Set (a, the), *see also under significant words following.*

Settling an island, In | the first building erected by a Spaniard will be a church; by a Frenchman, a fort; by a Dutchman, a warehouse; and by an Englishman, an alehouse.

1787 GROSE (*Glos., Eng.*) 149.

Seven deadly sins.

1340 *Ayenbite* 9 Lecheire . . . is one of þe ȝeuen dyadliche ȝennes. *c.* **1386** CHAUCER *Parson's T.* I. 387 Now is it bihovely thyng to telle whiche been the sevene deedly synnes, this is to seyn, chieftaynes of synnes. **1604–5** SHAKS. *Meas. for Meas.* III. i. 109 Sure it is no sin; Or of the deadly seven it is the least. *a.* **1711** KEN *Hymnotheo* Poet. Wks. (1721) III. 269 The Seven curs'd deadly Sins. . . . Pride, Envy, Sloth, Intemp'rance, Av'rice, Ire, And Lust.

Seven hours' sleep will make a clown (the husbandman) forget his design.

1732 FULLER no. 4112. **1846** DENHAM 5 (with 'the husbandman').

Seven Sleepers.

1633 DONNE *The Good-Morrow* Or snorted we in the Seven Sleepers' den? **1837** CARLYLE *Fr. Rev.* II. III. i The whole French people . . . bounce up . . . like amazed Seven-sleepers awakening. **1861** H. KINGSLEY *Ravenshoe* xxxviii He made noise enough to waken the seven sleepers. **1869** S. BARING-GOULD *Cur. Myths* 101 The Seven Sleepers of Ephesus, who had been slumbering two hundred years in a cavern of Mount Celion, . . . had . . . turned themselves over on their left sides.

Seven years, *see* Keep a thing s. y.

Seven(s), *see also* All in the s. (It is); Sixes and s.

Seventh heaven, The.

[= a state of bliss.] [By the Jews seven

heavens were recognized, the highest being the abode of God and the highest angels.] **1824** SCOTT *St. Ronans* xxvi He looked upon himself as approaching to the seventh heaven. **1844** KINGLAKE *Eothen* xvii The Sheik . . . rolled his eyes . . . between every draught, as though the drink . . . had come from the seventh heaven. **1883** RITA *After Long Grief* xxii Lady Ramsey was in the seventh heaven of delight.

Severn, Fixt thy pale in | Severn will be as before.

1662 FULLER (*Montgom.*) III. 549 'Fixt thy pale (with intent to force out his water) in Severn, Severn will be as before.' Appliable to such who undertake projects above their power to perform, or grapple in vain against Nature.

Severn, *see also* Blessed is the eye betwixt S. and Wye; Sip up the S. as soon.

Seville, He who has not seen | has not seen a wonder.

1748 SMOLLETT tr. *Gil. Blas* X. x. (1907) II. 269 Thou wilt not be sorry to see that capital of Andalusia. He that hath not Seville seen (saith the proverb[1]) Is no traveller, I ween. [[1] Quien no ha visto a Sevilla, No ha visto maravilla.]

Sew, *see* Little to s. when tailors true.

Sexton has shaked his shoo[1] at him, The.

1917 BRIDGE 120 . . . Said of any one who is ill and not likely to get better. [[1] shovel or spade.]

Shade, *see* Live in the s.

Shadow(s), *see* Catch not at the s.; Coming events cast their s.; Dispute about s. of an ass; Fight with s.; Hair so small but hath s. (No); Old wise man's s. better than buzzard's sword.

Shaft[1] or a bolt[2] of it, I will make a.

[= I will take the risk, whatever may come of it.] **1594** NASHE *Wks.* (Gros.) III. 254 (A) To make a shaft or a bolt of this drumbling subiect of dreames. **1600–1** SHAKS. *Merry W.* III. iv. 24 I'll make a shaft or a bolt on 't. 'Slid, 'tis but venturing. **1608** MIDDLETON *Trick to Catch* II. i *Freedom.* I'll quickly make a bolt or a shaft on 't. **1687** R. L'ESTRANGE *Answ. Dissenter* 46 One might have made a Bolt or a Shaft on 't. **1819** SCOTT *Ivanhoe* xxvii footnote Hence the English proverb 'I will either make . . .'. [[1] arrow for a longbow. [2] arrow for a cross-bow.]

Shake a bridle over a Yorkshireman's grave, and he'll rise and steal a horse.

1787 GROSE (*Yorks.*) 235 . . . An allusion to the fondness for horses, shown by almost every native of this county. **1821** SCOTT *Pirate* iv His father observed that Trip could be always silenced by jingling a bridle

P p

at his ear. From which he used to swear . . .
that the boy would prove true Yorkshire.

Shake a Leicestershire man by the collar, and you shall hear the beans rattle in his belly.

15th cent. *Rel. Antiq.* (1841) I. 269 (A)
Leicesterschir, full of benys. 1613–22
DRAYTON *Polyolb.* xxiii. 265 (1876) III. 95
Bean belly, Lestershire her attribute doth bear.
1662 FULLER (*Leic.*) II. 225 'Shake a Leicestershire yeoman by the collar, and you shall
hear the beans rattle in his belly'; but those
yeomen smile at what is said to rattle in their
bellies, whilst . . . good silver ringeth in their
pockets. 1818 SCOTT *Ht. Midl.* xxix An ye
touch her, I'll gie ye a shake by the collar
shall make the Leicester beans rattle. 1881
A. B. EVANS *Leicest. Wds.* 299 'Shake a
Leicestershire man by the collar, and you
shall hear the beans rattle in his belly' . . . is
still current, as is also the answer . . . ; 'Yoi,
lad, but 'ew doo'st?'

Shake a loose (*or* free) leg, To.

[= to lead an irregular life, live freely.] 1834
AINSWORTH *Rookwood* III. ix (1878) 233
While luck lasts, the highwayman shakes a
loose leg! 1856 MAYHEW *Gt. World Lond.* 87
Those who love to 'shake a free leg', and lead
a roving life, as they term it. 1876 MRS.
BANKS *Manch. Man* xxviii It was doubly
satisfactory to find the comforts of their
home appreciated . . . and to be able to refute
Mr. Ashton's theory that 'all young men like
to shake a loose leg'.

Shake in one's shoes, To.

[= to tremble with fear.] 1818 COBBETT
Polit. Reg. XXXIII. 497 This is quite enough
to make Corruption and all her tribe shake
in their shoes.

Shake the dust off one's feet, To.

[in allusion to *Matt.* x. 14, &c.] *c.* 1000 *Ags.
Gosp.* Matt. x. 14 Asceacaþ þæt dust of
eowrum fotum. 1382 WYCLIF *Matt.* x. 14
ȝee goynge forth fro that hous, or citee,
smytith awey the dust fro ȝoure feet.

Shake the elbow, To.

[= to play at dice.] 1705 HEARNE *Collect.*
26 Nov. (1885–6) I. 100 Money which . . . he
squander'd away in shaking his elbow. 1826
J. WILSON *Noct. Ambr.* Wks. (1855) I. 127
Many good and great men have shook the
elbow.

Shake the pagoda[1] tree, To.

[= to make a fortune rapidly in India.] 1836
T. HOOK *G. Gurney* I. 45 The amusing pursuit
of 'shaking the pagoda-tree' once so popular
in our oriental possessions. 1912 *Spectator*
17 Feb. 273 Rennell['s] . . . contemporaries
had won handsome fortunes by 'shaking the
Pagoda Tree', by the private trade that then
was permitted to John Company's servants.
[1 Indian gold coin.]

Shake your ears, You may go and.

[= to show contempt or displeasure.] 1573
G. HARVEY *Letter-bk.* (Camden Soc.) 42 As for

gentle M. Gawber, his Mastership may go
shake his eares elswhere. 1599–1600 SHAKS.
Twelfth N. II. iii. 134 *Mal.* She [my lady]
shall know of it, by this hand. *Maria* (to
Malvolio) Go shake your ears. *c.* 1645
HOWELL (1655) I, § i. xxi. 32 They shut their
Gates against him, and made him go shake
his ears, and to shift for his lodging. 1690
D'URFEY *Collin's W.* iv. 177 If this be true
as it appears, Why dost not rouse and shake
thy Ears? 1813 RAY 215 . . . Spoken to one
who has lost his money.

Shake(s), *see also* All that s. falls not

Shallow streams (waters) make most din.

1721 KELLY 289 *Shaal*[1] *waters make the
greatest sound.* And empty fellows make the
greatest noise. 1832 HENDERSON 87.
[1 shallow.]

Shallow, *see also* Water is s. (Where), no
vessel will ride.

Sham Abra(ha)m, To.

[Orig. *Naut. slang* = to feign sickness.] 1752
Gentl. Mag. Mar. 140/2 As he [Capt. Lowry]
went along some sailors cry'd out . . . that
He must not sham Abram (a cant sea phrase
when a sailor is unwilling to work on pretence
of sickness . . .). 1760 GOLDSMITH *Cit. World*
cxix The boatswain . . . swore . . . that I
shammed Abraham merely to be idle. 1827
SCOTT *Surg. Dau.* vi It's good enough . . . for
a set of lubbers, that lie shamming Abraham.
1863 C. READE *Hard Cash* xxxi (1868) 265
He's shamming Abraham.

Shame fall on him that speers[1] and kens sae weel.

1691 J. WILSON *Belphegor* v. ii (1874) 372
Mat. What are ye? *Jul.* Shame fa' him that
speers and kens sae weel. [1 inquires.]

Shame fall the gear and the blad'ry[1] o't.

1721 KELLY 296 . . . The turn of an old
Scottish song, spoken when a young, handsome girl marries an old man, upon the
account of his wealth. [1 trumpery.]

Shame in a kindred cannot be avoided.

1636 CAMDEN 305.

Shame is past the shedd[1] of your hair.

1641 FERGUSSON 90. 1721 KELLY 287 . . .
Spoken to people impudent, and past blushing. [1 parting.]

Shameful (Shameless) craving must have shameful nay.

1550 HEYWOOD I. xi. 29 (with 'shameful').
1670 RAY 141 (with 'shameless').

Shameful leaving is worse than shameful eating.

1721 KELLY 63. 1894 NORTHALL *Folk
Phrases* (E.D.S.) 22 (A).

Shames, He that | shall be shent.

1641 FERGUSSON 42. **1721** KELLY 159 *He that shames let him be shent.* . . . A wish that he who exposes his neighbour, may come to shame himself.

Shame take him, *see* Ill be to him . . . [*Honi soit qui mal y pense*].

Shame to steal, It is a | but a worse to carry home.

1639 CLARKE 190 (with 'a greater shame to bring again'). **1670** RAY 141. **1732** FULLER no. 2875.

Shame, *see also* Loss embraceth s.; Past s. past amendment; Pride goeth before, s. cometh after; Pride rides, s. lacqueys; Single long, s. at length.

Shank's (Shanks's) mare (nag, pony).

[= one's own legs as a means of conveyance.] *a.* **1774** FERGUSSON *Poems* (1808) 333 And auld shanks-naig wad tire, I dread, To pace to Berwick. *a.* **1795** s. BISHOP *Poet. Wks.* (1796) I. 204 I'd rather . . . ride on Shanks's mare. **1859** G. A. SALA *Twice Round Clock* (1878) 87 The humbler conveyances known as 'Shanks's mare', and the 'Marrowbone Stage'—in more refined language, walking. **1898** WATTS-DUNTON *Aylwin* XII. iii I'll start for Carnarvon on Shanks's pony.

Shape a coat for the moon, You may as soon.

1678 RAY 260.

Shape coat and sark[1] for them, We can | but we cannot shape their weird.

1721 KELLY 356 . . . Spoken when people of good education fall into misfortunes, or come to untimely ends. **1832** HENDERSON 3 We can shape our bairns' wyliecoat,[2] but canna shape their weird. (We can shape our children's clothes, but not their fate.) [[1] shirt. [2] a flannel vest.]

Shape, *see also* Good s. is in shears' mouth; Lick into s.

Shapes as Proteus, As many.

[A sea-deity of many shapes.] *c.* **1370** CHAUCER *Romaunt of the Rose* 6319 For Protheus, that cowde hym chaunge, In every shap homely and straunge. **1590–1** SHAKS. *3 Hen. VI* III. ii. 192 I can . . . change shapes with Proteus. **1600** *Sir J. Oldcastle* I. ii I have as many shapes as Proteus had. **1761** CHURCHILL *Rosciad* Wks. (1868) 14 The Proteus shifts, bawd, parson, auctioneer.

Share and share alike (some all, some never a whit).

1611 COTGRAVE s.v. 'Escot' Whereat every guest paies his part, or share and share like. **1634** WITHALS 562 Share and share like, some all, some never a whit. **1817** EDGEWORTH *Ormond* XXV The woman . . . was dividing the prize among the *lawful owners,* 'share and share alike'.

Share not pears with your master, either in jest or in earnest.

1732 FULLER no. 4117.

Shares, He who | has the worst share.

1855 BOHN 401. *Span.*

Shareth honey with the bear, He who | hath the least part of it.

1732 FULLER no. 2403.

Sharp as a needle, As.

1902 DOBSON *Richardson* 31 She [Pamela] is only fifteen, but she is as sharp as a needle.

Sharp as a razor, As.

c. **1370** CHAUCER *Romaunt of the Rose* B 1885 Kene grounde as ony rasour. **1519** HORMAN *Vulg.* f. 277 (A) My wodknyfe is as sharp as a rasur.

Sharp as vinegar.

1615 H. CROOKE *Microcosmographia* (1631) 632 Sowre and sharpe as Vineger. **1636** QUARLES *Elegie* Wks. (Gros.) III. 11/1 We . . . sadly rise With the sharp vinegre of suffused eyes.

Sharp stomach makes short devotion, A.

1639 CLARKE 112. **1721** KELLY 293 Sharp stomachs make short graces.

Sharp's the word and quick's the motion.

1709 CIBBER *Rival Fools* I (A) Sharp's the word! We'll have half ours too. **1712** ADDISON *Spect.* No. 403 Wks. (Bohn) III. 381 'Sharp's the word. Now or never boy. Up to the walls of Paris directly.' **1837** T. HOOK *Jack Brag* ii 'Be alive, my fine fellow! . . . no nonsense—sharp's the word and quick's the motion, eh ?'

Sharp, *see also* All things that are s. are short.

Sharper the storm, The | the sooner it's over.

9 June **1872** *Kilvert's Diary* ii. 207 The harder the storm the sooner 'tis over. **1913** *Folk-Lore* xxiv. 76 (A).

Shave an egg, It is very hard to.

1639 CLARKE 243. **1648** HERRICK *Hesper.* 558 (1893) I. 262 Eggs Ile not shave. **1670** RAY 84 . . . Where nothing is, nothing can be had. **1861** C. READE *Cloister & H.* lviii We Dutchmen are hard bargainers. We are the lads . . . 'to shave an egg'.

Shaving against the wool, It is ill.

1636 CAMDEN 300. **1670** RAY 141.

Shave(s, -ing), *see also* Barber learns to s. by s. fools; Barber s. another gratis; Beard will pay for s.

Sheaf of a stook[1] is enough, One.

1721 KELLY 34 ... An answer to those who propose to match twice into the same family: and hits the patter if the first match was not very fortunate. [1 group of sheaves.]

Shear sheep that have them.

1678 RAY 201.

Shear your sheep in May, and shear them all away.

1670 RAY 41. **1732** FULLER no. 6195 (with 'clear' for the second 'shear').

Shearer, *see* Bad s. never had good sickle.

Shears, *see* Pair of s. between them (Went but a).

Sheath, *see* Blade wears out s.; Leaden sword in ivory s.; Makes much of painted s.; Wooden dagger in painted s.

Shed riners with a whaver, To.

1826 WILBRAHAM *Chesh. Glos.* 68 'To shed riners with a whaver' ... means, to surpass anything skilful or adroit by something still more so. **1917** BRIDGE 143 To shed riners with a whaver. *Shed* = to divide or surpass. *Riner* = toucher. Used at Quoits. A *Riner* is when the quoit touches the peg or mark. *Whaver* is when it rests upon the peg and hangs over and consequently wins the cast.

Sheen, *see* Nun of Sion with friar of S.

Sheep and a cow, Now I have a | everybody bids me 'Good morrow'. (*Cf.* Ewe and a lamb, &c.)

1757 FRANKLIN *Poor Rich. Improved; Alm. for 1758* in ARBER *Garner* v. 581 Industry gives comfort, and plenty, and respect. ... *Now I have a sheep and a cow Everybody bids me 'Good morrow'.*

Sheep follows another, One.

1678 RAY *Adag. Hebr.* 405 ... So one thief, and any other evil doer, follows the ill example of his companion.

Sheep hang by his (its) own shank, Let every.

1721 KELLY 240 ... Every man must stand by his own endeavour, industry, and interest. **1818** SCOTT *Rob Roy* xxvi Na, na! let every herring hing by its ain head, and every sheep by its ain shank.

Sheep in the flock, He that has one | will like all the rest the better for it.

1721 KELLY 137 ... Spoken when we have a son at such a school, university, army, or society, we will wish the prosperity of these respective bodies, upon his account.

Sheep leap o'er the dyke[1], If one | all the rest will follow.

1721 KELLY 179 ... Shewing the influence of evil example. **1816** SCOTT *Old Mort.* xxxvi Call in the other fellow, who has some common sense. One sheep will leap the ditch when another goes first. [1 ditch.]

Sheep of Beery; it is marked on the nose, It is a.

1651 HERBERT 365. **1867** *N. & Q.* 3rd Ser. XII. 488 ... A sheep is often marked on the nose to show to what barn it belongs.

Sheep to shear, You have no more.

1678 RAY 344 ... *Somerset.*

Sheep's eye at (or upon), To cast (or throw) a.

[= to look amorously or longingly at.] **1529** SKELTON *Agst. Garnesche* iii. 54 When ye kyst a shepys ie, ... [At] mastres Andelby. *a.* **1586** SIDNEY *Arcadia* II (Sommer) 107 Mopsa throwing a great number of sheeps eyes vpon me. **1738** SWIFT (Dial. i) 335 *Lady S.* How do you like Mr. Spruce? I swear I have often seen him cast a sheep's eye out of a calf's head at you. **1809** MALKIN *Gil Blas* I. iv (Rtldg.) 9 I could not help casting a sheep's eye at the gold and silver plate peeping out of the different cupboards. **1848** THACKERAY *Vanity F.* xxvii The horrud old Colonel, ... was making sheep's eyes at a half-caste girl there.

Sheep's flesh, *see* Loveth well s. f. (mutton) that wets bread in wool.

Sheep, *see also* Better give the wool than the s.; Black s. is a biting beast; Black s. in every flock; Black s. keep the white (Let); Butcher does not fear many s.; Carrion crows bewail dead s.; Death of wolves is safety of flock; Dust raised by s. does not choke wolf; Every hand fleeceth (Where), s. goes naked; Every time s. bleats loses mouthful; Foolish s. makes wolf confessor; Hanged for a s. as a lamb; Keep s. by moonlight; Lazy s. thinks wool heavy; Lone s. in danger of wolf; Makes himself a s. (He that), eaten by wolf; Rich as a new-shorn s.; Scabbed s. will mar flock; Seek in a s. five feet; Shrew than a s. (Better to be *or* to marry); Some good some bad as s. come to fold; Soon goes the young s. to the pot; Steals a s. and gives back trotters; Troubles a wolf how many s. (Never); Wolf eateth the s. (By little); Wolf eats often s. that have been told; Wolf to keep the s. (Set the).

Sheet(s), *see* Difference is wide that s. will not decide; Makes much of his painted s.; Stand in a white s.; Three s. in the wind.

Sheffield Park is ploughed and sown, When | then little England hold thine own.

1678 RAY 340 Yorkshire. *When* Sheffield *Park is plowed and sown, Then little* England *hold thine own.* It hath been plow'd and sown these six or seven years.

Shelter, *see* Good tree is good s.

Sheltering under an old hedge, It is good.

1674 *Learne to lye Warm; or An Apology for that Proverb, 'Tis good sheltering under an Old Hedge* [title of tract] (A). **1678** RAY 351.

Shepherd's warning, *see* Rainbow in the morning; Sky red in the morning.

Shepherd(s), *see* Good s. must fleece ... not flay; Sike as the s. sike his sheep; Wolves rend sheep when s. fail.

Sherramuir (Sheriff-muir), *see* Mair lost at S.

Shield, *see* Cover yourself with your s.

Shift may serve long, A good | but it will not serve for ever.

1678 RAY 201.

Shift to want, It is no.

1721 KELLY 210 ... Spoken when in necessity we take what we have use for.

Shift(s), *see also* Bad s. better than none; Hang him that hath no s.; Make a s., as Macwhid with preaching.

Shilling, *see* Bad penny (s.) comes back; Cut off with a s.; Know by a penny how s. spends; Poor man's s. is but a penny; Take the (King's) s. *See also* Five shillings.

Shin(s), *see* Against the s.; Fast for fear of breaking your s. (Not too); Lies not in your gate breaks not your s. (It that).

Shine(s), *see* Bright that s. by himself; Burns most (He that) s. most.

Ship and a woman are ever repairing, A.

1602–3 MANNINGHAM *Diary* (Camden Soc.) 12 (A) To furnish a shipp requireth much trouble, But to furnishe a woman the charges are double. **1640** HERBERT 353 **1840** DANA *Two Years bef. Mast* iii As has often been said, a ship is like a lady's watch, always out of repair.

Ship comes home, When my.

[= when one comes into one's fortune.] **1851** MAYHEW *Lond. Labour* i. 175 One [customer] always says he'll give me a ton of taties when his ship comes home. **1857** MISS MULOCK *Jno. Halifax* xxii 'Perhaps we may manage it some time.' 'When our ship comes in.'

Ship, As broken a | has come to land.

1641 FERGUSSON 14. **1725** A. RAMSAY *Gentle Shep.* III. ii. **1732** FULLER no. 668. **1824** SCOTT *St. Ronans* ix 'My sister will never marry.' ... 'That's easily said, ... but as broken a ship's come to land.'

Ship (*orig. and prop.* Sheep, Ewe, Hog), To lose (*or* spoil) the | for a halfpennyworth of tar.

[= to lose an object, spoil an enterprise, or court failure, by trying to save in a small matter of detail, referring to the use of tar to protect sores or wounds on sheep from flies: *sheep* is dialectically pronounced *ship* over a great part of England.] **1600** DAY *Blind Beggar* v (A) To him, father; never lose a hog for a halfp'north of tar. **1623** CAMDEN 265 A man will not lose a hog, for a halfeperth of tarre. **1636** J. CRAWSHEY *Countryman's Instructor* Ep. ded. Hee that will loose a Sheepe (or a Hogge) for a pennyworth of Tarre, cannot deserve the name of a good husband. **1670** RAY 103 Ne're lose a *hog* for a half-penny-worth of tarre. [ed. 1678 154 *adds* Some have it, lose not a sheep, &c. Indeed **tarr** is more used about sheep then swine.] **1672** J. PHILLIPS *Moronides* VI. 22 And judge you now what fooles those are, Will lose a Hog for a ha'porth of tar. **1861** READE *Cloister & H.* i Gerard fell a thinking how he could spare her purse. ... 'Never tyne[1] the ship for want of a bit of tar, Gerard', said this changeable mother. **1886** E. J. HARDY *How to be Happy* xiii People are often saving at the wrong place, and spoil the ship for a halfpenny worth of tar. **1910** *Spectator* 19 Feb. 289 The ratepayers ... are accused of ... cheeseparing, of spoiling the ship for a ha'p'orth of tar, of being penny wise and pound foolish. [[1] lose.]

Ship of the desert, The.

[= the camel.] **1844** KINGLAKE *Eothen* xvii Gaza ... bears towards [the desert] the same kind of relation as a seaport bears to the sea. It is there that you *charter* your camels ('the ships of the Desert') ... for the voyage.

Ship(s), *see also* Crazy s. all winds contrary (To a); Dear s. long in haven; Every wind is ill to broken s.; Great s. asks deep waters; Leak will sink great s.; November ... let s. no more sail; Sands will sink s.; Simon and Jude all s. home crowd; Thresher take his flail, and s. no more sail; Venture (Take your) as many a good s.

Shipmate, *see* Messmate before s.

Shipped the devil, He that hath | must make the best of him.

1678 RAY 125. **1720** DEFOE *Capt. Singleton* (1906) 8 He that is shipped with the devil must sail with the devil. **1732** FULLER no. 2152 He that has purchas'd the Devil must make the most of him.

Ships fear fire more than water.

1640 HERBERT 359.

Shipshape and Bristol fashion.

1826 SCOTT *Chron. of Canongate* Introd. (A) Stretching our fair canvas to the breeze, all ship-shape and Bristol fashion. **1840** DANA *Two Years bef. Mast* xxii Her decks were wide and roomy. ... There was no foolish gilding and gingerbread work, ... but everything was 'ship-shape and Bristol fashion'.

Shipwreck be your sea-mark, Let another's.

1662 FULLER (*Derbysh.*) I. 372 Seeing *nocumenta, documenta*; and that the shipwrecks of some are sea-marks to others; even this knight's[1] miscarriage proved a direction to others. **1670** DRYDEN *Cong. Gran.* I. III. i (Merm.) 63 *Abdel.* I am your sea-mark; and, though wrecked and lost, My ruin stands to warn you from the coast. **1855** BOHN 440. **1910** *Times Lit. Sup.* 9 Dec. 491 If he[2] makes other's shipwrecks his sea-marks, . . . all will be well with the great Dependency. [[1] Sir Hugh Willoughby. [2] Lord Hardinge.]

Shipwreck, *see also* Complains wrongfully on sea that twice suffers s.; O Master Vier . . . no s. upon our coast; Slander is a s.

Shire, *see* Lost in the hundred found in s.

Shires, To come out of the.

1736 PEGGE *Kenticisms, Prov.* 71 (E.D.S.) 78 . . . A proverbial saying relative to any person who comes from a distance. . . . The word *shire* is not annexed to any one of the counties bordering upon Kent.

Shirt full of sore bones, I will give you a.

c. **1680** ROGER NORTH *Lives of the Norths* (Bohn) i. 179 Give him 'a serk full of sere benes', that is a shirt full of sore bones. **1732** FULLER no. 2637.

Shirt knew my design, If my | I'd burn it.

1592 G. DELAMOTHE (1647) 50 If our shirt would know our secrets, we ought to burn it. **1616** DRAXE 185 If our shirt knew our secrecie, it were to be burnt. **1633** JONSON *T. Tub* I. i *Hugh.* My cassock shall not know it; If I thought it did, I'd burn it. **1710** SWIFT *Jrnl. to Stella* 30 Nov. He know my secrets? No; as my Lord Mayor said, 'No; if I thought my shirt knew', &c. **1732** FULLER no. 2695.

Shirt of Nessus.

[The garment dipped in the blood of the centaur Nessus, sent by Deianeira to Hercules, whose flesh it consumed.] **1606-7** SHAKS. *Ant. & Cleop.* IV. x. 56 The shirt of Nessus is upon me. **1905** WEYMAN *Starvecrow F.* xxxii Remorse is the very shirt of Nessus. It is of all mental pains the worst. It seizes upon the whole mind.

Shirt(s), *see also* Near is my coat but nearer my s.; Near is my coat (s.) but nearer my skin; Purser's s. on a handspike (Like a); Smocks than s. in a bucking (He that hath more).

Shitten luck is good luck.

1639-61 *Rump Songs* (1662, repr. 1874) Pt. I. 137 (A). **1670** RAY 141. **1894** NORTHALL *Folk-phrases* (E.D.S.) 22 Sh . . . n luck is good luck. Said by one who treads accidentally into excrement, or is befouled by mischance. This . . . probably owes its existence to an ancient term for ordure—*gold* or *gold dust* . . . 'The name *gold finder* or *gold farmer*, [was] given as late as the seventeenth century to the cleaners of privies.'

Shive[1] of a cut loaf, It is safe taking a.

1593-4 SHAKS. *Titus Andron.* II. i. 87 Easy it is Of a cut loaf to steal a shive. **1670** RAY 52. [[1] slice.]

Shive[1] of my own loaf, A.

1670 RAY 188. [[1] slice of bread, &c.]

Shive(s), *see also* Cut large s. of another's loaf; Fiddle for s.

Shod in the cradle, barefoot in the stubble.

1641 FERGUSSON 88. **1721** KELLY 289 . . . Spoken of those who are tenderly used in their infancy, and after meet with harsher treatment.

Shod, *see also* Hosed and s. (He came in); More bare (Worse s.) than shoemaker's wife and smith's mare (None).

Shoe fits not every foot, Every.

1616 B. RICH *Looking Glasse* 21 Euery shooe is not fit for euery foote. **1721** KELLY 96 . . . Every condition of life, every behaviour, every speech and gesture becomes not every body; that will be decent in one, which will be ridiculous in another.

Shoe knows whether the stocking has holes, The.

1855 TRENCH iv. 84 This too with its keen appreciation of the fact that our faults may be hidden from others, but scarcely from those with whom we are brought into the nearness of daily life, . . . comes . . . from a Creole source: *The shoe knows whether the stocking has holes.*

Shoe the goose (gander, gosling), To. (*Cf.* Meddleth in all things, &c.)

[= to spend one's time in trifling or unnecessary labour. *Bodl. misc. 264, c.* 1340, shows a miniature: shoeing the swan (GREEN *Short Hist.* ill. ed. II. 481).] *c.* **1410** HOCCLEVE *Poems* (1796) 13 (A) Ye medle of al thyng, ye moot shoo the goos. **14**.. *Why I cant be Nun* 254 in *E.P.P.* (1862) 144 He schalle be put owte of company, and scho the gose. **1546** HEYWOOD II. iii. 49 Who medleth in all thyng, maie shooe the goslyng. **1583** STUBBES *Anat. Abus.* II. (1882) 31 Then may he go sue ye goose, for house gets he none. **1594** NASHE *Unf. Trav.* c 26 Galen might go shooe the Gander for any good he could doo. **1641** FERGUSSON 36 Go shoe the geese. **1804** EDGEWORTH *Pop. Tales, Lame Jervas* iii A blacksmith once said to me, when . . . asked why he was not both blacksmith and whitesmith, 'The smith that will meddle with all things may go shoe the goslings.'

Shoe the Pasha's horses, They came to | and the beetle stretched out its leg.

1875 BURCKHARDT *Arabic Prov.* 58 *They came to shoe the horses of the Pâshâ; the beetle* *then stretched out its leg (to be shod)*. On ridiculous pretensions. **1899** SIR ALG. WEST *Recoll.* (1908) ix The modesty of a few and the pretensions of many—who reminded me of the Persian proverb, 'They came to shoe the Pasha's horses, and the beetle stretched out his leg.'

Shoe (Ride) the wild (mockish) mare, To.

[A childish Christmas game.] *a.* **1529** SKELTON *Colin Clout* 180 For let see who that dare Shoe the mockish mare. **1597-8** SHAKS. *2 Hen. IV* II. iv. 268 [He] drinks off candles' ends for flap-dragons, and rides the wild mare with the boys. **1609** ARMIN *Maids of More-Cl.* (1880) 92 Christmas gambuls, father, shooing the wilde mare. **1611** COTGRAVE s.v. 'Asne' Desferer l'asne. To unshooe the asse; we say, to ride the wilde mare.

Shoe will hold with the sole, The.

1546 HEYWOOD II. v. 55 Folke say of olde, the shoe will holde with the sole. **1580** LYLY *Euph. & his Eng.* (Arb.) 308 I will stick as close to thee, as the soale doth to the shoe.

Shoe wringeth me (pinches), I know best where the.

[PLUTARCH *Vita Aemilii* c. 5; s. JEROME *Adv. Iov.* i. 48 *Nemo scit praeter me ubi me* (*soccus*) *premat.*] *c.* **1386** CHAUCER *Merch. T.* 1553 But I woot best where wryngeth me my sho. *c.* **1510** DUNBAR *Wks.* (Schipper) 356 Thow knawis best quhair bindis the thi scho. **1546** HEYWOOD II. v. 57 My selfe can tell best, where my shooe doth wryng mée. **1620** SHELTON *Quix.* IV. v (1908) I. 309 As though I knew not . . . where the shoe wrests me now. **1641** FERGUSSON 66 I wot where my awn shoe bindes me. **1749** SMOLLETT *Gil Blas* VIII. vi I did not feel where the shoe pinched. **1895** J. PAYN *In Market O.* xxvi Dives . . . does not see where the shoe of poverty pinches; and this ignorance . . . is often the cause of deplorable sins of omission.

Shoe(s), shoon, *see also* All feet tread not in one s.; Better cut the s.; Dead men's s.; Find fault with my s. and give no leather; Great s. fits not little foot; Higher the tree . . . better the s. blacker the thumb; Knows not whether s. awry; Mare's s. and horse's s. alike; Meal cheap and s. dear; One s. not fit all feet; Over s. over boots; Shake in one's s.; Want of a nail s. is lost; Worthy to wipe (buckle) his s. (Not). *See also* Wooden shoes.

Shoe-buckles, Not worth.

1670 RAY 192.

Shoe-buckles, *see also* Play with you for s.-b.

Shoeing, *see* Winter-time for s.

Shoeing-horn to help on his gloves, He calls for a.

c. **1700** B. E. *Dict. Cant. Crew* s.v. *Hobbist* Sir Posthumus Hobby, one that Draws on his

Breeches with a Shoeing-horn. **1732** FULLER no. 1816.

Shoeing horn, *see also* Nose will not make.

Shoemaker's stocks, In the.

1678 RAY 347. *a.* **1700** B. E. *Dict. Cant. Crew Shoemakers-stocks*, pincht with strait Shoes.

Shoemaker, *see also* More bare (Worse shod) than s.'s wife (Who goes); Six awls make a s.

Shoes be made of running leather, His.

1575 CHURCHYARD *Chippes* (Collier) 130 (A) My Minde could never rest at hoem, My shoes wear maed of running leather suer. **1639** CLARKE 159.

Shoes, *see also* Shoe(s).

Shoot a second arrow to find the first, To.

c. **1596-7** SHAKS. *Merch. V.* I. i. 140 When I had lost one shaft, I shot his fellow of the self-same flight The self-same way, with more advised watch To find the other forth, and by adventuring both, I oft found both. **1601** J. CHAMBERLAIN, *Letters* (McLure) i. 115. **1616** T. DEKKER, *Villainies Discovered* K 1 He shot a second Arrow to finde the first. **1659** HOWELL *Eng. Prov.* 19/2.

Shoot at a pigeon and kill a crow, To.

1639 CLARKE 2. **1670** RAY 189. **1830** LD. LYTTON *Brachylogia* in *Paul Clifford* (1848) 445 A law is a gun, which if it misses a pigeon always kills a crow;—if it does not strike the guilty it hits some one else. **1866** BLACKMORE *Cradock N.* xxvii You . . . must be prepared to meet some horrible accusations. . . . Very likely he is innocent. Perhaps they are shooting at the pigeon in order to hit the crow.

Shoot higher who shoots at the moon (sun) than he who aims at a tree, He will.

1590 SIDNEY *Arcadia* II. vi. 2 (1912) 184 Who shootes at the mid-day Sunne, though he be sure he shall never hit the marke; yet as sure he is he shall shoote higher, than who ayms but at a bush. **1632** HERBERT *Priest to Temple*, Auth. to Rdr. I have resolved to set down the Form and Character of a true Pastor, that I may have a Mark to aim at: which also I will set as high as I can, since he shoots higher that threatens the Moon, than he that aims at a Tree. **1655-62** GURNALL *Chrn. in Armour* (1865) I. 365 He that aims at the sky, shoots higher than he that means only to hit a tree. **1721** KELLY 136 *He will shoot higher that shoots at the moon, than he that shoots at the midding, though he never hit the mark.* Spoken as an encouragement to noble designs and endeavours.

Shoot Niagara, To.

[= attempt desperate adventure.] **1867**

CARLYLE *Shooting Niagara* (title) in *Macmil. Mag.* **1868** LES. STEPHEN in *Life & Lett.* (1906) xi. 203 The Reform Bill will change all this, it may be, and we shall shoot Niagara.

Shoot the cat, To.

[= to vomit, especially from too much drink.] **1830** MARRYAT *King's Own* xxxii I'm cursedly inclined to *shoot the cat.*

Shoot the moon, To.

[= to make a moonlight flitting.] **1837** COL. HAWKER *Diary* (1893) II. 123 He having just 'shot the moon', I had to follow him to a cockloft in St. Giles's. **1882** W. BESANT *All Sorts* iv I told him who were responsible tenants; I warned him when shooting of moons seemed likely.

Shoot with a silver gun, To.

1823 COBBETT *Rural Rides* 1 Aug. Shooting with *a silver gun* is a saying amongst game-eaters. That is to say, *purchasing* the game. A . . . fellow that does not know how to prime and load will, in this way, beat the best shot in the county.

Shoot zaftly,[1] doey now.

1787 GROSE (*Dorset*) 109 Shoot zaftly, doey now. A privateer of [Poole] having . . . loaded their guns, on their return to port, wished to draw out the shot, but . . . could [not] think of any other method, than that of firing them off, and receiving the shot in a kettle: the person employed to hold the kettle . . . prayed for his companion, who was to discharge the gun, to shoot zaftly. [1 softly.]

Shooteth well that hits the mark, He.

1656 L. PRICE *A Map of Merry Conceits* A 5ᵛ He shoots well that hits the mark. **1659** HOWELL *Eng. Prov.* 20/2.

Shooting, *see* Far s. never killed; Kittle s. at corbies and clergy; Short s. loseth game.

Shoots oft at last shall hit the mark, He that.

[CICERO *Div.* 2. 59. 121 *Quis est enim, qui totum diem iaculans, non aliquando collineat?*] **1551** ROBINSON tr. *More's Utop.* (Arb.) 52 He made the prouerbe true, which saieth: he that shoteth oft, at the last shal hit the mark. **1732** FULLER no. 2276 He that's always shooting, must sometimes hit.

Shop, *see* Fair s. and little gain; Keep thy s. and thy s. will keep thee. *See also* Shut up s.

Shop windows, *see* Shut up s.

Shopkeepers, *see* English are nation of.

Shore, *see* Lean to the wrong s. (To).

Shorn, *see* God tempers the wind; Wool (Go out for) and come home s.

Short acquaintance brings repentance.

1670 RAY 142.

Short and sweet.

1552 TAVERNER I₄ The Englysh prouerbe is thus pronounced. Short and swete. **1579–80** LODGE *Def. of Plays* 28 Shorte and sweete if I were judge, a peece surely worthy prayse. **1623** MIDDLETON *Span. Gip.* IV. iii *San.* Both short and sweet some say is best. **1721** KELLY 59 Better short and sweet, than long and lax. **1882** BLACKMORE *Christowell* xix 'Short, but not sweet', said Mr. Gaston, lifting his eyebrows, as he read indignantly— 'I beg to return your rigmarole.' **1902** F. VILLIERS *Pict. of Many Wars* 3 A short interview. But a very sweet one to me. I left . . . with a bag of sovereigns in my pocket.

Short and sweet, like a donkey's gallop.

1894 NORTHALL *Folk-phrases* (E.D.S.) 22 Short and sweet, like a donkey's gallop. Some say, like a roast maggot. **1914** K. F. PURDON *Folk of Furry F.* viii Dan . . . started the old donkey off as well as he could. Short and sweet like an ass's gallop, as the saying is, and she soon failed at it.

Short boughs, long vintage.

1573 SANDFORD 109 A short bow [*Ramo curto*], a long grape time, a store of grapes. **1640** HERBERT 341.

Short days and nights, *see* Discourse makes.

Short folk are soon angry.

1721 KELLY 285 . . . It is alleged that people of a low stature are pettish, passionate, and fiery.

Short folk's heart is soon at their mouth.

1721 KELLY 284 . . . It is alleged that people of a low stature are pettish, passionate, and fiery.

Short harvests make short adlings.[1]

1846 DENHAM 54 [1 earnings.]

Short horse is soon curried, A. (*See also* Bonny bride is soon buskit, &c.*)

c. **1350** Douce MS. 52 no. 17 Short hors is son j-curryed. *c.* **1500** *Sloane MS. 747* (ed Förster) in *Anglia* 42. 204 Short horse ys sone coryed. **1546** HEYWOOD I. x. 19. **1659** HOWELL *Eng. Prov.* 4 A little horse is soon curried. **1820** SCOTT *Abbot* xi A short tale is soon told—and a short horse soon curried.

Short Lent, He has but a | that must pay money at Easter.

1642 TORRIANO 34. **1658** *Comes Facundus* 23 He that would have a short Lent, let him take money to be paid at Easter. **1659** HOWELL *Ital.–Eng.* 11. **1732** FULLER no. 1865. **1758** FRANKLIN in ARBER *E. Garner* v. 585 TIME will seem to have added wings to his heels, as well as shoulders. *Those have a short Lent,* saith *Poor* RICHARD, *who owe money to be paid at Easter.*

Short life and a merry one, A.

1654 GAYTON *Pleasant Notes Don Q.* 101 (A) The indicted cry a merry life and a short. **1660** J. TATHAM *The Rump* I. i (1879) 204 A short life and a merry life. **1745** SWIFT *Dir. Servts.* IV. Wks. (1856) II. 363 Go upon the road . . . ; there you will . . . live a short life and a merry one. **1870** READE *Put Yourself* xxiv 'We prefer a short life and a merry one, Mr. Little', said the father of all file-cutters.

Short pleasure, long lament.

1468 *Coventry Plays* (Shaks. S.) 32 Schort lykyng xal be longe bought. **1556** G. COLVILE tr. *Boethius* (1897) 66 *Phil.* Or, as a man woulde saye: for a lytle pleasure, long payne. **1670** RAY 142 . . . De court plaisir long repentir, *Gall.* **1732** FULLER no. 4155 Short pleasures, long pains.

Short reckonings are soon cleared.

1732 FULLER no. 4156.

Short reckonings (accounts) make long friends.

1537 R. WHITFORD *Werke for Housholders* sig. A 6 The commune prouerbe is that ofte rekeninge holdeth longe felawshyppe. **1641** FERGUSSON 82 Oft compting makes good friends. **1721** KELLY 271 Oft counting keeps friends long together. **1804** EDGEWORTH *Pop. Tales; Out of Debt* ii (1892) 128 Short accounts, they say, make long friends; and . . . it would be very convenient if he could be got to settle with Mr. Ludgate. **1842** LOVER *Handy A.* viii There must be no nonsense about the wedding. . . . Just marry her off, and take her home. Short reckonings make long friends. **1892** HENLEY & STEVENSON *Adml. Guinea* II. i *Pew.* Short reckonings make long friends, hey? Where's my change?

Short rede,[1] good rede.

a. **1235** ROGER OF WENDOVER *Chron.* (E.H.S.) II. 18 Unus ex illis cujus arbitrium omnes exspectabant, præcipitanter patria lingua dixit, 'Schort red, god red; slea ye the bischop'. **1828** SCOTT *F. M. Perth* vii 'What shall we do?' 'Short rede, good rede', said the Smith. 'Let us to our Provost, and demand his . . . assistance.' **1888** FREEMAN *William the Conq.* x On May 14, 1080, a full Gemót . . . was held at Gateshead. . . . There was no vote, no debate; the shout was 'Short rede good rede, slay ye the Bishop.' And . . . Walcher himself and his companions . . . were slaughtered. [1 counsel.]

Short shooting loseth the game.

1546 HEYWOOD II. ix. 80 No hast but good (quoth she) Short shootyng léeseth your game, ye maie sée. *c.* **1580** G. HARVEY *Marginalia* (1913) 147 Lett not short shooting loose yor game . aime straight, draw home . risoluto per tutto.

Short views, Take.

1904 H. SIDGWICK *Misc. Ess. & Add.* 233 It is for most practical purposes wise to 'take short views' of the life of civilized society: . . . short compared with those of the aspiring constructors of social dynamics, from Auguste Comte downwards.

Short, *see also* All things that are sharp are s.

Shortest answer is doing, The.

1640 HERBERT 343.

Shortest day, *see* St. Thomas gray.

Shortly as a horse will lick his ear, As.

1546 HEYWOOD II. ix. 77 Ye will get it againe (quoth she) I feare, As shortly as a horse will licke his eare.

Shot my bolt, I have. (*Cf.* Fool's bolt soon shot.)

[= made my endeavour.] **1577** STANYHURST *Descr. Irel.* in Holinshed (1808) i. 11 But if I may craue your patience till time you see me shoot my bolt. **1901** *Daily Express* 28 Feb. 4/5 The home players had shot their bolt, and in thirty minutes the Birmingham team added two goals. **1944** *Times* 29 Dec. 4/1 All the indications now are that Rundstedt has shot his bolt in the Ardennes.

Shoulder of mutton and English beer, make the Flemings tarry here.

1617 MORYSON *Itin.* III. ii. 99 (1907–8) IV. 62 They [the Dutch] greatly esteeme English Beere. . . . So in the Sea townes of England they sing this English rime; Shoulder of mutton and English Beere, make the Flemmings tarry here.

Shoulder of mutton draws (drives) down another, One.

1670 RAY 128. **1738** SWIFT (Dial. ii) 346 *Col.* I think the more I eat the hungrier I am. *Spark.* Why, colonel, they say, one shoulder of mutton drives down another. **1811** JANE AUSTEN *Sense & Sensib.* xxx (Mrs. Jennings) 'One shoulder of mutton, you know, drives another down.' **1828** LYTTON *Pelham* xxv I am sure if you were to go there, you would cut and come again—one shoulder of mutton drives down another. **1833** TENNYSON to Spedding, 9 Feb. Are we not quits then, or in the language of Mrs. Jennings, 'Does not one shoulder of mutton drive down another?'

Shoulder of mutton for a sick horse, As fit as a.

1598 JONSON *Ev. Man in Humour* II. i But counsel to him is as good as a shoulder of mutton to a sick horse. **1670** RAY 204. **1732** FULLER no. 1179 Counsel is as welcome to him as a shoulder of mutton to a sick horse.

Shoulder of mutton is going, When the | 'tis good to take a slice.

1678 RAY 350.

Shoulder of veal, In a | there are twenty and two good bits.

1678 RAY 83 . . . This is a piece of country wit.

They mean by it, There are twenty (others say forty) bits in a shoulder of veal, and but two good ones. **1738** SWIFT (*Dial.* ii) 344 *Col.* They say there are thirty and two good bits in a shoulder of veal. *Lady S.* Ay, colonel, thirty bad bits and two good ones.

Shoulder to the wheel, Put your.

1621 BURTON *Anat. Mel.* II. i. II (1651) 222 Like him in Æsop, that, when his cart was stalled, lay flat on his back, and cryed aloud, 'Help, Hercules!' but that was to little purpose, except, as his friend advised him, ... he whipt his horses withal, and put his shoulder to the wheel. *a.* **1889** C. MACKAY *Cheer! Boys, cheer!* (Song). If you'll only put your shoulder to the wheel. **1907** *Spectator* 2 Mar. 333 National progress is impossible unless the individuals who compose the nation themselves put their own shoulders to the wheel.

Shoulder, *see also* Over the left s.; Ride with beard on s.; See not what sits on our s.

Shouting, *see* All is over but the s.

Shovel, *see* Put to bed with a s.

Shovelfuls of earth to bury the truth, It takes a good many.

1853 TRENCH vi. 128 The vitality of the truth ... is well expressed in a Swiss proverb: *It takes a good many shovelfuls of earth to bury the truth.* It ... will have a resurrection.

Show a fair (clean) pair of heels, To.

[= to run away.] **1546** HEYWOOD II. vii. 64 Except hir maide shewe a fayre paire of héeles, She haleth her by the boy rope. **1597–8** SHAKS. *1 Hen. IV* II. iv. 52 Darest thou ... play the coward with thy indenture and show it a fair pair of heels and run from it? **1737** RAY 70 He hath shewed them a fair pair of heels. **1819** SCOTT *Ivanhoe* xl Or Folly will show a clean pair of heels, and leave Valour to find out his way.

Show a good man his error, and he turns it to a virtue; but an ill, it doubles his fault.

1640 HERBERT 348.

Show me a liar, and I will show thee (you) a thief.

1607 R. WEST *Court of Conscience* F 1 (A) He that will lie will steal. **1629** T. ADAMS *Serm.* (1861–2) I. 284 The proverb gives the liar the inseparable society of another sin: *Da mihi mendacem, et ego ostendam tibi furem,*— Shew me a liar, and I will show thee a thief.

Show me not (Look not on) the meat, but show me (look on) the man.

1534 J. HEYWOOD *Play of Love* l. 1230 (Brandl *Quellen* 198) (A). **1546** HEYWOOD II. iv. 50 And though your pasture look barreinly and dull, Yet looke not on the meate, but looke on the man. **1639** CLARKE 84. **1650** FULLER *Pisgah-sight* II. x (1869) 201 Our English

proverb saith, 'Show me not the meat, but show me the man.' The well battling of the giants bred in Philistia ... sufficiently attests the fertility of their soil. **1721** KELLY 259 ... If a man be fat, plump, and in good liking, I shall not ask what keeping he has had.

Show me the man, and I'll show you the law.

1641 FERGUSSON 90. **1721** KELLY 289 ... The sentences of judges may vary, according to the measure of their fear, favour, or affection. **1819** SCOTT *Bride Lam.* ii A case of importance scarcely occurred, in which there was not some ground for bias or partiality on the part of the judges, who were so little able to withstand the temptation, that the adage 'Show me the man, and I will show you the law', became as prevalent as it was scandalous.

Show the bull-horn, To.

[= to make a show of resistance.] **1838** GALT in *Fraser's Mag.* VIII. 655 He shewed, when he durst, the bull-horn.

Show the gallows before they show the town, To.

1855 BOHN 543. *Span.*

Show (*noun*), *see* Flaming figure (**Fair s.**) in country church (It will make).

Show (*verb*), *see also* Cloven hoof (**To s.**); Dare not s. his head; Good manners to s. learning before ladies (Not); White feather (**To s.**).

Shower in July, A | when the corn begins to fill, is worth a plow of oxen, and all belongs there till.

1721 KELLY 43. **1732** FULLER no. 6468. **1893** INWARDS 30.

Shower(s), *see also* April s. ... May flowers; Every day of the week a s. of rain; Many drops make s.

Shows all his wit at once, He.

1616 DRAXE 71. **1670** RAY 199.

Shows his purse, He that | bribes the thief.

1721 KELLY 129.

Shows his purse, He that | longs to be rid of it.

1639 CLARKE 176. **1732** FULLER no. 2299 He that sheweth his wealth to a thief is the cause of his own pillage.

Shrew profitable may serve a man reasonable, A.

1616 BRETON *Cross. Prov.* (1879) II. App. iii A shrew profitable, is good for a man reasonable. **1623** CAMDEN 265. **1662** FULLER (*Shrops.*) III. 54 A profitable shrew may well content a reasonable man, the poets feigning

Juno chaste and thrifty, qualities which commonly attend a shrewd nature.

Shrew than a sheep, It is better to be (marry) a.

[*Cf. c. 1560 Tom Tyler* l. 710 Though some be sheep, yet some be shrowes.] **1573** TUSSER 157 Now be she lambe or be she eaw, Giue me the sheepe, take thou the shreaw. **1575** GASCOIGNE *Gl. Govt.* III. i. Wks. (1910) II. 44 It is an olde saying, one shrew is worth two sheep. **1614** CAMDEN 308. *c.* **1645** HOWELL *Lett.* (1650) I. 110 It is better to marry a Shrew than a Sheep; for though silence be the dumb Orator of beauty, ... yet a Phlegmatic dull Wife is fulsom and fastidious.

Shrew(s), *see also* Fair weather when the s. have dined; Leap an inch from a s. (She cannot); Rule a s. (Every man can); Stretton in the Street, where s. meet.

Shrift, He hath been at.

1528 TINDALE *Obed. Chrn. Man* (1888) 267 Of him that is betrayed, and wotteth not how, we say, 'He hath been at shrift'.

Shrine, *see* Saint (S.) (Like) like offering.

Shrub, *see* Pine wishes herself s.

Shrug, *see* Neapolitan s.

Shuffle, *see* Patience and s. the cards.

Shuns the man that knows him well, He.

a. **1250** *Owl & Night.* 235 For Alured King hit seide z wrot: 'He schunet þat hine [vu]l wot.'

Shut the stable-door when the steed is stolen, It is too late to.

[L. *Maxima pars pecore amisso praesepia claudit* (MARCELL. PALINGEN. *Zodiacus Vitae* ix. 287). *c.* **1190** *Li Proverbe au Vilain* (Tobler) 22 A tart ferme on l'estable, quant li chevauz est perduz, ci dit li vilains.] *c.* **1350** *Douce MS.* no. 22 When þe hors is stole steke þe stabull-dore. *c.* **1390** GOWER *Conf. Amantis* IV. 903 For whan the grete stiede Is stole, thanne he taketh hiede, And makth the stable dore fast. *c.* **1490** *Provs. in Sloane MS.* 747 (ed. Förster) in *Anglia* 42. 204 Whan the stede ys stole than shytte the stable-dore. *a.* **1530** *R. Hill's Commonpl. Bk.* (E.E.T.S.) 128 Whan the stede is stole, shit the stabill dore. **1546** HEYWOOD I. x. 21 To late (quoth mine aunt) this repentance shewd is, Whan the stéede is stolne shut the stable durre. **1579** LYLY *Euphues* 37 But things past, are past calling againe: it is too late to shutte the stable doore when the steede is stolne. **1602** *Narcissus* (1893) 264 It is too late, When steede is stolne to shutt the stable gate. **1719** DEFOE *Crusoe* II (Globe) 387 It was only shutting the Stable Door after the Stead was stoln. **1817** LAMB to the Kenneys, Oct. 'Tis too late when the steed is stole, to shut the stable door.

Shut up shop (windows), To.

c. **1514** A. BARCLAY *Egloges* IV. l. 493 Then may I . . . shet the shopwindowes for lacke of marchaundice. **1599** DEKKER *Shoem. Holiday* (1610) v. ii We may shut up our shop and make holiday. **1650** VAUGHAN *Silex Scint., Faith* 19 Stars shut up shop, mists pack away, And the Moon mourns. **1659** N. R. *Eng.–Fr.*, &c. 58 He that hath not his craft let him shut up shop. **1678** RAY 89 *A Bankrupt.* He has shut up shop-windows.

Shut up shop, *see also* Craft (He that hath not the); Wares be gone (When), **s. u. s.** windows.

Shuttle, *see* Life is a s.

Siamese twins.

[Two male natives of Siam, Chang and Eng (1814–74), who were united by a tubular band in the region of the waist.] **1899** *Daily News* 15 Mar. 4/4 The death of M. Erckmann . . . removes the last of the Siamese twins of French fiction. **1904** H. SIDGWICK *Misc. Ess. & Add.* 273 There seems no adequate reason why Latin and Greek should be regarded as a sort of linguistic Siamese twins, which nature has joined together, and which would wither if separated.

Sib[1] as sieve and riddle[2], As much | that grew in the same wood together.

a. **1530** DUNBAR *Test. of A. Kennedy* 55 Wks. (1907) 102 We were als sib as seue and riddill, In vna silua que creuerunt. **1670** RAY 207 As much sib'd as sieve and ridder, that grew both in a wood together. **1721** KELLY 31 *As sib as sive and riddle that grew both in one wood.* Spoken to them who groundlessly pretend kindred to great persons. **1824** SCOTT *Redg. Lr.* xiii Whilk . . . sounds as like being akin to a peatship & sherriffdom, as a sieve is sib to a riddle. [[1] related. [2] a coarse wire sieve.]

Sick and sorry.

1907 SIR W. BUTLER *From Naboth's V.* 182 The devil is sick and sorry to-day in South Africa, but his sorrow is for himself. It does not extend to others.

Sick, He who never was | dies the first fit.

1732 FULLER no. 2409.

Sick Man.

[*i.e.* Turkey.] [**1853** NICHOLAS I.] **1855** HAMLEY *War in Crimea* (ed. 3) 11 The true design of the Czar . . . had been made clear . . . in various conversations in . . . 1853. 'We have on our hands a sick man. . . . I repeat to you that the sick man is dying.' **1909** *Spectator* 2 Oct. The ambitions of Greeks, when Turkey was only the 'Sick Man', may have had a reasonable hope of being realized, . . . but . . . Turkey has rejuvenated herself.

Sick man is not to be pitied who hath his cure in his sleeve, That.

1732 FULLER no. 4371.

Sick nor sorry, Neither.

1894 NORTHALL *Folk-phrases* 20 . . . Said of one who has caused annoyance or trouble and takes the matter lightly. Some understand ' sorry' in the old sense of *sore*.

Sick of a fever lurden[1], He that is | must be cured by the hazel gelding.

c. **1500** HAZLITT *Early Pop. Poetry* i. 93 I trow he was infecte certeyn With the faitour, or the fever lordeyn. **1633** D. DYKE *Com. upon Philemon* 134 Yet sometimes, the fever-lurden having caught her, she begins to be lazy, and to have no list to work. **1678** RAY 172. [[1] laziness.]

Sick of the idle crick, and the belly-wark in the heel.

1678 RAY 254 . . . Bellywark, *i.e.* belly-ake. It is used when people complain of sickness for a pretence to be idle upon no apparent cause.

Sick of the idles.

1616 WITHALS 558. **1638** J. CLARKE *Phraseol. Puerilis* C 7 Sicke of the idle. **1639** CLARKE 144.

Sick of the Lombard fever.

[= a fit of idleness.] **1659** HOWELL *Eng. Prov.* 11/2. **1670** RAY 215 Sick o' th' *Lombard* feaver, or of the idles.

Sick of the mulligrubs with eating chopped hay.

[= ill-tempered and grumbling.] *c.* **1620** BEAUM. & FL. *Mons. Thomas* II. iii (A) Whose dog lies sick o' the mulligrubs? **1670** RAY 218. **1738** SWIFT (Dial. i) 339 *Lady S.* What! you are sick of the mulligrubs with eating chopped hay?

Sick of the silver dropsy.

[= inordinate desire for silver.] **1616** DRAXE 33 He hath the silver dropsie. **1639** CLARKE 40.

Sick of the slothful guise, loth to bed and loth to rise, Ever. (*See also* Sluggard's guise.)

1639 CLARKE 292.

Sick, *see also* Physic before he is s. (Takes).

Sicker, *see* Over fast (s.) over loose.

Sickle, *see* Marries between s. and scythe.

Sickness of the body may prove the health of the soul, The.

1855 BOHN 514.

Sickness shows (tells) us what we are.

1732 FULLER no. 4161. **1908** S. PAGET *Confessio Medici* 19 Sickness, as Lucretius says of impending death, shows us things as they are: the mask is torn off, the facts remain.

Sickness soaks the purse.

1616 BRETON *Cross. Prov.* Wks. (1879) II. App. iii.

Sickness, *see also* Chamber of s. is chapel of devotion; Foul dirty ways and long s. (Take heed of); Health and s. men's double enemies; Health is not valued till s.; No man was ever more healthful from s.

Side of the hedge, To be on the right (better, safe) *or* wrong.

1600 HOLLAND *Pliny* lxix. Epit. 1246 One who ever loved to be on the better side of the hedge. **1653** BAXTER *Worc. Petit. Def.* 24 If you say, We have too much in any of these particulars; then we are on the safer side of the hedge. **1816** AINSWORTH *Lat. Dict.* s.v. To be on the wrong side of the hedge, or mistaken, *hallucinor, erro.*

Side(s), *see also* Right s.; Rise on right (wrong) s.; Two s. to every question.

Sieve(s), *see* Blind enough who sees not through s.; Deals in the world (He that) needs four s.; Leak like s.; Sib as s. and riddle; Water in a s. (Carry).

Sift him grain by grain and he proveth but chaff.

1616 DRAXE 47.

Sigh (*verb*), *see* Never s. but send.

Sight for sore eyes, A.

1836 HAZLITT *Of Persons one Would Wish to have Seen* 347 What a sight for sore eyes that would be [viz. to see Garrick act].

Sight of a man hath the force of a lion, The.

1640 HERBERT 346.

Sight, *see also* Farther the s. nearer the rain; Out of s. out of languor; Out of s. out of mind.

Sign invites you in; The | but your money must redeem you out.

1642 TORRIANO 7 As you come in the signe inviteth you, but as you go out, you must have money or moneyes worth. **1732** FULLER no. 4746.

Sike[1] a man as thou wald[2] be, draw thee to sike[1] company.

1641 FERGUSSON 88. [[1] such. [2] would.]

Sike[1] as the shepherd, sike be his sheep.

1579 SPENSER *Shep. Cal.* Sept. Wks. (Globe) 474 *Dig.* Sike as the shepheards, sike bene her sheepe. [[1] such.]

Silence catches a mouse.

1639 CLARKE 302 Whist, and catch a mouse. **1721** KELLY 289 . . . Saying nothing, till you be ready to put in execution, is the way to shun prevention, and effect your business.

Silence doth seldom harm.

1630 BRATHWAITE *Eng. Gent. &c.* (1641) 51 (A) Silence . . . may doe good, but can doe little harme. **1670** RAY 24. **1732** FULLER no. 4170 Silence seldom hurts.

Silence gives consent.

c. **1380** WYCLIF *Sel. Wks.* III. 349 Oo maner of consent is, whanne a man is stille & tellip not. *c.* **1490** *Partonope* (E.E.T.S.) 467 This proverbe was seide full longe a-go: 'Who so holdeth hym still dothe assent.' **1591** LYLY *Endym.* v. iii *End.* Silence, madam, consents. **1611** COTGRAVE S.V. 'Consentir' . . . (Many, who know not much more Latine, can say, *Qui tacet consentire videtur.*[1]) **1651** HOBBES *Leviath.* II. xxxvi. 138 Silence is sometimes an argument of Consent. **1721** KELLY 299. **1847–9** *Friends in C.* 1 Ser. ix I have known a man in office bear patiently . . . a serious charge which a few lines would have entirely answered. . . . Silence does not give consent in these cases. **1883** FROUDE *Short Stud.* IV. I. vii. 77 The archbishop [Becket] answered that there was a proverb in England that silence gave consent. [*c.* 1200 in *Materials Hist. Becket* (Rolls) I. 68.] [[1] BONIFACE VIII. *Sexti Decret. Lib.* v. xii.]

Silence in the pigmarket, and let the old sow have a grunt.

1894 NORTHALL *Folk-phrases* (E.D.S.) 22.

Silence (is) the best ornament of a woman.

1539 TAVERNER (1545) I 3ᵛ *Mulierem ornat silentium.* Silence garnysheth a woman. **1547** BALDWIN *Treatise of Moral Phil.* (1550) K 7ᵛ Silence in a woman, is a great and a goodly vertue. *a.* **1619** DANIEL *To Lady Anne Clifford* 85 Through silence women never ill became. **1659** HOWELL *Eng. Prov.* 11/1.

Silence was never written down.

1853 TRENCH iv. 86 On the *safety* that is in silence, I know none happier than . . . one most truly characteristic of Italian caution: *Silence was never written down.*[1] [[1] Il tacer non fu mai scritto.]

Silence, *see also* Repented speech than s. (More); Sorrow makes s. best orator; Speech is silvern, s. golden; Wisdom like s. (No).

Silent as death (the grave).

1377 LANGLAND *P. Pl.* B. x. 137 As doumbe as deth. **1604–5** SHAKS. *Othello* V. ii. 93 Ha! no more moving? Still as the grave. **1829** SCOTT *Jrnl.* 1 July The house . . . became silent as the grave.

Silent deaths.

1898 ANSTED *Dict. Sea Terms* 253 Silent deaths.—A name given by fishermen to screw steam vessels. . . . Those . . . accidentally in too close proximity to large steamers, . . . will have discovered how silently these huge vessels creep along.

Silent, He that is | gathers stones.

1599 MINSHEU (1623) 2 X 3. **1813** RAY 159.

Silent Highway, The.

[= the Thames.] **1859** G. A. SALA *Twice Round Clock* (1878) 87 The Silent Highway has been their travelling route. On the broad . . . bosom of Father Thames, they have been borne in swift, grimy little steamboats.

Silent man, *see* Beware of a s. dog (man)

Silent Sister.

1834 FATHER PROUT in *Fraser* 1 Aug. The silent and unproductive Trinity College Dublin [at that time producing few books]. **1896** W. O'C. MORRIS *Ireland 1494–1868*, 245 The University of Dublin . . . was not supported by great public schools, . . . and it was long known by the name of the 'Silent Sister'.

Silent, *see also* Beware of a s. dog; Speak fitly or be s. wisely; Wise men s. fools talk.

Silk and scarlet walks many a harlot, In.

1869 HAZLITT 234. **1892** NORTHALL *Eng. Folk Rhymes* 547 A certain lady . . . observing a mason carefully working said, 'By line and rule, works many a fool, . . .' To which the man readily responded, 'In silk and scarlet walks many a harlot, . . .'

Silk, The fairest | is soonest stained.

1579 LYLY *Euphues* (Arb.) 39 The fairest silke is soonest soyled. **1639** CLARKE 83. **1670** RAY 88 . . . The handsomest women are soonest corrupted, because they are most tempted. It may also be applied to good natures, which are more easily drawn away by evil company.

Silk purse (Velvet) out of a sow's ear, You cannot make a.

c. **1514** A. BARCLAY *Eclogues* v. 360 None can . . . make goodly silke of a gotes flece. **1579** GOSSON *Ephemerides* 62 b Seekinge . . . too make a silke purse of a Sowes eare, that when it shoulde close, will not come togeather. **1659** HOWELL *Eng. Prov.* 13/1 You will never make a Sattin purse of a Sowes ear. **1670** RAY 152. You cannot make velvet of a sow's ear. **1738** SWIFT (*Dial.* ii) 349 *Col.* He fell asleep, and snored so hard that we thought he was driving his hogs to market. *Never.* . . . You can't make a silk purse out of a sow's ear. **1767** STERNE *T. Shandy* IV Slawkenburgius's Tale, As certainly as you can make a velvet-cap out of sow's ear. **1834** MARRYAT *P. Simple* xii The master, . . . having been brought up in a collier, he could not be expected to be very refined; . . . 'it was impossible to make a silk purse out of a sow's ear'. **1875** BROWNING *Inn Album* i Still silk purse Roughs finger with some bristle sow-ear-armed.

Silks and satins put out the fire in the chimney (kitchen fire).

1640 HERBERT 359. **1721** KELLY 293 (with 'kitchen fire'). Commonly spoken by servants, when they think that their masters' and mistresses' extravagant cloaths make their meat and drink something scarcer. **1758** FRANKLIN in ARBER *E. Garner* v. 583 Many a one, for the sake of finery on the back, has gone with a hungry belly, and half starved their families. *Silks and satins, scarlet and velvets,* as *Poor* RICHARD says, *put out the kitchen fire!*

Silk, *see also* Silver in his purse (He that has not), should have s. on tongue.

Sillier than a crab, that has all his brains in his belly, He is.

1732 FULLER no. 1944.

Silly Billy.

[1836] **1881** GOLDW. SMITH *Lect. & Ess.* 193 Old William, Duke of Gloucester, the King's uncle, being rather weak in intellect, was called 'Silly Billy'.

Silly[1] child is soon ylered.[2]

c. **1300** *Prov. of Hending* 9 Sely child is sone ylered. *c.* **1386** CHAUCER *Prior. T.* 1701, 2 And he forgate it naught, For sely child wol alday soone leere. *c.* **1400** *Latin MS. 394, John Rylands Libr.* (ed. Pantin) in *Bull. J. R. Libr.* XIV, f. 17a Sely chylde sone lerned. **1641** FERGUSSON 88 Sillie bairns are eith to lear. [[1] good, forward. [2] taught.]

Silly fish that is caught twice with the same bait, It is a.

1732 FULLER no. 2879.

Silly (Sairy, Sorry) flock where the ewe bears the bell, It is a.

1641 FERGUSSON 60 It is a sillie flock where the 30we[1] bears the bell. **1721** KELLY 181 *It is a sairy flock where the ewe bears the bell.* It is a bad house where the wife commands. **1732** FULLER no. 2885. [[1] ewe.]

Silly Jockey, There never was a | but there was as silly a Jenny.

1821 J. GALT *Annals of Par.* xxvii Take a lady of your own.... There never was a silly Jock, but there was as silly a Jenny'. **1832** HENDERSON 140 There ne'er was a silly Jockey but what there was a silly Jenny.

Silly man that can neither do good nor ill, He is a.

1721 KELLY 137 Used as a dissuasive from disobliging any, even the meanest, for some time or other it may be in his power to do you service, or disservice.

Silly pack that may not pay the custom, It is a.

1641 D. FERGUSSON 66. **1721** KELLY 178 *It's an ill pack that's no worth the custom.* It is a bad thing that is not worth any small pains, or cost, that it may require.

Silly season.

[August & Sept., when newspapers, for lack of real news, discussed trivial topics.] **1871** *Punch* 9 Sept. 102/2 The present time of the year has been named 'the silly season'. **1884** *Illustr. Lond. News* 23 Aug. 171/1 The 'silly season' having begun . . . , the newspapers are, as a necessary consequence, full of instructive and amusing matter.

Silly Suffolk.

1867 J. G. NALL *Gt. Yarm. & Glos. E. Angl.* 720 'Silly Suffolk' and 'Essex Calves' are local amenities liberally bestowed on each other by the natives.

Silly Sutton.

1892 *Eastern Ev. News,* Norwich 15/11 in LEAN I. 152 In this district we had . . . 'Silly Sutton' . . . Sutton is awarded its . . . title from the tradition that its aged natives . . . put their hands out of their bedroom windows to feel if it was daylight.

Silver in his purse, He that has not | should have silk on his tongue.

1659 HOWELL *Ital.–Eng.* 5 Who hath not money in his purse, let him have honey in his mouth. **1721** KELLY 143 . . . He that cannot pay his debts should at least give good words. **1732** FULLER no. 2149.

Silver key can open an iron lock, A.

1618 *The Owl's Almanack* 39 Siluer keyes open any doores. **1732** FULLER no. 400.

Silver streak.

[*i.e.* the English Channel.] **1879** *Even. Standard* 11 Nov. The answer of the citizens of London to the 'silver-streak' politicians. **1903** H. B. GEORGE *Relat. of Geog. & Hist.* 136 The value of the 'silver streak', as a defence for England against her enemies, scarcely needs demonstration in words. **1909** *Sphere* 27 Mar. 'The silver streak' can be crossed in little over an hour from Folkestone or Dover.

Silver will have a silver sound.

1594–5 SHAKS. *Rom. & Jul.* IV. v. 134 Silver hath a sweet sound. **1616** DRAXE 241 Siluer will haue a siluer sound.

Silver, *see also* Angle with s. hook; Born with a s. spoon; No s. no servant; No s. without dross; Shoot with s. gun; Sick of the s. dropsy; Tip the cow's horn with s.; White s. draws black lines.

Silvered pin, fair without but foul within, He is like a.

1813 RAY 237.

Simile runs on all fours, No.

[L. *Nullum simile quatuor pedibus czrrit*]. **1598** CHAPMAN *Iliad* ii (comm.) That a simile must *semper uno pede claudicare* [from Spondanus] . . . only sheweth how vain vulgar tradition is. **1629** T. ADAMS *Serm.* (1861–2) I. 376 No metaphor should of necessity run like a coach on four wheels. **1692** BENTLEY *Phalaris* (Bohn) 13 quotes 'the English proverb'. **1825** MACAULAY *Ess. on Milton* It is not easy to make a simile go on all fours.

1905 ALEX. MACLAREN *Expos., Matthew* III. 39
No metaphor of that sort goes on all fours,
and there has been a great deal of harm done
. . . by carrying out too completely the
analogy between money debts and our sins
against God.

Simon, *see* **Simple S.; Sup, S.**

Simon and Jude[1] all the ships on the sea home they do crowd.

1902–4 LEAN I. 381 [[1] SS. Simon & Jude,
Oct. 28.]

Simper-de-cocket.

[An affected, coquettish air; a woman charac-
terized by this; a flirt.] *a.* 1529 SKELTON *E.
Rummyng* 55 She wyll iet. . . . In her furred
flocket, And gray russet rocket, With symper
the cocket. *a.* 1530 J. HEYWOOD *Weather* 877
(Brandl), I saw you dally with your symper
de cokket. 1546 HEYWOOD II. i. 43 Vpright
as a candle standth in a socket, Stoode she
that daie, so simpre de cocket. 1707 tr. *Wks.
C'tess D'Anois* (1715) 384 I have here in my
Custody, said she, a little Simper de cockit
that will not let me be at quiet.

Simpers like a bride on her wedding-day, She.

1678 RAY 288.

Simpers like a furmity kettle, She.

1565 J. PHILLIP *Patient Grissil* C 3 l. 429
Symper like a fyrmentie pot. 1594 NASHE
Unf. Trav. (McKerrow) ii. 225 I sympered
with my countenance like a porredge pot on
the fire when it first begins to seethe. 1678
RAY 289. 1738 SWIFT (Dial. i) 337 *Lady S.*
Her tongue runs like the clapper of a mill. . . .
Never. And yet she simpers like a firmity
kettle.

Simpers like a riven dish, She.

1678 RAY 288.

Simple man is the beggar's brother, The.

1832 HENDERSON 90

Simple Simon.

1785 GROSE *Dict. Vulgar T.* s.v. Simple
Simon' a natural, a silly fellow. 1899 *Westm.
Gaz.* 12 June 5/1 A tall, ungainly Simple
Simon of a peasant.

Simples, *see* **Battersea; Cut for the s.**

Sin brings its punishment with it, Every.

1616 DRAXE 171 As a man sinneth, so is his
punishment. 1640 HERBERT 352. 1824
MARRYAT *Jacob Faith.* xiv That is the punishment of making free with the bottle, . . . but
if it is an offence, then it carries its own
punishment.

Sin that is hidden is half-forgiven.

1567 G. FENTON *Bandello* (T.T.) ii. 149 (A)
Me thinkes a falte don in secrett is halfe

perdoned. 1629 *Bk. Meery Riddles* (Halliwell)
97.

Sin to sell dear, It is no | but a sin to give ill measure.

1721 KELLY 189 . . . When you sell the buyers
are on their guard, but measures and weights
are left to your conscience. 1732 FULLER
no. 2993 It is not a sin to sell dear, but it is to
make ill measure.

Sin(s), *see also* **Charity covers s.; Fall into s.
is human; Fear nothing but s.; Four things
(Of) man has more than he knows;
Hospitality (S. against); Kiss (Do not
make me) and will not make me s.; Lie
against the devil (S. to); Old s. new shame;
Punishment (Many without), none without
s.; Seven deadly s.; Swims in s. shall sink
in sorrow; Ugly as s.** *See also* **Sins.**

Sinew, *see* **Tough s. in auld wife's heel.**

Sinews of war, *see* **Money is the s.**

Sing before breakfast, If you | you'll cry before night. (*Cf.* Laugh before breakfast.)

1530 PALSGRAVE 776 You waxe mery this
morning, God gyue grace you wepe nat or
nyght.

Sing *lachrymæ*, To.

[= to lament. Refers to John Dowland's
'Lachrimae or Seaven Teares', London,
1605.] 1614 SIR T. OVERBURY *Characters*
Wks. (1890) 155 *A Prison.* Every man here
sings *Lachrymæ* at first sight.

Sing like a lark, To.

1620 SHELTON *Quix.* II. xix (1908) II. 313
He . . . sings like a lark, plays upon a gittern
as if he made it speak. 1621 JONSON *Gypsies
Metam.* Wks. (Herford & Simpson) VII. 600.
1847–8 THACKERAY *Vanity F.* v Amelia
came . . . singing like a lark.

Sing (one's) *nunc dimittis*, To.

[= to declare glad acceptance of release from
life or some employment. The first words of
the Song of Simeon in *Luke* ii. 29.] 1642
NETHERSOLE *Consid. upon Affairs* 8 I should
. . . cheerfully sing my *Nunc dimittis.* 1776
J. ADAMS Wks. (1854) IX. 391 When these
things are once completed, I shall . . . sing
my *nunc dimittis,* return to my farm [&c.].
1825 HAN. MORE in W. ROBERTS *Mem.* (1834)
IV. 257 If I could see the abolition of the
slavery . . . in the West Indies . . . I could
sing my *nunc dimittis* with joy. 1859 DARWIN
Life & Lett. (1887) II. 232 I am now contented, and can sing my 'nunc dimittis'.

Sing *placebo*, To.

[= to play the sycophant, be time-serving.
L. *Placebo.* I shall be pleasing or acceptable.
Placebo Domino in regione vivorum, Ps. cxiv. 9
Vulg.] 1340 *Ayenb.* 60 þe uerþe zenne is þet
huanne hi alle zingeþ 'Placebo', þet is to
zigge: 'mi lhord zayþ zoþ, mi lhord deþ wel'.
c. 1386 CHAUCER *Pars. T.* I. 543 Flatereres

been the deueles Chapelleyns that syngen euere Placebo. **1607–8** BACON *Gen. Naturaliz.* Wks. (1879) I. 467 If any man shall think that I have sung a placebo, for mine own particular, I would have him know that I am not so unseen in the world. **1818** SCOTT *Let.* 12 Nov. in LOCKHART *Life* xliii He is too much addicted to the *placebo* . . . too apt to fear to give offence by contradiction.

Sing so merry a note, Who can | as he that cannot change a groat?

1546 HEYWOOD I. xii. 38 And who can syng so mery a note, As maie he, that can not chaunge a grote. Ye (quoth he) beggers maie syng before théeues.

Sing the same (another) song, To.

[TERENCE *Phormio* 3. 2. 10 *Cantilenam eandem canis.* You sing the same song.] **1390** GOWER *Conf. Amantis* I. 260 O thou, which hast desesed The Court of France be thi wrong, Now schalt thou singe an other song. **1588** J. UDALL *Diotrephes* (Arb.) 18 If they had euen my experience, they would sing another song. **1670** RAY 192 . . . Nothing more troublesome and ungrateful than the same thing over and over. **1711** W. KING tr. *Naude's Ref. Politics* iii. 91 The Jesuits began to play their part, and sing another song.

Sing(s, eth), *see also* Beggar may s. before thief; Dirt-bird s., we shall have rain; Learn to say before you s.; Little birds that can s.; Many a man s. that wife home bringeth; Robin s. in bush (If); Thorn against breast (S. with).

Singed cat, He is like the | better than he's likely.[1]

1737 RAMSAY 40. **1914** K. F. PURDON *Folk of Furry F.* ii Maybe I'm like the singed cat, better than I look! [[1] of good appearance.]

Singest like a bird called a swine, Thou.

1678 RAY 269.

Singing man keeps his shop in his throat, The.

1640 HERBERT 359.

Single long, shame at length.

1659 HOWELL *Brit. Prov.* 21.

Sings at a deaf man's door, He.

1616 DRAXE 39. **1631** T. DEKKER *Penny-Wise, Pound-Foolish* B 2 The musicke of their enchanting tongues but songs to the deafe. **1638** J. CLARKE *Phraseol. Puerilis* E 2[v].

Sings on Friday, He that | will weep on Sunday.

1640 HERBERT 336. **1642** FULLER *Fast Serm. on Innoc. Day* (1891) I. 241 Let not old men . . . be transported with their follies. . . . The French proverb saith, *They that laugh on Friday, shall cry on Sunday.* [Fr. *Tel qui rit vendredi, dimanche pleurera.*]

Sings, *see also* Sing(s).

Sink or swim.

c. **1368** CHAUCER *Compl. Pite* 110 Ye rekke not whethyr I flete or sinke. **1386** Id. *Knight's T.* 1539 She . . . reccheth neuere wher I synke or fleete. **1538** STARKEY *England* I. iii. 85 They care not (as hyt ys com mynly sayd) 'whether they synke or swyme'. **1668** R. STEELE *Husbandman's Calling* iii (1672) 29 I will be just and honest, sink or swim. **1818** SCOTT *Ht. Midl.* xxvi Sink or swim, I am determined to gang to Lunnon. **1889** 'R. BOLDREWOOD' *Robbery under Arms* xxiii It's sink or swim with all of us.

Sins and our debts are often more than we think, Our.

1642 TORRIANO 59. **1658** *Comes Facundus* 23. **1659** HOWELL *Ital.–Eng.* 1 Our sinnes and our debts are alwayes more then we take them to be. **1721** KELLY . . . We are too apt to have too good an opinion of our condition both in reference to this world, and another.

Sins are not known till they be acted.

1640 HERBERT 360.

Sins grow old, When all | covetousness is young.

1560 BECON *Catechism* (P.S.) 373 Covetous ness is a vice appropriated . . . to old men, according to this old saying: *Cum omnia vitia senescunt, sola avaritia juvenescit*: 'When all vices wax old, covetousness alone waxeth young.' **1640** HERBERT 318.

Sins, *see also* Sin(s).

Sion, *see* Nun of S.

Sip up the Severn and swallow Malvern as soon, You may.

1659 HOWELL *Eng. Prov.* 20/1 . . . *meant of impossibilities.* **1787** GROSE (*Worcs.*) 231 . . . That is, sip up a great river, and swallow a range of hills.

Sip, *see also* Blow first, s. afterwards.

Sir, *see* Call one s. and something else.

Sir Robert, *see* Robert.

Sire, *see* Litter is like to s. and dam.

Sirrah[1] your dogs, sirrah not me; for I was born before you could see.

1670 RAY 192. **1732** FULLER no. 6496 Sirrah your dog, but sirrah not me, For I was born before you could see. [[1] a contemptuous form of address.]

Sister of the Charterhouse,[1] She is a.

1528 TINDALE *Obed. Chrn. Man* (1888) 267 Of her that answereth her husband six words for one, we say, 'She is a sister of the Charter house': as who should say, 'She thinketh that she is not bound to keep silence; their silence shall be a satisfaction for her.' [[1] a Carthusian monastery with severe discipline.]

Sister(s), *see also* Silent S.; Three **s.**

Sisyphus, *see* Stone of S.

Sit awhile and go a mile.

1530 PALSGRAVE 436/2 Rest a whyle and roune a myle. **1639** CLARKE 235.

Sit in Rome and strive against the Pope, It is hard to.

1641 FERGUSSON 112 Ye may not sit in Rome and strive with the Pope. **1721** KELLY 194 ... It is foolish to strive with our governors, landlords, or those under whose distress we are. **1904–10** A. MACLAREN *Expos., Daniel* 58 'It is ill sitting at Rome and striving with the Pope'. Nebuchadnezzar's palace was not precisely the place to dispute with Nebuchadnezzar.

Sit in the chair that have malt to sell, They may.

1639 CLARKE 99.

Sit in your place, and none can make you rise.

1611 COTGRAVE s.v. 'Seoir' He need not fear to be chidden who sits where he is bidden. **1640** HERBERT 335. **1721** KELLY 299 *Sit in your seat, and none will raise you.* Spoken to those who have gotten an affront for presuming beyond their station. **1853** TRENCH v. 115 Genuine modesty and manly self-assertion are united in this: *Sit in your own place, and no man can make you rise.*

Sit near the fire when the chimney smokes, It is best to.

1779–81 JOHNSON *Lives of Poets* (Napier) I. 236 Roscommon, foreseeing that some violent concussion of the State was at hand, purposed to retire to Rome, alleging, that *it was best to sit near the chimney when the chamber smoaked.* **1826** SCOTT *Woodst.* xxi It is best sitting near the fire when the chimney smokes; ... Woodstock, ... in the vicinity of the soldiers, will be less suspected ... than more distant corners.

Sit on (upon *or* in) one's skirts, To.

[= to press hard upon one; punish severely.] **1546** HEYWOOD I. v. 10 Hold their noses to grinstone, and syt on theyr skurtis, That erst sate on mine. **1654** H. L'ESTRANGE *Chas. I* (1655) 184 Many began ... to sit upon the Bishops skirts, that is, to controvert the motes and bounds of their authority. **1755** SMOLLETT *Quix.* II. iii. xv (1803) IV. 75 If my government holds, ... I will sit upon the skirts of more than one of these men of business.

Sit on your thumb till more room do come.

1894 NORTHALL *Folk-phrases* (E.D.S.) 22 ... A reply to a child that continually says, 'Where shall I sit?'

Sits above that deals acres (land), He.

c. **1300** *Provs. of Hending* in *Anglia* **51.** 267

Heye he sit þat akeres deleþ. **1641** FERGUSSON 42. **1721** KELLY 162 ... An appeal to the divine providence, justice, and omniscience.

Sits full still that has riven breeks, He.

1641 FERGUSSON 44. **1721** KELLY 149 ... A man who is not very clamorous in his complaints, may lie under as great inconveniencies as they that do. It took its rise from the Earl of Angus, who being in an engagement,[1] ... stayed till all his men were drest, and then told them that he was wounded himself, by repeating this proverb. **1822** SCOTT *Nigel* xxxv Poortith takes away pith, and the man sits full still that has a rent in his breeks. **1852** E. FITZGERALD *Polonius* 63 The Guilty Man. May escape, but he cannot rest sure of doing so.—*Epicurus.* **Riven** breeks sit still.' [¹ Shrewsbury, 1403.]

Sits not sure that sits too high, He.

1611 COTGRAVE s.v. 'Asseuré'. He is not safe that's got too high. **1855** BOHN 382.

Sitteth well, He that | thinketh ill.

1573 SANDFORD (1576) 100 H 2ᵛ. **1578** FLORIO *First Fruites* f. 28. **1629** *Book of Meery Riddles* Prov. 10.

Sit(s, teth), *see also* Better rue **s.** than rue flit; Better **s.** still than rise and fall; Frog on chopping-block (S. like); Lowly **s.** richly warm; Patch and long **s.**; Thorn against **breast** (S. with); Wire-drawer (S. like).

Sitting, *see* Cheap **s.** as standing.

Six awls make a shoemaker.

1670 RAY 216.

Six days shalt thou labour and do all that thou art able, and on the seventh—holystone the decks and scrape the cable.

1840 DANA *Two Years bef. Mast* iii Some officers ... have set them to ... scraping the chain cables. The 'Philadelphia Catechism' is, 'Six days shalt thou labor and do all that thou art able, And on the seventh—holystone the decks and scrape the cable'.

Six feet of earth make all men equal.

1659 HOWELL *Ital.–Eng.* 8. **1855** BOHN 487.

Six hours' sleep for a man, seven for a woman, and eight for a fool.

1623 WODROEPHE 310 The Student sleepes six Howres, the Traueller seuen; the Workeman eight, and all Laizie Bodies sleepe nine houres and more. **1642** TORRIANO 38 (A) Five hours sleepeth a traveller, seven a scholar, eight a merchant, and eleven every knave. **1864** FRISWELL *Gentle Life* 259 John Wesley ... considered that five hours' sleep was enough for him or any man. ... The old English proverb, so often in the mouth of George III, was 'six hours for a man, seven

for a woman, and eight for a fool'. 1903
Spectator 19 Dec. Is there not a proverb that
a man requires six hours' sleep, a woman
seven, a child eight and only a fool more? If
this be true, thousands of great men were,
and are, fools.

Six of one and half a dozen of the other.

[= little or no difference between two (sets
of) persons or things.] 1836 MARRYAT *Pirate*
iv I never knows the children. It's just six
of one and half-a-dozen of the other. 1864
J. PAYN *Lost Sir M.* xvi 'There were faults on
both sides; it was six of one, and —.' 1889
'R. BOLDREWOOD' *Robbery under Arms* xi It's
six of one and half-a-dozen of the other, so
far as being on the square goes.

Six strings, *see* Whip with s. s.

Sixes and sevens, To be (set all) at.

[= To be careless of consequences, or let
things go to disorder: the original form, *on
six and seven*, is based on dicing.] *c.* 1340
Avowyne of Arthur (Camden Soc.) st. 65 (A)
Alle in Sundur hit brast in six or in seuyn.
c. 1374 CHAUCER *Troylus* IV. 622 Let nat this
wrechched wo thyn herte gnawe, But manly
set the world on sexe and seuene. *c.* 1410
Towneley Plays xvi, l. 128 I shall, and that
in hy set all on sex and seuen. 1535 JOYE
Apol. Tindale (Arb.) 43 Yet had he leuer
marre and destroy al, and (as they saye) set
all at six and seuen, then [&c.]. 1595–6
SHAKS. *Rich. II* II. ii. 121 All is uneven, And
everything is left at six and seven. 1629
T. ADAMS *Serm.* (1861–2) III. 61 He that sits
on the throne is not idle; to let all things in
the world run at sixes and sevens. 1655–62
GURNALL *Chrn. in Armour* (1865) I. 154
Calling left at six and sevens; yea, wife and
children crying, may be starving; while the
wretch is . . . wasting their livelihood. 1712
ARBUTHNOT *John Bull* II. i His Affairs went
on at sixes and sevens. 1843 MRS. CARLYLE in
New Lett. (1903) I. 219 With her departure
everything went to sixes and sevens. 1848
THACKERAY *Vanity F.* liv There 's a regular
shinty in the house; and everything at sixes
and sevens.

Sixpence, *see* Loseth his wife and s. (He that).

Size cinque will not, and deuce ace cannot, then quatre trey must, If.

[Taken from dicing.] 1602–3 *Diary of Jno.
Manningham* (Camden Soc.) 81 'Size ace
will not, deux ace cannot, quater tree must',
quothe Blackborne, when he sent for wine;
a common phrase of subsidies and such taxes,
the greate ones will not, the little ones cannot,
the meane men must pay for all. 1678 RAY
348 . . . The middle sort bear publick bur-
thens, taxes, &c. most. *Deux ace non possunt
& size cinque solvere nolunt: Est igitur notum
quatre trey solvere totum.*

Skaiths, *see* Better two s. than one sorrow.

Skeer your own fire.

1917 BRIDGE 109 . . . Skeer = to rake out.
Mind your own business.

Skein, *see* Tangled s. to wind off.

Skeleton at the feast, The.

[HDT. 2. 78. PETRON. 35.] 1651 JER. TAYLOR
Holy Dying ii, § 1 (1850) 330 All the wise and
good men of the world, . . . chose to throw
some ashes into their chalices . . . Such was
. . . the Egyptian skeleton served up at feasts.
1839 MRS. CARLYLE *Let.* 20 May, Poor Mrs.
Edward Irving . . . in her weeds, . . . seemed
to me . . . like the skeleton which the old
Egyptians placed at table, in their feasts, to
be a memorial of their latter end. 1909
E. PHILLPOTTS *The Haven* I. iii Dick . . . was
a skeleton at the feast of life in Brixham.

Skeleton in the closet (cupboard), The.

[A secret source of shame or pain to a family
or person.] 1855 THACKERAY *Newcomes* lv
Some particulars regarding the Newcome
family, which will show us that they have a
skeleton in their closets, as well as their
neighbours. 1859 W. COLLINS *Q. of Hearts*
(1875) 62 Our family had a skeleton in the
cupboard. 1884 'F. ANSTEY' *Giant's Robe* xxv
His skeleton came out of the cupboard and
gibbered at him. What right had he, with
this fraud on his soul, to be admitted . . . to
the . . . friendship of a high-minded girl?
1928 *Times* 20 Jan. 13/6 The skeleton of
religious division . . . came out of its cupboard yesterday and rattled its bones in the
Senate Chamber.

Skiddaw hath a cap, If | Scruffel [Criffel] wots full well of that.

1586 CAMDEN *Britann., Cumb.* (1722) I. 1006
*If Skiddaw hath a cap, Scruffel wots full well of
that.* 1662 FULLER (*Cumb.*) I. 340 'If Skiddaw hath a cap, Scruffell wots full well of
that'. These are two neighbour hills, the one
in this county, the other in Annandale in
Scotland. If the former be capped with
clouds and foggy mists, it will not be long
before rain falls on the other. 1791 I. DISRAELI
Curios. Lit. (1858) III. 55 When Scotland, in
the last century, felt its allegiance to England
doubtful, and when the French sent an
expedition to the Land of Cakes, a local
proverb was revived to show the identity of
interests which affected both nations: If
Skiddaw hath a cap, Scruffel wots full well of
that. 1818 SCOTT *Ht. Midl.* xl When a Sark-
foot wife gets on her broomstick, the dames
of Allonby are ready to mount, just as sure
as the byword gangs o' the hills—If Skiddaw hath a cap, Criffel wots full weel of that.

Skiddaw, Lauvellin, and Casticand, are the highest hills in all England.

1586 CAMDEN *Britannia, Cumb.* (1722) II.
1006 The Inhabitants . . . have this rhyme . . .
concerning the height of this and two other
mountains in those parts: *Skiddaw,*[1] *Lauvellin,* and *Casticand, Are the highest hills in
all England.* [[1] 3,054 ft.]

Skilfullest wanting money is scorned, The.

1670 RAY 18.

Skill and confidence are an uncon-
quered army.

1640 HERBERT 346.

Skill in horseflesh, He hath good |
to buy a goose to ride on.

1670 RAY 181. **1738** SWIFT (Dial. i) 340
*Spark. Is it possible she could take that
booby, Tom Blunder for love? Miss. She
had good skill in horse-flesh that could choose
a goose to ride on.*

Skill of man and beast, You have |
you were born between the Beltanes.[1]

1721 KELLY 372 . . . A ridicule on them that
pretend to skill. [[1] the 1st and 8th of May.]

Skill, *see also* All things require s. but appetite; Try your s. in gilt first.

Skimmington, To ride.

1609 C. BUTLER *Fem. Mon.* iv (1623) Ij Yet
when they have it [*sc.* their desire] let them
use poore Skimmington as best they may,
especially in publike, to hide his shame.
1633–4 HEYWOOD & BROME *Late Lancashire
Witches* iv. 230 A Skimmington, A Skimmington.

Skin a louse, and send the hide to
market, He would.

1813 RAY 323 He'd skin a louse, and send the
hide and fat to market.

Skin and bone, He is nothing but.

c. **1430** *Hymns Virgin* (1867) 73 Ful of
fleissche Y was to fele, Now . . . Me is lefte
But skyn & boon. **1562** HEYWOOD *Three
Hund. Epigr.* No. 42, 134 And yet art thou
skyn and bone. **1617** MORYSON *Itin.* I. 251
My self being nothing but skin and bone, as
one that languished in a Consumption.

Skin of one's teeth, With (By) the.

[= narrowly, barely.] **1560** BIBLE (Geneva)
Job xix. 20 I haue escaped with the skinne
of my tethe. **1647** CLARENDON *Contempl. Ps.*
Tracts (1727) 510 He reckoned himself only
escaped with the skin of his teeth, that he
had nothing left. **1894** SALA *Lond. Up to Date*
66 I got in by the skin of my teeth.

Skin (*noun*), *see also* Near is my coat but
nearer my s.; No more of a cat but s. (You
can have); No more of a fox than s. (You
can have); Sell the bear's s. before caught;
Sleeping in a whole s. (Good); Soon goeth
young lamb's s. to market (As); Tail
follow s. (Let); Wish your s. full of holes
(Long ere you).

Skin (*verb*), *see also* Flay (S.) a flint.

Skirts of straw, Who hath | needs
fear the fire.

1664 CODRINGTON 226. **1666** TORRIANO 184
Who hath a tail of straw is afraid of fire. **1670**
RAY 25.

Skirt(s), *see also* Sit on one's s.

Skulls, *see* Golgotha are s. of all sizes (In).

Sky falls we shall catch (have) larks,
If the.

[**1534** RABELAIS I. xi Si les nues tomboient
esperoyt prandre les alouettes.] *a.* **1530**
R. Hill's Commonpl. Bk. (1858) 140 And
hevyn fell we shall have meny larkys. **1546**
HEYWOOD I. iv. 9. **1567** *Appius & Virginia*
(Mal. Soc.) l. 407 If hap the skie fall, we hap
may haue Larkes. **1597** LYLY *Wom. in Moon*
IV. i. 290. **1611** DAVIES *Prov.* 294. *a.* **1619**
FLETCHER *Mad Lover* I. ii. 104. **1670**
RAY 143. **1721** KELLY 343 *What if the lift[1]
fall, you may gather laverocks.[2]* Spoken when
people make silly, frivolous excuses and
objections. **1837** CARLYLE *Fr. Rev.* I. vii. i
' If the King gets this Veto, what is the use of
National Assembly? . . .' Friends, if the sky
fall, there will be catching of larks! [[1] sky.
[2] larks.]

Sky red in the morning is a sailor's
(shepherd's) warning; sky red at
night is the sailor's (shepherd's)
delight.

[BIBLE *Matth.* xvi. 2 When it is evening, ye
say, It will be fair weather: for the sky is red.]
1551 T. WILSON *Rule of Reason* M 4 (A) The
skie was very red this morning, Ergo we are
like to have rayne or nyght. **1584** R. SCOT
Witchcraft XI. xv (A) The skie being red at
evening Foreshews a faire and clear morning;
But if the morning riseth red, Of wind or
raine we shall be sped. **1593** SHAKS. *Venus &
Adonis* 453–5 Like a red morn, that ever yet
betoken'd Wrack to the seaman, tempest to
the field, Sorrow to shepherds. **1893** INWARDS
53.

Slain that had warning, He was |
not he that took it.

1659 HOWELL *Brit. Prov.* 3.

Slander, It may be a | but it is no lie.

1546 HEYWOOD II. vii. 69 For sclaunder
perchaunce (quoth she) I do not denie. It
maie be a sclander, but it is no lie. **1612–13**
SHAKS. *Hen. VIII* II. i. 153 But that slander,
sir, Is found a truth now.

Slander is a shipwreck by a dry
tempest.

1651 HERBERT (Gros.) no. 135a.

Slander leaves a score[1] (scar) behind it.

1616 DRAXE 192 ('skarre'). **1670** RAY 24
('score'). *Calumniare fortiter, aliquid adhærebit.* **1721** KELLY 286 Slander always
leaves a slur. Eng. *Throw much dirt some will
stick.* Lat. *Calumniare audacter, aliquid
adhærebit.* [[1] mark.]

Slander one with a matter of truth,
To.

1603 *Bachelor's Banquet* (F. P. Wilson) 107.

1619 J. FAVOUR *Antiquity Triumphing over Novelty* 318. **1678** RAY 269.

Slander(s), *see also* Pardons . . . are revenges of s.; Truth is no s.

Slanning, *see* Charles's Wain.

Slave(s), *see* Give a s. a rod; Servants (S.) (So many), so many enemies.

Slavery, *see* Think no labour s. that brings penny.

Slay(s), slain, *see* Lie where he was s. (He will not).

Sleep is the brother (cousin) of death.

[HOMER *Iliad* 14. 231 Ἔνθ' Ὕπνῳ ξύμβλητο, κασιγνήτῳ Θανάτοιο. There she fell in with Sleep, brother of Death.] **1563** *Mirr. Mag.* Q iv By him lay heavy slepe, the cosin of death. **1718** POPE *Iliad* xiv 265 The cave of Death's half-brother, Sleep. **1813** SHELLEY *Queen Mab* i How wonderful is Death, Death and his brother Sleep!

Sleep is the image of death.

1639 CLARKE 322.

Sleep soundly, He who desireth to | let him buy the bed of a bankrupt. (*Cf.* Sleeps too sound, &c.)

1813 RAY 21. *Hisp.*

Sleep to all, I don't.

c. **1580** J. CONYBEARE 56 *Non omnibus dormio*, I sleepe not to all menne, I am not readye at euery mans challenge. **1725** BAILEY tr. *Erasmus' Colloq.* 487 (A) You know the old proverb, I don't sleep to all.

Sleep with one eye (one's eyes) open, To.

1581 PETTIE *Guazzo's Civ. Conv.* (1586) f. 140 Which sleepeth (as they say) her eies being open. **1732** FULLER no. 1947 He is so wary, that he sleeps like a Hare, with his Eyes open. **1836** MARRYAT *Midsh. Easy* xviii It may be as well to sleep with one eye open. . . . Suppose we keep watch and watch, and have our pistols out ready?

Sleep without rocking, I shall.

1631 R. BRATHWAIT *Whimzies* (1859) 106 (A) Hee sleepes soundly without rocking. **1738** SWIFT (Dial. iii) 352 *Lady S.* I'm sure I shall sleep without rocking.

Sleep without supping, and wake without owing.

1640 HERBERT 321.

Sleep (*noun*), *see also* Hour's sleep before midnight; Man is known mortal by s. and lust; Seven hours' s. make clown forget design; Six hours' s. for a man; Take it out in s.

Sleeper(s), *see* Net of the s. catches fish; Seven S.

Sleeping dogs, *see* Let s. d. lie; Waken s. d. (Ill to).

Sleeping enough in the grave, There will be.

1758 FRANKLIN in ARBER *E. Garner* v. 579 How much more than is necessary do we spend in sleep? forgetting that . . . *there will be sleeping enough in the grave, as Poor* RICHARD says.

Sleeping fox catches no poultry, The.

1758 FRANKLIN in ARBER *E. Garner* v. 579 How much more than is necessary do we spend in sleep? forgetting that *the sleeping fox catches no poultry.*

Sleeping in a whole skin, It is good.

1546 HEYWOOD II. v. 56 Sens by stryfe, ye maie lose, and can not wyn, Suffer. It is good slepyng in a whole skyn. **1620** SHELTON *Quix.* II. xli (1908) III. 97 'Tis good sleeping in a whole skin; I mean, I am very well at home in this house. **1684** BUNYAN *Pilgr.* II (1877) 210 Mrs. *Bat's-eyes* . . . If he was here again, he would rest him content in a whole skin, and never run so many hazards for nothing. **1745** A. SKIRVING *Johnnie Cope* Fy now, Johnnie, get up and rin; . . . It's best to sleep in a hale skin. **1837** CARLYLE *Fr. Rev.* III. I. iii Patriotism is good; but so is . . . sleeping in whole skin.

Sleeps as dogs do when wives sift meal, He.

1641 FERGUSSON 54 *Of hypocrites.* . . . He sleeps as dogs does, when wives sifts meal. **1721** KELLY 127 *He sleeps as dogs do, when wives bakes; or when wives sift meal.* Apply'd to those who pretend to be asleep, or unconcern'd, who are all the while making their remarks.

Sleeps too sound, Let him that | borrow the debtor's pillow. (*Cf.* Sleep soundly, &c.)

1659 J. HOWELL *Span. Proverbs*, Letter to Sir Lewis Dives, He who desires to sleep soundly, let him buy the boulster of one who died in debt. **1753** JOHNSON *Adventurer* no. 41 I never retired to rest without feeling the justness of the Spanish proverb, 'Let him who sleeps too much, borrow the pillow of a debtor'. **1910** *Times Lit. Sup.* 28 Oct. 398 The dun, the lawyer's letter, the writ, . . . are an old story in the annals of authors by trade. There is a Spanish proverb, 'Let him that sleeps too sound borrow the debtor's pillow'.

Sleep(s, ing), (*verb*), *see also* Child s. upon bones (Let not); Fern is as high (When the) . . . you may s.; Lubberland where they have half a crown for s.; Man s. (When), his head is in stomach; Walk groundly . . . s. soundly.

Sleepy master makes his servant a lout, A.

1640 HERBERT 352.

Sleeve, *see* Broken s. holdeth arm back; Stretch your arm no further than s.

Sleeveless[1] errand, A.

1546 HEYWOOD I. vii. 14 He tooke in hande, To make to my house, a sléeueles errande. **1601–2** SHAKS. *Troil. & Cres.* V. iv. 9 Might send that Greekish whoremasterly villain ... on a sleeveless errand. **1655** FULLER *Ch. Hist.* IV. iii (1868) I. 603 Warwick ... had taken so much pains about nothing, ... employed about a sleeveless errand. [[1] useless; Apperson quotes from Lady Charlotte Guest's tr. of the *Mabinogion* ('Dream of Mayen Wledig') an explanation of this word, relating to the sleeve worn by messengers on their caps as a sort of passport and protection.]

Slender in the middle as a cow in the waist, As.

1621 BURTON *Anat. Mel.* III. ii. III. 1 (A) She stoops, is lame, ... as slender in the middle as a cow in the waist. **1670** RAY 207. **1732** FULLER no. 727.

Slept well, He hath | that remembers not he hath slept ill.

1679 *Baconiana* 61 (from the *Mimi* of Publilius Syrus). **1732** FULLER no. 1897.

Slice, *see* Shoulder of mutton is going (When), good to take s.

Sliddery[1] stone before the hall[2] door, There is a.

1721 KELLY 305 ... Signifying the uncertainty of court favour, and the promises of great men. [[1] slippery. [2] great man's house.]

Slight, *see* Laird s. the lady (If the) so will kitchen boys.

Sling, *see* Killing a crow with empty s.

Slip(s), *see* Better the foot s. than the tongue; Cup and the lip (Many a s. between); Neck out of collar (S.); Stands not surely that never s.

Slippery as an eel, As.

[ERASMUS *Chil. Adag.* Ἀπ' οὐρᾶς τὴν ἐγχελυν ἔχεις. You have got the eel by the tail.] c. **1384** CHAUCER *Ho. Fame* III. 2154 And stampen, as men doon after eles. c. **1412** HOCCLEVE *Reg. Princes* l. 1985 Mi wit is also slippir as an eel. **1546** HEYWOOD I. x. 20 Her promise of fréendshipe, for any auayle, Is as sure to holde as an ele by the tayle. **1641** FERGUSSON 66 I have a sliddrie eill by the tail. **1670** RAY 173 There is as much hold of his word, as of a wet eel by the tail. **1728** POPE *Dunciad* i. 279 How index-learning turns no student pale, Yet holds the eel of science by the tail.

Sloe tree is as white as a sheet, When the | sow your barley whether it be dry or wet.

1678 RAY 49. **1732** FULLER no. 6482.

Sloes, *see* Many haws, many s., many cold toes.

Sloth, like rust, consumes faster than labour wears.

1758 FRANKLIN in ARBER *E. Garner* v. 579 Sloth, by bringing on diseases, absolutely shortens life. *Sloth, like Rust, consumes faster than Labour wears.*

Sloth must breed a scab.

1546 HEYWOOD I. iii. 7.

Sloth (is) the key of (to) poverty.

1669 *Politeuphuia* 306 (A) [with 'mother' for key']. **1853** TRENCH v. 114 To many languages another with its striking image, *Sloth, the key of poverty,*[1] belongs. [[1] *Pereza, llave de pobreza.*]

Sloth turneth the edge of wit.

1579 LYLY *Euphues* (Arb.) 126. **1670** RAY 24.

Slothful guise, *see* Sick of the s. g.

Slothful is the servant of the counters,[1] The.

1640 HERBERT 346. [[1] prisons.]

Slothful man is the beggar's brother, The.

1663 P. STAMPOY 2. **1707** MAPLETOFT 121. **1721** KELLY 315.

Slough of Despond.

1678 BUNYAN *Pilgr.* I (1877) 8 They drew near to a very miry *Slough*, that was in the midst of the plain. The name of the slough was Dispond. ... Wherfore *Christian* was left to tumble in the Slough of *Dispond* alone. **1929** *Times* 4 Oct. 16/4 During the last 12 months trade had come out of the 'Slough of Despond'.

Slovens, *see* Sluts are good enough to make s.' pottage.

Slow and (but) sure.

1606 MARSTON *The Fawn* III. 1. 95 This snail ['s] slow, but sure. c. **1608–9** MIDDLETON *Widow* II. ii *Brand.* Martino, we ride slow. *Mart.* But we ride sure, sir; Your hasty riders often come short home. **1639** CLARKE 325. **1692** L'ESTRANGE *Aesop's Fab.* ccclxix (1738) 388 Slow and sure in these cases, is good counsel. ... *He that will be rich before night, may be hanged before noon.* **1727** GAY *Fables* iv. 28 The hound is slow, but always sure. **1882** BLACKMORE *Christowell* xiv You go on so fast, when you want to slur a point. Slow and sure is my style of business.

Slow and sure, like Pedley's mare.

1732 FULLER no. 4188.

Slow and (but) sure (steady) wins the race.

1859 SMILES *Self-Help* 358 Provided the

dunce has persistency and application he will inevitably head the cleverer fellow without those qualities. Slow but sure wins the race. **1894** NORTHALL *Folk-phrases* (E.D.S.) 22 Slow and steady wins the race.

Slow to bed, *see* Sluggard's guise.

Sluggard must be clad in rags, The.
1636 CAMDEN 307.

Sluggard takes an hundred steps because he would not take one in due time, A.
1707 MAPLETOFT 22. **1855** BOHN 300.

Sluggard's convenient season never comes, The.
1732 FULLER no. 4750.

Sluggards' guise, slow to bed, and slow to rise. (*See also* Sick of the slothful guise.)
1639 J. SMYTH *Berkeley MSS.* (1885) III. 32 Hee is tainted with an evill guise, Loth to bed and lother to rise. **1855** BOHN 487.

Sluggards, *see also* Every day is holiday with s.

Slumber finds (invites) another, One.
1640 HERBERT 342. **1670** RAY 20 (with 'invites').

Sluts are good enough to make slovens' pottage.
1639 CLARKE 287. **1670** RAY 143. **1732** FULLER no. 4190.

Slut(s), *see also* Leap an inch from a s. (She cannot); Tame beasts (Of all) I hate s.

Small beer, *see* Chronicle s. b.; Good s. b. (There is no such thing as); Good things I do not love, good s. b.; Think no s. b. of oneself.

Small birds must have meat.
[**1611** BIBLE *Job* xxxviii. 41 Who provideth for the raven his food? *Ps.* cxlvii. 9 He giveth to the beast his food, and to the young ravens which cry.] **1600–1** SHAKS. *Merry W.* I. iii. 36 Young ravens must have food. **1639** CLARKE 246. **1670** RAY 63 ... Children must be fed, they cannot be maintained with nothing.

Small choice, *see* Choice in rotten apples (There is small)

Small game, *see* Play s. g. before he will sit out.

Small house has a wide throat, A, *see* Little house has a wide mouth.

Small invitation will serve a beggar.
1659 N. R. 92. **1855** BOHN 487.

Small pack becomes a small pedlar, A.
1592 DELAMOTHE (1639) 4. **1611** COTGRAVE s.v. 'Mercier' The little pedler a little pack doth serve. **1623** WODROEPHE 475 A litle pedler, a litle Packe. **1670** RAY 143 ... Petit mercier, petit panier, *Gall.* **1802** WOLCOT (P. Pindar) *Middl. Elect.* i *Little packs Become a little pedlar.*

Small profits and quick returns.
1899 SIR ALG. WEST xxxi His mission had been conducted on strictly commercial lines of small profits and quick returns.

Small riches hath most rest.
1514 A. BARCLAY *Eclogs* iii (Spen. Soc.) 28 *Corn.* Small riches hath most rest, In greatest seas moste sorest is tempest.

Small sorrows speak; great ones are silent.
[SENECA *Phaedra* 607 *Curae leves loquuntur, ingentes stupent.*] **1587** T. HUGHES *Misf. Arthur* (Clar. Press) IV. ii. 14 *Nunc.* Small griefes can speake: the great astonisht stand. **1605** SHAKS. *Macbeth* IV. iii. 209 The grief that does not speak whispers the o'erfraught heart and bids it break. *a.* **1642** KYNASTON in SAINTSBURY *Carol. Poets* ii. 142 Small sorrows speak, the greatest still are dumb.

Small sum will serve to pay a short reckoning, A.
1607–40 *Politeuphuia* s.v. 'Proverbs'. **1639** CLARKE 128. **1732** FULLER no. 413.

Small, *see also* Many s. make a great.

Small, *see also under significant words following.*

Smell a rat, To.
[= to have suspicions.] **1533** *Ballads from MSS.* (B.S.) i. 182 (A) For yf they smell a ratt ... *a.* **1550** *Image Hypocr.* I. 51 in *Skelton's Wks.* (1843) II. 414/2 Yf they smell a ratt, They grisely chide and chatt. **1603** T. HEYWOOD *Wom. K. Kindness* IV. iv *Jenkin.* Now you talk of a cat, Cicely, I smell a rat. **1663** BUTLER *Hudibras* I. i. 821 Quoth Hudibras, I smell a rat; Ralpho, thou dost prevaricate. **1712** ARBUTHNOT *John Bull* II. xi The good old gentlewoman was not so simple as to go into his projects—she began to smell a rat. **1874** G. J. WHYTE-MELVILLE *Uncle John* xx A young ... smelt a rat, and followed him out of the house.

Smell fire, Well may he | whose gown burns.
1640 HERBERT 323.

Smell of the baby, To.
[= to be childish.] **1618** BRETON *Courtier & Countryman* 19 (D.) So long in their horne booke that, doe what they can, they will smell of the Baby till they can not see to read.

Smell of the inkhorn, To.

[= to be pedantic.] 1587 GOLDING *De Mornay* xxvi. 396 Proclamations set forth in such a stile, ... smelling too much of the Inkehorne.

Smell, *see also* Best s. is bread.

Smells best that smells of nothing, He (She).

[PLAUT. *Most.* I. iii. 116 *Mulier tum bene olet ubi nihil olet.*] 1598 MERES *Palladis* f. 32 (A) As women do Smell well which smel of nothing. 1599 DAVIES *Nosce Teipsum* Sith they smell best that do of nothing smell. 1607 *Lingua* IV. iii None can weare Ciuet, but they are suspected of a proper badde sent, where the prouerbe springs, hee smelleth best, that doth of nothing smell. 1621 BURTON *Anat. Mel.* III. ii. III. iii (1651) 477 *Mulier recte olet, ubi nihil olet*; then a woman smells best, when she hath no perfume at all.

Smells of the lamp (oil), It.

[PYTHEAS (PLUTARCH, *Demosth.* 8. 2) Ἐλλυχνίων ὄζειν αὐτοῦ τα ἐνθυμήματα. His impromptus smell of the lamp. L. *Olet lucernam.*] 1542 UDALL tr. *Erasm. Apoph.* (1877) 370 One Pythias obiected to Demosthenes, that his argumentes ... smelled all of the candle: signifiyng, that he pronounced none oracion but out of writyng, and made with greate studie, by Candle in the night time. 1603 FLORIO tr. *Montaigne* I. x. (1897) I. 53 Some compositions ... smell of the oil, and of the lamp, by reason of a certain harshness, ... which long plodding labour imprints in them that be much elaborated. 1605 BACON *Adv. Learn.* I. ii. (Oxf. 1900) 16 Æschines[1] ... told him[2] That his orations did smell of the lamp. 1625 JONSON *Staple News* Prol. A work not smelling of the lamp to-night, But fitted for your Majesty's disport. 1907 *Times Wkly.* 8 Feb. Nothing but the rapt fervour which he brought to his researches could have saved 'John Inglesant' from the smell of the lamp. [[1] Pytheas, not Æschines. [2] Demosthenes.]

Smelt where all stink, One is not.

1629 T. ADAMS *Serm.* (1861–2) I. 76 They that will quarter themselves with the wicked must drink of their poison. If you ask how haps it that their infection is not smelt, Bernard answers: *Ubi omnes sordent, unus minime sentitur,*—One is not smelt, where all stink.

Smelts, *see also* Westward for s.

Smiles of a pretty woman are the tears of the purse, The.

1855 BOHN 515. *It.*

Smile(s) (*noun*), *see also* Better the last s. than first laughter; Rely on the ... s. of mother-in-law (Never).

Smile(s) (*verb*), *see* Laugh (S.) on the wrong side.

Smiling boy seldom proves a good servant, A.

1659 HOWELL *Eng. Prov. Rend. into Fr.* 8.

1670 RAY 24. 1721 KELLY 53 *A laughing fac'd lad makes a lither servant.* It is supposed such are too full of roguery to be diligent. 1852 FITZGERALD *Polonius* liii Softness of smile indicates softness of character.... 'A smiling boy is a bad servant.'

Smiling face, *see* Man without s. f. must not open shop.

Smith (*proper name*), *see* There or thereabouts, as Parson S. says.

Smith and his penny both are black, The.

1640 HERBERT 325. 1655–62 GURNALL *Chrn. in Armour* (1865) I. 504 'The smith', we say, 'and his penny, both are black.' So wert thou with all thy duties and performances, while unreconciled in his eye. 1875 SMILES *Thrift* 178 'The smith and his penny are both black'. But the penny earned by the smith is an honest one.

Smith forges a very weak knife, Often a full dexterous.

c. 1200 *Ancrene Riwle* (Camden Soc.) 52 Ofte a ful hawur smið smeoðið a ful woc knif.

Smith hath always a spark in his throat, The.

1678 RAY 90. 1721 KELLY 334 *The smith has ay a spark in his haise.*[1] And they often take pains to quench it, but to no purpose. 1865 G. MACDONALD *Alec Forbes* lxii 'Jist rax down the bottle, gudewife' ... 'Ye're a true smith, man: ye hae aye a spark i' yer throat.' [[1] throat.]

Smith of Nottingham, The little | who doth the work that no man can.

1609 c. BUTLER *Fem. Monarchie* B 3 The little smith of Nottingham (whose art is thought to excel al art of man). 1662 FULLER (*Notts.*) II. 570 'The little smith of Nottingham, who doth the work that no man can'.... I ... have cause to suspect that this ... is a periphrasis of *Nemo, Οὖτις*, or a person who never was. And the proverb ... is applied to such who, being conceited of their own skill, pretend to the achieving of impossibilities.

Smith's dog, Like the | —so well used to the sparks that he'll not burn.

1862 HISLOP 136 ... Spoken of people who are so much accustomed to tipple, that they never seem any the worse for it.

Smith's dog, Like the | that sleeps at the noise of the hammer, and wakes at the crashing (crunching) of teeth.

1692 L'ESTRANGE *Aesop's Fab.* cxvii (1738) 133 A blacksmith took notice of a cur he had, that would be perpetually sleeping, so long as his master was at his hammer; but whenever he went to dinner, the dog would be sure to make one. **1732** FULLER no. 3236.

Smith, *see also* More bare (Worse shod) than s.'s mare (Who goes); Water in a s.'s forge.

Smithfield bargain, A.

[= a roguish bargain; also, a marriage of interest, not love.] **1604** B. RICH *The Fruits of long Experience* H 2ᵛ Will you then fetch him [your soldier] from Bridewell? That were to buy a horse out of Smithfield. **1624** BURTON *Anat. Mel.* III. iii. iv. ii. 3 S 3ᵛ He that marries a wife out of a suspected Inne or Alehouse, buyes a horse in Smithfield . . . shall likely have a Jade to his horse. **1662** J. WILSON *Cheats* v. v. Your daughter has married a gentleman:—is not this better than a Smithfield bargain? **1710–11** SWIFT *Jrnl. to Stella* 10 Mar. He was such a fool as to offer him money . . . and a hundred pounds is too much in a Smithfield bargain. **1775** SHERIDAN *Rivals* v. i To find myself made a mere Smithfield bargain of at last!

Smithfield, *see also* Westminster for a wife (Who goes to) . . . S. for a horse.

Smithwick, You been like | either clemmed or borsten.

1678 RAY 291 . . . *Chesh.* **1917** BRIDGE 157 You bin like Smithwick, either clemmed or bossten. . . . Either starved or bursting.

Smock, *see* Near is my coat (petticoat) but nearer my s.

Smocks than shirts in a bucking, He that hath more | had need be a man of good forelooking.

1678 RAY 353.

Smoke follows the fairest, The.

[ARISTOPHAN. Fr. 4 Κονδύλους πλάττειν δὲ Τελαμών, τοὺς καλοὺς πειρᾶν καπνός.] **1639** *Berkeley MSS.* (1885) iii. 31 (A) If many Gossips will sit against a smokey chimney the smoke will bend to the fairest. **1646** SIR T. BROWNE *Enq. into Vulg. & Common Err.* in Wks. (1835) III. 166 That smoke doth follow the fairest, is an usual saying with us . . . yet is it the continuation of a very ancient opinion, as . . . observed from a passage in Athenæus; wherein a parasite thus describeth himself: . . . Like smoke unto the fair I fly. **1721** KELLY 314 *The reek follows the fairest. . . .* This is in Aristophanes, and signifies that envy is a concomitant of excellency. **1738** SWIFT (Dial. i) 335 *A puff of smoke comes down the chimney.* Lady A. . . . Does your ladyship's chimney smoke? *Col.* No, madam; but they say smoke always pursues the fair, and your ladyship sat nearest. **1832** HENDERSON 86 Reek follows the fairest, bear witness to the crook.¹ [¹ The chain and hooks by which vessels are hung over the fire.]

Smoke of a man's own country (house) is better than the fire of another's, The.

[ERASM. *Ad. Patriæ fumus igni alieno luculentior.* The smoke of our own country is

brighter than the fire of another.] **1539** TAVERNER 7 The smoke of a man's own country, is much dearer than the fire in a strange country. **1632** MASSINGER *City Madam* v. i (Merm.) 483 *Anne.* We desire A competence. *Mary.* And prefer our country's smoke Before outlandish fire. **1670** RAY 20 (with 'house'). *Hispan.* **1721** KELLY 307 The reek of my own house is better than the fire of another's.

Smoke of Charren.

1659 HOWELL *Eng. Prov.* 21/1 The smoak of Charren; *A Proverb relating to a wife who had beat her husband, and he going out weeping, said it was for the smoake that his eyes watered.*

Smoke(s), *see also* Chimneys (Many), little s.; Consume your own s.; Fire (Make no), raise no s.; No s. without fire; Pipe of peace (S.); Sit near the fire when chimney s.; Three things drive out of house, s. . . . .

Smooth as oil.

1596 SHAKS. *1 Henry IV* I. iii. 7 *a.* **1637** JONSON *Underwoods* (1640) 257.

Smooth, *see also* Still (s.) waters run deep.

Snacks, *see* Go s.

Snail slides up the tower at last, The | though the swallow mounteth it sooner.

1580 LYLY *Euph. & his Eng.* (Arb.) 419 (A) The slow snaile clymeth the tower at last, though the swift swallow mount it. **1595** *Locrine* II. i 1 (*Shaks. Apoc.*) 44 At length the snaile doth clime the highest tops, Ascending vp the stately castle walls. **1732** FULLER no. 4757.

Snail's gallop (*or* pace), To go (at) a.

a. **1400–50** *Alexander* 4095 þan snyʒes¹ þar, out of þat snyth² hill as with a snayles pas, A burly best. **1533** *Johan Johan* l. 419 As fast as a snayle. **1793** MME D'ARBLAY *Lett.* 12 Sept. That snail's pace with which business is done by letters. **1901** *Scotsman* 5 Nov. 6/8 For a time they were able to get along at a snail's gallop, men leading the horses with torches and lanterns. [¹ creeps. ² ? smooth.]

Snails on the road you see, When black | then on the morrow rain will be.

1883 ROPER 31. **1893** INWARDS 144.

Snail(s), *see also* Drive a s. to Rome; Haste like a s.; Tramp on a s., she'll shoot out horns.

Snake (Viper) in the bosom.

[Refers to the ingratitude and treachery of the snake in Aesop's Fable. (I. x).] *c.* **1386** CHAUCER *Summoner's T.* D 1993 Be war from hire that in thy bosom crepeth. Id. *Merch. T.* E² 1786 Lyk to the naddre in bosom sly untrewe. **1590–1** SHAKS. *2 Hen. VI* III. i. 343 I fear me you but warm the starved snake, Who, cherish'd in your breasts, will sting your hearts. **1595–6** *Rich. II* III. ii. 131 Snakes, in my heart-blood warm'd, that sting

my heart. **1671** MILTON *Samson* 763 Drawn
to wear out miserable days. Entangl'd with
a poysnous bosom snake. **1721** KELLY 61
Eng. Put a snake in your Bosom, and it will
sting when it is warm. **1732** FULLER no. 5210
To nourish a viper in one's bosom. **1763**
JOHNSON 8 Dec. in BOSWELL (1848) xviii. 162
Every desire is a viper in the bosom, who,
while he was chill, was harmless; but when
warmth give him strength, exerted it in
poison. **1865** KINGSLEY *Hereward* I. ix. 214
The wild Viking would have crushed the
growing snake in his bosom.

Snake in the grass.

[After VIRGIL *Ecl.* 3. 93 *Latet anguis in
herba.*] *c.* **1290** WRIGHT *Pol. Songs John to
Edw. II* (Camden Soc.) 172 (A) Cum totum
fecisse putas, latet anguis in herba. *c.* **1386**
CHAUCER *Summoner's T.* D 1994 War fro the
serpent that so slily crepeth Under the gras,
and styngeth subtilly. *c.* **1420** LYDGATE *Troy
Bk.* I. 185 Lyche an addre vnder flouris fayre.
1579–80 LODGE *Def. Poet.* (1853) 22 *Latet
anguis in herba*, under your fair show of
conscience take heed you cloak not your
abuse. **1590–1** SHAKS. *2 Hen. VI* III. i. 228
Or as the snake rolled in a flowering bank . . .
doth sting a child. **1594–5** *Rom. & Jul.* III.
ii. 73 O serpent heart, hid with a flower face.
1595–6 *Rich. II* III. ii. 19 And when they
from thy bosom pluck a flower. Guard it, I
pray thee, with a lurking adder. **1605–6** *Macbeth* I. v. 66 Look like the innocent flower,
But be the serpent under it. **1677** YARRANTON
Eng. Impr. 101 Hold, hold, you drive too
fast; there is a snake in the Bush. **1696**
[C. LESLIE] (*title*), The Snake in the Grass.
1709 HEARNE *Collect.* (O.H.S.) II. 173 There
is a Snake in the Grasse, and the designe is
mischievous. **1868** W. COLLINS *Moonstone* xiv
Those enquiries took him (in the capacity of
snake in the grass) among my fellow-servants.

Snake, *see also* Eaten a s.

Snakes in Iceland.

1778 JOHNSON in *Boswell* (1848) lxiv. 589 A
complete chapter of 'The Natural History
of Iceland', from the Danish of *Horrebow*, . . .
chap. lxii.—*Concerning Snakes.* 'There are
no snakes to be met with throughout the
whole island.' **1906** *Spectator* 5 May 'The
Value of a Public School Education' reminds
one of the chapter on the snakes in Iceland.
. . . 'So far as the school at large is concerned
every Greek and Latin book should be
destroyed'.

Snap, *see* Bite (S.) one's nose off.

Snapping so short makes you look so lean.

1678 RAY 345.

Sneck before one's snout, To put a.

1607 *Dobson's Dry Bobs* L 4 He found a
snecke before his snowt. *c.* **1770** PEGGE
Derbicisms (E.D.S.) 65 (A) The sneck is the
latch itself and not the string, Hence the
proverb: 'to put a sneck before one's snout'.

Sneeze, *see* Friend at a s. . . . God bless you.

Sneezed at, Not to be.

[= not to be under-valued.] **1813** SCOTT
24 Aug. in LOCKHART *Life* As I am situated,
£300 or £400 a-year is not to be sneezed at.
1860 SURTEES *Plain or Ringlets?* xxxv Their
Jasper was not a young man to be sneezed at.
1891 N. GOULD *Double Event* 82 A thousand
pounds . . . was not to be sneezed at.

Snipe, *see* Winter enough for the s.

Snite[1] need not the woodcock be-twite[2], The.

1581 J. BELL *Haddon's Answ. Osorius* 374 Ill
may the Snight the Woodcock twight, for
his long bill. **1678** RAY 344 . . . *Som.* [[1] snipe.
[2] upbraid.]

Snotty, *see* Better a s. child.

Snout, *see* Sneck before one's s.

Snow for a se'nnight is a mother to the earth, for ever after a step-mother.

1855 BOHN 40. [*Ital.*]

Snow in harvest, As welcome as.

c. **1568** WAGER *Longer thou livest* F 3 (A) As
snow in haruest is untimelie. **1641** FER-
GUSSON 52 *Of untymous persons.* . . . He is as
welcome as snaw in harvest.

Snow is white, and lieth in the dike, and every man lets it lie.

1546 HEYWOOD II. iv. 51.

Snow year, a rich year, A.

1580 J. FRAMPTON tr. MONARDES (T.T.) ii.
162 (A) For this it is said, The yeare of snow,
the yeare of fertilitie. **1640** HERBERT 322.

Snow(s), snaw(s), *see also* Boil s. or pound it,
can have but water; Candlemas-day is
come (When) s. lies; Corn hides itself in s.
as old man in furs; Filth under s. sun discovers; Many haws many s.; Seasonable
as s. in summer; Under water famine,
under s. bread.

Snowdon will yield sufficient pasture for all the cattle of Wales put together.

1586 CAMDEN *Britannia, Caernarvon* (1722)
II. 795 It is a common saying among the
Welsh, *That the mountains of* Eryreu *would,
in case of necessity, afford Pasture enough for
all the Cattel in Wales.* **1662** FULLER (*Carnarvon*) III. 527 'Craig Eriry, or Snow-don,
will yield sufficient pasture for all the cattle
of Wales put together' . . . importing, by help
of an hyperbole, the extraordinary fruitful-
ness of this place.

Snuff, To be up to.

[= knowing, sharp.] **1811** POOLE *Hamlet
Trav.* II. i He knows well enough The game

we're after: Zooks he's up to snuff. **1837**
DICKENS *Pickwick* xii Up to snuff and a pinch
or two over—eh? **1894** BLACKMORE *Perlycross* xxiv The Parson was up to snuff—if
the matter may be put upon so low a footing.

Snuff, To take (*or* take in).

[= to take offence at a thing.] **1560** DAUS
Sleidane's Comm. 463 A brute went that the
Pope toke it in snuffe [L. *indigne tulisse*] that
this truce was made. **1565** ALLEN *Def. Purg.*
xiv. 262 Aërius, . . . taking snoffe that he
could not get a bishoprike, fell in to the
hæresy of Arius. **1594–5** SHAKS. *L.L.L.* V. ii.
22 You'll mar the light by taking it in snuff.
1597–8 *1 Hen. IV* I. iii. 41 Who [the nose]
therewith angry . . . took it in snuff. **1617**
MORYSON *Itin.* III. 28 Englishmen, especially
being young and unexperienced, are apt to
take all things in snuffe. **1692** L'ESTRANGE
Aesop's Fab. I. clxxxv. 156 Jupiter took
Snuff at the Contempt, and Punish'd him
for't. **1716** T. WARD *Eng. Reform.* 129 Pray
take it not, you old Cur-mudgeon, So much
in snuff and evil dudgeon.

Snug as a bug in a rug, As.

1769 *Stratford Jubilee* II. i If she has the
mopus's, I'll have her, as snug as a bug in a
rug.

Snug as a pig in pea-straw, As.

1603 T. HEYWOOD *Wom. K. Kindness* IV. iv
To bed, . . . and let us sleep as snug as pigs
in pease-straw.

Snug's the word.

1714 STEELE *Lover* No. 7. 11 Mar. *Select.*
(Clar. Press) 279 I here lay *Incog.* for at least
three seconds; snug was the word. **1738**
POPE *Imit. Hor.* Ep. I. 146, 7 'Away, away!
take all your scaffolds down For *Snug's the
word*: My dear! we'll live in Town.'

So far, so good.

1721 KELLY 300 *So far, so good.* So much is
done to good purpose. **1753** RICHARDSON
Grandison v. x (1812) 389 'So far, so good',
said Aunt Eleanor. **1921** M. HEWLETT *Wiltshire
Ess.* 108 Not the most gallant way of putting
it, perhaps; but so far, so good.

So got, so gone.

1678 RAY 349.

So many, *see under significant words following.*

So much is mine as I enjoy.

1573 SANDFORD (1576) H 2ᵛ. **1629** *Book of
Meery Riddles* Prov. 17 So much is mine as I
possesse, and give, or lose, for God's sake.
1732 FULLER no. 4198 (with 'and give away
for God's sake'.)

So said so done.

1577 J. FITJOHN *A Diamond most Precious*
H 2ᵛ So sayd, and so done, is a thread well
spone. **1594** SHAKS. *Tam. Shrew* I. ii (A) So
said, so done, is well.

Sober, *see* Honest (S.) by Act of Parliament
(Cannot make people).

Sober men, *see* Royet lads make s. m.

Soberness conceals, What | drunken-ness reveals.

[L. *Quod in corde sobrii, id in linguâ ebrii.*]
c. **1386** CHAUCER *Man of Law's T.* B¹ 776
Ther dronkenesse regneth in any route, Ther
is no conseil hyd withouten doute. **1579**
LYLY *Euphues* (Arb.) 146 It is an old
Prouerbe, Whatsoeuer is in the heart of the
sober man, is in the mouth of the drunckarde.
1639 CLARKE 47.

Socket, *see* Body is s. of soul.

Sodom, *see* Apple of S.

Soft answer turneth away wrath, A.

1382 WYCLIF *Prov.* xv. 1 A soft answere
brekith ire. c. **1382** GOWER *Vox Clam.* l. 1509
Iram multociens frangit responsio mollis.
c. **1420** *Peter Idle's Instructions to his Son*
(Miessner) l. 190 A softe worde swagith Ire.
1586 *Maxwell Younger MS.* in HENDERSON
Scot. Prov. (1832) Pref. xli Ane meik answer
slokinnis melancholie. **1611** BIBLE *Prov.* xv.
1 A soft answer turneth away wrath: but
grievous words stir up anger. **1826** SOUTHEY
19 July *Lett.* (1912) 414 A soft answer turneth away wrath. There is no shield against
wrongs so effectual as an unresisting temper.

Soft fire makes sweet malt.

a. **1530** R. *Hill's Commonpl. Bk.* (1858) 140
A softe ffyre makyth swete malte. a. **1553**
UDALL *Royster D.* I. ii (Arb.) 20 Soft fire
maketh sweete malte, good Madge. **1599**
PORTER *Angry Wom. Abingd.* II. i (Merm.) 125
Nich. Haste makes waste; soft fire makes
sweet malt. **1648** HERRICK *Hesper., Con.
Flores* 50 (1921) 218 Extreames have still
their fault; *The softest Fire makes the sweetest
Mault.* **1663** BUTLER *Hudibras* I. iii. 1251
Hold, hold (quoth Hudibras), soft fire, They
say, does make sweet malt.

Soft pace goes far.

1576 DESAINLIENS D 8ᵛ Soft passe goeth
farre. **1598** MERES *Palladis* f. 259 (A). **1669**
Politeuphuia 182.

Soft place in one's head, To have a. (*Cf.* Sound head, &c.)

1670 RAY 193.

Soft words and hard arguments.

1670 RAY 158. **1766** *Goody Two-Shoes* [ed. 3]
ii Use soft words and hard arguments.

Softly, *see* Fair and s., as lawyers to heaven;
Fair and s. goes far.

Sold, *see* Pleasing ware is half s.

Soldier's wind—there and back again, A.

1855 KINGSLEY *Westward Ho!* xix The breeze
. . . was 'a soldier's wind, there and back
again', for either ship. **1899** J. K. LAUGHTON
From Howard to Nelson 114 The 'favourable
gale' which took the English ships in and out
of the harbour seems to have been . . . a
'soldier's wind', there and back again.

Soldiers and travellers may lie by authority. (*See also* **Old men and travellers**; **Traveller may lie**, &c.)

1659 HOWELL *Eng. Prov.* 21/1.

Soldiers in peace are like chimneys in summer.

1594 A. COPLEY *Wits, Fits, etc.* (1614) 34 (A). *a.* **1598** LD. BURLEIGH *Advice to Son in* KNIGHT *Half-Hours* IV. 75 Neither . . . shalt thou train them up in wars. . . . It is a science no longer in request than in use. For soldiers in peace are like chimneys in summer. **1732** FULLER no. 4207.

Soldier(s), *see also* **Love lost betwixt sailors and s.** (No); **Obedience is duty of s.**; **Old s. over one** (To come); **Water, fire, and s. make room.**

Sole, *see* **Shoe will hold with s.**

Solitary man.

1547 WM. BALDWIN *Moral Philosophy* (1550) O 6ᵛ. **1551** Id. *Beware the Cat* (1584) C 5 margin. **1624** BURTON *Anat. Mel.* 77 As the saying is, *homo solus aut Deus, aut Dæmon*: a man alone is either a Saint or a Diuell. **1732** FULLER no. 418 A solitary man is either a brute or an angel.

Solitude, *see* **Great city great s.**

Solomon was a wise man, and Sampson was a strong man, yet neither of them could pay money before they had it. (*Cf.* **Samson was a strong man**, &c.)

1659 HOWELL *Eng. Prov.* 21/1.

Solomon's wise, loath to go to bed, but ten times loather to rise.

1882 E. L. CHAMBERLAIN *West Worc. Wds.* 39.

Solomon, *see also* **Good wife's a prize** (saith S.); **Sampson than S. in him** (More of).

Solvitur ambulando.

[*i.e.* It is solved by walking.] **1863** CONINGTON *Horace Odes* xxviii How easily the *Solvitur ambulando* of an artist like Mr Tennyson may disturb a whole chain of ingenious reasoning on the possibilities of things. **1906** F. W. MAITLAND *Lesl. Stephen* xvii He would have to proceed empirically. *Solvitur ambulando*—the motto of the philosophic tramp—had also to be the motto of the editor. **1931** *Times* 16 Feb. 13/5 There has been nothing so perfect since Zeno's proof that motion is an impossibility and the answer in both cases is the same: *Solvitur ambulando*, or 'get a move on'.

Some are wise, and some are otherwise.

1601 JONSON *Poetaster* III. iv. 23 Some wiser then some. **1658** *Comes Facundus* 308. **1659** HOWELL *Eng. Prov.* 1. **1738** SWIFT (Dial. i)

335 *Never*. Some people take him for a wise man. *Lady S.* Ay, ay; some are wise, and some are otherwise.

Some good, some bad, as sheep come to the fold.

1577 J. FITJOHN *A Diamond most precious* G 3ᵛ They . . . are as the prouerb sayth, some good, some bad. **1678** RAY 247.

Somebody, *see* **Everybody's s.** (When).

Somerton ending.

1678 RAY 347 . . . *Somerset. i.e.* When the difference between two is divided.

Something (Somewhat) hath some savour.

[JUVENAL *Sat.* 14. 204 *Lucri bonus est odor, ex re Qualibet.* Good is the smell of gain, come from what it may.] **1576** U. FULWELL *Ars Adulandi* sig. C 2 As somewhat hath some sauor, so nothing doth no harme. **1634** WITHALS 563 Somewhat hath some savour, so we get the chincke,[1] we will beare with the stinke. **1738** SWIFT (Dial. i) 343 *Lady A.* Has he got a good fortune with his lady? for they say something has some savour, but nothing has no flavour. [1 coin.]

Something, *see also* **Always a s.**; **Somewhat (S.) is better than nothing.**

Somewhat (Something) is better than nothing.

1546 HEYWOOD I. ix. 24 And by this prouerbe apéerth this o thyng, That alwaie somwhat is better then nothyng. **1620** SHELTON *Quix.* II. 1 (1908) III. 169 A string of coral beads, . . . I could wish they had been oriental pearls, but something is better than nothing.

Son full and tattered, The | the daughter empty and fine.

1640 HERBERT 327.

Son is my son, My | till he hath got him a wife; but my daughter's my daughter all the days of her life.

1670 RAY 53. **1732** FULLER no. 6076. **1857** D. M. MULOCK *John Halifax* xxxii There is often a pitiful truth . . . in the foolish rhyme, . . .—'My son's my son till he gets him a wife, My daughter's my daughter all her life.' **1863** C. READE *Hard Cash* v 'Oh, mamma,' said Julia warmly, 'and do you think all the marriage in the world . . . can make me luke-warm to my . . . mother? . . . Your son is your son till he gets him a wife: but your daughter's your daughter, all the days of her life.'

Son of a bachelor, He is the.

1678 RAY 66 . . . i.e. a bastard.

Son(s) of a (the) white hen.

[= very fortunate.] [JUVENAL *Sat.* 13. 141 *Gallinæ filius albæ.*] **1540** PALSGRAVE

Acolastus L 2ᵛ May not I by ryghte be estemed the sonne of a whyte henne . i . maye not men . . . thinke, that I was borne in a good howre? **1631** JONSON *New Inn* I. i *Host.* Yet all, sir, are not sons of the white hen: Nor can we . . . all . . . be wrapt . . . in fortune's smock.

Son of his own works, Every man is the.

1620 SHELTON *Quix.* I. iv (1908) I. 23 There may be knights of the Haldudos; and what is more, every one is son of his works.

Son(s), *see also* Brings up his s. to nothing (He that); God gave no s. (He to whom); Great men's s.; One hog (He that hath) . . . one s. makes him fool.

Song, *see* Beginneth the s. (Let him that) make an end; End of an old s.; Made a s. of (She is not to be); No s. no supper.

Soon as man is born he begins to die, As.

[MANIL. 4. 16 *Nascentes morimur, finisque ab origine pendet. Cf.* AUG. *Civ. Dei* 13. 10.] **1596** *K. Edw. III* IV. iv For, from the instant we begin to live, We do pursue and hunt the time to die. **1629** T. ADAMS *Serm.* (1861–2) I. 292 As soon as we are born, we begin to draw to our end. **1742** YOUNG *Night Thoughts* v. 717 While man is growing, life is in decrease, And cradles rock us nearer to our tomb. Our birth is nothing but our death begun.

Soon deemeth, He that | soon repenteth (shall soon repent).

c. **1386** CHAUCER *Mel.* 2220 For the commune proverbe seith thus: 'He that soone deemeth, soone shal repente'.

Soon enough, if well enough.

[L. *Sat cito, si sat bene.*] **1545** ASCHAM *Toxoph.* (Arb.) 114 Men whiche labour more spedily to make manye bowes . . . then they woorke diligently to make good bowes, . . . not layinge before theyr eyes, thys wyse prouerbe. *Sone ynough, if wel ynough.* **1651** HERBERT 368 We do it soon enough, if that we do be well.

Soon enough to cry 'Chuck'[1] when it is out of the shell.

1721 KELLY 288 . . . It is time enough to reckon on a thing when you are sure of it. [[1] the hen's call to a chicken.]

Soon goes the young sheep to the pot as the old, As.

1599 T. PORTER *Angry Wom. Abingd.* II. i (Merm.) 127 Take heed, as soon goes the young sheep to the pot as the old.

Soon goeth the young lamb's skin to the market as the old ewe's, As.

c. **1520** *Calisto & Melibea* B 3 As sone goth to market the lambys fell As the shyppes. **1546** HEYWOOD II. iv. 49 As soone goth the yonge lamskyn to the market As tholde yewes. **1641** FERGUSSON 8. **1819** SCOTT *Bride Lam.* v I thought Sir William would have verified the auld Scottish saying, 'as soon comes the lamb's skin to market as the auld tup's'.

Soon gotten, soon spent.

1546 HEYWOOD II. vi. 62. **1639** CLARKE 115.

Soon hot, soon cold. (*See also* Hasty love, &c.)

c. **1450** BURGH (& LYDGATE) *Secrees* (E.E.T.S.) 60 (A). *a.* **1502** *Not-Browne Mayd* in PERCY *Reliques* It is sayd of olde, Sone hote, sone colde; And so is a womàn. **1639** CLARKE 116. **1732** FULLER no. 4228.

Soon in the goom,[1] quick in the womb.

1869 HAZLITT 354 (1882) . . . A saying relevant to children who cut their teeth early. [[1] gum.]

Soon learnt, soon forgotten.

c. **1374** CHAUCER *Troylus* II, l. 1238 Forwhy men seyth 'impressiones lighte Ful lightly been ay redy to the flighte'. **1855** BOHN 489.

Soon ripe, soon rotten.

[L. *Cito maturum cito putridum.*] **1393** LANGLAND *P. Pl.* C. xiii. 223 And that that rathest[1] rypeth . roteth most saunest.[2] **1546** HEYWOOD I. x. 22 In youth she was towarde and without euill. But soone rype soone rotten. **1594** GREENE *Fr. Bacon* Timely ripe is rotten too-too soon. **1642** D. ROGERS *Naaman* x. 288 Some indeed . . . are moved to . . . disdain by their inferiors' forwardness, calling them hastings, soon ripe, soon rotten. **1832** HENDERSON 136 Ripe fruit is soonest rotten. **1887** SMILES *Life & Labour* vi Very few prize boys and girls stand the test of wear. Prodigies are almost always uncertain; they illustrate the proverb of 'soon ripe, soon rotten'. [[1] earliest; [2] soonest.]

Soon up, soon down.

1642 D. ROGERS *Naaman* 229 Carnall reason is no torrent, soone up soone downe; but a gulfe.

Soon, *see also* Well done, s. done.

Sooner fall than rise, One may.

1670 RAY 9.

Sooner named, sooner come.

1581 *Conflict of Conscience* III. ii in HAZL. *O.E.P.* VI. 66 *Hyp.* But I marvel what doth him from hence so long stay, Sooner named, sooner come, as common proverbs say.

Sooner, *see also* Easier (S.) said than done.

Sooth as God is king.

c. **1386** CHAUCER *Merch. T.* E² 1267 As soth as God is king.

Sooth bourd is no bourd.

1386 CHAUCER *Cook's Prol.* A 4356 Thou seist ful sooth', quod Roger, 'by my fey!

But "sooth pley[1] quaad[2] pley", as the Flemyng seith.' **1546** HEYWOOD II. viii. 72 It is yll iestyng on the soothe. Sooth bourd is no bourd, in ought that mirth doothe. **1591** HARINGTON *Orl. Fur.* Apol. Poet. P vj As the old saying is (sooth boord is no boord). **1721** KELLY 3 ... Spoken when people reflect too satirically upon the real vices, follies, and miscarriages of their neighbours. **1824** SCOTT *Redg.* xii This sally did not take quite as well as former efforts of the Laird's wit. The lady drew up, and the Provost said, half aside, 'The sooth bourd is nae bourd'. [[1] play, jest. [2] evil, bad: Dutch *kwaad*.]

Sooth saws be to lords lothe.

c. **1412** HOCCLEVE *De Regim. Princ.* (Roxb. Cl.) 106 And, for sothe sawes ben to lordes lothe, Nought wole he sothe seyne, he hathe made his othe.

Sooth, *see* True (S.) as gospel.

Soothsayer, *see* Make me a diviner.

Sop to Cerberus, To give a.

[= to give something to stop for the moment the mouths of Cerberus, the three-headed dog, in mythology, which guards the entrance to Hades.] **1513** DOUGLAS *Æneis* VI. vi. 69 Cerberus, the hidduus hund. ... Quham till the prophetes. ... A sop stepit intill hunny ... gan cast. **1695** CONGREVE *Love for L.* I. iv. 17 If I can give that Cerberus a sop, I shall be at rest for one Day. **1825** HOR. SMITH *Gaieties & Grav.* I will throw down a napoleon, as a sop to Cerberus.

Sops, *see* Gangs up i' s. (When it), it'll fau down in drops.

Sore fight wrens as cranes, As.

1641 FERGUSSON 10. **1721** KELLY 36 ... Little people (if rightly match'd) will fight as bitterly ... as those who are stronger or bigger.

Sore foot, *see* Keep something for the s. f.

Sore heart, *see* Send you away with **s.** h. (He will never).

Sore heel, *see* Touch me not on s. h.

Sore toe, *see* Tread on a s. t. (Never).

Sore upon sore is not a salve.

1639 CLARKE 197.

Sore(s), *see also* Healing of an old s. (Ill); Old debts better than old s.; Rip not up old s.; Shirt full of s. bones. *See also* Sairs.

Sorrow and an evil (ill) life maketh soon an old wife.

1639 CLARKE 279. **1670** RAY 144. **1721** KELLY 286.

Sorrow be in the house that you're beguiled in.

1721 KELLY 298 ... Spoken to sharp expert people who have their interest in their eye.

Sorrow, Of thy | be not too sad, of thy joy be not too glad.

c. **1450** *Provs. of Wysdom* 51 Off þy sorow be nott to sad, Of þy ioy be not to glad.

Sorrow (and ill weather) comes (come) unsent for.

[L. *Mala ultro adsunt.* Misfortunes come unsought.] **1579** SPENSER *Shep. Cal.* May Wks. (Globe) 460 Sorrowe ne neede be hastened on, For he will come, without calling, anone. **1639** CLARKE 101 Sorrow comes unsent for. *Ibid.* 165 Like ill weather, sorrow comes unsent for. **1721** KELLY 290 *Sorrow and ill weather come unsent for.* Spoken when a person is coming to your house, whose company you do not care for.

Sorrow is always dry.

[Fr. **14** .. *Provs. communs.* Assez boit qui a deuil.] *c.* **1548** BALE *K. Johan* 2458, Sed. I woulde I were now at Rome at the sygne of the Cuppe, For heavynesse is drye. *c.* **1612** BEAUM. & FL. *Scornf. Lady* II. i. Wks. (C.U.P.) I. 251 *Y. Love.* Off with thy drink, thou hast a spice of sorrow makes thee dry. **1644** W. BROWNE *Lidford Journey* Wks. (Roxb. Lib.) II. 352 To see it thus much grieved was I, The proverb says, Sorrow is dry; So was I at this matter. **1714** GAY *Shep. Wk., Frid.* 151, 2 For Gaffer Treadwell told us, by the bye, Excessive sorrow is exceeding dry. **1885** D. C. MURRAY *Rainbow G.* V. vi That's a public-house. Sorrow's dry, and so am I.

Sorrow is asleep, When | wake it not.

1659 HOWELL *Eng. Prov.* 16/1. **1732** FULLER no. 5569. **1852** MISS M. A. STODDART Song, *When sorrow sleepeth wake it not.*

Sorrow is at parting if at meeting there be laughter.

c. **1460** *Towneley Myst., Proces. Talent* (Surtees) 243 Thus sorow is at partyng, at metyng if ther be laghter.

Sorrow is good for nothing but sin.

1605 CAMDEN (1637) 287 Sorrow is good for nothing save sin onely. **1658** *Comes Facundus* 194. **1659** HOWELL *Eng. Prov.* 2/1.

Sorrow is soon enough when it comes.

1576 PETTIE *Petite Pall.* (Gollancz) II. 70 Every evil bringeth grief enough with it when it comes. **1721** KELLY 291 ... Spoken to them who vex themselves with future dismal expectations.

Sorrow makes silence her best orator.

1595 S. DANIEL *Civil Wars* ii. 93. **1597** *Politeuphuia* 131 b Sorrow makes silence her best ayde, & her best Orator.

Sorrow rode in my cart.

1830 FORBY 429 ... I did ill, but I had reason to repent it afterwards.

Sorrow to his (my) sops.

1546 HEYWOOD II. viii. 72 But two daies after this came in vre,[1] I had sorow to my sops ynough be sure. **1788** GROSE *Dict. Vulg. T.* (ed. 2), Sorrow shall be his sops, he shall repent this. [¹ use.]

Sorrow will pay no debt.

1669 *New Help to Discourse* 310 (A) Sorrow quits no scores. **1670** RAY 144.

Sorrow wit you wat¹ where a blessing may light.

1721 KELLY 291 ... You know not but I may have a better fortune than you think, or expect. [¹ you can by no means know, equivalent to 'Deil Kens'.]

Sorrows gars¹ websters spin.

1641 FERGUSSON 88. [¹ makes.]

Sorrow(s) (*noun*), *see also* Better a little loss than long s.; Better two skaiths than one s.; Fat s. better than lean; God send you joy, for s. come fast enough; Good to be sent for s. (You are); Hundred pounds of s. pays not debt; Lay s. to your heart (Never); Much science much s.; Need makes ... and s. makes websters spin; Remembrance of past s. is joyful; Seill comes not while s. be gone; Small s. speak; Swims in sin shall sink in s.; Two in distress makes s. less; Two s. of one (Make not); Weal pricks (Whom) s. ... licks; Worth s. (He is) that buys it. *See also* Grief.

Sorrows (*verb*), *see* Lives not well one year (He that) s. seven.

Sorry for you, I am | but I cannot weep.

1584 *Three Ladies of Lond.* in HAZL. *O.E.P.* VI. 319 Alas! Lucre, I am sorry for thee, but I cannot weep. **1611** BEAUM. & FL. *Kt. Burn. P.* I. i *Luce.* Beshrew me, sir, I'm sorry for your losses, But as the proverb says, I cannot cry. **1827** SCOTT *Journ.* 4 June Sorry for it, but I can't cry.

Sorry, *see also* Better be sure than s.; Sick and s.; Sick nor s. (Neither).

Sorts, *see* All s. to make world.

Sough, *see* Keep a calm s.

Soul above buttons, To have a.

1795 G. COLMAN *Sylv. Daggerwood* i (1808) 10 My father was an eminent Button-Maker ... but I had a soul above buttons ... I panted for a liberal profession. **1833** MARRYAT *P. Simple* i My father, who was a clergyman ... had ... a 'soul above buttons', if his son had not.

Soul is not where it lives, but where it loves, The.

1580 LYLY *Euph. & his Eng.* (Arb.) 266 I feare my friends sore, will breed to a *Fistula*: for you may perceiue that he is not where he liues, but wher he loues. **1662** FULLER (*Westmor.*) III. 310 The proverb is, 'Homo non est ubi animat, sed amat' (One is not to

be reputed there where he lives, but where he loves). **1732** FULLER no. 4761. **1908** ALEX. MACLAREN *Expos., Acts* I. 139 In the inmost depth of reality, the soul that loves is where it loves, and has whom it loves ever with it.

Soul needs few things, The | the body many.

1640 HERBERT 347.

Soul(s), *see also* Body is more dressed than s.; Body is socket of s.; Charge of s. (He that hath); Corn is cleansed ... and the s. by chastenings; Counsellors (Though thou hast) do not forsake counsel of s.; Garby whose s. neither God nor devil would have; Holy habit cleanses not foul s.; Little body harbours great s.; Little troubles the eye, less the s.; Penniless s. maun pine in purgatory; Sickness of body ... health of soul.

Sound as a bell, As.

1598–9 SHAKS. *Much Ado* III. ii. 12 He hath a heart as sound as a bell. **1616** DRAXE 88.

Sound head that has not a soft piece in it, It is a. (*Cf.* Soft place in one's head.)

1721 KELLY 133.

Sound love is not soon forgotten.

1659 N. R. 91. **1664** CODRINGTON 210. **1894** NORTHALL *Folk Phrases* (E.D.S.) 23 (A).

Sound mind in a sound body, A.

[JUV. *Sat.* 10. 356 *Orandum est, ut sit mens sana in corpore sano.*] **1586** *Maxwell Younger MS.* no. 32 in HENDERSON *Scot. Prov.* (1832) Pref. The dispositioun of the mynd followeth the constitutioun of the body. **1692** L'ESTRANGE *Aesop's Fab.* (1738) cccxxv. 337 A sound mind in a sound body is the perfection of human bliss. **1749** FIELDING *T. Jones* XII. iv. **1912** *Times, Wkly.* 16 Feb. 127 Conditions which will give to the native a sound mind in a sound body.

Sound travelling far and wide, a stormy day will betide.

1883 ROPER 25 A good hearing day is a sign of wet *and* Much sound in the air is a sign of rain. **1893** INWARDS 106.

Sound, *see also* Empty vessels ... greatest s.

Soup and love, Of | the first is the best.

[Sp. *c.* **1627** CORREAS *Vocab.* (1906) 192 Las sopas y los amores, los primeros son los mejores.] **1732** FULLER no. 3699.

Sour as wer.¹

1616 DRAXE 195 As sowre as a crab. **1691** RAY *Words not Generally Used* (E.D.S.) 73 (A) As sour as wharre. **1917** BRIDGE As sour as wer (or wharre). [¹ = crab-apples.]

Sour apple-tree, *see* Tied to the s. a.-t.

Sour as whig.[1]

1589 LYLY *Pap with a Hatchet* Wks. (Bond) III. 406 More sower than wig. **1854** BAKER *Northants Gloss.* s.v. 'Whig' . . . a common proverbial simile (A). [[1] sour whey.]

Sour(er), *see also* Nothing turns s. than milk; Sell (If it will not), it will not s.

Source, *see* Stream cannot rise above s.

Souter gave the sow a kiss; The | Humph, quoth she, its for a birse.[1]

1721 KELLY 338 . . . Spoken of those whose service we suppose to be mercenary. **1815** SCOTT *Let.* to Dk. of Buc. in LOCKHART *Life* xxxvi The following lines are . . . from an ancient Scottish canzonetta . . . 'The sutor ga'e the sow a kiss: Grumph! quo' the sow, it's a' for my birss'. [[1] bristle.]

Souters shouldna be sailors, wha can neither steer nor row.

1832 HENDERSON 88.

South, *see* Wind is s. (When), it blows bait into fish's mouth; Wind's in the s. (When), it's in rain's mouth.

South Darne, *see* Sutton.

Southerly wind and a cloudy sky, A | proclaim a hunting morning.

1846 DENHAM 8. **1869** G. A. SALA *Rome & Venice* xxxii 'A southerly wind and a cloudy sky proclaim a hunting morning', to which I may venture to add that 'You all know Tom Moody, the whipper-in, well'.

Southerly wind with showers of rain will bring the wind from west again, A.

1883 ROPER 691. **1893** INWARDS 82.

Southwark ale.

c. **1386** CHAUCER *Miller's Prol.* 3140 If that I mysspeke or seye, Wyte it the ale of South-werk, I you preye. **1665** R. BRATHWAIT *Comments upon Chaucer's Tales* (1901) 6 Where the best Ale is . . . was made good long ago, as may appear by that overworn Proverb, *The nappy strong Ale of Southwirke Keeps many a Gossip fra the Kirke.*

Sow beans in the mud, and they'll grow like (a) wood.

1639 CLARKE 307. **1647** FULLER *Gd. Thoughts in Worse T.* viii (1863) 124 I saw in seedtime a husbandman at plough, in a very rainy day; asking . . . why he would not rather leave off than labour in such foul weather, his answer was . . . : Sow beans in the mud, And they'll come up like a wood. **1846** DENHAM 40.

Sow beans in the wind, To.

[= labour in vain.] **1568** *Marr. Wit. & Wisd.* 45 (N.) It is not for idlenis that men sow beanes in the wind.

Sow by the ear, To have (take) the right (wrong).

1546 HEYWOOD II. ix. 75 Ye tooke The wrong way to wood, and the wrong sow by theare. **1598** B. JONSON *Ev. Man in Humour* II. i *Dow.* When he is got into one o' your city pounds, the counters, he has the wrong sow by the ear. **1630** J. TAYLOR (Water-P.) *Wit & Mirth* Wks. II. 180/2 I knew when he first medled with your Ladyship, that hee had a wrong Sow by the eare. **1690** D'URFEY *Collin's Walk* iv. 168 Thought Strumpet, since the Wind sits there, I'le take the right Sow by the Ear. **1857** E. FITZGERALD in BENSON *Ed. FitzGerald* (1905) 98 I am not always quite certain of always getting the right sow by the ear.

Sow by the right ear, To have the.

1570 FOXE *A. & M.* (ed. 2) 2034/1 I perceiue . . . that that man hath the sow by the right eare. **1605** CHAPMAN, &c. *Eastw. Hoe* II. i Plays (1889) 460 You have the sow by the right ear, sir.

Sow dry and to set wet, This rule in gardening never forget, to.

1678 RAY 49.

Sow four beans in a row, one for cowscot[1] and one for crow, one to rot and one to grow.

1932 *Times* 23 May 20/6 Pigeons do attack beans. . . . A saying here[2] indicates how experience forestalls the mischief by a liberal sowing—Sow four beans in a row, one for cowscot and one for crow, One to rot and one to grow. [[1] Cushat. [2] Guisborough, Yorks.]

Sow in the slop, 'twill be heavy at top.

1823 MOOR *Suffolk Words* 376 (A). **1830** FORBY 417 . . . *i.e.* Wheat sown when the ground is wet, is most productive.

Sow is good mutton, Right, Roger, your.

1658 E. PHILLIPS *Mysteries of Love and Eloquence* 159. **1670** RAY 191. **1732** FULLER no. 4054.

Sow or set beans in Candlemas waddle.

1678 RAY 343 . . . *i.e.* Wane of the Moon. Somerset.

Sow peas and beans in the wane of the moon; who soweth them sooner, he soweth too soon.

1846 DENHAM 42.

Sow playing on a trump, Like a.

1721 KELLY 232 . . . Spoken when people do a thing ungracefully. **1818** SCOTT *Rob Roy* xxv Never look like a sow playing upon a trump for the luve o' that, man . . . ye'll cool and come to yoursell.

Sow, As they | so let them reap.

c. **1275** *Provs. of Alfred* (1907) A82 Hwych
so þe mon soweþ, al swuch he schal mowe.
1380 WYCLIF *Gal.* vi. 7 For tho thingis that a
man sowith: the thingis he schal repe. **14..**
Mankind 175 But such as thei haue sowyn,
such xall thei repe. **1664** BUTLER *Hudibras*
II. ii. 503 And look before you ere you leap;
For as you sow, you're like to reap. **1871**
FROUDE *Short Stud., Calvinism* (1900) II. 12
As men have sown they must still reap. The
profligate . . . may recover . . . peace of
mind . . . ; but no miracle takes away his
paralysis.

Sow (Swine) teaching Minerva, A.

[ERASM. *Ad. Sus Minervam.*] **1542** UDALL tr.
Erasm. Apoph. 342 *b* A swyne to teache
Minerua, was a prouerbe.

Sow the wind and reap the whirl-wind, To.

1611 BIBLE *Hosea* ix. 7 For they have sown
the wind, and they shall reap the whirlwind.
1837 CARLYLE *Fr. Rev.* III. v. i They . . . are
at work, *sowing the wind.* And yet, as God
lives, they shall *reap the whirlwind.* **1929**
DEAN INGE *Assessmts. & Anticip.* 144 Class-
hatred and class-warfare are preached . . . by
middle-class *enragés,* . . . These rascals sow
the wind; the next generation reaps the
whirlwind.

Sow thin and mow (shear) thin.

1641 FERGUSSON 90 Saw thin, and maw thin.
1721 KELLY 299. **1846** DENHAM 33 Sow thin
shear thin.

Sow to a fiddle, A.

[ERASM. *Ad. Asinus ad lyram*: An ass listening to a lyre.] *c.* **1380** CHAUCER *Tr. & Cress.*
i. 731 Or artowe [art thou] lyk an asse to the
harpe? **1616** WITHALS 552. **1639** CLARKE 5.
1670 RAY 193.

Sow to bear a saddle, As meet as a.

1546 HEYWOOD II. i. 43 She is nowe, To
become a bryde, as méete as a sowe To beare
a saddle. **1681** S. COLVIL *Whiggs Supp.* 39
Which them becomes, as all avow, As well as
a saddle doth a sow. **1738** SWIFT (Dial. ii)
346 *Sir J.* It became him, as a saddle becomes a sow.

Sow to her own trough, Every.

1678 RAY 204.

Sow wheat in dirt, and rye in dust.

1721 KELLY 298 . . . A wet season agrees with
the one, and a dry with the other.

Sow with the hand, and not with the whole sack.

[PLUTARCH τῇ χειρὶ δεῖ σπείρειν, ἀλλὰ μὴ
ὅλῳ τῷ θυλάκῳ. *One must sow with the hand,
not from the sack's mouth.* Corinna's advice to
Pindar.] **1591** SIR J. HARINGTON *Apol. Poet.*
in *Orl. Fur.* (1634) For as men use to sow
with the hand and not with the whole sacke,
so I would have the eare fed, but not cloyed

with these pleasing and sweet falling meeters.
1629 T. ADAMS *Serm.* (1861–2) II. 464 That
stock lasts that is neither hoarded miserably
nor dealt out indiscreetly. We sow the
furrow, not by the sack, but by the handful.
1853 TRENCH V. 112 The Greeks, who never
lost sight of measure and proportion, . . .
said, *Sow with the hand, and not with the whole
sack.*

Sowed cockle reaped no corn.

c. **1386** CHAUCER *C.T., Man of Law's End-link*
B¹ 1183 He wolde sowen som difficulte, Or
springen cokkel in our clene corn. **1594–5**
SHAKS. *L.L.L.* IV. iii. 383 Sow'd cockle
reap'd no corn; and justice always whirls in
equal measure. **1607–8** *Coriol.* III. i. 69 The
cockle of rebellion, insolence, sedition, Which
we ourselves have plough'd for, sow'd and
scatter'd.

Sower, *see* Rath s. never borroweth.

Soweth good seed, He that | shall reap good corn.

1616 DRAXE 12.

Soweth virtue, He that | shall reap fame.

1573 SANDFORD (1576) H 4ᵛ. **1629** *Book of
Meery Riddles* Prov. 48.

Sowing on the sand, He is.

c. **1580** SIDNEY First *Arcadia* Wks. (Feuillerat) iv. 69 Hee water plowes and soweth in
the sande. **1616** DRAXE He soweth on the
sand. **1813** RAY 75.

Sowlegrove sil lew.

1686–7 J. AUBREY *Rem. Gent. & Jud.* (1881)
9 The Shepheards, and vulgar people in
South Wilts call Februarie Sowlegrove: and
have this proverbe of it: viz. Sowlegrove sil
lew. February is seldome warme.

Sows, He that | trusts in God.

1640 HERBERT 333. **1670** RAY 24 Who sows
his corn in the field trusts in God.

Sows in the highway, He that | tires his oxen and loseth his corn.

1616 DRAXE 223 He that soweth in the high
way, wearieth his oxen, and looseth his
labour. **1732** FULLER no. 2305.

Sow(s) (*noun*), *see also* Barren s. was never
good to pigs; Grease the fat s.; Lay the
head of the s. to tail of grice; Little
knoweth fat s. what lean doth mean;
Love a woman (He that doth not) sucked
a s.; Nose to make poor man's s. (He
hath); Pretty pig makes ugly s.; Sailing
in a s.'s ear; Silence in the pig-market
and let s. grunt; Silk purse of a s.'s ear;
Souter gave the s. a kiss; Still s. eats up
draff.

Sow(s, eth), sowing, sown (*verb*), *see also*
David and Chad s. peas; Dragon's teeth;
Early s. early mow; Forbear not s. because

of birds; Many things grow in garden never s.; One s., another reapeth; Quiet s. quiet mow; St. Mattho take hopper and s.; Speaks (He that) s., holds his peace gathers; Thrush when he pollutes . . . s. seeds of woe; Wild oats.

Space cometh grace, In.

a. **1530** WOLSEY in *Letters & Papers Hen. VIII,* iv. 6182 (cited A. F. POLLARD *Wolsey* 323). **1546** HEYWOOD I. iv. **1591** HY. SMITH *Serm.* (1866) I. 22 He must not look to find a wife without a fault, . . . and if he find the proverb true, That in space cometh grace, he must rejoice . . . when she amendeth. **1641** FERGUSSON 60. **1670** RAY 144. **1732** FULLER no. 6167.

Spade, *see* Call a s. a s.

Spain, *see* Castles in S.; Death come to me from S.; Live in Italy, die in S.; Nothing ill in S. but that which speaks; Succours of S.

Spake an angel, There.

[An angel was a gold coin worth 10*s.*; often used, as here, in quibbles.] *c.* **1590–5** *Sir Thos. More* I. i (*Shaks. Apoc.*) 387 *Wil.* Lets freendly goe and drinke together. *Geo.* There spake an angell. **1605** CHAPMAN, &c. *Eastw. Hoe* II. i (1874) 460 *Qu.* The bloodhound, Security, will smell out ready money for you instantly. *Pe.* There spake an angel.

Span new, *see* Spick and span.

Span, *see also* Life is a s.; Spick and s.

Spaniard is a bad servant, but a worse master, The.

1629 T. ADAMS *Serm.* (1861–2) I. 116 He that serves the *flesh* serves his fellow. . . . We may say of him, as of the Spaniard, he is a bad servant, but a worse master.

Spaniard, *see also* Bad S. makes good Portuguese.

Spaniel, A | a woman, and a walnut-tree, the more they're beaten the better they be.

[L. *Nux, asinus, mulier verbere opus habent.*] **1586** PETTIE *Guazzo's Civ. Conv.* 139 I have read, I know not where, these verses, A woman, an ass, and a walnut-tree, Bring the more fruit, the more beaten they be. **1594–5** SHAKS. *Two Gent.* IV. ii. 14 Spaniel-like, the more she spurns my love, the more it grows and fawneth on her still. **1595–6** *Mids. N.* II. i. 202 I am your spaniel; and, Demetrius, The more you beat me, I will fawn on you. **1650** Letter to Sir Ralph Verney *Verney Memoirs* (1894) iii. 147 He [Tom Verney] is of the Spaniell kind, the more he is beaten the more he fawnes and per contra. **1670** RAY 50 A spaniel, a woman and a walnut tree, The more they're beaten the better still they be. **1692** L'ESTRANGE *Aesop's Fab.* (1738) cccxvi. 329 A company of young fellows were cudgelling a walnut tree. . . . Says one of the lads, ''Tis natural for asses, women, and walnut-trees to mend upon beating'. **1902–4** LEAN I. 455 A woman, a whelp, and a walnut-tree, the more you bash 'em the better they

be. **1913** *Spectator* 15 Mar. 440 If it were only a case of a spaniel, a wife or a walnut tree we might be capable of the ultimate brutality of the proverb.

Spaniels that fawn when beaten, will never forsake their masters.

1580 LYLY *Euph. & his Eng.* (Arb.) 392 The Spaniel that fawneth when he is beaten will neuer forsake his maister, the man that do[a]teth when he is disdained, will neuer foregoe his mistres. **1732** FULLER no. 4236. **1764** CHURCHILL *Independence* 327 He, like a thorough true-bred spaniel, licks The hand which cuffs him, and the foot which kicks.

Spaniel(s), *see also* Fawn like a s.; Flattering as a s.

Spare at the spigot, and let it out at the bung-hole.

1642 TORRIANO 50 He holdeth in at the spicket, but letteth out at the bung hole. **1670** RAY 193. **1721** KELLY 299 . . . Spoken to them who are careful and penurious in some trifling things, but neglective in the main chance. **1886** E. J. HARDY *How to be Happy* xiii People are often saving at the wrong place. . . . They spare at the spigot, and let all run away at the bunghole.

Spare the rod and spoil the child.

[BIBLE *Prov.* xiii. 24.] *c.* **1000** ÆLFRIC *Hom.* II. 324 Se ðe sparað his ȝyrde, he hatað his cild. **1377** LANGLAND *P. Pl.* B. v. 38–41 'Salamon seide . . . *Qui parcit virge, odit filium.* The English of this latyn is . . . Who-so spareth the sprynge[1]. spilleth his children.' **1382** WYCLIF *Prov.* xiii. 24 He that sparith the ȝerde, hatith his sone. **1577** *Misogonus* in BRANDL *Quellen* II. iii. 442 He that spareth the rode, hates the childe, as Solomon writes. **1639** CLARKE 161. **1664** BUTLER *Hudibras* II. i. 843 Love is a boy, by poets styled; Then spare the rod and spoil the child. **1876** MRS. BANKS *Manch. Man* xxiv 'Spare the rod and spoil the child' had not been abolished from the educational code fifty-five years back. [[1] rod.]

Spare to speak (and) spare to speed.

c. **1350** *Douce MS. 52* no. 27 Who-so sparyth to speke, sparyth to spede. *c.* **1390** GOWER *Conf. Amantis* i. 1293 For specheles may no man spede. **1546** HEYWOOD I. xi. 31. **1721** KELLY 5 . . . Unless a man make interest, and importune, he will not readily come to profit, honour, or advancement. **1788** BURNS *The Blue-eyed Lass* But spare to speak, and spare to speed. *a.* **1863** ARCHBP. WHATELY *Commonpl. Bk.* (1865) 201 Another goes on the maxim . . . of 'spare to speak and spare to speed'.

Spare well and have (spend) well.

1541 COVERDALE *Christ. State Matr.* sig. I 3 To spare that thou mayest haue to spend. **1832** HENDERSON 16. **1855** BOHN 490 ('spend').

Spare when the bottom is bare (all is spent), It is too late to.

[HESIOD *Op.* 367 δειλὴ δ' ἐνὶ πυθμένι φειδώ. SENECA *Epist.* I *Sera in fundo parsimonia.*]

1539 TAVERNER f. 32 It is too late sparynge at the bottome. **1639** CLARKE 283. 1662 FULLER (*Sussex*) III. 251 By his magnificent prodigality, he spent the greatest part, till he seasonably began to spare, growing near to the bottom of his estate. **1736** AINSWORTH *Thesaurus* I. s.v. It is too late to spare when all is spent. **1853** TRENCH V. 120 There is another ancient proverb,[1] which in English runs thus: *It is* too late to spare when all is spent. [[1] Sera in imo parsimonia.]

Spare when you're young, and spend when you're old.

1541 COVERDALE *Christ. State Matrim.* I 3 (A) Spare for thyne age. **1670** RAY 79 He that spares when he is young, may the better spend when he is old. **1721** KELLY 297.

Sparing is a great revenue.

1539 TAVERNER tr. *Erasm. Garden of Wisdom* B 8 Sparing is great rentes or reuenues. **1572** T. WILSON *Discourse upon Usury* (1925) 338 In sparing is great gettynge.

Sparing is the first gaining. (*Cf.* Saving (Of) cometh having.)

1573 SANDFORD 212. **1578** FLORIO *First Fruites* 30 The first gain or profit is to spare.

Spare(s, d, -ing), *see also* Better s. at brim; Better s. than ill spent; Better s. to have of thine own; Daft that has to do and s. for every speech; Know when to spend and when to s.; Lost the large coat for the hood (Oft for s.); Spend and God will send, s. ever bare; Spend not where may save, s. not where must spend; Up hill s. me.

Sparks, *see* Heart is a fire (When) some s. fly.

Sparrow(s), *see* Pert as a s.; Two s. on one ear of corn make ill agreement.

Speak and speed, ask and have.

1639 CLARKE 40 Speak and speed.

Speak as if you would creep into my mouth, You.

1546 HEYWOOD II. ix. 77 Ye speake now, as ye would créepe into my mouth, In pure peinted processe, as false as fayre.

Speak, You never | but your mouth opens.

1670 RAY 193.

Speak by the card, To.

[= to express oneself with care and nicety.] **1602** SHAKS. *Hamlet* V. i. 149 We must speak by the card, or equivocation will undo us. **1875** JOWETT *Plato* (ed. 2) IV. 315 I speak by the card in order to avoid entanglement of words.

Speak fair and think what you will.

1598 SIR R. BARCKLEY *Discourse of Felicity of Man* A 8 Farewell, and speake well, and thinke as ye list. **1611** GRUTER. **1614** CAMDEN 312.

Speak false Latin, To.

[*Fig.* to commit a breach of manners.] **1607** *Puritan Widow* I. i (*Shaks. Apoc.*) 222 *Mol.* I lou'd my father well, too; but to say, Nay, vow, I would not marry for his death—Sure, I should speake false Lattin, should I not? **1665** G. HAVERS *P. della Valle's Trav. E. India* 186 He (the King) bid us several times put on our Hats; but our Captain . . . answer'd that he would not, that they should not cause him to commit that false Latine.

Speak fitly, or be silent wisely.

1611 COTGRAVE s.v. 'Taire' Better no words then words unfitly placed. **1640** HERBERT 346.

Speak for yourself.

1902–4 LEAN IV. 99 . . . *i.e.* don't compromise others by unauthorized admissions.

Speak good of archers, for your father shot in a bow.

1721 KELLY 292 . . . Spoken to them who despise the trade, profession, or way of living, that their father had.

Speak good of pipers, your father was a fiddler.

1832 HENDERSON 137.

Speak ill of others is the fifth element, To.

1573 SANDFORD (1576) 210. **1578** FLORIO *First Fruites* f. 29.

Speak in clusters; You | you were begot in nutting.

1678 RAY 346. **1732** FULLER no. 6009.

Speak like an oracle, To.

1600 JONSON *Cynthia's Revels* III. iv. 16 One that will speake More darke and doubtful then six oracles. *c.* **1676** SOUTH *Serm.* (1715) 341 (A) He only now-a-days speaks like an oracle, who speaks tricks and ambiguities.

Speak much who cannot speak well, Many.

1616 DRAXE 11.

Speak not of a dead man at the table.

1640 HERBERT 348.

Speak not of my debts, unless you mean to pay them.

1640 HERBERT 363. **1902–4** LEAN IV. 57.

Speak of my drink, that never consider my drouth,[1] They. (*Cf. the following proverb.*)

1721 KELLY 312 . . . They censure my doing such a thing, who neither consider my occasions of doing it, or what provocations I had to do it. [[1] drought, thirst.]

Speak of my great drinking, Many | but few of my sore thirst.

1641 FERGUSSON 80 Mony speaks of my grit drinking bot few of my sore thirst.

Speak (Talk) of Robin Hood, Many | that never shot in his bow.

c. **1374** CHAUCER *Troilus* II. 861 Swich maner folk, I gesse, Defamen love, as no-thing of him knowe; They speken, but they bente never his bowe. **1401** *Reply of Friar Daw Topias in* T. WRIGHT *Pol. Poems* (1859–61) II. 59 Many men speken of Robyn Hood, and shot nevere in his bowe. **1546** HEYWOOD II. vi. 61. **1631** R. BRATHWAIT *Whimzies* (1859) 13 He cites . . . as if they were his familiars Euclid, Ptolemie . . . But many have spoke of Robin Hood, that never shot in his bow. **1670** RAY 137 . . . And many talk of Little John that never did him know.

Speak of the fair as things went with them there, Men.

1640 HERBERT 324.

Speak of what you understand.

1639 CLARKE 11.

Speak, spend, and speed, quoth Jon of Bathon.

[*c.* 1381] **1652** TWYSDEN *Hist. Angl. Script.* X. 2638 Speke, spende and spede, quoth Jon of Bathon.

Speak to a fasting man, Never.

1639 CLARKE 178.

Speak to the man at the wheel, Don't.

1897 BADEN-POWELL *Matabele Camp.* 235 The maxim, 'Do not speak to the man at the wheel', should ever be . . . acted up to, by those with a column who think they know better than the guide.

Speak well of the dead.

[CHILON *Diog. Laert.* 1. 3. 2. 70 Τὸν τεθνη-κότα μὴ κακολογεῖν. Speak no evil of the dead. L. *De mortuis nil nisi bonum.* Say nothing of the dead but what is good.] **1540** TAVERNER tr. *Erasm. Flores sententiarum* A. 6 Rayle not upon him that is deade. **1642** TORRIANO 6 One ought not to wrong the absent, or the dead. **1648** HERRICK *Hesper.*, *No despight to the dead.* Reproach we may the living; not the dead. **1669** PENN *No Cross, No Crown* xix Chilon . . . would say, . . . 'Speak well of the dead'. **1779–81** JOHNSON *Lives Poets* (Bohn) III. 321 He that has too much feeling to speak ill of the dead, . . . will not hesitate . . . to destroy . . . the reputation . . . of the living. **1902** *Spectator* 1 Nov. The dislike to speak ill of those lately dead has been proverbial for ages.

Speak well of your friend, of your enemy say nothing.

1707 MAPLETOFT 2. **1855** BOHN 490.

Speak well, He cannot | that cannot hold his tongue.

1547 WM. BALDWIN *Treatise Moral Philosophy* (1550) K 8 He knoweth not howe to speake that knoweth not howe to holde hys peace. **1553** *Precepts of Cato* (1560) Q 1ᵛ Pittacus He to speake wel shalbe nothynge connynge That wyll not know how to leaue his bablynge. **1666** TORRIANO 279. **1732** FULLER no. 1820.

Speak when you are spoken to.

1586 LA PRIMAUDAYE *French Academy* tr. T. Bowes (1589) A 5ᵛ It is unmanerly for a maid-servant to speake before she be spoken unto. **1599** PORTER *Angry Wom. Abingd.* II. i (Merm.) 127 *Nich.* Who speaks to you? you may speak when ye are spoken to. **1670** RAY 145 Speak when you are spoke to, come when you are call'd. **1721** KELLY 293 *Speak when you're spoken to, do what you're bidden. Come when you're call'd, and you'll not be chidden.* A cant of mistresses to their maid servants. **1876** MRS. BANKS *Manch. Man* xiii Girls of fifteen were then . . . taught only to 'speak when spoken to'.

Speak with your gold, You may | and make other tongues dumb.

1659 N. R. 126 Where gold speaks every tongue is silent. **1666** TORRIANO 179 *Where gold speaks, every tongue is silent.* **1670** RAY 12 . . . *Ital.*

Speak without the book, To.

[i.e. deviating from the text of the play-book.] **1599** PORTER *Angry Wom. Abingd.* III. ii (Merm.) 147 Methinks you speake without the book, To place a four-wheel waggon in my look.

Speaks as if every word would lift a dish, He.

1721 KELLY 154. **1732** FULLER no. 2024.

Speaks ill, Of him that | consider the life more than the word.

1640 HERBERT 352.

Speaks in his drink what he thought in his drouth,[1] He.

1721 KELLY 134 . . . Eng. *What sobriety conceals, drunkennes reveals.* Lat. *Quod in corde sobrii, more ebrii.* [1 thirst.]

Speaks lavishly, He that | shall hear as knavishly.

1540 TAVERNER tr. *Erasm. Flores Sententiarum* A 6ᵛ If thou speake what thou wilt thou shalt heare what thou wilt not. **1547** WM. BALDWIN *Treatise Moral Philosophy* (1550) N 8ᵛ. **1616** WITHALS 577. **1670** RAY 144. **1732** FULLER no. 6367.

Speaks me fair and loves me not, He that | I'll speak him fair and trust him not.

1616 DRAXE 68. **1670** RAY 24.

Speaks sows, He that | and he that holds his peace gathers.

1640 HERBERT 338. **1853** TRENCH iv. 86 *Speech is silvern, silence is golden*; with which we may compare the Italian: *Who speaks sows; who keeps silence, reaps.*

Speaks the thing he should not, He that | hears the things he would not.

[TER. *Qui pergit ea quae vult dicere, ea quae non vult audiet.* He who insists on saying what he pleases, will hear that which pleases him not.] **1641** FERGUSSON 38.

Speaks well, He that | fights well.

c. **1250** *Owl & Night.* 1074 Wel fiȝt þat wel specþ' seide Alured.

Speak(s), spoke(n), *see also* Ale will make cat s.; All men s. (When), no man hears; Bad cause that none s. in; Effect s., tongue need not; First think then s.; Good friend that s. well of us; Hears much and s. not at all (He that) shall be welcome; Knows most (Who) s. least; Leave to s. (Must have) who cannot hold tongue; Losers leave to s. (Give); Mickle s. part maun spill; Mouse in cheese (S. like); Read, try, s. as you find; Spare to s.; Think much s. little; Time to s. (There is a); Usurer at table (To s. of); Well-bred youth neither s. of himself; Well s. that is well taken.

Speaking, *see* Full man and fasting (Ill s. between).

Spear of Achilles, The.

[Telephus, king of Mysia, wounded by the spear of Achilles, was told by an oracle that he could only be cured by the weapon that gave the wound.] **1579** LYLY *Euphues* (Arb.) 107 Achilles' speare could as wel heale as hurt. **1590–1** SHAKS. *2 Hen. VI* V. i. 100 Like to Achilles' spear Is able . . . To kill and cure. **1621** BURTON *Anat. Mel.* III. ii. VI. iv (1651) 572 Many fly to . . . philters, amulets, . . . which as a wound with the spear of Achilles, if so made and caused, must so be cured. **1900** C. BIGG in *The Church, Past & Pres.* 40 Evolution may be compared to the spear of Achilles; it heals at any rate some of the wounds which it causes . . . by telling . . . how . . . the lower must always prepare the way for the higher.

Spear, *see also* Good s. (He that hath), let him try it.

Spectacles are death's harquebuze.

1640 HERBERT 360.

Spectators, *see* Sport is sweetest when no s.

Speech is silvern, silence is golden.

1831 CARLYLE *Sart. Res.* III. iii As the Swiss Inscription says: *Sprechen ist silbern, Schweigen ist golden* (Speech is silvern, Silence is golden). **1868** *Silent Hours* i. 4 Speech is, after all, not the silvern but the golden thing, when rightly used.

Speech is the picture of the mind.

[DION. HAL. 1. 1 Εἰκόνας εἶναι τῆς ἑκάστου ψυχῆς τοὺς λογόυς. ERASM. *Ad. Hominis figura oratione agnoscitur.*] **1616** DRAXE 197. **1670** RAY 19.

Speech shows what a man is.

1639 CLARKE 238.

Speech, *see also* Repented s. than silence (More).

Speed is in the spurs, All the.

1641 FERGUSSON 8. **1721** KELLY 24 . . . Spoken when a man rides a lazy horse, . . . or must ride hard or lose his business. **1732** FULLER no. 556.

Speed the plough, God.

1472 *Paston Letters* (Gairdner) iii. 50 (A) God sped the plowghe. *c.* **1500** *Spede the Plough* 8 I pray to God, spede wele the plough. **1602** DEKKER *Honest Wh.* xii *Mad.* God speed the Plow, thou shalt not speed me. **1891** J. E. T. ROGERS *Ind. & Commer. Hist.* II. iv The English farmer . . . wherever he may be . . . chronicles his opportunity of proposing the British toast of 'Speed the Plough'. **1896** SKEAT *Stud. Pastime* 79 'God speed the plough' does not mean 'God hasten the plough', but 'God prosper the plough'.

Speed (*noun*), *see also* More haste than s.; Speers all opinions comes ill s.

Speed, sped (*verb*), *see also* Spare to speak and spare to s.; Speak and s., ask and have; Speak, spend, s., quoth Jon of Bathon; Tod never s. better than own errand.

Speers all opinions, He that | comes ill speed.

1721 KELLY 167 . . . Because their different advices will confuse, and distract him.

Speers the gate he knows full well, Many a man.

1641 FERGUSSON 78.

Speer(s), *see also* Shame fall him that s. and kens.

Spell Yarmouth steeple right, You cannot.

1787 GROSE (*Norfolk*) 210 . . . This is a play on the word *right*. Yarmouth spire is awry or crooked, and cannot be set right or straight by spelling.

Spend a whole year's rent at one meal's meat, He will.

1640 HERBERT 331.

Spend and be free, but make no waste.

1616 WITHALS 564. **1639** CLARKE 129. **1670** RAY 24. **1732** FULLER no. 4247.

Spend, and God will send; spare, and ever bare.

c. **1350** *Douce MS. 52* no. 16 Spende and God wyl sende; spare and euer bare—Expendas late, mittet tibi Deus omnia grate. **1546** HEYWOOD II. v. 54 Euer spare and euer bare (saieth he) by and by. Spend, and god shall send (saieth he) saith tholde ballet. **1575** GASCOIGNE *Flowers* Wks. (1907) I. 64 The common speech is, spend and God will send. **1623** CAMDEN 268 Euer spare, and euer bare. **1721** KELLY 290 ... *Solomon* says, *There is that scattereth, and yet aboundeth: And there is some that withholdeth more than is meet, and it tendeth to poverty.*

Spend as you get.

1639 CLARKE 212.

Spend me and defend me.

1590 PAYNE *Brief Descr. Ireland* (1841) 4 They have a common saying which I am persuaded they speak vnfeinedly, which is, Defend me and Spend me. **1596** SPENSER *State Ireld.* Wks. (Globe) 624/1 They ... are very loth to yeld any certayne rent, but onely such spendinges, saying commonly, 'Spend me and defend me'. **1619** HOWELL *Lett.* 1 May (1903) I. 17 [In Amsterdam] monstrous exercises ... are imposed upon all sorts of commodities ... ; it goes ... to preserve them from the Spaniards, so that the saying is truly verified here, 'Defend me and spend me'. **1678** RAY 351 Defend me and spend me (*saith the* Irish *churle*). **1853** TRENCH iii. 61 *Spend me and defend me* ... expresses their idea of what they owed to their native chiefs, and what these owed in return to them.

Spend much, If you can | put the more to the fire.

1641 D. FERGUSSON 62. **1721** KELLY 181 ... That is, if you have a great income spend accordingly. Some have it *Put the more to the fore*, that is, lay up the more, and do accordingly.

Spend not where you may save; spare not where you must spend.

1678 RAY 348.

Spender, To a good | God is the treasurer.

1640 HERBERT 342.

Spenders are bad lenders, Great.

1639 CLARKE 262.

Spending lies the advantage, In.

1640 HERBERT 320.

Spends his Michaelmas rent in Midsummer moon, He.

1617 SWETNAM *School of Defence* 79 Spend not Michaelmasse rent in Midsummer quarter abroade. **1623** CAMDEN 270. **1670** RAY 186.

Spends more than he should, shall not have to spend when he would, Who.

1664 CODRINGTON 226. **1670** RAY 25. **1732** FULLER no. 6074.

Spends the traveller more than the abider, Much.

1640 HERBERT 330.

Spent we had; What we | what we gave, we have; what we left, we lost.

1579 Gloss to SPENSER *Shep. Cal.* May, Much like the epitaph of a good old Erle of Devonshire ... the rymes be these; Ho, ho! Who lies here? I the good Earle of Devonshere And Maulde my wife that was ful deare ... That we spent, we had; That we gave, we have: That we lefte we lost. **1669** *New Help to discourse* 250 (A) (with 'What we lent is lost').

Spend(s, -t), *see also* Better spared than ill s.; Covetous s. more than liberal; Do not all you can, s. not all you have; Gain teacheth to s.; Gains well and s. well (He that); House and land are s. (When), learning is excellent; Know when to s.; Little good is soon s.; More than he is worth doth s. (Who); Narrow gathered widely s.; Penny is well s. that saves; Spare well and s. well; Spare when young, s. when old; Speak, s., speed, quoth Jon of Bathon.

Spice is black, but it has a sweet smack.

1721 KELLY 296 ... An apology for black people.

Spice, He that hath the | may season as he list.

1640 HERBERT 337. **1670** RAY 25 Who hath spice enough may season his meat as he pleaseth.

Spice, *see also* Beat s., it will smell sweeter.

Spick and span, *or* Spick and span new (*formerly* Span new).

c. **1300** *Havelok* 968 The cok bigan of him to rewe, And bouthe him clopes, al spannewe. *c.* **1374** CHAUCER *Troylus* III. 1665 This tale was ay span-newe to bygynne. *a.* **1579–80** NORTH *Plutarch* (1895) II. 217 They were all in goodly gilt armours, and braue purple cassocks upon them, spicke, and spanne newe. *c.* **1590** Forewords to STUBBES' *Anat.* (1877) 38 A spicke and spanne new Geneua Bible. **1665** PEPYS *Diary* 15 Nov. My Lady Batten walking through the dirty lane with new spicke and span white shoes. **1691** RAY *S. & E. Co. Words* 114 *Span New*, very new: that was never worn or used. **1846** THACKERAY *Crit. Rev.* Wks. (1886) XXIII. 159 Benvenuto, spick and span in his very best clothes. **1886** 'MAXWELL GRAY' *Silence Dean Maitland* I. i. 9 A dog-cart, ... driven by a spick-and-span groom.

Spider lost her distaff, and is ever since forced to draw her thread through her tail, The.

1732 FULLER no. 4766.

Spider(s), *see also* Bee sacks honey (Where), s. sucks poison; Killed the blue s. in Blanch powder land; Swallowed a s.; Thrive (He who would wish) must let s. run alive.

Spies are the ears and eyes of princes.

1651 HERBERT 366.

Spies, The life of | is to know, not to be known.

1640 HERBERT 366.

Spigot, *see* Spare at the s.

Spill, *see* Mickle spoken part maun s.

Spilt wine is worse than water.

1721 KELLY 295 . . . Spoken when a thing is spoil'd and not put to its proper use.

Spin a fair (fine) thread, To.

c. **1412** HOCCLEVE *Reg. Princes* (E.E.T.S.) 64, l. 1763 Alasse! this likerous dampnable errour, In this londe hath so large a threde I-sponne, That wers peple is non vndir the sonne. *c.* **1545** *Jacob & Esau* C 3. **1546** HEY-WOOD II. v. 56 In beyng your owne foe, you spin a fayre threede. **1660** TATHAM *The Rump* IV. i. Wks. (1879) 246 Cain has kill'd his brother, Coll. Cordmayner. He has spun a fine thread to-day.

Spin and reel at the same time, A man cannot.

1678 RAY 205. **1732** FULLER no. 2591 (with 'weave' for 'reel').

Spin(s), *see also* Kiss than s. (She had rather); Labours and thrives s. gold; Spoil before you s. (Must).

Spindle and thy distaff ready, Get thy | and God will send thee flax.

1670 RAY 11. **1721** KELLY 119 *Get your spindle and roke ready, and God will send you tow.* Use proper means, and depend upon God for the blessing.

Spindles are made, By one and one.

1573 SANDFORD (1576) 206.

Spinner has a large shift, The diligent.

1659 HOWELL *Moral Prov.* (Spanish) 11 Who spins well hath a large smock. **1758** FRANKLIN in ARBER *E. Garner* v. 581 Industry gives comfort, and plenty, and respect. . . . *The diligent spinner has a large shift.*

Spinola's pleasure, *see* Kirkbie's castle.

Spins well that breeds her children, She.

1640 HERBERT 323.

Spirit is willing, The | but the flesh is weak.

[BIBLE *Matt.* xxvi. 41 The spirit indeed is willing. . . .] **1827** SCOTT *Journ.* 23 July The spirit is willing but the flesh is weak, so I must retreat into the invalided corps.

Spirit of building is come upon him, The.

1678 RAY 67.

Spirits, *see also* Raise no more devils (s.) than you can lay.

Spit in (on) his hand and do full ill, A man may.

1641 FERGUSSON 12. **1721** KELLY 26 . . . A man . . . will spit in his hand, that he may hold the cudgel the faster: meaning, that a man may make good offers to act stoutly, whose heart may yet misgive him after all.

Spit in his mouth, and make him a mastiff.

a. **1633** JONSON *T. Tub* II. iv. 10 A Spaniel, And scarce be spit i' th'mouth for 't. **1670** RAY 216.

Spit in your hand and take better hold (hold fast).

1546 HEYWOOD II. iv. 52. Naie, I will spyt in my handes, and take better holde. **1577** GRANGE *Gold. Aphrod.* H j b If I haue anoynted your palmes with hope, spitte on your handes and take good holde. **1670** RAY 194. **1721** KELLY 291 *Spit in your hand and hold fast.* Spoken to wives, when they speak of their husband's second marriage. **1738** SWIFT (Dial. i) 335 *Lady S.* Nought's never in danger. I warrant miss will spit in her hand, and hold fast. **1866** BLACKMORE *Cradock N.* xxxiii Spit on your grapples, my lads of wax, and better luck the cast after.

Spit of, The very.

[The exact image, likeness, or counterpart of (a person, &c.)] **1825** KNAPP & BALDWIN *Newgate Cal.* III. 497/2 A daughter, . . . the very spit of the old captain. **1836** T. HOOK *G. Gurney* I. 202 You are a queer fellow—the very spit of your father. [Cf. Fr. *tout craché* (LA FONTAINE, *Contes, Deux Amis*).]

Spit on a (the) stone, (and) it will be wet at last.

1641 FERGUSSON 88 Spit on the stane, it will be wet at the last. **1721** KELLY 300 . . . Constant and perpetual doing, though slow, yet may at last effect great things.

Spit one's venom, To.

c. **1200** *Ancrene Riwle* 86 The uorme cumeð al openliche, & seið vuel bi anoðer, & speoweð ut his atter[1]. *c.* **1386** CHAUCER *Pard. T. Prol.*

135 Thus spitte I out my venym vnder hewe Of hoolynesse, to semen hooly. *c.* 1450 *Myrr. our Ladye* 205 God gaue mankynde fowde of lyfe wherein the enemy spued venym by a worde of lesyng. 1639 CLARKE 54. 1701 FARQUHAR *Sir H. Wildair* I. i Let 'em spit their venom among themselves, and it hurts nobody. [¹ venom.]

Spit upon the same stone, To.

1777 BRAND *Pop. Antiq.* 101 *note* We have too a kind of popular Saying, when Persons are of the same Party, or agree in Sentiment, 'they spit upon the same stone'.

Spit (*noun*), *see also* God's blessing make . . . my s. go (Will); Roast meat (Give one) and beat him with s.

Spit(s) (*verb*), *see also* Bitter in his mouth (Who hath) s. not all sweet; Like one as if s. out of his mouth; Long as I live I'll s. in my parlour.

Spital, Spittle (i.e. hospital), *see* God keep me from . . . s.; One foot in the straw (He that hath) hath another in s.

Spite of the devil and Dick Senhouse,¹ It will do, in.

1794 W. HUTCHINSON *Hist. Cumberland* II. 269 They were a constant family of gamesters. . . . The doctor playing with a stranger, he tipped the die so pat, that the other exclaimed, *Surely it is either the devil or Dick Senhouse!*' A common saying, '*It will do in spight of the devil and Dick Senhouse*'. [¹ Richard Senhouse, Bishop of Carlisle, 1624–6.]

Spits against heaven (the wind), Who | it falls in his face.

1557 NORTH *Diall of Princes* f. 106 (A) As he whiche spitteth into the element and the spittel falleth againe into his eies. 1612 WEBSTER *White Devil* III. i (Merm.) 48 For your names Of whore and murderess, they proceed from you, As if a man should spit against the wind; The filth returns in 's face. 1629 T. ADAMS *Serm.* (1861–2) I. 391 God shall . . . at last despise you, that have despised him in us. *In expuentis recidit faciem, quod in cœlum expuit*—That which a man spits against heaven shall fall back on his own face. 1640 HERBERT 333.

Spits on his own blanket (sleeve), He.

1639 CLARKE 54 You spit on your owne sleeve. 1641 FERGUSSON 48 *Of misnurtured persons.* . . . He spits on his own blanket. 1721 KELLY 367 What you say reflects upon yourself, or family. Eng. *You spit on your own blanket* (*lap*). 1828 LYTTON *Pelham* lxxvii Mr. Pelham, who is a long-headed gentleman, and does not *spit on his own blanket,* knows well enough that one can't do all this for five thousand pounds.

Spits, *see also* Spit(s).

Spitting in the church, Some make a conscience of | yet rob the altar.

1591 FLORIO *Sec. Frutes* 13 (A) Who some-times make it a matter of conscience to spitt in the church, and at another time will beray the altar. 1640 HERBERT 347.

Spleen, *see* Good for the liver bad for s.

Splice the main-brace, To.

[= to serve out grog.] 1805 *Naval Chron.* XIII. 480 Now splice the main brace. 1833 MARRYAT *P. Simple* xv Mr. Falcon, splice the main-brace, and call the watch. 1841 CHAMIER *Tom Bowl.* xxvii I'm not going to splice the mainbrace, my lads; we must have no Dutch courage.

Split, *see* Cut (S.) the hair.

Spoil before you spin, You must.

1639 CLARKE 110. 1732 FULLER no. 5970 (with 'spin well').

Spoil the Egyptians, To.

1611 BIBLE *Exodus* xii. 35, 36 They borrowed [R.V. asked] of the Egyptians jewels of silver, and jewels of gold, and raiment. . . . And they spoiled the Egyptians. 1818 SCOTT *Rob Roy* xviii 'How does a man of your strict principles reconcile yourself to cheat the revenue?' 'It's a mere spoiling o' the Egyptians', replied Andrew. 1872 C. READE *Wand. Heir* iv But I doubt me whether that would be fair trade. . . . Is it lawful to spoil the Egyptians?

Spoke in his wheel, It is the best.

1721 KELLY 223.

Spoke in one's wheel, To put a.

1580 LYLY *Euph. & his Eng.* Wks. (Bond) II. 173 Camilla not thinking to be silent, put in hir spoke as she thought into the best wheele. 1601 JONSON *Poetaster* II. i. 47 You would haue your spoke in my cart!

Spoke, *see also* Worst s. breaks first.

Sponge, *see* Throw up s.

Spoon(s), *see* Born with a silver s.; Come after with salt and s.; Fill the mouth with empty s.; Gives fair words feeds with empty s.; Horn s. holds no poison; Long s. that sups with devil; Make a s. or spoil a horn; Sup with a cutty than want a s. (Better to).

Sport best pleases that does least know how, That.

1594–5 SHAKS. *L.L.L.* V. ii. 516 That sport best pleases that does least know how.

Sport is sweetest when there be no spectators.

1616 WITHALS 555 (with 'lookers on'). 1639 CLARKE 326.

Sport, The best of the | is to do the deed, and say nothing.

1640 HERBERT 354.

Sport, *see also* Age is jocund (When) it makes **s.** for death; Good **s.** that fills belly; Make **s.** (He that cannot) should mar none; Mischief (More) the better **s.**; No **s.** no pie.

Sports and journeys men are known, In.

1640 HERBERT 336.

Spots (even) in (on) the sun, There are.

1843–4 DICKENS *M. Chuz.* iv You are . . . a strange instance of the little frailties that beset a mighty mind . . . I should have been quite certain from my observation of you, Chiv, that there were spots on the sun. **1907** s. LEE *Gt. Eng. of 16th Cent.* 7 But in the case of Bacon and Shakespeare, such errors are spots on the sun.

Spot(s), *see also* Enemy (In an) **s.** soon seen; Ermine (In an) **s.** soon discovered; Leopard (In a) the **s.** not observed.

Sprat, Jack, *see* Jack S. he loved no fat; J. S. would teach grandame.

Sprat now-a-days calls itself a herring, Every.

1732 FULLER no. 1464.

Sprat to catch a mackerel (herring, whale), Throw out a.

1827 HONE *Ev. Day Book* ii. 1410 (A) It is but 'giving a sprat to catch a herring', as a body may say. **1832** MARRYAT *N. Forster* xliv 'Depend upon it, that's his plan. A sprat to catch a mackerel.' **1850** DICKENS *M. Chuz.* viii It was their custom . . . never to throw away sprats, but as bait for whales. **1926** *Times* 31 Mar. 5/7 The firm is doing that for a purpose. . . . That is in the nature of a sprat to catch a mackerel.

Sprat, *see also* Fish for herring and catch **s.**

Spread the table, and contention will cease.

1678 RAY *Adag. Hebr.* 413.

Spring in his elbow, He hath a.

1678 RAY 351 He hath a spring in his elbow. Spoken of a gamester.

Spring (*or* Be sprung) of a (the) stone, To.

[= to indicate the absence of any known ancestry of kinsfolk.] **1297** R. GLOUC. (Rolls) 6720 Seint Edward in normandie was þo bileued al one As bar, as wo seiþ, of þe kunde as he sprong of þe stone. *a.* **1300** *K. Horn* (Camb.) 1026 Horn him ʒede alone, Also he sprunge of stone. *a.* **1400** *Sir Perc.* 1043 Als he ware sprongene of a stane, Thare na mane hym kende.

Spring, *see also* Blossom in the **s.** (That which doth); Tread on nine daisies, **s.** has come.

Spring(s) (= tune), *see* Old **s.** give no price; Take a **s.** of his own fiddle (Let him).

Spun, If it will not be | bring it not to the distaff.

1640 HERBERT 348 That which will not be spun, let it not come between the spindle and the distaff. **1732** FULLER no. 2726. **1855** BOHN 416.

Spur a hamshackled[1] horse, It is idle to.

1828 SCOTT *F. M. Perth* xxxiii 'It is but idle to spur a horse when his legs are hamshackled', said the Highlander haughtily. 'Her own self cannot fight even now, and there is little gallantry in taunting her thus.' [[1] shackled, by having its head tied to one of its forelegs.]

Spur a jade a question, and [s]he'll kick you an answer.

1692 L'ESTRANGE *Aesop's Fab.* cccxvi (1738) 329 *Spur a jade a question, and he'll kick ye an answer.* . . . People should not be too inquisitive, without considering how far they themselves may be concerned in the answer to the question.

Spur and a whip for a dull horse, A.

1616 DRAXE 181. **1639** CLARKE 76.

Spur in the head is worth two in the heel, A.

1670 RAY 218. **1721** KELLY 49 . . . A man when drunk rides hard. **1738** SWIFT (Dial ii) 349 Stay till this bottle's out . . . a cup in the pate is a mile in the gate, and a spur in the head is worth two in the heel. **1812** EDGEWORTH *Absentee* x That's four good miles; but 'a spur in the head is worth two in the heel'.

Spur of the moment, On the.

1806 A. DUNCAN *Nelson's Funeral* 43 The contrivance of Mr. Wyatt, on the spur of the moment. **1831** BLAKEY *Free Will* 152 A speaker who gives us a ready reply upon the spur of the moment.

Spur(s), *see also* Bridle and **s.** makes good horse; Love in his breast (He that hath) hath **s.**; Reason lies between **s.** and bridle; Speed is in the **s.**; Win **s.**

Spurring a free horse, It is ill.

[OVID *Ars. Am.* 2. 732 *Nolle admisso subdere calcar equo.*] **1477** *Paston Lett.* (Gairdner) III. 200. It shall never neede to prykke nor threte a free horse. **1595–6** SHAKS. *Rich. II* IV. i. 72. How fondly dost thou spur a forward horse. **1599** JAMES VI *Basil. Dor.* (Arb.) 156 Pastimes, wherewith men by driving time, spur a free and fast enough running horse (as the proverb is). **1659** HOWELL *Eng. Prov.* 17/1. **1670** RAY 145.

Spurring, *see also* Untimeous **s.** spills the steed.

Spy faults if your eyes were out,
You would.

1678 RAY 271.

Square, *see* Inch breaks no s.; Just as a s.

Squeak, *see* Young one s. (Make the).

Squeeze a cork, you will get but little
juice, If you.

1732 FULLER no. 2791.

Squib, *see* Angry as an ass with s. in breech.

Squint-eyed, *see* Perverseness makes one s.

Squire, *see* Scald horse for scabbed s.

Squires and spires, *see* Northamptonshire.

Squirrels, *see* Hunt s. and make no noise.

Stabbed with a Bridport dagger.

1662 FULLER (*Dorset*) I. 453 'Stabb'd with a
Bridport dagger.' That is, hanged . . . at the
gallows; the best . . . hemp . . . growing about
Bridport, a market town in this county. **1910**
Times Lit. Sup. 21 Oct. 384 Leland . . . jots
down, 'At Bridporth be made good daggers'.
Nowadays, at any rate, a Bridport dagger is
a grimly humorous euphemism for a hangman's rope.

Stable-door, *see* Shut the s.-d. when steed
stolen (Too late to).

Staff be crooked, If the | the shadow cannot be straight.

1640 HERBERT 344.

Staff (Stick) is quickly (soon) found to beat a dog, A.

1563 BECON *Early Wks.* (P.S.) Pref. 28 (A)
How easy a thing it is to find a staff if a man
be minded to beat a dog. **1586** PETTIE
Guazzo's Civ. Conv. 178 It is an old proverb.
A staff is soon found to beat a dog. **1590–1**
SHAKS. *2 Hen. VI* III. i. 171 A staff is quickly
found to beat a dog. **1616** N. BRETON *Cross.
Prov.* Wks. (Gros.) II. e6 A staffe is soone
found to beat a dogge withall. **1692**
L'ESTRANGE *Aesop's Fab.* (1738) iii. 3 'Tis
an easy matter to find a staff to beat a dog.
Innocence is no protection against . . . a
tyrannical power. **1875** SMILES *Thrift* 328
Excuses were abundant. . . . It is easy to find
a stick to beat a sick dog. **1908** *Times Lit.
Sup.* 6 Nov. 391 The reviewer seems . . . predisposed to the view that any stick is good
enough to beat a dog with.

Staff to break his own head, He brings a.

c. **1510** STANBRIDGE *Vulg.* (E.E.T.S.) 23 He
hath ordeyned a staffe for his owne heed.
1641 FERGUSSON 52 He brings a staff to his
own head.

Staff, *see also* Broken reed (s.) (Lean upon);
End of the s. (To have the better *or* worse);
Keep the s. in own hand; Literature is
good s.; Set up one's s.

Stafford blue.

[= some kind of blue cloth.] *c.* **1460** *Towneley Myst.* iii. 200 Thou were worthi be cled
In stafford blew; ffor thou art alway adred.

Stafford law.

[= 'club law'.] **1557** *A merry Dialogue* B 1ᵛ
Yf that she woulde not be rewled by wordes
(a goddes name take Stafforde lawe). **1589**
Hay any Work A iij I threatned him with
blowes, and to deale by stafford law. **1611**
COTGRAVE He hath had a trial in Stafford
court (*Il a été au festin de Martin baston*). **1615**
BEDWELL *Moham. Impost.* 1, § 26 The Alkoran
of Mohammed established by Stafford law.
1634 T. HEYWOOD *Captives* III. ii.

Stag (= gander), *see* Full flock.

Stag(s), *see* Army of s. led by lion.

Stagger like a drunken man, To.

1611 BIBLE *Ps.* cvii 27 They reel to and fro,
and stagger like a drunken man. **1837**
CHAMIER *Saucy Areth.* xi The ship rolled
over the waves, but . . . as she recovered herself she seemed to stagger like a drunken
man.

Stained, *see* Silk is soonest s. (Fairest).

Stake, The low (An ill) | standeth long (longest).

1614 CAMDEN 313. **1670** RAY 14 An ill stake
standeth longest.

Stake that cannot stand one year in a hedge (the ground), It is an ill (poor).

1546 HEYWOOD II. iv. 49 So is it an yll stake
I haue heard among. That cannot stande one
yere in a hedge. **1640** HERBERT 343 It is a
poor stake that cannot stand one year in the
ground.

Stake (*noun*), *see also* Bear to the s. (Go like
a); Eaten (Swallowed) a s.; Water a s.

Stake (*verb*), *see* Nothing s. nothing draw;
Stopford law, no s. no draw.

Stalk (Streak) of carl hemp[1] in you, You have a.

1721 KELLY 373 . . . Spoken to sturdy and
stubborn boys. **1862** HISLOP 329 (with
'streak'). Figuratively this means that a
person possesses firmness, or strength of
mind. [[1] male hemp.]

Stamford, *see* Mad as the baiting bull of S.

Stamps like a ewe upon yeaning,[1] She.

1678 RAY 344 . . . *Somerset.* [[1] bringing forth
young.]

Stand in a white sheet, To.

[= to do penance.] **1587** HARRISON *England*
II. xi. 185/1 in *Holinshed* Harlots and their
mates by . . . doing of open penance in streets,

in churches and market steeds are ... put to rebuke. **1597** *Pilgr. Parnass.* v. 546 An honest man that nere did stande in sheete. **1607** MIDDLETON *Fam. Love* IV. iv I can describe how often a man may lie with another man's wife before 'a come to the white sheet.

Stand in one's own light, To.

[= to prejudice one's chances.] **1546** HEYWOOD II. iv. 51 How blindly ye stand in your own light. **1579** LYLY *Euph.* (Arb.) 46 Heere ye may behold Gentlemen, how leaudly wit standeth in his owne light. **1616** DRAXE 90 Hee standeth in his owne light. **1664** COTTON *Scarron.* iv. 65 Y'have ... stood too much in your own light. **1738** SWIFT (Dial. i) 334 *Lady S.* Mr. Neverout, methinks you stand in your own light. *Never.* Ah! madam, I have done so all my life.

Stand Moses (*slang*), To.

1796 GROSE *Dict. Vulg. T.* s.v. A man is said to stand *Moses* when he has another man's bastard child fathered upon him, and he is obliged by the parish to maintain it.

Stand to one's guns, To.

[= to maintain one's position.] **1769** BOSWELL *Johnson* xxii (1848) 201 Mrs. Thrale stood to her gun with great courage, in defence of amorous ditties. **1909** *Spectator* 24 Apr. 661 The Quakers ... stood to their guns (their principles) and, without any resort to brute force, finally won all along the line.

Standers-by (Lookers on) see more than gamesters (*See also* Lookers-on, &c.)

1597 BACON *Ess., Followers, &c.* (A) To take aduise of friends is euer honorable: For lookers on many times see more then gamesters. **1678** RAY 206. **1748** RICHARDSON *Clar. Harlowe* vii A stander-by may see more of the game than one that plays.

Standing pools (dubs[1]) gather filth.

1579 GOSSON *Sch. Abuse* (Arb.) 52 Standing streames geather filth; flowing riuers are euer sweet. **1597** *Politeuphuia* 167. **1639** CLARKE 144. **1721** KELLY 299 Standing pools gather mud. **1832** HENDERSON 13 Standing dubs gather dirt. [1 pools.]

Standing, *see also* Long s. ... maketh poor parsons.

Stands not surely that never slips, He.

1611 COTGRAVE s.v. 'Mescheoir' with 'did never slip'). **1640** HERBERT 320.

Stand(s), *see also* Stake that cannot s. one year; Tub must s. on own bottom.

Stare like a stuck pig, To.

1694 MOTTEUX *Rabelais* v. ix. 41 Panurge stared at him like a dead pig. **1720** GAY *New S. New Sim.* Like a stuck pig I gaping stare. **1837** DISRAELI *Corr. w. Sister* 21 Nov. Gibson Craig ... rose, stared like a stuck pig, and said nothing.

Staring, *see* Difference between s. and stark blind.

Stark dead, Nothing like. (*Cf.* Stone-dead hath no fellow.)

1721 KELLY 262 ... First used by Captain *James Stewart*, against the noble Earl of *Morton;*[1] and afterwards apply'd to ... *Strafford,* and ... *Laud.* Lat. *Mortui non mordent.* [1 *d.* 1581.]

Stark dead be thy comfort.

1659 HOWELL *Eng. Prov.* 11/2.

Stars than a pair, There are more.

c. **1382** CHAUCER *Parl. Foules* 595 'There ben mo sterrés, god wot, than a payre!'

Stars, *see* Sun, moon, and seven s. against us.

Starve in a cook's shop, To

1611 COTGRAVE s.v. 'Aimer' He that loves another better than himselfe starves in a cooks shop. **1629** T. ADAMS *Serm.* (1861–2) II. 535 We see others *esurientes in popina,* as the byword is, starving in a cook's shop—wretched in their highest fortunes. **1659** HOWELL *Eng. Prov.* 5/2 What, shall we starve in a Cooks-shop, and a shoulder of mutton by? **1738** SWIFT (Dial. ii) 346 *Smart.* I am very glad you like it; and pray don't spare it. *Col.* No, my lord; I'll never starve in a cook's shop.

Starv 'em, Rob 'em, and Cheat 'em.

1787 GROSE (*Kent*) 186 Starv 'em, Rob 'em, and Cheat 'em. Stroud, Rochester, and Chatham. A saying in the mouths of the soldiers and sailors, in allusion to the impositions practised upon them.

State, *see* Ounce of s. requires pound of gold.

States have their conversions and periods as well as natural bodies.

1651 HERBERT 372.

Stay a little, and news will find you.

1640 HERBERT 333.

Stay a while, that we may make an end the sooner.

1580 SIDNEY *Arcadia* (1893) i. 63 (A) His horse ... taught him that 'discreet stays make speedy journeys'. **1625** BACON *Apoph. Wks.* (Chandos) 365 Sir Amyas Pawlet, when he saw too much haste made in any matter, was wont to say, 'Stay a while, that we may make an end the sooner'. **1732** FULLER no. 4263 Stop a little, to make an end the sooner.

Stay, and drink of your browst.[1]

1721 KELLY 289 ... Take a share of the mischief that you have occasioned. [1 brewing.]

Stay, If any thing | let work stay.

1678 RAY 278.

Stay, He that can | obtains.

1611 COTGRAVE s.v. 'Attendre' He that can stay his time shall compasse any thing. **1640** HERBERT 356. *Ibid.* 325 He that stays does the business. **1721** KELLY 108 *He that well bides well betides.* He that waits patiently, may come to be well served at last.

Stay till the lame messenger come, if you will know the truth of the thing.

1640 HERBERT 333.

Stay, *see also* Nay, s., quoth Stringer.

Stays in the valley, He that | shall never get over the hill.

1616 DRAXE 42. **1670** RAY 152.

Steady, *see* Slow and s. wins race.

Steal a goose and give the giblets in alms, To.

1659 HOWELL *Eng. Prov.* 1/1. **1670** RAY 25.

Steal a goose and stick down a feather, To.

1546 HEYWOOD I. xi. 35 As dyd the pure penitent that stale a goose And stack downe a fether. **1658** J. SPENCER *Things New & Old* (1868) 574 Like those that steal a goose and stick down a feather, or those that have undone many, then build a hospital for some few. **1714** JNO. WALKER *Sufferings of Clergy* ii. 331 For the Managers of those times thought fit, when they *Stole the Goose, To stick down the Feather,* and allow the *Sequestred's Wife* and *Children* the *Fifths* To live on.

Steal a horse, One man may | while another may not look over a hedge.

1546 HEYWOOD II. ix. 75 This prouerbe, . . . Which saith, that some man maie steale a hors better, Than some other may stande and looke vpone. **1591** LYLY *Endym.* III. iii. Wks. (1902) III. 44 *Toph.* Some man may better steale a horse, then another looke ouer the hedge. **1670** RAY 128 . . . If we once conceive a good opinion of a man, we will not be perswaded he doth any thing amiss; but him whom we have a prejudice against, we are ready to suspect on the sleightest occasion. **1748** CHESTERFIELD 26 July, In that respect the vulgar saying is true. . . **1891** A. LANG *Ess. in Little* 30 Nobody has bellowed 'Plagiarist!' Some people may not look over a fence: Mr. Stevenson, if he liked, might steal a horse. **1894** LD. AVEBURY *Use of Life* ii The Graces help a man almost as much as the Muses . . . 'One man may steal a horse, while another may not look over a hedge'; . . . because the one does things pleasantly, the other disagreably.

Steal a march, To.

[= to get a secret advantage over a rival or opponent.] **1740** CIBBER *Apol.* (1756) I. 143 After we had stolen some few days march upon them. **1771** SMOLLETT *Humph. Clink.* 6 May (1815) 73 She yesterday wanted to steal a march of poor Liddy. **1856** READE *Never too Late* xxii Happening to awake earlier than usual, he stole a march on his nurses, and . . . walked out.

Steal a pin, He that will | will steal a better thing.

1537 R. WHITFORD *Werke for Housholders* D 7 (A) The chylde yᵗ beginneth to pike at a pynne or a poynte wyl after pyke a penny or a pounde. **1670** RAY 145. **1732** FULLER no. 6087.

Steal an egg, He that will | will steal an ox.

1639 CLARKE 148.

Steal for others, If you | you shall be hanged yourself.

1732 FULLER no. 2790.

Steal not my kail, If thou | break not my dyke.

1641 FERGUSSON 62.

Steal the hog and give the feet for alms, To. (*Cf.* Steals a sheep, &c.)

1640 HERBERT 328. **1670** RAY 25 They steal the hog and give away the feet in alms. *Hispan.* **1732** FULLER no. 2028 (He steals a hog, &c.)

Steal the horse, and carry home the bridle.

1678 RAY 342.

Steals a sheep and gives back the trotters, He. (*Cf.* Steal the hog, &c.)

1604 R. DALLINGTON *The View of France* R 2 Hee steales the sheepe, and giues the Tratters [*sic*] for Gods sake. **1655** FULLER *Ch. Hist.* VI. iv (1868) II. 287 The expression of a late Bishop of Norwich is complained of, . . . that 'King Henry took away the sheep from that cathedral, and did not restore so much as the trotters unto it'. **1891** J. E. T. ROGERS *Indust. & Com. Hist.* II. viii Mary Tudor . . . felt herself constrained to allow the alienation of the abbey lands. The nobles of the day, as the Spanish proverb goes, stole the sheep and kept it, but gave God the trotters.

Steals can hide, He that.

1642 TORRIANO 80 It is not enough to know how to steal, one must know how to hide too. **1721** KELLY 140 . . . Yes, and forswear too, a discouragement to search stolen goods. **1732** FULLER no. 2315.

Steals honey, He that | should beware of the sting.

1721 KELLY 163.

Steal(s, ing), stolen, *see also* Daughter is s.
(When) shut Pepper Gate; Friar preached
against s.; Knows what may be gained
(He that) never s.; Learned timely to s.
that could not say nay; Lie will s. (He that
will); Rich man s. (Why should); Shame
to s., but worse to carry home; Wit to . . .
s. horse, wisdom to let alone; Wrongs not
an old man that s. supper.

Steed, *see* Untimeous spurring spills the s.

Steel in my needle eye, There is | though there be little of it.

1721 KELLY 321 . . . Spoken when a thing,
commendable for its kind, is found fault with
for its quantity.

Steel to the back.

1579 LYLY *Euphues* Wks. (Bond) I. 247 I
knowe Curio to be steele to the backe.
c. **1591** SHAKS. *Titus Andron.* IV. iii (A) We
are . . . steele to the very backe.

Steel, *see also* True as s.; True s. as Ripon
rowels.

Steersman, *see* Gunner to his linstock.

Step after step the ladder is ascended.

1611 COTGRAVE s.v. 'Pas' Step after step
goes farre. **1640** HERBERT 336. **1732** FULLER
no. 4260.

Step, The greatest | is that out of doors.

1640 HERBERT 339. **1655–62** GURNALL *Chrn.
in Armour* (1865) I. 206 The greatest step
to heaven, is out of our own doors, over our
own threshold. **1659** HOWELL *Ital.–Eng.* 7.
1668 COWLEY *Ess.* x (1904) 105 Begin; the
getting out of doors is the greatest part of the
journey. Varro[1] teaches us that Latin proverb, *portam itineri longissimam esse.* [[1] *De
Re Rust.* Lib. i.]

Step is the only difficulty, The first.

1616 WITHALS 576 The first step is as good
as halfe over. **1639** CLARKE 171.

Stepped, *see also* Wheamow . . . when she
s. into milk bowl.

Stepmother: Take heed of a | the very name of her sufficeth.

1651 HERBERT 371.

Stern chase is a long chase, A.

1836 MARRYAT *Midsh. Easy* xxix The Aurora
. . . had neared the chase about two miles.
'This will be a long chase, a stern chase
always is.'

Stew, *see* Fry (S.) in one's own grease (juice).

Steward abroad when there is a wind-frost, There is a good.

1830 FORBY 431 . . . *i.e.* You have no occasion
to look to your labourers, they must work to
keep themselves warm.

Stick by the ribs, To.

1603 *The Bachelor's Banquet* (Wilson) 84
Some one . . . hath offred her such Kindnes,
as sticks by her ribs a good while after. **1670**
RAY 194.

Stick is the surest peacemaker, The.

1902–4 LEAN IV. 139 The stick is the surest
peacemaker. Baston porte paix [**1610** GRUTER
Prov. 189.]

Sticking[1] goes not by strength, but by guiding of the gully.[2]

1721 KELLY 292 . . . Matters are carried on
rather by art than strength. [[1] stabbing.
[2] knife.]

Sticks and stones will break my bones, but names will never hurt me.

1894 NORTHALL *Folk-phrases* (E.D.S.) 23 . . .
Said by one youngster to another calling
names.

Stick(s) (*noun*), *see also* Dress up a s. and
it does not appear a s.; End of the staff
(s.) (To have the wrong); Little s. kindle
fire; Staff (S.) is quickly found to beat dog;
Straight s. crooked in water; Trust to a
dry s. (No); Two dry s. kindle green one.

Stick(s) (*verb*), *see also* Ball does not s. to the
wall (If); Hap (Some have the), some s. in
gap; Put it on thick a little will s.

Stiff as a poker.

1792 *Letters of S. T. Coleridge* (ed. E. H.
Coleridge) i. 30. **1797** COLMAN JR. *Heir at
Law* III. ii (A) Stuck up as stiff as a poker.

Stiff upper lip, To keep (carry) a.

1833 J. NEAL *Down Easters* I. ii. 15 'What's
the use o' boo-hooin'? . . . keep a stiff upper
lip. **1837** HALIBURTON *Clockm.* Ser. I. xxv
She used to carry a stiff upper lip and make
him and the broomstick acquainted together.

Stile(s), *see* Best dog leap s. first; Go over the
s. (He that will not); Leap over hedge
before you come at s.; Over the s. ere you
are at it (You would be); Suffolk s.

Still him, Who hath none to | may weep out his eyes.

1640 HERBERT 318.

Still sow eats up all the draff, The.

c. **1225** *Trin. MS. O. 11. 45* (ed. Förster) in
Eng. Stud. **31.** 6 The stille sohghe het, þare
gruniende, mete. *Sus taciturna vorat, dum
garrula voce laborat. c.* **1250** *Digby MS. 53*, f. 8,
in *Eng. Stud.* **31.** 15 The stille sue æt gruniende hire mete. *c.* **1400** *MS. Latin no. 394*,
J. *Rylands Libr.* (ed. Pantin) in *Bull. J. R.
Libr.* XIV. 29 The stylle sowʒe etus alle þe
draffe. **1546** HEYWOOD I. x. 22. Well the still
sowe eats vp all the draffe. **1600–1** SHAKS.

Merry W. IV. ii. 109 'Tis old but true, Still Swine eats all the draugh. **1633** JONSON *T. Tub* III. v *Dame T.* I'll ne'er trust smooth-faced tileman for his sake. *Awd.* Mother, the still sow eats up all the draff. **1721** KELLY 313 . . . Spoken to persons who look demurely, but are roguish. **1828** LYTTON *Pelham* lxi 'You won't bet, Mr. Pelham? close and shy . . . ; well, *the silent sow sups up all the broth.'*

Still tongue makes a wise head, A.

1562 HEYWOOD *Sixth Hund. Epigr.* no. 83, 214 Hauyng a styll toung he had a besy head. **1892** QUILLER-COUCH *Three Ships* vii A still tongue makes a wise head, and 'twill be time enough to talk . . . when, &c.

Still (Smooth) waters run deep.

c. **1400** *Cato's Morals* in *Cursor M.* (E.E.T.S.) l. 1672 (A) There the flode is deppist the water standis stillist. *c.* **1430** LYDGATE *Churl & Bird* (Percy Soc.) 186 Smothe waters ben ofte sithes depe. *c.* **1435** *Burgh's Cato* v. 1050 In floodis stille is watir deep and hihe. **1580** LYLY *Euph. & his Eng.* (Arb.) 287 I perceiue *Issida* that where the streame runneth smoothest, the water is deepest. **1590–1** SHAKS. *2 Hen. VI* III. i. 53 Smooth runs the water where the brook is deep. **1616** DRAXE 178 Where riuers runne most stilly, they are the deepest. **1721** KELLY 387 Smooth waters run deep. **1858** MRS. CRAIK *A Woman's Thoughts* 291 In mature age, . . . the fullest, tenderest tide of which the loving heart is capable, may be described by those 'still waters' which 'run deep'. **1869** TROLLOPE *He knew he was right* xxxv 'What do you call Dorothy Stanbury? That's what I call still water. She runs deep enough. . . . So quiet, but so—clever.'

Still waters, Take heed of | the quick pass away.

1623 WODROEPHE 276 Flee from still waters, for in running water thou mayst enter assuredly. **1640** HERBERT (Gros.) no. 171.

Still, *see also* Be s. and have thy will; Beware of a silent dog and s. water.

Stillest humours are always the worst, The.

1664 CODRINGTON 216. **1670** RAY 25.

Sting is in the tail, The.

[**1534** TINDALE *Rev.* ix. 10 They had tayles lyke vnto scorpions, and there were stinges in their tayles.] **1593–4** SHAKS. *Tam. Shrew* II. i. 211 *Kath.* If I be waspish, best beware my sting. *Pet.* My remedy is, then, to pluck it out. *Kath.* Ay, if the fool could find out where it lies. *Pet.* Who knows not where a wasp does wear his sting? In his tail. **1615** T. ADAMS *England's Sickness* 17 Hee is like a Bee or an Epigram, all his sting is in his tail. **1657** in *Verney Mem.* (1907) II. 52 His letter to you I hope will be full of douceur without a stinge at the tayle of it. **1926** *Times* 7 Sept. 17/5 But the sting of this book is in its tail.

Sting of a reproach is the truth of it, The.

1732 FULLER no. 4769. **1909** *Times Lit. Sup.* 17 Dec. 491 This merciless exposition of American military weakness will prove very unpleasant reading for American citizens. The sting . . . lies in its truth.

Sting, *see also* After your fling watch for s.

Stink like a brock,[1] To.

c. **1400** *Ywaine & Gaw.* 98 It es ful semeli, als me think, A brok omang men forto stynk. *a.* **1528** SKELTON *Agst. Garnesche* 55 She seyd your brethe stank lyke a broke. [[1] badger.]

Stink like a goat, To.

c. **1386** CHAUCER *Can. Yeo. T.* 886 For al the world they stynken as a goot.

Stink like a polecat, To.

1533 J. HEYWOOD *Johan Johan* 73 That she shall stynke lyke a pole-kat. **1630** DEKKER *Honest Wh.*—Pt. II. iv. iii (Merm.) 263 Sh'as a breath Stinks worse than fifty polecats.

Stink (*noun*), *see* Chink (So we get) bear with s.

Stink(s) (*verb*), *see also* Proffered service s.; Smelt where all s. (One is not); Stir it (The more you), worse it s.; What serves dirt for if it do not s.?

Stinking fish, *see* No man cries s. f.

Stinking praise comes out of one's own mouth, It is a.

1737 RAMSAY III. 187.

Stir it (a turd), The more you | the worse it stinks.

1546 HEYWOOD II. vi. 63 Let him pas, for we thinke, The more we stur a tourde, the wurs it will stynke. **1620** SHELTON *Quix.* II. xiii (1908) II. 266 'I have spoken, . . . but let it alone; the more it is stirred, the more it will stink. **1639** CLARKE 200 The more you stirre it, the worse it stinkes. **1670** RAY 194. The more you stir, the worse you stink.

Stir one's stumps,[1] To.

[= to walk or dance briskly.] **1559** *Mirr. Mag., Jack Cade* xx But hope of money made him stur his stumpes, And to assault me valiauntly and bolde. **1596** COLSE *Penelope* (1880) 164 I doubt not but poore shepheards will stirre their stumps after my minstrelsie. **1832** MARRYAT *N. Forster* x Come this way, my hearty—stir your stumps. **1876** BLACKMORE *Cripps* xiii Look alive, woman! Stir your stumps! [[1] legs.]

Stirling gets a hat, When the castle of | the carse of Corntown pays for that.

1857 DEAN RAMSAY *Remin.* v (1911) 205 *When the castle of Stirling gets a hat, the carse of Corntown pays for that.* When the clouds descend so low as to envelop Stirling Castle, a deluge of rain may be expected in the adjacent country.

Stitch[1] against, To have (or take) a.

a. **1591** H. SMITH *Serm.* (1594) 224 Therefore his Maiestie hath a stitch against her, as Salomon had to Shimei. *a.* **1639** W. WHATELEY *Prototypes* II. xxx (1640) 100 We sometimes take such a stitch and spleene against those whom nature hath tyed to us. [[1] a grudge, dislike.]

Stitch in time saves nine, A.

1732 FULLER no. 6291 A stitch in time may save nine. **1793** *Friendly Addr. Poor* 14 A stitch in time may save nine. **1869** READE *Foul Play* ix Repairing the ship. Found a crack or two in her inner skin. . . . A stitch in time saves nine.

Stitch, *see also* Stop s. while I put needle in; Tailor that makes not knot loseth s.

Stock, lock, and barrel.

[= the entirety of any thing.] **1817** SCOTT in LOCKHART *Life* v. 238 Like the Highlandman's gun, she wants stock, lock, and barrel, to put her into repair. **1853** G. J. WHYTE-MELVILLE *Digby Grand* xxiv When a woman is a trump there is nothing like her; but when she does go to the bad, she goes altogether, 'stock, lock and barrel'. **1912** *Spectator* 6 Jan. 24 He condemns fiscal autonomy—lock, stock, and barrel—as ignoring the lessons of the past.

Stock(s), *see also* Buy no s.; Constable of Openshaw . . . s. at Manchester; Grafting on a good s.; Lacketh a s. (Who), his gain is not worth chip; Look to him gaoler . . . frog in s.; Shoemaker's s.

Stockfish, *see* Beat one like a s.

Stocking off a bare leg, It is hard to get a.

1641 FERGUSSON 62 It is ill to take a breik off a bair arse. **1917** BRIDGE 84 . . . Spoken of a bankrupt.

Stocking(s), *see also* Green s.; Shoe knows whether s. has holes; Yellow s.

Stolen waters (pleasures) are sweet.

[**1611** BIBLE *Prov.* ix. 17.] **1629** T. ADAMS *Serm.* (1862) I. 159 Sin shows you a fair picture—'Stolen waters are sweet'. **1632** MASSINGER *City Madam* II. i And pleasure stolen, being sweetest. **1721** KELLY 298 . . . People take great delight in that which they can get privately. **1824** SCOTT *Redg.* Letter 10 His eyes dancing with all the glee of a forbidden revel; and his features . . . confessing the full sweetness of stolen waters.

Stolen, *see also* Nothing is s. without hands.

Stomach, To have a | and lack meat: to have meat and lack a stomach: to lie in bed and cannot rest: are great miseries.

1636 CAMDEN 307.

Stomach (Digestion) like an ostrich, A.

1584 COGAN *Haven Health* ix (1636) 33 Rusticks, who have stomachs like ostriges, that can digest hard yron. **1590–1** SHAKS. *2 Hen. VI* IV. x. 27 I'll make thee eat iron like an ostrich . . . ere thou and I part. **1658** WALL *Comm. Times* 63 Estridge Consciences, that can digest Iron but not straw. **1819** SCOTT *Let.* 15 Apr. in LOCKHART *Life* xliv At least till my stomach recovers its tone and ostrich-like capacity of digestion.

Stomachs to eat, He has two | and one to work.

1813 RAY 104 . . . The Spaniards say, *Al hacer temblar y al comer sudar.* To quake at doing, and sweat at eating.

Stomach(s), *see also* Poor men seek meat for their s.; Sharp s. makes short devotion.

Stone, The lower | can do no good without the higher.

1519 HORMAN *Vulg.* (1530) xv. e. 1 The lower stone cä do no good without the hyer. [*i.e.* the upper millstone.]

Stone in a well is not lost, A.

1640 HERBERT 356.

Stone of Sisyphus.

[In Greek mythology, Sisyphus was condemned to roll daily to the top of a hill a huge stone, which thereupon rolled down again.] **1621** BURTON *Anat. Mel.* I. ii. III. xi (1652) 112 Commonly, they that, like Sisyphus, roll this restless stone of ambition, are in a perpetual agony. **1670** DRYDEN *Conq. Gran.* III. ii *Oz.* Whate'er I plot, like Sisyphus, in vain I heave a stone, that tumbles down again. **1909** *Times Lit. Sup.* 16 Jul. 260 'The task of Sisyphus has to be begun again by all . . rulers of empires; and the stone of civilization which has been painfully rolled up the mountain side tumbles back into the pit'.

Stone that is fit for the wall is not left in the way, A.

1853 TRENCH v. 116 How manful a lesson is contained in this Persian proverb: *A stone that is fit for the wall, is not left in the way.* . . . Only be *fit for the wall.* . . . Sooner or later the builders will be glad of thee.

Stone that lies not in your gate breaks not your toes, The.

1721 KELLY 308 . . . Spoken against meddling in the business in which we have no concern. **1732** FULLER no. 4770. The Stone, that lieth not in your Way, need not offend you.

Stone(s), *see also* Boil s. in butter; Constant dropping wears s.; Fells two dogs with one s.; Gently over the s.; Hard as a flint (s.); Holds his peace and gathers s. will find time to throw; Leave no s. unturned; Never take a s. to break egg; No man can flay a s.; Remove s. bruise fingers (Who);

Roast a s. Rolling s. no moss; Rugged s. grows smooth; Silent gathers s.; Sliddery s. before hall door; Spring of a s. (To); Stumbles twice at one s.; Tree loaded with fruit people throw s.; Trick for trick and a s. in thy foot besides; Water (Blood) from a s.; White s.; Word and a s. cannot be called back; Word (S.) to throw at a dog.

Stone wall, *see* Run one's head against s. w.

Stone-dead hath no fellow. (*Cf.* Stark dead, Nothing like.)

[1641] 1828 MACAULAY *Ess., Hallam* Wks. V. 185 Essex said, . . . with more truth than elegance, 'Stone-dead hath no fellow'. **1926** *Times* 27 Aug. 11/3 The execution of the death sentence had been postponed for a week, an unusual period in a country where the adage 'stone-dead hath no fellow' wins general support.

Stonham, *see* No cousin . . . at S.

Stool in the sun; Put a | when one knave rises, another comes.

1659 HOWELL *Eng. Prov.* 2/1 . . . *viz. To places of preferment.* **1732** FULLER no. 4105.

Stool of repentance.

[A stool formerly placed in Scottish churches for offenders (especially against chastity); also called *Cutty-stool*.] *a.* **1674** CLARENDON *Hist. Reb.* xiii § 48 To stand publickly in the Stool of Repentance, acknowledging their former transgressions. *a.* **1704** T. BROWN *Walk round London* Wks. (1709) III. 34 When the Fumes of Melancholy or Wine set them on the Stool of Repentance. **1884** *Christian World* 2 Oct. 737/1 *The Times* . . . seats itself as it were in shame on the stool of repentance.

Stool(s), *see also* Between two s.; Comb head with three-legged s.; Lay the s.'s foot in water.

Stool-foot, *see* Pottage of a s.-f. (With cost one may make).

Stoop for a pin, He that will not | shall never be worth a point (pound).

1668 PEPYS *Diary* 2 Jan. (Globe) 600 Sir W. Coventry answered: 'I see your Majesty do not remember the old English proverb, "He that will not stoop for a pin, will never be worth a pound".' **1670** RAY 131 (with 'point').

Stoop that hath a low door, He must.

1678 RAY 206. **1732** FULLER no. 1995.

Stoop when the head is off, It is no time to.

1470 HENRYSON *Moral Fab.* in *Wks.* (S.T.S.) II. 130 The nek to stoup, quhen it the straik sall get Is sone aneuch. **1641** FERGUSSON 62.

1721 KELLY 197 . . . That is, care, wariness, and saving, is to no purpose when all is gone. **1737** RAMSAY III. 183 It is past jouking[1] when the head's aff. [[1] bowing the head.]

Stooping, *see* Come, but come s.

Stop every man's mouth, He who will| must have a great deal of meal.

1509 A. BARCLAY *Ship of Fools* (1874) I. 208 One must have moche mele, to stoppe eche mannys mouthe. **1603** *Bachelor's Banquet* (Wilson) 23 Their mouthes will not be stopt with a bushell of wheat that speak it. **1707** MAPLETOFT 6. **1855** BOHN 401.

Stop gaps with rushes, To.

[= a futile effort.] 1550 HEYWOOD II. ix. 78 Ye will (quoth she) as soone stop gaps with rushes.

Stop stitch while I put a needle in.

1847 HALLIWELL *Dict.* (1889) II. 808 . . . a proverbial phrase applied to any one when one wishes him to do anything more slowly.

Stop two gaps with one bush, To.

1550 HEYWOOD II. ix. 78. **1600** HOLLAND *Livy* XXIII. iii. 474 Therefore with one bush (as they say) ye are to stop two gaps, and to do both at once. **1639** FULLER *Holy War* v. xxii (1840) 280 These Italians stopped two gaps with one bush; they were merchant pilgrims, and together applied themselves to profit and piety.

Stop two mouths with one morsel, To.

1616 WITHALS 556. **1639** CLARKE 45.

Stopford[1] law; no stake, no draw.

1678 RAY 301 *Cheshire.* **1787** GROSE (*Chesh.*) 157 . . . Commonly used to signify that only such as contribute to the liquor, are entitled to drink of it. **1917** BRIDGE 110 Stopport[1] law, no stake no draw. . . . Only those who contribute to an undertaking may reap any benefit from it. . . . Stockport is half in Lancashire and half in Cheshire. [[1] Stockport.]

Store is no sore.

1471 RIPLEY *Comp. Alch.* XII. viii in *Ashm.* (1652) 186 For wyse men done sey store ys no sore. **1546** HEYWOOD I. v. 10 Gredinesse, to drawe desyre to hir lore, Saieth, . . . store is no sore. **1633** MASSINGER *New Way* III. ii (Merm.) 149 *Over.* Let my dressers crack with the weight Of curious viands. *Greedy.* 'Store indeed's no sore', sir.

Store of butter, They that have got good | may lay it thick on their bread.

1639 CLARKE 49.

Store of oatmeal, Where there is | you may put enough in the crock.

1678 RAY 352 . . . *Somerset.*

Store, *see also* Worst s., maid unbestowed.

Stork, *see* Log nor a stork (Neither a).

Storm, As welcome as a.

1597 DELONEY *1 Gentle Craft* Wks. (Mann) 73 As welcome to me, as a storme to a distressed Mariner. **1732** FULLER no. 746.

Storm in a teacup, A.

[CICERO, *Leg.* 3. 16. 36 *Excitare fluctus in simpulo.*] **1678** DK. ORMONDE *Let. Earl Arlington* in *Hist. MSS. Comm., Ormonde MSS.* IV. 292 Our skirmish . . . compared with the great things now on foot, is but a storm in a cream bowl. **1854** B. BAYLE Title of farce. **1872** BLACK *Strange Adv. Ph.* xix She has raised a storm in a tea-cup by her . . . unwarranted assault. **1900** G. C. BRODRICK *Mem. & Impr.* 360 Here the storm in the Oxford tea-cup raged as furiously as in the open sea.

Storm(s), *see* After a s. a calm (*or vice versa*); Fair day in winter mother of s.; High regions never without s.; Sharper the s. sooner over; Stuffing holds out s; Vows made in s. forgotten in calms.

Stormy, *see* Sound travelling far and wide.

Story without sticklers,[1] No.

1659 HOWELL *Brit. Prov.* 35. [[1] strong supporters.]

Story, *see also* One tale (s.) is good till another told.

Stot(s), *see* Old oxen (s.) have stiff horns.

Stoup(s), *see* Pint s. hae lang lugs; Water s. hold no ale.

Stout (*or* Strong), As you are | be merciful.

1721 KELLY 39 . . . Spoken in a taunting manner to them that threaten us. **1738** SWIFT (Dial. i) 333 [*Col. offering, in jest, to draw his sword.*] *Never.* Colonel, as you are stout, be merciful. **1884** D. C. MURRAY *Way of World* xxix But, Clare, as you are strong be merciful.

Stout, *see* Hard (S.) heart against hard hap (to stey brae); I proud (s.) and thou proud (s.); Proud (S.) comes behind as goes before; Wight (S.) as a webster's (miller's) waistcoat.

Stow on the Wold,[1] where the wind blows cold.

1852 *N. & Q.* 1st Ser. v. 375 A particularly appropriate rhyme is that of 'Stow on the Wold Where the wind blows cold.' **1853** HALLIWELL *Nursery Rh. of Eng.* in LEAN I. 39 At Stow in the Wold the wind blows cold, I know no more than this. [[1] a small market-town in the Cotswold Hills.]

Straight as a line.

c. **1380** CHAUCER *Troylus* ii. 1461. **1412–20** LYDGATE *Troy Book* ii. 6739 (A) The wey hem ladde To the paleis, streight as any lyne.

Straight stick is crooked in the water, A.

1603 FLORIO tr. *Montaigne* I. xl To judge of high and great matters, a high and great mind is required. . . . A straight oar being under the water seemeth to be crooked. **1647** FULLER *Serm.* (1891) I. 546 Take a straight stick and put it into the water; then it will seem crooked. Why? Because we look upon it through two mediums, air and water. **1732** FULLER no. 425.

Straight trees have crooked roots.

1580 LYLY *Euph. & his Eng.* Wks. (Bond) II 99 For experience teacheth me, that straight trees haue crooked rootes. **1732** FULLER no. 4264.

Strain at (out) a gnat and swallow a camel, To.

c. **1200** *Ancrene Riwle* 8 ȝe beon ase sum deð . . . þe isihð þene gnet & swoluweð þe uliȝe. [fly]. **1526** TINDALE *Matt.* xxiii. 24 Ye blinde gydes, which strayne out a gnat, and swalowe a cammyll. **1594** J. KING *On Jonas* (1599) 284 They have verified the old proverbe in strayning at gnats and swallowing downe camells. **1611** BIBLE *Matt.* xxiii. 24 Ye blind guides, which straine at a gnat, and swallow a camel. **1612–15** BP. HALL *Contempl.* IV. xxxi (1825) II. 517 Do ye fear to be defiled with the touch of Pilate's pavement? doth so small a gnat stick in your throats, while ye swallow such a camel of flagitious wickedness? **1928** *Times* 31 Jan. 5/3 Factor said in effect: 'I will swallow all the camels you have said about me, but I strain at this gnat'.

Strand on the Green, thirteen houses, fourteen cuckolds, and never a house between.

1659 HOWELL *Eng. Prov.* 21/2 *Strand on the Green, thirteen houses, fourteen Cuckolds, and never a house between; For the father and son lay in one house.*

Strange beast that hath neither head nor tail, It is a.

1616 DRAXE 202. **1639** CLARKE 8.

Stranger is for the wolf, The.

1908 C. M. DOUGHTY *Wander. in Arabia* (1908) I. vii. 117 There is not . . . a man . . . had not slain thee. . . . The *stranger is for the wolf!* you heard not this proverb in your own country?

Stranger, *see also* Strew green rushes for s.

Strap, *see* Oil of whip (s.).

Strathbogie, *see* Miscall a Gordon.

Straw, Not worth a.

c. **1300** *Havelok* (E.E.T.S.) 10, l. 315 He let his oth al ouer-ga, Þerof ne yaf he nouth a stra. *c.* **1390** GOWER *Conf. Amantis* III. 666 And seith, that such an Housebonde Was to a wif noght worth a Stre. *c.* **1412** HOCCLEVE *De Reg. Princ.* 1670 Swiche vsage is Not

worþ a strawe. **1522** *Mundus et Infans* 355
(1903) 365 *Manh.* All thy techynge is not
worthe a straye. **1730** SWIFT *On Stephen
Duck* Wks. (1856) I. 637 Though 'tis confess'd that those who ever saw His poems
think them all not worth a straw!

Straw, To be in (out of) the.

[= in childbed: recovered after child bearing.] **1662** FULLER (*Lincs.*) II. 263 Our
English plain proverb, 'de puerperis' (they
are in the straw). **1705** [E. WARD] *Hudibras
Rediv.* IV. 18 We sipp'd our Fuddle, As
Women in the Straw do Caudle. **1772**
Grimston Papers (MS.) I hope your neighbour, Mrs. G., is safe out of the straw, and the
child well. **1832** MARRYAT *N. Forster* xv They
found the lady *in the straw.*

Straw to his dog and bones to his ass, He gives.

1813 RAY 75.

Straws show which way the wind blows.

1689 SELDEN *Table-Talk, Libels* (Arb.) 67
Take a straw and throw it up into the Air,
you shall see by that which way the Wind is
. . . More solid things do not show the Complexion of the times so well, as Ballads and
Libels. **1823** BYRON *D. Juan* XIV. viii You
know, or don't know that great Bacon saith
'Fling up a straw, 'twill show the way the
wind blows'. **1835** LYTTON *Rienzi* II. iii The
Provençal, who well knew how to construe
the wind by the direction of straws. **1861**
READE *Cloister & H.* lvi And such straws of
speech show how blows the wind. **1907** S. LEE
Gt. Eng. of 16th Cent. 224 Bacon set forth
these views as mere *ballons d'essai*, as straws
to show him which way the wind blew.

Straw(s), *see also* Care a s. (Not to); Corn lies
under the s. (Much); Cradle s. are scarce
out of his breech; Drowning man catch at
s.; Eyes draw s.; Fire of s.; Ill man lie in
thy s. (Let an); Last s.; Law for wagging
of s. (Will go to); Long journey (In a) s.
weighs; One foot in the s.; Pad in the s.;
Playing with s. before old cat (No); Skirts
of s. (Who hath) fear the fire; Stumble
at a s. and leap block; Time and s. make
medlars ripe; Wagging of a s.

Strawberry, *see* Cut down an oak.

Stream cannot rise above its source, The.

1700 DRYDEN *Wife of Bath* 388–9 Then what
can Birth, or mortal Men bestow, Since
Floods no higher than their Fountains flow?
1732 FULLER no. 4771 The Stream can never
rise above the Springhead. **1905** VACHELL
The Hill 84 Clever chap, . . . but one is reminded that a stream can't rise higher than
its source. **1921** T. R. GLOVER *The Pilgrim* 125
It is held that a stream cannot rise above its
source; but . . . [a] river may have many
tributaries, and one of them may change the
character of what we call the main stream.

Stream, *see also* Cross the s. where it is ebbest;
Little s. drives light mill; Striving against
s. (Ill).

Street of 'By-and-bye', By the | one arrives at the house of 'Never'.

1853 TRENCH iv. 88 In this Spanish [proverb]
the final issues of procrastination are well
set forth: *By the street of 'By-and-bye' one
arrives at the house of 'Never'.*

Strength enough to bear the misfortunes of one's friends, One has always.

1773 GOLDSMITH *She Stoops to C.* III. Wks.
(Globe) 661 *Mrs. Hard.* You must learn
resignation. . . . See me, how calm I am.
Miss Nev. Ay, people are generally calm at
the misfortunes of others. **1853** TRENCH v.
104 This Russian, . . . *The burden is light on
the shoulders of another*; with which the
French may be compared: *One has always
enough strength to bear the misfortunes of one's
friends* [*On a toujours assez de force pour
supporter le malheur de ses amis.*]

Strength, *see also* Sticking goes not by s.;
Wisdom goes beyond s.

Stretch without a halter, You.

1738 SWIFT (Dial. i) 338 COLONEL *stretching
himself. Lady S.* Why, colonel, you break the
King's laws; you stretch without a halter.

Stretch your arm (Put your hand) no further than your sleeve will reach.

1549 LATIMER *2nd Serm. bef. Edw. VI* (Arb.)
51 Mayntayn no greater port, then thou art
able to bear out and support of thyne owne
provision. Put thy hand no further then thy
sleue will reache. **1590** GREENE *Mourning
Garment* Wks. (Huth) IX. 216 My sutes were
silke, my talke was all of State, I stretcht
beyond the compasse of my sleeye. **1639**
CLARKE 211 Stretch your arm no further than
your sleeve will reach. **1721** KELLY 277 *Put
your hand no farther than your sleeve will
reach.* That is, spend no more than your
estate will bear. **1822** J. GALT *Provost* ii I
replied, 'Dinna try to stretch your arm,
gude-wife, further than your sleeve will let
you.' **1881** W. WESTALL *Old Factory* xxi It
would leave me short of working capital,
and . . . I mustn't stretch my arm further
than th' coat-sleeve will reach.

Stretch your legs according to your coverlet.

a. **1253** GROSTESTE *Bk. of Husbandry* in RILEY
Mem. of London 8, note 4 Whoso streket his
fot forthere than the whitel[1] wil reche, he
schal streken in the straw. **1393** LANGLAND
P. Pl. C. xvii. 76 When he streyneth hym to
strecche . the straw is hus whitel. **1640**
HERBERT 323 Everyone stretcheth his legs
according to his coverlet. **1670** RAY 25. **1897**
'H. S. MERRIMAN' *Kedar's Tents* iv 'Every
one stretches his legs according to the length
of his coverlet', he said. [[1] blanket.]

Stretching and yawning leadeth to bed.

1659 HOWELL *Eng. Prov.* 17/2. **1678** RAY 81.

Stretton in the Street, where shrews meet.

1678 RAY 333 Rutlandshire.

Strew green rushes for the stranger.

[Before the introduction of carpets the rushes on the floor were renewed for a visitor.] **1546** HEYWOOD II. iii. 48 She bad vs welcome and merily toward me, Gréene rushes for this straunger, strawe here (quoth she). **1589** GREENE *Menaphon* (Arb.) 85 When you come you shall have greene rushes, you are such a straunger. **1593–4** SHAK. *Tam. Shrew* IV. i. 48 Is supper ready, the house trimmed, rushes strewed, cobwebs swept? **1738** SWIFT (Dial. i) 333 *Lady S.* If we had known of your coming, we should have strewn rushes for you.

Stricken deer withdraws himself to die, The.

1583 MELBANCKE *Philot.* 167 The stricken Deare withdrawes himself to die. **1593–4** SHAKS. *Tit. Andron.* III. i. 89 Seeking to hide herself, as doth the deer, That hath receiv'd some unrecuring wound.

Stricken the ball under the line, Thou hast.

[*i.e.* not played according to the rules.] **1546** HEYWOOD I. xi. 35. **1611–12** SHAKS. *Tempest* IV. i. 237 Mistress line, is not this my jerkin? Now is the jerkin under the line. **1616** DRAXE 166 Hee hath strooke the ball vnder the line.

Stricken, see also Pryeth into every cloud may be s. (He that).

Strife, see Devil hath cast bone to set s.; God stint all s.; Want makes s. 'twixt man and wife; Weight and measure take away s.

Strike all of (on *obs.*) a heap, To.

[= to paralyse, to cause to collapse.] **1711** *Brit. Apollo* III. No. 133. 2/1 A Young Woman . . . struck me all on a heap. **1741** RICHARDSON *Pamela* I. 205 This alarm'd us both; and he seem'd quite struck of a Heap. **1818** SCOTT *Rob Roy* xxiv The interrogatory seemed to strike the honest magistrate, to use the vulgar phrase, 'all of a heap'. **1875** JOWETT *Plato* (ed.) III. 120 Some one who . . . will not be struck all of a heap like a child by the vain pomp of tyranny.

Strike as ye feed, and that's but soberly.

1721 KELLY 286 . . . A reproof to them that correct those over whom they have no power.

Strike, but hear.

[PLUTARCH *Themistocles* xi Πάταξον μὲν, ἄκουσον δέ. L. *Verbera sed audi.*] [480 B.C.] **1579** NORTH *Plutarch, Themistocles* (Dent) II. 18 Eurybiades[1] having a staff in his hand lift it up, as though he would have stricken him. Strike and thou wilt, said he,[2] so thou wilt hear me. [[1] Spartan commander of the Grecian fleet at Artemisium. [2] Themistocles.]

Strike, Dawkin; the devil is in the hemp.

1678 RAY 70.

Strike the serpent's head with your enemy's hand, It is good to.

1732 FULLER no. 2945.

Strike while the iron is hot.

c. **1374** CHAUCER *Troylus* II. 1275 Pandarē, which that stood hir fastē by, Felte iren hoot, and he began to smyte. *c.* **1386** Id. *Mel.* B² 2226 Whil that iren is hoot, men sholden smyte. **1546** HEYWOOD I. iii. 6 And one good lesson to this purpose I pike From the smithis forge, whan thyron is hot strike. **1580** LYLY *Euph. & his Eng.* (Arb.) 367 Omitting no time, least the yron should coole before he could strike, he presently went to *Camilla.* **1590–1** SHAKS. *3 Hen. VI* V. i. 49 Strike now, or else the iron cools. **1611** CHAPMAN *Il.* 16. 352 Patroclus then did strike while steel was hot. **1614** CAMDEN 309 It is good to strike while the iron is hot. **1682** BUNYAN *Holy War* ii. Wks. (Offor) III. 260 Finding . . . the affections of the people warmly inclining to him, he, as thinking it was best striking while the iron is hot, made this . . . speech unto them.

Strikes my dog, He that | would strike me if he durst.

1721 KELLY 143 . . . Spoken with resentment to them who injure any thing that belongs to us. **1732** FULLER no. 2318.

Strikes with his tongue, He that | must ward with his head.

1640 HERBERT 332. **1732** FULLER no. 2319.

Striketh with the sword, He that | shall be stricken with the scabbard.

1546 HEYWOOD II. vii. 63 The prouerbe saith he that striketh with the swoorde, Shalbe strikyn with the scaberde. **1599** PORTER *Angry Wom. Abingd.* III. ii (Merm.) 158 Blessed are the peace-makers; they that strike with the sword, shall be beaten with the scabbard.

Strike(s, th), see also Many s. on anvil (When) they must s. by measure; Mint ere you s.

String(s), see Go to heaven in a s.; Knot is loose (Where) s. slippeth; Two s. to one's bow; World in a s. (To have the).

Stringer, see Nay, stay, quoth S.

Strip it, Thou'lt | as Slack stript the cat, when he pull'd her out of the churn.

1678 RAY 289.

Striving against the stream, It is ill (evil).

[*Iesus Sirach* 4. 31. *Vulg. Ecclus.* 4. 22. ERASM. *Ad.* 3. 2. 9.] *c.* **1275** *Prov. of Alfred* (Skeat) A 145 Strong hit is to rowe ayeyn the see that floweth So hit is to swynke ayeyn un-ylimpe[1]. *c.* **1300** *Cato's Dist.* (Furnivall) iv. 585 Aȝeyn þe strem ne strive þou nouȝt. *c.* **1390** GOWER *Conf. Amantis* IV. 1780 Betre is to wayte upon the tyde than rowe ayein the stremes stronge. **1539** TAVERNER 15 It is euyll stryuyng against the streme, that is to saye, It is greate folye to struggle agaynste such thynges as thou canst not ouer come. **1593** SHAKS. *Venus & Adon.* 772 All in vain you strive against the stream. **1599** GREENE *Alphonsus* III. iii. (Merm.) 45 In vain it is to strive against the stream; Fates must be follow'd and the gods' decree Must needs take place. **1614** CAMDEN 308 It is hard striving against a stream. **1641** FERGUSSON 112 Ye strive against the stream. *a.* **1721** PRIOR *Dialog. of Dead* (1907) 250 *Vic. of Bray.* Never strive against the stream, always drive the nail that will go. [[1] misfortune.]

Strokes be good to give, If | they are good to get.

1721 KELLY 186 . . . Spoken to those whom we beat for beating others. **1732** FULLER no. 2700.

Strokes fell great (tall) oaks, Many (Little).

[ERASM. *Ad. Multis rigida quercus domatur ictibus.*] *c.* **1370** CHAUCER *Romaunt of the Rose* 3688 No man at fyrste stroke He maye nat fele down an oke. **1539** TAVERNER f. 26 Wyth many strokes is an oke ouerthrowne. **1579** LYLY *Euphues* (Arb.) 81 Many strokes ouerthrow the tallest Oke. **1590–1** SHAKS. *3 Hen. VI* II. i. 54 *Mer.* And many strokes, . . . Hew down, and fell the hardest-timber'd oak. By many hands your father was subdu'd. **1670** RAY 115 *Multis ictibus dejicitur quercus.* Many strokes fell, &c. Assiduity overcomes all difficulty. **1758** FRANKIN *Way to Wealth* (Crowell) 17 Stick to it steadily and you will see great effects; for . . . *Little strokes fell great oaks.*

Stroke(s), *see also* Great s. make not music; Oak is not felled at one s.; Redder's s.; Words go with the wind, but s. out of play.

Strong as a horse, As.

1703 WARD *Writings* ii. 81 (A).

Strong, *see also* Handsome at twenty, nor s. at thirty (He that is not); Stout (S.) be merciful (As you are).

Struck at Tib, but down fell Tom, He.

1639 CLARKE 1.

Strumpet, *see* Never was s. fair.

Stuarts, *see* All S. not sib to the king.

Stuck a knife to my heart, If you had | it would not have bled.

1721 KELLY 192 . . . Intimating that the thing was a great surprise. **1858** READE *Jack of All Trades* xii A chill came over me. If you had stuck a knife in me I shouldn't have bled.

Students, *see* Thrive as New College s.

Studied, *see* Whittington's College (He has s. at).

Studies his content, He that | wants it.

1611 COTGRAVE s.v. 'Aise' Hee that studies his contentment overmuch, ever wants it. **1640** HERBERT 317.

Studies pass into his character, A man's.

[OVID *Heroides* 15. 83 *Abeunt studia in mores.* **1612** BACON *Ess., Studies* (Arb.) 11 *Histories* make one wise, *Poets* wittie, . . . *Abeunt studia in mores.* **1889** J. W. HALES Introd. to Johnson *Lives of Poets* xxvi Perhaps we may invert. . . . 'Studia abeunt in mores', that is, 'A man's studies pass into his character', and read, 'Mores abeunt in studia', . . . 'A man's character passes into his studies', expresses itself inevitably in his writings.

Stuff a cold and starve a fever.

1852 E. FITZGERALD *Polonius* 9 In the case of . . . a Cold—'Stuff a cold and starve a fever', has been greatly misconstrued, so as to bring on the fever it was meant to prevent. **1881** *N. & Q.* 6th Ser. IV. 54 'Stuff a cold', &c. The expression is elliptical, for '[if you] stuff a cold, [you will have to] starve a fever'.

Stuffing holds out storm.

1721 KELLY 293 . . . Advising men to take some good thing, before they travel in a bad day.

Stumble at a straw and leap over a block, To.

1526 *Hund. Mer. Tales* v. B. iii As ye commen prouerb is they stumble at a straw & lepe ouer a blok. **1547** *Homilies, Works* D iv They were of so blynd iudgemente, that they stombled at a strawe, & leped ouer a blocke. **1653** W. RAMESEY *Astrol. Restored,* To Rdr. 17 To skip over blocks, and stumble at straws. **1721** KELLY 288 *Start at a straw, and loup o'er a bink.*[1] Scruple at small things, and be guilty of greater. [[1] bench.]

Stumble may prevent a fall, A.

1732 FULLER no. 424.

Stumbles and falls not, He that | mends his pace.

1611 COTGRAVE s.v. 'Choper' He that stumbles without falling gets the more forward. **1636** HOWELL *Lett.* 15 Aug. (1903) II. 105 We find that a stumble makes one take firmer footing. . . . Kit hath now overcome himself, therefore I think he will be too hard for the devil hereafter. **1640** HERBERT 317. **1655** FULLER *Ch. Hist.* VIII. i. (1868) II. 456 Archbishop Cranmer . . . recanted his subscription, and valiantly burned at the stake. Thus, he that stumbleth, and doth not fall down, gaineth ground thereby; as this good man's slip mended his pace to his martyrdom.

Stumbles twice over one stone, He who | deserves to break his shins.

[ZENOBIUS 3. 29 δὶς πρὸς τὸν αὐτὸν αἰσχρὸν προσκρούειν λίθον.] **1580** LYLY *Euph. & his Eng.* (Arb.) 319 A burnt childe dreadeth the fire, he that stumbleth twice at one stone is worthy to break his shins.

Stumps, *see* Stir one's s.

Stung by a nettle than pricked by a rose, It is better to be.

1580 LYLY *Euph. & his Eng.* (Arb.) 323 I can better take a blister of a Nettle, then a prick of a Rose. **1659** HOWELL *Eng. Prov.* 18/2 'Tis better to be stung by a Nettle, then prickt by a Rose; *viz. To be wronged by a foe, then a friend.* **1732** FULLER no. 878.

Stung by a serpent, She has been.

1855 BOHN 59 She has been stung, *i.e.* She is with child. *E stata beccata da una serpe.* Ital.

Stung like a tench, To be.

1597–8 SHAKS. *1 Hen. IV* II. i. 17 The most villainous house in all London road for fleas: I am stung like a tench.

Sturt[1] follows all extremes.

1721 KELLY 286. [[1] trouble.]

Sturt[1] pays no debt.

1641 FERGUSSON 88. **1721** KELLY 292 . . . Spoken with resentment, to them who storm when we crave of them our just debts. [[1] haughtiness, indignation.]

Style is the man, The.

[L. *Stylus virum arguit.* The style shows the man. ERASM. *Ad. Qualis vir, talis oratio.* **1753** BUFFON *Discours sur le style*, Le style est l'homme même.] **1621** BURTON *Anat. Mel.* To the Reader *Stylus virum arguit*, our style bewrays us. **1827–48** HARE *Gues. at Truth* (1859) ii. 343 Shakespeare was always alive . . . to the truth of the maxim, *le style est l'homme même.* **1901** ALEX. WHYTE *Bib. Char.*, Stephen, &c. civ. 72 If the style is the man in Holy Scripture also, . . . we feel a very great liking for Luke.

Subject's love is the king's lifeguard, The.

[SENECA *De Clementia* 1. 19. 6.] *c.* **1386** CHAUCER *Mel.* B[2] 2529 For thus seith Tullius, that 'there is a maner garnison that no man ne venquisse ne disconfite, and that is, a lord to be biloved of hise citezeins and of his peple.' **1616** DRAXE 119 The loue of the subiect, is the strongest pillar of the prince. **1721** KELLY 338.

Sublime to the ridiculous, There is but one step from the.

[*c.* **1799** MARMONTEL Le ridicule touche au sublime. **1812** NAPOLEON in DE PRADT, *Hist. de l'Ambassade dans le Grand-duché de Varsovie en 1812* Du sublime au ridicule il n'y a qu'un pas.] **1794** T. PAINE *Age of Reason* ii Note The sublime and the ridiculous are often so nearly related, that it is difficult to class them separately. One step above the sublime makes the ridiculous, and one step above the ridiculous makes the sublime again. **1879** M. PATTISON *Milton* 116 The Hague tittle-tattle . . . is set forth in the pomp of Milton's loftiest Latin. . . . The sublime and the ridiculous are here blended without the step between. **1909** *Times Lit. Sup.* 17 Dec. 492 In the case of Louis XVIII, indeed, the ridiculous was, as it is commonly said to be, only a step removed from sublime.

Submitting to one wrong brings on another, The.

[L. *Veterem injuriam ferendo, invitas novam.* By submitting to an old injury, you invite a new one.] **1692** L'ESTRANGE *Aesop's Fab.* cclxxxv (1738) 299 A snake . . . appealed to Jupiter . . . who told him . . . ' If you had but bit the first man that affronted ye, the second would have taken warning by't'. . . . *The putting up of one affront draws on another.* **1855** BOHN 515.

Substance, *see* Catch not at the shadow.

Subtlety is better than force.

1616 DRAXE 237. **1664** CODRINGTON 210. **1736** BAILEY *Dict.* s.v.

Success makes a fool seem wise.

1707 MAPLETOFT 111. **1855** BOHN 492.

Success, *see* Failure teaches s.; Nothing succeeds like s.

Succours of Spain, either late or never.

1853 TRENCH iii. 53 *Succours of Spain, either late or never.*[1] Any one who reads the despatches of England's Great Captain during the Peninsular War will find in almost every page of them justifications of this proverb. [[1] *Socorros de España, ó tarde, ó nunca.*]

Such, *see also* Sike.

Such . . . , such . . . , *see under significant words following.*

Sucked evil from the dug, He.

a. **1591** H. SMITH *Serm.* (1866) I. 32 We say *He sucked evil from the dug*; that is, as the nurse is affected in her body or in her mind, commonly the child draweth the like infirmity from her. **1592–3** SHAKS. *Rich. III* II. ii. 30 He is my son. . . . Yet from my dugs he drew not this deceit.

Sucked not this out of my fingers' ends, I.

1546 HEYWOOD I. xi. 35. **1588** E. BULKELEY *An*

Answer 23 You rather sucke that out of your owne fingers, then find it in *Luthers* works. **1616** DRAXE 123. **1670** RAY 25.

Suck(s, ed), *see also* Looks as if s. his dam through hurdle; Love a woman (He that does not) s. a sow; Pick (S.) a person's brains.

Sudden friendship, sure repentance.

1721 KELLY 285. **1732** FULLER no. 4281.

Suds, To be (leave, lie) in the.

[= in difficulties.] **1572** GASCOIGNE *Posies Fruites Warre* Wks. (1907) I. 161 He . . . sought with victuall to supplie Poore Myddleburgh which then in suddes did lie. **1653** H. MORE *Conject. Cabbal.* (1713) 230 After the hurry of his inordinate pleasures and passion, when he was for a time left in the suds, as they call it. **1730** SWIFT *Death & Daphne* Misc. (1735) v. 109 Away the frighted Spectre scuds And leaves my Lady in the Suds. **1775** S. J. PRATT *Liberal Opin.* cxxxiv (1783) IV. 216 This proves, *logicè*, that you are in the suds; which is *Anglicè*, that you will be hanged.

Sue a beggar, and get a louse.

1639 CLARKE 72. **1659** HOWELL *Eng. Prov.* 2/1 Goe to law with a beggar, thou shalt gett a lowse. **1819** SCOTT *Bride Lam.* iii I guess it is some law phrase—but sue a beggar, and —your honour knows what follows'.

Suffer a calf to be laid on thee, If thou | within a little they'll clap on the cow.

1853 TRENCH iii. 68 The Italian, *If thou suffer a calf to be laid on thee, within a little they'll clap on the cow.* . . . Undue liberties are best resisted at the outset.

Suffer and expect.

1640 HERBERT 350.

Suffer the ill and look for the good.

1573 SANDFORD 219 I suffer the yl, hoping for the good. *Ibid.* 221 Suffer the il, and loke for the good.

Suffer(s), *see also* Better s. ill than do ill; Do right nor s. wrong (He will neither); Lives long (He that) s.

Sufferance, Of | cometh ease (rest).

c. **1386** CHAUCER *Merchant's T.* E[2] 871 Passe over is an ese, I sey na-more. c. **1390** GOWER *Conf. Amantis* III. 1639 Suffrance haþ euere be þe beste To wissen him þat secheþ reste. **1546** HEYWOOD I. ix. 18 Sens ye can nought wyn, if ye can not please, Best is it to suffre: For of suffrance comth ease. a. **1591** HY. SMITH *Serm.* (1866) I. 229 Even those which cannot suffer that they might have rest, yet sing the patient proverb, In sufferance is rest. **1597–8** SHAKS. *2 Hen. IV* V. iv. 27 O, that right should thus overcome might! Well, of sufferance comes ease. **1607** MARSTON *What you will*, Prol. Ile give a proverbe—'Sufferance giveth ease'.

Sufferance, *see also* Forbearance.

Suffered to do more than is fitting, He that is | will do more than is lawful.

1664 CODRINGTON 195. **1670** RAY 9.

Suffering, It is not the | but the cause which makes a martyr.

1644 S. TORSHELL *Hypocrite Discovered* I. xii. 44 That saying which hath gone current through all Antiquity, That it is not the suffering but the cause which makes a Martyr, will hold good still. **1655** FULLER *Ch. Hist.* x. iv (1868) III. 284 To Smithfield he was brought to be burned . . . : it is neither the pain, nor the place, but only the cause, makes a martyr.

Sufficeth, That which | is not little.

1640 HERBERT 357.

Sufficient unto the day is the evil thereof.

[**1611** BIBLE *Matt.* vi. 34.] **1824** SCOTT *St. Ronan's* xi You must not . . . plague me with any of the ceremonial for your fête—'sufficient for the day is the evil thereof'. **1836** MRS. CARLYLE *Let.* to Miss Welsh, 1 Apr. In the meanwhile there were no sense in worrying over schemes for a future, which we may not live to see. 'Sufficient for the day is the evil thereof.' **1857** TROLLOPE *Barch. Tow.* xv 'We shall be poor enough, but you will have absolutely nothing.' 'Sufficient for the day is the evil thereof', said Bertie.

Suffolk, Old, *see* Read, try, speak as you find, quoth O. S.

Suffolk cheese.

1661 PEPYS *Diary* 4 Oct. (A) I found my wife vexed at her people for grumbling to eat Suffolk cheese. **1699** E. WARD *World Bewitched* 183 in LEAN I. 194 Many London prentices will be forced to eat Suffolk cheese that their master's daughters may be kept at a boarding school. **1787** GROSE (*Suffolk*) 224 Hunger will break through stone walls, or any thing except a Suffolk cheese. Suffolk cheese is . . . by some represented as only fit for making wheels for wheelbarrows. **1830** FORBY 424 *Suffolk Cheese.* . . . The cheese speaks: Those that made me were uncivil, for they made me harder than the d—l. Knives won't cut me; fire won't sweat me; Dogs bark at me, but can't eat me.

Suffolk fair maids.

1622 DRAYTON *Polyol.* xxiii (A) Fair Suffolk maids and milk. **1662** FULLER (*Suffolk*) III. 161 'Suffolk fair maids'. It seems the God of nature hath been bountiful in giving them beautiful complexions.

Suffolk is the land of churches.

1867 NALL *Gt. Yarmouth, &c.* 224 Suffolk has been called the land of churches. . . . In Domesday Book whilst only one church is recorded as existing in Cambridgeshire, and none in Lancashire, Cornwall, or Middlesex, 364 are enumerated in Suffolk.

Suffolk milk.

1622 *See quot. under* 'Suffolk fair maids' *supra.* **1662** FULLER (*Suffolk*) III. 160 'Suffolk milk' . . . No county in England affords better and sweeter of this kind. **1818** R. BLOOMFIELD in *Suffolk Garland* 374 Hence Suffolk dairy-wives run mad for cream, And leave their milk with nothing but its name; Its name derision and reproach pursue, And strangers tell of 'three times skimm'd sky-blue'.

Suffolk stiles.

1662 FULLER (*Suffolk*) III. 161   Suffolk stiles'. It is a measuring cast, whether this proverb pertaineth to Essex or this county; . . . both . . . abound with high stiles, troublesome to be clambered over.

Suffolk whine.

1787 GROSE (*Suff.*) 223 The Suffolk whine. The inhabitants of this county have a kind of whining tone in their speech, much resembling that of a person in great mental distress.

Suffolk, *see also* Silly S.

Sugar or salt, Not made of.

[= not to be disconcerted by wet weather.] **1733** SWIFT (Dial. i) 334 *Lady A.* Did you walk through the Park in the rain? *Spark.* Yes, madam, we were neither sugar nor salt; we were not afraid the rain would melt us. **1786** *Har'st Rig* (1794) 27 But Highlanders ne'er mind a douk, For they're na'e sawt. **1855** CARLYLE in *E. FitzGerald's Lett.* (1889) I. 235 I persist in believing the weather will clear, . . . at any rate I am not made of sugar or of salt.

Suit at law and a urinal bring a man to the hospital, A.

1616 DRAXE 112 Suites in Law, and oft taking of physicke undoeth many. **1664** CODRINGTON 184. **1670** RAY 15. **1732** FULLER no. 6238.

Suit is best that best fits me, That.

1639 CLARKE 16 (with 'suits' for 'fits'). **1670** RAY 146.

Suit of law, One | breeds twenty.

1640 HERBERT 328 The worst of law is, that one suit breeds twenty. **1732** FULLER no. 3796.

Suitor, *see* Last s. wins maid.

Suits hang half a year in Westminster Hall; at Tyburn, half an hour's hanging endeth all.

1562 HEYWOOD *Fifth Hund. Epig.* no. 12, 180 Sutes hange halfe a yere in Westminster hall, At Tyburne, halfe an houres hangyng endeth al.

Sullen man, *see* Keep out of . . . a s. m.'s way.

Sum, *see* Small s. will pay short reckoning.

Summer, There is no | but it has a winter.

1846 DENHAM 48.

Summer in winter, and a summer's flood, never boded England good.

1846 DENHAM 68.

Summer is a seemly time.

1721 KELLY 289.

Summer, *see also* Dry s. never made dear peck; English s. three hot days; Good winter good s.; Grass (S.) on the top of oak (Look for); Indian S.; Winter's thunder and s.'s flood never boded good.

Summerish, *see* January (A s.).

Summoned before the Mayor of Halgaver,[1] He is to be.

1602 CAREW *Survey of Cornwall* (1769) 126[v] Hence is sprung the prouerb, when we see one slouenly appareled, to say, He shall be presented in Halgaver Court. **1662** FULLER (*Cornwall*) I. 307 'He is to be summoned before the Mayor of Halgaver'. This is a jocular and imaginary court, wherewith men make merriment . . ., presenting such persons as go slovenly in their attire, . . . where judgment in formal terms is . . . executed more to the scorn than hurt of the persons. **1821** SCOTT *Kenilw.* iv We'll have you summoned before the Mayor of Halgaver. [[1] Halgaver Moor, Bodmin.]

Sun can be seen by nothing but its own light, The.

1732 FULLER no. 4774.

Sun does not shine on both sides of the hedge at once, The.

1879 R. JEFFERIES *Wild Life in South. County* xvii The hedge . . . forms the basis of many proverbs . . . such as, 'The sun does not shine on both sides of the hedge at once'.

Sun enters, Where the | the doctor does not.

1928 *Times* 6 June 12/4 There is an Italian proverb which says, 'Dove va il sole non va il medico' ('Where the sun enters the doctor does not'). . . . I saw gangs of Italian roadmen acting on that proverb by lying half-clad on the roadside after their midday meal.

Sun goes pale to bed, If the | 'twill rain tomorrow, it is said.

1883 ROPER 7. **1893** INWARDS 52.

Sun has set; The | no night has followed.

[a. **1220** GIRALDUS CAMBRENSIS. *Sol occubuit; nox nulla secuta est.*] a. **1626** SIR J. DAVIES Wks. (Gros.) 467 By that Eclipse which darken'd our Apollo, Our sunne did sett, and yett noe night did follow [James I's death]. **1860** RILEY *Dict. Lat. Quot.* 435 'The sun has set; no night has ensued'. A piece of flattery addressed to a son, and equally complimentary to his father. . . . Ascribed to Giraldus, and refers to the succession of Richard on the death of Henry II.

Sun in red should set, If the | the next day surely will be wet; if the sun should set in grey, the next will be a rainy day. (*Cf.* Sky red, &c.)

1846 DENHAM 10.

Sun is highest, When the | he casts the least shadow.

1580 LYLY *Euph. & his Eng.* Wks. (Bond) II. 179 When the Sunne is at the highest . . . then is my shadow at the shortest. 1608 CHAPMAN *Byron's Tragedy* v. i. 140 As the sun At height and passive o'er the crowns of men . . . Casts but a little or no shade at all. 1732 FULLER no. 5607.

Sun is never the worse for shining on a dunghill, The.

[TERTULL. *de Spect.* 20 *Sane sol et in cloacam radios suos defert, nec inquinatur.*] 1303 BRUNNE *Handl. Synne* l. 2299 The sunne, hys feyrnes neuer he tynes, þogh hyt on þe muk hepe shynes. *c.* 1386 CHAUCER *Parson's T.* 911 Though that holy writ speke of horrible sinne, certes, holy writ may nat been defouled, na-more than the sonne that shyneth on the mixen. 1579 LYLY *Euphues* (Arb.) 43 The Sunne shineth vpon the dounghil and is not corrupted. 1600–1 SHAKS. *Merry W.* I. iii. 68 *Fal.* Sometimes the beam of her view gilded my foot, sometimes my portly belly. *Pist.* Then did the sun on dunghill shine. 1633 PRYNNE *Histrio-Mastix* II. 961 If any here reply . . . : That the sun shines on a dung-hill, and yet its beams are not defiled by it: . . . for unto the pure all things are pure.

Sun may do its duty, The | though your grapes are not ripe.

1732 FULLER no. 4778.

Sun, moon, and seven stars are against us, The.

1601 A. DENT *Plain Man's Pathway* 285 Wee haue (as they say) the Sunne, Moone, and seuen Starres against vs. 1616 DRAXE 3.

Sun rises in the morning, In every country the.

1640 HERBERT 346.

Sun rises, When the | the disease will abate.

1678 RAY *Adag. Hebr.* 400 . . . It is said . . . there was a pretious stone which did hang on the neck of *Abraham*, which when the sick man looked on he was presently healed; And that when *Abraham* died God placed this stone in the Sun.

Sun seeth all things and discovereth all things, The.

1564 UDALL tr. *Erasm. Apoph.* (1877) 344 Cicero thought in his merie conceipte, that forasmuch as according to the prouerbe, *Sol omnia videt ac revelat*, the sunne seeth all thinges and discouereth all thinges, &c.

Sun sets bright and clear, When the | an easterly wind you need not fear.

1846 DENHAM 20.

Sun sets in a bank,[1] When the | a westerly wind we shall not want.

1846 DENHAM 12. [[1] a heavy, dark cloud.]

Sun shines upon all alike (everywhere), The.

1553 T. WILSON *Arte of Rhet.* (1909) 32 The Sunne shineth indifferently ouer all. 1580 LYLY *Euph. & his Eng.* (Arb.) 443 The Sunne when he is at his height shineth as wel vpon course carsie [Kersey] as cloth of tissue. 1599–1600 SHAKS. *Twelfth N.* III. i. 44 Foolery, sir, does walk about the orb like the sun; it shines everywhere. 1659 HOWELL *Span. Prov.* 3 The sergeant and the sun are everywhere. 1882 BESANT *All Sorts* vii The sun shines everywhere, even, as Mr. Bunker remarked, in an Almshouse.

Sun with a candle, To set forth the.

[ERASM. *Ad. Lumen soli mutuas.*] 1551 MORE *Utopia* tr. Robinson (Lupton) 23 Unles I wolde seme to shew and set furth the brightenes of the sonne wyth a candell, as the Prouerbe sayth. *c.* 1570 J. SAPARTON *Saparton's Alarum* (ballad) Match not the candle with the sun. 1596–7 SHAKS. *K. John* IV. ii. 14 With taper-light To seek the beauteous eye of heaven to garnish Is wasteful and ridiculous excess. 1616 T. DEKKER *Artillery Garden* C 4 Bringes but a candle to the mid-day light. 1667 *Life of Duke of Newcastle* 149. *a.* 1765 YOUNG *Satire* vii. 97 How commentators each dark passage shun, and hold their farthing candle to the sun.

Sun without a shadow, No.

1639 CLARKE 326.

Sun, *see also* Although the s. shine leave not thy cloak; Bride the s. shines on (Happy is); Day still while s. shines; Every light is not the s.; Filth under snow s. discovers; God take the s. . . . (Though), we must have patience; March s.; Moon's not seen where s. shines; Morning s. never lasts a day; Morning s. . . . seldom end well; Out of God's blessing into warm s.; Place in the s.; Red the s. begin his race (If); Spots in the s.; Stool in the s., when one knave rises other comes; Walk much in the s. will be tanned at last; Wind follows s.'s course; Worship the rising s.

Sunday comes it will be holy day, When.

1639 CLARKE 19.

Sunday's wooing draws to ruin.

1832 HENDERSON 9.

Sunday(s), *see also* Alike every day, clout on S.; Begin a journey on S.; Come day . . . God send S.; Every day braw makes S. a daw; Month of S.; Nutting on S. the devil will help; Saturday servants . . . S. servants run away; Saturday's new and S.'s full [sc. moon]; Two S. come together (When).

Sun-dial in the shade? What's the good of a.

1732 FULLER no. 5507 What's a Sun-dial in the Shade good for? 1750 FRANKLIN Oct. Hide not your Talents, they for Use were made. What's a Sun-Dial in the Shade?

Sung well before he broke his left shoulder with whistling, He could have.

1678 RAY 82.

Sunshine. *see* Heat (S.) that melts wax harden clay; Saturday without s. (Never a).

Sup kail with him, He would not | unless he broke the dish on his head.

1721 KELLY 134 . . . A disdainful answer to them who compare our friend to some unworthy inferior fellow.

Sup, Simon, the best is at the bottom (*or* here's good broth.)

1598 DELONEY *Thomas of Reading* Wks. (Mann) 232 Sup Simon, theres good broth. 1607 *The Puritan* III. v (A) Sup, Simon, now! eat porridge for a month. 1639 CLARKE 46. 1678 RAY 88 *Prov. Phrases . . . belonging to . . . drinking.* Sup Simon the best is at the bottom.

Sup with a cutty than want a spoon, It is better to.

1721 KELLY 210 . . . It is better to have a thing, not quite so good in its kind, than to want altogether.

Sup, *see also* No man can both s. and blow.

Supernaculum, see Pearl on your nail.

Superstition, *see* Devil divides . . . between atheism and s.

Supperless, *see* Better go to bed s.; Goes to bed s. all night tosses.

Suppers, By | more have been killed than *Galen*[1] ever cured.

1640 HERBERT 329. [[1] a Greek physician; c. A.D. 130–201.]

Supper(s), *see also* After dinner sit; Hole in the groat and s. to seek; Hunger makes dinners, pastime s.; No song no s.; Salad may be prologue to bad s.; Wrongs not an old man that steals s.

Supping, *see* Sleep without s.

Sups ill who eats all at dinner, He.

1611 COTGRAVE s.v. 'Disner' *Mal soupe qui tout disne*: He sups ill who dines all; after a gluttonous and disordinate youth, follows a needie and hungrie age (A). 1678 RAY 125.

Sure as a gun, As.

1622 BEAUM. & FL. *Propheless* I. iii (A) You are right master, Right as a gun. 1654 E. GAYTON *Festivous Notes on Don Quixote* 55 Sure as a gun. 1656 S. HOLLAND *Wit & Fancy in a Maze* 161 He is dead as sure as a Gun. 1730 FIELDING *T. Thumb* III. ii Sure as a gun I'll have thee laid. 1849–50 THACKERAY *Pendennis* lviii In every party of the nobility his name's down as sure as a gun.

Sure as a louse in Pomfret, As.

1638 BRATHWAIT *Barnabees Jrnl.* A *Louse* in *Pomfrait* is not surer, Then the Poor through Sloth securer.

Sure as eggs is eggs, As.

1699 B. E. *Dict. Cant. Crew* As sure as eggs be eggs. 1768 GOLDSMITH *Goodn. Man* iv And, as sure as eggs is eggs, the bridegroom and she had a miff. 1837 DICKENS *Pickwick* xliii (Romance) And the Bishop says 'Sure as eggs is eggs, This here's the bold Turpin!' 1857 HUGHES *T. Brown* II. vi I shall come out bottom of the form as sure as eggs is eggs!

Sure as fate, As.

1701 FARQUHAR *Sir H. Wildair* v. v *Wild.* 'Her Ghost! Ha, ha, ha. . . .' *Stand.* 'As sure as fate, it walks in my House.'

Sure as God's in Gloucestershire, As.

1655 FULLER *Ch. Hist.* VI. ii (1868) II. 212 Of all counties . . . Gloucestershire was most pestered with monks. . . . Hence the . . . proverb . . . : 'As sure as God is in Gloucestershire'. 1902–4 LEAN I. 86 As sure as God's in Gloucestershire . . . *i.e.* the relic of Christ's blood preserved at Hailes Abbey.

Sure as if it had been sealed with butter, As.

1546 HEYWOOD II. vii. 71 Euery promise that thou therein dost utter, Is as sure as it were sealed with butter.

Sure as the coat on one's back.

1601 A. DENT *Plain Man's Pathway* 128 As sure as the coate of our backe. 1607 *Dobson's Dry Bobs* C 3 Predestinate vnto him before either coat or shert. 1639 CLARKE 209. 1670 RAY 208.

Sure card, A.

?1560 *Interlude of Thersites* (1848) 87 Nowe thys is a sure carde, nowe I may well saye. 1579 LYLY *Euphues* (Arb.) 207 A cleere conscience is a sure carde, truth hath the prerogative to speake with plainenesse. 1593–4 SHAKS. *Tit. Andron.* V. i. 100 As sure a card as ever won the set. 1616 DRAXE 200 He hath a sure card.

Sure of your watch on deck, You are always | but never sure of your watch below.

1903 W. C. RUSSELL *Overdue* ii It's a true saying that you're always sure of your watch on deck, but never sure of your watch below.

Sure: It is good to be | toll it again, quoth the miller.

c. **1386** CHAUCER *Cant. T. Prol.* 562 Wel Koude he [the Miller] stelen corn and tollen thries. **1678** RAY 91. **1721** KELLY 189 It is good to be sure, quoth the miller, when he moultered[1] twice. [[1] took the toll.]

Sure, *see* Better be s. than sorry; Rides s. that never fell; Sits not s.; Slow and s.

Surety for another, He that is | is never sure himself (shall pay).

1539 TAVERNER 20 (A) Be suretie for another and harme is at hande. **1651** HERBERT 334 He that will be surety, shall pay. **1721** KELLY 272 *Oft times the cautioner[1] pays the debt.* Not only a caution against suretyship, but often a return to them who say they'll be cautioner (that is, bail) that we will come to some ill accident. **1855** BOHN 389. [[1] surety, bail.]

Surety wants a surety, Your.

1678 RAY *Adag. Hebr.* 404 . . . This Proverb is used of an infirm argument that is not sufficient to prove what it is alleged for. **1911** A. COHEN *Anct. Jew. Prov.* 114 Thy guarantee needs a guarantee. Applied to an unreliable authority.

Surety, *see also* Leaveth s. and leaneth to chance.

Surfeits of too much honesty, A man never.

1616 WITHALS 570. **1639** CLARKE 213 Too much honesty did never man harm. **1670** RAY 13. **1732** FULLER no. 3597. No man ever surfeited on too much honesty.

Surgeon must have an eagle's eye, a lion's heart, and a lady's hand, A good.

1589 L. WRIGHT *Display of Dutie* 37 (A) In a good chirurgian, a hawkes eye: a lyons heart: and a ladies hand. **1629** T. ADAMS *Serm.* (1861) I. 43 We say of the chirurgeon, that he should have a lady's hand and a lion's heart; but the Christian soldier should have a lady's heart and a lion's hand. **1670** RAY 36. **1837** T. HOOK *Jack Brag* ix A surgeon ought to have an eagle's eye, a lion's heart, and a lady's hand.

Surgeon, *see also* Pitiful s. spoileth sore.

Surnames, *see* 'Ford' (In), in 'ham' . . . most English s. run.

Surprised with the first frost, He that is | feels it all the winter after.

1640 HERBERT 362.

Surprised, *see also* Man assaulted is half taken.

Suspicion has double eyes.

1597–8 SHAKS. *1 Hen. IV* V. ii. 8 Suspicion all our lives shall be stuck full of eyes. *c.* **1680** in *Roxb. Ballads* (B.S.) VI. 317 It is a proverb of old 'Suspicion hath double eyes'.

Suspicion, *see also* Virtue of a coward is s.

Sussex moon.

1928 *Times* 7 Dec. 19/6 Even the old horn lantern, the 'Sussex moon' of the country jape, blurred the eyes to its mild splendours.

Sussex weeds.

1869 HAZLITT 348 Sussex weeds. *i.e.* Oaks, which are particularly common in that county.

Sutton for good mutton, Cheam for juicy beef, Croydon for a pretty girl, and Mitcham for a thief.

1852 *N. & Q.* 1st Ser. v. 374.

Sutton for mutton, Carshalton for beeves; Epsom for whores, and Ewell for thieves.

1787 GROSE (*Surrey*) 91 . . . The downs near Sutton . . . produce delicate small sheep, and the rich meadows about Cashalton are remarkable for fattening oxen. Epsom . . . mineral waters . . . were . . . resorted to . . . particularly by ladies of easy virtue. Ewel is a poor village, about a mile from Epsom.

Sutton[1] for mutton, Kirby[2] for beef, South Darne[3] for gingerbread, Dartford for a thief.

1902–4 LEAN I. 114. [[1] Sutton at Hone. [2] Horton Kirby. [3] S. Darenth (all on the river Darenth, in Kent).]

Sutton for mutton, Tamworth for beef, Walsall for bandy legs, and Brummagem[1] for a thief.

a. **1871** Higson's *MSS. Coll.* No. 175 in HAZLITT 361. [[1] Birmingham.]

Sutton Wall and Kentchester Hill, are able to buy London were it to sell.

1659 HOWELL *Eng. Prov.* 20/2 *Sutton* wall, and *Kenchister*, are able to buy *London* were it to sell; *Two fruitful places in Herefordshire.* **1678** RAY 311.

Sutton, *see also* Silly S.; York excels foul S.

Swallow a gudgeon, To.

[= to be made a fool of.] **1579** LYLY *Euphues* (Arb.) 97 You have made both me and *Philautus* to swallow a Gudgen. **1605** CHAPMAN *All Fools* III. i. 95 And do you think he'll swallow down the gudgeon? **1659** HOWELL *French Prov.* 19 He is cozened, or he hath swallowed a gudgeon. **1664** BUTLER *Hudibras* II. iii. 923 (1854) I. 197 To swallow gudgeons ere they're catch'd, And count their chickens ere they're hatch'd.

Swallow a tavern token, To.

1598 JONSON *Ev. Man in his Humour* I. iii. 45 Drunk Sir? . . . perhaps he swallow'd a tauerne token. **1604** *Meeting of Gallants* (Dekker's *Plague Pamphlets* ed. Wilson 122) This strange Wine-sucker . . . had swallowed downe many Tauerne-tokens. **1655** J. COT-GRAVE *Wit's Interpreter* 2 E 3ᵛ.

Swallow an ox, and be choked with the tail, To.

1659 HOWELL *Eng. Prov. Rend. into Fr.* 6. **1670** RAY 194. **1732** FULLER no. 5238.

Swallow, One | does not make a summer.

[Gk. Μία χελιδὼν ἔαρ οὐ ποιεῖ. ERASM. *Ad. Una hirundo non facit ver.* One swallow does not make spring.] **1539** TAVERNER 25 It is not one swalowe that bryngeth in somer. It is not one good qualitie that meketh a man good. **1546** HEYWOOD II. v. 57. **1636** CAMDEN 303. **1642** D. ROGERS *Matr. Hon.* 28 One swallow makes no summer, neither ought it to prescribe a precedent unto others. **1690** D'URFEY *Collin's W.* iii One Swallow makes ('tis true) no Summer, Yet one Tongue may create a Rumour.

Swallow (*noun*), *see also* Robin and the wren; Snail slides up tower though s. mounteth it sooner.

Swallowed a fly, He has.

1721 KELLY 175 . . . Spoken of sots who are always drunk, as if there was a fly in their throat which they endeavoured to wash down.

Swallowed a spider, He hath.

1659 HOWELL *Eng. Prov.* 6/1. **1678** RAY *Prov.* 89 *A Bankrupt.*

Swallowed the devil, If you have | you may swallow his horns.

1853 TRENCH vi. 151 In this too there speaks out a just scorn of those who, having enter-tained no scruple about a sin, reserve all their scruples for some trifling adjunct of the sin: *If you have swallowed the devil, you may swallow his horns.*

Swallow(s, ed) (*verb*), *see also* Eaten (S.) a stake; Say true (You), will you s. my knife.

Swan sings when death comes, The.

[CICERO *Tusc. Disp.* 1. 30. 73 (*Commemorat ut*) *cygni . . . providentes quid in morte boni sit, cum cantu et voluptate morian-tur.* The swan, foreseeing how much good there is in death, dies with song and rejoic-ing.] *c.* **1382** CHAUCER *Parl. Foules* 342 The jalous swan, ayens his deth that syngeth. *c.* **1430** LYDGATE *Against Self-love* in *Minor Poems* (Percy Soc.) 157 The yelwe swan famous and aggreable, Ageyn his dethe

melodyously syngyng. **1596–7** SHAKS. *K. John* V. vii. 21 I am the cygnet to this pale faint swan, Who chants a doleful hymn to his own death. **1604–5** *Othello* V. ii. 245 I will play the swan, And die in music. **1594** *Lucrece* 1611 And now this pale swan in her watery nest Begins the sad dirge of her certain ending. **1650** SIR T. BROWNE *Pseud. Ep.* III. xxvii (1894) 357 From great antiquity . . . the musical note of swans hath been commended, and that they sing most sweetly before their death. **1732** FULLER no. 4779.

Swan(s), *see also* Black s.; Geese are s. (All).

Swap horses when crossing a stream, Don't.

1864 ABRAHAM LINCOLN in E. R. JONES *Lincoln*, &c. (1876) 59 I am reminded . . . of a story of an old Dutch farmer, who remarked . . . 'that it was not best to swap horses when crossing a stream'. **1889** W. F. BUTLER *Gordon* 17 Clothing and equipment were then undergoing a vigorous process of 'swopping' at the moment the animals were in the mid-stream of the siege of Sebastopol.

Swarm of bees all in a churm (*or* Humble bee in a churn), Like a.

1863 J. R. WISE *New Forest* xvi 'Charm', or rather 'churm', signifying . . . noise or dis-turbance. . . . We meet it . . . in the common Forest proverb, 'Like a swarm of bees all in a churm'. **1894** NORTHALL *Folk-phrases* 19 Like a humble bee in a churn. Spoken of one whose voice is indistinct.

Swarm of bees in May, A | is worth a load of hay, but a swarm in July is not worth a fly.

1655 *Reformed Commonwealth of Bees* 26 (A) It being a proverb, that a swarm of bees in May is worth a cow and a bottle of hay, whereas a swarm in July is not worth a fly. **1670** RAY 41. **1879** R. JEFFERIES *Wild Life South. Co.* vii 'A swarm in May is worth a load of hay; a swarm in June is worth a silver spoon; but a swarm in July is not worth a fly'—for it is then too late . . . to store up honey before the flowers begin to fade.

Swarston Bridge, *see* Driving his hogs over S. B.

Swear dagger out of sheath, He will.

1678 RAY 271.

Swear like a carter, To.

1607 H. ESTIENNE *World of Wonders* tr. R. C. 70 He sweareth like a carter. **1611** COTGRAVE s.v. 'Chartier' He swears like a carter (we say, like a tinker).

Swear like a falconer, To.

1612 WEBSTER *White Devil* v. 1 (Merm.) 88 A new up-start; one that swears like a falconer.

Swear like a gentleman, To.

1607 H. ESTIENNE *World of Wonders* tr. R. C. 70 He sweareth like a gentleman. *c.* **1645** MS. Proverbs in *N. & Q.* 154. 27 (A).

Swear like a lord, To.

1531 ELYOT *Gov.* I. xxvi They wyll say he that swereth depe, swereth like a lorde.

Swear like a trooper, To.

1824 MOIR *Mansie W.* xiv He swore like a trooper that . . . he would run in spite of their teeth. **1896** M. A. S. HUME *Courtships of Q. Eliz.* 323 Calling Cecil as a witness to her words, she renewed her vows, swearing like a trooper.

Swear the devil out of hell, He will.

1678 RAY 271.

Swear through an inch board, He will.

1678 RAY 271. **1728** EARL OF AILESBURY *Mem.* (1890) 372 Then he went through thick and thin, according to an old English phrase, swore through a two-inch board.

Swear till one is black in the face, To.

1778 F. BURNEY *Evelina* (1920) II. 23 However, if you swear till you're black in the face, I shan't believe you. **1850** THACKERAY *Pendennis* lv I'd swear, till I was black in the face, he was innocent, rather than give that good soul pain. **1855** BOHN 179.

Swear Walsingham, To.

[= to swear by our Lady of Walsingham, in Norfolk, there being a noted shrine of the Virgin at that place.] **1599** PORTER *Angry Wom. Abingd.* IV. iii (Merm.) 175 I warrant, when he was in, he swore Walsingham, and chafed terrible for the time.

Swear, He that will | will lie.

1601 A. DENT *Plain Man's Pathway* 168 Swearing and lying, be of very neare kindred. **1606** *The . . . Murder committed by . . . Annis Dell* B 3 Who knowes not lying and swearing are partners, If you sweare you shall catch no fish. **1630** J. TAYLOR (Water-P.) Wks. (2nd pag.) 189 (A).

Swear, If you | you'll catch no fish.

1607 HEYWOOD *Fair Maid of Exchange* in Wks. (1874) II. 69 (A) What are you cursing too? then we catch no fish. *a.* **1625** J. FLETCHER *Mons. Thomas* I. iii No swearing; He'll catch no fish else. **1630** J. TAYLOR (Water-P.) Wks. I. 117/2 The Prouerbe sayes, If you sweare you shall catch no fish. **1790** WOLCOT (P. Pindar) *Benev. Ep. to Sylv. Urb.* Besides, a proverb, suited to my wish, Declares that swearing never catcheth fish.

Swearing came in at the head, and is going out at the heels (tail).

1812 J. BRADY *Clavis Calend.* I. 339 There was formerly an expression . . . that 'SWEARING CAME IN AT THE HEAD, BUT IS GOING OUT AT THE TAIL'; in allusion to its having once been the vice of the great, though . . . it had descended to the most low and vulgar of the people.

Sweat, *see* Ground s. cures all disorders; Sweet without s. (No).

Sweep before his own door, If each would | we should have a clean city (*or* street).

1629 T. ADAMS *Serm.* (1861–2) II. 307 When we would have the street cleansed, let every man sweep his own door, and it is quickly done. **1650** FULLER *Pisgah Sight* III. v. 327 How soon are those streets made clean, where every one sweeps against his own door? **1666** TORRIANO 41 If every one will sweep his own house, the City will be clean. **1732** FULLER no. 4296 Sweep before your own Door. **1856** ABP. WHATELY *Annot. Bacon's Ess.* (1876) 287 No one of us but what ought to engage in the important work of *self-reformation*. . . . 'If each would sweep before his own door, we should have a clean street.' **1930** *Times* 25 Mar. 10/5 It appears to be hard to draw a clear distinction between deciding a question of right and wrong for one's self and deciding it for others. . . .—'If every man would sweep his own doorstep the city would soon be clean.'

Sweeps, swept, *see* Tall maid is stooping (While) little one hath s.

Sweet appears sour when we pay.

1659 HOWELL *Brit. Prov.* 21.

Sweet as a nut.

c. **1599** *Club Law* I. iv. 13. **1685** N. THOMPSON *A Collection of 86 Loyal Poems* 23.

Sweet as honey.

c. **1475** *Mankind* l. 218 Swetere then hony. **1506** PYNSON *Kal. of Shepherds* (1892) 75 (A) Swete as hony in oure mouth.

Sweet beauty with sour beggary.

1546 HEYWOOD I. xiii. 40 Swéete beautie with soure beggery, naie I am gon, To the welthy wythered wydow.

Sweet in the bed, and sweir up in the morning, was never a good housewife.

1721 KELLY 290 . . . A jocose reproof to young maids, when they lie long a-bed.

Sweet in the on taking, but sour in the off putting.

1721 KELLY 297 . . . Spoken of debt for the most part, but applied to sin, sensual pleasure, and the like.

Sweet meat will have sour sauce.

c. **1400** *Beryn* (E.E.T.S.) 29 (A) ffor 'aftir swete, the soure comith, ful offt, in many a plase.' **1546** HEYWOOD I. viii. 16 And although it were swéete for a wéeke or twayne, Swéete meate will haue sowre sawce, I sée now playne. **1594–5** SHAKS. *Rom. & Jul.* II. iv. 85 *Merc.* Thy wit is a very bitter sweeting; it is a most sharp sauce. *Rom.* And is it not well served to a sweet goose? **1607** HIERON *Wks.* (1614) I. 20 The sweet meats of wickednesse will have the sowre sauce of wretchedness and misery.

Sweet nut if you were well cracked, You are a.

1583 MELBANCKE *Philotimus* 160 You are a swete nut, the Deuill cracke you. **1721** KELLY 389 ... Ironically spoken to bad boys.

Sweet sauce begins to wax sour.

1546 HEYWOOD II. i. 44 When she sawe swéete sauce began to waxe soure, She waxt as sowre as he.

Sweet things are bad for the teeth.

1607 DEKKER *Whore of Babylon* I 2 Sweet meates that rotte the eater. **1612** WEBSTER, *White Devil* III. ii. 84 Sweete meates which rot the eater. **1738** SWIFT (Dial. ii) 347 *Never*. Miss, I would have a bigger glass [of jelly]. ... *Miss*. But you know, sweet things are bad for the teeth.

Sweet tooth, To have a.

[= a liking for sweet things.] **1580** LYLY *Euph. & his Eng.* (Arb.) 308 I am glad that my *Adonis* hath a sweete tooth in his head. **1594–5** SHAKS. *Two Gent*. III. i. 333 *Item, She hath a sweet mouth*. **1629** T. ADAMS *Serm.* (1861–2) II. 354 Thou hast ... a sweet tooth in thy head, a liquorish appetite to delicate meats and intoxicating wines. **1876** MRS. BANKS *Manch. Man* xvii 'I know you've a sweet tooth, ... but ... nothing half so good as Mrs. Clowes's toffy takes you there'.

Sweet with the sour, Take the.

1509 A. BARCLAY *Ship of Fools* (1874) I. 39 Take ye in good worth the swetnes with the Sour. **1546** HEYWOOD II. iv. 51 Content ye (quoth she) take the swéete with the sowre.

Sweet without (some) sweat, No.

1576 PETTIE *Petite Pall.* (Gollancz) II. 138 (A) You ... live ... by the sweet of other men's sweat. **1639** CLARKE 87. **1667** FLAVEL *Saint Indeed* (1754) 129 He that will not have the sweat, must not expect the sweet of religion. **1670** RAY 146 No sweet without some sweat. Nul pain sans peine, *Gall.*

Sweet, *see also* Bitter to endure may be s. to remember; Deserves not the s. that will not taste the sour; Good in the maw that is s. in mouth; Lay the s. side of your tongue to it; Lost his taste (To him that has) s. is sour; White hath its black and s. its sour.

Sweet-heart and bag-pudding.

1659 HOWELL *Eng. Prov.* 6/1.

'Sweet-heart' and 'Honey-bird' keeps no house.

1678 RAY 57.

Sweetness, *see* Saying Honey, Honey (It is not with) s. will come.

Sweets to the sweet.

1600–1 SHAKS. *Hamlet* V. i. 265 What! the fair Ophelia? *Queen*. Sweets to the sweet: farewell! [*Scattering flowers*.]

Sweir, *see* Work for nought makes folk s.

Swell like a toad, To.

1546 HEYWOOD I. xi. 32 And streight as she sawe me, she swelde lyke a tode.

Swells in prosperity will shrink in adversity, He who.

1855 BOHN 401.

Swim like a cork, To.

1869 C. READE *Foul Play* x Throw that madman into the sea; then we can pick him up. He swims like a cork.

Swim like a duck, To.

1611–12 SHAKS. *Tempest* II. ii. 137 I can swim like a duck. **1866** BLACKMORE *Cradock N*. liv What a lovely deep pool! I can swim like a duck.

Swim like a fish, To.

1622 J. FLETCHER *Sea-Voyage* I. 1 I can swim like a fish. **1852** SMEDLEY *Lewis Arundel* lvi He follows the calling of a gondolier, ... and can swim like a fish.

Swim like a stone, To.

1866 BLACKMORE *Cradock N*. liv I can swim like a duck; and you like a stone, I suppose.

Swim, He must needs | that is held up by the chin.

a. **1530** R. *Hill's Commonpl. Bk.* (E.E.T.S.) 129 He mai lightli swim, that is hold up by þe chin. **1580** LYLY *Euph. & his Eng.* (Arb.) 216 If your Lordship with your lyttle finger doe but holde me vp by the chinne, I shall swimme. **1614** BEAUM. & FL. *Wit at S.W.* I. i Well he may make a padler i' th' world, ... but never a brave swimmer, Borne up by th' chin. **1655** FULLER *Ch. Hist.* IV. i (1868) I. 531 Whose safety, ... is not so much to be ascribed to his own strength in swimming, as to such as held him up by the chin. **1721** KELLY 129 *He may well swim that's held up by the chin*. Spoken of the thriving condition of those, who have some to support, assist, and raise them.

Swim without bladders, He can.

1649 HOWELL *Pre-em. Parl.* 17 My whole life (since I was left to my self to swim, as they say without bladders). **1732** FULLER no.1821.

Swim, *see also* Knows not to s. goes to bottom; Sink or s.; Taught you to s. (I) and now you'd drown me; Venture ... till you can s. (Never). *See also* Swims.

Swimmers, The best | are the oftenest drowned.

1902–4 LEAN IV. 110.

Swimmers, *see also* Good s. at length drowned.

Swims in sin shall sink in sorrow, Who.

1563 GOOGE *Eglogs* viii (Arb.) 67 The

wretched man . . . Whom Deth hymself flyngs ouer bord, amyd the Seas of syn, The place wher late, he swetly swam, now lyes he drowned in. **1579** LYLY *Euph.* (Arb.) 185 They that couet to swim in vice, shall sinke in vanitie. **1766** *Goody Two-Shoes* [ed. 3] v. i A Moral Lesson. He that swims in sin will sink in sorrow.

Swine (Pig), He is like a | he'll never do good while he lives. (*See also* Like a hog (swine), &c.)

1564 BULLEIN *Dial. agst. Fever* (1888) 9 Covetous usurers, which be like fat unclean swine, which do never good until they come to the dish. **1599** J. MINSHEU (1623) 2 T IV A dead hog tasteth best when he is eaten. **1629** T. ADAMS *Serm.* (1861–2) I. 482 The covetitious man is like a two-legged hog: while he lives he is ever rooting in the earth, and never doth good till he is dead. **1678** RAY 90 with 'until he comes to the knife'. **1733** FRANKLIN April A rich rogue is like a fat hog, who never does good till as dead as a log.

Swine over fat, is the cause of his own bane, A.

c. **1532** SIR ADRIAN FORTESCUE no. 33 A Swyne that is over fatte, is cause of his owne dedde. **1550** HEYWOOD II. vii. 67. **1614** CAMDEN 303.

Swine, women, and bees cannot be turned.

1678 RAY 212. **1732** FULLER no. 4299.

Swine's gone through it, The.

1721 KELLY 330 . . . Spoken when an intended marriage is gone back, out of a superstitious conceit, that if a swine come between a man and his mistress, they will never be married. **1809** SCOTT *Let. to Ellis* 23 Mar. in LOCKHART *Life* xviii (1860) 175 He suffered the pigs to run through the business, when he might in some measure have prevented them. **1823** GALT *Entail* II. 30 'If it's within the compass o' a possibility, get the swine driven through't, or it may work . . . as his father's moonlight marriage did.'

Swine. *see also* Draff is good enough for s.

Swing of the pendulum.

a. **1694** TILLOTSON in DOWDEN, *Puritan & Anglican* 335 Nothing was more natural than for extremes in religion to beget one another, like the vibrations of the pendulum, which the more violently you swing it one way, the farther it will return the other. **1851** HELPS *Compan. of Solit.* iii. 26 The pendulous folly of mankind oscillates as far in this direction as it has come from that. **1906** *Brit. Wkly.* 15 Nov. Mr. Watts-Dunton says: 'George Eliot's fame has suffered from the "swing of the pendulum" against that excessive laudation of which during life she was made the subject. . . . A reaction against her was inevitable.'

Swing (*verb*), *see* Room to s. a cat.

Swings, To lose on the | and make up on the roundabouts.

1912 P. R. CHALMERS *Green Days & Blue Days* 19 What's lost upon the roundabouts we pulls up on the swings! **1927** *Times* 24 Mar. 15/5 By screwing more money out of taxpayers he diminishes their savings, and the market for trustee securities loses on the swings what it gains on the roundabouts. **1929** *Times* 9 Aug. 11/6 The recent decision . . . to abolish all entrance fees into State galleries and museums will be appreciated. . . . What the Government may lose on the swings it will more than make up on the roundabouts.

Swiss, *see* No money no S.

Swoop, At one fell.

1605 SHAKS. *Macbeth* IV. iii. 219 Oh Hell-Kite! All? What, all my pretty chickens and their dam at one fell swoop? **1612** WEBSTER *White Devil* I. i. 6 If she [Fortune] give ought, she deales it in smal percels, That she may take away all at one swope. **1819** BYRON *D. Juan* I. 45 For there we have them all at one fell swoop.

Sword, One | keeps another in the sheath (scabbard).

1625 PURCHAS *Pilgrims* (1905–7) XIX. 254 Prudence . . . armeth herself against fears of war, forewarning and forearming men by the sword drawn to prevent the drawing of swords. **1640** HERBERT 351. **1836** F. CHAMIER *Ben Brace* i The proverb 'One sword drawn keeps the other in the scabbard' was verified, the hostile preparations led to negociations, and the question was settled without fighting. **1853** TRENCH iii. 70 *One sword keeps another in its scabbard;*—surely a far wiser . . . word than the puling . . . babble of our shallow Peace Societies.

Sword of Damocles.

[Dionysius I., of Syracuse (405–367 B.C.) allowed a courtier named Damocles to take his place at a banquet, but had a sword hung over him by a hair, to illustrate the insecurity of place and power. Used allusively.] **1594** *Selimus* 853–7 (Dent) 32 *Baj.* Too true that tyrant Dionysius Did picture out the image of a King, When Damocles was placed in his throne, And o'er his head a threat'ning sword did hang, Fastned up only by a horse's hair. **1882** 'F. ANSTEY' *Vice Versâ* i He was an old gentleman . . . of irreproachable character . . .; no Damocles' sword of exposure was swinging over his bald but blameless head.

Sword, *see also* Choosing a wife and . . . s. not trust to another; Draweth his s. against his prince (Who); Gluttony kills more than s.; Horse, a wife, and s. may be shewed, not lent; Leaden s. in ivory sheath; Naked s. in madman's hand; Old wise man's shadow better than buzzard's s.; Peace with s. in hand; Rusty s. and empty purse plead performance; Striketh with the s. (He that).

Sworn at Highgate, He has been.

c. 1720 J. SMEDLEY in *Somers Tracts* (1811) xiii. 825 (A) Dined, and was sworn at Highgate. 1787 GROSE (*Middx.*) 209 He has been sworn at Highgate. A saying used to express that a person preferred strong beer to small;

an allusion to an ancient custom . . . in this village, where the landlord of the Horns . . . used to swear . . . passengers, upon a pair of horns, stuck on a stick . . . They should not kiss the maid, when they could kiss the mistress; nor drink small beer when they could get strong.

T

Table robs more than a thief, The.

1640 HERBERT 347. 1732 FULLER no. 4782 The table is a great robber.

Table, *see also* Feet under another's t.; Good man from home (When) . . . t. soon spread; Poor man's t. soon spread; Round t. no dispute of place.

Table-cloth, *see* Dish-clout my t.-c. (Not make).

Tabor, *see* Hunt for hare with t.

Tace is Latin for a candle.

[*Tace* is the Latin for 'Be silent'. The saying is a hint to keep silent about something.] 1676 SHADWELL *Virtuoso* I (A) I took him up with my old repartee: Peace, said I, *Tace* is *Latin* for candle. 1697 *Dampier's Voy.* 356 Trust none of them for they are all Thieves, but Tace is Latin for a Candle. 1752 FIELDING *Amelia* I. x '*Tace*, Madam', answered Murphy, 'is Latin for a candle; I commend your prudence'. 1827 SCOTT *Journ.* 23 Mar. So *Tace* is Latin for a candle. 1897 STEVENSON *St. Ives* x 'Ye must tell me nothing of that. I am in the law, you know, and *tace* is the Latin for a candle.

Tacks, *see* Brass t. (To come down to).

Taffrail, *see* Whistle psalms to t.

Tag, rag, and bobtail (cut and long tail).

[A contemptuous term for people of all sorts.] 1553 *Vocacyon of John Bale* in *Harl. Miscell.* VI. 459 Than was all the rable of the shippe, hag, tag, and rag, called to the reckeninge. 1579 GOSSON *Sch. Abuse* (Arb.) 45 Euerye one which comes to buye their Iestes, shall haue an honest neighbour, tagge and ragge, cutte and longe tayle. 1599–1600 SHAKS. *Jul. Caes.* I. ii. 260 If the tag-rag people did not clap him and hiss him. 1607–8 *Coriol.* III. i. 247 Will you hence, Before the tag return? 1645 *Just Defence John Bastwick* 15 That rabble rout tag ragge and bobtaile. 1670 *Mod. Account of Scotland* in *Harl. Miscell.* VI. 138 The young couple, being attended with tagrag and bobtail, gang to kirk. 1850 THACKERAY *Pendennis* vii 'Fancy marrying a woman of a low rank of life, and having your house filled with her confounded tag-rag-and-bobtail relations!' 1883 LD. R. GOWER *My Remin.* I. xiii. 251 The mounted police charged the crowd . . . and our party had to fly before them along with tag, rag, and bob-tail.

Tail broader than thy wings, Make not thy.

1597 BACON *Ess., Follow* (Arb.) 32 Costly followers are not to be liked, least while a man maketh his traine longer, hee make his wings shorter. 1659 HOWELL *Eng. Prov.* 18/2 . . . *viz.* Keep not too many attendants.

Tail doth often catch the fox, The.

1573 SANDFORD (1576) 215 The tayle condemneth many tymes the Foxe to die, for being ouer long. 1611 DAVIES *Prov.* 70. 1616 DRAXE 73.

Tail follow the skin, Let the.

1721 KELLY 236 . . . Let the appurtenance follow the main bulk.

Tail will catch the chin-cough,[1] His.

1678 RAY 82 His tail will catch the kincough. Spoken of one that sits on the ground. [1 or kinkcough, whooping-cough.]

Tail(s), *see also* Better be the head of a dog (lizard, pike, ass, yeomanry) than t. of a lion (sturgeon, horse, gentry); Cow knows not what her t. is worth; Cow may want own t. yet; Cracked nuts with her t. (Goes as if she); Craw flies (When) her t. follows; Come cut and long t.; Fox that having lost its t.; Heads I win; Ride an inch behind the t.; Tag, rag, and bob-t.; Wite your teeth if your t. be small. *See also* Cow's t., Fox's t., Pig's t.

Tailor-like.

c. 1560 *Tom Tyler* l. 310 *Tiler.* Tom Tayler, how dost thou? *Tayler.* After the old sort, in mirth and jolly sport, Tayler-like I tell you. 1601 CORNWALLIS *Essayes* II (1610) Dd 6 (A) What is his gaine but the marke of an ideot? What his knowledge, but tailor-like and light?

Tailor makes the man, The.

[ERASM. *Ad.* (quoting Gk. Εἵματα ἀνήρ) *Vestis virum facit.* The garment makes the man.] 1605–6 SHAKS. *K. Lear* II. ii. 60 A tailor made thee. *Cor.* Thou art a strange fellow; a tailor make a man? 1609–10 *Cymb.* IV. ii. 81 *Clo.* Know'st me not by my clothes? *Gui.* No, nor thy tailor, rascal, Who is thy grandfather: he made those clothes, Which, as it seems, make thee. 1607 DEKKER *North. Hoe* II. i They say three Taylors go to the making vp of a man, but Ime sure I had foure Taylors and a halfe went to the making of me thus. **1625** JONSON *Staple of N.* I. i Believe it, sir, That clothes do much upon the wit, . . . and thence comes your proverb, The tailor makes the man. **1861** G. J. WHYTE-MELVILI E *Market Harbor.* xxiv Dress works wonders, and the tailor, . . . doubtless helps to make the man.

Tailor must cut three sleeves to every woman's gown, The.

1583 R. D. *The Mirror of Mirth* M 3ᵛ Tailor . . . would cut out . . . three sleeues in a cloke, and sowe on but twooe. **1662** *Common Cries of London* in COLLIER *Roxb. Ballads* (1847) 209 The weaver and the taylor, cozens they be sure, They cannot work but they must steal, to keep their hands in ure; For it is a common proverb thorowout the town, The taylor he must cut three sleeves to every womans gown.

Tailor that makes not a knot, The | loseth a stitch.

1732 FULLER no. 4786.

Tailor, Like the | that sewed for nothing, and found thread himself.

1732 FULLER no. 3237. **1885** J. ORMSBY *D. Quix.* IV. 391 *The tailor of El Campillo who stitched for nothing and found thread.*

Tailors and writers must mind the fashion.

1579 LYLY *Euphues* Wks. (Bond) I. 182 In my mynde Printers and Taylors are bound chiefely to pray for Gentlemen, the one hath so many fantasies to print, the other such divers fashions to make, that the pressing yron of the one is neuer out of the fyre, nor the printing presse of the other any tyme lyeth still. **1732** FULLER no. 4301.

Tailors of Tooley Street, Three.

[*a.* 1827 CANNING.] **1872** BREWER *Dict. Phr. & F.* 875 *The three tailors of Tooley Street.* Canning says that three tailors of Tooley Street, Southwark, addressed a petition of grievances to the House of Commons, beginning—'We, the people of England'. **1885** c. LOWE *Bismarck* ii (1898) 25 The second German parliament[1] . . . only contained delegates from Prussia and some of the other minor states . . . The Teutonic tailors of Tooley Street, so to speak, had again assembled. **1909** *Times Wkly.* 20 Aug. Our Correspondent 'has been misled into taking the clamours of the Toronto variety of the "three tailors of Tooley-street" for the voice of Canada'. [1 1850.]

Tailor(s), *see also* Knavery in all trades, most in t.; Little to sew when t. true; Nine t. make a man; Put a miller . . . and a t. in bag, first that comes out will be thief; Trust a t. that doesn't sing (Never).

Take a leaf out of (a person's) book, To.

[= to imitate one.] **1809** MALKIN *Gil Blas* VII. ii (Rtldg.) 12 I took a leaf out of their book. **1861** HUGHES *Tom Brown Oxf.* I. ii. 32 It is a great pity that some of our instructors . . . will not take a leaf out of the same book. **1926** *Times* 19 July 11/1 France . . . might well take a leaf out of Germany's discarded book.

Take a man by his word, and a cow by her horn.

1641 FERGUSSON 98. **1721** KELLY 320 . . . A reflection upon one who has broken his word to us.

Take a pain for a pleasure all wise men can.

1546 HEYWOOD I. v. 11.

Take a spring[1] of his own fiddle, and dance to it when he has done, Let him.

1721 KELLY 240 . . . Let him go in his own way, and bear the effects of it. **1818** SCOTT *Rob Roy* xxix 'Aweel, aweel, sir,' said the Bailie, 'you're welcome to a tune on your ain fiddle; but see if I dinna gar ye dance till't afore a's dune.' [1 tune.]

Take all and pay all.

1600–1 SHAKS. *Merry W.* II. ii. 124 Never a wife in Windsor leads a better life than she does: do what she will, . . . take all, pay all, . . . all is as she will. **1642** D. ROGERS *Matrim. Hon.* 92 Your heirs must be fain to take all, and pay all, and so fleece the rest.

Take all, and pay the baker.

1678 RAY 348. **1721** KELLY 331 *Take it all pay the Maltman (Baker).* Spoken jocosely when we give all of such a thing. **1732** FULLER no. 4303.

Take away my good name and take away my life.

1638 J. TAYLOR *Bull, Bear, and Horse* A 7 He that hath no good name is half hanged. **1670** RAY 124. **1732** FULLER no. 4306. **1790** TRUSLER *Prov. Exempl.* 60 What is life without a character? *Take away my good name, and take away my life.*

Take away the salt, If you | you may throw the flesh to the dogs.

1678 RAY *Adag. Hebr.* 402. **1911** A. COHEN *Anc. Jew. Prov.* 33 Shake the salt off and throw the meat to the dog. . . . When the soul leaves the body what remains is worthless. The soul is the preservative of the body in the same way as all salt is a preservative for meat.

Take by the hand, *see* Dance (When you), take heed whom you t. by the h.

Take care of Dowb.

c. **1854** MINCHIN *Our Pub. Sch.* (1901) 42 'Take care of Dowb' . . . has become a synonym for unblushing nepotism. . . . Dowbiggin joined the army and went out to the Crimea. His uncle, as Secretary for War, despatched a cablegram . . . 'Take care of

Dowbiggin etc. etc.' The cable . . . broke off at the first syllable, and Take care of Dowb' got into the papers. **1858** SURTEES *Ask Mamma* xl The next was larger, . . . urging him as before to take care of Dowb (meaning himself). **1890** W. F. BUTLER *Sir C. Napier* 187 'The world' thought he could do it a good turn in the matter of its brothers and sons and nephews . . . 'Dowb' had to be 'taken care of'.

Take care of the pence, and the pounds will take care of themselves.

[*a.* **1724**] **1750** LD. CHESTERFIELD *Lett.* 5 Feb. (1774) I. 551 Old Mr. Lowndes, the famous Secretary of the Treasury, . . . used to say, *take care of the pence, and the pounds will take care of themselves.* **1827** HARE *Gues. at Truth* (1859) i. 229 Thrift is the best means of thriving. . . . *Take care of the pence; and the pounds will take care of themselves.* **1846** JOWETT to R. R. W. Lingen 18 Aug. A tradesman's [emphatic] motto ought to be 'Take care . . .'

Take counsel of (or consult with) one's pillow, To.

[= to take a night to reflect.] **1540** PALSGRAVE *Acolastus* (Carver) 25. **1573** G. HARVEY *Letter-bk.* (Camden Soc.) 21 You counsel me to take counsel of mi pillow. **1642** FULLER *H. & P. State* v. xvi (1841) 394 Others . . . feared, there being so many privy to the plot, that, if they suffered them to consult with their pillows, their pillows would advise them to make much of their heads. **1709** STEELE *Tatler* No. 60. par. 1 [He] frequently consulted his Pillow to know how to behave himself, on such important Occasions.

Take from the right hand and give to the left, To.

1672 CODRINGTON 568 (with 'left side' 'right'). **1732** FULLER no. 5241.

Take half in hand and the rest by and by, It is best to.

1678 RAY 354 . . . (The tradesman that is for ready money.)

Take hares with foxes, To.

1577 STANYHURST *Descr. Irel.* in HOLINSHED (1807–8) VI. 52 But in deed it is hard to take hares with foxes.

Take heed doth surely speed, Good.

1670 RAY 147.

Take heed is a fair thing (good rede[1]).

c. **1374** CHAUCER *Troylus* II. 343 Avysëment is good before the nede. **1546** HEYWOOD II. viii. 72 Take héede is a faire thing. Beware this blindnesse. **1599** PORTER *Angry Wom. Abingd.* III. ii (Merm.) 158 *Nich.* I could have said to you, sir, Take heed is a good reed. **1614** CAMDEN 312 Take heede is a good reede. [[1] counsel.]

Take heed (of), *see also under significant words following.*

Take it or leave it.

1605–6 SHAKS. *K. Lear* I. i. 208 Will you . . . Take her, or leave her? . . . Then leave her, Sir. **1664** KILLIGREW *Thomaso* I. IV. ii That is the price, and less I know, in curtesie you cannot offer me; take it or leave it. **1930** *Times* 25 Mar. 17/2 The Commons . . . are informed of the result of each event after it is over, and have no option, as the saying is, to take it or leave it.

Take it out in sleep.

1902–4 LEAN IV. 106 . . . The consolation of the supperless. Qui dort dîne.

Take me not up before I fall.

1583 MELBANCKE *Philotimus* L 1 Thou louest me well that takest me up before I fall. **1617** J. SWETNAM *School of Defence* 183. **1655** FULLER *Ch. Hist.* III. viii (1868) I. 481 The pope . . . predisposed such places to such successors as he pleased . . . He took up churches before they fell, yea, before they ever stumbled. **1658** MARGARET ELMES to Sir R. Verney *Verney Memoirs* iii (1894) 431 I may justly make yous of the owlde fraise and say you tooke me up be foare I was downe. **1721** KELLY 336 . . . Do not . . . give an answer to my discourse, before you hear me out. **1738** SWIFT (Dial. i) 333 What! Mr. Neverout, you take me up before I'm down. **1818** SCOTT *Ht. Midl.* xviii 'Sir, . . . ye take me up before I fall down. I canna see why I suld be termed a Cameronian.'

Take no more on you than you're able to bear.

1721 KELLY 305.

Take one down a peg or two (a peg, or a button-hole, &c., lower), To.

[= to humble him.] *c.* **1550** BECON *Catechism, &c.* (P.S.) 561 (A) This doctrine plucketh them down one staff lower than they were before. **1589** ? LYLY *Pappe w. Hatchet* in Wks. (1902) III. To Huffe, Ruffe, &c., Now have at you all my gaffers of the rayling religion, tis I that must take you a peg lower. **1594–5** SHAKS. *L.L.L.* V. ii. 705 Master, let me take you a button-hole lower. **1664** BUTLER *Hudibras* II. ii. 522 We still have worsted all your holy Tricks, . . . And took your Grandees down a peg. **1781** C. JOHNSTON *Hist. J. Juniper* II. 247 An opportunity for letting him down a peg or two. **1886** G. A. SALA *America Revis.* 373 The Grand Pacific clerk . . . thought he would take him down a peg or two.

Take one's ease in one's inn, To.

[= to enjoy oneself as if one were at home.] **1546** HEYWOOD I. v. 10 To let the world wag, and take mine ease in mine in. **1597–8** SHAKS. *1 Hen. IV* III. iii. 91 Shall I not take mine ease in mine inn but I shall have my pocket picked?

Take (-ing) out, *see* Always t. o. of the mealtub . . . soon comes to bottom; New lease of life (To t. o.)

Take part of the pelf, when the pack is a-dealing.

1641 FERGUSSON 94.

Take pet, To.

1590 LODGE *Euphues Gold. Leg.* Wks. (Gros.) IV. 90 Some while they thought he had taken some word vnkindly, and had taken the pet. **1606** CHAPMAN *Mons. d'Olive* II. i Fled backe as it came and went away in Pett. **1660** PEPYS *Diary* 6 Dec. Which did vex me . . . and so I took occasion to go up and to bed in a pet. **1669** *New Help to Discourse* 252 (A) He thereupon took pet, and so did die.

Take tea in the kitchen, To.

1894 NORTHALL *Folk-phrases* (E.D.S.) 30 To take tea in the kitchen = To pour tea from the cup into the saucer, and drink it from this.

Take the bear by the tooth, To.

1601 DENT *Path. Heauen* 62 To put his finger into the Lion's mouth, and . . . take the Beare by the tooth. **1670** RAY 163 You dare as well take a bear by the tooth. **1736** BAILEY s.v. You dare as well take a Bear by the Tooth, That is, You dare not attempt it.

Take the bit in the teeth, To.

[= to be beyond restraint.] **1589** ? LYLY *Pappe w. Hatchet* in Wks. (1902) III. 410 But if like a resty iade thou wilt take the bit in thy mouth, and then run over hedge and ditch, thou shalt be broken as Prosper broke his horses. **1600** ABP. ABBOT *Exp. Jonah* 521 Neither yet taking the bit perversely in his teeth. **1927** *Times* 30 Jul. 10/2 If . . . Congress should take the bit in its teeth and authorize an imposing addition to the United States Naval strength, would he . . . intervene with his veto ?

Take the bread out of one's mouth, To.

[= take away his living by competition.] **1708** MOTTEUX *Rabelais* IV. xvi You little Prigs, will you offer to take the Bread out of my mouth? **1845** J. W. CROKER in *Papers* (1884) III. xxiv. 47 Lord Johnny dashed forward to take the bread out of his [Peel's] mouth.

Take the bull by the horns, To.

[= to meet a difficulty rather than to evade it.] **1816** SCOTT *Old Mort.* xxv (A). **1822** GALT *Provost* xxviii It would never do to take the bull by the horns in that manner. **1850** LYTTON *Caxtons* II. i Dr. Herman, in his theory of education, began at the beginning! he took the bull fairly by the horns. **1869** TROLLOPE *He knew he was right* xci Nora would have faced the difficulty, and taken the bull by the horns, and asked her father to sanction her engagement in the presence of her lover.

Take the fat with the lean, You must.

1813 RAY 218.

5017

Take the gilt off the gingerbread, To.

[= to deprive something of its attractive qualities.] **1830** FORBY 432 (A) It will take the gilding off the gingerbread. **1874** G. J. WHYTE-MELVILLE *Uncle John* xii He marvelled how this angel could have come down from heaven to be his own! For him the gilt was yet on the gingerbread, the paint on the toy, the dew on the flower. **1884** J. PAYN *Canon's W.* xi He . . . embarrassed his grandmother by his plain speaking. . . . He was always rubbing the gilt off some gingerbread theory which other children swallow without enquiry.

Take the law into one's own hands, To.

1606 DEKKER *Sev. Sinnes* 35 They . . . take the lawe into their owne handes, and doe what they list. **1840** MARRYAT *Poor Jack* xxviii He has taken the law into his own hands already by mast-heading me for eight hours, and now he makes a complaint to you. **1881** E. B. TYLOR *Anthropology* (1889) 418 The avenger of blood . . . would now be himself punished as a criminal for taking the law into his own hands.

Take the rue, To.

[= to repent.] **1789** *Shepherd's Wedding* 10 (E.D.D.) I own, indeed, I've ta'en the rue, My mind is fairly alter'd. **1816** SCOTT *Old Mort.* xxviii Tam Halliday took the rue, and tauld me a' about it. **1848** MRS. GASKELL *Mary Barton* xii It would be to give him a hint you'd taken the rue, and would be very glad to have him now.

Take the (King's) (Queen's) shilling, To.

[= to enlist as a soldier by accepting a shilling from a recruiting officer.] **1707** HEARNE *Collect.* 27 Mar. (O.H.S.) II. 2 He did take a shilling, but not with any intent of listing. **1852** THACKERAY *Esmond* III. v One fellow was jilted by his mistress, and took the shilling in despair. **1886** FARJEON *Three Times Tried* I I took the Queen's shilling, and became a soldier. **1901** *Scotsman* 4 Mar. 8/1 A contingent of Volunteer Engineers was sworn in for service in South Africa. Each was presented . . . with the King's shilling.

Take the wind out of the sails of, To.

[= to put at a disadvantage.] **1822** SCOTT *Nigel* ix He would take the wind out of the sail of every gallant. **1883** *Harper's Mag.* Feb. 339/2 A young upstart of a rival, Llanelly . . . which has taken a great deal of the wind out of the sails of its older neighbour. **1911** *Spectator* 30 Dec. 1141 Dr. . . . aims at taking the wind out of his critics' sails by giving the nation a lead in regard to relations with England.

Take things as they are (be) meant.

1571 R. EDWARDS *Damon & Pithias* Prol. in HAZL. *O.E.P.* IV. 13 But, worthy audience, we you pray, take things as they be meant.

Take things as they come.

1611 DAVIES Prov. 296 'Take all things as they come and be content.'

Take things as you find them.

1902–4 LEAN IV. 105.

Take to a thing like a duck to water, To.

1901 G. W. STEEVENS *In India* 94 In Bengal . . . the native took to European education as a duck to water.

Take up the cudgels (bucklers), To.

[= to attack or defend vigorously.] **1649** SELDEN *Laws Eng.* I. lix (1739) 109 The Clergy took up the bucklers, and beat both King and Commons to a retreat. **1662** FULLER (*Westmorld.*) III. 309 Mr. Chillingworth, a great master of defence in school divinity, took up the cudgels against him. **1691** WOOD *Ath. Oxon.* II. 61 John dying before he could make a reply . . . Dr. Franc. White took up the bucklers. **1788** WOLCOT (P. Pindar) *Sir J. Banks* Wks. (1816) I. 473 I must take up the cudgels for my client. **1826** SCOTT *Journ.* 4 Feb. Here I am taking up the cudgels and may expect a drubbing in return. **1876** SIR G. O. TREVELYAN *Life & Let. Macaulay* iii George Babington . . . was always ready to take up the Tory cudgels.

Take what you find or what you bring.

c. **1386** CHAUCER *Reeves T.* A 4129 I have herd seyd, man sal taa of twa thinges, Slyk as he fyndes, or taa slyk as he bringes. [A man must take (one) of two things, either such as he finds, or such as he brings. These lines imitate the dialect of the North of England.—Skeat.] **1599** GREENE *George a Greene* IV. iv. 1002 If this like you not, Take that you finde, or that you bring, for me. **1862** HISLOP 166 If ye dinna like what I gie ye, tak what ye brought wi' ye.

Take your thanks to feed your cat.

1862 HISLOP 271.

Taken by a morsel, I was | says the fish.

1640 HERBERT 346.

Taken my horse and left me the tether, He hath.

1672 WALKER 17.

Takes gifts, She that | herself she sells, and she that gives, does not else.

1641 FERGUSSON 90. **1721** KELLY 294.

Takes his wife, As a man | — for better, for worse.

1552 *Book of Common Prayer, Solemnization of Matrimony.* **1668** COWLEY *Essays* i (1904) 7 We enter into the bonds of it, like those of matrimony; . . . and take it for better or worse. **1738** SWIFT (Dial. i) 339. *Lady A.* Colonel, you must take it for better for worse, as a man takes his wife.

Takes not up a pin, He that | slights his wife.

1640 HERBERT 334. **1732** FULLER no. 2324.

Takes the devil into his boat, He that | must carry him over the sound.

1678 RAY 125. **1732** FULLER no. 2326.

Takes the raven for his guide, He that | will light on carrion.

1865 ABP. TRENCH *Poems* 302 Who doth the raven for a guide invite, Must marvel not on carcases to light.

Take(s, n), *see also* Everything is as it is t.; Give a thing and t. a thing; Give and t.; Things are as they be t.; Well spoken that is well t.

Take, To, *see also under significant words following.*

Taking (Getting) the breeks off a Hielandman, It is ill.

1546 HEYWOOD. I ix. 16 (A) There is nothing more vain . . . than to beg a breeche of a bare arst man. **1818** SCOTT *Rob Roy* xxvii It will be nonsense fining me, . . . that hasna a grey groat to pay a fine wi'—it's ill taking the breeks aff a Hielandman. **1857** DEAN RAMSAY *Remin.* v. (1911) 194 *It's ill getting the breeks aff the Highlandman* . . . savours . . . of a Lowland Scotch origin. Having suffered loss at the hands of their neighbours from the hills, . . . there was little hope of redress from those who had not the means of supplying it. **1863** C. READE *Hard Cash* xli What . . . was . . . poor Dr. Wolf to do? Could he sub-embezzle a Highlander's breeks?

Taking the wall of a dog, Not worth.

1639 CLARKE 228.

Tale ill told is marred in the telling, A good.

[L. *Male narrando fabula depravatur.*] c. **1532** SIR ADRIAN FORTESCUE no. 59 A good tale yll toldd is spyllt in the telling. **1550** HEYWOOD II. vii. 67. **1605–6** SHAKS. *K. Lear* I. iv. 35 I can . . . mar a curious tale in telling it. **1614** CAMDEN 302. **1721** KELLY 244 *Many a good tale is spoil'd in the telling.* Apply'd often when a good sermon is ill delivered.

Tale is none the worse for being twice told, A good.

1581 *Stationers' Register* (Arb.) ii. 388 A good tale cannot too often be told. **1681** S. COLVIL *Whiggs Suppl.* 42 It's not superfluous and vain To tell a good tale ov'r again. **1721** KELLY 33 . . . An apology for them that say grace twice, unawares. **1816** SCOTT *Old Mort.* vii It's very true the curates read aye the same words . . . ; and . . . what for no? A gude tale's no the waur o' being twice tauld.

Tale never loses (tines) in the telling, A.

1616 DRAXE 177 A tale in the carrying is made more. **1721** KELLY 55 . . . Fame or report . . . commonly receives an addition as it goes from hand to hand. **1907** *Spectator* 16 Nov. 773 A story never loses in the telling in the mouth of an Egyptian.

Tale of a roasted horse, A.

1575 GASCOIGNE *Cert. Notes Instruct.* in *Steele Glas, &c.* (Arb.) 36 The verse that is to easie is like a tale of a rosted horse. **1611** COTGRAVE s.v. 'Cicogne' *Contes de la cicogne*, idle histories ; . . . tales . . . of a rosted horse.

Tale of a tub, A.

1532 MORE *Confut. Tindale* Wks. 576/1 Thys is a fayre tale of a tubbe tolde vs of hys electes. **1633** JONSON *T. Tub* I. ii A mere Tale of a Tub. Lend it no ear, I pray you. **1724** DEFOE *Mem. Cavalier* (1840) 97 Having entertained the fellow with a tale of a tub.

Tale of bricks is doubled, When the | Moses comes.

[L. *Cum duplicantur lateres, Moses venit.*] **1853** TRENCH iii. 65 *When the tale of bricks is doubled, Moses comes* . . . [is] an allusion to Exod. v. 9–19. . . . This proverb was a favourite one with the German Protestants during the worst times of the Thirty Years War. Gustavus Adolphus was the Moses who should come in the hour of uttermost need.

Tale of two drinks, It is a.

1721 KELLY 177 . . . It is a thing that requires deliberation ; at least as long as the glass may go twice about.

Tale runs as it pleases the teller, The.

1732 FULLER no. 4783.

Tale(s), *see also* Believe no t. from enemy ; Half a t. enough ; Keep my mind . . . tell my t. to wind (I will) ; Old man never wants a t. ; Old wives' t. ; One t. is good till another told ; Poor man's t. cannot be heard ; Tell another t. when you are tried ; Tell you a t. and find you ears ; Thereby hangs a t.

Tale-bearer is worse than a thief, A.

1721 KELLY 37. **1736** BAILEY *Dict.* s.v.

Tale-bearers, *see* Put no faith in t.-b.

Tales of Robin Hood are good among fools.

1509 A. BARCLAY *Ship of Fools* (1874) II. 155 All of fables and Iestis of Robyn hode. **1546** HEYWOOD II. ix. 77. **1670** RAY 137 Tales of Robin Hood are good enough for fools. . . . [Robin] Hood was a famous robber in the time of King Richard the first.

Tales out of school, Tell no.

1530 TINDALE *Pract. of Prelates* (P.S.) 249 (A) So that what cometh once in may never out, for fear of telling tales out of school. **1550** HEYWOOD I. x. 19 To tell tales out of schoole, that is hir great lust. **1679** SHADWELL *True Widow* IV. i Fie, miss! fie! tell tales out of school. **1721** KELLY 303 *Tell no school tales.* Do not blab abroad what is said in drink, or among companions. **1876** MRS. BANKS *Manch. Man* xv All attempts to make known school troubles and grievances were met with 'Never tell tales out of school'.

Tales, *see also* Tale(s).

Talk as Dutch[1] as Daimport's[2] (Darnford's) dog, To.

1879 G. F. JACKSON *Shropshire Wordbk.* 129 ''E talks as *Dutch* as Darnford's dog': proverbial saying heard in the neighbourhood of Whitchurch. **1917** BRIDGE 144 To talk as Dutch as Daimport's dog. [[1] fine, affected. [2] Davenport.]

Talk is but talk ; but 'tis money buys lands. (*Cf.* Prate is but prate, &c.)

1678 RAY 346.

Talk like a book, To.

1821 SCOTT *Lives of Novelists* (1887) 412 His talk too stiffly complimentary, too like a printed book, to use a Scottish phrase. **1900** G. C. BRODRICK *Mem. & Impress.* 205 I do not mean that 'talking like a book' has ceased to be fashionable— . . . but that slang is the order of the day.

Talk like an apothecary, To.

1616 WITHALS 560 You speake like a Pottecary, such a reason pist my goose. **1639** CLARKE 133 (A) He prates like a poticary. **1670** RAY 195.

Talk much, and err much, says the Spaniard.

1640 HERBERT 347.

Talk of an angel and you'll hear his wings.

1902–4 LEAN IV. 106.

Talk of Christmas so long, that it comes, They.

1611 COTGRAVE s.v. 'Noel' So long is Christmas cryed that at length it comes. **1640** HERBERT 355.

Talk of the devil, and he is sure to appear.

1666 TORRIANO 134 The English say, Talk of the Devil, and he's presently at your elbow. **1721** PRIOR *Hans Carvel* 71 Forthwith the devil did appear (For name him, and he's always near). **1721** KELLY 299 *Speak of the Dee'l, and he'll appear.* Spoken when they, of whom we are speaking, come in by chance. **1830** MARRYAT *King's Own* xxv The unexpected appearance of Mrs. Rainscourt made him involuntarily exclaim, 'Talk of the devil—' 'And she appears, sir', replied the lady. **1853** TRENCH vi. 149 *Talk of the devil, and he is sure to appear . . . contains . . . a very needful warning against . . . curiosity about evil.*

Talk of the devil, and he'll either come or send.

1591 LYLY *Endymion* I. iii. 5 *Et ecce autem—Will you see the Devil?* **1678** RAY 125.

Talk than trouble, There is more.

1640 HERBERT 329.

Talk the hind leg off a donkey (horse), To.

1844 H. COCKTON *Sylvester S.* xxxi He'd talk a horse's hind leg off, sir; and then wouldn't be quiet. **1877** BESANT *This Son of V.* I. xiii I believe you'd talk a donkey's hind leg off, give you time. **1909** *Times Wkly.* 15 Jan. 41 Socialists . . . would argue the hind leg off a donkey, to drop into their own vernacular vein.

Talk(s), *see also* Hold your tongue and let me t.; Think with wise, t. with vulgar; Tongue t. at head's cost; Walk groundly, t. profoundly.

Talkers, The greatest | are (always) the least doers.

1592–3 SHAKS. *Rich. III* I. iii. 350 Talkers are no good doers: be assur'd We go to use our hands and not our tongues. **1614** CAMDEN 312. **1670** RAY 147 (with 'always').

Talking pays no toll.

1640 HERBERT 340. **1732** FULLER no. 4317.

Talks much of his happiness, He that | summons grief.

1640 HERBERT 356.

Talks to himself, He that | speaks to a fool.

1721 KELLY 139 . . . Because none but fools will do so. **1732** FULLER no. 2328.

Talks, *see also* Talk(s).

Tall maid is stooping, While the | the little one hath swept the house.

1666 TORRIANO 108 Whilst a tall Meg of Westminster is stooping, a short wench sweeps the house. **1855** BOHN 565.

Tame beasts, Of all | I hate sluts.

1678 RAY 81.

Tame (*verb*), *see* Tod's bairns ill to t.

Tammie Norie o' the Bass canna kiss a bonny lass.

1842 R. CHAMBERS *Pop. Rhymes Scot.* (1870) 190 The Puffin.—Tammie Norie o' the Bass Canna kiss a bonny lass. . . . Said jocularly, when a young man refuses to salute a rustic coquette. The puffin, which builds . . . on the Bass Rock, is a very shy bird. . . . It is also customary to call a stupid-looking man a *Tammie Norie.*

Tamworth, *see* Sutton.

Tangled skein of it to wind off, You have a.

1732 FULLER no. 2603. **1855** BOHN 577.

Tankard, *see* Tears of the t.

Tantallon, *see* Ding doun T.

Tantony, *see* St. Anthony.

Tap, *see* Run t. run tapster.

Tar, *see* Ship (To lose) for halfpennyworth of t.

Tar-box, *see* Capers like a fly in a t.-b.

Tarred with the same brush (stick), All.

1623 WODROEPHE 287 Ye are all stained with one Pitch. **1818** SCOTT *Ht. Midl.* xlii The worshipful gentleman was . . . tarred wi' the same stick . . . as mony of them, . . . a hasty . . . temper. **1880** BLACKMORE *Mary Aner.* xxix They are . . . all tarred with one brush—all stuffed with a heap of lies.

Tarrows, *see* Plaints (T.) early that plaints on his kail.

Tarry breeks pays no fraught.

1721 KELLY 318 . . . People of a trade assist one another mutually.

Tarrying, *see* Long t. takes thanks away.

Tarry-long brings little home.

1721 KELLY 389 You have tarried long and brought little home. **1732** FULLER no. 4230.

Tartar, *see* Catch a T.; Scratch a Russian.

Tastes differ.

1868 W. COLLINS *Moonstone* xv Tastes differ . . . I never saw a marine landscape that I admired less.

Taste(s), *see also* Accounting for t. (No); Every man to his t.; Lost his t. (To him that has) sweet is sour.

Tattered, *see* Son full and t.

Taught you to swim, I | and now you'd drown me.

1732 FULLER no. 2626.

Taught, *see also* Better fed than t.

Taunt one tit over thumb, To.

1546 HEYWOOD II. iv. 52 And ye taunt me tyt ouer thumb (quoth shée).

Taunton, *see* Nertown was a market town.

Taunton Dean, *see* 'Ch was bore at T. D.

Tavern, *see* God keep me from . . . t.; St. Peter's in the Poor, where no t.

Tavern token, *see* Swallow a t. t.

Tawse, *see* Never take the t. when a word will do.

Tax(es), *see* Nothing is certain but . . . t.

Taxation without representation, No.

1769 BURKE *Late St. Nat.* Wks. II. 138 We ought to be quite so ready with our taxes, until we can secure the desired representation in parliament. **1891** J. E. T. ROGERS *Indust. & Commer. Hist.* i Most people dwell on the successful struggle of a principle which that war [of American Independence] is said to have represented, that taxation without representation is tyranny. **1919** DEAN INGE *Outspoken Ess.* i. 11 The corruption of democracies proceeds directly from the fact that one class imposes the taxes and another class pays them. The constitutional principle, 'No taxation without representation', is utterly set at nought.

Te Deum, see Correct *Magnificat* before one has learnt *T.D.*

Tea, *see* Many estates are spent . . . for t.; Take t. in the kitchen.

Teach an old dog tricks, It is hard to.

1523 FITZHERBERT *Husbandry* (E.D.S.) 45 (A) The dogge must lerne it when he is a whelpe, or els it wyl not be; for it is harde to make an olde dogge to stoupe. **1546** HEYWOOD II. vii. 70 But it is harde to make an olde dog stoupe. **1636** CAMDEN 300. **1670** RAY 127 An old dog will learn no tricks. It's all one to physic the dead, as to instruct old men. **1760–7** STERNE *T. Shandy* III. xxxiv The same renitency against conviction which is observed in old dogs, 'of not learning new tricks'. **1819** SCOTT *Bride Lam.* xxvi I am ower auld a dog to learn new tricks, or to follow a new master. **1857** TROLLOPE *Barch. Tow.* xiii There can be nothing wrong in your wishing to make yourself useful . . . As for myself . . . 'It's bad teaching an old dog tricks.'

Teach the cat the way to the kirn,[1] To.

1721 KELLY 93 *Eith*[2] *to learn the Cat to the Kirn.* An ill custom is soon learn'd, but not so soon forgotten. **1820** SCOTT *Monast.* xxxv I gave her . . . a yard of that very black say,[3] to make her a couvre-chef; but I see it is ill done to teach the cat the way to the kirn. [1 churn. 2 easy. 3 silk.]

Teach your father to get children.

1641 FERGUSSON 112 Ye learn your father to get bairns. **1670** RAY 9.

Teach your grandame to grope[1] (her) ducks.

1611 COTGRAVE s.v. Apprendre' (An idle, vaine, or needlesse labour) we say, to teach his grandame to grope ducks. **1670** RAY 178 . . . Teach me to do that I know how to do much better then your self. [1 To handle (poultry) in order to find whether they have eggs.]

Teach your grandame to sup sour milk.

1670 RAY 178.

Teach your grandmother to suck eggs.

1707 J. STEVENS tr. *Quevedo's Com. Wks.* (1709) 348 You would have me teach my Grandame to suck eggs. **1738** SWIFT (Dial. i) 338 *Never.* I'll mend it, miss. *Miss.* You mend it! go, teach your grannam to suck eggs. **1797** WOLCOT (P. Pindar) *Ode to Liv. London* ii (1816) III. 140 Those fellows talk to *me*—. . . They teach, forsooth, their grannum to *suck eggs!* **1882** BLACKMORE *Christow.* xxi A . . . twinkle, which might have been interpreted—'instruct your grandfather in the suction of gallinaceous products'.

Teaches himself, He that | has a fool for his master.

a. **1637** JONSON *Discoveries* (*Consilia*) Wks. (1904) III. 390 But very few men are wise by their own counsel; or learned by their own teaching. For he that was only taught by himself, had a fool to his master. **1655–62** GURNALL *Chrn. in Armour* (1865) II. 225 'He that is his own teacher', saith Bernard, 'is sure to have a fool for his master.' **1741** FRANKLIN Jan. Learn of the skilful: He that teaches himself, hath a fool for his master.

Teacheth ill, He | who teacheth all.

1605 CAMDEN (1637) 157. **1659** HOWELL *Eng. Prov. Rend. into Fr.* 4/2. **1670** RAY 147. **1732** FULLER no. 2035.

Teach(eth, ing), *see also* Dead or t. school (He is either); Gain t. to spend.

Teague's cocks, Like | that fought one another, though all were of the same side.

1732 FULLER no. 3234.

Tears of the tankard, The.

1678 RAY 82.

Tear(s) (*noun*), *see also* Crocodile t.; Dainties of great, t. of poor; Lass with the t. in her eye; Nothing dries sooner than t.; Pleasures of mighty, t. of poor; Smiles of pretty woman are t. of purse.

Teeth are longer than your beard, Your.

1591 *A Wonderful Prognostication* in Nashe's *Wks.* (McKerrow) III. 394 Diuerse men shall haue their teeth longer than their beards. **1855** BOHN 582.

Teeth forward (outward), From the.

1584 R. WILSON *Three Ladies of London* E 2v

Thou canst not loue but from the teeth forward. **1595** LIPSIUS *Constancy* tr. Stradling D1ᵛ Speak you that from your heart, or onlie from the teeth outward? *c.* **1607** SHAKS. *Ant. & Cleop.* III. iv. 9 When the best hint was given him, he not took't, Or did it from his teeth. **1721** KELLY 105 . . . That is, not inwardly, and from my heart. **1898** CUNNINGHAME GRAHAM *Mogreb-El-Acksa* 25 Christ and Mohammed never will be friends. . . . Even the truce they keep is from the teeth outwards.

Tell a lie and find a (the) truth.

1605 BACON *Adv. Learn.* II. xxiii. 18 (1900) 231 There are few men so true to themselves and so settled, but that, . . . they open themselves; specially if they be put to it with a counter-dissimulation, according to the proverb of Spain, *Di mentira, y sacarás verdad: Tell a lie and find a truth.* **1678** RAY 75 Tell a lie and find the troth. **1732** FULLER no. 4324 ('find out the truth').

Tell another tale when you are tried, You will.

1678 RAY 348.

Tell how many holes be in a scummer, You.

1616 WITHALS 553. **1639** CLARKE 146.

Tell me it snows.

1639 CLARKE 8 Fiddle, faddle, tell me it snowes. **1670** RAY 193.

Tell me news.

1603 RALEIGH in *Criminal Trials* (1832) i. 408 (A) All this while you tell me news, Mr. Attorney. **1670** RAY 187.

Tell me with whom thou goest, and I'll tell thee what thou doest.

1586 PETTIE *Guazzo's Civ. Conv.* 22 Tell me with whom thou dost goe, and I shall know what thou doest. **1678** RAY 147.

Tell (Reckon) money after your own father (kin).

1604 S. HIERON *The Preacher's Plea* (1605) 236 We have a Prouerbe, that a man must tell mony euen after his owne father. **1616** DRAXE 209 A man must tell gold after his owne father. **1639** CLARKE 90. **1692** L'ESTRANGE *Aesop's Fab.* cccxl (1738) 353 One gave him a fee of forty broad pieces: he took 'em, and counted 'em (as *a man may count money after his father*, they say). **1721** KELLY 284 Reckon money after all your kin.

Tell not all you know, nor do all you can.

1739 FRANKLIN Oct. Proclaim not all thou knowest, all thou owest, all thou hast, nor all thou canst. **1855** BOHN 495 . . . *Ital.*

Tell that to the marines!

1805 J. DAVIS *Post Captain* ch. 5. **1823** BYRON *Island* II. xxi Right, quoth Ben, that will do for the marines. **1824** SCOTT *Redg.* xiv Tell that to the marines—the sailors won't believe it. **1850** THACKERAY *Pendennis* lxvii 'Tell that to the marines, Major', replied the valet, 'that cock won't fight with me'. **1928** *Times* 21 Jul. 17/5 He said that I should . . . most likely be shot. I ventured to suggest that he should tell that to the Marines.

Tell[1] thy cards, and then tell me what thou hast won.

1550 HEYWOOD I. xi. 29. **1732** FULLER no. 5628 When you have counted your cards, you'll find you have little left. [[1] count.]

Tell thy foe that thy foot acheth (sleeps), Never.

c. **1300** *Prov. of Hending* 12 Tel thou neuer thy fo that they fot aketh. **1641** FERGUSSON 100 Thou should not tell thy foe when thy fit slides. **1721** KELLY 317 Tell not thy foe when thy foot's sleeping, nor thy stepminny when thou'rt sore hungry. **1862** HISLOP 240 Ne'er tell your fae when your foot sleeps.

Tell truth and shame the devil.

1548 PATTEN *Exped. Scotl.* Pref. a v An epigram . . . , the which I had, or rather (to say truth and shame the devil, for out it will) I stale . . . from a friend of mine. **1576** GASCOIGNE *Grief of Joy* iv. 38 Wks. (1910) II. 555 I will tell trewth, the devyll hymselfe to shame, Although therby I seeme to purchase blame. **1597-8** SHAKS. *1 Hen. IV* III. i. 58 And I can teach thee, coz, to shame the devil By telling truth: tell truth and shame the devil. **1611** GRUTER. **1614** CAMDEN 313 Truth shameth the diuell. **1738** SWIFT (Dial. i) 341 *Miss.* Well, but who was your author? Come, tell truth and shame the devil. **1853** TRENCH vi. 129 *Tell the truth, and shame the devil.* . . . When once a man has brought himself to tell the truth to himself and to God, and, where need requires, to his fellowmen, . . . he has defied the devil.

Tell where to turn his nose, He cannot.

c. **1570** *A Balade of a Preist* in *Anct. Ballads & Broadsides* (1867) 211 The prouerbe is true in you, I suppose,—He cannot tell where to turne his nose.

Tell you a tale and find you ears too? Must I.

1546 HEYWOOD II. ix. 74 Who euer with you any tyme therin weares, He must both tell you a tale, and fynde you eares. **1670** RAY 195 Tell you a tale, and find you ears. **1738** SWIFT (Dial. i) 337 *Never.* What, miss! must I tell you a story and find you ears?

Tell you, you are an ass, If one, two, or three | put on a bridle (tail).

1678 RAY *Adag. Hebr.* 396 If any say that one of thine ears is the ear of an ass, regard it not: If he say so of them both, procure thyself a bridle: That is, it is time to arm ourselves with patience when we are greatly reproached. **1732** FULLER no. 2697. **1903**

Brit. Wkly, 9 Apr. 673 The outsider's judgment is usually safe. It is written in the Talmud, 'If thy friends agree in calling thee an ass, go and get the halter round thee'. **1911** A. COHEN *Anct. Jew. Prov.* 89 If one person tell thee thou hast ass's ears, take no notice; should two tell thee so, procure a saddle for thyself.

Tells a secret, He that | is another's servant.

1623 WODROEPHE 277 To him thou tellest thy Secret, thou giuest also thy Liberty. **1640** HERBERT 341. **1647** HOWELL *Lett.* 14 Feb. (1903) II. 257 I find it now true, that he who discovers his secrets to another sells him his liberty and becomes his slave.

Tells his wife news, He that | is but newly married.

c. **1275** *Provs. of Alfred* (Skeat) A 269 Ne wurth thu neuer so wod, ne so wyn-drunke, That euer segge thine wife alle thine wille. [Never be so mad or so drunken as to tell all thy counsel to thy wife.] **1640** HERBERT 362. **1642** FULLER *H. & P. State* I. iii He keeps her in the wholesome ignorance of unnecessary secrets. . . . He knows little, who will tell his wife all he knows. **1732** FULLER no. 2330 (omitting 'news').

Tell(s), told, *see also* Ass kicks you (When) never t. it; Do not all you can, t. not all you know; Glass t. you (What your) will not be t. by counsel; Know all (Since you) t. me what I dreamed.

Tell-truth, *see* Tom T.-t.

Temperance is the best physic.

1520 WHITTINTON *Vulg.* (E.E.T.S.) 45 He that foloweth temperaunce . . . nedeth no physicyons. **1855** BOHN 495.

Tempers (*verb*), *see* God t. the wind.

Tempest, *see* No t. good July.

Temple brough, *see* Winkabank.

Tempt(ed), *see* Busy (He that is) is t. by one devil; Open door may t. a saint.

Ten, *see* Commandments.

Tench, *see* Stung like a t.

Tender as a parson's leman, As.

1546 HEYWOOD I. x. 22. **1659** HOWELL *Eng. Prov.* 15.

Tender as Parnell, that broke her finger in a posset-curd, As.

1678 RAY 289.

Tender Gordons, You are one of the | that dow[1] not be hanged for galling their neck.

1721 KELLY 380 . . . Spoken to those who readily complain of hurts and hardships. [[1] could.]

Tenham, *see* Live a little while.

Tent[1] thee, I will | quoth Wood: if I can't rule my daughter, I'll rule my good.

1670 RAY 52 . . . *Chesh.* [[1] attend to, take heed.]

Tenterden steeple is the cause of Goodwin Sands.

[The land now represented by these quicksands, opposite Sandwich, was submerged, about 1100, because, it is said, the stones for its sea-wall were used by the abbot of St. Augustine's, Canterbury, for the tower of Tenterden church.] **1528** MORE *Dialogue* in Wks. (1557) p. 278 col. 1 (A). **1550** LATIMER *Last Serm. bef. Edw. VI* (P.S.) 251 'Forsooth, sir', quoth he, 'I am an old man; I think that Tenterton steeple is the cause of Goodwin sands'. **1662** FULLER (*Kent*) II. 125 'Tenterden's steeple is the cause of the breach in Goodwin Sands'. It is used commonly in derision of such who, being demanded to render a reason of some important accident, assign . . . a ridiculous and improbable cause thereof. . . . But . . . the old man had told a rational tale, had he found but the due favour to finish it.

Tenterhooks, To be on.

[= in a state of painful suspense.] **1748** SMOLLETT *Rod. Rand.* xlv I left him upon the tenter-hooks of impatient uncertainty. **1761** A. MURPHY *Old Maid* Wks. (1786) II.160 *Mrs. Har.* The heart . . . flutters upon the tenter-hooks of expectation. **1887** *Sat. Rev.* 25 Dec. 754/1 The author keeps . . . the reader . . . on tenterhooks.

Term time in the court of conscience, It is always.

1732 FULLER no. 2914.

Testament(s), *see* Nothing patent in New T.; Prosperity is blessing of Old T.; Tochers (The greatest) make not greatest t.; Weime (That which is in my) is not in my t.

Testoons are gone to Oxford to study in Brasenose.[1]

[Henry VIII debased the coins to ⅓ silver and ⅔ alloy. The testoons (shillings) having the king's full face soon began to show the inferior metal at the end of the nose.] **1562** HEYWOOD *Fifth Hund. Epig.* no. 63, 189 Testons be gone to Oxforde, god be their spéede: To studie in Brazennose there to procéede. **1662** FULLER (*Oxf.*) III. 6 'Testons are gone to Oxford, to study in Brazen-nose.' This proverb began about the end of the reign of King Henry the Eighth . . . . *Testons* especially . . . [were] *allayed* . . . with copper (which common people confound with brass). [[1]Brasenose College was founded in 1509.]

Tether, *see* Hair to make a t.

Tewkesbury mustard.

[**1500** ERASM. *Ad. Sinapi victitare.*] **1597-8** SHAKS. *2 Hen. IV* II. iv. 262 His wit is as thick as Tewkesbury mustard. **1662** FULLER

(*Glos.*) I. 353 He looks as if he had lived on Tewkesbury mustard. It is spoken partly of such who always have a sad, severe, and tetrick countenance.

Thames, *see* Ducks fare well in T.; Safe from the E. Indies, drowned in T.; Set the T. on fire.

Thanet, *see* England wrings (When), T. sings.

Thank God that your father was born before you, You may. (*Cf.* Happy is he whose friendship, &c.)

1721 KELLY 379 (with 'friends were'). **1855** BOHN 579.

Thank you for nothing.

1594 LYLY *Moth. Bomb.* II. iii. Wks. (1902) III. 191 I thank you for nothing, because I understand nothing. **1668** SHADWELL *Sullen Lov.* v. iii (Merm.) 110 *C. Gent.* Thank you for nothing. Is this the honour you have for me . . .? **1712** ADDISON *Spect.* No. 391 Wks. (Bohn) III. 366 One . . . promised Jupiter . . . a silver cup. Jupiter thanked him for nothing. **1847–8** THACKERAY *Vanity F.* xxiv It's you who want to introduce beggars into my family. Thank you for nothing, Captain.

Thank you for the next, I will | for this I am sure of.

1678 RAY 273. **1738** SWIFT (Dial. ii) 349 *Sir J.* [He gets a brimmer and drinks it off.] . . . Your wine is excellent good, so I thank you for the next, for I am sure of this.

Thankless, *see* Many a man serves t. master.

Thanks, *see also* Gets little t. for losing his own; Old t. pay not new debt; Rank courtesy when man forced give t. for own; Take your t. to feed your cat.

That is for that, and butter's for fish.

1721 KELLY 336 . . . Spoken when a thing fits nicely what it was design'd for. **1738** SWIFT (Dial. i) 340 *Spark.* Well, so much for that, and butter for fish.

Thatch Groby Pool[1] with pancakes, Then I'll.

1678 RAY 317 (*Leics.*). **1787** GROSE (*Leics.*) 192 . . . Spoken when something improbable is promised or foretold. **1818** SCOTT *Ht. Midl.* xxix 'I hope there is nae bad company on the road, sir?' . . . 'Why, when it's clean without them I'll thatch Groby pool wi' pancakes.' [1 a large sheet of water near Leicester.]

Thatched his house, When I have | he would throw me down.

1639 CLARKE 170. **1732** FULLER no. 5559 When I had thatch'd his house, he would have hurl'd me from the roof.

Thatches his house with turds, He that | shall have more teachers than reachers.

1678 RAY 209. **1721** KELLY 147 . . . He that

---

is engaged in a difficult and troublesome business, will have more to give him their advice than their assistance.

Thatch(ed, es), *see also* Head is down (When my), house is t.; Long as he is lither (If he were), he might t. a house.

Theologian, *see* Heart that makes t.

There or thereabouts, as Parson Smith says.

1678 RAY 343 . . . *Proverbial* about *Dunmow* in *Essex.*

Thereby hangs (lies) a tale.

1523 SKELTON *Garl. Laurel* 1200 Yet, thoughe I say it, therby lyeth a tale. **1593–4** SHAKS. *Tam. Shrew* IV. i. 60 Out of their saddles into the dirt, and thereby hangs a tale. **1599–1600** *A.Y.L.* II. vii. 28 And then from hour to hour we rot and rot, And thereby hangs a tale. **1600–1** *Merry W.* I. iv. 159 *Quick.* Have not your worship a wart above your eye? . . . Well, thereby hangs a tale. **1604–5** *Othello* III. i. 8 *Clo.* Are these, I pray you, wind-instruments? *First Mus.* Ay, marry, are they, sir. *Clo.* O! thereby hangs a tail. *First Mus.* Whereby hangs a tale, sir? *Clo.* Marry, sir, by many a wind-instrument that I know. *a.* **1642** SUCKLING *Ballad on Wed.* The maid (and thereby hangs a tale).

Therm, *see* Wide t. had never long arm.

'They say so', is half a lie (liar).

1666 TORRIANO 30 To have heard say is half a lye. **1732** FULLER no. 4970. **1853** TRENCH i. 13 '*They say so*', *is half a liar*; here is the better word with which *they* may arm themselves, who count it a primal duty to close their ears against . . . unauthenticated rumours to the discredit of their neighbours.

They say!—What say they?—Let them say.

[From a late engraved Roman gem: Λέγουσιν ἃ θέλουσιν· λεγέτωσαν· οὐ μέλ[ε]ι μοι.] *c.* **1593** KEITH, EARL MARISCHAL in W. WATT *Aberdeen & Banff* (1900) 179 The defiant motto which the fifth earl inscribed on . . . his college[1] in Aberdeen—'They haif said: Quhat say thay? Lat thame say.' [1 Marischall Coll. in the University of Aberdeen.]

Thick and thin, Through.

[= through everything that is in the way.] *c.* **1386** CHAUCER *Reeve's T.* 144–6 Whan the hors was loos, he ginneth gon Toward the fen, . . . thurgh thikke and thurgh thenne. **1543** GRAFTON *Contn. Harding* 544 Kyng Richard . . . purposed to goo thorow thicke and thinne in this mater. **1782** COWPER *Gilpin* 45 Six precious souls, and all agog to dash through thick and thin.

Thick and threefold.

1549 CHALONER tr. *Erasm. Praise of Folly* L4ᵛ. **1552** HULOET *Abced.* III (A). **1650** FULLER *Pisgah Sight* II. ix (A) Disaster . . . which afterwards fell thick and threefold upon it.

Thick as thieves, As.

1833 T. HOOK *Parson's Dau.* II. ii She and my wife are as thick as thieves, as the proverb goes.

Thick, *see also* Fast (T.) as hops; Put it on t., a little will stick.

Thief doth fear each bush an officer, The.

1583 MELBANCKE *Philot.* 166 Tush, thou art like a Thiefe, that thinkes euerye Tree a true man. **1590–1** SHAKS. *3 Hen. VI* V. vi. 12 Suspicion always haunts the guilty mind; The thief doth fear each bush an officer. **1594** NASHE *Unf. Trav.* (1920) 114 A theefe, they saie, mistakes euerie bush for a true man.

Thief for the widdy[1], It is as meet as a.

1641 FERGUSSON 66. [1 gallows.]

Thief is sorry he is to be hanged, but not that he is a thief, The.

1732 FULLER no. 4788.

Thief knows a thief as a wolf knows a wolf, A.

1539 TAVERNER (1545) E 3 The thefe Knoweth the thefe, and the wolfe the wolfe. **1616** DRAXE 107 One thiefe knoweth another. **1732** FULLER no. 430.

Thief passes for a gentleman when stealing has made him rich, A.

1732 T. FULLER no. 431. **1802** WOLCOT (P. Pindar) *Middl. Elect.* iii A thief may be a gentleman That git'th estates by stealing.

Thief robs another, One.

1600 *Sir J. Oldcastle* III. iv (*Shaks. Apoc.*) 146 *King.* Wel, if thou wilt needs haue it, there tis: iust the prouerb, one thiefe robs another.

Thief to catch (take) a thief, Set a.

1655 FULLER *Ch. Hist.* IX. iii (1868) II. 596 Many were his lime-twigs to this purpose. . . . Always set a —— to catch a ——; and the greatest deer-stealers make the best park-keepers. **1670** RAY 148. **1778** LANGTON in BOSWELL *Johnson* lxvi (1848) 611 'A fine surmise. Set a thief to catch a thief.' **1812** EDGEWORTH *Absentee* xvii 'You have been all your life evading the laws . . .; do you think this has qualified you peculiarly for being a guardian of the laws?' Sir Terence replied, 'Yes, sure; set a thief to catch a thief is no bad maxim.'

Thieves and rogues have the best luck, if they do but scape hanging.

1670 RAY 118.

Thieves fall out, When | true (honest) men come to their own.

1546 HEYWOOD II. ix. 76 Whan théeues fall out, true men come to their goode. **1616** BRETON *Cross. Prov.* II. Wks. (1879) II. App.

iii When thieves fall out, true men come by their own. **1629** T. ADAMS *Serm.* (1861–2) II. 395 This is eventually one good effect of many controverted points: the way is cleansed for others, though not for themselves. Thieves falling out, true men come by their goods. **1681** S. COLVIL *Whiggs Sup.* II. 53 When thieves reckon, it's oft-times known That honest people get their own. **1721** KELLY 345 When thieves reckon leal[1] folks come to their gear.[2] **1866** KINGSLEY *Hereward* xv The rogues have fallen out, and honest men may come by their own. [1 honest. 2 goods.]

Thieves, All are not | that dogs bark at.

1577 PEACHAM *Garden of Eloquence* (1593) 30 All are not theeues that dogges barke at. **1616** DRAXE 48. **1639** CLARKE 54. **1670** RAY 56.

Thief (-ves), *see also* Ask my fellow if I be t.; Beggar may sing before t.; Bolder than miller's neckcloth (What is); Brings up his son to nothing (He that); Careless hussy makes many t.; Ease makes t.; Every man gets his own (When), t. will get widdie; Great t. hang little ones; Hole calls the t.; Honour among t.; Hop whore pipe t.; Ill layers up make t.; Little t. are hanged; Looks as the wood were full of t.; Men of all trades (Of the) they hang t.; No receiver no t.; Old t. new halter; Opportunity makes the t.; Poor kin that has neither whore nor t.; Postern door makes t.; Put a miller . . . in a bag, the first will be t.; Receiver is as bad as t.; Rope enough (Give a t.); Rope for a thief (Meet as); Safe as a t. in a mill; Save a t. from the gallows and . . .; Show me a liar and I will show t.; Tale-bearer is worse than t.; Thick as t.; Thunders (When it) t. becomes honest; True man and a t. think not the same; War makes t., peace hangs them; Whores and t. go by clock; Worth it as a t. worth a rope.

Thimble, *see* Four farthings and a t.; Tine t. tine thrift.

Thin as Banbury cheese, As.

1562 HEYWOOD *Sixth Hund. Epig.* no. 24, 204 I neuer saw Banbury chéese thicke enough. **1600–1** SHAKS. *Merry W.* I. i. 130 *Bar.* (to Slender) You Banbery Cheese. **1601** *Pasquil & Kath.* III. 178 Put off your clothes, and you are like a Banbery cheese, Nothing but paring.

Thin end of the wedge is to be feared, The.

1884 BLACKMORE *Tom. Upmore* xvii My father kept calling him . . . the thin end of the wedge, and telling dear mother . . . not . . . to let him in. **1908** *Spectator* 15 Feb. 263 The Mission inserted the thin end of its wedge when it set up constant communications with a Legate from the Emperor.

Thin meadow is soon mowed, A.

a. **1659** FULLER *Serm.* (1891) II. 570 By his vastation to leave . . . footing for foreign enemies to fasten on this country. . . . And no wonder if a thin meadow were quickly mown. **1670** RAY 26.

Thing in it, There is a | (quoth the fellow when he drank the dish-clout).

1639 CLARKE 8. **1732** FULLER no. 4884 ('drunk dish-clout and all').

Thing that's done is na to do, The.

1855 BOHN *Scot. Prov.* 257.

Thing that's, *see also under significant words following.*

Things are as they be taken. (*Cf.* Everything is as it is taken.)

1639 CLARKE 214.

Things at the worst will mend.

1596–7 SHAKS. *K. John* III. iv. 114 Evils that take leave, On their departure most of all show evil. **1600** *Sir J. Oldcastle* IV. iii (*Shaks. Apoc.*) 153 *Harp.* Patience, good madame, things at worst will mend. **1605–6** SHAKS. *Macbeth* IV. ii. 24 Things at the worst will cease, or else climb upward To what they were before. **1623** WEBSTER *Duch. of M.* IV. i (Merm.) 200 *Bos.* Things being at the worst begin to mend. **1858** SURTEES *Ask Mamma* xxv Certainly, things got to their worst in the farming way, before they began to mend. **1901** R. G. MOULTON *Shaks. as Dram. Art.* 46 Proverbs like . . . 'When things come to the worst they are sure to mend', exactly express moral equilibrium.

Things of friends are in common, The.

[PYTHAGORAS Κοινὰ τὰ τῶν φίλων.] **1539** TAVERNER 70 Amicorum omnia sunt communia. Amongst friends all things be common. **1546** W. HUGH *Troub. Man's Med.* (1831) I. i. 3 As all things are common among them which are trusty and faithful friends, so, doubtless, are the very affections of the mind. **1853** TRENCH vi. 134 . . . Where does this find its exhaustive fulfilment, but in the communion of saints?

Things present are judged by things past.

1573 SANDFORD (1576) H 4. **1578** FLORIO *First Fruites* f. 30. **1629** *Book of Meery Riddles* Prov. 36.

Things that are above us, The | are nothing to us.

[ERASM. *Ad. Quae supra nos nihil ad nos.*] **1583** STUBBES *Anat.* (N. Sh. S.) II. i. 56 It is an olde saieng, . . . *Quae supra nos, nihil ad nos,* Those things that are aboue our reach, conserne vs not, and therefore we ought not to enter into the bowels and secrets of the Lord. **1616** GREENE *Mourn. Garm.* Wks. (Huth) IX. 185 His Aphorisms are too farre fetcht for me, and therefore, *Quae supra nos, nihil ad nos.* **1621** BURTON *Anat. Mel.* I. ii. I. ii But be they [sublunary devils] more or less, *Quod supra nos nihil ad nos* (what is beyond our comprehension does not concern us).

Things that are below us, The | are nothing to us.

1860 RILEY *Dict. Lat. Quot.* 353 *Quae infra nos nihil ad nos. Prov.* 'The things that are below us are nothing to us.' We must look upwards.

Things that are, Things of, *see also under significant words following.*

Things that must be, In | it is good to be resolute.

1732 FULLER no. 2830.

Thing(s), *see also* Good t. are hard; Good t. soon caught up; Little t.; One t. at a time.

Think a calf a muckle beast that never saw a cow, They.

1832 HENDERSON 93.

Think all is lost that goes beside your own mouth, You.

1633 D. DYKE *Wks. Philemon* 108 They . . . snatch it all to themselves, grudging another the least morsel, thinking all is lost that goes besides their own lips. **1738** SWIFT (Dial. iii) 352 *Miss.* I wish they would be quiet, and let me drink my tea. *Never.* What! I warrant you think all is lost that goes beside your own mouth.

Think much, speak little, and write less.

c. **1430** LYDGATE *Minor Poems* (Percy Soc.) 155 Take no quarelle, thynk mekyl and sey nought. *c.* **1450** *Prov. of Wysdom* (ed. Schleich) in *Anglia* 51, l. 94 Whateuer þou þenkest sey but lyte. **1666** TORRIANO 200 (18).

Think no labour (travail) slavery that brings in penny saverly.[1]

1573 TUSSER 17 To count no trauell slauerie, that brings in peny sauerlie. **1813** RAY 42 [[1] by saving.]

Think no small beer of oneself, To.

1837 SOUTHEY *Doctor* IV. 381 It is clear . . . that the Author does not in vulgar parlance, think Small Beer of himself. **1840** DE QUINCEY *Style* Wks. XI. 174 Should express her self-esteem by the popular phrase, that she did not 'think small beer of herself'.

Think none ill, They that | are soonest beguiled.

1546 HEYWOOD II. v. 60 I feare fals measures or els I were a chylde. For they that thinke none yll, are soonest begylde.

Think of ease, but work on.

1640 HERBERT 325.

Think, One may | that dares not speak.

1597 T. DELONEY *Thomas of Reading* Wks. (Mann) 230 Though he said little, hee thought the more. **1605–6** SHAKS. *Macbeth* V. i. 86 I think, but dare not speak. **1616** DRAXE 21. **1630** J. TAYLOR *Works* Qq 2ᵛ Though my Daw doe not speak, yet I am in good hope that he thinkes the more. **1639** CLARKE 34.

Think there is bacon, Where you | there is no chimney.

1640 HERBERT 321.

Think well of all men.

1659 HOWELL *Eng. Prov.* 10/1.

Think with the wise, but talk with the vulgar.

1545 ASCHAM *Toxoph.* (Arb.) 18 He that wyll wryte well in any tongue, muste folowe thys councel of Aristotle, to speake as the common people do, to thinke as wise men do. **1605** BACON *Adv. Learn.* II. xiv. 11 (Oxf. 1900) 163 Although we . . . prescribe it well *loquendum ut vulgus sentiendum ut sapientia.* **1662** FULLER (*Lond.*) II. 348 Common people (we must speak with the *volge*, and think with the wise) call it Gutturlane. *a.* **1682** Motto of SIR HENRY BLOUNT (1602–82, Aubrey's *Lives*). **1871** J. HAY *Pike County Ballads* Speak with the speech of the world, think with the thoughts of the few.

Thinketh his feet be, He | where his head shall never come.

1550 HEYWOOD I. xi. 29.

Thinking is very far from knowing.

1707 MAPLETOFT 50. **1855** BOHN 528.

Thinks amiss, He that | concludes worse.

1651 HERBERT 365.

Thinks every bush a boggard, He.

1579 GOSSON *Apology* (Arb.) 65 I am not so childishe to take euery bushe for a monster. **1594** SHAKS. *Lucrece* l. 972 Let . . . the dire thought of his committed evil Shape every bush a hideous shapeless devil. **1595–6** *Mids. N. V.* i. 22 Or in the night, imagining some fear, How easy is a bush suppos'd a bear! *c.* **1660** R. WATKYNS *The Righteous is Confident as a Lyon* The guilty conscience fears, when there's no fear, and thinks that every bush contains a bear. **1678** RAY 232 He thinks every bush a boggard, *i.e.* a bugbear or phantasm.

Thinks his business below him, He that | will always be above his business.

1732 FULLER no. 2333.

Thinks his penny (farthing, halfpenny) good silver, He.

[= has a good opinion of himself.] **1546**

HEYWOOD I. X. 22 She thinkth her farthyng good syluer I tell you. **1575** GASCOIGNE *Gl. Govt.* III. iv (1910) 49 I think my halfpenny as good silver as another doth. **1579** LYLY *Euphues* (Arb.) 46 He deemeth no penny good siluer but his owne, preferring . . . his owne wit before all mens wisedomes. **1590** SIDNEY *Arcadia* II. xiv I, simple though I sit here, thought once my penny as good silver, as some of you do. **1603** BRETON *Packet Mad Let.* liv (1879) 20/1 There are more Batchelors than Roger, and my peny is as good siluer as yours. **1721** KELLY 172 *He counts his halfpenny good silver.* That is, he thinks much of himself with little reason.

Thinks not well, He | that thinks not again.

1611 COTGRAVE s.v. 'Penser' He thinks not well that . . . thinks not more than once. **1640** HERBERT 355.

Think(s, eth, ing), thought (*verb*), *see also* First t. then speak; Fool saith, Who would have t. it; Fool that t. not that another t.; Ill be to him that t. ill; Mackissock's cow did (Will do as), I'll t. more than I say; One thing t. the bear; One thing t. the horse; Put on considering (t.) cap; Say as men say but t.; Say little but t. the more; Says nothing (Though he), he pays with t.; Sitteth well t. ill; Speak fair and t. what you will; Speaks in his drink what he t. in his drouth; Warm (He that is) t. all so; Weal or woe as he t. himself so.

Third is a charm, The.

1721 KELLY 331 . . . Spoken to encourage those who have attempted a thing once and again to try a third time.

Third of April, On the | comes in the cuckoo and nightingale.

1732 FULLER no. 6136. **1846** DENHAM 41.

Third pays for all, The.

1575 HIGGINS *Mirr. for Magist.* I 'Q. Elstride' st. 23 in *Brit. Bibliographer* 68 The third payes home, this prouerbe is to true. **1599–1600** SHAKS. *Twelfth N. V.* i. 40 *Primo, secundo, tertio,* is a good play; and the old saying is, 'the third pays for all'. **1917** BRIDGE 120 The third time pays for all. Never despair.

Third time's lucky, The.

1862 HISLOP [ed. 2] 297.

Thirst, *see* First glass for t.; Speak of my drinking (Many), but few of my t.

Thirsty, *see* Goes to bed t. (He that).

Thirteen of you may go to the dozen well enough.

1721 KELLY 323 . . . Spoken to worthless fellows.

Thistle is a fat salad for an ass's mouth, A.

1721 KELLY 241 (given as an English proverb).

1732 FULLER no. 435. **1802** WOLCOT (P. Pindar) *Middl. Elect.* iii A disell, by an ass's jaws, Is thoft a pretty sallet.

Thistle(s), *see also* Brain sows not corn (If), plants t.; Good harvest (He that hath) content with some t.; Need of a blessing that kneel to a t.

Thither as I would go, I can go late; thither as I would not go, I know not the gate.

1678 RAY 296.

Thole[1] well is good for burning.

1721 KELLY 312 ... Eng. *Patience and posset-drink cures all maladies.* [[1] bear.]

Thomson, *see* John T.'s man.

Thong(s), *see* Buckle and t.; Buckle and bare t.; Cut large t. of other men's leather (Men); Cut one's t. according to one's leather.

Thorn against the breast, To sing (or sit) with a.

1594 SHAKS. *Lucrece* 1135 Come, Philomel, ... And whiles against a thorn thou bear'st thy part To keep thy sharp woes waking, wretched I, . . . against my heart Will fix a sharp knife. **1599** *Passionate Pilgrim*, *Sonn. to Sund. Notes* vi. 10 She, poor bird, as all forlorn, Lean'd her breast upon a thorn, And there sung the dolefull'st ditty. **1610** G. FLETCHER *Christ's Vict. & Tri.* But leaning on a thorn her dainty chest, . . . Expresses in her song grief not to be expressed. **1629** T. ADAMS *Serm.* (1862) II. 154 The godly must be fain to sit, like the nightingale, with a thorn against her breast.

Thorn comes forth with the point forwards, The.

1640 HERBERT 328.

Thorn-bush, *see* Dwell (Wherever a man) t.-b. near his door.

Thorney, *see* Ramsey.

Thorns, To be (sit, stand) on (upon).

1528 MORE *Wks.* (1557) 234 col. 1 (A) I long by my trouth, quod he, and euen syt on thornes tyll I see that constitucion. **1561** T. HOBY tr. *Castiglione's Courtyer* II. (1900) 114 The poore gentilwoman stood upon thornes, and thought an houre a thousande yeare, till she were got from him. *c.* **1580** JEFFERIE *Bugbears* III. ii. in *Archiv. Stud. Neu. Spr.* (1897) I sytt all on thornes till that matter take effect. *a.* **1599** SHAKS. *Sonn.* 99 The Roses fearfully on thorns did stand. **1768** EARL CARLISLE in JESSE *Selwyn & Contemp.* (1843) II. 316 I should have been upon thorns till you had wrote.

Thorns make the greatest crackling.

[BIBLE *Eccles.* vii. 6 As the crackling of thorns under a pot, so is the laughter of the fool.] **1732** FULLER no. 5031.

Thorns whiten, yet do nothing.

1640 HERBERT 360.

Thorn(s), *see also* Barefoot must not plant t.; Early pricks that will be t.; Handles t. (He that); Honey that is licked from t.; Lie upon roses . . . upon t. when old; Pull the t. out of your foot (I will not); Truths and roses have t.

Thou thyself canst do it, If | attend no other's help or hand.

1541 COVERDALE *Christ. State Matrimony* I 3 (A) That whych thou cannest do conueniently thy selfe commytte it not to another. **1640** HERBERT 354.

Though I say it, that should not say it.

1594 LYLY *Moth. Bomb.* v. iii. Wks. (1902) III. 217 Though I say it that should not, haue bene a minstrell these thirtie yeeres. **1721** KELLY 316 *Though you say it, that should not say it, and must say it, if it be said.* A ridicule upon them that commend themselves. **1809** HANNAH MORE *Cœlebs* v Though I say it, who should not say it, they are as highly accomplished as any ladies at St. James's. **1818** SCOTT *Ht. Midl.* xxvii 'I am not able to dispute with you'. 'Few folk are—. . . though I say it that shouldna say it,' returned Bartoline, with great delight.

Thought hath good legs, The | and the quill a good tongue.

1640 HERBERT 346. **1732** FULLER no. 4790 (with 'wings' for 'legs').

Thought is free.

c. **1390** GOWER *Conf. Amantis* v. 4485 I have herd seid that thoght is fre. *c.* **1490** *Partonope* (E.E.T.S.) 440, l. 10884 Therfore þis proverbe is seide full truly: þought to a man is euer ffre. **1546** HEYWOOD II. ii. 47 I say little (said she) but I thinke more. Thought is frée. **1580** LYLY *Euph. & his Eng.* (Arb.) 281 Why then quoth he, doest thou thinke me a foole, thought is free my Lord quoth she. **1599–1600** SHAKS. *Twelfth N.* I. iii. 74 Now, sir, 'thought is free'. **1600–1** *Hamlet* III. ii. 225 Our thoughts are ours, their ends none of our own. **1604–5** *Meas. for Meas.* V. i. 454 Thoughts are no subjects. *Othello* III. iii. 135 I am not bound to that all slaves are free to. Utter my thoughts? **1611–12** *Tempest* III. ii. 134 Thought is free. **1874** G. MACDONALD *Malcolm* xxxix 'How do you come to think of such things?' 'Thocht 's free, my lord.'

Thoughts be free from toll.

1636 CAMDEN 307.

Thoughts close and your countenance loose, Your.

1612 CHARRON *Of Wisdom* tr. Lennard (1640) 335 *Frons aperta, lingua parca, mens clausa, nulli fidere*: His face open, his tongue silent, his mind secret, and to trust none. [**1638** Letter from SIR HENRY WOOTTON to John

Milton printed before *Comus*, *I pensieri stretti e il viso sciolto* will go safely over the whole World.] **1651** HERBERT no. 1183. **1707** MAPLETOFT 21. **1748** CHESTERFIELD 19 Oct. The height of abilities is to have *volto sciolto* and *pensieri stretti*. **1825** SCOTT *Journ.* 28 Nov. He [Lockhart] sometimes reverses the proverb and gives the *volte strette e pensiere sciolti* [sic].

Thought(s) (*noun*), *see also* Know your t. (I); Second t. are best. *For* Thought (*verb*) *see* Think.

Thousand pounds, A | and a bottle of hay, is all one thing at doomsday.

1659 HOWELL *Eng. Prov.* 1/2. **1670** RAY 26. **1732** FULLER no. 6398.

Thousand pounds (worth) of law, In a | there's not an ounce of love (a shilling's worth of pleasure).

1611 COTGRAVE s.v. 'Amour' In a hundred pound of law ther's not a half-peny weight of love. **1670** RAY 15. **1732** FULLER no. 2811.

Thraw[1] the wand[2] while it is green.

1641 FERGUSSON 94. [[1] twist. [2] rod.]

Thrawn[1] faced bairn that is gotten against the father's will, It is a.

1721 KELLY 188 . . . Kindness extorted come[s] always with an ill grace. [[1] distorted.]

Thread breaks where it is weakest, The.

1640 HERBERT 345. **1732** FULLER no. 5647 Where it's weakest, there the thread breaketh.

Thread is spun.

1605 JONSON *Volpone* v. iii. 11 Mosca? Is his thred spunne? **1681** *Roxb. Ballads* v. 45 (A) Give them what they deserve, their thread is spun.

Thread will tie an honest man better than a rape[1] will do a rogue, A.

1832 HENDERSON 32. [[1] rope.]

Thread, *see also* Put it together with . . . burnt t.; Rowan tree and red t.; Spin a fair t.

Threadneedle St., The old lady of.

[= the Bank of England.] **1864** J. PAYN *Lost Sir Massingb.* xxvii I trust you are not come about any fresh wrongs against the Old Lady of Threadneedle Street. I never see your face but I think of an invitation bank-note.

Threaten, *see* Easy to t. than to kill (More).

Threatened folk(s) (men) live long

c. **1555** COLLMAN *Ballads, &c.* (Roxb. Cl.) 69 (A) It is a true prouerbe: the threatned

man lyues long. **1599** PORTER *Angry Wom. Abingd.* IV. iii (Merm.) 176 *Nich.* Ay, Brag's a good dog; threatened folks live long. **1614** CAMDEN 313. **1655** FULLER *Ch. Hist.* VIII. iii (1868) II. 476 Gardiner . . . vowed . . . to stop the sending of all supplies unto them. . . . But threatened folk live long. **1865** THORNBURY *Haunted London* ii Temple Bar was doomed to destruction by the City as early as 1790. . . . 'Threatened men live long.' . . . Temple Bar[1] still stands. [1] taken down in 1878.]

Threatened men eat bread, says the Spaniard.

1651 HERBERT 367.

Threatened than stricken, There are more men.

1640 HERBERT 329.

Threatens many that hurts any, He.

1553 *Precepts of Cato* (1560) Ee 3 He who doeth to one man an iniury, Dothe thretten to do the same to many. **1572** SIR HUGH PLATT *Flowers of Philosophy* (cited G. Harvey, *Marginalia* 101) He threatenith many That hurtith any. **1604** JONSON *Sejanus* II. i. 476 He threatens many, that hath iniur'd one. **1642** TORRIANO 19. **1732** FULLER no. 2372.

Three, *see* One's too few, t. too many.

Three acres and a cow.

[1885] **1894** SIR H. MAXWELL *Life of W. H. Smith* 274 The anxiety to secure support from the newly enfranchised labourers gave prominence to Mr. Jesse Collings's formula of 'three acres and a cow', which became the battle-cry of the Liberal party. **1902** DEAN HOLE *Then & Now* (ed. 7) xi An honest man who had worked long and well should have 'three acres and a cow'.

Three blue beans in a blue bladder.

a. **1591** GREENE *Orlando Furioso* player's part of Orlando 11. 135. **1640** *Wit's Recreations* no. 684 As there are three blue . . . There are three Universities. **1715** PRIOR *Alma* c. i, l. 29 They say . . . That, putting all his words together, 'Tis three blue beans in one blue bladder. **1804** ANNA SEWARD *Mem. of Darwin* 310 It is to the ear no whit more agreeable than 'Three blue . . .' **1827** MOORE *Diary* 12 Sept. Porson's Greek version τοεῖς κύανοι κύαμοι.

Three classes of clergy: Nimrods, ramrods, and fishing-rods.

1902–4 LEAN IV. 159. [i.e. men fond of hunting, shooting, and fishing.]

Three cranes in the Vintry, *see* Patience in adversity.

Three dear years will raise a baker's daughter to a portion.

1678 RAY 86 . . . 'Tis not the smalness of the bread, but the knavery of the baker.

Three failures and a fire make a Scotsman's fortune.

1896 CHEVIOT 369.

Three flails and cuckoo.

1917 BRIDGE 123 . . . A farmer who at the return of the cuckoo can keep three flails at work cannot want for capital or be otherwise than prosperous.

Three halfpence, Not worth.

1576 AELIAN tr. A. Fleming E 1 Skarse woorth three halfpence. **1617** J. SWETNAM *School of Defence* 173 Not . . . worth two-pence. **1672** WALKER 26.

Three helping one another, bear the burthen of six.

1640 HERBERT 323.

Three ills come from the north, a cold wind, a shrinking cloth, and a dissembling man. (*See also under* North.)

1614 JONSON *Barth. Fair* IV. iii *Pup.* Do my northern cloth zhrink i' the wetting, ha? **1659** HOWELL *Eng. Prov.* 1/1. **1682** N.O. tr. BOILEAU *Le Lutrin* III. 28 Recall your wonted worth, new frights forgetting; 'Tis Yorkshire cloth, you know, that shrinks i' th' wetting!

Three L's.

1867 ADM. W. H. SMYTH *Sailor's Word-bk.* 427 The three L's were formerly vaunted by seamen who despised the use of nautical astronomy; viz. lead, latitude, and look-out.

Three letters, A man of.

[PLAUTUS *Aulularia* II. iv. 46 *Homo trium literarum.* A man of three letters (i.e. 'fur', a thief).] **1888** J. E. T. ROGERS *Econ. Interp. Hist.* II. xxii The various settlers, . . . the aggregate of whom is implied by Juvenal in his word of three letters.

Three Moors to a Portuguese; three Portuguese to an Englishman.

1625 PURCHAS *Pilgrims* (1905–7) I. 35 Even the Indians (which yield commonly in martial, always in Neptunian affairs to the Moors) have a proverb, three Moors to a Portugal, three Portugals to an Englishman.

Three pence, If you make not much of | you'll ne'er be worth a groat.

1678 RAY 210.

Three R's.

[Toast said to have been first given by Alder-man Curtis, hero of Peter Pindar's *Fat Knight and Petition.*] **1908** E. M. SNEYD-KYNNERSLEY *H.M.I.* (1910) vi It was seldom that the examination . . . went beyond the three elementary subjects commonly known as the Three R's. (What philosopher . . . first found out that reading, writing, and arithmetic all began with R?)

Three removes are as bad as a fire.

1758 FRANKLIN in ARBER *E. Garner* v. 581

As *Poor* RICHARD *says, I never saw an oft re-moved tree, Nor yet an oft removed family, That throve so well, as those that settled be.* And again, *Three Removes are as bad as a Fire.* **1852** MRS. CARLYLE *Let.* 25 Sept. Three flittings, they say, is equal to a fire; but a 'thorough repair' is equal to three fires. **1929** *Times* 16 Feb. 10/1 There used to be a saying that three removals were equal to a fire. This applies to householders . . . the handling of their furniture apparently having always involved a serious amount of destruction.

Three sheets in the wind.

[= very drunk.] **1821** EGAN *Real Life* I. xviii. 385 Old Wax and Bristles is about three sheets in the wind. **1840** R. H. DANA *Two Years Bef. Mast* xx He talked a great deal about . . . steadiness, . . . but seldom went up to the town without coming down 'three sheets in the wind'.

Three sisters.

[The Fates or Parcae.] *c.* **1374** CHAUCER *Troylus* III. 733 O fatale sustrin! which, or eny clothe Me shapyn was, my destyne me sponne. **1402** LYDGATE *Compl. Bl. Knight* 489 Or I was born, my desteny was sponne By Parcas sustren, to slee me, if they come. *c.* **1449** PECOCK *Repr.* II. iv. 155 This opin-ioun, that iij. sistris (whiche ben spiritis) comen to the cradilis of infants, forto sette to the babe what schal bifalle to him. **1559** *Mirr. Mag.* (1563) B ij Whose fatall threde false fortune needes would reele, Ere it were twisted by the sustiers thre. **1595–6** SHAKS. *Mids. N.* V. 344 O, Sisters Three, Come, come to me. **1596–7** *Merch. V.* II. ii. 68 The young gentleman,—according to . . . the Sisters Three and such branches of learning, —is, indeed, deceased. **1597–8** *2 Hen. IV* II. iv. 212 Why then, let grievous, ghastly, gaping wounds Untwine the Sisters Three!

Three things are insatiable, priests, monks, and the sea.

c. **1560** WRIGHT, *Songs, &c.* Philip and Mary (Roxb. Cl.) 208 (A). **1607** H. ESTIENNE, *World of Wonders* tr. R.C. 48 *Three things are vnsatiable, Priests, Monks, and the Sea* . . . Howbeit I haue heard old folkes name these three, *Priests, women, and the sea.*

Three things are thrown away in a bowling-green—time, money, and oaths.

1628 EARLE *Microcosmographie* no. xxx A bowl-alley is the place where there are three things thrown away beside bowls, to wit, time, money, and curses, and the last ten to one. **1822** SCOTT *Nigel* xii The field . . . soon resounded with . . . 'Run, run—rub, rub—hold bias, you infernal trundling timber! thus making good the saying, that three things are thrown away in a bowling-green, namely, time, money, and oaths.

Three things cost dear: the caresses of a dog, the love of a mistress, and the invasion of a host.

1659 N. R. 105. **1707** MAPLETOFT 3 (Ital.). **1855** BOHN 530.

Three things drive a man out of his house—smoke, rain, and a scolding wife.

[Perhaps the original form of this commonly quoted proverb is this:—'Tria sunt enim quae non sinunt hominem in domo permanere: fumus, stillicidium, et mala uxor'; Innocens Papa, *De Contemptu Mundi*, i. 18. [Compiled] from Prov. x. 26, xix. 13, and xxvii. 15. Note by SKEAT *P. Pl.* (1886) II. 246.] *c.* 1386 CHAUCER *Mel.* 2276 Three thinges dryven a man out of his hous; that is to seyn, smoke, dropping of reyn, and wikked wyves. 1393 LANGLAND *P. Pl.* C. xx. 297–304 Ac thre thynges ther beeth · that doth a man to sterte Out of his owene hous · . . . a wikkede wif · . . . and reyne on hus bedde, . . . Ac when smoke and smorthre · smerteth hus syghte. 1576 GASCOIGNE *Drum Dooms.* Wks. (1910) II. 227 There are three thinges that suffer not a man to abyde in his owne house. Smooke, Rayne, and an evil wyfe. 1597–8 SHAKS. *1 Hen. IV* III. i. 158 O! he's as tedious As a tired horse, a railing wife; Worse than a smoky house.

Three things there be full hard to be known.

1417 *Reliq. Antiquae* (1841) I. 233 (A) There ben thre thinges full hard to be knowen which waye they woll drawe. The first is of a birde sitting upon a bough. The second is of a vessell in the see. And the thirde is the waye of a yonge man. 1509 BARCLAY *Ship of Fools* (1874) II. 7–8 There be thynges the Right harde to knowe, . . . whan a byrde doth fle Alonge in the ayre . . . The way of a Shyp in the se . . . the way of a serpent ouer a stone.

Three ways: There are | the church (universities), the sea, the court.

1620 SHELTON *Quix.* IV. xii (1908) II. 39 There is an old proverb in this our Spain, . . . 'The Church, the Sea, or the Court'. 1640 HERBERT 335 There are three ways, the Universities, the Sea, the Court.

Three women (and a goose) make a market.

1586 PETTIE *Guazzo's Civ. Conv.* 115 Doe you not know the Prouerbe that three women make a market. 1665 J. WILSON *Projectors* III. i. Wks. (1874) 249 If two women and a goose make a market, I see no reason why three may not make a council. 1666 TORRIANO 76. 15 Three geese, and three women, make up a market. 1678 RAY 59 *Three women and a goose make a market.* This is an Italian one, Tre donne & un occa fan un mercato. 1738 SWIFT (Dial. iii) 352 *Col.* Miss, did you never hear that three women and a goose are enough to make a market?

Three words . . . , At.

1616 DRAXE 10 At three words he is at the top of the house. 1659 HOWELL *Eng. Prov.* 15/1 In three words she is at the roof of the house.

Threefold, *see* Thick and t.

Thresh(ed), *see* Barn's full (When), you may t. before door; I do what I can . . . when he t. in his cloak.

Thresher take his flail, Let the | and the ship no more sail. (*Cf.* November take flail.)

1626 BRETON *Fantasticks* (Gros.) 10 (A) It is now November, and according to the old prouerbe, Let the thresher &c. 1661 M. STEVENSON *The Twelve Moneths*, Nov. 51 Now wheels the Proverb about, *Let the* Thresher take his Flayl, and the Ship no more Sayl; for the high winds, and the rough seas will try the Ribs of the Ship, and the hearts of the Saylors.

Thrice, *see* All things thrive at t.

Thrift and he are at fray.

1546 HEYWOOD I. xi. 35 How be it whan thrift and you fell fyrst at a fray, You played the man for ye made thrift ren away. 1639 CLARKE 261.

Thrift goes by the profit of a yeld[1] hen, Your.

1721 KELLY 378 . . . A taunt upon them who boast of what they have wrought. 1862 HISLOP 349 Your thrift's as gude as the profit o' a yeld hen. [[1] barren.]

Thrift is a great revenue.

[CICERO *Paradoxa* 6. 3. 49 *Non intelligunt homines quam magnum vectigal sit parsimonia.* Men do not realize how great a revenue thrift is.] 1659 HOWELL *Fr.–Eng.* 15 Parsimony is the best revenue. 1855 BOHN 530. 1930 *Times* 10 Oct. 13/5 Thrift which is not only a great virtue but also 'a great revenue', as Tacitus told us long ago when he wrote *magnum vectigal est parsimonia.*

Thrift is in the town, When | you are in the field.

1546 HEYWOOD II. ix. 75 Whan thrift is in the towne, ye be in the féelde. But contrary, you made that sence to sowne, Whan thrift was in the féelde, ye were in the towne. 1670 RAY 196 When thrift's in the field, he's in town.

Thrift is the philosopher's stone.

1732 FULLER no. 5040.

Thrift of you, and the wool of a dog, would make a good web, The. (*Cf.* Wit of you, &c.)

1721 KELLY 331 . . . Spoken in jest to them that pretend to be thrifty.

Thrift, *see also* Inch of his will for span of his t. (He will not give).

Thrive as New College students, who are golden Scholars, silver Bachelors, and leaden Masters, They.

1659 HOWELL *Eng. Prov.* 20/2.

Thrive in all haste, You would.

1546 HEYWOOD II. ix. 78 Now thrifte is gone, now would ye thryue in all haste.

Thrive, He that will | must ask leave of his wife.

c. **1470** *Songs & Carols* (Percy Soc. No. 73) 87 (A) Fore he that cast hym for to thryve, he must ask off his wiffe leve. **1550** HEYWOOD I. xi. 28. **1641** FERGUSSON 12 A man cannot thrive except his wife let him. **1670** RAY 117 A man must ask his wife leave to thrive. **1858** R. S. SURTEES *Ask Mamma* x His wife, by whose permission men thrive, was a capital manager.

Thrive, He who would wish to | must let spiders run alive.

1867 *N. & Q.* 3rd Ser. XI. 32 The proverb so often used in Kent: 'He who would wish to thrive Must let spiders run alive.'

Thrive, He that will | must rise at five; he that hath thriven may lie till seven.

c. **1590** G. HARVEY *Marginalia* (1913) 102 (A). **1639** CLARKE 93. **1766** *Goody Two-Shoes* i. **1807** SCOTT *Let. to Southey* Nov. in LOCKHART *Life* xvi The only difference . . . is on the principle contained in the old proverb: *He that would thrive—must rise by five—He that has thriven—may lye till seven.*

Thrives he whom God loves, Well.

? **1597** *How the Goode Wif, &c.* 10 in HAZL. *Early Pop. Poet.* I. 180 Wele thryuethe that God loueth, my dere childe.

Thrive(s), *see also* All things t. at thrice; First t. then wive; Good man t. (If a), all t. with him; Leave to t. for throng (You cannot get); Office (He hath a good), he must t.; Plough would t. (He that by the); Wise with whom all things t. (Seemeth); Wive and t. in a year (Hard to).

Throat(s), *see* Belly thinks t. is cut; Cut one's own t.; Small house has wide t.; Tickle my t. with feather; Wash their t. before they washed their eyes; Whet a knife for own t.

Throng, *see* Leave to thrive for t. (You cannot get).

Throw (Send) good money after bad, To.

1884 J. PAYN *Canon's Ward* xxv If they would confess it, and forget it, and start free, instead of sending their good money after bad—how much happier would be this world of ours! **1931** *Times* 15 Jul. 14/3 It would be throwing good money after bad if France came to the rescue without very definite guarantees for the preservation of peace.

Throw him into the Nile and he will come up with a fish in his mouth.

1853 TRENCH i. 20 Of a man whose good luck seems never to forsake him, . . . the Arabs say: *Throw him into the Nile, and he will come up with a fish in his mouth.*

Throw no gift again at the giver's head.

1546 HEYWOOD I. xi. 30 Throw no gyft agayne at the geuers head, For better is halfe a lofe than no bread.

Throw of the dice, The best | is to throw them away.

a. **1591** HY. SMITH *Serm.* (1866) II. 242 If thou dost not only venture thy money, but hazard thy soul; then the best cast at dice is, to cast them quite away.

Throw up one's (the) cards, To.

[= to abandon a course.] **1639** FULLER *Holy War* II. xviii (1840) 73 Others, being crossed by the world by some misfortune, sought to cross the world again in renouncing of it. These, like furious gamesters, threw up their cards, not out of dislike of gaming but of their game. *a.* **1721** PRIOR *Dial. of Dead* (1907) 256 What think you of . . . Regulus, Cato, and Brutus? . . . Whenever the game did not go well they always threw up the cards.

Throw up the sponge, To.

[= to confess oneself beaten.] **1888** 'R. BOLDREWOOD' *Robbery under Arms* xxxi We must stand up to our fight now, or throw up the sponge. **1909** ALEX. MACLAREN *Philippians* 366 If ever you are tempted to say . . . 'I am beaten and I throw up the sponge', remember Paul's wise exhortation.

Throw, *see also* Dust in man's eyes (To t.); House out of windows (To t.); Thatched his house (When I have), he would t. me down.

Throw, To, *see also under significant words following.*

Thrown would ever wrestle, He that is.

1640 HERBERT 354.

Thrush when he pollutes the bough sows for himself the seeds of woe, The.

[L. *Turdus ipse sibi malum cacat.* The thrush voids evil for itself.] **1612–15** BP. HALL *Contempl.* IX. viii (1825) I. 248 The Shechemites . . . raised [Abimelech] unjustly to the throne, they are the first that feel the weight of his sceptre. The foolish bird limes herself with that which grew from her own excretion. **1635** SWAN *Spec. Mundi* (1665) 246 The berries . . . voided out again in her excrements, grow into a bush, the bush bringeth forth berries, and of the berries the fowler maketh birdlime, wherewith after he taketh the thrush: and thus, Turdus sibi cacat malum.

Thumb, To be under (a person's .

[= At the disposal of, subservient to.] **1754** RICHARDSON *Grandison* IV. xxix. 181 She . . .

is obliged to be silent. I have her under my thumb. 1809 MALKIN *Gil Blas* VII. xiii, par. 6 Authors . . . are under the thumb of booksellers and players. 1889 JESSOPP *Coming of Friars* ii. 65 The lord was a petty king, having his subjects very much under his thumb.

Thumb under one's belt, To have a man's.

1641 FERGUSSON 98 Thy thumb is under my belt.

Thumb(s), *see also* Bite one's t.; Bite the t. at; Biteth the mare by the t.; Cow's t.; Fingers are all t. (His); Hit one over t.; Miller hath golden t.; Sit on your t.; Taunt one tit over t.

Thunder lasted, While the | two bad men were friends.

1908 A. C. BENSON *At Large* iii. 42 'While the thunder lasted', says the old Indian proverb, 'two bad men were friends.' That means that a common danger will sometimes draw even malevolent people together.

Thunder, Dunder (*noun*), *see also* Black as t.; D. do gally the beans; Dying duck in t.; Escaped the t. and fell into lightning; Noise is so great, cannot hear God t.; Winter t. summer hunger; Winter's t. . . . never boded good; Winter's t. makes summer's wonder.

Thunderbolt hath but his clap, The.

1579 LYLY *Euphues* Wks. (Bond) I. 45. 1616 DRAXE 217. 1639 CLARKE 166. 1670 RAY 148. 1732 FULLER no. 4793.

Thunderbolt, *see also* Pryeth into every cloud (He that).

Thunders, When it | the thief becomes honest.

1640 HERBERT 349.

Thunders (*verb*), *see also* Lightens and t. (If it) beware of a tree.

Thursday at three, On | look out, and you'll see what Friday will be.

1883 ROPER 23. 1893 INWARDS 42.

Thursday come, and the week is gone.

1640 HERBERT 345.

Thwitten[1] a mill-post to a pudding-prick, He hath.

1528 MORE *Dialog. concernynge Heresyes* in Wks. (1557) Now forsoth . . . , here was a gret post wel thwyted to a pudding pricke. 1573 G. HARVEY *Letter-bk.* (Camden Soc.) 26 Meaning belike to . . . make a great monsterus milpost of his litle pudding prick. 1611 COTGRAVE s.v. 'Arbre' (We say of one that hath squandered away great wealth) hee hath

thwitten a mill-post to a pudding pricke. 1659 HOWELL *Eng. Prov.* I He hath brought a mill-post to a pudding-prick. [[1] whittled.]

Thyme, *see* Rue and t. grow in one garden; Rue in t. a maiden's posie.

Thynne, *see* Horner; Portman.

Thyrsus-bearers, Many are the | but the bacchants are few.

[Gk. Πολλοί τοι ναρθηκοφόροι, παῦροι δέ τε βάκχοι.] 1853 TRENCH vi. 144 *The thyrsus-bearers are many, but the bacchants few*; many assume the outward tokens of inspiration, whirling the thyrsus[1] aloft; but those whom the god indeed fills with his spirit are few. . . . And there is the classical Roman proverb: Non omnes qui habent citharam, sunt citharoedi. 1892 SIR H. MAXWELL *Meridiana* 244 'Many are the thyrsus-bearers, but few are the mystics'. There are plenty who take books in their hands, but few who care to commune with the writer. [[1] a staff which was the attribute of Bacchus.]

Tib, *see* Struck at T. down fell Tom.

Tib's (Tibb's) Eve.

[= never. See suggestions as to origin in *N. & Q.* 2nd Ser. XI. 269 and possibly cf. 1586 CAMDEN *Britannia* (1616) *Rutlandshire* 419 Tibbia, minorum gentium Diua, quasi Diana ab aucupibus, . . . colebatur.] 1785 GROSE *Dict. Vulg. T.* s.v. Saint Tibb's evening, the evening of the last day, or day of judgement; he will pay you on St. Tibb's eve (*Irish*). 1837 W. H. MAXWELL *Bivouac* III. iii He would return and claim her hand on 'Tib's eve'—an Irish festival which is stated to occur 'neither before nor after Christmas'. 1882 W. P. IAGO *Dialect of Cornwall* 323 St. Tibb's Eve, neither before nor after Christmas, i.e. at no time. 'I'll do et St. Tibb's Eve.'

Tickle it with a hoe and it will laugh into a harvest.

1907 SIR W. F. BUTLER *From Naboth's V.* 210 It used to be said of the Egyptian Delta that if you tickled it with a hoe it would laugh into a harvest.

Tickle my throat with a feather, and make a fool of my stomach.

1678 RAY 210.

Tickle(s), *see also* Nothing t. that pinches not.

Tide in the affairs of men, There is a | which, taken at the flood, leads on to fortune.

1599–1600 SHAKS. *Jul. Caes.* IV. iii. 217. 1830 MARRYAT *King's Own* xxiii 'There is a tide in the affairs of men', and it was on this decision . . . that depended the future misery or welfare of M'Elvina. 1868 H. SMART *Breezie Lang.* iv It is no use meditating on when 'the tide in your affairs' took place. . . . You did not take it at the turn.

Tide keeps its course, The.

1659 HOWELL *Eng. Prov.* 10/1.

Tide never goes out so far but it always comes in again, The.

1864 *N. & Q.* 3rd Ser. VI. 494 Cornish Proverbs.

Tide stayeth (tarrieth) for no man, The. (*Cf.* Time and tide tarry, &c.)

c. **1440** LYDGATE *Fall of Princes* III, l. 2801 The tid abit nat for no maner man, Nor stynt his cours for no creature. **1546** HEYWOOD I. 'ii. 6 The tide tarieth no man. *a.* **1553** UDALL *Royster D.* I. ii (Arb.) 13 Farewell . . . the tyme away dothe waste And the tide they say, tarieth for no man. **1580** LYLY *Euph. & his Eng.* (Arb.) 427 *Euphues* knowing the tyde would tarrye for no man, . . . determined sodeinly to departe. **1592-3** SHAKS. *Com. Err.* IV. i. 46 Both wind and tide stays for this gentleman. **1594-5** *Two Gent.* II. iii. 40 *Pant.* Away, ass! you'll lose the tide if you tarry any longer. **1614** CAMDEN 313.

Tide(s), *see also* Ebb will fetch off what t. brings; Time and t. tarry no man; Work double t.

Tie can oblige the perfidious, No.

1651 HERBERT 366.

Tie it well, and let it go.

1640 HERBERT 347.

Tied a knot with his tongue that he cannot untie with his teeth, He hath.

1580 LYLY *Euphues & his Eng.* (Arb.) 468 That before this good company, we might knit that knot with our tongues, that we shall neuer vndoe with our teeth. **1594** Id. *Moth. Bomb.* III. iii. Wks. (1902) III. 199 Accius tongue shall tie all Memphio's land to Silena's dowry, let his father's teeth undo them if he can. **1625** HOWELL *Lett.* 5 Feb. (1903) I. 249 Marriage . . . may make you or mar you. . . . The tongue useth to tie so hard a knot that the teeth can never untie. **1670** RAY 183. **1738** SWIFT (Dial. i) 343 *Ld. S.* Is . . . Ned Rattle married? *Never.* Yes, . . .; he has tied a knot with his tongue that he can never untie with his teeth. **1831** SCOTT *Diary* 6, 7, 8 May in *Life* X. 58 I cannot conceive that I should have tied a knot with my tongue which my teeth cannot untie. We shall see.

Tied by the tooth.

1624 BURTON *Anat. Mel.* III. i. II. i. 342 Friends were tied to thee [the rich man] by the teeth. **1917** BRIDGE 124 . . . Sheep and cattle will not break through fences or try to wander if the pasture in which they are grazing is very good. They are '*tied by the tooth*'.

Tied to the sour apple-tree, To be.

1670 RAY 193 . . . *i.e.* To be married to an ill husband.

Tiger, *see* Rides a t. afraid to dismount.

Timber, *see* Knotty t.

Time and art, With | the leaf of the mulberry-tree becomes satin.

1659 HOWELL *Eng. Prov., New Sayings,* 2 Cent. 3/2 With Time, and Art, the Mulberry leafs grow to be sattin. **1865** ABP. TRENCH *Poems*; *Provs., Turk. & Pers.* xxi. 303 What will not time and toil?—by these a worm Will into silk a mulberry leaf transform.

Time and I against any two.

1712 ARBUTHNOT *John Bull* [1727] *Postscript.* Wks. (1892) 290 Chap. xvi Commentary upon the Spanish proverb, 'time and I against any two'.

Time, He that hath | and looks for time, loseth time.

1573 SANDFORD (1576) 208 He that hath tyme, let him not loke for tyme. **1599** MINSHEU (1623) Tt 2[v]. **1636** CAMDEN 297.

Time and straw make medlars ripe.

1578 FLORIO *First Fruites* f. 14 With time and with straw, Medlers are made ripe. **1670** RAY 149.

Time and tide tarry (stay, wait for) no man. (*Cf.* Tide stayeth, &c.)

c. **1386** CHAUCER *Cant. T.* (Skeat) E 118 (A) For thogh we slepe or wake, or rome or ryde, Ay fleeth the tyme, it nil no man abyde. **1592** GREENE *Disput.* 22 Tyde nor time tarrieth no man. **1639** CLARKE 233. **1655** FULLER *Ch. Hist.* IV. iii (1868) I. 590 The press (like time and tide) staying for no man, I have not been so happy seasonably to receive it. **1816** SCOTT *Antiq.* i 'Time and tide tarry for no man; and so, . . . we'll have a snack here at the Hawes.' **1852** E. FITZGERALD *Polonius* 89 'Time and tide wait for no man', still to be seen on the Temple sundial.

Time (Occasion) by the forelock, Take | (for she is bald behind).

[The Greek God Καιρός, *Occasio,* used to be represented with a full forelock. ERASM. *Ad. Fronte capillata, post hæc occasio calva.*] **1578** PETTIE *Petite Pall.* (Gollancz) II. 185 Let not slip occasion, for it is bald behind, it cannot be pulled back again by the hair. **1587** MARLOWE *2 Tamburlaine* V. iii The nature of these proud rebelling jades Will take occasion by the slenderest hair. **1591** GREENE *Farewell to Folly* Wks. (Gros.) IX. 311 Take time now by the forehead, she is bald behinde. **1594** SPENSER *Amoretti* lxx The ioyous time will not be staid, Unlesse she doe him by the forelock take. **1602-3** SHAKS. *All's Well* V. iii. 39 Let's take the instant by the foremost top. **1604-5** *Othello* III. i. 52 To take the saf'st occasion by the front To bring you in again. **1606** BRYSKETT *Civ. Life* 9 If he may once lay hold upon that locke, which, men say, Occasion hath growing on her forehead, being bald behind. **1611** CHAPMAN *May Day* Occasion is bald, take her by the forelock. **1625** BACON *Ess., Delays* (Arb.) 525 Occasion . . . turneth a Bald Noddle, after she hath presented her locks in Front, and no hold taken. **1633** SHIRLEY *Witty Fair One* IV. iii (*Song*) Enforce time itself to stay, And by the forelock hold him fast, Lest occasion slip away. **1824** SCOTT *St. Ronan's* xxvi Time was—time is—and, if I catch it not by the forelock as it passes, time will be no more. **1882** BLACKMORE *Christowell* xlvii He had taken time by the forelock now, so far as to seize and hide the cash-box, before the intrusion of lawyers. **1909** ALEX. MACLAREN *Expos., Ephesians* v. 336 Occasion is bald behind, and is to be grasped by the forelock.

Time devours all things.

[OVID *Metam.* xv. 234 *Tempus edax rerum.* Time, the devourer of all things.] **1855** BOHN 531.

Time discloses (reveals) all things.

[ERASM. *Ad. Tempus omnia revelat.*] **1539** TAVERNER 37 *Tempus omnia reuelat.* Tyme dyscloseth all thynges. Nothinge is couered, but shalbe reueld, nothynge is hyd, that shal not be knowen, sayeth Christe. **1616** DRAXE 205 Time reuealeth all things.

'Time enough' lost the ducks.

1910 P. W. JOYCE *Eng. as we Speak* 114 'Time enough lost the ducks'. The ducks should have been secured at once, as it was known that a fox was prowling about.

Time flies.

[L. *Tempus fugit.*] c. **1386** CHAUCER *Clerk's T.* E[1] 118 For though we slepe or wake, or rome, or ryde, Ay fleeth the tyme, it nil no man abyde. **1807** CRABBE *Sir Eust. Grey* 44 Some twenty years, I think, are gone; (Time flies, I know not how, away). **1842** MARRYAT *Perc. K.* xx How time flies away . . . You have been afloat nearly three years.

Time flieth away without delay.

1639 CLARKE 308. **1732** FULLER no. 6090.

Time for all things (everything), There is a.

[BIBLE, VULGATE *Eccles.* iii. 1 *Omnia tempus habent.* **1382** WYCLIF *Eccles.* iii. 1 Alle thingis han tyme.] c. **1386** CHAUCER *Clk. of Oxf. T.* Prol. 6 But Salomon seith 'every thyng hath tyme' . . . It is no time for to studien heere. a. **1450** *Ratis Raving* III. 3497 (E.E.T.S. 100) Al thing has tyme wald men tak heid. **1592–3** SHAKS. *Com. Err.* II. ii. 67 Well, sir, learn to jest in good time: there's a time for all things. **1594** LYLY *Moth. Bomb.* v. iii. Wks. (1902) III. 217 Boy, no more words! theres a time for al things. **1671** MILTON *P.R.* iii. 183 And time there is for all things, Truth hath said. **1832** MACAULAY *Ess., Mirabeau* Wks. V. 620 The highest glory of the statesman is to construct. But there is a time for everything, — a time to set up, and a time to pull down.

Time for honest folks to be a-bed, It is.

1738 SWIFT (Dial. iii) 352 *Lady A.* I'm sure 'tis time for honest folks to be a-bed.

Time, He that has most | has none to lose.

1732 FULLER no. 2141.

Time, He that hath | hath life.

1573 SANDFORD (1576) H 2[v]. **1578** FLORIO *First Fruites* f. 28. **1629** *Book of Meery Riddles* Prov. 14.

Time hath turned white sugar to white salt.

1546 HEYWOOD I. ii. 5 Whan time hath tournd white surger to white salte, Than suche folke see, soft fire maketh sweete malte. **1580** LYLY *Euph. & his Eng.* (Arb.) 477 Until time might turne white salt into fine sugar.

Time is a file that wears and makes no noise.

1666 TORRIANO 282. 41 Time is a still file. **1855** BOHN 531.

Time is money.

[THEOPHR. in *D. Laert.* 5. 2. 10. 40: πολυτελὲς ἀνάλωμα εἶναι τὸν χρόνον.] **1572** T. WILSON *A Discourse upon Usury* (1925) 228 They saye tyme is precious. **1607–12** BACON *Essays* 'Despatch' Time is the measure of business, as money is of wares. **1748** BENJ. FRANKLIN *Adv. to Young Tradesman* in Wks. (1793) 2. 55 Remember that time is money. **1840** LYTTON *Money* III. vi. *Gloss.* You don't come often to the club, Stout? *Stout* No; time is money. **1859** SMILES *Self-Help* ix Men of business are accustomed to quote the maxim that Time is money. **1887** LD. AVEBURY *Pleas. of Life* I. vi Time is often said to be money, but it is more—it is life.

Time is the father of truth.

1573 SANDFORD H 4[v] Time is the father of truth. **1578** FLORIO *First Fruites* f. 32. **1629** *Book of Meery Riddles* Prov. 47.

Time is the rider that breaks youth.

1640 HERBERT 346. **1666** TORRIANO 282. 39 Time is the coult-breaker, which tames youth.

Time is tickle.[1]

1546 HEYWOOD I. iii. 7. **1616** DRAXE 206 Time is ticklish. [[1] uncertain.]

Time is, time was, and time is past.

1589 GREENE *Friar Bacon* xi. 55–76 (Ward) 94–5 *The Brazen Head.* Time is . . . Time was . . . Time is past. a. **1603** BACON *Apologie* in Spedding (1868) III. 152 I must speak to you as Friar Bacon's head spake, . . . *Time is*, and then *Time was*, and *Time would never be*: for certainly (said I) it is now far too late. **1614** SIR T. OVERBURY *Characters* Wks. (1890) 99 *A Bawde.* The burden of her song is like that of *Frier Bacons* head; time is, time was, and time is past. **1930** *Times* 7 Nov. 15/5 Cannot British statesmanship rise to the height of this great occasion? 'Time is.' I need not finish the quotation.

Time like the present, No.

1771 SMOLLETT *Humph. Clink.* 28 Sept. Wks.

(1871) 564 'There is no time like the present time', cried Mr. Bramble. **1790** TRUSLER *Prov. Exempl.* 152 *No time like the present,* a thousand unforeseen circumstances may interrupt you at a future time. **1888** MRS. OLIPHANT *Second Son* iv 'There's no time like the present', answered Roger.

Time lost (past) cannot be recalled (won again).

c. **1374** CHAUCER *Troylus* IV. 1283 For time y-lost may not recoverèd be. **1546** HEYWOOD II. i. 42 And that tyme loste, again we can not wyn. **1579** GASCOIGNE *Hemates* Wks. (1910) II. 476 Time past can not be called again. **1580** LYLY *Euph. & his Eng.* (Arb.) 297 And time lost [past] may well be repented, but neuer recalled. **1621** BURTON *Anat. Mel.* III. ii. VI. v (1651) 577 *Volat irrevocabile tempus,* time past cannot be recal'd. **1748** FRANKLIN Jan. Lost time is never found again.

Time stays not the fool's leisure.

1659 N.R. 112. **1855** BOHN 531.

Time (and thinking) tames the strongest grief.

[TERENCE *Heaut.* 3. 1. 13. ERASM. *Ad. Dies adimit ægritudinem.*] *c.* **1374** CHAUCER *Troylus* v. 350 As tyme hem hurt, a tyme doth hem cure. **1539** TAVERNER 38 *Dies adimit ægritudinem.* Tyme taketh awaye greuaunce. There is no displeasure so greate, . . . no sorow so immoderat, but tyme aswageth it. **1594–5** SHAKS. *Two Gent.* III. ii. 14 A little time, my lord, will kill that grief. **1721** KELLY 333 Time and thought tames the strongest grief. **1832** HENDERSON 55. **1887** BLACKMORE *Springhaven* xxxii Sad tidings, which would make the rest of her life flow on in shadow. So . . . she thought, forgetful . . . that time and the tide of years submerge the loftiest youthful sorrow.

Time to cock your hay and corn, It is | when the old donkey blows his horn.

1836 *Farmer's Mag.* IV. 447 in *N. & Q.* (1861) 2nd Ser. XII. 304 ''Tis time to cock your hay and corn When the old donkey blows his horn.' **1849** HALLIWELL *Pop. Rhymes* 157 It is time to cock your hay and corn, When the old donkey blows his horn. The braying of the ass is said to be an indication of rain or hail.

Time to set in, It is | when the oven comes to the dough.

1678 RAY 186 . . . *i.e.* Time to marry when the maid wooes the man.

Time to speak and a time to be silent, There is a.

[BIBLE *Eccles.* iii. 7 A time to keep silence, and a time to speak.] **1485** CAXTON *Charles the Grete* (E.E.T.S.) 56 The comyn prouerbe —sayth that there is a tyme of spekyng and tyme of beyng stylle. **1616** DRAXE 190 There is a time to speake, and a time to holde ones

peace. **1670** RAY 103 *Amyclas silentium perdidit.* . . . The Amycleans . . . disquieted with vain reports of the enemies coming, made a law that no man should bring . . . such news. . . . When the enemies did come indeed, they were surprised and taken. There is a time to speak as well as to be silent.

Time to wink as well as to see, There is a.

a. **1699** L'ESTRANGE *Aesop's Fab.* cxvii There's a Time to Sleep (says the Dog) and a Time to Wake. **1721** KELLY 339 *There's a time to glye,[1] and a time to look even.* There is a time when a man must overlook things. **1732** FULLER no. 4885. [[1] look a-squint.]

Time to yoke, It is | when the cart comes to the caples.

1670 RAY 48 It's time to yoke when the cart comes to the caples, *i.e.* horses. *Chesh.* That is, It's time to marry when the woman wooes the man.

Time tries all (things).

1553 *Republica* Prol. (A) Yet tyme trieth all. **1599** PORTER *Angry Wom. Abingd.* IV. iii (Merm.) 175 Time and truth tries all. **1599–1600** SHAKS. *A.Y.L.* IV. i. 211 Time is the old justice that examines all such offenders, and let time try. **1610–11** *Wint. T.* IV. i, Prol. 1 Time, I, that please some, try all. *a.* **1625** J. FLETCHER *Mons. Thomas* IV. ii *Seb.* Time tries all then. **1639** CLARKE 308 Time trieth all things.

Time tries (trieth) truth.

1546 HEYWOOD II. v. 59 Let tyme trie. Tyme tryeth trouth in euery doubt. **1589** PUTTENHAM (Arb.) 185 Time tried his truth, his travails and his trust. **1641** FERGUSSON 94.

Time undermines us.

1640 HERBERT 359.

Time when time cometh, Take | lest time steal away.

1546 HEYWOOD I. iii. 6. *a.* **1585** MONTGOMERIE *Cherrie & Slae* xxxvi (1821) 21 Tak time in time, or time be tint,[1] For tyme will not remaine. [[1] lost.]

Time while time is, Take | for time will away.

a. **1529** SKELTON *Wks.* (Dyce) I. 137 (A) Take tyme when tyme is, for tyme is ay mutable. **1670** RAY 149.

Time works wonders.

1845 D. W. JERROLD *Time Works Wonders* (Title of play). **1872** G. J. WHYTE-MELVILLE *Satanella* xxiv 'I want you to like me'. . . . 'They say time works wonders, . . . and I feel I shall.'

Time(s), *see also* **Best use of their t.** (Those that make) have none to spare; **Busiest men** have most t.; **Crutch of t.** . . . **club of Hercules; Done at any t.** will be done no t.;

Everything hath its t.; Gains t. gains all things; God will send t.; Good t. coming; Happiness takes no account of t.; Health (Chief box of) is t.; Lose your t. cannot get gain; Nature, t. . . . great physicians; Other t. other manners; Patience, t. and money; Truth is daughter of T.

Timely blossom, timely ripe.

1639 CLARKE 171 (with 'beare' for ripe'). 1670 RAY 149. 1732 FULLER no. 5057.

Tine[1] cat, tine game.

1721 KELLY 325 . . . An allusion to a play called *Cat i' the Hole*. . . . Spoken when men at law have lost their principal evidence. [[1] lose.]

Tine heart, tine all.

1721 KELLY 142 *Have you geer, have you none, tine heart and all is gone.* Spoken to dissuade people from desponding in any case. 1778 A. ROSS *Helenore* [ed. 2] 83 We manna[1] weary at thir rugged braes; Tyne heart, tyne a'. 1818 SCOTT *Ht. Midl.* 1 'When ye deal wi' thae folk, it's tyne heart tyne a'.' [[1] must not.]

Tine needle, tine darg[1] (dark[1]).

1721 KELLY 325 *Tine needle, tine dark.* Spoken to young girls, when they lose their needle. [[1] day's work.]

Tine[1] the tuppen[n]y belt for the twapenny[2] whang,[3] You.

1641 FERGUSSON 78 Monie tynes the halfe marke whinger, for the halfe pinnie whang. 1721 KELLY 360 . . . People lose often things of a great value, for not being at a small expense. [[1] lose. [2] one-sixth of a penny. [3] thong.]

Tine thimble, tine thrift.

1862 HISLOP 306.

Tinker(s), *see* Banbury t.; Cobblers and t. best ale-drinkers.

Tinsel (= loss), *see* Winning (Your) is not in my t.

Tint[1] a cow, He never | that grat[2] for a needle.

1641 FERGUSSON 44 He tint never a cow, that grate for a needle. 1721 KELLY 149 . . . It is a token that a man had never a great loss, who is immoderately griev'd for a small one. [[1] lost. [2] wept.]

Tint (Lost) thing, For a | care not.

1641 FERGUSSON 32. 1678 RAY 366.

Tip the cow's horn with silver, To.

1917 BRIDGE 144 When a butcher pays for the cow he has bought, he expects a 'luckpenny' to be returned to him which . . . is usually a shilling and is technically called '*tipping the cow's horn with silver*'.

Tit for tat.

[App. a variation of *tip for tap* = one stroke in return for another; retaliation.] 1546 HEYWOOD II. iv. 52. 1556 J. HEYWOOD *Spider & F.* xxxvii. 26 That is tit for tat in this altricacion. 1710 ADDISON *Tatler* No. 229, par. 3 I was threatened to be answered Weekly Tit for Tat. 1881 SAINTSBURY *Dryden* iv. 80 A fair literary tit-for-tat in return for the *Rehearsal*.

Tit, *see also* Little t. all tail; Taunt one t. over thumb.

Tithe and be rich.

1651 HERBERT 370.

Tither, *see* Good t. good thriver.

Tittle-tattle, give the goose more hay.

1659 HOWELL *Eng. Prov.* 11/1. 1678 RAY 82 (*Joculatory*). 1732 FULLER no. 5058.

Tiuidal [? = Teesdale].

1583 MELBANCKE *Philot.* Aa 2 It is a prouerbe in Englande that the men of Tiuidal borderers on y[e] English midle marches, haue likers, lemmons, and lyerbies.

Toad under a harrow, Like a.

c. 1380 WYCLIF *Sel. Engl. Wks.* ii. 280 (A) Christene men may seye, as the poete seith in proverbe, the frogge seide to the harwe, cursid be so many lordis. 1732 FULLER no. 3354 Many masters, quoth the toad to the harrow, when every tine turned her over. 1802–12 BENTHAM *Rationale of Evidence* (1827) I. 385 *Note*, Kept like toads under a harrow. 1859 SMILES *Self-Help* iv While in this employment he endured much hardship —living, as he used to say, 'like a toad under a harrow'. 1897 M. A. S. HUME *Sir W. Ralegh* 10 The country gentry had lived like toads under a harrow for the last three reigns.

Toad, *see also* Frog (T.) said to the harrow, Cursed be so many lords; Purse is made of a t.'s skin; Swell like a t.

Toast, *see* Second side bread less time to t.

Toasted cheese hath no master.

1678 RAY 82.

Tobacco-hic, if a man be well, it will make him sick; tobacco-hic, will make a man well if he be sick.

1678 RAY 296.

Tocherless[1] dame sits long at hame, A.

1721 KELLY 32 . . . A maid without a portion will be long unmarried. [[1] portionless.]

Tochers,[1] The greatest | make not the greatest testaments.[2]

1721 KELLY 333. [[1] portion, dowry. [2] will.]

Tochers, *see also* Maidens' t. are aye less than called.

Tod[1] gets to the wood, When the | he cares not who keek[2] in his tail.

1721 KELLY 345 ... Spoken when a villain has so cleanly escap'd that he cares not who look after him. [[1] fox. [2] peep.]

Tod[1] keeps his own hole clean, The.

1721 KELLY 320 ... Apply'd to batchelors who keep women servants, whom they ought not to meddle with. 1823 SCOTT *Peveril* iv Fear ye naething frae Christie; tods keep their ain holes clean. [[1] fox.]

Tod never sped better than when he went his own errand, The.

1721 KELLY 311 ... Every man is most zealous for his own interest; spoken to advise a man to go about such a business himself.

Tod's bairns (whelps) are ill to tame, The.

1721 KELLY 329 ... Apply'd to them who are descended of an ill parentage, or curs'd with a bad education: such are hard to be made good or virtuous.

Tod's bairns, *see also* Breed of the t.'s b., if one good all good.

Tod's whelp, Like the | aye the aulder the waur.

1823 J. GALT *Entail* iv Nae doubt, Cornie, the world's like the tod's whelp, aye the aulder the waur.

Tod(s), *see also* Hare (T.) or bracken bush; Proud t. that will not scrape own hole; Serve the t. (As long as you) bear up his tail.

To-day a man, to-morrow a mouse.

1666 TORRIANO 59. 1670 RAY 77. 1732 FULLER no. 5152.

To-day a man, to-morrow none.

a. 1500 R. Hill's *Commonpl. Bk.* (E.E.T.S.) 129 (A) This dai a man, to-morow non. 1539 TAVERNER 34 Nothynge is more frayle ... than y[e] lyfe of man. If ye requyre the english prouerbe it is this. To day a man to morrow none.

To-day is the scholar of yesterday.

[PUB. SYRUS 124 *Discipulus est prioris posterior dies.*] 1732 FULLER no. 5153 To-Day is Yesterday's Pupil. 1853 TRENCH v. 122 The Latin proverb, *To-day is the scholar of yesterday*.... Let our 'to-day' learn of our 'yesterday'.... There is a teaching in our blunders and our errors ... which is not anywhere else to be obtained. 1909 *Times* 7 Jan. The present has always to be read in the light of the past. To-day is what yesterday made it.

To-day, One | is worth two to-morrows.

1660 W. SECKER *Nonsuch Prof.* II (1891) 292 Many think not of living any holier, till they can live no longer: but one to-day is worth two to-morrows.

To-day will not, If | to-morrow may.

1591 W. STEPNEY *Span. Schoolmaster* L 3[v] That which is not done to day may be done to morrow. 1732 FULLER no. 2725.

To-day, *see also* I t., you to-morrow.

Toes, *see* Many haws ... many cold toes.

Toil of a pleasure, I will not make a | (quoth the good man when he buried his wife).

1603 N. BRETON *Dial. of Pitte* in Wks. (Gros.) II j7 I doo not loue so to make a toyle of a pleasure. 1721 KELLY 192 ... A man going under his wife's head to the grave, was bid go faster, because the way was long, and the day short; [he] answered, *I will not make a toil of a pleasure.*

Toil so for trash, If you | what would you do for treasure?

1639 CLARKE 194.

Toiling dog comes halting home, A.

1721 KELLY 27. 1732 FULLER no. 441.

Toils like a dog in a wheel, He | who roasts meat for other people's eating.

1614 SIR T. OVERBURY *Newes* Wks. (1890) 200 A covetous man is like a dog in a wheele, that toiles to roast meat for other mens eating. 1748 RICHARDSON *Clarissa H.* (1785) IV. 120 What is a covetous man to be likened to so fitly, as *to a dog in a wheel, which roasts meat for others?* 1813 RAY 72.

Told you so, I.

1604–5 SHAKS. *Meas. for Meas.* II. i. 262 If you live to see this come to pass, say, Pompey told you so. 1827–48 HARE *Gues. at Truth* If a misfortune which a man has prognosticated, befalls his friend, the monitor ... will often exclaim ... *Didn't I tell you so?* 1872 W. BLACK *Adv. Phaeton* xv The man who would triumph over the wife of his bosom merely to have the pleasure of saying 'I told you so', does not deserve ... such tender companionship.

Told, *see also* Tell(s).

Toll (*noun*), *see* Forsake not market for the t.; Hear a t. or knell (When thou dost) think on passing bell.

Toll (*verb*), *see* Sure (Good to be), t. it again.

Tom Fool, *see* More know T. F.

Tom of Lincoln, *see* Loud as T. of L.

Tom pitcher's broken, When | I shall have the shards.

1678 RAY 351 ... (*i.e.* Kindness after others have done with it; or refuse).

Tom Tell-truth.

1377 LANGLAND *P. Pl.* B III. 320 Thanne worth Trewe-tonge a tidy man. *Ibid.* B IV. 17 Tomme Trewe-tonge-tille-me-no-tales. **1550** LATIMER *Serm. Stamford* (P.S.) 289 Master, we know that thou art Tom Truth, and thou tellest the very truth. **1580** H. GIFFORD *Gilloflowers* (1875) 147 Is not Tom teltroath euerywhere, A busie cockcombe deem[d]e? **1639** CLARKE 308 Time is Tom Tell-truth. **1646** *Ex-ale-tation of Ale* 7 Tom tell troth lies hid in a [pot of good Ale]. **1721** KELLY 303 Tom Tell-truth lies without. **1738** SWIFT (Dial. iii) 351 You know, I'm old Telltruth; I love to call a spade a spade. **1862** HISLOP 271 Tam-tell-truth 's nae courtier.

Tom Tiddler's ground.

[= any place where money, &c., is 'picked up' readily.] **1848** DICKENS *Dombey* xxxvi The spacious dining-room with . . . the glittering table, . . . might have been taken for a grown-up exposition of Tom Tiddler's ground, where children pick up gold and silver. **1890** 'R. BOLDREWOOD' *Col. Reformer* (1891) 290 He . . . had come on to . . . Tom Tiddler's ground, . . . gold . . . was sticking out of the soil everywhere. **1907** A. C. BENSON *From Coll. Window* [ed. 4] 182 I would rather regard literature as a kind of Tom Tiddler's ground, where there is gold as well as silver to be picked up.

To-morrow come never.

1539 TAVERNER (1545) B 2 This to morow is euer commyng but neuer present. **1602** J. CHAMBERLAIN *Letters* 8 May (McLure) i. 142 Tomorrow comes not yet. **1639** *Stationers' Register* 28 June (Arb.) iv. 470 A book, Too late to call back yesterday and to-morrow comes not yet. **1678** RAY 343. **1738** SWIFT (Dial. i) 336 *Never.* I'll send it you to-morrow. *Miss.* . . . I suppose, you mean to-morrow come never. **1830** MARRYAT *King's Own* xxvi 'To-morrow you shall see that with your own eyes'. 'To-morrow come never!' muttered the coxswain.

To-morrow is a new day.

c. **1520** *Calisto & Mel.* in HAZL. *O.E.P.* I. 86 Well, mother, to-morrow is a new day. **1594** LYLY *Moth. Bomb.* III. iv. Wks. (1902) III. 217 Let vs not brabble but play: to morrow is a new daie. **1603** FLORIO tr. *Montaigne* II. iv (1897) III. 57 A letter . . . being delivered him . . . at supper, he[1] deferred the opening of it, pronouncing this by word: *To-morrow is a new day.* **1738** SWIFT (Dial. i) 336 *Never.* I'll send it you to-morrow. *Miss.* Well, well; to-morrow 's a new day. **1824** SCOTT *St. Ronan's* xxxiii We will say no more of it at present . . . , to-morrow is a new day. [1 Archias, at Thebes, 379 B.C.]

To-morrow morning I found a horse-shoe.

1620 SHELTON *Quix.* II. xliii (1908) III. 113 I bid thee leave thy proverbs, . . . that are as much to the purpose as To-morrow I found a horseshoe. **1732** FULLER no. 5208.

To-morrow, *see also* Business t.; Catch birds t. (Shall); Friend asks (When), there is no

t.; Put off till t. (Never); To-day will not (If), t. may; Trust (This day no), but come t.

Tomson, Tommy, *see* Contentibus.

Tomtit on a round of beef, Like a.

1849 NORTHALL *Folk-phrases* 19 . . . A little person is said to look so when situated on some coign of vantage.

Tong, *see* Live a little while . . . go to T.

Tongs, *see* Find it where Highlandman found t.; Touch him with a pair of t.

Tongue breaketh bone, and herself hath none.

[*Prov.* xxv. 15 A soft tongue breaketh the bone.] *c.* **1225** *Trin. MS. O. 11. 45* in *Eng. Stud.* **31.** 6 Tunge bregþ bon, þegh heo nabbe hire silf non. *a.* **1250** *Provs. of Alfred* A 425 (Skeat) 38 For ofte tunge brekeþ bon, þeyh heo seolf nabbe non. *c.* **1300** *Prov. of Hending* xix Tonge breketh bon, and nath hire-selue non. *c.* **1350** *Douce MS. 52* no. 42 The tonge brekyth bon, And hath hym sylfe non. *c.* **1390** GOWER *Conf. Amantis* III. 465 For men sein that the harde bon, Althogh himselven have non, A tunge brekth it al to pieces. *c.* **1425** *Eng. Conq. Irel.* 46 Tong breketh bon, thegh hym-self ne hawe none. *c.* **1470** *Harl. MS. 3362,* f. 1[b] Tunge brekyth bon, þat hyr self haue non. **1546** HEYWOOD II. v. 56 Tounge breaketh bone, it selfe hauyng none.

Tongue cut your throat, Let not your.

1855 BOHN 21. *Arabic.*

Tongue doth lie that speaks in haste, That.

1573 SANDFORD (1576) 216. **1611** DAVIES *Prov.* 74.

Tongue ever turns to the aching tooth, The.

1586 PETTIE *Guazzo's Civ. Conv.* 221 The more they are in loue, the more they tell things that are not apparentlie credible, and yet are most true, because according to the Prouerbe. The tongue rolles there where the teeth aketh. **1732** FULLER no. 4796.

Tongue is made of very loose leather, Your.

1721 KELLY 382 You have o'er mickle lose Leather about your Lips. **1732** FULLER no. 6062.

Tongue is no slander, His (Your).

1599–1600 SHAKS. *Twelfth N.* I. v. 101 There is no slander in an allowed fool, though he do nothing but rail. **1616** DRAXE 123. **1670** RAY 196. **1692** L'ESTRANGE *Aesop's Fab.* ccccc (1738) 547 The best on't is, sirrah, *Your tongue's no slander.* **1721** KELLY 390 . . . Because you are known to be a liar. **1738** SWIFT (Dial. i) 335 Well, my comfort is, your tongue is no slander.

Tongue is not steel yet it cuts, The.

c. 1386 CHAUCER *Manciple's T.* H. 342 Right as a swerd forkutteth and forkerveth. . . . A tonge kutteth freendshipe al a-two. 1546 HEYWOOD I. x. 20 Her tong is no edge toole, but yet it will cut. 1640 HERBERT 355. 1853 TRENCH vi. 146 In a discourse warning against sins of the tongue, we might produce many words . . . less likely to be remembered than . . . : *The tongue is not steel, but it cuts.*

Tongue is the rudder of our ship, The.

1664 TORRIANO 68. 1732 FULLER no. 4798.

Tongue run at rover, Let not your.

[= at random, unrestrained.] 1546 HEYWOOD II. v. 56 Be silent. Leat not your toung roon at rouer.

Tongue runs before his (your) wit, His (Your).

c. 1350 *Pearl* (1921) l. 294 Thy worde by-fore þy wytte con fle. 1546 HEYWOOD II. iv. 52. 1659 HOWELL *Eng. Prov.* 7/1. 1710 STEELE *Tatler* no. 235 If Mrs. Rebecca is not so talkative . . . she knows better what she says when she does speak. If her wit be slow, her tongue never runs before it.

Tongue runs like the clapper of a mill, Her.

1738 SWIFT (Dial. i) 337 Her tongue runs like the clapper of a mill; she talks enough for herself and all the company.

Tongue runs nineteen to the dozen, Your.

1785 GROSE *Dict. Vulg. T.* s.v. 'Chatterbox' one whose tongue runs twelve score to the dozen. 1854 BAKER *Northants Gloss.* s.v. 'Nineteen' A Common expression when any one talks too fast (A).

Tongue runs on pattens (wheels), Her.

c. 1450 *Partonope* (E.E.T.S.) l. 10123 Suche mennes tonges gone euer on wheles. 1546 HEYWOOD II. vii. 64. *a.* 1553 UDALL *Royster D.* I. iii. (Arb.) 20 Yet your tongue can renne on patins as well as mine. 1575 *Gam. Gurton's N.* II. iv. 34 How she began to scolde! The tonge it went on patins. 1639 CLARKE 133. 1670 RAY 196 His tongue runs on wheels (or at random).

Tongue talks at the head's cost, The.

1640 HERBERT 332. 1732 FULLER no. 4801.

Tongue walks where the teeth speed not, The.

1609 DEKKER *Gull's Hornbook* D 4ᵛ Let your tongue walke faster then your teeth. 1640 HERBERT 321.

Tongue(s), *see also* Arthur could not tame woman's t.; Blister upon t. that tells lie; Child hath red t. like father; Eat above t.

like calf; Effect speaks, t. need not; False t. hardly speak truth; Fool's t. long enough; Foolish t. talk by dozen; Good t. is good weapon; Good t. (Who has not) ought to have good hands; Good t. that says no ill; Heart is full (When) t. will speak; Heart thinketh (What the) t. speaketh; Hold one's t. in ill time; Honey t., heart of gall; Keep one's t. within teeth; Lame t. gets nothing; Lay the sweet side of t. to it; Lickerish of t.; Little can a long t. lein; Long t. short hand; Lost the t. of the trump; Nature has given . . . one t.; Nurse's t. privileged; Old as my t.; One t. is enough for woman; Ox is taken by horns, man by t.; Ox on his t.; Play with the ears than t. (Better); Speak with your gold and make other t. dumb; Still t. wise head; Strikes with his t. (He that); Thought hath good legs and quill good t.; Tied a knot with his t.; Two ears to one t., hear twice as much as you speak; Venom to that of t. (No); Wae's the wife that wants the t.; Wide ears short t. *See also* Hold his tongue, Woman's tongue.

Too big for one's boots, To be.

1894 SIR H. MAXWELL *Life W. H. Smith* 34 Sometimes a young man, 'too big for his boots', would . . . sniff at being put in charge of a railway bookstall.

Too clever by half.

1889 W. WESTALL *Birch Dene* (1891) 144 'He's a good scholar, and nobody can deny as he's clever'. 'Ay, too clever by half.'

Too far east is west.

1664 BUTLER *Hudibras* II. i. 271 Th' extremes of glory and of shame, Like east and west become the same. 1853 TRENCH (1905) 93 *Extremes meet*, or its parallel, *Too far East is West*, reaches very far into the heart and centre of things.

Too good is stark naught.

1738 SWIFT (Dial. ii) 348 *Lady A.* The only fault I find is, that they are too good. *Lady S.* O, madam, I have heard 'em say, that too good is stark naught.

Too good to be true.

1578 WHETSTONE *Promos & Cassandra* B 3 I thought thy talke was too sweete to be true. 1580 T. LUPTON *Sinquila. Too good to be true* (title). 1594 LYLY *Moth. Bomb.* IV. ii. Wks. (1902) III. 208 It was too good to be true. 1606 DANIEL *Queen's Arcadia* 2383 Besides 'tis too good to be true. 1638 T. HEYWOOD *Wise W. of Hogs.* IV. iv (Merm.) 310 The name of that news is called 'too good to be true'. 1908 W. S. CHURCHILL *My Afr. Jrny.* v It *is* too good to be true. One can hardly believe that such an attractive spot can be cursed with malignant attributes.

Too hasty to be a parish clerk.

1616 DRAXE 10. 1639 CLARKE 116. 1670 RAY 180.

Too hot to hold.

1639 CLARKE 178. **1678** RAY 346 . . . *Moderata durant.*

Too late to, *see* Grieve when chance past; Shut the stable-door; Spare when bottom bare.

Too many cooks spoil the broth.

1575 GASCOIGNE *Life Sir P. Carew* 33 There is the proverb, the more cooks the worse potage. **1662** GERBIER *Princ.* (1665) 24 Too many cooks spoils the broth. **1851** KINGSLEY *Yeast* iii 'Get out of the way, my men!' quoth the colonel. 'Too many cooks spoil the broth.'

Too much breaks the bag.

1664 CODRINGTON 214. **1666** TORRIANO 244. **1670** RAY 26 . . . *Hispan.* **1732** FULLER no. 5259.

Too much for one, and not enough for two, like the Walsall man's goose.

1880 POOLE *Arch. & Prov. Words of Staff.* 25 in NORTHALL *Folk-phrases* (1894) 31 A Walsall man, when asked if he and his wife were going to have a goose for their Christmas dinner, replied 'No ; . . . the goose was a silly bird—too much for one to eat, and not enough for two.'

Too much liberty spoils all.

1533 UDALL *Flowers for Latin Speaking* (1560) T 4ᵛ We be all the worse by hauying to much libertee. **1567** WM. BALDWIN *Moral Philos.* T 1ᵛ To muche lybertye turnithe into bondage. **1611** COTGRAVE s.v. 'Bandon' (A) Much liberty brings men to the gallowes. **1681** ROBERTSON *Phraseol. Generalis* 822.

Too much of a good thing.

1599–1600 SHAKS. *A.Y.L.* IV. i 128 Why then, can one desire too much of a good thing? **1901** R. G. MOULTON *Shaks. as Dram. Art.* 46 'Too much of a good thing' suggests that the Nemesis on departures from the golden mean applies to good things as well as bad.

Too much of nothing but of fools and asses.

1616 DRAXE 70. **1639** CLARKE 73.

Too much of one thing is not good (good for nothing).

c. **1386** CHAUCER *Canon's Yeom. Prol.* G. 645 That that is overdoon, it wol nat preeve Aright, as clerkes seyn ; it is a vice. **1546** HEYWOOD II. iv. 53 Well (quoth I) to muche of one thyng is not good, Leaue of this. **1616** BRETON *Cross. Prov. Wks.* (1879) II. App. iii Too much of any thing is good for nothing. **1738** SWIFT (*Dial.* i) 340 *Never.* Fie, miss ; you said that once before ; and, you know, too much of one thing is good for nothing.

Too much of ought is good for nought.

1871 *N. & Q.* 4th Ser. VIII. 506 Common Lancashire Proverbs.—'Too much of ought Is good for nought.'

Too much pudding will choke a dog.

1830 G. COLMAN, Younger *Random Records* in *Broad Grins* 421 'Too much pudding will choke a dog', which is a caution against excess. **1841** S. WARREN *Ten Thous. a Year* xvi All this might be very well in its way, began to think Miss Tagrag—but it was possible to choke a dog with pudding. **1917** BRIDGE 141 Too much pudding would sade[1] a dog. [1 sate or surfeit.]

Too much spoileth, too little is nothing.

1642 TORRIANO 64. **1659** HOWELL *Ital.–Eng.* 12 Too much spoiles, too little doth not satisfie. **1732** FULLER no. 5268.

Too much taking heed is loss.

1640 HERBERT 358.

Too much water drowns the miller.

1823 SCOTT *Peveril* xxi A jug of home-brewed ale . . . was warranted . . . as excellent ; 'for', said she, 'we know by practice that too much water drowns the miller, and we spare it on our malt as we would in our mill-dam'.

Too-too will in two.

1678 RAY 210 . . . *Chesh. i.e.* Strain a thing too much and it will not hold.

Too wise to live long.

1586 TIM. BRIGHT *Treat. Melancholy* xi. 52 Wherupon I take it, the prouerbe ariseth: that they bee of short life, who are of wit so pregnant: because their bodies doe receaue by nature so speedye a ripenes, as thereby age is hastened. **1592–3** SHAKS. *Rich. III* III. i. 79 So wise so young, they say, do never live long. **1607** MIDDLETON *Phœnix* I. i A little too wise, a little too wise to live long.

Too'd (= Toothed), *see* Quickly too'd and quickly go.

Took her for a rose, I | but she breedeth a burr.

1546 HEYWOOD I. x. 21 I toke hir for a rose, but she bréedth a burre. She comth to sticke to me nowe in hir lacke.

Tool(s), *see* Bad workman quarrels with t. ; Edged t. ; Workman without his t. (What is).

Tooley Street, *see* Tailors of T. S.

Toom[1] bags rattle.

1641 FERGUSSON 94. [1 empty.]

Toom pokes will strive.

1721 KELLY 313 . . . When a married couple are pinch'd with poverty they will be apt to jarr.

Toom[1] purse makes a blate[2] merchant, A.

1678 RAY 356. [1 empty. 2 bashful.]

Tooth, teeth, *see* Aching t. at one (To have an); Aching t. (Who hath) hath ill tenants; Any t., good barber; Cast in the t.; Colt's t.; Dragon's t.; Fight t. and nail; Never bite unless . . . t. meet; Old as my tongue, older than t.; Pull not out your t. but with leaden; Pull out one t. and pull out more; Sweet things bad for t.; Sweet t.; Take the bear by the t.; Take the bit in the t.; Tied by the t.; Tongue ever turns to aching t.; Trust not a horse's heel nor dog's t.; Wite your t. if your tail be small; Wolf may lose his t. but never memory.

Toothache is more ease than to deal with ill people, The.

1640 HERBERT 343.

Toothache, *see also* Music helps not t.; Pain like . . . t. (No).

Tooth-drawer, He looks like a.

1608 BEAUM. & FL. *Philas.* I. i Here is a fellow has some fire in 's veins; The outlandish prince looks like a tooth-drawer. **1678** RAY 83 . . . i.e. very thin and meager.

Top, *see* Drive a t. over tiled house; Parish t. (Like a).

Torch, *see* Light a t. gives (The more).

Tortoise to catch the hare, To set the.

1798 MALTHUS *Popul.* (1817) III. 117 It would appear to be setting the tortoise to catch the hare.

Tortoise wins the race while the hare is sleeping, The.

[From *Aesop's Fables.*] **1850** THACKERAY *Pendennis* xxi He had slept and the tortoise had won the race. He had marred at its outset what might have been a brilliant career.

Tortoise, *see also* Contempt pierces shell of t.

Totnes,[1] Here I sit and here I rest, and this town shall be called.

1850 *N. & Q.* 1st Ser. II. 511 When Brutus of Troy landed at Totnes, he gave the town its name; thus—'Here I sit, and here I rest, And this town shall be called Totnes'. [[1] Devon.]

Tottenham is turned French.

1536 NORFOLK to Cromwell, in *Cal. Lett. etc. Henry VIII* II, no. 233 (A) It is further written to me that a bruit doth run that I should be in the Tower of London. When I shall deserve to be there Totynham shall turn French. **1546** HEYWOOD I. vii. 14 Their faces told toies, that Totnam was tournd frenche. **1662** FULLER (*Middlesex*) II. 314 'Tottenham is turned French' . . . French mechanics swarmed in England, . . . which caused the insurrection in London, . . . anno Domini 1517. Nor was the city only, but country villages for four miles about, filled with French fashions and infections.

Tottenham wood is all on fire, When | then Tottenham street is nought but mire.

1631 W. BEDWELL *Brief Descrip. of Tottenham* iii *When Tottenham wood is all on fire, Then Tottenham streat is naught but mire.* . . . It is obserued, That whensoever a foggy thicke mist doth arise out of this wood, and hang ouer it . . . in maner of a smoake, That it's generally a signe of raine and foule weather.

Tottenham Wood, *see also* Remove T. W. (As easily).

Touch and go.

[= a risky or ticklish case or state of things.] **1815** R. WARDLAW *Let.* in ALEXANDER *Life* vi (1856) 166 'Twas touch and go—but I got my seat. **1831** MISS FERRIER *Destiny* iv So it was with Glenroy and his lady. It had been touch-and-go with them for many a day; and now . . . ended in a threatened separation. **1842–3** W. H. MAXWELL *Hector O'Halloran* xxv You had a close escape. Well, 'touch and go' is good pilotage they say.

Touch and take.

1591 FLORIO *Sec. Frutes* 197 Euery finger a limetwig, touch and take, take and holde. **1670** NARBOROUGH *Jrnl.* in *Acc. Sev. Late Voy.* I. (1694) 14 One blinded with a Cloth serv'd every Man as they were called to touch and take. **1805** NELSON *Let. to J. D. Thomson* 5 Sept. The Enemy have a shoal of frigates with their fleet. . . . My Motto shall be Touch and Take.

Touch him with a pair of tongs, I would not.

1639 CLARKE 34 Not to be handled with a pair of tongues. **1658** J. SMITH *Wit Restor'd* (Hotten) 281 Without a payre of tongs no man will touch her. **1670** RAY 196. **1688** BUNYAN *Jer. Sinner Saved* Wks. (1855) I. 98 We are scarce for touching of the poor ones that are left behind; no, not with a pair of tongs. **1801** EDGEWORTH *Out of Debt* i She, who had formerly been heard to say 'she would not touch him with a pair of tongs', now unreluctantly gave him her envied hand at a ball. **1854** DICKENS *Hard Times* I. iv I was so ragged and dirty, that you wouldn't have touched me with a pair of tongs.

Touch me not on the sore heel.

1641 D. FERGUSSON 98. **1721** KELLY 320 . . . Do not jest too near with my honour and interest.

Touch pot, If you | you must touch penny.

1654 GAYTON *Pleasant Notes Don Q.* 83 (A) Touch pot touch penny. **1678** RAY 351 . . . *Somers.* (Pay for what you have.) **1822** SCOTT *Nigel* xvi Every man . . . with his purse in his hand is as free to make new laws as he, . . . since touch pot touch penny makes every man equal.

Touch wood; it's sure to come good.

[To touch wood is supposed to be a charm to

avert misfortune, especially after untimely boasting.] **1906** *N. & Q.* 10th Ser. VI. 231 (A). **1908** *Westmr. Gaz.* 30 Dec. 2/3 On the next occasion when we read of Christmas with spring weather or of the changing seasons we shall 'touch wood'. **1909** *Times Wkly.* 11 June 377 I witnessed on June 2 a diligence accident . . . 'Have you ever had an accident?' . . . 'No signor, . . . and I have driven this coach for 15 years.' But he did not touch wood.

Touch your eye but with your elbow, You should never.

1640 HERBERT 340 Diseases of the eye are to be cured with the elbow. **1670** RAY 39. **1856** ABP. WHATELY *Annot. Bacon's Ess.* (1876) xxii. 252 The granting of some permission, coupled with some condition which . . . cannot or will not be fulfilled, is practically a prohibition. . . . According to the proverbial caution 'You should never rub your eye except with your elbow'.

Touch-box, *see* Glimmer in the t.

Touched him on the quick, He has.

1551 ROBINSON *Utopia* (1556. Arb.) 53 For he . . . beynge thus touched on the quicke, and hit on the gaule, . . . fumed and chafed. **1592-3** SHAKS. *Com. Err.* II. ii. 134 How dearly would it touch thee to the quick, Shouldst thou but hear I were licentious. **1593-4** *Tit. Andron.* IV. ii. 28 Lines, that wound, beyond their feeling, to the quick. *Ibid.* IV. iv. 36 But, Titus, I have touch'd thee to the quick. **1600-1** *Hamlet* II. ii. 634 I'll tent him to the quick: if he but blench I know my course. **1611-12** *Tempest* V. 25 With their high wrongs I am struck to the quick.

Toucheth pitch shall be defiled, He that.

[APOCRYPHA *Ecclus.* xiii. 1 He that toucheth pitch shall be defiled therewith.] *c.* **1300** BRUNNE *Handl. Synne* l. 6578 Who-so handlyth pycche wellyng hote, He shal haue fylthe therof sumdeyl. *c.* **1386** CHAUCER *Parson's T.* 854 As who-so toucheth warm pych, it shent his fyngres. **1579** LYLY *Euphues* (Arb.) 111 Hee that toucheth Pitch shall bee defiled. **1597-8** SHAKS. *I Hen. IV.* II. iv. 455 This pitch, as ancient writers report, doth defile. **1598-9** *Much Ado* III. iii. 60 I think they that touch pitch will be defiled. **1655** FULLER *Ch. Hist.* x. iv (1868) III. 278 Vorstius had . . . received several letters from certain Samosatenian heretics . . . and . . . had handled pitch so long that at last it stuck to his fingers. **1852** ED. FITZGERALD *Polonius* 157 'Touch pitch and be daubed'. Never wholly separate in your mind the merits of any political question from the Men who are concerned in it. *Burke.*

Touchstone tries gold, As the | so gold tries men.

1540 TAVERNER tr. *Erasm. Flores Sententiarum* A 7 The touche stone tryeth golde, gold tryeth man. **1579** LYLY *Euphues* Wks. (Bond) I. 58 But as the true gold is tried by

the touch . . . so the loyal heart of the faithful louer is known by the trial of his lady. **1593** GREENE *Wks.* (Gros.) II. 215 As the touchestone trieth the golde, so adversitie prooueth friends. **1625** BACON *Apophth.* Wks. (Chandos) 377 Chilon would say, 'That gold was tried with the touch-stone, and men with gold'. **1642** FULLER *Holy State* IV. vii (1841) 256 Integrity is the proper portion of a judge. Men have a touchstone whereby to try gold, but gold is the touchstone whereby to try men. **1732** FULLER no. 736.

Tough as leather, As.

1533 W. TINDALE (?) *Enchiridion* (1905) 161 As tough as white leather. **1611** COTGRAVE s.v. 'Corias'. **1678** RAY 290 As tough as whitleather.

Tough sinew in an auld wife's heel, There is a.

1737 RAMSAY III. 196.

Toulouse, *see* Gold of T.

Tout, *see* New t. in old horn.

Tow on one's distaff (rock), To have.

[= to have business to attend to.] *c.* **1386** CHAUCER *Miller's T.* A 3774 This Absolon . . . hadde moore tow on his distaf Than Gerueys knew. **1412** HOCCLEVE *Reg. of Princes* (E.E.T.S.) 45, l. 1226 Tow on my distaf haue I for to spynne, Morĕ, my fadir, than ye wot of yit. *c.* **1460** *Towneley Myst.* xiii. 389 I have tow on my rok more than euer I had. **1546** HEYWOOD II. v. 60 Some of them shall wyn More towe on their distaues, than they can well spyn. **1721** KELLY 182 I have other tow on my roke. **1756** MRS. CALDERWOOD in *Coltness Collect.* (Maitl. Club) 155 'In good faith', says John, . . . 'the Dutch has some other tow in their rock'. **1818** SCOTT *Fam. Letters* (1894) II. 4 Above all, I had too much flax on my distaff.

Tow, *see also* Fire and t. (All); Quenching of fire with t (No).

Town but had a mire at one end of it, There was never a good.

1721 KELLY 312 . . . The deficiency and unsatisfactoriness of every created being, has given occasion to this, and many other proverbs.

Town in May, He that is in a | loseth his Spring.

1640 HERBERT 362.

Town, *see also* Thrift is in the t. (When), you are in field.

Toy, John, *see* Lucky J. T.

Tracys have always the wind in their faces, The.

1662 FULLER (*Glouc.*) I. 552 'The Tracies have always the wind in their faces'. Tradition . . . reporteth, that, ever since Sir William Tracy was most active amongst the four knights which killed Thomas Becket,[1] it is imposed on Tracies for miraculous penance, that . . . the wind is ever in their faces. [[1] 1170.]

Trade follows the flag.

1888 J. E. T. ROGERS *Econ. Interp. of Hist.* (1894) II. xiii. 291 The English . . . began to build up a new colonial empire, . . . under a new . . . maxim, that trade follows the flag. **1902** H. J. MACKINDER *Britain & Brit. Seas* 345 Britain . . . derives profit from her daughter states. In Canada and Australia trade has undoubtedly tended to follow the flag.

Trade is better than service, A.

1640 HERBERT 363.

Trade is the mother of money.

1616 DRAXE 208. **1670** RAY 27. **1732** FULLER no. 5271.

Trades live, Let all.

1721 KELLY 241 . . . Spoken when we have broken an utensil, which must employ a tradesman to mend it, or make a new one. **1832** HENDERSON 129 'Let a' trades live', quo' the wife, when she burnt her besom.

Trade(s), *see also* Drives a subtle t.; Every man to his t.; Good t. (He that hath no), it is to his loss; Good t. (Who hath a) through waters may wade; Handful of t. handful of gold; Knavery in all t., most in tailors; Learns a t. hath a purchase; Many t. (Man of) begs; Two of a t. seldom agree; Virtue and a t. best for children.

Tradesmen, *see* Break or wear out (If things did not) how would t. live.

Traduttori, traditori (Translators, traitors).

1607 H. ESTIENNE *World of Wonders* tr. R.C. 13 He performed not the office of a *traduttore*, but of a *traditore*, that is, . . . he played not the part of a *translator*, but of a traitor. **1853** TRENCH i. 20 [An] Italian proverb . . . *Traduttori, traditori* . . . *Translators, traitors*; so untrue very often are they to the genius of their original. **1929** *Times* 7 Aug. 6/3 The visitor . . . ought to be able to speak fluently the language of the country visited. Working through an interpreter is roundabout and in many cases hopeless. As the Italian proverb says: *Traduttore traditore*.

Trail of the serpent, The.

[In reference to *Genesis* iii.] **1817** MOORE *Lalla R., Par. & Peri* 206 Some flow'rets of Eden ye still inherit, But the trail of the Serpent is over them all! **1909** *Spectator* 2 Oct. 488 These essays are avowedly an *olla podrida*, and . . . we are painfully conscious of the trail of the journalistic serpent.

Traitors at the table, Are there | that the loaf is turned the wrong side upwards?

1678 RAY 82. **1827–30** SCOTT *Tales Grandf.* vii

The signal . . . was when one of his pretended friends, who betrayed him,[1] should turn a loaf . . . with its bottom or flat side uppermost. [[1] Wallace, in 1305.]

Traitors' Bridge, *see* Loyal heart.

Traitor(s), *see also Traduttori*; Treason is loved but t. hated.

Tramp on a snail, and she'll shoot out her horns.

1721 KELLY 302 . . . The meanest, when injured, will show their resentment.

Tramp on a turd, The more you | the broader it grows.

1641 FERGUSSON 96. **1721** KELLY 316 . . . Spoken when people make a great stir about scandalous words which they are supposed to have deserv'd.

Tranent, *see* Salt to Dysart and puddings to T. (Carry).

Translators, *see Traduttori*.

Trap, He understands (is up to).

[i.e. knows his own interest.] **1681** T. FLATMAN *Heraclitus Ridens* No. 5 (1713) I. 30 Well, Brother, I understand Trap. **1785** COWPER *Let. to Lady Hesketh* 15 Dec. He understands booksellers' trap as well as any man. **1842** S. LOVER *Handy Andy* ii A clever, ready-witted fellow up to all sorts of trap.

Trap, *see also* Easy to fall into t.

Trash, *see* Toil so for t. (If you).

Travel makes a wise man better, but a fool worse.

1620–8 FELTHAM *Resolves* (1904) 240 Yet I think it not fit, that every man should travel. It makes a wise man better, and a fool worse. **1732** FULLER no. 5272.

Travel through the world, To | it is necessary to have the mouth of a hog, the legs of a stag, the eyes of a falcon, the ears of an ass, shoulders of a camel, and the face of an ape, and overplus, a satchel full of money and patience.

1591 FLORIO *Sec. Frutes* 93 (A) [with slight variations on above]. **1666** TORRIANO 157.

Travel (noun), *see also* Little wit meikle t.

Traveller may lie with authority, A. (*See also* Old men and travellers, Soldiers and travellers.)

c. **1362** LANGLAND *P. Pl.* A Prol. 46 Pilgrymes and palmers . . . hedden leue to lyȝen heere lyf aftir. **1594** MARLOWE *Edw. II* I. i *Gav.* What art thou? 2 *Man.* A traveller. *Gav.* . . . Thou would'st do well to . . . tell me lies at dinner-time. **1602–3** SHAKS. *All's Well* II. v. 31 A good traveller is something at the latter end of a dinner; but one that lies three thirds ... should be once heard and thrice beaten. **1611–12** *Temp.* III. iii. 26 Travellers ne'er did lie, Though fools at home condemn 'em. **1614** CAMDEN 303. **1706** FARQUHAR *Recruit. Off.* III. i Add but the traveller's privilege of lying; and even that he abuses. **1721** KELLY 23 A travelled man has leave to lie.

Traveller to Rome must have the back of an ass, the belly of a hog, and a conscience as broad as the king's highway, A.

1580 LYLY *Euph. & his Eng.* Wks. (Bond) II. 25 [A traveller] must haue the back of an Asse to beare all, and the snowt of a Swine to say nothing, thy hand on thy cap to shew reuerence to euery rascall. **1617** MORYSON *Itin.* III. i. 49 We in England vulgarly say, that a traveller to Rome must have the back of an ass, the belly of a hog, and a conscience as broad as the king's highway.

Travellers change climates, not conditions.

[HORACE *Epist.* 1. 11. 27 *Coelum non animum mutant, qui trans mare currunt.* Those who cross the sea, change their clime but not their character.] **1655** FULLER *Ch. Hist.* III. ii (1868) I. 366 *cœlum non animum.* 'Travellers change climates, not conditions.' Witness our Becket; stubborn he went over, stubborn he staid, stubborn he returned.

Traveller(s), *see also* Lame t. should get out betimes; Nothing so necessary for t. as languages; Old men and t. lie by authority; Put tricks upon t. (Don't); Soldiers and t. lie by authority; Spends the t. more than abider (Much).

Travelleth not by sea, He who | knows not what the fear of God is.

1573 SANDFORD (1576) 208. **1623** WODROEPHE *Spared Houres* 230 (A).

Travels far, He that | knows much.

1639 CLARKE 276. **1670** RAY 149.

Travel(s) (*verb*), *see also* Rides behind another does not t. when he pleases.

Tre, Pol, and Pen, you shall know the Cornish men, By.

1548 BORDE *Introduction* (E.E.T.S.) 122 To sew Tre poll pen, for wagging of a straw. **1602** CAREW *Survey of Cornwall* (1769) 55. **1662** FULLER (*Cornw.*) I. 306 'By Tre, Pol, and Pen, You shall know the Cornish men'. ... *Tre* signifieth a *town* ... *Pol* an *head* ... *Pen* a *top.* **1821** SCOTT *Kenilw.* i A worthy name ... of Cornish lineage; for ... 'By Pol, Tre, and Pen, You may know the Cornish men'. **1864** *N. & Q.* 3rd Ser. v. 208 Cornish Provs. ... By Tre, Pol, and Pen, Ros, Caer and Lan, You shall know all Cornish men. The second line of the old saw is frequently omitted.

Tread on a sore toe, Never.

1855 BOHN 459.

Tread on a worm and it will turn.

[Even the humblest will resent extreme ill-treatment.] **1546** HEYWOOD 52 Tread a woorme on the tayle, and it must turne agayne. **1590–1** SHAKS. *3 Hen. VI* II. ii. 17 The smallest worm will turn, being trodden on. **1611** DAVIES *Prov.* 115 Presse a worme on the taile, and t'will turne againe. **1748** RICHARDSON *Clar. H.* (1785) I. vii. 41 How can one be such a reptile as not to turn when trampled upon. **1864** BROWNING *Mr. Sludge* 72 Tread on a worm, it turns, sir! If I turn, Your fault!

Tread on nine daisies at once, When you can | spring has come.

1862 CHAMBERS *Bk. of Days* (1869) I. 312 Still we can now plant our 'foot upon nine daisies' and not until that can be done do the old-fashioned country people believe that spring is really come. **1910** *Spectator* 26 Mar. Spring is here when you can tread on nine daisies at once on the village green; so goes one of the country proverbs.

Treason is loved, The | but the traitor is hated.

[TACITUS *Annals* 1. 58 *Proditores etiam iis quos anteponunt invisi sunt.* Traitors are hated even by those whom they prefer.] **1594** *Selimus* 2122 (Dent) 79 *Sel.* O sir! I love the fruit that treason brings, But those that are the traitors, them I hate. *a.* **1627** MIDDLETON *Women Beware* II. ii (Merm.) 305 I'm like that great one, Who, making politic use of a base villain, He likes the treason well, but hates the traitor. **1692** L'ESTRANGE *Aesop's Fab.* cxciv (1738) 209 *We love the treason, but we hate the traitor.*

Treason, *see also* Trust is t. (In).

Tree, Up a.

[= in a difficulty or 'fix'.] **1825** J. NEAL *Bro. Jonathan* II. 103 If I didn't—I'm up a tree—that's a fact. **1839** THACKERAY *Maj. Gahagan* v I had her in my power—up a tree, as the Americans say.

Tree but bears (some) fruit, There is no.

c. **1514** A. BARCLAY *Eclogues* iv. 321 Euery tree hath fruit after his Kinde. **1616** BRETON *Cross. Prov.* Wks. (1879) II. App. iii There is no tree but beareth fruit. **1639** CLARKE 198.

Tree is fallen, When the | every one runs to it with his axe (hatchet).

[MENANDER *Monosticha* 123 Δρυὸς πεσούσης πᾶς ἀνὴρ ξυλεύεται. When an oak has fallen every man becomes a woodcutter. L. *Dejectâ arbore, quivis ligna colligit.* When the tree is fallen, every one runs to it with his axe.] **1586** PETTIE *Guazzo's Civ. Conv.* 206 This is a most true saying, That the tree is no sooner fallen downe to the grounde, but euerie one is readie to runne vppon it with his Hatchette. **1732** FULLER no. 4804 The tree is no sooner down but every one runs for his hatchet. **1791** I. DISRAELI *Curios. Lit.* (1858) III. 444 The dissolution of the foundations of deans and chapters would open an ample source to pay the king's debts, and scatter the streams of patronage. . . . He[1] quoted a Greek proverb, 'that when a great oak falls, every neighbour may scuffle for a faggot'. [[1] Preston, Master of Emmanuel Coll.]

Tree is known by its fruit, A.

1389 WYCLIF *Matt.* xii. 33 A tree is knowen of the fruyt. **1526** TINDALE *ibid.* The tree ys knowen by hys frute. **1573** TUSSER 160 How euer trée groweth, the fruit the trée showeth. **1597–8** SHAKS. *1 Hen. IV* II. iv. 470 If then the tree may be known by the fruit, as the fruit by the tree. **1670** RAY 11 A tree is known by the fruit, and not by the leaves. **1896** FROUDE *Council of Trent* iv. 77 Lutherans said the tree is known by its fruit. Teach a pure faith, and abuses will disappear, and a righteous life grow out of it as the fruit grows.

Tree, Like | like fruit.

c. **1300** *Cursor M.* l. 38 O gode pertre coms god peres, Wers tre, wers fruit it beres. *c.* **1386** CHAUCER *Cant. T. Mel.–Monk Link* B[2] 3146 Of fieble trees ther comen wrecched ympes [grafts]. Id. *Leg. Good Women* l. 2395 That wiked fruit cometh of a wiked tre, That may ye fynde, if that it like yow. **1402** HOCCLEVE *Minor Poems* (E.E.T.S.) 79 For swiche the frute ys as that is the tre. *a.* **1529** SKELTON *Replyc.* 155 For it is an auncyent brute, Suche apple tre, suche frute. **1639** CLARKE 224. **1670** RAY 149 Such as the tree is, such is the fruit.

Tree loaded with fruit, It is only at the | that people throw stones.

1865 ABP. TRENCH *Poems*; '*Proverbs*' xvi Be bold to bring forth fruit, though stick and stone At the fruit-bearing trees are flung alone.

Tree roots more fast, The | which has stood a rough blast.

1856 ABP. WHATELY *Annot. Bacon's Ess.* (1876) v. 76 'The tree roots more fast, which has stood a rough blast'. . . . The agitation of a tree . . . by winds . . . causes it to put out more and stronger roots. Even so, every temptation that has been withstood . . . strengthens the roots of good principle.

Tree that God plants, The | no wind hurts it.

1640 HERBERT 349.

Tree that grows slowly, The | keeps itself for another.

1640 HERBERT 326.

Trees eat but once.

1640 HERBERT 360.

Tree(s), *see also* Crooketh the t. (Timely) that

will good cammock be; Do these things in a green t. (If they); Good t. is good shelter; Good t. that hath neither knap nor gaw; Great t. are good for shade; Great t. keep down little ones; Higher the t. sweeter the plum; Highest t. has greatest fall; Lightens and thunders (If it), beware of a t.; Loves the t. loves branch; Man lives (As a) . . . as a t. falls so shall it lie; Remove an old t. and it will wither; See the wood for the t. (Cannot); Set. t. at All-hallontide; Set t. poor; Straight t. have crooked roots; Withy t. (Old) would have new gate.

Trelawny, *see* Never a Granville wanted.

Tremble, *see* Aspen leaf.

Trencher, *see* Little and good fills the t.; Trim as a t.

Trevannion, *see* Charles's Wain.

Treve, The, *see* Every man's man had a man . . . made the T. fall.

Tribe of Levi must have no mind to the tribe of Gad, The.

[A play upon the word *gad*.] **1629** T. ADAMS *Serm.* (1861–2) I. 455 Ministers must be like stars fixed in their orbs; ours is a stable profession, not a gadding ministry. . . . He spake merrily that said, the tribe of Levi must have no mind to the tribe of *Gad*. **1738** SWIFT (Dial. i) 341 *Col.* I think your ladyship is one of the tribe of Gad.

Trick for trick, and a stone in thy foot besides, quoth one pulling a stone out of his mare's foot, when she bit him upon the back, and he her upon the buttock.

1659 HOWELL *Eng. Prov.* 4/1.

Trick the colt gets at his first backing, The | will, while he continueth, never be lacking.

1721 KELLY 63. [*English.*]

Trick worth two of that, A.

1597–8 SHAKS. *1 Hen. IV* II. i. 41 Nay, soft, I pray ye: I know a trick worth two of that. **1608** DAY *Hum. out of Br.* IV. ii Tut, I can tell you a trick worth two of that. **1619** *Sir J. Barnavelt* IV. i. *fin.* I know a trick worth ten of that.

Tricks as a dancing bear, He hath as many.

1670 RAY 163. **1738** SWIFT (Dial. i) 338 I wish you would be quiet, you have more tricks than a dancing bear.

Trick(s), *see also* Fencer hath one t. in his budget; Put t. upon travellers (Don't); Teach an old dog t.

Trim as a trencher.

1542 UDALL tr. *Erasm. Apoph.* 246 b Fillyng vp as trymme as a trencher ye space that stood voide.

Trim tram, like master like man.

1617 MIDDLETON & ROWLEY *Fair Quarrel* II. ii (Merm.) 231 My name is Trimtram, forsooth; look, what my master does, I use to do the like. **1659** HOWELL *Eng. Prov.* 13/2 **1790** TRUSLER *Provs. Exempl.* 28 Even the slave who follows him, is infected with his master's pride; and . . . illustrates the proverb, *Trim tram, like Master like Man.*

Tring,[1] Wing,[2] and Ivinghoe,[2] for striking of a blow Hampden did forego, and glad he could escape so.

1830 SCOTT *Ivanhoe* Introd. A rhyme recording three names of the manors forfeited by the ancestor of the celebrated Hampden, for striking the Black Prince a blow with his racket, when they quarrelled at tennis:—Tring, Wing, and Ivanhoe, For striking of a blow, Hampden did forego, And glad he could escape so. **1864** *N. & Q.* 3rd Ser. v. 176 As the Messrs. Lysons remark, 'this tradition . . . will not bear the test of examination; for it appears, by record, that neither the manors of Tring, Wing, or Ivanhoe, ever were in the Hampden family'. (*Bucks*, vol. i, pt. iii, p. 571.) [[1] Herts. [2] Bucks.]

Tring,[1] Wing[2] and Ivinghoe,[2] three dirty villages all in a row, and never without a rogue or two. Would you know the reason why? Leighton Buzzard[3] is hard by.

1852 *N. & Q.* 1st Ser. v. 619. [[1] Herts. [2] Bucks. [3] Beds.]

Tripe's good meat if it be well wiped.

1678 RAY 50.

Tripoli, To come from.

['To vault and tumble with activity. It was, I believe, first applied to the tricks of an ape, or monkey, which might be supposed to come from that part of the world.' Nares. There may also be a pun on 'trip' = to caper or dance.] **1609** JONSON *Sil. Woman* V. i I protest, Sir John, you come as high from Tripoli as I do. *a.* **1625** FLETCHER *M. Thomas* IV. ii. 69 Get up to that window there, and presently . . . come from Tripoli. **1827** SCOTT *Journ.* 3 Apr. I drank a glass or two of wine more than usual, got into good spirits, and *came from Tripoli* for the amusement of the good company.

Triton of (among) minnows, To be a.

1607 SHAKS. *Cor.* III. i. 89 Heare you this Triton of the Minnowes? [Quoted by BYRON *Beppo* st. lxxiii.] **1796** LAMB to Coleridge 27 May Why, he is a very Leviathan of Bards!—the small minnow, I!

Trivet, *see* Right as a t.

Trojans became wise too late, The.

[ERASM. *Ad. Sero sapiunt Phryges.*] **1860** RILEY *Dict. Lat. Quot.* 418 'The Trojans became wise too late'. When their city was on the point of being taken, they began to think of restoring Helen. **1895** SIR H. MAXWELL *Post Meridiana* 49 *Sero sapiunt Phryges*—knowledge comes, but wisdom tarries,[1] as was said long ago. [[1] *Locksley Hall.*]

Trooper, *see* Young t. should have old horse.

Trot (*proper name*), *see* John T.

Trot (*verb*), *see* Need makes old wife t.

Trotters, *see* Steals a sheep, gives t.

Troubles a wolf how many the sheep be, It never.

1625 BACON *Ess., Great. of Kingd.* (Arb.) 473 Nay Number (it selfe) in Armies, importeth not much, where the People is of weake Courage: for (as *Virgil* saith) *It neuer troubles a Wolfe, how many the sheepe be.*[1] **1786** MRS. PIOZZI *Anec. of S. Johnson* (1892) 18 I said to him, 'Why there happens to be no less than five Cambridge men in the room now'. 'I did not (said he) think of that till you told me; but the wolf don't count the sheep.' [[1] VIRGIL *Ecl.* 7. 52.]

Trouble(s), *see also* Company in t. (Good to have); Meet t. half-way (Don't); Peck of t.; Seeks t. never misses; Seeks t. pity he should miss it; Talk than t. (More); War, hunting . . . full of t.; Young bear with his t. before him (Like a).

Troublesome, *see* Better be unmannerly than t.

Trout, *see* Chevin to the t. (Said the); Lose a fly to catch a t.; Whole (*or* Sound) as a t.

Trowel, *see* Lay it on with t.

Troy was.

[VIRGIL *Aen.* 3. 11 *Troja fuit.*] **1620** SHELTON *Quix.* II. lxvi (1908) III. 284 As they went out of Barcelona, Don Quixote beheld the place where he had his fall, and said, '"Hic Troja fuit"; here . . . my fortune fell, never to rise again'. **1754** WESLEY *Journ.* Jul. [at ruins of Old Sarum] Troy was. **1828** LAMB to Cowden Clarke, 25 Feb. They all live in my mind's eye . . . *Troja fuit.*

Truck (*noun*), *see* Muck and t.

Trucks (*verb*), *see* Fair chieve all where love t.

Trudge, *see* One thing said twice deserveth a t.

True as a turtle to her mate, As.

c. **1380** CHAUCER *Parl. of Foules* l. 355 (A) The wedded turtel with her herte trewe. **1601-2** SHAKS. *Troil. & Cres.* III. ii. 185 As true as . . . turtle to her mate. *c.* **1608-9** MIDDLETON *Widow* I. i Mine own wit this, and 'tis as true as turtle.

True as God is in heaven, As.

1600 DEKKER *The Shoemaker's Holiday* Dramatic Wks. (1873) I. 58. **1737** RAY 226.

True (Sooth) as gospel.

13. . *Minor Poems fr. Vernon MS.* xxiii. 796 Soþ as gospelle. *c.* **1380** *Romaunt of the Rose* l. 5453 And trowe been as the Evangile. *c.* **1440** *Partonope* 153 And that hit were as sothe as gospell. **1509** A. BARCLAY *Ship of Fools* (1874) I. 100. **1514** Id. *Eclogues* I. 637. *c.* **1520** SKELTON *Magnificence* l. 218 As trewe as the crede. *c.* **1520** J. RASTELL *Four Elements* E 2 As trewe as the gospell. **1538** J. BALE *Three Laws* E 4.

True as I am his uncle, That is as.

1678 RAY 83.

True as steel, As.

a. **1300** *Siriz* 95 in *Anec. Lit.* (1844) 5 Oure love is also trewe as stel, Withouten wou. *c.* **1300** BRUNNE *Handl. Synne* l. 2338 And to the ded was as trew as steyl. *c.* **1385** CHAUCER *L. G. W.* 334 That ben as trewe as euer was any steel. **1575** GASCOIGNE *Posies* (1907) 143 Though it have been thought as true as steel. **1594–5** SHAKS. *Rom. & Jul.* II. iv. 211 I warrant thee my man's as true as steel. **1595–6** *Mids. N.* II. i. 197 My heart Is true as steel. **1601–2** *Troil. & Cres.* III. ii. 184 As true as steel. **1705** DUNTON *Life & Err.* 244 He's as true as steel to his word.

True as that the cat crew, That is as | and the cock rocked the cradle.

1732 FULLER no. 4351.

True blue. (*See also quotations under the following proverb.*)

1600 JONSON *Cynth. Rev.* v. i Steal into his hat the colour whose blueness doth express trueness. **1650** COWLEY *Guardian* v. v Bess, poor wench, is married to a chandler; but she's true blue still. **1663** BUTLER *Hudibras* I. i. 191 'Twas Presbyterian true blue. **1890** W. F. BUTLER *Sir C. Napier* 95 A conspiracy among the . . . True Blues of their party to shut out the Princess Victoria from the throne.

True blue will never stain.

1659 HOWELL *Eng. Prov.* 11/1. **1670** RAY 166 . . . Coventry had formerly the reputation for dyeing of blues; insomuch that true blue became a proverb to signifie one that was always the same and like himself. **1721** KELLY 303 . . . A man of fix'd principles, and firm resolutions, will not be easily induc'd to do an ill, or mean thing.

True love kythes[1] in time of need.

1641 FERGUSSON 98. **1721** KELLY 326 . . . L. *Amicus certus in re incerta cernitur.* [[1] show itself.]

True man, A | and a thief think not the same.

1386 CHAUCER *Squire's T.* F[1] 537 A trewe wight and a theef thenken nat oon. **1598–9**

SHAKS. *Much Ado* III. iii. 53 If you meet a thief, you may suspect him . . . to be no true man.

True praise roots and spreads.

1640 HERBERT 347.

True steel as Ripon rowels, As.

1625 JONSON *Staple of News* I. i Why, there's an angel; if my spurs Be not right Ripon—. **1662** FULLER (*Yorks.*) III. 398 'As true steel as Ripon rowels'. It is said of trusty persons, men of metal, faithful in their employments. . . . The best spurs . . . are made at Ripon.

True that all men say, It is.

1520 WHITTINGTON *Vulg.* (E.E.T.S.) 72 It is lyke to be true that euery man sayth. **1545** TAVERNER H 1[v] The englyshe prouerbe . . . It is like to be true that euery man sayeth. **1546** HEYWOOD I. xi. 31 It must néedes be true, that euery man sayth. **1611** DAVIES *Prov.* 29. **1623** CAMDEN 272. **1670** RAY 150 . . . *Vox populi vox Dei.* **1721** KELLY 187 It may be true that some men say; but it must be true that all men say. **1840** MARRYAT *Poor Jack* xxxiii Every one declared that she was the handsomest creature that ever they had seen; and what every one says must be true. **1905** ALEX. MACLAREN *Matthew* II. 246 'What everybody says must be true' is a cowardly proverb . . . What most people say is usually false.

True word is spoken in jest, Many a.

c. **1386** CHAUCER *Monk-Nun's Priest Link* B[2] 1353 Be nat wrooth, my lord, for that I pleye. Ful ofte in game a soothe I have herd seye! **1605–6** SHAKS. *K. Lear* V. iii. 71 Jesters do oft prove prophets. **1641** FERGUSSON 94 There are many sooth words spoken in bourding.[1] **1738** SWIFT (*Dial.* i) 343 *Never.* Well, I . . . was a great puppy for my pains. *Miss* . . . They say, many a true word's spoken in jest. **1877** ABP. TRENCH *Med. Ch. Hist.* (1879) ix. 130 Damiani . . . fondly calls him[2] his *Sanctus Satanas*, . . . and . . . as the proverb tells us, many a true word has been uttered in jest. [[1] jesting. [2] Hildebrand.]

True, *see also* Velvet t. heart. *See also* Sooth.

Truest jests sound worst in guilty ears, The.

1664 CODRINGTON 215. **1670** RAY 14.

Trump, *see* Lost the tongue of the t.; Sow playing on t. (Like a).

Trump(s) (at cards), *see* Put one to his t.; Turn up t.

Trumpet, *see* Blow one's own t.

Trumpeter is dead, Your.

1721 KELLY 375 . . . Spoken when people commend themselves. **1785** GROSE *Dict. Vulg. T.* (1796) s.v. His trumpeter is dead, he is therefore forced to sound his own trumpet.

Trumpeter, *see also* Die (When you), your t. will be buried; Dry cough t. of death.

Trunch, *see* Gimmingham.

Truss up all his wit in an eggshell, You may.

1678 RAY 84 [*Joculatory*]. 1732 FULLER no. 5957.

Trust a tailor that does not sing at his work, Never.

1611 BEAUM. & FL. *Kt. Burn. P.* II. viii (Dent) 64 *Mer.* Never trust a tailor that does not sing at his work; his mind is of nothing but filching.

Trust before you try, If you | you may repent before you die.

c. 1560 HUTH *Ancient Ballads* (1867) 221 (A) Who trusts before he tries may soon his trust repent. 1670 RAY 149. 1732 FULLER no. 6084.

Trust, This day there is no | but come tomorrow.

1642 TORRIANO 58. 1658 *Comes Facundus in Via* 15–16. 1732 FULLER no. 4999.

Trust him no further than I can fling him (throw a mill-stone), I will.

1618 HARINGTON *Epigrams* bk. ii no. 74 (A) That he might scant trust him so farre as to throw him. 1670 RAY 197 I'll trust him no further than I can fling him. 1678 Id. 274 I'll trust him no further then I can throw a millstone. 1732 FULLER no. 5286 (with 'than you can throw him').

Trust him with untold gold (money), You may.

1616 DRAXE 210. 1639 CLARKE 116. 1670 RAY 197.

Trust in God, Put your | but keep your powder dry.

a. 1658 CROMWELL in HAYES *Ballads of Ireld.* (1855) I. 191 Cromwell . . . when his troops were about crossing a river . . . concluded an address . . . with these words—'put your trust in God; but mind to keep your powder dry.' 1908 *Times Lit. Sup.* 6 Nov. 383 In thus keeping his powder dry the bishop acted most wisely, though he himself ascribes the happy result entirely to observance of the other half of Cromwell's maxim.

Trust is the mother of deceit.

c. 1400 *Rom. Rose* 3932 For he may best, in every cost, Disceyve, that men tristen most. a. 1530 R. *Hill's Commonpl. Bk.* (E.E.T.S.) 130 In whom I trust most, soonest me deseyvith. 1611–12 SHAKS. *Tempest* I. ii. 93 My trust, Like a good parent, did beget of him A falsehood in its contrary as great As my trust was. 1636 CAMDEN 307.

Trust is treason, In.

c. 1450 *Mankind* 743 *Mercy.* In trust ys treson, this promes ys not credyble. 1531 SIR T. ELYOT *Governour* II. xii (Dent) 170 Ye,
your truste is the cause that I haue conspired agayne you this treason. 1546 HEYWOOD II. v. 55 Shall I trust him then? nay in trust is treason. 1614 CAMDEN 308.

Trust is truth, In.

1639 CLARKE 116.

Trust me, but look to thyself.

1721 KELLY 239. 1732 FULLER no. 5288.

Trust not a horse's heel, nor a dog's tooth.

[L. *Ab equinis pedibus procul recede.* Keep at a distance from a horse's heels.] 1577 PEACHAM *Garden of Eloquence* (1593) 87. 1678 RAY 158. 1910 P. W. JOYCE *Eng. as we Speak* 110 Three things are not to be trusted—a cow's horn, a dog's tooth, and a horse's hoof.

Trust not a new friend nor an old enemy.

a. 1450 *Ballad* 288 in *Ratis Raving, &c.* (E.E.T.S.) 9 Thi enemys auld trow neuer in. c. 1450 *Provs. of Wysdom* 21 Trust neuer in thyn enmy. 1721 KELLY 262 Never trust much to a new friend, or an old enemy. 1869 HAZLITT 459.

Trust not the praise of a friend, nor the contempt of an enemy.

1855 BOHN 546 *Ital.*

Trust to a dry stick, No.

1616 BRETON *Cross. Prov. Wks.* (1879) II. App. iii. 8.

Trust to the dog, While you | the wolf slips into the sheepfold.

1732 FULLER no. 5690.

Trusted (Get credit) with a house full of unbored millstones, He may be.

1641 FERGUSSON 48 *Of false persons.* He will get credit of a house full of unbored millstones. 1721 KELLY 151 . . . That is, only with what he cannot carry away.

Trusteth not, He who | is not deceived.

1616 DRAXE 210. 1642 TORRIANO 24. 1707 MAPLETOFT 66. 1732 FULLER no. 2406.

Trusts in a lie, He that | shall perish in truth.

1640 HERBERT 344.

Trusts much, He that | obliges much, says the Spaniard.

1651 HERBERT 365.

Trust(s, ed), *see also* Better known than t.; First try then t.; Put not your t. in princes; See your friend (Whensoever you), t. to yourself; Sows (He that) trusts in God; Speaks me fair and loves me not . . . t. him not; Try before you t.

Truth and oil are ever above.

1620 SHELTON *Quix.* II. 1 (1908) III. 174 I have told you the truth, which shall always prevail above lies, as the oil above the water. **1640** HERBERT 328.

Truth fears no colours. (*Cf.* Truth needs no colours).

[= fears no enemy.] *Cf.* **1594–5** SHAKS. *L.L.L.* IV. ii. 157 *Nath.* Sir, you have done this in the fear of God, very religiously; and, as a certain Father saith— *Hol.* Sir, tell me not of the Father; I do fear colourable colours. **1597–8** *2 Hen. IV* V. v. 94 *Fal.* Sir, I will be as good as my word . . . Fear no colours. **1599–1600** *Twelfth N.* I. v. 10 I can tell thee where that saying was born of, 'I fear no colours'. **1613** MARSTON *Insat. Count.* II. 1 Then came in after him one that, it seem'd, feared no colours. Must they go on fearing no colours? **1678** COTTON *Scarron.* RAY 347.

Truth finds foes, where it makes none.

[AUSONIUS *Ludus Septem Sapientum, Bias, Veritas odium parit.* Truth produces hatred.] **1572** T. WILSON *Discourse upon Usury* (1925) 188 (A) It is a common saying, *Veritas odium parit,* Truth purchaseth hatred. **1576** PETTIE *Petite Pall.* (Gollancz) II. 113 Truth getteth hatred. **1670** RAY 150.

Truth has a scratched face.

1584 LYLY *Campaspe* IV. iii. 26 Truth is neuer without a scratcht face. **1875** CHEALES *Proverb. Folk-Lore* 118 (A).

Truth hath a good face, but bad (ill) clothes.

1600 BODENHAM *Belvedere* (Spens. Soc.) Truth most delights, when shee goes meanest clad. **1639** FULLER *Holy War* III. xix Strange that any should fall in love with that profession, whose professors were so miserable! But truth hath always a good face, though often but bad clothes. **1659** HOWELL *Eng. Prov.* 3/2.

Truth hath always a fast bottom.

1678 RAY 211. **1732** FULLER no. 5300 (with 'sure' for 'fast').

Truth is always green, The.

1853 TRENCH iv. 76 There may be poetry in a play upon words . . . as . . . in that exquisite Spanish proverb: *La verdad es siempre verde* . . . The truth is always green. **1894** BLACKMORE *Perlycross* xiii Ivory—. . . which . . . whitens with the lapse of years, though green at first, as truth is.

Truth is lost, In too much dispute.

1653 A. WILSON *Hist. of Gt. Britain* 291 But *nimium altercando Veritas amittitur,* Truth may be lost in a croud. **1659** HOWELL *Fr.-Eng.* 1.

Truth is no slander, The.

1583 MELBANCKE *Philot.* 96 But I had better

slander them trulye, which is no Slaunder indeede, then flatter them falsely as thou doest. **1612–13** SHAKS. *Hen. VIII* II. i. 153 But that slander, sir, Is found a truth now.

Truth is stranger than fiction.

1823 BYRON *Juan* XIV. ci Truth is always strange; Stranger than fiction.

Truth is the daughter of God.

1732 FULLER no. 5301.

Truth is the daughter of Time.

[A. GELLIUS 1. 2. 9 *Veritatem Temporis filiam esse.*] **1553** *Respublica* 1. 33 Veritie, the daughter of sage old Father Tyme. **1567** WM. BALDWIN *Moral Philos.* Bb 8ᵛ Truth is the daughter of time. **1592** GREENE *Wks.* (Gros.) XI. 189 Now doo I proove that true by experience, which earst I held onelye for a bare prouerbe, that trueth is the daughter of time. **1597** *Politeuphuia* 9 Truth is the daughter of Time and the guide of all goodnesse. **1647** HOWELL *Fam. Lett.* (1903) III. 22 As Time begets her [Truth], so he doth the obstetritious office of a Midwife to bring her forth. **1663** BUTLER *Hudibras* II. iii. 663 'Tis not Antiquity, nor Author, that makes truth truth, although time's daughter.

Truth is truth to the end of the reckoning.

c. **1390** GOWER *Conf. Amantis* Prol. 1. 369 For trowthe mot stonde ate laste. c. **1400** *Beryn* 1. 2037 For, aftir comyn seying—evir atte ende The trowith woll be previd, how-so men evir trend. **1604–5** SHAKS. *Meas. for Meas.* V. i. 45 Truth is truth To the end of reckoning. **1855** BOHN 547.

Truth lies at the bottom of a well.

[DIOGENES LAERTIUS Ἐτεὸν δὲ οὐδὲν ἴδμεν ἐν βυθῷ γὰρ ἡ ἀλήθεια. We know nothing certain; for truth is hidden in the bottom of an abyss. LACTANTIUS *Inst.* 3. 28. 13 *In puteo . . . veritatem iacere submersam.*] **1547** WM. BALDWIN *Moral Philos.* (1550) N 1ᵛ Wysedome is lyke a thyng fallen into the water, whiche no man can fynde, excepte he searche in at the bottome. **1601** T. WRIGHT *The Passions of the Mind* 232 *Veritas in profundo latet,* veritie lieth in the bottome. **1625** BACON *Apoph.* no. 263 Truth lies in profound pits, and when it is got, it needs much refining. **1635** HOWELL *Fam. Lett.* (1903) II. 112 As if truth were got into some dungeon; or, as the old Wizard said, into some deep Pit. *a.* **1721** PRIOR *Dial. of Dead* (1907) 225 You know the ancient philosophers said Truth lay at the bottom of a well. **1822** SHELLEY in SYMONDS *Life* (1878) vi Trelawny fished him out, and when he had taken breath he said: 'I always find the bottom of the well, and they say Truth lies there'.

Truth may be blamed, but cannot be shamed.

c. **1450** *Coventry Myst.* (Shaks. Soc.) 367 Trewthe dyd nevyr his maystyr shame. **1655** FULLER *Ch. Hist.* IV. i (1868) I. 548 Here, if ever, did the proverb take effect, 'Truth may be blamed, but cannot be shamed'; for, although . . . condemned . . . he was beheld as loyalty's confessor, speaking . . . in discharge of his conscience. **1670** RAY 150 *Truth* may be blamed, but 't shall never be shamed.

Truth needs no colours. (*Cf.* Truth fears no colours.)

1519 HARMAN *Vulg.* (James) 91 Treuthe nedeth no peynted or colored termes. **1580** J. BARET P 925 Truth and honestie need no cloke. *c.* **1600** *Edmund Ironside* 1. 1198 Truth needes noe cullors.

Truth shows best being naked, The.

c. **1390** GOWER *Conf. Amantis* I. 284 For trowthe hise wordes wol noght peinte. *c.* **1613** J. TAYLOR (Water-P.) *Watermens Suit* Wks. (1872) 19 Thus (because the truth shows best being naked) I have plainly set down how far I proceeded in my suit. **1732** FULLER no. 5314 Truth's best Ornament is Nakedness.

Truth, The | the whole truth, and nothing but the truth.

1580 LYLY *Euph. & his Eng.* (Arb.) 329 Speake no more then the trueth, vtter no lesse. **1659** HEYLIN *Animadversions* in FULLER *Appeal Inj. Innoc.* (1840) 651 Let us see therefore what he saith of this prelate, and how far he saith truth, the whole truth, and nothing but the truth.

Truth will prevail.

c. **1390** GOWER *Conf. Amantis* Prol. 369 Trowthe mot stonde ate laste. *c.* **1580** FUL-WELL *Ars Adulandi* E 4 (A) Trueth in the ende shall preuayle.

Truths and roses have thorns about them.

1707 MAPLETOFT 61. **1855** BOHN 547.

Truths too fine spun are subtle fooleries.

1707 MAPLETOFT 52. **1855** BOHN 547.

Truth(s), *see also* All t. are not to be told; Better speak t. rudely; Craft must have clothes; Face to face, the t. comes out; Fact (T.) is stranger than fiction; Fair fall t.; Follow not t. too near the heels; Greater the t. greater the libel; Half the t. a great lie; Many words (In) the t. goeth by; Probabilities (Thousand) do not make t.; Shovelfuls to bury t.; Slander one with matter of t.; Sting of a reproach is the t.; Tell t. and shame devil; Time is the father of t.; Trust is t. (In); Wine in, t. out; Wine there is t. (In).

Try all ways to the wood, You.

1639 CLARKE 163.

Try (your friend) before you trust (him). (*Cf.* First try and then trust.)

c. **1460** *Good Wyfe wold a Pylgremage*

(E.E.T.S.) l. 118 (A) A-say [Assay] or euer thow trust. *a.* **1530** R. *Hill's Commonpl. Bk.* (E.E.T.S.) 132 Assay thy friend or thou haue nede. **1578** *Parad. D. Deuises* (repr.) 38 *Trye before you trust* (Title). **1580** LYLY *Euph. & his Eng.* (Arb.) 378 Friendes are tryed before they are to be trusted. *a.* **1600** TURBERVILLE *To Browne* Beware my Browne of light beliefe, trust not before you trie. **1616** BRETON *Cross. Prov.* Wks. (1879) II. App. iii Try and then trust. **1633** SHIRLEY *Witty Fair One* IV. ii (Merm.) 55 Try me, and trust me after. **1639** CLARKE 24 Try your friend before you trust him.

Try that bone on some other dog.

1620 SHELTON *Quix.* IV. v (1908) I. 309 'There were never such knights in the world, nor such adventures and ravings happened in it'. 'Cast that bone to another dog', quoth the innkeeper, 'as though I knew not how many numbers are five'.

Try your skill in gilt first, and then in gold.

1670 RAY 95 . . . Practise new and doubtful experiments in cheap commodities, or upon things of small value.

Try, *see also* First t. then trust; Know what you can do till you t. (You never).

Tu quoque, see You are another.

Tub (Vat) must stand on its own bottom, Every.

1564 BULLEIN *Dial. agst. Fever* (E.E.T.S.) 65 Let euerie Fatte stande vpon his owne bottome. **1639** CLARKE 66. **1670** RAY 102 . . . Every man must give an account for himself. **1678** BUNYAN *Pilgr.* I. (1877) 37 *Presumption* said, *Every Fat must stand upon his own bottom.* **1866** READE *Grif. Gaunt* vi There is an old saying, 'Let every tub stand on its own bottom'.

Tub to the whale, To throw out a.

[= to create a diversion.] **1651** JER. TAYLOR *Holy Dying* I. iii (Bohn) 313 He is at first entertained with trifles . . . and little images of things are laid before him, like a cock-boat to a whale, only to play withal. **1704** SWIFT *T. Tub* Author's Pref. 14 Sea-men have a Custom when they meet a Whale, to fling him out an empty Tub, . . . to divert him from laying violent Hands upon the Ship. **1810** W. B. RHODES *Bombastes Fur.* i (1873) 16 A tub thrown to a whale, To make the fish a fool. **1912** *Nation* 29 June 465/2 He throws a tub to the High Church whale.

Tubs, *see* Put out your t. when raining.

Tumult, *see* Wrath of . . . and t. of people (Take heed of).

Tune the old cow died of, The.

[**1732** FULLER no. 4360 That is the old Tune upon the Bag-Pipe.] **1859** C. READE *Love me Little* iii 'David, . . . that is enough of the tune the old cow died of; take and play something to keep our hearts up.'

Tune (-ing), *see also* Good t. on old fiddle (Many); Long a-tuning your pipes (You are as).

Tuppenny, *see* Tine the t. belt for the twapenny whang.

Turd(s), *see* Ill weed mars pottage; Stir it (The more you), the worse it stinks; Thatches his house with t. (He that); Tramp on a t. (The more you), the broader it grows. *See also* Horse-turd.

Turf, On the | all men are equal— and under it.

[i.e. on the race-course and in the grave.] **1854** SURTEES *Hand. Cross* lix 'On the turf and under the turf all men are obliged to be equal', mused our master. **1896** 'H. S. MERRIMAN' *Sowers* iii It appears that beneath the turf or on it all men are equal; so no one could object to the presence of Billy Bale, the man . . . who could give you the straight tip on any race.

Turf, *see also* Need of a besom that sweep with t. (They have).

Turk and the Pope, Here is a talk of the | but my next neighbour doth me more harm than either of them both.

1651 HERBERT 372.

Turk's horse doth once tread, Where the | the grass never grows.

1639 FULLER *Holy War* v. xxx (1840) 297 The Turkish empire is the greatest . . . the sun ever saw. . . . Populus it is not, for . . . it lieth waste, according to the old proverb, Grass springeth not where the grand signior's horse setteth his foot. **1659** HOWELL *Eng. Prov.* 6/2. **1902** F. VILLIERS *Pict. of Many Wars* 11 Each day's bloody work added to the night's lurid glow, for the Turks . . . destroyed everything . . . as they advanced, illustrating the aphorism: 'Where the hoof of the Turkish horse treads no blade of grass ever grows.'

Turk, *see also* Turn T.; Unspeakable T.

Turkey-cock, To strut (swell) like a.

1598–9 SHAKS. *Hen. V* V. i. 15 Why, here he comes, swelling like a turkey-cock. **1689** SHADWELL *Bury Fair* III. i (Merm.) 407 What, like one of those odious creatures, will you dress at me? . . . and strut like a turkey-cock, and prune yourself? **1857** TROLLOPE *Barch. Tow.* xxxix They all swelled into madam's drawing-room, like so many turkey cocks.

Turkey-cock, *see also* Red as a t.-c.

Turkeys, carps, hops, pickerel,[1] and beer came into England all in one year.

1643 BAKER *Chron.* (1660) 317 About [1524] it happened that divers things were newly brought into England, whereupon this

Rhyme was made: 'Turkeys, Carps, Hoppes, Piccarell, and Beer, Came into England all in one year.' [[1] young pike.]

Turkeys, *see also* Driving t. to market.

Turn (over) a (new) leaf, To.

[= to adopt a different line of conduct, now in a good sense.] **1546** HEYWOOD II. iv. 52 Naie she will tourne the leafe. **1592** *Arden of Fevers.* III. i. 7 (*Shaks. Apoc.*) 15 No question then but she would turn the leafe And sorrow for her desolation. **1597** BEARD *Theatre God's Judgem.* (1631) 92 But as soone as he was exalted to honor, he turned over a new leafe, and began . . . furiously to afflict . . . the . . . faithful servants of Christ. **1861** HUGHES *Tom B. at Oxford* xlii (1889) 411 I will turn over a new leaf, and write to you. **1909** ALEX. MACLAREN *Ephesians* iv. 22 How many times have you said . . . 'I have played the fool . . . but I now turn over a new leaf'.

Turn a narrow adlant, To.

1879 JACKSON *Shrops. Word-Book* 3 (A) To 'turn on a mighty narrow adlant' is a proverbial saying expressive of a very narrow escape. **1917** BRIDGE 145 To turn a narrow adlant. *To have a narrow escape from death or some calamity. . . . Adlant is the headland of a field.*

Turn about is fair play.

1892 STEVENSON *Wrecker* xxiv You had your chance then; seems to me it's mine now. Turn about's fair play.

Turn in his grave, To make a person.

1864 J. PAYN *Lost Sir Massingb.* xxxiv This holiday-making and mixture of high and low here, are themselves enough to make Sir Massingberd turn in his grave. **1888** BRYCE *Amer. Commonw.* I. xii. 159 Jefferson might turn in his grave if he knew of such an attempt to introduce European distinctions of rank into his democracy. **1927** *Times* 28 Nov. 15/5 If the tune is changed at that service I shall turn in my grave.

Turn one's coat (tippet), To.

[= to change sides, desert.] **1546** HEYWOOD II. i. 44 So turned they their typpets by way of exchaunge, From laughyng to lowryng. **1565** SHACKLOCK *Hatchet of Heresies* 74 How many times Melancthon hath turned his coat in this one opinion. **1650** TRAPP *Comm. Exod.* xii. 38 Strangers, that took hold of the skirts of these Jews . . . but afterwards turned tippet. **1655** FULLER *Ch. Hist.* IX. vii, § 24 That all the Protestants would either turn their coats, copies, arms, or fly away. **1819** SCOTT *Leg. Mont.* xvii Sir John Urrie, a soldier of fortune . . ., had already changed sides twice during the Civil War, and was destined to turn his coat a third time before it was ended.

Turn or burn.

1616 WITHALS 576 Rather turne then burne. **1639** CLARKE 222 Rather turne than burne. **1675** BUNYAN *Saved by Grace* Wks. (Offor) I. 351 They now began to see that they must either turn or burn. [*Footnote*. These terms are taken from Foxe's *Martyrology*. It was frequently the brutal remark of the Judges, You must turn or burn. Bunyan here applies it to turning from sin or burning in hell.— ED.] **1855** KINGSLEY *Westward Ho!* vii The Inquisition . . . claims the bodies and souls of all heretics . . . and none that it catches . . . but must turn or burn.

Turn (*or* Twist) (a person) round one's (little) finger, To.

1855 MOTLEY *Dutch Rep.* v. iii (1866) 698 Margaret . . . had already turned that functionary round her finger.

Turn the cat in the pan, To.

[= (*a*) to reverse the order of things so dexterously as to make them appear the very opposite of what they really are; to turn a thing right about; (*b*) to change one's position, change sides, from motives of interest, &c.] *a.* **1384** WYCLIF *Works* (Arnold) III. 332 Many men of lawe . . . bi here suteltes turnen the cat in the panne. **1532** *Use Dice Play* (1850) 18 These vile cheaters turned the cat in the pan, giving to diverse vile, patching thefts, an honest and goodly title, calling it by the name of a law. **1543** BECON *Invect. agst. Swearing* Wks. (1843) 353 God saith, 'Cry, cease not', but they turn cat in the pan, and say 'Cease, cry not'. **1622** T. STOUGHTON *Chr. Sacrif.* vii. 91 How do they shrinke? yea, how foully do they . . . turne cat in pan, and become themselves persecuters of others. **1675** CROWNE *City Polit.* II. 1 Come, Sirrah, you are a villain, have turn'd cat-in-pan, and are a Tory. *a.* **1720** *Song, Vicar of Bray* I turned the cat in pan once more, And so became a Whig, sir. **1816** SCOTT *Old Mort.* XXXV O, this precious Basil will turn cat in pan with any man.

Turn the money in your pocket when you hear the cuckoo.

1850 *N. & Q.* 1st Ser. II. 164 When the cry of the cuckoo is heard for the first time in the season, it is customary to turn the money in the pocket, and wish. **1869** HAZLITT 441 Turn your money when you hear the cuckoo, and you'll have money in your purse till the cuckoo come again.

Turn the (an honest) penny, To.

[= to employ one's money profitably; or, to gain money.] **1546** HEYWOOD 75 Towne ware was your ware, to tourne the peny. *c.* **1645** HOWELL *Lett.* (1754) 76 There is no State that winds the Penny more nimbly, and makes quicker returns. **1676** WYCHERLEY *Pl. Dealer* III. Wks. (Rtldg.) 125/2 You must call usury and extortion God's blessing, or the honest turning of the penny. **1838** DICKENS *Oliver T.* xxxvii I suppose, a married man . . . is not more averse to turning an honest penny when he can, than a single one. **1887** JESSOPP *Arcady* vii. 216 He turns an honest penny by horse hire.

Turn the tables, To.

[= to reverse the relation between two persons or parties, from the notion of players reversing the position of the board.] **1612** CHAPMAN *Widow's Tears* I. iii. 27 I may turn the tables with you ere long. **1634** SANDERSON *Serm.* II. 290 Whosoever thou art that dost another wrong, do but turn the tables; imagine thy neighbour were now playing thy game, and thou his. **1647** DIGGES *Unlawf. Taking Arms* iii. 70 The tables are quite turned, and your friends have undertaken the same bad game, and play it much worse. **1713** ADDISON *Guard.* No. 134, par. 4 In short, Sir, the tables are now quite turned upon me. **1893** SELOUS *Trav. S.E. Africa* 33 They had won the first match, though I hoped I might yet turn the tables on them in the return.

Turn Turk, To.

[= to change completely as from a Christian to an infidel.] **1598-9** SHAKS. *Much Ado* III. iv. 57 Well, an you be not turned Turk, there's no more sailing by the star. **1600-1** *Hamlet* III. ii. 287 If the rest of my fortunes turn Turk with me. **1629** J. M. tr. *Fonseca's Dev. Contempl.* 403 The Souldier, he will turne Turke vpon point either of profit, or of honor.

Turn up one's nose, To.

[= to show disdain.] **1579** TOMSON *Calvin's Serm. Tim.* 228/1 Let women holde vppe their noses no more: for all their presumption is sufficiently beaten downe here. **1779** MME D'ARBLAY *Diary* 20 Oct. Mr. Thrale . . . turned up his nose with an expression of contempt. **1836** MARRYAT *Midsh. Easy* xxiv Miss Julia, who turned up her nose at a midshipman.

Turn up trump(s), To.

1621 BURTON *Anat. Mel.* III. iii. I. ii (1651) 602 They turned up trumpe, before the cards were shuffled. **1642** FULLER *H. & P. State* IV. viii The cards were so shuffled that two kings were turned up trump at once, which amazed men how to play their game. **1862** W. W. COLLINS *No Name* IV. viii Instances . . . of short courtships and speedy marriages, which have turned up trumps—I beg your pardon—which have turned out well, after all.

Turn (*noun*), *see* Everything in t.; Good t.; Ill t.

Turn(s, ed, eth) (*verb*), *see also* Goes far that t. not again; Great businesses t. on little pin; Great engines t. on small pivots; Runneth far that never t.; Tell where to t. his nose (He cannot).

Turnagain Lane.

1531 TINDALE *Expos. St. John* (P.S.) 140 (A) It is become a turn-again lane with them. **1562** HEYWOOD 190 Finde meanes to take a house in turne againe lane. **1662** FULLER (*Lond.*) II. 348 'He must take him a house in Turn-again Lane'. This, in old records, is called Wind-again Lane, and lieth in the parish of St. Sepulchre's, going down to Fleet-dike; which men must turn again the same way they came, for there it is stopped. The proverb is applied to those who ... must seasonably alter their manners.

Turnips like a dry bed but a wet head.

1917 BRIDGE 147 Turnips like a dry bed but a wet head. They do not grow well on un-drained land.

Turnips, *see also* Given him t. (She has).

Turtle, *see* True as a t. to her mate.

Tweedledum and Tweedledee, The difference between.

[Used originally of two rival musicians, and now in reference to differences held to be insignificant.] **1725** BYROM *Handel & Bononcini Poems* (1773) I. 344 Strange all this Difference should be, 'Twixt Tweedle-dum and Tweedle-dee! **1851** THACKERAY *Eng. Hum.* v (1876) 304 Swift could not see the difference between tweedle-dee and tweedle-dum. **1911** *Chr. Endeavour Times* 10 Aug. 724/1 A ... war of words over tweedledees of subtle doctrinal differences and tweedledums of Church polity.

Twelfth Day the days are lengthened a cock's stride, At.

1678 RAY 52.

Twenty-four hours in the day, There are only.

1902–4 LEAN IV. 145 ... Against those who attempt too much.

Twenty-fourth of August be fair and clear, If the | then hope for a prosperous autumn that year.

1732 FULLER no. 6470.

Twice clogs, once boots.

1871 *N. & Q.* 4th Ser. VII. 472 (A) Clogs to clogs is only three generations. A Lancashire proverb implying that, however rich a poor man may eventually become, his great-grandson will certainly fall back to poverty and clogs. **1875** SMILES *Thrift* 306 Hence the Lancashire proverb, 'Twice clogs, once boots'. The first man wore clogs, and accumulated a 'power o' money'; his rich son spent it; and the third generation took up the clogs again.

Twice, *see also* Done t. (If things were to be); Look t. at a penny; One thing said t. deserveth trudge; War (In) it is not permitted t. to err; Well done is t. done.

Twig(s), *see* Bend while it is a t.; Birchen t. break no ribs; Hop the t.

'Twill not be why for thy.

1678 RAY 345 *Somerset*. Of a bad bargain or great loss for little profit.

Twinkling of a bedpost (bed-staff), In the.

1660 *Charac. Italy* 78 In the twinkling of a Bedstaff he disrobed himself. **1833** MARRYAT *P. Simple* xxxvi Won't I get you out of purgatory in the twinkling of a bedpost? **1871** M. COLLINS *Mrg. & Merch.* III. iii. 78 In the twinkling of a bedpost Is each savoury platter clear.

Twinkling of an eye, In the.

c. **1300** *Vernon MS.* (E.E.T.S.) 286 In a twynclyng of an eiȝe ffrom erþe to heuene þon maiȝt styȝe. **1380** WYCLIF *1 Cor.* xv. 52 In a moment in the twynkelynge of an yȝe. **1549** LATIMER *4th Serm. bef. Edw. VI* (Arb.) 117 I wyl not denye but that he maye in the twynkeling of an eye, saue a man. **1596–7** SHAKS. *Merch. V.* II. ii. 183 I'll take my leave of the Jew in the twinkling of an eye.

Twist, *see* Turn (T.) round one's finger.

Twittle twattle,[1] drink up your posset-drink.

1670 RAY 253 ... This proverb had its original in *Cambridge*, and is scarce known elsewhere. [1 idle talk.]

Two and thirty, *see* One and thirty.

Two and two make four.

1697 COLLIER *Ess. Mor. Subj.* II (1703) 85 The ... notion ... is as clear as that two and two makes four. **1779** JOHNSON in *Boswell* (1848) lxviii. 624 You may have a reason why two and two should make five; but they will still make but four. **1927** *Times* 1 Mar. 19/6 The rules of arithmetic—the law that two and two make four ... are the laws that sentimental economists are always uncon-sciously trying to evade.

Two anons and a by-and-bye, is an hour and a half.

1636 CAMDEN 308.

Two attorneys can live in a town, when one cannot.

1902–4 LEAN IV. 169 ... *i.e.* they make work for each other. Quoted by Pollock, barrister on circuit, Sept. 1880.

Two bachelors drinking to you at once; you'll soon be married.

1738 SWIFT (Dial. ii) 347 *Lady A.* Well, miss, you'll certainly be soon married; here's two bachelors drinking to you at once.

Two bigs will not go in one bag.

1659 HOWELL *Brit. Prov.* 22.

Two bites of a cherry, To make.

1694 MOTTEUX *Rabelais* v. xxviii By Jingo, I believe he wou'd make three bites of a cherry. **1827** SCOT *Two Drovers* Take it all, man—take it all—never make two bites of a cherry.

Two blacks do not make a white.

1721 KELLY 321 ... An answer to them who, being blam'd, say others have done as ill or worse. **1881** AINGER C. Lamb 136 As two blacks do not make a white, it was beside the mark to make laborious fun over Southey's youthful ballads.

Two cats and a mouse, two wives in one house, two dogs and a bone, never agree in one.

c. 1417 Lansdowne MS. 762 in Reliq. Antiq. (1841) I. 233 Two wymen in one howse, Two cattes and one mowce, Two dogges and one bone, Maye never accorde in one. **1670** RAY 151. **1732** FULLER no. 6095 Two cats and one mouse, Two wives in one house, Two dogs at one bone, Can never agree in one.

Two daughters and a back door are three arrant (stark) thieves.

1641 FERGUSSON 94. **1670** RAY 51. **1721** KELLY 304 ... Daughters are expensive, and backdoors give servants opportunity to purloyn their master's goods.

Two dogs strive for a bone, and a third runs away with it.

c. 1386 CHAUCER Knight's T. A 1177 We stryve as dide the houndes for the boon, ... Ther cam a kyte, whyl that they were wrothe, And bar away the boon. **1575** GASCOIGNE Posies (1907) 475 It hath been a eld saying, that whiles two dogs do strive for a bone, the third may come and carry it away. **1592** Arden of Fevers. III. vi. 30 (Shaks. Apoc.) 20 I pray you, sirs, list to Esops talk: Whilest two stout dogs were striuing for a bone, There comes a cur and stole it from them both. **1721** KELLY 308 ... Spoken when two, by their mutual contentions, hinder each other of a place, and preferment, and it has fallen to a third by that means.

Two dry sticks will kindle a green one.

1678 RAY 213.

Two ears to one tongue, therefore hear twice as much as you speak.

[ZENO Diogenes Laertius 7. 1. 19. 23 Διὰ τοῦτο, εἶπε, δύο ὦτα ἔχομεν, στόμα δὲ ἔν, ἵνα πλείω μὲν ἀκούωμεν ἥττονα δὲ λέγωμεν. The reason that we have two ears and only one mouth, is that we may hear more and speak less.] **1535** Dialogues of Creatures (1816) cclvi To euery creature longith but oon tonge and two erys. **1669** PENN No Cross, No Crown xix Demosthenes ... had these sentences: 'That wise men speak little, and that therefore nature hath given men two ears and one tongue, to hear more than they speak.'

Two eyes can see more than one.

1596 BACON Promus no. 946 (A) Two eyes are better than one. **1614** CAMDEN 313. **1642** FULLER H. & P. State IV. v (1841) 246 Matters of inferior consequence he will communicate to a fast friend, and crave his advice; for, two eyes see more than one.

Two faces (heads) in one hood, To bear (carry, have).

c. 1400 Rom. Rose 7388 With so gret devotion They made her confession, that they had ofte, for the nones, Two hedes in one hood at ones. **1550** LEVER Serm. (Arb.) 99 These flatterers be wonders perilous felowes, hauynge two faces under one hoode. **1639** CLARKE 140 He carrieth two faces under one hood. **1668** SHADWELL Sul. Lov. IV. i (Merm.) 83 Luce. Hypocrisy is an abominable vice. C. Gent. 'Tis indeed, to be a Pharisee, and carry two faces in a hood, as the saying is. **1888** 'R. BOLDREWOOD' Robbery under Arms ii We ... scorned to look pious and keep two faces under one hood.

Two fools in one house are too many.

1579 LYLY Euphues (Arb.) 283 Me thinketh it were no good match, for two fooles in one bed are too many. **1641** FERGUSSON 96 Twa fooles in ane house is over many. **1732** FULLER no. 5328 Two Fools in a House are too many by a Couple.

Two fools met, There.

1721 KELLY 338 ... Spoken to them that say they refused such a considerable price for such a pennyworth. That is, he was a fool that offered it, and you a fool that refus'd it. **1732** FULLER no. 5679 Where two fools meet the bargain goes off.

Two forenoons in the same day, You cannot have.

1854 N. & Q. 1st Ser. IX. 527 In answer to some remarks ... on the necessary infirmities of old age, one of them replied, 'You cannot have two forenoons in the same day'.

Two friends have a common purse, When | one sings and the other weeps.

1707 MAPLETOFT 59. **1855** BOHN 562.

Two friends with one gift, To make.

1616 WITHALS 555 To make two friends with one favour. **1642** TORRIANO 45 To make two friends with one gift. **1732** FULLER no. 5205.

Two hands in a dish, and one in a purse.

1623 CAMDEN 279. **1738** SWIFT (Dial. ii) 344 Col. Then pray, Tom, carve for yourself; they say, two hands in a dish, and one in a purse. **1809** MALKIN Gil Blas x. x There was my bag! Two hands in a dish and one in a purse, was not one of her proverbs; so that finding the contents in crowns and pistoles, she thought ... the money ... hers.

Two hares afoot, To have (or To run after two hares).

1580 LYLY Euph. & his Eng. (Arb.) 394 Yet one thing maketh [mee] to feare, that in running after two Hares, I catch neither. **1658–9** BURTON *Diary* 9 Mar. (1828) IV. 108 Keep to your debate. You have two hares a-foot. You will lose both. **1732** FULLER no. 2782 If you run after two Hares, you will catch neither.

Two (Many) heads (wits) are better than one.

c. **1390** GOWER *Conf. Amantis* Prol. 157 Althogh a man be wys himselue, Yit is the wisdome more of twelue. *Ibid.* i. 1020 Two han more wit then on. **1546** HEYWOOD I. ix. 18 But of these two thinges he woulde determine none Without ayde. For two heddis are better than one. **1591** SPENSER *M. Hubberd* 82 Two is better than one head. **1641** FERGUSSON 96 Twa wits is better nor ane. **1721** KELLY 247 Many heads are better than one. *Ibid.* 335 Two wits are better than one. *Plus vident oculi, quam oculus.* **1772** FOOTE *Nabob* i. Wks. (1799) II. 289 Here comes brother Thomas; two heads are better than one; let us take his opinion. **1818** SCOTT *Rob Roy* viii Oh, certainly; but two heads are better than one; you know.

Two heads are better than one, even if the one's a sheep's.

1864 'Cornish Proverbs' in *N. & Q.* 3rd Ser. VI. 494 (A) Two heads are better than one if only sheeps' heads. **1894** NORTHALL *Folkphrases* (E.D.S.) 32 Two heads are better than one, even if the one's a sheep's. . . . 'A sheep's' head in folk figure, means a daft or unreasoning head.

Two heads are better than one, quoth the woman, when she had her dog with her to the market.

1732 FULLER no. 5331.

Two in distress makes sorrow less.

1855 BOHN 548.

Two is company, but three is none.

1871 *N. & Q.* 4th Ser. VIII. 506 Common Lancashire Proverbs. . . . When a lover meets his intended with her companion, the latter will say, 'Two are company, but three are none', and pass on another road. **1876** J. PAYN *Halves* xxi The proverb that 'Two is company, but three is none', had great weight with me just then. **1880** MRS. PARR *Adam & Eve* ix. 124 'Two's company and three's trumpery, my dear'.

Two kings in one kingdom do not agree well together.

1542 UDALL tr. *Erasm. Apoph.* (1877) 209 Vnto Darius he [Alexander] made aunswere in this maner, that neither the yearth might endure or abyde two sonnes, nor the countree of Asia, two kinges. **1596** SHAKS. *1 Henry IV* V. iv. 65–6 Two stars keep not their motion in one sphere; Nor can one England brook a double reign. **1609** DEKKER *Work for Armourers* (Gros.) iv. 105 *Non capit Regnum duos*, A Kingdome is heauen, and loues not two suns shining in it.

Two men ride on a horse, If | one must ride behind.

1598–9 SHAKS. *Much Ado* III. v. 40 An two men ride of a horse, one must ride behind. **1874** WHYTE-MELVILLE *Uncle John* x An old adage . . . affirms . . . that 'when two people ride on a horse, one must ride behind'. In that sentence is condensed the whole science of domestic government. **1927** *Times* 16 Feb. 10/4 'When two men ride a horse, one must ride behind'. . . . It is . . . the wife who must yield when conflict arises.

Two men, *see also* Amongst good men t. m. suffice.

Two negatives make an affirmative.

c. **1580** SIDNEY *Astrophel & Stella* Wks. (Feuillerat) II. 377 For Grammer sayes (to Grammer who sayes nay) That in one speech, two negatives affirme. **1593** 6. HARVEY in Wks. (Gros.) I. 293 But euen those two Negatiues . . . would be conformable enough, to conclude an Affirmatiue. **1596** HARINGTON *Metam. of Ajax* (1814) 126 For in one speech two negatives affirm. **1599–1600** SHAKS. *Twelfth N.* V. i. 24 If your four negatives make your two affirmatives, why then, the worse for my friends and the better for my foes. **1647** FULLER *Gd. Thoughts in Worse T.* xvii (1863) 190 Two negatives make an affirmative.

Two of a trade seldom agree.

c. **1605** DEKKER *Honest Wh.* Pt. II. IV. i (Merm.) 255–6 It is a common rule, and 'tis most true, Two of one trade ne'er love: no more do you. **1678** RAY 212. **1727** GAY *Fables* I. xxi. 43 (1859) 197 In every age and clime we see, Two of a trade can ne'er agree.

Two peas, As like as.

1580 LYLY *Euph. & his Eng.* (Arb.) 215 The Twinnes of Harpocrates (who wer as lyke as one pease is to an other). **1778** FRANCES BURNEY *Evelina* xxi (1920) 104 Why it's as like the twelve-penny gallery at Drury-Lane . . . as two peas are to one another.

Two places at once, One cannot be in.

1655–62 GURNALL *Chrn. in Armour* (1865) I. 206 You cannot be found in two places at once. Choose whether you will be found in your own righteousness or in Christ's. **1842** W. H. MAXWELL *Hector O'H.* xii As . . . nothing can be in two places at once . . . it was quite clear that neither of the Prymes could be at one and the same time in bed and in the street.

Two sides to every question, There are.

1863 C. KINGSLEY *Water Bab.* vi Let them recollect this, that there are two sides to every question.

Two sorrows of one, Make not.

c. **1430** LYDGATE *Chorle & Bird* in *Minor Poems* (Percy Soc.) 187 For who takethe sorowe for losse in that degree, Reknethe first his losse & aftir rekyn his peyne, And of

oon sorowe, makethe he sorowes tweyne.
1546 HEYWOOD II. v. 59 And reason saieth,
make not two sorowes of one. **1609** JONSON
Case Altered I. ii *Ct. Fern.* Passion's dulled
eye can make two griefs of one.

Two sparrows on one ear of corn make an ill agreement.

1599 MINSHEU (1623) Tt 2. **1651** HERBERT
367.

Two (Many, &c.) strings to one's bow, To have.

c. **1477** CAXTON *Jason* (E.E.T.S.) 57 I wil wel
that euery man be amerous & loue . but that
he haue .ij. strenges on his bowe. **1546** HEY-
WOOD I. xi. 30 Ye haue many stryngis to the
bowe. **1579** LYLY *Euphues* (Arb.) 116 My
counsaile is that thou have more strings to
thy bow, than one. **1585** QUEEN ELIZABETH
Let. to James VI, June I . . . hope that you
wyl remember, that who seaketh two stringes
to one bowe, he may shute strong, but never
strait. **1678** BUTLER *Hudibras* III. i. 3 As he
that has two strings t' his bow, And burns for
love and money too. **1771** SMOLLETT *Humph.
Clink.* 8 June, Wks. (1871) 507 A right
Scotchman has always two strings to his
bow, and is *in utrumque paratus* [prepared for
either alternative]. **1857** TROLLOPE *Barch.
Tow.* xxvii It was hard to say which was the
old love and which the new. . . . But two
strings to Cupid's bow are always dangerous
to him on whose behalf they are to be used.

Two Sundays come together (meet), When.

1616 HAUGHTON *Englishman for my Money*
I. ii. in HAZLITT's *O.E.P.* X. 502 *Wal.* Art
thou so mad as to turn French? *Math.* Yes,
marry, when two Sundays come together.
1678 RAY 271 When two *Sundays* meet, *i.e.*
never.

Two things, *see* Never be angry at (T. t. a
man should).

Two (words) to make a bargain, It takes. (*Cf.* More words than one; Second (word) makes, &c.)

1579 LYLY *Euphues* Wks. (Bond) I. 228 As
ther can be no bargaine where both be not
agreed, neither any Indentures sealed where
the one will not consent. **1608-9** MIDDLETON
Widow V. i. (Merm.) II. 479 There's two
words to a bargain ever, . . . and, if love be
one, I'm sure money's the other. *a.* **1633**
JONSON *T. Tub* II. iv. 76. **1732** FULLER
no. 3465 More Words than one to a Bargain.
1766 GOLDSMITH *Vicar W.* xxxi (Globe) 79
'Hold, hold, Sir,' cried Jenkinson, 'there are
two words to that bargain'. **1858** R. S.
SURTEES *Ask Mamma* lxxv Unfortunately,
it requires two parties to these bargains, and
Mrs. Yammerton wouldn't agree to it.

Two to make a quarrel, It takes.

1859 H. KINGSLEY *Geof. Hamlyn* xxx It takes
two to make a quarrel, Cecil, and I will not
be one. **1912** A. MACLAREN *Expos., Romans*
298 'It takes two to make a quarrel', . . . ;

it takes two to make peace also. **1919** DEAN
INGE *Outspoken Ess.* (1920) 42 In spite of
the proverb, it takes in reality only one to
make a quarrel. It is useless for the sheep to
pass resolutions in favour of vegetarianism,
while the wolf remains of a different opinion.

Two to one in all things against the angry man.

1732 FULLER no. 5336.

Two to one is odds.

1616 N. BRETON *Wks.* (Gros.) I *t* 24 Twoe to
one is odds. **1670** RAY 151 . . . *Noli pugnare
duobus,* Catull. *& Ne Hercules quidem adversus duos.* It's no uncomely thing to give
place to multitude. . . . *Hercules* was too
little for the *Hydra* and *Cancer* together.

Two will, That which | takes effect.

c. **1386** CHAUCER *Pard. T.* C 825 And two of
us shal strenger be than oon. c. **1596** MAR-
LOWE *Ovid's Elegies* in Wks. (Dyce) II. cl. 3
327 What two determine never wants effect.
1640 HERBERT 250.

Two wives in one house, *see under* Two cats.

Two wolves may worry one sheep.

1641 FERGUSSON 96 Twa wolfs may worrie
ane sheep.

Two wrongs don't make a right.

1875 CHEALES *Proverb. Folk-Lore* 120 (A).
1905 S. WEYMAN *Starvecrow Fm.* xxiv After
all, two wrongs don't make a right. **1906**
Spectator 23 June Two wrongs can never
make a right, and therefore we cannot accept
the ill-doing of the Nonconformist extremists
as an excuse for Churchmen who have forgotten their duty.

Two, *see also* No man can do t. things at once.

Twyford; My name is | I know nothing of the matter.

1694 MOTTEUX *Rabelais* (1897) **v.** xiii Has
not the fellow told you he does not know a
word of the business? His name is Twyford.
1732 FULLER no. 3502.

Tyburn tippet, A.

[= hangman's rope: Tyburn was the place of
public execution for Middlesex until 1783.]
1549 LATIMER *2nd Serm. bef. Edw. VI* (Arb.)
63 He should haue had a Tiburne tippet, a
halpeny halter, and all suche proude prelates.
1680 C. NESSE *Church Hist.* 143 The cart at
Tyburn drives away when the tippet is fast
about the necks of the condemned.

Tyburn, *see also* Dance the T. jig; Low ebb
at Newgate, afloat at T.; Preach at T.
Cross; Suits hang . . . in Westminster
Hall, at T. . . . .

Tying the sack before it be full, It is good.

1640 HERBERT 356.

Tympany[1] with two heels, She hath (is cured of) a.

c. 1566 *The Bugbears* III. iii. 38 Her greatest disease is a spice of the timpanye. 1579 *Marr. of Wit & Wisdom* (Shak. Soc.) 15 Nay, by S. Anne, I am afraid it is a tympany with two legges! 1678 RAY 275 She is cured of a tympany with two heels. 1732 FULLER no. 4127 She hath a tympany with two heels. [1 swelling: a euphemism for pregnancy.]

Tyrant is most tyrant to himself, A.

1640 HERBERT 358.

Tyrants seem to kiss, 'Tis time to fear when.

1609 *Pericles* I. ii. 78. 1855 BOHN 534.

U

Ugly as sin, As.

1804 EDGEWORTH *Pop. Tales, Out of Debt* (1805) I. 315 Why, she is as ugly as sin!

Ugly, *see also* Old enough and u. enough.

Ulysses, *see* Bow of U.

Unbidden guest knoweth not where to sit (*or*, must bring his stool with him), An.

c. 1350 *Douce MS. 52* no. 53 Unboden gest not, where he shall sytte. 1546 HEYWOOD I. ix. 17. 1579 LYLY *Euphues* (Arb.) 52 I will either bring a stoole on mine arme for an vnbidden guest, or a vizard on my face. 1612 WEBSTER *White Devil* III. i An unbidden guest Should travel as Dutchwomen go to church, Bear their stools with them. 1659 HOWELL *Eng. Prov.* 15 An unbidden guest must bring his stool with him.

Unblessed, *see* Ungirt, u.

Unborn, *see* Better u. than unbred.

Uncalled, *see* Come not to counsel u.; Comes u. sits unserved.

Uncertainty of the law, The glorious.

1848 BROS. MAYHEW *Image of his Father* xxv. 285 'Being a lawyer, I don't like to advise parties to go to law. I know the glorious uncertainty of it, as it's called.'

Uncle, *see* Call the bear 'u.'; Dutch u. (Talk like a).

Uncouth, *see* Unknown (U.) unkissed.

Under the rose.

[= in secret: there is reason to believe that the phrase originated in Germany. L. *sub rosa*.] 1546 *State Papers Hen. VIII* XI. 200 The sayde questyons were asked with lysence, and that yt shulde remayn under the rosse, that is to say, to remayn under the bourde, and no more to be rehersyd. 1622 FLETCHER *Beggars' Bush* II. iii If this make us speak Bold words, anon, 'tis all under the Rose forgotten. 1654 GAYTON *Pleas. Notes* III. v. 93 What ever thou and the foul pusse did doe (*sub Rosa* as they say). 1708 *Brit. Apollo* no. 112. 3/1 But when we with caution a secret Disclose, We cry Be it spoken (Sir) under the Rose. 1899 A. W. WARD *Eng. Dram. Lit.* III. 298 *Hudibras* ... merely repeated ... the comments which during the rule of Puritanism men had been making 'under the rose'.

Under water, famine; under snow, bread.

1640 HERBERT 341. 1721 KELLY 358 *Under water dearth, under snow bread.* Great rains in winter wash and impoverish the ground; but snow is supposed to cherish it.

Understanding, Who has not | let him have legs.

1813 RAY 24. *Ital.*

Understands ill, Who | answers ill.

1642 TORRIANO 30 He who understandeth amisse, answereth worse. 1736 BAILEY *Dict.* s.v. 'Understand' (A).

Understand(s), *see also* Good language which all u. not (Not); Trap (He u.).

Unexpected, *see* Nothing is so certain as the u.; Unforeseen (U.) that happens (It is).

Unforeseen (Unexpected) that always happens, It is the.

[PLAUTUS *Most.* 1. 3. 40 *Insperata accidunt magis quam speres.*] 1886 E. J. HARDY *How to be Happy* xxv It is the unexpected that constantly happens. 1909 *Times, Wkly.* 12 Nov. No place in the world is more familiar than the House of Commons with 'the unforeseen that always happens'.

Unforeseen, *see also* Nothing is certain but the u.

Ungirt, unblessed.

c. 1477 CAXTON *Book of Curtesye* (E.E.T.S.) 45 Vngyrte . vnblyssed . seruyng atte table Me semeth hym a seruant nothing able. 1596 SPENSER *F. Q.* IV. v. 18 Fie on the man, that did it first inuent, To shame vs all with this, 'Vngirt vnblest'. 1612–15 BP. HALL *Contempl.* IV. xii (1825) II. 385 'Ungirt, unblest', was the old word; as not ready till they were girded, so not till they had prayed. 1690 *c.* NESSE *O. & N. Test.* I. 451 Here, if ever, doth that proverb Ungirt, Unblest, hold true.

Unhappy man's cart is eith[1] to tumble[2], An.

1641 FERGUSSON 6. 1721 KELLY 22 ... Spoken of an unfortunate man, when misfortunes follow him. [1 easy. 2 overturn.]

Union is strength.

1596-7 SHAKS. *K. John* II. i. 446 This union shall do more than battery can To our fast-closed gates. **1877** WALFORD *Tales of Gt. Fam.* (1890) 156 The prosperity of the House of Rothschild [is due to] the unity which has attended the co-partnership of its members, ... a fresh example of the saying that 'union is strength'.

Union, *see also* Henry was the u. of the roses (In); Mezentian u.

Universities, *see* Three ways, the church (u.), sea, court.

Unkind, *see* Unkissed, u.

Unkindness, *see* Cut to u. (No); No man may poind for u.

Unkissed, unkind.

1584 PEELE *Arraign. of Paris* I. ii *Œn.* And I will have a lover's fee; they say, unkissed, unkind.

Unkissed, *see also* Unknown u.

Unknown (Uncouth) unkissed.

1374 CHAUCER *Troylus* I. 809 Vnknowe vnkyst and lost that is vn-sought. **1401** *Pol. Poems* (Rolls) II. 59 On old Englis it is said, unkissid is unknowun. **1546** HEYWOOD I. xi. 31 Vnknowne vnkyst . it is loste that is vnsought. *c.* **1592** NASHE *Mar-Martine* xxii Thou caytif kerne, vncouth thou art, vnkist thou eke sal bee. *a.* **1697** AUBREY *Lives* (1898) II. 254 He . . . ransackt the MSS. of the church of Hereford (there were a great many that lay uncouth and unkiss).

Unknown, *see also* Ignotum.

Unmannerly, *see* Better be u. than troublesome.

Unminded, unmoaned.

1546 HEYWOOD I. ix. 17 Unminded, vnmoned, go make your mone.

Unmoaned, *see* Unminded u.

Unreasonable are never durable, Things.

1855 BOHN 528. *Ital.*

Unrighteous penny corrupts the righteous pound, The.

1855 BOHN 517. *Ger.*

Unsafely, *see* Lives u. that looks too near.

Unseyit, *see* All things are good u.

Unsonsy[1] fish aye gets the unlucky bait, The.

1832 HENDERSON 140. [[1] unlucky.]

Unsought, *see* Lost that is u.

Unsound minds, like unsound bodies, if you feed, you poison.

1651 HERBERT 367.

Unspeakable Turk, The.

1876 GLADSTONE in MAXWELL *Life of W. H. Smith* (1894) 151 Mr. Gladstone ... published an article in the 'Contemporary Review' advocating the expulsion of the 'unspeakable Turk, bag and baggage', from Europe. **1907** H. DE WINDT *Through Savage Europe* viii Nearly thirty years had now elapsed since Servia last fought to free herself from the yoke of the unspeakable Turk.

Unstable as water.

c. **1380** WYCLIF *Sel. Wks.* II. 90 þis Emperour . . . was vnstable as watir. **1604-5** SHAKS. *Othello* V. ii. 132 She was false as water. **1611** BIBLE *Gen.* xlix. 4 Unstable as water, thou shalt not excel. **1824** SCOTT *St. Ronan's* xv Ye have got an idea that every thing must be changed—Unstable as water, ye shall not excel.

Untaught, *see* Better u. than ill taught.

Unthankful, *see* Call a man no worse than u. (You can).

Unthrift, *see* Blames their wife for own u.

Untimeous[1] spurring spills[2] the steed.

a. **1585** MONTGOMERIE *Cherrie & Slae* 397 (1645) 29 (p. 15) (Quoth DANGER) Huilie,[3] Freind, take heed, Untymous spurring spills the Steed. **1721** KELLY 343 ... That is, too much haste spoils business. [[1] untimely. [2] spoils. [3] softly.]

Unwashed, The great.

1864 J. PAYN *Lost Sir Massingb.* I There were no such things as skilled workmen', or 'respectable artisans', in those days. The 'people' were 'the Great Unwashed'.

Unworthy of life that causes not life in another, He is.

1633 D. DYKE *Six Evangel. Hist.* 98 Life, when grown to strength, is generative. . . . *Nascitur indigne per quem non nascitur alter*; He is unworthy of life, that causes not life in another.

Unworthy to live who lives only for himself, He is.

1732 FULLER no. 1952.

Up and down, *see* Wants in u. and d. (What she).

Up hill, spare me; down hill bear (forbear) me; plain way, spare me not; let me not drink when I am hot.

1721 KELLY 358 ... A rule in jockeyship how to use a horse in a journey.

Up the hill favour me, down the hill beware thee.

1639 CLARKE 22. **1721** KELLY 359 *Up hill spare me, down hill take tent[1] to thee.* For if you ride fast down a hill the horse will be fair to stumble. [[1] heed.]

Up to one's gossip, To be.

1785 GROSE *Dict. Vulg. T. Up to their Gossip*,
to be a match for one who attempts to cheat,
or deceive, to be on a footing, or in the Secret.
1828 CARR *Craven Dialect.* i. 193 (A).

Up to the ears.

a. **1553** UDALL *Roister D.* I. i (Arb. 12) If any
woman smyle Vp is he to the harde eares in
love. **1594** BARNFIELD *Affect. Sheph.* (Percy
Soc.) 8 (A) But leave we him in love up to
the eares.

Up, *see also* Take me not up before I fall.

Upper ten thousand, The.

1860 JOWETT in *Life* iii. 170 The world, that
is to say the upper 10,000. **1878** J. PAYN *By
Proxy* xxxvi Warren . . . is a *novus homo*, and
only a Conservative on that account; it being
the quickest method to gain admission
among the Upper Ten. **1905** SIR. G. O.
TREVELYAN *Interludes* 286 A rout which . . .
embraces a tithe of the Upper Ten Thousand,
is conventionally described . . . by the epithets
'small' and 'early'.

Urinal, *see* Suit at law and u.

Use legs and have legs.

c. **1582** G. HARVEY *Marginalia* (1913) 188 Vse
Legges, & haue Legges: Vse Law and haue
Law. Vse nether & haue nether. **1636** S.
WARD *Sermons* (1862) 25 Graces, gifts,
virtues . . . the principal beauty and benefit
of them consists in use. . . . Use limbs, and
have limbs; the more thou dost, the more
thou mayest. **1670** RAY 153. **1721** KELLY 342
Work legs, and win legs; hain[1] legs, and tine[2]
legs. [[1] save, spare. [2] lose.]

Use makes (maketh) mastery.

1340 *Ayenbite* (E.E.T.S.) 178 (A) Uor wone
makeþ maister. **1477** NORTON *Ord. Alch.* vii
in ASHM. *Theat. Chem. Brit.* (1652) 105 Use
maketh Masterie. **1546** HEYWOOD II. ii. 45.

Use (*later* Practice) makes perfect (perfectness).

[L. *Usus promptum facit.* Practice makes
perfect.] **1560** T. WILSON *Arte of Rhet.* (1909)
5 (A) Eloquence was vsed, and through
practise made perfect. **1564** BULLEIN *Dial.
agst. Fever* (1888) 66 Use maketh perfectness; we will teach you to swim by art as well
as we do by Nature. **1599** PORTER *Angry
Wom. Abingd.* II. i (Merm.) 127 Forsooth, as
use makes perfectness, so seldom seen is soon
forgotten. **1810** CRABBE *The Borough* xix
(1908) 186 *Practice makes perfect*; when the
month came round, He dropp'd the cash, nor
listen'd for a sound. **1829** SCOTT *Jrnl.* 27
Jan. Use makes perfectness. **1863** C. READE
Hard Cash xliv He lighted seven fires, skil-
fully on the whole, for practice makes perfect.
1902 *Spectator* 10 May Practice never makes
perfect. It improves up to a point.

Use one like a dog, To.

1619 W. HORNBY *Scourge of Drunkennes* A 4
(A) Ile vse thee like a dogge, a Iew, a slave.
1688 SHADWELL *Squire Alsatia* I. i (Merm.)

242 I'll endure 't no longer! . . . I'll teach
him to use his son like a dog. **1714** STEELE
Lover, No. 7, 11 Mar. I was terribly afraid
that . . . if she caught me at such an advantage, she would use me like a dog.

Use one like a Jew, To.

1619 W. HORNBY *Scourge of Drunkennes* A 4
(A) Ile vse thee like a dogge, a Iew, a slave.
1662 FULLER (*Lond.*) II. 346 'I will use you as
bad as a Jew'. . . . That poor nation (especially on Shrove Tuesday) being intolerably
abused by the English. **1700** BP. PATRICK
Comm. Deut. xxviii. 37 Better we cannot
express the most cut-throat dealing, than
thus, You use me like a Jew.

Use (*noun*), *see also* Keep a thing seven
years, find u. for it; Old u. and wont, legs
about the fire; Once a u. ever a custom;
Worst u. can put man to is to hang him.

Use (*verb*), *see* Means (U. the) and God give
blessing; Once and u. it not.

Used key is always bright, The.

1758 FRANKLIN in ARBER *E. Garner* v. 579
*Sloth, like Rust, consumes faster than Labour
wears; while the used key is always bright.*

Used to, *see* Nothing when you are u. to it;
Youth is u. to (What), age remembers.

Useth me better than he is wont, He that | will betray me.

1573 SANDFORD (1576) H 2[v]. **1723** FULLER
no. 2180 He that is kinder than he was wont,
hath a design upon thee.

Usurer at the table, To speak of a | mars the wine.

1640 HERBERT 362.

Usurers are always good husbands.

1616 BRETON *Cross. Prov.* Wks. (1879) II.
App. iii Vsurers are alwaies good Husbands.

Usurers live by the fall of heirs, as swine by the dropping of acorns.

1607 G. WILKINS *Mis. of Enf. Marriage* III.
in HAZLITT *O.E.P.* IX. 509 To see that we
and usurers live by the fall of young heirs,
as swine by the dropping of acorns.

Usurer(s), *see also* God keep me from . . . u.'s
[house].

Uter-Pendragon[1] do what he can, Let | The river Eden will run as it ran.

1659 HOWELL *Eng. Prov.* 20/1. **1662** FULLER
(*Westm.*) III. 302 'Let Uter-Pendragon do what
he can, The River Eden will run as it ran'. . . .
Uter-Pendragon had a design to fortify the
castle of Pendragon in this county . . . whereunto, with much art and industry, he invited
. . . the river of Eden to forsake his old
channel, and all to no purpose . . . *Naturam
expellas furcâ licet, usque recurret.* [[1] a mythical
Welsh prince.]

Utopia.

[The title of the book published by Sir T. More, in 1516, describing an imaginary island with a perfect system of government, hence an ideally perfect place or state of things. (= nowhere, from Gk. οὐ not + τόπ-ος a place).] **1570** FOXE *Bk. Martyrs* (ed. 2) 1156/2 I do not . . . thinke, that . . . there is any such fourth place of Purgatory at all (vnles it be in M. More's Vtopia). **1613** PURCHAS *Pilgrimage* (1614) 708 The reports of this his voyage savour more of an Vtopia,

and Plato's Commonwealth, then of true Historie. **1621** BURTON *Anat. Mel.* To the Reader, I will yet, to satisfy and please myself, make an Utopia of mine own, a new Atlantis, a poetical Commonwealth of mine own. *a.* **1734** NORTH *Lives* II. 364 Young men, for want of experience, . . . create Utopias in their own imagination. **1837** MACAULAY *Ess.*, *Lord Bacon* (1903) 402 An acre in Middlesex is better than a principality in Utopia. The smallest actual good is better than the most magnificent promise of impossibilities.

V

Vain-glory blossoms but never bears.

1616 DRAXE 213 Vaine glory is a floure that beareth no corne. **1732** FULLER no. 5342.

Vale best discovereth the hill, The.

1594 BACON *Promus* no. 145 (A). **1597–8** Id. *Ess.*, *Followers* (Arb.) 38 To take aduise of friends is euer honorable: . . . *And the vale best discouereth the hill.*

Valentine's Day[1], On | will a good goose lay; if she be a good goose, her dame well to pay, she will lay two eggs before Valentine's Day.

1678 RAY 51. [[1] 14 Feb.]

Valet, *see* No man is a hero to v.

Valiant man's look is more than a coward's sword, A.

1640 HERBERT 350.

Valley, *see* Stays in the v. (He that).

Valour can do little without discretion.

1664 CODRINGTON 223. **1670** RAY 27.

Valour that parleys is near yielding.

1637 HOWELL *Lett.* 4 Dec. (1903) II. 106 Others . . . will endure . . . a siege; but will incline to parley at last, and . . . fort and female which begins to parley is half won. **1640** HERBERT 345.

Valour would fight, but discretion would run away.

1678 RAY 214. **1732** FULLER no. 5344.

Valour, *see also* Discretion.

Value, *see* Know the v. of a ducat (If you would).

Vanity Fair.

1678 BUNYAN *Pilgr. P.* (1900) 82 The name of that Town is Vanity; and at the town there is a Fair kept, called Vanity Fair. **1816** J. SCOTT *Vis. Paris* (ed. 5) 137 Such is the Palais Royal;—a vanity fair—a mart of sin and seduction! **1848** THACKERAY *Vanity F.* xxv The last scene of her dismal Vanity Fair comedy was fast approaching.

Variety is charming.

1822 COBBETT *Rural Rides* 24 Nov. They say that ' *variety* is charming', and this day I have had of scenes and of soils a variety indeed! **1861** G. J. WHYTE-MELVILLE *Tilbury N.* XXV ' Variety is charming', and that charm no one can deny to the different kinds of weather which successively constitute an English summer's day.

Varlet, *see* Ape's an ape, a v.'s a v.

Vat, *see* Tub (V.) must stand on own bottom.

Vaunter and a liar are near akin, A.

c. **1374** CHAUCER *Troylus* III. 309 A vauntor and a lier, al is on. **1641** FERGUSSON 4 A vaunter and a lier is both one thing. **1721** KELLY 36 . . . when a man once takes a humour of boasting . . . , he will not stop at the most palpable lies.

Veal will be cheap: calves fall.

1678 RAY 83 . . . A jeer for those who lose the calves of their legs.

Veal, *see also* Calf (Greatest) is not sweetest v.; Raw pulleyn, v., make churchyards fat; Shoulder of v. (In a) . . . good bits.

Vease thee, I will.

1678 RAY 345 I'll vease thee (i.e. *hunt, drive thee*). *Somerset.*

Velvet, On.

1769 BURKE *Obs. Pres. St. Nat.* Wks. II. 142 Not like our author, who is always on velvet, he is aware of some difficulties. **1785** GROSE *Dict. Vulg. T. To be upon velvet*, to have the best of a bet or match. **1826** SCOTT *Journ.* 4 March Though I have something to pay out of it, I shall be on velvet for expense. **1897** *Daily News* 1 June 3/5 Is that what you call being ' On velvet' when you are sure to win something?—Yes.

Velvet true heart, He is a.

1678 RAY 83 . . . *Chesh.*

Velvet, *see also* Iron hand in v. glove; Silk purse (V.) out of sow's ear.

Vengeance, The noblest | is to forgive.

1547 W. BALDWIN *Treatise of Moral Philos.* (1550) O 4 Forgiuenes is a valyaunte kynde of reuengeance. **1573** SANDFORD (1567) 19 Saith Seneca, *Nobilissimum vindictae genus est parcere.* The noblest kind of reuengeance is to forgive. **1580** LYLY *Euph. & his Eng.* (Arb.) 452 Thinking no reuenge more princely, then to spare when she might spill. **1666** TORRIANO 202 To pardon, is a divine revenge. **1853** TRENCH i. 13 *The noblest vengeance is to forgive*; here is the godlike proverb on the manner in which wrongs should be recompensed.

Vengeance of the law, The.

1881 E. B. TYLOR *Anthrop.* (1889) 417 Reading ... of a Corsican 'vendetta', we hardly ... think of it as a relic of ancient law . . ., as is still plain . . . [from] such phrases as 'the vengeance of the law'.

Vengeance, *see also* Vice is (Where), v. follows. *See also* Revenge.

Venice-glass broken, *see* Credit lost.

Venison, *see* Flesh (All) is not v.; Gentlemen and rich men v. in heaven; Princes are v. in heaven.

Venom to that of the tongue, There is no.

1659 HOWELL *Eng. Prov.* 11/2.

Venom, *see also* Spit one's v.

Venture a small fish to catch a great one.

1670 RAY 152 ... Il faut hazarder un petit poisson pour prendre un grand, *Gall.* **1796** EDGEWORTH *Par. Asst., Lit. Merch.* i (1903) 376 Venture a small fish, as the proverb says, to catch a great one.

Venture, Take your | as many a good ship has done.

1721 KELLY 304 ... Spoken when advice is asked in a case where the success may be dubious.

Venture it, I will | as Johnson did his wife, and she did well.

1678 RAY 83. **1732** FULLER no. 1367 E'en venture on, as Johnson did on his wife.

Venture not all in one bottom.[1]

[ERASM. *Ad. Ne uni navi facultates.*] **1579** LYLY *Euphues* (Arb.) 285 I adventured in one ship to put all my wealth. **1596–7** SHAKS. *Merch. V.* I. i. 42 My ventures are not in one bottom trusted. **1623** WEBSTER *Duch. Malfi* III. v (Merm.) 193 Let us not venture all this poor remainder In one unlucky bottom. **1639** CLARKE 95. **1732** FULLER no. 5349. [1 vessel.]

Venture out of your depth till you can swim, Never.

1855 BOHN 459.

Venture(s), *see also* Many v. make full freight; Nothing v. nothing have; Nothing v. nothing win.

Venus, *see* Ceres and Bacchus (Without), V. grows cold.

Verbum sap. See Word is enough.

Verdingales[1] to Broad-gates[2] in Oxford, Send.

1562 HEYWOOD *Fifth Hund. Epig.* no. 55, 188 Alas poor verdingales must lie in the streete: To house them, no doore in the citee made meete. Syns at our narow doores they in cannot win, Send them to Oxforde, at Brodegates to get in. **1662** FULLER (*Oxf.*) III. 7 'Send verdingales to Broad Gates in Oxford.' With these *verdingales* the gowns of women beneath their waists were pent-housed out far beyond their bodies; ... the first inventress ... a light house-wife, who, . . . sought to cover her shame and the fruits of her wantonness. ... Their wearers could not enter (except going sidelong) at any ordinary door; which gave the occasion to this proverb. [1 hooped petticoats (farthingales). 2 Broadgates Hall, Oxford, was superseded in 1624 by Pembroke College.]

Verify, *see* Always v. your references.

Vessel, The greatest | hath but its measure.

1732 FULLER no. 4580.

Vessel(s), *see also,* Ill v. seldom miscarry; Old v. must leak; Weaker v.

Vex a dog to see a pudding creep, It would.

1659 HOWELL *Eng. Prov.* 21/1. **1738** SWIFT (Dial. ii) 349 *Col.* I have a mind to eat a piece of that sturgeon, but fear it will make me sick. *Never* . . . Let it alone, and I warrant it won't hurt you. *Col.* Well, it would vex a dog to see a pudding creep.

Vicar of Bowdon, Every man cannot be.

1678 RAY 301 *Chesh.* . . . Bowden . . . is one of the greatest livings near Chester.

Vicar of Bray will be vicar of Bray still, The.

1662 FULLER (*Berks.*) I. 113 'The Vicar of Bray will be Vicar of Bray still'. The vivacious vicar hereof living under king Henry the Eighth, king Edward the Sixth, queen Mary, and queen Elizabeth, was first a Papist, then a Protestant, then a Papist, then a Protestant again. ... Being taxed . . . for being a turncoat . . .—'Not so', said he; 'for I always kept my principle, which is this, to live and die the vicar of Bray.' *c. 1720 Song, Vicar of Bray* That whatsoever King shall reign, I'll still be Vicar of Bray, Sir. **1735** BROME in *Lett. by Eminent Persons* (1813) II. 100 It is Simon Aleyn or Allen, who was Vicar of Bray about 1540 and died 1588.

Vicar of fools is his ghostly father, The.

1562 HEYWOOD *Fifth Hund. Epig.* no. 19, 182 (A) Whence come all these? From the vicar of saint fools. **1564** BULLEIN *Dial. agst. Fever* (1888) 27 *Medicus.* The vicar of S. Fooles be your ghostly father. Are you so wise? **1660** TATHAM *Rump.* v. i. Wks. (1879) 268 Sure the vicar of fools was his ghostly father. Be beat without a blow, there's a mystery indeed!

Vice is often clothed in virtue's habit.

1569 C. AGRIPPA *Vanity of Arts & Sciences* *2 Vices often times put on the coloure of vertue. *c.* **1590** HARVEY *Marginalia* 99 Eueri Vice hath a cloak: and preasith, or creepith in, under yͤ maske of A vertu. **1664** CODRINGTON 223.

Vice is, Where | vengeance follows.

[HORACE *Odes* 3. 2. 31 *Raro antecedentem scelestum Deseruit pede pœna claudo.* Rarely has punishment, with halting foot, failed to overtake the evil-doer in his flight.] **1639** CLARKE 325.

Vice, *see also* Hates not the person but the v.; Maintains one v. (What) would bring up two children.

Victory that comes without blood, It is a great.

1640 HERBERT 327.

Victory, *see also* Better a lean peace; Moors (The more), better v.; Pyrrhic v.

Victualled my camp, I have.

1678 RAY 345 I have victualled my camp (*filled my belly*).

Victuals, Of all | drink digests the quickest.

1721 KELLY 274 *Of all meat in the world, drink goes down the best.* A facetious bull when we drink heartily after meat. **1738** SWIFT (*Dial.* ii) 346 *Spark.* Of all vittles drink digests the quickest: give me a glass of wine.

Victuals in England, There is more good | than in seven other kingdoms.

1639 CLARKE 74.

Video meliora proboque, deteriora sequor, see See and approve the better course.

Vier, *see* O Master V.

Views, *see* Short v. (Take).

Village, *see* Better be first in a v.

Vine of a good soil, Take a | and the daughter of a good mother.

1813 RAY 45 Di buona terra to' la vigna, di buona madre to' la figlia. *Take a vine of a good soil, and the daughter of a good mother.*

Vine poor, Make the | and it will make you rich.

1813 RAY 44 . . . Prune off its branches.

Vinegar of sweet wine, Take heed of the.

1578 FLORIO *First Fruites* f. 30 (A) Beware of vinegar and sweete wine, and of the anger of a peaceable man. **1579** LYLY *Euph.* (Arb.) 48 For as the best Wine doth make the sharpest vinegar, so the deepest loue turneth to the deadlyest hate. **1612** WEBSTER *White Devil* IV. i (Merm.) 74 Best natures do commit the grossest faults, When they're given o'er to jealousy, as best wine, Dying, makes strongest vinegar. **1640** HERBERT 338 **1754** FRANKLIN *Jan.* Take heed of the Vinegar of sweet Wine, and the Anger of Goodnature. **1852** E. FITZGERALD *Polonius* 9 'It is . . . the sweet wine that makes the sharpest vinegar', says an old proverb.

Vinegar, *see also* Cries wine sells v.; Sharp as v.

Vintage, *see* Short boughs long v.

Vintry, Three Cranes in the, *see* Patience in adversity.

Violent, *see* Nothing that is v. is permanent.

Violet(s), *see* A-mothering (Who goes) finds v.

Viper so little, but hath its venom, No.

1666 TORRIANO 257 Every serpent hath it venom. **1732** FULLER no. 3639.

Viper, *see also* Snake (V.) in the bosom.

Virtue and a trade are the best portion for children.

1640 HERBERT 321.

Virtue flies from the heart of a mercenary man.

1651 HERBERT 370.

Virtue has all things in itself.

1594 LIPSIUS *6 Books of Politics* tr. Jones B 1ᵛ Vertue . . . in her selfe containeth all things. **1736** BAILEY *Dict.* s.v. 'Virtue' (A).

Virtue is a jewel of great price.

1616 BRETON *Cross. Prov.* Wks. (1879) II. App. iii.

Virtue is her own reward.

1642 SIR T. BROWNE *Relig. Med.* I. xlvii (1881) 74 *Ipsa sui pretium virtus sibi,*[1] that Vertue is her own reward, is but a cold principle. **1692** PRIOR *Ode in Imit. of Horace* 146 And virtue is her own reward. [[1] CLAUDIAN *De Mallii Theod. Consul.* v. 1.]

Virtue is the only true nobility.

1592 DELAMOTHE (1647) 6 It is vertue only that gives nobility. **1732** FULLER no. 5383.

Virtue never grows old.

1640 HERBERT 320.

Virtue of a coward is suspicion, The.

1651 HERBERT 373.

Virtue of necessity, Make a.

[QUINTIL. **1**. 5 *Laudem virtutis necessitati damus*. ST. JEROME *In Libros Rufini*, III. 2. *Facis de necessitate virtutem*. (You make a virtue of necessity.)] *c.* **1374** CHAUCER *Troylus* IV. 1586 Thus maketh vertu of necessité! *c.* **1412** HOCCLEVE *Reg. Princes* (E.E.T.S.) 46, l. 1252 Make of necessite, reed I, vertu. **1532** HENRYSON *Test. Cress.* 478 I counsale thee mak vertew of ane neid. *c.* **1586** *Maxwell Younger MS.* in HENDERSON (1832) xli, no. 172 Neide oft makis wertew. **1594–5** SHAKS. *Two Gent.* IV. i. 62 Are you content . . . To make a virtue of necessity And live, as we do, in this wilderness? **1595–6** *Rich. II* I. iii. 278 There is no virtue like necessity. **1641** FERGUSSON 80 Need makes vertue. **1642** J. HOWELL *Inst. For. Trav.* xiii (Arb.) 62 Industrious people . . . making a *rare vertue of necessity*, for the *same thing which makes a Parrot speake, makes them to labour.*

Virtue that poverty destroyeth not, There is no.

1573 SANDFORD (1576) 103 & 218. **1578** FLORIO *First Fruites* f. 32 (A) There is no vertue, but pouertie will marre it.

Virtue which parleys is near a surrender.

1721 BAILEY *Dict.* s.v. 'Virtue' (A). **1855** BOHN 550.

Virtue, *see also* Blushing is v.'s colour; Money, wit, and v. (Of) believe one fourth; Show a good man his error, he turns it to v.; Soweth v. shall reap fame; Vice is often clothed in v.'s habit; Youth (Who that in) no v. useth.

Virtuous, He cannot be | that is not rigorous.

1640 HERBERT 348.

Visible church, The.

[*i.e.* Harrow on the Hill.] *a.* **1685** CHARLES II in DEFOE *Tour through Gt. Brit.* (1748) II. iv. 214 *Harrow*; the Church of which standing on the Summit of an Hill, and having a very high Spire, they tell us, King Charles II, ridiculing the warm Disputes . . . concerning the *Visible* Church of *Christ* upon Earth, used to say, This was it. **1790** GROSE S.V. Middx. *The visible church; i.e. Harrow on the Hill.* King Charles II, speaking on a topic then much agitated among divines of different persuasions, namely, which was the visible church, gave it in favour of Harrow on the Hill, which, he said, he saw, go where he would.

Visit(s), *see* Angel v.

Vixere fortes ante Agamemnona, *see* Brave men before A.

Voice is the best music, The.

1639 CLARKE 57.

Voice of the people, the voice of God, The.

[L. *Vox populi, vox Dei*, a misunderstanding of *Isaiah* lxvi. 6 *Vox populi de civitate* . . . *vox Domini reddentis retributionem inimicis*.] *a.* **804** ALCUIN *Opp.* (Froben, 1777) cxxvii. t. 1, p. 191 (A) *Nec audiendi sunt ii qui volent dicere, vox populi vox Dei, cum tumultuositas vulgi semper insaniae proxima est. c.* **1378** GOWER *Mir. de l'Omme*, l. 12725 Au vois commune est acordant La vois de dieu. *c.* **1412** HOCCLEVE *Reg. Princes* (E.E.T.S.) 104, l. 2886 For peples vois is goddes voys, men seyne. **1575** GASCOIGNE *Posies, Dulce Bel. Inex.* (1907) 143 Yet could I never any reason feele, To thinke *Vox populi vox Dei est.* **1738** POPE *Imit. Hor.* II. i. 89, 90 All this may be; the people's voice is odd, It is, and it is not, the voice of God. **1827–48** HARE *Gues. at Truth* (1859) i. 164 That *vox populi*, which, when it bursts from the heaving depths of a nation's heart, is in truth *vox Dei.* **1853** TRENCH vi. 130 The Latin proverb, *The voice of the people, the voice of God* . . . rests on the assumption that the foundations of man's being are laid in the truth. . . . 'The general and perpetual voice of men is as the sentence of God himself.' [HOOKER *Eccles. Pol.* i, § 8.]

Volunteer, One | is worth two pressed[1] men.

1705 LD. SEYMOUR in HEARNE *Collect.* 31 Oct. (O.H.S.) I. 62, 100 Voluntiers are better than 200 press'd men. **1834** MARRYAT *Jacob Faith.* xiii 'Shall I give you a song?' 'That's right, Tom; a volunteer's worth two pressed men.' **1837** CHAMIER *Saucy Areth.* iii Don't fancy you will be detained against your will: one volunteer is worth two pressed men. [1 impressed for the King's or Government service.]

Vomit, *see* Dog returns to his v.

Vote, *see* Voyage never has luck where each one has v.

Vows made in storms are forgotten in calms.

1639 FULLER *Holy War* II. xlvi (1840) 114 The cardinals lamented out of measure. . . . But this their passion spent itself . . . , and these mariners' vows ended with the tempest. **1732** FULLER no. 5408.

Vox populi, vox Dei, *see* Voice of the people.

Voyage never has luck where each one has a vote, That.

a. **1585** MONTGOMERIE *Cherrie & Slae* li (1821) 28 'They say, that voyage never luckis, Quhar ilke ane hes ane vote'.

Voyage, *see also* Goes a great v. . . . to bottom of sea; Goes and comes maketh good v. (He that); No man was ever . . . better from v.

Vulgar will keep no account of your hits, but of your misses, The.

1732 FULLER no. 4816.

W

Wabster, Jock, *see* Devil goes ower J. W.

Wade's Mill, *see* Ware and W. M.

Wading in an unknown water, No safe.

c. **1552** *Manifest Detection* (Percy Soc.) 6 Ye seem to be a man that wadeth not so unadvisedly in the deep, but that always ye be sure of an anchor hold. **1588** GREENE *Wks.* (Gros.) IX. 67 Wade not too far where the foorde is vnknowne. **1589** *Ibid.* VII. 160 Wade not there where the ford hath no footing. **1612** T. ADAMS *Wks.* (1616) 50. **1639** CLARKE 250. **1670** RAY 153. **1721** KELLY 261 *No safe wading in uncouth[1] waters.* It is no wisdom to engage with dangers that we are not acquainted with. **1732** FULLER no. 3627. [[1] strange.]

Wae 's[1] the wife that wants the tongue, but weel 's the man that gets her.

1832 HENDERSON 62. [[1] woe's.]

Wag as the bush wags, He will.

1721 KELLY 140 *He'll wag as the bush wags with him.* That is, he will comply with all the changes of times, and parties.

Wage will get a page.

1721 KELLY 358 . . . If I be able to hire servants I will get them to hire.

Wagging of a straw, The.

[= a mere trifle.] *c.* **1374** CHAUCER *Troylus* II. 1745 In titeryng, and pursuyte, and delayes, The folk devyne at waggyng of a stree. *a.* **1529** SKELTON *Magnif.* 1026 Wks. (1843) I. 258 Sometyme I laughe at waggynge of a straw. **1592-3** SHAKS. *Rich. III* III. v. 7 I can . . . Tremble and start at wagging of a straw. **1639** CLARKE 34 Angry at the wagging of a straw. **1670** RAY 184 He will go to law for the wagging of a straw.

Wagon, *see* Hitch your w. to a star.

Wags a wand in the water, He.

1641 FERGUSSON 48 *Of unprofitable foolish persons. . . .*

Wagtail, *see* Makes his mistress a goldfinch.

Waistcoat, *see* Wight (Stout) as webster's (miller's) w.

Wait and see.

1839 DICKENS *N. Nickleby* lv Very good, my dear', replied Mrs. Nickleby, with great confidence, 'Wait and see'. *Ibid.* lxiii [Mrs. N. again] 'Never mind; wait and see'. **1915-16** A phrase generally associated with Asquith as Premier at that date, a catchword from the legal chambers of Sir Henry James, where he worked. G. Robey in his song 'In Other Words' (Asquith supposed speaking): Remain inert and dormant just like me, and cultivate spontaneous quiescence, In other words, Wait and See! **1945** A. J. CUMMINGS in *News Chron.* 24 Aug. They [the Labour party in Parliament] are prepared to 'wait and see'.

Wait till you're asked.

1888 MRS. OLIPHANT *Second Son* xiv 'I have never been at a dance. . . . Oh, papa, let me go'. 'You had better wait till you're asked,' said the Squire.

Wait(s), *see also* Everything comes to him who w.; Know what to do (When you don't), w.; Pulls with a long rope that w. another's death; Wash my hands and w. upon you.

Waiting for dead men's shoes, It is ill.

1815 SCOTT *Guy Man.* xxxvii That's but sma' gear, puir thing; she had a sair time o't with the auld leddy. But it's ill waiting for dead folk's shoon. **1853** TRENCH v. 113 What a warning . . . against . . . looking forward to certain advantages . . . is contained in that proverb: *It is ill standing in dead men's shoes.* **1870** C. READE *Put Yourself* xxix What, go into his house, and wait for dead men's shoes! Find myself some day wishing . . . that noble old fellow would die!

Wakefield, *see* Merry W.

Waken sleeping dogs, It is ill to. (*Cf.* Let sleeping dogs lie.)

c. **1374** CHAUCER *Troylus* III. 764 It is nought good a slepyng hound to wake. **1546** HEYWOOD I. x. 24 A sléepe by (quoth she) routyng lyke a hog. And it is euyll wakyng of a sléepyng dog. **1597-8** SHAKS. *2 Hen. IV* I. ii. 176 Since all is well, Keep it so: wake not a sleeping wolf. **1641** FERGUSSON 64. **1647** *Countryman's New Commonw.* 22 Wake not a sleeping Lyon. **1721** KELLY 85 . . . It is foolish to stir up a quarrel that has been long forgot; or provoke a person to whom you are not a match.

Waking men, *see* War must be waged by w. m.

Waldrons, *see* Clent (People of).

Wales, *see* Anglesea is the mother of W.; Knight of Cales; Powys is paradise of W.

Walk (*noun*), *see* Fisherman's w.

Walk, drab, walk!

[= begone.] **1525** *Widow Edyth* 11th Jest (HAZLITT iii. 91) No man can tel, Where she is become, with Walk queane walk. **1546** HEYWOOD II. iv. 52 Walke drab[1] walke. [[1] slut, harlot.]

Walk groundly; talk profoundly; drink roundly; sleep soundly.

1562 HEYWOOD *Sixth Hundred of Epigrams,* no. 29. **1869** HAZLITT 446.

Walk, knave, walk!

[= begone] **1529** MORE *Dyaloge* I. xiv. 18 b
He bad hym walk faytoure. **1530** TINDALE
Pract. Prelates G vb The Cardinall bad him
walcke a vilayne. **1546** HEYWOOD II. iv. 52
Nay (quoth she) walke knaue walke Saieth
that terme. *c.* **1655** *Roxburghe Ballads*
(Ballad Soc.) **VI. 211** 'Walk, knave!' is a
parrot's note.

Walk much in the sun, They that | will be tanned at last.

1553 T. WILSON *Arte of Rhet.* (1909) 5 They
that walke much in the Sunne, and thinke not
of it, are yet for the most part Sunne burnt.
1579 GOSSON *Sch. Abuse* (Arb.) 59 We walke
in the Sun many times for pleasure, but our
faces are tanned before we returne: though
you go to theaters to se sport, *Cupid* may
catche you ere you departe. **1579–80** E. KIRKE
Ded. of *Shep. Cal.* in Spenser Wks. (Globe)
441 How could it be, ... but that walking in
the sonne, ... he mought be sunburnt; and,
having the sound of those auncient Poetes
still ringing in his eares, he mought ... hit
out some of theyr tunes. **1670** RAY 146.

Walk(eth) (*verb*), *see also* Ground is not good
enough for her to w. on; Wisely w. that
safely go.

Walking over my grave, Some one is.

1738 SWIFT (Dial. i) 341 *Miss.* [*Shuddering.*]
Lord! there's somebody walking over my
grave.

Walking with a horse in one's hand, It is good.

1591 LYLY *Endym.* IV. ii *Epi.* Why, is it not
said: It is good walking when one hath his
horse in his hand? **1721** KELLY 196 ... It is
good when a man of any art, trade, or profession, has an estate to support him, if these
should fail. **1738** SWIFT (Dial. ii) 345 *Col.* ...
I hear you are a great walker.... *Sir J.* No,
...; I always love to walk with a horse in my
hand.

Wallet, *see* Kingdom of a cheater (In the);
See not what is in w. behind.

Wallflower, *see* Faint at the smell of a w.

Walls have ears. (*Cf.* Fields have eyes, &c.)

1566 GASCOIGNE *Supposes* I. i The tables ...
beds . portals, yea and the cupbords themselves have eares ... the windowes and the
doores. **1591** HARINGTON *Orl. Fur.* xxii. 32
(A) For posts have eares, and walls have eyes
to see. **1620** SHELTON *Quix.* IV. vii. 53 They
say Walls have ears.

Wall(s), *see also* Bare w. make giddy housewives; England's wooden w.; Further than
the w. he cannot go; Great without small,
bad w.; Hard with hard makes not w.;
Line to the w. (Bring your); Look on the
w. and it will not bite; Run one's head
against w.; Taking the w. of dog (Not
worth); White w. fool's paper.

Walnut-tree, *see* Plants a w.-t. expects not to
eat fruit (Who); Spaniel, a woman, and
a w.-t.

Walsall, *see* Sutton.

Walsall man's goose, *see* Too much for one.

Walsingham, *see* Swear W.

Waltham, *see* Wise as W.'s calf.

Wame, *see* Lay your w. to your winning. *See
also* Weime.

Wand[1] ding[2] him, Let his own.

1641 FERGUSSON 44 He is sairest dung when
his awn wand dings him. **1721** KELLY 233 ...
Let him reap the fruits of his own folly.
[[1] rod. [2] beat.]

Wand, *see also* Thraw the w. while green;
Wags a w. in the water.

Want a pretence to whip a dog, If you | it is enough to say he eat up the frying-pan.

1732 FULLER no. 2794.

Want a thing (well) done, If you | do it yourself.

[*Cf.* **1566** PAINTER *Pal. of Pleasure* i. 87
(Jacobs) This proverbe olde and true ...
The thing do not expect by frends for to
atchieue: which thou thyselfe canst doe, thy
selfe for to relieue.] **1616** DRAXE 163 If a
man will haue his business well done, he must
doe it himselfe. **1858** LONGFELLOW *Miles
Standish* ii That's what I always say; if you
want a thing to be well done, You must do it
yourself. **1902–4** LEAN IV. 3. **1927** *Times*
14 Nov. 15/3 Lastly there is the illustration
of the great principle: if you want a thing
done, do it yourself.

Want (wish) a thing done, If you | go; if not, send.

1743 FRANKLIN Nov. If you'd have it done,
Go: If not, send. **1858** MRS. CRAIK *A Woman's
Thoughts* ii 'If you want a thing done, go
yourself; if not send'. This pithy axiom, of
which most men know the full value, is by
no means so well appreciated by women.

Want in meat, What they | let them take out in drink.

1590 LODGE *Rosalynde* What they wanted in
meat, was supplyed with drinke. **1597–8**
SHAKS. *2 Hen. IV* V. iii. 28 What you want
in meat we'll have in drink. **1617** T. HEY-
WOOD *Fair Maid of W.* II. i (Merm.) 98
Clem. Make it four shillings wine, though you
bate it them in their meat. *Bess.* Why so,
I prithee? *Clem.* Because of the old proverb,
'What they want in meat, let them take out
in drink'.

Want is the worst of it.

1721 KELLY 347 ... Spoken when one must
take a mean thing or want all.

Want makes strife 'twixt man and wife. (*Cf.* Poverty breeds strife.)

1732 FULLER no. 6109. **1855** BOHN 551.

Want of a nail the shoe is lost; For | for want of a shoe the horse is lost; for want of a horse the rider is lost.

Cf. c. **1390** GOWER *Conf. Amantis* v. 4785 For sparinge of a litel cost Ful oftë time a man hath lost The largë cotë for the hod. **1629** T. ADAMS *Serm.* (1861–2) II. 359 The Frenchmen have a military proverb: 'The loss of a nail, the loss of an army.' The want of a nail loseth the shoe, the loss of a shoe troubles the horse, the horse endangereth the rider, the rider breaking his rank molests the company so far as to hazard the whole army. **1640** HERBERT 341. **1880** SMILES *Duty* 270 'Don't care' was the man who was to blame for the well-known catastrophe:—'For want of a nail the shoe was lost, for want of a shoe the horse was lost, and for want of a horse the man was lost.'

Want of a wise man (wise men), For | a fool is set in the chair (fools sit on benches).

c. **1400** *Wisdom of Solomon* (E.E.T.S.) 23, l. 765 I saw ful set one segis of honore, and wysmen set one lawar segis. *c.* **1450** HENRYSON *Want of Wise Men* 16 Poems & Fab. (1845) 36 Sen want of wyse men makis fulis sitt on bynkis. **1639** CLARKE 137 For want of a wise man, a fool is set in the chaire. **1721** KELLY 105 *For fault of wise men fools sit on benks.* Spoken when we see unworthy persons in authority.

Want of company, For | welcome trumpery.

1678 RAY 69. **1721** KELLY 54 *After company welcome thrump'ry.* Spoken by them who are not well pleas'd that you took not notice of them as soon as other company. Or when people come to visit us that we care not for.

Want of money, want of comfort.

1616 DRAXE 25. **1664** CODRINGTON 226. **1736** BAILEY *Dict.* s.v. 'Want' (A).

Want of wit is worse than want of gear.

1721 KELLY 357.

Want the thing you have, You.

1573 SANDFORD (1576) 223. **1629** *Book of Meery Riddles* Prov. 130 (A).

Want when I have, and when I haven't too, I will not.

1678 RAY 344 . . . *Somerset.* **1732** FULLER no. 2650 I will not want when I have it, and have it not too.

Want will be my (your) master.

1738 SWIFT (Dial. i) 338 *Never.* Miss, I want that diamond ring of yours. *Miss.* Why then,

want 's like to be your master. **1869** READE *Foul Play* 1 Wylie . . . replied stoutly that it was pretty well known . . . what he wanted in that quarter. 'Well, then,' said Nancy, 'want will be your master. . . . Get out o' my sight, do.'

Want (*noun*), see also Save while you may (For age and w.); Wealth is best known by w.; Woe to w. (No); Worth of a thing known by w. of it.

Wanted me and your meat, If you | you would want one good friend.

1641 FERGUSSON 66. **1721** KELLY 198 . . . Facetiously meaning, by the one good friend, his meat.

Want(s, ed) (*verb*), see also Leal folks never w. gear; Shift to w. (It is no).

Wanton as a calf with two dams, As.

1678 RAY 290. **1880** BLACKMORE *Mary Aner.* xiii Like the celebrated calf that sucked two cows, Carroway had drawn royal pay . . . upon either element.

Wanton kittens (may) make sober cats.

1732 FULLER no. 5415 Wanton Kitlins may make sober old Cats. **1832** HENDERSON 93 Wanton kittens mak douce[1] cats. [[1] sedate.]

Wants a mule without fault, He who | must walk on foot.

1854 R. SURTEES *Hand. Cross* xvii 'There is an old saying in Spain, that a man wot would buy a mule without a fault must not buy one at all, and faultless 'osses are equally rare.'

Wants in up and down, What she | she hath in round about.

[L. *Quod alibi diminutum, exsequatur alibi.* What is wanting in one way may be made up in another.] **1678** RAY 346. **1721** KELLY 346 *What you want up and down, you have to and fro.* Spoken to them who are low of stature, but broad and squat.

Wants, see also Want(s).

War and physic are governed by the eye.

1640 HERBERT 358.

War begins, When | then hell openeth.

1642 TORRIANO 87. **1651** HERBERT 370.

War, hunting, and law (love), are as full of trouble as pleasure.

1640 HERBERT 327 In war, hunting, and love, men for one pleasure a thousand griefs prove. **1670** RAY 28. **1732** FULLER no. 5416 War, hunting, and love have a thousand troubles for their pleasure.

War is death's feast.

1611 COTGRAVE s.v. 'Feste' Warre is the dead mans holy-day. **1640** HERBERT 355.

War is not done so long as my enemy lives, The.

1651 HERBERT 366.

War is sweet to them that know it not.

1539 TAVERNER 67 *Dulce bellum inexpertis.* Batell is a swete thynge to them that neuer essayed it. **1575** GASCOIGNE *Posies, Dulce Bel. Inex.* (1907) 170 Yet proves it still . . . That *war seems sweet to such as know it not.* **1621** BURTON *Anat. Mel.* III. ii. v. iii *Dulce bellum inexpertis,* as the proverb [Erasm.] is, 'tis fine talking of war . . . till it be tried. **1816** SCOTT *Antiq.* xxviii 'A soldier! then you have slain and burnt, and sacked and spoiled?' . . . 'It's a rough trade—war's sweet to them that never tried it.'

War is the sport of kings.

1906 A. T. QUILLER-COUCH *Mayor of Troy* v 'War is a terrible business'. 'It has been called the sport of kings', answered the Major.

War, In | it is not permitted twice to err.

[ERASM. *Ad. Bis peccare in bello non licet*; said of Lamachus, PLUT. *Apoph. Reg.*] **1777** JOHNSON in *Boswell* (1848) lxi. 564 Quoting the saying, '*In bello non licet bis errare*': and adding, 'this equally true in planting'.

War makes thieves, and peace hangs them.

1598 SIR R. BARCKLEY *Of the Felicity of Man* 370 'The Italian hath a prouerbe; warres make theeues, and peece hangeth them vp. **1640** HERBERT 339. **1721** KELLY 358 . . . This has relation to the Border Wars betwixt the two Nations, which was the great Nursery of Thieves. **1732** FULLER no. 5418.

War must be waged by waking men.

1639 CLARKE 318. **1732** FULLER no. 5419 War must not be waged by men asleep.

War(s), Of all | peace is the end.

1399 GOWER *In Praise of Peace* 66 Wks. (O.U.P.) III. 483 For of bataile the final ende is pees. **1641** FERGUSSON 84 Of all war peace is the finall end. **1721** KELLY 275 *Of all wars peace is the end.* Spoken by them who would compose a law suit, or reconcile those who have had an outfall.

War to the knife.

[= relentless war, after Sp. *guerra al cuchillo.*] **1812** BYRON *Ch. Har.* I. lxxxvi War, war is still the cry, 'War even to the Knife!' **1842** MARRYAT *Perc. Keene* xviii He was . . . very strict about the lights being put out. This was the occasion of war to the knife between the midshipmen and Mr. Culpepper. **1876** GLADSTONE *Relig. Thought* i in *Contemp. Rev.*

June 7 'Catholicism' has . . . declared war to the knife against modern culture.

War with all the world, and peace with England.

1659 HOWELL *Span. Prov.* 1 *With all the World have War, But with* England *do not jar.* Con todo el Mundo guerra, Y paz con Ingalatierra. **1913** *Spectator* 20 Sept. 413 The sixteenth-century Spaniards embodied a . . . maxim of State policy . . . in the following distisch, . . . 'Con todo el mundo guerra Y paz con Inglaterra'.

War without a woman, No.

1639 CLARKE 117.

War(s), *see also* Advise none to . . . go to w.; Clothe thee in w.; Just w. better than unjust peace; Keeps his own makes w.; Magnificent but not w.; Makes a good w., makes a good peace; Peace (In time of) prepare for w.; Preacheth w. is devil's chaplain.

Wardour-street English.

[**1861** TROLLOPE *Framley Pars.* viii The vast hall [of Gatherum Castle] adorned with trophies—with marble busts from Italy and armour from Wardour Street. **1918** F. MUIRHEAD *London* 161 *Wardour Street,* once noted for . . . its spurious antiques, extends from Coventry St. to Oxford St.] **1888** A. BALLANTYNE in *Longm. Mag.* Oct. 585 (*title*) *Wardour-Street English. Ibid.* 589 This is Wardour-Street Early English—a perfectly modern article with a sham appearance of the real antique about it. **1910** *Times Lit. Sup.* 18 Nov. Both this chapter and an excursion into Wardour-street English in describing the book trade in 1530, are blemishes in a book which is otherwise written with taste and care.

Wardrobe, *see* Carrieth all his w.

Ware and Wade's Mill are worth all London.

[A play on the name *Ware,* a town in Herts., as if it meant *goods*; 2 m. to the N. is the village of Wade's Mill.] **1588** A. FRAUNCE *Lawiers Logike* f. 27 (A) Ware and Wadesmill bee worth al London. **1662** FULLER (*Herts*) II. 39 'Ware and Wadesmill are worth all London'. This . . . is a master-piece of the vulgar wits in this county. . . . The fallacy lieth in the homonymy of Ware, here taken . . . appellatively for all vendible commodities.

Ware (the) hawk.

[A phrase applied to an officer of the law, who pounces upon criminals.] *a.* **1529** SKELTON (title) *Ware the Hauke.* **1673** S' *too him Bayes* 31 But now ware hawk!

Wares be gone, When the | shut up the shop windows.

c. **1514** BARCLAY *Eclogues* IV. 493 Shet the shopwindowes for lack of marchaundice. **1605** CAMDEN 255–6 Sir Thomas More *loq.*:

When the wares are gone, and the tooles taken away, we must shut vp shop. **1612** WEBSTER *White Devil* V. iv Now the wares are gone, we may shut up shop. **1639** CLARKE 119.

Ware(s), *see also* Good w. quick markets; Ill w. never cheap.

Warm one in his armour, It is absurd to.

1640 HERBERT 353.

Warm, He that is | thinks all so.

1640 HERBERT 320.

Warm (*adj.*), *see also* Head and feet keep w.; Lowly sit richly w.; Wise enough that can keep w.

Warms too near that burns, He.

1640 HERBERT 354.

Warm(s, eth) (*verb*), *see also* Leg w. (While), boot harmeth; Seest thine house in flames (When), w. thyself by it.

Warned folks may live.

1639 CLARKE 202.

Warning, *see* Scarborough w.; Rainbow in the morning; Sky red in the morning; Slain that had w.

Warp, *see* Make ab or w. of the business.

War-path, To be (go) on the.

1775 ADAIR *Hist. Amer. Ind.* 396 I often have rode that war path alone. **1841** J. F. COOPER *Deerslayer* xv The great serpent of the Mohicans must be worthy to go on the war-path with Hawkeye.

Warrant you for an egg at Easter, I will.

1670 RAY 214.

Warrant, *see also* Wrong has no w.

Wars bring scars.

1639 CLARKE 44. **1732** FULLER no. 6096. **1826** SCOTT *Woodst.* xxvii Myself am in some sort rheumatic—as war will leave its scars behind, sir.

Wars, He that is not in the | is not out of danger.

1640 HERBERT 363.

Wars, *see also* War(s).

Warsaw, *see* Order reigns at W.

Wary, *see* Happy whom other men's perils make w.

Wash a blackamoor (Ethiopian) white, To.

[LUCIAN *Adversus Indoctum* 28 Αἰθίοπα σμήχειν ἐπιχειρῶ. I am endeavouring to wash

an Ethiopian white. ERASM. *Ad. Æthiopem lavas* (or *dealbas*).] **1543** BECON *Early Wks.* (P.S.) 49 Here, therefore, do ye nothing else than, as the common proverb is, go about to make an Ethiop white. **1621** BRATHWAITE *Omphale* (1877) 275 'To wash the Moore, is labouring in vaine, For th' colour that he h'as, is d'id in graine'. **1684** BUNYAN *Pilgr. P.* II. (1877) 336 They saw one *Fool* and one *Want-wit* washing of an Ethiopian with intention to make him white, but the more they washed him the blacker he was. **1799** WOLCOT (P. Pindar) *Postscript to Nil Admirari* (1816) III. 430 I have exhibited my imbecility in trying to wash the blackamoor white.

Wash dirty linen in public, To.

[= to give publicity to family disputes or scandals.] **1886** E. J. HARDY *How to be Happy* i Married people . . . should remember the proverb about the home-washing of soiled linen. **1895** *Globe* 23 May People who ought to wash their dirty linen at home will not be satisfied with a less public laundry than Piccadilly. **1931** *Times* 3 Aug. 9/1 If the Government had made tactful . . . representations . . . to the Holy See, . . . the whole matter could have been quietly settled without any washing of dirty linen in public.

Wash my hands and wait upon you, I will.

1678 RAY 353.

Wash one's face in an ale-clout, To.

[= to get drunk.] **1550** HEYWOOD I. x. 22 As sober as she séemth, fewe daies come about But she will onece wasshe hir face in an ale clout.

Wash out ink with ink, You.

1616 WITHALS 563. **1639** CLARKE 197.

Wash their throats before they washed their eyes, Our fathers which were wondrous wise, did.

1613 WITHER *Abuses* II. i *Prethee let me intreat thee for to drinke. Before thou wash; Our fathers that were wise, Were wont to say, 'tis wholesome for the eyes.* **1659** HOWELL *Eng. Prov.* 6/1.

Wash your hands often, your feet seldom, and your head never.

1670 RAY 38.

Washeth an ass's head, He that | loseth both his lye[1] (soap) and his labour.

1592 LODGE *Euphues Shadow* (1882) 53 Who washeth the Asses eares, looseth both his Sope and his labour. **1639** CLARKE 155. **1789** WOLCOT (P. Pindar) *Expost. Odes* xiv To try to wash an ass's face, Is really labour to misplace; And really loss of time as well as sope. **1861** HUGHES *Tom B. at Oxford* xxiii Simon . . . summed up . . . by the remark that ' 'Twas waste of soap to lather an ass'. [[1] cleansing agent.]

Washing his hands, For | none sells his lands.

1611 COTGRAVE s.v. 'laver' *Pour laver ses mains on n'en vend pas sa terre*: Prov. Neuer did cleanlinesse any man vndoe. 1640 HERBERT 319.

Wasp, *see* Angry as a w.; Quiet as a w. in nose.

Waste (Wilful waste) makes (woeful) want.

1576 *Par. Dainty Dev.* in *Brit. Bibliogr.* (1812) III. 88 For want is next to waste and shame doeth synne ensue. 1721 KELLY 353 Wilful waste makes woeful want. 1732 FULLER no. 5423. 1835 J. M. WILSON *Tales of Borders* I. 202 She never suffered herself to forget ... that ... 'wilful waste makes woful want'.

Waste not, want not.

1796 EDGEWORTH *Par. Asst.* (1903) 232 The following words ... were written ... over the chimneypiece in his uncle's spacious kitchen. —'Waste not, want not.' 1855 KINGSLEY *Westward Ho!* viii Waste not want not is my doctrine; so you and I may have a somewhat to stay our stomachs.

Waste (*noun*), *see also* Haste makes w.; Spend and be free, but no w.

Watch one as a cat watches a mouse, To.

1579–80 LODGE *Def. Poetry* (Shaks. Soc.) 44 As the catte watcheth the praye of the mouse, so dilygentlye intendes hee to the compassing of some young novice. 1623 HOWELL *Lett.* 10 July (1903) I. 186 It was no handsome comparison of Olivarez, that he watched her as a cat doth a mouse. 1738 SWIFT (Dial. iii) 350 *Miss.* I am told she watches him as a cat would watch a mouse.

Watch (*noun*), *see* Good w. prevents misfortune; Sure of your w. on deck (You are always); Wise man though you can't make a w.

Watch (*verb*), *see also* Harm w. harm catch.

Watched pot (pan) is long in boiling, A.

1848 GASKELL *M. Barton* c. xxxi. 1908 *Spectator* 12 Dec. 988 He remarks to himself that a watched pot never boils.

Water a stake, To.

[= useless labour.] 1636 S. WARD *Serm.* (1862) 107 Who waters a dry stake with any heart? What comfort hath Peter to pray for Simon Magus in the gall of bitterness? 1732 FULLER no. 5897 You do but water a dead Stake.

Water afar quencheth not fire.

1581 PETTIE *Guazzo's Civ. Conv.* (1586) f. 191 Water a farre of doth [not] quench fier that is nigh. 1640 HERBERT 336.

Water bewitched.

[= excessively diluted liquor; now chiefly, very weak tea.] 1678 RAY 84 Water bewitch't. *i.e.* very thin beer. 1694 S. JOHNSON *Notes Past. Let. Bp. Burnet* I. Pref. 2 There was not one drop of Wine in it, it was all Water Bewitch't. 1699 T. BROWN *L'Estrange's Colloq. of Erasm.* Add. v. 53 The Broth was nothing in the world but Water bewitched [L. *mera aqua*], if it deserved so good a name. 1738 SWIFT (Dial. i) 335 *Miss.* Your ladyship is very sparing of your tea; I protest, the last I took was no more than water bewitch'd.

Water, fire, and soldiers, quickly make room.

1640 HERBERT 341.

Water (Blood) from a flint (stone), To get (or wring).

1580 LYLY *Euph. & his Eng.* Wks. (Bond) II. 139 But if thou attempt againe to wring water out of the Pommice, thou shalt but bewraye thy falshoode, and augment thy shame, and my seueritie. a. 1592 GREENE *George a Greene* Dram. Wks. II. 189 Faith, I see, it is hard to get water out of a flint, as to get him to have a bout with me. 1666 TORRIANO 161 There's no getting of bloud out of that wall. 1850 DICKENS *Dav. Cop.* xi Blood cannot be obtained from a stone, neither can anything on account be obtained ... from Mr. Micawber. 1881 A. JESSOP *Arcady* 157 If these ... Norfolk landlords have no more than their land, you may as well try to get blood out of a stone as try and make them build houses for other people's labourers.

Water goes by the mill that the miller knows not of, Much.

1546 HEYWOOD II. v. 60. 1593–4 SHAKS. *Tit. Andron.* II. i. 85 What, man! more water glideth by the mill Than wots the miller of. 1641 FERGUSSON 76 Meikle water runs where the miller sleeps. 1670 RAY 121. 1721 KELLY 256 ... That is, people who have much among their hands, will have things broken, lost, and purloined, of which they will not be sensible.

Water has run under the bridge since then, Much.

1927 *Times* 27 July 15/3 A good deal of water has flowed under the Thames bridges since the report of ... last December.

Water his horse at Highgate, I will make him.

1678 RAY 86 ... *i.e.* I'll sue him, and make him take a journey up to London.

Water in a sieve, To carry (draw, fetch).

[ERASM. *Ad. Cribro aquam haurire.*] 1477 NORTON *Ord. Alch.* i in Ashm. (1652) 17 As he that fetcheth Water in a Sive. 1509 A. BARCLAY *Ship of Fools* (1874) I. 245 Wymen ar no kepars of councell It goeth

through them as water trough a syue. **1589**
GREENE *Menaph.* (Arb.) 48 Suppose she were
a Vestall, . . . shee might carie water with
Amulia in a siue. **1598–9** SHAKS. *Much Ado*
V. i. 5 Thy counsel . . . falls into mine ears as
profitless As water in a sieve. **1602–3** *All's
Well* I. iii. 210 Yet, in this captious and in-
tenible sieve I still pour in the waters of my
love. **1686** HORNECK *Crucif. Jesus* xxii. 741
That's no better, than taking up water in a
sieve. **1732** FULLER no. 5979 You pour
water into a sieve. **1764** A. MURPHY *No One's
Enemy* I. Wks. (1786) II. 335 To trust him,
is taking up water with a sieve.

Water in a smith's forge, As | that serves rather to kindle than quench.

1576 PETTIE *Petite Pall.* (Gollancz) I. 154
But as the smith his forge, by casting on cold
water, burneth more fiercely, so their love
by those delays increased more vehemently.
1579 LYLY *Euphues* (Arb.) 61 (A) He that
casteth water on the fire in the smith's forge,
maketh it to flame fiercer. **1639** CLARKE 158.

Water into a ship, As welcome as.

1520 R. WHITTINTON *Vulg.* (E.E.T.S.) 88.
a. **1553** UDALL *Royster D.* III. ii (Arb.) 40
For it liked hir as well to tell you no lies,
As water in hir shyppe. **1580** LYLY *Euph. &
his Eng.* (Arb.) 381 My counsell is no more
welcome vnto thee then water into a ship.
1641 FERGUSSON 52 *Of untymous persons.* . . .
He is as welcome as water in a rivin ship.

Water into one's shoes, As welcome as.

1678 RAY 281.

Water into the sea (Thames), To cast.

1377 LANGLAND *P. Pl.* B. xv. 332 And went
forth with that water · to woke with Themese
[= to moisten the Thames with]. **1509** A.
BARCLAY *Ship of Fools* (1874) I. 166 Or in
the se cast water, thynkynge it to augment.
1546 HEYWOOD I. xi. 32 It is, to geue him,
as much almes or néede As cast water in
tems.[1] **1590** SWINBURNE *Testaments Pref.*
I may be thought to powre water into the
Sea, to carry owles to Athens, and to trouble
the reader with a matter altogether needlesse and superfluous. **1625** PURCHAS *Pilgrims*
(1905–7) II. 55 Foolishly do I further pour
water into this sea, into which Pope Alexander's bull hath brought me. [1 Thames.]

Water is as dangerous as com-modious.

1579 GOSSON *Sch. Abuse* (Arb.) 23 Water [is]
as daungerous, as it is commodious. **1669**
Politeuphuia 184.

Water is shallow, Where the | no vessel will ride.

1597 *Politeuphuia* 166. **1639** CLARKE 245.

Water is the eye of a landscape.

1902–4 LEAN IV. 175.

Water off (on) a duck's back, Like.

1824 MAGINN *Maxims of Sir M. O'Doherty*
(1849) 128 He only laughed . . . and the
thing passed off like water from a duck's
back. **1866** BLACKMORE *Cradock N.* xxxix
Irony . . . antithesis . . . metaphor . . . all
these are like water on a duck's back when
the heart won't let the brain work. **1912**
Spectator 20 July 82 No one would listen to
our arguments. They fell like water off a
duck's back.

Water stoups hold no ale.

1721 KELLY 339 . . . An apology for not
drinking strong liquor, because we have not
been accustomed to it.

Water trotted is as good as oats.

1640 HERBERT 323. **1867** *N. & Q.* 3rd Ser.
XII. 488 'Water trotted is as good as oats'.—
Giving a horse on a journey a drink of water,
provided you trot afterwards, is as good as a
feed of oats.

Water will never reave the widdy, The, *see* Born to be hanged, He that is | will never be drowned.

Water where the stirk[1] drowned, There was aye some.

1721 KELLY 309 . . . There was certainly
some occasion for so much talk, rumour, and
suspicion. [1 a young bullock.]

Water(s) (*noun*), *see also* Beware of . . . still w.; Carries fire in one hand and w. in other; Cast not out the foul w. till; Cost hot w. (It will); Deepest w. best fishing; Draw w. to mill; Drink w. (Let none say I will not); Fire and w. (Go through); Fire and w. good servants; Fire and w. have no mercy; Fish mars w.; Foul w. as soon as fair will quench; Go to the well against his will . . . w. will spill; Know the worth of w. till well dry (We never); Lay the stool's foot in w.; Look to (a person's) w.; Muckle w. rins while miller sleeps; Pour not w. on drowned mouse; Reeds (Where there are) there is w.; Ride the w. with (He is not man to); Send him to the sea, he will not get w.; Still w. (Take heed of); Still w. run deep; Too much w. drowns miller; Under w. famine; Wading in unknown w. (No safe).

Water (*verb*), *see also* Green cheese (You see no) but teeth w.

Watering-pot, *see* Although it rain throw not away.

Waterings, *see* St. Thomas à W.

Waveney, *see* Castle of Bungay.

Wavering as the wind.

1546 HEYWOOD II. i. 45 For in one state they
twayne could not yet settle. But waueryng
as the wynde, in docke out nettle.

Wax, *see* Head of w. (He that hath); Nose of w.

Way is an ill neighbour, The.

1640 HERBERT 359.

Way of all flesh, The.

1605 MARSTON *The Dutch Courtesan* I. 1. 88 **1606** CHAPMAN *Mons. D'Olive* I. i. 344 Send her the way of all flesh. **1607** DEKKER *Westward Hoe* D 1. **1609** Id. *Raven's Almanack* C 3ᵛ. **1611** HEYWOOD *Golden Age* III (A) If I go by land, and miscarry, then I go the way of all flesh. **1631** Id. *Fair Maid of West* II. IV (A) She . . . by this is gone the way of all flesh.

Way to an Englishman's heart is through his stomach, The.

1845 R. FORD *Handbk. Spain* i. 30 The way to many an honest heart lies through the belly. **1857** MRS. CRAIK *John Halifax* xxx 'Christmas dinners will be much in request'. 'There's a saying that the way to an Englishman's heart is through his stomach.'

Way to Babylon will never bring you to Jerusalem, The.

1732 FULLER no. 4819.

Way to be gone is not to stay here, The.

1678 RAY 72.

Way to be safe is never to be secure, The.

1732 FULLER no. 4820.

Way to heaven is alike in every place, The.

[CIC. *Tusc.* 1. 43. 104 *Undique ad inferos tantundem viae est.*] **1516** MORE *Utopia* (Arb.) 30 *Undique ad superos tantundem est viae.* **1669** PENN *No Cross, No Crown* xix To one bewailing himself that he should not die in his own country: 'Be of comfort', saith he,[1] 'for the way to heaven is alike in every place.' [1 Diogenes.]

Way to heaven is as ready by water as by land, The.

[1532] ELSTOWE in FROUDE *Hist. Eng.* (1856) I. 373 Essex told them they deserved to be . . . thrown into the Thames. 'Threaten . . . rich and dainty folk . . .', answered Elstowe . . . 'we know the way to heaven to be as ready by water as by land.' **1583** SIR HUM. GILBERT in FULLER (*Devon*) I. 418 A terrible tempest did arise; and Sir Humphrey said cheerfully . . . , 'We are as near heaven here at sea as at land'.

Ways of dressing a calf's head, There are many.

1902–4 LEAN IV. 145 There are many ways of dressing a calf's head (*i.e.* of showing your folly). At the Calf's Head Club it was served in every imaginable guise.

Ways to fame, There are many.

1640 HERBERT 342.

Ways to kill a dog (cat) than hanging (choking her with cream), There are more.

1678 RAY 127. **1721** KELLY 253 *Many ways to kill a dog, and not to hang him.* There be many ways to bring about one and the same thing, or business. **1855** KINGSLEY *West. Ho!* xx (A) (with 'cat . . . cream').

Ways to the wood than one, There are more.

1546 HEYWOOD II. ix. 77 What wife there be mo waies to the wood than one. **1659** HEYLIN *Animadv.* in FULLER *Appeal Inj. Innoc.* (1840) 524 But there are more ways to the wood than one; and they had wit enough to cast about for some other way, since the first had failed them.

Way(s), *see also* Every man in his w.; Fair w. (To be in a); Farthest w. about, nearest w. home; Foul dirty w. (Take heed of); Good land, evil w.; Half the w. to know the w.; Long w. long lies; Nearest w. commonly foulest; Once a w. and aye a w.; Try all w. to the wood; Wrong way to the wood (Go); Wrong w. to work (Go).

Waykenning, *see* Ill of his harbory good of w.

Wayside, *see* House built by w. too high or too low.

We hounds slew the hare, quoth the messan.[1]

1641 FERGUSSON 108. **1721** KELLY 349 . . . Spoken to insignificant persons, when they attribute to themselves any part of a great achievement. **1732** FULLER no. 5443 We hounds killed the hare, quoth the lap-dog. [1 lap-dog.]

Weabley, *see* Lemster bread and W. ale.

Weak men had need be witty.

1639 CLARKE 42.

Weak side, Every man hath his.

1692 L'ESTRANGE *Aesop's Fab.* cccxcii (1738) 415 Every man, in fine, has a weak side, if a body could but hit upon't. **1850** KINGSLEY *Alton Locke* xxiv But every man has his weak side; and . . . his was a sort of High-Church Radicalism.

Weak, *see also* Wiles help w. folk.

Weaker goeth to the pot, The.

1546 HEYWOOD II. v. 56 Where the small with the great, can not agrée, The weaker goeth to the potte, we all daie sée.

Weaker hath the worse, The.

1481 CAXTON *Reynard* xiv (Arb.) 31 Hit went with hem as it ofte doth the feblest hath the worst. **1546** HEYWOOD I. x. 19 But the weaker hath the wurs we all daie sée.

Weaker vessel, *see* Woman is.

Weakest goes to the wall, The.

a. **1500** *Coventry Plays* (E.E.T.S.) 47 The weykist gothe eyuer to the walle. **1579** LYLY *Euphues* (Arb.) 53 He that worst may is always enforced to holde the candell, the weakest must still to the wall. **1594–5** SHAKS. *Rom. & Jul.* I. i. 17 That shows thee a weak slave; for the weakest goes to the wall. **1623** CAMDEN 279 The weakest goe to the walles. **1833** MARRYAT *P. Simple* v You will be thrashed all day long . . . ; the weakest always goes to the wall there. **1867–77** FROUDE *Short Stud., Cat's Pilg.* (1890) I. 645 My good Cat, there is but one law in the world. The weakest goes to the wall.

Weal and women cannot pan, but woe and women can.

1639 CLARKE 118 Weale and women never sam, but sorrow and they can. **1678** RAY 355 *Northern Proverbs.* Weal and women cannot pan, i.e. *close together.* But woe and women can.

Weal (Well) or woe as he thinks himself so, A man is.

1721 KELLY 25 . . . A contented mind will sweeten every condition, and a repining heart will produce the contrary effects.

Weal pricks, Whom | sorrow comes after and licks.

1636 CAMDEN 305.

Weal, *see also* World (So goeth), now woe now w.; Worth no w. that can bide no woe.

Wealth is best known by want.

1631 DEKKER *Penny-wise, Pound-foolish* A 3 Wealth is not regarded till we come to Beggerie. **1732** FULLER no. 5463.

Wealth, The greatest | is contentment with a little.

1670 RAY 28.

Wealth is like rheum, it falls on the weakest parts.

a. **1633** G. HERBERT 'Confession' *Wks.* (Hutchinson) 126. **1640** HERBERT 340.

Wealth is not his who hath it, but his who enjoys it.

1642 TORRIANO 70. **1659** HOWELL *Ital.–Eng.* 12.

Wealth makes wit waver.

1641 FERGUSSON 108 Wealth gars[1] wit waver. **1721** KELLY 340] . . . Spoken when people have many advantageous offers, and are at a loss which to take. **1824** SCOTT *St. Ronan's* xv Weel, weel, . . . nae doubt wealth makes wit waver. [[1] makes.]

Wealth makes worship.

1639 CLARKE 99. **1732** FULLER no. 5464 Wealth wants not for worship.

Wealth, *see also* Bear w., poverty will bear itself; Bring home w. of the Indies; Knowledge makes one laugh, but w. dance; Little w. little care; Wisdom (Without) w. is worthless; Wit than w. (Better); World's w. (If we have not), we have ease.

Weapons of war (*or* Arms of England) will not arm fear, All the.

1573 SANDFORD (1576) H 2[v] All the weapons of *Brescia* can not arme feare. **1578** FLORIO *First Fruites* f. 32 (A) All the weapons of London wyl not arme feare. **1611** DAVIES *Prov.* 78. **1640** HERBERT 351 All the arms of England will not arm fear.

Weapon(s), *see also* Wight man never wanted w.; Wise man never wants w.

Wear a horn, and blow it not.

1639 CLARKE 142.

Wear clothes, Ever since we | we know not one another.

1640 HERBERT 324. **1667** MILTON *P.L.* iv. 740 These troublesome disguises which we wear.

Wear like a horseshoe, the longer the brighter, She will.

1721 KELLY 300 . . . Spoken of ill-coloured girls who they hope will clear up when they are married.

Wear the breeches, To.

[= where the wife rules the husband.] **15th** cent. *Songs and Carols of 15th Cent.* (Percy Soc.) 65 (A) Nova, Nova, sawe you euer such, The most mayster of the hows weryth no brych. **1546** HEYWOOD II. iii. 48 Shall the maister weare a breech or none? **1553** T. WILSON *Arte of Rhet.* 89 As though the good man of the house weare no breeches or that the Graye Mare were the better horse. **1590–1** SHAKS. *3 Hen. VI* V. v. 26 That you might still have worn the petticoat, And ne'er have stol'n the breech from Lancaster. **1606** *Choice, Chance & C.* (1881) 22 She that is master of her husband must weare the breeches. **1807** W. IRVING *Salmag.* (1824) 102 The violent inclination she felt to wear the breeches.

Wear the king's coat, To.

[= to serve as a soldier.] **1883** STEVENSON *Treasure Isl.* IV. xxi (1886) 166 I thought you had worn the king's coat!

Wear the willow, To.

[= to mourn loss or absence of one's beloved, formerly indicated by a garland of willow leaves.] **1563** B. GOOGE *Eglogs* vi (Arb.) 52 Let Wyllows wynde aboute my hed (a Wrethe for Wretches mete). **1590–1** SHAKS. *3 Hen. VI* III. iii. 228 Tell him . . . I'll wear the willow garland for his sake. *Ibid.* IV. i. 100. **1598–9** *Much Ado* II. i. 225 I offered him my company to a willow tree, . . . to make him a garland, as being forsaken. **1884** BLACKMORE *Tommy Up.* xxxiii You are quite wrong

... in supposing that I have any call ... to wear the willow.... Miss Windsor ... never has been to me more than a bubble.

Wears black must hang a brush at his back, He that.

1639 CLARKE 201. **1670** RAY 63. **1732** FULLER no. 6298.

Wears his heart upon his sleeve, He.

[= exposes his feelings, &c., to every one.] **1604–5** SHAKS. *Oth.* I. i. 64 'Tis not long after But I will wear my heart upon my sleeve For dawes to peck at. **1895** J. PAYN *In Market Ov.* xxiii He had not worn his heart on his sleeve, exactly, but it had been visible to men, and especially to women.

Wears the bull's feather, He.

1533 *Ballads from MSS.* (B.S.) i. 199 (A) Lyke cokold foles to-gether ... we wer an oxes fether. **1662** J. WILSON *The Cheats* II. iv Let no man disorder his rest, By believing bull's feathers in's crest. **1678** RAY 67 ... This is a French Proverb, for a cuckold.

Wear(s, ing), *see also* Better w. out than rust out; Break or w. out (If things did not); Everything is worse for w.; Wide will w., narrow will tear; Win and w.

Wearieth, *see* Doth well (He that) w. not.

Weary (-iest), *see* Every one is w.; Go a long way w. (One can); Never be w. of well doing; Ox when w. treads surest.

Weasel and the cat make a marriage, When the | it is a very ill presage.

1678 RAY *Adag. Hebr.* 406 When the weasil and the cat make a marriage it is a very ill presage. ... When evil men, who were formerly at variance, and are of great power, make agreement, it portends danger to the innocent. ... Thus upon the agreement of *Herod* and *Pilot* the most innocent bloud is shed.

Weasel, *see also* Catch a w. asleep.

Weather is ill, No | if the wind be still.

1623 CAMDEN 279. **1639** CLARKE 263. **1670** RAY 42.

Weather meet to set paddocks[1] abroad in.

1546 HEYWOOD I. xiii. 41 We haue had ... Weather, méete to sette paddockes[1] abroode in. Rain, more than enough. [1 toads, frogs.]

Weather, *see also* After black clouds clear w.; April w. rain and sunshine; Brook the w. that love not wind; Change of w. discourse of fools; Child (To a) all w. is cold; Cold w. ... come out of north; Fair w.; Farewell frost, fair w. next; Leeward for fine w. (Look not to); Queen's w.; Wind and w. do thy worst.

Weathercock in the wind, Like a.

c. **1340** *Ayenbite of Inwyt* (E.E.T.S.) 180 Hi byeth ase the wedercoc that is ope the steple, thet him went mid eche wynde. *c.* **1386** CHAUCER *Clerk's T.* E[1] 996 O stormy peple! unsad and evere untrewe! Ay undiscreet and chaungynge as a vane. *c.* **1598** *MS. Prov.* in FERGUSSON 57 He is lyk ane widder cok in the wind.

Weathercock, *see also* Woman is a w.

Weather-eye, *see* Keep your w. open.

Weavers' beef of Colchester, The.

1662 FULLER (*Essex*) I. 498 'The weavers' beef of Colchester'. These are sprats, caught hereabouts, ... in incredible abundance, whereon the poor weavers (numerous in this city) make much of their repast, ... as lasting in season well nigh a quarter of a year.

Weaver(s), *see also* Devil would have been w. but for Temples; Put a miller, a w. ... in a bag, first that comes out will be thief.

Web of a bottle[1] of hay, It is hard to make a good.

1670 RAY 154. [1 bundle.]

Web (Weft), *see also* Ill-spun w. will out.

Webley ale, Medley bells, Lemster ore.[1] (*See also* Lemster bread, &c.).

1610 P. HOLLAND tr. *Camden's Britannia* 620 (A) Lemster bread and Weabley Ale ... are growne unto a common proverbe. **1659** HOWELL *Eng. Prov.* 20/2 *Webley* Ale, *Medley* Bells, *Lemster* Ore; three things in Herefordshire, which are the best in that kind. [Weobley; Madeley, in Salop; Leominster; wool.]

Webster(s), *see* Need makes ... and sorrow makes w. spin; Sorrows gars w. spin; Wight as a w.'s waistcoat.

Wed(s), *see* Better w. over the mixen; Early w. early dead; Men are April ... December when they w.; More folks are w. than keep good houses; Nought is to w. with (Where) ... flee the clog; Old man who w.; Wiser now you're w.; Woo where he will, w. where his hap is.

Wedded to one's will, To be.

1546 HEYWOOD II. xi. 84 I was wedded vnto my wyll. How be it, I will be deuorst, and be wed to my wyt. **1594–5** SHAKS. *L.L.L.* II. i. 209 *Ber.* Is she wedded or no? *Boyet* To her will, sir, or so.

Wedding begets another, One.

1713 GAY *Wife of Bath* I. i *Alis.* One Wedding, the Proverb says, begets another. **1929** *Daily Mail* 19 Sept. 10/2 It is apparent that weddings do breed weddings, and that bridesmaids are particularly apt to find themselves early involved in matrimony.

Wedding ring wears, As your | your cares will wear away.

1678 RAY 344. *Somerset.* **1732** FULLER no. 6146 As your wedding ring wears, You'll wear off your cares.

Wedding, *see also* After a dream of a w.; Hanging and w. go by destiny; Wooing was day after w

Wedge, There goes the | where the beetle drives it.

1678 RAY 216. **1732** FULLER no. 4869.

Wedge(s), *see also* Blunt w. rive hard knots; Crabbed knot must have crabbed w.; Fool that makes a w. of fist; Thin end of w.

Wedlock is a padlock.

1678 RAY 56. **1732** FULLER no. 6261.

Wedlock, *see also* Age and w. tames.

Weeding, *see* One year's seeding.

Weeds overgrow the corn, The.

c. **1450** *MS. Harl. 5396* in *Reliq. Antiq.* (1843) II. 240 Therfor eny man may care, Lest the wede growe over the whete. a. **1534** *Hyckscorner* 545 *Pyte*. Lo, lordes, they may curs the tyme they were borne For the wedes that over-groweth the corne. **1641** FERGUSSON 94 The weeds overgaes the corn. **1721** KELLY 319 . . . The bad are the most numerous.

Weeds want no sowing.

1659 N. R. 127 You need not sow weeds. **1732** FULLER no. 5466.

Weed(s), *see also* Fat land grow w. (On); Ill w. grow apace; Ill w. mars a whole pot; Ill w. wax well; Sussex w.

Week, *see* Thursday come and w. is gone.

Weel bides, weel betides.

1641 FERGUSSON 180.

Weel kens the mouse (when) the cat's out of the house.

1641 FERGUSSON 108. **1721** KELLY 342. **1821** J. GALT *Annals of Parish* xxxvii I saw that it would be necessary . . . for me to take another wife . . . on account of the servant lasses, who grew out of all bounds, verifying the proverb, 'Well kens the mouse, when the cat's out of the house'.

Weel's him and wae's him that has a bishop in his kin.

1641 FERGUSSON 108. **1721** KELLY 347 . . . Because such may be advanc'd, and perhaps disappointed.

Weening is not measure.

1640 HERBERT 354.

Weep for joy is a kind of manna, To.

1640 HERBERT 339.

Weep Irish, To.

[= to feign sorrow.] **1586** STANYHURST *Descr. Irel.* viii. 44/2 in *Holinshed* They follow the dead corpse to the graue with howling and barbarous outcries . . .; whereof grew, as I suppose, the prouerbe: To weepe Irish [orig. Hibernice lacrimari]. **1612** WEBSTER *White Devil* IV. ii What! dost weep? Procure but ten of thy dissembling trade, Ye'd furnish all the Irish funerals With howling past wild Irish. **1681** ROBERTSON *Phraseol. Gen.* 1305 To weep Irish, or to feign sorrow.

Weep (Drop) millstones, To.

[= said of a hard-hearted person.] **1592–3** SHAKS. *Rich. III* I. iii. 353 Your eyes drop millstones, when fools' eyes fall tears. *Ibid.* I. iv. 248 *Clar.* He will weep. *First Murd.* Ay, millstones. **1601–2** *Troil. & Cres.* I. ii. 156 *Pan.* Queen Hecuba laughed that her eyes ran o'er. *Cres.* With millstones. **1632** MASSINGER *City Madam* IV. iii (Merm.) 469 *For.* He, good gentleman, Will weep when he hears how we are used. *1st Serj.* Yes, millstones. **1820** SHELLEY *Oed. Tyr.* 334 And every tear turned to a millstone.

Weep(s, ing), *see also* Better children w. than old men; Learn w. shall gain laughing; See a woman w. (No more pity than goose go barefoot); Still him (Who hath none to) may w. out eyes.

Weeping cross, *see* Goeth out with often loss.

Weevil in a biscuit, Like a.

1899 A. T. QUILLER-COUCH *Ship of Stars* xiii Suppose you put me to work in the vestry? There's only one window . . . : you can block that up with a curtain, and there I'll be like a weevil in a biscuit.

Weigh justly and sell dearly.

1573 SANDFORD (1576) 220 Make iust waight and sell deere. **1578** FLORIO *First Fruites* f. 33 Weigh iust, and sel deere. **1640** HERBERT 341.

Weigh(s), *see also* Carries well to whom it w. not.

Weight and measure take away strife.

1640 HERBERT 326. **1721** KELLY 247 *Met*[1] *and measure make all men wise.* Spoken when people would have what they buy weighed, or measured. **1732** FULLER no. 5468 Weight, measure, and tale take away strife. [[1] weight.]

Weight(s), *see also* Great w. on small wires.

Weime[1], That which is in my | is not in my testament.

1721 KELLY 324 . . . An excuse for eating rather than keeping what is before us. [[1] belly.]

Weird (noun), *see* Old wife that wats her w.; Shape coat and sark (We can) but not w

Welcome death, quoth the rat, when the trap fell down.

1659 HOWELL *Eng. Prov.* 10/1. **1732** FULLER no. 5469.

Welcome evil, if thou comest alone.

1620 SHELTON *Quix.* II. lv (1908) III. 206 I . . . think that every moment I shall fall into a deeper profundity than this former, that will swallow me downright. 'Tis a good ill that comes alone. **1640** HERBERT 323. **1732** FULLER no. 5471 (with 'mischief' for evil').

Welcome fares well, He that is.

1641 FERGUSSON 309. **1721** KELLY 158. **1736** BAILEY *Dict.* s.v. 'Welcome' (A).

Welcome (Good will and welcome) is the best cheer.

[Gk. Ξενίων δέ τε θυμὸς ἄριστος. In hospitality it is the spirit that is the chief thing.] *c.* **1430** LYDGATE *Isopes* (E.E.T.S.) l. 434 As men seyen & reporte, at þe leste, Nat many deyntees, but good chere makeþ a feste. **1592-3** SHAKS. *Com. Err.* III. i. 26 Small cheer and great welcome makes a merry feast. **1611** COTGRAVE s.v. 'Chere' a hearty welcome is worth halfe a feast. **1670** RAY 154. **1721** KELLY 349 Welcome is the best dish in the kitchen.

Welcome, Such | such farewell.

1546 HEYWOOD II. vii. 66.

Welcome that bring, They are.

1641 FERGUSSON 94.

Welcome when thou goest.

1546 HEYWOOD II. vii. 65 Welcom when thou goest . thus is thine errand sped.

Welcome, *see also* Bold than w. (More); Breams in his pond . . . friend w.; Come and w.; Ewe and a lamb (Now I have) everyone cries w. Peter.

Welcome as, *see* Flowers in May; Snow in harvest; Storm; Water into a ship; Water into one's shoes.

Well and them cannot, then ill and them can, If.

1670 RAY 155. *Yorksh.*

Well begun is half done (ended). (*Cf.* Good beginning, &c.)

[HORACE *Ep.* 1. 2. 40 *Dimidium facti, qui coepit, habet.* He who has made a beginning, has half done.] **1539** TAVERNER 9 *Principium dimidium totius.* The beginning is half the whole. **1597** BACON *Col. of G. & E.* 10 (Arb.) 153 Hence grew the common place of extolling the beginning of euery thing, *Dimidium qui bene coepit habet.* **1642** D. ROGERS *Naaman* ix. 256 A work well entered is truly said to be half done. **1908** ALEX. MACLAREN *Acts* I. 176 Satan spoils many a well-begun work.... Well begun is half—but only half—ended.

Well doing, *see* Never be weary of w. d.

Well done is twice (ever) done, That which is.

1606 DAY *Ile of Gulls* V For, saies my mother, a thinge once wel done is twice done. **1630** J. TAYLOR *Wks.* L 5ᵛ When a thing is well done (tis an old saying) it is twice done. **1658**

E. WILLIAMSON *J. Cleaveland Revived* (1668) A 3 There is a saying, *Once well done, and ever done.* **1659** HOWELL *Eng. Prov.* 9/1. **1670** RAY 154. **1732** FULLER no. 4381.

Well done, soon done.

1641 FERGUSSON 108.

Well fare nothing (nought) once a year.

1639 CLARKE 244 Well fare nought once by the yeere. **1659** HOWELL *Eng. Prov.* 18/2 ... *For then he is not subject to plundring.*

Well fitted abide, Things.

1640 HERBERT 340.

Well for him who feeds a good man.

c. **1300** *Havelok* 1693 Wel is him þat god man fedes!

Well for him who has a good child.

c. **1300** *Havelok* 2983 Him stondes wel þat god child strenes.[1] [[1] begets.]

Well, When you are | hold yourself so.

1721 KELLY 357 ... A discouragement from hazarding the alteration of our condition by new projects.

Well is full, When the | it will run over.

1721 KELLY 357 ... That is, when people are much wrong'd they will shew their resentments. **1736** BAILEY *Dict.* s.v. 'Well' (A).

Well is, that well does.

1707 MAPLETOFT 120 (Scotch proverb). **1721** KELLY 353.

Well married, She is | who has neither mother-in-law nor sister-in-law by her husband. (*Cf.* Happy is she who marries, &c.)

1855 BOHN 484.

Well, He that would be | needs not go from his own house.

1611 COTGRAVE s.v. 'bouger' *Qui bien est ne se bouge:* Prov. Let not him budge that finds himselfe well seated. **1640** HERBERT 338.

Well off, *see* Wise man who, when w. o., can keep so.

Well old, He that would be | must be old betimes.

1640 HERBERT 335.

Well rhymed, tutor, brains and stairs.

1639 CLARKE 70.

Well spoken that is well taken, That is.

1599 PORTER *Angry Wom. Abingd.* I. i (Merm.) 99 Things are well-spoken, if they be well-taken. **1600** JONSON *Cynth. Rev.* IV. iii. Aso.

Whatsoever they speak is well-taken; and whatsoever is well-taken is well-spoken. **1639** CLARKE 111. **1662** FULLER (*Som.*) III. 99 'Had I', said he, 'failed of my design, I would have killed the kings and all in the place'; words well spoken because well taken, all persons present being then highly in good humour.

Well that ends well, All is.

c. **1300** *Prov. of Hending* no. 1 Wel is him, þa wel ende mai. *a.* **1530** *R. Hill's Commonpl. Bk.* (E.E.T.S.) 110 'All ys well þat endyth well' said þe gud wyff. **1546** HEYWOOD I. x. 21 Well aunt (quoth Ales) all is well that endes well. **1602-3** SHAKS. *All's Well.* IV. iv. 35 All's well that ends well: still the fine's the crown. *Ibid.* V. i. 25 All's well that ends well yet. **1655** FULLER *Ch. Hist.* III. i (1868) I. 319 But all is well that ends well; and so did this contest. **1836** MARRYAT *Midsh. Easy* vi I had got rid of the farmer, ... dog, ... bull, and the bees—all's well that ends well.

Well to work and make a fire, it doth care and skill require.

1664 CODRINGTON 227. **1670** RAY 28.

Well used, Where men are | they'll frequent there.

1659 HOWELL *Eng. Prov.* 10/1. **1670** RAY 27. **1732** FULLER no. 5649 Where men are kindly used they will resort.

Well well, is a word of malice.

1670 RAY 154 ... *Chesh.* In other places, if you say *well well*, they will ask, whom you threaten.

Well with him who is beloved of his neighbours, All is.

1640 HERBERT 317.

Well with me, Where it is | there is my country.

[L. *Ubi bene, ibi patria.*] **1579** LYLY *Euphues* (Arb.) 187 He [Plato] noted that euery place was a country to a wise man, and al parts a pallace to a quiet mind. **1599** *Solyman & Perseda* IV. in HAZL. *O.E.P.* V. 342 Basil. My valour everywhere shall purchase friends; And where a man lives well, there is his country. **1639** CLARKE 121 A good heart may doe well any where. **1909** A. LLOYD *Every-day Japan* (1911) Pref. *Ubi bene est ibi patria.* The wonderful kindness I have always received in Japan has made me understand how true the phrase is.

Well worth aw (awe, all), it (that) makes (gars) the plough draw.

c. **1598** *MS. Proverbs* in FERGUSSON 109 Weill worth aw it gars the pleugh draw. **1639** CLARKE 93 Awe, makes Dun draw. **1641** FERGUSSON 108 Weill worth aw, that gars the plough draw. **1670** RAY 58. **1721** KELLY 354 ... Spoken when people are over-aw'd to do a thing, which otherways they would not do. **1862** HISLOP 313 Weel worth a' that gars the plough draw. *Anglice*, Good luck to

everything by which we earn money. **1881** EVANS *Leics. Words, &c.* (E.D.S.) 95 (A) Au Au! an exclamation to horses to bid them turn to the left or near side. 'Aw makes Dun draw' is a punning proverb quoted by Ray. [[1] makes.]

Well (*adj., adv.*), *see also* Do w. and doubt no man; Do w. and have w.; Doth w. (He that) wearieth not; Leave w. alone; Man hath his mare again (All is w.); Never w., full nor fasting; One thing at a time ... done w.; Say w. and do w. end with one letter; Say w. or be still; Want a thing w. done (If you); Weal (W.) or woe as he thinks (Man is); Wisdom counsels (W. goes case when); Wise that knows when he's w. enough.

Well(s) (*noun*), *see also* Dirt into the w. (Cast no); Dog in the w.; Drawn w. seldom dry; —— have sweetest water; Go the w. against his will ... water will spill; Know the worth of water till w. dry (We never); Many w. many buckets.

Well-bred youth neither speaks of himself, nor, being spoken to, is silent, A.

1640 HERBERT 330.

Wellington Roundheads.[1]

1678 RAY 353 ... Proverbial in *Taunton* for a violent fanatick. [[1] members of the Parliamentary party in the Civil War of the 17th century, who wore their hair cut short, Puritan fashion.]

Welly[1] brosten,[2] I am.

1738 SWIFT (Dial. ii) 348 *A footman brings a great whole cheese ... Sir J.* Well: I'm welly brosten, as they say in Lancashire. [[1] almost. [2] burst.]

Welsh ambassador.

[A name for '*a*) the cuckoo; (*b*) the owl.] **1608** MIDDLETON *Trick to catch Old One* iv. H 1 Thy Sound is like the cuckowe, the welch Embassador. *c.* **1620** *Welsh Embass.* iv. 1501 (Malone Soc.) Pray mr Reese ... what is the reason that wee english men when the Cuckoe is vppon entrance saie the welsh embassador is Cominge. **1683-4** in MACRAY *Reg. Magd. Coll.* N.S. IV (1904) 135 Mr. Clerke, commoner, complain'd of Sir Charnock, demy, for abusing him ..., calling him foole, Welsh ambassadour (an expression for an owle). **1917** BRIDGE 121 ... This is the general Cheshire name for the cuckoo which is heard first from the Welsh quarter.

Welsh bait.

[= a rest, without other refreshment, given to a horse on reaching the top of a hill; also *fig.*] **1603** T. POWELL (*title*) Welch Bayte to spare Prouender. Or, A looking backe vpon the Times past. **1658** HARRINGTON *Prerog. Pop. Govt.* I. vi. 32 In this place he takes a Welsh bait, and looking back makes a Muster of his Victories.

Welsh blood is up, His.

1631 SHIRLEY *Love Tricks* V. iii (A) Her Welsh blood is up. **1662** FULLER (*Wales*) III. 488 'His Welsh blood is up'. A double reason may be rendered why the Welsh are subject to anger.

Welsh mile.

[= a long and tedious mile, chiefly proverbial.] c. **1450** *Merlin* XV. 247 All the contrey was of hem covered the length of a walshe myle. **1652** J. TAYLOR (Water-P.) *Journ. Wales* (1859) 21 I hired a guide who brought me to Swansey (sixteen well stretch'd Welch mountainous miles). **1785** GROSE *Dict. Vulg. T.* (1796) 'Welch Mile' Like a Welch mile, long and narrow.

Welsh parsley.

a. **1625** FLETCHER *Elder Brother* I. ii In tough Welsh Parsly, which in our vulgar Tongue, is strong Hempen Halters. **1638** RANDOLPH *Hey for Honesty* IV. i (1651) 30 This is a Rascal deserves . . . To dance in Hemp *Derricks Caranto*: Lets choke him with Welch Parsley.

Welsh, *see also* Long as W. pedigree

Welshman had rather see his dam on the bier, than to see a fair Februeer, The.

1678 RAY 44.

Welshman keeps nothing until he hath lost it, The.

1662 FULLER (*Cardig.*) III. 520 'The Welchman keeps nothing until he hath lost it' . . . When the British recovered the lost castles from the English, they doubled their diligence and valour, keeping them more tenaciously than before.

Welshman, The older the | the more madman.

1659 HOWELL *Brit. Prov.* 31.

Welshman's cow, little and good, Like the.

1850 KINGSLEY *Alton Locke* XXVII We're just of a size, you know; little and good, like a Welshman's cow.

Welshman's hose of, To make.

[= to wrest the meaning of a word or sentence.] *a.* **1529** *Colin Cloute* 780 A thousand thousande other, That . . . make a Walshmans hose Of the texte and of the glose. **1559** *Mirr. Mag., Robt. Tresilian* xi And words that wer most plaine . . . we turned by construction lyke a welchmans hose.

Welshman, *see also* Heart of an Englishman towards W.; Irishman for a hand.

Welt or guard, Without.

[= without ornamentation or trimming; also used *fig.*] c. **1590** GREENE *Fr. Bacon* 2140 Marke you waisters, hears a plaine honest man, without welt or garde. **1592** Id. *Upst. Courtier* B 3b I sawe they were a plaine payre of Cloth breeches, without eyther welt or garde. **1594** NASH *Unf. Trav.* (1920) 8 He kept a plaine alehouse without welt or gard of anie iuybush. **1620** SHELTON *Quix.* II. v (1908) II. 220 I was christened Teresa, without welt or gard, nor additions of Don or Dona.

Wench(es), *see* Wine and w. empty men's purses; Young w. make old wrenches.

Wept when I was born, I | and every day shows why.

1605–6 SHAKS. *K. Lear* IV. vi. 187 When we are born, we cry that we are come To this great stage of fools. **1640** HERBERT 326. **1768** GOLDSMITH *Good-nat. Man* I (Globe) 613 *Hon.* Nothing can exceed the vanity of our existence, but the folly of our pursuits. We wept when we came into the world, and every day tells us why.

Wer, *see* Sour as w.

West (*proper name*), *see* Jack W.

West, *see* Wind is w. (When), fish bite best; Wind's in the w., weather at best.

Westminster for a wife, Who goes to | to Paul's for a man, and to Smithfield for a horse, may meet with a whore, a knave, and a jade.

1593 *Passionate Morrice* (N.Sh.S.) 83 (A) It is more vncertaine . . . whether a Smithfeelde horse will proue good or iadish. **1597–8** SHAKS. *2 Hen. IV* I. ii. 48 Where's Bardolph? . . . I bought him in Paul's, and he'll buy me a horse in Smithfield: an I could get me but a wife in the stews, I were manned, horsed, and wived. **1617** MORYSON *Itin.* III. i. 53 (1908) III. 463 The Londoners pronounce woe to him, that buys a horse in Smithfield, that takes a servant in Paul's church, that marries a wife out of Westminster. **1659** HOWELL *Eng. Prov.* 14/1.

Westminster Hall, *see* Suits hang half a year in W. H., at Tyburn . . .

Westward for smelts.

1607 DEKKER &c. *Westw. Hoe* II. iii But wenches, with what pullies shall we slide . . . out of our husbandes suspition, being gone Westward for smelts all night. **1608** *Great Frost* in ARBER *E. Garner* i. 85 (1877) Say, have none gone 'westward for smelts' as our proverbial phrase is? **1620** *Westward for Smelts, or the Waterman's Fare of Mad, Merry, Western Wenches, &c.* [title].

Wet finger, With a.

[= with the utmost ease.] **1519** HORMAN *Vulg.* f. 195 (A) I wyll helpe all this besines with a wete fynger. **1542** UDALL tr. *Erasm. Apoph.* To Rdr. Readie waie and recourse maie with a weate finger easily be found out. **1602** DEKKER *Honest Wh.*, Pt. I. v. i (Merm.) 170 Trust not a woman when she cries, For she'll pump water from her eyes With a wet finger. **1611** CHAPMAN *May Day* I. i. 315 I am able to pay it with a wet finger. **1748** RICHARDSON *Clarissa* (1750) v. 152 If thou likest her, I'll get her for thee with a wet finger, as the saying is. **1754** FOOTE *Knights* I. Wks. (1799) I. 69 If Dame Winifred were here she'd make them all out with a wet finger.

Wet one's whistle, To.

[= to take a drink.] *c.* **1386** CHAUCER *Reeve's T.* A 4155 So was hir ioly whistle wel y-wet. **1530** PALSGRAVE 780 I wete my whystell, as good drinkers do, *je crocque la pie.* **1653** WALTON *Angler* iii. 75 Lets . . . drink the other cup to wet our whistles, and so sing away all sad thought. **1787** WOLCOT (P. Pindar) *Ode upon Ode* Wks. (1812) I. 447 Nor damn thy precious soul to wet thy whistle.

Wether, *see* Belled w. break the snow (Let the).

Whale, Very like a.

1600–1 SHAKS. *Hamlet* III. ii. 406 Very like a whale. **1842–3** W. H. MAXWELL *Hector O'Hal.* viii 'I was endeavouring to make peace', returned Mr. French, with unblushing effrontery. 'Mighty like a whale!' observed the commander, in a side whisper. **1859** *Slang Dict.* 115 *Very like a whale,* said of anything that is very improbable.

Whale, *see also* Sprat to catch w.; Tub to the w. (Throw).

Wharlers, *see* Carleton w.

What d'ye lack?

[A salesman's cry.] **1563** NEWBERY *Dives Pragmaticus* A 3 (A) What lacke ye, sir what seke you, what wyll you bye? **1614** B. JONSON *Barth. Fair* II. i What do you lacke? what is't you buy? . . . rattles, drums, halberts [&c.]. **1668** DRYDEN *Evening's Love* v. i. Wks. (1883) III. 363 To draw us in, with a what-do-you-lack, as we passed by.

What has been, may be.

1603 FLORIO tr. *Montaigne,* To Reader What is that that hath beene? That that shall be. **1732** FULLER no. 5491.

What is he (she), It is not | but what has he (she).

1621 R. BRAITHWAIT *Sheph. Tales* II. Eg. 1 (1877) 233 *Dor.* Alas poor Swaine; 'tis true what th' prouerbe saith, We aske not what he is, but what he hath. **1721** KELLY 224 . . . Spoken of the choice of wives, where the portion is often more look'd after than either the person or the virtues. **1738** SWIFT (Dial. i) 340 *Lady A.* She's immensely rich. *Never.* . . . They say her father was a baker. *Lady S.* Ay; but it is not, What is she? but, What has she? now-a-days.

What rake[1] the feud where the friendship dow[2] not.

1641 FERGUSSON 108. **1721** KELLY 349 . . . Signifying our contempt of mean persons,

whose hatred we defy, and whose friendship we despise. [[1] signifies. [2] avails, profits.]

What serves dirt for if it do not stink?

1721 KELLY 354 . . . Spoken . . . when mean, base born people, speak proudly, or behave themselves saucily.

What will be, shall be.

c. **1386** CHAUCER *Knight's T.* 1466 As whan a thyng is shapen it shal be. **1546** HEYWOOD II. i. 43 That shalbe, shalbe. *c.* **1590** MARLOWE *Faustus* I. i. 75 What doctrine call you this, *Che sera, sera,* What will be, shall be?

Whaup in the rape, There is a.

1721 KELLY 305 . . . There is something amiss. **1862** A. HISLOP 289 . . . There is a knot in the rope—there is something wrong.

Whaver, *see* Shed riners with a w.

Wheamow, I am very | quoth the old woman, when she stepped into the milk bowl.

1678 RAY 84 I am very wheamow (*i.e.* nimble) quoth the old woman, when she step't into the milk-bowl. *Yorksh.* **1917** BRIDGE 79 I'm very wheamow (active) as the old woman said when she stept into the middle of the bittlin (milk-bowl). . . . As *wheamow* is not a common Cheshire word the proverb has doubtless come to us from a neighbouring county.

Wheat always lies best in wet sheets.

1830 FORBY 417.

Wheat will not have two praises.

1678 RAY 348 . . . (*Summer and Winter.*)

Wheat, *see also* May makes or mars w.; Sow w. in dirt.

Wheat-sowing, *see* First of November . . . an end of w.-s.

Wheatears, *see* May never goes without w.

Wheelbarrow, *see* Drunk as a w.; Go to heaven in w.; Music on a w. (Make as good).

Wheels within wheels, There are.

[A complexity of forces or influences. **1611** BIBLE *Ezek.* i. 16 Their work was as it were a wheel in the middle of a wheel.] **1642** D. ROGERS *Matrim. Honour,* To Reader (A) This wheele of our conversation . . . including many lesser wheeles in, and under it. **1709** SHAFTSB. *Charac.* (1711) I. 114 Thus we have Wheels within Wheels. And in some National Constitutions . . . we have one Empire within another. **1824** L. MURRAY *Engl. Gram.* (ed. 5) I. 457 They are wheels within wheels; sentences in the midst of sentences. **1900** 'H. S. MERRIMAN' *Isle of Unrest* vi There are wheels within wheels . . . in the social world of Paris.

Wheel(s), see also Fly sat upon the axletree; Fortune to be pictured on w. (Not only ought); Greases his w. helps oxen; Worst w. creaks most.

Whelp, see Expect a good w. from ill dog (We may not); First pig, last w. is the best; Tod's w., aye the aulder the waur.

Where one is bred, Not | but where he is fed.

1662 FULLER (xxi) I. 84 The Latins have a proverb, 'non ubi nascor, sed ubi pascor'; making that place their mother, not which bred but which fed them.

Whet a knife for one's own throat, To.

1639 FULLER *Holy War* II. xl (1840) 104 Thus princes who make their subjects overgreat, whet a knife for their own throats.

Whet brings no let.

1616 DRAXE 176 Whetting (viz. of knives and sithes) is no letting. **1639** CLARKE 271 Whetting is no letting. **1654** FULLER *Serm.* (1891) 1. 75 *A whet is no let,* saith the proverb: mowers lose not any time which they spend in whetting . . . their scythes. **1659** HOWELL *Eng. Prov.* 2/1 Whett brings no lett, *viz. When a mower whets his sithe.*

Whet his knife on the threshold of the Fleet, He may.

1662 FULLER (*Lond.*) II. 348 'He may whet his knife on the threshold of the Fleet'. The Fleet is . . . a prison, so called . . . from a brook running by. . . . The proverb is applicable to those who never owed ought; or else, having run into debt, have crept out of it; so . . . may defy danger and arrests.

Whetstone, To deserve (have, lie for) the.

[= to be a great liar: in allusion to the former custom of hanging a whetstone round the neck of a liar.] **1364** *Liber Albus* (Rolls) iv. 601 Juggement de Pillorie par iii heures, ove un ague pier entour soun col, pur mensonges controeves. *c.* **1410** *Towneley Plays* xxi. 80 A, good sir, lett hym oone; he lyes for the quetstone. **1418** *Cal. Let.-Bks. Lond., Let.-Bk. I* (1909) 197 He, as a fals lyere . . . shal stond . . . upon þe pillorye . . . wiþ a Westone aboute his necke. **1577** FULKE *Confut. Purg.* 437 You haue sayd enough, M. Allen, to winne the whetstone. **1616** DRAXE 123 He will lie for the whetstone. **1658** [H. EDMUNDSON] *Fellow-trav.* 285 A great Person . . . had in a frolick set on some wanton wits to lye for the Whetstone. **1678** RAY 89 He deserves the whetstone. He'll not let any body lye by him. **1778** *Exmoor Courtship* (E.D.S.) 79 What a gurt Lee es thate! . . . thek Man shou'd a had the Whitstone.

Whetstone, though it can't itself cut, makes tools cut, A.

[HOR. *A.P.* **304** *Fungar vice cotis acutum*

Reddere quae ferrum valet exsors ipse secandi, I will perform the function of a whetstone, which, itself incapable of cutting, can make iron sharp.] *c.* **1374** CHAUCER *Troylus* I. 631 A wheston is no kerving instrument, But yit it maketh sharpè kerving toles. **1621** BURTON *Anat. Mel.* III. iv. I. ii (1651) 648 Yet as so many whetstones to make other tools cut, but cut not themselves, though they be of no religion at all, they will make others most devout and superstitious. **1732** FULLER no. 455.

Which way to London? A poke[1] full of plums.

1580 J. BARET *Alveary* F 63 *Falces postulabas.* . . . A Prouerbe vsed, when a man asking a question, answere is made quite contrarie to his demand: as thus: which is the way to London? answere is made, A poke full of plumbes. **1639** CLARKE 19. [[1] bag, sack.]

Whig, see Sour as w.

Whiles[1] thou, whiles I, so goes the bailery.[2]

1721 KELLY 352 . . . Spoken when persons, and parties, get authority by turns. [[1] sometimes. [2] magistracy.]

Whin, see March wind . . . blooms the w.

Whine, see Suffolk w.

Whip and bell.

[= something that detracts from one's comfort or pleasure: the Romans attached a whip and a bell to the triumphal chariot of a general, to drive away evil.] **1644** CLEVELAND *Char. Lond. Diurn.* 4 In all this Triumph there is a whip and a Bell. **1684** OTWAY *Atheist* I. i To get rid of that Whip and a Bell, call'd thy Wife.

Whip and whirr never made good fur.[1]

a. **1553** UDALL *Royster D.* I. iii (Arb.) 20 No haste but good, . . . for whip and whurre The olde prouerbe doth say, neuer made good furre. [[1] furrow.]

Whip for a fool, A | and a rod for a school, is always in good season.

1613 S. ROWLEY *When you see me* F 1 (A) A rod in scoole, a whip for a foole, is alwaies in season. **1670** RAY 212.

Whip the cat, To.

[= to be drunk.] **1599** MINSHEU (1623) 2 X 2[v] Hunts the Fox, whips the cat, or is drunke. **1611** COTGRAVE s.v. 'Bertrand (Deschausser)' To be drunke . . . to whip the cat.

Whip with six strings.

[= the severe religious Act of the Six Articles, 1539.] *a.* **1548** HALL *Chron., Hen. VIII* 234 This act established chiefly sixe articles, wherof . . . of some it was named the whip with six strynges. **1655** FULLER *Ch.*

Hist. v. v (1868) ii. 112 The Six Articles . . . that whip with six knots, each one, as heavily laid on, fetching blood from the backs of poor protestants.

Whip(s), *see also* Chastise with scorpions; Oil of w.; Spur and a w. for dull horse; Want a pretence to w. a dog (If you).

Whip-hand of, To have the.

[= to have the advantage, upper hand of.] 1680 ALSOP *Mischief Impos.* ii. 8 When once they are got into the Saddle, and have the whip-hand of the poor Laity. 1690 CHILD *Disc. Trade* Pref. C. 8 Before the Dutch get too much the whip-hand of us. 1849 DE QUINCEY *Engl. Mail-Coach* Wks. (1890) XIII. 307 In the art of conversation, . . . he admitted that I had the whip-hand of him.

Whirl the eyes too much, shows a kite's brain, To.

1640 HERBERT 350.

Whisker, *see* Dam of that was a w.; March w. never good fisher.

Whispering but there is lying, There is no.

1678 RAY 348 Where there is whispering there is lying. 1738 SWIFT (Dial. i) 339 MISS *whispers Lady* SMART. *Never.* There's no whispering, but there's lying.

Whistle and drink at the same time, A man cannot.

1586 PETTIE *Guazzo's Civ. Conv.* 137 It is a common saying, that one cannot drink and whistle together.

Whistle for a wind (*or* breeze), To.

1834 MARRYAT *Jacob Faith.* xxxix We must whistle for a breeze. In the mean time, Mr. Knight, we will have the boats all ready.

Whistle like a blackbird, To.

1663 BUTLER *Hudibras* I. i. 53, 4 That Latin was no more difficile, Than to a blackbird 'tis to whistle. 1887 BLACKMORE *Springhaven* vi You can whistle like a blackbird when you choose.

Whistle psalms to the taffrail, To.

1898 ANSTED *Dict. Sea Terms* 310 *Whistling psalms to the taffrail.* An expression signifying the throwing away of good advice upon some person who may be about as susceptible to its influence as is the taffrail of his yacht.

Whistle (*noun***),** *see* Clean as a w.; Make an end of your w. though cart overthrow; Pay too dear for one's w.; Wet one's w.

Whistle(s, d) (*verb***),** *see* Gled w. (Never for nothing that the); Halloo (W.) until one is out of wood (Not to); Says anything but prayers and those he w.

Whistling maid, *see* Crooning cow.

Whistling to going to plough, There belongs more than.

1678 RAY 191.

Whistling, *see also* Sung well before he broke shoulder with w.

White black, To make.

[JUV. 3. 30: *Qui nigrum in candida vertunt.*] *a.* 1593 MARLOWE *Edwd. II* I, iv (Merm.) 344 Such reasons make white black, and dark night day. 1612–13 SHAKS. *Hen. VIII* I. i. 209 That dye is on me Which makes my whit'st part black.

White (*or* White-headed) boy.

[= a favourite.] 1539 TAVERNER (1545) F 7ᵛ He that can flatter and say as I saye, shalbe myne owne white sonne. 1541 COVERDALE *Confut. Standish* (1547) lii b Maruaill not . . . though . . . I call you . . . her owne whyte sonne. *a.* 1553 UDALL *Royster D.* I. i Be his nowne white sonne. 1599 PORTER *Angry Wom. Abingd.* (Percy Soc.) 69 Whose white boy is that same? *c.* 1600 *Timon* I. iii (1842) 10 *Gelas* . . . What speake the virgines of me? . . . *Pæd.* They terme you delight of men, white boye. 1639 FULLER *Holy War* I. xiii (1840) 22 The pope was loath to adventure his darlings into danger; those white boys were to stay at home with his holiness. 1690 C. NESSE *O. & N. Test.* I. 377 Joseph . . . was not only his earthly fathers white-boy, but his heavenly's also. 1823 LAMB *All Fools' Day* fin. So many darlings of absurdity, minions of the goddess, and her white boys. 1894 HALL CAINE *Manxman* II. xi He was always my white-headed boy, and I stuck to him with life.

White feather, To show the.

[= to betray cowardice, a white feather in a game-bird's tail being a mark of bad breeding.] 1824 SCOTT *St. Ronan's* viii 'To him, man . . . he shows the white feather.' 1850 THACKERAY *Pendennis* xl It was reported . . . he . . . had certainly shown the white feather in his regiment.

White foot, One | —buy him: two white feet—try him: three white feet—look well about him: four white feet—go without him.

1882 *N. & Q.* 6th Ser. v. 427. Horsedealing Proverb.

White hands cannot hurt.

1853 TRENCH iii. 52 We . . . meet in the proverbs of Spain a grave thoughtfulness, a stately humour. . . . How eminently chivalresque . . . : *White hands cannot hurt. Las manos blancas no ofenden.*

White hath its black, and every sweet its sour, Every.

c. 1400 *Beryn* (E.E.T.S.) 29 For 'aftir swete, the soure comyth, ful offt, in many a plase'. *a.* 1765 *Sir Cauline* II. i in PERCY *Reliques* I. 39 Everye white will have its blacke, And everye sweete its sowre. 1818 MISS FERRIER *Marriage* lv 'Every white will have its black, And every sweet its sour', as Lady Juliana experienced. Her daughter was Duchess of

Altamont, but Grizzy Douglas had arrived in Bath!

White hen, *see* Son of a w. h.

White horse and a fair wife, He that hath a | never wants trouble.

1586 PETTIE *Guazzo's Civ. Conv.* 124 It is yet an ordinary saying, That he that hath a white horse, and a fayre woman, is neuer without trouble.

White horse, *see also* Keep something for him that rides w. h.; Save something for man that rides w. h.

White legs would aye be rused.[1]

1721 KELLY 340 . . . Spoken when people fish for commendations, by disparaging a little their persons, or performances. [[1] praised.]

White Man's Grave, The.

[**1873**] SIR W. BUTLER *Autobiog.* (1911) ix. 143 What did it matter if the Gold Coast had been the White Man's Grave ever since Columbus had been there? One never dreamt of asking whether a climate was good or bad. **1910** *Times Lit. Sup.* 25 Feb. 65 The colony of Sierra Leone is happily no longer known as 'The White Man's Grave'. . . . Europeans can now live on the coast and in the hinterland under reasonably healthy conditions.

White silver draws black lines.

1579 GOSSON *Sch. Abuse* (Arb.) 23 Whyte siluer, drawes a blacke lyne. **1670** RAY 142.

White stone, *see* Mark with w. s.

White wall is a fool's paper, A.

1573 SANDFORD 218. **1611** DAVIES Prov. 77 'A fool's paper is a white wall:' But it was not so in Baltazar's hall. **1636** CAMDEN 292. **1662** FULLER (*Lancs.*) II. 191 'A wall is the fool's paper', whereon they scribble their fancies.

White, *see also* Grey (W.) hairs death's blossoms; Son of a w. hen; Wool so w. but dyer can make black (No).

Whither go you, *see* How doth your.

Whither goest, grief? Where I am wont.

1640 HERBERT 321.

Whiting, *see* Fine as if you had a w. hanging at your side; Leaped a haddock (w.).

Whittington's College, He has studied at.

1592 *The Defence of Conny catching . . . By Cuthbert Cunny-catcher, Licenciate in Whittington College* [title]. **1602** S. ROWLANDS 'Tis Merry when Gossips Meet A 2ᵛ Commence Bachelor in Whittington College. **1787** GROSE (*Lond.*) 204 . . . That is, he has been confined in Newgate, which was rebuilt A.D. 1423, according to the will of Sir Richard Whittington; by . . . his executors.

Whitworth (Madge), *see* Go here away.

Who are you for? I am for him whom I get most by.

1707 MAPLETOFT 33. **1855** BOHN 565.

Who's the fool now?

1588 *Stationers' Register* 9 Nov. (Arb.) ii. 506 Martyn said to his man, whoe is the foole now. **1600** 'C. SNUFFE' *Quips upon Questions* B 3ᵛ Who's the Foole now? **1600** DEKKER *Old Fortunatus* (1873) i. 101 Wise men . . . crie who's the foole now?

Who wats who may keep sheep another day.

1721 KELLY 345 . . . Who knows but it may be in my power to do you good or harm hereafter, and as you use me, so will I you.

Whole (*or* Sound) as a trout, As.

a. **1300** *Cursor M.* 11884 (Cott.) Bi þat þou par-of cum vte þou sal be hale sum ani trute [*v. r.* troute]. *c.* **1518** SKELTON *Magnyf.* 1624, I am forthwith as hole as a troute. **1592** SHAKS. *Two Gent.* II. v. 19. Both as whole as a fish. **1635** SWAN *Spec. M.* (1670) 347 When we speak of one who is sound indeed, we say that he is sound as a Trout. **1678** RAY 289 As sound as a trout.

Whole hog, *see* Go the w. h.

Whole, *see also* Lick w.

Wholesomest meal is at another man's cost, The.

1659 HOWELL *Eng. Prov.* 19/1. **1670** RAY 1.

Whooping, *see* Out of all w.

Whore in a fine dress is like a clean entry to a dirty house, A.

1721 KELLY 51. **1736** BAILEY *Dict.* S.V. (A).

Whoredom and grace, dwelt ne'er in one place.

1721 KELLY 355.

Whoredom, *see also* Opportunity is w.'s bawd.

Whores affect not you but your money.

1659 N. R. 120. **1664** CODRINGTON 225. **1670** RAY 28. **1732** FULLER no. 5726.

Whores and thieves go by the clock.

1607 DEKKER & WEBSTER *Northward Ho* C 2 They say Whores and bawdes go by clocks. **1678** RAY 68.

Whores in Hose than honest women in Long Clawson, There are more.

1787 GROSE (*Leic.*) 191 There are more whores in Hose, than honest women in Long Clawton. Hose and Long Clawton are neighbouring villages . . . : Howes, or Hose, is but a small place, Long Claxton, Clayston, or Clawston, is . . . near a mile long. . . . The entendre lies in the word Hose, which here is meant to signify stockings.

Whore(s), *see also* Drives an ass and leads a w.. (Who), hath toil; Hop w. pipe thief; Once a w. **ever** a w.; Plays the w. for apples, then bestows; Poor kin that has neither w. nor thief; Postern door makes w.

Whoring and bawdry do often end in beggary.

1664 CODRINGTON 230. **1670** RAY 28.

Whose mare is dead?

1595 *Maroccus Extaticus* (Percy Soc.) 5 Holla, Marocco, whose mare is dead, that you are thus melancholy? **1597–8** SHAKS. *2 Hen. IV* II. i. 47 How now? Whose mare's dead? What's the matter. **1738** SWIFT *Pol. Conv.* (1927) i. 71 What's the matter? whose mare's dead now?

Why hath a wherefore, Every.

1566 GASCOIGNE *Supp.* I. i. in Wks. (1907) I. 189 I have given you a wherefore for this why many times. **1592–3** SHAKS. *Com. Err.* II. ii. 45 Ay, sir, and wherefore; for they say every why hath a wherefore. **1678** RAY 348 There is never a why but there's a wherefore. **1822** SCOTT *Nigel* iii In troth, my lord, every *why* has its *wherefore.*

Why, *see also* 'Twill not be w. for thy.

Wicked book is the wickeder because it cannot repent, A.

1732 FULLER no. 457.

Wicked man is his own hell, A.

c. **1590** MARLOWE *Faustus* II. i Hell hath no limits, nor is circumscribed In one self place; but where we are is Hell. **1642** BROWNE *Rel. Med.* I (1881) 81 I feel sometimes a hell within my self. **1667** MILTON *Par. Lost* IV. 75 Which way I fly is hell; my self am hell. **1732** FULLER no. 460 . . . and his passions and lusts the fiends that torment him.

Wicked man's gift hath a touch of his master, A.

1640 HERBERT 324.

Wicked, The more | the more fortunate (lucky).

1552 LATIMER *Serm. Lincolnsh.* i (1562) 68 And therefore there is a common sayinge The more wicked, the more lucky.

Wicked thing to make a dearth one's garner, It is a.

1640 HERBERT 358. **1732** FULLER no. 2890.

Wicked woman and an evil is three halfpence worse than the devil, A.

1576 T. T. *The Schoolmaster* (1583) P 2 A wicked woman fraught with all euill is by three farthings worse then the Deuill. **1639** CLARKE 118. **1670** RAY 50. **1732** FULLER no. 6406.

Wicked world, It is a | and we make part of it.

1732 FULLER no. 5063.

Wicked, *see also* Love of w. more dangerous than hatred; Prayers of w. won't prevail.

Wickedly, *see* Liveth w. can hardly die honestly.

Widdie[1] hold thine own.

1721 KELLY 353 . . . Spoken when we see a bad man in danger, as if he owed his life to the gallows. [[1] gallows.]

Widdie or Widdy, *see* Every man gets his own (When), thief will get w.; Highest in court nearest the w.; Laughing to girn in a w. (It is nae); Water will never reave the w.

Wide ears and a short tongue.

1616 DRAXE 191. **1639** CLARKE 302.

Wide therm[1] had never a long arm, He that has a.

1721 KELLY 137 . . . Gluttonous people will not be liberal of their meat. [[1] gut.]

Wide will wear, but narrow will tear.

1678 RAY 217. **1732** FULLER no. 6097. **1856** ABP. WHATELY *Annot. Bacon's Ess.* (1876) 510 The rule should be . . . not a severe one; lest, like over-severe laws, . . . it should be violated; according to the Proverb, that 'Wide will wear, but tight will tear'.

Widecombe folks are picking their geese, faster, faster, faster.

1850 *N. & Q.* 1st Ser. II. 512 'Widdecombe folks are picking their geese, Faster, faster, faster'. A saying among the parishes of the south coast during a snowstorm. **1911** W. CROSSING *Folk Rhymes of Devon* 29 Widecombe folks are picking their geese, Faster, faster. Widecombe-in-the-Moor is an extensive Dartmoor parish. . . . The village of the same name lies in a deep valley. . . . A writer . . . has suggested that the name of the moorland village . . . is merely a corruption of . . . 'widdicote', an old Devonshire term for the sky.

Widows are always rich.

1678 RAY 57.

Widow(s), *see also* Keep yourself from . . . w. thrice married; Long a w. weds with shame; Marries a w. and three children (He that); Marries a w. and two daughters (He that); Marries a w. (He that), dead man's head in dish; Marry a w. before she leaves mourning; Marry a w. (Never), unless first husband hanged; Person marked (Take heed of) and w. thrice married; Wooers and w. never poor.

Wife, Next to no | a good wife is best.

1642 FULLER *H. & P. State* III. xxii (1841) 205 A bachelor was saying, 'Next to no wife, a good wife is best'. 'Nay,' said a gentle-woman, 'next to a good wife, no wife is the best.'

Wife an ass, If you make your | she will make you an ox.

1732 FULLER no. 2772.

Wife and children are bills of charges.

1607–12 BACON *Ess., Marriage* (Arb.) 266 There are some other that esteeme wife, and children but as Bills of Charges. **1659** HOWELL *Eng. Prov.* 18/1.

Wife and children, He that hath a | hath given hostages to fortune.

[LUCAN 7. 660 *Coniunx est mihi, sunt nati; dedimus tot pignora fatis.*] **1612** BACON *Ess., Mar. & Sing. Life* (Arb.) 264 He that hath wife, and children, hath given hostages to fortune, for they are impediments to great enterprizes. **1678** BUTLER *Hudibras* III. i. 809 For what secures the civil life But pawns of children, and a wife? That lie, like hostages, at stake, To pay for all men undertake. **1732** FULLER no. 5742 Wife and Children are Hostages given to Fortune.

Wife and children, He that hath a | wants not business.

1640 HERBERT 353. **1732** FULLER no. 2157.

Wife, He that hath no | beateth her oft.

1573 SANDFORD (1576) 208. **1629** *Book of Meery Riddles* Prov. 79 (A).

Wife cries five loaves a penny, My.

1678 RAY 71 My wife cryes *five* loaves a penny, *i.e.* She is in travel.[1] [[1] travail.]

Wife, He that has a | has a master.

1721 KELLY 138.

Wife is the key of the house, The.

1616 DRAXE 231 The wife is the key of the house. **1640** HERBERT 358. **1732** FULLER no. 4828.

Wife that kept her supper for her breakfast, There was a | and she died ere day.

1721 KELLY 317 ... Spoken when you are bid keep such a thing for another meal.

Wife that never cries for the ladle till the pot runs over, Like the.

1862 HISLOP 214 ... That is, never asks for an article until it is too late.

Wife (Wives), *see also* Bachelors' w. well taught; Best or worst ... is choosing good or ill w.; Better a portion in a w.; Blames w. for own unthrift; Blind man's w. needs no painting; Child's bird and knave's w.; Choose a w. on a Saturday; Choosing a w. not trust to another; Commend not your w.; Cunning w. makes husband apron; Dawted daughters daidling w.; Devil is dead (When) there's a w. for Humphrey; Ding the Deil into a w. (You may); Fair w. ... breed quarrels; Fair w. (Who hath) needs more than two eyes; Fault of a w. (He has) that marries mam's pet; First w. is matrimony; Go down ladder when marriest a w.; Good husband makes good w.; Good lasses, but whence bad w.; Good w. and health; Good w. in the country (There is one) and every man thinks; Good w. makes good husband; Good w.'s a goodly prize; Groaning horse and groaning w.; Hope better, quoth Benson, when w. bade him come in cuckold; Horse, a w., and a sword shewed not lent; Horse made and w. to make; House, a w., and fire to put her in; Husbands are in heaven whose w. scold not; Lack to a w. (No); Lack to lack w. (No); Lets his horse ... and w. to every wake; Little house ... little w. well willed; Long-tongued w. go long with bairn; Loses (Loseth) his w. and a farthing (six-pence); Many a man singeth that w. home bringeth; Mills and w. ever wanting; Nice w. ... make rich man poor; Prolong thy life, quiet heart loving w.; Proud eye ... light w. bring; Purse to your w. (If you sell your), give your breeks; Refuse a w. with one fault; Takes his w. (As a man), for better, for worse; Tells his w. news is newly married; Thrive (He that will) must ask his w.; Two cats ... two w. in a house never agree; Venture it, as Johnson did his w.; Wae's the w. that wants the tongue; White horse and a fair w. (He that hath); Wite yourself if w. with bairn; Women (W. and wind) are necessary evils. *See also* Old (Auld) wife (wives), Scolding wife.

Wight[1] (Stout) as a webster's (miller's) waistcoat, As | that every morning takes a thief by the neck.

1658 *Comes Facundus* 34 In *Germany* they say, when they speak of a stout man, that he is as bold as a Millers shirt, that every morning takes a theef by the neck. **1721** KELLY 34 *As wight as a webster's westcoat, that every morning takes a thief by the neck.* The Scots have but an ill opinion of weavers' honesty. Applied to them who brag of their stoutness. [[1] active.]

Wight[1] man never wanted a weapon, A. (*Cf.* Wise man never wants a weapon).

1641 FERGUSSON 4. **1721** KELLY 6 ... A man

of sense . . . will make a tool of the first thing that comes to his hands. [¹ strong, bold.]

Wigs on the green, There will be.

[A colloq. expression (orig. Irish) for coming to blows or sharp altercation.] **1856** *Chamb. Jrnl.* 1 Mar. 139/1 If a quarrel is foreseen as a probable contingency, it is predicted that 'there'll be wigs on the green'. **1893** STEVENSON *Catriona* xvii Mr. David Balfour has a very good ground of complaint, and . . . if his story were properly redd¹ out . . . there would be a number of wigs on the green. [¹ put in order.]

Wigs, *see also* Judges' w.

Wild boar, The rage of a | is able to spoil more than one wood.

1639 CLARKE 259.

Wild cat out of a bush, He looks like a.

1721 KELLY 173. **1732** FULLER no. 1973.

Wild goose chase, To run the.

[= a foolish, fruitless, or hopeless quest.] **1594–5** SHAKS. *Rom. & Jul.* II. iv. 75 Nay, if our wits run the wild-goose chase, I am done. **1606** CHAPMAN *Mons. D'Olive* I. i Plays (1889) 117 We may . . . talk satire, and let our wits run the wild-goose chase over Court and country. **1754** H. WALPOLE to Bentley 20 Nov. Don't let me think, that if you return, you will set out upon every wild-goose chase, sticking to nothing. **1876** F. E. TROLLOPE *Charming Fellow* xii His journey to London on such slender encouragement is a wild-goose chase! **1894** BLACKMORE *Perlycross* xxiv The English public . . . always exult in a wild-goose chase.

Wild goose never laid a tame egg, A.

1855 BOHN 303.

Wild mare, *see* Shoe the w. m.

Wild oats, To sow one's.

[= to indulge in youthful vices.] **1576** NEWTON *Lemnie's Complex* II. 99 That wilfull and vnruly age, which lacketh rypenes and discretion, and (as wee saye) hath not sowed all theyr wyeld Oates. **1638** T. HEYWOOD *Wise W. Hogsd.* II. i (Merm.) 268 And will these wild oats never be sown? **1829** COBBETT *Adv. to Y. Men* These vices of youth are varnished over by the saying, that there must be time for 'sowing the wild oats'. **1861** T. HUGHES *Tom B. at Oxford* vi 'A young fellow must sow his wild oats'. . . . You can make nothing but a devil's maxim of it.

Wiles help weak folk.

1641 FERGUSSON 108.

Wiles, *see also* Wise men are caught in w.

Wilful as a pig; As | he'll neither lead nor drive.

1678 RAY 291. **1864–5** DICKENS *Mut. Friend* III. ix I [Bella] am naturally as obstinate as a pig.

Wilful man had need be very wise, A.

[*Cf.* **1616** DRAXE 234 He is more wilful then wise.] **1721** KELLY 2. **1732** FULLER no. 465.

Wilful man will have his way, A.

1818 SCOTT *Rob Roy* xxviii The Hecate . . . ejaculated, 'A wilfu' man will hae his way'.

Will and wit strive with you.

1721 KELLY 347 . . . You are at a stand whether to do the pleasantest or the most profitable. Lat. *Aliud appetitus, aliud sapientia suadet.* **1736** BAILEY *Dict.* s.v. 'Wit' Wit and will strive for the victory (A).

Will buyeth and money payeth.

1573 SANDFORD (1576) 223. **1578** FLORIO *First Fruites* f. 34 (A) Wyl maketh the market but money maketh payment. **1629** *Book of Meery Riddles* Prov. 133.

Will for the deed, Take the.

[*ov. Ex Ponto* 4. 8. 5 *Meritum velle iuvare voco.*] *a.* **1450** *Ratis Raving* 294 (E.E.T.S.) 98 The wyll Is reput for the deid. **1576** PETTIE *Petite Pall.* (Gollancz) I. 135 Rather weigh the will of the speaker, than the worth of the words. **1606–7** SHAKS. *Ant. & Cleop.* II. v. 8 And when good will is show'd, though 't come too short, The actor may plead pardon. **1612–15** BP. HALL *Contempl.* I. iv (1825) I. 17 That God, which (in good) accepts the will for the deed, condemns the will for the deed in evil. **1738** SWIFT (Dial. ii) 344 *Lady S.* If we had known we should have such good company, we should have been better provided; but you must take the will for the deed. **1883** J. PAYN *Thicker than W.* xxxi The necessity for the self-sacrifice had not arisen, but by Beryl Paton the will was taken for the deed.

Will is a good boy when Will's at home.

1639 CLARKE 253.

Will is a good son, and will is a shrewd boy.

1546 HEYWOOD I. xi. 28 Will is a good sonne, and will is a shrewde boy. And wilfull shrewde will hath wrought thée this toy.

Will is ready, Where your | your feet are light.

1640 HERBERT 338.

Will is the cause of woe.

1639 CLARKE 253. **1732** FULLER no. 5757.

Will may win my heart.

1546 HEYWOOD I. iv. 9 Will maie wyn my herte, herein to consent, To take all thinges as it comth, and be content.

Will not, If one | another will; (so are all maidens married).

1546 HEYWOOD I. iii. 6 Sens that that one will not, on other will. **1639** CLARKE 17 What one will not, another will. **1670** RAY 158 The world was never so dull but if one will not another will. **1721** KELLY 182 If one will not, another will; so are all maidens married.

Will not, If one | another will; the morn's[1] the market day.

1721 KELLY 182. [[1] to-morrow.]

Will not when he may, He that | when he will (would) he shall have nay.

10th cent. A.-S. *Homily* quoted in SKEAT *Early Eng. Prov.* vi (A) þe læs, gif he nu nelle þa hwile þe he mæge, eft þonne he late wille, þæt he ne mæge. **a. 1180** ST. BASIL in JOHN OF SALISBURY *Polycrat.* viii. 17 *Qui non vult cum potest, non utique poterit cum volet.* **c. 1200** *Ancrene Riwle* (1853) 296 Hwo ne deth hwon he mei, he ne schal nout hwon he wolde. **1303** R. BRUNNE *Handl. Synne* 4795 Hyt ys seyd al day, for thys skyl, 'He that wyl nat whan he may He shal nat, when he wyl'. **c. 1350** *Douce MS. 52* no. 57 Who-so wylle not, when he may, He shall not, when he wylle. **a. 1506** HENRYSON *Rob. & Mak.* The man that will nocht quhen he may, Sall haif nocht quhen he wald. **1546** HEYWOOD I. iii. 6. **1621** BURTON *Anat. Mel.* III. ii. VI. V (1651) 576 But commonly they omit opportunities, . . . He that will not when he may, When he will he shall have nay. **1893** STEVENSON *Catriona* xix That young lady, with whom I so much desired to be alone again, sang . . . 'He that will not when he may, When he will he shall have nay'.

Will, Where there's a | there's a way.

1640 HERBERT 351 To him that will, ways are not wanting. **1886** M. SCOTT *Cruise Midge* I had no small difficulty . . . but I had set my heart on it, and 'where there's a will there's a way'. **1927** *Times* 9 Aug. 11/5 Great Britain . . . has shown a genuine desire to find a way. 'Where there's a will there's a way.'

Will will have will, though will woe win.

1546 HEYWOOD I. xi. 28 But lo, wyll wyll haue wyll, though will wo wyn. **1732** FULLER no. 5758 Will will have its will. . . .

'Will you' was never a good fellow.

1910 P. W. JOYCE *Eng. as we Speak* 114 *Will you* was never a good fellow'. The bad fellow says 'Will you have some lunch?' (while there is as yet nothing on the table); on the chance that the visitor will say 'No, thank you'.

Will (*noun*), *see also* Be still and have thy w.; Complies against his w. is of same opinion still; Go to the well against his w. (If the lad) . . . water will spill; Ill w. never said well; Inch of his w. (He will not give) for span of thrift; One man's w. another man's wit; Wedded to one's w.; Wit and w. strive for victory.

Will(s) (*verb*), *see also* Do what one's own self w. (Easy to); Two will (That which) takes effect. *See also* Wills.

Willing horse, All lay load on the.

1546 HEYWOOD I. xi. 34 Whan ought was to doo, I was common hackney, Folke call on the horse that will cary alwey. **1670** RAY 116. **1732** FULLER no. 532. **1926** *Times* 24 Apr. 16/6 He was . . . the 'willing horse' upon whom every one of the many duties . . . were laid.

Willing, *see also* Fate leads the w.

Willow will buy a horse before the oak will pay for a saddle, The.

1662 FULLER (*Cambs.*) I. 223 [The willow] groweth incredibly fast; it being a by-word in this county, 'that the profit by willows will buy the owner a horse, before that by other trees will pay for his saddle'.

Willows are weak, yet they bind other wood.

1640 HERBERT 345. **1754** FRANKLIN Aug. Willows are weak, but they bind the faggot. **1912** *Spectator* 2 Mar. 343 Ella Fuller Maitland . . . has written . . . —'Withy is weak', the proverb tells, 'But many woods he binds; And in the truth that therein dwells My heart some comfort finds.

Willow(s), *see also* Hang one's harp on w.; Wear the w.

Wills the end, He who | wills the means.

1679–1715 SOUTH *Sermons* (1842) I. 206 That most true aphorism, 'That he who wills the end, wills also the means'. **1910** *Spectator* 29 Oct. 677 We won at Trafalgar . . . because we not only meant to win, but knew how to win—because we understood . . . the maxim, 'He who wills the end wills the means'.

Wiltshire moonrakers.

1787 GROSE (*Wilts.*) 230 . . . Some Wiltshire rustics, as the story goes, seeing the figure of the moon in the pond, attempted to rake it out. **1819** J. C. HOBHOUSE *Let.* in SMILES *J. Murray* (1891) I. xvi. 409 I have been . . . immersed in the miserable provincial politics of my brother moon-rakers of this county. **1863** J. R. WISE *New Forest* (1895) xv. 170 'Hampshire and Wiltshire moon-rakers' had its origin in the Wiltshire peasants fishing up the contraband goods at night, brought through the Forest, and hid in the various ponds.

Wily beguiled with himself, He hath played.

1555 LATIMER in STRYPE *Eccl. Mem.* (1721) III. App. xxxvi. 103. **1616** DRAXE 40. **1678** RAY 84. **1732** FULLER no. 1895 He hath played a wily trick, and beguil'd himself.

Wimble,[1] The little | will let in the great auger.

1636 FEATLEY *Clavis Myst.* xxix. 377 As the wimble bores a hole for the auger. **1732** FULLER no. 4632. [[1] gimlet.]

Wimple[1] in a lawyer's clew,[2] There is aye a.

1818 SCOTT *Ht. Midl.* xxiv The Judge didna tell us a' . . . about the application for pardon . . . ; there is aye a wimple in a lawyer's clew. [[1] twist. [2] ball of thread.]

Win and Wear.

c. **1552** *Manifest Detection of Dice-Play* A 1[v] There is my xx. li. win it and weare it. **1573** G. HARVEY *Letter Bk.* (Camden Soc.) 114 Thou hast woone her—weare her. *c.* **1592** MARLOWE *Jew of M.* II. iii (Merm.) 268 *Lod.* This is thy diamond; tell me shall I have it? *Bar.* Win it and wear it, it is yet unsoiled. **1597–8** SHAKS. *2 Hen. IV* IV. v. 220 You won it, wore it, kept it, gave it me. **1598–9** *Much Ado* V. i. 82 Win me and wear me. **1622** J. FLETCHER *Span. Cur.* II. i. Wks. (1905) II. 75 I'l win this Diamond from the rock and wear her. **1847** MARRYAT *Childr. N. Forest* xxvii As for his daughter . . . you have yet to 'win her and wear her', as the saying is.

Win at first and lose at last.

1678 RAY 349.

Win gold and wear gold.

1583 MELBANCKE *Philot.* C 4 (A) Thou hast woon goulde, now weare gould. **1614** CAMDEN 315 Win gold and wear gold. **1660** TATHAM *The Rump* III. i. Wks. (1879) 244 He that wins gold, let him wear gold, I cry. **1748** RICHARDSON *Clarissa* III. 350 I, who have won the gold, am only fit to wear it.

Win purple and wear purple.

1650 FULLER *Pisgah Sight* IV. vi, § 1 Earned with her industry (and good reason—win purple and wear purple). **1853** TRENCH v. 114 Very few [proverbs] . . . would fain persuade you that 'luck is all', or that your fortunes are in any other hands, under God, except your own. This . . . *Win purple and wear purple*, proclaims.

Win (one's *or* the) spurs, To.

[= to gain knighthood; *fig.* gain distinction.] *c.* **1425** LYDGATE *Assembly of Gods* 759 These xiiii Knyghtes made Vyce that day; To wynne theyr spores they seyde they wold assay. **1551** T. WILSON *Logike* (1580) 74 b Sennacherib that wicked kyng, thought . . . to winne his spurres against Jerusalem. **1600** HOLLAND *Livy* XXX. xxxii. 762 Resolute that day either to winne the spurres or loose the saddle.

Win the horse or lose the saddle, Either.

1550 HEYWOOD II. ix Recover the horse or lese the saddle too. **1575** GASCOIGNE *Posies, Dulce Bel. Inex.* (1907) 169 It was my full entent, To loose the sadle or the horse to winne. **1670** RAY 199. **1721** KELLY 96 *Either win the horse, or tine the saddle.* Spoken as an encouragement to a noble attempt.

Win(s, won), *see also* Daughter w. (He that would the); Gear that is gifted . . . that is w.; Laugh that w.; Looks as if neither w. nor lost; Lost (W.) in the hundred found (lost) in the shire; Nought w. by the one.

Winchester goose.

[= a certain venereal disease; also, a prostitute.] **1554–5** H. HILARIE [= John Bale?] *Resurrection of the Mass* (cited in *The Library,* New Series, xxi. 150) A Wynchester goose to heale is my gyse. **1559** BECON in *Prayers, &c.* (P.S.) 284 (A) Making whole of a Winchester goose. **1591–2** SHAKS. *1 Hen. VI* I. iii. 53 *Winch.* Gloster, thou wilt answer this before the Pope. *Glost.* Winchester Goose, I cry, a Rope, a Rope. **1601–2** *Troil. & Cres.* V. x. 55 My fear is this, Some galled goose of Winchester would hiss. **1611** COTGRAVE s.v. 'Clapoir', a botch in the Groyne, or yard; a Winchester goose. **1630** J. TAYLOR (Water-P.) Wks. I. 105/2 Then ther's a goose that breeds at Winchester, And of all Geese, my mind is least to her. **1778** *Eng. Gazetteer* [ed. 2] s.v. *Southwark* In the times of popery here were no less than 18 houses on the Bankside, licensed by the Bishops of Winchester . . . to keep whores, who were, therefore, commonly called Winchester Geese.

Winchester, *see also* Canterbury is the higher rack.

Wind, To have one in the.

1546 HEYWOOD I. xi. 32 I smelde hir out, and had hir streight in the wynde. **1602–3** SHAKS. *All's Well* III. vi. 123 By this same coxcomb that we have i' the wind.

Wind and water, Between.

1588 *Cert. Advert. Losses Sp. Navie Irel.* B 2 One of the shot was betweene the winde and the water, whereof they thought she would have sonke. *c.* **1607** T. HEYWOOD & W. ROWLEY *Fortune by Land and Sea* IV. iii. You gave not one shot betwixt wind and water in all this skirmish. **1608** BEAUM. & FL. *Philas.* IV. i The wench has shot him between wind and water. **1639** FULLER *Holy War* IV. xxiv (1840) 222 Sea-fights are more bloody . . . since guns came up, whose shot betwixt wind and water . . . is commonly observed mortal. **1774** BURKE *Sp. on Amer. Tax.* 19 Apr. Charles Townshend . . . hit the house just between wind and water.

Wind and weather, do thy worst.

1678 RAY 277. **1732** FULLER no. 5743 . . . do your utmost.

Wind blew you hither? What.

c. **1374** CHAUCER *Troylus* II, l. 1104 What manere wyndes gydeth yow now here? *c.* **1489** CAXTON *Sonnes of Aymon* (E.E.T.S.) 106 Lordes, what ye be, and what wynde dryveth you hyther. **1546** HEYWOOD I. x. 20 Ye huswife, what wynde blowth ye hyther thus right? **1597-8** SHAKS. *2 Hen. IV* V. iii. 87 What wind blew you hither, Pistol? **1664** COTTON *Scarron*. iv. 1120 He ask'd what wind had blown her thither. **1824** SCOTT *Redg*. xxi Pengwinion, you Cornish chough, has this good wind blown you north?

Wind bloweth not down the corn, Every.

1546 HEYWOOD II. ix. 77.

Wind blows, As the | you must set your sail.

1846 DENHAM 3.

Wind follows sun's course, If | expect fair weather.

1883 ROPER 10. **1893** INWARDS 71.

Wind in one's face makes one wise, The.

1640 HERBERT 351.

Wind in that door (corner)? Is the.

1470-85 MALORY *Arthur* VII. xxxv 'What! neuewe, is the wynde in that dore?' **1546** HEYWOOD II. v. 56 If the winde stande in that doore, it standth awry. **1589** *Marprel. Epit.* B. iv Is the winde at that dore with you brother deane? **1597-8** SHAKS. *1 Hen. IV* III. iii. 102 Is the wind in that door, i' faith? **1598-9** *Much Ado* II. iii. 108 Sits the wind in that corner? *a*. **1625** BEAUM. & FL. *Coronation* II. i *Phil*. Is the wind in that corner? **1668** DRYDEN *Evening's Love* IV. i Is the Wind in that Door? Here's like to be fine doings.

Wind is in the north-west, Do business with men when the.

1883 ROPER 10. **1893** INWARDS 78.

Wind is north-east, If the | three days without rain, eight days will pass before south wind again.

1883 ROPER 9. **1893** INWARDS 78.

Wind is on Martinmas Eve, Where the | there it will be the rest of winter.

1883 ROPER 23 If the wind is south-west at Martinmas, It keeps there till after Christmas. **1893** INWARDS 37.

Wind is south, When the | it blows your bait into a fish's mouth.

1653 WALTON *Angler* v (Clar. Press) 115 For the wind . . . the south wind is said to be the best. One observes, that—When the wind is south, It blows your bait into a fish's mouth. **1732** FULLER no. 6226.

Wind is west, When the | the fish bite best.

1883 ROPER 11. **1893** INWARDS 77.

Wind keeps not always in one quarter, The.

1579 GOSSON *Ephemerides* 15 The wind is not euer in one quarter. **1616** WITHALS 586. **1639** CLARKE 124. **1670** RAY 1156. **1732** FULLER no. 4831.

Wind shakes no corn, All this.

1546 HEYWOOD I. xi. 30 What man all this winde shakis no corne. Let this winde ouerblow . a tyme I will spy, to take wynde and tyde with me. **1612-15** BP. HALL *Contempl.* VII. iii (1825) I. 168 What if he had been suffered to go and curse? What corn had this wind shaken, when God meant to bless them?

Wind that comes in at a hole, and a reconciled enemy, Take heed of. (*Cf.* Reconciled enemies, Take heed of.)

1651 HERBERT 371.

Wind up your bottom,[1] To.

[= to sum up, conclude.] **1639** CLARKE 46. **1698** S. CLARK *Script. Just.* 112 It's high Time now to wind up my Bottoms. **1826** SCOTT *Diary* 15 Mar. in LOCKHART *Life* lxx (1860) 617 Must work hard for a day or two. I wish I could wind up my bottom handsomely. [1 ball of thread.]

Wind up (*verb*), *see also* Good house-wife that will not w. u. her bottom (Not a).

Wind veers against the sun, When the | trust it not, for back 'twill run.

1883 ROPER 10. **1893** INWARDS 71.

Wind's in the east, When the | it's neither good for man nor beast.

1659 HOWELL *Eng. Prov.* 19/1. **1670** RAY 41 . . . The East-wind with us is commonly very sharp, because it comes off the Continent. **1927** *Times* 21 Nov. 15/4 Science is beginning a new incursion into . . . such wisdom as is contained in the lines When the wind is in the East 'Tis neither good for man nor beast.

Wind's in the east on Candlemas Day,[1] When the | there it will stick till the second of May.

1852 *N. & Q.* 1st Ser. v. 462. [1 2 Feb.]

Wind's in the north, When the | the skilful fisher goes not forth.

1846 DENHAM 17. **1869** INWARDS 48.

Wind's in the south, When the | it's in the rain's mouth.

1639 CLARKE 263. **1670** RAY 42. **1721** KELLY 353 When the wind is in the south, rain will be fouth.[1] [1 in abundance.]

Wind's in the west, When the | the weather's at the best.

1721 KELLY 353. **1732** FULLER no. 6223.

Wind(s), *see also* Blow the w. never so fast; Brook the weather that love not w.; Catch the w. in a net; Cold w. reach you through a hole; Come with the w., go with the water; Crazy ship all w. contrary (To a); Devil never sent w. but he would sail with it; Easterly w. and rain bring cockles; Easterly w. unkind; Every w. is ill to broken ship; Free as the w.; God tempers the w.; God will (When), no w. but brings rain; Good w. that blows to the wine; Great w. upon high hills; Hoist your sail when w. is fair; Ill w. that blows nobody good; Keep yourself from ... w. at a hole; Kick the w.; Know which way the w. blows; Little kens the wife ... the w. blows cold on Hurleburle-swyre; Little w. kindles fire; March sun causeth dust and w. blows in; North w. doth blow; Northern w. brings weather fair; North-west w. (Honest man and a); Pluck the grass to know where w. sits; Puff not against w.; Pull down your hat on w. side; Rain comes before the w.; Rain lays great w.; Raise the w.; Sail near w.; Sail, quoth the king, hold, quoth the w.; Soldier's wind, there and back; Southerly w. with showers of rain; Southerly w. hunting morning; Sow beans in the w.; Sow the w. and reap the whirlwind; Sun sets bright (When), easterly wind you need not fear; Sun sets in a bank (When), westerly w.; Take the w. out of the sails; Tracys have always w. in their faces; Tree that God plants no w. hurts; Wavering as the w.; Weather is ill (No) if w. still; Whistle for w.; Woman's mind and winter w. change oft; Women (Wives and w.) are necessary evils; Women change as often as w.; Words and feathers w. carries away; Words are but w.; Wroth as the w.

Wind-frost, *see* Steward abroad when there is w. (There is good).

Windlestraws, *see* Redd for w. (He that is) should not sleep in lees.

Windmill dwindles into a nutcrack, Your.

1678 RAY 277. **1732** FULLER no. 6064 (with 'nut-cracker').

Windmill go with a pair of bellows, You cannot make a.

1640 HERBERT 349.

Windmill, *see also* Bradshaw's w.

Windmills[1] in one's head, To have.

[Referring to Don Quixote's fight with the windmills (I. viii). Span. *acometer molinos de viento*.] **1622** MASSINGER & DEKKER *Virg. Mart.* II.iii Thy head is full of Windemils. **1639** CHAPMAN & SHIRLEY *The Ball* v. Chapman *Plays* (1874) 494 *Lady Luc.* I do love One that has windmills in his head. *Trav.* How, madam? *L. Luc.* Projects and proclamations.

1665 J. WILSON *Project.* I. i. Wks. (1874) 220 If they will set up windmills in their heads, contribute my assistance to cut out the sails. **1754** RICHARDSON 21 Aug. (*Corresp.* III. 212) But she had a windmill in her head, and away the air of it carried her upwards of one hundred miles from her Doctor. [[1] impossible or impracticable schemes.]

Window(s), *see* Air of a w. is as ... crossbow; Come in at the w.; Fair day (To a) open the w.; House out of w. (Throw the); Shop w.; Woman that loves to be at w.

Windy March and a rainy April make May beautiful, A.

1657 E. LEIGH *Select & Choice Observations* 270. **1732** FULLER no. 468.

Wine and wenches empty men's purses.

1639 CLARKE 28.

Wine and women.

[*Ecclus.* xix. 2 *Vinum et mulieres apostatare faciunt sapientes.*] *a.* **1532** *Rem. Love* xxxvi Chaucer's Wks. 367/1 Wyne and women in to apostasy Cause wyse men to fal. **1616** DRAXE 236 Wine and women make wisemen runagates. **1621** BURTON *Anat. Mel.* I. ii. III. xiii (1836) 193 Those two main plagues, and common dotages of humane kind, wine and women, which have infatuated and besotted myriads of people. They go commonly together. **1727** GAY *Begg. Op.* II. i Women and wine should Life employ. **1819** BYRON *Juan* II. clxxviii Let us have wine and women, mirth and laughter. **1862** THACKERAY *Philip* vii As Doctor Luther sang, Who loves not wine, woman, and song He is a fool his whole life long.

Wine and youth increase love.

c. **1386** CHAUCER *Phys. T.* C 59 For wyn and youthe doon Venus encrece, As men in fyr wol casten oile or grece.

Wine by the barrel, You cannot know.

1611 COTGRAVE s.v. 'Cercle' The goodnes of wine is not known by the fashion, or strength of the hoops that begird it. **1640** HERBERT (Gros.) no. 20. **1732** FULLER 5884 (with 'cask').

Wine by the savour, bread by the colour (heat).

1573 SANDFORD (1576) 212 Wyne by the Sauoure, bread by the colour. **1578** FLORIO *First Fruites* f. 29 Wine by the sauour, and bread by the heate. **1666** TORRIANO 186 Bread by the colour, and wine by the taste.

Wine counsels seldom prosper.

1640 HERBERT 354.

Wine ever pays for his lodging.

1640 HERBERT 360.

Wine in the bottle does not quench thirst.

1640 HERBERT 346. **1732** FULLER no. 5745 (with 'hogshead' for 'bottle').

Wine in, truth out.

1545 TAVERNER H 5[v]. **1611** COTGRAVE S.V. 'Mentir' Wine telleth truth and should not be belied. **1839** DICKENS *N. Nickleby* xxvii (A) 'Oh, ho!' thought that knowing Lady [Mrs. Nickleby]; 'Wine in, truth out.'

Wine is a turncoat (first a friend, then an enemy).

1640 HERBERT 360.

Wine is a whetstone to wit.

1647 *Countryman's New Commonwealth* 14. **1736** BAILEY *Dict.* s.v. 'Whetstone' (A).

Wine is drawn; The | it must be drunk.

1853 TRENCH ii. 43 At the siege of Douay, in 1667, Louis XIV ... under a heavy cannon-ade ... was about ... to retire; when M. de Charost ... whispered ... in his ear: *The wine is drawn; it must be drunk.* [Le vin est tiré; il faut le boire.] **1891** J. L. KIPLING *Beast & Man* 123 A Bengal saying recalling the French 'When the cork is drawn, the wine must be drunk' is, 'Milk once drawn from the dug never goes back'.

Wine is not common, Where | commons must be sent. (*Cf.* Coin is not common.)

1611 GRUTER. **1614** CAMDEN 314. **1659** HOWELL *Eng. Prov.* 10/1.

Wine is old men's milk.

1584 COGAN *Haven of Health* (1636) 244 To old men, wine is as sucke to young children, and is therefore called of some *Lac senum.* **1809** MALKIN *Gil Blas* x. i You reprobate the ignorance of those writers who dignify wine with the appellation of old men's milk.

Wine is the best liquor to wash glasses in.

1738 SWIFT (Dial. ii) 350 *Ld. S.* John, bring clean glasses. *Col.* I'll keep mine; for I think wine is the best liquor to wash glasses in.

Wine is the master's, The | the good-ness is the butler's (drawer's).

1639 CLARKE 209 (with 'drawers'). **1678** RAY *Adag. Hebr.* 401 The wine is the masters, but the goodness of it is the butlers.

Wine is the mirror of the mind.

[ERASM. *Ad.* quoting Aesch. fr. 288 Κάτο-πτρον εἴδους χαλκός ἐστ', οἶνος δὲ νοῦ.] **1579** LYLY *Euphues* (Arb.) 308 Wine is the glasse of the mind.

Wine makes all sorts of creatures at table.

1640 HERBERT 360.

Wine makes old wives wenches.

1639 CLARKE 192.

Wine savours (will taste) of the cask, The.

1579 LYLY *Euphues* (Arb.) 41 Season the woode neuer so well the wine will tast of the caske. **1621** BURTON *Anat. Mel.* I. ii. v. ii (1651) 173 As wine savours of the cask wherein it is kept, the soul receives a tincture from the body, through which it works. **1662** FULLER (*Wilts.*) III. 333 If any fustiness be found in his writings, it comes not from the grape, but from the cask. The smack of superstition in his books is ... to be im-puted ... to the age wherein he[1] lived. [[1] William of Malmesbury.]

Wine sinks, When | words swim.

1721 KELLY 354. **1732** FULLER no. 5622.

Wine that cost nothing is digested before it be drunk.

1640 HERBERT 360. **1732** FULLER no. 5750.

Wine, Of | the middle, of oil the top, and of honey the bottom, is the best.

[MACROB. *Saturn.* VII. 12. *Quaero igitur, Cur oleum quod in summo est, vinum quod in medio, mel quod in fundo optimum esse cre-dantur.*] **1580** LYLY *Euph. & his Eng.* Wks. (Bond) II. 219 The oyle that swimmeth in the top is the wholsomest ... the honny that lieth in the bottome is the sweetest ... the wine which is in the middest ... the finest. **1603** PLUTARCH *Moralia* tr. Holland 'Of Symposiaques' vii. 3 What is the cause, that the mids of wine, the top of oile, and the bottome of honie, is best. **1659** HOWELL *Ital.-Eng.* 15. **1662** FULLER (*Hants*) II. 3 It is an old and true rule, 'the best oil is in the top; the best wine in the middle; and the best honey in the bottom'. **1678** RAY 41 Vino di mezzo, oglio di sopra & miele di sotto. *Of wine the middle, of oil the top, and of honey the bottom is best.*

Wine there is truth, In.

[Gk. Ἐν οἴνῳ ἀλήθεια.—L. *In vino veritas.*] **1539** TAVENER (1545) H 4[v] *In uino ueritas.* In wyne is trouthe. c. **1590** LYLY *Moth. Bomb.* in Wks. (Bond) III. 199 I perceiue sober men tell most lies, for *in vino veritas.* If they had drunke wine, they would haue tolde the truth. **1597** DELONEY *1 Gentle Craft* Wks. (Mann) 129 Wine is the bewrayer of secrets. **1611** COTGRAVE s.v. 'Mentir' Wine telleth truth and should not be belied. **1772** BOSWELL in *Johnson* xxvii (1848) 242 I ... had recourse to the maxim, *in vino veritas*, a man who is well warmed with wine will speak truth. **1869** TROLLOPE *He knew he was right* li There is no saying truer than that ... there is truth in wine. Wine ... has the merit of forcing a man to show his true colours.

Wine washeth off the daub.

1732 FULLER no. 5752.

Wine wears no breeches.

1611 COTGRAVE s.v. 'Vin' Wine wanteth, or goeth without, breeches; *viz.* bewrayeth a mans infirmities. **1659** HOWELL *Eng. Prov.* 7/1.

Wine, *see also* Ale (W.) is in (When), wit is out; Best w. comes out of old vessel; Best wine is ... at another's cost; Commend not your w.; Cries w., sells vinegar; Drinks not w. after salad (He that); Gaming, women, and w.; Good wind that blows to w.; Good w. engendreth good blood; Good w. needs no bush; Know w. by the barrel (Cannot); Milk says to w. welcome; Old friends and old w. are best; Old wood is best ... old w. to drink; Play, women, and w. undo; Praise the w. before . . .; Spilt w. worse than water; Women and w. . . . . make the wealth small.

Wing (*proper name*), *see* Tring.

Wing(s), *see* Ant had w. to her hurt; Bill under w.; Clip the w. of; Flying without w. (No); Lies have no w.; Tail broader than thy w. (Make not).

Wink and choose.

c. **1614** WEBSTER *Duch. of Malfi* I. i. 390 Let old wives report I wincked and chose a husband. **1621** BURTON *Anat. Mel.* Democr. to Rdr. (1651) 46 Go backward or forward, choose out of the whole pack, wink and choose: you shall find them all alike. **1678** RAY 347 One may wink and choose.

Wink at small faults.

1598–9 SHAKS. *Hen. V* II. ii. 55 If little faults, . . . Shall not be wink'd at, how shall we stretch our eye When capital crimes, . . . Appear before us? **1639** CLARKE 225. **1721** KELLY 341 Wink at small faults, for you have great ones yourself.

Winkabank and Temple brough will buy all England through and through.

1678 RAY 340 *Yorkshire.* Winkabank *and* Temple brough, *Will buy all* England *through and through.* Winkabank is a wood upon a hill near Sheffield where there are some remainders of an old Camp. *Temple brough* stands between the *Rother* and the *Don.* . . . It is a square plat of ground encompassed by two trenches.

Winketh with one eye, He that | and looketh with the other, I will not trust him though he were my brother.

c. **1390** GOWER *Conf. Amantis* I. l. 384 Betre is to winke than to loke. **1530** PALSGRAVE 782 (A). **1550** HEYWOOD I. xi. 33. **1614** CAMDEN 307. **1721** KELLY 169 *He that looks with one eye, and winks with another, I will not believe him, though he was my brother.* If the man naturally squint, my countrymen have an aversion to him, and all who have any thing disagreeable, if he wink or nod they look upon him to be a false man.

Wink(eth), *see also* Cat w. (When), little wots mouse; Rain raineth and the goose w. (When), little wots gosling; Time to w. as well as to see.

Winner, *see* Games it is good leave off a w.

Winneral (Winnold), *see* First comes David.

Winning is not in my tinsel,[1] Your.

1721 KELLY 378. [[1] loss.]

Winning, *see also* Lay your wame to your w.

Winter enough for the snipe and woodcock too, There is.

1732 FULLER no. 4939.

Winter finds out what summer lays up.

c. 1460 *Good Wyfe wold a Pylgremage* (E.E.T.S.) l. 155 (A) Wynttur ettythe that somer gettyth. **1678** RAY 219.

Winter is summer's heir.

1678 RAY 218.

Winter never died in a ditch.

1883 ROPER 33. **1893** INWARDS 8.

Winter never rots in the sky.

1612–15 BP. HALL *Contempl.* XIII. i (1825) I. 368 God . . . chooses out a fit season for the execution. As we use to say of winter, the judgments of God do never rot in the sky, but shall fall, if late, yet surely, yet seasonably. **1642** D. ROGERS *Naaman* ix. 264 Beware therefore of extremities, and till the Lord hath truly brought down thy winter out of the sky, know it will never rot there.

Winter thunder (bodes) summer hunger.

1721 KELLY 353 Winter thunder, summer hunger. **1846** DENHAM 3 Winter thunder bodes summer hunger.

Winter's thunder and summer's flood never boded Englishman good.

1670 RAY 44. **1732** FULLER no. 6479.

Winter's thunder makes summer's wonder.

1605 R. VERSTEGAN *Restitution Decayed Intelligence* (1673) ch. 7, p. 217. **1611** COTGRAVE s.v. 'Tonner'. **1636** CAMDEN 310. **1658** T. WILLSFORD *Natures Secrets* 113 Thunder and lightning in Winter . . . is held ominous . . . and a thing seldome seen, according to the old Adigy, *Winters thunder, is the Sommers wonder.*

Winter, *see also* Age (W.) and wedlock tames; Good w. good summer; Green w. fat churchyard; Hard w. when wolf eats another; Life of man is a w. way; —— w.'s way and w.'s day; Passeth a w.'s day escapes an enemy; Summer but it has a w. (No); Woodcock does not make w. (One).

Winter-time for shoeing, peascod-time for wooing.

1841 BRAND *Pop. Antiq.* (Bohn) ii. 100 (A) [quoted as 'an old proverb in a MS.' Devon Glossary]. **1846** DENHAM 64.

Wipe one's nose with one's own sleeve, To.

c. **1436** *Libelle of Englyshe Polycye* in *Wright's Polit. Poems* II. 176 And thus they wold, if we will beleve, Wypen our nose with our owne sleve. **1659** HOWELL *French–Eng.* 22 He wiped his nose with his own sleeve, viz. he cousened him neatly.

Wiped his nose of (on) it, I.

[= deprived, defrauded of something.] **1598** R. BERNARD *Terence, Eunuch* I. i The very destruction of our substance: who wipes our noses of all that we should have. **1611** CHAPMAN *May Day* v. i. 267 Wilt thou suffer thy nose to be wiped of this great heir? **1667** PEPYS *Diary* 17 July That the King [might] own a marriage . . . with the Queen, and so wipe their noses of the Crown. **1678** RAY 343 I wip't his nose on it. **1721** CIBBER *Rival Fools* Wks. II. 1754 I. 29 I durst lay my life thou wipest this foolish knight's nose of his mistress at last.

Wipes the child's nose, He that | kisseth the mother's cheek.

1640 HERBERT 364.

Wipe(s), *see also* Never kiss a man's wife nor w. his knife.

Wire-drawer under his work, To sit like a.

1670 RAY 217. *Yorksh.*

Wires, *see* Death upon w.

Wisdom counsels, Well goes the case when.

1707 MAPLETOFT 126 (Welsh). **1736** BAILEY *Dict.* s.v. 'Wisdom' (A).

Wisdom goes beyond strength.

1616 DRAXE 237 Wisedome is better then strength. **1664** CODRINGTON 224 [as Draxe]. **1736** BAILEY *Dict.* s.v. 'Wisdom' (A).

Wisdom hath one foot on land, and another on sea.

1640 HERBERT 346.

Wisdom, What is not | is danger.

1707 MAPLETOFT 125 (Welsh). **1878** J. PLATT *Morality* 34 (A).

Wisdom like silence, No.

[PLUTARCH *De Liberis educ.* 14. 10 E Σοφὸν γὰρ εὔκαιρος σιγὴ καὶ παντὸς λόγου κρεῖττον. There is wisdom in timely silence which is better than all speech.] **1869** HAZLITT 296.

Wisdom peace, By | by peace plenty.

1611 GRUTER. **1614** CAMDEN 304.

Wisdom sometimes to seem a fool, It is.

1549 CHALENOR tr. *Erasm. Praise of Folly* Q 1ᵛ This verse of Cato . . . It is most wyse-dome for a man in place to countrefaicte Folie. **1732** FULLER no. 5125.

Wisdom to find out one's own folly, It is a great point of.

1732 FULLER no. 2860.

Wisdom, Without | wealth is worthless.

[**1611** BIBLE *Prov.* xvi. 16 How much better is it to get wisdom than gold!] *c.* **1275** *Provs. of Alfred* (Skeat) A 119 Wyþ-vte wysdome is weole wel vnwurþ. [Without wisdom wealth is of little value.]

Wisdom, *see* Haste and w. far odd; Hearing (From) comes w.; Learn w. by follies of others; Money, w., and good faith (Of) less than count upon; Wit and w.; Wit to pick lock and steal horse, w. to let alone.

Wise after the event, It is easy to be.

1609 JONSON *Silent Wom.* in Wks. III (Merm.) II. ii Away, thou strange justifier of thyself to be wiser than thou wert, by the event! **1900** A. LANG *Hist. Scot.* I. i To the wisdom which comes after the event the map of Scotland seems, in part, a prophecy of her history. **1900** A. C. DOYLE *Boer War* (1902) xix It is easy to be wise after the event, but it does certainly appear that . . . the action at Paardeberg was as unnecessary as it was expensive.

Wise and great, He that is truly | lives both too early and too late.

1856 ABP. WHATELY *Annot. Bacon's Ess.* (1876) 240 A man . . . will often be mortified at perceiving that he has come too late for some things, and too soon for others. . . . Hence the proverb—'He that is truly wise and great, Lives both too early and too late'.

Wise as a goose, As.

1509 A. BARCLAY *Ship of Fools* (1874) I. 179 As wyse as a gander. **1528** MORE *Wks.* (1557) p. 179 col. 2 (A) And all as wise as wilde geese.

Wise as a man of Gotham, As.

[Ironical.] *c.* **1410** *Towneley Plays* 106 Sagh I neuer none so fare bot the foles of gotham. **1526** *Hundr. Merry Tales* (Oesterley) no. xxiv. 45 (title) Of the III wyse men of gotam. **1659** HOWELL *Eng. Prov.* 6 You are as wise as the men of Gotham, who went to build a wall about the wood to keep out the cuckow. **1662** FULLER (*Notts.*) II. 569 'As wise as a man of Gotham'. It passeth publicly for the periphrasis of a fool; and a hundred fopperies are . . . fathered on the town-folk of Gotham, . . . in this county. **1770** SWIFT *Prop. for Univ. Use of Irish Manuf.* Wks. (1856) II. 63 A volume as large as the history of the Wise Men of Gotham. **1824** MOIR *Mansie W.* xii It was an agreed . . . thing among . . . these wise men of Gotham, to abolish all kings, clergy, and religion.

Wise as a woodcock, As.

c. **1512** *Hickscorner* C 3 I was as wyse as a woodcock. **1520** R. WHITTINTON *Vulg.* (E.E.T.S.) 60 He hath . . . as many braynes as a woodcok. **1670** RAY 203.

Wise as Waltham's calf, As.

[Ironical.] *c.* **1525** SKELTON *Col. Cloute* l. 811 As wyse as Waltom's calfe. **1546** HEYWOOD II. iii. 48. **1659** HEYLIN *Animadv. on Ch. Hist.* in FULLER's *Appeal Inj. Innoc.* (1840) 596 But certainly our author showed himself 'no wiser than Waltham's calf, who ran nine miles to suck a bull, and came home athirst', as the proverb saith.

Wise, None is so | but the fool overtakes him.

1640 HERBERT 351.

Wise child that knows its own father, It is a.

[HOM. *Od.* 1. 216 Οὐ γάρ πώ τις ἐὸν γόνον αὐτὸς ἀνέγνω.] **1589** GREENE *Wks.* (Gros.) VI. 92 (A) For wise are the children in these dayes that know their owne fathers. **1596–7** SHAKS. *Merch. V.* II. ii. 83 It is a wise father that knows his own child. **1607** TOURNEUR *Rev. Trag.* II. i The world's so changed one shape into another, It is a wise child now that knows her mother. **1613** WITHER *Abuses; Of Desire* v. 27 Is't not hence this common proverb grows, '*Tis a wise child that his own father knows?* **1762** GOLDSMITH *The Mystery Revealed* Wks. (1912) II. 472 She called her father John instead of Thomas, . . . but perhaps she was willing to verify the old proverb, that 'It is a wise child that knows its own father'. **1827** SCOTT *Surg. D.* ix It is not every child that knows its own father, so how can every man be so sure of his own name?

Wise enough that can keep himself warm, He is.

1537 *Thersites* C 4 Sonne, ye be wise, kepe ye warme. **1546** HEYWOOD II. ii. 46 Ye are wise inough (quoth he) if ye kéepe ye warme. **1593–4** SHAKS. *Tam. Shrew* II. i. 258 *Pet.* Am I not wise? *Kath.* Yes; keep you warm. **1598–9** *Much Ado* I. i. 68 If he have wit enough to keep himself warm. **1614** JONSON *Barth. Fair* v. iii In a scrivener's furred gown, which shews he is no fool: For therein he hath wit enough to keep himself warm. **1670** RAY 28.

Wise erred not, If the | it would go hard with fools.

1640 HERBERT 341.

Wise fear begets care.

1707 MAPLETOFT 8 Wise Distrust is the Parent of Security. **1732** FULLER no. 6355.

Wise hand doth not all that the foolish mouth speaks, The.

1640 HERBERT 328.

Wise head makes a close mouth, A.

c. **1386** CHAUCER *Miller's T.* A 3598 Men seyn thus 'sende the wise, and sey no thyng'. **1678** RAY 219. **1707** MAPLETOFT ('hath a close mouth to it'). **1732** FULLER no. 469 (as 1707).

Wise man by day is no fool by night, He that is a.

1855 BOHN 389.

Wise man cares not for what he cannot have, A.

1640 HERBERT 348. **1670** RAY 29.

Wise man is a great wonder, A.

1624 BURTON *Anat. Mel.* 36. **1732** FULLER no. 472.

Wise man is never less alone than when he is alone, A.

[CIC. *De Offic.* 3. 1, quoted by **1642** BROWNE *Rel. Med.* Pt. II (1881) 114.] **1669** PENN *No Cross, No Crown* xix Scipio Africanus . . . used to say, That he was never less alone, than when he was alone. **1707** SWIFT *Facult. of Mind* Wks. (1904) 416 Contemplation . . . exceeds action. And therefore a wise man is never less alone than when he is alone: *Nunquam minus solus, quam cum solus.*

Wise man must carry the fool upon his shoulders, The.

1573 SANDFORD (1576) 210. **1623** WODROEPHE 489.

Wise man needs not blush for changing his purpose, A.

1553 *Precepts of Cato* (1560) F 2ᵛ In a wyse manne it is no maner of cryme, Hys maners to chaunge, accordyng to the time. **1573** SANDFORD (1576) H 4ᵛ. **1640** HERBERT 346.

Wise man never wants a weapon, A. (*Cf.* Wight man, &c.)

1736 BAILEY *Dict.* s.v. 'Weapon' (A).

Wise man on an errand, Send a | and say nothing to him.

c. **1386** CHAUCER *Miller's T.* A 3598 Men seyn thus 'send the wyse, and sey no thyng'. **1640** HERBERT 327.

Wise man though you can't make a watch, You may be a.

1664 CODRINGTON 231. **1670** RAY 29.

Wise man, He is not a | who cannot play the fool on occasion.

1553 *Precepts of Cato* (1560) I 3ᵛ Some tyme to playe the foole is a poynt of wyt. **1597** *Politeuphuia* 29 To play the foole well, is a signe of wisdom. **1601** JONSON *Poetaster* IV. v. 46 I haue reade in a booke, that to play the foole wisely, is high wisdome. **1732** FULLER no. 1929.

Wise man, He is a | who, when he is well off, can keep so.

1641 FERGUSSON 40 He is wise when he is well, can had[1] him sa. **1855** BOHN 404. [[1] hold.]

Wise men are caught in (with) wiles.

1205 LAYAMON *Brut* (Madden) I. 32 Nis nawer nan so wis mon That me ne mai bi-swiken. [There is nowhere so wise a man that one may not deceive.] **1639** CLARKE 266. **1721** KELLY 360 . . . I have writ down this proverb as the *English* have it, because in *Scotch* it is smutty.

Wise men change their mind, fools never.

1631 MABBE *Celestina* (T.T.) 104 A wise man altreth his purpose, but a foole persevereth in his folly. **1855** BOHN 570.

Wise men have their mouth in their heart, fools their heart in their mouth.

1477 RIVERS *Dictes & Sayings* (1877) 140 And another said the tonge of a discrete man is in his herte & the herte of a foole is in his tonge. **1630** BRATHWAIT *Eng. Gent.* (1641) 47 These are those *fooles*, which carry their *Hearts* in their *Mouthes*; and farre from those *wise men*, which carry their Mouthes in their Hearts. **1855** BOHN 570.

Wise men learn by other men's harms (mistakes); fools, by their own.

[PLAUTUS *Mercator* IV. 7. 40 (interpolated) *Feliciter is sapit qui periculo alieno sapit.* He is happy in his wisdom, who is wise at the expense of another. ERASM. *Ad. Felix quem faciunt aliena pericula cautum.*] c. **1374** CHAUCER *Troylus* III. 329 For wysẻ ben by folẻs harm chastysed. **1732** FULLER no. 5779.

Wise men make proverbs and fools repeat them.

1710 S. PALMER *Moral Essays on Prov.* Pref. viii Wise men make Proverbs, but Fools Repeat 'em. **1857** DEAN RAMSAY *Remin.* V (1911) 198 *Fules mak' feasts, and wise men eat em* . . . was said to a Scottish nobleman . . . who readily answered, 'Ay, and *Wise men make proverbs and fools repeat 'em*'.

Wise men play the fool, If | they do it with a vengeance.

1707 MAPLETOFT 20. **1855** BOHN 419.

Wise men propose, and fools determine.

1625 BACON *Apophthegms* no. 231 (with 'dispose' for 'determine'). **1692** L'ESTRANGE *Aesop's Fab.* cxxii (1738) 139 Right reason deliberates. . . . The old saying is a shrewd one; that *Wise men propose, and fools determine.*

Wise men silent, fools talk.

1624 BURTON *Anat. Mel.* 30. **1639** CLARKE 5.

Wise man (men), *see also* Bridges were made for w. m.; Fool does in the end (What), w. m. in beginning; Fool doth think . . . but w. m. knows himself fool; Fool wanders, w. m. travels; No man can play fool as w. m.; Nod for a w. m.; Old w. m.'s shadow better than buzzard's sword; Oppression maketh w. m. mad; Riches serve a w. m.; Want of a w. m. (For) fool set in chair; Wit is folly unless w. m. hath keeping; Words are w. m.'s counters.

Wise that hath wit enough for his own affairs, He is.

c. **1386** CHAUCER *Monk's Tale* B² 3329 Ful wys is he that kan hymselven knowe! **1732** FULLER no. 1954.

Wise that is honest, He is.

1670 RAY 13.

Wise that is rich, He is.

1609 DEKKER *Work for Armourers* E 2ᵛ Hee is wise enough that hath wealth enough. **1616** BRETON *Cross. Prov.* Wks. (1879) II. App. iii. He is wise that is rich. **1629** T. ADAMS *Serm.* (1861–2) II. 128 It is even a maxim in common acceptation, 'He is wise that is rich'.

Wise that is ware, He is.

1303 R. BRUNNE *Handl. Synne* 8085 He wys is, that ware ys. c. **1374** CHAUCER *Troylus* II 343 Avysẽment is good before the nede. **1600–1** SHAKS. *Merry W.* II. iii. 10 *Caius.* He is dead already, if he be come. *Rug.* He is wise, Sir; he knew your worship would kill him if he came. **1641** FERGUSSON 40 He is wise that he is ware in time. **1721** KELLY 156 *He is wise that is wary in time.* That is, who foresees harm before it come, and provides against it.

Wise that knows when he's well enough, He is.

1493 *Dives et Pauper* sig. A 1 It is an olde prouerbe. He is well atte ease that hath ynough & can saye ho. **1546** HEYWOOD II. vii. 67 He that knoweth when he hath enough, is no foole. **1721** KELLY . . . That is a pitch of wisdom to which few attain. **1732** FULLER no. 2475.

Wise who first gave a reward, He was very.

12.. SIR TRISTREM 626 (1886) 18 He was ful wise, y say, þat first ʒaue ʒift in land. *c.* 1300 *Havelok* 1635 He was ful wis þat first yaf mede,[1] And **so** was hauelok ful wis here. [[1] reward.]

Wise, He is not | who is not wise for himself.

[Gk. Μισῶ σοφιστὴν ὅστις οὐχ αὑτῷ σοφός. I hate the wise man who is not wise for himself. CIC. *ad Fam.* 7. 6 *Qui ipsi sibi sapiens prodesse non quit, nequiquam sapit.*] **1539** TAVERNER 18 *Nequicquam sapit qui sibi non sapit.* He is in vain wise that is not wise for himself. **1590** LODGE *Rosalynde* Wks. (1883) I. 39 *Non sapit, qui non sibi sapit* is fondly spoken in such bitter extreames. **1594** GREENE *Looking-Glass* II. ii You know the old proverb, 'He is not wise that is not wise for himself'.

Wise with whom all things thrive, He seemeth.

1642 TORRIANO 2. **1658** *Comes Facundus* 309. **1721** KELLY 163. **1732** FULLER no. 2016.

Wise, *see also* Adversity makes man w.; Better be happy than w.; Few words to the w. suffice; Handsome at twenty nor w. at fifty (He that is not); Love and be w. (Cannot); Merry and w.; Mete and measure make all w.; More nice than w.; No man is w. all times; Pie-lid makes w.; Seldom is long man w.; Some are w., some otherwise; Think with the w., talk with the vulgar; Too w. to live long; Trojans became w. too late; Wind in one's face makes **w.**; Witty and w.; Word is enough to the w.

Wisely walketh that doth safely go, He.

1592 DANIEL *Complaint of Rosamond* l. 285. **1600** BODENHAM *Belvedere* (Spens. Soc.) 49 (A).

Wiser now you're wed, You will be.

1639 CLARKE 266.

Wisest, *see* Recks not who is rich (W. is he who).

Wisest men, *see* Clerks (The greatest) be not **w. m.**

Wish and wish on.

1852 E. FITZGERALD *Polonius* 13 Wish and wish on'. . . . Who has many wishes has generally but little will. Who has energy of will has few diverging wishes.

Wish is father to the thought, The, *see* Believe what we desire (We soon).

Wish one at Jericho, To.

[= **to** wish one elsewhere.] **1850** LYTTON *Caxtons* v. ii I wish Uncle Jack had been at Jericho before he had brought me up to London. **1878** J. PAYN *By Proxy* xxxiv She wishes you were . . . at Jericho—anywhere else, in short, than at Sandybeach.

Wish the burn dry because it weets our feet, We maunna.

1832 HENDERSON 19.

Wish your skin full of holes, It will be long enough ere you.

1678 RAY 219.

Wish(ed), *see also* Better to have than w.; Fared worse than when I w. for supper (I never); Want (W.) a thing done (If you).

Wishers and woulders be no good householders.

c. **1510** STANBRIDGE *Vulg.* (E.E.T.S.) 30 Wysshers and wolders be small housholders. **1546** HEYWOOD I. xi. 26 Sonne (quoth he) as I haue herd of myne olders, Wishers and wolders be no good householders. **1614–16** *Times Whistle* vii. 3276–8 But the olde proverbe is exceeding true, 'That these great wishers, & these common woulders, Are never (for the moste part) good householders'. **1641** FERGUSSON 108 Wishers and walders are poore householders. **1870** SCHAFF *Comm. Prov.* xxi. 25–6 Wishers and woulders are neither good householders nor long livers.

Wishes never can fill a sack.

1666 TORRIANO 29 By longing thou shalt never fill up thy sack. **1855** BOHN 570.

Wishes were butter-cakes, If | beggars might bite.

1678 RAY 219.

Wishes were horses, If | beggars would ride.

1721 KELLY 178 If wishes were horses, beggars would ride. **1844** HALLIWELL *Nursery Rhymes of Eng.* 217 If wishes were horses, Beggars would ride; If turnips were watches, I would wear one by my side. **1912** *Brit. Wkly.* 18 Jan. If wishes were horses Unionists would ride rapidly into office.

Wishes were thrushes (truths), If | then beggars would eat birds.

1623 CAMDEN 272 If wishes were truths beggars would eat birds. **1636** *Ibid.* 300 (thrushes).

Wishes would bide, If | beggars would ride.

1611 COTGRAVE s.v. 'Pastoureau' If wishes might succeed poore men would Princes be. **1670** RAY 157 . . . *Si souhaits furent vrais pastoureaux seroyent rois, Gall.* If wishes might prevail, shepherds would be kings.

Wist, *see* Had I w.

Wit and will strive for the victory.

1721 KELLY 347 with 'Will and wit . . .'.
1736 BAILEY *Dict.* s.v. 'Wit' (A).

Wit and wisdom is good warison.[1]

c. 1300 *Provs. of Hending* 3 (*Rel. Antiq.* (1841) i. 109) Wyt and wysdom is god warysoun. [[1] provision or store.]

Wit at will, He has | that with an angry heart can hold him still.

1641 FERGUSSON 44. 1738 SWIFT (*Dial.* i) She's very handsome, and has wit at will. 1821 SCOTT *Pirate* xiv 'He is an Orkney goose, if it please you, Mr. Dryden', said Tim, who had wit at will.

Wit in his head, He hath no more | than thou in both thy shoulders.

1601–2 SHAKS. *Troil. & Cres.* II. i. 48 Thou sodden-witted lord! thou hast no more brain than I have in mine elbows. 1670 RAY 217.

Wit in his little finger, He has more | than you have in your whole hand.

1721 KELLY 173.

Wit is folly unless a wise man hath the keeping of it.

1707 MAPLETOFT 114. 1766 *Goody Two-Shoes* (1881) 40. 1813 RAY 174.

Wit of a woman is a great matter, The.

1589 *Jane Anger her Protection for Women* C 2. 1599 BRETON *Wks.* II. ch. 59 (cited as 'the common proverbe') (A).

Wit of you, The | and the wool of a blue dog, will make a good medley. (*Cf.* Thrift of you, &c.)

1659 HOWELL *Eng. Prov.* 11/2. 1732 FULLER no. 4836.

Wit once bought is worth twice taught. (*Cf.* Bought wit, &c.)

1639 R. CHAMBERLAIN *Conceits, Clinches* no. 118. 1670 RAY 157.

Wit than a coot, No more.

c. 1548 BALE *K. Johan* 176 *K. Johan.* Thou semyste by thy wordes to have no more wytt than a coote.

Wit than wealth, Better.

1567 WM. BALDWIN *Treatise Moral Philos.* P 5 It is better to want ryches then witte. 1736 BAILEY *Dict.* s.v. 'Better' (A).

Wit to pick a lock and steal a horse, but wisdom to let them alone, It is.

1659 HOWELL *Eng. Prov. Rend. into Fr.* 3/1. 1670 RAY 30.

Wit, whither wilt thou?

[Phrase addressed to one who is talking too much or foolishly.] 1599–1600 SHAKS. *A.Y.L.* I. ii. 60 How now, wit! whither wander you? *Ibid.* IV. i. 174 A man that hath a wife with such a wit, he might say, 'Wit, whither wilt?' 1600 KEMP *Kemp's Nine Day's Wonder* (G. B. Harrison) 26. 1617 *Greene's Groat's W. Wit* Pref. A 2 This olde Ballad made in Hell: *Ingenio perij, qui miser ipse meo*: Wit, whither wilt thou? woe is me.

Wit will never worry you, Your.

1721 KELLY 383.

Wit without learning is like a tree without fruit.

1567 WM. BALDWIN *Treatise Moral Philos.* P 4. 1647 *Countryman's New Commonwealth*, 15.

Wit(s), *see also* Ale is in (When) w. is out; All the w. in the world (If you had), fools would fell you; Born when w. was scant; Bought w. is dear; Bought w. is the best; Bush natural, more hair than w.; Constable for your w. (You might be a); God send you more w.; Good w., if a wise man had keeping; Good w. jump; Great w. short memories; Little w. and it doth you good; Little w. in head, work for heel; Little w., meikle travel; Little w. serve fortunate; Men (So many), so many w.; Mickle head, little w.; Money, w. (Of), believe one fourth; Moon's in the full when w.'s in the wane; One man's will another man's w.; Ounce of discretion worth a pound of w.; Ounce of w. that's bought; Set your w. against child (Don't); Shows all his w. at once; Tongue runs before his w.; Truss up his w. in eggshell (You may); Two heads (w.) better than one; Want of w. worse than want of gear; Wealth makes w. waver; Will and w. strive with you; Wine is a whetstone to w.; Wise that hath w. enough for own affairs; Wood in wilderness . . . w. in poor man are little thought of. *See also* After wit.

Witch, I believe you are a.

1738 SWIFT (Dial. iii) II. 351 *Lady S.* Guess again. *Miss.* A girl, then. *Lady S.* You have hit it; I believe you are a witch.

Witch of Endor.

[(In allusion to *1 Sam.* xxviii. 7): a fanciful term for (*a*) a bewitching person; (*b*) a medium.] 1819 C'TESS SPENCER *Let.* 15 Nov. in *Sarah, Lady Lyttleton's Corr.* (1912) viii 217 That witch of Endor, the Duchess of Devon, has been doing mischief of another kind. 1919 R. R. MARETT in *Q. Rev.* Apr. 458 In the West End a *séance* with a Witch of Endor is doubtless to be obtained for a suitable fee.

Witches' Sabbath.

[A midnight meeting of witches, presided over by the Devil, held as an orgy or festival.]

a. 1660 F. BROOKE tr. *Le Blanc's Trav.* 312 Divers Sorcerers . . . have confessed that in their Sabbaths, . . . they feed on such fare. 1735 POPE *Ep. Lady* 239 As Hags hold Sabbaths, less for joy than spite, So these their merry, miserable Night. 1883 *Harper's Mag.* 831/2 It might have been . . . a veritable Witches' Sabbath.

Witch(es), *see also* Burn you for w. (They that) will lose coals; Go in God's name, so ride no w.; Rowan tree and red thread; Rynt you w., quoth Bessie Lockit.

Wite[1] God, You need not | if the Deil ding you over.[2]

1721 KELLY 384 . . . Spoken to them that have great big legs. [[1] blame. [2] throw you down.]

Wite[1] your teeth if your tail be small.

1721 KELLY 355 . . . Spoken to them that have good meat at their will. [[1] blame.]

Wite[1] yourself if your wife be with bairn.

1721 KELLY 357 . . . Spoken when people's misfortunes come by their own blame. [[1] blame.]

Witham eel, and Ancum (Ancolme) pike, in all the world there is none syke.

1587 HARRISON *Descr. of Britain* in Holinshed (cited *Wks.* Drayton V (1941) 243) Ancolme ele, and Witham pike Search all England and find not the like. 1613–22 DRAYTON *Polyolb.* xxv. 307–10 (1876) III. 151 As *Kestiven* doth boast, her *Wytham* so have I, My *Ancum* (only mine) whose fame as far doth fly, For fat and dainty *Eels*, as hers doth for her *Pyke*, Which makes the proverb up, the world hath not the like. (Selden's note:— *Wytham Eele*, and *Ancum Pyke*, In all the world there is none syke.)

Witham pike: England hath none like.

1662 FULLER (*Lincs.*) II. 262 English pikes, wherein this county is eminent, especially in that river which runneth by Lincoln, whence . . . 'Witham pike England hath none like'. 1896 BEALBY *Dau. of Fen* viii The fish fully justified the local saying, 'Witham pike, none like'. It was big and fat and beautifully marked.

Withdraw, *see* Choleric man w. a little (From a).

Within, *see* Better were w. (If), better would come out.

Withy tree would have a new gate hung at it, The old.

1678 RAY 184.

Witness everywhere, There is a.

[L. *Nullum locum putes sine teste: semper adesse Deum cogita.*] 1621 BURTON *Anat. Mel.*

II. iii. VII (1651) 360 Think no place without a witness. 1732 FULLER no. 4886.

Wits are a wool-gathering, Your.

[= absent-mindedness.] 1553 T. WILSON *Rhet.* II. 59 Hackyng & hemmyng as though our wittes and our senses were a woll gatheryng. 1621 BURTON *Anat. Mel.* I. ii. III. XV (1651) 129 Th. Aquinas, supping with King Lewis of France, upon a sudden . . . cryed, *conclusum est contra Manichæos*; his wits were a wool-gathering (as they say), and his head busied about other matters. 1677 YARRANTON *Eng. Improvement* 100 My Brains shall go with yours a Woolgathering this one bout. 1815 SCOTT *Guy Man.* xlvii 'I crave pardon, honourable sir! but my wits' —'Are gone a wool-gathering, I think.'

Wits' end, He is at his.

c. 1374 CHAUCER *Troylus* III. 931 At dulcarnon, right at my wittes ende. *c.* 1420 LYDGATE *Ass. of Gods* (E.E.T.S.) 49 They were dreuyn to her wyttes ende. *c.* 1510 STANBRIDGE *Vulg.* (E.E.T.S.) 22 I am at my wyttes ende. 1576 PETTIE *Petite Pall.* (Gollancz) I. 172 The learned physicians . . . were at their wits' end. 1641 FERGUSSON 46 *Of wilfull persons.* He is at his wits end.

Wits, *see also* Wit(s).

Witty and wise, It is good to be.

1567 *Trial of Treasure* in HAZL. *O.E.P.* (1874) III. 72 *Lust.* Therefore it is good to be witty and wise.

Witty, *see also* Every one is w. for own purpose; Weak men had need be w.

Wive and thrive both in a year, It is hard to.

c. 1410 *Towneley Plays* xii l. 97 It is sayde full ryfe 'a man may not wyfe' and also 'thryfe and all in a year.' 1573 TUSSER lvi. 153 It is too much we dailie heare, To wiue and thriue both in a yeare. 1580 LYLY *Euph. & his Eng.* (Arb.) 470 Although in one yeare to mar[r]ie and to thr[i]ue it be hard. 1614 CAMDEN 308. 1721 KELLY 49 *A man cannot wive and thrive in a year.* For courting, marriage, and their appurtenance, occasions an expense that one year cannot retrieve. 1738 SWIFT (*Dial.* i) 341 *Spark.* You can't expect to wive and thrive in the same year.

Wive, *see also* First thrive then w.

Wives must be had, be they good or bad.

1639 CLARKE 328.

Wives, *see also* Wife (Wives).

Wiving and thriving a man should take counsel of all the world, In.

a. 1591 HY. SMITH *Serm.* (1866) I. 9 They say, that in wiving and thriving a man should take counsel of all the world, lest he light upon a curse while he seeks for a blessing.

Wiving, *see also* Hanging and w. gr by destiny.

Woe to him that is alone.

[BIBLE (Latin Vulgate) *Eccles.* iv. 10 *Vae soli! quia cum ceciderit, non habet subleuantem se.* **1382** WYCLIF *Ibid.* Wo to hym that is aloone, for whanne he fallith, he hath noon reisynge him.] *c.* **1200** *Ancrene Riwle* (Camden Soc.) 252 Wo is him thet is euer one, uor hwon he ualleth he naueth hwo him areare.[1] *c.* **1374** CHAUCER *Troylus* i. 694–5 The wysè seyth, wo him that is allone, For, and he falle, he hath noon help to ryse. [[1] to raise.]

Woe to the house where there is no chiding.

1640 HERBERT 338. **1732** FULLER no. 5801.

Woe to want, No.

1590 R. GREENE *Wks.* (Gros.) IX. 312 He felt . . . that there was no greater woe than want. **1623** CAMDEN 278. **1639** CLARKE 244.

Woe worth ill company, quoth the kae[1] of Camnethen.

1721 KELLY 345 . . . Spoken when we have been drawn by ill company into an ill thing. A jack-daw in *Camnethen* learned this word from a guest in the house when he was upon his penitentials after hard drinking. [[1] Jack-daw.]

Woe's to them that have the cat's dish, and she aye mewing.

1721 KELLY 343 . . . Spoken when people owe a thing to, or detain a thing from needy people, who are always calling for it.

Woeful is the household that wants a woman.

c. **1460** *Towneley Myst., 2nd Shep. Play* 420 Ffull wofull is the householde That wantys a woman.

Woes unite foes.

1832 HENDERSON 20 Waes unite faes.

Woe(s), *see also* Weal and women cannot pan, but w. and women can; Will is the cause of w.; World (So goeth), now w. now weal.

Wogan, *see* King cometh to W. (Shall be done when).

Wolf, To see (*or* have seen) a.

[THEOCR. 14. 22, &c. λύκον ἰδεῖν = to be tongue-tied, from the belief that a man on seeing a wolf lost his voice. *Cf.* VERG. *Ecl.* 9. 53 *Lupi Moerin videre priores.*] **1697** DRYDEN *Virg. Past.* ix. 75 My Voice grows hoarse; I feel the Notes decay; As if the Wolves had seen me first to Day. **1823** SCOTT *Quentin D.* xviii Our young companion has seen a wolf, . . . and he has lost his tongue in consequence.

Wolf and fox are both privateers, The.

1732 FULLER no. 4837.

Wolf by the ears, To have (*or* hold) a.

[APOLLOD. CARYST. *Epid.* 5 Τῶν ὤτων ἔχω τὸν λύκον . . . I have got a wolf by the ears, I can neither hold him nor let go. TERENCE *Phormio* 3. 2. 21 *Auribus teneo lupum.*] *c.* **1386** CHAUCER *Mel.* B [2] 2732 And Salomon seith that 'he that entre metteth him of the noyse or stryf of another man is lyk to him that taketh an hound by the eres'. . . . For . . . he that taketh a straunge hound by the eres is outherwhyle biten with the hound. *c.* **1560** DAUS tr. *Sleidane's Comm.* 425 The Bishop of Rome, . . . as the prouerbe is, helde the woulfe by both eares, . . . he coueted to gratifie the Kyng, and also feared themperours displeasure. **1616** DRAXE 19 A medlar is as he that taketh a wolfe by the eares. **1621** BURTON *Anat. Mel.* Democr. to Rdr. (1651) 50 He that goes to law (as the proverb is) holds a wolf by the ears; . . . if he prosecute his cause, he is consumed: if he surcease his suit, he loseth all. **1631** QUARLES *Samson* xi. 63 I have a Wolfe by th' eares; I dare be bold, Neither with safety, to let goe, nor hold. **1884** *Times* 29 Oct. 9/3 These expressions come from a man who has a wolf by the ears, whose task is well-nigh desperate.

Wolf doth something every week that keeps him from going to church on Sunday, The.

1732 FULLER no. 4838.

Wolf eateth the sheep, By little and little the.

1611 COTGRAVE s.v. 'Manger'. **1616** DRAXE 13.

Wolf eats often the sheep that have been told[1] (warned), The.

1639 CLARKE 271. **1651** HERBERT 370 The wolf eats oft of the sheep that have been warned. **1666** TORRIANO 132, 21 The wolf worries sheep, for all that they are told. [[1] i.e. counted. Fr. *Brebis comptées, le loup les mange.*]

Wolf for his mate, Who hath a | needs a dog for his man.

1611 COTGRAVE s.v. 'Loup' He that hath a Wolfe to his mate, had need of a dog to his man. **1623** WODROEPHE 276 If thou makest the Wolfe thy Fellow, cary a Dog vnder thy Cloake. **1640** HERBERT 319.

Wolf from the door, Enough to keep the.

1546 HEYWOOD II. vii. 68 I would haue ye stur Honestly, to kepe the wolfe from the dur. **1645** HOWELL *Lett.* 28 Apr. (1903) I. 99 *He or she* should have wherewith . . . at least to keep the wolf from the door, otherwise it were a mere madness to marry. **1885** ORMSBY *Don Quix.* I. Introd. 30 He married . . . a lady . . . who brought him a fortune which may possibly have served to keep the wolf from the door, but if so, that was all.

Wolf in sheep's clothing (a lamb's skin), A.

1389 WYCLIF *Matt.* vii. 15 Fals prophetis, the whiche cummen to ʒou in clothingis of sheepis, bot wythynne thei ben rauyshynge wolues. **1546** HEYWOOD I. x. 23 Of trouth she is a wolfe in a lambes skyn. **1590–1** SHAKS. *2 Hen. VI* III. i. 77 Is he a lamb? His skin is surely lent him, For he's inclined as is the ravenous wolf. **1591–2** *1 Hen. VI* I. iii. 55 Thee I'll chase hence, thou wolf in sheep's array. **1641** FERGUSSON 54 *Of hypocrites* . . . He is a wolf in a lamb's skin.

Wolf, If it had been a | it would have worried you.

1721 KELLY 196 . . . Spoken when one hath, to no purpose, sought a thing, that was afterwards found hard by them.

Wolf knows what the ill beast thinks, The.

1611 COTGRAVE s.v. 'Loup' Le loup sçait bien que male beste pense: Prov. One lewd fellow is well acquainted with the purposes, or sleights of another. **1640** HERBERT 318.

Wolf may lose his teeth, but never his nature (memory), The.

1616 DRAXE 238 (wlth 'memory'). **1666** TORRIANO 132 The wolf loseth his tooth, but not his instinct. **1670** RAY 30 Wolves lose their teeth, but not their memory. **1732** FULLER no. 5802 (with 'nature'). **1832** HENDERSON 90.

Wolf must die in his own skin, The.

c. **1400** *Rom. Rose* C 7313 Men ne may in no manere Teren the wolf out of his hide Til he be flayn, bak and side. **1611** COTGRAVE s.v. 'Loup' A knave will die in a knaves skin, if he formerly lose it not. **1640** HERBERT 356.

Wolf to keep the sheep, To set the.

1576 F. PATRIZI *Civil Policy* tr. R. Robinson I 2ᵛ It is most dangerous as it is spoken in the Prouerbe: To betake a sheepe into the custodye of a wolfe. **1576** PETTIE *Petite Pall.* (Gollancz) I. 60. **1579** GOSSON *Sch. Abuse* (Arb.) 47. **1639** CLARKE 95 You have given the wolf the weather to keep.

Wolves rend sheep when the shepherds fail.

[*Cf.* BIBLE *John* x. 12. ALANUS DE INSULIS *Liber Parabolarum* i. 31 *Sub molli pastore capit lanam lupus, et grex Incustoditus dilaceratur eo.*] *c.* **1386** CHAUCER *Phys. T.* C 101 Under a shepherde softe and necligent The wolf hath many a sheep and lamb to-rent.

Wolf (-ves), *see also* Cry w.; Cut down the woods, catch w.; Death of a young w. never too soon; Death of w. safety of sheep; Dust raised by sheep not choke w.; Foolish sheep makes w. confessor; Give never the w. the wether; Growing youth hath w. in belly; Hard winter when w. eats another; Howl with the w.; Hunger fetches w. out of woods; Keep w. from door; Keeps company with w. (Who) will learn to howl; Kid that keeps above is in no danger of w.; Life of the w. is death of lamb; Lone sheep in danger of w.; Man is to man a w.; Man is to man either god or w.; Stranger is for the w.; Thief knows a thief as w. knows w.; Troubles a w. how many sheep (Never); Trust to dog (While you), w. slips into sheepfold; Two w. may worry one sheep.

Woman and a cherry are painted for their own harm, A.

1659 HOWELL *Span.–Eng.* 18 ('paint themselves for their own hurt'). **1666** TORRIANO 75 A woman and a cherry is coloured to its prejudice. **1855** BOHN 304.

Woman and a glass are ever in danger, A.

1640 HERBERT 328.

Woman, She is a | and therefore may be wooed, she is a woman and therefore may be won.

1588 GREENE *Wks.* (Gros.) VII. 68 Melissa was a woman and therefore to be woone. **1589** *Ibid.* XII. 31 and 78 Argentina is a woman, and therefore to be wooed, and so to be won. *c.* **1591–2** SHAKS. *1 Hen. VI* V. iii. 65. *c.* **1592–3** *Richard III* I. ii. 228. *c.* **1593–4** *Titus Andron.* II. i. 82.

Woman conceals what she knows not, A.

c. **1386** CHAUCER *Mel.* B² 2274 Ye seyn that 'the Ianglerie of wommen hath hid thinges that they woot not' as who seith, that 'a woman can nat hyde that she woot'. **1597–8** SHAKS. *1 Hen. IV* II. iii. 112 Constant you are, But yet a woman . . . for I well believe Thou wilt not utter what thou dost not know. **1640** HERBERT 364. **1721** KELLY 347 *Women and bairns lain¹ what they know not. But what they know they'll blab out.* [¹ conceal.]

Woman is a weathercock, A.

1607 MIDDLETON *Family of Love* I. ii. 59 Women . . . are but windy turning vanes. **1612** N. FIELD *A Woman is a Weathercock* [title]. **1616** W. HAUGHTON, *Englishmen for my Money* E 2ᵛ. **1616** DRAXE 239.

Woman is flax, A | man is fire, the devil comes and blows the bellows.

1666 TORRIANO 75. **1874** WHYTE-MELVILLE *Uncle John* vi The tow and tinder of which men and women are proverbially composed, only wait a chance spark, a rising breeze, to become a bonfire.

Woman is the confusion (woe) of man.

[VINCENT DE BEAUVAIS¹ *Spec. Hist.* x. 71 *Mulier est hominis confusio.*] *c.* **1386** CHAUCER *Mel.* B² 2294 If that woman were nat goode, . . . our lord god . . . wold never hav wroght hem, ne called hem help of man, but rather

confusioun of man. Id. *Nun's Priest's T.* B²
4354 *Mulier est hominis confusio.* 1546
HEYWOOD II. vii. 68 A woman. As who
saith, wo to the man. 1576 PETTIE *Petite Pall.*
(Gollancz) II. 126 I think them [women]
made of God only for a plague and woe unto
men, as their name importeth. *c.* 1637
WHITING in *Caroline Poets* iii. 479 She is woe
to man, a woman to me. 1667 MILTON *P.L.* xi
633 But still I see the tenor of man's woe
Holds on the same, from Woman to begin.
[¹ Died *c.* 1264.]

Woman is the weaker vessel, A.

[*1 Peter* iii. 7 Giving honour unto the wife,
as unto the weaker vessel.] 1594–5 SHAKS.
L.L.L. I. i. 271 Jaquenetta—so is the weaker
vessel called. 1594–5 *Rom. & Jul.* I. i. 19
Women, being the weaker vessels, are ever
thrust to the wall. 1597–8 *2 Hen. IV* II. iv.
64 You are the weaker vessel, as they say,
the emptier vessel. 1599–1600 *A.Y.L.* II. iv.
5 I must comfort the weaker vessel, as
doublet and hose ought to show itself
courageous to petticoat. 1639 CLARKE 118
A woman is the weaker vessel.

Woman need but look on her apron-string to find an excuse, A.

1738 SWIFT (Dial. iii) 351 They say, a woman
need but look on her apron-string to find an
excuse.

Woman she is fair, Tell a | and she will soon turn fool.

1664 CODRINGTON 219 The way to make a
Woman fool is to commend her beauty. 1707
MAPLETOFT 5 Tell a Woman she is wondrous
fair, and she will soon turn Fool.

Woman that deliberates is lost, The.

1713 ADDISON *Cato* IV. i *Marc.* When love
once pleads admission to our hearts (In spite
of all the virtue we can boast) The woman
that deliberates is lost. 1887 BLACKMORE
Springhaven xlii 'May I tell you my ideas
about that matter?'... Dolly hesitated, and
with the proverbial result.

Woman that loves to be at the window, A | is like a bunch of grapes on the highway.

1666 TORRIANO 74 A woman at a window,
as grapes on the highway. 1869 HAZLITT 39.

Woman that paints, A | puts up a bill to let.

1700 WARD *London Spy* (1924) 420 (A) For
she that paints will doubtless be a whore.
1732 FULLER no. 481. 1855 BOHN 304.

Woman, A | the more curious she is about her face, the more careless about her house.

1623 'J. DAWE' *Vox Graculi* G 1 (with the
Spanish). *a.* 1637 JONSON *Discoveries* (1640)
90.

Woman were as little as she is good, If a | a pease-cod would make her a gown and a hood.

1591 FLORIO *Sec. Frutes* 175 If women were
as little as they are good, a peas-cod would
make them a gowne and a hood. 1678 RAY
64 ... *Se la donna fosse piccola come è buona,
la minima foglia la farebbe una veste & una
corona.* Ital.

Woman's advice is best at a dead lift, A.

1659 HOWELL *Eng. Prov.* 6/2.

Woman's advice is no great thing, A | but he who won't take it is a fool.

1620 SHELTON *Quix.* II. vii (1908) II. 230 I
say a woman's advice is but slender, yet he
that refuseth it is a madman.

Woman's eye, *see* Black man is a pearl in fair
w.'s e.

Woman's mind and winter wind change oft, A.

1639 CLARKE 159. 1721 KELLY 17 *A woman's
mind is like the wind in a winter's night.* ...
The fickleness and inconstancy of women, in
which, ... they are very much rival'd by the
men. *a.* 1796 BURNS *Women's Minds* Tho'
women's minds like winter winds May shift
and turn, and a' that.

Woman's painting breed thy heart's (stomach's) fainting, Let no.

1664 CODRINGTON 204 (with 'Stomack').
1670 RAY 20. 1732 FULLER no. 6243.

Woman's tongue is the last thing about her that dies, A.

1612 CHAPMAN *Widow's Tears* IV. ii (A) When
a man dies the last thing that moves is his
heart; in a woman her tongue. 1738 SWIFT
(Dial. iii) 352 Well, miss, they say a woman's
tongue is the last thing about her that dies.

Woman's tongue wags like a lamb's tail, A.

1670 RAY 49. 1721 KELLY 387 *Your Tongue
goes like a lamb's tail.* Spoken to people that
talk too much, and to little purpose.

Woman's tongue, *see also* Arthur could not
tame w. t.

Woman's work is never at an end (never done), A.

1573 TUSSER (1878) 162 Some respit to
husbands the weather may send, But hus-
wiues affaires haue neuer an end. 1629 Title
of ballad entered *Stationers' Register* 1 June
(Arb.) iv. 213. 1670 RAY 50. 1678 *Ibid.* 60
A woman's work and washing of dishes is
never at an end. 1721 KELLY 356 ... So
much care and the management of a family
requires. 1920 *Times Wkly.* 12 Mar. 209
'Women's work is never done'.... We shall
never hear the whole of woman's work during
the war.

Women and dogs set men together by the ears (cause much strife).

1541 *Schoolho. of Women* 689, in HAZLITT *Early Pop. Poet.* IV. 131 The prouerb olde accordeth right: Women and dogges cause much strife. **1639** CLARKE 117.

Women and geese, Where there are | there wants no noise.

1616 DRAXE 239 Where there are women, there is much tatling. **1659** HOWELL *Ital.-Eng.* 16. **1678** RAY 64. **1732** FULLER no. 5684 Where women are and geese there wants no gagling.

Women and hens through too much gadding are lost.

1611 COTGRAVE s.v. 'Poule' Women and hennes, that gad overmuch, are quickly lost. **1620** SHELTON *Quix.* II. xlix (1908) III. 165 The honest maid [is] better at home with a bone broken than a-gadding; the woman and the hen are lost with straggling. **1666** TORRIANO 10.

Women and music should never be dated.

1773 GOLDSMITH *She Stoops to C.* III (Globe) 663 *Miss Hard.* I must not tell my age. They say women and music should never be dated.

Women and wine, game and deceit, make the wealth small, and the wants great.

1591 FLORIO *Sec. Frutes* 73 (A) Women, wine, and dice will bring a man to lice. **1721** KELLY 353 . . . This is the translation of an old monkish rhyme. *Pisces, perdices, vinum, nec non meritrices Corrumpunt cistam, & quicquid ponis in istam.* **1732** FULLER no. 6416.

Women are always in extremes.

1639 CLARKE 118.

Women are born in Wiltshire, brought up in Cumberland, lead their lives in Bedfordshire, bring their husbands to Buckingham, and die in Shrewsbury.

1658 *Wit Restor'd* 99 Women are borne in *Wilsheire*, Brought up in *Cumberland*, Lead their lives in *Bedfordsheire*, Bring their husbands to *Buckingame*, and dye in *Shrewsbury*. **1662** FULLER (Shrops.) III. 54 'He that fetcheth a wife from Shrewsbury must carry her into Staffordshire, or else shall live in Cumberland.' The staple-wit of this vulgar proverb, consisting solely in similitude of sound, is scarce worth the inserting. **1738** FRANKLIN *Mar.* Jack's wife was born in *Wiltshire*, brought up in *Cumberland*, led much of her life in *Bedfordshire*, sent her husband into *Huntingdonshire* in order to send him into *Buckinghamshire*. But he took courage in *Hartfordshire*, and carried her into *Staffordshire*, or else he might have lived and died in *Shrewsbury*.

Women are like wasps in their anger.

1616 BRETON *Cross. Prov.* Wks. (1879) II. App. iii Woemen are like Waspes in their anger. **1639** CLARKE 217 Women be waspes if angered.

Women (Wives and wind) are necessary evils.

[MENANDER *Minor Fragments* 651 K (Loeb) Tὸ γαμεῖν, ἐάν τις τὴν ἀλήθειαν σκοπῇ, κακὸν μέν ἐστιν, ἀλλ' ἀναγκαῖον κακόν. Marriage if one will face the truth, is an evil but a necessary evil.] **1547** WM. BALDWIN *Treatise Moral Philos.* (1550) O 5. **1576** PETTIE *Petite Pall.* (Gollancz) II. 166 You, Gentlemen, may learn hereby . . . to use them [women] as necessary evils. **1639** CLARKE 118. **1721** KELLY 355 Wives and wind are necessary evils.

Women are the devil's nets.

1520 *Calisto & Melib.* A iij b Yt is an old sayeing That women be the deuells netts, and hed of syn.

Women change as often as the wind. (*Cf.* Woman is a weathercock.)

c. **1560** L. WAGER *Mary Magdalen* G 3 Womens heartes turne oft as doth the wynde. *c.* **1566** *The Bugbears* v. ii You know women's Clackes will walke with euery winde. **1579** LYLY *Euphues* Wks. (Bond) I. 203 Women are to be wonne with every wynde. **1639** CLARKE 159 A woman's mind and winter wind change oft. **1670** RAY 50 [as 1639].

Women in mischief are wiser than men.

1547 WM. BALDWIN *Treatise Moral Philos.* (1550) O 5ᵛ. **1647** *Countryman's New Commonwealth* 11.

Women in state affairs are like monkeys in glass-shops.

1659 HOWELL *Eng. Prov.* 12/2.

Women laugh when they can, and weep when they will.

1611 COTGRAVE s.v. 'Femme (rit quand elle peut).' **1640** HERBERT 355.

Women look in their glass, The more | the less they look to their house.

1640 HERBERT 328.

Women must have their wills while they live, because they make none when they die. (*Cf.* Women will have, &c.)

1602-3 MANNINGHAM *Diary* (Camden Soc.) 92 (A) Women, because they cannot have their wills when they dye, they will have their wills while they live. **1678** RAY 63.

Women naturally deceive, weep and spin.

[Med. L. *Fallere, flere, nere, dedit Deus in muliere.*] *c.* 1386 CHAUCER *W. of Bath's Prol.* D 401 Deceite, weping, spinning god hath yive To wommen kindely, whyl they may live. *c.* 1430 LYDGATE *Of Deceitful Women* 29–33 in SKEAT *E.E.P.* 113 Women, of kinde, have condicions three; The first is, that that they be fulle of deceit; To spinne also it is hir propertee; And women have a wonderful conceit, They wepen oft, and al is but a sleight. 1589 PUTTENHAM *Eng. Poesie* I. vii (Arb.) 29 This . . . was written (no doubt by some forlorne louer, or els some old malicious Monke). . . . *Fallere flere nere mentiri nilque tacere Hæc quinque vere statuit Deus in muliere.*

Women, priests, and poultry, have never enough.

1659 HOWELL *Ital.–Eng.* 7. 1670 RAY 30.

Women think *place* a sweet fish.

1678 RAY 59.

Women will have the last word.

1541 *Schoolho. of Wom.* 75 in HAZLITT *Early Pop. Poet.* IV. 108 That be their reason not worth a t—de, Yet wil the woman haue the last woord.

Women will have their wills. (*Cf.* Women must have, &c.)

1547 A. BORDE *Brev. of Helthe* (1557) f. lxxxii Let euery man please his wyfe in all matters, and . . . let her haue her owne wyll, for that she wyll haue who so euer say nay. 1639 CLARKE 329.

Women will say anything.

1610–11 SHAKS. *Wint. T.* I. ii. 131 Women say so, That will say anything.

Women's counsel is cold.

[Icelandic prov. Köld eru opt kvenna-ráð (cold, *i.e.* fatal, are often women's counsels).] *c.* 1275 *Provs. of Alfred* (Skeat) A 336 Cold red is quene red (cold advice is women's advice). *c.* 1386 CHAUCER *Nun's Priest's T.* 4446 Wommennes counseils been ful ofte colde; Wommannes counseil broghte us first to wo, And made Adam fro paradys to go.

Woman (Women), *see also* All w. are good; Ass climbs a ladder (When), may find wisdom in w.; Bad w. is worse than bad man; Because is w.'s reason; Choose neither a w. by candle-light; City (W.) that parleys; Dally not with w.; Dead w. will have four to carry her; Discreet w. have neither eyes; Fair w. and a slashed gown; Fair w. without virtue; Find a w. without an excuse; First advice of a w. (Take); Gaming w. and wine; Honest w.; Man is as old as he feels, w. as she looks; Man of straw worth w. of gold; Man, w., and devil are three degrees; Many w. many words; Married w. has nothing of her own but; Meat and good drink (If it wasn't for) w.

might gnaw sheets; Morning sun . . . and Latin-bred w.; Mother's (W.'s) side is surest; No man is a match for a w.; No mischief but a w. is at bottom; Old w.; Old w. in wooden ruff; One tongue is enough for w.; Peas (The smaller the) . . . the fairer the w. the more the giglot; Play, w., and wine undo; See a w. weep (No more pity to) than goose go barefoot; Ship and a w. ever repairing; Silence is best ornament of w.; Spaniel, a w., and a walnut-tree; Swine, w., and bees cannot be turned; War without a w. (No); Weal and w. cannot pan; Wicked w. worse than devil; Wine and w.; Wit of a w. a great matter; Woeful is a household that wants a w.; Wonders of England (Three).

Won with the egg and lost with the shell.

1575 GASCOIGNE *Posies*; *Advent. of Master F. J.* (1907) 450 Nor woman true but even as stories tell, Wonne with an egge, and lost againe with shell.

Wonder at nothing, *see Nil admirari.*

Wonder is the daughter of ignorance.

1573 SANDFORD Maruell is the daughter of ignoraunce. 1629 *Book of Meery Riddles* Prov. 44 (A) (as 1573). 1629 T. ADAMS *Serm.* (1861–2) I. 444 Wonder you at this? Wonder is the daughter of ignorance, ignorance of nature.

Wonder lasts but nine days, A.

c. 1374 CHAUCER *Troylus* IV. 588 For wonder last but nine night nevere in toune! 1546 HEYWOOD II. i. 44 This wonder (as wonders last) lasted nine daies. 1590–1 SHAKS. *2 Hen. VI* II. iv. 69 These few days' wonder will be quickly worn. 1590–1 *3 Hen. VI* III. ii. 114 *Glos.* That would be ten days' wonder at the least. *Clar.* That's a day longer than a wonder lasts. 1599–1600 *A.Y.L.* III. ii. 184 I was seven of the nine days out of the wonder before you came. 1633 MASSINGER *New Way* IV. ii That were but nine day wonder. 1764 CHURCHILL *Ghost* III. 547 He would be found . . . A nine day's wonder at the most. 1879 W. MINTO *Defoe* 135 Selkirk, whose solitary residence on . . . Juan Fernandez was a nine days' wonder.

Wonders of England, Three | the churches, the women, the wool.

1612–15 BP. HALL *Contempl.* IV. xi (1825) II. 378 There were wont to be reckoned three wonders of England, ecclesia, fœmina, lana; 'the churches, the women, the wool'.

Wonders will never cease.

1776 *Garrick Corresp.* (1832) ii. 174 (A). 1842 LEVER *Jack Hinton* xx The bystanders . . . looked from one to the other, with expressions of mingled surprise and dread . . . 'Blessed hour, . . . wonders will never cease'. 1885 C. LOWE *Bismarck* (1898) x. 339 Bismarck had . . . been kissed and hugged by his Majesty. . . . The world had been again reminded . . . that wonders, truly, would never cease.

Wont, *see* Useth me better than he is w. (He that) will betray me.

Woo but[1] cost? Who may.

1721 KELLY 352 . . . That is, no great matter can be easily attain'd or achiev'd. [[1] without.]

Woo, To | is a pleasure in a young man, a fault in an old.

1664 CODRINGTON 217. **1670** RAY 30. **1732** FULLER no. 5254 (with 'phrenzy' for 'fault').

Woo where he will, A man may | but he will wed where his hap is.

1641 FERGUSSON 12. **1721** KELLY 27 *A man may woo where he will, but wed where his wife is.* Spoken of a man who having courted many mistresses, has at last married to his disadvantage.

Woo, *see also* Men are April when they w.; Petticoats w. (When), breeks may come speed.

Wood (*proper name*), *see* Hunt's (W.'s) dog (Like); Peter of W., church and mills are his; Tent thee, quoth W.

Wood, To be in a.

[= to be bewildered.] **1608** DAY *Law Tricks* v. i Ime in a wood. **1608** MIDDLETON *Mad World* v. ii. 143. *c.* **1616** BEAUM. & FL. *Mad Lover* IV (A) Help the boy; He's in a wood, poor child.

Wood half-burnt is easily kindled.

1557 G. CAVENDISH *Life of Card. Wolsey* (1893) 142 Nowe ye may perceyve the old malice begynnyth to breake owt, & newely to kyndell the brand that after proved to a great fier. **1640** HERBERT 345.

Wood in a wilderness, moss in a mountain, and wit in a poor man's breast, are little thought of.

1641 FERGUSSON 108 Wit in a poore mans head, mosse in a mountain availes nothing. **1721** KELLY 347.

Wood, Like | like arrows.

1616 DRAXE 114.

Wood(s), *see also* Arrows (Not to know of what w. to make); Crab of the w. . . . w. of the crab; Cut down the w., catch wolf; Cut Falkland w. with penknife; Fields have eyes; Green w. makes hot fire; Halloo until out of the w. (Not to); Lay on more w., ashes give money; Little w. heat little oven; Lived too near a w. to be frightened by owls; Lives longest must fetch w. farthest; Looks as the w. were full of thieves; New beer . . . green w. makes hair grow through hood; Old w. is best to burn; Red w. makes gude spindles; Sairy w. that has never withered bough; Sap and heart are best of w.; See the w. for trees (Cannot); Touch w.; Ways to the w. than one (More).

Wood (= mad), *see* Horn mad (w.); Once w. and aye the waur.

Woodcock does not make a winter, One.

1617 J. SWETNAM *School of Defence* 171 One Swallow maketh not a Summer, nor two Woodcocks a Winter. **1636** CAMDEN 203. **1659** N. R. 84. **1662** J. WILSON *Cheats* I. ii *Folly* One woodcock makes no winter. **1670** RAY 128 One swallow makes not a spring, nor one woodcock a winter.

Woodcock, *see also* Partridge had w.'s thigh (If); Snite need not w. betwite; Winter enough for the snipe and w.; Wise as a w.

Wooden bell, *see* Counsel of fools (To).

Wooden dagger, I will not wear the.

1670 RAY 198 I'll not wear the wooden dagger, *i.e.* lose my winnings.

Wooden dagger in a painted sheath, A.

1616 WITHALS 560. **1639** CLARKE 6.

Wooden legs, *see* Runs in the blood like w. l.

Wooden shoes, *see* No Jews, no w. s.

Wood-pile, *see* Nigger in the w.-p.

Wooers and widows are never poor.

a. **1553** UDALL *Royster D.* I. ii (Arb.) 16 Hir Thousande pound. . . . Is muche neere about two hundred and fiftie, Howebeit wowers and Widows are neuer poore.

Wooing for woeing; banna for banning.

1546 HEYWOOD II. vii. 68 Had I not béene witcht, . . . The termes that longe to weddyng had warnde mée. First wooyng for woing, banna for bannyng.

Wooing that is not long a-doing, Happy is the.

1576 *Parad. of D. Devices* in *Brit. Bibliog.* (1812) iii. 71 (A) Thrise happie is that woying That is not long a doyng. **1621** BURTON *Anat. Mel.* III. ii. VI. v (1651) 578 Blessed is the wooing, That is not long a-doing. As the saying is, when the parties are sufficiently known to each other, . . . let her means be what they will, take her without any more ado. **1670** RAY 48. **1721** KELLY 153 . . . I have seldom seen . . . a sudden match prove comfortable or prosperous. **1753** RICHARDSON *Grandison* I. ix (1812) 13 What signifies shilly-shally? What says the old proverb?— 'Happy is the wooing, That is not long a-doing.'

Wooing was a day after the wedding, The.

1579 LYLY *Euphues* (Arb.) 84 I cannot but smyle to hear that . . . the wooing should be a daye after the wedding. **1732** FULLER no. 4840.

Wooing, see also Courting and w. bring dallying; Sunday's w. draws to ruin.

Wool, Many go out for | and come home shorn.

1599 MINSHEU (1623) 3 A 5. **1612** SHELTON *Quix*. I. vii (1908) I. 43 To wander through the world, ... without once considering how many there go to seek for wool that return again shorn themselves? **1678** RAY 220. **1824** SCOTT *St. Ronan's* xxxvi You are one of the happy sheep that go out for wool, and come home shorn. **1910** G. W. E. RUSSELL *Sketches & Snap*. 315 Some go [to Ascot] intent on repairing the ravages of Epsom or Newmarket; and in this speculative section not a few ... who go for wool come away shorn.

Wool over (a person's) eyes, To draw (pull).

1855 FRANCES M. WHITCHER *Widow Bedott* (1883) xv. 55 He ain't so big a fool as to have the wool drawd over his eyes in that way. **1884** HOWELLS *Silas Lapham* vii I don't propose he shall pull the wool over my eyes.

Wool so white but a dyer can make it black, There is no.

1576 PETTIE *Pet. Pall*. (Gollancz) II. 69 (A) I see there is no wool so coarse but it will take some colour. **1580** LYLY *Euph. & his Eng*. (Arb.) 330 There is no wool so white but the Diar can make blacke. **1732** FULLER no. 4927. **1802** WOLCOT (P. Pindar) *Middl. Elect*. iii. Wks. (1816) IV. 194 E'en let mun all their poison spit, My lord, there is no wooll zo whit, That a dyer caan't make *black*.

Wool, see also Better give the w. than the sheep; Cap be made of w. (If his); Feet of deities shod with w.; Go to a goat for w.; Great cry little w.; Loveth well sheep's flesh who ... bread in w.; Shaving against the w.; Thrift of you and w. of dog good web; Wit of you and w. of blue dog good medley; Wonders of England (Three).

Wool-gathering, see Wits are w.-g.

Woolpack(s), see London Bridge.

Wool-seller knows a wool-buyer, A.

1641 FERGUSSON no. 52. **1670** RAY 159. **1721** KELLY 341 *Wool sellers ken ay wool buyers*. Roguish people know their own consorts.

Woolward, To go.

[= without linen]. c. **1315** SHOREHAM *Poems* i. 1024 Baruot go, Wolle-ward and wakynge. **1377** LANGLAND *P. Pl*. B xviii. 1 Wolleward and wete-shoed went I forth after. c. **1489** Id. *Sonnes of Aymon* xxvii. 574 He is goon his wayes wulwarde and barefote. c. **1594** SHAKS. *L.L.L.* V. ii. 697.

Woos a maid, He that | must seldom come in her sight; but he that woos a widow must woo her day and night.

1639 CLARKE 27 He that will win a maid must seldom come in her sight. **1670** RAY 49. **1732** FULLER no. 6403.

Woos for cake and pudding, He.

1721 KELLY 172 ... Spoken when people pretend courtship, to promote another interest.

Word and a blow, A.

c. **1568** WAGER *Longer thou Livest* D 1 (A) This is manhoode to make thee bolde, Let there be but a worde and a blow. **1594–5** SHAKS. *Rom. & Jul*. III. i. 44 Make it a word and a blow. **1678** BUNYAN *Pilgr*. I. (1877) 74 He was but a word and a blow, for down he knocked me, and laid me for dead.

Word and a stone let go cannot be called back, A.

1616 DRAXE 241. **1732** FULLER no. 485.

Word before is worth two behind, A.

1641 FERGUSSON 8.

Word is enough to the wise, A.

[L. *Verbum sat sapienti*.] **1577** RHODES *Boke of Nature* in *Babees Book* (E.E.T.S.) 88 (A) For few wordes to wise men is best. **1609** JONSON *Case is Altered* I. i *Presto*. Go to, a word to the wise. **1662** FULLER (*Westmor*.) III. 302 I hope the townsmen thereof (a word is enough to the wise) will make their commodities ... substantial. **1837–47** BARHAM *Ingol. Leg*. (1898) 488 Which some learned Chap ... perhaps would translate by the words '*Verbum Sap!*'

Word is in your mouth, While the | it is your own; when 'tis once spoken 'tis another's.

1509 A. BARCLAY *Ship of Fools* (1874) I. 110 Whan a worde is nat sayd, the byrde is in the cage ... whan thy worde is spoken ... Thou arte nat mayster but he that hath it harde. **1547** WM. BALDWIN *Treatise Moral Philos*. (1550) K 8 A man hath power ouer hys wordes till they bee spoken, but after they be vttered they haue power over hym. **1646** A. BROME *Roxb. Ballads* (B.S.) viii. 109 (A) Our words are our own if we keep them within.

Word spoken is past recalling, A.

[HOR. *Ep*. 1. 18. 71 *Semel amissum volat irrevocabile verbum*.] c. **1386** CHAUCER *Manc. T*. H 355 Thing that is seyd, is seyd; and forth it gooth Though him repente, or be him leef or looth. **1509** A. BARCLAY *Ship of Fools* (1874) I. 108 A worde ones spokyn reuoked can nat be. **1639** CLARKE 51.

Word (Stone) to throw at a dog, He hasn't a.

1599–1600 SHAKS. *A.Y.L.* I. iii. 3 *Cel*. Not a word? *Ros*. Not one to throw at a dog. *Cel*. No, thy words are too precious to be cast away upon curs. **1600–1** *Merry W*. I. iv. 118 He shall not have a stone to trow at his dog. **1639** CLARKE 302 He hath not a word to cast at a dog. **1738** SWIFT (Dial. i) 333 Here's poor miss has not a word to throw at a dog. **1837** LOVER *Rory O'More* xxii This last monosyllable 'annihilated' the Frenchman, ... 'he hadn't a word to throw to a dog'.

1890 HENLEY & STEVENSON *Beau Austin* I. i
She falls away, has not a word to throw at a
dog, and is ridiculously pale.

Words and feathers the wind carries away.

1591 STEPNEY *Span. Schoolmaster* E 3ᵛ
Words are more light than feathers, that are
caried with euery swift winde. **1599** MINSHEU
2 T 2ᵛ. **1651** HERBERT 368.

Words and not of deeds, A man of | is like a garden full of weeds.

1670 RAY 211.

Words are but sands, but 'tis money buys lands.

1659 HOWELL *Eng. Prov.* 11/2.

Words are but wind.

c. **1200** *Ancrene Riwle* 122 Hwat is word bute
wind? *c.* **1390** GOWER *Conf. Amantis* III. 2768
For word is wynd, bot the maistrie Is that a
man himself defende Of thing which is noght
to commende. **1509** A. BARCLAY *Ship of
Fools* (Jamieson) I. 207 Wordes ar but
wynde. **1592-3** SHAKS. *Com. Err.* III. i. 75
A man may break a word with you, sir, and
words are but wind. **1594-5** *L.L.L.* IV. iii. 68
Vows are but breath, and breath a vapour is.
1598-9 *Much Ado* V. ii. 53 Foul words is but
foul wind. **1616** DRAXE 204. **1650** COWLEY
Guardian I. iii I'm . . . given to jeering: but
what, man? words are but wind. **1652**
FULLER *Com. on Christ's Tempt.* in *Sel. Serm.*
(1891) II. 44 Some will say, *Words are but
wind*; but God's are real words, such as fill
and fat those that depend upon them.

Words are but wind, but blows unkind (dunts[1] are the devil).

1616 DRAXE 102. **1641** FERGUSSON 108
Words are but wind, but dunts are the devil.
1659 HOWELL *Eng. Prov.* 14/2. **1721** KELLY
340 Words go with the wind, but dunts are
the devil. [¹ hard blows.]

Words are but words.

c. **1595** *Sir Thomas More* vii. 107 Woords are
but wordes and payes not what men owe.
c. **1620** BEAUM. & FL. *Little Fr. Lawyer* I. i (A).

Words are wise men's counters, the money of fools.

1651 HOBBES *Leviathan* I. iv (1904) 18 Words
are wise mens counters, they do but reckon
by them: but they are the mony of fooles, that
value them by the authority of an *Aristotle*,
a *Cicero*, or a *Thomas*. **1903** JAS. BRYCE
Biograph. Stud., *Ld. Beaconsfield* 40 In his
fondness for particular words and phrases
there was a touch . . . of the cynical view that
words are the counters with which the wise
play their game.

Words bind men.

[L. *Verba ligant homines, taurorum cornua
funes.*] **1621** BURTON *Anat. Mel.* III. ii. III. iv
(1651) 484 It was Cleopatras sweet voice,
and pleasant speech which inveagled
Anthony. . . . *Verba ligant hominem, ut
taurorum cornua funes*, as bulls horns are
bound with ropes, so are mens hearts with
pleasant words.

Words cut (hurt) more than swords.

[PHOCYLIDES *Sententiae* 124 Ὅπλον τοι
λόγος ἀνδρὶ τομώτερόν ἐστι σιδήρου. The
tongue is a sharper weapon than the sword.]
c. **1200** *Ancrene Riwle* 74 Mo sleað word þene
sweord. **1621** BURTON *Anat. Mel.* I. ii. IV. iv.
(1651) 196 It is an old saying, *a blow with a
word strikes deeper than a blow with a sword.*
1659 HOWELL *Eng. Prov.* 13/1. **1670** RAY
158 Many words hurt more then swords.
1878 J. A. SYMONDS *Sidney* 13, 15 A letter
written by Sir Henry Sidney to his son . . .
may here be cited . . . 'A wound given by a
word is oftentimes harder to be cured than
that which is given with the sword.'

Words ending in *ique*, The | do mock the physician; as hectique, paralitique, apoplectique, lethargique.

1651 HERBERT 365.

Words go with the wind, but strokes are out of play.

1721 KELLY 340.

Words have long tails, and have no tails.

1678 RAY 221.

Words may pass, but blows fall heavy.

1678 RAY 354. *Somerset.*

Words to deeds is a great space, From.

1573 SANDFORD 210 From worde to dede is a
great space. **1642** TORRIANO 44 From the
word to the deed, there is a great distance.

Words will not fill a bushel (fill not the firlot[1]), Many.

1641 FERGUSSON 78 Mony words fils not the
furlot. **1659** HOWELL *Eng. Prov.* 9/1. **1692**
BUNYAN *Christ a Complete Sav.* Wks. (1855)
I. 213 For the more compliment, the less
sincerity. Many words will not fill a bushel.
1721 KELLY 251 Many words fill not the
farlet. [¹ a dry measure.]

Words would have much drink, Many.

1641 FERGUSSON 76 Mony words wald have
meikle drink. **1824** SCOTT *St. Ronan's* xxxii
Ye hae garr'd the poor wretch speak till she
swarfs.¹ . . . Let me till her wi' the dram—
mony words mickle drought, ye ken.
[¹ swoons.]

Word(s), *see also* Actions speak louder; Bare w. no bargain; Changing of w.; Deeds are fruits, w. are leaves; Deeds are males, w. females; Deeds, not w.; Evening w. not

like morning; Fair w. and foul deeds cheat; —— and foul play cheat; —— butter no parsnips; —— in flyting (Never a). Few w., many deeds; Few w. to the wise suffice; Fine w. dress ill deeds; First w. of flyting (You have got); First w. stand (Let the); Gives fair w.; Good word costs no more; Good words and ill deeds deceive; Good w. anoint us; ——cool more; ——cost nought; —— fill not a sack; —— good cheap; ——without deeds; Hard w. break no bones; Honest man's w.; Ill w. asketh another; Ill w. meets another; Keep off and give fair w.; King of your w. (Ye should be); Last w.; Live by selling ware for w. (One cannot); Mad w. deaf ears; Many w.; More w. than one to bargain; Never take the tawse when w. will do; Nine w. at once; Second w. makes bargain; Soft w. hard arguments; Speaks as if every w. would lift dish; Take a man by his w.; Three w. (At); True w. spoken in jest; Two (w.) to a bargain; Wine sinks (When) w. swim.

Work and no play makes Jack a dull boy, All.

1670 RAY 158. 1859 SMILES Self-Help xi 'All work and no play makes Jack a dull boy'; but all play and no work makes him something greatly worse.

Work double tides, To.

1788 MME D'ARBLAY Diary 1 July I was most content to work double tides for the pleasure of his company. 1832 Examiner 745/2 The artisans work double tides, that is, they perform two days' labour in one. 1852 MISS YONGE Cameos (1877) II. vii. 95 There is not a spinster in Brittany who will not spin double tides until my purchase-money be raised.

Work (&c.) for a dead horse, To.

1638 BROME Antipodes I. Wks. (1873) III. 234 His land . . . 'twas sold to pay his debts; All went that way, for a dead horse, as one would say. 1670 RAY 171 . . . To work out an old debt, or without hope of future reward. 1857 N. & Q. 2nd Ser. IV. 192/1 . . . He has so much unprofitable work to get through in the ensuing week, which is called 'dead horse'.

Work for nought makes folk dead sweir.[1]

1721 KELLY 341 [[1] lazy.]

Work hard, To | live hard, die hard, and go to hell after all, would be hard indeed!

1840 R. H. DANA Two Years bef. Mast vi Sailors . . . seldom get beyond the common phrase which seems to imply that their sufferings and hard treatment here will excuse them hereafter—'To work hard, live hard, die hard and go to hell after all, would be hard indeed!'

Work in the morning may trimly be done, Some | that all the day after may hardly be won.

1573 TUSSER 75 (E.D.S.) 167.

Work like a galley-slave, To.

1841 F. CHAMIER Tom Bowl. ii I made up my mind to be contented in my situation, and . . . worked away like a galley-slave.

Work like a horse, To.

1710 SWIFT Jrnl. to Stella 9 Sept. Lord Wharton . . . is working like a horse for elections. 1857 HUGHES Tom Brown II. viii The Marylebone men played carelessly in their second innings, but they are working like horses now to save the match.

Work, He that will not | shall not eat.

[2 Thessalonians 3. 10] c. 1535 LYNDSAY Three Estates 2600 Qui non laborat non manducet, . . . Quha labouris nocht he sall not eit. 1616 DRAXE 109. 1639 CLARKE 163.

Work that kills, It is not | but worry.

1908 E. M. SNEYD-KYNNERSLEY H.M.I. xviii The work is often very heavy, but it is not work that kills: it is worry. 1909 Brit. Wkly. 8 July 333 It is worry that kills, they say, and not work. . . . The canker of care seems to eat the life away.

Work to-day, for you know not how much you may be hindered to-morrow.

1664 CODRINGTON 224 Work wisely, lest you be prevented. 1846 DENHAM 3.

Work with the Government (dockyard) stroke, To.

1873 W. ALLINGHAM Rambles II. 60 'Working with a dockyard stroke' . . . means . . . taking the longest time to do as little as possible. 1909 Spectator 22 May 807 Working with 'the Government stroke' . . . mean[s] that when a man is working for the Government he works less strenuously than when working for a private employer.

Work(s) (noun), see also All in the day's w.; Cobble and clout (They that) shall have w.; Day is short, w. is much; Fools and bairns . . . half-done w.; Great gain makes w. easy; Little wit in head makes w.; Son of his own w.; Stay (If anything) let w. stay; Woman's w. never done.

Work(s, ed) (verb), see Corn him well, he'll w. the better; Eat till you sweat, w. till you freeze; Think of ease but w. on; Well to w. and make a fire doth care require.

Workers, see Ill w. are aye good to-putters.

Work-hard, see Forecast is better.

Working and making a fire doth discretion require.

1640 HERBERT 327.

Workman, The better | the worse husband.

1616 DRAXE 63. **1670** RAY 158 . . . It is an observation generally true (the more the pity) and therefore . . . I put it down.

Workman without his tools? What is a.

1546 HEYWOOD II. ix. 77. **1559** BACON *Prayers &c.* (P.S.) 260 Ye cannot consecrate aright. Ye have not all your tools. . . . For what is a workman without his tools? **1614** CAMDEN 314.

Workman, *see also* Bad w. quarrels with tools; Good w. seldom rich; Little let lets an ill w.

Works after his own manner, He that | his head aches not at the matter.

1640 HERBERT 337.

Works, *see also* Work(s).

World and his wife, All the.

1738 SWIFT (Dial. iii) II. 350 *Miss.* Who were the company? *Lady S.* Why there was all the world and his wife. **1816** BYRON to Moore 29 Feb. I am at war with all the world and his wife.

World, This is the | and the other is the country.

1678 RAY 84. (*Joculatory.*)

World in a string, To have the.

[= to have it under control.] **1583** MEL-BANCKE *Philot.* I j Those that walke as they will, . . . perswading themselues that they haue the worlde in a string, are like the ruffian Capaney, who [&c.]. **1681** H. MORE *Exp. Dan.* 162 He [Alex. the Great] had the world in a string, as our English Proverbial Phrase is. **1894** F. BARRETT *Justif. Lebrun* viii. 66 When they believed they had the world on a string.

World is a ladder for some to go up and some down, The.

1642 TORRIANO 63. **1659** HOWELL *Ital.-Eng.* 1 The world is like a ladder, one goeth up, the other down. **1732** FULLER no. 4841.

World is a long journey, The.

1616 BRETON *Cross. Prov.* Wks. (1879) II. App. iii.

World is a wide parish (place), The.

1659 HOWELL *Brit. Prov.* 12. **1738** SWIFT (Dial. ii) 347 *Miss.* I believe there is not such another in the varsal[1] world. *Lady A.* O, miss, the world's a wide place. [[1] universal.]

World is bound to no man, The.

1855 BOHN 257.

World is but a little place, after all, The.

1886 G. A. SALA *America Revisited* [ed. 6] 431 Thirty-one years afterwards I find him in San Francisco . . . ; and yet it is not such a large world after all. **1902–4** LEAN IV. 143 The world is but a little place, after all (or, The world is round). Spoken when two casually meet, and find that they have many mutual friends.

World is his that enjoys it, The, *see* Gown is his that wears it.

World is naught, The.

1639 CLARK 219.

World is nothing, This | except it tend to another.

1640 HERBERT 335. **1909** ALEX. MACLAREN *Ephesians* i. 18 This world means nothing worthy, except as an introduction to another.

World is nowadays, God save the conqueror, The.

1651 HERBERT 367.

World is unstable, This | so saith sage: therefore gather in time, ere thou fall into age.

[Prov. attached to Caxton's ed. of Lydgate's *Stans Puer ad Mensam.* HAZLITT (1907) 455.]

World is well amended with him, The.

1562–3 *Stationers' Register* (Arb.) i. 205 'The world is well amended quoth little Jack a Lent' (ballad). **1594** NASHE *Unfor. Trav.* Wks. (McKerrow) II. 214. **1599** J. CHAMBERLAIN *Letters* (McLure) 23 Aug. i. 82. **1616** DRAXE 4 The world is somewhat amended for him. **1670** RAY 200.

World is wiser than it was, The.

1794 WOLCOT (P. Pindar) *Ode* (in *Pindariana*) Wks. (1816) III. 274 As everybody says, 'the world grows wiser'.

World: So goeth the | now woe, now weal.

c. **1390** GOWER *Conf. Amantis* viii (1889) 427 Fortúne hath sworne To set him upward on the whele; So goth the world; now wo, now wele.

World on your chessboard, Had you the | you could not fill all to your mind.

1640 HERBERT 350.

World runs on wheels, The.

1546 HEYWOOD II. vii. 64. **1603** FLORIO tr. *Montaigne* III. ii (1897) V. 26 The world runs all on wheels. All things therein move

without intermission. **1629** T. ADAMS *Serm.*
(1861–2) I. 87 The proud gallant . . . and his
adorned lady . . . are riders too. . . . The world
with them runs upon wheels; and they . . .
outrun it.

World, Thus fareth the | that one goeth up and another goeth down.

1481 CAXTON *Reynard* xxxii (Arb.) 97 I
wente dounward and ye cam vpward . . .
thou saidest thus fareth the world that one
goth vp and another goth doun.

World, the flesh, and the devil, The.

[BOOK OF COMMON PRAYER, *Athanasian
Creed. Collect for 18th Sunday after Trinity.*]
1621 BURTON *Anat. Mel.* I. ii. III. xv [Where
the learned clerk has acquired a small
benefice] our misery begins afresh, we are
suddenly encountered with the flesh, world,
and devil, with a new onset.

World to see, It is a.

c. **1475** *Assembly of Ladies* in SKEAT'S *Chaucer*
VII. 397 For yonge and olde, and every
maner age, It was a world to loke on her
visage. **1519** *The Four Elements* in HAZL.
O.E.P. (1874–6) I. 35 *Ta.* It is a world to see
her whirl, Dancing in a round. **1579** LYLY
Euphues (Arb.) 116 It is a world to see howe
commonly we are blinded with the collusions
of women. **1593–4** SHAKS. *Tam. Shrew* II. 305
'Tis a world to see, How tame. . . . A meacock
wretch can make the curstest shrew. **1598–9**
Much Ado III. v. 38 *Dogb.* God help us! it
is a world to see.

World wag (slide, shog[1]), Let the.

a. **1529** SKELTON *Sp. Parrot* 90 In flattryng
fables men fynde but lyttyl fayth: But *moveatur
terra*, let the world wag. **1550** CROWLEY
Epigr. 361 Let the worlde wagge, we must
neades haue drynke. **1593–4** SHAKS. *Tam.
Shrew* Ind. I. vi Therefore . . . Let the world
slide. *Ibid.* Ind. II. 146 Come, madam wife,
sit by my side, And let the world slip. **1611**
COTGRAVE s.v. 'Chargé' To take no thought,
passe the time merrily, let the world slide.
1616 DRAXE 185 He letteth the world wag,
or slide. **1637** SANDERSON *Serm.* (1681) II. 73
Solomons sluggard, . . . who foldeth his hands
together, and letteth the world wag as it will.
1719 RAMSAY *Ep. Hamilton* Answ. iii. 20 Be
blythe, and let the Warld e'en shog, as it
thinks fit. **1721** KELLY 240 *Let the world shogg.*
Spoken by them who have a mind to do as
they have resolv'd, be the issue what will.
1877 W. BLACK *Green Past.* xlii Let the world
wag on as it may. [[1] shake, roll from side to
side.]

World wags, I wot well how the | he is best loved that hath most bags.

1538 LATIMER *Let. to Cromwell* Serm. & Rem.
(1845) By this bill enclosed your lordship
can perceive how the world doth wag with
Warwick College. **1639** CLARKE 97. **1887**
BLACKMORE *Springhaven* xxxi We must wag
as the world does; and you know the proverb,
'What makes the world wag, but the weight
of the bag?'

World will be gulled, If the | let it be gulled.

[J. A. DE THOU *Historia* 17. 7 *Quandoquidem
populus iste vult decipi, decipiatur.* Remark
by Cardinal Caraffa on his entry into Paris
(1556) greeted with reverence. (King's
Classical Quot.).] **1621** BURTON *Anat. Mel.*
III. iv. I. ii (1632) 646 Austin . . . censures
Scævola saying . . . that it was a fit thing
cities should be deceived by religion, according
to the diverbe, *Si mundus vult decipi,
decipiatur,* if the world will be gulled, let it
be gulled.

World will not last alway, The.

c. **1384** CHAUCER *Hc. Fame* III. 1147 But men
seyn 'what may ever laste?' **1639** CLARKE
233. **1641** FERGUSSON 100 This warld will
not last ay.

World's end, *see* Great journey to.

World's wealth, If we have not the | we have the world's ease.

1721 KELLY 213 . . . Spoken by those who
live happily, in a mean condition.

World, *see also* All sorts to make w.; Best
thing in w. is to live above it; Die (When
I), w. dies with me; Every man is master
(Where), w. goes to wrack; Good w., but
they are ill that are on it; Good w. if it
hold; Gown is his . . . and w. is his that
enjoys it; Half the w. knows not; Long
time to know w.'s pulse; Out of the w. out
of fashion; Travel through the w. (To) . . .
money and patience; War with all the w.,
peace with England; Wicked w. and we
make part of it; Worst w. that ever was,
some man won; ——, malt-man got his
sack again.

Worm in his brain, He has a.

1678 RAY 278.

Worm, *see also* Tread on a w. and it will turn.

Worry, *see* Kings and bears oft w. keepers;
Work that kills (Not) but w.

Worse appear the better cause (or reason), To make the.

[PLATO *Apol.* 18 B τὸν ἥττω λόγον κρείττω
ποιεῖν, charge against Socrates.] **1605** BACON
Adv. Learning I. ii. 1 To make the worse
matter seem the better, and to suppress truth
by force of eloquence and speech. **1749** LD.
CHESTERFIELD *Lett.* clxxv (1774) I. 517 Like
Belial, in Milton[1], 'he made the worse appear
the better cause'. [[1] *P.L.* ii. 113.]

Worse luck now, The | the better another time.

1721 KELLY 323 . . . Spoken to hearten
losing gamesters. **1732** FULLER no. 4847.

Worse the passage, The | the more welcome the port.

1732 FULLER no. 4848.

Worse, *see also* Everything is w. for wearing; More bare (W. shod) than the shoemaker's wife.

Worship the rising sun, Men use to.

[L. *Plures adorant solem orientem quam occidentem.* More worship the rising than the setting sun.] **1553** T. WILSON *Arte of Rhet.* (1909) 67 All men commonly more reioyce in the Sunne rising, then they doe in the Sunne setting. **1639** CLARKE 12. **1655** FULLER *Ch. Hist.* VIII. i (1868) II. 428 Some are so desirous to worship the rising sun, that . . . they will adore the dawning day. **1670** RAY 137 . . . *Plures adorant solem orientem quam occidentem.* They that are young and rising have more followers, then they that are old and decaying. This consideration . . . withheld Queen *Elizabeth* . . . from declaring her successour. **1738** GAY *Fables* II. ix. 109 (1859) 282 In shoals the servile creatures run, To bow before the rising sun. **1754** GARRICK on Pelham's death, Let others hail the rising sun.

Worship, *see also* Forecasts all perils will win no w. (He that); Good bearing beginneth w. (In); Love (W.) the ground he treads on; More cost more w.; Wealth makes w.

Worst carver in the world: I am the | I should never make a good chaplain.

1738 SWIFT (Dial. ii) 345 I can just carve pudding and that's all; I am the worst carver in the world; I should never make a good chaplain.

Worst dog that is waggeth his tail, The.

1578 FLORIO *First Fruites* f. 33 (A). **1611** DAVIES Prov. 190.

Worst goes foremost, The.

a. **1640** MASSINGER *Old Law* III. ii *Lys.* You shall be first; I'll observe court rules: Always the worst goes foremost. **1902–4** LEAN IV. 144 . . . *i.e.* is produced and put forward first, as the lowest in rank is in a procession.

Worst is behind, The.

1546 HEYWOOD II. ii. 47 The woorst is behynd, we come not where it grew. **1600–1** SHAKS. *Hamlet* III. iv. 179 Thus bad begins and worse remains behind. **1659** HOWELL *Eng. Prov.* 6/2.

Worst may, He that | shall (must) hold the candle.

c. **1534** *Coventry Plays* (Craig) 47 He thatt ma wast of all The candyll ys lyke to holde. **1546** HEYWOOD II. ii. 46. **1594–5** SHAKS. *Rom. & Jul.* I. iv. 38 For I am proverb'd with a grandsire phrase; I'll be a candle-holder, and look on. **1614** CAMDEN 307 He that worst may must hold the candle. **1670** RAY 159 He that worst may, still holds the candle. *Au plus debile la chandelle a la main. Gall.*

Worst misfortunes are those which never befall us, Our.

1885 E. P. HOOD *World of Prov.* 131 'Our worst misfortunes are those which never befall us'. It is Emerson who says—'. . . What torments of pain you endured From the griefs that never arrived'. **1907** A. C. BENSON *From Coll. Wind.* 35 Lord Beaconsfield once said that the worst evil one has to endure is the anticipation of the calamities that do not happen.

Worst pig often gets the best pear, The.

1666 TORRIANO 212 The worst hog lights on the best pear. **1855** BOHN 519.

Worst spoke in a cart breaks first, The.

1678 RAY 205. **1732** FULLER no. 4851.

Worst store, The | a maid unbestowed.

1659 HOWELL *Brit. Prov.* 15.

Worst use you can put a man to is to hang him, The.

a. **1639** SIR H. WOTTON in *Reliq. Wotton.* (1651) 69 And he believed doubtlesse, that Hanging was the worse use man could be put to. **1830** LYTTON *Paul Clif.* XXXVI Mark this truth . . . 'The very worst use to which you can put a man is to hang him!'

Worst wheel of a cart creaks most (makes most noise), The.

c. **1400** *MS. Latin no. 394*, J. Rylands Libr. (ed. Pantin) in *Bull. J. R. Libr.* XIV. 106 Euer þe worst spoke of þe cart krakes. **1586** PETTIE *Guazzo's Civ. Conv.* 106 Those which know least, speake, contend, and crie the loudest. Whereof belike ariseth this Prouerbe, That the brokenest wheele of the charriot maketh alwaies the greatest noise. **1659** FULLER *Appeal Inj. Innoc.* in *Hist. Camb. Univ.* (1840) 305 That spoke in the wheel which creaketh most doth not bear the greatest burden in the cart. The greatest complainers are not always the greatest sufferers. **1692** L'ESTRANGE *Aesop's Fab.* CCCXXXVI (1738) 349 A waggoner took notice upon the creaking of a wheel, that it was the worst wheel of the four that made most noise. . . . 'They that are sickly are ever the most piping and troublesome.' **1737** FRANKLIN July The worst wheel of the cart makes the most noise.

Worst world that ever was, The | some man won.[1]

1641 FERGUSSON 94. [[1] got advantage by it.]

Worst world that ever was, The | the maltman got his sack again.

1721 KELLY 308.

Worst, *see also* Fear the w.; Know the w. (To) is good; Provide for the w.; Things at w. mend.

Worth a Jew's eye, To be.

[= to be of much value: *orig.* worth while for a Jewess's eye to look at.] **1593** G. HARVEY *Wks.* (Gros.) II. 146 As dear as a Iewes eye. **1596–7** SHAKS. *Merch. V.* II. v. 43 There will come a Christian by, Will be worth a Jewess's eye. **1833** MARRYAT *P. Simple* ii Although the journey . . . would cost twice the value of a gold seal, . . . in the end it might be worth a Jew's eye.

Worth doing at all, What is | is worth doing well.

1875 CHEALES *Prov. Folk-Lore* 138 (A). **1893** *Lett. of C. Dickens* Pref. [Dickens] would take as much pains about the hanging of a picture . . . as . . . about the more serious business of his life; thus carrying out . . . his favourite motto of 'What is worth doing at all is worth doing well'.

Worth gold that can win it, He is.

1721 KELLY 128 . . . Spoken to them who grudge the thriving condition of some neighbour, his decent apparel, or plentiful estate.

Worth his weight in gold, He is.

c. **1500** MEDWALL *Nature* l. 936 (A) Nay ye ar worth thy weyght of gold. **1636** S. WARD *Serm.* (1862) 146 A thankful man is worth his weight in the gold of Ophir. **1923** A. RAWLINSON *Advent. in Near East* 158 A railway officer and twenty men, who now were worth their weight in gold.

Worth it as a thief is worth a rope, As well.

1678 RAY 290.

Worth no weal that can bide no woe, He is.

1641 FERGUSSON 42. **1721** KELLY 133.

Worth of a thing is best known by the want of it, The.

1598–9 SHAKS. *Much Ado* IV. 1. 220 It so falls out That what we have we prize not to the worth Whiles we enjoy it, but being lack'd and lost . . . we find The virtue that possession would not show us Whiles it was ours. **1611** COTGRAVE s.v. 'Cogneu' The worth of things is knowne when they be lost. **1616** DRAXE 2 A man knoweth not the worth of a thing before that he wanteth it. **1670** RAY 159 . . . The cow knows not what her tail is worth, till she hath lost it. **1850** LYTTON *Caxtons* XVII. i Ay, one don't know the worth of a thing till one has lost it.

Worth of a thing is what it will bring, The.

1569 C. AGRIPPA *Vanity of Arts & Sciences* (1575) 160 The thinge is so muche worthy as it maye be solde for. **1664** BUTLER *Hudibras* II. i. 465 (1854) I. 126 For what is worth in any thing, But so much money as 'twill bring? **1813** SOUTHEY *Nelson* ii Vouchers, he found in that country were no check whatever; the principle was, that 'a thing was

always worth what it would bring'. **1818** *Letters of Keats* (M. B. Forman 1935) 111 Tradesmen say every thing is worth what it will fetch. **1908** *Spectator* 4 Apr. 'The real worth of anything, is just as much as it will bring'. You cannot get beyond that piece of ancient wisdom as to the determination of value.

Worth one's salt, To be.

[= efficient, capable.] **1830** MARRYAT *King's Own* lii The captain . . . is not worth his salt. **1857** HUGHES *Tom Brown* II. v Every one who is worth his salt has his enemies.

Worth sorrow, He is well | that buys it with his silver.

1641 FERGUSSON 62 It is weill warit they have sorrow that buys with their silver. **1721** KELLY 130 . . . Spoken to them that have been at some pains to inconvene themselves.

Worth, *see also* Man is w. (As the), his land is w.; Threepence (If you make not much of), ne'er w. a groat. *See also* Not worth.

Worthies, *see* Nine W.

Worthy to be named the same day, Not.

1642 D. ROGERS *Naaman* 139 Not worthy to be named the same day . . . with God.

Worthy to bear (carry) his books after him, Not.

1639 CLARKE 72.

Worthy to wipe (buckle, unbuckle) his shoes, Not.

[BIBLE *John* i. 27 He it is, who coming after me is preferred before me, whose shoe's latchet I am not worthy to unloose.] *c.* **1386** CHAUCER *Squire's T.* F[1] 555 Ne were worthy unbokelen his galoche. *c.* **1410** *Towneley Plays* (E.E.T.S.) 196 I am not worthy for to lawse the leste thwong that longys to his shoyne. **1569** HUTH *Anc. Ballads* (1867) 21 For I . . . , Vnworthie most maie seeme to bee, To undoo the lachet of her shooe. **1670** RAY 200. **1826** SCOTT *Journ.* 11 Dec. The blockheads talk of my being like Shakespeare—not fit to tie his brogues. **1829** LAMB to Gilman 26 Oct. He [Thomas Aquinas] comes to greet Coleridge's acceptance, for his shoe-latchets I am unworthy to unloose.

Wots not whether he bears the earth, or the earth him, He.

1721 KELLY 174 . . . Spoken of excessive proud people.

Wotton under Weaver, where God came never.

1610 CAMDEN *Britannia* tr. Holland 587 This *Moreland* . . . keepeth snow lying upon it a long while: in so much as that of a little country village named *Wotton* lying here under *Woverhil* the neighbour inhabitants haue this rime rife in their mouth . . . *Wotton* under *Wever*, Where God came never.

Would *No, I thank you* had never been made.

1678 RAY 77.

Would, *see also* Young man w. (If the) and old man could.

Would have, *see* Lack what they w. h. in their pack (Many men).

Wound be healed, Though the | yet a scar remains.

a. **1542** SIR T. WYATT 'Wyatt being in prison, to Bryan', 'Sure am I, Brian, this wound shall heale again: But yet, alas, the skarre shall still remaign. **1575** GASCOIGNE *Posies, Dulce Bel.* (1907) 159 *Bellum* . . . striketh with a sting, And leaves a skarre although the wound be heald. **1594** SHAKS. *Lucrece* 732 Bearing away the wound that nothing healeth, The scar that will despite of cure remain. **1612–15** BP. HALL *Contempl.* III. v (1825) I. 65 As wounds once healed leave a scar behind them, so remitted injuries leave commonly in the actors a guilty remembrance. **1660** W. SECKER *Nonsuch Prof.* II (1891) 358 It is best that dissension should never be born among brethren. . . . Members rent and torn cannot be healed without a scar.

Wound that bleedeth inwardly is most dangerous, The.

1579 LYLY *Euphues* (Arb.) 63 Seeing the wound that bleedeth inwardly is most daungerous, . . . it is hyghe tyme to vnfolde my secret loue to my secret friend. **1732** FULLER no. 4852.

Wound(s), *see also* Afraid of w. (He that is); Green w. is soon healed; Ill w. is cured, not ill name.

Wranglers are never in the wrong.

1616 DRAXE 244 A wrangler neuer wanteth words. **1670** RAY 31 ('never want words'). **1732** FULLER no. 5833.

Wrap (a thing) up in clean linen, To.

1678 RAY 84 . . . To deliver sordid or uncleanly matter in decent language.

Wrapped, *see* Lapped (W.) in mother's smock (He was).

Wrath of a mighty man, Take heed of the | and the tumult of the people.

1651 HERBERT 371.

Wrath, *see also* God gives his w. by weight; Soft answer turneth away w.

Wrekin, *see* Friends round the W.

Wren(s), *see* Robin and w. God's cock and hen; Sore fight w. as cranes.

Wrestle, *see* Thrown would ever w.

Wretched, It is hard to be | but worse to be known so.

1640 HERBERT 344.

Wrinkle(s), *see* Nicks (W.) in her horn (She has).

Write down the advice of him who loves you, though you like it not at present.

1666 TORRIANO 51 The counsel of one who wisheth thee well, write it down, though it seem cross. **1855** BOHN 572.

Write like an angel, To.

1774 GARRICK in *Mem. of Goldsmith* (Globe) lv Here lies Poet Goldsmith, . . . Who wrote like an angel, but talked like poor Poll. **1908** *Times* 30 Nov. Ruskin . . . wrote like an angel when he was not provoked to scream like a child.

Write, *see also* Think much . . . w. less.

Writers, *see* Tailors and w. must mind fashion.

Writes a hand like a foot, He.

1738 SWIFT (Dial. i) 335 *Lady A.* That's a billet-doux from your mistress. *Col.* . . . I don't know whence it comes; but who'er writ it, writes a hand like a foot.

Writing (Handwriting) on the wall, The.

[BIBLE *Daniel* v. 5.] **1837** LOCKHART *Scott* xxvii (1845) 256/1 This hand which, like the writing on Belshazzar's wall, disturbed his hour of hilarity. **1866** KINGSLEY *Hereward* xviii William went back to France. . . . But . . . the handwriting was on the wall, unseen by man; and he, and his policy, and his race, were weighed in the balance, and found wanting. **1878** J. PAYN *By Proxy* xxxviii He stared at those pregnant words till . . . they seemed to be written, like Belshazzar's warning on the wall, in letters of fire.

Writing you learn to write, By.

[L. *Scribendo disces scribere.*] **1763** JOHNSON *Let.* 16 Apr. in BOSWELL *Life* xiv (1847) 130 If at the end of seven years you write good Latin, you will excel most of your contemporaries: Scribendo disces scribere. It is only by writing ill that you can attain to write well.

Writing, *see also* Reading maketh a full man, w. an exact man.

Written letter remains, *see Littera scripta manet.*

Wrong box, To be in the.

[= awkwardly placed.] **1546** HEYWOOD II. ix. 75 And therby in the wrong boxe to thryue ye weare. *a.* **1555** RIDLEY *Wks.* 163 (D.) If you will hear how St. Augustine expoundeth that place, you shall perceive that you are in a wrong box. *a.* **1659** CLEVELAND *Coachman* 12 Sir, faith you were in the wrong Box. **1734** CAREY *Chronon.* iii Egad, we're in the wrong box. **1836** MARRYAT *Midsh. Easy* x. 31 Take care your rights of man don't get you in the wrong box.

Wrong has no warrant.

1641 FERGUSSON 108. **1721** KELLY 349 . . . No man can pretend authority to do an ill thing.

Wrong hears, wrong answer gives.

1641 FERGUSSON 108.

Wrong horse, *see* Put one's money on w. h.

Wrong laws maketh short governance.

c. **1470** HARDING *Chron.* lxxxvi. v.

Wrong man, *see* Claps his dish at w. m.'s door.

Wrong never comes right.

1853 TRENCH i. 8. **1882** BLACKMORE *Christowel* xxii Bad work cannot be turned into good; any more than wrong can be turned into right, in this world. **1888** MRS. OLIPHANT *Second Son* ii 'Then it all comes right again.' 'What's wrong can never be right,' said Pax.

Wrong side of the blanket, Born on the.

[= of illegitimate birth.] **1771** SMOLLETT *Humph. Clink.* II 185 I didn't come on the wrong side of the blanket, girl. **1815** SCOTT *Guy Man.* ix Frank Kennedy, he said, was a gentleman, though on the wrang side of the blanket.

Wrong tree, *see* Bark up w. t.

Wrong way to the wood, You go (take) the.

1546 HEYWOOD II. ix. 75 In mistakyng me, ye may sée, ye tooke The wrong way to wood. **1580** LYLY *Euph. & his Eng.* (Arb.) 288 *Fidus* you goe the wrong way to the Woode, in making a gappe, when the gate is open.

Wrong way to work, You go the.

1639 CLARKE 8.

Wrong without a remedy, No.

[L. *Ubi jus, ibi remedium.* Law Max.— Where there is a right, there is a remedy.] **1910** *Spectator* 10 Dec. 1016 Again and again . . . English judges have invented artifices in order to give effect to the excellent legal maxim that there shall be no wrong without a remedy.

Wrongs not an old man that steals his supper from him, He.

1640 HERBERT 331. **1737** FRANKLIN Jan. He that steals the old man's supper do's him no wrong. **1855** BOHN 31 Who steals an old man's supper, does him no wrong. *Span.*

Wrongs of a husband or master are not reproached, The.

1640 HERBERT 323.

Wrong(s), *see also* Beg at the w. door; Do w. once and never hear the end; Extremity of right is w.; Losers are always in w.; Morally w. cannot be politically right; Oweth (Who) is in all the w.; Revenged all w. (Had I); Right (He that hath) fears, w. hopes; Rise on the w. side; Submitting to one w. brings another; Two w. don't make a right.

Wroth as the wind.

13. . *E. E. Allit. P. C.* 410 He wex[1] as wroth as þe wynde towarde oure lorde. **1393** LANGLAND *P. Pl. C.* iv. 486 As wroth as the wynd. wex[1] Mede ther-after. [[1] became.]

Wroth, *see also* Cometh last . . . soonest w.

Wry mouth, To make a.

1605 DEKKER *2 The Honest Whore* II. i I should ha made a wry mouth at the World like a Playce. **1611** COTGRAVE s.v. 'Moue' We say of one that's hanged, he makes a wry mouth.

Wych-waller, *see* Scold like a w.-w.

Wye, *see* Blessed is the eye betwixt Severn and W.; Naughty Ashford, surly W.

Wyndham, *see* Horner.

Y

Yarmouth, *see* Spell Y. steeple right (Cannot).

Yate for another, good fellow, One.

1678 RAY 263 The Earl [of Rutland] riding by himself one day . . . a Countreyman . . . open'd him the first gate they came to, not knowing who the Earl was. When they came to the next gate the Earl expecting . . . the same again, Nay soft, saith the Countreyman, *One yate for another, Good fellow.*

Yawning, *see* Stretching and y. leadeth to bed.

Year doth nothing else but open and shut, The.

1640 HERBERT 358.

Year is, As the | your pot must seethe.

1640 HERBERT 333.

Year sooner to the begging, It is but a.

1721 KELLY 217 . . . Facetiously spoken,

when we design to be at a little more expense than we thought.

Year, A good | will not make him, and an ill year will not break him.

1658 *Comes Facundus* 24. **1721** KELLY 36.

Yeared, It is.

1678 RAY 344 . . . *Spoken of a desperate debt.*

Years know more than books.

1640 HERBERT 359.

Year(s), *see also* All one a hundred y. hence; Cherry y. merry y.; Fewer his y. fewer his tears; Four things (Of) man has more than he knows . . . y.; Good y. corn is hay; Ill y.; Let your house to enemy (First y.); Men's y. and faults are more than they own; Old (None so) that he hopes not for a y.; One y. a nurse; One y. of joy; One y.'s seeding; Pear y.; Say no ill of the y. till; Snow y. a rich y.; Spend a whole y.'s rent at one meal.

Yellow as a kite's foot, As.

1509 A. BARCLAY *Ship of Fools* (1874) I. 287 Though he be yelowe as kyte Is of his fete. **1630** DAVENANT *Just Italian* I (A) Yellow as foot of kite.

Yellow as a paigle,[1] As.

a. **1697** G. MERITON *Yorks. Ale* 83 As Blake [= yellow] as a paigle. **1735** PEGGE *Kenticisms* in E.D.S. no. 12, p. 40 (A). **1791** Id. *Derbicisms* (E.D.S.) 114 (A). [[1] cowslip.]

Yellow as the golden noble, As.

1587 HARRISON *Descr. of England* (New Sh. Soc.) i. 160 The beere . . . yellow as the gold noble, as our potknights call it. **1678** RAY 350.

Yellow bellies.

1787 GROSE (*Linc.*) 193 . . . This is an appellation given to persons born in the Fens, who, it is jocularly said, have yellow bellies, like their eels. **1895** ADDY *Household Tales* Introd. xxix Dr. Morton . . . who was born in a Lincolnshire village, . . . never thought that the Yellow Bellies 'were . . . yellow, but something of a bronze shade'. **1896** BEALBY *Daughter of Fen* xiii 'That's allus the waay wi' you yaller-bellies, I noätice', chimed in Brewster Bletherwell.

Yellow Jack.

[= yellow fever.] **1833** MARRYAT *P. Simple* xxix With regard to Yellow Jack, as we calls the Yellow fever, it's a devil incarnate.

Yellow peril.

[= a supposed danger of invasion of Europe by Asiatic peoples.] **1900** *Daily News* 21 July 3/5 The 'yellow peril' in its most serious form. **1911** *Spectator* 2 Dec. 936 In . . . *The Air Scout* . . . [the] 'Yellow Peril' has come upon the White World'. It is not Japan that is threatening the West. . . . It is China that has awoke.

Yellow Press, The.

[Applied to newspapers of a sensational character. Derived from the figure of a child in a yellow dress in a cartoon issued in 1895 by the *New York World*.] **1898** *Daily News* 2 Mar. 7/2 The yellow Press is for a war with Spain at all costs. **1906** A. T. QUILLER-COUCH *Cornish W.* 52 Whatever nation your Yellow Press happens to be insulting at this moment.

Yellow stockings, To wear.

[= to be jealous.] *c.* **1590** *Tarlton's News out of Purgatory* D 2 He resolues with the crue of the Yellow hosde companions . . . that *Mulier* . . . is a woorde of vnconstancie. *c.* **1598** DELONEY *Thomas of Reading* Wks. (Mann) 217 Fie, vpon these yellow hose. **1606** DEKKER *News from Hell* C 1ᵛ If he put on yellow stockings. **1736** BAILEY *Dict.* s.v. 'Yellow'.

Yellow's forsaken, and green's forsworn, but blue and red ought to be worn.

1862 HISLOP 334 . . . In allusion to the superstitious notions formerly held regarding these colours.

Yellow, *see also* Jaundiced eye (To) all things y.

Yellow-hammer, *see* Dead shot at.

Yelping curs will raise mastiffs.

1721 KELLY 360 . . . Spoken when mean and unworthy people, by their private contentions, cause differences among greater persons.

Yeoman's service.

1603 SHAKS. *Hamlet* V. ii. 36 It did me yeoman's service. **1824** SCOTT *St. Ronan's* xix I have wanted it [your help] already, and that when it might have done me yeoman's service. **1826** Id. *Journ.* 16 Nov. It [note by Wellington] is furiously scrawled . . . but it *shall* do me yeoman's service.

Yesterday will not be called again.

a. **1529** SKELTON *Magnif.* 2057 *Pouer.* Ye, syr, yesterday wyll not be callyd agayne. **1546** HEYWOOD II. ix. 74 Well well (quoth she) what euer ye now saie, It is too late to call again yesterdaie. **1616** N. BRETON *Cross. Prov.* Wks. (1879) II, App. iii No man can call again yesterday. **1692** L'ESTRANGE *Aesop's Fab.* ccv (1738) 221 'Tis to no purpose to think of recalling yesterday.

Yew bow in Chester, There is more than one.

1662 FULLER (*Flint.*) III. 537 'Mwy nag un bwa yro Ynghaer'. That is, more than one yugh-bow in Chester. Modern use applieth this proverb to such who seize on other folk's goods . . . mistaken with similitude thereof to their own goods. **1917** BRIDGE 118 . . . Mwy nag un bwa yew ynghaer. Many a Welshman on the border has found out the truth of this saying, and . . . the Welsh . . . were not allowed to carry bows themselves when they visited the City.... Now if a man boasts of some unique possession, he is sometimes told that 'there is more than one yew bow in Chester', *i.e.* it is not so rare as he thinks.

Yoke, *see* Time to y. when cart comes to caples.

York excels foul Sutton, As much as.

1607 R. CAREW in Epistle to Reader before H. ESTIENNE *A World of Wonders* A l[V] If the life of our Ministers be compared with that of their triers, it will be found to exceed theirs as farre as *Yorke* doth foule *Sutton*, to vse a Northerne phrase. **1732** FULLER no. 715.

York, you're wanted.

1816 T. MORTON *The Slave* I. 1 *Fog.* (*To Sailors*). . . . What, you won't go? Holloa, York you're wanted. *Enter* SAM SHARPSET ... *Miss V. F.* Who is that? *Gov.* His name is Sharpset: he's his Yorkshire mentor. **1866** *N. & Q.* 3rd Ser. x. 355 'York, you're wanted.'—This phrase is commonly used on board a man-of-war when something goes wrong by reason of the absence of 'the right man' from the 'right place'.

York, *see also* Lincoln was; Oxford for learning ... Y. for a tit.

Yorkshire (= a sharp fellow), He is.

1790 GROSE s.v. 'Yorkshire' Master's Yorkshire too. *a.* **1806** WOLCOT (P. Pindar) *Pitt's Flight* Wks. (1816) III. 64 But, hang the fellow, '*he was Yorkshire too*'. **1813** RAY 223 The Italians say, *E Spoletino.* He's of Spoleto: intimating, he's a cunning blade.

Yorkshire on one, To come (*or* put).

[= to cheat, dupe, overreach him.] **1700** *Step to the Bath* 10 I ask'd what Countrey-Man my Landlord was? Answer was made full North ; and Faith 'twas very Evident ; for he had put the Yorkshire most Damnably upon us.

Yorkshire, *see also* Master's Y. too.

Yorkshireman, *see* Give a Y. a halter; Shake a bridle over Y.'s grave.

You are another.

[L. *Tu quoque*, 'thou also' = Eng. slang you're another!', a retort upon one's accuser.] **1553** UDALL *Roister D.* III. v R. If it were an other but thou, it were a knaue. *M.* Ye are an other your selfe, sir. **1614** J. COOKE (*title*) Greenes Tu Quoque. **1749** FIELDING *Tom Jones* IX. vi 'I only said your conclusion was a non sequitur.' 'You are another,' cries the sergeant. **1838** LYTTON *Alice* III. iv No man knew better the rhetorical effect of the *tu quoque* form of argument.

Young are not always with their bow bent, The.

1678 RAY 353 ... *i.e.* Under rule.

Young barber and an old physician, A. (*Cf.* Old physician, young lawyer.)

1573 SANDFORD (1576) 103. **1578** FLORIO *First Fruites* f. 32 (A). **1666** TORRIANO 21.

Young bear, Like a | with all his troubles before him.

1833 MARRYAT *P. Simple* ii I replied that I had never been at sea . . . but that I was going. 'Well, then, you're like a young bear, all your sorrows to come'.

Young cocks love no coops.

1636 CAMDEN 310.

Young colts will canter.

1824 SCOTT *St. Ronan's* i 'They were daft callants,'[1] she said, . . . ; 'a young cowt will canter, be it up hill or down'. [[1] youths.]

Young courtier, A | an old beggar. (*Cf.* Young serving-man, &c.)

c. **1510** BARCLAY *Eclogues* 2. 1056. **1577** J. FIT JOHN *Diamond most Precious* B 2 The old Prouerbe is true, A yong Courtier, an old Begger. **1579** LYLY *Euphues* (Arb.) 185 It is an olde saying that who so liueth in the court, shall dye in the strawe. **1598** *Health to the Gentlemanly Prof.* C 4 For, I holde it an infallible rule, an olde Seruing man, a young Beggar. **1607** TOURNEUR *Rev. Trag.* IV. iv O, when women are young courtiers, They are sure to be old beggars. **1616** BRETON *Cross. Prov.* Wks. (1879) II App. iii A young courtier an old beggar. **1642** FULLER *Holy State* I. vii. 6 Hadst thou an occupation (for service is no heritage ; a young courtier, an old beggar), I could find it in my heart to cast her away upon thee. **1659** HOWELL *Eng. Prov.* 12 An old Serving-man, a young beggar.

Young enough to mend, Ye be | but I am too old to see it.

1546 HEYWOOD II. ix. 74.

Young man idle, A | an old man needy, *see* Idle youth, &c., 1642 quotn.

Young man should not marry yet, A | an old man not at all.

1546 UDALL tr. *Erasm. Apoph.* (1877) 139 To one demanding when best season were to wedde a wife: For a young man, (quoth he[1]) it is too soone, and for an olde manne ouerlate. **1602–3** SHAKS. *All's Well* II. iii. 314 A young man married is a man that's marr'd. [[1] Diogenes.]

Young man would, If the | and the old man could, there would be nothing undone.

1642 TORRIANO 91 If the young man did but know, and the old man were but able, there is nothing but might be effected. **1736** BAILEY *Dict.* s.v. 'Would' (A).

Young man, *see also* **Woo** is a pleasure in a y. m. (To).

Young men die many, Of | of old men scape not any. (*Cf.* Young men may die, &c.)

1659 N. R. 83. **1666** TORRIANO 105 (A) Of young people many dye, of the old none escapes. **1670** RAY 127. **1732** FULLER no. 6379.

Young men may die, but old must die. (*Cf.* Young men die many, &c.)

1534 MORE *Dial. of Comforte* in *Works* (1557) 1139/2 For as we will wot, that a young man may dye soone: so be we very sure that an olde man cannot liue long. **1593–4** SHAKS. *Tam. Shrew* II. i.385 May not young men die as well as old? **1623** CAMDEN 276. **1670** RAY 127 Of young men die many, of old men scape not any. De giovane ne muoiono di molti, di vecchi ne scampa nessuno. *Ital.*

Young men think old men fools, and old men know young men to be so.

1577 J. GRANGE *Golden Aphroditis* O 2 (A). **1580** LYLY *Euph. & his Eng.* (Arb.) 241 Such a quarrel hath ther alwaies bin betweene the graue and the cradle, that he yat is young thinketh the olde man fond, and the olde knoweth the young man to be a foole. **1605** CAMDEN (1637) 281 quoted as the saying of Dr. (Nicholas) Metcalfe (d. 1539). **1605** CHAPMAN *All Fools* v. i (1874) 75 *Go.* What, I say! Young men think old men are fools; but old men know young men are fools. **1639** CLARKE 181. **1710** STEELE *Tatler* No. 132 11 Feb. He is constantly told by his uncle, . . . 'Ay, ay, Jack, you young men think us fools; but we old men know you are.'

Young men's knocks old men feel.

[L. *Quae peccamus juvenes ea luimus senes.* We pay when we are old for the misdeeds of our youth.] **1670** RAY 38.

Young one squeak, Make the | and you'll catch the old one.

1732 FULLER no. 3326.

Young pig grunts like the old sow, The.

1678 RAY 184.

Young saint, old devil.

c. **1470** *Harl. MS. 3362* (ed. Förster) in *Anglia* 42 ʒoung seynt, old deuyl. *a.* **1530** DUNBAR *Merle & Nycht.* 35 Of yung sanctis growis auld feyndis but faill. **1546** HEYWOOD I. x. 22 But soone rype, soone rotten, yong seynt olde deuill. **1552** LATIMER *7th Serm. Lord's Prayer* (P.S.) 431 The old proverb, 'Young saints, old devils' . . . is . . . the devil's own invention; which would have parents negligent in bringing up their children in goodness. **1636** S. WARD *Serm.* (1862) 81 Young saints will prove but old devils. . . . But . . . such were never right bred. Such as prove falling stars never were aught but meteors.

Young serving-man, A | an old beggar. (*Cf.* Young courtier, &c.)

1587 HARRISON *Descr. of England* (New Sh. S.) i. 134 There runneth a prouerbe; Yoong seruing men, old beggars. **1598** *Servingmans Comfort* in *Inedited Tracts* (Hazlitt) 117 (A).

Young trooper should have an old horse, A.

1611 COTGRAVE s.v. 'Soldat' A young souldier would be fitted with an old horse. **1642** TORRIANO 3. **1732** FULLER 493.

Young wenches make old wrenches.

1639 CLARKE 174.

Young when they are old, They who would be | must be old when they are young.

1670 RAY 34.

Younger brother hath the more wit, The.

1607 SHARPHAM *Cupid's Whirligig* (1926) III. 42 The younger brothers (according to the old wiues tailes) alwaie prooued the wisest men. **1678** RAY 85.

Younger brother is the better gentleman, The.

1642 FULLER *Holy State* xv (1840) 37 The Younger Brother. Some account him the better gentleman of the two, because son to the more ancient gentleman. **1678** RAY 85 The younger brother is the ancienter Gentleman. **1738** SWIFT (Dial. i) 340 *Lady A.* You are a younger brother. *Col.* Well, madam, the younger brother is the better gentleman.

Younger brother of him, He has made a.

1597 *Discouerie of Knights of the Poste* C 2 Thou must not thinke to make a younger brother of me. **1599–1600** SHAKS. *A.Y.L.* III. iii. 402 *Orl.* What were his marks? *Ros.* . . . A beard neglected, which you have not: but I pardon you that, for, simply, your having in beard is a younger brother's revenue. **1678** RAY 85.

Young(er), *see also* **Labour** younger (Ye shall never); **Learneth** y. (Whoso) forgets not; **Offspring** of . . . very y. lasts not; **Quite** y. and all alive; **Soon** goeth the y. lamb's skin to market (As).

Youth and age will never agree.

c. **1390** CHAUCER *Miller's Tale* 3229 Youthe and elde is often at debaat. *c.* **1450** *Towneley Plays* x. 170 It is ill cowpled of youth and elde. **1562** HEYWOOD *First Hundred of Epigrams,* no. 33 Age and youth together can seeld agree. *c.* **1599** SHAKS. *Pass. Pilgr.* xii. 1 Crabbed age and youth cannot live together. **1641** FERGUSSON 112.

Youth and white paper take any impression.

1579 LYLY *Euphues* (Arb.) 37 (A) The tender youth of a child is ... apt to receive any form. **1594–5** SHAKS. *Two Gent.* III. i. 34 Tender youth is soon suggested. **1670** RAY 31 Youth and white paper take any impression. **1796** EDGEWORTH *Par. Asst., Lit. Merch.* i (1903) 374 Youth and white paper, as the proverb says, take all impressions. The boy profited much by his father's precepts, and more by his example.

Youth is used to, What | age remembers.

1303 BRUNNE *Handl. Synne* 7674 (Yn a proverbe of olde Englys)—That yougthe wones, Yn age mones; That thou dedyst ones, Thou dedyst eftsones. (That which youth is used to, in age (one) remembers; that which thou didst once, thou didst again.) [Skeat.]

Youth knew what age would crave, If | it would both get and save.

1670 RAY 160.

Youth never casts for peril (is reckless).

c. **1400** *Beryn* 1052 ʒowith is recheles. **1641** FERGUSSON 112. **1721** KELLY 374 ... Signifying that youth is rash and headstrong.

Youth, Who that in | no virtue useth, in age all honour him refuseth.

c. **1450** *Provs. of Wysdom* 9, 10 Who that in youth no vertew vsyþe, In age all honowre hym refusythe.

Youth will be served.

1851 BORROW *Lavengro* iii. 291 (A) Youth will be served, every dog has his day, and mine has been a fine one. **1900** A. C. DOYLE *Green Flag &c.* 125 There were ... points in his favour. ... There was age—twenty-three against forty. There was an old ring proverb that 'Youth will be served'. **1928** *Times* 30 Aug. 15/6 This visit was to initiate a novice in the mysteries of the dry fly. And, as youth must be served, it would never have done to begin his education ... where ... there is no rise till the evening.

Youth will have its course (*or* swing).

1579 LYLY *Euphues* (Arb.) 124 We haue an olde (prouerbe) youth wil haue his course. **1639** CLARKE 183 Youth will have its swing.

Youth, *see also* Abundance of money ruins y.; Growing y. has wolf in belly; Idle y. needy age; Lazy y., lousy age; *Maxima debetur*; Reckless y. makes rueful age; Rule y. well; Wine and y. increase love.

Yowe, *see* Ewe.

Yule feast may be done (or quit) at Pasch,[1] A.

1641 FERGUSSON 14 A ʒule feast may be quat at Pasche. **1662** FULLER (*Northumb.*) II. 544 'A Yule feast may be quat at Pasche'. That is, Christmas cheer may be digested, and the party hungry again, at Easter. **1721** KELLY 27 ... A good office, done at one time, may be requit at another. **1857** DEAN RAMSAY *Remin.* V (1911) 198 *A Yule feast may be done at Pasch.* Festivities ... need not ... be confined to any season. [[1] Easter.]

Yule is come, and Yule is gone, and we have feasted well; so Jack must to his flail again, and Jenny to her wheel.

1846 DENHAM 67.

Yule is good on Yule even.

1639 CLARKE 307.

Yule is young in Yule even, and as old in Saint Stephen.[1]

1721 KELLY 378 ... Spoken when people are much taken with novelties, and as soon weary of them. [26 Dec.]

Yule, *see also* Cry Y. at other men's cost; Fool that marries wife at Y.; Green Y. ... fat churchyard; Now is now and Y.'s in winter.

Yule-day, *see* Every day's no Y.-d.

Z

Zeal like that of a pervert, No.

1872 *N. & Q.* 4th Ser. x. 108 Those who are likest in disposition disagree most hotly when a difference arises. ... 'There is no hate like that of a brother'; no zeal like that of a pervert.

Zeal, when it is a virtue, is a dangerous one.

1732 FULLER no. 6071.

Zeal without knowledge.

[**1611** BIBLE *Romans* x. 2 They haue a zeale of God, but not according to knowledge.] **1611** DAVIES *Prov.* 57 'Zeale without knowledge is sister of Folly': But though it be witlesse, men hold it most holly. **1732** FULLER no. 6069 Zeal without Knowledge is Fire without Light.